··LEGACIES··

Fiction · Poetry · Drama · Nonfiction
Third Edition

Jan Zlotnik Schmidt
SUNY New Paltz

Carley Rees Bogarad
SUNY New Paltz

with Lynne Crockett
SUNY New Paltz

W9-AAH-517

THOMSON

WADSWORTH

Australia Brazil Canada Mexico Singapore Spain United Kingdom United States

THOMSON
✦ ™
WADSWORTH

Legacies: Fiction, Poetry, Drama, Nonfiction, Third Edition
Jan Zlotnik Schmidt/Carley Rees Bogarad

Publisher: *Michael Rosenberg*
Acquisitions Editor: *Aron Keesbury*
Development Editor: *Mary Beth Walden*
Editorial Assistant: *Cheryl Forman*
Technology Project Manager: *Joe Gallagher*
Senior Marketing Manager: *Mary Jo Southern*
Marketing Assistant: *Dawn Giovanniello*
Associate MarCom Manager: *Patrick Rooney*
Associate Project Manager, Editorial Production:
  Karen Stocz

Manufacturing Manager: *Marcia Locke*
Permissions Editor: *Karyn Morrison*
Project Manager: *Laura Horowitz, Hearthside*
  Publishing Services
Photo Manager: *Sheri Blaney*
Cover Designer: *Diane Levy*
Cover Printer: *Phoenix Color Corp.*
Compositor: *ATLIS Graphics & Design*
Text Printer: *Malloy Incorporated*

Cover photos: HIP / Art Resource, NY; Victoria &
Albert Museum, London / Art Resource, NY; Image
Select / Art Resource, NY; Réunion des Musées
Nationaux / Art Resource, NY; © Hulton-Deutsch
Collection/CORBIS

For more information about our products, contact us at:
Thomson Learning Academic Resource Center
1-800-423-0563
For permission to use material from this text
or product, submit a request online at
http://www.thomsonrights.com
Any additional questions about permissions can be
submitted by
e-mail to **thomsonrights@thomson.com**

Library of Congress Control Number: 2005926360

Student Edition: ISBN 1-4130-1126-8

Thomson Higher Education
25 Thomson Place
Boston, MA 02210-1202
USA

Asia (including India)
Thomson Learning
5 Shenton Way
#01-01 UIC Building
Singapore 068808

Australia/New Zealand
Thomson Learning Australia
102 Dodds Street
Southbank, Victoria 3006
Australia

Canada
Thomson Nelson
1120 Birchmount Road
Toronto, Ontario M1K 5G4
Canada

UK/Europe/Middle East/Africa
Thomson Learning
High Holborn House
50–51 Bedford Road
London WC1R 4LR
United Kingdom

Latin America
Thomson Learning
Seneca, 53
Colonia Polanco
11560 Mexico
D.F. Mexico

■ IN MEMORIAM ■

Dr. Carley Rees Bogarad

An Inspirational Teacher and Colleague

·BRIEF CONTENTS·

· CONTENTS ·

vii

PART TWO ■ Thematic Anthology

Chapter 4 ■ The Heroic Journey

· THEMATIC · CLUSTERS in *LEGACIES*

· ALTERNATE · CONTENTS

POETRY

DRAMA

NONFICTION

▪ PREFACE ▪

Legacies challenges students to enter the world of the new millennium, a culturally diverse place in which people's fates are crucially interconnected. It also introduces students to the analysis of literature and to critical thinking. The readings—fiction, poetry, drama, and non-fiction—represent complex and exciting traditions from 500 B.C. to the first decade of the twenty-first century. They include both global masterpieces and contemporary works from Lao-tzu to Luisa Valenzuela, from Sophocles to Rita Dove, from Rabindranath Tagore to Ernest Hemingway. As a thematic exploration of the individual in social, political, and cultural contexts, *Legacies* engages us in intellectual inquiry and provides the personal pleasures associated with the arts.

By reading and responding to fiction, poetry, drama, and nonfiction, we discover more about ourselves and others; we expand our thinking as conscious human beings. We develop moral imagination so that we can envision the views, experiences, and beliefs of others. Reading and writing about literature involves us in a process of critical analysis involving the same faculties we use in our everyday lives, but the process becomes directed, focused, and intensified. Interpretation of literary works encourages us to question, to observe keenly, to probe, and to critique—habits of mind that are central to liberal education.

Because we agree with Wittgenstein's statement that "the limits of [our] language mean the limits of [our] world," we have written and edited this textbook with excellence and expansiveness as guiding principles. We have divided the book into three major sections and two appendixes. In part 1, Acts of Interpretation, the first chapter defines types of critical thinking and critical reading and then connects these ideas to the analysis of literature. Chapter 2 contains a discussion of forms of reader response to literature. Chapter 3 presents the process of writing about literary works and the forms of the essay. Part 2, Thematic Anthology, features readings organized by genre around five themes that progress from exploration of the self to larger issues: The Heroic Journey, Haunted Houses, Gender and Sexuality, Sites of Conflict, and Strange New Worlds. We hope that each work will open and illuminate the others to inspire dynamic and complex inquiry and insight in every reader. Part 3, Reading and Writing about the Genres, introduces forms and elements of the four genres of fiction, poetry, drama, and nonfiction. The appendixes include a full description of the research process and MLA documentation and an overview of contemporary approaches to literary criticism.

Each anthology chapter of part 2 opens with an evocative image and provocative quotations designed as prompts for prewriting, questioning, and exploration. Next, each chapter has an introduction that articulates generative ideas about the theme, selections, and connections among the texts. We intend our comments not as definitive interpretations but as starting points for discussion. The initial Crossing the Genres clusters in the chapters combine works from the four genres to offer various possibilities for analysis, and the clusters that follow also suggest thematic connections across the genres. In addition, thematically linked short stories and poems are included for comparison/contrast. Biographical headnotes precede most selections, and exploratory questions, suggestions for reader response, and formal writing activities follow the texts. Extensive, process-oriented writing assignments and model student essays appear at the end of each chapter.

New to this edition are:

- Expanded treatment of the critical thinking, critical reading, and reader response process, including discussion of creative responses to literature.
- Expanded discussion of writing the argumentative essay about literature.
- Expanded discussion of the research process, including use and evaluation of online sources and a new model research paper that ventures into social, historical and textual analysis.
- Addition of more authors from the traditional canon (e.g., Herman Melville, John Steinbeck, and F. Scott Fitzgerald) as well as new pieces by multicultural authors (e.g., Julia Alvarez, Chang-rae Lee, and Naomi Shihab Nye) and by new contemporary writers (e.g., Dan Chaon, ZZ Packer, and Nathan Englander).
- More innovative thematic clusters treating such current themes as gender and sexual identity, sites of conflict, terror and terrorism, and environmental issues.
- Addition of web clusters and resources centered on such topics as fairy tales, gothic tales (featuring Edgar Allan Poe short stories), and responses to 9/11.
- Expanded selection of classic and contemporary drama (e.g., Henrik Ibsen's *A Doll's House,* David Henry Hwang's *M Butterfly,* and Rebecca Gilman's *Boy Gets Girl*).
- New essays that provide contexts for the readings (e.g., Bruno Bettelheim's "Introduction" from *The Uses of Enchantment* and Elie Wiesel's "Why I Write: Making No Become Yes").
- Expanded treatment of forms of creative nonfiction including such authors as Joan Didion, Gretel Ehrlich, Scott Russell Sanders, and David Sedaris.
- Expanded and updated appendix on critical approaches to literature.

Legacies engages students in the indivisible activities of reading and writing, and it enlarges their capacities to develop ideas and to appreciate the richness and depth of responding to literature through the following important features:

- **Emphasis on Critical Thinking and on the Reading and Writing Processes.** Chapters 1 to 3 present numerous examples of student responses, formal writing, and a profile of one student's writing process: notes and initial and final drafts of an essay on Gloria Anzaldúa's "horse."
- **A Wide Variety of Readings from Traditional and Nontraditional Canons.** Selections represent the best of new voices and of classic writers. These diverse readings, which prompt us to consider issues of gender, ethnicity, class, and sexual orientation, embody our heritage, our literary legacies. Note the number of Nobel Prize laureates.
- **Juxtapositions of Readings within Themes.** In each chapter, readings are organized by clusters and by genre, but they also can be studied by juxtaposing a number of works according to subtopics of the major theme, gender, new and traditional voices, or regions of the world, to name only a few possibilities. This process leads naturally to contrastive analysis, to questioning, and to examination of issues from multiple perspectives.

- **Crossing the Genres.** These sets of suggested readings from each genre introduce each anthology chapter and exemplify the principle of juxtaposition. In each cluster, the poem may serve, for example, as motivation for discussion; the essay may provide a framework for analysis; and the fiction and/or drama may play against or complement each other. Together, these works can stimulate a dynamic process of critical inquiry. Additional thematic clusters are suggested at the beginning of each anthology chapter.

- **Extensive Questions for Explorations of the Text.** These questions may be used for individual study, for guided class discussion, for lesson plans, or for collaborative (group) work. The questions begin with issues intrinsic to a given work (both textual and interpretive) and then consider thematic connections with other works. Questions have been field-tested: The number and nature of the exploratory questions represent the suggestions of students in classes.

- **Variety of Writing Activities.** Possibilities for reader response and ideas for writing follow each reading. They provide opportunities for personal reaction, creative expression, practice in various modes of exposition and argument, analysis and interpretation of literature, and consideration of formal elements of the genres.

- **Sample Student Essays.** Each anthology chapter offers at least one model student writing that illustrates a different form of the essay about literature: thematic analysis; comparison/contrast; critical analysis; explication; argument; cultural, historical, or social analysis; and creative responses to literature.

- **Interesting and Ample Writing Assignments.** At the end of each anthology chapter, many of the assignments require a number of stages that encourage thorough exploration of topics. Many others are traditional. Some contain directed research topics. Included are debate topics focused on literary texts.

- **Extensive Treatment of the Forms and Features of Each Genre.** Chapters 9 to 12 feature comprehensive discussions of the genres with lively examples. The models of student writing in each chapter offer a wide range of approaches to all aspects of the reading and writing processes: reader response, explication, critical analysis, and evaluation.

- **Research, MLA Documentation, and Student Essay with Editorial Comments (Appendix A).** This appendix introduces a complete study of the research process and documentation; all major forms of MLA citation; an example of a student research paper with comments; and an additional research essay combining argument, explication, and historical, social, and cultural analysis. No handbook should be necessary for the research process.

- **Critical Theory (Appendix B).** *Legacies* presents a concise explanation of current approaches to literature and demonstrates these theories through multiple interpretations of Kate Chopin's "The Story of an Hour."

- **Extensive Definitions of Literary Terms.** Definitions of terms appear in the text as well as in the Glossary. Terms are printed in boldface type when they first appear in the text.

- **Comprehensive Instructor's Manual.** Our Instructor's Manual, based on materials that have been tested and developed in the classroom, includes sample syllabi (with readings organized by theme or genre), answers to the "Explorations of the Text" for each selection, suggested further works and films to complement the readings in each chapter, lesson plans, and a brief bibliography of books helpful to teachers of writing.

Eduardo Galeano suggests that "one writes out of a need to communicate and to commune with others. . . . One assumes that literature transmits knowledge and affects the behavior and language of those who read, thus helping us to know ourselves better and to save ourselves collectively." We hope that this book will prompt readers to "communicate and to commune." In large measure, we have based this volume on what our students have told us that they want to "know." It reflects their choices of texts and presents examples of their thoughts and writing. It is their book, their legacy.

• ACKNOWLEDGMENTS •

Thanks must go to everyone who contributed to this third edition of *Legacies*. First, we thank our students for their cooperation and contributions to this project. We also acknowledge colleagues who contributed their insights, suggestions, and proofreading skills. At the State University of New York, New Paltz, Donna Baumler, Mark Bellomo, Danielle Bienvenue, William Boyle, Stella Deen, Michelle Diana, Mary Fakler, Ernelle Fife, Penny Freel, Joan Perisse, Jenica Shapiro, Vika Shock, Stefan Spezio, Doris Stewart, and Any Washburn.

Several other faculty members at the State University of New York, New Paltz, served as consultants for the anthology. Professor Kenneth Moss offered advice about drama, and Professor Pauline Uchmanowicz recommended several outstanding ethnic writers and selected texts. We learned a great deal from her and profited from her expertise. As our Shakespeare consultant, Professor Thomas G. Olsen was particularly helpful in providing scholarly perspectives and in thoroughly editing and revising the apparatus for *Hamlet*. His assistance was invaluable. We are deeply indebted to Mark Bellomo for his extraordinary work as author of the Instructor's Manual.

More specifically, we want to acknowledge the efforts of those who contributed particular sections to *Legacies*:

- Michael Dougherty, for the apparatus for John Steinbeck's "Flight."
- Sarah Gardner, for the apparatus for F. Scott Fitzgerald's "Letter to his Daughter"
- Meri Weiss, for suggestions and the apparatus for Kim Ficera's "All in the Family" and "Bi-Bye."
- Kathena Hasbrouck, for her support and advice and for the apparatus and sample student portfolio for *Boy Gets Girl*.
- Robert Waugh, for his expertise in science fiction, his research on Galway Kinnell's "When the Towers Fell," and for his superb translation of Paul Celan's "Death Fugue."
- Carrie Holligan, for the apparatus for Tim O'Brien's "How to Tell a True War Story."
- Rachel Rigolino, for her class project—the online assignment, student creative work, and discussion forum for "horse."
- Abigail Robin, for her suggestions for essays by Emma Goldman and the apparatus for "Minorities vs. Majorities."
- Ken Moss, for the apparatus for Isabel Allende's "And of Clay Are We Created."
- Fiona Paton and John Langan, for their collaboration on the second edition of *Legacies* and for their revision of Appendix B.

This book truly was a collaborative effort.

We also extend our thanks to Neil C. Trager, Director, Samuel Dorsky Museum of Art, and Wayne Lempka, Art Collections Manager, Samuel Dorsky Museum of Art, at the State

University of New York, New Paltz, for their suggestions and for their assistance in securing images for the text.

For their work on *Legacies,* for their commitment and dedication to this project, we also express our gratitude to Ethel Wesdorp, Meredith VanEtten, and Jennifer Smits. This volume could not have come to fruition without their dedicated efforts.

Finally, and most importantly, Harold A. Zlotnik—a consummate teacher, poet, and mentor—contributed his insights, as well as proofreading and editing skills, in addition to work on William Faulkner's "A Rose For Emily." He provides a model of excellence in teaching that continues to inspire.

We also are grateful for the many productive suggestions and comments from the following reviewers, though, of course, any remaining shortcomings of the volume are our responsibility alone:

Mary Bayer, *Grand Rapids Community College*
Michelle Diana, *SUNY New Paltz*
Michelle Doss, *Lubbock Christian University*
Clovia Feldman, *William Paterson University*
David Siar, *Winston-Salem State University*
Jan Smith, *Greenville Technical College*
Tija Spitsberg, *University of Michigan*
Susan Blassingame, *Lubbock Christian University*
Mary Ann DiEdwardo, *Northampton Community College*
Caterina Feldmann, *William Paterson University*
Jim Hayes, *Grand Rapids Community College*
Sabine Klein, *Purdue University*
Don S. Lawson, *Lander University*
M. Leighty, *J. Sargeant Reynolds Community College*
Miles McCrimmon, *J. Sargeant Reynolds Community College*
Andrea Patterson, *Winston-Salem State University*
Ronna Privett, *Lubbock Christian University*
Julie Stevenson, *Grand Rapids Community College*
Shannon Stewart, *Coastal Carolina University*
David Sudol, *Arizona State University*
Fred VanHartesveldt, *Grand Rapids Community College*

We also thank Aron Keesbury, a brilliant and imaginative acquisitions editor at Thomson Wadsworth, who has a passion for literature and who believed in this book, and Mary Beth Walden, a supportive, energetic, and thoughtful developmental editor.

And we are indebted to Karen Stocz, project manager, and Laura Horowitz, project editor, for turning our manuscript into a beautiful book.

Finally, we acknowledge friends and family who contributed their suggestions, insights, proofreading skills, and most importantly, their support: Barbara and Michael Adams, Arthur Cash, Judith Dorney, Phyllis R. Freeman, Mary Gordon, Patricia Phillips, Deborah Roth, Robert and Katherine Waugh. Most of all, we thank our families—Donald Gardeski, Peter and Maggie Crockett, and Kyung-Sook Boo; Marilyn Zlotnik, Peter Hultberg, Samantha, and Gabriel; Adrienne Todd, Jared, Dylan, and Mechelle; Gayle, Segev, and Yotam Guistizia; Philip and Reed Schmidt; and Mae and Harold Zlotnik—for their unending encouragement and unwavering love. They have been our best readers. We dedicate this book to them and to our students.

Jan Zlotnik Schmidt
Lynne Crockett

·· PART ONE ··

Acts of Interpretation

· CHAPTER 1 ·

Critical Thinking and Critical Analysis of Literature

[The mysterious] is the fundamental emotion which stands at the cradle of true art and science. He [she] who knows it not and can no longer wonder, no longer feel amazement, is as good as dead, a snuffed out candle.

Albert Einstein

Two girls discover
the secret of life
in a sudden line of
poetry.

I who don't know the
secret wrote
the line. They
told me

(through a third person)
they had found it
but not what it was,
not even

what line it was. No doubt
by now, more than a week
later, they have forgotten
the secret,

the line, the name of
the poem. I love them

for finding what
I can't find

and for loving me
for the line I wrote
and for forgetting it
so that

a thousand times, til death
find them, they may
discover it again, in other
lines,

in other
happenings. And for
wanting to know it,
for

assuming there is
such a secret, yes
for that
most of all.

                    Denise Levertov, "The Secret"

As human beings, when we "read" the world around us, whether we realize it or not, we delve into the world's secrets. From our vantage point, we may look at a beautiful mountain scene and ask ourselves if a fog is on the mountain, what wildflowers would grow there, or whether a hiking path leads to the summit. Or we may take a bus ride, observe the passengers, and construct visions of their lives: An elderly woman in a dark housedress lives alone in a depressing New York apartment; a young boy with a baseball cap is going to a little league game; a college student with a book bag is on her way to take a final exam that will determine whether she passes or fails a class. We observe, question, and construct visions of the "secrets" of a place and/or of a person. Then, as quickly as we create meanings, the scene disappears from view, and we may begin the process again to "discover" meanings "in other happenings." The ways in which we respond to the texts of our world are not qualitatively different from the ways in which we read literary works. When we read, we look more deeply, and we "discover" and construct a work's "secret[s]"—visions of experience—and share these mysteries with other readers. And then, as Denise Levertov suggests, we may forget our interpretations, reread a work, and discover new meanings. The study of literature gives us this vital process—opportunities to find "the secret of life" in a "sudden line of poetry."

THE CRITICAL THINKING PROCESS

This ability to wonder, to be curious, to probe, to observe, to question, to look below the surface, to reflect, to discover, and to create meanings constitutes our capacity for critical thinking. As human beings, we constantly seek meaning from—and impose meaning upon—our experiences. In our desire to comprehend, we reflect on our perceptions, feelings, experiences, and ideas, and in the process, we create interpretations of our world.

THE CRITICAL THINKING/CRITICAL READING CONNECTION

In critical analysis of literature, certain aspects of the thinking process that we use in daily life are heightened and intensified: reaction and response, analysis, interpretation, and evaluation and judgment. According to Ellin Oliver Keene and Susan Zimmerman in *Mosaics of Thought,* we read on several levels. We make **text-to-self**, **text-to-text**, and **text-to-world** connections. In **text-to-self** connections, we read a work, react, create associations between the work and our own lives, and explore our feelings and responses. We may ask how we respond to the world of the reading. For example, if we are reacting to a short story, we may analyze our responses to setting, to character, and to the plot. We may ask ourselves if we are involved in the world of the reading, if the experiences of the characters resonate with our own, if we come to realizations as a result of our reading, and if our own experiences are illuminated by the ideas represented in the literary work. We assess the impact of the work upon our inner lives, and we determine if the author's vision will enlarge or change our views of self and of the world. We wonder if the work's "secret[s]" will lead us to understand our own.

We also read, observe, and ask ourselves about the meaning and the effect of the words on the page. We create **text-to-text** connections to form an interpretation of the work. We look beneath the surface of the words to find implied meaning. We consider the ideas that are implicit in the words. In this process, we ask ourselves the following questions:

1. What is stated?
2. What exists beyond the surface level? What is implied?
3. What information do we need to make inferences?
4. What are our biases? How does our perspective shape our views?
5. How does the writer's perspective shape the work?
6. What conclusions do we form as to meaning?

We form conclusions about our inferences and develop patterns of meaning—**text-to-text** connections that constitute interpretations of a work.

Finally we create **text-to-world** connections. We ask ourselves if, through reading, we will comprehend another world, another culture, or another time in history. We also make connections between ideas in the work and issues in our world and, consequently, gain insights about our own life and times. Extratextual material also includes biographical information, historical background, cultural and social contexts and issues, and critical views. All these perspectives expand our understanding of the "secret[s]" of a work, and they enlarge our own view of the world.

We also read to discern if the ideas presented in a work have value. We evaluate the language of the text, assess the words for evidence of a writer's bias and assumptions, and draw conclusions about a writer's attitude toward his or her subject and beliefs. We may compare the author's stance with our own beliefs. We may criticize, argue with, and debate the meanings and views of a text—accepting or rejecting its ideas and embracing or disdaining its author's point of view.

In addition, we may judge the language to determine its worth. If the text is an argument, we may ask if the writer is persuasive. If it is a descriptive piece, we may examine our involvement in the world of the reading. If it is a political speech, we may ask how the politician wants us to respond. We may wonder if we are being manipulated by the words of the speech; we may analyze the slant of the speaker, the use of evidence, and the logic of the approach. To determine the effectiveness of a literary work, we may focus intensively on a study of language and explore the effects of words: the **denotations** (dictionary definitions) and **connotations** (associations, suggested and implied meanings) of the words; the author's **tone** (attitude) and **point of view** (perspective) toward his or her subject; the **structure** (organization) of the work; **style** (detail, imagery, word choice); and the nature of the themes presented. Finally, we may ask ourselves if the work seems effective and worthwhile and determine its merits according to our standards of judgment.

Consider student responses during a class discussion of Lorna Dee Cervantes's poem "Refugee Ship" as an illustration of the critical thinking/critical reading connection.

Lorna Dee Cervantes

REFUGEE SHIP

> like wet cornstarch
> I slide past mi abuelita's[1] eyes
> bible placed by her side
> she removes her glasses
> 5 the pudding thickens
>
> mama raised me with no language
> I am an orphan to my spanish name
> the words are foreign, stumbling on my tongue
> I stare at my reflection in the mirror
> 10 brown skin, black hair
>
> I feel I am a captive
> aboard the refugee ship
> a ship that will never dock
> a ship that will never dock

First the students made text-to-self connections. They reacted to the title and stated that the poem made them feel sad and that it invoked comparisons with the plight of the Vietnamese, with the predicament of other immigrant groups who came earlier to the United States, and with the tragedy of the Haitian and Chinese boat people. As they pondered the significance of the title in relation to the story of a grandmother and a granddaughter, they expressed feelings, discovered personal associations, and asked questions about the text.

They also realized that they needed to step back, to cast their personal associations aside, and to develop an interpretation of the work that focused on the relationship of the grandmother and her granddaughter and the speaker's connection to her heritage. They made text-to-text connections. They gathered information from the poem and focused first on understanding the grandmother's character through analyzing the objects associated with her: "glasses," "bible," and her gesture of taking off her spectacles. They concluded that

---

[1] **mi abuelita's eyes:** my grandmother's eyes.

she was a traditional Latina grandmother, unable to understand the speaker, her grand-daughter. Some descriptive details (the images of "cornstarch" and "pudding [that] thickens") puzzled them. They wondered, "What is 'like wet cornstarch'?"; "What does the image have to do with the portrayal of the granddaughter?"; "What is the speaker like?" "Why is she described as an 'orphan' and as a 'captive'?" They began by making observations, and then they started analyzing the stated and implied meanings of the words and images of the poem.

The students concluded that the grandmother and granddaughter exist in separate worlds. The granddaughter, the speaker, cannot communicate with her grandmother because the latter cannot speak or understand English. The persona (the speaker in the poem) has learned "no language"; she has not learned Spanish and, therefore, she finds herself with "words [that] are foreign, stumbling on [her] tongue," her Spanish heritage lost. The granddaughter yearns to know Spanish, to communicate with her grandmother, and to learn more about her people. As the students began deciphering the meaning of the words and images, they realized that "wet cornstarch" is a necessary ingredient that "thick[ens]" a pudding; and that the "pudding" then suggests the emotional distance between grandmother and granddaughter, a distance that the speaker cannot dissolve or resolve.

Lastly they made text-to-world connections. As the students formed interpretations about the meaning of the work, they also realized that the speaker feels as if she lives like a "captive" on a "refugee ship/a ship that will never dock." One student exclaimed, "The movement of the ship—anxiety—never to be able to dock, to find stability, to understand her roots, to have a home"; and another reflected, "The repetition of the last line adds emphasis and sadness." Finally, a student concluded, "Both people are lost, not at home in America, and lost to each other."

The class discussion dynamically progressed from text-to-self, to text-to-text, to text-to-world connections. The students moved beyond their first impressions of the work and discovered multiple layers of implied meanings. They also evaluated the work and determined that each word, phrase, and image evoked vivid and significant ideas. A deceptively simple poem presented to them a compelling vision of loss of heritage, language, and connection with one's past.

CRITICAL ANALYSIS OF LITERATURE: A CLASSROOM EXPERIENCE

Examine this more expansive model of the critical reading process that emerged during a class discussion of Theodore Roethke's "My Papa's Waltz."

THEODORE ROETHKE

MY PAPA'S WALTZ

The whiskey on your breath
Could make a small boy dizzy;
But I hung on like death:
Such waltzing was not easy.

5 We romped until the pans
Slid from the kitchen shelf;
My mother's countenance
Could not unfrown itself.

The hand that held my wrist
10 Was battered on one knuckle;
At every step you missed
My right ear scraped a buckle.

You beat time on my head
With a palm caked hard by dirt,
15 Then waltzed me off to bed
Still clinging to your shirt.

Text-to-Self Connections

The teacher asked students to record their initial responses to the poem in the form of a cluster that she put on the board:

First Impressions
Emotional Responses and Associations

Very sad
Mother is passive

Hardworking man
Does he do physical labor?

Dysfunctional family ← "My Papa's Waltz" → Sadness
Boy is abused

Anger at the father
Father is a bully

Vision of abuse?

Confusion
Is the father always drunk?

Text-to-Text Connections

Next she had students focus on key words and questions and group their observations into patterns of meaning. The students asked, for example, whether the waltz suggested a moment of closeness, albeit tainted, between father and son or a relationship between an abusive parent and child. Witness the next cluster that they formed and their list of several patterns of meaning.

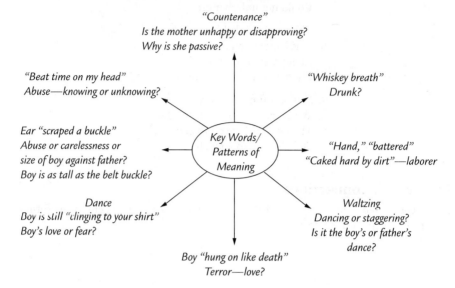

The basic facts: Drunken father, a dance between father and child
Scene: The kitchen—The dance creates a mess—pans fall down
Fun or Frenzy?

"Countenance"
Is the mother unhappy or disapproving?
Why is she passive?

"Beat time on my head"
Abuse—knowing or unknowing?

"Whiskey breath"
Drunk?

Ear "scraped a buckle"
Abuse or carelessness or
size of boy against father?
Boy is as tall as the belt buckle?

Key Words/
Patterns of
Meaning

"Hand," "battered"
"Caked hard by dirt"—laborer

Dance
Boy is still "clinging to your shirt"
Boy's love or fear?

Waltzing
Dancing or staggering?
Is it the boy's or father's
dance?

Boy "hung on like death"
Terror—love?

Patterns of Meaning/Questions and Interpretations

- Is the boy hoping that the dance will never end? (Is it a moment of closeness, or is the boy clinging to an abusive father?)
- Why is the "waltzing . . . not easy"? Is the boy struggling to hold on, afraid to let go, or is he "clinging" affectionately to a staggering father?
- Is the father too drunk to notice that he is wounding his child?
- Is the father deliberately abusing his son or is he drunk and careless, carried away by the moment of dancing? Is he happy dancing with his son?
- Is he actually "waltzing" or does the dance imply both the predictable pattern of the relationship and the father's unpredictable treatment of his child?
- Does the child predictably return to the same parent for punishment or affection?
- What is the source of the mother's anger? Is the mother frowning because her husband is creating a ruckus and keeping her son up too long? Or because he is abusive and she can't stop him? Is there a distance between mother and father?

The class in the process of analyzing the poem for meaning also noted these effective poetic techniques:

- The rhythm, rhyme, and four-line stanzas are unobtrusive and fit the waltzing motif.
- The images of the dance are powerful.
- The perspective of the child works.

Finally, the class formed interpretations of the poem. The class was divided in its analysis of the meaning of the work. Some students believed that the speaker was presenting a moment between an alcoholic father who was negligent and careless but who loved his child. This group of students thought that the poem depicts a moment of bonding between father and son, represented in the boy's "clinging" to the father's shirt as he was danced "off to bed." However, the other group of students determined that the father was abusive. They pointed to the images of cruelty in the poem: The boy's ear "scraped a buckle"; The father was "beat[ing] time on [the boy's] head" while the boy "hung on like death." Both groups examined the work carefully, dissecting word and image, constructing patterns of meaning and interpretations. "Who was right?" they asked. The teacher assured students that several interpretations of a work were valid as long as they returned to the text to test their evolving interpretation and to find evidence to support their ideas.

At this point she also suggested the possibility of turning to extra-textual materials, **(text-to-world information),** of doing biographical research, or of reading criticism of the work. Although biographical information may be misleading, it also may illuminate a writer's choices: a portrayal of a character's dilemma, a plot element, or a symbolic motif. It is important to realize, the teacher suggested, that his poem is based on Roethke's memory of a "dance" with his father, that the poet's father was a florist and owned a greenhouse (hence, "the palm caked hard by dirt"), and, therefore, that the ambiguities in the poem may reflect the ambivalent response of a son to a father and the fuzziness of memory.

As the students examined their responses to "My Papa's Waltz," they began to understand the various processes involved in critical reading. Many of the analyses and evaluations they agreed upon. Then they uncovered disagreements. Ultimately, they decided that the poem had multiple layers of meaning and that they could entertain several points of view at once as they tested their conclusions against the words on the page, the words of others in the class and critical sources. They learned that class discussion, dialogue, and research enhanced the critical reading process. Finally, in the course of discussion, they also discovered the wholeness of the process. In reading any text, we do not separate modes of feeling and thinking, but simultaneously engage in many critical acts of interpretation. We react, remember, associate, observe, infer from information, form conclusions, analyze, interpret, evaluate, and judge. These processes lead to a deepened appreciation of the phenomena and texts of our world.

· CHAPTER 2 ·

The Reading Process

READER RESPONSE

To be frank, not every reading experience becomes a full, rich, interpretation of a text. Many times we read simply to garner information, as when we survey road signs, food labels, or sets of instructions. We may read newspapers, letters, and textbooks in our college classes; and the main aim may be solely to summarize information. At other times, we may wish to read a book on a level approaching pure emotional response and appreciation. Often, while we read, our minds are wandering, not concentrating on the work. However, the process of critical reading that we wish to emphasize is one in which the reader is fully involved, responding on many levels of feeling and thinking. We do not simply scan words on a page; we form emotional reactions, gather information, construct patterns of meaning, analyze, interpret, and evaluate a work to determine its effectiveness and its worth.

THE READING/WRITING CONNECTION

Writing helps develop the reading process, keeping it active and critical. Writing also inspires fuller text-to-self, text-to-text, and text-to-world connections. The following are some procedures for reading and reacting to a text, called *reader response strategies,* all of which involve writing. These procedures include *glossing* and *annotating, brainstorming* and *questioning, freewriting, journal writing, notetaking, "think" writings,* and *creative responses to literature.*

Glossing and Annotating

Examine a series of reader responses written by students about Gloria Anzaldúa's poem, "horse," from her autobiography, *Borderlands: La Frontera—The New Mestiza.* You may react to this poem in many ways. Reading theorists suggest that you first preview the work by looking at the title and by scanning the poem to gain an overview of it. Then read the passage again to learn content and to write notes about your reactions to the text. This process is called *glossing* and *annotating.* When you gloss a work, you read it to understand content; and you take notes, called *annotations,* as you read. You may make comments in the margins, underline the title and key words, and record reactions or questions. You create a map of the reading so that you know its structure and key points. You also discover your own questions, reactions, and initial responses. After you have completed your marginal annotations, you might make *end comments* that include the key ideas and describe the impact of the work on you. Analyze this annotation and end comment for "horse":

horse
(para la gente de Hargill, Texas[1])

Why the title?
Why small letters?

Is this a true story? What does the dedication mean?

Horse is free, powerful.

Great horse running in the fields
come thundering toward
the outstretched hands
nostrils flaring at the corn

Look at ing verbs: power-action

5 only it was knives in the hidden hands
can a horse smell tempered steel?

*Shift to death and destruction

Anoche[2] some kids cut up a horse
it was night and the pueblo[3] slept
the Mexicans mutter among themselves:

Contrast Spanish words vs. anglos Spanish gringo

Key: hobbled crippled horse

10 they hobbled the two front legs
the two hind legs, kids aged sixteen
but they're gringos
and the sheriff won't do a thing
he'd just say boys will be boys

Mexican World Narrative form Build up of story

15 just following their instincts.

Horse— Soul of people

But it's the mind that kills
the animal the mexicanos murmur
killing it would have been a mercy
black horse running in the dark

Horse— symbol of Mexican identity

20 came thundering toward
the outstretched hands
nostrils flaring at the smell
only it was knives in the hidden hands
did it pray all night for morning?

Repetition— Contrast Power of horse vs. crippling

Mexican people?

25 It was the owner came running
30.30 in his hand
put the caballo[4] out of its pain
the Chicanos shake their heads
turn away some rich father

A Mexican must put horse out of pain. Mexican people go home to die.

30 fished out his wallet
held out the folds of green

Strong images of blood. Graphic. Is the horse castrated?

as if green could staunch red
pools dripping from the ribbons
on the horse's flanks

Boys "get off." Money is power.

35 could cast up testicles
grow back the ears on the horse's head

---

[1] **para la gente de Hargill, Texas:** for the people of Hargill, Texas.

[2] **Anoche:** last night

[3] **pueblo:** town or village.

[4] **caballo:** horse.

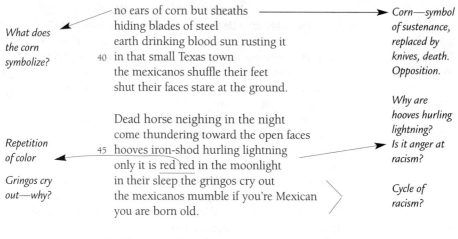

What does the corn symbolize?

no ears of corn but sheaths
hiding blades of steel
earth drinking blood sun rusting it
40 in that small Texas town
the mexicanos shuffle their feet
shut their faces stare at the ground.

Corn—symbol of sustenance, replaced by knives, death. Opposition.

Repetition of color

Gringos cry out—why?

Dead horse neighing in the night
come thundering toward the open faces
45 hooves iron-shod hurling lightning
only it is red red in the moonlight
in their sleep the gringos cry out
the mexicanos mumble if you're Mexican
you are born old.

Why are hooves hurling lightning? Is it anger at racism?

Cycle of racism?

End Comment: Does this poem use a true story of boys crippling and mutilating a horse to suggest the pain and suffering of Mexicans in Texas facing prejudice and racism?

Brainstorming and Questioning

Another notetaking process is *brainstorming*, a process in which you write down ideas and comments in any order without attention to sequence, logic, or sentence structure. Register as many of your reactions as you can as your mind "storms" through a work. Jot single words or phrases without worrying about creating coherent, grammatical sentences and without worrying about organization and development. This technique allows you to sketch the range of your responses; later you can select certain ideas to compose your essay. One focused form of brainstorming is generating a list of questions concerning the work. You may use the reporter's questions (Who? What? When? Where? Why? How?) to trigger your explorations. Examine Mark Greenberg's brainstorming exercise for "horse":

> *Who is the "great horse"? Symbol?*
> *Who is the speaker?*
> *Who has the knives?*
> *Why are they hidden?*
> *Why did they do it?*
> *The sheriff is hateful.*
> *How can he use such lame excuses—"boys will be boys?" I'm a man, and I would never participate in such a terrible act.*
> *Why does the father cover for the son? My dad would kill me.*
> *The dead horse can thunder, can hurl lightning?*
> *Is this the poet's retelling of the story? Autobiographical?*
> *The horse, in many images, has many meanings.*
> *Social tensions—inequalities between gringos and Mexicans.*
> *Finally something about race relations.*
> *A true story?*

In his exercise, Greenberg's questions focus on the events of the poem, on the cruelty, and on his reactions to the sheriff who excuses and to the father who covers for the barbaric actions of the "boys." His responses direct Greenberg to the beginning of an interpretation: a poem about "inequalities between gringos and Mexicans" and "race relations."

Freewriting

Another method to express your responses, reactions, questions, associations, and analysis of the work is to freewrite immediately after you finish reading. *Freewriting* is a process in which you give yourself a certain amount of time, say, five minutes, to compose sentences without stopping and without censoring your thoughts. Write without stopping, without worrying, and without rereading—just keep going. Do not worry about grammar, spelling, punctuation, or meaning. Freewriting is a way to unleash ideas, to discover your own responses and ideas. It is a way to bypass the part of the writer's self who is the editor and critic, that part of the self that blocks and censors the process of discovery. Often it is helpful not only to freewrite immediately after a first reading, but also to freewrite after several readings. You can compose a first sample, then isolate one idea from that work, and draft another version based on that idea. This second activity is called *focused freewriting*. You may create a series of freewritings that prompt you to discover your full reactions and to develop your thoughts into an essay.

Here are two examples of freewriting about "horse":

horse
Frances Gonzalez

The poem presents a powerful set of contrasts between the soul of the Mexican people and what happens to people when there is racism. The horse is powerful, black, free. The "thundering" gives a feeling of strength and force. Then the horse is "hobbled"; racism cripples. The black horse "running" "thundering" is contrasted with the impotence of, the powerlessness of the Mexicans who "mumble" "shake their heads" "shuffle" "stare at the ground" and "mumble." They seem weak, yet there is some hope. For the "dead horse" in the night "comes thundering" "hurling lightning"—that "lightning" is "red red." Does that mean that the Mexicans will rebel against injustice—that eventually justice will be done? Is the poet "hurling lightning" hoping to cry out—hoping her words will be heard that people will learn and speak "from the mind" in a different way? Not a way that kills?

horse
Julie Miller

I love the feeling of freedom at the beginning of the poem. There are such powerful images of the horse—running, "thundering"—"nostrils flaring." The horse is powerful and alive— then I knew danger was coming in the image of the knives. Why did the boys cut up the horse? Why would anyone do anything that senseless? I thought that it was so brutal and cruel that the horse was mutilated. It was hard to read. What did the horse symbolize? Did it symbolize the Mexicans? The "gringos" just think nothing of cutting up the horse. In the same way the white world in Texas is stopping Mexicans from having opportunities. The poem is asking people to feel the way the Mexicans are treated unfairly. The way they are being oppressed. The white world wins—The "rich father" pays off the owner. The boys aren't punished. The gringos have power. I understand the lines "if you're Mexican/you are born old." You are born with the knowledge of prejudice. This poem makes a powerful plea for understanding injustice.

Journal Writing

You may chart your reading responses by keeping a journal: an informal record of your thoughts and impressions. Your instructor already may have asked you to write a personal journal. A *reader response journal* provides an opportunity for you to write informally about the works that you read and encourages an expansion of the process of personal writing. The methods previously discussed are appropriate for a reader response journal in which you may include glosses and annotations (if you include the works), brainstorming notes and questions, freewrites, and responses to texts. In your reader response journal, you may write significant ideas and quotations. You may focus on any one of the following subjects:

Explication, analyses (explanations of the works)

Personal response (feelings-reactions to the works)

Likes/dislikes

Associations with other characters, other works, other readings, themes, issues, current events, materials in other classes

Associations with events in your life

Responses to characters

Responses to key events

Responses to key passages or to quotations

Responses to issues presented (social, political)

Judgments of characters

Arguments with the writer, with key ideas, with characters' views

Arguments with positions presented in class discussion

Creative writing (stories, poems, plays)

Imitations of style

Monologues in the voices of characters

Again, as in freewriting, you need not worry about grammar, punctuation, spelling, or logical presentation of subject matter. Follow your own responses, ideas, and questions; and let them take over. A journal entry, however, may be more developed and more structured than a freewrite. You may be asked to revise your reactions as developed paragraphs. Your journal may become the source of ideas for essays. In your journal, you may have a record not only of your reading responses, but also of your emotional and intellectual development.

In this entry about "horse," Mark Greenberg summarizes information, reacts to descriptive language, begins to respond to details in the poem, and ends with his feelings about the message of the work.

horse

The black horse "thundered" toward the boys because they beckoned it. How could they summon a "great horse," the Mexican, only to cut it to pieces with knives, knives hidden in their hands? They tortured the animal because they believed that they had a right to do so. The "red red" blood, the flaying, excited them. They expected their fathers to pay for their cruelty and the owner of the horse to kill it—to finish their game. They exercised rights which they believed came with the color of their skin, with their social and economic positions. Little did they know that the dark horse would invade their dreams and make them "cry out," the dead horse—"red red"—"hurling lightning" through their dreams forever.

Notetaking and the Double-Entry Notebook

Another method of becoming an active reader is to keep a *double-entry notebook,* a form of notetaking adapted from theorist Ann Berthoff, who contends that writing and reading processes involve us in continually "interpreting our interpretations." Berthoff suggests that readers sometimes recognize only one level of reaction to a text—summary of main information—and neglect other levels of thinking provoked by the words: reactions, associations, questionings, analysis, synthesis, and theorizing. The double-entry notebook, or *dialectical notebook* as Berthoff calls it, prompts readers to be aware of all acts of interpretation and creates what Berthoff calls "the continuing audit of meaning." The journal entries provide readers with records of what they think about their own thinking.

For a double-entry notebook, we recommend that you write on the left-hand page of a notebook the facts, key points, and main information from a work. On the right-hand page, write all of your other responses, feelings, associations, questions, comparisons with other ideas, and interpretations. The notes need to be recorded as the reading takes place so that you capture your mind in action. Alternate from the left-hand page to the right-hand page. Keep writing back and forth from fact to reaction, analysis, questions, and comments. The double-entry notebook results in a more complex and complete response to a work. You are, therefore, much better prepared to write an essay about the text.

Examine the beginning and the conclusion of Mark Greenberg's double-entry notebook concerning "horse":

horse
Gloria Anzaldúa

Title "horse"	Symbolic. Why no caps?
para la gente de Hargill	I don't know Spanish, but I can guess that the words mean—"For the people of Hargill." Why does she dedicate the poem? Is it a true story?

Great horse
  running
  thundering
  nostrils flaring
	The horse is powerful, beautiful, expectant. Progressives add power and action. Good parallel constructions.

Knives in hidden hands	Why offer corn and hide knives? Who?
Question about smelling steel	Rhetorical? Good sounds. Does steel have a smell?
"Anoche"	"Night"? "Last night"? "The night before"? "At night"?
The Mexicans slept, and boys cut up a horse	The straight story. Incredible cruelty. A narrative poem.
The Mexicans "mutter"	They cannot protest aloud.
The "gringos" hobbled the legs	How did they conceive of such cruelty? The horse is like the Mexicans—hobbled.
Sheriff "boys will be boys" following instincts	The law does not apply to gringos. What is wrong with us? This racism is blatant.
It's the mind that kills the animal	This statement is like a thesis sentence. It clearly emphasizes the situation of the Mexicans.
Mexicans "murmur"	Again, they cannot speak loudly.
Killing would have been mercy	These boys feel no sadness, have no mercy. The suffering seems unbearable. The writer must want me to feel this pain.

Repetition of images and event
  black horse thundering
  outstretched hands
  flaring nostrils
  corn—knives

Now that I know about the knives, the repetition is incredibly effective. The horse represents everything and everyone who was ever destroyed by promises of kindness and who was nurtured only to be conquered, tortured, or killed. This poem is difficult to read, to face, and to accept. The horse symbolizes the Mexicans.

Dead horse neighing in night
  thundering hooves
  "iron-shod"
  hurling lightning
"red red in moonlight"

Paradox—unravels in dreams Retribution for the knives.

The horse has turned red, transformation. Blood, anger, revenge?

"gringos" "cry out"

The horse enters their dreams; they are not absolved; they have not triumphed. They have received a life sentence of nightmares.

The Mexicanos "mumble" "If you're Mexican/you are born old."

They do not speak. They are not empowered by the horse which hurls lightning. They are born old in a corrupt and oppressive environment. I want racism to disappear. I want a world which includes everyone. I want it now.

Note the writer's questions, analysis of the portrait and the symbolism of the horse, and inferences about the knife and the central action of the poem. Notice also the judgments about the boys' behavior and about the effectiveness of the verbs and images. The double-entry exercise prompted the writer to engage in all aspects of critical thinking and analysis.

"Think" Writings

Your instructor may assign as homework informal paragraphs or mini-essays with designated topics or questions that relate to the readings. Some instructors prefer not to incorporate freewriting or journals in a course because they think that these forms of writing are too subjective and unstructured and will not necessarily provoke in-depth analysis of works. They concentrate, instead, on more objective and formal modes of response to the assigned works. These "think" writings, however, like the more personal forms of reaction, prompt you to explore your responses to a literary work, direct your thinking, prepare you for participating in class discussion and for writing the essay about literature, and stimulate analysis and reflection. The questions may focus on a particular issue or theme of the work or a specific literary technique (for example, the symbolism in "horse"). Your instructor may collect these writings on a weekly or monthly basis or may ask you to select several of them as part of a writing portfolio. In addition, your instructor may ask you to frame these "think" questions yourself, to become a class discussion leader, and to present these topics as the opening to class discussion or as the basis of collaborative work. Finally, your instructor may ask you to participate in an online discussion group and to respond to "think" questions as part of your work in the course. (See chapter 7 for an example of an online exercise in response to "horse.")

Possibilities for "think" writing topics include the following:

First and final impressions of a work

In-depth analysis of a key passage

Treatment of a literary technique

Selection and response to a quotation

Focus on a particular theme

Debate with a position suggested by a reading

Letter to an author or to a character

Note Esther Martinez's short paragraph written in response to this "think" question: "What does the poem suggest about the American dream?" Note how she connects the horse with the identity of Mexican Americans and then compares the mutilation of the horse with the destruction of the American dream for Mexican Americans.

> *This is a poem about racism. Whites against Mexicans. There are a lot of ways that the poet shows the "inferiority" of the Mexicans. "horse" is not capitalized. Although the horse is a powerful, passionate animal, "thundering," "nostrils flaring," the horse is treated as inferior. The description of the kids hacking away at the horse symbolizes the Mexicans being beaten down, harassed. The castration symbolizes the Mexicans' shame. Their culture, way of life, traditions are seen as less special, their lifestyle as inferior. Is it wrong just because gringos say it's wrong? Are they not entitled to opportunity? What happens to their dreams for themselves, for their lives?*

Creative Responses to Literature

Another way to write about a work is to respond imaginatively through creative writing exercises. Imaginative writing gives you a different perspective on a work. Some possible approaches include the following:

- Write a letter to a character.
- Write a prequel or a sequel to a story.
- Add a scene to a drama.
- Turn a scene from a short story or drama into a film script.
- Cast the characters in a work as if you were directing a film. Explain your choices.
- Compose another stanza to a poem.
- Create a parody or imitation of a poem.
- Create a response to a poem using a different voice.
- Create a dialogue between characters from different works.
- Create a talk show featuring characters from different works.
- Change the genre of a work—for example, turn a realistic story into a horror story.
- Add another character to a work, and tell the story from his or her perspective.
- Change the point of view of a work—for example, if it is told in first person, shift to third person.
- Change the narrative perspective—for example, tell the story from the point of view of a minor character in the text.

- Create a poem or work of art in response to a text.
- Create a book cover, portrait of a character, or scene from a work.
- Create a new rhetorical situation for information in the text, such as a newspaper account, biography or obituary for a character, eyewitness report, or psychological case study.
- Create a poem or short story in response to a work, and then evaluate your text, suggesting how it reveals your responses to the work and/or specific themes of the work.

What follows is a creative response to "horse," a last stanza to the poem written by Emily Kate Hertzberg:

memory like explosives in a feather pillow
hundreds of missing lines
horrible mouths torn from old
they melted the horse from their minds
like photographs taken by dead people with cameras without film
black out-of-tune notes playing a death dirge on a violin strung with barbwire
at a loss for a reason
surrounded by danger and uncertainty
hallucinating that the horse still rode in the night
breaking the mirror of silence
badly beaten by invisible things
water boiling underground
remember to remember
time to turn somebody in
it's now and never
never seen or heard from again

Critical analysis requires your active involvement in the process. These forms of reader response—glossing and annotating, brainstorming and questioning, freewriting, journal writing, keeping a double-entry notebook, "think" writings, and creative responses—will help you become a more involved reader and lead to richer, fuller, more complex interpretations and judgments of literary works.

SOME FINAL CONSIDERATIONS ABOUT THE READING PROCESS

These methods of reader response enable us to discover ideas and to unpeel the layers of our reactions to a work. They also validate our approaches to literature. They remind us that the reading process is both objective and subjective—objective, because we interpret verifiable texts; subjective, because we are unique in our reactions to those texts. We create meanings as a result of our own perspectives, gender, ethnic and class backgrounds, cultural contexts, personalities, and values. Reading is an interactive process. The writer, who has a particular perspective, personality, and background and who is part of a particular culture at a specific time in history, creates a work and invests it with a set of meanings. The reader, who, likewise, is a product of individual traits and cultural influences at a particular point in history, brings ideas and values to the work and derives meaning from the work. The text acts on the reader; the reader creates a particular version (interpretation) of the text.

Certain aspects of literature, however, may be more widely comprehended. *Hamlet's famous soliloquy* generally may be understood as an exploration of questions concerning suicide. "Do Not Go Gentle into That Good Night" by Dylan Thomas generally will be considered a meditation on mortality. Yet each period's writers, each culture's writers, reinterpret these objective judgments, guided by emotional, personal, and social concerns. Each literary work, then, represents both a moment in history and in culture and a moment in an individual reader's and writer's life.

Would Harriet Beecher Stowe have written her antislavery novel, *Uncle Tom's Cabin,* if she had not been the daughter of an abolitionist minister, if she had not been driven by moral outrage and financial need, if she had not known the patterns of slave narratives, if she had not herself seen a place where runaway slaves had crossed the Ohio River to freedom? In each century, readers interpret Stowe's fiction differently. During her lifetime, readers in New England were moved by her novel to struggle to abolish slavery; her book was a bestseller. However, some present readers criticize her sentimentality and her depiction of the black slave.

Interpretations will vary, but some analyses of a work seem more valid than others. To justify our interpretations, we return continually to the work as the primary source, and we share our views with others in a community of readers in order to discuss and to compare ideas. In dialogue with others, we may critique; and we may change our ideas and impressions. We may agree with an interpretation that differs from our original conclusion. We can enlarge our understanding of a work as we engage in the cyclic activities required by thinking, reading, and writing. Through these processes, which are *recursive,* to which we continuously return, we develop new perspectives on a work. For example, we may reread "Refugee Ship" and suddenly decide to study the poem from the point of view of the grandmother who cannot understand her granddaughter. The "glasses," the "bible," and the "pudding" assume new connotations as we shift attention from the speaker to the situation of another character in the work. In the process, we recognize that critical reading activities lead to a more comprehensive understanding of literature.

· CHAPTER 3 ·

The Writing Process: Writing the Essay about Literature

When you approach the task of writing about literature, you may worry that you will not understand the text, that you will miss its secrets, and that you will not give the responses the instructor expects. You might believe that you have nothing to say. Such anxieties are natural—and groundless. Keep in mind that writing essays about literature evolves from the processes of critical thinking and reader response described in chapters 1 and 2. These multifaceted activities provide no right or wrong answers.

You will not be asked to write papers that pose correct answers, although you will be expected to provide thoughtful interpretations supported by careful reading of a work. As you learn to trust your own thinking, you also will learn to trust your own acts of interpretation. Remember that you have valuable insights to contribute and that you will have opportunities to question, to test ideas with your peers and instructor, and to construct more developed interpretations that confirm, deny, or expand your initial views of a work.

INTERRELATED STAGES OF WRITING

Writing essays about literature follows directly from procedures for reader response. You should realize, however, that an essay is not composed in a short burst of reader reaction or in moments of brilliant creative insights. Rather, the best essays result from many, many hours of thinking; and they take shape on paper in interrelated stages that include the following:

1. **Prewriting:** Discovering and planning ideas for writing.
2. **Shaping:** Organizing, outlining, and structuring ideas with an audience in mind.
3. **Drafting:** Composing and concentrating on organization, development, and fluency.
4. **Revising and Editing:** Sharpening wording, sentence structure, and style; rearranging, deleting, and clarifying; checking for sentence variety and correct usage.
5. **Proofreading:** Correcting grammar, spelling, and punctuation.

These stages do not always occur in this sequential order; they vary from person to person and from writing task to writing task. Some people draft, edit, and proofread as they work. Others quickly write a first draft and check spelling, grammar, and punctuation later. Different writing situations dictate different processes: a laboratory report, a meditative essay, a journal, and a research paper all require distinct approaches to writing. Whatever your task, you will probably engage in many of these activities before you submit the final version of your essay. Consider each of these stages in detail.

Prewriting

Prewriting, the first stage of the process, takes place even before beginning a first draft and involves finding ideas for composing. As you prewrite, you discover subject matter, approach, and **point of view** (attitude toward the subject matter). Various prewriting strategies include these techniques—annotating, brainstorming, taking notes, listing, freewriting, clustering, mapping, journal writing, and talking with others. You also will select the form of your essay: think about the requirements of your assignment (page length and designated rhetorical mode—exposition, argument, research—for example). Then consider the purpose of your assignment, your main goal in writing. Some central purposes for writing are the following: to express yourself, to inform, to argue, or to create a literary work. You will begin to define your audience. In writing about literary subjects, you may assume that your audience is your instructor and your classmates—people who are familiar with the works that you discuss. Your instructor may designate such different audiences for your material as the campus newspaper or some group interested in the subject. Considerations of point of view, purpose, and audience constitute the **rhetorical situation** of a writing.

Shaping

The second stage of the writing process involves clear definition of focus, point of view, tone, tentative **thesis** (main idea), and topics for discussion. In terms of point of view and tone, you need to decide how you want your essay to sound to the reader. Will you write formally or informally? Will you sound sympathetic, involved, or angry? Will you be lyrical, meditative, or persuasive? These decisions fall into place as you determine your thesis, topics, method of organization, and relationship to audience. At this point, you assess your audience, determine the direction of thesis and topics, and develop and shape supporting evidence with your audience in mind. Then you map ideas, plan your writing, and create informal or formal outlines.

Drafting

The third stage of the writing process is drafting. In creating versions of essays, you still consider not only purpose, requirements of the assignment, and audience, but also development and organization. You may recast your thesis, alter points, delete and add supporting information (quotations, facts, and specific paraphrased examples from the text), and sharpen language.

Revising and Editing

The fourth stage of the writing process involves revising and editing your essay. Consider your relationship with your audience, and ask yourself if you have organized and developed points with a particular audience in mind. Ask yourself if your tone and point of view are appropriate, if they are likely to interest your readers, and if they are convincing and strong. Examine your introduction to determine if it will capture your readers' attention and establish your purpose and thesis. Determine whether you have sufficiently developed your thesis and supporting points. Evaluate your conclusion and decide if it conveys the proper emphasis. Rewriting sometimes requires reviewing ideas and clarifying points—perhaps, even rethinking the entire piece—but it also involves fine tuning through editing, through changes in word choice, and through small alterations of order and structure.

Proofreading

Proofreading is the final stage of the writing process. Check your final draft for grammatical, punctuation, spelling, and typographical errors. For example, if you have trouble with sentence fragments, review sentence structure. If you tend to confuse "it's" and "its," reread your paper with this problem in mind. Examine the manuscript to ensure that it still follows the original requirements of the assignment.

Composing on a Computer

Many students compose directly on a computer. After jotting down some preliminary notes, they may draft immediately on the computer and embed the processes of prewriting, shaping, drafting, revising, and editing. If you work in this manner, here are some useful strategies to consider:

- Create a file folder; then enter and save prewriting (e.g., brainstorming, notes, and outlines). You may want to refer to this work later on in the process.
- Archive versions of your essay. Again, you don't want to lose important information that may not be contained in your final draft. You may want to refer to it later.
- If you work from a single paragraph, exploratory draft and then use your cut-and-paste function to block out separate introductory, body, and concluding paragraphs, make sure these paragraphs and sentences within a paragraph proceed logically from point to point. Check the progression of ideas. As you rearrange and delete text, you should make sure your ideas still cohere. Check your transitional expressions; add transition words or sentences as necessary to create a fluid essay.
- As you expand and develop ideas, take the time to return to the text for further evidence. Note significant facts, quotes, and specifics in the margins of a draft. Then revise. It is difficult to draft and to find supporting evidence at the same time. (See Esther Martinez's work in chapter 3.)
- Leave time to evaluate a version of your essay. Print out a penultimate copy for review. It is crucial to see your work as a whole in order to assess it.
- And, of course, use your spell check and proofread thoroughly.
- Always save your work on disk.

Summary

There are as many composing processes as there are students and writing situations. You need to work through the process in *your* own way; however, the omission of stages of composing can lead to weaknesses in your final draft. For example, if you do not spend enough time planning your writing, your essay may be disorganized and unconvincing. If you do not spend enough time prewriting and exploring ideas, you may submit a final draft that is lifeless and undeveloped. If you do not spend enough time editing and proofreading, you may create a work so riddled with distracting grammatical errors and spelling mistakes that your essay will fail to convince your readers of the merit of your ideas. Each stage of the writing process is necessary to the development of a strong essay.

THE WRITING PROCESS: AN EXAMPLE

As an exercise in reading, responding, and writing, assume that your instructor has asked you to create a short essay, a literary analysis of a poem, building on one of your "think" writings. Esther Martinez chose to expand her treatment of "horse," concentrating on such specific literary techniques as symbolism, diction, and imagery.

Esther began her paper by doing the assigned "think" writing (presented in chapter 2). She next jotted down some notes and observations and created a thesis and a mini-outline.

Notes on "horse"

What are the words for literary essays? Diction, word choice, irony, imagery.

Diction: Repetition

"Great horse"

"Thundering"

"Mexicans mutter"

Thesis: Through diction, repetition, imagery, the author clearly portrays the injustice experienced by Mexican Americans.

Diction

Repetition

Imagery

Symbolism

Additional Notes:

Tone changes from awe to disgust and frenzy

There is tension, craziness

Money is power

White man rules

Instead of killing the horse—they watch it suffer in a pool of blood

Description of kids works. Testicles—shame

Title—'horse'—lowercase

After jotting down these notes and developing a thesis, she wrote a short exploratory draft and noted details that she wanted to include. In her second draft, she more systematically focused on symbolism, diction, and imagery. Following her instructor's suggestions, she treated each technique in a separate paragraph and she developed the symbolism of the horse and compared it with the state of the Mexican Americans. In her third draft she more clearly organized and developed the essay, devoting a paragraph to each literary technique, and she included an historical reference that places the boys' actions within a particular historical context. This context explains and deepens the symbolic motif in the poem. The boys' actions not only represent the aberrant, violent, and racist behavior of adolescents, but they also mirror the prejudice directed at Mexican Americans and experienced by those who have been on the margins in this country from its inception. Perhaps what is most significant is that Esther's involvement with the work began with her own connection to her Mexican American heritage. Notice how her passion fuels her analysis, yet she retains the capacity to "stand back" and objectively analyze the work. What emerges is a complex and thoughtful treatment of a powerful poem.

Esther Martinez's First Exploratory Draft and Notes (Written at Home)

In the poem entitled, "horse" by Gloria Anzaldúa, the poet describes a symbolic situation of teenage boys killing a horse and the consequences of their action.

imagery
Through the title, syntax, diction, and immagry and
symbolism   *poet*
foreshadowing the peot makes a statement about the power of money and the white man by showing the injustice shown to Mexicans.

Action   Through diction, the Mexican people are characterized along with their suffering. The "great horse" gallops and "some kids" follow as "Mexicans mutter among
(knowing)
themselves" in anticipation and knowing. This powerful horse racing through the field symbolizes the Mexican people and their culture. Great care is taken in describing the power of the horse as it races through the field symbolizing the Mexican people and their culture. On the other hand, the white teens are simply "some kids" showing the Mexican people are threatened and at-
because
tacked mentally and physically by the—it doesn't matter who killed the horse and their identity won't matter because whites don't get in trouble for lashing out at Mexicans. The Mexicans are aware of what is going on, but are unable to stop what is happening. The tension of the poem mounts . . . "Hidden hands" await the horse that "cast up testicles." The hidden hands
connote   *Imagery*
conotate the . . . ? Immagery creates a powerful pic-
helplessness of the
ture of the oppressed Mexican people and their reaction to the situation. The "mexicanos murmur" and "shuffle their feet" as their "faces stare at the ground." The image created shows the inferiority felt by the Mexicans who shuffle their feet in nervous anticipation and a desire to lash out at their oppres-
allowed
sor. However, they aren't alowed to speak out or act, so in shame and helplessness they listen, wait, watch,

The poem can be related to all races

tempered steel— unbreakable, unbendable, powerful, strong

whisper
wisper. The "folds of green" cover the stain of the
"earth drinking blood."

　　Symbolism is used throughout the poem to help show
the brutality of racism.

- boys pretending to feed horse

- weapon hidden in corn

- money

- can money replace/make all injury to Mexicans
  in the U.S. go away?

Second Draft
(Turned in to Instructor)

In the poem "horse" by Gloria Anzaldúa, the poet describes a symbolic situation of teenage boys killing a
horse and the consequences of their action. Through symbolism, diction and imagery the poet makes a statement
about the power of money and the white man by demonstrating the injustice shown to Mexicans.

Excellent opening

Commas

Excellent thesis

Solid topics

Symbolism is used throughout the poem to help show
the brutality of racism. In the poem a "horse [runs]" toward open palms holding tempting "ears of corn," not
knowing there is "tempered steel" hidden within. The situation symbolizes the characteristic injustice of whites
that in past history have been known to befriend a foe
and gain trust in order to defeat "the enemy." This tactic was used when the whites coaxed the Indians out of
hiding by declaring peace and giving them land to live
on. When the Native Americans settled, the Europeans
slaughtered the people, burnt the village, and destroyed
the corn. The tempered steel symbolizes, not only the
weapons used to mutilate the horse, but also the
Americans who are powerful, cold, and unjust.

Could you give more pointed historical information?

Vague—too general

You could expand with historical references and explanations.

Diction and imagery create a powerful picture of the
oppressed Mexican people and their reaction to the situation in the poem. "Folds of green" sneak out of a father's wallet, money that is to correct the injustice
performed on the "great horse" that "some kids" mutilated. Much care is taken in describing the "great horse"
as it races through the field. There is a passion and
power behind it's "thundering" gallop, "flaring" "nostrils" and "iron-shod" hooves. The white teens, however,
are simply described as "some kids" — showing that the
identity of the whites doesn't and won't matter, because
whites don't get in trouble for racism. Money is used to
resolve the situation, however, money isn't capable
of wiping away the pain, suffering, shame felt by the

Divide into two para-graphs—separate topics

its
it's = it is

Excellent discussion of imagery of the horse

Good use of particular details from text

Excellent analysis of wording

Careful, no comma!

comma splice

Solid focus on verbs to describe Mexicanos

victims. The "*mexicanos* murmur" and "shuffle their feet" and "their faces stare at the ground." The images created show the inferiority felt by the Mexicans who desire to defend their lifestyle and culture. However, they aren't allowed to speak out or act, so in shame and helplessness they listen, wait, watch, whisper.

Excellent interpretation and portrayal of the Mexicanos

solid parallelism in wording

Careful, format for including lines of poetry; use slash between lines

Excellent point

"If you're Mexican you are born old," the poem concludes. From birth, Mexicans must struggle for their lives—not only against the injustice of racism, but also
against poverty. Their childhood is snatched away as quickly as it's given. The poem "horse" can be related
       or   with a particular
to any race people ~~or~~ lifestyle suffering from persecution. The title itself—in all lowercase letters—signifies a people looked at as inferior.

Focus on closing image. How can the image of the "dead horse" contrast with the image of Mexicanos who are born old? Expand analysis of closing. Is this an emphatic closing sentence?

INSTRUCTOR'S COMMENTS

I am impressed with your process of revision. You revise beautifully—what a difference between your initial "think" writing and drafts. This essay has a solid thesis, is well-organized, well-developed, and persuasive. Work on the concluding images in the poem and your conclusion.

QUESTION

How does the image of the "dead horse" contrast with the image of Mexicanos who are "born old"? Develop your conclusion further.

Final Draft

Add comma

In the poem "horse" by Gloria Anzaldúa the poet describes a symbolic situation of teenage boys' killing a horse and the consequences of their action. Through symbolism, diction and imagery the poet makes a statement about the power of money and the white man by demonstrating the injustice shown to Mexicans.

Careful, add commas!

Solid thesis

Symbolism is used throughout the poem to help show the brutality of racism. In the poem, a "horse [runs]" toward open palms holding tempting ears of "corn," not knowing there is "tempered steel" hidden within. The situation symbolizes the characteristic injustice of whites that in past history have been known to befriend a foe and gain trust in order to defeat "the enemy." This tactic was used when the whites coaxed the Indians out of hiding by declaring peace and giving them land to live on. When the Native Americans settled, the Europeans slaughtered the people, burnt the village, and destroyed the corn. In *American Slavery, American Freedom* Edmund Morgan wrote:

Excellent use of historical reference

Again add comma

> Since the Indians were better woodsmen than the English and virtually impossible to track down, the method was to feign peaceful intentions, let them settle down and plant their corn wherever they chose, and then just before harvest, fall upon them, killing as many as possible and burning the corn.
>
> (Zinn 13)

Excellent inclusion of a quote

The tempered steel symbolizes not only the weapons used to mutilate the horse, but also the Americans who are powerful, cold, and unjust.

Diction is used to reveal the arrogance of the whites, and the cruelty shown to the Mexicans. The father "[fishes] out his wallet" intending to correct the injustice performed on the "great horse" that "some

the spirit of the Mexicans,

Again, add —comma

kids" mutilated. Much care is taken in describing the "great horse" as it races through the field. There is a passion and power behind it's "thundering" gallop, "flaring" nostrils, and "iron-shod" hooves. The white ~~teens, however,~~ adolescents are simply described as "some kids"—showing that the identity of the whites doesn't and won't matter, because whites don't get punished for racism. The father lightly and carelessly pulls out his wallet —confident that money will resolve the situation. Money, however, isn't capable of wiping away the pain, suffering, and shame felt by the victims.

Transition needed.

However, that power doesn't protect the Mexicans. The teens have the power to destroy.

its again!

No comma

Through imagery, a powerful picture is painted of the reactions of both the perpetrators and the oppressed Mexican people. The neighing horse hurtles toward the "open faces" of the sleeping gringos who "cry out" in desperation. The reader can clearly see the white boys waking up night after night—faces pale and clammy with perspiration, mouths open in shock and terror after having yet another nightmare. The whites are forever haunted by the images and brutality of their actions —an inadequate penance. With the *mexicanos* in lowercase and italicized, the reader feels compelled to whisper the phrase, and, in turn, to experience the same anxiety, tension, and anticipation felt by the tormented people. The image created also shows the inferiority felt by the Mexicans who desire to defend their lifestyle and culture. However, they aren't allowed to speak out or act, so in shame and helplessness they listen, wait, watch, whisper.

Excellent expanded treatment

Because "mexicanos" is written in

wording needs to be clearer

comma again

"If you're Mexican/you are born old," the poem concludes. From birth, Mexicans must struggle for their lives—not only against the injustice of racism, but also against poverty. ↓Their childhood is snatched away as quickly as it's given. The phrase "dead horse *, however,* neighing in the night"—shows that although the

Change the order of sentences for greater emphasis in conclusion

```
Mexicans' voices are stifled, they will not give up in
their struggle for equality and justice. The poem
"horse" can be related to any race, people, or
lifestyle suffering from persecution. [The title it-
self—in all lowercase letters —signifies a people
viewed as inferior.]
```

*Again—
re-order
closing
sentences*

Work Cited

Zinn, Howard. *A People's History of the United States: 1492–Present.* New York: Harper Perennial, 1995.

INSTRUCTOR'S COMMENTS

A wonderful essay, Esther. You analyze the themes of the poem beautifully. Excellent added treatment of the imagery.
Work on:

- *Transitions*
- *Progression of thought from sentence to sentence*
- *Commas*

STUDENT'S COMMENTS

I chose to analyze the poem "horse" because I was able to relate to the message. I felt anger and frustration as I read the poem and wanted to expose the truth of the poem. My family is Hispanic and has suffered because of racism and oppression, and because of the personal experience, I thought, with my emotions raging, I would be able to write an effective paper. I was also able to relate to the past suffering the Native Americans experienced. It was remarkable and horrifying to see the hatred and cruelty that hasn't died in America, but, instead, is thriving.

Peer Evaluation

Be aware that you may exchange early drafts of your essays with a peer for feedback if your instructor so desires, or your instructor may read and comment on drafts of your writing. Three levels of peer critique are helpful:

1. *Provide Initial Reaction.* A peer may give you an initial emotional response and react to specific sections of the work in terms of his or her feelings and thoughts about the work.
2. *Indicate Organizational Strengths and Weaknesses.* A peer reader can outline the work—pinpointing thesis, key points, and details—to check the progression and development of the writer's arguments. A peer editor also may single out examples that are most convincing and vivid and note areas that are confusing and/or need further development.
3. *Provide an Evaluative Response.* Your instructor or your peer reviewers can provide a detailed evaluation of your essay's focus, thesis, organization, paragraph development, logic, transitions, style, and sentence structure.

It is helpful to evaluate a draft with a set of questions in mind so that the critical responses might provide pointed, productive feedback. Here is a checklist for evaluating a draft of writing:

THE READING/WRITING CONNECTION

1. Have I used some form of reader response first to gain ideas?
2. What is the focus of my response? What is my purpose?

CONTENT

3. What is my perspective? My point of view? Tone?
4. What is my main idea? My thesis? Who is my audience? Have I structured my thesis and topics with my audience in mind?
5. Do my major points follow from the thesis? Are they appropriate for the audience?

ORGANIZATION

6. Are my major points arranged in a logical order? Do they build? Do I emphasize my most convincing point?
7. Does my essay have an introduction, middle paragraphs, and a conclusion?
8. Will my introduction interest a reader and give the reader a sense of the direction of my essay?
9. Does my conclusion end emphatically and reinforce my main idea and points? Do I leave the reader with something to consider?

DEVELOPMENT

10. Have I included enough evidence (reasons, details, quotations, and examples) from the work to explain my points? Have I explained the examples sufficiently?
11. Have I included this evidence properly? Have I used proper quoting techniques and proper techniques for paraphrasing?

GRAMMAR, STYLE, SENTENCE SENSE

12. Have I written about the work in the present tense?
13. Have I maintained a consistent tone? (e.g., objective? personal? persuasive? meditative?)
14. Am I satisfied with wording, sentence structure, patterns of sentences (emphasis, variety)? Have I avoided repetitive wording and phrasing?
15. Have I created coherence by repeating key words, by creating transitions from point to point, and by using parallelism?
16. Have I shifted levels of diction?
17. Is my word choice specific, pointed, not vague?
18. Have I checked the final draft for grammar, punctuation, and spelling errors?

SPECIAL REQUIREMENTS FOR WRITING ABOUT LITERATURE

Several special requirements for writing about literature are important to note. First, compose primarily in the present tense. Use the past tense to refer only to events in a text that clearly took place in the past. For example, in "horse," you would use the present tense to describe the horse's mythic running in the night, but you would use the past tense to describe the animal's mutilation because that event occurred before the speaker begins her story.

Another important feature of writing about literature is the inclusion of quotations from the work. When you quote, be careful to cite the exact quotation and to insert ellipses (. . .) for any information that you delete within a quotation; use four periods (. . . .) for any part of a sentence that you delete at the end of the quotation. Block and indent quotations of more than four lines of prose or three lines of poetry. You also must make the quotation consistent with the preceding discussion. Use brackets to insert any changes in wording so that the quotation fits content and presentation of ideas and so that it makes sense. For example, consider this sentence from Martinez's essay: "In the poem, a 'horse [runs]' toward open palms." The writer changed "ran" to "runs" to keep the tense consistent.

Select sufficient quotations from the work as evidence. Your writing will be more persuasive if you include specifics from the work. Remember the student's weaving of quotations into her discussion of "horse." Be aware, however, that it is disastrous to overload your analysis with unexplained or extensive quotations. This technique could lead a reader to assume that you have not understood the work fully.

Another important aspect of using evidence from a text is to **paraphrase** correctly. Where you do not use quotations, you still might want to support your points with descriptions, examples, or events in the text by phrasing them in your own words—that is, by paraphrasing the original work. Be careful to choose only your own words in such cases; any of the original language must be placed within quotation marks. Consider this additional example from Martinez's essay: "Much care is taken in describing the 'great horse' as it races through the field." She paraphrases the action of the horse as she also uses a direct quotation from the poem to add emphasis and to name the creature.

FORMS OF THE ESSAY ABOUT LITERATURE

In critical analysis of literature, you experience a complicated process of response. In writing about literature, you focus your energies on one aspect, one strand of your reading experience. Depending on your particular reading and on your goals in writing, you may then compose an essay in response to literature that may assume any of several different forms: response; explication; comparison-contrast; argumentation; critical analysis; historical, social, or cultural analysis; review; research; and creative responses to literature.

Response Essay

A response essay is an analysis of a reader's emotional response to a work. In this kind of paper, you explain both your reading experience and the parts of the work that evoke your reaction. For example, you might respond to Luisa Valenzuela's story "I'm Your Horse in the Night" (chapter 7) by discussing your mounting horror and disgust as the characters suffer torture and death at the hands of the government police in Argentina. You may want to proceed sequentially through the story to discuss the stages and aspects of your response. Or you may focus on one main emotional reaction and explore its components: the elements of the story that provoke your reaction.

Explication Essay

Another form of response, explication, is a careful analysis of the work to examine its meaning. In this type of essay, the writer proceeds through the text methodically and analyzes those aspects of the work and the writer's technique that create the themes. Usually explications of meaning are done on short texts so that the work can be analyzed in depth and treated fully. For example, a student may explore a theme of Emily Dickinson's "My Life Had Stood—" (chapter 4) by carefully examining each line, each image, and each stanza and by finding the strands of connection revealed by this process. Such analysis demonstrates aspects of the poem (wording, imagery, figurative language, point of view, tone, rhythm, and rhyme) that develop Dickinson's message. You may organize the essay by treating each part of the text as a separate paragraph or by organizing in terms of poetic techniques; that is, have each technique serve as a topic for a middle paragraph.

Comparison/Contrast Essay

In this form of essay, you may compare and/or contrast two works to find similarities and differences. Then you may have to decide to concentrate on treatment of theme, character, style, or technique. Instructors often specify the subject of the comparison and ask students to compare two characters in two different stories, to evaluate two poems with similar themes, or to assess two plays to determine which treatment of character or theme seems more effective.

There are two major organizational patterns for a comparison/contrast essay. You may treat first one text and then the other in successive paragraphs: this format is labeled *block* or *side-by-side* organization. For example, you might devote several paragraphs to a given theme, such as coming of age in "A White Heron," followed immediately by several paragraphs on the same theme in "Barn Burning" (chapter 4). This type of pattern is sometimes not effective because it separates the discussion of the two works and confuses or loses the reader. The other pattern relies on *point-by-point* or *alternating* organization. In this form of the essay, each of the middle (body) paragraphs presents the treatment of a key topic (point) in both of the works. For example, in a discussion of coming of age in "A White Heron" and in "Barn Burning," one middle paragraph might focus on the innocence of the main protagonist. The next paragraph might explain each protagonist's capability for moral decision making as a prerequisite for growing beyond childhood. In every paragraph, the writer would consider first "A White Heron" and then "Barn Burning." This method keeps the topics for comparison foremost in the reader's mind and allows the reader to weigh and compare the evidence from each story.

Argumentation Essay

An argument presents your point of view, your opinion (position), reasons, and supporting evidence. For an argumentative paper on literature, you take a particular position regarding the text; and then you defend your position by providing reasons and supporting evidence from the text. As in other forms of argument, you will need to create a sound thesis, defend your thesis with logical reasoning, and provide sufficient evidence to prove your points and to convince the reader. In addition, you need to consider the opposing point of view: to evaluate and to analyze arguments in opposition to yours.

There are various ways to structure argumentative essays about literature. In classical argument, you state your thesis (your main position), present reasons and evidence, acknowledge and refute opposition arguments, and then restate and emphasize your argumentative position. In Toulmin logic, the main argumentative position is labeled as the

Patterns for Comparison/Contrast Essays

Block or Side-by-Side		Point-by-Point	
Introduction—Thesis		Introduction—Thesis	
Middle Paragraphs		Middle Paragraphs	
Work A	"A White Heron"	**Topic 1**	Innocence of protagonist
Topic 1	Innocence of protagonist	**Work A**	"A White Heron"
Topic 2	Capacity for moral decisions	**Work B**	"Barn Burning"
Work B	"Barn Burning"	**Topic 2**	Capacity for moral decisions
Topic 1	Innocence of protagonist	**Work A**	"A White Heron"
Topic 2	Capacity for moral decisions	**Work B**	"Barn Burning"
Conclusion		Conclusion	

"claim," the evidence as "the data," and the underlying reasons that link evidence to the claim as the "warrants." In Rogerian argument, the emphasis is not on asserting your thesis and defeating the opposition; rather, the emphasis is on listening and being open to divergent points of view. In a Rogerian argument, you state an argumentative question, consider and evaluate reasons for one side of the controversial position and then the other, and finally come to a compromise position in your conclusion.

What follows are three argumentative thesis statements in response to the following question: In Sarah Orne Jewett's "A White Heron," does Sylvia do the right thing in rejecting the huntsman's offer?

1. **Classical Argument:** Despite her grandmother's and her own need for the money, Sylvia rejects the huntsman's offer because of her desire not to violate her principles—her care for wildlife and respect for nature.

2. **Toulmin Argument:** Sylvia rightly rejects the huntsman's offer, because her value system places greater emphasis on the sacredness of nature than on materialistic concerns. At the moment of decision, Sylvia cannot reveal the bird's location as she remembers "[t]he murmur of the pine's green branches . . . in her ears . . . [and] how the white heron came flying through the golden air and how they watched the sea and the morning together. . . . Sylvia cannot speak; she cannot tell the heron's secret and give its life away." For in giving its life away, she would give away what is most central to her character: her sense of the sacred, and her tie with nature.

3. **Rogerian Argument:** Should Sylvia have rejected the huntsman's offer? On the one hand, her family needs the money. On the other hand, she realizes that in accepting the money, she will betray her principles.

Here are organizational patterns for these forms of argument:

Classical Argument	Toulmin Argument	Rogerian Argument
Introduction—State Main Position (Thesis)	Introduction—State Main Claim	Introduction—Ask Argumentative Question
Middle Paragraphs—Present Reasons and Evidence Middle Paragraph—Refute the Opposition	Middle Paragraphs—Present Warrants and Evidence Middle Paragraph—Refute the Opposition	Middle Paragraphs—Evaluate Pro and Con Arguments
Conclusion—Restate and Emphasize Main Position	Conclusion—Restate Main Position	Conclusion—Come to a Compromise Position

Logical Fallacies in Literary Arguments

When you construct literary arguments, some common logical fallacies are important to avoid, for they will weaken your presentation of ideas. Knowing these fallacies will help you to develop more effective, reasoned argumentative thesis statements and critical judgments about a work. What follows are illogical and then rephrased argumentative theses or critical comments for an essay about Joyce Carol Oates's "Where Are You Going, Where Have You Been?" (chapter 4), a story about a young teenager stalked by a possible serial killer.

SWEEPING GENERALIZATION

Avoid overgeneralizing. Limit your argumentative thesis to a debatable point about the work.

Illogical Thesis: In "Where Are You Going, Where Have You Been?" Connie, like all teenagers, has "two sides" to her nature.

Comment: Do all teenagers have "two sides"? How could you prove this?

Rephrased Thesis: Like many teenagers, Connie has "two sides" to her nature.

HASTY GENERALIZATION

Make sure your thesis is a claim supported by evidence throughout the work, not by one quotation or specific example.

Illogical Thesis: Like many schizophrenics, Connie has a divided self.

Comment: Other than the surreal, dream sequence at the end of the story, is there evidence throughout the text to support the contention that Connie is schizophrenic? Are there any other reasons for this stylistic turn at the end of the work?

Rephrased Thesis: Connie's divided self reaches its heightened state in her final interaction with Arnold Friend at the end of the story.

FALSE CAUSAL RELATIONSHIPS

Make sure that your argumentative points, your conclusion about motivations for a character's actions or a cause-and-effect relationship in the plot, can be supported by specifics from the text.

Illogical Thesis:	In "Where Are you Going, Where Have You Been?" Connie's downfall is caused by her "two sides."
Comment:	Are the "two sides" the actual cause of her demise? Or does her behavior outside of the house lead her to the fast-food place where Arnold spies her?
Rephrased Thesis:	Connie's two-sidedness is a contributing factor but not a direct cause of her downfall.

FALSE CONTEXT

Be careful to examine the context of a work—its specific historical, cultural, social, and biographical frame of reference. Do not attribute characteristics or behavior to a character or present an explanation of a theme that is not consistent with these factors.

Illogical Thesis:	Connie is a flower child of the 1960s.
Comment:	The story was published in 1970 but set in the early 1960s, before the late 1960s youth culture.
Rephrased Thesis:	At the root of Connie's character is a restlessness that gets her into trouble.

SUMMARY RATHER THAN CRITICAL COMMENT

Avoid an argumentative thesis that is a summary rather than a critical response, claim, or evaluation of a work.

Illogical Thesis:	Connie is threatened by Arnold Friend, who stalks her at her house.
Comment:	This is a one-sentence summary of part of the plot.
Rephrased Thesis:	Arnold Friend is symbolically portrayed as a demon lover, a figure that dominates European mythology.

The above thesis presents an interpretation of Arnold Friend's symbolic character rather than plot details.

Critical Analysis Essay

In a *critical analysis,* you are asked to analyze a literary work according to a single principle: theme, character, style, or a particular technique of fiction, poetry, drama, or nonfiction. For example, you may be asked to explore one theme of "Hills Like White Elephants" (chapter 6); or you might be asked to analyze the character of the woman in that story; your instructor may ask you to analyze Hemingway's style; or you might be asked to focus on the imagery of the hills or the symbolism of the title. In each case, you isolate one level of a work and explore its function and its impact. Critical analysis often leads to judgments of effectiveness. Is the theme treated compellingly? Is the character portrayal moving? Believable? Is the imagery powerful? Is Hemingway's style effective?

Historical, Social, or Cultural Analysis Essay

The *historical, social, or cultural analysis essay* involves a study of how the work reveals historical, social, or cultural realities or trends. In this essay, you concentrate on how the work mirrors, comments on, or critiques particular historical, social, or cultural phenomena. For example, Esther Martinez, in her essay about "horse," views the poem as a critical examination of the oppression faced by Mexicans in the United States and then relates the work to larger issues—the way "any race . . . or people . . . [suffer] from persecution." She locates the poem in a particular time and place, connects it to the past history of minorities in this country, and analyzes the social, political, and cultural forces portrayed in the work.

In another instance, in an historical analysis of Charlotte Gilman Perkins's "The Yellow Wallpaper," an autobiographically inspired work of fiction about a woman at the turn of the century who has a nervous breakdown after the birth of her child (chapter 6), you may be asked to research the autobiographical roots of the work and learn more about the historical context and background of the work, particularly the treatment for postpartum depression. In a social analysis, you may evaluate how the work presents gender roles for men and women at the turn of the century; in a cultural analysis, you may consider if the work critiques such roles. In historical, social, or cultural analyses, your reading would extend beyond the text to encompass the author's biography, letters, or autobiography; historical background information; and other texts of the time, such as advertisements, documents, historical tracts, or other cultural artifacts. You would consider the relevance of such information to your reading of the work.

Evaluation and Review Essay

Evaluation and *review* are forms of critical analysis that focus on determining the effectiveness of a work. When you are asked to evaluate a text, you compare the text with chosen standards and come to conclusions about its worth and effectiveness. You might evaluate Athol Fugard's *"Master Harold" . . . and the Boys* (chapter 8), for example, and conclude that its characters, dialogue, conflict, and themes create a drama of great power.

A *review* is a particular form of evaluative response that often follows this set pattern:

Paragraph One:	General assessment of a work. Relevant background information.
Paragraph Two:	Summary of key features of the work.
	(The reviewer assumes that the reader has not yet seen or read the work.)
Paragraph Three:	Strengths
Paragraph Four:	Weaknesses
Conclusion:	A general recommendation

Reviews are a common form of both academic and journalistic prose. Many instructors in college courses require book, magazine, or film reviews. Consequently, this form is a valuable one to learn.

Creative Essay

The *creative essay* about literature presents an imaginative response to a literary work. The approaches explained in chapter 2, "Creative Responses to Literature," may be used to develop this kind of essay. In addition, your instructor may ask you to analyze your creative work, concentrating on your composing process, an analysis of character or theme, or particular literary elements (e.g., use of figurative language or symbolism). Note the extended online forum about "horse" presented in chapter 7—the creative responses and comment on the works.

Research Essay

The *research paper* is a writing assignment that involves searching beyond the text to find information that expands your understanding of the work. Research opens the text to different interpretations and enriches the reading experience. Research may move in different directions. You may explore any one of the following areas:

- *Biographical research:* Research on the writer's life. Exploration of the connections between the writer's life and art.
- *Research on the historical, cultural, political, philosophical, or sociological background or context of the work.*
- *Reading of criticism that treats the work.* This reading of another's exploration of the text will help you understand it and, perhaps, explain aspects that are puzzling. Critics provide you with alternative interpretations.
- *Reading of specific forms of literary criticism.* Historical, cultural, social, formalist, feminist, deconstructive. (See Appendix B.) These particular schools of literary criticism will provide you with frameworks and theories that will help you read the work in particular ways and place it in new intellectual contexts.

In each instance, once you write about secondary sources, you must cite the sources of the information and give adequate documentation for the works that you quote or paraphrase. One accepted method of documenting information in essays about literature is MLA (Modern Language Association of America) citation form as recommended in the *MLA Handbook for Writers of Research Papers.* The MLA citation form involves two steps: citations of references in the work itself and a "Works Cited" page that contains all of your primary and secondary sources in alphabetical order by author's last name. The MLA citations within the discussion sections of your paper include two parts: author, page. If the author's name is presented in your essay, you only indicate page number. If an author has written two books, you should include an abbreviated title in the citation. Note the following excerpt from a rough draft of a student research essay on Sylvia Plath's theme of transcendence. The writer, Kevin Stoffel, contends that an examination of the drafts of Plath's poems reveals a transformation of suffering into images of power, autonomy, and purity. Note the correct form of MLA citation. You can find a complete discussion of MLA documentation and of this research paper in Appendix B.

> Plath's poems were an outlet for her constant pain. From her swings and fits of mania and depression, she drew on the theme of transcendence. The transformation of this theme, from its early stages to its final state, can be seen in the drafts of the poems, "Fever 103˙," "Ariel," and "Edge."
>
> In a statement prepared for a BBC reading, Plath wrote of "Fever 103˙":
>
>> This poem is about two kinds of fire—the fires of hell, which merely agonize, and the fires of heaven which purify. During the poem, the first

```
                   sort  of  fire  suffers  into  the  second.  (Newman
                62)
                   "Fever  103'"  is  one  of  several  poems  in  which
                fire  serves  to  bring  about  a  sense  of  purity  equivalent
                to  a  type  of  transcendence,  a  movement  to  a  higher
                plane.
```

SUMMARY

The recursive processes of critical thinking, reader response, and composing the essay about literature develop new capacities for understanding texts in different genres—fiction, poetry, drama, and nonfiction. As you read, analyze, and write about selections in the thematic anthology that follows, you not only will find yourself more interested in issues like those presented in Gloria Anzaldúa's poem, "horse," but you also will find your life enriched by the insights and ideas provided by the study of these works.

··PART TWO··

Thematic Anthology

· CHAPTER 4 ·

The Heroic Journey

For a man needs only to be turned around once with his eyes shut in this world to be lost. . . Not til we are lost . . . do we begin to find ourselves.

HENRY DAVID THOREAU, *Walden*

"Old woman, what is this freedom you love so well?" . . . "I guess now, it ain't nothing but knowing how to say what I got up in my head."

RALPH ELLISON, *The Invisible Man*

Growth demands a temporary surrender of security.

GAIL SHEEHY

The road to psychological maturity is twisting, hilly, and poorly surfaced.

ROBERT E. NIXON

Frederick Childe Hassam "Marie at the Window," 1923

■ *Introduction* ■

I came to explore the wreck.
The words are purposes.
The words are maps.
I came to see the damage that was done
and the treasures that prevail.

Adrienne Rich, "Diving into the Wreck"

It is not possible to define the self without acts of consciousness, without surveying "the damage that was done/and the treasures that prevail." Similarly, it is not possible to grow without being challenged by experience and cultural mores. When we are young, we live in a seemingly idyllic world. As we mature, we experience those rites of passage that take away our innocence, that complicate our lives, and that provide the basis for growth and for the development of identity. These rites of passage also enrich us, endowing our lives with depth and greater meaning.

For children and adolescents, loss of innocence often comes from an exposure to danger—to a threatening, violent, and often unpredictable world that brings with it the dissolution of a sense of a secure existence. This movement from innocence to experience can also take on other dimensions. For figures in literary works, loss of innocence also comes from facing the transitory nature of life, the facts of birth and death.

Adolescence is not necessarily a dangerous phase of life; it also may be a time of great growth, challenge, and joy. Many works affirmatively portray the physical energy and vitality of adolescence. In some cases, the vitality of adolescence emerges from a drive to rebel. Members of ethnic groups who experience alienation in North American culture often use rebellion to gain an understanding of prejudice and to reject societal mores. Experiencing discrimination also can lead to an awareness of difference and to confusion about cultural heritage, as many of the works in this chapter illustrate. Should we aspire to assimilate or to embrace our cultural legacies, or are we caught between worlds? The process of coming of age differs for women and for men as well as from culture to culture.

One outcome of these challenges is the consolidation of identity—"the treasures that prevail": the movement from confusion to a surer, albeit not necessarily static, sense of the adult self. Certainly the development of selfhood is not solidified when we reach adulthood; rather, confusion and identity crises persist into our twenties, thirties, and forties. We continue to face experiences that challenge us to define and to redefine self, to examine our relationship with our past, and to find our place in the world.

As readers we are cognizant that acts of writing, acts of communication, are revelatory. Like Adrienne Rich, we know that words are the "purposes," the "maps," by which we come to know ourselves and to find our ways in the world.

Crossing the Genres
DANGERS OF ADOLESCENCE

JOYCE CAROL OATES

Joyce Carol Oates (1938–   ), born in Lockport, New York, studied at Syracuse University and the University of Wisconsin. With the publication of The Garden of Earthly Delights *(1967) and* Expensive People *(1968), she became famous. In 1969, her novel,* them, *won the National Book Award. Known for her prolific and varied writing, Oates, Professor of Humanities at Princeton University, has published almost fifty books: novels, short fiction, poetry, essays, and literary criticism. Recent works include Oates's novel* What I Lived For *(1994), which was a 1995 Pulitzer Prize finalist;* Blonde *(2000), a fictionalization of Marilyn Monroe's life, which also won the National Book Award; and* The Falls *(2004). Oates based her most famous story, "Where Are You Going, Where Have You Been?" on a article in* Life *magazine about a murderer, Charles Schmid of Tucson, Arizona.*

1970

WHERE ARE YOU GOING, WHERE HAVE YOU BEEN?

To Bob Dylan

Her name was Connie. She was fifteen and she had a quick nervous giggling habit of craning her neck to glance into mirrors or checking other people's faces to make sure her own was all right. Her mother, who noticed everything and knew everything and who hadn't much reason any longer to look at her own face, always scolded Connie about it. "Stop gawking at yourself, who are you? You think you're so pretty?" she would say. Connie would raise her eyebrows at these familiar complaints and look right through her mother, into a shadowy vision of herself as she was right at that moment: she knew she was pretty and that was everything. Her mother had been pretty once too, if you could believe those old snapshots in the album, but now her looks were gone and that was why she was always after Connie. "Why don't you keep your room clean like your sister? How've you got your hair fixed—what the hell stinks? Hair spray? You don't see your sister using that junk."

Her sister June was twenty-four and still lived at home. She was a secretary in the high school Connie attended, and if that wasn't bad enough—with her in the same building— she was so plain and chunky and steady that Connie had to hear her praised all the time by her mother and her mother's sisters. June did this, June did that, she saved money and helped clean the house and cooked and Connie couldn't do a thing, her mind was all filled with trashy daydreams. Their father was away at work most of the time and when he came home he wanted supper and he read the newspaper at supper and after supper he went to bed. He didn't bother talking much to them, but around his bent head Connie's mother kept picking at her until Connie wished her mother were dead and she herself were dead and it were all over. "She makes me want to throw up sometimes," she complained to her friends. She had a high, breathless, amused voice which made everything she said sound a little forced, whether it was sincere or not.

There was one good thing: June went places with girlfriends of hers, girls who were just as plain and steady as she, and so when Connie wanted to do that her mother had no objections. The father of Connie's best girlfriend drove the girls the three miles to town and left them off at a shopping plaza, so that they could walk through the stores or go to a movie, and when he came to pick them up again at eleven he never bothered to ask what they had done.

They must have been familiar sights, walking around that shopping plaza in their shorts and flat ballerina slippers that always scuffed the sidewalk, with charm bracelets jingling on their thin wrists; they would lean together to whisper and laugh secretly if someone passed by who amused or interested them. Connie had long dark blond hair that drew anyone's eye to it, and she wore part of it pulled up on her head and puffed out and the rest of it she let fall down her back. She wore a pullover jersey blouse that looked one way when she was at home and another way when she was away from home. Everything about her had two sides to it, one for home and one for anywhere that was not home: her walk that could be childlike and bobbing, or languid enough to make anyone think she was hearing music in her head, her mouth which was pale and smirking most of the time, but bright and pink on these evenings out, her laugh which was cynical and drawling at home—"Ha, ha, very funny"—but high-pitched and nervous anywhere else, like the jingling of the charms on her bracelet.

5   Sometimes they did go shopping or to a movie, but sometimes they went across the highway, ducking fast across the busy road, to a drive-in restaurant where older kids hung out. The restaurant was shaped like a big bottle, though squatter than a real bottle, and on its cap was a revolving figure of a grinning boy who held a hamburger aloft. One night in midsummer they ran across, breathless with daring, and right away someone leaned out a car window and invited them over, but it was just a boy from high school they didn't like. It made them feel good to be able to ignore him. They went up through the maze of parked and cruising cars to the bright-lit, fly-infested restaurant, their faces pleased and expectant as if they were entering a sacred building that loomed out of the night to give them what haven and what blessing they yearned for. They sat at the counter and crossed their legs at the ankles, their thin shoulders rigid with excitement, and listened to the music that made everything so good: the music was always in the background like music at a church service, it was something to depend upon.

A boy named Eddie came in to talk with them. He sat backward on his stool, turning himself jerkily around in semicircles and then stopping and turning again, and after a while he asked Connie if she would like something to eat. She said she did and so she tapped her friend's arm on her way out—her friend pulled her face up into a brave droll look—and Connie said she would meet her at eleven, across the way. "I just hate to leave her like that," Connie said earnestly, but the boy said that she wouldn't be alone for long. So they went out to his car and on the way Connie couldn't help but let her eyes wander over the windshields and faces all around her, her face gleaming with a joy that had nothing to do with Eddie or even this place; it might have been the music. She drew her shoulders up and sucked in her breath with the pure pleasure of being alive, and just at that moment she happened to glance at a face just a few feet from hers. It was a boy with shaggy black hair, in a convertible jalopy painted gold. He stared at her and then his lips widened into a grin. Connie slit her eyes at him and turned away, but she couldn't help glancing back and there he was still watching her. He wagged a finger and laughed and said, "Gonna get you, baby," and Connie turned away again without Eddie noticing anything.

She spent three hours with him, at the restaurant where they ate hamburgers and drank Cokes in wax cups that were always sweating, and then down an alley a mile or so away, and when he left her off at five to eleven only the movie house was still open at the plaza. Her girlfriend was there, talking with a boy. When Connie came up and the two girls smiled at each other and Connie said, "How was the movie?" and the girl said, "*You* should know." They rode off with the girl's father, sleepy and pleased, and Connie couldn't help but look at the darkened shopping plaza with its big empty parking lot and its signs that were faded and ghostly now, and over at the drive-in restaurant where cars were still circling tirelessly. She couldn't hear the music at this distance.

Next morning June asked her how the movie was and Connie said, "So-so."

She and that girl and occasionally another girl went out several times a week that way, and the rest of the time Connie spent around the house—it was summer vacation—getting in her mother's way and thinking, dreaming, about the boys she met. But all the boys fell back and dissolved into a single face that was not even a face, but an idea, a feeling, mixed up with the urgent insistent pounding of the music and the humid night air of July. Connie's mother kept dragging her back to the daylight by finding things for her to do or saying, suddenly, "What's this about the Pettinger girl?"

10   And Connie would say nervously, "Oh, her. That dope." She always drew thick clear lines between herself and such girls, and her mother was simple and kindly enough to believe her. Her mother was so simple, Connie thought, that it was maybe cruel to fool her so much. Her mother went scuffling around the house in old bedroom slippers and complained over the telephone to one sister about the other, then the other called up and the two of them complained about the third one. If June's name was mentioned her mother's tone was approving, and if Connie's name was mentioned it was disapproving. This did not really mean she disliked Connie and actually Connie thought that her mother preferred her to June because she was prettier, but the two of them kept up a pretense of exasperation, a sense that they were tugging and struggling over something of little value to either of them. Sometimes, over coffee, they were almost friends, but something would come up—some vexation that was like a fly buzzing suddenly around their heads—and their faces went hard with contempt.

One Sunday Connie got up at eleven—none of them bothered with church—and washed her hair so that it could dry all day long, in the sun. Her parents and sisters were going to a barbecue at an aunt's house and Connie said no, she wasn't interested, rolling her eyes to let her mother know just what she thought of it. "Stay home alone then," her mother said sharply. Connie sat out back in a lawn chair and watched them drive away, her father quiet and bald, hunched around so that he could back the car out, her mother with a look that was still angry and not at all softened through the windshield, and in the back seat poor old June all dressed up as if she didn't know what a barbecue was, with all the running yelling kids and the flies. Connie sat with her eyes closed in the sun, dreaming and dazed with the warmth about her as if this were a kind of love, the caresses of love, and her mind slipped over onto thoughts of the boy she had been with the night before and how nice he had been, how sweet it always was, not the way someone like June would suppose but sweet, gentle, the way it was in movies and promised in songs; and when she opened her eyes she hardly knew where she was, the back yard ran off into weeds and a fence line of trees and behind it the sky was perfectly blue and still. The asbestos "ranch house" that was now three years old startled her—it looked small. She shook her head as if to get awake.

It was too hot. She went inside the house and turned on the radio to drown out the quiet. She sat on the edge of her bed, barefoot, and listened for an hour and a half to a program called XYZ Sunday Jamboree, record after record of hard, fast, shrieking songs she sang along with, interspersed by exclamations from "Bobby King": "An' look here you girls at Napoleon's—Son and Charley want you to pay real close attention to this song coming up!"

And Connie paid close attention herself, bathed in a glow of slow-pulsed joy that seemed to rise mysteriously out of the music itself and lay languidly about the airless little room, breathed in and breathed out with each gentle rise and fall of her chest.

After a while she heard a car coming up the drive. She sat up at once, startled, because it couldn't be her father so soon. The gravel kept crunching all the way in from the road—the driveway was long—and Connie ran to the window. It was a car she didn't know. It was an open jalopy, painted a bright gold that caught the sunlight opaquely. Her heart began to pound and her fingers snatched at her hair, checking it, and she whispered "Christ, Christ," wondering how bad she looked. The car came to a stop at the side door and the horn sounded four short taps as if this were a signal Connie knew.

15   She went into the kitchen and approached the door slowly, then hung out the screen door, her bare toes curling down off the step. There were two boys in the car and now she recognized the driver: he had shaggy, shabby black hair that looked crazy as a wig and he was grinning at her.

"I ain't late, am I?" he said.

"Who the hell do you think you are?" Connie said.

"Toldja I'd be out, didn't I?"

"I don't even know who you are."

20   She spoke sullenly, careful to show no interest or pleasure, and he spoke in a fast bright monotone. Connie looked past him to the other boy, taking her time. He had fair brown hair, with a lock that fell onto his forehead. His sideburns gave him a fierce, embarrassed look, but so far he hadn't even bothered to glance at her. Both boys wore sunglasses. The driver's glasses were metallic and mirrored everything in miniature.

"You wanta come for a ride?" he said.

Connie smirked and let her hair fall loose over one shoulder.

"Don'tcha like my car? New paint job," he said. "Hey."

"What?"

25   "You're cute."

She pretended to fidget, chasing flies away from the door.

"Don'tcha believe me, or what?" he said.

"Look, I don't even know who you are," Connie said in disgust.

"Hey, Ellie's got a radio, see. Mine's broke down." He lifted his friend's arm and showed her the little transistor the boy was holding, and now Connie began to hear the music. It was the same program that was playing inside the house.

30   "Bobby King?" she said.

"I listen to him all the time. I think he's great."

"He's kind of great," Connie said reluctantly.

"Listen, that guy's *great*. He knows where the action is."

Connie blushed a little, because the glasses made it impossible for her to see just what this boy was looking at. She couldn't decide if she liked him or if he was just a jerk, and so she dawdled in the doorway and wouldn't come down or go back inside. She said, "What's all that stuff painted on your car?"

35   "Can'tcha read it?" He opened the door very carefully, as if he was afraid it might fall off. He slid out just as carefully, planting his feet firmly on the ground, the tiny metallic world in his glasses slowing down like gelatine hardening and in the midst of it Connie's bright green blouse. "This here is my name, to begin with," he said. ARNOLD FRIEND was written in tarlike black letters on the side, with a drawing of a round grinning face that reminded Connie of a pumpkin, except it wore sunglasses. "I wanta introduce myself, I'm Arnold Friend and that's my real name and I'm gonna be your friend, honey, and inside the car's Ellie Oscar, he's kinda shy." Ellie brought his transistor radio up to his shoulder and balanced it there. "Now these numbers are a secret code, honey," Arnold Friend explained. He read off the numbers 33, 19, 17 and raised his eyebrows at her to see what she thought of that, but she didn't think much of it. The left rear fender had been smashed and around it

was written, on the gleaming gold background: DONE BY CRAZY WOMAN DRIVER. Connie had to laugh at that. Arnold Friend was pleased at her laughter and looked up at her. "Around the other side's a lot more—you wanta come and see them?"

"No."

"Why not?"

"Why should I?"

"Don'tcha wanta see what's on the car? Don'tcha wanta go for a ride?"

40   "I don't know."

"Why not?"

"I got things to do."

"Like what?"

"Things."

45   He laughed as if she had said something funny. He slapped his thighs. He was standing in a strange way, leaning back against the car as if he were balancing himself. He wasn't tall, only an inch or so taller than she would be if she came down to him. Connie liked the way he was dressed, which was the way all of them dressed: tight faded jeans stuffed into black, scuffed boots, a belt that pulled his waist in and showed how lean he was, and a white pullover shirt that was a little soiled and showed the hard small muscles of his arms and shoulders. He looked as if he probably did hard work, lifting and carrying things. Even his neck looked muscular. And his face was a familiar face, somehow: the jaw and chin and cheeks slightly darkened, because he hadn't shaved for a day or two, and the nose long and hawklike, sniffing as if she were a treat he was going to gobble up and it was all a joke.

"Connie, you ain't telling the truth. This is your day set aside for a ride with me and you know it," he said, still laughing. The way he straightened and recovered from his fit of laughing showed that it had been all fake.

"How do you know what my name is?" she said suspiciously.

"It's Connie."

"Maybe and maybe not."

50   "I know my Connie," he said, wagging his finger. Now she remembered him even better, back at the restaurant, and her cheeks warmed at the thought of how she sucked in her breath just at the moment she passed him—how she must have looked at him. And he had remembered her. "Ellie and I come out here especially for you," he said. "Ellie can sit in back. How about it?"

"Where?"

"Where what?"

"Where're we going?"

He looked at her. He took off the sunglasses and she saw how pale the skin around his eyes was, like holes that were not in shadow but instead in light. His eyes were like chips of broken glass that catch the light in an amiable way. He smiled. It was as if the idea of going for a ride somewhere, to some place, was a new idea to him.

55   "Just for a ride, Connie sweetheart."

"I never said my name was Connie," she said.

"But I know what it is. I know your name and all about you, lots of things," Arnold Friend said. He had not moved yet but stood still leaning back against the side of his jalopy. "I took a special interest in you, such a pretty girl, and found out all about you like I know your parents and sister are gone somewheres and I know where and how long they're going to be gone, and I know who you were with last night, and your best girlfriend's name is Betty. Right?"

He spoke in a simple lilting voice, exactly as if he were reciting the words to a song. His smile assured her that everything was fine. In the car Ellie turned up the volume on his radio and did not bother to look around at them.

"Ellie can sit in the back seat," Arnold Friend said. He indicated his friend with a casual jerk of his chin, as if Ellie did not count and she should not bother with him.

60   "How'd you find out all that stuff?" Connie said.

"Listen: Betty Schultz and Tony Fitch and Jimmy Pettinger and Nancy Pettinger," he said, in a chant. "Raymond Stanley and Bob Hutter—"

"Do you know all those kids?"

"I know everybody."

"Look, you're kidding. You're not from around here."

65   "Sure."

"But—how come we never saw you before?"

"Sure you saw me before," he said. He looked down at his boots, as if he were a little offended. "You just don't remember."

"I guess I'd remember you," Connie said.

"Yeah?" He looked up at this, beaming. He was pleased. He began to mark time with the music from Ellie's radio, tapping his fists lightly together. Connie looked away from his smile to the car, which was painted so bright it almost hurt her eyes to look at it. She looked at that name. ARNOLD FRIEND. And up at the front fender was an expression that was familiar—MAN THE FLYING SAUCERS. It was an expression kids had used the year before, but didn't use this year. She looked at it for a while as if the words meant something to her that she did not yet know.

70   "What're you thinking about? Huh?" Arnold Friend demanded. "Not worried about your hair blowing around in the car, are you?"

"No."

"Think I maybe can't drive good?"

"How do I know?"

"You're a hard girl to handle. How come?" he said. "Don't you know I'm your friend? Didn't you see me put my sign in the air when you walked by?"

75   "What sign?"

"My sign." And he drew an X in the air, leaning out toward her. They were maybe ten feet apart. After his hand fell back to his side the X was still in the air, almost visible. Connie let the screen door close and stood perfectly still inside it, listening to the music from her radio and the boy's blend together. She stared at Arnold Friend. He stood there so stiffly relaxed, pretending to be relaxed, with one hand idly on the door handle as if he were keeping himself up that way and had no intention of ever moving again. She recognized most things about him, the tight jeans that showed his thighs and buttocks and the greasy leather boots and the tight shirt, and even that slippery friendly smile of his, that sleepy dreamy smile that all the boys used to get across ideas they didn't want to put into words. She recognized all this and also the singsong way he talked, slightly mocking, kidding, but serious and a little melancholy, and she recognized the way he tapped one fist against the other in homage of the perpetual music behind him. But all these things did not come together.

She said suddenly, "Hey, how old are you?"

His smile faded. She could see then that he wasn't a kid, he was much older—thirty, maybe more. At this knowledge her heart began to pound faster.

"That's a crazy thing to ask. Can'tcha see I'm your own age?"

80   "Like hell you are."

"Or maybe a coupla years older, I'm eighteen."

"Eighteen?" she said doubtfully.

He grinned to reassure her and lines appeared at the corners of his mouth. His teeth were big and white. He grinned so broadly his eyes became slits and she saw how thick the lashes were, thick and black as if painted with a black tarlike material. Then he seemed to become embarrassed, abruptly, and looked over his shoulder at Ellie. "*Him*, he's crazy," he said. "Ain't he a riot, he's a nut, a real character." Ellie was still listening to the music. His sunglasses told nothing about what he was thinking. He wore a bright orange shirt unbuttoned halfway to show his chest, which was a pale, bluish chest and not muscular like Arnold Friend's. His shirt collar was turned up all around and the very tips of the collar pointed out past his chin as if they were protecting him. He was pressing the transistor radio up against his ear and sat there in a kind of daze, right in the sun.

"He's kinda strange," Connie said.

85   "Hey, she says you're kinda strange! Kinda strange!" Arnold Friend cried. He pounded on the car to get Ellie's attention. Ellie turned for the first time and Connie saw with shock that he wasn't a kid either—he had a fair, hairless face, cheeks reddened slightly as if the veins grew too close to the surface of his skin, the face of a forty-year-old baby. Connie felt a wave of dizziness rise in her at this sight and she stared at him as if waiting for something to change the shock of the moment, make it all right again. Ellie's lips kept shaping words, mumbling along with the words blasting in his ear.

"Maybe you two better go away," Connie said faintly.

"What? How come?" Arnold Friend cried. "We come out here to take you for a ride. It's Sunday." He had the voice of the man on the radio now. It was the same voice, Connie thought. "Don'tcha know it's Sunday all day and honey, no matter who you were with last night today you're with Arnold Friend and don't you forget it!—Maybe you better step out here," he said, and this last was in a different voice. It was a little flatter, as if the heat was finally getting to him.

"No. I got things to do."

"Hey."

90   "You two better leave."

"We ain't leaving until you come with us."

"Like hell I am—"

"Connie, don't fool around with me. I mean, I mean, don't fool *around*," he said, shaking his head. He laughed incredulously. He placed his sunglasses on top of his head, carefully, as if he were indeed wearing a wig, and brought the stems down behind his ears. Connie stared at him, another wave of dizziness and fear rising in her so that for a moment he wasn't even in focus but was just a blur, standing there against his gold car, and she had the idea that he had driven up the driveway all right but had come from nowhere before that and belonged nowhere and that everything about him and even about the music that was so familiar to her was only half real.

"If my father comes and sees you—"

95   "He ain't coming. He's at a barbecue."

"How do you know that?"

"Aunt Tillie's. Right now they're—uh—they're drinking. Sitting around," he said vaguely, squinting as if he were staring all the way to town and over to Aunt Tillie's back yard. Then the vision seemed to get clear and he nodded energetically. "Yeah. Sitting around. There's your sister in a blue dress, huh? And high heels, the poor sad bitch—nothing like you, sweetheart! And your mother's helping some fat woman with the corn, they're cleaning the corn— husking the corn—"

"What fat woman?" Connie cried.

"How do I know what fat woman, I don't know every goddam fat woman in the world!" Arnold laughed.

100   "Oh, that's Mrs. Hornby . . . Who invited her?" Connie said. She felt a little light-headed. Her breath was coming quickly.

"She's too fat. I don't like them fat. I like them the way you are, honey," he said, smiling sleepily at her. They stared at each other for a while, through the screen door. He said softly, "Now what you're going to do is this: you're going to come out that door. You're going to sit up front with me and Ellie's going to sit in the back, the hell with Ellie, right? This isn't Ellie's date. You're my date. I'm your lover, honey."

"What? You're crazy—"

"Yes, I'm your lover. You don't know what that is, but you will," he said. "I know that too. I know all about you. But look: it's real nice and you couldn't ask for nobody better than me, or more polite. I always keep my word. I'll tell you how it is, I'm always nice at first, the first time. I'll hold you so tight you won't think you have to try to get away or pretend anything because you'll know you can't. And I'll come inside you where it's all secret and you'll give in to me and you'll love me—"

"Shut up! You're crazy!" Connie said. She backed away from the door. She put her hands against her ears as if she'd heard something terrible, something not meant for her. "People don't talk like that, you're crazy," she muttered. Her heart was almost too big now for her chest and its pumping made sweat break out all over her. She looked out to see Arnold Friend pause and then take a step toward the porch lurching. He almost fell. But, like a clever drunken man, he managed to catch his balance. He wobbled in his high boots and grabbed hold of one of the porch posts.

105   "Honey?" he said. "You still listening?"

"Get the hell out of here!"

"Be nice, honey. Listen."

"I'm going to call the police—"

He wobbled again and out of the side of his mouth came a fast spat curse, an aside not meant for her to hear. But even this "Christ!" sounded forced. Then he began to smile again. She watched this smile come, awkward as if he were smiling from inside a mask. His whole face was a mask, she thought wildly, tanned down onto his throat but then running out as if he had plastered makeup on his face but had forgotten about his throat.

110   "Honey—? Listen, here's how it is. I always tell the truth and I promise you this: I ain't coming in that house after you."

"You better not! I'm going to call the police if you—if you don't—"

"Honey," he said, talking right through her voice, "honey, I'm not coming in there but you are coming out here. You know why?"

She was panting. The kitchen looked like a place she had never seen before, some rooms she had run inside but which wasn't good enough, wasn't going to help her. The kitchen window had never had a curtain, after three years, and there were dishes in the sink for her to do—probably—and if you ran your hand across the table you'd probably feel something sticky there.

"You listening, honey? Hey?"

115   "—going to call the police—"

"Soon as you touch the phone I don't need to keep my promise and can come inside. You won't want that."

She rushed forward and tried to lock the door. Her fingers were shaking. "But why lock it," Arnold Friend said gently, talking right into her face. "It's just a screen door. It's just nothing." One of his boots was at a strange angle, as if his foot wasn't in it. It pointed out to the left, bent at the ankle. "I mean, anybody can break through a screen door and glass and wood and iron or anything else if he needs to, anybody at all and specially Arnold Friend. If the place got lit up with a fire honey you'd come runnin' out into my arms, right into my arms an' safe at home—like you knew I was your lover and'd stopped fooling around. I don't mind a nice shy girl but I don't like no fooling around." Part of those words were spoken with a slight rhythmic lilt, and Connie somehow recognized them—the echo of a song from last year, about a girl rushing into her boyfriend's arms and coming home again—

Connie stood barefoot on the linoleum floor, staring at him. "What do you want?" she whispered.

"I want you," he said.

120   "What?"

"Seen you that night and thought, that's the one, yes sir. I never needed to look any more."

"But my father's coming back. He's coming to get me. I had to wash my hair first—" She spoke in a dry, rapid voice, hardly raising it for him to hear.

"No, your Daddy is not coming and yes, you had to wash your hair and you washed it for me. It's nice and shining and all for me, I thank you, sweetheart," he said, with a mock bow, but again he almost lost his balance. He had to bend and adjust his boots. Evidently his feet did not go all the way down; the boots must have been stuffed with something so that he would seem taller. Connie stared out at him and behind him Ellie in the car, who seemed to be looking off toward Connie's right into nothing. This Ellie said, pulling the words out of the air one after another as if he were just discovering them, "You want me to pull out the phone?"

"Shut your mouth and keep it shut," Arnold Friend said, his face red from bending over or maybe from embarrassment because Connie had seen his boots. "This ain't none of your business."

125   "What—what are you doing? What do you want?" Connie said. "If I call the police they'll get you, they'll arrest you—"

"Promise was not to come in unless you touch the phone, and I'll keep that promise," he said. He resumed his erect position and tried to force his shoulders back. He sounded like a hero in a movie, declaring something important. He spoke too loudly and it was as if he were speaking to someone behind Connie. "I ain't made plans for coming in that house where I don't belong but just for you to come out to me, the way you should. Don't you know who I am?"

"You're crazy," she whispered. She backed away from the door but did not want to go into another part of the house, as if this would give him permission to come through the door. "What do you . . . You're crazy, you . . ."

"Huh? What're you saying, honey?"

Her eyes darted everywhere in the kitchen. She could not remember what it was, this room.

130   "This is how it is, honey; you come out and we'll drive away, have a nice ride. But if you don't come out we're gonna wait till your people come home and then they're all going to get it."

"You want that telephone pulled out?" Ellie said. He held the radio away from his ear and grimaced, as if without the radio the air was too much for him.

"I toldja shut up, Ellie," Arnold Friend said, "you're deaf, get a hearing aid, right? Fix yourself up. This little girl's no trouble and's gonna be nice to me, so Ellie keep to yourself, this ain't your date—right? Don't hem in on me. Don't hog. Don't crush. Don't bird dog. Don't trail me," he said in a rapid meaningless voice, as if he were running through all the expressions he'd learned but was no longer sure which one of them was in style, then rushing on to new ones, making them up with his eyes closed, "Don't crawl under my fence, don't squeeze in my chipmunk hole, don't sniff my glue, suck my popsicle, keep your own greasy fingers on yourself!" He shaded his eyes and peered in at Connie, who was backed against the kitchen table. "Don't mind him honey he's just a creep. He's a dope. Right? I'm the boy for you and like I said you come out here nice like a lady and give me your hand, and nobody else gets hurt, I mean, your nice old bald-headed daddy and your mummy and your sister in her high heels. Because listen: why bring them in this?"

"Leave me alone," Connie whispered.

"Hey, you know that old woman down the road, the one with the chickens and stuff— you know her?"

135   "She's dead!"

"Dead? What? You know her?" Arnold Friend said.

"She's dead—"

"Don't you like her?"

"She dead—she's—she isn't there any more—"

140   "But don't you like her, I mean, you got something against her? Some grudge or something?" Then his voice dipped as if he were conscious of a rudeness. He touched the sunglasses perched on top of his head as if to make sure they were still there. "Now you be a good girl."

"What are you going to do?"

"Just two things, or maybe three," Arnold Friend said. "But I promise it won't last long and you'll like me the way you get to like people you're close to. You will. It's all over for you here, so come on out. You don't want your people in any trouble, do you?"

She turned and bumped against a chair or something, hurting her leg, but she ran into the back room and picked up the telephone. Something roared in her ear, a tiny roaring, and she was so sick with fear that she could do nothing but listen to it—the telephone was clammy and very heavy and her fingers groped down to the dial but were too weak to touch it. She began to scream into the phone, into the roaring. She cried out, she cried for her mother, she felt her breath start jerking back and forth in her lungs as if it were something Arnold Friend were stabbing her with again and again with no tenderness. A noisy sorrowful wailing rose all about her and she was locked inside it the way she was locked inside this house.

After a while she could hear again. She was sitting on the floor with her wet back against the wall.

145   Arnold Friend was saying from the door, "That's a good girl. Put the phone back."

She kicked the phone away from her.

"No, honey. Pick it up. Put it back right."

She picked it up and put it back. The dial tone stopped.

"That's a good girl. Now you come outside."

150   She was hollow with what had been fear, but what was now just an emptiness. All that screaming had blasted it out of her. She sat, one leg cramped under her, and deep inside her brain was something like a pinpoint of light that kept going and would not let her relax. She thought, I'm not going to see my mother again. She thought, I'm not going to sleep in my bed again. Her bright green blouse was all wet.

Arnold Friend said, in a gentle-loud voice that was like a stage voice. "The place where you came from ain't there any more, and where you had in mind to go is canceled out. This place you are now—inside your daddy's house—is nothing but a cardboard box I can knock down any time. You know that and always did know it. You hear me?"

She thought, I have got to think. I have to know what to do.

"We'll go out to a nice field, out in the country here where it smells so nice and it's sunny," Arnold Friend said. "I'll have my arms tight around you so you won't need to try to get away and I'll show you what love is like, what it does. The hell with this house! It looks solid all right," he said. He ran a fingernail down the screen and the noise did not make Connie shiver, as it would have the day before. "Now put your hand on your heart, honey. Feel that? That feels solid too, but we know better, be nice to me, be sweet like you can because what else is there for a girl like you but to be sweet and pretty and give in?—and get away before her people come back?"

She felt her pounding heart. Her hand seemed to enclose it. She thought for the first time in her life that it was nothing that was hers, that belonged to her, but just a pounding, living thing inside this body that wasn't really hers either.

155 "You don't want them to get hurt," Arnold Friend went on. "Now get up, honey. Get up all by yourself."

She stood.

"Now turn this way. That's right. Come over here to me—Ellie, put that away, didn't I tell you? You dope. You miserable creepy dope," Arnold Friend said. His words were not angry but only part of an incantation. The incantation was kindly. "Now come out through the kitchen to me honey, and let's see a smile, try it, you're a brave sweet little girl and now they're eating corn and hot dogs cooked to bursting over an outdoor fire, and they don't know one thing about you and never did and honey you're better than them because not a one of them would have done this for you."

Connie felt the linoleum under her feet; it was cool. She brushed her hair back out of her eyes. Arnold Friend let go of the post tentatively and opened his arms for her, his elbows pointing in toward each other and his wrists limp, to show that this was an embarrassed embrace and a little mocking, he didn't want to make her self-conscious.

She put out her hand against the screen. She watched herself push the door slowly open as if she were safe back somewhere in the other doorway, watching this body and this head of long hair moving out into the sunlight where Arnold Friend waited.

160 "My sweet little blue-eyed girl," he said, in a half-sung sigh that had nothing to do with her brown eyes but was taken up just the same by the vast sunlit reaches of the land behind him and on all sides of him, so much land that Connie had never seen before and did not recognize except to know that she was going to it.

JOHN STEINBECK

John Steinbeck (1902–68) was born in Salinas, California, a location that provided the setting for many of his novels. Steinbeck attended Stanford University from 1919 until 1925, though he never earned a degree. His first novel, Cup of Gold: A Life of Sir Henry Morgan, Buccaneer, with Occasional Reference to History, *a fictional biography of a seventeenth-century pirate, was rejected by seven publishers before finally being printed in 1929. Despite this inauspicious introduction to the world of writing, Steinbeck went on to publish thirty-one books, three plays, six screenplays, and numerous works of fiction and essays, the most famous of which include* Tortilla Flat *(1935), the novel and play* Of Mice and Men *(1937),* The Grapes of Wrath *(1939),* Cannery Row *(1945),* East of Eden *(1952), and* Travels with Charley *(1962). Steinbeck received several awards for his writing, including a Pulitzer Prize for* The Grapes of Wrath *in 1940 and the Nobel Prize for Literature in 1962. Steinbeck is known for his portrayal of common people who struggle to find meaning in their difficult lives and a recognition of the importance of human responsibility, themes considered by many to be quintessentially American.*

1938

FLIGHT

Out fifteen miles below Monterey, on the wild coast, the Torres family had their farm, a few sloping acres above a cliff that dropped to the brown reefs and to the hissing white waters of the ocean. Behind the farm the stone mountains stood up against the sky.

The farm buildings huddled like the clinging aphids[1] on the mountain skirts, crouched low to the ground as though the wind might blow them into the sea. The little shack, the rattling, rotting barn were gray-bitten with sea salt, beaten by the damp wind until they had taken on the color of the granite hills. Two horses, a red cow and a red calf, half a dozen pigs and a flock of lean, multicolored chickens stocked the place. A little corn was raised on the sterile slope, and it grew short and thick under the wind, and all the cobs formed on the landward sides of the stalks.

Mama Torres, a lean, dry woman with ancient eyes, had ruled the farm for ten years, ever since her husband tripped over a stone in the field one day and fell full length on a rattlesnake. When one is bitten on the chest there is not much that can be done.

Mama Torres had three children, two undersized black ones of twelve and fourteen, Emilio and Rosy, whom Mama kept fishing on the rocks below the farm when the sea was kind and when the truant officer was in some distant part of Monterey County. And there was Pepé, the tall smiling son of nineteen, a gentle, affectionate boy, but very lazy. Pepé had a tall head, pointed at the top, and from its peak coarse black hair grew down like a thatch all around. Over his smiling little eyes Mama cut a straight bang so he could see. Pepé had sharp Indian cheek bones and an eagle nose, but his mouth was as sweet and shapely as a girl's mouth, and his chin was fragile and chiseled. He was loose and gangling, all legs and feet and wrists, and he was very lazy. Mama thought him fine and brave, but she never told him so. She said, "Some lazy cow must have got into thy father's family, else how could I have a son like thee." And she said, "When I carried thee, a sneaking lazy coyote came out of the brush and looked at me one day. That must have made thee so."

Pepé smiled sheepishly and stabbed at the ground with his knife to keep the blade sharp and free from rust. It was his inheritance, that knife, his father's knife. The long heavy blade folded back into the black handle. There was a button on the handle. When Pepé pressed the button, the blade leaped out ready for use. The knife was with Pepé always, for it had been his father's knife.

5   One sunny morning when the sea below the cliff was glinting and blue and the white surf creamed on the reef, when even the stone mountains looked kindly, Mama Torres called out the door of the shack, "Pepé, I have a labor for thee."

There was no answer. Mama listened. From behind the barn she heard a burst of laughter. She lifted her full long skirt and walked in the direction of the noise.

Pepé was sitting on the ground with his back against a box. His white teeth glistened. On either side of him stood the two black ones, tense and expectant. Fifteen feet away a redwood post was set in the ground. Pepé's right hand lay limply in his lap, and in the palm the big black knife rested. The blade was closed back into the handle. Pepé looked smiling at the sky.

Suddenly Emilio cried, "Ya!"

Pepé's wrist flicked like the head of a snake. The blade seemed to fly open in mid-air, and with a thump the point dug into the redwood post, and the black handle quivered. The three burst into excited laughter. Rosy ran to the post and pulled out the knife and brought it back to Pepé. He closed the blade and settled the knife carefully in his listless palm again. He grinned self-consciously at the sky.

10   "Ya!"

The heavy knife lanced out and sunk into the post again. Mama moved forward like a ship and scattered the play.

---

[1] Small insects that live on plants.

"All day you do foolish things with the knife, like a toy baby," she stormed. "Get up on thy huge feet that eat up shoes. Get up!" She took him by one loose shoulder and hoisted at him. Pepé grinned sheepishly and came halfheartedly to his feet. "Look!" Mama cried. "Big lazy, you must catch the horse and put on him thy father's saddle. You must ride to Monterey. The medicine bottle is empty. There is no salt. Go thou now, Peanut! Catch the horse."

A revolution took place in the relaxed figure of Pepé. "To Monterey, me? Alone? Si, Mama."

She scowled at him. "Do not think, big sheep, that you will buy candy. No, I will give you only enough for the medicine and the salt."

15   Pepé smiled. "Mama, you will put the hatband on the hat?"

She relented then. "Yes, Pepé. You may wear the hatband."

His voice grew insinuating. "And the green handkerchief, Mama?"

"Yes, if you go quickly and return with no trouble, the silk green handkerchief will go. If you make sure to take off the handkerchief when you eat so no spot may fall on it."

"Si, Mama. I will be careful, I am a man."

20   "Thou? A man? Thou art a peanut."

He went to the rickety barn and brought out a rope, and he walked agilely enough up the hill to catch the horse. When he was ready and mounted before the door, mounted on his father's saddle that was so old that the oaken frame showed through torn leather in many places, then Mama brought out the round black hat with the tooled leather band, and she reached up and knotted the green silk handkerchief about his neck. Pepé's blue denim coat was much darker than his jeans, for it had been washed much less often.

Mama handed up the big medicine bottle and the silver coins. "That for the medicine," she said, "and that for the salt. That for a candle to burn for the papa. That for dulces[2] for the little ones. Our friend Mrs. Rodriguez will give you dinner and maybe a bed for the night. When you go to the church, say only ten paternosters[3] and only twenty-five Ave Marias.[4] Oh! I know, big coyote. You would sit there flapping your mouth over Aves all day while you looked at the candles and the holy pictures. That is not good devotion to stare at the pretty things."

The black hat, covering the high pointed head and black thatched hair of Pepé, gave him dignity and age. He sat the rangy horse well. Mama thought how handsome he was, dark and lean and tall. "I would not send thee now alone, thou little one, except for the medicine," she said softly, "It is not good to have no medicine, for who knows when the toothache will come, or the sadness of the stomach. These things are."

"Adios, Mama," Pepé cried. "I will come back soon. You may send me often alone. I am a man."

25   "Thou art a foolish chicken."

He straightened his shoulders, flipped the reins against the horse's shoulder, and rode away. He turned once and saw that they still watched him. Emilio and Rosy and Mama. Pepé grinned with pride and gladness and lifted the tough buckskin horse to a trot.

When he had dropped out of sight over a little dip in the road, Mama turned to the black ones, but she spoke to herself. "He is nearly a man now," she said. "It will be a nice thing to have a man in the house again." Her eyes sharpened on the children. "Go to the rocks now. The tide is going out. There will be abalones[5] to be found." She put the iron

---

[2] Sweets.

[3] Ten repetitions of the Lord's Prayer.

[4] Twenty-five prayers to the Virgin Mary.

[5] Large snail whose flesh is used for eating and whose shell is used for ornaments and as a source of mother-of-pearl.

hooks into their hands and saw them down the steep trail to the reefs. She brought the smooth stone metate[6] to the doorway and sat grinding her corn to flour and looking occasionally at the road over which Pepé had gone. The noonday came and then the afternoon, when the little ones beat the abalones on a rock to make them tender and Mama patted the tortillas to make them thin. They ate dinner as the red sun was plunging down toward the ocean. They sat on the doorsteps and watched a big white moon come over the mountain tops.

Mama said. "He is now at the house of our friend Mrs. Rodriguez. She will give him nice things to eat and maybe a present."

Emilio said. "Someday I, too, will ride to Monterey for medicine. Did Pepé come to be a man today?"

30   Mama said wisely, "A boy gets to be a man when a man is needed. Remember this thing. I have known boys forty years old because there was no need for a man."

Soon afterward they retired, Mama in her big oak bed on one side of the room, Emilio and Rosy in their boxes full of straw and sheepskins on the other side of the room.

The moon went over the sky and the surf roared on the rocks. The roosters crowed the first call. The surf subsided to a whispering surge against the reef. The moon dropped toward the sea. The roosters crowed again.

The moon was near down to the water when Pepé rode on a winded horse to his home flat. His dog bounced out and circled the horse, yelping with pleasure. Pepé slid off the saddle to the ground. The weathered little shack was silver in the moonlight and the square shadow of it was black to the north and east. Against the east the piling mountains were misty with light; their tops melted into the sky.

Pepé walked wearily up the three steps and into the house. It was dark inside. There was a rustle in the corner.

35   Mama cried out from her bed. "Who comes? Pepé, is it thou?"

"Si, Mama."

"Did you get the medicine?"

"Si, Mama"

"Well, go to sleep, then. I thought you would be sleeping at the house of Mrs. Rodriguez." Pepé stood silently in the dark room. "Why do you stand there, Pepé? Did you drink wine?"

40   "Si, Mama"

"Well, go to bed then and sleep out the wine."

His voice was tired and patient, but very firm. "Light the candle, Mama. I must go away into the mountains."

"What is this, Pepé? You are crazy." Mama struck a sulfur match and held the little blue burr until the flame spread up the stick. She set light to the candle on the floor beside her bed. "Now, Pepé, what is this you say?" She looked anxiously into his face.

He was changed. The fragile quality seemed to have gone from his chin. His mouth was less full than it had been, the lines of the lip were straighter, but in his eyes the greatest change had taken place. There was no laughter in them anymore, nor any bashfulness. They were sharp and bright and purposeful.

45   He told her in a tired monotone, told her everything just as it had happened. A few people came into the kitchen of Mrs. Rodriguez. There was wine to drink. Pepé drank wine. The little quarrel—the man started toward Pepé and then the knife—it went almost by itself. It flew, it darted before Pepé knew it. As he talked, Mama's face grew stern, and it

---

[6] Stone used for grinding.

seemed to grow more lean. Pepé finished. "I am a man now, Mama. The man said names to me I could not allow."

Mama nodded, "Yes, thou art a man, my poor little Pepé. Thou art a man. I have seen it coming on thee. I have watched you throwing the knife into the post, and I have been afraid." For a moment her face had softened, but now it grew stern again. "Come! We must get you ready. Go. Awaken Emilio and Rosy. Go quickly."

Pepé stepped over to the corner where his brother and sister slept among the sheepskins. He leaned down and shook them gently. "Come, Rosy! Come, Emilio! The mama says you must arise."

The little black ones sat up and rubbed their eyes in the candlelight. Mama was out of bed now, her long black skirt over her nightgown. "Emilio," she cried. "Go up and catch the other horse for Pepé. Quickly, now! Quickly." Emilio put his legs in his overalls and stumbled sleepily out the door.

"You heard no one behind you on the road?" Mama demanded.

50   "No, Mama. I listened carefully. No one was on the road."

Mama darted like a bird about the room. From a nail on the wall she took a canvas bag and threw it on the floor. She stripped a blanket from her bed and rolled it into a tight tube and tied the ends with string. From a box beside the stove she lifted a flour sack half full of black string jerky ."Your father's black coat, Pepé. Here, put it on."

Pepé stood in the middle of the floor watching her activity. She reached behind the door and brought out the rifle, a long 38-56, worn shiny the whole length of the barrel. Pepé took it from her and held it in the crook of his elbow. Mama brought a little leather bag and counted the cartridges into his hand. "Only ten left," she warned. "You must not waste them."

Emilio put his head in the door. "'Qui 'st'I caballo,[7] Mama."

"Put on the saddle from the other horse. Tie on the blanket. Here, tie the jerky to the saddle horn."

55   Still Pepé stood silently watching his mother's frantic activity. His chin looked hard, and his sweet mouth was drawn and thin. His little eyes followed Mama about the room almost suspiciously.

Rosy asked softly. "Where goes Pepé?"

Mama's eyes were fierce, "Pepé goes on a journey. Pepé is a man now. He has a man's thing to do."

Pepé straightened his shoulders. His mouth changed until he looked very much like Mama.

At last the preparation was finished. The loaded horse stood outside the door. The water bag dripped a line of moisture down the bay shoulder,

60   The moonlight was being thinned by the dawn and the big white moon was near down to the sea. The family stood by the shack. Mama confronted Pepé. "Look, my son! Do not stop until it is dark again. Do not sleep even though you are tired. Take care of the horse in order that he may not stop of weariness. Remember to be careful with the bullets—there are only ten. Do not fill thy stomach with jerky or it will make thee sick. Eat a little jerky and fill thy stomach with grass. When thou comest to the high mountains, if thou seest any of the dark watching men, go not near to them nor try to speak to them. And forget not thy prayers." She put her lean hands on Pepé's shoulders, stood on her toes and kissed him formally on both cheeks, and Pepé kissed her on both cheeks. Then he went to Emilio and Rosy and kissed both of their cheeks.

---

[7] **'Qui 'st'l caballo:** Here is the horse.

Pepé turned back to Mama. He seemed to look for a little softness, a little weakness in her. His eyes were searching, but Mama's face remained fierce. "Go now," she said. "Do not wait to be caught like a chicken."

Pepé pulled himself into the saddle. "I am a man," he said.

It was the first dawn when he rode up the hill toward the little canyon which let a trail into the mountains. Moonlight and daylight fought with each other, and the two warring qualities made it difficult to see. Before Pepé had gone a hundred yards, the outlines of his figure were misty; and long before he entered the canyon, he had become a gray, indefinite shadow.

Mama stood stiffly in front of her doorstep, and on either side of her stood Emilio and Rosy. They cast furtive glances at Mama now and then.

65   When the gray shape of Pepé melted into the hillside and disappeared, Mama relaxed. She began the high, whining keen of the death wail. "Our beautiful—our brave," she cried. "Our protector, our son is gone." Emilio and Rosy moaned beside her. "Our beautiful—our brave, he is gone." It was the formal wail. It rose to a high piercing whine and subsided to a moan. Mama raised it three times and then she turned and went into the house and shut the door.

Emilio and Rosy stood wondering in the dawn. They heard Mama whimpering in the house. They went out to sit on the cliff above the ocean. They touched shoulders. "When did Pepé come to be a man?" Emilio asked.

"Last night," said Rosy. "Last night in Monterey." The ocean clouds turned red with the sun that was behind the mountains.

"We will have no breakfast," said Emilio." Mama will not want to cook." Rosy did not answer him. "Where is Pepé gone?" he asked.

Rosy looked around at him. She drew her knowledge from the quiet air. "He has gone on a journey. He will never come back."

70   "Is he dead? Do you think he is dead?"

Rosy looked back at the ocean again. A little steamer, drawing a line of smoke, sat on the edge of the horizon. "He is not dead," Rosy explained. "Not yet."

Pepé rested the big rifle across the saddle in front of him. He let the horse walk up the hill and he didn't look back. The stony slope took on a coat of short brush so that Pepé found the entrance to a trail and entered it.

When he came to the canyon opening, he swung once in his saddle and looked back, but the houses were swallowed in the misty light. Pepé jerked forward again. The high shoulder of the canyon closed in on him. His horse stretched out its neck and sighed and settled to the trail.

It was a well-worn path, dark soft leaf-mold earth strewn with broken pieces of sandstone. The trail rounded the shoulder of the canyon and dropped steeply into the bed of the stream. In the shallows the water ran smoothly, glinting in the first morning sun. Small round stones on the bottom were as brown as rust with sun moss. In the sand along the edges of the stream the tall, rich wild mint grew, while in the water itself the cress,[8] old and tough, had gone to heavy seed.

75   The path went into the stream and emerged on the other side. The horse sloshed into the water and stopped. Pepé dropped his bridle and let the beast drink of the running water.

Soon the canyon sides became steep and the first giant sentinel redwoods guarded the trail, great round red trunks bearing foliage as green and lacy as ferns. Once Pepé was among the trees, the sun was lost. A perfumed and purple light lay in the pale green of the

---

[8] Watercress.

underbrush. Gooseberry bushes and blackberries and tall ferns lined the stream, and over-head the branches of the redwoods met and cut off the sky.

Pepé drank from the water bag, and he reached into the flour sack and brought out a black string of jerky. His white teeth gnawed at the string until the tough meat parted. He chewed slowly and drank occasionally from the water bag. His little eyes were slumberous and tired, but the muscles of his face were hard-set. The earth of the trail was black now. It gave up a hollow sound under the walking hoofbeats.

The stream fell more sharply. Little waterfalls splashed on the stones. Five-fingered ferns hung over the water and dropped spray from their fingertips. Pepé rode half over his saddle, dangling one leg loosely. He picked a bay leaf from a tree beside the way and put it into his mouth for a moment to flavor the dry jerky. He held the gun loosely across the pommel.

Suddenly he squared in his saddle, swung the horse from the trail and kicked it hurriedly up behind a big redwood tree. He pulled up the reins tight against the bit to keep the horse from whinnying. His face was intent and his nostrils quivered a little.

80 A hollow pounding came down the trail, and a horseman rode by, a fat man with red cheeks and a white stubble beard. His horse put down his head and blubbered at the trail when it came to the place where Pepé had turned off. "Hold up!" said the man, and he pulled up his horse's head.

When the last sound of the hooves died away, Pepé came back into the trail again. He did not relax in the saddle any more. He lifted the big rifle and swung the lever to throw a shell into the chamber, and then he let down the hammer to half cock.

The trail grew very steep. Now the redwood trees were smaller and their tops were dead, bitten dead where the wind reached them. The horse plodded on; the sun went slowly overhead and started down toward the afternoon.

Where the stream came out of a side canyon, the trail left it. Pepé dismounted and watered his horse and filled up his water bag. As soon as the trail had parted from the stream, the trees were gone and only the thick brittle sage and manzanita[9] and the chaparral[10] edged the trail. And the soft black earth was gone, too, leaving only the light tan broken rock for the trail bed. Lizards scampered away into the brush as the horse rattled over the little stones.

Pepé turned in his saddle and looked back. He was in the open now: he could be seen from a distance. As he ascended the trail the country grew more rough and terrible and dry. The way wound about the bases of great square rocks. Little gray rabbits skittered in the brush. A bird made a monotonous high creaking. Eastward the bare rock mountaintops were pale and powder-dry under the dropping sun. The horse plodded up and up the trail toward the little V in the ridge which was the pass.

85 Pepé looked suspiciously back every minute or so, and his eyes sought the tops of the ridges ahead. Once, on a white barren spur, he saw a black figure for a moment; but he looked quickly away, for it was one of the dark watchers. No one knew who the watchers were, nor where they lived, but it was better to ignore them and never to show interest in them. They did not bother one who stayed on the trail and minded his own business.

The air was parched and full of light dust blown by the breeze from the eroding mountains. Pepé drank sparingly from his bag and corked it tightly and hung it on the horn again. The trail moved up the dry shale hillside, avoiding rocks, dropping under clefts, climbing in and out of old water scars. When he arrived at the little pass he stopped and looked back for a

---

[9] Shrubs.

[10] A dense thicket.

long time. No dark watchers were to be seen now. The trail behind was empty. Only the high tops of the redwoods indicated where the stream flowed.

Pepé rode on through the pass. His little eyes were nearly closed with weariness, but his face was stern, relentless, and manly. The high mountain wind coasted sighing through the pass and whistled on the edges of the big blocks of broken granite. In the air, a red-tailed hawk sailed over close to the ridge and screamed angrily. Pepé went slowly through the broken jagged pass and looked down on the other side.

The trail dropped quickly, staggering among broken rock. At the bottom of the slope there was a dark crease, thick with brush, and on the other side of the crease a little flat, in which a grove of oak trees grew. A scar of green grass cut across the flat. And behind the flat another mountain rose, desolate with dead rocks and starving little black bushes. Pepé drank from the bag again, for the air was so dry that it encrusted his nostrils and burned his lips. He put the horse down the trail. The hoofs slipped and struggled on the steep way, starting little stones that rolled off into the brush. The sun was gone behind the westward mountain now, but still it glowed brilliantly on the oaks and on the grassy flat. The rocks and the hillsides still sent up waves of the heat they had gathered from the day's sun.

Pepé looked up to the top of the next dry withered ridge. He saw a dark form against the sky, a man's figure standing on top of a rock, and he glanced away quickly not to appear curious. When a moment later he looked up again, the figure was gone.

90   Downward the trail was quickly covered. Sometimes the horse floundered for footing, sometimes set his feet and slid a little way. They came at last to the bottom where the dark chaparral was higher than Pepé's head. He held up his rifle on one side and his arm on the other to shield his face from the sharp brittle fingers of the brush.

Up and out of the crease he rode, and up a little cliff. The grassy flat was before him, and the round comfortable oaks. For a moment he studied the trail down which he had come, but there was no movement and no sound from it. Finally he rode out over the flat, to the green streak, and at the upper end of the damp he found a little spring welling out of the earth and dropping into a dug basin before it seeped out over the flat.

Pepé filled his bag first, and then he let the thirsty horse drink out of the pool. He led the horse to the clump of oaks, and in the middle of the grove, fairly protected from sight on all sides, he took off the saddle and the bridle and laid them on the ground. The horse stretched his jaws sideways and yawned. Pepé knotted the lead rope about the horse's neck and tied him to a sapling among the oaks, where he could graze in a fairly large circle.

When the horse was gnawing hungrily at the dry grass, Pepé went to the saddle and took a black string of jerky from the sack and strolled to an oak tree on the edge of the grove, from under which he could watch the trail. He sat down in the crisp dry oak leaves and automatically felt for his big black knife to cut the jerky, but he had no knife. He leaned back on his elbow and gnawed at the tough strong meat. His face was blank, but it was a man's face.

The bright evening light washed the eastern ridge, but the valley was darkening. Doves flew down from the hills to the spring, and the quail came running out of the brush and joined them, calling clearly to one another.

95   Out of the corner of his eye Pepé saw a shadow grow out of the bushy crease. He turned his head slowly. A big spotted wildcat was creeping toward the spring, belly to the ground, moving like thought.

Pepé cocked his rifle and edged the muzzle slowly around. Then he looked apprehensively up the trail and dropped the hammer again. From the ground beside him he picked an oak twig and threw it toward the spring. The quail flew up with a roar and the doves whistled away. The big cat stood up; for a long moment he looked at Pepé with cold yellow eyes, and then fearlessly walked back into the gulch.

The dusk gathered quickly in the deep valley. Pepé muttered his prayers, put his head down on his arm and went instantly to sleep.

The moon came up and filled the valley with cold blue light, and the wind swept rustling down from the peaks. The owls worked up and down the slopes looking for rabbits. Down in the brush of the gulch a coyote gabbled. The oak trees whispered softly in the night breeze.

Pepé started up, listening. His horse had whinnied. The moon was just slipping behind the western ridge, leaving the valley in darkness behind it. Pepé sat tensely gripping his rifle. From far up the trail he heard an answering whinny and the crash of shod hooves on the broken rock. He jumped to his feet, ran to his horse and led it under the trees. He threw on the saddle and cinched it tight for the steep trail, caught the unwilling head and forced the bit into the mouth. He felt the saddle to make sure the water bag and the sack of jerky were there. Then he mounted and turned up the hill.

100   It was velvet-dark. The horse found the entrance to the trail where it left the flat, and started up, stumbling and slipping on the rocks. Pepé's hand rose up to his head. His hat was gone. He had left it under the oak tree.

The horse had struggled far up the trail when the first change of dawn came into the air, a steel grayness as light mixed thoroughly with dark. Gradually the sharp snaggled edge of the ridge stood out above them, rotten granite tortured and eaten by the winds of time. Pepé had dropped his reins on the horn, leaving direction to the horse. The brush grabbed at his legs in the dark until one knee of his jeans was ripped.

Gradually the light flowed down over the ridge. The starved brush and rocks stood out in the half-light, strange and lonely in high perspective. Then there came warmth into the light. Pepé drew up and looked back, but he could see nothing in the darker valley below. The sky turned blue over the coming sun. In the waste of the mountainside, the poor dry brush grew only three feet high. Here and there, big outcroppings of unrotted granite stood up like moldering houses. Pepé relaxed a little. He drank from his water bag and bit off a piece of jerky. A single eagle flew over, high in the light.

Without warning Pepé's horse screamed and fell on its side. He was almost down before the rifle crash echoed up from the valley. From a hole behind the struggling shoulder, a stream of bright crimson blood pumped and stopped and pumped and stopped. The hooves threshed on the ground. Pepé lay half stunned beside the horse. He looked slowly down the hill. A piece of sage clipped off beside his head and another crash echoed up from side to side of the canyon. Pepé flung himself frantically behind a bush.

He crawled up the hill on his knees and one hand. His right hand held the rifle up off the ground and pushed it ahead of him. He moved with the instinctive care of an animal. Rapidly he wormed his way toward one of the big outcroppings of granite on the hill above him. Where the brush was high he doubled up and ran, but where the cover was slight he wriggled forward on his stomach, pushing the rifle ahead of him. In the last little distance there was no cover at all. Pepé poised and then he darted across the space and flashed around the corner of the rock.

105   He leaned panting against the stone. When his breath came easier he moved along behind the big rock until he came to a narrow split that offered a thin section of vision down the hill. Pepé lay on his stomach and pushed the rifle barrel through the slit and waited.

The sun reddened the western ridges now. Already the buzzards were settling down toward the place where the horse lay. A small brown bird scratched in the dead sage leaves directly in front of the rifle muzzle. The coasting eagle flew back toward the rising sun.

Pepé saw a little movement in the brush far below. His grip tightened on the gun. A little brown doe stepped daintily out on the trail arid crossed it and disappeared into the brush again. For a long time Pepé waited. Far below he could see the little flat and the oak trees and the slash of green. Suddenly his eyes flashed back at the trail again. A quarter of a mile down there had been a quick movement in the chaparral. The rifle swung over. The front sight nestled in the V of the rear sight. Pepé studied for a moment and then raised the rear sight a notch. The little movement in the brush came again. The sight settled on it. Pepé squeezed the trigger. The explosion crashed down the mountain and up the other side, and came rattling back. The whole side of the slope grew still. No more movement. And then a white streak cut into the granite of the slit and a bullet whined away and a crash sounded up from below. Pepé felt a sharp pain in his right hand. A sliver of granite was sticking out from between his first and second knuckles and the point protruded from his palm. Carefully he pulled out the sliver of stone. The wound bled evenly and gently. No vein or artery was cut.

Pepé looked into a little dusty cave in the rock and gathered a handful of spider web, and he pressed the mass into the cut, plastering the soft web into the blood. The flow stopped almost at once.

The rifle was on the ground. Pepé picked it up, levered a new shell into the chamber. And then he slid into the brush on his stomach. Far to the right he crawled, and then up the hill, moving slowly and carefully, crawling to cover and resting and then crawling again.

110   In the mountains the sun is high in its arc before it penetrates the gorges. The hot face looked over the hill and brought instant heat with it. The white light beat on the rocks and reflected from them and rose up quivering from the earth again, and the rocks and bushes seemed to quiver behind the air.

Pepé crawled in the general direction of the ridge peak, zigzagging for cover. The deep cut between his knuckles began to throb. He crawled close to a rattlesnake before he saw it, and when it raised its dry head and made a soft beginning whir, he backed up and took another way. The quick gray lizards flashed in front of him, raising a tiny line of dust. He found another mass of spider web and pressed it against his throbbing hand.

Pepé was pushing the rifle with his left hand now. Little drops of sweat ran to the ends of his coarse black hair and rolled down his cheeks. His lips and tongue were growing thick and heavy. His lips writhed to draw saliva into his mouth. His little dark eyes were uneasy and suspicious. Once when a gray lizard paused in front of him on the parched ground and turned its head sideways, he crushed it flat with a stone.

When the sun slid past noon he had not gone a mile. He crawled exhaustedly a last hundred yards to a patch of high sharp manzanita, crawled desperately, and when the patch was reached he wriggled in among the tough gnarly trunks and dropped his head on his left arm. There was little shade in the meager brush, but there was cover and safety. Pepé went to sleep as he lay and the sun beat on his back. A few little birds hopped close to him and peered and hopped away, Pepé squirmed in his sleep and he raised and dropped his wounded hand again and again.

The sun went down behind the peaks and the cool evening came, and then the dark; A coyote yelled from the hillside. Pepé started awake and looked about with misty eyes. His hand was swollen and heavy; a little thread of pain ran up the inside of his arm and settled in a pocket in his armpit. He peered about and then stood up, for the mountains were black and the moon had not yet risen. Pepé stood up in the dark. The coat of his father pressed on his arm. His tongue was swollen until it nearly filled his mouth. He wriggled out of the coat and dropped it in the brush, and then he struggled up the hill, falling over rocks and tearing his way through the brush. The rifle knocked against stones as he went. Little dry avalanches of gravel and shattered stone went whispering down the hill behind him.

115   After a while the old moon came up and showed the jagged ridgetop ahead of him. By moonlight Pepé traveled more easily. He bent forward so that his throbbing arm hung away from his body. The journey uphill was made in dashes and rests, a frantic rush up a few

yards and then a rest. The wind coasted down the slope, rattling the dry stems of the bushes.

The moon was at meridian when Pepé came at last to the sharp backbone of the ridgetop. On the last hundred yards of the rise no soil had clung under the wearing winds. The way was on solid rock. He clambered to the top and looked down on the other side. There was a draw like the last below him, misty with moonlight, brushed with dry struggling sage and chaparral. On the other side the hill rose up sharply and at the top the jagged rotten teeth of the mountain showed against the sky. At the bottom of the cut the brush was thick and dark.

Pepé stumbled down the hill. His throat was almost closed with thirst. At first he tried to run, but immediately he fell and rolled. After that he went more carefully. The moon was just disappearing behind the mountains when he came to the bottom. He crawled into the heavy brush, feeling with his fingers for water. There was no water in the bed of the stream, only damp earth. Pepé laid his gun down and scooped up a handful of mud and put it in his mouth, and then he spluttered and scraped the earth from his tongue with his finger, for the mud drew at his mouth like a poultice. He dug a hole in the stream bed with his fingers, dug a little basin to catch water; but before it was very deep his head fell forward on the damp ground and he slept.

The dawn came and the heat of the day fell on the earth, and still Pepé slept. Late in the afternoon his head jerked up. He looked slowly around. His eyes were slits of weariness. Twenty feet away in the heavy brush a big tawny mountain lion stood looking at him. Its long thick tail waved gracefully; its ears were erect with interest, not laid back dangerously. The lion squatted down on its stomach and watched him.

Pepé looked at the hole he had dug in the earth. A half-inch of muddy water had collected in the bottom. He tore the sleeve from his hurt arm, with his teeth ripped out a little square, soaked it in the water and put it in his mouth. Over and over he filled the cloth and sucked it.

120 Still the lion sat and watched him. The evening came down but there was no movement on the hills. No birds visited the dry bottom of the cut. Pepé looked occasionally at the lion. The eyes of the yellow beast drooped as though he were about to sleep. He yawned and his long thin red tongue curled out. Suddenly his head jerked around and his nostrils quivered. His big tail lashed. He stood up and slunk like a tawny shadow into the thick brush.

A moment later Pepé heard the sound, the faint far crash of horses' hooves on gravel. And he heard something else, a high whining yelp of a dog.

Pepé took his rifle in his left hand and he glided into the brush almost as quietly as the lion had. In the darkening evening he crouched up the hill toward the next ridge. Only when the dark came did he stand up. His energy was short. Once it was dark he fell over the rocks and slipped to his knees on the steep slope, but he moved on and on up the hill, climbing and scrambling over the broken hillside.

When he was far up toward the top, he lay down and slept for a little while. The withered moon, shining on his face, awakened him. He stood up and moved up the hill. Fifty yards away he stopped and turned back, for he had forgotten his rifle. He walked heavily down and poked about in the brush, but he could not find his gun. At last he lay down to rest. The pocket of pain in his armpit had grown more sharp. His arm seemed to swell out and fall with every heartbeat. There was no position lying down where the heavy arm did not press against his armpit.

With the effort of a hurt beast, Pepé got up and moved again toward the top of the ridge. He held his swollen arm away from his body with his left hand. Up the steep hill he dragged himself, a few steps and a rest, and a few more steps. At last he was nearing the top. The moon showed the uneven sharp back of it against the sky.

125   Pepé's brain spun in a big spiral up and away from him. He slumped to the ground and lay still. The rock ridgetop was only a hundred feet above him.

The moon moved over the sky. Pepé half turned on his back. His tongue tried to make words, but only a thick hissing came from between his lips.

When the dawn came, Pepé pulled himself up. His eyes were sane again. He drew his great puffed arm in front of him and looked at the angry wound. The black line ran up from his wrist to his armpit. Automatically he reached in his pocket for the big black knife, but it was not there. His eyes searched the ground. He picked up a sharp blade of stone and scraped at the wound, sawed at the proud flesh and then squeezed the green juice out in big drops. Instantly he threw back his head and whined like a dog. His whole right side shuddered at the pain, but the pain cleared his head.

In the gray light he struggled up the last slope to the ridge and crawled over and lay down behind a line of rocks. Below him lay a deep canyon exactly like the last, waterless and desolate. There was no flat, no oak trees, not even heavy brush in the bottom of it And on the other side a sharp ridge stood up, thinly brushed with starving sage, littered with broken granite. Strewn over the hill there were giant outcroppings, and on the top the granite teeth stood out against the sky.

The new day was light now. The flame of the sun came over the ridge and fell on Pepé where he lay on the ground. His coarse black hair was littered with twigs and bits of spider web. His eyes had retreated back into his head. Between his lips the tip of his black tongue showed.

130   He sat up and dragged his great arm into his lap and nursed it, rocking his body and moaning in his throat. He threw back his head and looked up into the pale sky. A big black bird circled nearly out of sight, and far to the left another was sailing near.

He lifted his head to listen, for a familiar sound had come to him from the valley he had climbed out of; it was the crying yelp of hounds, excited and feverish, on a trail.

Pepé bowed his head quickly. He tried to speak rapid words but only a thick hiss came from his lips. He drew a shaky cross on his breast with his left hand. It was a long struggle to get to his feet. He crawled slowly and mechanically to the top of a big rock on the ridge peak. Once there, he arose slowly, swaying to his feet, and stood erect. Far below he could see the dark brush where he had slept. He braced his feet and stood there, black against the morning sky.

There came a ripping sound at his feet A piece of stone flew up and a bullet droned off into the next gorge. The hollow crash echoed up from below. Pepé looked down for a moment and then pulled himself straight again.

His body jarred back. His left hand fluttered helplessly toward his breast. The second crash sounded from below. Pepé swung forward and toppled from the rock. His body struck and rolled over and over, starting a little avalanche. And when at last he stopped against a bush, the avalanche slid slowly down and covered up his head.

MARIE HOWE

Marie Howe (1950–   ) was born in Rochester, New York, and was educated at the University of Windsor and Columbia University. She presently teaches writing at Columbia University and Sarah Lawrence College. The oldest of nine children, Howe entertained herself and her siblings by telling stories, an activity that she claims led to her career as a poet. Her publications include two books of poetry, The Good Thief *(1988) and* What the Living Do *(1997). With Michael Klein, she edited a collection of writing about AIDS entitled* In the Company of My Solitude: American Writing from the AIDS Pandemic *(1994). Howe received both a*

Guggenheim and a National Endowment for the Arts fellowship, and her poems have appeared in The New Yorker, *the* Atlantic, Agni, Harvard Review, *and* New England Review. *"The Attic," written after her brother's death from AIDS, is from* What the Living Do, *a collection of poems about people who survive the death of those they love.*

1998

THE ATTIC

Praise to my older brother, the seventeen-year-old boy, who lived
in the attic with me an exiled prince grown hard in his confinement,

bitter, bent to his evening task building the imaginary building
on the drawing board they'd given him in school. His tools gleam

5 under the desk lamp. He is as hard as the pencil he holds,
drawing the line straight along the ruler.

Tower prince, young king, praise to the boy
who has willed his blood to cool and his heart to slow. He's building

a structure with so many doors it's finally quiet,
10 so that when our father climbs heavily up the attic stairs, he doesn't

at first hear him pass down the narrow hall. My brother is rebuilding
the foundation. He lifts the clear plastic of one page

to look more closely at the plumbing,
—he barely hears the springs of my bed when my father sits down—

15 he's imagining where the boiler might go, because
where it is now isn't working. Not until I've slammed the door behind

the man stumbling down the stairs again
does my brother look up from where he's working. I know it hurts him

to rise, to knock on my door and come in. And when he draws his
20   skinny arm
around my shaking shoulders,

I don't know if he knows he's building a world where I can one day
love a man—he sits there without saying anything.

Praise him.
I know he can hardly bear to touch me.

WILLIAM S. KOWINSKI

A poet, fiction writer, and critic, William Severini Kowinski studied at Knox College and has been a writer and editor for the Boston Phoenix *and* Washington Newsworks. *He has published in numerous magazines including* Esquire, New Times, *and* The New York Times Magazine. *His book,* The Malling of America: An Inside Look at the Great Consumer Paradise *(1985), was reissued in 2002 with a new introduction and memoir about the publication of the first edition. This excerpt from Kowinski's book is an investigation of the effects of shopping malls on the lives of adolescents.*

1985

KIDS IN THE MALL

> *Butch heaved himself up and loomed over the group. "Like it was different for me," he piped. "My folks used to drop me off at the shopping mall every morning and leave me all day. It was like a big free babysitter, you know? One night they never came back for me. Maybe they moved away. Maybe there's some kind of Bureau of Missing Parents I could check with."*
>
> —Richard Peck
> Secrets of the Shopping Mall
> *a novel for teenagers*

From his sister at Swarthmore, I'd heard about a kid in Florida whose mother picked him up after school every day, drove him straight to the mall, and left him there until it closed—all at his insistence. I'd heard about a boy in Washington who, when his family moved from one suburb to another, pedaled his bicycle five miles every day to get back to his old mall, where he once belonged.

These stories aren't unusual. The mall is a common experience for the majority of American youth; they have probably been going there all their lives. Some ran within their first large open space, saw their first fountain, bought their first toy, and read their first book in a mall. They may have smoked their first cigarette or first joint or turned them down, had their first kiss or lost their virginity in the mall parking lot. Teenagers in America now spend more time in the mall than anywhere else but home and school. Mostly it is their choice, but some of that mall time is put in as the result of two-paycheck and single-parent households, and the lack of other viable alternatives. But are these kids being harmed by the mall?

I wondered first of all what difference it makes for adolescents to experience so many important moments in the mall. They are, after all, at play in the fields of its little world and they learn its ways; they adapt to it and make it adapt to them. It's here that these kids get their street sense, only it's mall sense. They are learning the ways of a large-scale artificial environment: its subtleties and flexibilities, its particular pleasures and resonances, and the attitudes it fosters.

The presence of so many teenagers for so much time was not something mall developers planned on. In fact, it came as a big surprise. But kids became a fact of mall life very early, and the International Council of Shopping Centers found it necessary to commission a study, which they published along with a guide to mall managers on how to handle the teenage incursion.

5   The study found that "teenagers in suburban centers are bored and come to the shopping centers mainly as a place to go. Teenagers in suburban centers spent more time fighting, drinking, littering and walking than did their urban counterparts, but presented fewer overall problems." The report observed that "adolescents congregated in groups of two to four and predominantly at locations selected by them rather than management." This probably had something to do with the decision to install game arcades, which allow management to channel these restless adolescents into naturally contained areas away from major traffic points of adult shoppers.

The guide concluded that mall management should tolerate and even encourage the teenage presence because, in the words of the report, "The vast majority support the same set of values as does shopping center management." *The same set of values* means simply that mall kids are already preprogrammed to be consumers and that the mall can put the finishing touches to them as hard-core, lifelong shoppers just like everybody else. That, after all, is what the mall is about. So it shouldn't be surprising that in spending a lot of time there, adolescents find little that challenges the assumption that the goal of life is to make money and buy products, or that just about everything else in life is to be used to serve those ends.

Growing up in a high-consumption society already adds inestimable pressure to kids' lives. Clothes consciousness has invaded the grade schools, and popularity is linked with having the best, newest clothes in the currently acceptable styles. Even what they read has been affected. "Miss [Nancy] Drew wasn't obsessed with her wardrobe," noted *The Wall Street Journal,* "but today the mystery in teen fiction for girls is what outfit the heroine will wear next." Shopping has become a survival skill and there is certainly no better place to learn it than the mall, where its importance is powerfully reinforced and certainly never questioned.

The mall as a university of suburban materialism, where Valley Girls and Boys from coast to coast are educated in consumption, has its other lessons in this era of change in family life and sexual mores and their economic and social ramifications. The plethora of products in the mall, plus the pressure on teens to buy them, may contribute to the phenomenon that psychologist David Elkind calls "the hurried child": kids who are exposed to too much of the adult world too quickly, and must respond with a sophistication that belies their still-tender emotional development. Certainly the adult products marketed for children—form-fitting designer jeans, sexy tops for preteen girls—add to the social pressure to look like an adult, along with the home-grown need to understand adult finances (why mothers must work) and adult emotions (when parents divorce).

Kids spend so much time at the mall partly because their parents allow it and even encourage it. The mall is safe, it doesn't seem to harbor any unsavory activities, and there is adult supervision; it is, after all, a controlled environment. So the temptation, especially for working parents, is to let the mall be their babysitter. At least the kids aren't watching TV. But the mall's role as a surrogate mother may be more extensive and more profound.

10   Karen Lansky, a writer living in Los Angeles, has looked into the subject and she told me some of her conclusions about the effects on its teenaged denizens of the mall's controlled and controlling environment. "Structure is the dominant idea, since true 'mall rats' lack just that in their home lives," she said, "and adolescents about to make the big leap into growing up crave more structure than our modern society cares to acknowledge." Karen pointed out some of the elements malls supply that kids used to get from their families, like warmth (Strawberry Shortcake dolls and similar cute and cuddly merchandise), old-fashioned mothering ("We do it all for you," the fast-food slogan), and even home cooking (the "homemade" treats at the food court).

The problem in all this, as Karen Lansky sees it, is that while families nurture children by encouraging growth through the assumption of responsibility and then by letting them rest in the bosom of the family from the rigors of growing up, the mall as a structural mother encourages passivity and consumption, as long as the kid doesn't make trouble. Therefore all they learn about becoming adults is how to act and how to consume.

Kids are in the mall not only in the passive role of shoppers—they also work there, especially as fast-food outlets infiltrate the mall's enclosure. There they learn how to hold a job and take responsibility, but still within the same value context. When *CBS Reports* went to Oak Park Mall in suburban Kansas City, Kansas, to tape part of their hour-long consideration of malls, "After the Dream Comes True," they interviewed a teenaged girl who worked in a fast-food outlet there. In a sequence that didn't make the final program, she described the major goal of her present life, which was to perfect the curl on top of the ice-cream cones that were her store's speciality. If she could do that, she would be moved from the lowly soft-drink dispenser to the more prestigious ice-cream division, the curl on top of the status ladder at her restaurant. These are the achievements that are important at the mall.

Other benefits of such jobs may also be overrated, according to Laurence D. Steinberg of the University of California at Irvine's social ecology department, who did a study on teenage employment. Their jobs, he found, are generally simple, mindlessly repetitive and boring. They don't really learn anything, and the jobs don't head anywhere. Teenagers also work primarily with other teenagers; even their supervisors are often just a little older than they are. "Kids need to spend time with adults," Steinberg told me. "Although they get benefits from peer relationships, without parents and other adults it's a one-sided socialization. They hang out with each other, have age-segregated jobs, and watch TV."

Perhaps much of this is not so terrible or even so terribly different. Now that they have so much more to contend with in their lives, adolescents probably need more time to spend with other adolescents without adult impositions, just to sort things out. Though it is more concentrated in the mall (and therefore perhaps a clearer target), the value system there is really the dominant one of the whole society. Attitudes about curiosity, initiative, self-expression, empathy, and disinterested learning aren't necessarily made in the mall; they are mirrored there, perhaps a bit more intensely—as through a glass brightly.

15   Besides, the mall is not without its educational opportunities. There are bookstores, where there is at least a short shelf of classics at great prices, and other books from which it is possible to learn more than how to do sit-ups. There are tools, from hammers to VCRs, and products, from clothes to records, that can help the young find and express themselves. There are older people with stories, and places to be alone or to talk one-on-one with a kindred spirit. And there is always the passing show.

The mall itself may very well be an education about the future. I was struck with the realization, as early as my first forays into Greengate, that the mall is only one of a number of enclosed and controlled environments that are part of the lives of today's young. The mall is just an extension, say, of those large suburban schools—only there's Karmelkorn instead of chem lab, the ice rink instead of the gym: It's high school without the impertinence of classes.

Growing up, moving from home to school to the mall—from enclosure to enclosure, transported in cars—is a curiously continuous process, without much in the way of contrast or contact with unenclosed reality. Places must tend to blur into one another. But whatever differences and dangers there are in this, the skills these adolescents are learning may turn out to be useful in their later lives. For we seem to be moving inexorably into an age of preplanned and regulated environments, and this is the world they will inherit.

Still, it might be better if they had more of a choice. One teenaged girl confessed to *CBS Reports* that she sometimes felt she was missing something by hanging out at the mall so much. "But I'm here," she said, "and this is what I have."

■ EXPLORATIONS OF THE TEXT

1. In Oates's "Where Are You Going, Where Have You Been?" Connie is described as having "two sides" to her personality. Do other characters portrayed in works in this cluster have "two sides" to their personalities? Analyze the personalities of the main protagonists in two other pieces.

2. What forces support the development of identity and selfhood? What forces thwart personal growth? Do the protagonists in Oates's and Steinbeck's stories and the persona in Howe's poem find eventual redemption? Explain.

3. "Flight" contains many references to Pepé's being a man, looking like a man, and having reached manhood. What does it mean to be a man in North American society? Examine how the authors in this cluster treat this theme.

4. Some critics see aspects of Steinbeck's "Flight" as projections of a human, psychological landscape. If this is the case, what part of the human psyche could "the dark watchers" represent? How does this critical interpretation fit Oates's "Where Are You Going, Where Have You Been?" or Howe's "The Attic"? What are "the dark watchers" in those works?

5. Discuss how the symbolism in the selected works in this cluster enhances the development of theme (for example: music and fairy tale motifs in Oates's "Where Are You Going, Where Have You Been?"; color imagery and directions in "Flight"; the fairy tale motifs of "Little Red Riding Hood" and "Rapunzel"; or the prince and the castle in Howe's "The Attic").

6. In Oates's, Steinbeck's, and Howe's works, the writers allude to, but do not graphically describe, violent events. As in Greek tragedy, the central acts of violence take place off-stage. What is the impact of this artistic choice? Is it effective?

7. Using Hollis's stages of the heroic journey (from "The Heroic Journey") or Bettelheim's concept of the "existential predicament" (from "The Uses of Enchantment"), analyze the journeys taken by characters in this thematic cluster.

■ THE READING/WRITING CONNECTION

1. Does Connie or one of the other characters featured in works in this cluster lack inner resources? Respond to this question in a paragraph.

2. "Think" Topic: What is a major theme or lesson that one may learn from one of the protagonist's experiences? Relate that lesson to your own life. What were some difficult, painful, or damaging lessons that you or someone you know had to learn?

3. Compose a letter written by Pepé to his mother and family shortly before his death, or choose a protagonist from a different work and write a letter or monologue in his or her voice.

■ IDEAS FOR WRITING

1. Write a critical analysis essay that presents a central theme from one of the stories in this cluster. Demonstrate how setting, character development, plot, or symbolism develop the theme.

2. Both Steinbeck's "Flight" and Oates's "Where Are You Going, Where Have You Been?" are among their most frequently anthologized stories. What makes them effective? Evaluate one of the works, and consider such elements of fiction as point of view, conflict, character development, language, and tone (chapter 9).

3. Is Oates's "Where Are You Going, Where Have you Been?" still relevant to contemporary teenage culture? Using Kowinski's "Kids in the Mall" or Elkind's "Our Hurried Children" as a resource, construct an argument that addresses this question.

■ FICTION ■

SARAH ORNE JEWETT

Born in South Berwick, Maine, Theodora Sarah Orne Jewett (1849–1909) graduated from Berwick Academy. She began writing stories under a pseudonym for the Atlantic *magazine. In 1877, she published her first collection,* Deephaven. *It was followed by the story* collections, *A White Heron, and Other Stories (1886) and The King of Folly Island (1888), and the novels,* A Country Doctor *(1988) and* The Country of Pointed Firs *(1896). Jewett stated that she wrote about those "country characters and landscapes to which (she herself) belonged, and which (she) had been taught to love with all (her) heart."*

1886

A WHITE HERON

I

The woods were already filled with shadows one June evening, just before eight o'clock, though a bright sunset still glimmered faintly among the trunks of the trees. A little girl was driving home her cow, a plodding, dilatory, provoking creature in her behavior, but a valued companion for all that. They were going away from the western light, and striking deep into the dark woods, but their feet were familiar with the path, and it was no matter whether their eyes could see it or not.

There was hardly a night the summer through when the old cow could be found waiting at the pasture bars; on the contrary, it was her greatest pleasure to hide herself away among the high huckleberry bushes, and though she wore a loud bell she had made the discovery that if one stood perfectly still it would not ring. So Sylvia had to hunt for her until she found her, and call Co'! Co'! with never an answering Moo, until her childish patience was quite spent. If the creature had not given good milk and plenty of it, the case would have seemed very different to her owners. Besides, Sylvia had all the time there was, and very little use to make of it. Sometimes in pleasant weather it was a consolation to look upon the cow's pranks as an intelligent attempt to play hide and seek, and as the child had no playmates she lent herself to this amusement with a good deal of zest. Though this chase had been so long that the wary animal herself had given an unusual signal of her whereabouts, Sylvia had only laughed when she came upon Mistress Moolly at the swamp-side, and urged her affectionately homeward with a twig of birch leaves. The old cow was not inclined to wander farther, she even turned in the right direction for once as they left the pasture, and stepped along the road at a good pace. She was quite ready to be milked now, and seldom stopped to browse. Sylvia wondered what her grandmother would say because they were so late. It was a great while since she had left home at half past five o'clock, but everybody knew the difficulty of making this errand a short one. Mrs. Tilley had chased the horned torment too many summer evenings herself to blame any one else for lingering, and was only thankful as she waited that she had Sylvia, nowadays, to give such valuable assistance. The good woman suspected that Sylvia loitered occasionally on her own account; there never was such a child for straying about out-of-doors since the world was made! Everybody said that it was a good change for a little maid who had tried to grow for eight years in a crowded manufacturing town, but, as for Sylvia herself, it seemed as if she never had been alive at all before she came to live at the farm. She thought often with wistful compassion of a wretched dry geranium that belonged to a town neighbor.

"'Afraid of folks,'" old Mrs. Tilley said to herself, with a smile, after she had made the unlikely choice of Sylvia from her daughter's houseful of children, and was returning to the farm. " 'Afraid of folks,' they said! I guess she won't be troubled no great with 'em up to the old place!" When they reached the door of the lonely house and stopped to unlock it, and the cat came to purr loudly, and rub against them, a deserted pussy, indeed, but fat with young robins, Sylvia whispered that this was a beautiful place to live in, and she never should wish to go home.

* * *

The companions followed the shady wood-road, the cow taking slow steps, and the child very fast ones. The cow stopped long at the brook to drink, as if the pasture were not half a swamp, and Sylvia stood still and waited, letting her bare feet cool themselves in the shoal water, while the great twilight moths struck softly against her. She waded on through the brook as the cow moved away, and listened to the thrushes with a heart that beat fast with pleasure. There was a stirring in the great boughs overhead. They were full of little birds and beasts that seemed to be wide-awake, and going about their world, or else saying good-night to each other in sleepy twitters. Sylvia herself felt sleepy as she walked along. However, it was not much farther to the house, and the air was soft and sweet. She was not often in the woods so late as this, and it made her feel as if she were a part of the gray shadows and the moving leaves. She was just thinking how long it seemed since she first came to the farm a year ago, and wondering if everything went on in the noisy town just the same as when she was there; the thought of the great red-faced boy who used to chase and frighten her made her hurry along the path to escape from the shadow of the trees.

5   Suddenly this little woods-girl was horror-stricken to hear a clear whistle not very far away. Not a bird's whistle, which would have a sort of friendliness, but a boy's whistle, determined, and somewhat aggressive. Sylvia left the cow to whatever sad fate might await her, and stepped discreetly aside into the bushes, but she was just too late. The enemy had discovered her, and called out in a very cheerful and persuasive tone. "Halloa, little girl, how far is it to the road?" and trembling Sylvia answered almost inaudibly, "A good ways."

She did not dare to look boldly at the tall young man, who carried a gun over his shoulder, but she came out of her bush and again followed the cow, while he walked alongside.

"I have been hunting for some birds," the stranger said kindly, "and I have lost my way, and need a friend very much. Don't be afraid," he added gallantly. "Speak up and tell me what your name is, and whether you think I can spend the night at your house, and go out gunning early in the morning."

Sylvia was more alarmed than before. Would not her grandmother consider her much to blame? But who could have foreseen such an accident as this? It did not appear to be her fault, and she hung her head as if the stem of it were broken, but managed to answer, "Sylvy," with much effort when her companion again asked her name.

Mrs. Tilley was standing in the doorway when the trio came into view. The cow gave a loud moo by way of explanation.

10   "Yes, you'd better speak up for yourself, you old trial! Where'd she tucked herself away this time, Sylvy?" Sylvia kept an awed silence; she knew by instinct that her grandmother did not comprehend the gravity of the situation. She must be mistaking the stranger for one of the farmer-lads of the region.

The young man stood his gun beside the door, and dropped a heavy game-bag beside it; then he bade Mrs. Tilley good evening, and repeated his wayfarer's story, and asked if he could have a night's lodging.

"Put me anywhere you like," he said. "I must be off early in the morning, before day; but I am very hungry, indeed. You can give me some milk at any rate, that's plain."

"Dear sakes, yes," responded the hostess, whose long slumbering hospitality seemed to be easily awakened. "You might fare better if you went out on the main road a mile or so, but you're welcome to what we've got. I'll milk right off, and you make yourself at home. You can sleep on husks or feathers," she proffered graciously. "I raised them all myself. There's good pasturing for geese just below here towards the ma'sh. Now step round and set a plate for the gentleman, Sylvy!" And Sylvia promptly stepped. She was glad to have something to do, and she was hungry herself.

It was a surprise to find so clean and comfortable a little dwelling in this New England wilderness. The young man had known the horrors of its most primitive housekeeping, and the dreary squalor of that level of society which does not rebel at the companionship of hens. This was the best thrift of an old-fashioned farmstead, though on such a small scale that it seemed like a hermitage. He listened eagerly to the old woman's quaint talk, he watched Sylvia's pale face and shining gray eyes with ever growing enthusiasm, and insisted that this was the best supper he had eaten for a month; then, afterward, the new-made friends sat down in the doorway together while the moon came up.

15   Soon it would be berry time, and Sylvia was a great help at picking. The cow was a good milker, though a plaguy thing to keep track of, the hostess gossiped frankly, adding presently that she had buried four children, so that Sylvia's mother, and a son (who might be dead) in California were all the children she had left. "Dan, my boy, was a great hand to go gunning," she explained sadly. "I never wanted for pa'tridges or gray squer'ls while he was to home. He's been a great wand'rer, I expect, and he's no hand to write letters. There, I don't blame him, I'd ha' seen the world myself if it had been so I could."

"Sylvia takes after him," the grandmother continued affectionately, after a minute's pause. "There ain't a foot o' ground she don't know her way over, and the wild creatur's counts her one o' themselves. Squer'ls she'll tame to come an' feed right out o' her hands, and all sorts o' birds. Last winter she got the jay-birds to bangeing here, and I believe she'd 'a' scanted herself of her own meals to have plenty to throw out amongst 'em, if I hadn't kep' watch. Anything but crows, I tell her, I'm willin' to help support,—though Dan he went an' tamed one o' them that did seem to have reason same as folks. It was round here a good spell after he went away. Dan an' his father they didn't hitch,—but he never held up his head ag'in after Dan had dared him an' gone off."

The guest did not notice this hint of family sorrows in his eager interest in something else.

"So Sylvy knows all about birds, does she?" he exclaimed, as he looked round at the little girl who sat, very demure but increasingly sleepy, in the moonlight. "I am making a collection of birds myself. I have been at it ever since I was a boy." (Mrs. Tilley smiled.) "There are two or three very rare ones I have been hunting for these five years. I mean to get them on my own ground if they can be found."

"Do you cage 'em up?" asked Mrs. Tilley doubtfully, in response to this enthusiastic announcement.

20   "Oh, no, they're stuffed and preserved, dozens and dozens of them," said the ornithologist, "and I have shot or snared every one myself. I caught a glimpse of a white heron three miles from here on Saturday, and I have followed it in this direction. They have never been found in this district at all. The little white heron, it is," and he turned again to look at Sylvia with the hope of discovering that the rare bird was one of her acquaintances.

But Sylvia was watching a hop toad in the narrow footpath.

"You would know the heron if you saw it," the stranger continued eagerly. "A queer tall white bird with soft feathers and long thin legs. And it would have a nest perhaps in the top of a high tree, made of sticks, something like a hawk's nest."

Sylvia's heart gave a wild beat; she knew that strange white bird, and had once stolen softly near where it stood in some bright green swamp grass, away over at the other side of the woods. There was an open place where the sunshine always seemed strangely yellow and hot, where tall, nodding rushes grew, and her grandmother had warned her that she might sink in the soft black mud underneath and never be heard of more. Not far beyond were the salt marshes and beyond those was the sea, the sea which Sylvia wondered and dreamed about, but never had looked upon, though its great voice could often be heard above the noise of the woods on stormy nights.

"I can't think of anything I should like so much as to find that heron's nest," the handsome stranger was saying. "I would give ten dollars to anybody who could show it to me," he added desperately, "and I mean to spend my whole vacation hunting for it if need be. Perhaps it was only migrating, or had been chased out of its region by some bird of prey."

25   Mrs. Tilley gave amazed attention to all this, but Sylvia still watched the toad, not divining, as she might have done at some calmer time, that the creature wished to get to its hole under the doorstep, and was much hindered by the unusual spectators at that hour of the evening. No amount of thought, that night, could decide how many wished-for treasures the ten dollars, so lightly spoken of, would buy.

The next day the young sportsman hovered about the woods, and Sylvia kept him company, having lost her first fear of the friendly lad, who proved to be most kind and sympathetic. He told her many things about the birds and what they knew and where they lived and what they did with themselves. And he gave her a jackknife, which she thought as great a treasure as if she were a desert-islander. All day long he did not once make her troubled or afraid except when he brought down some unsuspecting singing creature from its bough. Sylvia would have liked him vastly better without his gun; she could not understand why he killed the very birds he seemed to like so much. But as the day waned, Sylvia still watched the young man with loving admiration. She had never seen anybody so charming and delightful: the woman's heart, asleep in the child, was vaguely thrilled by a dream of love. Some premonition of that great power stirred and swayed these young foresters who traversed the solemn woodlands with soft-footed silent care. They stopped to listen to a bird's song; they pressed forward again eagerly, parting the branches—speaking to each other rarely and in whispers; the young man going first and Sylvia following, fascinated, a few steps behind, with her gray eyes dark with excitement.

She grieved because the longed-for white heron was elusive, but she did not lead the guest, she only followed, and there was no such thing as speaking first. The sound of her own unquestioned voice would have terrified her—it was hard enough to answer yes or no when there was need of that. At last evening began to fall, and they drove the cow home together, and Sylvia smiled with pleasure when they came to the place where she heard the whistle and was afraid only the night before.

II

Half a mile from home, at the farther edge of the woods, where the land was highest, a great pine-tree stood, the last of its generation. Whether it was left for a boundary mark, or for what reason, no one could say; the woodchoppers who had felled its mates were dead and gone long ago, and a whole forest of sturdy trees, pines and oaks and maples, had grown again. But the stately head of this old pine towered above them all and made a landmark for sea and shore miles and miles away. Sylvia knew it well. She had always believed that whoever climbed to the top of it could see the ocean; and the little girl had often laid her hand on the great rough trunk and looked up wistfully at those dark boughs that the wind always stirred, no matter how hot and still the air might be below. Now she thought of the tree with a new excitement, for why, if one climbed it at break of day, could not one see all the world, and easily discover whence the white heron flew, and mark the place, and find the hidden nest?

What a spirit of adventure, what wild ambition! What fancied triumph and delight and glory for the later morning when she could make known the secret! It was almost too real and too great for the childish heart to bear.

30   All night the door of the little house stood open, and the whippoorwills came and sang upon the very step. The young sportsman and his old hostess were sound asleep, but

Sylvia's great design kept her broad awake and watching. She forgot to think of sleep. The short summer night seemed as long as the winter darkness, and at last when the whippoor-wills ceased, and she was afraid the morning would after all come too soon, she stole out of the house and followed the pasture path through the woods, hastening toward the open ground beyond, listening with a sense of comfort and companionship to the drowsy twitter of a half-awakened bird, whose perch she had jarred in passing. Alas, if the great wave of human interest which flooded for the first time this dull little life should sweep away the satisfactions of an existence heart to heart with nature and the dumb life of the forest!

There was the huge tree asleep yet in the paling moonlight, and small and hopeful Sylvia began with utmost bravery to mount to the top of it, with tingling, eager blood coursing the channels of her whole frame, with her bare feet and fingers, that pinched and held like bird's claws to the monstrous ladder reaching up, up, almost to the sky itself. First she must mount the white oak tree that grew alongside, where she was almost lost among the dark branches and the green leaves heavy and wet with dew; a bird fluttered off its nest, and a red squirrel ran to and fro and scolded pettishly at the harmless housebreaker. Sylvia felt her way easily. She had often climbed there, and knew that higher still one of the oak's upper branches chafed against the pine trunk, just where its lower boughs were set close together. There, when she made the dangerous pass from one tree to the other, the great enterprise would really begin.

She crept out along the swaying oak limb at last, and took the daring step across into the old pine-tree. The way was harder than she thought; she must reach far and hold fast, the sharp dry twigs caught and held her and scratched her like angry talons, the pitch made her thin little fingers clumsy and stiff as she went round and round the tree's great stem, higher and higher upward. The sparrows and robins in the woods below were beginning to wake and twitter to the dawn, yet it seemed much lighter there aloft in the pine-tree, and the child knew that she must hurry if her project were to be of any use.

The tree seemed to lengthen itself out as she went up, and to reach farther and farther upward. It was like a great main-mast to the voyaging earth; it must truly have been amazed that morning through all its ponderous frame as it felt this determined spark of human spirit creeping and climbing from higher branch to branch. Who knows how steadily the least twigs held themselves to advantage this light, weak creature on her way! The old pine must have loved his new dependent. More than all the hawks, and bats, and moths, and even the sweet-voiced thrushes, was the brave, beating heart of the solitary gray-eyed child. And the tree stood still and held away the winds that June morning while the dawn grew bright in the east.

Sylvia's face was like a pale star, if one had seen it from the ground, when the last thorny bough was past, and she stood trembling and tired but wholly triumphant, high in the tree-top. Yes, there was the sea with the dawning sun making a golden dazzle over it, and toward that glorious east flew two hawks with slow-moving pinions.[1] How low they looked in the air from that height when before one had only seen them far up, and dark against the blue sky. Their gray feathers were as soft as moths; they seemed only a little way from the tree, and Sylvia felt as if she too could go flying away among the clouds. Westward, the woodlands and farms reached miles and miles into the distance; here and there were church steeples, and white villages; truly it was a vast and awesome world.

35   The birds sang louder and louder. At last the sun came up bewilderingly bright. Sylvia could see the white sails of ships out at sea, and the clouds that were purple and rose-colored and yellow at first began to fade away. Where was the white heron's nest in the sea of green branches, and was this wonderful sight and pageant of the world the only reward

---

[1] Parts of a bird's wing; wings or feathers.

for having climbed to such a giddy height? Now look down again, Sylvia, where the green marsh is set among the shining birches and dark hemlocks; there where you saw the white heron once you will see him again; look, look! a white spot of him like a single floating feather comes up from the dead hemlock and grows larger, and rises, and comes close at last, and goes by the landmark pine with steady sweep of wing and outstretched slender neck and crested head. And wait! wait! do not move a foot or a finger, little girl, do not send an arrow of light and consciousness from your two eager eyes, for the heron has perched on a pine bough not far beyond yours, and cries back to his mate on the nest, and plumes his feathers for the new day!

The child gives a long sigh a minute later when a company of shouting cat-birds comes also to the tree, and vexed by their fluttering and lawlessness the solemn heron goes away. She knows his secret now, the wild, light, slender bird that floats and wavers, and goes back like an arrow presently to his home in the green world beneath. Then Sylvia, well satisfied, makes her perilous way down again, not daring to look far below the branch she stands on, ready to cry sometimes because her fingers ache and her lamed feet slip. Wondering over and over again what the stranger would say to her, and what he would think when she told him how to find his way straight to the heron's nest.

"Sylvy, Sylvy!" called the busy old grandmother again and again, but nobody answered, and the small husk bed was empty, and Sylvia had disappeared.

The guest waked from a dream, and remembering his day's pleasure hurried to dress himself that it might sooner begin. He was sure from the way the shy little girl looked once or twice yesterday that she had at least seen the white heron, and now she must really be persuaded to tell. Here she comes now, paler than ever, and her worn old frock is torn and tattered, and smeared with pine pitch. The grandmother and the sportsman stand in the door together and question her, and the splendid moment has come to speak of the dead hemlock-tree by the green marsh.

But Sylvia does not speak after all, though the old grandmother fretfully rebukes her, and the young man's kind appealing eyes are looking straight in her own. He can make them rich with money; he has promised it, and they are poor now. He is so well worth making happy, and he waits to hear the story she can tell.

40 No, she must keep silence! What is it that suddenly forbids her and makes her dumb? Has she been nine years growing, and now, when the great world for the first time puts out a hand to her, must she thrust it aside for a bird's sake? The murmur of the pine's green branches is in her ears, she remembers how the white heron came flying through the golden air and how they watched the sea and the morning together, and Sylvia cannot speak; she cannot tell the heron's secret and give its life away.

Dear loyalty, that suffered a sharp pang as the guest went away disappointed later in the day, that could have served and followed him and loved him as a dog loves! Many a night Sylvia heard the echo of his whistle haunting the pasture path as she came home with the loitering cow. She forgot even her sorrow at the sharp report of his gun and the piteous sight of thrushes and sparrows dropping silent to the ground, their songs hushed and their pretty feathers stained and wet with blood. Were the birds better friends than their hunter might have been,—who can tell? Whatever treasures were lost to her, woodlands and summertime, remember! Bring your gifts and graces and tell your secrets to this lonely country child!

■ **EXPLORATIONS OF THE TEXT**

1. What is the relationship of landscapes to character? What is the significance of the girl's name?

2. Characterize the ornithologist. Why does Sylvia want to please the young man? What are the complications?
3. What is the relationship between the grandmother and Sylvia?
4. Why does Sylvia save the bird? How does she decide?
5. How does this story differ in theme and style from Faulkner's "Barn Burning?" What elements are similar?

■ **THE READING/WRITING CONNECTION**

1. In a journal entry, describe female initiation in Jewett's story. What does Sylvia learn?
2. Freewrite and react to the depiction of nature in this work.
3. Write a monologue in the voice of the ornithologist.
4. "Think" Topic: Does Sylvia do the right thing in not revealing the location of the heron?

■ **IDEAS FOR WRITING**

1. Write about the conflict between love and principle in "A White Heron."
2. Compare the depiction of hunting and violence in "A White Heron" and in Cervantes's "Uncle's First Rabbit."

JOHN UPDIKE

John Updike (1932–   ) was born in Shillington, Pennsylvania. In 1950, Updike attended Harvard University, where he wrote for and eventually edited the Harvard Lampoon. *His first short story, "Friends from Philadelphia," was sold to* The New Yorker *the year he graduated from Harvard, 1954, and fifty years later, his stories, poems, and essays are still regularly printed in that magazine. Updike has published more than 200 stories, fifty-six novels, and a great number of poems and essays. Although he has won many awards for his short stories, Updike may be best known for his* Rabbit *novels—*Rabbit, Run *(1960),* Rabbit Redux *(1971),* Rabbit Is Rich *(1981), and* Rabbit at Rest *(1990)—which depict Rabbit Angstrom's life through youth, marriage, middle age, and death. He received a Pulitzer Prize and National Book Critics Circle Award for both* Rabbit Is Rich *and* Rabbit at Rest *and a National Book Critics Circle Award for* Hugging the Shore *(1983). Updike was elected to the National Institute of Arts and Letters in 1964 and the American Academy of Arts and Letters in 1977, and he was honored with the National Medal of the Arts in 1989. More recently he has been awarded the Harvard Arts First Medal and the 1998 National Book Foundation Medal for Distinguished Contribution to American Arts and Letters. Updike's stories depict the moral dilemmas that confront humans even in the most common of situations.*

1961

A&P

In walks these three girls in nothing but bathing suits. I'm in the third checkout slot, with my back to the door, so I don't see them until they're over by the bread. The one that caught my eye first was the one in the plaid green two-piece. She was a chunky kid, with a good tan and a sweet broad soft-looking can with those two crescents of white just under it, where the sun never seems to hit, at the top of the backs of her legs. I stood there with my hand on a box of HiHo crackers trying to remember if I rang it up or not. I ring it up again and the customer starts giving me hell. She's one of these cash-register-watchers, a witch about fifty with rouge on her cheekbones and no eyebrows, and I know it made her day to trip me up. She'd been watching cash registers forty years and probably never seen a mistake before.

By the time I got her feathers smoothed and her goodies into a bag—she gives me a little snort in passing, if she'd been born at the right time they would have burned her over in Salem—by the time I get her on her way the girls had circled around the bread and were coming back, without a pushcart, back my way along the counters, in the aisle between the checkouts and the Special bins. They didn't even have shoes on. There was this chunky one, with the two-piece—it was bright green and the seams on the bra were still sharp and her belly was still pretty pale so I guessed she just got it (the suit)—there was this one, with one of those chubby berry-faces, the lips all bunched together under her nose, this one, and a tall one, with black hair that hadn't quite frizzed right, and one of these sunburns right across under the eyes, and a chin that was too long—you know, the kind of girl other girls think is very "striking" and "attractive" but never quite makes it, as they very well know, which is why they like her so much—and then the third one, that wasn't quite so tall. She was the queen. She kind of led them, the other two peeking around and making their shoulders round. She didn't look around, not this queen, she just walked straight on slowly, on these long white primadonna legs. She came down a little hard on her heels, as if she didn't walk in her bare feet that much, putting down her heels and then letting the weight move along to her toes as if she was testing the floor with every step, putting a little deliberate extra action into it. You never know for sure how girls' minds work (do you really think it's a mind in there or just a little buzz like a bee in a glass jar?) but you got the idea she had talked the other two into coming in here with her, and now she was showing them how to do it, walk slow and hold yourself straight.

She had on a kind of dirty-pink—beige maybe, I don't know—bathing suit with a little nubble all over it and, what got me, the straps were down. They were off her shoulders looped loose around the cool tops of her arms, and I guess as a result the suit had slipped a little on her, so all around the top of the cloth there was this shining rim. If it hadn't been there you wouldn't have known there could have been anything whiter than those shoulders. With the straps pushed off, there was nothing between the top of the suit and the top of her head except just *her,* this clean bare plane of the top of her chest down from the shoulder bones like a dented sheet of metal tilted in the light. I mean, it was more than pretty. ▪

She had sort of oaky hair that the sun and salt had bleached, done up in a bun that was unravelling, and a kind of prim face. Walking into the A & P with your straps down, I suppose it's the only kind of face you *can* have. She held her head so high her neck, coming up out of those white shoulders, looked kind of stretched, but I didn't mind. The longer her neck was, the more of her there was.

5   She must have felt in the corner of her eye me and over my shoulder Stokesie in the second slot watching, but she didn't tip. Not this queen. She kept her eyes moving across the racks, and stopped, and turned so slow it made my stomach rub the inside of my apron, and buzzed to the other two, who kind of huddled against her for relief, and they all three of them went up the cat-and-dog-food-breakfast-cereal-macaroni-rice-raisins-seasonings-spreads-spaghetti-soft-drinks-crackers-and-cookies aisle. From the third slot I look straight up this aisle to the meat counter, and I watched them all the way. The fat one with the tan sort of fumbled with the cookies, but on second thought she put the package back. The sheep pushing their carts down the aisle—the girls were walking against the usual traffic (not that we have one-way signs or anything)—were pretty hilarious. You could see them, when Queenie's white shoulders dawned on them, kind of jerk, or hop, or hiccup, but their eyes snapped back to their own baskets and on they pushed. I bet you could set off dynamite in an A & P and the people would by and large keep reaching and checking oatmeal off their lists and muttering "Let me see, there was a third thing, began with A, asparagus, no, ah, yes, applesauce!" or whatever it is they do mutter. But there was no doubt, this jiggled them. A few houseslaves in pin curlers even looked around after pushing their carts past to make sure what they had seen was correct.

You know, it's one thing to have a girl in a bathing suit down on the beach, where what with the glare nobody can look at each other much anyway, and another thing in the cool of the A & P, under the fluorescent lights, against all those stacked packages, with her feet paddling along naked over our checkerboard green-and-cream rubber-tile floor.

"Oh Daddy," Stokesie said beside me. "I feel so faint."

"Darling," I said. "Hold me tight." Stokesie's married, with two babies chalked up on his fuselage already, but as far as I can tell that's the only difference. He's twenty-two, and I was nineteen this April.

"Is it done?" he asks, the responsible married man finding his voice. I forgot to say he thinks he's going to be manager some sunny day, maybe in 1990 when it's called the Great Alexandrov and Petrooshki Tea Company or something.

10   What he meant was, our town is five miles from a beach, with a big summer colony out on the Point, but we're right in the middle of town, and the women generally put on a shirt or shorts or something before they get out of the car into the street. And anyway these are usually women with six children and varicose veins mapping their legs and nobody, including them, could care less. As I say, we're right in the middle of town, and if you stand at our front doors you can see two banks and the Congregational church and the newspaper store and three real-estate offices and about twenty-seven old free-loaders tearing up Central Street because the sewer broke again. It's not as if we're on the Cape; we're north of Boston and there's people in this town haven't seen the ocean for twenty years.

The girls had reached the meat counter and were asking McMahon something. He pointed, they pointed, and they shuffled out of sight behind a pyramid of Diet Delight peaches. All that was left for us to see was old McMahon patting his mouth and looking after them sizing up their joints. Poor kids, I began to feel sorry for them, they couldn't help it.

Now here comes the sad part of the story, at least my family says it's sad, but I don't think it's so sad myself. The store's pretty empty, it being Thursday afternoon, so there was nothing much to do except lean on the register and wait for the girls to show up again. The whole store was like a pinball machine and I didn't know which tunnel they'd come out of. After a while they come around out of the far aisle, around the light bulbs, records at discount of the Caribbean Six or Tony Martin Sings or some such gunk you wonder they waste the wax on, sixpacks of candy bars, and plastic toys done up in cellophane that fall apart when a kid looks at them anyway. Around they come, Queenie still leading the way, and holding a little gray jar in her hand. Slots Three through Seven are unmanned and I could see her wondering between Stokes and me, but Stokesie with his usual luck draws an old party in baggy gray pants who stumbles up with four giant cans of pineapple juice (what do these bums *do* with all that pineapple juice? I've often asked myself) so the girls come to me. Queenie puts down the jar and I take it into my fingers icy cold. Kingfish Fancy Herring Snacks in Pure Sour Cream: 49¢. Now her hands are empty, not a ring or a bracelet, bare as God made them, and I wonder where the money's coming from. Still with that prim look she lifts a folded dollar bill out of the hollow at the center of her nubbled pink top. The jar went heavy in my hand. Really, I thought that was so cute.

Then everybody's luck begins to run out. Lengel comes in from haggling with a truck full of cabbages on the lot and is about to scuttle into that door marked MANAGER behind which he hides all day when the girls touch his eye. Lengel's pretty dreary, teaches Sunday school and the rest, but he doesn't miss that much. He comes over and says, "Girls, this isn't the beach."

Queenie blushes, though maybe it's just a brush of sunburn I was noticing for the first time, now that she was so close. "My mother asked me to pick up a jar of herring snacks." Her voice kind of startled me, the way voices do when you see the people first, coming out so flat and dumb yet kind of tony, too, the way it ticked over "pick up" and "snacks." All of a sudden I slid right down her voice into her living room. Her father and the other men were standing around in icecream coats and bow ties and the women were in sandals picking up herring snacks on toothpicks off a big plate and they were all holding drinks the color of water with olives and sprigs of mint in them. When my parents have somebody over they get lemonade and if it's a real racy affair Schlitz in tall glasses with "They'll Do It Every Time" cartoons stencilled on.

15   "That's all right," Lengel said. "But this isn't the beach." His repeating this struck me as funny, as if it had just occurred to him, and he had been thinking all these years the A & P was a great big dune and he was the head lifeguard. He didn't like my smiling—as I say he doesn't miss much—but he concentrates on giving the girls that sad Sunday-school-superintendent stare.

Queenie's blush is no sunburn now, and the plump one in plaid, that I liked better from the back—a really sweet can—pipes up, "We weren't doing any shopping. We just came in for the one thing."

"That makes no difference," Lengel tells her, and I could see from the way his eyes went that he hadn't noticed she was wearing a two-piece before. "We want you decently dressed when you come in here."

"We *are* decent," Queenie says suddenly, her lower lip pushing, getting sore now that she remembers her place, a place from which the crowd that runs the A & P must look pretty crummy. Fancy Herring Snacks flashed in her very blue eyes.

"Girls, I don't want to argue with you. After this come in here with your shoulders covered. It's our policy." He turns his back. That's policy for you. Policy is what the kingpins want. What the others want is juvenile delinquency.

20   All this while, the customers had been showing up with their carts but, you know, sheep, seeing a scene, they had all bunched up on Stokesie, who shook open a paper bag as gently as peeling a peach, not wanting to miss a word. I could feel in the silence everybody getting nervous, most of all Lengel, who asks me, "Sammy, have you rung up this purchase?"

I thought and said "No" but it wasn't about that I was thinking. I go through the punches, 4, 9, GROC, TOT—it's more complicated than you think, and after you do it often enough, it begins to make a little song, that you hear words to, in my case "Hello (*bing*) there, you (*gung*) happy *pee*-pul (*splat*)!"—the *splat* being the drawer flying out. I uncrease the bill, tenderly as you may imagine, it just having come from between the two smoothest scoops of vanilla I had ever known were there, and pass a half and a penny into her narrow pink palm, and nestle the herrings in a bag and twist its neck and hand it over, all the time thinking.

The girls, and who'd blame them, are in a hurry to get out, so I say "I quit" to Lengel quick enough for them to hear, hoping they'll stop and watch me, their unsuspected hero. They keep right on going, into the electric eye; the door flies open and they flicker across the lot to their car, Queenie and Plaid and Big Tall Goony-Goony (not that as raw material she was so bad), leaving me with Lengel and a kink in his eyebrow.

"Did you say something, Sammy?"

"I said I quit."

25   "I thought you did."

"You didn't have to embarrass them."

"It was they who were embarrassing us."

I started to say something that came out "Fiddle-de-doo." It's a saying of my grandmother's, and I know she would have been pleased.

"I don't think you know what you're saying," Lengel said.

30   "I know you don't," I said. "But I do." I pull the bow at the back of my apron and start shrugging it off my shoulders. A couple customers that had been heading for my slot begin to knock against each other, like scared pigs in a chute.

Lengel sighs and begins to look very patient and old and gray. He's been a friend of my parents for years. "Sammy, you don't want to do this to your Mom and Dad," he tells me. It's true, I don't. But it seems to me that once you begin a gesture it's fatal not to go through with it. I fold the apron, "Sammy" stitched in red on the pocket, and put it on the counter, and drop the bow tie on top of it. The bow tie is theirs, if you've ever wondered. "You'll feel this for the rest of your life," Lengel says, and I know that's true, too, but remembering how he made that pretty girl blush makes me so scrunchy inside I punch the No Sale tab and the machine whirs "pee-pul" and the drawer splats out. One advantage to this scene taking place in summer, I can follow this up with a clean exit, there's no fumbling around getting your coat and galoshes, I just saunter into the electric eye in my white shirt that my mother ironed the night before, and the door heaves itself open, and outside the sunshine is skating around on the asphalt.

I look around for my girls, but they're gone, of course. There wasn't anybody but some young married screaming with her children about some candy they didn't get by the door of a powder-blue Falcon station wagon. Looking back in the big windows, over the bags of peat moss and aluminum lawn furniture stacked on the pavement, I could see Lengel in my place in the slot, checking the sheep through. His face was dark gray and his back stiff, as if he'd just had an injection of iron, and my stomach kind of fell as I felt how hard the world was going to be to me hereafter.

■ EXPLORATIONS OF THE TEXT

1. How does the point of view—Sammy's perspective—develop the narrative? How would the story change if it were told from Queenie's, Stokesie's, or Lengel's perspective or if there were an omniscient narrator?
2.. Analyze Sammy's character. Consider his background, his attitudes, his values, and his interactions with the customers and with the girls. Compare and contrast his character with that of Stokesie, Lengel, or Queenie.
3. Why does Sammy quit?
4. Explore the significance of this statement: "I felt how hard the world was going to be to me hereafter." Discuss the significance of such word choices as "hard" and "to me" as opposed to "for me." Is the ending optimistic or pessimistic? Critics are divided on this point.
5. How does the setting enlarge the scope of the work? Explicate the imagery used to depict the store. What critique is Updike presenting of this early 1960s world?
6. Explore the class differences presented in the work. How do these differences explain the behavior of the characters?
7. Compare Sammy's coming-of-age experience with Rosaura's in "The Stolen Party." What do these characters learn about the state of the world? Alternatively, compare Sammy's moral decision with Sarty's in "Barn Burning."

■ THE READING/WRITING CONNECTION

1. Freewrite in response to this statement: "There's people in this town haven't seen the ocean for twenty years."
2. Write a monologue in Queenie's or one of the other girl's voices. Tell the story from her perspective.
3. Continue the narrative. What happens to Sammy?

■ IDEAS FOR WRITING

1. This story is set in the early 1960s. Is the story still relevant? How would it change if it were set in a supermarket today? Write a new version of the story, and then in a short essay, explain your changes.

2. In an earlier version of this story, Updike described what happens after Sammy quits his job. In the final version, Updike deleted this ending, later using it as the basis of another work, "Lifeguard." Find a copy of "Lifeguard," and compare the two stories, focusing on such elements of fiction as setting, character development, plot, and theme.

LILIANA HEKER

Born in Argentina, Liliana Heker (1943-   ) published her first volume of short stories, Those Who Beheld the Burning Bush *(1966), when she was still a teenager. She served as the editor of the literary journal* The Platypus *during the years of Argentina's dictatorship, when many writers "disappeared" and many who objected to oppression were tortured and killed by death squads. Since then Heker has published several books, most recently a collection of essays entitled* Las hermanas de Shakespeare *("The Sisters of Shakespeare," 1999) and* La crueldad de la vida *("The Cruelty of Life," 2001).*

1982

THE STOLEN PARTY

As soon as she arrived she went straight to the kitchen to see if the monkey was there. It was: what a relief! She wouldn't have liked to admit that her mother had been right. *Monkeys at a birthday? Get away with you, believing any nonsense you're told!* She was cross, but not because of the monkey, the girl thought; it's just because of the party.

"I don't like you going," she told her. "It's a rich people's party."

"Rich people go to Heaven too," said the girl, who studied religion at school.

"Get away with Heaven," said the mother. "The problem with you, young lady, is that you like to fart higher than your ass."

5   The girl didn't approve of the way her mother spoke. She was barely nine, and one of the best in her class.

"I'm going because I've been invited," she said. "And I've been invited because Luciana is my friend. So there."

"Ah yes, your friend," her mother grumbled. She paused. "Listen, Rosaura," she said at last. "That one's not your friend. You know what you are to them? The maid's daughter, that's what."

Rosaura blinked hard: she wasn't going to cry. Then she yelled: "Shut up! You know nothing about being friends!"

Every afternoon she used to go to Luciana's house and they would both finish their homework while Rosaura's mother did the cleaning. They had their tea in the kitchen and they told each other secrets. Rosaura loved everything in the big house, and she also loved the people who lived there.

10   "I'm going because it will be the most lovely party in the whole world, Luciana told me it would. There will be a magician, and he will bring a monkey and everything."

The mother swung around to take a good look at her child, and pompously put her hands on her hips.

"Monkeys at a birthday?" she said. "Get away with you, believing any nonsense you're told!"

Rosaura was deeply offended. She thought it unfair of her mother to accuse other people of being liars simply because they were rich. Rosaura too wanted to be rich, of course. If one day she managed to live in a beautiful palace, would her mother stop loving her? She felt very sad. She wanted to go to that party more than anything else in the world.

"I'll die if I don't go," she whispered, almost without moving her lips.

15 And she wasn't sure whether she had been heard, but on the morning of the party she discovered that her mother had starched her Christmas dress. And in the afternoon, after washing her hair, her mother rinsed it in apple vinegar so that it would be all nice and shiny. Before going out, Rosaura admired herself in the mirror, with her white dress and glossy hair, and thought she looked terribly pretty.

Señora Ines seemed to notice. As soon as she saw her, she said:

"How lovely you look today, Rosaura."

Rosaura gave her starched skirt a slight toss with her hands and walked into the party with a firm step. She said hello to Luciana and asked about the monkey. Luciana put on a secretive look and whispered into Rosaura's ear: "He's in the kitchen. But don't tell anyone, because it's a surprise."

Rosaura wanted to make sure. Carefully she entered the kitchen and there she saw it: deep in thought, inside its cage. It looked so funny that the girl stood there for while, watching it, and later, every so often, she would slip out of the party unseen and go and admire it. Rosaura was the only one allowed into the kitchen. Señora Ines had said: "You yes, but not the others, they're much too boisterous, they might break something." Rosaura had never broken anything. She even managed the jug of orange juice, carrying it from the kitchen into the dining room. She held it carefully and didn't spill a single drop. And Señora Ines had said: "Are you sure you can manage a jug as big as that?" Of course she could manage. She wasn't a butterfingers, like the others. Like that blonde girl with the bow in her hair. As soon as she saw Rosaura, the girl with the bow had said:

20 "And you? Who are you?"

"I'm a friend of Luciana," said Rosaura.

"No," said the girl with the bow, "you are not a friend of Luciana because I'm her cousin and I know all her friends. And I don't know you."

"So what," said Rosaura. "I come here every afternoon with my mother and we do our homework together."

"You and your mother do your homework together?" asked the girl, laughing.

25 "I and Luciana do our homework together," said Rosaura, very seriously.

The girl with the bow shrugged her shoulders.

"That's not being friends," she said. "Do you go to school together?"

"No."

"So where do you know her from?" said the girl, getting impatient.

30 Rosaura remembered her mother's words perfectly. She took a deep breath.

"I'm the daughter of the employee," she said.

Her mother had said very clearly: "If someone asks, you say you're the daughter of the employee; that's all." She also told her to add: "And proud of it." But Rosaura thought that never in her life would she dare say something of the sort.

"What employee?" said the girl with the bow. "Employee in a shop?"

"No," said Rosaura angrily. "My mother doesn't sell anything in any shop, so there."

35 "So how come she's an employee?" said the girl with the bow.

Just then Señora Ines arrived saying shh shh, and asked Rosaura if she wouldn't mind helping serve out the hotdogs, as she knew the house so much better than the others.

"See?" said Rosaura to the girl with the bow, and when no one was looking she kicked her in the shin.

Apart from the girl with the bow, all the others were delightful. The one she liked best was Luciana, with her golden birthday crown; and then the boys. Rosaura won the sack race, and nobody managed to catch her when they played tag. When they split into two teams to play charades, all the boys wanted her for their side. Rosaura felt she had never been so happy in all her life.

But the best was still to come. The best came after Luciana blew out the candles. First the cake. Señora Ines had asked her to help pass the cake around, and Rosaura had enjoyed the task immensely, because everyone called out to her, shouting "Me, me!" Rosaura remembered a story in which there was a queen who had the power of life or death over her subjects. She had always loved that, having the power of life or death. To Luciana and the boys she gave the largest pieces, and to the girl with the bow she gave a slice so thin one could see through it.

40   After the cake came the magician, tall and bony, with a fine red cape. A true magician: he could untie handkerchiefs by blowing on them and make a chain with links that had no openings. He could guess what cards were pulled out from a pack, and the monkey was his assistant. He called the monkey "partner." "Let's see here, partner," he would say, "turn over a card." And, "Don't run away, partner: time to work now."

The final trick was wonderful. One of the children had to hold the monkey in his arms and the magician said he would make him disappear.

"What, the boy?" they all shouted.

"No, the monkey!" shouted back the magician.

Rosaura thought that this was truly the most amusing party in the whole world.

45   The magician asked a small fat boy to come and help, but the small fat boy got frightened almost at once and dropped the monkey on the floor. The magician picked him up carefully, whispered something in his ear, and the monkey nodded almost as if he understood.

"You mustn't be so unmanly, my friend," the magician said to the fat boy.

"What's unmanly?" said the fat boy.

The magician turned around as if to look for spies.

"A sissy," said the magician. "Go sit down."

50   Then he stared at all the faces, one by one. Rosaura felt her heart tremble.

"You, with the Spanish eyes," said the magician. And everyone saw that he was pointing at her.

She wasn't afraid. Neither holding the monkey, nor when the magician made him vanish; not even when, at the end, the magician flung his red cape over Rosaura's head and uttered a few magic words . . . and the monkey reappeared, chattering happily, in her arms. The children clapped furiously. And before Rosaura returned to her seat, the magician said:

"Thank you very much, my little countess."

She was so pleased with the compliment that a while later, when her mother came to fetch her, that was the first thing she told her.

55   "I helped the magician and he said to me, 'Thank you very much, my little countess.'"

It was strange because up to then Rosaura had thought that she was angry with her mother. All along Rosaura had imagined that she would say to her: "See that the monkey wasn't a lie?" But instead she was so thrilled that she told her mother all about the wonderful magician.

Her mother tapped her on the head and said: "So now we're a countess!"

But one could see that she was beaming.

And now they both stood in the entrance, because a moment ago Señora Ines, smiling, had said: "Please wait here a second."

60   Her mother suddenly seemed worried.

"What is it?" she asked Rosaura.

"What is what?" said Rosaura. "It's nothing; she just wants to get the presents for those who are leaving, see?"

She pointed at the fat boy and at a girl with pigtails who were also waiting there, next to their mothers. And she explained about the presents. She knew, because she had been watching those who left before her. When one of the girls was about to leave, Señora Ines would give her a bracelet. When a boy left, Señora Ines gave him a yo-yo. Rosaura preferred the yo-yo because it sparkled, but she didn't mention that to her mother. Her mother might have said: "So why don't you ask for one, you blockhead?" That's what her mother was like. Rosaura didn't feel like explaining that she'd be horribly ashamed to be the odd one out. Instead she said:

"I was the best-behaved at the party."

65　And she said no more because Señora Ines came out into the hall with two bags, one pink and one blue.

First she went up to the fat boy, gave him a yo-yo out of the blue bag, and the fat boy left with his mother. Then she went up to the girl and gave her a bracelet out of the pink bag, and the girl with the pigtails left as well.

Finally she came up to Rosaura and her mother. She had a big smile on her face and Rosaura liked that. Señora Ines looked down at her, then looked up at her mother, and then said something that made Rosaura proud:

"What a marvelous daughter you have, Herminia."

For an instant, Rosaura thought that she'd give her two presents: the bracelet and the yo-yo. Señora Ines bent down as if about to look for something. Rosaura also leaned forward, stretching out her arm. But she never completed the movement.

70　Señora Ines didn't look in the pink bag. Nor did she look in the blue bag. Instead she rummaged in her purse. In her hand appeared two bills.

"You really and truly earned this," she said handing them over. "Thank you for all your help, my pet."

Rosaura felt her arms stiffen, stick close to her body, and then she noticed her mother's hand on her shoulder. Instinctively she pressed herself against her mother's body. That was all. Except her eyes. Rosaura's eyes had a cold, clear look that fixed itself on Señora Ines's face.

Señora Ines, motionless, stood there with her hand outstretched. As if she didn't dare draw it back. As if the slightest change might shatter an infinitely delicate balance.

■ EXPLORATIONS OF THE TEXT

1. What is the central conflict between the mother and Rosaura?
2. What fantasies does Rosaura invent about herself and about her life?
3. How does Heker weave a subtle pattern of servitude into Rosaura's participation in the party?
4. In the episode with the monkey, what is the role of the fat boy? What does the incident symbolize?
5. Why does Señora Ines offer Rosaura money? What does Rosaura's "cold, clear look" suggest? What is the "infinitely delicate balance" at the end?
6. Two pairs of mothers and daughters appear in this story. What do you learn about the social status and world views of these characters?
7. How would you characterize the tone of this story? Why?
8. How do details contribute to the theme of the story? What can you learn about subtlety, about irony, and about organization from Liliana Heker?

■ THE READING/WRITING CONNECTION

1. How is the party "stolen"? Respond to this question in a journal entry.
2. Write a paragraph, and continue the story.
3. "Think" Topic: What characterizes children's perceptions of prejudice or stereotyping in the works by Heker and by Countee Cullen?

■ **IDEAS FOR WRITING**

1. How does point of view contribute to the development of the themes in this work?
2. Write about a "stolen party" from your childhood or adolescence. What did you realize? Or compare a party that you attended as a child with Rosaura's experience.

WILLIAM FAULKNER

William Faulkner (1897–1962) lived most of his life in Oxford, Mississippi. His literary career began in New Orleans, where he wrote newspaper stories for the Times-Picayune. *With the assistance of the writer Sherwood Anderson, whom he met in New Orleans, Faulkner published his first novel,* Soldier's Pay *(1926). In his major novels, considered among the greatest of the twentieth century, he created an imaginary region near Oxford called Yoknapatawpha County, chronicling its history in* The Sound and the Fury *(1929), As* I Lay Dying *(1930),* Light in August *(1932),* Absalom, Absalom! *(1936),* The Hamlet *(1940), and* Go Down, Moses *(1942). His short fiction can be found in* The Collected Stories of William Faulkner *(1951). Faulkner received the Nobel Prize for Literature in 1949.*

1938

BARN BURNING

The store in which the Justice of the Peace's court was sitting smelled of cheese. The boy, crouched on his nail keg at the back of the crowded room, knew he smelled cheese, and more; from where he sat he could see the ranked shelves close-packed with the solid, squat, dynamic shapes of tin cans whose labels his stomach read, not from the lettering which meant nothing to his mind but from the scarlet devils and the silver curve of fish—this, the cheese which he knew he smelled and the hermetic meat[1] which his intestines believed he smelled coming in intermittent gusts momentary and brief between the other constant one, the smell and sense just a little of fear because mostly of despair and grief, the old fierce pull of blood. He could not see the table where the Justice sat and before which his father and his father's enemy (*our enemy* he thought in that despair; *ourn! mine and his both! He's my father!*) stood, but he could hear them, the two of them that is, because his father had said no word yet:

"But what proof have you, Mr. Harris?"

"I told you. The hog got into my corn. I caught it up and sent it back to him. He had no fence that would hold it. I told him so, warned him. The next time I put the hog in my pen. When he came to get it I gave him enough wire to patch up his pen. The next time I put the hog up and kept it. I rode down to his house and saw the wire I gave him still rolled on to the spool in his yard. I told him he could have the hog when he paid me a dollar pound fee. That evening a nigger came with the dollar and got the hog. He was a strange nigger. He said, 'He say to tell you wood and hay kin burn.' I said, 'What?' 'That what he say to tell you,' the nigger said. 'Wood and hay kin burn.' That night my barn burned. I got the stock out but I lost the barn."

"Where is the nigger? Have you got him?"

5   "He was a strange nigger, I tell you. I don't know what became of him."

"But that's not proof. Don't you see that's not proof?"

---

[1] Canned meat.

"Get that boy up here. He knows." For a moment the boy thought too that the man meant his older brother until Harris said. "Not him. The little one. The boy," and, crouching, small for his age, small and wiry like his father, in patched and faded jeans even too small for him, with straight, uncombed, brown hair and eyes gray and wild as storm scud, he saw the men between himself and the table part and become a lane of grim faces, at the end of which he saw the Justice, a shabby, collarless, graying man in spectacles, beckoning him. He felt no floor under his bare feet; he seemed to walk beneath the palpable weight of the grim turning faces. His father, stiff in his black Sunday coat donned not for the trial but for the moving, did not even look at him. *He aims for me to lie,* he thought, again with that frantic grief and despair. *And I will have to do hit.*

"What's your name, boy?" the Justice said.

"Colonel Sartoris Snopes," the boy whispered.

10 "Hey?" the Justice said. "Talk louder. Colonel Sartoris? I reckon anybody named for Colonel Sartoris in this country can't help but tell the truth, can they?" The boy said nothing. *Enemy! Enemy!* he thought; for a moment he could not even see, could not see that the Justice's face was kindly nor discern that his voice was troubled when he spoke to the man named Harris: "Do you want me to question this boy?" But he could hear, and during those subsequent long seconds there was absolutely no sound in the crowded little room save that of quiet and intent breathing it was as if he had swung outward at the end of a grape vine, over a ravine, and at the top of the swing had been caught in a prolonged instant of mesmerized gravity, weightless in time.

"No!" Harris said violently, explosively. "Damnation! Send him out of here!" Now time, the fluid world, rushed beneath him again, the voices coming to him again through the smell of cheese and sealed meat, the fear and despair and the old grief of blood:

"This case is closed. I can't find against you, Snopes, but I can give you advice. Leave this country and don't come back to it."

His father spoke for the first time, his voice cold and harsh, level, without emphasis: "I aim to. I don't figure to stay in a country among people who . . ." he said something unprintable and vile, addressed to no one.

"That'll do," the Justice said, "Take your wagon and get out of this country before dark. Case dismissed."

15 His father turned, and he followed the stiff black coat, the wiry figure walking a little stiffly, from where a Confederate provost's man's musket ball had taken him in the heel on a stolen horse thirty years ago, followed the two backs now, since his older brother had appeared from somewhere in the crowd, no taller than the father but thicker, chewing tobacco steadily, between the two lines of grim-faced men and out of the store and across the worn gallery and down the sagging steps and among the dogs and half-grown boys in the mild May dust, where as he passed a voice hissed:

"Barn burner!"

Again he could not see, whirling; there was a face in a red haze, moonlike, bigger than the full moon, the owner of it half again his size, he leaping in the red haze toward the face, feeling no blow, feeling no shock when his head struck the earth, scrabbling up and leaping again, feeling no blow this time either and tasting no blood, scrabbling up to see the other boy in full flight and himself already leaping into pursuit as his father's hand jerked him back, the harsh, cold voice speaking above him: "Go get in the wagon."

It stood in a grove of locusts and mulberries across the road. His two hulking sisters in their Sunday dresses and his mother and her sister in calico and sunbonnets were already in it, sitting on and among the sorry residue of the dozen and more movings which even the boy could remember—the battered stove, the broken beds and chairs, the clock inlaid with mother-of-pearl, which would not run, stopped at some fourteen minutes past two o'clock of a dead and forgotten day and time, which had been his mother's dowry. She was crying, though when she saw him she drew her sleeve across her face and began to descend from the wagon. "Get back," the father said.

"He's hurt, I got to get some water and wash his . . ."

20 "Get back in the wagon," his father said. He got in too, over the tail-gate. His father mounted to the seat where the older brother already sat and struck the gaunt mules two savage blows with the peeled willow, but without heat. It was not even sadistic; it was exactly that same quality which in later years would cause his descendants to over-run the engine before putting a motor car into motion, striking and reining back in the same movement. The wagon went on, the store with its quiet crowd of grimly watching men dropped behind; a curve in the road hid it. *Forever* he thought. *Maybe he's done satisfied now, now that he has . . .* stopping himself, not to say it aloud even to himself. His mother's hand touched his shoulder.

"Does hit hurt?" she said.

"Naw," he said. "Hit don't hurt. Lemme be."

"Can't you wipe some of the blood off before hit dries?"

"I'll wash tonight," he said. "Lemme be, I tell you."

25 The wagon went on. He did not know where they were going. None of them ever did or ever asked, because it was always somewhere, always a house of sorts waiting for them a day or two days or even three days away. Likely his father had already arranged to make a crop on another farm before he . . . Again he had to stop himself. He (the father) always did. There was something about his wolflike independence and even courage when the advantage was at least neutral which impressed strangers, as if they got from his latent ravening ferocity not so much a sense of dependability as a feeling that his ferocious conviction in the rightness of his own actions would be of advantage to all whose interest lay with his.

That night they camped, in a grove of oaks and beeches where a spring ran. The nights were still cool and they had a fire against it, of a rail lifted from a nearby fence and cut into lengths—a small fire, neat, niggard almost, a shrewd fire; such fires were his father's habit and custom always, even in freezing weather. Older, the boy might have remarked this and wondered why not a big one; why should not a man who had not only seen the waste and extravagance of war, but who had in his blood an inherent voracious prodigality with material not his own, have burned everything in sight? Then he might have gone a step farther and thought that that was the reason; that niggard blaze was the living fruits of nights passed during those four years in the woods hiding from all men, blue or grey, with his strings of horses (captured horses, he called them). And older still, he might have divined the true reason: that the element of fire spoke to some deep mainspring of his father's being, as the element of steel or of powder spoke to other men, as the one weapon for the preservation of integrity, else breath were not worth the breathing, and hence to be regarded with respect and used with discretion.

But he did not think this now and he had seen those same niggard blazes all his life. He merely ate his supper beside it and was already half asleep over his iron plate when his father called him, and once more he followed the stiff back, the stiff and ruthless limp, up the slope and on to the starlit road where, turning, he could see his father against the stars but without face or depth—a shape black, flat, and bloodless as though cut from tin in the iron folds of the frockcoat which had not been made for him, the voice harsh like tin and without heat like tin:

"You were fixing to tell them. You would have told him." He didn't answer. His father struck him with the flat of his hand on the side of the head, hard but without heat, exactly as he had struck the two mules at the store, exactly as he would strike either of them with any stick in order to kill a horse fly, his voice still without heat or anger: "You're getting to be a man. You got to learn. You got to learn to stick to your own blood or you ain't going to have any blood to stick to you. Do you think either of them, any man there this morning, would? Don't you know all they wanted was a chance to get at me because they knew I had them beat? Eh?" Later, twenty years later, he was to tell himself, "If I had said they wanted only truth, justice, he would have hit me again." But now he said nothing. He was not crying. He just stood there. "Answer me," his father said.

"Yes," he whispered. His father turned.

30   "Get on to bed. We'll be there tomorrow."

Tomorrow they were there. In the early afternoon the wagon stopped before a paintless two-room house identical almost with the dozen others it had stopped before even in the boy's ten years, and again, as on the other dozen occasions, his mother and aunt got down and began to unload the wagon, although his two sisters and his father and brother had not moved.

"Likely hit ain't fitten for hawgs," one of the sisters said.

"Nevertheless, fit it will and you'll hog it and like it," his father said. "Get out of them chairs and help your Ma unload."

The two sisters got down, big, bovine, in a flutter of cheap ribbons; one of them drew from the jumbled wagon bed a battered lantern, the other a worn broom. His father handed the reins to the older son and began to climb stiffly over the wheel. "When they get unloaded, take the team to the barn and feed them." Then he said, and at first the boy thought he was still speaking to his brother: "Come with me."

35   "Me?" he said.

"Yes," his father said. "You."

"Abner," his mother said. His father paused and looked back—the harsh level stare beneath the shaggy, graying, irascible brows.

"I reckon I'll have a word with the man that aims to begin tomorrow owning me body and soul for the next eight months."

They went back up the road. A week ago—or before last night, that is—he would have asked where they were going, but not now. His father had struck him before last night but never before had he paused afterward to explain why; it was as if the blow and the following calm, outrageous voice still rang, repercussed, divulging nothing to him save the terrible handicap of being young, the light weight of his few years, just heavy enough to prevent his soaring free of the world as it seemed to be ordered but not heavy enough to keep footed solid in it, to resist it and try to change the course of its events.

40   Presently he could see the grove of oaks and cedars and the other flowering trees and shrubs where the house would be, though not the house yet. They walked beside a fence massed with honeysuckle and Cherokee roses and came to a gate swinging open between two brick pillars, and now, beyond sweep of drive, he saw the house for the first time and at that instant he forgot his father and the terror and despair both, and even when he remembered his father again (who had stopped) the terror and despair did not return. Because, for all the twelve movings, they had sojourned until now in a poor country, a land of small farms and fields and houses, and he had never seen a house like this before. *Hit's big as a courthouse* he thought quietly, with a surge of peace and joy whose reason he could not have thought into words, being too young for that: *They are safe from him. People whose lives are a part of this peace and dignity are beyond his touch, he no more to them than a buzzing wasp: capable of stinging for a little moment but that's all; the spell of this peace and dignity rendering even the barns and stable and cribs which belong to it impervious to the puny flames he might contrive . . .* this, the peace and joy, ebbing for an instant as he looked again at the stiff black back, the stiff and implacable limp of the figure which was not dwarfed by the house, for the reason that it had never looked big anywhere and which now, against the serene

columned backdrop, had more than ever that impervious quality of something cut ruth-lessly from tin, depthless, as though, sidewise to the sun, it would cast no shadow. Watching him, the boy remarked the absolutely undeviating course which his father held and saw the stiff foot come squarely down in a pile of fresh droppings where a horse had stood in the drive and which his father could have avoided by a simple change of stride. But it ebbed only for a moment, though he could not have thought this into words either, walking on in the spell of the house, which he could even want but without envy, without sorrow, cer-tainly never with that ravening and jealous rage which unknown to him walked in the iron-like black coat before him: *Maybe he will feel it too. Maybe it will even change him now from what maybe he couldn't help but be.*

They crossed the portico. Now he could hear his father's stiff foot as it came down on the boards with clocklike finality, a sound out of all proportion to the displacement of the body it bore and which was not dwarfed either by the white door before it, as though it had attained to a sort of vicious and ravening minimum not to be dwarfed by anything—the flat, wide, black hat, the formal coat of broadcloth which had once been black but which had now that friction-glazed greenish cast of the bodies of old house flies, the lifted sleeve which was too large, the lifted hand like a curled claw. The door opened so promptly that the boy knew the Negro must have been watching them all the time, an old man with neat grizzled hair, in a linen jacket, who stood barring the door with his body, saying "Wipe yo foots, white man, fo you come in here. Major ain't home nohow."

"Get out of my way, nigger," his father said, without heat too, flinging the door back and the Negro also and entering, his hat still on his head. And now the boy saw the prints of the stiff foot on the doorsill and saw them appear on the pale rug behind the machinelike deliberation of the foot which seemed to bear (or transmit) twice the weight which the body compassed. The Negro was shouting "Miss Lula! Miss Lula!" somewhere behind them, then the boy, deluged as though by a warm wave by a suave turn of carpeted stair and a pendant glitter of chandeliers and a mute gleam of gold frames, heard the swift feet and saw her too, a lady—perhaps he had never seen her like before either—in a gray, smooth gown with lace at the throat and an apron tied at the waist and the sleeves turned back, wiping cake or bis-cuit dough from her hands with a towel as she came up the hall, looking not at his father at all but at the tracks on the blond rug with an expression of incredulous amazement.

"I tried," the Negro cried. "I tole him to . . ."

"Will you please go away?" she said in a shaking voice. "Major de Spain is not at home. Will you please go away?"

45   His father had not spoken again. He did not speak again. He did not even look at her. He just stood stiff in the center of the rug, in his hat, the shaggy iron-gray brows twitching slightly above the pebble-colored eyes as he appeared to examine the house with brief delib-eration. Then with the same deliberation he turned; the boy watched him pivot on the good leg and saw the stiff foot drag round the arc of the turning, leaving a final long and fading smear. His father never looked at it, he never once looked down at the rug. The Negro held the door. It closed behind them, upon the hysteric and indistinguishable woman-wail. His father stopped at the top of the steps and scraped his boot clean on the edge of it. At the gate he stopped again. He stood for a moment, planted stiffly on the stiff foot, looking back at the house. "Pretty and white, ain't it?" he said. "That's sweat. Nigger sweat. Maybe it ain't white enough yet to suit him. Maybe he wants to mix some white sweat with it."

Two hours later the boy was chopping wood behind the house within which his mother and aunt and the two sisters (the mother and aunt, not the two girls, he knew that; even at this distance and muffled by walls the flat loud voices of the two girls emanated an incorrigible idle inertia) were setting up the stove to prepare a meal, when he heard the hooves and saw the linen-clad man on a fine sorrel mare, whom he recognized even before he saw the rolled rug in front of the Negro youth following on a fat bay carriage horse—a suffused, angry face vanishing, still at full gallop, beyond the corner of the house where his father and brother were sitting in the two tilted chairs; and a moment later, almost before he could have put the axe down, he heard the hooves again and watched the sorrel mare go back out of the yard, already galloping again. Then his father began to shout one of the sisters' names, who presently emerged backward from the kitchen door dragging the rolled rug along the ground by one end while the other sister walked behind it.

"If you ain't going to tote, go on and set up the wash pot," the first said.

"You, Sarty!" the second shouted. "Set up the wash pot!" His father appeared at the door, framed against that shabbiness, as he had been against that other bland perfection, impervious to either, the mother's anxious face at his shoulder.

"Go on," the father said. "Pick it up." The two sisters stooped, broad, lethargic; stooping, they presented an incredible expanse of pale cloth and a flutter of tawdry ribbons.

50   "If I thought enough of a rug to have to git hit all the way from France I wouldn't keep hit where folks coming in would have to tromp on hit," the first said. They raised the rug.

"Abner," the mother said. "Let me do it."

"You go back and git dinner," his father said. "I'll tend to this."

From the woodpile through the rest of the afternoon the boy watched them, the rug spread flat in the dust beside the bubbling wash pot, the two sisters stooping over it with that profound and lethargic reluctance, while the father stood over them in turn, implacable and grim, driving them though never raising his voice again. He could smell the harsh homemade lye they were using; he saw his mother come to the door once and look toward them with an expression not anxious now but very like despair; he saw his father turn, and he fell to with the axe and saw from the corner of his eye his father raise from the ground a flattish fragment of field stone and examine it and return to the pot, and this time his mother actually spoke: "Abner. Abner. Please don't. Please, Abner."

Then he was done too. It was dusk; the whippoorwills had already begun. He could smell coffee from the room where they would presently eat the cold food remaining from the mid-afternoon meal, though when he entered the house he realized they were having coffee again because there was a fire on the hearth, before which the rug now lay spread over the backs of the two chairs. The tracks of his father's foot were gone. Where they had been were now long, water-cloudy scoriations resembling the sporadic course of a Lilliputian[2] mowing machine.

55   It still hung there while they ate the cold food and then went to bed, scattered without order or claim up and down the two rooms, his mother in one bed, where his father would later lie, the older brother in the other, himself, the aunt, and the two sisters on pallets on the floor. But his father was not in bed yet. The last thing the boy remembered was the depthless, harsh silhouette of the hat and coat bending over the rug and it seemed to him that he had not even closed his eyes when the silhouette was standing over him, the fire almost dead behind it, the stiff foot prodding him awake. "Catch up the mule," his father said.

When he returned with the mule his father was standing in the black door, the rolled rug over his shoulder. "Ain't you going to ride?" he said.

"No. Give me your foot."

He bent his knee into his father's hand, the wiry, surprising power flowed smoothly, rising, he rising with it, on to the mule's bare back (they had owned a saddle once; the boy could remember it though not when or where) and with the same effortlessness his father

---

[2] Referring to Lilliput, an imaginary island in Jonathan Swift's *Gulliver's Travels,* the inhabitants of which were six inches tall; diminutive.

swung the rug up in front of him. Now in the starlight they retraced the afternoon's path, up the dusty road rife with honeysuckle, through the gate and up the black tunnel of the drive to the lightless house, where he sat on the mule and felt the rough warp of the rug drag across his thighs and vanish.

"Don't you want me to help?" he whispered. His father did not answer and now he heard again that stiff foot striking the hollow portico with that wooden and clocklike deliberation, that outrageous overstatement of the weight it carried. The rug, hunched, not flung (the boy could tell that even in the darkness) from his father's shoulder, struck the angle of wall and floor with a sound unbelievably loud, thunderous, then the foot again, unhurried and enormous; a light came on in the house and the boy sat, tense, breathing steadily and quietly and just a little fast, though the foot itself did not increase its beat at all, descending the steps now; now the boy could see him.

60 "Don't you want to ride now?" he whispered. "We kin both ride now," the light within the house altering now, flaring up and sinking. *He's coming down the stairs now,* he thought. He had already ridden the mule up beside the horse block; presently his father was up behind him and he doubled the reins over and slashed the mule across the neck, but before the animal could begin to trot the hard, thin arm came round him, the hard, knotted hand jerking the mule back to a walk.

In the first red rays of the sun they were in the lot, putting plow gear on the mules. This time the sorrel mare was in the lot before he heard it at all, the rider collarless and even bareheaded, trembling, speaking in a shaking voice as the woman in the house had done, his father merely looking up once before stooping again to the hame he was buckling, so that the man on the mare spoke to his stooping back:

"You must realize you have ruined that rug. Wasn't there anybody here, any of your women . . ." He ceased, shaking, the boy watching him, the older brother leaning now in the stable door, chewing, blinking slowly and steadily at nothing apparently. "It cost a hundred dollars. But you never had a hundred dollars. You never will. So I'm going to charge you twenty bushels of corn against your crop. I'll add it in your contract and when you come to the commissary you can sign it. That won't keep Mrs. de Spain quiet but maybe it will teach you to wipe your feet off before you enter her house again."

Then he was gone. The boy looked at his father, who still had not spoken or even looked up again, who was now adjusting the logger-head in the hame.

"Pap," he said. His father looked at him—the inscrutable face, the shaggy brows beneath which the gray eyes glinted coldly. Suddenly the boy went toward him, fast, stopping as suddenly. "You done the best you could!" he cried. "If he wanted hit done different why didn't he wait and tell you how? He won't git no twenty bushels! He won't git none! We'll get hit and hide hit! I kin watch . . ."

65 "Did you put the cutter back in that straight stock like I told you?"

"No, sir," he said.

"Then go do it."

That was Wednesday. During the rest of that week he worked steadily, at what was within his scope and some which was beyond it, with an industry that did not need to be driven nor even commanded twice; he had this from his mother, with the difference that some at least of what he did he liked to do, such as splitting wood with the half-size axe which his mother and aunt had earned, or saved money somehow, to present him with at Christmas. In company with the two older women (and on one afternoon even one of the sisters), he built pens for the shoat and the cow which were a part of his father's contract with the landlord, and one afternoon, his father being absent, gone somewhere on one of the mules, he went to the field.

They were running a middle buster now, his brother holding the plow straight while he handled the reins, and walking beside the straining mule, the rich black soil shearing cool and damp against his bare ankles, he thought *Maybe this is the end of it. Maybe even that twenty bushels that seems hard to have to pay for just a rug will be a cheap price for him to stop forever and always from being what he used to be;* thinking, dreaming now, so that his brother had to speak sharply to him to mind the mule: *Maybe he even won't collect the twenty bushels. Maybe it will all add up and balance and vanish—corn, rug, fire; the terror and grief, the being pulled two ways like between two teams of horses—gone, done with forever and ever.*

70   Then it was Saturday; he looked up from beneath the mule he was harnessing and saw his father in the black coat and hat. "Not that," his father said. "The wagon gear." And then, two hours later, sitting in the wagon bed behind his father and brother on the seat, the wagon accomplished a final curve, and he saw the weathered paintless store with its tattered tobacco- and patent-medicine posters and the tethered wagons and saddle animals below the gallery. He mounted the gnawed steps behind father and brother, and there again was the lane of quiet, watching faces for the three of them to walk through. He saw the man in spectacles sitting at the plank table and he did not need to be told this was Justice of the Peace; he sent one glare of fierce, exultant, partisan defiance at the man in collar and cravat now, whom he had seen but twice in his life, and that on a galloping horse, who now wore on his face an expression not of rage but of amazed unbelief which the boy could not have known was at the incredible circumstance of being sued by one of his own tenants, and came and stood against his father and cried at the Justice: "He ain't done it! He ain't burnt . . ."

"Go back to the wagon," his father said.

"Burnt?" the Justice said. "Do I understand this rug was burned too?"

"Does anybody here claim it was?" his father said. "Go back to the wagon." But he did not, he merely retreated to the rear of the room, crowded as that other had been, but not to sit down this time, instead, to stand pressing among the motionless bodies, listening to the voices:

"And you claim twenty bushels of corn is too high for the damage you did to the rug?"

75   "He brought the rug to me and said he wanted the tracks washed out of it. I washed the tracks out and took the rug back to him."

"But you didn't carry the rug back to him in the same condition it was in before you made the tracks on it."

His father did not answer, and now for perhaps half a minute there was no sound at all save that of breathing, the faint, steady suspiration of complete and intent listening.

"You decline to answer that, Mr. Snopes?" Again his father did not answer. "I'm going to find against you, Mr. Snopes. I'm going to find that you were responsible for the injury to Major de Spain's rug and hold you liable for it. But twenty bushels of corn seems a little high for a man in your circumstances to have to pay. Major de Spain claims it cost a hundred dollars. October corn will be worth about fifty cents. I figure that if Major de Spain can stand a ninety-five-dollar loss on something he paid cash for, you can stand a five-dollar loss you haven't earned yet. I hold you in damages to Major de Spain to the amount of ten bushels of corn over and above your contract with him, to be paid to him out of your crop at gathering time. Court adjourned."

It had taken no time hardly, the morning was but half begun. He thought they would return home and perhaps back to the field, since they were late, far behind all other farmers. But instead his father passed on behind the wagon, merely indicating with his hand for the older brother to follow with it, and crossed the road toward the blacksmith shop opposite, pressing on after his father, overtaking him, speaking, whispering up at the harsh, calm face beneath the weathered hat: "He won't git no ten bushels neither. He won't git one. We'll . . ." until his father glanced for an instant down on him, the face absolutely calm, the grizzled eyebrows tangled above the cold eyes, the voice almost pleasant, almost gentle:

80   "You think so? Well, we'll wait till October anyway."

The matter of the wagon—the setting of a spoke or two and the tightening of the tires—did not take long either, the business of the tires accomplished by driving the wagon into the spring branch behind the shop and letting it stand there, the mules nuzzling into the water from time to time, and the boy on the seat with the idle reins, looking up the slope and through the sooty tunnel of the shed where the slow hammer rang and where his father sat on an upended cypress bolt, easily, either talking or listening, still sitting there when the boy brought the dripping wagon up out of the branch and halted it before the door.

"Take them on to the shade and hitch," his father said. He did so and returned. His father and the smith and a third man squatting on his heels inside the door were talking, about crops and animals; the boy, squatting too in the ammoniac dust and hoof-parings and scales of rust, heard his father tell a long and unhurried story out of the time before the birth of the older brother even when he had been a professional horsetrader. And then his father came up beside him where he stood before a tattered last year's circus poster on the other side of the store, gazing rapt and quiet at the scarlet horses, the incredible poisings and convolutions of tulle and tights and the painted leers of comedians, and said, "It's time to eat."

But not at home. Squatting beside his brother against the front wall, he watched his father emerge from the store and produce from a paper sack a segment of cheese and divided it carefully and deliberately into three with his pocket knife and produce crackers from the same sack. They all three squatted on the gallery and ate slowly, without talking; then in the store again, they drank from a tin dipper tepid water smelling of the cedar bucket and of living beech trees. And still they did not go home. It was a horse lot this time, a tall rail fence upon and along which men stood and sat and out of which one by one horses were led, to be walked and trotted and then cantered back and forth along the road while the slow swapping and buying went on and the sun began to slant westward, they—the three of them—watching and listening, the older brother with his muddy eyes and his steady inevitable tobacco, the father commenting now and then on certain of the animals, to no one in particular.

It was after sundown when they reached home. They ate supper by lamplight, then, sitting on the doorstep, the boy watched the night fully accomplish, listening to the whippoorwills and the frogs, when he heard his mother's voice: "Abner! No! No! Oh, God, Oh, God, Abner!" and he rose, whirled, and saw the altered light through the door where a candle stub now burned in a bottle neck on the table and his father, still in the hat and coat, at once formal and burlesque as though dressed carefully for some shabby and ceremonial violence, emptying the reservoir of the lamp back into the five-gallon kerosene can from which it had been filled, while the mother tugged at his arm until he shifted the lamp to the other hand and flung her back, not savagely or viciously, just hard, into the wall, her hands flung out against the wall for balance, her mouth open and in her face the same quality of hopeless despair as had been in her voice. Then his father saw him standing in the door.

85   "Go to the barn and get that can of oil we were oiling the wagon with," he said. The boy did not move. Then he could speak.

"What . . ." he cried. "What are you . . ."

"Go get that oil," his father said. "Go."

Then he was moving, running, outside the house, toward the stable: this the old habit, the old blood which he had not been permitted to choose for himself, which had been bequeathed him willy nilly and which had run for so long (and who knew where, battening on what of outrage and savagery and lust) before it came to him. *I could keep on,* he thought, *I could run on and on and never look back, never need to see his face again. Only I can't. I can't,* the rusted can in his hand now, the liquid sloshing in it as he ran back to the house and into it, into the sound of his mother's weeping in the next room, and handed the can to his father.

"Ain't you going to even send a nigger?" he cried. "At least you sent a nigger before!"

90   This time his father didn't strike him. The hand came even faster than the blow had, the same hand which had set the can on the table with almost excruciating care flashing from the can toward him too quick for him to follow it, gripping him by the back of his shirt and on to tiptoe before he had seen it quit the can, the face stooping at him in breathless and frozen ferocity, the cold, dead voice speaking over him to the older brother who leaned against the table, chewing with that steady, curious, sidewise motion of cows:

"Empty the can into the big one and go on. I'll catch up with you."

"Better tie him up to the bedpost," the brother said.

"Do like I told you," the father said. Then the boy was moving, his bunched shirt and the hard, bony hand between his shoulder-blades, his toes just touching the floor, across the room and into the other one, past the sisters sitting with spread heavy thighs in the two chairs over the cold hearth, and to where his mother and aunt sat side by side on the bed, the aunt's arms about the mother's shoulders.

"Hold him," the father said. The aunt made a startled movement. "Not you," the father said. "Lennie. Take hold of him. I want to see you do it." His mother took him by the wrist. "You'll hold him better than that. If he gets loose don't you know what he is going to do? He will go up yonder." He jerked his head toward the road. "Maybe I'd better tie him."

95   "I'll hold him," his mother whispered.

"See you do then." Then his father was gone, the stiff foot heavy and measured upon the boards, ceasing at last.

Then he began to struggle. His mother caught him in both arms, he jerking and wrenching at them. He would be stronger in the end, he knew that. But he had not time to wait for it. "Lemme go!" he cried. "I don't want to have to hit you!"

"Let him go!" the aunt said. "If he don't go, before God, I am going up there myself!"

"Don't you see I can't?" his mother cried. "Sarty! Sarty! No! No! Help me, Lizzie!"

100   Then he was free. His aunt grasped at him but it was too late. He whirled, running, his mother stumbled forward on to her knees behind him, crying to the nearer sister: "Catch him, Net! Catch him!" But that was too late too, the sister (the sisters were twins, born at the same time, yet either of them now gave the impression of being, encompassing as much living meat and volume and weight as any other two of the family) not yet having begun to rise from the chair, her head, face, alone merely turned, presenting to him in the flying instant an astonishing expanse of young female features untroubled by any surprise even, wearing only an expression of bovine interest. Then he was out of the room, out of the house, in the mild dust of the starlit road and the heavy rifeness of honeysuckle, the pale ribbon unspooling with terrific slowness under his running feet, reaching the gate at last and turning in, running, his heart and lungs drumming, on up the drive toward the lighted house, the lighted door. He did not knock, he burst in, sobbing for breath, incapable for the moment of speech; he saw the astonished face of the Negro in the line jacket without knowing when the Negro had appeared.

"De Spain!" he cried, panted. "Where's . . ." then he saw the white man too emerging from a white door down the hall. "Barn!" he cried. "Barn!"

"What?" the white man said. "Barn?"

"Yes!" the boy cried. "Barn!"

"Catch him!" the white man shouted.

105   But it was too late this time too. The Negro grasped his shirt, but the entire sleeve, rotten with washing, carried away, and he was out that door too and in the drive again, and had actually never ceased to run even while he was screaming into the white man's face.

Behind him the white man was shouting. "My horse! Fetch my horse!" and he thought for an instant of cutting across the park and climbing the fence into the road, but he did not know the park nor how high the vine-massed fence might be and he dared not risk it. So he ran on down the drive, blood and breath roaring; presently he was in the road again though he could not see it. He could not hear either: the galloping mare was almost upon him before he heard her, and even then he held his course, as if the very urgency of his wild grief and need must in a moment more find him wings, waiting until the ultimate instant to hurl himself aside and into the weed-choked roadside ditch as the horse thundered past and on, for an instant in furious silhouette against the stars, the tranquil early summer night sky which, even before the shape of the horse and rider vanished, strained abruptly and violently upward: a long, swirling roar incredible and soundless, blotting the stars, and he springing up and into the road again, running again, knowing it was too late yet still running even after he heard the shot and, an instant later, two shots, pausing now without knowing he had ceased to run, crying "Pap! Pap!," running again before he knew he had begun to run, stumbling, tripping over something and scrabbling up again without ceasing to run, looking backward over his shoulder at the glare as he got up, running on among the invisible trees, panting, sobbing, "Father! Father!"

At midnight he was sitting on the crest of a hill. He did not know it was midnight and he did not know how far he had come. But there was no glare behind him now and he sat now, his back toward what he had called home for four days anyhow, his face toward the dark woods which he would enter when breath was strong again, small, shaking steadily in the chill darkness, hugging himself into the remainder of his thin, rotten shirt, the grief and despair now no longer terror and fear but just grief and despair. *Father. My father,* he thought. "He was brave!" he cried suddenly, aloud but not loud, no more than a whisper: "He was! He was in the war! He was in Colonel Sartoris' cav'ry!" not knowing that his father had gone to that war a private in the fine old European sense, wearing no uniform, admitting the authority of and giving fidelity to no man or army or flag, going to war as Malbrouck[3] himself did: for booty—it meant nothing and less than nothing to him if it were enemy booty or his own.

The slow constellations wheeled on. It would be dawn and then sun-up after a while and he would be hungry. But that would be tomorrow and now he was only cold, and walking would cure that. His breathing was easier now and he decided to get up and go on, and then he found that he had been asleep because he knew it was almost dawn, the night almost over. He could tell that from the whippoorwills. They were everywhere now among the dark trees below him, constant and inflectioned and ceaseless, so that, as the instant for giving over to the day birds drew nearer and nearer, there was no interval at all between them. He got up. He was a little stiff, but walking would cure that too as it would the cold, and soon there would be the sun. He went on down the hill, toward the dark woods within which the liquid silver voices of the birds called unceasing—the rapid and urgent beating of the urgent and quiring heart of the late spring night. He did not look back.

■ **EXPLORATIONS OF THE TEXT**
1. Describe the courtroom scene at the beginning of the story. How does Sarty feel and react?
2. Why does the boy feel "peace and joy" when he sees Major de Spain's house?
3. What are the father's values? Does the boy renounce them? Does the boy really betray the father?
4. What image characterizes the women in the story? What do you conclude?

---

[3] Hero of an old French ballad ("Malbrouck s'en va-t-en guerre"); the original Malbrouck was the English Duke of Marborough (1650–1722), accused of profiteering during wartime (1702–13)

5. What concepts of justice emerge in "Barn Burning"? What is implied about the evolution of justice from rudimentary to more civilized ideas?
6. Trace the changes in Sarty's character. Be specific.
7. Read the last two paragraphs carefully. Is the ending pessimistic or optimistic? Which words give evidence for a conclusion?
8. Faulkner is noted for his complex style. Is the style appropriate in this story?

■ THE READING/WRITING CONNECTION

1. "Think" Topic: In a paragraph, discuss the logic of each participant in the courtroom scene.
2. Evaluate Faulkner's technique in the opening of the story.

■ IDEAS FOR WRITING

1. Describe the father's past and explain his actions in the story. Does the reader have any sympathy for him?
2. How does Faulkner portray women in "Barn Burning"?"
3. Write on one of the following themes: betrayal, guilt and redemption, or sins of the father.

BARBARA KINGSOLVER

Barbara Kingsolver (1955–   ) was born in Kentucky and educated at DePauw University and the University of Arizona. She published her first novel, The Bean Trees, *in 1989. Subsequent novels include* Animal Dreams *(1990), for which she was awarded the PEN fiction prize and Edward Abbey Ecofiction Award in 1991, and* The Poisonwood Bible *(1998), winner of the National Humanities Medal in 2000. She has also published a collection of short stories,* Homeland and Other Stories *(1989); a collection of essays,* High Tide in Tuscon: Essays for Now and Never *(1995); a collection of poems,* Another America *(1992); and a nonfiction book,* Holding the Line: Women in the Great Arizona Mine Strike of 1983 *(1989), and most recently a collection of essays,* Small Wonder *(2002). Kingsolver has described the goal of her fiction as first to entertain and second to educate.*

1989

ROSE-JOHNNY

Rose-Johnny wore a man's haircut and terrified little children, although I will never believe that was her intention. For her own part she inspired in us only curiosity. It was our mothers who took this fascination and wrung it, through daily admonitions, into the most irresistible kind of horror. She was like the old wells, covered with ancient rotting boards and overgrown with weeds, that waited behind the barns to swallow us down: our mothers warned us time and again not to go near them, and still were certain that we did.

My own mother was not one of those who had a great deal to say about her, but Walnut Knobs was a small enough town so that a person did not need to be told things directly. When I had my first good look at her, at close range, I was ten years old. I fully understood the importance of the encounter.

What mattered to me at the time, though, was that it was something my sister had not done before me. She was five years older, and as a consequence there was hardly an achievement in my life, nor even an article of clothing, that had not first been Mary Etta's. But, because of the circumstances of my meeting Rose-Johnny, I couldn't tell a living soul about it, and so for nearly a year I carried the secret torment of a great power that can't be used. My agitation was not relieved but made worse when I told the story to myself, over and over again.

She was not, as we always heard, half man and half woman, something akin to the pagan creatures whose naked torsos are inserted in various shocking ways into parts of animal bodies. In fact, I was astonished by her ordinariness. It is true that she wore Red Wing boots like my father. And also there was something not quite womanly in her face, but maybe any woman's face would look the same with that haircut. Her hair was coal black, cut flat across the top of her round head, so that when she looked down I could see a faint pale spot right on top where the scalp almost surfaced.

5   But the rest of her looked exactly like anybody's mother in a big flowered dress without a waistline and with two faded spots in front, where her bosom rubbed over the counter when she reached across to make change or wipe away the dust.

People say there is a reason for every important thing that happens. I was sent to the feed store, where I spoke to Rose-Johnny and passed a quarter from my hand into hers, because it was haying time. And because I was small for my age. I was not too small to help with tobacco setting in the spring, in fact I was better at it than Mary Etta, who complained about the stains on her hands, but I was not yet big enough to throw a bale of hay onto the flatbed. It was the time of year when Daddy complained about not having boys. Mama said that at least he oughtn't to bother going into town for the chicken mash that day because Georgeann could do it on her way home from school.

Mama told me to ask Aunt Minnie to please ma'am give me a ride home. "Ask her nice to stop off at Lester Wall's store so you can run in with this quarter and get five pound of laying mash."[1]

I put the quarter in my pocket, keeping my eye out to make certain Mary Etta understood what I had been asked to do. Mary Etta had once told me that I was no better than the bugs that suck on potato vines, and that the family was going to starve to death because of my laziness. It was one of the summer days when we were on our knees in the garden picking off bugs and dropping them into cans of coal oil. She couldn't go into town with Aunt Minnie to look at dress patterns until we finished with the potato bugs. What she said, exactly, was that if I couldn't work any harder than that, then she might just as well throw *me* into a can of coal oil. Later she told me she hadn't meant it, but I intended to remember it nonetheless.

Aunt Minnie taught the first grade and had a 1951 Dodge. That is how she referred to her car whenever she spoke of it. It was the newest automobile belonging to anyone related to us, although some of the Wilcox cousins had once come down to visit from Knoxville in a Ford they were said to have bought the same year it was made. But I saw that car and did not find it nearly as impressive as Aunt Minnie's, which was white and immense and shone like glass. She paid a boy to polish it every other Saturday.

10   On the day she took me to Wall's, she waited in the car while I went inside with my fist tight around the quarter. I had never been in the store before, and although I had passed by it many times and knew what could be bought there, I had never imagined what a wonderful combination of warm, sweet smells of mash and animals and seed corn it would contain. The dust lay white and thin on everything like a bridal veil. Rose-Johnny was in the back with a water can, leaning over into one of the chick tubs. The steel rang with the sound of

---

[1] A type of boiled grain, bran, or meal, fed warm to horses, cattle, and chickens.

confined baby birds, and a light bulb shining up from inside the tub made her face glow white. Mr. Wall, Rose-Johnny's Pa, was in the front of the store talking to two men about a horse. He didn't notice me as I crept up to the counter. It was Rose-Johnny who came forward to the cash register.

"And what for you, missy?"

She is exactly like anybody's mama, was all I could think, and I wanted to reach and touch her flowered dress. The two men were looking at me.

"My mama needs five pound of laying mash and here's a quarter for it." I clicked the coin quickly onto the counter.

"Yes, ma'am." She smiled at me, but her boots made heavy, tired sounds on the floor. She made her way slowly, like a duck in water, over to the row of wooden bins that stood against the wall. She scooped the mash into a paper bag and weighed it, then shoved the scoop back into the bin. A little cloud of dust rose out of the mash up into the window. I watched her from the counter.

15   "Don't your mama know she's wasting good money on chicken mash? Any fool chicken will eat corn." I jumped when the man spoke. It was one of the two, and they were standing so close behind me I would have had to look right straight up to see their faces. Mr. Wall was gone.

"No sir, they need mash," I said to the man's boots.

"What's that?" It was the taller man doing the talking.

"They need mash," I said louder. "To lay good sturdy eggs for selling. A little mash mixed in with the corn. Mama says it's got oster shells in it."

"Is that a fact," he said. "Did you hear that, Rose-Johnny?" he called out. "This child says you put oster shells in that mash. Is that right?"

20   When Rose-Johnny came back to the cash register she was moon-eyed. She made quick motions with her hands and pushed the bag at me as if she didn't know how to talk.

"Do you catch them osters yourself, Rose-Johnny? Up at Jackson Crick?" The man was laughing. The other man was quiet.

Rose-Johnny looked all around and up at the ceiling. She scratched at her short hair, fast and hard, like a dog with ticks.

When the two men were gone I stood on my toes and leaned over the counter as far as I could. "Do you catch the osters yourself?"

She hooked her eyes right into mine, the way the bit goes into the mule's mouth and fits just so, one way and no other. Her eyes were the palest blue of any I had ever seen. Then she threw back her head and laughed so hard I could see the wide, flat bottoms of her back teeth, and I wasn't afraid of her.

25   When I left the store, the two men were still outside. Their boots scuffed on the front-porch floorboards, and the shorter one spoke.

"Child, how much did you pay that woman for the chicken mash?"

"A quarter," I told him.

He put a quarter in my hand. "You take this here, and go home and tell your daddy something. Tell him not never to send his little girls to Wall's feed store. Tell him to send his boys if he has to, but not his little girls." His hat was off, and his hair lay back in wet orange strips. A clean line separated the white top of his forehead from the red-burned hide of his face. In this way, it was like my father's face.

"No, sir, I can't tell him, because all my daddy's got is girls."

30   "That's George Bowles's child, Bud," the tall man said. "He's just got the two girls."

"Then tell him to come for hisself," Bud said. His eyes had the sun in them, and looked like a pair of new pennies.

Aunt Minnie didn't see the man give me the quarter because she was looking at herself in the side-view mirror of the Dodge. Aunt Minnie was older than Mama, but everyone mistook her for the younger because of the way she fixed herself up. And, of course, Mama was married. Mama said if Aunt Minnie ever found a man she would act her age.

When I climbed in the car she was pulling gray hairs out of her part. She said it was teaching school that caused them, but early gray ran in my mama's family.

She jumped when I slammed the car door. "All set?"

35 "Yes, ma'am," I said. She put her little purple hat back on her head and slowly pushed the long pin through it. I shuddered as she started up the car.

Aunt Minnie laughed. "Somebody walked over your grave."

"I don't have a grave," I said. "I'm not dead."

"No, you most certainly are not. That's just what they say when a person shivers like that." She smiled. I liked Aunt Minnie most of the time.

"I don't think they mean your real grave, with you in it," she said after a minute. "I think it means the place where your grave is going to be someday."

40 I thought about this for a while. I tried to picture the place, but could not. Then I thought about the two men outside Wall's store. I asked Aunt Minnie why it was all right for boys to do some things that girls couldn't.

"Oh, there's all kinds of reasons," she said. "Like what kinds of things, do you mean?"

"Like going into Wall's feed store."

"Who told you that?"

"Somebody."

45 Aunt Minnie didn't say anything.

Then I said, "It's because of Rose-Johnny, isn't it?"

Aunt Minnie raised her chin just a tiny bit. She might have been checking her lipstick in the mirror, or she might have been saying yes.

"Why?" I asked.

"Why what?"

50 "Why because of Rose-Johnny?"

"I can't tell you that, Georgeann."

"Why can't you tell me?" I whined. "Tell me."

The car rumbled over a cattle grate. When we came to the crossing, Aunt Minnie stepped on the brake so hard we both flopped forward. She looked at me. "Georgeann, Rose-Johnny is a Lebanese. That's all I'm going to tell you. You'll understand better when you're older."

When I got home I put the laying mash in the henhouse. The hens were already roosting high above my head, clucking softly into their feathers and shifting back and forth on their feet. I collected the eggs as I did every day, and took them into the house. I hadn't yet decided what to do about the quarter, and so I held on to it until dinnertime.

55 Mary Etta was late coming down, and even though she had washed and changed she looked pale as a haunt from helping with the haying all day. She didn't speak and she hardly ate.

"Here, girls, both of you, eat up these potatoes," Mama said after a while. "There's not but just a little bit left. Something to grow on."

"I don't need none then," Mary Etta said. "I've done growed all I'm going to grow."

"Don't talk back to your mama," Daddy said.

"I'm not talking back. It's the truth." Mary Etta looked at Mama. "Well, it is."

60 "Eat a little bite, Mary Etta. Just because you're in the same dresses for a year don't mean you're not going to grow no more."

"I'm as big as you are, Mama."

"All right then." Mama scraped the mashed potatoes onto my plate. "I expect now you'll be telling me you don't want to grow no more either," she said to me.

"No, ma'am, I won't," I said. But I was distressed, and looked sideways at the pink shirtwaist I had looked forward to inheriting along with the grown-up shape that would have to be worn inside it. Now it appeared that I was condemned to my present clothes and potato-shaped body; keeping these forever seemed to me far more likely than the possibility of having clothes that, like the Wilcox automobile, had never before been owned. I ate my potatoes quietly. Dinner was almost over when Daddy asked if I had remembered to get the laying mash.

"Yes, sir. I put it in the henhouse." I hesitated. "And here's the quarter back. Mr. Wall gave me the mash for nothing."

65 "Why did he do that?" Mama asked.

Mary Etta was staring like the dead. Even her hair looked tired, slumped over the back of her chair like a long black shadow.

"I helped him out," I said. "Rose-Johnny wasn't there, she was sick, and Mr. Wall said if I would help him clean out the bins and dust the shelves and water the chicks, then it wouldn't cost me for the laying mash."

"And Aunt Minnie waited while you did all that?"

"She didn't mind," I said. "She had some magazines to look at."

70 It was the first important lie I had told in my life, and I was thrilled with its power. Every member of my family believed I had brought home the laying mash in exchange for honest work.

I was also astonished at how my story, once I had begun it, wouldn't finish. "He wants me to come back and help him again the next time we need something," I said.

"I don't reckon you let on like we couldn't pay for the mash?" Daddy asked sternly.

"No, sir. I put the quarter right up there on the counter. But he said he needed the help. Rose-Johnny's real sick."

He looked at me like he knew. Like he had found the hole in the coop where the black snake was getting in. But he just said, "All right. You can go, if Aunt Minnie don't mind waiting for you."

75 "You don't have to say a thing to her about it," I said. "I can walk home the same as I do ever day. Five pound of mash isn't nothing to carry."

"We'll see," Mama said.

That night I believed I would burst. For a long time after Mary Etta fell asleep I twisted in my blankets and told the story over to myself, both the true and false versions. I talked to my doll, Miss Regina. She was a big doll, a birthday present from my Grandma and Grandpa Bowles, with a tiny wire crown and lovely long blond curls.

"Rose-Johnny isn't really sick," I told Miss Regina. "She's a Lebanese."

I looked up the word in Aunt Minnie's Bible dictionary after school. I pretended to be looking up St. John the Baptist but then turned over in a hurry to the *L*'s while she was washing her chalkboards. My heart thumped when I found it, but I read the passage quickly, several times over, and found it empty. It said the Lebanese were a seafaring people who built great ships from cedar trees. I couldn't believe that even when I was older I would be able, as Aunt Minnie promised, to connect this with what I had seen of Rose-Johnny. Nevertheless, I resolved to understand. The following week I went back to the store, confident that my lie would continue to carry its own weight.

80 Rose-Johnny recognized me. "Five pounds of laying mash," she said, and this time I followed her to the feed bins. There were flecks of white dust in her hair.

"Is it true you come from over the sea?" I asked her quietly as she bent over with the scoop.

She laughed and rolled her eyes. "A lot of them says I come from the moon," she said, and I was afraid she was going to be struck dumb and animal-eyed as she was the time before. But, when she finished weighing the bag, she just said, "I was born in Slate Holler, and that's as far from here as I ever been or will be."

"Is that where you get the osters from?" I asked, looking into the mash and trying to pick out which of the colored flecks they might be.

Rose-Johnny looked at me for a long time, and then suddenly laughed her big laugh. "Why, honey child, don't you know? Osters comes from the sea."

85   She rang up twenty-five cents on the register, but I didn't look at her.

"That was all, wasn't it?"

I leaned over the counter and tried to put tears in my eyes, but they wouldn't come. "I can't pay," I said. "My daddy said to ask you if I could do some work for it. Clean up or something."

"Your daddy said to ask me that? Well, bless your heart," she said. "Let me see if we can't find something for you to do. Bless your little heart, child, what's your name?"

"Georgeann," I told her.

90   "I'm Rose-Johnny," she said, and I did not say that I knew it, that like every other child I had known it since the first time I saw her in town, when I was five or six, and had to ask Mama if it was a man or a lady.

"Pleased to meet you," I said.

We kept it between the two of us: I came in every week to help with the pullets and the feed, and took home my mash. We did not tell Mr. Wall, although it seemed it would not have mattered one whit to him. Mr. Wall was in the store so seldom that he might not have known I was there. He kept to himself in the apartment at the back where he and Rose-Johnny lived.

It was she who ran the store, kept the accounts, and did the orders. She showed me how to feed and water the pullets and ducklings and pull out the sick ones. Later I learned how to weigh out packages of seed and to mix the different kinds of mash. There were lists nailed to the wall telling how much cracked corn and oats and grit to put in. I followed the recipes with enormous care, adding tiny amounts at a time to the bag on the hanging scales until the needle touched the right number. Although she was patient with me, I felt slow next to Rose-Johnny, who never had to look at the lists and used the scales only to check herself. It seemed to me she knew how to do more things than anyone I had ever known, woman or man.

She also knew the names of all the customers, although she rarely spoke to them. Sometimes such a change came over her when the men were there that it wasn't clear to me whether she was pretending or had really lost the capacity to speak. But afterward she would tell me their names and everything about them. Once she told me about Ed Charney, Sr. and Bud Mattox, the two men I had seen the first day I was in the store. According to Rose-Johnny, Ed had an old red mule he was in the habit of mistreating. "But even so," she said, "Ed's mule don't have it as bad as Bud's wife." I never knew how she acquired this knowledge.

95   When she said "Bud Mattox," I remembered his penny-colored eyes and connected him then with all the Mattox boys at school. It had never occurred to me that eyes could run in families, like early gray.

Occasionally a group of black-skinned children came to the store, always after hours. Rose-Johnny opened up for them. She called each child by name, and asked after their families and the health of their mothers' laying hens.

The oldest one, whose name was Cleota, was shaped like Mary Etta. Her hair was straight and pointed, and smelled to me like citronella candles. The younger girls had plaits that curved out from their heads like so many handles. Several of them wore dresses made from the same bolt of cloth, but they were not sisters. Rose-Johnny filled a separate order for each child.

I watched, but didn't speak. The skin on their heels and palms was creased, and as light as my own. Once, after they had left, I asked Rose-Johnny why they only came into the store when it was closed.

"People's got their ways," she said, stoking up the wood stove for the night. Then she told me all their names again, starting with Cleota and working down. She looked me in the eye. "When you see them in town, you speak. Do you hear? By *name*. I don't care who is watching."

∽

100 I was allowed to spend half an hour or more with Rose-Johnny nearly every day after school, so long as I did not neglect my chores at home. Sometimes on days that were rainy or cold Aunt Minnie would pick me up, but I preferred to walk. By myself, without Mary Etta to hurry me up.

As far as I know, my parents believed I was helping Mr. Wall because of Rose-Johnny's illness. They had no opportunity to learn otherwise, though I worried that some-day Aunt Minnie would come inside the store to fetch me, instead of just honking, or that Daddy would have to go to Wall's for something and see for himself that Rose-Johnny was fit and well. Come springtime he would be needing to buy tobacco seed.

It was soon after Christmas when I became consumed with a desire to confess. I felt the lies down inside me like cold, dirty potatoes in a root cellar, beginning to sprout and crowd. At night I told Miss Regina of my dishonesty and the things that were likely to happen to me be-cause of it. In so doing, there were several times I nearly confessed by accident to Mary Etta.

"Who's going to wring your neck?" she wanted to know, coming into the room one night when I thought she was downstairs washing the supper dishes.

"Nobody," I said, clutching Miss Regina to my pillow. I pretended to be asleep. I could hear Mary Etta starting to brush her hair. Every night before she went to bed she sat with her dress hiked up and her head hung over between her knees, brushing her hair all the way down to the floor. This improved the circulation to the hair, she told me, and would prevent it turning. Mary Etta was already beginning to get white hairs.

105 "Is it because Mama let you watch Daddy kill the cockerels? Did it scare you to see them jump around like that with their necks broke?"

"I'm not scared," I murmured, but I wanted so badly to tell the truth that I started to cry. I knew, for certain, that something bad was going to happen. I believe I also knew it would happen to my sister, instead of me.

"Nobody's going to hurt you," Mary Etta said. She smoothed my bangs and laid my pig-tails down flat on top of the quilt. "Give me Miss Regina and let me put her up for you now, so you won't get her hair all messed up."

I let her have the doll. "I'm not scared about the cockerels, Mary Etta. I promise." With my finger, under the covers, I traced a cross over my heart.

∽

When Rose-Johnny fell ill I was sick with guilt. When I first saw Mr. Wall behind the counter instead of Rose-Johnny, so help me God, I prayed this would be the day Aunt Minnie would come inside to get me. Immediately after, I felt sure God would kill me for my wickedness. I pictured myself falling dead beside the oat bin. I begged Mr. Wall to let me see her.

110   "Go on back, littl'un. She told me you'd be coming in," he said.

I had never been in the apartment before. There was little in it beyond the necessary things and a few old photographs on the walls, all of the same woman. The rooms were cold and felt infused with sickness and an odor I incorrectly believed to be medicine. Because my father didn't drink, I had never before encountered the smell of whiskey.

Rose-Johnny was propped on the pillows in a lifeless flannel gown. Her face changed when she saw me, and I remembered the way her face was lit by the light bulb in the chick tub, the first time I saw her. With fresh guilt I threw myself on her bosom.

"I'm sorry. I could have paid for the mash. I didn't mean to make you sick." Through my sobs I heard accusing needly wheezing sounds in Rose-Johnny's chest. She breathed with a great pulling effort.

"Child, don't talk foolish."

115   As weeks passed and Rose-Johnny didn't improve, it became clear that my lie was prophetic. Without Rose-Johnny to run the store, Mr. Wall badly needed my help. He seemed mystified by his inventory and was rendered helpless by any unusual demand from a customer. It was March, the busiest time for the store. I had turned eleven, one week before Mary Etta turned sixteen. These seven days out of each year, during which she was only four years older, I considered to be God's greatest gifts to me.

The afternoon my father would come in to buy the vegetable garden and tobacco seed was an event I had rehearsed endlessly in my mind. When it finally did transpire, Mr. Wall's confusion gave such complete respectability to my long-standing lie that I didn't need to say a word myself in support of it. I waited on him with dignity, precisely weighing out his tobacco seed, and even recommended to him the white runner beans that Mr. Wall had accidentally overstocked, and which my father did not buy.

Later on that same afternoon, after the winter light had come slanting through the dusty windows and I was alone in the store cleaning up, Cleota and the other children came pecking at the glass. I let them in. When I had filled all the orders Cleota unwrapped their coins, knotted all together into a blue handkerchief. I counted, and counted again. It was not the right amount, not even half.

"That's what Miss Rose-Johnny ast us for it," Cleota said. "Same as always." The smaller children—Venise, Anita, Little-Roy, James—shuffled and elbowed each other like fighting cocks, paying no attention. Cleota gazed at me calmly, steadily. Her eyebrows were two perfect arches.

"I thank you very much," I said, and put the coins in their proper places in the cash drawer.

120   During that week I also discovered an epidemic of chick droop in the pullets. I had to pull Mr. Wall over by the hand to make him look. There were more sick ones than well.

"It's because it's so cold in the store," I told him. "They can't keep warm. Can't we make it warmer in here?"

Mr. Wall shrugged at the wood stove, helpless. He could never keep a fire going for long, the way Rose-Johnny could.

"We have to try. The one light bulb isn't enough," I said. The chicks were huddled around the bulb just the way the men would collect around the stove in the mornings to say howdy-do to Mr. Wall and warm up their hands on the way to work. Except the chicks were more ruthless: they climbed and shoved, and the healthy ones pecked at the eyes and feet of the sick ones, making them bleed.

I had not noticed before what a very old man Mr. Wall was. As he stared down at the light, I saw that his eyes were covered with a film. "How do we fix them up?" he asked me.

125   "We can't. We've got to take the sick ones out so they won't all get it. Rose-Johnny puts them in that tub over there. We give them water and keep them warm, but it don't do any good. They've got to die."

     He looked so sad I stood and patted his old freckled hand.

     I spent much more time than before at the store, but no longer enjoyed it particularly. Working in the shadow of Rose-Johnny's expertise, I had been a secret witness to a wondrous ritual of counting, weighing, and tending. Together we created little packages that sailed out like ships to all parts of the country, giving rise to gardens and barnyard life in places I had never even seen. I felt superior to my schoolmates, knowing that I had had a hand in the creation of their families' poultry flocks and their mothers' kitchen gardens. By contrast, Mr. Wall's bewilderment was pathetic and only increased my guilt. But each day I was able to spend a little time in the back rooms with Rose-Johnny.

     There were rumors about her illness, both before and after the fact. It did not occur to me that I might have been the source of some of the earlier rumors. But, if I didn't think of this, it was because Walnut Knobs was overrun with tales of Rose-Johnny, and not because I didn't take notice of the stories. I did.

     The tales that troubled me most were those about Rose-Johnny's daddy. I had heard many adults say that he was responsible for her misfortune, which I presumed to mean her short hair. But it was also said that he was a colored man, and this I knew to be untrue. Aunt Minnie, when I pressed her, would offer nothing more than that if it were up to her I wouldn't go near either one of them, advice which I ignored. I was coming to understand that I would not hear the truth about Rose-Johnny from Aunt Minnie or anyone else. I knew, in a manner that went beyond the meanings of words I could not understand, that she was no more masculine than my mother or aunt, and no more lesbian than Lebanese. Rose-Johnny was simply herself, and alone.

130   And yet she was such a capable woman that I couldn't believe she would be sick for very long. But as the warm weather came she grew sluggish and pale. Her slow, difficult breathing frightened me. I brought my schoolbooks and read to her from the foot of the bed. Sometimes the rather ordinary adventures of the boy in my reader would make her laugh aloud until she choked. Other times she fell asleep while I read, but then would make me read those parts over again.

     She worried about the store. Frequently she would ask about Mr. Wall and the customers, and how he was managing. "He does all right," I always said. But eventually my eagerness to avoid the burden of further lies, along with the considerable force of my pride, led me to confess that I had to tell him nearly everything. "He forgets something awful," I told her.

     Rose-Johnny smiled. "He used to be as smart as anything, and taught me. Now I've done taught you, and you him again." She was lying back on the pillows with her eyes closed and her plump hands folded on her stomach.

     "But he's a nice man," I said. I listened to her breathing. "He don't hurt you does he? Your pa?"

     Nothing moved except her eyelids. They opened and let the blue eyes out at me. I looked down and traced my finger over the triangles of the flying-geese patch on the quilt. I whispered, "Does he make you cut off your hair?"

135   Rose-Johnny's eyes were so pale they were almost white, like ice with water running underneath. "He cuts it with a butcher knife. Sometimes he chases me all the way down to the river." She laughed a hissing laugh like a boy, and she had the same look the yearling calves get when they are cornered and jump the corral and run to the woods and won't be butchered. I understood then that Rose-Johnny, too, knew the power of a lie.

∞

It was the youngest Mattox boy who started the fight at school on the Monday after Easter. He was older than me, and a boy, so nobody believed he would hit me, but when he started the name calling I called them right back, and he threw me down on the ground. The girls screamed and ran to get the teacher, but by the time she arrived I had a bloody nose and had bitten his arm wonderfully hard.

Miss Althea gave me her handkerchief for my nose and dragged Roy Mattox inside to see the principal. All the other children stood in a circle, looking at me.

"It isn't true, what he said," I told them. "And not about Rose-Johnny either. She isn't a pervert. I love her."

"Pervert," one of the boys said.

140   I marveled at the sight of my own blood soaking through the handkerchief. "I love her," I said.

I did not get to see Rose-Johnny that day. The door of Wall's store was locked. I could see Mr. Wall through the window, though, so I banged on the glass with the flats of my hands until he came. He had the strong medicine smell on his breath.

"Not today, littl'un." The skin under his eyes was dark blue.

"I need to see Rose-Johnny." I was irritated with Mr. Wall, and did not consider him important enough to prevent me from seeing her. But evidently he was.

"Not today," he said. "We're closed." He shut the door and locked it.

145   I shouted at him through the glass. "Tell her I hit a boy and bit his arm, that was calling her names. Tell her I fought with a boy, Mr. Wall."

The next day the door was open, but I didn't see him in the store. In the back, the apartment was dark except for the lamp by Rose-Johnny's bed. A small brown bottle and a glass stood just touching each other on the night table. Rose-Johnny looked asleep but made a snuffing sound when I climbed onto the bottom of the bed.

"Did your daddy tell you what I told him yesterday?"

She said nothing.

"Is your daddy sick?"

150   "My daddy's dead," she said suddenly, causing me to swallow a little gulp of air. She opened her eyes, then closed them again. "Pa's all right, honey, just stepped out, I imagine." She stopped to breathe between every few words. "I didn't mean to give you a fright. Pa's not my daddy, he's my mama's daddy."

I was confused. "And your real daddy's dead?"

She nodded. "Long time."

"And your mama, what about her? Is she dead too?"

"Mm-hmm," she said, in the same lazy sort of way Mama would say it when she wasn't really listening.

155   "That her?" I pointed to the picture over the bed. The woman's shoulders were bare except for a dark lace shawl. She was looking backward toward you, over her shoulder.

Rose-Johnny looked up at the picture, and said yes it was.

"She's pretty," I said.

"People used to say I looked just like her." Rose-Johnny laughed a wheezy laugh, and coughed.

"Why did she die?"

160   Rose-Johnny shook her head. "I can't tell you that."

"Can you when I'm older?"

She didn't answer.

"Well then, if Mr. Wall isn't your daddy, then the colored man is your daddy," I said mostly to myself.

She looked at me. "Is that what they say?"

165 I shrugged.

"Does no harm to me. Every man is some color," she said.

"Oh," I said.

"My daddy was white. After he died my mama loved another man and he was brown."

"What happened then?"

170 "What happened then," she said. "Then they had a sweet little baby Johnny." Her voice was more like singing than talking, and her eyes were so peacefully closed I was afraid they might not open again. Every time she breathed there was the sound of a hundred tiny birds chirping inside her chest.

"Where's he?"

"Mama's Rose and sweet little baby Johnny," she sang it like an old song. "Not nothing bad going to happen to them, not nobody going to take her babies." A silvery moth flew into the lamp and clicked against the inside of the lampshade. Rose-Johnny stretched out her hand toward the night table. "I want you to pour me some of that bottle."

I lifted the bottle carefully and poured the glass half full. "That your medicine?" I asked. No answer. I feared this would be another story without an end, without meaning. "Did somebody take your mama's babies?" I persisted.

"Took her man, is what they did, and hung him up from a tree." She sat up slowly on her elbows, and looked straight at me. "Do you know what lynched is?"

175 "Yes, ma'am," I said, although until that moment I had not been sure.

"People will tell you there's never been no lynchings north of where the rivers don't freeze over. But they done it. Do you know where Jackson Crick is, up there by Floyd's Mill?" I nodded. "They lynched him up there, and drowned her baby Johnny in Jackson Crick, and it was as froze as you're ever going to see it. They had to break a hole in the ice to do it." She would not stop looking right into me. "In that river. Poor little baby in that cold river. Poor Mama, what they did to Mama. And said they would do to me, when I got old enough."

She didn't drink the medicine I poured for her, but let it sit. I was afraid to hear any more, and afraid to leave. I watched the moth crawl up the outside of the lampshade.

And then, out of the clear blue, she sat up and said, "But they didn't do a thing to me!" The way she said it, she sounded more like she ought to be weighing out bags of mash than sick in bed. "Do you want to know what Mama did?"

I didn't say.

180 "I'll tell you what she did. She took her scissors and cut my hair right off, every bit of it. She said, 'From now on, I want you to be Rose and Johnny both.' And then she went down to the same hole in the crick where they put baby Johnny in."

I sat with Rose-Johnny for a long time. I patted the lump in the covers where her knees were, and wiped my nose on my sleeve. "You'd better drink your medicine, Rose-Johnny," I said. "Drink up and get better now," I told her. "It's all over now."

∞

It was the last time I saw Rose-Johnny. The next time I saw the store, more than a month later, it was locked and boarded up. Later on, the Londroski brothers took it over. Some people said she had died. Others thought she and Mr. Wall had gone to live somewhere up in the Blue Ridge, and opened a store there. This is the story I believed. In the years since, when passing through that part of the country, I have never failed to notice the Plymouth Rocks and Rhode Islands scratching in the yards, and the tomato vines tied up around the back doors.

∞

I would like to stop here and say no more, but there are enough half-true stories in my past. This one will have to be heard to the end.

Whatever became of Rose-Johnny and her grandfather, I am certain that their going away had something to do with what happened on that same evening to Mary Etta. And I knew this to be my fault.

185   It was late when I got home. As I walked I turned Rose-Johnny's story over and over, like Grandpa Bowles's Indian penny with the head on both sides. You never could stop turning it over.

When I caught sight of Mama standing like somebody's ghost in the front doorway I thought she was going to thrash me, but she didn't. Instead she ran out into the yard and picked me up like she used to when I was a little girl, and carried me into the house.

"Where's Daddy?" I asked. It was suppertime, but there was no supper.

"Daddy's gone looking for you in the truck. He'll be back directly, when he don't find you."

"Why's he looking for me? What did I do?"

190   "Georgeann, some men tried to hurt Mary Etta. We don't know why they done it, but we was afraid they might try to hurt you."

"No, ma'am, nobody hurt me," I said quietly. "Did they kill her?" I asked.

"Oh Lordy no," Mama said, and hugged me. "She's all right. You can go upstairs and see her, but don't bother her if she don't want to be bothered."

Our room was dark, and Mary Etta was in bed crying. "Can I turn on the little light?" I asked. I wanted to see Mary Etta. I was afraid that some part of her might be missing.

"If you want to."

195   She was all there: arms, legs, hair. Her face was swollen, and there were marks on her neck.

"Don't stare at me," she said.

"I'm sorry." I looked around the room. Her dress was hanging over the chair. It was her best dress, the solid green linen with covered buttons and attached petticoat that had taken her all winter to make. It was red with dirt and torn nearly in half at the bodice.

"I'll fix your dress, Mary Etta. I can't sew as good as you, but I can mend," I said.

"Can't be mended," she said, but then tried to smile with her swollen mouth. "You can help me make another one."

200   "Who was it that done it?" I asked.

"I don't know." She rolled over and faced the wallpaper. "Some men. Three or four of them. Some of them might have been boys, I couldn't tell for sure. They had things over their faces."

"What kind of things?"

"I don't know. Just bandanners and things." She spoke quietly to the wall. "You know how the Mattoxes have those funny-colored eyes? I think some of them might of been Mattoxes. Don't tell, Georgeann. Promise."

I remembered the feeling of Roy Mattox's muscle in my teeth. I did not promise.

205   "Did you hit them?"

"No. I screamed. Mr. Dorsey come along the road."

"What did they say, before you screamed?"

"Nothing. They just kept saying, 'Are you the Bowles girl, are you the Bowles girl?' And they said nasty things."

"It was me they was looking for," I said. And no matter what anyone said, I would not believe otherwise. I took to my bed and would not eat or speak to anyone. My convalescence was longer than Mary Etta's. It was during that time that I found my sister's sewing scissors and cut off all my hair and all of Miss Regina's. I said that my name was George-Etta, not Georgeann, and I called my doll Rose-Johnny.

210   For the most part, my family tolerated my distress. My mother retrimmed my hair as neatly as she could, but there was little that could be done. Every time I looked in the mirror I was startled and secretly pleased to see that I looked exactly like a little boy. Mama said that when I went back to school I would have to do the explaining for myself. Aunt Minnie said I was going through a stage and oughtn't to be pampered.

But there was only a month left of school, and my father let Mary Etta and me stay home to help set tobacco. By the end of the summer my hair had grown out sufficiently so that no explanations were needed. Miss Regina's hair, of course, never grew back.

■ **EXPLORATIONS OF THE TEXT**

1. How is suspense created at the beginning of the story?
2. Why do you think Georgeann tells the lie about the quarter?
3. Why does she want to work at the feed store? What attracts her to Rose-Johnny?
4. Characterize Rose-Johnny. What do you learn about her from her appearance, gestures, actions, dialogue?
5. What repetitions of plot occur in the story? Why do the men assault Mary Etta?
6. Why does Georgeann say her name is George-Etta?
7. What is the significance of the last line—of the doll's hair staying cut?
8. What is the narrative perspective? What are the aspects of a child's perspective? Of an adult looking back and recalling a child's experiences?
9. Compare Georgeann's coming of age with Rosaura's in "The Stolen Party." What do these characters learn about life and the world?

■ **THE READING/WRITING CONNECTION**

1. "Think" Topic: In an interview Barbara Kingsolver revealed that she "often [chose] to tell stories in the voices of fairly unsophisticated people. Children are . . . [a] good choice because they haven't lived long enough yet to get sophisticated." What is the impact of her point of view? Is it successful?
2. Journal Entry: Write about a moment when you felt different from others or when you observed or experienced prejudice.

■ **IDEAS FOR WRITING**

1. In that same interview, Kingsolver suggested that she "invented this story, which got wilder and wilder but had everything to do with prejudices of small towns in the South and how they rein people in or cut them free." Discuss the theme of conformity in this work and in "Barn Burning."
2. Analyze the character of Rose-Johnny or of Georgeann.

FLANNERY O'CONNOR

Flannery O'Connor (1925–64) was born in Savannah, Georgia. After being educated at Georgia State College for Women and the University of Iowa, O'Connor published her first novel, Wise Blood, *in 1952. Afflicted by lupus, the same disease that killed her father, O'Connor lived most her life with her mother on the family farm in Milledgeville, Georgia. She is best known for short stories, collected in* A Good Man Is Hard to Find *(1955), the posthumous* Everything

That Rises Must Converge (1965), and The Complete Stories *(1971), which won the National Book Award. Considered by many critics to be one of the finest American short story writers, O'Connor wrote stories distinguished by their violence, their use of the grotesque, and their deep spiritual concerns.*

1955

A GOOD MAN IS HARD TO FIND

The grandmother didn't want to go to Florida. She wanted to visit some of her connections in east Tennessee and she was seizing at every chance to change Bailey's mind. Bailey was the son she lived with, her only boy. He was sitting on the edge of his chair at the table, bent over the orange sports section of the *Journal*. "Now look here, Bailey," she said, "see here, read this," and she stood with one hand on her thin hip and the other rattling the newspaper at his bald head. "Here this fellow that calls himself The Misfit is aloose from the Federal Pen and headed toward Florida and you read here what it says he did to these people. Just you read it. I wouldn't take my children in any direction with a criminal like that aloose in it. I couldn't answer to my conscience if I did."

Bailey didn't look up from his reading so she wheeled around then and faced the children's mother, a young woman in slacks, whose face was as broad and innocent as a cabbage and was tied around with a green head-kerchief that had two points on the top like a rabbit's ears. She was sitting on the sofa, feeding the baby his apricots out of a jar. "The children have been to Florida before," the old lady said. "You all ought to take them somewhere else for a change so they would see different parts of the world and be broad. They never have been to east Tennessee."

The children's mother didn't seem to hear her but the eight-year-old boy, John Wesley, a stocky child with glasses, said, "If you don't want to go to Florida, why dontcha stay at home?" He and the little girl, June Star, were reading the funny papers on the floor.

"She wouldn't stay at home to be queen for a day," June Star said without raising her yellow head.

5   "Yes and what would you do if this fellow, The Misfit, caught you?" the grandmother asked.

"I'd smack his face," John Wesley said.

"She wouldn't stay at home for a million bucks," June Star said. "Afraid she'd miss something. She has to go everywhere we go."

"All right, Miss," the grandmother said. "Just remember that the next time you want me to curl your hair."

June Star said her hair was naturally curly.

10   The next morning the grandmother was the first one in the car, ready to go. She had her big black valise that looked like the head of a hippopotamus in one corner, and underneath it she was hiding a basket with Pitty Sing, the cat, in it. She didn't intend for the cat to be left alone in the house for three days because he would miss her too much and she was afraid he might brush against one of the gas burners and accidentally asphyxiate himself. Her son, Bailey, didn't like to arrive at a motel with a cat.

She sat in the middle of the back seat with John Wesley and June Star on either side of her. Bailey and the children's mother and the baby sat in front and they left Atlanta at eight forty-five with the mileage on the car at 55890. The grandmother wrote this down because she thought it would be interesting to say how many miles they had been when they got back. It took them twenty minutes to reach the outskirts of the city.

The old lady settled herself comfortably, removing her white cotton gloves and putting them up with her purse on the shelf in front of the back window. The children's mother still had on slacks and still had her head tied up in a green kerchief, but the grandmother had on a navy blue straw sailor hat with a bunch of white violets on the brim and a navy blue dress with a small white dot in the print. Her collars and cuffs were white organdy trimmed with lace and at her neckline she had pinned a purple spray of cloth violets containing a sachet. In case of an accident, anyone seeing her dead on the highway would know at once that she was a lady.

She said she thought it was going to be a good day for driving, neither too hot nor too cold, and she cautioned Bailey that the speed limit was fifty-five miles an hour and that the patrolmen hid themselves behind billboards and small clumps of trees and sped out after you before you had a chance to slow down. She pointed out interesting details of the scenery: Stone Mountain; the blue granite that in some places came up to both sides of the highway; the brilliant red clay banks slightly streaked with purple; and the various crops that made rows of green lace-work on the ground. The trees were full of silver-white sunlight and the meanest of them sparkled. The children were reading comic magazines and their mother had gone back to sleep.

"Let's go through Georgia fast so we won't have to look at it much," John Wesley said.

15   "If I were a little boy," said the grandmother, "I wouldn't talk about my native state that way. Tennessee has the mountains and Georgia has the hills."

"Tennessee is just a hillbilly dumping ground," John Wesley said, "and Georgia is a lousy state too."

"You said it," June Star said.

"In my time," said the grandmother, folding her thin veined fingers, "children were more respectful of their native states and their parents and everything else. People did right then. Oh look at the cute little pickaninny!" she said and pointed to a Negro child standing in the door of a shack. "Wouldn't that make a picture, now?" she asked and they all turned and looked at the little Negro out of the back window. He waved.

"He didn't have any britches on," June Star said.

20   "He probably didn't have any," the grandmother explained. "Little niggers in the country don't have things like we do. If I could paint, I'd paint that picture," she said.

The children exchanged comic books.

The grandmother offered to hold the baby and the children's mother passed him over the front seat to her. She set him on her knee and bounced him and told him about the things they were passing. She rolled her eyes and screwed up her mouth and stuck her leathery thin face into his smooth bland one. Occasionally he gave her a faraway smile. They passed a large cotton field with five or six graves fenced in the middle of it, like a small island. "Look at the graveyard!" the grandmother said, pointing it out. "That was the old family burying ground. That belonged to the plantation."

"Where's the plantation?" John Wesley asked.

"Gone With the Wind," said the grandmother. "Ha. Ha."

25   When the children finished all the comic books they had brought, they opened the lunch and ate it. The grandmother ate a peanut butter sandwich and an olive and would not let the children throw the box and the paper napkins out the window. When there was nothing else to do they played a game by choosing a cloud and making the other two guess what shape it suggested. John Wesley took one the shape of a cow and June Starr guessed a cow and John Wesley said, no, an automobile, and June Star said he didn't play fair, and they began to slap each other over the grandmother.

The grandmother said she would tell them a story if they would keep quiet. When she told a story, she rolled her eyes and waved her head and was very dramatic. She said once when she was a maiden lady she had been courted by a Mr. Edgar Atkins Teagarden from Jasper, Georgia. She said he was a very good-looking man and a gentleman and that he brought her a watermelon every Saturday afternoon with initials cut in it, E. A. T. Well, one Saturday, she said, Mr. Teagarden brought the watermelon and there was nobody at home and he left it on the front porch and returned in his buggy to Jasper, but she never got the watermelon, she said, because a nigger boy ate it when he saw the initials, E. A. T.! This story tickled John Wesley's funny bone and he giggled and giggled but June Star didn't think it was any good. She said she wouldn't marry a man that just brought her a watermelon on Saturday. The grandmother said she would have done well to marry Mr. Teagarden because he was a gentleman and had bought Coca-Cola stock when it first came out and that he had died only a few years ago, a very wealthy man.

They stopped at The Tower for barbecued sandwiches. The Tower was a part stucco and part wood filling station and dance hall set in a clearing outside of Timothy. A fat man named Red Sammy Butts ran it and there were signs stuck here and there on the building and for miles up and down the highway saying, TRY RED SAMMY'S FAMOUS BARBECUE. NONE LIKE FAMOUS RED SAMMY'S! RED SAM! THE FAT BOY WITH THE HAPPY LAUGH! A VETERAN! RED SAMMY'S YOUR MAN!

Red Sammy was lying on the bare ground outside The Tower with his head under a truck while a gray monkey about a foot high, chained to a small chinaberry tree, chattered nearby. The monkey sprang back into the tree and got on the highest limb as soon as he saw the children jump out of the car and run toward him.

Inside, The Tower was a long dark room with a counter at one end and tables at the other and dancing space in the middle. They all sat down at a board table next to the nickelodeon and Red Sam's wife, a tall burnt-brown woman with hair and eyes lighter than her skin, came and took their order. The children's mother put a dime in the machine and played "The Tennessee Waltz," and the grandmother said that tune always made her want to dance. She asked Bailey if he would like to dance but he only glared at her. He didn't have a naturally sunny disposition like she did and trips made him nervous. The grandmother's brown eyes were very bright. She swayed her head from side to side and pretended she was dancing in her chair. June Star said play something she could tap to so the children's mother put in another dime and played a fast number and June Star stepped out onto the dance floor and did her tap routine.

30   "Ain't she cute?" Red Sam's wife said, leaning over the counter. "Would you like to come be my little girl?"

"No I certainly wouldn't," June Star said. "I wouldn't live in a broken-down place like this for a million bucks!" and she ran back to the table.

"Ain't she cute?" the woman repeated, stretching her mouth politely.

"Aren't you ashamed?" hissed the grandmother.

Red Sam came in and told his wife to quit lounging on the counter and hurry up with these people's order. His khaki trousers reached just to his hip bones and his stomach hung over them like a sack of meal swaying under his shirt. He came over and sat down at a table nearby and let out a combination sign and yodel. "You can't win," he said. "You can't win," and he wiped his sweating red face off with a gray handkerchief. "These days you don't know who to trust," he said. "Ain't that the truth?"

35   "People are certainly not nice like they used to be," said the grandmother.

"Two fellers come in here last week," Red Sammy said, "driving a Chrysler. It was a old beat-up car but it was a good one and these boys looked all right to me. Said they worked at the mill and you know I let them fellers charge the gas they bought? Now why did I do that?"

"Because you're a good man!" the grandmother said at once.

"Yes'm, I suppose so," Red Sam said as if he were struck with this answer.

His wife brought the orders, carrying the five plates all at once without a tray, two in each hand and one balanced on her arm. "It isn't a soul in this green world of God's that you can trust," she said. "And I don't count nobody out of that, not nobody," she repeated, looking at Red Sammy.

40   "Did you read about the criminal, The Misfit, that's escaped?" asked the grandmother.

"I wouldn't be a bit surprised if he didn't attact this place right here," said the woman. "If he hears about it being here, I wouldn't be none surprised to see him. If he hears it's two cent in the cash register, I wouldn't be a tall surprised if he . . ."

"That'll do," Red Sam said. "Go bring these people their Co'-Colas," and the woman went off to get the rest of the order.

"A good man is hard to find," Red Sammy said. "Everything is getting terrible. I remember the day you could go off and leave your screen door unlatched. Not no more."

He and the grandmother discussed better times. The old lady said that in her opinion Europe was entirely to blame for the way things were now. She said the way Europe acted you would think we were made of money and Red Sam said it was no use talking about it, she was exactly right. The children ran outside into the white sunlight and looked at the monkey in the lacy chinaberry tree. He was busy catching fleas on himself and biting each one carefully between his teeth as if it were a delicacy.

45   They drove off again into the hot afternoon. The grandmother took cat naps and woke up every few minutes with her own snoring. Outside of Toombsboro she woke up and recalled an old plantation that she had visited in this neighborhood once when she was a young lady. She said the house had six white columns across the front and that there was an avenue of oaks leading up to it and two little wooden trellis arbors on either side in front where you sat down with your suitor after a stroll in the garden. She recalled exactly which road to turn off to get to it. She knew that Bailey would not be willing to lose any time looking at an old house, but the more she talked about it, the more she wanted to see it once again and find out if the little twin arbors were still standing. "There was a secret panel in this house," she said craftily, not telling the truth but wishing that she were, "and the story went that all the family silver was hidden in it when Sherman[1] came through but it was never found . . ."

"Hey!" John Wesley said. "Let's go see it! We'll find it! We'll poke all the woodwork and find it! Who lives there? Where do you turn off at? Hey Pop, can't we turn off there?"

"We never have seen a house with a secret panel!" June Star shrieked. "Let's go to the house with the secret panel! Hey Pop, can't we go see the house with the secret panel!"

"It's not far from here, I know," the grandmother said. "It wouldn't take over twenty minutes."

Bailey was looking straight ahead. His jaw was as rigid as a horseshoe. "No," he said.

50   The children began to yell and scream that they wanted to see the house with the secret panel. John Wesley kicked the back of the front seat and June Star hung over her mother's shoulder and whined desperately into her ear that they never had any fun even on their vacation, that they could never do what THEY wanted to do. The baby began to scream and John Wesley kicked the back of the seat so hard that his father could feel the blows in his kidney.

"All right!" he shouted and drew the car to a stop at the side of the road. "Will you all shut up? Will you just shut up for one second? If you don't shut up, we won't go anywhere."

"It would be very educational for them," the grandmother murmured.

"All right," Bailey said, "but get this: this is the only time we're going to stop for anything like this. This is the one and only time."

---

[1] William Tecumseh Sherman (1820–1891). Union general during the Civil War.

"The dirt road that you have to turn down is about a mile back," the grandmother directed. "I marked it when we passed."

55 "A dirt road," Bailey groaned.

After they had turned around and were headed toward the dirt road, the grandmother recalled other points about the house, the beautiful glass over the front doorway and the candle-lamp in the hall. John Wesley said that the secret panel was probably in the fireplace.

"You can't go inside this house," Bailey said. "You don't know who lives there."

"While you all talk to the people in front, I'll run around behind and get in a window," John Wesley suggested.

"We'll all stay in the car," his mother said.

60 They turned onto the dirt road and the car raced roughly along in a swirl of pink dust. The grandmother recalled the times when there were no paved roads and thirty miles was a day's journey. The dirt road was hilly and there were sudden washes in it and sharp curves on dangerous embankments. All at once they would be on a hill, looking down over the blue tops of trees for miles around, then the next minute, they would be in a red depression with the dust-coated trees looking down on them.

"This place had better turn up in a minute," Bailey said, "or I'm going to turn around."

The road looked as if no one had traveled on it in months.

"It's not much farther," the grandmother said and just as she said it, a horrible thought came to her. The thought was so embarrassing that she turned red in the face and her eyes dilated and her feet jumped up, upsetting her valise in the corner. The instant the valise moved, the newspaper top she had over the basket under it rose with a snarl and Pitty Sing, the cat, sprang onto Bailey's shoulder.

The children were thrown to the floor and their mother, clutching the baby, was thrown out the door onto the ground; the old lady was thrown into the front seat. The car turned over once and landed right-side-up in a gulch off the side of the road. Bailey remained in the driver's seat with the cat—gray-striped with a broad white face and an orange nose—clinging to his neck like a caterpillar.

65 As soon as the children saw they could move their arms and legs, they scrambled out of the car, shouting, "We've had an ACCIDENT!" The grandmother was curled up under the dashboard, hoping she was injured so that Bailey's wrath would not come down on her all at once. The horrible thought she had had before the accident was that the house she had remembered so vividly was not in Georgia but in Tennessee.

Bailey removed the cat from his neck with both hands and flung it out the window against the side of a pine tree. Then he got out of the car and started looking for the children's mother. She was sitting against the side of the red gutted ditch, holding the screaming baby, but she only had a cut down her face and a broken shoulder. "We've had an ACCIDENT!" the children screamed in a frenzy of delight.

"But nobody's killed," June Star said with disappointment as the grandmother limped out of the car, her hat still pinned to her head but the broken front brim standing up at a jaunty angle and the violet spray hanging off the side. They all sat down in the ditch, except the children, to recover from the shock. They were all shaking.

"Maybe a car will come along," said the children's mother hoarsely.

"I believe I have injured an organ," said the grandmother, pressing her side, but no one answered her. Bailey's teeth were clattering. He had on a yellow sport shirt with bright blue parrots designed in it and his face was as yellow as the shirt. The grandmother decided that she would not mention that the house was in Tennessee.

70 The road was about ten feet above and they could see only the tops of the trees on the other side of it. Behind the ditch they were sitting in there were more woods, tall and dark and deep. In a few minutes they saw a car some distance away on top of a hill, coming slowly

as if the occupants were watching them. The grandmother stood up and waved both arms dramatically to attract their attention. The car continued to come on slowly, disappeared around a bend and appeared again, moving even slower, on top of the hill they had gone over. It was a big black battered hearse-like automobile. There were three men in it.

It came to a stop just over them and for some minutes, the driver looked down with a steady expressionless gaze to where they were sitting, and didn't speak. Then he turned his head and muttered something to the other two and they got out. One was a fat boy in black trousers and a red sweat shirt with a silver stallion embossed on the front of it. He moved around on the right side of them and stood staring, his mouth partly open in a kind of loose grin. The other had on khaki pants and a blue striped coat and a gray hat pulled down very low, hiding most of his face. He came around slowly on the left side. Neither spoke.

The driver got out of the car and stood by the side of it, looking down at them. He was an older man than the other two. His hair was just beginning to gray and he wore silver-rimmed spectacles that gave him a scholarly look. He had a long creased face and didn't have on any shirt or undershirt. He had on blue jeans that were too tight for him and was holding a black hat and a gun. The two boys also had guns.

"We've had an ACCIDENT!" the children screamed.

The grandmother had the peculiar feeling that the bespectacled man was someone she knew. His face was as familiar to her as if she had known him all her life but she could not recall who he was. He moved away from the car and began to come down the embankment, placing his feet carefully so that he wouldn't slip. He had on tan and white shoes and no socks, and his ankles were red and thin. "Good afternoon," he said. "I see you all had you a little spill."

75 "We turned over twice!" said the grandmother.

"Oncet," he corrected. "We seen it happen. Try their car and see will it run, Hiram," he said quietly to the boy with the gray hat.

"What you got that gun for?" John Wesley asked. "Whatcha gonna do with that gun?"

"Lady," the man said to the children's mother, "would you mind calling them children to sit down by you? Children make me nervous. I want all you all to sit down right there together where you're at."

"What are you telling US what to do for?" June Star asked.

80 Behind them the line of woods gaped like a dark open mouth. "Come here," said their mother.

"Look here now," Bailey began suddenly, "We're in a predicament! We're in . . ."

The grandmother shrieked. She scrambled to her feet and stood staring. "You're The Misfit!" she said. "I recognized you at once!"

"Yes'm," the man said, smiling slightly as if he were pleased in spite of himself to be known, "but it would have been better for all of you, lady, if you hadn't of recker-nized me."

Bailey turned his head sharply and said something to his mother that shocked even the children. The old lady began to cry and The Misfit reddened.

85 "Lady," he said, "don't you get upset. Sometimes a man says things he don't mean. I don't reckon he meant to talk to you thataway."

"You wouldn't shoot a lady, would you?" the grandmother said and removed a clean handkerchief from her cuff and began to slap at her eyes with it.

The Misfit pointed the toe of his shoe into the ground and made a little hole and then covered it up again. "I would hate to have to," he said.

"Listen," the grandmother almost screamed, "I know you're a good man. You don't look a bit like you have common blood. I know you must come from nice people!"

"Yes mam," he said, "finest people in the world." When he smiled he showed a row of strong white teeth. "God never made a finer woman than my mother and my daddy's heart was pure gold," he said. The boy with the red sweat shirt had come around behind them and was standing with his gun at his hip. The Misfit squatted down on the ground. "Watch them children, Bobby Lee," he said. "You know they make me nervous." He looked at the six of them huddled together in front of him and he seemed to be embarrassed as if he couldn't think of anything to say. "Ain't a cloud in the sky," he remarked, looking up at it. "Don't see no sun but don't see no cloud either."

90   "Yes, it's a beautiful day," said the grandmother. "Listen," she said, "you shouldn't call yourself The Misfit because I know you're a good man at heart. I can just look at you and tell."

"Hush!" Bailey yelled. "Hush! Everybody shut up and let me handle this!" He was squatting in the position of a runner about to sprint forward but he didn't move.

"I pre-chate that, lady," The Misfit said and drew a little circle in the ground with the butt of his gun.

"It'll take a half a hour to fix this here car," Hiram called, looking over the raised hood of it.

"Well, first you and Bobby Lee get him and that little boy to step over yonder with you," The Misfit said, pointing to Bailey and John Wesley. "The boys want to ast you something," he said to Bailey. "Would you mind stepping back in them woods there with them?"

95   "Listen," Bailey began, "we're in a terrible predicament! Nobody realizes what this is," and his voice cracked. His eyes were as blue and intense as the parrots in his shirt and he remained perfectly still.

The grandmother reached up to adjust her hat brim as if she were going to the woods with him but it came off in her hand. She stood staring at it and after a second she let it fall on the ground. Hiram pulled Bailey up by the arm as if he were assisting an old man. John Wesley caught hold of his father's hand and Bobby Lee followed. They went off toward the woods and just as they reached the dark edge, Bailey turned and supporting himself against a gray naked pine trunk, he shouted, "I'll be back in a minute, Mama, wait on me!"

"Come back this instant!" his mother shrilled but they all disappeared into the woods.

"Bailey Boy!" the grandmother called in a tragic voice but she found she was looking at The Misfit squatting on the ground in front of her. "I just know you're a good man," she said desperately. "You're not a bit common!"

"Nome, I ain't a good man," The Misfit said after a second as if he had considered her statement carefully, "but I ain't the worst in the world neither. My daddy said I was a different breed of dog from my brothers and sisters. 'You know,' Daddy said, 'it's some that can live their whole life out without asking about it and it's others has to know why it is, and this boy is one of the latters. He's going to be into everything!'" He put on his black hat and looked up suddenly and then away deep into the woods as if he were embarrassed again. "I'm sorry I don't have on a shirt before you ladies," he said, hunching his shoulders slightly. "We buried our clothes that we had on when we escaped and we're just making do until we can get better. We borrowed these from some folks we met," he explained.

100   "That's perfectly all right," the grandmother said. "Maybe Bailey has an extra shirt in his suitcase."

"I'll look and see terrectly," The Misfit said.

"Where are they taking him?" the children's mother screamed.

"Daddy was a card himself," The Misfit said. "You couldn't put anything over on him. He never got in trouble with the Authorities though. Just had the knack of handling them."

"You could be honest too if you'd only try," said the grandmother. "Think how wonderful it would be to settle down and live a comfortable life and not have to think about somebody chasing you all the time."

105   The Misfit kept scratching in the ground with the butt of his gun as if he were thinking about it. "Yes'm, somebody is always after you," he murmured.

    The grandmother noticed how thin his shoulder blades were just behind his hat because she was standing up looking down on him. "Do you ever pray?" she asked.

    He shook his head. All she saw was the black hat wiggle between his shoulder blades. "Nome," he said.

    There was a pistol shot from the woods, followed closely by another. Then silence. The old lady's head jerked around. She could hear the wind move through the tree tops like a long satisfied insuck of breath. "Bailey Boy!" she called.

    "I was a gospel singer for a while," The Misfit said. "I been most everything. Been in the arm service, both land and sea, at home and abroad, been twict married, been an undertaker, been with the railroads, plowed Mother Earth, been in a tornado, seen a man burnt alive oncet," and looked up at the children's mother and the little girl who were sitting close together, their faces white and their eyes glassy; "I even seen a woman flogged," he said.

110   "Pray, pray," the grandmother began, "pray, pray . . ."

    "I never was a bad boy that I remember of," The Misfit said in an almost dreamy voice, "but somewheres along the line I done something wrong and got sent to the penitentiary. I was buried alive," and he looked up and held her attention to him by a steady stare.

    "That's when you should have started to pray," she said. "What did you do to get sent to the penitentiary that first time?"

    "Turn to the right, it was a wall," The Misfit said, looking up again at the cloudless sky. "Turn to the left, it was a wall. Look up it was a ceiling, look down it was a floor. I forget what I done, lady. I set there and set there, trying to remember what it was I done and I ain't recalled it to this day. Oncet in a while, I would think it was coming to me, but it never come."

    "Maybe they put you in by mistake," the old lady said vaguely.

115   "Nome," he said. "It wasn't no mistake. They had the papers on me."

    "You must have stolen something," she said.

    The Misfit sneered slightly. "Nobody had nothing I wanted," he said. "It was a head-doctor at the penitentiary said what I had done was kill my daddy but I known that for a lie. My daddy died in nineteen ought nineteen of the epidemic flu and I never had a thing to do with it. He was buried in the Mount Hopewell Baptist churchyard and you can go there and see for yourself."

    "If you would pray," the old lady said, "Jesus would help you."

    "That's right," The Misfit said.

120   "Well then, why don't you pray?" she asked trembling with delight suddenly.

    "I don't want no hep," he said. "I'm doing all right by myself."

    Bobby Lee and Hiram came ambling back from the woods. Bobby Lee was dragging a yellow shirt with bright blue parrots in it.

    "Thow me that shirt, Bobby Lee," The Misfit said. The shirt came flying at him and landed on his shoulder and he put it on. The grandmother couldn't name what the shirt reminded her of. "No, lady," The Misfit said while he was buttoning it up, "I found out the crime don't matter. You can do one thing or you can do another, kill a man or take a tire off his car, because sooner or later you're going to forget what it was you done and just be punished for it."

    The children's mother had begun to make heaving noises as if she couldn't get her breath. "Lady," he asked, "would you and that little girl like to step off yonder with Bobby Lee and Hiram and join your husband?"

125   "Yes, thank you," the mother said faintly. Her left arm dangled helplessly and she was holding the baby, who had gone to sleep, in the other. "Hep that lady up, Hiram," The

Misfit said as she struggled to climb out of the ditch, "and Bobby Lee, you hold onto that little girl's hand."

"I don't want to hold hands with him," June Star said. "He reminds me of a pig."

The fat boy blushed and laughed and caught her by the arm and pulled her off into the woods after Hiram and her mother.

Alone with The Misfit, the grandmother found that she had lost her voice. There was not a cloud in the sky nor any sun. There was nothing around her but woods. She wanted to tell him that he must pray. She opened and closed her mouth several times before anything came out. Finally she found herself saying, "Jesus, Jesus," meaning, Jesus will help you, but the way she was saying it, it sounded as if she might be cursing.

"Yes'm," The Misfit said as if he agreed. "Jesus thown everything off balance. It was the same case with Him as with me except He hadn't committed any crime and they could prove I had committed one because they had the papers on me. Of course," he said, "they never shown me my papers. That's why I sign myself now. I said long ago, you get you a signature and sign everything you do and keep a copy of it. Then you'll know what you done and you can hold up the crime to the punishment and see do they match and in the end you'll have something to prove you ain't been treated right. I call myself The Misfit," he said, "because I can't make what all I done wrong fit what all I gone through in punishment."

130   There was a piercing scream from the woods, followed closely by a pistol report. "Does it seem right to you, lady, that one is punished a heap and another ain't punished at all?"

"Jesus!" the old lady cried. "You've got good blood! I know you wouldn't shoot a lady! I know you come from nice people! Pray! Jesus, you ought not to shoot a lady. I'll give you all the money I've got!"

"Lady," The Misfit said, looking beyond her far into the woods, "there never was a body that give the undertaker a tip."

There were two more pistol reports and the grandmother raised her head like a parched old turkey hen crying for water and called, "Bailey Boy, Bailey Boy!" as if her heart would break.

"Jesus was the only One that ever raised the dead," The Misfit continued, "and He shouldn't have done it. He thrown everything off balance. If He did what He said, then it's nothing for you to do but throw away everything and follow Him, and if He didn't, then it's nothing for you to do but enjoy the few minutes you got left the best way you can—by killing somebody or burning down his house or doing some other meanness to him. No pleasure but meanness," he said and his voice had become almost a snarl.

135   "Maybe He didn't raise the dead," the old lady mumbled, not knowing what she was saying and feeling so dizzy that she sank down in the ditch with her legs twisted under her.

"I wasn't there so I can't say He didn't," The Misfit said. "I wisht I had of been there," he said, hitting the ground with his fist. "It ain't right I wasn't there because if I had of been there I would of known. Listen lady," he said in a high voice, "if I had of been there I would of known and I wouldn't be like I am now." His voice seemed about to crack and the grandmother's head cleared for an instant. She saw the man's face twisted close to her own as if he were going to cry and she murmured, "Why you're one of my babies. You're one of my own children!" She reached out and touched him on the shoulder. The Misfit sprang back as if a snake had bitten him and shot her three times through the chest. Then he put his gun down on the ground and took off his glasses and began to clean them.

Hiram and Bobby Lee returned from the woods and stood over the ditch, looking down at the grandmother who half sat and half lay in a puddle of blood with her legs crossed under her like a child's and her face smiling up at the cloudless sky.

Without his glasses, The Misfit's eyes were red-rimmed and pale and defenseless-looking. "Take her off and throw her where you thrown the others," he said, picking up the cat that was rubbing itself against his leg.

"She was talker, wasn't she?" Bobby Lee said, sliding down the ditch with a yodel.

140 "She would of been a good woman," The Misfit said, "if it had been somebody there to shoot her every minute of her life."

"Some fun!" Bobby Lee said.

"Shut up, Bobby Lee," The Misfit said. "It's no real pleasure in life."

■ **EXPLORATIONS OF THE TEXT**

1. Analyze the grandmother's character. Examine her relationship with her grandchildren, her son, and with her daughter-in-law. Discuss her concept of being a lady.
2. Discuss the episode in The Tower restaurant and the symbolism of the monkey.
3. What causes the accident?
4. What is your view of The Misfit? Is he a homicidal serial killer or a demented prophet?
5. Does the grandmother change? Does The Misfit change? Examine the grandmother's final confrontation with The Misfit.
6. Explore the significance of The Misfit statement: " 'She would of been a good woman,' . . . 'if it had been somebody there to shoot her every minute of her life.' "
7. Discuss the significance of the title.

■ **THE READING/WRITING CONNECTION**

1. List your questions about this story. Then answer one of them in a paragraph.
2. "Think" Topic: Is this a story about salvation or damnation?
3. Journal Entry: React to Red Sam's statement: " 'These days you don't know who to trust.' "
4. Debate Topic: "The grandmother has become a good woman." Argue pro or con.

■ **IDEAS FOR WRITING**

1. Compare the treatment of violence in this story with "Where Are You Going, Where Have You Been?" or compare the endings of both stories.
2. Compare the grandmother's "coming of age" with the narrator's in "Cathedral."
3. Compare the spiritual vision in "Cathedral" with that of "A Good Man Is Hard to Find." Refer to the student essay anthologized in this chapter.

RAYMOND CARVER

Raymond Carver (1938–89) grew up in Oregon. He studied creative writing with John Gardner at Chico State College, earned his B.A. from Humboldt State College, and studied at the University of Iowa. He taught at a number of colleges, principally Syracuse University. He achieved fame for his short stories, a form of which he was a master. His first collection of stories, Will You Please Be Quiet, Please? *was nominated for the National Book Award in 1976. He subsequently published ten more collections of stories and poetry, including* What We Talk About When We Talk About Love *(1981),* Cathedral *(1984), and* Where I'm Calling From *(1988). With Richard Ford and Tobias Wolff, Carver was considered one of the leading members of the literary school of "dirty realism," fiction that focused on the minute, and frequently unpleasant, details of people's daily lives.*

1984

CATHEDRAL

This blind man, an old friend of my wife's, he was on his way to spend the night. His wife had died. So he was visiting the dead wife's relatives in Connecticut. He called my wife from his in-laws'. Arrangements were made. He would come by train, a five-hour trip, and my wife would meet him at the station. She hadn't seen him since she worked for him one summer in Seattle ten years ago. But she and the blind man had kept in touch. They made tapes and mailed them back and forth. I wasn't enthusiastic about his visit. He was no one I knew. And his being blind bothered me. My idea of blindness came from the movies. In the movies, the blind moved slowly and never laughed. Sometimes they were led by seeing-eye dogs. A blind man in my house was not something I looked forward to.

That summer in Seattle she had needed a job. She didn't have any money. The man she was going to marry at the end of the summer was in officers' training school. He didn't have any money, either. But she was in love with the guy, and he was in love with her, etc. She'd seen something in the paper: HELP WANTED—*Reading to Blind Man,* and a telephone number. She phoned and went over, was hired on the spot. She'd worked with this blind man all summer. She read stuff to him, case studies, reports, that sort of thing. She helped him organize his little office in the county social-service department. They'd become good friends, my wife and the blind man. How do I know these things? She told me. And she told me something else. On her last day in the office, the blind man asked if he could touch her face. She agreed to this. She told me he touched his fingers to every part of her face, her nose—even her neck! She never forgot it. She even tried to write a poem about it. She was always trying to write a poem. She wrote a poem or two every year, usually after something really important had happened to her.

When we first started going out together, she showed me the poem. In the poem, she recalled his fingers and the way they had moved around over her face. In the poem, she talked about what she had felt at the time, about what went through her mind when the blind man touched her nose and lips. I can remember I didn't think much of the poem. Of course, I didn't tell her that. Maybe I just don't understand poetry. I admit it's not the first thing I reach for when I pick up something to read.

Anyway, this man who'd first enjoyed her favors, the officer-to-be, he'd been her childhood sweetheart. So okay. I'm saying that at the end of the summer she let the blind man run his hands over her face, said goodbye to him, married her childhood etc., who was now a commissioned officer, and she moved away from Seattle. But they'd kept in touch, she and the blind man. She made the first contact after a year or so. She called him up one night from an Air Force base in Alabama. She wanted to talk. They talked. He asked her to send him a tape and tell him about her life. She did this. She sent the tape. On the tape, she told the blind man about her husband and about their life together in the military. She told the blind man she loved her husband but she didn't like it where they lived and she didn't like it that he was a part of the military-industrial thing. She told the blind man she'd written a poem and he was in it. She told him that she was writing a poem about what it was like to be an Air Force officer's wife. The poem wasn't finished yet. She was still writing it. The blind man made a tape. He sent her the tape. She made a tape. This went on for years. My wife's officer was posted to one base and then another. She sent tapes from Moody AFB, McGuire, McConnell, and finally Travis, near Sacramento, where one night she got to feeling lonely and cut off from people she kept losing in that moving-around life. She got to feeling she couldn't go it another step. She went in and swallowed all the pills and capsules in the medicine chest and washed them down with a bottle of gin. Then she got into a hot bath and passed out.

5 But instead of dying, she got sick. She threw up. Her officer—why should he have a name? he was the childhood sweetheart, and what more does he want?—came home from somewhere, found her, and called the ambulance. In time, she put it all on a tape and sent the tape to the blind man. Over the years, she put all kinds of stuff on tapes and sent the tapes off lickety-split. Next to writing a poem every year, I think it was her chief means of recreation. On one tape, she told the blind man she'd decided to live away from her officer for a time. On another tape, she told him about her divorce. She and I began going out, and

of course she told her blind man about it. She told him everything, or so it seemed to me. Once she asked me if I'd like to hear the latest tape from the blind man. This was a year ago. I was on the tape, she said. So I said okay, I'd listen to it. I got us drinks and we settled down in the living room. We made ready to listen. First she inserted the tape into the player and adjusted a couple of dials. Then she pushed a lever. The tape squeaked and someone began to talk in this loud voice. She lowered the volume. After a few minutes of harmless chitchat, I heard my own name in the mouth of this stranger, this blind man I didn't even know! And then this: "From all you've said about him, I can only conclude—" But we were interrupted, a knock at the door, something, and we didn't ever get back to the tape. Maybe it was just as well. I'd heard all I wanted to.

Now this same blind man was coming to sleep in my house.

"Maybe I could take him bowling," I said to my wife. She was at the draining board do-ing scalloped potatoes. She put down the knife she was using and turned around.

"If you love me," she said, "you can do this for me. If you don't love me, okay. But if you had a friend, any friend, and the friend came to visit, I'd make him feel comfortable." She wiped her hands with the dish towel.

"I don't have any blind friends," I said.

10   "You don't have *any* friends," she said. "Period. Besides," she said, "goddamn it, his wife's just died! Don't you understand that? The man's lost his wife!"

I didn't answer. She'd told me a little about the blind man's wife. Her name was Beulah. Beulah! That's a name for a colored woman.

"Was his wife a Negro?" I asked.

"Are you crazy?" my wife said. "Have you just flipped or something?" She picked up a potato. I saw it hit the floor, then roll under the stove. "What's wrong with you?" she said. "Are you drunk?"

"I'm just asking," I said.

15   Right then my wife filled me in with more detail than I cared to know. I made a drink and sat at the kitchen table to listen. Pieces of the story began to fall into place.

Beulah had gone to work for the blind man the summer after my wife had stopped working for him. Pretty soon Beulah and the blind man had themselves a church wedding. It was a little wedding—who'd want to go to such a wedding in the first place?—just the two of them, plus the minister and the minister's wife. But it was a church wedding just the same. It was what Beulah had wanted, he's said. But even then Beulah must have been car-rying the cancer in her glands. After they had been inseparable for eight years—my wife's word, *inseparable*—Beulah's health went into a rapid decline. She died in a Seattle hospital room, the blind man sitting beside the bed and holding on to her hand. They'd married, lived and worked together, slept together—had sex, sure—and then the blind man had to bury her. All this without his having ever seen what the goddamned woman looked like. It was beyond my understanding. Hearing this, I felt sorry for the blind man for a little bit. And then I found myself thinking what a pitiful life this woman must have led. Imagine a woman who could never see herself as she was seen in the eyes of her loved one. A woman who could go on day after day and never receive the smallest compliment from her beloved. A woman whose husband could never read the expression on her face, be it misery or some-thing better. Someone who could wear makeup or not—what difference to him? She could, if she wanted, wear green eye-shadow around one eye, a straight pin in her nostril, yellow slacks and purple shoes, no matter. And then to slip off into death, the blind man's hand on her hand, his blind eyes streaming tears—I'm imagining now—her last thought maybe this: that he never even knew what she looked like, and she on an express to the grave. Robert was left with a small insurance policy and half of a twenty-peso Mexican coin. The other half of the coin went into the box with her. Pathetic.

So when the time rolled around, my wife went to the depot to pick him up. With nothing to do but wait—sure, I blamed him for that—I was having a drink and watching the TV when I heard the car pull into the drive. I got up from the sofa with my drink and went to the window to have a look.

I saw my wife laughing as she parked the car. I saw her get out of the car and shut the door. She was still wearing a smile. Just amazing. She went around to the other side of the car to where the blind man was already starting to get out. This blind man, feature this, he was wearing a full beard! A beard on a blind man! Too much, I say. The blind man reached into the back seat and dragged out a suitcase. My wife took his arm, shut the car door, and, talking all the way, moved him down the drive and then up the steps to the front porch. I turned off the TV. I finished my drink, rinsed the glass, dried my hands. Then I went to the door.

My wife said, "I want you to meet Robert. Robert, this is my husband. I've told you all about him." She was beaming. She had this blind man by his coat sleeve.

20   The blind man let go of his suitcase and up came his hand.

I took it. He squeezed hard, held my hand, and then he let it go.

"I feel like we've already met," he boomed.

"Likewise," I said. I didn't know what else to say. Then I said, "Welcome. I've heard a lot about you." We began to move then, a little group, from the porch into the living room, my wife guiding him by the arm. The blind man was carrying his suitcase in his other hand. My wife said things like, "To your left here, Robert. That's right. Now watch it, there's a chair. That's it. Sit down right here. This is the sofa. We just bought this sofa two weeks ago."

I started to say something about the old sofa. I'd liked that old sofa. But I didn't say anything. Then I wanted to say something else, small-talk, about the scenic ride along the Hudson. How going *to* New York, you should sit on the right-hand side of the train, and coming *from* New York, the left-hand side.

25   "Did you have a good train ride?" I said. "Which side of the train did you sit on, by the way?"

"What a question, which side!" my wife said. "What's it matter which side?" she said.

"I just asked," I said.

"Right side," the blind man said. "I hadn't been on a train in nearly forty years. Not since I was a kid. With my folks. That's been a long time. I'd nearly forgotten the sensation. I have winter in my beard now," he said. "So I've been told, anyway. Do I look distinguished, my dear?" the blind man said to my wife.

"You look distinguished, Robert," she said. "Robert," she said. "Robert, it's just so good to see you."

30   My wife finally took her eyes off the blind man and looked at me. I had the feeling she didn't like what she saw. I shrugged.

I've never met, or personally known, anyone who was blind. This blind man was late forties, a heavy-set, balding man with stooped shoulders, as if he carried a great weight there. He wore brown slacks, brown shoes, a light-brown shirt, a tie, a sports coat. Spiffy. He also had this full beard. But he didn't use a cane and he didn't wear dark glasses. I'd always thought dark glasses were a must for the blind. Fact was, I wished he had a pair. At first glance, his eyes looked like anyone else's eyes. But if you looked close, there was something different about them. Too much white in the iris, for one thing, and the pupils seemed to move around in the sockets without his knowing it or being able to stop it. Creepy. As I stared at his face, I saw the left pupil turn in toward his nose while the other made an effort to keep in one place. But it was only an effort, for that eye was on the roam without his knowing it or wanting it to be.

I said, "Let me get you a drink. What's your pleasure? We have a little of everything. It's one of our pastimes."

"Bub, I'm a Scotch man myself," he said fast enough in this big voice.

"Right," I said. Bub! "Sure you are. I knew it."

35 He let his fingers touch his suitcase, which was sitting alongside the sofa. He was taking his bearings. I didn't blame him for that.

"I'll move that up to your room," my wife said.

"No, that's fine," the blind man said loudly. "It can go up when I go up."

"A little water with the Scotch?" I said.

"Very little," he said.

40 "I knew it," I said.

He said, "Just a tad. The Irish actor, Barry Fitzgerald? I'm like that fellow. When I drink water, Fitzgerald said, I drink water. When I drink whiskey, I drink whiskey." My wife laughed. The blind man brought his hand up under his beard. He lifted his beard slowly and let it drop.

I did the drinks, three big glasses of Scotch with a splash of water in each. Then we made ourselves comfortable and talked about Robert's travels. First the long flight from the West Coast to Connecticut, we covered that. Then from Connecticut up here by train. We had another drink concerning that leg of the trip.

I remembered having read somewhere that the blind didn't smoke because, as speculation had it, they couldn't see the smoke they exhaled. I thought I knew that much and that much only about blind people. But this blind man smoked his cigarette down to the nubbin and then lit another one. This blind man filled his ashtray and my wife emptied it.

When we sat down at the table for dinner, we had another drink. My wife heaped Robert's plate with cube steak, scalloped potatoes, green beans. I buttered him up two slices of bread. I said, "Here's bread and butter for you." I swallowed some of my drink. "Now let us pray," I said, and the blind man lowered his head. My wife looked at me, her mouth agape. "Pray the phone won't ring and the food doesn't get cold," I said.

45 We dug in. We ate everything there was to eat on the table. We ate like there was no tomorrow. We didn't talk. We ate. We scarfed. We grazed that table. We were into serious eating. The blind man had right away located his foods, he knew just where everything was on his plate. I watched with admiration as he used his knife and fork on the meat. He'd cut two pieces of meat, fork the meat into his mouth, and then go all out for the scalloped potatoes, the beans next, and then he'd tear off a hunk of buttered bread and eat that. He'd follow this up with a big drink of milk. It didn't seem to bother him to use his fingers once in a while, either.

We finished everything, including half a strawberry pie. For a few moments, we sat as if stunned. Sweat beaded on our faces. Finally, we got up from the table and left the dirty plates. We didn't look back. We took ourselves into the living room and sank into our places again. Robert and my wife sat on the sofa. I took the big chair. We had us two or three more drinks while they talked about the major things that had come to pass for them in the past ten years. For the most part, I just listened. Now and then I joined in. I didn't want him to think I'd left the room, and I didn't want her to think I was feeling left out. They talked of things that had happened to them—to them!—these past ten years. I waited in vain to hear my name on my wife's sweet lips: "And then my dear husband came into my life"—something like that. But I heard nothing of the sort. More talk of Robert. Robert had done a little of everything, it seemed, a regular blind jack-of-all-trades. But most recently he and his wife had had an Amway distributorship, from which, I gathered, they'd earned their living, such as it was. The blind man was also a ham radio operator. He talked in his loud voice about conversations he'd had with fellow operators in Guam, in the Philippines, in Alaska, and even in Tahiti. He said he'd have a lot of friends there if he ever wanted to go visit those places. From time to time, he'd turn his blind face toward me, put his hand under his beard, ask me something. How long had I been in my present position? (Three years.) Did I like my work? (I didn't.) Was I going to stay with it? (What were the options?) Finally, when I thought he was beginning to run down, I got up and turned on the TV.

My wife looked at me with irritation. She was heading toward a boil. Then she looked at the blind man and said, "Robert, do you have a TV?"

The blind man said, "My dear, I have two TVs. I have a color set and a black-and-white thing, an old relic. It's funny, but if I turn the TV on, and I'm always turning it on, I turn on the color set. It's funny, don't you think?"

I didn't know what to say to that. I had absolutely nothing to say to that. No opinion. So I watched the news program and tried to listen to what the announcer was saying.

50 "This is a color TV," the blind man said. "Don't ask me how, but I can tell."

"We traded up a while ago," I said.

The blind man had another taste of his drink. He lifted his beard, sniffed it, and let it fall. He leaned forward on the sofa. He positioned his ashtray on the coffee table, then put the lighter to his cigarette. He leaned back on the sofa and crossed his legs at the ankles.

My wife covered her mouth, and then she yawned. She stretched. She said, "I think I'll go upstairs and put on my robe. I think I'll change into something else. Robert, you make yourself comfortable," she said.

"I'm comfortable," the blind man said.

55 "I want you to feel comfortable in this house," she said.

"I am comfortable," the blind man said.

After she'd left the room, he and I listened to the weather report and then to the sports roundup. By that time, she'd been gone so long I didn't know if she was going to come back. I thought she might have gone to bed. I wished she'd come back downstairs. I didn't want to be left alone with a blind man. I asked him if he wanted another drink, and he said sure. Then I asked if he wanted to smoke some dope with me. I said I'd just rolled a number. I hadn't, but I planned to do so in about two shakes.

"I'll try some with you," he said.

"Damn right," I said. "That's the stuff."

60 I got our drinks and sat down on the sofa with him. Then I rolled us two fat numbers. I lit one and passed it. I brought it to his fingers. He took it and inhaled.

"Hold it as long as you can," I said. I could tell he didn't know the first thing.

My wife came back downstairs wearing her pink robe and her pink slippers.

"What do I smell?" she said.

"We thought we'd have us some cannabis," I said.

65 My wife gave me a savage look. Then she looked at the blind man and said, "Robert, I didn't know you smoked."

He said, "I do now, my dear. There's a first time for everything. But I don't feel anything yet."

"This stuff is pretty mellow," I said. "This stuff is mild. It's dope you can reason with," I said. "It doesn't mess you up."

"Not much it doesn't, bub," he said, and laughed.

My wife sat on the sofa between the blind man and me. I passed her the number. She took it and toked and then passed it back to me. "Which way is this going?" she said. Then she said, "I shouldn't be smoking this. I can hardly keep my eyes open as it is. That dinner did me in. I shouldn't have eaten so much."

70   "It was the strawberry pie," the blind man said. "That's what did it," he said, and he laughed his big laugh. Then he shook his head.

     "There's more strawberry pie," I said.

     "Do you want some more, Robert?" my wife said.

     "Maybe in a little while," he said.

     We gave our attention to the TV. My wife yawned again. She said, "Your bed is made up when you feel like going to bed, Robert. I know you must have had a long day. When you're ready to go to bed, say so." She pulled his arm. "Robert?"

75   He came to and said, "I've had a real nice time. This beats tapes, doesn't it?"

     I said, "Coming at you," and I put the number between his fingers. He inhaled, held the smoke, and then let it go. It was like he'd been doing it since he was nine years old.

     "Thanks, bub," he said. "But I think this is all for me. I think I'm beginning to feel it," he said. He held the burning roach out for my wife.

     "Same here," she said. "Ditto. Me, too." She took the roach and passed it to me. "I may just sit here for a while between you two guys with my eyes closed. But don't let me bother you, okay? Either one of you. If it bothers you, say so. Otherwise, I may just sit here with my eyes closed until you're ready to go to bed," she said. "Your bed's made up, Robert, when you're ready. It's right next to our room at the top of the stairs. We'll show you up when you're ready. You wake me up now, you guys, if I fall asleep." She said that and then she closed her eyes and went to sleep.

     The news program ended. I got up and changed the channel. I sat back down on the sofa. I wished my wife hadn't pooped out. Her head lay across the back of the sofa, her mouth open. She'd turned so that her robe had slipped away from her legs, exposing a juicy thigh. I reached to draw her robe back over her, and it was then that I glanced at the blind man. What the hell! I flipped the robe open again.

80   "You say when you want some strawberry pie," I said.

     "I will," he said.

     I said, "Are you tired? Do you want me to take you up to your bed? Are you ready to hit the hay?"

     "Not yet," he said. "No, I'll stay up with you, bub. If that's all right. I'll stay up until you're ready to turn in. We haven't had a chance to talk. Know what I mean? I feel like me and her monopolized the evening." He lifted his beard and he let it fall. He picked up his cigarettes and his lighter.

     "That's all right," I said. Then I said, "I'm glad for the company."

85   And I guess I was. Every night I smoked dope and stayed up as long as I could before I fell asleep. My wife and I hardly ever went to bed at the same time. When I did go to sleep, I had these dreams. Sometimes I'd wake up from one of them, my heart going crazy.

     Something about the church and the Middle Ages was on the TV. Not your run-of-the-mill TV fare. I wanted to watch something else. I turned to the other channels. But there was nothing on them, either. So I turned back to the first channel and apologized.

     "Bub, it's all right," the blind man said. "It's fine with me. Whatever you want to watch is okay. I'm always learning something. Learning never ends. It won't hurt me to learn something tonight. I got ears," he said.

We didn't say anything for a time. He was leaning forward with his head turned at me, his right ear aimed in the direction of the set. Very disconcerting. Now and then his eyelids drooped and then they snapped open again. Now and then he put his fingers into his beard and tugged, like he was thinking about something he was hearing on the television.

     On the screen, a group of men wearing cowls was being set upon and tormented by men dressed in skeleton costumes and men dressed as devils. The men dressed as devils wore devil masks, horns, and long tails. This pageant was part of a procession. The Englishman who was narrating the thing said it took place in Spain once a year. I tried to explain to the blind man what was happening.

90   "Skeletons," he said. "I know about skeletons," he said, and he nodded.

The TV showed this one cathedral. Then there was a long, slow look at another one. Finally, the picture switched to the famous one in Paris, with its flying buttresses and its spires reaching up to the clouds. The camera pulled away to show the whole of the cathedral rising above the skyline.

There were times when the Englishman who was telling the thing would shut up, would simply let the camera move around over the cathedrals. Or else the camera would tour the countryside, men in fields walking behind oxen. I waited as long as I could. Then I felt I had to say something. I said, "They're showing the outside of this cathedral now. Gargoyles. Little statues carved to look like monsters. Now I guess they're in Italy. Yeah, they're in Italy. There's paintings on the walls of this one church."

"Are those fresco paintings, bub?" he asked, and he sipped from his drink.

I reached for my glass. But it was empty. I tried to remember what I could remember. "You're asking me are those frescoes?" I said. "That's a good question. I don't know."

95   The camera moved to a cathedral outside Lisbon. The differences in the Portuguese cathedral compared with the French and Italian were not that great. But they were there. Mostly the interior stuff. Then something occurred to me, and I said, "Something has occurred to me. Do you have any idea what a cathedral is? What they look like, that is? Do you follow me? If somebody says cathedral to you, do you have any notion what they're talking about? Do you know the difference between that and a Baptist church, say?"

He let the smoke dribble from his mouth. "I know they took hundreds of workers fifty or a hundred years to build," he said. "I just heard the man say that, of course. I know generations of the same families worked on a cathedral. I heard him say that, too. The men who began their life's work on them, they never lived to see the completion of their work. In that wise, bub, they're no different from the rest of us, right?" He laughed. Then his eyelids drooped again. His head nodded. He seemed to be snoozing. Maybe he was imagining himself in Portugal. The TV was showing another cathedral now. This one was in Germany. The Englishman's voice droned on. "Cathedrals," the blind man said. He sat up and rolled his head back and forth. "If you want the truth, bub, that's about all I know. What I just said. What I heard him say. But maybe you could describe one to me? I wish you'd do it. I'd like that. If you want to know, I really don't have a good idea."

I stared hard at the shot of the cathedral on the TV. How could I even begin to describe it? But say my life depended on it. Say my life was being threatened by an insane guy who said I had to do it or else.

I stared some more at the cathedral before the picture flipped off into the countryside. There was no use. I turned to the blind man and said, "To begin with, they're very tall." I was looking around the room for clues. "They reach way up. Up and up. Toward the sky. They're so big, some of them, they have to have these supports. To help hold them up, so to speak. These supports are called buttresses. They remind me of viaducts, for some reason. But maybe you don't know viaducts, either? Sometimes the cathedrals have devils and such carved into the front. Sometimes lords and ladies. Don't ask me why this is," I said.

He was nodding. The whole upper part of his body seemed to be moving back and forth.

100   "I'm not doing so good, am I?" I said.

He stopped nodding and leaned forward on the edge of the sofa. As he listened to me, he was running his fingers through his beard. I wasn't getting through to him, I could see that. But he waited for me to go on just the same. He nodded, like he was trying to encourage me. I tried to think what else to say. "They're really big," I said. "They're massive. They're built of stone. Marble, too, sometimes. In those olden days, when they built cathedrals, men wanted to be close to God. In those olden days, God was an important part of everyone's life. You could tell this from their cathedral-building. I'm sorry," I said, "but it looks like that's the best I can do for you. I'm just no good at it."

"That's all right, bub," the blind man said. "Hey, listen. I hope you don't mind my asking you. Can I ask you something? Let me ask you a simple question, yes or no. I'm just curious and there's no offense. You're my host. But let me ask if you are in any way religious? You don't mind my asking?"

I shook my head. He couldn't see that, though. A wink is the same as a nod to a blind man. "I guess I don't believe in it. In anything. Sometimes it's hard. You know what I'm saying?"

"Sure, I do," he said.

105 "Right," I said.

The Englishman was still holding forth. My wife sighed in her sleep. She drew a long breath and went on with her sleeping.

"You'll have to forgive me," I said. "But I can't tell you what a cathedral looks like. It just isn't in me to do it. I can't do any more than I've done."

The blind man sat very still, his head down, as he listened to me.

I said, "The truth is, cathedrals don't mean anything special to me. Nothing. Cathedrals. They're something to look at on late-night TV. That's all they are."

110 It was then that the blind man cleared his throat. He brought something up. He took a handkerchief from his back pocket. Then he said, "I get it, bub. It's okay. It happens. Don't worry about it," he said. "Hey, listen to me. Will you do me a favor? I got an idea. Why don't you find us some heavy paper? And a pen. We'll do something. We'll draw one together. Get us a pen and some heavy paper. Go on, bub, get the stuff," he said.

So I went upstairs. My legs felt like they didn't have any strength in them. They felt like they did after I'd done some running. In my wife's room, I looked around. I found some ballpoints in a little basket on her table. And then I tried to think where to look for the kind of paper he was talking about.

Downstairs, in the kitchen, I found a shopping bag with onion skins in the bottom of the bag. I emptied the bag and shook it. I brought it into the living room and sat down with it near his legs. I moved some things, smoothed the wrinkles from the bag, spread it out on the coffee table.

The blind man got down from the sofa and sat next to me on the carpet.

He ran his fingers over the paper. He went up and down the sides of the paper. The edges, even the edges. He fingered the corners.

115 "All right," he said. "All right, let's do her."

He found my hand, the hand with the pen. He closed his hand over my hand. "Go ahead, bub, draw," he said. "Draw. You'll see. I'll follow along with you. It'll be okay. Just begin now like I'm telling you. You'll see. Draw," the blind man said.

So I began. First I drew a box that looked like a house. It could have been the house I lived in. Then I put a roof on it. At either end of the roof, I drew spires. Crazy.

"Swell," he said. "Terrific. You're doing fine," he said. "Never thought anything like this could happen in your lifetime, did you, bub? Well, it's a strange life, we all know that. Go on now. Keep it up."

I put in windows with arches. I drew flying buttresses.[1] I hung great doors. I couldn't stop. The TV station went off the air. I put down the pen and closed and opened my fingers.

---

[1] A crucial part of the architecture of Gothic cathedrals; an external support arch that carries an outward and downward thrust to a solid buttress, thereby creating a vertical thrust against a masonry wall to help hold the structure.

The blind man felt around over the paper. He moved the tips of his fingers over the paper, all over what I had drawn, and he nodded.

120 "Doing fine," the blind man said.

I took up the pen again, and he found my hand. I kept at it. I'm no artist. But I kept drawing just the same.

My wife opened up her eyes and gazed at us. She sat up on the sofa, her robe hanging open. She said, "What are you doing? Tell me, I want to know."

I didn't answer her.

The blind man said, "We're drawing a cathedral. Me and him are working on it. Press hard," he said to me. "That's right. That's good," he said. "Sure. You got it, bub. I can tell. You didn't think you could. But you can, can't you? You're cooking with gas now. You know what I'm saying? We're going to really have us something here in a minute. How's the old arm?" he said. "Put some people in there now. What's a cathedral without people?"

125 My wife said, "What's going on? Robert, what are you doing? What's going on?"

"It's all right," he said to her. "Close your eyes now," the blind man said to me.

I did it. I closed them just like he said.

"Are they closed?" he said. "Don't fudge."

"They're closed," I said.

130 "Keep them that way," he said. He said, "Don't stop now. Draw."

So we kept on with it. His fingers rode my fingers as my hand went over the paper. It was like nothing else in my life up to now.

Then he said, "I think that's it. I think you got it," he said. "Take a look. What do you think?"

But I had my eyes closed. I thought I'd keep them that way for a little longer. I thought it was something I ought to do.

"Well?" he said. "Are you looking?"

135 My eyes were still closed. I was in my house. I knew that. But I didn't feel like I was inside anything.

"It's really something," I said.

■ EXPLORATIONS OF THE TEXT

1. Examine the character of the speaker: his attitudes, values, actions, speech.
2. Why does only the blind man have a name? Describe his attitudes, his physical characteristics, and his capacity for friendship.
3. What is the nature of the relationship between the wife and Robert? Between the wife and the narrator?
4. Why does the woman leave Robert and the narrator together? Is her action deliberate?
5. Does the incident concerning the cathedral have religious meaning? What is the symbolism of the title? In what way does the narrator change at the end of the story?

■ THE READING/WRITING CONNECTION

1. "Think" Topic: What does the narrator mean when he says, "I didn't feel like I was inside anything"?
2. Journal Entry: extend the narrative: write about possible changes in the narrator when the blind man leaves.

■ IDEAS FOR WRITING

1. Write a character analysis of the wife that takes into account her first marriage, her suicide attempt, her friendship with Robert, and her present life.
2. Explore the symbolism of the cathedral.
3. Carver mentions television numerous times in the opening paragraphs of the story. Why? Use evidence from the story to support your thesis.

Stories for Comparison/Contrast: Fairy Tales

NADINE GORDIMER (1923–)   1989

ONCE UPON A TIME

Someone has written to ask me to contribute to an anthology of stories for children. I reply that I don't write children's stories; and he writes back that at a recent congress/book fair/seminar a certain novelist said every writer ought to write at least one story for children. I think of sending a postcard saying I don't accept that I "ought" to write anything.

And then last night I woke up—or rather was awakened without knowing what had roused me.

A voice in the echo-chamber of the subconscious?

A sound.

5   A creaking of the kind made by the weight carried by one foot after another along a wooden floor. I listened. I felt the apertures of my ears distend with concentration. Again: the creaking. I was waiting for it; waiting to hear if it indicated that feet were moving from room to room, coming up the passage—to my door. I have no burglar bars, no gun under my pillow, but I have the same fears as people who do take these precautions, and my windowpanes are thin as rime, could shatter like a wineglass. A woman was murdered (how do they put it) in broad daylight in a house two blocks away, last year, and the fierce dogs who guarded an old widower and his collection of antique clocks were strangled before he was knifed by a casual laborer he had dismissed without pay.

I was staring at the door, making it out in my mind rather than seeing it, in the dark. I lay quite still—a victim already—but the arrhythmia of my heart was fleeing, knocking this way and that against its body-cage. How finely tuned the senses are, just out of rest, sleep! I could never listen intently as that in the distractions of the day; I was reading every faintest sound, identifying and classifying its possible threat.

But I learned that I was to be neither threatened nor spared. There was no human weight pressing on the boards, the creaking was a buckling, an epicenter of stress. I was in it. The house that surrounds me when I sleep is built on undermined ground; far beneath my bed, the floor, the house's foundations, the stopes and passages of gold mines have hollowed the rock, and when some face trembles, detaches and falls, three thousand feet below, the whole house shifts slightly, bringing uneasy strain to the balance and counterbalance of brick, cement, wood and glass that hold it as a structure around me. The misbeats of my heart tailed off like the last muffled flourishes on one of the wooden xylophones made by the Chopi and Tsonga[1] migrant miners who might have been down there, under me in the earth at that moment. The stope where the fall was could have been disused, dripping water from its ruptured veins; or men might now be interred there in the most profound of tombs.

I couldn't find a position in which my mind would let go of my body—release me to sleep again. So I began to tell myself a story; a bedtime story.

In a house, in a suburb, in a city, there were a man and his wife who loved each other very much and were living happily ever after. They had a little boy, and they loved him very

---

[1] **Chopi and Tsonga:** two peoples from Mozambique, northeast of South Africa.

much. They had a cat and a dog that the little boy loved very much. They had a car and a caravan trailer for holidays, and a swimming-pool which was fenced so that the little boy and his playmates would not fall in and drown. They had a housemaid who was absolutely trustworthy and an itinerant gardener who was highly recommended by the neighbors. For when they began to live happily ever after they were warned by that wise old witch, the husband's mother, not to take on anyone off the street. They were inscribed in a medical benefit society, their pet dog was licensed, they were insured against fire, flood damage and theft, and they subscribed to the local Neighborhood Watch, which supplied them with a plaque for their gates lettered YOU HAVE BEEN WARNED over the silhouette of a would-be intruder. He was masked; it could not be said if he was black or white, and therefore proved the owner was no racist.

10   It was not possible to insure the house, the swimming-pool or the car against riot damage. There were riots, but these were outside the city, where people of another color were quartered. These people were not allowed into the suburb except as reliable housemaids and gardeners, so there was nothing to fear, the husband told the wife. Yet she was afraid that some day such people might come up the street and tear off the plaque YOU HAVE BEEN WARNED and open the gates and stream in . . . Nonsense, my dear, said the husband, there are police and soldiers and tear-gas and guns to keep them away. But to please her—for he loved her very much and buses were being burned, cars stoned, and school-children shot by the police in those quarters out of sight and hearing of the suburb—he had electronically controlled gates fitted. Anyone who pulled off the sign YOU HAVE BEEN WARNED and tried to open the gates would have to announce his intentions by pressing a button and speaking into a receiver relayed to the house. The little boy was fascinated by the device and used it as a walkie-talkie in cops and robbers play with his small friends.

The riots were suppressed, but there were many burglaries in the suburb and some-body's trusted housemaid was tied up and shut in a cupboard by thieves while she was in charge of her employers' house. The trusted housemaid of the man and wife and little boy was so upset by this misfortune befalling a friend left, as she herself often was, with respon-sibility for the possessions of the man and his wife and the little boy that she implored her employers to have burglar bars attached to the doors and windows of the house, and an alarm system installed. The wife said, She is right, let us take heed of her advice. So from every window and door in the house where they were living happily ever after they now saw the trees and sky through bars, and when the little boy's pet cat tried to climb in by the fan-light to keep him company in his little bed at night, as it customarily had done, it set off the alarm keening through the house.

The alarm was often answered—it seemed—by other burglar alarms, in other houses, that had been triggered by pet cats or nibbling mice. The alarms called to one another across the gardens in shrills and bleats and wails that everyone soon became accustomed to, so that the din aroused the inhabitants of the suburb no more than the croak of frogs and mu-sical grating of cicadas' legs. Under cover of the electronic harpies' discourse, intruders sawed the iron bars and broke into homes, taking away hi-fi equipment, television sets, cas-sette players, cameras and radios, jewelry and clothing, and sometimes were hungry enough to devour everything in the refrigerator or paused audaciously to drink the whisky in the cabinets or patio bars. Insurance companies paid no compensation for single malt,[2] a loss made keener by the property owner's knowledge that the thieves wouldn't even have been able to appreciate what it was they were drinking.

---

[2] Expensive Scotch whisky.

Then the time came when many of the people who were not trusted housemaids and gardeners hung about the suburb because they were unemployed. Some importuned for a job: weeding or painting a roof; anything, *baas*,[3] madam. But the man and his wife remembered the warning about taking on anyone off the street. Some drank liquor and fouled the street with discarded bottles. Some begged, waiting for the man and his wife to drive the car out of the electronically operated gates. They sat about with their feet in the gutters, under the jacaranda trees that made a green tunnel of the street—for it was a beautiful suburb, spoiled only by their presence—and sometimes they fell asleep lying right before the gates in the midday sun. The wife could never see anyone go hungry. She sent the trusted housemaid out with bread and tea, but the trusted housemaid said these were loafers and *tsotsis*,[4] who would come and tie her up and shut her up in a cupboard. The husband said. She's right. Take heed of her advice. You only encourage them with your bread and tea. They are looking for their chance . . . And he brought the little boy's tricycle from the garden into the house every night, because if the house was surely secure, once locked and with the alarm set, someone might still be able to climb over the wall or the electronically closed gates into the garden.

You are right, said the wife, then the wall should be higher. And the wise old witch, the husband's mother, paid for the extra bricks as her Christmas present to her son and his wife—the little boy got a Space Man outfit and a book of fairy tales.

15 But every week there were more reports of intrusion: in broad daylight and the dead of night, in the early hours of the morning, and even in the lovely summer twilight—a certain family was at dinner while the bedrooms were being ransacked upstairs. The man and his wife, talking of the latest armed robbery in the suburb, were distracted by the sight of the little boy's pet cat effortlessly arriving over the seven-foot wall, descending first with a rapid bracing of extended forepaws down on the sheer vertical surface, and then a graceful launch, landing with swishing tail within the property. The whitewashed wall was marked with the cat's comings and goings; and on the street side of the wall there were larger red-earth smudges that could have been made by the kind of broken running shoes, seen on the feet of unemployed loiterers, that had no innocent destination.

When the man and wife and little boy took the pet dog for a walk round the neighborhood streets, they no longer paused to admire this show of roses or that perfect lawn; these were hidden behind an array of different varieties of security fences, walls, and devices. The man, wife, little boy and dog passed a remarkable choice: there was the low-cost option of pieces of broken glass embedded in cement along the top of walls, there were iron grilles ending in lance-points, there were attempts at reconciling the aesthetics of prison architecture with the Spanish Villa style (spikes painted pink) and with the plaster urns of neoclassical façades (twelve-inch pikes finned like zigzags of lightning and painted pure white). Some walls had a small board affixed, giving the name and telephone number of the firm responsible for the installation of the devices. While the little boy and the pet dog raced ahead, the husband and wife found themselves comparing the possible effectiveness of each style against its appearance; and after several weeks when they paused before this barricade or that without needing to speak, both came out with the conclusion that only one was worth considering. It was the ugliest but the most honest in its suggestion of the pure concentration-camp style, no frills, all evident efficacy. Placed the length of walls, it consisted of a continuous coil of stiff and shining metal serrated into jagged blades, so that there would be no way of climbing over it and no way through its tunnel without getting entangled in its fangs. There

---

[3] Boss.

[4] Hooligans.

would be no way out, only a struggle getting bloodier and bloodier, a deeper and sharper hooking and tearing of flesh. The wife shuddered to look at it. You're right, said the husband, anyone would think twice. . . And they took heed of the advice on the small board fixed to the wall: Consult DRAGON'S TEETH The People for Total Security.

Next day a gang of workmen came and stretched the razor-bladed coils all round the walls of the house where the husband and wife and little boy and pet dog and cat were living happily ever after. The sunlight flashed and slashed off the serrations; the cornice of razor thorns encircled the home, shining. The husband said, Never mind. It will weather. The wife said. You're wrong. They guarantee it's rust-proof. And she waited until the little boy had run off to play before she said, I hope the cat will take heed . . . The husband said, Don't worry, my dear, cats always look before they leap. And it was true that from that day on the cat slept in the little boy's bed and kept to the garden, never risking a try at breaching security.

One evening, the mother read the little boy to sleep with a fairy story from the book the wise old witch had given him at Christmas. Next day he pretended to be the Prince who braves the terrible thicket of thorns to enter the palace and kiss the Sleeping Beauty back to life: he dragged a ladder to the wall, the shining coiled tunnel was just wide enough for his body to creep in, and with the first fixing of its razor-teeth in his knees and hands and head he screamed and struggled deeper into its tangle. The trusted housemaid and itinerant gardener, whose "day" it was, came running, the first to see and to scream with him, and the itinerant gardener tore his hands trying to get at the little boy. Then the man and his wife burst wildly into the garden and for some reason (the cat, probably) the alarm set up wailing against the screams while the bleeding mass of the little boy was hacked out of the security coil with saws, wire-cutters, choppers, and they carried it—the man, the wife, the hysterical trusted housemaid, and the weeping gardener—into the house.

ANGELA CARTER (1940–1992)   1979

THE COMPANY OF WOLVES

Ope beast and only one howls in the woods by night.

The wolf is carnivore incarnate and he's as cunning as he is ferocious; once he's had a taste of flesh then nothing else will do.

At night, the eyes of wolves shine like candle flames, yellowish, reddish, but that is because the pupils of their eyes fatten on darkness and catch the light from your lantern to flash it back to you—red for danger; if a wolf's eyes reflect only moonlight, then they gleam a cold and unnatural green, a mineral, a piercing color. If the benighted traveller spies those luminous, terrible sequins stitched suddenly on the black thickets, then he knows he must run, if fear has not struck him stock-still.

But those eyes are all you will be able to glimpse of the forest assassins as they cluster invisibly round your smell of meat as you go through the wood unwisely late. They will be like shadows, they will be like wraiths, grey members of a congregation of nightmare; hark! his long, wavering howl . . . an aria of fear made audible.

5   The wolfsong is the sound of the rending you will suffer, in itself a murdering.

It is winter and cold weather. In this region of mountain and forest, there is now nothing for the wolves to eat. Goats and sheep are locked up in the byre, the deer departed for the remaining pasturage on the southern slopes—wolves grow lean and famished. There is so little flesh on them that you could count the starveling ribs through their pelts, if they gave you time before they pounced. Those slavering jaws; the lolling tongue; the rime of saliva on the grizzled chops—of all the teeming perils of the night and the forest, ghosts, hob-goblins, ogres that grill babies upon gridirons, witches that fatten their captives in cages for cannibal tables, the wolf is worst for he cannot listen to reason.

You are always in danger in the forest, where no people are. Step between the portals of the great pines where the shaggy branches tangle about you, trapping the unwary traveller in nets as if the vegetation itself were in a plot with the wolves who live there, as though the wicked trees go fishing on behalf of their friends—step between the gateposts of the forest with the greatest trepidation and infinite precautions, for if you stray from the path for one instant, the wolves will eat you. They are grey as famine, they are as unkind as plague.

The grave-eyed children of the sparse villages always carry knives with them when they go out to tend the little flocks of goats that provide the homesteads with acrid milk and rank, maggoty cheeses. Their knives are half as big as they are, the blades are sharpened daily.

But the wolves have ways of arriving at your own hearthside. We try and try but some-times we cannot keep them out. There is no winter's night the cottager does not fear to see a lean, grey, famished snout questing under the door, and there was a woman once bitten in her own kitchen as she was straining the macaroni.

10   Fear and flee the wolf; for, worst of all, the wolf may be more than he seems.

There was a hunter once, near here, that trapped a wolf in a pit. This wolf had massa-cred the sheep and goats; eaten up a mad old man who used to live by himself in a hut halfway up the mountain and sing to Jesus all day; pounced on a girl looking after the sheep, but she made such a commotion that men came with rifles and scared him away and tried to track him into the forest but he was cunning and easily gave them the slip. So this hunter dug a pit and put a duck in it, for bait, all alive-oh; and he covered the pit with straw smeared with wolf dung. Quack, quack! went the duck and a wolf came slinking out of the forest, a big one, a heavy one, he weighed as much as a grown man and the straw gave way beneath him—into the pit he tumbled. The hunter jumped down after him, slit his throat, cut off all his paws for a trophy.

And then no wolf at all lay in front of the hunter but the bloody trunk of a man, head-less, footless, dying, dead.

A witch from up the valley once turned an entire wedding party into wolves because the groom had settled on another girl. She used to order them to visit her, at night, from spite, and they would sit and howl around her cottage for her, serenading her with their misery

Not so very long ago, a young woman in our village married a man who vanished clean away on her wedding night. The bed was made with new sheets and the bride lay down in it; the groom said, he was going out to relieve himself, insisted on it, for the sake of decency, and she drew the coverlet up to her chin and she lay there. And she waited and she waited and then she waited again—surely he's been gone a long time? Until she jumps up in bed and shrieks to hear a howling, coming on the wind from the forest.

15   That long-drawn, wavering howl has, for all its fearful resonance, some inherent sad-ness in it, as if the beasts would love to be less beastly if only they knew how and never cease to mourn their own condition. There is a vast melancholy in the canticles of the wolves, melancholy infinite as the forest, endless as these long nights of winter and yet that ghastly sadness, that mourning for their own, irremediable appetites, can never move the heart for not one phrase in it hints at the possibility of redemption; grace could not come to the wolf from its own despair, only through some external mediator, so that, sometimes, the beast will look as if he half welcomes the knife that despatches him.

The young woman's brothers searched the outhouses and the haystacks but never found any remains so the sensible girl dried her eyes and found herself another husband not too shy to piss into a pot who spent the nights indoors. She gave him a pair of bonny babies and all went right as a trivet until, one freezing night, the night of the solstice, the hinge of the year when things do not fit together as well as they should, the longest night, her first good man came home again.

A great thump on the door announced him as she was stirring the soup for the father of her children and she knew him the moment she lifted the latch to him although it was years since she'd worn black for him and now he was in rags and his hair hung down his back and never saw a comb, alive with lice.

"Here I am again, missus," he said. "Get me my bowl of cabbage and be quick about it."

Then her second husband came in with wood for the fire and when the first one saw she'd slept with another man and, worse, clapped his red eyes on her little children who'd crept into the kitchen to see what all the din was about, he shouted: "I wish I were a wolf again, to teach this whore a lesson!" So a wolf he instantly became and tore off the eldest boy's left foot before he was chopped up with the hatchet they used for chopping logs. But when the wolf lay bleeding and gasping its last, the pelt peeled off again and he was just as he had been, years ago, when he ran away from his marriage bed, so that she wept and her second husband beat her.

20   They say there's an ointment the Devil gives you that turns you into a wolf the minute you rub it on. Or, that he was born feet first and had a wolf for his father and his torso is a man's but his legs and genitals are a wolf's. And he has a wolf's heart.

Seven years is a werewolf's natural span but if you burn his human clothing you condemn him to wolfishness for the rest of his life, so old wives hereabouts think it some protection to throw a hat or an apron at the werewolf, as if clothes made the man. Yet by the eyes, those phosphorescent eyes, you know him in all his shapes; the eyes alone unchanged by metamorphosis.

Before he can become a wolf, the lycanthrope strips stark naked. If you spy a naked man among the pines, you must run as if the Devil were after you.

It is midwinter and the robin, the friend of man, sits on the handle of the gardener's spade and sings. It is the worst time in all the year for wolves but this strong-minded child insists she will go off through the wood. She is quite sure the wild beasts cannot harm her although, well-warned, she lays a carving knife in the basket her mother has packed with cheeses. There is a bottle of harsh liquor distilled from brambles; a batch of flat oatcakes baked on the hearthstone; a pot or two of jam. The flaxen-haired girl will take these delicious gifts to a reclusive grandmother so old the burden of her years is crushing her to death. Granny lives two hours' trudge through the winter woods; the child wraps herself up in her thick shawl, draws it over her head. She steps into her stout wooden shoes; she is dressed and ready and it is Christmas Eve. The malign door of the solstice still swings upon its hinges but she has been too much loved ever to feel scared.

Children do not stay young for long in this savage country There are no toys for them to play with so they work hard and grow wise but this one, so pretty and the youngest of her family, a little late-comer, had been indulged by her mother and the grandmother who'd knitted her the red shawl that, today, has the ominous if brilliant look of blood on snow. Her breasts have just begun to swell; her hair is like lint, so fair it hardly makes a shadow on her pale forehead; her cheeks are an emblematic scarlet and white and she has just started her woman's bleeding, the clock inside her that will strike, henceforward, once a month.

25   She stands and moves within the invisible pentacle[1] of her own virginity She is an unbroken egg; she is a sealed vessel; she has inside her a magic space the entrance to which is

---

[1] A figure of a five-pointed star within a circle.

shut tight with a plug of membrane; she is a closed system; she does not know how to shiver. She has her knife and she is afraid of nothing,

Her father might forbid her, if he were home, but he is away in the forest, gathering wood, and her mother cannot deny her.

The forest closed upon her like a pair of jaws.

There is always something to look at in the forest, even in the middle of winter—the huddled mounds of birds, succumbed to the lethargy of the season, heaped on the creaking boughs and too forlorn to sing; the bright frills of the winter fungi on the blotched trunks of the trees; the cuneiform slots of rabbits and deer, the herringbone tracks of the birds, a hare as lean as a rasher of bacon streaking across the path where the thin sunlight dapples the russet brakes of last year's bracken.

When she heard the freezing howl of a distant wolf, her practised hand sprang to the handle of her knife, but she saw no sign of a wolf at all, nor of a naked man, neither, but then she heard a clattering among the brushwood and there sprang on to the path a fully clothed one, a very handsome young one, in the green coat and wide-awake hat of a hunter, laden with carcasses of game birds. She had her hand on her knife at the first rustle of twigs but he laughed with a flash of white teeth when he saw her and made her a comic yet flattering little bow; she'd never seen such a fine fellow before, not among the rustic clowns of her native village. So on they went together, through the thickening light of the afternoon.

30   Soon they were laughing and joking like old friends. When he offered to carry her basket, she gave it to him although her knife was in it because he told her his rifle would protect them. As the day darkened, it began to snow again; she felt the first flakes settle on her eyelashes but now there was only half a mile to go and there would be a fire, and hot tea, and a welcome, a warm one, surely, for the dashing huntsman as well as for herself.

This young man had a remarkable object in his pocket. It was a compass. She looked at the little round glass face in the palm of his hand and watched the wavering needle with a vague wonder. He assured her this compass had taken him safely through the wood on his hunting trip because the needle always told him with perfect accuracy where the north was. She did not believe it; she knew she should never leave the path on the way through the wood or else she would be lost instantly. He laughed at her again; gleaming trails of spittle clung to his teeth. He said, if he plunged off the path into the forest that surrounded them, he could guarantee to arrive at her grandmother's house a good quarter of an hour before she did, plotting his way through the undergrowth with his compass, while she trudged the long way, along the winding path.

I don't believe you. Besides, aren't you afraid of the wolves?

He only tapped the gleaming butt of his rifle and grinned.

Is it a bet? he asked her. Shall we make a game of it? What will you give me if I get to your grandmother's house before you?

35   What would you like? she asked disingenuously.

A kiss.

Commonplaces of a rustic seduction; she lowered her eyes and blushed. He went through the undergrowth and took her basket with him but she forgot to be afraid of the beasts, although now the moon was rising, for she wanted to dawdle on her way to make sure the handsome gentleman would win his wager.

Grandmother's house stood by itself a little way out of the village. The freshly falling snow blew in eddies about the kitchen garden and the young man stepped delicately up the snowy path to the door as if he were reluctant to get his feet wet, swinging his bundle of game and the girl's basket and humming a little tune to himself.

There is a faint trace of blood on his chin; he has been snacking on his catch.

40   He rapped upon the panels with his knuckles.

Aged and frail, granny is three-quarters succumbed to the mortality the ache in her bones promises her and almost ready to give in entirely. A boy came out from the village to build up her hearth for the night an hour ago and the kitchen crackles with busy firelight. She has her Bible for company, she is a pious old woman. She is propped up on several pillows in the bed set into the wall peasant-fashion, wrapped up in the patchwork quilt she made before she was married, more years ago than she cares to remember. Two china spaniels with liver-coloured blotches on their coats and black noses sit on either side of the fireplace. There is a bright rug of woven rags on the pantiles. The grandfather clock ticks away her eroding time.

We. keep the wolves outside by living well.

He rapped upon the panels with his hairy knuckles.

It is your granddaughter, he mimicked in a high soprano.

45   Lift up the latch and walk in, my darling.

You can tell them by their eyes, eyes of a beast of prey, nocturnal, devastating eyes as red as a wound; you can hurl your Bible at him and your apron after, granny, you thought that was a sure prophylactic against these infernal vermin . . . now call on Christ and his mother and all the angels in heaven to protect you but it won't do you any good.

His feral muzzle is sharp as a knife; he drops his golden burden of gnawed pheasant on the table and puts down your dear girl's basket, too. Oh, my God, what have you done with her?

Off with his disguise, that coat of forest-coloured cloth, the hat with the feather tucked into the ribbon; his matted hair streams down his white shirt and she can see the lice moving in it. The sticks in the hearth shift and hiss; night and the forest has come into the kitchen with darkness tangled in its hair.

He strips off his shirt. His skin is the colour and texture of vellum. A crisp stripe of hair runs down his belly, his nipples are ripe and dark as poison fruit but he's so thin you could count the ribs under his skin if only he gave you the time. He strips off his trousers and she can see how hairy his legs are. His genitals, huge. Ah! huge.

50   The last thing the old lady saw in all this world was a young man, eyes like cinders, naked as a stone, approaching her bed.

The wolf is carnivore incarnate.

When he had finished with her, he licked his chops and quickly dressed himself again, until he was just as he had been when he came through her door. He burned the inedible hair in the fireplace and wrapped the bones, up in a napkin that he hid away under the bed in the wooden chest in which he found a clean pair of sheets. These he carefully put on the bed instead of the tell-tale stained ones he stowed away in the laundry basket. He plumped up the pillows and shook out the patchwork quilt, he picked up the Bible from the floor, closed it and laid it on the table. All was as it had been before except that grandmother was gone. The sticks twitched in the grate, the clock ticked and the young man sat patiently, deceitfully beside the bed in granny's nightcap.

Rat-a-tap-tap.

Who's there, he quavers in granny's antique falsetto.

55   Only your granddaughter.

So she came in, bringing with her a flurry of snow that melted in tears on the tiles, and perhaps she was a little disappointed to see only her grandmother sitting beside the fire. But then he flung off the blanket and sprang to the door, pressing his back against it so that she could not get out again.

The girl looked round the room and saw there was not even the indentation of a head on the smooth cheek of the pillow and how, for the first time she'd seen it so, the Bible lay closed on the table. The tick of the clock cracked like a whip. She wanted her knife from her basket but she did not dare reach for it because his eyes were fixed upon her—huge eyes that now seemed to shine with a unique, interior light, eyes the size of saucers, saucers full of Greek fire, diabolic phosphorescence.

What big eyes you have.

All the better to see you with.

60   No trace at all of the old woman except for a tuft of white hair that had caught in the bark of an unburned log. When the girl saw that, she knew she was in danger of death.

Where is my grandmother?

There's nobody here but we two, my darling.

Now a great howling rose up all around them, near, very near, as close as the kitchen garden, the howling of a multitude of wolves; she knew the worst wolves are hairy on the inside and she shivered, in spite of the scarlet shawl she pulled more closely round herself as if it could protect her although it was as red as the blood she must spill.

Who has come to sing us carols, she said.

65   Those are the voices of my brothers, darling; I love the company of wolves. Look out of the window and you'll see them.

Snow half-caked the lattice and she opened it to look into the garden. It was a white night of moon and snow; the blizzard whirled round the gaunt, grey beasts who squatted on their haunches among the rows of winter cabbage, pointing their sharp snouts to the moon and howling as if their hearts would break. Ten wolves; twenty wolves—so many wolves she could not count them, howling in concert as if demented or deranged. Their eyes reflected the light from the kitchen and shone like a hundred candles.

It is very cold, poor things, she said; no wonder they howl so.

She closed the window on the wolves' threnody[2] and took off her scarlet shawl, the colour of poppies, the colour of sacrifices, the colour of her menses, and, since her fear did her no good, she ceased to be afraid.

What shall I do with my shawl?

70   Throw it on the fire, dear one. You won't need it again.

She bundled up her shawl and threw it on the blaze, which instantly consumed it. Then she drew her blouse over her head; her small breasts gleamed as if the snow had invaded the room.

What shall I do with my blouse?

Into the fire with it, too, my pet.

The thin muslin went flaring up the chimney like a magic bird and now off came her skirt, her woollen stockings, her shoes, and on to the fire they went, too, and were gone for good. The firelight shone through the edges of her skin; now she was clothed only in her untouched integument of flesh. This dazzling, naked she combed out her hair with her fingers; her hair looked white as the snow outside. Then went directly to the man with red eyes in whose unkempt mane the lice moved; she stood up on tiptoe and unbuttoned the collar of his shirt.

75   What big arms you have.

All the better to hug you with.

Every wolf in the world now howled a prothalamion[3] outside the window as she freely gave the kiss she owed him.

---

[2] A lamentation song; a dirge.

[3] A song in celebration of a marriage.

What big teeth you have!

She saw how his jaw began to slaver and the room was full of the clamour of the forest's Liebestod[4] but the wise child never flinched, even when he answered:

80   All the better to eat you with.

The girl burst out laughing; she knew she was nobody's meat. She laughed at him full in the face, she ripped off his shirt for him and flung it into the fire, in the fiery wake of her own discarded clothing. The flames danced like dead souls on Walpurgisnacht[5] and the old bones under the bed set up a terrible clattering but she did not pay them any heed.

Carnivore incarnate, only immaculate flesh appeases him.

She will lay his fearful head on her lap and she will pick out the lice from his pelt and perhaps she will put the lice into her mouth and eat them, as he will bid her, as she would do in a savage marriage ceremony.

The blizzard will die down.

85   The blizzard died down, leaving the mountains as randomly covered with snow as if a blind woman had thrown a sheet over them, the upper branches of the forest pines limed, creaking, swollen with the fall.

Snowlight, moonlight, a confusion of paw-prints.

All silent, all still.

Midnight; and the clock strikes. It is Christmas Day, the werewolves' birthday, the door of the solstice stands wide open; let them all sink through.

See! sweet and sound she sleeps in granny's bed, between the paws of the tender wolf.

ON THE WEB

Introduction to Fairy Tales

The Children's Literature Association
http://ebbs.english.vt.edu/chla/.index.html

---

[4] Literally, love-death.

[5] The eve of May Day, when, according to legend, witches rendezvous.

■ POETRY ■

DIANE WAKOSKI

Diane Wakoski (1937–   ) was born in Whittier, California. Wakoski, educated at the University of California, Berkeley, has held a number of jobs, including working in a bookstore, teaching high school English, and teaching at universities. Her more than twenty volumes of poetry include Coins and Coffins *(1962),* The Man Who Shook Hands *(1978),* Medea the Sorceress *(1991) and* Argonaut Rose *(1998). Her collection of poetry,* Emerald Ice: Selected Poems, 1962–1987, *won the William Carlos Williams Prize in 1989, and she was granted the Michigan Library Association's Author of the Year award in 2003. Much of Wakoski's poetry concerns itself with creating a personal mythology for the writer.*

1966

WIND SECRETS

I like the wind
with its puffed cheeks and closed eyes.
Nice wind.
I like its gentle sounds
5 and fierce bites.
When I was little
I used to sit by the black, potbellied stove and stare
at a spot on the ceiling,
while the wind breathed and blew
10 outside.

"Nice wind,"
I murmured to myself.

I would ask mother when she kneeled to tie my shoes
what the wind said.

15 Mother knew.

And the wind whistled and roared outside
while the coals opened their eyes in anger
at me.
I would hear mother crying under the wind.
20 "Nice wind," I said,
But my heart leapt like a darting fish.
I remember the wind better than any sound.
It was the first thing I heard
with blazing ears,
25 a sound that didn't murmur and coo,
and the sounds wrapped round my head
and huffed open my eyes.
It was the first thing I heard
besides my father beating my mother.

30 The sounds slashed at my ears like scissors.
Nice wind.

The wind blows
while the glowing coals from the stove look at me
with angry eyes.
Nice wind.
35 Nice wind.
Oh, close your eyes.
There was nothing I could do.

■ EXPLORATIONS OF THE TEXT
1. Discuss the speaker's point of view. Is it a child's or an adult's voice? Explain.
2. What comparisons create the dramatic effects and momentum in the poem? What do they suggest about the child's state of mind?
3. Explore the symbolism of the "eyes." Whose "eyes" are they?

■ THE READING/WRITING CONNECTION
1. Do a freewrite response to this poem.
2. Journal Entry: Create a moment from childhood in which you use nature imagery to suggest your state of mind (You may create a poem or a drawing for this entry).

■ IDEAS FOR WRITING
1. Write a monologue in the voice of the mother.
2. Discuss the use of figurative language in this poem. How does the language develop the theme?
3. Compare this poem with "Incident." Focus on loss of innocence.

COUNTEE CULLEN

Born in New York City, Countee Cullen (1903–46) was a central figure in the Harlem Renaissance. He published his first collection of poems, Color, *in 1925 when he was a student at New York University. He received a Guggenheim Fellowship and published* Black Christ and Other Poems *in France in 1929. Cullen also wrote a novel and children's stories. He collaborated with his friend Arna Bontemps on a play,* St. Louis Woman, *which became a popular Broadway musical in 1946.*

1925

INCIDENT

Once riding in old Baltimore,
    Heart-filled, head-filled with glee,
I saw a Baltimorean
    Keep looking straight at me.

5 Now I was eight and very small,
    And he was no whit bigger,
And so I smiled, but he poked out
    His tongue and called me, "Nigger."

I saw the whole of Baltimore
10   From May until December:

Of all the things that happened there
That's all that I remember.

▪ **EXPLORATIONS OF THE TEXT**
1. What is the nature of the interaction between the two boys?
2. Why does the speaker remember nothing more than the incident, even though he stayed in Baltimore from "May until December"?
3. What aspects of this poem are similar to the story by Heker?

▪ **THE READING/WRITING CONNECTION**
1. In a paragraph compare your experience of prejudice with the persona in the poem.
2. "Think" Topic: Compare the reactions of the persona with those in the works by Heker and Erdrich.

▪ **IDEAS FOR WRITING**
1. What do its form and rhyme add to this poem?
2. What is the power of language? What are the effects of the use of the term *nigger?*

LORNA DEE CERVANTES

Born in San Francisco and educated in California, Lorna Dee Cervantes (1954–) is active in the Chicano community and in literary affairs. In 1976, she founded Mango Publications, a small press that publishes a literary journal and both Mexican American and multicultural books. Her first volume of poetry, Emplumada *(1981), won the American Book Award in 1982. Her second volume of poems,* From the Cables of Genocide, *was published in 1991.*

1981

UNCLE'S FIRST RABBIT

He was a good boy
making his way through
the Santa Barbara[1] pines,
sighting the blast of fluff
5   as he leveled the rifle,
and the terrible singing began.
He was ten years old,
hunting my grandpa's supper.
He had dreamed of running,
10 shouldering the rifle to town,
selling it, and taking the next
train out.
       Fifty years
have passed and he still hears
15 that rabbit "just like a baby."
He remembers how the rabbit
stopped keening under the butt

---

[1] A city in California.

of his rifle, how he brought
it home with tears streaming
20 down his blood soaked jacket.
"That bastard. That bastard."
He cried all night and the week
after, remembering that voice
like his dead baby sister's,
25 remembering his father's drunken
kicking that had pushed her
into birth. She had a voice
like that, growing faint
at its end; his mother rocking,
30 softly, keening. He dreamed
of running, running
the bastard out of his life.
He would forget them, run down
the hill, leave his mother's
35 silent waters, and the sounds
of beating night after night,
    When war came,
he took the man's vow. He was
finally leaving and taking
40 the bastard's last bloodline
with him. At war's end, he could
still hear her, her soft
body stiffening under water
like a shark's. The color
45 of the water, darkening, soaking,
as he clung to what was left
of a ship's gun. Ten long hours
off the coast of Okinawa,[2] he sang
so he wouldn't hear them.
50 He pounded their voices out
of his head, and awakened
to find himself slugging the bloodied
face of his wife.
    Fifty years
55 have passed and he has not run
the way he dreamed. The Paradise
pines shadow the bleak hills
to his home. His hunting hounds,
dead now. His father, long dead.
60 His wife, dying, hacking in the bed
she has not let him enter for the last
thirty years. He stands looking,
he mouths the words, "Die you bitch.

---

[2] One of the islands of the Ryukyu group, part of Japan, occupied by the United States from 1945 to 1972,
when it was returned to Japan.

I'll live to watch you die." He turns,
65 entering their moss-soft livingroom.
He watches out the picture window
and remembers running: how he'll
take the new pickup to town, sell it,
and get the next train out.

■ EXPLORATIONS OF THE TEXT

1. What events relate to the killing of the rabbit? Why is it compared to a baby?
2. What is the narrator's point of view?
3. How has the uncle changed in fifty years?
4. Why does the uncle not leave? Will he ever leave?
5. What connections can you find between this poem and "Barn Burning"?

■ THE READING/WRITING CONNECTION

1. Paraphrase this poem in a paragraph.
2. Respond to the actions of the uncle. Freewrite.

■ IDEAS FOR WRITING

1. Gloss the poem, focusing on the speaker's attitude toward killing the rabbit. Which words provide clues or evidence for your position?
2. Analyze the uncle's character.
3. Compare this presentation of hunting with the hunting scene in Alberto Moravia's "The Chase" (chapter 6).

WALT WHITMAN

Walt Whitman (1819–92) was born on Long Island. Until the early 1850s, he moved among printing, writing, and teaching jobs in New York. The first edition of his Leaves of Grass *was published in 1855 and consisted of twelve untitled poems, including the work eventually titled "Song of Myself." Whitman spent the rest of his life revising* Leaves of Grass, *editing the poems in it and adding new ones. The spacious, unconventional verse patterns in* Leaves of Grass *have had a profound and lasting effect on North and South American poetry.*

1859

OUT OF THE CRADLE ENDLESSLY ROCKING

Out of the cradle endlessly rocking,
Out of the mocking-bird's throat, the musical shuttle,
Out of the Ninth-month[1] midnight,
Over the sterile sands and the fields beyond, where the child leaving his bed
    wander'd alone, bareheaded, barefoot,
5 Down from the shower'd halo,
Up from the mystic play of shadows twining and twisting as if they were alive,
Out from the patches of briers and blackberries,

---

[1] Quaker name for September.

From the memories of the bird that chanted to me,
From your memories sad brother, from the fitful risings and fallings I heard,
10 From under that yellow half-moon late-risen and swollen as if with tears,
From those beginning notes of yearning and love there in the mist,
From the thousand responses of my heart never to cease,
From the myriad thence-arous'd words,
From the word stronger and more delicious than any,
15 For such as now they start the scene revisiting,
As a flock, twittering, rising, or overhead passing,
Borne hither, ere all eludes me, hurriedly,
A man, yet by these tears a little boy again,
Throwing myself on the sand, confronting the waves,
20 I, chanter of pains and joys, uniter of here and hereafter,
Taking all hints to use them, but swiftly leaping beyond them,
A reminiscence sing.

Once Paumanok,
When the lilac-scent was in the air and Fifth-month grass was growing,
25 Up this seashore in some briers,
Two feather'd guests from Alabama, two together,
And their nest, and four light-green eggs spotted with brown,
And every day the he-bird to and fro near at hand,
And every day the she-bird crouch'd on her nest, silent, with bright eyes,
30 And every day I, a curious boy, never too close, never disturbing them,
Cautiously peering, absorbing, translating.

Shine! shine! shine!
Pour down your warmth, great sun!
While we bask, we two together.

35 *Two together!*
Winds blow south, or winds blow north,
Day come white, or night come black,
Home, or rivers and mountains from home,
Singing all time, minding no time,
40 *While we two keep together.*

Till of a sudden,
May-be kill'd, unknown to her mate,
One forenoon the she-bird crouch'd not on the nest,
Nor return'd that afternoon, nor the next,
45 Nor ever appear'd again.

And thenceforward all summer in the sound of the sea,
And at night under the full of the moon in calmer weather,
Over the hoarse surging of the sea,
Or flitting from brier to brier by day,
50 I saw, I heard at intervals the remaining one, the he-bird,
The solitary guest from Alabama.

Blow! blow! blow!
Blow up sea-winds along Paumanok's shore;
I wait and I wait till you blow my mate to me.

55 Yes, when the stars glisten'd,
   All night long on the prong of a moss-scallop'd stake,
   Down almost amid the slapping waves,
   Sat the lone singer wonderful causing tears.
   He call'd on his mate,
60 He pour'd forth the meanings which I of all men know.

   Yes my brother I know,
   The rest might not, but I have treasur'd every note,
   For more than once dimly down to the beach gliding,
   Silent, avoiding the moonbeams, blending myself with the shadows,
65 Recalling now the obscure shapes, the echoes, the sounds and sights after
      their sorts,
   The white arms out in the breakers tirelessly tossing,
   I, with bare feet, a child, the wind wafting my hair,
   Listen'd long and long.

   Listen'd to keep, to sing, now translating the notes,
70 Following you my brother.

   Soothe! soothe! soothe!
   Close on its wave soothes the wave behind,
   And again another behind embracing and lapping, every one close,
   But my love soothes not me, not me.

75 *Low hangs the moon, it rose late,*
   It is lagging—O I think it is heavy with love, with love.

   O madly the sea pushes upon the land,
   With love, with love.

   O night! do I not see my love fluttering out among the breakers?
80 *What is that little black thing I see there in the white?*

   Loud! loud! loud!
   Loud I call to you, my love!
   High and clear I shoot my voice over the waves,
   Surely you must know who is here, is here,
85 *You must know who I am, my love.*

   Low-hanging moon!
   What is that dusky spot in your brown yellow?
   O it is the shape, the shape of my mate!
   O moon do not keep her from me any longer.

90 *Land! land! O land!*
   Whichever way I turn, O I think you could give me my mate back again if you
      only would,
   For I am almost sure I see her dimly whichever way I look.

   O rising stars!
   Perhaps the one I want so much will rise, will rise with some of you.

95 *O throat! O trembling throat!*
   Sound clearer through the atmosphere!

Pierce the woods, the earth,
Somewhere listening to catch you must be the one I want.

Shake out carols!
100 *Solitary here, the night's carols!*
Carols of lonesome love! death's carols!
Carols under that lagging, yellow, waning moon!
O under that moon where she droops down into the sea!
O reckless despairing carols.

105 *But soft! sink low!*
Soft! let me just murmur,
And do you wait a moment you husky-nois'd sea,
For somewhere I believe I heard my mate responding to me,
So faint, I must be still, be still to listen,
110 *But not altogether still, for then she might not come immediately to me.*

Hither my love!
Here I am! here!
With this just-sustain'd note I announce myself to you,
This gentle call is for you my love, for you.

115 *Do not be decoy'd elsewhere,*
That is the whistle of the wind, it is not my voice,
That is the fluttering, the fluttering of the spray,
Those are the shadows of leaves.

O darkness! O in vain!
120 *O I am very sick and sorrowful.*

O brown halo in the sky near the moon, drooping upon the sea!
O troubled reflection in the sea!

O throat! O throbbing heart!
And I singing uselessly, uselessly all the night.

125 *O past! O happy life! O songs of joy!*
In the air, in the woods, over fields,
Loved! loved! loved! loved! loved!
But my mate no more, no more with me!
We two together no more.

130 The aria[2] sinking,
All else continuing, the stars shining,
The winds blowing, the notes of the bird continuous echoing,
With angry moans the fierce old mother incessantly moaning,
On the sands of Paumanok's shore gray and rustling,
135 The yellow half-moon enlarged, sagging down, drooping, the face of the
    sea almost touching
The boy ecstatic, with his bare feet the waves, with his hair the atmosphere
    dallying,

---

[2] A song performed by a single voice in opera.

The love in the heart long pent, now loose, now at last tumultuously
    bursting,
The aria's meaning, the ears, the soul, swiftly depositing,
The strange tears down the cheeks coursing,
140 The colloquy there, the trio, each uttering,
The undertone, the savage old mother incessantly crying,
To the boy's soul's questions sullenly timing, some drown'd secret hissing,
To the outsetting bard.[3]

Demon or bird! (said the boy's soul,)
145 Is it indeed toward your mate you sing? or is it really to me?
For I, that was a child, my tongue's use sleeping, now I have heard you,
Now in a moment I know what I am for, I awake,
And already a thousand singers, a thousand songs, clearer, louder and
    more sorrowful than yours,
A thousand warbling echoes have started to live within me, never to die.

150 O you singer solitary, singing by yourself, projecting me,
O solitary me listening, never more shall I cease perpetuating you,
Never more shall I escape, never more the reverberations,
Never more the cries of unsatisfied love be absent from me,
Never again leave me to be the peaceful child I was before what there in the
    night,
155 By the sea under the yellow and sagging moon,
The messenger there arous'd, the fire, the sweet hell within,
The unknown want, the destiny of me.

O give me the clew! (it lurks in the night here somewhere,)
O if I am to have so much, let me have more!

160 A word then, (for I will conquer it,)
The word final, superior to all,
Subtle, sent up—what is it?—I listen;
Are you whispering it, and have been all the time, you sea waves?
Is that it from your liquid rims and wet sands?

165 Whereto answering, the sea,
Delaying not, hurrying not,
Whisper'd me through the night, and very plainly before daybreak,
Lisp'd to me the low and delicious word death,
And again death, death, death, death,
Hissing melodious, neither like the bird nor like my arous'd child's heart,
170 But edging near as privately for me rustling at my feet,
Creeping thence steadily up to my ears and laving me softly all over,
Death, death, death, death, death.

Which I do not forget,
175 But fuse the song of my dusky demon and brother,
That he sang to me in the moonlight on Paumanok's gray beach,
With the thousand responsive songs at random,

---

[3] A poet

My own songs awaked from that hour,
And with them the key, the word up from the waves,
180 The word of the sweetest song and all songs,
The strong and delicious word which, creeping to my feet,
(Or like some old crone rocking the cradle, swathed in sweet garments,
    bending aside,)
The sea whisper'd me.

■ EXPLORATIONS OF THE TEXT

1. About what does the speaker reminisce? What is the speaker's motivation for this "reminiscence" song?
2. What is the mood of the prologue?
3. What is the message of the he-bird's lament? Is the personification effective?
4. What does the boy learn of life through the "reminiscence" song? What does the adult speaker learn?
5. Explore the connections of birth, love, and death expressed in this poem.
6. Whitman is known for his organic free verse (poetry that has music, form, and rhythm, but not a standard metric or rhythmic pattern); see the Glossary and chapter 10. How does Whitman's free verse work in this poem?
7. How does Whitman make use of musical form?

■ THE READING/WRITING CONNECTION

1. Choose one line from the poem, and in a journal entry respond to the line.
2. Freewrite about one of the following symbols: star, bird, or sea.
3. Study the he-bird's song. Create a free verse monologue spoken by a bird or other creature. In a concrete manner, convey an abstract idea, such as loss, betrayal, death, or love.

■ IDEAS FOR WRITING

1. Analyze the persona. (See lines 1–21 and 130–182.)
2. What do the repeated symbols of the star, bird, and sea suggest?

GARY SOTO

Gary Soto (1952–), born in Fresno, California, won the Before Columbus Foundation 1985 American Book Award for his volume of autobiographical essays, Living Up the Street *(1984). His volumes of poetry include* The Element of San Joaquin *(1977),* The Tale of Sunlight *(1978),* Black Hair *(1985), and* Shadow of the Plum: Poems *(2002). He has edited* Pieces of the Heart: New Chicano Fiction *(1993). Soto teaches Chicano Studies and English at the University of California at Berkeley. Among other honors, he has received a Guggenheim Fellowship and the Academy of American Poets Award. Soto now serves as Young People's Ambassador for the California Rural Legal Assistance (CRLA) and the United Farm Workers of America (UFW).*

1985

BLACK HAIR

At eight I was brilliant with my body.
In July, that ring of heat
We all jumped through, I sat in the bleachers

Of Romain Playground, in the lengthening
5 Shade that rose from our dirty feet.
The game before us was more than baseball.
It was a figure—Hector Moreno
Quick and hard with turned muscles,
His crouch the one I assumed before an altar
10 Of worn baseball cards, in my room.

I came here because I was Mexican, a stick
Of brown light in love with those
Who could do it—the triple and hard slide,
The gloves eating balls into double plays.
15 What could I do with 50 pounds, my shyness,
My black torch of hair, about to go out?
Father was dead, his face no longer
Hanging over the table or our sleep,
And mother was the terror of mouths
20 Twisting hurt by butter knives.

In the bleachers I was brilliant with my body,
Waving players in and stomping my feet,
I chewed sunflower seeds. I drank water
And bit my arm through the late innings.
25 When Hector lined balls into deep
Center, in my mind I rounded the bases
With him, my face flared, my hair lifting
Beautifully, because we were coming home
To the arms of brown people.

■ EXPLORATIONS OF THE TEXT

1. What is the speaker's view of Hector Moreno? What does Hector Moreno represent?
2. How are the speaker's attitudes toward being Mexican and toward baseball intertwined?
3. What is the nature of the narrator's relationship with his father and his mother?
4. What is the significance of the image of "black hair"?
5. Contrast the speaker's position in this poem with the experience of the teenagers in "Indian Boarding School: The Runaways."

■ THE READING/WRITING CONNECTION

1. Why are sports important to teenagers? Respond to this question in a journal entry.
2. "Think" Topic: What ways have ethnic groups found to break cultural barriers in the United States? How has North American culture changed as a result?

■ IDEAS FOR WRITING

1. Write about the possible meanings and connotations of the word *brilliant* in "Black Hair."
2. Hector Moreno is the speaker's hero. Write about a hero in your own life.

GARY SOTO

1985

ORANGES

The first time I walked
With a girl, I was twelve,
Cold, and weighted down
With two oranges in my jacket.
5 December. Frost cracking
Beneath my steps, my breath
Before me, then gone,
As I walked toward
Her house, the one whose
10 Porch light burned yellow
Night and day, in any weather.
A dog barked at me, until
She came out pulling
At her gloves, face bright
15 With rouge. I smiled,
Touched her shoulder, and led
Her down the street, across
A used car lot and a line
Of newly planted trees,
20 Until we were breathing
Before a drugstore. We
Entered, the tiny bell
Bringing a saleslady
Down a narrow aisle of goods.
25 I turned to the candies
Tiered like bleachers,
And asked what she wanted—
Light in her eyes, a smile
Starting at the corners
30 Of her mouth. I fingered
A nickel in my pocket,
And when she lifted a chocolate
That cost a dime,
I didn't say anything.
35 I took the nickel from
My pocket, then an orange,
And set them quietly on
The counter. When I looked up,
The lady's eyes met mine,
40 And held them, knowing
Very well what it was all
About.

Outside,
A few cars hissing past,
45 Fog hanging like old
Coats between the trees.
I took my girl's hand
In mine for two blocks,
Then released it to let
50 Her unwrap the chocolate.
I peeled my orange
That was so bright against
The gray of December
That, from some distance,
55 Someone might have thought
I was making a fire in my hands.

■ **EXPLORATIONS OF THE TEXT**
1. Discuss the significance of the purchase at the drugstore.
2. Explore the symbolism of peeling the paper from the chocolate, peeling the orange, and the last line. What do these images suggest?
3. Examine the images associated with weather. How does the time of year enhance the mood of the poem?

■ **THE READING/WRITING CONNECTION**
1. In a journal entry, write about your first date.
2. Write a monologue in the voice of the young girl.
3. "Think" Topic: How does the outside world, the environment, influence the speaker's experience? Are there clues in the poem?

■ **IDEAS FOR WRITING**
1. What do the last two lines of the poem mean? Do they present a satisfying conclusion?
2. Compare the state of mind of the speaker with that of Audre Lorde's adolescent girl in "Hanging Fire."

Louise Glück

Louise Glück (1943–) was born in New York City and raised on Long Island. Glück studied at Columbia University with the poet Stanley Kunitz. Since her first book of poetry, Firstborn, *was printed in 1968, Glück has published nine books of poetry and two books of essays, and she has received many awards for her writing, including the Pulitzer Prize for her book of poetry,* The Wild Iris *(1992). In 1999 she was named a chancellor of the Academy of American Poets. Glück's poems reflect the conflicting emotions that accompany people from childhood through adulthood regarding their bodies, sexuality, and families.*

2001

SUMMER AT THE BEACH

Before we started camp, we went to the beach.

Long days, before the sun was dangerous.
My sister lay on her stomach, reading mysteries.
I sat in the sand, watching the water.

5   You could use the sand to cover
parts of your body that you didn't like.
I covered my feet, to make my legs longer;
the sand climbed over my ankles.

I looked down at my body, away from the water.
10 I was what the magazines told me to be:
coltish. I was a frozen colt.

My sister didn't bother with these adjustments.
When I told her to cover her feet, she tried a few times,
but she got bored; she didn't have enough willpower
15 to sustain a deception.

I watched the sea; I listened to the other families.
Babies everywhere: what went on in their heads?
I couldn't imagine myself as a baby;
I couldn't picture myself not thinking.

20 I couldn't imagine myself as an adult either.
They all had terrible bodies: lax, oily, completely
committed to being male and female.

The days were all the same.
When it rained, we stayed home.
25 When the sun shone, we went to the beach with my mother.
My sister lay on her stomach, reading her mysteries.
I sat with my legs arranged to resemble
what I saw in my head, what I believed was my true self.

Because is *was* true: when I didn't move I was perfect.

■ EXPLORATIONS OF THE TEXT

1. Characterize the persona's voice. How does she see herself in contrast to her sister? Analyze the imagery used to describe the two sisters. How do the sisters differ in regard to their sense of themselves?
2. Why is the word "before" important?
3. Discuss the significance of the closing three lines.
4. Compare and contrast the persona's view of her body with that of the speaker in Soto's "Black Hair," Dove's "Adolescence I, II, III," and Lorde's "Hanging Fire."

■ THE READING/WRITING CONNECTION

1. "Think" Topic: The "sister lay on her stomach, reading mysteries." Why does Glück change the repeated line from "reading mysteries" to "reading her mysteries"? What is the "myste[ry]" in the poem?
2. Freewrite about the symbolism of the sea in the poem.
3. Freewrite about a vacation with family.

■ IDEAS FOR WRITING

1. Analyze the theme of the adolescent's relation to his or her body, to sexuality, and/or to self-image in this work, in Soto's "Oranges," Lorde's "Hanging Fire," and Shihab Nye's "Biography of an Armenian Schoolgirl."
2. Freewrite about your memories of early adolescence: your self-doubts, fears, and insecurities. Then compare your own adolescent struggles with Glück's persona.

3. Compare the sibling relationship in this work with that of Connie and June in "Where Are You Going, Where Have You Been?" or Georgeann or Mary-Etta in "Rose-Johnny."

RITA DOVE

Rita Dove (1952–) was born in Akron, Ohio. She began teaching at Arizona State University and is currently a professor at the University of Virginia. In 1987, she was awarded the Pulitzer Prize for poetry for Thomas and Beulah, *poems based loosely on the lives of Dove's maternal grandparents. In 1993, her* Selected Poems *was published, and she was appointed Poet Laureate of the United States, not only the first African American, but also the youngest person ever to receive this honor. Dove's book* On the Bus with Rosa Parks: Poems *(1999) won a National Book Critics Circle Award nomination (2000).*

1980

ADOLESCENCE—I
ADOLESCENCE—II
ADOLESCENCE—III

Adolescence—I

In water-heavy nights behind grandmother's porch
We knelt in the tickling grasses and whispered:
Linda's face hung before us, pale as a pecan,
And it grew wise as she said:
5   "A boy's lips are soft,
   As soft as baby's skin."
The air closed over her words.
A firefly whirred near my ear, and in the distance
I could hear streetlamps ping
10 Into miniature suns
Against a feathery sky.

Adolescence—II

Although it is night, I sit in the bathroom, waiting.
Sweat prickles behind my knees, the baby-breasts are alert.
Venetian blinds slice up the moon; the tiles quiver in pale strips.

Then they come, the three seal men with eyes as round
5 As dinner plates and eyelashes like sharpened tines.
They bring the scent of licorice. One sits in the washbowl,

One on the bathtub edge; one leans against the door.
"Can you feel it yet?" they whisper.
I don't know what to say, again. They chuckle,

10 Patting their sleek bodies with their hands.
"Well, maybe next time." And they rise,
Glittering like pools of ink under moonlight,

And vanish. I clutch at the ragged holes
They leave behind, here at the edge of darkness.
15 Night rests like a ball of fur on my tongue.

Adolescence—III

With Dad gone, Mom and I worked
The dusky rows of tomatoes.
As they glowed orange in sunlight
And rotted in shadow, I too
5 Grew orange and softer, swelling out
Starched cotton slips.

The texture of twilight made me think of
Lengths of Dotted Swiss.[1] In my room
I wrapped scarred knees in dresses
10 That once went to big-band dances;
I baptized my earlobes with rosewater.
Along the window-sill, the lipstick stubs
Glittered in their steel shells.

Looking out at the rows of clay
15 And chicken manure, I dreamed how it would happen:
He would meet me by the blue spruce,
A carnation over his heart, saying,
"I have come for you, Madam;
I have loved you in my dreams."

20 At his touch, the scabs would fall away.
Over his shoulder, I see my father coming toward us:
He carries his tears in a bowl,
And blood hangs in the pine-soaked air.

■ EXPLORATIONS OF THE TEXT

I.

1. What is the focus of the girls' gatherings?
2. What are the mood and tone of the poem? What images create the mood and tone?
3. What is the meaning of the images of "suns," "firefly," and "feathers"?

II.

1. Who are the "seal men"? Explore their symbolic significance.
2. For what does she wait?
3. How does the mood change in this section?
4. Explain the line, "Night rests like a ball of fur on my tongue."

III.

1. What are the roles of the mother and the father?
2. Explore the symbolism of "tomatoes," "sunlight," and "twilight."

---

[1] A muslin material with raised dots.

3. What is the meaning of the closing lines concerning the father: "He carries his tears in a bowl" and "blood hangs in the pine-soaked air"? What are the consequences of sexual awakening?

■ THE READING/WRITING CONNECTION

1. "Think" Topic: How do the views of female sexuality change in these three poems?

■ IDEAS FOR WRITING

1. Characterize the stages of adolescence in the three poems.
2. Compare Dove's view of coming of age as a female with Soto's view of coming in age in "Oranges" and in "Black Hair."

AUDRE LORDE

Audre Lorde (1934–92) was born in New York City of West Indian parents. She attended National University of Mexico, Hunter College, and Columbia University, where she received her M.L.S. She subsequently worked as a librarian and taught school, and she spent a year at Tougaloo College, Mississippi, as poet-in-residence. Lorde taught writing and English at several colleges before becoming professor of English at Hunter College in 1980. Her volumes of poetry include Cables to Rage *(1970),* Coal *(1976), and* The Black Unicorn *(1978). She also wrote an account of her courageous struggle with breast cancer and mastectomy,* The Cancer Journals *(1980), and a prose autobiography,* Zami: A New Spelling of My Name *(1982).*

1978

HANGING FIRE

I am fourteen
and my skin has betrayed me
the boy I cannot live without
still sucks his thumb
5   in secret
how come my knees are
always so ashy
what if I die
before morning
10 and momma's in the bedroom
with the door closed.

I have to learn how to dance
in time for the next party
my room is too small for me
15 suppose I die before graduation
they will sing sad melodies
but finally
tell the truth about me
There is nothing I want to do
20 and too much
that has to be done
and momma's in the bedroom
with the door closed.

                    Nobody even stops to think
          25   about my side of it
                    I should have been on Math Team
                    my marks were better than his
                    why do I have to be
                    the one
          30   wearing braces
                    I have nothing to wear tomorrow
                    will I live long enough
                    to grow up
                    and momma's in the bedroom
          35   with the door closed.

■ EXPLORATIONS OF THE TEXT
1. Characterize the voice and the tone of the speaker.
2. Discuss the speaker's conflict. What is her view of her body?
3. What is "momma's" role in her life?
4. Discuss the impact of the repetition in the poem.
5. What does the poem reveal about being "fourteen"? Explore the meaning of the title.
6. Compare and contrast this persona's sense of herself with Glück's speaker in "Summer at the Beach."

■ THE READING/WRITING CONNECTION
1. Freewrite about being an adolescent.
2. "Think" Topic: Does the poem present a realistic portrait of early adolescence?

■ IDEAS FOR WRITING
1. Compare the vision of adolescence in this work with those in "Oranges," "Black Hair," and "Adolescence I, II, III."
2. How can parents help adolescents negotiate this difficult stage of life? Write a letter to the mother in this poem.

NIKKI GIOVANNI

Nikki Giovanni (1943–   ), born and educated in Tennessee, has taught creative writing at Rutgers University and other colleges. Currently, she teaches at Virginia Polytechnic University. A prolific poet, her volumes of poetry include Ego Tripping and Other Poems *(1973),* Cotton Candy on a Rainy Day *(1978),* Spin a Soft Black Song *(1985),* Sacred Cows and Other Edibles *(1988),* Blues: For All the Changes: New Poems *(1999), and* Quilting the Black-Eyed Pea: Poems and Not Quite Poems *(2002). Since college Giovanni has been actively involved in the African-American struggle for equality, and in 2002 she was presented with the first Rosa Parks Woman of Courage Award.*

1973

EGO TRIPPING

(there may be a reason why)

          I was born in the congo

I walked to the fertile crescent and built
   the sphinx[1]
I designed a pyramid so tough that a star
5   that only glows every one hundred years falls
   into the center giving divine perfect light
I am bad

I sat on the throne
   drinking nectar with allah[2]
10 I got hot and sent an ice age to europe
   to cool my thirst
My oldest daughter is nefertiti[3]
   the tears from my birth pains
   created the nile[4]
15 I am a beautiful woman

I gazed on the forest and burned
   out the sahara desert
   with a packet of goat's meat
   and a change of clothes
20 I crossed it in two hours
I am a gazelle so swift
   so swift you can't catch me

For a birthday present when he was three
I gave my son hannibal[5] an elephant
25   He gave me rome for mother's day
My strength flows ever on
My son noah built new/ark and
I stood proudly at the helm
   as we sailed on a soft summer day
30 I turned myself into myself and was
   jesus
   men intone my loving name

All praises All praises
I am the one who would save

35 I sowed diamonds in my back yard
My bowels deliver uranium
   the filings from my fingernails are
   semi-precious jewels
   On a trip north
40 I caught a cold and blew
My nose giving oil to the arab world

---

[1] A mythical creature with the head of a human or animal, the body of a lion, and the wings of an eagle. One of the famous monuments in ancient Egypt, near the pyramids. In Greek mythology, the Sphinx proposed a riddle to Oedipus; and when he answered it, she killed herself.

[2] In Islam, the name of God; Supreme Being.

[3] An Egyptian queen (fourteenth century B.C.), known for her beauty.

[4] Longest river in Africa, flowing north from Lake Victoria to the Mediterranean.

[5] A Carthaginian general who crossed the Mediterranean and the Alps and attacked Italy. Carthage—a country in North Africa.

I am so hip even my errors are correct
I sailed west to reach east and had to round off
    the earth as I went
45 The hair from my head thinned and gold was laid
    across three continents

I am so perfect so divine so ethereal so surreal
I cannot be comprehended
    except by my permission

50 I mean . . . I . . . can fly
    like a bird in the sky . . .

■ EXPLORATIONS OF THE TEXT

1. What is the speaker's view of herself? What character traits does she attribute to herself?
2. How is the title a clue to the meaning of the poem? In what ways does the poem extend its themes beyond the ego?
3. How does the poet use such devices from oral tradition as exaggeration and **anaphora** (repetition) to create an impact?
4. How does humor contribute to the poem's effect?
5. Identify the historical and anthropological references in the poem. How do these allusions enrich this work?
6. Contrast the speaker's sense of self with the persona's identity in "Suicide Note."

■ THE READING/WRITING CONNECTION

1. Do a double-entry for a section of the poem as preparation for one of the assigned ideas for writing.
2. "Think" Topic: What are the advantages and disadvantages of **hyperbole** (exaggeration)? Use details from this poem to support your position.

■ IDEAS FOR WRITING

1. Analyze the voice and tone of the speaker.
2. Write a short essay that explicates one of the allusions in the poem.

ANNE SEXTON

Anne Sexton (1928–74) was born in Newton, Massachusetts. She attended Garland Junior College in Massachusetts and taught high school and college. After suffering one of many nervous breakdowns, Sexton was urged by a psychiatrist to try writing poetry. She did so with immediate success: the poet Robert Lowell was one of her mentors. She published her first book of poems, To Bedlam and Part Way Back, *in 1960. In 1967, she won the Pulitzer Prize for Poetry for* Live or Die. *With Lowell, Sexton is associated with the Confessional school of poetry, drawing on intensely personal subject matter for her poems. She committed suicide in 1974. Sexton's* Complete Poems *were published in 1981.*

1971

CINDERELLA

You always read about it:
the plumber with twelve children
who wins the Irish Sweepstakes.
From toilets to riches.
5 That story.

Or the nursemaid,
some luscious sweet from Denmark
who captures the oldest son's heart.
From diapers to Dior.
10 That story.

Or a milkman who serves the wealthy,
eggs, cream, butter, yogurt, milk,
the white truck like an ambulance
who goes into real estate
15 and makes a pile.
From homogenized to martinis at lunch.

Or the charwoman
who is on the bus when it cracks up
and collects enough from the insurance.
20 From mops to Bonwit Teller.[1]
That story.

Once
the wife of a rich man was on her deathbed
and she said to her daughter Cinderella:
25 Be devout. Be good. Then I will smile
down from heaven in the seam of a cloud.
The man took another wife who had
two daughters, pretty enough
but with hearts like blackjacks.
30 Cinderella was their maid.
She slept on the sooty hearth each night
and walked around looking like Al Jolson.
Her father brought presents home from town,
jewels and gowns for the other women
35 but the twig of a tree for Cinderella.
She planted that twig on her mother's grave
and it grew to a tree where a white dove sat.
Whenever she wished for anything the dove
would drop it like an egg upon the ground.
40 The bird is important, my dears, so heed him.

Next came the ball, as you all know.
It was a marriage market.
The prince was looking for a wife.
All but Cinderella were preparing
45 and gussying up for the big event.
Cinderella begged to go too.
Her stepmother threw a dish of lentils
into the cinders and said: Pick them
up in an hour and you shall go.

---

[1] An exclusive department store in New York City.

50 The white dove brought all his friends;
   all the warm wings of the fatherland came,
   and picked up the lentils in a jiffy.
   No, Cinderella, said the stepmother,
   you have no clothes and cannot dance.
55 That's the way with stepmothers.

   Cinderella went to the tree at the grave
   and cried forth like a gospel singer:
   Mama! Mama! My turtledove,
   send me to the prince's ball!
60 The bird dropped down a golden dress
   and delicate little gold slippers.
   Rather a large package for a simple bird.
   So she went. Which is no surprise.
   Her stepmother and sisters didn't
65 recognize her without her cinder face
   and the prince took her hand on the spot
   and danced with no other the whole day.

   As nightfall came she thought she'd better
   get home. The prince walked her home
70 and she disappeared into the pigeon house
   and although the prince took an axe and broke
   it open she was gone. Back to her cinders.
   These events repeated themselves for three days.
   However on the third day the prince
75 covered the palace steps with cobbler's wax
   and Cinderella's gold shoe stuck upon it.
   Now he would find whom the shoe fit
   and find his strange dancing girl for keeps.
   He went to their house and the two sisters
80 were delighted because they had lovely feet.
   The eldest went into a room to try the slipper on
   but her big toe got in the way so she simply
   sliced it off and put on the slipper.
   The prince rode away with her until the white dove
85 told him to look at the blood pouring forth.
   That is the way with amputations.
   They don't just heal up like a wish.
   The other sister cut off her heel
   but the blood told as blood will.
90 The prince was getting tired.
   He began to feel like a shoe salesman.
   But he gave it one last try.
   This time Cinderella fit into the shoe
   like a love letter into its envelope.

95 At the wedding ceremony
   the two sisters came to curry favor
   and the white dove pecked their eyes out.

Two hollow spots were left
like soup spoons.

100 Cinderella and the prince
lived, they say, happily ever after,
like two dolls in a museum case
never bothered by diapers or dust,
never arguing over the timing of an egg,
105 never telling the same story twice,
never getting a middle-aged spread,
their darling smiles pasted on for eternity.
Regular Bobbsey Twins.[2]
That story.

■ EXPLORATIONS OF THE TEXT

1. Characterize the speaker's point of view and tone. List the particular words that convey tone. What is their impact?
2. Why does Sexton introduce the Cinderella story with the "toilet to riches" stories in the first four stanzas? What purpose do they serve? Why does she repeat "that story"?
3. Research Perrault's "Cinderella." How does Sexton change the story through her use of figurative language and imagery? Contrast the original text with Sexton's imaginative rendering of the tale.
4. Analyze the closing stanza's commentary on the "rags to riches" theme. Discuss Sexton's use of irony.
5. Compare and contrast Hecht's treatment of fairy tale motifs with Sexton's treatment.

■ THE READING/WRITING CONNECTION

1. Do a double-entry notebook for one section of the poem. What is the impact of the imagery, figurative language, form, and diction?
2. This poem is drawn from Sexton's poetry volume, *Transformations,* which contains her imaginative retellings of many other fairy tales. You may consult that volume as inspiration. Using Sexton's work as a model, create your own retelling of a fairy tale or a children's story with which you are familiar.

■ IDEAS FOR WRITING

1. How do the writers in the fairy tale cluster in this chapter depict the mythic battle between good and evil?
2. Compare Sexton's treatment of romance with a selected poem about love in chapter 6.

ANTHONY HECHT

Anthony Hecht (1923–2004) was born in New York City and was educated at Bard College and Columbia University. His publications consist of twenty-five books of poetry, lectures, essays, and translations for which he has won numerous awards, including the Pulitzer Prize in

---

[2] Twins in a series of children's books published in the 1950s.

poetry for The Hard Hours *(1968) and, most recently, the Los Angeles Times Book Award (2003) for* Collected Later Poems. *In addition to his many fellowships and awards, Hecht has been granted five honorary doctorates. "It Out-Herods Herod. Pray You, Avoid It"[1] is from Hecht's collection* The Hard Hours *(1968). A member of the New School of Formalism, Hecht artfully illustrates in his poems the balance between life's beauty and darkness.*

1968

IT OUT-HEROD'S HEROD. PRAY YOU, AVOID IT.

Tonight my children hunch
Toward their Western, and are glad
As, with a Sunday punch,
The Good casts out the Bad.

5 And in their fairy tales
The warty giant and witch
Get sealed in doorless jails
And the match-girl strikes it rich.

I've made myself a drink.
10 The giant and witch are set
To bust out of the clink
When my children have gone to bed.

All frequencies are loud
With signals of despair;
15 In flash and morse[2] they crowd
The rondure[3] of the air.

For the wicked have grown strong,
Their numbers mock at death,
Their cow brings forth its young,
20 Their bull engendereth.

Their very fund of strength,
Satan, bestrides the globe;
He stalks its breadth and length
And finds out even Job.

25 Yet by quite other laws
My children make their case;
Half God, half Santa Claus,
But with my voice and face,

---

[1] The title refers to *Hamlet,* Act III, scene ii, lines 1–20, Hamlet's speech about the players.
[2] Bit.
[3] Circle.

A hero comes to save
30 The poorman, beggarman, thief,
And make the world behave
And put an end to grief.

And that their sleep be sound
I say this childermas
35 Who could not, at one time,
Have saved them from the gas.

■ **EXPLORATIONS OF THE TEXT**

1. Analyze the speaker's point of view. Does he believe in a "fairy tale" world? Isolate specific words that create the speaker's tone, and discuss their impact.
2. Contrast the speaker's attitude toward good and evil with that of his children. How does he view his parental role?
3. How do the stanzaic form, rhythm, and rhyme develop the themes of the poem?
4. The poem is not only about the battle between good and evil but also about constructing narratives, stories about our world. How do the narratives that he composes for his children compare with the reality of the world?

■ **THE READING/WRITING CONNECTION**

1. Debate Topic: Are parents powerless to protect their children? Present your views on this issue.
2. Freewrite: What fairy tales, children stories, or animated films were your favorites? Why were they important to you?

■ **IDEAS FOR WRITING**

1. Compare Hecht's treatment of fairy tale motifs with Sexton's in "Cinderella" and/or Gordimer's in "Once Upon a Time." How do the writers use irony to develop their themes?
2. Hecht uses several allusions in the poem, particularly the reference to *Hamlet,* to develop the theme of the work. Research one allusion, and then comment on its significance in the work.

Poems for Comparison/Contrast: Transitions

JUDITH ORTIZ COFER (1952–)   **1993**

LATIN WOMEN PRAY

Latin women pray
In incense sweet churches
They pray in Spanish
To an Anglo God
5 With a Jewish heritage.
And this Great White Father
Imperturbable
In his marble pedestal

Looks down upon
10 His brown daughters
Votive candles shining like lust
In his all seeing eyes
Unmoved
By their persistent prayers.
15 Yet year after year
Before his image they kneel
Margarita Josefina Maria and Isabel
All fervently hoping
That if not omnipotent
20 At least He be bilingual.

CATHY SONG (1955–   )   1983

LOST SISTER

1

In China,
even the peasants
named their first daughters
Jade—
5 the stone that in the far fields
could moisten the dry season,
could make men move mountains
for the healing green of the inner hills
glistening like slices of winter melon.

10 And the daughters were grateful:
They never left home.
To move freely was a luxury
stolen from them at birth.
Instead, they gathered patience,
15 learning to walk in shoes
the size of teacups,
without breaking—
the arc of their movements
as dormant as the rooted willow,
20 as redundant as the farmyard hens.
But they traveled far
in surviving,
learning to stretch the family rice,
to quiet the demons,
25 the noisy stomachs.

2

There is a sister
across the ocean,
who relinquished her name,
diluting jade green

30 with the blue of the Pacific.
Rising with a tide of locusts,
she swarmed with others
to inundate another shore.
In America,
35 there are many roads
and women can stride along with men.

But in another wilderness,
the possibilities,
the loneliness,
40 can strangulate like jungle vines.
The meager provisions and sentiments
of once belonging—
fermented roots, Mah-Jong[1] tiles and firecrackers—set but
a flimsy household
45 in a forest of nightless cities.
A giant snake rattles above,
spewing black clouds into your kitchen.
Dough-faced landlords
slip in and out of your keyholes,
50 making claims you don't understand,
tapping into your communication systems
of laundry lines and restaurant chains.

You find you need China:
your one fragile identification,
55 a jade link
handcuffed to your wrist.
You remember your mother
who walked for centuries,
footless—
60 and like her,
you have left no footprints,
but only because
there is an ocean in between,
the unremitting space of your rebellion.

Naomi Shihab Nye (1952–   )   **1993**

BIOGRAPHY OF AN ARMENIAN SCHOOLGIRL

I have lived in the room of stone
where voices become bones
buried under us long ago.
You could dig for years
uncovering the same sweet dust.   5

---

[1] Chinese game, similar to dominoes.

My hands dream crescent-shaped cakes,
trapped moons on a narrow veined earth.
All day I am studying my hands—giving them
   new things to hold.

Travel, I say. They become boats.   10
Go—the bird squirms to detach from the arm.
Across the courtyards, a radio rises up and explodes.

What is the history of Europe to us if we cannot
   choose our own husbands?
Yesterday my father met with the widower,   15
   the man with no hair.
How will I sleep with him, I who have never slept
   away from my mother?

Once I bought bread from the vendor with the
   humped back.   20
I carried it home singing,
the days had doors in them
that would swing open in front of me.

Now I copy the alphabets of three languages,
imagining the loops in my Arabic letters are eyes.   25
What you do when you are tired of what you see,

what happens to the gray body
when it is laid in the earth,
these are the subjects which concern me.
But they teach algebra.   30
They pull our hair back and examine our nails.

Every afternoon, predictable passage of sun
   across a wall.
I would fly out of here. Travel, I say.
I would go so far away my life would be   35
   a small thing behind me.

They teach physics, chemistry.
I throw my book out the window,
watch the pages scatter like wings.
I stitch the professor's[1] jacket   40
to the back of his chair.

There is something else we were born for.
I almost remember it. While I write,
a ghost writes on the same tablet,
achieves a different sum.   45

---

[1] A high school teacher.

LOUISE ERDRICH (1954–)   **1984**

INDIAN BOARDING SCHOOL: THE RUNAWAYS

Home's the place we head for in our sleep.
Boxcars stumbling north in dreams
don't wait for us. We catch them on the run.
The rails, old lacerations that we love,
5 shoot parallel across the face and break
just under Turtle Mountains.[1] Riding scars
you can't get lost. Home is the place they cross.

The lame guard strikes a match and makes the dark
less tolerant. We watch through cracks in boards
10 as the land starts rolling, rolling till it hurts
to be here, cold in regulation clothes.
We know the sheriff's waiting at midrun
to take us back. His car is dumb and warm.
The highway doesn't rock, it only hums
15 like a wing of long insults. The worn-down welts
of ancient punishments lead back and forth.
All runaways wear dresses, long green ones,
the color you would think shame was. We scrub
the sidewalks down because it's shameful work.
20 Our brushes cut the stone in watered arcs
and in the soak frail outlines shiver clear
a moment, things us kids pressed on the dark
face before it hardened, place, remembering
delicate old injuries, the spines of names and leaves.

JANICE MIRIKITANI (1942–)   **1983**

SUICIDE NOTE

. . An Asian American college student was reported to have jumped to her death from her dormitory window. Her body was found two days later under a deep cover of snow. Her suicide note contained an apology to her parents for having received less than a perfect four point grade average . . .

How many notes written . . .
ink smeared like birdprints in snow.

not good enough   not pretty enough   not smart enough
dear mother and father.

---

[1] The location of a Chippewa Indian reservation in North Dakota

5 I apologize
   for disappointing you.
   I've worked very hard,
                   not good enough
   harder, perhaps to please you.
10 If only I were a son, shoulders broad
   as the sunset threading through pine,
   I would see the light in my mother's
   eyes, or the golden pride reflected
   in my father's dream
15 of my wide, male hands worthy of work
   and comfort.
   I would swagger through life
   muscled and bold and assured,
   drawing praises to me
20 like currents in the bed of wind, virile
   with confidence.
       not good enough   not strong enough   not good enough

   I apologize.
   Tasks do not come easily.
25 Each failure, a glacier.
   Each disapproval, a bootprint.
   Each disappointment,
   ice above my river.
   So I have worked hard.
30   not good enough
   My sacrifice I will drop
   bone by bone, perched
   on the ledge of my womanhood,
   fragile as wings.
35   not strong enough
   It is snowing steadily
   surely not good weather
   for flying—this sparrow
   sillied and dizzied by the wind
40 on the edge.
                   not smart enough
   I make this ledge my altar
   to offer penance.
   This air will not hold me,
45 The snow burdens my crippled wings,
   my tears drop like bitter cloth
   softly into the gutter below.
       not good enough   not strong enough   not smart enough
                   Choices thin as shaved
50   ice. Notes shredded
                   drift like snow
   on my broken body,

covers me like whispers
of sorries
55 sorries.
Perhaps when they find me
they will bury
my bird bones beneath
a sturdy pine
60 and scatter my feathers like
unspoken song
over this white and cold and silent
breast of earth.

Poems for Comparison/Contrast: Metamorphoses

JOHN MILTON (1608–1674)   **1655**

WHEN I CONSIDER HOW MY LIGHT IS SPENT

When I consider how my light is spent
        Ere half my days, in this dark world and wide,
        And that one talent which is death to hide[1]
        Lodged with me useless, though my soul more bent
5 To serve therewith my Maker, and present
        My true account, lest he returning chide;
        "Doth God exact day-labor, light denied?"
        I fondly[2] ask; but Patience to prevent[3]
That murmur, soon replies, "God doth not need
10   Either man's work or his own gifts; who best
        Bear his mild yoke, they serve him best. His state
Is kingly. Thousands at his bidding speed
        And post o'er land and ocean without rest:
        They also serve who only stand and wait."

---

[1] Reference to Christ's "Parable of the Talents" (Matthew 25:14ff) in which a servant is chastised for not using his talent (a monetary unit): an intended pun. Note also play on words in "use," meaning using or interest.

[2] Foolishly.

[3] To forestall.

WALT WHITMAN (1819–1892)   **1855**

THERE WAS A CHILD WENT FORTH

There was a child went forth every day,
And the first object he look'd upon, that object he became,
And that object became part of him for the day or a certain part of the day,
Or for many years or stretching cycles of years.
5   The early lilacs became part of this child,
And grass and white and red morning-glories, and white and red clover,
    and the song of the phoebe-bird,
And the Third-month lambs and the sow's pink-faint litter, and the mare's
    foal and the cow's calf,
And the noisy brood of the barnyard or by the mire of the pond-side,
And the fish suspending themselves so curiously below there, and the
    beautiful curious liquid,
10   And the water-plants with their graceful flat heads, all became part of him.
The field-sprouts of Fourth-month and Fifth-month became part of him,
Winter-grain sprouts and those of the light-yellow corn, and the esculent
    roots of the garden,
And the apple-trees cover'd with blossoms and the fruit afterward, and
    wood-berries, and the commonest weeds by the road,
And the old drunkard staggering home from the outhouse of the tavern
    whence he had lately risen,
15   And the schoolmistress that pass'd on her way to the school,
And the friendly boys that pass'd, and the quarrelsome boys,
And the tidy and fresh-cheek'd girls, and the barefoot negro boy and girl,
And all the changes of city and country wherever he went.

His own parents, he that had father'd him and she that had conceiv'd him
    in her womb and birth'd him,
20   They gave this child more of themselves than that,
They gave him afterward every day, they became part of him.

The mother at home quietly placing the dishes on the supper-table,
The mother with mild words, clean her cap and gown, a wholesome odor
    falling off her person and clothes as she walks by,
The father, strong, self-sufficient, manly, mean, anger'd, unjust,
25   The blow, the quick loud word, the tight bargain, the crafty lure,
The family usages, the language, the company, the furniture, the yearning
    and swelling heart,
Affection that will not be gainsay'd, the sense of what is real, the thought if
    after all it should prove unreal,
The doubts of day-time and the doubts of night-time, the curious whether and
    how,
Whether that which appears so is so, or is it all flashes and specks?
30   Men and women crowding fast in the streets, if they are not flashes and
    specks what are they?
The streets themselves and the façades of houses, and goods in the windows,

Vehicles, teams, the heavy-plank'd wharves, the huge crossing at the ferries,
The village on the highland seen from afar at sunset, the river between,
Shadows, aureola and mist, the light falling on roofs and gables of white or
    brown two miles off,
35 The schooner near by sleepily dropping down the tide, the little boat slack-
    tow'd astern,
The hurrying tumbling waves, quick-broken crests, slapping,
The strata of color'd clouds, the long bar of maroon-tint away solitary by
    itself, the spread of purity it lies motionless in,
The horizon's edge, the flying sea-crow, the fragrance of salt marsh and
    shore mud,
These became part of that child who went forth every day, and who now
    goes, and will always go forth every day.

EMILY DICKINSON (1830–1886)

c. 1863

MY LIFE HAD STOOD—

My Life had stood—a Loaded Gun—
In Corners—till a Day
The Owner passed—identified—
And carried Me away—

5 And now We roam in Sovereign Woods—
And now We hunt the Doe—
And every time I speak for Him—
The Mountains straight reply—

And do I smile, such cordial light
10 Upon the Valley glow—
It is as a Vesuvian[1] face
Had let its pleasure through—

And when at Night—Our good Day done—
I guard My Master's Head—
15 'Tis better than the Eider-Duck's
Deep Pillow[2]—to have shared—

To foe of His—I'm deadly foe—
None stir the second time—
On whom I lay a Yellow Eye—
20 Or an emphatic Thumb—

---

[1] Resembling Mount Vesuvius, a volcano in Italy.
[2] Eider down; referring to soft feathers from the female Eider-Duck.

Though I than He—may longer live
He longer must—than I—
For I have but the power to kill,
Without—the power to die—

Dylan Thomas (1914–1953)   **1946**

FERN HILL

Now as I was young and easy under the apple boughs
About the lilting house and happy as the grass was green,
    The night above the dingle[1] starry,
      Time let me hail and climb
5   Golden in the heydays of his eyes,
And honoured among wagons I was prince of the apple towns
And once below a time I lordly had the trees and leaves
      Trail with daisies and barley
    Down the rivers of the windfall light.

10 And as I was green and carefree, famous among the barns
About the happy yard and singing as the farm was home,
    In the sun that is young once only,
      Time let me play and be
    Golden in the mercy of his means,
15 And green and golden I was huntsman and herdsman, the calves
Sang to my horn, the foxes on the hills barked clear and cold,
      And the sabbath rang slowly
    In the pebbles of the holy streams.

All the sun long it was running, it was lovely, the hay
20 Fields high as the house, the tunes from the chimneys, it was air
    And playing, lovely and watery
      And fire green as grass.
    And nightly under the simple stars
As I rode to sleep the owls were bearing the farm away,
25 All the moon long I heard, blessed among stables, the night-jars[2]
      Flying with the ricks,[3] and the horses
      Flashing into the dark.

---

[1] A narrow valley or shady dell.
[2] Any old world goat-sucker (a nocturnal European bird).
[3] A pile of straw or hay.

And then to awake, and the farm, like a wanderer white
With the dew, come back, the cock on his shoulder: it was all
30   Shining, it was Adam and maiden,
        The sky gathered again
     And the sun grew round that very day.
So it must have been after the birth of the simple light
In the first, spinning place, the spellbound horses walking warm
35   Out of the whinnying green stable
        On to the fields of praise.

And honoured among foxes and pheasants by the gay house
Under the new made clouds and happy as the heart was long,
     In the sun born over and over,
40   I ran my heedless ways,
        My wishes raced through the house high hay
And nothing I cared, at my sky blue trades, that time allows
In all his tuneful turning so few and such morning songs
        Before the children green and golden
45   Follow him out of grace,

Nothing I cared, in the lamb white days, that time would take me
Up to the swallow thronged loft by the shadow of my hand,
     In the moon that is always rising,
        Nor that riding to sleep
50   I should hear him fly with the high fields
And wake to the farm forever fled from the childless land.
Oh as I was young and easy in the mercy of his means,
        Time held me green and dying
     Though I sang in my chains like the sea.

Judith Ortiz Cofer (1952–   )   **1993**

THE LESSON OF THE SUGARCANE

        My mother opened her eyes wide
        at the edge of the field
        ready for cutting
        "Take a deep breath,"
5   she whispered,
        "There is nothing as sweet:
        Nada más dulce."
            Overhearing,
        Father left the flat he was changing
10   in the road-warping sun,
        and grabbing my arm, broke my sprint
        toward a stalk:
        "Cane can choke a little girl: snakes hide
        where it grows over your head."

15 And he led us back to the crippled car
   where we sweated out our penitence,
   for having craved more sweetness
   than we were allowed,
   more sweetness than we could handle.

LISEL MUELLER (1924–   )   **1980**

NOT ONLY THE ESKIMOS

We have only one noun
but as many different kinds:

the grainy snow of the Puritans
and snow of soft, fat flakes,

5 guerrilla snow, which comes in the night
   and changes the world by morning,

rabbinical snow, a permanent skullcap
on the highest mountains,

snow that blows in like the Long Ranger,[1]
10 riding hard from out of the West,

surreal snow in the Dakotas,
when you can't find your house, your street,
though you are not in a dream
or a science-fiction movie,

15 snow that tastes good to the sun
   when it licks black tree limbs,
   leaving us only one white stripe,
   a replica of a skunk,

unbelievable snows:
20 the blizzard that strikes on the tenth of April,
   the false snow before Indian summer,
   the Big Snow on Mozart's birthday,
   when Chicago became the Elysian Fields[2]
   and strangers spoke to each other,

---

[1] Here in a television western from the 1950s.
[2] In classical myth, the abode of the blessed after death; a perfect state of happiness.

25 paper snow, cut and taped
to the inside of grade-school windows,

in an old tale, the snow
that covers a nest of strawberries,
small hearts, ripe and sweet,
30 the special snow that goes with Christmas,
whether it falls or not,

the Russian snow we remember
along with the warmth and smell of our furs,
though we have never traveled
35 to Russia or worn furs,

Villon's snows of yesteryear,[3]
lost with ladies gone out like matches,
the snow in Joyce's "The Dead,"
the silent, secret snow
40 in a story by Conrad Aiken,[4]
which is the snow of first love,

the snowfall between the child
and the spacewoman on TV,

snow as idea of whiteness,
45 as in *snowdrop, snow goose, snowball bush,*

the snow that puts stars in your hair,
and your hair, which has turned to snow,

the snow Elinor Wylie[5] walked in
in velvet shoes,

50 the snow before her footprints
and the snow after,

the snow in the back of our heads,
whiter than white, which has to do
with childhood again each year.

---

[3] French poet (1431–63).
[4] American writer (1889–1973).
[5] American poet and novelist (1885–1928).

Ha Jin (1956–)   1996

THE PAST

I have supposed my past is a part of myself.
As my shadow appears whenever I'm in the sun
the past cannot be thrown off and its weight
must be borne, or I will become another man.

5 But I saw someone wall his past into a garden
whose produce is always in fashion.
If you enter his property without permission
he will welcome you with a watchdog or a gun.

I saw someone set up his past as a harbor.
10 Wherever it sails, his boat is safe—
if a storm comes, he can always head for home.
His voyage is the adventure of a kite.

I saw someone drop his past like trash.
He buried it and shed it altogether.
15 He has shown me that without the past
one can also move ahead and get somewhere.

Like a shroud my past surrounds me,
but I will cut it and stitch it,
to make good shoes with it,
20 shoes that fit my feet.

Aron Keesbury (1971–)   2005

WHO PLACES THINGS EXACTLY

where they
don't belong

is he who knows
how hard

5 it is to find
things, gone

from where
he knows to look.

▪ DRAMA ▪

WILLIAM SHAKESPEARE

William Shakespeare (1564–1616), the most widely known writer of English literature, was born in Stratford-on-Avon, England. By 1592, Shakespeare had become an accomplished actor and playwright in London. With several other actors, Shakespeare formed a syndicate to build a new playhouse, The Globe, one of the most famous theaters of its time. Shakespeare wrote almost forty plays, sonnets, and narrative poems and is believed to have played such supporting roles as the ghost of Hamlet's father. The dramas in the accepted canon—works authentically Shakespeare's—are usually arranged into four categories: comedies, histories, tragedies, and romances. Of the tragedies, Hamlet remains the most frequently staged and analyzed.

1603

HAMLET

Dramatis Personae

Claudius, King of Denmark
Hamlet, son to the late, and nephew to the present King
Polonius, Lord Chamberlain
Horatio, friend to Hamlet
Laertes, son to Polonius
Voltimand ⎫
Cornelius ⎪
Rosencrantz ⎬ courtiers
Guildenstern ⎪
Osric ⎪
A Gentleman ⎭
A Priest
Marcellus ⎫
Bernardo ⎬ officers
Francisco, a soldier
Reynaldo, servant to Polonius
Players
Two Clowns, gravediggers
Fortinbras, Prince of Norway
A Captain
English Ambassadors
Gertrude, Queen of Denmark, and mother to Hamlet
Ophelia, daughter to Polonius
Lords, Ladies, Officers, Soldiers, Sailors, Messengers, and other Attendants
Ghost of Hamlet's father
Scene—Denmark.

Act I

Scene I. Elsinore. A platform[1] before the castle.

(Francisco at his post. Enter to him Bernardo.)

Bernardo: Who's there?
Francisco: Nay, answer me. Stand, and unfold yourself.[2]
Bernardo: Long live the King![3]
Francisco: Bernardo?
5 **Bernardo:**   He.
Francisco: You come most carefully upon your hour.
Bernardo: 'Tis now struck twelve. Get thee to bed, Francisco.
Francisco: For this relief much thanks. 'Tis bitter cold,
    And I am sick at heart.
10 **Bernardo:** Have you had quiet guard?
Francisco: Not a mouse stirring.
Bernardo: Well, good night.
    If you do meet Horatio and Marcellus,
    The rivals[4] of my watch, bid them make haste.
15 **Francisco:** I think I hear them. Stand, ho! Who is there!

(Enter Horatio and Marcellus.)

Horatio: Friends to this ground.
Marcellus: And liegemen[5] to the Dane.
Francisco: Give you good night.
Marcellus: Oh, farewell, honest soldier!
20   Who hath relieved you?
Francisco: Bernardo hath my place.
    Give you good night.

    (Exit.)

Marcellus: Holla! Bernardo!
Bernardo: Say—
25   What, is Horatio there?
Horatio: A piece of him.
Bernardo: Welcome, Horatio. Welcome, good Marcellus.
Marcellus: What, has this thing appeared again tonight?
Bernardo: I have seen nothing.
30 **Marcellus:** Horatio says 'tis but our fantasy,[6]
    And will not let belief take hold of him
    Touching this dreaded sight twice seen of us.
    Therefore I have entreated him along
    With us to watch the minutes of this night,
35   That if again this apparition come,
    He may approve our eyes[7] and speak to it.
Horatio: Tush, tush, 'twill not appear.

---

[1] **platform:** the level space on the ramparts where the cannon were mounted.   [2] **unfold yourself:** reveal who you are.   [3] **Long . . . King:** probably the password for the night.   [4] **rivals:** partners.   [5] **liegemen:** loyal subjects.   [6] **fantasy:** imagination.   [7] **approve our eyes:** verify what we have seen.

Bernardo: Sit down awhile,
And let us once again assail your ears,
40   That are so fortified against our story,
What we have two nights seen.
Horatio: Well, sit we down,
And let us hear Bernardo speak of this.
Bernardo: Last night of all,
45   When yond same star that's westward from the pole[8]
Had made his course to illume[9] that part of heaven
Where now it burns, Marcellus and myself,
The bell then beating one—

(Enter Ghost.)

Marcellus: Peace, break thee off. Look where it comes again!
50 **Bernardo:** In the same figure, like the King that's dead.
Marcellus: Thou art a scholar.[10] Speak to it, Horatio.
Bernardo: Looks it not like the King? Mark it, Horatio.
Horatio: Most like. It harrows[11] me with fear and wonder.
Bernardo: It would be spoken to.
55 **Marcellus:**   Question it, Horatio.
Horatio: What art thou that usurp'st this time of night,
Together with[12] that fair and warlike form
In which the majesty of buried Denmark[13]
Did sometimes march? By Heaven I charge thee, speak!
60 **Marcellus:** It is offended.
Bernardo: See, it stalks away!
Horatio: Stay! Speak, speak! I charge thee, speak!

(Exit Ghost.)

Marcellus: 'Tis gone, and will not answer.
Bernardo: How now, Horatio! You tremble and look pale.
65   Is not this something more than fantasy?
What think you on 't?
Horatio: Before my God, I might not this believe
Without the sensible and true avouch
Of mine own eyes.[14]
70 **Marcellus:**   Is it not like the King?
Horatio: As thou art to thyself.
Such was the very armor he had on
When he the ambitious Norway combated.
So frowned he once when, in an angry parle,[15]
75   He smote the sledded Polacks[16] on the ice.
'Tis strange.

---

[8] **pole:** Polestar.   [9] **illume:** light.   [10] **scholar:** As Latin was the proper language in which to address and exorcise evil spirits, a scholar was necessary.   [11] **harrows:** distresses; lit., plows up.   [12] **Together with:** i.e., appearing in.   [13] **majesty . . . Denmark:** the dead King.   [14] **Without . . . eyes:** unless my own eyes had vouched for it.   [15] **parle:** parley [Editor's note: confrontation].   [16] **sledded Polacks:** There has been much controversy about this phrase. Q^1 and Q_2 read "sleaded Pollax." F_1 reads "sledded Pollax." Either the late King smote his heavy (leaded) poleax on the ice, or else he attacked the Poles in their sledges. There is no further reference to this incident.

Marcellus: Thus twice before, and jump at this dead hour,[17]
    With martial stalk hath he gone by our watch.
Horatio: In what particular thought to work I know not,
80   But in the gross and scope[18] of my opinion
    This bodes some strange eruption[19] to our state.
Marcellus: Good now, sit down and tell me, he that knows,
    Why this same strict and most observant watch
    So nightly toils[20] the subject[21] of the land;
85   And why such daily cast of brazen cannon
    And foreign mart[22] for implements of war;
    Why[23] such impress[24] of shipwrights, whose sore task
    Does not divide the Sunday from the week;
    What might be toward,[25] that this sweaty haste
90   Doth make the night joint laborer with the day.
    Who is 't that can inform me?
Horatio: That can I,
    At last the whisper goes so. Our last king,
    Whose image even but now appeared to us,
95   Was, as you know, by Fortinbras of Norway,
    Thereto pricked[26] on by a most emulate[27] pride,
    Dared to the combat, in which our valiant Hamlet—
    (For so this side of our known world esteemed him)
    Did slay this Fortinbras. Who[28] by a sealed compact,[29]
100   Well ratified by law and heraldry,[30]
    Did forfeit, with his life, all those his lands
    Which he stood seized of[31] to the conqueror;
    Against the which, a moiety competent[32]
    Was gagéd[33] by our King, which had returned
105   To the inheritance of Fortinbras
    Had he been vanquisher, as by the same covenant
    And carriage of the article designed[34]
    His fell to Hamlet. Now, sir, young Fortinbras,
    Of unimprovèd mettle[35] hot and full,
110   Hath in the skirts[36] of Norway here and there
    Sharked[37] up a list of lawless resolutes,[38]
    For food and diet[39] to some enterprise
    That hath a stomach[40] in 't. Which is no other,
    As it doth well appear unto our state,
115   But to recover of us, by strong hand

---

[17] **jump . . . hour:** just at deep midnight. [18] **gross . . . scope:** general conclusion. [19] **eruption:** violent disturbance. [20] **toils:** wearies. [21] **subject:** subjects. [22] **foreign mart:** purchase abroad.
[23] **Why . . . day:** i.e., workers in shipyards and munition factories are working night shifts and Sundays.
[24] **impress:** conscription. [25] **toward:** in preparation. [26] **pricked:** spurred. [27] **emulate:** jealous.
[28] **Who . . . Hamlet:** i.e., before the combat it was agreed that the victor should win the land of the vanquished. [29] **sealed compact:** formal agreement. [30] **heraldry:** The heralds were responsible for arranging formal combats [Editor's note: "laws of chivalry"]. [31] **seized of:** possessed of, a legal term. [32] **moiety competent:** adequate portion. [33] **gaged:** pledged. [34] **carriage . . . designed:** fulfillment of the clause in the agreement. [35] **unimproved mettle:** untutored, wild material, nature. [36] **skirts:** outlying parts.
[37] **Sharked:** collected indiscriminately, as a shark bolts its prey [Editor's note: gobbles its prey.]. [38] **lawless resolutes:** gangsters. [39] **diet:** maintenance. [40] **stomach:** resolution.

	And terms compulsatory,[41] those foresaid lands
	So by his father lost. And this, I take it,
	Is the main motive of our preparations,
	The source of this our watch and the chief head[42]
120	Of this posthaste and romage[43] in the land.

Bernardo: I think it be no other but e'en so.
Well may it sort[44] that this portentous figure
Comes armèd through our watch, so like the King
That was and is the question of these wars.

125 **Horatio:** A mote[45] it is to trouble the mind's eye.
In the most high and palmy[46] state of Rome,
A little ere the mightiest Julius fell,
The graves stood tenantless, and the sheeted[47] dead
Did squeak and gibber[48] in the Roman streets.

130 As stars[49] with trains of fire and dews of blood,
Disasters[50] in the sun, and the moist star[51]
Upon whose influence Neptune's empire stands
Was sick almost to doomsday with eclipse.
And even the like precurse[52] of fierce events,

135 As harbingers[53] preceding still the fates
And prologue to the omen[54] coming on,
Have heaven and earth together demonstrated
Unto our climatures[55] and countrymen.

(Re-enter Ghost.)

But soft, behold! Lo where it comes again!

140 I'll cross it,[56] though it blast me. Stay, illusion!
If thou hast any sound, or use of voice,
Speak to me.
If[57] there be any good thing to be done
That may to thee do ease, and grace to me,[58]

145 Speak to me.
If thou art privy to[59] thy country's fate,
Which, happily,[60] foreknowing may avoid,
O, speak!
Or if thou hast uphoarded in thy life

150 Extorted[61] treasure in the womb of earth,

---

[41] **terms compulsatory:** force. [42] **chief head:** main purpose. [43] **posthaste . . . romage:** urgency and bustle. [44] **Well . . . sort:** it would be a natural reason. [45] **mote:** speck of dust. [46] **palmy:** flourishing. [47] **sheeted:** in their shrouds. [48] **gibber:** utter strange sounds. [49] **As stars:** The sense of the passage is here broken; possibly a line has been omitted after l. 116. [50] **Disasters:** unlucky signs. [51] **moist star:** the moon, which influences the tides. [52] **precurse:** forewarning. [53] **harbingers:** forerunners. The harbinger was an officer of the Court who was sent ahead to make the arrangements when the Court went on progress. [54] **omen:** disaster. [55] **climatures:** regions. [56] **cross it:** stand in its way [Editor's note: "I will confront it, though it may destroy me."]. [57] **If . . . speak:** In popular belief there were four reasons why the spirit of a dead man should *walk:* (a) to reveal a secret, (b) to utter a warning, (c) to reveal concealed treasure, (d) to reveal the manner of its death. Horatio thus adjures the ghost by three potent reasons, but before he can utter the fourth the cock crows. [58] **grace to me:** bring me into a state of spiritual grace. [59] **privy to:** have secret knowledge of. [60] **happily:** by good luck. [61] **Extorted:** evilly acquired.

For which, they say, you spirits oft walk in death,
Speak of it. Stay, and speak! (*The cock crows.*[62]) Stop it, Marcellus.
Marcellus: Shall I strike at it with my partisan?[63]
Horatio: Do, if it will not stand.
155 **Bernardo:** 'Tis here!
Horatio: 'Tis here!
Marcellus: 'Tis gone!

(*Exit Ghost.*)

We do it wrong, being so majestical,
To offer it the show of violence,
160 For it is as the air invulnerable,
And our vain blows malicious mockery.
Bernardo: It was about to speak when the cock crew.
Horatio: And then it started like a guilty thing
Upon a fearful[64] summons. I have heard
165 The cock, that is the trumpet to the morn,
Doth with his lofty and shrill-sounding throat
Awake the god of day, and at his warning,
Whether in sea or fire, in earth or air,
The extravagant and erring[65] spirit hies
170 To his confine.[66] And of the truth herein
This present object made probation.[67]
Marcellus: It faded on the crowing of the cock.
Some say that ever 'gainst[68] that season comes
Wherein Our Saviour's birth is celebrated,
175 This bird of dawning singeth all night long.
And then, they say, no spirit dare stir abroad,
The nights are wholesome, then no planets[69] strike,
No fairy takes[70] nor witch hath power to charm,
So hallowed and so gracious is the time.
180 **Horatio:** So have I heard and do in part believe it.
But look, the morn, in russet mantle clad,
Walks o'er the dew of yon high eastward hill.
Break we our watch up, and by my advice
Let us impart what we have seen tonight
185 Unto young Hamlet, for upon my life,
This spirit, dumb to us, will speak to him.
Do you consent we shall acquaint him with it,
As needful in our loves, fitting our duty?
Marcellus: Let's do 't, I pray. And I this morning know
190 Where we shall find him most conveniently.

(*Exeunt.*)

---

[62] s.d., **cock crows:** i.e., a sign that dawn is at hand. See ll. 162–179.   [63] **partisan:** spear-like weapon.
[64] **fearful:** causing fear.   [65] **extravagant . . . erring:** both words mean "wandering."   [66] **confine:** place of
confinement.   [67] **probation:** proof.   [68] **'gainst:** in anticipation of.   [69] **planets:** Planets were supposed to
bring disaster.   [70] **takes:** bewitches.

Scene II. A room of state in the castle.

(Flourish.[1] Enter the King, Queen, Hamlet, Polonius, Laertes, Voltimand, Cornelius, Lords, and Attendants.)

King: Though yet of Hamlet our dear brother's death
The memory be green,[2] and that it us befitted
To bear our hearts in grief and our whole kingdom
To be contracted in one brow of woe,[3]
5   Yet so far hath discretion[4] fought with nature[5]
That we with wisest sorrow think of him,
Together with remembrance of ourselves.
Therefore our sometime sister,[6] now our Queen,
The imperial jointress[7] to this warlike state,
10   Have we, as 'twere with a defeated joy—
With an auspicious and a dropping eye,[8]
With mirth in funeral and with dirge in marriage,
In equal scale weighing delight and dole[9]—
Taken to wife. Nor have we herein barred
15   Your better wisdoms,[10] which have freely gone
With this affair along. For all, our thanks.
Now follows that you know. Young Fortinbras,
Holding a weak supposal[11] of our worth,
Or thinking by our late dear brother's death
20   Our state to be disjoint and out of frame,
Colleaguéd with the dream of his advantage,[12]
He hath not failed to pester us with message
Importing the surrender of those lands
Lost by his father, with all bonds of law,[13]
25   To our most valiant brother. So much for him.
Now for ourself, and for this time of meeting.
Thus much the business is: We have here writ
To Norway, uncle of young Fortinbras—
Who, impotent and bedrid, scarcely hears
30   Of this his nephew's purpose—to suppress
His further gait[14] herein, in that the levies,
The lists[15] and full proportions,[16] are all made
Out of his subject.[17] And we here dispatch
You, good Cornelius, and you, Voltimand,
35   For bearers of this greeting to old Norway,
Giving to you no further personal power
To business with the King more than the scope[18]

---

[1] **Flourish:** fanfare of trumpets. [2] **green:** fresh. [3] **contracted . . . woe:** i.e., every subject's forehead should be puckered with grief. [4] **discretion:** common sense. [5] **nature:** natural sorrow. [6] **sister:** sister-in-law. [7] **jointress:** partner by marriage. [8] **auspicious . . . eye:** an eye at the same time full of joy and tears. [9] **dole:** grief. [10] **barred . . . wisdoms:** i.e., in taking this step we have not shut out your advice. As is obvious throughout the play, the Danes chose their King by election and not by right of birth. [11] **weak supposal:** poor opinion. [12] **Colleagued . . . advantage:** uniting himself with this dream that here was a good opportunity. [13] **with . . . law:** legally binding. [14] **gait:** progress. [15] **lists:** rosters [Editor's note: roster of troops]. [16] **proportions:** military establishments. [17] **subject:** subjects. [18] **scope:** limit.

Of these delated articles[19] allow.
Farewell, and let your haste commend[20] your duty.

40 **Cornelius & Voltimand:** In that and all things will we show our duty.
King: We doubt it nothing. Heartily farewell.

(Exeunt Voltimand and Cornelius.)

And now, Laertes, what's the news with you?
You told us of some suit[21]—what is 't, Laertes?
You cannot speak of reason to the Dane
45 And lose your voice. What wouldst thou beg, Laertes,
That shall not be my offer, not thy asking?
The head is not more native[22] to the heart,
The hand more instrumental[23] to the mouth,
Than is the throne of Denmark to thy father.
50 What wouldst thou have, Laertes?

Laertes: My dread[24] lord,
Your leave and favor to return to France,
From whence, though willingly, I came to Denmark
To show my duty in your coronation,
55 Yet now, I must confess, that duty done,
My thoughts and wishes bend again toward France
And bow them to your gracious leave and pardon.

King: Have you your father's leave? What says Polonius?
Polonius: He hath, my lord, wrung from me my slow leave
60 By laborsome petition, and at last
Upon his will[25] I sealed my hard consent.[26]
I do beseech you give him leave to go.

King: Take thy fair hour, Laertes, time be thine,
And thy best graces spend[27] it at thy will!
65 But now, my cousin[28] Hamlet, and my son—
Hamlet: *(Aside.)* A little more than kin and less than kind.[29]
King: How is it that the clouds still hang on you?
Hamlet: Not so, my lord. I am too much in the sun.
Queen: Good Hamlet, cast thy nighted color[30] off.
70 And let thine eye look like a friend on Denmark.
Do not forever with thy vailèd lids[31]
Seek for thy noble father in the dust.
Thou know'st 'tis common—all that lives must die,
Passing through nature to eternity.
75 **Hamlet:** Aye, madam, it is common.

---

[19] **delated articles:** detailed instructions. Claudius is following usual diplomatic procedure. Ambassadors sent on a special mission carried with them a letter of introduction and greeting to the King of the foreign Court and detailed instructions to guide them in the negotiations.   [20] **commend:** display; lit., recommend.
[21] **suit:** petition.   [22] **native:** closely related.   [23] **instrumental:** serviceable.   [24] **dread:** dreaded, much respected.   [25] **will:** desire.   [26] **sealed . . . consent:** agreed to, but with great reluctance.   [27] **best . . . spend:** i.e., use your time well.   [28] **cousin:** kinsman. The word was used for any near relation.
[29] **A . . . kind:** too near a relation (uncle-father) and too little natural affection. **kind:** affectionate.
[30] **nighted color:** black. Hamlet alone is in deep mourning; the rest of the Court wear gay clothes. [Editor's note: bright clothes].   [31] **vailèd lids:** lowered eyelids.

Queen: If it be,
    Why seems it so particular with thee?
Hamlet: Seems, madam? Nay, it is. I know not "seems."
    'Tis not alone my inky cloak, good Mother,
80   Nor customary suits of solemn black,
    Nor windy suspiration of forced breath—
    No, nor the fruitful river[32] in the eye,
    Nor the dejected havior of the visage,[33]
    Together with all forms, moods, shapes of grief—
85   That can denote me truly. These indeed seem,
    For they are actions that a man might play.[34]
    But I have that within which passeth show,
    These but the trappings[35] and the suits of woe.
King: 'Tis sweet and commendable in your nature, Hamlet,
90   To give these mourning duties to your father.
    But you must know your father lost a father,
    That father lost, lost his, and the survivor bound
    In filial obligation for some term
    To do obsequious sorrow.[36] But to perséver
95   In obstinate condolement[37] is a course
    Of impious stubbornness, 'tis unmanly grief.
    It shows a will most incorrect to Heaven,
    A heart unfortified,[38] a mind impatient,
    An understanding simple and unschooled.
100   For what we know must be and is as common
    As any the most vulgar[39] thing to sense,
    Why should we in our peevish opposition
    Take it to heart? Fie! 'Tis a fault to Heaven,
    A fault against the dead, a fault to nature,
105   To reason most absurd, whose common theme
    Is death of fathers, and who still hath cried,
    From the first corse[40] till he that died today,
    "This must be so." We pray you throw to earth
    This unprevailing[41] woe, and think of us
110   As of a father. For let the world take note
    You are the most immediate[42] to our throne,
    And with no less nobility of love
    Than that which dearest father bears his son
    Do I impart toward you. For your intent
115   In going back to school[43] in Wittenberg,
    It is most retrograde[44] to our desire.
    And we beseech you bend you[45] to remain
    Here in the cheer and comfort of our eye,
    Our chiefest courtier, cousin, and our son.

---

[32] **fruitful river:** stream of tears.   [33] **dejected . . . visage:** downcast countenance.   [34] **play:** act, as in a play.   [35] **trappings:** ornaments.   [36] **obsequious sorrow:** the sorrow usual at funerals.   [37] **obstinate condolement:** lamentation disregarding the will of God.   [38] **unfortified:** not strengthened with the consolation of religion.   [39] **vulgar:** common.   [40] **corse:** corpse. There is unconscious irony in this remark, for the first corpse was that of Abel, also slain by his brother.   [41] **unprevailing:** futile.   [42] **most immediate:** next heir.   [43] **school:** university.   [44] **retrograde:** contrary.   [45] **bend you:** incline.

120 **Queen:** Let not thy mother lose her prayers, Hamlet.
　　　　I pray thee, stay with us, go not to Wittenberg.
　　Hamlet: I shall in all my best obey you, Madam.
　　King: Why, 'tis a loving and a fair reply.
　　　　Be as ourself in Denmark. Madam, come,
125　　This gentle and unforced accord of Hamlet
　　　　Sits smiling to my heart. In grace whereof,
　　　　No jocund health that Denmark drinks today
　　　　But the great cannon[46] to the clouds shall tell,
　　　　And the King's rouse[47] the Heaven shall bruit[48] again,
130　　Respeaking earthly thunder. Come away.

　　(Flourish. Exeunt all but Hamlet.)

　　Hamlet: O, that this too too solid flesh would melt,
　　　　Thaw, and resolve itself into a dew,
　　　　Or that the Everlasting had not fixed
　　　　His canon[49] 'gainst self-slaughter! Oh, God! God!
135　　How weary, stale, flat, and unprofitable
　　　　Seem to me all the uses[50] of this world!
　　　　Fie on 't, ah, fie! 'Tis an unweeded garden,
　　　　That grows to seed. Things rank[51] and gross in nature
　　　　Possess it merely.[52] That it should come to this!
140　　But two months dead! Nay, not so much, not two.
　　　　So excellent a King, that was, to this,
　　　　Hyperion[53] to a satyr.[54] So loving to my mother
　　　　That he might not beteem[55] the winds of heaven
　　　　Visit her face too roughly. Heaven and earth!
145　　Must I remember? Why, she would hang on him
　　　　As if increase of appetite had grown
　　　　By what it fed on. And yet within a month—
　　　　Let me not think on 't.—Frailty, thy name is woman!—
　　　　A little month, or ere those shoes were old
150　　With which she followed my poor father's body,
　　　　Like Niobe[56] all tears.—Why she, even she—
　　　　O, God! A beast that wants discourse of reason[57]
　　　　Would have mourned longer—married with my uncle,
　　　　My father's brother, but no more like my father
155　　Than I to Hercules. Within a month,
　　　　Ere yet the salt of most unrighteous tears
　　　　Had left the flushing in her gallèd[58] eyes,
　　　　She married. O, most wicked speed, to post[59]
　　　　With such dexterity[60] to incestuous sheets!

---

[46] **great cannon:** This Danish custom of discharging cannon when the King proposed a toast was much noted by Englishmen. [47] **rouse:** deep drink. [48] **bruit:** sound loudly, echo. [49] **canon:** rule, law. [50] **uses:** ways. [51] **rank:** coarse. [52] **merely:** entirely. [53] **Hyperion:** the sun god. [54] **satyr:** a creature half man, half goat—ugly and lecherous. [55] **beteem:** allow. [56] **Niobe:** She boasted of her children, to the annoyance of the goddess Artemis, who slew them all. Thereafter Niobe became so sorrowful that she changed into a rock everlastingly dripping water. [57] **wants . . . reason:** is without ability to reason. [58] **gallèd:** sore. [59] **post:** hasten. [60] **dexterity:** nimbleness.

160 It is not, nor it cannot, come to good.
But break, my heart, for I must hold my tongue!

(Enter Horatio, Marcellus, and Bernardo.)

Horatio: Hail to your lordship!
Hamlet: I am glad to see you well.
Horatio—or I do forget myself.
165 **Horatio:** The same, my lord, and your poor servant ever.
Hamlet: Sir, my good friend—I'll change that name[61] with you.
And what make you from Wittenberg, Horatio?
Marcellus?
Marcellus: My good lord?
Hamlet: I am very glad to see you. *(To Bernardo.)* Good even, sir—
170 But what, in faith, make you from Wittenberg?
Horatio: A truant disposition, good my lord.
Hamlet: I would not hear your enemy say so,
Nor shall you do my ear that violence
To make it truster of your own report
175 Against yourself. I know you are no truant.
But what is your affair in Elsinore?
We'll teach you to drink deep[62] ere you depart.
Horatio: My lord, I came to see your father's funeral.
Hamlet: I pray thee do not mock me, fellow student.
180 I think it was to see my mother's wedding.
Horatio: Indeed, my lord, it followed hard upon.
Hamlet: Thrift, thrift, Horatio! The funeral baked meats
Did coldly furnish forth the marriage tables.[63]
Would I had met my dearest[64] foe in Heaven
185 Or ever I had seen that day, Horatio!
My father!—Methinks I see my father.
Horatio: Oh, where, my lord?
Hamlet: In my mind's eye, Horatio.
Horatio: I saw him once. He was a goodly King.
190 **Hamlet:** He was a man, take him for all in all.
I shall not look upon his like again.
Horatio: My lord, I think I saw him yesternight.
Hamlet: Saw? Who?
Horatio: My lord, the King your father.
195 **Hamlet:**   The King my father!
Horatio: Season your admiration[65] for a while
With an attent[66] ear till I may deliver,
Upon the witness of these gentlemen,
This marvel to you.
200 **Hamlet:** For God's love, let me hear!

---

[61] **that name:** i.e., friend.   [62] **drink deep:** For more on the drunken habits of the Danes, see I.iv. 11–40.
[63] **Thrift . . . tables:** they hurried on the wedding for economy's sake, so that the remains of food served at the funeral might be used cold for the wedding. **baked meats:** feast.   [64] **dearest:** best-hated.
[65] **Season . . . admiration:** moderate your wonder.   [66] **attent:** attentive.

Horatio: Two nights together had these gentlemen,
Marcellus and Bernardo, on their watch
In the dead vast and middle of the night,[67]
Been thus encountered. A figure like your father,
205 Armed at point exactly, cap-a-pe,[68]
Appears before them and with solemn march
Goes slow and stately by them. Thrice he walked
By their oppressed and fear-surprisèd eyes
Within his truncheon's[69] length, whilst they, distilled[70]
210 Almost to jelly with the act of fear,
Stand dumb, and speak not to him. This to me
In dreadful secrecy impart they did,
And I with them the third night kept the watch.
Where, as they had delivered, both in time,
215 Form of the thing, each word made true and good,
The apparition comes. I knew your father.
These hands are not more like.
Hamlet: But where was this?
Marcellus: My lord, upon the platform where we watched.
220 **Hamlet:** Did you not speak to it?
Horatio: My lord, I did,
But answer made it none. Yet once methought
It lifted up it[71] head and did address
Itself to motion, like as it would speak.
225 But even then the morning cock crew loud,
And at the sound it shrunk in haste away
And vanished from our sight.
Hamlet: 'Tis very strange.
Horatio: As I do live, my honored lord, 'tis true,
230 And we did think it writ down in our duty
To let you know of it.
Hamlet: Indeed, indeed, sirs, but this troubles me.
Hold you the watch tonight?
Marcellus & Bernardo: We do, my lord.
235 **Hamlet:** Armed, say you?
Marcellus & Bernardo: Armed, my lord.
Hamlet: From top to toe?
Marcellus & Bernardo: My lord, from head to foot.
Hamlet: Then saw you not his face?
240 **Horatio:** O yes, my lord, he wore his beaver[72] up.
Hamlet: What, looked he frowningly?
Horatio: A countenance more in sorrow than in anger.
Hamlet: Pale, or red?
Horatio: Nay, very pale.
245 **Hamlet:** And fixed his eyes upon you?
Horatio: Most constantly.

---

[67] **dead . . . night:** deep, silent midnight. [68] **at . . . cap-a-pe:** complete in every detail, head to foot.
[69] **truncheon:** a general's staff. [70] **distilled:** melted. [71] **it:** its. [72] **beaver:** front part of the helmet,
which could be raised.

Hamlet: I would I had been there.

Horatio: It would have much amazed you.

Hamlet: Very like.

250   Stayed it long?

Horatio: While one with moderate haste might tell[73] a hundred.

Marcellus & Bernardo: Longer, longer.

Horatio: Not when I saw 't.

Hamlet: His beard was grizzled?[74] No?

255 **Horatio:** It was as I have seen it in his life,
      A sable silvered.[75]

Hamlet: I will watch tonight.
      Perchance 'twill walk again.

Horatio: I warrant it will.

260 **Hamlet:** If it assume my noble father's person,
      I'll speak to it though Hell itself should gape
      And bid me hold my peace. I pray you all,
      If you have hitherto concealed this sight,
      Let it be tenable[76] in your silence still,

265   And whatsoever else shall hap tonight,
      Give it an understanding, but no tongue.
      I will requite[77] your loves. So fare you well.
      Upon the platform, 'twixt eleven and twelve,
      I'll visit you.

270 **All:**   Our duty to your honor.

Hamlet: Your loves, as mine to you. Farewell.

(Exeunt all but Hamlet.)

My father's spirit in arms! All is not well.
I doubt[78] some foul play. Would the night were come!
Till then sit still, my soul. Foul deeds will rise.

275 Though all the earth o'erwhelm them, to men's eyes.

(Exit.)

Scene III. A room in Polonius's house.

(Enter Laertes and Ophelia.)

Laertes: My necessaries[1] are embarked. Farewell.
      And, sister, as the winds give benefit
      And convoy is assistant,[2] do not sleep,
      But let me hear from you.

5 **Ophelia:**   Do you doubt that?

Laertes: For Hamlet, and the trifling of his favor,[3]
      Hold it a fashion and a toy in blood,[4]
      A violet in the youth of primy[5] nature,
      Forward, not permanent, sweet, not lasting,

---

[73] **tell:** count. [74] **grizzled:** gray. [75] **sable silvered:** black mingled with white. [76] **tenable:** held fast.
[77] **requite:** repay. [78] **doubt:** suspect. [1] **necessaries:** baggage. [2] **convoy . . . assistant:** means of conveyance is available. [3] **favor:** i.e., toward you. [4] **toy in blood:** trifling impulse [Editor's note: a trifling sexual impulse]. [5] **primy:** springtime; i.e., youthful.

10   The perfume and suppliance of a minute[6]—
          No more.

Ophelia: No more but so?

Laertes: Think it no more.
          For Nature crescent does not grow alone

15   In thews and bulk,[7] but as this temple[8] waxes
          The inward service of the mind and soul
          Grows wide withal. Perhaps he loves you now,
          And now no soil nor cautel[9] doth besmirch
          The virtue of his will.[10] But you must fear,

20   His greatness weighed,[11] his will is not his own.
          For he himself is subject to his birth.
          He may not, as unvalued persons do,
          Carve[12] for himself, for on his choice depends
          The safety and health of this whole state,

25   And therefore must his choice be circumscribed[13]
          Unto the voice and yielding of that body
          Whereof he is the head. Then if he says he loves you,
          It fits your wisdom so far to believe it
          As he in his particular act and place

30   May give his saying deed, which is no further
          Than the main voice of Denmark goes withal.
          Then weigh what loss your honor may sustain
          If with too credent[14] ear you list his songs,
          Or lose your heart, or your chaste treasure[15] open

35   To his unmastered importunity.
          Fear it, Ophelia, fear it, my dear sister,
          And keep you in the rear[16] of your affection,
          Out of the shot and danger of desire.
          The chariest maid is prodigal enough

40   If she unmask her beauty to the moon.
          Virtue itself 'scapes not calumnious strokes.
          The canker galls the infants[17] of the spring
          Too oft before their buttons[18] be disclosed,
          And in the morn and liquid dew of youth

45   Contagious blastments[19] are most imminent.
          Be wary, then, best safety lies in fear.
          Youth to itself rebels, though none else near.[20]

Ophelia: I shall the effect of this good lesson keep
          As watchman to my heart. But, good my brother,

50   Do not, as some ungracious pastors do,
          Show me the steep and thorny way to heaven
          Whilst, like a puffed[21] and reckless libertine,

---

[6] **perfume . . . minute:** perfume which lasts only for a minute.   [7] **For . . . bulk:** for natural growth is not only in bodily bulk.   [8] **temple:** i.e., the body.   [9] **cautel:** deceit.   [10] **will:** desire.   [11] **His . . . weighed:** when you consider his high position.   [12] **Carve:** choose.   [13] **circumscribed:** restricted.   [14] **credent:** credulous.   [15] **chaste treasure:** the treasure of your chastity.   [16] **in . . . rear:** i.e., farthest from danger.   [17] **canker . . . infants:** maggot harms the unopened buds.   [18] **buttons:** buds.   [19] **Contagious blastments:** infectious blasts.   [20] **though . . . near:** without anyone else to encourage it.   [21] **puffed:** panting.

Himself the primrose path of dalliance[22] treads
And recks not his own rede.[23]

55 **Laertes:** O, fear me not.
I stay too long. But here my father comes.

(Enter Polonius.)

A double blessing is a double grace,
Occasion smiles[24] upon a second leave.

Polonius: Yet here, Laertes! Aboard, aboard, for shame!
60 The wind sits in the shoulder of your sail
And you are stayed[25] for. There, my blessing with thee!
And these few precepts in thy memory
Look thou chárácter.[26] Give thy thoughts no tongue,
Nor any unproportioned[27] thought his act.
65 Be thou familiar, but by no means vulgar.
Those friends thou hast, and their adoption tried,[28]
Grapple them to thy soul with hoops of steel,
But do not dull thy palm with entertainment[29]
Of each new-hatched unfledged[30] comrade. Beware
70 Of entrance to a quarrel, but being in,
Bear 't that the opposèd may beware of thee.
Give every man thy ear, but few thy voice.[31]
Take each man's censure,[32] but reserve thy judgment.
Costly thy habit[33] as thy purse can buy,
75 But not expressed in fancy[34]—rich, not gaudy.
For the apparel oft proclaims the man,
And they in France of the best rank and station
Are of a most select and generous chief in that.[35]
Neither a borrower nor a lender be,
80 For loan oft loses both itself and friend
And borrowing dulls the edge of husbandry.[36]
This above all: To thine own self be true,
And it must follow, as the night the day,
Thou canst not then be false to any man.
85 Farewell. My blessing season[37] this in thee!

Laertes: Most humbly do I take my leave, my lord.

Polonius: The time invests you. Go, your servants tend.[38]

Laertes: Farewell, Ophelia, and remember well
What I have said to you.

---

[22] **primrose . . . dalliance:** i.e., the pleasant way of love-making. [23] **recks . . . rede:** takes no heed of his own advice. [24] **Occasion smiles:** i.e., here is a happy chance. [25] **stayed:** waited. [26] **chárácter:** inscribe. [27] **unproportioned:** unsuitable. [28] **adoption tried:** friendship tested by experience. [29] **dull . . . entertainment:** let your hand grow callous with welcome. [30] **unfledged:** lit., newly out of the egg, immature. [31] **Give . . . voice:** listen to everyone but commit yourself to few. [32] **censure:** opinion. [33] **habit:** dress. [34] **expressed in fancy:** fantastic. [35] **Are. . . that:** A disputed line; this is the F reading. Q_2 reads "Or of the most select and generous, chief in that"; i.e., the best noble and gentle families are very particular in their dress. **generous:** of gentle birth. [36] **husbandry:** economy. [37] **season:** bring to fruit. [38] **tend:** attend.

90 **Ophelia:**   'Tis in my memory locked,
    And you yourself shall keep the key of it.
Laertes: Farewell.

    (*Exit.*)

Polonius: What is 't, Ophelia, he hath said to you?
Ophelia: So please you, something touching the Lord Hamlet.
95 **Polonius:** Marry,[39] well bethought.[40]
    'Tis told me he hath very oft of late
    Given private time to you, and you yourself
    Have of your audience been most free and bounteous.
    If it be so—as so 'tis put on me,
100   And that in way of caution—I must tell you
    You do not understand yourself so clearly
    As it behooves[41] my daughter and your honor.
    What is between you? Give me up the truth.
Ophelia: He hath, my lord, of late made many tenders[42]
105   Of his affection to me.
Polonius: Affection? Pooh! You speak like a green girl,
    Unsifted[43] in such perilous circumstance.
    Do you believe his tenders, as you call them?
Ophelia: I do not know, my lord, what I should think.
110 **Polonius:** Marry, I'll teach you. Think yourself a baby
    That you have ta'en these tenders[44] for true pay,
    Which are not sterling.[45] Tender yourself more dearly,
    Or—not to crack the wind of[46] the poor phrase,
    Running it thus—you'll tender me a fool.
115 **Ophelia:** My lord, he hath importuned me with love
    In honorable fashion.
Polonius: Aye, fashion[47] you may call it. Go to, go to.
Ophelia: And hath given countenance to his speech,[48] my lord,
    With almost all the holy vows of heaven.
120 **Polonius:** Aye, springes[49] to catch woodcocks.[50] I do know,
    When the blood burns, how prodigal[51] the soul
    Lends the tongue vows. These blazes,[52] daughter,
    Giving more light than heat, extinct in both,
    Even in their promise as it is a-making,
125   You must not take for fire. From this time
    Be something scanter of your maiden presence,
    Set your entreatments at a higher rate
    Than a command to parle.[53] For Lord Hamlet,
    Believe so much in him, that he is young,

---

[39] **Marry:** Mary, by the Virgin Mary.   [40] **well bethought:** well remembered.   [41] **behooves:** is the duty of.
[42] **tenders:** offers.   [43] **Unsifted:** untried.   [44] **tenders . . . tender:** Polonius puns on "tenders," counters (used for money in games); "tender," value; "tender," show.   [45] **sterling:** true currency.   [46] **crack . . . of:** i.e., ride to death.   [47] **fashion:** mere show.   [48] **given . . . speech:** confirmed his words.   [49] **springes:** snares.   [50] **woodcocks:** foolish birds.   [51] **prodigal:** extravagantly.   [52] **blazes:** flashes, quickly extinguished (*extinct*).   [53] **Set . . . parley:** when you are asked to see him do not regard it as a command to negotiate.   **parle:** meeting to discuss terms.

130 And with a larger tether[54] may he walk
 Than may be given you. In few,[55] Ophelia,
 Do not believe his vows, for they are brokers,[56]
 Not of that dye which their investments[57] show,
 But mere implorators[58] of unholy suits,
135 Breathing like sanctified and pious bawds[59]
 The better to beguile. This is for all:
 I would not, in plain terms, from this time forth
 Have you so slander any moment leisure[60]
 As to give words or talk with the Lord Hamlet.
140 Look to 't, I charge you. Come your ways.
 Ophelia: I shall obey, my lord.

 (*Exeunt.*)

Scene IV. The platform

(*Enter Hamlet, Horatio, and Marcellus.*)

Hamlet: The air bites shrewdly.[1] It is very cold.
Horatio: It is a nipping and an eager[2] air.
Hamlet: What hour now?
Horatio: I think it lacks of twelve.
5 **Marcellus:** No, it is struck.
Horatio: Indeed? I heard it not.
 It then draws near the season
 Wherein the spirit held his wont to walk.

(*A flourish of trumpets, and ordnance shot off within.[3]*)

 What doth this mean, my lord?
10 **Hamlet:** The King doth wake[4] tonight and takes his rouse,[5]
 Keeps wassail,[6] and the swaggering upspring reels.[7]
 And as he drains his draughts of Rhenish[8] down,
 The kettledrum and trumpet thus bray out
 The triumph of his pledge.
15 **Horatio:**   Is it a custom?
Hamlet: Aye, marry, is 't.
 But to my mind, though I am native here
 And to the manner born, it is a custom
 More honored in the breach than the observance.
20 This heavy-headed revel[9] east and west
 Makes us traduced and taxed of[10] other nations.
 They clepe[11] us drunkards, and with swinish phrase
 Soil our addition,[12] and indeed it takes

---

[54] **tether:** rope by which a grazing animal is fastened to its peg. [55] **In few:** in short. [56] **brokers:** traveling salesmen. [57] **investments:** garments. [58] **implorators:** men who solicit. [59] **bawds:** keepers of brothels. F₁ and Q₂ read "bond," an easy misprint for "baud"—the Elizabethan spelling of "bawd." [60] **slander . . . leisure:** misuse any moment of leisure. [1] **shrewdly:** bitterly. [2] **eager:** sharp. [3] **within:** off stage. [4] **wake:** "makes a night of it." [5] **rouse:** See I.ii. 129, n. [6] **wassail:** revelry.
[7] **swaggering . . . reels:** reel in a riotous dance. [8] **Rhenish:** Rhine wine. [9] **heavy-headed revel:** drinking that produces a thick head. [10] **traduced . . . of:** disgraced and censured by. [11] **clepe:** call.
[12] **soil . . . addition:** smirch our honor. **addition:** lit., title of honor added to a man's name.

From our achievements, though performed at height,[13]
The pith and marrow of our attribute.[14]
So oft it chances in particular men,
That for some vicious mole[15] of nature in them,
As in their birth—wherein they are not guilty,
(Since nature cannot choose his origin),
By the o'ergrowth of some complexion,[16]
Oft breaking down the pales[17] and forts of reason,
Or by some habit that too much o'erleavens[18]
The form of plausive[19] manners, that these men—
Carrying, I say, the stamp of one defect,
Being nature's livery,[20] or fortune's star[21]—
Their virtues else—be they as pure as grace,
As infinite as man may undergo—
Shall in the general censure take corruption
From that particular fault. The dram of evil
Doth all the noble substance of a doubt
To his own scandal.[22]

(Enter Ghost.)

Horatio: Look, my lord, it comes!
Hamlet: Angels and ministers of grace defend us!
Be thou a spirit of health or goblin damned,[23]
Bring with thee airs from heaven or blasts from hell,
Be thy intents wicked or charitable,
Thou comest in such a questionable[24] shape
That I will speak to thee. I'll call thee Hamlet,
King, Father, royal Dane. Oh, answer me!
Let me not burst in ignorance, but tell
Why thy canónized[25] bones, hearsèd[26] in death,
Have burst their cerements,[27] why the sepulcher
Wherein we saw thee quietly inurned[28]
Hath oped his ponderous and marble jaws
To cast thee up again. What may this mean,
That thou, dead corse, again, in complete steel,[29]

---

[13] **though . . . height:** though of the highest merit.   [14] **pith . . . attribute:** essential part of our honor; i.e., we lose the honor due to our achievements because of our reputation for drunkenness.   [15] **mole:** blemish. [16] **o'ergrowth . . . complexion:** some quality allowed to overbalance the rest.   [17] **pales:** defenses.   [18] **o'erleavens:** mixes with.   [19] **plausive:** agreeable.   [20] **Nature's livery:** i.e., inborn.   [21] **Fortune's star:** the result of ill luck.   [22] **The . . . scandal:** This is the most famous of all disputed passages in Shakespeare's plays. The general meaning is clear: "a small portion of evil brings scandal on the whole substance, however noble." "Eale" is an Elizabethan spelling and pronunciation of "evil," as later in Q₂; "deale" is the spelling and pronunciation of "Devil." The difficulty lies in "of a doubt," which is obviously a misprint for some such word as "corrupt"; but to be satisfactory it must fit the meter and be a plausible misprint. So far, although many guesses have been made, none is wholly convincing. The best is perhaps "often dout"—often put out.   [23] **spirit . . . damned:** a holy spirit or damned fiend. Hamlet, until convinced at the end of the play scene (III.ii.), is perpetually in doubt whether the ghost which he sees is a good spirit sent to warn him, a devil sent to tempt him into some damnable action, or a hallucination created by his own diseased imagination.   [24] **questionable:** inviting question.   [25] **canónized:** buried with full rites according to the canon of the Church.   [26] **hearsed:** buried. [27] **cerements:** waxen shroud, used to wrap the bodies of the illustrious dead.   [28] **inurned:** buried.   [29] **complete steel:** full armor.

Revisit'st thus the glimpses of the moon,
Making night hideous, and we fools[30] of nature
So horridly to shake our disposition[31]
60   With thoughts beyond the reaches of our souls?
Say, why is this? Wherefore? What should we do?

(Ghost beckons Hamlet.)

Horatio: It beckons you to go away with it,
As if it some impartment[32] did desire
To you alone.
65 **Marcellus:**   Look with what courteous action
It waves you to a more removèd ground.
But do not go with it.
Horatio: No, by no means.
Hamlet: It will not speak. Then I will follow it.
70 **Horatio:** Do not, my lord.
Hamlet: Why, what should be the fear?
I do not set my life as a pin's fee,[33]
And for my soul, what can it do to that,
Being a thing immortal as itself?
75   It waves me forth again. I'll follow it.
Horatio: What if it tempt you toward the flood, my lord,
Or to the dreadful summit of the cliff
That beetles o'er[34] his base into the sea,
And there assume some other horrible form
80   Which might deprive your sovereignty of reason[35]
And draw you into madness? Think of it.
The very place puts toys of desperation,[36]
Without more motive, into every brain
That looks so many fathoms to the sea
85   And hears it roar beneath.
Hamlet: It waves me still.
Go on. I'll follow thee.
Marcellus: You shall not go, my lord.
Hamlet: Hold off your hands.
90 **Horatio:** Be ruled. You shall not go.
Hamlet: My fate cries out,
And makes each petty artery in this body
As hardy as the Nemean lion's nerve.[37]
Still am I called. Unhand me, gentlemen.
95   By heaven, I'll make a ghost of him that lets[38] me!
I say, away! Go on. I'll follow thee.

(Exeunt Ghost and Hamlet.)

---

[30] **fools:** dupes. [31] **disposition:** nature. [32] **impartment:** communication. [33] **fee:** value. [34] **beetles o'er:** juts out over. [35] **sovereignty of reason:** control of your reason over your actions. [36] **toys of desperation:** desperate fancies. [37] **Nemean . . . nerve:** sinew of a fierce beast slain by Hercules. [38] **lets:** hinders.

Horatio: He waxes desperate with imagination.

Marcellus: Let's follow. 'Tis not fit thus to obey him.

Horatio: Have after. To what issue will this come?

100 **Marcellus:** Something is rotten in the state of Denmark.

Horatio: Heaven will direct it.

Marcellus: Nay, let's follow him.

(Exeunt.)

Scene V. Another part of the platform.

(Enter Ghost and Hamlet.)

Hamlet: Whither wilt thou lead me? Speak. I'll go no further.

Ghost: Mark me.

Hamlet: I will.

Ghost: My hour is almost come

5   When I to sulphurous and tormenting flames

    Must render up myself.

Hamlet: Alas, poor ghost!

Ghost: Pity me not, but lend thy serious hearing

    To what I shall unfold.

10 **Hamlet:** Speak. I am bound to hear.

Ghost: So art thou to revenge, when thou shalt hear.

Hamlet: What?

Ghost: I am thy father's spirit,

    Doomed for a certain term to walk the night

15   And for the day confined to fast in fires

    Till the foul crimes done in my days of nature

    Are burnt and purged away. But that I am forbid

    To tell the secrets of my prison house,

    I could a tale unfold whose lightest word

20   Would harrow up thy soul, freeze thy young blood,

    Make thy two eyes, like stars, start from their spheres,[1]

    Thy knotted and combinèd[2] locks to part

    And each particular[3] hair to stand an[4] end

    Like quills upon the fretful porpentine.[5]

25   But this eternal blazon[6] must not be

    To ears of flesh and blood. List, list, oh, list!

    If thou didst ever thy dear father love—

Hamlet: O, God!

Ghost: Revenge his foul and most unnatural murder.

30 **Hamlet:** Murder!

Ghost: Murder most foul, as in the best[7] it is,

    But this most foul, strange, and unnatural.

---

[1] **spheres:** the circles in which the planets and stars were supposed to move [Editor's Note: The eyes would start from the eyeballs or orbits of the skull]. [2] **knotted . . . locks:** the hair that lies together in a mass.
[3] **particular:** individual. [4] **an:** on. [5] **porpentine:** porcupine. [6] **eternal blazon:** description of eternity.
[7] **in . . . best:** i.e., murder is foul even when there is a good excuse.

Hamlet: Haste me to know 't, that I, with wings as swift
  As meditation or the thoughts of love,
35   May sweep to my revenge.
Ghost: I find thee apt,
  And duller shouldst thou be than the fat[8] weed
  That roots itself in ease[9] of Lethe wharf[10]
  Wouldst thou not stir in this. Now, Hamlet, hear.
40   'Tis given out that, sleeping in my orchard,
  A serpent stung me—so the whole ear of Denmark
  Is by a forgèd process[11] of my death
  Rankly abused. But know, thou noble youth,
  The serpent that did sting thy father's life
45   Now wears his crown.
Hamlet: O, my prophetic soul!
  My uncle!
Ghost: Aye, that incestuous, that adulterate beast,
  With witchcraft of his wit, with traitorous gifts—
50   O, wicked wit and gifts, that have the power
  So to seduce!—won to his shameful lust
  The will of my most seeming-virtuous queen.
  O Hamlet, what a falling-off was there!
  From me, whose love was of that dignity
55   That it went hand in hand even with the vow
  I made to her in marriage, and to decline
  Upon a wretch whose natural gifts were poor
  To those of mine!
  But virtue, as it never will be moved
60   Though lewdness court it in a shape of heaven,[12]
  So Lust, though to a radiant angel linked,
  Will sate itself[13] in a celestial bed
  And prey on garbage.
  But soft! Methinks I scent the morning air.
65   Brief let me be. Sleeping within my orchard,
  My custom always of the afternoon,
  Upon my secure hour[14] thy uncle stole
  With juice of cursèd hebenon[15] in a vial,
  And in the porches[16] of my ears did pour
70   The leperous distillment,[17] whose effect
  Holds such an enmity with blood of man
  That swift as quicksilver it courses through
  The natural gates and alleys of the body,
  And with a sudden vigor it doth posset[18]
75   And curd, like eager[19] droppings into milk,
  The thin and wholesome blood. So did it mine,

---

[8] **fat:** thick, slimy, motionless.   [9] **in ease:** undisturbed.   [10] **Lethe wharf:** the bank of Lethe, the river of forgetfulness in the underworld.   [11] **forged process:** false account.   [12] **lewdness . . . Heaven:** though wooed by Lust disguised as an angel.   [13] **state itself:** gorge.   [14] **secure hour:** time of relaxation.   [15] **hebenon:** probably henbane, a poisonous plant.   [16] **porches:** entrances.   [17] **leperous distillment:** distillation causing leprosy.   [18] **posset:** curdle.   [19] **eager:** acid.

And a most instant tetter barked[20] about,
Most lazarlike,[21] with vile and loathsome crust,
All my smooth body.
80 Thus was I, sleeping, by a brother's hand
Of life, of crown, of queen, at once dispatched—
Cut off even in the blossoms of my sin,[22]
Unhouseled, disappointed, unaneled,[23]
No reckoning made, but sent to my account
85 With all my imperfections on my head.
O, horrible! O, horrible, most horrible!
If thou hast nature[24] in thee, bear it not.
Let not the royal bed of Denmark be
A couch for luxury[25] and damned incest.
90 But, howsoever thou pursuest this act,
Taint not thy mind, nor let thy soul contrive
Against thy mother aught. Leave her to heaven
And to those thorns that in her bosom lodge
To prick and sting her. Fare thee well at once!
95 Thy glowworm shows the matin[26] to be near,
And 'gins to pale his uneffectual[27] fire.
Adieu, adieu, adieu! Remember me.

(Exit.)

Hamlet: O all you host of heaven! O earth! What else?
And shall I couple hell? Oh, fie! Hold, hold, my heart,
100 And you, my sinews, grow not instant old
But bear me stiffly up. Remember thee?
Aye, thou poor ghost, while memory holds a seat
In this distracted globe.[28] Remember thee?
Yea, from the table[29] of my memory
105 I'll wipe away all trivial fond[30] records,
All saws[31] of books, all forms,[32] all pressures[33] past,
That youth and observation copied there,
And thy commandment all alone shall live
Within the book and volume of my brain,
110 Unmixed with baser matter. Yes, by heaven!
O most pernicious woman!
O villain, villain, smiling, damnèd villain!
My tables—meet it is I set it down

(Writing.)

That one may smile, and smile, and be a villain.
115 At least I'm sure it may be so in Denmark.

---

[20] **tetter barked:** eruption formed a bark.   [21] **lazarlike:** like leprosy.   [22] **Cut . . . sin:** cut off in a state of sin and so in danger of damnation.   [23] **Unhouseled . . . unaneled:** without receiving the sacrament, not properly prepared, unanointed—without extreme unction.   [24] **nature:** natural feelings.   [25] **luxury:** lust.   [26] **matin:** morning.   [27] **uneffectual:** made ineffectual by daylight.   [28] **globe:** i.e., head.   [29] **table:** notebook. Intellectual young men carried notebooks in which they recorded good sayings and notable observations.   [30] **fond:** trifling.   [31] **saws:** wise sayings.   [32] **forms:** images in the mind.   [33] **pressures:** impressions.

So, uncle, there you are. Now to my word.[34]
It is "Adieu, adieu! Remember me."
I have sworn 't.

Horatio & Marcellus: *(Within.)* My lord, my lord!

(Enter Horatio and Marcellus.)

120 **Marcellus:** Lord Hamlet!
Horatio: Heaven secure him!
Hamlet: So be it!
Marcellus: Illo, ho, ho,[35] my lord!
Hamlet: Hillo, ho, ho, boy! Come, bird, come.
125 **Marcellus:** How is 't, my noble lord?
Horatio: What news, my lord?
Hamlet: O, wonderful!
Horatio: Good my lord, tell it.
Hamlet: No, you will reveal it.
130 **Horatio:** Not I, my lord, by heaven.
Marcellus: Nor I, my lord.
Hamlet: How say you, then, would heart of man once think it?
But you'll be secret?
Horatio & Marcellus: Aye, by Heaven, my lord.
135 **Hamlet:** There's ne'er a villain dwelling in all Denmark
But he's an arrant[36] knave.
Horatio: There needs no ghost, my lord, come from the grave
To tell us this.
Hamlet: Why, right, you are i' the right.
140 And so, without more circumstance[37] at all,
I hold it fit that we shake hands and part—
You as your business and desire shall point you,
For every man hath business and desire,
Such as it is. And for my own poor part,
145 Look you, I'll go pray.
Horatio: These are but wild and whirling[38] words, my lord.
Hamlet: I'm sorry they offend you, heartily,
Yes, faith, heartily.
Horatio: There's no offense, my lord.
150 **Hamlet:** Yes, by Saint Patrick, but there is, Horatio,
And much offense too. Touching this vision here,
It is an honest[39] ghost, that let me tell you.
For your desire to know what is between us,
O'ermaster 't as you may. And now, good friends,
155 As you are friends, scholars, and soldiers,
Give me one poor request.
Horatio: What is 't, my lord? We will.
Hamlet: Never make known what you have seen tonight.
Horatio & Marcellus: My lord, we will not.

---

[34] **word:** cue. [35] **Illo . . . ho:** the falconer's cry to recall the hawk. [36] **arrant:** out-and-out. [37] **circumstance:** ceremony. [38] **whirling:** violent. [39] **honest:** true.

| 160 | **Hamlet:** | Nay, but swear 't. |
| | **Horatio:** | In faith, |

     My lord, not I.

Marcellus: Nor I, my lord, in faith.

Hamlet: Upon my sword.

165 **Marcellus:**   We have sworn, my lord, already.

Hamlet: Indeed, upon my sword,[40] indeed.

Ghost: (*Beneath.*) Swear.

Hamlet: Ah, ha, boy! Say'st thou so? Art thou there, truepenny?[41]
     Come on. You hear this fellow in the cellarage.

170   Consent to swear.

Horatio: Propose the oath, my lord.

Hamlet: Never to speak of this that you have seen,
     Swear by my sword.

Ghost: (*Beneath.*) Swear.

175 **Hamlet:** *Hic et ubique?*[42] Then we'll shift our ground.
     Come hither, gentlemen,
     And lay your hands again upon my sword.
     Swear by my sword.
     Never to speak of this that you have heard,

180 **Ghost:** (*Beneath.*) Swear by his sword.

Hamlet: Well said, old mole! Canst work i' the earth so fast?
     A worthy pioner![43] Once more remove,[44] good friends.

Horatio: O, day and night, but this is wondrous strange!

Hamlet: And therefore as a stranger give it welcome.

185   There are more things in heaven and earth, Horatio,
     Than are dreamt of in your philosophy.
     But come,
     Here, as before, never, so help you mercy,
     How strange or odd soe'er I bear myself

190   (As I perchance hereafter shall think meet
     To put an antic disposition[45] on),
     That you, at such times seeing me, never shall,
     With arms encumbered[46] thus, or this headshake,
     Or by pronouncing of some doubtful phrase,

195   As "Well, well, we know," or "We could an if we would,"
     Or "If we list to speak," or "There be, an if they might,"
     Or such ambiguous giving out, to note
     That you know aught of me. This do swear,
     So grace and mercy at your most need help you.

200 **Ghost:** (*Beneath.*) Swear.

Hamlet: Rest, rest, perturbèd spirit! (*They swear.*) So, gentlemen,
     With all my love I do commend me to you.
     And what so poor a man as Hamlet is
     May do to express his love and friending[47] to you,

---

[40] **upon . . . sword:** on the cross made by the hilt of the sword; but for soldiers the sword itself was a sacred object. [41] **truepenny:** old boy. [42] **Hic et ubique:** here and everywhere. [43] **pioner:** miner. [44] **remove:** move. [45] **antic disposition:** mad behavior. [46] **encumbered:** folded. [47] **friending:** friendship.

205 God willing, shall not lack. Let us go in together.
And still your fingers on your lips, I pray.
The time is out of joint. Oh, cursèd spite
That ever I was born to set it right!
Nay, come, let's go together.

(*Exeunt.*)

Act II

Scene I. A room in Polonius's house.

(*Enter Polonius and Reynaldo.*)

Polonius: Give him this money and these notes, Reynaldo.
Reynaldo: I will, my lord.
Polonius: You shall do marvelous wisely, good Reynaldo.
Before you visit him, to make inquire
5 Of his behavior.
Reynaldo: My lord, I did intend it.
Polonius: Marry, well said, very well said. Look you, sir,
Inquire me first what Danskers[1] are in Paris,
And how, and who, what means,[2] and where they keep,[3]
10 What company, at what expense, and finding
By this encompassment and drift of question[4]
That they do know my son, come you more nearer
Than your particular demands will touch it.[5]
Take you, as 'twere, some distant knowledge of him,
15 As thus, "I know his father and his friends,
And in part him." Do you mark this, Reynaldo?
Reynaldo: Aye, very well, my lord.
Polonius: "And in part him, but," you may say, "not well.
But if 't be he I mean, he's very wild,
20 Addicted so and so"—and there put on him
What forgeries[6] you please. Marry, none so rank[7]
As may dishonor him, take heed of that,
But, sir, such wanton, wild, and usual slips
As are companions noted and most known
25 To youth and liberty.
Reynaldo: As gaming, my lord.
Polonius: Aye, or drinking, fencing,[8] swearing,
Quarreling, drabbing.[9] You may go so far.
Reynaldo: My lord, that would dishonor him.
30 **Polonius:** Faith, no, as you may season[10] it in the charge.
You must not put another scandal on him,
That he is open to incontinency.[11]

---

[1] **Danskers:** Danes. [2] **what means:** what their income is. [3] **keep:** live. [4] **encompassment . . . question:** roundabout method of questioning. [5] **your . . . it:** i.e., you won't get at the truth by straight questions. [6] **forgeries:** inventions. [7] **rank:** gross. [8] **fencing:** A young man who haunted fencing schools would be regarded as quarrelsome and likely to belong to the sporting set. [9] **Drabbing:** whoring. [10] **season:** qualify. [11] **open . . . incontinency:** So long as Laertes does his drabbing inconspicuously Polonius would not be disturbed.

That's not my meaning. But breathe his faults so quaintly[12]
That they may seem the taints of liberty,
35 The flash and outbreak of a fiery mind,
A savageness in unreclaimèd[13] blood,
Of general assault.[14]

Reynaldo: But, my good lord—
Polonius. Wherefore should you do this?
40 **Reynaldo:**   Aye, my lord,
I would know that.
Polonius: Marry, sir, here's my drift,[15]
And I believe it is a fetch of warrant.[16]
You laying these slight sullies[17] on my son,
45 As 'twere a thing a little soiled i' the working,
Mark you,
Your party in converse, him you would sound,
Having ever seen[18] in the prenominate[19] crimes
The youth you breathe of guilty, be assured
50 He closes with you in this consequence[20]—
"Good sir," or so, or "friend," or "gentleman,"
According to the phrase or the addition[21]
Of man and country.
Reynaldo: Very good, my lord.
55 **Polonius:** And then, sir, does he this—he does—What was I about to say?
By the mass, I was about to say something.
Where did I leave?
Reynaldo: At "closes in the consequence."
Polonius: At "closes in the consequence," aye, marry,
60 He closes with you thus: "I know the gentleman.
I saw him yesterday, or t'other day,
Or then, or then, with such, or such, and, as you say,
There was a' gaming, there o'ertook in 's rouse,
There falling out at tennis."[22] Or perchance,
65 "I saw him enter such a house of sale,"
Videlicet,[23] a brothel, or so forth.
See you now,
Your bait of falsehood takes this carp of truth.
And thus do we of wisdom and of reach,[24]
70 With windlasses[25] and with assays of bias,[26]
By indirections find directions out.[27]
So, by my former lecture and advice,
Shall you my son. You have me, have you not?

---

[12] **quaintly:** skillfully.   [13] **unreclaimed:** naturally wild.   [14] **Of . . . assault:** common to all men.   [15] **drift:** intention.   [16] **fetch . . . warrant:** trick warranted to work.   [17] **sullies:** blemishes.   [18] **Having . . . seen:** if ever he has seen.   [19] **prenominate:** aforementioned.   [20] **closes . . . consequence:** follows up with this reply.   [21] **addition:** title.   [22] **tennis:** Visitors to France were much impressed by the enthusiasm of all classes of Frenchmen for tennis, which in England was mainly a courtier's game.   [23] **Videlicet:** namely, "viz."   [24] **wisdom . . . reach:** of far-reaching wisdom.   [25] **windlasses:** roundabout methods.   [26] **assays of bias:** making our bowl take a curved course [Editor's Note: Taking a curved course].   [27] **indirections . . . out:** by indirect means come at the direct truth.

Reynaldo: My lord, I have.

75 **Polonius:** God be wi' ye, fare ye well.

Reynaldo: Good my lord!

Polonius: Observe his inclination in[28] yourself.

Reynaldo: I shall, my lord.

Polonius: And let him ply his music.

80 **Reynaldo:** Well, my lord.

Polonius: Farewell!

(Exit Reynaldo.)

(Enter Ophelia.)

How now, Ophelia! What's the matter?

Ophelia: Oh, my lord, my lord, I have been so affrighted!

Polonius: With what, i' the name of God?

85 **Ophelia:** My lord, as I was sewing in my closet,[29]

Lord Hamlet, with his doublet[30] all unbraced,

No hat upon his head, his stockings fouled,

Ungartered and down-gyved[31] to his ankle,

Pale as his shirt, his knees knocking each other,

90 And with a look so piteous in purport

As if he had been loosèd out of hell

To speak of horrors, he comes before me.

Polonius: Mad for thy love?

Ophelia: My lord, I do not know,

95 But truly I do fear it.

Polonius: What said he?

Ophelia: He took me by the wrist and held me hard.

Then goes he to the length of all his arm,

And with his other hand thus o'er his brow,

100 He falls to such perusal of my face

As he would draw it. Long stayed he so.

At last, a little shaking of mine arm,

And thrice his head thus waving up and down,

He raised a sigh so piteous and profound

105 As it did seem to shatter all his bulk

And end his being. That done, he lets me go.

And with his head over his shoulder turned,

He seemed to find his way without his eyes;

For out o' doors he went without their helps,

110 And to the last bended their light on me.

Polonius: Come, go with me. I will go seek the king.

This is the very ecstasy[32] of love,

Whose violent property fordoes[33] itself

And leads the will to desperate undertakings

---

[28] **in:** for.   [29] **closet:** private room.   [30] **doublet:** the short close-fitting coat which was braced to the hose by laces. When a man was relaxing or careless of appearance, he *unbraced*, as a modern man takes off his coat or unbuttons his waistcoat.   [31] **down-gyved:** hanging around his ankles like fetters.   [32] **ecstasy:** frenzy.   [33] **property fordoes:** natural quality destroys.

115 As oft as any passion under heaven
   That does afflict our natures. I am sorry.
   What, have you given him any hard words of late?
Ophelia: No, my good lord, but, as you did command,
   I did repel his letters and denied
120 His access to me.
Polonius: That hath made him mad.
   I am sorry that with better heed and judgment
   I had not quoted[34] him. I feared he did but trifle
   And meant to wreck thee, but beshrew[35] my jealousy!
125 By Heaven, it is as proper[36] to our age
   To cast beyond ourselves[37] in our opinions
   As it is common for the younger sort
   To lack discretion. Come, go we to the king.
   This must be known, which, being kept close, might move
130 More grief to hide than hate to utter love.[38]
   Come.

(*Exeunt.*)

Scene II. A room in the castle.

(*Flourish. Enter King, Queen, Rosencrantz, Guildenstern, and Attendants.*)

King: Welcome, dear Rosencrantz and Guildenstern!
   Moreover[1] that we much did long to see you,
   The need we have to use you did provoke
   Our hasty sending. Something have you heard
5 Of Hamlet's transformation—so call it,
   Sith[2] nor the exterior nor the inward man
   Resembles that it was. What it should be,
   More than his father's death, that thus hath put him
   So much from the understanding of himself
10 I cannot dream of. I entreat you both
   That, being of so young days brought up with him
   And sith so neighbored to his youth and havior[3]
   That you vouchsafe your rest[4] here in our court
   Some little time, so by your companies
15 To draw him on to pleasures, and to gather
   So much as from occasion you may glean,
   Whether aught to us unknown afflicts him thus
   That opened lies within our remedy.[5]
Queen: Good gentlemen, he hath much talked of you,
20 And sure I am two men there art not living
   To whom he more adheres.[6] If it will please you

---

[34] **quoted:** observed carefully.   [35] **beshrew:** a plague on.   [36] **proper:** natural.   [37] **cast . . . ourselves:** be too clever.   [38] **which . . . love:** by being kept secret it may cause more sorrow than it will cause anger by being revealed; i.e., the King and Queen may be angry at the thought of the Prince's marrying beneath his proper rank.   [1] **Moreover:** in addition to the fact that.   [2] **Sith:** since.   [3] **neighbored . . . havior:** so near to his youthful manner of living.   [4] **vouchsafe . . . rest:** consent to stay.   [5] **opened . . . remedy:** if revealed, might be put right by us.   [6] **To . . . adheres:** whom he regards more highly.

To show us so much gentry[7] and goodwill
As to expend your time with us a while
For the supply and profit of our hope,[8]
25   Your visitation shall receive such thanks
As fits a king's remembrance.

Rosencrantz: Both your majesties
Might, by the sovereign power you have of us,
Put your dread pleasures more into command
30   Than to entreaty.

Guildenstern: But we both obey,
And here give up ourselves, in the full bent[9]
To lay our service freely at your feet,
To be commanded.

35 **King:** Thanks, Rosencrantz and gentle Guildenstern.

Queen: Thanks, Guildenstern and gentle Rosencrantz.
And I beseech you instantly to visit
My too-much-changed son. Go, some of you,
And bring these gentlemen where Hamlet is.

40 **Guildenstern:** Heavens make our presence and our practices
Pleasant and helpful to him!

Queen: Aye, amen!

(Exeunt Rosencrantz, Guildenstern, and some Attendants.)

(Enter Polonius.)

Polonius: The ambassadors from Norway, my good lord,
Are joyfully returned.

45 **King:** Thou still[10] hast been the father of good news.

Polonius: Have I, my lord? I assure my good liege
I hold my duty as I hold my soul,
Both to my God and to my gracious king.
And I do think, or else this brain of mine
50   Hunts not the trail of policy so sure
As it hath used to do,[11] that I have found
The very cause of Hamlet's lunacy.

King: O, speak of that. That do I long to hear.

Polonius: Give first admittance to the ambassadors.
55   My news shall be the fruit[12] to that great feast.

King: Thyself do grace[13] to them and bring them in.

(Exit Polonius.)

He tells me, my dear Gertrude, he hath found
The head and source of all your son's distemper.[14]

Queen: I doubt it is no other but the main,[15]
60   His father's death and our o'erhasty marriage.

---

[7] **gentry:** courtesy.   [8] **supply . . . hope:** to bring a profitable conclusion to our hope.   [9] **in . . . bent:** stretched to our uttermost.   [10] **still:** always.   [11] **Hunts . . . do:** is not so good at following the scent of political events as it used to be.   [12] **fruit:** the dessert, which comes at the end of the feast.   [13] **do grace:** honor; i.e., by escorting them into the royal presence.   [14] **distemper:** mental disturbance.   [15] **main:** principal cause.

King: Well, we shall sift him.

(Re-enter Polonius, with Voltimand and Cornelius.)

Welcome, my good friends!
Say, Voltimand, what from our brother Norway?

Voltimand: Most fair return of greetings and desires.

65   Upon our first,[16] he sent out to suppress
His nephew's levies, which to him appeared
To be a preparation 'gainst the Polack,
But better looked into, he truly found
It was against your highness, whereat, grieved

70   That so his sickness, age, and impotence
Was falsely borne in hand,[17] sends out arrests
On Fortinbras; which he, in brief, obeys,
Receives rebuke from Norway, and in fine[18]
Makes vow before his uncle never more

75   To give the assay of arms[19] against your majesty.
Whereon old Norway, overcome with joy,
Gives him three thousand crowns in annual fee
And his commission to employ those soldiers,
So levied as before, against the Polack.

80   With an entreaty, herein further shown,

(Giving a paper.)

That it might please you to give quiet pass[20]
Through your dominions for this enterprise,
On such regards of safety and allowance[21]
As therein are set down.

85 **King:**   It likes[22] us well,
And at our more considered time we'll read,
Answer, and think upon this business.
Meantime we thank you for your well-took labor.
Go to your rest. At night we'll feast together.

90   Most welcome home!

(Exeunt Voltimand and Cornelius.)

Polonius: This business is well ended.
My liege, and madam, to expostulate[23]
What majesty should be, what duty is,
Why day is day, night night, and time is time,

95   Were nothing but to waste night, day, and time.
Therefore, since brevity is the soul of wit
And tediousness the limbs and outward flourishes,[24]
I will be brief. Your noble son is mad.
Mad call I it, for to define true madness,

---

[16] **first:** i.e., audience.   [17] **borne in hand:** imposed upon.   [18] **in fine:** in the end.   [19] **give . . . arms:** make an attack.   [20] **quiet pass:** unmolested passage.   [21] **regards . . . allowance:** safeguard and conditions.   [22] **likes:** pleases.   [23] **expostulate:** indulge in an academic discussion.   [24] **flourishes:** ornaments.

100 What is 't but to be nothing else but mad?
   But let that go.
  Queen: More matter, with less art.[25]
  Polonius: Madam, I swear I use no art at all.
   That he is mad, 'tis true. 'Tis true 'tis pity,
105 And pity 'tis 'tis true—a foolish figure,[26]
   But farewell it, for I will use no art.
   Mad let us grant him, then. And now remains
   That we find out the cause of this effect,
   Or rather say the cause of this defect,
110 For this effect defective comes by cause.
   Thus it remains and the remainder thus.
   Perpend.[27]
   I have a daughter—have while she is mine—
   Who in her duty and obedience, mark,
115 Hath given me this. Now gather and surmise.[28]

   (Reads.)

   "To the celestial, and my soul's idol, the most beautified[29]
   "Ophelia."—That's an ill phrase, a vile phrase, "beautified" is a
     vile phrase. But you shall hear. Thus:

   (Reads.)

   "In her excellent white bosom, these," and so forth.
120 **Queen:** Came this from Hamlet to her?
  Polonius: Good madam, stay awhile, I will be faithful.

   (Reads.)

      "Doubt thou the stars are fire,
       Doubt that the sun doth move,
      Doubt truth to be a liar,
125   But never doubt I love.

   "O dear Ophelia, I am ill at these numbers,[30] I have not art to reckon my groans, but
     that I love thee best, O most best, believe it.
   Adieu.
      "Thine evermore, most dear lady, whilst this machine[31] is to him, Hamlet."
130 This in obedience hath my daughter shown me,
   And more above, hath his solicitings,
   As they fell out by time, by means and place,
   All given to mine ear.
  King: But how hath she
135 Received his love?
  Polonius: What do you think of me?
  King: As of a man faithful and honorable.

---

[25] **art:** ornament. [26] **figure:** i.e., a figure of speech. [27] **Perpend:** note carefully. [28] **surmise:** guess the meaning. [29] **beautified:** beautiful. [30] **numbers:** verses. [31] **machine:** i.e., body, an affected phrase.

Polonius: I would fain prove so. But what might you think,
When I had seen this hot love on the wing,
140   (As I perceived it, I must tell you that,
Before my daughter told me), what might you
Or my dear majesty your Queen here think
If I had played the desk or table book,[32]
Or given my heart awinking, mute and dumb,
145   Or looked upon this love with idle sight—
What might you think? No, I went round[33] to work,
And my young mistress thus I did bespeak:[34]
"Lord Hamlet is a Prince, out of thy star.[35]
This must not be." And then I prescripts[36] gave her
150   That she should lock herself from his resort,
Admit no messengers, receive no tokens.
Which done, she took the fruits of my advice.
And he, repulsèd, a short tale to make,
Fell into a sadness, then into a fast,
155   Thence to a watch, thence into a weakness,
Thence to a lightness,[37] and by this declension[38]
Into the madness wherein now he raves
And all we mourn for.
King: Do you think this?
160 **Queen:** It may be, very like.
Polonius: Hath there been such a time, I'd fain know that,
That I have positively said "'Tis so"
When it proved otherwise?
King: Not that I know.
165 **Polonius:** *(Pointing to his head and shoulder.)* Take this from this, if this be otherwise.
If circumstances lead me, I will find
Where truth is hid, though it were hid indeed
Within the center.[39]
King: How may we try it further?
170 **Polonius:** You know sometimes he walks four hours together.
Here in the lobby.
Queen: So he does indeed.
Polonius: At such a time I'll loose[40] my daughter to him.
Be you and I behind an arras[41] then.
175   Mark the encounter. If he love her not,
And be not from his reason fall'n thereon,
Let me be no assistant for a state,
But keep a farm and carters.[42]
King: We will try it.

---

[32] **desk . . . book:** i.e., acted as silent go-between (desks and books being natural post offices for a love letter), or been a recipient of secrets but took no action (as desks and notebooks are the natural but inanimate place for keeping secrets).   [33] **round:** straight.   [34] **bespeak:** address.   [35] **out . . . star:** above your destiny.   [36] **prescripts:** instructions.   [37] **Fell . . . lightness:** Hamlet's case history, according to Polonius, develops by stages—melancholy, loss of appetite, sleeplessness, physical weakness, mental instability, and finally madness.   [38] **declension:** decline.   [39] **center:** the very center of the earth.   [40] **loose:** turn loose.   [41] **arras:** tapestry hanging.   [42] **keep . . . carters:** i.e., turn country squire.

180   **Queen:** But look where sadly the poor wretch comes reading.

     Polonius: Away, I do beseech you, both away.

        I'll board[43] him presently.

     (Exeunt King, Queen, and Attendants.)

     (Enter Hamlet, reading.)

                             O, give me leave,

     How does my good Lord Hamlet?

185   **Hamlet:** Well, God-a-mercy.

     Polonius: Do you know me, my lord?

     Hamlet: Excellent well. You are a fishmonger.[44]

     Polonius: Not I, my lord.

     Hamlet: Then I would you were so honest a man.

190   **Polonius:** Honest, my lord!

     Hamlet: Aye, sir, to be honest, as this world goes, is to be one man picked out of ten
        thousand.

     Polonius: That's very true, my lord.

     Hamlet: For if the sun breed maggots[45] in a dead dog, being a god[46] kissing carrion[47]—

195   Have you a daughter?

     Polonius: I have, my lord.

     Hamlet: Let her not walk i' the sun. Conception is a blessing, but not as your daughter
        may conceive—friend, look to 't.

     Polonius: How say you by that? *(Aside.)* Still harping on my daughter. Yet he knew me not

200   at first, he said I was a fishmonger. He is far gone, far gone. And truly in my youth I
        suffered much extremity for love, very near this. I'll speak to him again.—What do
        you read, my lord?

     Hamlet: Words, words, words.

     Polonius: What is the matter, my lord?

205   **Hamlet:** Between who?

     Polonius: I mean the matter that you read, my lord.

     Hamlet: Slanders, sir. For the satirical rogue says here that old men have gray beards, that
        their faces are wrinkled, their eyes purging thick amber and plum-tree gum, and that
        they have a plentiful lack of wit, together with most weak hams.[48] All which, sir,

210   though I most powerfully and potently believe, yet I hold it not honesty to have it t
        hus set down; for yourself, sir, should be old as I am if like a crab you could go
        backward.

     Polonius: *(Aside.)* Though this be madness, yet there is method[49] in 't.—Will you walk out
        of the air, my lord?

215   **Hamlet:** Into my grave?

     Polonius: Indeed, that's out of the air. *(Aside.)* How pregnant[50] sometimes his replies are! A
        happiness[51] that often madness hits on, which reason and sanity could not so prosper-
        ously be delivered of. I will leave him, and suddenly contrive the means of meeting
        between him and my daughter.—My honorable lord, I will most humbly take my

220   leave of you.

     Hamlet: You cannot, sir, take from me anything that I will more willingly part withal—ex-
        cept my life, except my life, except my life.

---

[43] board: accost.   [44] **fishmonger:** Hamlet is now in his "antic disposition," enjoying himself by fooling
Polonius.   [45] **sun . . . maggots:** a general belief.   [46] **god:** Q_2 and F_1 read "good."   [47] **carrion:** flesh.
[48] **hams:** knee joints.   [49] **method:** order, sense.   [50] **pregnant:** apt, meaningful.   [51] **happiness:** good
turn of phrase.

Polonius: Fare you well, my lord.

Hamlet: These tedious old fools!

(Enter Rosencrantz and Guildenstern.)

225 **Polonius:** You go to seek the Lord Hamlet. There he is.

Rosencrantz: *(To Polonius.)* God save you, sir!

(Exit Polonius.)

Guildenstern: My honored lord!

Rosencrantz: My most dear lord!

Hamlet: My excellent good friends![52] How dost thou, Guildenstern?

230 Ah, Rosencrantz! Good lads, how do you both?

Rosencrantz: As the indifferent[53] children of the earth.

Guildenstern: Happy in that we are not overhappy.

On Fortune's cap we are not the very button.[54]

Hamlet: Nor the soles of her shoe?

235 **Rosencrantz:** Neither, my lord.

Hamlet: Then you live about her waist, or in the middle of her favors?

Guildenstern: Faith, her privates[55] we.

Hamlet: In the secret parts of Fortune? Oh, most true, she is a strumpet. What's the news?

Rosencrantz: None, my lord, but that the world's grown honest.

240 **Hamlet:** Then is Doomsday near. But your news is not true. Let me question more in particular. What have you, my good friends, deserved at the hands of Fortune, that she sends you to prison hither?

Guildenstern: Prison, my lord!

Hamlet: Denmark's a prison.

245 **Rosencrantz:** Then is the world one.

Hamlet: A goodly one, in which there are many confines,[56] wards,[57] and dungeons, Denmark being one o' the worst.

Rosencrantz: We think not so, my lord.

Hamlet: Why, then 'tis none to you, for there is nothing either good or bad but thinking

250 makes it so. To me it is a prison.

Rosencrantz: Why, then your ambition[58] makes it one. 'Tis too narrow for your mind.

Hamlet: O, God, I could be bounded in a nutshell and count myself a king of infinite space were it not that I have bad dreams.

Guildenstern: Which dreams indeed are ambition, for the very substance of the

255 ambitious[59] is merely the shadow of a dream.

Hamlet: A dream itself is but a shadow.

Rosencrantz: Truly, and I hold ambition of so airy and light a quality that it is but a shadow's shadow.

Hamlet: Then are our beggars bodies, and our monarchs and outstretched heroes the beg-

260 gars' shadows.[60] Shall we to the Court? For, by my fay,[61] I cannot reason.[62]

---

[52] **My . . . friends:** As soon as Polonius has gone, Hamlet drops his assumed madness and greets Rosencrantz and Guildenstern naturally. [53] **indifferent:** neither too great nor too little. [54] **button:** i.e., at the top. [55] **privates:** with a pun on "private parts" and "private," not concerned with politics. [56] **confines:** places of confinement. [57] **wards:** cells. [58] **your ambition:** Rosencrantz is feeling after one possible cause of Hamlet's melancholy—thwarted ambition. [59] **substance . . . ambitious:** that on which an ambitious man feeds his fancies. [60] **Then . . . shadows:** i.e., by your reasoning beggars are the only men of substance, for kings and heroes are by nature ambitious and therefore "the shadows of a dream." **outstretched:** of exaggerated reputation. [61] **fay:** faith. [62] **reason:** argue.

Rosencrantz & Guildenstern: We'll wait upon you.[63]

Hamlet: No such matter. I will not sort[64] you with the rest of my servants, for, to speak to you like an honest man, I am most dreadfully attended.[65] But in the beaten way of friendship, what make you at Elsinore?

265 **Rosencrantz:** To visit you, my lord, no other occasion.

Hamlet: Beggar that I am, I am even poor in thanks, but I thank you. And sure, dear friends, my thanks are too dear a halfpenny.[66] Were you not sent for? Is it your own inclining? Is it a free visitation?[67] Come, deal justly with me. Come, come. Nay, speak.

270 **Guildenstern:** What should we say, my lord?

Hamlet: Why, anything, but to the purpose.[68] You were sent for, and there is a kind of confession in your looks which your modesties have not craft enough to color.[69] I know the good king and queen have sent for you.

Rosencrantz: To what end, my lord?

275 **Hamlet:** That you must teach me. But let me conjure[70] you, by the rights of our fellowship,[71] by the consonancy[72] of our youth, by the obligation of our ever preserved love, and by what more dear a better proposer could charge you withal, be even[73] and direct with me, whether you were sent for, or no.

Rosencrantz: *(Aside to Guildenstern.)* What say you?

280 **Hamlet:** *(Aside.)* Nay, then, I have an eye of you.—If you love me, hold not off.

Guildenstern: My lord, we were sent for.

Hamlet: I will tell you why. So shall my anticipation prevent your discovery, and your secrecy to the king and queen molt no feather.[74] I have of late—but wherefore I know not—lost all my mirth, forgone all custom of exercises, and indeed it goes so heavily

285 with my disposition that this goodly frame the earth seems to me a sterile promontory. This most excellent canopy,[75] the air, look you, this brave o'erhanging firmament,[76] this majestical roof fretted[77] with golden fire—why, it appears no other thing to me than a foul and pestilent congregation of vapors. What a piece of work is a man! How noble in reason! How infinite in faculty![78] In form and moving[79] how express[80] and

290 admirable! In action how like an angel! In apprehension how like a god! The beauty of the world! The paragon of animals! And yet, to me, what is this quintessence[81] of dust? Man delights not me—no, nor woman neither, though by your smiling you seem to say so.

Rosencrantz: My lord, there was no such stuff in my thoughts.

295 **Hamlet:** Why did you laugh, then, when I said "Man delights not me"?

Rosencrantz: To think, my lord, if you delight not in man, what lenten entertainment[82] the players shall receive from you. We coted[83] them on the way, and hither are they coming to offer you service.

Hamlet: He that plays the king shall be welcome, His majesty shall have tribute of me. The

300 adventurous knight shall use his foil and target,[84] the lover shall not sigh gratis, the humorous man[85] shall end his part in peace, the clown shall make those laugh whose

---

[63] **wait . . . you:** be your servants. [64] **sort:** class. [65] **dreadfully attended:** my attendants are a poor crowd. [66] **too . . . halfpenny:** not worth a halfpenny. [67] **free visitation:** voluntary visit.
[68] **anything . . . purpose:** anything so long as it is not true. [69] **color:** conceal. [70] **conjure:** make solemn appeal to. [71] **fellowship:** comradeship. [72] **consonancy:** concord. [73] **even:** straight.
[74] **So . . . feather:** i.e., so by my telling you first you will not be obliged to betray the secrets of the King. **prevent:** forestall. **molt no feather:** be undisturbed. [75] **canopy:** covering. [76] **firmament:** sky. [77] **fretted:** ornamented. [78] **faculty:** power of the mind. [79] **moving:** movement. [80] **express:** exact. [81] **quintessence:** perfection; the fifth essence, which would be left if the four elements were taken away. [82] **lenten entertainment:** meager welcome. [83] **coted:** overtook. [84] **foil . . . target:** rapier and small shield.
[85] **humorous man:** the man who specializes in character parts.

lungs are tickle o' the sere,[86] and the lady shall say her mind freely or the blank verse
shall halt[87] for 't. What players are they?

Rosencrantz: Even those you were wont to take such delight in, the tragedians of the city.

305 **Hamlet:** How chances it they travel? Their residence, both in reputation and profit, was
better both ways.[88]

Rosencrantz: I[89] think their inhibition[90] comes by the means of the late innovation.[91]

Hamlet: Do they hold the same estimation they did when I was in the city? Are they so
followed?

310 **Rosencrantz:** No, indeed are they not.

Hamlet: How comes it? Do they grow rusty?

Rosencrantz: Nay, their endeavor keeps in the wonted pace.[92] But there is, sir, an eyrie[93] of
children, little eyases,[94] that cry out on the top of question[95] and are most
tyrannically[96] clapped for 't. These are now the fashion, and so berattle[97] the common

315 stages[98]—so they call them—that many wearing rapiers are afraid of goose quills[99] and
dare scare come thither.

Hamlet: What, are they children? Who maintains 'em? How are they escoted?[100] Will they
pursue the quality[101] no longer than they can sing? Will they not say afterward, if they
should grow themselves to common players—as it is most like if their means are

320 no better—their writers do them wrong to make them exclaim against their own
succession?[102]

Rosencrantz: Faith, there has been much to-do on both sides, and the nation holds it no
sin to tarre[103] them to controversy. There was for a while no money bid for argument[104] unless the poet and the player went to cuffs[105] in the question.

325 **Hamlet:** Is 't possible?

Guildenstern: O, there has been much throwing-about of brains.

Hamlet: Do the boys carry it away?

Rosencrantz: Aye, that they do, my lord, Hercules and his load[106] too.

Hamlet: It is not very strange, for my uncle is King of Denmark, and those that would

330 make mows[107] at him while my father lived give twenty, forty, fifty, a hundred ducats
apiece for his picture in little. 'Sblood,[108] there is something in this more than natural,
if philosophy could find it out.

(Flourish of trumpets within.)

Guildenstern: There are the players.

Hamlet: Gentlemen, you are welcome to Elsinore. Your hands. Come then. The appurte-

335 nance of welcome is fashion and ceremony.[109] Let me comply[110] with you in this
garb,[111] lest my extent[112] to the players—which, I tell you, must show fairly outward—

---

86 **are . . . sere:** explode at a touch. The *sere* is part of the trigger mechanism of a gun which if "ticklish" will
go off at a touch.   87 **halt:** limp.   88 **Their . . . ways:** i.e., if they stayed in the city, it would bring them
more profit and fame.   89 **I . . . too** (ll. 307–328): This reference to the stage war between the Children's
Companies is one of the several topical references in *Hamlet*.   90 **inhibition:** formal prohibition.   91 **innovation:** riot.   92 **endeavor . . . pace:** they try as hard as ever.   93 **eyrie:** nest.   94 **eyases:** young hawks.
95 **cry . . . question:** either "cry in a shrill voice" or perhaps "cry out the latest detail of the dispute."
96 **tyrannically:** outrageously.   97 **berattle:** abuse.   98 **common stages:** the professional players. The boys
acted in "private" playhouses.   99 **goose quills:** pens; i.e., of such as Ben Jonson.   100 **escoted:** paid.
101 **quality:** acting profession.   102 **exclaim . . . succession:** abuse the profession to which they will afterward belong.   103 **tarre:** urge on to fight; generally used of encouraging a dog.   104 **argument:** plot of a
play.   105 **went to cuffs:** boxed each others' ears.   106 **Hercules . . . load:** Hercules carrying the globe on
his shoulders was the sign of the Globe Playhouse.   107 **mows:** grimaces.   108 **'Sblood:** by God's blood.
109 **appurtenance . . . ceremony:** that which pertains to welcome is formal ceremony.   110 **comply:** use the
formality of welcome; i.e., shake hands with you.   111 **garb:** fashion.   112 **extent:** outward behavior.

should more appear like entertainment[113] than yours. You are welcome. But my uncle-
father and aunt-mother are deceived.

Guildenstern: In what, my dear lord?

340 **Hamlet:** I am but mad north-northwest.[114] When the wind is southerly,[115]
I know a hawk from a handsaw.[116]

(Re-enter Polonius.)

Polonius: Well be with you, gentlemen!

Hamlet: Hark you, Guildenstern, and you too—at each ear a hearer.
That great baby you see there is not yet out of his swaddling clouts.[117]

345 **Rosencrantz:** Happily he's the second time come to them, for they say an old man is twice
a child.

Hamlet: I will prophesy he comes to tell me of the players, mark it.
You say right, sir. O' Monday morning, 'twas so indeed.

Polonius: My lord, I have news to tell you.

350 **Hamlet:** My lord, I have news to tell you.
When Roscius[118] was an actor in Rome—

Polonius: The actors are come hither, my lord.

Hamlet: Buzz, buzz![119]

Polonius: Upon my honor—

355 **Hamlet:** Then came each actor on his ass—

Polonius: The[120] best actors in the world, either for tragedy, comedy, history, pastoral, pastoral-
comical, historical pastoral, tragical-historical, tragical-comical-historical-pastoral, scene
individable[121] or poem unlimited.[122] Seneca cannot be too heavy, nor Plautus[123] too light.
For the law of writ[124] and the liberty,[125] these are the only men.

360 **Hamlet:** O Jephthah,[126] judge of Israel, what a treasure hadst thou!

Polonius: What a treasure had he, my lord?

Hamlet: Why,

> "One[127] fair daughter, and no more,
> The which he loved passing well."

365 **Polonius:** *(Aside.)* Still[128] on my daughter.

Hamlet: Am I not i' the right, old Jephthah?

Polonius: If you call me Jephthah, my lord, I have a daughter that I love passing well.

Hamlet: Nay, that follows not.

Polonius: What follows, then, my lord?

370 **Hamlet:** Why,

> "As by lot, God wot,"[129]

and then you know,

> "It came to pass, as most like it was."

---

[113] **entertainment:** welcome. [114] **north-northwest:** i.e., 327° (out of 360°) of the compass. [115] **wind is
southerly:** The south wind was considered unhealthy. [116] **hawk . . . handsaw:** Either "handsaw" is a corruption of "heronshaw," heron, or a hawk is a tool like a pickax. The phrase means "I'm not so mad as you
think." [117] **clouts:** clothes. [118] **Roscius:** the most famous of Roman actors. [119] **Buzz, buzz:** slang for
"stale news." [120] **The . . . men:** Polonius reads out the accomplishments of the actors from the license
which they have presented him. [121] **scene individable:** i.e., a play preserving the unities. [122] **poem unlimited:** i.e., a play that disregards the rules. [123] **Seneca . . . Plautus:** the Roman writers of tragedy and
comedy with whose plays every educated man was familiar. [124] **law of writ:** the critical rules; i.e., classical
plays. [125] **liberty:** plays freely written; i.e., "modern" drama. [126] **Jephthah:** The story of Jephthah is told
in Judges, Chapter II. He vowed that if successful against the Ammonites he would sacrifice the first creature
to meet him on his return, which was his daughter. [127] **One . . . was:** Quotations from a ballad of Jephthah.
[128] **Still:** always. [129] **wot:** knows.

The first row[130] of the pious chanson[131] will show you more, for look where my abridge-
375 ment[132] comes. (*Enter four or five Players.*) You are welcome, masters, welcome all. I am
glad to see thee well. Welcome, good friends. Oh, my old friend![133] Why, thy face is
valanced[134] since I saw thee last. Comest thou to beard[135] me in Denmark? What, my
young lady[136] and mistress! By 'r Lady, your ladyship is nearer to Heaven than when I saw
you last, by the altitude of a chopine.[137] Pray God your voice, like a piece of uncurrent
380 gold, be not cracked within the ring.[138] Masters, you are all welcome. We'll e'en to 't like
French falconers,[139] fly at anything we see. We'll have a speech straight. Come, give us a
taste of your quality[140]—come, a passionate speech.

1. Player: What speech, my good lord?

Hamlet: I heard thee speak me a speech once, but it was never acted, or if it was, not
385 above once; for the play, I remember, pleased not the million, 'twas caviar[141] to the
general.[142] But it was—as I received it, and others, whose judgments in such matters
cried in the top of mine[143]—an excellent play, well digested[144] in the scenes, set
down with as much modesty[145] as cunning. I remember one said there were no sallets[146] in the lines to make the matter savory, nor no matter in the phrase that might
390 indict the author of affection,[147] but called it an honest method, as wholesome as
sweet, and by very much more handsome than fine.[148] One speech in it I chiefly
loved. 'Twas Aeneas' tale to Dido,[149] and thereabout of it especially where he speaks of
Priam's[150] slaughter. If it lives in your memory, begin at this line—let me see, let me
see—

395   "The rugged Pyrrhus,[151] like th' Hyrcanian beast,[152]—"

It is not so. It begins with "Pyrrhus."

         "The[153] rugged Pyrrhus, he whose sable[154] arms,
         Black as his purpose, did the night resemble
         When he lay couchèd in the ominous[155] horse,[156]
400   Hath now this dread and black complexion smeared
         With heraldry[157] more dismal. Head to foot
         Now is he total gules, horridly tricked
         With blood of fathers, mothers, daughters, sons,
         Baked and impasted[158] with the parching streets
405   That lend a tyrannous and a damnèd light

---

[130] **row:** line. [131] **pious chanson:** godly poem. [132] **abridgement:** entertainment. [133] **old friend:** i.e., the
leading player. [134] **valanced:** bearded. A valance is a fringe hung round the sides and bottom of a bed.
[135] **beard:** dare, with a pun on "valanced." [136] **young lady:** i.e., the boy who takes the woman's parts.
[137] **chopine:** lady's shoe with thick cork sole. [138] **cracked ... ring:** Before coins were milled on the rim they
were liable to crack. When the crack reached the ring surrounding the device, the coin was no longer valid.
[139] **French falconers:** They were famous for their skill in hawking. [140] **quality:** skill as an actor.
[141] **caviar:** sturgeon's roe, a Russian delicacy not then appreciated (or known) by any but gourmets. [142] **general:** common herd. [143] **cried ... mine:** surpassed mine. [144] **digested:** composed. [145] **modesty:** moder-
ation. [146] **sallets:** tasty bits. [147] **phrase ... affection:** nothing in the language which could charge the
author with affectation. [148] **fine:** subtle. [149] **Aeneas' ... Dido:** the story of the sack of Troy as told by Aeneas to Dido, Queen of Carthage. The original is in Virgil's *Aeneid*. A similar speech occurs in Marlowe's play
Dido, Queen of Carthage. [150] **Priam:** the old King of Troy. [151] **Pyrrhus:** the son of Achilles, one of the Greeks
concealed in the Wooden Horse. [152] **Hyrcanian beast:** the tiger. [153] **The ... gods:** The speech may be from
some lost play of *Dido* and *Aeneas,* but more likely it is Shakespeare's own invention. It is written in the heavy
elaborate style still popular in the dramas of the Admiral's Men. The first player delivers it with excessive gesture
and emotion. [154] **sable:** black. [155] **ominous:** fateful. [156] **horse:** the Wooden Horse by which a small Greek
force was enabled to make a secret entry into Troy. [157] **heraldry:** painting. The image of heraldic painting is
kept up in *gules* (the heraldic term for red) and *tricked* (painted). [158] **impasted:** turned into a crust by the heat
of the burning city.

> To their lord's murder. Roasted in wrath and fire,
> And thus o'ersized with coagulate gore,[159]
> With eyes like carbuncles, the hellish Pyrrhus
> Old grandsire Priam seeks."

410   So proceed you.

Polonius: 'Fore God, my lord, well spoken, with good accent and good discretion.

1. Player: "Anon he finds him

> Striking too short at Greeks. His antique sword,
> Rebellious to his arm, lies where it falls,
415   Repugnant to command.[160] Unequal matched,
> Pyrrhus at Priam drives, in rage strikes wide,
> But with the whiff and wind of his fell sword
> The unnerved father falls. Then senseless Ilium,[161]
> Seeming to feel this blow, with flaming top
420   Stoops to his base,[162] and with a hideous crash
> Takes prisoner Pyrrhus' ear. For lo! his sword,
> Which was declining[163] on the milky[164] head
> Of reverend Priam, seemed i' the air to stick.
> So as a painted tyrant[165] Pyrrhus stood,
425   And like a neutral to his will and matter,[166]
> Did nothing.
> But as we often see, against[167] some storm
> A silence in the heavens, the rack[168] stand still,
> The bold winds speechless and the orb[169] below
430   As hush as death, anon the dreadful thunder
> Doth rend the region[170]—so after Pyrrhus' pause
> Arousèd vengeance sets him new awork.
> And never did the Cyclops'[171] hammers fall
> On Mars's armor, forged for proof eterne,[172]
435   With less remorse[173] than Pyrrhus' bleeding sword
> Now falls on Priam.
> Out, out, thou strumpet, Fortune! All you gods,
> In general synod[174] take away her power,
> Break all the spokes and fellies[175] from her wheel,
440   And bowl the round nave[176] down the hill of heaven
> As low as to the fiends!"

Polonius: This is too long.

Hamlet: It shall to the barber's, with your beard. Prithee, say on. He's for a jig[177] or a tale of bawdry, or he sleeps. Say on. Come to Hecuba.

445   **1. Player:** "But who, oh, who had seen the mobléd[178] Queen—"

---

[159] **o'ersized . . . gore:** covered over with congealed blood.   [160] **Repugnant to command:** refusing to be used.   [161] **Ilium:** the citadel of Troy.   [162] **stoops . . . base:** collapses.   [163] **declining:** bending toward.   [164] **milky:** milk-white.   [165] **painted tyrant:** as in the painting of a tyrant.   [166] **neutral . . . matter:** one midway (*neutral*) between his desire (*will*) and action (*matter*).   [167] **against:** just before.   [168] **rack:** the clouds in the upper air.   [169] **orb:** world.   [170] **region:** the country round.   [171] **Cyclops':** of Titans, giants who aided Vulcan, the blacksmith god, to make armor for Mars, the war god.   [172] **proof eterne:** everlasting protection.   [173] **remorse:** pity.   [174] **synod:** council.   [175] **fellies:** the pieces forming the circumference of a wooden wheel.   [176] **nave:** center of the wheel.   [177] **jig:** bawdy dance.   [178] **mobléd:** muffled.

Hamlet: "The mobléd Queen"?

Polonius: That's good, "mobléd Queen" is good.

1. Player: "Run barefoot up and down, threatening the flames

    With bisson rheum,[179] a clout[180] upon that head

450   Where late the diadem stood, and for a robe,

    About her lank and all o'erteemed[181] loins

    A blanket, in the alarm of fear caught up.

    Who this had seen, with tongue in venom steeped

    'Gainst Fortune's state would treason have pronounced.[182]

455   But if the gods themselves did see her then,

    When she saw Pyrrhus make malicious sport

    In mincing with his sword her husband's limbs,

    The instant burst of clamor that she made,

    Unless things mortal move them not at all,

460   Would have made milch[183] the burning eyes of heaven

    And passion in the gods."

Polonius: Look whether he has not turned his color and has tears in 's eyes. Prithee, no more.

Hamlet: 'Tis well; I'll have thee speak out the rest of this soon. Good my lord, will you see

465 the players well bestowed?[184] Do you hear, let them be well used, for they are the abstract and brief chronicles of the time.[185] After your death you were better have a bad epitaph than their ill report while you live.

Polonius: My lord, I will use them according to their desert.[186]

Hamlet: God's bodkin,[187] man, much better. Use every man after his desert and who shall

470 'scape whipping? Use them after your own honor and dignity. The less they deserve, the more merit is in your bounty. Take them in.

Polonius: Come, sirs.

Hamlet: Follow him, friends. We'll hear a play tomorrow.

(Exit Polonius with all the Players but the First.)

    Dost thou hear me, old friend? Can you play *The Murder of Gonzago*?

475 **1. Player:** Aye, my lord.

Hamlet: We'll ha 't tomorrow night. You could, for a need, study a speech of some dozen or sixteen lines which I would set down and insert in 't, could you not?

1. Player: Aye, my lord.

Hamlet: Very well. Follow that lord, and look you mock him not.

(Exit First Player.)

480   My good friends, I'll leave you till night. You are welcome to Elsinore.

Rosencrantz: Good my lord!

Hamlet: Aye, so, God be wi' ye! *(Exeunt Rosencrantz and Guildenstern.)* Now I am alone.

    O, what a rogue and peasant slave am I!

    Is it not monstrous that this player here,

---

[179] **bisson rheum:** blinding moisture.   [180] **clout:** rag.   [181] **o'erteemed:** exhausted by bearing children; she had borne fifty-two.   [182] **Who . . . pronounced:** anyone who had seen this sight would with bitter words have uttered treason against the tyranny of Fortune.   [183] **milch:** milky, i.e., dripping moisture.   [184] **bestowed:** housed.   [185] **abstract . . . time:** they summarize and record the events of our time. Elizabethan players were often in trouble for too saucily commenting on their betters in plays dealing with history or contemporary events and persons.   [186] **desert:** rank.   [187] **God's bodkin:** by God's little body.

485   But in a fiction, in a dream of passion,[188]
             Could force his soul so to his own conceit[189]
             That from her working[190] all his visage wanned,[191]
             Tears in his eyes, distraction[192] in 's aspect,[193]
             A broken voice, and his whole function[194] suiting

490   With forms to his conceit? And all for nothing!
             For Hecuba!
             What's Hecuba to him or he to Hecuba,
             That he should weep for her? What would he do
             Had he the motive and the cue for passion

495   That I have? He would drown the stage with tears
             And cleave the general ear[195] with horrid speech,
             Make mad the guilty and appal the free,[196]
             Confound the ignorant, and amaze indeed
             The very faculties of eyes and ears.

500   Yet I,
             A dull and muddy-mettled[197] rascal, peak,[198]
             Like John-a-dreams,[199] unpregnant of my cause,[200]
             And can say nothing—no, not for a king
             Upon whose property[201] and most dear life

505   A damned defeat[202] was made. Am I a coward?
             Who[203] calls me villain? Breaks my pate across?
             Plucks off my beard and blows it in my face?
             Tweaks me by the nose? Gives me the lie i' the throat
             As deep as to the lungs? Who does me this?

510   Ha! 'Swounds,[204] I should take it. For it cannot be
             But I am pigeon-livered[205] and lack gall[206]
             To make oppression bitter, or ere this
             I should have fatted all the region kites
             With this slave's offal.[207] Bloody, bawdy villain!

515   Remorseless, treacherous, lecherous, kindless[208] villain!
             O, vengeance!
             Why, what an ass am I! This is most brave,
             That I, the son of a dear father murdered,
             Prompted to my revenge by heaven and hell,

520   Must, like a whore, unpack my heart with words
             And fall a-cursing like a very drab,[209]
             A scullion![210] Fie upon 't! Foh!
             About, my brain! Hum, I have heard
             That guilty creatures sitting at a play,

---

[188] **dream of passion:** imaginary emotion. [189] **conceit:** imagination. [190] **her working:** i.e., the effect of imagination. [191] **wanned:** went pale. [192] **distraction:** frenzy. [193] **aspect:** countenance. [194] **function:** behavior. [195] **general ear:** ears of the audience. [196] **free:** innocent. [197] **muddy-mettled:** made of mud, not iron. [198] **peak:** mope. [199] **John-a-dreams:** "Sleepy Sam" [Editor's Note: sleepy fellow]. [200] **unpregnant . . . cause:** barren of plans for vengeance. [201] **property:** personality, life. [202] **defeat:** ruin. [203] **Who . . . this:** Hamlet runs through all the insults which provoked a resolute man to mortal combat. **pate:** head. **lie . . . throat:** the bitterest of insults. [204] **'Swounds:** by God's wounds. [205] **pigeon-livered:** "as gentle as a dove." [206] **gall:** spirit. [207] **I . . . offal:** before this I would have fed this slave's (i.e., the King's) guts to the kites. **fatted:** made fat. [208] **kindless:** unnatural. [209] **drab:** "moll" [Editor's Note: whore]. [210] **scullion:** the lowest of the kitchen servants.

525 Have by the very cunning of the scene
Been struck so to the soul that presently[211]
They have proclaimed their malefactions;[212]
For murder, though it have no tongue, will speak
With most miraculous organ. I'll have these players
530 Play something like the murder of my father
Before mine uncle. I'll observe his looks,
I'll tent[213] him to the quick. If he but blench,[214]
I know my course. The spirit that I have seen
May be the devil, and the devil hath power
535 To assume a pleasing shape. Yea, and perhaps
Out of my weakness and my melancholy,
As he is very potent with such spirits,
Abuses me to damn me.[215] I'll have grounds[216]
More relative than this.[217] The play's the thing
540 Wherein I'll catch the conscience of the king.

(*Exit.*)

Act III

Scene I. A room in the castle.

(*Enter King, Queen, Polonius, Ophelia, Rosencrantz, and Guildenstern.*)

King: And can you, by no drift of circumstance,[1]
Get from him why he puts on this confusion,
Grating[2] so harshly all his days of quiet
With turbulent and dangerous lunacy?
5 **Rosencrantz:** He does confess he feels himself distracted,
But from what cause he will by no means speak.
Guildenstern: Nor do we find him forward to be sounded,[3]
But, with a crafty madness, keeps aloof
When we would bring him on to some confession
10 Of his true state.
Queen: Did he receive you well?
Rosencrantz: Most like a gentleman.
Guildenstern: But with much forcing of his disposition.[4]
Rosencrantz: Niggard of question,[5] but of our demands
15 Most free in his reply.
Queen: Did you assay him
To any pastime?[6]
Rosencrantz: Madam, it so fell out that certain players
We o'erraught[7] on the way. Of these we told him,
20 And there did seem in him a kind of joy

---

[211] **presently:** immediately.   [212] **proclaimed . . . malefactions:** shouted out their crimes.   [213] **tent:** probe.   [214] **blench:** flinch.   [215] **Abuses . . . me:** i.e., deceives me so that I may commit the sin of murder that will bring me to damnation.   [216] **grounds:** reasons for actions.   [217] **relative . . . this:** i.e., more convincing than the appearance of a ghost.   [1] **drift of circumstance:** circumstantial evidence, hint.   [2] **grating:** disturbing.   [3] **forward . . . sounded:** eager to be questioned.   [4] **much . . . disposition:** making a great effort to be civil to us.   [5] **Niggard of question:** not asking many questions.   [6] **Did . . . pastime:** did you try to interest him in any amusement.   [7] **o'erraught:** overtook.

To hear of it. They are about the court,
And, as I think, they have already order
This night to play before him.

Polonius: 'Tis most true.
25   And he beseeched me to entreat your majesties
To hear and see the matter.

King: With all my heart, and it doth much content me
To hear him so inclined.
Good gentlemen, give him a further edge,[8]
30   And drive his purpose on to these delights.

Rosencrantz: We shall, my lord.

(Exeunt Rosencrantz and Guildenstern.)

King: Sweet Gertrude, leave us too,
For we have closely[9] sent for Hamlet hither,
That he, as 'twere by accident, may here
35   Affront[10] Ophelia.
Her father and myself, lawful espials,[11]
Will so bestow ourselves that, seeing unseen,
We may of their encounter frankly judge
And gather by him, as he is behaved,[12]
40   If 't be the affliction of his love or no
That thus he suffers for.

Queen: I shall obey you.—
And for your part, Ophelia, I do wish
That your good beauties be the happy cause
45   Of Hamlet's wildness. So shall I hope your virtues
Will bring him to his wonted way[13] again,
To both your honors.

Ophelia: Madam, I wish it may.

(Exit Queen.)

Polonius: Ophelia, walk you here.—Gracious,[14] so please you,
50   We will bestow outselves. *(To Ophelia.)* Read on this book,[15]
That show of such an exercise may color
Your loneliness. We are oft to blame in this—
'Tis too much proved—that with devotion's visage[16]
And pious action we do sugar o'er
55   The Devil himself.

King: *(Aside.)*   O, 'tis too true!
How smart a lash that speech doth give my conscience!
The harlot's cheek, beautied with plastering art,
Is not more ugly to the thing that helps it[17]
60   Than is my deed to my most painted[18] word.
O, heavy burden!

---

[8] **edge:** encouragement.   [9] **closely:** secretly.   [10] **Affront:** encounter.   [11] **lawful espials:** who are justified in spying on him.   [12] **by . . . behaved:** from him, from his behavior.   [13] **wonted way:** normal state.   [14] **Gracious:** your Majesty—addressed to the King.   [15] **book:** i.e., of devotions.   [16] **devotion's visage:** an outward appearance of religion.   [17] **ugly . . . it:** i.e., lust, which is the cause of its artificial beauty.   [18] **painted:** i.e., false.

Polonius: I hear him coming. Let's withdraw, my lord.

(Exeunt King and Polonius.)

(Enter Hamlet.[19])

Hamlet: To be, or not to be—that is the question:
Whether 'tis nobler in the mind to suffer
65 The slings and arrows of outrageous[20] fortune,
Or to take arms against a sea[21] of troubles,
And by opposing end them. To die, to sleep—
No more, and by a sleep to say we end
The heartache and the thousand natural shocks
70 That flesh is heir to. 'Tis a consummation[22]
Devoutly to be wished. To die, to sleep,
To sleep—perchance to dream. Aye, there's the rub,[23]
For in that sleep of death what dreams may come
When we have shuffled off this mortal coil[24]
75 Must give us pause. There's the respect[25]
That makes calamity of so long life.[26]
For who would bear the whips and scorns of time,
The oppressor's wrong, the proud man's contumely[27]
The pangs of déspised love, the law's delay,
80 The insolence of office[28] and the spurns
That patient merit of the unworthy takes,[29]
When he himself might his quietus[30] make
With a bare bodkin?[31] Who would fardels[32] bear,
To grunt and sweat under a weary life,
85 But that the dread of something after death,
The undiscovered country from whose bourn[33]
No traveler returns, puzzles the will,[34]
And makes us rather bear those ills we have
Than fly to others that we know not of?
90 Thus[35] conscience does make cowards of us all,
And thus the native hue[36] of resolution
Is sicklied o'er with the pale cast[37] of thought,
And enterprises of great pitch[38] and moment
With this regard their currents turn awry
95 And lose the name of action.[39]—Soft you now!
The fair Ophelia! Nymph, in thy orisons[40]
Be all my sins remembered.

---

[19] **Enter Hamlet:** In Q_1 the King draws attention to Hamlet's approach with the words "See where he comes poring upon a book." Hamlet is again reading, and is too much absorbed to notice Ophelia. [20] **outrageous:** cruel. [21] **sea:** i.e., an endless turmoil. [22] **consummation:** completion. [23] **rub:** impediment. [24] **shuffled . . . coil:** cast off this fuss of life. [25] **respect:** reason. [26] **makes . . . life:** makes it a calamity to have to live so long. [27] **contumely:** insulting behavior. [28] **insolence of office:** insolent behavior of government officials. [29] **spurns . . . takes:** insults which men of merit have patiently to endure from the unworthy. [30] **quietus:** discharge. [31] **bodkin:** dagger. [32] **fardels:** burdens, the coolie pack. [33] **bourn:** boundary. [34] **will:** resolution, ability to act. [35] **Thus . . . action:** the religious fear that death may not be the end makes men shrink from heroic actions. [36] **native hue:** natural color. [37] **cast:** color. [38] **pitch:** height; used of the soaring flight of a hawk. [39] **With . . . action:** by brooding on this thought great enterprises are diverted from their course and fade away. [40] **orisons:** prayers.

Ophelia: Good my lord,
How does your honor for this many a day?

100 **Hamlet:** I humbly thank you—well, well, well.

Ophelia: My lord, I have remembrances of yours
That I have longed long to redeliver.
I pray you now receive them.

Hamlet: No, not I.

105 I never gave you aught.

Ophelia: My honored lord, you know right well you did,
And with them words of so sweet breath composed
As made the things more rich. Their perfume lost,
Take these again, for to the noble mind

110 Rich gifts wax poor when givers prove unkind.
There, my lord.

Hamlet: Ha, ha! Are you honest?[41]

Ophelia: My lord?

Hamlet: Are you fair?

115 **Ophelia:** What means your lordship?

Hamlet: That if you be honest and fair, your honesty should admit no discourse to your beauty.[42]

Ophelia: Could beauty, my lord, have better commerce than with honesty?

Hamlet: Aye, truly, for the power of beauty will sooner transform honesty from what it is to

120 a bawd[43] than the force of honesty can translate beauty into his likeness. This was sometime a paradox,[44] but now the time gives it proof. I did love you once.

Ophelia: Indeed, my lord, you made me believe so.

Hamlet: You should not have believed me, for virtue cannot so inoculate our old stock but we shall relish[45] of it. I loved you not.

125 **Ophelia:** I was the more deceived.

Hamlet: Get thee to a nunnery. Why wouldst thou be a breeder of sinners? I am myself indifferent honest,[46] but yet I could accuse me of such things that it were better my mother had not borne me. I am very proud, revengeful, ambitious, with more offenses at my beck[47] than I have thoughts to put them in, imagination to give them shape, or

130 time to act them in. What should such fellows as I do crawling between heaven and earth? We are arrant knaves all. Believe none of us. Go thy ways to a nunnery.[48] Where's your father?

Ophelia: At home, my lord.

Hamlet: Let the doors be shut upon him, that he may play the fool nowhere but in 's own

135 house. Farewell.

Ophelia: O, help him, you sweet heavens!

Hamlet: I thou dost marry, I'll give thee this plague for thy dowry: Be thou as chaste as ice, as pure as snow—thou shalt not escape calumny.[49] Get thee to a nunnery, go. Farewell. Or if thou wilt needs marry, marry a fool, for wise men know well

140 enough what monsters[50] you make of them. To a nunnery, go, and quickly too. Farewell.

---

[41] **honest:** chaste. [42] **That . . . beauty:** if you are chaste and beautiful your chastity should have nothing to do with your beauty—because (so Hamlet thinks in his bitterness) beautiful women are seldom chaste. [43] **bawd:** brothel-keeper. [44] **paradox:** statement contrary to accepted opinion. [45] **relish:** have some trace. [46] **indifferent honest:** moderately honorable. [47] **at . . . beck:** waiting to come when I beckon. [48] **nunnery:** i.e., a place where she will be removed from temptation. [49] **calumny:** slander. [50] **monsters:** horned beasts, cuckolds.

Ophelia: O heavenly powers, restore him!

Hamlet: I have heard of your paintings[51] too, well enough. God hath given you one face and you make yourselves another. You jig,[52] you amble,[53] and you lisp,[54] and nick-
145 name God's creatures, and make your wantonness your ignorance.[55] Go to, I'll no more on 't—it hath made me mad. I say we will have no more marriages. Those that are married already, all but one, shall live; the rest shall keep as they are. To a nunnery, go. (*Exit.*)

Ophelia: O, what a noble mind is here o'erthrown!
150 The courtier's, soldier's, scholar's, eye, tongue, sword—
The expectancy and rose[56] of the fair state,
The glass[57] of fashion and the mold of form,[58]
The observed of all observers—quite, quite down!
And I, of ladies most deject and wretched,
155 That sucked the honey of his music vows,
Now see that noble and most sovereign reason,
Like sweet bells jangled, out of tune and harsh,
That unmatched[59] form and feature of blown[60] youth
Blasted with ecstasy.[61] O, woe is me,
160 To have seen what I have seen, see what I see!

(*Re-enter King and Polonius.*)

King: Love! His affections[62] do not that way tend,
Nor what he spake, though it lacked form a little,
Was not like madness. There's something in his soul
O'er which his melancholy sits on brood,[63]
165 And I do doubt the hatch and the disclose[64]
Will be some danger. Which for to prevent,
I have in quick determination
Thus set it down: He shall with speed to England,
For the demand of our neglected tribute.
170 Haply[65] the seas and countries different
With variable objects[66] shall expel
This something-settled[67] matter in his heart
Whereon his brains still beating puts him thus
From fashion of himself.[68] What think you on 't?
175 **Polonius:** It shall do well. But yet do I believe
The origin and commencement of his grief
Sprung from neglected love. How now, Ophelia!
You need not tell us what Lord Hamlet said,
We heard it all. My lord, do as you please,
180 But, if you hold it fit, after the play

---

[51] **paintings:** using make-up.   [52] **jig:** dance lecherously.   [53] **amble:** walk artificially.   [54] **lisp:** talk affectedly.   [55] **nickname . . . ignorance:** give things indecent names and pretend to be too simple to understand
their meanings.   [56] **expectancy . . . rose:** bright hope. The rose is used as a symbol for beauty and perfection.   [57] **glass:** mirror.   [58] **mold of form:** perfect pattern of manly beauty.   [59] **unmatched:** unmatchable.
[60] **blown:** perfect, like an open flower at its best.   [61] **Blasted . . . ecstasy:** ruined by madness.   [62] **affections:** state of mind.   [63] **sits . . . brood:** sits hatching.   [64] **doubt . . . disclose:** suspect the brood which
will result.   [65] **Haply:** perhaps.   [66] **variable objects:** novel sights.   [67] **something-settled:** somewhat settled; i.e., not yet incurable.   [68] **puts . . . himself:** i.e., separates him from his normal self.

Let his queen mother all alone entreat him
To show his grief. Let her be round[69] with him,
And I'll be placed, so please you, in the ear
Of all their conference. If she find him not,
185 To England send him, or confine him where
Your wisdom best shall think.

King: It shall be so.
Madness in great ones must not unwatched go.

(Exeunt.)

Scene II. A hall in the castle.

(Enter Hamlet and Players.)

Hamlet: Speak the speech,[1] I pray you, as I pronounced it to you, trippingly[2] on the tongue. But if you mouth[3] it, as many of your players do, I had as lief[4] the town crier spoke my lines. Nor do not saw the air too much with your hand, thus, but use all gently. For in the very torrent, tempest, and, as I may say, whirlwind of
5 passion, you must acquire and beget a temperance that may give it smoothness. Oh, it offends me to the soul to hear a robustious[5] periwig-pated[6] fellow tear a passion to tatters, to very rags, to split the ears of the groundlings,[7] who for the most part are capable of nothing but inexplicable dumb shows[8] and noise. I would have such a fellow whipped for o'erdoing Termagant[9]—it out-Herods
10 Herod. Pray you, avoid it.

1. Player: I warrant your honor.

Hamlet: Be not too tame neither, but let your own discretion be your tutor. Suit the action to the word, the word to the action, with this special observance, that you o'erstep not the modesty of nature. For anything so overdone is from[10] the purpose of playing,
15 whose end, both at the first and now, was and is to hold as 'twere the mirror up to Nature—to show Virtue her own feature, scorn her own image, and the very age and body of the time his form and pressure.[11] Now this overdone or come tardy off, though it make the unskillful laugh, cannot but make the judicious grieve, the censure of the which one[12] must in your allowance o'erweigh a whole theater of others. Oh,
20 there be players[13] that I have seen play, and heard others praise—and that highly, not to speak it profanely—that neither having the accent of Christians nor the gait of Christian, pagan, nor man, have so strutted and bellowed that I have thought some of Nature's journeymen[14] had made men, and not made them well, they imitated humanity so abominably.

25 **1. Player:** I hope we have reformed that indifferently[15] with us, sir.

---

[69] **round:** direct. [1] **the speech:** which he has written. The whole passage which follows is Shakespeare's own comment on the actor's art and states the creed and practice of his company as contrasted with the more violent methods of Edward Alleyn and his fellows. [2] **trippingly:** smoothly, easily. [3] **mouth:** "ham" it. [4] **lief:** soon. [5] **robustious:** ranting. [6] **periwig-pated:** wearing a wig. [7] **groundlings:** the poorer spectators, who stood in the yard of the playhouse. [8] **dumb shows:** an old-fashioned dramatic device, still being used by the Admiral's Men: before a tragedy, and sometimes before each act, the characters mimed the action which was to follow. [9] **Termagant:** God of the Saracens, who, like Herod, was presented in early stage plays as a roaring tyrant. [10] **from:** contrary to. [11] **very . . . pressure:** an exact reproduction of the age. **form:** shape. **pressure:** imprint (of a seal). [12] **the . . . one:** i.e., the judicious spectator. [13] **there . . . players:** An obvious attack on Alleyn. [14] **journeymen:** hired workmen, not masters of the trade. [15] **indifferently:** moderately.

Hamlet: O, reform it altogether. And let those that play your clowns[16] speak no more than is set down for them. For there be of them that will themselves laugh, to set on some quantity of barren spectators to laugh too, though in the meantime some necessary question of the play be then to be considered. That's villainous, and shows a most piti-
30   ful[17] ambition in the fool that uses it. Go, make you ready.

(Exeunt Players. Enter Polonius, Rosencrantz, and Guildenstern.)

How now, my lord! Will the king hear this piece of work?
Polonius: And the queen too, and that presently.
Hamlet: Bid the players make haste.

(Exit Polonius.)

Will you two help to hasten them?
35 **Rosencrantz & Guildenstern:** We will, my lord.

(Exeunt Rosencrantz and Guildenstern.)

Hamlet: What ho! Horatio!

(Enter Horatio.)

Horatio: Here, sweet lord, at your service.
Hamlet: Horatio, thou art e'en as just a man
         As e'er my conversation coped[18] withal.
40 **Horatio:** Oh, my dear lord—
Hamlet: Nay, do not think I flatter,
         For what advancement[19] may I hope from thee,
         That no revénue hast but thy good spirits
         To feed and clothe thee? Why should the poor be flattered?
45   No, let the candied[20] tongue lick absurd pomp
         And crook the pregnant hinges of the knee
         Where thrift may follow fawning.[21] Dost thou hear?
         Since my dear soul was mistress of her choice
         And could of men distinguish her election
50   Hath sealed[22] thee for herself. For thou hast been
         As one in suffering all that suffers nothing,
         A man that fortune's buffets and rewards
         Hast ta'en with equal thanks. And blest are those
         Whose blood and judgment are so well commingled
55   That they are not a pipe[23] for Fortune's finger
         To sound what stop she please. Give me that man
         That is not passion's slave, and I will wear him

---

[16] **those . . . clowns:** A hit at Will Kempe, the former clown of Shakespeare's company. Q_1 adds the passage "And then you have some again that keep one suit of jests, as a man is known by one suit of apparel, and gentlemen quote his jests down in their tables before they come to the play, as thus: 'Cannot you stay till I eat my porridge?' and 'You owe me a quarter's wages,' and 'My coat wants a cullison,' and 'Your beer is sour,' and blabbering with his lips, and thus keeping in his cinquepace of jests, when God knows the warm clown cannot make a jest unless by chance, as the blind man catcheth a hare. Masters tell him of it."   [17] **pitiful:** contemptible.   [18] **coped:** met.   [19] **advancement:** promotion.   [20] **candied:** sugared over with hypocrisy.   [21] **crook . . . fawning:** bend the ready knees whenever gain will follow flattery.   [22] **sealed:** set a mark on.   [23] **pipe:** an instrument that varies its notes.

In my heart's core—aye, in my heart of heart,
As I do thee. Something too much of this.

60 There is a play tonight before the king.
One scene of it comes near the circumstance
Which I have told thee of my father's death.
I prithee when thou seest that act afoot,
Even with the very comment[24] of thy soul

65 Observe my uncle. If his occulted[25] guilt
Do not itself unkennel[26] in one speech
It is a damnéd ghost[27] that we have seen
And my imaginations are as foul
As Vulcan's[28] stithy.[29] Give him heedful note,[30]

70 For I mine eyes will rivet to his face,
And after we will both our judgments join
In censure of his seeming.[31]

Horatio: Well, my lord.
If he steal aught the whilst this play is playing,

75 And 'scape detecting, I will pay the theft.

Hamlet: They are coming to the play. I must be idle.[32]
Get you a place.

(*Danish march. A flourish. Enter King, Queen, Polonius, Ophelia, Rosencrantz, Guildenstern, and other Lords attendant, with the Guard carrying torches.*)

King: How fares our cousin Hamlet?

Hamlet: Excellent, i' faith, of the chameleon's dish. I eat the air, promise crammed. You can-

80 not feed capons so.[33]

King: I have nothing with this answer,[34] Hamlet. These words are not mine.

Hamlet: No, nor mine now.[35] (*To Polonius.*) My lord, you played once i' the university, you say?

Polonius: That did I, my lord, and was accounted a good actor.

85 **Hamlet:** What did you enact?

Polonius: I did enact Julius Caesar. I was killed i' the Capitol. Brutus killed me.

Hamlet: It was a brute part of him to kill so capital a calf there. Be the players ready?

Rosencrantz: Aye, my lord, they stay upon your patience.[36]

Queen: Come hither, my dear Hamlet, sit by me.

90 **Hamlet:** No, good Mother, here's metal more attractive.

Polonius: (*To the King.*) O ho! Do you mark that?

Hamlet: Lady, shall I lie in your lap?

(*Lying down at Ophelia's feet.*)

Ophelia: No, my lord.

Hamlet: I mean, my head upon your lap?

95 **Ophelia:** Aye, my lord.

---

[24] **comment:** close observation.   [25] **occulted:** concealed.   [26] **unkennel:** come to light; lit., force a fox from his hole.   [27] **damned ghost:** evil spirit.   [28] **Vulcan:** the blacksmith god.   [29] **stithy:** smithy. [30] **heedful note:** careful observation.   [31] **censure . . . seeming:** judgment on his looks.   [32] **be idle:** seem crazy.   [33] **Excellent . . . so:** Hamlet takes "fare" literally as "what food are you eating." The chameleon was supposed to feed on air. **promise-crammed:** stuffed, like a fattened chicken (*capon*)—but with empty promises.   [34] **I . . . answer:** I cannot make any sense of your answer.   [35] **nor . . . now:** i.e., once words have left the lips they cease to belong to the speaker.   [36] **stay . . . patience:** wait for you to be ready.

Hamlet: Do you think I meant country matters?[37]
Ophelia: I think nothing, my lord.
Hamlet: That's a fair thought to lie between maids' legs.
Ophelia: What is, my lord?
100 **Hamlet:** Nothing.
Ophelia: You are merry, my lord.
Hamlet: Who, I?
Ophelia: Aye, my lord.
Hamlet: Oh God, your only jig-maker.[38] What should a man do but be merry? For
105   look you how cheerfully my mother looks, and my father died within 's two
          hours.
Ophelia: Nay, 'tis twice two months, my lord.
Hamlet: So long? Nay, then, let the devil wear black, for I'll have a suit of sables.[39] O
          heavens! Die two months ago, and not forgotten yet? Then there's hope a great man's
110   memory may outlive his life half a year. But, by 'r Lady, he must build churches then,
          or else shall he suffer not thinking on, with the hobbyhorse,[40] whose epitaph is "For,
          oh, for oh, the hobbyhorse is forgot."

          (*Hautboys*[41] *play. The dumb show enters.*[42] *Enter a King and a Queen very lovingly, the
          Queen embracing him and he her. She kneels, and makes show of protestation unto him. He
          takes her up, and declines his head upon her neck, lays him down upon a bank of flowers. She,
          seeing him asleep, leaves him. Anon comes in a fellow, takes off his crown, kisses it, and pours
          poison in the King's ears, and exit. The Queen returns, finds the King dead, and makes pas-
          sionate action. The Poisoner, with some two or three Mutes, comes in again, seeming to lament
          with her. The dead body is carried away. The Poisoner woos the Queen with gifts. She seems
          loath and unwilling awhile, but in the end accepts his love.*
          Exeunt.)

Ophelia: What means this, my lord?
Hamlet: Marry, this is miching mallecho.[43] It means mischief.
115 **Ophelia:** Belike this show imports the argument[44] of the play.

          (*Enter Prologue.*)

Hamlet: We shall know by this fellow. The players cannot keep counsel, they'll tell all.
Ophelia: Will he tell us what this show meant?
Hamlet: Aye, or any show that you'll show him. Be not you ashamed to show, he'll not
          shame to tell you what it means.
120 **Ophelia:** You are naught,[45] you are naught. I'll mark the play.
Prologue: For us, and for our tragedy,
          Here stooping to your clemency,
          We beg your hearing patiently.

---

[37] **country matters:** something indecent.   [38] **jig-maker:** composer of jigs.   [39] **suit of sables:** a quibble on
"sable," black, and "sable," gown trimmed with sable fur, worn by wealthy old gentlemen.   [40] **hobbyhorse:**
imitation horse worn by performers in a morris dance, an amusement much disapproved of by the godly.
[41] **Hautboys:** oboes.   [42] **The dumb show enters:** Critics have been disturbed because this dumb show
cannot be exactly paralleled in any other Elizabethan play, and because the King is apparently not disturbed
by it. Shakespeare's intention, however, in presenting a play within a play is to produce something stagy and
artificial compared with the play proper. Moreover, as Hamlet has already complained, dumb shows were
often inexplicable.   [43] **miching mallecho:** slinking mischief.   [44] **argument:** plot. She too is puzzled by
the dumb show.   [45] **naught:** i.e., disgusting.

Hamlet: Is this a prologue, or the posy of a ring?[46]
125 **Ophelia:** 'Tis brief, my lord.
Hamlet: As woman's love.

(Enter two Players, King and Queen.)

Player King: Full[47] thirty times hath Phoebus' cart[48] gone round
    Neptune's[49] salt wash and Tellus'[50] orbèd ground,
    And thirty dozen moons with borrowed sheen[51]
130   About the world have times twelve thirties been,
    Since love our hearts and Hymen[52] did our hands
    Unite commutual[53] in most sacred bands.
Player Queen: So many journeys may the sun and moon
    Make us again count o'er ere love be done!
135   But, woe is me, you are so sick of late,
    So far from cheer and from your former state,
    That I distrust[54] you. Yet, though I distrust,
    Discomfort you, my lord, it nothing must.
    For women's fear and love holds quantity[55]
140   In neither aught or in extremity.[56]
    Now what my love is, proof hath made you know,
    And as my love is sized, my fear is so.
    Where love is great, the littlest doubts are fear;
    Where little fears grow great, great love grows there.
145 **Player King:** Faith, I must leave thee,[57] love, and shortly too,
    My operant powers[58] their functions leave to do.
    And thou shalt live in this fair world behind,
    Honored, beloved, and haply one as kind
    For husband shalt thou—
150 **Player Queen:**   Oh, confound the rest!
    Such love must needs be treason in my breast.
    In second husband let me be accurst!
    None wed the second but who killed the first.
Hamlet: *(Aside.)* Wormwood,[59] wormwood.
155 **Player Queen:** The instances[60] that second marriage move
    Are base respects of thrift,[61] but none of love.
    A second time I kill my husband dead
    When second husband kisses me in bed.
Player King: I do believe you think what now you speak,
160   But what we do determine oft we break.
    Purpose is but the slave to memory,
    Of violent birth but poor validity,
    Which now, like fruit unripe, sticks on the tree

---

[46] **posy . . . ring:** It was a custom to inscribe rings with little mottoes or messages, which were necessarily brief.   [47] **Full . . . twain:** The play is deliberately written in crude rhyming verse, full of ridiculous and bombastic phrases.   [48] **Phoebus' cart:** the chariot of the sun.   [49] **Neptune:** the sea god.   [50] **Tellus:** the earth goddess.   [51] **borrowed sheen:** light borrowed from the sun.   [52] **Hymen:** god of marriage. [53] **commutual:** mutually.   [54] **distrust:** am anxious about.   [55] **quantity:** proportion.   [56] **In . . . extremity:** either nothing or too much.   [57] **leave thee:** i.e., die.   [58] **operant powers:** bodily strength. [59] **Wormwood:** bitterness.   [60] **instances:** arguments [Editor's Note: arguments for remarrying].   [61] **respects of thrift:** considerations of gain.

But fall unshaken when they mellow be.
165 Most necessary 'tis that we forget
To pay ourselves what to ourselves is debt.
What to ourselves in passion we propose,
That passion ending, doth the purpose lose.
The violence of either grief or joy
170 Their own enactures[62] with themselves destroy.
Where joy most revels, grief doth most lament,
Grief joys, joy grieves, on slender accident.
This world is not for aye,[63] nor 'tis not strange
That even our loves should with our fortunes change,
175 For 'tis a question left us yet to prove
Whether love lead fortune or else fortune love.
The great man down, you mark his favorite flies,
The poor advanced makes friends of enemies.
And hitherto doth love on fortune tend,
180 For who not needs shall never lack a friend,
And who in want a hollow friend doth try
Directly seasons[64] him his enemy.
But, orderly to end where I begun,
Our wills and fates do so contráry run
185 That our devices still are overthrown,
Our thoughts are ours, their ends none of our own.
So think thou wilt no second husband wed,
But die thy thoughts when thy first lord is dead.
Player Queen: Nor earth to me give food nor heaven light!
190 Sport and repose lock from me day and night!
To desperation turn my trust and hope!
An anchor's[65] cheer in prison be my scope!
Each opposite that blanks[66] the face of joy
Meet what I would have well and it destroy!
195 Both here and hence pursue me lasting strife
If, once a widow, ever I be wife!
Hamlet: If she should break it now!
Player King: 'Tis deeply sworn. Sweet, leave me here a while.
My spirits grow dull, and fain I would beguile
200 The tedious day with sleep. *(Sleeps.)*
Player Queen: Sleep rock thy brain,
And never come mischance betwéen us twain!

(Exit.)

Hamlet: Madam, how like you this play?
Queen: The lady doth protest too much, methinks.
205 **Hamlet:** O, but she'll keep her word.
King: Have you heard the argument?[67] Is there no offense in 't?

---

[62] **enactures:** performance.   [63] **aye:** ever.   [64] **seasons:** ripens into.   [65] **anchor:** anchorite, hermit.
[66] **blanks:** makes pale.   [67] **argument:** plot [Editor's note: plot summary]. When performances were given at Court it was sometimes customary to provide a written or printed synopsis of the story for the distinguished spectators.

Hamlet: No, no, they do but jest, poison in jest—no offense i' the world.

King: What do you call the play?

Hamlet: The Mousetrap.[68] Marry, how? Tropically.[69] This play is the image of a murder
210 done in Vienna. Gonzago is the Duke's name, his wife, Baptista. You shall see anon.
'Tis a knavish piece of work, but what o' that? Your majesty, and we that have free[70]
souls, it touches us not. Let the galled jade wince, our withers are unwrung.[71]

(Enter Lucianus.)

This is one Lucianus, nephew to the king.

Ophelia: You are as good as a chorus,[72] my lord.

215 **Hamlet:** I could interpret between you and your love, if I could see the puppets
dallying.[73]

Ophelia: You are keen, my lord, you are keen.

Hamlet: I would cost you a groaning to take off mine edge.

Ophelia: Still better, and worse.

220 **Hamlet:** So you must take your husbands.[74] Begin, murderer. Pox, leave thy damnable
faces and begin. Come, the croaking raven doth bellow for revenge.

Lucianus: Thoughts black, hands apt, drugs fit, and time agreeing,
Confederate season, else no creature[75] seeing,
Thou mixture rank of midnight weeds collected,
225 With Hecate's ban[76] thrice blasted, thrice infected,
Thy natural magic and dire property[77]
On wholesome life usurp immediately.

(Pours the poison into the sleeper's ear.)

Hamlet: He poisons him i' the garden for his estate.[78] His name's Gonzago. The story is extant, and written in very choice Italian. You shall see anon how the murderer gets the
230 love of Gonzago's wife.

Ophelia: The king rises.

Hamlet: What, frighted with false fire![79]

Queen: How fares my lord?

Polonius: Give o'er the play.

235 **King:** Give me some light. Away!

Polonius: Lights, lights, lights!

(Exeunt all but Hamlet and Horatio.)

Hamlet:

"Why, let the stricken deer go weep,
The hart ungallèd play,
240 For some must watch while some must sleep.
Thus runs the world away."

---

[68] **Mousetrap:** The phrase was used of a device to entice a person to his own destruction (OED). [69] **Tropically:** figuratively, with a pun on "trap." [70] **free:** innocent. [71] **galled . . . unwrung:** let a nag with a sore
back flinch when the saddle is put on; our shoulders (being ungalled) feel no pain. [72] **chorus:** the chorus
sometimes introduced the characters and commented on what was to follow. [73] **puppets dallying:** Elizabethan puppets were crude marionettes, popular at fairs. While the figures were put through their motions, the
puppet master explained what was happening. [74] **So . . . husbands:** i.e., as the marriage service expresses it,
"for better, for worse." [75] **confederate . . . creature:** the opportunity conspiring with me, no other creature. [76] **Hecate's ban:** the curse of Hecate, goddess of witchcraft. [77] **property:** nature. [78] **estate:** kingdom. [79] **false fire:** a mere show.

Would not this, sir, and a forest of feathers[80]—if the rest of my fortunes turn
Turk[81] with me—with two Provincial roses[82] on my razed[83] shoes, get me a
fellowship[84] in a cry[85] of players, sir?

245 **Horatio:** Half a share.
Hamlet: A whole one, I.

> "For thou dost know, O Damon[86] dear,
> This realm dismantled[87] was
> Of Jove himself, and now reigns here
250 > A very, very—pajock."[88]

Horatio: You might have rhymed.
Hamlet: O good Horatio, I'll take the ghost's word for a thousand pound.
Didst perceive?
Horatio: Very well, my lord.
255 **Hamlet:** Upon the talk of the poisoning?
Horatio: I did very well note him.
Hamlet: Ah, ha! Come, some music! Come, the recorders![89]

> "For if the king like not the comedy,
> Why then, belike, he likes it not, perdy."[90]

260 Come, some music!

(Re-enter Rosencrantz and Guildenstern.)

Guildenstern: Good my lord, vouchsafe me a word with you.
Hamlet: Sir, a whole history.
Guildenstern: The king, sir—
Hamlet: Aye, sir, what of him?
265 **Guildenstern:** Is in his retirement marvelous distempered.[91]
Hamlet: With drink, sir?
Guildenstern: No, my lord, rather with choler.[92]
Hamlet: Your wisdom should show itself more richer to signify this to the doctor, for me to
put him to his purgation[93] would perhaps plunge him into far more choler.
270 **Guildenstern:** Good my lord, put your discourse into some frame,[94] and start not so
wildly from my affair.
Hamlet: I am tame, sir. Pronounce.
Guildenstern: The Queen your mother, in most great affliction of spirit, hath sent me to
you.
275 **Hamlet:** You are welcome.
Guildenstern: Nay, good my lord, this courtesy is not of the right breed. If it shall please
you to make me a wholesome answer, I will do your mother's commandment. If not,
your pardon and my return shall be the end of my business.
Hamlet: Sir, I cannot.

---

[80] **forest of feathers:** set of plumes, much worn by players.   [81] **turn Turk:** turn heathen, and treat me cruelly.   [82] **Provincial roses:** rosettes, worn on the shoes.   [83] **razed:** slashed, ornamented with cuts.   [84] **fellowship:** partnership.   [85] **cry:** pack.   [86] **Damon:** Damon and Pythias were types of perfect friends.
[87] **dismantled:** robbed.   [88] **pajock:** peacock, a strutting, lecherous bird. These verses, and the lines above, may have come from some ballad, otherwise lost.   [89] **recorders:** wooden pipes.   [90] **perdy:** by God.
[91] **distempered:** disturbed: but Hamlet takes the word in its other sense of "drunk."   [92] **choler:** anger, which Hamlet again pretends to understand as meaning "biliousness."   [93] **put . . . purgation:** "give him a dose of salts."   [94] **frame:** shape; i.e., "please talk sense."

280 **Guildenstern:** What, my lord?

Hamlet: Make you a wholesome answer, my wit's diseased. But, sir, such answer as I can make you shall command, or rather, as you say, my mother. Therefore no more, but to the matter. My mother, you say—

Rosencrantz: Then thus she says. Your behavior hath struck her into amazement and ad-
285 miration.[95]

Hamlet: Oh, wonderful son that can so astonish a mother! But is there no sequel at the heels of this mother's admiration? Impart.

Rosencrantz: She desires to speak with you in her closet ere you go to bed.

Hamlet: We shall obey, were she ten times our mother. Have you any further trade with
290 us?

Rosencrantz: My lord, you once did love me.

Hamlet: So I do still, by these pickers and stealers.[96]

Rosencrantz: Good my lord, what is your cause of distemper? You do surely bar the door upon your own liberty if you deny your griefs[97] to your friend.

295 **Hamlet:** Sir, I lack advancement.[98]

Rosencrantz: How can that be when you have the voice of the king himself for your succession in Denmark?

Hamlet: Aye, sir, but "While the grass grows"[99]—the proverb is something musty.

(Re-enter Players with recorders.)

Oh, the recorders![100] Let me see one. To withdraw[101] with you—why do you go
300 about to recover the wind[102] of me, as if you would drive me into a toil?[103]

Guildenstern: O my lord, if my duty be too bold, my love is too unmannerly.[104]

Hamlet: I do not well understand that. Will you play upon this pipe?

Guildenstern: My lord, I cannot.

Hamlet: I pray you.

305 **Guildenstern:** Believe me, I cannot.

Hamlet: I do beseech you.

Guildenstern: I know no touch of it, my lord.

Hamlet: It is as easy as lying. Govern these ventages[105] with your fingers and thumb, give it breath with your mouth, and it will discourse most eloquent music. Look you, these
310 are the stops.

Guildenstern: But these cannot I command to any utterance of harmony, I have not the skill.

Hamlet: Why, look you now, how unworthy a thing you make of me! You would play upon me, you would seem to know my stops, you would pluck out the heart of my
315 mystery, you would sound me from my lowest note to the top of my compass—and there is much music, excellent voice, in this little organ—yet cannot you make it speak. 'Sblood, do you think I am easier to be played on than a pipe? Call me what instrument you will, though you can fret[106] me, you cannot play upon me.

---

[95] **admiration:** wonder.   [96] **pickers . . . stealers:** i.e., hands—an echo from the Christian's duty in the catechism to keep his hands "from picking and stealing."   [97] **deny . . . griefs:** refuse to tell your troubles.
[98] **advancement:** promotion. Hamlet harks back to his previous interview with Rosencrantz and Guildenstern.   [99] **While . . . grows:** the proverb ends "the steed starves."   [100] **recorders:** wooden pipes.
[101] **withdraw:** go aside. Hamlet leads Guildenstern to one side of the stage.   [102] **recover . . . wind:** a hunting metaphor; approach me with the wind against you.   [103] **toil:** net.   [104] **if . . . unmannerly:** if I exceed my duty by asking these questions, then my affection for you shows lack of manners; i.e., forgive me if I have been impertinent.   [105] **ventages:** holes, stops.   [106] **fret:** annoy, with a pun on the frets or bars on stringed instruments by which the fingering is regulated.

(Re-enter Polonius.)

God bless you, sir!

320 **Polonius:** My lord, the queen would speak with you, and presently.
Hamlet: Do you see yonder cloud that's almost in shape of a camel?
Polonius: By the mass, and 'tis like a camel indeed.
Hamlet: Methinks it is like a weasel.
Polonius: It is backed like a weasel.
325 **Hamlet:** Or like a whale?
Polonius: Very like a whale.
Hamlet: Then I will come to my mother by and by. *(Aside)* They fool me to the top of my
bent.[107]—I will come by and by.
Polonius: I will say so.

(Exit Polonius.)

330 **Hamlet:** "By and by" is easily said. Leave me, friends.

(Exeunt all but Hamlet.)

'Tis now the very witching time[108] of night,
When churchyards yawn and hell itself breathes out
Contagion[109] to this world. Now could I drink hot blood,
And do such bitter business as the day
335 Would quake to look on. Soft! Now to my mother.
O heart, lose not thy nature, let not ever
The soul of Nero[110] enter this firm bosom.
Let me be cruel, not unnatural.
I will speak daggers to her, but use none.
340 My tongue and soul in this be hypocrites,
How in my words soever she be shent,[111]
To give them seals[112] never, my soul, consent!

(Exit.)

Scene III. A room in the castle.

(Enter King, Rosencrantz, and Guildenstern.)

King: I like him not, nor stands it safe with us
To let his madness range.[1] Therefore prepare you.
I your commission will forthwith dispatch,
And he to England shall along with you.
5 The terms of our estate[2] may not endure
Hazard so near us as doth hourly grow
Out of his lunacies.
Guildenstern: We will ourselves provide.[3]
Most holy and religious fear[4] it is

---

[107] **top . . . bent:** to the utmost.   [108] **witching time:** when witches perform their foul rites.   [109] **Contagion:** infection.   [110] **Nero:** Nero killed his own mother. Hamlet is afraid that in the interview to come he will lose all self-control.   [111] **shent:** rebuked.   [112] **give . . . seals:** ratify words by actions.   [1] **range:** roam freely.   [2] **terms . . . estate:** i.e., one in my position.   [3] **ourselves provide:** make our preparations.   [4] **fear:** anxiety.

10   To keep those many many bodies safe
       That live and feed upon your majesty.
Rosencrantz: The single and peculiar[5] life is bound
       With all the strength and armor of the mind
       To keep itself from noyance,[6] but much more
15   That spirit upon whose weal[7] depends and rests
       The lives of many. The cease of majesty[8]
       Dies not alone, but like a gulf[9] doth draw
       What's near it with it. It is a massy[10] wheel
       Fixed on the summit of the highest mount,
20   To whose huge spokes ten thousand lesser things
       Are mortised[11] and adjoined; which, when it falls,
       Each small annexment, petty consequence,[12]
       Attends[13] the boisterous ruin. Never alone
       Did the king sigh but with a general groan.
25 **King:** Arm you, I pray you, to this speedy voyage,
       For we will fetters put upon this fear,
       Which now goes too free-footed.
Rosencrantz & Guildenstern: We will haste us.

(Exeunt Rosencrantz and Guildenstern.)

(Enter Polonius.)

Polonius: My lord, he's going to his mother's closet.
30   Behind the arras I'll convey myself
       To hear the process.[14] I'll warrant she'll tax[15] him home.
       And, as you said,[16] and wisely was it said,
       'Tis meet that some more audience than a mother,
       Since nature makes them partial, should o'erhear
35   The speech, of vantage.[17] Fare you well, my liege.
       I'll call upon you ere you go to bed
       And tell you what I know.
King: Thanks, dear my lord.

(Exit Polonius.)

       O, my offense is rank,[18] it smells to heaven.
40   It hath the primal eldest curse[19] upon 't,
       A brother's murder. Pray can I not,
       Though inclination be as sharp as will.[20]
       My stronger guilt defeats my strong intent,
       And like a man to double business bound,
45   I stand in pause where I shall first begin,
       And both neglect. What if this cursèd hand
       Were thicker than itself with brother's blood,

---

[5] **peculiar:** individual. [6] **noyance:** injury. [7] **weal:** welfare. [8] **cease of majesty:** death of a king.
[9] **gulf:** whirlpool. [10] **massy:** massive. [11] **mortised:** firm. [12] **annexment . . . consequence:** attachment, smallest thing connected with it. [13] **Attends:** waits on, is involved in. [14] **process:** proceeding.
[15] **tax:** censure. [16] **as . . . said:** Actually Polonius himself had said it. [17] **of vantage:** from a place of vantage; i.e., concealment. [18] **rank:** foul. [19] **primal . . . curse:** the curse laid upon Cain, the first murderer, who also slew his brother. [20] **will:** desire.

Is there not rain enough in the sweet heavens
To wash it white as snow? Whereto serves mercy
50 But to confront the visage of offense?[21]
And what's in prayer but this twofold force,
To be forestalled[22] ere we come to fall
Or pardoned being down? Then I'll look up,
My fault is past. But, O, what form of prayer
55 Can serve my turn? "Forgive me my foul murder"?
That cannot be, since I am still possessed
Of those effects[23] for which I did the murder—
My crown, mine own ambition, and my queen.
May one be pardoned and retain the offense?[24]
60 In the corrupted currents[25] of this world
Offense's gilded hand may shove by justice,
And oft 'tis seen the wicked prize[26] itself
Buys out the law. But 'tis not so above.
There is no shuffling, there the action lies
65 In his true nature,[27] and we ourselves compelled
Even to the teeth and forehead[28] of our faults
To give in evidence. What then? What rests?
Try what repentance can. What can it not?
Yet what can it when one cannot repent?
70 O, wretched state! O, bosom black as death!
O, limèd[29] soul, that struggling to be free
Art more engaged![30] Help, angels! Make assay![31]
Bow, stubborn knees, and heart with strings of steel,
Be soft as sinews of the newborn babe!
75 All may be well. (Retires and kneels.)

(Enter Hamlet.)

Hamlet: Now might I do it pat, now he is praying,
And now I'll do 't. And so he goes to heaven,[32]
And so am I revenged. That would be scanned:
A villain kills my father, and for that
80 I, his sole son, do this same villain send
To heaven.
O, this is hire and salary,[33] not revenge.
He took my father grossly,[34] full of bread,
With all his crimes broad blown, as flush[35] as May,
85 And how his audit[36] stands who knows save heaven?
But in our circumstance and course of thought,[37]
'Tis heavy with him. And am I then revenged,

---

[21] **confront . . . offense:** look crime in the face.   [22] **forestalled:** prevented.   [23] **effects:** advantages.
[24] **offense:** i.e., that for which he has offended.   [25] **currents:** courses, ways.   [26] **wicked prize:** the proceeds of the crime.   [27] **there . . . nature:** in Heaven the case is tried on its own merits.   [28] **teeth . . . forehead:** i.e., face to face.   [29] **limed:** caught as in birdlime.   [30] **engaged:** stuck fast.   [31] **assay:** attempt.
[32] **And . . . Heaven:** Praying, Claudius is in a state of grace.   [33] **hire . . . salary:** i.e., a kind of action deserving pay.   [34] **grossly:** i.e., when he was in a state of sin.   [35] **broad . . . flush:** in full blossom, as luxuriant.   [36] **audit:** account.   [37] **circumstance . . . thought:** as it appears to my mind.

To take him in the purging of his soul,
When he is fit and seasoned,[38] for his passage?
90 No.
Up, sword, and know thou a more horrid hent.[39]
When he is drunk asleep, or in his rage,
Or in the incestuous pleasure of his bed—
At gaming, swearing, or about some act
95 That has no relish of salvation in 't—
Then trip him, that his heels may kick at heaven
And that his soul may be as damned and black
As hell, whereto it goes. My mother stays.
This physic but prolongs thy sickly days. (*Exit.*)
100 **King:** (*Rising.*) My words fly up, my thoughts remain below.
Words without thoughts never to heaven go.

(*Exit.*)

Scene IV. The Queen's closet.

(*Enter Queen and Polonius.*)

Polonius: He will come straight. Look you lay home to[1] him.
Tell him his pranks have been too broad[2] to bear with,
And that your grace hath screened and stood between
Much heat and him. I'll sconce me[3] even here.
5 Pray you, be round with him.
Hamlet: (*Within.*) Mother, Mother, Mother!
Queen: I'll warrant you,
Fear me not. Withdraw, I hear him coming.

(*Polonius hides behind the arras.*)

(*Enter Hamlet.*)

Hamlet: Now, Mother, what's the matter?
10 **Queen:** Hamlet, thou hast thy father much offended.
Hamlet: Mother, you have my father much offended.
Queen: Come, come, you answer with an idle[4] tongue.
Hamlet: Go, go, you question with a wicked tongue.
Queen: Why, how now, Hamlet!
15 **Hamlet:** What's the matter now?
Queen: Have you forgot me?
Hamlet: No, by the rood,[5] not so.
You are the queen, your husband's brother's wife,
And—would it were not so!—you are my mother.
20 **Queen:** Nay, then, I'll set those to you that can speak.
Hamlet: Come, come, and sit you down. You shall not budge,
You go not till I set you up a glass[6]
Where you may see the inmost part of you.

---

[38] **seasoned:** ripe.   [39] **hent:** opportunity.   [1] **lay . . . to:** be strict with.   [2] **broad:** unrestrained. Polonius is thinking of the obvious insolence of the remarks about second marriage in the play scene.   [3] **sconce me:** hide myself.   [4] **idle:** foolish.   [5] **rood:** crucifix.   [6] **glass:** looking-glass.

Queen: What wilt thou do? Thou wilt not murder me?
25   Help, help, ho!
Polonius: (*Behind.*) What ho! Help, help, help!
Hamlet: (*Drawing.*) How now! A rat?
    Dead, for a ducat, dead! (*Makes a pass through the arras.*)
Polonius: (*Behind.*) O, I am slain! (*Falls and dies.*)
30 **Queen:** O me, what hast thou done?
Hamlet: Nay, I know not.
    Is it the King?
Queen: O, what a rash and bloody deed is this!
Hamlet: A bloody deed! Almost as bad, good mother,
35   As kill a king and marry with his brother.
Queen: As kill a king!
Hamlet: Aye, lady, 'twas my word.

(*Lifts up the arras and discovers Polonius.*)

    Thou wretched, rash, intruding fool, farewell!
    I took thee for thy better. Take thy fortune.
40   Thou find 'st to be too busy is some danger.
    Leave wringing of your hands. Peace! Sit you down,
    And let me wring your heart. For so I shall
    If it be made of penetrable stuff,
    If damnèd custom have not brassed[7] it so
45   That it be proof and bulwark against sense.
Queen: What have I done that thou darest wag thy tongue
    In noise so rude against me?
Hamlet: Such an act
    That blurs the grace and blush of modesty,
50   Calls virtue hypocrite, takes off the rose
    From the fair forehead of an innocent love,
    And sets a blister[8] there—makes marriage vows
    As false as dicers' oaths. O, such a deed
    As from the body of contraction[9] plucks
55   The very soul, and sweet religion makes
    A rhapsody of words.[10] heaven's face doth glow,
    Yea, this solidity and compound mass,[11]
    With tristful visage, as against the doom,[12]
    Is thought-sick at the act.
60 **Queen:**   Aye me, what act
    That roars so loud and thunders in the index?[13]
Hamlet: Look here upon this picture,[14] and on this,
    The counterfeit presentment[15] of two brothers.
    See what a grace was seated on this brow—

---

[7] **brassed:** made brazen; i.e., impenetrable. [8] **sets a blister:** brands as a harlot. [9] **contraction:** the marriage contract. [10] **rhapsody of words:** string of meaningless words. [11] **solidity . . . mass:** i.e., solid earth. [12] **tristful . . . doom:** sorrowful face, as in anticipation of Doomsday. [13] **in . . . index:** i.e., if the beginning (*index*, i.e., table of contents) is so noisy, what will follow? [14] **picture:** Modern producers usually interpret the pictures as miniatures, Hamlet wearing one of his father, Gertrude one of Claudius. In the eighteenth century, wall portraits were used. [15] **counterfeit presentment:** portrait.

65 Hyperion's curls, the front[16] of Jove himself,
  An eye like Mars, to threaten and command,
  A station[17] like the herald Mercury[18]
  New-lighted[19] on a heaven-kissing hill,
  A combination[20] and a form indeed
70 Where every god did seem to set his seal[21]
  To give the world assurance of a man.
  This was your husband. Look you now what follows.
  Here is your husband, like a mildewed ear,
  Blasting his wholesome brother. Have you eyes?
75 Could you on this fair mountain leave to feed
  And batten[22] on this moor? Ha! Have you eyes?
  You cannot call it love, for at your age
  The heyday[23] in the blood is tame, it's humble,
  And waits upon the judgment. And what judgment
80 Would step from this to this? Sense[24] sure you have,
  Else could you not have motion.[25] But sure that sense
  Is apoplexed;[26] for madness would not err,
  Nor sense to ecstasy[27] was ne'er so thralled[28]
  But it reserved some quantity of choice
85 To serve in such a difference.[29] What devil was 't
  That thus hath cozened[30] you at hoodman-blind?[31]
  Eyes without feeling, feeling without sight,
  Ears without hands or eyes, smelling sans[32] all,
  Or but a sickly part of one true sense
90 Could not so mope.[33] O, shame! Where is thy blush?
  Rebellious[34] hell,
  If thou canst mutine[35] in a matron's bones,
  To flaming youth let virtue be as wax
  And melt in her own fire. Proclaim no shame
95 When the compulsive ardor[36] gives the charge,
  Since frost itself as actively doth burn,
  And reason panders[37] will.
 Queen: O Hamlet, speak no more.
  Thou turn'st mine eyes into my very soul,
100 And there I see such black and grainèd[38] spots
  As will not leave their tinct.[39]

---

[16] **front:** forehead. [17] **station:** figure; lit., standing. [18] **Mercury:** messenger of the gods, and one of the most beautiful. [19] **New-lighted:** newly alighted. [20] **combination:** i.e., of physical qualities.
[21] **set . . . seal:** guarantee as a perfect man. [22] **batten:** glut yourself. [23] **heyday:** excitement. [24] **Sense:** feeling. [25] **Motion:** desire. [26] **apoplexed:** paralyzed. [27] **ecstasy:** excitement, passion. [28] **thralled:** enslaved. [29] **serve . . . difference:** to enable you to see the difference between your former and your present husband. [30] **cozened:** cheated. [31] **hoodman-blind:** blindman's-buff. [32] **sans:** without. [33] **mope:** be dull. [34] **Rebellious . . . will:** i.e., if the passion (*Hell*) of a woman of your age is uncontrollable (*rebellious*), youth can have no restraints; there is no shame in a young man's lust when the elderly are just as eager and their reason (which should control desire) encourages them. [35] **mutine:** mutiny. [36] **compulsive ardor:** compelling lust. [37] **panders:** acts as go-between. [38] **grainèd:** dyed in the grain. [39] **tinct:** color.

Hamlet: Nay, but to live
    In the rank sweat of an enseamèd[40] bed,
    Stewed in corruption, honeying and making love
105   Over the nasty sty—
Queen: Oh, speak to me no more,
    These words like daggers enter in my ears.
    No more, sweet Hamlet!
Hamlet: A murderer and a villain,
110   A slave that is not twentieth part the tithe[41]
    Of your precedent[42] lord, a vice of kings,[43]
    A cutpurse[44] of the empire and the rule,
    That from a shelf the precious diadem stole
    And put it in his pocket!
115 **Queen:**   No more!
Hamlet: A king of shreds and patches—

(Enter Ghost.)

    Save me, and hover o'er me with your wings,
    You heavenly guards! What would your gracious figure?
Queen: Alas, he's mad!
120 **Hamlet:** Do you not come your tardy son to chide
    That, lapsed in time and passion, lets go by
    The important acting of your dread command?[45]
    O, say!
Ghost: Do not forget. This visitation
125   Is but to whet thy almost blunted purpose.
    But look, amazement on thy mother sits.
    O, step between her and her fighting soul.
    Conceit[46] in weakest bodies strongest works.
    Speak to her, Hamlet.
130 **Hamlet:** How is it with you, lady?
Queen: Alas, how is 't with you
    That you do bend your eye on vacancy[47]
    And with the incorporal[48] air do hold discourse?
    Forth at your eyes your spirits wildly peep,
135   And as the sleeping soldiers in the alarm,
    Your bedded[49] hairs, like life in excrements,[50]
    Start up and stand an[51] end. O gentle son,
    Upon the heat and flame of thy distemper[52]
    Sprinkle cool patience. Whereon do you look?
140 **Hamlet:** On him, on him! Look you how pale he glares!
    His form and cause conjoined,[53] preaching to stones,
    Would make them capable.[54] Do not look upon me,

---

[40] **enseamed:** greasy.   [41] **tithe:** tenth part.   [42] **precedent:** former.   [43] **vice of kings:** caricature of a king.
[44] **cutpurse:** thief.   [45] **That . . . command:** who has allowed time to pass and passion to cool and neglects
the urgent duty of obeying your dread command.   [46] **Conceit:** imagination.   [47] **vacancy:** empty space.
[48] **incorporal:** bodiless.   [49] **bedded:** evenly laid.   [50] **excrements:** anything that grows out of the body,
such as hair or fingernails: here hair.   [51] **an:** on.   [52] **distemper:** mental disturbance.   [53] **form . . . con-
joined:** his appearance and the reason for his appearance joined.   [54] **capable:** i.e., of feeling.

Lest with this piteous action you convert
My stern effects.[55] Then what I have to do
145   Will want true color—tears perchance for blood.
Queen: To whom to you speak this?
Hamlet: Do you see nothing there?
Queen: Nothing at all, yet all that is I see.
Hamlet: Nor did you nothing hear?
150 **Queen:** No, nothing but ourselves.
Hamlet: Why, look you there! Look how it steals away!
My father, in his habit as he lived!
Look where he goes, even now, out at the portal!

(Exit Ghost.)

Queen: This is the very coinage of your brain.
155   This bodiless creation ecstasy[56]
Is very cunning in.
Hamlet: Ecstasy!
My pulse, as yours, doth temperately keep time,
And makes as healthful music. It is not madness
160   That I have uttered. Bring me to the test
And I the matter will reword, which madness
Would gambol[57] from. Mother, for love of grace,
Lay not that flattering unction[58] to your soul,
That not your trespass but my madness speaks.
165   It will but skin and film the ulcerous place,
Whiles rank corruption, mining[59] all within,
Infects unseen. Confess yourself to heaven,
Repent what's past, avoid what is to come,
And do not spread the compost[60] on the weeds
170   To make them ranker. Forgive me this my virtue,
For in the fatness[61] of these pursy[62] times
Virtue itself of vice must pardon beg—
Yea, curb[63] and woo for leave to do him good.
Queen: O Hamlet, thou hast cleft my heart in twain.
175 **Hamlet:** Oh, throw away the worser part of it,
And live the purer with the other half.
Good night. But go not to my uncle's bed.
Assume a virtue if you have it not.
That[64] monster, custom, who all sense doth eat,
180   Of habits devil,[65] is angel yet in this,
That to the use[66] of actions fair and good
He likewise gives a frock or livery
That aptly[67] is put on. Refrain tonight,

---

[55] **convert . . . effects:** change the stern action which should follow.   [56] **ecstasy:** madness.   [57] **gambol:** start away.   [58] **unction:** healing ointment.   [59] **mining:** undermining.   [60] **compost:** manure.   [61] **fatness:** grossness.   [62] **pursy:** bloated.   [63] **curb:** bow low.   [64] **That . . . on:** i.e., custom (bad habits) like an evil monster destroys all sense of good and evil, but yet can become an angel (good habits) when it makes us perform good actions as mechanically as we put on our clothes.   [65] **devil:** This is the Q_2 reading; the passage is omitted in F_1. Probably the word should be "evil."   [66] **use:** practice.   [67] **aptly:** readily.

And that shall lend a kind of easiness
185   To the next abstinence, the next more easy.
For use almost can change the stamp[68] of nature,
And either curb the Devil,[69] or throw him out
With wondrous potency. Once more, good night.
And when you are desirous to be blest,
190   I'll blessing beg of you. For this same lord,

(Pointing to Polonius.)

I do repent; but heaven hath pleased it so,
To punish me with this, and this with me,
That I must be their scourge and minister.
I will bestow[70] him, and will answer well
195   The death I gave him. So again good night.
I must be cruel only to be kind.
Thus bad begins, and worse remains behind.
One word more, good lady.
    Queen: What shall I do?
200 **Hamlet:** Not this, by no means, that I bid you do.
Let the bloat[71] king tempt you again to bed,
Pinch wanton[72] on your cheek, call you his mouse,
And let him, for a pair of reechy[73] kisses
Or paddling in your neck with his damned fingers,
205   Make you to ravel[74] all this matter out,
That I essentially am not in madness,
But mad in craft. 'Twere good you let him know.
For who that's but a queen, fair, sober, wise,
Would from a paddock,[75] from a bat, a gib,[76]
210   Such dear concernings[77] hide? Who would do so?
No, in despite[78] of sense and secrecy,
Unpeg the basket on the house's top,
Let the birds fly, and like the famous ape,[79]
To try conclusions,[80] in the basket creep
215   And break your own neck down.
    Queen: Be thou assured if words be made of breath
And breath of life, I have no life to breathe
What thou hast said to me.
    Hamlet: I must to England. You know that?
220 **Queen:**   Alack,
I had forgot. 'Tis so concluded on.
    Hamlet: There's letters sealed, and my two school fellows,
Whom I will trust as I will adders fanged,
They bear the mandate.[81] They must sweep my way,

---

[68] **stamp**: impression.   [69] **either the Devil**: some verb such as "shame" or "curb" has been omitted.   [70] **bestow**: get rid of.   [71] **bloat**: bloated.   [72] **wanton**: lewdly.   [73] **reechy**: foul.   [74] **ravel**: unravel, reveal.   [75] **paddock**: toad.   [76] **gib**: tomcat.   [77] **dear concernings**: important matters.   [78] **despite**: spite.   [79] **famous ape**: The story is not known, but evidently told of an ape that let the birds out of their cage and, seeing them fly, crept into the cage himself and jumped out, breaking his own neck.   [80] **try conclusions**: repeat the experiment.   [81] **mandate**: command.

225   And marshal me to knavery. Let it work,
       For 'tis the sport to have the enginer[82]
       Hoist with his own petar.[83] And 't shall go hard
       But I will delve one yard below their mines
       And blow them at the moon: O, 'tis most sweet
230   When in one line two crafts[84] directly meet.
       This man shall set me packing.
       I'll lug the guts into the neighbor room.
       Mother, good night. Indeed this counselor
       Is now most still, most secret, and most grave
235   Who was in life a foolish prating knave.
       Come, sir, to draw toward an end with you.
       Good night, mother.

(Exeunt severally,[85] Hamlet dragging in Polonius.)

Act IV

Scene I. A room in the castle.

(Enter King, Queen, Rosencrantz, and Guildenstern.)

King: There's matter[1] in these sighs, these profound heaves,
       You must translate. 'Tis fit we understand them.
       Where is your son?
Queen: Bestow this place[2] on us a little while.

(Exeunt Rosencrantz and Guildenstern.)

5   Ah, mine own lord, what have I seen tonight!
King: What, Gertrude? How does Hamlet?
Queen: Mad as the sea and wind when both contend
       Which is the mightier. In his lawless fit,
       Behind the arras hearing something stir,
10   Whips out his rapier, cries "A rat, a rat!"
       And in this brainish apprehension[3] kills
       The unseen good old man.
King: Oh, heavy deed!
       It had been so with us had we been there.
15   His liberty is full of threats to all,
       To you yourself, to us, to everyone.
       Alas, how shall this bloody deed be answered?
       It will be laid to us, whose providence[4]
       Should have kept short,[5] restrained and out of haunt,[6]
20   This mad young man. But so much was our love
       We would not understand what was most fit,
       But, like the owner of a foul disease,

---

[82] **enginer:** engineer.   [83] **petar:** petard, land mine.   [84] **crafts:** devices.   [85] **Exeunt severally:** i.e., by separate exits. In F₁ there is no break here. The King enters as soon as Hamlet has dragged the body away. Q₂ marks the break. The act division was first inserted in a quarto of 1676.   [1] **matter:** something serious.   [2] **Bestow . . . place:** give place, leave us.   [3] **brainish apprehension:** mad imagination.   [4] **providence:** foresight.   [5] **short:** confined.   [6] **out of haunt:** away from others.

To keep it from divulging[7] let it feed
Even on the pith[8] of life. Where is he gone?
25 **Queen:** To draw apart the body he hath killed,
O'er whom his very madness, like some ore
Among a mineral of metals base,
Shows itself pure. He weeps for what is done.
King: O Gertrude, come away!
30 The sun no sooner shall the mountains touch
But we will ship him hence. And this vile deed
We must, with all our majesty and skill,
Both countenance[9] and excuse. Ho, Guildenstern!

(Re-enter Rosencrantz and Guildenstern.)

Friends both, go join you with some further aid.
35 Hamlet in madness hath Polonius slain,
And from his mother's closet hath he dragged him.
Go seek him out, speak fair, and bring the body
Into the chapel. I pray you, haste in this.

(Exeunt Rosencrantz and Guildenstern.)

Come, Gertrude, we'll call up our wisest friends,
40 And let them know both what we mean to do
And what's untimely done,[10]
Whose whisper o'er the world's diameter
As level as the cannon to his blank[11]
Transports his poisoned shot, may miss our name
45 And hit the woundless air. Oh, come away!
My soul is full of discord and dismay.

(Exeunt.)

Scene II. Another room in the castle.

(Enter Hamlet.)

Hamlet: Safely stowed.
Rosencrantz & Guildenstern: *(Within)* Hamlet! Lord Hamlet!
Hamlet: But soft, what noise? Who calls on Hamlet?
Oh, here they come.

(Enter Rosencrantz and Guildenstern.)

5 **Rosencrantz:** What have you done, my lord, with the dead body?
Hamlet: Compounded it with dust, whereto 'tis kin.
Rosencrantz: Tell us where 'tis, that we may take it thence
And bear it to the chapel.
Hamlet: Do not believe it.
10 **Rosencrantz:** Believe what?

---

[7] **divulging:** becoming known.   [8] **pith:** marrow.   [9] **countenance:** take responsibility for.   [10] **done:** A half-line has been omitted. Some editors fill the gap with "So, haply slander."   [11] **blank:** target.

Hamlet: That I can keep your counsel and not mine own. Besides, to be demanded of a sponge! What replication[1] should be made by the son of a king?

Rosencrantz: Take you me for a sponge, my lord?

Hamlet: Aye, sir, that soaks up the king's countenance,[2] his rewards, his authorities. But such officers do the king best service in the end. He keeps them, like an ape, in the corner of his jaw, first mouthed, to be last swallowed. When he needs what you have gleaned, it is but squeezing you and, sponge, you shall be dry again.

Rosencrantz: I understand you not, my lord.

Hamlet: I am glad of it. A knavish speech sleeps in a foolish ear.[3]

Rosencrantz: My lord, you must tell us where the body is; and go with us to the king.

Hamlet: The body is with the king, but the king is not with the body.[4]
    The king is a thing—

Guildenstern: A thing, my lord?

Hamlet: Of nothing. Bring me to him. Hide fox, and all after.[5]

(Exeunt.)

Scene III. Another room in the castle.

(Enter King, attended.)

King: I have sent to seek him, and to find the body.
    How dangerous is it that this man goes loose!
    Yet must not we put the strong law on him.
    He's loved of the distracted[1] multitude,
    Who like not in their judgment but their eyes;[2]
    And where 'tis so, the offender's scourge[3] is weighed,
    But never the offense. To bear[4] all smooth and even,
    This sudden sending him away must seem
    Deliberate pause.[5] Diseases desperate grown
    By desperate appliance are relieved,
    Or not at all.

(Enter Rosencrantz.)

                How now! What hath befall'n?

Rosencrantz: Where the dead body is bestowed, my lord,
    We cannot get from him.

King: But where is he?

Rosencrantz: Without, my lord, guarded, to know your pleasure.

King: Bring him before us.

Rosencrantz: Ho, Guildenstern! Bring in my lord.

(Enter Hamlet and Guildenstern.)

King: Now, Hamlet, where's Polonius?

Hamlet: At supper.

King: At supper! Where?

---

[1] **replication:** answer. [2] **countenance:** favor. [3] **A . . . ear:** a fool never understands the point of a sinister speech. [4] **The . . . body:** Hamlet deliberately bewilders his companions. [5] **Hide . . . after:** a form of the game of hide-and-seek. With these words Hamlet runs away from them. [1] **distracted:** bewildered.
[2] **like . . . eyes:** whose likings are swayed not by judgment but by looks. [3] **scourge:** punishment.
[4] **bear:** make. [5] **Deliberate pause:** the result of careful planning.

Hamlet: Not where he eats, but where he is eaten. A certain convocation of politic worms[6] are e'en at him. Your worm is your only emperor for diet. We fat all creatures else to fat us, and we fat ourselves for maggots. Your fat king and your lean beggar is but vari-
25 able service,[7] two dishes, but to one table. That's the end.

King: Alas, alas!

Hamlet: A man may fish with the worm that hath eat of a king, and eat of the fish that hath fed of that worm.

King: What dost thou mean by this?

30 **Hamlet:** Nothing but to show you how a king may go a progress[8] through the guts of a beggar.

King: Where is Polonius?

Hamlet: In heaven—send thither to see. If your messenger find him not there, seek him i' the other place yourself. But indeed if you find him not within this month, you shall
35 nose him as you go up the stairs into the lobby.

King: (*To some Attendants*) Go seek him there.

Hamlet: He will stay till you come.

(*Exeunt Attendants.*)

King: Hamlet, this deed, for thine especial safety,
Which we do tender,[9] as we dearly grieve
40 For that which thou hast done, must send thee hence
With fiery quickness. Therefore prepare thyself.
The bark is ready and the wind at help,[10]
The associates tend,[11] and every thing is bent[12]
For England.

45 **Hamlet:**   For England?

King: Aye, Hamlet.

Hamlet: Good.

King: So is it if thou knew'st our purposes.

Hamlet: I see a cherub that sees them. But, come, for England!
50 Farewell, dear Mother.

King: Thy loving father, Hamlet.

Hamlet: My mother. Father and mother is man and wife, man and wife is one flesh, and so, my mother. Come, for England!

(*Exit.*)

King: Follow him at foot,[13] tempt[14] him with speed aboard.
55 Delay it not, I'll have him hence tonight.
Away! For everything is sealed and done
That else leans on the affair. Pray you make haste.

(*Exeunt Rosencrantz and Guildenstern.*)

And, England, if my love thou hold'st at aught—
As my great power thereof may give thee sense,
60 Since yet thy cicatrice[15] looks raw and red

---

[6] **convocation . . . worms:** an assembly of political-minded worms.   [7] **variable service:** choice of alternatives.   [8] **go a progress:** make a state journey.   [9] **tender:** regard highly.   [10] **at help:** favorable.   [11] **associates tend:** your companions are waiting.   [12] **bent:** ready.   [13] **at foot:** at his heels.   [14] **tempt:** entice.
[15] **cicatrice:** scar. There is nothing in the play to explain this incident.

After the Danish sword, and thy free awe[16]
Pays homage to us—thou mayst not coldly set
Our sovereign process,[17] which imports at full,
By letters congruing[18] to that effect,
65   The present[19] death of Hamlet. Do it, England,
For like the hectic[20] in my blood he rages,
And thou must cure me. Till I know 'tis done,
Howe'er my haps,[21] my joys were ne'er begun.

(Exit.)

Scene IV. A plain in Denmark.

(Enter Fortinbras, a Captain and Soldiers, marching.)

Fortinbras: Go, Captain, from me greet the Danish king.
Tell him that by his license Fortinbras
Craves the conveyance of a promised march[1]
Over his kingdom. You know the rendezvous.
5   If that His majesty would aught with us,
We shall express our duty in his eye,[2]
And let him know so.
Captain: I will do 't, my lord.
Fortinbras: Go softly on.

(Exeunt Fortinbras and Soldiers.)

(Enter Hamlet, Rosencrantz, Guildenstern, and others.)

10 **Hamlet:** Good sir, whose powers[3] are these?
Captain: They are of Norway, sir.
Hamlet: How purposed, sir, I pray you?
Captain: Against some part of Poland.
Hamlet: Who commands them, sir?
15 **Captain:** The nephew to old Norway, Fortinbras.
Hamlet: Goes it against the main[4] of Poland, sir,
Or for some frontier?
Captain: Truly to speak, and with no addition,[5]
We go to gain a little patch of ground
20   That hath in it no profit but the name.
To pay five ducats, five, I would not farm it,
Nor will it yield to Norway or the Pole
A ranker[6] rate should it be sold in fee.[7]
Hamlet: Why, then the Polack never will defend it.
25 **Captain:** Yes, it is already garrisoned.
Hamlet: Two thousand souls and twenty thousand ducats
Will not debate the question of this straw.

---

[16] **free awe:** voluntary submission. [17] **coldly . . . process:** hesitate to carry out our royal command.
[18] **congruing:** agreeing. [19] **present:** immediate. [20] **hectic:** fever. [21] **Howe'er my haps:** whatever may happen to me. [1] **Craves . . . march:** asks for permission to transport his army, as had already been promised. [2] **in . . . eye:** before his eyes; i.e., in person. [3] **powers:** forces. [4] **main:** mainland. [5] **addition:** exaggeration. [6] **ranker:** richer. [7] **in fee:** with possession as freehold.

This is the imposthume of[8] much wealth and peace,
That inward breaks, and shows no cause without
30   Why the man dies. I humbly thank you, sir.

Captain: God be wi' you, sir. *(Exit.)*

Rosencrantz: Will 't please you go, my lord?

Hamlet: I'll be with you straight. Go a little before.

(Exeunt all but Hamlet.)

How[9] all occasions do inform against[10] me
35   And spur my dull revenge! What is a man
If his chief good and market[11] of his time
Be but to sleep and feed? A beast, no more.
Sure. He that made us with such large discourse,
Looking before and after,[12] gave us not
40   That capability and godlike reason
To fust[13] in us unused. Now whether it be
Bestial oblivion, or some craven scruple
Of thinking too precisely on the event—
A thought which, quartered, hath but one part wisdom
45   And ever three parts coward—I do not know
Why yet I live to say "This thing's to do,"
Sith I have cause, and will, and strength, and means
To do 't. Examples gross[14] as earth exhort me.
Witness this army, of such mass and charge,[15]
50   Led by a delicate and tender prince
Whose spirit with divine ambition puffed
Makes mouths at the invisible event,[16]
Exposing what is mortal and unsure
To all that fortune, death, and danger dare,
55   Even for an eggshell.[17] Rightly to be great
Is not to stir without great argument,
But greatly to find quarrel in a straw
When honor's at the stake.[18] How stand I then,
That have a father killed, a mother stained,
60   Excitements of my reason and my blood,
And let all sleep while to my shame I see
The imminent death of twenty thousand men
That for a fantasy and trick[19] of fame
Go to their graves like beds, fight for a plot
65   Whereon the numbers cannot try the cause,[20]
Which is not tomb enough and continent[21]

---

[8] **imposthume of:** inward swelling caused by. [9] **How . . . worth:** The soliloquy and all the dialogue after the exit of Fortinbras are omitted in F$_1$. [10] **inform against:** accuse. [11] **market:** profit. [12] **such . . . after:** intelligence that enables us to consider the future and the past. [13] **fust:** grow musty. [14] **gross:** large. [15] **charge:** expense. [16] **Makes . . . event:** mocks at the unseen risk. [17] **eggshell:** i.e., worthless trifle. [18] **Rightly . . . stake:** true greatness is a matter of fighting not for a mighty cause but for the merest trifle when honor is concerned. [19] **fantasy . . . trick:** illusion and whim. [20] **Whereon . . . cause:** a piece of ground so small that it would not hold the combatants. [21] **continent:** large enough to contain.

To hide the slain? O, from this time forth,
My thoughts be bloody or be nothing worth!

(Exit.)

Scene V. Elsinore. A room in the castle.

(Enter Queen, Horatio, and a Gentleman.)

Queen: I will not speak with her.
Gentleman: She is importunate, indeed distract.[1]
    Her mood will needs be pitied.
Queen: What would she have?
5 **Gentleman:** She speaks much of her father, says she hears
    There's tricks[2] i' the world, and hems[3] and beats her heart,
    Spurns enviously[4] at straws, speaks things in doubt
    That carry but half-sense. Her speech is nothing,
    Yet the unshaped use[5] of it doth move
10   The hearers to collection.[6] They aim[7] at it,
    And botch[8] the words up fit to their own thoughts,
    Which, as her winks and nods and gestures yield them,
    Indeed would make one think there might be thought,
    Though nothing sure, yet much unhappily.
15 **Horatio:** 'Twere good she were spoken with, for she may strew
    Dangerous conjectures in ill-breeding minds.
Queen: Let her come in.

(Exit Gentleman.)

(Aside) To my sick soul, as sin's true nature is,
Each toy[9] seems prologue to some great amiss.[10]
20 So full of artless jealousy[11] is guilt,
It spills itself in fearing to be spilt.[12]

(Re-enter Gentleman, with Ophelia.[13]

Ophelia: Where is the beauteous majesty of Denmark?
Queen: How now, Ophelia!
Ophelia: (Sings.)

25   "How should I your truelove know
        From another one?
    By his cockle hat[14] and staff
        And his sandal shoon."[15]

Queen: Alas, sweet lady, what imports this song?
30 **Ophelia:** Say you? Nay, pray you, mark.

(Sings.)

---

[1] **distract:** out of her mind. [2] **tricks:** trickery. [3] **hems:** makes significant noises. [4] **Spurns enviously:** kicks spitefully. [5] **unshaped use:** disorder. [6] **collection:** i.e., attempts to find a sinister meaning. [7] **aim:** guess. [8] **botch:** patch. [9] **toy:** trifle. [10] **amiss:** calamity. [11] **artless jealousy:** clumsy suspicion. [12] **It . . . spilt:** guilt reveals itself by its efforts at concealment. [13] **Re-enter . . . Ophelia:** Q₁ notes "Enter Ophelia playing on a lute, and her hair down, singing." [14] **cockle hat:** a hat adorned with a cockleshell worn by pilgrims. [15] **sandal shoon:** sandals, the proper footwear of pilgrims.

"He is dead and gone, lady,
    He is dead and gone,
At his head a grass-green turf,
    At his heels a stone."

35   Oh, oh!

Queen: Nay, but, Ophelia—

Ophelia: Pray you, mark.

(Sings.)

"White his shroud as the mountain snow—"

(Enter King.)

Queen: Alas, look here, my lord.

40 **Ophelia:** *(Sings.)*

"Larded[16] with sweet flowers,
Which bewept to the grave did go
With truelove showers."[17]

King: How do you, pretty lady?

45 **Ophelia:** Well, God 'ild[18] you! They say the owl was a baker's daughter.[19] Lord, we know
what we are but know not what we may be. God be at your table!

King: Conceit upon her father.

Ophelia: Pray you let's have no words of this, but when they ask you what it means, say
you this

(Sings.):

50   "Tomorrow is Saint Valentine's day,[20]
      All in the morning betime,
And I a maid at your window,
      To be your Valentine.

"Then up he rose, and donned his clothes,
55   And dupped[21] the chamber door,
Let in the maid, that out a maid
      Never departed more."

King: Pretty Ophelia!

Ophelia: Indeed, la, without an oath, I'll make an end on 't.

(Sings.):

60   "By Gis[22] and by Saint Charity,
      Alack, and fie for shame!
Young men will do 't, if they come to 't,
      By cock, they are to blame.

---

[16] **Larded:** garnished.   [17] **truelove showers:** the tears of his faithful love.   [18] **'ild (yield):** reward.
[19] **owl . . . daughter:** An allusion to a legend that Christ once went into a baker's shop and asked for bread.
The baker's wife gave him a piece but was rebuked by her daughter for giving him too much. Thereupon the
daughter was turned into an owl.   [20] **Saint . . . day:** February 14, the day when birds are supposed to mate.
According to the old belief the first single man then seen by a maid is destined to be her husband.
[21] **dupped:** opened.   [22] **Gis . . . cock:** for "Jesus" and "God," both words being used instead of the sacred
names, like the modern "Jeez" and "Gee."

Quoth she, before you tumbled me,
> You promised me to wed."
He answers:
"So would I ha' done, by yonder sun,
> An thou hadst not come to my bed."

King: How long hath she been thus?

70 **Ophelia:** I hope all will be well. We must be patient. But I cannot choose but weep to think they should lay him i' the cold ground. My brother shall know of it. And so I thank you for your good counsel. Come, my coach! Good night, ladies, good night, sweet ladies, good night, good night. (*Exit.*)

King: Follow her close,[23] give her good watch, I pray you.

(Exit Horatio.)

75 Oh, this is the poison of deep grief. It springs
All from her father's death. O Gertrude, Gertrude.
When sorrows come, they come not single spies,[24]
But in battalions! First, her father slain.
Next, your son gone, and he most violent author[25]
80 Of his own just remove. The people muddied,
Thick and unwholesome in their thoughts and whispers,
For good Polonius' death. And we have done but greenly[26]
In huggermugger[27] to inter him. Poor Ophelia
Divided from herself and her fair judgment,[28]
85 Without the which we are pictures,[29] or mere beasts.
Last, and as much containing as all these,
Her brother is in secret come from France,
Feeds on his wonder, keeps himself in clouds,
And wants not buzzers[30] to infect his ear
90 With pestilent speeches of his father's death,
Wherein necessity, of matter beggared,
Will nothing stick our person to arraign[31]
In ear and ear. O my dear Gertrude, this,
Like to a murdering piece,[32] in many places
95 Gives me superfluous death.

(A noise within.)

Queen: Alack, what noise is this?
King: Where are my Switzers?[33] Let them guard the door.

(Enter another Gentleman.)

What is the matter?
Gentleman: Save yourself, my lord!
100 The ocean, overpeering of his list,[34]

---

[23] **close:** closely. [24] **spies:** scouts. [25] **author:** cause. [26] **done . . . greenly:** shown immature judgment.
[27] **hugger-mugger:** secret haste, "any which way." [28] **Divided . . . judgment:** no longer able to use her judgment. [29] **pictures:** lifeless imitations. [30] **buzzers:** scandalmongers. [31] **herein . . . arraign:** in which, knowing nothing of the true facts, he may necessarily accuse us. [32] **murdering piece:** cannon loaded with grapeshot. [33] **Switzers:** Swiss bodyguard. [34] **overpeering . . . list:** looking over its boundary; i.e., flooding the mainland.

Eats not the flats[35] with more impetuous haste
Than young Laertes, in a riotous head,[36]
O'erbears your officers. The rabble call him lord.
And as the world were now but to begin,
105   Antiquity forgot, custom not known,
The ratifiers and props of every word,[37]
They cry "Choose we—Laertes shall be king!"
Caps, hands, and tongues applaud it to the clouds—
"Laertes shall be king, Laertes king!"
110 **Queen:** How cheerfully on the false trail they cry!
O, this is counter,[38] you false Danish dogs!

(Noise within.)

King: The doors are broke.

(Enter Laertes, armed, Danes following.)

Laertes: Where is this king? Sirs, stand you all without.
Danes: No, let's come in.
115 **Laertes:**   I pray you, give me leave.
Danes: We will, we will.

(They retire without the door.)

Laertes: I thank you. Keep the door.
                                  O thou vile King,
Give me my father!
120 **Queen:**   Calmly, good Laertes.
Laertes: That drop of blood that's calm proclaims me bastard,
Cries cuckold[39] to my father, brands the harlot[40]
Even here, between the chaste unsmirchèd brows
Of my true mother.
125 **King:**   What is the cause, Laertes,
That thy rebellion looks so giantlike?
Let him go, Gertrude. Do not fear[41] our person.
There's such divinity doth hedge a king[42]
That treason can but peep[43] to what it would,
130   Acts little of his will. Tell me, Laertes,
Why thou art thus incensed. Let him go, Gertrude.
Speak, man.
Laertes: Where is my father?
King: Dead.
135 **Queen:** But not by him.
King: Let him demand his fill.
Laertes: How came he dead? I'll not be juggled with.
To hell, allegiance! Vows, to the blackest devil!
Conscience and grace, to the profoundest pit!

---

[35] **Eats . . . flats:** floods not the flat country. [36] **in . . . head:** with a force of rioters.
[37] **Antiquity . . . word:** forgetting ancient rule and ignoring old custom, by which all promises must be maintained. [38] **counter:** in the wrong direction of the scent. [39] **cuckold:** a husband deceived by his wife. [40] **brands . . . harlot:** Convicted harlots were branded with a hot iron. [41] **fear:** fear for. [42] **divinity . . . king:** divine protection surrounds a king as with a hedge. [43] **peep:** look over, not break through.

140   I dare damnation. To this point I stand,
          That both the worlds I give to negligence.[44]
          Let come what comes, only I'll be revenged
          Most throughly[45] for my father.
King: Who shall stay you?

145 **Laertes:**   My will, not all the world.
          And for my means, I'll husband[46] them so well
          They shall go far with little.
King: Good Laertes,
          If you desire to know the certainty

150   Of your dear father's death, is 't writ in your revenge
          That, swoopstake,[47] you will draw both friend and foe,
          Winner and loser?
Laertes: None but his enemies.
King: Will you know them, then?

155 **Laertes:** To his good friends thus wide I'll ope my arms,
          And like the kind life-rendering pelican,[48]
          Repast[49] them with my blood.
King: Why, now you speak
          Like a good child and a true gentleman.

160   That I am guiltless of your father's death,
          And am most sensibly[50] in grief for it,
          It shall as level[51] to your judgment pierce
          As day does to your eye.
Danes: *(Within.)*   Let her come in.
Laertes: How now! What noise is that?

          (Re-enter Ophelia.)

165   O heat, dry up my brains! Tears seven times salt
          Burn out the sense and virtue of mine eye!
          By Heaven, thy madness shall be paid with weight
          Till our scale turn the beam.[52] O rose of May![53]

170   Dear maid, kind sister, sweet Ophelia!
          Oh heavens! Is 't possible a young maid's wits
          Should be as mortal as an old man's life?
          Nature is fine in love, and where 'tis fine
          It sends some precious instance of itself

175   After the thing it loves.[54]
Ophelia: *(Sings.)*

          "They bore him barefaced on the bier,
            Hey non nonny, nonny, hey nonny,
          And in his grave rained many a tear—"

---

[44] **That . . . negligence:** I do not care what happens to me in this world or the next.   [45] **throughly:** thoroughly.   [46] **husband:** use economically.   [47] **swoopstake:** "sweeping the board" [Editors note: "sweepstake; taking all the stakes].   [48] **life-rendering pelican:** The mother pelican was supposed to feed her young with blood from her own breast.   [49] **Repast:** feed.   [50] **sensibly:** feelingly.   [51] **level:** clearly.
[52] **turn . . . beam:** weigh down the beam of the scale.   [53] **rose of May:** perfection of young beauty.
[54] **Nature . . . loves:** i.e., her love for her father was so exquisite that she has sent her sanity after him. Laertes, especially in moments of emotion, is prone to use highly exaggerated speech.

180   Fare you well, my dove!

Laertes: Hadst thou thy wits and didst persuade revenge,
      It could not move thus.
Ophelia: (*Sings.*)

      "You must sing down a-down
185   An you call him a-down-a."
      Oh, how the wheel[55] becomes it! It is the false steward, that stole his master's daughter.

Laertes: This nothing's more than matter.[56]
Ophelia: There's[57] rosemary, that's for remembrance—pray you, love, remember. And there
      is pansies, that is for thoughts.
190 **Laertes:** A document[58] in madness, thoughts and remembrance fitted.
Ophelia: There's fennel for you, and columbines. There's rue for you, and here's some for
      me—we may call it herb of grace o' Sundays. Oh, you must wear your rue with a differ-
      ence. There's a daisy. I would give you some violets, but they withered all when my fa-
      ther died. They say a' made a good end.

      (*Sings.*)

195   "For bonny sweet Robin is all my joy."

Laertes: Thought and affliction, passion, hell itself,
      She turns to favor[59] and to prettiness.
Ophelia: (Sings.)

      "And will a' not come again?
200   And will a' not come again?
          No, no, he is dead,
          Go to thy deathbed,
      He never will come again.

      "His beard was as white as snow,
205   All flaxen was his poll.[60]
          He is gone, he is gone,
          And we cast away moan.
      God ha' mercy on his soul!"

      And of all Christian souls, I pray God. God be wi' you. (*Exit.*)
210 **Laertes:** Do you see this, O God?
King: Laertes, I must commune with your grief,
      Or you deny me right. Go but apart,
      Make choice of whom your wisest friends you will,
      And they shall hear and judge 'twixt you and me.
215   If by direct or by collateral[61] hand

---

[55] **wheel:** explained variously as the spinning wheel, Fortune's wheel, or the refrain. The likeliest explanation is that she breaks into a little dance at the words "You must sing," and that the **wheel** is the turn as she
circles round.   [56] **This . . . matter:** this nonsense means more than sense.   [57] **There's . . . died:** In the
language of flowers, each has its peculiar meaning, and Ophelia distributes them appropriately: for her
brother rosemary (remembrance) and pansies (thoughts); for the King fennel (flattery) and columbine
(thanklessness); for the Queen rue, called also herb o' grace (sorrow), and daisy (light of love). Neither is
worthy of violets (faithfulness).   [58] **document:** instruction.   [59] **favor:** charm.   [60] **flaxen . . . poll:** white
as flax was his head.   [61] **collateral:** i.e., as an accessory.

They find us touched,[62] we will our kingdom give,
Our crown, our life, and all that we call ours,
To you in satisfaction. But if not,
Be you content to lend your patience to us
220 And we shall jointly labor with your soul
To give it due content.

Laertes: Let this be so.
His means of death, his obscure funeral,[63]
No trophy, sword, nor hatchment[64] o'er his bones,
225 No noble rite nor formal ostentation,[65]
Cry to be heard, as 'twere from heaven to earth,
That I must call 't in question.

King: So you shall,
And where the offense is let the great ax fall.
230 I pray you, go with me.

(Exeunt.)

Scene VI. Another room in the castle.

(Enter Horatio and a Servant.)

Horatio: What are they that would speak with me?
Servant: Seafaring men, sir. They say they have letters for you.
Horatio: Let them come in.

(Exit Servant.)

I do not know from what part of the world
5 I should be greeted, if not from Lord Hamlet.

(Enter Sailors.)

1. Sailor: God bless you, sir.
Horatio: Let him bless thee too.
1. Sailor: He shall, sir, an 't please him. There's a letter for you, sir. It comes from the ambassador that was bound for England—if your name be Horatio, as I am let to know
10   it is.
Horatio: *(Reads.)* "Horatio, when thou shalt have overlooked[1] this, give these fellows some means[2] to the king. They have letters for him. Ere we were two days old at sea, a pirate of very warlike appointment[3] gave us chase. Finding ourselves too slow of sail, we put on a compelled valor, and in the grapple I boarded them. On the instant they got
15   clear of our ship, so I alone became their prisoner. They have dealt with me like thieves of mercy; but they knew what they did—I am to do a good turn for them. Let the king have the letters I have sent, and repair thou to me with as much speed as thou wouldest fly death. I have words to speak in thine ear will make thee dumb, yet are they much too light for the bore of the matter.[4] These good fellows will bring thee

---

[62] **touched:** implicated.   [63] **obscure funeral:** Men of rank were buried with much ostentation. To bury Polonius "huggermugger" was thus an insult to his memory and to his family.   [64] **hatchment:** device of the coat of arms carried in a funeral and hung up over the tomb.   [65] **formal ostentation:** ceremony properly ordered.   [1] **overlooked:** read.   [2] **means:** access.   [3] **appointment:** equipment.   [4] **too . . . matter:** i.e., words fall short, like a small shot fired from a cannon with too wide a bore.

20   where I am. Rosencrantz and Guildenstern hold their course for England. Of them I
have much to tell thee. Farewell.

"He that thou knowest thine.

"Hamlet"

Come, I will make you way for these your letters,
25   And do 't the speedier that you may direct me
To him from whom you brought them.

(Exeunt.)

Scene VII. Another room in the castle.

(Enter King and Laertes.)

King: Now must your conscience my acquittance seal,[1]
    And you must put me in your heart for friend,
    Sith you have heard, and with a knowing ear,
    That he which hath your noble father slain
5   Pursued my life.
Laertes: It well appears. But tell me
    Why you proceeded not against these feats,[2]
    So crimeful and so capital[3] in nature,
    As by your safety, wisdom, all things else,
10   You mainly were stirred up.
King: O, for two special reasons,
    Which may to you perhaps seem much unsinewed,[4]
    But yet to me they're strong. The queen his mother
    Lives almost by his looks, and for myself—
15   My virtue or my plague, be it either which—
    She's so conjunctive[5] to my life and soul
    That as the star moves not but[6] in his sphere,
    I could not but by her. The other motive
    Why to a public count[7] I might not go
20   Is the great love the general gender[8] bear him,
    Who, dipping all his faults in their affection,[9]
    Would, like the spring that turneth wood to stone,[10]
    Convert his gyves to graces.[11] So that my arrows,
    Too slightly timbered[12] for so loud a wind,
25   Would have reverted to my bow again
    And not where I had aimed them.
Laertes: And so have I a noble father lost,
    A sister driven into desperate terms,[13]
    Whose worth, if praises may go back again,[14]

---

[1] **my . . . seal:** acquit me.   [2] **feats:** acts.   [3] **capital:** deserving death.   [4] **unsinewed:** weak, flabby.
[5] **conjunctive:** joined inseparably.   [6] **moves . . . but:** moves only in.   [7] **count:** trial.   [8] **general gender:**
common people.   [9] **dipping . . . affection:** gilding his faults with their love.   [10] **like . . . stone:** In several
places in England there are springs of water so strongly impregnated with lime that they will quickly cover
with stone anything placed under them.   [11] **Convert . . . graces:** regard his fetters as honorable ornaments.   [12] **timbered:** shafted. A light arrow is caught by the wind and blown back.   [13] **terms:** condition.
[14] **if . . . again:** if one may praise her for what she used to be.

30   Stood challenger on mount of all the age
        For her perfections.[15] But my revenge will come.
  King: Break not your sleeps for that. You must not think
        That we are made of stuff so flat and dull
        That we can let our beard be shook with danger
35   And think it pastime. You shortly shall hear more.[16]
        I loved your father, and we love ourself,
        And that, I hope, will teach you to imagine—

        (Enter a Messenger, with letters.)

        How now! What news!
  Messenger: Letters, my lord, from Hamlet.
40   This to your majesty, this to the queen.
  King: From Hamlet! Who brought them?
  Messenger: Sailors, my lord, they say—I saw them not.
        They were given me by Claudio, he received them
        Of him that brought them.
45 **King:**   Laertes, you shall hear them.
        Leave us.

        (Exit Messenger.)

        (Reads.) "High and Mighty, you shall know I am set naked[17] on your kingdom. Tomorrow shall I beg leave to see your kingly eyes, when I shall, first asking your pardon thereunto, recount the occasion of my sudden and more strange return.
50   "Hamlet"
        What should this mean? Are all the rest come back?
        Or is it some abuse,[18] and no such thing?
  Laertes: Know you the hand?
  King: 'Tis Hamlet's character.[19] "Naked!"
55   And in a postscript here, he says "alone."
        Can you advise me?
  Laertes: I'm lost in it, my lord. But let him come.
        It warms the very sickness in my heart
        That I shall live and tell him to his teeth
60   "Thus didest thou."
  King: If it be so, Laertes—
        As how should it be so, how otherwise?—
        Will you be ruled by me?
  Laertes: Aye, my lord,
65   So you will not o'errule[20] me to a peace.
  King: To thine own peace. If he be now returned,
        As checking at[21] his voyage, and that he means
        No more to undertake it, I will work him
        To an exploit now ripe in my device,
70   Under the which he shall not choose but fall.

---

[15] **Stood . . . perfections:** i.e., her worth challenged the whole world to find one as perfect.   [16] **hear more:** i.e., when news comes from England that Hamlet is dead.   [17] **naked:** destitute.   [18] **abuse:** attempt to deceive.   [19] **character:** handwriting.   [20] **o'errule:** command.   [21] **checking at:** swerving aside from, like a hawk that leaves the pursuit of its prey.

And for his death no wind of blame shall breathe,
But even his mother shall uncharge the practice[22]
And call it accident.

Laertes: My lord, I will be ruled,
75   The rather if you could devise it so
That I might be the organ.[23]

King: It falls right.
You have been talked of since your travel much,
And that in Hamlet's hearing, for a quality
80   Wherein they say you shine. Your sum of parts[24]
Did not together pluck such envy from him
As did that one, and that in my regard
Of the unworthiest siege.[25]

Laertes: What part is that, my lord?

85 **King:** A very ribbon in the cap of youth,
Yet needful too; for youth no less becomes
The light and careless livery that it wears
Than settled age his sables and his weeds,[26]
Importing health and graveness. Two months since,
90   Here was a gentleman of Normandy.
I've seen myself, and served against, the French,
And they can well[27] on horseback; but this gallant
Had witchcraft in 't, he grew unto his seat,
And to such wondrous doing brought his horse
95   As had he been incorpsed and deminatured[28]
With the brave beast. So far he topped my thought[29]
That I, in forgery of shapes and tricks,[30]
Come short of what he did.

Laertes: A Norman was 't?
100 **King:** A Norman.

Laertes: Upon my life, Lamond.

King: The very same.

Laertes: I know him well. He is the brooch[31] indeed
And gem of all the nation.

105 **King:** He made confession[32] of you,
And gave you such a masterly report
For art and exercise in your defense,
And for your rapier most especial,
That he cried out 'twould be a sight indeed
110   If one could match you. The scrimers[33] of their nation,
He swore, had neither motion, guard, nor eye
If you opposed them. Sir, this report of his
Did Hamlet so envenom[34] with his envy
That he could nothing do but wish and beg

---

[22] **uncharge . . . practice:** not suspect that his death was the result of the plot.   [23] **organ:** instrument.
[24] **sum of parts:** accomplishments as a whole.   [25] **siege:** seat, place.   [26] **sables . . . weeds:** dignified
roles.   [27] **can well:** can do well.   [28] **incorpsed . . . deminatured:** of one body.   [29] **topped my thoughts:**
surpassed what I could imagine.   [30] **forgery . . . tricks:** imagination of all kinds of fancy tricks. **shapes:**
fancies.   [31] **brooch:** ornament.   [32] **confession:** report.   [33] **scrimers:** fencers.   [34] **envenom:** poison.

115   Your sudden coming o'er, to play with him.
        Now, out of this—
Laertes: What out of this, my lord?
King: Laertes, was your father dear to you?
        Or are you like the painting[35] of a sorrow,
120   A face without a heart?
Laertes: Why ask you this?
King: Not that I think you did not love your father,
        But that I know love is begun by time,
        And that I see, in passages of proof,[36]
125   Time qualifies[37] the spark and fire of it.
        There lives within the very flame of love
        A kind of wick or snuff[38] that will abate it.
        And nothing is at a like goodness still,[39]
        For goodness, growing to a pleurisy,[40]
130   Dies in his own too much. That we would do
        We should do when we would; for this "would" changes
        And hath abatements and delays as many
        As there are tongues, are hands, are accidents,
        And then this "should" is like a spendthrift[41] sigh
135   That hurts by easing. But to the quick o' the ulcer.[42]
        Hamlet comes back. What would you undertake
        To show yourself your father's son in deed
        More than in words?
Laertes: To cut his throat i' the church.[43]
140 **King:** No place indeed should murder sanctuarize,[44]
        Revenge should have no bounds. But, good Laertes,
        Will you do this, keep close within your chamber.
        Hamlet returned shall know you are come home.
        We'll put on those[45] shall praise your excellence
145   And set a double varnish on the fame
        The Frenchman gave you, bring you in fine[46] together
        And wager on your heads. He, being remiss,[47]
        Most generous[48] and free from all contriving,[49]
        Will not peruse the foils, so that with ease,
150   Or with a little shuffling, you may choose
        A sword unbated,[50] and in a pass of practice[51]
        Requite him for your father.
Laertes: I will do 't,
        And for that purpose I'll anoint my sword.
155   I bought an unction[52] of a mountebank[53]

---

[35] **painting:** i.e., imitation.   [36] **passages of proof:** experiences which prove.   [37] **qualifies:** diminishes.
[38] **snuff:** Before the invention of self-consuming wicks for candles, the wick smoldered and formed a ball of soot which dimmed the light and gave out a foul smoke.   [39] **still:** always.   [40] **pleurisy:** fullness [Editor's note: a diseased swelling or fullness].   [41] **spendthrift:** wasteful, because sighing was supposed to be bad for the blood.   [42] **quick . . . ulcer:** i.e., to come to the real issue. **quick:** flesh, sensitive part.
[43] **cut . . . church:** i.e., to commit murder in a holy place, which would bring Laertes in danger of everlasting damnation; no crime could be worse.   [44] **sanctuarize:** give sanctuary to.   [45] **put . . . those:** set on some.   [46] **fine:** short.   [47] **remiss:** careless.   [48] **generous:** noble.   [49] **contriving:** plotting.   [50] **unbated:** not blunted, with a sharp point.   [51] **pass of practice:** treacherous thrust.   [52] **unction:** poison.   [53] **mountebank:** quack doctor.

So mortal that but dip a knife in it,
Where it draws blood no cataplasm[54] so rare,
Collected from all simples[55] that have virtue
Under the moon,[56] can save the thing from death
160   That is but scratched withal. I'll touch my point
With this contagion, that if I gall[57] him slightly,
It may be death.
King: Let's further think of this,
Weigh what convenience both of time and means
165   May fit us to our shape.[58] If this should fail,
And that our drift look through our bad performance,[59]
'Twere better not assayed. Therefore this project
Should have a back or second, that might hold
If this did blast in proof.[60] Soft! Let me see—
170   We'll make a solemn wager on your cunnings.
I ha 't.
When in your motion you are hot and dry—
As make your bouts[61] more violent to that end—
And that he calls for drink, I'll have prepared him
175   A chalice[62] for the nonce,[63] whereon but sipping,
If he by chance escape your venomed stuck,[64]
Our purpose may hold there. But stay, what noise?

(Enter Queen.)

                              How now, Sweet Queen!
Queen: One woe doth tread upon another's heel.
180   So fast they follow. Your sister's drowned, Laertes.
Laertes: Drowned! Oh, where?
Queen: There is a willow grows aslant a brook
That shows his hoar[65] leaves in the glassy stream.
There with fantastic garlands did she come
185   Of crowflowers, nettles, daises, and long purples
That liberal[66] shepherds give a grosser name,
But our cold maids do dead-men's-fingers call them.
There on the pendent[67] boughs her coronet weeds[68]
Clambering to hang, an envious sliver[69] broke,
190   When down her weedy trophies and herself
Fell in the weeping brook. Her clothes spread wide,
And mermaidlike awhile they bore her up—
Which time she chanted snatches of old tunes,
As one incapable[70] of her own distress,
195   Or like a creature native and indued[71]

---

[54] **cataplasm:** poultice.   [55] **simples:** herbs.   [56] **Under . . . moon:** herbs collected by moonlight were regarded as particularly potent.   [57] **gall:** break the skin.   [58] **Weigh . . . shape:** consider the best time and method of carrying out a plan.   [59] **drift . . . performance:** intention be revealed through bungling.
[60] **blast in proof:** break in trial, like a cannon which bursts when being tested.   [61] **bouts:** attacks, in the fencing match.   [62] **chalice:** cup.   [63] **nonce:** occasion.   [64] **stuck:** thrust.   [65] **hoar:** gray. The underside of the leaves of the willow are silver-gray.   [66] **liberal:** coarse-mouthed.   [67] **pendent:** hanging over the water.
[68] **coronet weeds:** wild flowers woven into a crown.   [69] **envious sliver:** malicious branch.   [70] **incapable:** not realizing.   [71] **indued:** endowed; i.e., a creature whose natural home is the water (*element*).

Unto that element. But long it could not be
Till that her garments, heavy with their drink,
Pulled the poor wretch from her melodious lay[72]
To muddy death.
200 **Laertes:**   Alas, then, she is drowned!
Queen: Drowned, drowned.
Laertes: Too much of water hast thou, poor Ophelia,
And therefore I forbid my tears. But yet
It is our trick[73]—Nature her custom holds,
205 Let shame say what it will. When these[74] are gone,
The woman will be out.[75] Adieu, my lord.
I have a speech of fire that fain[76] would blaze
But that this folly douts[77] it.

(*Exit.*)

King: Let's follow, Gertrude.
210 How much I had to do to calm his rage!
Now fear I this will give it start again,
Therefore let's follow

(*Exeunt.*)

Act V

Scene I. A churchyard.

(*Enter two Clowns,[1] with spades, etc.*)

1. Clown: Is she to be buried in Christian burial[2] that willfully seeks her own salvation?

2. Clown: I tell thee she is, and therefore make her grave straight.[3] The crowner[4] hath sat on her, and finds it Christian burial.

1. Clown: How can that be, unless she drowned herself in her own defense?

5 **2. Clown:** Why, 'tis found so.

1. Clown: It must be "se offendendo,"[5] it cannot be else. For here lies the point. If I drown myself wittingly,[6] it argues an act, and an act hath three branches—it is to act, to do, and to perform. Argal,[7] she drowned herself wittingly.

2. Clown: Nay, but hear you, goodman delver.[8]

10 **1. Clown:** Give me leave. Here lies the water, good. Here stands the man, good. If the man go to this water and drown himself, it is will he, nill he[9] he goes, mark you that; but if the water come to him and drown him, he drowns not himself. Argal, he that is not guilty of his own death shortens not his own life.

2. Clown: But is this law?

15 **1. Clown:** Aye, marry, is 't, crowner's quest[10] law.

---

[72] **lay:** song. [73] **But . . . trick:** it is our habit; i.e., to break into tears of great sorrow. [74] **these:** i.e., my tears. [75] **woman . . . out:** I shall be a man again. [76] **fain:** willingly. [77] **douts:** puts out. [1] **Clowns:** countrymen. [2] **Christian burial:** Suicides were not allowed burial in consecrated ground, but were buried at crossroads. The gravediggers and the priest are professionally scandalized that Ophelia should be allowed Christian burial solely because she is a lady of the Court. [3] **straight:** straightway. [4] **crowner:** coroner. [5] **se offendendo:** for **defendendo,** in self-defense. [6] **wittingly:** with full knowledge. [7] **Argal:** for the Latin ergo, therefore. [8] **delver:** digger. [9] **will he, nill he:** willy-nilly, whether he wishes or not. [10] **quest:** inquest.

2. Clown: Will you ha' the truth on 't? If this had not been a gentlewoman, she should have been buried out o' Christian burial.

1. Clown: Why, there thou say'st. And the more pity that great folks should have countenance[11] in this world to drown or hang themselves more than their even[12] Christian. Come, my spade. There is no ancient gentlemen but gardeners, ditchers, and grave-makers. They hold up[13] Adam's profession.

20

2. Clown: Was he a gentleman?

1. Clown: A' was the first that ever bore arms.[14]

2. Clown: Why, he had none.

25 **1. Clown:** What, art a heathen? How dost thou understand·the Scripture? The Scripture says Adam digged. Could he dig without arms? I'll put another question to thee. If thou answerest me not to the purpose, confess thyself—

2. Clown: Go to.

1. Clown: What is he that builds stronger than either the mason, the shipwright, or the carpenter?

30

2. Clown: The gallows-maker, for that frame outlives a thousand tenants.

1. Clown: I like thy wit well, in good faith. The gallows does well, but how does it well? It does well to those that do ill. Now thou dost ill to say the gallows is built stronger than the church; argal, the gallows may do well to thee. To 't again, come.

35 **2. Clown:** Who builds stronger than a mason, a shipwright, or a carpenter?

1. Clown: Aye, tell me that, and unyoke.[15]

2. Clown: Marry, now I can tell.

1. Clown: To 't.

2. Clown: Mass,[16] I cannot tell.

(Enter Hamlet and Horatio, afar off.)

40 **1. Clown:** Cudgel thy brains no more about it, for your dull ass will not mend his pace with beating, and when you are asked this question next, say "A gravemaker." The houses that he makes last till Doomsday. Go, get thee to Yaughan,[17] fetch me a stoup[18] of liquor.

(Exit Second Clown.)

(First Clown digs, and sings.)

"In youth,[19] when I did love, did love,
    Methought it was very sweet,
45 To contract; oh, the time, for-a my behoove,[20]
    Oh, methought, there-a was nothing- a meet."

Hamlet: Has this fellow no feeling for his business, that he sings at grave-making?

Horatio: Custom hath made it in him a property of easiness.[21]

50 **Hamlet:** 'Tis e'en so. The hand of little employment hath the daintier sense.[22]

---

[11] **countenance:** favor. [12] **even:** fellow. [13] **hold up:** support. [14] **bore arms:** had a coat of arms—the outward sign of a gentleman. [15] **unyoke:** finish the job, unyoking the plow oxen being the end of the day's work. [16] **Mass:** by the mass. [17] **Yaughan:** apparently an innkeeper near the Globe Theatre. [18] **stoup:** large pot. [19] **In youth . . . meet:** The song which the gravedigger sings without much care for accuracy or sense was first printed in **Tottel's Miscellany,** 1558. [20] **behoove:** benefit. [21] **property of easiness:** careless habits. [22] **hand . . . sense:** those who have little to do are the most sensitive.

1. Clown: (*Sings.*)

> "But age, with his stealing steps,
> > Hath clawed me in his clutch,
> And hath shipped me intil the land[23]
> > As if I had never been such."

55

(*Throws up a skull.*)

Hamlet: That skull had a tongue in it, and could sing once. How the knave jowls[24] it to the ground, as if it were Cain's jawbone, that did the first murder! It might be the pate of a politician which this ass now o'erreaches[25]—one that would circumvent[26] God, might it not?

60 **Horatio:** It might, my lord.

Hamlet: Or of a courtier, which could say "Good morrow, sweet lord! How dost thou, good lord?" This might be my lord Such-a-one that praised my lord Such-a-one's horse when he meant to beg it, might it not?

Horatio: Aye, my lord.

65 **Hamlet:** Why, e'en so. And now my Lady Worm's chapless,[27] and knocked about the mazzard[28] with a sexton's spade. Here's fine revolution, an we had the trick to see 't. Did these bones cost no more the breeding but to play at loggats[29] with 'em? Mine ache to think on 't.

1. Clown: (*Sings.*)

> "A pickax and a spade, a spade,
> > For and a shrouding sheet—
> Oh, a pit of clay for to be made
> > For such a guest is meet."

70

(*Throws up another skull.*)

Hamlet: There's another. Why may not that be the skull of a lawyer?[30] Where be his quiddities now, his quillets, his cases, his tenures, and his tricks? Why does he suffer this rude knave now to knock him about the sconce[31] with a dirty shovel, and will not tell him of his action of battery? Hum! This fellow might be in 's time a great buyer of land, with his statutes, his recognizances, his fines, his double vouchers, his recoveries. Is this the fine[32] of his fines and the recovery of his recoveries, to have his fine pate full of fine dirt? Will his vouchers vouch him no more of his purchase, and double ones too, than the length and breadth of a pair of indentures? The very conveyances of his lands will hardly lie in this box,[33] and must the interior himself have no more, ha?

75

80

Horatio: Not a jot more, my lord.

Hamlet: Is not parchment made of sheepskins?

Horatio: Aye, my lord, and of calfskins too.

85 **Hamlet:** They are sheep and calves which seek out assurance in that. I will speak to this fellow. Whose grave's this, sirrah?

---

[23] **shipped . . . land:** shoved me into the ground.   [24] **jowls:** dashes.   [25] **o'erreaches:** gets the better of.
[26] **circumvent:** get around.   [27] **chapless:** without jaws.   [28] **mazzard:** head, a slang word; lit., drinking-bowl.   [29] **loggats:** a game in which billets [Editor's note: carved pieces] of wood or bones were stuck in the ground and knocked over by throwing at them.   [30] **lawyer . . . indentures:** Hamlet strings out a number of the legal phrases loved by lawyers: *quiddities:* subtle arguments; *quillets:* quibbles; *tenures:* titles to property; *tricks:* knavery; *statutes:* bonds; *recognizances:* obligation; *fines:* conveyances; *vouchers:* guarantors; *recoveries:* transfers; *indentures:* agreements.   [31] **sconce:** head; lit., blockhouse.   [32] **fine:** ending.   [33] **box:** coffin.

1. Clown: Mine, sir. *(Sings.)*

> "Oh, a pit of clay for to be made
> For such a guest is meet."

90 **Hamlet:** I think it be thine indeed, for thou liest in 't.

1. Clown: You lie out on 't, sir, and therefore 'tis not yours. For my part, I do not lie in 't, and yet it is mine.

Hamlet: Thou does lie in 't, be in 't and say it is thine. 'Tis for the dead, not for the quick, therefore thou liest.

95 **1. Clown:** 'Tis a quick lie, sir, 'twill away again, from me to you.

Hamlet: What man dost thou dig it for?

1. Clown: For no man, sir.

Hamlet: What woman, then?

1. Clown: For none, neither.

100 **Hamlet:** Who is to be buried in 't?

1. Clown: One that was a woman, sir, but, rest her soul, she's dead.

Hamlet: How absolute[34] the knave is! We must speak by the card,[35] or equivocation[36] will undo us. By the Lord, Horatio, this three years I have taken note of it—the age is grown so picked[37] that the toe of the peasant comes so near the heel of the courtier, he
105 galls his kibe.[38] How long hast thou been a gravemaker?

1. Clown: Of all the days i' the year, I came to 't that day that our last King Hamlet o'ercame Fortinbras.

Hamlet: How long is that since?

1. Clown: Cannot you tell that? Every fool can tell that. It was that very day that young
110 Hamlet was born, he that is mad, and sent into England.

Hamlet: Aye, marry, why was he sent into England?

1. Clown: Why, because a' was mad. A' shall recover his wits there, or, if a' do not, 'tis no great matter there.

Hamlet: Why?

115 **1. Clown:** 'Twill not be seen in him there—there the men are as mad as he.

Hamlet: How came he mad?

1. Clown: Very strangely, they say.

Hamlet: How "strangely"?

1. Clown: Faith, e'en with losing his wits.

120 **Hamlet:** Upon what ground?

1. Clown: Why, here in Denmark. I have been sexton here, man and boy, thirty years.[39]

Hamlet: How long will a man lie i' the earth ere he rot?

1. Clown: I' faith, if a' be not rotten before a' die—as we have many pocky[40] corses nowadays that will scarce hold the laying in—a' will last you some eight year or nine year. A
125 tanner will last you nine year.

Hamlet: Why he more than another?

---

[34] **absolute:** exact. [35] **by . . . card:** exactly. The card is the mariner's compass. [36] **equivocation:** speaking with a double sense. The word was much discussed when *Hamlet* was written. [37] **picked:** refined.
[38] **toe . . . kibe:** i.e., the peasant follows the courtier so closely that he rubs the courtier's heel into a blister. From about 1598 onward, writers, especially dramatists, often satirized the practice of yeoman farmers grown rich from war profits in sending their awkward sons to London to learn gentlemanly manners. Ben Jonson portrays two specimens in Stephen in *Every Man in His Humour* and Sogliardo in *Every Man out of His Humour.* [39] **thirty years:** The Clown's chronology has puzzled critics, for the general impression is that Hamlet was much younger. [40] **pocky:** suffering from the pox (venereal disease).

1. Clown: Why, sir, his hide is so tanned with his trade that a' will keep out water a great while, and your water is a sore decayer of your whoreson[41] dead body. Here's a skull now. This skull has lain in the earth three and twenty years.

130 **Hamlet:** Whose was it?

1. Clown: A whoreson mad fellow's it was. Whose do you think it was?

Hamlet: Nay, I know not.

1. Clown: A pestilence on him for a mad rogue! A' poured a flagon of Rhenish on my head once. This same skull, sir, was Yorick's skull, the king's jester.

135 **Hamlet:** This?

1. Clown: E'en that.

Hamlet: Let me see. (*Takes the skull.*) Alas, poor Yorick! I knew him, Horatio—a fellow of infinite jest, of most excellent fancy. He hath borne me on his back a thousand times, and now how abhorred in my imagination it is! My gorge rises[42] at it. Here
140 hung those lips that I have kissed I know not how oft. Where be your gibes now? Your gambols? Your songs? Your flashes of merriment that were wont to set the table on a roar? Not one now, to mock your own grinning? Quite chop-fallen?[43] Now get you to my lady's chamber and tell her, let her paint an inch thick, to this favor[44] she must come—make her laugh at that. Prithee, Horatio, tell me one
145 thing.

Horatio: What's that, my lord?

Hamlet: Dost thou think Alexander looked o' this fashion i' the earth?

Horatio: E'en so.

Hamlet: And smelt so? Pah!

(*Puts down the skull.*)

150 **Horatio:** E'en so, my lord.

Hamlet: To what base uses we may return, Horatio! Why may not imagination trace the noble dust of Alexander till he find it stopping a bunghole?[45]

Horatio: 'Twere to consider too curiously[46] to consider so.

Hamlet: No, faith, not a jot, but to follow him thither with modesty[47] enough and likeli-
155 hood to lead it. As thus: Alexander died, Alexander was buried, Alexander returneth into dust; the dust is earth; of earth we make loam;[48] and why of that loam, whereto he was converted, might they not stop a beer barrel?

"Imperious Caesar, dead and turned to clay,
Might stop a hole to keep the wind away.
160 Oh, that that earth which kept the world in awe
Should patch a wall to expel the winter's flaw!"[49]

But soft! But soft! Aside— re comes the king.
The Queen, the courtiers.

---

[41] **whoreson:** bastard, "son of a bitch." [42] **My . . . rises:** I feel sick. **gorge:** throat. [43] **chop-fallen:**
downcast, with a pun on "chapless." [44] **favor:** appearance, especially in the face. [45] **bunghole:** the hole
in a beer barrel. [46] **curiously:** precisely. [47] **with modesty:** without exaggeration. [48] **loam:** mixture of
clay and sand, used in plastering walls. [49] **flaw:** blast.

(Enter Priests,[50] *etc., in procession; the corpse of Ophelia, Laertes and Mourners following; King, Queen, their trains, etc.)*

Who is this they follow?

165 And with such maimèd[51] rites? This doth betoken[52]
The corse they follow did with desperate hand
Fordo[53] its own life. 'Twas of some estate.[54]
Couch[55] we awhile, and mark.

(Retiring with Horatio.)

Laertes: What ceremony else?
170 **Hamlet:** That is Laertes, a very noble youth. Mark.
Laertes: What ceremony else?
1. Priest: Her obsequies have been as far enlarged
    As we have warranty.[56] Her death was doubtful,
    And but that great command o'ersways the order,[57]
175   She should in ground unsanctified have lodged
    Till the last trumpet; for[58] charitable prayers,
    Shards,[59] flints, and pebbles should be thrown on her.
    Yet here she is 'lowed her virgin crants,[60]
    Her maiden strewments[61] and the bringing home
180   Of bell and burial.
Laertes: Must there no more be done?
1. Priest: No more be done.
    We should profane the service of the dead
    To sing a requiem and such rest to her
185   As to peace-parted souls.[62]
Laertes: Lay her i' the earth.
    And from her fair and unpolluted flesh
    May violets spring! I tell thee, churlish priest,
    A ministering angel shall my sister be
190   When thou liest howling.
Hamlet: What, the fair Ophelia!
Queen: *(Scattering flowers.)* Sweets to the sweet. Farewell!
    I hoped thou shouldst have been my Hamlet's wife,
    I thought thy bride bed to have decked, sweet maid,
195   And not have strewed thy grave.
Laertes: Oh, treble woe
    Fall ten times treble on that cursèd head
    Whose wicked deed thy most ingenious sense[63]

---

[50] **Enter Priests:** The stage directions in early texts are less elaborate. Q_2 notes, curtly, **Enter K.Q. Laertes and the corse.** F_1 has *Enter King, Queen, Laertes, and a coffin, with Lords attendant.* Q_1 prints *Enter King and Queen, Laertes and other lords, with a Priest after the coffin.* This probably was how the scene was originally staged. The modern directions ignore the whole significance of the "maimed rites"—Ophelia's funeral is insultingly simple. [51] **maimed:** curtailed. [52] **betoken:** indicate. [53] **Fordo:** destroy. [54] **estate:** high rank. [55] **Couch:** lie down. [56] **Her . . . warranty:** the funeral rites have been as complete as may be allowed. [57] **but . . . order:** if the King's command had not overruled the proper procedure. [58] **for:** instead of. [59] **Shards:** pieces of broken crockery. [60] **crants:** wreaths of flowers—a sign that she had died unwed. [61] **maiden strewments:** the flowers strewn on the corpse of a maiden. [62] **peace-parted souls:** souls which departed in peace, fortified with the rites of the Church. [63] **most . . . sense:** lively intelligence.

Deprived thee of! Hold off the earth a while
200   Till I have caught her once more in mine arms.

(Leaps into the grave.)

Now pile your dust upon the quick[64] and dead
Till of this flat a mountain you have made
To o'ertop old Pelion[65] on the skyish[66] head
Of blue Olympus.
205 **Hamlet:** *(Advancing.)* What is he whose grief
Bears such an emphasis? Whose phrase of sorrow
Conjures the wandering stars and makes them stand[67]
Like wonder-wounded hearers? This is I,
Hamlet the Dane. *(Leaps into the grave.)*
210 **Laertes:** The devil take thy soul!

(Grappling with him.)

Hamlet: Thou pray'st not well.
I prithee, take thy fingers from my throat,
For though I am not splenitive[68] and rash,
Yet have I in me something dangerous,
215   Which let thy wisdom fear. Hold off thy hand.
King: Pluck them asunder.
Queen: Hamlet, Hamlet!
All: Gentlemen—
Horatio: Good my lord, be quiet.

(The Attendants part them, and they come out of the grave.)

220 **Hamlet:** Why, I will fight with him upon this theme
Until my eyelids will no longer wag.
Queen: O my son, what theme?
Hamlet: I loved Ophelia. Forty thousand brothers
Could not, with all their quantity of love,
225   Make up my sum. What wilt thou do for her?
King: O, he is mad, Laertes.
Queen: For love of God, forbear him.[69]
Hamlet: 'Swounds,[70] show me that thou'lt do.
Woo 't weep? Woo 't fight? Woo 't fast? Woo 't tear thyself?
230   Woo 't drink up eisel?[71] Eat a crocodile?
I'll do 't. Dost thou come here to whine?
To outface[72] me with leaping in her grave?
Be buried quick with her, and so will I.
And if thou prate of mountains, let them throw
235   Millions of acres on us, till our ground,
Singeing his pate against the burning zone,

---

[64] **quick:** living. [65] **Pelion:** When the giants fought against the gods in order to reach Heaven, they tried to pile Mount Pelion and Mount Ossa on Mount Olympus, the highest mountain in Greece. [66] **skyish:** reaching the sky. [67] **stand:** stand still. [68] **splenitive:** hot-tempered. [69] **forbear him:** leave him alone. [70] **'Swounds . . . thou:** Hamlet in his excitement cries out that if Laertes wishes to make extravagant boasts of what he will do to show his sorrow, he will be even more extravagant. [71] **eisel:** vinegar. [72] **outface:** brow beat.

Make Ossa[73] like a wart! Nay, an thou 'lt mouth,
I'll rant as well as thou.

Queen: This is mere madness.
240   And thus awhile the fit will work on him.
Anon, as patient as the female dove
When that her golden couplets[74] are disclosed,[75]
His silence will sit drooping.

Hamlet: Hear you, sir.
245   What is the reason that you use me thus?
I loved you ever. But it is no matter,
Let Hercules himself do what he may,
The cat will mew and dog will have his day.[76] (*Exit.*)

King: I pray thee, good Horatio, wait upon him.

(*Exit Horatio.*)

250   (*To Laertes*) Strengthen your patience in our last night's speech.
We'll put the matter to the present push.[77]
Good Gertrude, set some watch over your son.
This grave shall have a living monument.[78]
An hour of quiet shortly shall we see,
255   Till then, in patience our proceeding be.

(*Exeunt.*)

Scene II. A hall in the castle.

(*Enter Hamlet and Horatio.*)

Hamlet: So much for this, sir. Now shall you see the other.
You do remember all the circumstance?
Horatio: Remember it, my lord!
Hamlet: Sir, in my heart there was a kind of fighting
5   That would not let me sleep. Methought I lay
Worse than the mutines in the bilboes.[1] Rashly,
And praised be rashness for it, let us know,
Our indiscretion sometime serves us well
When our deep plots do pall.[2] And that should learn[3] us
10   There's a divinity that shapes our ends,
Roughhew them how we will.[4]
Horatio: That is most certain.
Hamlet: Up from my cabin,
My sea gown[5] scarfed[6] about me, in the dark
15   Groped I to find out them,[7] had my desire,
Fingered their packet, and in fine withdrew
To mine own room again, making so bold,

---

[73] **Ossa:** See l. 208, n.   [74] **couplets:** eggs, of which the dove lays two only.   [75] **disclosed:** hatched.
[76] **Let . . . day:** i.e., let this ranting hero have his turn; mine will come sometime.   [77] **push:** test; lit., thrust
of a pike.   [78] **living monument:** with the double meaning of "lifelike memorial" and "the death of Hamlet."
[1] **mutines . . . bilboes:** mutineers in the shackles used on board ship.   [2] **pall:** fail.   [3] **learn:** teach.
[4] **There's . . . will:** though we may make the rough beginning, God finishes our designs.   [5] **sea gown:** a
thick coat with a high collar worn by seamen.   [6] **scarfed:** wrapped.   [7] **them:** i.e., Rosencrantz and
Guildenstern.

My fears forgetting manners, to unseal
Their grand commission where I found, Horatio—
20   O royal knavery!—an exact command,
Larded[8] with many several sorts of reasons,
Importing Denmark's health and England's too,
With, ho! such bugs[9] and goblins in my life[10]
That, on the supervise,[11] no leisure bated,[12]
25   No, not to stay the grinding of the ax,
My head should be struck off.
Horatio: Is 't possible?
Hamlet: Here's the commission. Read it at more leisure
But wilt thou hear me how I did proceed?
30 **Horatio:** I beseech you.
Hamlet: Being thus benetted round with villainies—
Ere I could make a prologue to my brains,
They had begun the play—I sat me down,
Devised a new commission, wrote it fair.
35   I once did hold it, as our statists[13] do,
A baseness to write fair, and labored much
How to forget that learning, but, sir, now
It did me yeoman's service.[14] Wilt thou know
The effect of what I wrote?
40 **Horatio:**   Aye, good my lord.
Hamlet: An earnest conjuration from the King,
As England was his faithful tributary,
As love between them like the palm might flourish,
As peace should still her wheaten garland wear
45   And stand a comma 'tween their amities,[15]
And many suchlike "Ases"[16] of great charge,[17]
That, on the view and knowing of these contents,
Without debatement[18] further, more or less,
He should the bearers put to sudden death,
50   Not shriving time allowed.[19]
Horatio: How was this sealed?
Hamlet: Why, even in that was heaven ordinant.[20]
I had my father's signet in my purse,
Which was the model[21] of that Danish seal—
55   Folded the writ[22] up in the form of the other,
Subscribed[23] it, gave 't the impression,[24] placed it safely,
The changeling[25] never known. Now the next day

---

[8] **Larded:** garnished.   [9] **bugs:** bugbears.   [10] **in my life:** so long as I was alive.   [11] **supervise:** reading.
[12] **bated:** allowed.   [13] **statists:** statesmen. As scholars who have had to read Elizabethan documents know,
the more exalted the writer, the worse his handwriting. As a girl Queen Elizabeth wrote a beautiful script; as
Queen her letters are as illegible as any. All but the most confidential documents were copied out in a fair
hand by a secretary.   [14] **yeoman's service:** faithful service. The most reliable English soldiers were
yeomen—farmers and their men.   [15] **stand . . . amities:** be a connecting link of their friendship.
[16] **"Ases":** Official documents were written in flowery language full of metaphorical clauses beginning with
"As." Hamlet puns on "asses."   [17] **great charge:** "great weight" and "heavy burden."   [18] **debatement:** argument.   [19] **Not . . . allowed:** without giving them time even to confess their sins.   [20] **ordinant:** directing, in control.   [21] **model:** copy.   [22] **writ:** writing.   [23] **Subscribed:** signed.   [24] **impression:** of the seal.
[25] **changeling:** lit., an ugly child exchanged by the fairies for a fair one.

Was our sea fight, and what to this was sequent[26]
    Thou know'st already.
60 **Horatio:** So Guildenstern and Rosencrantz go to 't.
Hamlet: Why, man, they did make love to this employment.
    They are not near my conscience, their defeat[27]
    Does by their own insinuation[28] grow.
    'Tis dangerous when the baser nature comes
65   Between the pass and fell incensèd points
    Of mighty opposites.[29]
Horatio: Why, what a king is this!
Hamlet: Does it not, think'st thee, stand me now upon—
    He that hath killed my king and whored my mother,
70   Popped in between the election and my hopes,[30]
    Thrown out his angle[31] for my proper[32] life,
    And with such cozenage[33]—is 't not perfect conscience,
    To quit[34] him with this arm? And is 't not to be damned,
    To let this canker[35] of our nature come
75   In further evil?
Horatio: It must be shortly known to him from England
    What is the issue of the business there.
Hamlet: It will be short. The interim[36] is mine,
    And a man's life's no more than to say "One."
80   But I am very sorry, good Horatio,
    That to Laertes I forgot myself,
    For by the image of my cause I see
    The portraiture of his. I'll court his favors.
    But, sure, the bravery[37] of his grief did put me
85   Into a towering passion.
Horatio: Peace! Who comes here?

(Enter Osric.)

Osric: Your lordship is right welcome back to Denmark.
Hamlet: I humbly thank you, sir. Dost know this water fly?[39]
Horatio: No, my good lord.
90 **Hamlet:** Thy state is the more gracious,[40] for 'tis a vice to know him. He hath much land,
    and fertile. Let a beast be lord of beasts and his crib shall stand at the king's mess.[41]
    'Tis a chough,[42] but, as I say, spacious[43] in the possession of dirt.
Osric: Sweet lord, if your lordship were at leisure, I should impart a thing to you from his
    majesty.

---

[26] **sequent:** following.   [27] **defeat:** destruction.   [28] **by . . . insinuation:** because they insinuated themselves into this business.   [29] **'Tis . . . opposites:** it is dangerous for inferior men to interfere in a duel between mighty enemies. **pass:** thrust. **fell:** fierce.   [30] **Popped . . . hopes:** As is from time to time shown in the play, the Danes chose their King by election.   [31] **angle:** fishing rod and line.   [32] **proper:** own. [33] **cozenage:** cheating.   [34] **quit:** pay back.   [35] **canker:** maggot.   [36] **interim:** interval; between now and the news from England.   [37] **bravery:** excessive [Editor's note: or boastful] show.   [38] **Osric:** Osric is a specimen of the fashionable, effeminate courtier. He dresses prettily and talks the jargon of his class, which at this time affected elaborate and allusive metaphors and at all costs avoided saying plain things plainly. [39] **water fly:** a useless little creature that flits about.   [40] **Thy . . . gracious:** you are in the better state. [41] **Let . . . mess:** i.e., any man, however low, who has wealth enough will find a good place at Court. **crib:** manger. **mess:** table.   [42] **chough:** jackdaw.   [43] **spacious:** wealthy.

95 **Hamlet:** I will receive it, sir, with all diligence of spirit. Put your bonnet to his right use,[44] 'tis for the head.

Osric: I thank your lordship, it is very hot.

Hamlet: No, believe me, 'tis very cold. The wind is northerly.

Osric: It is indifferent[45] cold, my lord, indeed.

100 **Hamlet:** But yet methinks it is very sultry and hot, for my complexion—

Osric: Exceedingly, my lord. It is very sultry, as 'twere—I cannot tell how. But, my lord, his majesty bade me signify to you that he has laid a great wager on your head. Sir, this is the matter—

Hamlet: I beseech you, remember—

(Hamlet moves him to put on his hat.)

105 **Osric:** Nay, good my lord, for mine ease, in good faith. Sir, here is newly come to Court Laertes—believe me, an absolute[46] gentleman, full of most excellent differences,[47] of very soft society[48] and great showing.[49] Indeed, to speak feelingly[50] of him, he is the card or calendar of gentry,[51] for you shall find in him the continent of what part a gentleman would see.[52]

110 **Hamlet:** Sir,[53] his definement suffers no perdition in you, though I know to divide him inventorially would dizzy the arithmetic of memory, and yet but yaw neither, in respect of his quick sail. But in the verity of extolment, I take him to be a soul of great article, and his infusion of such dearth and rareness as, to make true diction of him, his semblable is his mirror, and who else would trace him, his umbrage—nothing

115 more.

Osric: Your lordship speaks most infallibly of him.

Hamlet: The concernancy,[54] sir? Why do we wrap the gentleman in our more rawer breath?[55]

Osric: Sir?[56]

120 **Horatio:** Is 't not possible to understand in another tongue? You will do 't, sir, really.

Hamlet: What imports the nomination[57] of this gentleman?

Osric: Of Laertes?

Horatio: His purse is empty already, all's golden words are spent.

Hamlet: Of him, sir.

125 **Osric:** I know you are not ignorant—

Hamlet: I would you did, sir. Yet, in faith, if you did, it would not much approve[58] me. Well, sir?

Osric: You are not ignorant of what excellence Laertes is—

---

[44] **Put . . . use:** i.e., put your hat on your head. Osric is so nice-mannered that he cannot bring himself to wear his hat in the presence of the Prince. [45] **indifferent:** moderately. [46] **absolute:** perfect. [47] **differences:** qualities peculiar to himself. [48] **soft society:** gentle breeding. [49] **great showing:** distinguished appearance. [50] **feelingly:** with proper appreciation. [51] **card . . . gentry:** the very fashion plate of what a gentleman should be. [52] **continent . . . see:** all the parts that should be in a perfect gentleman.
[53] **Sir . . . more:** Hamlet retorts in similar but even more extravagant language. This is too much for Osric (and for most modern readers). Hamlet's words may be paraphrased: "Sir, the description of this perfect gentleman loses nothing in your account of him; though I realize that if one were to try to enumerate his excellences, it would exhaust our arithmetic, and yet"—here he changes the image to one of sailing—"we should still lag behind him as he outsails us. But in the true vocabulary of praise, I take him to be a soul of the greatest worth, and his perfume"—i.e., his personal essence—"so scarce and rare that to speak truly of him, the only thing like him is his own reflection in his mirror, and everyone else who tries to follow him merely his shadow." **yaw:** fall off from the course laid. **verity . . . extolment:** in true praise. **infusion:** essence. **semblable:** resemblance. **trace:** follow. **umbrage:** shadow. [54] **concernancy:** i.e., what is all this talk about? [55] **Why . . . breath:** why do we discuss the gentleman with our inadequate voices? [56] **Sir:** Osric is completely baffled. [57] **nomination:** naming. [58] **approve:** commend.

Hamlet: I dare not confess that, lest I should compare with him in excellence, but to know
130   a man well were to know himself.

Osric: I mean, sir, for his weapon,[59] but in the imputation[60] laid on him by them, in his
meed[61] he's unfellowed.[62]

Hamlet: What's his weapon?

Osric: Rapier and dagger.

135 **Hamlet.** That's two of his weapons, but, well.

Osric: The king, sir, hath wagered with him six Barbary horses, against the which he has
imponed,[63] as I take it, six French rapiers and poniards, with their assigns,[64] as girdle,
hanger,[65] and so—three of the carriages, in faith, are very dear to fancy,[66] very responsive to[67] the hilts, most delicate carriages, and of very liberal conceit.[68]

140 **Hamlet:** What call you the carriages?

Horatio: I knew you must be edified by the margent[69] ere you had done.

Osric: The carriages, sir, are the hangers.

Hamlet: The phrase would be more germane[70] to the matter if we could carry a cannon
by our sides. I would it might be hangers till then. But, on—six Barbary horses
145   against six French swords, their assigns, and three liberal-conceited carriages.
That's the French bet against the Danish. Why is this "imponed," as you
call it?

Osric: The King, sir, hath laid, sir, that in a dozen passes between yourself and him, he
shall not exceed you three hits. He hath laid on twelve for nine,[71] and it would come
150   to immediate trial if your lordship would vouchsafe the answer.

Hamlet: How if I answer no?

Osric: I mean, my lord, the opposition of your person in trial.

Hamlet: Sir, I will walk here in the hall. If it please his majesty, it is the breathing-time of
day with me.[72] Let the foils be brought, the gentleman willing, and the king hold his
155   purpose, I will win for him an I can. If not, I will gain nothing but my shame and the
odd hits.

Osric: Shall I redeliver you e'en so?

Hamlet: To this effect, sir, after what flourish[73] your nature will.

Osric: I commend my duty to your lordship.

160 **Hamlet:** Yours, yours. *(Exit Osric.)* He does well to commend it himself, there are no
tongues else for 's turn.

Horatio: This lapwing[74] runs away with the shell on his head.

Hamlet: He did comply with his dug[75] before he sucked it. Thus has he—and many more
of the same breed that I know the drossy[76] age dotes on—only got the tune of the time
165   and outward habit of encounter,[77] a kind of yesty collection[78] which carries them
through and through the most fond[79] and winnowed[80] opinions—and do but blow
them to their trial, the bubbles are out.[81]

(Enter a Lord.)

---

[59] **his weapon:** i.e., skill with his weapon.   [60] **imputation:** reputation.   [61] **meed:** merit.   [62] **unfellowed:**
without an equal.   [63] **imponed:** laid down as a stake.   [64] **assigns:** that which goes with them.   [65] **hanger:**
straps by which the scabbard was hung from the belt, for specimens.   [66] **dear to fancy:** of beautiful design.
[67] **responsive to:** matching.   [68] **liberal conceit:** elaborately artistic.   [69] **edified . . . margent:** informed by
the notes. In Shakespeare's time the notes were often printed in the margin.   [70] **germane:** related.
[71] **twelve . . . nine:** Laertes has bet the King he will hit Hamlet twelve times before Hamlet hits him nine.
[72] **breathing-time . . . me:** time when I take exercise.   [73] **flourish:** fanfare, elaborate phrasing.   [74] **lapwing:**
a pretty, lively little bird. It is so lively that it can run about the moment it is hatched.   [75] **did . . . dug:** was
ceremonious with the nipple; i.e., behaved in this . . . [Editor's note: courteous] way from his infancy.
[76] **drossy:** scummy, frivolous.   [77] **tune . . . encounter:** i.e., they sing the same tune as everyone else and
have the same society manners.   [78] **yesty collection:** frothy catchwords.   [79] **fond:** foolish.   [80] **winnowed:**
light as chaff. Winnowing is the process of fanning the chaff from the grain.   [81] **do . . . out:** force them to
make sense of their words and they are deflated, as Hamlet has just deflated Osric.

Lord: My lord, his majesty commended him to you by young Osric, who brings back to
him that you attend him in the hall. He sends to know if your pleasure hold to play
170   with Laertes, or that you will take longer time.

Hamlet: I am constant to my purpose, they follow the king's pleasure. If his fitness speaks,
mine is ready, now or whensoever, provided I be so able as now.

Lord: The king and queen and all are coming down.

Hamlet: In happy time.[82]

175   **Lord:** The queen desires you to use some gentle entertainment[83] to Laertes before you fall
to play.

Hamlet: She well instructs me.

(Exit Lord.)

Horatio: You will lose this wager, my lord.

Hamlet: I do not think so. Since he went into France I have been in continual practice, I
180   shall win at the odds. But thou wouldst not think how ill all's here about my heart—
but it is no matter.

Horatio: Nay, good my lord—

Hamlet: It is but foolery, but it is such a kind of gaingiving[84] as would perhaps trouble a
woman.

185   **Horatio:** If your mind dislike anything, obey it. I will forestall their repair hither and say
you are not fit.

Hamlet: Not a whit, we defy augury.[85] There's special providence in the fall of a sparrow.[86]
If it be now, 'tis not to come; if it be not to come, it will be now; if it be not now, yet it
will come. The readiness is all. Since no man has aught of what he leaves, what is 't to
190   leave betimes? Let be.

*(Enter King, Queen, Laertes, and Lords, Osric and other Attendants with foils; a table and
flagons of wine on it.)*

King: Come, Hamlet, come, and take this hand from me.

(The King puts Laertes' hand into Hamlet's.)

Hamlet: Give me your pardon, sir. I've done you wrong,
But pardon 't, as you are a gentleman.
This presence[87] knows, And you must needs have heard,
195   How I am punished with sore distraction.
What I have done
That might your nature, honor, and exception[88]
Roughly awake, I here proclaim was madness.
Was 't Hamlet wronged Laertes? Never Hamlet.
200   If Hamlet from himself be ta'en away,[89]
And when he's not himself does wrong Laertes,
Then Hamlet does it not, Hamlet denies it.
Who does it, then? His madness. If 't be so,
Hamlet is of the faction that is wronged,

---

[82] **In . . . time:** at a good moment.   [83] **gentle entertainment:** kindly treatment; i.e., be reconciled after the
brawl in the churchyard.   [84] **gaingiving:** misgiving.   [85] **augury:** omens.   [86] **special . . . sparrow.** The
idea comes from Matthew 10:29, "Are not two sparrows sold for a farthing? and one of them shall not fall to
the ground without your Father."   [87] **presence:** the whole Court.   [88] **exception:** resentment.
[89] **If . . . away:** i.e., Hamlet mad is not Hamlet.

205   His madness is poor Hamlet's enemy.
          Sir, in this audience
          Let my disclaiming from a purposed evil[90]
          Free me so far in your most generous thoughts
          That I have shot mine arrow o'er the house,
210   And hurt my brother.
     Laertes: I am satisfied in nature,
          Whose motive, in this case, should stir me most
          To my revenge. But in my terms of honor
          I stand aloof, and will no reconcilement
215   Till by some elder masters of known honor
          I have a voice and precedent of peace
          To keep my name ungored.[91] But till that time
          I do receive your offered love like love
          And will not wrong it.
220 **Hamlet:**   I embrace it freely,
          And will this brother's wager frankly play.
          Give us the foils. Come on.
     Laertes: Come, one for me.
     Hamlet: I'll be your foil,[92] Laertes. In mine ignorance
225   Your skill shall, like a star i' the darkest night,
          Stick[93] fiery off indeed.
     Laertes: You mock me, sir.
     Hamlet: No, by this hand.
     King: Give them the foils, young Osric. Cousin Hamlet,
230   You know the wager?
     Hamlet: Very well, my lord.
          Your Grace has laid the odds o' the weaker side.
     King: I do not fear it, I have seen you both.
          But since he is bettered,[94] We have therefore odds.
235 **Laertes:** This is too heavy, let me see another.
     Hamlet: This likes[95] me well. These foils have all a length?[96]

     (They prepare to play.)

     Osric: Aye, my good lord.
     King: Set me the stoups[97] of wine upon that table.
          If Hamlet give the first or second hit,
240   Or quit[98] in answer of the third exchange,
          Let all the battlements their ordnance fire.
          The king shall drink to Hamlet's better breath,
          And in the cup a union[99] shall he throw

---

[90] **Let . . . evil:** let my declaration that I did not intend any harm.   [91] **I . . . ungored:** I bear you no grudge so far as concerns my personal feelings, which would most readily move me to vengeance; but as this matter touches my honor, I cannot accept your apology until I have been assured by those expert in matters of honor that I may so do without loss of reputation.   [92] **foil:** Hamlet puns on the other meaning of foil—tin foil set behind a gem to give it luster.   [93] **Stick . . . off:** Shine out.   [94] **bettered:** considered your superior. [95] **likes:** pleases.   [96] **have . . . length:** are all of equal length.   [97] **stoups:** drinking vessels.   [98] **quit:** strike back.   [99] **union:** a large pearl.

Richer than that which four successive kings
245 In Denmark's crown have worn. Give me the cups,
And let the kettle[100] to the trumpet speak,
The trumpet to the cannoneer without,
The cannon to the heavens, the heaven to earth,
"Now the king drinks to Hamlet." Come, begin,
250 And you, the judge, bear a wary eye.
Hamlet: Come on, sir.
Laertes: Come, my lord.

(They play.)

Hamlet: One.
Laertes: No.
255 **Hamlet:**   Judgment.
Osric: A hit, a very palpable[101] hit.
Laertes: Well, again.
King: Stay, give me drink. Hamlet, this pearl is thine[102]—
Here's to thy health. Give him the cup.

(Trumpets sound, and cannon shot off within.)

260 **Hamlet:** I'll play this bout first. Set it by a while.
Come.

(They play.)

Another hit, what say you?
Laertes: A touch, a touch, I do confess.
King: Our son shall win.
265 **Queen:**   He's fat[103] and scant of breath.
Here, Hamlet, take my napkin, rub thy brows.
The Queen carouses to thy fortune, Hamlet.
Hamlet: Good madam!
King: Gertrude, do not drink.
270 **Queen:** I will, my lord, I pray you pardon me.

(She drinks.)

King: *(Aside.)* It is the poisoned cup, it is too late.
Hamlet: I dare not drink yet, madam—by and by.
Queen: Come, let me wipe thy face.
Laertes: My lord, I'll hit him now.
275 **King:**   I do not think 't.
Laertes: *(Aside.)* And yet 'tis almost against my conscience.
Hamlet: Come, for the third, Laertes. You but dally.[104]
I pray you pass with your best violence,
I am afeard you make a wanton of me.[105]

---

[100] **kettle:** kettledrum.   [101] **palpable:** clear.   [102] **this . . . thine:** With these words the King drops the poisoned pearl into the cup intended for Hamlet.   [103] **fat:** out of condition.   [104] **dally:** play.
[105] **make . . . me:** treat me like a child by letting me win.

280 **Laertes:** Say you so? Come on.

(*They play.*)

Osric: Nothing, neither way.

Laertes: Have at you now!

(*Laertes wounds Hamlet; then, in scuffling, they change rapiers,*[106] *and Hamlet wounds Laertes.*)

King: Part them, they are incensed.

Hamlet: Nay, come, again. (*The Queen falls.*)

285 **Osric:** Look to the queen there, ho!

Horatio: They bleed on both sides. How is it, my lord?

Osric: How is 't, Laertes?

Laertes: Why, as a woodcock to mine own springe,[107] Osric,

 I am justly killed with mine own treachery.

290 **Hamlet:** How does the Queen?

King: She swounds to see them bleed.

Queen: No, no, the drink, the drink!—O my dear Hamlet—

 The drink, the drink! I am poisoned. (*Dies.*)

Hamlet: Oh, villainy! Ho! Let the door be locked.

295 Treachery! Seek it out. (*Laertes falls.*)

Laertes: It is here, Hamlet. Hamlet, thou art slain.

 No medicine in the world can do thee good,

 In thee there is not half an hour of life.

 The treacherous instrument is in thy hand,

300 Unbated and envenomed. The foul practice

 Hath turned itself on me. Lo, here I lie

 Never to rise again. Thy mother's poisoned.

 I can no more. The king, the king's to blame.

Hamlet: The point envenomed too!

305 Then, venom, to thy work. (*Stabs the King.*)

All: Treason! Treason!

King: Oh, yet defend me, friends, I am but hurt.

Hamlet: Here, thou incestuous, murderous, damnèd Dane,

 Drink off this potion. Is thy union[108] here?

310 Follow my mother. (*King dies.*)

Laertes: He is justly served.

 It is a poison tempered[109] by himself.

 Exchange forgiveness with me, noble Hamlet.

 Mine and my father's death come not upon thee,[110]

315 Nor thine on me! (*Dies.*)

Hamlet: Heaven make thee free of it![111] I follow thee,

 I am dead, Horatio. Wretched queen, adieu!

 You that look pale and tremble at this chance,

 That are but mutes or audience to this act,

---

[106] **they . . . rapiers:** With the exchange of rapiers, Hamlet wounds Laertes with the pointed and poisoned weapon. [107] **springe:** snare. [108] **union:** pearl. [109] **tempered:** mixed. [110] **come . . . thee:** are not on your head. [111] **Heaven . . . it:** God forgives you.

320   Had I but time—as this fell[112] sergeant,[113] Death,
    Is strict in his arrest—O, I could tell you—
    But let it be. Horatio, I am dead,
    Thou livest. Report me and my cause aright
    To the unsatisfied.[114]

325 **Horatio:**   Never believe it.
    I am more an antique Roman[115] than a Dane.
    Here's yet some liquor left.

    Hamlet: As thou 'rt a man,
    Give me the cup. Let go—by Heaven, I'll have 't.

330   O good Horatio, what a wounded name,
    Things standing thus unknown, shall live behind me!
    If thou didst ever hold me in thy heart,
    Absent thee from felicity a while,
    And in this harsh world draw thy breath in pain

335   To tell my story.

    (March afar off, and shot within.)

          What warlike noise is this?

    Osric: Young Fortinbras, with conquest come from Poland,
    To the ambassadors of England gives
    This warlike volley.

340 **Hamlet:**   Oh, I die, Horatio,
    The potent poison quite o'ercrows[116] my spirit.
    I cannot live to hear the news from England,
    But I do prophesy the election[117] lights
    On Fortinbras. He has my dying voice.[118]

345   So tell him, with the occurrents, more and less,
    Which have solicited.[119] The rest is silence. *(Dies.)*

    Horatio: Now cracks a noble heart. Good night, sweet prince,
    And flights of angels sing thee to thy rest!

    (March within.)

    Why does the drum come hither?

    (Enter Fortinbras, and the English Ambassadors, with drum, colors, and Attendants.)

350 **Fortinbras:** Where is this sight?

    Horatio: What is it you would see?
    If aught of woe or wonder, cease your search.

    Fortinbras: This quarry cries on havoc.[120] O proud death,
    What feast is toward[121] in thine eternal cell

355   That thou so many princes at a shot
    So bloodily hast struck?

---

[112] **fell:** dread. [113] **sergeant:** the officer of the Court who made arrests. [114] **unsatisfied:** who do not know the truth. [115] **antique Roman:** like Cato and Brutus, who killed themselves rather than survive in a world which was unpleasing to them. [116] **o'ercrows:** overpowers. [117] **election:** as King of Denmark. [118] **voice:** support. [119] **occurrents . . . solicited:** events great and small which have caused me to act. [120] **quarry . . . havoc:** heap of slain denotes a pitiless slaughter. [121] **toward:** being prepared.

1. Ambassador: The sight is dismal,
And our affairs from England come too late.
The ears are senseless that should give us hearing,
360   To tell him his commandment is fulfilled,
That Rosencrantz and Guildenstern are dead.
Where should we have our thanks?

Horatio: Not from his mouth
Had it the ability of life to thank you.
365   He never gave commandment for their death.
But since, so jump[122] upon this bloody question,[123]
You from the Polack wars, and you from England,
Are here arrived, give order that these bodies
High on a stage be placèd to the view,
370   And let me speak to the yet unknowing world
How these things came about. So shall you hear
Of carnal, bloody, and unnatural acts,
Of accidental judgments, casual slaughters,
Of deaths put on by cunning and forced cause,
375   And, in this upshot, purposes mistook
Fall'n on the investors' heads.[124] All this can I
Truly deliver.

Fortinbras: Let us haste to hear it,
And call the noblest to the audience.
380   For me, with sorrow I embrace my fortune.
I have some rights of memory[125] in this kingdom,
Which now to claim my vantage[126] doth invite me.

Horatio: Of that I shall have also cause to speak,
And from his mouth whose voice will draw on more.[127]
385   But let this same be presently performed,
Even while men's minds are wild, lest more mischance
On plots and errors happen.

Fortinbras: Let four captains
Bear Hamlet, like a soldier, to the stage.
390   For he was likely, had he been put on,[128]
To have proved most royally. And for his passage
The soldiers' music and the rites of war
Speak loudly for him.
Take up the bodies. Such a sight as this
395   Becomes the field, but here shows much amiss.
Go, bid the soldiers shoot.

(A dead march. Exeunt, bearing off the bodies; after which a peal of ordnance is shot off.)

---

[122] **jump:** exactly.   [123] **question:** matter.   [124] **carnal . . . heads:** These lines sum up the whole tragedy.
[125] **rights of memory:** rights that will be remembered; i.e., with the disappearance of all the family of the original King Hamlet the situation reverts to what it was before the death of Fortinbras' father.   [126] **vantage:** i.e., my advantage, there being none to dispute my claim.   [127] **voice . . . more:** i.e., Hamlet's dying voice will strengthen your claim.   [128] **had . . . on:** had he become King.

■ EXPLORATIONS OF THE TEXT

Act I

1. What do we learn from the first scene of Act I concerning the tense situation in Denmark? Which character seems to have all the answers?
2. What do we learn about Hamlet's feelings toward his mother and stepfather from his first appearance in scene ii and, especially, from the soliloquy that begins at line 131?
3. In scene iii, we see Laertes, Ophelia, and Polonius interacting as a family unit. Why do you think it is important that we see them in this relatively unguarded, informal moment?
4. What sort of character does Hamlet seem to be when he first encounters the Ghost? What makes you say so? (Hint: come back to this question when you have read the play to the end.)

Act II

1. In Act II, we witness several different forms of spying, snooping, and subterfuge. How important are these various forms of indirection to the plot that is unfolding before us?
2. Reflect upon the appearance of "the tragedians of the city" in this play (Act II, scene ii, line 304). Does Shakespeare seem to be making any comment upon the profession of the theater of his own day?
3. How does Hamlet actually involve the players in his emerging revenge plot?
4. Read Hamlet's soliloquy that begins "Now I am alone" (Act II, scene ii, lines 481–540). What sorts of passions and inhibitions do we see revealed in these lines? Compare and contrast this speech with the soliloquy that he delivers in Act I, scene ii.

Act III

1. Perhaps the most famous and widely quoted words in the English language are those that begin Hamlet's soliloquy in Act III, scene i (lines 63–97). In light of the soliloquy as a whole, what does the phrase "to be or not to be" actually mean? What does the speech tell us about Hamlet's emotional and mental state at this point in the play?
2. In the same soliloquy, look closely at the way Hamlet constructs his phrases and sentences. To whom is he speaking? About whom is he speaking? Is there anything unusual about the way this speech is worded?
3. In Act III, scene ii, Hamlet gives some advice to the players before they perform *The Murder of Gonzago*. What are his main points?
4. One of the few times that we actually see Hamlet and Ophelia interact is in Act III, scene ii, as they are preparing to watch the play and while they watch the play begin. What kinds of tensions do you notice as they converse with each other?
5. Does Act III, scene iii, tell us anything important about guilt, motives, fears, and courage in the unfolding drama?
6. Do you feel that Polonius dies in a fitting way? Why, or why not?
7. Many readers, critics, actors, and directors have considered the "closet scene" between Hamlet and Gertrude (Act III, scene iv) to be one of the most important moments in the play. What do we learn about Gertrude, Hamlet, Claudius, and the Ghost in this encounter?

Act IV

1. Act IV, scene i, allows us to witness a brief, intimate moment between Claudius and Gertrude. What do we learn about their states of mind and emotions at this point in the play?
2. Rosencrantz and Guildenstern, minor characters who periodically appear throughout the play, now begin to have a more central importance in Act IV. In what ways do they become more important?

3. Act IV contains seven scenes and multiple actions. Is there a reason that this act is so crowded with so many different plot strands?

4. With Polonius dead, Laertes returns, vowing to avenge his dead father. Do his rage and firm sense of purpose reveal anything about Hamlet?

5. What conclusions do you draw about the manner and circumstances of Ophelia's death?

6. How would you characterize the interaction between Claudius and Laertes in Act IV, scenes v and vii?

Act V

1. Does the action of Act V, scene i, lines 1–167 reveal anything important about Hamlet?

2. A final swordfight, much like the gunfight of Westerns and action movies, always makes for exciting spectacle. In reality, however, the contest between Hamlet and Laertes is not what it appears to be to those who are watching. What aspects of this sword fight are unusual or notable? What is "behind the scenes," as it were?

3. Make a tally of all the characters who have died by the end of the play. Are there any patterns or themes to all this carnage? Who, do you think, is ultimately responsible for the bloodshed? Do you feel that we can draw any overarching moral lesson from the play?

4. What sort of leader does Fortinbras promise to be? Does he have any just claim to the throne of Denmark?

5. A play that begins with questions of state politics ends with a scene featuring state politics. Do you feel that the play offers any resolution to the political and personal problems that set the plot in motion?

■ THE READING/WRITING CONNECTION

1. Select a line or an image from the play that has particular meaning for you. Then write either a poem or lyrics to a song inspired by your choice. In your poem or lyrics, consider who is speaking: Is it the same character who speaks in the play? Is it someone else?

2. Imagine that the characters in *Hamlet* live in your own age, with all the advantages of modern electronic communication: What would an instant-message or text-message exchange between two important characters contain? How would the personal traits or motives of the characters you chose be revealed in this exchange?

3. Imagine a sixth act of *Hamlet*: Fortinbras is now in command and he is trying to pick up the pieces of a badly broken kingdom. Write a twenty- to forty-line speech in the style of Shakespeare in which Fortinbras addresses his court. Does he sound like Claudius did in Act I, scene ii, or does he take a different approach?

4. You are given the opportunity to direct a production of *Hamlet*. At the first meeting with the cast, you are going to work on Act I, scene ii, lines 1–161. You have to tell Claudius, Gertrude, Polonius, Laertes, and Hamlet how you want them to play the scene. What do you tell them?

5. For the same production of *Hamlet*, you are asked to write a 300-word introduction to the play that will be included in the theater program that all patrons receive as they enter the theater. Write that 300-word introduction for the program; then write a separate essay in which you explain why you included the points that you did and how you targeted your readers.

■ IDEAS FOR WRITING

1. Discuss one key relationship between characters in *Hamlet*. Good pairings might include Hamlet and Gertrude, Hamlet and Ophelia, Hamlet and Claudius, Hamlet and Laertes, Hamlet and Horatio, Gertrude and Ophelia, Gertrude and Claudius, Polonius and Claudius, Polonius and Gertrude, Polonius and Ophelia, or Laertes and Ophelia. Other pairings also might prove interesting to explore. What does the relationship you chose tell us about the play as a whole?

2. After reading the play, choose two film versions of *Hamlet,* and watch them carefully for their different portrayals of one major character. What does this comparison tell you about the depths and dramatic possibilities of the character you chose?

3. Is revenge made to seem justified in this play? Why, or why not? Write an expository essay in which you consider the essential nature of revenge in light of both current events and this play.

4. Research the physical and artistic conditions of the Elizabethan theater. How might these conditions have influenced the earliest performances of *Hamlet?*

5. Read James Hollis's "The Heroic Journey." Do you feel that James Hollis's ideas about heroism have any relevance to the character of Hamlet?

■ FILMS

Hamlet has been filmed many times, in many languages, but the following list includes widely distributed versions that should be generally available in libraries, video stores, and for sale. Be sure to look for other versions, too!

Hamlet (1948). Directed by Laurence Olivier. Stars Olivier, Jean Simmons, Eileen Herlie, and Basil Sydney.

Hamlet (1990). Directed by Franco Zeffirelli. Stars Mel Gibson, Glenn Close, Helena Bonham-Carter, Paul Scofield, and Ian Holm.

Hamlet (1996). Directed by Kenneth Branagh. Stars Branagh, Kate Winslet, Derek Jacobi, and Julie Christie.

Hamlet (2000). Directed by Michael Almereyda. Stars Ethan Hawke, Julia Stiles, Bill Murray, Kyle MacLachlan, Diane Venora, Liev Schreiber, and Sam Shepard.

ON THE WEB

Shakespeare and His Times

Mr. William Shakespeare and the Internet:
http://daphne.palomar.edu/shakespeare
Shakespeare Resource Center: http://www.bardweb.net
Globe Theatre: http://www.shakespeares-globe.org

HENRIK IBSEN   Translated and edited by James Walter McFarlane

Henrik Ibsen (1828–1906) was born in Norway and was educated at the University of Christiania (now Oslo). Noted for his many plays (more than twenty-five), Ibsen also published poetry and essays. Ibsen's drama writing is viewed as having had three stages—the romantic historical tragedies (Love's Comedy, 1862; Peer Gynt, 1867), those that portrayed social realism (A Doll's House, 1879; Hedda Gabler, 1890), and those that illustrated the conflict between life and art (The Master Builder, 1892; When We Dead Awaken, 1899). Ibsen is best known for having broken out of the Romantic mold of nineteenth-century drama to portray realistic characters in psychologically tense situations, offering at the end no clear moral solution to life's difficulties.

1879

A DOLL'S HOUSE

Characters

Torvald Helmer, *a lawyer*
Nora, *his wife*
Dr. Rank
Mrs. Kristine Linde
Nils Krogstad
Anne Marie, *the nursemaid*
Helene, *the maid*
The Helmers' three children
A Porter

Scene

The action takes place in the Helmers' flat.

Act I

A pleasant room, tastefully but not expensively furnished. On the back wall, one door on the right leads to the entrance hall, a second door on the left leads to Helmer's study. Between these two doors, a piano. In the middle of the left wall, a door; and downstage from it, a window. Near the window a round table with armchairs and a small sofa. In the right wall, upstage, a door; and on the same wall downstage, a porcelain stove with a couple of armchairs and a rocking chair. Between the stove and the door a small table. Etchings on the walls. A whatnot with china and other small objets d'art; a small bookcase with books in handsome bindings. Carpet on the floor; a fire burns in the stove. A winter's day.

The front door-bell rings in the hall; a moment later; there is the sound of the front door being opened. Nora comes into the room, happily humming to herself. She is dressed in her outdoor things, and is carrying lots of parcels which she then puts down on the table, right. She leaves the door into the hall standing open; a Porter can be seen outside holding a Christmas tree and a basket; he hands them to the Maid who has opened the door for them.

Nora: Hide the Christmas tree away carefully, Helene. The children mustn't see it till this evening when it's decorated. *[To the Porter, taking out her purse.]* How much?
Porter: Fifty öre.
Nora: There's a crown. Keep the change.

[The Porter thanks her and goes. Nora shuts the door. She continues to laugh quietly and happily to herself as she takes off her things. She takes a bag of macaroons out of her pocket and eats one or two; then she walks stealthily across and listens at her husband's door.]

Nora: Yes, he's in.

[She begins humming again as she walks over to the table, right.]

5   **Helmer:** *[In his study].* Is that my little sky-lark chirruping out there?
Nora: *[busy opening some of the parcels].* Yes, it is.
Helmer: Is that my little squirrel frisking about?
Nora: Yes!
Helmer: When did my little squirrel get home?
10   **Nora:** Just this minute. *[She stuffs the bag of macaroons in her pocket and wipes her mouth.]* Come on out, Torvald, and see what I've bought.

Helmer: I don't want to be disturbed! *[A moment later, he opens the door and looks out, his pen in his hand.]* "Bought," did you say? All that? Has my little spendthrift been out squandering money again?

Nora: But, Torvald, surely this year we can spread ourselves just a little. This is the first Christmas we haven't had to go carefully.

Helmer: Ah, but that doesn't mean we can afford to be extravagant, you know.

Nora: Oh yes, Torvald, surely we can afford to be just a little bit extravagant now, can't we? Just a teeny-weeny bit. You are getting quite a good salary now, and you are going to earn lots and lots of money.

15 **Helmer:** Yes, after the New Year. But it's going to be three whole months before the first pay check comes in.

Nora: Pooh! We can always borrow in the meantime.

Helmer: Nora! *[Crosses to her and takes her playfully by the ear.]* Here we go again, you and your frivolous ideas! Suppose I went and borrowed a thousand crowns today, and you went and spent it over Christmas, then on New Year's Eve a slate fell and hit me on the head and there I was. . . .

Nora: *[putting her hand over his mouth].* Sh! Don't say such horrid things.

Helmer: Yes, but supposing something like that did happen . . . what then?

20 **Nora:** If anything as awful as that did happen, I wouldn't care if I owed anybody anything or not.

Helmer: Yes, but what about the people I'd borrowed from?

Nora: Them? Who cares about them! They are only strangers!

Helmer: Nora, Nora! Just like a woman! Seriously though, Nora, you know what I think about these things. No debts! Never borrow! There's always something inhibited, something unpleasant, about a home built on credit and borrowed money. We two have managed to stick it out so far, and that's the way we'll go on for the little time that remains.

Nora: *[walks over to the store].* Very well, just as you say, Torvald.

25 **Helmer:** *[following her].* There, there! My little singing bird mustn't go drooping her wings, eh? Has it got the sulks, that little squirrel of mine? *[Takes out his wallet.]* Nora, what do you think I've got here?

Nora: *[quickly turning around].* Money!

Helmer: There! *[He hands her some notes.]* Good heavens, I know only too well how Christmas runs away with the housekeeping.

Nora: *[counts].* Ten, twenty, thirty, forty. Oh, thank you, thank you. Torvald! This will see me quite a long way.

Helmer: Yes, it'll have to.

30 **Nora:** Yes, yes, I'll see that it does. But come over here, I want to show you all the things I've bought. And so cheap! Look, some new clothes for Ivar . . . and a little sword. There's a horse and a trumpet for Bob. And a doll and a doll's cot for Emmy. They are not very grand but she'll have them all broken before long anyway. And I've got some dress material and some handkerchiefs for the maids. Though, really, dear old Anne Marie should have had something better.

Helmer: And what's in this parcel here?

Nora: *[shrieking].* No, Torvald! You mustn't see that till tonight!

Helmer: All right. But tell me now, what did my little spendthrift fancy for herself?

Nora: For me? Pooh, I don't really want anything.

35 **Helmer:** Of course you do. Anything reasonable that you think you might like, just tell me.

Nora: Well, I don't really know. As a matter of fact, though, Torvald . . .

Helmer: Well?

Nora: [*toying with his coat buttons, and without looking at him*]. If you did want to give me something, you could . . . you could always . . .

Helmer: Well, well, out with it!

40 **Nora:** [*quickly*]. You could always give me money, Torvald. Only what you think you could spare. And then I could buy myself something with it later on.

Helmer: But Nora . . .

Nora: Oh, please, Torvald dear! Please! I beg you. Then I'd wrap the money up in some pretty gilt paper and hang it on the Christmas tree. Wouldn't that be fun?

Helmer: What do we call my pretty little pet when it runs away with all the money?

Nora: I know, I know, we call it a spendthrift. But please let's do what I said, Torvald. Then I'll have a bit of time to think about what I need most. Isn't that awfully sensible, now, eh?

45 **Helmer:** [*smiling*]. Yes, it is indeed—that is, if only you really could hold on to the money I gave you, and really did buy something for yourself with it. But it just gets mixed up with the housekeeping and frittered away on all sorts of useless things, and then I have to dig into my pocket all over again.

Nora: Oh but, Torvald . . .

Helmer: You can't deny it, Nora dear. [*Puts his arm around her waist.*] My pretty little pet is very sweet, but it runs away with an awful lot of money. It's incredible how expensive it is for a man to keep such a pet.

Nora: For shame! How can you say such a thing? As a matter of fact I save everything I can.

Helmer: [*laughs*]. Yes, you are right there. Everything you *can*. But you simply can't.

50 **Nora:** [*hums and smiles quietly and happily*]. Ah, if you only knew how many expenses the likes of us sky-larks and squirrels have, Torvald!

Helmer: What a funny little one you are! Just like your father. Always on the look-out for money, wherever you can lay your hands on it; but as soon as you've got it, it just seems to slip through your fingers. You never seem to know what you've done with it. Well, one must accept you as you are. It's in the blood. Oh yes, it is, Nora. That sort of thing is hereditary.

Nora: Oh, I only wish I'd inherited a few more of Daddy's qualities.

Helmer: And I wouldn't want my pretty little song-bird to be the least bit different from what she is now. But come to think of it, you look rather . . . rather . . . how shall I put it? . . . rather guilty today. . . .

Nora: Do I?

55 **Helmer:** Yes, you do indeed. Look me straight in the eye.

Nora: [*looks at him*]. Well?

Helmer: [*wagging his finger at her*]. My little sweet-tooth surely didn't forget herself in town today?

Nora: No, whatever makes you think that?

Helmer: She didn't just pop into the confectioner's for a moment?

60 **Nora:** No, I assure you, Torvald . . . !

Helmer: Didn't try sampling the preserves?

Nora: No, really I didn't.

Helmer: Didn't go nibbling a macaroon or two?

Nora: No, Torvald, honestly, you must believe me . . . !

65 **Helmer:** All right then! It's really just my little joke. . . .

Nora: [*crosses to the table*]. I would never dream of doing anything you didn't want me to.

Helmer: Of course not, I know that. And then you've given me your word. . . . [*Crosses to her.*] Well then, Nora dearest, you shall keep your little Christmas secrets. They'll all come out tonight, I dare say, when we light the tree.

Nora: Did you remember to invite Dr. Rank?

Helmer: No. But there's really no need. Of course he'll come and have dinner with us. Anyway, I can ask him when he looks in this morning. I've ordered some good wine. Nora, you can't imagine how I am looking forward to this evening.

70 **Nora:** So am I. And won't the children enjoy it, Torvald!

Helmer: Oh, what a glorious feeling it is, knowing you've got a nice, safe job, and a good fat income. Don't you agree? Isn't it wonderful, just thinking about it?

Nora: Oh, it's marvelous!

Helmer: Do you remember last Christmas? Three whole weeks beforehand you shut yourself up every evening till after midnight making flowers for the Christmas tree and all the other splendid things you wanted to surprise us with. Ugh, I never felt so bored in all my life.

Nora: I wasn't the least bit bored.

75 **Helmer:** *[smiling].* But it turned out a bit of an anticlimax, Nora.

Nora: Oh, you are not going to tease me about that again! How was I to know the cat would get in and pull everything to bits?

Helmer: No, of course you couldn't. Poor little Nora! All you wanted was for us to have a nice time—and it's the thought behind it that counts, after all. All the same, it's a good thing we've seen the back of those lean times.

Nora: Yes, really it's marvelous.

Helmer: Now there's no need for me to sit here all on my own, bored to tears. And you don't have to strain your dear little eyes, and work those dainty little fingers to the bone. . . .

80 **Nora:** *[clapping her hands].* No, Torvald, I don't do I? Not any more. Oh, how marvelous it is to hear that! *[Takes his arm.]* Now I want to tell you how I've been thinking we might arrange things, Torvald. As soon as Christmas is over. . . . *[The door-bell rings in the hall.]* Oh, there's the bell. *[Tidies one or two things in the room.]* It's probably a visitor. What a nuisance!

Helmer: Remember I'm not at home to callers.

Maid: *[in the doorway].* There's a lady to see you, ma'am.

Nora: Show her in, please.

Maid: *[to Helmer].* And the doctor's just arrived, too, sir.

85 **Helmer:** Did he go straight into my room?

Maid: Yes, he did, sir.

[Helmer goes into his study. The Maid shows in Mrs. Linde, who is in traveling clothes, and closes the door after her.]

Mrs. Linde: *[subdued and rather hesitantly].* How do you do, Nora?

Nora: *[uncertainly].* How do you do?

Mrs. Linde: I'm afraid you don't recognize me.

90 **Nora:** No, I don't think I . . . And yet I seem to. . . . *[Bursts out suddenly.]* Why! Kristine! Is it really you?

Mrs. Linde: Yes, it's me.

Nora: Fancy not recognizing you again! But how was I to, when . . . *[Gently.]* How you've changed, Kristine!

Mrs. Linde: I dare say I have. In nine . . . ten years. . . .

Nora: Is it so long since we last saw each other? Yes, it must be. Oh, believe me these last eight years have been such a happy time. And now you've come up to town, too? All that long journey in wintertime. That took courage.

95 **Mrs. Linde:** I just arrived this morning on the steamer.

Nora: To enjoy yourself over Christmas, of course. How lovely! Oh, we'll have such fun, you'll see. Do take off your things. You are not cold, are you? *[Helps her.]* There now! Now let's sit down here in comfort beside the stove. No, here, you take the armchair,

I'll sit here on the rocking chair. *[Takes her hands.]* Ah, now you look a bit more like your old self again. It was just that when I first saw you. . . . But you are a little paler, Kristine . . . and perhaps even a bit thinner!

Mrs. Linde: And much, much older, Nora.

Nora: Yes, perhaps a little older . . . very, very little, not really very much. *[Stops suddenly and looks serious.]* Oh, what a thoughtless creature I am, sitting here chattering on like this! Dear, sweet Kristine, can you forgive me?

Mrs. Linde: What do you mean, Nora?

100 **Nora:** *[gently].* Poor Kristine, of course you're a widow now.

Mrs. Linde: Yes, my husband died three years ago.

Nora: Oh, I remember now. I read about it in the papers. Oh, Kristine, believe me I often thought at the time of writing to you. But I kept putting it off, something always seemed to crop up.

Mrs. Linde: My dear Nora, I understand so well.

Nora: No, it wasn't very nice of me, Kristine. Oh, you poor thing, what you must have gone through. And didn't he leave you anything?

105 **Mrs. Linde:** No.

Nora: And no children?

Mrs. Linde: No.

Nora: Absolutely nothing?

Mrs. Linde: Nothing at all . . . not even a broken heart to grieve over.

110 **Nora:** *[looks at her incredulously].* But, Kristine, is that possible?

Mrs. Linde: *[smiles sadly and strokes Nora's hair].* Oh, it sometimes happens, Nora.

Nora: So utterly alone. How terribly sad that must be for you. I have three lovely children. You can't see them for the moment, because they're out with their nanny. But now you must tell me all about yourself. . . .

Mrs. Linde: No, no, I want to hear about you.

Nora: No, you start. I won't be selfish today. I must think only about your affairs today. But there's just one thing I really must tell you. Have you heard about the great stroke of luck we've had in the last few days?

115 **Mrs. Linde:** No. What is it?

Nora: What do you think? My husband has just been made Bank Manager!

Mrs. Linde: Your husband? How splendid!

Nora: Isn't it tremendous! It's not a very steady way of making a living, you know, being a lawyer, especially if he refuses to take on anything that's the least bit shady—which of course is what Torvald does, and I think he's quite right. You can imagine how pleased we are! He starts at the bank straight after New Year, and he's getting a big salary and lots of commission. From now on we'll be able to live quite differently . . . we'll do just what we want. Oh, Kristine, I'm so happy and relieved. I must say it's lovely to have plenty of money and not have to worry. Isn't it?

Mrs. Linde: Yes. It must be nice to have enough, at any rate.

120 **Nora:** No, not just enough, but pots and pots of money.

Mrs. Linde: *[smiles].* Nora, Nora, haven't you learned any sense yet? At school you used to be an awful spendthrift.

Nora: Yes, Torvald still says I am. *[Wags her finger.]* But little Nora isn't as stupid as everybody thinks. Oh, we haven't really been in a position where I could afford to spend a lot of money. We've both had to work.

Mrs. Linde: You too?

Nora: Yes, odd jobs—sewing, crochet-work, embroidery and things like that. *[Casually.]* And one or two other things, besides. I suppose you know that Torvald left the

Ministry when we got married. There weren't any prospects of promotion in his department, and of course he needed to earn more money than he had before. But the first year he wore himself out completely. He had to take on all kinds of extra jobs, you know, and he found himself working all hours of the day and night. But he couldn't go on like that, and he became seriously ill. The doctors said it was essential for him to go South.

125 **Mrs. Linde:** Yes, I believe you spent a whole year in Italy, didn't you?

Nora: That's right. It wasn't easy to get away, I can tell you. It was just after I'd had Ivar. But of course we had to go. Oh, it was an absolutely marvelous trip. And it saved Torvald's life. But it cost an awful lot of money, Kristine.

Mrs. Linde: That I can well imagine.

Nora: Twelve hundred dollars. Four thousand eight hundred crowns. That's a lot of money, Kristine.

Mrs. Linde: Yes, but in such circumstances, one is very lucky if one has it.

130 **Nora:** Well, we got it from Daddy, you see.

Mrs. Linde: Ah, that was it. It was just about then your father died, I believe, wasn't it?

Nora: Yes, Kristine, just about then. And do you know, I couldn't even go and look after him. Here was I expecting Ivar any day. And I also had poor Torvald, gravely ill, on my hands. Dear, kind Daddy! I never saw him again, Kristine. Oh, that's the saddest thing that has happened to me in all my married life.

Mrs. Linde: I know you were very fond of him. But after that you left for Italy?

Nora: Yes, we had the money then, and the doctors said it was urgent. We left a month later.

135 **Mrs. Linde:** And your husband came back completely cured?

Nora: Fit as a fiddle!

Mrs. Linde: But . . . what about the doctor?

Nora: How do you mean?

Mrs. Linde: I thought the maid said something about the gentleman who came at the same time as me being a doctor.

140 **Nora:** Yes, that was Dr. Rank. But this isn't a professional visit. He's our best friend and he always looks in at least once a day. No, Torvald has never had a day's illness since. And the children are fit and healthy, and so am I. *[Jumps up and claps her hands.]* Oh God, oh God, isn't it marvelous to be alive, and to be happy, Kristine! . . . Oh but I ought to be ashamed of myself . . . Here I go on talking about nothing but myself. *[She sits on a low stool near Mrs. Linde and lays her arms on her lap.]* Oh, please, you mustn't be angry with me! Tell me, is it really true that you didn't love your husband? What made you marry him, then?

Mrs. Linde: My mother was still alive; she was bedridden and helpless. And then I had two young brothers to look after as well. I didn't think I would be justified in refusing him.

Nora: No, I dare say you are right. I suppose he was fairly wealthy then?

Mrs. Linde: He was quite well off, I believe. But the business was shaky. When he died, it went all to pieces, and there just wasn't anything left.

Nora: What then?

145 **Mrs. Linde:** Well, I had to fend for myself, opening a little shop, running a little school, anything I could turn my hand to. These last three years have been one long relentless drudge. But now it's finished, Nora. My poor dear mother doesn't need me any more, she's passed away. Nor the boys either; they're at work now, they can look after themselves.

Nora: What a relief you must find it. . . .

Mrs. Linde: No, Nora! Just unutterably empty. Nobody to live for any more. *[Stands up restlessly.]* That's why I couldn't stand it any longer being cut off up there. Surely it must be a bit easier here to find something to occupy your mind. If only I could manage to find a steady job of some kind, in an office perhaps. . . .

Nora: But, Kristine, that's terribly exhausting; and you look so worn out even before you start. The best thing for you would be a little holiday at some quiet little resort.

Mrs. Linde: *[crosses to the window].* I haven't any father I can fall back on for the money, Nora.

150 **Nora:** *[rises].* Oh, please, you mustn't be angry with me!

Mrs. Linde: *[goes to her].* My dear Nora, you mustn't be angry with me either. That's the worst thing about people in my position, they become so bitter. One has nobody to work for, yet one has to be on the look-out all the time. Life has to go on, and one starts thinking only of oneself. Believe it or not, when you told me the good news about your step up, I was pleased not so much for your sake as for mine.

Nora: How do you mean? Ah, I see. You think Torvald might be able to do something for you.

Mrs. Linde: Yes, that's exactly what I thought.

Nora: And so he shall, Kristine. Just leave things to me. I'll bring it up so cleverly. . . . I'll think up something to put him in a good mood. Oh, I do so much want to help you.

155 **Mrs. Linde:** It is awfully kind of you, Nora, offering to do all this for me, particularly in your case, where you haven't known much trouble or hardship in your own life.

Nora: When I . . . ? I haven't known much . . . ?

Mrs. Linde: *[smiling].* Well, good heavens, a little bit of sewing to do and a few things like that. What a child you are, Nora!

Nora: *[tosses her head and walks across the room].* I wouldn't be too sure of that, if I were you.

Mrs. Linde: Oh?

160 **Nora:** You're just like the rest of them. You all think I'm useless when it comes to anything really serious. . . .

Mrs. Linde: Come, come. . . .

Nora: You think I've never had anything much to contend with in this hard world.

Mrs. Linde: Nora dear, you've only just been telling me all the things you've had to put up with.

Nora: Pooh! They were just trivialities! *[Softly.]* I haven't told you about the really big thing.

165 **Mrs. Linde:** What big thing? What do you mean?

Nora: I know you rather tend to look down on me, Kristine. But you shouldn't, you know. You are proud of having worked so hard and so long for your mother.

Mrs. Linde: I'm sure I don't look down on anybody. But it's true what you say: I am both proud and happy when I think of how I was able to make Mother's life a little easier towards the end.

Nora: And you are proud when you think of what you have done for your brothers, too.

Mrs. Linde: I think I have every right to be.

170 **Nora:** I think so too. But now I'm going to tell you something, Kristine. I too have something to be proud and happy about.

Mrs. Linde: I don't doubt that. But what is it you mean?

Nora: Not so loud. Imagine if Torvald were to hear! He must never on any account . . . nobody must know about it, Kristine, nobody but you.

Mrs. Linde: But what is it?

Nora: Come over here. *[She pulls her down on the sofa beside her.]* Yes, Kristine, I too have something to be proud and happy about. I was the one who saved Torvald's life.

175 **Mrs. Linde:** Saved . . . ? How . . . ?

Nora: I told you about our trip to Italy. Torvald would never have recovered but for that. . . .

Mrs. Linde: Well? Your father gave you what money was necessary.

Nora: [smiles]. That's what Torvald thinks, and everybody else. But . . .

Mrs. Linde: But . . . ?

180 **Nora:** Daddy never gave us a penny. I was the one who raised the money.

Mrs. Linde: You? All that money?

Nora: Twelve hundred dollars. Four thousand eight hundred crowns. What do you say to that!

Mrs. Linde: But, Nora, how was it possible? Had you won a sweepstake or something?

Nora: [contemptuously]. A sweepstake? Pooh! There would have been nothing to it then.

185 **Mrs. Linde:** Where did you get it from, then?

Nora: [hums and smiles secretively]. H'm, tra-la-la!

Mrs. Linde: Because what you couldn't do was borrow it.

Nora: Oh? Why not?

Mrs. Linde: Well, a wife can't borrow without her husband's consent.

190 **Nora:** [tossing her head]. Ah, but when it happens to be a wife with a bit of a sense for business . . . a wife who knows her way about things, then. . . .

Mrs. Linde: But, Nora, I just don't understand. . . .

Nora: You don't have to. I haven't said I did borrow the money. I might have got it some other way. [Throws herself back on the sofa.] I might even have got it from some admirer. Anyone as reasonably attractive as I am. . . .

Mrs. Linde: Don't be so silly!

Nora: Now you must be dying of curiosity, Kristine.

195 **Mrs. Linde:** Listen to me now, Nora dear—you haven't done anything rash, have you?

Nora: [sitting up again]. Is it rash to save your husband's life?

Mrs. Linde: I think it was rash to do anything without telling him. . . .

Nora: But the whole point was that he mustn't know anything. Good heavens, can't you see! He wasn't even supposed to know how desperately ill he was. It was me the doctors came and told his life was in danger, that the only way to save him was to go South for a while. Do you think I didn't try talking him into it first? I began dropping hints about how nice it would be if I could be taken on a little trip abroad, like other young wives. I wept, I pleaded. I told him he ought to show some consideration for my condition, and let me have a bit of my own way. And then I suggested he might take out a loan. But at that he nearly lost his temper, Kristine. He said I was being frivolous, that it was his duty as a husband not to give in to all these whims and fancies of mine—as I do believe he called them. All right, I thought, somehow you've got to be saved. And it was then I found a way. . . .

Mrs. Linde: Did your husband never find out from your father that the money hadn't come from him?

200 **Nora:** No, never. It was just about the time Daddy died. I'd intended letting him into the secret and asking him not to give me away. But when he was so ill . . . I'm sorry to say it never became necessary.

Mrs. Linde: And you never confided in your husband?

Nora: Good heavens, how could you ever imagine such a thing! When he's so strict about such matters! Besides, Torvald is a man with a good deal of pride—it would be terribly embarrassing and humiliating for him if he thought he owed anything to me. It would spoil everything between us; this happy home of ours would never be the same again.

Mrs. Linde: Are you never going to tell him?

Nora: [reflectively, half-smiling]. Oh yes, some day perhaps . . . in many years' time, when I'm no longer as pretty as I am now. You mustn't laugh! What I mean of course is when Torvald isn't quite so much in love with me as he is now, when he's lost interest in watching me dance, or get dressed up, or recite. Then it might be a good thing to have something in reserve. . . . [*Breaks off.*] What nonsense! That day will never come. Well, what have you got to say to my big secret, Kristine? Still think I'm not much good for anything? One thing, though, it's meant a lot of worry for me, I can tell you. It hasn't always been easy to meet my obligations when the time came. You know in business there is something called quarterly interest, and other things called installments, and these are always terribly difficult things to cope with. So what I've had to do is save a little here and there, you see, wherever I could. I couldn't really save anything out of the housekeeping, because Torvald has to live in decent style. I couldn't let the children go about badly dressed either—I felt any money I got for them had to go on them alone. Such sweet little things!

205   **Mrs. Linde:** Poor Nora! So it had to come out of your own allowance?

  Nora: Of course. After all, I was the one it concerned most. Whenever Torvald gave me money for new clothes and such-like, I never spent more than half. And always I bought the simplest and cheapest things. It's a blessing most things look well on me, so Torvald never noticed anything. But sometimes I did feel it was a bit hard, Kristine, because it is nice to be well dressed, isn't it?

  Mrs. Linde: Yes, I suppose it is.

  Nora: I have had some other sources of income, of course. Last winter I was lucky enough to get quite a bit of copying to do. So I shut myself up every night and sat and wrote through to the small hours of the morning. Oh, sometimes I was so tired, so tired. But it was tremendous fun all the same, sitting there working and earning money like that. It was almost like being a man.

  Mrs. Linde: And how much have you been able to pay off like this?

210   **Nora:** Well, I can't tell exactly. It's not easy to know where you are with transactions of this kind, you understand. All I know is I've paid off just as much as I could scrape together. Many's the time I was at my wit's end. [*Smiles*] Then I used to sit here and pretend that some rich old gentleman had fallen in love with me. . . .

  Mrs. Linde: What! What gentleman?

  Nora: Oh, rubbish! . . . and that now he had died, and when they opened his will, there in big letters were the words: "My entire fortune is to be paid over, immediately and in cash, to charming Mrs. Nora Helmer."

  Mrs. Linde: But my dear Nora—who *is* this man?

  Nora: Good heavens, don't you understand? There never was any old gentleman; it was just something I used to sit here pretending, time and time again, when I didn't know where to turn next for money. But it doesn't make very much difference; as far as I'm concerned the old boy can do what he likes, I'm tired of him; I can't be bothered any more with him or his will. Because now all my worries are over. [*Jumping up.*] Oh God, what a glorious thought, Kristine! No more worries! Just think of being without a care in the world . . . being able to romp with the children, and making the house nice and attractive, and having things just as Torvald likes to have them? And then spring will soon be here, and blue skies. And maybe we can go away somewhere. I might even see something of the sea again. Oh yes! When you're happy, life is a wonderful thing!

[*The door-bell is heard in the hall.*]

215   **Mrs. Linde:** [*gets up*]. There's the bell. Perhaps I'd better go.

  Nora: No, do stay, please. I don't suppose it's for me; it's probably somebody for Torvald. . . .

  Maid: [*in the doorway*]. Excuse me, ma'am, but there's a gentleman here wants to see Mr. Helmer, and I didn't quite know . . . because the Doctor is in there. . . .

  Nora: Who is the gentleman?

Krogstad: [in the doorway]. It's me, Mrs. Helmer.

[Mrs. Linde starts, then turns away to the window.]

220 **Nora:** [tense, takes a step towards him and speaks in a low voice]. You? What is it? What do you want to talk to my husband about?

Krogstad: Bank matters . . . in a manner of speaking. I work at the bank, and I hear your husband is to be the new manager. . . .

Nora: So it's . . .

Krogstad: Just routine business matters, Mrs. Helmer. Absolutely nothing else.

[She nods impassively and shuts the hall door behind him; then she walks across and sees to the stove.]

Mrs. Linde: Nora . . . who was that man?

225 **Nora:** His name is Krogstad.

Mrs. Linde: So it really was him.

Nora: Do you know the man?

Mrs. Linde: I used to know him . . . a good many years ago. He was a solicitor's clerk in our district for a while.

Nora: Yes, so he was.

230 **Mrs. Linde:** How he's changed!

Nora: His marriage wasn't a very happy one, I believe.

Mrs. Linde: He's a widower now, isn't he?

Nora: With a lot of children. There, it'll burn better now.

[She closes the stove door and moves the rocking chair a little to one side.]

Mrs. Linde: He does a certain amount of business on the side, they say?

235 **Nora:** Oh? Yes, it's always possible. I just don't know. . . . But let's not think about business . . . it's all so dull.

[Dr. Rank comes in from Helmer's study.]

Dr. Rank: [still in the doorway]. No, no, Torvald, I won't intrude. I'll just look in on your wife for a moment. [Shuts the door and notices Mrs. Linde.] Oh, I beg your pardon. I'm afraid I'm intruding here as well.

Nora: No, not at all! [Introduces them.] Dr. Rank . . . Mrs. Linde.

Rank: Ah! A name I've often heard mentioned in this house. I believe I came past you on the stairs as I came in.

Mrs. Linde: I have to take things slowly going upstairs. I find it rather a trial.

240 **Nora:** Ah, some little disability somewhere, eh?

Mrs. Linde: Just a bit run down, I think, actually.

Rank: Is that all? Then I suppose you've come to town for a good rest—doing the rounds of the parties?

Mrs. Linde: I have come to look for work.

Rank: Is that supposed to be some kind of sovereign remedy for being run down?

245 **Mrs. Linde:** One must live, Doctor.

Rank: Yes, it's generally thought to be necessary.

Nora: Come, come, Dr. Rank. You are quite as keen to live as anybody.

Rank: Quite keen, yes. Miserable as I am, I'm quite ready to let things drag on as long as possible. All my patients are the same. Even those with a moral affliction are no different. As a matter of fact, there's a bad case of that kind in talking with Helmer at this very moment. . . .

Mrs. Linde: [softly]. Ah!

250 **Nora:** Whom do you mean?

Rank: A person called Krogstad—nobody you would know. He's rotten to the core. But even he began talking about having to *live*, as though it were something terribly important.

Nora: Oh? And what did he want to talk to Torvald about?

Rank: I honestly don't know. All I heard was something about the Bank.

Nora: I didn't know that Krog . . . that this Mr. Krogstad had anything to do with the Bank.

255 **Rank:** Oh yes, he's got some kind of job down there. [To Mrs. Linde.] I wonder if you've got people in your part of the country too who go rushing round sniffing out cases of moral corruption, and then installing the individuals concerned in nice, well-paid jobs where they can keep them under observation. Sound, decent people have to be content to stay out in the cold.

Mrs. Linde: Yet surely it's the sick who most need to be brought in.

Rank: [shrugs his shoulders]. Well, there we have it. It's that attitude that's turning society into a clinic.

[Nora, lost in her own thoughts, breaks into smothered laughter and claps her hands.]

Rank: Why are you laughing at that? Do you know in fact what society is?

Nora: What do I care about your silly old society? I was laughing about something quite different . . . something frightfully funny. Tell me, Dr. Rank, are all the people who work at the bank dependent on Torvald now?

260 **Rank:** Is *that* what you find so frightfully funny?

Nora: [smiles and hums]. Never you mind! Never you mind! [Walks about the room.] Yes, it really is terribly amusing to think that we . . . that Torvald now has power over so many people. [She takes the bag out of her pocket.] Dr. Rank, what about a little macaroon?

Rank: Look at this, eh? Macaroons. I thought they were forbidden here.

Nora: Yes, but these are some Kristine gave me.

Mrs. Linde: What? I . . . ?

265 **Nora:** Now, now, you needn't be alarmed. You weren't to know that Torvald had forbidden them. He's worried in case they ruin my teeth, you know. Still . . . what's it matter once in a while! Don't you think so, Dr. Rank? Here! [She pops a macaroon into his mouth.] And you too, Kristine. And I shall have one as well; just a little one . . . or two at the most. [She walks about the room again.] Really I am so happy. There's just one little thing I'd love to do now.

Rank: What's that?

Nora: Something I'd love to say in front of Torvald.

Rank: Then why can't you?

Nora: No, I daren't. It's not very nice.

270 **Mrs. Linde:** Not very nice?

Rank: Well, in that case it might not be wise. But to us, I don't see why. . . . What is this you would love to say in front of Helmer?

Nora: I would simply love to say: "Damn."

Rank: Are you mad!

Mrs. Linde: Good gracious, Nora . . . !

275 **Rank:** Say it! Here he is!

Nora: [hiding the bag of macaroons]. Sh! Sh!

[Helmer comes out of his room, his overcoat over his arm and his hat in his hand.]

Nora: [going over to him]. Well, Torvald dear, did you get rid of him?

Helmer: Yes, he's just gone.

Nora: Let me introduce you. This is Kristine, who has just arrived in town. . . .

280 **Helmer:** Kristine . . . ? You must forgive me, but I don't think I know . . .

Nora: Mrs. Linde, Torvald dear. Kristine Linde.

Helmer: Ah, indeed. A school-friend of my wife's, presumably.

Mrs. Linde: Yes, we were girls together.

Nora: Fancy, Torvald, she's come all this long way just to have a word with you.

285 **Helmer:** How is that?

Mrs. Linde: Well, it wasn't really. . . .

Nora: The thing is, Kristine is terribly clever at office work, and she's frightfully keen on finding a job with some efficient man, so that she can learn even more. . . .

Helmer: Very sensible, Mrs. Linde.

Nora: And then when she read you'd been made Bank Manager—there was a bit in the paper about it—she set off at once. Torvald, please! You *will* try and do something for Kristine, won't you? For my sake?

290 **Helmer:** Well, that's not altogether impossible. You are a widow, I presume?

Mrs. Linde: Yes.

Helmer: And you've had some experience in business?

Mrs. Linde: A fair amount.

Helmer: Well, it's quite probable I can find you a job, I think. . . .

295 **Nora:** *[clapping her hands].* There, you see!

Helmer: You have come at a fortunate moment, Mrs. Linde. . . .

Mrs. Linde: Oh, how can I ever thank you . . . ?

Helmer: Not a bit. *[He puts on his overcoat.]* But for the present I must ask you to excuse me. . . .

Rank: Wait. I'm coming with you.

[He fetches his fur coat from the hall and warms it at the stove.]

300 **Nora:** Don't be long, Torvald dear.

Helmer: Not more than an hour, that's all.

Nora: Are you leaving too, Kristine?

Mrs. Linde: *[putting on her things].* Yes, I must go and see if I can't find myself a room.

Helmer: Perhaps we can all walk down the road together.

305 **Nora:** *[helping her].* What a nuisance we are so limited for space here. I'm afraid it just isn't possible. . . .

Mrs. Linde: Oh, you mustn't dream of it! Goodbye, Nora dear, and thanks for everything.

Nora: Goodbye for the present. But . . . you'll be coming back this evening, of course. And you too, Dr. Rank? What's that? If you are up to it? Of course you'll be up to it. Just wrap yourself up well.

[They go out, talking, into the hall; Children's voices can be heard on the stairs.]

Nora: Here they are! Here they are! *[She runs to the front door and opens it. Anne Marie, the nursemaid, enters with the Children.]* Come in! Come in! *[She bends down and kisses them.]* Ah! my sweet little darlings. . . . You see them, Kristine? Aren't they lovely!

Rank: Don't stand here chattering in this draft!

310 **Helmer:** Come along, Mrs. Linde. The place now becomes unbearable for anybody except mothers.

[Dr. Rank, Helmer, and Mrs. Linde go down the stairs: the Nursemaid comes into the room with the Children, then Nora, shutting the door behind her.]

Nora: How fresh and bright you look! My, what red cheeks you've got! Like apples and roses. *[During the following, the Children keep chattering away to her.]* Have you had a nice time? That's splendid. And you gave Emmy and Bob a ride on your sledge? Did you now! Both together! Fancy that! There's a clever boy, Ivar. Oh, let me take her a little while, Anne Marie. There's my sweet little baby-doll! *[She takes the youngest of the Children from the Nursemaid and dances with her.]* All right, Mummy will dance with Bobby too. What? You've been throwing snowballs? Oh, I wish I'd been there. No, don't bother, Anne Marie, I'll help them off with their things. No, please let me—I like doing it. You go on in, you look frozen. You'll find some hot coffee on the stove. *[The Nursemaid goes into the room, left. Nora takes off the Children's coats and hats and throws them down anywhere, while the Children all talk at once.]* Really! A great big dog came running after you? But he didn't bite. No, the doggies wouldn't bite my pretty little dollies. You mustn't touch the parcels, Ivar! What are they? Wouldn't you like to know! No, no, that's nasty. Now? Shall we play something? What shall we play? Hide and seek? Yes, let's play hide and seek. Bob can hide first. Me first? All right, let me hide first.

[She and the other Children play, laughing and shrieking, in this room and in the adjacent room on the right. Finally Nora hides under the table; the Children come rushing in to look for her but cannot find her; they hear her stifled laughter, rush to the table, lift up the tablecloth and find her. Tremendous shouts of delight. She creeps out and pretends to frighten them. More shouts. Meanwhile there has been a knock at the front door, which nobody has heard. The door half opens, and Krogstad can be seen. He waits a little; the game continues.]

Krogstad: I beg your pardon, Mrs. Helmer. . . .

Nora: *[turns with a stifled cry and half jumps up]*. Ah! What do you want?

Krogstad: Excuse me. The front door was standing open. Somebody must have forgotten to shut it. . . .

315 **Nora:** *[standing up]*. My husband isn't at home, Mr. Krogstad.

Krogstad: I know.

Nora: Well . . . what are you doing here?

Krogstad: I want a word with you.

Nora: With . . . ? *[Quietly, to the Children.]* Go to Anne Marie. What? No, the strange man won't do anything to Mummy. When he's gone we'll have another game. *[She leads the Children into the room, left, and shuts the door after them; tense and uneasy.]* You want to speak to me?

320 **Krogstad:** Yes, I do.

Nora: Today? But it isn't the first of the month yet. . . .

Krogstad: No, it's Christmas Eve. It depends entirely on you what sort of Christmas you have.

Nora: What do you want? Today I can't possibly . . .

Krogstad: Let's not talk about that for the moment. It's something else. You've got a moment to spare?

325 **Nora:** Yes, I suppose so, though . . .

Krogstad: Good. I was sitting in Olsen's cafe, and I saw your husband go down the road . . .

Nora: Did you?

Krogstad: . . . with a lady.

Nora: Well?

330 **Krogstad:** May I be so bold as to ask whether that lady was Mrs. Linde?

Nora: Yes.

Krogstad: Just arrived in town?

Nora: Yes, today.

Krogstad: And she's a good friend of yours?

335 **Nora:** Yes, she is. But I can't see . . .

Krogstad: I also knew her once.

Nora: I know.

Krogstad: Oh? So you know all about it. I thought as much. Well, I want to ask you straight: is Mrs. Linde getting a job in the Bank?

Nora: How dare you cross-examine me like this, Mr. Krogstad? You, one of my husband's subordinates? But since you've asked me, I'll tell you. Yes, Mrs. Linde *has* got a job. And I'm the one who got it for her, Mr. Krogstad. Now you know.

340 **Krogstad:** So my guess was right.

Nora: *[walking up and down].* Oh, I think I can say that some of us have a little influence now and again. Just because one happens to be a woman, that doesn't mean. . . . People in subordinate positions ought to take care they don't offend anybody . . . who . . . hm . . .

Krogstad: . . . has influence?

Nora: Exactly.

Krogstad: *[changing his tone].* Mrs. Helmer, will you have the goodness to use your influence on my behalf?

345 **Nora:** What? What do you mean?

Krogstad: Will you be so good as to see that I keep my modest little job at the Bank?

Nora: What do you mean? Who wants to take it away from you?

Krogstad: Oh, you needn't try and pretend to me you don't know. I can quite see that this friend of yours isn't particularly anxious to bump up against me. And I can also see now whom I can thank for being given the sack.

Nora: But I assure you. . . .

350 **Krogstad:** All right, all right. But to come to the point: there's still time. And I advise you to use your influence to stop it.

Nora: But, Mr. Krogstad, I *have* no influence.

Krogstad: Haven't you? I thought just now you said yourself . . .

Nora: I didn't mean it that way, of course. Me? What makes you think I've got any influence of that kind over my husband?

Krogstad: I know your husband from our student days. I don't suppose he is any more steadfast than other married men.

355 **Nora:** You speak disrespectfully of my husband like that and I'll show you the door.

Krogstad: So the lady's got courage.

Nora: I'm not frightened of you any more. After New Year I'll soon be finished with the whole business.

Krogstad: *[controlling himself].* Listen to me, Mrs. Helmer. If necessary I shall fight for my little job in the bank as if I were fighting for my life.

Nora: So it seems.

360 **Krogstad:** It's not just for the money, that's the last thing I care about. There's something else . . . well, I might as well out with it. You see it's like this. You know as well as anybody that some years ago I got myself mixed up in a bit of trouble.

Nora: I believe I've heard something of the sort.

Krogstad: It never got as far as the courts; but immediately it was as if all paths were barred to me. So I started going in for the sort of business you know about. I had to do something, and I think I can say I haven't been one of the worst. But now I have to get out of it. My sons are growing up; for their sake I must try and win back what respectability I can. That job in the bank was like the first step on the ladder for me. And now your husband wants to kick me off the ladder again, back into the mud.

Nora: But in God's name, Mr. Krogstad, it's quite beyond my power to help you.

Krogstad: That's because you haven't the will to help me. But I have ways of making you.

365 **Nora:** You wouldn't go and tell my husband I owe you money?

Krogstad: Suppose I did tell him?

Nora: It would be a rotten shame. [*Half choking with tears.*] That secret is all my pride and joy—why should he have to hear about it in this nasty, horrid way . . . hear about it from *you.* You would make things horribly unpleasant for me. . . .

Krogstad: Merely unpleasant?

Nora: [*vehemently*]. Go on, do it then! It'll be all the worse for you. Because then my husband will see for himself what a bad man you are, and then you certainly won't be able to keep your job.

370 **Krogstad:** I asked whether it was only a bit of domestic unpleasantness you were afraid of?

Nora: If my husband gets to know about it, he'll pay off what's owing at once. And then we'd have nothing more to do with you.

Krogstad: [*taking a pace towards her*]. Listen, Mrs. Helmer, either you haven't a very good memory, or else you don't understand much about business. I'd better make the position a little bit clearer for you.

Nora: How do you mean?

Krogstad: When your husband was ill, you came to me for the loan of twelve hundred dollars.

375 **Nora:** I didn't know of anybody else.

Krogstad: I promised to find you the money. . . .

Nora: And you did find it.

Krogstad: I promised to find you the money on certain conditions. At the time you were so concerned about your husband's illness, and so anxious to get the money for going away with, that I don't think you paid very much attention to all the incidentals. So there is perhaps some point in reminding you of them. Well, I promised to find you the money against an IOU which I drew up for you.

Nora: Yes, and which I signed.

380 **Krogstad:** Very good. But below that I added a few lines, by which your father was to stand security. This your father was to sign.

Nora: Was to . . . ? He did sign it.

Krogstad: I had left the date blank. The idea was that your father was to add the date himself when he signed it. Remember?

Nora: Yes, I think. . . .

Krogstad: I then gave you the IOU to post to your father. Wasn't that so?

385 **Nora:** Yes.

Krogstad: Which of course you did at once. Because only about five or six days later you brought it back to me with your father's signature. I then paid out the money.

Nora: Well? Haven't I paid the installments regularly?

Krogstad: Yes, fairly. But . . . coming back to what we were talking about . . . that was a pretty bad period you were going through then, Mrs. Helmer.

Nora: Yes, it was.

390 **Krogstad:** Your father was seriously ill, I believe.

Nora: He was very near the end.

Krogstad: And died shortly afterwards?

Nora: Yes.

Krogstad: Tell me, Mrs. Helmer, do you happen to remember which day your father died? The exact date, I mean.

395 **Nora:** Daddy died on 29 September.

Krogstad: Quite correct. I made some inquiries. Which brings up a rather curious point *[takes out a paper]* which I simply cannot explain.

Nora: Curious . . . ? I don't know . . .

Krogstad: The curious thing is, Mrs. Helmer, that your father signed this document three days after his death.

Nora: What? I don't understand. . . .

400 **Krogstad:** Your father died on 29 September. But look here. Your father has dated his signature 2 October. Isn't that rather curious, Mrs. Helmer? *[Nora remains silent.]* It's also remarkable that the words "2 October" and the year are not in your father's handwriting, but in a handwriting I rather think I recognize. Well, perhaps that could be explained. Your father might have forgotten to date his signature, and then somebody else might have made a guess at the date later, before the fact of your father's death was known. There is nothing wrong in that. What really matters is the signature. And *that* is of course genuine, Mrs. Helmer? It really was your father who wrote his name here?

Nora: *[after a moment's silence, throws her head back and looks at him defiantly].* No, it wasn't. It was me who signed father's name.

Krogstad: Listen to me. I suppose you realize that that is a very dangerous confession?

Nora: Why? You'll soon have all your money back.

Krogstad: Let me ask you a question: why didn't you send that document to your father?

405 **Nora:** It was impossible. Daddy was ill. If I'd asked him for his signature, I'd have had to tell him what the money was for. Don't you see, when he was as ill as that I couldn't go and tell him that my husband's life was in danger. It was simply impossible.

Krogstad: It would have been better for you if you had abandoned the whole trip.

Nora: No, that was impossible. This was the thing that was to save my husband's life. I couldn't give it up.

Krogstad: But did it never strike you that this was fraudulent . . . ?

Nora: That wouldn't have meant anything to me. Why should I worry about you? I couldn't stand you, not when you insisted on going through with all those cold-blooded formalities, knowing all the time what a critical state my husband was in.

410 **Krogstad:** Mrs. Helmer, it's quite clear you still haven't the faintest idea what it is you've committed. But let me tell you, my own offense was no more and no worse than that, and it ruined my entire reputation.

Nora: You? Are you trying to tell me that you once risked everything to save your wife's life?

Krogstad: The law takes no account of motives.

Nora: Then they must be very bad laws.

Krogstad: Bad or not, if I produce this document in court, you'll be condemned according to them.

415 **Nora:** I don't believe it. Isn't a daughter entitled to try and save her father from worry and anxiety on his deathbed? Isn't a wife entitled to save her husband's life? I might not know very much about the law, but I feel sure of one thing: it must say somewhere that things like this are allowed. You mean to say you don't know that—you, when it's your job? You must have been a rotten lawyer, Mr. Krogstad.

Krogstad: That may be. But when it comes to business transactions—like the sort between us two—perhaps you'll admit I know something about them? Good. Now you must please yourself. But I tell you this: if I'm pitched out a second time, you are going to keep me company.

[He bows and goes out through the hall.]

Nora: *[stands thoughtfully for a moment, then tosses her head].* Rubbish! He's just trying to scare me. I'm not such a fool as all that. *[Begins gathering up the Children's clothes; after a moment she stops.]* Yet . . . ? No, it's impossible! I did it for love, didn't I?

The Children: *[in the doorway, left].* Mummy, the gentleman's just gone out of the gate.

Nora: Yes, I know. But you mustn't say anything to anybody about that gentleman. You hear? Not even to Daddy!

420 **The Children:** All right, Mummy. Are you going to play again?

Nora: No, not just now.

The Children: But Mummy, you promised!

Nora: Yes, but I can't just now. Off you go now, I have a lot to do. Off you go, my darlings. *[She herds them carefully into the other room and shuts the door behind them. She sits down on the sofa, picks up her embroidery and works a few stitches, but soon stops.]* No! *[She flings her work down, stands up, goes to the hall door and calls out.]* Helene! Fetch the tree in for me, please. *[She walks across to the table, left, and opens the drawer; again pauses.]* No, really, it's quite impossible!

Maid: *[with the Christmas tree].* Where shall I put it, ma'am?

425 **Nora:** On the floor there, in the middle.

Maid: Anything else you want me to bring?

Nora: No, thank you. I've got what I want.

[The Maid has put the tree down and goes out.]

Nora: *[busy decorating the tree].* Candles here . . . and flowers here.—Revolting man! It's all nonsense! There's nothing to worry about. We'll have a lovely Christmas tree. And I'll do anything you want me to, Torvald; I'll sing for you, dance for you. . . .

[Helmer, with a bundle of documents under his arm, comes in by the hall door.]

Nora: Ah, back again already?

430 **Helmer:** Yes. Anybody been?

Nora: Here? No.

Helmer: That's funny. I just saw Krogstad leave the house.

Nora: Oh? O yes, that's right. Krogstad was here a minute.

Helmer: Nora, I can tell by your face he's been asking you to put a good word in for him.

435 **Nora:** Yes.

Helmer: And you were to pretend it was your own idea? You were to keep quiet about his having been here. He asked you to do that as well, didn't he?

Nora: Yes, Torvald. But . . .

Helmer: Nora, Nora, what possessed you to do a thing like that? Talking to a person like him, making him promises? And then on top of everything, to tell me a lie!

Nora: A lie . . . ?

440 **Helmer:** Didn't you say that nobody had been here? *[Wagging his finger at her.]* Never again must my little song-bird do a thing like that! Little song-birds must keep their pretty little beaks out of mischief; no chirruping out of tune! *[Puts his arm around her waist.]* Isn't that the way we want things to be? Yes, of course it is. *[Lets her go.]* So let's say no more about it. *[Sits down by the stove.]* Ah, nice and cozy here!

[He glances through his papers.]

Nora: *[busy with the Christmas tree, after a short pause].* Torvald!

Helmer: Yes.

Nora: dress ball at the Stenborgs' on Boxing Day.[1]

Helmer: And I'm terribly curious to see what sort of surprise you've got for me.

445 **Nora:** Oh, it's too silly.

---

[1] The first weekday after Christmas.

Helmer: Oh?

Nora: I just can't think of anything suitable. Everything seems so absurd, so pointless.

Helmer: Has my little Nora come to *that* conclusion?

Nora: *[behind his chair, her arms on the chairback].* Are you very busy, Torvald?

450 **Helmer:** Oh . . .

Nora: What are all those papers?

Helmer: Bank matters.

Nora: Already?

Helmer: I have persuaded the retiring manager to give me authority to make any changes in organization or personnel I think necessary. I have to work on it over the Christmas week. I want everything straight by the New Year.

455 **Nora:** So that was why that poor Krog-stad. . . .

Helmer: Hm!

Nora: *[still leaning against the back of the chair, running her fingers through his har].* If you hadn't been so busy, Torvald, I'd have asked you to do me an awfully big favor.

Helmer: Let me hear it. What's it to be?

Nora: Nobody's got such good taste as you. And the thing is I do so want to look my best at the fancy dress ball. Torvald, couldn't you give me some advice and tell me what you think I ought to go as, and how I should arrange my costume?

460 **Helmer:** Aha! So my impulsive little woman is asking for somebody to come to her rescue, eh?

Nora: Please Torvald, I never get anywhere without your help.

Helmer: Very well, I'll think about it. We'll find something.

Nora: That's sweet of you. *[She goes across to the tree again; pause.]* How pretty these red flowers look.—Tell me, was it really something terribly wrong this man Krogstad did?

Helmer: Forgery. Have you any idea what that means?

465 **Nora:** Perhaps circumstances left him no choice?

Helmer: Maybe. Or perhaps, like so many others, he just didn't think. I am not so heartless that I would necessarily want to condemn a man for a single mistake like that.

Nora: Oh no, Torvald, of course not!

Helmer: Many a man might be able to redeem himself, if he honestly confessed his guilt and took his punishment.

Nora: Punishment?

470 **Helmer:** But that wasn't the way Krogstad chose. He dodged what was due to him by a cunning trick. And that's what has been the cause of his corruption.

Nora: Do you think it would . . . ?

Helmer: Just think how a man with a thing like that on his conscience will always be having to lie and cheat and dissemble; he can never drop the mask, not even with his own wife and children. And the children—*that's* the most terrible part of it, Nora.

Nora: Why?

Helmer: A fog of lies like that in a household, and it spreads disease and infection to every part of it. Every breath the children take in that kind of house is reeking with evil germs.

475 **Nora:** *[closer to him].* Are you sure of that?

Helmer: My dear Nora, as a lawyer I know what I'm talking about. Practically all juvenile delinquents come from homes where the mother is dishonest.

Nora: Why mothers particularly?

Helmer: It's generally traceable to the mothers, but of course fathers can have the same influence. Every lawyer knows that only too well. And yet there's Krogstad been poisoning his own children for years with lies and deceit. That's the reason I call him morally depraved. *[Holds out his hands to her.]* That's why my sweet little Nora must promise me not to try putting in any more good words for him. Shake hands on it. Well? What's this? Give me your hand. There now! That's settled. I assure you I would have found it impossible to work with him. I quite literally feel physically sick in the presence of such people.

Nora: *[draws her hand away and walks over to the other side of the Christmas tree]*. How hot it is in here! And I still have such a lot to do.

480 **Helmer:** *[stands up and collects his papers together]*. Yes, I'd better think of getting some of this read before dinner. I must also think about your costume. And I might even be able to lay my hands on something to wrap in gold paper and hang on the Christmas tree. *[He lays his hand on her head.]* My precious little singing bird.

[He goes into his study and shuts the door behind him.]

Nora: *[quietly, after a pause]*. Nonsense! It can't be. It's impossible. It *must* be impossible.

Maid: *[in the doorway, left]*. The children keep asking so nicely if they can come in and see Mummy.

Nora: No, no, don't let them in! You stay with them, Anne Marie.

Maid: Very well, ma'am.

[She shuts the door.]

485 **Nora:** *[pale with terror]*. Corrupt my children . . . ! Poison my home? *[Short pause; she throws back her head.]* It's not true! It could never, never be true!

Act II

The same room. In the corner beside the piano stands the Christmas tree, stripped, bedraggled and with its candles burnt out. Nora's outdoor things lie on the sofa. Nora, alone there, walks about restlessly; at last she stops by the sofa and picks up her coat.

Nora: *[putting her coat down again]*. Somebody's coming! *[Crosses to the door, listens.]* No, it's nobody. Nobody will come today, of course, Christmas Day—nor tomorrow, either. But perhaps. . . . *[She opens the door and looks out.]* No, nothing in the letter box; quite empty. *[Comes forward.]* Oh, nonsense! He didn't mean it seriously. Things like that can't happen. It's impossible! Why, I have three small children.

[The Nursemaid comes from the room, left, carrying a big cardboard box.]

Nursemaid: I finally found it, the box with the fancy dress costumes.

Nora: Thank you. Put it on the table, please.

Nursemaid: *[does this]*. But I'm afraid they are in an awful mess.

5 **Nora:** Oh, if only I could rip them up into a thousand pieces!

Nursemaid: Good heavens, they can be mended all right, with a bit of patience.

Nora: Yes, I'll go over and get Mrs. Linde to help me.

Nursemaid: Out again? In this terrible weather? You'll catch your death of cold, Ma'am.

Nora: Oh, worse things might happen.—How are the children?

10 **Nursemaid:** Playing with their Christmas presents, poor little things, but . . .

Nora: Do they keep asking for me?

Nursemaid: They are so used to being with their Mummy.

Nora: Yes, Anne Marie, from now on I can't be with them as often as I was before.

Nursemaid: Ah well, children get used to anything in time.

15 **Nora:** Do you think so? Do you think they would forget their Mummy if she went away for good?

Nursemaid: Good gracious—for good?

Nora: Tell me, Anne Marie—I've often wondered—how on earth could you bear to hand your children over to strangers?

Nursemaid: Well, there was nothing else for it when I had to come and nurse my little Nora.

Nora: Yes but . . . how could you *bring* yourself to do it?

20 **Nursemaid:** When I had the chance of such a good place? When a poor girl's been in trouble she must make the best of things. Because *he* didn't help, the rotter.

Nora: But your daughter will have forgotten you.

Nursemaid: Oh no, she hasn't. She wrote to me when she got confirmed, and again when she got married.

Nora: *[putting her arms around her neck].* Dear old Anne Marie, you were a good mother to me when I was little.

Nursemaid: My poor little Nora never had any other mother but me.

25 **Nora:** And if my little ones only had you, I know you would . . . Oh, what am I talking about! *[She opens the box.]* Go in to them. I must . . . Tomorrow I'll let you see how pretty I am going to look.

[She goes into the room, left.]

Nora: *[begins unpacking the box, but soon throws it down].* Oh, if only I dare go out. If only I could be sure nobody would come. And that nothing would happen in the meantime here at home. Rubbish—nobody's going to come. I mustn't think about it. Brush this muff. Pretty gloves, pretty gloves! I'll put it right out of my mind. One, two, three, four, five, six. . . . *[Secreams.]* Ah, they are coming. . . . *[She starts towards the door, but stops irresolute. Mrs. Linde comes from the hall, where she has taken off her things.]* Oh, it's you, Kristine. There's nobody else out there, is there? I'm so glad you've come.

Mrs. Linde: I heard you'd been over looking for me.

Nora: Yes, I was just passing. There's something you must help me with. Come and sit beside me on the sofa here. You see, the Stenborgs are having a fancy dress party upstairs tomorrow evening, and now Torvald wants me to go as a Neapolitan fisher lass and dance the tarantella. I learned it in Capri, you know.

Mrs. Linde: Well, well! So you are going to do a party piece?

30 **Nora:** Torvald says I should. Look, here's the costume, Torvald had it made for me down there. But it's got all torn and I simply don't know. . . .

Mrs. Linde: We'll soon have that put right. It's only the trimming come away here and there. Got a needle and thread? Ah, here's what we are after.

Nora: It's awfully kind of you.

Mrs. Linde: So you are going to be all dressed up tomorrow, Nora? Tell you what—I'll pop over for a minute to see you in all your finery. But I'm quite forgetting to thank you for the pleasant time we had last night.

Nora: *[gets up and walks across the room].* Somehow I didn't think yesterday was as nice as things generally are.—You should have come to town a little earlier, Kristine.—Yes, Torvald certainly knows how to make things pleasant about the place.

35 **Mrs. Linde:** You too, I should say. You are not your father's daughter for nothing. But tell me, is Dr. Rank always as depressed as he was last night?

Nora: No, last night it was rather obvious. He's got something seriously wrong with him, you know. Tuberculosis of the spine, poor fellow. His father was a horrible man, who used to have mistresses and things like that. That's why the son was always ailing, right from being a child.

Mrs. Linde: *[lowering her sewing].* But my dear Nora, how do you come to know about things like that?

Nora: *[walking about the room].* Huh! When you've got three children, you get these visits from . . . women who have had a certain amount of medical training. And you hear all sorts of things from them.

Mrs. Linde: *[begins sewing again; short silence].* Does Dr. Rank call in every day?

40 **Nora:** Every single day. He was Torvald's best friend as a boy, and he's a good friend of *mine,* too. Dr. Rank is almost like one of the family.

Mrs. Linde: But tell me—is he really genuine? What I mean is: doesn't he sometimes rather turn on the charm?

Nora: No, on the contrary. What makes you think that?

Mrs. Linde: When you introduced me yesterday, he claimed he'd often heard my name in this house. Afterwards I noticed your husband hadn't the faintest idea who I was. Then how is it that Dr. Rank should. . . .

Nora: Oh yes, it was quite right what he said, Kristine. You see Torvald is so terribly in love with me that he says he wants me all to himself. When we were first married, it even used to make him sort of jealous if I only as much as mentioned any of my old friends from back home. So of course I stopped doing it. But I often talk to Dr. Rank about such things. He likes hearing about them.

45 **Mrs. Linde:** Listen, Nora! In lots of ways you are still a child. Now, I'm a good deal older than you, and a bit more experienced. I'll tell you something: I think you ought to give up all this business with Dr. Rank.

Nora: Give up what business?

Mrs. Linde: The whole thing, I should say. Weren't you saying yesterday something about a rich admirer who was to provide you with money. . . .

Nora: One who's never existed, I regret to say. But what of it?

Mrs. Linde: Has Dr. Rank money?

50 **Nora:** Yes, he has.

Mrs. Linde: And no dependents?

Nora: No, nobody. But . . . ?

Mrs. Linde: And he comes to the house every day?

Nora: Yes, I told you.

55 **Mrs. Linde:** But how can a man of his position want to pester you like this?

Nora: I simply don't understand.

Mrs. Linde: Don't pretend, Nora. Do you think I don't see now who you borrowed the twelve hundred from?

Nora: Are you out of your mind? Do you really think that? A friend of ours who comes here every day? The whole situation would have been absolutely intolerable.

Mrs. Linde: It *really* isn't him?

60 **Nora:** No, I give you my word. It would never have occurred to me for one moment. . . . Anyway, he didn't have the money to lend then. He didn't inherit it till later.

Mrs. Linde: Just as well for you, I'd say, my dear Nora.

Nora: No, it would never have occurred to me to ask Dr. Rank. . . . All the same I'm pretty certain if I were to ask him . . .

Mrs. Linde: But of course you won't.

Nora: No, of course not. I can't ever imagine it being necessary. But I'm quite certain if ever I were to mention it to Dr. Rank . . .

65 **Mrs. Linde:** Behind your husband's back?

Nora: I have to get myself out of that other business. That's also behind his back. I *must* get myself out of that.

Mrs. Linde: Yes, that's what I said yesterday. But . . .

Nora: [*walking up and down*]. A man's better at coping with these things than a woman. . . .

Mrs. Linde: Your own husband, yes.

70 **Nora:** Nonsense! [*Stops.*] When you've paid everything you owe, you do get your IOU back again, don't you?

Mrs. Linde: Of course.

Nora: And you can tear it up into a thousand pieces and burn it—the nasty, filthy thing!

Mrs. Linde: [*looking fixedly at her, puts down her sewing and slowly rises*]. Nora, you are hiding something from me.

Nora: Is it so obvious?

75 **Mrs. Linde:** Something has happened to you since yesterday morning. Nora, what is it?

Nora: [*going towards her*]. Kristine! [*Listens.*] Hush! There's Torvald back. Look, you go and sit in there beside the children for the time being. Torvald can't stand the sight of mending lying about. Get Anne Marie to help you.

Mrs. Linde: [*gathering a lot of things together*]. All right, but I'm not leaving until we have thrashed this thing out.

[*She goes into the room, left; at the same time Helmer comes in from the hall.*]

Nora: [*goes to meet him*]. I've been longing for you to be back, Torvald, dear.

Helmer: Was that the dressmaker . . . ?

80 **Nora:** No, it was Kristine; she's helping me with my costume. I think it's going to look very nice. . . .

Helmer: Wasn't that a good idea of mine, now?

Nora: Wonderful! But wasn't it also nice of me to let you have your way?

Helmer: [*taking her under the chin*]. Nice of you—because you let your husband have his way? All right, you little rogue, I know you didn't mean it that way. But I don't want to disturb you. You'll be wanting to try the costume on, I suppose.

Nora: And I dare say you've got work to do?

85 **Helmer:** Yes. [*Shows her a bundle of papers.*] Look at this. I've been down at the Bank. . . .

[*He turns to go into his study.*]

Nora: Torvald!

Helmer: [*stopping*]. Yes.

Nora: If a little squirrel were to ask ever so nicely . . . ?

Helmer: Well?

90 **Nora:** Would you do something for it?

Helmer: Naturally I would first have to know what it is.

Nora: Please, if only you would let it have its way, and do what it wants, it'd scamper about and do all sorts of marvelous tricks.

Helmer: What is it?

Nora: And the pretty little sky-lark would sing all day long. . . .

95 **Helmer:** Huh! It does that anyway.

Nora: I'd pretend I was an elfin child and dance a moonlight dance for you, Torvald.

Helmer: Nora—I hope it's not that business you started on this morning?

Nora: [*coming closer*]. Yes, it is, Torvald. I implore you!

Helmer: You have the nerve to bring that up again?

100 **Nora:** Yes, yes, you *must* listen to me. You must let Krogstad keep his job at the Bank.

Helmer: My dear Nora, I'm giving his job to Mrs. Linde.

Nora: Yes, it's awfully sweet of you. But couldn't you get rid of somebody else in the office instead of Krogstad?

Helmer: This really is the most incredible obstinacy! Just because you go and make some thoughtless promise to put in a good word for him, you expect me . . .

Nora: It's not that, Torvald. It's for your own sake. That man writes in all the nastiest papers, you told me that yourself. He can do you no end of harm. He terrifies me to death. . . .

105   **Helmer:** Aha, now I see. It's your memories of what happened before that are frightening you.

Nora: What do you mean?

Helmer: It's your father you are thinking of.

Nora: Yes . . . yes, that's right. You remember all the nasty insinuations those wicked people put in the papers about Daddy? I honestly think they would have had him dismissed if the Ministry hadn't sent you down to investigate, and you hadn't been so kind and helpful.

Helmer: My dear little Nora, there is a considerable difference between your father and me. Your father's professional conduct was not entirely above suspicion. Mine is. And I hope it's going to stay that way as long as I hold this position.

110   **Nora:** But nobody knows what some of these evil people are capable of. Things could be so nice and pleasant for us here, in the peace and quiet of our home—you and me and the children, Torvald! That's why I implore you. . . .

Helmer: The more you plead for him, the more impossible you make it for me to keep him on. It's already known down at the bank that I am going to give Krogstad his notice. If it ever got around that the new manager had been talked over by his wife. . . .

Nora: What of it?

Helmer: Oh, nothing! As long as the little woman gets her own stubborn way . . . ! Do you want me to make myself a laughing stock in the office? . . . Give the people the idea that I am susceptible to any kind of outside pressure? You can imagine how soon I'd feel the consequences of that! Anyway, there's one other consideration that makes it impossible to have Krogstad in the bank as long as I am manager.

Nora: What's that?

115   **Helmer:** At a pinch I might have overlooked his past lapses. . . .

Nora: Of course you could, Torvald!

Helmer: And I'm told he's not bad at his job, either. But we knew each other rather well when we were younger. It was one of those rather rash friendships that prove embarrassing in later life. There's no reason why you shouldn't know we were once on terms of some familiarity. And he, in his tactless way, makes no attempt to hide the fact, particularly when other people are present. On the contrary, he thinks he has every right to treat me as an equal, with his "Torvald this" and "Torvald that" every time he opens his mouth. I find it extremely irritating, I can tell you. He would make my position at the bank absolutely intolerable.

Nora: Torvald, surely you aren't serious?

Helmer: Oh? Why not?

120   **Nora:** Well, it's all so petty.

Helmer: What's that you say? Petty? Do you think I'm petty?

Nora: No, not at all, Torvald dear! And that's why . . .

Helmer: Doesn't make any difference! . . . You call my motives petty; so I must be petty too. Petty! Indeed! Well, we'll put a stop to that, once and for all. [*He opens the hall door and calls.*] Helene!

Nora: What are you going to do?

125 **Helmer:** *[searching among his papers]*. Settle things. *[The Maid comes in.]* See this letter? I
want you to take it down at once. Get hold of a messenger and get him to deliver it.
Quickly. The address is on the outside. There's the money.

Maid: Very good, sir. *[She goes with the letter.]*

Helmer: *[putting his papers together]*. There now, my stubborn little miss.

Nora: *[breathless]*. Torvald . . . what was that letter?

Helmer: Krogstad's notice.

130 **Nora:** Get it back, Torvald! There's still time! Oh, Torvald, get it back! Please for my sake,
for your sake, for the sake of the children! Listen, Torvald, please! You don't realize
what it can do to us.

Helmer: Too late.

Nora: Yes, too late.

Helmer: My dear Nora, I forgive you this anxiety of yours, although it is actually a bit of an
insult. Oh, but it is, I tell you! It's hardly flattering to suppose that anything this miserable pen-pusher wrote could frighten *me*! But I forgive you all the same, because it is
rather a sweet way of showing how much you love me. *[He takes her in his arms.]* This
is how things must be, my own darling Nora. When it comes to the point, I've enough
strength and enough courage, believe me, for whatever happens. You'll find I'm man
enough to take everything on myself.

Nora: *[terrified]*. What do you mean?

135 **Helmer:** Everything, I said. . . .

Nora: *[in command of herself]*. That is something you shall never, never do.

Helmer: All right, then we'll share it, Nora—as man and wife. That's what we'll do. *[Caressing
her.]* Does that make you happy now? There, there, don't look at me with those eyes, like
a little frightened dove. The whole thing is sheer imagination.—Why don't you run
through the tarantella and try out the tambourine? I'll go into my study and shut both the
doors, then I won't hear anything. You can make all the noise you want. *[Turns in the doorway.]* And when Rank comes, tell him where he can find me.

[He nods to her, goes with his papers into his room, and shuts the door behind him.]

Nora: *[wild-eyed with terror, stands as though transfixed]*. He's quite capable of doing it! He
would do it! No matter what, he'd do it.—No, never in this world! Anything but that!
Help? Some way out . . . ? *[The door-bell rings in the hall.]* Dr. Rank . . . ! Anything but that,
anything! *[She brushes her hands over her face, pulls herself together and opens the door into the
hall. Dr. Rank is standing outside hanging up his fur coat. During what follows it begins to grow
dark.]* Hello, Dr. Rank. I recognized your ring. Do you mind not going in to Torvald just
yet, I think he's busy.

Rank: And you?

[Dr. Rank comes into the room and she closes the door behind him.]

140 **Nora:** Oh, you know very well I've always got time for you.

Rank: Thank you. A privilege I shall take advantage of as long as I am able.

Nora: What do you mean—as long as you are able?

Rank: Does that frighten you?

Nora: Well, its just that it sounds so strange. Is anything likely to happen?

145 **Rank:** Only what I have long expected. But I didn't think it would come quite so
soon.

Nora: *[catching at his arm]*. What have you found out? Dr. Rank, you must tell me!

Rank: I'm slowly sinking. There's nothing to be done about it.

Nora: *[with a sigh of relief]*. Oh, it's *you* you're . . . ?

Rank: Who else? No point in deceiving oneself. I am the most wretched of all my patients, Mrs. Helmer. These last few days I've made a careful analysis of my internal economy. Bankrupt! Within a month I shall probably be lying rotting up there in the churchyard.

150 **Nora:** Come now, what a ghastly thing to say!

Rank: The whole damned thing is ghastly. But the worst thing is all the ghastliness that has to be gone through first. I only have one more test to make; and when that's done I'll know pretty well when the final disintegration will start. There's something I want to ask you. Helmer is a sensitive soul; he loathes anything that's ugly. I don't want him visiting me. . . .

Nora: But Dr. Rank. . . .

Rank: On no account must he. I won't have it. I'll lock the door on him.—As soon as I'm absolutely certain of the worst, I'll send you my visiting card with a black cross on it. You'll know then the final horrible disintegration has begun.

Nora: Really, you are being quite absurd today. And here I was hoping you would be in a thoroughly good mood.

155 **Rank:** With death staring me in the face? Why should I suffer for another man's sins? What justice is there in that? Somewhere, somehow, every single family must be suffering some such cruel retribution. . . .

Nora: [stopping up her ears]. Rubbish! Do cheer up!

Rank: Yes, really the whole thing's nothing but a huge joke. My poor innocent spine must do penance for my father's gay subaltern life.

Nora: [by the table, left]. Wasn't he rather partial to asparagus and pâté de foie gras?

Rank: Yes, he was. And truffles.

160 **Nora:** Truffles, yes. And oysters, too, I believe?

Rank: Yes, oysters, oysters, of course.

Nora: And all the port and champagne that goes with them. It does seem a pity all these delicious things should attack the spine.

Rank: Especially when they attack a poor spine that never had any fun out of them.

Nora: Yes, that is an awful pity.

165 **Rank:** [looks at her sharply]. Hm . . .

Nora: [after a pause]. Why did you smile?

Rank: No, it was you who laughed.

Nora: No, it was you who smiled, Dr. Rank!

Rank: [getting up]. You are a bigger rascal than I thought you were.

170 **Nora:** I feel full of mischief today.

Rank: So it seems.

Nora: [putting her hands on his shoulders]. Dear, dear Dr. Rank, you mustn't go and die on Torvald and me.

Rank: You wouldn't miss me for long. When you are gone, you are soon forgotten.

Nora: [looking at him anxiously]. Do you think so?

175 **Rank:** People make new contacts, then . . .

Nora: Who make new contacts?

Rank: Both you and Helmer will, when I'm gone. You yourself are already well on the way, it seems to me. What was this Mrs. Linde doing here last night?

Nora: Surely you aren't jealous of poor Kristine?

Rank: Yes, I am. She'll be my successor in this house. When I'm done for, I can see this woman . . .

180 **Nora:** Hush! Don't talk so loud, she's in there.

Rank: Today as well? There you are, you see!

Nora: Just to do some sewing on my dress. Good Lord, how absurd you are! *[She sits down on the sofa.]* Now Dr. Rank, cheer up. You'll see tomorrow how nicely I can dance. And you can pretend I'm doing it just for you—and for Torvald as well, of course. *[She takes various things out of the box.]* Come here, Dr. Rank. I want to show you something.

Rank: *[sits]*. What is it?

Nora: Look!

185 **Rank:** Silk stockings.

Nora: Flesh-colored! Aren't they lovely! Of course, it's dark here now, but tomorrow. . . . No, no, no, you can only look at the feet. Oh well, you might as well see a bit higher up, too.

Rank: Hm . . .

Nora: Why are you looking so critical? Don't you think they'll fit?

Rank: I couldn't possibly offer any informed opinion about that.

190 **Nora:** *[looks at him for a moment]*. Shame on you. *[Hits him lightly across the ear with the stockings.]* Take that! *[Folds them up again.]*

Rank: And what other delights am I to be allowed to see?

Nora: Not another thing. You are too naughty. *[She hums a little and searches among her things.]*

Rank: *[after a short pause]*. Sitting here so intimately like this with you, I can't imagine . . . I simply cannot conceive what would have become of me if I had never come to this house.

Nora: *[smiles]*. Yes, I rather think you do enjoy coming here.

195 **Rank:** *[in a low voice, looking fixedly ahead]*. And the thought of having to leave it all . . .

Nora: Nonsense. You aren't leaving.

Rank: *[in the same tone]*. . . . without being able to leave behind even the slightest token of gratitude, hardly a fleeting regret even . . . nothing but an empty place to be filled by the first person that comes along.

Nora: Supposing I were to ask you to . . . ? No . . .

Rank: What?

200 **Nora:** . . . to show me the extent of your friendship . . .

Rank: Yes?

Nora: I mean . . . to do me a tremendous favor. . . .

Rank: Would you really, for once, give me that pleasure?

Nora: You have no idea what it is.

205 **Rank:** All right, tell me.

Nora: No, really I can't, Dr. Rank. It's altogether too much to ask . . . because I need your advice and help as well. . . .

Rank: The more the better. I cannot imagine what you have in mind. But tell me anyway. You do trust me, don't you?

Nora: Yes, I trust you more than anybody I know. You are my best and my most faithful friend. I know that. So I will tell you. Well then, Dr. Rank, there is something you must help me to prevent. You know how deeply, how passionately Torvald is in love with me. He would never hesitate for a moment to sacrifice his life for my sake.

Rank: *[bending towards her]*. Nora . . . do you think he's the only one who . . . ?

210 **Nora:** *[stiffening slightly]*. Who . . . ?

Rank: Who wouldn't gladly give his life for your sake.

Nora: *[sadly]*. Oh!

Rank: I swore to myself you would know before I went. I'll never have a better opportunity. Well, Nora! Now you know. And now you know too that you can confide in me as in nobody else.

Nora: [rises and speaks evenly and calmly]. Let me past.

215 **Rank:** [makes way for her, but remains seated]. Nora . . .

Nora: [in the hall doorway]. Helene, bring the lamp in, please. [Walks over to the stove.] Oh, my dear Dr. Rank, that really was rather horrid of you.

Rank: [getting up]. That I have loved you every bit as much as anybody? Is that horrid?

Nora: No, but that you had to go and tell me. When it was all so unnecessary. . . .

Rank: What do you mean? Did you know . . . ?

[The Maid comes in with the lamp, puts in on the table, and goes out again.]

220 **Rank:** Nora . . . Mrs. Helmer . . . I'm asking you if you knew?

Nora: How can I tell whether I did or didn't. I simply can't tell you. . . . Oh, how could you be so clumsy, Dr. Rank! When everything was so nice.

Rank: Anyway, you know now that I'm at your service, body and soul. So you can speak out.

Nora: [looking at him]. After this?

Rank: I beg you to tell me what it is.

225 **Nora:** I can tell you nothing now.

Rank: You must. You can't torment me like this. Give me a chance—I'll do anything that's humanly possible.

Nora: You can do nothing for me now. Actually, I don't really need any help. It's all just my imagination, really it is. Of course! [She sits down in the rocking chair, looks at him and smiles.] I must say, you are a nice one, Dr. Rank! Don't you feel ashamed of yourself, now the lamp's been brought in?

Rank: No, not exactly. But perhaps I ought to go—for good?

Nora: No, you mustn't do that. You must keep coming just as you've always done. You know very well Torvald would miss you terribly.

230 **Rank:** And you?

Nora: I always think it's tremendous fun having you.

Rank: That's exactly what gave me the wrong ideas. I just can't puzzle you out. I often used to feel you'd just as soon be with me as with Helmer.

Nora: Well, you see, there are those people you love and those people you'd almost rather be with.

Rank: Yes, there's something in that.

235 **Nora:** When I was a girl at home, I loved Daddy best, of course. But I also thought it great fun if I could slip into the maids' room. For one thing they never preached at me. And they always talked about such exciting things.

Rank: Aha! So it's their role I've taken over!

Nora: [jumps up and crosses to him]. Oh, my dear, kind Dr. Rank, I didn't mean that at all. But you can see how it's a bit with Torvald as it was with Daddy. . . .

[The Maid comes in from the hall.]

Maid: Please, ma'am . . . !

[She whispers and hands her a card.]

Nora: [glances at the card]. Ah!

[She puts it in her pocket.]

240 **Rank:** Anything wrong?

Nora: No, no, not at all. It's just . . . it's my new costume. . . .

Rank: How is that? There's your costume in there.

Nora: That one, yes. But this is another one. I've ordered it. Torvald mustn't hear about it. . . .

Rank: Ah, so that's the big secret, is it!

245 **Nora:** Yes, that's right. Just go in and see him, will you? He's in the study. Keep him occu-
     pied for the time being. . . .

Rank: Don't worry. He shan't escape me.

   [He goes into Helmer's study.]

Nora: *[to the Maid].* Is he waiting in the kitchen?

Maid: Yes, he came up the back stairs. . . .

Nora: But didn't you tell him somebody was here?

250 **Maid:** Yes, but it was no good.

Nora: Won't he go?

Maid: No, he won't till he's seen you.

Nora: Let him in, then. But quietly. Helene, you mustn't tell anybody about this. It's a sur-
     prise for my husband.

Maid: I understand, ma'am. . . .

   [She goes out.]

255 **Nora:** Here it comes! What I've been dreading! No, no, it can't happen, it *can't* happen.

   [She walks over and bolts Helmer's door. The Maid opens the hall door for Krogstad and shuts
   it again behind him. He is wearing a fur coat, overshoes, and a fur cap.]

Nora: *[goes towards him].* Keep your voice down, my husband is at home.

Krogstad: What if he is?

Nora: What do you want with me?

Krogstad: To find out something.

260 **Nora:** Hurry, then. What is it?

Krogstad: You know I've been given notice.

Nora: I couldn't prevent it, Mr. Krogstad. I did my utmost for you, but it was no use.

Krogstad: Has your husband so little affection for you? He knows what I can do to you, yet
     he dares. . . .

Nora: You don't imagine he knows about it!

265 **Krogstad:** No, I didn't imagine he did. It didn't seem a bit like my good friend Torvald
     Helmer to show that much courage. . . .

Nora: Mr. Krogstad, I must ask you to show some respect for my husband.

Krogstad: Oh, sure! All due respect! But since you are so anxious to keep this business
     quiet, Mrs. Helmer, I take it you now have a rather clearer idea of just what it is you've
     done, than you had yesterday.

Nora: Clearer than *you* could ever have given me.

Krogstad: Yes, being as I am such a rotten lawyer. . . .

270 **Nora:** What do you want with me?

Krogstad: I just wanted to see how things stood, Mrs. Helmer. I've been thinking about
     you all day. Even a mere money-lender, a hack journalist, a—well, even somebody like
     me has a bit of what you might call feeling.

Nora: Show it then. Think of my little children.

Krogstad: Did you or your husband think of mine? But what does it matter now? There
     was just one thing I wanted to say: you needn't take this business too seriously. I shan't
     start any proceedings, for the present.

Nora: Ah, I knew you wouldn't.

275 **Krogstad:** The whole thing can be arranged quite amicably. Nobody need know. Just the
     three of us.

Nora: My husband must never know.

Krogstad: How can you prevent it? Can you pay off the balance?

Nora: No, not immediately.

Krogstad: Perhaps you've some way of getting hold of the money in the next few days.

280 **Nora:** None I want to make use of.

Krogstad: Well, it wouldn't have been very much help to you if you had. Even if you stood there with the cash in your hand and to spare, you still wouldn't get your IOU back from me now.

Nora: What are you going to do with it?

Krogstad: Just keep it—have it in my possession. Nobody who isn't implicated need know about it. So if you are thinking of trying any desperate remedies . . .

Nora: Which I am. . . .

285 **Krogstad:** . . . if you happen to be thinking of running away . . .

Nora: Which I am!

Krogstad: . . . or anything worse . . .

Nora: How did you know?

Krogstad: . . . forget it!

290 **Nora:** How did you know I was thinking of *that?*

Krogstad: Most of us think of *that,* to begin with. I did, too; but I didn't have the courage. . . .

Nora: [*tonelessly*]. I haven't either.

Krogstad: [*relieved*]. So you haven't the courage either, eh?

Nora: No, I haven't! I haven't!

295 **Krogstad:** It would also be very stupid. There'd only be the first domestic storm to get over. . . . I've got a letter to your husband in my pocket here. . . .

Nora: And it's all in there?

Krogstad: In as tactful a way as possible.

Nora: [*quickly*]. He must never read that letter. Tear it up. I'll find the money somehow.

Krogstad: Excuse me, Mrs. Helmer, but I've just told you. . . .

300 **Nora:** I'm not talking about the money I owe you. I want to know how much you are demanding from my husband, and I'll get the money.

Krogstad: I want no money from your husband.

Nora: What do you want?

Krogstad: I'll tell you. I want to get on my feet again, Mrs. Helmer; I want to get to the top. And your husband is going to help me. For the last eighteen months I've gone straight; all that time it's been hard going; I was content to work my way up, step by step. Now I'm being kicked out, and I won't stand for being taken back again as an act of charity. I'm going to get to the top, I tell you. I'm going back into that bank—with a better job. Your husband is going to create a new vacancy, just for me. . . .

Nora: He'll never do that!

305 **Krogstad:** He will do it. I know him. He'll do it without so much as a whimper. And once I'm in there with him, you'll see what's what. In less than a year I'll be his right-hand man. It'll be Nils Krogstad, not Torvald Helmer, who'll be running that bank.

Nora: You'll never live to see that day!

Krogstad: You mean you . . . ?

Nora: Now I have the courage.

Krogstad: You can't frighten me! A precious pampered little thing like you. . . .

310 **Nora:** I'll show you! I'll show you!

Krogstad: Under the ice, maybe? Down in the cold, black water? Then being washed up in the spring, bloated, hairless, unrecognizable. . . .

Nora: You can't frighten me.

Krogstad: You can't frighten me, either. People don't do that sort of thing, Mrs. Helmer. There wouldn't be any point to it, anyway, I'd still have him in my pocket.

Nora: Afterwards? When I'm no longer . . .

315 **Krogstad:** Aren't you forgetting that your reputation would then be entirely in my hands? *[Nora stands looking at him, speechless.]* Well, I've warned you. Don't do anything silly. When Helmer gets my letter, I expect to hear from him. And don't forget: it's him who is forcing me off the straight and narrow again, your own husband! That's something I'll never forgive him for. Goodbye, Mrs. Helmer.

[He goes out through the hall. Nora crosses to the door, opens it slightly, and listens.]

Nora: He's going. He hasn't left the letter. No, no, that would be impossible! *[Opens the door further and further.]* What's he doing? He's stopped outside. He's not going down the stairs. Has he changed his mind? Is he . . . ? [A letter falls into the letter-box. Then Krogstad's footsteps are heard receding as he walks downstairs. Nora gives a stifled cry, runs across the room to the sofa table; pause.] In the letter-box. *[She creeps stealthily across to the hall door.]* There it is! Torvald, Torvald! It's hopeless now!

Mrs. Linde: *[comes into the room, left, carrying the costume]*. There, I think that's everything. Shall we try it on?

Nora: *[in a low, hoarse voice]*. Kristine, come here.

Mrs. Linde: *[throws the dress down on the sofa]*. What's wrong with you? You look upset.

320 **Nora:** Come here. Do you see that letter? *There*, look! Through the glass in the letter-box.

Mrs. Linde: Yes, yes, I can see it.

Nora: It's a letter from Krogstad.

Mrs. Linde: Nora! It was Krogstad who lent you the money!

Nora: Yes. And now Torvald will get to know everything.

325 **Mrs. Linde:** Believe me, Nora, it's best for you both.

Nora: But there's more to it than that. I forged a signature. . . .

Mrs. Linde: Heavens above!

Nora: Listen, I want to tell you something, Kristine, so you can be my witness.

Mrs. Linde: What do you mean "witness"? What do you want me to . . . ?

330 **Nora:** If I should go mad . . . which might easily happen . . .

Mrs. Linde: Nora!

Nora: Or if anything happened to me . . . which meant I couldn't be here. . . .

Mrs. Linde: Nora, Nora! Are you out of your mind?

Nora: And if somebody else wanted to take it all upon himself, the whole blame, you understand. . . .

335 **Mrs. Linde:** Yes, yes. But what makes you think . . . ?

Nora: Then you must testify that it isn't true, Kristine. I'm not out of my mind; I'm quite sane now. And I tell you this: nobody else knew anything, I alone was responsible for the whole thing. Remember that!

Mrs. Linde: I will. But I don't understand a word of it.

Nora: Why should you? You see something miraculous is going to happen.

Mrs. Linde: Something miraculous?

340 **Nora:** Yes, a miracle. But something so terrible as well, Kristine—oh, it must *never* happen, not for anything.

Mrs. Linde: I'm going straight over to talk to Krogstad.

Nora: Don't go. He'll only do you harm.

Mrs. Linde: There was a time when he would have done anything for me.

Nora: Him!

345   **Mrs. Linde:** Where does he live?

      Nora: How do I know . . . ? Wait a minute. *[She feels in her pocket.]* Here's his card. But the letter, the letter . . . !

      Helmer: *[from his study, knocking on the door].* Nora!

      Nora: *[cries out in terror].* What's that? What do you want?

      Helmer: Don't be frightened. We're not coming in. You've locked the door. Are you trying on?

350   **Nora:** Yes, yes, I'm trying on. It looks so nice on me, Torvald.

      Mrs. Linde: *[who has read the card].* He lives just round the corner.

      Nora: It's no use. It's hopeless. The letter is there in the box.

      Mrs. Linde: Your husband keeps the key?

      Nora: Always.

355   **Mrs. Linde:** Krogstad must ask for his letter back unread, he must find some sort of excuse. . . .

      Nora: But this is just the time that Torvald generally . . .

      Mrs. Linde: Put him off! Go in and keep him busy. I'll be back as soon as I can.

[She goes out hastily by the hall door. Nora walks over to Helmer's door, opens it, and peeps in.]

      Nora: Torvald!

      Helmer: *[in the study].* Well, can a man get into his own living room again now? Come along, Rank, now we'll see . . . *[In the doorway.]* But what's this?

360   **Nora:** What, Torvald dear?

      Helmer: Rank led me to expect some kind of marvelous transformation.

      Rank: *[in the doorway].* That's what I thought too, but I must have been mistaken.

      Nora: I'm not showing myself off to anybody before tomorrow.

      Helmer: Nora dear, you look tired. You haven't been practicing too hard?

365   **Nora:** No, I haven't practiced at all yet.

      Helmer: You'll have to, though.

      Nora: Yes, I certainly must, Torvald. But I just can't get anywhere without your help: I've completely forgotten it.

      Helmer: We'll soon polish it up.

      Nora: Yes, do help me, Torvald. Promise? I'm so nervous. All those people. . . . You must devote yourself exclusively to me this evening. Pens away! Forget all about the office! Promise me, Torvald dear!

370   **Helmer:** I promise. This evening I am wholly and entirely at your service . . . helpless little thing that you are. Oh, but while I remember, I'll just look first . . .

[He goes towards the hall door.]

      Nora: What do you want out there?

      Helmer: Just want to see if there are any letters.

      Nora: No, don't, Torvald!

      Helmer: Why not?

375   **Nora:** Torvald, *please!* There aren't any.

      Helmer: Just let me see.

[He starts to go. Nora, at the piano, plays the opening bars of the tarantella.]

      Helmer: *[at the door, stops].* Aha!

      Nora: I shan't be able to dance tomorrow if I don't rehearse it with you.

      Helmer: *[walks to her].* Are you really so nervous, Nora dear?

380 **Nora:** Terribly nervous. Let me run through it now. There's still time before supper. Come and sit here and play for me, Torvald dear. Tell me what to do, keep me right—as you always do.

Helmer: Certainly, with pleasure, if that's what you want.

[*He sits at the piano. Nora snatches the tambourine out of the box, and also a long gaily-colored shawl which she drapes around herself, then with a bound she leaps forward.*]

Nora: [*shouts*]. Now play for me! Now I'll dance!

[*Helmer plays and Nora dances; Dr. Rank stands at the piano behind Helmer and looks on.*]

Helmer: [*playing*]. Not so fast! Not so fast!

Nora: I can't help it.

385 **Helmer:** Not so wild, Nora!

Nora: This is how it has to be.

Helmer: [*stops*]. No, no, that won't do at all.

Nora: [*laughs and swings the tambourine*]. Didn't I tell you?

Rank: Let me play for her.

390 **Helmer:** [*gets up*]. Yes, do. Then I'll be better able to tell her what to do.

[*Rank sits down at the piano and plays. Nora dances more and more wildly. Helmer stands by the stove giving her repeated directions as she dances; she does not seem to hear them. Her hair comes undone and falls about her shoulders; she pays no attention and goes on dancing. Mrs. Linde enters.*]

Mrs. Linde: [*standing as though spellbound in the doorway*]. Ah . . . !

Nora: [*dancing*]. See what fun we are having, Kristine.

Helmer: But my dear darling Nora, you are dancing as though your life depended on it.

Nora: It does.

395 **Helmer:** Stop, Rank! This is sheer madness. Stop, I say.

[*Rank stops playing and Nora comes to a sudden halt.*]

Helmer: [*crosses to her*]. I would never have believed it. You have forgotten everything I ever taught you.

Nora: [*throwing away the tambourine*]. There you are, you see.

Helmer: Well, some more instruction is certainly needed there.

Nora: Yes, you see how necessary it is. You must go on coaching me right up to the last minute. Promise me, Torvald?

400 **Helmer:** You can rely on me.

Nora: You mustn't think about anything else but me until after tomorrow . . . mustn't open any letters . . . mustn't touch the letter-box.

Helmer: Ah, you are still frightened of what that man might . . .

Nora: Yes, yes, I am.

Helmer: I can see from your face there's already a letter there from him.

405 **Nora:** I don't know. I think so. But you mustn't read anything like that now. We don't want anything horrid coming between us until all this is over.

Rank: [*softly to Helmer*]. I shouldn't cross her.

Helmer: [*puts his arm around her*]. The child must have her way. But tomorrow night, when your dance is done. . . .

Nora: Then you are free.

Maid: [*in the doorway, right*]. Dinner is served, madam.

410 **Nora:** We'll have champagne, Helene.

Maid: Very good, madam.

[She goes.]

Helmer: Aha! It's to be quite a banquet, eh?

Nora: With champagne flowing until dawn. *[Shouts.]* And some macaroons, Helene . . . lots of them, for once in a while.

Helmer: *[seizing her hands].* Now, now, not so wild and excitable! Let me see you being my own little singing bird again.

415 **Nora:** Oh yes, I will. And if you'll just go in . . . you, too, Dr. Rank. Kristine, you must help me to do my hair.

Rank: *[softly, as they leave].* There isn't anything . . . anything as it were, impending, is there?

Helmer: No, not at all, my dear fellow. It's nothing but these childish fears I was telling you about.

[They go out to the right.]

Nora: Well?

Mrs. Linde: He's left town.

420 **Nora:** I saw it in your face.

Mrs. Linde: He's coming back tomorrow evening. I left a note for him.

Nora: You shouldn't have done that. You must let things take their course. Because really it's a case for rejoicing, waiting like this for the miracle.

Mrs. Linde: What is it you are waiting for?

Nora: Oh, you wouldn't understand. Go and join the other two. I'll be there in a minute.

[Mrs. Linde goes into the dining-room. Nora stands for a moment as though to collect herself, then looks at her watch.]

425 **Nora:** Five. Seven hours to midnight. Then twenty-four hours till the next midnight. Then the tarantella will be over. Twenty-four and seven? Thirty-one hours to live.

Helmer: *[in the doorway, right].* What's happened to our little sky-lark?

Nora: *[running towards him with open arms].* Here she is!

Act III

The same room. The round table has been moved to the center of the room, and the chairs placed round it. A lamp is burning on the table. The door to the hall stands open. Dance music can be heard coming from the floor above. Mrs. Linde is sitting by the table, idly turning over the pages of a book; she tries to read, but does not seem able to concentrate. Once or twice she listens, tensely, for a sound at the front door.

Mrs. Linde: *[looking at her watch].* Still not here. There isn't much time left. I only hope he hasn't . . . *[She listens again.]* Ah, there he is. *[She goes out into the hall, and cautiously opens the front door. Soft footsteps can be heard on the stairs. She whispers.]* Come in. There's nobody here.

Krogstad: *[in the doorway].* I found a note from you at home. What does it all mean?

Mrs. Linde: I *had* to talk to you.

Krogstad: Oh? And did it have to be here, in this house?

5 **Mrs. Linde:** It wasn't possible over at my place, it hasn't a separate entrance. Come in. We are quite alone. The maid's asleep and the Helmers are at a party upstairs.

Krogstad: *[comes into the room].* Well, well! So the Helmers are out dancing tonight! Really?

Mrs. Linde: Yes, why not?

Krogstad: Why not indeed!

Mrs. Linde: Well then, Nils. Let's talk.

10 **Krogstad:** Have we two anything more to talk about?

Mrs. Linde: We have a great deal to talk about.

Krogstad: I shouldn't have thought so.

Mrs. Linde: That's because you never really understood me.

Krogstad: What else was there to understand, apart from the old, old story? A heartless
woman throws a man over the moment something more profitable offers itself.

15 **Mrs. Linde:** Do you really think I'm so heartless? Do you think I found it easy to break
it off?

Krogstad: Didn't you?

Mrs. Linde: You didn't really believe that?

Krogstad: If that wasn't the case, why did you write to me as you did?

Mrs. Linde: There was nothing else I could do. If I had to make the break, I felt in duty
bound to destroy any feeling that you had for me.

20 **Krogstad:** *[clenching his hands]*. So that's how it was. And all that . . . was for money!

Mrs. Linde: You mustn't forget I had a helpless mother and two young brothers. We couldn't
wait for you, Nils. At that time you hadn't much immediate prospect of anything.

Krogstad: That may be. But you had no right to throw me over for somebody else.

Mrs. Linde: Well, I don't know. Many's the time I've asked myself whether I was justified.

Krogstad: *[more quietly]*. When I lost you, it was just as if the ground had slipped away
from under my feet. Look at me now: a broken man clinging to the wreck of his life.

25 **Mrs. Linde:** Help might be near.

Krogstad: It was near. Then you came along and got in the way.

Mrs. Linde: Quite without knowing, Nils. I only heard today it's you I'm supposed to be
replacing at the bank.

Krogstad: If you say so, I believe you. But now you do know, aren't you going to
withdraw?

Mrs. Linde: No, that wouldn't benefit you in the slightest.

30 **Krogstad:** Benefit, benefit . . . ! I would do it just the same.

Mrs. Linde: I have learned to go carefully. Life and hard, bitter necessity have taught me
that.

Krogstad: And life has taught me not to believe in pretty speeches.

Mrs. Linde: Then life has taught you a very sensible thing. But deeds are something you
surely must believe in?

Krogstad: How do you mean?

35 **Mrs. Linde:** You said you were like a broken man clinging to the wreck of his life.

Krogstad: And I said it with good reason.

Mrs. Linde: And I am like a broken woman clinging to the wreck of her life. Nobody to
care about, and nobody to care for.

Krogstad: It was your own choice.

Mrs. Linde: At the time there was no other choice.

40 **Krogstad:** Well, what of it?

Mrs. Linde: Nils, what about us two castaways joining forces?

Krogstad: What's that you say?

Mrs. Linde: Two of us on *one* wreck surely stand a better chance than each on his own.

Krogstad: Kristine!

45 **Mrs. Linde:** Why do you suppose I came to town?

Krogstad: You mean, you thought of me?

Mrs. Linde: Without work I couldn't live. All my life I have worked, for as long as I can re-member; that has always been my one great joy. But now I'm completely alone in the world, and feeling horribly empty and forlorn. There's no pleasure in working only for yourself. Nils, give me somebody and something to work for.

Krogstad: I don't believe all this. It's only a woman's hysteria, wanting to be all magnani-mous and self-sacrificing.

Mrs. Linde: Have you ever known me hysterical before?

50 **Krogstad:** Would you really do this? Tell me—do you know all about my past?

Mrs. Linde: Yes.

Krogstad: And you know what people think about me?

Mrs. Linde: Just now you hinted you thought you might have been a different person with me.

Krogstad: I'm convinced I would.

55 **Mrs. Linde:** Couldn't it still happen?

Krogstad: Kristine! You know what you are saying, don't you? Yes, you do. I can see you do. Have you really the courage . . . ?

Mrs. Linde: I need someone to mother, and your children need a mother. We two need each other. Nils, I have faith in what, deep down, you are. With you I can face anything.

Krogstad: [seizing her hands]. Thank you, thank you, Kristine. And I'll soon have every-body looking up to me, or I'll know the reason why. Ah, but I was forgetting. . . .

Mrs. Linde: Hush! The tarantella! You must go!

60 **Krogstad:** Why? What is it?

Mrs. Linde: You hear that dance upstairs? When it's finished they'll be coming.

Krogstad: Yes, I'll go. It's too late to do anything. Of course, you know nothing about what steps I've taken against the Helmers.

Mrs. Linde: Yes, Nils, I do know.

Krogstad: Yet you still want to go on. . . .

65 **Mrs. Linde:** I know how far a man like you can be driven by despair.

Krogstad: Oh, if only I could undo what I've done!

Mrs. Linde: You still can. Your letter is still there in the box.

Krogstad: Are you sure?

Mrs. Linde: Quite sure. But . . .

70 **Krogstad:** [regards her searching]. Is that how things are? You want to save your friend at any price? Tell me straight. Is that it?

Mrs. Linde: When you've sold yourself *once* for other people's sake, you don't do it again.

Krogstad: I shall demand my letter back.

Mrs. Linde: No, no.

Krogstad: Of course I will, I'll wait here till Helmer comes. I'll tell him he has to give me my letter back . . . that it's only about my notice . . . that he mustn't read it. . . .

75 **Mrs. Linde:** No, Nils, don't ask for it back.

Krogstad: But wasn't that the very reason you got me here?

Mrs. Linde: Yes, that was my first terrified reaction. But that was yesterday, and it's quite incredible the things I've witnessed in this house in the last twenty-four hours. Helmer must know everything. This unhappy secret must come out. Those two must have the whole thing out between them. All this secrecy and deception, it just can't go on.

Krogstad: Well, if you want to risk it. . . . But one thing I can do, and I'll do it at once. . . .

Mrs. Linde: [listening]. Hurry! Go, go! The dance has stopped. We aren't safe a moment longer.

80 **Krogstad:** I'll wait for you downstairs.

Mrs. Linde: Yes, do. You must see me home.

Krogstad: I've never been so incredibly happy before.

[He goes out by the front door. The door out into the hall remains standing open.]

Mrs. Linde: *[tidies the room a little and gets her hat and coat ready].* How things change! How things change! Somebody to work for . . . to live for. A home to bring happiness into. Just let me get down to it. . . . I wish they'd come. . . . *[Listens.]* Ah, there they are. . . . Get my things.

[She takes her coat and hat. The voices of Helmer and Nora are heard outside. A key is turned and Helmer pushes Nora almost forcibly into the hall. She is dressed in the Italian costume, with a big black shawl over it. He is in evening dress, and over it a black cloak, open.]

Nora: *[still in the doorway, reluctantly].* No, no, not in here! I want to go back up again. I don't want to leave so early.

85 **Helmer:** But my dearest Nora . . .

Nora: Oh, please, Torvald, I beg you. . . . *Please,* just for another hour.

Helmer: Not another minute, Nora my sweet. You remember what we agreed. There now, come along in. You'll catch cold standing there.

[He leads her, in spite of her resistance, gently but firmly into the room.]

Mrs. Linde: Good evening.

Nora: Kristine!

90 **Helmer:** Why, Mrs. Linde, You here so late?

Mrs. Linde: Yes. You must forgive me but I did so want to see Nora all dressed up.

Nora: Have you been sitting here waiting for me?

Mrs. Linde: Yes, I'm afraid I wasn't in time to catch you before you went upstairs. And I felt I couldn't leave again without seeing you.

Helmer: *[removing Nora's shawl].* Well, take a good look at her. I think I can say she's worth looking at. Isn't she lovely, Mrs. Linde?

95 **Mrs. Linde:** Yes, I must say. . . .

Helmer: Isn't she quite extraordinarily lovely? That's what everybody at the party thought, too. But she's dreadfully stubborn . . . the sweet little thing! And what shall we do about that? Would you believe it, I nearly had to use force to get her away.

Nora: Oh Torvald, you'll be sorry you didn't let me stay, even for half an hour.

Helmer: You hear that, Mrs. Linde? She dances her tarantella, there's wild applause—which was well deserved, although the performance was perhaps rather realistic . . . I mean, rather more so than was strictly necessary from the artistic point of view. But anyway! The main thing is she was a success, a tremendous success. Was I supposed to let her stay after that? Spoil the effect? No, thank you! I took my lovely little Capri girl—my capricious little Capri girl, I might say—by the arm, whisked her once round the room, a curtsey all round, and then—as they say in novels—the beautiful vision vanished. An exit should always be effective, Mrs. Linde. But I just can't get Nora to see that. Phew! It's warm in here. *[He throws his cloak over a chair and opens the door to his study.]* What? It's dark. Oh yes, of course. Excuse me. . . .

[He goes in and lights a few candles.]

Nora: *[quickly, in a breathless whisper].* Well?

100   **Mrs. Linde:** *[softly].* I've spoken to him.
     Nora: And . . . ?
     Mrs. Linde: Nora . . . you must tell your husband everything.
     Nora: *[tonelessly].* I knew it.
     Mrs. Linde: You've got nothing to fear from Krogstad. But you must speak.
105   **Nora:** I won't.
     Mrs. Linde: Then the letter will.
     Nora: Thank you, Kristine. Now I know what's to be done. Hush . . . !
     Helmer: *[comes in again].* Well, Mrs. Linde, have you finished admiring her?
     Mrs. Linde: Yes. And now I must say good night.
110   **Helmer:** Oh, already? Is this yours, this knitting?
     Mrs. Linde: *[takes it].* Yes, thank you. I nearly forgot it.
     Helmer: So you knit, eh?
     Mrs. Linde: Yes.
     Helmer: You should embroider instead, you know.
115   **Mrs. Linde:** Oh? Why?
     Helmer: So much prettier. Watch! You hold the embroidery like this in the left hand, and
         then you take the needle in the right hand, like this, and you describe a long, graceful
         curve. Isn't that right?
     Mrs. Linde: Yes, I suppose so. . . .
     Helmer: Whereas knitting, on the other hand, just can't help being ugly. Look! Arms
         pressed into the sides, the knitting needles going up and down—there's something
         Chinese about it. . . . Ah, that was marvelous champagne they served tonight.
     Mrs. Linde: Well, good night, Nora! And stop being so stubborn.
120   **Helmer:** Well said, Mrs. Linde!
     Mrs. Linde: Good night, Mr. Helmer.
     Helmer: *[accompanying her to the door].* Good night, good night! You'll get home all right, I
         hope? I'd be only too pleased to . . . But you haven't far to walk. Good night, good
         night! *[She goes; he shuts the door behind her and comes in again.]* There we are, got rid of
         her at last. She's a frightful bore, that woman.
     Nora: Are you very tired, Torvald?
     Helmer: Not in the least.
125   **Nora:** Not sleepy?
     Helmer: Not at all. On the contrary, I feel extremely lively. What about you? Yes, you look
         quite tired and sleepy.
     Nora: Yes, I'm very tired. I just want to fall straight off to sleep.
     Helmer: There you are, you see! Wasn't I right in thinking we shouldn't stay any longer.
     Nora: Oh, everything you do is right.
130   **Helmer:** *[kissing her forehead].* There's my little sky-lark talking common sense. Did you no-
         tice how gay Rank was this evening?
     Nora: Oh, was he? I didn't get a chance to talk to him.
     Helmer: I hardly did either. But it's a long time since I saw him in such a good mood.
         [Looks at Nora for a moment or two, then comes nearer her.] Ah, it's wonderful to be back
         in our own home again, and quite alone with you. How irresistibly lovely you are,
         Nora!
     Nora: Don't look at me like that, Torvald!
     Helmer: Can't I look at my most treasured possession? At all this loveliness that's mine and
         mine alone, completely and utterly mine.
135   **Nora:** *[walks round to the other side of the table].* You mustn't talk to me like that tonight.

Helmer: *[following her].* You still have the tarantella in your blood, I see. And that makes you even more desirable. Listen! The guests are beginning to leave now. *[Softly.]* Nora . . . soon the whole house will be silent.

Nora: I should hope so.

Helmer: Of course you do, don't you, Nora my darling? You know, whenever I'm out at a party with you . . . do you know why I never talk to you very much, why I always stand away from you and only steal a quick glance at you now and then . . . do you know why I do that? It's because I'm pretending we are secretly in love, secretly engaged and nobody suspects there is anything between us.

Nora: Yes, yes. I know your thoughts are always with me, of course.

140 **Helmer:** And when it's time to go, and I lay your shawl round those shapely, young shoulders, round the exquisite curve of your neck . . . I pretend that you are my young bride, that we are just leaving our wedding, that I am taking you to our new home for the first time . . . to be alone with you for the first time . . . quite alone with your young and trembling loveliness! All evening I've been longing for you, and nothing else. And as I watched you darting and swaying in the tarantella, my blood was on fire . . . I couldn't bear it any longer . . . and that's why I brought you down here with me so early. . . .

Nora: Go away, Torvald! Please leave me alone. I won't have it.

Helmer: What's this? It's just your little game isn't it, my little Nora. Won't Won't! Am I not your husband . . . ?

[There is a knock on the front door.]

Nora: *[startled].* Listen . . . !

Helmer: *[going towards the hall].* Who's there?

145 **Rank:** *[outside].* It's me. Can I come in for a minute?

Helmer: *[in a low voice, annoyed].* Oh, what does he want now? *[Aloud.]* Wait a moment. *[He walks across and opens the door.]* How nice of you to look in on your way out.

Rank: I fancied I heard your voice and I thought I would just look in. *[He takes a quick glance round.]* Ah yes, this dear, familiar old place! How cozy and comfortable you've got things here, you two.

Helmer: You seemed to be having a pretty good time upstairs yourself.

Rank: Capital! Why shouldn't I? Why not make the most of things in this world? At least as much as one can, and for as long as one can. The wine was excellent. . . .

150 **Helmer:** Especially the champagne.

Rank: You noticed that too, did you? It's incredible the amount I was able to put away.

Nora: Torvald also drank a lot of champagne this evening.

Rank: Oh?

Nora: Yes, and that always makes him quite merry.

155 **Rank:** Well, why shouldn't a man allow himself a jolly evening after a day well spent?

Helmer: Well spent? I'm afraid I can't exactly claim that.

Rank: *[clapping him on the shoulder].* But I can, you see!

Nora: Dr. Rank, am I right in thinking you carried out a certain laboratory test today?

Rank: Exactly.

160 **Helmer:** Look at our little Nora talking about laboratory tests!

Nora: And may I congratulate you on the result?

Rank: You may indeed.

Nora: So it was good?

Rank: The best possible, for both doctor and patient—certainty!

165 **Nora:** *[quickly and searchingly].* Certainty?

Rank: Absolute certainty. So why shouldn't I allow myself a jolly evening after that?
Nora: Quite right, Dr. Rank.
Helmer: I quite agree. As long as you don't suffer for it in the morning.
Rank: Well, you never get anything for nothing in this life.
170 **Nora:** Dr. Rank . . . you are very fond of masquerades, aren't you?
Rank: Yes, when there are plenty of amusing disguises. . . .
Nora: Tell me, what shall we two go as next time?
Helmer: There's frivolity for you . . . thinking about the next time already!
Rank: We two? I'll tell you. You must go as Lady Luck. . . .
175 **Helmer:** Yes, but how do you find a costume to suggest *that*?
Rank: Your wife could simply go in her everyday clothes. . . .
Helmer: That was nicely said. But don't you know what you would be?
Rank: Yes, my dear friend, I know exactly what I shall be.
Helmer: Well?
180 **Rank:** At the next masquerade, I shall be invisible.
Helmer: That's a funny idea!
Rank: There's a big black cloak . . . haven't you heard of the cloak of invisibility? That
comes right down over you, and then nobody can see you.
Helmer: [*suppressing a smile*]. Of course, that's right.
Rank: But I'm clean forgetting what I came for. Helmer, give me a cigar, one of the dark
Havanas.
185 **Helmer:** With the greatest of pleasure.

[*He offers his case.*]

Rank: [*takes one and cuts the end off*]. Thanks.
Nora: [*strikes a match*]. Let me give you a light.
Rank: Thank you. [*She holds out the match and he lights his cigar.*] And now, goodbye!
Helmer: Goodbye, goodbye, my dear fellow!
190 **Nora:** Sleep well, Dr. Rank.
Rank: Thank you for that wish.
Nora: Wish me the same.
Rank: You? All right, if you want me to. . . . Sleep well. And thanks for the light.

[*He nods to them both, and goes.*]

Helmer: [*subdued*]. He's had a lot to drink.
195 **Nora:** [*absently*]. Very likely.

[*Helmer takes a bunch of keys out of his pocket and goes out into the hall.*]

Nora: Torvald . . . what do you want there?
Helmer: I must empty the letter-box, it's quite full. There'll be no room for the papers in
the morning. . . .
Nora: Are you going to work tonight?
Helmer: You know very well I'm not. Hello, what's this? Somebody's been at the lock.
200 **Nora:** At the lock?
Helmer: Yes, I'm sure of it. Why should that be? I'd hardly have thought the maids . . . ?
Here's a broken hair-pin. Nora, it's one of yours. . . .
Nora: [*quickly*]. It must have been the children. . . .
Helmer: Then you'd better tell them not to. Ah . . . there . . . I've managed to get it open.
[*He takes the things out and shouts into the kitchen.*] Helene! . . . Helene, put the light out
in the hall. [*He comes into the room again with the letters in his hand and shuts the hall
door.*] Look how it all mounts up. [*Runs through them.*] What's this?

Nora: The letter! Oh no, Torvald, no!

205 **Helmer:** Two visiting cards . . . from Dr. Rank.

Nora: From Dr. Rank?

Helmer: *[looking at them].* Dr. Rank, Medical Practitioner. They were on top. He must have put them in as he left.

Nora: Is there anything on them?

Helmer: There's a black cross above his name. Look. What an uncanny idea. It's just as if he were announcing his own death.

210 **Nora:** He is.

Helmer: What? What do you know about it? Has he said anything to you?

Nora: Yes. He said when these cards came, he would have taken his last leave of us. He was going to shut himself up and die.

Helmer: Poor fellow! Of course I knew we couldn't keep him with us very long. But so soon. . . . And hiding himself away like a wounded animal.

Nora: When it has to happen, it's best that it should happen without words. Don't you think so, Torvald?

215 **Helmer:** *[walking up and down].* He had grown so close to us. I don't think I can imagine him gone. His suffering and his loneliness seemed almost to provide a background of dark cloud to the sunshine of our lives. Well, perhaps it's all for the best. For him at any rate. *[Pauses.]* And maybe for us as well, Nora. Now there's just the two of us. *[Puts his arms around her.]* Oh, my darling wife, I can't hold you close enough. You know, Nora . . . many's the time I wish you were threatened by some terrible danger so I could risk everything, body and soul, for your sake.

Nora: *[tears herself free and says firmly and decisively].* Now you must read your letters, Torvald.

Helmer: No, no, not tonight. I want to be with you, my darling wife.

Nora: Knowing all the time your friend is dying . . . ?

Helmer: You are right. It's been a shock to both of us. This ugly thing has come between us . . . thoughts of death and decay. We must try to free ourselves from it. Until then . . . we shall go our separate ways.

220 **Nora:** *[her arms round his neck].* Torvald . . . good night! Good night!

Helmer: *[kisses her forehead].* Goodnight, my little singing bird. Sleep well, Nora, I'll just read through my letters.

[He takes the letters into his room and shuts the door behind him.]

Nora: *[gropes around her, wild-eyed, seizes Helmer's cloak, wraps it round herself, and whispers quickly, hoarsely, spasmodically].* Never see him again. Never, never, never. *[Throws her shawl over her head.]* And never see the children again either. Never, never. Oh, that black icy water. Oh, that bottomless . . . ! If only it were all over! He's got it now. Now he's reading it. Oh no, no! Not yet! Torvald, goodbye . . . and my children. . . .

[She rushes out in the direction of the hall; at the same moment Helmer flings open his door and stands there with an open letter in his hand.]

Helmer: Nora!

Nora: *[shrieks].* Ah!

225 **Helmer:** What is this? Do you know what is in this letter?

Nora: Yes, I know. Let me go! Let me out!

Helmer: *[holds her back].* Where are you going?

Nora: *[trying to tear herself free].* You mustn't try to save me, Torvald!

Helmer: [reels back]. True! Is it true what he writes? How dreadful! No, no, it can't possibly be true.

230 **Nora:** It *is* true. I loved you more than anything else in the world.

Helmer: Don't come to me with a lot of paltry excuses!

Nora: [taking a step towards him]. Torvald . . . !

Helmer: Miserable woman . . . what is this you have done?

Nora: Let me go. I won't have you taking the blame for me. You mustn't take it on yourself.

235 **Helmer:** Stop play-acting! [Locks the front door]. You are staying here to give an account of yourself. Do you understand what you have done? Answer me! Do you understand?

Nora: [looking fixedly at him, her face hardening]. Yes, now I'm really beginning to understand.

Helmer: [walking up and down]. Oh, what a terrible awakening this is. All these eight years . . . this woman who was my pride and joy . . . a hypocrite, a liar, worse than that, a criminal! Oh, how utterly squalid it all is! Ugh! Ugh! [Nora remains silent and looks fixedly at him.] I should have realized something like this would happen. I should have seen it coming. All your father's irresponsible ways . . . Quiet! All your father's irresponsible ways are coming out in you. No religion, no morals, no sense of duty . . . Oh, this is my punishment for turning a blind eye to him. It was for your sake I did it, and this is what I get for it.

Nora: Yes, this.

Helmer: Now you have ruined my entire happiness, jeopardized my whole future. It's terrible to think of. Here I am, at the mercy of a thoroughly unscrupulous person; he can do whatever he likes with me, demand anything he wants, order me about just as he chooses . . . and I daren't even whimper. I'm done for, a miserable failure, and it's all the fault of a feather-brained woman!

240 **Nora:** When I've left this world behind, you will be free.

Helmer: Oh, stop pretending! Your father was just the same, always ready with fine phrases. What good would it do me if you left this world behind, as you put it? Not the slightest bit of good. He can still let it all come out, if he likes; and if he does, people might even suspect me of being an accomplice in these criminal acts of yours; they might even think I was the one behind it all, that it was I who pushed you into it! And it's you I have to thank for this . . . and when I've taken such good care of you, all our married life. Now do you understand what you have done to me?

Nora: [coldly and calmly]. Yes.

Helmer: I just can't understand it, it's so incredible. But we must see about putting things right. Take that shawl off. Take it off, I tell you! I must see if I can't find some way or other of appeasing him. The thing must be hushed up at all costs. And as far as you and I are concerned, things must appear to go on exactly as before. But only in the eyes of the world, of course. In other words you'll go on living here; that's understood. But you will not be allowed to bring up the children; I can't trust you with them. . . . Oh, that I should have to say this to the woman I loved so dearly, the woman I still . . . Well, that must be all over and done with. From now on, there can be no question of happiness. All we can do is save the bits and pieces from the wreck, preserve appearances . . . [The front door-bell rings. Helmer gives a start.] What's that? So late? How terrible, supposing . . . If he should . . . ? Hide, Nora! Say you are not well.

[Nora stands motionless. Helmer walks across and opens the door into the hall.]

Maid: [half dressed, in the hall]. It's a note for Mrs. Helmer.

245 **Helmer:** Give it to me. *[He snatches the note and shuts the door.]* Yes, it's from him. You can't have it. I want to read it myself.

Nora: You read it then.

Helmer: *[by the lamp]*. I hardly dare. Perhaps this is the end, for both of us. Well, I *must* know. *[He opens the note hurriedly, reads a few lines, looks at another enclosed sheet, and gives a cry of joy.]* Nora! *[Nora looks at him inquiringly.]* Nora! I must read it again. Yes, yes, it's true! I am saved! Nora, I am saved!

Nora: And me?

Helmer: You too, of course, we are both saved, you as well as me. Look, he's sent your IOU back. He sends his regrets and apologies for what he has done. . . . His luck has changed. . . . Oh, what does it matter what he says. We are saved, Nora! Nobody can do anything to you now. Oh, Nora, Nora . . . but let's get rid of this disgusting thing first. Let me see. . . . *[He glances at the IOU.]* No, I don't want to see it. I don't want it to be anything but a dream. *[He tears up the IOU and both letters, throws all the pieces into the stove and watches them burn.]* Well, that's the end of that. He said in his note you'd known since Christmas Eve. . . . You must have had three terrible days of it, Nora.

250 **Nora:** These three days haven't been easy.

Helmer: The agonies you must have gone through! When the only way out seemed to be. . . . No, let's forget the whole ghastly thing. We can rejoice and say: It's all over! It's all over! Listen to me, Nora! You don't seem to understand: it's all over! Why this grim look on your face? Oh, poor little Nora, of course I understand. You can't bring yourself to believe I've forgiven you. But I have. Nora, I swear it. I forgive you everything. I know you did what you did because you loved me.

Nora: That's true.

Helmer: You loved me as a wife should love her husband. It was simply that you didn't have the experience to judge what was the best way of going about things. But do you think I love you any the less for that; just because you don't know how to act on your own responsibility? No, no, you just lean on me. I shall give you all the advice and guidance you need. I wouldn't be a proper man if I didn't find a woman doubly attractive for being so obviously helpless. You mustn't dwell on the harsh things I said in the first moment of horror, when I thought everything was going to come crashing down about my ears. I have forgiven you, Nora, I swear it! I have forgiven you!

Nora: Thank you for your forgiveness.

[She goes out through the door, right.]

255 **Helmer:** No, don't go! *[He looks through the doorway.]* What are you doing in the spare room?

Nora: Taking off this fancy dress.

Helmer: *[standing at the open door]*. Yes, do. You try and get some rest, and set your mind at peace again, my frightened little song-bird. Have a good long sleep; you know you are safe and sound under my wing. *[Walks up and down near the door.]* What a nice, cozy little home we have here, Nora! Here you can find refuge. Here I shall hold you like a hunted dove I have rescued unscathed from the cruel talons of the hawk, and calm your poor beating heart. And that will come, gradually, Nora, believe me. Tomorrow you'll see everything quite differently. Soon everything will be just as it was before. You won't need me to keep on telling you I've forgiven you: you'll feel convinced of it in your own heart. You don't really imagine me ever thinking of turning you out, or even of reproaching you? Oh, a real man isn't made that way, you know, Nora. For a man, there's something indescribably moving and very satisfying in knowing that he has forgiven his wife—forgiven her, completely and genuinely, from the depths of his heart. It's as though it made her his property in a double sense: he has, as it were, given her a new life, and she becomes in a way both his wife and at the same time his child. That is how you will seem to me after today, helpless, perplexed little thing that you are. Don't you worry your pretty little head about anything, Nora. Just you be frank with me, and I'll make all the decisions for you. . . . What's this? Not in bed? You've changed your things?

Nora: *[in her everyday dress].* Yes, Torvald, I've changed.

Helmer: What for? It's late.

260 **Nora:** I shan't sleep tonight.

Helmer: But my dear Nora. . . .

Nora: *[looks at her watch].* It's not so terribly late. Sit down, Torvald. We two have a lot to talk about.

[She sits down at one side of the table.]

Helmer: Nora, what is all this? Why so grim?

Nora: Sit down. It'll take some time. I have a lot to say to you.

265 **Helmer:** *[sits down at the table opposite her].* You frighten me, Nora. I don't understand you.

Nora: Exactly. You don't understand me. And I have never understood you, either—until tonight. No, don't interrupt. I just want you to listen to what I have to say. We are going to have things out, Torvald.

Helmer: What do you mean?

Nora: Isn't there anything that strikes you about the way we two are sitting here?

Helmer: What's that?

270 **Nora:** We have now been married eight years. Hasn't it struck you this is the first time you and I, man and wife, have had a serious talk together?

Helmer: Depends what you mean by "serious."

Nora: Eight whole years—no, more, ever since we first knew each other—and never have we exchanged one serious word about serious things.

Helmer: What did you want me to do? Get you involved in worries that you couldn't possibly help me to bear?

Nora: I'm not talking about worries. I say we've never once sat down together and seriously tried to get to the bottom of anything.

275 **Helmer:** But, my dear Nora, would that have been a thing for you?

Nora: That's just it. You have never understood me . . . I've been greatly wronged, Torvald. First by my father, and then by you.

Helmer: What! Us two! The two people who loved you more than anybody?

Nora: *[shakes her head].* You two never loved me. You only thought how nice it was to be in love with me.

Helmer: But, Nora, what's this you are saying?

280 **Nora:** It's right, you know, Torvald. At home, Daddy used to tell me what he thought, then I thought the same. And if I thought differently, I kept quiet about it, because he wouldn't have liked it. He used to call me his baby doll, and he played with me as I used to play with my dolls. Then I came to live in your house. . . .

Helmer: What way is that to talk about our marriage?

Nora: *[imperturbably].* What I mean is: I passed out of Daddy's hands into yours. You arranged everything to your tastes, and I acquired the same tastes. Or pretended to . . . I don't really know . . . I think it was a bit of both, sometimes one thing and sometimes the other. When I looked back, it seems to me I have been living here like a beggar, from hand to mouth. I lived by doing tricks for you, Torvald. But that's the way you wanted it. You and Daddy did me a great wrong. It's your fault that I've never made anything of my life.

Helmer: Nora, how unreasonable . . . how ungrateful you are! Haven't you been happy here?

Nora: No, never. I thought I was, but I wasn't really.

285 **Helmer:** Not . . . not happy!

Nora: No, just gay. And you've always been so kind to me. But our house has never been anything but a play-room. I have been your doll wife, just as at home I was Daddy's doll child. And the children in turn have been my dolls. I thought it was fun when you came and played with me, just as they thought it was fun when I went and played with them. That's been our marriage, Torvald.

Helmer: There is some truth in what you say, exaggerated and hysterical though it is. But from now on it will be different. Play-time is over; now comes the time for lessons.

Nora: Whose lessons? Mine or the children's?

Helmer: Both yours and the children's, my dear Nora.

290 **Nora:** Ah, Torvald, you are not the man to teach me to be a good wife for you.

Helmer: How can you say that?

Nora: And what sort of qualifications have I to teach the children?

Helmer: Nora!

Nora: Didn't you say yourself, a minute or two ago, that you couldn't trust me with that job.

295 **Helmer:** In the heat of the moment! You shouldn't pay any attention to that.

Nora: On the contrary, you were quite right. I'm not up to it. There's another problem needs solving first. I must take steps to educate myself. You are not the man to help me there. That's something I must do on my own. That's why I'm leaving you.

Helmer: [*jumps up*]. What did you say?

Nora: If I'm ever to reach any understanding of myself and the things around me, I must learn to stand alone. That's why I can't stay here with you any longer.

Helmer: Nora! Nora!

300 **Nora:** I'm leaving here at once. I dare say Kristine will put me up for tonight. . . .

Helmer: You are out of your mind! I won't let you! I forbid you!

Nora: It's no use forbidding me anything now. I'm taking with me my own personal belongings. I don't want anything of yours, either now or later.

Helmer: This is madness!

Nora: Tomorrow I'm going home—to what used to be my home, I mean. It will be easier for me to find something to do there.

305 **Helmer:** Oh, you blind, inexperienced . . .

Nora: I must set about *getting* experience, Torvald.

Helmer: And leave your home, your husband and your children? Don't you care what people will say?

Nora: That's no concern of mine. All I know is that this is necessary for *me*.

Helmer: This is outrageous! You are betraying your most sacred duty.

310 **Nora:** And what do you consider to be my most sacred duty?

Helmer: Does it take me to tell you that? Isn't it your duty to your husband and your children?

Nora: I have another duty equally sacred.

Helmer: You have not. What duty might *that* be?

Nora: My duty to myself.

315 **Helmer:** First and foremost, you are a wife and mother.

Nora: That I don't believe any more. I believe that first and foremost I am an individual, just as much as you are—or at least I'm going to try to be. I know most people agree with you, Torvald, and that's also what it says in books. But I'm not content any more with what most people say, or with what it says in books. I have to think things out for myself, and get things clear.

Helmer: Surely you are clear about your position in your own home? Haven't you an infallible guide in questions like these? Haven't you your religion?

Nora: Oh, Torvald, I don't really know what religion is.

Helmer: What do you say?

320   **Nora:** All I know is what Pastor Hansen said when I was confirmed. He said religion was this, that and the other. When I'm away from all this and on my own, I'll go into that, too. I want to find out whether what Pastor Hansen told me was right—or at least whether it's right for *me*.

Helmer: This is incredible talk from a young woman! But if religion cannot keep you on the right path, let me at least stir your conscience. I suppose you do have some moral sense? Or tell me—perhaps you don't?

Nora: Well, Torvald, that's not easy to say. I simply don't know. I'm really confused about such things. All I know is my ideas about such things are very different from yours. I've also learned that the law is different from what I thought; but I simply can't get it into my head that that particular law is right. Apparently a woman has no right to spare her old father on his death-bed, or to save her husband's life, even. I just don't believe it.

Helmer: You are talking like a child. You understand nothing about the society you live in.

Nora: No, I don't. But I shall go into that too. I must try to discover who is right, society or me.

325   **Helmer:** You are ill, Nora. You are delirious. I'm half inclined to think you are out of your mind.

Nora: Never have I felt so calm and collected as I do tonight.

Helmer: Calm and collected enough to leave your husband and children?

Nora: Yes.

Helmer: Then only one explanation is possible.

330   **Nora:** And that is?

Helmer: You don't love me any more.

Nora: Exactly.

Helmer: Nora! Can you say that!

Nora: I'm desperately sorry, Torvald. Because you have always been so kind to me. But I can't help it. I don't love you any more.

335   **Helmer:** [*struggling to keep his composure*]. Is that also a "calm and collected" decision you've made?

Nora: Yes, absolutely calm and collected. That's why I don't want to stay here.

Helmer: And can you also account for how I forfeited your love?

Nora: Yes, very easily. It was tonight, when the miracle didn't happen. It was then I realized you weren't the man I thought you were.

Helmer: Explain yourself more clearly. I don't understand.

340   **Nora:** For eight years I have been patiently waiting. Because, heavens, I knew miracles didn't happen every day. Then this devastating business started, and I became absolutely convinced the miracle *would* happen. All the time Krogstad's letter lay there, it never so much as crossed my mind that you would ever submit to that man's conditions. I was absolutely convinced you would say to him: Tell the whole wide world if you like. And when that was done . . .

Helmer: Yes, then what? After I had exposed my wife to dishonor and shame . . . !

Nora: When that was done, I was absolutely convinced you would come forward and take everything on yourself, and say: I am the guilty one.

Helmer: Nora!

Nora: You mean I'd never let you make such a sacrifice for my sake? Of course not. But what would my story have counted for against yours?—That was the miracle I went in hope and dread of. It was to prevent it that I was ready to end my life.

345 **Helmer:** I would gladly toil day and night for you, Nora, enduring all manner of sorrow and distress. But nobody sacrifices his *honor* for the one he loves.

Nora: Hundreds and thousands of women have.

Helmer: Oh, you think and talk like a stupid child.

Nora: All right. But you neither think nor talk like the man I would want to share my life with. When you had got over your fright—and you weren't concerned about me but only about what might happen to you—and when all danger was past, you acted as though nothing had happened. I was your little sky-lark again, your little doll, exactly as before; except you would have to protect it twice as carefully as before, now that it had shown itself to be so weak and fragile. *[Rises.]* Torvald, that was the moment I realized that for eight years I'd been living with a stranger, and had borne him three children. . . . Oh, I can't bear to think about it! I could tear myself to shreds.

Helmer: *[sadly].* I see. I see. There is a tremendous gulf dividing us. But, Nora, is there no way we might bridge it?

350 **Nora:** As I am now, I am no wife for you.

Helmer: I still have it in me to change.

Nora: Perhaps . . . if you have your doll taken away.

Helmer: And be separated from you! No, no, Nora, the very thought of it is inconceivable.

Nora: *[goes into the room, right].* All the more reason why it must be done.

[She comes back with her outdoor things and a small traveling bag which she puts on the chair beside the table.]

355 **Helmer:** Nora, Nora, not now! Wait till the morning.

Nora: *[putting on her coat].* I can't spend the night in a strange man's room.

Helmer: Couldn't we go on living here like brother and sister . . . ?

Nora: *[tying on her hat].* You know very well that wouldn't last. *[She draws the shawl round her.]* Goodbye, Torvald. I don't want to see the children. I know they are in better hands than mine. As I am now, I can never be anything to them.

Helmer: But some day, Nora, some day . . . ?

360 **Nora:** How should I know? I've no idea what I might turn out to be.

Helmer: But you are my wife, whatever you are.

Nora: Listen, Torvald, from what I've heard, when a wife leaves her husband's house as I am doing now, he is absolved by law of all responsibility for her. I can, at any rate, free you from all responsibility. You must not feel in any way bound, any more than I shall. There must be full freedom on both sides. Look, here's your ring back. Give me mine.

Helmer: That too?

Nora: That too.

365 **Helmer:** There it is.

Nora: Well, that's the end of that. I'll put the keys down here. The maids know where everything is in the house—better than I do, in fact. Kristine will come in the morning after I've left to pack up the few things I brought with me from home. I want them sent on.

Helmer: The end! Nora, will you never think of me?

Nora: I dare say I'll often think about you and the children and this house.

Helmer: May I write to you, Nora?

370 **Nora:** No, never. I won't let you.

Helmer: But surely I can send you . . .

Nora: Nothing, nothing.

Helmer: Can't I help you if ever you need it?

Nora: I said "no." I don't accept things from strangers.

375 **Helmer:** Nora, can I never be anything more to you than a stranger?

Nora: *[takes her bag].* Ah, Torvald, only by a miracle of miracles. . . .

Helmer: Name it, this miracle of miracles!

Nora: Both you and I would have to change to the point where . . . Oh, Torvald, I don't believe in miracles any more.

Helmer: But I *will* believe. Name it! Change to the point where . . . ?

380 **Nora:** Where we could make a real marriage of our lives together. Goodbye!

> *[She goes out through the hall door.]*

Helmer: *[sinks down on a chair near the door, and covers his face with his hands].* Nora! Nora! *[He rises and looks round.]* Empty! She's gone! *[With sudden hope.]* The miracle of miracles . . . ?

> *[The heavy sound of a door being slammed is heard from below.]*

THE CURTAIN FALLS.

■ EXPLORATIONS OF THE TEXT

1. What are your first impressions of Nora's and Torvald's personalities? Of their relationship? Why does Torvald call Nora "my pretty little pet" or "my little squirrel"? What do these nicknames suggest about his attitude toward her?

2. Do you think that Nora was justified in taking out the loan, breaking the law and forging her father's signature? Consider Krogstad's statement: "The law takes no account of motives." Should she have revealed her "secret" to Torvald right away?

3. Discuss Nora's relationship with her children in Act I. What is significant about her actions?

4. How does the conflict between Nora and Torvald escalate in Act II? What motivates each character's behavior? Examine their interaction in the dance scene at the end of Act II. What is the significance of the tarantella?

5. List the other conflicts in the drama. How do they evolve in Acts II and III?

6. How do Mrs. Linde, Krogstad, and Dr. Rank serve as character foils? What roles do they play in determining Nora's fate?

7. The conflict between Nora and Torvald reaches its climax in Act III. Examine Torvald's and Nora's differing moral positions. Is Torvald justified in condemning her? With whom are you more sympathetic?

8. How does Nora change from the beginning to the end of the play?

9. Why does Nora leave? Do you think that Nora should have left her children?

10. Compare and contrast Nora with the narrator in "The Yellow Wallpaper."

11. Compare Nora's stages of growth with Hollis's "hero's journey." What do you conclude?

■ THE READING/WRITING CONNECTION

1. "Think" Topic: What is the meaning of the title?

2. Choose one scene featuring Nora and Torvald. Examine their relationship.

3. Freewrite: What do you think is the basis for a successful marriage?
4. What do you think happens to Nora after the end of the play?

■ **IDEAS FOR WRITING**

1. Write a character analysis of Nora or of Torvald.
2. Choose one symbolic element of setting or of gesture, and demonstrate how it develops themes of the play.
3. Should Nora have left Torvald and her children? Compose an argumentative essay that presents your position on this question. Use specific evidence from the text to support your views.
4. Both Hamlet and Nora are trapped by the past. In what ways?

■ **NONFICTION** ■

DAVID ELKIND

David Elkind (1931–   ) was born in Detroit, Michigan. Elkind, educated at the University of California, Los Angeles, where he received his undergraduate degree and his doctorate in psychology, is a practicing child psychologist. He has written several books concerned with child development and the factors influencing it. Currently, Elkind is a professor in the Child Development Department at Tufts University.

1981

OUR HURRIED CHILDREN

From *The Hurried Child: Growing Up Too Fast Too Soon*

The concept of childhood, so vital to the traditional American way of life, is threatened with extinction in the society we have created. Today's child has become the unwilling, unintended victim of overwhelming stress—the stress borne of rapid, bewildering social change and constantly rising expectations. The contemporary parent dwells in a pressure-cooker of competing demands, transitions, role changes, personal and professional uncertainties, over which he or she exerts slight direction. We seek release from stress whenever we can, and usually the one sure ambit of our control is the home. Here, if nowhere else, we enjoy the fact (or illusion) of playing a determining role. If child-rearing necessarily entails stress, then by hurrying children to grow up, or by treating them as adults, we hope to remove a portion of our burden of worry and anxiety and to enlist our children's aid in carrying life's load. We do not mean our children harm in acting thus—on the contrary, as a society we have come to imagine that it is good for young people to mature rapidly. Yet we do our children harm when we hurry them through childhood.

The principal architect of our modern notion of childhood was the French philosopher Jean-Jacques Rousseau. It was he who first criticized the educational methods for presenting materials from a uniquely adult perspective, reflecting adult values and interests. Classical *paideia*—that is, the value of transmitting a cultural-social heritage—was a good thing, said

Rousseau, but the learning process must take the child's perceptions and stage of development into account. In his classic work *Emile,* Rousseau wrote, "Childhood has its own way of seeing, thinking, and feeling, and nothing is more foolish than to try to substitute ours for theirs." More specifically, he observed that children matured in four stages, and just as each stage had its own characteristics, it should also have a corresponding set of appropriate educational objectives.

This idea of childhood as a distinct phase preceding adult life became inextricably interwoven with the modern concepts of universal education and the small, nuclear family (mother, father, children—not the extended family of earlier eras) in the late eighteenth and early nineteenth centuries, the heyday of the original Industrial Revolution. The transition is well explained by futurologist Alvin Toffler: "As work shifted out of the fields and the home, children had to be prepared for factory life. . . . If young people could be prefitted in the industrial system, it would vastly ease the problems of industrial discipline later on. The result was another central structure of all [modern] societies: mass education."

In addition to free, universal, public education, the emergent society tended to create smaller family units. Toffler writes, "To free workers for factory labor, key functions of the family were parcelled out to new specialized institutions. Education of the child was turned over to schools. Care of the aged was turned over to the poor houses or old-age homes or nursing homes. Above all, the new society required mobility. It needed workers who would follow jobs from place to place. . . . Torn apart by migration to the cities, battered by economic storms, families stripped themselves of unwanted relatives, grew smaller, more mobile, more suited to the needs of the [work place]."

5   While industrialization proceeded apace, the cultural recognition of childhood as a discrete life phase was given strong social reinforcement in the late nineteenth century with the establishment of child psychology as a scientific discipline. Work in this field began with the so-called baby biographies—minutely detailed accounts by observant parents of their infants' behavior. Bronson Alcott, father of Louisa May, contributed one such study, as did Milicent Shinn. Jean Piaget, the celebrated Swiss psychologist, carried on the tradition when he took time off from his collective studies of children to observe at close range (and write about) his own three offspring.

Around the turn of the century, G. Stanley Hall, generally regarded as the founder of the laboratory study of children, initiated the ill-fated "Child Study Movement." The extensive questionnaires he designed that parents and teachers administered to children by the thousands proved to be terribly error-prone and inexact. However, Hall had more success in founding Clark University, and the school's department of child psychology, carefully cultivated by Hall, led the nation in research and training in the new field, producing scientists of the eminence of Arnold Gessell and Lewis Terman.

After the Second World War, child psychology entered its boom period. Whereas before the war there were only two scientific journals reporting research in child development, today there are more than a dozen. All university departments of psychology include psychologists who are studying topics as varied as adolescence, learning in infants, socialization, peer interaction, sexual development, attachment and loss, the measurement of intelligence, learning disabilities, language acquisition, and so on. In short, we have accumulated a large library of data and knowledge about the period of life we call childhood. It is indeed no small irony that at the very time the stress of social life and change is threatening the existence of childhood, we know far more about childhood than we have ever known in the past.

What is even more curious is the degree to which this scientific knowledge is available to and consumed by the general public, for the research explosion in child study has been matched by a corresponding blaze of popular books about children. Often, well-known child psychologists undertake to "translate" scientific finds into useful applications. As early as 1894, the renowned psychologist T. Emmet Holt informed readers of his book *Care and Feeding of Children* how to prevent chafing: "First, not too much or too strong soap should be used; secondly, careful rinsing of the body, thirdly, not too vigorous rubbing, either during or after the bath; fourthly, the very free use of dusting powder in all the folds of the skin. . . . This is of the utmost importance in very fat infants." Holt was merely the first in a seemingly endless line of distinguished (and not so distinguished) "translators" of scientific child psychology into a popular idiom. Perhaps the two best-known are Arnold Gesell's *The Child from Birth to Five* and the incomparably influential *Infant and Child Care* by Benjamin Spock. Yet each year an awesome number of books, some very well written and others less so, appear with titles like (to consider just 1977) *Raising Happy Healthy Children, For Love of Children, Parenting, The Parent Book, Living with Your Hyperactive Children,* and *Helping Your Child Learn Right from Wrong.* Workshops and courses are available in every community in the country to guide and assist adults involved with the rearing of young people. If we hurry children to grow up too fast today, then, it is surely not done out of ignorance.

Miniature Adults

Today's pressures on middle-class children to grow up fast begin in early childhood. Chief among them is the pressure for early intellectual attainment, deriving from a changed perception of precocity. Several decades ago precocity was looked upon with great suspicion. The child prodigy, it was thought, turned out to be a neurotic adult; thus the phrase "early ripe, early rot!" Trying to accelerate children's acquisition of academic skills was seen as evidence of bad parenting.

10   A good example of this type of attitude is provided by the case of William James Sidis, the son of a psychiatrist. Sidis was born at the turn of the century and became a celebrated child prodigy who entered Harvard College at the age of eleven. His papers on higher mathematics gave the impression that he would make major contributions in this area. Sidis soon attracted the attention of the media, who celebrated his feats as a child. But Sidis never went further and seemed to move aimlessly from one job to another. In 1930 James Thurber wrote a profile of Sidis in *The New Yorker* magazine entitled "Where Are They Now?"; he described Sidis's lonely and pitiful existence in which his major preoccupation was collecting streetcar transfers from all over the world.

Such attitudes, however, changed markedly during the 1960s when parents were bombarded with professional and semiprofessional dicta on the importance of learning in the early years. If you did not start teaching children when they were young, parents were told, a golden opportunity for learning would be lost. Today, tax-supported kindergartens are operating in almost every state, and children are admitted at increasingly earlier ages. (In many cities a child born before January 1 can enter kindergarten the preceding September, making his or her effective entrance age four.) Once enrolled in kindergarten, children are now often presented with formal instruction in reading and math once reserved for the later grades.

How did this radical turnabout in attitudes happen? There are probably many reasons, but a major one was the attack on "progressive" education that occurred in the fifties and that found much education material dated. The Russian launching of the Sputnik in 1957 drove Americans into a frenzy of self-criticism about education and promoted the massive curriculum movement of the 1960s that brought academics from major universities into curriculum writing. Unfortunately, many academics knew their discipline but didn't know children and were unduly optimistic about how fast and how much children could learn. This optimism was epitomized in Jerome Bruner's famous phrase, "That any subject can be taught effectively in some intellectually honest form to any child at any stage of development." What a shift from "early ripe, early rot"!

The trend toward early academic pressure was further supported by the civil rights movement, which highlighted the poor performance of disadvantaged children in our schools. Teachers were under attack by avant-garde educators such as John Holt, Jonathan Kozol, and Herbert Kohl, and they were forced to defend their lack of success by shifting the blame. Their children did not do well because they came inadequately prepared. It was not what was going on in the classroom but what had not gone on at home that was the root of academic failure among the disadvantaged; hence Head Start, hence busing, which by integrating students would equalize background differences.

One consequence of all this concern for the early years was the demise of the "readiness" concept. The concept of readiness had been extolled by developmental psychologists such as Arnold Gesell who argues for the biological limitations on learning. Gesell believed that children were not biologically ready for learning to read until they had attained a Mental Age (a test score in which children are credited with a certain number of months for each correct answer) of six and one-half years. But the emphasis on early intervention and early intellectual stimulation (even of infants) made the concept of readiness appear dated and old-fashioned. In professional educational circles readiness, once an honored educational concept, is now in disrepute.

15   The pressure for early academic achievement is but one of many contemporary pressures on children to grow up fast. Children's dress is another. Three or four decades ago, prepubescent boys wore short pants and knickers until they began to shave; getting a pair of long pants was a true rite of passage. Girls were not permitted to wear makeup or sheer stockings until they were in their teens. For both sexes, clothing set children apart. It signaled adults that these people were to be treated differently, perhaps indulgently; it made it easier for children to act as children. Today even preschool children wear miniature versions of adult clothing. From overalls to LaCoste shirts to scaled-down designer fashions, a whole range of adult costumes is available to children. (Along with them is a wide choice of corresponding postures such as those of young teenagers modeling designer jeans.) Below is an illustration from a recent article by Susan Ferraro entitled "Hotsy Totsy."

> It was a party like any other: ice cream and cake, a donkey poster and twelve haphazard tails, and a door prize for everyone including Toby, the birthday girl's little brother who couldn't do anything but smear icing.
>
> "Ooh," sighed seven-year-old Melissa as she opened her first present. It was Calvin Klein jeans. "Aah," she gasped at the second box revealed a bright new top from Gloria Vanderbilt. There were Christian Dior undies from grandma—a satiny little chemise and matching bloomer bottoms—and mother herself had fallen for a marvelous party outfit from Yves St. Laurent. Melissa's best friend gave her an Izod sports shirt, complete with alligator emblem. Added to that a couple of books were, indeed, very nice and predictable—except for the fancy doll one guest's eccentric mother insisted on bringing.

When children dress like adults they are more likely to behave as adults do, to imitate adult actions. It is hard to walk like an adult male wearing corduroy knickers that make an awful noise. But boys in long pants can walk like men, and little girls in tight jeans can walk like women. It is more difficult today to recognize that children are children and not miniature adults, because children dress and move like adults.

Another evidence of the pressure to grow up fast is the change in the programs of summer camps for children. Although there are still many summer camps that offer swimming, sailing, horseback riding, archery, and camp fires—activities we remember from our own childhood—an increasing number of summer camps offer specialized training in many different areas, including foreign languages, tennis, baseball, dance, music, and even computers.

Among such camps the most popular seem to be those that specialize in competitive sports: softball, weight training, tennis, golf, football, basketball, hockey, soccer, lacrosse, gymnastics, wrestling, judo, figure skating, surfing. "Whatever the sport there's a camp (or ten or a hundred of them) dedicated to teaching the finer points. Often these camps are under the direction, actual or nominal, of a big name in a particular sport, and many have professional athletes on their staffs. The daily routine is rigorous, with individual and/or group lessons, practice sessions and tournaments, complete with trophies. And, to cheer the athletes on with more pep and polish, cheerleaders and song girls can also attend."

The change in the programs of summer camps reflects the new attitude that the years of childhood are not to be frittered away by engaging in activities merely for fun. Rather, the years are to be used to perfect skills and abilities that are the same as those of adults. Children are early initiated into the rigors of adult competition. Competitive sports for children are becoming ever more widespread and include everything from Little League to Pee Wee hockey. The pressure to engage in organized, competitive sports at camp and at home is one of the most obvious pressures on contemporary children to grow up fast.

20   There are many other pressures as well. Many children today travel across the country, and indeed across the world, alone. The so-called unaccompanied minor has become so commonplace that airlines have instituted special rules and regulations for them. The phenomenon is a direct result of the increase in middle-class divorces and the fact that one or the other parent moves to another part of the country or world. Consequently, the child travels to visit one parent or the other. Children also fly alone to see grandparents or to go to special camps or training facilities.

While some children really do not like to travel alone, others enjoy it. This young man's story is illustrative:

> Louic Villeneuve, nine, who lives in Cambridge, flies to Montreal alone each summer to visit his mother and to stay in the city where he spent the first five years of his life. "He loves it," said his father. "Once there weren't enough seats in the back of the plane so I had to go first class," Louic said, "there was so much food." The only problem Louic finds is adults who ask him which he likes better, Montreal or Boston. No matter which he answers, Louic has found, someone is unhappy. When his father flew with him recently, Louic commented, "I wish you weren't with me." A child alone, he seems to have discovered, gets more attention, more crayons, and more food than one travelling with a parent.

Although airline personnel take good care of unaccompanied children and some children like Louic enjoy traveling alone, it is very stressful for other children. Young children in particular may feel that they are abandoning their parent, or are being abandoned, or both. Being in an airplane with strange people and going to a different living arrangement, children are required to make adaptations that are more appropriate to older children and adults.

Other facets of society also press children to grow up fast. Lawyers, for example, are encouraging children to sue their parents for a variety of grievances. In California, four-and-one-half-year-old Kimberely Ann Alpin, who was born out of wedlock, is suing her father for the right to visit with him. The father, who provides support payments, does not want to see Kimberely. Whatever the decision, or the merits of the case, it illustrates the tendency of child-advocates to accord adult legal right to children. In West Hartford, Connecticut, David Burn, age 16, legally "divorced" his parents under a new state law in 1980. While such rights may have some benefits, they also put children in a difficult and often stressful position vis-à-vis their parents.

The media too, including music, books, films, and television, increasingly portray young people as precocious and present them in more or less explicit sexual or manipulative situations. Such portrayals force children to think they should act grown up before they are ready. In the movie *Little Darlings* the two principals—teenage girls—are in competition as to who will lose her virginity first. Similarly, teen music extols songs such as "Take Your Time (Do It Right)" and "Do That to Me One More Time," which are high on the charts of teen favorites. Television also promotes teenage erotica with features detailing such themes as teenage prostitution. According to some teenagers, the only show on television where playing hard to get is not regarded as stupid is "Laverne and Shirley."

25   The media promote not only teenage sexuality but also the wearing of adult clothes and the use of adult behaviors, language, and interpersonal strategies. Sexual promotion occurs in the context of other suggestions and models for growing up fast. A Jordache jean commercial, which depicts a young girl piggyback on a young boy, highlights clothing and implicit sexuality as well as adult expressions, hairstyles, and so on. Likewise, in the film *Foxes,* four teenage girls not only blunder into sexual entanglements but also model provocative adult clothing, makeup, language, and postures. Thus the media reinforce the pressure on children to grow up fast in their language, thinking, and behavior.

But can young people be hurried into growing up fast emotionally as well? Psychologists and psychiatrists recognize that emotions and feelings are the most complex and intricate part of development. Feelings and emotions have their own timing and rhythm and cannot be hurried. Young teenagers may look and behave like adults but they usually don't feel like adults. (Watch a group of teenagers in a children's playground as they swing on the swings and teeter on the teeter-totters.) Children can grow up fast in some ways but not in others. Growing up emotionally is complicated and difficult under any circumstances but may be especially so when children's behavior and appearance speak "adult" while their feelings cry "child."

The Child Inside

Some of the more negative consequences of hurrying usually become evident in adolescence, when the pressures to grow up fast collide with institutional prohibitions. Children pushed to grow up fast suddenly find that many adult prerogatives—which they assumed would be their prerogative—such as smoking, drinking, driving, and so on, are denied them until they reach a certain age. Many adolescents feel betrayed by a society that tells them to grow up fast but also to remain a child. Not surprisingly, the stresses of growing up fast often result in troubled and troublesome behavior during adolescence.

In a recent article, Patricia O'Brien gave some examples of what she called "the shrinking of childhood." Her examples reflect a rush to experiment that is certainly one consequence of growing up fast:

> Martin L (not his real name) confronted his teenager who had stayed out very late the night before. The son replied, "Look, Dad, I've done it all—drugs, sex, and booze, there is nothing left I don't know about." This young man is twelve years old!

> In Washington, D.C., area schools administrators estimate that many thousands of teenagers are alcoholics, with an estimated 30,000 such young people in Northern Virginia alone.

The rush to experiment is perhaps most noticeable in teenage sexual behavior. Although survey data are not always as reliable as one might wish, the available information suggests that there has been a dramatic increase in the number of sexually active teenage girls in the last decade. Melvin Zelnick and John F. Kanther, professors of public health at Johns Hopkins University in Baltimore, conclude that nearly 50 percent of the total population of teenage girls between the ages of fifteen and nineteen (about 10.3 million females) have had premarital sex. The percentage has nearly doubled since the investigators first undertook their study in 1971. "Things that supported remaining a virgin in the past—the fear of getting pregnant, being labelled the 'town pump,' or whatever have disappeared," observes Zelnick.

30   Young people themselves are very much aware of this trend. "I'd say half the girls in my graduating class are virgins," says an eighteen-year-old high school senior from New Iberia, Louisiana. "But you wouldn't believe those freshmen and sophomores. By the time they graduate there aren't going to be any virgins left."

There are a number of disturbing consequences of this sexual liberation. The number of teenage pregnancies is growing at a startling rate. About 10 percent of all teenage girls, one million in all, get pregnant each year and the number keeps increasing. About 600,000 teenagers give birth each year, and the sharpest increase in such births is for girls under fourteen! In addition, venereal disease is a growing problem among teenagers, who accout for 25 percent of the one million or so cases of gonorrhea each year.

The causes of this enhanced sexual activity among young people today are many and varied. The age of first menstruation, for example, has dropped from age seventeen about a century ago to age twelve and half today. Fortunately this seems to be the lower limit made possible by good health care and nutrition. However, this age of first menstruation has remained stable over the past decade, so it cannot account for the increased sexual activity of young women during this period. Other contributing factors include rapid changes in social values, women's liberation, the exploding divorce rate, the decline of parental and institutional authority, and the fatalistic sense, not often verbalized, that we are all going to die in a nuclear holocaust anyway, so "what the hell, have a good time."

Although the media are quick to pick up these sexual trends and exploit them for commercial purposes (for example, the cosmetics for girls four to nine years old currently being marketed by toy manufacturers), the immediate adult model is perhaps the most powerful and the most pervasive. Married couples are generally discreet about their sexuality in front of their offspring—in part because of a natural tendency to avoid exposing children to what they might not understand, but also because by the time the children are born, much of the romantic phase of the relationship for many couples is in the past.

But single parents who are dating provide a very different model for children. Quite aside from confrontations such as that in *Kramer vs. Kramer* wherein the son encounters the father's naked girlfriend, single parents are likely to be much more overtly sexual than married couples. With single parents, children may witness the romantic phase of courtship— the hand-holding, the eye-gazing, the constant touching and fondling. This overt sexuality, with all the positive affection it demonstrates, may encourage young people to look for something similar.

35   It is also true, as Professor Mavis Hetherington of the University of Virginia has found in her research, that daughters of divorced women tend to be more sexually oriented, more flirtatious with men than daughters of widowed mothers or daughters from two-parent homes. Because there are more teenage daughters from single-parent homes today than ever before, this too could contribute to enhanced sexual activity of contemporary teenage girls.

While it is true that some young people in every past generation have engaged in sex at an early age, have become pregnant, contracted venereal disease, and so on, they were always a small proportion of the population. What is new today are the numbers, which indicate that pressures to grow up fast are social and general rather than familial and specific (reflecting parental biases and needs). The proportion of young people who are abusing drugs, are sexually active, and are becoming pregnant is so great that we must look to the society as a whole for a full explanation, not to just the parents who mirror it.

Parallelling the increased sexuality of young people is an increase in children of what in adults are known as stress diseases. Pediatricians report a greater incidence of such ailments as headaches, stomachaches, allergic reactions, and so on in today's youngsters than in previous generations. Type A behavior (high-strung, competitive, demanding) has been identified in children and associated with heightened cholesterol levels. It has also been associated with parental pressure for achievement.

Another negative reflection of the pressure to grow up fast is teenage (and younger) crime. During 1980, for example, New York police arrested 12,762 children aged sixteen and under on felony charges. In Chicago the figure for the same period was 18,754 charges. Having worked for juvenile courts, I am sure that these figures are underestimated. Many children who have committed felonies are released without a formal complaint so that they will not have a police record. The children who are "booked" have usually had several previous encounters with the law.

The following examples, recent cases from the New York Police Department, illustrate the sort of activities for which children get arrested:

- On 27 February 1981, a boy who had to stand on tiptoes to speak to the bank teller made off with $118 that he had secured at gunpoint. He was nine years old, the youngest felon ever sought by the F.B.I.
- A ten-year-old Brooklyn girl was apprehended in December after she snatched a wallet from a woman's purse. Police said it was the girl's nineteenth arrest.
- One of four suspects captured in the murder of a policeman in Queens on 12 January 1981 was a fifteen-year-old youth.
- A thirteen-year-old Bronx boy was arrested in March 1981 on charges that he killed two elderly women during attempted purse snatchings.
- Another thirteen-year-old boy had a record of thirty-two arrests when seized last year on a charge of attempted murder. He later confessed to an incredible 200 plus felonies.

40   Such crimes are not being committed just by poor disadvantaged youth who are acting out against a society prejudiced against them. Much teenage crime is committed by middle-class youngsters. However, it tends to be concealed because police and parents try to protect the children; but sometimes this is not possible. One case involved a thirteen-year-old Long Island boy who was killed by three teenagers who stomped on him and strangled him by stuffing stones down his throat. He was attacked because he accidentally discovered that the other boys had stolen an old dirt bike worth only a couple of dollars. It was one of the most brutal and gruesome murders to be committed on Long Island.

How can pressure to grow up fast contribute to crime among teenagers from affluent backgrounds? Consider the case of John Warnock Hinckley, Jr., the young man who shot President Reagan and others on March 31, 1981. Unlike other assassins such as Lee Harvey Oswald, who shot President Kennedy, John Hinckley came from a respected upper-class family. Young Hinckley's father had built a prosperous business, and he and his wife had brought up three bright children. The family was religious, law-abiding, and socially conscious. Before and after the family moved from Dallas to Denver, Mrs. Hinckley made it a point to stay home to raise the children. Mr. Hinckley, though busy with his business, always made it a point to take his children camping, on family outings, and the like.

> In line with this model upbringing, the three children—especially Scott, the eldest, now 32—and Diane, now 29—were viewed as popular, intelligent and good looking. Scott, for example, was a scholarly athlete at Highland Park High School, the most prestigious public high school in the Dallas area. He was a member of an academic honorary group, the student council and the chess club and he was a varsity tennis player. At Vanderbilt University in Nashville, Tenn., Scott the fraternity man earned academic honors in mechanical engineering and went on to become the Singapore branch manager of Reading & Bates Inc. a Tulsa based oil company.

Diane is just as memorable. The blond beauty was the head cheerleader, a home-coming princess, an honor student, and a member of the choir and of the student council during her years at Highland Park High. At well-heeled Southern Methodist University in Dallas, she joined a sorority, majored in education, and met her future husband, Stephen Sims, who now is a Dallas insurance executive. Friends describe her today as a "model housewife" with two small children, a red brick house, and a two-car garage.

John Hinckley also did well in his early school career. He was active in sports and in the Cub Scouts. In the eighth grade, he was too small to make the basketball team but he handed out towels and led cheers from the bench. In the seventh and ninth grades he was elected president of his homeroom. But the pressure of Highland Park High School was apparently too much for John. From an outgoing cheerful boy, he became progressively more quiet and withdrawn, eventually preferring to practice his guitar alone at home than to be out with his friends.

Unlike his brother and sister, who went to expensive private schools, John elected to go to Texas Tech, a public institution. But he did not fraternize and often enrolled in courses that he never attended. Tendencies toward political extremism began to emerge. John joined and was eventually expelled from the Naturalist Socialist Party of America (a neo-Nazi party). He was expelled from the group because, according to another member, "We thought he was either deranged or could become an agent provocateur of violence."

John left college, was out of touch with his parents, and began the aimless drifting that was suddenly given direction and motivation by the desire to shoot the President. That this act was to gain the attention of a movie actress may be true in part, but the actress also had the same first name as his mother—Jodi.

45   John Hinckley's case shows how the pressure to achieve and to achieve early can bring about personality disorder and emotional disturbance. Had John been born into a different family, had his brother and sister not been so successful, he might have found himself. But in Erik Erikson's terms, John's older brother—by being at the same time athlete, scholar, and social leader—preempted all of the personal identities held out as valuable by his parents. Consequently, John adopted a negative identity—one of extremism, aloneness, social disruption—the negative of what his parents valued.

The pressure to grow up fast, to achieve early in the area of sports, academics, and social interaction, is very great in middle-class America. There is no room today for the "late bloomers," the children who come into their own later in life rather than earlier (John might have been one of these). Children have to achieve success early or they are regarded as losers. It has gone so far that many parents refuse to have their children repeat or be retained in kindergarten—despite all the evidence that this is the best possible time to retain a child. "But," the parents say, "how can we tell our friends that our son failed kindergarten?"

John Hinckley's solution to the problem of early achievement and success was attaining notoriety, catching people's attention with negative rather than positive accomplishments. But there are many other solutions to this pressure to achieve early. One such solution is to join a cult, such as the "Moonies." What characterizes such cults is that they accept young people unconditionally, regardless of academic success or failure. The cults, in effect, provide an accepting family that does not demand achievement in return for love, although cults do demand obedience and adherence to a certain moral ethic. Even rebellious young people find it easy to adhere to these rules in the atmosphere of acceptance and lack of pressure and competition offered by the cult group. Cult membership is another form of negative identity in which young people adopt a group identity rather than an individual one.

A case in point is the Christ Commune (a pseudonym), a branch of the best-organized and most rapidly growing sect of what has been called the Jesus movement. The Commune is a summer camp where members come from their homes for a few months each year. The population (about one hundred) consists of young adults between the ages of fifteen and thirty (average age twenty-one) who are white and come from large (four to eight children), middle-class families. Most have completed high school and some have done college work. One gets the impression they are young people who have not distinguished themselves socially, academically, or athletically and who have held boring, low-paying jobs.

The group offers a strict moral code, a rigid behavioral program, and a sense of mission, of being chosen by and working for God through the mediation of Christ. The members work hard—they get up at 4:30 A.M. and go to sleep at 11:00 P.M. They seem happy with simple food (little meat, water to drink, peanut butter sandwiches for lunch) and strenuous work six days a week. Entertainment and recreation are limited to sitting in a common room, talking, singing spirituals, and engaging in spontaneous prayer.

50   Such communes, the Jesus movement, and other religious groups are attractive to young people whose personal styles are at variance with those of the larger society. Such groups offer recognition and status to young people who tend to be noncompetitive, anti-intellectual, and spiritual in orientation. Thus the groups provide a needed haven from the pressure to grow up fast, to achieve early, and to make a distinctive mark in life.

The last phenomenon in relation to hurrying to be discussed here is teenage suicide. Currently, suicide is the third leading cause of death during the teen years—preceded only by death via accidents and homicide. An American Academy of Pediatrics report on teenage suicide indicates a large increase in the number of suicides by adolescents in the last decade—the number is now about 5000 per year. For young people between the ages of fifteen to nineteen, the number of suicides per year doubled during the period from 1968 to 1976. The data for young adolescents of ages ten to fourteen are even more distressing: the number of suicides was 116 in 1968 and rose to 158 by 1976.

For every suicide completed, some 50 to 200 are attempted but not successful. Adolescents from all walks of life, all races, religions, and ethnic groups commit or attempt to commit suicide. Boys are generally more successful than girls because they use more lethal methods—boys tend to shoot or hang themselves whereas girls are more likely to overdose on pills or to cut their wrists. "For most adolescents," the pediatric report concludes, "suicide represents an attempt to resolve a difficult conflict, escape an intolerable living arrangement or punish important individuals in their lives."

To illustrate how hurrying can contribute to teenage suicide, consider the data from the most affluent suburbs of Chicago, a ten-mile stretch of communities along Chicago's north-side lakefront that is one of the richest areas in the country. It is the locale chosen by director Robert Redford for the movie *Ordinary People*. The median income per family is about $60,000. Children in these areas attend excellent schools, travel about the world on vacations, are admitted to the best and most prestigious private colleges, and often drive their own cars (which can sometimes be a Mercedes). These are children of affluence who would seem to have it made.

And yet, this cluster of suburbs has the highest number of teenage suicides per year in the state, and almost in the nation. There has been a 250 percent increase in suicides per year over the past decade. These figures are dismaying not only in and of themselves but because the community has made serious efforts at suicide prevention, including the training of teachers in suicide detection and the provision of a twenty-four-hour hot line. One hot line, provided by Chicago psychoanalyst Joseph Pribyl, receives some 150 calls per month. But the suicides continue.

55   A nineteen-year-old from Glencoe, Illinois, says, "We have an outrageous number of suicides for a community our size." One of this teenager's friends cut her wrist and two others drove their cars into trees. "Growing up here you are handed everything on a platter,

but something else is missing. The one thing parents don't give is love, understanding, and acceptance of you as a person." And Isadora Sherman, of Highland Park's Jewish Family and Community Service says, "People give their kids a lot materially, but expect a lot in return. No one sees his kids as average, and those who don't perform are made to feel like failures."

Chicago psychiatrist Harold Visotsky succinctly states how pressure to achieve at an early age, to grow up and be successful fast can contribute to teenage suicide: "People on the lower end of the social scale expect less than these people. Whatever anger the poor experience is acted out in antisocial ways—vandalism, homicide, riots—and the sense of shared misery in the lower income groups prevents people from feeling so isolated. With well-to-do kids, *the rattle goes in the mouth and the foot goes on the social ladder.* The competition ethic takes over, making a child feel even more alone. He's more likely to take it out on himself than society."

Adolescents are very audience conscious. Failure is a public event, and the adolescent senses the audience's disapproval. It is the sense that "everyone knows" that is so painful and that can lead to attempted and successful suicides in adolescents who are otherwise so disposed. Hurrying our children has, I believe, contributed to the extraordinary rise in suicide rates among young people over the past decade.

All Grown Up and No Place to Go

Sigmund Freud was once asked to describe the characteristics of maturity, and he replied: *lieben und arbeiten* ("loving and working"). The mature adult is one who can love and allow himself or herself to be loved and who can work productively, meaningfully, and with satisfaction. Yet most adolescents, and certainly all children, are really not able to work or to love in the mature way that Freud had in mind. Children love their parents in a far different way from how they will love a real or potential mate. And many, probably most, young people will not find their life work until they are well into young adulthood.

When children are expected to dress, act, and think as adults, they are really being asked to playact, because all of the trappings of adulthood do not in any way make them adults in the true sense of *lieben und arbeiten.* It is ironic that the very parents who won't allow their children to believe in Santa Claus or the Easter Bunny (because they are fantasy and therefore dishonest) allow their children to dress and behave as adults without any sense of the tremendous dishonesty involved in allowing children to present themselves in this grown-up way.

60   It is even more ironic that practices once considered the province of lower-class citizens now have the allure of middle-class chic. Divorce, single parenting, dual-career couples, and unmarried couples living together were common among the lower class decades ago. Such arrangements were prompted more often than not by economic need, and the children of low-income families were thus pressured to grow up fast out of necessity. They were pitied and looked down upon by upper- and middle-class parents, who helped provide shelters like the Home for Little Wanderers in Boston.

Today the middle class has made divorce its status symbol. And single parenting and living together without being married are increasingly commonplace. Yet middle-class children have not kept pace with the adjustments these adult changes require. In years past a child in a low-income family could appreciate the need to take on adult responsibilities early; families needed the income a child's farm or factory labor would bring, and chores and child-rearing tasks had to be allocated to even younger members of the family. But for the middle-income child today, it is hard to see the necessity of being relegated to a baby sitter or sent to a nursery school or a day care center when he or she has a perfectly nice playroom and yard at home. It isn't the fact of parents' being divorced that is so distressing to middle-class children, but rather that often it seems so unnecessary, so clearly a reflection of parent and not child need. As we shall see, it is the feeling of being used, of being exploited by parents, of losing the identity and uniqueness of childhood without just cause that constitute the major stress of hurrying and account for so much unhappiness among affluent young people today.

It is certainly true that the trend toward obscuring the divisions between children and adults is part of a broad egalitarian movement in this country that seeks to overcome the barriers separating the sexes, ethnic and racial groups, and the handicapped. We see these trends in unisex clothing and hairstyles, in the call for equal pay for equal work, in the demands for affirmative action, and in the appeals and legislation that provide the handicapped with equal opportunities for education and meaningful jobs.

From this perspective, the contemporary pressure for children to grow up fast is only one symptom of a much larger social phenomenon in this country—a movement toward true equality, toward the ideal expressed in our Declaration of Independence. While one can only applaud this movement with respect to the sexes, ethnic and racial groups, and the handicapped, its unthinking extension to children is unfortunate.

Children need time to grow, to learn, and to develop. To treat them differently from adults is not to discriminate against them but rather to recognize their special estate. Similarly, when we provide bilingual programs for Hispanic children, we are not discriminating against them but are responding to the special needs they have, which, if not attended to, would prevent them from attaining a successful education and true equality. In the same way, building ramps for handicapped students is a means to their attaining equal opportunity. Recognizing special needs is not discriminatory; on the contrary, it is the only way that true equality can be attained.

65 All children have, vis-à-vis adults, special needs—intellectual, social, and emotional. Children do not learn, think, or feel in the same way as adults. To ignore these differences, to treat children as adults, is really not democratic or egalitarian. If we ignore the special needs of children, we are behaving just as if we denied Hispanic or Indian children bilingual programs, or denied the handicapped their ramps and guideposts. In truth, the recognition of a group's special needs and accommodation to those needs are the only true ways to insure equality and true equal opportunity.

■ EXPLORATIONS OF THE TEXT

1. Paraphrase Elkind's central thesis in paragraph 1. Do you agree with him?
2. According to Elkind, what are the reasons for this change in the view of "childhood" and child rearing? What "pressures" do children in North American society face?
3. What are the "negative consequences" for today's children of "grow[ing] up fast"?
4. What does Elkind propose as a solution?
5. What forms of evidence does Elkind include to support his points? Is his argument persuasive?
6. Connect Elkind's views of childhood with Connie's situation in "Where Are You Going, Where Have You Been?" with the personae in "Suicide Note" or in "Twilight Bey" (See chapter 7).

■ THE READING/WRITING CONNECTION

1. Outline Elkind's argument as preparation for class discussion.
2. "Think" Topic: Choose one statement from the essay. Write a paragraph response, agreeing or disagreeing with Elkind's views.
3. Debate Topic: "Are children's lives today too hurried?"

■ IDEAS FOR WRITING

1. Do you agree with Elkind's view of childhood? What solutions would you propose?
2. Choose a character from one of the works in this chapter (for example, the speaker in "Suicide Note"). Have that character write a letter to Elkind. Or choose a character from a popular television show and have that character write a letter to Elkind in which he/she responds to Elkind's argument.

GRETEL EHRLICH

Gretel Ehrlich (1946–   ) was born in Santa Barbara, California and was raised in Montecito on the California coast. After high school she moved east to attend college in Bennington, Vermont, then changed her mind and returned to California's University of Los Angeles. She soon returned east to New York, where she worked as an editor while attending the New School for Social Research, then the next year came back to California to write screenplays and direct documentaries for PBS. Since then, Ehrlich has traveled to and written about China, Greenland, the Canadian Arctic, and Wyoming, the state she chose to make her home. When walking with her two dogs in 1991, Ehrlich was badly injured by a lightning strike, an event that is captured in her book, A Match to the Heart: One Woman's Story of Being Struck by Lightning *(1994). Ehrlich's first published collection of poems,* Geode/Rock/Body *(1970), reflects the disintegration of boundaries between the landscape and the human, a theme that has solidified her reputation as a nature writer. She has written sixteen books, six scripts for television, has contributed numerous works to anthologies and periodicals, and has received several awards for her writing, including a Whiting Foundation grant and a Guggenheim fellowship.*

1995

LOOKING FOR A LOST DOG

The most valuable thoughts which I entertain are anything but what I thought. Nature abhors a vacuum, and if I can only walk with sufficient carelessness I am sure to be filled.

—Henry David Thoreau

I started off this morning looking for my lost dog. He's a red heeler, blotched brown and white, and I tell people he looks like a big saddle shoe. Born at Christmas on a thirty-below-zero night, he's tough, though his right front leg is crooked where it froze to the ground.

It's the old needle-in-the-haystack routine: small dog, huge landscape, and rugged terrain. While moving cows once, he fell in a hole and disappeared. We heard him whining but couldn't see him. When we put our ears to the ground, we could hear the hole that had swallowed him.

It's no wonder human beings are so narcissistic. The way our ears are constructed, we can only hear what's right next to us or else the internal monologue inside. I've taken to cupping my hands behind my ears—mule-like—and pricking them all the way forward or back to hear what's happened or what's ahead.

"Life is polyphonic," a Hungarian friend in her eighties said. She was a child prodigy from Budapest who had soloed on the violin in Paris and Berlin by the time she was twelve. "Childishly, I once thought hearing had mostly to do with music," she said. "Now that I'm too old to play the fiddle, I know it has to do with the great suspiration of life everywhere."

5 But back to the dog. I'm walking and looking and listening for him, though there is no trail, no clue, no direction to the search. Whimsically, I head north toward the falls. They're set in a deep gorge where Precambrian rock piles up to ten thousand feet on either side. A raven creaks overhead, flies into the cleft, glides toward a panel of white water splashing over a ledge, and comes out cawing.

To find what is lost is an art in some cultures. The Navajos employ "hand tremblers," usually women, who go into a trance and "see" where the lost article or person is located. When I asked one such diviner what it was like when she was in trance, she said, "Lots of noise, but noise that's hard to hear."

Near the falls the ground flattens into a high-altitude valley before the mountains rise vertically. The falls roar, but they're overgrown with spruce, pine, willow, and wild rose, and the closer I get, the harder it is to see the water. Perhaps that is how it will be in my search for the dog.

We're worried about Frenchy because last summer he was bitten three times by rattlesnakes. After the first bite he walked toward me, reeled dramatically, and collapsed. I could see the two holes in his nose where the fangs went in, and I felt sure he was dying. I drove him twenty miles to the vet; by the time we arrived, Frenchy resembled a monster. His nose and neck had swollen as though a football had been sewn under the skin.

I walk and walk. Past the falls, through a pass, toward a larger, rowdier creek. The sky goes black. In the distance snow on the Owl Creek Mountains glares. A blue ocean seems to stretch between, and the black sky hangs over like a frown. A string of cottonwoods whose new, tender leaves are the color of limes pulls me downstream. I come into the meadow with the abandoned apple orchard. The trees have leaves but have lost most of their blossoms. I feel as if I had caught strangers undressed.

10   The sun comes back, and the wind. It brings no dog, but ducks slide overhead. An Eskimo from Barrow, Alaska, told me the reason spring has such fierce winds is so birds coming north will have something to fly on.

To find what's lost; to lose what's found. Several times I've thought I might be "losing my mind." Of course, minds aren't literally misplaced—on the contrary, we live too much under them. As with viewing the falls, we can lose sight of what is too close. It is between the distant and close-up views that the struggle between impulse and reason, logic and passion takes place.

The feet move; the mind wanders. In his journals Thoreau wrote: "The saunterer, in the good sense, is no more vagrant than the meandering river, which is all the while sedulously seeking the shortest course to the sea."

Today I'm filled with longings—for what I'm not, for what is impossible, for people I love who can't be in my life. Passions of all sorts struggle soundlessly, or else, like the falls, they are all noise but can't be seen. My hybrid anguish spends itself as recklessly and purposefully as water.

Now I'm following a game trail up a sidehill. It's a mosaic of tracks—elk, deer, rabbit, and bird. If city dwellers could leave imprints in cement, it would look this way: tracks would overlap, go backward and forward like the peregrine saunterings of the mind.

15   I see a dog's track, or is it a coyote's? I get down on my hands and knees to sniff out a scent. What am I doing? I entertain expectations of myself as preposterous as when I landed in Toyko—I felt so at home there that I thought I would break into fluent Japanese. Now I sniff the ground and smell only dirt. If I spent ten years sniffing, would I learn scents?

The tracks veer off the trail and disappear. Descending into a dry wash whose elegant, tortured junipers and tumbled boulders resemble a Japanese garden, I trip on a sagebrush root. I look. Deep in the center of the plant there is a bird's nest, but instead of eggs, a locust stares up at me.

Some days I think this one place isn't enough. That's when nothing is enough, when I want to live multiple lives and be allowed to love without limits. Those days, like today, I walk with a purpose but no destination. Only then do I see, at least momentarily, that everything is here. To my left a towering cottonwood is lunatic with birdsong. Under it I'm a listening post while its great gray trunk—like a baton or the source of something—heaves its green symphony into the air.

I walk and walk: from the falls, over Grouse Hill, to the dry wash. Today it is enough to make a shadow.

■ **EXPLORATIONS OF THE TEXT**

1. How does the Henry David Thoreau quotation establish the direction of the essay? What do you predict the essay will be about?
2. Is the essay about "looking for a lost dog"? What is Ehrlich's subject matter? What is the narrator's internal conflict?
3. What is "lost"? Isolate several passages that provide clues.
4. Explain the significance of the following statements: "My hybrid anguish spends itself as recklessly and purposefully as water," and "I walk with a purpose but no destination."
5. What is the final revelation in the essay? Examine the last two paragraphs.

■ **THE READING/WRITING CONNECTION**

1. Freewrite: Discuss Ehrlich's inner conflict. What does she mean by "today it is enough to make a shadow." What does the "shadow" signify?
2. Compare Ehrlich's journey with Hollis's stages of "the heroic journey."
3. Select a significant passage in the essay, and use it as the starting point for a freewrite.
4. "Think" Topic: Ehrlich uses allusions and quotations to enlarge the scope of her argument. Choose one allusion or quotation, and discuss how it develops her point. Is this technique effective?
5. Make a list of the sense details in this work. What is the impact of the sensory language? How does it contribute to the development of Ehrlich's message?

■ **IDEAS FOR WRITING**

1. Write about a journey that you have taken—a hike, a car trip, or travel abroad or at home. Create a short synopsis of the event, and then write as descriptively as possible. Finally, jot down any discoveries about the event that have emerged through writing. Use this writing as the basis of a descriptive essay.
2. Compare Ehrlich's journey with Sedaris's "I Like Guys."

BRUNO BETTELHEIM

Bruno Bettelheim (1903–90) was born in Vienna, Austria, and in 1938 received his Ph.D. in Psychology from the University of Vienna. Soon after, the Nazis annexed Austria, and Bettelheim was arrested and sent to concentration camps at Dachau and Buchenwald, an experience that influenced his study of human psychology. He moved to the United States in 1939 after having been released from Buchenwald. Bettelheim was an authority on childhood emotional disorders, especially autism and juvenile psychosis. He published more than twenty-five books, essays, and lectures on psychology and the survival of trauma. Bettelheim's writing brings psychological theory to laypeople in an accessible and interesting form.

1975

INTRODUCTION: THE STRUGGLE FOR MEANING

From *The Uses of Enchantment*

If we hope to live not just from moment to moment, but in true consciousness of our existence, then our greatest need and most difficult achievement is to find meaning in our lives. It is well known how many have lost the will to live, and have stopped trying, because such meaning has evaded them. An understanding of the meaning of one's life is not suddenly acquired at a particular age, not even when one has reached chronological maturity. On the contrary, gaining a secure understanding of what the meaning of one's life may or ought to be—this is what constitutes having attained psychological maturity. And this achievement is the end result of a long development: at each age we seek, and must be able to find, some modicum of meaning congruent with how our minds and understanding have already developed.

Contrary to the ancient myth, wisdom does not burst forth fully developed like Athena out of Zeus's head; it is built up, small step by small step, from most irrational beginnings. Only in adulthood can an intelligent understanding of the meaning of one's existence in this world be gained from one's experiences in it. Unfortunately, too many parents want their children's minds to function as their own do—as if mature understanding of ourselves and the world, and our ideas about the meaning of life, did not have to develop as slowly as our bodies and minds.

Today, as in times past, the most important and also the most difficult task in raising a child is helping him to find meaning in life. Many growth experiences are needed to achieve this. The child, as he develops, must learn step by step to understand himself better; with this he becomes more able to understand others, and eventually can relate to them in ways which are mutually satisfying and meaningful.

To find deeper meaning, one must become able to transcend the narrow confines of a self-centered existence and believe that one will make a significant contribution to life—if not right now, then at some future time. This feeling is necessary if a person is to be satisfied with himself and with what he is doing. In order not to be at the mercy of the vagaries of life, one must develop one's inner resources, so that one's emotions, imagination, and intellect mutually support and enrich one another. Our positive feelings give us the strength to develop our rationality; only hope for the future can sustain us in the adversities we unavoidably encounter.

5   As an educator and therapist of severely disturbed children, my main task was to restore meaning to their lives. This work made it obvious to me that if children were reared so that life was meaningful to them, they would not need special help. I was confronted with the problem of deducing what experiences in a child's life are most suited to promote his ability to find meaning in his life; to endow life in general with more meaning. Regarding this task, nothing is more important than the impact of parents and others who take care of the child; second in importance is our cultural heritage, when transmitted to the child in the right manner. When children are young, it is literature that carries such information best.

Given this fact, I became deeply dissatisfied with much of the literature intended to develop the child's mind and personality, because it fails to stimulate and nurture those resources he needs most in order to cope with his difficult inner problems. The preprimers and primers from which he is taught to read in school are designed to teach the necessary skills, irrespective of meaning. The overwhelming bulk of the rest of so-called "children's literature" attempts to entertain or to inform, or both. But most of these books are so shallow in substance that little of significance can be gained from them. The acquisition of skills, including the ability to read, becomes devalued when what one has learned to read adds nothing of importance to one's life.

We all tend to assess the future merits of an activity on the basis of what it offers now. But this is especially true for the child, who, much more than the adult, lives in the present and, although he has anxieties about his future, has only the vaguest notions of what it may require or be like. The idea that learning to read may enable one later to enrich one's life is experienced as an empty promise when the stories the child listens to, or is reading at the moment, are vacuous. The worst feature of these children's books is that they cheat the child of what he ought to gain from the experience of literature: access to deeper meaning, and that which is meaningful to him at his stage of development.

For a story truly to hold the child's attention, it must entertain him and arouse his curiosity. But to enrich his life, it must stimulate his imagination; help him to develop his intellect and to clarify his emotions; be attuned to his anxieties and aspirations; give full recognition to his difficulties, while at the same time suggesting solutions to the problems which perturb him. In short, it must at one and the same time relate to all aspects of his personality—and this without ever belittling but, on the contrary, giving full credence to the seriousness of the child's predicaments, while simultaneously promoting confidence in himself and in his future.

In all these and many other respects, of the entire "children's literature"—with rare exceptions—nothing can be as enriching and satisfying to child and adult alike as the folk fairy tale. True, on an overt level fairy tales teach little about the specific conditions of life in modern mass society; these tales were created long before it came into being. But more can be learned from them about the inner problems of human beings, and of the right solutions to their predicaments in any society, than from any other type of story within a child's comprehension. Since the child at every moment of his life is exposed to the society in which he lives, he will certainly learn to cope with its conditions, provided his inner resources permit him to do so.

10   Just because his life is often bewildering to him, the child needs even more to be given the chance to understand himself in this complex world with which he must learn to cope. To be able to do so, the child must be helped to make some coherent sense out of the turmoil of his feelings. He needs ideas on how to bring his inner house into order, and on that basis be able to create order in his life. He needs—and this hardly requires emphasis at this moment in our history—a moral education which subtly, and by implication only, conveys to him the advantages of moral behavior, not through abstract ethical concepts but through that which seems tangibly right and therefore meaningful to him.

The child finds this kind of meaning through fairy tales. Like many other modern psychological insights, this was anticipated long ago by poets. The German poet Schiller wrote: "Deeper meaning resides in the fairy tales told to me in my childhood than in the truth that is taught by life." (*The Piccolomini*, III, 4.)

Through the centuries (if not millennia) during which, in their retelling, fairy tales became ever more refined, they came to convey at the same time overt and covert meanings—came to speak simultaneously to all levels of the human personality, communicating in a manner which reaches the uneducated mind of the child as well as that of the sophisticated adult. Applying the psychoanalytic model of the human personality, fairy tales carry important messages to the conscious, the preconscious, and the unconscious mind, on whatever level each is functioning at the time. By dealing with universal human problems, particularly those which preoccupy the child's mind, these stories speak to his budding ego and encourage its development, while at the same time relieving preconscious and unconscious pressures. As the stories unfold, they give conscious credence and body to id pressures and show ways to satisfy these that are in line with ego and superego requirements.

But my interest in fairy tales is not the result of such a technical analysis of their merits. It is, on the contrary, the consequence of asking myself why, in my experience, children—normal and abnormal alike, and at all levels of intelligence—find folk fairy tales more satisfying than all other children's stories.

The more I tried to understand why these stories are so successful at enriching the inner life of the child, the more I realized that these tales, in a touch deeper sense than any other reading material, start where the child really is in his psychological and emotional being. They speak about his severe inner pressures in a way that the child unconsciously understands, and—without belittling the most serious inner struggles which growing up entails—offer examples of both temporary and permanent solutions to pressing difficulties.

15   When a grant from the Spencer Foundation provided the leisure to study what contributions psychoanalysis can make to the education of children—and since reading and being read to are essential means of education—:it seemed appropriate to use this opportunity to explore in greater detail and depth why folk fairy tales are so valuable in the upbringing of children. My hope is that a proper understanding of the unique merits of fairy tales will induce parents and teachers to assign them once again to that central role in the life of the child they held for centuries.

Fairy Tales and the Existential Predicament

In order to master the psychological problems of growing up—overcoming narcissistic disappointments, oedipal dilemmas, sibling rivalries; becoming able to relinquish childhood dependencies; gaining a feeling of selfhood and of self-worth, and a sense of moral obligation—a child needs to understand what is going on within his conscious self so that he can also cope with that which goes on in his unconscious. He can achieve this understanding, and with it the ability to cope, not through rational comprehension of the nature and content of his unconscious, but by becoming familiar with it through spinning out daydreams—ruminating, rearranging, and fantasizing about suitable story elements in response to unconscious pressures. By doing this, the child fits unconscious content into conscious fantasies, which then enable him to deal with that content. It is here that fairy tales have unequaled value, 'because they offer new dimensions to the child's imagination which would be impossible for him to discover as truly on his own. Even more important, the form and structure of fairy tales suggest images to the child by which he can structure his daydreams and with them give better direction to his life.

     In child or adult, the unconscious is a powerful determinant of behavior. When the unconscious is repressed and its content denied entrance into awareness, then eventually the person's conscious mind will be partially overwhelmed by derivatives of these unconscious elements, or else he is forced to keep such rigid, compulsive control over them that his personality may become severely crippled. But when unconscious material *is* to some degree permitted to come to awareness and worked through in imagination, its potential for causing harm—to ourselves or others—is much reduced; some of its forces can then be made to serve positive purposes. However, the prevalent parental belief is that a child must be diverted from what troubles him most: his formless, nameless anxieties, and his chaotic, angry, and even violent fantasies. Many parents believe that only conscious reality or pleasant and wish-fulfilling images should be presented to the child—that he should be exposed only to the sunny side of things. But such one-sided fare nourishes the mind only in a one-sided way, and real life is not all sunny.

     There is a widespread refusal to let children know that the source of much that goes wrong in life is due to our very own natures—the propensity of all men for acting aggressively, asocially, selfishly, out of anger and anxiety. Instead, we want our children to believe that, inherently, all men are good. But children know that *they* are not always good; and often, even when they are, they would prefer not to be. This contradicts what they are told by their parents, and therefore makes the child a monster in his own eyes.

     The dominant culture wishes to pretend, particularly where children are concerned, that the dark side of man does not exist, and professes a belief in an optimistic meliorism. Psychoanalysis itself is viewed as having the purpose of making life easy—but this is not what its founder intended. Psychoanalysis was created to enable man to accept the problematic nature of life without being defeated by it, or giving in to escapism. Freud's prescription is that only by struggling courageously against what seem like overwhelming odds can man succeed in wringing meaning out of his existence.

20   This is exactly the message that fairy tales get across to the child in manifold form: that a struggle against severe difficulties in life is unavoidable, is an intrinsic part of human existence—but that if one does not shy away, but steadfastly meets unexpected and often unjust hardships, one masters all obstacles and at the end emerges victorious.

Modern stories written for young children mainly avoid these existential problems, although they are crucial issues for all of us. The child needs most particularly to be given suggestions in symbolic form about how he may deal with these issues and grow safely into maturity. "Safe" stories mention neither death nor aging, the limits to our existence, nor the wish for eternal life. The fairy tale, by contrast, confronts the child squarely with the basic human predicaments.

For example, many fairy stories begin with the death of a mother or father; in these tales the death of the parent creates the most agonizing problems, as it (or the fear of it) does in real life. Other stories tell about an aging parent who decides that the time has come to let the new generation take over. But before this can happen, the successor has to prove himself capable and worthy. The Brothers Grimm's story "The Three Feathers" begins: "There was once upon a time a king who had three sons. . . . When the king had become old and weak, and was thinking of his end, he did not know which of his sons should inherit the kingdom after him." In order to decide, the king sets all his sons a difficult task; the son who meets it best "shall be king after my death."

It is characteristic of fairy tales to state an existential dilemma briefly and pointedly. This permits the child to come to grips with the problem in its most essential form, where a more complex plot would confuse matters for him. The fairy tale simplifies all situations. Its figures are clearly drawn; and details, unless very important, are eliminated. All characters are typical rather than unique.

Contrary to what takes place in many modern children's stories, in fairy tales evil is as omnipresent as virtue. In practically every fairy tale good and evil are given body in the form of some figures and their actions, as good and evil are omnipresent in life and the propensities for both are present in every man. It is this duality which poses the moral problem, and requires the struggle to solve it.

25   Evil is not without its attractions—symbolized by the mighty giant or dragon, the power of the witch, the cunning queen in "Snow White"—and often it is temporarily in the ascendancy. In many fairy tales a usurper succeeds for a time in seizing the place which rightfully belongs to the hero—as the wicked sisters do in "Cinderella." It is not that the evildoer is punished at the story's end which makes immersing oneself in fairy stories an experience in moral education, although this is part of it. In fairy tales, as in life, punishment or fear of it is only a limited deterrent to crime. The conviction that crime does not pay is a much more effective deterrent, and that is why in fairy tales the bad person always loses out. It is not the fact that virtue wins out at the end which promotes morality, but that the hero is most attractive to the child, who identifies with the hero in all his struggles. Because of this identification the child imagines that he suffers with the hero his trials and tribulations, and triumphs with him as virtue is victorious. The child makes such identifications all on his own, and the inner and outer struggles of the hero imprint morality on him.

The figures in fairy tales are not ambivalent—not good and bad at the same time, as we all are in reality. But since polarization dominates the child's mind, it also dominates fairy tales. A person is either good or bad, nothing in between. One brother is stupid, the other is clever. One sister is virtuous and industrious, the others are vile and lazy. One is beautiful, the others are ugly. One parent is all good, the other evil. The juxtaposition of opposite characters is not for the purpose of stressing right behavior, as would be true for cautionary tales. (There are some amoral fairy tales where goodness or badness, beauty or ugliness play no role at all.) Presenting the polarities of character permits the child to comprehend easily the difference between the two, which he could not do as readily were the figures drawn more true to life, with all the complexities that characterize real people. Ambiguities must wait until a relatively firm personality has been established on the basis of positive identifications. Then the child has a basis for understanding that there are great differences between people, and that therefore one has to make choices about who one wants to be. This basic decision, on which all later personality development will build, is facilitated by the polarizations of the fairy tale.

Furthermore, a child's choices are based, not so much on right versus wrong, as on who arouses his sympathy and who his antipathy. The more simple and straightforward a good character, the easier it is for a child to identify with it and to reject the bad other. The child identifies with the good hero not because of his goodness, but because the hero's condition makes a deep positive appeal to him. The question for the child is not "Do I want to be good?" but "Who do I want to be like?" The child decides this on the basis of projecting himself wholeheartedly into one character. If this fairy-tale figure is a very good person, then the child decides that he wants to be good, too.

Amoral fairy tales show no polarization or juxtaposition of good and bad persons; that is because these amoral stories serve an entirely different purpose. Such tales or type figures as "Puss in Boots," who arranges for the hero's success through trickery, and Jack, who steals the giant's treasure, build character not by promoting choices between good and bad, but by giving the child the hope that even the meekest can succeed in life. After all, what's the use of choosing to become a good person when one feels so insignificant that he fears he will never amount to anything? Morality is not the issue in these tales, but rather, assurance that one can succeed. Whether one meets life with a belief in the possibility of mastering its difficulties or with the expectation of defeat is also a very important existential problem.

The deep inner conflicts originating in our primitive drives and our violent emotions are all denied in much of modern children's literature, and so the child is not helped in coping with them. But the child is subject to desperate feelings of loneliness and isolation, and he often experiences mortal anxiety. More often than not, he is unable to express these feelings in words, or he can do so only by indirection: fear of the dark, of some animal, anxiety about his body. Since it creates discomfort in a parent to recognize these emotions in his child, the parent tends to overlook them, or he belittles these spoken fears out of his own anxiety, believing this will cover over the child's fears.

30   The fairy tale, by contrast, takes these existential anxieties and dilemmas very seriously and addresses itself directly to them: the need to be loved and the fear that one is thought worthless; the love of life, and the fear of death. Further, the fairy tale offers solutions in ways that the child can grasp on his level of understanding. For example, fairy tales pose the dilemma of wishing to live eternally by occasionally concluding: "If they have not died, they are still alive." The other ending—"And they lived happily ever after"—does not for a moment fool the child that eternal life is possible. But it does indicate that which alone can take the sting out of the narrow limits of our time on this earth: forming a truly satisfying bond to another. The tales teach that when one has done this, one has reached the ultimate in emotional security of existence and permanence of relation available to man; and this alone can dissipate the fear of death. If one has found true adult love, the fairy story also tells, one doesn't need to wish for eternal life. This is suggested by another ending found in fairy tales: "They lived for a long time afterward, happy and in pleasure."

An uninformed view of the fairy tale sees in this type of ending an unrealistic wish-fulfillment, missing completely the important message it conveys to the child. These tales tell him that by forming a true interpersonal relation, one escapes the separation anxiety which haunts him (and which sets the stage for many fairy tales, but is always resolved at the story's ending). Furthermore, the story tells, this ending is not made possible, as the child wishes and believes, by holding on to his mother eternally. If we try to escape separation anxiety and death anxiety by desperately keeping our grasp on our parents, we will only be cruelly forced out, like Hansel and Gretel.

Only by going out into the world can the fairy-tale hero (child) find himself there; and as he does, he will also find the other with whom he will be able to live happily ever after; that is, without ever again having to experience separation anxiety. The fairy tale is future-oriented and guides the child—in terms he can understand in both his conscious and his unconscious mind—to relinquish his infantile dependency wishes and achieve a more satisfying independent existence.

Today children no longer grow up within the security of an extended family, or of a well-integrated community. Therefore, even more than at the times fairy tales were invented, it is important to provide the modern child with images of heroes who have to go out into the world all by themselves and who, although originally ignorant of the ultimate things, find secure places in the world by following their right way with deep inner confidence.

The fairy-tale hero proceeds for a time in isolation, as the modern child often feels isolated. The hero is helped by being in touch with primitive things—a tree, an animal, nature—as the child feels more in touch with those things than most adults do. The fate of these heroes convinces the child that, like them, he may feel outcast and abandoned in the world, groping in the dark, but, like them, in the course of his life he will be guided step by step, and given help when it is needed. Today, even more than in past times, the child needs the reassurance offered by the image of the isolated man who nevertheless is capable of achieving meaningful and rewarding relations with the world around him.

■ EXPLORATIONS OF THE TEXT

1. According to Bettelheim, what is the main reason to read fairy tales? What is the difference for children between reading these tales and other forms of children's literature?
2. What are the differences between the ways in which children and adults gain meaning from experience? According to Bettelheim, what is "the most difficult task in raising a child"?
3. How do children benefit from reading fairy tales? Do you agree with Bettelheim's conclusions?
4. What does Bettelheim mean by the "existential predicament"?
5. Do you agree with Bettelheim's contention that reading fairy tales provides a way for children to deal with "deep inner conflicts"?
6. Compare and contrast Bettelheim's view of the developmental journey with Hollis's conception of the "hero's journey."
7. How do Gordimer and Carter portray what Bettelheim labels as "the existential predicament"?

■ THE READING/WRITING CONNECTION

1. Bettelheim's essay is in the form of an argument. Gloss and annotate the text, pinpointing the main claim, reasons, and evidence. Do you think that the work is persuasive?
2. Select one statement about the function of fairy tales, and relate it to your own experience of reading a fairy tale or seeing an animated version of a tale as a child. What do you learn?

■ IDEAS FOR WRITING

1. Web Research: Find one fairy tale to consider. Some popular ones include "Rapunzel," "Snow White," "Hansel and Gretel," and "Jack and the Beanstalk." Then apply Bettelheim's theory of reading to the work. What do you conclude?
2. View the movie *Shrek* or *Shrek 2*. How does the movie allude to and subvert fairy tale motifs? Write a short essay.
3. Do you agree with one of the following of Bettelheim's contentions:

Much of the literature intended to develop the child's mind and personality . . . fails to stimulate and nurture those resources he needs most in order to cope with his difficult inner problems. The preprimer and primers from which he is taught to read in school are designed to teach the necessary skills irrespective of meaning.

OR

Today, even more than in past times, the child needs the reassurance offered [in fairy tales of] the image of the isolated man who nevertheless is capable of achieving meaningful and rewarding relations with the world around him.

Bettelheim wrote *The Uses of Enchantment* in the mid-1970s. Are these arguments still relevant today? Refer to your own experience of schooling or of reading of children's literature.

4. Bettelheim suggests that it is important for people to find "meaning" in their lives. Relate this idea to the character development in the following works: the grandmother in O'Connor's "A Good Man Is Hard to Find," the unnamed narrator in Carver's "Cathedral," or Hamlet in *Hamlet*.

5. Bettelheim points out a predominant motif in fairy tales: heroines who are saved by men. Compare and contrast the fates of female characters in such works as Oates's "Where Are You Going, Where Have You Been?"; Kingsolver's "Rose-Johnny"; Jewett's "A White Heron"; or the animated film *Shrek* or *Mulan*.

JAMES HOLLIS

James Hollis is a Jungian analyst who earned his Ph.D. at the C. G. Jung Institute in Zurich, Switzerland. An executive director of the Jung Educational Center in Houston, Texas, and a member of the Omega Institute's faculty, he travels around the United States giving lectures on theories of human development. Hollis is the author of ten books, including The Middle Passage: From Misery to Meaning in Midlife *(1993) and* Under Saturn's Shadow: The Wounding and Healing of Men *(1994). The following is an excerpt from* Tracking the Gods: The Place of Myth in Modern Life *(1995). Hollis's work helps people to live more meaningful lives through providing an understanding of their own needs within the context of a complex society, or what he calls "the meeting place of psyche and soul."*

1995

THE HEROIC JOURNEY

From "The Eternal Return and the Heroic Quest" in
Tracking the Gods: The Place of Myth in Modern Life

No single legend will contain all of the motifs of the journey as described herein, but all will illustrate at least one aspect. For example, the hero is always "called," although he or she may not initially understand this as a call or even wish to be called. Odysseus,[1] for example, feigned madness in order to avoid going on the expedition against Troy. He sowed his field with salt, but when his children were placed in front of his plow and he had to exercise rational choice to save them, he was then dragged to his destiny.

---

[1] The hero of *The Odyssey,* a Greek epic poem written by Homer in the eighth or ninth century B.C. *The Odyssey* concerns the hero's struggle to return home after the Trojan War.

The call or summons represents a need for some older value, personal or tribal, to be overthrown. Seldom is the way clear. Certainly it is never easy. The hero must persist, with the greatest obstacle being his own lethargy, fear and longing for home.

Sometimes the hero will receive critical aid from another—an old crone, a gnome in the forest, a helpful animal, advice remembered from a wise elder, or strengths to draw upon from the tribal memory. The path is strewn with various temptations—the devil of doubt, hope for an easier way, seductions of wealth, power, hedonism. Odysseus, on the long voyage back to Ithaca, had to wrench his men away from the Isle of the Lotus Eaters, whose sweet poppies would ease their pain, and the enchantments of Circe, who would turn them into sensual swine. All of these temptations caused his crew to forget the journey.

Often the hero of such stories sets out on an adventure in the world; sometimes the journey is internal as the hero descends into the depths of the unconscious. If the hero survives the descent—and typically many predecessors did not—and the battle with whatever monsters await in the depths, then he or she is able to undertake the ascent and be transformed. This transformation constitutes a death and rebirth experience. Who the person was, and what his or her conscious world was like, is no more. All is transformed.

5   Often these struggles have wounded the person. Think of the wounds of Christ and Wotan and Odysseus,[2] for example, wounds through which they were later recognized as heroes. Wounds quicken consciousness and, as we recall from the mythology of the eternal return, are the necessary quid pro quo for enlargement. Frequently there are tokens of this new state—a pot of gold, the hand of the beloved, a new homeland—but these are only the outward vestiges of a changed relationship of soul to cosmos.

The hero attains a new consciousness of the possible and a new relationship to the tribe and to the gods. As token of this change are irrelevant to the worth of the transformation of consciousness, such trophies need to be seen metaphorically. Any quest for the trophies themselves would be materialism, seeking the icon instead of the god, and losing the point of it all. While the journey of the hero may take the form of outer adventures, the goal is inner transformation. While the heroic adventures of our tribal memory take some outer form, the same motifs of summons, descent, struggle, wounding and return are part of the everyday life of the individual. To discern that each of us is part of such a rich pattern on a daily basis is to recover the depth principle.

The Psychological Meaning of the Journey

Tom Stoppard wrote an interesting play a number of years ago titled *Rosencrantz and Guildenstern Are Dead.*[3] Rosencrantz and Guildenstern are familiar as very minor characters in *Hamlet.* In Shakespeare's version, Hamlet is of course the tragic hero who is summoned and encounters overwhelming inner resistance to his duty to avenge his father. Finally, at the end of the longest play Shakespeare ever wrote, Hamlet overcomes his lethargy and acts. In the meantime, the transient passages of Rosencrantz and Guildenstern are concluded with the simple remark that they are dead—unimportant if the play is called *Hamlet,* but very important if one is in a play called *Rosencrantz* or *Guildenstern.*

Stoppard follows the thought that each of us is cast into a great drama, a drama in which we may be following an uncertain script but in which, surely, we are summoned to be the protagonist. The denouement of the play is certain—we die. But the meaning of Stoppard's play derives from how and in what fashion the protagonist can come to con-

---

[2] **Wotan:** Scandinavian God.
[3] See *Hamlet.*

sciousness and make heroic choices. Certainly Stoppard's twin figures are in the anti-hero mold as they wander about in the uncertain play of their lives, not clear about who they are or what is going on, interrupted once in awhile by some guy named Hamlet who crosses their stage with a sense of his own importance.

Rosencrantz and Guildenstern are prototypes for modern individuals, who, feeling no heroic stature, no sustaining mythos, wander from idea to idea, impulse to impulse, morosely changing channels in the hope of finding something better to watch.

10 In each of us there is a Hamlet, adrift in the cross-currents of ambivalence, and in each of us a Rosencrantz or Guildenstern. In each of us is the archetype of the hero, the capacity to rise to the challenge of life. If we have an outer hero it is only to remind us of our own imperative. In the acts of another—the one who scales the impossible slope, the one who discovers the new vaccine, the one who articulates a transformative idea, the one who brings beauty into the world—we are reminded of our own calling, our heroic vocation.

Surely the only measure by which we can judge ourselves in the end, or be judged by others, is the degree to which we have heard and responded to the imperative to become ourselves in the face of what would hold us back. The stories of heroes may inspire and guide us, but it is up to each to answer our own call, to individuate. As the old Zen parable has it, "I am looking for the face I had before the world was made." Throughout the land there are those who quietly, daily, answer this call, taking care of their children, going to their burdensome but necessary jobs, fighting self-doubt and fear. Such persons, in their unsung ways, are worthier of admiration than celebrities; heroic others are not meant to divert us from our own journey but rather to remind us of it.

The recurrent leitmotif of the hero's quest implies a voyage from unconsciousness toward consciousness, from tenebrous depths to luminous heights, from dependency to self-sufficiency. That force, that patterning energy (which is what an archetype is), seeks to overthrow the domination of chaos, the sweet seductions of unconsciousness, to achieve ever greater differentiation.

Each morning two grinning gremlins sit at the foot of the bed. One is named Lethargy and one is called Fear. Either will gladly eat us alive.It scarcely matters what one did yesterday in combat with them, for they daily renew their interest in possessing the soul. The energy available to take them on is part and parcel of the hero archetype. In this fashion one can see, then, how universal the hero drama is, for each of us has come to recognize the subtle seduction of comfort and the fears that paralyze like Medusa's gaze.[4] Our life's journey is a series of defeats by these demons, a daily-renewed summons to take them on and play the protagonist in the drama that is our life.

Joseph Campbell's classic, *The Hero With a Thousand Faces,* documents the ubiquity of what he considered the mono-myth of the hero.[5] This central myth seems to have three stages: departure, initiation and return. The departure stage arises when the person is expelled from the community or has outgrown the old dispensation. Then he or she is obliged to wander in strange lands. Descents, ascents and wounding initiate the neophyte into the mysteries of nature and of relationship. The return is seldom back to the old land and never back to the old psychology. Such a return would obviate the journey and annihilate consciousness. Rather the return involves circling back at a higher level. Thus the informing image of the quest motif is not a linear movement once and for all time, but rather an evolutionary movement akin to a spiral. This voyage necessarily differentiates a person, develops a new being who may no longer be recognizable by the old tribe or the old

---

[4] Chief of the Gorgons, serpent-headed monsters of Greek mythology who turned men into stone.

[5] North American leading scholar (1904–87) of mythology.

values. The hero must bear the burden of loneliness and guilt and, as Jung notes, must give something back:

> Individuation cuts one off from personal conformity and hence from collectivity. Thai is the guilt which the individuant leaves behind him for the world, that is the guilt which he must endeavour to redeem. He must offer a ransom in place of himself, that is, he must bring forth values which are an equivalent substitute for his absence in the collective personal sphere.[6]

15   In this way we see that the heroic imperative summons us all, for not only is the individual created thereby, but such a person becomes a treasure to the tribe. Many have thought that individuation is a form of narcissistic preoccupation. Rather the enlarged person, the one who undertakes and returns from the quest, serves the tribe through challenge, redemption and reinvigoration.

The archetype of the journey is the formalization of the life force, that is, the activation and channeling of libido toward greater development. The greatest risk a person will ever encounter is the subtle seduction of the unconscious, the longing to abide in the known and comfortable. Jung describes such a person:

> Always he imagines his worst enemy in front of him, yet he carries the enemy within himself—a deadly longing for the abyss, a longing to drown in his own source. . . . This regressive tendency has been consistently opposed from the most primitive times by the great psychotherapeutic systems which we know as the religions. They seek to create an autonomous consciousness by weaning mankind away from the sleep of childhood.[7]

If it is true that the great myths and myth-making institutions sought to activate and channel the libido of the individual, then the erosion of such powerful guiding images acts as a psychological abandonment. So we are obliged to be even more conscious of our developmental task, since we must often undertake it in solitude and silence.

The "deadly longing for the abyss" that Jung speaks of is the grinning gremlin Lethargy. The other one, Fear, is natural to the fragile human who works so hard to achieve a measure of security only to find that it is a trap, a stultification of the life force. To grow, to individuate, obliges us to reject that security and move into the unknown. Jung puts it dramatically:

> The spirit of evil is fear, negation. . . . he is the spirit of regression, who threatens us with bondage to the mother and with dissolution and extinction in the unconscious. . . . For the hero, fear is a challenge and a task, because only boldness can deliver from fear. And if the risk is not taken, the meaning of life is somehow violated, and the whole future is condemned to hopeless staleness, to a drab grey lit only by will-o'-the-wisps.[8]

These, then, are the two great ideas contemporary Westerners must keep in mind—the eternal return and the hero's journey. They must be made all the more conscious in our lives because we are not positioned in a sustaining mythological tradition that activates such imperatives, channels libido and mediates the woe and wonder of it all. Those whose traditions presented them with images of the Great Mother were sustained by "great winds across the sky." We are not.

---

[6] "Adaptation, Individuation, Collectivity," *The Symbolic Life,* collected works 18, par. 1095.

[7] *Symbols of Transformation,* collected works 5, par. 553.

[8] Ibid., par. 551.

20   Perhaps nowhere are we more neurotic, that is, split internally, than over the question of mortality. The culture we have evolved is focused on acquisition, fueled by the power complex and sustained by denial. Mortality is the ultimate in personal loss, before which we are powerless, and that will not in the end be denied. Thus mortality serves as the grand affront to modern Western culture and so we call current medical interventions "heroic measures," as if death were the enemy.

The Tibetan tradition has long seen the transitions between life, death, the period after life, and the period of rebirth as a *bardo,* that is, a time of revelation, of transformation of consciousness. In this tradition the daily meditation on one's mortality is understood not as morbidity but as soul work. The more soul work, the greater the achievement of transformative consciousness. How alien this mindfulness of mortality seems in the midst of the wealth and neurotic preoccupations of modernism. Yet to see one's own life as a chip in the mosaic, a spark in the great fire, a drop in the cosmic sea, is not to deny the individual but to relocate oneself in a divine setting.

For an age of wanderers, such relocation is the final homecoming. Secretary of War Edwin Stanton must have felt this at the moment of Lincoln's passing when he said, "Now he belongs to the ages."[9] The memory of the Great Mother, her cycle of sacrifice, the great round, eternal return, serves as both fate and destiny for all humans. Those who can assimilate this image in their bones will transcend much of the alienation that characterizes our culture.

The other great idea, the hero's journey, reminds us of the. countertruth, that a person best serves the great mystery of nature by becoming an individual. The paradox is that the person must be subsumed into the great round and yet is incarnated here in order to differentiate and to develop. In this process the tribe is served, the individual is served, and, in ways we can only surmise, the divine is served as well.

It is folly to identify either of these great truths with gender roles, for both women and men are part of the same universal cycle and have the same imperative to individuate. Both have of course been constrained by the ideologies of gender roles, and hurt in body and soul as a result.

25   It may be unsettling to feel the wind of existential freedom, solitude and terror, but in that climate choices are made. The modern condition is that of deracination, wandering from ideology to ideology, from fad and fashion to ennui and depression, but the meaning of these two eternal mythological patterns is there to be embraced on an individual basis.

We are each obliged to suffer, to meditate upon, to incarnate, our unique experience of the cycle of sacrifice-death-rebirth, and, equally, to overthrow the gremlins of lethargy and fear to become that which nature so mysteriously offered. When we have taken on this unique yet absolute requirement that we become the protagonist in our own life drama, then we are living heroically. Though we may admire another, we need no hero to live for our vicarious satisfaction. Two characters in Bertolt Brecht's *Galileo* express it:

Unhappy the land that has no heroes.
No, unhappy the land that needs heroes:[10]

The poet Rilke eloquently summarized both our peril and our promise in his fourth "Sonnet to Orpheus":

You have been chosen, you are sound and whole. . . .
Do not be afraid to suffer, give
the heaviness back to the weight of the earth;
mountains are heavy, seas are heavy.

---

[9] Noah Andre Trudeau, *Out of the Storm,* p. 226.
[10] *Galileo,* scene 13.

Even those trees you planted as children
became too heavy long ago—you couldn't carry them now.
But you can cany the winds . . . and the open spaces[11]

Bibliography

Bly, Robert; Hillman, James; and Meade, Michael, eds. *The Rag and the Bone Shop of the Heart:* New York: HarperCollins, 1992.

Brecht, Berthold. *Galileo.* New York: Grove 1966.

Jung, C. G. *The Collected Works* (Bollingen Series XX), 20 vols. Trans. R. F. C. Hull. Ed. H. Read, M. Fordham, G. Adler, Wm. McGuire. Princeton: Princeton University Press, 1953–1979.

Trudeau, Noah Andre. *Out of the Storm.* New York: Little Brown, 1994.

▪ EXPLORATIONS OF THE TEXT

1. Gloss and annotate the work, summarizing the stages of "the heroic journey." What is Hollis's thesis? Subtopics? Are his examples persuasive?
2. Provide your own explanations and examples for the external and "internal" journey.
3. What does Hollis mean by "inner transformation"?
4. Explore the significance of the demons of "fear" and "lethargy." Can you identify these disruptive forces in your own life? How do they hinder individuation?
5. Explore the paradox at the heart of the essay: "The person must be subsumed into the great round and yet it is incarnated here in order to differentiate and to develop. In this process the tribe is served, the individual is served, and, in ways we can only surmise, the divine is served as well." How through "the heroic journey" is "the tribe . . . served, the individual . . . served"?

▪ THE READING/WRITING CONNECTION

1. "Think" Topic: Do you agree with Hollis's contention that gender roles do not play a significant role in influencing "the heroic journey," that "women and men are part of the same universal cycle and have the same imperative to individuate"? Using Hollis's theory as a context, compare and contrast "the heroic journey[s]" in Jewett's "A White Heron" and Steinbeck's "Flight." You also may consider the journeys of men and women whom you know.
2. Using Hollis's vision of the journey, freewrite about a particular time in your life when you felt that your sense of self was challenged. How did you respond? What did you learn? How did you grow?
3. Have you had a time in your life when you had to "overthrow the gremlins of lethargy and fear to become that which nature so mysteriously offered"?

▪ IDEAS FOR WRITING

1. Concentrate on the theme of the individual versus society in three works in the thematic cluster, "The Quest." Do the protagonists need to break away from the social world? Do they have opportunities for growth and reintegration, for what Hollis describes in another part of this selected text as the pattern of "departure, initiation, and return"?
2. Based on your observations and experiences, do you concur with Hollis's depiction of people in contemporary society: "modern individuals who, feeling no heroic stature,

---

[11] Trans. Robert Bly, in Robert Bly, James Hillman and Michael Meade, eds., *The Rag and Bone Shop of the Heart,* p. 100.

no sustaining mythos, wander from idea to idea, impulse to impulse, morosely changing channels in the hope of finding something better to watch"? Write a short essay that
presents your argumentative response.

DAVID SEDARIS

*Davis Sedaris (1957–   ) was born in Raleigh, North Carolina, and presently resides in New
York City and Paris, France. In* Me Talk Pretty One Day *(2000), Sedaris claims he moved to
France because it is still socially acceptable in that country to smoke in public. Sedaris was educated at the School of the Art Institute of Chicago, where he taught writing. He is known as
an essayist, short-story writer, and radio commentator. He is the author of seven books, including his first,* Origins of the Underclass, and Other Stories *(1992) and, most recent,* Dress
Your Family in Corduroy and Denim *(2004). Sedaris's dry humor and quirky perspective of
life have quickly earned him popularity as a writer and humorist. "I Like Guys" is taken from*
Naked *(1997), a collection of autobiographical essays.*

1997

I LIKE GUYS

Shortly before I graduated from eighth grade, it was announced that, come fall, our
county school system would adopt a policy of racial integration by way of forced busing. My Spanish teacher broke the news in a way she hoped might lead us to a greater understanding of her beauty and generosity.

"I remember the time I was at the state fair, standing in line for a Sno-Kone," she said,
fingering the kiss curls that framed her squat, compact face. "And a little colored girl ran up
and tugged at my skirt, asking if she could touch my hair. 'Just once,' she said. 'Just one
time for good luck.'

"Now, I don't know about the rest of you, but my hair means a lot to me." The members of my class nodded to signify that their hair meant a lot to them as well. They inched
forward in their seats, eager to know where this story might be going. Perhaps the little Negro girl was holding a concealed razor blade. Maybe she was one of the troublemakers out
for a fresh white scalp.

I sat marveling at their naïveté. Like all her previous anecdotes, this woman's story was
headed straight up her ass.

5   "I checked to make sure she didn't have any candy on her hands, and then I bent down
and let this little colored girl touch my hair." The teacher's eyes assumed the dewy, faraway
look she reserved for such Hallmark moments. "Then this little fudge-colored girl put her
hand on my cheek and said, 'Oh,' she said, 'I wish I could be white and pretty like you.'"
She paused, positioning herself on the edge of the desk as though she were posing for a portrait the federal government might use on a stamp commemorating gallantry. "The thing to
remember," she said, "is that more than anything in this world, those colored people wish
they were white."

I wasn't buying it. This was the same teacher who when announcing her pregnancy
said, "I just pray that my firstborn is a boy. I'll have a boy and then maybe later I'll have a
girl, because when you do it the other way round, there's a good chance the boy will turn
out to be funny."

" 'Funny,' as in having no arms and legs?" I asked.

"That," the teacher said, "is far from funny. That is tragic, and you, sir, should have
your lips sewn shut for saying such a cruel and ugly thing. When I say 'funny,' I mean funny

as in . . ." She relaxed her wrist, allowing her hand to dangle and flop. "I mean 'funny' as in *that* kind of funny." She minced across the room, but it failed to illustrate her point, as this was more or less her natural walk, a series of gamboling little steps, her back held straight, giving the impression she was balancing something of value atop her empty head. My seventh-period math teacher did a much better version. Snatching a purse off the back of a student's chair, he would prance about the room, batting his eyes and blowing kisses at the boys seated in the front row. "So fairy nice to meet you," he'd say.

Fearful of drawing any attention to myself, I hooted and squawked along with the rest of the class, all the while thinking, *That's me he's talking about.* If I was going to make fun of people, I had to expect a little something in return, that seemed only fair. Still, though, it bothered me that they'd found such an easy way to get a laugh. As entertainers, these teachers were nothing, zero. They could barely impersonate themselves. "Look at you!" my second-period gym teacher would shout, his sneakers squealing against the basketball court. "You're a group of ladies, a pack of tap-dancing queers."

10   The other boys shrugged their shoulders or smiled down at their shoes. They reacted as if they had been called Buddhists or vampires; sure, it was an insult, but no one would ever mistake them for the real thing. Had they ever chanted in the privacy of their backyard temple or slept in a coffin, they would have felt the sting of recognition and shared my fear of discovery.

I had never done anything with another guy and literally prayed that I never would. As much as I fantasized about it, I understood that there could be nothing worse than making it official. You'd seen them on television from time to time, the homosexuals, maybe on one of the afternoon talk shows. No one ever came out and called them a queer, but you could just tell by their voices as they flattered the host and proclaimed great respect for their fellow guests. These were the celebrities never asked about their home life, the comedians running scarves beneath their toupees or framing their puffy faces with their open palms in an effort to eliminate the circles beneath their eyes. "The poor man's face lift," my mother called it. Regardless of their natty attire, these men appeared sweaty and desperate, willing to play the fool in exchange for the studio applause they seemed to mistake for love and acceptance. I saw something of myself in their mock weary delivery, in the way they crossed their legs and laughed at their own jokes. I pictured their homes: the finicky placement of their throw rugs and sectional sofas, the magazines carefully fanned just so upon the coffee tables with no wives or children to disturb their order. I imagined the pornography hidden in their closets and envisioned them powerless and sobbing as the police led them away in shackles, past the teenage boy who stood bathed in the light of the television news camera and shouted, "That's him! He's the one who touched my hair!"

It was my hope to win a contest, cash in the prizes, and use the money to visit a psychiatrist who might cure me of having homosexual thoughts. Electroshock, brain surgery, hypnotism—I was willing to try anything. Under a doctor's supervision, I would buckle down and really change, I swore I would.

My parents knew a couple whose son had killed a Presbyterian minister while driving drunk. They had friends whose eldest daughter had sprinkled a Bundt cake with Comet, and knew of a child who, high on spray paint, had set fire to the family's cocker spaniel. Yet, they spoke of no one whose son was a homosexual. The odds struck me as bizarre, but the message was the same: this was clearly the worst thing that could happen to a person. The day-to-day anxiety was bad enough without my instructors taking their feeble little potshots. If my math teacher were able to subtract the alcohol from his diet, he'd still be on the football field where he belonged; and my Spanish teacher's credentials were based on nothing more than a long weekend in Tijuana, as far as I could tell. I quit taking their tests and completing their homework assignments, accepting Fs rather than delivering the grades I thought might promote their reputations as good teachers. It was a strategy that hurt only me, but I thought it cunning. We each had our self-defeating schemes, all the boys I had come to identify as homosexuals. Except for a few transfer students, I had known most of them since the third grade. We'd spent years gathered together in cinder-block offices as one speech therapist after another tried to cure us of our lisps. Had there been a walking specialist, we probably would have met there, too. These were the same boys who carried poorly forged notes to gym class and were the first to raise their hands when the English teacher asked for a volunteer to read aloud from *The Yearling* or *Lord of the Flies.* We had long ago identified one another and understood that because of everything we had in common, we could never be friends. To socialize would have drawn too much attention to ourselves. We were members of a secret society founded on self-loathing. When a teacher or classmate made fun of a real homosexual, I made certain my laugh was louder than anyone else's. When a club member's clothing was thrown into the locker-room toilet, I was always the first to cheer. When it was my clothing, I watched as the faces of my fellows broke into recognizable expressions of relief. *Faggots,* I thought. *This should have been you.*

Several of my teachers, when discussing the upcoming school integration, would scratch at the damp stains beneath their arms, pulling back their lips to reveal every bit of tooth and gum. They made monkey noises, a manic succession of ohhs and ahhs meant to suggest that soon our school would be no different than a jungle. Had a genuine ape been seated in the room, I guessed he might have identified their calls as a cry of panic. Anything that caused them suffering brought me joy, but I doubted they would talk this way come fall. From everything I'd seen on television, the Negros would never stand for such foolishness. As a people, they seemed to stick together. They knew how to fight, and I hoped that once they arrived, the battle might come down to the gladiators, leaving the rest of us alone.

15   At the end of the school year, my sister Lisa and I were excused from our volunteer jobs and sent to Greece to attend a month-long summer camp advertised as "the Crown Jewel of the Ionian Sea." The camp was reserved exclusively for Greek Americans and featured instruction in such topics as folk singing and something called "religious prayer and flag." I despised the idea of summer camp but longed to boast that I had been to Europe. "It changes people!" our neighbor had said. Following a visit to Saint-Tropez, she had marked her garden with a series of tissue-sized international flags. A once discreet and modest woman, she now paraded about her yard wearing nothing but clogs and a flame-stitched bikini. "Europe is the best thing that can happen to a person, especially if you like wine!"

I saw Europe as an opportunity to re-invent myself. I might still look and speak the same way, but having walked those cobblestoned streets, I would be identified as Continental. "He has a passport," my classmates would whisper. "Quick, let's run before he judges us!"

I told myself that I would find a girlfriend in Greece. She would be a French tourist wandering the beach with a loaf of bread beneath her arm. Lisette would prove that I wasn't a homosexual, but a man with refined tastes. I saw us holding hands against the silhouette of the Acropolis, the girl begging me to take her accordian as a memento of our love. "Silly you," I would say, brushing the tears from her eyes, "just give me the beret, that will be enough to hold you in my heart until the end of time."

In case no one believed me, I would have my sister as a witness. Lisa and I weren't getting along very well, but I hoped that the warm Mediterranean waters might melt the icicle she seemed to have mistaken for a rectal thermometer. Faced with a country of strangers, she would have no choice but to appreciate my company.

Our father accompanied us to New York, where we met our fellow campers for the charter flight to Athens. There were hundreds of them, each one confident and celebratory. They tossed their complimentary Aegean Airlines tote bags across the room, shouting and jostling one another. This would be the way I'd act once we'd finally returned from camp, but not one moment before. Were it an all-girl's camp, I would have been able to work up some enthusiasm. Had they sent me alone to pry leeches off the backs of bloodthirsty Pygmies, I might have gone bravely—but spending a month in a dormitory full of boys, that was asking too much. I'd tried to put it out of my mind, but faced with their boisterous presence, I found myself growing progressively more hysterical. My nervous tics shifted into their highest gear, and a small crowd gathered to watch what they believed to be an exotic folk dance. If my sister was anxious about our trip, she certainly didn't show it. Prying my fingers off her wrist, she crossed the room and introduced herself to a girl who stood picking salvageable butts out of the standing ashtray. This was a tough-looking Queens native named Stefani Heartattackus or Testicockules. I recall only that her last name had granted her a lifelong supply of resentment. Stefani wore mirrored aviator sunglasses and carried an oversized comb in the back pocket of her hiphugger jeans. Of all the girls in the room, she seemed the least likely candidate for my sister's friendship. They sat beside each other on the plane, and by the time we disembarked in Athens, Lisa was speaking in a very bad Queens accent. During the long flight, while I sat cowering beside a boy named Seamen, my sister had undergone a complete physical and cultural transformation. Her shoulder-length hair was now parted on the side, covering the left half of her face as if to conceal a nasty scar. She cursed and spat, scowling out the window of the chartered bus as if she'd come to Greece with the sole intention of kicking its dusty ass. "What a shithole," she yelled. "Jeez, if I'd knowed it was gonna be dis hot, I woulda stayed home wit my head din da oven, right, girls!"

20   It shamed me to hear my sister struggle so hard with an accent that did nothing but demean her, yet I silently congratulated her on the attempt. I approached her once we reached the camp, a cluster of whitewashed buildings hugging the desolate coast, far from any neighboring village.

"Listen, asshole," she said, "as far as this place is concerned, I don't know you and you sure as shit don't know me, you got that?" She spoke as if she were auditioning for a touring company of *West Side Story*, one hand on her hip and the other fingering her pocket comb as if it were a switchblade.

"Hey, Carolina!" one of her new friends called.

"A righta ready," she brayed. "I'm comin', I'm comin'."

That was the last time we spoke before returning home. Lisa had adjusted with remarkable ease, but something deep in my stomach suggested I wouldn't thrive nearly as well. Camp lasted a month, during which time I never once had a bowel movement. I was used to having a semiprivate bathroom and could not bring myself to occupy one of the men's room stalls, fearful that someone might recognize my shoes or, even worse, not see my shoes at all and walk in on me. Sitting down three times a day for a heavy Greek meal became an exercise akin to packing a musket. I told myself I'd sneak off during one of our field trips, but those toilets were nothing more than a hole in the floor, a hole I could have filled with no problem whatsoever. I considered using the Ionian Sea, but for some unexplained reason, we were not allowed to swim in those waters. The camp had an Olympic-size pool that was fed from the sea and soon grew murky with stray bits of jellyfish that had been pulverized by the pump. The tiny tentacles raised welts on campers' skin, so shortly after arriving, it was announced that we could photograph both the pool *and* the ocean but could swim in neither. The Greeks had invented democracy, built the Acropolis, and then called it a day. Our swimming period was converted into "contemplation hour" for the girls and an extended soccer practice for the boys.

25   "I really think I'd be better off contemplating," I told the coach, massaging my distended stomach. "I've got a personal problem that's sort of weighing me down."

Because we were first and foremost Americans, the camp was basically an extension of junior high school except that here everyone had an excess of moles or a single eyebrow. The attractive sports-minded boys ran the show, currying favor from the staff and ruining our weekly outdoor movie with their inane heckling. From time to time the rented tour buses would carry us to view one of the country's many splendors, and we would raid the gift shops, stealing anything that wasn't chained to the shelf or locked in a guarded case. These were cheap, plated puzzle rings and pint-size vases, little pom-pommed shoes, and coffee mugs reading SPARTA IS FOR A LOVER. My shoplifting experience was the only thing that gave me an edge over the popular boys. "Hold it like this," I'd whisper. "Then swivel around and slip the statue of Diana down the back of your shorts, covering it with your T-shirt. Remember to back out the door while leaving and never forget to wave good-bye."

There was one boy at camp I felt I might get along with, a Detroit native named Jason who slept on the bunk beneath mine. Jason tended to look away when talking to the other boys, shifting his eyes as though he were studying the weather conditions. Like me, he used his free time to curl into a fetal position, staring at the bedside calendar upon which he'd x-ed out all the days he had endured so far. We were finishing our 7:15 to 7:45 wash-and-rinse segment one morning when our dormitory counselor arrived for inspection shouting, "What are you, a bunch of goddamned faggots who can't make your beds?"

I giggled out loud at his stupidity. If anyone knew how to make a bed, it was a faggot. It was the others he needed to worry about. I saw Jason laughing, too, and soon we took to mocking this counselor, referring to each other first as "faggots" and then as "stinking faggots." We were "lazy faggots" and "sunburned faggots" before we eventually became "faggoty faggots." We couldn't protest the word, as that would have meant acknowledging the truth of it. The most we could do was embrace it as a joke. Embodying the term in all its clichéd glory, we minced and pranced about the room for each other's entertainment when the others weren't looking. I found myself easily outperforming my teachers, who had failed to capture the proper spirit of loopy bravado inherent to the role. *Faggot,* as a word, was always delivered in a harsh, unforgiving tone befitting those weak or stupid enough to act upon their impulses. We used it as a joke, an accusation, and finally as a dare. Late at night I'd feel my bunk buck and sway, knowing that Jason was either masturbating or beating eggs for an omelette. *Is it me he's thinking about?* I'd follow his lead and wake the next morning to find our entire iron-frame unit had wandered a good eighteen inches away from the wall. Our love had the power to move bunks.

Having no willpower, we depended on circumstances to keep us apart. *This cannot happen* was accompanied by the sound of bedsprings whining, *Oh, but maybe just this once.* There came an afternoon when, running late for flag worship, we found ourselves alone in the dormitory. What started off as name-calling escalated into a series of mock angry slaps. We wrestled each other onto one of the lower bunks, both of us longing to be pinned. "You kids think you invented sex," my mother was fond of saying. But hadn't we? With no instruction manual or federally enforced training period, didn't we all come away feeling we'd discovered something unspeakably modern? What produced in others a feeling of exhilaration left Jason and me with a mortifying sense of guilt. We fled the room as if, in our fumblings, we had uncapped some virus we still might escape if we ran fast enough. Had one of the counselors not caught me scaling the fence, I felt certain I could have made it back to Raleigh by morning, skittering across the surface of the ocean like one of those lizards often featured on television wildlife programs.

30 When discovered making out with one of the Greek bus drivers, a sixteen-year-old camper was forced to stand beside the flagpole dressed in long pants and thick sweaters. We watched her cook in the hot sun until, fully roasted, she crumpled to the pavement and passed out.

"That," the chief counselor said, "is what happens to people who play around."

If this was the punishment for a boy and a girl, I felt certain the penalty for two boys somehow involved barbed wire, a team of donkeys, and the nearest volcano. Nothing, however, could match the cruelty and humiliation Jason and I soon practiced upon each other. He started a rumor that I had stolen an athletic supporter from another camper and secretly wore it over my mouth like a surgical mask. I retaliated, claiming he had expressed a desire to become a dancer. "That's nothing," he said to the assembled crowd, "take a look at what I found on David's bed!" He reached into the pocket of his tennis shorts and withdrew a sheet of notebook paper upon which were written the words I LIKE GUYS. Presented as an indictment, the document was both pathetic and comic. Would I supposedly have written the note to remind myself of that fact, lest I forget? Had I intended to wear it taped to my back, advertising my preference the next time our rented buses carried us off to yet another swinging sexual playground?

I LIKE GUYS. He held the paper above his head, turning a slow circle so that everyone might get a chance to see. I supposed he had originally intended to plant the paper on my bunk for one of the counselors to find. Presenting it himself had foiled the note's intended effect. Rather than beating me with sticks and heavy shoes, the other boys simply groaned and looked away, wondering why he'd picked the thing up and carried it around in his pants pocket. He might as well have hoisted a glistening turd, shouting, "Look what he did!" Touching such a foul document made him suspect and guilty by association. In attempting to discredit each other, we wound up alienating ourselves even further.

Jason—even his name seemed affected. During meals I studied him from across the room. Here I was, sweating onto my plate, my stomach knotted and cramped, when *he* was the one full of shit. Clearly he had tricked me, cast a spell or slipped something into my food. I watched as he befriended a girl named Theodora and held her hand during a screening of *A Lovely Way to Die,* one of the cave paintings the head counselor offered as a weekly movie.

35   She wasn't a bad person, Theodora. Someday the doctors might find a way to transplant a calf's brain into a human skull, and then she'd be just as lively and intelligent as he was. I tried to find a girlfriend of my own, but my one possible candidate was sent back home when she tumbled down the steps of the Parthenon, causing serious damage to her leg brace.

Jason looked convincing enough in the company of his girlfriend. They scrambled about the various ruins, snapping each other's pictures while I hung back fuming, watching them nuzzle and coo. My jealousy stemmed from the belief that he had been cured. One fistful of my flesh and he had lost all symptoms of the disease.

Camp ended and I flew home with my legs crossed, dropping my bag of stolen souvenirs and racing to the bathroom, where I spent the next several days sitting on the toilet and studying my face in a hand mirror. *I like guys.* The words had settled themselves into my features. I was a professional now, and it showed.

I returned to my volunteer job at the mental hospital, carrying harsh Greek cigarettes as an incentive to some of the more difficult patients.

"Faggot!" a woman shouted, stooping to protect her collection of pinecones. "Get your faggoty hands away from my radio transmitters."

40   "Don't mind Mary Elizabeth," the orderly said. "She's crazy."

Maybe not, I thought, holding a pinecone up against my ear. She's gotten the faggot part right, so maybe she was onto something.

The moment we boarded our return flight from Kennedy to Raleigh, Lisa re-arranged her hair, dropped her accent, and turned to me saying, "Well, I thought that was very nice, how about you?" Over the course of five minutes, she had eliminated all traces of her reckless European self. Why couldn't I do the same?

In late August my class schedule arrived along with the news that I would not be bused. There had been violence in other towns and counties, trouble as far away as Boston;

but in Raleigh the transition was peaceful. Not only students but many of the teachers had been shifted from one school to another. My new science teacher was a black man very adept at swishing his way across the room, mocking everyone from Albert Einstein to the dweebish host of a popular children's television program. Black and white, the teachers offered their ridicule as though it were an olive branch. "Here," they said, "this is something we each have in common, proof that we're all brothers under the skin."

■ EXPLORATIONS OF THE TEXT

1. How do the opening anecdotes about Sedaris's eighth-grade teacher set the stage for the narrative? What social issues are introduced?
2. The essay is set in a Southern town during the late 1960s. How do the townspeople's attitudes and media images of homosexuality influence the adolescent persona's emerging sense of sexual identity and self-concept? Does he experience confusion about his sexual orientation?
3. Compare and contrast Lisa's, Jason's, and the persona's experience at the summer camp.
4. Analyze the "first" sexual encounter depicted in the work. How do Jason's and the persona's response to the experience differ?
5. How does Sedaris handle the idea of role playing? Consider his treatment of the change in his sister's personality.
6. How does Sedaris's point of view and humor contribute to the effectiveness of the essay?
7. Human beings have a need for acceptance. Compare and contrast Sedaris's self-loathing and desire to belong with the speaker's in Mirikitani's "Suicide Note."

■ THE READING/WRITING CONNECTION

1. "Think" Topic: Compare Sedaris's treatment of gayness in this work with that of Ficera's in "Bi-Bye" (chapter 6). How does the difference in time periods figure in their representations of sexual identity?
2. Write about a sexual encounter or a "first" in your life—perhaps your first kiss.

■ IDEAS FOR WRITING

1. Explore the journey motif in this work with that in one other work in "The Quest" thematic cluster.
2. David Sedaris has written several best-selling volumes of essays, including *Naked, Barrel Fever,* and *Me Talk Pretty One Day.* Examine another essay by this writer. What makes his work effective? Consider such elements of nonfiction as point of view, organization, use of detail, figurative language, and humor.

■ WRITING ASSIGNMENTS ■

1. a. What makes you proud of your background? Freewrite.
    b. Compare your view of cultural pride and identity with the views in two of the following poems: "Ego Tripping," "Indian Boarding School: The Runaways," "Lost Sister," and "Suicide Note."
2. a. Compare the view of gaining sexual awareness and identity for men and for women in any of the works in this chapter.
    b. Interview several people about their experiences in gaining sexual awareness.
    c. Based on the works in this chapter and/or your interviews, write an essay that classifies ways in which adolescents acquire sexual knowledge.

3. Rites of passage may be characterized as those that involve loss, those that entail facing death, those that include isolation, and those that involve gaining new knowledge. Analyze two or three of the works in the chapter according to one of these categories.

4. Compare Elkind's view of adolescence with that of one of the other works in this chapter.

5. Coming of age and initiation experiences prompt adolescents either to accept or to reject adult responsibilities. Analyze the conflicts of a character in one of the works in this chapter in light of this idea.

6. Use one of these topic areas as the basis for an essay on a rite of passage: driving, flying, running, being caged, facing the self, hunting, lying.

7. a. Freewrite on a coming-of-age ritual you have experienced, for example, a bar mitzvah.
   b. Read about coming-of-age rituals in a particular culture. Take notes. Examine the origins, the evolution, and the current practice of the ritual (for example, bar mitzvah in Jewish culture). Write an outline, draft, revision, and final version of a research paper concerning one such ritual.

8. Contrast views of cultural identity in this chapter.

9. a. List the ways in which you have conformed and the ways in which you have rebelled.
   b. Write about a single event that symbolizes the conflict between conformity and rebellion.
   c. Coming of age involves coming to terms with one's culture. Discuss the struggle between acceptance and rejection of cultural roots as it is presented in several works in the chapter.

10. Discuss how a scene or vignette from a story or play functions in the development of a particular character.

11. Many of the works in this chapter depend on *irony*. Choose two or three selections, and discuss the function and effects of irony. (Suggestions: "Barn Burning," "The Stolen Party," "Cinderella," "Rose-Johnny," and/or *Hamlet*.)

12. a. Write a journal entry on your search for selfhood.
    b. Compare your process of individuation with the struggles of a character in a work in this chapter.
    c. Discuss the themes concerning the search for self.

13. a. Write a journal entry on a coming-of-age experience.
    b. Compare your experience with the conflict concerning the coming of age of a character in one of the works in this chapter.

14. Discuss the connection between "Kids in the Mall" or "Our Hurried Children" and "Where Are You Going, Where Have You Been?"

15. Initiation stories often involve the spilling of blood. Using examples from the works in this chapter, argue in support or refutation of such an assertion.

16. Choose two or three works that exemplify the theme of initiation at different ages. What similarities and differences are apparent?

17. a. Interview your parents or other adults about conflicts between parents and children in adolescence.
    b. Interview several teenagers about their perspectives concerning conflicts between parents and adolescents.
    c. Write a summary of these responses.
    d. Write an essay that compares these perspectives.

18. Explore the connection between danger and adolescence in the works in the Crossing the Genres section.

19. Discuss stages of coming of age presented in Robert Frost's "Birches" (see chapter 8), and then apply these rites of passage to the situations of two characters in two works in this chapter.

20. Choose several stories in this chapter and discuss whether those stories' portrayal of adolescence is still relevant today.
21. Analyze the search for self experienced by one character in one of the works in this chapter.
22. Explore your personal responses to one of the works in this chapter. You may frame your response as a letter to the writer. (See Staci Ferris's essay, "Response to Greg Delanty's 'Leavetaking.'")
23. Fairy tales often end with the promise of a "happily ever after" life. Do the stories in this chapter conclude in this manner? Compare the endings of several works in this chapter. Are the conclusions unexpected, or are they the predictable outcomes of characters' plights?
24. Much of what goes wrong in life is caused by our own natures. Relate this idea to such works as "Flight," "Rose-Johnny," "A Good Man Is Hard to Find," *A Doll's House,* and/or *Hamlet.*
25. It is important for people to find meaning in their lives.
    a. Write about a time in your life that challenged you, that pushed you beyond your own comfort level and prompted you to find new meanings in life.
    b. Focus on this same struggle for protagonists in such works as "A Good Man Is Hard to Find," "Cathedral," *A Doll's House,* or *Hamlet.*
    c. Compare and contrast you own search for meaning with that of one or several of the protagonists in the above works.
26. Bettelheim discusses the "images of heroes who have to go out into the world all by themselves," like Pepé in "Flight," the adolescent protagonist in Sedaris's piece, or Sarty in "Barn Burning." Discuss how or why these characters achieve or fail to achieve meaningful relations with the world around them.
27. "Treasures" and "Loss": Both of these words characterize our relationships with our pasts.
    a. Use each word as the basis of a freewrite. What were the treasures and the losses of your childhood and adolescence?
    b. Compare your complex relationship with your own past with that of several characters from works in this chapter. (Suggestions: "The Attic," "Biography of an Armenian Schoolgirl," and "Black Hair.")
28. Create a character analysis in creative or analytic form of one of the protagonists in one of the works in this chapter. See Jean Thompson's "Journal for Sylvia: 'A White Heron'" or Leigh Grimm's "The Jilting of Granny Weatherall" (chapter 6).

■ STUDENT ESSAYS ■

Student Essay: Personal Response

GREG DELANTY (1958–   )   1992

LEAVETAKING

After you board the train, you sit & wait,
  to begin your first real journey alone.
You read to avoid the window's awkwardness,
  knowing he's anxious to catch your eye,
    loitering out in never-ending rain,

> to wave, a bit shy, another final goodbye;
> you are afraid of having to wave too soon.
>
> 5 And for the moment you think it's the train
>   next to you has begun, but it is yours,
> and your face, pressed to the windowpane,
>   is distorted & numbed by the icy glass,
>   pinning your eyes upon your father,
> as he cranes to defy your disappearing train.
> Both of you waving, eternally, to each other.

STACI ANNA MARIE FERRIS

Response to Greg Delanty's "Leavetaking"

Dear Greg,

   Your poem "Leavetaking" brought memories flowing back into my mind. Memories of the day that I left my home and family in Switzerland and headed to college on a train. Memories of many tears and yet memories of excitement. Reading your poem was like having someone read my mind and put the memories of that day on paper. I am amazed at how much alike our feelings and experiences were about leaving home.

   The first thing about the poem that struck me as a coincidence was the train. I also left home a little more than two months ago on a train. When you talk about "sit[ting] and wait[ing]/to begin your first real journey alone," as I read, memories of the day of leavetaking began to flow back into my mind as vividly as the day I left. I remember stepping on the train and taking my seat next to the window. On the other side of the window was my family. I felt as if I were already over the ocean, and they still were at home in Switzerland. I felt the window's "awkwardness." The window of the train was like a barrier between home and the future, my future. I could not look at them out the window for fear that I would break out into tears.

   But yet at the same time I wanted to look at them, to capture the memory of every line of my family's faces, hair, the clothes that they were wearing, and, most importantly, the look in their eyes. Everyone had looks of sadness on their faces and tears in their eyes, except my little cousins who were too young to understand what was happening—that I was going to be away for a long time. My cousins were all standing there with ice cream in their hands, smiling and waving. All I could think was how I wished that I was that little again and wasn't on the train about to leave. I only looked at them at short glances thinking what would happen if I just jumped off the train and decided to stay home. But I continued to sit on the train for what seemed an eternity.

   Another line that struck me was "you are afraid of having to wave too soon." I remember that I was too afraid to wave because I thought that once I began to wave the train would move, and I would be slowly moving down the track away from my family and home. I kept thinking—my "face pressed to the windowpane"—that if I didn't wave, then the train wouldn't move; I could just sit there forever taking short glances at my family. However, finally the train began to move, and I got a funny feeling in the pit of my stomach, a sick feeling perhaps. I began to wave out the window at my family, and they waved back. They were crying and waving, and I was doing the same. All of us waving, "eternally, to each other," hoping that I wasn't really leaving and that they could still see me. As the miles passed and the mountains became practically invisible, I realized that I had left home and my family to start this new journey, new beginning, a new chapter of my life: a chapter filled with new people and places, but still containing my family and my home. However, I would be living at a distance from them and not seeing them as much.

Greg, your poem took me back to a very important and vivid day in my life. Thank you for reminding me of that day and the moment that the train started to move on the tracks.

Yours truly,
Staci Ferris

Student Essay: Creative Response to Literature and Character Analysis

JEAN THOMPSON

Journal for Sylvia: "A White Heron"

June 14

When I looked in the mirror tonight, I was surprised to see the same girl with the "pale face and shining gray eyes" that I always see. I feel so different on the inside that I thought it would be fitting for my physical appearance to be different as well. I wonder if anyone else can sense that something has changed.

Today started out just like any other day. I completed my chores and explored the wonderful forest. It took a particularly long time to find the cow, but that is not very surprising. Then I heard the whistle of a human being and was immediately frightened. I find comfort in the sound of a bird's whistle, but I never have been too fond of people. I attempted to hide in the bushes, but the stranger came upon me too quickly. I tried to calmly answer his questions, but my heart was beating rapidly and I struggled to form words. I always have had difficulty communicating with people. I find it so much easier to communicate with the forest creatures.

I am not sure exactly how it all happened. It seemed quick and out of my control, but somehow I ended up walking home with two companions rather than arriving with only the cow. I was worried that my grandmother would be angry with me. I always do what she tells me to without a question, and I thought that I had somehow let her down by allowing this stranger to accompany me home. Surprisingly, my grandmother was not angry at all. In fact, she seemed pleased to have a guest. Fortunately, she told me to set a place for the guest, so I was able to escape from the discomfort of being with a strange man.

My grandmother and the sportsman talked for a long while. I paid close attention to what they were saying, but I tried not to make my interest obvious. When the stranger began talking about the white heron, I felt sure that they could both hear that my heart started beating faster. This young man really wants to find a white heron, and I have seen one before. I am sure that I could find the heron again. I know every inch of the forest so well. The man said he would pay ten dollars to anyone who could lead him to this rare and beautiful bird. Ten dollars!

I wonder what it would be like to have that much money. There are so many little treasures that I could buy.

Now all I can think about is the stranger and the money. I am so used to spending the majority of my day playing in the wilderness. I do not usually have much interaction with other humans. I moved out here and away from town so that I could get away from all of the people. It really was not so bad meeting this young man today though. It was actually quite exciting, and I just cannot stop imagining what I could do with ten dollars.

June 15

I spent the whole day with the sportsman, hunting for various kinds of birds. It was such an incredible day. I listened carefully to all that he said, but I found it so hard to even answer yes or no. I definitely never spoke first; the sound of my "own unquestioned voice would have terrified" me. I do not really think that I had anything that important to say, and he says so many wonderful things. He even gave me a jackknife. I think it is the best present I have ever received, and I will treasure it always.

Everything about him is wonderful except that he kills birds. It hurt me so much to watch him shoot all of those beautiful creatures. Just the thought of it makes me want to cry. These creatures are my companions. They understand me, and I understand them. I do not know what to do about this situation. I really admire the sportsman and have enjoyed spending time with him, but I also feel that I should be loyal to the birds because they have been my companions for much longer than he has.

June 16

Last night I could not sleep because I thought of an incredible idea. I thought that I could climb the majestic old pine tree, and then I could find the white heron and lead the sportsman to it. I got up early this morning before anyone else was awake and made my way to the large tree. I climbed the smaller oak tree beside it first and then stepped across to the pine tree. I felt so daring and adventurous. I was a little scared, but there was so much excitement inside me that I was able to overcome my fear. The climbing was harder than I thought it would be, but it was definitely worth the effort.

When I finally reached the top of the tree, I experienced the most triumphant moment of my life. I forgot about my physical exhaustion and took in all of the sights and sounds that surrounded me. The sea was just as glorious as I had imagined. The sun had started its ascent through the sky, and its brilliant rays sparkled on the vast expanse of water. I watched two hawks soar across the sky and felt like I was flying as well. I loved looking down upon the world from this viewpoint, and I savored every sight, sound, and feeling.

Then the most magical event occurred. I spotted the exquisite white heron making its way toward the "landmark pine." I held my breath and made sure not to move even a finger, and the magnificent bird landed on a pine branch not too far from mine. Only a minute later a group of "shouting cat-birds" came along and the heron disappeared. As I made the long difficult journey back down the tree, I only wished that my time with the heron had lasted longer. I believe that moment is one that I will never forget.

By the time I got down from the tree, my clothes were ripped and torn, and I was covered with pine pitch. As I hurried back toward home, part of me truly believed that I was going to tell the guest what I had discovered. There was also a part of me that knew that this was not true. Something had happened inside of me when I had encountered the heron so closely. My love for the heron and all of the forest creatures was renewed. I could no longer ignore how much it hurt me to watch the stranger kill birds. There were many thoughts running through my mind during the journey back to the house. I thought about my respect for the heron and my respect for the stranger. At that point I may have known deep down inside me what was about to happen, but I was still fighting within myself to determine who would receive my loyalty.

The events that occurred after that are still painful and confusing. I found myself unable to tell the stranger what I had learned about the heron. I thought about the ten dollars and my admiration for this young man, but for some reason I just could not bring myself to tell him what I knew. I have been silent for almost all of my life, but before I always chose to keep quiet because of fear or simply because I had no desire to speak. This silence was different. I felt that something was stopping me, and whatever this force was it was out of my control. I watched the stranger walk away until he disappeared among the trees. I felt a "sharp pang" as I realized that I had lost this special friend.

Loyalty to the heron kept me from making a friend and receiving enough money to buy all the treasures I could want. After my encounter with the heron this morning, I felt a special bond with him, and even though the guest and I had shared a day full of adventures, the bond I had with the guest could not compare with the respect and admiration I had for this bird. I just could not bear to think about this incredible creature being shot down. Before I came to live here with my grandmother, I lived in a house crowded with children that was in a town crowded with people. I was never happy there; I never like being around so many people. I love being here though, especially when I am out-of-doors in the wilderness. I love all nature, and all nature loves me. I am not sure that I will ever have a special bond with human beings as I do with forest creatures.

· CHAPTER 5 ·

Haunted Houses

Your family is the void you emerge from and the place you
    return to when you die. And that is the paradox; the closer
    you're drawn back in, the deeper into the void you go.

The Ice Storm

Happy or unhappy, families are all mysterious. We have only to imagine
    how differently we would be described—and will be, after our deaths—
    by each of the family members who believe they know us. The only
    question is, Why are some mysteries more important than others?

Gloria Steinem

No people are ever as divided as those of the same blood.

Mavis Gallant

In search of my mother's garden, I found my own.

Alice Walker

Federico Castellón, "Rendezvous in a Landscape," n.d. (20th century)

▪ *Introduction* ▪

*We live our lives like chips in a kaleidoscope, always
part of patterns that are larger than ourselves and somehow
more than the sum of their parts.*

Salvadore Minuchin, *Family Kaleidoscope*

We live as part of a kaleidoscope that is "larger than ourselves." The "chips" of the pattern are variegated, beautiful, and complex. The fundamental pieces of the pattern upon which the others depend are family members. They provide the initial forms of bonding: the crucial experiences of security and insecurity, of love and hate. These early relationships of intimacy, connection, and conflict with parents and siblings influence our responses to the world.

Perhaps one of the enduring facts of family life is that family members exist in separate worlds. Each person in the kaleidoscope harbors secret thoughts, wishes, dreams—an inner life of which others have no knowledge. Another is that we often are haunted by the ghosts of the past: personal, familial, historical, and cultural traumatic events. Family dynamics, the relationships between parents and children, inevitably are complicated. Literature is replete, for example, with images of the father as the authority figure, as the protector, and as the provider. What happens when fathers fail to fulfill these obligations? A number of works in this chapter explore the question. Of course, relationships with fathers not only are destructive but also life-giving and nurturing. Literature also represents fathers who demonstrate their values and teach their children to live in the world as several works in chapter 5 illustrate. Like the bonds of fathers with their children, the relationships of mothers with their sons and daughters not only are fraught with anxiety, but also are life-giving, and nurturing.

The works in this chapter concerning parents and children, then, are stories of love and nurture as well as of loss and recognition of loss. As some stories demonstrate complex and positive relationships between parents and children, some demonstrate the failings of parents, and they record the anger of children who perceive that their parents have failed them—failed them because of their own limits, failed them because of desire for their children to be perfect, to be like them, and to compensate for their deficiencies.

We not only are members of a nuclear family but also of an extended family, of a tribe, and of a community. We are the products of personal, familial, and cultural histories. The same kaleidoscope of relationships that characterize parents and children exists among siblings and friends. Several poems and essays affirm kinship ties, those bonds with others that become sources of strength. As Etheridge Knight's persona reveals: "I am all of them,/they are all of me, I am me, they are they, and I have no children/to float in the space between." These bonds exist as our "lineage," our roots, as Margaret Walker suggests in "Lineage".

Thematic Clusters

More Themes that Cross the Genres

Crossing the Genres

FAMILY SECRETS

NATHANIEL HAWTHORNE

Nathaniel Hawthorne (1804–64) was born in Salem, Massachusetts, and educated at Bowdoin College. Twenty-two years separate his first novel, Fanshawe *(1828), from his second,* The Scarlet Letter *(1850), time during which he honed his skills as a writer by working on the short stories that were collected in* Twice-Told Tales *(1837) and* Mosses from an Old Manse *(1846). Hawthorne wrote three other novels:* The House of the Seven Gables *(1851),* The Blithedale Romance *(1853), and* The Marble Faun *(1860). Hawthorne's fiction is marked by its use of symbol and allegory and its concern with sin.*

1846

RAPPACCINI'S DAUGHTER

A young man, named Giovanni Guasconti, came, very long ago, from the more southern region of Italy, to pursue his studies at the University of Padua. Giovanni, who had but a scanty supply of gold ducats[1] in his pocket, took lodgings in a high gloomy chamber of an old edifice which looked not unworthy to have been the palace of a Paduan noble, and which, in fact, exhibited over its entrance the armorial bearings of a family long since extinct. The young stranger, who was not unstudied in the great poem of his country, recollected that one of the ancestors of this family, and perhaps an occupant of this very mansion, had been pictured by Dante as a partaker of the immortal agonies of his Inferno.[2] These reminiscences and associations, together with the tendency to heartbreak natural to a young man for the first time out of his native sphere, caused Giovanni to sigh heavily as he looked around the desolate and ill-furnished apartment.

"Holy Virgin, signor!" cried old Dame Lisabetta, who, won by the youth's remarkable beauty of person was kindly endeavoring to give the chamber a habitable air, "what a sigh was that to come out of a young man's heart! Do you find this old mansion gloomy? For the love of Heaven, then, put your head out of the window, and you will see as bright sunshine as you have left in Naples."

Guasconti mechanically did as the old woman advised, but could not quite agree with her that the Paduan sunshine was as cheerful as that of southern Italy. Such as it was, however, it fell upon a garden beneath the window and expended its fostering influences on a variety of plants, which seemed to have been cultivated with exceeding care.

"Does this garden belong to the house?" asked Giovanni.

5 "Heaven forbid, signor, unless it were fruitful of better pot herbs than any that grow there now," answered old Lisabetta. "No; that garden is cultivated by the own hands of Signor Giacomo Rappaccini, the famous doctor, who, I warrant him, has been heard of as far as Naples. It is said that he distils these plants into medicines that are as potent as a

---

[1] Gold coins.

[2] In *Inferno* 18:71, Dante mentions an unnamed Paduan nobleman among those who have committed crimes against Nature.

charm. Oftentimes you may see the signor doctor at work, and perchance the signora, his daughter, too, gathering the strange flowers that grow in the garden."

The old woman had now done what she could for the aspect of the chamber; and, commending the young man to the protection of the saints, took her departure.

Giovanni still found no better occupation than to look down into the garden beneath his window. From its appearance, he judged it to be one of those botanic gardens which were of earlier date in Padua than elsewhere in Italy or in the world. Or, not improbably, it might once have been the pleasure-place of an opulent family; for there was the ruin of a marble fountain in the centre, sculptured with rare art, but so wofully shattered that it was impossible to trace the original design from the chaos of remaining fragments. The water, however, continued to gush and sparkle into the sunbeams as cheerfully as ever. A little gurgling sound ascended to the young man's window and made him feel as if the fountain were an immortal spirit that sung its song unceasingly and without heeding the vicissitudes around it, while one century imbodied it in marble and another scattered the perishable garniture on the soil. All about the pool into which the water subsided grew various plants, that seemed to require a plentiful supply of moisture for the nourishment of gigantic leaves, and, in some instances, flowers gorgeously magnificent. There was one shrub in particular, set in a marble vase in the midst of the pool, that bore a profusion of purple blossoms, each of which had the lustre and richness of a gem; and the whole together made a show so resplendent that it seemed enough to illuminate the garden, even had there been no sunshine. Every portion of the soil was peopled with plants and herbs, which, if less beautiful, still bore tokens of assiduous care, as if all had their individual virtues, known to the scientific mind that fostered them. Some were placed in urns, rich with old carving, and others in common garden pots; some crept serpent-like along the ground or climbed on high, using whatever means of ascent was offered them. One plant had wreathed itself round a statue of Vertumnus,[3] which was thus quite veiled and shrouded in a drapery of hanging foliage, so happily arranged that it might have served a sculptor for a study.

While Giovanni stood at the window he heard a rustling behind a screen of leaves, and became aware that a person was at work in the garden. His figure soon emerged into view, and showed itself to be that of no common laborer, but a tall, emaciated, sallow, and sickly-looking man, dressed in a scholar's garb of black. He was beyond the middle term of life, with gray hair, a thin, gray beard, and a face singularly marked with intellect and cultivation, but which could never, even in his more youthful days, have expressed much warmth of heart.

Nothing could exceed the intentness with which this scientific gardener examined every shrub which grew in his path: it seemed as if he was looking into their inmost nature, making observations in regard to their creative essence, and discovering why one leaf grew in this shape and another in that, and wherefore such and such flowers differed among themselves in hue and perfume. Nevertheless, in spite of this deep intelligence on his part, there was no approach to intimacy between himself and these vegetable existences. On the contrary, he avoided their actual touch or the direct inhaling of their odors with a caution that impressed Giovanni most disagreeably; for the man's demeanor was that of one walking among malignant influences, such as savage beasts, or deadly snakes, or evil spirit, which, should he allow them one moment of license, would wreak upon him some terrible fatality. It was strangely frightful to the young man's imagination to see this air of insecurity in a person cultivating a garden, that most simple and innocent of human toils, and which has been alike the joy and labor of the unfallen parents of the race. Was this garden, then, the Eden of

---

[3] The Roman god of the seasons

the present world? And this man, with such a perception of harm in what his own hands caused to grow,—was he the Adam?

10   The distrustful gardener, while plucking away the dead leaves or pruning the too luxuriant growth of the shrubs, defended his hands with a pair of thick gloves. Nor were these his only armor. When, in his walk through the garden, he came to the magnificent plant that hung its purple gems beside the marble fountain, he placed a kind of mask over his mouth and nostrils, as if all this beauty did but conceal a deadlier malice; but, finding his task still too dangerous, he drew back, removed the mask, and called loudly, but in the infirm voice of a person affected with inward disease,—

"Beatrice! Beatrice!"

"Here am I, my father. What would you?" cried a rich and youthful voice from the window of the opposite house—a voice as rich as a tropical sunset, and which made Giovanni, though he knew not why, think of deep hues of purple or crimson and of perfumes heavily delectable. "Are you in the garden?"

"Yes, Beatrice," answered the gardener; "and I need your help."

Soon there emerged from under a sculptured portal the figure of a young girl, arrayed with as much richness of taste as the most splendid of the flowers, beautiful as the day, and with a bloom so deep and vivid that one shade more would have been too much. She looked redundant with life, health, and energy; all of which attributes were bound down and compressed, as it were, and girdled tensely, in their luxuriance, by her virgin zone.[4] Yet Giovanni's fancy must have grown morbid while he looked down into the garden; for the impression which the fair stranger made upon him was as if here were another flower, the human sister of those vegetable ones, as beautiful as they, more beautiful than the richest of them, but still to be touched only with a glove, nor to be approached without a mask. As Beatrice came down the garden path, it was observable that she handled and inhaled the odor of several of the plants which her father had most sedulously avoided.

15   "Here, Beatrice," said the latter, "see how many needful offices require to be done to our chief treasure. Yet, shattered as I am, my life might pay the penalty of approaching it so closely as circumstances demand. Henceforth, I fear, this plant must be consigned to your sole charge."

"And gladly will I undertake it," cried again the rich tones of the young lady, as she bent towards the magnificent plant and opened her arms as if to embrace it. "Yes, my sister, my splendor, it shall be Beatrice's task to nurse and serve thee; and thou shalt reward her with thy kisses and perfumed breath, which to her is as the breath of life."

Then, with all the tenderness in her manner that was so strikingly expressed in her words, she busied herself with such attentions as the plant seemed to require; and Giovanni, at his lofty window, rubbed his eyes, and almost doubted whether it were a girl tending her favorite flower, or one sister performing the duties of affection to another. The scene soon terminated. Whether Dr. Rappaccini had finished his labors in the garden, or that his watchful eye had caught the stranger's face, he now took his daughter's arm and retired. Night was already closing in; oppressive exhalations seemed to proceed from the plants and steal upward past the open window; and Giovanni, closing the lattice, went to this couch and dreamed of a rich flower and beautiful girl. Flower and maiden were different, and yet the same, and fraught with some strange peril in either shape.

But there is an influence in the light of morning that tends to rectify whatever errors of fancy, or even of judgment, we may have incurred during the sun's decline, or among the shadows of the night, or in the less wholesome glow of moonshine. Giovanni's first movement,

---

[4] Her belt, "virgin" because Beatrice appears to be an unmarried girl.

on starting from sleep, was to throw open the window and gaze down into the garden which his dreams had made so fertile of mysteries. He was surprised, and a little ashamed, to find how real and matter-of-fact an affair it proved to be, in the first rays of the sun which gilded the dewdrops that hung upon leaf and blossom, and while giving a brighter beauty to each rare flower, brought every thing within the limits of ordinary experience. The young man rejoiced that, in the heart of the barren city, he had the privilege of over-looking this spot of lovely and luxuriant vegetation. It would serve, he said to himself, as a symbolic language to keep him in communion with Nature. Neither the sickly and thoughtworn Dr. Giacomo Rappaccini, it is true, nor his brilliant daughter, were now visible; so that Giovanni could not determine how much of the singularity which he attributed to both was due to their own qualities and how much to his wonder-working fancy; but he was inclined to take a most rational view of the whole matter.

In the course of the day he paid his respects to Signor Pietro Baglioni, professor of medicine in the university, a physician of eminent repute, to whom Giovanni had brought a letter of introduction. The professor was an elderly personage, apparently of genial nature and habits that might almost be called jovial. He kept the young man to dinner, and made himself very agreeable by the freedom and liveliness of his conversation, especially when warmed by a flask or two of Tuscan wine. Giovanni, conceiving that men of science, inhabitants of the same city, must needs be on familiar terms with one another, took an opportunity to mention the name of Dr. Rappaccini. But the professor did not respond with so much cordiality as he had anticipated.

20   "Ill would it become a teacher of the divine art of medicine," said Professor Pietro Baglioni, in answer to a question of Giovanni, "to withhold due and well-considered praise of a physician so eminently skilled as Rappaccini; but, on the other hand, I should answer it but scantily to my conscience were I to permit a worthy like yourself, Signor Giovanni, the son of an ancient friend, to imbibe erroneous ideas respecting a man who might hereafter chance to hold your life and death in his hands. The truth is, our worshipful Dr. Rappaccini has as much science as any member of the faculty—with perhaps one single exception—in Padua, or all Italy; but there are certain grave objections to his professional character."

"And what are they?" asked the young man.

"Has my friend Giovanni any disease of body or heart, that he is so inquisitive about physicians?" said the professor, with a smile. "But as for Rappaccini, it is said of him—and I, who know the man well, can answer for its truth—that he cares infinitely more for science than for mankind. His patients are interesting to him only as subjects for some new experiment. He would sacrifice human life, his own among the rest, or whatever else was dearest to him, for the sake of adding so much as a grain of mustard seed to the great heap of his accumulated knowledge."

"Methinks he is an awful[5] man indeed," remarked Guasconti, mentally recalling the cold and purely intellectual aspect of Rappaccini. "And yet, worshipful professor, is it not a noble spirit? Are there many men capable of so spiritual a love or science?"

"God forbid," answered the professor, somewhat testily; "at least, unless they take sounder views of the healing art than those adopted by Rappaccini. It is his theory that all medicinal virtues are comprised within those substances which we term vegetable poisons. These he cultivates with his own hands, and is said even to have produced new varieties of poison, more horribly deleterious than Nature, without the assistance of this learned person, would ever have plagued the world withal. That the signor doctor does less mischief than might be expected with such dangerous substances, is undeniable. Now and then, it

---

[5] Frightful, inspiring fear; dreadful.

must be owned, he has effected, or seemed to effect, a marvellous cure; but, to tell you my private mind, Signor Giovanni, he should receive little credit for such instances of success,—they being probably the work of chance,—but should be held strictly accountable for his failures, which may justly be considered his own work."

25   The youth might have taken Baglioni's opinions with many grains of allowance had he known that there was a professional warfare of long continuance between him and Dr. Rappaccini, in which the latter was generally thought to have gained the advantage. If the reader be inclined to judge for himself, we refer him to certain black-letter tracts on both sides, preserved in the medical department of the University of Padua.

"I know not, most learned professor," returned Giovanni, after musing on what had been said of Rappaccini's exclusive zeal for science,—"I know not how dearly this physician may love his art; but surely there is one object more dear to him. He has a daughter."

"Aha!" cried the professor, with a laugh. "So now our friend Giovanni's secret is out. You have heard of this daughter, whom all the young men in Padua are wild about, though not half a dozen have ever had the good hap to see her face. I know little of the Signora Beatrice save that Rappaccini is said to have instructed her deeply in his science, and that, young and beautiful as fame reports her, she is already qualified to fill a professor's chair. Perchance her father destines her for mine! Other absurd rumors there be, not worth talking about or listening to. So now, Signor Giovanni, drink off your glass of lachryma."[6]

Guasconti returned to his lodgings somewhat heated with the wine he had quaffed, and which caused his brain to swim with strange fantasies in reference to Dr. Rappaccini and the beautiful Beatrice. On his way, happening to pass by a florist's, he bought a fresh bouquet of flowers.

Ascending to his chamber, he seated himself near the window, but within the shadow thrown by the depth of the wall, so that he could look down into the garden with little risk of being discovered. All beneath his eye was a solitude. The strange plants were basking in the sunshine, and now and then nodding gently to one another, as if in acknowledgment of sympathy and kindred. In the midst, by the shattered fountain, grew the magnificent shrub, with its purple gems clustering all over it; they glowed in the air, and gleamed back again out of the depths of the pool, which thus seemed to overflow with colored radiance from the rich reflection that was steeped in it. At first, as we have said, the garden was a solitude. Soon, however,—as Giovanni had half hoped, half feared, would be the case,—a figure appeared beneath the antique sculptured portal, and came down between the rows of plants, inhaling their various perfumes as if she were one of those beings of old classic fable that lived upon sweet odors. On again beholding Beatrice, the young man was even startled to perceive how much her beauty exceeded his recollection of it; so brilliant, so vivid, was its character, that she glowed amid the sunlight, and, as Giovanni whispered to himself, positively illuminated the more shadowy intervals of the garden path. Her face being now more revealed than on the former occasion, he was struck by its expression of simplicity and sweetness—qualities that had not entered into his idea of her character, and which made him ask anew what manner of mortal she might be. Nor did he fail again to observe, or imagine, an analogy between the beautiful girl and the gorgeous shrub that hung its gemlike flowers over the fountain—a resemblance which Beatrice seemed to have indulged a fantastic humor in heightening, both by the arrangement of her dress and the selection of its hues.

30   Approaching the shrub, she threw open her arms, as with a passionate ardor, and drew its branches into an intimate embrace—so intimate that her features were hidden in its leafy bosom and her glistening ringlets all intermingled with the flowers.

---

[6] Italian wine, grown near Mount Vesuvius; lachrymal also pertains to tears.

"Give me thy breath, my sister," exclaimed Beatrice; "for I am faint with common air. And give me this flower of thine, which I separate with gentlest fingers from the stem and place it close beside my heart."

With these words the beautiful daughter of Rappaccini plucked one of the richest blossoms of the shrub, and was about to fasten it in her bosom. But now, unless Giovanni's draughts of wine had bewildered his senses, a singular incident occurred. A small orange-colored reptile, of the lizard or chameleon species, chanced to be creeping along the path, just at the feet of Beatrice. It appeared to Giovanni,—but, at the distance from which he gazed, he could scarcely have seen any thing so minute,—it appeared to him, however, that a drop or two of moisture from the broken stem of the flower descended upon the lizard's head. For an instant the reptile contorted itself violently, and then lay motionless in the sunshine. Beatrice observed this remarkable phenomenon, and crossed herself, sadly, but without surprise; nor did she therefore hesitate to arrange the fatal flower in her bosom. There it blushed, and almost glimmered with the dazzling effect of a precious stone, adding to her dress and aspect the one appropriate charm which nothing else in the world could have supplied. But Giovanni, out of the shadow of his window, bent forward and shrank bank, and murmured and trembled.

"Am I awake? Have I my senses?" said he to himself. "What is this being? Beautiful shall I call her, or inexpressibly terrible?"

Beatrice now strayed carelessly through the garden, approaching closer beneath Giovanni's window, so that he was compelled to thrust his head quite out of its concealment in order to gratify the intense and painful curiosity which she excited. At this moment there came a beautiful insect over the garden wall: it had, perhaps, wandered through the city, and found no flowers or verdure among those antique haunts of men until the heavy perfumes of Dr. Rappaccini's shrubs had lured it from afar. Without alighting on the flowers, this winged brightness seemed to be attracted by Beatrice, and lingered in the air and fluttered about her head. Now, here it could not be but that Giovanni Guasconti's eyes deceived him. Be that as it might, he fancied that, while Beatrice was gazing at the insect with childish delight, it grew faint and fell at her feet; its bright wings shivered; it was dead—from no cause that he could discern, unless it were the atmosphere of her breath. Again Beatrice crossed herself and sighed heavily as she bent over the dead insect.

35   An impulsive movement of Giovanni drew her eyes to the window. There she beheld the beautiful head of the young man—rather a Grecian than an Italian head, with fair, regular features, and a glistening of gold among his ringlets—gazing down upon her like a being that hovered in mid air. Scarcely knowing what he did, Giovanni threw down the bouquet which he had hitherto held in his hand.

"Signora," said he, "there are pure and healthful flowers. Wear them for the sake of Giovanni Guasconti."

"Thanks, signor," replied Beatrice, with her rich voice, that came forth as it were like a gush of music, and with a mirthful expression half childish and half womanlike. "I accept your gift, and would fain recompense it with this precious purple flower; but, if I toss it into the air, it will not reach you. So Signor Guasconti must even content himself with my thanks."

She lifted the bouquet from the ground, and then, as if inwardly ashamed at having stepped aside from her maidenly reserve to respond to a stranger's greeting, passed swiftly homeward through the garden. But, few as the moments were, it seemed to Giovanni, when she was on the point of vanishing beneath the sculptured portal, that his beautiful bouquet was already beginning to wither in her grasp. It was an idle thought; there could be no possibility of distinguishing a faded flower from a fresh one at so great a distance.

For many days after this incident the young man avoided the window that looked into Dr. Rappaccini's garden, as if something ugly and monstrous would have blasted his eyesight had he been betrayed into a glance. He felt conscious of having put himself, to a certain extent, within the influence of an unintelligible power by the communication which he had opened with Beatrice. The wisest course would have been, if his heart were in any real danger, to quit his lodging and Padua itself at once; the next wiser, to have accustomed himself, as far as possible, to the familiar and daylight view of Beatrice—thus bringing her rigidly and systematically within the limits of ordinary experience. Least of all, while avoiding her sight, ought Giovanni to have remained so near this extraordinary being that the proximity and possibility even of intercourse should give a kind of substance and reality to the wild vagaries which his imagination ran riot continually in producing. Guasconti had not a deep heart—or, at all events, its depths were not sounded now; but he had a quick fancy, and an ardent southern temperament, which rose every instant to a higher fever pitch. Whether or not Beatrice possessed those terrible attributes, that fatal breath, the affinity with those so beautiful and deadly flowers which were indicated by what Giovanni had witnessed, she had at least instilled a fierce and subtle poison in his system. It was not love, although her rich beauty was a madness to him; nor horror, even while he fancied her spirit to be imbued with the same baneful essence that seemed to pervade her physical frame; but a wild offspring of both love and horror that had each parent in it, and burned like one and shivered like the other. Giovanni knew not what to dread; still less did he know what to hope; yet hope and dread kept a continual warfare in his breast, alternately vanquishing one another and starting up afresh to renew the contest. Blessed are all simple emotions, be they dark or bright! It is the lurid intermixture of the two that produces the illuminating blaze of the infernal regions.

40   Sometimes he endeavored to assuage the fever of his spirit by a rapid walk through the streets of Padua or beyond its gates: his footsteps kept time with the throbbings of his brain, so that the walk was apt to accelerate itself to a race. One day he found himself arrested; his arm was seized by a portly personage, who had turned back on recognizing the young man and expended much breath in overtaking him.

"Signor Giovanni! Stay, my young friend!" cried he. "Have you forgotten me? That might well be the case if I were as much altered as yourself."

It was Baglioni, whom Giovanni had avoided ever since their first meeting, from a doubt that the professor's sagacity would look too deeply into his secrets. Endeavoring to recover himself, he stared forth wildly from his inner world into the outer one and spoke like a man in a dream.

"Yes; I am Giovanni Guasconti. You are Professor Pietro Baglioni. Now let me pass!"

"Not yet, not yet, Signor Giovanni Guasconti," said the professor, smiling, but at the same time scrutinizing the youth with an earnest glance. "What! did I grow up side by side with your father? and shall his son pass me like a stranger in these old streets of Padua? Stand still, Signor Giovanni; for we must have a word or two before we part."

45   "Speedily, then, most worshipful professor, speedily," said Giovanni, with feverish impatience. "Does not your worship see that I am in haste?"

Now, while he was speaking there came a man in black along the street, stooping and moving feebly like a person in inferior health. His face was all overspread with a most sickly and sallow hue, but yet so pervaded with an expression of piercing and active intellect that an observer might easily have overlooked the merely physical attributes and have seen only this wonderful energy. As he passed, this person exchanged a cold and distant salutation with Baglioni, but fixed his eyes upon Giovanni with an intentness that seemed to bring out whatever was within him worthy of notice. Nevertheless, there was a peculiar quietness in the look, as if taking merely a speculative, not a human, interest in the young man.

"It is Dr. Rappaccini!" whispered the professor when the stranger had passed. "Has he ever seen your face before?

"Not that I know," answered Giovanni, starting at the name.

He *has* seen you! he must have seen you!" said Baglioni, hastily. "For some purpose or other, this man of science is making a study of you. I know that look of his! It is the same that coldly illuminates his face as he bends over a bird, a mouse, or a butterfly; which, in pursuance of some experiment, he has killed by the perfume of a flower; a look as deep as Nature itself, but without Nature's warmth of love. Signor Giovanni, I will stake my life upon it, you are the subject of one of Rappaccini's experiments!"

50   "Will you make a fool of me?" cried Giovanni, passionately. "*That,* signor professor, were an untoward experiment."

"Patience! patience!" replied the imperturbable professor. "I tell thee, my poor Giovanni, that Rappaccini has a scientific interest in thee. Thou hast fallen into fearful hands! And the Signora Beatrice,—what part does she act in this mystery?"

But Guasconti, finding Baglioni's pertinacity intolerable, here broke away, and was gone before the professor could again seize his arm. He looked after the young man intently and shook his head.

"This must not be," said Baglioni to himself. "The youth is the son of my old friend, and shall not come to any harm from which the arcana[7] of medical science can preserve him. Besides, it is too insufferable an impertinence in Rappaccini thus to snatch the lad out of my own hands, as I may say, and make use of him for his infernal experiments. This daughter of his! It shall be looked to. Perchance, most learned Rappaccini, I may foil you where you little dream of it!"

Meanwhile Giovanni had pursued a circuitous route, and at length found himself at the door of his lodgings. As he crossed the threshold he was met by old Lisabetta, who smirked and smiled, and was evidently desirous to attract his attention; vainly, however, as the ebullition of his feelings had momentarily subsided into a cold and dull vacuity. He turned his eyes full upon the withered face that was puckering itself into a smile, but seemed to behold it not. The old dame, therefore, laid her grasp upon his cloak.

55   "Signor! signor!" whispered she, still with a smile over the whole breadth of her visage, so that it looked not unlike a grotesque carving in wood, darkened by centuries. "Listen, signor! There is a private entrance into the garden!"

"What do you say?" exclaimed Giovanni, turning quickly about, as if an inanimate thing should start into feverish life. "A private entrance into Dr. Rappaccini's garden?"

"Hush, hush! not so loud!" whispered Lisabetta, putting her hand over his mouth. "Yes; into the worshipful doctor's garden, where you may see all his fine shrubbery. Many a young man in Padua would give gold to be admitted among those flowers."

Giovanni put a piece of gold into her hand.

"Show me the way," said he.

60   A surmise, probably excited by his conversation with Baglioni, crossed his mind, that this interposition of old Lisabetta might perchance be connected with the intrigue, whatever were its nature, in which the professor seemed to suppose that Dr. Rappaccini was involving him. But such a suspicion, though it disturbed Giovanni, was inadequate to restrain him. The instant that he was aware of the possibility of approaching Beatrice, it seemed an absolute necessity of his existence to do so. It mattered not whether she were angel or demon; he was irrevocably within her sphere, and must obey the law that whirled him onward, in ever-lessening circles, towards a result which he did not attempt to foreshadow; and yet, strange to say, there came across him a sudden doubt whether this intense interest on his part were not delusory; whether it were really of so deep and positive a nature as to justify

---

[7] Secrets

him in now thrusting himself into an incalculable position; whether it were not merely the fantasy of a young man's brain, only slightly or not at all connected with his heart.

He paused, hesitated, turned half about, but again went on. His withered guide led him along several obscure passages, and finally undid a door, through which, as it was opened, there came the sight and sound of rustling leaves, with the broken sunshine glimmering among them. Giovanni stepped forth, and, forcing himself through the entanglement of a shrub that wreathed its tendrils over the hidden entrance, stood beneath his own window in the open area of Dr. Rappaccini's garden.

How often is it the case that, when impossibilities have come to pass and dreams have condensed their misty substance into tangible realities, we find ourselves calm, and even coldly self-possessed, amid circumstances which it would have been a delirium of joy or agony to anticipate! Fate delights to thwart us thus. Passion will choose his own time to rush upon the scene, and lingers sluggishly behind when an appropriate adjustment of events would seem to summon his appearance. So was it now with Giovanni. Day after day his pulses had throbbed with feverish blood at the improbably idea of an interview with Beatrice, and of standing with her, face to face, in this very garden, basking in the Oriental sunshine of her beauty, and snatching from her full gaze the mystery which he deemed the riddle of his own existence. But now there was a singular and untimely equanimity within this breast. He threw a glance around the garden to discover if Beatrice or her father were present, and, perceiving that he was alone, began a critical observation of the plants.

The aspect of one and all of them dissatisfied him; their gorgeousness seemed fierce, passionate, and even unnatural. There was hardly an individual shrub which a wanderer, straying by himself through a forest, would not have been startled to find growing wild, as if an unearthly face had glared at him out of the thicket. Several also would have shocked a delicate instinct by an appearance of artificialness indicating that there had been such commixture, and, as it were, adultery of various vegetable species, that the production was not longer of God's making, but the monstrous offspring of man's depraved fancy, glowing with only an evil mockery of beauty. They were probably the result of experiment, which in one or two cases had succeeded in mingling plants individually lovely into a compound possessing the questionable and ominous character that distinguished the whole growth of the garden. In fine, Giovanni recognized but two or three plants in the collection, and those of a kind that he well knew to be poisonous. While busy with these contemplations he heard the rustling of a silken garment, and, turning, beheld Beatrice emerging from beneath the sculptured portal.

Giovanni had not considered with himself what should be his deportment; whether he should apologize for his intrusion into the garden, or assume that he was there with the privity at least, if not by the desire, of Dr. Rappaccini or his daughter; but Beatrice's manner placed him at his ease, though leaving him still in doubt by what agency he had gained admittance. She came lightly along the path and met him near the broken fountain. There was surprise in her face, but brightened by a simple and kind expression of pleasure.

65 "You are a connoisseur in flowers, signor," said Beatrice, with a smile, alluding to the bouquet which he had flung her from the window. "It is no marvel, therefore, if the sight of my father's rare collection has tempted you to take a nearer view. If he were here, he could tell you many strange and interesting facts as to the nature and habits of these shrubs; for he has spent a lifetime in such studies, and this garden is his world."

"And yourself, lady," observed Giovanni, "if fame says true,—you likewise are deeply skilled in the virtues indicated by these rich blossoms and these spicy perfumes. Would you deign to be my instructress, I should prove an apter scholar than if taught by Signor Rappaccini himself."

"Are there such idle rumors?" asked Beatrice, with the music of a pleasant laugh. "Do people say that I am skilled in my father's science of plants? What a jest is there! No; though

I have grown up among these flowers, I know no more of them than their hues and perfume; and sometimes methinks I would fain rid myself of even that small knowledge. There are many flowers here, and those not the least brilliant, that shock and offend me when they meet my eye. But pray, signor, do not believe these stories about my science. Believe nothing of me save what you see with your own eyes."

"And must I believe all that I have seen with my own eyes?" asked Giovanni, pointedly, while the recollection of former scenes made him shrink. "No, signora; you demand too little of me. Bid me believe nothing save what comes from your own lips."

It would appear that Beatrice understood him. There came a deep flush to her cheek; but she looked full into Giovanni's eyes, and responded to his gaze of uneasy suspicion with a queenlike haughtiness.

70   "I do so bid you, signor," she replied. "Forget whatever you may have fancied in regard to me. If true to the outward senses, still it may be false in its essence; but the words of Beatrice Rappaccini's lips are true from the depths of the heart outward. Those you may believe."

A fervor glowed in her whole aspect and beamed upon Giovanni's consciousness like the light of truth itself; but while she spoke there was a fragrance in the atmosphere around her, rich and delightful, though evanescent, yet which the young man, from an indefinable reluctance, scarcely dared to draw into his lungs. It might be the odor of the flowers. Could it be Beatrice's breath which thus embalmed her words with a strange richness, as if by steeping them in her heart? A faintness passed like a shadow over Giovanni and flitted away; he seemed to gaze through the beautiful girl's eyes into her transparent soul, and felt no more doubt or fear.

The tinge of passion that had colored Beatrice's manner vanished; she became gay, and appeared to derive a pure delight from her communion with the youth not unlike what the maiden of a lonely island might have felt conversing with a voyager from the civilized world. Evidently her experience of life had been confined within the limits of that garden. She talked now about matters as simple as the daylight or summer clouds, and now asked questions in reference to the city, or Giovanni's distant home, his friends, his mother, and his sisters—questions indicating such seclusion, and such lack of familiarity with modes and forms, that Giovanni responded as if to an infant. Her spirit gushed out before him like a fresh rill that was just catching its first glimpse of the sunlight and wondering at the reflections of earth and sky which were flung into its bosom. There came thoughts, too, from a deep source, and fantasies of a gemlike brilliancy, as if diamonds and rubies sparkled upward among the bubbles of the fountain. Ever and anon there gleamed across the young man's mind a sense of wonder that he should be walking side by side with the being who had so wrought upon his imagination, whom he had idealized in such hues of terror, in whom he had positively witnessed such manifestations of dreadful attributes—that he should be conversing with Beatrice like a brother, and should find her so human and so maidenlike. But such reflections were only momentary; the effect of her character was too real not to make itself familiar at once.

In this free intercourse they had strayed through the garden, and now, after many turns among its avenues, were come to the shattered fountain, beside which grew the magnificent shrub, with its treasury of flowing blossoms. A fragrance was diffused from it which Giovanni recognized as identical with that which he had attributed to Beatrice's breath, but incomparably more powerful. As her eyes fell upon it, Giovanni beheld her press her hand to her bosom as if her heart were throbbing suddenly and painfully.

"For the first time in my life," murmured she, addressing the shrub, "I had forgotten thee."

75   "I remember, signora," said Giovanni, "that you once promised to reward me with one of these living gems for the bouquet which I had the happy boldness to fling to your feet. Permit me now to pluck it as a memorial of this interview."

He made a step towards the shrub with extended hand; but Beatrice darted forward, uttering a shriek that went through his heart like a dagger. She caught his hand and drew it back with the whole force of her slender figure. Giovanni felt her touch thrilling through his fibres.

"Touch it not!" exclaimed she, in a voice of agony. "Not for thy life! It is fatal!"

Then, hiding her face, she fled from him and vanished beneath the sculptured portal. As Giovanni followed her with his eyes, he beheld the emaciated figure and pale intelligence of Dr. Rappaccini, who had been watching the scene, he knew not how long, within the shadow of the entrance.

No sooner was Guasconti alone in his chamber than the image of Beatrice came back to his passionate musings, invested with all the witchery that had been gathering around it ever since his first glimpse of her, and now likewise imbued with a tender warmth of girlish womanhood. She was human; her nature was endowed with all gentle and feminine qualities; she was worthiest to be worshipped; she was capable, surely, on her part, of the height and heroism of love. Those tokens which he had hitherto considered as proofs of a frightful peculiarity in her physical and moral system were now either forgotten or by the subtle sophistry of passion transmitted into a golden crown of enchantment, rendering Beatrice the more admirable by so much as she was the more unique. Whatever had looked ugly was not beautiful; or, if incapable of such a change, it stole away and hid itself among those shapeless half ideas which throng the dim region beyond the daylight of our perfect consciousness. Thus did he spend the night, nor fell asleep until the dawn had begun to awake the slumbering flowers in Dr. Rappaccini's garden, whither Giovanni's dreams doubtless led him. Up rose the sun in his due season, and, flinging his beams upon the young man's eyelids, awoke him to a sense of pain. When thoroughly aroused, he became sensible of a burning and tingling agony in his hand—in his right hand—the very hand which Beatrice had grasped in her own when he was on the point of plucking one of the gemlike flowers. On the back of that hand there was now a purple print like that of four small fingers, and the likeness of a slender thumb upon his wrist.

80 　　O, how stubbornly does love,—or even that cunning semblance of love which flourishes in the imagination, but strikes no depth of root into the heart,—how stubbornly does it hold its faith until the moment comes when it is doomed to vanish into thin mist! Giovanni wrapped a handkerchief about his hand and wondered what evil thing had stung him, and soon forgot his pain in a revery of Beatrice.

After the first interview, a second was in the inevitable course of what we call fate. A third; a fourth; and a meeting with Beatrice in the garden was no longer an incident in Giovanni's daily life, but the whole space in which he might be said to live; for the anticipation and memory of that ecstatic hour made up the remainder. Nor was it otherwise with the daughter of Rappaccini. She watched for the youth's appearance and flew to his side with confidence as unreserved as if they had been playmates from early infancy—as if they were such playmates still. If, by any unwonted chance, he failed to come at the appointed moment, she stood beneath the window and sent up the rich sweetness of her tones to float around him in his chamber and echo and reverberate throughout his heart—"Giovanni! Giovanni! Why tarriest thou? Come down!" And down he hastened into that Eden of poisonous flowers.

But, with all this intimate familiarity, there was still a reserve in Beatrice's demeanor, so rigidly and invariably sustained that the idea of infringing it scarcely occurred to his imagination. By all appreciable signs, they loved; they had looked love with eyes that conveyed the holy secret from the depths of one soul into the depths of the other, as if it were too sacred to be whispered by the way; they had even spoken love in those gushes of passion when their spirits darted forth in articulated breath like tongues of long hidden flame; and yet there had been no seal of lips, no clasp of hands, nor any slightest caress such as love

claims and hallows. He had never touched one of the gleaming ringlets of her hair; her garment—so marked was the physical barrier between them—had never been waved against
him by a breeze. On the few occasions when Giovanni had seemed tempted to overstep the
limit, Beatrice grew so sad, so stern, and withal wore such a look of desolate separation,
shuddering at itself, that not a spoken word was requisite to repel him. At such times he was
startled at the horrible suspicions that rose, monster-like, out of the caverns of his heart and
stared him in the face; his love grew thin and faint as the morning mist; his doubts alone
had substance. But, when Beatrice's face brightened again after the momentary shadow, she
was transformed at once from the mysterious, questionable being whom he had watched
with so much awe and horror; she was now the beautiful and unsophisticated girl whom he
felt that his spirit knew with a certainty beyond all other knowledge.

A considerable time had now passed since Giovanni's last meeting with Baglioni. One
morning, however, he was disagreeably surprised by a visit from the professor, whom he
had scarcely thought of for whole weeks, and would willingly have forgotten still longer.
Given up as he had long been to a pervading excitement, he could tolerate no companions
except upon condition of their perfect sympathy with his present state of feeling. Such sympathy was not to be expected from Professor Baglioni.

The visitor chatted carelessly for a few moments about the gossip of the city and the
university, and then took up another topic.

85   "I have been reading an old classic author lately," said he, "and met with a story that
strangely interested me. Possibly you may remember it. It is of an Indian prince, who sent a
beautiful woman as a present to Alexander the Great. She was as lovely as the dawn and
gorgeous as the sunset; but what especially distinguished her was a certain rich perfume in
her breath—richer than a garden of Persian roses. Alexander, as was natural to a youthful
conqueror, fell in love at first sight with this magnificent stranger; but a certain sage physician, happening to be present, discovered a terrible secret in regard to her."

"And what was that?" asked Giovanni, turning his eyes downward to avoid those of the
professor.

"That this lovely woman," continued Baglioni, with emphasis, "had been nourished
with poisons from her birth upward, until her whole nature was so imbued with them that
she herself had become the deadliest poison in existence. Poison was her element of life.
With that rich perfume of her breath she blasted the very air. Her love would have been poison—her embrace death. Is not this a marvellous tale?"

"A childish fable," answered Giovanni, nervously starting from his chair. "I marvel how
your worship finds time to read such nonsense among your graver studies."

"By the by," said the professor, looking uneasily about him, "what singular fragrance is
this in your apartment? Is it the perfume of your gloves? It is faint, but delicious; and yet, after all, by no means agreeable. Were I to breathe it long, methinks it would make me ill. It is
like the breath of a flower; but I see no flowers in the chamber."

90   "Nor are there any," replied Giovanni, who had turned pale as the professor spoke; "nor, I
think, is there any fragrance except in your worship's imagination. Odors, being a sort of element combined of the sensual and the spiritual, are apt to deceive us in this matter. The recollection of a perfume, the bare idea of it, may easily be mistaken for a present reality."

"Ay; but my sober imagination does not often play such tricks," said Baglioni; "and, were
I to fancy any kind of odor, it would be that of some vile apothecary drug, wherewith my fingers are likely enough to be imbued. Our worshipful friend Rappaccini, as I have heard, tinctures his medicaments with odors richer than those of Araby.[8] Doubtless, likewise, the fair

---

[8] Arabia.

and learned Signora Beatrice would minister to her patients with draughts as sweet as a maiden's breath; but woe to him that sips them!"

Giovanni's face evinced many contending emotions. The tone in which the professor alluded to the pure and lovely daughter of Rappaccini was a torture to his soul; and yet the intimation of a view of her character, opposite to his own, gave instantaneous distinctness to a thousand dim suspicions, which now grinned at him like so many demons. But he strove hard to quell them and to respond to Baglioni with a true lover's perfect faith.

"Signor professor," said he, "you were my father's friend; perchance, too, it is your purpose to act a friendly part towards his son. I would fain feel nothing towards you save respect and deference; but I pray you to observe, signor, that there is one subject on which we must not speak. You know not the Signora Beatrice. You cannot, therefore, estimate the wrong—the blasphemy, I may even say—that is offered to her character by a light or injurious word."

"Giovanni! my poor Giovanni!" answered the professor, with a calm expression of pity. "I know this wretched girl far better than yourself. You shall hear the truth in respect to the poisoner Rappaccini and his poisonous daughter; yes, poisonous as she is beautiful. Listen; for, even should you do violence to my gray hairs, it shall not silence me. That old fable of the Indian woman has become a truth by the deep and deadly science of Rappaccini and in the person of the lovely Beatrice."

95   Giovanni groaned and hid his face.

"Her father," continued Baglioni, "was not restrained by natural affection from offering up his child in this horrible manner as the victim of his insane zeal for science; for, let us do him justice, he is as true a man of science as ever distilled his own heart in an alembic. What, then, will be your fate? Beyond a doubt you are selected as the material of some new experiment. Perhaps the result is to be death; perhaps a fate more awful still. Rappaccini, with what he calls the interest of science before his eyes, will hesitate at nothing."

"It is a dream," muttered Giovanni to himself; "surely it is a dream."

"But," resumed the professor, "be of good cheer, son of my friend. It is not yet too late for the rescue. Possibly we may even succeed in bringing back this miserable child within the limits of ordinary nature, from which her father's madness has estranged her. Behold this little silver vase! It was wrought by the hands of the renowned Benvenuto Cellini,[9] and is well worthy to be a love gift to the fairest dame in Italy. But its contents are invaluable. One little sip of this antidote would have rendered the most virulent poisons of the Borgias[10] innocuous. Doubt not that it will be as efficacious against those of Rappaccini. Bestow the vase, and the precious liquid within it, on your Beatrice, and hopefully await the result."

Baglioni laid a small, exquisitely wrought silver vial on the table and withdrew, leaving what he had said to produce its effect upon the young man's mind.

100   "We will thwart Rappaccini yet," thought he, chuckling to himself, as he descended the stairs; "but, let us confess the truth of him, he is a wonderful man—a wonderful man indeed; a vile empiric,[11] however, in his practice, and therefore not to be tolerated by those who respect the good old rules of the medical profession."

Throughout Giovanni's whole acquaintance with Beatrice, he had occasionally, as we have said, been haunted by dark surmises as to her character; yet so thoroughly had she

---

[9] Benvenuto Cellini (1500–71), an Italian sculptor.
[10] Notorious, powerful Italian Renaissance family, noted for cruelty and political intrigues.
[11] Charlatan.

made herself felt by him as a simple, natural, most affectionate, and guileless creature, that the image now held up by Professor Baglioni looked as strange and incredible as if it were not in accordance with his own original conception. True, there were ugly recollections connected with his first glimpses of the beautiful girl; he could not quite forget the bouquet that withered in her grasp, and the insect that perished amid the sunny air, by no ostensible agency save the fragrance of her breath. These incidents, however, dissolving in the pure light of her character, had no longer the efficacy of facts, but were acknowledged as mistaken fantasies, by whatever testimony of the senses they might appear to be substantiated. There is something truer and more real than what we can see with the eyes and touch with the finger. On such better evidence had Giovanni founded his confidence in Beatrice, though rather by the necessary force of her high attributes than by any deep and generous faith on his part. But now his spirit was incapable of sustaining itself at the height to which the early enthusiasm of passion had exalted it; he fell down, grovelling among earthly doubts, and defiled therewith the pure whiteness of Beatrice's image. Not that he gave her up; he did but distrust. He resolved to institute some decisive test that should satisfy him, once for all, whether there were those dreadful peculiarities in her physical nature which could not be supposed to exist without some corresponding monstrosity of soul. His eyes, gazing down afar, might have deceived him as to the lizard, the insect, and the flowers; but if he could witness, at the distance of a few paces, the sudden blight of one fresh and healthful flower in Beatrice's hand, there would be room for no further question. With this idea he hastened to the florist's and purchased a bouquet that was still gemmed with the morning dewdrops.

It was now the customary hour of his daily interview with Beatrice. Before descending into the garden, Giovanni failed not to look at his figure in the mirror—a vanity to be expected in a beautiful young man, yet, as displaying itself at that troubled and feverish moment, the token of a certain shallowness of feeling and insincerity of character. He did gaze, however, and said to himself that his features had never before possessed so rich a grace, nor his eyes such vivacity, nor his cheeks so warm a hue of superabundant life.

"At least," thought he, "her poison has not yet insinuated itself into my system. I am no flower to perish in her grasp."

With that thought he turned his eyes on the bouquet, which he had never once laid aside from his hand. A thrill of indefinable horror shot through his frame on perceiving that those dewy flowers were already beginning to droop; they wore the aspect of things that had been fresh and lovely yesterday. Giovanni grew white as marble, and stood motionless before the mirror, staring at his own reflection there as at the likeness of something frightful. He remembered Baglioni's remark about the fragrance that seemed to pervade the chamber. It must have been the poison in his breath! Then he shuddered—shuddered at himself. Recovering from his stupor, he began to watch with curious eye a spider that was busily at work hanging its web from the antique cornice of the apartment, crossing and recrossing the artful system of interwoven lines—as vigorous and active a spider as ever dangled from an old ceiling. Giovanni bent towards the insect, and emitted a deep, long breath. The spider suddenly ceased its toil; the web vibrated with a tremor originating in the body of the small artisan. Again Giovanni sent forth a breath, deeper, longer, and imbued with a venomous feeling out of his heart: he knew not whether he were wicked, or only desperate. The spider made a convulsive gripe with his limbs and hung dead across the window.

105   "Accursed! accursed!" muttered Giovanni, addressing himself. "Hast thou grown so poisonous that this deadly insect perishes by thy breath?"

At that moment a rich, sweet voice came floating up from the garden.

"Giovanni! Giovanni! It is past the hour! Why tarriest thou? Come down!"

"Yes," muttered Giovanni again. "she is the only being whom my breath may not slay! Would that it might!"

He rushed down, and in an instant was standing before the bright and loving eyes of Beatrice. A moment ago his wrath and despair had been so fierce that he could have desired nothing so much as to wither her by a glance; but with her actual presence there came influences which had too real an existence to be at once shaken off; recollections of the delicate and benign power of her feminine nature, which had so often enveloped him in a religious calm; recollections of many a holy and passionate outgush of her heart, when the pure fountain had been unsealed from its depths and made visible in its transparency to his mental eye; recollections which, had Giovanni known how to estimate them, would have assured him that all this ugly mystery was but an earthly illusion, and that, whatever mist of evil might seem to have gathered over her, the real Beatrice was a heavenly angel. Incapable as he was of such high faith, still her presence had not utterly lost its magic. Giovanni's rage was quelled into an aspect of sullen insensibility. Beatrice, with a quick spiritual sense, immediately felt that there was a gulf of blackness between them which neither he nor she could pass. They walked on together, sad and silent, and came thus to the marble fountain and to its pool of water on the ground, in the midst of which grew the shrub that bore gem-like blossoms. Giovanni was affrighted at the eager enjoyment—the appetite, as it were—with which he found himself inhaling the fragrance of the flowers.

110   "Beatrice," asked he, abruptly, "whence came this shrub?"

"My father created it," answered she, with simplicity.

"Created it! created it!" repeated Giovanni. "What mean you, Beatrice?"

"He is a man fearfully acquainted with the secrets of Nature," replied Beatrice; "and, at the hour when I first drew breath, this plant sprang from the soil, the offspring of his science, of his intellect, while I was but his earthly child. Approach it not!" continued she, observing with terror that Giovanni was drawing nearer to the shrub. "It has qualities that you little dream of. But I, dearest Giovanni,—I grew up and blossomed with the plant and was nourished with its breath. It was my sister, and I loved it with a human affection; for, alas!—hast thou not suspected it?—there was an awful doom."

Here Giovanni frowned so darkly upon her that Beatrice paused and trembled. But her faith in his tenderness reassured her, and made her blush that she had doubted for an instant.

115   "There was an awful doom," she continued, "The effect of my father's fatal love of science, which estranged me from all society of my kind. Until Heaven sent thee, dearest Giovanni, O, how lonely was thy poor Beatrice!"

"Was it a hard doom?" asked Giovanni, fixing his eyes upon her.

"Only of late have I known how hard it was," answered she, tenderly. "O, yes; but my heart was torpid, and therefore quiet."

Giovanni's rage broke forth from his sullen gloom like a lightning flash out of a dark cloud.

"Accursed one!" cried he, with venomous scorn and anger. "And, finding thy solitude wearisome, thou hast severed me likewise from all the warmth of life and enticed me into thy region of unspeakable horror!"

120   "Giovanni!" exclaimed Beatrice, turning her large bright eyes upon his face. The force of his words had not found it way into her mind; she was merely thunderstruck.

"Yes, poisonous thing!" repeated Giovanni, beside himself with passion. "Thou hast done it! Thou hast blasted me! Thou hast filled my veins with poison! Thou hast made me as hateful, as ugly, as loathsome and deadly a creature as thyself—a world's wonder of hideous monstrosity! Now, if our breath be happily as fatal to ourselves as to all other, let us join our lips in one kiss of unutterable hatred, and so die!"

"What has befallen me?" murmured Beatrice, with a low moan out of her heart. "Holy Virgin, pity me, a poor heart-broken child!"

"Thou, —dost thou pray?" cried Giovanni, still with the same fiendish scorn. "Thy very prayers, as they come from thy lips, taint the atmosphere with death. Yes, yes; let us pray! Let us to church and dip our fingers in the holy water at the portal! They that come after us will perish as by a pestilence! Let us sign crosses in the air! It will be scattering curses abroad in the likeness of holy symbols!"

"Giovanni," said Beatrice, calmly, for her grief was beyond passion, "why dost thou join thyself with me thus in those terrible words? I, it is true, am the horrible thing thou namest me. But thou,—what hast thou to do, save with one other shudder at my hideous misery to go forth out of the garden and mingle with thy race, and forget that there ever crawled on earth such a monster as poor Beatrice?"

125 Dost thou pretend ignorance?" asked Giovanni, scowling upon her. "Behold! this power have I gained from the pure daughter of Rappaccini."

There was a swarm of summer insects flitting through the air in search of the food promised by the flower odors of the fatal garden. They circled round Giovanni's head, and were evidently attracted towards him by the same influence which had drawn them for an instant within the sphere of several of the shrubs. He sent forth a breath among them, and smiled bitterly at Beatrice as at least a score of the insects fell dead upon the ground.

"I see it! I see it!" shrieked Beatrice. "It is my father's fatal science! No, no, Giovanni; it was not I! Never! never! I dreamed only to love thee and be with thee a little time, and so to let thee pass away, leaving but thine image in mine heart; for, Giovanni, believe it, though my body be nourished with poison, my spirit is God's creature, and craves love as its daily food. But my father,—he has united us in this fearful sympathy. Yes; spurn me, tread upon me, kill me! O, what is death after such words as thine? But it was not I. Not for a world of bliss would I have done it."

Giovanni's passion had exhausted itself in its outburst from his lips. There now came across him a sense, mournful, and not without tenderness, of the intimate and peculiar relationship between Beatrice and himself. They stood, as it were, in an utter solitude, which would be made none the less solitary by the densest throng of human life. Ought not, then, the desert of humanity around them to press this insulated pair closer together? If they should be cruel to one another, who was there to be kind to them? Besides, thought Giovanni, might there not still be a hope of his returning within the limits of ordinary nature, and leading Beatrice, the redeemed Beatrice, by the hand? O, weak, and selfish, and unworthy spirit, that could dream of an earthly union and earthly happiness as possible, after such deep love had been so bitterly wronged as was Beatrice's love by Giovanni's blighting words! No, no; there could be no such hope. She must pass heavily, with that broken heart, across the borders of Time—she must bathe her hurts in some fount of paradise, and forget her grief in the light of immortality, and *there* be well.

But Giovanni did not know it.

130 "Dear Beatrice," said he, approaching her, while she shrank away as always at his approach, but now with a different impulse, "dearest Beatrice, our fate is not yet so desperate. Behold! there is a medicine, potent, as a wise physician has assured me, and almost divine in its efficacy. It is composed of ingredients the most opposite to those by which thy awful father has brought this calamity upon thee and me. It is distilled of blessed herbs. Shall we not quaff it together, and thus be purified from evil?"

"Give it me!" said Beatrice, extending her hand to receive the little silver vial which Giovanni took from his bosom. She added, with a peculiar emphasis, "I will drink; but do thou await the result."

She put Baglioni's antidote to her lips; and, at the same moment, the figure of Rappaccini emerged from the portal and came slowly towards the marble fountain. As he drew near, the pale man of science seemed to gaze with a triumphant expression at the beautiful youth and maiden, as might an artist who should spend his life in achieving a picture or a group of statuary and finally be satisfied with his success. He paused; his bent form grew erect with conscious power; he spread out his hands over them in the attitude of a father imploring a blessing upon his children; but those were the same hands that had thrown poison into the stream of their lives. Giovanni trembled. Beatrice shuddered nervously, and pressed her hand upon her heart.

"My daughter," said Rappaccini, "thou art no longer lonely in the world. Pluck one of those precious gems from thy sister shrub and bid thy bridegroom wear it in his bosom. It will not harm him now. My science and the sympathy between thee and him have so wrought within his system that he now stands apart from common men, as thou dost, daughter of my pride and triumph, from ordinary women. Pass on, then, through the world, most dear to one another and dreadful to all besides!"

"My father," said Beatrice, feebly—and still as she spoke she kept her hand upon her heart,—"wherefore didst thou inflict this miserable doom upon thy child?"

135 "Miserable!" exclaimed Rappaccini. "What mean you, foolish girl." Dost thou deem it misery to be endowed with marvellous gifts against which no power nor strength could avail an enemy—misery, to be able to quell the mightiest with a breath—misery, to be as terrible as thou art beautiful? Wouldst thou, then, have preferred the condition of a weak woman, exposed to all evil and capable of none?"

"I would fain have been loved, not feared," murmured Beatrice, sinking down upon the ground. "But now it matters not. I am going, father, where the evil which thou hast striven to mingle with my being will pass away like a dream—like the fragrance of these poisonous flowers, which will no longer taint my breath among the flowers of Eden. Farewell, Giovanni! Thy words of hatred are like lead within my heart; but they, too, will fall away as I ascend. O, was there not, from the first, more poison in thy nature than in mine?"

To Beatrice,—so radically had her earthly part been wrought upon by Rappaccini's skill,—as poison had been life, so the powerful antidote was death; and thus the poor victim of man's ingenuity and of thwarted nature, and of the fatality that attends all such efforts of perverted wisdom, perished there, at the feet of her father and Giovanni. Just at that moment Professor Pietro Baglioni looked forth from the window, and called loudly, in a tone of triumph mixed with horror, to the thunderstricken man of science,—

"Rappaccini! Rappaccini! and is *this* the upshot of your experiment?"

EDWIDGE DANTICAT

Edwidge Danticat (1969–   ) was born in Haiti but has lived from the age of twelve in New York. Educated at Barnard College and Brown University, Danticat published her first collection of short stories, Krik? Krak!, *in 1996. Her first novel,* Breath, Eyes, Memory, *appeared in 1994 and was followed by* The Farming of Bones *(1998),* Behind the Mountains *(2002), and* The Dew Breaker *(2004). Danticat's awards include a Granta Regional Award for Best Young American Novelist and a Pushcart Prize. In her writing, Danticat explores the history and lives of Haitians living in Haiti and in the United States.*

2004

THE BOOK OF THE DEAD

My father is gone. I'm slouched in a cast-aluminum chair across from two men, one the manager of the hotel where we're staying and the other a policeman. They're both waiting for me to explain what's become of him, my father.

The hotel manager—MR. FLAVIO SALINAS, the plaque on his office door reads—has the most striking pair of chartreuse eyes I've ever seen on a man with an island Spanish lilt to his voice.

The police officer, .Officer Bo, is a baby-faced, short, white Floridian with a potbelly.

"Where are you and your daddy from, Ms. Bienaimé?" Officer Bo asks, doing the best he can with my last name. He does such a lousy job that, even though he and I and Salinas are the only people in Salinas' office, at first I think he's talking to someone else.

5   I was born and raised in East Flatbush, Brooklyn, and have never even been to my parents' birthplace. Still, I answer "Haiti" because it is one more thing I've always longed to have in common with my parents.

Officer Bo plows forward with, "You all the way down here in Lakeland from Haiti?"

"We live in New York," I say. "We were on our way to Tampa."

"To do what?" Officer Bo continues. "Visit?"

"To deliver a sculpture," I say. "I'm an artist, a sculptor."

10   I'm really not an artist, not in the way I'd like to be. I'm more of an obsessive woodcarver with a single subject thus far—my father.

My creative eye finds Manager Salinas' office gaudy. The walls are covered with orange-and-green wallpaper, briefly interrupted by a giant gold leaf–bordered print of a Victorian cottage that resembles the building we're in.

Patting his light green tie, which brings out even more the hallucinatory shade of his eyes, Manager Salinas reassuringly tells me, "Officer Bo and I will do our best."

We start out with a brief description of my father: "Sixty-five, five feet eight inches, one hundred and eighty pounds, with a widow's peak, thinning salt-and-pepper hair, and velvet-brown eyes—"

"Velvet?" Officer Bo interrupts.

15   "Deep brown, same color as his complexion," I explain.

My father has had partial frontal dentures since he fell off his and my mother's bed and landed on his face ten years ago when he was having one of his prison nightmares. I mention that too. Just the dentures, not the nightmares. I also bring up the blunt, ropelike scar that runs from my father's right cheek down to the corner of his mouth, the only visible reminder of the year he spent in prison in Haiti.

"Please don't be offended by what I'm about to ask," Officer Bo says. "I deal with an older population here, and this is something that comes up a lot when they go missing. Does your daddy have any kind of mental illness, senility?"

I reply, "No, he's not senile."

"You have any pictures of your daddy?" Officer Bo asks.

20   My father has never liked having his picture taken. We have only a few of him at home, some awkward shots at my different school graduations, with him standing between my mother and me, his hand covering his scar. I had hoped to take some pictures of him on this trip, but he hadn't let me. At one of the rest stops I bought a disposable camera and pointed it at him anyway. As usual, he protested, covering his face with both hands like a little boy protecting his cheeks from a slap. He didn't want any more pictures taken of him for the rest of his life, he said, he was feeling too ugly.

"That's too bad," Officer Bo offers at the end of my too lengthy explanation. "He speaks English, your daddy? Can he ask for directions, et cetera?"

"Yes," I say

"Is there anything that might make your father run away from you, particularly here in Lakeland?" Manager Salinas asks. "Did you two have a fight?"

I had never tried to tell my father's story in words before now, but my first completed sculpture of him was the reason for our trip: a three-foot mahogany figure of my father naked, kneeling on a half-foot-square base, his back arched like the curve of a crescent moon, his downcast eyes fixed on his very long fingers and the large palms of his hands. It was hardly revolutionary, rough and not too detailed, minimalist at best, but it was my favorite of all my attempted representations of my father. It was the way I had imagined him in prison.

25　The last time I had seen my father? The previous night, before falling asleep. When we pulled our rental car into the hotel's hedge-bordered parking lot, it was almost midnight. All the restaurants in the area were closed. There was nothing to do but shower and go to bed.

"It's like paradise here," my father had said when he'd seen our tiny room. It had the same orange-and-green wallpaper as Salinas' office, and the plush emerald carpet matched the walls. "Look, Ka," he said, his deep, raspy voice muted with exhaustion, "the carpet is like grass under our feet."

He'd picked the bed closest to the bathroom, removed the top of his gray jogging suit, and unpacked his toiletries. Soon after, I heard him humming loudly, as he always did, in the shower.

I checked on the sculpture, just felt it a little bit through the bubble padding and carton wrapping to make sure it was still whole. I'd used a piece of mahogany that was naturally flawed, with a few superficial cracks along what was now the back. I'd thought these cracks beautiful and had made no effort to sand or polish them away, as they seemed like the wood's own scars, like the one my father had on his face. But I was also a little worried about the cracks. Would they seem amateurish and unintentional, like a mistake? Could the wood come apart with simple movements or with age? Would the client be satisfied?

I closed my eyes and tried to picture the client to whom I was delivering the sculpture: Gabrielle Fonteneau, a Haitian American woman about my age, the star of a popular television series and an avid art collector. My friend Céline Benoit, a former colleague at the junior high school where I'm a substitute art teacher, had grown up with Gabrielle Fonteneau in Tampa and, at my request, on a holiday visit home had shown Gabrielle Fonteneau a snapshot of my *Father* piece and had persuaded her to buy it.

30　Gabrielle Fonteneau was spending the week away from Hollywood at her parents' house in Tampa. I took some time off, and both my mother and I figured that my father, who watched a lot of television, both at home and at his Nostrand Avenue barbershop, would enjoy meeting Gabrielle Fonteneau too. But when I woke up, my father was gone and so was the sculpture.

I stepped out of the room and onto the balcony overlooking the parking lot. It was a hot and muggy morning, the humid air laden with the smell of the freshly mowed tropical grass and sprinkler-showered hibiscus bordering the parking lot. My rental car too was gone. I hoped my father was driving around trying to find us some breakfast and would explain when he got back why he'd taken the sculpture with him, so I got dressed and waited. I watched a half hour of local morning news, smoked five mentholated cigarettes even though we were in a nonsmoking room, and waited some more.

All that waiting took two hours, and I felt guilty for having held back so long before going to the front desk to ask, "Have you seen my father?"

I feel Officer Bo's fingers gently stroking my wrist, perhaps to tell me to stop talking. Up close Officer Bo smells like fried eggs and gasoline, like breakfast at the Amoco.

"I'll put the word out with the other boys," he says. "Salinas here will be in his office. Why don't you go on back to your hotel room in case your daddy shows up there?"

35　Back in the room, I lie in my father's unmade bed. The sheets smell like his cologne, an odd mix of lavender and lime that I've always thought too pungent, but that he likes nonetheless.

I jump up when I hear the click from the electronic key in the door. It's the maid. She's a young Cuban woman who is overly polite, making up for her lack of English with deferential gestures: a great big smile, a nod, even a bow as she backs out of the room. She reminds me of my mother when she has to work on non-Haitian clients at her beauty shop, how she pays much more attention to those clients, forcing herself to laugh at jokes she barely understands and smiling at insults she doesn't quite grasp, all to avoid being forced into a conversation, knowing she couldn't hold up her end very well.

It's almost noon when I pick up the phone and call my mother at the salon. One of her employees tells me that she's not yet returned from the Mass she attends every day. After the Mass, if she has clients waiting, she'll walk the twenty blocks from the church to the salon. If she has no appointments, then she'll let her workers handle the walk-ins and go home for lunch. This was as close to retirement as my mother would ever come. This routine was her dream when she first started the shop. She had always wanted a life with room for daily Mass and long walks and the option of sometimes not going to work

I call my parents' house. My mother isn't there either, so I leave the hotel number on the machine.

"Please call as soon as you can, Manman," I say. "It's about Papa."

40   It's early afternoon when my mother calls back, her voice cracking with worry. I had been sitting in that tiny hotel room, eating chips and candy bars from the vending machines, chain-smoking and waiting for something to happen, either for my father, Officer Bo, or Manager Salinas to walk into the room with some terrible news or for my mother or Gabrielle Fonteneau to call. I took turns imagining my mother screaming hysterically, berating both herself and me for thinking this trip with my father a good idea, then envisioning Gabrielle Fonteneau calling to say that we shouldn't have come on the trip. It had all been a joke. She wasn't going to buy a sculpture from me after all, especially one I didn't have.

"Where Papa?" Just as I expected, my mother sounds as though she's gasping for breath. I tell her to calm down, that nothing bad has happened. Papa's okay. I've just lost sight of him for a little while.

"How you lost him?" she asks.

"He got up before I did and disappeared," I say.

"How long he been gone?"

45   I can tell she's pacing back and forth in the kitchen, her slippers flapping against the Mexican tiles. I can hear the faucet when she turns it on, imagine her pushing a glass underneath it and filling it up. I hear her sipping the water as I say, "He's been gone for hours now. I don't even believe it myself."

"You call police?"

Now she's probably sitting at the kitchen table, her eyes closed, her fingers sliding back and forth across her forehead. She clicks her tongue and starts humming one of those mournful songs from the Mass, songs that my father, who attends church only at Christmas, picks up from her and also hums to himself in the shower.

My mother stops humming just long enough to ask, 'What the police say?"

"To wait, that he'll come back."

50   There's a loud tapping on the line, my mother thumping her fingers against the phone's mouthpiece; it gives me a slight ache in my ear.

"He come back," she says with more certainty than either Officer Bo or Manager Salinas. "He not leave you like that."

I promise to call my mother hourly with an update, but I know she'll call me sooner than that, so I dial Gabrielle Fonteneau's cell phone. Gabrielle Fonteneau's voice sounds just as it does on television, but more silken, nuanced, and seductive without the sitcom laugh track.

"To think," my father once said while watching her show, in which she plays a smart-mouthed nurse in an inner-city hospital's maternity ward. "A Haitian-born actress with her own American television show. We have really come far."

"So nice of you to come all this way to personally deliver the sculpture," Gabrielle Fonteneau says. She sounds like she's in a place with cicadas, waterfalls, palm trees, and citronella candles to keep the mosquitoes away. I realize that I too am in such a place, but I'm not able to enjoy it.

55   "Were you told why I like this sculpture so much?" Gabrielle Fonteneau asks. "It's regal and humble at the same time. It reminds me of my own father."

I hadn't been trying to delve into the universal world of fathers, but I'm glad my sculpture reminds Gabrielle Fonteneau of her father, for I'm not beyond the spontaneous fanaticism inspired by famous people, whose breezy declarations seem to carry so much more weight than those of ordinary mortals. I still had trouble believing I had Gabrielle Fonteneau's cell number, which Céline Benoit had made me promise not to share with anyone else, not even my father.

My thoughts are drifting from Gabrielle Fonteneau's father to mine when I hear her say, "So when will you get here? You have the directions, right? Maybe you can join us for lunch tomorrow, at around twelve."

"We'll be there," I say

But I'm no longer so certain.

60   My father loves museums. When he's not working at his barbershop, he's often at the Brooklyn Museum. The Ancient Egyptian rooms are his favorites.

"The Egyptians, they was like us," he likes to say. The Egyptians worshiped their gods in many forms, fought among themselves, and were often ruled by foreigners. The pharaohs were like the dictators he had fled, and their queens were as beautiful as Gabrielle Fonteneau. But what he admires most about the Ancient Egyptians is the way they mourn their dead.

"They know how to grieve," he'd say, marveling at the mummification process that went on for weeks but resulted in corpses that survived thousands of years.

My whole adult life, I have struggled to find the proper manner of sculpting my father, a quiet and distant man who only came alive while standing with me most of the Saturday mornings of my childhood, mesmerized by the golden masks, the shawabtis, and the schist tablets, Isis, Nefertiti, and Osiris, the jackal-headed ruler of the underworld.

The sun is setting and my mother has called more than a dozen times when my father finally appears in the hotel room doorway. He looks like a much younger man and appears calm and rested, as if bronzed after a long day at the beach.

65   "Too smoky in here," he says.

I point to my makeshift ashtray, a Dixie cup filled with tobacco-dyed water and cigarette butts.

"Ka, let your father talk to you." He fans the smoky air with his hands, walks over to the bed, and bends down to unlace his sneakers. "Yon ti koze, a little chat."

"Where were you?" I feel my eyelids twitching, a nervous reaction I inherited from my epileptic mother. "Why didn't you leave a note? And Papa, where is the sculpture?"

"That is why we must chat," he says, pulling off his sand-filled sneakers and rubbing the soles of his large, calloused feet each in turn. "I have objections."

70   He's silent for a long time, concentrating on his foot massage, as though he'd been looking forward to it all day.

"I'd prefer you not sell that statue," he says at last. Then he turns away, picks up the phone, and calls my mother.

"I know she called you," he says to her in Creole. "She panicked. I was just walking, thinking."

I hear my mother loudly scolding him, telling him not to leave me again. When he hangs up, he grabs his sneakers and puts them back on.

"Where's the sculpture?" My eyes are twitching so badly now I can barely see.

75　　"We go," he says. "I take you to it."

We walk out to the parking lot, where the hotel sprinkler is once more at work, spouting water onto the grass and hedges like centrifugal rain. The streetlights are on now, looking brighter and brighter as the dusk deepens around them. New hotel guests are arriving. Others are leaving for dinner, talking loudly as they walk to their cars.

As my father maneuvers our car out of the parking lot, I tell myself that he might be ill, mentally ill, even though I'd never detected any signs of it before, beyond his prison nightmares.

When I was eight years old and my father had the measles for the first time in his life, I overheard him say to a customer on the phone, "Maybe serious. Doctor tell me, at my age, measles can kill."

This was the first time I realized that my father could die. I looked up the word "kill" in every dictionary and encyclopedia at school, trying to understand what it really meant, that my father could be eradicated from my life.

80　My father stops the car on the side of the highway near a man-made lake, one of those marvels of the modern tropical city, with curved stone benches surrounding a stagnant body of water. There's scant light to see by except a half-moon. Stomping the well-manicured grass, my father heads toward one of the benches. I sit down next to him, letting my hands dangle between my legs.

Here I am a little girl again, on some outing with my father, like his trips to the botanic garden or the zoo or the Egyptian statues at the museum. Again, I'm there simply because he wants me to be. I knew I was supposed to learn something from these childhood outings, but it took me years to realize that ultimately my father was doing his best to be like other fathers, to share as much of himself with me as he could.

I glance over at the lake. It's muddy and dark, and there are some very large pink fishes bobbing back and forth near the surface, looking as though they want to leap out and trade places with us.

"Is this where the sculpture is?" I ask.

"In the water," he says.

85　　"Okay," I say calmly. But I know I'm already defeated. I know the piece is already lost. The cracks have probably taken in so much water that the wood has split into several chunks and plunged to the bottom. All I can think of saying is something glib, something I'm not even sure my father will understand.

"Please know this about yourself," I say. "You're a very harsh critic."

My father attempts to smother a smile. He scratches his chin and the scar on the side of his face, but says nothing. In this light the usually chiseled and embossed-looking scar appears deeper than usual, yet somehow less threatening, like a dimple that's spread out too far.

Anger is a wasted emotion, I've always thought. My parents would complain to each other about unjust politics in New York, but they never got angry at my grades, at all the Cs I got in everything but art classes, at my not eating my vegetables or occasionally vomiting my daily spoonful of cod-liver oil. Ordinary anger, I've always thought, is useless. But now I'm deeply angry. I want to hit my father, beat the craziness out of his head.

"Ka," he says, "I tell you why I named you Ka."

90 Yes, he'd told me, many, many times before. Now does not seem like a good time to remind me, but maybe he's hoping it will calm me, keep me from hating him for the rest of my life.

"Your mother not like the name at all," he says. "She say everybody tease you, people take pleasure repeating your name, calling you Kaka, Kaka, Kaka."

This too I had heard before.

"Okay," I interrupt him with a quick wave of my hands. "I've got it."

"I call you Ka," he says, "because in Egyptian world—"

95 A ka is a double of the body, I want to complete the sentence for him—the body's companion through life and after life. It guides the body through the kingdom of the dead. That's what I tell my students when I overhear them referring to me as Teacher Kaka.

"You see, ka is like soul," my father now says. "In Haiti is what we call good angel, ti bon anj. When you born, I look at your face, I think, here is my ka, my good angel."

I'm softening a bit. Hearing my father call me his good angel is the point at which I often stop being apathetic.

"I say rest in Creole," he prefaces, "because my tongue too heavy in English to say things like this, especially older things."

"Fine," I reply defiantly in English.

100 "Ka," he continues in Creole, "when I first saw your statue, I wanted to be buried with it, to take it with me into the other world."

"Like the Ancient Egyptians," I continue in English.

He smiles, grateful, I think, that in spite of everything, I can still appreciate his passions.

"Ka," he says, "when I read to you, with my very bad accent, from *The Book of the Dead*, do you remember how I made you read some chapters to me too?"[1]

But this recollection is harder for me to embrace. I had been terribly bored by *The Book of the Dead*. The images of dead hearts being placed on scales and souls traveling aimlessly down fiery underground rivers had given me my own nightmares. It had seemed selfish of him not to ask me what I wanted to listen to before going to bed, what I wanted to read and have read to me. But since he'd recovered from the measles and hadn't died as we'd both feared, I'd vowed to myself to always tolerate, even indulge him, letting him take me places I didn't enjoy and read me things I cared nothing about, simply to witness the joy they gave him, the kind of bliss that might keep a dying person alive. But maybe he wasn't going to be alive for long. Maybe this is what *this* outing is about. Perhaps my "statue," as he called it, is a sacrificial offering, the final one that he and I would make together before he was gone.

105 "Are you dying?" I ask my father. It's the one explanation that would make what he's done seem insignificant or even logical. "Are you ill? Are you going to die?"

What would I do now, if this were true? I'd find him the best doctor, move back home with him and my mother. I'd get a serious job, find a boyfriend, and get married, and I'd never complain again about his having dumped my sculpture in the lake.

Like me, my father tends to be silent a moment too long during an important conversation and then say too much when less should be said. I listen to the wailing of crickets and cicadas, though I can't tell where they're coming from. There's the highway, and the cars

---

[1] *The Egyptian Book of the Dead* can be viewed as a deceased's guide to a happy afterlife. It was intended to be read during the deceased's journey to the underworld.

racing by, the half-moon, the lake dug up from the depths of the ground—with my sculpture now at the bottom of it, the allée of royal palms whose shadows intermingle with the giant fishes on the surface of that lake, and there is me and my father.

"Do you recall the judgment of the dead," my father speaks up at last, "when the heart of a person is put on a scale? If it's heavy, the heart, then this person cannot enter the other world."

It is a testament to my upbringing, and perhaps the Kaka and good angel story has something to do with this as well, that I remain silent now, at this particular time.

110 "I don't deserve a statue," my father says. But at this very instant he does look like one, like the Madonna of humility, contemplating her losses in the dust, or an Ancient Egyptian funerary priest, kneeling with his hands prayerfully folded on his lap.

"Ka," he says, "when I took you to the Brooklyn Museum, I would stand there for hours admiring them. But all you noticed was how there were pieces missing from them, eyes, noses, legs, sometimes even heads. You always noticed more what was not there than what was."

Of course, this way of looking at things was why I ultimately began sculpting in the first place, to make statues that would amaze my father even more than these ancient relics.

"Ka, I am like one of those statues," he says.

"An Ancient Egyptian?" I hear echoes of my loud, derisive laugh only after I've been laughing for a while. It's the only weapon I have now, the only way I know to take my revenge on my father.

115 "Don't do that," he says, frowning, irritated, almost shouting over my laughter. "Why do that? If you are mad, let yourself be mad. Why do you always laugh like a clown when you are angry?"

I tend to wave my hands about wildly when I laugh, but I don't notice I'm doing that now until he reaches over to grab them. I quickly move them away, but he ends up catching my right wrist, the same wrist Officer Bo had stroked earlier to make me shut up. My father holds on to it so tightly now that I feel his fingers crushing the bone, almost splitting it apart, and I can't laugh anymore.

"Let go," I say, and he releases my wrist quickly. He looks down at his own fingers, then lowers his hand to his lap.

My wrist is still throbbing. I keep stroking it to relieve some of the pain. It's the ache there that makes me want to cry more than anything, not so much this sudden, uncharacteristic flash of anger from my father.

"I'm sorry," he says. "I did not want to hurt you. I did not want to hurt anyone."

120 I keep rubbing my wrist, hoping he'll feel even sorrier, even guiltier for grabbing me so hard, but even more for throwing away my work.

"Ka, I don't deserve a statue," he says again, this time much more slowly, "not a whole one, at least. You see, Ka, your father was the hunter, he was not the prey."

I stop stroking my wrist, sensing something coming that might hurt much more. He's silent again. I don't want to prod him, feed him any cues, urge him to speak, but finally I get tired of the silence and feel I have no choice but to ask, "What are you talking about?"

I immediately regret the question. Is he going to explain why he and my mother have no close friends, why they've never had anyone over to the house, why they never speak of any relatives in Haiti or anywhere else, or have never returned there or, even after I learned Creole from them, have never taught me anything else about the country beyond what I could find out on my own, on the television, in newspapers, in books? Is he about to tell me why Manman is so pious? Why she goes to daily Mass? I am not sure I want to know anything more than the little they've chosen to share with me all these years, but it is clear to me that he needs to tell me, has been trying to for a long time.

"We have a proverb," he continues. "One day for the hunter, one day for the prey. Ka, your father was the hunter, he was not the prey."

125　　Each word is now hard-won as it leaves my father's mouth, balanced like those hearts on the Ancient Egyptian scales.

"Ka, I was never in prison," he says.

"Okay," I say, sounding like I am fourteen again, chanting from what my mother used to call the meaningless adolescent chorus, just to sound like everyone else my age.

"I was working in the prison," my father says. And I decide not to interrupt him again until he's done.

Stranded in the middle of this speech now, he has to go on. "It was one of the prisoners inside the prison who cut my face in this way," he says.

130　　My father now points to the long, pitted scar on his right cheek. I am so used to his hands covering it up that this new purposeful motion toward it seems dramatic and extreme, almost like raising a veil.

"This man who cut my face," he continues, "I shot and killed him, like I killed many people."

I'm amazed that he managed to say all of this in one breath, like a monologue. I wish I too had had some rehearsal time, a chance to have learned what to say in response.

There is no time yet, no space in my brain to allow for whatever my mother might have to confess. Was she huntress or prey? A thirty-year-plus disciple of my father's coercive persuasion? She'd kept to herself even more than he had, like someone who was nurturing a great pain that she could never speak about. Yet she had done her best to be a good mother to me, taking charge of feeding and clothing me and making sure my hair was always combed, leaving only what she must have considered my intellectual development to my father.

When I was younger, she'd taken me to Mass with her on Sundays. Was I supposed to have been praying for my father all that time, the father who was the hunter and not the prey?

135　　I think back to "The Negative Confession" ritual from *The Book of the Dead,* a ceremony that was supposed to take place before the weighing of hearts, giving the dead a chance to affirm that they'd done only good things in their lifetime. It was one of the chapters my father read to me most often. Now he was telling me I should have heard something beyond what he was reading. I should have removed the negatives.

"I am not a violent man," he had read. "I have made no one weep. I have never been angry without cause. I have never uttered any lies. I have never slain any men or women. I have done no evil."

And just so I will be absolutely certain of what I'd heard, I ask my father, "And those nightmares you were always having, what were they?"

"Of what I," he says, "your father, did to others."

Another image of my mother now fills my head, of her as a young woman, a woman my age, taking my father in her arms. At what point did she decide that she loved him? When did she know that she was supposed to have despised him?

140　　"Does Manman know?" I ask.

"Yes," he says. "I explained, after you were born."

I am the one who drives the short distance back to the hotel. The ride seems drawn out, the cars in front of us appear to be dawdling. I honk impatiently, even when everyone except me is driving at a normal speed. My father is silent, not even telling me, as he has always done whenever he's been my passenger, to calm down, to be careful, to take my time.

As we are pulling into the hotel parking lot, I realize that I haven't notified Officer Bo and Manager Salinas that my father has been found. I decide that I will call them from my room. Then, before we leave the car, my father says, "Ka, no matter what, I'm still your father, still your mother's husband. I would never do these things now."

And this to me is as meaningful a declaration as his other confession. It was my first inkling that maybe my father was wrong in his own representation of his former life, that maybe his past offered more choices than being either hunter or prey.

When we get back to the hotel room, I find messages from both Officer Bo and Manager Salinas. Their shifts are over, but I leave word informing them that my father has returned.

145   While I'm on the phone, my father slips into the bathroom and runs the shower at full force. He is not humming.

When it seems he's never coming out, I call my mother at home in Brooklyn.

"Manman, how do you love him?" I whisper into the phone.

My mother is clicking her tongue and tapping her fingers against the mouthpiece again. Her soft tone makes me think I have awakened her from her sleep.

"He tell you?" she asks.

150   "Yes;" I say.

"Everything?"

"Is there more?"

"What he told you he want to tell you for long time." she says, "you, his good angel."

It has always amazed me how much my mother and father echo each other, in their speech, their actions, even in their businesses. I wonder how much more alike they could possibly be. But why shouldn't they be alike? Like all parents, they were a society of two, sharing a series of private codes and associations, a past that even if I'd been born in the country of their birth, I still wouldn't have known, couldn't have known, thoroughly. I was a part of them. Some might say I belonged to them. But I wasn't them.

155   "I don't know, Ka." My mother is whispering now, as though there's a chance she might also be overheard by my father. "You and me, we save him. When I meet him, it made him stop hurt the people. This how I see it. He a seed thrown in rock. You, me, we make him take root."

As my mother is speaking, this feeling comes over me that I sometimes have when I'm carving, this sensation that my hands don't belong to me at all, that something else besides my brain and muscles is moving my fingers, something bigger and stronger than myself, an invisible puppetmaster over whom I have no control. I feel as though it's this same puppetmaster that now forces me to lower the phone and hang up, in midconversation, on my mother.

As soon as I put the phone down, I tell myself that I could continue this particular conversation at will, in a few minutes, a few hours, a few days, even a few years. Whenever I'm ready.

My father walks back into the room, his thinning hair wet, his pajamas on. My mother does not call me back. Somehow she must know that she has betrayed me by not sharing my confusion and, on some level, my feeling that my life could have gone on fine without my knowing these types of things about my father.

When I get up the next morning, my father's already dressed. He's sitting on the edge of the bed, his head bowed, his face buried in his palms, his forehead shadowed by his fingers. If I were sculpting him at this moment, I would carve a praying mantis, crouching motionless, seeming to pray, while actually waiting to strike.

160   With his back to me now, my father says, "Will you call that actress and tell her we have it no more, the statue?"

"We were invited to lunch there," I say. "I believe we should go and tell her in person."

He raises his shoulders and shrugs.

"Up to you," he says.

We start out for Gabrielle Fonteneaus house after breakfast. Its not quite as hot as the previous morning, but it's getting there. I crank up the AC at full blast, making it almost impossible for us to have a conversation, even if we wanted to.

165 The drive seems longer than the twenty-four hours it took to get to Lakeland from New York. I quickly grow tired of the fake lakes, the fenced-in canals, the citrus groves, the fan-shaped travelers' palms, the highway so imposingly neat. My father turns his face away from me and takes in the tropical landscape, as though he will never see it again. I know he's enjoying the live oaks with Spanish moss and bromeliads growing in their shade, the yellow trumpet flowers and flame vines, the tamarinds and jacaranda trees we speed by, because he expressed his admiration for them before, on the first half of our journey.

As we approach Gabrielle Fonteneau's house, my father breaks the silence in the car by saying, "Now you see, Ka, why your mother and me, we have never returned home,"

The Fonteneaus' house is made of bricks and white coral, on a cul-de-sac with a row of banyans separating the two sides of the street.

My father and I get out of the car and follow a concrete path to the front door. Before we can knock, an older woman appears in the doorway. It's Gabrielle Fonteneau's mother. She resembles Gabrielle Fonteneau, or the way Gabrielle looks on television, with stunning almond eyes, skin the color of sorrel and spiraling curls brushing the sides of her face.

"We've been looking out for you," she says with a broad smile.

170 When Gabrielle's father joins her in the doorway, I realize where Gabrielle Fonteneau gets her height. He's more than six feet tall.

Mr. Fonteneau extends his hands, first to my father and then to me. They're relatively small, half the size of my father's.

We move slowly through the living room, which has a cathedral ceiling and walls covered with Haitian paintings with subjects ranging from market scenes and first communions to weddings and wakes. Most remarkable is a life-size portrait of Gabrielle Fonteneau sitting on a canopy-covered bench in what seems like her parents' garden.

Out on the back terrace, which towers over a nursery of azaleas, hibiscus, dracaenas, and lemongrass, a table is set for lunch.

Mr. Fonteneau asks my father where he is from in Haiti, and my father lies. In the past, I thought he always said he was from a different province each time because he'd really lived in all of those places, but I realize now that he says this to reduce the possibility of anyone identifying him, even though thirty-seven years and a thinning head of widow-peaked salt-and-pepper hair shield him from the threat of immediate recognition.

175 When Gabrielle Fonteneau makes her entrance, in an off-the-shoulder ruby dress, my father and I both rise from our seats.

"Gabrielle," she coos, extending her hand to my father, who leans forward and kisses it before spontaneously blurting out, "My dear, you are one of the most splendid flowers of Haiti."

Gabrielle Fonteneau looks a bit flustered. She tilts her head coyly and turns toward me.

"Welcome," she says.

During the meal of conch fried plantains, and mushroom rice, Mr Fonteneau tries to draw my father into conversation by asking him, in Creole, when he was last in Haiti.

180 "Thirty-seven years," my father answers with a mouthful of food.

"No going back for you?" asks Mrs. Fonteneau.

"I have not yet had the opportunity," my father replies.

"We go back every year," says Mrs. Fonteneau, "to a beautiful place overlooking the ocean, in the mountains of Jacmel."

"Have you ever been to Jacmel?" Gabrielle Fonteneau asks me.

185   I shake my head no.

"We're fortunate," Mrs. Fonteneau says, "that we have a place to go where we can say the rain is sweeter, the dust is lighter, our beaches prettier."

"So now we are tasting rain and weighing dust?" Mr. Fonteneau says and laughs.

"There's nothing like drinking the sweet juice from a coconut fetched from your own tree." Mrs. Fonteneau's eyes are lit up now as she puts her fork down to better paint the picture for us. She's giddy; her voice grows louder and higher, and even her daughter is absorbed, smiling and recollecting with her mother.

"There's nothing like sinking your hand in sand from the beach in your own country," Mrs, Fonteneau is saying. "It's a wonderful feeling, wonderful."

190   I imagine my father's nightmares. Maybe he dreams of dipping his hands in the sand on a beach in his own country and finding that what he comes up with is a fistful of blood.

After lunch, my father asks if he can have a closer look at the Fonteneaus' garden. While he's taking the tour, I make my confession about the sculpture to Gabrielle Fonteneau.

She frowns as she listens, fidgeting, shifting her weight from one foot to the other, as though she's greatly annoyed that so much of her valuable time had been so carelessly squandered on me. Perhaps she's wondering if this was just an elaborate scheme to meet her, perhaps she wants us out of her house as quickly as possible.

"I don't usually have people come into my house like this," she says, "I promise you."

"I appreciate it," I say. "I'm grateful for your trust and I didn't mean to violate it."

195   "I guess if you don't have it, then you don't have it," she says. "But I'm very disappointed. I really wanted to give that piece to my father."

"I'm sorry," I say

"I should have known something was off." she says, looking around the room, as if for something more interesting to concentrate on. "Usually when people come here to sell us art, first of all they're always carrying it with them and they always show it to us right away. But since you know Céline, I overlooked that."

"There was a sculpture," I say, aware of how stupid my excuse was going to sound. "My father didn't like it, and he threw it away."

She raises her perfectly arched eyebrows, as if out of concern for my father's sanity, or for my own. Or maybe it's another indirect signal that she now wants us out of her sight.

200   "We're done, then," she says, looking directly at my face. "I have to make a call. Enjoy the rest of your day."

Gabrielle Fonteneau excuses herself, disappearing behind a closed door. Through the terrace overlooking the garden, I see her parents guiding my father along rows of lemongrass. I want to call Gabrielle Fonteneau back and promise her that I will make her another sculpture, but I can't. I don't know that I will be able to work on anything for some time. I have lost my subject, the prisoner father I loved as well as pitied.

In the garden Mr. Fonteneau snaps a few sprigs of lemongrass from one of the plants, puts them in a plastic bag that Mrs. Fonteneau is holding. Mrs. Fonteneau hands the bag of lemongrass to my father.

Watching my father accept with a nod of thanks, I remember the chapter "Driving Back Slaughters" from *The Book of the Dead,* which my father sometimes read to me to drive away my fear of imagined monsters. It was a chapter full of terrible lines like "My mouth is the keeper of both speech and silence. I am the child who travels the roads of yesterday, the one who has been wrought from his eye."

I wave to my father in the garden to signal that we should leave now, and he slowly comes toward me, the Fonteneaus trailing behind him.

205   With each step forward, he rubs the scar on the side of his face, and out of a strange reflex I scratch my face in the same spot.

Maybe the last person my father harmed had dreamed moments like this into my father's future, strangers seeing that scar furrowed into his face and taking turns staring at it and avoiding it, forcing him to conceal it with his hands, pretend it's not there, or make up some lie about it, to explain.

Out on the sidewalk in front of the Fonteneaus' house, before we both take our places in the car, my father and I wave good-bye to Gabrielle Fonteneau's parents, who are standing in their doorway. Even though I'm not sure they understood the purpose of our visit, they were more than kind, treating us as though we were old friends of their daughter's, which maybe they had mistaken us for.

As the Fonteneaus turn their backs to us and close their front door, I look over at my father, who's still smiling and waving. When he smiles the scar shrinks and nearly disappears into the folds of his cheek, which used to make me make wish he would never stop smiling.

Once the Fonteneaus are out of sight, my father reaches down on his lap and strokes the plastic bag with the lemongrass the Fonteneaus had given him. The car is already beginning to smell too much like lemongrass, like air freshener overkill.

210   "What will you use that for?" I ask.

"To make tea," he says, "for Manman and me."

I pull the car away from the Fonteneaus' curb, dreading the rest stops, the gas station, the midway hotels ahead for us. I wish my mother were here now, talking to us about some miracle she'd just heard about in a sermon at the Mass. I wish my sculpture were still in the trunk. I wish I hadn't met Gabrielle Fonteneau, that I still had that to look forward to somewhere else, sometime in the future. I wish I could give my father whatever he'd been seeking in telling me his secret. But my father, if anyone could, must have already understood that confessions do not lighten living hearts.

I had always thought that my father's only ordeal was that he'd left his country and moved to a place where everything from the climate to the language was so unlike his own, a place where he never quite seemed to fit in, never appeared to belong. The only thing I can grasp now, as I drive way beyond the speed limit down yet another highway, is why the unfamiliar might have been so comforting, rather than distressing, to my father. And why he has never wanted the person he was, is, permanently documented in any way. He taught himself to appreciate the enormous weight of permanent markers by learning about the Ancient Egyptians. He had gotten to know them, through their crypts and monuments, in a way that he wanted no one to know him, no one except my mother and me, we, who are now his kas, his good angels, his masks against his own face.

Robyn Joy Leff

Robyn Joy Leff (1964–   ) was born in Ohio and grew up in Cleveland, Chicago, California, and Tennessee before heading to Hampshire College in Massachusetts at age sixteen. She later received a degree in Media Studies from the University of California, Santa Cruz. Her short stories have appeared in such publications as The Atlantic Monthly, Quarterly West, *and* Zyzzyva. *She currently lives in Los Angeles, where she writes marketing materials for motion pictures to make a living and is at work on a novel. Leff's physicist father and artistic mother became polar opposite influences in her life.*

2003

BURN YOUR MAPS

Six days after Halloween my nine-year-old, Wes, is still dressing in the furry, puffed-out uniform of a Mongolian nomad. He goes to school in the bushy fake fez he ordered off the Internet, tromps across the light Portland snow in his bloated felt boots. What seemed impossibly clever at the end of October has by November grown a bit disconcerting. We threw the gap-toothed pumpkin out two days ago, and Wes merely yawned. But just try to touch his hat—say, to wash his hair—and he turns all claws and parental condemnations.

Wes's father, Connor, is more annoyed than troubled by this unexpected detour into Ulan Bator. Connor, who sells next-generation CAT- and PET-scan equipment to major medical centers, survives on his ability to make up other people's minds, to blunt dissent with reason.

At dinner he shouts at our son, one word at a time: "Who are you?"

"I'm a yak herder, sir."

5 "Who are you really, though?"

Wes considers the question carefully. "For now," he says, "you can call me Baltnai."

Connor refuses to call his son Baltnai. On the seventh day, at breakfast, we all sit in silence and glare: I at Connor, Connor at Wes, Wes at no one in particular. When Wes is in the bathroom, Connor seriously suggests that we stage a midnight raid, rip off the kid's costume while he's asleep, and toss it in the trash compactor. End of Mongolian story.

"A fledgling imagination is at stake here," I say. "We can't just crush it."

"I've got this weird stomach thing again," Connor says, tossing away his pumpernickel bagel. "Every morning."

10 "Connor, he's only nine. The developing brain is wacky."

"Wes is not going to be wacky."

I touch my hand to his shoulder. "What I'm saying is, he has a lot of good reasons."

Wes comes out of the bathroom dragging a huge ball of toilet paper, at least three quarters of the roll, wrapped into an amorphous blob and hitched to his wrist with mint-flavored floss.

"What in the world are you doing?" Connor asks.

15 "Now I have a flock," Wes says. "A little lamb."

"What about Ethel?" I worry all the time about my son's fading allegiance to our elderly dachshund, about his breaking her very fine heart.

"She's a dog. This is a lamb."

"You're not dragging that pile of crap to school," Connor says with a snort.

"It's not a pile of crap," Wes states, entirely cool. "And Dad, even in Mongolia sheep don't go to school."

20 In our usual routine, Connor drops Wes in front of Hawkins Elementary and me at the equally dour-looking community center. Wes gets a kiss, but I don't.

"Why don't you ask one of your freaky child-psych friends," he says when I'm already halfway out of the car.

"Connor, you're making too big a deal. Do you know my brother swore he was Spider-Man for a month? One day he started up our garage and he actually thought his hands would stick. The fricking moron broke his leg, pissed off my dad, and ended the superhero summer."

"Lovely. Your brother. Alise, let me ask you something." Connor doesn't even turn off NPR. "You ever had any Mongolian students?"

"Probably. We cover the globe here in the Pacific Northwest."

25 "You think that has anything to do with it?"

"It's going to be my fault now—is that the concept?" I zip my jacket high over my throat.

"It's just a question," Connor says. "A line of inquiry."

"It was a National Geographic special, Con. That's what Wes says. Ask him yourself, Mr. Inquiry."

"That damned Discovery Channel," Connor says. "They act as if all information is equal."

30 "I think it's TBS," I say.

"He watches too much TV as it is," Connor says.

"Con, it's not like we let him watch *Wild Police Videos*."

"Let's review this later," he says.

"Have a nice day," I say.

35 I teach English as a Second Language. My students come from Mongolia or Turkey or Laos, yet I rarely know it. They are the tired, the huddled, the oddly uniform masses who yearn for Oprah and Wolfgang Puck and Intel. They all wear Gap-ish clothing, even if it's second-hand or Kmart. They bring lunches that have nothing to do with where they come from— the Polish woman eats supermarket sushi, the Japanese teenager downs a burger, the Somali carries in boxes of Chinese takeout and snakes cold spicy noodles into his mouth with his equally serpentine fingers.

I used to love all this, used to get off on the very odor of the classroom—a volatile magic of knockoff perfumes, ethnic spices, and cheap wet leather. I could smell the hunger to fit in, to regenerate into fatter, tanner, more legend-worthy versions of themselves, and it aroused me intellectually. I wanted to feed that hunger, wanted to snake American customs and social niceties and the correct use of adjectives into their heads like so many cold spicy noodles. But that was before burnout set in, before I saw too many of my students get nowhere or get terminally frustrated or get deported, their well-taught English turned to spite.

This year, for the first time in a long while, I have a favorite. I actually find myself bouncing to class, pleased to sit authoritatively behind my desk waiting for Ismail to walk in, always with that loose neon-blue backpack bumping toward his high ass, always with the slightest, smoothest shift of the eyes, always catching my eyes with the very corner of his.

He is a Pakistani in his forties, short, and lean. He was an engineer in his former life— something to do with mines, I believe, though I fantasize that he is a bridge builder. Earlier in the quarter I asked my students to write a short essay titled "My Advice to New Immigrants Coming to the USA." I got a lot of funny answers—"There are many bad drivers." "Bring earplugs." "You must have some lucky." "Eat ketchup, yum."—but Ismail's actually stopped me in my tracks. He wrote,

> Throw out all maps. Rip them from your books. Rip them from your heart. Or they will break it. I guarantee. Toss all globes from the roof until you have plastic pieces. Burn any atlas. You can't understand them anyway. They are offensive, like fairy tales from another tribe. The lines make no sense and no longer make mountains. You have come to the land where no one looks back. Remember, don't look back. Don't look out the window. Don't dare turn your head. You could grow dizzy. You could fall down. Throw out all your maps. Burn them.

I asked him to stay after class the day I returned the papers. I underlined the A on his essay twice.

40 "Your essay was so poetic and so sad," I said. "Your written English is quite excellent."

"Yes, it is for crying," he said. "I am this year forty-five, but I am learning like an American boy. Every day I see MTV. Now I rap better than talk. You enjoy Snoop Doggy Dogg, teacher?"

I snorted. He wasn't the gloomy or downtrodden sort I'd expected. "I don't know, we're more into 'NSync at my house. Tell me, Ismail, what are you hoping to do here in America? Return to engineering?"

"No, not one chance. I want to have a coffee shop. Coffee makes all the world happy."

"Not me, actually. Burns my stomach."

45 He frowned. "For you, for you then, teacher, we have something very special. We have sweet milk, or mint tea, or a drink of almonds. No worries. We make you happy. We will. No doubts."

For some reason in that moment I believed him, and we became friends after that, talking after class about the vagaries of Portland's traffic laws, about the cultural accuracy of *The Godfather*, sometimes even about Connor and Wes. Ismail never talked about his own family, and I didn't push in that area. After all, he was a man who advocated throwing away all maps—and what were families if not sharp demarcations in the flesh?

But on this day, when all the others have shuffled from the room with their admittedly cushy assignment to write a New Year's party menu, I sit on the floor next to Ismail's folding chair and say, "I've never asked, but do you have children?"

"What do you mean with 'have'?" He smiles slyly. It is impossible to know if he is teasing, playing the coy student.

"Are you a father?"

50 "Of course," he answers. "But my children, they are not with me in my home. So I think I do not 'have' them, as you say."

"Oh," I say. "I'm sorry, then."

"That's no problem," he says. "But you. I think you look very bad. Unhappy."

"No sleep. My son is acting a little weird, and my husband is angry."

"Anger is for husbands," Ismail says with a shrug. "That is the way."

55 "I know, but this is different. We disagree about Wes. About how best to raise him. You understand?"

Ismail, perched above me in his chair, lowers a hand, seemingly toward my hair, and then lets it slide away. "In this country," he says, "I cannot imagine to be a father. Your problems, they are so—" I think he's going to say "ridiculous"—"decadent."

"Well, Wes wants to be a Mongolian."

"What do you mean by this?" Ismail is no less confused than I.

"He wears a little tunic and pretends he's from Inner Asia. I don't know why—something he saw on TV or read on the Internet. It struck him as, I don't know, a kind of home."

60 "Mongolia? Like, as in, Mongolia?"

"Yeah, Mongolia."

"Shitty Mongolia?" Ismail shouts. "Dirty, ugly, poor Mongolia?"

We both start to laugh, the kind of musical laughter that feeds on itself, until Ismail puts a long finger to his stilled top lip and settles himself deep into the impossibly flimsy-looking chair beneath him.

It always ends this way. No matter how Ismail and I begin our conversations, they always complete themselves just like this. We both shut up and just sit together. We don't look in each other's eyes. We don't touch. We just slump, staring into space, breathing lightly, together. At first I found it quite odd, disturbing, indefinite; but now I'm beginning to wonder if it isn't some previously undiscovered form of love.

65 Wes leads his toilet-paper sheep to the dinner table on night number seven. Connor makes strange faces at me, curling and crushing his lips.

"I met a neurosurgeon from the Ukraine today," he begins, spinning yet another tale of MD heroics for Wes's future benefit. "He was all of five-foot-one, ugly little guy, but they say he has magical hands. He can make precise movements of a millimeter or less. You know how big that is?"

"Has he been to Mongolia?" Wes asks.

"Didn't ask. He uses something called a gamma knife. To blast right through tumors. Is that cool or what?"

"Mongolia isn't that far from the Ukraine," Wes points out.

70 "How was it in Mongolia today?" I ask.

Connor clicks his tongue at me.

"It was cold," Wes says, "but then, it always is. It was windy, too. It's almost time for *dzud*."

"What's *dzud*?"

"It means the slow white death," Wes says.

75 "Jesus," Connor says. "Are you okay with this?" He is pointing his fork at me, a piece of spinach waving limply.

"Wes," I say, ignoring Connor, "what is it you like so much about being Mongolian?"

He squints at me. "Can I sleep on the stairs tonight?"

"Why, Wes?"

"Baltnai," he corrects. "Because that's where the Mongolians live. On the steps."

80 "That's s-t-e-p-p-e, you know. It means a plateau, like a high, flat piece of land."

"I know what it is, Mom," he says, in the fierce way of smart boys. "But since I'm here, I got to do what I can to be there."

"Name me one reason," Connor says before bed.

I could name him three, not the least of which is that we are on the verge of separation. On the verge, we say, as if it were a bungee-jumping platform, as if we could just step backward at any point and laugh at what we almost did. But I don't want to start that talk tonight, so I say, "Grandpa Firth."

"Absurd," Connor says. He is lying on top of the covers in his briefs, fingertips jammed just under the band, which incongruously screams JOE BOXER. He doesn't look as if he could sell firewood to an Eskimo. He looks like a little boy himself. He turns to the right and hugs the bottom of his naked ribs. I toss his half of the blanket over him. He shrinks to a lump beneath it.

85 "Slow white death," I say. "You think that's a coincidence?"

"Alise," he says.

Two months ago Connor's father died in our television room, surrounded by hospital equipment and cases of Ensure. Before that we saw Grandpa Firth maybe once every other year, guilted into occasional holidays. Wes barely knew him. Hell, I barely knew him. Connor used to say he didn't want him spreading his lies to Wes. I knew only that Connor was like a nine-year-old himself in the old man's presence.

"You don't see the connection?"

"Between my old man and Mongolia? You're just pushing any button you can find."

90 "No—I mean, maybe there's something there. About the incredible transience of human contact. Or something. I mean, I don't know what I mean."

"No shit, Sherlock."

He shuffles and moves in closer, his skin sharp with cold, igniting that lingering instinct to warm what's next to you. It's almost though we could drop this whole pretense of so many years, wiggle into one another, make sweat-happy teenage love. Instead I slide the sole of a foot onto his icy calf.

"I think Grandpa Firth told Wes that he used to be a CIA agent in Singapore."

"I'd say it was the chemo talking, but that was him. In translation, he meant he once had too many drinks in a bar in Singapore."

95 "I'm just saying that Wes liked his stories. He's got that storytelling thing now. It's like an addiction."

"My dad was real good with addictions."

"It kills you that anyone could like Will Firth, doesn't it?"

Connor wriggles a little. "You're so wrong it's hilarious, Alise. That's the only thing around here I'm happy about. Wes was the only one who ever made my dad—" He clears his throat as if he's going to cry, but of course he doesn't. "But you know," he goes on, "maybe it's you, and the way you give him so much freedom. He lacks a sense of that one thing Will Firth gave me—boundaries."

I snort, but then suddenly I'm the one who's crying. Lightly, but still crying.

100 Boundaries. Borders. Maps. I retreat fully from Connor's body, drop my foot off his warming leg, tuck into full fetal position. It could be worse, I suppose. I have a friend, a child psychologist as it happens, who keeps separate bedrooms with her artist husband. He has sleep issues, Krista tells me, and he can't fall asleep if someone else is in the room. So once every two weeks or so they come to each other to make love, but she tells me it's like visiting a stranger's bed: they are awkward and silly, and when they're done, they wipe up and return to their separate islands.

Separate islands, my brain sings near sleep. Then, before I drop off, I begin to wonder just how many young nomad boys in the heart of Inner Mongolia—*most? 50 percent?*—are lying in their yurts right now humming to the Backstreet Boys on some Walkman a tourist left behind, fully engaged in the reverse of Wes's fantasy, certain they were meant to be born American.

I'm sure I have plenty of culpability. Unlike Connor, I don't consider myself that free a parent. Wes may watch some TV shows but not others. A 9:00 P.M. bed curfew is enforced. I've spanked him several times, but never with premeditation. My worst sin may be that I have spent so many nights on Wes's bedcovers, my favorite globe spinning under my fingers. Ismail's nightmare, our little game.

"It's all so close together," Wes said, giggling, in September, because that's what happens when all you do is trace your finger from one land to another: the very shape of distance falls away, becomes an impossible geometry.

"That's just an illusion," I said.

105 It was a huge error. People of my generation feel we have good excuses for our loneliness. But what about Wes? He flicks through dozens of search-engine hits for Mongolia, and learns that the world's millions are within his reach. So how can he know it's still okay to feel that no one on Earth can understand him, that no one can comfort him if he sits in his room, a micro-lump in the middle of Oregon in the middle of America in the middle of the world, losing it?

Connor doesn't speak at breakfast. He just clutches his slight paunch. "Are you going to call the doctor?" I ask.

"About Wes?"

"About your bellyache, Con. You see a million doctors every day."

"They're head guys. I need a GI man."

110 "Like GI Joe," Wes says.

"'GI' means 'gastrointestinal' in medical talk. Like guts."

"Ew, that's gross," Wes says. He rubs his nubby wool hat violently.

"Bet your hair really itches," Connor teases.

"When it does, I meditate. It's like praying, only you do it to Buddha"—Wes says
115 *"Butt-ah"*—"instead of God."

"Where do you get this stuff?" Connor asks.

"I don't know. Encarta and stuff."

"You know, nomads don't really have the Internet or CD-ROMs."

"Duh, Dad. They don't need it, anyway."

120 "Why not?"

"Everything they need is right there. They don't have to order stuff from UPS." He is
unflinching, standing up to his father. Connor must secretly be proud.

"And where is everything you need, Wes?"

Wes shrugs and squints, making his features so small and pointed that I want to put
him back to my breast, grow him all over again. "I don't know," he says. "Where?"

So much purpling blood pours into Connor's face that I am certain he is going to
scream. But instead he shuffles quickly toward the bathroom, where he remains until we are
all going to be late.

Thank God it is Friday. I'm not exactly looking forward to the weekend, with everything
building to a head over Mongolia, but Friday is my student-conference day, when I meet with
125 anyone who makes an appointment to see me. Ismail always makes an appointment.

My Friday slots are almost always filled. Most of my students come desperately seeking
help—but not with their English. Today a tall, balding Sri Lankan inquires whether I know
any performing-arts agents. His son has an Asian-techno hip-hop band, and if the kid can
just snag a record contract, they'll be able to afford a bigger apartment. I tell him to try a
book at the library, which makes him belly laugh for a good long minute. At least I'm useful
for something.

Sometimes I think I am a fraud, because I myself can barely speak a second language. I
can squeak by with some Spanish and a tad of Farsi, and I have painstakingly memorized
certain Chinese characters, but I lack that magical ability some annoying linguists have to
slide simply between two tongues, easing back and forth between one way of speaking and
another. I admit that I am attached to the shapes my tongue makes, to the comforting way
my throat opens and closes day after day.

I didn't mean to do this kind of teaching. First I wanted to be a ballet dancer, but my
hips bloomed round; then I wanted to be in the Peace Corps, but I met Con; then I fantasized about becoming one of those brilliant private school matrons who mold little geniuses
into men and women of the world, only that was just silly. Of course, it was the same for
Connor, who wanted to be a brain surgeon but kept failing chemistry. Nothing quite turns
out in our lives. But that's what gets me: there might still be a very few remote places in the
world—deepest Mongolia, maybe—where a person comes to live exactly the life expected,
exactly as offered. I didn't. None of my students has. Wes, child of his times already, doesn't
even have a shot at it. And yet somehow it thrills me—and maybe Wes as well—to know
that such a thing remains imaginable.

By 3:00 P.M. Ismail should have arrived, but he is late. In his absence I draw thin, mal-
formed yaks on my doodle pad and think about Connor's stomach. Mostly I imagine it's a
problem of emptiness. He has lost twenty pounds in the past six months, has started taking
a kickboxing class on the weekends, has stopped buying ice cream. I wonder if this has affected Wes at all—his father's slipping away, disappearing, reducing himself. I wonder also if
Connor is doing it for me. Is that possible? Is it wicked to hope that his ill health is rooted in
thwarted passion?

When Ismail arrives, he is breathless, agitated. He walks right across my office to the
window, which looks on a parking lot overgrown with peeling, rusted Subarus.

130   "You think *you* have some trouble," he says.

"Is something wrong?"

"Lahore has called. A son may be arrested."

I think of going to him, but I know that's not what he wants. His skin—what I can see of it—seems to sag, pulled toward the window and away from me.

"Why?"

135   "It is not known. Maybe some drugs, maybe some politics, maybe, I don't know how to say, crazy, crazy, crazy."

"Will you go there?"

At last he turns around, and I can see his face, which looks no different—as soft and yielding around the lips and jawline as ever, eyes still shifted to the side.

"I cannot, you see."

"Can I do anything? To help?"

140   He saunters back to my desk, forcing a slow grin.

"Let us discuss the *Austin Powers*," he says. "I do not get this one."

"Ismail," I say, "I can't talk about *Austin Powers* right now."

"Why so?"

"You've upset me. You're upset. It's outrageous."

145   He sits on top of my desk, the way a boy with a crush would. "Everything is what you say: outrageous," he says.

He's so damn glib it infuriates me. I scrunch up my doodle page, yaks and all, and throw it at him. Hard.

He glares at me, finally revealing a glint of hurt. Then he grabs a slim paperback off a shelf and hurls it at my shoulder.

I return fire with a catapulted rubber band. Ismail takes up chalk from my board and strafes my side of the desk with several pieces. One hits me square in the cheek, smarting immediately. I rise and move toward the bookshelves. A paper clip ricochets off my breast. Blindly I grab at a stapler. He takes my wrist. I take his waist.

We crumple into each other, almost hugging. But not. Our arms fall to our sides, the stapler falls to the floor, and we tremble. But we say nothing. We do not touch. We do not look in each other's eyes. We do nothing but stand there.

150   Finally he steps back and says, "Thank you. You are a good teacher."

"Ismail," I say.

"Shush—we cross no line," he says.

We cross no line, he says. Or at least we pretend not to. You choose your home and you burn all your maps, but that doesn't mean you might not find yourself lost and speechless where the lines fall away and the mountains blur and the silence feels better than years and years of conversation.

Ismail and I walk casually to the parking lot, talking of *Austin Powers*. "Okay," he says. "But why is this funny?"

155   "Analysis kills humor," I tell him.

"Why does joy break so easy? This is one shitty substance."

I see Connor in the Toyota, biting his nails. I imagine him winking at me. "Try *Groundhog Day*," I say. "And please, your son, if there's anything—"

He laughs, just like the Sri Lankan—the most frequent response to offers of assistance these days.

In the car Connor says, "That your Mongolian?"

160   "Oh, Lord. He's Pakistani, Con. He was wondering why *Austin Powers* is funny."

"Wrong person to ask."

"What does that mean?"

"Alise. Let's not. Hey, I talked to a doctor today."

"About your stomach?"

165 "About Wes. A neuropsychologist, top gun, Harvard, the whole schmeer. He says we're in trouble. We have to nip it in the bud."

"Nip what? What about your stomach?"

"He says that obsessions can literally reshape the landscape of the brain. Neurons get stuck in little pathways, draw new maps. It can be permanent."

"Does he have kids?"

"What?"

170 "Does he have a nine-year-old son on whom he experiments?"

"I don't know, Alise. The point is he knows the brain."

"The brain is just a bit."

"The most important bit," Connor says.

I exhale into my fist. "So what does he say we should do?"

175 "Take the costume."

"Take the costume," I repeat.

"Throw it away, bury it, burn it. Free Wes of the compulsion."

"Oh, Connor, that seems needlessly cruel."

"Are you saying I'm cruel?"

180 "Not you, Con. The idea of it."

"Just like that, you know more than the experts, huh?"

"I know my son," I say.

"I know my son too," he says.

The Toyota pulls hard to a halt in front of the library, where Wes waits inside, no doubt reading up on Mongolia. I find myself unable to undo my seat belt. Connor doesn't take his off either. We just sit there a moment, strapped in, he tapping on the dashboard, I fiddling in the cavern of my handbag for something I cannot name.

185 Saturday afternoon, day nine, Wes walks Ethel the dachshund up and down my back. This is a ritual we began about a year ago, when I started getting fierce cramps in my trapezius. Wes told me he'd read that Gypsies used to walk pet bears up and down people's backs for money. He has always been that kind of kid—digging up weird facts and anecdotes wherever he could find them. Nondiscriminatory about information, I guess, all of it worth paying out.

The truth is that a lot of his info is crap. But with Ethel he hit gold. She loves being the masseuse, and I can tell by the way her sweeping tail draws broad smiles up and down my torso. I, in turn, love the feeling of the paws pressing into my sinews, their animal motion so much more random and unflinching than a human rubdown. Just a walk on the back. Pure, motiveless attention.

I am grateful, as usual, after the mini-hound massage, so I brew Wes a pot of tea, since that is what he says Mongolians drink. Tea and lots of vodka, he says pointedly, but I roll my eyes, so we have Celestial Seasonings Cranberry Cove instead.

Connor is at his kickboxing class, which means that Wes and I can talk about his idea of building a *ger* in the back yard.

"It's like a tent, but it's round," he tells me. "I just need sticks and animal skins."

190 "Your father will have a cow," I say.

"A cow skin would be good," he says. I wish his smile would last longer.

"Wes," I say. "Are you mad at us?"

"At who?"

"At me. Or your father."

195 "Not really." He wrinkles his perfectly smooth face. "Not exactly."

"Are you still sad about Grandpa Firth?"

"It's okay, you know. I think he'll be reincarnated. Maybe as a Javanese rhino, but he'll be born in a zoo, because they're almost extinct."

"Wes," I say, "you've got to tell me the truth. Do you hate your life?"

"You're freaking, Mom."

200 "Really. You can tell me. Do you hate your life with us, with me and your dad, here in America?"

He takes a sloppy sip of tea and then smiles sympathetically at me, as if I'm a hundred moves behind him. "Silly worrywart," he says. "You guys always think it's 'cause of you. But sometimes that's not true. Sometimes a person just wants to be a Mongolian, okay?"

"Okay," I say. "If that's what you feel like."

But it's not okay, because when Connor comes home from his kickboxing class, his forehead is taut and shiny, his cheeks are fat and ruddy, and he stands in the foyer huffing.

"Are you all right?" I ask.

205 "Stop it with the stomach."

"You seem a little off is all."

"I'm good. I had a great workout." He smells salty and smoky, like winter air.

"Good," I say. "Tougher and stronger every day."

"Are you mocking me?"

210 "Jesus," I say. "Can't I say something nice?" But I am thinking, *Mocking, the bane of our times,* and *Why don't I ever feel the instinct for niceness first anymore?*

"Let's go to the movies," he says. "It's icy as hell out there, so it won't be crowded. We'll get hot cocoa and popcorn, be a real fam."

"Okay," I say. "Let's be a real fam."

He stands there for a second. "Where's Wes?"

"In his room. On the computer, I think."

215 "Wes," Connor calls.

"I think he's going to be okay," I say suddenly. I don't know why.

"Wes," Connor calls in a louder voice.

"He's really such a smart kid."

He appears in front of us, a smart kid in a tunic, felt boots, and a wool fez, dragging crumpled toilet paper.

220 "Do you want to go to the movies?" Connor asks. "That thing with Keanu Reeves?"

"Really?"

"It's not R?" I interrupt.

"Really," Connor says.

"That's so radical, Dad. It's all CGI—computer animation, you know."

225 "Great. Why don't you put on your jeans and a sweater, and we'll go get the tickets."

"What do you mean?" Wes asks.

"Connor, please," I say.

"I mean, just go change into something normal, and we'll go."

"I'm a nomad, Dad. Take it or leave it."

230 "I'll leave it," Connor says. The edge has taken over his entire voice, lopped off the soft bits. "You can wear the hat, but the rest is history. That's my final deal."

"I'm going upstairs," Wes says, and shrugs. "I'll be on the modem. 'Night, Mommy."

"No computer," Connor says.

"What?"

"No computer until you take that stuff off."

235 "Mom?" Wes looks at me urgently.

"Con, let's just rent a video and have a nice night," I plead. I feel like an envoy to the Middle East, my centrist position as dangerous as any.

"I want to see a movie," Connor says.

"Well, I want to see a video," I say.

"Well, I want to have a loving wife and a sane son, but you can't always get what you want."

240   "Take that back." Wes jumps in his father's face now, looking fierce and ancient in his little nomad uniform. If he had a scimitar, somebody would get hurt.

"Listen, Wes—" Connor says.

"No," Wes says. "I won't. Not till you take it back."

"Take what back?"

"You know what. Take it back."

245   Connor bends slightly at the waist, and his knees seem to make small circles. I can see how badly he wants to take it back, how the very pull is shredding his innards. But he can't. He can't take it back because he has no more room to stash anything.

"Take it back, Dad," Wes says again in a hoarse whisper.

But his father, my husband, is paralyzed where he stands, in the foyer, at the base of the stairs. Wes pushes past us and races out the front door, whipping it shut on the beat of a sharp sniffle.

I want to say something to Connor, something he won't ever forget, but he looks so bereft that I can't imagine doing further damage. So I button my shirt to the neck and head out into air that has the essence of conscious razor blades, cutting you just for having the gall to breathe it in.

What I find first, on the Swenson's lawn, is a fur cap laced with strands of greasy hair. Then I see the tunic on a tree stump across Ashford Avenue, and the sash and the fat yellow boots near the bus stop. They have been violently strewn, ripped away. Bits of thread are everywhere in the snow, like shrapnel. I follow the line of them, contemplating just how cold it really is, just how long it would take a naked nine-year-old boy to develop hypothermia.

250   It's amazing how fast he can run in the snow, as if he was born to it. My lungs are like meat in a freezer, all elasticity gone. I am forced to crawl at the bus-stop corner, because the sidewalks are far too icy to get traction with my sneakers.

I almost lose him, but near the school I find a footprint rarely seen in the snow—light as a snow angel, with individual little ellipses of toe shapes. They lead me to an anemic bush inside whose silver arms Wes is huddled, snorting snot into his trembling hands. His body is bright red, but it looks strong. As I get closer, I see that what I thought were white blisters on his belly are actually frail bubbles of water. He looks more inviolate than I ever imagined he could be.

I grab at him anyway, search his limbs for wounds, feel his baby-thin skin for aberrations. Then I catch his eyes, the whites expanding like the universe, and I see him searching for something in mine, for some reason or explanation or even just a nanoglimmer of hope that will set this all back to bearable. He begins to laugh.

"It's not funny," I protest. "You could die out here like this."

"I'm naked in the snow," he giggles. "I'm a naked Mongolian. My butt has ice on it."

255   This part is true. He is in shockingly dirty blue Gap briefs, which are soaked with snow and sagging off him. I start to laugh too.

We both look up and see Connor approaching, lurching and sliding and completely off-kilter. When he reaches us, his chest heaves; his breath steams out his mouth.

"What in the hell are you two—" he starts, but then he stops.

That's what gets me. He stops.

260 "Oh, Christ, you both must be freezing," he says. "Come here."

I scoop Wes in my arms, his wet bottom drenching my shirt. Connor has had the presence of mind to take a wool coat on his way out, and now he wraps it around all three of us, making a kind of mobile cave. For the first time I realize that I am freezing, that my fingers, nipples, and nose are buzzing near numb. Inside the coat Wes and I cling to each other and to Connor's almost fiery warmth. We start walking home, three bodies moving through the night under one cloak, picking up pieces of Mongolia the whole way.

It's very quiet out. The night is so cold and so amply hushed that I can hear the constellations hum like halogen lamps. We say nothing to one another. When we get to the house, before we separate and rush for the door, for a single moment I almost speak. I almost say, "We're home."

But I cannot tell a lie. I don't know that we're home, because it's as if we don't belong anyplace on this Earth, in any country, or any house, or anywhere, really, but in this ragged circle of wool.

ROBERT HAYDEN

Robert Hayden (1913–80) was born in Detroit, Michigan. He attended Detroit City College (now Wayne State University) and the University of Michigan. He garnered many honors and fellowships and in 1976 became the first African American poet to be chosen Consultant in Poetry to the Library of Congress. His works include Heart-Shape in the Dust *(1940),* Words in Mourning Time *(1970), and* Robert Hayden: Collected Poems *(1982).*

1962

THOSE WINTER SUNDAYS

Sundays too my father got up early
and put his clothes on in the blueblack cold,
then with cracked hands that ached
from labor in the weekday weather made
5 banked fires blaze. No one ever thanked him.

I'd wake and hear the cold splintering, breaking.
When the rooms were warm, he'd call,
and slowly I would rise and dress,
fearing the chronic angers of that house,

10 Speaking indifferently to him,
who had driven out the cold
and polished my good shoes as well.
What did I know, what did I know
of love's austere and lonely offices?

BELL HOOKS

bell hooks (1955–   ), born Gloria Watkins in Kentucky and educated at Stanford University, published her first book, Ain't I a Woman: Black Women and Feminism, *in 1981. A prolific writer, hooks has pursued the role of public intellectual, seeking to bring her concerns with matters of race and gender to a broad audience. Her books include* Talking Back: Thinking Feminist, Thinking Black *(1989),* Teaching to Transgress: Education as the Price of Freedom *(1994),* We Real Cool: Black Men and Masculinity *(2003), and* Teaching Community: A Pedagogy of Hope *(2003).*

1996

BONE BLACK

Chapters 49, 50 and 51

49

They have never heard their mama and daddy fussing or fighting. They have heard him be harsh, complain that the house should be cleaner, that he should not have to come home from work to a house that is not cleaned just right. They know he gets mad. When he gets mad about the house he begins to clean it himself to show that he can do better. Although he never cooks he knows how. He would not be able to judge her cooking if he did not cook himself. They are afraid of him when he is mad. They go upstairs to get out of his way. He does not come upstairs. Taking care of children is not a man's work. It does not concern him. He is not even interested—that is, unless something goes wrong. Then he can show her that she is not very good at parenting. They know they have a good mama, the best. Even though they fear him they are not moved by his opinions. She tries to remember a time when she felt loved by him. She remembers it as being the time when she was a baby girl, a small girl. She remembers him taking her places, taking her to the world inhabited by black men, the barbershop, the pool hall. He took his affections away from her abruptly. She never understood why, only that they went and did not come back. She remembered trying to do whatever she could to bring them back, only they never came. Growing up she stopped trying. He mainly ignored her. She mainly tried to stay out of his way. In her own way she grew to hate wanting his love and not being able to get it. She hated that part of herself that kept wanting his love or even just his approval long after she could see that he was never, never going to give it.

Out of nowhere he comes home from work angry. He reaches the porch yelling and screaming at the woman inside—yelling that she is his wife, he can do with her what he wants. They do not understand what is happening. He is pushing, hitting, telling her to shut up. She is pleading—crying. He does not want to hear, to listen. They catch his angry words in their hands like lightning bugs—store them in a jar to sort them out later. Words about other men, about phone calls, about how he had told her. They do not know what he has told her. They have never heard them talk in an angry way.

She thinks of all the nights she lies awake in her bed hearing the woman's voice, her mother's voice, hearing his voice. She wonders if it is then that he is telling her everything—warning her. Yelling, screaming, hitting: they stare at the red blood that trickles through the crying mouth. They cannot believe this pleading, crying woman, this woman who does not fight back, is the same person they know. The person they know is strong, gets things done, is a woman of ways and means, a woman of action. They do not know her still, paralyzed, waiting for the next blow, pleading. They do not know their mama afraid. Even if she does not hit back they want her to run, to run and to not stop running. She wants her to hit him with the table light, the ashtray, the one near her hand. She does not want to see her like this, not fighting back. He notices them, long enough to tell them to get out, go upstairs. She refuses to move. She cannot move. She cannot leave her mama alone. When he says What are you staring at, do you want some, too? she is afraid enough to move. She will not take her orders from him. She asks the woman if it is right to leave her alone. The woman—her mother—nods her head yes. She still stands still. It is his movement in her direction that sends her up the stairs. She cannot believe all her sisters and her brother are not taking a stand, that they go to sleep. She cannot bear their betrayal. When the father is not looking she creeps down the steps. She wants the woman to know that she is not alone. She wants to bear witness.

They say she is near death, that we must go and see her because it may be the last time. I will not go. I have my own ideas about death. I see her all the time. I see her as she moves about the house doing things, cooking, cleaning, fussing. I refuse to go. I cannot tell them why, that I do not want to have the last sight of her be there in the white hospital bed, surrounded by strangers and the smell of death. She does not die. She comes home angry, not wanting to see the uncaring daughter, the one who would not even come to say good-bye. She is in control. She is not yet ready to love. She does not understand. Upstairs in my hiding place I cry. They tell her she is upstairs crying and will not stop. She sends me orders to stop crying right this minute, that I have nothing to cry about, that she should be crying to have such a terrible daughter. When I go to her, sitting on the bed, with my longing and my tears she knows that she breaks my heart a little. She thinks I break her heart a little. She cannot know the joy we feel that she is home, alive.

50

5 All that she does not understand about marriage, about men and women, is explained to her one night. In her dark place on the stairs she is seeing over and over again the still body of the woman pleading, crying, the moving body of the man angry, yelling. She sees that the man has a gun. She hears him tell the woman that he will kill her. She sits in her place on the stair and demands to know of herself is she able to come to the rescue, is she willing to fight, is she ready to die. Her body shakes with the answers. She is fighting back the tears. When he leaves the room she comes to ask the woman if she is all right, if there is anything she can do. The woman's voice is full of tenderness and hurt. She is in her role as mother. She tells her daughter to go upstairs and go to sleep, that everything will be all right. The daughter does not believe her. Her eyes are pleading. She does not want to be told to go. She hovers in the shadows. When he returns he tells her that he has told her to get her ass upstairs. She does not look at him. He turns to the woman, tells her to leave, tells her to take the daughter with her.

The woman does not protest. She moves like a robot, hurriedly throwing things into suitcases, boxes. She says nothing to the man. He is still screaming, muttering. When she tries to say to him he is wrong, so wrong, he is more angry, threatening. All the neat drawers are emptied out on the bed, all the precious belongings that can be carried, stuffed, are to be taken. There is sorrow in every gesture, sorrow and pain—like a dust collecting on everything, so thick she can gather it in her hands. She is seeing that the man owns everything, that the woman has only her clothes, her shoes, and other personal belongings. She is seeing that the woman can be told to go, can be sent away in the silent, long hours of the night. She is hearing in her head the man's threats to kill. She can feel the cool metal as if it is resting against her cheek. She can hear the click, the blast. She can see the woman's body falling. No, it is not her body, it is the body of love. She witnesses the death of love. If love were alive she believes it would stop everything. It would steady the man's voice, calm his rage. Love would take the woman's hand, caress her cheek and with a clean handkerchief wipe her eyes. The gun is pointed at love. He lays it on the table. He wants his wife to finish her packing, to go.

She is again in her role as mother. She tells the daughter that she does not have to flee in the middle of the night, that it is not her fight. The daughter is silent, staring into the woman's eyes. She is looking for the bright lights, the care and adoration she has shown the man. The eyes are dark with grief, swollen. She feels that a fire inside the woman is dying out, that she is cold. She is sure the woman will freeze to death if she goes out into the night alone. She takes her hand, ready to go with her. Yet she hopes there will be no going. She hopes when the mother's brother comes he will be strong enough to take love's body and give it, mouth-to-mouth, the life it has lost. She hopes he will talk to the man, guide him. When he finally comes, her mother's favorite brother, she cannot believe the calm way he lifts suitcase, box, sack, carries them to the car without question. She cannot bear his silent agreement that the man is right, that he has done what men are able to do. She cannot take the bits and pieces of her mother's heart and put them together again.

51

I am always fighting with mama. Everything has come between us. She no longer stands between me and all that would hurt me. She is hurting me. This is my dream of her—that she will stand between me and all that hurts me, that she will protect me at all cost. It is only a dream. In some way I understand that it has to do with marriage, that to be the wife to the husband she must be willing to sacrifice even her daughters for his good. For the mother it is not simple. She is always torn. She works hard to fulfill his needs, our needs. When they are not the same she must maneuver, manipulate, choose. She has chosen. She has decided in his favor. She is a religious woman. She has been told that a man should obey god, that a woman should obey man, that children should obey their fathers and mothers, particularly their mothers. I will not obey.

She says that she punishes me for my own good. I do not know what it is I have done this time. I know that she is ready with her switches, that I am to stand still while she lashes out again and again. In my mind there is the memory of a woman sitting still while she is being hit, punished. In my mind I am remembering how much I want that woman to fight back. Before I can think clearly my hands reach out, grab the switches, are raised as if to hit her back. For a moment she is stunned, unbelieving. She is shocked. She tells me that I must never *ever* as long as I live raise my hand against my mother. I tell her I do not have a mother. She is even more shocked. Enraged, she lashes out again. This time I am still. This time I cry. I see the hurt in her eyes when I say I do not have a mother. I am ready to be punished. My desire was to stop the pain, not to hurt. I am ashamed and torn. I do not want to stand still and be punished but I never want to hurt mama. It is better to hurt than to cause her pain. She warns me that she will tell daddy when he comes home, that I will be punished again. I cannot understand her acts of betrayal. I cannot understand that she must be against me to be for him. He and I are strangers. Deep in the night we parted from one another, knowing that nothing would ever be the same. He did not say good-bye. I did not look him in the face. Now we avoid one another. He speaks to me through her.

10   Although they act as if everything between them is the same, that life is as it was. It is only a game. They pretend. There is no pain in the pretense. Everything is hidden. Secrets find a way out in sleep. My sisters say to mama She cries in her sleep, calls out. In her sleep is the place of remembering. It is the place where there is no pretense. She is dreaming always the same dream. A movie is showing. It is a tragic story of jealousy and lost love. It is called *Crime of Passion*. In the movie a man has killed his wife and daughter. He has killed his wife because he believes she has lovers. He has killed the daughter because she witnesses the death of the wife. When they go to trial all the remaining family come to speak on behalf of the man. At his job he is calm and quiet, a hardworking man, a family man.

Neighbors come to testify that the dead woman was young and restless, that the daughter was wild and rebellious. Everyone sympathizes with the man. His story is so sad that they begin to weep. All their handkerchiefs are clean and white. Like flags waving, they are a signal of peace, of surrender. They are a gesture to the man that he can go on with life.

■ EXPLORATIONS OF THE TEXT

1. Examine the relationships between parents and children. What are the children's roles in the families?
2. Discuss the failure to communicate—what Leff in "Burn Your Maps" describes as the "transience of human contact"—portrayed in these works. Analyze the silences in family life.
3. What are the secrets of the main characters? How do the protagonists live on "separate islands" (as suggested in Leff's "Burn Your Maps")? What do the protagonists yearn for? What losses do they experience? Do the children absorb the anxieties, insecurities, suppressed emotions, dreams, and desires of their parents? Do family secrets damage the children?
4. How would each work in this cluster change if the point of view were different? (Example: What if the third person narrative in hooks's work were changed to first person?)
5. Explore the theme of the dysfunctional family in these works. How do these works redefine "home"?
6. How does setting in these works serve as a symbol of family life?
7. How do parental power and control shape the destinies of children?
8. Danticat's work is entitled "The Book of the Dead." Indeed, that title would fit many of the works in this cluster. Why? Categorize the confrontations with forms of death represented in these works. What are the results for the characters?

■ THE READING/WRITING CONNECTION

1. Freewrite. Respond to this line from "Burn Your Maps": "Throw out all maps. Rip them out from your books. Rip them from your heart." Does this statement convey truths about the dynamics of family relationships, of other intimate relationships (e.g., friendship or love relationships)? Argue pro or con.
2. Journal Entry: As a child, did you have imaginary friends? As an alternative, construct a fantasy world as Wes does in "Burn Your Maps."
3. Have your parents disappointed you? When did you realize that your parents were not perfect human beings? Answer either or both questions in a journal entry.
4. Write a letter to one of your parents expressing your feelings concerning an issue or an experience about which you have kept silent, or say something (positive or negative) that you always have wanted to express to them.
5. Create a monologue or a journal entry for one of the characters that reveals the character's inner life.
6. Create a new title for one of the works, and then justify your choice. As an alternative, create an artwork or collage that represents your response to the work, and then explain what it signifies about the work.

■ IDEAS FOR WRITING

1. How do the secrets or obsessions of parents have consequences for their children? How do the secrets shape the children's destinies? Once the secrets are revealed, what are the consequences? Analyze this thematic motif in works in this cluster.

2. In the excerpt from *bone black,* hooks observes that "the silent agreement that the man is right" is operative in the marriage of her parents. How are the dynamics of the marital relationships portrayed in the works in this cluster governed by social conditioning? Create a feminist critique of one of the marital relationships. As an alternative, based on your observations and experience, do you believe the roles in marriage have changed? Present your views on this issue.

3. In Synge's "Riders to the Sea," Maurya bows to the power of the sea, stating, "'What more can we want . . . . No man at all can be living forever, and we must be satisfied.'" Compare the view of fate in this work with themes of Hawthorne's "Rappaccini's Daughter" or Danticat's "The Book of the Dead."

4. Interpret this quotation from Paul Simon's song "The Sound of Silence": "Silence like a cancer grows." Connect it with the conflicts of several protagonists in these works.

■ FICTION ■

TILLIE OLSEN

Tillie Olsen (1913–), born in Omaha, Nebraska, is the daughter of blue-collar workers who fled czarist Russia after the 1905 revolution. She grew up in poverty and at age fifteen quit high school to help support her family during the Depression. Celebrated as a crusader for the feminist movement and other causes, Olsen was presented the O. Henry Award in 1961 for Tell Me a Riddle. *Her first novel,* Yonnondio, *started in 1934, finally was published in 1974;* Silences, *a study exploring circumstances that interfere with women's creativity, appeared in 1978.*

1953

I STAND HERE IRONING

I stand here ironing, and what you asked me moves tormented back and forth with the iron.

"I wish you would manage the time to come and talk with me about your daughter. I'm sure you can help me understand her. She's a youngster who needs help and whom I'm deeply interested in helping."

"Who needs help." . . . Even if I came, what good would it do? You think because I am her mother I have a key, or that in some way you could use me as a key? She has lived for nineteen years. There is all that life that has happened outside of me, beyond me.

And when is there time to remember, to sift, to weigh, to estimate, to total? I will start and there will be an interruption and I will have to gather it all together again. Or I will become engulfed with all I did or did not do, with what should have been and what cannot be helped.

5   She was a beautiful baby. The first and only one of our five that was beautiful at birth. You do not guess how new and uneasy her tenancy in her now-loveliness. You did not know her all those years she was thought homely, or see her poring over her baby pictures, making me tell her over and over how beautiful she had been—and would be, I would tell her—and was now, to the seeing eye. But the seeing eyes were few or nonexistent. Including mine.

I nursed her. They feel that's important nowadays. I nursed all the children, but with her, with all the fierce rigidity of first motherhood, I did like the books then said. Though her cries battered me to trembling and my breasts ached with swollenness, I waited till the clock decreed.

Why do I put that first? I do not even know if it matters, or if it explains anything.

She was a beautiful baby. She blew shining bubbles of sound. She loved motion, loved light, loved color and music and textures. She would lie on the floor in her blue overalls patting the surface so hard in ecstasy her hands and feet would blur. She was a miracle to me, but when she was eight months old I had to leave her daytimes with the woman downstairs to whom she was no miracle at all, for I worked or looked for work and for Emily's father, who "could no longer endure" (he wrote in his good-bye note) "sharing want with us."

I was nineteen. It was the pre-relief, pre-WPA[1] world of the Depression. I would start running as soon as I got off the streetcar, running up the stairs, the place smelling sour, and awake or asleep to startle awake, when she saw me she would break into a clogged weeping that could not be comforted, a weeping I can hear yet.

10 After a while I found a job hashing at night so I could be with her days, and it was better. But it came to where I had to bring her to his family and leave her.

It took a long time to raise the money for her fare back. Then she got chicken pox and I had to wait longer. When she finally came, I hardly knew her, walking quick and nervous like her father, looking like her father, thin, and dressed in a shoddy red that yellowed her skin and glared at the pockmarks. All the baby loveliness gone.

She was two. Old enough for nursery school they said, and I did not know then what I know now—the fatigue of the long day, and the lacerations of group life in the kinds of nurseries that are only parking places for children.

Except that it would have made no difference if I had known. It was the only place there was. It was the only way we could be together, the only way I could hold a job.

And even without knowing, I knew. I knew the teacher that was evil because all these years it has curdled into my memory, the little boy hunched in the corner, her rasp, "why aren't you outside, because Alvin hits you? that's no reason, go out, scaredy." I knew Emily hated it even if she did not clutch and implore "don't go Mommy" like the other children, mornings.

15 She always had a reason why we should stay home. Momma, you look sick. Momma, I feel sick. Momma, the teachers aren't there today, they're sick. Momma, we can't go, there was a fire there last night. Momma, it's a holiday today, no school, they told me.

But never a direct protest, never rebellion. I think of our others in their three-, four-year-oldness—the explosions, the tempers, the denunciations, the demands—and I feel suddenly ill. I put the iron down. What in me demanded that goodness in her? And what was the cost, the cost to her of such goodness?

The old man living in the back once said in his gentle way: "You should smile at Emily more when you look at her." What *was* in my face when I looked at her? I loved her. There were all the acts of love.

It was only with the others I remembered what he said, and it was the face of joy, and not of care or tightness or worry I turned to them—too late for Emily. She does not smile easily, let alone almost always as her brothers and sisters do. Her face is closed and sombre, but when she wants, how fluid. You must have seen it in her pantomimes, you spoke of her rare gift for comedy on the stage that rouses a laughter out of the audience so dear they applaud and applaud and do not want to let her go.

---

[1] Works Progress Administration: a federal agency that administered public works to relieve unemployment from 1935 to 1943.

Where does it come from, that comedy? There was none of it in her when she came back to me that second time, after I had had to send her away again. She had a new daddy now to learn to love, and I think perhaps it was a better time.

20   Except when we left her alone nights, telling ourselves she was old enough.

"Can't you go some other time, Mommy, like tomorrow?" she would ask. "Will it be just a little while you'll be gone? Do you promise?"

The time we came back, the front door open, the clock on the floor in the hall. She rigid awake. "It wasn't just a little while. I didn't cry. Three times I called you, just three times, and then I ran downstairs to open the door so you could come faster. The clock talked loud. I threw it away, it scared me what it talked."

She said the clock talked loud again that night I went to the hospital to have Susan. She was delirious with the fever that comes before red measles, but she was fully conscious all the week I was gone and the week after we were home when she could not come near the new baby or me.

She did not get well. She stayed skeleton thin, not wanting to eat, and night after night she had nightmares. She would call for me, and I would rouse from exhaustion to sleepily call back: "You're all right, darling, go to sleep, it's just a dream," and if she still called, in a sterner voice, "now go to sleep, Emily, there's nothing to hurt you." Twice, only twice, when I had to get up for Susan anyhow, I went in to sit with her.

25   Now when it is too late (as if she would let me hold and comfort her like I do the others) I get up and go to her at once at her moan or restless stirring. "Are you awake, Emily? Can I get you something?" And the answer is always the same: "No, I'm all right, go back to sleep, Mother."

They persuaded me at the clinic to send her away to a convalescent home in the country where "she can have the kind of food and care you can't manage for her, and you'll be free to concentrate on the new baby." They still send children to that place. I see pictures on the society page of sleek young women planning affairs to raise money for it, or dancing at the affairs, or decorating Easter eggs or filling Christmas stockings for the children.

They never have a picture of the children so I do not know if the girls still wear those gigantic red bows and the ravaged looks on the every other Sunday when parents can come to visit "unless otherwise notified"—as we were notified the first six weeks.

Oh it is a handsome place, green lawns and tall trees and fluted flower beds. High up on the balconies of each cottage the children stand, the girls in their red bows and white dresses, the boys in white suits and giant red ties. The parents stand below shrieking up to be heard and the children shriek down to be heard, and between them the invisible wall "Not to Be Contaminated by Parental Germs or Physical Affection."

There was a tiny girl who always stood hand in hand with Emily. Her parents never came. One visit she was gone. "They moved her to Rose Cottage," Emily shouted in explanation. "They don't like you to love anybody here."

30   She wrote once a week, the labored writing of a seven-year-old. "I am fine. How is the baby. If I write my leter nicly I will have a star. Love" There never was a star. We wrote every other day, letters she could never hold or keep but only hear read—once. "We simply do not have room for children to keep any personal possessions," they patiently explained when we pieced one Sunday's shrieking together to plead how much it would mean to Emily, who loved so to keep things, to be allowed to keep her letters and cards.

Each visit she looked frailer. "She isn't eating," they told us.

(They had runny eggs for breakfast or mush with lumps, Emily said later, I'd hold it in my mouth and not swallow. Nothing ever tasted good, just when they had chicken.)

It took us eight months to get her released home, and only the fact that she gained back so little of her seven lost pounds convinced the social worker.

I used to try to hold and love her after she came back, but her body would stay stiff, and after a while she'd push away. She ate little. Food sickened her, and I think much of life too. Oh she had physical lightness and brightness, twinkling by on skates, bouncing like a ball up and down up and down over the jump rope, skimming over the hill; but these were momentary.

35   She fretted about her appearance, thin and dark and foreign-looking at a time when every little girl was supposed to look or thought she should look a chubby blonde replica of Shirley Temple. The doorbell sometimes rang for her, but no one seemed to come and play in the house or be a best friend. Maybe because we moved so much.

There was a boy she loved painfully through two school semesters. Months later she told me how she had taken pennies from my purse to buy him candy. "Licorice was his favorite and I brought him some every day, but he still liked Jennifer better'n me. Why, Mommy?" The kind of question for which there is no answer.

School was a worry to her. She was not glib or quick in a world where glibness and quickness were easily confused with ability to learn. To her overworked and exasperated teachers she was an overconscientious "slow learner" who kept trying to catch up and was absent entirely too often.

I let her be absent, though sometimes the illness was imaginary. How different from my now-strictness about attendance with the others. I wasn't working. We had a new baby, I was home anyhow. Sometimes, after Susan grew old enough, I would keep her home from school, too, to have them all together.

Mostly Emily had asthma, and her breathing, harsh and labored, would fill the house with a curiously tranquil sound. I would bring the two old dresser mirrors and her boxes of collections to her bed. She would select beads and single earrings, bottle tops and shells, dried flowers and pebbles, old postcards and scraps, all sorts of oddments; then she and Susan would play Kingdom, setting up landscapes and furniture, peopling them with action.

40   Those were the only times of peaceful companionship between her and Susan. I have edged away from it, that poisonous feeling between them, that terrible balancing of hurts and needs I had to do between the two, and did so badly, those earlier years.

Oh there are conflicts between the others too, each one human, needing, demanding, hurting, taking—but only between Emily and Susan, no, Emily toward Susan that corroding resentment. It seems so obvious on the surface, yet it is not obvious. Susan, the second child, Susan, golden- and curly-haired and chubby, quick and articulate and assured, everything in appearance and manner Emily was not; Susan, not able to resist Emily's precious things, losing or sometimes clumsily breaking them; Susan telling jokes and riddles to company for applause while Emily sat silent (to say to me later: that was *my* riddle, Mother, I told it to Susan); Susan, who for all the five years' difference in age was just a year behind Emily in developing physically.

I am glad for that slow physical development that widened the difference between her and her contemporaries, though she suffered over it. She was too vulnerable for that terrible world of youthful competition, of preening and parading, of constant measuring of yourself against every other, of envy, "If I had that copper hair," "If I had that skin. . . ." She tormented herself enough about not looking like the others, there was enough of the unsureness, the having to be conscious of words before you speak, the constant caring—what are they thinking of me? without having it all magnified by the merciless physical drives.

Ronnie is calling. He is wet and I change him. It is rare there is such a cry now. That time of motherhood is almost behind me when the ear is not one's own but must always be racked and listening for the child cry, the child call. We sit for a while and I hold him, looking out over the city spread in charcoal with its soft aisles of light. *"Shoogily,"* he breathes and curls closer. I carry him back to bed, asleep. *Shoogily*. A funny word, a family word, inherited from Emily, invented by her to say: *comfort*.

In this and other ways she leaves her seal, I say aloud. And startle at my saying it. What do I mean? What did I start to gather together, to try and make coherent? I was at the terrible, growing years. War years. I do not remember them well. I was working, there were four smaller ones now, there was not time for her. She had to help be a mother, and housekeeper, and shopper. She had to set her seal. Mornings of crisis and near hysteria trying to get lunches packed, hair combed, coats and shoes found, everyone to school or Child Care on time, the baby ready for transportation. And always the paper scribbled on by a smaller one, the book looked at by Susan then mislaid, the homework not done. Running out to that huge school where she was one, she was lost, she was a drop; suffering over the unpreparedness, stammering and unsure in her classes.

45 There was so little time left at night after the kids were bedded down. She would struggle over books, always eating (it was in those years she developed her enormous appetite that is legendary in our family) and I would be ironing, or preparing food for the next day, or writing V-mail to Bill, or tending the baby. Sometimes, to make me laugh, or out of her despair, she would imitate happenings or types at school.

I think I said once: "Why don't you do something like this in the school amateur show?" One morning she phoned me at work, hardly understandable through the weeping: "Mother, I did it. I won, I won; they gave me first prize; they clapped and clapped and wouldn't let me go."

Now suddenly she was Somebody, and as imprisoned in her difference as she had been in anonymity.

She began to be asked to perform at other high schools, even in colleges, then at city and statewide affairs. The first one we went to, I only recognized her that first moment when thin, shy, she almost drowned herself into the curtains. Then: Was this Emily? The control, the command, the convulsing and deadly clowning, the spell, then the roaring, stamping audience, unwilling to let this rare and precious laughter out of their lives.

Afterwards: You ought to do something about her with a gift like that—but without money or knowing how, what does one do? We have left it all to her, and the gift has as often eddied inside, clogged and clotted, as been used and growing.

50 She is coming. She runs up the stairs two at a time with her light graceful step, and I know she is happy tonight. Whatever it was that occasioned your call did not happen today.

"Aren't you ever going to finish the ironing, Mother? Whistler[2] painted his mother in a rocker. I'd have to paint mine standing over an ironing board." This is one of her communicative nights and she tells me everything and nothing as she fixes herself a plate of food out of the icebox.

She is so lovely. Why did you want me to come in at all? Why were you concerned? She will find her way.

She starts up the stairs to bed. "Don't get me up with the rest in the morning." "But I thought you were having midterms." "Oh, those," she comes back in, kisses me, and says quite lightly, "in a couple of years when we'll all be atom-dead they won't matter a bit."

She has said it before. She *believes* it. But because I have been dredging the past, and all that compounds a human being is so heavy and meaningful in me, I cannot endure it tonight.

55 I will never total it all. I will never come in to say: She was a child seldom smiled at. Her father left me before she was a year old. I had to work her first six years when there was

---

[2] James (Abbott) McNeill Whistler (1834–1903), United States painter and etcher.

work, or I sent her home and to his relatives. There were years she had care she hated. She was dark and thin and foreign-looking in a world where the prestige went to blondeness and curly hair and dimples, she was slow where glibness was prized. She was a child of anxious, not proud, love. We were poor and could not afford for her the soil of easy growth. I was a young mother, I was a distracted mother. There were other children pushing up, demanding. Her younger sister seemed all that she was not. There were years she did not want me to touch her. She kept too much in herself, her life was such she had to keep too much in herself. My wisdom came too late. She has much to her and probably little will come of it. She is a child of her age, of depression, of war, of fear.

Let her be. So all that is in her will not bloom—but in how many does it? There is still enough left to live by. Only help her to know—help make it so there is cause for her to know—that she is more than this dress on the ironing board, helpless before the iron.

■ EXPLORATIONS OF THE TEXT

1. How does the mother view her daughter Emily as a baby?
2. How do economic and social circumstances affect the mother's ability to take care of Emily?
3. Characterize Emily as a baby and at different stages in her life. According to the narrator, what needs, yearnings, and conflicts shape the daughter's view of herself?
4. Analyze the images describing Emily's body. How do societal conceptions of beauty figure in Emily's development?
5. What are reasons for the conflict between Emily and Susan?
6. How does the mother feel about herself as a parent? Is she a "good mother"? Is she to blame for what has happened to Emily?
7. Explore the significance of the title and the symbol of ironing. Discuss Tillie Olsen's critique of woman's position in society.
8. How does the opening, the interchange between the unnamed social worker and the mother, develop the story?
9. What vision of parenting is presented in the story? How much control do parents possess? How much depends on fate or circumstance?

■ THE READING/WRITING CONNECTION

1. "Think" Topic: What effect does the first-person point of view have on the story? Rewrite several passages in third person. How does the perspective change?
2. Write a monologue in the voice of Emily, and present her version of her upbringing. Or write a letter from Emily to her mother.

■ IDEAS FOR WRITING

1. Compare this story with "Scar" and/or "Burn Your Maps."
2. Some psychologists suggest that "wounds" in childhood may later become sources of creativity. Is there support for this theory in the story?
3. Continue the story. What is going to happen to Emily?

JUNOT DÍAZ

Junot Díaz (1968–) was born in Santo Domingo, Dominican Republic, and educated at Rutgers and Cornell universities. He has published his fiction in many magazines, including The New Yorker, Story, *and* Paris Review. *His first collection of stories,* Drown, *was published in 1996. He is a professor in the Program of Writing and Humanistic Studies at Massachusetts Institute of Technology and is a fellow at Radcliffe Institute for Advanced Study at Harvard University.*

1996

FIESTA 1980

Mami's youngest sister—my tía[1] Yrma—finally made it to the United States that year. She and tío[2] Miguel got themselves an apartment in the Bronx, off the Grand Concourse and everybody decided that we should have a party. Actually, my pops decided, but everybody—meaning Mami, tía Yrma, tío Miguel and their neighbors—thought it a dope idea. On the afternoon of the party Papi came back from work around six. Right on time. We were all dressed by then, which was a smart move on our part. If Papi had walked in and caught us lounging around in our underwear, he would have kicked our asses something serious.

He didn't say nothing to nobody, not even my moms. He just pushed past her, held up his hand when she tried to talk to him and headed right into the shower. Rafa gave me the look and I gave it back to him; we both knew Papi had been with that Puerto Rican woman he was seeing and wanted to wash off the evidence quick.

Mami looked really nice that day. The United States had finally put some meat on her; she was no longer the same flaca[3] who had arrived here three years before. She had cut her hair short and was wearing tons of cheap-ass jewelry which on her didn't look too lousy. She smelled like herself, like the wind through a tree. She always waited until the last possible minute to put on her perfume because she said it was a waste to spray it on early and then have to spray it on again once you got to the party.

We—meaning me, my brother, my little sister and Mami—waited for Papi to finish his shower. Mami seemed anxious, in her usual dispassionate way. Her hands adjusted the buckle of her belt over and over again. That morning, when she had gotten us up for school, Mami told us that she wanted to have a good time at the party. I want to dance, she said, but now, with the sun sliding out of the sky like spit off a wall, she seemed ready just to get this over with.

5   Rafa didn't much want to go to no party either, and me, I never wanted to go anywhere with my family. There was a baseball game in the parking lot outside and we could hear our friends, yelling, Hey, and, Cabrón, to one another. We heard the pop of a ball as it sailed over the cars, the clatter of an aluminum bat dropping to the concrete. Not that me or Rafa loved baseball; we just liked playing with the local kids, thrashing them at anything they were doing. By the sounds of the shouting, we both knew the game was close, either of us could have made a difference. Rafa frowned and when I frowned back, he put up his fist. Don't you mirror me, he said.

Don't you mirror me, I said.

He punched me—I would have hit him back but Papi marched into the living room with his towel around his waist, looking a lot smaller than he did when he was dressed. He had a few strands of hair around his nipples and a surly closed-mouth expression, like maybe he'd scalded his tongue or something.

Have you eaten? he asked Mami.

She nodded. I made you something.

10   You didn't let him eat, did you?

Ay, Dios mío,[4] she said, letting her arms fall to her side.

Ay, Dios mío is right, Papi said.

---

[1] Aunt.

[2] Uncle.

[3] Thin woman.

[4] My God.

I was never supposed to eat before our car trips, but earlier, when she had put out our dinner of rice, beans and sweet platanos, guess who had been the first one to clean his plate? You couldn't blame Mami really, she had been busy—cooking, getting ready, dressing my sister Madai. I should have reminded her not to feed me but I wasn't that sort of son.

Papi turned to me. Coño, muchacho,[5] why did you eat?

15   Rafa had already started inching away from me. I'd once told him I considered him a low-down chickenshit for moving out of the way every time Papi was going to smack me.

Collateral damage, Rafa had said. Ever heard of it?

No.

Look it up.

Chickenshit or not, I didn't dare glance at him. Papi was old-fashioned; he expected your undivided attention when you were getting your ass whupped. You couldn't look him in the eye either—that wasn't allowed. Better to stare at his belly button, which was perfectly round and immaculate. Papi pulled me to my feet by my ear.

20   If you throw up—

I won't, I cried, tears in my eyes, more out of reflex than pain.

Ya, Ramón, ya. It's not his fault, Mami said.

They've known about this party forever. How did they think we were going to get there? Fly?

He finally let go of my ear and I sat back down. Madai was too scared to open her eyes. Being around Papi all her life had turned her into a major-league wuss. Anytime Papi raised his voice her lip would start trembling, like some specialized tuning fork. Rafa pretended that he had knuckles to crack and when I shoved him, he gave me a *Don't start* look. But even that little bit of recognition made me feel better.

25   I was the one who was always in trouble with my dad. It was like my God-given duty to piss him off, to do everything the way he hated. Our fights didn't bother me too much. I well wanted him to love me, something that never seemed strange or contradictory until years later, when he was out of our lives.

By the time my ear stopped stinging Papi was dressed and Mami was crossing each one of us, solemnly, like we were heading off to war. We said, in turn, Bendición,[6] Mami, and she poked us in our five cardinal spots while saying, Que Dios te bendiga.[7]

This was how all our trips began, the words that followed me every time I left the house.

None of us spoke until we were inside Papi's Volkswagen van. Brand-new, lime-green and bought to impress. Oh, we were impressed, but me, every time I was in that VW and Papi went above twenty miles an hour, I vomited. I'd never had trouble with cars before—that van was like my curse. Mami suspected it was the upholstery. In her mind, American things—appliances, mouthwash, funny-looking upholstery—all seemed to have an intrinsic badness about them. Papi was careful about taking me anywhere in the VW, but when he had to, I rode up front in Mami's usual seat so I could throw up out a window.

¿Cómo te sientas?[8] Mami asked over my shoulder when Papi pulled onto the turnpike. She had her hand on the base of my neck. One thing about Mami, her palms never sweated.

30   I'm OK, I said, keeping my eyes straight ahead. I definitely didn't want to trade glances with Papi. He had this one look, furious and sharp, that always left me feeling bruised.

---

[5] Boy.

[6] Benediction.

[7] May God bless you.

[8] How do you feel?

Toma. Mami handed me four mentas.[9] She had thrown three out of her window at the beginning of our trip, an offering to Eshú; the rest were for me.

I took one and sucked it slowly, my tongue knocking it up against my teeth. We passed Newark Airport without any incident. If Madai had been awake she would have cried because the planes flew so close to the cars.

How's he feeling? Papi asked.

Fine, I said. I glanced back at Rafa and he pretended like he didn't see me. That was the way he was, at school and at home. When I was in trouble, he didn't know me. Madai was solidly asleep, but even with her face all wrinkled up and drooling she looked cute, her hair all separated into twists.

35   I turned around and concentrated on the candy. Papi even started to joke that we might not have to scrub the van out tonight. He was beginning to loosen up, not checking his watch too much. Maybe he was thinking about that Puerto Rican woman or maybe he was just happy that we were all together. I could never tell. At the toll, he was feeling positive enough to actually get out of the van and search around under the basket for dropped coins. It was something he had once done to amuse Madai, but now it was habit. Cars behind us honked their horns and I slid down in my seat. Rafa didn't care; he grinned back at the other cars and waved. His actual job was to make sure no cops were coming. Mami shook Madai awake and as soon as she saw Papi stooping for a couple of quarters she let out this screech of delight that almost took off the top of my head.

That was the end of the good times. Just outside the Washington Bridge, I started feeling woozy. The smell of the upholstery got all up inside my head and I found myself with a mouthful of saliva. Mami's hand tensed on my shoulder and when I caught Papi's eye, he was like, No way. Don't do it.

The first time I got sick in the van Papi was taking me to the library. Rafa was with us and he couldn't believe I threw up. I was famous for my steel-lined stomach. A third-world childhood could give you that. Papi was worried enough that just as quick as Rafa could drop off the books we were on our way home. Mami fixed me one of her honey-and-onion concoctions and that made my stomach feel better. A week later we tried the library again and on this go-around I couldn't get the window open in time. When Papi got me home, he went and cleaned out the van himself, an expression of askho on his face. This was a big deal, since Papi almost never cleaned anything himself. He came back inside and found me sitting on the couch feeling like hell.

It's the car, he said to Mami. It's making him sick.

This time the damage was pretty minimal, nothing Papi couldn't wash off the door with a blast of the hose. He was pissed, though; he jammed his finger into my cheek, a nice solid thrust. That was the way he was with his punishments: imaginative. Earlier that year I'd written an essay in school called "My Father the Torturer," but the teacher made me write a new one. She thought I was kidding.

40   We drove the rest of the way to the Bronx in silence. We only stopped once, so I could brush my teeth. Mami had brought along my toothbrush and a tube of toothpaste and while every car known to man sped by us she stood outside with me so I wouldn't feel alone.

Tío Miguel was about seven feet tall and had his hair combed up and out, into a demi-fro. He gave me and Rafa big spleen-crushing hugs and then kissed Mami and finally ended up with Madai on his shoulder. The last time I'd seen Tío was at the airport, his first day in the

---

[9] Candies.

United States. I remembered how he hadn't seemed all that troubled to be in another country.

He looked down at me. Carajo,[10] Yunior, you look horrible!

He threw up, my brother explained.

I pushed Rafa. Thanks a lot, ass-face.

45 Hey, he said. Tío asked.

Tío clapped a bricklayer's hand on my shoulder. Everybody gets sick sometimes, he said. You should have seen me on the plane over here. Dios mío! He rolled his Asian-looking eyes for emphasis. I thought we were all going to die.

Everybody could tell he was lying. I smiled like he was making me feel better.

Do you want me to get you a drink? Tío asked. We got beer and rum.

Miguel, Mami said. He's young.

50 Young? Back in Santo Domingo, he'd be getting laid by now.

Mami thinned her lips, which took some doing.

Well, it's true, Tío said.

So, Mami, I said. When do I get to go visit the D.R.?

That's enough, Yunior.

55 It's the only pussy you'll ever get, Rafa said to me in English.

Not counting your girlfriend, of course.

Rafa smiled. He had to give me that one.

Papi came in from parking the van. He and Miguel gave each other the sort of hand-shakes that would have turned my fingers into Wonder bread.

Coño, compa'i,[11] ¿cómo va todo? they said to each other.

60 Tía came out then, with an apron on and maybe the longest Lee Press-On Nails I've ever seen in my life. There was this one guru motherfucker in the *Guinness Book of World Records* who had longer nails, but I tell you, it was close. She gave everybody kisses, told me and Rafa how guapo we were—Rafa, of course, believed her—told Madai how bella[12] she was, but when she got to Papi, she froze a little, like maybe she'd seen a wasp on the tip of his nose, but then kissed him all the same.

Mami told us to join the other kids in the living room. Tío said, Wait a minute, I want to show you the apartment. I was glad Tía said, Hold on, because from what I'd seen so far, the place had been furnished in Contemporary Dominican Tacky. The less I saw, the better. I mean, I liked plastic sofa covers but damn, Tío and Tía had taken it to another level. They had a disco ball hanging in the living room and the type of stucco ceilings that looked like stalactite heaven. The sofas all had golden tassels dangling from their edges. Tía came out of the kitchen with some people I didn't know and by the time she got done introducing every-body, only Papi and Mami were given the guided tour of the four-room third-floor apart-ment. Me and Rafa joined the kids in the living room. They'd already started eating. We were hungry, one of the girls explained, a pastelito in hand. The boy was about three years younger than me but the girl who'd spoken, Leti, was my age. She and another girl were on the sofa together and they were cute as hell.

Leti introduced them: the boy was her brother Wilquins and the other girl was her neighbor Mari. Leti had some serious tetas and I could tell that my brother was going to gun for her. His taste in girls was predictable. He sat down right between Leti and Mari and by the way they were smiling at him I knew he'd do fine. Neither of the girls gave me more

---

[10] Darn.

[11] Darn, compadre. How are you all? How's everything?

[12] *Guapo*—handsome; *bella*—beautiful.

than a cursory one-two, which didn't bother me. Sure, I liked girls but I was always too terrified to speak to them unless we were arguing or I was calling them stupidos, which was one of my favorite words that year. I turned to Wilquins and asked him what there was to do around here. Mari, who had the lowest voice I'd ever heard, said, He can't speak.

What does that mean?

He's mute.

I looked at Wilquins incredulously. He smiled and nodded, as if he'd won a prize or something.

Does he understand? I asked.

Of course he understands, Rafa said. He's not dumb.

I could tell Rafa had said that just to score point with the girls. Both of them nodded. Low-voice Mari said, He's the best student in his grade.

I thought, Not bad for a mute. I sat next to Wilquins. After about two seconds of TV Wilquins whipped out a bag of dominos and motioned to me. Did I want to play? Sure. Me and him played Rafa and Leti and we whupped their collective asses twice, which put Rafa in a real bad mood. He looked at me like maybe he wanted to take a swing, just one to make him feel better. Leti kept whispering into Rafa's ear, telling him it was OK.

70   In the kitchen I could hear my parents slipping into their usual modes. Papi's voice was loud and argumentative; you didn't have to be anywhere near him to catch his drift. And Mami, you had to put cups to your ears to hear hers. I went into the kitchen a few times— once so the tíos could show off how much bullshit I'd been able to cram in my head the last few years; another time for a bucket-sized cup of soda. Mami and Tía were frying tostones and the last of the pastelitos. She appeared happier now and the way her hands worked on our dinner you would think she had a life somewhere else making rare and precious things. She nudged Tía every now and then, shit they must have been doing all their lives. As soon as Mami saw me though, she gave me the eye. Don't stay long, that eye said. Don't piss your old man off.

Papi was too busy arguing about Elvis to notice me. Then somebody mentioned María Montez and Papi barked, María Montez? Let me tell *you* about María Montez, compa'i.[13]

Maybe I was used to him. His voice—louder than most adults'—didn't bother me none, though the other kids shifted uneasily in their seats. Wilquins was about to raise the volume on the TV, but Rafa said, I wouldn't do that. Muteboy had balls, though. He did it anyway and then sat down. Wilquins's pop came into the living room a second later, a bottle of Presidente in hand. That dude must have had Spider-senses or something. Did you raise that? he asked Wilquins and Wilquins nodded.

Is this your house? his pops asked. He looked ready to beat Wilquins silly but he lowered the volume instead.

See, Rafa said. You nearly got your ass *kicked*.

75 I met the Puerto Rican woman right after Papi had gotten the van. He was taking me on short trips, trying to cure me of my vomiting. It wasn't really working but I looked foward to our trips, even though at the end of each one I'd be sick. These were the only times me and Papi did anything together. When we were alone he treated me much better, like maybe I was his son or something.

Before each drive Mami would cross me.

Bendición, Mami, I'd say.

---

[13] A Hispanic actress.

She'd kiss my forehead. Que Dios te bendiga. And then she would give me a handful of mentas because she wanted me to be OK. Mami didn't think these excursions would cure anything, but the one time she had brought it up to Papi he had told her to shut up, what did she know about anything anyway?

Me and Papi didn't talk much. We just drove around our neighborhood. Occasionally he'd ask, How is it?

80   And I'd nod, no matter how I felt.

One day I was sick outside of Perth Amboy. Instead of taking me home he went the other way on Industrial Avenue, stopping a few minutes later in front of a light blue house I didn't recognize. It reminded me of the Easter eggs we colored at school, the ones we threw out the bus windows at other cars.

The Puerto Rican woman was there and she helped me clean up. She had dry papery hands and when she rubbed the towel on my chest, she did it hard, like I was a bumper she was waxing. She was very thin and had a cloud of brown hair rising above her narrow face and the sharpest blackest eyes you've ever seen.

He's cute, she said to Papi.

Not when he's throwing up, Papi said.

85   What's your name? she asked me. Are you Rafa?

I shook my head.

Then it's Yunior, right?

I nodded.

You're the smart one, she said, suddenly happy with herself. Maybe you want to see my books?

90   They weren't hers. I recognized them as ones my father must have left in her house. Papi was a voracious reader, couldn't even go cheating without a paperback in his pocket.

Why don't you go watch TV? Papi suggested. He was looking at her like she was the last piece of chicken on earth.

We got plenty of channels, she said. Use the remote if you want.

The two of them went upstairs and I was too scared of what was happening to poke around. I just sat there, ashamed, expecting something big and fiery to crash down on our heads. I watched a whole hour of the news before Papi came downstairs and said, Let's go.

About two hours later the women laid out the food and like always nobody but the kids thanked them. It must be some Dominican tradition or something. There was everything I liked—chicharrones,[14] fried chicken, tostones,[15] sancocho,[16] rice, fried cheese, yuca, avocado, potato salad, a meteor-sized hunk of pernil,[17] even a tossed salad which I could do without—but when I joined the other kids around the serving table, Papi said, Oh no you don't, and took the paper plate out of my hand. His fingers weren't gentle.

95   What's wrong now? Tía asked, handing me another plate.

He ain't eating, Papi said. Mami pretended to help Rafa with the pernil.

Why can't he eat?

Because I said so.

I nodded.

---

[14] Pork fritters.

[15] Thick, fried plantains.

[16] Soup, beef broth with potato, corn, yuca.

[17] Pork leg.

100   And if your brother gives you any food, I'll beat him too. Right here in front of everybody. ¿Entiendes?[18]

      I nodded again. I wanted to kill him and he must have sensed it because he gave my
head a little shove.

      All the kids watched me come in and sit down in front of the TV.

      What's wrong with your dad? Leti asked.

      He's a dick, I said.

105   Rafa shook his head. Don't say that shit in front of people.

      Easy for you to be nice when you're eating, I said.

      Hey, if I was a pukey little baby, I wouldn't get no food either.

      I almost said something back but I concentrated on the TV. I wasn't going to start it. No
fucking way. So I watched Bruce Lee beat Chuck Norris into the floor of the Colosseum and
tried to pretend that there was no food anywhere in the house. It was Tía who finally saved
me. She came into the living room and said, Since you ain't eating, Yunior, you can at least
help me get some ice.

      I didn't want to, but she mistook my reluctance for something else.

110   I already asked your father.

      She held my hand while we walked; Tía didn't have any kids but I could tell she wanted
them. She was the sort of relative who always remembered your birthday but who you only
went to visit because you had to. We didn't get past the first-floor landing before she opened
her pocketbook and handed me the first of three pastelitos[19] she had smuggled out of the
apartment.

      Go ahead, she said. And as soon as you get inside make sure you brush your teeth.

      Thanks a lot, Tía, I said.

      Those pastelitos didn't stand a chance.

115   She sat next to me on the stair and smoked her cigarette. All the way down on the first
floor and we could still hear the music and the adults and the television. Tía looked a ton
like Mami; the two of them were both short and light-skinned. Tía smiled a lot and that was
what set them apart the most.

      How is it at home, Yunior?

      What do you mean?

      How's it going in the apartment? Are you kids OK?

      I knew an interrogation when I heard one, no matter how sugar-coated it was. I didn't
say anything. Don't get me wrong, I loved my tía, but something told me to keep my mouth
shut. Maybe it was family loyalty, maybe I just wanted to protect Mami or I was afraid that
Papi would find out—it could have been anything really.

120   Is your mom all right?

      I shrugged.

      Have there been lots of fights?

      None, I said. Too many shrugs would have been just as bad as an answer. Papi's at work
too much.

      Work, Tía said, like it was somebody's name she didn't like.

125 Me and Rafa we didn't talk much about the Puerto Rican woman. When we ate dinner at
her house, the few times Papi had taken us over there, we still acted like nothing was out of
the ordinary. Pass the ketchup, man. No sweat, bro. The affair was like a hole in our living

---

[18] Understand?

[19] Round, small empanadas or meatpies.

room floor, one we'd gotten so used to circumnavigating that we sometimes forgot it was there.

By midnight all the adults were crazy dancing. I was sitting outside Tía's bedroom—where Madai was sleeping—trying not to attract attention. Rafa had me guarding the door; he and Leti were in there too, with some of the other kids, getting busy no doubt. Wilquins had gone across the hall to bed so I had me and the roaches to mess around with.

When I peered into the main room I saw about twenty moms and dads dancing and drinking beers. Every now and then somebody yelled, Quisqueya! And then everybody else would yell and stomp their feet. From what I could see my parents seemed to be enjoying themselves.

Mami and Tía spent a lot of time side by side, whispering, and I kept expecting something to come of this, a brawl maybe. I'd never once been out with my family when it hadn't turned to shit. We weren't even theatrical or straight crazy like other families. We fought like sixth-graders, without any real dignity. I guess the whole night I'd been waiting for a blowup, something between Papi and Mami. This was how I always figured Papi would be exposed, out in public, where everybody would know.

You're a cheater!

130   But everything was calmer than usual. And Mami didn't look like she was about to say anything to Papi. The two of them danced every now and then but they never lasted more than a song before Mami joined Tía again in whatever conversation they were having.

I tried to imagine Mami before Papi. Maybe I was tired, or just sad, thinking about the way my family was. Maybe I already knew how it would all end up in a few years, Mami without Papi, and that was why I did it. Picturing her alone wasn't easy. It seemed like Papi had always been with her, even when we were waiting in Santo Domingo for him to send for us.

The only photograph our family had of Mami as a young woman, before she married Papi, was the one that somebody took of her at an election party that I found one day while rummaging for money to go to the arcade. Mami had it tucked into her immigration papers. In the photo, she's surrounded by laughing cousins I will never meet, who are all shiny from dancing, whose clothes are rumpled and loose. You can tell it's night and hot and that the mosquitos have been biting. She sits straight and even in a crowd she stands out, smiling quietly like maybe she's the one everybody's celebrating. You can't see her hands but I imagined they're knotting a straw or a bit of thread. This was the woman my father met a year later on the Malecón,[20] the woman Mami thought she'd always be.

Mami must have caught me studying her because she stopped what she was doing and gave me a smile, maybe her first one of the night. Suddenly I wanted to go over and hug her, for no other reason than I loved her, but there were about eleven fat jiggling bodies between us. So I sat down on the tiled floor and waited.

I must have fallen asleep because the next thing I knew Rafa was kicking me and saying, Let's go. He looked like he'd been hitting those girls off; he was all smiles. I got to my feet in time to kiss Tía and Tío good-bye. Mami was holding the serving dish she had brought with her.

135   Where's Papi? I asked.

He's downstairs, bringing the van around. Mami leaned down to kiss me.

You were good today, she said.

---

[20] Embankment (literally): Walk by the ocean.

And then Papi burst in and told us to get the hell downstairs before some pendejo[21] cop gave him a ticket. More kisses, more handshakes and then we were gone.

I don't remember being out of sorts after I met the Puerto Rican woman, but I must have been because Mami only asked me questions when she thought something was wrong in my life. It took her about ten passes but finally she cornered me one afternoon when we were alone in the apartment. Our upstairs neighbors were beating the crap out of their kids, and me and her had been listening to it all afternoon. She put her hand on mine and said, Is everything OK, Yunior? Have you been fighting with your brother?

140   Me and Rafa had already talked. We'd been in the basement, where our parents couldn't hear us. He told me that yeah, he knew about her.

Papi's taken me there twice now, he said.

Why didn't you tell me? I asked.

What the hell was I going to say? *Hey, Yunior, guess what happened yesterday? I met Papi's sucia!*[22]

I didn't say anything to Mami either. She watched me, very very closely. Later I would think, maybe if I had told her, she would have confronted him, would have done something, but who can know these things? I said I'd been having trouble in school and like that everything was back to normal between us. She put her hand on my shoulder and squeezed and that was that.

145 We were on the turnpike, just past Exit 11, when I started feeling it again. I sat up from leaning against Rafa. His fingers smelled and he'd gone to sleep almost as soon as he got into the van. Madai was out too but at least she wasn't snoring.

In the darkness, I saw that Papi had a hand on Mami's knee and that the two of them were quiet and still. They weren't slumped back or anything; they were both wide awake, bolted into their seats. I couldn't see either of their faces and no matter how hard I tried I could not imagine their expressions. Neither of them moved. Every now and then the van was filled with the bright rush of somebody else's headlights. Finally I said, Mami, and they both looked back, already knowing what was happening.

■ EXPLORATIONS OF THE TEXT

1. Analyze the point of view and tone of the narrator. Discuss the narrator's role in his family. Discuss his relationship with his siblings. Why does his father single him out for punishment?
2. What main impression do you gain of Papi's and Mami's characters? What distinguishes their relationship? What are the reasons for the breakdown of their marriage?
3. Why does the story center on the fiesta? What is the significance of the last encounter between Mami and Papi?
4. Why does the narrator vomit in the car? Explore the symbolism of this action.
5. What is the impact of the inclusion of Spanish words and colloquial language?
6. Compare the father-son relationship in this story with the one in "This Is What It Means to Say Phoenix, Arizona."

■ THE READING/WRITING CONNECTION

1. Journal Entry: "What is unspoken in family life wields great power." Relate this quotation to your own life experiences.

---

[21] Idiot.
[22] Lover.

2. Gloss and annotate the text; note images of words versus silence. Then freewrite about the work and concentrate on this theme.

■ IDEAS FOR WRITING
1. Write a character analysis of the narrator or of Papi.
2. Compare Mami to Elena, the speaker in Pat Mora's poem.
3. Write an essay on themes of estrangement and loss in this story.

JAMES BALDWIN

James Baldwin (1924–87) was born and raised in Harlem, a district on New York's Manhattan Island. He grew up in a large family, and his stepfather was an evangelical preacher. An excellent student, Baldwin wrote from an early age. Although several well-known publications accepted his essays and short stories and although Richard Wright helped him win a fellowship, it was not until he moved to Europe in 1948 that Baldwin's creative powers came to fruition. His first novel, Go Tell It on the Mountain *(1953), is about a Harlem teenager's conflicts with a repressive father; his first play,* The Amen Corner *(1955), which deals with the pentecostal faith, represents Baldwin's search for his racial heritage. These were followed by* Notes of a Native Son *(1955), the 1956 novel* Giovanni's Room, Nobody Knows My Name: More Notes of a Native Son *(1961), and* The Fire Next Time *(1963).*

1957

SONNY'S BLUES

I read about it in the paper, in the subway, on my way to work. I read it, and I couldn't believe it, and I read it again. Then perhaps I just stared at it, at the newsprint spelling out his name, spelling out the story. I stared at it in the swinging lights of the subway car, and in the faces and bodies of the people, and in my own face, trapped in the darkness which roared outside.

It was not to be believed and I kept telling myself that, as I walked from the subway station to the high school. And at the same time I couldn't doubt it. I was scared, scared for Sonny. He became real to me again. A great block of ice got settled in my belly and kept melting there slowly all day long, while I taught my classes algebra. It was a special kind of ice. It kept melting, sending trickles of ice water all up and down my veins, but it never got less. Sometimes it hardened and seemed to expand until I felt my guts were going to come spilling out or that I was going to choke or scream. This would always be at a moment when I was remembering some specific thing Sonny had once said or done.

When he was about as old as the boys in my classes his face had been bright and open, there was a lot of copper in it; and he'd had wonderfully direct brown eyes, and great gentleness and privacy. I wondered what he looked like now. He had been picked up, the evening before, in a raid on an apartment downtown, for peddling and using heroin.

I couldn't believe it: but what I mean by that is that I couldn't find any room for it anywhere inside me. I had kept it outside me for a long time. I hadn't wanted to know. I had had suspicions, but I didn't name them, I kept putting them away. I told myself that Sonny was wild, but he wasn't crazy. And he'd always been a good boy, he hadn't ever turned hard or evil or disrespectful, the way kids can, so quick, so quick, especially in Harlem. I didn't want to believe that I'd ever see my brother going down, coming to nothing, all that light in his face gone out, in the condition I'd already seen so many others. Yet it had happened and here I was, talking about algebra to a lot of boys who might, every one of them for all I knew, be popping off needles every time they went to the head. Maybe it did more for them than algebra could.

5   I was sure that the first time Sonny had ever had horse, he couldn't have been much older than these boys were now. These boys, now, were living as we'd been living then, they were growing up with a rush and their heads bumped abruptly against the low ceiling of their actual possibilities. They were filled with rage. All they really knew were two darknesses, the darkness of their lives, which was now closing in on them, and the darkness of the movies, which had blinded them to that other darkness, and in which they now, vindictively, dreamed, at once more together than they were at any other time, and more alone.

When the last bell rang, the last class ended, I let out my breath. It seemed I'd been holding it for all that time. My clothes were wet—I may have looked as though I'd been sitting in a steam bath, all dressed up, all afternoon. I sat alone in the classroom a long time. I listened to the boys outside, downstairs, shouting and cursing and laughing. Their laughter struck me for perhaps the first time. It was not the joyous laughter which—God knows why—one associates with children. It was mocking and insular, its intent was to denigrate. It was disenchanted, and in this, also, lay the authority of their curses. Perhaps I was listening to them because I was thinking about my brother and in them I heard my brother. And myself.

One boy was whistling a tune, at once very complicated and very simple, it seemed to be pouring out of him as though he were a bird, and it sounded very cool and moving through all that harsh, bright air, only just holding its own through all those other sounds.

I stood up and walked over to the window and looked down into the courtyard. It was the beginning of the spring and the sap was rising in the boys. A teacher passed through them every now and again, quickly, as though he or she couldn't wait to get out of that courtyard, to get those boys out of their sight and off their minds. I started collecting my stuff. I thought I'd better get home and talk to Isabel.

The courtyard was almost deserted by the time I got downstairs. I saw this boy standing in the shadow of a doorway, looking just like Sonny. I almost called his name. Then I saw that it wasn't Sonny, but somebody we used to know, a boy from around our block. He'd been Sonny's friend. He'd never been mine, having been too young for me, and, anyway, I'd never liked him. And now, even though he was a grown-up man, he still hung around that block, still spent hours on the street corners, was always high and raggy. I used to run into him from time to time and he'd often work around to asking me for a quarter or fifty cents. He always had some real good excuse, too, and I always gave it to him, I don't know why.

10   But now, abruptly, I hated him. I couldn't stand the way he looked at me, partly like a dog, partly like a cunning child. I wanted to ask him what the hell he was doing in the school courtyard.

He sort of shuffled over to me, and he said, "I see you got the papers. So you already know about it."

"You mean about Sonny? Yes, I already know about it. How come they didn't get you?"

He grinned. It made him repulsive and it also brought to mind what he'd looked like as a kid. "I wasn't there. I stay away from them people."

"Good for you." I offered him a cigarette and I watched him through the smoke. "You come all the way down here just to tell me about Sonny?"

15   "That's right." He was sort of shaking his head and his eyes looked strange, as though they were about to cross. The bright sun deadened his damp dark brown skin and it made his eyes look yellow and showed up the dirt in his kinked hair. He smelled funky. I moved a little away from him and I said, "Well, thanks. But I already know about it and I got to get home."

"I'll walk you a little ways," he said. We started walking. There were a couple of kids still loitering in the courtyard and one of them said goodnight to me and looked strangely at the boy beside me.

"What're you going to do?" he asked me. "I mean, about Sonny?"

"Look. I haven't seen Sonny for over a year, I'm not sure I'm going to do anything. Anyway, what the hell *can* I do?"

"That's right," he said quickly, "ain't nothing you can do. Can't much help old Sonny no more, I guess."

20   It was what I was thinking and so it seemed to me he had no right to say it.

"I'm surprised at Sonny, though," he went on—he had a funny way of talking, he looked straight ahead as though he were talking to himself—"I thought Sonny was a smart boy, I thought he was too smart to get hung."

"I guess he thought so too," I said sharply, "and that's how he got hung. And now about you? You're pretty goddamn smart, I bet."

Then he looked directly at me, just for a minute. "I ain't smart," he said. "If I was smart, I'd have reached for a pistol a long time ago."

"Look. Don't tell *me* your sad story, if it was up to me, I'd give you one." Then I felt guilty—guilty, probably, for never having supposed that the poor bastard *had* a story of his own, much less a sad one, and I asked, quickly, "What's going to happen to him now?"

25   He didn't answer this. He was off by himself some place. "Funny thing," he said, and from his tone we might have been discussing the quickest way to get to Brooklyn, "when I saw the papers this morning, the first thing I asked myself was if I had anything to do with it. I felt sort of responsible."

I began to listen more carefully. The subway station was on the corner, just before us, and I stopped. He stopped, too. We were in front of a bar and he ducked slightly, peering in, but whoever he was looking for didn't seem to be there. The juke box was blasting away with something black and bouncy and I half watched the barmaid as she danced her way from the juke box to her place behind the bar. And I watched her face as she laughingly responded to something someone said to her, still keeping time to the music. When she smiled one saw the little girl, one sensed the doomed, still-struggling woman beneath the battered face of the semi-whore.

"I never give Sonny nothing," the boy said finally, "but a long time ago I come to school high and Sonny asked me how it felt." He paused, I couldn't bear to watch him, I watched the barmaid, and I listened to the music which seemed to be causing the pavement to shake. "I told him it felt great." The music stopped, the barmaid paused and watched the juke box until the music began again. "It did."

All this way carrying me some place I didn't want to go. I certainly didn't want to know how it felt. It filled everything, the people, the houses, the music, the dark, quick-silver barmaid, with menace: and this menace was their reality.

"What's going to happen to him now?" I asked again.

30   "They'll send him away some place and they'll try to cure him." He shook his head. "Maybe he'll even think he's kicked the habit. Then they'll let him loose"—he gestured, throwing his cigarette into the gutter. "That's all."

"What do you mean, that's *all*?"

But I knew what he meant.

"I mean, that's *all*." He turned his head and looked at me, pulling down the corners of his mouth. "Don't you know what I mean?" he asked, softly.

"How the hell would I know what you mean?" I almost whispered it. I don't know why.

35   "That's right," he said to the air, "how would he know what I mean?" He turned toward me again, patient and calm, and yet I somehow felt him shaking, shaking as though he were

going to fall apart. I felt that ice in my guts again, the dread I'd felt all afternoon; and again I watched the barmaid, moving about the bar, washing glasses, and singing. "Listen. They'll let him out and then it'll just start all over again. That's what I mean."

"You mean—they'll let him out. And then he'll just start working his way back in again. You mean he'll never kick the habit. Is that what you mean?"

"That's right," he said, cheerfully. "You see what I mean."

"Tell me," I said at last, "why does he want to die? He must want to die, he's killing himself, why does he want to die?"

He looked at me in surprise. He licked his lips. "He don't want to die. He wants to live. Don't nobody want to die, ever."

40   Then I wanted to ask him—too many things. He could not have answered, or if he had, I could not have borne the answers. I started walking. "Well, I guess it's none of my business."

"It's going to be rough on old Sonny," he said. We reached the subway station. "This is your station?" he asked. I nodded. I took one step down. "Damn!" he said, suddenly. I looked up at him. He grinned again. "Damn it if I didn't leave all my money home. You ain't got a dollar on you, have you? Just for a couple of days, is all."

All at once something inside gave and threatened to come pouring out of me. I didn't hate him any more, I felt that in another moment I'd start crying like a child.

"Sure," I said. "Don't swear." I looked in my wallet and didn't have a dollar, I only had a five. "Here," I said. "That hold you?"

He didn't look at it—he didn't want to look at it. A terrible, closed look came over his face, as though he were keeping the number on the bill a secret from him and me. "Thanks," he said, and now he was dying to see me go. "Don't worry about Sonny. Maybe I'll write him or something."

45   "Sure," I said. "You do that. So long."

"Be seeing you," he said. I went down the steps.

And I didn't write Sonny or send him anything for a long time. When I finally did, it was just after my little girl died, he wrote me back a letter which made me feel like a bastard.

Here's what he said:

Dear Brother,

You don't know how much I needed to hear from you. I wanted to write you many a time but I dug how much I must have hurt you and so I didn't write. But now I feel like a man who's been trying to climb up out of some deep, real deep and funky hole and just saw the sun up there, outside. I got to get outside.

I can't tell you much about how I got here. I mean I don't know how to tell you. I guess I was afraid of something or I was trying to escape from something and you know I have never been very strong in the head (smile). I'm glad Mama and Daddy are dead and can't see what's happened to their son and I swear if I'd known what I was doing I would never have hurt you so, you and a lot of other fine people who were nice to me and who believed in me.

I don't want you to think it had anything to do with me being a musician. It's more than that. Or maybe less than that. I can't get anything straight in my head down here and I try not to think about what's going to happen to me when I get outside again. Sometime I think I'm going to flip and never get outside and some-time I think I'll come straight back, I tell you one thing, though. I'd rather blow my brains out than go through this again. But that's what they all say, so they tell me. If I tell you when I'm coming to New York and if you could meet me, I sure would appreciate it. Give my love to Isabel and the kids and I was sure sorry to hear about little Gracie. I wish I could be like Mama and say the Lord's will be done, but I don't know it seems to me that trouble is the one thing that never does get stopped and I don't know what good it does to blame it on the Lord. But maybe it does some good if you believe it.

Your brother,
Sonny

Then I kept in constant touch with him and I sent him whatever I could and I went to meet him when he came back to New York. When I saw him many things I thought I had forgotten came flooding back to me. This was because I had begun, finally, to wonder about Sonny, about the life that Sonny lived inside. This life, whatever it was, had made him older and thinner and it had deepened the distant stillness in which he had always moved. He looked very unlike my baby brother. Yet, when he smiled, when we shook hands, the baby brother I'd never known looked out from the depths of his private life, like an animal waiting to be coaxed into the light.

50 "How you been keeping?" he asked me.

"All right. And you?"

"Just fine." He was smiling all over his face. "It's good to see you again."

"It's good to see you."

The seven years' difference in our ages lay between us like a chasm: I wondered if these years would ever operate between us as a bridge. I was remembering, and it made it hard to catch my breath, that I had been there when he was born; and I had heard the first words he had ever spoken. When he started to walk, he walked from our mother straight to me. I caught him just before he fell when he took the first steps he ever took in this world.

55 "How's Isabel?"

"Just fine. She's dying to see you."

"And the boys?"

"They're fine, too. They're anxious to see their uncle."

"Oh, come on. You know they don't remember me."

60 "Are you kidding? Of course they remember you."

He grinned again. We got into a taxi. We had a lot to say to each other, far too much to know how to begin.

As the taxi began to move, I asked, "You still want to go to India?"

He laughed. "You still remember that. Hell, no. This place is Indian enough for me."

"It used to belong to them," I said.

65 And he laughed again. "They damn sure knew what they were doing when they got rid of it."

Years ago, when he was around fourteen, he'd been all hipped on the idea of going to India. He read books about people sitting on rocks, naked, in all kinds of weather, but mostly bad, naturally, and walking barefoot through hot coals and arriving at wisdom. I used to say that it sounded to me as though they were getting away from wisdom as fast as they could. I think he sort of looked down on me for that.

"Do you mind," he asked, "if we have the driver drive alongside the park? On the west side—I haven't seen the city in so long."

"Of course not," I said. I was afraid that I might sound as though I were humoring him, but I hoped he wouldn't take it that way.

So we drove along, between the green of the park and the stony, lifeless elegance of hotels and apartment buildings, toward the vivid, killing streets of our childhood. These streets hadn't changed, though housing projects jutted up out of them now like rocks in the middle of a boiling sea. Most of the houses in which we had grown up had vanished, as had the stores from which we had stolen, the basements in which we had first tried sex, the rooftops from which we had hurled tin cans and bricks. But houses exactly like the houses of our past yet dominated the landscape, boys exactly like the boys we once had been found themselves smothering in these houses, came down into the streets for light and air and found themselves encircled by disaster. Some escaped the trap, most didn't. Those who got out always left something of themselves behind, as some animals amputate a leg and leave it in the trap. It might be said, perhaps, that I had escaped, after all, I was a school teacher; or that Sonny had, he hadn't lived in Harlem for years. Yet, as the cab moved uptown through streets which seemed, with a rush, to darken with dark people, and as I covertly studied Sonny's face, it came to me that what we both were seeking through our separate cab windows was that part of ourselves which had been left behind. It's always at the hour of trouble and confrontation that the missing member aches.

70   We hit 110th Street and started rolling up Lenox Avenue. And I'd known this avenue all my life, but it seemed to me again, as it had seemed on the day I'd first heard about Sonny's trouble, filled with a hidden menace which was its very breath of life.

"We almost there," said Sonny.

"Almost." We were both too nervous to say anything more.

We live in a housing project. It hasn't been up long. A few days after it was up it seemed uninhabitably new, now, of course, it's already rundown. It looks like a parody of the good, clean, faceless life—God knows the people who live in it do their best to make it a parody. The beat-looking grass lying around isn't enough to make their lives green, the hedges will never hold out the streets, and they know it. The big windows fool no one, they aren't big enough to make space out of no space. They don't bother with the windows, they watch the TV screen instead. The playground is most popular with the children who don't play at jacks, or skip rope, or roller skate, or swing, and they can be found in it after dark. We moved in partly because it's not too far from where I teach, and partly for the kids; but it's really just like the houses in which Sonny and I grew up. The same things happen, they'll have the same things to remember. The moment Sonny and I started into the house I had the feeling that I was simply bringing him back into the danger he had almost died trying to escape.

    Sonny has never been talkative. So I don't know why I was sure he'd be dying to talk to me when supper was over the first night. Everything went fine, the oldest boy remembered him, and the youngest boy liked him, and Sonny had remembered to bring something for each of them; and Isabel, who is really much nicer than I am, more open and giving, had gone to a lot of trouble about dinner and was genuinely glad to see him. And she's always been able to tease Sonny in a way that I haven't. It was nice to see her face so vivid again and to hear her laugh and watch her make Sonny laugh. She wasn't, or, anyway, she didn't seem to be, at all uneasy or embarrassed. She chatted as though there were no subject which had to be avoided and she got Sonny past his first, faint stiffness. And thank God she was there, for I was filled with that icy dread again. Everything I did seemed awkward to me, and everything I said sounded freighted with hidden meaning. I was trying to remember everything I'd heard about dope addiction and I couldn't help watching Sonny for signs. I wasn't doing it out of malice. I was trying to find out something about my brother. I was dying to hear him tell he was safe.

75   "Safe!" my father grunted, whenever Mama suggested trying to move to a neighborhood which might be safer for children. "Safe, hell! Ain't no place safe for kids, nor nobody."

He always went on like this, but he wasn't, ever, really as bad as he sounded, not even on weekends, when he got drunk. As a matter of fact, he was always on the lookout for "something a little better," but he died before he found it. He died suddenly, during a drunken weekend in the middle of the war, when Sonny was fifteen. He and Sonny hadn't ever got on too well. And this was partly because Sonny was the apple of his father's eye. It was because he loved Sonny so much and was frightened for him, that he was always fighting with him. It doesn't do any good to fight with Sonny. Sonny just moves back, inside himself, where he can't be reached. But the principal reason that they never hit it off is that they were so much alike. Daddy was big and rough and loud-talking, just the opposite of Sonny, but they both had—that same privacy.

Mama tried to tell me something about this, just after Daddy died. I was home on leave from the army.

This was the last time I ever saw my mother alive. Just the same, this picture gets all mixed up in my mind with pictures I had of her when she was younger. The way I always see her is the way she used to be on a Sunday afternoon, say, when the old folks were talking after the big Sunday dinner. I always see her wearing pale blue. She'd be sitting on the sofa. And my father would be sitting in the easy chair, not far from her. And the living room would be full of church folks and relatives. There they sit, in chairs all around the living room, and the night is creeping up outside, but nobody knows it yet. You can see the darkness growing against the windowpanes and you hear the street noises every now and again, or maybe the jangling beat of a tambourine from one of the churches close by, but it's real quiet in the room. For a moment nobody's talking, but every face looks darkening, like the sky outside. And my mother rocks a little from the waist, and my father's eyes are closed. Everyone is looking at something a child can't see. For a minute they've forgotten the children. Maybe a kid is lying on the rug, half asleep. Maybe somebody's got a kid in his lap and is absent-mindedly stroking the kid's head. Maybe there's a kid, quiet and big-eyed, curled up on a big chair in the corner. The silence, the darkness coming, and the darkness in the faces frightens the child obscurely. He hopes that the hand which strokes his forehead will never stop—will never die. He hopes that there will never come a time when the old folks won't be sitting around the living room, talking about where they've come from, and what they've seen, and what's happened to them and their kinfolk.

But something deep and watchful in the child knows that this is bound to end, is already ending. In a moment someone will get up and turn on the light. Then the old folks will remember the children and they won't talk any more that day. And when light fills the room, the child is filled with darkness. He knows that every time this happens he's moved just a little closer to that darkness outside. The darkness outside is what the old folks have been talking about. It's what they've come from. It's what they endure. The child knows that they won't talk any more because if he knows too much about what's happened to *them,* he'll know too much too soon, about what's going to happen to *him.*

80 The last time I talked to my mother, I remember I was restless. I wanted to get out and see Isabel. We weren't married then and we had a lot to straighten out between us.

There Mama sat, in black, by the window. She was humming an old church song, *Lord, you brought me from a long ways off.* Sonny was out somewhere. Mama kept watching the streets.

"I don't know," she said, "if I'll ever see you again, after you go off from here. But I hope you'll remember the things I tried to teach you."

"Don't talk like that," I said, and smiled. "You'll be here a long time yet."

She smiled, too, but she said nothing. She was quiet for a long time. And I said, "Mama, don't you worry about nothing. I'll be writing all the time, and you be getting the checks. . . ."

85 "I want to talk to you about your brother," she said, suddenly. "If anything happens to me he ain't going to have nobody to look out for him."

"Mama," I said, "ain't nothing going to happen to you *or* Sonny. Sonny's all right. He's a good boy and he's got good sense."

"It ain't a question of his being a good boy," Mama said, "nor of his having good sense. It ain't only the bad ones, nor yet the dumb ones that gets sucked under." She stopped, looking at me. "Your Daddy once had a brother," she said, and she smiled in a way that made me feel she was in pain. "You didn't never know that, did you?"

"No," I said, "I never knew that," and I watched her face.

"Oh, yes," she said, "your Daddy had a brother." She looked out of the window again. "I know you never saw your Daddy cry. But I did—many a time, through all these years."

90   I asked her, "What happened to his brother? How come nobody's ever talked about him?"

This was the first time I ever saw my mother look old.

"His brother got killed," she said, "when he was just a little younger than you are now. I knew him. He was a fine boy. He was maybe a little full of the devil, but he didn't mean nobody no harm."

Then she stopped and the room was silent, exactly as it had sometimes been on those Sunday afternoons. Mama kept looking out into the streets.

"He used to have a job in the mill," she said, "and, like all young folks, he just liked to perform on Saturday nights. Saturday nights, him and your father would drift around to different places, go to dances and things like that, or just sit around with people they knew, and your father's brother would sing, he had a fine voice, and play along with himself on his guitar. Well, this particular Saturday night, him and your father was coming home from some place, and they were both a little drunk and there was a moon that night, it was bright like day. Your father's brother was feeling kind of good, and he was whistling to himself, and he had his guitar slung over this shoulder. They was coming down a hill and beneath them was a road that turned off from the highway. Well, your father's brother, being always kind of frisky, decided to run down this hill, and he did, with that guitar banging and clanging behind him, and he ran across the road, and he was making water behind a tree. And your father was sort of amused at him and he was still coming down the hill, kind of slow. Then he heard a car motor and that same minute his brother stepped from behind the tree, into the road, in the moonlight. And he started to cross the road. And your father started to run down the hill, he says he don't know why. This car was full of white men. They was all drunk, and when they seen your father's brother they let out a great whoop and holler and they aimed the car straight at him. They was having fun, they just wanted to scare him, the way they do sometimes, you know. But they was drunk. And I guess the boy, being drunk, too, and scared, kind of lost his head. By the time he jumped it was too late. Your father says he heard his brother scream when the car rolled over him, and he heard the wood of that guitar when it give, and he heard them strings go flying, and he heard them white men shouting, and the car kept on a-going and it ain't stopped till this day. And, time your father got down the hill, his brother weren't nothing but blood and pulp."

95   Tears were gleaming on my mother's face. There wasn't anything I could say.

"He never mentioned it," she said, "because I never let him mention it before you children. Your Daddy was like a crazy man that night and for many a night thereafter. He says he never in his life seen anything as dark as that road after the lights of that car had gone away. Weren't nothing, weren't nobody on that road, just your Daddy and his brother and that busted guitar. Oh, yes. Your Daddy never did really get right again. Till the day he died he weren't sure but that every white man he saw was the man that killed his brother."

She stopped and took out her handkerchief and dried her eyes and looked at me.

"I ain't telling you all this," she said, "to make you scared or bitter or to make you hate nobody. I'm telling you this because you got a brother. And the world ain't changed."

I guess I didn't want to believe this. I guess she saw this in my face. She turned away from me, toward the window again, searching those streets.

100   "But I praise my Redeemer," she said at last, "that He called your Daddy home before me. I ain't saying it to throw no flowers at myself, but, I declare, it keeps me from feeling too cast down to know I helped your father get safely through this world. Your father always acted like he was the roughest, strongest man on earth. And everybody took him to be like that. But if he hadn't had *me* there—to see his tears!"

She was crying again. Still, I couldn't move. I said, "Lord, Lord, Mama, I didn't know it was like that."

"Oh, honey," she said, "there's a lot that you don't know. But you are going to find it out." She stood up from the window and came over to me. "You got to hold on to your brother," she said, "and don't let him fall, no matter what it looks like is happening to him and no matter how evil you gets with him. You going to be evil with him many a time. But don't you forget what I told you, you hear?"

"I won't forget," I said. "Don't you worry, I won't forget. I won't let nothing happen to Sonny."

My mother smiled as though she were amused at something she saw in my face. Then, "You may not be able to stop nothing from happening. But you got to let him know you's *there*."

105   Two days later I was married, and then I was gone. And I had a lot of things on my mind and I pretty well forgot my promise to Mama until I got shipped home on a special furlough for her funeral.

And after the funeral, with just Sonny and me alone in the empty kitchen, I tried to find out something about him.

"What do you want to do?" I asked him.

"I'm going to be a musician," he said.

For he had graduated, in the time I had been away, from dancing to the juke box to finding out who was playing what, and what they were doing with it, and he had bought himself a set of drums.

110   "You mean, you want to be a drummer?" I somehow had the feeling that being a drummer might be all right for other people but not for my brother Sonny.

"I don't think," he said, looking at me very gravely, "that I'll ever be a good drummer. But I think I can play a piano."

I frowned. I'd never played the role of the older brother quite so seriously before, had scarcely ever, in fact, *asked* Sonny a damn thing. I sensed myself in the presence of something I didn't really know how to handle, didn't understand. So I made my frown a little deeper as I asked: "What kind of musician do you want to be?"

He grinned, "How many kinds do you think there are?"

"Be *serious*," I said.

115   He laughed, throwing his head back, and then looked at me. "I *am* serious."

"Well, then, for Christ's sake, stop kidding around and answer a serious question. I mean, do you want to be a concert pianist, you want to play classical music and all that, or—or what?" Long before I finished he was laughing again. "For Christ's *sake*, Sonny!"

He sobered, but with difficulty. "I'm sorry, But you sound so—*scared!*" and he was off again.

"Well, you may think it's funny now, baby, but it's not going to be so funny when you have to make your living at it, let me tell you *that*." I was furious because I knew he was laughing at me and I didn't know why.

"No," he said, very sober now, and afraid, perhaps, that he'd hurt me. "I don't want to be a classical pianist. That isn't what interests me. I mean"—he paused, looking hard at me, as though his eyes would help me to understand, and then gestured helplessly, as though perhaps his hand would help—"I mean, I'll have a lot of studying to do, and I'll have to study *everything,* but, I mean, I want to play *with*—jazz musicians." He stopped, "I want to play jazz," he said.

120   Well, the word had never before sounded as heavy, as real, as it sounded that afternoon in Sonny's mouth. I just looked at him and I was probably frowning a real frown by this time. I simply couldn't see why on earth he'd want to spend his time hanging around night-clubs, clowning around on bandstands, while people pushed each other around a dance floor. It seemed—beneath him, somehow. I had never thought about it before, had never been forced to, but I suppose I had always put jazz musicians in a class with what Daddy called "good-time people."

    "Are you *serious?*"

    "Hell, *yes,* I'm serious."

    He looked more helpless than ever, and annoyed, and deeply hurt.

    I suggested, helpfully: "You mean—like Louis Armstrong?"[1]

125   His face closed as though I'd struck him. "No. I'm not talking about none of that old-time, down home crap."

    "Well, look, Sonny, I'm sorry, don't get mad. I just don't altogether get it, that's all. Name somebody—you know, a jazz musician you admire."

    "Bird."

    "Who?"

    "Bird! Charlie Parker![2] Don't they teach you nothing in the goddamn army?"

130   I lit a cigarette. I was surprised and then a little amused to discover that I was trembling. "I've been out of touch," I said. "You'll have to be patient with me. Now. Who's this Parker character?"

    "He's just one of the greatest jazz musicians alive," said Sonny, sullenly, his hands in his pockets, his back to me. "Maybe *the* greatest," he added, bitterly, "that's probably why *you* never heard of him."

    "All right," I said, "I'm ignorant. I'm sorry. I'll go out and buy all the cat's records right away, all right?"

    "It don't," said Sonny, with dignity, "make any difference to me. I don't care what you listen to. Don't do me no favors."

    I was beginning to realize that I'd never seen him so upset before. With another part of my mind I was thinking that this would probably turn out to be one of those things kids go through and that I shouldn't make it seem important by pushing it too hard. Still, I didn't think it would do any harm to ask: "Doesn't all this take a lot of time? Can you make a living at it?"

135   He turned back to me and half leaned, half sat, on the kitchen table. "Everything takes time," he said, "and—well, yes, sure, I can make a living at it. But what I don't seem to be able to make you understand is that it's the only thing I want to do."

    "Well, Sonny," I said, gently, "you know people can't always do exactly what they *want* to do—"

    "*No,* I don't know that," said Sonny, surprising me. "I think people *ought* to do what they want to do, what else are they alive for?"

    "You getting to be a big boy," I said desperately, "it's time you started thinking about your future."

---

[1] Famous jazz trumpet player.

[2] Famous jazz musician, nicknamed Bird.

"I'm thinking about my future," said Sonny, grimly. "I think about it all the time."

140   I gave up. I decided, if he didn't change his mind, that we could always talk about it later. "In the meantime," I said, "you got to finish school." We had already decided that he'd have to move in with Isabel and her folks. I knew this wasn't the ideal arrangement because Isabel's folks are inclined to be dicty[3] and they hadn't especially wanted Isabel to marry me. But I didn't know what else to do. "And we have to get you fixed up at Isabel's."

There was a long silence. He moved from the kitchen table to the window. "That's a terrible idea. You know it yourself."

"Do you have a *better* idea?"

He just walked up and down the kitchen for a minute. He was as tall as I was. He had started to shave. I suddenly had the feeling that I didn't know him at all.

He stopped at the kitchen table and picked up my cigarettes. Looking at me with a kind of mocking, amused defiance, he put one between his lips. "You mind?"

145   "You smoking already?"

He lit the cigarette and nodded, watching me through the smoke. "I just wanted to see if I'd have the courage to smoke in front of you." He grinned and blew a great cloud of smoke to the ceiling. "It was easy." He looked at my face. "Come on, now. I bet you was smoking at my age, tell the truth."

I didn't say anything but the truth was on my face, and he laughed. But now there was something very strained in his laugh. "Sure. And I bet that ain't all you was doing."

He was frightening me a little. "Cut the crap," I said. "We already decided that you was going to go and live at Isabel's. Now what's got into you all of a sudden?"

"*You* decided it," he pointed out. "*I* didn't decide nothing." He stopped in front of me, leaning against the stove, arms loosely folded. "Look, brother. I don't want to stay in Harlem no more, I really don't." He was very earnest. He looked at me, then over toward the kitchen window. There was something in his eyes I'd never seen before, some thoughtfulness, some worry all his own. He rubbed the muscle of one arm. "It's time I was getting out of here."

150   "Where do you want to *go,* Sonny?"

"I want to join the army. Or the navy, I don't care. If I say I'm old enough, they'll believe me."

Then I got mad. It was because I was so scared. "You must be crazy. You goddamn fool, what the hell do you want to go and join the *army* for?"

"I just told you. To get out of Harlem."

"Sonny, you haven't even finished *school.* And if you really want to be a musician, how do you expect to study if you're in the *army?*"

155   He looked at me, trapped, and in anguish. "There's ways. I might be able to work out some kind of deal. Anyway, I'll have the G.I. Bill when I come out."

"*If* you come out." We stared at each other. "Sonny, please. Be reasonable. I know the setup is far from perfect. But we got to do the best we can."

"I ain't learning nothing in school," he said. "Even when I go." He turned away from me and opened the window and threw his cigarette out into the narrow alley. I watched his back. "At least, I ain't learning nothing you'd want me to learn." He slammed the window so hard I thought the glass would fly out, and turned back to me. "And I'm sick of the stink of these garbage cans!"

"Sonny," I said, "I know how you feel. But if you don't finish school now, you're going to be sorry later that you didn't." I grabbed him by the shoulders. "And you only got another

---

[3] Putting on fine airs.

year. It ain't so bad. And I'll come back and I swear I'll help you do *whatever* you want to do. Just try to put up with it till I come back. Will you please do that? For me?"

He didn't answer and he wouldn't look at me.

160 "Sonny. You hear me?"

He pulled away. "I hear you. But you never hear anything *I* say."

I didn't know what to say to that. He looked out of the window and then back at me. OK," he said, and sighed. "I'll try."

Then I said, trying to cheer him up a little, "They got a piano at Isabel's. You can practice on it."

And as a matter of fact, it did cheer him up for a minute. "That's right," he said to himself. "I forgot that." His face relaxed a little. But the worry, the thoughtfulness, played on it still, the way shadows play on a face which is staring into the fire.

165 But I thought I'd never hear the end of that piano. At first, Isabel, would write me, saying how nice it was that Sonny was so serious about his music and how, as soon as he came in from school, or wherever he had been when he was supposed to be at school, he went straight to that piano and stayed there until suppertime. And, after supper, he went back to that piano and stayed there until everybody went to bed. He was at the piano all day Saturday and all day Sunday. Then he bought a record player and started playing records. He'd play one record over and over again, all day long sometimes, and he'd improvise along with it on the piano. Or he'd play one section of the record, one chord, one change, one progression, then he'd do it on the piano. Then back to the record. Then back to the piano.

Well, I really don't know how they stood it. Isabel finally confessed that it wasn't like living with a person at all, it was like living with sound. And the sound didn't make any sense to her, didn't make any sense to any of them—naturally. They began, in a way, to be afflicted by this presence that was living in their home. It was as though Sonny were some sort of god, or monster. He moved in an atmosphere which wasn't like theirs at all. They fed him and he ate, he washed himself, he walked in and out of their door; he certainly wasn't nasty or unpleasant or rude, Sonny isn't any of those things; but it was as though he were all wrapped up in some cloud, some fire, some vision all his own; and there wasn't any way to reach him.

At the same time, he wasn't really a man yet, he was still a child, and they had to watch out for him in all kinds of ways. They certainly couldn't throw him out. Neither did they dare to make a great scene about that piano because even they dimly sensed, as I sensed, from so many thousands of miles away, that Sonny was at that piano playing for his life.

But he hadn't been going to school. One day a letter came from the school board and Isabel's mother got it—there had, apparently, been other letters but Sonny had torn them up. This day, when Sonny came in, Isabel's mother showed him the letter and asked where he'd been spending his time. And she finally got it out of him that he'd been down in Greenwich Village, with musicians and other characters, in a white girl's apartment. And this scared her and she started to scream at him and what came up, once she began—though she denies it to this day—was what sacrifices they were making to give Sonny a decent home and how little he appreciated it.

Sonny didn't play the piano that day. By evening, Isabel's mother had calmed down but then there was the old man to deal with, and Isabel herself. Isabel says she did her best to be calm but she broke down and started crying. She says she just watched Sonny's face. She could tell, by watching him, what was happening with him. And what was happening was that they penetrated his cloud, they had reached him. Even if their fingers had been a thousand times more gentle than human fingers ever are, he could hardly help feeling that they had stripped him naked and were spitting on that nakedness. For he also had to see that his presence, that music, which was life or death to him, had been torture for them and that they had endured it, not at all for his sake, but only for mine. And Sonny couldn't take that. He can take it a little better today than he could then but he's still not very good at it and, frankly, I don't know anybody who is.

170   The silence of the next few days must have been louder than the sound of all the music ever played since time began. One morning, before she went to work, Isabel was in his room for something and she suddenly realized that all of his records were gone. And she knew for certain that he was gone. And he was. He went as far as the navy would carry him. He finally sent me a postcard from some place in Greece and that was the first I knew that Sonny was still alive. I didn't see him any more until we were both back in New York and the war had long been over.

He was a man by then, of course, but I wasn't willing to see it. He came by the house from time to time, but we fought almost every time we met. I didn't like the way he carried himself, loose and dreamlike all the time, and I didn't like his friends, and his music seemed to be merely an excuse for the life he led. It sounded just that weird and disordered.

Then we had a fight, a pretty awful fight, and I didn't see him for months. By and by I looked him up, where he was living, in a furnished room in the Village, and I tried to make it up. But there were lots of other people in the room and Sonny just lay on his bed, and he wouldn't come downstairs with me, and he treated these other people as though they were his family and I weren't. So I got mad and then he got mad, and then I told him that he might just as well be dead as live the way he was living. Then he stood up and he told me not to worry about him any more in life, that he *was* dead as far as I was concerned. Then he pushed me to the door and the other people looked on as though nothing were happening, and he slammed the door behind me. I stood in the hallway, staring at the door. I heard somebody laugh in the room and then the tears came to my eyes. I started down the steps, whistling to keep from crying. I kept whistling to myself, *You going to need me, baby, one of these cold, rainy days.*

I read about Sonny's trouble in the spring. Little Grace died in the fall. She was a beautiful little girl. But she only lived a little over two years. She died of polio and she suffered. She had a slight fever for a couple of days, but it didn't seem like anything and we just kept her in bed. And we would certainly have called the doctor, but the fever dropped, and she seemed to be all right. So we thought it had just been a cold. Then, one day, she was up, playing, Isabel was in the kitchen fixing lunch for the two boys when they'd come in from school, and she heard Grace fall down in the living room. When you have a lot of children you don't always start running when one of them falls, unless they start screaming or something. And, this time, Grace was quiet. Yet, Isabel says that when she heard that *thump* and then that silence, something happened in her to make her afraid. And she ran to the living room and there was little Grace on the floor, all twisted up, and the reason she hadn't screamed was that she couldn't get her breath. And when she did scream, it was the worst sound, Isabel says, that she'd ever heard in all her life, and she still hears it sometimes in her dreams. Isabel will sometimes wake me up with a low, moaning, strangled sound and I have to be quick to awaken her and hold her to me and where Isabel is weeping against me seems a mortal wound.

I think I may have written Sonny the very day that little Grace was buried. I was sitting in the living room in the dark, by myself, and I suddenly thought of Sonny. My trouble made his real.

175   One Saturday afternoon, when Sonny had been living with us, or, anyway, been in our house, for nearly two weeks, I found myself wandering aimlessly about the living room, drinking from a can of beer, and trying to work up the courage to search Sonny's room. He

was out, he was usually out whenever I was home, and Isabel had taken the children to see their grandparents. Suddenly I was standing still in front of the living room window, watching Seventh Avenue. The idea of searching Sonny's room made me still. I scarcely dared to admit to myself what I'd be searching for. I didn't know what I'd do if I found it. Or if I didn't.

On the sidewalk across from me, near the entrance to a barbecue joint, some people were holding an old-fashioned revival meeting. The barbecue cook, wearing a dirty white apron, his conked hair reddish and metallic in the pale sun, and a cigarette between his lips, stood in the doorway, watching them. Kids and older people paused in their errands and stood there, along with some older men and a couple of very tough-looking women who watched everything that happened on the avenue, as though they owned it, or were maybe owned by it. Well, they were watching this, too. The revival was being carried on by three sisters in black, and a brother. All they had were their voices and their Bibles and a tambourine. The brother was testifying and while he testified two of the sisters stood together, seeming to say, amen, and the third sister walked around with the tambourine outstretched and a couple of people dropped coins into it. Then the brother's testimony ended and the sister who had been taking up the collection dumped the coins into her palm and transferred them to the pocket of her long black robe. Then she raised both hands, striking the tambourine against the air, and then against one hand, and she started to sing. And the two other sisters and the brother joined in.

It was strange, suddenly, to watch, though I had been seeing these street meetings all my life. So, of course, had everybody else down there. Yet, they paused and watched and listened and I stood still at the window. *"Tis the old ship of Zion,"* they sang, and the sister with the tambourine kept a steady, jangling beat, *"it has rescued many a thousand!"* Not a soul under the sound of their voices was hearing this song for the first time, not one of them had been rescued. Nor had they seen much in the way of rescue work being done around them. Neither did they especially believe in the holiness of the three sisters and the brother, they knew too much about them, knew where they lived, and how. The woman with the tambourine, whose voice dominated the air, whose face was bright with joy, was divided by very little from the woman who stood watching her, a cigarette between her heavy, chapped lips, her hair a cuckoo's nest, her face scarred and swollen from many beatings, and her black eyes glittering like coal. Perhaps they both knew this, which was why, when, as rarely, they addressed each other, they addressed each other as Sister. As the singing filled the air the watching, listening faces underwent a change, and eyes focusing on something within; the music seemed to soothe a poison out of them; and time seemed, nearly, to fall away from the sullen, belligerent, battered faces, as though they were fleeing back to their first condition, while dreaming of their last. The barbecue cook half shook his head and smiled, and dropped his cigarette and disappeared into his joint. A man fumbled in his pockets for change and stood holding it in his hand impatiently, as though he had just remembered a pressing appointment further up the avenue. He looked furious. Then I saw Sonny, standing on the edge of the crowd. He was carrying a wide, flat notebook with a green cover, and it made him look, from where I was standing, almost like a schoolboy. The coppery sun brought out the copper in his skin, he was very faintly smiling, standing very still. Then the singing stopped, the tambourine turned into a collection plate again. The furious man dropped in his coins and vanished, so did a couple of the women, and Sonny dropped some change in the plate, looking directly at the woman with a little smile. He started across the avenue, toward the house. He has a slow, loping walk, something like the way Harlem hipsters walk, only he's imposed on this his own half-beat. I had never really noticed it before.

I stayed at the window, both relieved and apprehensive. As Sonny disappeared from my sight, they began singing again. And they were still singing when his key turned in the lock.

"Hey," he said.

180 "Hey, yourself. You want some beer?"

"No. Well, maybe." But he came up to the window and stood beside me, looking out. "What a warm voice," he said.

They were singing *If I could only hear my mother pray again!*

"Yes," I said, "and she can sure beat that tambourine."

"But what a terrible song," he said, and laughed. He dropped his notebook on the sofa and disappeared into the kitchen. "Where's Isabel and the kids?"

185 "I think they went to see their grandparents. You hungry?"

"No." He came back into the living room with his can of beer. "You want to come some place with me tonight?"

I sensed, I don't know how, that I couldn't possibly say no. "Sure. Where?"

He sat down on the sofa and picked up his notebook and started leafing through it. "I'm going to sit in with some fellows in a joint in the Village."

"You mean, you're going to play, tonight?"

190 "That's right." He took a swallow of his beer and moved back to the window. He gave me a sidelong look. "If you can stand it."

"I'll try," I said.

He smiled to himself and we both watched as the meeting across the way broke up. The three sisters and the brother, heads bowed, were singing *God be with you till we meet again*. The faces around them were very quiet. Then the song ended. The small crowd dispersed. We watched the three women and the lone man walk slowly up the avenue.

"When she was singing before," said Sonny, abruptly, "her voice reminded me for a minute of what heroin feels like sometimes—when it's in your veins. It makes you feel sort of warm and cool at the same time. And distant. And—and sure." He sipped his beer, very deliberately not looking at me. I watched his face. "It makes you feel—in control. Sometimes you've got to have that feeling."

"Do you?" I sat down slowly in the easy chair.

195 "Sometimes." He went to the sofa and picked up his notebook again. "Some people do."

"In order," I asked, "to play?" And my voice was very ugly, full of contempt and anger.

"Well"—he looked at me with great, troubled eyes, as though, in fact, he hoped his eyes would tell me things he could never otherwise say—"they *think* so. And *if* they think so—!"

"And what do *you* think?" I asked.

He sat on the sofa and put his can of beer on the floor. "I don't know," he said, and I couldn't be sure if he were answering my question or pursuing his thoughts. He face didn't tell me. "It's not so much to *play*. It's to *stand* it, to be able to make it at all. On any level." He frowned and smiled: "In order to keep from shaking to pieces."

200 "But these friends of yours," I said, "they seem to shake themselves to pieces pretty goddamn fast."

"Maybe." He played with the notebook. And something told me that I should curb my tongue, that Sonny was doing his best to talk, that I should listen. "But of course you only know the ones that've gone to pieces. Some don't—or at least they haven't *yet* and that's just about all *any* of us can say." He paused. "And then there are some who just live, really, in hell, and they know it and they see what's happening and they go right on. I don't know." He sighed, dropped the notebook, folded his arms. "Some guys, you can tell from the way they play, they on something *all* the time. And you can see that, well, it makes something real for them. But of course," he picked up his beer from the floor and sipped it and put the can down again, "they *want* to, too, you've got to see that. Even some of them that say they don't—*some*, not all.

"And what about you?" I asked—I couldn't help it. "What about you? Do *you* want to?"

He stood up and walked to the window and remained silent for a long time. Then he sighed. "Me," he said. Then: "While I was downstairs before, on my way here, listening to that woman sing, it struck me all of a sudden how much suffering she must have had to go through—to sing like that. It's *repulsive* to think you have to suffer that much."

I said: "But there's no way not to suffer—is there, Sonny?"

205   "I believe not," he said and smiled, "but that's never stopped anyone from trying." He looked at me. "Has it?" I realized, with this mocking look, that there stood between us, forever, beyond the power of time or forgiveness, the fact that I had held silence—so long!—when he had needed human speech to help him. He turned back to the window. "No, there's no way not to suffer. But you try all kinds of ways to keep from drowning in it, to keep on top of it, and to make it seem—well, like *you*. Like you did something, all right, and now you're suffering for it. You know?" I said nothing. "Well you know," he said, impatiently, "why *do* people suffer? Maybe it's better to do something to give it a reason, *any* reason."

"But we just agreed," I said, "that there's no way not to suffer. Isn't it better, then, just to—take it?"

"But nobody just takes it," Sonny cried, "that's what I'm telling you! *Everybody* tries not to. You're just hung up on the *way* some people try—it's not *your* way!"

The hair on my face began to itch, my face felt wet. "That's not true," I said, "that's not true. I don't give a damn what other people do, I don't even care how they suffer. I just care how *you* suffer." And he looked at me. "Please believe me," I said, "I don't want to see you—die—trying not to suffer."

"I won't," he said, flatly, "die trying not to suffer. At least, not any faster than anybody else."

210   "But there's no need," I said, trying to laugh, "is there? in killing yourself."

I wanted to say more, but I couldn't. I wanted to talk about will power and how life could be—well, beautiful. I wanted to say that it was all within; but was it? or, rather, wasn't that exactly the trouble? And I wanted to promise that I would never fail him again. But it would all have sounded—empty words and lies.

So I made the promise to myself and prayed that I would keep it.

"It's terrible sometimes, inside," he said, "that's what's the trouble. You walk these streets, black and funky and cold, and there's not really a living ass to talk to, and there's nothing shaking, and there's no way of getting it out—that storm inside. You can't talk it and you can't make love with it, and when you finally try to get with it and play it, you realize *nobody's* listening. So *you've* got to listen. You got to find a way to listen."

And then he walked away from the window and sat on the sofa again, as though all the wind had suddenly been knocked out of him. "Sometimes you'll do *anything* to play, even cut your mother's throat." He laughed and looked at me. "Or your brother's." Then he sobered. "Or your own." Then: "Don't worry. I'm all right now and I think I'll *be* all right. But I can't forget—where I've been. I don't mean just the physical place I've been, I mean where I've *been*. And *what* I've been."

215   "What have you been, Sonny?" I asked.

He smiled—but sat sideways on the sofa, his elbow resting on the back, his fingers playing with his mouth and chin, not looking at me. "I've been something I didn't recognize, didn't know I could be. Didn't know anybody could be." He stopped, looking inward, looking helplessly young, looking old. "I'm not talking about it now because I feel *guilty* or anything like that—maybe it would be better if I did, I don't know. Anyway, I can't really talk about it. Not to you, not to anybody," and now he turned and faced me. "Sometimes, you know, and it was actually when I was most *out* of the world, I felt that I was in it, that I was *with* it, really, and I could play or I didn't really have to *play*, it just came out of me, it was there. And I don't know how I played, thinking about it now, but I know I did awful things, those times, sometimes, to people. Or it wasn't that I *did* anything to them—it was that they weren't real." He picked up the beer can; it was empty; he rolled it between his palms: "And other times—well, I needed a fix, I needed to find a place to lean, I needed to clear a space to *listen*—and I couldn't find it, and I—went crazy, I did terrible things to *me*, I was terrible *for* me." He began pressing the beer can between his hands, I watched the metal begin to give. It glittered, as he played with it, like a knife, and I was afraid he would cut himself, but I said nothing. "Oh well, I can never tell you. I was all by myself at the bottom of something, stinking and sweating and crying and shaking, and I smelled it, you know? *my* stink, and I thought I'd die if I couldn't get away from it and yet, all the same, I knew that everything I was doing was just locking me in with it. And I didn't know," he paused, still flattening the beer can, "I didn't know, I still *don't* know, something kept telling me that maybe it was good to smell your own stink, but I didn't think that *that* was what I'd been trying to do—and—who can stand it?" and he abruptly dropped the ruined beer can, looking at me with a small, still smile, and then rose, walking to the window as though it were the lodestone rock. I watched his face, he watched the avenue. "I couldn't tell you when Mama died—but the reason I wanted to leave Harlem so bad was to get away from drugs. And then, when I ran away, that's what I was running from—really. When I came back, nothing had changed, *I* hadn't changed, I was just—older." And he stopped, drumming with his fingers on the windowpane. The sun had vanished, soon darkness would fall. I watched his face. "It can come again," he said, almost as though speaking to himself. Then he turned to me. "It can come again," he repeated. "I just want you to know that."

"All right," I said, at last. "So it can come again, All right."

He smiled, but the smile was sorrowful. "I had to try to tell you," he said.

"Yes," I said. "I understand that."

220   "You're my brother," he said, looking straight at me, and not smiling at all.

"Yes," I repeated, "yes. I understand that."

He turned back to the window, looking out. "All that hatred down there," he said, "all that hatred and misery and love. It's a wonder it doesn't blow the avenue apart."

We went to the only nightclub on a short, dark street, downtown. We squeezed through the narrow, chattering, jampacked bar to the entrance of the big room, where the bandstand was. And we stood there for a moment, for the lights were very dim in this room and we couldn't see. Then, "Hello, boy," said a voice and an enormous black man, much older than Sonny or myself, erupted out of all that atmospheric lighting and put an arm around Sonny's shoulder. "I been sitting right here," he said, "waiting for you."

He had a big voice, too, and heads in the darkness turned toward us.

225   Sonny grinned and pulled a little away, and said, "Creole, this is my brother. I told you about him."

Creole shook my hand. "I'm glad to meet you, son," he said, and it was clear that he was glad to meet me *there,* for Sonny's sake. And he smiled, "You got a real musician in *your* family," and he took his arm from Sonny's shoulder and slapped him, lightly, affectionately, with the back of his hand.

"Well. Now I've heard it all," said a voice behind us. This was another musician, and a friend of Sonny's, a coal-black, cheerful-looking man, built close to the ground. He immediately began confiding to me, at the top of his lungs, the most terrible things about Sonny, his teeth gleaming like a lighthouse and his laugh coming up out of him like the beginning of an earthquake. And it turned out that everyone at the bar knew Sonny, or almost everyone; some were musicians, working there, or nearby, or not working, some were simply hangers-on, and some were there to hear Sonny play. I was introduced to all of them and they were all very polite to me. Yet it was clear that, for them, I was only Sonny's brother. Here, I was in Sonny's world. Or, rather: his kingdom. Here, it was not even a question that his veins bore royal blood.

They were going to play soon and Creole installed me, by myself, at a table in a dark corner. Then I watched them, Creole, and the little black man, and Sonny, and the others, while they horsed around, standing just below the bandstand. The light from the bandstand spilled just a little short of them and, watching them laughing and gesturing and moving about, I had the feeling that they, nevertheless, were being most careful not to step into that circle of light too suddenly: that if they moved into the light too suddenly, without thinking, they would perish in flame. Then, while I watched, one of them, the small, black man, moved into the light and crossed the bandstand and started fooling around with his drums. Then—being funny and being, also, extremely ceremonious—Creole took Sonny by the arm and led him to the piano. A woman's voice called Sonny's name and a few hands started clapping. And Sonny, also being funny and being ceremonious, and so touched, I think, that he could have cried, but neither hiding it nor showing it, riding it like a man, grinned, and put both hands to his heart and bowed from the waist.

Creole then went to the bass fiddle and a lean, very bright-skinned brown man jumped up on the bandstand and picked up his horn. So there they were, and the atmosphere on the bandstand and in the room began to change and tighten. Someone stepped up to the microphone and announced them. Then there were all kinds of murmurs. Some people at the bar shushed others. The waitress ran around, frantically getting in the last orders, guys and chicks got closer to each other, and the lights on the bandstand, on the quartet, turned to a kind of indigo. Then they all looked different there. Creole looked about him for the last time, as though he were making certain that all his chickens were in the coop, and then he—jumped and struck the fiddle. And there they were.

230   All I know about music is that not many people ever really hear it. And even then, on the rare occasions when something opens within, and the music enters, what we mainly hear, or hear corroborated, are personal, private, vanishing evocations. But the man who creates the music is hearing something else, is dealing with the roar rising from the void and imposing order on it as it hits the air. What is evoked in him, then, is of another order, more terrible because it has no words, and triumphant, too, for that same reason. And his triumph, when he triumphs, is ours. I just watched Sonny's face. His face was troubled, he was working hard, but he wasn't with it. And I had the feeling that, in a way, everyone on the bandstand was waiting for him, both waiting for him and pushing him along. But as I began to watch Creole, I realized that it was Creole who held them all back. He had them on a short rein. Up there, keeping the beat with his whole body, wailing on the fiddle, with his eyes half closed, he was listening to everything, but he was listening to Sonny. He was having a dialogue with Sonny. He wanted Sonny to leave the shoreline and strike out for the deep water. He was Sonny's witness that deep water and drowning were not the same thing—he had been there, and he knew. And he wanted Sonny to know. He was waiting for Sonny to do the things on the keys which would let Creole know that Sonny was in the water.

And, while Creole listened, Sonny moved, deep within, exactly like someone in torment. I had never before thought of how awful the relationship must be between the musician and his instrument. He has to fill it, this instrument, with the breath of life, his own. He has to make it do what he wants it to do. And a piano is just a piano. It's made out of so much wood and wires and little hammers and big ones, and ivory. While there's only so much you can do with it, the only way to find this out is to try; to try and make it do everything.

And Sonny hadn't been near a piano for over a year. And he wasn't on much better terms with his life, not the life that stretched before him now. He and the piano stammered, started one way, got scared, stopped; started another way, panicked, marked time, started again; then seemed to have found a direction, panicked again, got stuck. And the face I saw on Sonny I'd never seen before. Everything had been burned out of it, and, at the same time, things usually hidden were being burned in, by the fire and fury of the battle which was occurring in him up there.

Yet, watching Creole's face as they neared the end of the first set, I had the feeling that something had happened, something I hadn't heard. Then they finished, there was scattered applause, and then, without an instant's warning, Creole started into something else, it was almost sardonic, it was *Am I Blue*. And, as though he commanded, Sonny began to play. Something began to happen. And Creole let out the reins. The dry, low, black man said something awful on the drums, Creole answered, and the drums talked back. Then the horn insisted, sweet and high, slightly detached perhaps, and Creole listened, commenting now and then, dry, and driving, beautiful and calm and old. Then they all came together again, and Sonny was part of the family again. I could tell this from his face. He seemed to have found, right there beneath his fingers, a damn brand-new piano. It seemed that he couldn't get over it. Then, for awhile, just being happy with Sonny, they seemed to be agreeing with him that brand-new pianos certainly were a gas.

Then Creole stepped forward to remind them that what they were playing was the blues. He hit something in all of them, he hit something in me, myself, and the music tightened and deepened, apprehension began to beat the air. Creole began to tell us what the blues were all about. They were not about anything very new. He and his boys up there were keeping it new, at the risk of ruin, destruction, madness, and death, in order to find new ways to make us listen. For, while the tale of how we suffer, and how we are delighted, and how we may triumph is never new, it always must be heard. There isn't any other tale to tell, it's the only light we've got in all this darkness.

235   And this tale, according to that face, that body, those strong hands on those strings, has another aspect in every country, and a new depth in every generation. Listen, Creole seemed to be saying, listen. Now these are Sonny's blues. He made the little black man on the drums know it, and the bright, brown man on the horn. Creole wasn't trying any longer to get Sonny in the water. He was wishing him Godspeed. Then he stepped back, very slowly, filling the air with the immense suggestion that Sonny speak for himself.

Then they all gathered around Sonny and Sonny played. Every now and again one of them seemed to say, amen. Sonny's fingers filled the air with life, his life. But that life contained so many others. And Sonny went all the way back, he really began with the spare, flat statement of the opening phrase of the song. Then he began to make it his. It was very beautiful because it wasn't hurried and it was no longer a lament. I seemed to hear with what burning he had made it his, with what burning we had yet to make it ours, how we could cease lamenting. Freedom lurked around us and I understood, at last, that he could help us to be free if we would listen, that he would never be free until we did. Yet, there was no battle in his face now. I heard what he had gone through, and would continue to go through until he came to rest in earth. He had made it his: that long line, of which we knew only Mama and Daddy. And he was giving it back, as everything must be given back, so that, passing through death, it can live forever. I saw my mother's face again, and felt, for the first time, how the stones of the road she had walked on must have bruised her feet. I saw the moonlit road where my father's brother died. And it brought something else back to me, and carried me past it, I saw my little girl again and felt Isabel's tears again, and I felt my own tears begin to rise. And I was yet aware that this was only a moment, that the world waited outside, as hungry as a tiger, and that trouble stretched above us, longer than the sky.

Then it was over. Creole and Sonny let out their breath, both soaking wet, and grinning. There was a lot of applause and some of it was real. In the dark, the girl came by and I asked her to take drinks to the bandstand. There was a long pause, while they talked up there in the indigo light and after awhile I saw a girl put a Scotch and milk on top of the piano for Sonny. He didn't seem to notice it, but just before they started playing again, he sipped from it and looked toward me, and nodded. Then he put it back on top of the piano. For me, then, as they began to play again, it glowed and shook above my brother's head like the very cup of trembling.[4]

■ **EXPLORATIONS OF THE TEXT**

1. After reading the first paragraph, what do you predict about the **narrator** and about the **plot** of the story? Why is the narrator's face "trapped in the darkness which roared outside"? What does the "darkness . . . outside" signify to the children? To the adult narrator? To us as readers?
2. Explore the metaphor of "the block of ice." What does the metaphor reveal about the narrator's feelings for Sonny?
3. What characterizes the narrator's relationship with his brother at the beginning of the story?
4. Characterize the narrator. What is revealed about his personality in his constant position as an onlooker (at the window in the schoolroom, at the window in his apartment, at the jazz club)?
5. Compare and contrast the narrator and Sonny. Why have they grown up differently?
6. Why does Sonny turn to the life of the streets? drugs? What importance does music play in his life?
7. Why does the relationship between the narrator and Sonny change? What are the narrator's feelings for his brother at the end of the story?
8. What is the meaning of the scene in the club at the end? What does the narrator realize? What does the scotch and milk cocktail that the narrator sends up to Sonny symbolize?
9. The story is told through a series of **flashbacks**. What would the story lose if it were structured chronologically?

■ **THE READING/WRITING CONNECTION**

1. Baldwin published this story in 1957 about life in Harlem. Does this vision of life still seem real? What might Baldwin write about today?
2. Freewrite and respond to a nonverbal art form (a photograph, a painting, a piece of music) so that someone unfamiliar with the work can share your feelings.
3. "Think" Topic: Will Sonny be saved by music?

■ **IDEAS FOR WRITING**

1. Is violence part of the life of the nuclear family? Explore this **theme** in the works of Hayden, Diaz, and/or Baldwin.
2. How do the images of light and darkness function in this story? What do they suggest about growing up in Harlem?
3. Imagine Sonny's future.
4. What are the causes of Sonny's problems? Propose possible solutions. (Use the "Think" topic as a beginning.)

---

[4] An allusion to the Bible, Isaiah 51:22; "I have taken out of thine hand the cup of trembling . . . thou shalt no more drink it again. . . ."

SHERMAN ALEXIE

Sherman Alexie (1966–   ), a Spokane/Coeur d'Alene Indian, was born on the Spokane Indian Reservation in Wellpinit, Washington. He graduated from Washington State University. By the time his first novel, Reservation Blues *(1995), was published, Alexie had published over three hundred poems, stories, essays, and reviews. His other works include a novel,* Indian Killer *(1996), and the short story collections,* The Lone Ranger and Tonto Fistfight in Heaven *(1993), which served as the basis for the 1998 film* Smoke Signals, The Toughest Indian in the World *(2000), and* Ten Little Indians *(2003).*

1993

THIS IS WHAT IT MEANS TO SAY PHOENIX, ARIZONA

Just after Victor lost his job at the Bureau of Indian Affairs, he also found out that his father had died of a heart attack in Phoenix, Arizona. Victor hadn't seen his father in a few years, had only talked to him on the telephone once or twice, but there still was a genetic pain, which was as real and immediate as a broken bone. Victor didn't have any money. Who does have money on a reservation, except the cigarette and fireworks salespeople? His father had a savings account waiting to be claimed, but Victor needed to find a way to get from Spokane to Phoenix. Victor's mother was just as poor as he was, and the rest of the family didn't have any use at all for him. So Victor called the tribal council.

"Listen," Victor said. "My father just died. I need some money to get to Phoenix to make arrangements."

"Now, Victor," the council said, "you know we're having a difficult time financially."

"But I thought the council had special funds set aside for stuff like this."

5   "Now, Victor, we do have some money available for the proper return of tribal members' bodies. But I don't think we have enough to bring your father all the way back from Phoenix."

"Well," Victor said. "It ain't going to cost all that much. He had to be cremated. Things were kind of ugly. He died of a heart attack in his trailer and nobody found him for a week. It was really hot, too. You get the picture."

"Now, Victor, we're sorry for your loss and the circumstances. But we can really only afford to give you one hundred dollars."

"That's not even enough for a plane ticket."

"Well, you might consider driving down to Phoenix."

10   "I don't have a car. Besides, I was going to drive my father's pickup back up here."

"Now, Victor," the council said, "we're sure there is somebody who could drive you to Phoenix. Or could anybody lend you the rest of the money?"

"You know there ain't nobody around with that kind of money."

"Well, we're sorry, Victor, but that's the best we can do."

Victor accepted the tribal council's offer. What else could he do? So he signed the proper papers, picked up his check, and walked over to the Trading Post to cash it.

15   While Victor stood in line, he watched Thomas Builds-the-Fire standing near the magazine rack talking to himself. Like he always did. Thomas was a storyteller whom nobody wanted to listen to. That's like being a dentist in a town where everybody has false teeth.

Victor and Thomas Builds-the-Fire were the same age, had grown up and played in the dirt together. Ever since Victor could remember, it was Thomas who had always had something to say.

Once, when they were seven years old, when Victor's father still lived with the family, Thomas closed his eyes and told Victor this story: "Your father's heart is weak. He is afraid of his own family. He is afraid of you. Late at night, he sits in the dark. Watches the television until there's nothing but that white noise. Sometimes he feels like he wants to buy a motorcycle and ride away. He wants to run and hide. He doesn't want to be found."

Thomas Builds-the-Fire had known that Victor's father was going to leave, known it before anyone. Now Victor stood in the Trading Post with a one-hundred-dollar check in his hand, wondering if Thomas knew that Victor's father was dead, if he knew what was going to happen next.

Just then, Thomas looked at Victor, smiled, and walked over to him.

20   "Victor, I'm sorry about your father," Thomas said.

"How did you know about it?" Victor asked.

"I heard it on the wind. I heard it from the birds. I felt it in the sunlight. Also, your mother was just in here crying."

"Oh," Victor said and looked around the Trading Post. All the other Indians stared, surprised that Victor was even talking to Thomas. Nobody talked to Thomas anymore because he told the same damn stories over and over again. Victor was embarrassed, but he thought that Thomas might be able to help him. Victor felt a sudden need for tradition.

"I can lend you the money you need," Thomas said suddenly. "But you have to take me with you."

25   "I can't take your money," Victor said. "I mean, I haven't hardly talked to you in years. We're not really friends anymore."

"I didn't say we were friends. I said you had to take me with you."

"Let me think about it."

Victor went home with his one hundred dollars and sat at the kitchen table. He held his head in his hands and thought about Thomas Builds-the-Fire, remembered little details, tears and scars, the bicycle they shared for a summer, so many stories.

Thomas Builds-the-Fire sat on the bicycle, waiting in Vector's yard. He was ten years old and skinny. His hair was dirty because it was the Fourth of July.

30   "Victor," Thomas yelled. "Hurry up. We're going to miss the fireworks."

After a few minutes, Victor ran out of his family's house, vaulted over the porch railing, and landed gracefully on the sidewalk.

Thomas gave him the bike and they headed for the fireworks. It was nearly dark and the fireworks were about to start.

"You know," Thomas said, "it's strange how us Indians celebrate the Fourth of July. It ain't like it was our independence everybody was fighting for."

"You think about things too much," Victor said. "It's just supposed to be fun. Maybe Junior will be there."

35   "Which Junior? Everybody on this reservation is named Junior."

The fireworks were small, hardly more than a few bottle rockets and a fountain. But it was enough for two Indian boys. Years later, they would need much more.

Afterward, sitting in the dark, fighting off mosquitoes, Victor turned to Thomas Builds-the-Fire.

"Hey," Victor said. "Tell me a story."

Thomas closed his eyes and told this story: "There were these two Indian boys who wanted to be warriors. But it was too late to be warriors in the old way. All the horses were gone. So the two Indian boys stole a car and drove to the city. They parked the stolen car in the front of the police station and then hitchhiked back home to the reservation. When they got back, all their friends cheered and their parents' eyes shone with pride. 'You were very brave,' everybody said to the two Indian boys. 'Very brave.' "

40   "Ya-hey," Victor said. "That's a good one. I wish I could be a warrior."

"Me too." Thomas said.

Victor sat at his kitchen table. He counted his one hundred dollars again and again. He knew he needed more to make it to Phoenix and back. He knew he needed Thomas Builds-the-Fire. So he put his money in his wallet and opened the front door to find Thomas on the porch.

"Ya-hey, Victor," Thomas said. "I knew you'd call me."

Thomas walked into the living room and sat down in Victor's favorite chair.

45 "I've got some money saved up," Thomas said. "It's enough to get us down there, but you have to get us back."

"I've got this hundred dollars," Victor said. "And my dad had a savings account I'm going to claim."

"How much in your dad's account?"

"Enough. A few hundred."

"Sounds good. When we leaving?"

50 When they were fifteen and had long since stopped being friends, Victor and Thomas got into a fistfight. That is, Victor was really drunk and beat Thomas up for no reason at all. All the other Indian boys stood around and watched it happen. Junior was there and so were Lester, Seymour, and a lot of others.

The beating might have gone on until Thomas was dead if Norma Many Horses hadn't come along and stopped it.

"Hey, you boys," Norma yelled and jumped out of her car. "Leave him alone."

If it had been someone else, even another man, the Indian boys would've just ignored the warnings. But Norma was a warrior. She was powerful. She could have picked up any two of the boys and smashed their skulls together. But worse than that, she would have dragged them all over to some tepee and made them listen to some elder tell a dusty old story.

The Indian boys scattered, and Norma walked over to Thomas and picked him up.

55 "Hey, little man, are you O.K.?" she asked.

Thomas gave her a thumbs-up.

"Why they always picking on you?"

Thomas shook his head, closed his eyes, but no stories came to him, no words or music. He just wanted to go home, to lie in his bed and let his dreams tell the stories for him.

Thomas Builds-the-Fire and Victor sat next to each other in the airplane, coach section. A tiny white woman had the window seat. She was busy twisting her body into pretzels. She was flexible.

60 "I have to ask," Thomas said, and Victor closed his eyes in embarrassment.

"Don't," Victor said.

"Excuse me, miss," Thomas asked. "Are you a gymnast or something?"

"There's no something about it," she said. "I was first alternate on the 1980 Olympic team."

"Really?" Thomas asked.

65 "Really."

"I mean, you used to be a world-class athlete?" Thomas asked.

"My husband thinks I still am."

Thomas Builds-the-Fire smiled. She was a mental gymnast too. She pulled her leg straight up against her body so that she could've kissed her kneecap.

"I wish I could do that," Thomas said.

70 Victor was ready to jump out of the plane. Thomas, that crazy Indian storyteller with ratty old braids and broken teeth, was flirting with a beautiful Olympic gymnast. Nobody back home on the reservation would ever believe it.

"Well," the gymnast said. "It's easy. Try it."

Thomas grabbed at his leg and tried to pull it up into the same position as the gymnast's. He couldn't even come close, which made Victor and the gymnast laugh.

"Hey," she asked. "You two are Indian, right?"

"Full-blood," Victor said.

75 "Not me," Thomas said. "I'm half magician on my mother's side and half clown on my father's."

They all laughed.

"What are your names?" she asked.

"Victor and Thomas."

"Mine is Cathy. Pleased to meet you all."

80 The three of them talked for the duration of the flight. Cathy the gymnast complained about the government, how they screwed the 1980 Olympic team by boycotting the games.[1]

"Sounds like you all got a lot in common with Indians," Thomas said.

Nobody laughed.

After the plane landed in Phoenix and they had all found their way to the terminal, Cathy the gymnast smiled and waved goodbye.

"She was really nice," Thomas said.

85 "Yeah, but everybody talks to everybody on airplanes," Victor said.

"You always used to tell me I think too much," Thomas said. "Now it sounds like you do."

"Maybe I caught it from you."

"Yeah."

Thomas and Victor rode in a taxi to the trailer where Victor's father had died.

90 "Listen," Victor said as they stopped in front of the trailer. "I never told you I was sorry for beating you up that time."

"Oh, it was nothing. We were just kids and you were drunk."

"Yeah, but I'm still sorry."

"That's all right."

Victor paid for the taxi, and the two of them stood in the hot Phoenix summer. They could smell the trailer.

95 "This ain't going to be nice," Victor said. "You don't have to go in."

"You're going to need help."

Victor walked to the front door and opened it. The stink rolled out and made them both gag. Victor's father had lain in that trailer for a week in hundred-degree temperatures before anyone had found him. And the only reason anyone found him was the smell. They needed dental records to identify him. That's exactly what the coroner said. They needed dental records.

"Oh, man," Victor said. "I don't know if I can do this."

"Well, then don't."

100 "But there might be something valuable in there."

"I thought his money was in the bank."

"It is. I was talking about pictures and letters and stuff like that."

"Oh," Thomas said as he held his breath and followed Victor into the trailer.

---

[1] To protest the Soviet military action in Afghanistan, sixty-two nations including the United States boycotted the 1980 Olympics held in Moscow.

When Victor was twelve, he stepped into an underground wasps' nest. His foot was caught in the hole and no matter how hard he struggled, Victor couldn't pull free. He might have died there, stung a thousand times, if Thomas Builds-the-Fire had not come by.

105 "Run," Thomas yelled and pulled Victor's foot from the hole. They ran then, hard as they ever had, faster than Billy Mills, faster than Jim Thorpe,[2] faster than the wasps could fly.

Victor and Thomas ran until they couldn't breathe, ran until it was cold and dark outside, ran until they were lost and it took hours to find their way home. All the way back, Victor counted his stings.

"Seven," Victor said. "My lucky number."

Victor didn't find much to keep in the trailer. Only a photo album and a stereo. Everything else had that smell stuck in it or was useless anyway. "I guess this is all," Victor said. "It ain't much."

"Better than nothing," Thomas said.

110 "Yeah, and I do have the pickup."

"Yeah," Thomas said. "It's in good shape."

"Dad was good about that stuff."

"Yeah, I remember your dad."

"Really?" Victor asked. "What do you remember?"

115 Thomas Builds-the-Fire closed his eyes and told this story: "I remember when I had this dream that told me to go to Spokane, to stand by the falls in the middle of the city and wait for a sign. I knew I had to go there but I didn't have a car. Didn't have a license. I was only thirteen. So I walked all the way, took me all day, and I finally made it to the falls. I stood there for an hour waiting. Then your dad came walking up. 'What the hell are you doing here?' he asked me. I said, 'Waiting for a vision.' Then your father said, 'All you're going to get here is mugged.' So he drove me over to Denny's bought me dinner, and then drove me home to the reservation. For a long time, I was mad because I thought my dreams had lied to me. But they hadn't. Your dad was my vision. *Take care of each other* is what my dreams were saying. *Take care of each other.*"

Victor was quiet for a long time. He searched his mind for memories of his father, found the good ones, found a few bad ones, added it all up, and smiled.

"My father never told me about finding you in Spokane," Victor said.

"He said he wouldn't tell anybody. Didn't want me to get in trouble. But he said I had to watch out for you as part of the deal."

"Really?"

120 "Really. Your father said you would need the help. He was right."

"That's why you came down here with me, isn't it?" Victor asked.

"I came because of your father."

Victor and Thomas climbed into the pickup, drove over to the bank, and claimed the three hundred dollars in the savings account.

Thomas Builds-the-Fire could fly.

125 Once, he jumped off the roof of the tribal school and flapped his arms like a crazy eagle. And he flew. For a second he hovered, suspended above all the other Indian boys, who were too smart or too scared to jump too.

---

[2] U.S. athletes who were Native American.

"He's flying," Junior yelled, and Seymour was busy looking for the trick wires or mirrors. But it was real. As real as the dirt when Thomas lost altitude and crashed to the ground.

He broke his arm in two places.

"He broke his wing, he broke his wing, he broke his wing," all the Indian boys chanted as they ran off, flapping their wings, wishing they could fly too. They hated Thomas for his courage, his brief moment as a bird. Everybody has dreams about flying. Thomas flew.

One of his dreams came true for just a second, just enough to make it real.

130 Victor's father, his ashes, fit in one wooden box with enough left over to fill a cardboard box.

"He always was a big man," Thomas said.

Victor carried part of his father out to the pickup, and Thomas carried the rest. They set him down carefully behind the seats, put a cowboy hat on the wooden box and a Dodgers cap on the cardboard box. That was the way it was supposed to be.

"Ready to head back home?" Victor asked.

"It's going to be a long drive."

135 "Yeah, take a couple days, maybe."

"We can take turns," Thomas said.

"O.K.," Victor said, but they didn't take turns. Victor drove for sixteen hours straight north, made it halfway up Nevada toward home before he finally pulled over.

"Hey, Thomas," Victor said. "You got to drive for a while."

"O.K."

140 Thomas Builds-the-Fire slid behind the wheel and started off down the road. All through Nevada, Thomas and Victor had been amazed at the lack of animal life, at the absence of water, of movement.

"Where is everything?" Victor had asked more than once.

Now, when Thomas was finally driving, they saw the first animal, maybe the only animal in Nevada. It was a long-eared jackrabbit.

"Look," Victor yelled. "It's alive."

Thomas and Victor were busy congratulating themselves on their discovery when the jackrabbit darted out into the road and under the wheels of the pickup.

145 "Stop the goddamn car," Victor yelled, and Thomas did stop and backed the pickup to the dead jackrabbit.

"Oh, man, he's dead," Victor said as he looked at the squashed animal.

"Really dead."

"The only thing alive in this whole state and we just killed it."

"I don't know," Thomas said. "I think it was suicide."

150 Victor looked around the desert, sniffed the air, felt the emptiness and loneliness, and nodded his head.

"Yeah," Victor said. "It had to be suicide."

"I can't believe this," Thomas said. "You drive for a thousand miles and there ain't even any bugs smashed on the windshield. I drive for ten seconds and kill the only living thing in Nevada."

"Yeah," Victor said. "Maybe I should drive."

"Maybe you should."

155 Thomas Builds-the-Fire walked through the corridors of the tribal school by himself. Nobody wanted to be anywhere near him because of all those stories. Story after story.

Thomas closed his eyes and this story came to him: "We are all given one thing by which our lives are measured, one determination. Mine are the stories that can change or not change the world. It doesn't matter which, as long as I continue to tell the stories. My father, he died on Okinawa in World War II,[3] died fighting for this country, which had tried to kill him for years. My mother, she died giving birth to me, died while I was still inside her: She pushed me out into the world with her last breath. I have no brothers or sisters. I have only my stories, which came to me before I even had the words to speak. I learned a thousand stories before I took my first thousand steps. They are all I have. It's all I can do."

Thomas Builds-the-Fire told his stories to all those who would stop and listen. He kept telling them long after people had stopped listening.

Victor and Thomas made it back to the reservation just as the sun was rising. It was the beginning of a new day on earth, but the same old shit on the reservation.

"Good morning," Thomas said.

160   "Good morning."

The tribe was waking up, ready for work, eating breakfast, reading the newspaper, just like everybody else does. Willene LeBret was out in her garden, wearing a bathrobe. She waved when Thomas and Victor drove by.

"Crazy Indians made it," she said to herself and went back to her roses.

Victor stopped the pickup in front of Thomas Build-the-Fire's HUD house. They both yawned, stretched a little, shook dust from their bodies.

"I'm tired," Victor said.

165   "Of everything," Thomas added.

They both searched for words to end the journey. Victor needed to thank Thomas for his help and for the money, and to make the promise to pay it all back.

"Don't worry about the money," Thomas said. "It don't make any difference anyhow."

"Probably not, enit?"

"Nope."

170   Victor knew that Thomas would remain the crazy storyteller who talked to dogs and cars, who listened to the wind and pine trees. Victor knew that he couldn't really be friends with Thomas, even after all that had happened. It was cruel but it was real. As real as the ash, as Victor's father, sitting behind the seats.

"I know how it is," Thomas said. "I know you ain't going to treat me any better than you did before. I know your friends would give you too much shit about it."

Victor was ashamed of himself. Whatever happened to the tribal ties, the sense of community? The only real thing he shared with anybody was a bottle and broken dreams. He owed Thomas something, anything.

"Listen," Victor said and handed Thomas the cardboard box that contained half of his father. "I want you to have this."

Thomas took the ashes and smiled, closed his eyes, and told this story: "I'm going to travel to Spokane Falls one last time and toss these ashes into the water. And your father will rise like a salmon, leap over the bridge, over me, and find his way home. It will be beautiful. His teeth will shine like silver, like a rainbow. He will rise, Victor, he will rise."

175   Victor smiled.

"I was planning on doing the same thing with my half," Victor said. "But I didn't imaging my father looking anything like a salmon. I thought it'd be like cleaning the attic or something. Like letting things go after they've stopped having any use."

"Nothing stops, cousin," Thomas said. "Nothing stops."

---

[3] Okinawa, one of the largest of the Ryukyu Islands, occupied by U.S. forces 1945–72 and returned to Japan in 1972.

Thomas Builds-the-Fire got out of the pickup and walked up his driveway. Victor started the pickup and began the drive home.

"Wait," Thomas yelled suddenly from his porch. "I just got to ask one favor."

180 Victor stopped the pickup, leaned out the window, and shouted back.

"What do you want?" he asked.

"Just one time when I'm telling a story somewhere, why don't you stop and listen?" Thomas asked.

"Just once?"

"Just once."

185 Victor waved his arms to let Thomas know that the deal was good. It was a fair trade. That's all Thomas had ever wanted from his whole life. So Victor drove his father's pickup toward home while Thomas went into his house, closed the door behind him, and heard a new story come to him in the silence afterward.

■ EXPLORATIONS OF THE TEXT

1. How do the settings—real and imagined—create the context, atmosphere, and mood of the story (i.e., the Indian reservation; the plane; the trailer in Phoenix, Arizona; the desert in Nevada; and the falls in Spokane)?

2. Analyze Thomas's and Victor's characters. Why weren't they friends in childhood? How do they differ?

3. Discuss the stages of the journey. What do the two protagonists learn by the end of the trip? How does the gymnast function as a character foil?

4. Interpret the symbolism of the falls in Spokane and of Thomas's dream.

5. Explore the significance of storytelling as a motif in the story.

6. Are the flashbacks and dream sequences an effective means of exposition? Does the structure of the story work?

7. Compare the views of heritage presented in this work with those ideas expressed in "Heritage" and "The Idea of Ancestry."

8. Compare the father-son relationships in "My Father's Song," "Persimmons," "Digging," and this work.

■ THE READING/WRITING CONNECTION

1. List questions that you have about this story. After class discussion of the work, return to your questions and answer one of them.

2. Freewrite about your initial impression of the work. After class discussion, write a second freewrite. Compare your first and final impressions. How have your views of the work changed?

3. "Think" Topic: Who is the true "warrior"—Victor or Thomas?

4. Journal Entry: Read this poetic excerpt from the film script for Smoke Signals—Sherman Alexie's film adaptation of this story—then answer this question: "Do we forgive our fathers?" You may substitute "mothers" for "fathers." Respond.

> Do we forgive our fathers for leaving us too often or
> forever when we were little? Maybe for scaring us with
> unexpected rage or making us nervous because there never
> seemed to be any rage there at all?
>
> Do we forgive our fathers for marrying or not marrying
> our mother? For divorcing or not divorcing our mothers?
> And shall we forgive them for their excesses of warmth or
> coldness?

Shall we forgive them for pushing or leaning? For shutting
doors? For speaking only through layers of cloth, or never
speaking, or never being silent?

Do we forgive our fathers in our age or in theirs? Or in
their deaths? Saying it to them or not saying it? If we
forgive our fathers what is left?

■ **IDEAS FOR WRITING**
1. Connect themes of the poem with those of the story.
2. Watch *Smoke Signals*. Compare the story and the film. Or compare the poetic excerpt
    (which is the conclusion of the script) with the story's ending. Which has more
    power—the written or visual form?

Amy Tan

*Amy Tan (1952–   ) was born in Oakland, California, shortly after her parents immigrated to the
United States from China. She was educated at San Francisco State University and San Jose University. In 1989, she published her first book of fiction,* The Joy Luck Club. *Her work includes
several novels,* The Kitchen God's Wife *(1991),* The Hundred Secret Senses *(1996), and* The
Bonesetter's Daughter *(2001), and a collection of essays,* The Opposite of Fate: A Book of
Musings *(2003). In her work, Tan explores her Chinese heritage and the relationships between
generations, especially those between Chinese immigrants to America and their children.*

1989

SCAR

From *The Joy Luck Club*

When I was a young girl in China, my grandmother told me my mother was a ghost.
This did not mean my mother was dead. In those days, a ghost was anything we
were forbidden to talk about. So I knew Popo wanted me to forget my mother on purpose,
and this is how I came to remember nothing of her. The life that I knew began in the large
house in Ningpo with the cold hallways and tall stairs. This was my uncle and auntie's family house, where I lived with Popo and my little brother.

But I often heard stories of a ghost who tried to take children away, especially strong-
willed little girls who were disobedient. Many times Popo said aloud to all who could hear
that my brother and I had fallen out of the bowels of a stupid goose, two eggs that nobody
wanted, not even good enough to crack over rice porridge. She said this so that the ghosts
would not steal us away. So you see, to Popo we were also very precious.

All my life, Popo scared me. I became even more scared when she grew sick. This was
in 1923, when I was nine years old. Popo had swollen up like an overripe squash, so full
her flesh had gone soft and rotten with a bad smell. She would call me into her room with
the terrible stink and tell me stories. "An-mei," she said, calling me by my school name.
"Listen carefully." She told me stories I could not understand.

One was about a greedy girl whose belly grew fatter and fatter. This girl poisoned herself after refusing to say whose child she carried. When the monks cut open her body, they
found inside a large white winter melon.

5   "If you are greedy, what is inside you is what makes you always hungry," said Popo.

    Another time, Popo told me about a girl who refused to listen to her elders. One day this bad girl shook her head so vigorously to refuse her auntie's simple request that a little white ball fell from her ear and out poured all her brains, as clear as chicken broth.

    "Your own thoughts are so busy swimming inside that everything else gets pushed out," Popo told me.

    Right before Popo became so sick she could no longer speak, she pulled me close and talked to me about my mother. "Never say her name," she warned. "To say her name is to spit on your father's grave."

    The only father I knew was a big painting that hung in the main hall. He was a large, unsmiling man, unhappy to be so still on the wall. His restless eyes followed me around the house. Even from my room at the end of the hall, I could see my father's watching eyes. Popo said he watched me for any signs of disrespect. So sometimes, when I had thrown pebbles at other children at school, or had lost a book through carelessness, I would quickly walk by my father with a know-nothing look and hide in a corner of my room where he could not see my face.

10   I felt our house was so unhappy, but my little brother did not seem to think so. He rode his bicycle through the courtyard, chasing chickens and other children, laughing over which ones shrieked the loudest. Inside the quiet house, he jumped up and down on Uncle and Auntie's best feather sofas when they were away visiting village friends.

    But even my brother's happiness went away. One hot summer day when Popo was already very sick, we stood outside watching a village funeral procession marching by our courtyard. Just as it passed our gate, the heavy framed picture of the dead man toppled from its stand and fell to the dusty ground. An old lady screamed and fainted. My brother laughed and Auntie slapped him.

    My auntie, who had a very bad temper with children, told him he had no *shou,* no respect for ancestors or family, just like our mother. Auntie had a tongue like hungry scissors eating silk cloth. So when my brother gave her a sour look, Auntie said our mother was so thoughtless she had fled north in a big hurry, without taking the dowry furniture from her marriage to my father, without bringing her ten pairs of silver chopsticks, without paying respect to my father's grave and those of our ancestors. When my brother accused Auntie of frightening our mother away, Auntie shouted that our mother had married a man named Wu Tsing who already had a wife, two concubines, and other bad children.

    And when my brother shouted that Auntie was a talking chicken without a head, she pushed my brother against the gate and spat on his face.

    "You throw strong words at me, but you are nothing," Auntie said. "You are the son of a mother who has so little respect she has become *ni,* a traitor to our ancestors. She is so beneath others that even the devil must look down to see her."

15   That is when I began to understand the stories Popo taught me, the lessons I had to learn for my mother. "When you lose your face, An-mei," Popo often said, "it is like dropping your necklace down a well. The only way you can get it back is to fall in after it."

    Now I could imagine my mother, a thoughtless woman who laughed and shook her head, who dipped her chopsticks many times to eat another piece of sweet fruit, happy to be free of Popo, her unhappy husband on the wall, and her two disobedient children. I felt unlucky that she was my mother and unlucky that she had left us. These were the thoughts I had while hiding in the corner of my room where my father could not watch me.

I was sitting at the top of the stairs when she arrived. I knew it was my mother even though I had not seen her in all my memory. She stood just inside the doorway so that her face became a dark shadow. She was much taller than my auntie, almost as tall as my uncle. She looked strange, too, like the missionary ladies at our school who were insolent and bossy in their too-tall shoes, foreign clothes, and short hair.

My auntie quickly looked away and did not call her by name or offer her tea. An old servant hurried away with a displeased look. I tried to keep very still, but my heart felt like crickets scratching to get out of a cage. My mother must have heard, because she looked up. And when she did, I saw my own face looking back at me. Eyes that stayed wide open and saw too much.

In Popo's room my auntie protested, "Too late, too late," as my mother approached the bed. But this did not stop my mother.

20   "Come back, stay here," murmured my mother to Popo. "*Nuyer* is here. Your daughter is back." Popo's eyes were open, but now her mind ran in many different directions, not staying long enough to see anything. If Popo's mind had been clear she would have raised her two arms and flung my mother out of the room.

I watched my mother, seeing her for the first time, this pretty woman with her white skin and oval face, not too round like Auntie's or sharp like Popo's. I saw that she had a long white neck, just like the goose that had laid me. That she seemed to float back and forth like a ghost, dipping cool cloths to lay on Popo's bloated face. As she peered into Popo's eyes, she clucked soft worried sounds. I watched her carefully, yet it was her voice that confused me, a familiar sound from a forgotten dream.

When I returned to my room later that afternoon, she was there, standing tall. And because I remember Popo told me not to speak her name, I stood there, mute. She took my hand and led me to the settee. And then she also sat down as though we had done this every day.

My mother began to loosen my braids and brush my hair with long sweeping strokes.

"An-mei, you have been a good daughter?" she asked, smiling a secret look.

25   I looked at her with my know-nothing face, but inside I was trembling. I was the girl whose belly held a colorless winter melon.

"An-mei, you know who I am," she said with a small scold in her voice. This time I did not look for fear my head would burst and my brains would dribble out of my ears.

She stopped brushing. And then I could feel her long smooth fingers rubbing and searching under my chin, finding the spot that was my smooth-neck scar. As she rubbed this spot, I became very still. It was as though she were rubbing the memory back into my skin. And then her hand dropped and she began to cry, wrapping her hands around her own neck. She cried with a wailing voice that was so sad. And then I remembered the dream with my mother's voice.

I was four years old. My chin was just above the dinner table, and I could see my baby brother sitting on Popo's lap, crying with an angry face. I could hear voices praising a steaming dark soup brought to the table, voices murmuring politely, "*Ching! Ching!*"—Please, eat!

And then the talking stopped. My uncle rose from his chair. Everyone turned to look at the door, where a tall woman stood. I was the only one who spoke.

30   "Ma," I had cried, rushing off my chair, but my auntie slapped my face and pushed me back down. Now everyone was standing up and shouting, and I heard my mother's voice crying, "An-mei! An-mei!" Above this noise, Popo's shrill voice spoke.

"Who is this ghost? Not an honored widow. Just a number-three concubine. If you take your daughter, she will become like you. No face. Never able to lift up her head."

Still my mother shouted for me to come. I remember her voice so clearly now. An-mei! An-mei! I could see my mother's face across the table. Between us stood the soup pot on its heavy chimney-pot stand—rocking slowly, back and forth. And then with one shout this dark boiling soup spilled forward and fell all over my neck. It was as though everyone's anger were pouring all over me.

This was the kind of pain so terrible that a little child should never remember it. But it is still in my skin's memory. I cried out loud only a little, because soon my flesh began to burst inside and out and cut off my breathing air.

I could not speak because of this terrible choking feeling. I could not see because of all the tears that poured out to wash away the pain. But I could hear my mother's crying voice. Popo and Auntie were shouting. And then my mother's voice went away.

35 Later that night Popo's voice came to me.

"An-mei, listen carefully." Her voice had the same scolding tone she used when I ran up and down the hallway. "An-mei, we have made your dying clothes and shoes for you. They are all white cotton."

I listened, scared.

"An-mei," she murmured, now more gently. "Your dying clothes are very plain. They are not fancy, because you are still a child. If you die, you will have a short life and you will still owe your family a debt. Your funeral will be very small. Our mourning time for you will be very short."

And then Popo said something that was worse than the burning on my neck.

40 "Even your mother has used up her tears and left. If you do not get well soon, she will forget you."

Popo was very smart. I came hurrying back from the other world to find my mother.

Every night I cried so that both my eyes and my neck burned. Next to my bed sat Popo. She would pour cool water over my neck from the hollowed cup of a large grapefruit. She would pour and pour until my breathing became soft and I could fall asleep. In the morning, Popo would use her sharp fingernails like tweezers and peel off the dead membranes.

In two years' time, my scar became pale and shiny and I had no memory of my mother. That is the way it is with a wound. The wound begins to close in on itself, to protect what is hurting so much. And once it is closed, you no longer see what is underneath, what started the pain.

I worshipped this mother from my dream. But the woman standing by Popo's bed was not the mother of my memory. Yet I came to love this mother as well. Not because she came to me and begged me to forgive her. She did not. She did not need to explain that Popo chased her out of the house when I was dying. This I knew. She did not need to tell me she married Wu Tsing to exchange one unhappiness for another. I knew this as well.

45 Here is how I came to love my mother. How I saw in her my own true nature. What was beneath my skin. Inside my bones.

It was late at night when I went to Popo's room. My auntie said it was Popo's dying time and I must show respect. I put on a clean dress and stood between my auntie and uncle at the foot of Popo's bed. I cried a little, not too loud.

I saw my mother on the other side of the room. Quiet and sad. She was cooking a soup, pouring herbs and medicines into the steaming pot. And then I saw her pull up her sleeve and pull out a sharp knife. She put this knife on the softest part of her arm. I tried to close my eyes, but could not.

And then my mother cut a piece of meat from her arm. Tears poured from her face and blood spilled to the floor.

My mother took her flesh and put it in the soup. She cooked magic in the ancient tradition to try to cure her mother this one last time. She opened Popo's mouth, already too tight from trying to keep her spirit in. She fed her this soup, but that night Popo flew away with her illness.

50   Even though I was young, I could see the pain of the flesh and the worth of the pain.
This is how a daughter honors her mother. It is *shou* so deep it is in your bones. The
pain of the flesh is nothing. The pain you must forget. Because sometimes that is the only
way to remember what is in your bones. You must peel off your skin, and that of your
mother, and her mother before her. Until there is nothing. No scar, no skin, no flesh.

■ **EXPLORATIONS OF THE TEXT**

1. Why is An-Mei Hsu's mother considered a "ghost" by the family? Why is she a "ghost"
    to the little girl?
2. Why does Popo tell the child scary stories?
3. What are An-Mei's feelings about her father? Explain the symbolism of the portrait.
4. What motivates Auntie's behavior? What effect do her actions have on An-Mei and on
    her brother?
5. What are the connotations of "luck" in this story?
6. Does An-Mei feel that her mother loves her when her mother returns?
7. What are the symbolic implications of the scenes in which An-Mei becomes sick be-
    cause the soup spilled and in which An-Mei's mother cuts her own flesh and puts it
    into the soup for her mother, Popo?

■ **THE READING/WRITING CONNECTION**

1. "Think" Topic: What is the importance of the scar? Discuss the meaning of this passage:
    "In two years' time, my scar became pale and shiny and I had no memory of my
    mother. That is the way it is with a wound. The wound begins to close in on itself, to
    protect what is hurting so much. And once it is closed, you no longer see what is un-
    derneath, what started the pain."
2. What does the closing paragraph reveal? What is meant by "You must peel off your
    skin, and that of your mother, and her mother before her. Until there is nothing. No
    scar, no skin, no flesh"? Create a double-entry for the ending of the work.

■ **IDEAS FOR WRITING**

1. What does "Scar" imply about the relationships between parents and children in Chi-
    nese society? How are children supposed to behave? What values are important?
2. Explore the theme of intense connectedness between mothers and their daughters in
    "Girl," "Ruth's Song," and/or "Scar."
3. Explore the theme of loss between parents and children in "Scar," "Elena," "Persim-
    mons," "Daddy," and/or "Ruth's Song."
4. What do images or dreams suggest about the hold of the past in "Scar," "This Is What It
    Means to say Phoenix, Arizona," "Making the Jam Without You," and/or "Ruth's Song"?

LOUISE ERDRICH   **2001**

THE SHAWL

Among the Anishinaabeg on the road where I live, it is told how a woman loved a man
other than her husband and went off into the bush and bore his child. Her name was
Aanakwad, which means cloud, and like a cloud she was changeable. She was moody and
sullen one moment, her lower lip jutting and her eyes flashing, filled with storms. The next,
she would shake her hair over her face and blow it straight out in front of her to make her
children scream with laughter. For she also had two children by her husband, one a yearning boy of five years and the other a capable daughter of nine.

When Aanakwad brought the new baby out of the trees that autumn, the older girl was like a second mother, even waking in the night to clean the baby and nudge it to her mother's breast. Aanakwad slept through its cries, hardly woke. It wasn't that she didn't love her baby; no, it was the opposite—she loved it too much, the way she loved its father, and not her husband. This passion ate away at her, and her feelings were unbearable. If she could have thrown off that wronghearted love, she would have, but the thought of the other man, who lived across the lake, was with her always. She became a gray sky, stared monotonously at the walls, sometimes wept into her hands for hours at a time. Soon, she couldn't rise to cook or keep the cabin neat, and it was too much for the girl, who curled up each night exhausted in her red-and-brown plaid shawl, and slept and slept, until the husband had to wake her to awaken her mother, for he was afraid of his wife's bad temper, and it was he who roused Aanakwad into anger by the sheer fact that he was himself and not the other.

At last, even though he loved Aanakwad, the husband had to admit that their life together was no good anymore. And it was he who sent for the other man's uncle. In those days, our people lived widely scattered, along the shores and in the islands, even out on the plains. There were no roads then, just trails, though we had horses and wagons and, for the winter, sleds. When the uncle came around to fetch Aanakwad, in his wagon fitted out with sled runners, it was very hard, for she and her husband had argued right up to the last about the children, argued fiercely until the husband had finally given in. He turned his face to the wall, and did not move to see the daughter, whom he treasured, sit down beside her mother, wrapped in her plaid robe in the wagon bed. They left right away, with their bundles and sacks, not bothering to heat up the stones to warm their feet. The father had stopped his ears, so he did not hear his son cry out when he suddenly understood that he would be left behind.

As the uncle slapped the reins and the horse lurched forward, the boy tried to jump into the wagon, but his mother pried his hands off the boards, crying, *Gego.gego,* and he fell down hard. But there was something in him that would not let her leave. He jumped up and, although he was wearing only light clothing, he ran behind the wagon over the packed drifts. The horses picked up speed. His chest was scorched with pain, and yet he pushed himself on. He'd never run so fast, so hard and furiously, but he was determined, and he refused to believe that the increasing distance between him and the wagon was real. He kept going until his throat closed, he saw red, and in the ice of the air his lungs shut. Then, as he fell onto the board-hard snow, he raised his head. He watched the back of the wagon and the tiny figures of his mother and sister disappear, and something failed in him. Something broke. At that moment he truly did not care if he was alive or dead. So when he saw the gray shapes, the shadows, bounding lightly from the trees to either side of the trail, far ahead, he was not afraid.

5   The next the boy knew, his father had him wrapped on a blanket and was carrying him home. His father's chest was broad and, although he already spat the tubercular blood that would write the end of his story, he was still a strong man. It would take him many years to die. In those years, the father would tell the boy, who had forgotten this part entirely, that at first when he talked about the shadows the father thought he'd been visited by *manidoog.* But then, as the boy described the shapes, his father had understood that they were not spirits. Uneasy, he had decided to take his gun back along the trail. He had built up the fire in the cabin, and settled his boy near it, and gone back out into the snow. Perhaps the story spread through our settlements because the father had to tell what he saw, again and again, in order to get rid of it. Perhaps as with all frightful dreams, *amaniso,* he had to talk about it to destroy its power—though in this case nothing could stop the dream from being real.

The shadows' tracks were the tracks of wolves, and in those days, when our guns had taken all their food for furs and hides to sell, the wolves were bold and had abandoned the old agreement between them and the first humans. For a time, until we understood and let the game increase, the wolves hunted us. The father bounded forward when he saw the tracks. He could see where the pack, desperate, had tried to slash the tendons of the horses' legs. Next, where they'd leaped for the back of the wagon. He hurried on to where the trail gave out at the broad empty ice of the lake. There, he saw what he saw, scattered, and the ravens, attending to the bitter small leavings of the wolves.

For a time, the boy had no understanding of what had happened. His father kept what he knew to himself, at least that first year, and when his son asked about his sister's torn plaid shawl, and why it was kept in the house, his father said nothing. But he wept when the boy asked if his sister was cold. It was only after his father had been weakened by the disease that he began to tell the story, far too often and always the same way: he told how when the wolves closed in Aanakwad had thrown her daughter to them.

When his father said those words, the boy went still. What had his sister felt? What had thrust through her heart? Had something broken inside her, too, as it had in him? Even then, he knew that this broken place inside him would not be mended, except by some terrible means. For he kept seeing his mother put the baby down and grip his sister around the waist. He saw Aanakwad swing the girl lightly out over the side of the wagon. He saw the brown shawl with its red lines flying open. He saw the shadows, the wolves, rush together, quick and avid, as the wagon with sled runners disappeared into the distance—forever, for neither he nor his father saw Aanakwad again.

When I was little, my own father terrified us with his drinking. This was after we lost our mother, because before that the only time I was aware that he touched the *ishkode waaboo* was on an occasional weekend when they got home late, or sometimes during berry-picking gatherings when we went out to the bush and camped with others. Not until she died did he start the heavy sort of drinking, the continuous drinking, where we were left alone in the house for days. The kind where, when he came home, we'd jump out the window and hide in the woods while he barged around, shouting for us. We'd go back only after he had fallen dead asleep.

10 There were three of us: me, the oldest at ten, and my little sister and brother, twins, and only six years old. I was surprisingly good at taking care of them, I think, and because we learned to survive together during those drinking years we have always been close, Their names are Doris and Raymond, and they married a brother and sister. When we get together, which is often, for we live on the same road, there come times in the talking and card-playing, and maybe even in the light beer now and then, when we will bring up those days. Most people understand how it was. Our story isn't uncommon. But for us it helps to compare our points of view.

How else would I know, for instance, that Raymond saw me the first time I hid my father's belt? I pulled it from around his waist while he was passed out, and then I buried it in the woods. I kept doing it after that. Our father couldn't understand why his belt was always stolen when he went to town drinking. He even accused his *shkwebii* buddies of the theft. But I had good reasons. Not only was he embarrassed, afterward, to go out with his pants held up by rope, but he couldn't snake his belt out in anger and snap the hooked buckle end in the air. He couldn't hit us with it. Of course, being resourceful, he used other things. There was a board. A willow wand. And there was himself—his hands and fists and boots—and things he could throw. But eventually it became easy to evade him, and after a while we rarely suffered a bruise or a scratch. We had our own place in the woods, even a little campfire for the cold nights. And we'd take money from him every chance we got, slip it from his shoe, where he thought it well hidden. He became, for us, a thing to be avoided, outsmarted, and exploited. We survived off him as if he were a capricious and dangerous line of work. I suppose we stopped thinking of him as a human being, certainly as a father.

I got my growth earlier than some boys, and, one night when I was thirteen and Doris and Raymond and I were sitting around wishing for something besides the oatmeal and commodity canned milk I'd stashed so he couldn't sell them, I heard him coming down the road. He was shouting and making noise all the way to the house, and Doris and Raymond looked at me and headed for the back window. When they saw that I wasn't coming, they stopped. C'mon, *ondaas,* get with it—they tried to pull me along. I shook them off and told them to get out quickly—I was staying. I think I can take him now is what I said.

He was big; he hadn't yet wasted away from the alcohol. His nose had been pushed to one side in a fight, then slammed back to the other side, so now it was straight. His teeth were half gone, and he smelled the way he had to smell, being five days drunk. When he came in the door, he paused for a moment, his eyes red and swollen, tiny slits. Then he saw that I was waiting for him, and he smiled in a bad way. My first punch surprised him. I had been practicing on a hay-stuffed bag, then on a padded board, toughening my fists, and I'd got so quick I flickered like fire. I still wasn't as strong as he was, and he had a good twenty pounds on me. Yet I'd do some damage, I was sure of it. I'd teach him not to mess with me. What I didn't foresee was how the fight itself would get right into me.

There is something terrible about fighting your father. It came on suddenly, with the second blow—a frightful kind of joy. A power surged up from the center of me, and I danced at him, light and giddy, full of a heady rightness. Here is the thing: I wanted to waste him, waste him good. I wanted to smack the living shit out of him. Kill him, if I must. A punch for Doris, a kick for Raymond. And all the while I was silent, then screaming, then silent again, in this rage of happiness that filled me with a simultaneous despair so that, I guess you could say, I stood apart from myself.

15   He came at me, crashed over a chair that was already broken, then threw the pieces. I grabbed one of the legs and whacked him on the ear so that his head spun and turned back to me, bloody, I watched myself striking him again and again. I knew what I was doing, but not really, not in the ordinary sense. It was as if I were standing calm, against the wall with my arms folded, pitying us both. I saw the boy, the chair leg, the man fold and fall, his hands held up in begging fashion. Then I also saw that, for a while now, the bigger man had not even bothered to fight back.

Suddenly, he was my father again. And when I knelt down next to him, I was his son. I reached for the closest rag, and picked up this piece of blanket that my father always kept with him for some reason. And as I picked it up and wiped the blood off his face, I said to him. Your nose is crooked again. He looked at me, steady and quizzical, as though he had never had a drink in his life, and I wiped his face again with that frayed piece of blanket. Well, it was a shawl, really, a kind of old-fashioned woman's blanket-shawl. Once, maybe, it had been plaid. You could still see lines, some red, the background a faded brown. He watched intently as my hand brought the rag to his face. I was pretty sure, then, that I'd clocked him too hard, that he'd really lost it now. Gently, though, he clasped one hand around my wrist. With the other hand he took the shawl. He crumpled it and held it to the middle of his forehead. It was as if he were praying, as if he were having thoughts he wanted to collect in that piece of cloth. For a while he lay like that, and I, crouched over, let him be, hardly breathing. Something told me to sit there, still. And then at last he said to me, in the sober new voice I would hear from then on, *Did you know I had a sister once?*

There was a time when the government moved everybody off the farthest reaches of the reservation, onto roads, into towns, into housing. It looked good at first, and then it all went sour. Shortly afterward, it seemed that anyone who was someone was either drunk, killed, near suicide, or had just dusted himself. None of the old sort were left, it seemed—the old kind of people, the Geteanishinaabeg, who are kind beyond kindness and would do anything for others. It was during that time that my mother died and my father hurt us, as I have said.

Now, gradually, that term of despair has lifted somewhat and yielded up its survivors. But we still have sorrows that are passed to us from early generations, sorrows to handle in addition to our own, and cruelties lodged where we cannot forget them. We have the need to forget. We are always walking on oblivion's edge.

Some get away, like my brother and sister, married now and living quietly down the road. And me, to some degree, though I prefer to live alone. And even my father, who recently found a woman. Once, when he brought up the old days, and we went over the story again, I told him at last the two things I had been thinking.

20   First, I told him that keeping his sister's shawl was wrong, because we never keep the clothing of the dead. Now's the time to burn it, I said. Send it off to cloak her spirit. And he agreed.

The other thing I said to him was in the form of a question. Have you ever considered, I asked him, given how tenderhearted your sister was, and how brave, that she looked at the whole situation? She saw that the wolves were only hungry. She knew that their need was only need. She knew that you were back there, alone in the snow. She understood that the baby she loved would not live without a mother, and that only the uncle knew the way. She saw clearly that one person on the wagon had to be offered up, or they all would die. And in that moment of knowledge, don't you think, being who she was, of the old sort of Anishinaabeg, who thinks of the good of the people first, she jumped, my father, *n'dede,* brother to that little girl? Don't you think she lifted her shawl and flew?

■ EXPLORATIONS OF THE TEXT

1. Why does Erdrich begin the story with the Anishinaabeg tale? How does the tale relate to the narrator's life story? Discuss the symbolism of the wolves.
2. Analyze the narrator's role in the family. How does he differ from his brother and his sister? Characterize the children's relationship with their father.
3. How does the power dynamic, the relationship between father and son, shift in the climactic scene of the narrator's confrontation with his father? What do the descriptive details of the fight suggest about their relationship?
4. What does the father reveal about his past life? Interpret the symbolism of the shawl.
5. How does the talk-story relate to the fate of the narrator's family?
6. Consider the theme of generational legacies in the story. How does the narrator retell both the Anishinaabeg tale and his father's story? How does it continue the life of the tribe?
7. Explore the concept of bearing witness in this work and in hooks's autobiographical narrative.

■ THE READING/WRITING CONNECTION

1. Freewrite about a treasured object from your childhood. What does it signify in your life?
2. "Think" Topic: Compare the symbolism of wolves in this work with Carter's "The Company of Wolves" (chapter 4).
3. Journal Entry: Write about a family story that has been handed down from one generation to the next, or write about an incident from the past. Ask several family members to relate the same event. How do their versions differ? What do you conclude?

■ IDEAS FOR WRITING

1. In an essay entitled, "Language and Literature from a Pueblo Indian Perspective," Leslie Silko suggests that storytelling is vital to the survival of a community. How does this vision of talk-story apply to Erdrich's "The Shawl"? To Hongo's "Kubota"? To Silko's "Yellow Woman" (chapter 6)? To Kingston's "No Name Woman" (chapter 6)?
2. Compare and contrast the symbolism of the shawl in this work with that of Ozick's "The Shawl" (chapter 7).

Stories for Comparison/Contrast: Alienation in Families

DAN CHAON (1964–)   **1995**

FITTING ENDS

There is a story about my brother Del that appears in a book called *More True Tales of the Weird and Supernatural.* The piece on Del is about three pages long, full of exclamation points and supposedly eerie descriptions. It is based on what the writer calls "true facts."

The writer spends much of the first few paragraphs setting the scene, trying to make it sound spooky. "The tiny, isolated village of Pyramid, Nebraska," is what the author calls the place where I grew up. I had never thought of it as a village. It wasn't much of anything, really—it wasn't even on the map, and hadn't been since my father was a boy, when it was a stop on the Union Pacific railroad line. Back then, there was a shantytown for the railroad workers, a dance hall, a general store, a post office. By the time I was growing up, all that was left was a cluster of mostly boarded-up, rundown houses. My family—my parents and grandparents and my brother and I—lived in the only occupied buildings. There was a grain elevator, which my grandfather had run until he retired and my father took over. PYRAMID was painted in peeling block letters on one of the silos.

The man who wrote the story got fixated on that elevator. He talks of it as "a menacing, hulking structure"and says it is like "Childe Roland's ancient dark tower, presiding over the barren fields and empty, sentient houses." He even goes so far as to mention "the soundless flutter of bats flying in and out of the single eyelike window at the top of the elevator" and "the distant, melancholy calls of coyotes from the hills beyond," which are then drowned out by "the strange echoing moan of a freight train as it passes in the night."

There really are bats, of course; you find them in every country place. Personally, I never heard coyotes, though it is true they were around. I saw one once when I was about twelve. I was staring from my bedroom window late one night and there he was. He had come down from the hills and was crouched in our yard, licking drops of water off the propeller of the sprinkler. As for the trains, they passed through about every half-hour, day and night. If you lived there, you didn't even hear them—or maybe only half-heard them, the way, now that I live in a town, I might vaguely notice the bells of the nearby Catholic church at noon.

5   But anyway, this is how the writer sets things up. Then he begins to tell about some of the train engineers, how they dreaded passing through this particular stretch. He quotes one man as saying he got goose bumps every time he started to come up on Pyramid. "There was just something about that place," says this man. There were a few bad accidents at the crossing—a carload of drunken teenagers who tried to beat the train, an old guy who had a heart attack as his pickup bumped across the tracks. That sort of thing. Actually, this happens anywhere that has a railroad crossing.

Then came the sightings. An engineer would see "a figure" walking along the tracks in front of the train, just beyond the Pyramid elevator. The engineer would blow his horn, but the person, "the figure," would seem not to notice. The engineer blasted the horn several more times, more and more insistent. But the person kept walking; pretty soon the train's headlights glared onto a tall, muscular boy with shaggy dark hair and a green fatigue jacket. They tried to brake the train, but it was too late. The boy suddenly fell to his knees, and the engineer was certain he'd hit him. But of course when the train was stopped, they could find nothing. "Not a trace," says our author. This happened to three different engineers; three different incidents in a two-year period.

You can imagine the ending, of course: that was how my brother died, a few years after these supposed sightings began. His car had run out of gas a few miles from home, and he was walking back. He was drunk. Who knows why he was walking along the tracks? Who knows why he suddenly kneeled down? Maybe he stumbled, or had to throw up. Maybe he did it on purpose. He was killed instantly.

The whole ghost stuff came out afterward. One of the engineers who'd seen the ghost recognized Del's picture in the paper and came forward or something. I always believed it was made up. It was stupid, I always thought, like a million campfire stories you'd heard or some cheesy program on TV. But the author of *More True Tales of the Weird and Supernatural* found it "spine-tingling." "The strange story of the boy whose ghost appeared—two years before he died!" says a line on the back cover.

This happened when I was fourteen. My early brush with tragedy, I guess you could call it, though by the time I was twenty-one I felt I had recovered. I didn't think the incident had shaped my life in any particular way, and in fact I'd sometimes find myself telling the story, ghost and all, to girls I met at fraternity parties. I'd take a girl up to my room, show her the *More True Tales* book. We'd smoke some marijuana and talk about it, my voice taking on an intensity and heaviness that surprised both of us. From time to time, we'd end up in bed. I remember this one girl, Lindsey, telling me how moved she was by the whole thing. It gave me, she said, a Heathcliff quality; I had turned brooding and mysterious; the wheat fields had turned to moors. "I'm not mysterious," I said, embarrassed, and later, after we'd parted ways, she agreed. "I thought you were different," she said, "deeper." She cornered me one evening when I was talking to another girl and wanted to know if I wasn't a little ashamed, using my dead brother to get laid. She said that she had come to realize that I, like Heath-cliff, was just another jerk.

10　After that I stopped telling the story for a while. There would be months when I wouldn't speak of my brother at all, and even when I was home in Pyramid, I could spend my whole vacation without once mentioning Del's name. My parents never spoke of him, at least not with me.

Of course, this only made him more present than ever. He hovered there as I spoke of college, my future, my life, my father barely listening. When we would argue, my father would stiffen sullenly, and I knew he was thinking of arguments he'd had with Del. I could shout at him, and nothing would happen. He'd stare as I tossed some obscene word casually toward him, and I'd feel it rattle and spin like a coin I'd flipped on the table in front of him. But he wouldn't say anything.

I actually wondered back then why they put up with this sort of thing. It was surprising, even a little unnerving, especially given my father's temper when I was growing up, the old violence-promising glares that once made my bones feel like wax, the ability he formerly had to make me flinch with a gesture or a well-chosen phrase.

Now I was their only surviving child, and I was gone—more thoroughly gone than Del was, in a way. I'd driven off to college in New York, and it was clear I wasn't ever coming back. Even my visits became shorter and shorter—summer trimmed down from three months to less than two weeks over the course of my years at college; at Christmas, I'd stay on campus after finals, wandering the emptying passageways of my residence hall, loitering in the student center, my hands clasped behind my back, staring at the ragged bulletin boards as if they were paintings in a museum. I found excuses to keep from going back. And then, when I got there, finally, I was just another ghost.

About a year before he died, Del saved my life. It was no big deal, I thought. It was summer, trucks were coming to the grain elevator, and my brother and I had gone up to the roof to fix a hole. The elevator was flat on top, and when I was little, I used to imagine that being up there was like being in the turret of a lighthouse. I used to stare out over the expanse of prairie, across the fields and their flotsam of machinery, cattle, men, over the rooftops of houses, along the highways and railroad tracks that trailed off into the horizon. "When I was small, this would fill me with wonder. My father would stand there with me, holding my hand,.and the wind would ripple our clothes.

15   I was thinking of this, remembering, when I suddenly started to do a little dance. I didn't know why I did such things: my father said that ever since I started junior high school I'd been like a "-holic" of some sort, addicted to making an ass out of myself. Maybe this was true, because I started to caper around, and Del said, "I'd laugh if you fell, you idiot," stern and condescending, as if I were the juvenile delinquent. I ignored him. With my back turned to him, I began to sing "Ain't No Mountain High Enough" in a deep corny voice like my father's. I'd never been afraid of heights, and I suppose I was careless. Too close to the edge, I slipped, and my brother caught my arm.

I was never able to recall exactly what happened in that instant. I remember being surprised by the sound that came from my throat, a high scream like a rabbit's that seemed to ricochet downward, a stone rattling through a long drainpipe. I looked up and my brother's mouth was wide open, as if he'd made the sound. The tendons on his neck stood out.

I told myself that if I'd been alone, nothing would have happened. I would've just teetered a little, then gained my balance again. But when my brother grabbed me, I lost my equilibrium, and over the edge I went. There were a dozen trucks lined up to have their loads weighed, and all the men down there heard that screech, looked up startled to see me dangling there with two hundred feet between me and the ground. They all watched Del yank me back up to safety.

I was on the ground before it hit me. Harvesters were getting out of their trucks and ambling toward us, and I could see my father pushing his way through the crowd. It was then that my body took heed of what had happened. The solid earth kept opening up underneath me, and Del put his arm around me as I wobbled. Then my father loomed. He got hold of me, clenching my shoulders, shaking me. "My sore neck!" I cried out. "Dad, my neck!" The harvesters' faces jittered, pressing closer; I could see a man in sunglasses with his black, glittering eyes fixed on me.

"Del pushed me," I cried out as my father's gritted teeth came toward my face. Tears slipped suddenly out of my eyes. "Del pushed me, Dad! It wasn't my fault."

20   My father had good reason to believe this lie, even though he and some twelve or more others had been witness to my singing and careless prancing up there. The possibility still existed that Del might have given me a shove from behind. My father didn't want to believe Del was capable of such a thing. But he knew he was.

Del had only been back home for about three weeks. Prior to that, he'd spent several months in a special program for juvenile delinquents. The main reason for this was that he'd become so belligerent, so violent, that my parents didn't feel they could control him. He'd also, over the course of things, stolen a car.

For much of the time that my brother was in this program, I wore a neck brace. He'd tried to strangle me the night before he was sent away. He claimed he'd seen me smirking at him, though actually I was only thinking of something funny I'd seen on TV. Del was the furthest thing from my thoughts until he jumped on me. If my father hadn't separated us, Del probably would have choked me to death.

This was one of the things that my father must have thought of. He must have remembered the other times that Del might have killed me: the time when I was twelve and he threw a can of motor oil at my head when my back was turned; the time when I was seven and he pushed me off the tailgate of a moving pickup, where my father had let us sit when he was driving slowly down a dirt road. My father was as used to hearing these horror stories as I was to telling them.

Though he was only three and a half years older than me, Del was much larger. He was much bigger than I'll ever be, and I was just starting to realize that. Six foot three, 220-pound defensive back, my father used to tell people when he spoke of Del. My father used to believe that Del would get a football scholarship to the state university. Never mind that once he started high school he wouldn't even play on the team. Never mind that all he seemed to want to do was vandalize people's property and drink beer and cause problems at home. My father still talked about it like there was some hope.

25   When my brother got out of his program, he told us that things would be different from now on. He had changed, he said, and he swore that he would make up for the things that he'd done. I gave him a hug. He stood there before us with his hands clasped behind his back, posed like the famous orator whose picture was in the library of our school. We all smiled, the visions of the horrible family fights wavering behind our friendly expressions.

So here was another one, on the night of my almost-death.

Before very long, my brother had started crying. I hadn't seen him actually shed tears in a very long time; he hadn't even cried on the day he was sent away.

"He's a liar," my brother shouted. We had all been fighting and carrying on for almost an hour. I had told my version of the story five or six times, getting better at it with each repetition. I could have almost believed it myself. "You fucking liar," my brother screamed at me. "I wish I had pushed you. I'd never save your ass now." He stared at me suddenly, wild-eyed, like I was a dark shadow that was bending over his bed when he woke at night. Then he sat down at the kitchen table. He put his face in his hands, and his shoulders began to shudder.

Watching him—this giant, broad-shouldered boy, my brother, weeping—I could have almost taken it back. The whole lie, I thought, the words I spoke at first came out of nowhere, sprang to my lips as a shield against my father's red face and bared teeth, his fingernails cutting my shoulder as everyone watched. It was really my father's fault. I could have started crying myself.

30   But looking back on it, I have to admit that there was something else, too—a heat at the core of my stomach, spreading through my body like a stain. It made my skin throb, my face a mask of innocence and defiance. I sat there looking at him and put my hand to my throat. After years of being on the receiving end, it wasn't in my nature to see Del as someone who could be wronged, as someone to feel pity for. This was something Del could have done, I thought. It was not so unlikely.

At first I thought it would end with my brother leaving, barreling out of the house with the slamming of doors and the circling whine of the fan belt in my father's old beater pickup, the muffler retorting all the way down the long dirt road, into the night. Once, when he was drunk, my brother tried to drive his truck off a cliff on the hill out behind our house. But the embankment wasn't steep enough, and the truck just went bump, bump down the side of the hill, all four wheels staying on the ground until it finally came to rest in the field below. Del pointed a shotgun at my father that night, and my father was so stunned and upset that my mother thought he was having a heart attack. She was running around hysterical, calling police, ambulance, bawling. In the distance, Del went up the hill, down the hill, up, down. You could hear him revving the motor. It felt somehow like one of those slapstick moments in a comedy movie, where everything is falling down at once and all the actors run in and out of doorways. I sat, shivering, curled up on the couch while all this was going on, staring at the television.

But the night after I'd almost fallen, my brother did not try to take off. We all knew that if my parents had to call the police on him again, it would be the end. He would go to a foster home or even back to the juvenile hall, which he said was worse than prison. So instead, he and my father were in a shoving match; there was my mother between them, screaming, "Oh, stop it I can't stand it I can't stand it," turning her deadly, red-eyed stare abruptly upon me; there was my brother crying. But he didn't try to leave. He just sat there, with his face in his hands. "God-damn all of you," he cried suddenly. "I hate all your guts. I wish I was fucking dead."

My father hit him then, hit him with the flat of his hand alongside the head, and Del tilted in his chair with the force of it. He made a small, high-pitched sound, and I watched as he folded his arms over his ears as my father descended on him, a blow, a pause, a blow, a pause. My father stood over him, breathing hard. A tear fell from Del's nose.

"Don't you ever say that," my father roared. "Don't you dare ever say that." He didn't mean the f-word—he meant wishing you were dead, the threats Del had made in the past. That was the worst thing, my father had told us once, the most terrible thing a person could do. My father's hands fell to his sides. I saw that he was crying also.

35   After a time, Del lifted his head. He seemed to have calmed—everything seemed to have grown quiet, a dull, wavery throb of static. I saw that he looked at me. I slumped my shoulders, staring down at my fingernails.

"You lie," Del said softly. "You can't even look me in the face." He got up and stumbled a few steps, as if my father would go after him again. But my father just stood there.

"Get out of my sight," he said. "Go on."

I heard Del's tennis shoes thump up the stairs, the slam of our bedroom door. But just as I felt my body start to untense, my father turned to me. He wiped the heel of his hand over his eyes, gazing at me without blinking. After all of Del's previous lies, his denials, his betrayals, you would think they would never believe his side of things again. But I could see a slowly creaking hinge of doubt behind my father's expression. I looked down.

"If I ever find out you're lying to me, boy," my father said.

40   He didn't ever find out. The day I almost fell was another one of those things we never got around to talking about again. It probably didn't seem very significant to my parents, in the span of events that had happened before and came after. They dwelt on other things.

On what, I never knew. My wife found this unbelievable: "Didn't they say anything after he died?" she asked me, and I had to admit that I didn't remember. They were sad, I told her. I recalled my father crying. But they were country people. I tried to explain this to my wife, good Boston girl that she is, the sort of impossible grief that is like something gnarled and stubborn and underground. I never really believed it myself. For years, I kept expecting things to go back to normal, waiting for whatever was happening to them to finally be over.

My parents actually became quite mellow in the last years of their lives. My mother lost weight, was often ill. Eventually, shortly after her sixtieth birthday, she went deaf. Her hearing slipped away quickly, like a skin she was shedding, and all the tests proved inconclusive. That was the year that my son was born. In January, when my wife discovered that she was pregnant, my parents were in the process of buying a fancy, expensive hearing aid. By the time the baby was four months old, the world was completely soundless for my mother, hearing aid or not.

The problems of my college years had passed away by that time. I was working at a small private college in upstate New York, in alumni relations. My wife and I seldom went back to Nebraska; we couldn't afford the money or the time. .But I talked to my parents regularly on the phone, once or twice a month.

We ended up going back that Christmas after Ezra was born. My mother's letters had made it almost impossible to avoid. "It breaks my heart that I can't hear my grandson's voice, now that he is making his little sounds," she had written. "But am getting by O.K. and will begin lip-reading classes in Denver after Xmas. It will be easier for me then." She would get on the phone when I called my father. "I can't hear you talking, but I love you," she'd say.

45 "We have to work to make her feel involved in things," my father told us as we drove from the airport, where he'd picked us up. "The worst thing is that they start feeling isolated," he told us. "We got little pads so we can write her notes." He looked over at me, strangely academic-looking in the new glasses he had for driving. In the last few years he had begun to change, his voice turning slow and gentle, as if he were watching something out in the distance beyond the window or something sad and mysterious on TV as we talked. His former short temper had vanished, leaving only a soft reproachfulness in its place. But even that was muted. He knew that he couldn't really make me feel guilty. "You know how she is," he said to my wife and me, though of course we did not, either one of us, really know her. "You know how she is. The hardest part is, you know, we don't want her to get depressed."

She looked awful. Every time I had seen her since I graduated from college, this had stunned me. I came in, carrying my sleeping son, and she was sitting at the kitchen table, her spine curved a little bit more than the last time, thinner, so skinny that her muscles seemed to stand out against the bone. Back in New York, I worked with alumni ladies older than her who played tennis, who dressed in trendy clothes, who walked with a casual and still sexy ease. These women wouldn't look like my mother for another twenty years, if ever. I felt my smile pull awkwardly on my face.

"Hello!" I called, but of course she didn't look up. My father flicked on the porch light. "She hates it when you surprise her," he said softly, as if there were still some possibility of her overhearing. My wife looked over at me. Her eyes said that this was going to be another holiday that was like work for her.

My mother lifted her head. Her shrewdness was still intact, at least, and she was ready for us the moment the porch light hit her consciousness. That terrible, monkeyish dullness seemed to lift from her expression as she looked up.

"Well, howdy," she called, in the same jolly, slightly ironic way she always did when she hadn't seen me in a long time. She came over to hug us, then peered down at Ezra, who stirred a little as she pushed back his parka hood to get a better look. "Oh, what an angel," she whispered. "It's about killing me, not being able to see this boy." Then she stared down at Ezra again. How he'd grown, she told us. She thought he looked like me, she said, and I was relieved. Actually, I'd begun to think that Ezra somewhat resembled the pictures I'd seen of Del as a baby. But my mother didn't say that, at least.

50 I had planned to have a serious talk with them on this trip. Or maybe "planned" is the wrong word—"considered" might be closer, though even that doesn't express the vague, unpleasantly anxious urge that I could feel at the back of my neck. I didn't really know what I wanted to know. And the truth was, these quiet, fragile, distantly tender people bore little resemblance to the mother and father in my mind. It had been ten years since I'd lived at home. Ten years!—which filled the long, snowy evenings with a numbing politeness. My father sat in his easy chair after dinner, watching the news. My wife read. My mother and I did the dishes together, silently, nodding as the plate she had rinsed passed from her hand to mine, to be dried and put away. When a train passed, the little window above the sink vibrated, humming like a piece of cellophane. But she did not notice this.

We did have a talk of sorts that trip, my father and I. It was on the third day after our arrival, a few nights before Christmas Eve. My wife and my mother were both asleep. My father and I sat out on the closed-in porch, drinking beer, watching the snow drift across the yard, watching the wind send fingers of snow slithering along low to the ground. I had drunk more than he had. I saw him glance sharply at me for a second when I came back from the refrigerator a fourth time and popped open the can. But the look faded quickly. Outside, beyond the window, I could see the blurry shape of the elevator through the falling snow, its outlines indistinct, wavering like a mirage.

"Do you remember that time," I said, "when I almost fell off the elevator?"

It came out like that, abrupt, stupid. As I sat there in my father's silence, I realized how impossible it was, how useless to try to patch years of ellipsis into something resembling dialogue. I looked down, and he cleared his throat.

"Sure," he said at last, noncommittal. "Of course I remember."

55 "I think about that sometimes," I said. Drunk—I felt the alcohol edge into my voice as I spoke. "It seems," I said, "significant." That was the word that came to me. "It seems significant sometimes," I said.

My father considered this for a while. He stiffened formally, as if he were being interviewed. "Well," he said, "I don't know. There were so many things like that. It was all a mess by then, anyway. Nothing could be done. It was too late for anything to be done." He looked down to his own beer, which must have gone warm by that time, and took a small sip. "It should have been taken care of earlier—when you were kids. That's where I think things must have gone wrong. I was too hard on you both. But Del—I was harder on him. He was the oldest. Too much pressure. Expected too much."

He drifted off at that, embarrassed. We sat there, and I could not even imagine what he meant—what specifics he was referring to. What pressure? What expectations? But I didn't push any further.

"But you turned out all right," my father said. "You've done pretty well, haven't you?"

There were no signs in our childhood, no incidents pointing the way to his eventual end. None that I could see, at least, and I thought about it quite a bit after his death. "It should have been taken care of earlier," my father said, but what was "it"? Del seemed to have been happy, at least up until high school.

60 Maybe things happened when they were alone together. From time to time, I remember Del coming back from helping my father in the shop with his eyes red from crying. Once, I remember our father coming into our room on a Saturday morning and cuffing the top of Del's sleeping head with the back of his hand: he had stepped in dog dirt on the lawn. The dog was Del's responsibility. Del must have been about eight or nine at the time, and I remember him kneeling on our bedroom floor in his pajamas, crying bitterly as he cleaned off my father's boot. When I told that story later on, I was pleased by the ugly, almost fascist overtones it had. I remember recounting it to some college friends—handsome, suburban kids—lording this little bit of squalor from my childhood over them. Child abuse and family violence were enjoying a media vogue at that time, and I found I could mine this memory to good effect. In the version I told, I was the one cleaning the boots.

But the truth was, my father was never abusive in an especially spectacular way. He was more like a simple bully, easily eluded when he was in a short-tempered mood. He used to get so furious when we avoided him. I recall how he used to grab us by the hair on the back of our necks, tilting our heads so we looked into his face. "You don't listen," he would hiss. "I want you to look at me when I talk to you." That was about the worst of it, until Del started getting into trouble. And by that time my father's blows weren't enough. Del would laugh, he would strike back. It was then that my father finally decided to turn him over to the authorities. He had no other choice, he said.

He must have believed it. He wasn't, despite his temper, a bad man, a bad parent. He'd seemed so kindly sometimes, so fatherly—especially with Del. I remember watching them from my window some autumn mornings, watching them wade through the high weeds in the stubble field out behind our house, walking toward the hill with their shotguns pointing at the ground, their steps slow, synchronized. Once I'd gone upstairs and heard them laughing in Del's and my bedroom. I just stood there outside the doorway, watching as my father and Del put a model ship together, sharing the job, their talk easy, happy.

This was what I thought of, that night we were talking. I thought of my own son, the innocent baby I loved so much, and it chilled me to think that things could change so much—that Del's closeness to my father could turn in on itself, transformed into the kind of closeness that thrived on their fights, on the different ways Del could push my father into a rage. That finally my father would feel he had no choices left. We looked at each other, my father and I. "What are you thinking?" I said softly, but he just shook his head.

Del and I had never been close. We had never been like friends, or even like brothers. Yet after that day on the elevator I came to realize that there had been something between us. There had been something that could be taken away.

65 He stopped talking to me altogether for a while. In the weeks and months that followed my lie, I doubt if we even looked at each other more than two or three times, though we shared the same room.

For a while I slept on the couch. I was afraid to go up to our bedroom. I can remember those first few nights, waiting in the living room for my father to go to bed, the television hissing with laughter. The furniture, the table, the floors, seemed to shudder as I touched them, as if they were just waiting for the right moment to burst apart.

I'd go outside sometimes, though that was really no better. It was the period of late summer when thunderstorms seemed to pass over every night. The wind came up. The shivering tops of trees bent in the flashes of heat lightning.

There was no way out of the situation I'd created. I could see that. Days and weeks stretched out in front of me, more than a month before school started. By that time, I thought, maybe it would all blow over. Maybe it would melt into the whole series of bad things that had happened, another layer of paint that would eventually be covered over by a new one, forgotten.

If he really had pushed me, that was what would have happened. It would have been like the time he tried to choke me, or the time he tried to drive the car off the hill. Once those incidents were over, there was always the possibility that this was the last time. There was always the hope that everything would be better now.

70 In retrospect, it wouldn't have been so hard to recant. There would have been a big scene, of course. I would have been punished, humiliated. I would have had to endure my brother's triumph, my parents' disgust. But I realize now that it wouldn't have been so bad.

I might have finally told the truth, too, if Del had reacted the way I expected. I imagined that there would be a string of confrontations in the days that followed, that he'd continue to protest with my father. I figured he wouldn't give up.

But he did. After that night, he didn't try to deny it anymore. For a while I even thought that maybe he had begun to believe that he pushed me. He acted like a guilty person, eating his supper in silence, walking noiselessly through the living room, his shoulders hunched like a traveler on a snowy road.

My parents seemed to take this as penitence. They still spoke sternly, but their tone began to be edged by gentleness, a kind of forgiveness. "Did you take out the trash?" they would ask. "Another potato?"—and they would wait for him to quickly nod. He was truly sorry, they thought. Everything was finally going to be O.K. He was shaping up.

At these times I noticed something in his eyes—a kind of sharpness, a subtle shift of the iris. He would lower his head, and the corners of his mouth would move slightly. To me, his face seemed to flicker with hidden, mysterious thoughts.

75   When I finally began to sleep in our room again, he pretended I wasn't there. I would come in, almost as quiet as he himself had become, to find him sitting at our desk or on his bed, peeling off a sock with such slow concentration that it might have been his skin. It was as if there were an unspoken agreement between us—I no longer existed. He wouldn't look at me, but I could watch him for as long as I wanted. I would pull the covers over myself and just lie there, observing, as he went about doing whatever he was doing as if oblivious. He listened to a tape on his headphones; flipped through a magazine; did sit-ups; sat staring out the window; turned out the light. And all that time his face remained neutral, impassive. Once he even chuckled to himself at a book he was reading, a paperback anthology of *The Far Side* cartoons.

When I was alone in the room, I found myself looking through his things, with an interest I'd never had before. I ran my fingers over his models, the monster-wheeled trucks and B-10 bombers. I flipped through his collection of tapes. I found some literature he'd brought home from the detention center, brochures with titles like *Teens and Alcohol: What You Should Know!* and *Rap Session, Talking About Feelings.* Underneath this stuff I found the essay he'd been working on.

He had to write an essay so that they would let him back into high school. There was a letter from the guidance counselor explaining the school's policy, and then there were several sheets of notebook paper with his handwriting on them. He'd scratched out lots of words, sometimes whole paragraphs. In the margins he'd written little notes to himself: "(sp.)" or "?" or "No." He wrote in scratchy block letters.

His essay told of the Outward Bound program. "I had embarked on a sixty-day rehabilitation program in the form of a wilderness survival course name of Outward Bound," he had written. "THESIS: The wilderness has allowed for me to reach deep inside my inner self and grasp ahold of my morals and values that would set the standard and tell the story of the rest of my life."

I would go into our room when my brother was out and take the essay out of the drawer where he'd hidden it. He was working on it, off and on, all that month; I'd flip it open to discover new additions or deletions —whole paragraphs appearing as if overnight. I never saw him doing it.

80   The majority of the essay was a narrative, describing their trip. They had hiked almost two hundred miles, he said. "Up by sun and down by moon," he wrote. There were obstacles they had to cross. Once they had to climb down a hundred-foot cliff. "The repelling was very exciting but also scary," he'd written. "This was meant to teach us trust and confidence in ourselves as well as our teammates, they said. Well as I reached the peak of my climb I saw to my despair that the smallest fellow in the group was guiding my safety rope. Now he was no more than one hundred and ten pounds and I was tipping the scales at about two twenty five needless to say I was reluctant."

But they made it. I remember reading this passage several times; it seemed very vivid in my mind. In my imagination, I was in the place of the little guy holding the safety rope. I saw my brother hopping lightly, bit by bit, down the sheer face of the cliff to the ground below, as if he could fly, as if there were no gravity anymore.

"My experience with the Outward Bound program opened my eyes to such values as friendship, trust, responsibility and sharing," Del wrote in his conclusion. "Without the understanding of these I would not exist as I do now but would probably instead be another statistic. With these values I will purely succeed. Without I would surely fail." Next to this he'd written: "Sounds like bullshit (?)."

I don't know that I recognized that distinct ache that I felt on reading this, or understood why his sudden distance, the silent, moody aura he trailed after him in those weeks, should have affected me in such a way. Years later, I would recall that feeling— standing over my son's crib, a dark shape leaning over him as he stirred with dreams—waiting at the window for the headlights of my wife's car to turn into our driveway. That sad, trembly feeling was a species of love—or at least a symptom of it.

I thought of this a long time after the fact. I loved my brother, I thought. Briefly.

85   None of this lasted. By the time he died, a year later, he'd worked his way back to his normal self, or a slightly modified, moodier version. Just like before, money had begun to disappear from my mother's purse; my parents searched his room for drugs. He and my father had argued that morning about the friends he was hanging around with, about his wanting to take the car every night. Del claimed that he was dating a girl, said he only wanted to see a movie in town. He'd used that one before, often lying ridiculously when he was asked the next day about the plot of the film. I remember him telling my mother that the war film *Apocalypse Now* was set in the future, which I knew was not true from an article I'd read in the paper. I remember making some comment in reference to this as he was getting ready to go out, and he looked at me in that careful, hooded way, reminiscent of the time when he was pretending I didn't exist. "Eat shit and die, Stewart," he murmured, without heat. Unfortunately, I believe that this was the last thing he ever said to me.

Afterward, his friends said that he had seemed like he was in a good mood. They had all been in his car, my father's car, driving up and down the main street in Scottsbluff. They poured a little rum into their cans of Coke, cruising from one end of town to the other, calling out the window at a earful of passing teenage girls, revving the engine at the stoplights. He wasn't that drunk, they said.

I used to imagine that there was a specific moment when he realized that he was going to die. I don't believe he knew it when he left our house, or even at the beginning of his car ride with his friends. If that were true, I have to assume that there would have been a sign, some gesture or expression, something one of us would have noticed. If it was planned, then why on that particular, insignificant day?

Yet I wondered. I used to think of him in his friend Sully's car, listening to his buddies laughing, making dumb jokes, running red lights. It might have been sometime around then, I thought. Time seemed to slow down. He would sense a long, billowing delay in the spaces between words; the laughing faces of the girls in a passing car would seem to pull by forever, their expressions frozen.

Or I thought about his driving home. I could see the heavy, foglike darkness of those country roads, the shadows of weeds springing up when the headlights touched them, I could imagine the halt and sputter of the old pickup as the gas ran out, that moment when you can feel the power lift up out of the machine like a spirit. It's vivid enough in my mind that it's almost as if I were with him as the pickup rolled lifelessly on—slowing, then stopping at last on the shoulder where it would be found the next day, the emergency lights still blinking dimly. He and I stepped out into the thick night air, seeing the shape of the elevator in the distance, above the tall sunflowers and pigweed. And though we knew we were outdoors, it felt like we were inside something. The sky seemed to close down on us like the lid of a box.

90   No one in my family ever used the word "suicide." When we referred to Del's death, if we referred to it, we spoke of "the accident." To the best of our knowledge, that's what it was.

There was a time, right before I left for college, when I woke from a dream to the low wail of a passing train. I could see it when I sat up in bed—through the branches of trees outside my window I could see the boxcars shuffling through flashes of heat lightning, trailing past the elevator and into the distance, rattling, rattling.

And there was another time, my senior year in college, when I saw a kid who looked like Del coming out of a bar, a boy melting into the crowded, carnival atmosphere of this particular strip of saloons and dance clubs where students went on a Saturday night. I followed this person a few blocks before I lost sight of him. All those cheerful, drunken faces seemed to loom as I passed by them, blurring together like an expressionist painting. I leaned against a wall, breathing.

And there was that night when we came to Pyramid with my infant son, the night my father and I stayed up talking. I sat there in the dark long after he'd gone to bed, finishing another beer. I remember looking up to see my mother moving through the kitchen, at first only clearly seeing the billowy whiteness of her nightgown hovering in the dark, a shape floating slowly through the kitchen toward me. I had a moment of fear before I realized it was her. She did not know I was there. She walked slowly, delicately, thinking herself alone in this room at night. I would have had to touch her to let her know that I was there, and that would have probably startled her badly. So I didn't move. I watched as she lit a cigarette and sat down at the kitchen table, her head turned toward the window, where the snow was still falling. She watched it drift down. I heard her breathe smoke, exhaling in a long, thoughtful sigh. She was remembering something, I thought.

It was at these moments that everything seemed clear to me. I felt that I could take all the loose ends of my life and fit them together perfectly, as easily as a writer could write a spooky story, where all the details add up and you know the end even before the last sentence. This would make a good ending, you think at such moments. You'll go on living, of course. But at the same time you recognize, in that brief flash of clarity and closure, you realize that everything is summed up. It's not really worth becoming what there is left for you to become.

GISH JEN (1956–   )   **1998**

CHIN

I wasn't his friend, but I wasn't one of the main kids who hounded him up onto the shed roof, either. Sure I'd lob a rock or two, but this was our stage of life back then, someplace between the arm and the fist. Not to chuck nothing would have been against nature, and I never did him one he couldn't duck easy, especially being as fast as he was—basically the fastest kid in the ninth grade, and one of the smartest besides, smarter even than yours truly, the official class underachiever. I tested so high on my IQ that the school psychologists made me take the test over, nobody could believe it. They've been hounding me to apply myself ever since. But Chin was smart, too—not so much in math and science as in stuff like history and English. How's that for irony? And he was a good climber, you had to give him that, the only kid who could scale that shed wall, period. Because that wall didn't have no handholds or footholds. In fact, the naked eye would've pronounced that wall plain concrete; you had to wonder if the kid had some kind of special vision, so that he could look at that wall and see a way up. Maybe where we saw wall, he saw cracks, or maybe there was something he knew in his body about walls; or maybe they didn't have walls in China, besides the Great Wall, that is, so that he knew a wall was only a wall because we thought it was a wall. That might be getting philosophical. But you know, I've seen guys do that in basketball, find the basket in ways you can't account for. You can rewind the tape and watch the replay until your eyeballs pop, but finally you've got to say that obstacles are not always obstacles for these guys. Things melt away for them.

Gus said it was on account of there was monkey feet inside his sneakers that the kid could get up there. That was the day the kid started stockpiling the rocks we threw and raining them back down on us. A fall day, full of the crack and smell of people burning leaves illegally. It was just like the monkeys in the zoo when they get mad at the zookeepers, that's what I said. I saw that on TV once. But Gus blew a smoke ring and considered it like a sunset, then said even though you couldn't see the kid's monkey feet, they were like hands and could grip onto things. He said you've never seen such long toes, or such weird toenails, either, and that the toenails were these little bitty slits, like his eyes. And that, he said, was why he was going to drown me in a douche bag if I threw any more rocks without paying attention. He said I was fucking arming the ape.

We didn't live in the same building, that kid and me. His name was Chin or something, like chin-up we used to say, and his family lived in the garden apartment next door to ours. This was in scenic Yonkers, New York, home of Central Avenue. We were both stuck on the ground floor, where everyone could look right into your kitchen. It was like having people look up your dress, my ma said, and they were smack across the alley from us. So you see, if I'd really wanted to nail him with a rock, I could've done it any time their windows were open if I didn't want to break any glass. And I could've done it any time at all if I didn't care about noise and commotion and getting a JD card like the Beyer kid got for climbing the water tower. Of course, they didn't open their windows much, the Chins. My ma said it was because they were Chinese people—you know, like Chinese food, from China, she said, and then she cuffed me for playing dumb and getting her to explain what a Chinese was when they were getting to be a fact of life. Not like in California or Queens, but they were definitely proliferating, along with a lot of other people who could tell you where they came from, if they spoke English. They weren't like us who came from Yonkers and didn't have no special foods, unless you wanted to count fries. Gus never could see why we couldn't count fries. My own hunch, though, guess why, was that they just might be French. Not that I said so I was more interested in why everybody suddenly had to have a special food. And why was everybody asking what your family was? First time somebody asked me that, I had no idea what they were talking about But after a while, I said, Vanilla. I said that because I didn't want to say we were nothing, my family was nothing.

My ma said that the Chins kept their windows shut because they liked their apartment hot, seeing as how it was what they were used to. People keep to what they're used to, she liked to say, though she also liked to say, Wait and see, you know your taste changes. Especially to my big sister she was always saying that, because my sis was getting married for real this time, to this hair dresser who had suddenly started offering her free bang trims anytime. Out of the blue, this was. He was a thinker, this Ray. He had it all figured out, how from doing the bang trim he could get to talking about her beautiful blue eyes. And damned if he wasn't right that a lot of people, including yours truly, had never particularly noticed her eyes, what with the hair hanging in them. A real truth-teller, that Ray was, and sharp as a narc. It was all that practice with women all day long, my ma said. He knows how to make a woman feel like a queen, not like your pa, who knows how to make her feel like shit. She was as excited as my sis, that's the truth, now that this Ray and her Debi were hitting the aisle sure enough. Ray was doing my ma's hair free, too, every other day just about, trying to fine-tune her do for the wedding, and in between she was trying to pitch a couple of last You knows across to Debi while she could. Kind of a cram course.

5 But my pa said the Chins did that with their windows because somebody put a cherry bomb in their kitchen for fun one day, and it upset them. Maybe they didn't know it was just a cherry bomb. Who knows what they thought it was, but they beat up Chin over it; that much we did know, because we could see everything and hear everything they did over there, especially if we turned the TV down, which we sometimes did for a fight. If only more was in English, we could've understood everything, too. Instead all we caught was that Chin got beat up over the cherry bomb, as if they thought it was owing to him that somebody put the bomb in the window. Go figure.

Chin got beat up a lot—this wasn't the first time. He got beat up on account of he played hooky from school sometimes, and he got beat up on account of he mouthed off to his pa, and he got beat up on account of he once got a C in math, which was why right near the bomb site there was a blackboard in the kitchen. Nights he wasn't getting beaten up, he was parked in front of the blackboard doing equations with his pa, who people said was not satisfied with Chin plain getting the correct answer in algebra, he had to be able to get it two or three ways. Also he got beat up because he liked to find little presents for himself and his sis and his ma. He did this in scores without paying for them, and that pissed the hell out of his pa. On principle, people said, but maybe he just felt left out. I always thought Chin should've known enough to get something for his pa, too.

But really Chin got beat up, my pa said, because Mr. Chin had this weird cheek. He had some kind of infection in some kind of hole, and as a result, the cheek shook and for a long time he wouldn't go to the doctor, seeing as how in China he used to be a doctor himself. Here he was a cab driver—the worst driver in the city, we're talking someone who would sooner puke on the Pope than cut across two lanes of traffic. He had a little plastic sleeve on the passenger-side visor where he displayed his driver's license; that's how much it meant to him that he'd actually gotten one. But in China he'd been a doctor, and as a result, he refused to go to a doctor here until his whole cheek was about gone. Thought he should be able to cure himself with herbs. Now even with the missus out working down at the dry cleaners, they were getting cleaned out themselves, what with the bills. They're going to need that boy for their old age, that's what my pa said. Cabbies don't have no pension plan like firemen and policemen and everybody else. They can't afford for him to go wrong, he's going to have to step up to the plate and hit that ball into the bleachers for them. That's why he gets beat, so he'll grow up to be a doctor who can practice in America. They want that kid to have his M.D. hanging up instead of his driver's license.

That was our general theory of why Chin got the treatment. But this time was maybe different. This time my pa wondered if maybe Chin's pa thought he was in some kind of a gang. He asked me if Chin was or wasn't, and I said no way was he in anything. Nobody hung with Chin, why would anybody hang with the guy everyone wanted to break? Unless you wanted them to try and break you, too. That's when my pa nodded in that captain of the force way you see on TV, and I was glad I told him. It made me feel like I'd forked over valuable information to the guy who ought to know. I felt like I could relax after I'd told him, even though maybe it was Mr. Chin who really should've known. Who knows but maybe my pa should've told Mr. Chin. Though what was he going to do, call him up and say, This is our theory next door? The truth is, I understood my pa. Like maybe I should've told Gus that Chin didn't actually have monkey feet, because I've seen his feet top and bottom through my pa's binoculars, and they were just regular. But let's face it, people don't want to be told much. And what difference did it make that I didn't think his toes were even that long, or that I could see them completely plain because his pa used to make him kneel when he wanted to beat him? What difference does it make what anybody's seen?

Sometimes I think I should've kept my eyes on the TV where they belonged, instead of watching stuff I couldn't turn off. Chin's pa used to use a belt mostly, but sometimes he used a metal garden stake, and with every single whack, I used to think how glad I was that it was Chin and not me that had those big welts rising up out of his back skin. They looked like some great special effect, these oozy red caterpillars crawling over some older pinkish ones. Chin never moved or said anything, and that just infuriated his pa more. You could see it so clear, you almost felt sorry for him. Here he had this garden stake and there was nothing he could do. What with his cheek all wrapped up, he had to stop the beating every now and then to readjust his bandage.

My pa used a ruler on me once, just like the one they used at school—Big Bertha, we called it, a solid eighteen inches, and if you flinched, you got hit another three times on the hands. Naturally, Chin never did, as a result of the advanced training he got at home. People said he didn't feel nothing; he was like a horse you had to kick with heel spurs, your plain heel just tickled. But I wasn't used to torture instruments. We didn't believe in that sort of thing in my house. Even that time my pa did get out the ruler, it broke and he had to go back to using his hand. That was bad enough. My pa was a fireman, meaning he was a lot stronger than Chin's pa was ever going to be, which maybe had nothing to do with anything. But my theory was, it was on account of that he knew he wasn't that strong that Mr. Chin used the garden stake on Chin, and once on the sister, too.

10   She wasn't as old as my sister, and she wasn't that pretty, and she wasn't that smart, and you were just glad when you looked at her that you weren't her gym teacher. She wore these glasses that looked like they were designed to fall off, and she moseyed down the school halls the way her pa did the highway—keeping all the way to the right and hesitating dangerously in the intersections. But she had a beautiful voice and was always doing the solo at school assembly. Some boring thing—the songs at school were all worse than ever since Mr. Reardon, the math teacher, had to take over music. He was so musical, people had to show him how to work those black stands; he didn't know you could adjust them, he thought they came in sizes. To be fair, he asked three times if he couldn't do study hall instead. But Chin's sister managed to wring something out of the songs he picked somehow. Everything she sang sounded like her. It was funny—she never talked, this girl, and everybody called her quiet, but when she sang, she filled up the whole auditorium and you completely forgot she wore these glasses people said were bulletproof.

It wasn't the usual thing that the sister got hit. But one day she threatened to move out of the house, actually stomped out into the snow, saying that she could not stand to watch what was going on anymore. Then her pa hauled her back and beat her, too. At least he left her clothes on and didn't make her kneel. She got to stand and only fell on the floor, curled up, by choice. But here was the sad thing: It turned out you could hear her singing voice when she cried; she still sounded like herself. She didn't look like herself with her glasses off, though, and nobody else did, either. Chin the unflinching turned so red in the face, he looked as though blood beads were going to come busting straight out of his pores, and he started pounding the wall so hard, he put craters in it. His ma told him to stop, but he kept going, until finally she packed a suitcase and put the sister's glasses back on for her. Ma Chin had to tape the suitcase with duct tape to get it to stay shut. Then Ma Chin and the sister both put on their coats and headed for the front door. The snowflakes by then were so giant, you'd think there was a closeout sale on underwear going on up in heaven. Still the dynamic duo marched out into the neighborhood and up our little hill without any boots. Right up the middle of the street, they went; I guess there being two of them bucked up the sister. Ma Chin started out with the suitcase, but by the time they'd reached the hill, the sister'd wrestled it away from her. Another unexpected physical feat. It was cold out, and so dark that what with all the snow, the light from the streetlights appeared to be falling down too, and kind of drifting around. My pa wondered out loud if he should give our neighbors a friendly lift someplace. After all, the Chins had no car, and it was a long walk over to the bus stop. But what would he say? Excuse me, I just happened to be out driving?

He was trying to work this out with my ma, but she had to tell him first how Ray would know what to say without having to consult nobody and how glad she was that her Debi wasn't marrying nobody like him. Ray, Ray, Ray! my pa said finally. Why don't you go fuck him yourself instead of using your daughter? Then he sat right in the kitchen window, where anybody who bothered to look could see him, and watched as Ma Chin and the sister stopped and had themselves a little conference. They were up to their ankles in snow, neither in one streetlight cone or the next, but smack in between. They jawed for a long time. Then they moved a little farther up the incline and stopped and jawed again, sheltering their glasses from the snow with their hands. They almost looked like lifeguards out there, trying to keep the sun out of their eyes, except that they didn't seem to know that they were supposed to be looking for something. Probably their glasses were all fogged up. Still my pa watched them and watched them while I had a look at Chin. and his pa back at the ranch, and saw the most astounding thing of all: They were back at the blackboard, working problems out. Mr. Chin had a cup of tea made, and you couldn't see his face on account of his bandage, but he was gesturing with the eraser and Chin was nodding. How do you figure? I half-wanted to say something to my pa, to point out this useless fact. But my pa was too busy sitting in the window with the lights on, waiting for the Chin women to shout Fire! or something, I guess. He wanted them to behold him there, all lit up, their rescuer. Unfortunately, though, it was snowing out, not burning, and their heads were bent and their eyes were on the ground as they dragged their broken suitcase straight back across our view.

ON THE WEB

Visions of Hauntings: The Works of Edgar Allan Poe

"The Fall of the House of Usher," The Edgar Allan Poe Society, http://bau2.uibk.ac.at/sg/poe/poe.html
"The Tell-Tale Heart," The Edgar Allan Poe Society, http://www.eapoe.org/works

▪ POETRY ▪

BEN JONSON

Ben Jonson (1572–1637) was born in London, attended Westminster School, then became apprenticed as a bricklayer. For a short time, he served as a soldier in the Netherlands, before returning to England, marrying, and working as an actor and playwright. Jonson's first original play, Every Man in His Humor, *was performed in 1598. Jonson wrote satirical plays that assailed Elizabethan and Jacobean morals and his fellow playwrights, including* Volpone, or The Fox *(1605) and* The Alchemist *(1610). Among Jonson's* Epigrams *(1616) is a poem mourning the death of his seven-year-old son Benjamin, who died of the plague in 1603 while Jonson was away.*

ON MY FIRST SON[1]

Farewell, thou child of my right hand,[2] and joy;
My sin was too much hope of thee, loved boy;
Seven years thou wert lent to me, and I thee pay,
Exacted by thy fate, on the just day.
5 Oh, could I lose all father, now! For why
Will man lament the state he should envy?
To have so soon scaped world's, and flesh's rage,
And, if no other misery, yet age?
Rest in soft peace, and, asked, say here doth lie
10 Ben Jonson his best piece of poetry,
For whose sake, henceforth, all his vows be such,
As what he loves may never like too much.

■ EXPLORATIONS OF THE TEXT

1. How does the **allusion** to the Hebrew source of the child's name create an effect in the opening?
2. What **metaphoric reference** does Jonson make in lines 3 and 4? How does the metaphor strengthen the lament?
3. Explain the lines: "Oh, could I lose all father, now! For why/Will man lament the state he should envy?/To have so soon scaped world's and flesh's rage."
4. What poetic device is evident in "soft peace"? What is its effect upon a reader?
5. Why does the speaker call his son "his best piece of poetry"?
6. What is revealed in the closing couplet?
7. What is the rhyme scheme? How does rhyme reinforce meaning?

■ THE READING/WRITING CONNECTION

1. Discuss the responses of a parent who has lost a child as they are revealed in the poem.

■ IDEAS FOR WRITING

1. **Explicate** this poem.
2. Discuss the grief of the loss of children in "On My First Son" and "Elena."

AMIRI BARAKA

Born Everett LeRoi Jones in Newark, New Jersey, Amiri Baraka (1934–   ) changed his name in 1967. He attended Rutgers and Howard Universities before serving two and a half years in the U.S. Air Force. During the early 1960s, Baraka lived in Greenwich Village, obtained master's degrees in philosophy and German, and socialized with writers of the Beat movement. His first book of poetry, Preface to a Twenty Volume Suicide Note, *was published in 1961. Famous for his poetry and his plays, Baraka has received the Obie Award; fellowships from the Guggenheim, Rockefeller, and John Whitney Foundations; an American Book Award; and prizes from the International Art Festival, the National Endowment of the Arts, and the New Jersey Council for the Arts. Baraka was named Poet Laureate of New Jersey in 2002.*

---

[1] Jonson's oldest son, Benjamin, died in 1603 on his seventh birthday.
[2] Translated literally from the Hebrew, the name means Ben—"son of"—and Jamin—"my right hand."

1961

PREFACE TO A TWENTY VOLUME SUICIDE NOTE

For **Kellie Jones, born 16 May 1959**

Lately, I've become accustomed to the way
The ground opens up and envelops me
Each time I go out to walk the dog.
Or the broad-edged silly music the wind
5   Makes when I run for a bus . . .

Things have come to that.

And now, each night I count the stars,
And each night I get the same number.
And when they will not come to be counted,
10 I count the holes they leave.

Nobody sings anymore.

And then last night, I tiptoed up
To my daughter's room and heard her
Talking to someone, and when I opened
15 The door, there was no one there . . .
Only she on her knees, peeking into

Her own clasped hands.

■ **EXPLORATIONS OF THE TEXT**
1. What is the mood of the speaker in the opening lines? What images suggest his feelings?
2. What is the significance of music—the absence of song—in this poem?
3. What is the significance of the daughter's gesture of peeking into "her own clasped hands"?
4. What does the title mean? How does it explain the closing line?
5. Why does Baraka have three short lines, separated as stanzas? How do they convey the message of the poem?
6. Why does Baraka begin stanzas with "Lately," "And now," and "And then"? What do these transition words accomplish?
7. How does the speaker feel about his daughter? What does she represent to him?

■ **THE READING/WRITING CONNECTION**
1. "Think" Topic: Do you think that the experience of parenting differs for mothers and for fathers? Refer to two works that you have read.

■ **IDEAS FOR WRITING**
1. How does Baraka use figurative language in this poem? Is the figurative language effective?
2. What do children represent and give to their parents in two of the following poems: "Preface to a Twenty Volume Suicide Note," "Heart's Needle," "Making the Jam Without You," "My Little Girl, My Stringbean, My Lovely Woman"?

Linda Pastan

Linda Pastan (1932–) was born in New York City and attended Radcliffe College, where in her senior year, like her contemporary Sylvia Plath, she won the Mademoiselle *poetry contest. Pastan temporarily gave up writing to raise a family and later returned to composing poetry while her children were in school. She has published fifteen books of poetry, including her first,* A Perfect Circle of Sun *(1971), and more recently,* Carnival Evening *(1998) and* The Last Uncle: Poems *(2002). Her work appears in many periodicals, including* Atlantic Monthly, The New Yorker, The New Republic, *and* The Paris Review. *Beginning with the* Mademoiselle *Dylan Thomas Poetry Award in 1958, Pastan has been honored with several prestigious awards, including the role of Maryland's poet laureate from 1991 to 1995. "In the Old Guerilla War" is from Pastan's 1983 collection,* PM/AM: New and Selected Poems. *Pastan's poetry frequently portrays the complexity of domestic life.*

1978

IN THE OLD GUERILLA WAR

In the old guerilla war
between father and son
I am the no-man's-land.
When the moon shows
5 over my scorched breast
they fire across me.
If a bullet ricochets
and I bleed, they say
it is my time of month.
10 Sometimes I iron
handkerchiefs
into flags of truce,
hide them in pockets;
or humming, I roll socks
15 instead of bandages.
Then we sit down together
breaking only bread.
The family tree
shades us, the snipers
20 waiting in its branches
sleep between green leaves.
I think of the elm
sending its roots
like spies underground
25 through any rough terrain
in search of water; or Noah
sending out the dove
to find land.
Only survive long enough;
30 the triggers will rust into rings
around both their fingers.
I will be a field

where all the flowers
on my housedress
35 bloom at once.

■ EXPLORATIONS OF THE TEXT

1. Pastan uses an extended metaphor of a "guerilla war" to depict family relationships in this work. List the battle and war images. What vision of family dynamics do they convey?
2. What defines the relationship between father and son? What is the speaker's role in the family? Why is she in "no-man's land"? Compare and contrast her position with that of An-mei in Tan's "Scar."
3. Contrast the battle imagery with the natural imagery. What does this contrast suggest? Explicate the closing lines in the poem; "I will be a field/where all the flowers/on my housedress/bloom at once."
4. Compare and contrast the mother's role in this poem with that of the mother in Leff's "Burn Your Maps" or in Hansberry's *A Raisin in the Sun*.

■ THE READING/WRITING CONNECTION

1. Use an extended metaphor to describe your relationship with a family member. You may write a poem or a journal entry.
2. The poem uses metaphors to describe the conflicts between father and son. What do you think is the source of the trouble? Provide specifics that pinpoint sources of strife.
3. Write a poetic sequel to this poem. Does the relationship between father and son change?
4. Write a monologue for the father or the son, or write a dialogue between them about a conflict situation (e.g., use of the family car, curfews).

■ IDEAS FOR WRITING

1. Compare and contrast the father's relationship with his son in this work with that of Jen's "Chin" or Chaon's "Fitting Ends."

SYLVIA PLATH

Sylvia Plath (1932–63) was born in Boston, Massachusetts, the daughter of German immigrants who both taught at Boston University. Plath attended Smith College in Massachusetts, where she won a contest that sent her to work for a national magazine in New York, much like the protagonist of her novel, The Bell Jar *(1963). Plath won a Fullbright Scholarship to Cambridge University in England, where she met the poet Ted Hughes. They were married in 1956 and moved to Smith College, where Plath taught for a short time. The couple returned to England, where they had two children before separating. Plath's first volume of poems,* The Colossus, *appeared in 1960. She committed suicide in 1963 at the age of thirty, leaving the manuscript containing the highly acclaimed posthumous collection of poems,* Ariel *(1965). Like Anne Sexton and Robert Lowell, she is considered a Confessional poet. When Plath was eight years old, her father died, an event from which she never seemed to recover. Biographical accounts show some connection between the man in "Daddy" and her father; however, Plath herself stated that the two should not be confused. When she read the poem for the BBC, she suggested that the poem's speaker suffers from an Electra complex.*

DADDY

You do not do, you do not do
Any more, black shoe
In which I have lived like a foot
For thirty years, poor and white,
5 Barely daring to breathe or Achoo.

Daddy, I have had to kill you.
You died before I had time—
Marble-heavy, a bag full of God,
Ghastly statue[1] with one grey toe
10 Big as a Frisco seal

And a head in the freakish Atlantic
Where it pours bean green over blue
In the waters off beautiful Nauset.[2]
I used to pray to recover you.
15 Ach, du.[3]

In the German tongue, in the Polish town
Scraped flat by the roller
Of wars, wars, wars.
But the name of the town is common.
20 My Polack friend

Says there are a dozen or two.
So I never could tell where you
Put your foot, your root,
I never could talk to you.
25 The tongue stuck in my jaw.

It stuck in a barb wire snare.
Ich, ich, ich, ich,[4]
I could hardly speak.
I thought every German was you.
30 And the language obscene

An engine, an engine
Chuffing me off like a Jew.
A Jew to Dachau, Auschwitz, Belsen.[5]
I began to talk like a Jew.
35 I think I may well be a Jew.

---

[1] The Colossus at Rhodes, a gigantic statue of Apollo protecting the harbor at Rhodes; the Colossus was known as one of the seven wonders of the world.

[2] A place on the shore on Cape Cod in Massachusetts.

[3] "Oh, you" (translation from German).

[4] "I, I, I, I" (translation from German).

[5] Locations of concentration camps.

The snows of the Tyrol,[6] the clear beer of Vienna
Are not very pure or true.
With my gypsy ancestress and my weird luck
And my Taroc pack and my Taroc pack
40 I may be a bit of a Jew.

I have always been scared of *you,*
With your Luftwaffe,[7] your gobbledygoo.
And your neat moustache
And your Aryan[8] eye, bright blue.
45 Panzer-man,[9] panzer-man, O You—

Not God but a swastika
So black no sky could squeak through.
Every woman adores a Fascist,
The boot in the face, the brute
50 Brute heart of a brute like you.

You stand at the blackboard, daddy,
In the picture I have of you,
A cleft in your chin instead of your foot
But no less a devil for that, no not
55 Any less the black man who

Bit my pretty red heart in two.
I was ten when they buried you.
At twenty I tried to die
And get back, back, back to you.
60 I thought even the bones would do.

But they pulled me out of the sack,
And they stuck me together with glue.
And then I knew what to do.
I made a model of you,
65 A man in black with a Meinkampf[10] look

And a love of the rack and the screw.[11]
And I said I do, I do.
So daddy, I'm finally through.
The black telephone's off at the root,
70 The voices just can't worm through.

---

[6] Region of the Alps in West Austria and Northern Italy.

[7] The German air force.

[8] Of or pertaining to a presumed ethnic type descended from early speakers of Indo-European languages; a term used by the Nazi party in World War II to denote racial purity.

[9] A *panzer* is a "tank" (translation from German).

[10] Book written by Hitler; *My Struggle* (translation from German).

[11] Instruments of torture.

If I've killed one man, I've killed two—
The vampire who said he was you
And drank my blood for a year,
Seven years, if you want to know.
75 Daddy, you can lie back now.

There's a stake in your fat black heart
And the villagers never liked you.
They are dancing and stamping on you.
They always *knew* it was you.
80 Daddy, daddy, you bastard, I'm through.

■ EXPLORATIONS OF THE TEXT

1. What is the significance of the "black shoe"?
2. To what nursery rhyme does the poet allude? How does the allusion dictate the rhyme scheme? What is the emotional effect of the dominant sounds of the rhyme scheme?
3. How does the speaker first present her father? Why does she envision him as "Marble-heavy, a bag full of God"?
4. Why does she compare her father to a German? a Nazi? Why does she compare herself to a Jew?
5. Why does she compare her father to a "devil"?
6. Why does the speaker try to kill herself at twenty?
7. Why does the speaker state: "If I've killed one man, I've killed two"?
8. To what does the movie imagery in the last stanza refer? What is the effect of Plath's use of black humor?
9. Compare Plath's vision with the characterization of the father in "Rappaccini's Daughter."

■ THE READING/WRITING CONNECTION

1. "Think" Topic: Plath described the persona as a girl with an Electra complex. What is an Electra complex? Is this an adequate explanation for the behavior of the persona in the poem?

■ IDEAS FOR WRITING

1. How does Plath use sound and rhyme in "Daddy"? How do these techniques develop themes of the poem?
2. Why is the persona so angry at "Daddy"? Is the conflict resolved? Is she "through"?
3. Compare the point of view and tone of the speaker in this poem with that of one speaker in another poem in this chapter.

SIMON ORTIZ

Simon Ortiz (1941–   ), an Acoma Pueblo Indian, was born in Albuquerque, New Mexico. Between 1961 and 1969 Ortiz attended college, interrupting his education to serve in the U.S. Army in Vietnam from 1963 to 1966. In 1969, he won a Discovery Award from the National Endowment for the Arts. In 1976, Going for the Rain, *his first major collection of poems, was published. Subsequent volumes include* A Good Journey *(1977),* Fight Back: For the Sake of the People, For the Sake of the Land *(1980),* From Sand Creek: Rising in This House Which Is Our America *(1981) and* Out There Somewhere *(2002). Ortiz's work focuses on the entwined destinies of the Native Americans and other cultures, alienation of human beings from their roots, and his dream for producing harmony between humans and nature.*

1976

MY FATHER'S SONG

Wanting to say things,
I miss my father tonight.
His voice, the slight catch,
the depth from his thin chest,
5 the tremble of emotion
in something he has just said
to his son, his song:

We planted corn one Spring at Acu—
we planted several times
10 but this one particular time
I remember the soft damp sand
in my hand.

My father had stopped at one point
to show me an overturned furrow;
15 the plowshare had unearthed
the burrow nest of a mouse
in the soft moist sand.

Very gently, he scooped tiny pink animals
into the palm of his hand
20 and told me to touch them.
We took them to the edge
of the field and put them in the shade
of a sand moist clod.

I remember the very softness
25 of cool and warm sand and tiny alive mice
and my father saying things.

■ **EXPLORATIONS OF THE TEXT**

1. Who is the speaker in the first stanza of the poem? Who is the speaker in the last four stanzas?
2. What picture emerges of the father in the first stanza? What images give you clues?
3. What does "his song" suggest about the speaker, his father, and his grandfather?
4. Why does the poet repeat the image of "damp sand"? How do the associations of "sand" change or build?
5. What is the significance of the central images of "cool and warm sand" and "tiny alive mice"? What do the furrows and the ploughing suggest?
6. What inheritance does the grandfather want to give to his son? What does the father want to leave to the speaker?

■ **THE READING/WRITING CONNECTION**

1. Freewrite. Respond to the philosophy of life presented in the poem.

2. Contrast the inability to communicate in "Daddy" with the memory of voice in "My Father's Song."

■ **IDEAS FOR WRITING**

1. Explicate and evaluate this poem. (See chapter 10.)
2. What is the relation of human beings to the earth in "My Father's Song"?

LI-YOUNG LEE

Li-Young Lee (1957–) was born in Indonesia to Chinese parents. In 1957, his father was jailed by then-dictator Sukarno for nineteen months, sixteen of which were spent in a leper colony. After his father escaped, the family fled the country, settling in western Pennsylvania. Lee's culturally diverse background is evident in his love of both the Chinese poetry and Bible verses recited to him by his classically educated parents. His autobiography, The Winged Seed *(1995), won the American Book award and the Before Columbus Foundation award. His first volume of poetry,* Rose, *was published in 1986; his second volume,* The City in Which I Love You, *won the Lamont Prize for Poetry in 1990; and his third,* Book of My Nights, *was published in 2001.*

1986

PERSIMMONS

In sixth grade Mrs. Walker
slapped the back of my head
and made me stand in the corner
for not knowing the difference
5 between *persimmon* and *precision*.
How to choose
persimmons. This is precision.
Ripe ones are soft and brown-spotted.
Sniff the bottoms. The sweet one
10 will be fragrant. How to eat:
put the knife away, lay down newspaper.
Peel the skin tenderly, not to tear the meat.
Chew the skin, suck it,
and swallow. Now, eat
15 the meat of the fruit,
so sweet,
all of it, to the heart.

Donna undresses, her stomach is white.
In the yard, dewy and shivering
20 with crickets, we lie naked,
face-up, face-down.
I teach her Chinese.
Crickets: *chiu chiu.* Dew: I've forgotten.
Naked: I've forgotten.
25 *Ni, wo:*   you and me.
I part her legs,
remember to tell her
she is beautiful as the moon.

Other words
30 that got me into trouble were
fight and *fright, wren* and *yarn.*
Fight was what I did when I was frightened,
fright was what I felt when I was fighting.
Wrens are small, plain birds,
35 yarn is what one knits with.
Wrens are soft as yarn.
My mother made birds out of yarn.
I loved to watch her tie the stuff;
a bird, a rabbit, a wee man.

40 Mrs. Walker brought a persimmon to class
and cut it up
so everyone could taste
a *Chinese apple.* Knowing
it wasn't ripe or sweet, I didn't eat
45 but watched the other faces.

My mother said every persimmon has a sun
inside, something golden, glowing,
warm as my face.

Once, in the cellar, I found two wrapped in newspaper,
50 forgotten and not yet ripe.
I took them and set both on my bedroom windowsill,
where each morning a cardinal
sang, *The sun, the sun.*

Finally understanding
55 he was going blind,
my father sat up all one night
waiting for a song, a ghost.
I gave him the persimmons,
swelled, heavy as sadness,
60 and sweet as love.

This year, in the muddy lighting
of my parent's cellar, I rummage, looking
for something I lost.
My father sits on the tired, wooden stairs,
65 black cane between his knees,
hand over hand, gripping the handle.

He's so happy that I've come home.
I ask how his eyes are, a stupid question.
All gone, he answers.

70 Under some blankets, I find a box.
Inside the box I find three scrolls.
I sit beside him and untie
three paintings by my father:
Hibiscus leaf and a white flower.

75 Two cats preening.
Two persimmons, so full they want to drop from the cloth.

He raises both hands to touch the cloth,
asks, *Which is this?*

This is persimmons, Father.

80 *Oh, the feel of the wolftail on the silk,*
the strength, the tense
precision in the wrist.
I painted them hundreds of times
eyes closed. These I painted blind.
85 *Some things never leave a person:*
scent of the hair of one you love,
the texture of persimmons,
in your palm, the ripe weight.

■ EXPLORATIONS OF THE TEXT

1. Characterize the voice and the tone of the speaker.
2. What does the symbolism of persimmons suggest about the speaker's background? Attitude toward his heritage? Relationship with his father?
3. Why does the poet insert the love scene in stanza 2?
4. List the words that the speaker confuses and then discuss their significance.
5. Explore the meaning of the dialogue between father and son in the last six stanzas. What does the son learn about their relationship? Analyze the play on words of "sun" and "son."
6. What gifts of mind and spirit does the father give to his son? What values does the father want to pass on to his child?

■ THE READING/WRITING CONNECTION

1. Write a monologue in the voice of the father.
2. Journal Entry: Imagine other incidents between father and son. Create a series of scenes and narrative moments.
3. Gloss and annotate the poem; focus on images of China. What do you learn?

■ IDEAS FOR WRITING

1. "Think" Topic: Are the fathers in "Persimmons" and in "Those Winter Sundays" good fathers? Do they nurture their sons? Are the speakers good sons? Do they relate to and know their fathers?
2. In a journal entry discuss how cultural expectations have shaped the father's and son's lives in "Persimmons."

SEAMUS HEANEY

Seamus Heaney (1939–) was born into a Roman Catholic family in predominantly Protestant Northern Ireland. Educated at Queen's University, Belfast, Heaney became part of a group of young Northern Irish poets. His first book of poems, Digging, *was published in 1966. Subsequent volumes include* North *(1975),* Station Island *(1984),* Seeing Things *(1991), and* Electric Light *(2001). Despite Heaney's commitment to the Catholic cause in Northern Island, he moved to the Republic of Ireland in 1972 and divides his time with the United States, where he teaches at Harvard University. He was awarded the Nobel Prize for Literature in 1995. His poetry is marked by its concern with the natural world, with Irish history, and with the language of everyday speech.*

1966

DIGGING

Between my finger and my thumb
The squat pen rests; snug as a gun.

Under my window, a clean rasping sound
When the spade sinks into gravelly ground:
5 My father, digging. I look down

Till his straining rump among the flowerbeds
Bends low, comes up twenty years away
Stooping in rhythm through potato drills
Where he was digging.

10 The coarse boot nestled on the lug, the shaft
Against the inside knee was levered firmly.
He rooted out tall tops, buried the bright edge deep
To scatter new potatoes that we picked
Loving their cool hardness in our hands.

15 By God, the old man could handle a spade.
Just like his old man.

My grandfather cut more turf in a day
Than any other man on Toner's bog.
Once I carried him milk in a bottle
20 Corked sloppily with paper. He straightened up

To drink it, then fell to right away
Nicking and slicing neatly, heaving sods
Over his shoulder, going down and down
For the good turf. Digging.

25 The cold smell of potato mould, the squelch and slap
Of soggy peat, the curt cuts of an edge
Through living roots awaken in my head.
But I've no spade to follow men like them.

Between my finger and my thumb
30 The squat pen rests.
I'll dig with it.

■ EXPLORATIONS OF THE TEXT

1. Contrast the speaker's sense of vocation with his representation of his father's and grandfather's work. Explicate the line: "The squat pen rests." Why does he use the word "squat"?
2. How does the poet describe the father's and grandfather's "digging"? What metaphors
   are used to describe their labors?
3. What does the speaker realize about his ancestry?
4. Explore the multiple meanings of the title, "Digging."

■ THE READING/WRITING CONNECTION

1. Journal Entry: Contrast a physical act or gesture that you associate with a grandparent
   or with a parent and one of your own. What do you learn about your connection with
   your past?
2. "Think" Topic: What views of labor and of artistry are expressed in this work?

■ IDEAS FOR WRITING
1. Create a dialogue among three fathers presented in three poems in this chapter.
2. Explicate this poem: Focus on point of view, tone, imagery, structure, and word choice.

MARTIN ESPADA

Martin Espada (1957–), born in Brooklyn, New York, has worked at jobs ranging from bouncer to tenant lawyer. Espada, a professor at the University of Massachusetts, Amherst, has won two National Endowment of the Arts Fellowships, a Massachusetts Artists' Fellowship, a PEN/Revson Fellowship, and the Patterson Poetry Price. His volumes of poetry include Immigrant Iceboy's Bolero *(1982),* Rebellion Is the Circle of a Lover's Hand *(1990), and* Imagine the Angels of Bread *(1996). Espada's writing and life are devoted to improving the social conditions of Hispanic and other marginalized people.*

1996

THE SIGN IN MY FATHER'S HANDS

for Frank Espada

> The beer company
> did not hire Blacks or Puerto Ricans,
> so my father joined the picket line
> at the Schaefer Beer Pavilion, New York World's Fair,
> 5 amid the crowds glaring with canine hostility.
> But the cops brandished nightsticks
> and handcuffs to protect the beer,
> and my father disappeared.
>
> In 1964, I had never tasted beer,
> 10 and no one told me about the picket signs
> torn in two by the cops of brewery.
> I knew what dead was: dead was a cat
> overrun with parasites and dumped
> in the hallway incinerator.
> 15 I knew my father was dead.
> I went mute and filmy-eyed, the slow boy
> who did not hear the question in school.
> I sat studying his framed photograph
> like a mirror, my darker face.
>
> 20 Days later, he appeared in the doorway
> grinning with his gilded tooth.
> Not dead, though I would come to learn
> that sometimes Puerto Ricans die
> in jail, with bruises no one can explain
> 25 swelling their eyes shut.
> I would learn too that "boycott"

is not a boy's haircut,
that I could sketch a picket line
on the blank side of a leaflet.
30 That day my father returned
from the netherworld
easily as riding the elevator to apartment 14-F,
and the brewery cops could only watch
in drunken disappointment.
35 I searched my father's hands
for a sign of the miracle.

■ **EXPLORATIONS OF THE TEXT**

1. Discuss the point of view and perspective of the speaker. How does the speaker view his father?
2. Paraphrase the action of the poem. What has happened to the speaker's father?
3. Explore the connotations of the word "gilded." How does this particular word choice suggest a theme of the work?
4. What is "the miracle"?
5. Discuss the symbolism of the title.
6. Compare the persona's father with the speaker's father in "My Father's Song."

■ **THE READING/WRITING CONNECTION**

1. "Think" Topic: What is the father's mythic journey?

■ **IDEAS FOR WRITING**

1. Compare the use of mythic allusions in this work and in "Persimmons."

LYN LIFSHIN

Lyn Lifshin (1944–   ), born in Burlington, Vermont, published her first collection of poems,
Why Is the House Dissolving? *in 1968, although she had been writing poetry since age three.*
Many critics consider her finest work to be about historical subjects. In the Shaker House Poems *(1976), Lifshin captures the essence of early American Shaker religious communities; her*
poetic reflections on early Eskimo culture of the Arctic are contained in Leaning South
(1977). During her prolific career, Lifshin has published more than 100 volumes of poetry, in-
cluding her most recent, A New Film by a Woman in Love with the Dead *(2002) and* Another Woman Who Looks Like Me *(2003). During her career, Lifshin has taught writing and*
poetry at universities and colleges throughout the United States and has received numerous
awards for her poetry. She also has edited an important collection of women's autobiograph-
ical writing, Ariadne's Thread: A Collection of Contemporary Women's Journals *(1982).*

1968

MY MOTHER AND THE BED

No, not that way she'd
say when I was 7, pulling
the bottom sheet smooth,
you've got to   saying
5   hospital corners

I wet the bed much later
than I should, until
just writing this I
hadn't thought of
10 the connection

My mother would never
sleep on sheets someone
else had   I never
saw any stains on hers
15 tho her bedroom was

a maze of powder   hair
pins   black dresses
Sometimes she brings her
own sheets to my house,
20 carries toilet seat covers

Did anybody sleep
in my   she always asks
Her sheets   her hair
she says the rooms here
25 smell funny

We drive at 3 am
slowly into Boston and
strip what looks like
two clean beds as the
30 sky gets light   I

smooth on the form
fitted flower bottom,
she redoes it

She thinks of my life
35 as a bed only she
can make right

■ EXPLORATIONS OF THE TEXT

1. What does the symbol of the bed reveal about each stage of the speaker's life? What does it suggest about the relationship of the speaker and her mother?
2. What conclusions do you draw about the character of the mother?
3. What is the significance of the closing stanza of the poem?
4. Does the humor in the poem add to or detract from the message?
5. Do you think the lack of punctuation enhances the poem? Why? In what ways?

■ THE READING/WRITING CONNECTION

1. "Think" Topic: Based on your own experience and observations, what truths about the mother-daughter relationship does the poem suggest? Is the poem realistic? Why? Why not?
2. Gloss the poem; note examples of humor. What role does humor play in this poem?

■ IDEAS FOR WRITING

1. Write a humorous portrayal of your relationship with a family member. You may write a poem. Use a thematic motif (e.g., the bed).
2. Analyze your essay. Is the humor effective?

Jamaica Kincaid

*Jamaica Kincaid (1949–   ) was born in Antigua in the West Indies. Kincaid emigrated to the United States to attend college, which she found "a dismal failure." She is now a naturalized citizen, living in New York City and in Burlington, Vermont. Her first collection of short sto-*ries, At the Bottom of the River *(1983), won the Morton Dauwen Zabel Award of the Amer-ican Academy and Institute of Arts and Letters. Her subsequent volumes have included* Annie John *(1985),* The Autobiography of My Mother *(1996),* My Brother *(1997), and* Mr. Potter *(2002).*

"Girl" was Kincaid's first published piece of fiction (in The New Yorker*), written in 1977 af-ter reading Elizabeth Bishop's "In the Waiting Room." She drafted it in one rush of energy, and it is one long sentence.*

1977

GIRL

Wash the white clothes on Monday and put them on the stone heap; wash the color clothes on Tuesday and put them on the clothesline to dry; don't walk barehead in the hot sun; cook pumpkin fritters in very hot sweet oil; soak your little cloths right after you take them off; when buying cotton to make yourself a nice blouse, be sure that it doesn't have gum on it, because that way it won't hold up well after a wash; soak salt fish overnight before you cook it; is it true that you sing benna[1] in Sunday school?; always eat your food in such a way that it won't turn someone else's stomach; on Sundays try to walk like a lady and not like the slut you are so bent on becoming; don't sing benna in Sunday school; you mustn't speak to wharf-rat boys, not even to give directions; don't eat fruits on the street—flies will follow you; *but I don't sing benna on Sundays at all and never in Sunday school;* this is how to sew on a button; this is how to make a button-hole for the button you have just sewed on; this is how to hem a dress when you see the hem coming down and so to prevent yourself from looking like the slut I know you are so bent on becoming; this is how you iron your father's khaki shirt so that it doesn't have a crease; this is how you iron your father's khaki pants so that they don't have a crease, this is how you grow okra—far from the house, because okra tree harbors red ants: when you are growing dasheen,[2] make sure it gets plenty of water or else it makes your throat itch when you are eating it; this is how you sweep a corner; this is how you sweep a whole house; this is how you sweep a yard; this is how you smile to someone you don't like too much; this is how you smile to someone you don't like at all; this is how you smile to someone you like completely; this is how you set a table for tea; this is how you set a table for dinner; this is how you set a table for dinner with an important guest; this is how you set a table for lunch; this is how you set a table for breakfast; this is how to behave in the presence of men who don't know you very well, and this way they won't recognize immediately the slut I have warned you against be-coming; be sure to wash every day, even if it is with your own spit; don't squat down to play marbles—you are not a boy, you know; don't pick people's flowers—you might catch some-thing; don't throw stones at blackbirds, because it might not be a blackbird at all; this is how to make a bread pudding; this is how to make doukona,[3] this is how to make pepper pot;[4]

---

[1] Calypso music.

[2] A kind of potato.

[3] A spicy pudding made of plantains.

[4] A kind of stew.

this is how to make a good medicine for a cold; this is how to make a good medicine to throw away a child before it even becomes a child; this is how to catch a fish; this is how to throw back a fish you don't like, and that way something bad won't fall on you; this is how to bully a man; this is how a man bullies you; this is how to love a man, and if this doesn't work there are other ways, and if they don't work don't feel too bad about giving up; this is how to spit up in the air if you feel like it, and this is how to move quick so that it doesn't fall on you; this is how to make ends meet; always squeeze bread to make sure it's fresh; *but what if the baker won't let me feel the bread?;* you mean to say that after all you are really going to be the kind of woman who the baker won't let near the bread?

■ EXPLORATIONS OF THE TEXT

1. Who speaks which lines in the poem?
2. The speech is a single sentence filled with commands. What do they suggest about the main speaker's intentions? Characterize the speaker.
3. What is the main speaker's tone? What is the significance of the variations of the phrase, "not like the slut you are so bent on becoming"?
4. What do the girl's lines reveal about her character? about her relationship with the speaker?
5. Why does the speaker say, "You mean to say that after all you are really going to be the kind of woman who the baker won't let near the bread?"
6. What vision of female roles emerges in this piece?
7. What is the impact of the repeated phrasing, of the parallel structure, and of its form as a single sentence?

■ THE READING/WRITING CONNECTION

1. Create an imitation of this speech as a mother/father giving advice to a child in North America. You may create the voice of your parent talking to you.
2. Become a representative figure and give advice (e.g., a teenager giving advice about how to be a "teen" in North America to a foreign student; a senior giving advice to a college freshman).
3. Create a comparable version of "Girl" for a "Boy."

■ IDEAS FOR WRITING

1. What motivates the mother's speech? Is her approach effective? Why? Why not?

MARIE HOWE (1950–   )   **1998**

THE BOY

My older brother is walking down the sidewalk into the suburban
    summer night:
white T-shirt, blue jeans—to the field at the end of the street.

Hangers Hideout the boys called it, an undeveloped plot, a pit
    overgrown
with weeds, some old furniture thrown down there,

5 and some metal hangers clinking in the trees like wind chimes.
He's running away from home because our father wants to cut his hair.

And in two more days our father will convince me to go to him—you know
where he is—and talk to him: No reprisals. He promised. A small parade
   of kids

in feet pajamas will accompany me, their voices like the first peepers
   in spring.
10 And my brother will walk ahead of us home, and my father

will shave his head bald, and my brother will not speak to anyone the next
month, not a word, not *pass the milk,* nothing.

What happened in our house taught my brothers how to leave, how to walk
down a sidewalk without looking back.

15 I was the girl. What happened taught me to follow him, whoever he was,
calling and calling his name.

■ EXPLORATIONS OF THE TEXT

1. What is the speaker's role in her family? How does she relate to both her father and her brother?
2. What do the boy's clothes, "hideout," and hair suggest about his identity and rebelliousness?
3. Discuss the father-son relationship in the poem. What does the relationship reveal about socially conditioned gender roles for men and women in North American society?
4. Explore the use of force in this poem and in Pastan's "The Old Guerilla War." What are the consequences for the development of boys?

■ THE READING/WRITING CONNECTION

1. Freewrite: What have you been taught about how to be a boy or a girl in North American society? How have you conformed to societal expectations? How have you rebelled?
2. Write about a conflict with one of your parents over appearance or choice of clothing.
3. Write a poetic response in the voice of the boy, or write a letter from the boy to his father.

■ IDEAS FOR WRITING

1. Ortiz's "My Father's Song," Sexton's "My Little Girl, My Stringbean, My Lovely Woman," Pastan's "In the Old Guerilla War," and Howe's "The Boy" use nature imagery to suggest theme. What is the impact of this word choice? What does it suggest about family relationships? About gender roles? Compare and contrast the use of this technique by several of the writers.
2. Compare and contrast gender roles for women presented in this work with those in Kincaid's "Girl."

ANNE SEXTON

Anne Sexton (1928–74) was born in Newton, Massachusetts. She attended Garland Junior College in Massachusetts and taught high school and college. After suffering one of many nervous breakdowns, Sexton was urged by a psychiatrist to try writing poetry. She did so with immediate success; the poet Robert Lowell was one of her mentors. She published her first book of poems, To Bedlam and Part Way Back, *in 1960. In 1967, she won the Pulitzer Prize for Poetry for* Live or Die. *With Lowell, Sexton is associated with the Confessional school of poetry, drawing on intensely personal subject matter for her poems. She committed suicide in 1974. Sexton's* Complete Poems *were published in 1981.*

1964

MY LITTLE GIRL, MY STRINGBEAN,
MY LOVELY WOMAN

My daughter, at eleven
(almost twelve), is like a garden.

Oh, darling! Born in that sweet birthday suit
and having owned it and known it for so long,
5   now you must watch high noon enter—
noon, that ghost hour.
Oh, funny little girl—this one under a blueberry sky,
this one! How can I say that I've known
just what you know and just where you are?

10   It's not a strange place, this odd home
where your face sits in my hand
so full of distance,
so full of its immediate fever.
The summer has seized you,
15   as when, last month in Amalfi,[1] I saw
lemons as large as your desk-side globe—
that miniature map of the world—
and I could mention, too,
the market stalls of mushrooms
20   and garlic buds all engorged.
Or I think even of the orchard next door,
where the berries are done
and the apples are beginning to swell.
And once, with our first backyard,
25   I remember I planted an acre of yellow beans
we couldn't eat.

Oh, little girl,
my stringbean,
how do you grow?
30   *You grow this way.*
You are too many to eat.

I hear
as in a dream
the conversation of the old wives
35   speaking of *womanhood.*
I remember that I heard nothing myself.

---

[1] Town in Italy.

I was alone.
I waited like a target.

Let high noon enter—
40 the hour of the ghosts.
Once the Romans believed
that noon was the ghost hour,
and I can believe it, too,
under that startling sun,
45 and someday they will come to you,
someday, men bare to the waist, young Romans
at noon where they belong,
with ladders and hammers
while no one sleeps.

50 But before they enter
I will have said,
Your bones are lovely,
and before their strange hands
there was always this hand that formed.

55 Oh, darling, let your body in,
let it tie you in,
in comfort.
What I want to say, Linda,
is that women are born twice.
60 If I could have watched you grow
as a magical mother might,
if I could have seen through my magical transparent belly,
there would have been such ripening within:
your embryo,
65 the seed taking on its own,
life clapping the bedpost,
bones from the pond,
thumbs and two mysterious eyes,
the awfully human head,
70 the heart jumping like a puppy,
the important lungs,
the becoming—
while it becomes!
as it does now,
75 a world of its own,
a delicate place.

I say hello
to such shakes and knockings and high jinks,
such music, such sprouts,
80 such dancing-mad-bears of music,
such necessary sugar,
such goings-on!

Oh, little girl,
my stringbean,
85 *how do you grow?*
You grow this way.
You are too many to eat.

What I want to say, Linda,
is that there is nothing in your body that lies.
90 All that is new is telling the truth.
I'm here, that somebody else,
an old tree in the background.

Darling,
stand still at your door,
95 sure of yourself, a white stone, a good stone—
as exceptional as laughter
you will strike fire,
that new thing!

■ EXPLORATIONS OF THE TEXT

1. What is the significance of the garden imagery? What is the meaning of the refrain?
2. The poem shifts from garden imagery to birth imagery. What do "birth" and "womb" images suggest about the speaker's view of her daughter's imminent adolescence?
3. What does "high noon" signify?
4. What does the speaker envision as her role in her daughter's life?
5. Explore the significance of the statement that "women are born twice."
6. What are the speaker's final wishes for her daughter expressed in the last two stanzas? How will she help her daughter in adolescence?
7. Contrast the image of the mother who "waited like a target" with the image of the daughter who "will strike fire."
8. Compare the speaker's relationship with her daughter with relationships in poems by Baraka and Kumin.

■ THE READING/WRITING CONNECTION

1. "Think" Topic: How does Sexton use nursery and children's rhymes? How do the rhymes develop the poem's themes?
2. Journal Entry: Based on your experience, develop advice about growing up and about sexuality, and write it in the form of a letter to an adolescent.

■ IDEAS FOR WRITING

1. What are the speaker's feelings toward her daughter? How does the tone of the poem reveal her attitude? Which specific words and phrases create the tone?
2. Sexton's, Lifshin's, Lorde's, and Kincaid's works portray intense bonds between mothers and daughters. What differences appear in these writers' treatments of mother-daughter relationships?

MAXINE KUMIN

Maxine Kumin (1925–   ) was born in Philadelphia and educated at Radcliffe College. Kumin married, had three children, then enrolled in writing workshops at the Boston Center for Adult Education. There she met Anne Sexton, with whom she had a celebrated friendship, collaborating on four children's books with her. In 1973, Kumin received the Pulitzer Price for Poetry for her fourth volume, Up Country: Poems of New England. *Along with five other poetry collections, including her* Selected Poems: 1960–1990 *(1997), and her most recent volume,* The Long Marriage *(2001), Kumin has published several novels, twenty-two children's books, a collection of short stories, and several volumes of essays. She has lectured at universities across the country.*

1970

MAKING THE JAM WITHOUT YOU

for Judy

Old daughter, small traveler
asleep in a German featherbed
under the eaves in a postcard town
of turrets and towers,
5 I am putting a dream in your head.
Listen! Here it is afternoon.
The rain comes down like bullets.
I stand in the kitchen,
that harem of good smells
10 where we have bumped hips and
cracked the cupboards with our talk
while the stove top danced with pots
and it was not clear who did
the mothering. Now I am
15 crushing blackberries
to make the annual jam
in a white cocoon of steam.

Take it, my sleeper. Redo it
in any of your three
20 languages and nineteen years.
Change the geography.
Let there be a mountain,
the fat cows on it belled
like a cathedral. Let

25 there be someone beside you
as you come upon the ruins
of a schloss,[1] all overgrown
with a glorious thicket,
its brambles soft as wool.
30 Let him bring the buckets
crooked on his angel arms
and may the berries, vaster
than any forage in

---

[1] Castle.

the mild hills of New Hampshire,
35 drop in your pail, plum size,
heavy as the eyes
of any honest dog
and may you bear them
home together to a square
40 white unreconstructed kitchen
not unlike this one.
Now may your two heads
touch over the kettle,
over the blood of the berries
45 that drink up sugar and sun,
over that tar-thick boil
love cannot stir down.
More plainly than
the bric-a-brac of shelves
50 filling with jelly glasses,
more surely than
the light driving through them
trite as rubies, I see him
as pale as paraffin beside you.
55 I see you cutting
fresh baked bread to spread it
with the bright royal fur.

At this time
I lift the flap of your dream
60 and slip out thinner than a sliver
as your two mouths open
for the sweet stain of purple.

■ EXPLORATIONS OF THE TEXT

1. What mood and tone are established by the speaker's imagined scene of the girl asleep "under the eaves in a postcard town"?
2. What is the mother's dream? What is the effect of the dream images (fanciful, mysterious)?
3. What is the significance of the **simile,** "the rain comes down like bullets"?
4. How does the poet develop the symbol of the berries? In what ways do the meanings of the berries change and build?
5. What is the speaker's position in the last stanza? Why does she "slip out thinner than a sliver"?
6. What is the speaker's final wish for her daughter?

■ THE READING/WRITING CONNECTION

1. Write a monologue in the speaker's voice, and make explicit her dreams for her daughter. As a parent, would you have similar hopes?
2. "Think" Topic: How does Kumin use the imagery of the berries?

■ IDEAS FOR WRITING

1. What images indicate a symbiotic relationship between mother and daughter? Which images evoke the mother's letting go of the daughter?
2. Compare this poem with Lifshin's, Synge's, and Lorde's visions.

PAT MORA

Pat Mora (1942–   ) was born in El Paso, Texas. She has written poetry, Chants *(1984),* Borders *(1986),* Communion *(1991), and* Aunt Carmen's Book of Practical Saints *(1997); essays,* Napantla: Essays from the Land in the Middle *(1993); and children's books,* A Birthday Basket for Tia *(1992),* Pablo's Tree *(1994),* Tomas and the Library Lady *(1997) and* Maria Paints the Hills *(2002). Mora, awarded a Kellogg Fellowship in 1986, has worked as a teacher and as a museum curator.*

1984

ELENA

My Spanish isn't enough
I remember how I'd smile
listening to my little ones,
understanding every word they'd say,
5   their jokes, their songs, their plots.
    Vamos a pedirle dulces a mamá. Vamos.[1]
But that was in Mexico.
Now my children go to American high schools.
They speak English. At night they sit around
10 the kitchen table, laugh with one another.
I stand by the stove and feel dumb, alone.
I bought a book to learn English.
My husband frowned, drank more beer.
My oldest said, "Mamá, he doesn't want you
15 to be smarter than he is." I'm forty,
    embarrassed at mispronouncing words,
    embarrassed at the laughter of my children,
    the grocer, the mailman. Sometimes I take
    my English book and lock myself in the bathroom,
20 say the thick words softly,
    for if I stop trying, I will be deaf
    when my children need my help.

■ **EXPLORATIONS OF THE TEXT**

1. What is the speaker's conflict in "Elena"?
2. Discuss images of power and powerlessness in the poem. Explore the connotation of the words "deaf" and "dumb" in the poem.
3. Explore the theme of silencing in the work.

■ **THE READING/WRITING CONNECTION**

1. Journal Entry: Write a letter, monologue, or diary entry in Elena's voice.
2. "Think" Topic: Create a dialogue between Elena and the father in "Persimmons" on the subject of living in North America.

■ **IDEAS FOR WRITING**

1. Compare the character of Elena with that of the speaker in "Refugee Ship."
2. Explore themes of exile in this poem with that of "Lost Sister" (chapter 4).

---

[1] "Let's go ask mama for sweets. Let's go."

Poems for Comparison/Contrast: Lineage

MARGARET WALKER (1915–1998)   **1942**

LINEAGE

My grandmothers were strong.
They followed plows and bent to toil.
They moved through fields sowing seed.
They touched earth and grain grew.
5 They were full of sturdiness and singing.
My grandmothers were strong.

My grandmothers are full of memories
Smelling of soap and onions and wet clay
With veins rolling roughly over quick hands
10 They have many clean words to say.
My grandmothers were strong.
Why am I not as they?

ETHERIDGE KNIGHT (1931–1991)   **1968**

THE IDEA OF ANCESTRY

1

Taped to the wall of my cell are 47 pictures: 47 black
faces: my father, mother, grandmothers (1 dead), grandfathers (both dead), brothers, sisters, uncles, aunts,
cousins (1st & 2nd), nieces, and nephews. They stare
5 across the space at me sprawling on my bunk. I know
their dark eyes, they know mine. I know their style,
they know mine. I am all of them, they are all of me;
they are farmers, I am a thief, I am me, they are thee.

I have at one time or.other been in love with my mother,
10 1 grandmother, 2 sisters, 2 aunts (1 went to the asylum),
and 5 cousins. I am now in love with a 7 yr old niece
(she sends me letters written in large block print, and
her picture is the only one that smiles at me).

I have the same name as 1 grandfather, 3 cousins, 3 nephews,
15 and 1 uncle. The uncle disappeared when he was 15, just took
off and caught a freight (they say). He's discussed each year
when the family has a reunion, he causes uneasiness in
the clan, he is an empty space. My father's mother, who is 93

and who keeps the Family Bible with everybody's birth dates
20 (and death dates) in it, always mentions him. There is no
   place in her Bible for "whereabouts unknown."

Each fall the graves of my grandfathers call me, the brown
hills and red gullies of mississippi send out their electric
messages, galvanizing my genes. Last yr / like a salmon quitting
25 the cold ocean-leaping and bucking up his birthstream / I
   hitchhiked my way from L.A. with 16 caps[1] in my pocket and a
   monkey on my back.[2] And I almost kicked it with the kinfolks.
   I walked barefooted in my grandmother's backyard / I smelled the old
   land and the woods / I sipped cornwhiskey from fruit jars with the men /
30 I flirted with the women / I had a ball till the caps ran out
   and my habit came down. That night I looked at my grandmother
   and split / my guts were screaming for junk[3] / but I was almost
   contented / I had almost caught up with me.
   (The next day in Memphis I cracked a croaker's crib for a fix.)

35 This yr there is a gray stone wall damming my stream, and when
   the falling leaves stir my genes, I pace my cell or flop on my bunk
   and stare at 47 black faces across the space. I am all of them,
   they are all of me, I am me, they are thee, and I have no children
   to float in the space between.

AGHA SHAHID ALI (1949–   )   1987

SNOWMEN

My ancestor, a man
of Himalayan snow,
came to Kashmir from Samarkand,
carrying a bag
5 of whale bones:
heirlooms from sea funerals.
His skeleton
carved from glaciers, his breath
arctic,
10 he froze women in his embrace.
His wife thawed into stony water,

---

[1] Capsules or vials of drugs.
[2] Being high; having a drug habit.
[3] Heroin.

her old age a clear
evaporation.

This heirloom,
15 his skeleton under my skin, passed
from son to grandson,
generations of snowmen on my back.
They tap every year on my window,
their voices hushed to ice.

20 No, they won't let me out of winter,
and I've promised myself,
even if I'm the last snowman,
that I'll ride into spring
on their melting shoulders.

Poems for Comparison/Contrast: Loss and Family

ANNE BRADSTREET (1612?–1672)   1678

TO MY DEAR AND LOVING HUSBAND

If ever two were one, then surely we.
If ever man were loved by wife, then thee;
If ever wife was happy in a man,
Compare with me, ye women, if you can.
5 I prize thy love more than whole mines of gold
Or all the riches that the East doth hold.
My love is such that rivers cannot quench,
Nor ought but love from thee, give recompense.
Thy love is such I can no way repay,
10 The heavens reward thee manifold, I pray.
Then while we live, in love let's so persevere
That when we live no more, we may live ever.

WILLIAM WORDSWORTH (1770–1850)   1807

THE SAILOR'S MOTHER

One morning (raw it was and wet—
A foggy day in winter time)
A Woman on the road I met,

      Not old, though something past her prime:
5   Majestic in her person, tall and straight;
And like a Roman matron's was her mien and gait.

      The ancient spirit is not dead;
      Old times, thought I, are breathing there;
      Proud was I that my country bred
10   Such strength, a dignity so fair:
      She begged an alms, like one in poor estate;
I looked at her again, nor did my pride abate.

      When from these lofty thoughts I woke,
      "What is it," said I, "that you bear,
15   Beneath the covert of your Cloak,
      Protected from this cold damp air?"
      She answered, soon as she the question heard,
"A simple burthen, Sir, a little Singing-bird."

      And, thus continuing, she said,
20   "I had a Son, who many a day
      Sailed on the seas, but he is dead;
      In Denmark he was cast away:
      And I have travelled weary miles to see
If aught which he had owned might still remain for me.

25   "The bird and cage they both were his:
      'Twas my Son's bird; and neat and trim
      He kept it: many voyages
      The singing-bird had gone with him;
      When last he sailed, he left the bird behind;
30 From bodings, as might be, that hung upon his mind.

      "He to a fellow-lodger's care
      Had left it, to be watched and fed,
      And pipe its song in safety;—there
      I found it when my Son was dead;
35   And now, God help me for my little wit!
I bear it with me, Sir;—he took so much delight in it."

FRANCES ELLEN WATKINS HARPER (1825–1911)   **1854**

THE SLAVE MOTHER

      Heard you that shriek? It rose
        So wildly on the air.
      It seemed as if a burden'd heart
        Was breaking in despair.

5 Saw you those hands so sadly clasped—
        The bowed the feeble head—
      The shuddering of that fragile form—
        That look of grief and dread?

Saw you the sad, imploring eye?
10   Its every glance was pain,
As if a storm of agony
     Were sweeping through the brain.

She is a mother, pale with fear,
     Her boy clings to her side,
15 And in her kirtle[1] vainly tries
     His trembling form to hide.

He is not hers, although she bore
     For him a mother's pains;
He is not hers, although her blood
20   Is coursing through his veins!

He is not hers, for cruel hands
     May rudely tear apart
The only wreath of household love
     That binds her breaking heart.

25 His love has been a joyous light
     That o'er her pathway smiled,
A fountain gushing ever new,
     Amid life's desert wild.

His lightest word has been a tone
30   Of music round her heart,
Their lives a streamlet blent in one—
     Oh, Father! must they part?

They tear him from her circling arms,
     Her last and fond embrace.
35 Oh! never more may her sad eyes
     Gaze on his mournful face.

No marvel, then, these bitter shrieks
     Disturb the listening air:
She is a mother, and her heart
40   Is breaking in despair.

D. H. Lawrence (1885–1930)   1918

PIANO

Softly, in the dusk, a woman is singing to me;
Taking me back down the vista of years, till I see
A child sitting under the piano, in the boom of the tingling strings
And pressing the small, poised feet of a mother who smiles as she sings.

---

[1] Loose-fitting gown.

5 In spite of myself, the insidious mastery of song
  Betrays me back, till the heart of me weeps to belong
  To the old Sunday evenings at home, with winter outside
  And hymns in the cozy parlour, the tinkling piano our guide.

  So now it is vain for the singer to burst into clamour
10 With the great black piano appassionato. The glamour
  Of childish days is upon me, my manhood is cast
  Down in the flood of remembrance, I weep like a child for the past.

HAROLD A. ZLOTNIK (1914–)   **1948**

ODYSSEY

(For My Daughter)

Take this, my child, O World, and
    give her strength
As durable as grass that hugs the
    earth
5 In its vicissitudes; insure the length
Of summer days, uncradling from
    birth
A sky of living with that pine ter-
    rain
10 Of solitude; and let forgiveness,
    grow
Pervasive as the democratic rain
In hostile moments. Just as others
    know
15 Compassion past their grief, let her
    receive
That night-wind as the balm for
    desert heat
Her cool, diurnal hope, and soon
20   perceive
The beacon stars in crisis or retreat,
And mix her blood divinely with the
    sun
For faith to burn in glory and be
25   won.

LINDA HOGAN (1947–)   **1979**

HERITAGE

From my mother, the antique mirror
where I watch my face take on her lines.

She left me the smell of baking bread
to warm fine hairs in my nostrils,
5 she left the large white breasts that weigh down
my body.

From my father I take his brown eyes,
the plague of locusts that leveled our crops,
they flew in formation like buzzards.

10 From my uncle the whittled wood
that rattles like bones
and is white
and smells like all our old houses
that are no longer there. He was the man
15 who sang old chants to me, the words
my father was told not to remember.

From my grandfather who never spoke
I learned to fear silence.
I learned to kill a snake
20 when you're begging for rain.

And grandmother, blue-eyed woman
whose skin was brown,
she used snuff.[1]
When her coffee can full of black saliva
25 spilled on me
it was like the brown cloud of grasshoppers
that leveled her fields.
It was the brown stain
that covered my white shirt,
30 my whiteness a shame.
That sweet black liquid like the food
she chewed up and spit into my father's mouth
when he was an infant.
It was the brown earth of Oklahoma
35 stained with oil.
She said tobacco would purge your body of poisons.
It has more medicine than stones and knives
against your enemies.

That tobacco is the dark night that covers me.
40 She said it is wise to eat the flesh of deer
so you will be swift and travel over many miles.
She told me how our tribe has always followed a stick
that pointed west
that pointed east.

45 From my family I have learned the secrets
of never having a home.

---

[1] Finally ground tobacco that can be inhaled through the nose.

MARTIN ESPADA (1957–   )   **1993**

COCA-COLA AND COCO FRÍO

On his first visit to Puerto Rico,
island of family folklore,
the fat boy wandered
from table to table
5 with his mouth open.
At every table, some great-aunt
would steer him with cool spotted hands
to a glass of Coca-Cola.
One even sang to him, in all the English
10 she could remember, a Coca-Cola jingle
from the forties. He drank obediently, though
he was bored with this potion, familiar
from soda fountains in Brooklyn.

Then, at a roadside stand off the beach, the fat boy
15 opened his mouth to coco frío, a coconut
chilled, then scalped by a machete
so that a straw could inhale the clear milk.
The boy tilted the green shell overhead
and drooled coconut milk down his chin;
20 suddenly, Puerto Rico was not Coca-Cola
or Brooklyn, and neither was he.

For years afterward, the boy marveled at an island
where the people drank Coca-Cola
and sang jingles from World War II
25 in a language they did not speak,
while so many coconuts in the trees
sagged heavy with milk, swollen
and unsuckled.

DWIGHT OKITA (1958–   )   **1992**

THE NICE THING ABOUT COUNTING STARS

for my parents Fred and Patsy Okita

In 1942, over 100,000 Americans of Japanese descent were evacuated from their homes by the American government and forced to relocate in internment camps. They wound up staying for three years. My mother, Patsy Takeyo Okita, was one of them. This poem includes excerpts from her memoirs.

"In the hot summers of the 30's, we would
sit on the steps and sing for hours. We
even counted the stars in the sky and it
was always beautiful."

5 So my mother begins
    writing her life down, Jackie Onassis
    thinking in the car behind dark glasses.
    She recalls the luxury
    of growing up—she and her sisters
10 buying jelly bismarcks on Sundays
    and eating them in the back seat
    of their father's Packard
    parked on the drive.
    Pretending they were going
15 somewhere, and they were.
    Not knowing years later they would
    be headed for just such an exotic place.
    Somewhere far from Fresno, their white stone house
    on F Street, the blackboard in the kitchen
20 where they learned math,
                      long division, remainders,
        what is left
        after you divide something.

        "When Executive Order 9066 came telling
25   all Japanese-Americans to leave their
        houses, we cleared out of Fresno real
        fast. They gave us three days. I remember
        carrying a washboard to the camp. I don't
        know how it got in my hands. Someone must
30   have told me—Here, take this."

They were given three days to move
what had taken them years to acquire—
sewing machines, refrigerators, pianos, expensive fishing
rods from Italy. A war was on—Japs
35 had bombed Pearl Harbor.
Burma Shave billboards littered the highways:

    SLAP
           THE JAP

"Take only what you can carry"
40 My mother's family left the Packard
and with it left Sundays in the back seat.
Others walked away from acres of land,
drugstores, photo albums.

I think of turtles.
45 How they carry their whole lives
on their backs. My neighbor Jimmy
told me one night how they
make turtle soup down south.
A huge sea turtle—take a sledge hammer
50 to the massive shell, wedge it open
with one simple, solid blow
till the turtle can feel
no home above him, till everything

is taken away
55 and there is nothing
he will carry away from this moment.

My parents had three days
to relocate.
"Take only what you can carry."
60 One simple, solid blow—
They felt no home above them.

> *Dear Sirs:*
> *Of course I'll come. I've packed my galoshes*
> *and three packets of tomato seeds. Janet calls them*
> 65 *"love apples." My father says where we're going*
> *they won't grow.*
>
> *I am a fourteen-year-old girl with bad spelling*
> *and a messy room. If it helps any, I will tell you*
> *I have always felt funny using chopsticks*
> 70 *and my favorite food is hot dogs.*
> *My best friend is a white girl named Denise—*
> *we look at boys together. She sat in front of me*
> *all through grade school because of our names:*
> *O'Connor, Ozawa. I know the back of Denise's head very well.*
> 75 *I tell her she's going bald. She tells me I copy on tests.*
> *We are best friends.*
>
> *I saw Denise today in Geography class,*
> *She was sitting on the other side of the room.*
> *"You're trying to start a war," she said, "giving secrets away*
> 80 *to the Enemy, Why can't you keep your big mouth shut?"*
> *I didn't know what to say.*
> *I gave her a packet of tomato seeds*
> *and asked her to plant them for me, told her*
> *when the first tomato ripens*
> 85 *to miss me.*

> "We were sent to Jerome, Arkansas.
> Arriving there, I wondered how long
> we would be fenced in."

The nice thing about counting stars is
90 you can do it just about anywhere.
Even in a relocation camp
miles from home, even in Jerome, Arkansas
where a barbed wire fence crisscrosses itself
making stars of its own—but nothing
95 worth counting, nothing worth singing to.

My father remembers only two things:

> washing dishes in the mess hall each morning
> beside George Kaminishi and

> listening to Bing Crosby sing "White Christmas"
> 100 on the radio in the barracks late at night.

One morning, George looked up from a greasy skillet
at my dad and said Yosh, you're a happy-go-lucky guy.
What do you want to do with your life?
It was the first time he realized he had a life
105 to do things with. He was fifteen. He didn't know.
It was only later that Dad found out George
had colon cancer and had no life to do things with.
And when Bing sang late at night that song
Dad could only think, He's not singing to me he's
110 singing to white people.

    "I'm dreaming of a white Christmas,
    just like the ones I used to know."

My mother meanwhile was in a different camp
and hadn't met my father. At night, she'd lie
115 in bed and think about the old family car
back in the driveway—were the windows smashed
and broken into, the thing driven away by thieves?

Or was the grass a foot tall now, erasing the
Goodyear tires that were so shiny and new?
120 There was a hole in the week where Sunday
used to be, and she *wanted* jelly bismarcks
more than ever.

    "Somehow we adjusted. There were weekly
    dances for the young. Dad sent away
125   for a huge rice paper umbrella of vivid colors,
    and Peg and I hugged it during the stormy
    days."

Tonight, almost half a century later,
my father celebrates his 60th birthday.
130 He sits marking papers in the orange chair
in the living room, my mother enters grades
in the gradebook. In one corner
a brass gooseneck umbrella stand has been turned
into a planter—an ivy climbing its way
135 out. The oscillating fan shakes its head.

He remembers high school, Mrs. Barnett in Latin class,
himself at the head of it. A few days
before relocation, she took him aside.
So you'll be leaving us? she asked.
140 My father nodded.
She looked out the window at a maple tree
giving its leaves back to the earth,
at the chalky swirls of dust
on the blackboard for some good word
145 at the end of it all:

    Look on it as an adventure, she said.

JULIA ALVAREZ (1950–)   **1984**

HOMECOMING

When my cousin Carmen married, the guards
at her father's *finca*[1] took the guests' bracelets
and wedding rings and put them in an armored truck
for safekeeping while wealthy, dark-skinned men,
5 their plump, white women and spoiled children
bathed in a river whose bottom had been cleaned
for the occasion. She was Uncle's only daughter,
and he wanted to show her husband's family,
a bewildered group of sunburnt Minnesotans,
10 that she was valued. He sat me at their table
to show off my English, and when he danced with me,
fondling my shoulder blades beneath my bridesmaid's gown
as if they were breasts, he found me skinny
but pretty at seventeen, and clever.
15 *Come back from that cold place, Vermont,* he said,
all this is yours! Over his shoulder
a dozen workmen hauled in blocks of ice
to keep the champagne lukewarm and stole
glances at the wedding cake, a dollhouse duplicate
20 of the family *rancho,* the shutters marzipan,
the cobbles almonds. A maiden aunt housekept,
touching up whipped cream roses with a syringe
of eggwhites, rescuing the groom when the heat
melted his chocolate shoes into the frosting.
25 On too much rum Uncle led me across the dance floor,
dusted with talcum for easy gliding, a smell
of babies underfoot. He twirled me often,
excited by my pleas of dizziness, teasing me,
saying that my merengue had lost its Caribbean.
30 Above us, Chinese lanterns strung between posts
came on and one snapped off and rose
into a purple postcard sky.
A grandmother cried: *The children all grow up too fast.*
The Minnesotans finally broke loose and danced a Charleston
35 and were pronounced good gringos with latino hearts.
The little sister, freckled with a week of beach,
her hair as blonde as movie stars, was asked
by maids if they could touch her hair or skin,
and she backed off, until it was explained to her,
40 they meant no harm. *This is all yours,*
Uncle whispered, pressing himself into my dress.

---

[1] Plantation; farm.

The workmen costumed in their workclothes danced
a workman's jig. The maids went by with trays
of wedding bells and matchbooks monogrammed
45 with Dick's and Carmen's names. It would be years
before I took the courses that would change my mind
in schools paid for by sugar from the fields around us,
years before I could begin to comprehend
how one does not see the maids when they pass by. . . .
50 —It was too late, or early, to be wise—
The sun was coming up beyond the amber waves
of cane, the roosters crowed, the band struck up
Las Mañanitas, a morning serenade. I had a vision
that I blamed on the champagne:
55 the fields around us were burning. At last
a yawning bride and groom got up and cut
the wedding cake, but everyone was full
of drink and eggs, roast pig, and rice and beans.
Except the maids and workmen,
60 sitting on stoops behind the sugar house,
ate with their fingers from their open palms
windows, shutters, walls, pillars, doors,
made from the cane they had cut in the fields.

■ DRAMA ■

LORRAINE HANSBERRY

Lorraine Hansberry (1930–65) was born in Chicago. After attending the University of Wisconsin, she moved to New York City, where she married and wrote A Raisin in the Sun *(1959), which was an instant success. When* A Raisin in the Sun *appeared on Broadway in 1959, Hansberry became the first African American, the fifth woman, and the youngest playwright to win the New York Drama Critics Circle Award for Best Play of the Year. Actively involved in the civil rights movement, Hansberry was much in demand as a speaker. Her subsequent plays failed to equal the fame of her first, until the posthumously produced* To Be Young, Gifted, and Black *(1968), which was adapted from her earlier writing and which enjoyed a successful run off-Broadway.*

1959

A RAISIN IN THE SUN

A RAISIN IN THE SUN *was first presented by Philip Rose and David J. Cogan at the Ethel Barrymore Theatre, New York City, March 11, 1959, with the following cast:*

(In order of appearance)

Ruth Younger	Ruby Dee
Travis Younger	Glynn Turman
Walter Lee Younger (Brother)	Sidney Poitier

Beneatha Younger	Diana Sands
Lena Younger (Mama)	Claudia McNeil
Joseph Asagai	Ivan Dixon
George Murchison	Louis Gossett
Karl Lindner	John Fiedler
Bobo	Lonne Elder III
Moving Men	Ed Hall, Douglas Turner

The action of the play is set in Chicago's Southside,
sometime between World War II and the present.

Act One
Scene I. Friday morning.
Scene 2. The following morning.

Act Two
Scene I. Later, the same day.
Scene 2. Friday night, a few weeks later.
Scene 3. Moving day, one week later.

Act Three
An hour later.

Directed by Lloyd Richards
Designed and lighted by Ralph Alswang
Costumes by Virginia Volland

Act One
Scene I

The Younger living room would be a comfortable and well-ordered room if it were not for a number of indestructible contradictions to this state of being. Its furnishings are typical and undistinguished and their primary feature now is that they have clearly had to accommodate the living of too many people for too many years—and they are tired. Still, we can see that at some time, a time probably no longer remembered by the family (except perhaps for Mama), the furnishings of this room were actually selected with care and love and even hope—and brought to this apartment and arranged with taste and pride.

That was a long time ago. Now the once loved pattern of the couch upholstery has to fight to show itself from under acres of crocheted doilies and couch covers which have themselves finally come to be more important than the upholstery. And here a table or a chair has been moved to disguise the worn places in the carpet; but the carpet has fought back by showing its weariness, with depressing uniformity, elsewhere on its surface.

Weariness has, in fact, won in this room. Everything has been polished, washed, sat on, used, scrubbed too often. All pretenses but living itself have long since vanished from the very atmosphere of this room.

Moreover, a section of this room, for it is not really a room unto itself, though the landlord's lease would make it seem so, slopes backward to provide a small kitchen area, where the family prepares the meals that are eaten in the living room proper, which must also serve as dining room. The single window that has been provided for these "two" rooms is located in this kitchen area. The sole natural light the family may enjoy in the course of a day is only that which fights its way through this little window.

At left, a door leads to a bedroom which is shared by Mama and her daughter, Beneatha. At right, opposite, is a second room (which in the beginning of the life of this

*apartment was probably a breakfast room) which serves as a bedroom for Walter and his
wife, Ruth.*

    Time: Sometime between World War II and the present.

    Place: Chicago's Southside.

    *At Rise: It is morning dark in the living room. Travis is asleep on the make-down bed
at center. An alarm clock sounds from within the bedroom at right, and presently Ruth
enters from that room and closes the door behind her. She crosses sleepily toward the
window. As she passes her sleeping son she reaches down and shakes him a little. At the
window she raises the shade and a dusky Southside morning light comes in feebly. She
fills a pot with water and puts it on to boil. She calls to the boy, between yawns, in a
slightly muffled voice.*

    *Ruth is about thirty. We can see that she was a pretty girl, even exceptionally so, but
now it is apparent that life has been little that she expected, and disappointment has
already begun to hang in her face. In a few years, before thirty-five even, she will be
known among her people as a "settled woman."*

    She crosses to her son and gives him a good, final, rousing shake.

Ruth: Come on now, boy, it's seven-thirty! *(Her son sits up at last, in a stupor of sleepiness.)* I
    say hurry up, Travis! You ain't the only person in the world got to use a bathroom!
    *(The child, a sturdy, handsome little boy of ten or eleven, drags himself out of the bed and
    almost blindly takes his towels and "today's clothes" from drawers and a closet and goes out
    to the bathroom, which is in an outside hall and which is shared by another family or families
    on the same floor. Ruth crosses to the bedroom door at right and opens it and calls in to her
    husband.)* Walter Lee! . . . It's after seven-thirty! Lemme see you do some waking up in
    there now! *(She waits.)* You better get up from there, man! It's after seven-thirty I tell
    you. *(She waits again.)* All right, you just go ahead and lay there and next thing you
    know Travis be finished and Mr. Johnson'll be in there and you'll be fussing and
    cussing round here like a mad man! And be late too! *(She waits, at the end of patience.)*
    Walter Lee—it's time for you to get up!

*(She waits another second and then starts to go into the bedroom but is apparently satisfied that
her husband has begun to get up. She stops, pulls the door to, and returns to the kitchen area.
She wipes her face with a moist cloth and runs her fingers through her sleep-disheveled hair in a
vain effort and ties an apron around her housecoat. The bedroom door at right opens and her
husband stands in the doorway in his pajamas, which are rumpled and mismated. He is a lean,
intense young man in his middle thirties, inclined to quick nervous movements and erratic
speech habits—and always in his voice there is a quality of indictment.)*

Walter: Is he out yet?

Ruth: What you mean *out*? He ain't hardly got in there good yet.

Walter *(Wandering in, still more oriented to sleep than to a new day.):* Well, what was you
    doing all that yelling for if I can't even get in there yet? *(Stopping and thinking.)* Check
    coming today?

5 **Ruth:** They *said* Saturday and this is just Friday and I hopes to God you ain't going to get
    up here first thing this morning and start talking to me 'bout no money 'cause I 'bout
    don't want to hear it.

Walter: Something the matter with you this morning?

Ruth: No—I'm just sleepy as the devil. What kind of eggs you want?

Walter: Not scrambled. *(Ruth starts to scramble eggs.)* Paper come? *(Ruth points impatiently
    to the rolled up Tribune on the table, and he gets it and spreads it out and vaguely reads the
    front page.)* Set off another bomb yesterday.

Ruth (*Maximum indifference.*): Did they?

10 **Walter** (*Looking up.*): What's the matter with you?

Ruth: Ain't nothing the matter with me. And don't keep asking me that this morning.

Walter: Ain't nobody bothering you. (*Reading the news of the day absently again.*) Say Colonel McCormick is sick.

Ruth (*Affecting tea-party interest.*): Is he now? Poor thing.

Walter (*Sighing and looking at his watch.*): Oh, me. (*He waits.*) Now what is that boy doing in that bathroom all this time? He just going to have to start getting up earlier. I can't be being late to work on account of him fooling around in there.

15 **Ruth** (*Turning on him.*): Oh, no he ain't going to be getting up no earlier no such thing! It ain't his fault that he can't get to bed no earlier nights 'cause he got a bunch of crazy good-for-nothing clowns sitting up running their mouths in what is supposed to be his bedroom after ten o'clock at night . . .

Walter: That's what you mad about, ain't it? The things I want to talk about with my friends just couldn't be important in your mind, could they?

(*He rises and finds a cigarette in her handbag on the table and crosses to the little window and looks out, smoking and deeply enjoying this first one.*)

Ruth (*Almost matter of factly, a complaint too automatic to deserve emphasis.*): Why you always got to smoke before you eat in the morning?

Walter (*At the window.*): Just look at 'em down there . . . Running and racing to work . . . (*He turns and faces his wife and watches her a moment at the stove, and then, suddenly.*) You look young this morning, baby.

Ruth (*Indifferently.*): Yeah?

20 **Walter:** Just for a second—stirring them eggs. It's gone now—just for a second it was— you looked real young again. (*Then, drily.*) It's gone now—you look like yourself again.

Ruth: Man, if you don't shut up and leave me alone.

Walter (*Looking out to the street again.*): First thing a man ought to learn in life is not to make love to no colored woman first thing in the morning. You all some evil people at eight o'clock in the morning.

(*Travis appears in the hall doorway, almost fully dressed and quite wide awake now, his towels and pajamas across his shoulders. He opens the door and signals for his father to make the bathroom in a hurry.*)

Travis (*Watching the bathroom.*): Daddy, come on!

(*Walter gets his bathroom utensils and flies out to the bathroom.*)

Ruth: Sit down and have your breakfast, Travis.

25 **Travis:** Mama, this is Friday. (*Gleefully.*) Check coming tomorrow, huh?

Ruth: You get your mind off money and eat your breakfast.

Travis (*Eating.*): This is the morning we supposed to bring the fifty cents to school.

Ruth: Well, I ain't got no fifty cents this morning.

Travis: Teacher say we have to.

30 **Ruth:** I don't care what teacher say. I ain't got it. Eat your breakfast, Travis.

Travis: I *am* eating.

Ruth: Hush up now and just eat!

(*The boy gives her an exasperated look for her lack of understanding and eats grudgingly.*)

Travis: You think Grandmama would have it?

Ruth: No! And I want you to stop asking your grandmother for money, you hear me?

35 **Travis** (*Outraged.*): Gaaaleee! I don't ask her, she just gimme it sometimes!

Ruth: Travis Willard Younger—I got too much on me this morning to be—

Travis: Maybe Daddy—

Ruth: *Travis!*

(*The boy hushes abruptly. They are both quiet and tense for several seconds.*)

Travis (*Presently.*): Could I maybe go carry some groceries in front of the supermarket for a little while after school then?

40 **Ruth:** Just hush, I said. (*Travis jabs his spoon into his cereal bowl viciously, and rests his head in anger upon his fists.*) If you through eating, you can get over there and make up your bed.

(*The boy obeys stiffly and crosses the room, almost mechanically, to the bed and more or less carefully folds the covering. He carries the bedding into his mother's room and returns with his books and cap.*)

Travis (*Sulking and standing apart from her unnaturally.*): I'm gone.

Ruth (*Looking up from the stove to inspect him automatically.*): Come here. (*He crosses to her and she studies his head.*) If you don't take this comb and fix this here head, you better! (*Travis puts down his books with a great sign of oppression, and crosses to the mirror. His mother mutters under her breath about his "slubbornness."*) 'Bout to march out of here with that head looking just like chickens slept in it! I just don't know where you get your slubborn ways . . . And get your jacket, too. Looks chilly out this morning.

Travis (*With conspicuously brushed hair and jacket.*): I'm gone.

Ruth: Get carfare and milk money— (*Waving one finger.*) and not a single penny for no caps, you hear me?

45 **Travis:** (*With sullen politeness.*): Yes'm.

(*He turns in outrage to leave. His mother watches after him as in his frustration he approaches the door almost comically. When she speaks to him, her voice has become a very gentle tease.*)

Ruth (*Mocking; as she thinks he would say it.*): Oh, Mama makes me so mad sometimes, I don't know what to do! (*She waits and continues to his back as he stands stock-still in front of the door.*) I wouldn't kiss that woman good-bye for nothing in this world this morning! (*The boy finally turns around and rolls his eyes at her, knowing the mood has changed and he is vindicated; he does not, however, move toward her yet.*) Not for nothing in this world! (*She finally laughs aloud at him and holds out her arms to him and we see that it is a way between them, very old and practiced. He crosses to her and allows her to embrace him warmly but keeps his face fixed with masculine rigidity. She holds him back from her presently and looks at him and runs her fingers over the features of his face. With utter gentleness—.*) Now—whose little old angry man are you?

Travis (*The masculinity and gruffness start to fade at last.*): Aw gaalee—Mama . . .

Ruth (*Mimicking.*): Aw—gaaaaalleeeee, Mama! (*She pushes him, with rough playfulness and finality, toward the door.*) Get on out of here or you going to be late.

Travis (*In the face of love, new aggressiveness.*): Mama, could I *please* go carry groceries?

50 **Ruth:** Honey, it's starting to get so cold evenings.

Walter (*Coming in from the bathroom and drawing a make-believe gun from a make-believe holster and shooting at his son.*): What is it he wants to do?

Ruth: Go carry groceries after school at the supermarket.

Walter: Well, let him go . . .

Travis (*Quickly, to the ally.*): I have to—she won't gimme the fifty cents . . .

55 **Walter** (*To his wife only.*): Why not?

Ruth (*Simply, and with flavor.*): 'Cause we don't have it.

Walter (*To Ruth only.*): What you tell the boy things like that for? (*Reaching down into his pants with a rather important gesture.*) Here, son—

(*He hands the boy the coin, but his eyes are directed to his wife's. Travis takes the money happily.*)

Travis: Thanks, Daddy.

(*He starts out. Ruth watches both of them with murder in her eyes. Walter stands and stares back at her with defiance, and suddenly reaches into his pocket again on an afterthought.*)

Walter (*Without even looking at his son, still staring hard at his wife.*): In fact, here's another fifty cents . . . Buy yourself some fruit today—or take a taxi cab to school or something!

60 **Travis:** Whoopee—

(*He leaps up and clasps his father around the middle with his legs, and they face each other in mutual appreciation; slowly Walter Lee peeks around the boy to catch the violent rays from his wife's eyes and draws his head back as if shot.*)

Walter: You better get down now—and get to school, man.

Travis (*At the door.*): O.K. Good-bye.

(*He exits.*)

Walter (*After him, pointing with pride.*): That's my boy. (*She looks at him in disgust and turns back to her work.*) You know what I was thinking 'bout in the bathroom this morning?

Ruth: No.

65 **Walter:** How come you always try to be so pleasant!

Ruth: What is there to be pleasant 'bout!

Walter: You want to know what I was thinking 'bout in the bathroom or not!

Ruth: I know what you was thinking 'bout.

Walter (*Ignoring her.*): 'Bout what me and Willy Harris was talking about last night.

70 **Ruth** (*Immediately—a refrain.*): Willy Harris is a good-for-nothing loud mouth.

Walter: Anybody who talks to me has got to be a good-for-nothing loud mouth, ain't he? And what you know about who is just a good-for-nothing loud mouth? Charlie Atkins was just a "good-for-nothing loud mouth" too, wasn't he! When he wanted me to go in the dry-cleaning business with him. And now—he's grossing a hundred thousand a year. A hundred thousand dollars a year! You still call *him* a loud mouth!

Ruth (*Bitterly.*): Oh, Walter Lee . . .

(*She folds her head on her arms over on the table.*)

Walter (*Rising and coming to her and standing over her.*): You tired, ain't you? Tired of every-thing. Me, the boy, the way we live—this beat-up hole—everything. Ain't you? (*She doesn't look up, doesn't answer.*) So tired—moaning and groaning all the time, but you wouldn't do nothing to help, would you? You couldn't be on my side that long for nothing, could you?

Ruth: Walter, please leave me alone.

75 **Walter:** A man needs for a woman to back him up . . .

Ruth: Walter—

Walter: Mama would listen to you. You know she listen to you more than she do me and Bennie. She think more of you. All you have to do is just sit down with her when you drinking your coffee one morning and talking 'bout things like you do and— *(He sits down beside her and demonstrates graphically what he thinks her methods and tone should be.)*—you just sip your coffee, see, and say easy like that you been thinking 'bout that deal Walter Lee is so interested in, 'bout the store and all, and sip some more coffee, like what you saying ain't really that important to you— And the next thing you know, she be listening good and asking you questions and when I come home—I can tell her the details. This ain't no fly-by-night proposition, baby. I mean we figured it out, me and Willy and Bobo.

Ruth *(With a frown.)*: Bobo?

Walter: Yeah. You see, this little liquor store we got in mind cost seventy-five thousand and we figured the initial investment on the place be 'bout thirty thousand, see. That be ten thousand each. Course, there's a couple of hundred you got to pay so's you don't spend your life just waiting for them clowns to let your license get approved—

80 **Ruth:** You mean graft?

Walter *(Frowning impatiently.)*: Don't call it that. See there, that just goes to show you what women understand about the world. Baby, don't *nothing* happen for you in this world 'less you pay *somebody* off!

Ruth: Walter, leave me alone! *(She raises her head and stares at him vigorously—then says, more quietly.)* Eat your eggs, they gonna be cold.

Walter *(Straightening up from her and looking off.)*: That's it. There you are. Man say to his woman: I got me a dream. His woman say: Eat your eggs. *(Sadly, but gaining power.)* Man say: I got to take hold of this here world, baby! And a woman will say: Eat your eggs and go to work. *(Passionately now.)* Man say: I got to change my life, I'm choking to death, baby! And his woman say—*(In utter anguish as he brings his fists down on his thighs.)*—Your eggs is getting cold!

Ruth *(Softly.)*: Walter, that ain't none of our money.

85 **Walter** *(Not listening at all or even looking at her.)*: This morning, I was lookin' in the mirror and thinking about it . . . I'm thirty-five years old; I been married eleven years and I got a boy who sleeps in the living room—*(Very, very quietly.)*—and all I got to give him is stories about how rich white people live . . .

Ruth: Eat your eggs, Walter.

Walter: *Damn my eggs . . . damn all the eggs that ever was!*

Ruth: Then go to work.

Walter *(Looking up at her.)*: See—I'm trying to talk to you 'bout myself—*(Shaking his head with the repetition.)*—and all you can say is eat them eggs and go to work.

90 **Ruth** *(Wearily.)*: Honey, you never say nothing new. I listen to you every day, every night and every morning, and you never say nothing new. *(Shrugging.)* So you would rather *be* Mr. Arnold than be his chauffeur. So—I would *rather* be living in Buckingham Palace.

Walter: That is just what is wrong with the colored woman in this world . . . Don't understand about building their men up and making 'em feel like they somebody. Like they can do something.

Ruth *(Drily, but to hurt.)*: There *are* colored men who do things.

Walter: No thanks to the colored woman.

Ruth: Well, being a colored woman, I guess I can't help myself none.

(She rises and gets the ironing board and sets it up and attacks a huge pile of rough-dried clothes, sprinkling them in preparation for the ironing and then rolling them into tight fat balls.)

95 **Walter** (*Mumbling.*): We one group of men tied to a race of women with small minds.

(*His sister Beneatha enters. She is about twenty, as slim and intense as her brother. She is not as pretty as her sister-in-law, but her lean, almost intellectual face has a handsomeness of its own. She wears a bright-red flannel nightie, and her thick hair stands wildly about her head. Her speech is a mixture of many things; it is different from the rest of the family's insofar as education has permeated her sense of English—and perhaps the Midwest rather than the South has finally—at last—won out in her inflection; but not altogether, because over all of it is a soft slurring and transformed use of vowels which is the decided influence of the Southside. She passes through the room without looking at either Ruth or Walter and goes to the outside door and looks, a little blindly, out to the bathroom. She sees that it has been lost to the Johnsons. She closes the door with a sleepy vengeance and crosses to the table and sits down a little defeated.*)*

Beneatha: I am going to start timing those people.

Walter: You should get up earlier.

Beneatha (*Her face in her hands. She is still fighting the urge to go back to bed.*): Really—would you suggest dawn? Where's the paper?

Walter (*Pushing the paper across the table to her as he studies her almost clinically, as though he has never seen her before.*): You a horrible-looking chick at this hour.

100 **Beneatha** (*Drily.*): Good morning, everybody.

Walter (*Senselessly.*): How is school coming?

Beneatha (*In the same spirit.*): Lovely. Lovely. And you know, biology is the greatest. (*Looking up at him.*) I dissected something that looked just like you yesterday.

Walter: I just wondered if you've made up your mind and everything.

Beneatha (*Gaining in sharpness and impatience.*): And what did I answer yesterday morning—and the day before that?

105 **Ruth** (*From the ironing board, like someone disinterested and old.*): Don't be so nasty, Bennie.

Beneatha (*Still to her brother.*): And the day before that and the day before that!

Walter (*Defensively.*): I'm interested in you. Something wrong with that? Ain't many girls who decide—

Walter *and* **Beneatha** (*In unison.*): —"to be a doctor."

(*Silence.*)

Walter: Have we figured out yet just exactly how much medical school is going to cost?

110 **Ruth:** Walter Lee, why don't you leave that girl alone and get out of here to work?

Beneatha (*Exits to the bathroom and bangs on the door.*): Come on out of there, please!

Walter (*Looking at his sister intently.*): You know the check is coming tomorrow.

Beneatha (*Turning on him with a sharpness all her own.*): That money belongs to Mama, Walter, and it's for her to decide how she wants to use it. I don't care if she wants to buy a house or a rocket ship or just nail it up somewhere and look at it. It's hers. Not ours—*hers.*

Walter (*Bitterly.*): Now ain't that fine! You just got your mother's interest at heart, ain't you, girl? You such a nice girl—but if Mama got that money she can always take a few thousand and help you through school too—can't she?

115 **Beneatha:** I have never asked anyone around here to do anything for me!

Walter: No! And the line between asking and just accepting when the time comes is big and wide—ain't it!

Beneatha (*With fury.*): What do you want from me, Brother—that I quit school or just drop dead, which!

Walter: I don't want nothing but for you to stop acting holy 'round here. Me and Ruth done made some sacrifices for you—why can't you do something for the family?

Ruth: Walter, don't be dragging me in it.

120 **Walter:** You are in it—Don't you get up and go work in somebody's kitchen for the last three years to help put clothes on her back?

Ruth: Oh, Walter—that's not fair . . .

Walter: It ain't that nobody expects you to get on your knees and say thank you, Brother; thank you, Ruth; thank you, Mama—and thank you, Travis, for wearing the same pair of shoes for two semesters—

Beneatha (*Dropping to her knees.*): Well—I *do*—all right?—thank everybody . . . and forgive me for ever wanting to be anything at all . . . forgive me, forgive me!

Ruth: Please stop it! Your mama'll hear you.

125 **Walter:** Who the hell told you you had to be a doctor? If you so crazy 'bout messing 'round with sick people—then go be a nurse like other women—or just get married and be quiet . . .

Beneatha: Well—you finally got it said . . . It took you three years but you finally got it said. Walter, give up; leave me alone—it's Mama's money.

Walter: *He was my father, too!*

Beneatha: So what? He was mine, too—and Travis' grandfather—but the insurance money belongs to Mama. Picking on me is not going to make her give it to you to invest in any liquor stores—(*Underbreath, dropping into a chair.*)—and I for one say, God bless Mama for that!

Walter (*To Ruth.*): See—did you hear? Did you hear!

130 **Ruth:** Honey, please go to work.

Walter: Nobody in this house is ever going to understand me.

Beneatha: Because you're a nut.

Walter: Who's a nut?

Beneatha: You—you are a nut. Thee is mad, boy.

135 **Walter** (*Looking at his wife and his sister from the door, very sadly.*): The world's most backward race of people, and that's a fact.

Beneatha (*Turning slowly in her chair.*): And then there are all those prophets who would lead us out of the wilderness—(*Walter slams out of the house.*)—into the swamps!

Ruth: Bennie, why you always gotta be pickin' on your brother? Can't you be a little sweeter sometimes? (*Door opens. Walter walks in.*)

Walter (*To Ruth.*): I need some money for carfare.

Ruth (*Looks at him, then warms; teasing, but tenderly.*): Fifty cents? (*She goes to her bag and gets money.*) Here, take a taxi.

(*Walter exits. Mama enters. She is a woman in her early sixties, full-bodied and strong. She is one of those women of a certain grace and beauty who wear it so unobtrusively that it takes a while to notice. Her dark-brown face is surrounded by the total whiteness of her hair, and, being a woman who has adjusted to many things in life and overcome many more, her face is full of strength. She has, we can see, wit and faith of a kind that keep her eyes lit and full of interest and expectancy. She is, in a word, a beautiful woman. Her bearing is perhaps most like the noble bearing of the women of the Hereros of Southwest Africa—rather as if she imagines that as she walks she still bears a basket or a vessel upon her head. Her speech, on the other hand, is as careless as her carriage is precise—she is inclined to slur everything— but her voice is perhaps not so much quiet as simply soft.*)

140 **Mama:** Who that 'round here slamming doors at this hour?

(*She crosses through the room, goes to the window, opens it, and brings in a feeble little plant growing doggedly in a small pot on the window sill. She feels the dirt and puts it back out.*)

Ruth: That was Walter Lee. He and Bennie was at it again.

Mama: My children and they tempers. Lord, if this little old plant don't get more sun than it's been getting it ain't never going to see spring again. (*She turns from the window.*) What's the matter with you this morning, Ruth? You looks right peaked. You aiming to iron all them things? Leave some for me. I'll get to 'em this afternoon. Bennie honey, it's too drafty for you to be sitting 'round half dressed. Where's your robe?

Beneatha: In the cleaners.

Mama: Well, go get mine and put it on.

145 **Beneatha:** I'm not cold, Mama, honest.

Mama: I know—but you so thin . . .

Beneatha (*Irritably.*): Mama, I'm not cold.

Mama (*Seeing the make-down bed as Travis has left it.*): Lord have mercy, look at that poor bed. Bless his heart—he tries, don't he?

(*She moves to the bed Travis has sloppily made up.*)

Ruth: No—he don't half try at all 'cause he knows you going to come along behind him and fix everything. That's just how come he don't know how to do nothing right now—you done spoiled that boy so.

150 **Mama:** Well—he's a little boy. Ain't supposed to know 'bout housekeeping. My baby, that's what he is. What you fix for his breakfast this morning?

Ruth (*Angrily.*): I feed my son, Lena!

Mama: I ain't meddling—(*Underbreath; busy-bodyish.*) I just noticed all last week he had cold cereal, and when it starts getting this chilly in the fall a child ought to have some hot grits or something when he goes out in the cold—

Ruth (*Furious.*): I gave him hot oats—is that all right!

Mama: I ain't meddling. (*Pause.*) Put a lot of nice butter on it? (*Ruth shoots her an angry look and does not reply.*) He likes lots of butter.

155 **Ruth** (*Exasperated.*): Lena—

Mama (*To Beneatha. Mama is inclined to wander conversationally sometimes.*): What was you and your brother fussing 'bout this morning?

Beneatha: It's not important, Mama.

(*She gets up and goes to look out at the bathroom, which is apparently free, and she picks up her towels and rushes out.*)

Mama: What was they fighting about?

Ruth: Now you know as well as I do.

160 **Mama** (*Shaking her head.*): Brother still worrying hisself sick about that money?

Ruth: You know he is.

Mama: You had breakfast?

Ruth: Some coffee.

Mama: Girl, you better start eating and looking after yourself better. You almost thin as Travis.

165 **Ruth:** Lena—

Mama: Un-hunh?

Ruth: What are you going to do with it?

Mama: Now don't you start, child. It's too early in the morning to be talking about money. It ain't Christian.

Ruth: It's just that he got his heart set on that store—

170 **Mama:** You mean that liquor store that Willy Harris want him to invest in?

Ruth: Yes—

Mama: We ain't no business people, Ruth. We just plain working folks.

Ruth: Ain't nobody business people till they go into business. Walter Lee say colored people ain't never going to start getting ahead till they start gambling on some different kinds of things in the world—investments and things.

Mama: What done got into you, girl? Walter Lee done finally sold you on investing.

175 **Ruth:** No. Mama, something is happening between Walter and me. I don't know what it is—but he needs something—something I can't give him any more. He needs this chance, Lena.

Mama (*Frowning deeply.*): But liquor, honey—

Ruth: Well—like Walter say—I spec people going to always be drinking themselves some liquor.

Mama: Well—whether they drinks it or not ain't none of my business. But whether I go into business selling it to 'em *is,* and I don't want that on my ledger this late in life. (*Stopping suddenly and studying her daughter-in-law.*) Ruth Younger, what's the matter with you today? You look like you could fall over right there.

Ruth: I'm tired.

180 **Mama:** Then you better stay home from work today.

Ruth: I can't stay home. She'd be calling up the agency and screaming at them, "My girl didn't come in today—send me somebody! My girl didn't come in!" Oh, she just have a fit . . .

Mama: Well, let her have it. I'll just call her up and say you got the flu—

Ruth (*Laughing.*): Why the flu?

Mama: 'Cause it sounds respectable to 'em. Something white people get, too. they know 'bout the flu. Otherwise they think you been cut up or something when you tell 'em you sick.

185 **Ruth:** I got to go in. We need the money.

Mama: Somebody would of thought my children done all but starved to death the way they talk about money here late. Child, we got a great big old check coming tomorrow.

Ruth (*Sincerely, but also self-righteously.*): Now that's your money. It ain't got nothing to do with me. We all feel like that—Walter and Bennie and me—even Travis.

Mama (*Thoughtfully, and suddenly very far away.*): Ten thousand dollars—

Ruth: Sure is wonderful.

190 **Mama:** Ten thousand dollars.

Ruth: You know what you should do, Miss Lena? You should take yourself a trip somewhere. To Europe or South America or someplace—

Mama (*Throwing up her hands at the thought.*): Oh, child!

Ruth: I'm serious. Just pack up and leave! Go on away and enjoy yourself some. Forget about the family and have yourself a ball for once in your life—

Mama (*Drily.*): You sound like I'm just about ready to die. Who'd go with me? What I look like wandering 'round Europe by myself?

195 **Ruth:** Shoot—these here rich white women do it all the time. They don't think nothing of packing up they suitcases and piling on one of them big steamships and—swoosh!— they gone, child.

Mama: Something always told me I wasn't no rich white woman.

Ruth: Well—what are you going to do with it then?

Mama: I ain't rightly decided. (*Thinking. She speaks now with emphasis.*) Some of it got to be put away for Beneatha and her schoolin'—and ain't nothing going to touch that part of it. Nothing. (*She waits several seconds, trying to make up her mind about something, and looks at Ruth a little tentatively before going on.*) Been thinking that we maybe could meet the notes on a little old two-story somewhere, with a yard where Travis could play in the summertime, if we use part of the insurance for a down payment and everybody kind of pitch in. I could maybe take on a little day work again, few days a week—

Ruth (*Studying her mother-in-law furtively and concentrating on her ironing, anxious to encourage without seeming to.*): Well, Lord knows, we've put enough rent into this here rat trap to pay for four houses by now . . .

200 **Mama** (*Looking up at the words "rat trap" and then looking around and leaning back and sighing—in a suddenly reflective mood—.*): "Rat trap"—yes, that's all it is. (*Smiling.*) I remember just as well the day me and Big Walter moved in here. Hadn't been married but two weeks and wasn't planning on living here no more than a year. (*She shakes her head at the dissolved dream.*) We was going to set away, little by little, don't you know, and buy a little place out in Morgan Park. We had even picked out the house. (*Chuckling a little.*) Looks right dumpy today. But Lord, child, you should know all the dreams I had 'bout buying that house and fixing it up and making me a little garden in the back— (*She waits and stops smiling.*) And didn't none of it happen.

(*Dropping her hands in a futile gesture.*)

Ruth (*Keeps her head down, ironing.*): Yes, life can be a barrel of disappointments, sometimes.

Mama: Honey, Big Walter would come in here some nights back then and slump down on that couch there and just look at the rug, and look at me and look at the rug and then back at me—and I'd know he was down then . . . really down. (*After a second very long and thoughtful pause; she is seeing back to times that only she can see.*) And then, Lord, when I lost that baby—little Claude—I almost thought I was going to lose Big Walter too. Oh, that man grieved hisself! He was one man to love his children.

Ruth: Ain't nothin' can tear at you like losin' your baby.

Mama: I guess that's how come that man finally worked hisself to death like he done. Like he was fighting his own war with this here world that took his baby from him.

205 **Ruth:** He sure was a fine man, all right. I always liked Mr. Younger.

Mama: Crazy 'bout his children! God knows there was plenty wrong with Walter Younger—hard-headed, mean, kind of wild with women—plenty wrong with him. But he sure loved his children. Always wanted them to have something—be something. That's where Brother gets all these notions, I reckon. Big Walter used to say, he'd get right wet in the eyes sometimes, lean his head back with the water standing in his eyes and say, "Seem like God didn't see fit to give the black man nothing but dreams—but He did give us children to make them dreams seem worth while." (*She smiles.*) He could talk like that, don't you know.

Ruth: Yes, he sure could. He was a good man, Mr. Younger.

Mama: Yes, a fine man—just couldn't never catch up with his dreams, that's all.

(*Beneatha comes in, brushing her hair and looking up to the ceiling, where the sound of a vacuum cleaner has started up.*)

Beneatha: What could be so dirty on that woman's rugs that she has to vacuum them every single day?

210 **Ruth:** I wish certain young women 'round here who I could name would take inspiration about certain rugs in a certain apartment I could also mention.

Beneatha (*Shrugging.*): How much cleaning can a house need, for Christ's sakes.

Mama (*Not liking the Lord's name used thus.*): Bennie!

Ruth: Just listen to her—just listen!

Beneatha: Oh, God!

215 **Mama:** If you use the Lord's name just one more time—

Beneatha (*A bit of a whine.*): Oh, Mama—

Ruth: Fresh—just fresh as salt, this girl!

Beneatha (*Drily.*): Well—if the salt loses its savor—

Mama: Now that will do. I just ain't going to have you 'round here reciting the scriptures in vain—you hear me?

220 **Beneatha:** How did I manage to get on everybody's wrong side by just walking into a room?

Ruth: If you weren't so fresh—

Beneatha: Ruth, I'm twenty years old.

Mama: What time you be home from school today?

Beneatha: Kind of late. (*With enthusiasm.*) Madeline is going to start my guitar lessons today.

(*Mama and Ruth look up with the same expression.*)

225 **Mama:** Your *what* kind of lessons?

Beneatha: Guitar.

Ruth: Oh, Father!

Mama: How come you done taken it in your mind to learn to play the guitar?

Beneatha: I just want to, that's all.

230 **Mama** (*Smiling.*): Lord, child, don't you know what to do with yourself? How long it going to be before you get tired of this now—like you got tired of that little play-acting group you joined last year? (*Looking at Ruth.*) And what was it the year before that?

Ruth: The horseback-riding club for which she bought that fifty-five-dollar riding habit that's been hanging in the closet ever since!

Mama (*To Beneatha.*): Why you got to flit so from one thing to another, baby?

Beneatha (*Sharply.*): I just want to learn to play the guitar. Is there anything wrong with that?

Mama: Ain't nobody trying to stop you. I just wonders sometimes why you has to flit so from one thing to another all the time. You ain't never done nothing with all that camera equipment you brought home—

235 **Beneatha:** I don't flit! I—I experiment with different forms of expression—

Ruth: Like riding a horse?

Beneatha: —People have to express themselves one way or another.

Mama: What is it you want to express?

Beneatha (*Angrily.*): Me! (*Mama and Ruth look at each other and burst into raucous laughter.*) Don't worry—I don't expect you to understand.

240 **Mama** (*To change the subject.*): Who you going out with tomorrow night?

Beneatha (*With displeasure.*): George Murchison again.

Mama (*Pleased.*): Oh—you getting a little sweet on him?

Ruth: You ask me, this child ain't sweet on nobody but herself—(*Underbreath.*) Express herself!

(*They laugh.*)

Beneatha: Oh—I like George all right, Mama. I mean I like him enough to go out with him and stuff, but—

245 **Ruth** (*For devilment.*): What does *and stuff* mean?

Beneatha: Mind your own business.

Mama: Stop picking at her now, Ruth. (*A thoughtful pause, and then a suspicious sudden look at her daughter as she turns in her chair for emphasis.*) What *does* it mean?

Beneatha (*Wearily.*): Oh, I just mean I couldn't ever really be serious about George. He's—he's so shallow.

Ruth: Shallow—what do you mean he's shallow? He's *Rich!*

250 **Mama:** Hush, Ruth.

Beneatha: I know he's rich. He knows he's rich, too.

Ruth: Well—what other qualities a man got to have to satisfy you, little girl?

Beneatha: You wouldn't even begin to understand. Anybody who married Walter could not possibly understand.

Mama (*Outraged.*): What kind of way is that to talk about your brother?

255 **Beneatha:** Brother is a flip—let's face it.

Mama (*To Ruth, helplessly.*): What's a flip?

Ruth (*Glad to add kindling.*): She's saying he's crazy.

Beneatha: Not crazy. Brother isn't really crazy yet—he—he's an elaborate neurotic.

Mama: Hush your mouth!

260 **Beneatha:** As for George. Well. George looks good—he's got a beautiful car and he takes me to nice places and, as my sister-in-law says, he is probably the richest boy I will ever get to know and I even like him sometimes—but if the Youngers are sitting around waiting to see if their little Bennie is going to tie up the family with the Murchisons, they are wasting their time.

Ruth: You mean you wouldn't marry George Murchison if he asked you someday? That pretty, rich thing? Honey, I knew you was odd—

Beneatha: No I would not marry him if all I felt for him was what I feel now. Besides, George's family wouldn't really like it.

Mama: Why not?

Beneatha: Oh, Mama—the Murchisons are honest-to-God-real-*live*-rich colored people, and the only people in the world who are more snobbish than rich white people are rich colored people. I thought somebody knew that. I've met Mrs. Murchison. She's a scene!

265 **Mama:** You must not dislike people 'cause they well off, honey.

Beneatha: Why not? It makes just as much sense as disliking people 'cause they are poor, and lots of people do that.

Ruth (*A wisdom-of-the-ages manner. To Mama.*): Well, she'll get over some of this—

Beneatha: Get over it? What are you talking about, Ruth? Listen, I'm going to be a doctor. I'm not worried about who I'm going to marry yet—if I ever get married.

Mama *and* **Ruth:** *If!*

270 **Mama:** Now, Bennie—

Beneatha: Oh, I probably will . . . but first I'm going to be a doctor, and George, for one, still thinks that's pretty funny. I couldn't be bothered with that. I am going to be a doctor and everybody around here better understand that!

Mama (*Kindly.*): 'Course you going to be a doctor, honey, God willing.

Beneatha (*Drily.*): God hasn't got a thing to do with it.

Mama: Beneatha—that just wasn't necessary.

275 **Beneatha:** Well—neither is God. I get sick of hearing about God.

Mama: Beneatha!

Beneatha: I mean it! I'm just tired of hearing about God all the time. What has He got to do with anything? Does he pay tuition?

Mama: You 'bout to get your fresh little jaw slapped!

Ruth: That's just what she needs, all right!

280 **Beneatha:** Why? Why can't I say what I want to around here, like everybody else?

Mama: It don't sound nice for a young girl to say things like that—you wasn't brought up that way. Me and your father went to trouble to get you and Brother to church every Sunday.

Beneatha: Mama, you don't understand. It's all a matter of ideas, and God is just one idea I don't accept. It's not important. I am not going out and be immoral or commit crimes because I don't believe in God. I don't even think about it. It's just that I get tired of Him getting credit for all the things the human race achieves through its own stubborn effort. There simply is no blasted God—there is only man and it is he who makes miracles!

(Mama absorbs this speech, studies her daughter and rises slowly and crosses to Beneatha and slaps her powerfully across the face. After, there is only silence and the daughter drops her eyes from her mother's face, and Mama is very tall before her.)

Mama: Now—you say after me, in my mother's house there is still God. *(There is a long pause and Beneatha stares at the floor wordlessly. Mama repeats the phrase with precision and cool emotion.)* In my mother's house there is still God.

Beneatha: In my mother's house there is still God.

(A long pause.)

285 **Mama** *(Walking away from Beneatha, too disturbed for triumphant posture. Stopping and turning back to her daughter.):* There are some ideas we ain't going to have in this house. Not long as I am at the head of this family.

Beneatha: Yes, ma'am.

(Mama walks out of the room.)

Ruth *(Almost gently, with profound understanding.):* You think you a woman, Bennie—but you still a little girl. What you did was childish—so you got treated like a child.

Beneatha: I see. *(Quietly.)* I also see that everybody thinks it's all right for Mama to be a tyrant. But all the tyranny in the world will never put a God in the heavens!

(She picks up her books and goes out.)

Ruth *(Goes to Mama's door.):* She said she was sorry.

290 **Mama** *(Coming out, going to her plant.):* They frightens me, Ruth. My children.

Ruth: You got good children, Lena. They just a little off sometimes—but they're good.

Mama: No—there's something come down between me and them that don't let us understand each other and I don't know what it is. One done almost lost his mind thinking 'bout money all the time and the other done commence to talk about things I can't seem to understand in no form or fashion. What is it that's changing, Ruth?

Ruth *(Soothingly, older than her years.):* Now . . . you taking it all too seriously. You just got strong-willed children and it takes a strong woman like you to keep 'em in hand.

Mama *(Looking at her plant and sprinkling a little water on it.):* They spirited all right, my children. Got to admit they got spirit—Bennie and Walter. Like this little old plant that ain't never had enough sunshine or nothing—and look at it . . .

(She has her back to Ruth, who has had to stop ironing and lean against something and put the back of her hand to her forehead.)

295 **Ruth** *(Trying to keep Mama from noticing.):* You . . . sure . . . loves that little old thing, don't you? . . .

Mama: Well, I always wanted me a garden like I used to see sometimes at the back of the houses down home. This plant is close as I ever got to having one. *(She looks out of the window as she replaces the plant.)* Lord, ain't nothing as dreary as the view from this window on a dreary day, is there? Why ain't you singing this morning, Ruth? Sing that "No Ways Tired." That song always lifts me up so—(She turns at last to see that

Ruth has slipped quietly into a chair, in a state of semiconsciousness.) Ruth! Ruth honey—
what's the matter with you . . . Ruth!

(Curtain.)

Act One
Scene 2

*It is the following morning; a Saturday morning, and house cleaning is in progress at the
Youngers. Furniture has been shoved hither and yon and Mama is giving the kitchen-
area walls a washing down. Beneatha, in dungarees, with a handkerchief tired around
her face, is spraying insecticide into the cracks in the walls. As they work, the radio is on
and a Southside disk-jockey program is inappropriately filling the house with a rather
exotic saxophone blues. Travis, the sole idle one, is leaning on his arms, looking out of the
window.*

1 **Travis:** Grandmama, that stuff Bennie is using smells awful. Can I go downstairs, please?
Mama: Did you get all them chores done already? I ain't seen you doing much.
Travis: Yes'm—finished early. Where did Mama go this morning?
Mama *(Looking at Beneatha.)*: She had to go on a little errand.
5 **Travis:** Where?
Mama: To tend to her business.
Travis: Can I go outside then?
Mama: Oh, I guess so. You better stay right in front of the house, though . . . and keep a
  good lookout for the postman.
Travis: Yes'm. *(He starts out and decides to give his Aunt Beneatha a good swat on the legs as he
  passes her.)* Leave them poor little old cockroaches alone, they ain't bothering you
  none.

*(He runs as she swings the spray gun at him both viciously and playfully. Walter enters from
the bedroom and goes to the phone.)*

10 **Mama:** Look out there, girl, before you be spilling some of that stuff on that child!
Travis *(Teasing.)*: That's right—look out now!

(He exits.)

Beneatha *(Drily.)*: I can't imagine that it would hurt him—it has never hurt the roaches.
Mama: Well, little boys' hides ain't as tough as Southside roaches.
Walter *(Into phone.)*: Hello—Let me talk to Willy Harris.
15 **Mama:** You better get over there behind the bureau. I seen one marching out of there like
  Napoleon yesterday.
Walter: Hello, Willy? It ain't come yet. It'll be here in a few minutes. Did the lawyer give
  you the papers?
Beneatha: There's really only one way to get rid of them, Mama—
Mama: How?
Beneatha: Set fire to this building.
20 **Walter:** Good. Good. I'll be right over.
Beneatha: Where did Ruth go, Walter?
Walter: I don't know.

(He exits abruptly.)

Beneatha: Mama, where did Ruth go?
Mama *(Looking at her with meaning.)*: To the doctor, I think.

25 **Beneatha:** The doctor? What's the matter? *(They exchange glances.)* You don't think—
Mama *(With her sense of drama.)*: Now I ain't saying what I think. But I ain't never been wrong 'bout a woman neither.

(The phone rings.)

Beneatha *(At the phone.)*: Hay-lo . . . *(Pause, and a moment of recognition.)* Well—when did you get back! . . . And how was it? . . . Of course I've missed you—in my way . . . This morning? No . . . house cleaning and all that and Mama hates it if I let people come over when the house is like this . . . You *have?* Well, that's different . . . What is it— Oh, what the hell, come on over . . . Right, see you then.

(She hangs up.)

Mama *(Who has listened vigorously, as is her habit.)*: Who is that you inviting over here with this house looking like this? You ain't got the pride you was born with!
Beneatha: Asagai doesn't care how houses look, Mama—he's an intellectual.
30 **Mama:** *Who?*
Beneatha: Asagai—Joseph Asagai. He's an African boy I met on campus. He's been studying in Canada all summer.
Mama: What's his name?
Beneatha: Asagai, Joseph. Ah-sah-guy . . . He's from Nigeria.
Mama: Oh, that's the little country that was founded by slaves way back . . .
35 **Beneatha:** No, Mama—that's Liberia.
Mama: I don't think I never met no African before.
Beneatha: Well, do me a favor and don't ask him a whole lot of ignorant questions about Africans. I mean, do they wear clothes and all that—
Mama: Well, now, I guess if you think we so ignorant 'round here maybe you shouldn't bring your friends here—
Beneatha: It's just that people ask such crazy things. All anyone seems to know about when it comes to Africa is Tarzan—
40 **Mama** *(Indignantly.)*: Why should I know anything about Africa?
Beneatha: Why do you give money at church for the missionary work?
Mama: Well, that's to help save people.
Beneatha: You mean save them from *heathenism*—
Mama *(Innocently.)*: Yes.
45 **Beneatha:** I'm afraid they need more salvation from the British and the French.

(Ruth comes in forlornly and pulls off her coat with dejection. They both turn to look at her.)

Ruth *(Dispiritedly.)*: Well, I guess from all the happy faces—everybody knows.
Beneatha: You pregnant?
Mama: Lord have mercy, I sure hope it's a little old girl. Travis ought to have a sister.

(Beneatha and Ruth give her a hopeless look for this grandmotherly enthusiasm.)

Beneatha: How far along are you?
50 **Ruth:** Two months.
Beneatha: Did you mean to? I mean did you plan it or was it an accident?
Mama: What do you know about planning or not planning?
Beneatha: Oh, Mama.
Ruth *(Wearily.)*: She's twenty years old, Lena.
55 **Beneatha:** Did you plan it, Ruth?

Ruth: Mind your own business.

Beneatha: It's my business—where is he going to live, on the *roof? (There is silence follow-ing the remark as the three women react to the sense of it.)* Gee—I didn't mean that, Ruth, honest. Gee, I don't feel like that at all. I—I think it is wonderful.

Ruth *(Dully.):* Wonderful.

Beneatha: Yes—really.

60 **Mama** *(Looking at Ruth, worried.):* Doctor say everything going to be all right?

Ruth *(Far away.):* Yes—she says everything is going to be fine . . .

Mama *(Immediately suspicious.):* "She"— What doctor you went to?

(Ruth folds over, near hysteria.)

Mama *(Worriedly hovering over Ruth.):* Ruth honey—what's the matter with you—you sick?

(Ruth has her fists clenched on her thighs and is fighting hard to suppress a scream that seems to be rising in her.)

Beneatha: What's the matter with her, Mama?

65 **Mama** *(Working her fingers in Ruth's shoulder to relax her.):* She be all right. Women gets right depressed sometimes when they get her way. *(Speaking softly, expertly, rapidly.)* Now you just relax. That's right . . . just lean back, don't think 'bout nothing at all . . . nothing at all—

Ruth: I'm all right . . .

(The glass-eyed look melts and then she collapses into a fit of heavy sobbing. The bells rings.)

Beneatha: Oh, my God—that must be Asagai.

Mama (To Ruth.): Come on now, honey. You need to lie down and rest awhile . . . then have some nice hot food.

(They exit, Ruth's weight on her mother-in-law. Beneatha, herself profoundly disturbed, opens the door to admit a rather dramatic-looking young man with a large package.)

Asagai: Hello, Alaiyo—

70 **Beneatha** *(Holding the door open and regarding him with pleasure.):* Hello . . . *(Long pause.)* Well—come in. And please excuse everything. My mother was very upset about my letting anyone come here with the place like this.

Assagai *(Coming into the room.):* You look disturbed too . . . Is something wrong?

Beneatha *(Still at the door, absently.):* Yes . . . we've all got acute ghetto-itus. *(She smiles and comes toward him, finding a cigarette and sitting.)* So—sit down! How was Canada?

Asagai *(A sophisticate.):* Canadian.

Beneatha *(Looking at him.):* I'm very glad you are back.

75 **Asagai** *(Looking back at her in turn.):* Are you really?

Beneatha: Yes—very.

Asagai: Why—you were quite glad when I went away. What happened?

Beneatha: You went away.

Asagai: Ahhhhhhhh.

80 **Beneatha:** Before—you wanted to be so serious before there was time.

Asagai: How much time must there be before one knows what one feels?

Beneatha: *(Stalling this particular conversation. Her hands pressed together, in a deliberately childish gesture.):* What did you bring me?

Asagai *(Handing her the package.):* Open it and see.

Beneatha: *(Eagerly opening the package and drawing out some records and the colorful robes of a Nigerian woman.):* Oh, Asagai! . . . You got them for me! . . . How beautiful . . . and the records too! (*She lifts out the robes and runs to the mirror with them and holds the drapery up in front of herself.*)

85 **Asagai** (*Coming to her at the mirror.*): I shall have to teach you how to drape it properly. (*He flings the material about her for the moment and stands back to look at her.*) Ah—*Oh-pay-gay-day, oh-gbah-mu-shay.* (*A Yoruba exclamation for admiration.*) You wear it well . . . very well . . . mutilated hair and all.

Beneatha (*Turning suddenly.*): My hair—what's wrong with my hair?

Asagai (*Shrugging.*): Were you born with it like that?

Beneatha (*Reaching up to touch it.*): No . . . of course not.

(*She looks back to the mirror, disturbed.*)

Asagai (*Smiling.*): How then?

90 **Beneatha:** You know perfectly well how . . . as crinkly as yours . . . that's how.

Asagai: And it is ugly to you that way?

Beneatha: (*Quickly.*): Oh, no—not ugly . . . (*More slowly, apologetically.*) But it's so hard to manage when it's, well—raw.

Asagai: And so to accommodate that—you mutilate it every week?

Beneatha: It's not mutilation!

95 **Asagai** (*Laughing aloud at her seriousness.*): Oh . . . please! I am only teasing you because you are so very serious about these things. (*He stands back from her and folds his arms across his chest as he watches her pulling at her hair and frowning in the mirror.*) Do you remember the first time you met me at school? . . . (*He laughs.*) You came up to me and you said—and I thought you were the most serious little thing I had ever seen— you said: (*He imitates her.*) "Mr. Asagai—I want very much to talk with you. About Africa. You see, Mr. Asagai, I am looking for my *identity!*"

(*He laughs.*)

Beneatha (*Turning to him, not laughing.*): Yes—

(*Her face is quizzical, profoundly disturbed.*)

Asagai (*Still teasing and reaching out and taking her face in his hands and turning her profile to him.*): Well . . . it is true that this is not so much a profile of a Hollywood queen as perhaps as a queen of the Nile— (*A mock dismissal of the important of the question.*) But what does it matter? Assimilationism is so popular in your country.

Beneatha (*Wheeling, passionately, sharply.*): I am not an assimilationist!

Asagai (*The protest hangs in the room for a moment and Asagai studies her, his laughter fading.*): Such a serious one. (*There is a pause.*) So—you like the robes? You must take excellent care of them—they are from my sister's personal wardrobe.

100 **Beneatha** (*With incredulity.*): You—you sent all the way home—for me?

Asagai (*With charm.*): For you—I would do much more . . . Well, that is what I came for. I must go.

Beneatha: Will you call me Monday?

Asagai: Yes . . . We have a great deal to talk about. I mean about identity and time and all that.

Beneatha: Time?

105 **Asagai:** Yes. About how much time one needs to know what one feels.

Beneatha: You never understood that there is more than one kind of feeling which can exist between a man and a woman—or, at least, there should be.

Asagai (*Shaking his head negatively but gently.*): No. Between a man and a woman there need be only one kind of feeling. I have that for you . . . Now even . . . right this moment . . .

Beneatha: I know—and by itself—it won't do. I can find that anywhere.

Asagai: For a woman it should be enough.

110 **Beneatha:** I know—because that's what it says in all the novels that men write. But it isn't. Go ahead and laugh—but I'm not interested in being someone's little episode in America or—(*With feminine vengeance.*)—one of them! (*Asagai has burst into laughter again.*) That's funny as hell, huh!

Asagai: It's just that every American girl I have known has said that to me. White— black—in this you are all the same. And the same speech, too!

Beneatha (*Angrily.*): Yuk, yuk, yuk!

Asagai: It's how you can be sure that the world's most liberated women are not liberated at all. You all talk about it too much!

(*Mama enters and is immediately all social charm because of the presence of a guest.*)

Beneatha: Oh—Mama—this is Mr. Asagai.

115 **Mama:** How do you do?

Asagai (*Total politeness to an elder.*): How do you do, Mrs. Younger. Please forgive me for coming at such an outrageous hour on a Saturday.

Mama: Well, you are quite welcome. I just hope you understand that our house don't always look like this. (*Chatterish.*) You must come again. I would love to hear all about—(*Not sure of the name*)—your country. I think it's so sad the way our American Negroes don't know nothing about Africa 'cept Tarzan and all that. And all that money they pour into these churches when they ought to be helping you people over there drive out them French and Englishmen done taken away your land.

(*The mother flashes a slightly superior look at her daughter upon completion of the recitation.*)

Asagai (*Taken aback by this sudden and acutely unrelated expression of sympathy.*): Yes . . . yes . . .

Mama (*Smiling at him suddenly and relaxing and looking him over.*): How many miles is it from here to where you come from?

120 **Asagai:** Many thousands.

Mama (*Looking at him as she would Walter.*): I bet you don't half look after yourself, being away from your mama either. I spec you better come 'round here from time to time and get yourself some decent home-cooked meals . . .

Asagai (*Moved.*): Thank you. Thank you very much. (*They are all quiet, then—*) Well . . . I must go. I will call you Monday, Alaiyo.

Mama: What's that he call you?

Asagai: Oh—"Alaiyo." I hope you don't mind. It is what you would call a nickname, I think. It is a Yoruba word. I am a Yoruba.

125 **Mama** (*Looking at Beneatha.*): I—I thought he was from—

Asagai (*Understanding.*): Nigeria is my country. Yoruba is my tribal origin—

Beneatha: You didn't tell us what Alaiyo means . . . for all I know, you might be calling me Little Idiot or something . . .

Asagai: Well . . . let me see . . . I do not know how just to explain it . . . The sense of a thing can be so different when it changes languages.

Beneatha: You're evading.

130 **Asagai:** No—really it is difficult . . . (*Thinking.*) It means . . . it means One for Whom Bread—Food—Is Not Enough. (*He looks at her.*) Is that all right?

Beneatha (*Understanding, softly.*): Thank you.

Mama (*Looking from one to the other and not understanding any of it.*): Well . . . that's nice . . . You must come see us again—Mr.—

Asagai: Ah-sah-guy . . .
Mama: Yes . . . Do come again.
135 **Asagai:** Good-bye.

(He exits.)

Mama (After him.): Lord, that's a pretty thing just went out here! (Insinuatingly, to her daughter.) Yes, I guess I see why we done commence to get so interested in Africa 'round here. Missionaries my aunt Jenny!

(She exits.)

Beneatha: Oh, Mama! . . .

(She picks up the Nigerian dress and holds it up to her in front of the mirror again. She sets the headdress on haphazardly and then notices her hair again and clutches at it and then replaces the headdress and frowns at herself. Then she starts to wriggle in front of the mirror as she thinks a Nigerian woman might. Travis enters and regards her.)

Travis: You cracking up?
Beneatha: Shut up.

(She pulls the headdress off and looks at herself in the mirror and clutches at her hair again and squinches her eyes as if trying to imagine something. Then, suddenly, she gets her raincoat and kerchief and hurriedly prepares for going out.)

140 **Mama** (Coming back into the room.): She's resting now. Travis, baby, run next door and ask Miss Johnson to please let me have a little kitchen cleanser. This here can is empty as Jacob's kettle.
Travis: I just came in.
Mama: Do as you told. (He exits and she looks at her daughter.) Where you going?
Beneatha (Halting at the door.): To become a queen of the Nile!

(She exits in a breathless blaze of glory. Ruth appears in the bedroom doorway.)

Mama: Who told you to get up?
145 **Ruth:** Ain't nothing wrong with me to be lying in no bed for. Where did Bennie go?
Mama (Drumming her fingers.): Far as I could make out—to Egypt. (Ruth just looks at her.) What time is it getting to?
Ruth: Ten twenty. And the mailman going to ring that bell this morning just like he done every morning for the last umpteen years.

(Travis comes in with the cleanser can.)

Travis: She say to tell you that she don't have much.
Mama (Angrily.): Lord, some people I could name sure is tight-fisted! (Directing her grandson.) Mark two cans of cleanser down on the list there. If she that hard up for kitchen cleanser, I sure don't want to forget to get her none!
150 **Ruth:** Lena—maybe the woman is just short on cleanser—
Mama (Not listening.): —Much baking powder as she done borrowed from me all these years, she could of done gone into the baking business!

(The bell sounds suddenly and sharply and all three are stunned—serious and silent—mid-speech. In spite of all the other conversations and distractions of the morning, this is what they have been waiting for, even Travis, who looks helplessly from his mother to his grandmother. Ruth is the first to come to life again.)

Ruth (*To Travis.*): Get down them steps, boy!

(*Travis snaps to life and flies out to get the mail.*)

Mama (*Her eyes wide, her hand to her breast.*): You mean it done really come?

Ruth (*Excited.*) Oh, Miss Lena!

155   **Mama** (*Collecting herself.*): Well . . . I don't know what we all so excited about 'round here for. We known it was coming for months.

Ruth: That's a whole lot different from having it come and being able to hold it in your hands . . . a piece of paper worth ten thousand dollars . . .(*Travis bursts back into the room. He holds the envelope high above his head, like a little dancer, his face is radiant and he is breathless. He moves to his grandmother with sudden slow ceremony and puts the envelope into her hands. She accepts it, and then merely holds it and looks at it.*) Come on! Open it . . . Lord have mercy, I wish Walter Lee was here!

Travis: Open it, Grandmama!

Mama (*Staring at it.*): Now you all be quiet. It's just a check.

Ruth: Open it . . .

160   **Mama** (*Still staring at it.*): Now don't act silly . . . We ain't never been no people to act silly 'bout no money—

Ruth (*Swiftly.*): We ain't never had none before—*open it!*

(*Mama finally makes a good strong tear and pulls out the thin blue slice of paper and inspects it closely. The boy and his mother study it raptly over Mama's shoulders.*)

Mama: *Travis!* (*She is counting off with doubt.*) Is that the right number of zeros.

Travis: Yes'm . . . ten thousand dollars. Gaalee, Grandmama, you rich.

Mama (*She holds the check away from her, still looking at it. Slowly her face sobers into a mask of unhappiness.*): Ten thousand dollars. (*She hands it to Ruth.*) Put it away somewhere, Ruth. (*She does not look at Ruth; her eyes seem to be seeing something somewhere very far off.*) Ten thousand dollars they give you. Ten thousand dollars.

165   **Travis** (*To his mother, sincerely.*): What's the matter with Grandmama—don't she want to be rich?

Ruth (*Distractedly.*): You go on out and play now, baby. (*Travis exits. Mama start wiping dishes absently, humming intently to herself. Ruth turns to her, with kind exasperation.*) You've gone and got yourself upset.

Mama (*Not looking at her.*): I spec if it wasn't for you all . . . I would just put that money away or give it to the church or something.

Ruth: Now what kind of talk is that. Mr. Younger would just be plain mad if he could hear you talking foolish like that.

Mama (*Stopping and staring off.*): Yes . . . he sure would. (*Sighing.*) We got enough to do with that money, all right. (*She halts then, and turns and looks at her daughter-in-law hard; Ruth avoids her eyes and Mama wipes her hands with finality and starts to speak firmly to Ruth.*) Where did you go today, girl?

170   **Ruth:** To the doctor.

Mama (*Impatiently.*): Now, Ruth . . . you know better than that. Old Doctor Jones is strange enough in his way but there ain't nothing 'bout him make somebody slip and call him "she"—like you done this morning.

Ruth: Well, that's what happened—my tongue slipped.

Mama: You went to see that woman, didn't you?

Ruth (*Defensively, giving herself away.*): What woman you talking about?

175   **Mama** (*Angrily.*): That woman who—

(*Walter enters in great excitement.*)

Walter: Did it come?

Mama *(Quietly.):* Can't you give people a Christian greeting before you start asking about money?

Walter *(To Ruth.):* Did it come? *(Ruth unfolds the check and lays it quietly before him, watching him intently with thoughts of her own. Walter sits down and grasps it close and counts off the zeros.)* Ten thousand dollars— *(He turns suddenly, frantically to his mother and draws some papers out of his breast pocket.)* Mama—look. Old Willy Harris put everything on paper—

Mama: Son—I think you ought to talk to your wife . . . I'll go on out and leave you alone if you want—

180 **Walter:** I can talk to her later—Mama, look—

Mama: Son—

Walter: WILL SOMEBODY PLEASE LISTEN TO ME TODAY!

Mama *(Quietly.):* I don't 'low no yellin' in this house, Walter Lee, and you know it—*(Walter stares at them in frustration and starts to speak several times.)* And there ain't going to be no investing in no liquor stores. I don't aim to have to speak on that again.

(A long pause.)

Walter: Oh—so you don't aim to have to speak on that again? So *you* have decided . . . *(Crumpling his papers.)* Well, *you* tell that to my boy tonight when you put him to sleep on the living-room couch . . . *(Turning to Mama and speaking directly to her.)* Yeah—and tell it to my wife, Mama, tomorrow when she has to go out of here to look after somebody else's kids. And tell it to *me,* Mama, every time we need a new pair of curtains and I have to watch *you* go out and work in somebody's kitchen. Yeah, you tell me then!

(Walter starts out.)

185 **Ruth:** Where you going?

Walter: I'm going out!

Ruth: Where?

Walter: Just out of this house somewhere—

Ruth *(Getting her coat.):* I'll come too.

190 **Walter:** I don't want you to come!

Ruth: I got something to talk to you about, Walter.

Walter: That's too bad.

Mama *(Still quietly.):* Walter Lee—*(She waits and he finally turns and looks at her.)* Sit down.

Walter: I'm a grown man, Mama.

195 **Mama:** Ain't nobody said you wasn't grown. But you still in my house and my presence. And as long as you are—you'll talk to your wife civil. Now sit down.

Ruth *(Suddenly.):* Oh, let him go on out and drink himself to death! He makes me sick to my stomach! *(She flings her coat against him and exits to bedroom.)*

Walter *(Violently, flinging the coat after her.):* And you turn mine too, baby! *(Ruth goes into their bedroom and slam the door behind her.)* That was my greatest mistake—

Mama *(Still quietly.):* Walter, what is the matter with you?

Walter: Matter with me? Ain't nothing the matter with *me!*

200 **Mama:** Yes there is. Something eating you up like a crazy man. Something more than me not giving you this money. The past few years I been watching it happen to you. You get all nervous acting and kind of wild in the eyes—*(Walter jumps up impatiently at her words.)* I said sit there now, I'm talking to you!

Walter: Mama—I don't need no nagging at me today.

Mama: Seem like you getting to a place where you always tied up in some kind of knot about something. But if anybody ask you 'bout it you just yell at 'em and bust out the house and go out and drink somewheres. Walter Lee, people can't live with that. Ruth's a good, patient girl in her way—but you getting to be too much. Boy, don't make the mistake of driving that girl away from you.

Walter: Why—what she do for me?

Mama: She loves you

205 **Walter:** Mama—I'm going out. I want to go off somewhere and be by myself for a while.

Mama: I'm sorry 'bout your liquor store, son. It just wasn't the thing for us to do. That's what I want to tell you about—

Walter: I got to go out, Mama—

(He rises.)

Mama: It's dangerous, son.

Walter: What's dangerous?

210 **Mama:** When a man goes outside his home to look for peace.

Walter (Beseechingly.): Then why can't there never be no peace in this house then?

Mama: You done found it in some other house?

Walter: No—there ain't no woman! Why do women always think there's a woman somewhere when a man gets restless. (Coming to her.) Mama—Mama—I want so many things . . .

Mama: Yes, son—

215 **Walter:** I want so many things that they are driving me kind of crazy . . . Mama—look at me.

Mama: I'm looking at you. You a good-looking boy. You got a job, a nice wife, a fine boy and—

Walter: A job. (Looks at her.) Mama, a job? I open and close car doors all day long. I drive a man around in his limousine and I say, "Yes, sir: no, sir; very good, sir; shall I take the Drive, sir?" Mama, that ain't no kind of job . . . that ain't nothing at all. (Very quietly.) Mama, I don't know if I can make you understand.

Mama: Understand what, baby?

Walter (Quietly.): Sometimes it's like I can see the future stretched out in front of me—just plain as day. The future, Mama. Hanging over there at the edge of my days. Just waiting for me—a big, looming blank space—full of nothing. Just waiting for me. (Pause.) Mama—sometimes when I'm downtown and pass them cool, quiet-looking restaurants where them white boys are sitting back and talking 'bout things . . . sitting there turning deals worth millions of dollars . . . sometimes I see guys don't look much older than me—

220 **Mama:** Son—how come you talk so much 'bout money?

Walter (With immense passion.): Because it is life, Mama!

Mama (Quietly.): Oh—(Very quietly.) So now it's life. Money is life. Once upon a time freedom used to be life—now it's money. I guess the world really do change . . .

Walter: No—it was always money, Mama. We just didn't know about it.

Mama: No . . . something has changed. (She looks at him.) You something new, boy. In my time we was worried about not being lynched and getting to the North if we could and how to stay alive and still have a pinch of dignity too . . . Now here come you and Beneatha—talking 'bout things we ain't never even thought about hardly, me and your daddy. You ain't satisfied or proud of nothing we done. I mean that you had a home; that we kept you out of trouble till you was grown; that you don't have to ride to work on the back of nobody's streetcar— You my children—but how different we done become.

225 **Walter:** You just don't understand, Mama, you just don't understand.

Mama: Son—do you know your wife is expecting another baby? (*Walter stands, stunned, and absorbs what his mother has said.*) That's what she wanted to talk to you about. (*Walter sinks down into a chair.*) This ain't for me to be telling—but you ought to know. (*She waits.*) I think Ruth is thinking 'bout getting rid of that child.

Walter (*Slowly understanding.*): No—no—Ruth wouldn't do that.

Mama: When the world gets ugly enough—a woman will do anything for her family. *The part that's already living.*

Walter: You don't know Ruth, Mama, if you think she would do that.

(*Ruth opens the bedroom door and stands there a little limp.*)

230 **Ruth** (*Beaten.*): Yes I would too, Walter. (*Pause.*) I gave her a five-dollar down payment.

(*There is total silence as the man stares at his wife and the mother stares at her son.*)

Mama (*Presently.*): Well—(*Tightly.*) Well—son, I'm waiting to hear you say something . . . I'm waiting to hear how you be your father's son. Be the man he was . . . (*Pause.*) Your wife say she going to destroy your child. And I'm waiting to hear you talk like him and say we a people who give children life, not who destroys them—(*She rises.*) I'm waiting to see you stand up and look like your daddy and say we done give up one baby to poverty and that we ain't going to give up nary another one . . . I'm waiting.

Walter: Ruth—

Mama: If you a son of mine, tell her! (*Walter turns, looks at her and can say nothing. She continues, bitterly.*) You . . . you are a disgrace to your father's memory. Somebody get me my hat.

(*Curtain.*)

Act Two

Scene I

Time: Later the same day.
At rise: Ruth is ironing again. She has the radio going. Presently Beneatha's bedroom door opens and Ruth's mouth falls and she puts down the iron in fascination.

1 **Ruth:** What have we got on tonight!

Beneatha (*Emerging grandly from the doorway so that we can see her thoroughly robed in the costume Asagai brought.*): You are looking at what a well-dressed Nigerian woman wears—(*She parades for Ruth, her hair completely hidden by the headdress; she is coquettishly fanning herself with an ornate oriental fan, mistakenly more like Butterfly than any Nigerian that ever was.*) Isn't it beautiful? (*She promenades to the radio and, with an arrogant flourish, turns off the good loud blues that is playing.*) Enough of this assimilationist junk! (*Ruth follows her with her eyes as she goes to the phonograph and puts on a record and turns and waits ceremoniously for the music to come up. Then, with a shout—*) OCOMOGOSIAY!

(*Ruth jumps. The music comes up, a lovely Nigerian melody. Beneatha listens, enraptured, her eyes far away—"back to the past." She begins to dance. Ruth is dumbfounded.*)

Ruth: What kind of dance is that?

Beneatha: A folk dance.

5 **Ruth** (*Pearl Bailey.*): What kind of folks do that, honey?

Beneatha: It's from Nigeria. It's a dance of welcome.

Ruth: Who you welcoming?

Beneatha: The men back to the village.

Ruth: Where they been?

10 **Beneatha:** How should I know—out hunting or something. Anyway, they are coming back now . . .

Ruth: Well, that's good.

Beneatha *(With the record.):*

Alundi, alundi
Alundi alunya
Jop pu a jeepua
Ang gu sooooooooooo

Ai yai yae . . .
Ayehaye—alundi . . .

(Walter comes in during this performance; he has obviously been drinking. He leans against the door heavily and watches his sister, at first with distaste. Then his eyes look off—"back to the past"—as he lifts both his fists to the roof, screaming.)

Walter: YEAH . . . AND ETHIOPIA STRETCH FORTH HER HANDS AGAIN! . . .

Ruth *(Drily, looking at him.):* Yes—and Africa sure is claiming her own tonight. *(She gives them both up and starts ironing again.)*

15 **Walter** *(All in a drunken, dramatic shout.):* Shut up! . . . I'm digging them drums . . . them drums move me! . . . *(He makes his weaving way to his wife's face and leans in close to her.)* In my *heart of hearts—(He thumps his chest.)*—I am much warrior!

Ruth *(Without even looking up.):* In your heart of hearts you are much drunkard.

Walter *(Coming away from her and starting to wander around the room, shouting.):* Me and Jomo . . . *(Intently, in his sister's face. She has stopped dancing to watch him in this unknown mood.)* That's my man, Kenyatta. *(Shouting and thumping his chest.)* FLAMING SPEAR! HOT DAMN! *(He is suddenly in possession of an imaginary spear and actively spearing enemies all over the room.)* OCOMOGOSIAY . . . THE LION IS WAKING . . . OWIMOWEH! *(He pulls his shirt open and leaps up on a table and gestures with his spear. The bell rings. Ruth goes to answer.)*

Beneatha *(To encourage Walter, thoroughly caught up with this side of him.):* OCOMOGOSIAY, FLAMING SPEAR!

Walter *(On the table, very far gone, his eyes pure glass sheets. He sees what we cannot, that he is a leader of his people, a great chief, a descendant of Chaka, and that the hour to march has come.):* Listen, my black brothers—

20 **Beneatha:** OCOMOGOSIAY!

Walter: —Do you hear the waters rushing against the shores of the coastlands—

Beneatha: OCOMOGOSIAY!

Walter: —Do you hear the screeching of the cocks in yonder hills beyond where the chiefs meet in council for the coming of the mighty war—

Beneatha: OCOMOGOSIAY!

25 **Walter:** —Do you hear the beating of the wings of the birds flying over the mountains and the low places of our land—

(Ruth opens the door. George Murchison enters.)

Beneatha: OCOMOGOSIAY!

Walter: —Do you hear the singing of the women, singing the war songs of our fathers to the babies in the great houses . . . singing the sweet war songs? OH, DO YOU HEAR, MY BLACK BROTHERS!

Beneatha (*Completely gone.*): We hear you, Flaming Spear—
Walter: Telling us to prepare for the greatness of the time— (*To George.*) Black Brother!

(*He extends his hand for the fraternal clasp.*)

30 **George:** Black Brother, hell!
Ruth (*Having had enough, and embarrassed for the family.*): Beneatha, you got company—
   what's the matter with you? Walter Lee Younger, get down off that table and stop
   acting like a fool . . .

(*Walter comes down off the table suddenly and makes a quick exit to the bathroom.*)

Ruth: He's had a little to drink . . . I don't know what her excuse is.
George (*To Beneatha.*): Look honey, we're going *to* the theatre—we're not going to be *in*
   it . . . so go change, huh?
Ruth: You expect this boy to go out with you looking like that?
35 **Beneatha** (*Looking at George.*): That's up to George. If he's ashamed of his heritage—
George: Oh, don't be so proud of yourself, Bennie—just because you look eccentric.
Beneatha: How can something that's natural be eccentric?
George: That's what being eccentric means—being natural. Get dressed.
Beneatha: I don't like that, George.
40 **Ruth:** Why must you and your brother make an argument out of everything people
   say?
Beneatha: Because I hate assimilationist Negroes!
Ruth: Will somebody please tell me what assimila-whoever means!
George: Oh, it's just a college girl's way of calling people Uncle Toms—but that isn't what
   it means at all.
Ruth: Well, what does it mean?
45 **Beneatha** (*Cutting George off and staring at him as she replies to Ruth.*): It means someone
   who is willing to give up his own culture and submerge himself completely in the
   dominant, and in this case, *oppressive* culture!
George: Oh, dear, dear, dear! Here we go! A lecture on the African past! On our Great
   West African Heritage! In one second we will hear all about the great Ashanti empires; the great Songhay civilizations; and the great sculpture of Bénin—and then
   some poetry in the Bantu—and the whole monologue will end with the world *heritage*! (*Nastily.*) Let's face it, baby, your heritage is nothing but a bunch of raggedy-
   assed spirituals and some grass huts!
Beneatha: Grass huts! (*Ruth crosses to her and forcibly pushes her toward the bedroom.*) See
   there . . . you are standing there in your splendid ignorance talking about people who
   were the first to smelt iron on the face of the earth! (*Ruth is pushing her through the
   door.*) The Ashanti were performing surgical operations when the English—*Ruth pulls
   the door to, with Beneatha on the other side, and smiles graciously at George. Beneatha
   opens the door and shouts the end of the sentence defiantly at George.*)—were still tattoo-
   ing themselves with blue dragons . . . (*She goes back inside.*)
Ruth: Have a seat, George. (*They both sit. Ruth folds her hands rather primly on her lap, determined to demonstrate the civilization of the family.*) Warm, ain't it? I mean for
   September. (*Pause.*) Just like they always say about Chicago weather: If it's too hot or
   cold for you, just wait a minute and it'll change. (*She smiles happily at this cliché of
   clichés.*) Everybody say it's got to do with them bombs and things they keep setting
   off. (*Pause.*) Would you like a nice cold beer?
George: No, thank you. I don't care for beer. (*He looks at his watch.*) I hope she hurries up.
50 **Ruth:** What time is the show?

George: It's an eight-thirty curtain. That's just Chicago, though. In New York standard curtain time is eight forty.

(*He is rather proud of this knowledge.*)

Ruth (*Properly appreciating it.*): You get to New York a lot?
George (*Offhand.*): Few times a year.
Ruth: Oh—that's nice. I've never been to New York.

(*Walter enters. We feel he has relieved himself, but the edge of unreality is still with him.*)

55 **Walter:** New York ain't got nothing Chicago ain't. Just a bunch of hustling people all squeezed up together—being "Eastern."

(*He turns his face into a screw of displeasure.*)

George: Oh—you've been?
Walter: *Plenty* of times.
Ruth (*Shocked at the lie.*): Walter Lee Younger!
Walter (*Staring her down.*): Plenty! (*Pause.*) What we got to drink in this house? Why don't you offer this man some refreshment. (*To George.*) They don't know how to entertain people in this house, man.

60 **George:** Thank you—I don't really care for anything.
Walter (*Feeling his head; sobriety coming.*): Where's Mama?
Ruth: She ain't come back yet.
Walter (*Looking Murchison over from head to toe, scrutinizing his carefully casual tweed sports jacket over cashmere V-neck sweater over soft eyelet shirt and tie, and soft slacks, finished off with white buckskin shoes.*): Why all you college boys wear them fairyish-looking white shoes?
Ruth: Walter Lee!

(*George Murchison ignores the remark.*)

65 **Walter** (*To Ruth.*): Well, they look crazy as hell—white shoes, cold as it is.
Ruth (*Crushed.*): You have to excuse him—
Walter: No he don't! Excuse me for what? What you always excusing me for! I'll excuse myself when I needs to be excused! (*A pause.*) They look as funny as them black knee socks Beneatha wears out of here all the time.
Ruth: It's the college *style*, Walter.
Walter: Style, hell. She looks like she got burnt legs or something!
70 **Ruth:** Oh, Walter—
Walter (*An irritable mimic.*): Oh, Walter! Oh, Walter! (*To Murchison.*) How's your old man making out? I understand you all going to buy that big hotel on the Drive? (*He finds a beer in the refrigerator, wanders over to Murchison, sipping and wiping his lips with the back of his hand, and straddling a chair backwards to talk to the other man.*) Shrewd move. Your old man is all right, man. (*Tapping his head and half winking for emphasis.*) I mean he knows how to operate. I mean he thinks *big*, you know what I mean, I mean for a *home*, you know? But I think he's kind of running out of ideas now. I'd like to talk to him. Listen, man, I got some plans that could turn this city upside down. I mean I think like he does. *Big*. Invest big, gamble big, hell, lose *big* if you have to, you know what I mean. It's hard to find a man on this whole Southside who understands my kind of thinking—you dig? (*He scrutinizes Murchison again, drinks his beer, squints his eyes, and leans in close, confidential, man to man.*) Me and you ought to sit down and talk sometimes, man. Man, I got me some ideas . . .

Murchison (*With boredom.*): Yeah—sometimes we'll have to do that, Walter.

Walter (*Understanding the indifference, and offended.*): Yeah—well, when you get the time, man. I know you a busy little boy.

Ruth: Walter, please—

75 **Walter** (*Bitterly, hurt.*): I know ain't nothing in this world as busy as you colored college boys with your fraternity pins and white shoes . . .

Ruth (*Covering her face with humiliation.*): Oh, Walter Lee—

Walter: I see you all all the time—with the books tucked under your arms—going to your (*British A—a mimic.*) "clahsses." And for what! What the hell you learning over there? Filling up your heads—(*Counting off on his fingers.*)—with the sociology and the psychology—but they teaching you how to be a man? How to take over and run the world? They teaching you how to run a rubber plantation or a steel mill? Naw—just to talk proper and read books and wear white shoes . . .

George (*Looking at him with distaste, a little above it all.*): You're all wacked up with bitterness, man.

Walter (*Intently, almost quietly, between the teeth, glaring at the boy.*): And you—ain't you bitter, man? Ain't you just about had it yet? Don't you see no stars gleaming that you can't reach out and grab? You happy—you contented son-of-a-bitch—you happy? You got it made? Bitter? Man, I'm a volcano. Bitter? Here I am a giant—surrounded by ants! Ants who can't even understand what it is the giant is talking about.

80 **Ruth** (*Passionately and suddenly.*) Oh, Walter—ain't you with nobody!

Walter (*Violently.*): No! 'Cause ain't nobody with me! Not even my own mother!

Ruth: Walter, that's a terrible thing to say!

(*Beneatha enters, dressed for the evening in a cocktail dress and earrings.*)

George: Well—hey, you look great.

Beneatha: Let's go, George. See you all later.

85 **Ruth:** Have a nice time.

George: Thanks. Good night. (*To Walter, sarcastically.*) Good night, *Prometheus.*

(*Beneatha and George exit.*)

Walter (*To Ruth.*): Who is Prometheus?

Ruth: I don't know. Don't worry about it.

Walter (*In fury, pointing after George.*): See there—they get to a point where they can't insult you man to man—they got to go talk about something ain't nobody never heard of!

90 **Ruth:** How you know it was an insult? (*To humor him.*) Maybe Prometheus is a nice fellow.

Walter: Prometheus! I bet there ain't even no such thing! I bet that simple-minded clown—

Ruth: Walter—

(*She stops what she is doing and looks at him.*)

Walter (*Yelling.*): Don't start!

Ruth: Start what?

95 **Walter:** Your nagging! Where was I? Who was I with? How much money did I spend?

Ruth (*Plaintively.*): Walter Lee—why don't we just try to talk about it . . .

Walter (*Not listening.*): I been out talking with people who understand me. People who care about the things I got on my mind.

Ruth (*Wearily.*): I guess that means people like Willy Harris.

Walter: Yes, people like Willy Harris.

100 **Ruth** (*With a sudden flash of impatience.*): Why don't you all just hurry up and go into the banking business and stop talking about it!

Walter: Why? You want to know why? 'Cause we all tied up in a race of people that don't know how to do nothing but moan, pray, and have babies!

(The line is too bitter even for him and he looks at her and sits down.)

Ruth: Oh, Walter . . . *(Softly.)* Honey, why can't you stop fighting me?
Walter *(Without thinking.)*: Who's fighting you? Who even cares about you?

(This line begins the retardation of his mood).

Ruth: Well—*(She waits a long time, and then with resignation starts to put away her things.)* I guess I might as well go on to bed . . . *(More or less to herself.)* I don't know where we lost it . . . but we have . . . *(Then, to him.)* I—I'm sorry about this new baby, Walter. I guess maybe I better go on and do what I started . . . I guess I just didn't realize how bad things was with us . . . I guess I just didn't really realize—*(She starts out to the bedroom and stops.)* You want some hot milk?
105 **Walter:** Hot milk?
Ruth: Yes—hot milk.
Walter: Why hot milk?
Ruth: 'Cause after all that liquor you come home with you ought to have something hot in your stomach.
Walter: I don't want no milk.
110 **Ruth:** You want some coffee then?
Walter: No, I don't want no coffee. I don't want nothing hot to drink. *(Almost plaintively.)* Why you always trying to give me something to eat?
Ruth *(Standing and looking at him helplessly.)*: What else can I give you, Walter Lee Younger?

(She stands and looks at him and presently turns to go out again. He lifts his head and watches her going away from him in a new mood which began to emerge when he asked her "Who cares about you?")

Walter: It's been rough, ain't it, baby? *(She hears and stops but does not turn around and he continues to her back.)* I guess between two people there ain't never as much understood as folks generally thinks there is. I mean like between me and you—*(She turns to face him.)* How we gets to the place where we scared to talk softness to each other. *(He waits, thinking hard himself.)* Why you think it got to be like that? *(He is thoughtful, almost as a child would be.)* Ruth, what is it gets into people ought to be close?
Ruth: I don't know, honey. I think about it a lot.
115 **Walter:** On account of you and me, you mean? The way things are with us. The way something done come down between us.
Ruth: There ain't so much between us, Walter . . . Not when you come to me and try to talk to me. Try to be with me . . . a little even.
Walter *(Total honesty.)*: Sometimes . . . sometimes . . . I don't even know how to try.
Ruth: Walter—
Walter: Yes?
120 **Ruth** *(Coming to him, gently and with misgiving, but coming to him.)*: Honey . . . life don't have to be like this. I mean sometimes people can do things so that things are better . . . You remember how we used to talk when Travis was born . . . about the way we were going to live . . . the kind of house . . . *(She is stroking his head.)* Well, it's all starting to slip away from us . . .

(Mama enters, and Walter jumps up and shouts at her.)

Walter: Mama, where have you been?

Mama: My—them steps is longer than they used to be. Whew! *(She sits down and ignores him.)* How you feeling this evening, Ruth?

(Ruth shrugs, disturbed some at having been prematurely interrupted and watching her husband knowingly.)

Walter: Mama, where have you been all day?

Mama *(Still ignoring him and leaning on the table and changing to more comfortable shoes.):* Where's Travis?

125 **Ruth:** I let him go out earlier and he ain't come back yet. Boy, is he going to get it!

Walter: Mama!

Mama *(As if she heard him for the first time.):* Yes, son?

Walter: Where did you go this afternoon?

Mama: I went downtown to tend to some business that I had to tend to.

130 **Walter:** What kind of business?

Mama: You know better than to question me like a child, Brother.

Walter *(Rising and bending over the table.):* Where were you, Mama? *(Bringing his fists down and shouting.)* Mama, you didn't go do something with that insurance money, something crazy?

(The front door opens slowly, interrupting him, and Travis peeks his head in, less than hopefully.)

Travis *(To his mother.):* Mama, I—

Ruth: "Mama I" nothing! You're going to get it, boy! Get on in that bedroom and get yourself ready!

135 **Travis:** But I—

Mama: Why don't you all never let the child explain hisself.

Ruth: Keep out of it now, Lena.

(Mama clamps her lips together, and Ruth advances toward her son menacingly.)

Ruth: A thousand times I have told you not to go off like that—

Mama *(Holding out her arms to her grandson.):* Well—at least let me tell him something. I want him to be the first one to hear . . . Come here, Travis. *(The boy obeys, gladly.)* Travis—*(She takes him by the shoulders and looks into his face.)*—you know that money we got in the mail this morning?

140 **Travis:** Yes'm—

Mama: Well—what you think your grandmama gone and done with that money?

Travis: I don't know, Grandmama.

Mama *(Putting her finger on his nose for emphasis.):* She went out and she bought you a house! *(The explosion comes from Walter at the end of the revelation and he jumps up and turns away from all of them in a fury. Mama continues, to Travis.)* You glad about the house? It's going to be yours when you get to be a man.

Travis: Yeah—I always wanted to live in a house.

145 **Mama:** All right, gimme some sugar then—*(Travis puts his arms around her neck as she watches her son over the boy's shoulder. Then, to Travis, after the embrace.)* Now when you say your prayers tonight, you thank God and your grandfather—'cause it was him who give you the house—in his way.

Ruth *(Taking the boy from Mama and pushing him toward the bedroom.):* Now you get out of here and get ready for your beating.

Travis: Aw, Mama—

Ruth: Get on in there—(*Closing the door behind him and turning radiantly to her mother-in-law.*) So you went and did it!

Mama (*Quietly, looking at her son with pain.*): Yes, I did.

150 **Ruth** (*Raising both arms classically.*): Praise God! (*Looks at Walter a moment, who says nothing. She crosses rapidly to her husband.*) Please, honey—let me be glad . . . you be glad too. (*She has laid her hands on his shoulders, but he shakes himself free of her roughly, without turning to face her.*) Oh, Walter . . . a home . . . a home. (*She comes back to Mama.*) Well—where is it? How big is it? How much it going to cost?

Mama: Well—

Ruth: When we moving?

Mama (*Smiling at her.*): First of the month.

Ruth (*Throwing back her head with jubilation.*): Praise God!

155 **Mama** (*Tentatively, still looking at her son's back turned against her and Ruth.*): It's—it's a nice house too . . . (*She cannot help speaking directly to him. An imploring quality in her voice, her manner, makes her almost like a girl now.*) Three bedrooms—nice big one for you and Ruth . . . Me and Beneatha still have to share our room, but Travis have one of his own—and—(*With difficulty.*) I figures if the—new baby—is a boy, we could get one of the double-decker outfits . . . And there's a yard with a little patch of dirt where I could maybe get to grow me a few flowers . . . And a nice big basement . . .

Ruth: Walter honey, be glad—

Mama (*Still to his back, fingering things on the table.*): 'Course I don't want to make it sound fancier than it is . . . It's just a plain little old house—but it's made good and solid—and it will be *ours*. Walter Lee—it makes a difference in a man when he can walk on floors that belong to *him* . . .

Ruth: Where is it?

Mama (*Frightened at this telling.*): Well—well—it's out there in Clybourne Park—

(*Ruth's radiance fades abruptly, and Walter finally turns slowly to face his mother with incredulity and hostility.*)

160 **Ruth:** Where?

Mama (*Matter of factly.*): Four o six Clybourne Street, Clybourne Park.

Ruth: Clybourne Park? Mama, there ain't no colored people living in Clybourne Park.

Mama (*Almost idiotically.*): Well, I guess there's going to be some now.

Walter (*Bitterly.*) So that's the peace and comfort you went out and bought for us today!

165 **Mama** (*Raising her eyes to meet his finally.*): Son—I just tried to find the nicest place for the least amount of money for my family.

Ruth (*Trying to recover from the shock.*): Well—well—'course I ain't one never been 'fraid of no crackers, mind you—but—well, wasn't there no other houses nowhere?

Mama: Them houses they put up for colored in them areas way out all seem to cost twice as much as other houses. I did the best I could.

Ruth (*Struck senseless with the news, in its various degrees of goodness and trouble, she sits a moment, her fists propping her chin in thought, and then she starts to rise, bringing her fists down with vigor, the radiance spreading from cheek to cheek again.*): Well—well!—All I can say is—if this is my time in life—*my time*—to say good-bye—(*And she builds with momentum as she starts to circle the room with an exuberant, almost tearfully happy release.*)—to these God-damned cracking walls!—(*She pounds the walls.*)—and these marching roaches!—(*She wipes at an imaginary army of marching roaches.*)—and this cramped little closet which ain't now or never was no kitchen! . . . then I say it loud and good, *Hallelujah!* and good-bye misery . . . I don't never want to see your ugly face again! (*She laughs joyously, having practically destroyed the apartment, and flings her arms* *up and lets them come down happily, slowly, reflectively, over her abdomen, aware for the first time perhaps that the life therein pulses with happiness and not despair.)* Lena?

Mama *(moved, watching her happiness.):* Yes, honey?

170 **Ruth** *(Looking off.):* Is there—is there a whole lot of sunlight?

Mama *(Understanding.):* Yes, child, there's a whole lot of sunlight.

(Long pause.)

Ruth *(Collecting herself and going to the door of the room Travis is in.):* Well—I guess I better see 'bout Travis. *(To Mama.)* Lord, I sure don't feel like whipping nobody today!

(She exits.)

Mama *(The mother and son are left alone now and the mother waits a long time, considering deeply, before she speaks.):* Son—you—you understand what I done, don't you? *(Walter is silent and sullen.)* I—I just seen my family falling apart today . . . just falling to pieces in front of my eyes . . . We couldn't of gone on like we was today. We was going backwards 'stead of forwards—talking 'bout killing babies and wishing each other was dead . . . When it gets like that in life—you just got to do something different, push on out and do something bigger . . . *(She waits.)* I wish you say something, son . . . I wish you'd say how deep inside you, you think I done the right thing.

Walter *(Crossing slowly to his bedroom door and finally turning there and speaking measuredly.):* What you need me to say you done right for? *You* the head of this family. You run our lives like you want to. It was your money and you did what you wanted with it. So what you need for me to say it was all right for? *(Bitterly, to hurt her as deeply as he knows is possible.)* So you butchered up a dream of mine—you—who always talking 'bout your children's dreams . . .

175 **Mama:** Walter Lee—

(He just closes the door behind him. Mama sits alone, thinking heavily.)

(Curtain.)

Act Two
Scene 2

Time: Friday night. A few weeks later.
At rise: Packing crates mark the intention of the family to move. Beneatha and George come in, presumably from an evening out again.

1 **George:** O.K. . . . O.K., whatever you say . . . *(They both sit on the couch. He tries to kiss her. She moves away.)* Look, we've had a nice evening; let's not spoil it, huh? . . .

(He again turns her head and tries to nuzzle in and she turns away from him, not with distaste but with momentary lack of interest; in a mood to pursue what they were talking about.)

Beneatha: I'm *trying* to talk to you.

George: We always talk.

Beneatha: Yes—and I love to talk.

5 **George** *(Exasperated; rising.):* I know it and I don't mind it sometimes . . . I want you to cut it out, see— The moody stuff, I mean. I don't like it. You're a nice-looking girl . . . all over. That's all you need, honey, forget the atmosphere. Guys aren't going to go for the atmosphere—they're going to go for what they see. Be glad for that.

Drop the Garbo routine. It doesn't go with you. As for myself, I want a nice—
(*Groping.*)—simple—(*Thoughtfully.*) sophisticated girl . . . not a poet—O.K.?

(*She rebuffs him again and he starts to leave.*)

Beneatha: Why are you angry?

George: Because this is stupid! I don't go out with you to discuss the nature of "quiet
desperation" or to hear all about your thoughts—because the world will go on
thinking what it thinks regardless—

Beneatha: Then why read books? Why go to school?

George (*With artificial patience, counting on his fingers.*): It's simple. You read books—to
learn facts—to get grades—to pass the course—to get a degree. That's all—it has
nothing to do with thoughts.

(*A long pause.*)

10 **Beneatha:** I see. (*A longer pause as she looks at him.*) Good night, George.

(*George looks at her a little oddly, and starts to exit. He meets Mama coming in.*)

George: Oh—hello, Mrs. Younger.

Mama: Hello, George, how you feeling?

George: Fine—fine, how are you?

Mama: Oh, a little tired. You know them steps can get you after a day's work. You all have
a nice time tonight?

15 **George:** Yes—a fine time. Well, good night.

Mama: Good night. (*He exits. Mama closes the door behind her.*) Hello, honey. What you
sitting like that for?

Beneatha: I'm just sitting.

Mama: Didn't you have a nice time?

Beneatha: No.

20 **Mama:** No? What's the matter?

Beneatha: Mama, George is a fool—honest. (*She rises.*)

Mama (*Hustling around unloading the packages she has entered with. She stops.*): Is he, baby?

Beneatha: Yes.

(*Beneatha makes up Travis' bed as she talks.*)

Mama: You sure?

25 **Beneatha:** Yes.

Mama: Well—I guess you better not waste your time with no fools.

(*Beneatha looks up at her mother, watching her put groceries in the refrigerator. Finally, she
gathers up her things and starts into the bedroom. At the door she stops and looks back at her
mother.*)

Beneatha: Mama—

Mama: Yes, baby—

Beneatha: Thank you.

30 **Mama:** For what?

Beneatha: For understanding me this time.

(*She exits quickly and the mother stands, smiling a little, looking at the place where Beneatha
just stood. Ruth enters.*)

Ruth: Now don't you fool with any of this stuff, Lena—

Mama: Oh, I just thought I'd sort a few things out.

(*The phone rings. Ruth answers.*)

Ruth (*At the phone.*): Hello—Just a minute. (*Goes to door.*) Walter, it's Mrs. Arnold. (*Waits. Goes back to the phone. Tense.*) Hello. Yes, this is his wife speaking . . . He's lying down now. Yes . . . well, he'll be in tomorrow. He's been very sick. Yes—I know we should have called, but we were so sure he'd be able to come in today. Yes—yes, I'm very sorry. Yes . . . Thank you very much. (*She hangs up. Walter is standing in the doorway of the bedroom behind her.*) That was Mrs. Arnold.

35 **Walter** (*Indifferently.*): Was it?

Ruth: She said if you don't come in tomorrow that they are getting a new man . . .

Walter: Ain't that sad—ain't that crying sad.

Ruth: She said Mr. Arnold has had to take a cab for three days . . . Walter, you ain't been to work for three days! (*This is a revelation to her.*) Where you been, Walter Lee Younger? (*Walter looks at her and starts to laugh.*) You're going to lose your job.

Walter: That's right . . .

40 **Ruth:** Oh, Walter, and with your mother working like a dog every day—

Walter: That's sad too— Everything is sad.

Mama: What you been doing for these three days, son?

Walter: Mama—you don't know all the things a man what got leisure can find to do in this city . . . What's this—Friday night? Well—Wednesday I borrowed Willy Harris' car and I went for a drive . . . just me and myself and I drove and drove . . . Way out . . . way past South Chicago, and I parked the car and I sat and looked at the steel mills all day long. I just sat in the car and looked at them big black chimneys for hours. Then I drove back and I went to the Green Hat. (*Pause.*) And Thursday— Thursday I borrowed the car again and I got in it and I pointed it the other way and I drove the other way—for hours—way, way up to Wisconsin, and I looked at the farms. I just drove and looked at the farms. Then I drove back and I went to the Green Hat. (*Pause.*) And today—today I didn't get the car. Today I just walked. All over the Southside. And I looked at the Negroes and they looked at me and finally I just sat down on the curb at Thirty-ninth and South Parkway and I just sat there and watched the Negroes go by. And then I went to the Green Hat. You all sad? You all depressed? And you know where I am going right now—

(*Ruth goes out quietly.*)

Mama: Oh, Big Walter, is this the harvest of our days?

45 **Walter:** You know what I like about the Green Hat? (*He turns the radio on and a steamy, deep blues pours into the room.*) I like this little cat they got there who blows a sax . . . He blows. He talks to me. He ain't but 'bout five feet tall and he's got a conked head and his eyes is always closed and he's all music—

Mama (*Rising and getting some papers out of her handbag.*): Walter—

Walter: And there's this other guy who plays the piano . . . and they got a sound. I mean they can work on some music . . . They got the best little combo in the world in the Green Hat . . . You can just sit there and drink and listen to them three men play and you realize that don't nothing matter worth a damn, but just being there—

Mama: I've helped do it to you, haven't I, son? Walter, I been wrong.

Walter: Naw—you ain't never been wrong about nothing, Mama.

50 **Mama:** Listen to me, now. I say I been wrong, son. That I been doing to you what the rest of the world been doing to you. (*She stops and he looks up slowly at her and she meets his eyes pleadingly.*) Walter—what you ain't never understood is that I ain't got nothing,

don't own nothing, ain't never really wanted nothing that wasn't for you. There ain't nothing as precious to me . . . There ain't nothing worth holding on to, money, dreams, nothing else—if it means—if it means it's going to destroy my boy. (*She puts her papers in front of him and he watches her without speaking or moving.*) I paid the man thirty-five hundred dollars down on the house. That leaves sixty-five hundred dollars. Monday morning I want you to take this money and take three thousand dollars and put it in a savings account for Beneatha's medical schooling. The rest you put in a checking account—with your name on it. And from now on any penny that come out of it or that go in it is for you to look after. For you to decide. (*She drops her hands a little helplessly.*) It ain't much, but it's all I got in the world and I'm putting it in your hands. I'm telling you to be the head of this family from now on like you supposed to be.

Walter (*Stares at the money.*): You trust me like that, Mama?

Mama: I ain't never stop trusting you. Like I ain't never stop loving you.

(*She goes out, and Walter sits looking at the money on the table as the music continues in its idiom, pulsing in the room. Finally, in a decisive gesture, he gets up and, in a furious action, flings the bedclothes wildly from his son's makeshift bed to all over the floor—with a cry of desperation. Then he picks up the money and goes out in a hurry.*)

(*Curtain.*)

Act Two
Scene 3

Time: Saturday, moving day, one week later.

Before the curtain rises, Ruth's voice, a strident, dramatic church alto, cuts through the silence.

It is, in the darkness, a triumphant surge, a penetrating statement of expectation: "Oh, Lord, I don't feel no ways tired! Children, oh, glory hallelujah!"

As the curtain rises we see that Ruth is alone in the living room, finishing up the family's packing. It is moving day. She is nailing crates and tying cartons. Beneatha enters, carrying a guitar case, and watches her exuberant sister-in-law.

1 **Ruth:** Hey!

Beneatha (*Putting away the case.*): Hi.

Ruth (*Pointing at a package.*): Honey—look in that package there and see what I found on sale this morning at the South Center. (*Ruth gets up and moves to the package and draws out some curtains.*) Lookahere—hand-turned hems!

Beneatha: How do you know the window size out there?

5 **Ruth** (*Who hadn't thought of that.*): Oh— Well, they bound to fit something in the whole house. Anyhow, they was too good a bargain to pass up. (*Ruth slaps her head, suddenly remembering something.*) Oh, Bennie—I meant to put a special note on that carton over there. That's your mama's good china and she wants 'em to be very careful with it.

Beneatha: I'll do it.

(*Beneatha finds a piece of paper and starts to draw large letters on it.*)

Ruth: You know what I'm going to do soon as I get in that new house?

Beneatha: What?

Ruth: Honey—I'm going to run me a tub of water up to here . . . (*With her fingers practically up to her nostrils.*) And I'm going to get in it—and I am going to sit . . . and sit . . . and sit in that hot water and the first person who knocks to tell *me* to hurry up and come out—

10 **Beneatha:** Gets shot at sunrise.

Ruth (*Laughing happily.*): You said it, sister! (*Noticing how large Beneatha is absent-mindedly making the note.*) Honey, they ain't going to read that from no airplane.

Beneatha (*Laughing herself.*): I guess I always think things have more emphasis if they are big, somehow.

Ruth (*Looking up at her and smiling.*): You and your brother seem to have that as a philosophy of life. Lord, that man—done changed so 'round here. You know—you know what we did last night? Me and Walter Lee?

Beneatha: What?

15 **Ruth** (*Smiling to herself.*): We went to the movies. (*Looking at Beneatha to see if she understands.*) We went to the movies. You know the last time me and Walter went to the movies together?

Beneatha: No.

Ruth: Me neither. That's how long it been. (*Smiling again.*) But we went last night. The picture wasn't much good, but that didn't seem to matter. We went—and we held hands.

Beneatha: Oh, Lord!

Ruth: We held hands—and you know what?

20 **Beneatha:** What?

Ruth: When we come out of the show it was late and dark and all the stores and things was closed up . . . and it was kind of chilly and there wasn't many people on the streets . . . and we was still holding hands, me and Walter.

Beneatha: You're killing me.

(*Walter enters with a large package. His happiness is deep in him; he cannot keep still with his new-found exuberance. He is singing and wiggling and snapping his fingers. He puts his package in a corner and puts a phonograph record, which he has brought in with him, on the record player. As the music comes up he dances over to Ruth and tries to get her to dance with him. She gives in at last to his raunchiness and in a fit of giggling allows herself to be drawn into his mood and together they deliberately burlesque an old social dance of their youth.*)

Beneatha (*Regarding them a long time as they dance, then drawing in her breath for a deeply exaggerated comment which she does not particularly mean.*): Talk about— olddddddddddd-fashionedddddddd—Negroes!

Walter (*Stopping momentarily.*): What kind of Negroes?

(*He says this in fun. He is not angry with her today, nor with anyone. He starts to dance with his wife again.*)

25 **Beneatha:** Old-fashioned.

Walter (*As he dances with Ruth.*): You know, when these *New Negroes* have their convention— (*Pointing at his sister.*)—that is going to be the chairman of the Committee on Unending Agitation. (*He goes on dancing, then stops.*) Race, race, race! . . . Girl, I do believe you are the first person in the history of the entire human race to successfully brainwash yourself. (*Beneatha breaks up and he goes on dancing. He stops again, enjoying his tease.*) Damn, even the N double A C P takes a holiday sometimes! (*Beneatha and Ruth laugh. He dances with Ruth some more and starts to laugh and stops and pantomimes someone over an operating table.*) I can just see that chick someday looking down at some poor cat on an operating table before she starts to slice him, saying . . . (*Pulling his sleeves back maliciously.*) "By the way, what are your views on civil rights down there? . . ."

(*He laughs at her again and starts to dance happily. The bell sounds.*)

Beneatha: Sticks and stones may break my bones but . . . words will never hurt me!

(*Beneatha goes to the door and opens it as Walter and Ruth go on with the clowning. Beneatha is somewhat surprised to see a quiet-looking middle-aged white man in a business suit holding his hat and a briefcase in his hand and consulting a small piece of paper.*)

Man: Uh—how do you do, miss. I am looking for a Mrs.—(*He looks at the slip of paper.*) Mrs. Lena Younger?

Beneatha (*Smoothing her hair with slight embarrassment.*): Oh—yes, that's my mother. Excuse me. (*She closes the door and turns to quiet the other two.*) Ruth! Brother! Somebody's here. (*Then she opens the door. The man casts a curious quick glance at all of them.*) Uh—come in please.

30 **Man** (*Coming in.*): Thank you.

Beneatha: My mother isn't here just now. Is it business?

Man: Yes . . . well, of a sort.

Walter (*Freely, the Man of the House.*): Have a seat. I'm Mrs. Younger's son. I look after most of her business matters.

(*Ruth and Beneatha exchange amused glances.*)

Man (*Regarding Walter, and sitting.*): Well— My name is Karl Lindner . . .

35 **Walter** (*Stretching out his hand.*): Walter Younger. This is my wife—(*Ruth nods politely.*)— and my sister.

Lindner: How do you do.

Walter (*Amiably, as he sits himself easily on a chair, leaning with interest forward on his knees and looking expectantly into the newcomer's face.*): What can we do for you, Mr. Lindner!

Lindner (*Some minor shuffling of the hat and briefcase on his knees.*): Well—I am a representative of the Clybourne Park Improvement Association—

Walter (*Pointing.*): Why don't you sit your things on the floor?

40 **Lindner:** Oh—yes. Thank you. (*He slides the briefcase and hat under the chair.*) And as I was saying—I am from the Clybourne Park Improvement Association and we have had it brought to our attention at the last meeting that you people—or at least your mother—has bought a piece of residential property at—(*He digs for the slip of paper again.*)—four o six Clybourne Street . . .

Walter: That's right. Care for something to drink? Ruth, get Mr. Lindner a beer.

Lindner (*Upset for some reason.*): Oh—no, really. I mean thank you very much, but no thank you.

Ruth (*Innocently.*): Some coffee?

Lindner: Thank you, nothing at all.

(*Beneatha is watching the man carefully.*)

45 **Lindner:** Well, I don't know how much you folks know about our organization. (*He is a gentle man; thoughtful and somewhat labored in his manner.*) It is one of these community organizations set up to look after—oh, you know, things like block upkeep and special projects and we also have what we call our New Neighbors Orientation Committee . . .

Beneatha (*Drily.*): Yes—and what do they do?

Lindner (*Turning a little to her and then returning the main force to Walter.*): Well—it's what you might call a sort of welcoming committee, I guess. I mean they, we, I'm the chair-man of the committee—go around and see the new people who move into the neigh-borhood and sort of give them the lowdown on the way we do things out in Clybourne Park.

Beneatha (*With appreciation of the two meanings, which escape Ruth and Walter.*): Un-huh.

Lindner: And we also have the category of what the association calls—(*He looks elsewhere.*)—uh—special community problems . . .

50 **Beneatha:** Yes—and what are some of those?

Walter: Girl, let the man talk.

Lindner (*With understated relief.*): Thank you. I would sort of like to explain this thing in my own way. I mean I want to explain to you in a certain way.

Walter: Go ahead.

Lindner: Yes. Well. I'm going to try to get right to the point. I'm sure we'll all appreciate that in the long run.

55 **Beneatha:** Yes.

Walter: Be still now!

Lindner: Well—

Ruth (*Still innocently.*): Would you like another chair—you don't look comfortable.

Lindner (*More frustrated than annoyed.*): No, thank you very much. Please. Well—to get right to the point I—(*A great breath, and he is off at last.*) I am sure you people must be aware of some of the incidents which have happened in various part of the city when colored people have moved into certain areas—(*Beneatha exhales heavily and starts tossing a piece of fruit up and down in the air.*) Well—because we have what I think is going to be a unique type of organization in American community life—not only do we deplore that kind of thing—but we are trying to do something about it. (*Beneatha stops tossing and turns with a new and quizzical interest to the man.*) We feel—(*gaining confidence in his mission because of the interest in the faces of the people he is talking to.*)—we feel that most of the trouble in this world, when you come right down to it—(*He hits his knee for emphasis.*)—most of the trouble exists because people just don't sit down and talk to each other.

60 **Ruth** (*Nodding as she might in church, pleased with the remark.*): You can say that again, mister.

Lindner (*More encouraged by such affirmation.*): That we don't try hard enough in this world to understand the other fellow's problem. The other guy's point of view.

Ruth: Now that's right.

(*Beneatha and Walter merely watch and listen with genuine interest.*)

Lindner: Yes—that's the way we feel out in Clybourne Park. And that's why I was elected to come here this afternoon and talk to you people. Friendly like, you know, the way people should talk to each other and see if we couldn't find some way to work this thing out. As I say, the whole business is a matter of *caring* about the other fellow. Anybody can see that you are a nice family of folks, hard working and honest I'm sure. (*Beneatha frowns slightly, quizzically, her head tilted regarding him.*) Today everybody knows what it means to be on the outside of *something*. And of course, there is always somebody who is out to take the advantage of people who don't always understand.

Walter: What do you mean?

65 **Lindner:** Well—you see our community is made up of people who've worked hard as the dickens for years to build up that little community. They're not rich and fancy people; just hard-working, honest people who don't really have much but those little homes and a dream of the kind of community they want to raise their children in. Now, I don't say we are perfect and there is a lot wrong in some of the things they want. But you've got to admit that a man, right or wrong, has the right to want to have the neighborhood he lives in a certain kind of way. And at the moment the overwhelming majority of our people out there feel that people get along better, take more of a common interest in the life of the community, when they share a common background. I want you to believe me when I tell you that race prejudice simply

doesn't enter into it. It is a matter of the people of Clybourne Park believing, rightly or wrongly, as I say, that for the happiness of all concerned that our Negro families are happier when they live in their *own* communities.

Beneatha (*With a grand and bitter gesture.*): This, friends, is the Welcoming Committee!

Walter (*Dumbfounded, looking at Lindner.*): Is this what you came marching all the way over here to tell us?

Lindner: Well, now we've been having a fine conversation. I hope you'll hear me all the way through.

Walter (*Tightly.*): Go ahead, man.

70 **Lindner:** You see—in the face of all things I have said, we are prepared to make your family a very generous offer . . .

Beneatha: Thirty pieces and not a coin less!

Walter: Yeah?

Lindner (*Putting on his glasses and drawing a form out of the briefcase.*): Our association is prepared, through the collective effort of our people, to buy the house from you at a financial gain to your family.

Ruth: Lord have mercy, ain't this the living gall!

75 **Walter:** All right, you through?

Lindner: Well, I want to give you the exact terms of the financial arrangement—

Walter: We don't want to hear no exact terms of no arrangement. I want to know if you got any more to tell us 'bout getting together?

Lindner (*Taking off his glasses.*): Well—I don't suppose that you feel . . .

Walter: Never mind how I feel—you got any more to say 'bout how people ought to sit down and talk to each other? . . . Get out of my house, man.

(*He turns his back and walks to the door.*)

80 **Lindner** (*Looking around at the hostile faces and reaching and assembling his hat and briefcase.*): Well—I don't understand why you people are reacting this way. What do you think you are going to gain by moving into a neighborhood where you just aren't wanted and where some elements—well—people can get awful worked up when they feel that their whole way of life and everything they've ever worked for is threatened.

Walter: Get out.

Lindner (*At the door, holding a small card.*): Well—I'm sorry it went like this.

Walter: Get out.

Lindner (*Almost sadly regarding Walter.*): You just can't force people to change their hearts, son.

(*He turns and puts his card on a table and exits. Walter pushes the door to with stinging hatred, and stands looking at it. Ruth just sits and Beneatha just stands. They say nothing. Mama and Travis enter.*)

85 **Mama:** Well—this all the packing got done since I left out of here this morning. I testify before God that my children got all the energy of the dead. What time the moving men due?

Beneatha: Four o'clock. You had a caller, Mama.

(*She is smiling, teasingly.*)

Mama: Sure enough—who?

Beneatha (*Her arms folded saucily.*): The Welcoming Committee.

(*Walter and Ruth giggle.*)

Mama (*Innocently.*): Who?

90 **Beneatha:** The Welcoming Committee. They said they're sure going to be glad to see you when you get there.

Walter (*Devilishly.*): Yeah, they said they can't hardly wait to see your face.

(*Laughter.*)

Mama (*Sensing their facetiousness.*): What's the matter with you all?

Walter: Ain't nothing the matter with us. We just telling you 'bout the gentleman who came to see you this afternoon. From the Clybourne Park Improvement Association.

Mama: What he want?

95 **Ruth** (*In the same mood as Beneatha and Walter.*): To welcome you, honey.

Walter: He said they can't hardly wait. He said the one thing they don't have, that they just *dying* to have out there is a fine family of colored people! (*To Ruth and Beneatha.*) Ain't that right!

Ruth and **Beneatha** (*Mockingly.*): Yeah! He left his card in case—

(*They indicate the card, and Mama picks it up and throws it on the floor—understanding and looking off as she draws her chair up to the table on which she has put her plant and some sticks and some cord.*)

Mama: Father, give us strength. (*Knowingly—and without fun.*) Did he threaten us?

Beneatha: Oh—Mama—they don't do it like that any more. He talked Brotherhood. He said everybody ought learn how to sit down and hate each other with good Christian fellowship.

(*She and Walter shake hands to ridicule the remark.*)

100 **Mama** (*Sadly.*): Lord, protect us . . .

Ruth: You should hear the money those folks raised to buy the house from us. All we paid and then some.

Beneatha: What they think we going to do—eat 'em?

Ruth: No, honey, marry 'em.

Mama (*Shaking her head.*): Lord, Lord, Lord . . .

105 **Ruth:** Well—that's the way the crackers crumble. Joke.

Beneatha (*Laughingly noticing what her mother is doing.*): Mama, what are you doing?

Mama: Fixing my plant so it won't get hurt none on the way . . .

Beneatha: Mama, you going to take *that* to the new house?

Mama: Un-huh—

110 **Beneatha:** That raggedy-looking old thing?

Mama (*Stopping and looking at her.*): It expresses *me*.

Ruth (*With delight, to Beneatha.*): So there, Miss Thing!

(*Walter comes to Mama suddenly and bends down behind her and squeezes her in his arms with all his strength. She is overwhelmed by the suddenness of it and, though delighted, her manner is like that of Ruth with Travis.*)

Mama: Look out now, Boy! You make me mess up my thing here!

Walter (*His face lit, he slips down on his knees beside her, his arms still about her.*): Mama . . . you know what it means to climb up in the chariot?

115 **Mama** (*Gruffly, very happy.*): Get on away from me now . . .

Ruth (*Near the gift-wrapped package, trying to catch Walter's eye.*): Psst—

Walter: What the old song say, Mama . . .

Ruth: Walter— Now?

(*She is pointing at the package.*)

Walter (*Speaking the lines, sweetly, playfully, in his mother's face.*):
    I got wings . . . you got wings . . .
    All God's children got wings . . .

120 **Mama:** Boy—get out of my face and do some work . . .

Walter:
    When I get to heaven gonna put on my wings,
    Gonna fly all over God's heaven . . .

Beneatha (*Teasingly, from across the room.*): Everybody talking 'bout heaven ain't going there!

Walter (*To Ruth, who is carrying the box across to them.*): I don't know, you think we ought to give her that . . . Seems to me she ain't been very appreciative around here.

Mama (*Eying the box, which is obviously a gift.*): What is that?

125 **Walter** (*Taking it from Ruth and putting it on the table in front of Mama.*): Well—what you all think. Should we give it to her?

Ruth: Oh—she was pretty good today.

Mama: I'll good you—

(*She turns her eyes to the box again.*)

Beneatha: Open it, Mama.

(*She stand up, looks at it, turns and looks at all of them, and then presses her hands together and does not open the package.*)

Walter (*Sweetly.*): Open it, Mama. It's for you. (*Mama looks in his eyes. It is the first present in her life without its being Christmas. Slowly she opens her package and lifts out, one by one, a brand-new sparkling set of gardening tools. Walter continues, prodding.*) Ruth made up the note—read it . . .

130 **Mama** (*Picking up the card and adjusting her glasses.*): "To our own Mrs. Miniver—Love from Brother, Ruth and Beneatha." Ain't that lovely . . .

Travis (*Tugging at his father's sleeve.*): Daddy, can I give her mine now?

Walter: All right, son. (*Travis flies to get his gift.*) Travis didn't want to go in with the rest of us, Mama. He got his own. (*Somewhat amused.*) We don't know what it is . . .

Travis (*Racing back in the room with a large hatbox and putting it in front of his grandmother.*): Here!

Mama: Lord have mercy, baby. You done gone and bought your grandmother a hat?

135 **Travis** (*Very proud.*): Open it!

(*She does and lifts out an elaborate, but very elaborate, wide gardening hat, and all the adults break up at the sight of it.*)

Ruth: Travis, honey, what is that?

Travis (*Who thinks it is beautiful and appropriate.*): It's a gardening hat! Like the ladies always have on in the magazines when they work in their gardens.

Beneatha (*Giggling, fiercely.*): Travis—we were trying to make Mama Mrs. Miniver—not Scarlett O'Hara!

Mama (*Indignantly.*): What's the matter with you all! This here is a beautiful hat! (*Absurdly.*) I always wanted me one just like it!

(*She pops it on her head to prove it to her grandson, and the hat is ludicrous and considerably oversized.*)

140 **Ruth:** Hot dog! Go, Mama!

Walter (*Doubled over with laughter.*): I'm sorry, Mama—but you look like you ready to go out and chop you some cotton sure enough!

(*They all laugh except Mama, out of deference to Travis' feelings.*)

Mama (*Gathering the boy up to her.*): Bless your heart—this is the prettiest hat I ever owned— (*Walter, Ruth and Beneatha chime in—noisily, festively and insincerely congratulating Travis on his gift.*) What are we all standing around here for? We ain't finished packin' yet. Bennie, you ain't packed one book.

(*The bell rings.*)

Beneatha: That couldn't be the movers . . . it's not hardly two good yet—

(*Beneatha goes into her room. Mama starts for door.*)

Walter (*Turning, stiffening.*): Wait—wait—I'll get it.

(*He stands and looks at the door.*)

145 **Mama:** You expecting company, son?
Walter (*Just looking at the door.*): Yeah—yeah . . .

(*Mama looks at Ruth, and they exchange innocent and unfrightened glances.*)

Mama (*Not understanding.*): Well, let them in, son.
Beneatha (*From her room.*): We need some more string.
Mama: Travis—you run to the hardware and get me some string cord.

(*Mama goes out and Walter turns and looks at Ruth. Travis goes to a dish for money.*)

150 **Ruth:** Why don't you answer the door, man?
Walter (*Suddenly bounding across the floor to her.*): 'Cause sometimes it hard to let the future begin! (*Stooping down in her face.*)
I got wings! You got wings!
All God's children got wings!

(*He crosses to the door and throws it open. Standing there is a very slight little man in a not too prosperous business suit and with haunted frightened eyes and a hat pulled down tightly, brim up, around his forehead. Travis passes between the men and exits. Walter leans deep in the man's face, still in his jubilance.*)

When I get to heaven gonna put on my wings,
Gonna fly all over God's heaven . . .

(*The little man just stares at him.*)

Heaven—

(*Suddenly he stops and looks past the little man into the empty hallway.*) Where's Willy, man?

Bobo: He ain't with me.
Walter (*Not disturbed.*): Oh—come on in. You know my wife.
Bobo (*Dumbly, taking off his hat.*): Yes—h'you, Miss Ruth.
155 **Ruth** (*Quietly, a mood apart from her husband already, seeing Bobo.*): Hello, Bobo.
Walter: You right on time today . . . Right on time. That's the way! (*He slaps Bob on his back.*) Sit down . . . lemme hear.

(*Ruth stands stiffly and quietly in back of them, as though somehow she senses death, her eyes fixed on her husband.*)

Bobo (*His frightened eyes on the floor, his hat in his hands.*): Could I please get a drink a water, before I tell you about it, Walter Lee?

(*Walter does not take his eyes off the man. Ruth goes blindly to the tap and gets a glass of water and brings it to Bobo.*)

Walter: There ain't nothing wrong, is there?

Bobo: Lemme tell you—

160 **Walter:** Man—didn't nothing go wrong?

Bobo: Lemme tell you—Walter Lee. (*Looking at Ruth and talking to her more than to Walter.*) You know how it was. I got to tell you how it was. I mean first I got to tell you how it was all the way . . . I mean about the money I put in, Walter Lee . . .

Walter (*With taut agitation now.*): What about the money you put in?

Bobo: Well—it wasn't much as we told you—me and Willy— (*He stops.*) I'm sorry, Walter. I got a bad feeling about it. I got a real bad feeling about it . . .

Walter: Man, what you telling me about all this for? . . . Tell me what happened in Springfield . . .

165 **Bobo:** Springfield.

Ruth (*Like a dead woman.*): What was supposed to happen in Springfield?

Bobo (*To her.*): This deal that me and Walter went into with Willy— Me and Willy was going to go down to Springfield and spread some money 'round so's we wouldn't have to wait so long for the liquor license . . . That's what we were going to do. Everybody said that was the way you had to do, you understand, Miss Ruth?

Walter: Man—what happened down there?

Bobo (*A pitiful man, near tears.*): I'm trying to tell you, Walter.

170 **Walter** (*Screaming at him suddenly.*): THEN TELL ME, GODDAMNIT . . . WHAT'S THE MATTER WITH YOU?

Bobo: Man . . . I didn't go to no Springfield, yesterday.

Walter (*Halted, life hanging in the moment.*): Why not?

Bobo (*The long way, the hard way to tell.*): 'Cause I didn't have no reasons to . . .

Walter: Man, what are you talking about!

175 **Bobo:** I'm talking about the fact that when I got to the train station yesterday morning—eight o'clock like we planned . . . Man—*Willy didn't never show up.*

Walter: Why . . . where was he . . . where is he?

Bobo: That's what I'm trying to tell you . . . I don't know . . . I waited six hours . . . I called his house . . . and I waited . . . six hours . . . I waited in that train station six hours . . . (*Breaking into tears.*) That was all the extra money I had in the world . . . (*Looking up at Walter with the tears running down his face.*) Man, Willy is gone.

Walter: Gone, what you mean Willy is gone? Gone where? You mean he went by himself. You mean he went off to Springfield by himself—to take care of getting the license—(*Turns and looks anxiously at Ruth.*) You mean maybe he didn't want too many people in on the business down there? (*Looks to Ruth again, as before.*) You know Willy got his own ways. (*Looks back to Bobo.*) Maybe you was late yesterday and he just went on down there without you. Maybe—maybe—he's been callin' you at home tryin' to tell you what happened or something. Maybe—maybe—he just got sick. He's somewhere—he's got to be somewhere. (*Grabs Bobo senselessly by the collar and starts to shake him.*) We just got to find him—me and you got to find him. We got to!

Bobo (*In sudden angry, frightened agony.*): What's the matter with you, Walter! When a cat take off with your money he don't leave you no maps!

180 **Walter** (*Turning madly, as though he is looking for Willy in the very room.*): Willy! . . . Willy . . . don't do it . . . Please don't do it . . . Man, not with that money . . . Man, please, not with that money . . . Oh, God . . . Don't let it be true . . . (*He is wandering around, crying out for Willy and looking for him or perhaps for help from God.*) Man . . . I trusted you . . . Man, I put my life in your hands . . . (*He starts to crumple down on the floor as Ruth just covers her face in horror. Mama opens the door and comes into the room, with Beneatha behind her.*) Man . . . (*He starts to pound the floor with his fists, sobbing wildly.*) That money is made out of my father's flesh . . .

Bobo (*Standing over him helplessly.*): I'm sorry, Walter . . . (*Only Walter's sobs reply. Bobo puts on his hat.*) I had my life staked on this deal, too . . .

(*He exits.*)

Mama (*To Walter.*): Son—(*She goes to him, bends down to him, talks to his bent head.*) Son . . . Is it gone? Son, I gave you sixty-five hundred dollars. Is it gone? All of it? Beneatha's money too?

Walter (*Lifting his head slowly.*): Mama . . . I never . . . went to the bank at all . . .

Mama (*Not wanting to believe him.*): You mean . . . your sister's school money . . . you used that too . . . Walter? . . .

185 **Walter:** Yessss! . . . All of it . . . It's all gone . . .

(*There is total silence. Ruth stands with her face covered with her hands; Beneatha leans forlornly against a wall, fingering a piece of red ribbon from the mother's gift. Mama stops and looks at her son without recognition and then, quite without thinking about it, starts to beat him senselessly in the face. Beneatha goes to them and stops it.*)

Beneatha: Mama!

(*Mama stops and looks at both of her children and rises slowly and wanders vaguely, aimlessly away from them.*)

Mama: I see . . . him . . . night after night . . . come in . . . and look at that rug . . . and then look at me . . . the red showing in his eyes . . . the veins moving in his head . . . I see him grow thin and old before he was forty . . . working and working like somebody's old horse . . . killing himself . . . and you—you give it all away in a day . . .

Beneatha: Mama—

Mama: Oh, God . . . (*She looks up to Him.*) Look down here—and show me the strength.

190 **Beneatha:** Mama—

Mama (*Folding over.*): Strength . . .

Beneatha (*Plaintively.*): Mama . . .

Mama: Strength!

(*Curtain.*)

Act Three

An hour later.

At curtain, there is a sullen light of gloom in the living room, gray light not unlike that which began the first scene of Act One. At left we can see Walter within his room, alone with himself. He is stretched out on the bed, his shirt out and open, his arms under his head. He does not smoke, he does not cry out, he merely lies there, looking up at the ceiling, much as if he were alone in the world.

In the living room Beneatha sits at the table, still surrounded by the now almost ominous packing crates. She sits looking off. We feel that this is a mood struck perhaps an hour before, and it lingers now, full of the empty sound of profound disappointment. We see on a line from her brother's bedroom the sameness of their attitudes. Presently the bell rings and Beneatha rises without ambition or interest in answering. It is Asagai, smiling broadly, striding into the room with energy and happy expectation and conversation.

1 **Asagai:** I came over . . . I had some free time. I thought I might help with the packing. Ah, I like the look of packing crates! A household in preparation for a journey! It

depresses some people . . . but for me . . . it is another feeling. Something full of the flow of life, do you understand? Movement, progress . . . It makes me think of Africa.

Beneatha: Africa!

Asagai: What kind of a mood is this? Have I told you how deeply you move me?

Beneatha: He gave away the money, Asagai . . .

5   **Asagai:** Who gave away what money?

Beneatha: The insurance money. My brother gave it away.

Asagai: Gave it away?

Beneatha: He made an investment! With a man even Travis wouldn't have trusted.

Asagai: And it's gone?

10   **Beneatha:** Gone!

Asagai: I've very sorry . . . And you, now?

Beneatha: Me? . . . Me? . . . Me I'm nothing . . . Me. When I was very small . . . we used to take our sleds out in the wintertime and the only hills we had were the ice-covered stone steps of some houses down the street. And we used to fill them in with snow and make them smooth and slide down them all day . . . and it was very dangerous you know . . . far too steep . . . and sure enough one day a kid named Rufus came down too fast and hit the sidewalk . . . and we saw his face just split open right there in front of us . . . And I remember standing there looking at his bloody open face thinking that was the end of Rufus. But the ambulance came and they took him to the hospital and they fixed the broken bones and they sewed it all up . . . and the next time I saw Rufus he just had a little line down the middle of his face . . . I never got over that . . .

Asagai: What?

Beneatha: That that was what one person could do for another, fix him up—sew up the problem, make him all right again. That was the most marvelous thing in the world . . . I wanted to do that. I always thought it was the one concrete thing in the world that a human being could do. Fix up the sick, you know—and make them whole again. This was truly being God . . .

15   **Asagai:** You wanted to be God?

Beneatha: No—I wanted to cure. It used to be so important to me. I wanted to cure. It used to matter. I used to care. I mean about people and how their bodies hurt . . .

Asagai: And you've stopped caring?

Beneatha: Yes—I think so.

Asagai: Why?

20   **Beneatha:** Because it doesn't seem deep enough, close enough to the truth.

Asagai: Truth? Why is it that you despairing ones always think that only you have the truth? I never thought to see *you* like that. You! Your brother made a stupid, childish mistake—and you are grateful to him. So that now you can give up the ailing human race on account of it. You talk about what good is struggle; what good is anything? Where are we all going? And why are we bothering?

Beneatha: *And you cannot answer it!* All your talk and dreams about Africa and Independence. Independence and then what? What about all the crooks and petty thieves and just plain idiots who will come into power to steal and plunder the same as before—only now they will be black and do it in the name of the new Independence— You cannot answer that.

Asagai (*Shouting over her.*): *I live the answer!* (*Pause.*) In my village at home it is the exceptional man who can even read a newspaper . . . or who ever *sees* a book at all. I will go home and much of what I will have to say will seem strange to the people of my village . . . But I will teach and work and things will happen, slowly and swiftly. At times it will seem that nothing changes at all . . . and then again . . . the sudden dramatic events which make history leap into the future. And then quiet again. Retrogression even. Guns, murder, revolution. And I even will have moments when I wonder if the quiet was not better than all that death and hatred. But I will look about my village at the illiteracy and disease and ignorance, and I will not wonder long. And perhaps . . . perhaps I will be a great man . . . I mean perhaps I will hold on to the substance of truth and find my way always with the right course . . . and perhaps for it I will be butchered in my bed some night by the servants of empire . . .

Beneatha: *The martyr!*

25 **Asagai:** . . . or perhaps I shall live to be a very old man respected and esteemed in my new nation . . . And perhaps I shall hold office and this is what I'm trying to tell you, Alaiyo; perhaps the things I believe now for my country will be wrong and outmoded, and I will not understand and do terrible things to have things my way or merely to keep my power. Don't you see that there will be young men and women, not British soldiers then, but my own black countrymen . . . to step out of the shadows some evening and slit my then useless throat? Don't you see they have always been there . . . that they always will be. And that such a thing as my own death will be an advance? They who might kill me even . . . actually replenish me!

Beneatha: Oh, Asagai, I know all that.

Asagai: Good! Then stop moaning and groaning and tell me what you plan to do.

Beneatha: Do?

Asagai: I have a bit of a suggestion.

30 **Beneatha:** What?

Asagai (*Rather quietly for him.*): That when it is all over—that you come home with me—

Beneatha (*Slapping herself on the forehead with exasperation born of misunderstanding.*): Oh— Asagai—at this moment you decide to be romantic!

Asagai (*Quickly understanding the misunderstanding.*): My dear, young creature of the New World—I do not mean across the city—I mean across the ocean; home—to Africa.

Beneatha (*Slowly understanding and turning to him with murmured amazement.*): To—to Nigeria?

35 **Asagai:** Yes! . . . (*Smiling and lifting his arms playfully.*) Three hundred years later the African Prince rose up out of the seas and swept the maiden back across the middle passage over which her ancestors had come—

Beneatha (*Unable to play.*): Nigeria?

Asagai: Nigeria. Home. (*Coming to her with genuine romantic flippancy.*) I will show you our mountains and our stars; and give you cool drinks from gourds and teach you the old songs and the ways of our people—and, in time, we will pretend that—(*Very softly.*)— you have only been away for a day—

(*She turns her back to him, thinking. He swings her around and takes her full in his arms in a long embrace which proceeds to passion.*)

Beneatha (*Pulling away.*): You're getting me all mixed up—

Asagai: Why?

40 **Beneatha:** Too many things—too many things have happened today. I must sit down and think. I don't know what I feel about anything right this minute.

(*She promptly sits down and props her chin on her fist.*)

Asagai (*Charmed.*): All right, I shall leave you. No—don't get up. (*Touching her, gently, sweetly.*) Just sit awhile and think . . . Never be afraid to sit awhile and think. (*He goes to door and looks at her.*) How often I have looked at you and said, "Ah—so this is what the New World hath finally wrought . . ."

(*He exits. Beneatha sits on alone. Presently Walter enters from his room and starts to rummage through things, feverishly looking for something. She looks up and turns in her seat.*)

Beneatha (*Hissingly.*): Yes—just look at what the New World hath wrought! . . . Just look! (*She gestures with bitter disgust.*) There he is! Monsieur le petit bourgeois noir—himself! There he is—Symbol of a Rising Class! Entrepreneur! Titan of the system! (*Walter ignores her completely and continues frantically and destructively looking for something and hurling things to floor and tearing things out of their place in his search. Beneatha ignores the eccentricity of his actions and goes on with the monologue of insult.*) Did you dream of yachts on Lake Michigan, Brother? Did you see yourself on that Great Day sitting down at the Conference Table, surrounded by all the mighty bald-headed men in America? All halted, waiting, breathless, waiting for your pronouncements on industry? Waiting for you—Chairman of the Board? (*Walter finds what he is looking for—a small piece of white paper—and pushes it in his pocket and puts on his coat and rushes out without ever having looked at her. She shouts after him.*) I look at you and I see the final triumph of stupidity in the world!

(*The door slams and she returns to just sitting again. Ruth comes quickly out of Mama's room.*)

Ruth: Who was that?
Beneatha: Your husband.
45 **Ruth:** Where did he go?
Beneatha: Who knows—maybe he has an appointment at U.S. Steel.
Ruth (*Anxiously, with frightened eyes.*): You didn't say nothing bad to him, did you?
Beneatha: Bad? Say anything bad to him? No—I told him he was a sweet boy and full of dreams and everything is strictly peachy keen, as the ofay kids say!

(*Mama enters from her bedroom. She is lost, vague, trying to catch hold, to make some sense of her former command of the world, but it still eludes her. A sense of waste overwhelms her gait; a measure of apology rides on her shoulders. She goes to her plant, which has remained on the table, looks at it, picks it up and takes it to the window sill and sits it outside, and she stands and looks at it a long moment. Then she closes the window, straightens her body with effort and turns around to her children.*)

Mama: Well—ain't it a mess in here, though? (*A false cheerfulness, a beginning of something.*) I guess we all better stop moping around and get some work done. All this unpacking and everything we got to do. (*Ruth raises her head slowly in response to the sense of the line; and Beneatha in similar manner turns very slowly to look at her mother.*) One of you all better call the moving people and tell 'em not to come.
50 **Ruth:** Tell 'em not to come?
Mama: Of course, baby. Ain't no need in 'em coming all the way here and having to go back. They charges for that too. (*She sits down, fingers to her brow, thinking.*) Lord, ever since I was a little girl, I always remembers people saying, "Lena—Lena Eggleston, you aims too high all the time. You needs to slow down and see life a little more like it is. Just slow down some." That's what they always used to say down home—"Lord, that Lena Eggleston is a high-minded thing. She'll get her due one day!"
Ruth: No, Lena . . .
Mama: Me and Big Walter just didn't never learn right.
Ruth: Lena, no! We gotta go. Bennie—tell her . . . (*She rises and crosses to Beneatha with her arms outstretched. Beneatha doesn't respond.*) Tell her we can still move . . . the notes

ain't but a hundred and twenty-five a month. We got four grown people in this house—we can work . . .

55 **Mama** *(To herself.):* Just aimed too high all the time—

Ruth *(Turning and going to Mama fast—the words pouring out with urgency and desperation.):* Lena—I'll work . . . I'll work twenty hours a day in all the kitchens in Chicago . . . I'll strap my baby on my back if I have to and scrub all the floors in America and wash all the sheets in America if I have to—but we got move . . . We got to get out of here . . .

(Mama reaches out absently and pats Ruth's hand.)

Mama: No—I sees things differently now. Been thinking 'bout some of the things we could do to fix this place up some. I seen a second-hand bureau over on Maxwell Street just the other day that could fit right there. *(She points to where the new furniture might go. Ruth wanders away from her.)* Would need some new handles on it and then a little varnish and then it look like something brand-new. And—we can put up them new curtains in the kitchen . . . Why this place be looking fine. Cheer us all up so that we forget trouble ever came . . . *(To Ruth.)* And you could get some nice screens to put up in your room round the baby's bassinet . . . *(She looks at both of them, pleadingly.)* Sometimes you just got to know when to give up some things . . . and hold on to what you got.

(Walter enters from the outside, looking spent and leaning against the door, his coat hanging from him.)

Mama: Where you been, son?

Walter *(Breathing hard.):* Made a call.

60 **Mama:** To who, son?

Walter: To The Man.

Mama: What man, baby?

Walter: The Man, Mama. Don't you know who The Man is?

Ruth: Walter Lee?

65 **Walter:** *The Man.* Like the guys in the streets say—The Man. Captain Boss—Mistuh Charley . . . Old Captain Please Mr. Bossman . . .

Beneatha *(Suddenly.):* Lindner!

Walter: That's right! That's good. I told him to come right over.

Beneatha *(Fiercely, understanding.):* For what? What do you want to see him for!

Walter *(Looking at his sister.):* We going to do business with him.

70 **Mama:** What you talking 'bout, son?

Walter: Talking 'bout life, Mama. You all always telling me to see life like it is. Well—I laid in there on my back today . . . and I figured it out. Life just like it is. Who gets and who don't get. *(He sits down with his coat on and laughs.)* Mama, you know it's all divided up. Life is. Sure enough. Between the takers and the "tooken." *(He laughs.)* I've figured it out finally. *(He looks around at them.)* Yeah. Some of us always getting "tooken." *(He laughs.)* People like Willy Harris, they don't never get "tooken." And you know why the rest of us do? 'Cause we all mixed up. Mixed up bad. We get to looking 'round for the right and the wrong; and we worry about it and cry about it and stay up nights trying to figure out 'bout the wrong and the right of things all the time . . . And all the time, man, them takers is out there operating, just taking and taking. Willy Harris? Shoot—Willy Harris don't even count. He don't even count in the big scheme of things. But I'll say one thing for old Willy Harris . . . he's taught me something. He's taught me to keep my eye on what counts in this world. Yeah—*(Shouting out a little.)* Thanks, Willy!

Ruth: What did you call that man for, Walter Lee?

Walter: Called him to tell him to come on over to the show. Gonna put on a show for the man. Just what he wants to see. You see, Mama, the man came here today and he told us that them people out there where you want us to move—well they so upset they willing to pay us not to move out there. (*He laughs again.*) And—and oh, Mama—you would of been proud of the way me and Ruth and Bennie acted. We told him to get out . . . Lord have mercy! We told the man to get out. Oh, we was some proud folks this afternoon, yeah. (*He lights a cigarette.*) We were still full of that old-time stuff . . .

Ruth (*Coming toward him slowly.*): You talking 'bout taking them people's money to keep us from moving in that house?

75 **Walter:** I ain't just talking 'bout it, baby—I'm telling you that's what's going to happen.

Beneatha: Oh, God! Where is the bottom! Where is the real honest-to-God bottom so he can't go any farther!

Walter: See—that's the old stuff. You and that boy that was here today. You all want everybody to carry a flag and a spear and sing some marching songs, huh? You wanna spend your life looking into things and trying to find the right and the wrong part, huh? Yeah. You know what's going to happen to that boy someday—he'll find himself sitting in a dungeon, locked in forever—and the takers will have the key! Forget it, baby! There ain't no causes—there ain't nothing but taking in this world, and he who takes most is smartest—and it don't make a damn bit of difference *how*.

Mama: You making something inside me cry, son. Some awful pain inside me.

Walter: Don't cry, Mama. Understand. That white man is going to walk in that door able to write checks for more money than we ever had. It's important to him and I'm going to help him . . . I'm going to put on the show, Mama.

80 **Mama:** Son—I come from five generations of people who was slaves and sharecroppers—but ain't nobody in my family never let nobody pay 'em no money that was a way of telling us we wasn't fit to walk the earth. We ain't never been that poor. (*Raising her eyes and looking at him.*) We ain't never been that dead inside.

Beneatha: Well—we are dead now. All the talk about dreams and sunlight that goes on in this house. All dead.

Walter: What's the matter with you all! I didn't make this world! It was give to me this way! Hell, yes, I want me some yachts someday! Yes, I want to hang some real pearls 'round my wife's neck. Ain't she supposed to wear no pearls? Somebody tell me—tell me, who decides which women is supposed to wear pearls in this world. I tell you I am a *man*—and I think my wife should wear some pearls in this world!

(*This last line hangs a good while and Walter begins to move about the room. The word "Man" has penetrated his consciousness; he mumbles it to himself repeatedly between strange agitated pauses as he moves about.*)

Mama: Baby, how you going to feel on the inside?

Walter: Fine! . . . Going to feel fine . . . a man . . .

85 **Mama:** You won't have nothing left then, Walter Lee.

Walter (*Coming to her.*): I'm going to feel fine, Mama. I'm going to look that son-of-a-bitch in the eyes and say—(*He falters.*)—and say, "All right, Mr. Lindner—(*He falters even more.*)—that's your neighborhood out there. You got the right to keep it like you want. You got the right to have it like you want. Just write the check and—the house is yours." And, and I am going to say—(*His voice almost breaks.*) And you—you people just put the money in my hand and you won't have to live next to this bunch of stinking niggers! . . . (*He straightens up and moves away from his mother, walking around the room.*) Maybe—maybe I'll get down on my black knees . . . (*He does so; Ruth and*

Bennie and Mama watch him in frozen horror.) Captain, Mistuh, Bossman. *(He starts crying.)* A-hee-hee-hee! *(Wringing his hands in profoundly anguished imitation.)* Yasssssuh! Great White Father, just gi' ussen de money, fo' God's sake, and we's ain't gwine come out deh and dirty up yo' white folks neighborhood . . .

(He breaks down completely, then gets up and goes into the bedroom.)

Beneatha: That is not a man. That is nothing but a toothless rat.

Mama: Yes—death done come in this here house. *(She is nodding, slowly, reflectively.)* Done come walking in my house. On the lips of my children. You what supposed to be my beginning again. You—what supposed to be my harvest. *(To Beneatha.)* You—you mourning your brother?

Beneatha: He's no brother of mine.

90 **Mama:** What you say?

Beneatha: I said that that individual in that room is no brother of mine.

Mama: That's what I thought you said. You feeling like you better than he is today? *(Beneatha does not answer.)* Yes? What you tell him a minute ago? That he wasn't a man? Yes? You give him up for me? You done wrote his epitaph too—like the rest of the world? Well, who give you the privilege?

Beneatha Be on my side for once! You saw what he just did, Mama! You saw him—down on his knees. Wasn't it you who taught me—to despise any man who would do that. Do what he's going to do.

Mama: Yes—I taught you that. Me and your daddy. But I thought I taught you something else too . . . I thought I taught you to love him.

95 **Beneatha:** Love him? There is nothing left to love.

Mama: There is always something left to love. And if you ain't learned that, you ain't learned nothing. *(Looking at her.)* Have you cried for that boy today? I don't mean for yourself and for the family 'cause we lost the money. I mean for him; what he been through and what it done to him. Child, when do you think is the time to love somebody the most; when they done good and made things easy for everybody? Well then, you ain't through learning—because that ain't the time at all. It's when he's at his lowest and can't believe in hisself 'cause the world done whipped him so. When you starts measuring somebody, measure him right, child, measure him right. Make sure you done taken into account what hills and valleys he come through before he got to wherever he is.

(Travis bursts into the room at the end of the speech, leaving the door open.)

Travis: Grandmama—the moving men are downstairs! The truck just pulled up.

Mama *(Turning and looking at him.):* Are they, baby? They downstairs?

(She sighs and sits. Lindner appears in the doorway. He peers in and knocks lightly, to gain attention, and comes in. All turn to look at him.)

Lindner *(Hat and briefcase in hand):* Uh—hello . . .

(Ruth crosses mechanically to the bedroom door and opens it and lets it swing open freely and slowly as the lights come up on Walter within, still in his coat, sitting at the far corner of the room. He looks up and out through the room to Lindner.)

100 **Ruth:** He's here.

(A long minute passes and Walter slowly gets up.)

Lindner *(Coming to the table with efficiency, putting his briefcase on the table and starting to unfold papers and unscrew fountain pens.):* Well, I certainly was glad to hear from you people. (*Walter has begun the trek out of the room, slowly and awkwardly, rather like a small boy, passing the back of his sleeve across his mouth from time to time.*) Life can really be so much simpler than people let it be most of the time. Well—with whom do I negotiate? You, Mrs. Younger, or your son here? (*Mama sits with her hands folded on her lap and her eyes closed as Walter advances. Travis goes close to Lindner and looks at the papers curiously.*) Just some official papers, sonny.

Ruth: Travis, you go downstairs.

Mama (*Opening her eyes and looking into Walter's.*): No. Travis, you stay right here. And you make him understand what you doing, Walter Lee. You teach him good. Like Willy Harris taught you. You show where our five generations done come to. Go ahead, son—

Walter (*Looks down into his boy's eyes. Travis grins at him merrily and Walter draws him beside him with his arm lightly around his shoulders.*): Well, Mr. Lindner. (*Beneatha turns away.*) We called you—(*There is a profound, simple groping quality in his speech.*)—because, well, me and my family (*He looks around and shifts from one foot to the other.*) Well—we are very plain people . . .

105 **Lindner:** Yes—

Walter: I mean—I have worked as a chauffeur most of my life—and my wife here, she does domestic work in people's kitchens. So does my mother. I mean—we are plain people . . .

Lindner: Yes, Mr. Younger—

Walter (*Really like a small boy, looking down at his shoes and then up at the man.*): And—uh—well, my father, well, he was a laborer most of his life.

Lindner (*Absolutely confused.*): Uh, yes—

110 **Walter** (*Looking down at his toes once again.*): My father almost beat a man to death once because this man called him a bad name or something, you know what I mean?

Lindner: No, I'm afraid I don't.

Walter (*Finally straightening up.*): Well, what I mean is that we come from people who had a lot of pride. I mean—we are very proud people. And that's my sister over there and she's going to be a doctor—and we are very proud—

Lindner: Well—I am sure that is very nice, but—

Walter (*Starting to cry and facing the man eye to eye.*): What I am telling you is that we called you over here to tell you that we are very proud and that this is—this is my son, who makes the sixth generation of our family in this country, and that we have all thought about your offer and we have decided to move into our house because my father—my father—he earned it. (*Mama has her eyes closed and is rocking back and forth as though she were in church, with her head nodding the amen yes.*) We don't want to make no trouble for nobody or fight no causes—but we will try to be good neighbors. That's all we got to say. (*He looks the man absolutely in the eyes.*) We don't want your money.

(*He turns and walks away from the man.*)

115 **Lindner** (*Looking around at all of them.*): I take it then that you have decided to occupy.

Beneatha: That's what the man said.

Lindner (*To Mama in her reverie.*): Then I would like to appeal to you, Mrs. Younger. You are older and wiser and understand things better I am sure . . .

Mama (*Rising.*): I am afraid you don't understand. My son said we was going to move and there ain't nothing left for me to say. (*Shaking her head with double meaning.*) You know how these young folks is nowadays, mister. Can't do a thing with 'em. Good-bye.

Lindner (*Folding up his materials.*): Well—if you are that final about it . . . There is nothing left for me to say. (*He finishes. He is almost ignored by the family, who are concentrating* *on Walter Lee. At the door Lindner halts and looks around.)* I sure hope you people know what you're doing.

(He shakes his head and exits.)

120 **Ruth** *(Looking around and coming to life.):* Well, for God's sake—if the moving men are here—LET'S GET THE HELL OUT OF HERE!

Mama *(Into action.):* Ain't it the truth! Look at all this here mess. Ruth, put Travis' good jacket on him . . . Walter Lee, fix your tie and tuck your shirt in, you look just like somebody's hoodlum. Lord have mercy, where is my plant? *(She flies to get it amid the general bustling of the family, who are deliberately trying to ignore the nobility of the past moment.)* You all start on down . . . Travis child, don't go empty-handed . . . Ruth, where did I put that box with my skillets in it? I want to be in charge of it myself . . .I'm going to make us the biggest dinner we ever ate tonight . . . Beneatha, what's the matter with them stockings? Pull them things up, girl . . .

(The family starts to file out as two moving men appear and begin to carry out the heavier pieces of furniture, bumping into the family as they move about.)

Beneatha: Mama, Asagai—asked me to marry him today and go to Africa—

Mama *(In the middle of her getting-ready activity.):* He did? You ain't old enough to marry nobody—*(Seeing the moving men lifting one of her chairs precariously.)* Darling, that ain't no bale of cotton, please handle it so we can sit in it again. I had that chair twenty-five years . . .

(The movers sigh with exasperation and go on with their work.)

Beneatha *(Girlishly and unreasonably trying to pursue the conversation.):* To go to Africa, Mama—be a doctor in Africa . . .

125 **Mama** *(Distracted.):* Yes, baby—

Walter: Africa! What he want you to go to Africa for?

Beneatha: To practice there . . .

Walter: Girl, if you don't get all them silly ideas out your head! You better marry yourself a man with some loot . . .

Beneatha *(Angrily, precisely as in the first scent of the play.):* What have you got to do with who I marry!

130 **Walter:** Plenty. Now I think George Murchison—

(He and Beneatha go out yelling at each other vigorously; Beneatha is heard saying that she would not marry George Murchison if he were Adam and she were Eve, etc. The anger is loud and real till their voices diminish. Ruth stands at the door and turns to Mama and smiles knowingly.)

Mama *(Fixing her hat at last.):* Yeah—they something all right, my children . . .

Ruth: Yeah—they're something. Let's go, Lena.

Mama *(Stalling, starting to look around at the house.):* Yes—I'm coming. Ruth—

Ruth: Yes?

135 **Mama** *(Quietly, woman to woman.):* He finally come into his manhood today, didn't he? Kind of like a rainbow after the rain . . .

Ruth *(Biting her lip lest her own pride explode in front of Mama.):* Yes, Lena.

(Walter's voice calls for them raucously.)

Mama *(Waving Ruth out vaguely.):* All right, honey—go on down. I be down directly.

(Ruth hesitates, then exits. Mama stands, at last alone in the living room, her plant on the table before her as the lights start to come down. She looks around at all the walls and ceilings and suddenly, despite herself, while the children call below, a great heaving thing rises in her an she puts her fist to her mouth, takes a final desperate look, pulls her coat about her, pats her hat and goes out. The lights dim down. The door opens and she comes back in, grabs her plant, and goes out for the last time.)

(Curtain.)

■ EXPLORATIONS OF THE TEXT

1. How does the urban setting establish the atmosphere and mood of the play?
2. Characterize Mama. Discuss her relationships with her children. What expectations does she have for their futures?
3. Explore the primary conflicts of the play. What escalates the tension among the characters?
4. What do the two men with whom Beneatha is involved symbolize as directions for her life? What is their thematic significance?
5. How does Walter change in Act Three? What other conflicts within characters are resolved in this act?
6. Concentrate on an aspect of setting or on a stage prop. Is it symbolic? Explain.
7. Is the ending of the play effective?
8. Relate Langston Hughes's "Harlem," which serves as the epigraph to the play, to the characters' situations and states of mind (see chapter 7).
9. Does *A Raisin in the Sun* present timeless issues?

■ THE READING/WRITING CONNECTION

1. "Think" Topic: Lorraine Hansberry's play was written in the 1950s about problems for a family in urban Chicago. Do you relate to the characters, to the issues presented in the play? Are the events portrayed still relevant today? Argue pro or con.
2. Journal Entry: Write about Beneatha's choices. Have you faced a similar decision?

■ IDEAS FOR WRITING

1. Discuss a central theme of the play. Use evidence from the text to support your interpretation.
2. Compare the poem "Harlem" by Langston Hughes with the states of the main characters, or connect the poem with themes of the play.
3. View the film version of this drama. Compare the two works.

JOHN MILLINGTON SYNGE

John Millington Synge (1871–1909), the youngest of five children, was born to Protestant English parents near Dublin, Ireland. He graduated from Trinity College, Dublin, and spent ten years traveling the Continent. In Paris, he met William Butler Yeats, who suggested Synge visit the Aran Islands off the west coast of Ireland, which Synge did in 1899. The trip had a profound and lasting effect on him. Synge's first play, In the Shadow of the Glen, *was produced at Dublin's Abbey Theater in 1905. It was followed by* Riders to the Sea *(1904), and Synge's masterpiece,* The Playboy of the Western World *(1907). With Yeats and other playwrights and artists, Synge created a legendary Irish theater at the Abbey and was responsible for the renaissance of Irish literature at the beginning of the twentieth century.*

1904

RIDERS TO THE SEA

Characters

Maurya, an old woman
Bartley, her son
Cathleen, her daughter
Nora, a younger daughter
Men and Women

> *An island off the west of Ireland.*
> *Cottage kitchen, with nets, oil-skins, spinning-wheel, some new boards standing by the wall, etc. Cathleen, a girl of about twenty, finishes kneading cake, and puts it down on the pot-oven by the fire; then wipes her hands, and begins to spin at the wheel. Nora, a young girl, puts her head in at the door.*

Nora (*In a low voice.*): Where is she?
Cathleen: She's lying down, God help her, and may be sleeping, if she's able.

(*Nora comes in softly, and takes a bundle from under her shawl.*)

Cathleen (*Spinning the wheel rapidly.*): What is it you have?
Nora: The young priest is after bringing them. It's a shirt and a plain stocking were got off a drowned man in Donegal.[1]

(*Cathleen stops her wheel with a sudden movement, and leans out to listen.*)

5 **Nora:** We're to find out if it's Michael's they are, some time herself will be down looking by the sea.
Cathleen: How would they be Michael's, Nora? How would he go the length of that way to the Far North?
Nora: The young priest says he's known the like of it. "If it's Michael's they are," says he, "you can tell herself he's got a clean burial by the grace of God, and if they're not his, let no one say a word about them, for she'll be getting her death," says he, "with crying and lamenting."

(*The door which Nora half closed is blown open by a gust of wind.*)

Cathleen (*Looking out anxiously.*): Did you ask him would he stop Bartley going this day with the horses to the Galway[2] fair?
Nora: "I won't stop him," says he, "but let you not be afraid. Herself does be saying prayers half through the night, and the Almighty God won't leave her destitute," says he, "with no son living."
10 **Cathleen:** Is the sea bad by the white rocks, Nora?
Nora: Middling bad, God help us. There's a great roaring in the west, and it's worse it'll be getting when the tide's turned to the wind. (*She goes over to the table with the bundle.*) Shall I open it now?
Cathleen: Maybe she'd wake up on us, and come in before we'd done. (*Coming to the table.*) It's a long time we'll be, and the two of us crying.

---

[1] County in Northwestern Ireland; in Ulster.   [2] City in West Central Ireland.

Nora (*Goes to the inner door and listens.*): She's moving about on the bed. She'll be coming in a minute.

Cathleen: Give me the ladder, and I'll put them up in the turf-loft, the way she won't know of them at all, and maybe when the tide turns she'll be going down to see would he be floating from the east.

(*They put the ladder against the gable of the chimney; Cathleen goes up a few steps and hides the bundle in the turf-loft. Maurya comes from the inner room.*)

15 **Maurya** (*Looking up at Cathleen and speaking querulously.*): Isn't it turf enough you have for this day and evening?

Cathleen: There's a cake baking at the fire for a short space (*Throwing down the turf.*) and Bartley will want it when the tide turns if he goes to Connemara.[3]

(*Nora picks up the turf and puts it round the pot-oven.*)

Maurya (*Sitting down on a stool at the fire.*): He won't go this day with the wind rising from the south and west. He won't go this day, for the young priest will stop him surely.

Nora: He'll not stop him, Mother, and I heard Eamon Simon and Stephen Pheety and Colum Shawn saying he would go.

Maurya: Where is he itself?

20 **Nora:** He went down to see would there be another boat sailing in the week, and I'm thinking it won't be long till he's here now, for the tide's turning at the green head, and the hooker's[4] tacking from the east.

Cathleen: I hear some one passing the big stones.

Nora (*Looking out.*): He's coming now, and he in a hurry.

Bartley (*Comes in and looks round the room; speaking sadly and quietly.*): Where is the bit of new rope, Cathleen, was bought in Connemara?

Cathleen (*Coming down.*): Give it to him, Nora; it's on a nail by the white boards. I hung it up this morning, for the pig with the black feet was eating it.

25 **Nora** (*Giving him a rope.*): Is that it, Bartley?

Maurya: You'd do right to leave that rope, Bartley, hanging by the boards. (*Bartley takes the rope.*) It will be wanting in this place, I'm telling you, if Michael is washed up to-morrow morning, or the next morning, or any morning in the week, for it's a deep grave we'll make him by the grace of God.

Bartley (*Beginning to work with the rope.*): I've no halter the way I can ride down on the mare, and I must go now quickly. This is the one boat going for two weeks or beyond it, and the fair will be a good fair for horses I heard them saying below.

Maurya: It's a hard thing they'll be saying below if the body is washed up and there's no man in it to make the coffin, and I after giving a big price for the finest white boards you'd find in Connemara. (*She looks round at the boards.*)

Bartley How would it be washed up, and we after looking each day for nine days, and a strong wind blowing a while back from the west and south?

30 **Maurya:** If it wasn't found itself, that wind is raising the sea, and there was a star up against the moon, and it rising in the night. If it was a hundred horses, or a thousand horses you had itself, what is the price of a thousand horses against a son where there is one son only?

Bartley (*Working at the halter, to Cathleen.*): Let you go down each day, and see the sheep aren't jumping in on the rye, and if the jobber[5] comes you can sell the pig with the black feet if there is a good price going.

---

[3] Region of West Ireland.   [4] One-masted fishing boat used on the English and Irish coast.   [5] Wholesaler.

Maurya: How would the like of her get a good price for a pig?

Bartley *(To Cathleen.)*: If the west wind holds with the last bit of the moon let you and Nora get up weed enough for another cock[6] for the kelp. It's hard set we'll be from this day with no one in it but one man to work.

Maurya: It's hard set we'll be surely the day you're drowned'd with the rest. What way will I live and the girls with me, and I an old woman looking for the grave?

(Bartley lays down the halter, takes off his old coat, and puts on a newer one of the same flannel.)

35 **Bartley** *(To Nora.)*: Is she coming to the pier?

Nora *(Looking out.)*: She's passing the green head and letting fall her sails.

Bartley *(Getting his purse and tobacco.)*: I'll have half an hour to go down, and you'll see my coming again in two days, or in three days, or maybe in four days if the wind is bad.

Maurya *(Turning round to the fire, and putting her shawl over her head.)*: Isn't it a hard and cruel man won't hear a word from an old woman, and she holding him from the sea?

Cathleen: It's the life of a young man to be going on the sea, and who would listen to an old woman with one thing and she saying it over?

40 **Bartley** *(Taking the halter.)*: I must go now quickly. I'll ride down on the red mare, and the gray pony'll run behind me. . . . The blessing of God on you. *(He goes out.)*

Maurya *(Crying out as he is in the door.)*: He's gone now, God spare us, and we'll not see him again. He's gone now, and when the black night is falling I'll have no son left me in the world.

Cathleen: Why wouldn't you give him your blessing and he looking round in the door? Isn't it sorrow enough is on every one in this house without your sending him out with an unlucky word behind him and a hard word in his ear?

(Maurya takes up the tongs and begins raking the fire aimlessly without looking round.)

Nora *(Turning toward her.)*: You're taking away the turf from the cake.

Cathleen *(Crying out.)*: The Son of God forgive us, Nora, we're after forgetting his bit of bread. *(She comes over to the fire.)*

45 **Nora:** And it's destroyed he'll be going till dark night, and he after eating nothing since the sun went up.

Cathleen *(Turning the cake out of the oven.)*: It's destroyed he'll be, surely. There's no sense left on any person in a house where an old woman will be talking forever.

(Maurya sways herself on her stool.)

Cathleen *(Cutting off some of the bread and rolling it in a cloth; to Maurya.)*: Let you go down now to the spring well and give him this and he passing. You'll see him then and the dark word will be broken, and you can say "God speed you," the way he'll be easy in his mind.

Maurya *(Taking the bread.)*: Will I be in it as soon as himself?

Cathleen: If you go now quickly.

50 **Maurya** *(Standing up unsteadily.)*: It's hard set I am to walk.

Cathleen *(Looking at her anxiously.)*: Give her the stick, Nora, or maybe she'll slip on the big stones.

Nora: What stick?

---

[6] A small pile for burning seaweed into kelp (used as fertilizer).

Cathleen: The stick Michael brought from Connemara.

Maurya (*Taking a stick Nora gives her.*): In the big world the old people do be leaving
things after them for their sons and children, but in this place it is the young men do
be leaving things behind for them that do be old.

(*She goes out slowly. Nora goes over to the ladder.*)

55 **Cathleen:** Wait, Nora, maybe she'd turn back quickly. She's that sorry, God help her, you
wouldn't know the thing she'd do.

Nora: Is she gone round by the bush?

Cathleen (*Looking out.*): She's gone now. Throw it down quickly, for the Lord knows when
she'll be out of it again.

Nora (*Getting the bundle from the loft.*): The young priest said he'd be passing tomorrow,
and we might go down and speak to him below if it's Michael's they are surely.

Cathleen (*Taking the bundle.*): Did he say what way they were found?

60 **Nora** (*Coming down.*): "There were two men," says he, "and they rowing round with po-
teen[7] before the cocks crowed, and the oar of one of them caught the body, and they
passing the black cliffs of the north."

Cathleen (*Trying to open the bundle.*): Give me a knife, Nora, the string's perished with the
salt water, and there's a black knot on it you wouldn't loosen in a week.

Nora (*Giving her a knife.*): I've heard tell it was a long way to Donegal.

Cathleen (*Cutting the string.*): It is surely. There was a man in here a while ago—the man
sold us that knife—and he said if you set off walking from the rocks beyond, it would
be seven days you'd be in Donegal.

Nora: And what time would a man take, and he floating?

(*Cathleen opens the bundle and takes out a bit of a stocking. They look at them eagerly.*)

65 **Cathleen** (*In a low voice.*): The Lord spare us, Nora! isn't it a queer hard thing to say if it's
his they are surely?

Nora: I'll get his shirt off the hook the way we can put the one flannel on the other. (*She
looks through some clothes hanging in the corner.*) It's not with them, Cathleen, and
where will it be?

Cathleen: I'm thinking Bartley put it on him in the morning, for his own shirt was heavy
with the salt in it. (*Pointing to the corner.*) There's a bit of a sleeve was of the same
stuff. Give me that and it will do.

(*Nora brings it to her and they compare the flannel.*)

Cathleen: It's the same stuff, Nora; but if it is itself aren't there great rolls of it in the shops
of Galway, and isn't it many another man may have a shirt of it as well as Michael
himself?

Nora (*Who has taken up the stocking and counted the stitches, crying out.*): It's Michael,
Cathleen, it's Michael; God spare his soul, and what will herself say when she hears
this story, and Bartley on the sea?

70 **Cathleen** (*Taking the stocking.*): It's a plain stocking.

Nora: It's the second one of the third pair I knitted, and I put up threescore stitches, and I
dropped four of them.

---

[7] Illegally distilled whiskey.

Cathleen (*Counts the stitches.*): It's that number is in it. (*Crying out.*) Ah, Nora, isn't it a bitter thing to think of him floating that way to the Far North, and no one to keen[8] him but the black hags that do be flying on the sea?

Nora (*Swinging herself round, and throwing out her arms on the clothes.*): And isn't it a pitiful thing when there is nothing left of a man who was a great rower and fisher, but a bit of an old shirt and a plain stocking?

Cathleen (*After an instant.*): Tell me is herself coming, Nora? I hear a little sound on the path.

75 **Nora** (*Looking out.*): She is, Cathleen. She's coming up to the door.

Cathleen: Put these things away before she'll come in. Maybe it's easier she'll be after giving her blessing to Bartley, and we won't let on we've heard anything the time he's on the sea.

Nora (*Helping Cathleen to close the bundle.*): We'll put them here in the corner.

(*They put them into a hole in the chimney corner. Cathleen goes back to the spinning-wheel.*)

Nora: Will she see it was crying I was?

Cathleen: Keep your back to the door the way the light'll not be on you.

(*Nora sits down at the chimney corner, with her back to the door. Maurya comes in very slowly, without looking at the girls, and goes over to her stool at the other side of the fire. The cloth with the bread is still in her hand. The girls look at each other, and Nora points to the bundle of bread.*)

80 **Cathleen** (*After spinning for a moment.*): You didn't give him his bit of bread? (*Maurya begins to keen softly, without turning round.*)

Cathleen: Did you see him riding down?

(*Maurya goes on keening.*)

Cathleen (*A little impatiently.*): God forgive you; isn't it a better thing to raise your voice and tell what you seen, than to be making lamentation for a thing that's done? Did you see Bartley, I'm saying to you.

Maurya (*With a weak voice.*): My heart's broken from this day.

Cathleen (*As before.*): Did you see Bartley?

85 **Maurya:** I seen the fearfulest thing.

Cathleen (*Leaves her wheel and looks out.*): God forgive you; he's riding the mare now over the green head, and the gray pony behind him.

Maurya (*Starts, so that her shawl falls back from her head and shows her white tossed hair. With a frightened voice.*): The gray pony behind him.

Cathleen (*Coming to the fire.*): What is it ails you, at all?

Maurya (*Speaking very slowly.*): I've seen the fearfulest thing any person has seen, since the day Bride Dara seen the dead man with a child in his arms.

90 **Cathleen and Nora:** Uah.

(*They crouch down in front of the old woman at the fire.*)

Nora: Tell us what it is you seen.

Maurya: I went down to the spring well, and I stood there saying a prayer to myself. Then Bartley came along, and he riding on the red mare with the gray pony behind him. (*She puts up her hands, as if to hide something from her eyes.*) The Son of God spare us, Nora!

---

[8] Ritualized lamentation for the dead; wailing with deep sorrow about the dead.

Cathleen: What is it you seen?

Maurya: I seen Michael himself.

95 **Cathleen** (*Speaking softly.*): You did not, Mother; it wasn't Michael you seen for his body is after being found in the Far North, and he's got a clean burial by the grace of God.

Maurya (*A little defiantly.*): I'm after seeing him this day, and he riding and galloping. Bartley came first on the red mare; and I tried to say, "God speed you," but something choked the words in my throat. He went by quickly; and "the blessing of God on you," says he, and I could say nothing. I looked up then, and I crying, at the gray pony, and there was Michael upon it—with fine clothes on him, and new shoes on his feet.

Cathleen (*Begins to keen.*): It's destroyed we are from this day. It's destroyed, surely.

Nora: Didn't the young priest say the Almighty God wouldn't leave her destitute with no son living?

Maurya (*In a low voice, but clearly.*): It's little the like of him knows of the sea. . . . Bartley will be lost now, and let you call in Eamon and make me a good coffin out of the white boards, for I won't live after them. I've had a husband, and a husband's father, and six sons in this house—six fine men, though it was a hard birth I had with every one of them and they coming to the world—and some of them were found and some of them were not found, but they're gone now the lot of them. . . . There was Stephen, and Shawn, were lost in the great wind, and found after in the Bay of Gregory of the Golden Mouth, and carried up the two of them on the one plank, and in by that door.

(*She pauses for a moment, the girls start as if they heard something through the door that is half open behind them.*)

100 **Nora** (*In a whisper.*): Did you hear that, Cathleen? Did you hear a noise in the northeast?

Cathleen (*In a whisper.*): There's some one after crying out by the seashore.

Maurya (*Continues without hearing anything.*): There was Sheamus and his father, and his own father again, were lost in a dark night, and not a stick or sign was seen of them when the sun went up. There was Patch after was drowned out of a curagh that turned over. I was sitting here with Bartley, and he a baby, lying on my two knees, and I seen two women, and three women, and four women coming in, and they crossing themselves, and not saying a word. I looked out then, and there were men coming after them, and they holding a thing in the half of a red sail, and water dripping out of it—it was a dry day, Nora—and leaving a track to the door.

(*She pauses again with her hand stretched out toward the door. It opens softly and old women begin to come in, crossing themselves on the threshold, and kneeling down in front of the stage with red petticoats over their heads.*)

Maurya (*Half in a dream, to Cathleen.*): Is it Patch, or Michael, or what is it at all?

Cathleen: Michael is after being found in the Far North, and when he is found there how could he be here in this place?

105 **Maurya:** There does be a power of young men floating round in the sea, and what way would they know if it was Michael they had, or another man like him, for when a man is nine days in the sea, and the wind blowing, it's hard set his own mother would be to say what man was it.

Cathleen: It's Michael, God spare him, for they're after sending us a bit of his clothes from the Far North.

(*She reaches out and hands Maurya the clothes that belonged to Michael. Maurya stands up slowly, and takes them in her hands. Nora looks out.*)

Nora: They're carrying a thing among them and there's water dripping out of it and leaving a track by the big stones.

Cathleen (*In a whisper to the women who have come in.*): Is it Bartley it is?

One of the Women: It is surely, God rest his soul.

(*Two younger women come in and pull out the table. Then men carry in the body of Bartley, laid on a plank, with a bit of a sail over it, and lay it on the table.*)

110 **Cathleen** (*To the women, as they are doing so.*): What way was he drowned?

One of the Women: The gray pony knocked him into the sea, and he was washed out where there is a great surf on the white rocks.

(*Maurya has gone over and knelt down at the head of the table. The women are keening softly and swaying themselves with a slow movement. Cathleen and Nora kneel at the other end of the table. The men kneel near the door.*)

Maurya (*Raising her head and speaking as if she did not see the people around her.*): They're all gone now, and there isn't anything more the sea can do to me. . . . I'll have no call now to be up crying and praying when the wind breaks from the south, and you can hear the surf is in the east, and the surf is in the west, making a great stir with the two noises, and they hitting one on the other. I'll have no call now to be going down and getting Holy Water in the dark nights after Samhain,[9] and I won't care what way the sea is when the other women will be keening. (*To Nora.*) Give me the Holy Water, Nora, there's a small sup still on the dresser.

(*Nora gives it to her.*)

Maurya (*Drops Michael's clothes across Bartley's feet, and sprinkles the Holy Water over him.*): It isn't that I haven't prayed for you, Bartley, to the Almighty God. It isn't that I haven't said prayers in the dark night till you wouldn't know what I'd be saying; but it's a great rest I'll have now, and it's time surely. It's a great rest I'll have now, and great sleeping in the long nights after Samhain, if it's only a bit of wet flour we do have to eat, and maybe a fish that would be stinking.

(*She kneels down again, crossing herself, and saying prayers under her breath.*)

Cathleen (*To an old man.*): Maybe yourself and Eamon would make a coffin when the sun rises. We have fine white boards herself bought. God help her, thinking Michael would be found, and I have a new cake you can eat while you'll be working.

115 **The Old Man** (*Looking at the boards.*): Are there nails with them?

Cathleen: There are not, Colum; we didn't think of the nails.

Another Man: It's a great wonder she wouldn't think of the nails, and all the coffins she's seen made already.

Cathleen: It's getting old she is, and broken.

(*Maurya stands up again very slowly and spreads out the pieces of Michael's clothes beside the body, sprinkling them with the last of the Holy Water.*)

Nora (*In a whisper to Cathleen.*): She's quiet now and easy; but the day Michael was drowned you could hear her crying out from this to the spring well. It's fonder she was of Michael, and would any one have thought that?

---

[9] Similar to all hallows, a holiday which falls on November 1 and marks the beginning of winter; it is celebrated with harvest rites and a Feast of the Dead.

120 **Cathleen** (*Slowly and clearly.*): An old woman will be soon tired with anything she will do, and isn't it nine days herself is after crying and keening, and making great sorrow in the house?

Maurya (*Puts the empty cup mouth downwards on the table, and lays her hands together on Bartley's feet.*): They're all together this time, and the end is come. May the Almighty God have mercy on Bartley's soul, and on Michael's soul, and on the souls of Sheamus and Patch, and Stephen and Shawn; (*Bending her head.*) and may He have mercy on my soul, Nora, and on the soul of every one is left living in the world.

(*She pauses, and the keen rises a little more loudly from the women, then sinks away.*)

Maurya (*Continuing.*): Michael has a clean burial in the Far North, by the grace of the Almighty God. Bartley will have a fine coffin out of the white boards, and a deep grave surely. What more can we want than that? No man at all can be living forever, and we must be satisfied.

(*She kneels down again and the curtain falls slowly.*)

■ EXPLORATIONS OF THE TEXT

1. What does the initial dialogue between Nora and Cathleen reveal about the protagonists' world? What do they fear?
2. Dicuss the characters of Nora, Cathleen, and Bartley as individuals and as family members. How are they different from each other?
3. How do the sisters realize their brother is dead? Interpret the symbolism of Michael's clothes.
4. What is the meaning of Maurya's vision of Michael "on the red mare with the gray pony behind him"? Why is Maurya so concerned with a proper burial and coffin?
5. Consider Maurya's character. What has been her role as a mother? How does she handle the deaths of her sons?
6. Why does Maurya claim: "They're all gone now, and there isn't anything more the sea can do to me"? Do you believe her when she claims, "No man at all can be living forever, and we must be satisfied"?
7. Do the images of sea, surf, and wind change in the play? Are they negative or positive?
8. Compare the view of fate in this work with themes of Hawthorne's "Rappaccini's Daughter."

■ THE READING/WRITING CONNECTION

1. "Think" Topic: Synge's play is about people living on a small island off the coast of Ireland in the early 1900s. Does the fate of these people have relevance for us today? Why?
2. Discuss rituals of mourning and experiences of grief in a journal entry. (You may wish to refer to your own experience.)

■ IDEAS FOR WRITING

1. Choose a detail of the play—a stage direction, a gesture, an aspect of scene, a prop, an image—and analyze its relationship to theme.
2. Distinguish between the roles and concerns of men and of women in the play.
3. What does Synge believe about the power of the sea?
4. Synge has been quoted as saying, "The drama, like the symphony, does not teach or prove anything." After reading *Riders to the Sea*, do you agree with him?

■ NONFICTION ■

GLORIA STEINEM

Gloria Steinem (1934–   ) was born in Toledo, Ohio. She attended Smith College and the universities of Delhi and Calcutta in India. After her return to the United States, she worked for the civil rights and peace movements throughout the 1960s. Steinem's best-known article from her early career, "I Was a Playboy Bunny," resulted from an undercover assignment for the 1963 opening of New York City's Playboy Club. In 1968, she co-founded New York *magazine; in 1972 she co-founded* Ms. *magazine. She has been a leading spokesperson for the women's movement. Gloria Steinem has won many awards and fellowships, among them the Ceres Medal from the United Nations and a Woodrow Wilson International Center for Scholars award. Her writings include* The Beach Book *(1963),* Outrageous Acts and Everyday Rebellions *(1983), and* Revolution from Within *(1992). Steinem recently coedited* The Reader's Companion to U.S. Women's History *(1998), and she continues to work for social change.*

1983

RUTH'S SONG

Happy or unhappy, families are all mysterious. We have only to imagine how differently we would be described—and will be, after our deaths—by each of the family members who believe they know us. The only question is, Why are some mysteries more important than others?

The fate of my Uncle Ed was a mystery of importance in our family. We lavished years of speculation on his transformation from a brilliant young electrical engineer to the town handyman. What could have changed this elegant, Lincolnesque student voted "Best Dressed" by his classmates to the gaunt, unshaven man I remember? Why did he leave a young son and a first wife of the "proper" class and religion, marry a much less educated woman of the "wrong" religion, and raise a second family in a house near an abandoned airstrip; a house whose walls were patched with metal signs to stop the wind? Why did he never talk about his transformation?

For years, I assumed that some secret and dramatic events of a year he spent in Alaska had made the difference. Then I discovered that the trip had come after his change and probably been made because of it. Strangers he worked for as a much-loved handyman talked about him as one more tragedy of the Depression, and it was true that Uncle Ed's father, my paternal grandfather, had lost his money in the stockmarket Crash and died of (depending on who was telling the story) pneumonia or a broken heart. But the Crash of 1929 also had come long after Uncle Ed's transformation. Another theory was that he was afflicted with a mental problem that lasted most of his life, yet he was supremely competent at his work, led an independent life, and asked for help from no one.

Perhaps he had fallen under the spell of a radical professor in the early days of the century, the height of this country's romance with socialism and anarchism. That was the theory of another uncle on my mother's side. I do remember that no matter how much Uncle Ed needed money, he would charge no more for his work than materials plus 10 percent, and I never saw him in anything other than ancient boots and overalls held up with strategic safety pins. Was he really trying to replace socialism-in-one-country with socialism-in-one-man? If so, why did my grandmother, a woman who herself had run for the school board in coalition with anarchists and socialists, mistrust his judgment so much that she left his share of her estate in trust, even though he was over fifty when she died? And why did Uncle Ed seem uninterested in all other political words and acts? Was it true instead that, as another relative insisted, Uncle Ed had chosen poverty to disprove the myths of Jews and money?

5   Years after my uncle's death, I asked a son in his second family if he had the key to his family mystery. No, he said. He had never known his father any other way. For that cousin, there had been no question. For the rest of us, there was to be no answer.

For many years I also never imagined my mother any way other than the person she had become before I was born. She was just a fact of life when I was growing up; someone to be worried about and cared for; an invalid who lay in bed with eyes closed and lips moving in occasional response to voices only she could hear; a woman to whom I brought an endless stream of toast and coffee, bologna sandwiches and dime pies, in a child's version of what meals should be. She was a loving, intelligent, terrorized woman who tried hard to clean our littered house whenever she emerged from her private world, but who could rarely be counted on to finish one task. In many ways, our roles were reversed: I was the mother and she was the child. Yet that didn't help her, for she still worried about me with all the intensity of a frightened mother, plus the special fears of her own world full of threats and hostile voices.

Even then I suppose I must have known that, years before she was thirty-five and I was born, she had been a spirited adventurous young woman who struggled out of a working-class family and into college, who found work she loved and continued to do, even after she was married and my older sister was there to be cared for. Certainly, our immediate family and nearby relatives, of whom I was by far the youngest, must have remembered her life as a whole and functioning person. She was thirty before she gave up her own career to help my father run the Michigan summer resort that was the most practical of his many dreams, and she worked hard there as everything from bookkeeper to bar manager. The family must have watched this energetic, fun-loving, book-loving woman turn into someone who was afraid to be alone, who could not hang on to reality long enough to hold a job, and who could rarely concentrate enough to read a book.

Yet I don't remember any family speculation about the mystery of my mother's transformation. To the kind ones and those who liked her, this new Ruth was simply a sad event, perhaps a mental case, a family problem to be accepted and cared for until some natural process made her better. To the less kind or those who had resented her earlier independence, she was a willful failure, someone who lived in a filthy house, a woman who simply would not pull herself together.

Unlike the case of my Uncle Ed, exterior events were never suggested as reason enough for her problems. Giving up her own career was never cited as her personal parallel of the Depression. (Nor was there discussion of the Depression itself, though my mother, like millions of others, had made potato soup and cut up blankets to make my sister's winter clothes.) Her fears of dependence and poverty were no match for my uncle's possible political beliefs. The real influence of newspaper editors who had praised her reporting was not taken as seriously as the possible influence of one radical professor.

10   Even the explanation of mental illness seemed to contain more personal fault when applied to my mother. She had suffered her first "nervous breakdown," as she and everyone else called it, before I was born and when my sister was about five. It followed years of trying to take care of a baby, be the wife of a kind but financially irresponsible man with show business dreams, and still keep her much-loved job as reporter and newspaper editor. After many months in a sanatorium, she was pronounced recovered. That is, she was able to take care of my sister again, to move away from the city and the job she loved, and to work with

my father at the isolated rural lake in Michigan he was trying to transform into a resort worthy of the big dance bands of the 1930s.

But she was never again completely without the spells of depression, anxiety, and visions into some other world that eventually were to turn her into the nonperson I remember. And she was never again without a bottle of dark, acrid-smelling liquid she called "Doc Howard's medicine": a solution of chloral hydrate that I later learned was the main ingredient of "Mickey Finns" or "knockout drops," and that probably made my mother and her doctor the pioneers of modern tranquilizers. Though friends and relatives saw this medicine as one more evidence of weakness and indulgence, to me it always seemed an embarrassing but necessary evil. It slurred her speech and slowed her coordination, making our neighbors and my school friends believe she was a drunk. But without it, she would not sleep for days, even a week at a time, and her feverish eyes began to see only that private world in which wars and hostile voices threatened the people she loved.

Because my parents had divorced and my sister was working in a far-away city, my mother and I were alone together then, living off the meager fixed income that my mother got from leasing her share of the remaining land in Michigan. I remember a long Thanksgiving weekend spent hanging on to her with one hand and holding my eighth-grade assignment of *Tale of Two Cities*[1] in the other, because the war outside our house was so real to my mother that she had plunged her hand through a window, badly cutting her arm in an effort to help us escape. Only when she finally agreed to swallow the medicine could she sleep, and only then could I end the terrible calm that comes with crisis and admit to myself how afraid I had been.

No wonder that no relative in my memory challenged the doctor who prescribed this medicine, asked if some of her suffering and hallucinating might be due to overdose or withdrawal, or even consulted another doctor about its use. It was our relief as well as hers.

But why was she never returned even to that first sanatorium? Or to help that might come from other doctors? It's hard to say. Partly, it was her own fear of returning. Partly, it was too little money, and a family's not-unusual assumption that mental illness is an inevitable part of someone's personality. Or perhaps other family members had feared something like my experience when, one hot and desperate summer between the sixth and seventh grade, I finally persuaded her to let me take her to the only doctor from those sanatorium days whom she remembered without fear.

15 Yes, this brusque old man told me after talking to my abstracted, timid mother for twenty minutes: She definitely belongs in a state hospital. I should put her there right away. But even at that age, *Life* magazine and newspaper exposés had told me what horrors went on inside those hospitals. Assuming there to be no other alternative, I took her home and never tried again.

In retrospect, perhaps the biggest reason my mother was cared for but not helped for twenty years was the simplest: her functioning was not that necessary to the world. Like women alcoholics who drink in their kitchens while costly programs are constructed for executives who drink, or like the homemakers subdued with tranquilizers while male patients get therapy and personal attention instead, my mother was not an important worker. She was not even the caretaker of a very young child, as she had been when she was hospitalized the first time. My father had patiently brought home the groceries and kept our odd household going until I was eight or so and my sister went away to college. Two years later when wartime gas rationing closed his summer resort and he had to travel to buy and sell in summer as well as winter, he said: How can I travel and take care of your mother? How

---

[1] Novel by Charles Dickens, a nineteenth-century English writer.

can I make a living? He was right. It was impossible to do both. I did not blame him for leaving once I was old enough to be the bringer of meals and answerer of my mother's questions. ("Has your sister been killed in a car crash?" "Are there German soldiers outside?") I replaced my father, my mother was left with one more way of maintaining a sad status quo, and the world went on undisturbed.

That's why our lives, my mother's from forty-six to fifty-three, and my own from ten to seventeen, were spent alone together. There was one sane winter in a house we rented to be near my sister's college in Massachusetts, then one bad summer spent house-sitting in suburbia while my mother hallucinated and my sister struggled to hold down a summer job in New York. But the rest of those years were lived in Toledo where both my mother and father had been born, and on whose city newspapers an earlier Ruth had worked.

First we moved into a basement apartment in a good neighborhood. In those rooms behind a furnace, I made one last stab at being a child. By pretending to be much sicker with a cold than I really was, I hoped my mother would suddenly turn into a sane and cheerful woman bringing me chicken soup à la Hollywood. Of course, she could not. It only made her feel worse that she could not. I stopped pretending.

But for most of those years, we lived in the upstairs of the house my mother had grown up in and her parents left her—a deteriorating farm house engulfed by the city, with poor but newer houses stacked against it and a major highway a few feet from its sagging front porch. For a while, we could rent the two downstairs apartments to a newlywed factory worker and a local butcher's family. Then the health department condemned our ancient furnace for the final time, sealing it so tight that even my resourceful Uncle Ed couldn't produce illegal heat.

20   In that house, I remember:

. . . lying in the bed my mother and I shared for warmth, listening on the early morning radio to the royal wedding of Princess Elizabeth and Prince Philip being broadcast live, while we tried to ignore and thus protect each other from the unmistakable sounds of the factory worker downstairs beating up and locking up his pregnant wife.

. . . hanging paper drapes I had bought in the dime store; stacking books and papers in the shape of two armchairs and covering them with blankets; evolving my own dishwashing system (I waited until all the dishes were dirty, then put them in the bathtub); and listening to my mother's high praise for these housekeeping efforts to bring order from chaos, though in retrospect I think they probably depressed her further.

. . . coming back from one of the Eagles' Club shows where I and other veterans of a local tap-dancing school made ten dollars a night for two shows, and finding my mother waiting with a flashlight and no coat in the dark cold of the bus stop, worried about my safety walking home.

. . . in a good period, when my mother's native adventurousness came through, answering a classified ad together for an amateur acting troupe that performed Biblical dramas in churches, and doing several very corny performances of *Noah's Ark* while my proud mother shook metal sheets backstage to make thunder.

25   . . . on a hot summer night, being bitten by one of the rats that shared our house and its back alley. It was a terrifying night that turned into a touching one when my mother, summoning courage from some unknown reservoir of love, became a calm, comforting parent who took me to a hospital emergency room despite her terror at leaving home.

. . . coming home from a local library with the three books a week into which I regularly escaped, and discovering that for once there was no need to escape. My mother was calmly planting hollyhocks in the vacant lot next door.

But there were also times when she woke in the early winter dark, too frightened and disoriented to remember that I was at my usual after-school job, and so called the police to find me. Humiliated in front of my friends by sirens and policemen, I would yell at her—and she would bow her head in fear and say "I'm sorry, I'm sorry, I'm sorry," just as she had done so often when my otherwise-kindhearted father had yelled at her in frustration. Perhaps the worst thing about suffering is that it finally hardens the hearts of those around it.

And there were many, many times when I badgered her until her shaking hands had written a small check to cash at the corner grocery and I could leave her alone while I escaped to the comfort of well-heated dime stores that smelled of fresh doughnuts, or to air-conditioned Saturday-afternoon movies that were windows on a very different world.

But my ultimate protection was this: I was just passing through, a guest in the house; perhaps this wasn't my mother at all. Though I knew very well that I was her daughter, I sometimes imagined that I had been adopted and that my real parents would find me, a fantasy I've since discovered is common. (If children wrote more and grownups less, being adopted might be seen not only as a fear but also as a hope.) Certainly, I didn't mourn the wasted life of this woman who was scarcely older than I am now. I worried only about the times when she got worse.

30   Pity takes distance and a certainty of surviving. It was only after our house was bought for demolition by the church next door, and after my sister had performed the miracle of persuading my father to give me a carefree time before college by taking my mother with him to California for a year, that I could afford to think about the sadness of her life. Suddenly, I was far away in Washington, living with my sister and sharing a house with several of her friends. While I finished high school and discovered to my surprise that my classmates felt sorry for me because my mother *wasn't* there, I also realized that my sister, at least in her early childhood, had known a very different person who lived inside our mother, an earlier Ruth.

She was a woman I met for the first time in a mental hospital near Baltimore, a humane place with gardens and trees where I visited her each weekend of the summer after my first year away in college. Fortunately, my sister hadn't been able to work and be our mother's caretaker, too. After my father's year was up, my sister had carefully researched hospitals and found the courage to break the family chain.

At first, this Ruth was the same abstracted, frightened woman I had lived with all those years, though now all the sadder for being approached through long hospital corridors and many locked doors. But gradually she began to talk about her past life, memories that doctors there must have been awakening. I began to meet a Ruth I had never known.

. . . A tall, spirited, auburn-haired high-school girl who loved basketball and reading; who tried to drive her uncle's Stanley Steamer when it was the first car in the neighborhood; who had a gift for gardening and who sometimes, in defiance of convention, wore her father's overalls; a girl with the courage to go to dances even though her church told her that music itself was sinful, and whose sense of adventure almost made up for feeling gawky and unpretty next to her daintier, dark-haired sister.

. . . A very little girl, just learning to walk, discovering the body places where touching was pleasurable, and being punished by her mother who slapped her hard across the kitchen floor.

35   . . . A daughter of a handsome railroad-engineer and a schoolteacher who felt she had married "beneath her"; the mother who took her two daughters on Christmas trips to far-away New York on an engineer's free railroad pass and showed them the restaurants and theaters they should aspire to—even though they could only stand outside them in the snow.

. . . A good student at Oberlin College, whose freethinking traditions she loved, where friends nicknamed her "Billy"; a student with a talent for both mathematics and poetry, who was not above putting an invisible film of Karo syrup on all the john seats in her dormitory the night of a big prom; a daughter who had to return to Toledo, live with her family, and go to a local university when her ambitious mother—who had scrimped and saved, ghost-written a minister's sermons, and made her daughters' clothes in order to get them to college at all—ran out of money. At home, this Ruth became a part-time bookkeeper in a lingerie shop for the very rich, commuting to classes and listening to her mother's harsh lectures on the security of becoming a teacher; but also a young woman who was still rebellious enough to fall in love with my father, the editor of her university newspaper, a funny and charming young man who was a terrible student, had no intention of graduating, put on all the campus dances, and was unacceptably Jewish.

I knew from family lore that my mother had married my father twice: once secretly, after he invited her to become the literary editor of his campus newspaper, and once a year later in a public ceremony, which some members of both families refused to attend as the "mixed marriage" of its day.

And I knew that my mother had gone on to earn a teaching certificate. She had used it to scare away truant officers during the winters when, after my father closed the summer resort for the season, we lived in a house trailer and worked our way to Florida or California and back by buying and selling antiques.

But only during those increasingly adventurous weekend outings from the hospital—going shopping, to lunch, to the movies—did I realize that she had taught college calculus for a year in deference to her mother's insistence that she have teaching "to fall back on." And only then did I realize she had fallen in love with newspapers along with my father. After graduating from the university paper, she wrote a gossip column for a local tabloid, under the name "Duncan MacKenzie," since women weren't supposed to do such things, and soon had earned a job as society reporter on one of Toledo's two big dailies. By the time my sister was four or so, she had worked her way up to the coveted position of Sunday editor.

40 It was a strange experience to look into those brown eyes I had seen so often and realize suddenly how much they were like my own. For the first time, I realized that she might really be my mother.

I began to think about the many pressures that might have led up to that first nervous breakdown: leaving my sister who she loved very much with a grandmother whose values my mother didn't share; trying to hold on to a job she loved but was being asked to leave by her husband; wanting very much to go with a woman friend to pursue their own dreams in New York; falling in love with a co-worker at the newspaper who frightened her by being more sexually attractive, more supportive of her work than my father, and perhaps the man she should have married; and finally, nearly bleeding to death with a miscarriage because her own mother had little faith in doctors and refused to get help.

Did those months in the sanatorium brainwash her in some Freudian or very traditional way into making what were, for her, probably the wrong choices? I don't know. It almost doesn't matter. Without extraordinary support to the contrary, she was already convinced that divorce was unthinkable. A husband could not be left for another man, and certainly not for a reason as selfish as a career. A daughter could not be deprived of her father and certainly not be uprooted and taken off to an uncertain future in New York. A bride was supposed to be virginal (not "shop-worn," as my euphemistic mother would have said), and if your husband turned out to be kind, but innocent of the possibility of a woman's pleasure, then just be thankful for kindness.

Of course, other women have torn themselves away from work and love and still survived. But a story my mother told me years later has always symbolized for me the formidable forces arrayed against her.

It was early spring, nothing was open yet. There was nobody for miles around. We had stayed at the lake that winter, so I was alone a lot while your father took the car and traveled around on business. You were a baby. Your sister was in school, and there was no phone. The last straw was that the radio broke. Suddenly it seemed like forever since I'd been able to talk with anyone—or even hear the sound of another voice.

45   *I bundled you up, took the dog, and walked out to the Brooklyn road. I thought I'd walk the four or five miles to the grocery store, talk to some people, and find somebody to drive me back. I was walking along with Fritzie running up ahead in the empty road— when suddenly a car came out of nowhere and down the hill. It hit Fritzie head on and threw him over to the side of the road. I yelled and screamed at the driver, but he never slowed down. He never looked at us. He never even turned his head.*

    Poor Fritzie was all broken and bleeding, but he was still alive. I carried him and sat down in the middle of the road, with his head cradled in my arms. I was going to make the next car stop and help.

    But no car ever came. I sat there for hours, I don't know how long, with you in my lap and holding Fritzie, who was whimpering and looking up at me for help. It was dark by the time he finally died. I pulled him over to the side of the road and walked back home with you and washed the blood out of my clothes.

    I don't know what it was about that one day—it was like a breaking point. When your father came home, I said: "From now on, I'm going with you. I won't bother you. I'll just sit in the car. But I can't bear to be alone again."

I think she told me that story to show she had tried to save herself, or perhaps she wanted to exorcise a painful memory by saying it out loud. But hearing it made me understand what could have turned her into the woman I remember: a solitary figure sitting in the car, perspiring through the summer, bundled up in winter, waiting for my father to come out of this or that antique shop, grateful just not to be alone. I was there, too, because I was too young to be left at home, and I loved helping my father wrap and unwrap the newspaper around the china and small objects he had bought at auctions and was selling to dealers. It made me feel necessary and grown-up. But sometimes it was hours before we came back to the car again and to my mother who was always patiently, silently waiting.

50   At the hospital and later when Ruth told me stories of her past, I used to say, "But why didn't you leave? Why didn't you take the job? Why didn't you marry the other man?" She would always insist it didn't matter, she was lucky to have my sister and me. If I pressed hard enough, she would add, "If I'd left you never would have been born."

    I always thought but never had the courage to say: *But you might have been born instead.*

I'd like to tell you that this story has a happy ending. The best I can do is one that is happier than its beginning.

    After many months in that Baltimore hospital, my mother lived on her own in a small apartment for two years while I was in college and my sister married and lived nearby. When she felt the old terrors coming back, she returned to the hospital at her own request. She was approaching sixty by the time she emerged from there and from a Quaker farm that served as a halfway house, but she confounded her psychiatrists' predictions that she would be able to live outside for shorter and shorter periods. In fact, she never returned. She lived more than another twenty years, and for six of them, she was well enough to stay in a rooming house that provided both privacy and company. Even after my sister and her husband moved to a larger house and generously made two rooms into an apartment for her, she continued to have some independent life and many friends. She worked part-time as a "salesgirl" in a china shop; went away with me on yearly vacations and took one trip to Europe with relatives; went to women's club meetings; found a multiracial church that she loved; took meditation courses; and enjoyed many books. She still could not bear to see a sad movie, to stay alone with any of her six grandchildren while they were babies, to live without many tranquilizers, or to talk about those bad years in Toledo. The old terrors were still in the back of her mind, and each day was a fight to keep them down.

It was the length of her illness that had made doctors pessimistic. In fact, they could not identify any serious mental problem and diagnosed her only as having "an anxiety neurosis": low self-esteem, a fear of being dependent, a terror of being alone, a constant worry about money. She also had spells of what now would be called agoraphobia, a problem almost entirely confined to dependent women: fear of going outside the house, and incapacitating anxiety attacks in unfamiliar or public places.

55   Would you say, I asked one of her doctors, that her spirit had been broken? "I guess that's as good a diagnosis as any," he said. "And it's hard to mend anything that's been broken for twenty years."

But once out of the hospital for good, she continued to show flashes of the different woman inside; one with a wry kind of humor, a sense of adventure, and a love of learning. Books on math, physics, and mysticism occupied a lot of her time. ("Religion," she used to say firmly, "begins in the laboratory.") When she visited me in New York during her sixties and seventies, she always told taxi drivers that she was eighty years old ("so they will tell me how young I look"), and convinced theater ticket sellers that she was deaf long before she really was ("so they'll give us seats in the front row"). She made friends easily, with the vulnerability and charm of a person who feels entirely dependent on the approval of others. After one of her visits, every shopkeeper within blocks of my apartment would say, "Oh yes, I know your mother!" At home, she complained that people her own age were too old and stodgy for her. Many of her friends were far younger than she. It was as if she were making up for her own lost years.

She was also overly appreciative of any presents given to her—and that made giving them irresistible. I loved to send her clothes, jewelry, exotic soaps, and additions to her collection of tarot cards. She loved receiving them, though we both knew they would end up stored in boxes and drawers. She carried on a correspondence in German with our European relatives, and exchanges with many other friends, all written in her painfully slow, shaky handwriting. She also loved giving gifts. Even as she worried about money and figured out how to save pennies, she would buy or make carefully chosen presents for grandchildren and friends.

Part of the price she paid for this much health was forgetting. A single reminder of those bad years in Toledo was enough to plunge her into days of depression. There were times when this fact created loneliness for me, too. Only two of us had lived most of my childhood. Now, only one of us remembered. But there were also times in later years when, no matter how much I pled with reporters *not* to interview our friends and neighbors in Toledo, *not* to say that my mother had been hospitalized, they published things that hurt her very much and sent her into a downhill slide.

One the other hand, she was also her mother's daughter, a person with a certain amount of social pride and pretension, and some of her objections had less to do with depression than false pride. She complained bitterly about one report that we had lived in a house trailer. She finally asked angrily: "Couldn't they at least say 'vacation mobile home'?" Divorce was still a shame to her. She might cheerfully tell friends, "I don't know *why* Gloria says her father and I were divorced—we never were." I think she justified this to herself with the idea that they had gone through two marriage ceremonies, one in secret and one in public, but been divorced only once. In fact, they were definitely divorced, and my father had briefly married someone else.

60   She was very proud of my being a published writer, and we generally shared the same values. After her death, I found a mother-daughter morals quiz I once had written for a women's magazine. In her unmistakably shaky writing, she had recorded her own answers, her entirely accurate imagination of what my answers would be, and a score that concluded our differences were less than those "normal for women separated by twenty-odd years." Nonetheless, she was quite capable of putting a made-up name on her name tag when going to a conservative women's club where she feared our shared identity would bring controversy or even just questions. When I finally got up the nerve to tell her I was signing a 1972 petition of women who publicly said we had had abortions and were demanding the repeal of laws that made them illegal and dangerous, her only reply was sharp and aimed to hurt back. "Every starlet says she's had an abortion," she said. "It's just a way of getting publicity." I knew she agreed that abortion should be a legal choice, but I also knew she would never forgive me for embarrassing her in public.

In fact, her anger and a fairly imaginative ability to wound with words increased in her last years when she was most dependent, most focused on herself, and most likely to need the total attention of others. When my sister made a courageous decision to go to law school at the age of fifty, leaving my mother in a house that not only had many loving teenage grandchildren in it but a kindly older woman as a paid companion besides, my mother reduced her to frequent tears by insisting that this was a family with no love in it, no home-cooked food in the refrigerator; not a real family at all. Since arguments about home cooking wouldn't work on me, my punishment was creative and different. She was going to call up *The New York Times,* she said, and tell them that this was what feminism did: it left old sick women all alone.

Some of this bitterness brought on by failing faculties was eventually solved by a nursing home near my sister's house where my mother not only got the twenty-four-hour help her weakening body demanded, but the attention of affectionate nurses besides. She charmed them, they loved her, and she could still get out for an occasional family wedding. If I ever had any doubts about the debt we owe to nurses, those last months laid them to rest.

When my mother died just before her eighty-second birthday in a hospital room where my sister and I were alternating the hours in which her heart wound slowly down to its last sounds, we were alone together for a few hours while my sister slept. My mother seemed bewildered by her surroundings and the tubes that invaded her body, but her consciousness cleared long enough for her to say: "I want to go home. Please take me home." Lying to her one last time, I said I would. "Okay, honey," she said. "I trust you." Those were her last understandable words.

The nurses let my sister and me stay in the room long after there was no more breath. She had asked us to do that. One of her many fears came from a story she had been told as a child about a man whose coma was mistaken for death. She also had made out a living will requesting that no extraordinary measures be used to keep her alive, and that her ashes be sprinkled in the same stream as my father's.

65   Her memorial service was in the Episcopalian church that she loved because it fed the poor, let the homeless sleep in its pews, had members of almost every race, and had been sued by the Episcopalian hierarchy for having a woman priest. Most of all, she loved the affection with which its members had welcomed her, visited her at home, and driven her to services. I think she would have liked the Quaker-style informality with which people rose to tell their memories of her. I know she would have loved the presence of many friends. It was to this church that she had donated some of her remaining Michigan property in the hope that it could be used as a multiracial camp, thus getting even with those people in the tiny nearby town who had snubbed my father for being Jewish.

I think she also would have been pleased with her obituary. It emphasized her brief career as one of the early women journalists and asked for donations to Oberlin's scholarship fund so others could go to this college she loved so much but had to leave.

I know I will spend the next years figuring out what her life has left in me.

I realize that I've always been more touched by old people than by children. It's the talent and hopes locked up in a failing body that gets to me; a poignant contrast that reminds me of my mother, even when she was strong.

I've always been drawn to any story of a mother and a daughter on their own in the world. I saw *A Taste of Honey* several times as both a play and a film, and never stopped feeling it. Even *Gypsy* I saw over and over again, sneaking in backstage for the musical and going to the movies as well. I told myself that I was learning the tap-dance routines, but actually my eyes were full of tears.

70   I once fell in love with a man only because we both belonged to that large and secret club of children who had "crazy mothers." We traded stories of the shameful houses to which we could never invite our friends. Before he was born, his mother had gone to jail for her pacifist convictions. Then she married the politically ambitious young lawyer who had defended her, stayed home and raised many sons. I fell out of love when he confessed that he wished I wouldn't smoke or swear, and he hoped I wouldn't go on working. His mother's plight had taught him self-pity—nothing else.

I'm no longer obsessed, as I was for many years, with the fear that I would end up in a house like that one in Toledo. Now, I'm obsessed instead with the things I could have done for my mother while she was alive, or the things I should have said.

I still don't understand why so many, many years passed before I saw my mother as a person and before I understood that many of the forces in her life are patterns women share. Like a lot of daughters, I suppose I couldn't afford to admit that what had happened to my mother was not all personal or accidental, and therefore could happen to me.

One mystery has finally cleared. I could never understand why my mother hadn't been helped by Pauline, her mother-in-law; a woman she seemed to love more than her own mother. This paternal grandmother had died when I was five, before my mother's real problems began but long after that "nervous breakdown," and I knew Pauline was once a suffragist who addressed Congress, marched for the vote, and was the first woman member of a school board in Ohio. She must have been a courageous and independent woman, yet I could find no evidence in my mother's reminiscences that Pauline had encouraged or helped my mother toward a life of her own.

I finally realized that my grandmother never changed the politics of her own life, either. She was a feminist who kept a neat house for a husband and four antifeminist sons, a vegetarian among five male meat eaters, and a woman who felt so strongly about the dangers of alcohol that she used only paste vanilla; yet she served both meat and wine to the men of the house and made sure their lives and comforts were continued undisturbed. After the vote was won, Pauline seems to have stopped all feminist activity. My mother greatly admired the fact that her mother-in-law kept a spotless house and prepared a week's meals at a time. Whatever her own internal torments, Pauline was to my mother a woman who seemed able to "do it all." "Whither thou goest, I shall go," my mother used to say to her much-loved mother-in-law, quoting the Ruth of the Bible. In the end, her mother-in-law may have added to my mother's burdens of guilt.

75   Perhaps like many later suffragists, my grandmother was a public feminist and a private isolationist. That may have been heroic in itself, the most she could be expected to do, but the vote and a legal right to work were not the only kind of help my mother needed.

The world still missed a unique person named Ruth. Though she longed to live in New York and in Europe, she became a woman who was afraid to take a bus across town. Though she drove the first Stanley Steamer, she married a man who never let her drive.

I can only guess what she might have become. The clues are in moments of spirit or humor.

After all the years of fear, she still came to Oberlin with me when I was giving a speech there. She remembered everything about its history as the first college to admit blacks and the first to admit women, and responded to students with the dignity of a professor, the accuracy of a journalist, and a charm that was all her own.

When she could still make trips to Washington's wealth of libraries, she became an expert genealogist, delighting especially in finding the rogues and rebels in our family tree.

80 Just before I was born, when she had cooked one more enormous meal for all the members of some famous dance band at my father's resort and they failed to clean their plates, she had taken a shotgun down from the kitchen wall and held it over their frightened heads until they had finished the last crumb of strawberry shortcake. Only then did she tell them the gun wasn't loaded. It was a story she told with great satisfaction.

Though sex was a subject she couldn't discuss directly, she had a great appreciation of sensuous men. When a friend I brought home tried to talk to her about cooking, she was furious. ("He came out in the kitchen and talked to me about *stew!*") But she forgave him when we went swimming. She whispered, "He has wonderful legs!"

On her seventy-fifth birthday, she played softball with her grandsons on the beach, and took pride in hitting home runs into the ocean.

Even in the last year of her life, when my sister took her to visit a neighbor's new and luxurious house, she looked at the vertical stripes of a very abstract painting in the hallway and said, tartly, "Is that the price code?"

She worried terribly about being socially accepted herself, but she never withheld her own approval for the wrong reasons. Poverty or style or lack of education couldn't stand between her and a new friend. Though she lived in a mostly white society and worried if I went out with a man of the "wrong" race, just as she had once married a man of the "wrong" religion, she always accepted each person as an individual.

85 "Is he *very* dark?" she once asked worriedly about a friend. But when she met this very dark person, she only said afterward, "What a kind and nice man!"

My father was the Jewish half of the family, yet it was my mother who taught me to have pride in that tradition. It was she who encouraged me to listen to a radio play about a concentration camp when I was little. "You should know that this can happen," she said. Yet she did it just enough to teach, never enough to frighten.

It was she who introduced me to books and a respect for them, to poetry that she knew by heart, and to the idea that you could never criticize someone unless you "walked miles in their shoes."

It was she who sold that Toledo house, the only home she had, with the determination that the money be used to start me in college. She gave both her daughters the encouragement to leave home for four years of independence that she herself had never had.

After her death, my sister and I found a journal she had kept of her one cherished and belated trip to Europe. It was a trip she had described very little when she came home: she always deplored people who talked boringly about their personal travels and showed slides. Nonetheless, she had written a descriptive essay called "Grandma Goes to Europe." She still must have thought of herself as a writer. Yet she showed this long journal to no one.

90 I miss her, but perhaps no more in death than I did in life. Dying seems less sad than having lived too little. But at least we're now asking questions about all the Ruths and all our family mysteries.

If her song inspires that, I think she would be the first to say: It was worth the singing.

5 ▪ **EXPLORATIONS OF THE TEXT**

1. "Happy or unhappy, families are all mysterious." Does this opening statement provide clues about Steinem's possible purposes in writing?
2. How does Steinem's discussion of her Uncle Ed provide the framework for the portrait of her mother?
3. What are some of the "mysteries" in the life of Steinem's mother?
4. What role must Steinem assume? How does she react to it? What do her short anecdotes reveal about her childhood with her mother?
5. To what possible causes does Steinem trace her mother's breakdown?
6. How has Steinem's life as a child and as an adult been shaped by her mother's life? by her relationship with her mother?
7. Steinem states: "But at least we're now asking questions about all the Ruths and all our family mysteries." How does her mother become a representative figure? What does she represent?
8. Steinem gains control of her material through explicit and implicit comparisons. Examine this structural device. What comparisons guide this essay?
9. The essay begins in "mystery." Does it end in "mystery"?

▪ **THE READING/WRITING CONNECTION**

1. In a mini-essay, explore how the story of Steinem's mother on the road represents (as Steinem suggests) "the formidable forces arrayed against" her mother.
2. "Think" Topic: Does Steinem's process of remembering and writing lead to discovery? Does it lead to a happier ending?

▪ **IDEAS FOR WRITING**

1. Compare the mothers in Lee's "Coming Home Again," Synge's "Riders to the Sea," and this essay.
2. What revelations about family do you gain from Steinem's essay?
3. Using this work as a model, write about a mysterious relationship in your life.

F. SCOTT FITZGERALD

F. Scott Fitzgerald (1896–1940) was born in St. Paul, Minnesota, and attended Princeton University from 1913 to 1917. He left Princeton to join the U.S. Army from 1917 to 1919. Fitzgerald was a novelist, playwright, screenwriter, and short-story writer. He is best known for his novel The Great Gatsby *(1925), voted by the British public as one of the nation's 100 best-loved novels as part of the BBC's* The Big Read *in 2003. Fitzgerald's goal after college was to become one of the world's greatest writers, and the continued popularity of his novels and short stories indicates that he successfully achieved this dream. Other well-known novels include* This Side of Paradise *(1920),* Tender is the Night *(1934), and his unfinished work,* The Last Tycoon, *which was published posthumously in 1941. The following excerpt from* Scott Fitzgerald: Letters to His Daughter *is from his correspondence.*

1933

LETTER TO HIS DAUGHTER

From *Scott Fitzgerald: Letters to His Daughter*

La Paix, Rodgers' Forge
Towson, Maryland

AUGUST 8, 1933

Dear Pie:

   I feel very strongly about you doing [your] duty. Would you give me a little more documentation about your reading in French? I am glad you are happy but I never believe much in happiness. I never believe in misery either. Those are things you see on the stage or the
5 screen or the printed page, they never really happen to you in life.

   All I believe in in life is the rewards for virtue (according to your talents) and the *punishments* for not fulfilling your duties, which are doubly costly. If there is such a volume in the camp library, will you ask Mrs. Tyson to let you look up a sonnet of Shakespeare's in which the line occurs *"Lilies that fester smell far worse than weeds."*

10 Have had no thoughts today, life seems composed of getting up a *Saturday Evening Post* story. I think of you, and always pleasantly; but if you call me "Pappy" again I am going to take the White Cat out and beat his bottom *hard, six times for every time you are impertinent.* Do you react to that?

   I will arrange the camp bill.

15 Halfwit, I will conclude.

Things to worry about:
      Worry about courage
      Worry about cleanliness
      Worry about efficiency
20   Worry about horsemanship
      Worry about...
Things not to worry about:
      Don't worry about popular opinion
      Don't worry about dolls
25   Don't worry about the past
      Don't worry about the future
      Don't worry about growing up
      Don't worry about anybody getting ahead of you
      Don't worry about triumph
30   Don't worry about failure unless it comes through your own fault
      Don't worry about mosquitoes
      Don't worry about flies
      Don't worry about insects in general
      Don't worry about parents
35   Don't worry about boys
      Don't worry about disappointments
      Don't worry about pleasures
      Don't worry about satisfactions
Things to think about:
40   What am I really aiming at?
      How good am I really in comparison to my contemporaries in regard to:
      (a) Scholarship
      (b) Do I really understand about people and am I able to get along with them?
      (c) Am I trying to make my body a useful instrument or am I neglecting it?

45   With dearest love,
                                 [Daddy]

P.S. My come-back to your calling me Pappy is christening you by the word Egg, which implies that you belong to a very rudimentary state of life and that I could break you up and

50 crack you open at my will and I think it would be a word that would hang on if I ever told it to your contemporaries. "Egg Fitzgerald." How would you like that to go through life with—"Eggie Fitzgerald" or "Bad Egg Fitzgerald" or any form that might occur to fertile minds? Try it once more and I swear to God I will hang it on you and it will be up to you to shake it off. Why borrow trouble?

Love anyhow.

■ EXPLORATIONS OF THE TEXT

1. The writer begins his letter with, "I feel very strongly about you doing [your] duty." Based on inferences from the letter as a whole, what is Fitzgerald's definition of duty?
2. What is the effect of the writer's use of opposites, such as past and future, disappointments and pleasures?
3. In what parts of the letter does Fitzgerald use humor to soften the dictatorial tone?

■ THE READING/WRITING CONNECTION

1. Imagine that you are Fitzgerald's daughter, age twelve, and write a letter in reply.
2. Freewrite about your own ideas about duty.
3. Journal entry: Write about what you worry about and what you want not to worry about.

■ IDEAS FOR WRITING

1. Contrast the tone and content of Fitzgerald's letter with the tone and content of Kincaid's "Girl."
2. Write a letter of advice directed to your own child (real or imagined) or a letter of advice that one of your own parents might address to you.

GARRETT HONGO

Garrett Hongo (1951–   ) was born in Volcano, Hawaii, and moved to California when he was six years old. He was educated at Pomona College, the University of Michigan, and the University of California, Irvine, where he graduated with an M.F.A. in 1980. The author of seven books, Hongo presently teaches creative writing at the University of Oregon in Eugene. His work has been published in the American Poetry Review, Antaeus, Crazyhorse, Field, Ploughshares, Tri-Quarterly, *and* The New Yorker. *Of Japanese descent, Hongo attended a racially diverse high school in Los Angeles, an experience that colors his work. His writing explores the treatment of Japanese Americans during World War II and the cultural alienation that still afflicts Asian Americans living in the United States. "Kubota," first published in* Ploughshares, *is a selection from* Volcano: A Memoir of Hawaii *(1995).*

1990

KUBOTA

On December 8, 1941, the day after the Japanese attack on Pearl Harbor in Hawaii, my grandfather barricaded himself with his family—my grandmother, my teenage mother, her two sisters and two brothers—inside of his home in La'ie, a sugar plantation village on Oahu's North Shore. This was my maternal grandfather, a man most villagers called by his last name, Kubota. It could mean either "Wayside Field" or else "Broken Dreams," depending on which ideograms he used. Kubota ran La'ie's general store, and the previous night, after a long day of bad news on the radio, some locals had come by, pounded on the front door, and made threats. One was said to have brandished a machete. They were angry and shocked, as the whole nation was in the aftermath of the surprise attack. Kubota was one of the few Japanese Americans in the village and president of the local Japanese language school. He had become a target for their rage and suspicion. A wise man, he locked all his doors and windows and did not open his store the next day, but stayed closed and waited for news from some official.

He was a *kibei*, a Japanese American born in Hawaii (a U.S. territory then, so he was thus a citizen) but who was subsequently sent back by his father for formal education in Hiroshima, Japan, their home province. *Kibei* is written with two ideograms in Japanese: one is the word for "return" and the other is the word for "rice." Poetically, it means one who returns from America, known as the Land of Rice in Japanese (by contrast, Chinese immigrants called their new home Mountain of Gold).

Kubota was graduated from a Japanese high school and then came back to Hawaii as a teenager. He spoke English—and a Hawaiian Creole version of it at that—with a Japanese accent. But he was well liked and good at numbers, scrupulous and hard working like so many immigrants and children of immigrants. Castle & Cook, a grower's company that ran the sugarcane business along the North Shore, hired him on first as a stock boy and then appointed him to run one of its company stores. He did well, had the trust of management and labor—not an easy accomplishment in any day—married, had children, and had begun to exert himself in community affairs and excel in his own recreations. He put together a Japanese community organization that backed a Japanese language school for children and sponsored teachers from Japan. Kubota boarded many of them, in succession, in his own home. This made dinners a silent affair for his talkative, Hawaiian-bred children, as their stern *sensei*, or teacher, was nearly always at the table and their own abilities in the Japanese language were as delinquent as their attendance. While Kubota and the *sensei* rattled on about things Japanese, speaking Japanese, his children hurried through their suppers and tried to run off early to listen to the radio shows.

After dinner, while the *sensei* graded exams seated in a wicker chair in the spare room and his wife and children gathered around the radio in the front parlor, Kubota sat on the screened porch outside, reading the local Japanese newspapers. He finished reading about the same time as he finished the tea he drank for his digestion—a habit he'd learned in Japan—and then he'd get out his fishing gear and spread it out on the plank floors. The wraps on his rods needed to be redone, gears in his reels needed oil, and, once through with those tasks, he'd painstakingly wind on hundreds of yards of new line. Fishing was his hobby and his passion. He spent weekends camping along the North Shore beaches with his children, setting up umbrella tents, packing a rice pot and hibachi along for meals. And he caught fish. *Ulu'a* mostly, the huge surf-feeding fish known on the mainland as the jack crevalle, but he'd go after almost anything in its season. In Kawela, a plantation-owned bay nearby, he fished for mullet Hawaiian-style with a throw net, stalking the bottom-hugging, gray-backed schools as they gathered at the stream mouths and in the freshwater springs. In an outrigger out beyond the reef, he'd try for *aku*—the skipjack tuna prized for steaks and, sliced raw and mixed with fresh seaweed and cut onions, for *sashimi* salad. In Kahaluu and Ka'awa and on an off-shore rock locals called Goat Island, he loved to go torching, stringing lanterns on bamboo poles stuck in the sand to attract *kumu'u*, the red goatfish, as they schooled at night just inside the reef. But in Lai'e on Laniloa Point near Kahuku, the northernmost tip of Oahu, he cast twelve- and fourteen-foot surf rods for the huge, varicolored, and fast-running *ulu'a* as they ran for schools of squid and baitfish just beyond the biggest breakers and past the low sand flats wadable from the shore to nearly a half mile out. At sunset, against the western light, he looked as if he walked on water as he came back, fish and rods slung over his shoulders, stepping along the rock and coral path just inches under the surface of a running tide.

5   When it was torching season, in December or January, he'd drive out the afternoon before and stay with old friends, the Tanakas or Yoshikawas, shopkeepers like him who ran stores near the fishing grounds. They'd have been preparing for weeks, selecting and cutting their bamboo poles, cleaning the hurricane lanterns, tearing up burlap sacks for the cloths they'd soak with kerosene and tie onto sticks they'd poke into the soft sand of the shallows. Once lit, touched off with a Zippo lighter, these would be the torches they'd use as beacons to attract the schooling fish. In another time, they might have made up a dozen paper lanterns of the kind mostly used for decorating the summer folk dances outdoors on the grounds of the Buddhist church during O-Bon, the Festival for the Dead. But now, wealthy and modern and efficient killers of fish, Tanaka and Kubota used rag torches and Colemans and cast rods with tips made of Tonkin bamboo and butts of American-spun fiberglass. After just one good night, they might bring back a prize bounty of a dozen burlap bags filled with scores of bloody, rigid fish delicious to eat and even better to give away as gifts to friends, family, and special customers.

     It was a Monday night, the day after Pearl Harbor, and there was a rattling knock at the front door. Two FBI agents presented themselves, showed identification, and took my grandfather in for questioning in Honolulu. He didn't return home for days. No one knew what had happened or what was wrong. But there was a roundup going on of all those in the Japanese-American community suspected of sympathizing with the enemy and worse. My grandfather was suspected of espionage, of communicating with offshore Japanese submarines launched from the attack fleet days before war began. Torpedo planes and escort fighters, decorated with the insignia of the Rising Sun, had taken an approach route from northwest of Oahu directly across Kahuku Point and on toward Pearl. They had strafed an auxiliary air station near the fishing grounds my grandfather loved and destroyed a small gun battery there, killing three men. Kubota was known to have sponsored and harbored Japanese nationals in his own home. He had a radio. He had wholesale access to firearms. Circumstances and an undertone of racial resentment had combined with wartime hysteria in the aftermath of the tragic naval battle to cast suspicion on the loyalties of my grandfather and all other Japanese Americans. The FBI reached out and pulled hundreds of them in for questioning in dragnets cast throughout the West Coast and Hawaii.

     My grandfather was lucky; he'd somehow been let go after only a few days. Others were not as fortunate. Hundreds, from small communities in Washington, California, Oregon, and Hawaii, were rounded up and, after what appeared to be routine questioning, shipped off under Justice Department orders to holding centers in Leuppe on the Navaho reservation in Arizona, in Fort Missoula in Montana, and on Sand Island in Honolulu Harbor. There were other special camps on Maui in Ha'iku and on Hawaii—the Big Island—in my own home village of Volcano.

     Many of these men -it was exclusively the Japanese-American men suspected of ties to Japan who were initially rounded up—did not see their families again for more than four years. Under a suspension of due process that was only after the fact ruled as warranted by military necessity, they were, if only temporarily, "disappeared" in Justice Department prison camps scattered in particularly desolate areas of the United States designated as militarily "safe." These were grim forerunners of the assembly centers and concentration camps for the 120,000 Japanese-American evacuees that were to come later.

     I am Kubota's eldest grandchild, and I remember him as a lonely, habitually silent old man who lived with us in our home near Los Angeles for most of my childhood and adolescence. It was the fifties, and my parents had emigrated from Hawaii to the mainland in the hope of a better life away from the old sugar plantation. After some success, they had sent back for my grandparents and taken them in. And it was my grandparents who did the work of the household while my mother and father worked their salaried city jobs. My grandmother cooked and sewed, washed our clothes, and knitted in the front room under the light of a huge lamp with a bright three-way bulb. Kubota raised a flower garden, read up on soils and grasses in gardening books, and planted a zoysia lawn in front and a dichondra one in back. He planted a small patch near the rear block wall with green onions, eggplant, white Japanese radishes, and cucumber. While he hoed and spaded the loamless, clayey earth of Los Angeles, he sang particularly plangent songs in Japanese about plum blossoms and bamboo groves.

10   Once, in the mid-sixties, after a dinner during which, as always, he had been silent while he worked away at a meal of fish and rice spiced with dabs of Chinese mustard and catsup thinned with soy sauce, Kubota took his own dishes to the kitchen sink and washed them up. He took a clean jelly jar out of the cupboard—the glass was thick and its shape squatty like an old-fashioned. He reached around to the hutch below where he kept his bourbon. He made himself a drink and retired to the living room where I was expected to join him for "talk story," the Hawaiian idiom for chewing the fat.

I was a teenager and, though I was bored listening to stories I'd heard often enough before at holiday dinners, I was dutiful. I took my spot on the couch next to Kubota and heard him out. Usually, he'd tell me about his schooling in Japan where he learned judo along with mathematics and literature. He'd learned the *soroban* there—the abacus, which was the original pocket calculator of the Far East—and that, along with his strong, judo-trained back, got him his first job in Hawaii. This was the moral. "Study *ha-ahd*," he'd say with pidgin emphasis. "Learn read good. Learn speak da kine *good* English." The message is the familiar one taught to any children of immigrants: succeed through education. And imitation. But this time, Kubota reached down into his past and told me a different story. I was thirteen by then, and I suppose he thought me ready for it. He told me about Pearl Harbor, how the planes flew in wing after wing of formations over his old house in La'ie in Hawaii, and how, the next day, after Roosevelt had made his famous "Day of Infamy" speech about the treachery of the Japanese, the FBI agents had come to his door and taken him in, hauled him off to Honolulu for questioning, and held him without charge for several days. I thought he was lying. I thought he was making up a kind of horror story to shock me and give his moral that much more starch. But it was true. I asked around. I brought it up during history class in junior high school, and my teacher, after silencing me and stepping me off to the back of the room, told me that it was indeed so. I asked my mother and she said it was true. I asked my schoolmates, who laughed and ridiculed me for being so ignorant. We lived in a Japanese-American community, and the parents of most of my classmates were the *nisei* who had been interned as teenagers all through the war. But there was a strange silence around all of this. There was a hush, as if one were invoking the ill powers of the dead when one brought it up. No one cared to speak about the evacuation and relocation for very long. It wasn't in our history books, though we were studying World War II at the time. It wasn't in the family albums of the people I knew and whom I'd visit staying over weekends with friends. And it wasn't anything that the family talked about or allowed me to keep bringing up either. I was given the facts, told sternly and pointedly that "it was war" and that "nothing could be done." "*Shikatta ga nai*" is the phrase in Japanese, a kind of resolute and determinist pronouncement on how to deal with inexplicable tragedy. I was to know it but not to dwell on it. Japanese Americans were busy trying to forget it ever happened and were having a hard enough time building their new lives after "camp." It was as if we had no history for four years and the relocation was something unspeakable.

But Kubota would not let it go. In session after session, for months it seemed, he pounded away at his story. He wanted to tell me the names of the FBI agents. He went over their questions and his responses again and again. He'd tell me how one would try to act friendly toward him, offering him cigarettes while the other, who hounded him with accusations and threats, left the interrogation room. Good cop, bad cop, I thought to myself, already superficially streetwise from stories black classmates told of the Watts riots and from my having watched too many episodes of *Dragnet* and *The Mod Squad*. But Kubota was not interested in my experiences. I was not made yet, and he was determined that his stories be part of my making. He spoke quietly at first, mildly, but once into his narrative and after his drink was down, his voice would rise and quaver with resentment and he'd make his accusations. He gave his testimony to me and I held it at first cautiously in my conscience like it was an heirloom too delicate to expose to strangers and anyone outside of the world Kubota made with his words. "I give you story now," he once said, "and you learn speak good, eh?" It was my job, as the disciple of his preaching I had then become, Ananda to his Buddha, to reassure him with a promise. "You learn speak good like the Dillingham," he'd say another time, referring to the wealthy scion of the grower family who had once run, unsuccessfully, for one of Hawaii's first senatorial seats. Or he'd then invoke a magical name, the name of one of his heroes, a man he thought particularly exemplary and righteous. "Learn speak dah good Ing-rish like *Mistah Inouye*," Kubota shouted. "He *lick* dah Dillingham even in debate. I saw on *terrebision* myself." He was remembering the debates before the first senatorial election just before Hawaii was admitted to the Union as its fiftieth state. "You *tell* story," Kubota would end. And I had my injunction.

The town we settled in after the move from Hawaii is called Gardena, the independently incorporated city south of Los Angeles and north of San Pedro harbor. At its northern limit, it borders on Watts and Compton, black towns. To the southwest are Torrance and Redondo Beach, white towns. To the rest of L.A., Gardena is primarily famous for having legalized five-card draw poker after the war. On Vermont Boulevard, its eastern border, there is a dingy little Vegas-like strip of card clubs with huge parking lots and flickering neon signs that spell out "The Rainbow" and "The Horseshoe" in timed sequences of varicolored lights. The town is only secondarily famous as the largest community of Japanese Americans in the United States outside of Honolulu, Hawaii. When I was in high school there, it seemed to me that every *sansei* kid I knew wanted to be a doctor, an engineer, or a pharmacist. Our fathers were gardeners or electricians or nurserymen or ran small businesses catering to other Japanese Americans. Our mothers worked in civil service for the city or as cashiers for Thrifty Drug. What the kids wanted was a good job, good pay, a fine home, and no troubles. No one wanted to mess with the law—from either side—and no one wanted to mess with language or art. They all talked about getting into the right clubs so that they could go to the right schools. There was a certain kind of sameness, an intensely enforced system of conformity. Style was all. Boys wore moccasin-sewn shoes from Flagg Brothers, black A-1 slacks, and Kensington shirts with high collars. Girls wore their hair up in stiff bouffants solidified in hairspray and knew all the latest dances from the slauson to the funky chicken. We did well in chemistry and in math, no one who was Japanese but me spoke in English class or in history unless called upon, and no one talked about World War II. The day after Robert Kennedy was assassinated, after winning the California Democratic primary, we worked on calculus and elected class coordinators for the prom, featuring the 5th Dimension. We avoided grief. We avoided government. We avoided strong feelings and dangers of any kind. Once punished, we tried to maintain a concerted emotional and social discipline and would not willingly seek to fall out of the narrow margin of protective favor again.

But when I was thirteen, in junior high, I'd not understood why it was so difficult for my classmates, those who were themselves Japanese American, to talk about the relocation. They had cringed, too, when I tried to bring it up during our discussions of World War II. I was Hawaiian-born. They were mainland-born. Their parents had been in camp, had been the ones to suffer the complicated experience of having to distance themselves from their own history and all things Japanese in order to make their way back and into the American social and economic mainstream. It was out of this sense of shame and a fear of stigma I was only beginning to understand that the *nisei* had silenced themselves. And, for their children, among whom I grew up, they wanted no heritage, no culture, no contact with a defiled history. I recall the silence very well. The Japanese-Americarn children around me were burdened in a way I was not. Their injunction was silence. Mine was to speak.

15   Away at college, in another protected world in its own way as magical to me as the Hawaii of my childhood, I dreamed about my grandfather. Tired from studying languages, practicing German conjugations or scripting an army's worth of Chinese ideograms on a single sheet of paper, Kubota would come to me as I drifted off into sleep. Or I would walk across the newly mown ball field in back of my dormitory, cutting through a street-side phalanx of ancient eucalyptus trees on my way to visit friends off campus, and I would think of him, his anger, and his sadness.

I don't know myself what makes someone feel that kind of need to have a story they've lived through be deposited somewhere, but I can guess. I think about *The Iliad, The Odyssey, The Peloponnesian Wars* of Thucydides, and a myriad of the works of literature I've studied. A character, almost a *topoi* he occurs so often, is frequently the witness who gives personal testimony about an event the rest of his community cannot even imagine. The sibyl is such a character. And Procne, the maid whose tongue is cut out so that she will not tell that she has been raped by her own brother-in-law, the king of Thebes. There are the dime novels, the epic blockbusters Hollywood makes into miniseries, and then there are the plain, relentless stories of witnesses who have suffered through horrors major and minor that have marked and changed their lives. I myself haven't talked to Holocaust victims. But I've read their survival stories and their stories of witness and been revolted and moved by them. My father-in-law, Al Thiessen, tells me his war stories again and again and I listen. A Mennonite who set aside the strictures of his own church in order to serve, he was a Marine code-man in the Pacific during World War II, in the Signal Corps on Guadalcanal, Morotai, and Bougainville. He was part of the island-hopping maneuver MacArthur had devised to win the war in the Pacific. He saw friends die from bombs which exploded not ten yards away. When he was with the 298th Signal Corps attached to the Thirteenth Air Force, he saw plane after plane come in and crash, just short of the runway, killing their crews, setting the jungle ablaze with oil and gas fires. Emergency wagons would scramble, bouncing over newly bulldozed land men used just the afternoon before for a football game. Every time we go fishing together, whether it's in a McKenzie boat drifting for salmon in Tillamook Bay or taking a lunch break from wading the riffles of a stream in the Cascades, he tells me about what happened to him and the young men in his unit. One was a Jewish boy from Brooklyn. One was a foul-mouthed kid from Kansas. They died. And he *has* to tell me. And I *have* to listen. It's a ritual payment the young owe their elders who have survived. The evacuation and relocation is something like that.

Kubota, my grandfather, had been ill with Alzheimer's disease, for some time before he died. At the house he'd built on Kamehameha Highway in Hau'ula, a seacoast village just down the road from La'ie where he had his store, he'd wander out from the garage or greenhouse where he'd set up a workbench, and trudge down to the beach or up toward the line of pines he'd planted while employed by the Work Projects Administration during the thirties. Kubota thought he was going fishing. Or he thought he was back at work for Roosevelt, planting pines as a windbreak or soilbreak on the windward flank of the Ko'olau Mountains, emerald monoliths rising out of sea and cane fields from Waialua to Kaneohe. When I visited, my grandmother would send me down to the beach to fetch him. Or I'd run down Kam Highway a quarter mile or so and find him hiding in the cane field by the roadside, counting stalks, measuring circumferences in the claw of his thumb and forefinger. The look on his face was confused or concentrated, I didn't know which. But I guessed he was going fishing again. I'd grab him and walk him back to his house on the highway. My grandmother would shut him in a room.

Within a few years, Kubota had a stroke and survived it, then he had another one and was completely debilitated. The family decided to put him in a nursing home in Kahuku, just set back from the highway, within a mile or so of Kahuku Point and the Tanaka Store where he had his first job as a stock boy. He lived there three years, and I visited him once with my aunt. He was like a potato that had been worn down by cooking. Everything on him—his eyes, his teeth, his legs and torso—seemed like it had been sloughed away. What he had been was mostly gone now and I was looking at the nub of a man. In a wheelchair, he grasped my hands and tugged on them—violently. His hands were still thick and, I believed, strong enough to lift me out of my own seat into his lap. He murmured something in Japanese— he'd long ago ceased to speak any English. My aunt and I cried a little, and we left him.

I remember walking out on the black asphalt of the parking lot of the nursing home. It was heat-cracked and eroded already, and grass had veined itself into the interstices. There were coconut trees around, a cane field I could see across the street, and the ocean I knew was pitching a surf just beyond it. The green Ko'o-laus came up behind us. Somewhere nearby, alongside the beach, there was an abandoned airfield in the middle of the canes. As a child, I'd come upon it playing one day, and my friends and I kept returning to it, day after day, playing war or sprinting games or coming to fly kites. I recognize it even now when I see it on TV—it's used as a site for action scenes in the detective shows Hollyweod always sets in the islands: a helicopter chasing the hero racing away in a Ferrari, or gun dealers making a clandestine rendezvous on the abandoned runway. It was the old airfield strafed by Japanese planes the day the major flight attacked Peral Harbor. It was the airfield the FBI thought my grandfather had targeted in his night fishing and signaling with the long surf poles he'd stuck in the sandy bays near Kahuku Point.

20   Kubota died a short while after I visited him, but not, I thought, without giving me a final message. I was on the mainland, in California studying for Ph.D. exams, when my grandmother called me with the news. It was a relief. He'd suffered from his debilitation a long time and I was grateful he'd gone. I went home for the funeral and gave the eulogy. My grandmother and I took his ashes home in a small, heavy metal box wrapped in a black *furoshiki,* a large silk scarf. She showed me the name the priest had given to him on his death, scripted with a calligraphy brush on a long, narrow talent of plain wood. Buddhist commoners, at death, are given priestly names, received symbolically into the clergy. The idea is that, in their next life, one of scholarship and leisure, they might meditate and attain the enlightenment the religion is aimed at. *"Shaku Shūchi,"* the ideuograms read. It was Kubota's Buddhist name, incorporating characters from his family and given names. It meant "Shining Wisdom of the Law." He died on Pearl Harbor Day, December 7, 1983.

After years, after I'd finally come. back to live in Hawaii again, only once did I dream of Kubota, my grandfather. It was the same night I'd heard HR 442, the redress bill for Japanese Americans, had been signed into law. In my dream that night Kubota was "torching," and he sang a Japanese song, a querulous and wavery folk ballad, as he hung paper lanterns on bamboo poles stuck into the sand in the shallow water of the lagoon behind the reef near Kahuku Point. Then he was at a work table, smoking a hand-rolled cigarette, letting it dangle from his lips Bogart-style as he drew, daintily and skillfully, with a narrow trim brush, ideogram after ideogram on a score of paper lanterns he had hung in a dark shed to dry. He had painted a talismanic mantra onto each lantern, the ideogram for the word "red" in Japanese, a bit of art blended with some superstition, a piece of sympathetic magic appealing to the magenta coloring on the rough skins of the schooling, night-feeding fish he wanted to attract to his baited hooks. He strung them from pole to pole in the dream then, hiking up his khaki worker's pants so his white ankles showed and wading through the shimmering black waters of the sand flats and then the reef. "The moon is leaving, leaving," he sang in Japanese. "Take me deeper in the savage sea." He turned and crouched like an ice racer then, leaning forward so that his unshaven face almost touched the light film of water. I could see the light stubble of beard like a fine, gray ash covering the lower half of his face. I could see his gold-rimmed spectacles. He held a small wooden boat in his cupped hands and placed it lightly on the sea and pushed it away. One of his lanterns was on it and, written in small neat rows like a sutra scroll, it had been decorated with the silvery names of all our dead.

■ **EXPLORATIONS OF THE TEXT**

1. Why does Hongo not depict the events of his grandfather's life in chronological order? What is the impact of this technique?

2. Analyze the grandfather's character at several phases of his life (e.g., as a "kibei," as an adolescent in Japan and Hawaii, as a successful businessman before Pearl Harbor, as a "lonely . . . silent old man"). Focus on his appearance, behavior, actions, attitudes, and values.

3. What knowledge does his grandfather want to pass on to Hongo? What does the former hope to accomplish through his "talk-story"? Why does Hongo refer to "a myriad of the works of literature" that he studied in his discussion of his grandfather's storytelling?

4. In "The Smile of Accomplishment," Patricia Hampl suggests that the witness's survival is not the redemptive act but, rather, that it is the act of telling "that can approach transcendence." Apply this statement to Kubota. What do you learn?

5. Why does Hongo end his autobiographical essay with a dream? Explore the symbolism of "torching" and the Festival of O-Bon. What does the imagery suggest about his grandfather's legacy?

6. Compare Hongo's relationship to his heritage with that of Ali's speaker in "Snowmen" or Walker's persona in "Heritage."

■ **THE READING/WRITING CONNECTION**

1. Journal Entry: Describe a moment when you experienced or witnessed injustice.

2. "Think" Topic: What family stories are "part of [your] making"? Describe the stories and their impact upon you.

■ **IDEAS FOR WRITING**

1. Interview one of your grandparents or an elderly relative or person whom you know. Question them about significant moments in history that they experienced and/or remember (e.g., World War II, the assassination of John Kennedy, or the March on Washington). Record their reminiscences. What do you learn about cultural history? As an alternative, discuss the family stories—perhaps told many times—that you have resisted listening to. Why do you think that they are repeated? Do you think that your resistance is similar to that of Sonny's brother in Baldwin's "Sonny's Blues"; of An-mei, the narrator in Tan's "Scar"; or of the narrator in Hongo's "Kubota"?

2. Compose an autobiographical essay about your relationship with a grandparent or with an elderly relative. How has the person influenced your life? As an alternative, create a character sketch of a grandparent or someone who has influenced you. (Focus on their appearance, actions, gestures, relationships with others, and speech. Use Hongo's essay as a model.)

3. Compare and contrast Kubota with Mama in *A Raisin in the Sun.*

CHANG-RAE LEE

*Chang-rae Lee (1965–   ) was born in Seoul, Korea, and moved to the United States when he was three years old. Lee was educated at Yale University and the University of Oregon, where he received an M.F.A. in 1993. He has taught creative writing at the University of Oregon in Eugene, Hunter College, and Princeton University. Lee has published three books—*Native Speaker *(1995),* A Gesture of Life *(1999), and* Aloft *(2004)—and has won several awards for his writing, including the Hemingway Foundation/PEN award, the "New Voices" award from QPB, the Barnes & Noble Discover Great New Writers award, the American Book Award from the Before Columbus Foundation, the Oregon Books Award, the American Library Association Notable Book of the Year Award, all for* Native Speaker, *which was also a finalist for the PEN West award. In 1999 Lee was selected by* The New Yorker *magazine as one of the twenty best writers under forty. Lee's work focuses on the complex search for identity in Asian-American immigrants who feel alienated from both the United States and the culture of their parents. "Coming Home Again" was first published in* The New Yorker *and was anthologized in* The Best American Essays, 1996.*

1996

COMING HOME AGAIN

When my mother began using the electronic pump that fed her liquids and medication, we moved her to the family room. The bedroom she shared with my father was upstairs, and it was impossible to carry the machine up and down all day and night. The pump itself was attached to a metal stand on casters, and she pulled it along wherever she went. From anywhere in the house, you could hear the sound of the wheels clicking out a steady time over the grout lines of the slate-tiled foyer, her main thoroughfare to the bathroom and the kitchen. Sometimes you would hear her halt after only a few steps, to catch her breath or steady her balance, and whatever you were doing was instantly suspended by a pall of silence.

I was usually in the kitchen, preparing lunch or dinner, poised over the butcher block with her favorite chef's knife in my hand and her old yellow apron slung around my neck. I'd be breathless in the sudden quiet, and, having ceased my mincing and chopping, would stare blankly at the brushed sheen of the blade. Eventually, she would clear her throat or call out to say she was fine, then begin to move again, starting her rhythmic *ka-jug;* and only then could I go on with my cooking, the world of our house turning once more, wheeling through the black.

I wasn't cooking for my mother but for the rest of us. When she first moved downstairs she was still eating, though scantily, more just to taste what we were having than from any genuine desire for food. The point was simply to sit together at the kitchen table and array ourselves like a family again. My mother would gently set herself down in her customary chair near the stove. I sat across from her, my father and sister to my left and right, and crammed in the center was all the food I had made—a spicy codfish stew, say, or a casserole of gingery beef, dishes that in my youth she had prepared for us a hundred times.

It had been ten years since we'd all lived together in the house, which at fifteen I had left to attend boarding school in New Hampshire. My mother would sometimes point this out, by speaking of our present time as being "just like before Exeter," which surprised me, given how proud she always was that I was a graduate of the school.

5   My going to such a place was part of my mother's not so secret plan to change my character, which she worried was becoming too much like hers. I was clever and able enough,

but without outside pressure I was readily given to sloth and vanity. The famous school—
which none of us knew the first thing about—would prove my mettle. She was right, of
course, and while I was there I would falter more than a few times, academically and otherwise. But I never thought that my leaving home then would ever be a problem for her, a private quarrel she would have even as her life waned.

Now her house was full again. My sister had just resigned from her job in New York
City, and my father, who typically saw his psychiatric patients until eight or nine in the
evening, was appearing in the driveway at four-thirty. I had been living at home for nearly a
year and was in the final push of work on what would prove a dismal failure of a novel.
When I wasn't struggling over my prose, I kept occupied with the things she usually did—
the daily errands, the grocery shopping, the vacuuming and the cleaning, and, of course, all
the cooking.

When I was six or seven years old, I used to watch my mother as she prepared our favorite meals. It was one of my daily pleasures. She shooed me away in the beginning, telling
me that the kitchen wasn't my place, and adding, in her half-proud, half-deprecating way,
that her kind of work would only serve to weaken me. "Go out and play with your friends,"
she'd snap in Korean, "or better yet, do your reading and homework." She knew that I had
already done both, and that as the evening approached there was no place to go save her
small and tidy kitchen, from which the clatter of her mixing bowls and pans would ring
through the house.

I would enter the kitchen quietly and stand beside her, my chin lodging upon the point
of her hip. Peering through the crook of her arm, I beheld the movements of her hands. For
kalbi, she would take up a butchered short rib in her narrow hand, the flinty bone shaped
like a section of an airplane wing and deeply embedded in gristle and flesh, and with the
point of her knife cut so that the bone fell away, though not completely, leaving it connected
to the meat by the barest opaque layer of tendon. Then she methodically butterflied the
flesh, cutting and unfolding, repeating the action until the meat lay out on her board, glistening and ready for seasoning. She scored it diagonally, then sifted sugar into the crevices
with her pinched fingers, gently rubbing in the crystals. The sugar would tenderize as well
as sweeten the meat. She did this with each rib, and then set them all aside in a large shallow bowl. She minced a half-dozen cloves of garlic, a stub of ginger-root, sliced up a few
scallions, and spread it all over the meat. She wiped her hands and took out a bottle of
sesame oil, and, after pausing for a moment, streamed the dark oil in two swift circles
around the bowl. After adding a few splashes of soy sauce, she thrust her hands in and
kneaded the flesh, careful not to dislodge the bones. I asked her why it mattered that they
remain connected, "The meat needs the bone nearby," she said, "to borrow its richness." She
wiped her hands clean of the marinade, except for her little finger, which she would flick
with her tongue from time to time, because she knew that the flavor of a good dish developed not at once but in stages.

Whenever I cook, I find myself working just as she would, readying the ingredients—a
mash of garlic, a julienne of red peppers, fantails of shrimp—and piling them in little
mounds about the cutting surface. My mother never left me any recipes, but this is how I
learned to make her food, each dish coming not from a list or a card but from the aromatic
spread of a board.

10   I've always thought it was particularly cruel that the cancer was in her stomach, and that
for a long time at the end she couldn't eat. The last meal I made for her was on New Year's
Eve, 1990. My sister suggested that instead of a rib roast or a bird, or the usual overflow of
Korean food, we make all sorts of finger dishes that our mother might fancy and pick at.

We set the meal out on the glass coffee table in the family room. I prepared a tray of
smoked-salmon canapés, fried some Korean bean cakes, and made a few other dishes I

thought she might enjoy. My sister supervised me, arranging the platters, and then with some pomp carried each dish in to our parents. Finally, I brought out a bottle of champagne in a bucket of ice. My mother had moved to the sofa and was sitting up, surveying the low table. "It looks pretty nice," she said. "I think I'm feeling hungry."

This made us all feel good, especially me, for I couldn't remember the last time she had felt any hunger or had eaten something I cooked. We began to eat. My mother picked up a piece of salmon toast and took a tiny corner in her mouth. She rolled it around for a moment and then pushed it out with the tip of her tongue, letting it fall back onto her plate. She swallowed hard, as if to quell a gag, then glanced up to see if we had noticed. Of course we all had. She attempted a bean cake, some cheese, and then a slice of fruit, but nothing was any use.

She nodded at me anyway, and said, "Oh, it's very good." But I was already feeling lost and I put down my plate abruptly, nearly shattering it on the thick glass. There was an ugly pause before my father asked me in a weary, gentle voice if anything was wrong, and I answered that it was nothing, it was the last night of a long year, and we were together, and I was simply relieved. At midnight, I poured out glasses of champagne, even one for my mother, who took a deep sip. Her manner grew playful and light, and I helped her shuffle to her mattress, and she lay down in the place where in a brief week she was dead.

My mother could whip up most anything, but during our first years of living in this country we ate only Korean foods. At my harangue-like behest, my mother set herself to learning how to cook exotic American dishes. Luckily, a kind neighbor, Mrs. Churchill, a tall, florid young woman with flaxen hair, taught my mother her most trusted recipes, Mrs. Churchill's two young sons, palish, weepy boys with identical crew cuts, always accompanied her, and though I liked them well enough, I would slip away from them after a few minutes, for I knew that the real action would be in the kitchen, where their mother was playing guide. Mrs. Churchill hailed from the state of Maine, where the finest Swedish meatballs and tuna casserole and angel food cake in America are made. She readily demonstrated certain techniques—how to layer wet sheets of pasta for a lasagna or whisk up a simple roux, for example. She often brought gift shoeboxes containing curious ingredients like dried oregano, instant yeast, and cream of mushroom soup. The two women, though at ease and jolly with each other, had difficulty communicating, and this was made worse by the often confusing terminology of Western cuisine ("corned beef," "deviled eggs"). Although I was just learning the language myself, I'd gladly play the interlocutor, jumping back and forth between their places at the counter, dipping my fingers into whatever sauce lay about.

15   I was an insistent child, and, being my mother's firstborn, much too prized. My mother could say no to me, and did often enough, but anyone who knew us—particularly my father and sisters—could tell how much the denying pained her. And if I was overconscious of her indulgence even then, and suffered the rushing pangs of guilt that she could inflict upon me with the slightest wounded turn of her lip, I was too happily obtuse and venal to let her cease. She reminded me daily that I was her sole son, her reason for living, and that if she were to lose me, in either body or spirit, she wished that God would mercifully smite her, strike her down like a weak branch.

In the traditional fashion, she was the house accountant, the maid, the launderer, the disciplinarian, the driver, the secretary, and, of course, the cook. She was also my first basketball coach. In South Korea, where girls' high school basketball is a popular spectator sport, she had been a star, the point guard for the national high school team that once won the all-Asia championships. I learned this one Saturday during the summer, when I asked my father if he would go down to the schoolyard and shoot some baskets with me. I had just finished the fifth grade, and wanted desperately to make the middle school team the coming fall. He called for my mother and sister to come along. When we arrived, my sister immediately ran off to the swings, and I recall being annoyed that my mother wasn't following her. I dribbled clumsily around the key, on the verge of losing control of the ball, and flung a flat shot that caromed wildly off the rim. The ball bounced to my father, who took a few not so graceful dribbles and made an easy layup. He dribbled out and then drove to the hoop for a layup on the other side. He rebounded his shot and passed the ball to my mother, who had been watching us from the foul line. She turned from the basket and began heading the other way.

"*Um-mah,*" I cried at her, my exasperation already bubbling over, "the basket's over *here!*"

After a few steps she turned around, and from where the professional three-point line must be now, she effortlessly flipped the ball up in a two-handed set shot, its flight truer and higher than I'd witnessed from any boy or man. The ball arced cleanly into the hoop, stiffly popping the chain-link net. All afternoon, she rained in shot after shot, as my father and I scrambled after her.

When we got home from the playground, my mother showed me the photograph album of her team's championship run. For years I kept it in my room, on the same shelf that housed the scrapbooks I made of basketball stars, with magazine clippings of slick players like Bubbles Hawkins and Pistol Pete and George (the Iceman) Gervin.

20   It puzzled me how much she considered her own history to be immaterial, and if she never patently diminished herself, she was able to finesse a kind of self-removal by speaking of my father whenever she could. She zealously recounted his excellence as a student in medical school and reminded me, each night before I started my homework, of how hard he drove himself in his work to make a life for us. She said that because of his Asian face and imperfect English, he was "working two times the American doctors." I knew that she was building him up, buttressing him with both genuine admiration and her own brand of anxious braggadocio, and that her overarching concern was that I might fail to see him as she wished me to—in the most dawning light, his pose steadfast and solitary.

In the year before I left for Exeter, I became weary of her oft-repeated accounts of my father's success. I was a teenager, and so ever inclined to be dismissive and bitter toward anything that had to do with family and home. Often enough, my mother was the object of my derision. Suddenly, her life seemed so small to me. She was there, and sometimes, I thought, *always* there, as if she were confined to the four walls of our house. I would even complain about her cooking. Mostly, though, I was getting more and more impatient with the difficulty she encountered in doing everyday things. I was afraid for her. One day, we got into a terrible argument when she asked me to call the bank, to question a discrepancy she had discovered in the monthly statement. I asked her why she couldn't call herself. I was stupid and brutal, and I knew exactly how to wound her.

"Whom do I talk to?" she said. She would mostly speak to me in Korean, and I would answer in English.

"The bank manager, who else?"

"What do I say?"

25   "Whatever you want to say."

"Don't speak to me like that!" she cried.

"It's just that you should be able to do it yourself," I said.

"You know how I feel about this!"

"Well, maybe then you should consider it *practice,*" I answered lightly, using the Korean word to make sure she understood.

30   Her face blanched, and her neck suddenly became rigid, as if I were throttling her. She nearly struck me right then, but instead she bit her lip and ran upstairs. I followed her,

pleading for forgiveness at her door. But it was the one time in our life that I couldn't convince her, melt her resolve with the blandishments of a spoiled son.

When my mother was feeling strong enough, or was in particularly good spirits, she would roll her machine into the kitchen and sit at the table and watch me work. She wore pajamas day and night, mostly old pairs of mine.

She said, "I can't tell, what are you making?"

"*Mahn-doo* filling."

"You didn't salt the cabbage and squash."

35 "Was I supposed to?"

"Of course. Look, it's too wet. Now the skins will get soggy before you can fry them."

"What should I do?"

"It's too late. Maybe it'll be OK if you work quickly. Why didn't you ask me?"

"You were finally sleeping."

40 "You should have woken me."

"No way."

She sighed, as deeply as her weary lungs would allow.

"I don't know how you were going to make it without me."

"I don't know, either. I'll remember the salt next time."

45 "You better. And not too much."

We often talked like this, our tone decidedly matter-of-fact, chin up, just this side of being able to bear it. Once, while inspecting a potato fritter batter I was making, she asked me if she had ever done anything that I wished she hadn't done. I thought for a moment, and told her no. In the next breath, she wondered aloud if it was right of her to have let me go to Exeter, to live away from the house while I was so young. She tested the batter's thickness with her finger and called for more flour. Then she asked if, given a choice, I would go to Exeter again.

I wasn't sure what she was getting at, and I told her that I couldn't be certain, but probably yes, I would. She snorted at this and said it was my leaving home that had once so troubled our relationship. "Remember how I had so much difficulty talking to you? Remember?"

She believed back then that I had found her more and more ignorant each time I came home. She said she never blamed me, for this was the way she knew it would be with my wonderful new education. Nothing I could say seemed to quell the notion. But I knew that the problem wasn't simply the *education;* the first time I saw her again after starting school, barely six weeks later, when she and my father visited me on Parents Day, she had already grown nervous and distant. After the usual campus events, we had gone to the motel where they were staying in a nearby town and sat on the beds in our room. She seemed to sneak looks at me, as though I might discover a horrible new truth if our eyes should meet.

My own secret feeling was that I had missed my parents greatly, my mother especially, and much more than I had anticipated. I couldn't tell them that these first weeks were a mere blur to me, that I felt completely overwhelmed by all the studies and my much brighter friends and the thousand irritating details of living alone, and that I had really learned nothing, save perhaps how to put on a necktie while sprinting to class. I felt as if I had plunged too deep into the world, which, to my great horror, was much larger than I had ever imagined.

50 I welcomed the lull of the motel room. My father and I had nearly dozed off when my mother jumped up excitedly, murmured how stupid she was, and hurried to the closet by the door. She pulled out our old metal cooler and dragged it between the beds. She lifted the top and began unpacking plastic containers, and I thought she would never stop. One after the other they came out, each with a dish that traveled well—a salted stewed meat,

rolls of Korean-style sushi. I opened a container of radish kimchi and suddenly the room bloomed with its odor, and I reveled in the very peculiar sensation (which perhaps only true kimchi lovers know) of simultaneously drooling and gagging as I breathed it all in. For the next few minutes, they watched me eat. I'm not certain that I was even hungry. But after weeks of pork parmigiana and chicken patties and wax beans, I suddenly realized that I had lost all the savor in my life. And it seemed I couldn't get enough of it back. I ate and I ate, so much and so fast that I actually went to the bathroom and vomited. I came out dizzy and sated with the phantom warmth of my binge.

And beneath the face of her worry, I thought, my mother was smiling.

From that day, my mother prepared a certain meal to welcome me home. It was always the same. Even as I rode the school's shuttle bus from Exeter to Logan airport, I could already see the exact arrangement of my mother's table.

I knew that we would eat in the kitchen, the table brimming with plates. There was the *kalbi*, of course, broiled or grilled depending on the season. Leaf lettuce, to wrap the meat with. Bowls of garlicky clam broth with miso and tofu and fresh spinach. Shavings of cod dusted in flour and then dipped in egg wash and fried. Glass noodles with onions and shiitake. Scallion-and-hot-pepper pancakes. Chilled steamed shrimp. Seasoned salads of bean sprouts, spinach, and white radish. Crispy squares of seaweed. Steamed rice with barley and red beans. Homemade kimchi. It was all there—the old flavors I knew, the beautiful salt, the sweet, the excellent taste.

After the meal, my father and I talked about school, but I could never say enough for it to make any sense. My father would often recall his high school principal, who had gone to England to study the methods and traditions of the public schools, and regaled students with stories of the great Eton man. My mother sat with us, paring fruit, not saying a word but taking everything in. When it was time to go to bed, my father said good night first. I usually watched television until the early morning. My mother would sit with me for an hour or two, perhaps until she was accustomed to me again, and only then would she kiss me and head upstairs to sleep.

55   During the following days, it was always the cooking that started our conversations. She'd hold an inquest over the cold leftovers we ate at lunch, discussing each dish in terms of its balance of flavors or what might have been prepared differently. But mostly I begged her to leave the dishes alone. I wish I had paid more attention. After her death, when my father and I were the only ones left in the house, drifting through the rooms like ghosts, I sometimes tried to make that meal for him. Though it was too much for two, I made each dish anyway, taking as much care as I could. But nothing turned out quite right—not the color, not the smell. At the table, neither of us said much of anything. And we had to eat the food for days.

I remember washing rice in the kitchen one day and my mother's saying in English, from her usual seat, "I made a big mistake."

"About Exeter?"

"Yes. I made a big mistake. You should be with us for that time. I should never let you go there."

"So why did you?" I said.

60   "Because I didn't know I was going to die."

I let her words pass. For the first time in her life, she was letting herself speak her full mind, so what else could I do?

"But you know what?" she spoke up. "It was better for you. If you stayed home, you would not like me so much now."

I suggested that maybe I would like her even more.

She shook her head. "Impossible."

65   Sometimes I still think about what she said, about having made a mistake. I would have left home for college, that was never in doubt, but those years I was away at boarding school grew more precious to her as her illness progressed. After many months of exhaustion and pain and the haze of the drugs, I thought that her mind was beginning to fade, for more and more it seemed that she was seeing me again as her fifteen-year-old boy, the one she had dropped off in New Hampshire on a cloudy September afternoon.

     I remember the first person I met, another new student, named Zack, who walked to the welcome picnic with me. I had planned to eat with my parents—my mother had brought a coolerful of food even that first day—but I learned of the cookout and told her that I should probably go. I wanted to go, of course. I was excited, and no doubt fearful and nervous, and I must have thought I was only thinking ahead. She agreed wholeheartedly, saying I certainly should. I walked them to the car, and perhaps I hugged them, before saying goodbye. One day, after she died, my father told me what happened on the long drive home to Syracuse.

     He was driving the car, looking straight ahead. Traffic was light on the Massachusetts Turnpike, and the sky was nearly dark. They had driven for more than two hours and had not yet spoken a word. He then heard a strange sound from her, a kind of muffled chewing noise, as if something inside her were grinding its way out.

     "So, what's the matter?" he said, trying to keep an edge to his voice.

     She looked at him with her ashen face and she burst into tears. He began to cry himself, and pulled the car over onto the narrow shoulder of the turnpike, where they stayed for the next half hour or so, the blank-faced cars droning by them in the cold, onrushing; night.

70   Every once in a while, when I think of her, I'm driving alone somewhere on the highway. In the twilight, I see their car off to the side, a blue Olds coupe with a landau top, and as I pass them by I look back in the mirror and I see them again, the two figures huddling together in the front seat. Are they sleeping? Or kissing? Are they all right?

■ EXPLORATIONS OF THE TEXT

1. How does Lee define his relationship with his mother through the cooking anecdotes? In what ways are the mother and son similar? Different?
2. Discuss Lee's mother's place in North American society. How is she hampered as a non-native speaker of English? How is she caught between worlds? How do her language difficulties and ethnic background create a gulf between mother and son?
3. Explore the significance of the last scene (the last five paragraphs in the essay).
4. Why does Lee entitle the essay "Coming Home Again"? In tending to her in her final illness, in coping with her death, what does the narrator learn to appreciate about his mother? What does he discover through acts of autobiographical writing and reminiscing? Compare Lee's process of discovery with Steinem's in "Ruth's Song." Do both writers come to terms with their pasts?
5. Compare and contrast the situation for first-generation women in North American society in Song's "Lost Sister" (chapter 4), Cervantes's "Refugee Ship" (chapter 1), and Mora's "Elena" with Lee's mother.

■ THE READING/WRITING CONNECTION

1. Journal Entry: Write about your first few weeks in college or in high school.
2. Have your attitudes toward one of your parents changed over the years? Freewrite about this subject.
3. Write about foods of your childhood. What do they represent?
4. "Think" Topic: How does the symbolism of food function in the essay? What are the multiple ways that Lee uses this symbol?

■ **IDEAS FOR WRITING**

1. Create a character analysis of Lee's mother. Focus on her background, actions, attitudes, values, gestures, relationships with others, and speech.
2. Lee's work is an example of creative nonfiction. Analyze his style and approach. Consider such elements of creative nonfiction as point of view, use of descriptive detail, and figurative language. (Refer to chapter 12 for ideas.)

■ WRITING ASSIGNMENTS ■

1. a. Based on the selections in this chapter, freewrite about what you learned regarding the experience of parenting or of childhood that was revelatory to you.
   b. Write a journal entry comparing one example of the parent/child relationship presented in the works in this chapter with your own experience.
   c. Make a list of questions that emerge from these explorations of parent/child relationships. Write an answer to one of these questions. Refer to three works in this chapter.
2. a. Diagram a family tree for the central relationships in your life. Include extended family and friends. Draw straight lines for the relationships that represent solidity and broken lines (– – – –) for those that seem fragile or negative.
   b. Write your conclusions in your journal.
   c. Compare the positive and negative aspects of family dynamics in your life with one work in this chapter.
3. a. Think of a moment from your past—a moment of conflict or of closeness. Write a point-of-view piece, a monologue, for each family member.
   b. After you write these pieces, construct several freewrites about characters' conflicts within family settings presented in three works in this chapter. Then create monologues for these characters.
   c. Write an essay about sources of closeness or of conflict between parents and their children. Choose three works from this chapter. Include specific evidence from the texts.
4. Analyze the impact of mothers on their children. What are major issues in mother/daughter relationships evident in works in this chapter? Choose several works for discussion.
5. One important aspect of mothering is the issue of separation from the mother. Is this issue a pattern in the works in this chapter? Are other patterns evident?
6. a. Our views of family change at different stages in our lives. Do a freewrite about several changes in your views of a particular family member. You may begin: "When I was (ten), I thought. . . ."
   b. Find two works by the same writer about the same family member. Compare them.
7. Based on selections in this chapter, compare the relationships of fathers and sons to those of fathers and daughters. What conclusions can you draw about the nature of these relationships? See Castillo and Ing's "Fathers and Sons."
8. a. Define a good parent. (You may do this as either a freewrite or a journal entry.)
   b. Watch several situation comedies about families. What images of parents appear?
   c. Do any television programs present a realistic view of family life? Your analysis may become an argumentative essay.

     d. Compare a comedy from the fifties or sixties with one that is contemporary.

9. a. Interview several people with backgrounds different from your own. Concentrate on family life, particularly on the roles and responsibilities of parents and of children. What do you conclude?

    b. Based on your interviews and the selections in this chapter, compare the roles of parents or children in two different cultures. Do parents' roles differ? Are there different cultural expectations for children?

    c. Write an analysis of cultural roles for parents and/or children in such works as Tan's "Scar," Baldwin's "Sonny's Blues," or Ortiz's "My Father's Song." (Choose two.)

10. a. Using "Ruth's Song" as a model, write a character sketch about someone who has encouraged the best in you. Make that person come alive.

    b. If you wish, try this inventory for your character: Name, Sex, Age, Height, Weight, Color of Hair and Eyes, Occupation, Mannerisms, Birthplace and Family, Hobbies, Eating Habits, Major Personality Traits, Clothing, Dialogue, Relationships, Key Events That Reveal Character.

    c. To write this sketch, you may want to organize in one of the following ways: by personality traits, by physical description and key events, by monologue or dialogue.

11. a. Freewrite about which work in this chapter has affected you most intensely.

    b. Which work is the most powerful representation of family life? Why?

    c. Which piece is the least successful? Why?

    d. Write an essay about one of your entries. Direct the essay to the writers of the text.

12. Discuss water imagery in three works.

13. Explore the use of allusions to myth, fable, and fairy tale as a literary technique in "My Little Girl, My Stringbean, My Lovely Woman," "Kubota," and/or "Sonny's Blues."

14. a. Catalogue the qualities of "the good mother" and "the bad mother." What do you conclude?

    b. Compare several works which present visions of good and bad mothers.

    c. Write an essay about a work or works in which the mother's character is stereotypical. Evaluate each portrayal.

    d. You may write about fathers and follow the assignments in a, b, and c above.

15. Explore the idea of kinship, of extended family, and of community as these ideas are depicted in several works in this chapter.

16. Is the idea of the nuclear family in North America being redefined? Defend your position. You may use evidence from the works you have read or do research on this topic to support your argument.

17. Conceive of a definition of the family in the year 2010. What are its attributes? You may use evidence from the works you have read in this chapter, or you may research information to develop your definition.

18. Choose three characters from works in this chapter and create a conversation about family life.

19. Explicate one of the poems in this chapter. Concentrate on point of view, tone, imagery, figurative language, and form. How do these aspects of the work develop theme?

20. Several of the essays in this chapter are autobiographical. Reread these works and determine what creates effective autobiographical writing. (Refer to chapter 12 for directions for analysis.)

21. a. Interview one of your family members. What knowledge, attitudes, and values have been passed down from generation to generation?

    b. Compare your family legacies with that of a protagonist in one of the works in the "Generational Legacies" cluster.

22. Both intimacy and distance—closeness and separation—exist in family life. Explore this theme in several works in this chapter.

23. Parents inscribe traditional gender roles on their children. Consider this theme in relation to such works as Tan's "The Scar," Lifshin's "My Mother and the Bed," "Kincaid's "Girl," Howe's "The Boy," and Jen's "Chin."

24. How do the expectations of parents shape their children's lives? You may return to chapter 4 and consider Faulkner's "Barn Burning," Mirikitani's "Suicide Note," and Shakespeare's *Hamlet*.

25. In the excerpt from *bone black*, the autobiographical persona reveals: "She hated that part of herself that kept wanting . . . love or even his [her father's] approval long after she could see that he was never, never going to give it." How is the child's desire for approval portrayed in works in this chapter?

26. Many of these stories in this chapter end ambivalently. Write sequels to several of the stories. What happens to the characters? (Suggestions: Danticat's "The Book of the Dead," Baldwin's "Sonny's Blues," and Diaz's "Fiesta 1980.") Compare and contrast your endings. What do they reveal about characters and theme of the works?

27. "The family is the void to which we return" is a quotation from the film *The Ice Storm*. Explore the process of individuation and reintegration in family in Erdrich's "The Shawl," Hansberry's *A Raisin in the Sun,* or Ali's "Snowmen." You may choose other works from this chapter.

28. Home may be viewed as a site of conflict—a site of a cycle of family violence. Consider this theme in relation to Cervantes's "Uncle's First Rabbit" (chapter 4) and selected works from this chapter.

29. In Baldwin's "Sonny's Blues," the narrator's mother tells her son about the white men who killed his father's brother. This death, witnessed by the father, haunted him throughout his life. Similarly, in Erdrich's "The Shawl," the father is haunted by witnessing the death of his daughter. The loss of family deeply affects characters in works in this chapter (e.g., Chaon's "Fitting Ends," Plath's "Daddy," Alexie's "This is What it Means to Say Phoenix, Arizona," and in chapter 7, Busch's "Ralph the Duck," Ozick's "The Shawl," and Sophocles's *Antigone*).

    a. Compare and contrast one character from each work. How are the lives of these characters changed by the death of a family member?

    b. Choose a work in which the family remains intact, in which no one dies. Compare and contrast it with a depiction of a family that has lost someone to death. How does the death of one person alter the family dynamic and affect every person within?

30. In the excerpt from *bone black,* bell hooks reveals that "she wants to bear witness." How do characters in the works in this chapter "bear witness" to the tragedies of family life? What larger social issues are revealed?

31. Children or parents caught between family members is a state portrayed in several works in this chapter. Analyze this family dynamic.

32. In "Ruth's Song," Gloria Steinem suggests that "happy or unhappy, families are all mysterious." How do these "mysteries" manifest themselves in familial interactions? What is it we do not know about family members? What are the superficial ways in which we behave within family? What are the deeper, often unspoken connections?

    a. With these questions in mind, examine the family dynamics in several works in this chapter (Suggestions: Baldwin's "Sonny Blues," Lee's "Persimmons," Lee's "Coming Home Again," Leff's "Burn Your Maps," and in chapter 6, Leavitt's "Territory").

    b. Compare the family dynamics in one of these works to those in your family.

■ STUDENT ESSAYS ■

Student Essay: Comparison/Contrast

Mᴇʟɪssᴀ Dᴇʟ Cᴀsᴛɪʟʟᴏ
Mɪᴄʜᴇʟʟᴇ Iɴɢ

Fathers and Sons

In every society, fathers treat their children differently. In some societies, fathers respect their children and care about them and for them while in other societies, fathers don't believe that the children deserve respect. In the poem, "My Father's Song," a father explains to his son how he looks up to his own father and how he learned to respect the things of this world from his father. In the poem, "My Papa's Waltz," a boy explains that he loves his father despite all of his father's abuse. These poems present different kinds of relationships between fathers and sons.

In "My Father's Song," the father, the main speaker in the poem, relates to his son an experience that he had had with his own father. The father and son were walking in a field "one Spring at Acu" when the father noticed "tiny pink animals" in the furrows of a plough. The speaker states: "The plowshare had unearthed/the burrow nest of a mouse/in the soft moist sand." He began talking to his son, relating his "song" to his son, and teaching him to respect nature. The speaker states: "Very gently, he scooped tiny pink animals/into the palm of his hand/and told me to touch them." His father had enough respect for these animals that he carried them to safety. "We took them to the edge/of the field and put them in the shade/of a sand moist clod." His father, a very gentle man, taught his son love and respect for all creatures, and the speaker hopes that he can do the same for his son. He teaches his son to cherish life, and the son feels his father's love, and learns his grandfather's and father's values. He "miss[es]" a father whom he loves and who loves him. The son hopes that he can do the same thing for his children.

In the poem, "My Papa's Waltz," the father-son relationship appears to be a shaky and uncertain one. Although the father is an abusive alcoholic, the son does indeed love him and clings to him seeking affection. There is evidence of the father's abuse in the speaker's statement: "The whiskey on your breath/could make a small boy dizzy." But because the boy loves his father, he is not deterred by the alcohol. The father's behavior is revealed in the images of the boy's dance with the father. The dance is wild and then becomes violent: "We romped until the pans/slid from the kitchen shelf." The pans' sliding from the shelves indicates the father's becoming angry and throwing things. "The hand that held [the son's] wrist" which "was battered on one knuckle" became "battered" perhaps because the father was hitting the mother and son. Even after he beat the boy, the son was still attached to the father because he needed his love. The father "beat time on [his] head" and then "waltzed [him] off to bed/still clinging to [the father's] shirt." The boy will take the abuse as long as he can to be close to his father. The boy will hold on and dance with his papa to gain love. The waltz that the son talks about is like the dance of life—the son "clinging" to the father.

In "My Father's Song," the son respected his father, learned about love and caring from the latter, and hoped he could be a good father; meanwhile, in "My Papa's Waltz," the son, the speaker in the poem, remembers a dance with his father, a moment which represented the whole relationship, his father's lack of respect for him. The father didn't care about him, but his son loved him despite the abuse. In both poems, the sons love their fathers, but the difference is that one father cares, and the other doesn't.

· CHAPTER 6 ·

Gender and Sexuality

Adam's diary:

"This new creature with the long hair is a good deal in the way. It is always hanging around and
   following me about . . . I wish it would not talk; it is always talking."

Eve's diary:

"He talks very little. Perhaps it is because he is not bright, and is sensitive about it and wishes
   to conceal it."

* * *

Adam's diary:

"After all these years, I see that I was mistaken about Eve in the beginning; it is much better to
   live outside the Garden with her than inside it without her. At first I thought she talked too
   much; but now I should be sorry to have that voice fall silent and pass out of my life."

MARK TWAIN, "The Diary of Adam and Eve"

A good marriage is that in which each appoints the other the guardian of his solitude.

Rainer Maria Rilke

*Each friend represents a world in us, a world possibly not born until they arrive, and it is only
   by this meeting that a new world is born.*

Anaïs Nin

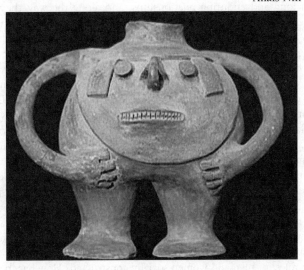

Unknown Pre-Columbian Artisan "Anthropomorphic Vessel" ca. 900–1300

Introduction

It is other people who have separated
You and me
Come, my lord!
Do not dream of listening
To the between-words of people.
My heart, thinking
"How beautiful he is"
Is like a swift river
[Which] though one dams it and dams it,
Will still break through.

"The Lady of Sakanoye," from the Manyō Shū
(compiled A.D. 760)

From the words of the Manyō Shū, from the love songs of Sappho, from Kalidosa's *Shakuntala*, from "The Song of Solomon," from William Shakespeare's sonnets to Anna Akhmatova's poetry, works have expressed the longing for love. This yearning represents a need deeper than sexual attraction or survival of the species; it represents the desire for connection that emerges as strongly as the urge for food or drink.

Intimacy takes on many forms: friendship, platonic love, passion, regret over lost or diminished love. Inevitably, lovers face challenges and obstacles in relationships, but they also discover the pleasures and the fulfillment that love offers. People fall in and out of love, remain in long and enduring relationships, and along the way, they discern more about themselves and continue a process of growth borne out of bonds with others.

The works in Crossing the Genres, "The Elusive Sexual Self," present the struggles inherent in gender and sexual identity formation and the conflicts apparent in same-sex relationships and the intimacy that prevails in such unions. Other questions about love are posed in many of the works. What is romantic love? What constitutes romantic fantasy? Passion? These questions are implied in such works as Anton Chekhov's "Lady with Lapdog," Leslie Marmon Silko's "Yellow Woman," and Octavio Paz's "My Life with the Wave." Some works ask why love fails and portray the obstacles in relationships and the distance between lovers. Other works explore the risks of sexual encounters. The desire for union may turn into an obsessive and dangerous quest for the other.

Experiencing passion, of course, need not always lead to danger. Many of the works in this chapter celebrate the joys of passion. Desire—of the young and old, of the married and unmarried—remains central to the experience of loving.

Other dimensions of love are the expectations, shaped by social mores, that men and women have of roles and behaviors in relationships. Are men and women doomed to reach out and yet misunderstand each other?

Are gender roles for men and women socially constructed? How has the lack of equality affected women's existences? Indeed, the questions of what it means to have an identity

614

as a woman and what it means to live in the body of a woman still seem as relevant today as they did for Virginia Woolf seventy-five years ago. Ultimately, however, the experience of love on some level will remain mysterious, but throughout the centuries, philosophers and writers have tried to explain and to analyze the human need to bond with another.

■ *Thematic Clusters* ■

■ *More Themes that Cross the Genres* ■

Crossing the Genres
THE ELUSIVE SEXUAL SELF

ZZ PACKER

ZZ Packer (1973–) was born in Chicago, Illinois, and raised in Atlanta, Georgia, and Louisville, Kentucky. Packer was named Zuwena—Swahili for "good"—but has been called ZZ by her family since childhood. Packer received a B.A. from Yale University (1994), an M.A. from Johns Hopkins University (1995), and an M.F.A. from the University of Iowa Writer's Workshop (1999). Packer's short stories have appeared in anthologies, magazines, and literary journals, including the Best American Short Stories 2000, Harper's, Story, *and* The New Yorker. *The following story is taken from her first book,* Drinking Coffee Elsewhere *(2003). Packer claims that her protagonists often struggle to understand their roles within their communities and that a reoccurring theme in her fiction is that of the outsider.*

2003

DRINKING COFFEE ELSEWHERE

Orientation games began the day I arrived at Yale from Baltimore. In my group we played heady, frustrating games for smart people. One game appeared to be charades reinterpreted by existentialists; another involved listening to rocks. Then a freshman counsellor made everyone play Trust. The idea was that if you had the faith to fall backward and wait for four scrawny former high-school geniuses to catch you, just before your head cracked on the slate sidewalk, then you might learn to trust your fellow-students. Russian roulette sounded like a better game.

"No way," I said. The white boys were waiting for me to fall, holding their arms out for me, sincerely, gallantly. "No fucking way."

"It's all cool, it's all cool," the counsellor said. Her hair was a shade of blond I'd seen only on *Playboy* covers, and she raised her hands as though backing away from a growling dog. "Sister," she said, in an I'm-down-with-the-struggle voice, "you don't have to play this game. As a person of color, you shouldn't have to fit into any white, patriarchal system."

I said, "It's a bit too late for that."

5   In the next game, all I had to do was wait in a circle until it was my turn to say what inanimate object I wanted to be. One guy said he'd like to be a gadfly, like Socrates. "Stop me if I wax Platonic," he said. The girl next to him was eating a rice cake. She wanted to be the Earth, she said. Earth with a capital "E."

There was one other black person in the circle. He wore an Exeter T-shirt and his overly elastic expressions resembled a series of facial exercises. At the end of each person's turn, he smiled and bobbed his head with unfettered enthusiasm. "Oh, that was good," he said, as if the game were an experiment he'd set up and the results were turning out better than he'd expected. "Good, good good!"

When it was my turn I said, "My name is Dina, and if I had to be any object, I guess I'd be a revolver." The sunlight dulled as if on cue. Clouds passed rapidly overhead, presaging rain. I don't know why I said it. Until that moment I'd been good in all the ways that were meant to matter. I was an honor-roll student—though I'd learned long ago not to mention it in the part of Baltimore where I lived. Suddenly I was hard-bitten and recalcitrant, the kind of kid who took pleasure in sticking pins into cats; the kind who chased down smart kids to spray them with mace.

"A revolver," a counsellor said, stroking his chin, as if it had grown a rabbinical beard. "Could you please elaborate?"

The black guy cocked his head and frowned, as if the beakers and Erlenmeyer flasks of his experiment had grown legs and scurried off.

10   "You were just kidding," the dean said, "about wiping out all of mankind. That, I suppose, was a joke." She squinted at me. One of her hands curved atop the other to form a pink, freckled molehill on her desk.

"Well," I said, "maybe I meant it at the time." I quickly saw that was not the answer she wanted. "I don't know. I think it's the architecture."

Through the dimming light of the dean's-office window, I could see the fortress of the old campus. On my ride from the bus station to the campus, I'd barely glimpsed New Haven—a flash of crumpled building here, a trio of straggly kids there. A lot like Baltimore. But everything had changed when we reached those streets hooded by the Gothic buildings, I imagined how the college must have looked when it was founded, when most of the students owned slaves. I pictured men wearing tights and knickers, smoking pipes.

"The architecture," the dean repeated. She bit her lip and seemed to be making a calculation of some sort. I noticed that she blinked less often than most people. I sat there, waiting to see how long it would be before she blinked again.

My revolver comment won me a year's worth of psychiatric counselling, weekly meetings with Dean Guest, and—since the parents of the roommate I'd never met weren't too hip on the idea of their Amy sharing a bunk bed with a budding homicidal loony—my very own room.

15   Shortly after getting my first D, I also received the first knock on my door. The female counsellors never knocked. The dean had spoken to them; I was a priority. Every other day, right before dinnertime, they'd look in on me, unannounced. "Just checking up," a counsellor would say. It was the voice of a suburban mother in training. By the second week, I had made a point of sitting in a chair in front of the door, just when I expected a counsellor to pop her head around. This was intended to startle them. I also made a point of being naked. The unannounced visits ended.

The knocking persisted. Through the peephole I saw a white face, distorted and balloonish.

"Let me in." The person looked like a boy but sounded like a girl. "Let me in," the voice repeated.

"Not a chance," I said.

Then the person began to sob, and I heard a back slump against the door. If I hadn't known the person was white from the peephole, I'd have known it from a display like this. Black people didn't knock on strangers' doors, crying. Not that I understood the black people at Yale. There was something pitiful in how cool they were. Occasionally one would reach out to me with missionary zeal, but I'd rebuff that person with haughty silence.

20   "I don't have anyone to talk to!" the person on the other side of the door cried.

"That is correct."

"When I was a child," the person said, "I played by myself in a corner of the schoolyard all alone. I hated dolls and I hated games, animals were not friendly and birds flew away. If anyone was looking for me I hid behind a tree and cried out 'I am an orphan—' "

I opened the door. It was a she.

"Plagiarist!" I yelled. She had just recited a Frank O'Hara poem[1] as though she'd thought it up herself. I knew the poem because it was one of the few things I'd been forced to read that I wished I'd written myself.

25   The girl turned to face me, smiling weakly, as though her triumph were not in getting me to open the door but in the fact that she was able to smile at all when she was so accustomed to crying. She was large but not obese, and crying had turned her face the color of raw chicken. She blew her nose into the waist end of her T-shirt, revealing a pale belly.

"How do you know that poem?"

She sniffed. "I'm in your Contemporary Poetry class."

She was Canadian and her name was Heidi, although she said she wanted people to call her Henrik. "That's a guy's name," I said. "What do you want? A sex change?"

She looked at me with so little surprise that I suspected she hadn't discounted this as an option. Then her story came out in teary, hiccup-like bursts. She had sucked some "cute guy's dick" and he'd told everybody and now people thought she was "a slut."

30   "Why'd you suck his dick? Aren't you a lesbian?"

She fit the bill. Short hair, hard, roach-stomping shoes. Dressed like an aspiring plumber. The lesbians I'd seen on TV were wiry, thin strips of muscle, but Heidi was round and soft and had a moonlike face. Drab mud-colored hair. And lesbians had cats. "Do you have a cat?" I asked.

Her eyes turned glossy with new tears. "No," she said, her voice wavering, "and I'm not a lesbian. Are you?"

"Do I look like one?" I said.

She didn't answer.

35   "O.K.," I said. "I could suck a guy's dick, too, if I wanted. But I don't. The human penis is one of the most germ-ridden objects there is." Heidi looked at me, unconvinced. "What I meant to say," I began again, "is that I don't like anybody. Period. Guys or girls. I'm a misanthrope."

"I am, too."

"No," I said, guiding her back through my door and out into the hallway. "You're not."

"Have you had dinner?" she asked. "Let's go to Commons."

I pointed to a pyramid of ramen noodle packages on my windowsill. "See that? That means I never have to go to Commons. Aside from class, I have contact with no one."

40   "I hate it here, too," she said. "I should have gone to McGill, eh."

"The way to feel better," I said, "is to get some ramen and lock yourself in your room. Everyone will forget about you and that guy's dick and you won't have to see anyone ever again. If anyone looks for you—"

"I'll hide behind a tree."

"A revolver?" Dr. Raeburn said, flipping through a manila folder. He looked up at me as if to ask another question, but he didn't.

Dr. Raeburn was the psychiatrist. He had the gray hair and whiskers of a Civil War general. He was also a chain smoker with beige teeth and a navy wool jacket smeared with ash. He asked about the revolver at the beginning of my first visit. When I was unable to explain myself he smiled, as if this were perfectly respectable.

45   "Tell me about your parents."

I wondered what he already had on file. The folder was thick, though I hadn't said a thing of significance since Day One.

"My father was a dick and my mother seemed to like him."

---

[1] Frank O'Hara (1926–1966), part of the New York School of poets in the 1950s.

He patted his pockets for his cigarettes. "That's some heavy stuff," he said. "How do you feel about Dad?" The man couldn't say the word "father." "Is Dad someone you see often?"

"I hate my father almost as much as I hate the word 'Dad.' "

50   He started tapping his cigarette.

"You can't smoke in here."

"That's right," he said, and slipped the cigarette back into the packet. He smiled, widening his eyes brightly. "Don't ever start."

I thought that that first encounter would be the last of Heidi, but then her head appeared in a window of Linsly-Chit during my Chaucer class. Next, she swooped down a flight of stairs in Harkness. She hailed me from across Elm Street and found me in the Sterling Library stacks. After one of my meetings with Dr. Raeburn, she was waiting for me outside Health Services, legs crossed, cleaning her fingernails.

"You know," she said, as we walked through Old Campus, "you've got to stop eating ramen. Not only does it lack a single nutrient but it's full of MSG."

55   "I like eating chemicals," I said. "It keeps the skin radiant."

"There's also hepatitis." She already knew how to get my attention—mention a disease.

"You get hepatitis from unwashed lettuce," I said. "If there's anything safe from the perils of the food chain, it's ramen."

"But you refrigerate what you don't eat. Each time you reheat it, you're killing good bacteria, which then can't keep the bad bacteria in check. A guy got sick from reheating Chinese noodles, and his son died from it. I read it in the *Times*." With this, she put a jovial arm around my neck. I continued walking, a little stunned. Then, just as quickly, she dropped her arm and stopped walking. I stopped, too.

"Did you notice that I put my arm around you?"

60   "Yes," I said. "Next time, I'll have to chop it off."

"I don't want you to get sick," she said. "Let's eat at Commons."

In the cold air, her arm had felt good.

The problem with Commons was that it was too big; its ceiling was as high as a cathedral's, but below it there were no awestruck worshippers, only eighteen-year-olds at heavy wooden tables, chatting over veal patties and Jell-0.

We got our food, tacos stuffed with meat substitute, and made our way through the maze of tables. The Koreans had a table. Each singing group had a table. The crew team sat at a long table of its own. We passed the black table. The sheer quantity of Heidi's flesh accentuated just how white she was.

65   "How you doing, sista?" a guy asked, his voice full of accusation, eyeballing me as though I were clad in a Klansman's sheet and hood. "I guess we won't see you till graduation."

"If," I said, "you graduate."

The remark was not well received. As I walked past, I heard protests, angry and loud, as if they'd discovered a cheat at their poker game. Heidi and I found an unoccupied table along the periphery, which was isolated and dark. We sat down. Heidi prayed over her tacos.

"I thought you didn't believe in God," I said.

"Not in the God depicted in the Judeo-Christian Bible, but I do believe that nature's essence is a spirit that—"

70   "All right," I said. I had begun to eat, and cubes of diced tomato fell from my mouth when I spoke. "Stop right there. Tacos and spirits don't mix."

"You've always got to be so flip," she said. "I'm going to apply for another friend."

"There's always Mr. Dick," I said. "Slurp, slurp."

"You are so lame. So unbelievably lame. I'm going out with Mr. Dick. Thursday night at Atticus. His name is Keith."

Heidi hadn't mentioned Mr. Dick since the day I'd met her. That was more than a month ago and we'd spent a lot of that time together. I checked for signs that she was lying, her habit of smiling too much, her eyes bright and cheeks full, so that she looked like a chipmunk. But she looked normal. Pleased, even, to see me so flustered.

75 "You're insane! What are you going to do this time?" I asked. "Sleep with him? Then when he makes fun of you, what? Come pound your head on my door reciting the 'Collected Poems of Sylvia Plath'?"

"He's going to apologize for before. And don't call me insane. You're the one going to the psychiatrist."

"Well, I'm not going to suck his dick, that's for sure."

She put her arm around me in mock comfort, but I pushed it off, and ignored her. She touched my shoulder again, and I turned, annoyed, but it wasn't Heidi after all; a sepia-toned boy dressed in khakis and a crisp plaid shirt was standing behind me. He handed me a hot-pink square of paper without a word, then briskly made his way toward the other end of Commons, where the crowds blossomed. Heidi leaned over and read it: "Wear Black Leather—the Less, the Better."

"It's a gay party," I said, crumpling the card. "He thinks we're fucking gay."

80 Heidi and I signed on to work at the Saybrook Dining Hall as dishwashers. The job consisted of dumping food from plates and trays into a vat of rustling water. It seemed straightforward, but then I learned better. You wouldn't believe what people could do with food until you worked in a dish room. Lettuce and crackers and soup would be bullied into a pulp in the bowl of some bored anorexic; ziti would be mixed with honey and granola; trays would appear heaped with mashed-potato snow women with melted chocolate ice cream for hair. Frat boys arrived at the dish-room window, en masse. They liked to fill glasses with food, then seal them, airtight, onto their trays. If you tried to prize them off, milk, Worcestershire sauce, peas, chunks of bread vomited onto your dish-room uniform.

When this happened one day in the middle of the lunch rush; for what seemed like the hundredth time, I tipped the tray toward one of the frat boys, popping the glasses off so that the mess spurted onto his Shetland sweater.

He looked down at his sweater. "Lesbo bitch!"

"No," I said, "that would be your mother."

Heidi, next to me, clenched my arm in support, but I remained motionless, waiting to see what the frat boy would do. He glared at me for a minute, then walked away.

85 "Let's take a smoke break," Heidi said.

I didn't smoke, but Heidi had begun to, because she thought it would help her lose weight. As I hefted a stack of glasses through the steamer, she lit up.

"Soft packs remind me of you," she said. "Just when you've smoked them all and you think there's none left, there's always one more, hiding in that little crushed corner." Before I could respond she said, "Oh, God. Not another mouse. You know whose job that is."

By the end of the rush, the floor mats got full and slippery with food. This was when mice tended to appear, scurrying over our shoes; more often than not, a mouse got caught in the grating that covered the drains in the floor. Sometimes the mouse was already dead by the time we noticed it. This one was alive.

"No way," I said. "This time you're going to help. Get some gloves and a trash bag."

90 "That's all I'm getting. I'm not getting that mouse out of there."

"Put on the gloves," I ordered. She winced, but put them on. "Reach down," I said. "At an angle, so you get at its middle. Otherwise, if you try to get it by its tail, the tail will break off."

"This is filthy, eh."

"That's why we're here," I said. "To clean up filth. Eh."

She reached down, but would not touch the mouse. I put my hand around her arm and pushed it till her hand made contact. The cries from the mouse were soft, songlike. "Oh, my God," she said. "Oh, my God, ohmigod." She wrestled it out of the grating and turned her head away.

95   "Don't you let it go," I said.

"Where's the food bag? It'll smother itself if I drop it in the food bag. Quick," she said, her head still turned away, her eyes closed. "Lead me to it."

"No. We are not going to smother this mouse. We've got to break its neck."

"You're one heartless bitch."

I wondered how to explain that if death is unavoidable it should be quick and painless. My mother had died slowly. At the hospital, they'd said it was kidney failure, but I knew that, in the end, it was my father. He made her scared to live in her own home, until she was finally driven away from it in an ambulance.

100   "Breaking its neck will save it the pain of smothering," I said. "Breaking its neck is more humane. Take the trash bag and cover it so you won't get any blood on you, then crush."

The loud jets of the steamer had shut off automatically and the dish room grew quiet. Heidi breathed in deeply, then crushed the mouse. She shuddered, disgusted. "Now what?"

"What do you mean, 'Now what?' Throw the little bastard in the trash."

At our third session, I told Dr. Raeburn I didn't mind if he smoked. He sat on the sill of his open window, smoking behind a jungle screen of office plants.

We spent the first ten minutes discussing the Iliad, and whether or not the text actually states that Achilles had been dipped in the River Styx. He said it did, and I said it didn't. After we'd finished with the Iliad, and with my new job in what he called "the scullery," he asked more questions about my parents. I told him nothing. It was none of his business. Instead, I talked about Heidi. I told him about that day in Commons, Heidi's plan to go on a date with Mr. Dick, and the invitation we'd been given to the gay party.

105   "You seem preoccupied by this soirée." He arched his eyebrows at the word "soirée."

"Wouldn't you be?"

"Dina," he said slowly, in a way that made my name seem like a song title, "have you ever had a romantic interest?"

"You want to know if I've ever had a boyfriend?" I said. "Just go ahead and ask if I've ever fucked anybody."

This appeared to surprise him. "I think that you are having a crisis of identity," he said.

110   "Oh, is that what this is?"

His profession had taught him not to roll his eyes. Instead, his exasperation revealed itself with a tiny pursing of his lips, as though he'd just tasted something awful and were trying very hard not to offend the cook.

"It doesn't have to be, as you say, someone you've fucked, it doesn't have to be a boyfriend," he said.

"Well, what are you trying to say? If it's not a boy, then you're saying it's a girl—"

"Calm down. It could be a crush, Dina" He lit one cigarette off another. "A crush on a male teacher, a crush on a dog, for heaven's sake. An interest. Not necessarily a relationship."

115   It was sacrifice time. If I could spend the next half hour talking about some boy, then I'd have given him what he wanted.

So I told him about the boy with the nice shoes.

I was sixteen and had spent the last few coins in my pocket on bus fare to buy groceries. I didn't like going to the Super Fresh two blocks away from my house, plunking government food stamps into the hands of the cashiers.

"There she go reading," one of them once said, even though I was only carrying a book. "Don't your eyes get tired?"

On Greenmount Avenue you could read schoolbooks—that was understandable. The government and your teachers forced you to read them. But anything else was anti-social. It meant you'd rather submit to the words of some white dude than shoot the breeze with your neighbors.

120   I hated those cashiers, and I hated them seeing me with food stamps, so I took the bus and shopped elsewhere. That day, I got off the bus at Govans, and though the neighborhood was black like my own—hair salon after hair salon of airbrushed signs promising arabesque hair styles and inch-long fingernails—the houses were neat and orderly, nothing at all like Greenmount, where every other house had at least one shattered window. The store was well swept, and people quietly checked long grocery lists—no screaming kids, no loud cashier-customer altercations. I got the groceries and left the store.

I decided to walk back. It was a fall day, and I walked for blocks. Then I sensed someone following me. I walked more quickly, my arms around the sack, the leafy lettuce tickling my nose. I didn't want to hold the sack so close that it would break the eggs or squash the hamburger buns, but it was slipping, and as I looked behind a boy my age, maybe older, rushed toward me.

"Let me help you," he said.

"That's all right." I set the bag on the sidewalk. Maybe I saw his face, maybe it was handsome enough, but what I noticed first, splayed on either side of the bag, were his shoes. They were nice shoes, real leather, a stitched design like a widow's peak on each one, or like birds' wings, and for the first time in my life I understood what people meant when they said "wing-tip shoes."

"I watched you carry them groceries out that store, then you look around, like you're lost, but like you liked being lost, then you walk down the sidewalk for blocks and blocks. Rearranging that bag, it almost gone to slip, then hefting it back up again."

125   "Huh, huh," I said.

"And then I passed my own house and was still following you. And then your bag really look like it was gone crash and everything. So I just thought I'd help." He sucked in his bottom lip, as if to keep it from making a smile. "What's your name?" When I told him, he said, "Dina, my name is Cecil." Then he said, " 'D' comes right after 'C.' "

"Yes," I said, "it does, doesn't it."

Then, half question, half statement, he said, "I could carry your groceries for you? And walk you home?"

I stopped the story there. Dr. Raeburn kept looking at me. "Then what happened?"

130   I couldn't tell him the rest: that I had not wanted the boy to walk me home, that I didn't want someone with such nice shoes to see where I lived.

Dr. Raeburn would only have pitied me if I'd told him that I ran down the sidewalk after I told the boy no, that I fell, the bag slipped, and the eggs cracked, their yolks running all over the lettuce. Clear amniotic fluid coated the can of cinnamon rolls. I left the bag there on the sidewalk, the groceries spilled out randomly like cards loosed from a deck. When I returned home, I told my mother that I'd lost the food stamps.

"Lost?" she said. I'd expected her to get angry, I'd wanted her to get angry, but she hadn't. "Lost?" she repeated. Why had I been so clumsy and nervous around a harmless boy? I could have brought the groceries home and washed off the egg yolk, but, instead, I'd just left them there. "Come on," Mama said, snuffing her tears, pulling my arm, trying to get me to join her and start yanking cushions off the couch. "We'll find enough change here. We got to get something for dinner before your father gets back."

We'd already searched the couch for money the previous week, and I knew there'd be nothing now, but I began to push my fingers into the couch's boniest corners, pretending that it was only a matter of time before I'd find some change or a lost watch or an earring. Something pawnable, perhaps.

"What happened next?" Dr. Raeburn asked again. "Did you let the boy walk you home?"

135   "My house was far, so we went to his house instead." Though I was sure Dr. Raeburn knew that I was making this part up, I continued. "We made out on his sofa. He kissed me."

Dr. Raeburn lit his next cigarette like a detective. Cool, suspicious. "How did it feel?"

"You know," I said. "Like a kiss feels. It felt nice. The kiss felt very, very nice."

Raeburn smiled gently, though he seemed unconvinced. When he called time on our session his cigarette had become one long pole of ash. I left his office, walking quickly down the corridor, afraid to look back. It would be like him to trot after me, his navy blazer flapping, just to eke the truth out of me. *You never kissed anyone.* The words slid from my brain, and knotted in my stomach.

When I reached my dorm, I found an old record player blocking my door and a Charles Mingus, LP[2] propped beside it. I carried them inside and then, lying on the floor, I played the Mingus over and over again until I fell asleep. I slept feeling as though Dr. Raeburn had attached electrodes to my head, willing into my mind a dream about my mother. I saw the lemon meringue of her skin, the long bone of her arm as she reached down to clip her toenails. I'd come home from a school trip to an aquarium, and I was explaining the differences between baleen and sperm whales according to the size of their heads, the range of their habitats, their feeding patterns.

140   I awoke remembering the expression on her face after I'd finished my dizzying whale lecture. She looked like a tourist who'd asked for directions to a place she thought was simple enough to get to only to hear a series of hypothetical turns, alleys, one-way streets. Her response was to nod politely at the perilous elaborateness of it all; to nod in the knowledge that she would never be able to get where she wanted to go.

The dishwashers always closed down the dining hall. One night, after everyone else had punched out, Heidi and I took a break, and though I wasn't a smoker, we set two milk crates upside down on the floor and smoked cigarettes.

The dishwashing machines were off, but steam still rose from them like a jungle mist. Outside in the winter air, students were singing carols in their groomed and tailored singing-group voices. The Whiffenpoofs were back in New Haven after a tour around the world, and I guess their return was a huge deal. Heidi and I craned our necks to watch the year's first snow through an open window.

"What are you going to do when you're finished?" Heidi asked. Sexy question marks of smoke drifted up to the windows before vanishing.

"Take a bath."

145   She swatted me with her free hand. "No, silly. Three years from now. When you leave Yale."

"I don't know. Open up a library. Somewhere where no one comes in for books. A library in a desert."

---

[2] Charlie Mingus (1922–1979), bassist, jazz musician, and composer.

She looked at me as though she'd expected this sort of answer and didn't know why she'd asked in the first place.

"What are you going to do?" I asked her.

"Open up a psych clinic. In a desert. And my only patient will be some wacko who runs a library."

150   "Ha," I said. "Whatever you do, don't work in a dish room ever again. You're no good." I got up from the crate. "C'mon. Let's hose the place down."

We put out our cigarettes on the floor, since it was our job to clean it, anyway. We held squirt guns in one hand and used the other to douse the floors with the standard-issue, eye-burning cleaning solution. We hosed the dish room, the kitchen, the serving line, sending the water and crud and suds into the drains. Then we hosed them again so the solution wouldn't eat holes in our shoes as we left. Then I had an idea. I unbuckled my belt.

"What the hell are you doing?" Heidi said.

"Listen, it's too cold to go outside with our uniforms all wet. We could just take a shower right here. There's nobody but us."

"What the fuck, eh?"

155   I let my pants drop, then took off my shirt and panties. I didn't wear a bra, since I didn't have much to fill one. I took off my shoes and hung my clothes on the stepladder.

"You've flipped," Heidi said. "I mean, really, psych-ward flipped."

I soaped up with the liquid hand soap until I felt as glazed as a ham. "Stand back and spray me."

"Oh, my God," she said. I didn't know whether she was confused or delighted, but she picked up the squirt gun and sprayed me. She was laughing. Then she got too close and the water started to sting.

"God damn it!" I said. "That hurt!"

160   "I was wondering what it would take to make you say that."

When all the soap had been rinsed off, I put on my regular clothes and said, "O.K. You're up next."

"No way," she said.

"Yes way"

She started to take off her uniform shirt, then stopped.

165   "What?"

"I'm too fat."

"You goddam right." She always said she was fat. One time, I'd told her that she should shut up about it, that large black women wore their fat like mink coats. "You're big as a house," I said now. "Frozen yogurt may be low in calories but not if you eat five tubs of it. Take your clothes off. I want to get out of here."

She began taking off her uniform, then stood there, hands cupped over her breasts, crouching at the pubic bone.

"Open up," I said, "or we'll never get done."

170   Her hands remained where they were. I threw the bottle of liquid soap at her, and she had to catch it, revealing herself as she did.

I turned on the squirt gun, and she stood there, stiff, arms at her sides, eyes closed, as though awaiting mummification. I began with the water on low, and she turned around in a full circle, hesitantly, letting the droplets from the spray fall on her as if she were submitting to a death by stoning.

When I increased the water pressure, she slipped and fell on the sudsy floor. She stood up and then slipped again. This time she laughed and remained on the floor, rolling around on it as I sprayed.

I think I began to love Heidi that night in the dish room, but who is to say that I hadn't begun to love her the first time I met her? I sprayed her and sprayed her, and she turned over and over like a large beautiful dolphin, lolling about in the sun.

Heidi started sleeping at my place. Sometimes she slept on the floor; sometimes we slept sardinelike, my feet at her head, until she complained that my feet were "taunting" her. When we finally slept head to head, she said, "Much better." She was so close I could smell her toothpaste. "I like your hair," she told me, touching it through the darkness. "You should wear it out more often."

175   "White people always say that about black people's hair. The worse it looks, the more they say they like it."

I'd expected her to disagree, but she kept touching my hair, her hands passing through it till my scalp tingled. When she began to touch the hair around the edge of my face, I felt myself quake. Her fingertips stopped for a moment, as if checking my pulse, then resumed.

"I like how it feels right here. See, mine just starts with the same old texture as the rest of my hair." She found my hand under the blanket and brought it to her hairline. "See," she said.

It was dark. As I touched her hair, it seemed as though I could smell it, too. Not a shampoo smell. Something richer, murkier. A bit dead, but sweet, like the decaying wood of a ship. She guided my hand.

"I see," I said. The record she'd given me was playing in my mind, and I kept trying to shut it off. I could also hear my mother saying that this is what happens when you've been around white people: things get weird. So weird I could hear the stylus etching its way into the flat vinyl of the record. "Listen," I said finally, when the bass and saxes started up. I heard Heidi breathe deeply, but she said nothing.

180   We spent the winter and some of the spring in my room—never hers—missing tests, listening to music, looking out my window to comment on people who wouldn't have given us a second thought. We read books related to none of our classes. I got riled up by "The Autobiography of Malcolm X" and "The Chomsky Reader";[3] Heidi read aloud passages from "The Anxiety of Influence."[4] We guiltily read mysteries and "Clan of the Cave Bear,"[5] then immediately threw them away. Once, we looked up from our books at exactly the same moment, as though trapped at a dinner table with nothing to say. A pleasant trap of silence.

Then one weekend I went back to Baltimore. When I returned, to a sleepy, tree-scented spring, a group of students were holding what was called "Coming Out Day." I watched it from my room.

The m.c. was the sepia boy who'd invited us to that party months back. His speech was strident but still smooth, and peppered with jokes. There was a speech about AIDS, with lots of statistics: nothing that seemed to make "coming out" worth it. Then the women spoke. One girl pronounced herself "out" as casually as if she'd announced the time. Another said nothing at all: she appeared at the microphone accompanied by a woman who began cutting off her waist-length, bleached-blond hair. The woman doing the cutting tossed the shorn hair in every direction as she cut. People were clapping and cheering and catching the locks of hair.

---

[3] Noam Chomsky (1928–   ) is Professor of Linguistics at Massachusetts Institute of Technology and author of works on linguistics, intellectual history, international affairs, and U.S. foreign policy

[4] Work of literary criticism by Harold Bloom, published in 1973.

[5] The first in Jean Auel's series of novels about prehistoric humans, published in 1980.

And then there was Heidi. She was proud that she liked girls, she said when she reached the microphone. She loved them, wanted to sleep with them. She was a dyke, she said repeatedly, stabbing her finger to her chest in case anyone was unsure to whom she was referring. She could not have seen me. I was across the street, three stories up. And yet, when everyone clapped for her, she seemed to be looking straight at me.

Heidi knocked. "Let me in."

185   It was like the first time I met her. The tears, the raw pink of her face.

We hadn't spoken in weeks. Outside, pink-and-white blossoms hung from the Old Campus trees. Students played hackeysack in T-shirts and shorts. Though I was the one who'd broken away after she went up to that podium, I still half expected her to poke her head out a window in Linsly-Chit, or tap on my back in Harkness, or even join me in the Commons dining hall, where I'd asked for my dish-room shift to be transferred. She did none of these.

"Well" I said, "what is it?"

She looked at me. "My mother," she said.

She continued to cry, but it seemed to have grown so silent in my room I wondered if I could hear the numbers change on my digital clock.

190   "When my parents were getting divorced," she said, "my mother bought a car. A used one. An El Dorado. It was filthy. It looked like a huge crushed can coming up the street. She kept trying to clean it out. I mean—"

I nodded and tried to think what to say in the pause she left behind. Finally I said, "We had one of those," though I was sure ours was an Impala.

She looked at me, eyes steely from trying not to cry. "Anyway she'd drive me around in it and although she didn't like me to eat in it, I always did. One day, I was eating cantaloupe slices, spitting the seeds on the floor. Maybe a month later, I saw this little sprout, growing right up from the car floor. I just started laughing and she kept saying what, what? I was laughing and then I saw she was so—"

She didn't finish. So what? So sad? So awful? Heidi looked a me with what seemed to be a renewed vigor. "We could have gotten a better car, eh?"

"It's all right. It's not a big deal," I said.

195   Of course, that was the wrong thing to say. And I really didn't mean it to sound the way it had come out.

I told Dr. Raeburn about Heidi's mother having cancer and how I'd said it wasn't a big deal, though I'd wanted to say exactly the opposite. I meant that I knew what it was like to have a parent die. My mother had died. I knew how eventually one accustoms oneself to the physical world's lack of sympathy: the buses that still run on time, the kids who still play in the street, the clocks that won't stop ticking for the person who's gone.

"You're pretending," Dr. Raeburn said, not sage or professional but a little shocked by the discovery, as if I'd been trying to hide a pack of his cigarettes behind my back.

"I'm pretending?" I shook my head. "All those years of psych grad," I said. "And to tell me *that*?"

"You construct stories about yourself and dish them out—one for you, one for you—" Here he reenacted the process, showing me handing out lies as if they were apples.

200   "Pretending. I believe the professional name for it might be denial," I said. "Are you calling me gay?"

He pursed his lips noncommittally. "No, Dina. I don't think you're gay."

I checked his eyes. I couldn't read them.

"No. Not at all," he said, sounding as if he were telling a subtle joke. "But maybe you'll finally understand."

"Understand what?"

205 "That constantly saying what one doesn't mean accustoms the mouth to meaningless phrases." His eyes narrowed. "Maybe you'll understand that when you need to express something truly significant, your mouth will revert to the insignificant nonsense it knows so well." He looked at me, his hands sputtering in the air in a gesture of defeat. "Who knows?" he asked, with a glib, psychiatric smile I'd never seen before. "Maybe its your survival mechanism. Black living in a white world."

I heard him, but only vaguely. I'd hooked on to that one word, pretending. What Dr. Raeburn would never understand was that pretending was what had got me this far. I remembered the morning of my mother's funeral. I'd been given milk to settle my stomach; I'd pretended it was coffee. I imagined I was drinking coffee elsewhere. Some Arabic-speaking country where the thick coffee served in little cups was so strong it could keep you awake for days. Some Arabic country where I'd sit in a tented café and be more than happy to don a veil.

Heidi wanted me to go with her to the funeral. She'd sent this message through the dean. "We'll pay for your ticket to Vancouver," the dean said.

"What about my ticket back?" I asked. "Maybe the shrink will pay for that."

The dean looked at me as though I were an insect she'd like to squash. "We'll pay for the whole thing. We might even pay for some lessons in manners."

210 So I packed my suitcase and walked from my suicide-single dorm to Heidi's room. A thin wispy girl in ragged cutoffs and a shirt that read "LSBN!" answered the door. A group of short-haired girls in thick black leather jackets, bundled up despite the summer heat, encircled Heidi in a protective fairy ring. They looked at me critically, clearly wondering if Heidi was too fragile for my company.

"You've got our numbers," one said, holding onto Heidi's shoulder. "And Vancouver's got a great gay community."

"Oh God," I said. "She's going to a funeral, not a 'Save the Dykes' rally."

One of the girls stepped in front of me.

"It's O.K., Cynthia," Heidi said. Then she ushered me into her bedroom and closed the door. A suitcase was on her bed, half packed. She folded a polka-dotted T-shirt that was wrong for any occasion. "Why haven't you talked to me?" she said. "Why haven't you talked to me in two months?"

215 "I don't know," I said.

"You don't know," she said, each syllable seeped in sarcasm. "You don't know. Well, I know. You thought I was going to try to sleep with you."

"Try to? We slept together all winter!"

"Smelling your feet is not 'sleeping together.' You've got a lot to learn." She seemed thinner and meaner.

"So tell me," I said. "What can you show me that I need to learn?" But as soon as I said it I somehow knew that she still hadn't slept with anyone.

220 "Am I supposed to come over there and sweep your enraged self into my arms?" I said. "Like in the movies? Is this the part where we're both so mad we kiss each other?"

She shook her head and smiled weakly. "You don't get it," she said. "My mother is dead." She closed her suitcase, clicking shut the old-fashioned locks. "My mother is dead," she said again, this time reminding herself. She set the suitcase upright on the floor and sat on it. She looked like someone waiting for a train.

"Fine," I said. "And she's going to be dead for a long time." Though it sounded stupid, I felt good saying it. As though I had my own locks to click shut.

Heidi went to Vancouver for her mother's funeral. I didn't go. Instead, I went back to Baltimore and moved in with an aunt I barely knew. Every day was the same: I read and smoked outside my aunt's apartment, studying the row of hair salons across the street, where girls in denim cut-offs and tank tops would troop in and come out hours later, a flash of neon nails, coifs the color and sheen of patent leather. And every day I imagined visiting Heidi in Vancouver. Her house would not be large, but it would be clean. Flowery shrubs would line the walks. The Canadian wind would whip us about like pennants. I'd be visiting her at some vague time in the future, deliberately vague, for people like me, who realign past events to suit themselves. In that future time, you always have a chance to catch the groceries before they fall, your words can always be rewound and erased, rewritten and revised.

But once I imagined Heidi visiting me. There would be no psychiatrists or deans. No boys with nice shoes or flip cashiers. Just me in my single room. She would knock on the door and say, "Open up."

DAVID LEAVITT

David Leavitt (1961–) was born in Pittsburgh, Pennsylvania, and received a B.A. in English from Yale University in 1983. He is the author of thirteen books and the editor of two, and he has contributed stories and essays to Esquire, Harper's, The New Yorker, The New York Times Book Review, The New York Times Magazine, *and* The Village Voice. *His novel* The Lost Language of Cranes *(1986) was made into a movie by the BBC in 1991, and* The Page Turner *(1998) was adapted for film as* Food of Love *by Spanish director Ventura Pons (2002). Leavitt published "Territory" in* The New Yorker *in 1982—the first openly gay story to be printed in that magazine. "Territory" was later included in Leavitt's collection of stories,* Family Dancing *(1984), which was nominated for the best fiction award by the National Book Critics Circle (1984) and was a finalist for the PEN/Faulkner Award (1985). Leavitt is known not only for his fictional portrayal of gays and lesbians but also for his depiction of complex family relationships.*

1983

TERRITORY

Neil's mother, Mrs. Campbell, sits on her lawn chair behind a card table outside the food co-op. Every few minutes, as the sun shifts, she moves the chair and table several inches back so as to remain in the shade. It is a hundred degrees outside, and bright white. Each time someone goes in or out of the co-op a gust of air-conditioning flies out of the automatic doors, raising dust from the cement.

Neil stands just inside, poised over a water fountain, and watches her. She has on a sun hat, and a sweatshirt over her tennis dress; her legs are bare, and shiny with cocoa butter. In front of her, propped against the table, a sign proclaims: MOTHERS, FIGHT FOR YOUR CHILDREN'S RIGHTS—SUPPORT A NON-NUCLEAR FUTURE. Women dressed exactly like her pass by, notice the sign, listen to her brief spiel, finger pamphlets, sign petitions or don't sign petitions, never give money. Her weary eyes are masked by dark glasses. In the age of Reagan, she has declared, keeping up the causes of peace and justice is a futile, tiresome, and unrewarding effort; it is therefore an effort fit only for mothers to keep up. The sun bounces off the window glass through which Neil watches her. His own reflection lines up with her profile.

∞

Later that afternoon, Neil spreads himself out alongside the pool and imagines he is being watched by the shirtless Chicano gardener. But the gardener, concentrating on his pruning, is neither seductive nor seducible. On the lawn, his mother's large Airedales—Abigail, Lucille, Fern—amble, sniff, urinate. Occasionally, they accost the gardener, who yells at them in Spanish.

After two years' absence, Neil reasons, he should feel nostalgia, regret, gladness upon returning home. He closes his eyes and tries to muster the proper background music for the cinematic scene of return. His rhapsody, however, is interrupted by the noises of his mother's trio—the scratchy cello, whining violin, stumbling piano—as she and Lillian Havalard and Charlotte Feder plunge through Mozart. The tune is cheery, in a Germanic sort of way, and utterly inappropriate to what Neil is trying to feel. Yet it *is* the music of his adolescence; they have played it for years, bent over the notes, their heads bobbing in silent time to the metronome.

5   It is getting darker. Every few minutes, he must move his towel so as to remain within the narrowing patch of sunlight. In four hours, Wayne, his lover of ten months and the only person he has ever imagined he could spend his life with, will be in this house, where no lover of his has ever set foot. The thought fills him with a sense of grand terror and curiosity. He stretches, tries to feel seductive, desirable. The gardener's shears whack at the ferns; the music above him rushes to a loud, premature conclusion. The women laugh and applaud themselves as they give up for the day. He hears Charlotte Feder's full nasal twang, the voice of a fat woman in a pink pants suit—odd, since she is a scrawny, arthritic old bird, rarely clad in anything other than tennis shorts and a blouse. Lillian is the fat woman in the pink pants suit; her voice is thin and warped by too much crying. Drink in hand, she calls out from the porch, "Hot enough!" and waves. He lifts himself up and nods to her.

The women sit on the porch and chatter; their voices blend with the clink of ice in glasses. They belong to a small circle of ladies all of whom, with the exception of Neil's mother, are widows and divorcées. Lillian's husband left her twenty-two years ago, and sends her a check every month to live on; Charlotte has been divorced twice as long as she was married, and has a daughter serving a long sentence for terrorist acts committed when she was nineteen. Only Neil's mother has a husband, a distant sort of husband, away often on business. He is away on business now. All of them feel betrayed—by husbands, by children, by history.

Neil closes his eyes, tries to hear the words only as sounds. Soon, a new noise accosts him: his mother arguing with the gardener in Spanish. He leans on his elbows and watches them; the syllables are loud, heated, and compressed, and seem on the verge of explosion. But the argument ends happily; they shake hands. The gardener collects his check and walks out the gate without so much as looking at Neil.

He does not know the gardener's name; as his mother has reminded him, he does not know most of what has gone on since he moved away. Her life has gone on, unaffected by his absence. He flinches at his own egoism, the egoism of sons.

"Neil! Did you call the airport to make sure the plane's coming in on time?"

10   "Yes," he shouts to her. "It is."

"Good. Well, I'll have dinner ready when you get back."

"Mom—"

"What?" The word comes out in a weary wail that is more of an answer than a question.

"What's wrong?" he says, forgetting his original question.

15   "Nothing's wrong," she declares in a tone that indicates that everything is wrong. "The dogs have to be fed, dinner has to be made, and I've got people here. Nothing's wrong."

"I hope things will be as comfortable as possible when Wayne gets here."

"Is that a request or a threat?"

"Mom—"

Behind her sunglasses, her eyes are inscrutable. "I'm tired," she says. "It's been a long day. I . . . I'm anxious to meet Wayne. I'm sure he'll be wonderful, and we'll all have a wonderful, wonderful time. I'm sorry. I'm just tired."

20   She heads up the stairs. He suddenly feels an urge to cover himself; his body embarrasses him, as it has in her presence since the day she saw him shirtless and said with delight, "Neil! You're growing hair under your arms!"

Before he can get up, the dogs gather round him and begin to sniff and lick at him. He wriggles to get away from them, but Abigail, the largest and stupidest, straddles his stomach and nuzzles his mouth. He splutters and, laughing, throws her off. "Get away from me, you goddamn dogs," he shouts, and swats at them. They are new dogs, not the dog of his childhood, not dogs he trusts.

He stands, and the dogs circle him, looking up at his face expectantly. He feels renewed terror at the thought that Wayne will be here so soon: Will they sleep in the same room? Will they make love? He has never had sex in his parents' house. How can he be expected to be a lover here, in this place of his childhood, of his earliest shame, in this household of mothers and dogs?

"Dinnertime! Abbylucyferny, Abbylucyferny, dinnertime!" His mother's litany disperses the dogs, and they run for the door.

"Do you realize," he shouts to her, "that no matter how much those dogs love you they'd probably kill you for the leg of lamb in the freezer?"

25   Neil was twelve the first time he recognized in himself something like sexuality. He was lying outside, on the grass, when Rasputin—the dog, long dead, of his childhood—began licking his face. He felt a tingle he did not recognize, pulled off his shirt to give the dog access to more of him. Rasputin's tongue tickled coolly. A wet nose started to sniff down his body, toward his bathing suit. What he felt frightened him, but he couldn't bring himself to push the dog away. Then his mother called out, "Dinner," and Rasputin was gone, more interested in food than in him.

It was the day after Rasputin was put to sleep, years later, that Neil finally stood in the kitchen, his back turned to his parents, and said, with unexpected ease, "I'm a homosexual." The words seemed insufficient, reductive. For years, he had believed his sexuality to be detachable from the essential him, but now he realized that it was part of him. He had the sudden, despairing sensation that though the words had been easy to say, the fact of their having been aired was incurably damning. Only then, for the first time, did he admit that they were true, and he shook and wept in regret for what he would not be for his mother, for having failed her. His father hung back, silent; he was absent for that moment as he was mostly absent—a strong absence. Neil always thought of him sitting on the edge of the bed in his underwear, captivated by something on television. He said, "It's O.K., Neil." But his mother was resolute; her lower lip didn't quaver. She had enormous reserves of strength to which she only gained access at moments like this one. She hugged him from behind, wrapped him in the childhood smells of perfume and brownies, and whispered, "It's O.K., honey." For once, her words seemed as inadequate as his. Neil felt himself shrunk to an embarrassed adolescent, hating her sympathy, not wanting her to touch him. It was the way he would feel from then on whenever he was in her presence—even now, at twenty-three, bringing home his lover to meet her.

All through his childhood, she had packed only the most nutritious lunches, had served on the PTA, had volunteered at the children's library and at his school, had organized a successful campaign to ban a racist history textbook. The day after he told her, she located and got in touch with an organization called the Coalition of Parents of Lesbians and Gays. Within a year, she was president of it. On weekends, she and the other mothers drove their station wagons to San Francisco, set up their card tables in front of the Bulldog Baths, the Liberty Baths, passed out literature to men in leather and denim who were loath to admit they even had mothers. These men, who would habitually do violence to each other, were strangely cowed by the suburban ladies with their informational booklets, and bent their heads. Neil was a sophomore in college then, and lived in San Francisco. She brought him pamphlets detailing the dangers of bathhouses and back rooms, enemas and poppers, wordless sex in alleyways. His excursion into that world had been brief and lamentable, and was over. He winced at the thought that she knew all his sexual secrets, and vowed to move to the East Coast to escape her. It was not very different from the days when she had campaigned for a better playground, or tutored the Hispanic children in the audiovisual room. Those days, as well, he had run away from her concern. Even today, perched in front of the co-op, collecting signatures for nuclear disarmament, she was quintessentially a mother. And if the lot of mothers was to expect nothing in return, was the lot of sons to return nothing?

Driving across the Dumbarton Bridge on his way to the airport, Neil thinks, I have returned nothing; I have simply returned. He wonders if she would have given birth to him had she known what he would grow up to be.

Then he berates himself: Why should he assume himself to be the cause of her sorrow? She has told him that her life is full of secrets. She has changed since he left home—grown thinner, more rigid, harder to hug. She has given up baking, taken up tennis; her skin has browned and tightened. She is no longer the woman who hugged him and kissed him, who said, "As long as you're happy, that's all that's important to us."

30   The flats spread out around him; the bridge floats on purple and green silt, and spongy bay fill, not water at all. Only ten miles north, a whole city has been built on gunk dredged up from the bay.

He arrives at the airport ten minutes early, to discover that the plane has landed twenty minutes early. His first view of Wayne is from behind, by the baggage belt. Wayne looks as he always looks—slightly windblown—and is wearing the ratty leather jacket he was wearing the night they met. Neil sneaks up on him and puts his hands on his shoulders; when Wayne turns around, he looks relieved to see him.

They hug like brothers; only in the safety of Neil's mother's car do they dare to kiss. They recognize each other's smells, and grow comfortable again. "I never imagined I'd actually see you out here," Neil says, "but you're exactly the same here as there."

"It's only been a week."

They kiss again. Neil wants to go to a motel, but Wayne insists on being pragmatic. "We'll be there soon. Don't worry."

35   "We could go to one of the bathhouses in the city and take a room for a couple of aeons," Neil says. "Christ, I'm hard up. I don't even know if we're going to be in the same bedroom."

"Well, if we're not," Wayne says, "we'll sneak around. It'll be romantic."

They cling to each other for a few more minutes, until they realize that people are looking in the car window. Reluctantly, they pull apart. Neil reminds himself that he loves this man, that there is a reason for him to bring this man home.

He takes the scenic route on the way back. The car careens over foothills, through forests, along white four-lane highways high in the mountains. Wayne tells Neil that he sat next to a woman on the plane who was once Marilyn Monroe's psychiatrist's nurse. He slips his foot out of his shoe and nudges Neil's ankle, pulling Neil's sock down with his toe.

"I have to drive," Neil says. "I'm very glad you're here."

40   There is a comfort in the privacy of the car. They have a common fear of walking hand in hand, of publicly showing physical affection, even in the permissive West Seventies of New York—a fear that they have admitted only to one another. They slip through a pass between two hills, and are suddenly in residential Northern California, the land of expensive ranch-style houses.

As they pull into Neil's mother's driveway, the dogs run barking toward the car. "When Wayne opens the door, they jump and lap at him, and he tries to close it again. "Don't worry. Abbylucyferny! Get in the house, damn it!"

His mother descends from the porch. She has changed into a blue flower-print dress, which Neil doesn't recognize. He gets out of the car and half-heartedly chastises the dogs. Crickets chirp in the trees. His mother looks radiant, even beautiful, illuminated by the headlights, surrounded by the now quiet dogs, like a Circe with her slaves. When she walks over to Wayne, offering her hand, and says, "Wayne, I'm Barbara," Neil forgets that she is his mother.

"Good to meet you, Barbara," Wayne says, and reaches out his hand. Craftier than she, he whirls her around to kiss her cheek.

Barbara! He is calling his mother Barbara! Then he remembers that Wayne is five years older than he is. They chat by the open car door, and Neil shrinks back—the embarrassed adolescent, uncomfortable, unwanted.

45   So the dreaded moment passes and he might as well not have been there. At dinner, Wayne keeps the conversation smooth, like a captivated courtier seeking Neil's mother's hand. A faggot son's sodomist—such words spit into Neil's head. She has prepared tiny meatballs with fresh coriander, fettucine with pesto. Wayne talks about the street people in New York; El Salvador is a tragedy; if only Sadat had lived; Phyllis Schlafly—what can you do?

"It's a losing battle," she tells him. "Every day I'm out there with my card table, me and the other mothers, but I tell you, Wayne, it's a losing battle. Sometimes I think us old ladies are the only ones with enough patience to fight."

Occasionally, Neil says something, but his comments seem stupid and clumsy. Wayne continues to call her Barbara. No one under forty has ever called her Barbara as long as Neil can remember. They drink wine; he does not.

Now is the time for drastic action. He contemplates taking Wayne's hand, then checks himself. He has never done anything in her presence to indicate that the sexuality he confessed to five years ago was a reality and not an invention. Even now, he and Wayne might as well be friends, college roommates. Then Wayne, his savior, with a single, sweeping gesture, reaches for his hand, and clasps it, in the midst of a joke he is telling about Saudi Arabians. By the time he is laughing, their hands are joined. Neil's throat contracts; his heart begins to beat violently. He notices his mother's eyes flicker, glance downward; she never breaks the stride of her sentence. The dinner goes on, and every taboo nurtured since childhood falls quietly away.

She removes the dishes. Their hands grow sticky; he cannot tell which fingers are his and which Wayne's. She clears the rest of the table and rounds up the dogs.

50   "Well, boys, I'm very tired, and I've got a long day ahead of me tomorrow, so I think I'll hit the sack. There are extra towels for you in Neil's bathroom, Wayne. Sleep well."

"Good night, Barbara," Wayne calls out. "It's been wonderful meeting you."

They are alone. Now they can disentangle their hands.

"No problem about where we sleep, is there?"

"No," Neil says. "I just can't imagine sleeping with someone in this house."

55   His leg shakes violently. Wayne takes Neil's hand in a firm grasp and hauls him up.

Later that night, they lie outside, under redwood trees, listening to the hysteria of the crickets, the hum of the pool cleaning itself. Redwood leaves prick their skin. They fell in love in bars and apartments, and this is the first time that they have made love outdoors. Neil is not sure he has enjoyed the experience. He kept sensing eyes, imagined that the neighborhood cats were staring at them from behind a fence of brambles. He remembers he once hid in this spot when he and some of the children from the neighborhood were playing sardines, remembers the intoxication of small bodies packed together, the warm breath of suppressed laughter on his neck. "The loser had to go through the spanking machine," he tells Wayne.

"Did you lose often?"

"Most of the time. The spanking machine never really hurt—just a whirl of hands. If you moved fast enough, no one could actually get you. Sometimes, though, late in the afternoon, we'd get naughty. We'd chase each other and pull each other's pants down. That was all. Boys and girls together!"

"Listen to the insects," Wayne says, and closes his eyes.

60 Neil turns to examine Wayne's face, notices a single, small pimple. Their love-making usually begins in a wrestle, a struggle for dominance, and ends with a somewhat confusing loss of identity—as now, when Neil sees a foot on the grass, resting against his leg, and tries to determine if it is his own or Wayne's.

From inside the house, the dogs begin to bark. Their yelps grow into alarmed falsettos. Neil lifts himself up. "I wonder if they smell something," he says.

"Probably just us," says Wayne.

"My mother will wake up. She hates getting waked up."

Lights go on in the house; the door to the porch opens.

65 "What's wrong, Abby? What's wrong?" his mother's voice calls softly.

Wayne clamps his hand over Neil's mouth. "Don't say anything," he whispers.

"I can't just—" Neil begins to say, but Wayne's hand closes over his mouth again. He bites it, and Wayne starts laughing.

"What was that?" Her voice projects into the garden. "Hello?" she says.

The dogs yelp louder. "Abbylucyferny, it's O.K., it's O.K." Her voice is soft and panicked. "Is anyone there?" she asks loudly.

70 The brambles shake. She takes a flashlight, shines it around the garden. Wayne and Neil duck down; the light lands on them and hovers for a few seconds. Then it clicks off and they are in the dark—a new dark, a darker dark, which their eyes must readjust to.

"Let's go to bed, Abbylucyferny," she says gently. Neil and Wayne hear her pad into the house. The dogs whimper as they follow her, and the lights go off.

Once before, Neil and his mother had stared at each other in the glare of bright lights. Four years ago, they stood in the arena created by the headlights of her car, waiting for the train. He was on his way back to San Francisco, where he was marching in a Gay Pride Parade the next day. The train station was next door to the food co-op and shared its parking lot. The co-op, familiar and boring by day, took on a certain mystery in the night. Neil recognized the spot where he had skidded on his bicycle and broken his leg. Through the glass doors, the brightly lit interior of the store glowed, its rows and rows of cans and boxes forming their own horizon, each can illuminated so that even from outside Neil could read the labels. All that was missing was the ladies in tennis dresses and sweatshirts, pushing their carts past bins of nuts and dried fruits.

"Your train is late," his mother said. Her hair fell loosely on her shoulders, and her legs were tanned. Neil looked at her and tried to imagine her in labor with him—bucking and struggling with his birth. He felt then the strange, sexless love for women which through his whole adolescence he had mistaken for heterosexual desire.

A single bright light approached them; it preceded the low, haunting sound of the whistle. Neil kissed his mother, and waved goodbye as he ran to meet the train. It was an old train, with windows tinted a sort of horrible lemon-lime. It stopped only long enough for him to hoist himself on board, and then it was moving again. He hurried to a window, hoping to see her drive off, but the tint of the window made it possible for him to make out only vague patches of light—street lamps, cars, the co-op.

75   He sank into the hard, green seat. The train was almost entirely empty; the only other passenger was a dark-skinned man wearing bluejeans and a leather jacket. He sat directly across the aisle from Neil, next to the window. He had rough skin and a thick mustache. Neil discovered that by pretending to look out the window he could study the man's reflection in the lemon-lime glass. It was only slightly hazy—the quality of a bad photograph. Neil felt his mouth open, felt sleep closing in on him. Hazy red and gold flashes through the glass pulsed in the face of the man in the window, giving the curious impression of muscle spasms. It took Neil a few minutes to realize that the man was staring at him, or, rather, staring at the back of his head—staring at his staring. The man smiled as though to say, I know exactly what you're staring at, and Neil felt the sickening sensation of desire rise in his throat.

Right before they reached the city, the man stood up and sat down in the seat next to Neil's. The man's thigh brushed deliberately against his own. Neil's eyes were watering; he felt sick to his stomach. Taking Neil's hand, the man said, "Why so nervous, honey? Relax."

Neil woke up the next morning with the taste of ashes in his mouth. He was lying on the floor, without blankets or sheets or pillows. Instinctively, he reached for his pants, and as he pulled them on came face to face with the man from the train. His name was Luis; he turned out to be a dog groomer. His apartment smelled of dog.

"Why such a hurry?" Luis said.

"The parade. The Gay Pride Parade. I'm meeting some friends to march."

80   "I'll come with you," Luis said. "I think I'm too old for these things, but why not?"

Neil did not want Luis to come with him, but he found it impossible to say so. Luis looked older by day, more likely to carry diseases. He dressed again in a torn T-shirt, leather jacket, bluejeans. "It's my everyday apparel," he said, and laughed. Neil buttoned his pants, aware that they had been washed by his mother the day before. Luis possessed the peculiar combination of hypermasculinity and effeminacy which exemplifies faggotry. Neil wanted to be rid of him, but Luis's mark was on him, he could see that much. They would become lovers whether Neil liked it or not.

They joined the parade midway. Neil hoped he wouldn't meet anyone he knew; he did not want to have to explain Luis, who clung to him. The parade was full of shirtless men with oiled, muscular shoulders. Neil's back ached. There were floats carrying garishly dressed prom queens and cheerleaders, some with beards, some actually looking like women. Luis said, "It makes me proud, makes me glad to be what I am." Neil supposed that by darting into the crowd ahead of him he might be able to lose Luis forever, but he found it difficult to let him go; the prospect of being alone seemed unbearable.

Neil was startled to see his mother watching the parade, holding up a sign. She was with the Coalition of Parents of Lesbians and Gays; they had posted a huge banner on the wall behind them proclaiming: OUR SONS AND DAUGHTERS, WE ARE PROUD OF YOU. She spotted him; she waved, and jumped up and down.

"Who's that woman?" Luis asked.

85   "My mother. I should go say hello to her."

"O.K.," Luis said. He followed Neil to the side of the parade. Neil kissed his mother. Luis took off his shirt, wiped his face with it, smiled.

"I'm glad you came," Neil said.

"I wouldn't have missed it, Neil. I wanted to show you I cared."

He smiled, and kissed her again. He showed no intention of introducing Luis, so Luis introduced himself.

90   "Hello, Luis," Mrs. Campbell said. Neil looked away. Luis shook her hand, and Neil wanted to warn his mother to wash it, warned himself to check with a V.D. clinic first thing Monday.

"Neil, this is Carmen Bologna, another one of the mothers," Mrs. Campbell said. She introduced him to a fat Italian woman with flushed cheeks, and hair arranged in the shape of a clamshell.

"Good to meet you, Neil, good to meet you," said Carmen Bologna. "You know my son, Michael? I'm so proud of Michael! He's doing so well now. I'm proud of him, proud to be his mother I am, and your mother's proud, too!"

The woman smiled at him, and Neil could think of nothing to say but "Thank you." He looked uncomfortably toward his mother, who stood listening to Luis. It occurred to him that the worst period of his life was probably about to begin and he had no way to stop it.

A group of drag queens ambled over to where the mothers were standing. "Michael! Michael!" shouted Carmen Bologna, and embraced a sticklike man wrapped in green satin. Michael's eyes were heavily dosed with green eye-shadow, and his lips were painted pink.

95   Neil turned and saw his mother staring, her mouth open. He marched over to where Luis was standing, and they moved back into the parade. He turned and waved to her. She waved back; he saw pain in her face, and then, briefly, regret. That day, he felt she would have traded him for any other son. Later, she said to him, "Carmen Bologna really was proud, and, speaking as a mother, let me tell you, you have to be brave to feel such pride."

Neil was never proud. It took him a year to dump Luis, another year to leave California. The sick taste of ashes was still in his mouth. On the plane, he envisioned his mother sitting alone in the dark, smoking. She did not leave his mind until he was circling New York, staring down at the dawn rising over Queens. The song playing in his earphones would remain hovering on the edges of his memory, always associated with her absence. After collecting his baggage, he took a bus into the city. Boys were selling newspapers in the middle of highways, through the windows of stopped cars. It was seven in the morning when he reached Manhattan. He stood for ten minutes on East Thirty-fourth Street, breathed the cold air, and felt bubbles rising in his blood.

Neil got a job as a paralegal—a temporary job, he told himself. When he met Wayne a year later, the sensations of that first morning returned to him. They'd been up all night, and at six they walked across the park to Wayne's apartment with the nervous, deliberate gait of people aching to make love for the first time. Joggers ran by with their dogs. None of them knew what Wayne and he were about to do, and the secrecy excited him. His mother came to mind, and the song, and the whirling vision of Queens coming alive below him. His breath solidified into clouds, and he felt happier than he had ever felt before in his life.

The second day of Wayne's visit, he and Neil go with Mrs. Campbell to pick up the dogs at the dog parlor. The grooming establishment is decorated with pink ribbons and photographs of the owner's champion pit bulls. A fat, middle-aged woman appears from the back, leading the newly trimmed and fluffed Abigail, Lucille, and Fern by three leashes. The dogs struggle frantically when they see Neil's mother, tangling the woman up in their leashes. "Ladies, behave!" Mrs. Campbell commands, and collects the dogs. She gives Fern to Neil and Abigail to Wayne. In the car on the way back, Abigail begins pawing to get on Wayne's lap.

"Just push her off," Mrs. Campbell says. "She knows she's not supposed to do that."

100   "You never groomed Rasputin," Neil complains.

"Rasputin was a mutt."

"Rasputin was a beautiful dog, even if he did smell."

"Do you remember when you were a little kid, Neil, you used to make Rasputin dance with you? Once you tried to dress him up in one of my blouses."

"I don't remember that," Neil says.

105   "Yes. I remember," says Mrs. Campbell. "Then you tried to organize a dog beauty contest in the neighborhood. You wanted to have runners-up—everything."

"A dog beauty contest?" Wayne says.

"Mother, do we have to—"

"I think it's a mother's privilege to embarrass her son," Mrs. Campbell says, and smiles.

When they are about to pull into the driveway, Wayne starts screaming, and pushes Abigail off his lap. "Oh, my God!" he says. "The dog just pissed all over me."

110   Neil turns around and sees a puddle seeping into Wayne's slacks. He suppresses his laughter, and Mrs. Campbell hands him a rag.

"I'm sorry, Wayne," she says. "It goes with the territory."

"This is really disgusting," Wayne says, swatting at himself with the rag.

Neil keeps his eyes on his own reflection in the rearview mirror and smiles.

At home, while Wayne cleans himself in the bathroom, Neil watches his mother cook lunch—Japanese noodles in soup. "When you went off to college," she says, "I went to the grocery store. I was going to buy you ramen noodles, and I suddenly realized you weren't going to be around to eat them. I started crying right then, blubbering like an idiot."

115   Neil clenches his fists inside his pockets. She has a way of telling him little sad stories when he doesn't want to hear them—stories of dolls broken by her brothers, lunches stolen by neighborhood boys on the way to school. Now he has joined the ranks of male children who have made her cry.

"Mama, I'm sorry," he says.

She is bent over the noodles, which steam in her face. "I didn't want to say anything in front of Wayne, but I wish you had answered me last night. I was very frightened—and worried."

"I'm sorry," he says, but it's not convincing. His fingers prickle. He senses a great sorrow about to be born.

"I lead a quiet life," she says. "I don't want to be a disciplinarian. I just don't have the energy for these—shenanigans. Please don't frighten me that way again."

120   "If you were so upset, why didn't you say something?"

"I'd rather not discuss it. I lead a quiet life. I'm not used to getting woken up late at night. I'm not used—"

"To my having a lover?"

"No, I'm not used to having other people around, that's all. Wayne is charming. A wonderful young man."

"He likes you, too."

125   "I'm sure we'll get along fine."

She scoops the steaming noodles into ceramic bowls. Wayne returns, wearing shorts. His white, hairy legs are a shocking contrast to hers, which are brown and sleek.

"I'll wash those pants, Wayne," Mrs. Campbell says. "I have a special detergent that'll take out the stain."

She gives Neil a look to indicate that the subject should be dropped. He looks at Wayne, looks at his mother; his initial embarrassment gives way to a fierce pride—the arrogance of mastery. He is glad his mother knows that he is desired, glad it makes her flinch.

Later, he steps into the back yard; the gardener is back, whacking at the bushes with his shears. Neil walks by him in his bathing suit, imagining he is on parade.

130   That afternoon, he finds his mother's daily list on the kitchen table:

> TUESDAY
> 7:00—breakfast
> Take dogs to groomer
> Groceries(?)

Campaign against Draft—4–7

Buy underwear
Trios—2:00
Spaghetti
Fruit
Asparagus if sale
Peanuts
Milk

Doctor's Appointment (make)
Write Cranston/Hayakawa
re disarmament

Handi-Wraps
Mozart
Abigail
Top Ramen
Pedro

Her desk and trash can are full of such lists; he remembers them from the earliest days of his childhood. He had learned to read from them. In his own life, too, there have been endless lists—covered with check marks and arrows, at least one item always spilling over onto the next day's agenda. From September to November, "Buy plane ticket for Christmas" floated from list to list to list.

The last item puzzles him: Pedro. Pedro must be the gardener. He observes the accretion of names, the arbitrary specifics that give a sense of his mother's life. He could make a list of his own selves: the child, the adolescent, the promiscuous faggot son, and finally the good son, settled, relatively successful. But the divisions wouldn't work; he is today and will always be the child being licked by the dog, the boy on the floor with Luis; he will still be everything he is ashamed of. The other lists—the lists of things done and undone—tell their own truth: that his life is measured more properly in objects than in stages. He knows himself as "jump rope," "book," "sunglasses," "underwear."

"Tell me about your family, Wayne," Mrs. Campbell says that night, as they drive toward town. They are going to see an Esther Williams movie at the local revival house: an underwater musical, populated by mermaids, underwater Rockettes.

"My father was a lawyer," Wayne says. "He had an office in Queens, with a neon sign. I think he's probably the only lawyer in the world who had a neon sign. Anyway, he died when I was ten. My mother never remarried. She lives in Queens. Her great claim to fame is that when she was twenty-two she went on 'The $64,000 Question.' Her category was mystery novels. She made it to sixteen thousand before she got tripped up."

"When I was about ten, I wanted you to go on 'Jeopardy,'" Neil says to his mother. "You really should have, you know. You would have won."

"You certainly loved 'Jeopardy,'" Mrs. Campbell says. "You used to watch it during dinner. Wayne, does your mother work?"

"No," he says. "She lives off investments."

"You're both only children," Mrs. Campbell says. Neil wonders if she is ruminating on the possible connection between that coincidence and their "alternative life style."

The movie theater is nearly empty. Neil sits between Wayne and his mother. There are pillows on the floor at the front of the theater, and a cat is prowling over them. It casts a

135

monstrous shadow every now and then on the screen, disturbing the sedative effect of water ballet. Like a teenager, Neil cautiously reaches his arm around Wayne's shoulder. Wayne takes his hand immediately. Next to them, Neil's mother breathes in, out, in, out. Neil timorously moves his other arm and lifts it behind his mother's neck. He does not look at her, but he can tell from her breathing that she senses what he is doing. Slowly, carefully, he lets his hand drop on her shoulder; it twitches spasmodically, and he jumps, as if he had received an electric shock. His mother's quiet breathing is broken by a gasp; even Wayne notices. A sudden brightness on the screen illuminates the panic in her eyes, Neil's arm frozen above her, about to fall again. Slowly, he lowers his arm until his fingertips touch her skin, the fabric of her dress. He has gone too far to go back now; they are all too far.

Wayne and Mrs. Campbell sink into their seats, but Neil remains stiff, holding up his arms, which rest on nothing. The movie ends, and they go on sitting just like that.

140   "I'm old," Mrs. Campbell says later, as they drive back home. "I remember when those films were new. Your father and I went to one on our first date. I loved them, because I could pretend that those women underwater were flying—they were so graceful. They really took advantage of Technicolor in those days. Color was something to appreciate. You can't know what it was like to see a color movie for the first time, after years of black-and-white. It's like trying to explain the surprise of snow to an East Coaster. Very little is new anymore, I fear."

Neil would like to tell her about his own nostalgia, but how can he explain that all of it revolves around her? The idea of her life before he was born pleases him. "Tell Wayne how you used to look like Esther Williams," he asks her.

She blushes. "I was told I looked like Esther Williams, but really more like Gene Tierney," she says. "Not beautiful, but interesting. I like to think I had a certain magnetism."

"You still do," Wayne says, and instantly recognizes the wrongness of his comment. Silence and a nervous laugh indicate that he has not yet mastered the family vocabulary.

When they get home, the night is once again full of the sound of crickets. Mrs. Campbell picks up a flashlight and calls the dogs. "Abbylucyferny, Abbylucyferny," she shouts, and the dogs amble from their various corners. She pushes them out the door to the back yard and follows them. Neil follows her. Wayne follows Neil, but hovers on the porch. Neil walks behind her as she tramps through the garden. She holds out her flashlight, and snails slide from behind bushes, from under rocks, to where she stands. When the snails become visible, she crushes them underfoot. They make a wet, cracking noise, like eggs being broken.

145   "Nights like this," she says, "I think of children without pants on, in hot South American countries. I have nightmares about tanks rolling down our street."

"The weather's never like this in New York," Neil says. "When it's hot, it's humid and sticky. You don't want to go outdoors."

"I could never live anywhere else but here. I think I'd die. I'm too used to the climate."

"Don't be silly."

"No, I mean it," she says. "I have adjusted too well to the weather."

150   The dogs bark and howl by the fence. "A cat, I suspect," she says. She aims her flashlight at a rock, and more snails emerge—uncountable numbers, too stupid to have learned not to trust light.

"I know what you were doing at the movie," she says.

"What?"

"I know what you were doing."

"What? I put my arm around you."

155   "I'm sorry, Neil," she says. "I can only take so much. Just so much."

"What do you mean?" he says. "I was only trying to show affection."

"Oh, affection—I know about affection."

He looks up at the porch, sees Wayne moving toward the door, trying not to listen.

"What do you mean?" Neil says to her.

160   She puts down the flashlight and wraps her arms around herself. "I remember when you were a little boy," she says. "I remember, and I have to stop remembering. I wanted you to grow up happy. And I'm very tolerant, very understanding. But I can only take so much."

His heart seems to have risen into his throat. "Mother," he says, "I think you know my life isn't your fault. But for God's sake, don't say that your life is my fault."

"It's not a question of fault," she says. She extracts a Kleenex from her pocket and blows her nose. "I'm sorry, Neil. I guess I'm just an old woman with too much on her mind and not enough to do." She laughs halfheartedly. "Don't worry. Don't say anything," she says. "Abbylucyferny, Abbylucyferny, time for bed!"

He watches her as she walks toward the porch, silent and regal. There is the pad of feet, the clinking of dog tags as the dogs run for the house.

He was twelve the first time she saw him march in a parade. He played the tuba, and as his elementary-school band lumbered down the streets of their then small town she stood on the sidelines and waved. Afterward, she had taken him out for ice cream. He spilled some on his red uniform, and she swiped at it with a napkin. She had been there for him that day, as well as years later, at that more memorable parade; she had been there for him every day.

165   Somewhere over Iowa, a week later, Neil remembers this scene, remembers other days, when he would find her sitting in the dark, crying. She had to take time out of her own private sorrow to appease his anxiety. "It was part of it," she told him later. "Part of being a mother."

"The scariest thing in the world is the thought that you could unknowingly ruin someone's life," Neil tells Wayne. "Or even change someone's life. I hate the thought of having such control. I'd make a rotten mother."

"You're crazy," Wayne says, "You have this great mother, and all you do is complain. I know people whose mothers have disowned them."

"Guilt goes with the territory," Neil says.

"Why?" Wayne asks, perfectly seriously.

170   Neil doesn't answer. He lies back in his seat, closes his eyes, imagines he grew up in a house in the mountains of Colorado, surrounded by snow—endless white snow on hills. No flat places, and no trees; just white hills. Every time he has flown away, she has come into his mind, usually sitting alone in the dark, smoking. Today she is outside at dusk, skimming leaves from the pool.

"I want to get a dog," Neil says.

Wayne laughs. "In the city? It'd suffocate."

The hum of the airplane is druglike, dazing. "I want to stay with you a long time," Neil says.

"I know." Imperceptibly, Wayne takes his hand.

175   "It's very hot there in the summer, too. You know, I'm not thinking about my mother now."

"It's O.K."

For a moment, Neil wonders what the stewardess or the old woman on the way to the bathroom will think, but then he laughs and relaxes.

Later, the plane makes a slow circle over New York City, and on it two men hold hands, eyes closed, and breathe in unison.

C. P. Cavafy

Constantine Peter Cavafy (1863–1933) was born in Alexandria, Egypt. Cavafy spent his child-hood in England and moved to Greece in his late teens before returning to Alexandria. Al-though as an adult Cavafy lived in Egypt, he was born to Greek parents and is considered to be a Greek poet. Besides writing poetry, Cavafy worked as a journalist, on the Egyptian Stock Exchange, and for the Ministry of Public Works in Alexandria. During his life he published sev-enteen volumes of poetry, most of which have been translated into English, including Four-teen Poems *(1966),* Passions and Ancient Days *(1971), and* The Essential Cavafy *(1995). Cavafy is considered to be one of the predominant Greek poets of the twentieth century, and his gay love poems are especially haunting because of the illicit nature of the relationships depicted.*

1918

THE NEXT TABLE

He must be barely twenty-two years old—
yet I'm certain just about that long ago
I enjoyed the very same body.

It isn't erotic fever at all.
5   And I came into the casino only a few minutes ago,
so I haven't had time to drink very much.
I enjoyed that very same body.

And if I don't remember where, this one lapse of memory doesn't mean
   a thing.

There, now that he's sitting down at the next table,
10   I recognize every motion he makes—and under his clothes
I see again the limbs that I loved, naked.

1904

ON THE STAIRS

As I was going down those ill-famed stairs
you were coming in the door, and for a second
I saw your unfamiliar face and you saw mine.
Then I hid so you wouldn't see me again,
5   and you hurried past me, hiding your face,
and slipped inside the ill-famed house
where you couldn't have found pleasure any more than I did.

And yet the love you were looking for, I had to give you;
the love I was looking for—so your tired, knowing eyes implied—
10   you had to give me.
Our bodies sensed and sought each other;
our blood and skin understood.

But we both hid ourselves, flustered.

DAVID HENRY HWANG

David Henry Hwang (1957–   ) was born in Los Angeles, California, and educated at Stanford and Yale Universities. Hwang has written close to twenty plays and has received awards for many of them, including an Obie Award for his first play, F.O.B. (1980), and for Golden Child *(1998) and the Antoinette Perry "Tony" Award, the Outer Critics Circle Award, the John Gassner Award, the Drama Desk Award, and the Pulitzer Prize nomination for* M Butterfly *(1989). Although Hwang considers his ethnicity to be as insignificant as his hair color, many of his plays focus on the experiences of Asians living in the United States. As is clear in* M But- terfly *(1989), Hwang's work also examines Western attitudes toward gender and culture.*

1986

M BUTTERFLY

The Characters

Rene Gallimard
Song Liling
Marc/Man No. 2/Consul Sharpless
Renee/Woman at Party/Pinup Girl
Comrade Chin/Suzuki/Shu-Fang
Helga
Toulon/Man No. 1/Judge
Dancers

Time and Place

The action of the play takes place in a Paris prison in the present, and, in recall, during the decade 1960–1970 in Beijing, and from 1966 to the present in Paris.

Playwright's Notes

A former French diplomat and a Chinese opera singer have been sentenced to six years in jail for spying for China after a two-day trial that traced a story of clandestine love and mistaken sexual identity. . . .

    Mr. Boursicot was accused of passing information to China after he fell in love with Mr. Shi, whom he believed for twenty years to be a woman.

—The New York Times, May 11, 1986

This play was suggested by international newspaper accounts of a recent espionage trial. For purposes of dramatization, names have been changed, characters created, and incidents devised or altered, and this play does not purport to be a factual record of real events or real people.

> *I could escape this feeling*
> *With my China girl . . .*
> *—David Bowie & Iggy Pop*

Act One
Scene 1
M. Gallimard's prison cell. Paris. 1988.

    Lights fade up to reveal Rene Gallimard, sixty-five, in a prison cell. He wears a comfort- able bathrobe and looks old and tired. The sparsely furnished cell contains a wooden crate, upon which sits a hot plate with a kettle and a portable tape recorder. Gallimard sits on the crate staring at the recorder, a sad smile on his face.

Upstage Song, who appears as a beautiful woman in traditional Chinese garb, dances a traditional piece from the Peking Opera, surrounded by the percussive clatter of Chinese music.

Then, slowly, lights and sound cross-fade; the Chinese opera music dissolves into a Western opera, the "Love Duet" from Puccini's Madame Butterfly. *Song continues dancing, now to the Western accompaniment. Though her movements are the same, the difference in music now gives them a balletic quality.*

Gallimard rises, and turns upstage towards the figure of Song, who dances without acknowledging him.

Gallimard: Butterfly, Butterfly . . .

He forces himself to turn away, as the image of Song fades out, and talks to us.

Gallimard: The limits of my cell are as such: four-and-a-half meters by five. There's one window against the far wall; a door, very strong, to protect me from autograph hounds. I'm responsible for the tape recorder, the hot plate, and this charming coffee table.

When I want to eat, I'm marched off to the dining room—hot, steaming slop appears on my plate. When I want to sleep, the light bulb turns itself off—the work of fairies. It's an enchanted space I occupy. The French—we know how to run a prison.

But, to be honest, I'm not treated like an ordinary prisoner. Why? Because I'm a celebrity. You see, I make people laugh.

I never dreamed this day would arrive. I've never been considered witty or clever. In fact, as a young boy, in an informal poll among my grammar school classmates, I was voted "least likely to be invited to a party." It's a title I managed to hold on to for many years. Despite some stiff competition.

But now, how the tables turn! Look at me: the life of every social function in Paris. Paris? Why be modest: My fame has spread to Amsterdam, London, New York. Listen to them! In the world's smartest parlors. I'm the one who lifts their spirits!

With a flourish, Gallimard directs our attention to another part of the stage.

Scene 2
A party, 1988.

Lights go up on a chic-looking parlor, where a well-dressed trio, two men and one woman, make conversation. Gallimard also remains lit; he observes them from his cell.

Woman: And what of Gallimard?
Man 1: Gallimard?
Man 2: Gallimard!
Gallimard *(to us):* You see? They're all determined to say my name, as if it were some new dance.
5 **Woman:** He still claims not to believe the truth.
Man 1: What? Still? Even since the trial?
Woman: Yes. Isn't it mad?
Man 2 *(laughing):* He says . . . it was dark . . . and she was very modest!

The trio break into laughter.

Man 1: So—what? He never touched her with his hands?

10 **Man 2:** Perhaps he did, and simply misidentified the equipment. A compelling case for sex
education in the schools.

Woman: To protect the National Security—the Church can't argue with that.

Man 1: That's impossible! How could he not know?

Man 2: Simple ignorance.

Man 1: For twenty years?

15 **Man 2:** Time flies when you're being stupid.

Woman: Well, I thought the French were ladies' men.

Man 2: It seems Monsieur Gallimard was overly anxious to live up to his national reputation.

Woman: Well, he's not very good-looking.

Man 1: No, he's not.

20 **Man 2:** Certainly not.

Woman: Actually, I feel sorry for him.

Man 2: A toast! To Monsieur Gallimard!

Woman: Yes! To Gallimard!

Man 1: To Gallimard!

25 **Man 2:** *Vive la différence!*

They toast, laughing. Lights down on them.

Scene 3

M. Gallimard's cell.

Gallimard *(smiling):* You see? They toast me. I've become a patron saint of the socially
inept. Can they really be so foolish? Men like that—they should be scratching at my
door, begging to learn my secrets! For I, Rene Gallimard, you see, I have known, and
been loved by . . . the Perfect Woman.

   Alone in this cell, I sit night after night, watching our story play through my
head, always searching for a new ending, one which redeems my honor, where she
returns at last to my arms. And I imagine you—my ideal audience—who come to
understand and even, perhaps just a little, to envy me.

*He turns on his tape recorder. Over the house speakers, we hear the opening phrases of
Madame Butterfly.*

Gallimard: In order for you to understand what I did and why, I must introduce you to my
favorite opera: *Madame Butterfly*. By Giacomo Puccini. First produced at La Scala,
Milan, in 1904, it is now beloved throughout the Western world.

As Gallimard describes the opera, the tape segues in and out to sections he may be describing.

Gallimard: And why not? Its heroine, Cio-Cio-San, also known as Butterfly, is a feminine
ideal, beautiful and brave. And its hero, the man for whom she gives up everything,
is—(*He pulls out a naval officer's cap from under his crate, pops it on his head, and struts
about.*)—not very good-looking, not too bright, and pretty much a wimp: Benjamin
Franklin Pinkerton of the U.S. Navy. As the curtain rises, he's just closed on two great
bargains: one on a house, the other on a woman—call it a package deal.

   Pinkerton purchased the rights to Butterfly for one hundred yen—in modern
currency, equivalent to about . . . sixty-six cents. So, he's feeling pretty pleased with
himself as Sharpless, the American consul, arrives to witness the marriage.

Marc, wearing an official cap to designate Sharpless, enters and plays the character.

Sharpless/Marc: Pinkerton!

Pinkerton/Gallimard: Sharpless! How's it hangin'? It's a great day, just great. Between my house, my wife, and the rickshaw ride in from town, I've saved nineteen cents just this morning.

Sharpless: Wonderful. I can see the inscription on your tombstone already: "I saved a dollar, here I lie." *(He looks around.)* Nice house.

5 **Pinkerton:** It's artistic. Artistic, don't you think? Like the way the shoji screens slide open to reveal the wet bar and disco mirror ball? Classy, huh? Great for impressing the chicks.

Sharpless: "Chicks"? Pinkerton, you're going to be a married man!

Pinkerton: Well, sort of.

Sharpless: What do you mean?

Pinkerton: This country—Sharpless, it is okay. You got all these geisha girls running around—

10 **Sharpless:** I know! I live here!

Pinkerton: Then, you know the marriage laws, right? I split for one month, it's annulled!

Sharpless: Leave it to you to read the fine print. Who's the lucky girl?

Pinkerton: Cio-Cio-San. Her friends call her Butterfly. Sharpless, she eats out of my hand!

Sharpless: She's probably very hungry.

15 **Pinkerton:** Not like American girls. It's true what they say about Oriental girls. They want to be treated bad!

Sharpless: Oh, please!

Pinkerton: It's true!

Sharpless: Are you serious about this girl?

Pinkerton: I'm marrying her, aren't I?

20 **Sharpless:** Yes—with generous trade-in terms.

Pinkerton: When I leave, she'll know what it's like to have loved a real man. And I'll even buy her a few nylons.

Sharpless: You aren't planning to take her with you?

Pinkerton: Huh? Where?

Sharpless: Home!

25 **Pinkerton:** You mean, America? Are you crazy? Can you see her trying to buy rice in St. Louis?

Sharpless: So, you're not serious.

Pause.

Pinkerton/Gallimard *(as Pinkerton):* Consul, I am a sailor in port. *(As Gallimard.)* They then proceed to sing the famous duet, "The Whole World Over."

The duet plays on the speakers. Gallimard, as Pinkerton, lip-syncs his lines from the opera.

Gallimard: To give a rough translation: "The whole world over, the Yankee travels, casting his anchor wherever he wants. Life's not worth living unless he can win the hearts of the fairest maidens, then hotfoot it off the premises ASAP." *(He turns towards Marc.)* In the preceding scene, I played Pinkerton, the womanizing cad, and my friend Marc from school . . . *(Marc bows grandly for our benefit.)* played Sharpless, the sensitive soul of reason. In life, however, our positions were usually—no, always—reversed.

Scene 4
École Nationale.[1] Aix-en-Provence. 1947.

---

[1] **École Nationale:** National School.

Gallimard: No, Marc, I think I'd rather stay home.

Marc: Are you crazy?! We are going to Dad's condo in Marseilles! You know what happened last time?

Gallimard: Of course I do.

Marc: Of course you don't! You never know. . . . They stripped, Rene!

5 **Gallimard:** Who stripped?

Marc. The girls!

Gallimard: Girls? Who said anything about girls?

Marc: Rene, we're a buncha university guys goin' up to the woods. What are we gonna do—talk philosophy?

Gallimard: What girls? Where do you get them?

10 **Marc:** Who cares? The point is, they come. On trucks. Packed in like sardines. The back flips open, babes hop out, we're ready to roll.

Gallimard: You mean, they just—?

Marc: Before you know it, every last one of them—they're stripped and splashing around my pool. There's no moon out, they can't see what's going on, their boobs are flapping, right? You close your eyes, reach out—it's grab bag, get it? Doesn't matter whose ass is between whose legs, whose teeth are sinking into who. You're just in there, going at it, eyes closed, on and on for as long as you can stand. (*Pause.*) Some fun, huh?

Gallimard: What happens in the morning?

Marc: In the morning, you're ready to talk some philosophy. (*Beat.*) So how 'bout it?

15 **Gallimard:** Marc, I can't . . . I'm afraid they'll say no—the girls. So I never ask.

Marc: You don't have to ask! That's the beauty—don't you see? They don't have to say yes. It's perfect for a guy like you, really.

Gallimard: You go ahead . . . I may come later.

Marc: Hey, Rene—it doesn't matter that you're clumsy and got zits—they're not looking!

Gallimard: Thank you very much.

20 **Marc:** Wimp.

Marc walks over to the other side of the stage, and starts waving and smiling at women in the audience.

Gallimard (*to us*): We now return to my version of *Madame Butterfly* and the events leading to my recent conviction for treason.

Gallimard notices Marc making lewd gestures.

Gallimard: Marc, what are you doing?

Marc: Huh? (*Sotto voce.*) Rene, there're a lotta great babes out there. They're probably lookin' at me and thinking, "What a dangerous guy."

Gallimard: Yes—how could they help but be impressed by your cool sophistication?

Gallimard pops the Sharpless cap on Marc's head, and points him offstage. Marc exits, leering.

Scene 5

M. Gallimard's cell.

Gallimard: Next, Butterfly makes her entrance. We learn her age—fifteen . . . but very mature for her years.

Lights come up on the area where we saw Song dancing at the top of the play. She appears there again, now dressed as Madame Butterfly, moving to the "Love Duet." Gallimard turns upstage slightly to watch, transfixed.

Gallimard: But as she glides past him, beautiful, laughing softly behind her fan, don't we who are men sigh with hope? We, who are not handsome, nor brave, nor powerful, yet somehow believe, like Pinkerton, that we deserve a Butterfly. She arrives with all her possessions in the folds of her sleeves, lays them all out, for her man to do with as he pleases. Even her life itself—she bows her head as she whispers that she's not even worth the hundred yen he paid for her. He's already given too much, when we know he's really had to give nothing at all.

Music and lights on Song out. Gallimard sits at his crate.

Gallimard: In real life, women who put their total worth at less than sixty-six cents are quite hard to find. The closest we come is in the pages of these magazines. (*He reaches into his crate, pulls out a stack of girlie magazines, and begins flipping through them.*) Quite a necessity in prison. For three or four dollars, you get seven or eight women.

I first discovered these magazines at my uncle's house. One day, as a boy of twelve. The first time I saw them in his closet . . . all lined up—my body shook. Not with lust—no, with power. Here were women—a shelfful—who would do exactly as I wanted.

The "Love Duet" creeps in over the speakers. Special comes up, revealing, not Song this time, but a pinup girl in a sexy negligee, her back to us. Gallimard turns upstage and looks at her.

Girl: I know you're watching me.
Gallimard: My throat . . . it's dry.
Girl: I leave my blinds open every night before I go to bed.
5 **Gallimard:** I can't move.
Girl: I leave my blinds open and the lights on.
Gallimard: I'm shaking. My skin is hot, but my penis is soft. Why?
Girl: I stand in front of the window.
Gallimard: What is she going to do?
10 **Girl:** I toss my hair, and I let my lips part . . . barely.
Gallimard: I shouldn't be seeing this. It's so dirty. I'm so bad.
Girl: Then, slowly, I lift off my nightdress.
Gallimard: Oh, god. I can't believe it. I can't—
Girl: I toss it to the ground.
15 **Gallimard:** Now, she's going to walk away. She's going to—
Girl: I stand there, in the light, displaying myself.
Gallimard: No. She's—why is she naked?
Girl: To you.
Gallimard: In front of a window? This is wrong. No—
20 **Girl:** Without shame.
Gallimard: No, she must . . . like it.
Girl: I like it.
Gallimard: She . . . she wants me to see.
Girl: I want you to see.
25 **Gallimard:** I can't believe it! She's getting excited!
Girl: I can't see you. You can do whatever you want.
Gallimard: I can't do a thing. Why?
Girl: What would you like me to do . . . next?

Lights go down on her. Music off. Silence, as Gallimard puts away his magazines. Then he resumes talking to us.

Gallimard: Act Two begins with Butterfly staring at the ocean. Pinkerton's been called back to the U.S., and he's given his wife a detailed schedule of his plans. In the column marked "return date," he's written "when the robins nest." This failed to ignite her suspicions. Now, three years have passed without a peep from him. Which brings a response from her faithful servant, Suzuki.

Comrade Chin enters, playing Suzuki.

30 **Suzuki:** Girl, he's a loser. What'd he ever give you? Nineteen cents and those ugly Day-Glo stockings? Look, it's finished! Kaput! Done! And you should be glad! I mean, the guy was a woofer! He tried before, you know—before he met you, he went down to geisha central and plunked down his spare change in front of the usual candidates—everyone else gagged! These are hungry prostitutes, and they were not interested, get the picture? Now, stop slathering when an American ship sails in, and let's make some bucks—I mean, yen! We are broke!

Now, what about Yamadori? Hey, hey—don't look away—the man is a prince—figuratively, and, what's even better, literally. He's rich, he's handsome, he says he'll die if you don't marry him—and he's even willing to overlook the little fact that you've been deflowered all over the place by a foreign devil. What do you mean, "But he's Japanese"? What do you think you are? You think you've been touched by the whitey god? He was a sailor with dirty hands!.

Suzuki stalks offstage.

Gallimard: She's also visited by Consul Sharpless, sent by Pinkerton on a minor errand.

Marc enters, as Sharpless.

Sharpless: I hate this job.
Gallimard: This Pinkerton—he doesn't show up personally to tell his wife he's abandoning her. No, he sends a government diplomat . . . at taxpayers' expense.
Sharpless: Butterfly? Butterfly? I have some bad—I'm going to be ill. Butterfly, I came to tell you—
35 **Gallimard:** Butterfly says she knows he'll return and if he doesn't she'll kill herself rather than go back to her own people. *(Beat.)* This causes a lull in the conversation.
Sharpless: Let's put it this way . . .
Gallimard: Butterfly runs into the next room, and returns holding—

Sound cue: a baby crying. Sharpless, "seeing" this, backs away.

Sharpless: Well, good. Happy to see things going so well. I suppose I'll be going now. Ta ta. Ciao. *(He turns away. Sound cue out.)* I hate this job. *(He exits.)*
Gallimard: At that moment, Butterfly spots in the harbor an American ship—the *Abramo Lincoln*!

Music cue: "The Flower Duet." Song, still dressed as Butterfly, changes into a wedding kimono, moving to the music.

Gallimard: This is the moment that redeems her years of waiting. With Suzuki's help, they cover the room with flowers—

Chin, as Suzuki, trudges onstage and drops a lone flower without much enthusiasm.

Gallimard: —and she changes into her wedding dress to prepare for Pinkerton's arrival.

Suzuki helps Butterfly change. Helga enters, and helps Gallimard change into a tuxedo.

Gallimard: I married a woman older than myself—Helga.

40 **Helga:** My father was ambassador to Australia. I grew up among criminals and kangaroos.

Gallimard: Hearing that brought me to the altar—

Helga exits.

Gallimard: —where I took a vow renouncing love. No fantasy woman would ever want me, so, yes, I would settle for a quick leap up the career ladder. Passion, I banish, and in its place—practicality!

But my vows had long since lost their charm by the time we arrived in China. The sad truth is that all men want a beautiful woman, and the uglier the man, the greater the want.

Suzuki makes final adjustments of Butterfly's costume, as does Gallimard of his tuxedo.

Gallimard: I married late, at age thirty-one. I was faithful to my marriage for eight years. Until the day when, as a junior-level diplomat in puritanical Peking, in a parlor at the German ambassador's house, during the "Reign of a Hundred Flowers,"[2] I first saw her . . . singing the death scene from *Madame Butterfly*.

Suzuki runs offstage.

Scene 6

German ambassador's house. Beijing, 1960.

The upstage special area now becomes a stage. Several chairs face upstage, representing seating for some twenty guests in the parlor. A few "diplomats"—Renee, Marc, Toulon—in formal dress enter and take seats.

Gallimard also sits down, but turns towards us and continues to talk. Orchestral accompaniment on the tape is now replaced by a simple piano. Song picks up the death scene from the point where Butterfly uncovers the hara-kiri knife.

Gallimard: The ending is pitiful. Pinkerton, in an act of great courage, stays home and sends his American wife to pick up Butterfly's child. The truth, long deferred, has come up to her door.

Song, playing Butterfly, sings the lines from the opera in her own voice—which, though not classical, should be decent.

Song: "Con onor muore / chi non puo serbar / vita con onore."

Gallimard (*simultaneously*): "Death with honor / Is better than life / Life with dishonor."

The stage is illuminated; we are now completely within an elegant diplomat's residence. Song proceeds to play out an abbreviated death scene. Everyone in the room applauds. Song, shyly, takes her bows. Others in the room rush to congratulate her. Gallimard remains with us.

Gallimard: They say in opera the voice is everything. That's probably why I'd never before enjoyed opera. Here . . . here was a Butterfly with little or no voice—but she had the grace, the delicacy . . . I believed this girl. I believed her suffering. I wanted to take her in my arms—so delicate, even I could protect her, take her home, pamper her until she smiled.

Over the course of the preceding speech, Song has broken from the upstage crowd and moved directly upstage of Gallimard.

---

[2] **Reign of a Hundred Flowers:** A time in 1957 when there was freedom of expression in China.

Song: Excuse me. Monsieur . . . ?

Gallimard turns upstage, shocked.

5   **Gallimard:** Oh! Gallimard. Mademoiselle . . . ? A beautiful. . . .
Song: Song Liling.
Gallimard: A beautiful performance.
Song: Oh, please.
Gallimard: I usually—
10 **Song:** You make me blush. I'm no opera singer at all.
Gallimard: I usually don't like *Butterfly*.
Song: I can't blame you in the least.
Gallimard: I mean, the story—
Song: Ridiculous.
15 **Gallimard:** I like the story, but . . . what?
Song: Oh, you like it?
Gallimard: I . . . what I mean is, I've always seen it played by huge women in so much bad
   makeup.
Song: Bad makeup is not unique to the West.
Gallimard: But, who can believe them?
20 **Song:** And you believe me?
Gallimard: Absolutely. You were utterly convincing. It's the first time—
Song: Convincing? As a Japanese woman? The Japanese used hundreds of our people for
   medical experiments during the war, you know. But I gather such an irony is lost on you.
Gallimard: No! I was about to say, it's the first time I've seen the beauty of the story.
Song: Really?
25 **Gallimard:** Of her death. It's a . . . a pure sacrifice. He's unworthy, but what can she do?
   She loves him . . . so much. It's a very beautiful story.
Song: Well, yes, to a Westerner.
Gallimard: Excuse me?
Song: It's one of your favorite fantasies, isn't it? The submissive Oriental woman and the
   cruel white man.
Gallimard: Well, I didn't quite mean . . .
30 **Song:** Consider it this way: what would you say if a blonde homecoming queen fell in love
   with a short Japanese businessman? He treats her cruelly, then goes home for three
   years, during which time she prays to his picture and turns down marriage from a
   young Kennedy. Then, when she learns he has remarried, she kills herself. Now, I believe you would consider this girl to be a deranged idiot, correct? But because it's an
   Oriental who kills herself for a Westerner—ah!—you find it beautiful.

Silence.

Gallimard: Yes . . . well . . . I see your point . . .
Song: I will never do Butterfly again, Monsieur Gallimard. If you wish to see some real theater, come to the Peking Opera sometime. Expand your mind.

Song walks offstage. Other guests exit with her.

Gallimard (*to us*): So much for protecting her in my big Western arms.

Scene 7
M. Gallimard's apartment. Beijing. 1960.
   Gallimard changes from his tux into a casual suit. Helga enters.

Gallimard: The Chinese are an incredibly arrogant people.

Helga: They warned us about that in Paris, remember?

Gallimard: Even Parisians consider them arrogant. That's a switch.

Helga: What is it that Madame Su says? "We are a very old civilization." I never know if she's talking about her country or herself.

5 **Gallimard:** I walk around here, all I hear every day, everywhere is how *old* this culture is. The fact that "old" may be synonymous with "senile" doesn't occur to them.

Helga: You're not going to change them. "East is east, west is west, and . . ." whatever that guy said.

Gallimard: It's just that—silly. I met . . . at Ambassador Koening's tonight—you should've been there.

Helga: Koening? Oh god, no. Did he enchant you all again with the history of Bavaria?

Gallimard: No. I met, I suppose, the Chinese equivalent of a diva. She's a singer in the Chinese opera.

10 **Helga:** They have an opera, too? Do they sing in Chinese? Or maybe—in Italian?

Gallimard: Tonight, she did sing in Italian.

Helga: How'd she manage that?

Gallimard: She must've been educated in the West before the Revolution. Her French is very good also. Anyway, she sang the death scene from *Madame Butterfly.*

Helga: *Madame Butterfly!* Then I should have come. (*She begins humming, floating around the room as if dragging long kimono sleeves.*) Did she have a nice costume? I think it's a classic piece of music.

15 **Gallimard:** That's what *I* thought, too. Don't let her hear you say that.

Helga: What's wrong?

Gallimard: Evidently the Chinese hate it.

Helga: She hated it, but she performed it anyway? Is she perverse?

Gallimard: They hate it because the white man gets the girl. Sour grapes if you ask me.

20 **Helga:** Politics again? Why can't they just hear it as a piece of beautiful music? So, what's in their opera?

Gallimard: I don't know. But, whatever it is, I'm sure it must be *old.*

Helga exits.

Scene 8

Chinese opera house and the streets of Beijing. 1960.
   The sound of gongs clanging fills the stage.

Gallimard: My wife's innocent question kept ringing in my ears. I asked around, but no one knew anything about the Chinese opera. It took four weeks, but my curiosity overcame my cowardice. This Chinese diva—this unwilling Butterfly—what did she do to make her so proud?

   The room was hot, and full of smoke. Wrinkled faces, old women, teeth missing—a man with a growth on his neck, like a human toad. All smiling, pipes falling from their mouths, cracking nuts between their teeth, a live chicken pecking at my foot—all looking, screaming, gawking . . . at her.

The upstage area is suddenly hit with a harsh white light. It has become the stage for the Chinese opera performance. Two dancers enter, along with Song. Gallimard stands apart, watching. Song glides gracefully amidst the two dancers. Drums suddenly slam to a halt. Song strikes a pose, looking straight at Gallimard. Dancers exit. Light change. Pause, then Song walks right off the stage and straight up to Gallimard.

Song: Yes. You. White man. I'm looking straight at you.

Gallimard: Me?

Song: You see any other white men? It was too easy to spot you. How often does a man in my audience come in a tie?

Song starts to remove her costume. Underneath, she wears simple baggy clothes. They are now backstage. The show is over.

5 **Song:** So, you are an adventurous imperialist?

Gallimard: I . . . thought it would further my education.

Song: It took you four weeks. Why?

Gallimard: I've been busy.

Song: Well, education has always been undervalued in the West, hasn't it?

10 **Gallimard** *(laughing):* I don't think that's true.

Song: No, you wouldn't. You're a Westerner. How can you objectively judge your own values?

Gallimard: I think it's possible to achieve some distance.

Song: Do you? *(Pause.)* It stinks in here. Let's go.

Gallimard: These are the smells of your loyal fans.

15 **Song:** I love them for being my fans, I hate the smell they leave behind. I too can distance myself from my people. *(She looks around, then whispers in his ear.)* "Art for the masses" is a shitty excuse to keep artists poor. *(She pops a cigarette in her mouth.)* Be a gentleman, will you? And light my cigarette.

Gallimard fumbles for a match.

Gallimard: I don't . . . smoke.

Song *(lighting her own):* Your loss. Had you lit my cigarette, I might have blown a puff of smoke right between your eyes. Come.

They start to walk about the stage. It is a summer night on the Beijing streets. Sounds of the city play on the house speakers.

Song: How I wish there were even a tiny café to sit in. With cappuccinos, and men in tuxedos and bad expatriate jazz.

Gallimard: If my history serves me correctly, you weren't even allowed into the clubs in Shanghai before the Revolution.

Song: Your history serves you poorly, Monsieur Gallimard. True, there were signs reading "No dogs and Chinamen." But a woman, especially a delicate Oriental woman—we always go where we please. Could you imagine it otherwise? Clubs in China filled with pasty, big-thighed white women, while thousands of slender lotus blossoms wait just outside the door? Never. The clubs would be empty. *(Beat.)* We have always held a certain fascination for you Caucasian men, have we not?

20 **Gallimard:** But . . . that fascination is imperialist, or so you tell me.

Song: Do you believe everything I tell you? Yes. It is always imperialist. But sometimes . . . sometimes, it is also mutual. Oh—this is my flat.

Gallimard: I didn't even—

Song: Thank you. Come another time and we will further expand your mind.

Song exits. Gallimard continues roaming the streets as he speaks to us.

Gallimard: What was that? What did she mean, "Sometimes . . . it is mutual"? Women do not flirt with me. And I normally can't talk to them. But tonight, I held up my end of the conversation.

Scene 9

Gallimard's bedroom. Beijing. 1960.
    Helga enters.

Helga: You didn't tell me you'd be home late.

Gallimard: I didn't intend to. Something came up.

Helga: Oh? Like what?

Gallimard: I went to the . . . to the Dutch ambassador's home.

5 **Helga:** Again?

Gallimard: There was a reception for a visiting scholar. He's writing a six-volume treatise on the Chinese revolution. We all gathered that meant he'd have to live here long enough to actually write six volumes, and we all expressed our deepest sympathies.

Helga: Well, I had a good night too. I went with the ladies to a martial arts demonstration. Some of those men—when they break those thick boards—*(she mimes fanning herself)* whoo-whoo!

Helga exits. Lights dim.

Gallimard: I lied to my wife. Why? I've never had any reason to lie before. But what reason did I have tonight? I didn't do anything wrong. That night, I had a dream. Other people, I've been told, have dreams when angels appear. Or dragons, or Sophia Loren in a towel. In my dream, Marc from school appeared.

Marc enters, in a nightshirt and cap.

Marc: Rene! You met a girl!

Gallimard and Marc stumble down the Beijing streets. Night sounds over the speakers.

10 **Gallimard:** It's not that amazing, thank you.

Marc: No! It's so monumental, I heard about it halfway around the world in my sleep!

Gallimard: I've met girls before, you know.

Marc: Name one. I've come across time and space to congratulate you. *(He hands Gallimard a bottle of wine.)*

Gallimard: Marc, this is expensive.

15 **Marc:** On those rare occasions when you become a formless spirit, why not steal the best?

Marc pops open the bottle, begins to share it with Gallimard.

Gallimard: You embarrass me. She . . . there's no reason to think she likes me.

Marc: "Sometimes, it is mutual"?

Gallimard: Oh.

Marc: "Mutual"? "Mutual"? What does that mean?

20 **Gallimard:** You heard?

Marc: It means the money is in the bank, you only have to write the check!

Gallimard: I am a married man!

Marc: And an excellent one too. I cheated after . . . six months. Then again and again, until now—three hundred girls in twelve years.

Gallimard: I don't think we should hold that up as a model.

25 **Marc:** Of course not! My life—it is disgusting! Phooey! Phooey! But, you—you are the model husband.

Gallimard: Anyway, it's impossible. I'm a foreigner.

Marc: Ah, yes. She cannot love you, it is taboo, but something deep inside her heart . . . she cannot help herself . . . she must surrender to you. It is her destiny.

Gallimard: How do you imagine all this?

Marc: The same way you do. It's an old story. It's in our blood. They fear us, Rene. Their women fear us. And their men—their men hate us. And, you know something? They are all correct.

They spot a light in a window.

30 **Marc:** There! There, Rene!

Gallimard: It's her window.

Marc: Late at night—it burns. The light—it burns for you.

Gallimard: I won't look. It's not respectful.

Marc: We don't have to be respectful. We're foreign devils.

Enter Song, in a sheer robe, her face completely swathed in black cloth. The "One Fine Day" aria creeps in over the speakers. With her back to us, Song mimes attending to her toilette. Her robe comes loose, revealing her white shoulders.

Marc: All your life you've waited for a beautiful girl who would lay down for you. All your life you've smiled like a saint when it's happened to every other man you know. And you see them in magazines and you see them in movies. And you wonder, what's wrong with me? Will anyone beautiful ever want me? As the years pass, your hair thins and you struggle to hold on to even your hopes. Stop struggling, Rene. The wait is over. *(He exits.)*

35 **Gallimard:** Marc? Marc?

At that moment, Song, her back still towards us, drops her robe. A second of her naked back, then a sound cue: a phone ringing, very loud. Blackout, followed in the next beat by a special up on the bedroom area, where a phone now sits. Gallimard stumbles across the stage and picks up the phone. Sound cue out. Over the course of his conversation, area lights fill in the vicinity of his bed. It is the following morning.

Gallimard: Yes? Hello?

Song *(offstage):* Is it very early?

Gallimard: Why, yes.

Song *(offstage):* How early?

Gallimard: It's . . . it's 5:30. Why are you—?

40 **Song** *(offstage):* But it's light outside. Already.

Gallimard: It is. The sun must be in confusion today.

Over the course of Song's next speech, her upstage special comes up again. She sits in a chair, legs crossed, in a robe, telephone to her ear.

Song: I waited until I saw the sun. That was as much discipline as I could manage for one night. Do you forgive me?

Gallimard: Of course . . . for what?

Song: Then I'll ask you quickly. Are you really interested in the opera?

45 **Gallimard:** Why, yes. Yes I am.

Song: Then come again next Thursday. I am playing *The Drunken Beauty*. May I count on you?

Gallimard: Yes. You may.

Song: Perfect. Well, I must be getting to bed. I'm exhausted. It's been a very long night for me.

Song hangs up; special on her goes off. Gallimard begins to dress for work.

Scene 10

Song Liling's apartment. Beijing. 1960.

Gallimard: I returned to the opera that next week, and the week after that . . . she keeps our meetings so short—perhaps fifteen, twenty minutes at most. So I am left each week with a thirst which is intensified. In this way, fifteen weeks have gone by. I am starting to doubt the words of my friend Marc. But no, not really. In my heart, I know she has . . . an interest in me. I suspect this is her way. She is outwardly bold and out-spoken, yet her heart is shy and afraid. It is the Oriental in her at war with her Western education.

Song *(offstage):* I will be out in an instant. Ask the servant for anything you want.

Gallimard: Tonight, I have finally been invited to enter her apartment. Though the idea is almost beyond belief, I believe she is afraid of me.

Gallimard looks around the room. He picks up a picture in a frame, studies it. Without his noticing, Song enters, dressed elegantly in a black gown from the twenties. She stands in the doorway looking like Anna May Wong.[3]

Song: That is my father.

5 **Gallimard** *(surprised):* Mademoiselle Song . . .

She glides up to him, snatches away the picture.

Song: It is very good that he did not live to see the Revolution. They would, no doubt, have made him kneel on broken glass. Not that he didn't deserve such a punishment. But he is my father. I would've hated to see it happen.

Gallimard: I'm very honored that you've allowed me to visit your home.

Song curtseys.

Song: Thank you. Oh! Haven't you been poured any tea?

Gallimard: I'm really not—

10 **Song** *(to her offstage servant):* Shu-Fang! Cha! Kwai-lah! *(To Gallimard.)* I'm sorry. You want everything to be perfect—

Gallimard: Please.

Song:—and before the evening even begins—

Gallimard: I'm really not thirsty.

Song: —it's ruined.

15 **Gallimard** *(sharply):* Mademoiselle Song!

Song sits down.

Song: I'm sorry.

Gallimard: What are you apologizing for now?

Pause; Song starts to giggle.

Song: I don't know!

Gallimard laughs.

Gallimard: Exactly my point.

20 **Song:** Oh, I am silly. Light-headed. I promise not to apologize for anything else tonight, do you hear me?

---

[3] **Anna May Wong** (1905–1961): First actress of Chinese descent to become famous in Hollywood.

Gallimard: That's a good girl.

Shu-Fang, a servant girl, comes out with a tea tray and starts to pour.

Song *(to Shu-Fang):* No! I'll pour myself for the gentleman!

Shu-Fang, staring at Gallimard, exits.

Gallimard: You have a beautiful home.
Song: No, I . . . I don't even know why I invited you up.
25 **Gallimard:** Well, I'm glad you did.

Song looks around the room.

Song: There is an element of danger to your presence.
Gallimard: Oh?
Song: You must know.
Gallimard: It doesn't concern me. We both know why I'm here.
30 **Song:** It doesn't concern me either. No . . . well perhaps . . .
Gallimard: What?
Song: Perhaps I am slightly afraid of scandal.
Gallimard: What are we doing?
Song: I'm entertaining you. In my parlor.
35 **Gallimard:** In France, that would hardly—
Song: France. France is a country living in the modern era. Perhaps even ahead of it. China
    is a nation whose soul is firmly rooted two thousand years in the past. What I do, even
    pouring the tea for you now . . . it has . . . implications. The walls and windows say
    so. Even my own heart, strapped inside this Western dress . . . even it says things—
    things I don't care to hear.

Song hands Gallimard a cup of tea. Gallimard puts his hand over both the teacup and Song's hand.

Gallimard: This is a beautiful dress.
Song: Don't.
Gallimard: What?
40 **Song:** I don't even know if it looks right on me.
Gallimard: Believe me—
Song: You are from France. You see so many beautiful women.
Gallimard: France? Since when are the European women—?
Song: Oh! What am I trying to do, anyway?!

Song runs to the door, composes herself, then turns towards Gallimard.

Song: Monsieur Gallimard, perhaps you should go.
45 **Gallimard:** But . . . why?
Song: There's something wrong about this.
Gallimard: I don't see what.
Song: I feel . . . I am not myself.
Gallimard: No. You're nervous.
50 **Song:** Please. Hard as I try to be modern, to speak like a man, to hold a Western woman's
    strong face up to my own . . . in the end, I fail. A small, frightened heart beats too
    quickly and gives me away. Monsieur Gallimard, I'm a Chinese girl. I've never . . .
    never invited a man up to my flat before. The forwardness of my actions makes my
    skin burn.
Gallimard: What are you afraid of? Certainly not me, I hope.

Song: I'm a modest girl.

Gallimard: I know. And very beautiful. (*He touches her hair.*)

Song: Please—go now. The next time you see me, I shall again be myself.

55 **Gallimard:** I like you the way you are right now.

Song: You are a cad.

Gallimard: What do you expect? I'm a foreign devil.

Gallimard walks downstage. Song exits.

Gallimard (*to us*): Did you hear the way she talked about Western women? Much differently than the first night. She does—she feels inferior to them—and to me.

Scene 11

The French embassy. Beijing. 1960.
Gallimard moves towards a desk.

Gallimard: I determined to try an experiment. In *Madame Butterfly*, Cio-Cio-San fears that the Western man who catches a butterfly will pierce its heart with a needle, then leave it to perish. I began to wonder: had I, too, caught a butterfly who would writhe on a needle?

Marc enters, dressed as a bureaucrat, holding a stack of papers. As Gallimard speaks, Marc hands papers to him. He peruses, then signs, stamps, or rejects them.

Gallimard: Over the next five weeks, I worked like a dynamo. I stopped going to the opera, I didn't phone or write her. I knew this little flower was waiting for me to call, and, as I wickedly refused to do so, I felt for the first time that rush of power—the absolute power of a man.

Mark continues acting as the bureaucrat, but he now speaks as himself.

Mark: Rene! It's me.

Gallimard: Marc—I hear your voice everywhere now. Even in the midst of work.

Marc: That's because I'm watching you—all the time.

5 **Gallimard:** You were always the most popular guy in school.

Marc: Well, there's no guarantee of failure in life like happiness in high school. Somehow I knew I'd end up in the suburbs working for Renault and you'd be in the Orient picking exotic women off the trees. And they say there's no justice.

Gallimard: That's why you were my friend?

Marc: I gave you a little of my life, so that now you can give me some of yours. (*Pause.*) Remember Isabelle?

Gallimard: Of course I remember! She was my first experience.

10 **Marc:** We all wanted to ball her. But she only wanted me.

Gallimard: I had her.

Marc: Right. You balled her.

Gallimard: You were the only one who ever believed me.

Marc: Well, there's a good reason for that. (*Beat.*) C'mon. You must've guessed.

15 **Gallimard:** You told me to wait in the bushes by the cafeteria that night. The next thing I knew, she was on me. Dress up in the air.

Marc: She never wore underwear.

Gallimard: My arms were pinned to the dirt

Marc: She loved the superior position. A girl ahead of her time.

Gallimard: I looked up, and there was this woman . . . bouncing up and down on my loins.

20 **Marc:** Screaming, right?

Gallimard: Screaming, and breaking off the branches all around me, and pounding my butt up and down into the dirt.

Marc: Huffing and puffing like a locomotive.

Gallimard: And in the middle of all this, the leaves were getting into my mouth, my legs were losing circulation, I thought, "God. So this is *it?*"

Marc: You thought that?

25 **Gallimard:** Well, I was worried about my legs falling off.

Marc: You didn't have a good time?

Gallimard: No, that's not what I—I had a great time!

Marc: You're sure?

Gallimard: Yeah. Really.

30 **Marc:** 'Cuz I wanted you to have a good time.

Gallimard: I did.

> *Pause.*

Marc: Shit. (*Pause.*) When all is said and done, she was kind of a lousy lay, wasn't she? I mean, there was a lot of energy there, but you never knew what she was doing with it. Like when she yelled "I'm coming!"—hell, it was so loud, you wanted to go, "Look, it's not that big a deal."

Gallimard: I got scared. I thought she meant someone was actually coming. (*Pause.*) But, Marc?

Marc: What?

35 **Gallimard:** Thanks.

Marc: Oh, don't mention it.

Gallimard: It was my first experience.

Marc: Yeah. You got her.

Gallimard: I got her.

40 **Marc:** Wait! Look at that letter again!

> *Gallimard picks up one of the papers he's been stamping, and rereads it.*

Gallimard (*to us*): After six weeks, they began to arrive. The letters.

> *Upstage special on Song, as Madame Butterfly. The scene is underscored by the "Love Duet."*

Song: Did we fight? I do not know. Is the opera no longer of interest to you? Please come—my audiences miss the white devil in their midst.

> *Gallimard looks up from the letter, towards us.*

Gallimard (*to us*): A concession, but much too dignified. (*Beat; he discards the letter.*) I skipped the opera again that week to complete a position paper on trade.

> *The bureaucrat hands him another letter.*

Song: Six weeks have passed since last we met. Is this your practice—to leave friends in the lurch? Sometimes I hate you, sometimes I hate myself, but always I miss you.

45 **Gallimard** (*to us*): Better, but I don't like the way she calls me "friend." When a woman calls a man her "friend," she's calling him a eunuch or a homosexual. (*Beat; he discards the letter.*) I was absent from the opera for the seventh week, feeling a sudden urge to clean out my files.

> *Bureaucrat hands him another letter.*

Song: Your rudeness is beyond belief. I don't deserve this cruelty. Don't bother to call. I'll have you turned away at the door.

Gallimard (*to us*): I didn't. (*He discards the letter; bureaucrat hands him another.*) And then finally, the letter that concluded my experiment.

Song: I am out of words. I can hide behind dignity no longer. What do you want? I have already given you my shame.

Gallimard gives the letter back to Marc, slowly. Special on Song fades out.

Gallimard (*to us*): Reading it, I became suddenly ashamed. Yes, my experiment had been a success. She was turning on my needle. But the victory seemed hollow.

50 **Marc:** Hollow?! Are you crazy?

Gallimard: Nothing, Marc. Please go away.

Marc (*exiting, with papers*): Haven't I taught you anything?

Gallimard: "I have already given you my shame." I had to attend a reception that evening. On the way, I felt sick. If there is a God, surely he would punish me now. I had finally gained power over a beautiful woman, only to abuse it cruelly. There must be justice in the world. I had the strange feeling that the ax would fall this very evening.

Scene 12

Ambassador Toulon's residence. Beijing. 1960.
Sound cue: party noises. Light change. We are now in a spacious residence. Toulon, the French ambassador, enters and taps Gallimard on the shoulder.

Toulon: Gallimard? Can I have a word? Over here.

Gallimard (*to us*): Manuel Toulon. French ambassador to China. He likes to think of us all as his children. Rather like God.

Toulon: Look, Gallimard, there's not much to say. I've liked you. From the day you walked in. You were no leader, but you were tidy and efficient.

Gallimard: Thank you, sir.

5 **Toulon:** Don't jump the gun. Okay, our needs in China are changing. It's embarrassing that we lost Indochina. Someone just wasn't on the ball there. I don't mean you personally, of course.

Gallimard: Thank you, sir.

Toulon: We're going to be doing a lot more information-gathering in the future. The nature of our work here is changing. Some people are just going to have to go. It's nothing personal.

Gallimard: Oh.

Toulon: Want to know a secret? Vice-Consul LeBon is being transferred.

10 **Gallimard** (*to us*): My immediate superior!

Toulon: And most of his department.

Gallimard (*to us*): Just as I feared! God has seen my evil heart—

Toulon: But not you.

Gallimard (*to us*): —and he's taking her away just as . . . (*To Toulon.*) Excuse me, sir?

15 **Toulon:** Scare you? I think I did. Cheer up, Gallimard. I want you to replace LeBon as vice-consul.

Gallimard: You—? Yes, well, thank you, sir.

Toulon: Anytime.

Gallimard: I . . . accept with great humility.

Toulon: Humility won't be part of the job. You're going to coordinate the revamped intelligence division. Want to know a secret? A year ago, you would've been out. But the past few months, I don't know how it happened, you've become this new aggressive confident . . . thing. And they also tell me you get along with the Chinese. So I think you're a lucky man, Gallimard. Congratulations.

They shake hands. Toulon exits. Party noises out. Gallimard stumbles across a darkened stage.

20 **Gallimard:** Vice-consul? Impossible! As I stumbled out of the party, I saw it written across the sky: There is no God. Or, no—say that there is a God. But that God . . . understands. Of course! God who creates Eve to serve Adam, who blesses Solomon with his harem but ties Jezebel to a burning bed—that God is a man. And he understands! At age thirty-nine, I was suddenly initiated into the way of the world.

Scene 13

Song Liling's apartment. Beijing. 1960.
Song enters, in a sheer dressing gown.

Song: Are you crazy?
Gallimard: Mademoiselle Song—
Song: To come here—at this hour? After . . . after eight weeks?
Gallimard: It's the most amazing—
5 **Song:** You bang on my door? Scare my servants, scandalize the neighbors?
Gallimard: I've been promoted. To vice-consul.

Pause.

Song: And what is that supposed to mean to me?
Gallimard: Are you my Butterfly?
Song: What are you saying?
10 **Gallimard:** I've come tonight for an answer: are you my Butterfly?
Song: Don't you know already?
Gallimard: I want you to say it.
Song: I don't want to say it.
Gallimard: So, that is your answer?
15 **Song:** You know how I feel about—
Gallimard: I do remember one thing.
Song: What?
Gallimard: In the letter I received today.
Song: Don't.
20 **Gallimard:** "I have already given you my shame."
Song: It's enough that I even wrote it.
Gallimard: Well, then—
Song: I shouldn't have it splashed across my face.
Gallimard:—if that's all true—
25 **Song:** Stop!
Gallimard: Then what is one more short answer?
Song: I don't want to!
Gallimard: Are you my Butterfly? (*Silence; he crosses the room and begins to touch her hair.*) I want from you honesty. There should be nothing false between us. No false pride.

Pause.

Song: Yes, I am. I am your Butterfly.

30 **Gallimard:** Then let me be honest with you. It is because of you that I was promoted tonight. You have changed my life forever. My little Butterfly, there should be no more secrets: I love you.

He starts to kiss her roughly. She resists slightly.

Song: No . . . no . . . gently . . . please, I've never . . .
Gallimard: No?
Song: I've tried to appear experienced, but . . . the truth is . . . no.
Gallimard: Are you cold?
35 **Song:** Yes. Cold.
Gallimard: Then we will go very, very slowly.

He starts to caress her; her gown begins to open.

Song: No . . . let me . . . keep my clothes . . .
Gallimard: But . . .
Song: Please . . . it all frightens me. I'm a modest Chinese girl.
40 **Gallimard:** My poor little treasure.
Song: I am your treasure. Though inexperienced, I am not . . . ignorant. They teach us things, our mothers, about pleasing a man.
Gallimard: Yes?
Song: I'll do my best to make you happy. Turn off the lights.

Gallimard gets up and heads for a lamp. Song, propped up on one elbow, tosses her hair back and smiles.

Song: Monsieur Gallimard?
45 **Gallimard:** Yes, Butterfly?
Song: *"Vieni, vieni!"*
Gallimard: "Come, darling."
Song: *"Ah! Dolce notte!"*
Gallimard: "Beautiful night."
50 **Song:** *"Tutto estatico d'amor ride il ciel!"*
Gallimard: "All ecstatic with love, the heavens are filled with laughter."

He turns off the lamp. Blackout.

Act Two
Scene 1
M. Gallimard's cell. Paris. 1988.
   Lights up on Gallimard. He sits in his cell, reading from a leaflet.

Gallimard: This, from a contemporary critic's commentary on *Madame Butterfly:* "Pinkerton suffers from . . . being an obnoxious bounder whom every man in the audience itches to kick." Bully for us men in the audience! Then, in the same note: "Butterfly is the most irresistibly appealing of Puccini's 'Little Women.' Watching the succession of her humiliations is like watching a child under torture." (*He tosses the pamphlet over his shoulder.*) I suggest that, while we men may all want to kick Pinkerton, very few of us would pass up the opportunity to *be* Pinkerton.

Gallimard moves out of his cell.

Scene 2
Gallimard and Butterfly's flat. Beijing. 1960.

We are in a simple but well-decorated parlor. Gallimard moves to sit on a sofa, while Song, dressed in a cheongsam,[1] enters and curls up at his feet.

Gallimard *(to us):* We secured a flat on the outskirts of Peking. Butterfly, as I was calling her now, decorated our "home" with Western furniture and Chinese antiques. And there, on a few stolen afternoons or evenings each week, Butterfly commenced her education.

Song: The Chinese men—they keep us down.

Gallimard: Even in the "New Society"?

Song: In the "New Society," we are all kept ignorant equally. That's one of the exciting things about loving a Western man. I know you are not threatened by a woman's education.

5 **Gallimard:** I'm no saint, Butterfly.

Song: But you come from a progressive society.

Gallimard: We're not always reminding each other how "old" we are, if that's what you mean.

Song: Exactly. We Chinese—once, I suppose, it is true, we ruled the world. But so what? How much more exciting to be part of the society ruling the world today. Tell me— what's happening in Vietnam?

Gallimard: Oh, Butterfly—you want me to bring my work home?

10 **Song:** I want to know what you know. To be impressed by my man. It's not the particulars so much as the fact that you're making decisions which change the shape of the world.

Gallimard: Not the world. At best, a small corner.

Toulon enters, and sits at a desk upstage.

Scene 3

French embassy. Beijing. 1961.
Gallimard moves downstage, to Toulon's desk. Song remains upstage, watching.

Toulon: And a more troublesome corner is hard to imagine.

Gallimard: So, the Americans plan to begin bombing?

Toulon: This is very secret, Gallimard: yes. The Americans don't have an embassy here. They're asking us to be their eyes and ears. Say Jack Kennedy signed an order to bomb North Vietnam, Laos. How would the Chinese react?

Gallimard: I think the Chinese will squawk—

5 **Toulon:** Uh-huh

Gallimard: —but, in their hearts, they don't even like Ho Chi Minh.[2]

Pause.

Toulon: What a bunch of jerks. Vietnam was *our* colony. Not only didn't the Americans help us fight to keep them, but now, seven years later, they've come back to grab the territory for themselves. It's very irritating,

Gallimard: With all due respect, sir, why should the Americans have won our war for us back in fifty-four if we didn't have the will to win it ourselves?

Toulon: You're kidding, aren't you?

Pause.

---

[1] **cheongsamz:** A dress with a slit skirt and mandarin collar.
[2] **Ho Chi Minh** (1890–1969): First president of North Vietnam (1945–1969).

10 **Gallimard:** The Orientals simply want to be associated with whoever shows the most strength and power. You live with the Chinese, sir. Do you think they like Communism?

Toulon: I live in China. Not with the Chinese.

Gallimard: Well, I—

Toulon: *You* live with the Chinese.

Gallimard: Excuse me?

15 **Toulon:** I can't keep a secret.

Gallimard: What are you saying?

Toulon: Only that I'm not immune to gossip. So, you're keeping a native mistress? Don't answer. It's none of my business. *(Pause.)* I'm sure she must be gorgeous.

Gallimard: Well . . .

Toulon: I'm impressed. You had the stamina to go out into the streets and hunt one down. Some of us have to be content with the wives of the expatriate community.

20 **Gallimard:** I do feel . . . fortunate.

Toulon: So, Gallimard, you've got the inside knowledge—what *do* the Chinese think?

Gallimard: Deep down, they miss the old days. You know, cappuccinos, men in tuxedos—

Toulon: So what do we tell the Americans about Vietnam?

Gallimard: Tell them there's a natural affinity between the West and the Orient.

25 **Toulon:** And that you speak from experience?

Gallimard: The Orientals are people too. They want the good things we can give them. If the Americans demonstrate the will to win, the Vietnamese will welcome them into a mutually beneficial union.

Toulon: I don't see how the Vietnamese can stand up to American firepower.

Gallimard: Orientals will always submit to a greater force.

Toulon: I'll note your opinions in my report. The Americans always love to hear how "welcome" they'll be. *(He starts to exit.)*

30 **Gallimard:** Sir?

Toulon: Mmmm?

Gallimard: This . . . rumor you've heard.

Toulon: Uh-huh?

Gallimard: How . . . widespread do you think it is?

35 **Toulon:** It's only widespread within this embassy. Where nobody talks because everybody is guilty. We were worried about you, Gallimard. We thought you were the only one here without a secret. Now you go and find a lotus blossom . . . and top us all. *(He exits.)*

Gallimard *(to us):* Toulon knows! And he approves! I was learning the benefits of being a man. We form our own clubs, sit behind thick doors, smoke—and celebrate the fact that we're still boys. *(He starts to move downstage, towards Song.)* So, over the—

Suddenly Comrade Chin enters. Gallimard backs away.

Gallimard *(to Song):* No! Why does she have to come in?

Song: Rene, be sensible. How can they understand the story without her? Now, don't embarrass yourself.

Gallimard moves down center.

Gallimard *(to us):* Now, you will see why my story is so amusing to so many people. Why they snicker at parties in disbelief. Please—try to understand it from my point of view. We are all prisoners of our time and place. *(He exits.)*

Scene 4

Gallimard and Butterfly's flat. Beijing. 1961

Song (*to us*): 1961. The flat Monsieur Gallimard rented for us. An evening after he has gone.

Chin: Okay, see if you can find out when the Americans plan to start bombing Vietnam. If you can find out what cities, even better.

Song: I'll do my best, but I don't want to arouse his suspicions.

Chin: Yeah, sure, of course. So, what else?

5 **Song:** The Americans will increase troops in Vietnam to 170,000 soldiers with 120,000 militia and 11,000 American advisors.

Chin (*writing*): Wait, wait, 120,000 militia and—

Song: —11,000 American—

Chin: —American advisors. (*Beat.*) How do you remember so much?

Song: I'm an actor.

10 **Chin:** Yeah. (*Beat.*) Is that how come you dress like that?

Song: Like what, Miss Chin?

Chin: Like that dress! You're wearing a dress. And every time I come here, you're wearing a dress. Is that because you're an actor? Or what?

Song: It's a . . . disguise. Miss Chin.

Chin: Actors, I think they're all weirdos. My mother tells me actors are like gamblers or prostitutes or—

15 **Song:** It helps me in my assignment.

Pause.

Chin: You're not gathering information in any way that violates Communist Party principles, are you?

Song: Why would I do that?

Chin: Just checking. Remember; when working for the Great Proletarian State, you represent our Chairman Mao in every position you take.

Song: I'll try to imagine the Chairman taking my positions.

20 **Chin:** We all think of him this way. Good-bye, comrade. (*She starts to exit.*) Comrade?

Song: Yes?

Chin: Don't forget: there is no homosexuality in China!

Song: Yes, I've heard.

Chin: Just checking. (*She exits.*)

25 **Song** (*to us*): What passes for a woman in modern China.

Gallimard sticks his head out from the wings.

Gallimard: Is she gone?

Song: Yes, Rene. Please continue in your own fashion.

Scene 5

Beijing. 1961–1963.

Gallimard moves to the couch where Song still sits. He lies down in her lap, and she strokes his forehead.

Gallimard (*to us*): And so, over the years 1961, '62, '63, we settled into our routine, Butterfly and I. She would always have prepared a light snack and then, ever so delicately, and only if I agreed, she would start to pleasure me. With her hands, her mouth . . . too many ways to explain, and too sad, given my present situation. But mostly we would talk. About my life. Perhaps there is nothing more rare than to find a woman who passionately listens.

Song remains upstage, listening, as Helga enters and plays a scene downstage with Gallimard.

Helga: Rene, I visited Dr. Bolleart this morning.

Gallimard: Why? Are you ill?

Helga: No, no. You see, I wanted to ask him . . . that question we've been discussing.

5 **Gallimard:** And I told you, it's only a matter of time. Why did you bring a doctor into this? We just have to keep trying—like a crapshoot, actually.

Helga: I went, I'm sorry. But listen: he says there's nothing wrong with me.

Gallimard: You see? Now, will you stop—?

Helga: Rene, he says he'd like you to go in and take some tests.

Gallimard: Why? So he can find there's nothing wrong with both of us?

10 **Helga:** Rene, I don't ask for much. One trip! One visit! And then, whatever you want to do about it—you decide.

Gallimard: You're assuming he'll find something defective!

Helga: No! Of course not! Whatever he finds—if he finds nothing, we decide what to do about nothing! But go!

Gallimard: If he finds nothing, we keep trying. Just like we do now.

Helga: But at least we'll know! *(Pause.)* I'm sorry. *(She starts to exit.)*

15 **Gallimard:** Do you really want me to see Dr. Bolleart?

Helga: Only if you want a child, Rene. We have to face the fact that time is running out. Only if you want a child. *(She exits.)*

Gallimard *(to Song):* I'm a modern man, Butterfly. And yet, I don't want to go. It's the same old voodoo. I feel like God himself is laughing at me if I can't produce a child.

Song: You men of the West—you're obsessed by your odd desire for equality. Your wife can't give you a child, and *you're* going to the doctor?

Gallimard: Well, you see, she's already gone.

20 **Song:** And because this incompetent can't find the defect, you now have to subject yourself to him? It's unnatural.

Gallimard: Well, what is the "natural" solution?

Song: In Imperial China, when a man found that one wife was inadequate, he turned to another—to give him his son.

Gallimard: What do you—? I can't . . . marry you, yet.

Song: Please. I'm not asking you to be my husband. But I am already your wife.

25 **Gallimard:** Do you want to . . . have my child?

Song: I thought you'd never ask.

Gallimard: But, your career . . . your—

Song: Phooey on my career! That's your Western mind, twisting itself into strange shapes again. Of course I love my career. But what would I love most of all? To feel something inside me—day and night—something I know is yours. *(Pause.)* Promise me . . . you won't go to this doctor. Who is this Western quack to set himself as judge over the man I love? I know who is a man, and who is not. *(She exits.)*

Gallimard *(to us):* Dr. Bolleart? Of course I didn't go. What man would?

Scene 6

Beijing. 1963.

> *Party noises over the house speakers. Renee enters, wearing, a revealing gown.*

Gallimard: 1963. A party at the Austrian embassy. None of us could remember the Austrian ambassador's name, which seemed somehow appropriate. *(To Renee.)* So, I tell the

Americans, Diem[3] must go. The U.S. wants to be respected by the Vietnamese, and yet they're propping up this nobody seminarian as her president. A man whose claim to fame is his sister-in-law imposing fanatic "moral order" campaigns? Oriental women— when they're good, they're very good, but when they're bad, they're Christians.

Renee: Yeah.

Gallimard: And what do you do?

Renee: I'm a student. My father exports a lot of useless stuff to the Third World.

5 **Gallimard:** How useless?

Renee: You know. Squirt guns, confectioner's sugar, Hula Hoops . . .

Gallimard: I'm sure they appreciate the sugar.

Renee: I'm here for two years to study Chinese.

Gallimard: Two years!

10 **Renee:** That's what everybody says.

Gallimard: When did you arrive?

Renee: Three weeks ago.

Gallimard: And?

Renee: I like it. Its primitive, but . . . well, this is the place to learn Chinese, so here I am.

15 **Gallimard:** Why Chinese?

Renee: I think it'll be important someday.

Gallimard: You do?

Renee: Don't ask me when, but . . . that's what I think.

Gallimard: Well, I agree with you. One hundred percent. That's very farsighted.

20 **Renee:** Yeah. Well of course, my father thinks I'm a complete weirdo.

Gallimard: He'll thank you someday.

Renee: Like when the Chinese start buying Hula Hoops?

Gallimard: There're a billion bellies out there.

Renee: And if they end up taking over the world—well, then I'll be lucky to know Chinese too, right?

Pause.

25 **Gallimard:** At this point, I don't see how the Chinese can possibly take—

Renee: You know what I *don't* like about China?

Gallimard: Excuse me? No—what?

Renee: Nothing to do at night.

Gallimard: You come to parties at embassies like everyone else.

30 **Renee:** Yeah, but they get out at ten. And then what?

Gallimard: I'm afraid the Chinese idea of a dance hall is a dirt floor and a man with a flute.

Renee: Are you married?

Gallimard: Yes. Why?

Renee: You wanna . . . fool around?

Pause.

35 **Gallimard:** Sure.

Renee: I'll wait for you outside. What's your name?

Gallimard: Gallimard. Rene.

---

[3] **Diem:** Ngo Dinh Diem (1901–1963), Vietnamese political leader and president of South Vietnam (1955–1963), assassinated in a coup d'état orchestrated by Vietnamese generals and supported by the United States.

Renee: Weird. I'm Renee too. *(She exits.)*

Gallimard *(to us):* And so, I embarked on my first extra-extramarital affair. Renee was picture perfect. With a body like those girls in the magazines. If I put a tissue paper over my eyes, I wouldn't have been able to tell the difference. And it was exciting to be with someone who wasn't afraid to be seen completely naked. But is it possible for a woman to be *too* uninhibited, *too* willing, so as to seem almost too . . . masculine?

Chuck Berry[4] blares from the house speakers, then comes down in volume as Renee enters, toweling her hair.

40 **Renee:** You have a nice weenie.

Gallimard: What?

Renee: Penis. You have a nice penis.

Gallimard: Oh. Well, thank you. That's very . . .

Renee : What—can't take a compliment?

45 **Gallimard:** No, it's very . . . reassuring.

Renee: But most girls don't come out and say it, huh?

Gallimard: And also . . . what did you call it?

Renee: Oh. Most girls don't call it a "weenie," huh?

Gallimard: It sounds very—

50 **Renee:** Small, I know.

Gallimard: I was going to say, "young."

Renee: Yeah. Young, small, same thing. Most guys are pretty, uh, sensitive about that. Like, you know, I had a boyfriend back home in Denmark. I got mad at him once and called him a little weeniehead. He got so mad! He said at least I should call him a great big weeniehead.

Gallimard: I suppose I just say "penis."

Renee: Yeah. That's pretty clinical. There's "cock," but that sounds like a chicken. And "prick" is painful, and "dick" is like you're talking about someone who's not in the room.

55 **Gallimard:** Yes. It's a . . . bigger problem than I imagined.

Renee: I—I think maybe it's because I really don't know what to do with them—that's why I call them "weenies."

Gallimard: Well, you did quite well with . . . mine.

Renee: Thanks, but I mean, really *do* with them. Like, okay, have you ever looked at one? I mean, really?

Gallimard: No, I suppose when it's part of you, you sort of take it for granted.

60 **Renee:** I guess. But, like, it just hangs there. This little . . . flap of flesh. And there's so much fuss that we make about it. Like, I think the reason we fight wars is because we wear clothes. Because no one knows—between the men, I mean—who has the biggest . . . weenie. So, if I'm a guy with a small one, I'm going to build a really big building or take over a really big piece of land or write a really long book so the other men don't know, right? But, see, it never really works, that's the problem. I mean, you conquer the country, or whatever, but you're still wearing clothes, so there's no way to prove absolutely whose is bigger or smaller. And that's what we call a civilized society. The whole world run by a bunch of men with pricks the size of pins. *(She exits.)*

Gallimard *(to us):* This was simply not acceptable.

---

[4] **Chuck Berry** (b. 1926): American rock 'n' roll musician.

A high-pitched chime rings through the air. Song, dressed as Butterfly, appears in the upstage special. She is obviously distressed. Her body swoons as she attempts to clip the stems of flowers she's arranging in a vase.

Gallimard: But I kept up our affair, wildly, for several months. Why? I believe because of Butterfly. She knew the secret I was trying to hide. But, unlike a Western woman, she didn't confront me, threaten, even pout. I remembered the words of Puccini's *Butterfly:*

Song: *"Noi siamo gente avvezza/alle piccole cose / umili e silenziose."*

Gallimard: "I come from a people / Who are accustomed to little / Humble and silent." I saw Pinkerton and Butterfly, and what she would say if he were unfaithful . . . nothing. She would cry, alone, into those wildly soft sleeves, once full of possessions, now empty to collect her tears. It was her tears and her silence that excited me, every time I visited Renee.

65   **Toulon** *(offstage):* Gallimard!

Toulon enters. Gallimard turns towards him. During the next section, Song, up center, begins to dance with the flowers. It is a drunken, reckless dance, where she breaks small pieces off the stems.

Toulon: They're killing him.

Gallimard: Who? I'm sorry? What?

Toulon: Bother you to come over at this late hour?

Gallimard: No . . . of course not.

70   **Toulon:** Not after you hear my secret. Champagne?

Gallimard: Um . . . thank you.

Toulon: You're surprised. There's something that you've wanted, Gallimard, No, not a promotion. Next time. Something in the world. You're not aware of this, but there's an informal gossip circle among intelligence agents. And some of ours heard from some of the Americans—

Gallimard: Yes?

Toulon: That the U.S. will allow the Vietnamese generals to stage a coup . . . and assassinate President Diem.

The chime rings again. Toulon freezes. Gallimard turns upstage and looks at Butterfly, who slowly and deliberately clips a flower off its stem. Gallimard turns back towards Toulon.

75   **Gallimard:** I think . . . that's a very wise move!

Toulon unfreezes.

Toulon: It's what you've been advocating. A toast?

Gallimard: Sure. I consider this a vindication.

Toulon: Not exactly. "To the test. Let's hope you pass."

They drink. The chime rings again. Toulon freezes. Gallimard turns upstage, and Song clips another flower.

Gallimard *(to Toulon):* The test?

80   **Toulon** *(unfreezing):* It's a test of everything you've been saying. I personally think the generals probably will stop the Communists. And you'll be a hero. But if anything goes wrong, then your opinions won't be worth a pig's ear. I'm sure that won't happen. But sometimes it's easier when they don't listen to you.

Gallimard: They're your opinions too, aren't they?

Toulon: Personally, yes.

Gallimard: So we agree.

Toulon: But my opinions aren't on that report. Yours are. Cheers.

Toulon turns away from Gallimard and raises his glass. At that instant Song picks up the vase and hurls it to the ground. It shatters. Song sinks down amidst the shards of the vase, in a calm, childlike trance. She sings softly, as if reciting a child's nursery rhyme.

85 **Song** *(repeat as necessary):* "The whole world over, the white man travels, setting anchor, wherever he likes. Life's not worth living, unless he finds, the finest maidens, of every land . . ."

Gallimard turns downstage towards us. Song continues singing.

Gallimard: I shook as I left his house. That coward! That worm! To put the burden for his decisions on my shoulders!

I started for Renee's. But no, that was all I needed. A schoolgirl who would question the role of the penis in modern society. What I wanted was revenge. A vessel to contain my humiliation. Though I hadn't seen her in several weeks, I headed for Butterfly's.

Gillimard enters Song's apartment.

Song: Oh! Rene . . . I was dreaming!

Gallimard: You've been drinking?

Song: If I can't sleep, then yes, I drink. But then, it gives me these dreams which—Rene, it's been almost three weeks since you visited me last.

90 **Gallimard:** I know. There's been a lot going on in the world.

Song: Fortunately I am drunk. So I can speak freely. It's not the world, it's you and me. And an old problem. Even the softest skin becomes like leather to a man who's touched it too often. I confess I don't know how to stop it. I don't know how to become another woman.

Gallimard: I have a request.

Song: Is this a solution? Or are you ready to give up the flat?

Gallimard: It may be a solution. But I'm sure you won't like it.

95 **Song:** Oh well, that's very important. "Like it?" Do you think I "like" lying here alone, waiting, always waiting for your return? Please—don't worry about what I may not "like."

Gallimard: I want to see you . . . naked.

Silence.

Song: I thought you understood my modesty. So you want me to—what—strip? Like a big cowboy girl? Shiny pasties on my breasts? Shall I fling my kimono over my head and yell "ya-hoo" in the process? I thought you respected my shame!

Gallimard: I believe you gave me your shame many years ago.

Song: Yes—and it is just like a white devil to use it against me. I can't believe it. I thought myself so repulsed by the passive Oriental and the cruel white man. Now I see—we are always most revolted by the things hidden within us.

100 **Gallimard:** I just mean—

Song: Yes?

Gallimard: —that it will remove the only barrier left between us.

Song: No, Rene. Don't couch your request in sweet words. Be yourself—a cad—and know that my love is enough, that I submit—submit to the worst you can give me. *(Pause.)* Well, come. Strip me. Whatever happens, know that you have willed it. Our love, in your hands. I'm helpless before my man,

Gallimard starts to cross the room.

Gallimard: Did I not undress her because I knew, somewhere deep down, what I would find? Perhaps. Happiness is so rare that our mind can turn somersaults to protect it.

At the time, I only knew that I was seeing Pinkerton stalking towards his Butterfly, ready to reward her love with his lecherous hands. The image sickened me, pulled me to my knees, so I was crawling towards her like a worm. By the time I reached her, Pinkerton . . . had vanished from my heart. To be replaced by something new, something unnatural, that flew in the face of all I'd learned in the world—something very close to love.

He grabs her around the waist; she strokes his hair.

105 **Gallimard:** Butterfly, forgive me.
Song: Rene . . .
Gallimard: For everything. From the start.
Song: I'm . . .
Gallimard: I want to—
110 **Song:** I'm pregnant. *(Beat.)* I'm pregnant. *(Beat.)* I'm pregnant.

Beat.

Gallimard: I want to marry you!

Scene 7

Gallimard and Butterfly's flat. Beijing. 1963.

Downstage, Song paces as Comrade Chin reads from her notepad. Upstage, Gallimard is still kneeling. He remains on his knees throughout the scene, watching it.

Song: I need a baby.
Chin *(from pad):* He's been spotted going to a dorm.
Song: I need a baby.
Chin: At the Foreign Language Institute.
5 **Song:** I need a baby.
Chin: The room of a Danish girl. . . . What do you mean, you need a baby?!
Song: Tell Comrade Kang—last night, the entire mission, it could've ended.
Chin: What do you mean?
Song: Tell Kang—he told me to strip.
10 **Chin:** Strip?!
Song: Write!
Chin: I tell you, I don't understand nothing about this case anymore. Nothing.
Song: He told me to strip, and I took a chance. Oh, we Chinese, we know how to gamble.
Chin *(writing,):* " . . . told him to strip."
15 **Song:** My palms were wet, I had to make a split-second decision.
Chin: Hey! Can you slow down?!

Pause.

Song: You write faster, I'm the artist here. Suddenly, it hit me—"All he wants is for her to submit. Once a woman submits, a man is always ready to become 'generous.'"
Chin: You're just gonna end up with rough notes.
Song: And it worked! He gave in! Now, if I can just present him with a baby. A Chinese baby with blond hair—he'll be mine for life!
20 **Chin:** Kang will never agree! The trading of babies has to be a counterrevolutionary act!
Song: Sometimes, a counterrevolutionary act is necessary to counter a counterrevolutionary act.

Pause.

Chin: Wait.

Song: I need one . . . in seven months. Make sure it's a boy.

Chin: This doesn't sound like something the Chairman would do. Maybe you'd better talk to Comrade Kang yourself.

25 **Song:** Good. I will.

Chin gets up to leave.

Song: Miss Chin? Why, in the Peking Opera, are women's roles played by men?

Chin: I don't know. Maybe, a reactionary remnant of male—

Song: No. *(Beat.)* Because only a man knows how a woman is supposed to act.

Chin exits. Song, turns upstage, towards Gallimard.

Gallimard *(calling after Chin):* Good riddance! *(To Song.)* I could forget all that betrayal in an instant, you know. If you'd just come back and become Butterfly again.

30 **Song:** Fat chance. You're here in prison, rotting in a cell. And I'm on a plane, winging my way back to China. Your President pardoned me of our treason, you know.

Gallimard: Yes, I read about that.

Song: Must make you feel . . . lower than shit.

Gallimard: But don't you, even a litle bit, wish you were here with me?

Song: I'm an artist, Rene. You were my greatest . . . acting challenge. *(She laughs.)* It doesn't matter how rotten I answer, does it? You still adore me. That's why I love you, Rene. *(She points to us.)* So—you were telling your audience about the night I announced I was pregnant.

Gallimard puts his arms around Song's waist. He and Song are in the positions they were in at the end of Scene 6.

Scene 8

Same.

Gallimard: I'll divorce my wife. We'll live together here, and then later in France.

Song: I feel so . . . ashamed.

Gallimard: Why?

Song: I had begun to lose faith. And now, you shame me with your generosity.

5 **Gallimard:** Generosity? No, I'm proposing for very selfish reasons.

Song: Your apologies only make me feel more ashamed. My outburst a moment ago!

Gallimard: Your outburst? What about my request?!

Song: You've been very patient dealing with my . . . eccentricities. A Western man, used to women freer with their bodies—

Gallimard: It was sick! Don't make excuses for me.

10 **Song:** I have to. You don't seem willing to make them for yourself.

Pause.

Gallimard: You're crazy.

Song: I'm happy. Which often looks like crazy.

Gallimard: Then make me crazy. Marry me.

Pause.

Song: No.

15 **Gallimard:** What?

Song: Do I sound silly, a slave, if I say I'm not worthy?

Gallimard: Yes. In fact you do. No one has loved me like you.

Song: Thank you. And no one ever will. I'll see to that.

Gallimard: So what is the problem?

20 **Song:** Rene, we Chinese are realists. We understand rice, gold, and guns. You are a diplomat. Your career is skyrocketing. Now, what would happen if you divorced your wife to marry a Communist Chinese actress?

Gallimard: That's not being realistic. That's defeating yourself before you begin.

Song: We conserve our strength for the battles we can win.

Gallimard: That sounds like a fortune cookie!

Song: Where do you think fortune cookies come from!

25 **Gallimard:** I don't care.

Song: You do. So do I. And we should. That is why I say I'm not worthy. I'm worthy to love and even to be loved by you. But I am not worthy to end the career of one of the West's most promising diplomats.

Gallimard: It's not that great a career! I made it sound like more than it is!

Song: Modesty will get you nowhere. Flatter yourself, and you flatter me. I'm flattered to decline your offer. (*She exits.*)

Gallimard (*to us*): Butterfly and I argued all night. And, in the end, I left, knowing I would never be her husband. She went away for several months—to the countryside, like a small animal. Until one night I received her call.

A baby's cry from offstage. Song enters, carrying a child.

30 **Song:** He looks like you.

Gallimard: Oh! (*Beat; he approaches the baby.*) Well, babies are never very attractive at birth.

Song: Stop!

Gallimard: I'm sure he'll grow more beautiful with age. More like his mother.

Song: "*Chi vide mai / a bimbo del Giappon . . .*"

35 **Gallimard:** "What baby, I wonder, was ever born in Japan"—or China, for that matter—

Song: "*. . . occhi azzurrini?*"

Gallimard: "With azure eyes"—they're actually sort of brown, wouldn't you say?

Song: "*E il labbro.*"

Gallimard: "And such lips!" (*He kisses Song.*) And such lips.

40 **Song:** "*E i ricciolini d'oro schietto?*"

Gallimard: "And such a head of golden"—if slightly patchy—"curls?"

Song: I'm going to call him "Peepee."

Gallimard: Darling, could you repeat that because I'm sure a rickshaw just flew by overhead.

Song: You heard me.

45 **Gallimard:** "Song Peepee"? May I suggest Michael, or Stephan, or Adolph?

Song: You may, but I won't listen.

Gallimard: You can't be serious. Can you imagine the time this child will have in school?

Song: In the West, yes.

Gallimard: It's worse than naming him Ping Pong or Long Dong or—

50 **Song:** But he's never going to live in the West, is he?

Pause.

Gallimard: That wasn't my choice.

Song: It is mine. And this is my promise to you: I will raise him, he will be our child, but he will never burden you outside of China.

Gallimard: Why do you make these promises? I want to be burdened! I want a scandal to cover the papers!

Song *(to us):* Prophetic.

55 **Gallimard:** I'm serious.

Song: So am I. His name is as I registered it. And he will never live in the West.

> *Song exits with the child.*

Gallimard *(to us):* Is it possible that her stubbornness only made me want her more? That drawing back at the moment of my capitulation was the most brilliant strategy she could have chosen? It is possible. But it is also possible that by this point she could have said, could have done . . . anything, and I would have adored her still.

Scene 9

Beijing. 1966.
> *A driving rhythm of Chinese percussion fills the stage.*

Gallimard: And then, China began to change. Mao became very old, and his cult became very strong. And, like many old men, he entered his second childhood. So he handed over the reins of state to those with minds like his own. And children ruled the Middle Kingdom[5] with complete caprice. The doctrine of the Cultural Revolution[6] implied continuous anarchy. Contact between Chinese and foreigners became impossible. Our flat was confiscated. Her fame and my money now counted against us.

> *Two dancers in Mao suits and red-starred caps enter, and begin crudely mimicking revolutionary violence, in an agitprop fashion.*

Gallimard: And somehow the American war went wrong, too. Four hundred thousand dollars were being spent for every Viet Cong[7] killed; so General Westmoreland's[8] remark that the Oriental does not value life the way Americans do was oddly accurate. Why weren't the Vietnamese people giving in? Why were they content instead to die and die and die again?

> *Toulon enters. Percussion and dancers continue upstage.*

Toulon: Congratulations, Gallimard.

Gallimard: Excuse me, sir?

5 **Toulon:** Not a promotion. That was last time. You're going home.

Gallimard: What?

Toulon: Don't say I didn't warn you.

Gallimard: I'm being transferred . . . because I was wrong about the American war?

---

[5] **Middle Kingdom:** The Middle Empire (581–960).

[6] **Cultural Revolution:** Mao's reform campaign of 1965–1967 to purge counterrevolutionary thought and rekindle revolutionary fervor in China. He did so with the help of the Red Guards, young followers who operated on the provincial level to purge China of capitalist elements.

[7] **Viet Cong:** Member of the National Liberation Front of South Vietnam, against which U.S. forces were fighting.

[8] **General Westmoreland** (b. 1914); Commanded American troops in Vietnam from 1964 to 1968.

Toulon: Of course not. We don't care about the Americans. We care about your mind. The quality of your analysis. In general, everything you've predicted here in the Orient . . . just hasn't happened.

10 **Gallimard:** I think that's premature.

Toulon: Don't force me to be blunt. Okay, you said China was ready to open to Western trade. The only thing they're trading out there are Western heads. And, yes, you said the Americans would succeed in Indochina. You were kidding, right?

Gallimard: I think the end is in sight.

Toulon: Don't be pathetic. And don't take this personally. You were wrong. It's not your fault.

Gallimard: But I'm going home.

15 **Toulon:** Right. Could I have the number of your mistress? (*Beat.*) Joke! Joke! Eat a croissant for me.

Toulon exits. Song, wearing a Mao suit, is dragged in from the wings as part of the upstage dance. They "beat" her, then lampoon the acrobatics of the Chinese opera, as she is made to kneel onstage.

Gallimard (*simultaneously*): I don't care to recall how Butterfly and I said our hurried farewell. Perhaps it was better to end our affair before it killed her.

Gallimard exits. Percussion rises in volume. The lampooning becomes faster, more frenetic. At its height. Comrade Chin walks across the stage with a banner reading: "The Actor Renounces His Decadent Profession!" She reaches the kneeling Song. At the moment Chin touches Song's chin, percussion stops with a thud. Dancers strike poses.

Chin: Actor-oppressor, for years you have lived above the common people and looked down on their labor. While the farmer ate millet—

Song: I ate pastries from France and sweetmeats from silver trays.

Chin: And how did you come to live in such an exalted position?

20 **Song:** I was a plaything for the imperialists!

Chin: What did you do?

Song: I shamed China by allowing myself to be corrupted by a foreigner . . .

Chin: What does this mean? The People demand a full confession!

Song: I engaged in the lowest perversions with China's enemies!

25 **Chin:** What perversions? Be more clear!

Song: I let him put it up my ass!

Dancers look over, disgusted.

Chin: Aaaa-ya! How can you use such sickening language?!

Song: My language . . . is only as foul as the crimes I committed . . .

Chin: Yeah. That's better. So—what do you want to do . . . now?

30 **Song:** I want to serve the people!

Percussion starts up, with Chinese strings.

Chin: What?

Song: I want to serve the people!

Dancers regain their revolutionary smiles, and begin a dance of victory.

Chin: What?!

Song: I want to serve the people!!

Dancers unveil a banner: "The Actor Is Re-Habilitated!" Song remains kneeling before Chin, as the dancers bounce around them, then exit. Music out.

Scene 10

A commune. Hunan Province. 1970.

Chin: How you planning to do that?

Song: I've already worked four years in the fields of Hunan, Comrade Chin.

Chin: So? Farmers work all their lives. Let me see your hands.

Song holds them out for her inspection.

Chin: Goddamn! Still so smooth! How long does it take to turn you actors into good any-things? Hunh. You've just spent too many years in luxury to be any good to the Revolution.

5   **Song:** I served the Revolution.

Chin: Serve the Revolution? Bullshit! You wore dresses! Don't tell me—I was there. I saw you! You and your white vice-consul! Stuck up there in your flat, living off the People's Treasury! Yeah, I knew what was going on! You two . . . homos! Homos! Homos! *(Pause; she composes herself.)* Ah! Well . . . you will serve the people, all right. But not with the Revolution's money. This time, you use your own money.

Song: I have no money.

Chin: Shut up! And you won't stink up China anymore with your pervert stuff. You'll pollute the place where pollution begins—the West.

Song: What do you mean?

10 **Chin:** Shut up! You're going to France. Without a cent in your pocket. You find your consul's house, you make him pay your expenses—

Song: No.

Chin: And you give us weekly reports! Useful information!

Song: That's crazy. It's been four years.

Chin: Either that, or back to rehabilitation center!

15 **Song:** Comrade Chin, he's not going to support me! Not in France! He's a white man! I was just his plaything—

Chin: Oh yuck! Again with the sickening language? Where's my stick?

Song: You don't understand the mind of a man.

Pause.

Chin: Oh no? No I don't? Then how come I'm married, huh? How come I got a man? Five, six years ago, you always tell me those kind of things, I felt very bad. But not now! Because what does the Chairman say? He tells us *I'm* now the smart one, you're now the nincompoop! *You're* the blockhead, the harebrain, the nitwit! You think you're so smart? You understand "The Mind of a Man"? Good! Then *you* go to France and be a pervert for Chairman Mao!

Chin and Song exit in opposite directions.

Scene 11

Paris. 1968–1970.
   Gallimard enters.

Gallimard: And what was waiting for me back in Paris? Well, better Chinese food than I'd eaten in China. Friends and relatives. A little accounting, regular schedule, keeping track of traffic violations in the suburbs. . . . And the indignity of students shouting the slogans of Chairman Mao at me—in French.

Helga: Rene? Rene? *(She enters, soaking wet.)* I've had a . . . problem.

(She sneezes.)

Gallimard: You're wet.

Helga: Yes, I . . . coming back from the grocer's. A group of students, waving red flags, they—

Gallimard fetches a towel.

Helga: —they ran by, I was caught up along with them. Before I knew what was happening—

Gallimard gives her the towel.

Helga: Thank you. The police started firing water cannons at us. I tried to shout, to tell them I was the wife of a diplomat, but—you know how it is . . . *(Pause.)* Needless to say, I lost the groceries. Rene, what's happening to France?

5 **Gallimard:** What's—? Well, nothing, really.

Helga: Nothing?! The storefronts are in flames, there's glass in the streets, buildings are toppling—and I'm wet!

Gallimard: Nothing! . . . that I care to think about.

Helga: And is that why you stay in this room?

Gallimard: Yes, in fact.

10 **Helga:** With the incense burning? You know something? I hate incense. It smells so sickly sweet.

Gallimard: Well, I hate the French. Who just smell—period!

Helga: And the Chinese were better?

Gallimard: Please—don't start.

Helga: When we left, this exact same thing, the riots—

15 **Gallimard:** No, no . . .

Helga: Students screaming slogans, smashing down doors—

Gallimard: Helga—

Helga: It was all going on in China, too. Don't you remember?!

Gallimard: Helga! Please! *(Pause.)* You have never understood China, have you? You walk in here with these ridiculous ideas, that the West is falling apart, that China was spitting in our faces. You come in, dripping of the streets, and you leave water all over my floor. *(He grabs Helga's towel, begins mopping up the floor.)*

20 **Helga:** But it's the truth!

Gallimard: Helga, I want a divorce.

Pause; Gallimard continues mopping the floor.

Helga: I take it back. China is . . . beautiful. Incense, I like incense.

Gallimard: I've had a mistress.

Helga: So?

25 **Gallimard:** For eight years.

Helga: I knew you would. I knew you would the day I married you. And now what? You want to marry her?

Gallimard: I can't. She's in China.

Helga: I see. You know that no one else is ever going to marry me, right?

Gallimard: I'm sorry.

30 **Helga:** And you want to leave. For someone who's not here, is that right?

Gallimard: That's right.

Helga: You can't live with her, but still you don't want to live with me.

Gallimard: That's right.

Pause.

Helga: Shit. How terrible that I can figure that out. *(Pause.)* I never thought I'd say it. But, in China, I was happy. I knew, in my own way, I knew that you were not everything you pretended to be. But the pretense—going on your arm to the embassy ball, visiting your office and the guards saying, "Good morning, good morning, Madame Gallimard"—the pretense . . . was very good indeed. *(Pause.)* I hope everyone is mean to you for the rest of your life. *(She exits.)*

35 **Gallimard** *(to us):* Prophetic.

Marc enters with two drinks.

Gallimard *(to Marc):* In China, I was different from all other men.

Marc: Sure. You were white. Here's your drink.

Gallimard: I felt . . . touched.

Marc: In the head? Rene, I don't want to hear about the Oriental love goddess. Okay? One night—can we just drink and throw up without a lot of conversation?

40 **Gallimard:** You still don't believe me, do you?

Marc: Sure I do. She was the most beautiful, et cetera, et cetera, blasé, blasé.

Pause.

Gallimard: My life in the West has been such a disappointment.

Marc: Life in the West is like that. You'll get used to it. Look, you're driving me away. I'm leaving. Happy, now? *(He exits, then returns.)* Look, I have a date tomorrow night. You wanna come? I can fix you up with—

Gallimard: Of course. I would love to come.

Pause.

45 **Marc:** Uh—on second thought, no. You'd better get ahold of yourself first.

He exits; Gallimard nurses his drink.

Gallimard *(to us):* This is the ultimate cruelty, isn't it? That I can talk and talk and to anyone listening, it's only air—too rich a diet to be swallowed by a mundane world. Why can't anyone understand? That in China, I once loved, and was loved by, very simply, the Perfect Woman.

Song enters, dressed as Butterfly in wedding dress.

Gallimard *(to Song):* Not again. My imagination is hell. Am I asleep this time? Or did I drink too much?

Song: Rene!

Gallimard: God, it's too painful! That you speak?

50 **Song:** What are you talking about? Rene—touch me.

Gallimard: Why?

Song: I'm real. Take my hand.

Gallimard: Why? So you can disappear again and leave me clutching at the air? For the entertainment of my neighbors who—?

Song touches Gallimard.

Song: Rene?

Gallimard takes Song's hand. Silence.

55 **Gallimard:** Butterfly? I never doubted you'd return.

Song: You hadn't . . . forgotten—?

Gallimard: Yes, actually, I've forgotten everything. My mind, you see—there wasn't enough room in this hard head—not for the world *and* for you. No, there was only room for one. *(Beat.)* Come, look. See? Your bed has been waiting, with the Klimt[9] poster you like, and—see? The *xiang lu*[10] you gave me?

Song: I . . . I don't know what to say.

Gallimard: There's nothing to say. Not at the end of a long trip. Can I make you some tea?

60 **Song:** But where's your wife?

Gallimard: She's by my side. She's by my side at last.

Gallimard reaches to embrace Song. Song sidesteps, dodging him.

Gallimard: Why?!

Song *(to us):* So I did return to Rene in Paris. Where I found—

Gallimard: Why do you run away? Can't we show them how we embraced that evening?

Song: Please. I'm talking.

65 **Gallimard:** You have to do what I say! I'm conjuring you up in *my* mind!

Song: Rene, I've never done what you've said. Why should it be any different in your mind? Now split—the story moves on, and I must change.

Gallimard: I welcomed you into my home! I didn't have to, you know! I could've left you penniless on the streets of Paris! But I took you in!

Song: Thank you.

Gallimard: So . . . please . . . don't change.

70 **Song:** You know I have to. You know I will. And anyway, what difference does it make? No matter what your eyes tell you, you can't ignore the truth. You already know too much.

Gallimard exits. Song turns to us.

Song: The change I'm going to make requires about five minutes. So I thought you might want to take this opportunity to stretch your legs, enjoy a drink, or listen to the musicians. I'll be here, when you return, right where you left me.

Song goes to a mirror in front of which is a wash basin of water. She starts to remove her makeup as stagelights go to half and houselights come up.

Act Three
Scene 1

A courthouse in Paris. 1986.

As he promised, Song has completed the bulk of his transformation onstage by the time the houselights go down and the stagelights come up full. As he speaks to us, he removes his wig and kimono, leaving them on the floor. Underneath, he wears a well-cut suit.

Song: So I'd done my job better than I had a right to expect. Well, give him some credit, too. He's right—I was in a fix when I arrived in Paris. I walked from the airport into town, then I located, by blind groping, the Chinatown district. Let me make one thing clear: whatever else may be said about the Chinese, they are stingy! I slept in doorways three days until I could find a tailor who would make me this kimono on credit.

---

[9] **Klimt:** Gustav Klimt (1863–1918), Austrian painter.

[10] **xiang lu:** Incense burner

As it turns out, maybe I didn't even need it. Maybe he would've been happy to see me in a simple shift and mascara. But . . . better safe than sorry.

That was 1970, when I arrived in Paris. For the next fifteen years, yes, I lived a very comfy life. Some relief, believe me, after four years on a fucking commune in Nowheresville, China. Rene supported the boy and me, and I did some demonstrations around the country as part of my "cultural exchange" cover. And then there was the spying.

Song moves upstage, to a chair. Toulon enters as a judge, wearing the appropriate wig and robes. He sits near Song. It's 1986, and Song is testifying in a courtroom.

Song: Not much at first. Rene had lost all his high-level contacts. Comrade Chin wasn't very interested in parking-ticket statistics. But finally, at my urging, Rene got a job as a courier, handling sensitive documents. He'd photograph them for me, and I'd pass them on to the Chinese embassy.

Judge: Did he understand the extent of his activity?

Song: He didn't ask. He knew that I needed those documents, and that was enough.

Judge: But he must've known he was passing classified information.

5 **Song:** I can't say.

Judge: He never asked what you were going to do with them?

Song: Nope.

Pause.

Judge: There is one thing that the court—indeed, that all of France—would like to know.

Song: Fire away.

10 **Judge:** Did Monsieur Gallimard know you were a man?

Song: Well, he never saw me completely naked. Ever.

Judge: But surely, he must've . . . how can I put this?

Song: Put it however you like. I'm not shy. He must've felt around?

Judge: Mmmmm.

15 **Song:** Not really. I did all the work. He just laid back. Of course we did enjoy more . . . complete union, and I suppose he *might* have wondered why I was always on my stomach, but. . . . But what you're thinking is, "Of course a wrist must've brushed . . . a hand hit . . . over twenty years!" Yeah. Well, Your Honor, it was my job to make him think I was a woman. And chew on this: it wasn't all that hard. See, my mother was a prostitute along the Bundt before the Revolution. And, uh, I think it's fair to say she learned a few things about Western men. So I borrowed her knowledge. In service to my country.

Judge: Would you care to enlighten the court with this secret knowledge? I'm sure we're all very curious.

Song: I'm sure you are. *(Pause.)* Okay, Rule One is: Men always believe what they want to hear. So a girl can tell the most obnoxious lies and the guys will believe them every time—"This is my first time"—"That's the biggest I've ever seen"—or *both*, which, if you really think about it, is not possible in a single lifetime. You've maybe heard those phrases a few times in your own life, yes, Your Honor?

Judge: It's not my life, Monsieur Song, which is on trial today.

Song: Okay, okay, just trying to lighten up the proceedings. Tough room.

20 **Judge:** Go on.

Song: Rule Two: As soon as a Western man comes into contact with the East—he's already confused. The West has sort of an international rape mentality towards the East. Do you know rape mentality?

Judge: Give us your definition, please.

Song: Basically, "Her mouth says no, but her eyes say yes."

The West thinks of itself as masculine—big guns, big industry, big money—so the East is feminine—weak, delicate, poor . . . but good at art, and full of inscrutable wisdom—the feminine mystique.

Her mouth says no, but her eyes say yes. The West believes the East, deep down, wants to be dominated—because a woman can't think for herself.

Judge: What does this have to do with my question?

25 **Song:** You expect Oriental countries to submit to your guns, and you expect Oriental women to be submissive to your men. That's why you say they make the best wives.

Judge: But why would that make it possible for you to fool Monsieur Gallimard? Please—get to the point.

Song: One, because when he finally met his fantasy woman, he wanted more than anything to believe that she was, in fact, a woman. And second, I am an Oriental. And being an Oriental, I could never be completely a man.

Pause.

Judge: Your armchair political theory is tenuous, Monsieur Song.

Song: You think so? That's why you'll lose in all your dealings with the East.

30 **Judge:** Just answer my question: did he know you were a man?

Pause.

Song: You know, Your Honor, I never asked.

Scene 2

Same.

Music from the "Death Scene" from Butterfly blares over the house speakers. It is the loudest thing we've heard in this play.

Gallimard enters, crawling towards Song's wig and kimono.

Gallimard: Butterfly? Butterfly?

Song remains a man, in the witness box, delivering a testimony we do not hear.

Gallimard *(to us):* In my moment of greatest shame, here, in this courtroom—with that . . . person up there, telling the world. . . . What strikes me especially is how shallow he is, how glib and obsequious . . . completely . . . without substance! The type that prowls around discos with a gold medallion stinking of garlic. So little like my Butterfly.

Yet even in this moment my mind remains agile, flip-flopping like a man on a trampoline. Even now, my picture dissolves, and I see that . . . witness . . . talking to me.

Song suddenly stands straight up in his witness box, and looks at Gallimard.

Song: Yes. You. White man.

Song steps out of the witness box, and moves downstage towards Gallimard. Light change.

Gallimard *(to Song):* Who? Me?

Song: Do you see any other white men?

5 **Gallimard:** Yes. There're white men all around. This is a French courtroom.

Song: So you are an adventurous imperialist. Tell me, why did it take you so long? To come back to this place?

Gallimard: What place?

Song: This theater in China. Where we met many years ago. . . .

Gallimard *(to us)*: And once again, against my will, I am transported.

Chinese opera music comes up on the speakers. Song begins to do opera moves, as he did the night they met.

10   **Song:** Do you remember? The night you gave your heart?

Gallimard: It was a long time ago.

Song: Not long enough. A night that turned your world upside down.

Gallimard: Perhaps.

Song: Oh, be honest with me. What's another bit of flattery when you've already given me twenty years' worth? It's a wonder my head hasn't swollen to the size of China.

15   **Gallimard:** Who's to say it hasn't?

Song: Who's to say? And what's the shame? In pride? You think I could've pulled this off if I wasn't already full of pride when we met? No, not just pride. Arrogance. It takes arrogance, really—to believe you can will, with your eyes and your lips, the destiny of another. *(He dances.)* C'mon. Admit it. You still want me. Even in slacks and a button-down collar.

Gallimard: I don't see what the point of—

Song: You don't? Well maybe, Rene, just maybe—I want you.

Gallimard: You do?

20   **Song:** Then again, maybe I'm just playing with you. How can you tell? *(Reprising his feminine character, he sidles up to Gallimard.)* "How I wish there were even a small café to sit in. With men in tuxedos, and cappuccinos, and bad expatriate jazz." Now you want to kiss me, don't you?

Gallimard *(pulling away)*: What makes you—?

Song: —so sure? See? I take the words from your mouth. Then I wait for you to come and retrieve them. *(He reclines on the floor.)*

Gallimard: Why?! Why do you treat me so cruelly?

Song: Perhaps I *was* treating you cruelly. But now—I'm being nice. Come here, my little one.

25   **Gallimard:** I'm not your little one!

Song: My mistake. It's I who am *your* little one, right?

Gallimard: Yes, I—

Song: So come get your little one. If you like, I may even let you strip me.

Gallimard: I mean, you were! Before . . . but not like this!

30   **Song:** I was? Then perhaps I still am. If you look hard enough. *(He starts to remove his clothes.)*

Gallimard: What—what are you doing?

Song: Helping you to see through my act.

Gallimard: Stop that! I don't want to! I don't—

Song: Oh, but you asked me to strip, remember?

35   **Gallimard:** What? That was years ago! And I took it back!

Song: No. You postponed it. Postponed the inevitable. Today, the inevitable has come calling.

From the speakers, cacophony: Butterfly mixed in with Chinese gongs.

Gallimard: No! Stop! I don't want to see!

Song: Then look away.

Gallimard: You're only in my mind! All this is in my mind! I order you! To stop!

40 **Song:** To what? To strip? That's just what I'm—

Gallimard: No! Stop! I want you—!

Song: You want me?

Gallimard: To stop!

Song: You know something, Rene? Your mouth says no, but your eyes say yes. Turn them away. I dare you.

45 **Gallimard:** I don't have to! Every night, you say you're going to strip, but then I beg you and you stop!

Song: I guess tonight is different.

Gallimard: Why? Why should that be?

Song: Maybe I've become frustrated. Maybe I'm saying "Look at me, you fool!" Or maybe I'm just feeling . . . sexy. *(He is down to his briefs.)*

Gallimard: Please. This is unnecessary. I know what you are.

50 **Song:** You do? What am I?

Gallimard: A—a man.

Song: You don't really believe that.

Gallimard: Yes I do! I knew all the time somewhere that my happiness was temporary, my love a deception. But my mind kept the knowledge at bay. To make the wait bearable.

Song: Monsieur Gallimard—the wait is over.

Song drops his briefs. He is naked. Sound cue out. Slowly, we and Song came to the realization that what we had thought to be Gallimard's sobbing is actually his laughter.

55 **Gallimard:** Oh god! What an idiot! Of course!

Song: Rene—what?

Gallimard: Look at you! You're a man! *(He bursts into laughter again.)*

Song: I fail to see what's so funny!

Gallimard: "You fail to see—!" I mean, you never did have much of a sense of humor, did you? I just think it's ridiculously funny that I've wasted so much time on just a man!

60 **Song:** Wait. I'm not "just a man."

Gallimard: No? Isn't that what you've been trying to convince me of?

Song: Yes, but what I mean—

Gallimard: And now, I finally believe you, and you tell me it's not true? I think you must have some kind of identity problem.

Song: Will you listen to me?

65 **Gallimard:** Why?! I've been listening to you for twenty years. Don't I deserve a vacation?

Song: I'm not just any man!

Gallimard: Then, what exactly are you?

Song: Rene, how can you ask—? Okay, what about this?

He picks up Butterfly's robes, starts to dance around. No music.

Gallimard: Yes, that's very nice. I have to admit.

Song holds out his arm to Gallimard.

70 **Song:** It's the same skin you've worshipped for years. Touch it.

Gallimard: Yes, it does feel the same.

Song: Now—close your eyes.

Song covers Gallimard's eyes with one hand. With the other, Song draws Gallimard's hand up to his face. Gallimard, like a blind man, lets his hands run over Song's face.

Gallimard: This skin, I remember. The curve of her face, the softness of her cheek, her hair against the back of my hand . . .

Song: I'm your Butterfly. Under the robes, beneath everything, it was always me. Now, open your eyes and admit it—you adore me. (*He removes his hand from Gallimard's eyes.*)

75 **Gallimard:** You, who knew every inch of my desires—how could you, of all people, have made such a mistake?

Song: What?

Gallimard: You showed me your true self. When all I loved was the lie. A perfect lie, which you let fall to the ground—and now, it's old and soiled.

Song: So—you never really loved me? Only when I was playing a part?

Gallimard: I'm a man who loved a woman created by a man. Everything else—simply falls short.

Pause.

80 **Song:** What am I supposed to do now?

Gallimard: You were a fine spy, Monsieur Song, with an even finer accomplice. But now I believe you should go. Get out of my life!

Song: Go where? Rene, you can't live without me. Not after twenty years.

Gallimard: I certainly can't live with you—not after twenty years of betrayal.

Song: Don't be stubborn! Where will you go?

85 **Gallimard:** I have a date . . . with my Butterfly.

Song: So, throw away your pride. And come . . .

Gallimard: Get away from me! Tonight, I've finally learned to tell fantasy from reality. And, knowing the difference, I choose fantasy.

Song: *I'm* your fantasy!

Gallimard: You? You're as real as hamburger. Now get out! I have a date with my Butterfly and I don't want your body polluting the room! (*He tosses Song's suit at him.*) Look at these—you dress like a pimp.

90 **Song:** Hey! These are Armani slacks and—! (*He puts on his briefs and slacks.*) Let's just say . . . I'm disappointed in you, Rene. In the crush of your adoration, I thought you'd become something more. More like . . . a woman.

But no. Men. You're like the rest of them. It's all in the way we dress, and make up our faces, and bat our eyelashes. You really have so little imagination!

Gallimard: You, Monsieur Song? Accuse me of too little imagination? You, if anyone, should know—I am pure imagination. And in imagination I will remain. Now get out!

Gallimard bodily removes Song from the stage, taking his kimono.

Song: Rene! I'll never put on those robes again! You'll be sorry!

Gallimard (*to Song*): I'm already sorry! (*Looking at the kimono in his hands.*) Exactly as sorry . . . as a Butterfly.

Scene 3

M. Gallimard's prison cell. Paris. 1988.

Gallimard: I've played out the events of my life night after night, always searching for a new ending to my story, one where I leave this cell and return forever to my Butterfly's arms.

Tonight I realize my search is over. That I've looked all along in the wrong place. And now, to you, I will prove that my love was not in vain—by returning to the world of fantasy where I first met her.

He picks up the kimono; dancers enter.

Gallimard: There is a vision of the Orient that I have. Of slender women in cheongsams and kimonos who die for the love of unworthy foreign devils. Who are born and raised to be the perfect women. Who take whatever punishment we give them, and bounce back, strengthened by love, unconditionally. It is a vision that has become my life.

Dancers bring the washbasin to him and help him make up his face.

Gallimard: In public, I have continued to deny that Song Liling is a man. This brings me headlines, and is a source of great embarrassment to my French colleagues, who can now be sent into a coughing fit by the mere mention of Chinese food. But alone, in my cell, I have long since faced the truth.

And the truth demands a sacrifice. For mistakes made over the course of a lifetime. My mistakes were simple and absolute—the man I loved was a cad, a bounder. He deserved nothing but a kick in the behind, and instead I gave him . . . all my love.

Yes—love. Why not admit it all? That was my undoing, wasn't it? Love warped my judgment, blinded my eyes, rearranged the very lines on my face . . . until I could look in the mirror and see nothing but . . . a woman.

Dancers help him put on the Butterfly wig.

Gallimard: I have a vision. Of the Orient. That, deep within its almond eyes, there are still women. Women willing to sacrifice themselves for the love of a man. Even a man whose love is completely without worth.

Dancers assist Gallimard in donning the kimono. They hand him a knife.

Gallimard: Death with honor is better than life . . . life with dishonor. (*He sets himself center stage, in a seppuku position.*) The love of a Butterfly can withstand many things—unfaithfulness, loss, even abandonment. But how can it face the one sin that implies all others? The devastating knowledge that, underneath it all, the object of her love was nothing more, nothing less than . . . a man. (*He sets the tip of the knife against his body.*) It is 1988. And I have found her at last. In a prison on the outskirts of Paris. My name is Rene Gallimard—also known as Madame Butterfly.

Gallimard turns upstage and plunges the knife into his body, as music from the "Love Duet" blares over the speakers. He collapses into the arms of the dancers, who lay him reverently on the floor. The image holds for several beats. Then a tight special up on Song, who stands as a man, staring at the dead Gallimard. He smokes a cigarette; the smoke filters up through the lights. Two words leave his lips.

Song: Butterfly? Butterfly?

Smoke rises as lights fade slowly to black.

KIM FICERA

Kim Ficera (1959–   ) was born in Connecticut, where she worked for many years as a free-lance journalist before moving with her partner to California. Ficera received a B.F.A. in Creative Writing from Emerson College. Ficera's humorous column, "From Hell to Breakfast," has earned her awards for the Best Columnist and Best Writer/Reporter in the Fairfield and Westchester County Weeklies's annual Reader's Polls (April 2001) and Second-Best Resident Celebrity in the Fairfield County Weekly's 2003 Reader's Poll (April 2003). Ficera also publishes an online soap opera, "Gays of Our Lives." Her writing has appeared in Girlfriends Magazine, *the* Stamford Advocate, *the* Greenwich Times, Flagpole Magazine, *and online. The following essay from Ficera's book,* Sex, Lies, and Stereotypes: An Uncon-ventional Life Uncensored *(2003), illustrates the humor that has led to her success as a journalist.*

2003

ALL IN THE FAMILY

As I write this essay, I'm preparing to break bread with the people I hope will one day be my in-laws. By the time you read it, Thanksgiving 2001 will have come and gone and my indelible mark on my babe's Republican family will have been made. Henceforth, they will regard me as either the creep their daughter sleeps with or that lovely Democrat with the antipasto whom they can't wait to see again.

Since I know I'll only get one chance to make a good impression, I plan on leaving my denim and leather at home and showing up for dinner dressed in something I'd likely wear to a wake. I won't wear anything too flashy or revealing because I don't want to call an un-usual amount of attention to myself or remind her father of Courtney Love. And even though I don't plan on switching political parties, I will leave my "Fuck Jesse Helms" T-shirt at home and borrow shoes that suggest I own a dress—shoes without tongues, laces, or soles with treads. I will not borrow said dress however, because I'm pretty sure that looking like a clown won't benefit me. I will be on my best behavior without appearing as though possessed by Ann Taylor. I will also wear earrings only in my ears, and will not make imma-ture jokes about the cranberry sauce during grace, no matter how badly I want to make those sitting at the kids' table laugh, to feel like they're part of the holiday and not outcasts from snobby adult society. I will be a charm-schooled version of myself.

I've already begun practicing saying "yes" instead of "damn straight!" and "thank you" instead of "groovy, Marcia." My babe has told me that her mom's pet peeve is bad grammar and that if I want to get on Mom's good side, I should quickly learn the rules concerning the usage of "who" and "whom" and "that" and "which." I should also refrain from saying "fart" in her presence. But since I've been given that instruction, "fart" is all I can think about. I know I'm going to blow it. I fear one will slip out—not an actual fart, but the word. I will have to try very hard not to say, "Please pass the artichoke farts . . . er . . . I mean hearts."

I will have an easier time with my babe's dad, I think. He, I'm told, not only has a sense of humor, but also smokes. I hope to bond with Dad by telling him jokes on cigarette breaks. The only problem is, I know a lot of fart jokes.

5   Perhaps if I get in good with her siblings, they will be able to influence their parents on my behalf should I fail to do so on my own. One sister is a writer, the other works at the Gap. We have words and jeans in common. But will our similarities run deep enough to fos-ter the kind of love I'd like to receive and give an extended family? Will my admiration for

David Sedaris and appreciation for button-fly pants assure that I'll be invited south for Christmas? I won't buy my ticket yet.

Although I've known for months about this weeklong family visit and I'm looking forward to meeting my babe's clan, I'm a little nervous. Both the calendar and my gut tell me that our relationship is still fairly new and that perhaps my future in-laws aren't ready to get to know me. Right now, I'm just a name they've heard mentioned in phone conversations. All they know of me is that I write, golf, eat, and didn't vote for George Bush. They don't know that I hate brussels sprouts, that I love *Moonstruck,* or that I once saved a child from drowning. They aren't aware of my desire to go to the moon before I go to France. And, most importantly, they don't have a clue as to exactly how much I care for their daughter. They've never even seen my picture, so, in their minds, I don't have a face. To them, I'm probably just a nontangible dyke who might resemble the mullet-headed, Camaro-driving, beer-guzzling freak they saw the first, and last, time they went to Red Lobster.

Naturally, I'm eager to drive up to the house with my normal hair in my Honda and prove them wrong, but I doubt they're ready for even a mild dose of reality. Although I've never been in their position, I have a family of my own and am aware that it's one thing for parents to know that their daughter is a lesbian and it's quite another to acknowledge it over bean casserole.

For ten years my father referred to an ex-girlfriend of mine as "what's-her-name." Of course, he knew and could pronounce her two-syllable name. And he liked her, really liked her, despite the lack of respect his refusal to utter her name suggested. But, apparently, referring to her by name would have told whoever was listening—namely me—that he approved of our relationship. She and I both knew better than to take his shame personally, but his discourtesy in the face of our love was difficult to accept.

As a result, I know I don't want to be the "what's-her-name" in my babe's life. I fear I will be, though, regardless of how polite I am to her family or how much I adore her, because I've been to this kind of dinner party before. Only when I met the parents of an ex-girlfriend whose siblings and exes were all drug addicts or convicts did I look fabulous in comparison.

10   If I'm going to win this family's affection, it won't be by default. Aside from being very blonde and well spoken, they're also all pretty stable, from what I hear. So, I'll be on my own. And that scares me, because I'm not sure I'll be able to survive the day with my charming personality and Strunk & White alone. I think I'll ask José Cuervo to join us. With him in the room, if I do accidentally say fart, there's a good chance no one will remember it.

BERNARD COOPER

Bernard Cooper (1951–　) was born in Oklahoma City and received an M.F.A. from the California Institute of the Arts (1975). Cooper's work has been printed in several magazines, including Harper's, The New York Times Magazine, *and* The Paris Review, *and has been anthologized in* The Best American Essays *(1988) and* The O. Henry Prize Collection *(1995). He won the Ernest Hemingway Foundation/PEN Award for his collection of autobiographical essays and poems,* Maps to Anywhere *(1990). "Burl's," which is told from the perspective of a child whose view of the world broadens during a family outing, comes from Cooper's book,* Truth Serum: A Memoir *(1996).*

1996

BURL'S

I

Iloved the restaurant's name, a compact curve of a word. Its sign, five big letters rimmed in neon, hovered above the roof. I almost never saw the sign with its neon lit; my parents took me there for early summer dinners, and even by the time we left—father cleaning his teeth with a toothpick, mother carrying steak bones in a doggie bag—the sky was still bright. Heat rippled off the cars parked along Hollywood Boulevard, the asphalt gummy from hours of sun.

With its sleek architecture, chrome appliances, and arctic temperature, Burl's offered a refuge from the street. We usually sat at one of the booths in front of the plate-glass windows. During our dinner, people came to a halt before the news-vending machine on the corner and burrowed in their pockets and purses for change.

The waitresses at Burl's wore brown uniforms edged in checked gingham. From their breast pockets frothed white lace handkerchiefs. In between reconnaissance missions to the table, they busied themselves behind the counter and shouted "Tuna to travel" or "Scorch that patty" to a harried short-order cook who manned the grill. Miniature pitchers of cream and individual pats of butter were extracted from an industrial refrigerator. Coca-Cola shot from a glinting spigot. Waitresses dodged and bumped one another, frantic as atoms,

My parents usually lingered after the meal, nursing cups of coffee while I played with the beads of condensation on my glass of ice water, tasted Tabasco sauce, or twisted pieces of my paper napkin into mangled animals. One evening, annoyed with my restlessness, my father gave me a dime and asked me to buy him a *Herald Examiner* from the vending machine in front of the restaurant.

5   Shouldering open the heavy glass door, I was seared by a sudden gust of heat. Traffic roared past me and stirred the air. Walking toward the newspaper machine, I held the dime so tightly it seemed to melt in my palm. Duty made me feel large and important. I inserted the dime and opened the box, yanking a *Herald* from the spring contraption that held it as tight as a mousetrap. When I turned around, paper in hand, I saw two women walking toward me.

Their high heels clicked on the sun-baked pavement. They were tall, broad-shouldered women who moved with a mixture of haste and defiance. They'd teased their hair into nearly identical black beehives. Dangling earrings flashed in the sun, brilliant as prisms. Each of them wore the kind of clinging, strapless outfit my mother referred to as a cocktail dress. The silky fabric—one dress was purple, the other pink—accentuated their breasts and hips and rippled with insolent highlights. The dresses exposed their bare arms, the slope of their shoulders, and the smooth, powdered plane of flesh where their cleavage began.

I owned at the time a book called *Things for Boys and Girls to Do*. There were pages to color, intricate mazes, and connect-the-dots. But another type of puzzle came to mind as I watched those women walking toward me: What's Wrong With This Picture? Say the drawing of a dining room looked normal at first glance; on closer inspection, a chair was missing its leg and the man who sat atop it wore half a pair of glasses.

The women had Adam's apples.

The closer they came, the shallower my breathing was. I blocked the sidewalk, an incredulous child stalled in their path. When they saw me staring, they shifted their purses and linked their arms. There was something sisterly and conspiratorial about their sudden closeness. Though their mouths didn't move, I thought they might have been communicating without moving their lips, so telepathic did they seem as they joined arms and pressed together, synchronizing their heavy steps. The pages of the *Herald* fluttered in the wind. I felt them against my arm, light as batted lashes.

10   The woman in pink shot me a haughty glance and yet she seemed pleased that I'd taken notice, hungry to be admired by a man, or even an awestruck eight-year-old boy. She tried to stifle a grin, her red lipstick more voluptuous than the lips it painted. Rouge deepened her cheekbones. Eye shadow dusted her lids, a clumsy abundance of blue. Her face was like a page in *Things for Boys and Girls to Do,* colored by a kid who went outside the lines.

At close range, I saw that her wig was slightly askew. I was certain it was a wig because my mother owned several; three Styrofoam heads lined a shelf in my mother's closet; upon them were perched a Page-Boy, an Empress, and a Baby-Doll, all in shades of auburn. The woman in the pink dress wore her wig like a crown of glory.

But it was the woman in the purple dress who passed nearest me, and I saw that her jaw was heavily powdered, a half-successful attempt to disguise the telltale shadow of a beard. Just as I noticed this, her heel caught on a crack in the pavement and she reeled on her stilettos. It was then that I witnessed a rift in her composure, a window through which I could glimpse the shades of maleness that her dress and wig and makeup obscured. She shifted her shoulders and threw out her hands like a surfer riding a curl. The instant she re-gained her balance, she smoothed her dress, patted her hair, and sauntered onward.

Any woman might be a man. The fact of it clanged through the chambers of my brain. In broad day, in the midst of traffic, with my parents drinking coffee a few feet away, I felt as if everything I understood, everything I had taken for granted up to that moment—the curve of the earth, the heat of the sun, the reliability of my own eyes—had been squeezed out of me. Who were those men? Did they help each other get inside those dresses? How many other people and things were not what they seemed? From the back, the impostors looked like women once again, slinky and curvaceous, purple and pink. I watched them disappear into the distance, their disguises so convincing that other people on the street seemed to take no notice, and for a moment I wondered if I had imagined the whole en-counter, a visitation by two unlikely muses.

Frozen in the middle of the sidewalk, I caught my reflection in the window of Burl's, a sil-houette floating between his parents. They faced one another across a table. Once the solid embodiments of woman and man, pedestrians and traffic appeared to pass through them.

II

15   There were some mornings, seconds before my eyes opened and my senses gathered into con-sciousness, that the child I was seemed to hover above the bed, and I couldn't tell what form my waking would take—the body of a boy or the body of a girl. Finally stirring, I'd blink against the early light and greet each incarnation as a male with mild surprise. My sex, in other words, didn't seem to be an absolute fact so much as a pleasant, recurring accident.

By the age of eight, I'd experienced this groggy phenomenon several times. Those ethe-real moments above my bed made waking up in the tangled blankets, a boy steeped in body heat, all the more astonishing. That this might be an unusual experience never occurred to me; it was one among a flood of sensations I could neither name nor ignore.

And so, shocked as I was when those transvestites passed me in front of Burl's, they confirmed something about which I already had an inkling: the hazy border between the sexes. My father, after all, raised his pinky when he drank from a teacup, and my mother looked as faded and plain as my father until she fixed her hair and painted her face.

Like most children, I once thought it possible to divide the world into male and female columns. Blue/Pink. Rooster/Hens. Trousers/Skirts. Such divisions were easy, not to men-tion comforting, for they simplified matter into compatible pairs. But there also existed a vast range of things that didn't fit neatly into either camp: clocks, milk, telephones, grass. There were nights I fell into a fitful sleep while trying to sex the world correctly.

Nothing typified the realms of male and female as clearly as my parents' walk-in closets. Home alone for any length of time, I always found my way inside them. I could stare at my parents' clothes for hours, grateful for the stillness and silence, haunting the very heart of their privacy.

20 The overhead light in my father's closet was a bare bulb. Whenever I groped for the chain in the dark, it wagged back and forth and resisted my grasp. Once the light clicked on, I saw dozens of ties hanging like stalactites. A monogrammed silk bathrobe sagged from a hook, a gift my father had received on a long-ago birthday and, thinking it fussy, rarely wore. Shirts were cramped together along the length of an aluminum pole, their starched sleeves sticking out as if in a halfhearted gesture of greeting. The medicinal odor of mothballs permeated the boxer shorts that were folded and stacked in a built-in drawer. Immaculate underwear was proof of a tenderness my mother couldn't otherwise express; she may not have touched my father often, but she laundered his boxers with infinite care. Even back then, I suspected that a sense of duty was the final erotic link between them.

Sitting in a neat row on the closet floor were my father's boots and slippers and dress shoes. I'd try on his wingtips and clomp around, slipping out of them with every step. My wary, unnatural stride made me all the more desperate to effect some authority. I'd whisper orders to imagined lackeys and take my invisible wife in my arms. But no matter how much I wanted them to fit, those shoes were as cold and hard as marble.

My mother's shoes were just as uncomfortable, but a lot more fun. From a brightly colored array of pumps and slingbacks, I'd pick a pair with the glee and deliberation of someone choosing a chocolate. Whatever embarrassment I felt was overwhelmed by the exhilaration of being taller in a pair of high heels. Things will look like this someday, I said to myself, gazing out from my new and improved vantage point as if from a crow's nest. Calves elongated, arms akimbo, I gauged each step so that I didn't fall over and moved with what might have passed for grace had someone seen me, a possibility I scrupulously avoided by locking the door.

Back and forth I went. The longer I wore a pair of heels, the better my balance. In the periphery of my vision, the shelf of wigs looked like a throng of kindly bystanders. Light streamed down from a high window, causing crystal bottles to glitter, the air ripe with perfume. A makeup mirror above the dressing table invited my self-absorption. Sound was muffled. Time slowed. It seemed as if nothing bad could happen as long as I stayed within those walls.

Though I'd never been discovered in my mother's closet, my parents knew that I was drawn toward girlish things—dolls and jump rope and jewelry—as well as to the games and preoccupations that were expected of a boy. I'm not sure now if it was my effeminacy itself that bothered them as much as my ability to slide back and forth, without the slightest warning, between male and female mannerisms. After I'd finished building the model of an F-17 bomber, say, I'd sit back to examine my handiwork, pursing my lips in concentration and crossing my legs at the knee.

III

25 One day my mother caught me standing in the middle of my bedroom doing an imitation of Mary Injijikian, a dark, overeager Armenian girl with whom I believed myself to be in love, not only because she was pretty but because I wanted to be like her. Collector of effortless A's, Mary seemed to know all the answers in class. Before the teacher had even finished asking a question, Mary would let out a little grunt and practically levitate out of her seat, as if her hand were filled with helium. "Could we please hear from someone else today besides Miss Injijikian," the teacher would say. *Miss Injijikian.* Those were the words I was repeating over and over to myself when my mother caught me. To utter them was rhythmic, delicious,

and under their spell I raised my hand and wiggled like Mary. I heard a cough and spun around. My mother froze in the doorway. She clutched the folded sheets to her stomach and turned without saying a word. My sudden flush of shame confused me. Weren't boys supposed to swoon over girls? Hadn't I seen babbling, heartsick men in a dozen movies?

Shortly after the Injijikian incident, my parents decided to send me to gymnastics class at the Los Angeles Athletic Club, a brick relic of a building on Olive Street. One of the oldest establishments of its kind in Los Angeles, the club prohibited women from the premises. My parents didn't have to say it aloud: they hoped a fraternal atmosphere would toughen me up and tilt me toward the male side of my nature.

My father drove me downtown so I could sign up for the class, meet the instructor, and get a tour of the place. On the way there, he reminisced about sports. Since he'd grown up in a rough Philadelphia neighborhood, sports consisted of kick-the-can or rolling a hoop down the street with a stick. The more he talked about his physical prowess, the more convinced I became that my daydreams and shyness were a disappointment to him.

The hushed lobby of the athletic club was paneled in dark wood. A few solitary figures were hidden in wing chairs. My father and I introduced ourselves to a man at the front desk who seemed unimpressed by our presence. His aloofness unnerved me, which wasn't hard considering that no matter how my parents put it, I knew their sending me here was a form of disapproval, a way of banishing the part of me they didn't care to know.

A call went out over the intercom for someone to show us around. While we waited, I noticed that the sand in the standing ashtrays had been raked into perfect furrows. The glossy leaves of the potted plants looked as if they'd been polished by hand. The place seemed more like a well-tended hotel than an atheletic club. Finally, a stoop-shouldered old man hobbled toward us, his head shrouded in a cloud of white hair. He wore a T-shirt that said "Instructor"; his arms were so wrinkled and anemic, I thought I might have misread it. While we followed him to the elevator, I readjusted my expectations, which had involved fantasies of a hulking drill sergeant barking orders at a flock of scrawny boys.

30   The instructor, mumbling to himself and never turning around to see if we were behind him, showed us where the gymnastics class took place. I'm certain the building was big, but the size of the room must be exaggerated by a trick of memory, because when I envision it, I picture a vast and windowless warehouse. Mats covered the wooden floor. Here and there, in remote and lonely pools of light, stood a pommel horse, a balance beam, and parallel bars. Tiers of bleachers rose into darkness. Unlike the cloistered air of a closet, the room seemed incomplete without a crowd.

Next we visited the dressing room, empty except for a naked middle-aged man. He sat on a narrow bench and clipped his formidable toenails. Moles dotted his back. He glistened like a fish.

We continued to follow the instructor down an aisle lined with numbered lockers. At the far end, steam billowed from the doorway that led to the showers. Fresh towels stacked on a nearby table made me think of my mother; I knew she liked to have me at home with her—I was often her only companion—and I resented her complicity in the plan to send me here.

The tour ended when the instructor gave me a sign-up sheet. Only a few names preceded mine. They were signatures, or so I imagined, of other soft and wayward sons.

IV

When the day of the first gymnastics class arrived, my mother gave me money and a gym bag and sent me to the corner of Hollywood and Western to wait for a bus. The sun was bright, the traffic heavy. While I sat there, an argument raged inside my head, the familiar, battering debate between the wish to be like other boys and the wish to be like myself. Why shouldn't I simply get up and go back home, where I'd be left alone to read and think? On the other hand, wouldn't life be easier if I liked athletics, or learned to like them?

35   No sooner did I steel my resolve to get on the bus than I thought of something better: I could spend the morning wandering through Woolworth's, then tell my parents I'd gone to the class. But would my lie stand up to scrutiny? As I practiced describing phantom gymnastics, I became aware of a car circling the block. It was a large car in whose shaded interior I could barely make out the driver, but I thought it might be the man who owned the local pet store. I'd often gone there on the pretext of looking at the cocker spaniel puppies huddled together in their pen, but I really went to gawk at the owner, whose tan chest, in the V of his shirt, was the place I most wanted to rest my head. Every time the man moved, counting stock or writing a receipt, his shirt parted, my mouth went dry, and I smelled the musk of sawdust and dogs.

    I found myself hoping that the driver was the man who ran the pet store. I was thrilled by the unlikely possibility that the sight of me, slumped on a bus bench in my T-shirt and shorts, had caused such a man to circle the block. Up to that point in my life, lovemaking hovered somewhere in the future, an impulse a boy might aspire to but didn't indulge. And there I was, sitting on a bus bench in the middle of the city, dreaming I could seduce an adult. I showered the owner of the pet store with kisses and, as aquariums bubbled, birds sang, and mice raced in a wire wheel, slipped my hand beneath his shirt. The roar of traffic brought me to my senses. I breathed deeply and blinked against the sun. I crossed my legs at the knee in order to hide an erection. My fantasy left me both drained and changed. The continent of sex had drifted closer.

    The car made another round. This time the driver leaned across the passenger seat and peered at me through the window. He was a complete stranger, whose gaze filled me with fear. It wasn't the surprise of not recognizing him that frightened me, it was what I did recognize—the unmistakable shame in his expression, and the weary temptation that drove him in circles. Before the car behind him honked, he mouthed "hello" and cocked his head. What now, he seemed to be asking. A bold, unbearable question.

    I bolted to my feet, slung the gym bag over my shoulder, and hurried toward home. Now and then I turned around to make sure he wasn't trailing me, both relieved and disappointed when I didn't see his car. Even after I became convinced that he wasn't at my back—my sudden flight had scared him off—I kept turning around to see what was making me so nervous, as if I might spot the source of my discomfort somewhere on the street. I walked faster and faster, trying to outrace myself. Eventually, the bus I was supposed to have taken roared past. Turning the corner, I watched it bob eastward.

    Closing the kitchen door behind me, I vowed never to leave home again. I was resolute in this decision without fully understanding why, or what it was I hoped to avoid; I was only aware of the need to hide and a vague notion, fading fast, that my trouble had something to do with sex. Already the mechanism of self-deception was at work. By the time my mother rushed into the kitchen to see why I'd returned so early, the thrill I'd felt while waiting for the bus had given way to indignation.

40   I poured out the story of the man circling the block and protested, with perhaps too great a passion, my own innocence. "I was just sitting there," I said again and again. I was so determined to deflect suspicion away from myself, and to justify my missing the class, that I portrayed the man as a grizzled pervert who drunkenly veered from lane to lane as he followed me halfway home.

    My mother cinched her housecoat. She seemed moved and shocked by what I told her, if a bit incredulous, which prompted me to be more dramatic. "It wouldn't be safe," I insisted, "for me to wait at the bus stop again."

    No matter how overwrought my story, I knew my mother wouldn't question it, wouldn't bring the subject up again; sex of any kind, especially sex between a man and a boy, was simply not discussed in our house. The gymnastics class, my parents agreed, was something I could do another time.

And so I spent the remainder of that summer at home with my mother, stirring cake batter, holding the dustpan, helping her fold the sheets. For a while I was proud of myself for engineering a reprieve from the athletic club. But as the days wore on, I began to see that my mother had wanted me with her all along, and forcing that to happen wasn't such a feat. Soon a sense of compromise set in; by expressing disgust for the man in the car, I'd expressed disgust for an aspect of myself. Now I had all the time in the world to sit around and contemplate my desire for men. The days grew long and stifling and hot, an endless sentence of self-examination.

Only trips to the pet store offered any respite. Every time I went there, I was too electrified with longing to think about longing in the abstract. The bell tinkled above the door, animals stirred within their cages, and the handsome owner glanced up from his work.

V

45 I handed my father the *Herald*. He opened the paper and disappeared behind it. My mother stirred her coffee and sighed. She gazed at the sweltering passersby and probably thought herself lucky. I slid into the vinyl booth and took my place beside my parents.

For a moment, I considered asking them about what had happened on the street, but they would have reacted with censure and alarm, and I sensed there was more to the story than they'd ever be willing to tell me. Men in dresses were only the tip of the iceberg. Who knew what other wonders existed—a boy, for example, who wanted to kiss a man—exceptions the world did its best to keep hidden.

It would be years before I heard the word "transvestite," so I struggled to find a word for what I'd seen. "He-she" came to mind, as lilting as "Injijikian." "Burl's" would have been perfect, like "boys" and "girls" spliced together, but I can't claim to have thought of this back then.

I must have looked stricken as I tried to figure it all out, because my mother put down her coffee cup and asked if I was O.K. She stopped just short of feeling my forehead. I assured her I was fine, but something within me had shifted, had given way to a heady doubt. When the waitress came and slapped down our check—"Thank You," it read, "Dine out more often"—I wondered if her lofty hairdo or the breasts on which her nametag quaked were real. Wax carnations bloomed at every table. Phony wood paneled the walls. Plastic food sat in a display case: fried eggs, a hamburger sandwich, a sundae topped with a garish cherry.

■ EXPLORATIONS OF THE TEXT

1. How do societal and familial expectations concerning gender roles shape the identities and actions of the protagonists?

2. How are the struggles of the protagonists with their sexual identities similar or different? Which characters seem to be most comfortable with their sexual orientation? With their sexual selves?

3. In "Burl's" Cooper's eight-year-old persona perceives the "hazy border between the sexes," stating that "sex . . . didn't seem to be an absolute fact so much as a pleasant, recurring accident." In what ways does *M Butterfly* portary this "hazy border"? How do other works in this cluster depict the fluidity of sexual identity?

4. Several of the works present the idea of pretense and role playing as a predominant force in relationships. What roles do characters adopt? What roles do the charactors reject?

5. How do longing and desire exert their hold on the protagonists?

6. In "Drinking Coffee Elsewhere," in "Territory," and in *M Butterfly*, character foils exist: Heidi in "Drinking Coffee Elsewhere," Wayne in "Territory," and Song Liling in *M Butterfly*. What are their roles in these works? What do they reveal about the personalities, attitude, and internal struggles of the main characters?

7. In "Drinking Coffee Elsewhere," the main character, Dina, retreats to a world of her own—her words—"always rewound and erased, rewritten and revised." How do other

characters in the works in this cluster live in fantasy worlds? What purpose do these constructed worlds serve in their lives? How do the fantasy worlds collide with reality?

8. How do class and race figure in the internal conflicts of the protagonists?

9. In "Arts of the Contact Zone," Mary Louise Pratt defines a "contact zone" as a "social space where cultures meet, clash, and grapple with each other, often in contexts of highly asymmetrical relations of power, such as colonialism, slavery, or their aftermaths as they are lived out in many parts of the world today." In such a space, patterns of domination and submission exist. Explore this motif in several works in this cluster.

■ **THE READING/WRITING CONNECTION**

1. "Think" Topic: Explore the theme of the outsider as presented in several works in this cluster.

2. Freewrite about a time when you brought a new partner home to meet your family.

■ **IDEAS FOR WRITING**

1. List your past and present selves. How do they edge into each other? Conflict with each other? Exist simultaneously? Which selves seem to be most formative? Which seem to be least important in your life? Which childhood selves persist in adulthood? Compare and contrast your cluster of selves with Neil's in "Territory," with Dina's in "Drinking Coffee Elsewhere," or with the autobiographical persona in "Bi Bi Hua."

2. Explore the tension between reality and illusion as presented in several works in this cluster.

■ FICTION ■

ANTON CHEKHOV   Translated by David Magarshack

Anton Chekhov (1860–1904) was born in southern Russia. His short stories and plays were formative in the development of modern, realistic literature. His major plays are The Sea Gull *(1898);* Uncle Vanya *(1899);* The Three Sisters *(1901); and* The Cherry Orchard *(1904). One theme dominates these plays: the protagonists' inabilities to change the circumstances of their lives—their imprisonment in the world of their failed dreams. During the last phase of his life, Chekhov also wrote several volumes of short stories:* Motley Stories *(1886),* Innocent Speeches *(1887),* In The Twilight *(1887), and* Stories *(1889).*

1899

LADY WITH LAPDOG

I

The appearance on the front of a new arrival—a lady with a lapdog—became the topic of general conversation. Dmitry Dmitrich Gurov, who had been a fortnight in Yalta[1] and got used to its ways, was also interested in new arrivals. One day, sitting on the terrace of Vernet's restaurant, he saw a young woman walking along the promenade; she was fair, not very tall, and wore a toque;[2] behind her trotted a white pomeranian.

---

[1] A seaport in the Ukraine on the Black Sea.
[2] A kind of hat.

Later he came across her in the park and in the square several times a day. She was always alone, always wearing the same toque, followed by the white pomeranian. No one knew who she was, and she became known simply as the lady with the lapdog.

"If she's here without her husband and without any friends," thought Gurov, "it wouldn't be a bad idea to strike up an acquaintance with her."

He was not yet forty, but he had a twelve-year-old daughter and two schoolboy sons. He had been married off when he was still in his second year at the university, and his wife seemed to him now to be almost twice his age. She was a tall, black-browed woman, erect, dignified, austere, and, as she liked to describe herself, a "thinking person." She was a great reader, preferred the new "advanced" spelling, called her husband by the more formal "Dimitry" and not the familiar "Dmitry"; and though he secretly considered her not particularly intelligent, narrow-minded, and inelegant, he was afraid of her and disliked being at home. He had been unfaithful to her for a long time, he was often unfaithful to her, and that was why, perhaps, he almost always spoke ill of women, and when men discussed women in his presence, he described them as *the lower breed.*

5   He could not help feeling that he had had enough bitter experience to have the right to call them as he pleased, but all the same without *the lower breed* he could not have existed a couple of days. He was bored and ill at ease among men, with whom he was reticent and cold, but when he was among women he felt at ease, he knew what to talk about with them and how to behave, even when he was silent in their company he experienced no feeling of constraint. There was something attractive, something elusive in his appearance, in his character and his whole person that women found interesting and irresistible; he was aware of it, and was himself drawn to them by some irresistible force.

Long and indeed bitter experience had taught him that every new affair, which at first relieved the monotony of life so pleasantly and appeared to be such a charming and light adventure, among decent people and especially among Muscovites, who are so irresolute and so hard to rouse, inevitably developed into an extremely complicated problem and finally the whole situation became rather cumbersome. But at every new meeting with an attractive woman he forgot all about this experience, he wanted to enjoy life so badly and it all seemed so simple and amusing.

And so one afternoon, while he was having dinner at a restaurant in the park, the woman in the toque walked in unhurriedly and took a seat at the table next to him. The way she looked, walked and dressed, wore her hair, told him that she was of good social standing, that she was married, that she was in Yalta for the first time, that she was alone and bored. . . . There was a great deal of exaggeration in the stories about the laxity of morals among the Yalta visitors, and he dismissed them with contempt, for he knew that such stories were mostly made up by people who would gladly have sinned themselves if they had had any idea how to go about it; but when the woman sat down at the table three yards away from him he remembered these stories of easy conquests and excursions to the mountains and the tempting thought of a quiet and fleeting affair, an affair with a strange woman whose very name he did not know, suddenly took possession of him.

He tried to attract the attention of the dog by calling softly to it, and when the pomeranian came up to him he shook a finger at it. The pomeranian growled. Gurov again shook a finger at it.

The woman looked up at him and immediately lowered her eyes.

10   "He doesn't bite," she said and blushed.

"May I give him a bone?" he asked, and when she nodded, he said amiably: "Have you been long in Yalta?"

"About five days."

"And I am just finishing my second week here."

They said nothing for the next few minutes.

15 "Time flies," she said without looking at him, "and yet it's so boring here."

"That's what one usually hears people saying here. A man may be living in Belev and Zhiz-dra or some other God-forsaken hole and he isn't bored, but the moment he comes here all you hear from him is 'Oh, it's so boring! Oh, the dust!' You'd think he'd come from Granada!"

She laughed. Then both went on eating in silence, like complete strangers; but after dinner they strolled off together, and they embarked on the light playful conversation of free and contented people who do not care where they go or what they talk about. They walked, and talked about the strange light that fell on the sea: the water was of such a soft and warm lilac, and the moon threw a shaft of gold across it. They talked about how close it was after a hot day. Gurov told her that he lived in Moscow, that he was a graduate in philology but worked in a bank, that he had at one time thought of singing in a private opera company but had given up the idea, that he owned two houses in Moscow. . . . From her he learnt that she had grown up in Petersburg, but had got married in the town of S——— , where she had been living for the past two years, that she would stay another month in Yalta, and that her husband, who also needed a rest, might join her. She was quite unable to tell him what her husband's job was, whether he served in the offices of the provincial governor or the rural council, and she found this rather amusing herself. Gurov also found out that her name and patronymic were Anna Sergeyevna.

Later, in his hotel room, he thought about her and felt sure that he would meet her again the next day. It had to be. As he went to bed he remembered that she had only recently left her boarding school, that she had been a schoolgirl like his own daughter; he recalled how much diffidence and angularity there was in her laughter and her conversation with a stranger—it was probably the first time in her life she had found herself alone, in a situation when men followed her, looked at her, and spoke to her with only one secret intention, an intention she could hardly fail to guess. He remembered her slender, weak neck, her beautiful grey eyes.

"There's something pathetic about her, all the same," he thought as he fell asleep.

II

20 A week had passed since their first meeting. It was a holiday. It was close indoors, while in the streets a strong wind raised clouds of dust and tore off people's hats. All day long one felt thirsty, and Gurov kept going to the terrace of the restaurant, offering Anna Sergeyevna fruit drinks and ices. There was nowhere to go.

In the evening, when the wind had dropped a little, they went to the pier to watch the arrival of the steamer. There were a great many people taking a walk on the landing pier; some were meeting friends, they had bunches of flowers in their hands. It was there that two peculiarities of the Yalta smart set at once arrested attention: the middle-aged women dressed as if they were still young girls and there was a great number of generals.

Because of the rough sea the steamer arrived late, after the sun had set, and she had to swing backwards and forwards several times before getting alongside the pier. Anna Sergeyevna looked at the steamer and the passengers through her lorgnette, as though trying to make out some friends, and when she turned to Gurov her eyes were sparkling. She talked a lot, asked many abrupt questions, and immediately forgot what it was she had wanted to know; then she lost her lorgnette in the crowd of people.

The smartly dressed crowd dispersed; soon they were all gone, the wind had dropped completely, but Gurov and Anna were still standing there as though waiting to see if someone else would come off the boat. Anna Sergeyevna was no longer talking. She was smelling her flowers without looking at Gurov.

"It's a nice evening," he said. "Where shall we go now? Shall we go for a drive?"

25 She made no answer.

Then he looked keenly at her and suddenly put his arms round her and kissed her on the mouth. He felt the fragrance and dampness of the flowers and immediately looked around him fearfully; had anyone seen them?

"Let's go to your room," he said softly.

And both walked off quickly.

It was very close in her hotel room, which was full of the smell of the scents she had bought in a Japanese shop. Looking at her now, Gurov thought: "Life is full of strange encounters!" From his past he preserved the memory of carefree, good-natured women, whom love had made gay and who were grateful to him for the happiness he gave them, however short-lived; and of women like his wife, who made love without sincerity, with unnecessary talk, affectedly, hysterically, with such an expression, as though it were not love or passion, but something much more significant; and of two or three very beautiful, frigid women, whose faces suddenly lit up with a predatory expression, an obstinate desire to take, to snatch from life more than it could give; these were women no longer in their first youth, capricious, unreasoning, despotic, unintelligent women, and when Gurov lost interest in them, their beauty merely aroused hatred in him and the lace trimmings on their négligés looked to him then like the scales of a snake.

30 But here there was still the same diffidence and angularity of inexperienced youth—an awkward feeling; and there was also the impression of embarrassment, as if someone had just knocked at the door. Anna Sergeyevna, this lady with the lapdog, apparently regarded what had happened in a peculiar sort of way, very seriously, as though she had become a fallen woman—so it seemed to him, and he found it odd and disconcerting. Her features lengthened and drooped, and her long hair hung mournfully on either side of her face; she sank into thought in a despondent pose, like a woman taken in adultery in an old painting.

"It's wrong," she said. "You'll be the first not to respect me now."

There was a water-melon on the table. Gurov cut himself a slice and began to eat it slowly. At least half an hour passed in silence.

Anna Sergeyevna was very touching; there was an air of pure, decent, naïve woman about her, a woman who had very little experience of life; the solitary candle burning on the table scarcely lighted up her face, but it was obvious that she was unhappy.

"But, darling, why should I stop respecting you?" Gurov asked. "You don't know yourself what you're saying."

35 "May God forgive me," she said, and her eyes filled with tears. "It's terrible."

"You seem to wish to justify yourself."

"How can I justify myself? I am a bad, despicable creature. I despise myself and have no thought of justifying myself. I haven't deceived my husband, I've deceived myself. And not only now. I've been deceiving myself for a long time. My husband is, I'm sure, a good and honest man, but, you see, he is a flunkey. I don't know what he does at his office, all I know is that he is a flunkey. I was only twenty when I married him, I was eaten up by curiosity, I wanted something better. There surely must be a different kind of life, I said to myself. I wanted to live. To live, to live! I was burning with curiosity. I don't think you know what I am talking about, but I swear I could no longer control myself, something was happening to me. I could not be held back. I told my husband I was ill, and I came here. . . . Here too I was going about as though in a daze, as though I was mad, and now I've become a vulgar worthless woman whom everyone has a right to despise."

Gurov could not help feeling bored as he listened to her; he was irritated by her naïve tone of voice and her repentance, which was so unexpected and so out of place; but for the tears in her eyes, he might have thought that she was joking or play-acting.

"I don't understand," he said gently, "what it is you want."

40   She buried her face on his chest and clung close to him.

"Please, please believe me," she said. "I love a pure, honest life. I hate immorality. I don't know myself what I am doing. The common people say 'the devil led her astray,' I too can now say about myself that the devil has led me astray."

"There, there . . ." he murmured.

He gazed into her staring, frightened eyes, kissed her, spoke gently and affectionately to her, and gradually she calmed down and her cheerfulness returned; both of them were soon laughing.

Later, when they went out, there was not a soul on the promenade, the town with its cypresses looked quite dead, but the sea was still roaring and dashing itself against the shore; a single launch tossed on the waves, its lamp flickering sleepily.

45   They hailed a cab and drove to Oreanda.

"I've just found out your surname, downstairs in the lobby," said Gurov. "Von Diederitz. Is your husband a German?"

"No. I believe his grandfather was German. He is of the Orthodox faith himself."

In Oreanda they sat on a bench not far from the church, looked down on the sea, and were silent. Yalta could scarcely be seen through the morning mist. White clouds lay motionless on the mountain tops. Not a leaf stirred on the trees, the cicadas chirped, and the monotonous, hollow roar of the sea, coming up from below, spoke of rest, of eternal sleep awaiting us all. The sea had roared like that down below when there was no Yalta or Oreanda, it was roaring now, and it would go on roaring as indifferently and hollowly when we were here no more. And in this constancy, in this complete indifference to life and death of each one of us, there is perhaps hidden the guarantee of our eternal salvation, the never-ceasing movement of life on earth, the never-ceasing movement towards perfection. Sitting beside a young woman who looked so beautiful at the break of day, soothed and enchanted by the sight of all that fairy-land scenery—the sea, the mountains, the clouds, the wide sky—Gurov reflected that, when you came to think of it, everything in the world was really really beautiful, everything but our own thoughts and actions when we lose sight of the higher aims of existence and our dignity as human beings.

Someone walked up to them, a watchman probably, looked at them, and went away. And there seemed to be something mysterious and also beautiful in this fact, too. They could see the Theodosia boat coming towards the pier, lit up by the sunrise, and with no lights.

50   "There's dew on the grass," said Anna Sergeyevna, breaking the silence.

"Yes. Time to go home."

They went back to town.

After that they met on the front every day at twelve o'clock, had lunch and dinner together, went for walks, admired the sea. She complained of sleeping badly and of her heart beating uneasily, asked the same questions, alternately worried by feelings of jealousy and by fear that he did not respect her sufficiently. And again and again in the park or in the square, when there was no one in sight, he would draw her to him and kiss her passionately. The complete idleness, these kisses in broad daylight, always having to look round for fear of someone watching them, the heat, the smell of the sea, and the constant looming into sight of idle, well-dressed, and well-fed people seemed to have made a new man of him; he told Anna Sergeyevna that she was beautiful, that she was desirable, made passionate love to her, never left her side, while she was often lost in thought and kept asking him to admit that he did not really respect her, that he was not in the least in love with her and only saw in her a vulgar woman. Almost every night they drove out of town, to Oreanda or to the waterfall; the excursion was always a success, and every time their impressions were invariably grand and beautiful.

They kept expecting her husband to arrive. But a letter came from him in which he wrote that he was having trouble with his eyes and implored his wife to return home as soon as possible. Anna Sergeyevna lost no time in getting ready for her journey home.

55 "It's a good thing I'm going," she said to Gurov. "It's fate."

She took a carriage to the railway station, and he saw her off. The drive took a whole day. When she got into the express train, after the second bell, she said:

"Let me have another look at you. . . . One last look. So."

She did not cry, but looked sad, just as if she were ill, and her face quivered.

"I'll be thinking of you, remembering you," she said. "Good-bye. You're staying, aren't you? Don't think badly of me. We are parting for ever. Yes, it must be so, for we should never have met. Well, good-bye. . . ."

60 The train moved rapidly out of the station; its lights soon disappeared, and a minute later it could not even be heard, just as though everything had conspired to put a quick end to this sweet trance, this madness. And standing alone on the platform gazing into the dark distance, Gurov listened to the chirping of the grasshoppers and the humming of the telegraph wires with a feeling as though he had just woken up. He told himself that this had been just one more affair in his life, just one more adventure, and that it too was over, leaving nothing but a memory. He was moved and sad, and felt a little penitent that the young woman, whom he would never see again, had not been happy with him; he had been amiable and affectionate with her, but all the same in his behavior to her, in the tone of his voice and in his caresses, there was a suspicion of light irony, the somewhat coarse arrogance of the successful male, who was, moreover, almost twice her age. All the time she called him good, wonderful, high-minded; evidently she must have taken him to be quite different from what he really was, which meant that he had involuntarily deceived her.

At the railway station there was already a whiff of autumn in the air; the evening was chilly.

"Time I went north, too," thought Gurov, as he walked off the platform. "High time!"

III

At home in Moscow everything was already like winter: the stoves were heated, and it was still dark in the morning when the children were getting ready to go to school and having breakfast, so that the nurse had to light the lamp for a short time. The frosts had set in. When the first snow falls and the first day one goes out for a ride in a sleigh, one is glad to see the white ground, the white roofs, the air is so soft and wonderful to breathe, and one remembers the days of one's youth. The old lime trees and birches, white with rime, have such a benignant look, they are nearer to one's heart than cypresses and palms, and beside them one no longer wants to think of mountains and the sea.

Gurov had been born and bred in Moscow, and he returned to Moscow on a fine frosty day; and when he put on his fur coat and warm gloves and took a walk down Petrovka Street, and when on Saturday evening he heard the church bells ringing, his recent holiday trip and the places he had visited lost their charm for him. Gradually he became immersed in Moscow life, eagerly reading three newspapers a day and declaring that he never read Moscow papers on principle. Once more, he could not resist the attraction of restaurants, clubs, banquets, and anniversary celebrations, and once more he felt flattered that well-known lawyers and actors came to see him and that in the Medical Club he played cards with a professor as his partner. Once again he was capable of eating a whole portion of the Moscow speciality of sour cabbage and meat served in a frying-pan. . . .

65 Another month and, he thought, nothing but a memory would remain of Anna Sergeyevna; he would remember her as through a haze and only occasionally dream of her

with a wistful smile, as he did of the others before her. But over a month passed, winter was at its height, and he remembered her as clearly as though he had only parted from her the day before. His memories haunted him more and more persistently. Every time the voices of his children doing their homework reached him in his study in the stillness of the evening, every time he heard a popular song or some music in a restaurant, every time the wind howled in the chimney—it all came back to him: their walks on the pier, early morning with the mist on the mountains, the Theodosia boat, and the kisses. He kept pacing the room for hours remembering it all and smiling, and then his memories turned into daydreams and the past mingled in his imagination with what was going to happen. He did not dream of Anna Sergeyevna, she accompanied him everywhere like his shadow and followed him wherever he went. Closing his eyes, he saw her as clearly as if she were before him, and she seemed to him lovelier, younger, and tenderer than she had been; and he thought that he too was much better than he had been in Yalta. In the evenings she gazed at him from the bookcase, from the fireplace, from the corner—he heard her breathing, the sweet rustle of her dress. In the street he followed women with his eyes, looking for anyone who resembled her. . . .

He was beginning to be overcome by an overwhelming desire to share his memories with someone. But at home it was impossible to talk of his love, and outside his home there was no one he could talk to. Not the tenants who lived in his house, and certainly not his colleagues in the bank. And what was he to tell them? Had he been in love then? Had there been anything beautiful, poetic, edifying, or even anything interesting about his relations with Anna Sergeyevna? So he had to talk in general terms about love and women, and no one guessed what he was driving at, and his wife merely raised her black eyebrows and said:

"Really, Dimitry, the role of a coxcomb doesn't suit you at all!"

One evening, as he left the Medical Club with his partner, a civil servant, he could not restrain himself, and said:

"If you knew what a fascinating woman I met in Yalta!"

70 The civil servant got into his sleigh and was about to be driven off, but suddenly he turned round and called out:

"I say!"

"Yes?"

"You were quite right; the sturgeon *was* a bit off."

These words, so ordinary in themselves, for some reason hurt Gurov's feelings: they seemed to him humiliating and indecent. What savage manners! What faces! What stupid nights! What uninteresting, wasted days! Crazy gambling at cards, gluttony, drunkenness, endless talk about one and the same thing. Business that was of no use to anyone and talk about one and the same thing absorbed the greater part of one's time and energy, and what was left in the end was a sort of dock-tailed, barren life, a sort of nonsensical existence, and it was impossible to escape from it, just as though you were in a lunatic asylum or a convict chaingang!

75 Gurov lay awake all night, fretting and fuming, and had a splitting headache the whole of the next day. The following nights too he slept badly, sitting up in bed thinking, or walking up and down his room. He was tired of his children, tired of the bank, he did not feel like going out anywhere or talking about anything.

In December, during the Christmas holidays, he packed his things, told his wife that he was going to Petersburg to get a job for a young man he knew, and set off for the town of S_____ . Why? He had no very clear idea himself. He wanted to see Anna Sergeyevna, to talk to her, to arrange a meeting, if possible.

He arrived in S_____ in the morning and took the best room in a hotel, with a fitted carpet of military grey cloth and an inkstand grey with dust on the table, surmounted by a horseman with raised hand and no head. The hall porter supplied him with all the necessary information: Von Diederitz lived in a house of his own in Old Potter's Street, not far from the hotel. He lived well, was rich, kept his own carriage horses, the whole town knew him. The hall porter pronounced the name: Dridiritz.

Gurov took a leisurely walk down Old Potter's Street and found the house. In front of it was a long grey fence studded with upturned nails.

"A fence like that would make anyone wish to run away," thought Gurov, scanning the windows and the fence.

80   As it was a holiday, he thought, her husband was probably at home. It did not matter either way, though, for he could not very well embarrass her by calling at the house. If he were to send in a note it might fall into the hands of the husband and ruin everything. The best thing was to rely on chance. And he kept walking up and down the street and along the fence, waiting for his chance. He watched a beggar enter the gate and the dogs attack him; then, an hour later, he heard the faint indistinct sounds of a piano. That must have been Anna Sergeyevna playing. Suddenly the front door opened and an old woman came out, followed by the familiar white pomeranian. Gurov was about to call to the dog, but his heart began to beat violently and in his excitement he could not remember its name.

He went on walking up and down the street, hating the grey fence more and more, and he was already saying to himself that Anna Sergeyevna had forgotten him and had perhaps been having a good time with someone else, which was indeed quite natural for a young woman who had to look at that damned fence from morning till night. He went back to his hotel room and sat on the sofa for a long time, not knowing what to do, then he had dinner and after dinner a long sleep.

"How stupid and disturbing it all is," he thought, waking up and staring at the dark windows: it was already evening. "Well, I've had a good sleep, so what now? What am I going to do tonight?"

He sat on a bed covered by a cheap grey blanket looking exactly like a hospital blanket, and taunted himself in vexation:

"A *lady* with a lapdog! Some adventure, I must say! Serves you right!"

85   At the railway station that morning he had noticed a poster announcing in huge letters the first performance of *The Geisha Girl* at the local theatre. He recalled it now, and decided to go to the theatre.

"Quite possibly she goes to first nights," he thought.

The theatre was full. As in all provincial theatres, there was a mist over the chandeliers and the people in the gallery kept up a noisy and excited conversation; in the first row of the stalls stood the local dandies with their hands crossed behind their backs; here, too, in the front seat of the Governor's box, sat the Governor's daughter, wearing a feather boa, while the Governor himself hid modestly behind the portière so that only his hands were visible; the curtain stirred, the orchestra took a long time tuning up. Gurov scanned the audience eagerly as they filed in and occupied their seats.

Anna Sergeyevna came in too. She took her seat in the third row, and when Gurov glanced at her his heart missed a beat and he realized clearly that there was no one in the world nearer and dearer or more important to him than that little woman with the stupid lorgnette in her hand, who was in no way remarkable. That woman lost in a provincial crowd now filled his whole life, was his misfortune, his joy, and the only happiness that he wished for himself. Listening to the bad orchestra and the wretched violins played by second-rate musicians, he thought how beautiful she was. He thought and dreamed.

A very tall, round-shouldered young man with small whiskers had come in with Anna Sergeyevna and sat down beside her; he nodded at every step he took and seemed to be continually bowing to someone. This was probably her husband, whom in a fit of bitterness

at Yalta she had called a flunkey. And indeed there was something of a lackey's obsequious-
ness in his lank figure, his whiskers, and the little bald spot on the top of his head. He
smiled sweetly, and the gleaming insignia of some scientific society which he wore in his
buttonhole looked like the number on a waiter's coat.

90   In the first interval the husband went out to smoke and she was left in her seat. Gurov,
who also had a seat in the stalls, went up to her and said in a trembling voice and with a
forced smile:

"Good evening!"

She looked up at him and turned pale, then looked at him again in panic, unable to believe her eyes, clenching her fan and lorgnette in her hand and apparently trying hard not to
fall into a dead faint. Both were silent. She sat and he stood, frightened by her embarrassment and not daring to sit down beside her. The violinists and the flautist began tuning
their instruments, and they suddenly felt terrified, as though they were being watched from
all the boxes. But a moment later she got up and walked rapidly towards one of the exits; he
followed her, and both of them walked aimlessly along corridors and up and down stairs.
Figures in all sorts of uniforms—lawyers, teachers, civil servants, all wearing badges—
flashed by them: ladies, fur coats hanging on pegs, the cold draught bringing with it the
odour of cigarette-ends. Gurov, whose heart was beating violently, thought:

"Oh, Lord, what are all these people, that orchestra, doing here?"

At that moment, he suddenly remembered how after seeing Anna Sergeyevna off he had
told himself that evening at the station that all was over and that they would never meet
again. But how far they still were from the end!

95   She stopped on a dark, narrow staircase with a notice over it: "To the Upper Circle."

"How you frightened me!" she said, breathing heavily, still looking pale and stunned.
"Oh, dear, how you frightened me! I'm scarcely alive. Why did you come? Why?"

"But, please, try to understand, Anna," he murmured hurriedly. "I beg you, please, try
to understand. . . ."

She looked at him with fear, entreaty, love, looked at him intently, so as to fix his features firmly in her mind.

"I've suffered so much," she went on, without listening to him. "I've been thinking of
you all the time. The thought of you kept me alive. And yet I tried so hard to forget you—
why, oh, why did you come?"

100   On the landing above two schoolboys were smoking and looking down, but Gurov did not
care. He drew Anna Sergeyevna towards him and began kissing her face, her lips, her hands.

"What are you doing? What are you doing?" she said in horror, pushing him away.
"We've both gone mad. You must go back tonight, this minute. I implore you, by all that's
sacred . . . Somebody's coming!"

Somebody was coming up the stairs.

"You must go back," continued Anna Sergeyevna in a whisper. "Do you hear? I'll come
to you in Moscow. I've never been happy, I'm unhappy now, and I shall never be happy,
never! So please don't make me suffer still more. I swear I'll come to you in Moscow. But
now we must part. Oh, my sweet, my darling, we must part!"

She pressed his hand and went quickly down the stairs, looking back at him all the time,
and he could see from the expression in her eyes that she really was unhappy. Gurov stood listening for a short time, and when all was quiet he went to look for his coat and left the theatre.

IV

105 Anna Sergeyevna began going to Moscow to see him. Every two or three months she left the
town of S_____ , telling her husband that she was going to consult a Moscow gynaecologist,

and her husband believed and did not believe her. In Moscow she stayed at the Slav Bazaar and immediately sent a porter in a red cap to inform Gurov of her arrival. Gurov went to her hotel, and no one in Moscow knew about it.

One winter morning he went to her hotel as usual (the porter had called with his message at his house the evening before, but he had not been in). He had his daughter with him, and he was glad of the opportunity of taking her to school, which was on the way to the hotel. Snow was falling in thick wet flakes.

"It's three degrees above zero," Gurov was saying to his daughter, "and yet it's snowing. But then, you see, it's only warm on the earth's surface, in the upper layers of the atmosphere the temperature's quite different."

"Why isn't there any thunder in winter, Daddy?"

He explained that, too. As he was speaking, he kept thinking that he was going to meet his mistress and not a living soul knew about it. He led a double life: one for all who were interested to see, full of conventional truth and conventional deception, exactly like the lives of his friends and acquaintances; and another which went on in secret. And by a kind of strange concatenation of circumstances, possibly quite by accident, everything that was important, interesting, essential, everything about which he was sincere and did not deceive himself, everything that made up the quintessence of his life, went on in secret, while everything that was a lie, everything that was merely the husk in which he hid himself to conceal the truth, like his work at the bank, for instance, his discussions at the club, his ideas of the lower breed, his going to anniversary functions with his wife—all that happened in the sight of all. He judged others by himself, did not believe what he saw, and was always of the opinion that every man's real and most interesting life went on in secret, under cover of night. The personal, private life of an individual was kept a secret, and perhaps that was partly the reason why civilized man was so anxious that his personal secrets should be respected.

110   Having seen his daughter off to her school, Gurov went to the Slav Bazaar. He took off his fur coat in the cloakroom, went upstairs, and knocked softly on the door. Anna Sergeyevna, wearing the grey dress he liked most, tired out by her journey and by the suspense of waiting for him, had been expecting him since the evening before; she was pale, looked at him without smiling, but was in his arms the moment he went into the room. Their kiss was long and lingering, as if they had not seen each other for two years.

"Well," he asked, "how are you getting on there? Anything new?"

"Wait, I'll tell you in a moment. . . . I can't . . ."

She could not speak because she was crying. She turned away from him and pressed her handkerchief to her eyes.

"Well, let her have her cry," he thought, sitting down in an armchair. "I'll wait."

115   Then he rang the bell and ordered tea; while he was having his tea, she was still standing there with her face to the window. She wept because she could not control her emotions, because she was bitterly conscious of the fact that their life was so sad: they could only meet in secret, they had to hide from people, like thieves! Was not their life ruined?

"Please stop crying!" he said.

It was quite clear to him that their love would not come to an end for a long time, if ever. Anna Sergeyevna was getting attached to him more and more strongly, she worshipped him, and it would have been absurd to tell her that all this would have to come to an end one day. She would not have believed it, anyway.

He went up to her and took her by the shoulders, wishing to be nice to her, to make her smile; and at that moment he caught sight of himself in the looking glass.

His hair was already beginning to turn grey. It struck him as strange that he should have aged so much, that he should have lost his good looks in the last few years. The shoulders on which his hands lay were warm and quivering. He felt so sorry for this life, still so warm and beautiful, but probably soon to fade and wilt like his own. Why did she love him so? To women he always seemed different from what he was, and they loved in him not himself, but the man their imagination conjured up and whom they had eagerly been looking for all their lives; and when they discovered their mistake they still loved him. And not one of them had ever been happy with him. Time had passed, he had met women, made love to them, parted from them, but not once had he been in love; there had been everything between them, but no love.

120   It was only now, when his hair was beginning to turn grey, that he had fallen in love properly, in good earnest for the first time in his life.

He and Anna Sergeyevna loved each other as people do who are very dear and near, as man and wife or close friends love each other; they could not help feeling that fate itself had intended them for one another, and they were unable to understand why he should have a wife and she a husband; they were like two migrating birds, male and female, who had been caught and forced to live in separate cages. They had forgiven each other what they had been ashamed of in the past, and forgave each other everything in their present, and felt that this love of theirs had changed them both.

Before, when he felt depressed, he had comforted himself by all sorts of arguments that happened to occur to him on the spur of the moment, but now he had more serious things to think of, he felt profound compassion, he longed to be sincere, tender. . . .

"Don't cry, my sweet," he said. "That'll do, you've had your cry. . . . Let's talk now, let's think of something."

Then they had a long talk. They tried to think how they could get rid of the necessity of hiding, telling lies, living in different towns, not seeing one another for so long. How were they to free themselves from their intolerable chains?

125   "How? How?" he asked himself, clutching at his head. "How?"

And it seemed to them that in only a few more minutes a solution would be found and a new, beautiful life would begin; but both of them knew very well that the end was still a long, long way away and that the most complicated and difficult part was only just beginning.

▪ EXPLORATIONS OF THE TEXT

1. Analyze Dmitry Gurov's attitude toward women in Part I. Why has he been "unfaithful" to his wife? Why does he describe women as the "lower breed"?
2. Discuss Anna Sergeyevna's character. Why does she have an affair with Gurov?
3. After lovemaking, why does Anna consider herself "a bad, despicable creature"? Is Gurov sympathetic to her?
4. Explain the symbolism of the landscape of Oreanda.
5. After they return to their homes and spouses, do the feelings of Anna and Gurov for each other change?
6. Interpret the ending. Do Anna and Gurov have a deep commitment to each other? Are they deluded?
7. What critique of Russian society and culture is apparent in the story?

▪ THE READING/WRITING CONNECTION

1. "Think" Topic: With which character do you most sympathize? Why?
2. In a journal entry, explore a love relationship that changed your life or that changed you.

▪ IDEAS FOR WRITING

1. Chekhov said about his fictional method that he was not a judge of human character; he simply presented problems. Does this story support his view of his fictional strategy?

2. Chekhov is considered a master of the short story. What are his strengths as a fiction writer? (See the evaluation checklist in chapter 9.)

3. Explore the theme of delusion in love or of fatal attraction in this story. You also may refer to another work from this chapter (or *Boy Gets Girl*).

ERNEST HEMINGWAY

Ernest Hemingway (1899–1961), born in Oak Park, Illinois, served as an ambulance driver during World War I and was severely wounded. After the war, he lived in Paris among many artists and intellectuals who comprised the "Lost Generation." In 1926, Hemingway published The Sun Also Rises, *which made him famous. He was known for his condensed, allusive style, which was tremendously influential. Hemingway famously compared his writing to the movement of an iceberg, which, he noted, floated largely out of sight, hidden beneath the water but very much there. His subsequent works include* A Farewell to Arms *(1929),* For Whom the Bell Tolls *(1940), and* The Old Man and the Sea *(1952), for which he was awarded the Pulitzer Prize. In 1954, he was awarded the Nobel Prize for Literature.*

1927

HILLS LIKE WHITE ELEPHANTS

The hills across the valley of the Ebro[1] were long and white. On this side there was no shade and no trees and the station was between two lines of rails in the sun. Close against the side of the station there was the warm shadow of the building and a curtain, made of strings of bamboo beads, hung across the open door into the bar, to keep out flies. The American and the girl with him sat at a table in the shade, outside the building. It was very hot and the express from Barcelona would come in forty minutes. It stopped at this junction for two minutes and went on to Madrid.

"What should we drink?" the girl asked. She had taken off her hat and put it on the table.

"It's pretty hot," the man said.

"Let's drink beer."

5   "Dos cervezas,"[2] the man said into the curtain.

"Big ones?" a woman asked from the doorway.

"Yes. Two big ones."

The woman brought two glasses of beer and two felt pads. She put the felt pads and the beer glasses on the table and looked at the man and the girl. The girl was looking off at the line of hills. They were white in the sun and the country was brown and dry.

"They look like white elephants," she said.

10   "I've never seen one," the man drank his beer.

"No, you wouldn't have."

"I might have," the man said. "Just because you say I wouldn't have doesn't prove anything."

The girl looked at the bead curtain. "They've painted something on it," she said. "What does it say?"

---

[1] River in Spain.

[2] Two beers.

"Anis del Toro. It's a drink."

15   "Could we try it?"

The man called "Listen" through the curtain. The woman came out from the bar.

"Four reales."

"We want two Anis del Toro."

"With water?"

20   "Do you want it with water?"

"I don't know," the girl said. "Is it good with water?"

"It's all right."

"You want them with water?" asked the woman.

"Yes, with water."

25   "It tastes like licorice," the girl said and put the glass down.

"That's the way with everything."

"Yes," said the girl. "Everything tastes of licorice. Especially all the things you've waited so long for, like absinthe."

"Oh, cut it out."

"You started it," the girl said. "I was being amused. I was having a fine time."

30   "Well, let's try and have a fine time."

"All right. I was trying. I said the mountains looked like white elephants. Wasn't that bright?"

"That was bright."

"I wanted to try this new drink. That's all we do, isn't it—look at things and try new drinks?"

"I guess so."

35   The girl looked across the hills.

"They're lovely hills," she said. "They don't really look like white elephants. I just meant the coloring of their skin through the trees."

"Should we have another drink?"

"All right."

The warm wind blew the bead curtain against the table.

40   "The beer's nice and cool," the man said.

"It's lovely," the girl said.

"It's really an awfully simple operation, Jig," the man said. "It's not really an operation at all."

The girl looked at the ground the table legs rested on.

"I know you wouldn't mind it, Jig. It's really not anything. It's just to let the air in."

45   The girl did not say anything.

"I'll go with you and I'll stay with you all the time. They just let the air in and then it's all perfectly natural."

"Then what will we do afterward?"

"We'll be fine afterward. Just like we were before."

"What makes you think so?"

50   "That's the only thing that bothers us. It's the only thing that's made us unhappy."

The girl looked at the bead curtain, put her hand out and took hold of two of the strings of beads.

"And you think then we'll be all right and be happy."

"I know we will. You don't have to be afraid. I've known lots of people that have done it."

"So have I," said the girl. "And afterward they were all happy."

55   "Well," the man said, "if you don't want to you don't have to. I wouldn't have you do it if you didn't want to. But I know it's perfectly simple."

"And you really want to?"

"I think it's the best thing to do. But I don't want you to do it if you don't really want to."

"And if I do it you'll be happy and things will be like they were and you'll love me?"

"I love you now. You know I love you."

60 "I know. But if I do it, then it will be nice again if I say things are like white elephants, and you'll like it?"

"I'll love it. I love it now but I just can't think about it. You know how I get when I worry."

"If I do it you won't ever worry?"

"I won't worry about that because it's perfectly simple."

"Then I'll do it. Because I don't care about me."

65 "What do you mean?"

"I don't care about me."

"Well, I care about you."

"Oh, yes. But I don't care about me. And I'll do it and then everything will be fine."

The girl stood up and walked to the end of the station. Across, on the other side, were fields of grain and trees along the banks of the Ebro. Far away, beyond the river, were mountains. The shadow of a cloud moved across the field of grain and she saw the river through the trees.

70 "And we could have all this," she said. "And we could have everything and every day we make it more impossible."

"What did you say?"

"I said we could have everything."

"We can have everything."

"No, we can't."

75 "We can have the whole world."

"No, we can't."

"We can go everywhere."

"No, we can't. It isn't ours any more."

"It's ours."

80 "No, it isn't. And once they take it away, you never get it back."

"But they haven't taken it away."

"We'll wait and see."

"Come on back in the shade," he said. "You mustn't feel that way."

"I don't feel any way," the girl said. "I just know things."

85 "I don't want you to do anything that you don't want to do—"

"Nor that isn't good for me," she said. "I know. Could we have another beer?"

"All right. But you've got to realize—"

"I realize," the girl said. "Can't we maybe stop talking?"

They sat down at the table and the girl looked across at the hills on the dry side of the valley and the man looked at her and at the table.

90 "You've got to realize," he said, "that I don't want you to do it if you don't want to. I'm perfectly willing to go through with it if it means anything to you."

"Doesn't it mean anything to you? We could get along."

"Of course it does. But I don't want anybody but you. I don't want any one else. And I know it's perfectly simple."

"Yes, you know it's perfectly simple."

"It's all right for you to say that, but I do know it."

95 "Would you do something for me now?"

"I'd do anything for you."

"Would you please please please please please please please stop talking?"

He did not say anything but looked at the bags against the wall of the station. There were labels on them from all the hotels where they had spent nights.

"But I don't want you to," he said, "I don't care anything about it."

100   "I'll scream," the girl said.

The woman came out through the curtains with two glasses of beer and put them down on the damp felt pads. "The train comes in five minutes," she said.

"What did she say?" asked the girl.

"That the train is coming in five minutes."

The girl smiled brightly at the woman, to thank her.

105   "I'd better take the bags over to the other side of the station," the man said. She smiled at him.

"All right. Then come back and we'll finish the beer."

He picked up the two heavy bags and carried them around the station to the other tracks. He looked up the tracks but could not see the train. Coming back, he walked through the barroom, where people waiting for the train were drinking. He drank an Anis at the bar and looked at the people. They were all waiting reasonably for the train. He went out through the bead curtain. She was sitting at the table and smiled at him.

"Do you feel better?" he asked.

"I feel fine," she said. "There's nothing wrong with me. I feel fine."

■ EXPLORATIONS OF THE TEXT

1. What mood is created at the beginning of the story?
2. Examine Jig's and the man's dialogue before the discussion of the operation. What can you infer about the woman's and the man's characters?
3. What is "it"? "the operation"? How does the symbol of the "white elephant" relate to the operation?
4. What is the source of the conflict between Jig and the man?
5. Discuss Jig's state of mind. What are her concerns? Isolate statements that reveal her feelings.
6. What are the man's reasons for wanting her to have "the operation"? Discuss his attitudes toward the woman and their relationship.
7. Why does she want him to "please . . . please stop talking"?
8. Explain the irony of Jig's last statement: "I feel fine. . . . There's nothing wrong with me. I feel fine."
9. Analyze the symbolism of the setting. How does setting develop themes of the story?

■ THE READING/WRITING CONNECTION

1. In a journal entry, write about what you would say to them if you were a marriage counselor.
2. Does Hemingway sympathize with either character? How can you tell?
3. Create a **monologue** in the voice of Jig or of the man several months or years later.

■ IDEAS FOR WRITING

1. Compare Hemingway's view of relationships with Paz's in "My Life with the Wave."
2. Why does Hemingway choose to present the story almost totally in **dialogue**? Evaluate this technique.
3. Compare Jig's possible feelings about love with the feeling of "the wave" in Paz's "My Life with the Wave."

James Joyce

James Joyce (1882–1941) was the eldest child of a poor, Catholic family in Dublin, Ireland. After graduating from University College, Dublin, he moved to Paris. Joyce lived on the Continent for the rest of his life, returning to Ireland only three times. In 1914, he published his famous collection of short stories, Dubliners. *It was followed by* A Portrait of the Artist as a Young Man *(1916);* Ulysses *(1922), his masterpiece; and* Finnegan's Wake *(1939). Joyce is considered one of the great literary innovators: developing the form of the modern short story and novel, experimenting with stream-of-consciousness, with narrative form, with language, with myth, and with symbol.*

1914

EVELINE

She sat at the window watching the evening invade the avenue. Her head was leaned against the window curtains and in her nostrils was the odour of dusty cretonne.[1] She was tired.

Few people passed. The man out of the last house passed on his way home; she heard his footsteps clacking along the concrete pavement and afterwards crunching on the cinder path before the new red houses. One time there used to be a field there in which they used to play every evening with other people's children. Then a man from Belfast[2] bought the field and built houses in it—not like their little brown houses but bright brick houses with shining roofs. The children of the avenue used to play together in that field—the Devines, the Waters, the Dunns, little Keogh the cripple, she and her brothers and sisters. Ernest, however, never played: he was too grown up. Her father used often to hunt them in out of the field with his blackthorn stick; but usually little Keogh used to keep *nix*[3] and call out when he saw her father coming. Still they seemed to have been rather happy then. Her father was not so bad then; and besides, her mother was alive. That was a long time ago; she and her brothers and sisters were all grown up; her mother was dead. Tizzie Dunn was dead, too, and the Waters had gone back to England. Everything changes. Now she was going to go away like the others, to leave her home.

Home! She looked round the room, reviewing all its familiar objects which she had dusted once a week for so many years, wondering where on earth all the dust came from. Perhaps she would never see again those familiar objects from which she had never dreamed of being divided. And yet during all those years she had never found out the name of the priest whose yellowing photograph hung on the wall above the broken harmonium beside the coloured print of the promises made to Blessed Margaret Mary Alacoque. He had been a school friend of her father. Whenever he showed the photograph to a visitor her father used to pass it with a casual word:

"He is Melbourne now."

5   She had consented to go away, to leave her home. Was that wise? She tried to weigh each side of the question. In her home anyway she had shelter and food; she had those whom she had known all her life about her. Of course she had to work hard both in the house and at business. What would they say of her in the Stores when they found out that

---

[1] A heavy cotton material used for draperies and slipcovers.

[2] Capital of present-day Northern Ireland; a city in Ireland before the partition.

[3] Keep watch (slang expression).

she had run away with a fellow? Say she was a fool, perhaps; and her place would be filled up by advertisement. Miss Gavan would be glad. She had always had an edge on her, especially whenever there were people listening.

"Miss Hill, don't you see these ladies are waiting?"

"Look lively, Miss Hill, please."

She would not cry many tears at leaving the Stores.

But in her new home, in a distant unknown country, it would not be like that. Then she would be married—she, Eveline. People would treat her with respect then. She would not be treated as her mother had been. Even now, though she was over nineteen, she sometimes felt herself in danger of her father's violence. She knew it was that that had given her the palpitations. When they were growing up he had never gone for her, like he used to go for Harry and Ernest, because she was a girl; but latterly he had begun to threaten her and say what he would do to her only for her dead mother's sake. And now she had nobody to protect her. Ernest was dead and Harry, who was in the church decorating business, was nearly always down somewhere in the country. Besides, the invariable squabble for money on Saturday nights had begun to weary her unspeakably. She always gave her entire wages—seven shillings—and Harry always sent up what he could but the trouble was to get any money from her father. He said she used to squander the money, that she had no head, that he wasn't going to give her his hard-earned money to throw about the streets, and much more, for he was usually fairly bad of a Saturday night. In the end he would give her the money and ask her had she any intention of buying Sunday's dinner. Then she had to rush out as quickly as she could and do her marketing, holding her black leather purse tightly in her hand as she elbowed her way through the crowds and returning home late under her load of provisions. She had hard work to keep the house together and to see that the two young children who had been left to her charge went to school regularly and got their meals regularly. It was hard work—a hard life—but now that she was about to leave it she did not find it a wholly undesirable life.

10   She was about to explore another life with Frank. Frank was very kind, manly, open-hearted. She was to go away with him by the night-boat to be his wife and to live with him in Buenos Ayres where he had a home waiting for her. How well she remembered the first time she had seen him; he was lodging in a house on the main road where she used to visit. It seemed a few weeks ago. He was standing at the gate, his peaked cap pushed back on his head and his hair tumbled forward over a face of bronze. Then they had come to know each other. He used to meet her outside the Stores every evening and see her home. He took her to see *The Bohemian Girl* and she felt elated as she sat in an unaccustomed part of the theatre with him. He was awfully fond of music and sang a little. People knew that they were courting and, when he sang about the lass that loves a sailor, she always felt pleasantly confused. He used to call her Poppens out of fun. First of all it had been an excitement for her to have a fellow and then she had begun to like him. He had tales of distant countries. He had started as a deck boy at a pound a month on a ship of the Allan Line going out to Canada. He told her the names of the ships he had been on and the names of the different services. He had sailed through the Straits of Magellan[4] and he told her stories of the terrible Patagonians.[5] He had fallen on his feet in Buenos Ayres, he said, and had come over to the old country just for a holiday. Of course, her father had found out the affair and had forbidden her to have anything to say to him.

"I know these sailor chaps," he said.

One day he had quarrelled with Frank and after that she had to meet her lover secretly.

---

[4] Channel linking the Atlantic and Pacific oceans at the tip of South America.

[5] People inhabiting the region of Patagonia in southern Argentina and Chile.

The evening deepened in the avenue. The white of two letters in her lap grew indistinct. One was to Harry; the other was to her father. Ernest had been her favourite but she liked Harry too. Her father was becoming old lately, she noticed; he would miss her. Sometimes he could be very nice. Not long before, when she had been laid up for a day, he had read her out a ghost story and made toast for her at the fire. Another day, when their mother was alive, they had all gone for a picnic to the Hill of Howth. She remembered her father putting on her mother's bonnet to make the children laugh.

Her time was running out but she continued to sit by the window, leaning her head against the window curtain, inhaling the odour of dusty cretonne. Down far in the avenue she could hear a street organ playing. She knew the air. Strange that it should come that very night to remind her of the promise to her mother, her promise to keep the home together as long as she could. She remembered the last night of her mother's illness; she was again in the close dark room at the other side of the hall and outside she heard a melancholy air of Italy. The organ-player had been ordered to go away and given sixpence. She remembered her father strutting back into the sickroom saying:

15   "Damned Italians! coming over here!"

As she mused the pitiful vision of her mother's life laid its spell on the very quick of her being—that life of commonplace sacrifices closing in final craziness. She trembled as she heard again her mother's voice saying constantly with foolish insistence:

"Derevaun Seraun! Derevaun Seraun!"[6]

She stood up in a sudden impulse of terror. Escape! She must escape! Frank would save her. He would give her life, perhaps love, too. But she wanted to live. Why should she be unhappy? She had a right to happiness. Frank would take her in his arms, fold her in his arms. He would save her.

She stood among the swaying crowd in the station at the North Wall. He held her hand and she knew that he was speaking to her, saying something about the passage over and over again. The station was full of soldiers with brown baggages. Through the wide doors of the sheds she caught a glimpse of the black mass of the boat, lying in beside the quay[7] wall, with illumined portholes. She answered nothing. She felt her cheek pale and cold and, out of a maze of distress, she prayed to God to direct her, to show her what was her duty. The boat blew a long mournful whistle into the mist. If she went, tomorrow she would be on the sea with Frank, steaming toward Buenos Ayres. Their passage had been booked. Could she still draw back after all he had done for her? Her distress awoke a nausea in her body and she kept moving her lips in silent fervent prayer.

20   A bell clanged upon her heart. She felt him seize her hand:

"Come!"

All the seas of the world tumbled about her heart. He was drawing her into them: he would drown her. She gripped with both hands at the iron railing.

"Come!"

No! no! No! It was impossible. Her hands clutched the iron in frenzy. Amid the seas she sent a cry of anguish!

25   "Eveline! Evvy!"

He rushed beyond the barrier and called to her to follow. He was shouted at to go on but he still called to her. She set her white face to him, passive, like a helpless animal. Her eyes gave him no sign of love or farewell or recognition.

---

[6] **Derevaun Seraun!** This exclamation, according to scholars, has never been completely understood; it is assumed to be gibberish spoken by the mother in her delirium.

[7] A landing place beside a body of water; a wharf.

■ EXPLORATIONS OF THE TEXT

1. How do the first two paragraphs create the setting and mood of the story? What details are most significant? What do the details suggest about Eveline's situation?
2. Why is Eveline drawn to Frank? Discuss Eveline's inner conflict.
3. Analyze the symbol of the cretonne curtain and the window.
4. Discuss the conclusion of the story. What is Eveline's epiphany? Do you think that she leaves with Frank?
5. Discuss images of entrapment in this story and/or in "The Wave."

■ THE READING/WRITING CONNECTION

1. "Think" Topic: Does Eveline leave with Frank? Create a debate in class based on this question. As preparation for the debate, list pros and cons.
2. Journal Entry: Write about leaving home. Consult Greg Delanty's poem, "Leavetaking," and Staci Ferris's Response Essay in chapter 4. What are the challenges? Rewards?
3. Continue the narrative. Write a monologue in Frank's or Eveline's voice.

■ IDEAS FOR WRITING

1. Write an essay on risk taking. Use your own experiences and that of two other protagonists in works from this chapter. (Consider, for example, Norma Jean in "Shiloh," or the unnamed wife in "The Chase.")
2. Joyce is considered a master of the modern short story. How do the elements of the story (consult the checklist for fiction in chapter 9) develop themes of the work?
3. Using criteria that you create for a successful short story, evaluate this work.
4. Write an argumentative essay that presents your position about Eveline's leaving home. Use the "Think" topic as prewriting material.

WILLIAM FAULKNER (1897–1962)   **1931**

A ROSE FOR EMILY

I

When Miss Emily Grierson died, our whole town went to her funeral: the men through a sort of respectful affection for a fallen monument, the women mostly out of curiosity to see the inside of her house, which no one save an old manservant—a combined gardener and cook—had seen in at least ten years.

It was a big, squarish frame house that had once been white, decorated with cupolas and spires and scrolled balconies in the heavily lightsome style of the seventies, set on what had once been our most select street. But garages and cotton gins had encroached and obliterated even the august names of that neighborhood; only Miss Emily's house was left, lifting its stubborn and coquettish decay above the cotton wagons and the gasoline pumps—an eyesore among eyesores. And now Miss Emily had gone to join the representatives of those august names where they lay in the cedar-bemused cemetery among the ranked and anonymous graves of Union and Confederate soldiers who fell at the battle of Jefferson.

Alive, Miss Emily had been a tradition, a duty, and a care; a sort of hereditary obligation upon the town, dating from that day in 1894 when Colonel Sartoris, the mayor—he who fathered the edict that no Negro woman should appear on the streets without an apron—remitted her taxes, the dispensation dating from the death of her father on into perpetuity. Not that Miss Emily would have accepted charity. Colonel Sartoris invented an involved tale to the effect that Miss Emily's father had loaned money to the town, which the town, as a matter of business, preferred this way of repaying. Only a man of Colonel Sartoris' generation and thought could have invented it, and only a woman could have believed it.

When the next generation, with its more modern ideas, became mayors and aldermen, this arrangement created some little dissatisfaction. On the first of the year they mailed her a tax notice. February came, and there was no reply. They wrote her a formal letter, asking her to call at the sheriff's office at her convenience. A week later the mayor wrote her himself, offering to call or to send his car for her, and received in reply a note on paper of an archaic shape, in a thin, flowing calligraphy in faded ink, to the effect that she no longer went out at all. The tax notice was also enclosed, without comment.

5   They called a special meeting of the Board of Aldermen. A deputation waited upon her, knocked at the door through which no visitor had passed since she ceased giving chinapainting lessons eight or ten years earlier. They were admitted by the old Negro into a dim hall from which a stairway mounted into still more shadow. It smelled of dust and disuse— a close, dank smell. The Negro led them into the parlor. It was furnished in heavy, leathercovered furniture. When the Negro opened the blinds of one window, they could see that the leather was cracked; and when they sat down, a faint dust rose sluggishly about their thighs, spinning with slow motes in the single sun-ray. On a tarnished gilt easel before the fireplace stood a crayon portrait of Miss Emily's father.

They rose when she entered—a small, fat woman in black, with a thin gold chain descending to her waist and vanishing into her belt, leaning on an ebony cane with a tarnished gold head. Her skeleton was small and spare; perhaps that was why what would have been merely plumpness in another was obesity in her. She looked bloated, like a body long submerged in motionless water, and of that pallid hue. Her eyes, lost in the fatty ridges of her face, looked like two small pieces of coal pressed into a lump of dough as they moved from one face to another while the visitors stated their errand.

She did not ask them to sit. She just stood in the door and listened quietly until the spokesman came to a stumbling halt. Then they could hear the invisible watch ticking at the end of the gold chain.

Her voice was dry and cold. "I have no taxes in Jefferson. Colonel Sartoris explained it to me. Perhaps one of you can gain access to the city records and satisfy yourselves."

"But we have. We are the city authorities, Miss Emily. Didn't you get a notice from the sheriff, signed by him?"

10   "I received a paper, yes," Miss Emily said. "Perhaps he considers himself the sheriff. . . . I have no taxes in Jefferson."

"But there is nothing on the books to show that, you see. We must go by the—"

"See Colonel Sartoris. I have no taxes in Jefferson."

"But, Miss Emily —"

"See Colonel Sartoris." (Colonel Sartoris had been dead almost ten years.) "I have no taxes in Jefferson. Tobe!" The Negro appeared. "Show these gentlemen out."

II

15 So she vanquished them, horse and foot, just as she had vanquished their fathers thirty years before about the smell. That was two years after her father's death and a short time after her sweetheart—the one we believed would marry her—had deserted her. After her father's death she went out very little; after her sweetheart went away, people hardly saw her at all. A few of the ladies had the temerity to call, but were not received, and the only sign of life about the place was the Negro man—a young man then—going in and out with a market basket.

"Just as if a man—any man—could keep a kitchen properly," the ladies said; so they were not surprised when the smell developed. It was another link between the gross, teeming world and the high and mighty Griersons.

A neighbor, a woman, complained to the mayor, Judge Stevens, eighty years old.

"But what will you have me do about it, madam?" he said.

"Why, send her word to stop it," the woman said. "Isn't there a law?"

20   I'm sure that won't be necessary," Judge Stevens said. "It's probably just a snake or a rat that nigger of hers killed in the yard. I'll speak to him about it."

The next day he received two more complaints, one from a man who came in diffident deprecation. "We really must do something about it, Judge. I'd be the last one in the world to bother Miss Emily, but we've got to do something." That night the Board of Aldermen met—three graybeards and one younger man, a member of the rising generation.

"It's simple enough," he said. "Send her word to have her place cleaned up. Give her a certain time to do it in, and if she don't. . . ."

"Dammit, sir," Judge Stevens said, "will you accuse a lady to her face of smelling bad?"

So the next night, after midnight, four men crossed Miss Emily's lawn and slunk about the house like burglars, sniffing along the base of the brickwork and at the cellar openings while one of them performed a regular sowing motion with his hand out of a sack slung from his shoulder. They broke open the cellar door and sprinkled lime there, and in all the outbuildings. As they recrossed the lawn, a window that had been dark was lighted and Miss Emily sat in it, the light behind her, and her upright torso motionless as that of an idol. They crept quietly across the lawn and into the shadow of the locusts that lined the street. After a week or two the smell went away.

25   That was when people had begun to feel really sorry for her. People in our town, remembering how old lady Wyatt, her great-aunt, had gone completely crazy at last, believed that the Griersons held themselves a little too high for what they really were. None of the young men were quite good enough for Miss Emily and such. We had long thought of them as a tableau, Miss Emily a slender figure in white in the background, her father a spraddled silhouette in the foreground, his back to her and clutching a horsewhip, the two of them framed by the backflung front door. So when she got to be thirty and was still single, we were not pleased exactly, but vindicated; even with insanity in the family she wouldn't have turned down all of her chances if they had really materialized.

When her father died, it got about that the house was all that was left to her; and in a way, people were glad. At last they could pity Miss Emily. Being left alone, and a pauper, she had become humanized. Now she too would know the old thrill and the old despair of a penny more or less.

The day after his death all the ladies prepared to call at the house and offer condolence and aid, as is our custom. Miss Emily met them at the door, dressed as usual and with no trace of grief on her face. She told them that her father was not dead. She did that for three days, with the ministers calling on her, and the doctors, trying to persuade her to let them dispose of the body. Just as they were about to resort to law and force, she broke down, and they buried her father quickly.

We did not say she was crazy then. We believed she had to do that. We remembered all the young men her father had driven away, and we knew that with nothing left, she would have to cling to that which had robbed her, as people will.

III

She was sick for a long time. When we saw her again, her hair was cut short, making her look like a girl, with a vague resemblance to those angels in colored church windows—sort of tragic and serene.

30   The town had just let the contracts for paving the sidewalks, and in the summer after her father's death they began the work. The construction company came with niggers and mules and machinery, and a foreman named Homer Barron, a Yankee—a big, dark, ready man, with a big voice and eyes lighter than his face. The little boys would follow in groups to hear him cuss the niggers, and the niggers singing in time to the rise and fall of picks. Pretty soon he knew everybody in town. Whenever you heard a lot of laughing anywhere about the square, Homer Barron would be in the center of the group. Presently, we began to see him and Miss Emily on Sunday afternoons driving in the yellow-wheeled buggy and the matched team of bays from the livery stable.

      At first we were glad that Miss Emily would have an interest, because the ladies all said, "Of course a Grierson would not think seriously of a Northerner, a day laborer." But there were still others, older people, who said that even grief could not cause a real lady to forget *noblesse oblige*—without calling it *noblesse oblige*. They just said, "Poor Emily. Her kinsfolk should come to her." She had some kin in Alabama; but years ago her father had fallen out with them over the estate of old lady Wyatt, the crazy woman, and there was no communication between the two families. They had not even been represented at the funeral.

      And as soon as the old people said, "Poor Emily," the whispering began. "Do you suppose it's really so?" they said to one another. "Of course it is. What else could. . . ." This behind their hands; rustling of craned silk and satin behind jalousies closed upon the sun of Sunday afternoon as the thin, swift clop-clop-clop of the matched team passed: "Poor Emily."

      She carried her head high enough—even when we believed that she was fallen. It was as if she demanded more than ever the recognition of her dignity as the last Grierson; as if it had wanted that touch of earthiness to reaffirm her imperviousness. Like when she bought the rat poison, the arsenic. That was over a year after they had begun to say "Poor Emily," and while the two female cousins were visiting her.

      "I want some poison," she said to the druggist. She was over thirty then, still a slight woman, though thinner than usual, with cold, haughty black eyes in a face the flesh of which was strained across the temples and about the eye-sockets as you imagine a lighthouse-keeper's face ought to look. "I want some poison," she said.

35   "Yes, Miss Emily. What kind? For rats and such? I'd recom—"

      "I want the best you have. I don't care what kind."

      The druggist named several. "They'll kill anything up to an elephant. But what you want is—"

      "Arsenic," Miss Emily said. "Is that a good one?"

      "Is . . . arsenic? Yes, ma'am. But what you want—"

40   "I want arsenic."

      The druggist looked down at her. She looked back at him, erect, her face like a strained flag. "Why, of course," the druggist said. "If that's what you want. But the law requires you to tell what you are going to use it for."

      Miss Emily just stared at him, her head tilted back in order to look him eye for eye, until he looked away and went and got the arsenic and wrapped it up. The Negro delivery boy brought her the package; the druggist didn't come back. When she opened the package at home there was written on the box, under the skull and bones: "For rats."

IV

So the next day we all said, "She will kill herself"; and we said it would be the best thing. When she had first begun to be seen with Homer Barron, we had said, "She will marry him." Then we said, "She will persuade him yet," because Homer himself had remarked—he liked men, and it was known that he drank with the younger men in the Elks' Club—that he was not a marrying man. Later we said, "Poor Emily" behind the jalousies as they passed on Sunday afternoon in the glittering buggy, Miss Emily with her head high and Homer Barron with his hat cocked and a cigar in his teeth, reins and whip in a yellow glove.

Then some of the ladies began to say that it was a disgrace to the town and a bad example to the young people. The men did not want to interfere, but at last the ladies forced the Baptist minister—Miss Emily's people were Episcopal—to call upon her. He would never divulge what happened during that interview, but he refused to go back again. The next Sunday they again drove about the streets, and the following day the minister's wife wrote to Miss Emily's relations in Alabama.

45   So she had blood-kin under her roof again and we sat back to watch developments. At first nothing happened. Then we were sure that they were to be married. We learned that Miss Emily had been to the jeweler's and ordered a man's toilet set in silver, with the letters H.B. on each piece. Two days later we learned that she had bought a complete outfit of men's clothing, including a nightshirt, and we said, "They are married." We were really glad. We were glad because the two female cousins were even more Grierson than Miss Emily had ever been.

So we were not surprised when Homer Barron—the streets had been finished some time since—was gone. We were a little disappointed that there was not a public blowing-off, but we believed that he had gone on to prepare for Miss Emily's coming, or to give her a chance to get rid of the cousins. (By that time it was a cabal, and we were all Miss Emily's allies to help circumvent the cousins.) Sure enough, after another week they departed. And, as we had expected all along, within three days Homer Barron was back in town. A neighbor saw the Negro man admit him at the kitchen door at dusk one evening.

And that was the last we saw of Homer Barron. And of Miss Emily for some time. The Negro man went in and out with the market basket, but the front door remained closed. Now and then we would see her at the window for a moment, as the men did that night when they sprinkled the lime, but for almost six months she did not appear on the streets. Then we knew that this was to be expected too; as if that quality of her father which had thwarted her woman's life so many times had been too virulent and too furious to die.

When we next saw Miss Emily, she had grown fat and her hair was turning gray. During the next few years it grew grayer and grayer until it attained an even pepper-and-salt iron-gray when it ceased turning. Up to the day of her death at seventy-four it was still that vigorous iron-gray, like the hair of an active man.

From that time on her front door remained closed, save during a period of six or seven years, when she was about forty, during which she gave lessons in china-painting. She fitted up a studio in one of the downstairs rooms, where the daughters and granddaughters of Colonel Sartoris' contemporaries were sent to her with the same regularity and in the same spirit that they were sent to church on Sundays with a twenty-five-cent piece for the collection plate. Meanwhile her taxes had been remitted.

50   Then the newer generation became the backbone and the spirit of the town, and the painting pupils grew up and fell away and did not send their children to her with boxes of color and tedious brushes and pictures cut from the ladies' magazines. The front door closed upon the last one and remained closed for good. When the town got free postal delivery, Miss Emily alone refused to let them fasten the metal numbers above her door and attach a mailbox to it. She would not listen to them.

Daily, monthly, yearly we watched the Negro grow grayer and more stooped, going in and out with the market basket. Each December we sent her a tax notice, which would be returned by the post office a week later, unclaimed. Now and then we would see her in one of the downstairs windows—she had evidently shut up the top floor of the house—like the carven torso of an idol in a niche, looking or not looking at us, we could never tell which.

Thus she passed from generation to generation—dear, inescapable, impervious, tranquil, and perverse.

And so she died. Fell ill in the house filled with dust and shadows, with only a doddering Negro man to wait on her. We did not even know she was sick; we had long since given up trying to get any information from the Negro. He talked to no one, probably not even to her, for his voice had grown harsh and rusty, as if from disuse.

She died in one of the downstairs rooms, in a heavy walnut bed with a curtain, her gray head propped on a pillow yellow and moldy with age and lack of sunlight.

V

The Negro met the first of the ladies at the front door and let them in, with their hushed, sibilant voices and their quick, curious glances, and then he disappeared. He walked right through the house and out the back and was not seen again.

55   The two female cousins came at once. They held the funeral on the second day, with the town coming to look at Miss Emily beneath a mass of bought flowers, with the crayon face of her father musing profoundly above the bier and the ladies sibilant and macabre; and the very old men—some in their brushed Confederate uniforms—on the porch and the lawn, talking of Miss Emily as if she had been a contemporary of theirs, believing that they had danced with her and courted her perhaps, confusing time with its mathematical progression, as the old do, to whom all the past is not a diminishing road but, instead, a huge meadow which no winter ever quite touches, divided from them now by the narrow bottleneck of the most recent decade of years.

Already we knew that there was one room in that region above stairs which no one had seen in forty years, and which would have to be forced. They waited until Miss Emily was decently in the ground before they opened it.

The violence of breaking down the door seemed to fill this room with pervading dust. A thin, acrid pall as of the tomb seemed to lie everywhere upon this room decked and furnished as for a bridal: upon the valance curtains of faded rose color, upon the rose-shaded lights, upon the dressing table, upon the delicate array of crystal and the man's toilet things backed with tarnished silver, silver so tarnished that the monogram was obscured. Among them lay a collar and tie, as if they had just been removed, which, lifted, left upon the surface a pale crescent in the dust. Upon a chair hung the suit, carefully folded; beneath it the two mute shoes and the discarded socks.

The man himself lay in the bed.

For a long while we just stood there, looking down at the profound and fleshless grin. The body had apparently once lain in the attitude of an embrace, but now the long sleep that outlasts love, that conquers even the grimace of love, had cuckolded him. What was left of him, rotted beneath what was left of the nightshirt, had become inextricable from the bed in which he lay; and upon him and upon the pillow beside him lay that even coating of the patient and biding dust.

60   Then we noticed that in the second pillow was the indentation of a head. One of us lifted something from it, and leaning forward, that faint and invisible dust dry and acrid in the nostrils, we saw a long strand of iron-gray hair.

■ EXPLORATIONS OF THE TEXT

1. The story is told through a narrator: Why does the narrator refer to Miss Emily throughout the text (Faulkner's title just refers to Emily.)?

2. Are there any clues from the narrator's telling in the first-person plural (the community) that he was personally involved with Emily or with her family? How old is the

narrator? Do you think that he was ever Emily's suitor? Why, or why not? Does the text of the story reveal any clues for us? Could the narrator be a woman? Why, or why not? Defend your point of view with evidence from the text.

3. Describe the relationship between Emily and her father. She did have opportunities to love and to be loved while her father was living. Why didn't Emily strike out for her own happiness?

4. Did Emily have any love for Homer? Why, or why not? Does the narrator give us any clues about this relationship?

5. The story has been classified as grotesque, as Gothic in atmosphere, in its unfolding. What evidence is there throughout the tale for this judgment?

6. Do you feel sympathy for Emily? Why, or why not? Support your point of view by referring to her actions in the story.

7. At a seminar with students, William Faulker denied that he was writing the story centering around two symbols in conflict: the North (Homer Barron) and the South (Emily): "It was a conflict not between the North and the South so much as between, well, you might say, God and Satan." In your reading of the story, which one of the two views do you take?

8. What is different in "A Rose for Emily" about the chronology of the events that occurred? Why do you think Faulkner used this approach in writing the story?

9. Compare and contrast Emily with Granny Weatherall.

■ THE READING/WRITING CONNECTION

1. The two female cousins show up at crucial times in the Grierson's family life. Imagine what these two people are like, and have them write a joint letter to Emily offering advice and help.

2. Write an entry in Colonel Sartoris's diary about Emily's attitude in dealing with the taxes.

3. "Think" Topic: What is the meaning of the title?

■ IDEAS FOR WRITING

1. Write two obituary columns for the local paper—one on Emily's father's death, and a second one on Emily's.

2. Create a feminist analysis of the story.

CHARLOTTE PERKINS GILMAN

Charlotte Perkins Gilman (1860–1935), born in Hartford, Connecticut, was raised by her mother. After divorcing her first husband, Gilman began to write, to lecture, and to teach. "The Yellow Wallpaper," her most famous story, appeared in 1892 in New England Magazine *and was based on her experience with treatment for postpartum depression. Gilman remarried in 1900. She wrote books about alternate social structures, including* The Home *(1903) and the feminist utopia,* Herland *(1915). She spoke at national and international women's conferences. Gilman committed suicide in 1935, stating that she preferred "chloroform to breast cancer" and that she felt it was her right to do so. Although she suffered from depression all her life, she was a remarkably productive writer and lecturer.*

1892

THE YELLOW WALLPAPER

It is very seldom that mere ordinary people like John and myself secure ancestral halls for the summer.

A colonial mansion, a hereditary estate, I would say a haunted house and reach the height of romantic felicity—but that would be asking too much of fate!

Still I will proudly declare that there is something queer about it.

Else, why should it be let so cheaply? And why have stood so long untenanted?

5   John laughs at me, of course, but one expects that.

John is practical in the extreme. He has no patience with faith, an intense horror of superstition, and he scoffs openly at any talk of things not to be felt and seen and put down in figures.

John is a physician, and *perhaps*—(I would not say it to a living soul, of course, but this is dead paper and a great relief to my mind)—*perhaps* that is one reason I do not get well faster.

You see he does not believe I am sick! And what can one do?

If a physician of high standing, and one's own husband, assures friends and relatives that there is really nothing the matter with one but temporary nervous depression—a slight hysterical tendency[1]—what is one to do?

10   My brother is also a physician, and also of high standing, and he says the same thing.

So I take phosphates[2] or phosphites—whichever it is—and tonics, and air and exercise, and journeys, and am absolutely forbidden to "work" until I am well again.

Personally, I disagree with their ideas.

Personally, I believe that congenial work, with excitement and change, would do me good.

But what is one to do?

15   I did write for a while in spite of them; but it *does* exhaust me a good deal—having to be so sly about it, or else meet with heavy opposition.

I sometimes fancy that in my condition, if I had less opposition and more society and stimulus—but John says the very worst thing I can do is to think about my condition, and I confess it always makes me feel bad.

So I will let it alone and talk about the house.

The most beautiful place! It is quite alone, standing well back from the road, quite three miles from the village. It makes me think of English places that you read about, for there are hedges and walls and gates that lock, and lots of separate little houses for the gardeners and people.

There is a *delicious* garden! I never saw such a garden—large and shady, full of box-bordered paths, and lined with long grape-covered arbors with seats under them.

20   There were greenhouses, but they are all broken now.

There was some legal trouble, I believe, something about the heirs and co-heirs; anyhow, the place has been empty for years.

That spoils my ghostliness, I am afraid, but I don't care—there is something strange about the house—I can feel it.

I even said so to John one moonlight evening, but he said what I felt was a draught, and shut the window.

I get unreasonably angry with John sometimes. I'm sure I never used to be so sensitive. I think it is due to this nervous condition.

25   But John says if I feel so I shall neglect proper self-control; so I take pains to control myself—before him, at least, and that makes me very tired.

---

[1] Hysteria was a general nervous condition, often diagnosed in women in the late nineteenth century. Symptoms included tension, anxiety, nervousness, and depression.

[2] A carbonated beverage made of water, fruit syrup, and phosphoric acid, used for medicinal purposes.

I don't like our room a bit. I wanted one downstairs that opened onto the piazza and had roses all over the window, and such pretty old-fashioned chintz hangings! But John would not hear of it.

He said there was only one window and not room for two beds, and no near room for him if he took another.

He is very careful and loving, and hardly lets me stir without special direction.

I have a schedule prescription for each hour in the day; he takes all care from me, and so I feel basely ungrateful not to value it more.

30   He said we came here solely on my account, that I was to have perfect rest and all the air I could get. "Your exercise depends on your strength, my dear," said he, "and your food somewhat on your appetite; but air you can absorb all the time." So we took the nursery at the top of the house.

It is a big, airy room, the whole floor nearly, with windows that look all ways, and air and sunshine galore. It was nursery first, and then playroom and gymnasium, I should judge, for the windows are barred for little children, and there are rings and things in the walls.

The paint and paper look as if a boys' school had used it. It is stripped off—the paper—in great patches all around the head of my bed, about as far as I can reach, and in a great place on the other side of the room low down. I never saw a worse paper in my life. One of those sprawling, flamboyant patterns committing every artistic sin.

It is dull enough to confuse the eye in following, pronounced enough to constantly irritate and provoke study, and when you follow the lame uncertain curves for a little distance they suddenly commit suicide—plunge off at outrageous angles, destroy themselves in unheard-of contradictions.

The color is repellent, almost revolting: a smouldering unclean yellow, strangely faded by the slow-turning sunlight. It is a dull yet lurid orange in some places, a sickly sulphur tint in others.

35   No wonder the children hated it! I should hate it myself if I had to live in this room long.

There comes John, and I must put this away—he hates to have me write a word.

We have been here two weeks, and I haven't felt like writing before, since that first day.

I am sitting by the window now, up in this atrocious nursery, and there is nothing to hinder my writing as much as I please, save lack of strength.

John is away all day, and even some nights when his cases are serious.

40   I am glad my case is not serious!

But these nervous troubles are dreadfully depressing.

John does not know how much I really suffer. He knows there is no reason to suffer, and that satisfies him.

Of course it is only nervousness. It does weigh on me so not to do my duty in any way!

I meant to be such a help to John, such a real rest and comfort, and here I am a comparative burden already!

45   Nobody would believe what an effort it is to do what little I am able—to dress and entertain, and order things.

It is fortunate Mary is so good with the baby. Such a dear baby!

And yet I *cannot* be with him, it makes me so nervous.

I suppose John never was nervous in his life. He laughs at me so about this wallpaper!

At first he meant to repaper the room, but afterward he said that I was letting it get the better of me, and that nothing was worse for a nervous patient than to give way to such fancies.

50   He said that after the wallpaper was changed it would be the heavy bedstead, and then the barred windows, and then that gate at the head of the stairs, and so on.

"You know the place is doing you good," he said, "and really, dear, I don't care to renovate the house just for a three months' rental."

"Then do let us go downstairs," I said. "There are such pretty rooms there."

Then he took me in his arms and called me a blessed little goose, and said he would go down to the cellar, if I wished, and have it whitewashed into the bargain.

But he is right enough about the beds and windows and things.

55   It is as airy and comfortable room as anyone need wish, and, of course, I would not be so silly as to make him uncomfortable just for a whim.

I'm really getting quite fond of the big room, all but that horrid paper.

Out of one window I can see the garden—those mysterious deep-shaded arbors, the riotous old-fashioned flowers, and bushes and gnarly trees.

Out of another I get a lovely view of the bay and a little private wharf belonging to the estate. There is a beautiful shaded lane that runs down there from the house. I always fancy I see people walking in these numerous paths and arbors, but John has cautioned me not to give way to fancy in the least. He says that with my imaginative power and habit of story-making, a nervous weakness like mine is sure to lead to all manner of excited fancies, and that I ought to use my will and good sense to check the tendency. So I try.

I think sometimes that if I were only well enough to write a little it would relieve the press of ideas and rest me.

60   But I find I get pretty tired when I try.

It is so discouraging not to have any advice and companionship about my work. When I get really well, John says we will ask Cousin Henry and Julia down for a long visit; but he says he would as soon put fireworks in my pillow-case as to let me have those stimulating people about now.

I wish I could get well faster.

But I must not think about that. This paper looks to me as if it *knew* what a vicious influence it had!

There is a recurrent spot where the pattern lolls like a broken neck and two bulbous eyes stare at you upside down.

65   I get positively angry with the impertinence of it and the everlastingness. Up and down and sideways they crawl, and those absurd unblinking eyes are everywhere. There is one place where two breadths didn't match, and the eyes go all up and down the line, one a little higher than the other.

I never saw so much expression in an inanimate thing before, and we all know how much expression they have! I used to lie awake as a child and get more entertainment and terror out of blank walls and plain furniture than most children could find in a toy-store.

I remember what a kindly wink the knobs of our big old bureau used to have, and there was one chair that always seemed like a strong friend.

I used to feel that if any of the other things looked too fierce I could always hop into that chair and be safe.

The furniture in this room is no worse than inharmonious, however, for we had to bring it all from downstairs. I suppose when this was used as a playroom they had to take the nursery things out, and no wonder! I never saw such ravages as the children have made here.

70   The wallpaper, as I said before, is torn off in spots, and it sticketh closer than a brother—they must have had perseverance as well as hatred.

Then the floor is scratched and gouged and splintered, the plaster itself is dug out here and there, and this great heavy bed, which is all we found in the room, looks as if it had been through the wars.

But I don't mind it a bit—only the paper.

There comes John's sister. Such a dear girl as she is, and so careful of me! I must not let her find me writing.

She is a perfect and enthusiastic housekeeper, and hopes for no better profession. I verily believe she thinks it is the writing which made me sick!

75   But I can write when she is out, and see her a long way off from these windows.

There is one that commands the road, a lovely shaded winding road, and one that just looks off over the country. A lovely country, too, full of great elms and velvet meadows.

This wallpaper has a kind of sub-pattern in a different shade, a particularly irritating one, for you can only see it in certain lights, and not clearly then.

But in the places where it isn't faded and where the sun is just so—I can see a strange, provoking, formless sort of figure that seems to skulk about behind that silly and conspicuous front design.

There's sister on the stairs!

80   Well, the Fourth of July is over! The people are all gone, and I am tired out. John thought it might do me good to see a little company, so we just had mother and Nellie and the children down for a week.

Of course I didn't do a thing. Jennie sees to everything now.

But it tired me all the same.

John says if I don't pick up faster he shall send me to Weir Mitchell[3] in the fall.

But I don't want to go there at all. I had a friend who was in his hands once, and she says he is just like John and my brother, only more so!

85   Besides, it is such an undertaking to go so far.

I don't feel as if it was worthwhile to turn my hand over for anything, and I'm getting dreadfully fretful and querulous.

I cry at nothing, and cry most of the time.

Of course I don't when John is here, or anybody else, but when I am alone.

And I am alone a good deal just now. John is kept in town very often by serious cases, and Jennie is good and lets me alone when I want her to.

90   So I walk a little in the garden or down that lovely lane, sit on the porch under the roses, and lie down up here a good deal.

I'm getting really fond of the room in spite of the wallpaper. Perhaps *because* of the wallpaper.

It dwells in my mind so!

I lie here on this great immovable bed—it is nailed down, I believe—and follow that pattern about by the hour. It is as good as gymnastics, I assure you. I start, we'll say, at the bottom, down in the corner over there where it has not been touched, and I determine for the thousandth time that I *will* follow that pointless pattern to some sort of a conclusion.

I know a little of the principle of design, and I know this thing was not arranged on any laws of radiation, or alternation, or repetition, or symmetry, or anything else that I ever heard of.

95   It is repeated, of course, by the breadths, but not otherwise.

---

[3] American neurologist who invented the "rest cure" for hysteria and who treated Gilman herself.

Looked at in one way, each breadth stands alone; the bloated curves and flourishes—a kind of "debased Romanesque"[4] with *delirium tremens*[5]—go waddling up and down in isolated columns of fatuity.

But, on the other hand, they connect diagonally, and the sprawling outlines run off in great slanting waves of optic horror, like a lot of wallowing sea-weeds in full chase.

The whole thing goes horizontally, too, at least it seems so, and I exhaust myself in trying to distinguish the order of its going in that direction.

They have used a horizontal breadth for a frieze,[6] and that adds wonderfully to the confusion.

100   There is one end of the room where it is almost intact, and there, when the crosslights fade and the low sun shines directly upon it, I can almost fancy radiation after all—the interminable grotesque seems to form around a common center and rush off in headlong plunges of equal distraction.

It makes me tired to follow it. I will take a nap, I guess.

I don't know why I should write this.

I don't want to.

I don't feel able.

105   And I know John would think it absurd. But I *must* say what I feel and think in some way—it is such a relief!

But the effort is getting to be greater than the relief.

Half the time now I am awfully lazy, and lie down ever so much. John says I mustn't lose my strength, and has me take cod liver oil and lots of tonics and things, to say nothing of ale and wine and rare meat.

Dear John! He loves me very dearly, and hates to have me sick. I tried to have a real earnest reasonable talk with him the other day, and tell him how I wish he would let me go and make a visit to Cousin Henry and Julia.

But he said I wasn't able to go, nor able to stand it after I got there; and I did not make out a very good case for myself, for I was crying before I had finished.

110   It is getting to be a great effort for me to think straight. Just this nervous weakness, I suppose.

And dear John gathered me up in his arms, and just carried me upstairs and laid me on the bed, and sat by me and read to me till it tired my head.

He said I was his darling and his comfort and all he had, and that I must take care of myself for his sake, and keep well.

He says no one but myself can help me out of it, that I must use my will and self-control and not let any silly fancies run away with me.

There's one comfort—the baby is well and happy, and does not have to occupy this nursery with the horrid wallpaper.

115   If we had not used it, that blessed child would have! What a fortunate escape! Why, I wouldn't have a child of mine, an impressionable little thing, live in such a room for worlds.

I never thought of it before, but it is lucky that John kept me here after all; I can stand it so much easier than a baby, you see.

---

[4] Style of architecture prevalent from the ninth to twelfth centuries in Europe, characterized by rounded arches and heavy masonry and design.

[5] Condition caused by excessive use of alcohol and characterized by physical trembling and hallucinations.

[6] A decorative band with lettering or sculpture.

Of course I never mention it to them any more—I am too wise—but I keep watch for it all the same.

There are things in that wallpaper that nobody knows about but me, or ever will.

Behind that outside pattern the dim shapes get clearer every day.

120 It is always the same shape, only very numerous.

And it is like a woman stooping down and creeping about behind that pattern. I don't like it a bit. I wonder—I begin to think—I wish John would take me away from here!

It is so hard to talk with John about my case, because he is so wise, and because he loves me so.

But I tried it last night.

It was moonlight. The moon shines in all around just as the sun does.

125 I hate to see it sometimes, it creeps so slowly, and always comes in by one window or another.

John was asleep and I hated to waken him, so I kept still and watched the moonlight on that undulating wallpaper till I felt creepy.

The faint figure behind seemed to shake the pattern, just as if she wanted to get out.

I got up softly and went to feel and see if the paper *did* move, and when I came back John was awake.

"What is it, little girl?" he said. "Don't go walking about like that—you'll get cold."

130 I thought it was a good time to talk, so I told him that I really was not gaining here, and that I wished he would take me away.

"Why, darling!" said he. "Our lease will be up in three weeks, and I can't see how to leave before.

"The repairs are not done at home, and I cannot possibly leave town just now. Of course, if you were in any danger, I could and would, but you really are better, dear, whether you can see it or not. I am a doctor, dear, and I know. You are gaining flesh and color, your appetite is better, I feel really much easier about you."

"I don't weigh a bit more," said I, "nor as much; and my appetite may be better in the evening when you are here but it is worse in the morning when you are away!"

"Bless her little heart!" said he with a big hug. "She shall be as sick as she pleases! But now let's improve the shining hours by going to sleep, and talk about it in the morning!"

135 "And you won't go away?" I asked gloomily.

"Why, how can I, dear? It is only three weeks more and then we will take a nice little trip of a few days while Jennie is getting the house ready. Really, dear, you are better!"

"Better in body perhaps—" I began, and stopped short, for he sat up straight and looked at me with such a stern, reproachful look that I could not say another word.

"My darling," said he, "I beg of you, for my sake and for our child's sake, as well as for your own, that you will never for one instant let that idea enter your mind! There is nothing so dangerous, so fascinating, to a temperament like yours. It is a false and foolish fancy. Can you not trust me as a physician when I tell you so?"

So of course I said no more on that score, and we went to sleep before long. He thought I was asleep first, but I wasn't, and lay there for hours trying to decide whether that front pattern and the back pattern really did move together or separately.

140 On a pattern like this, by daylight, there is a lack of sequence, a defiance of law, that is a constant irritant to a normal mind.

The color is hideous enough, and unreliable enough, and infuriating enough, but the pattern is torturing.

You think you have mastered it, but just as you get well under way in following, it turns a back-somersault and there you are. It slaps you in the face, knocks you down, and tramples upon you. It is like a bad dream.

The outside pattern is a florid arabesque, reminding one of a fungus. If you can imagine a toadstool in joints, an interminable string of toadstools, budding and sprouting in endless convolutions—why, that is something like it.

That is, sometimes!

145 There is one marked peculiarity about this paper, a thing nobody seems to notice but myself, and that is that it changes as the light changes.

When the sun shoots in through the east window—I always watch for that first long, straight ray—it changes so quickly that I never can quite believe it.

That is why I watch it always.

By moonlight—the moon shines in all night when there is a moon—I wouldn't know it was the same paper.

At night in any kind of light, in twilight, candlelight, lamplight, and worst of all by moonlight, it becomes bars! The outside pattern, I mean, and the woman behind it is as plain as can be.

150 I didn't realize for a long time what the thing was that showed behind, that dim subpattern, but now I am quite sure it is a woman.

By daylight she is subdued, quiet. I fancy it is the pattern that keeps her so still. It is so puzzling. It keeps me quiet by the hour.

I lie down ever so much now. John says it is good for me, and to sleep all I can.

Indeed he started the habit by making me lie down for an hour after each meal.

It is a very bad habit, I am convinced, for you see, I don't sleep.

155 And that cultivates deceit, for I don't tell them I'm awake—oh, no!

The fact is I am getting a little afraid of John.

He seems very queer sometimes, and even Jennie has an inexplicable look.

It strikes me occasionally, just as a scientific hypothesis, that perhaps it is the paper!

I have watched John when he did not know I was looking, and come into the room suddenly on the most innocent excuses, and I've caught him several times *looking at the paper!* And Jennie too. I caught Jennie with her hand on it once.

160 She didn't know I was in the room, and when I asked her in a quiet, a very quiet voice, with the most restrained manner possible, what she was doing with the paper, she turned around as if she had been caught stealing, and looked quite angry—asked me why I should frighten her so!

Then she said that the paper stained everything it touched, that she had found yellow smooches on all my clothes and John's, and she wished we would be more careful!

Did not that sound innocent? But I know she was studying that pattern and I am determined that nobody shall find it out but myself!

Life is very much more exciting now than it used to be. You see, I have something more to expect, to look forward to, to watch. I really do eat better, and am more quiet than I was.

John is so pleased to see me improve! He laughed a little the other day, and said I seemed to be flourishing in spite of my wallpaper.

165 I turned it off with a laugh. I had no intention of telling him it was *because* of the wallpaper—he would make fun of me. He might even want to take me away.

I don't want to leave now until I have found it out. There is a week more, and I think that will be enough.

I'm feeling so much better!

I don't sleep much at night, for it is so interesting to watch developments; but I sleep a good deal during the daytime.

In the daytime it is tiresome and perplexing.

170   There are always new shoots on the fungus, and new shades of yellow all over it. I cannot keep count of them, though I have tried conscientiously. It is the strangest yellow, that wallpaper! It makes me think of all the yellow things I ever saw—not beautiful ones like buttercups, but old, foul, bad yellow things.

But there is something else about that paper—the smell! I noticed it the moment we came into the room, but with so much air and sun it was not bad. Now we have had a week of fog and rain, and whether the windows are open or not, the smell is here.

It creeps all over the house.

I find it hovering in the dining-room, skulking in the parlor, hiding in the hall, lying in wait for me on the stairs.

It gets into my hair.

175   Even when I go to ride, if I turn my head suddenly and surprise it—there is that smell!

Such a peculiar odor, too! I have spent hours in trying to analyze it, to find what it smelled like.

It is not bad—at first—and very gentle, but quite the subtlest, most enduring odor I ever met.

In this damp weather it is awful. I wake up in the night and find it hanging over me.

It used to disturb me at first. I thought seriously of burning the house—to reach the smell.

180   But now I am used to it. The only thing I can think of that it is like is the *color* of the paper! A yellow smell.

There is a very funny mark on this wall, low down, near the mopboard. A streak that runs round the room. It goes behind every piece of furniture, except the bed, a long, straight, even *smooch,* as if it had been rubbed over and over.

I wonder how it was done and who did it, and what they did it for. Round and round and round—round and round and round—it makes me dizzy!

I really have discovered something at last.

Through watching so much at night, when it changes so, I have finally found out.

185   The front pattern *does* move—and no wonder! The woman behind shakes it!

Sometimes I think there are a great many women behind, and sometimes only one, and she crawls around fast, and her crawling shakes it all over.

Then in the very bright spots she keeps still, and in the very shady spots she just takes hold of the bars and shakes them hard.

And she is all the time trying to climb through. But nobody could climb through that pattern—it strangles so; I think that is why it has so many heads.

They get through, and then the pattern strangles them off and turns them upside down, and makes their eyes white!

190   If those heads were covered or taken off it would not be half so bad.

I think that woman gets out in the daytime!

And I'll tell you why—privately—I've seen her!

I can see her out of every one of my windows!

It is the same woman, I know, for she is always creeping, and most women do not creep by daylight.

195   I see her in that long shaded lane, creeping up and down. I see her in those dark grape arbors, creeping all around the garden.

I see her on that long road under the trees, creeping along, and when a carriage comes she hides under the blackberry vines.

I don't blame her a bit. It must be very humiliating to be caught creeping by daylight!

I always lock the door when I creep by daylight. I can't do it at night, for I know John would suspect something at once.

And John is so queer now that I don't want to irritate him. I wish he would take another room! Besides, I don't want anybody to get that woman out at night but myself.

200   I often wonder if I could see her out of all the windows at once.

But, turn as fast as I can, I can only see out of one at one time.

And though I always see her, she *may* be able to creep faster than I can turn! I have watched her sometimes away off in the open country, creeping as fast as a cloud shadow in a wind.

If only that top pattern could be gotten off from the under one! I mean to try it, little by little.

I have found out another funny thing, but I shan't tell it this time! It does not do to trust people too much.

205   There are only two more days to get this paper off, and I believe John is beginning to notice. I don't like the look in his eyes.

And I heard him ask Jennie a lot of professional questions about me. She had a very good report to give.

She said I slept a good deal in the daytime.

John knows I don't sleep very well at night, for all I'm so quiet!

He asked me all sorts of questions, too, and pretended to be very loving and kind.

210   As if I couldn't see through him!

Still, I don't wonder he acts so, sleeping under this paper for three months.

It only interests me, but I feel sure John and Jennie are secretly affected by it. Hurrah! This is the last day, but it is enough. John to stay in town over night, and won't be out until this evening.

Jennie wanted to sleep with me—the sly thing; but I told her I should undoubtedly rest better for a night all alone.

That was clever, for really I wasn't alone a bit! As soon as it was moonlight and that poor thing began to crawl and shake the pattern, I got up and ran to help her.

215   I pulled and she shook. I shook and she pulled, and before morning we had peeled off yards of that paper.

A strip about as high as my head and half around the room.

And then when the sun came and that awful pattern began to laugh at me, I declared I would finish it today!

We go away tomorrow, and they are moving all my furniture down again to leave things as they were before.

Jennie looked at the wall in amazement, but I told her merrily that I did it out of pure spite at the vicious thing.

220   She laughed and said she wouldn't mind doing it herself, but I must not get tired.

How she betrayed herself that time!

But I am here, and no person touches this paper but Me—not *alive!*

She tried to get me out of the room—it was too patent! But I said it was so quiet and empty and clean now that I believed I would lie down again and sleep all I could, and not to wake me even for dinner—I would call when I woke.

So now she is gone, and the servants are gone, and the things are gone, and there is nothing left but that great bedstead nailed down, with the canvas mattress we found on it.

225   We shall sleep downstairs tonight, and take the boat home tomorrow.

I quite enjoy the room, now it is bare again.

How those children did tear about here!

This bedstead is fairly gnawed!

But I must get to work.

230   I have locked the door and thrown the key down into the front path.

I don't want to go out, and I don't want to have anybody come in, till John comes.

I want to astonish him.

I've got a rope up here that even Jennie did not find. If that woman does get out, and tries to get away, I can tie her!

But I forgot I could not reach far without anything to stand on!

235   This bed will *not* move!

I tried to lift and push it until I was lame, and then I got so angry I bit off a little piece at one corner—but it hurt my teeth.

Then I peeled off all the paper I could reach standing on the floor. It sticks horribly and the pattern just enjoys it! All those strangled heads and bulbous eyes and waddling fungus growths just shriek with derision!

I am getting angry enough to do something desperate. To jump out of the window would be admirable exercise, but the bars are too strong even to try.

Besides I wouldn't do it. Of course not. I know well enough that a step like that is improper and might be misconstrued.

240   I don't like to *look* out of the windows even—there are so many of those creeping women, and they creep so fast.

I wonder if they all come out of that wallpaper as I did?

But I am securely fastened now by my well-hidden rope—you don't get *me* out in the road there!

I suppose I shall have to get back behind the pattern when it comes night, and that is hard!

It is so pleasant to be out in this great room and creep around as I please!

245   I don't want to go outside. I won't, even if Jennie asks me to.

For outside you have to creep on the ground, and everything is green instead of yellow.

But here I can creep smoothly on the floor, and my shoulder just fits in that long smooch around the wall, so I cannot lose my way.

Why, there's John at the door!

It is no use, young man, you can't open it!

250   How he does call and pound!

Now he's crying to Jeannie for an axe.

It would be a shame to break down that beautiful door!

"John dear!" said I in the gentlest voice. "The key is down by the front steps, under a plantain leaf!"

That silenced him for a few moments.

255   Then he said, very quietly indeed. "Open the door, my darling!"

"I can't," said I. "The key is down by the front door under a plantain leaf!" And then I said it again, several times, very gently and slowly, and said it so often that he had to go and see, and he got it of course, and came in. He stopped short by the door.

"What is the matter?" he cried. "For God's sake, what are you doing!"

I kept on creeping just the same, but I looked at him over my shoulder.

"I've got out at last," said I, "in spite of you and Jane. And I've pulled off most of the paper, so you can't put me back!"

260   Now why should that man have fainted? But he did, and right across my path by the wall, so that I had to creep over him every time!

■ EXPLORATIONS OF THE TEXT

1. What attitudes characterize John's treatment of his wife? Do his attitudes contribute to the narrator's situation? Look carefully at terms of endearment.

2. Is the narrator correct in her suspicions about her husband? about her brother? How do her attitudes change in the story?

3. What is the significance of the fact that the narrator's room was originally a nursery?
4. Why does John not want her to write? Why does she want to write?
5. What are the stages in the narrator's psychological breakdown? How are these stages reflected in her obsession with the wallpaper?
6. Who is the "woman" in the wallpaper? Discuss the symbolism of the figure. What does the yellow wallpaper finally symbolize?
7. What does the ending mean? What happens to the narrator? What is the husband's reaction?
8. Explore the point of view and the imagery in this story. How do they contribute to the story's emotional impact?
9. Compare character and theme in this story with those in "A Rose for Emily."

■ THE READING/WRITING CONNECTION

1. Create a character sketch of the narrator or John. Incorporate specifics from the story.

■ IDEAS FOR WRITING

1. Charlotte Perkins Gilman's doctor, treating her for nervous depression, once told her "never to touch pen, brush or pencil again." Why does Gilman imply that the treatment worsens the condition?
2. "The Yellow Wallpaper" was anthologized as a horror or ghost story for many years. Write a defense of "The Yellow Wallpaper" either as a horror story or as more serious fiction.

OCTAVIO PAZ

Born in Mexico City, Octavio Paz (1914–98) was educated in Catholic schools and graduated from the National University of Mexico. At nineteen, he published his first volume of poetry. His volumes of poetry include Sylvan Moon *(1933),* Salamandra *(1958–61), and* Configurations *(1971). A collected edition of his poems 1957 to 1987 appeared in 1987. He also wrote many volumes of prose. Paz was awarded the Nobel Prize for Literature in 1990. He was an outspoken social critic, a philosopher, an essayist, and a leading figure in the renaissance of Latin American literature.*

1949

MY LIFE WITH THE WAVE

When I left that sea, a wave moved ahead of the others. She was tall and light. In spite of the shouts of the others who grabbed her by her floating clothes, she clutched my arm and went off with me leaping. I didn't want to say anything to her, because it hurt me to shame her in front of her friends. Besides, the furious stares of the elders paralyzed me. When we got to town, I explained to her that it was impossible, that life in the city was not what she had been able to imagine with the ingenuity of a wave that had never left the sea. She watched me gravely: "No, your decision is made. You can't go back." I tried sweetness, hardness, irony. She cried, screamed, hugged, threatened. I had to apologize.

The next day my troubles began. How could we get on the train without being seen by the conductor, the passengers, the police? Certainly the rules say nothing in respect to the transport of waves on the railroad, but this same reserve was an indication of the severity with which our act would be judged. After much thought I arrived at the station an hour before departure, took my seat, and, when no one was looking, emptied the water tank for the passengers; then, carefully, poured in my friend.

The first incident came about when the children of a nearby couple declared their noisy thirst. I stopped them and promised them refreshments and lemonade. They were at the point of accepting when another thirsty passenger approached. I was about to invite her also, but the stare of her companion stopped me. The lady took a paper cup, approached the tank, and turned the faucet. Her cup was barely half full when I leaped between the woman and my friend. She looked at me astonished. While I apologized, one of the children turned the faucet again. I closed it violently. The lady brought the cup to her lips:

"Agh, this water is salty."

5   The boy echoed her. Various passengers rose. The husband called the conductor:

"This man put salt in the water."

The conductor called the Inspector:

"So you put substances in the water?"

The Inspector in turn called the police:

10   "So you poisoned the water?"

The police in turn called the Captain:

"So you're the poisoner?"

The Captain called three agents. The agents took me to an empty car, amid the stares and whispers of the passengers. At the next station they took me off and pushed and dragged me to the jail. For days no one spoke to me, except during the long interrogations. When I explained my story no one believed me, not even the jailer, who shook his head, saying: "The case is grave, truly grave. You didn't want to poison the children?" One day they brought me before the Magistrate.

"Your case is difficult," he repeated. "I will assign you to the Penal Judge."

15   A year passed. Finally they judged me. As there were no victims, my sentence was light. After a short time, my day of liberty arrived.

The Chief of the Prison called me in:

"Well, now you're free. You were lucky. Lucky there were no victims. But don't do it again, because the next time won't be so short . . ."

And he stared at me with the same grave stare with which everyone watched me.

The same afternoon I took the train and after hours of uncomfortable traveling arrived in Mexico City. I took a cab home. At the door of my apartment I heard laughter and singing. I felt a pain in my chest, like the smack of a wave of surprise when surprise smacks us across the chest: my friend was there, singing and laughing as always.

20   "How did you get back?"

"Simple: in the train. Someone, after making sure that I was only salt water, poured me in the engine. It was a rough trip: soon I was a white plume of vapor, soon I fell in a fine rain on the machine. I thinned out a lot. I lost many drops."

Her presence changed my life. The house of dark corridors and dusty furniture was filled with air, with sun, with sounds and green and blue reflections, a numerous and happy populace of reverberations and echoes. How many waves is one wave, and how it can make a beach or a rock or jetty out of a wall, a chest, a forehead that it crowns with foam! Even the abandoned corners, the abject corners of dust and debris were touched by her light hands. Everything began to laugh and everywhere shined with teeth. The sun entered the old rooms with pleasure and stayed in my house for hours, abandoning the other houses, the district, the city, the country. And some nights, very late, the scandalized stars watched it sneak from my house.

Love was a game, a perpetual creation. All was beach, sand, a bed of sheets that were always fresh. If I embraced her, she swelled with pride, incredibly tall, like the liquid stalk of a poplar; and soon that thinness flowered into a fountain of white feathers, into a plume of smiles that fell over my head and back and covered me with whiteness. Or she stretched out in front of me, infinite as the horizon, until I too became horizon and silence. Full and sinuous, it enveloped me like music or some giant lips. Her presence was a going and coming of caresses, of murmurs, of kisses. Entered in her waters, I was drenched to the socks and in a wink of an eye I found myself up above, at the height of vertigo, mysteriously suspended, to fall like a stone and feel myself gently deposited on the dryness, like a feather. Nothing is comparable to sleeping in those waters, to wake pounded by a thousand happy light lashes, by a thousand assaults that withdrew laughing.

But never did I reach the center of her being. Never did I touch the nakedness of pain and of death. Perhaps it does not exist in waves, that secret site that renders a woman vulnerable and mortal, that electric button where all interlocks, twitches, and straightens out to then swoon. Her sensibility, like that of women, spread in ripples, only they weren't concentric ripples, but rather excentric, spreading each time farther, until they touched other galaxies. To love her was to extend to remote contacts, to vibrate with far-off stars we never suspected. But her center . . . no, she had no center, just an emptiness as in a whirlwind, that sucked me in and smothered me.

25   Stretched out side by side, we exchanged confidences, whispers, smiles. Curled up, she fell on my chest and there unfolded like a vegetation of murmurs. She sang in my ear, a little snail. She became humble and transparent, clutching my feet like a small animal, calm water. She was so clear I could read all of her thoughts. Certain nights her skin was covered with phosphorescence and to embrace her was to embrace a piece of night tattooed with fire. But she also became black and bitter. At unexpected hours she roared, moaned, twisted. Her groans woke the neighbors. Upon hearing her, the sea wind would scratch at the door of the house or rave in a loud voice on the roof. Cloudy days irritated her; she broke furniture, said bad words, covered me with insults and green and gray foam. She spit, cried, swore, prophesied. Subject to the moon, to the stars, to the influence of the light of other worlds, she changed her moods and appearance in a way that I thought fantastic, but it was as fatal as the tide.

She began to miss solitude. The house was full of snails and conches, of small sailboats that in her fury she had shipwrecked (together with the others, laden with images, that each night left my forehead and sank in her ferocious or pleasant whirlwinds). How many little treasures were lost in that time! But my boats and the silent song of the snails was not enough. I had to install in the house a colony of fish. I confess that it was not without jealousy that I watched them swimming in my friend, caressing her breasts, sleeping between her legs, adorning her hair with light flashes of color.

Among all those fish there were a few particularly repulsive and ferocious ones, little tigers from the aquarium, with large fixed eyes and jagged and bloodthirsty mouths. I don't know by what aberration my friend delighted in playing with them, shamelessly showing them a preference whose significance I preferred to ignore. She passed long hours confined with those horrible creatures. One day I couldn't stand it any more; I threw open the door and launched after them. Agile and ghostly they escaped my hands while she laughed and pounded me until I fell. I thought I was drowning. And when I was at the point of death, and purple, she deposited me on the bank and began to kiss me, saying I don't know what things. I felt very weak, fatigued and humiliated. And at the same time her voluptuousness made me close my eyes, because her voice was sweet and she spoke to me of the delicious death of the drowned. When I recovered, I began to fear and hate her.

I had neglected my affairs. Now I began to visit friends and renew old and dear relations. I met an old girlfriend. Making her swear to keep my secret, I told her of my life with the wave. Nothing moves women so much as the possibility of saving a man. My redeemer employed all of her arts, but what could a woman, master of a limited number of souls and bodies, do in front of my friend who was always changing—and always identical to herself in her incessant metamorphoses.

Winter came. The sky turned gray. Fog fell on the city. Frozen drizzle rained. My friend cried every night. During the day she isolated herself, quiet and sinister, stuttering a single syllable, like an old woman who grumbles in a corner. She became cold; to sleep with her was to shiver all night and to feel freeze, little by little, the blood, the bones, the thoughts. She turned deep, impenetrable, restless. I left frequently and my absences were each time more prolonged. She, in her corner, howled loudly. With teeth like steel and a corrosive tongue she gnawed the walls, crumbled them. She passed the nights in mourning, reproaching me. She had nightmares, deliriums of the sun, of warm beaches. She dreamt of the pole and of changing into a great block of ice, sailing beneath black skies in nights long as months. She insulted me. She cursed and laughed; filled the house with guffaws and phantoms. She called up the monsters of the depths, blind ones, quick ones, blunt. Charged with electricity, she carbonized all she touched; full of acid, she dissolved whatever she brushed against. Her sweet embraces became knotty cords that strangled me. And her body, greenish and elastic, was an implacable whip that lashed, lashed, lashed. I fled. The horrible fish laughed with ferocious smiles.

30   There in the mountains, among the tall pines and precipices, I breathed the cold thin air like a thought of liberty. At the end of a month I returned. I had decided. It had been so cold that over the marble of the chimney, next to the extinct fire, I found a statue of ice. I was unmoved by her weary beauty. I put her in a big canvas sack and went out to the streets with the sleeper on my shoulders. In a restaurant in the outskirts I sold her to a waiter friend who immediately began to chop her into little pieces, which he carefully deposited in the buckets where bottles are chilled.

■ **EXPLORATIONS OF THE TEXT**

1. What merger of the real and the fantastic propels this story? Why does the narrator compare the sea and an elusive lover?
2. How is the wave like a woman? like a man's fantasy of a woman?
3. Explore the incident of the water fountain. Why is the water "salty"? What does the narrator's imprisonment suggest?
4. Once he returns home, how does her presence at first change his life? What stage of love is depicted?
5. What are the implications of these statements: "But never did I reach the center of her being," and "She had no center, just an emptiness as in a whirlwind, that sucked me in and smothered me"?
6. Why does the narrator have to install a colony of fish? Why does she prefer the "little tigers . . . with large fixed eyes and jagged and bloodthirsty mouths"?
7. Explore the sign of the "drowning" episode. Why does he begin "to fear and hate her"?
8. What is the outcome of their relationship? Explore the symbolic dimension of the wave's association with ice.
9. What visions of romantic love, of sexuality, and of relationships does the story present?
10. Why does Paz depict human love through an affair with a wave instead of an affair with a real lover? What is the impact of this metaphor? Is it effective?

■ **THE READING/WRITING CONNECTION**

1. Write a parable, fable, or story in magical realism for men's and women's relationships. Or write a feminist fable or fairy tale.
2. "Think" Topic: Why is the woman characterized as a "wave" rather than as an ocean?

■ **IDEAS FOR WRITING**

1. Examine the text to determine how Paz created the metamorphosis of the woman as ocean lover. Does it lie in the choice of details? verbs? adjectives? figurative language? Comment on Paz's style.
2. Categorize the stages of romantic love in this story.

ALBERTO MORAVIA

Alberto Moravia (1907–90) was born in Rome. He gained early fame for his first novel, The Time of Indifference *(1929). During the 1930s and 1940s, he earned international acclaim for his novels, which include* Wheel of Fortune *(1937) and* Agostino *(1944). His short story volumes include* Roman Tales *(1956) and* Command and I Will Obey You *(1969). Moravia is known for his penetrating portraits of men and women in love and their struggle to escape the isolation and sterility symptomatic of a materialistic age.*

1967

THE CHASE

I have never been a sportsman—or, rather, I have been a sportsman only once, and that was the first and last time. I was a child, and one day, for some reason or other, I found myself together with my father, who was holding a gun in his hand, behind a bush, watching a bird that had perched on a branch not very far away. It was a large, gray bird—or perhaps it was brown—with a long—or perhaps a short—beak; I don't remember. I only remember what I felt at that moment as I looked at it. It was like watching an animal whose vitality was rendered more intense by the very fact of my watching it and of the animal's not knowing that I was watching it.

At that moment, I say, the notion of wildness entered my mind, never again to leave it: everything is wild which is autonomous and unpredictable and does not depend upon us. Then all of a sudden there was an explosion; I could no longer see the bird and I thought it had flown away. But my father was leading the way, walking in front of me through the undergrowth. Finally he stooped down, picked up something, and put it in my hand. I was aware of something warm and soft and I lowered my eyes: there was the bird in the palm of my hand, its dangling, shattered head crowned with a plume of already-thickening blood. I burst into tears and dropped the corpse on the ground, and that was the end of my shooting experience.

I thought again of this remote episode in my life this very day after watching my wife, for the first and also the last time, as she was walking through the streets of the city. But let us take things in order.

What had my wife been like; what was she like now? She once had been, to put it briefly, "wild"—that is, entirely autonomous and unpredictable; latterly she had become "tame"—that is, predictable and dependent. For a long time she had been like the bird that, on that far-off morning in my childhood, I had seen perching on the bough; latterly, I am sorry to say, she had become like a hen about which one knows everything in advance—how it moves, how it eats, how it lays eggs, how it sleeps, and so on.

5   Nevertheless I would not wish anyone to think that my wife's wildness consisted of an uncouth, rough, rebellious character. Apart from being extremely beautiful, she is the gentlest, politest, most discreet person in the world. Rather her wildness consisted of the air of charming unpredictability, of independence in her way of living, with which during

the first years of our marriage she acted in my presence, both at home and abroad. Wildness signified intimacy, privacy, secrecy. Yes, my wife as she sat in front of her dressing table, her eyes fixed on the looking glass, passing the hairbrush with a repeated motion over her long, loose hair, was just as wild as the solitary quail hopping forward along a sun-filled furrow or the furtive fox coming out into a clearing and stopping to look around before running on. She was wild because I, as I looked at her, could never manage to foresee when she would give a last stroke with the hairbrush and rise and come toward me; wild to such a degree that sometimes when I went into our bedroom the smell of her, floating in the air, would have something of the acrid quality of a wild beast's lair.

Gradually she became less wild, tamer. I had had a fox, a quail, in the house, as I have said; then one day I realized that I had a hen. What effect does a hen have on someone who watches it? It has the effect of being, so to speak, an automaton in the form of a bird; automatic are the brief, rapid steps with which it moves about; automatic its hard, terse pecking; automatic the glance of the round eyes in its head that nods and turns; automatic its ready crouching down under the cock; automatic the dropping of the egg wherever it may be and the cry with which it announces that the egg has been laid. Good-by to the fox; good-by to the quail. And her smell—this no longer brought to my mind, in any way, the innocent odor of a wild animal; rather I detected in it the chemical suavity of some ordinary French perfume.

Our flat is on the first floor of a big building in a modern quarter of the town; our windows look out on a square in which there is a small public garden, the haunt of nurses and children and dogs. One day I was standing at the window, looking in a melancholy way at the garden. My wife, shortly before, had dressed to go out; and once again, watching her, I had noticed the irrevocable and, so to speak, invisible character of her gestures and personality; something which gave one the feeling of a thing already seen and already done and which therefore evaded even the most determined observation. And now, as I stood looking at the garden and at the same time wondering why the adorable wildness of former times had so completely disappeared, suddenly my wife came into my range of vision as she walked quickly across the garden in the direction of the bus stop. I watched her and then I almost jumped for joy; in a movement she was making to pull down a fold of her narrow skirt and smooth it over her thigh with the tips of her long, sharp nails, in this movement I recognized the wildness that in the past had made me love her. It was only an instant, but in that instant I said to myself: She's become wild again because she's convinced that I am not there and am not watching her. Then I left the window and rushed out.

But I did not join her at the bus stop; I felt that I must not allow myself to be seen. Instead I hurried to my car, which was standing nearby, got in, and waited. A bus came and she got in together with some other people; the bus started off again and I began following it. Then there came back to me the memory of that one shooting expedition in which I had taken part as a child, and I saw that the bus was the undergrowth with its bushes and trees, my wife the bird perching on the bough while I, unseen, watched it living before my eyes. And the whole town, during this pursuit, became, as though by magic, a fact of nature like the countryside: the houses were hills, the streets valleys, the vehicles hedges and woods, and even the passersby on the pavements had something unpredictable and autonomous—that is, wild—about them. And in my mouth, behind my clenched teeth, there was the acrid, metallic taste of gunfire; and my eyes, usually listless and wandering, had become sharp, watchful, attentive.

These eyes were fixed intently upon the exit door when the bus came to the end of its run. A number of people got out, and then I saw my wife getting out. Once again I recognized, in the manner in which she broke free of the crowd and started off toward a neighboring street, the wildness that pleased me so much. I jumped out of the car and started following her.

10   She was walking in front of me, ignorant of my presence, a tall woman with an elegant figure, long-legged, narrow-hipped, broad-backed, her brown hair falling on her shoulders.

Men turned around as she went past; perhaps they were aware of what I myself was now sensing with an intensity that quickened the beating of my heart and took my breath away: the unrestricted, steadily increasing, irresistible character of her mysterious wildness.

She walked hurriedly, having evidently some purpose in view, and even the fact that she had a purpose of which I was ignorant added to her wildness; I did not know where she was going, just as on that far-off morning I had not known what the bird perching on the bough was about to do. Moreover I thought the gradual, steady increase in this quality of wildness came partly from the fact that as she drew nearer to the object of this mysterious walk there was an increase in her—how shall I express it?—of biological tension, of existential excitement, of vital effervescence. Then, unexpectedly, with the suddenness of a film, her purpose was revealed.

A fair-haired young man in a leather jacket and a pair of corduroy trousers was leaning against the wall of a house in that ancient, narrow street. He was idly smoking as he looked in front of him. But as my wife passed close to him, he threw away his cigarette with a decisive gesture, took a step forward, and seized her arm. I was expecting her to rebuff him, to move away from him, but nothing happened: evidently obeying the rules of some kind of erotic ritual, she went on walking beside the young man. Then after a few steps, with a movement that confirmed her own complicity, she put her arm around her companion's waist and he put his around her.

I understood then that this unknown man who took such liberties with my wife was also attracted by wildness. And so, instead of making a conventional appointment with her, instead of meeting in a café with a handshake, a falsely friendly and respectful welcome, he had preferred, by agreement with her, to take her by surprise—or, rather, to pretend to do so—while she was apparently taking a walk on her own account. All this I perceived by intuition, noticing that at the very moment when he stepped forward and took her arm her wildness had, so to speak, given an upward bound. It was years since I had seen my wife so alive, but alas, the source of this life could not be traced to me.

15   They walked on thus entwined and then, without any preliminaries, just like two wild animals, they did an unexpected thing: they went into one of the dark doorways in order to kiss. I stopped and watched them from a distance, peering into the darkness of the entrance. My wife was turned away from me and was bending back with the pressure of his body, her hair hanging free. I looked at that long, thick mane of brown hair, which as she leaned back fell free of her shoulders, and I felt at that moment her vitality reached its diapason, just as happens with wild animals when the couple and their customary wildness is redoubled by the violence of love. I watched for a long time and then, since the kiss went on and on and in fact seemed to be prolonged beyond the limits of my power of endurance, I saw that I would have to intervene.

I would have to go forward, seize my wife by the arm—or actually by that hair, which hung down and conveyed so well the feeling of feminine passivity—then hurl myself with clenched fists upon the blond young man. After this encounter I would carry off my wife, weeping, mortified, ashamed, while I was raging and brokenhearted, upbraiding her and pouring scorn upon her.

But what else would this intervention amount to but the shot my father fired at that free, unknowing bird as it perched on the bough? The disorder and confusion, the mortification, the shame, that would follow would irreparably destroy the rare and precious moment of wildness that I was witnessing inside the dark doorway. It was true that this wildness was directed against me; but I had to remember that wildness, always and everywhere, is directed against everything and everybody. After the scene of my intervention it might be possible for me to regain control of my wife, but I should find her shattered and lifeless in my arms like the bird that my father placed in my hand so that I might throw it into the shooting bag.

The kiss went on and on: well, it was a kiss of passion—that could not be denied. I waited until they finished, until they came out of the doorway, until they walked on again still linked together. Then I turned back.

■ EXPLORATIONS OF THE TEXT

1. Why does the story begin with the incident of the bird? What do you learn about the narrator and his view of his maleness?
2. What does the narrator mean by "wildness"?
3. How has the narrator's wife changed? Explore the significance of the wife's transformation into a "hen about which one knows everything in advance."
4. What is the meaning of "the chase"? the narrator's pursuit of his wife?
5. Why does the narrator decide not to intervene?
6. Consider the narrator's statement in the beginning, when he watches his wife "for the first and also the last time." Why is it the "first" and "the last time"? What will happen after the story ends?
7. How does the hunting anecdote advance the narrative? What does it reveal about the narrator?
8. What critique of marriage, of sexual roles, and of male/female relations emerges in the story?
9. Compare the woman in "The Chase" with the narrator in "Yellow Woman." Who will be happier in her relationship? Why?

■ THE READING/WRITING CONNECTION

1. "Think" Topic: Compare the narrators in this story and in "My Life with the Wave." Are they reliable narrators? Why or why not?
2. Create a monologue spoken by the wife in "The Chase."
3. Does romantic love require a sense of intrigue? In a paragraph, argue pro or con.

■ IDEAS FOR WRITING

1. Rewrite the story with the woman as narrator. Why does the woman have an affair?
2. How is the hunting image central to the development of character, conflict, and theme in "The Chase"?
3. "The one who loves less has the power in a relationship." Use this statement as the basis for a discussion of "The Chase." Cite other stories and/or personal observations and experience if you wish.

LESLIE MARMON SILKO

Leslie Marmon Silko (1948–   ), born in Albuquerque, New Mexico, grew up on the Laguna Pueblo Reservation. Her heritage—Laguna, Mexican, European—provides the material and the inspiration for her writing. A graduate of the University of New Mexico, she taught until 1981 at the University of Arizona in Tucson, at which time a five-year MacArthur

Foundation Grant allowed her to write full time. Silko published her first novel, Ceremony, *in 1977. Subsequent works include* Storyteller *(1981),* Almanac of the Dead *(1991),* Yellow Woman and a Beauty of the Spirit: Essays on Native American Life Today *(1996), and* Gardens in the Dunes *(1999). Her fiction and poetry have earned her a grant from the National Endowment for the Arts, a poetry award from the* Chicago Review, *the Pushcart Prize for poetry, and the John D. and Catherine T. MacArthur Foundation Grant.*

1992

YELLOW WOMAN

I

My thigh clung to his with dampness, and I watched the sun rising up through the tamaracks and willows. The small brown water birds came to the river and hopped across the mud, leaving brown scratches in the alkali-white crust. They bathed in the river silently. I could hear the water, almost at our feet where the narrow fast channel bubbled and washed green ragged moss and fern leaves. I looked at him beside me, rolled in the red blanket on the white river sand. I cleaned the sand out of the cracks between my toes, squinting because the sun was above the willow trees. I looked at him for the last time, sleeping on the white river sand.

I felt hungry and followed the river south the way we had come the afternoon before, following our footprints that were already blurred by lizard tracks and bug trails. The horses were still lying down, and the black one whinnied when he saw me but he did not get up— maybe it was because the corral was made out of thick cedar branches and the horses had not yet felt the sun like I had. I tried to look beyond the pale red mesas to the pueblo. I knew it was there, even if I could not see it, on the sandrock hill above the river, the same river that moved past me now and had reflected the moon last night.

The horse felt warm underneath me. He shook his head and pawed the sand. The bay whinnied and leaned against the gate trying to follow, and I remembered him asleep in the red blanket beside the river. I slid off the horse and tied him close to the other horse. I walked north with the river again, and the white sand broke loose in footprints over footprints.

"Wake up."

5 He moved in the blanket and turned his face to me with his eyes still closed. I knelt down to touch him.

"I'm leaving."

He smiled now, eyes still closed. "You are coming with me, remember?" He sat up now with his bare dark chest and belly in the sun.

"Where?"

"To my place."

10 "And will I come back?"

He pulled his pants on. I walked away from him, feeling him behind me and smelling the willows.

"Yellow Woman," he said.

I turned to face him. "Who are you?" I asked.

He laughed and knelt on the low, sandy bank, washing his face in the river. "Last night you guessed my name, and you knew why I had come."

15 I stared past him at the shallow moving water and tried to remember the night, but I could only see the moon in the water and remember his warmth around me.

"But I only said that you were him and that I was Yellow Woman—I'm not really her—I have my own name and I come from the pueblo on the other side of the mesa. Your name is Silva and you are a stranger I met by the river yesterday afternoon."

He laughed softly. "What happened yesterday has nothing to do with what you will do today, Yellow Woman."

"I know—that's what I'm saying—the old stories about the ka'tsina spirit and Yellow Woman can't mean us."

My old grandpa liked to tell those stories best. There is one about Badger and Coyote who went hunting and were gone all day, and when the sun was going down they found a house. There was a girl living there alone, and she had light hair and eyes and she told them that they could sleep with her. Coyote wanted to be with her all night so he sent Badger into a prairie-dog hole, telling him he thought he saw something in it. As soon as Badger crawled in, Coyote blocked up the entrance with rocks and hurried back to Yellow Woman.

20   "Come here," he said gently.

He touched my neck and I moved close to him to feel his breathing and to hear his heart. I was wondering if Yellow Woman had known who she was—if she knew that she would become part of the stories. Maybe she'd had another name that her husband and relatives called her so that only the ka'tsina from the north and the storytellers would know her as Yellow Woman. But I didn't go on; I felt him all around me, pushing me down into the white river sand.

"Yellow Woman went away with the spirit from the north and lived with him and his relatives. She was gone for a long time, but then one day she came back and she brought twin boys.

"Do you know the story?"

"What story?" He smiled and pulled me close to him as he said this. I was afraid lying there on the red blanket. All I could know was the way he felt, warm, damp, his body beside me. This is the way it happens in the stories. I was thinking, with no thought beyond the moment she meets the ka'tsina spirit and they go.

25   "I don't have to go. What they tell in stories was real only then, back in time immemorial, like they say."

He stood up and pointed at my clothes tangled in the blanket. "Let's go," he said.

I walked beside him, breathing hard because he walked fast, his hand around my wrist. I had stopped trying to pull away from him, because his hand felt cool and the sun was high, drying the river bed into alkali. I will see someone, eventually I will see someone, and then I will be certain that he is only a man—some man from nearby—and I will be sure that I am not Yellow Woman. Because she is from out of time past and I live now and I've been to school and there are highways and pickup trucks that Yellow Woman never saw.

It was an easy ride north on horseback. I watched the change from the cottonwood trees along the river to the junipers that brushed past us in the foothills, and finally there were only piñons, and when I looked up at the rim of the mountain plateau I could see pine trees growing on the edge. Once I stopped to look down, but the pale sandstone had disappeared and the river was gone and the dark lava hills were all around. He touched my hand, not speaking, but always singing softly a mountain song and looking into my eyes.

I felt hungry and wondered what they were doing at home now—my mother, my grandmother, my husband, and the baby. Cooking breakfast, saying, "Where did she go?—maybe kidnapped," and Al going to the tribal police with the details: "She went walking along the river."

30   The house was made with black lava rock and red mud. It was high above the spreading miles of arroyos and long mesas. I smelled a mountain smell of pitch and buck brush. I stood there beside the black horse, looking down on the small, dim country we had passed, and I shivered.

"Yellow Woman, come inside where it's warm."

II

He lit a fire in the stove. It was an old stove with a round belly and an enamel coffeepot on top. There was only the stove, some faded Navajo blankets, and a bedroll and cardboard box. The floor was made of smooth adobe plaster, and there was one small window facing east. He pointed at the box.

"There's some potatoes and the frying pan." He sat on the floor with his arms around his knees pulling them close to his chest and he watched me fry the potatoes. I didn't mind him watching me because he was always watching me—he had been watching me since I came upon him sitting on the river bank trimming leaves from a willow twig with his knife. We ate from the pan and he wiped the grease from his fingers on his Levis.

"Have you brought women here before?" He smiled and kept chewing, so I said, "Do you always use the same tricks?"

35   "What tricks?" He looked at me like he didn't understand.

"The story about being a ka'tsina from the mountains. The story about Yellow Woman." Silva was silent, his face was calm.

"I don't believe it. Those stories couldn't happen now," I said.

He shook his head and said softly, "But someday they will talk about us, and they will say, 'Those two lived long ago when things like that happened.'"

40   He stood up and went out. I ate the rest of the potatoes and thought about things— about the noise the stove was making and the sound of the mountain wind outside. I remembered yesterday and the day before, and then I went outside.

I walked past the corral to the edge where the narrow trail cut through the black rim rock. I was standing in the sky with nothing around me but the wind that came down from the mountain peak behind me. I could see faint mountain images in the distance miles across the vast spread of mesa and valleys and plains. I wondered who was over there to feel the mountain wind on those sheer blue edges—who walks on the pine needles in those blue mountains.

"Can you see the pueblo?" Silva was standing behind me.

I shook my head. "We're too far away."

"From here I can see the world." He stepped out on the edge. "The Navajo reservation begins over there." He pointed to the east. "The Pueblo boundaries are over here." He looked below us to the south, where the narrow trail seemed to come from. "The Texans have their ranches over there, starting with that valley, the Concho Valley. The Mexicans run some cattle over there too."

45   "Do you ever work for them?"

"I steal from them," Silva answered. The sun was dropping behind us and shadows were filling the land below. I turned away from the edge that dropped forever into the valleys below.

"I'm cold," I said; "I'm going inside." I started wondering about this man who could speak the Pueblo language so well but who lived on a mountain and rustled cattle. I decided that this man Silva must be Navajo, because Pueblo men didn't do things like that.

"You must be a Navajo."

Silva shook his head gently. "Little Yellow Woman," he said, "you never give up, do you? I have told you who I am. The Navajo people know me, too." He knelt down and unrolled the

bedroll and spread the extra blankets out on a piece of canvas. The sun was down, and the
only light in the house came from outside—the dim orange light from sundown.

50   I stood there and waited for him to crawl under the blankets.

"What are you waiting for?" he said, and I lay down beside him. He undressed me
slowly like the night before beside the river—kissing my face gently and running his hands
up and down my belly and legs. He took off my pants and then he laughed.

"Why are you laughing?"

"You are breathing so hard."

I pulled away from him and turned my back to him.

55   He pulled me around and pinned me down with his arms and chest. "You don't understand, do you, little Yellow Woman? You will do what I want."

And again he was all around me with his skin slippery against mine, and I was afraid
because I understood that his strength could hurt me. I lay beneath him and I knew that he
could destroy me. But later, while he slept beside me, I touched his face and had a feeling—
the kind of feeling for him that overcame me that morning along the river. I kissed him on
the forehead and he reached out for me.

When I woke up in the morning he was gone. It gave me a strange feeling because for a
long time I sat there on the blankets and looked around the little house for some object of
his—some proof that he had been there or maybe that he was coming back. Only the blanket and the cardboard box remained. The .30-30 that had been leaning in the corner was
gone, and so was the knife I had used the night before. He was gone, and I had my chance
to go now. But first I had to eat, because I knew it would be a long walk home.

I found some dried apricots in the cardboard box, and I sat down on a rock at the edge
of the plateau rim. There was no wind and the sun warmed me. I was surrounded by silence. I drowsed with apricots in my mouth, and I didn't believe that there were highways
or railroads or cattle to steal.

When I woke up, I stared down at my feet in the black mountain dirt. Little black ants
were swarming over the pine needles around my foot. They must have smelled the apricots.
I thought about my family far below me. They would be wondering about me, because this
had never happened to me before. The tribal police would file a report. But if old Grandpa
weren't dead he would tell them what happened—he would laugh and say, "Stolen by a
ka'tsina, a mountain spirit. She'll come home—they usually do." There are enough of them
to handle things. My mother and grandmother will raise the baby like they raised me. Al will
find someone else, and they will go on like before, except that there will be a story about the
day I disappeared while I was walking along the river. Silva had come for me; he said he had.
I did not decide to go. I just went. Moonflowers blossom in the sand hills before dawn just as
I followed him. That's what I was thinking as I wandered along the trail through the pine
trees.

60   It was noon when I got back. When I saw the stone house I remembered that I had to
go home. But that didn't seem important any more, maybe because there were little blue
flowers growing in the meadow behind the stone house and the gray squirrels were playing
in the pines next to the house. The horses were standing in the corral, and there was a beef
carcass hanging on the shady side of a big pine in front of the house. Flies buzzed around
the clotted blood that hung from the carcass. Silva was washing his hands in a bucket full of
water. He must have heard me coming because he spoke to me without turning to face me.

"I've been waiting for you."

"I went walking in the big pine trees."

I looked into the bucket full of bloody water with brown-and-white animal hairs floating in it. Silva stood there letting his hand drip, examining me intently.

"Are you coming with me?"

65   "Where?" I asked him.

"To sell the meat in Marquez."

"If you're sure it's O.K."

"I wouldn't ask you if it wasn't," he answered.

He sloshed the water around in the bucket before he dumped it out and set the bucket upside down near the door. I followed him to the corral and watched him saddle the horses. Even beside the horses he looked tall, and I asked him again if he wasn't Navajo. He didn't say anything; he just shook his head and kept cinching up the saddle.

70   "But Navajos are tall."

"Get on the horse," he said, "and let's go."

The last thing he did before we started down the steep trail was to grab the .30-30 from the corner. He slid the rifle into the scabbard that hung from his saddle.

"Do they ever try to catch you?" I asked.

"They don't know who I am."

75   "Then why did you bring the rifle?"

"Because we are going to Marquez where the Mexicans live."

III

The trail leveled out on a narrow ridge that was steep on both sides like an animal spine. On one side I could see where the trail went around the rocky gray hills and disappeared into the southeast where the pale sandrock mesas stood in the distance near my home. On the other side was a trail that went west, and as I looked far into the distance I thought I saw the little town. But Silva said no, that I was looking in the wrong place, that I just thought I saw houses. After that I quit looking off into the distance; it was hot and the wildflowers were closing up their deep-yellow petals. Only the waxy cactus flowers bloomed in the bright sun, and I saw every color that a cactus blossom can be: the white ones and the red ones were still buds, but the purple and the yellow were blossoms, open full and the most beautiful of all.

Silva saw him before I did. The white man was riding a big gray horse, coming up the trail toward us. He was traveling fast and the gray horse's feet sent rocks rolling off the trail into the dry tumbleweeds. Silva motioned for me to stop and we watched the white man. He didn't see us right away, but finally his horse whinnied at our horses and he stopped. He looked at us briefly before he loped the gray horse across the three hundred yards that separated us. He stopped his horse in front of Silva, and his young fat face was shadowed by the brim of his hat. He didn't look mad, but his small, pale eyes moved from the blood-soaked gunny sacks hanging from my saddle to Silva's face and then back to my face.

"Where did you get the fresh meat?" the white man asked.

80   "I've been hunting," Silva said, and when he shifted his weight in the saddle the leather creaked.

"The hell you have, Indian. You've been rustling cattle. We've been looking for the thief for a long time."

The rancher was fat, and sweat began to soak through his white cowboy shirt and the wet cloth stuck to the thick rolls of belly fat. He almost seemed to be panting from the exertion of talking, and he smelled rancid, maybe because Silva scared him.

Silva turned to me and smiled. "Go back up the mountain, Yellow Woman."

The white man got angry when he heard Silva speak in a language he couldn't understand. "Don't try anything, Indian. Just keep riding to Marquez. We'll call the state police from there."

85   The rancher must have been unarmed because he was very frightened and if he had a gun he would have pulled it out then. I turned my horse around and the rancher yelled, "Stop!" I looked at Silva for an instant and there was something ancient and dark—something I could

feel in my stomach—in his eyes, and when I glanced at his hand I saw his finger on the trigger of the .30-30 that was still in the saddle scabbard. I slapped my horse across the flank and the sacks of raw meat swung against my knees as the horse leaped up the trail. It was hard to keep my balance, and once I thought I felt the saddle slipping backward; it was because of this that I could not look back.

I didn't stop until I reached the ridge where the trail forked. The horse was breathing deep gasps and there was a dark film of sweat on its neck. I looked down in the direction I had come from, but I couldn't see the place. I waited. The wind came up and pushed warm air past me. I looked up at the sky, pale blue and full of thin clouds and fading vapor trails left by jets.

I think four shots were fired—I remember hearing four hollow explosions that reminded me of deer hunting. There could have been more shots after that, but I couldn't have heard them because my horse was running again and the loose rocks were making too much noise as they scattered around his feet.

Horses have a hard time running downhill, but I went that way instead of uphill to the mountain because I thought it was safer. I felt better with the horse running southeast past the round gray hills that were covered with cedar trees and black lava rock. When I got to the plain in the distance I could see the dark green patches of tamaracks that grew along the river; and beyond the river I could see the beginning of the pale sandrock mesas. I stopped the horse and looked back to see if anyone was coming; then I got off the horse and turned the horse around, wondering if it would go back to its corral under the pines on the mountain. It looked back at me for a moment and then plucked a mouthful of green tumbleweeds before it trotted back up the trail with its ears pointed forward, carrying its head daintily to one side to avoid stepping on the dragging reins. When the horse disappeared over the last hill, the gunny sacks full of meat were still swinging and bouncing.

IV

I walked toward the river on a wood-hauler's road that I knew would eventually lead to the paved road. I was thinking about waiting beside the road for someone to drive by, but by the time I got to the pavement I had decided it wasn't very far to walk if I followed the river back the way Silva and I had come.

90   The river water tasted good, and I sat in the shade under a cluster of silvery willows. I thought about Silva, and I felt sad at leaving him; still, there was something strange about him, and I tried to figure it out all the way back home.

I came back to the place on the river bank where he had been sitting the first time I saw him. The green willow leaves that he had trimmed from the branch were still lying there, wilted in the sand. I saw the leaves and I wanted to go back to him—to kiss him and to touch him—but the mountains were too far away now. And I told myself, because I believe it, he will come back sometime and be waiting again by the river.

I followed the path up from the river into the village. The sun was getting low, and I could smell supper cooking when I got to the screen door of my house. I could hear their voices inside—my mother was telling my grandmother how to fix the Jell-o and my husband, Al, was playing with the baby. I decided to tell them that some Navajo had kidnapped me, but I was sorry that old Grandpa wasn't alive to hear my story because it was the Yellow Woman stories he liked to tell best.

■ **EXPLORATIONS OF THE TEXT**

1. How does the story of Yellow Woman and the ka'tsina function in this work?
2. Describe the relationship between the speaker and Silva. How does it change in each section?
3. How do details about the setting and about the horses emphasize the mythic elements of the story? How do the same details emphasize the sexual fascination between the two characters?
4. Discuss Silva's character. Why does he live a solitary life? Why does he steal horses? Why does he have a gun?
5. Why does Yellow Woman agree to help Silva sell the meat? What does the symbolism of the dead animal and of the blood signify?
6. Analyze the encounter between Silva and the rancher. Why does the narrator ride down the mountain? Does she make conscious choices?
7. Is the ending optimistic or pessimistic? What roles do imagination and fantasy play in the narrator's actions? What does the story suggest about the power of sexual fantasy?
8. Discuss the depiction of sexual roles in the story. Compare with Maxine Hong Kingston's "No Name Woman."

■ **THE READING/WRITING CONNECTION**

1. Extend the story to part five. Imitate Silko's style.
2. Freewrite about Silva.
3. "Think" Topic: Does the narrator return to her husband?

■ **IDEAS FOR WRITING**

1. Analyze the love relationship in this story. Are the male and female roles stereotypical?
2. Compare this vision of love with Senghor's "Nuit de Sine," Mason's "Shiloh," or Paz's "My Life with the Wave."

BOBBIE ANN MASON

Born in Mayfield, Kentucky, Bobbie Ann Mason (1940–   ) was educated at the University of Kentucky, the State University of New York at Binghamton, and the University of Connecticut. Her first collection of stories, Shiloh and Other Stories *(1982), won the Ernest Hemingway Award for First Fiction. Subsequent works include* Love Life: Stories *(1988),* In Country *(1985),* Spence and Lila *(1988),* Feather Crowns *(1994), and* Zigzagging Down a Wild Trail *(2001). Mason has also written a memoir,* Clear Springs *(1999), and a nonfiction book,* Elvis Presley *(2003). Mason is associated with so-called Kmart realism, which is to say, the use in fiction of icons of popular culture, particularly lower-class culture, to make serious points. She has been awarded fellowships by the National Endowment of the Arts and the Guggenheim Foundation.*

1982

SHILOH

Leroy Moffitt's wife, Norma Jean, is working on her pectorals. She lifts three-pound dumbbells to warm up, then progresses to a twenty-pound barbell. Standing with her legs apart, she reminds Leroy of Wonder Woman.

"I'd give anything if I could just get these muscles to where they're real hard," says Norma Jean. "Feel this arm. It's not as hard as the other one."

"That's 'cause you're right-handed," says Leroy, dodging as she swings the barbell in an arc.

"Do you think so?"

5   "Sure."

Leroy is a truckdriver. He injured his leg in a highway accident four months ago, and his physical therapy, which involves weights and a pulley, prompted Norma Jean to try building herself up. Now she is attending a body-building class. Leroy has been collecting temporary disability since his tractor-trailer jackknifed in Missouri, badly twisting his left leg in its socket. He has a steel pin in his hip. He will probably not be able to drive his rig again. It sits in the backyard, like a gigantic bird that has flown home to roost. Leroy has been home in Kentucky for three months, and his leg is almost healed, but the accident frightened him and he does not want to drive any more long hauls. He is not sure what to do next. In the meantime, he makes things from craft kits. He started by building a miniature log cabin from notched Popsicle sticks. He varnished it and placed it on the TV set, where it remains. It reminds him of a rustic Nativity scene. Then he tried string art (sailing ships on black velvet), a macramé owl kit, a snap-together B-17 Flying Fortress,[1] and a lamp made out of a model truck, with a light fixture screwed in the top of the cab. At first the kits were diversions, something to kill time, but now he is thinking about building a full-scale log house from a kit. It would be considerably cheaper than building a regular house, and besides, Leroy has grown to appreciate how things are put together. He has begun to realize that in all the years he was on the road he never took time to examine anything. He was always flying past scenery.

"They won't let you build a log cabin in any of the new subdivisions," Norma Jean tells him.

"They will if I tell them it's for you," he says, teasing her. Ever since they were married, he has promised Norma Jean he would build her a new home one day. They have always rented, and the house they live in is small and nondescript. It does not even feel like a home, Leroy realizes now.

Norma Jean works at the Rexall drugstore, and she has acquired an amazing amount of information about cosmetics. When she explains to Leroy the three stages of complexion care, involving creams, toners, and moisturizers, he thinks happily of other petroleum products— axle grease, diesel fuel. This is a connection between him and Norma Jean. Since he has been home, he has felt unusually tender about his wife and guilty over his long absences. But he can't tell what she feels about him. Norma Jean has never complained about his traveling; she has never made hurtful remarks, like calling his truck a "widow-maker." He is reasonably certain she has been faithful to him, but he wishes she would celebrate his permanent homecoming more happily. Norma Jean is often startled to find Leroy at home, and he thinks she seems a little disappointed about it. Perhaps he reminds her too much of the early days of their marriage, before he went on the road. They had a child who died as an infant, years ago. They never speak about their memories of Randy, which have almost faded, but now that Leroy is home all the time, they sometimes feel awkward around each other, and Leroy wonders if one of them should mention the child. He has the feeling that they are waking up out of a dream together—that they must create a new marriage, start afresh. They are lucky they are still married. Leroy has read that for most people losing a child destroys the marriage—or else he heard this on *Donahue*.[2] He can't always remember where he learns things anymore.

10   At Christmas, Leroy bought an electric organ for Norma Jean. She used to play the piano when she was in high school. "It don't leave you," she told him once. "It's like riding a bicycle."

---

[1] A model of a heavy bomber used by the U.S. Army in World War II.

[2] Popular television talk show hosted by Phil Donahue.

The new instrument had so many keys and buttons that she was bewildered by it at first. She touched the keys tentatively, pushed some buttons, then pecked out "Chopsticks." It came out in an amplified fox-trot rhythm, with marimba sounds.

"It's an orchestra!" she cried.

The organ had a pecan-look finish and eighteen preset chords, with optional flute, violin, trumpet, clarinet, and banjo accompaniments. Norma Jean mastered the organ almost immediately. At first she played Christmas songs. Then she bought *The Sixties Songbook* and learned every tune in it, adding variations to each with the rows of brightly colored buttons.

"I didn't like these old songs back then," she said. "But I have this crazy feeling I missed something."

15   "You didn't miss a thing," said Leroy.

Leroy likes to lie on the couch and smoke a joint and listen to Norma Jean play "Can't Take My Eyes Off You" and "I'll Be Back." He is back again. After fifteen years on the road, he is finally settling down with the woman he loves. She is still pretty. Her skin is flawless. Her frosted curls resemble pencil trimmings.

Now that Leroy has come home to stay, he notices how much the town has changed. Subdivisions are spreading across western Kentucky like an oil slick. The sign at the edge of town says "Pop: 11,500"—only seven hundred more than it said twenty years before. Leroy can't figure out who is living in all the new houses. The farmers who used to gather around the courthouse square on Saturday afternoons to play checkers and spit tobacco juice have gone. It has been years since Leroy has thought about the farmers, and they have disappeared without his noticing.

Leroy meets a kid named Stevie Hamilton in the parking lot at the new shopping center. While they pretend to be strangers meeting over a stalled car, Stevie tosses an ounce of marijuana under the front seat of Leroy's car. Stevie is wearing orange jogging shoes and a T-shirt that says CHATTAHOOCHEE SUPER-RAT. His father is a prominent doctor who lives in one of the expensive subdivisions in a new white-columned brick house that looks like a funeral parlor. In the phone book under his name there is a separate number, with the listing "Teenagers."

"Where do you get this stuff?" asks Leroy. "From your pappy?"

20   "That's for me to know and you to find out," Stevie says. He is slit-eyed and skinny.

"What else you got?"

"What you interested in?"

"Nothing special. Just wondered."

Leroy used to take speed on the road. Now he has to go slowly. He needs to be mellow. He leans back against the car and stays, "I'm aiming to build me a log house, soon as I get time. My wife, though, I don't think she likes the idea."

25   "Well, let me know when you want me again," Stevie says. He has a cigarette in his cupped palm, as though sheltering it from the wind. He takes a long drag, then stomps it on the asphalt and slouches away.

Stevie's father was two years ahead of Leroy in high school. Leroy is thirty-four. He married Norma Jean when they were both eighteen, and their child Randy was born a few months later, but he died at the age of four months and three days. He would be about Stevie's age now. Norma Jean and Leroy were at the drive-in, watching a double feature (*Dr. Strangelove* and *Lover Come Back*), and the baby was sleeping in the back seat. When the first movie ended, the baby was dead. It was the sudden infant death syndrome. Leroy remembers handing Randy to a nurse at the emergency room, as though he were offering her a large doll as a present. A dead baby feels like a sack of flour. "It just happens sometimes," said the doctor, in what Leroy always recalls as a nonchalant tone. Leroy can hardly remember the child anymore, but he still sees vividly a scene from *Dr. Strangelove* in which the President of the United States was talking in a folksy voice on the hot line to the Soviet premier about the bomber accidentally headed toward Russia. He was in the War Room, and the world map was lit up. Leroy remembers Norma Jean standing catatonically beside him in the hospital and himself thinking: Who is this strange girl? He had forgotten who she was. Now scientists are saying that crib death is caused by a virus. Nobody knows anything, Leroy thinks. The answers are always changing.

When Leroy gets home from the shopping center, Norma Jean's mother, Mabel Beasley, is there. Until this year, Leroy has not realized how much time she spends with Norma Jean. When she visits, she inspects the closets and then the plants, informing Norma Jean when a plant is droopy or yellow. Mabel calls the plants "flowers," although there are never any blooms. She also notices if Norma Jean's laundry is piling up. Mabel is a short, overweight woman whose tight, brown-dyed curls look more like a wig than the actual wig she sometimes wears. Today she has brought Norma Jean an off-white dust ruffle she made for the bed; Mabel works in a custom-upholstery shop.

"This is the tenth one I made this year," Mabel says. "I got started and couldn't stop."

"It's real pretty," says Norma Jean.

30 "Now we can hide things under the bed," says Leroy, who gets along with his mother-in-law primarily by joking with her. Mabel has never really forgiven him for disgracing her by getting Norma Jean pregnant. When the baby died, she said that fate was mocking her.

"What's that thing?" Mabel says to Leroy in a loud voice, pointing to a tangle of yarn on a piece of canvas.

Leroy holds it up for Mabel to see. "It's my needlepoint," he explains. "This is a *Star Trek* pillow cover."

"That's what a woman would do," says Mabel. "Great day in the morning!"

"All the big football players on TV do it," he says.

35 "Why, Leroy, you're always trying to fool me. I don't believe you for one minute. You don't know what to do with yourself—that's the whole trouble. Sewing!"

"I'm aiming to build us a log house," says Leroy. "Soon as my plans come."

"Like *heck* you are," says Norma Jean. She takes Leroy's needlepoint and shoves it into a drawer. "You have to find a job first. Nobody can afford to build now anyway."

Mabel straightens her girdle and says, "I still think before you get tied down y'all ought to take a little run to Shiloh."

"One of these days, Mama," Norma Jean says impatiently.

40 Mabel is talking about Shiloh, Tennessee. For the past few years, she has been urging Leroy and Norma Jean to visit the Civil War battleground there. Mabel went there on her honeymoon—the only real trip she ever took. Her husband died of a perforated ulcer when Norma Jean was ten, but Mabel, who was accepted into the United Daughters of the Confederacy in 1975, is still preoccupied with going back to Shiloh.

"I've been to kingdom come and back in that truck out yonder," Leroy says to Mabel, "but we never yet set foot in that battleground. Ain't' that something? How did I miss it?"

"It's not even that far," Mabel says.

After Mabel leaves, Norma Jean reads to Leroy from a list she has made. "Things you could do," she announces. "You could get a job as a guard at Union Carbide, where they'd let you set on a stool. You could get on at the lumberyard. You could do a little carpenter work, if you want to build so bad. You could—"

"I can't do something where I'd have to stand up all day."

45 "You ought to try standing up all day behind a cosmetics counter. It's amazing that I have strong feet, coming from two parents that never had strong feet at all." At the moment Norma Jean is holding on to the kitchen counter, raising her knees one at a time as she talks. She is wearing two-pound ankle weights.

"Don't worry," says Leroy. "I'll do something."

"You could truck calves to slaughter for somebody. You wouldn't have to drive any big old truck for that."

"I'm going to build you this house," says Leroy. "I want to make you a real home."

"I don't want to live in any log cabin."

50 "It's not a cabin. It's a house."

"I don't care. It looks like a cabin."

"You and me together could lift those logs. It's just like lifting weights."

Norma Jean doesn't answer. Under her breath, she is counting. Now she is marching through the kitchen. She is doing goose steps.

Before his accident, when Leroy came home he used to stay in the house with Norma Jean, watching TV in bed and playing cards. She would cook fried chicken, picnic ham, chocolate pie—all his favorites. Now he is home alone much of the time. In the mornings, Norma Jean disappears, leaving a cooling place in the bed. She eats a cereal called Body Buddies, and she leaves the bowl on the table, with the soggy tan balls floating in a milk puddle. He sees things about Norma Jean that he never realized before. When she chops onions, she stares off into a corner, as if she can't bear to look. She puts on her house slippers almost precisely at nine o'clock every evening and nudges her jogging shoes under the couch. She saves bread heels for the birds. Leroy watches the birds at the feeder. He notices the peculiar way goldfinches fly past the window. They close their wings, then fall, then spread their wings to catch and lift themselves. He wonders if they close their eyes when they fall. Norma Jean closes her eyes when they are in bed. She wants the lights turned out. Even then, he is sure she closes her eyes.

55 He goes for long drives around town. He tends to drive a car rather carelessly. Power steering and an automatic shift make a car feel so small and inconsequential that his body is hardly involved in the driving process. His injured leg stretches out comfortably. Once or twice he has almost hit something, but even the prospect of an accident seems minor in a car. He cruises the new subdivisions, feeling like a criminal rehearsing for a robbery. Norma Jean is probably right about a log house being inappropriate here in the new subdivision. All the houses look grand and complicated. They depress him.

One day when Leroy comes home from a drive he finds Norma Jean in tears. She is in the kitchen making a potato and mushroom-soup casserole, with grated cheese topping. She is crying because her mother caught her smoking.

"I didn't hear her coming. I was standing here puffing away pretty as you please," Norma Jean says, wiping her eyes.

"I knew it would happen sooner or later," says Leroy, putting his arm around her.

"She don't know the meaning of the word 'knock,' " says Norma Jean. "It's a wonder she hadn't caught me years ago."

60 "Think of it this way," Leroy says. "What if she caught me with a joint?"

"You better not let her!" Norma Jean shrieks. "I'm warning you, Leroy Moffitt!"

"I'm just kidding. Here, play me a tune. That'll help you relax."

Norma Jean puts the casserole in the oven and sets the timer. Then she plays a ragtime tune, with horns and banjo, as Leroy lights up a joint and lies on the couch, laughing to himself about Mabel's catching him at it. He thinks of Stevie Hamilton—a doctor's son pushing grass. Everything is funny. The whole town seems crazy and small. He is reminded of Virgil Mathis, a boastful policeman Leroy used to shoot pool with. Virgil recently led a drug bust in a back room at a bowling alley, where he seized ten thousand dollars' worth of marijuana. The newspaper had a picture of him holding up the bags of grass and grinning widely. Right now, Leroy can imagine Virgil breaking down the door and arresting him with a lungful of smoke. Virgil would probably have been alerted to the scene because of all the racket Norma Jean is making. Now she sounds like a hard-rock band. Norma Jean is terrific. When she switches to a Latin-rhythm version of "Sunshine Superman," Leroy hums along. Norma Jean's foot goes up and down, up and down.

"Well, what do you think?" Leroy says, when Norma Jean pauses to search through her music.

65   "What do I think about what?"

His mind has gone blank. Then he says, "I'll sell my rig and build us a house." That wasn't what he wanted to say. He wanted to know what she thought—what she *really* thought—about them.

"Don't start in on that again," says Norma Jean. She begins playing "Who'll Be the Next in Line?"

Leroy used to tell hitchhikers his whole life story—about his travels, his hometown, the baby. He would end with a question: "Well, what do you think?" It was just a rhetorical question. In time, he had the feeling that he'd been telling the same story over and over to the same hitchhikers. He quit talking to hitchhikers when he realized how his voice sounded—whining and self-pitying, like some teenage-tragedy song. Now Leroy has the sudden impulse to tell Norma Jean about himself, as if he had just met her. They have known each other so long they have forgotten a lot about each other. They could become reacquainted. But when the oven timer goes off and she runs to the kitchen, he forgets why he wants to do this.

The next day, Mabel drops by. It is Saturday and Norma Jean is cleaning. Leroy is studying the plans of his log house, which have finally come in the mail. He has them spread out on the table—big sheets of stiff blue paper, with diagrams and numbers printed in white. While Norma Jean runs the vacuum, Mabel drinks coffee. She sets her coffee cup on a blueprint.

70   "I'm just waiting for time to pass," she says to Leroy, drumming her fingers on the table.

As soon as Norma Jean switches off the vacuum, Mabel says in a loud voice, "Did you hear about the datsun dog that killed the baby?"

Norma Jeans says, "The word is 'dachshund.' "

"They put the dog on trial. It chewed the baby's legs off. The mother was in the next room all the time." She raises her voice. "They thought it was neglect."

Norma Jean is holding her ears. Leroy manages to open the refrigerator and get some Diet Pepsi to offer Mabel. Mabel still has some coffee and she waves away the Pepsi.

75   "Datsuns are like that," Mabel says. "They're jealous dogs. They'll tear a place to pieces if you don't keep an eye on them."

"You better watch out what you're saying, Mabel," says Leroy.

"Well, facts is facts."

Leroy looks out the window at his rig. It is like a huge piece of furniture gathering dust in the backyard. Pretty soon it will be an antique. He hears the vacuum cleaner. Norma Jean seems to be cleaning the living room rug again.

Later, she says to Leroy, "She just said that about the baby because she caught me smoking. She's trying to pay me back."

80   "What are you talking about?" Leroy says, nervously shuffling blueprints.

"You know good and well," Norma Jean says. She is sitting in a kitchen chair with her feet up and her arms wrapped around her knees. She looks small and helpless. She says, "The very idea, her bringing up a subject like that! Saying it was neglect."

"She didn't mean that," Leroy says.

"She might not have *thought* she meant it. She always says things like that. You don't know how she goes on."

"But she didn't really mean it. She was just talking."

85   Leroy opens a king-sized bottle of beer and pours it into two glasses, dividing it carefully. He hands a glass to Norma Jean and she takes it from him mechanically. For a long
time, they sit by the kitchen window watching the birds at the feeder.

Something is happening. Norma Jean is going to night school. She has graduated from her
six-week body-building course and now she is taking an adult-education course in composition at Paducah Community College. She spends her evenings outlining paragraphs.

"First, you have a topic sentence," she explains to Leroy. "Then you divide it up. Your
secondary topic has to be connected to your primary topic."

To Leroy, this sounds intimidating. "I never was any good in English," he says.

"It makes a lot of sense."

90   "What are you doing this for, anyhow?"

She shrugs. "It's something to do." She stands up and lifts her dumbbells a few times.

"Driving a rig, nobody cared about my English."

"I'm not criticizing your English."

Norma Jean used to say, "If I lose ten minutes' sleep, I just drag all day." Now she
stays up late, writing compositions. She got a B on her first paper—a how-to theme on
soup-based casseroles. Recently Norma Jean has been cooking unusual foods—tacos,
lasagna, Bombay chicken. She doesn't play the organ anymore, though her second paper
was called "Why Music Is Important to Me." She sits at the kitchen table, concentrating
on her outlines, while Leroy plays with his log house plans, practicing with a set of Lincoln logs. The thought of getting a truckload of notched, numbered logs scares him, and
he wants to be prepared. As he and Norma Jean work together at the kitchen table, Leroy
has the hopeful thought that they are sharing something, but he knows he is a fool to
think this. Norma Jean is miles away. He knows he is going to lose her. Like Mabel, he is
just waiting for time to pass.

95   One day, Mabel is there before Norma Jean gets home from work, and Leroy finds himself confiding in her. Mabel, he realizes, must know Norma Jean better than he does.

"I don't know what's got into that girl," Mabel says. "She used to go to bed with the
chickens. Now you say she's up all hours. Plus her a-smoking. I like to died."

"I want to make her this beautiful house," Leroy says, indicating the Lincoln Logs. "I
don't think she even wants it. Maybe she was happier with me gone."

"She don't know what to make of you, coming home like this."

"Is that it?"

100   Mabel takes the roof off his Lincoln Log cabin. "You couldn't get *me* in a log cabin," she
says. "I was raised in one. It's no picnic, let me tell you."

"They're different now," says Leroy.

"I tell you what," Mabel says, smiling oddly at Leroy.

"What?"

"Take her on down to Shiloh. Y'all need to get out together, stir a little. Her brain's all
balled up over them books."

105   Leroy can see traces of Norma Jean's features in her mother's face. Mabel's worn face has
the texture of crinkled cotton, but suddenly she looks pretty. It occurs to Leroy that Mabel
has been hinting all along that she wants them to take her with them to Shiloh.

"Let's all go to Shiloh," he says. "You and me and her. Come Sunday."

Mabel throws up her hand in protest. "Oh, no, not me. Young folks want to be by
theirselves."

When Norma Jean comes in with groceries, Leroy says excitedly, "Your mama here's
been dying to go to Shiloh for thirty-five years. It's about time we went, don't you think?"

"I'm not going to butt in on anybody's second honeymoon," Mabel says.

110 "Who's going on a honeymoon, for Christ's sake?" Norma Jean says loudly.

"I never raised no daughter of mine to talk that-a-way," Mabel says.

"You ain't seen nothing yet," says Norma Jean. She starts putting away boxes and cans, slamming cabinet doors.

"There's a log cabin at Shiloh," Mabel says. "It was there during the battle. There's bullet holes in it."

"When are you going to *shut up* about Shiloh, Mama?" asks Norma Jean.

115 "I always thought Shiloh was the prettiest place, so full of history," Mabel goes on. "I just hoped y'all could see it once before I die, so you could tell me about it." Later, she whispers to Leroy, "You do what I said. A little change is what she needs."

"Your name means 'the king,'" Norma Jean says to Leroy that evening. He is trying to get her to go to Shiloh, and she is reading a book about another century.

"Well, I reckon I ought to be right proud."

"I guess so."

"Am I still king around here?"

120 Norma Jean flexes her biceps and feels them for hardness. "I'm not fooling around with anybody, if that's what you mean," she says.

"Would you tell me if you were?"

"I don't know."

"What does *your* name mean?"

"It was Marilyn Monroe's real name."

125 "No kidding!"

"Norma comes from the Normans. They were invaders," she says. She closes her book and looks hard at Leroy. "I'll go to Shiloh with you if you'll stop staring at me."

On Sunday, Norma Jean packs a picnic and they go to Shiloh.[3] To Leroy's relief Mabel says she does not want to come with them. Norma Jean drives, and Leroy, sitting beside her, feels like some boring hitchhiker she has picked up. He tries some conversation, but she answers him in monosyllables. At Shiloh, she drives aimlessly through the park, past bluffs and trails and steep ravines. Shiloh is an immense place, and Leroy cannot see it as a battleground. It is not what he expected. He thought it would look like a golf course. Monuments are everywhere, showing through the thick clusters of trees. Norma Jean passes the log cabin Mabel mentioned. It is surrounded by tourists looking for bullet holes.

"That's not the kind of log house I've got in mind," says Leroy apologetically.

"I know *that*."

130 "This is a pretty place. Your mama was right."

"It's O.K.," says Norma Jean. "Well, we've seen it. I hope she's satisfied."

They burst out laughing together.

At the park museum, a movie on Shiloh is shown every half hour, but they decide that they don't want to see it. They buy a souvenir Confederate flag for Mabel, and then they find a picnic spot near the cemetery. Norma Jean has brought a picnic cooler, with pimento sandwiches, soft drinks, and Yodels. Leroy eats a sandwich and then smokes a joint, hiding

---

[3] Site of a famous Civil War battle fought in southwestern Tennessee, April 6–7, 1862. The battle resulted in a victory for the North, but there were large numbers of casualties on both sides.

it behind the picnic cooler. Norma Jean has quit smoking altogether. She is picking cake crumbs from the cellophane wrapper, like a fussy bird.

Leroy says, "So the boys in gray ended up in Corinth. The Union soldiers zapped 'em finally. April 7, 1862."

135 They both know that he doesn't know any history. He is just talking about some of the historical plaques they have read. He feels awkward, like a boy on a date with an older girl. They are still just making conversation.

"Corinth is where Mama eloped to," says Norma Jean.

They sit in silence and stare at the cemetery for the Union dead and, beyond, at a tall cluster of trees. Campers are parked nearby, bumper to bumper, and small children in bright clothing are cavorting and squealing. Norma Jean wads up the cake wrapper and squeezes it tightly in her hand. Without looking at Leroy, she says, "I want to leave you."

Leroy takes a bottle of Coke out of the cooler and flips off the cap. He holds the bottle poised near his mouth but cannot remember to take a drink. Finally he says, "No, you don't."

"Yes, I do."

140 "I won't let you."

"You can't stop me."

"Don't do me that way."

Leroy knows Norma Jean will have her own way. "Didn't I promise to be home from now on?" he says.

"In some ways, a woman prefers a man who wanders," says Norma Jean. "That sounds crazy, I know."

145 "You're not crazy."

Leroy remembers to drink from his Coke. Then he says, "Yes, you *are* crazy. You and me could start all over again. Right back at the beginning."

"We *have* started all over again," says Norma Jean. "And this is how it turned out."

"What did I do wrong?"

"Nothing."

150 "Is this one of those women's lib things?" Leroy asks.

"Don't be funny."

The cemetery, a green slope dotted with white markers, looks like a subdivision site. Leroy is trying to comprehend that his marriage is breaking up, but for some reason he is wondering about white slabs in a graveyard.

"Everything was fine till Mama caught me smoking," says Norma Jean, standing up. "That set something off."

"What are you talking about?"

155 "She won't leave me alone—*you* won't leave me alone." Norma Jean seems to be crying, but she is looking away from him. "I feel eighteen again. I can't face that all over again." She starts walking away. "No, it *wasn't* fine. I don't know what I'm saying. Forget it."

Leroy takes a lungful of smoke and closes his eyes as Norma Jean's words sink in. He tries to focus on the fact that thirty-five hundred soldiers died on the grounds around him. He can only think of that war as a board game with plastic soldiers. Leroy almost smiles, as he compares the Confederates' daring attack on the Union camps and Virgil Mathis's raid on the bowling alley. General Grant, drunk and furious, shoved the Southerners back to Corinth,[4] where Mabel and Jet Beasley were married years later, when Mabel was still thin and good-looking. The next day, Mabel and Jet visited the battleground, and then Norma

---

[4] Corinth, Mississippi.

Jean was born, and then she married Leroy and they had a baby, which they lost, and now Leroy and Norma Jean are here at the same battleground. Leroy knows he is leaving out a lot. He is leaving out the insides of history. History was always just names and dates to him. It occurs to him that building a house of logs is similarly empty—too simple. And the real inner workings of a marriage, like most of history, have escaped him. Now he sees that building a log house is the dumbest idea he could have had. It was clumsy of him to think Norma Jean would want a log house. It was a crazy idea. He'll have to think of something else, quickly. He will wad the blueprints into tight balls and fling them into the lake. Then he'll get moving again. He opens his eyes. Norma Jean has moved away and is walking through the cemetery, following a serpentine⁵ brick path.

Leroy gets up to follow his wife, but his good leg is asleep and his bad leg still hurts him. Norma Jean is far away, walking rapidly toward the bluff by the river, and he tries to hobble toward her. Some children run past him, screaming noisily. Norma Jean has reached the bluff, and she is looking out over the Tennessee River. Now she turns toward Leroy and waves her arms. Is she beckoning to him? She seems to be doing an exercise for her chest muscles. The sky is unusually pale—the color of the dust ruffle Mabel made for their bed.

■ EXPLORATIONS OF THE TEXT

1. What does the opening scene with the barbells reveal about Leroy's and Norma Jean's characters?
2. Why is Leroy building the log house? How has Leroy changed since his accident? How has Norma Jean changed since Leroy first married her?
3. What is Mabel's role in the story?
4. Discuss the significance of the trip to Shiloh. Closely examine the last two paragraphs. Relate the following quotation to themes of the story: "History was always just names and dates to him. . . . And the real inner workings of a marriage, like most of history, have escaped him."
5. Explore the conclusion of the story. What is happening? Does Norma Jean leave Leroy? What are possible interpretations of the ending?
6. Compare the endings of this story and "Eveline."

■ THE READING/WRITING CONNECTION

1. Journal Entry: Continue the story. What happens to Norma Jean and to Leroy?
2. Create an exchange of letters between Norma Jean and another character in this chapter. Here is one possible scenario: Have Norma Jean ask this character for advice about her relationship with Leroy.
3. "Think" Topic: Does the story present a realistic view of relationships?
4. Imagine that you are a marriage counselor. What advice would you give Leroy and Norma Jean?

■ IDEAS FOR WRITING

1. Who is responsible for the disintegration of the marriage: Leroy or Norma Jean? Write an argumentative essay defending your position.
2. Bobbie Ann Mason's work is noted for its minimalist style. The story seems straightforward and simply written, yet if one probes, one realizes that every detail builds the symbolic subtext of the work and the themes of the story. Choose one symbolic detail and explore its significance in building theme (e.g., the dust ruffle or the battle of Shiloh).

---

⁵ A winding path.

MARY GORDON

Mary Gordon (1950–   ), born on Long Island, New York, has written six novels, including Final
Payments *(1978),* Men and Angels *(1985),* Spending *(1998), and* Pearl *(2005). Her shorter fiction has been collected in* Temporary Shelter *(1987) and* The Rest of Life *(1993). Her nonfiction writings have been collected in* Good Boys and Dead Girls *(1991) and* Seeing Through
Places: Reflections on Geography and Identity *(1999). She has written a memoir,* The
Shadow Man *(1996), and a biography of Joan of Arc (2000). Winner of the Kafka Prize for fiction, she holds the McIntosh Chair as Professor of English at Barnard College. Her writing is
marked by its relentless scrutiny of experience.*

1986

VIOLATION

I suppose that in a forty-five-year life, I should feel grateful to have experienced only two
instances of sexual violation. Neither of them left me physically damaged and I cannot in
truth say they have destroyed my joy of men. I have been happily married for fifteen years
before which I had several blissful and some ordinary disappointing times with lovers. In
addition, I am the mother of two sons, my passion for whom causes me to draw inward,
away, when I hear the indiscriminate castigation of all males, so common and so understandable within the circles I frequent. I rarely think of my two experiences, and I'm grateful
for that, for I don't like what they suggest to me about a world which I must, after all, go on
inhabiting. And I don't like it when I start to feel in danger in my house, the Federalist
house we've been so careful in restoring, in the town not far from Hartford where we've
lived now for ten years, and when I wonder if, perhaps, safety is a feeling open to men
alone. It is then, especially that I am glad to be the mother only of sons.

I am thinking of all that now as I stand at the wooden counter cutting celery, carrots,
water chestnuts, so un-vegetative in their texture, radishes that willingly compose themselves in slices decorative as shells. Courageously, we've kept the kitchen faithful to its period: We have not replaced the small windows by large sheets of glass that would allow a
brightness our ancestors would have shunned. Leaves make a border at the windows; farther out—beech, locust—they become a net that breaks up the white sky. I arrange the vegetables, green, orange white, white circled by a ring of red on the dark wood of the
chopping board, as if I had to make decisions like a painter, purely on the basis of looks. As
I handle the slices of vegetable, cool and admirably dry, I think about myself as a young
woman, traveling abroad or "overseas" as my parents then called it, truly away from home
for the first time.

At twenty-two, I must have thought myself poetical. This is the only thing I can surmise when I look at the itinerary of that trip—my parents' present to me after college graduation—that I took with my college roommate and best friend. Lydia had majored in
economics like me, although like me she had adopted it as a practical measure, rejecting a
first love (for her it had been Art History, for me English). But we both prided ourselves on
being tough-minded and realistic; we knew the value of a comfortable life, and we didn't
want to feel we had to be dependent on a lucky marriage to achieve it. We'd both got jobs,
through our fathers' connections, at large Manhattan banks; we'd take them up in the fall,
and the knowledge of this gave us a sense of safety. We could be daring and adventurous all
summer, have experiences, talk to people (men) we never would have talked to at home,
reap the rewards of our secret devotion to the art and poetry we hadn't quite the confidence
to give our lives to. We considered ourselves in the great line of student pilgrims admiring
ourselves for our self-denial, traveling as we did with backpacks and hostel cards and a few

volumes of poetry. Not for a moment did we understand the luxury of a journey made on money we had never had to earn, and that the line we followed was that of young people on the grand tour: a look at the best pictures, the best buildings, some introduction to Continental manners, the collision of which with our young natures would rub off the rough edges but leave our idealism smooth. We would return then to the place that had been held for us in the real life that had been going on without us, not forgetting us, but not requiring us yet.

Our plane landed in Amsterdam. We saw the Rembrandts and Vermeers, and the Van Goghs my friend thought, by comparison, jejune, and then we took an all-night train to Florence. We stayed in a cheap *pensione* with marble floors and huge mirrors and painted ceilings above the iron cots that were our beds. And in Piazzole Michaelangelo, I met Giovanni, who sold Electrolux vacuum cleaners. Poor Italian, he was over-mastered by the consonants of his employer's name and pronounced his product E-LAY-TRO-LOO. Luckily, he worked all day so my friend and I could see the *Ufizzi,* the *Palazzo Pitti,* the *Duomo,* the *Museo San Marco,* and I need leave her alone only at night when Giovanni drove me around Florence at breakneck speed and snuck me into his *pensione* until midnight, then miraculously got me back into mine. (Now I see he must have bribed the concierge.) He agreed to drive us to Ravenna, where I could do homage to Dante and my friend to the mosaics, but even after he'd done this nice thing for the both of us and paid for both our lunches, my friend was put out with me. She felt that I'd abandoned her for a man. She hadn't met anybody possible, the friends that Giovanni had introduced her to were coarse, she said, and she was afraid to go out alone at night, she was always being followed by soldiers. It wasn't her idea of a vacation, she said, sitting in her room reading Kenneth Clark. Punitively, she suggested that when we got to England, where we both could speak the language, we should split up and travel alone. It would open us up to experiences, she said. Clearly she felt she hadn't had hers yet, and I'd had more than my share.

5   I left Giovanni tearfully, vowing to write. He bought us chocolates and bottles of *acqua minerale* for the train. Then we were off, heartlessly, to our next adventure. We were both sick crossing the channel; it made us tenderer to each other as we parted at Dover and hugged each other earnestly, awkward in our backpacks. She would go to Scotland, I to Ireland; in two weeks we would meet in London, stay there for a week, then travel home.

I decided to cross the Irish Sea from Wales, the home of poets. I would spend the day in Swansea and cross over at Fishguard to Rosslare. From Dylan Thomas' home, I would proceed on a pilgrimage to Yeats'. I felt ennobled but a bit lonely. It might be a long time, I knew, before I found someone to talk to.

Swansea was one of the least prepossessing cities I had ever seen: it might, despite the hints left by the poets, have been some place in Indiana or worse, Ohio, where I was from. I decided to look for a pub where Thomas must have got his inspiration. I found one that looked appropriate, ordered bread and sausages and beer and read my Yeats.

So I was not entirely surprised to hear an Irish voice ask if it could join me, and was pleased to look up and see a red-haired sailor standing with a pint of beer. I was abroad, after all, for experience, to do things I wouldn't do at home. I would never have spoken to a sailor in Cleveland, but then he wouldn't have been Irish. I thought he'd noticed me because he saw that I was reading Yeats.

"Yer American, then," he said.

10   "Yes."

"Great place, America. What yer doin' in this part of the world?"

"I'm traveling," I said.

"On yer own?"

"Yes."

15   "Brave, aren't ye?"

"No, not especially," I said. "I just don't see that much to be afraid of. And an awful lot that's fun and exciting. I'd hate to think I'd let fear hold me back."

"It's a great attitude. Great. Ye have people over here in Swansea?"

"No."

"What brings ye here?"

20   "Dylan Thomas, the poet. You've heard of him?"

"I have, of course. You're a great poetry lover, aren't ye? I seen ye with the Yeats. I'm from the Yeats country myself."

"That's where I'm going," I said, excitedly. "To Sligo."

"Yer takin' the ferry?"

"Nine o'clock."

25   "What a shame. I won't have much time to show ye Swansea. But we could have a drink or two."

"Okay," I said, anxious for talk. "You must have traveled a lot of places."

"Oh, all over," he said. "It's a great life, the sailor's."

He brought us drinks and I tried to encourage him to talk about himself, his home, his travels. I don't remember what he said, only that I was disappointed that he wasn't describing his life more colorfully, so I was glad when he suggested going for a walk to show me what he could of the town.

There really wasn't much to see in Swansea; he took me to the Catholic Church, the post office, the city hall. Then he suggested another pub. I said I had to be going, I didn't want to be late for the boat. He told me not to worry, he knew a shortcut; we could go there now.

30   I don't know when I realized I was in danger, but at some point I knew the path we were on was leading nowhere near other people. When he understood that I was not deceived, he felt no more need to hesitate. He must have known I would not resist, he didn't have to threaten. He merely spoke authoritatively, as if he wanted to get on with things.

"Sit down," he said. "And take that thing off your back."

I unbuckled my backpack and sat among the stalky weeds.

"Now take yer things off on the bottom."

I did what he said, closing my eyes. I didn't want to look at him. I could hear the clank of his belt as it hit the ground.

35   "What's this," he said, "One of yer American tricks?"

I had forgotten I was wearing a Tampax. Roughly, he pulled it out. I was more embarrassed by the imagination of it lying on the grass, so visible, than I was by my literal exposure.

"Yer not a virgin?" he said worriedly.

I told him I was not.

"All right then," he said, "then you know what's what."

40   In a few seconds, everything was finished, and he was on his feet. He turned his back to me to dress.

"I want ye to know one thing," he said. "I've just been checked out by the ship's doctor. Ye won't get no diseases from me, that's for sure. If ye come down with something, it's not my fault."

I thanked him.

"Yer all right?" he said.

"Yes," I told him.

45   He looked at his watch.

"Ye missed yer ferry."

"It's all right," I said, trying to sound polite. "There's another one in the morning." I was afraid that if I showed any trace of fear, any sense that what had happened was out of the ordinary, he might kill me to shut my mouth.

"I'll walk ye to the town."

I thanked him again.

50 "I'm awful sorry about yer missing the boat. It's too bad ye'll have to spend the night in this godforsaken town." He said this with genuine unhappiness, as though he had just described what was the genuine offense.

We walked on silently, looking at hotels blinking their red signs FULL.

"I'll be fine now," I said, hoping now we were in public, I could safely get him to leave.

"As long as yer all right."

"I'm fine, thank you."

55 "Would you give me yer name and address in the States? I could drop you a line. I'm off to South America next."

I wrote a false name and address on a page in my notebook, ripped it out and handed it to him.

He kissed me on the cheek, "Now don't go on like all these American ladies about how terrible we are to ye. Just remember, treat a man right, he'll treat you right."

"Okay," I said.

"Adios," he said, and waved.

60 I stepped into the foyer of the hotel we were standing in front of and stood there a while. Then I looked out onto the street to be sure he was gone. There was no sign of him, so I asked the hotel clerk for a room. I wanted one with a private bath, and he told me the only room available like that was the highest priced in the house. I gladly paid the money. I couldn't bear the idea of sharing a bathtub. It wasn't for myself I minded; I cared for the other people. I knew myself to be defiled, and I didn't want the other innocent, now sleeping guests, exposed to my contamination.

I traveled through Ireland for ten days, speaking to no one. It wasn't what I had expected, a country made up of bards and harpists and passionate fine-limbed women tossing their dark red hair. Unlike the other countries of Europe, there was nothing one really *had* to look at, and the beauty of the landscape seemed to wound, over and over, my abraded feelings; it made me feel even more alone. The greasy banisters of the urban hotels I stayed in sickened me; the glowing pictures of the Sacred Heart in the rooms of the private houses that, in the country, took in guests, disturbed my sleep. I felt that I was being stared at and found out.

And that, of course, was the last thing I wanted, to be found out. I've never said anything about the incident to anyone, not that there's much reason to keep it from people. Except, I guess, my shame at having been ravished, my dread of the implication, however slight, that I had "asked for what had happened," that my unwisdom was simply a masked desire for a coupling anonymous and blank. And so I have been silent about that time without good cause; how, then, could I ever speak of the second incident, which could, if I exposed it, unravel the fabric of my family's life?

My Uncle William was my father's only brother. He was two years older, handsomer, more flamboyant, more impatient, and it was said that though he lacked my father's steadiness, my father hadn't got his charm. Their mother had died when they were children, and their father drowned before their eyes when my father was seventeen and William nineteen. They agreed between them, teenage orphans, that my father should go off to college—he would study engineering at Purdue—and my uncle would stay home and run the family business, a successful clothing store my grandfather had built up and expanded as the town's prosperity increased and its tastes became more daring. When my father left for school it was a thriving business and it was assumed that with William's way with people, women especially (he planned to build his line of women's clothing; his first move was to enlarge the millinery department) it could only flourish. But in two years, everything was lost and my father had to leave college. The truly extraordinary aspect of the affair, to my mind, is that it was always my father who was apologetic about the situation. He felt it had been unfair, a terrible position to put Uncle William in, making him slave alone in the hometown he had never liked, while my father had been able to go away. William was really smarter, my father always said. (It wasn't true; even my mother, a great fan of Uncle William's and a stark critic of my father, corrected him, always, at this point in the story.) My father and my uncle agreed that it would be better for my uncle to go away; he'd put in his time and it was my father's turn; there was no reason for Uncle William to stick around and endure the petty insults and suspicions of uncomprehending minds.

In five years, my father had paid all the debts, a feat that so impressed the president of the local bank that he offered him a job. His rise in the bank was immediate, and it led to his move to Cleveland and his continued steady climb and marriage to my mother, the daughter of a bank president. I've never understood my father's success; he seems to trust everyone; wrongdoing not only shocks but seems genuinely to surprise him; yet he's made a career lending people money. I can only imagine that inside those cool buildings he always worked in, he assumed a new identity; the kind eyes grew steely, the tentative, apologetic yet protective posture hardened into something wary and astute. How else can I explain the fact that somebody so lovable made so much money?

65   In the years that my father was building his career, my uncle was traveling. We got letters from around the country; there was a reference in one, after the fact, to a failed marriage that lasted only sixteen months. And occasionally, irregularly, perhaps once every five years, there would be a visit, sudden, shimmering, like a rocket illumining our ordinary home and lives, making my father feel he had made all the right decisions, he was safe, yet not removed from glamour. For here it was, just at his table, in the presence of the brother whom he loved.

I, too, felt illumined by the visits. In middle age, William was dapper, anecdotal and offhand. He could imitate perfectly Italian tailors, widows of Texas oilmen, Mexican Indians who crossed the border every spring. In high school, my friends were enchanted by him; he was courtly and praising and gave them a sense of what they were going away to college for. But by the time we had all been away a couple of years, his stories seemed forced and repetitious, his autodidact's store of information suspect, his compliments something to be, at best, endured. For my father, however, my Uncle William never lost his luster. He hovered around his older brother, strangely maternal, as if my uncle were a rare, invalid *jeune fille*, possessed of delicate and special talents which a coarse world would not appreciate. And while my father hovered, my mother leaned toward my uncle flirtatious and expectant and alight.

Once, when I was living in New York, his visit and my visit to Ohio coincided. I was put on the living-room couch to sleep since my uncle had inhabited my room for two weeks and I would be home for only three days. At twenty-five, any visit home is a laceration, a gesture meanly wrought from a hard heart and an ungiving spirit. No one in town did I find worth talking to, my parents were darlings, but they would never understand my complicated and exciting life. Uncle William, in this context, was a relief; I had, of course, to condescend to him, but then he condescended to my parents, and he liked to take me out for drinks and hear me talk about my life.

One night, I had gone to dinner at a high school friend's. She had recently married, and I had all the single woman's contempt for her Danish Modern furniture, her silver pattern, her china with its modest print of roses. But it was one of those evenings that is so boring it's impossible to leave; one is always afraid that in rising from the chair, one is casting too pure a light on the whole fiasco. I drove into my parents' driveway at one-thirty, feeling ill-used and restless, longing for my own bed in my own apartment and the sound of Lexington

Avenue traffic. In five minutes, I was crankily settling onto the made-up couch, and I must have fallen instantly to sleep. I have always been a good sleeper.

It was nearly four when I realized there was someone near me, kneeling on the floor. Only gradually, I understood that it was my Uncle William, stroking my arm and breathing whiskey in my face.

70   "I couldn't sleep," he said. "I was thinking about you."

I lay perfectly still; I didn't know what else to do. I couldn't wake my parents, I could see behind my eyes years of my father's proud solicitude for the man now running his hand toward my breast, scene after scene of my mother's lively and absorbed attentions to him. As I lay there, I kept remembering the feeling of being a child sitting on the steps watching my parents and their guests below me as they talked and held their drinks and nibbled food I didn't recognize as coming from my mother's kitchen or her hand. A child transgressing, I was frozen into my position; any move would mean exposure and so punishment. At the same time that the danger of my situation stiffened me into immobility, I was paralyzed by the incomprehensibility of the behavior that went on downstairs. Could these be people I had known, laughing in these dangerous, sharp, unprovoked ways, leaning so close into one another, singing snatches of songs, then breaking off to compliment each other on their looks, their clothes, their business or community success. My childish sense of isolation from the acts of these familiars now grown strangers made me conscious of the nerves that traveled down my body's trunk, distinct, electric, and my eyes, wide as if they were set out on stalks, now lidless and impossibly alert. Twenty years later as I lay, desperately strategizing, watching my uncle I knew the memory was odd, but it stayed with me as I simulated flippancy, the only tactic I could imagine that would lead to my escape. My uncle had always called me his best audience when I'd forced laughter at one of his jokes; he'd say I was the only one in the family with a sense of humor.

"Well, unlike you, Uncle William, I *could* sleep, I *was* sleeping," I said, trying to sound like one of those thirties comedy heroines, clever in a jam.

"And that's what I want to do again."

"Ssh," he said, running his hand along my legs. "Don't be provincial. Have some courage, girl, some imagination. Besides I'm sure I'm not the first to have the privilege. I just want to see what all the New York guys are getting."

75   He continued to touch me, obsessive now and furtive, like an animal in a dark box.

"I'm not going to hurt you," he said. "I could make you happy. Happier than those young guys."

"What would make me really happy is to get some sleep," I said, in a tone I prayed did not reveal all my stiff desperation.

But, miraculously, he rose from his knees. "You really are a little prude at heart, aren't you? Just like everybody else in this stinking town."

And suddenly, he was gone. In the false blue light of four o'clock, I felt the animal's sheer gratitude for escape. I kept telling myself that nothing, after all, had happened, that I wasn't injured, it was rather funny really, I'd see that in time.

80   My great fear was that I would betray, by some lapse of warmth or interest in the morning, my uncle's drunken act. I longed for my parents' protection, yet I saw that it was I who must protect them. It had happened, that thing between parents and children: the balance had shifted; I was stronger. I was filled with a clean, painful love for them, which strikes me now each time I see them. They are gallant; they are innocent, and I must keep them so.

And I must do it once again today. They are coming to lunch with my Uncle William. I will be alone with them: my husband is working; my children are at school. In twenty years, I've only seen him twice, both times at my parents' house. I was able to keep up the tone: jocular, tough-minded, that would make him say, "You're my best audience," and make my father say, "They're cut from the same cloth, those two." It was one of those repayments the grown middle-class child must make, the overdue bill for the orthodontists, the dance lessons, the wardrobe for college, college itself. No one likes repayment; it is never a pure act, but for me it was a possible one. Today, though, it seems different. Today they are coming to my house, they will sit at my table. And as I stand at the kitchen window where I have been happy, where I have nurtured children and a husband's love and thought that I was safe, I rage as I look at the food I'd planned to serve them. The vegetables which minutes ago pleased me look contaminated to me now. Without my consent it seems, the side of my hand has moved toward them like a knife and shoved them off the cutting board. They land, all their distinction gone, in a heap in the sink. I know that I should get them out of there; I know I will; for I would never waste them, but for now it pleases me to see them ugly and abandoned and in danger, as if their fate were genuinely imperiled and unsure.

What is it that I want from Uncle William? I want some hesitation at the door, as if he isn't sure if he is welcome. I want him to take me aside and tell me he knows that he has done me harm. I want him to sit, if he must sit, at my table, silent and abashed. I don't demand that he be hounded; I don't even want him to confess. I simply want him to know, as I want the Irish sailor to know, that a wrong has been done me. I want to believe that they remember it with at the least regret. I know that things cannot be taken back, the forced embraces, the caresses brutal underneath the mask of courtship, but what I do want taken back are the words, spoken by those two men, that suggest that what they did was all right, no different from what other men had done, that it is all the same, the touch of men and women; nothing of desire or consent has weight, body parts touch body parts; that's all there is. I want them to know that because of them I cannot ever feel about the world the way I might have felt had they never come near me.

But the Irishman is gone and Uncle William, here before me, has grown old and weak. I can see him from the window, I can see the three of them. Him and my parents. They lean on one another, playful, tender; they have been together a lifetime. In old age, my parents have taken to traveling; I can hear them asking my uncle's advice about Mexico, where they will go this winter, where he once lived five years. They are wearing the youth-endowing clothing of the comfortably retired: windbreakers, sneakers, soft, light-colored sweaters, washable dun-colored pants. They have deliberately kept their health, my parents, so that they will not be a burden to me; for some other reason my uncle has kept his. Groaning, making exaggerated gestures, they complain about the steepness of my steps. But it is real, my father's muscular uncertainty as he grabs for the rail. They stand at my front door.

What happened happened twenty years ago. I've had a good life. I am a young and happy woman. And now I see the three of them, the old ones, frail, expectant, yearning toward me. So there is nothing for it; I must give them what they want. I open my arms to the embrace they offer. Heartily, I clap my uncle on the back.

85 "Howdy, stranger," I say in a cowboy voice. "Welcome to these parts."

▪ EXPLORATIONS OF THE TEXT
1. How does the setting establish the mood of the work?
2. Why does the work open with a flashback?
3. Characterize the narrator. Examine her attitudes, values, family background, interests, European experiences, and present state.
4. One of the motifs in nineteenth-century American literature is that of the innocent American abroad. How does this motif serve as the symbolic context for the drama? What do the tourist sites symbolize? How do they contrast with the sexual encounter?

5. Why does the narrator submit to the sailor's demand for sex? Does she have any choice? What is the impact of the "violation" upon her? How does the earlier experience with her uncle mirror the rape?
6. Does the narrator, as an adult, come to terms with her "violation"?
7. Compare and contrast the seduction scenes in this work and in Mar's "Bi Bi Hua." What do they reveal about male force and male sexuality?

■ THE READING/WRITING CONNECTION

1. The narrator theorizes that "safety is a feeling open to men alone." Do you agree? Respond in a freewrite.
2. "Think" Topic: Explore the theme of choice and agency in this work and in Mar's "Bi Bi Hua."
3. Have you, or has someone you know, been a victim of a sexual assault or a potential act of sexual aggression? You may write your response in the form of a journal entry or a fictional account.

■ IDEAS FOR WRITING

1. Discuss the dangers of sexual encounters in this work, in Gilman's *Boy Gets Girl,* and in Faulkner's "A Rose for Emily." Who are the aggressors? What are potential reasons for their actions? What are the consequences for the victims?
2. Compare the treatment of male power and sexuality in this work with that in Mar's "Bi Bi Hua," Paz's "My Life with the Wave," and/or Cervantes's "My Uncle's First Rabbit" (chapter 4).

LÊ THI DIEM THÚY

lê thi diem thúy (1972–   ) was born in Phan Thiet, South Vietnam, and left Vietnam with her father in a boat in 1978. After spending time in a refugee camp in Singapore, thúy and her father settled in California near San Diego. She graduated from Hampshire College in 1994 and presently lives in Northampton, Massachusetts, where she works as a writer and performance artist. "The Gangster We Are All Looking For" is taken from a book of the same name and explores her experience as a child in the United States.

2003

THE GANGSTER WE ARE ALL LOOKING FOR

Vietnam is a black-and-white photograph of my grandparents sitting in bamboo chairs in their front courtyard. They are sitting tall and proud, surrounded by chickens and a rooster. Between their feet and the dirt of the courtyard are thin sandals. My grandfather's broad forehead is shining. So too are my grandmother's famous sad eyes. The animals are oblivious, pecking at the ground. This looks like a wedding portrait though it is actually a photograph my grandparents had taken late in life, for their children, especially for my mother. When I think of this portrait of my grandparents in their last years, I always envision a beginning. To or toward what, I don't know, but always a beginning.

When my mother, a Catholic schoolgirl from the South, decided to marry my father, a Buddhist gangster from the North, her parents disowned her. This is in the photograph, though it is not visible to the eye. If it were, it would be a deep impression across the soft dirt of my grandparents' courtyard. Her father chased her out of the house, beating her with the same broom she had used every day of her life, from the time she could stand up and sweep until that very morning that she was chased away.

The year my mother met my father, there were several young men working at her parents' house, running errands for her father, pickling vegetables with her mother. It was understood by everyone that these men were courting my mother. My mother claims she had no such understanding.

She treated these men as brothers, sometimes as uncles even, later exclaiming in self-defense: I didn't even know about love then!

5   Ma says love came to her in a dark movie theater. She doesn't remember what movie it was or why she'd gone to see it, only that she'd gone alone and found herself sitting beside him. In the dark, she couldn't make out his face but noticed that his profile was handsome. She wondered if he knew she was watching him out of the corner of her eye. Watching him without embarrassment or shame. Watching him with a strange curiosity, a feeling that made her want to trace and retrace his silhouette with her fingertips until she'd memorized every feature and could call his face to mind in any dark place she passed through. Later, in the shadow of the beached fishing boats on the blackest nights of the year, she would call him to mind, his face a warm companion for her body on the edge of the sea.

In the early days of my parents' courtship, my mother told stories. She confessed elaborate dreams about the end of war: foods she'd eat (a banquet table, mangoes piled to the ceiling); songs she'd make up and sing, clapping her hands over her head and throwing her hair like a horse's mane; dances she'd dance, hopping from one foot to the other. Unlike the responsible favorite daughter or sister she was to her family, with my father, in the forest, my mother became reckless, drunk on her youth and the possibilities of love. Ignoring the chores to be done at home, she rolled her pants up to her knees, stuck her bare feet in puddles, and learned to smoke a cigarette.

She tied a vermilion ribbon in her hair. She became moody. She did her chores as though they were favors to her family, forgetting that she ate the same rice, was dependent on the same supply of food. It seemed to her the face that now stared back at her from deep inside the family well was the face of a woman she had never seen before. At night she lay in bed and thought of his hands, the way his thumb nicked down on the lighter and brought fire to her cigarette. She began to wonder what the forests were like before the American planes had come, flying low, raining something onto the trees that left them bare and dying. She remembered her father had once described to her the smiling broadness of leaves, jungles thick in the tangle of rich soil.

One evening, she followed my father in circles through the forest, supposedly in search of the clearing that would take them to his aunt's house. They wandered in darkness, never finding the clearing much less the aunt she knew he never had.

"You're not from here," she said.

10   "I know."

"So tell me, what's your aunt's name?"

"Xuan."

"Spring?"

"Yes."

15   She laughed. I can't be here, she thought.

"My father will be looking for me—"

"It's not too late. I'll walk you home."

In the dark, she could feel his hand extending toward her, filling the space between them. They had not touched once the entire evening and now he stood offering his hand to her. She stared at him for a long time. There was a small scar on his chin, curved like her fingernail. It was too dark to see this. She realized she had memorized his face.

My first memory of my father's face is framed by the coiling barbed wire of a military camp in South Vietnam. My mother's voice crosses through the wire. She is whispering his name and with this utterance, caressing him. Over and over, she calls him to her, "Anh Minh, Anh Minh." His name becomes a tree she presses her body against. The calling blows around them like a warm breeze and when she utters her own name, it is the second half of a verse that begins with his. She drops her name like a pebble into a well. She wants to be engulfed by him, "Anh Minh, em My. Anh Minh, em My."

20   The barbed wire gates open and she crosses through to him. She arrives warm, the slightest film of sweat on her bare arms. To his disbelieving eyes she says, "It's me, it's me." Shy and formal and breathless, my parents are always meeting for the first time, savoring the sound of a name, marveling at the bones of the face cupped by the bones of the hand.

I trail behind them, the tip of their dragon's tail. I am drawn along, like a silken banner on the body of a kite.

For a handful of pebbles and my father's sharp profile, my mother left home and never truly returned. Picture a handful of pebbles. Imagine the casual way he tossed them at her as she was walking home from school with her girlfriends. He did this because he liked her. Boys are dumb that way, my mother told me. A handful of pebbles, to be thrown in anger, in desperation, in joy. My father threw them in love. Ma says they touched her like warm kisses, these pebbles he had been holding in the sun. Warm kisses on the curve of her back, sliding down the crook of her arm, grazing her ankles and landing around her feet in the hot sand.

What my father told her could have been a story. There was no one in the South to confirm the details of his life. He said he came from a semi-aristocratic northern family. Unlacing his boot, he pulled out his foot and directed her close attention to how his second toe was significantly longer than the others. "A sure sign of aristocracy," he claimed. His nose was high, he said, because his mother was French, one of the many mistresses his father had kept. He found this out when he was sixteen. That year, he ran away from home and came south.

"There are thieves, gamblers, drunks I've met who remind me of people in my family. It's the way they're dreamers. My family's a garden full of dreamers lying on their backs, staring at the sky, drunk and choking on their dreams." He said this while leaning against a tree, his arms folded across his bare chest, his eyes staring at the ground, his shoulders golden.

25   She asked her mother, "What does it mean if your second toe is longer than your other toes?"

"It means . . . your mother will die before your father," her mother said.

"I heard somewhere it's a sign of aristocracy."

"Huh!"

When my mother looked at my father's bare feet she saw ten fishing boats, two groups of five. Within each group, the second boat ventured ahead, leading the others. She would climb a tree, stand gripping the branch with her own toes and stare down at his. She directed him to stand in the mud. There, she imagined what she saw to be ten small boats surrounded by black water, a fleet of junks journeying in the dark.

30   She would lean back and enjoy this vision, never explaining to him what it was she saw. She left him to wonder about her senses as he stood, cigarette in hand, staring at her trembling ankles, and not moving until she told him to.

I was born in the alley behind my grandparents' house. At three in the morning, my mother dragged herself out of the bed in the smaller house where she and my father lived after they married. My father was away, fighting in the war. Ma's youngest sister had come to live with her, helping her with my older brother, who was just a baby then. Ma left the two of them sleeping in the hammock, my brother lying in the crook of my aunt's arm, and set out alone.

She cut a crooked line on the beach. Moving in jerky steps, like a ball tossed on the waves, she seemed to be bounced along without direction. She walked to the schoolhouse and sat on the ground before it, leaning against the first step. She felt grains of sand pressing against her back. Each grain was a minute pinprick, and the pain grew and grew. Soon she felt as though her back would erupt, awash in blood. She thought, I am going to bleed to death. She put her hands on her belly. We are going to die.

In front of the schoolhouse lay a long metal tube. No one knew where it came from. It seemed to have been there always. Children hid inside it, crawled through it, spoke to each other from either ends of it, marched across it, sat upon it and confided secrets beside it. There had been so little to play with during the school recess. This long metal tube became everything. A tarp was suspended over it, to shield it from the sun. The tube looked like a blackened log in a room without walls. When the children sat in a line on the tube, their heads bobbing this way and that in conversation, it seemed they were sitting on a canopied raft.

The night I was born, my mother, looking at the tube, imagined it to be the badly burnt arm of a dying giant buried in the sand. She could not decide whether he had been buried and was trying to get out or whether he had tried to bury himself in the sand but had failed to cover his arm in time. In time for what? She had heard a story about a girl in a neighboring town who was killed during a napalm bombing. The bombing happened on an especially hot night, when this girl had walked to the beach to cool her feet in the water. They found her floating on the sea. The phosphorus from the napalm made her body glow, like a lantern. In her mind, my mother built a canopy for this girl. She started to cry, thinking of the buried giant, the floating girl, these bodies stopped in mid-stride, on their way somewhere.

35   She began to walk toward the tube. She had a sudden urge to be inside it. The world felt dangerous to her and she was alone. At the mouth of the tube, she bent down, her belly blocking the mouth. She tried the other side, the other mouth. Again, her belly stopped her. "But I remember," she muttered out loud, "as a girl I sometimes slept in here." This was what she wanted now, to sleep inside the tube.

"Tall noses come from somewhere—"
"Not from here."
"Not tall noses."

Eyes insinuate, moving from her nose to mine then back again. Mouths suck in air, color it into the darkest shade of contempt, then spit it at her feet as she walks by. I am riding on her hip. I am the new branch that makes the tree bend but she walks with her head held high. She knows where she pulled me from. No blue eye.

40   Ma says war is a bird with a broken wing flying over the countryside, trailing blood and burying crops in sorrow. If something grows in spite of this, it is both a curse and a miracle. When I was born, she cried to know that it was war I was breathing in, and she could never shake it out of me. Ma says war makes it dangerous to breathe, though she knows you die if you don't. She says she could have thrown me against the wall, until I broke or coughed up this war that is killing us all. She could have stomped on it in the dark, and danced on it like a madwoman dancing on gravestones. She could have ground it down to powder and spat on it, but didn't I know? War has no beginning and no end. It crosses oceans like a splintered boat filled with people singing a sad song.

    Every morning Anh wakes up in the house next to mine, a yellow duplex she and I call a town house since we found out from a real estate ad that a town house is a house with an upstairs and a downstairs. My father calls Anh "the chicken egg girl." Early each morning Anh's mother loads a small pushcart with stacks of eggs and Anh walks all over Linda Vista selling eggs before school. Her backyard is full of chickens and one rooster. Sometimes you can see the rooster fly up and balance himself on the back gate. From his perch, he'll crow and crow, on and off, all day long, until dark comes.

    We live in the country of California, the province of San Diego, the village of Linda Vista. We live in old Navy Housing bungalows built in the 1940s. Since the 1980s, these bungalows house Vietnamese, Cambodian, and Laotian refugees from the Vietnam War. When we moved in, we had to sign a form promising not to put fish bones in the garbage disposal.

    We live in a yellow house on Westinghouse Street. Our house is one story, made of wood and plaster. Between our house and another one-story house are six two-story houses. Facing our row of houses, across a field of brown dirt, sits another row of yellow houses, same as ours, watching us like a sad twin. Linda Vista is full of houses like ours, painted in peeling shades of olive green, baby blue, and sun-baked yellow.

    There's new Navy Housing on Linda Vista Road, the long street that takes you out of here. We see the Navy people watering their lawns, their children riding pink tricycles up and down the culs-de-sac. We see them in Victory Supermarket, buying groceries with cash. In Kelley Park they have picnics and shoot each other with water guns. At school their kids are Most Popular, Most Beautiful, Most Likely to Succeed. Though there are more Vietnamese, Cambodian, and Laotian kids at the school, in the yearbook we are not the most of anything. They call us Yang because one year a bunch of Laotian kids with the last name Yang came to our school. The Navy Housing kids started calling all the refugee kids "Yang."

45   Yang. Yang. Yang.

    Ma says living next to Anh's family reminds her of Vietnam because the blue tarp suspended above Anh's backyard is the bright blue of the South China Sea. Ma says, isn't it funny how sky and sea follow you from place to place as if they too were traveling.

    Thinking of my older brother, who was still in Vietnam, I ask Ma, "If the sky and the sea can follow us here, why can't people?"

    Ma ignores my question and says even Anh reminds her of Vietnam, the way she sets out for market each morning.

    Ba becomes a gardener. Overnight. He buys a truck full of equipment and a box of business cards from Uncle Twelve, who is moving to Texas to become a fisherman. The business cards read "Tom's Professional Gardening Service" and have a small green picture embossed on them, a man pushing a lawn mower. The man has his back to you, so no one holding the card can tell it's not Ba, no one who doesn't already know. He says I can be his secretary because I speak the best English. If you call us on the business phone, you will hear me say: "Hello, you have reached Tom's Professional Gardening Service. We are not here right now, but if you leave us a message, we will get back to you as soon as possible. Thank you."

50   It is hot and dusty where we live. Some people think it's dirty but they don't know much about us. They haven't seen our gardens full of lemongrass, mint, cilantro, and basil. Driving by with their windows rolled up, they've only seen the pigeons pecking at day-old rice and the skinny cats and dogs sitting in the skinny shade of skinny trees. Have they seen the berries that we pick, that turn our lips and fingertips red? How about the small staircase Ba built from our bedroom window to the backyard so I would have a shortcut to the clothesline? How about the Great Wall of China that snakes like a river from the top of the steep hill off Crandall Drive to the slightly curving bottom? Who has seen this?

It was so different at the Green Apartment. We had to close the gate behind us every time we came in. It clanged heavily, and I imagined a host of eyes, upstairs and down, staring at me from behind slightly parted curtains. There were four palm trees planted at the four corners of the courtyard and a central staircase that was narrow at the top and broad at the bottom. The steps were covered in fake grass, like the set of an old Hollywood movie, the kind that stars an aging beauty who wakes up to find something is terribly wrong.

"We moved out of the Green Apartment after we turned on the TV one night and heard that our manager and his brother had hacked a woman to pieces and dumped the parts of her body into the Pacific Ocean in ten-gallon garbage bags that washed up onshore. Ma said she didn't want to live in a place haunted by a murdered lady. So we moved to Linda Vista, where she said there were a lot of Vietnamese people like us, people whose only sin was a little bit of gambling and sucking on fish bones and laughing hard and arguing loudly.

Ma shaved her head in Linda Vista because she got mad at Ba for gambling away her money and getting drunk every week during *Monday Night Football*. Ba gave her a blue baseball cap to wear until her hair grew back and she wore it backward, like a real badass.

After that, some people in Linda Vista said that Ma was crazy and Ba was crazy for staying with her. But what do some people know?

55   When the photograph came, Ma and Ba got into a fight. Ba threw the fish tank out the front door and Ma broke all the dishes. They said they never should've got together.

Ma's sister sent her the photograph from Vietnam. It came in a stiff envelope. There was nothing else inside, as if anything more would be pointless. Ma held the photograph in her hands. She started to cry. "Child," she sobbed, over and over again. She wasn't talking about me. She was talking about herself.

Ba said, "Don't cry. Your parents have forgiven you."

Ma kept crying anyway and told him not to touch her with his gangster hands. Ba clenched his hands into tight fists and punched the walls.

"What hands?! What hands?!" he yelled. "Let me see the gangster! Let me see his hands!" I see his hands punch hands punch hands punch blood.

60   Ma is in the kitchen. She has torn the screen off the window. She is punctuating the pavement with dishes, plates, cups, rice bowls. She sends them out like birds gliding through the sky with nowhere in particular to go. Until they crash. Then she exhales "Huh!" in satisfaction.

I am in the hallway gulping air. I breathe in the breaking and the bleeding. When Ba plunges his hands into the fish tank, I detect the subtle tint of blood in water. When he throws the fish tank out the front door, yelling, "Let me see the gangster!" I am drinking up the spilt water and swallowing whole the beautiful tropical fish, their brilliant colors gliding across my tongue, before they can hit the ground, to cover themselves in dirt until only the whites of their eyes remain, blinking at the sun.

All the hands are in my throat, cutting themselves on broken dishes, and the fish swim in circles; they can't see for all the blood.

Ba jumps in his truck and drives away.

When I grow up I am going to be the gangster we are all looking for.

65   The neighborhood kids are standing outside our house, staring in through the windows and the open door. Even Anh, the chicken egg girl. I'm sure their gossiping mothers have sent them to spy on us. I run out front and dance like a crazy lady, dance like a fish, wiggle my head and whip my body around. At first they laugh but then they stop, not knowing what to think. Then I stop to stare them down, each one of them.

"What're you looking at?" I ask.

"Lookin' at you," one boy says, half giggling.

"Well," I say, with my hand on my hip, my head cocked to one side, "I'm looking at you too," and I give him my evil one-eyed look, focusing all my energy into my left eye. I stare at him hard as if my eye is a bullet and he can be dead.

I turn my back on them and walk into the house.

70   Ma is sitting in the window frame. The curve of her back is inside the bedroom while the rest of her body hangs outside, on the first of the steps Ba built from the bedroom to the garden. Without turning to look at me, she says, "Let me lift you into the attic."

"Why?"

"We have to move your grandparents in."

I don't really know what she is talking about, but I say O.K. anyway.

We have never needed the attic for anything. In fact, we have never gone up there. When we moved my grandparents in, Ma simply lifted me up and I pushed open the attic door with one hand while, with the other, I slipped the stiff envelope with the photograph of my grandparents into the crawl space above. I pushed the envelope the length of my arm and down to my fingertips. I pushed it so far it was beyond reach. Ma said that was all right; they had come to live with us, and sometimes you don't need to see or touch people to know they're there.

75   Ba came home drunk that night and asked to borrow my blanket. I heard him climbing the tree in the backyard. It took him a long time. He kept missing the wooden blocks that run up the tree like a ladder. Ba had put them in himself when he built the steps going from the bedroom window into the garden. If you stood on the very top block, your whole body would be hidden by tree branches. Ba put those blocks in for me, so I could win at hide-and-go-seek.

When Ba had finally made it onto the roof, he lay down over my room and I could hear him rolling across my ceiling. Rolling and crying. I was scared he would roll off the edge and kill himself, so I went to wake Ma.

She was already awake. She said it would be a good thing if he rolled off. But later I heard someone climb the tree, and all night two bodies rolled across my ceiling. Slowly and firmly they pressed against my sleep, the Catholic schoolgirl and the Buddhist gangster, two dogs chasing each other's tails. They have been running like this for so long, they have become one dog, one tail.

Without any hair and looking like a man, my mother is still my mother, though sometimes I can't see her even when I look and look and look so long all the colors of the world begin to swim and bob around me. Her hands always bring me up, her big peasant hands with the flat, wide nails, wide like her nose and just as expressive. I will know her by her hands and by her walk, at once slow and urgent, the walk of a woman going to market with her goods bound securely to her side. Even walking empty-handed, my mother's gait suggests invisible bundles whose contents no one but she can reveal. And if I never see her again, I will know my mother by the smell of the sea salt and the prints of my own bare feet crossing sand, running to and away from, to and away from, family.

When the eviction notice came, we didn't believe it so we threw it away. It said we had a month to get out. The houses on our block had a new owner who wanted to tear everything down and build better housing for the community. It said we were priority tenants for the new complex, but we couldn't afford to pay the new rent so it didn't matter. The notice also said that if we didn't get out in time, all our possessions would be confiscated in accordance with some section of a law book or manual we were supposed to have known about but had never seen. We couldn't believe the eviction notice so we threw it away.

80 The fence is tall, silver, and see-through. Chain-link, it rattles when you shake it and wobbles when you lean against it. It circles our block like a bad dream. It is not funny like the clothesline whose flying shirts and empty pants suggest human birds and vanishing acts. This fence presses sharply against your brain. We three stand still as posts. Looking at it, then at one another—this side and that—out of the corners of our eyes. What are we thinking?

At night we come back with three uncles. Ba cuts a hole in the fence and we step through. Quiet, we break into our own house through the back window. Quiet, we steal back everything that is ours. We fill ten-gallon garbage bags with clothes, pots and pans, flip-flops, the porcelain figure of Mary, the wooden Buddha and the Chinese fisherman lamp. In the arc of our flashlights we find our favorite hairbrushes behind bedposts. When we are done, we clamber, breathless. Though it's quiet, we can hear police cars coming to get us.

We tumble out the window like people tumbling across continents. We are time traveling, weighed down by heavy furniture and bags of precious junk. We find ourselves leaning against Ba's yellow truck. Ma calls his name, her voice reaching like a hand feeling for a tree trunk in darkness.

In the car, Ma starts to cry. "What about the sea?" she asks. "What about the garden?" Ba says we can come back in the morning and dig up the stalks of lemongrass and fold the sea into a blue square. Ma is sobbing. She is beating the dashboard with her fists. "I want to know," she says, "I want to know, I want to know . . . who is doing this to us?" Hiccupping she says, "I want to know, why—why there's always a fence. Why there's always someone on the outside wanting someone . . . something on the inside and between them . . . this . . . sharp fence. Why are we always leaving like this?"

Everyone is quiet when Ma screams.

85 "Take me back!" she says. "I can't go with you. I've forgotten my mother and father. I can't believe . . . Anh Minh, we've left them to die. Take me back."

Ma wants Ba to stop the car, but Ba doesn't know why. The three uncles, sitting in a row in the bed of the truck, think Ma is crazy. They yell in through the rear window, "My, are you going to walk back to Vietnam?"

"Yeah, are you going to walk home to your parents' house?"

In the silence another shakes his head and reaches into his shirt pocket for his cigarettes.

Ba puts his foot on the gas pedal. Our car jerks forward, and then plunges down the Crandall Drive hill. Ma says, "I need air, water . . ." I roll the window down. She puts her head in her hands. She keeps crying, "Child." Outside, I see the Great Wall of China. In the glare of the streetlamps, it is just a long strip of cardboard.

90   In the morning, the world is flat. Westinghouse Street is lying down like a jagged brushstroke of sun-burnt yellow. There is a big sign within the fence that reads

COMING SOON:
CONDOMINIUMS
TOWN HOUSES
FAMILY HOMES

Below these words is a copy of a watercolor drawing of a large pink complex.

We stand on the edge of the chain-link fence, sniffing the air for the scent of lemongrass, scanning this flat world for our blue sea. A wrecking ball dances madly through our house. Everything has burst wide open and sunk down low. Then I hear her calling them. She is whispering, "Ma/Ba, Ma/Ba." The whole world is two butterfly wings rubbing against my ear.

Listen . . . they are sitting in the attic, sitting like royalty. Shining in the dark, buried by a wrecking ball. Paper fragments floating across the surface of the sea.

There is not a trace of blood anywhere except here, in my throat, where I am telling you all this.

■ **EXPLORATIONS OF THE TEXT**

1. Why does the work open with the description of a photograph of the narrator's grandparents?
2. How does the narrator's mother rebel against her Vietnamese upbringing? What is her husband's allure? What sacrifices does the protagonist's mother make because of her love for the "gangster"?
3. How does the Vietnam war function in the narrative? How does the war influence the lives of the protagonists? Discuss the contrasts of love and war in the work.
4. According to the *New York Times,* this work is as "allusive as a poem." Examine the writer's use of such symbols as the pebbles, the tube, the forest, the sea, fences, and blood. How do these symbols develop themes of the work?
5. Explore the vision of cultural inheritance/cultural legacies presented in this work. How is the narrator shaped by her mother's love story?
6. Compare and contrast the depiction of passion in this work with several other works in this cluster.

■ **THE READING/WRITING CONNECTION**

1. Look at a photograph of your parents. Imagine what they were like before you were born. Write a journal or a poem based on your observations.
2. In a journal entry, write about a first experience of love.
3. Using Atwood's "Happy Endings" as a model, write several scenarios for the mother's marriage.

■ **IDEAS FOR WRITING**

1. Compare and contrast the depiction of the female body in this work, in Mar's "Bi Bi Hua," and in Hwang's *M Butterfly.*
2. Discuss the consequences of passion in this work and in Faulkner's "A Rose for Emily."

Margaret Atwood

Margaret Atwood (1939–   ) was born in Ottawa, Canada, and was educated at the University of Toronto, Radcliffe College, and Harvard University. Atwood is the author of twenty volumes of poetry, thirteen novels, and six short-story collections. She has contributed to many anthologies and has edited numerous other books, including The Best American Short Stories *(1989). Atwood is best known for her novel* The Handmaid's Tale *(1986), which won the Governor General's Award (1986), the* Los Angeles Times *Book Award (1986), the Arthur C. Clarke Award for Best Science Fiction (1987), and the Commonwealth Literature Prize (1987). She is the recipient of numerous other Canadian, American, and international awards, and she has received honorary degrees from fourteen universities. Other novels include her first,* The Edible Woman *(1969), and, more recently,* The Blind Assassin *(2000) and* Oryx and Crake *(2003). Atwood is known as a feminist writer because her work analyzes the shortcomings of women's lives in present-day society. She has said that the suffering of her female characters reflects that of the women she meets.*

1983

HAPPY ENDINGS

John and Mary meet.
What happens next?
If you want a happy ending, try A.

A

John and Mary fall in love and get married. They both have worthwhile and remunerative jobs which they find stimulating and challenging. They buy a charming house. Real estate values go up. Eventually, when they can afford live-in help, they have two children, to whom they are devoted. The children turn out well. John and Mary have a stimulating and challenging sex life and worthwhile friends. They go on fun vacations together. They retire. They both have hobbies which they find stimulating and challenging. Eventually they die. This is the end of the story.

B

5   Mary falls in love with John but John doesn't fall in love with Mary. He merely uses her body for selfish pleasure and ego gratification of a tepid kind. He comes to her apartment twice a week and she cooks him dinner, you'll notice that he doesn't even consider her worth the price of a dinner out, and after he's eaten the dinner he fucks her and after that he falls asleep, while she does the dishes so he won't think she's untidy, having all those dirty dishes lying around, and puts on fresh lipstick so she'll look good when he wakes up, but when he wakes up he doesn't even notice, he puts on his socks and his shorts and his pants and his shirt and his tie and his shoes, the reverse order from the one in which he took them off. He doesn't take off Mary's clothes, she takes them off herself, she acts as if she's dying for it every time, not because she likes sex exactly, she doesn't, but she wants John to think she does because if they do it often enough surely he'll get used to her, he'll come to depend on her and they will get married, but John goes out the door with hardly so much as a good-night and three days later he turns up at six o'clock and they do the whole thing over again.

Mary gets run-down. Crying is bad for your face, everyone knows that and so does Mary but she can't stop. People at work notice. Her friends tell her John is a rat, a pig, a dog, he isn't good enough for her, but she can't believe it. Inside John, she thinks, is another John, who is much nicer. This other John will emerge like a butterfly from a cocoon, a Jack from a box, a pit from a prune, if the first John is only squeezed enough.

One evening John complains about the food. He has never complained about the food before. Mary is hurt.

Her friends tell her they've seen him in a restaurant with another woman, whose name is Madge. It's not even Madge that finally gets to Mary: it's the restaurant. John has never taken Mary to a restaurant. Mary collects all the sleeping pills and aspirins she can find, and takes them and a half a bottle of sherry. You can see what kind of a woman she is by the fact that it's not even whiskey. She leaves a note for John. She hopes he'll discover her and get her to the hospital in time and repent and then they can get married, but this fails to happen and she dies.

John marries Madge and everything continues as in A.

C

10   John, who is an older man, falls in love with Mary, and Mary, who is only twenty-two, feels sorry for him because he's worried about his hair falling out. She sleeps with him even though she's not in love with him. She met him at work. She's in love with someone called James, who is twenty-two also and not yet ready to settle down.

John on the contrary settled down long ago: this is what is bothering him. John has a steady, respectable job and is getting ahead in his field, but Mary isn't impressed by him, she's impressed by James, who has a motorcycle and a fabulous record collection. But James is often away on his motorcycle, being free. Freedom isn't the same for girls, so in the meantime Mary spends Thursday evenings with John. Thursdays are the only days John can get away.

John is married to a woman called Madge and they have two children, a charming house which they bought just before the real estate values went up, and hobbies which they find stimulating and challenging, when they have the time. John tells Mary how important she is to him, but of course he can't leave his wife because a commitment is a commitment. He goes on about this more than is necessary and Mary finds it boring, but older men can keep it up longer so on the whole she has a fairly good time.

One day James breezes in on his motorcycle with some top-grade California hybrid and James and Mary get higher than you'd believe possible and they climb into bed. Everything becomes very underwater, but along comes John, who has a key to Mary's apartment. He finds them stoned and entwined. He's hardly in any position to be jealous, considering Madge, but nevertheless he's overcome with despair. Finally he's middle-aged, in two years he'll be bald as an egg and he can't stand it. He purchases a handgun, saying he needs it for target practice —this is the thin part of the plot, but it can be dealt with later—and shoots the two of them and himself.

Madge, after a suitable period of mourning, marries an understanding man called Fred and everything continues as in A, but under different names.

D

15   Fred and Madge have no problems. They get along exceptionally well and are good at working out any little difficulties that may arise. But their charming house is by the seashore and

one day a giant tidal wave approaches. Real estate values go down. The rest of the story is about what caused the tidal wave and how they escape from it. They do, though thousands drown, but Fred and Madge are virtuous and lucky. Finally on high ground they clasp each other, wet and dripping and grateful, and continue as in A.

E

Yes, but Fred has a bad heart. The rest of the story is about how kind and understanding they both are until Fred dies. Then Madge devotes herself to charity work until the end of A. If you like, it can be "Madge," "cancer," "guilty and confused," and "bird watching."

F

If you think this is all too bourgeois, make John a revolutionary and Mary a counterespionage agent and see how far that gets you. Remember, this is Canada. You'll still end up with A, though in between you may get a lustful brawling saga of passionate involvement, a chronicle of our times, sort of.

You'll have to face it, the endings are the same however you slice it. Don't be deluded by any other endings, they're all fake, either deliberately fake, with malicious intent to deceive, or just motivated by excessive optimism if not by downright sentimentality.

The only authentic ending is the one provided here:

20   *John and Mary die. John and Mary die. John and Mary die.*

So much for endings. Beginnings are always more fun. True connoisseurs, however, are known to favor the stretch in between, since it's the hardest to do anything with.

That's about all that can be said for plots, which anyway are just one thing after another, a what and a what and a what.

Now try How and Why.

■ **EXPLORATIONS OF THE TEXT**
 1. Compare and contrast the versions of John and Mary's love story. What do they suggest about love and marriage?
 2. Explore the significance of the last four paragraphs. Analyze and interpret the following: "The only authentic ending is the one provided here. John and Mary die. John and Mary die. John and Mary die." Why does Atwood repeat the sentence three times? Why are "beginnings . . . more fun"? What does "the stretch in between . . ." suggest?
 3. Is this a story about love, about writing fiction, or both?
 4. Discuss the critique of relationships and women's roles presented in the work. Discuss the criticism of bourgeois culture.
 5. How does the humor convey Atwood's theme?

■ **THE READING/WRITING CONNECTION**
 1. Write several different versions of a relationship in which you have been involved. What do you learn?
 2. Atwood's work is an example of metafiction (see glossary). How does Atwood handle this genre?

■ **IDEAS FOR WRITING**
 1. Compare and contrast the feminist critique of relationships in this work and in Gilman's "The Yellow Wallpaper."

MARGARET ATWOOD (1939–)   **1983**

THE FEMALE BODY

. . . entirely devoted to the subject of "The Female Body." Knowing how well you have written on this topic . . . this capacious topic . . .

—letter from Michigan Quarterly Review

1.

I agree, it's a hot topic. But only one? Look around, there's a wide range. Take my own, for instance.

I get up in the morning. My topic feels like hell. I sprinkle it with water, brush parts of it, rub it with towels, powder it, add lubricant. I dump in the fuel and away goes my topic, my topical topic, my controversial topic, my capacious topic, my limping topic, my nearsighted topic, my topic with back problems, my badly behaved topic, my vulgar topic, my outrageous topic, my aging topic, my topic that is out of the question and anyway still can't spell, in its oversized coat and worn winter boots, scuttling along the sidewalk as if it were flesh and blood, hunting for what's out there, an avocado, an alderman, an adjective, hungry as ever.

2.

The basic Female Body comes with the following accessories: garter belt, panti-girdle, crino-line, camisole, bustle, brassiere, stomacher, chemise, virgin zone, spike heels, nose ring, veil, kid gloves, fishnet stockings, fichu, bandeau, Merry Widow, weepers, chokers, bar-rettes, bangles, beads, lorgnette, feather boa, basic black, compact, Lycra stretch one-piece with modesty panel, designer peignoir, flannel nightie, lace teddy, bed, head.

3.

The Female Body is made of transparent plastic that lights up when you plug it in. You press a button to illuminate the different systems. The circulatory system is red, for the heart and arteries, purple for the veins; the respiratory system is blue; the lymphatic system is yellow; the digestive system is green, with liver and kidneys in aqua. The nerves are done in orange and the brain is pink. The skeleton, as you might expect, is white.

5   The reproductive system is optional, and can be removed. It comes with or without a miniature embryo. Parental judgment can thereby be exercised. We do not wish to frighten or offend.

4.

He said, I won't have one of those things in the house. It gives a young girl a false notion of beauty, not to mention anatomy. If a real woman was built like that she'd fall on her face.

She said, If we don't let her have one like all the other girls she'll feel singled out. It'll become an issue. She'll long for one and she'll long to turn into one. Repression breeds sub-limation. You know that.

He said, It's not just the pointy plastic tits, it's the wardrobes. The wardrobes and that stupid male doll, what's his name, the one with the underwear glued on.

She said, Better to get it over with when she's young. He said, All right, but don't let me see it.

10   She came whizzing down the stairs, thrown like a dart. She was stark naked. Her hair had been chopped off, her head was turned back to front, she was missing some toes and she'd been tattooed all over her body with purple ink in a scrollwork design. She hit the potted azalea, trembled there for a moment like a botched angel, and fell.

     He said, I guess we're safe.

5.

The Female Body has many uses. It's been used as a door knocker, a bottle opener, as a clock with a ticking belly, as something to hold up lampshades, as a nutcracker, just squeeze the brass legs together and out comes your nut. It bears torches, lifts victorious wreaths, grows copper wings and raises aloft a ring of neon stars; whole buildings rest on its marble heads.

     It sells cars, beer, shaving lotion, cigarettes, hard liquor; it sells diet plans and diamonds, and desire in tiny crystal bottles. Is this the face that launched a thousand products? You bet it is, but don't get any funny big ideas, honey, that smile is a dime a dozen.

     It does not merely sell, it is sold. Money flows into this country or that country, flies in, practically crawls in, suitful after suitful, lured by all those hairless pre-teen legs. Listen, you want to reduce the national debt, don't you? Aren't you patriotic? That's the spirit. That's my girl.

15   She's a natural resource, a renewable one luckily, because those things wear out so quickly. They don't make 'em like they used to. Shoddy goods.

6.

One and one equals another one. Pleasure in the female is not a requirement. Pair-bonding is stronger in geese. We're not talking about love, we're talking about biology. That's how we all got here, daughter.

     Snails do it differently. They're hermaphrodites, and work in threes.

7.

Each Female Body contains a female brain. Handy. Makes things work. Stick pins in it and you get amazing results. Old popular songs. Short circuits. Bad dreams.

     Anyway: each of these brains has two halves. They're joined together by a thick cord; neural pathways flow from one to the other, sparkles of electric information washing to and fro. Like light on waves. Like a conversation. How does a woman know? She listens. She listens in.

20   The male brain, now, that's a different matter. Only a thin connection. Space over here, time over there, music and arithmetic in their own sealed compartments. The right brain doesn't know what the left brain is doing. Good for aiming though, for hitting the target when you pull the trigger. What's the target? Who's the target? Who cares? What matters is hitting it. That's the male brain for you. Objective.

     This is why men are so sad, why they feel so cut off, why they think of themselves as orphans cast adrift, footloose and stringless in the deep void. What void? she asks. What are you talking about? The void of the universe, he says, and she says Oh and looks out the window and tries to get a handle on it, but it's no use, there's too much going on, too many rustlings in the leaves, too many voices, so she says, Would you like a cheese sandwich, a piece of cake, a cup of tea? And he grinds his teeth because she doesn't understand, and wanders off, not just alone but Alone, lost in the dark, lost in the skull, searching for the other half, the twin who could complete him.

Then it comes to him: he's lost the Female Body! Look, it shines in the gloom, far ahead, a vision of wholeness, ripeness, like a giant melon, like an apple, like a metaphor for "breast" in a bad sex novel; it shines like a balloon, like a foggy noon, a watery moon, shimmering in its egg of light.

Catch it. Put it in a pumpkin, in a higl tower, in a compound, in a chamber, in a house, in a room. Quick, stick a leash on it, a lock, a chain, some pain, settle it down, so it can never get away from you again.

■ EXPLORATIONS OF THE TEXT
1. Gloss and annotate each section of the text, noting the details used to portray the female body. What visions of the body do they convey?
2. In section 7, Atwood describes the differences in the male and female brain, body, and experiences. Do you agree with her vision of gender roles?
3. Compare her portrayal of the female body with that of Paz's "My Life with the Wave," Moravia's "The Chase," and Piercy's "Barbie Doll."
4. How does Atwood's segmented essay form develop the portrayal of the female body?

■ THE READING/WRITING CONNECTION
1. Compose a short work entitled "The Male Body," modeled after Atwood's essay.
2. "Think" Topic: Compare and contrast Atwood's concept of the female body and sexuality with the portrayal of male and female roles in thúy's "The Gangster We Are All Looking For" and with McDermott's "Enough."

■ IDEAS FOR WRITING
1. Atwood, Ficera, and McDermott use humor to convey social critiques. What is the impact of this stylistic choice?

KATHERINE ANNE PORTER

Katherine Anne Porter (1890–1980) was born in Indian Creek, Texas. She worked for a time as a newspaperwoman in Chicago and Denver and as a freelance writer in New York. Her first book of stories, Flowering Judas *(1930), was followed by other short story collections and short novels, among them* Noon Wine *(1937),* Pale Horse, Pale Rider *(1939), and* Collected Short Stories *(1965). Porter's only novel,* Ship of Fools, *based on the growth of Nazism, which she had witnessed in Germany, appeared in 1962. Porter's work brought her many honors, including the Pulitzer Prize and the National Book Award.*

1930

THE JILTING OF GRANNY WEATHERALL

She flicked her wrist neatly out of Doctor Harry's pudgy careful fingers and pulled the sheet up to her chin. The brat ought to be in knee breeches. Doctoring around the country with spectacles on his nose! "Get along now, take your schoolbooks and go. There's nothing wrong with me."

Doctor Harry spread a warm paw like a cushion on her forehead where the forked green vein danced and made her eyelids twitch. "Now, now, be a good girl, and we'll have you up in no time."

"That's no way to speak to a woman nearly eighty years old just because she's down. I'd have you respect your elders, young man."

"Well, Missy, excuse me." Doctor Harry patted her cheek. "But I've got to warn you, haven't I? You're a marvel, but you must be careful or you're going to be good and sorry."

5   "Don't tell me what I'm going to be. I'm on my feet now, morally speaking. It's Cornelia. I had to go to bed to get rid of her."

Her bones felt loose, and floated around in her skin, and Doctor Harry floated like a balloon around the foot of the bed. He floated and pulled down his waistcoat and swung his glasses on a cord. "Well, stay where you are, it certainly can't hurt you."

"Get along and doctor your sick," said Granny Weatherall. "Leave a well woman alone. I'll call for you when I want you. . . . Where were you forty years ago when I pulled through milk-leg[1] and double pneumonia? You weren't even born. Don't let Cornelia lead you on," she shouted, because Doctor Harry appeared to float up to the ceiling and out. "I pay my own bills, and I don't throw my money away on nonsense!"

She meant to wave good-by, but it was too much trouble. Her eyes closed of themselves, it was like a dark curtain drawn around the bed. The pillow rose and floated under her, pleasant as a hammock in a light wind. She listened to the leaves rustling outside the window. No, somebody was swishing newspapers: no, Cornelia and Doctor Harry were whispering together. She leaped broad awake, thinking they whispered in her ear.

"She was never like this, *never* like this!" "Well, what can we expect?" "Yes, eighty years old. . . ."

10   Well, and what if she was? She still had ears. It was like Cornelia to whisper around doors. She always kept things secret in such a public way. She was always being tactful and kind. Cornelia was dutiful; that was the trouble with her. Dutiful and good: "So good and dutiful," said Granny, "that I'd like to spank her." She saw herself spanking Cornelia and making a fine job of it.

"What'd you say, Mother?"

Granny felt her face tying up in hard knots.

"Can't a body think, I'd like to know?"

"I thought you might want something."

15   "I do. I want a lot of things. First off, go away and don't whisper."

She lay and drowsed, hoping in her sleep that the children would keep out and let her rest a minute. It had been a long day. Not that she was tired. It was always pleasant to snatch a minute now and then. There was always so much to be done, let me see: tomorrow.

Tomorrow was far away and there was nothing to trouble about. Things were finished somehow when the time came; thank God there was always a little margin over for peace: then a person could spread out the plan of life and tuck in the edges orderly. It was good to have everything clean and folded away, with the hair brushes and tonic bottles sitting straight on the white embroidered linen: the day started without fuss and the pantry shelves laid out with rows of jelly glasses and brown jugs and white stone-china jars with blue whirligigs and words painted on them: coffee, tea, sugar, ginger, cinnamon, allspice: and the bronze clock with the lion on top nicely dusted off. The dust that lion could collect in twenty-four hours! The box in the attic with all those letters tied up, well she'd have to go through that tomorrow. All those letters—George's letters and John's letters and her letters to them both—lying around for the children to find afterwards made her uneasy. Yes, that would be tomorrow's business. No use to let them know how silly she had been once.

---

[1] Swelling of the legs, sometimes occurring in women after childbirth.

While she was rummaging around she found death in her mind and it felt clammy and unfamiliar. She had spent so much time preparing for death there was no need for bringing it up again. Let it take care of itself now. When she was sixty she had felt very old, finished, and went around making farewell trips to see her children and grandchildren, with a secret in her mind: This is the very last of your mother, children! Then she made her will and came down with a long fever. That was all just a notion like a lot of other things, but it was lucky too, for she had once for all got over the idea of dying for a long time. Now she couldn't be worried. She hoped she had better sense now. Her father had lived to be one hundred and two years old and had drunk a noggin of strong hot toddy on his last birthday. He told the reporters it was his daily habit, and he owed his long life to that. He had made quite a scandal and was very pleased about it. She believed she'd just plague Cornelia a little.

"Cornelia! Cornelia!" No footsteps, but a sudden hand on her cheek. "Bless you, where have you been?"

20   "Here, mother."

"Well, Cornelia, I want a noggin of hot toddy."

"Are you cold, darling?"

"I'm chilly, Cornelia. Lying in bed stops the circulation. I must have told you that a thousand times."

Well, she could just hear Cornelia telling her husband that Mother was getting childish and they'd have to humor her. The thing that most annoyed her was that Cornelia thought she was deaf, dumb, and blind. Little hasty glances and tiny gestures tossed around her and over her head saying, "Don't cross her, let her have her way, she's eighty years old," and she sitting there as if she lived in a thin glass cage. Sometimes Granny almost made up her mind to pack up and move back to her own house where nobody could remind her every minute that she was old. Wait, wait, Cornelia, till your own children whisper behind your back!

25   In her day she had kept a better house and had got more work done. She wasn't too old yet for Lydia to be driving eighty miles for advice when one of the children jumped the track, and Jimmy still dropped in and talked things over: "Now, Mammy, you've a good business head, I want to know what you think of this? . . ." Old. Cornelia couldn't change the furniture around without asking. Little things, little things! They had been so sweet when they were little. Granny wished the old days were back again with the children young and everything to be done over. It had been a hard pull, but not too much for her. When she thought of all the food she had cooked, and all the clothes she had cut and sewed, and all the gardens she had made—well, the children showed it. There they were, made out of her, and they couldn't get away from that. Sometimes she wanted to see John again and point to them and say, Well, I didn't do so badly, did I? But that would have to wait. That was for tomorrow. She used to think of him as a man, but now all the children were older than their father, and he would be a child beside her if she saw him now. It seemed strange and there was something wrong in the idea. Why, he couldn't possibly recognize her. She had fenced in a hundred acres once, digging the post holes herself and clamping the wires with just a negro boy to help. That changed a woman. John would be looking for a young woman with the peaked Spanish comb in her hair and the painted fan. Digging post holes changed a woman. Riding country roads in the winter when women had their babies was another thing: sitting up nights with sick horses and sick negroes and sick children and hardly ever losing one. John, I hardly ever lost one of them! John would see that in a minute, that would be something he could understand, she wouldn't have to explain anything!

It made her feel like rolling up her sleeves and putting the whole place to rights again. No matter if Cornelia was determined to be everywhere at once, there were a great many things left undone on this place. She would start tomorrow and do them. It was good to be strong enough for everything, even if all you made melted and changed and slipped under your hands, so that by the time you finished you almost forgot what you were working for. What was it I set out to do? she asked herself intently, but she could not remember. A fog rose over the valley, she saw it marching across the creek swallowing the trees and moving up the hill like an army of ghosts. Soon it would be at the near edge of the orchard, and then it was time to go in and light the lamps. Come in children, don't stay out in the night air.

Lighting the lamps had been beautiful. The children huddled up to her and breathed like little calves waiting at the bars in the twilight. Their eyes followed the match and watched the flame rise and settle in a blue curve, then they moved away from her. The lamp was lit, they didn't have to be scared and hang on to mother any more. Never, never, never more. God, for all my life I thank Thee. Without Thee, my God, I could never have done it. Hail, Mary, full of grace.

I want you to pick all the fruit this year and see that nothing is wasted. There's always someone who can use it. Don't let good things rot for want of using. You waste life when you waste good food. Don't let things get lost. It's bitter to lose things. Now, don't let me get to thinking, not when I am tired and taking a little nap before supper. . . .

The pillow rose about her shoulders and pressed against her heart and the memory was being squeezed out of it: oh, push down the pillow, somebody: it would smother her if she tried to hold it. Such a fresh breeze blowing and such a green day with no threats in it. But he had not come, just the same. What does a woman do when she has put on the white veil and set out the white cake for a man and he doesn't come? She tried to remember. No, I swear he never harmed me but in that. He never harmed me but in that . . . and what if he did? There was the day, the day, but a whirl of dark smoke rose and covered it, crept up and over into the bright field where everything was planted so carefully in orderly rows. That was hell, she knew hell when she saw it. For sixty years she had prayed against remembering him and against losing her soul in the deep pit of hell, and now the two things were mingled in one and the thought of him was a smoky cloud from hell that moved and crept in her head when she had just got rid of Doctor Harry and was trying to rest a minute. Wounded vanity, Ellen, said a sharp voice in the top of her mind. Don't let your wounded vanity get the upper hand of you. Plenty of girls get jilted. You were jilted, weren't you? Then stand up to it. Her eyelids wavered and let in streamers of blue-gray light like tissue paper over her eyes. She must get up and pull the shades down or she'd never sleep. She was in bed again and the shades were not down. How could that happen? Better turn over, hide from the light, sleeping in the light gave you nightmares. "Mother, how do you feel now?" and a stinging wetness on her forehead. But I don't like having my face washed in cold water!

30   Hapsy? George? Lydia? Jimmy? No, Cornelia, and her features were swollen and full of little puddles. "They're coming, darling, they'll all be here soon." Go wash your face, child, you look funny.

Instead of obeying, Cornelia knelt down and put her head on the pillow. She seemed to be talking but there was no sound. "Well, are you tongue-tied? Whose birthday is it? Are you going to give a party?"

Cornelia's mouth moved urgently in strange shapes. "Don't do that, you bother me, daughter."

"Oh, no. Mother, oh, no . . ."

Nonsense. It was strange about children. They disputed your every word. "No what, Cornelia?"

35   "Here's Doctor Harry."

"I won't see that boy again. He just left five minutes ago."

"That was this morning, Mother. It's night now. Here's the nurse."

"This is Doctor Harry, Mrs. Weatherall. I never saw you look so young and happy!"

"Ah, I'll never be young again—but I'd be happy if they'd let me lie in peace and get rested."

40   She thought she spoke up loudly, but no one answered. A warm weight on her forehead, a warm bracelet on her wrist, and a breeze went on whispering, trying to tell her something. A shuffle of leaves in the everlasting hand of God. He blew on them and they danced and rattled. "Mother, don't mind, we're going to give you a little hypodermic." "Look here, daughter, how do ants get in this bed? I saw sugar ants yesterday." Did you send for Hapsy too?

It was Hapsy she really wanted. She had to go a long way back through a great many rooms to find Hapsy standing with a baby on her arm. She seemed to herself to be Hapsy also, and the baby on Hapsy's arm was Hapsy and himself and herself, all at once, and there was no surprise in the meeting. Then Hapsy melted from within and turned flimsy as gray gauze and the baby was a gauzy shadow, and Hapsy came up close and said, "I thought you'd never come," and looked at her very searchingly and said, "You haven't changed a bit!" They leaned forward to kiss, when Cornelia began whispering from a long way off, "Oh, is there anything you want to tell me? Is there anything I can do for you?"

Yes, she had changed her mind after sixty years and she would like to see George. I want you to find George. Find him and be sure to tell him I forgot him. I want him to know I had my husband just the same and my children and my house like any other woman. A good house too and a good husband that I loved and fine children out of him. Better than I hoped for even. Tell him I was given back everything he took away and more. Oh, no, oh, God, no, there was something else besides the house and the man and the children. Oh, surely they were not all? What was it? Something not given back. . . . Her breath crowded down under her ribs and grew into a monstrous frightening shape with cutting edges; it bored up into her head, and the agony was unbelievable: Yes, John, get the Doctor now, no more talk, my time has come.

When this one was born it should be the last. The last. It should have been born first, for it was the one she had truly wanted. Everything came in good time. Nothing left out, left over. She was strong, in three days she would be as well as ever. Better. A woman needed milk in her to have her full health.

"Mother, do you hear me?"

45   "I've been telling you—"

"Mother, Father Connolly's here."

"I went to Holy Communion only last week. Tell him I'm not so sinful as all that."

"Father just wants to speak to you."

He could speak as much as he pleased. It was like him to drop in and inquire about her soul as if it were a teething baby, and then stay on for a cup of tea and a round of cards and gossip. He always had a funny story of some sort, usually about an Irishman who made his little mistakes and confessed them, and the point lay in some absurd thing he would blurt out in the confessional showing his struggles between native piety and original sin. Granny felt easy about her soul. Cornelia, where are your manners? Give Father Connolly a chair. She had her secret comfortable understanding with a few favorite saints who cleared a straight road to God for her. All as surely signed and sealed as the papers for the new Forty Acres. Forever . . . heirs and assigns forever. Since the day the wedding cake was not cut, but thrown out and wasted. The whole bottom dropped out of the world, and there she was blind and sweating with nothing under her feet and the walls falling away. His hand had caught her under the breast, she had not fallen, there was the freshly polished floor with the green rug on it, just as before. He had cursed like a sailor's parrot and said, "I'll kill him for you." Don't lay a hand on him, for my sake leave something to God. "Now, Ellen, you must believe what I tell you. . . ."

50   So there was nothing, nothing to worry about any more, except sometimes in the night one of the children screamed in a nightmare, and they both hustled out shaking and hunting for the matches and calling, "There, wait a minute, here we are!" John, get the doctor now, Hapsy's time has come. But there was Hapsy standing by the bed in a white cap. "Cornelia, tell Hapsy to take off her cap. I can't see her plain."

Her eyes opened very wide and the room stood out like a picture she had seen somewhere. Dark colors with the shadow rising towards the ceiling in long angles. The tall black dresser gleamed with nothing on it but John's picture, enlarged from a little one, with John's eyes very black when they should have been blue. You never saw him, so how do you know how he looked? But the man insisted the copy was perfect, it was very rich and handsome. For a picture, yes, but it's not my husband. The table by the bed had a linen cover and a candle and a crucifix. The light was blue from Cornelia's silk lampshades. No sort of light at all, just frippery. You had to live forty years with kerosene lamps to appreciate honest electricity. She felt very strong and she saw Doctor Harry with a rosy nimbus around him.

"You look like a saint, Doctor Harry, and I vow that's as near as you'll ever come to it."

"She's saying something."

"I heard you, Cornelia. What's all this carrying-on?"

55   "Father Connolly's saying—"

Cornelia's voice staggered and bumped like a cart in a bad road. It rounded corners and turned back again and arrived nowhere. Granny stepped up in the cart very lightly and reached for the reins, but a man sat beside her and she knew him by his hands, driving the cart. She did not look in his face, for she knew without seeing, but looked instead down the road where the trees leaned over and bowed to each other and a thousand birds were singing a Mass. She felt like singing too, but she put her hand in the bosom of her dress and pulled out a rosary, and Father Connolly murmured Latin in a very solemn voice and tickled her feet. My God, will you stop that nonsense? I'm a married woman. What if he did run away and leave me to face the priest by myself? I found another a whole world better. I wouldn't have exchanged my husband for anybody except St. Michael himself, and you may tell him that for me with a thank you in the bargain.

Light flashed on her closed eyelids, and a deep roaring shook her. Cornelia, is that lightning? I hear thunder. There's going to be a storm. Close all the windows. Call the children in . . . "Mother, here we are, all of us." "Is that you, Hapsy?" "Oh, no, I'm Lydia. We drove as fast as we could." Their faces drifted above her, drifted away. The rosary fell out of her hands and Lydia put it back. Jimmy tried to help, their hands fumbled together, and Granny closed two fingers around Jimmy's thumb. Beads wouldn't do, it must be something alive. She was so amazed her thoughts ran round and round. So, my dear Lord, this is my death and I wasn't even thinking about it. My children have come to see me die. But I can't, it's not time. Oh, I always hated surprises. I wanted to give Cornelia the amethyst set—Cornelia, you're to have the amethyst set, but Hapsy's to wear it when she wants, and, Doctor Harry, do shut up. Nobody sent for you. Oh, my dear Lord, do wait a minute. I meant to do something about the Forty Acres, Jimmy doesn't need it and Lydia will later on with that worthless husband of hers. I meant to finish the altar cloth and send six bottles of wine to Sister Borgia for her dyspepsia.[2] I want to send six bottles of wine to Sister Borgia, Father Connolly, now don't let me forget.

Cornelia's voice made short turns and tilted over and crashed. "Oh, Mother, oh, Mother, oh, Mother. . . ."

"I'm not going, Cornelia. I'm taken by surprise. I can't go."

---

[2] Indigestion.

60   You'll see Hapsy again. What about her? "I thought you'd never come." Granny made a long journey outward, looking for Hapsy. What if I don't find her? What then? Her heart sank down and down, there was no bottom to death, she couldn't come to the end of it. The blue light from Cornelia's lampshade drew into a tiny point in the center of her brain, it flickered and winked like an eye, quietly it fluttered and dwindled. Granny lay curled down within herself, amazed and watchful, staring at the point of light that was herself; her body was now only a deeper mass of shadow in an endless darkness and this darkness would curl around the light and swallow it up. God, give a sign!

For the second time there was no sign. Again no bridegroom and the priest in the house. She could not remember any other sorrow because this grief wiped them all away. Oh, no, there's nothing more cruel than this—I'll never forgive it. She stretched herself with a deep breath and blew out the light.

■ **EXPLORATIONS OF THE TEXT**
1. Describe the point of view and voice of Granny Weatherall.
2. What do the interchanges between Granny Weatherall and both Cornelia and the doctor reveal about Granny's nature?
3. Analyze Granny's character as a young wife.
4. On her deathbed, whom does Granny Weatherall remember? What has happened to Hapsy?
5. Examine the symbolism of light, lamplight, shadow, and darkness. How does the symbolism develop themes of the story?
6. Explain the conclusion of the story. Discuss the allusion to the bridegroom. What is the final jilting?
7. Compare Granny Weatherall with the main character in McDermott's "Enough."

■ **THE READING/WRITING CONNECTION**
1. "Think" Topic: Explore the symbolism of Granny's name as a starting point for character analysis.
2. Freewrite and react to the portrayal of Granny Weatherall.
3. Write a letter in the voice of George (a letter taken from the box in the attic).

■ **IDEAS FOR WRITING**
1. Contrast the external (real) and internal (remembered) worlds in the story. How does Porter create a vision of these two worlds?
2. How does first love affect the rest of Granny Weatherall's life? Norma Jean's life in "Shiloh"? Compare the two women's lives.

Stories for Comparison/Contrast: Appetites

T. C. BOYLE (1948–)   **1987**

MODERN LOVE

There was no exchange of body fluids on the first date, and that suited both of us just fine. I picked her up at seven, took her to Mee Grop, where she meticulously separated each sliver of meat from her Phat Thai, watched her down four bottles of Singha at three dollars per, and then gently stroked her balsam-smelling hair while she snoozed through *The Terminator* at the Circle Shopping Center theater. We had a late-night drink at Rigoletto's Pizza Bar (and two slices, plain cheese), and I dropped her off. The moment we pulled up in front of her apartment she had the door open. She turned to me with the long, elegant, mournful face of her Puritan ancestors and held out her hand.

"It's been fun," she said.

"Yes," I said, taking her hand.

She was wearing gloves.

5   "I'll call you," she said,

"Good," I said, giving her my richest smile. "And I'll call you."

On the second date we got acquainted.

"I can't tell you what a strain it was for me the other night," she said, staring down into her chocolate-mocha-fudge sundae. It was early afternoon, we were in Helmut's Olde Tyme Ice Cream Parlor in Mamaroneck, and the sun streamed through the thick frosted windows and lit the place like a convalescent home. The fixtures glowed behind the counter, the brass rail was buffed to a reflective sheen, and everything smelled of disinfectant. We were the only people in the place.

"What do you mean?" I said, my mouth glutinous with melted marshmallow and caramel.

10   "I mean Thai food, the seats in the movie theater, the *ladies' room* in that place for god's sake . . ."

"Thai food?" I wasn't following her. I recalled the maneuver with the strips of pork and the fastidious dissection of the glass noodles. "You're a vegetarian?"

She looked away in exasperation, and then gave me the full, wide-eyed shock of her ice-blue eyes. "Have you seen the Health Department statistics on sanitary conditions in ethnic restaurants?"

I hadn't.

Her eyebrows leapt up. She was earnest. She was lecturing. "These people are refugees. They have—well, different standards. They haven't even been inoculated." I watched her dig the tiny spoon into the recesses of the dish and part her lips for a neat, foursquare morsel of ice cream and fudge.

15   "The illegals, anyway. And that's half of them." She swallowed with an almost imperceptible movement, a shudder, her throat dipping and rising like a gazelle's. "I got drunk from fear," she said. "Blind panic. I couldn't help thinking I'd wind up with hepatitis or dysentery or dengue fever or something."

"Dengue fever?"

"I usually bring a disposable sanitary sheet for public theaters—just think of who might have been in that seat before you, and how many times, and what sort of nasty festering little cultures of this and that there must be in all those ancient dribbles of taffy and Coke and extra-butter popcorn—but I didn't want you to think I was too extreme or anything on the first date, so I didn't. And then the *ladies' room* . . .You don't think I'm overreacting, do you?"

As a matter of fact, I did. Of course I did. I liked Thai food—and sushi and ginger crab and greasy souvlaki at the corner stand too. There was the look of the mad saint in her eye, the obsessive, the mortifier of the flesh, but I didn't care. She was lovely, wilting, clear-eyed, and pure, as cool and matchless as if she'd stepped out of a Pre-Raphaelite painting, and I was in love. Besides, I tended a little that way myself. Hypochondria. Anal retentiveness. The ordered environment and alphabetized books. I was a thirty-three-year-old bachelor, I carried some scars and I read the newspapers—herpes, AIDS, the Asian clap that foiled every antibiotic in the book. I was willing to take it slow. "No," I said, "I don't think you're overreacting at all."

I paused to draw in a breath so deep it might have been a sigh. "I'm sorry," I whispered, giving her a doglike look of contrition. "I didn't know."

20   She reached out then and touched my hand—touched it, skin to skin—and murmured that it was all right, she'd been through worse. "If you want to know," she breathed, "I like places like this."

I glanced around. The place was still empty, but for Helmut, in a blinding white jump-suit and toque, studiously polishing the tile walls. "I know what you mean," I said.

We dated for a month—museums, drives in the country, French and German restaurants, ice-cream emporia, fern bars—before we kissed. And when we kissed, after a showing of *David and Lisa* at a revival house all the way up in Rhinebeck and on a night so cold no run-of-the-mill bacterium or commonplace virus could have survived it, it was the merest brushing of the lips. She was wearing a big-shouldered coat of synthetic fur and a knit hat pulled down over her brow and she hugged my arm as we stepped out of the theater and into the blast of the night. "God," she said, "did you see him when he screamed 'You touched me!'? Wasn't that priceless?" Her eyes were big and she seemed weirdly excited. "Sure," I said, "yeah, it was great," and then she pulled me close and kissed me. I felt the soft flicker of her lips against mine. "I love you," she said, "I think."

A month of dating and one dry fluttering kiss. At this point you might begin to wonder about me, but really, I didn't mind. As I say, I was willing to wait—I had the patience of Sisyphus—and it was enough just to be with her. Why rush things? I thought. This is good, this is charming, like the slow sweet unfolding of the romance in a Frank Capra movie, where sweetness and light always prevail. Sure, she had her idiosyncrasies, but who didn't? Frankly, I'd never been comfortable with the three-drinks-dinner-and-bed sort of thing, the girls who come on like they've been in prison for six years and just got out in time to put on their makeup and jump into the passenger seat of your car. Breda—that was her name, Breda Drumhill, and the very sound and syllabification of it made me melt—was different.

Finally, two weeks after the trek to Rhinebeck, she invited me to her apartment. Cocktails, she said. Dinner. A quiet evening in front of the tube.

25   She lived in Croton, on the ground floor of a restored Victorian, half a mile from the Harmon station, where she caught the train each morning for Manhattan and her job as an editor of *Anthropology Today*. She'd held the job since graduating from Barnard six years earlier (with a double major in Rhetoric and Alien Cultures), and it suited her temperament perfectly. Field anthropologists living among the River Dyak of Borneo or the Kurds of Kurdistan would send her rough and grammatically tortured accounts of their observations and she would whip them into shape for popular consumption. Naturally, filth and exotic disease, as well as outlandish customs and revolting habits, played a leading role in her rewrites. Every other day or so she'd call me from work and in a voice that could barely contain its joy give me the details of some new and horrific disease she'd discovered.

She met me at the door in a silk kimono that featured a plunging neckline and a pair of dragons with intertwined tails. Her hair was pinned up as if she'd just stepped out of the bath and she smelled of Noxzema and pHisoHex. She pecked my cheek, took the bottle of Vouvray I held out in offering, and led me into the front room. "Chagas' disease," she said, grinning wide to show off her perfect, outsized teeth.

"Chagas' disease?" I echoed, not quite knowing what to do with myself. The room was as spare as a monk's cell. Two chairs, a loveseat, and a coffee table, in glass, chrome, and hard black plastic. No plants ("God knows what sort of insects might live on them—and the *dirt*, the dirt has got to be crawling with bacteria, not to mention spiders and worms and things") and no rug ("A breeding ground for fleas and ticks and chiggers").

Still grinning, she steered me to the hard black plastic loveseat and sat down beside me, the Vouvray cradled in her lap. "South America," she whispered, her eyes leaping with excitement. "In the jungle. These bugs—assassin bugs, they're called—isn't that wild? These bugs bite you and then, after they've sucked on you a while, they go potty next to the wound. When you scratch, it gets into your bloodstream, and anywhere from one to twenty years later you get a disease that's like a cross between malaria and AIDS."

"And then you die," I said.

30 "And then you die."

Her voice had turned somber. She wasn't grinning any longer. What could I say? I patted her hand and flashed a smile. "Yum," I said, mugging for her. "What's for dinner?"

She served a cold cream-of-tofu-carrot soup and little lentil-paste sandwiches for an appetizer and a garlic soufflé with biologically controlled vegetables for the entrée. Then it was snifters of cognac, the big-screen TV, and a movie called *The Boy in the Bubble*, about a kid raised in a totally antiseptic environment because he was born without an immune system. No one could touch him. Even the slightest sneeze would have killed him. Breda sniffled through the first half-hour, then pressed my hand and sobbed openly as the boy finally crawled out of the bubble, caught about thirty-seven different diseases, and died before the commercial break. "I've seen this movie six times now," she said, fighting to control her voice, "and it gets to me every time. What a life," she said, waving her snifter at the screen, "what a perfect life. Don't you envy him?"

I didn't envy him. I envied the jade pendant that dangled between her breasts and I told her so.

She might have giggled or gasped or lowered her eyes, but she didn't. She gave me a long slow look, as if she were deciding something, and then she allowed herself to blush, the color suffusing her throat in a delicious mottle of pink and white. "Give me a minute," she said mysteriously, and disappeared into the bathroom.

35 I was electrified. This was it. Finally. After all the avowals, the pressed hands, the little jokes and routines, after all the miles driven, meals consumed, museums paced, and movies watched, we were finally, naturally, gracefully going to come together in the ultimate act of intimacy and love.

I felt hot. There were beads of sweat on my forehead. I didn't know whether to stand or sit. And then the lights dimmed, and there she was at the rheostat.

She was still in her kimono, but her hair was pinned up more severely, wound in a tight coil to the crown of her head, as if she'd girded herself for battle. And she held something in her hand—a slim package, wrapped in plastic. It rustled as she crossed the room.

"When you're in love, you make love," she said, easing down beside me on the rocklike settee, "—it's only natural." She handed me the package. "I don't want to give you the wrong impression," she said, her voice throaty and raw, "just because I'm careful and modest and because there's so much, well, filth in the world, but I have my passionate side too. I do. And I love you, I think."

"Yes," I said, groping for her, the package all but forgotten.

40 We kissed. I rubbed the back of her neck, felt something strange, an odd sag and ripple, as if her skin had suddenly turned to Saran Wrap, and then she had her hand on my chest. "Wait," she breathed, "the, the thing."

I sat up. "Thing?"

The light was dim but I could see the blush invade her face now. She was sweet. Oh, she was sweet, my Little Em'ly, my Victorian princess. "It's Swedish," she said.

I looked down at the package in my lap. It was a clear, skin-like sheet of plastic, folded up in its transparent package like a heavy-duty garbage bag. I held it up to her huge, trembling eyes. A crazy idea darted in and out of my head. No, I thought.

"It's the newest thing," she said, the words coming in a rush, "the safest . . . I mean, nothing could possibly—"

45   My face was hot. "No," I said.

"It's a condom," she said, tears starting up in her eyes, "my doctor got them for me they're . . . they're Swedish." Her face wrinkled up and she began to cry. "It's a condom," she sobbed, crying so hard the kimono fell open and I could see the outline of the thing against the swell of her nipples, "a full-body condom."

I was offended. I admit it. It wasn't so much her obsession with germs and contagion, but that she didn't trust me after all that time. I was clean. Quintessentially clean. I was a man of moderate habits and good health, I changed my underwear and socks daily—sometimes twice a day—and I worked in an office, with clean, crisp, unequivocal numbers, managing my late father's chain of shoe stores (and he died cleanly himself, of a myocardial infarction, at seventy-five). "But Breda," I said, reaching out to console her and brushing her soft, plastic-clad breast in the process, "don't you trust me? Don't you believe in me? Don't you, don't you love me?" I took her by the shoulders, lifted her head, forced her to look me in the eye. "I'm clean," I said. "Trust me."

She looked away. "Do it for me," she said in her smallest voice, "if you really love me."

In the end, I did it. I looked at her, crying, crying for me, and I looked at the thin sheet of plastic clinging to her, and I did it. She helped me into the thing, poked two holes for my nostrils, zipped the plastic zipper up the back, and pulled it tight over my head. It fit like a wetsuit. And the whole thing—the stroking and the tenderness and the gentle yielding—was everything I'd hoped it would be.

50   Almost.

She called me from work the next day. I was playing with sales figures and thinking of her. "Hello," I said, practically cooing into the receiver.

"You've got to hear this." Her voice was giddy with excitement.

"Hey," I said, cutting her off in a passionate whisper, "last night was really special."

"Oh, yes," she said, "yes, last night. It was. And I love you, I do . . ." She paused to draw in her breath. "But listen to this: I just got a piece from a man and his wife living among the Tuareg of Nigeria—these are the people who follow cattle around, picking up the dung for their cooking fires?"

55   I made a small noise of awareness.

"Well, they make their huts of dung too—isn't that wild? And guess what—when times are hard, when the crops fail and the cattle can barely stand up, you know what they eat?"

"Let me guess," I said. "Dung?"

She let out a whoop. "Yes! Yes! Isn't it too much? They *eat* dung!"

I'd been saving one for her, a disease a doctor friend had told me about. "Onchocerciasis," I said. "You know it?"

60   There was a thrill in her voice. "Tell me."

"South America and Africa both. A fly bites you and lays its eggs in your bloodstream and when the eggs hatch, the larvae—these little white worms—migrate to your eyeballs, right underneath the membrane there, so you can see them wriggling around."

There was a silence on the other end of the line.

"Breda?"

"That's sick," she said. "That's really sick."

65   But I thought—? I trailed off. "Sorry," I said.

"Listen," and the edge came back into her voice, "the reason I called is because I love you, I think I love you, and I want you to meet somebody."

"Sure," I said.

"I want you to meet Michael. Michael Maloney."

"Sure. Who's he?"

70   She hesitated, paused just a beat, as if she knew she was going too far. "My doctor," she said.

You have to work at love. You have to bend, make subtle adjustments, sacrifices—love is nothing without sacrifice. I went to Dr. Maloney. Why not? I'd eaten tofu, bantered about leprosy and bilharziasis as if I were immune, and made love in a bag. If it made Breda happy—if it eased the nagging fears that ate at her day and night—then it was worth it.

The doctor's office was in Scarsdale, in his home, a two-tone mock Tudor with a winding drive and oaks as old as my grandfather's Chrysler. He was a young man—late thirties, I guessed—with a red beard, shaved head, and a pair of oversized spectacles in clear plastic frames. He took me right away—the very day I called—and met me at the door himself. "Breda's told me about you," he said, leading me into the floodlit vault of his office. He looked at me appraisingly a moment, murmuring "Yes, yes" into his beard, and then, with the aid of his nurses, Miss Archibald and Miss Slivovitz, put me through a battery of tests that would have embarrassed an astronaut.

First, there were the measurements, including digital joints, maxilla, cranium, penis, and earlobe. Next, the rectal exam, the EEG and urine sample. And then the tests. Stress tests, patch tests, reflex tests, lung-capacity tests (I blew up yellow balloons till they popped, then breathed into a machine the size of a Hammond organ), the X-rays, sperm count, and a closely printed, twenty-four-page questionnaire that included sections on dream analysis, genealogy, and logic and reasoning. He drew blood too, of course—to test vital-organ function and exposure to disease. "We're testing for antibodies to over fifty diseases," he said, eyes dodging behind the walls of his lenses. "You'd be surprised how many people have been infected without even knowing it." I couldn't tell if he was joking or not. On the way out he took my arm and told me he'd have the results in a week.

That week was the happiest of my life. I was with Breda every night, and over the weekend we drove up to Vermont to stay at a hygiene center her cousin had told her about. We dined by candlelight—on real food—and afterward we donned the Saran Wrap suits and made joyous, sanitary love. I wanted more, of course—the touch of skin on skin—but I was fulfilled and I was happy. Go slow, I told myself. All things in time. One night, as we lay entwined in the big white fortress of her bed, I stripped back the hood of the plastic suit and asked her if she'd ever trust me enough to make love in the way of the centuries, raw and unprotected, She twisted free of her own wrapping and looked away, giving me that matchless patrician profile. "Yes," she said, her voice pitched low, "yes, of course. Once the results are in."

75   "Results?"

She turned to me, her eyes searching mine. "Don't tell me you've forgotten?"

I had. Carried away, intense, passionate, brimming with love, I'd forgotten.

"Silly you," she murmured, tracing the line of my lips with a slim, plastic-clad finger, "Does the name Michael Maloney ring a bell?"

And then the roof fell in.

80   I called and there was no answer. I tried her at work and her secretary said she was out. I left messages. She never called back. It was as if we'd never known one another, as if I were a stranger, a door-to-door salesman, a beggar on the street.

I took up a vigil in front of her house. For a solid week I sat in my parked car and watched the door with all the fanatic devotion of a pilgrim at a shrine. Nothing. She neither

came nor went. I rang the phone off the hook, interrogated her friends, haunted the elevator, the hallway, and the reception room at her office. She'd disappeared.

Finally, in desperation, I called her cousin in Larchmont. I'd met her once—she was a
homely, droopy-sweatered, baleful-looking girl who represented everything gone wrong in
the genes that had come to such glorious fruition in Breda—and barely knew what to say to
her. I'd made up a speech, something about how my mother was dying in Phoenix, the
business was on the rocks, I was drinking too much and dwelling on thoughts of suicide,
destruction, and final judgment, and I had to talk to Breda just one more time before the
end, and did she by any chance know where she was? As it turned out, I didn't need the
speech. Breda answered the phone.

"Breda, it's me," I choked. "I've been going crazy looking for you."

Silence.

85   "Breda, what's wrong? Didn't you get my messages?"

Her voice was halting, distant. "I can't see you anymore," she said.

"Can't see me?" I was stunned, hurt, angry. "What do you mean?"

"All those feet," she said.

"Feet?" It took me a minute to realize she was talking about the shoe business. "But I
don't deal with anybody's feet—I work in an office. Like you. With air-conditioning and
sealed windows. I haven't touched a foot since I was sixteen."

90   "Athlete's foot," she said. "Psoriasis. Eczema. Jungle rot."

"What is it? The physical?" My voice cracked with outrage. "Did I flunk the damn physical? Is that it?"

She wouldn't answer me.

A chill went through me. "What did he say? What did the son of a bitch say?"

There was a distant ticking over the line, the pulse of time and space, the gentle sway of
Bell Telephone's hundred million miles of wire.

95   "Listen," I pleaded, "see me one more time, just once—that's all I ask. We'll talk it over.
We could go on a picnic. In the park. We could spread a blanket and, and we could sit on
opposite corners—"

"Lyme disease," she said.

"Lyme disease?"

"Spread by tick bite. They're seething in the grass. You get Bell's palsy, meningitis, the
lining of your brain swells up like dough."

"Rockefeller Center then," I said. "By the fountain."

100   Her voice was dead. "Pigeons," she said. "They're like flying rats."

"Helmut's. We can meet at Helmut's. Please. I love you."

"I'm sorry."

"Breda, please listen to me. We were so close—"

"Yes," she said, "we were close," and I thought of that first night in her apartment, the
boy in the bubble and the Saran Wrap suit, thought of the whole dizzy spectacle of our romance till her voice came down like a hammer on the refrain, "but not that close."

ALICE MCDERMOTT (1953–)   **2002**

ENOUGH

B egin, then, with the ice-cream dishes, carried from the dining room into the narrow
kitchen on a Sunday night, the rest of the family still sitting contented around the
lace-covered table, her father's cigarette smoke just beginning to drift into the air that was

still rich from the smell of the roast, and the roasted potatoes, the turnips and carrots and green beans, the biscuits and the Sunday-only perfume of her mother and sisters. Carried just two dishes at a time because this was the good set, cabbage roses with gold trim. Two bowls at a time, silver spoons inside, carried carefully and carefully placed on the drain-board beside the soapy water where the dinner plates were already soaking, her mother be-ing a great believer in soaking, whether children or dishes or clothes, or souls. Let it soak: the stained blouse, the bruised knee, the sin —sending them into their rooms with a whole rosary to pray, on their knees, and a full hour in which to do it.

She was the youngest child, the third girl with three brothers, and since the boys were excused and the kitchen too small, their mother said, to hold a pair of sisters in it together, this final task, the clearing of the ice-cream dishes, was hers alone. Two at a time, she gath-ered the plates while the others sat, contented, limp, stupefied with food, while she herself felt her stomach straining against the now tight waist of her good dress, felt her legs grown heavy from all she had eaten. Sunday dinner was the only meal they had with their father, who worked two jobs to keep them all fed (that was the way it was put by mother and fa-ther both, without variance), and the bounty of the spread seemed to be their parents' defi-ant proof of the man's long week of labor. They always ate too much at Sunday dinner and they always had dessert. Pie on the first Sunday of the month, then cake, ice cream, stewed fruit—one Sunday after the other and always in that same rotation. Ice cream being the pin-nacle for her, stewed fruit the depths from which she would have to rise, through pie (if mincemeat, hardly a step in the right direction, if blueberry, more encouraging), then cake—always yellow with eggs and dusted with powdered sugar—and then at last, again, ice cream, store-bought or homemade, it hardly made a difference to she who was told once a month that a lady takes a small spoonful, swallows it, and then takes another. She does *not* load the spoon up and then run the stuff in and out of her mouth, studying each time the shape her lips have made ("Look how cross-eyed she gets when she's gazing at it"). A lady doesn't want to show her tongue at the dinner table.

Carefully, she collected the bowls and carried them two by two into the narrow kitchen. She placed one on the drainboard and then lifted the spoon out of the other and, always, with a glance over her shoulder, licked the spoon, front and back, and then raised the delicate bowl to her chin and licked that, too, licked the cabbage roses and the pale spaces in between, long strokes of the tongue from gold-edged rim to gold-edged rim and then another tour around the middle. Place it down softly and pick up the next. The creamy dregs spotting her nose and her cheeks, vanilla or chocolate, peach or strawberry—straw-berry the best because her brothers and a sister always left behind any big pieces of the fruit. Heel of her hand to the sticky tip of her nose (lick that, too) and then back into the dining room again for the next two bowls. Oh, it was good, as good as the whole heaping bowl that had been filled by her father at the head of the table, passed hand to hand by her sisters and brothers, and set before her.

Extrapolate, then, from the girlhood ritual (not to say, of course, that it ended with her girl-hood) to what came to be known as her trouble with the couch. Trouble *on* the couch would have been more accurate, she understood later, when she had a sense of humor about these things that at the time had no humor in them at all. But such precision was the last thing her family would have sought, not in these matters. Her trouble with the couch, it was called. Mother walking into what should have been the empty apartment except that the boiler at the school had broken and the pastor had sent them all home and here she was with the boy from upstairs, side by side on the couch, her two cheeks flushed fever pink and her mouth a bleary, full-blown rose, and her mother would have her know (once the boy had slipped out the door) that she wasn't born yesterday and Glory Be to God fourteen years old was a fine age to be starting this nonsense and wasn't it a good thing that tomorrow was Saturday and the confessionals at church would be fully manned. She'd had a good soaking in recriminations all that evening and well into Saturday afternoon when she finished the rosary the priest himself had prescribed, the end coming only after she returned from the Communion rail on Sunday morning and her mother caught and held her eye. A stewed-fruit Sunday no doubt.

5   Her oldest sister found her next, on the couch with her high-school sweetheart, midafternoon once again—their mother, widowed now, off working in an office—and the first four buttons of her dress undone, the lace bodice of her pale-pink slip all exposed. And then not a month or two later that same sister found her there with another boy, his head in her lap and his hand brushing up and down from her ankle to her knees.

Then there was that Saturday night during the war when her oldest brother, too drunk to go home to his new wife on the next block, let himself in and found her stretched out on the couch in the embrace of some midshipman who, it was clear, despite their quick rearranging of clothes, had his fingers tangled up in her garter. There were buttons undone that time, too, and yet again when she was spied on by the second sister, who never did marry herself but who had an eyeful, let me tell you—a marine, this time, his mouth, to put it delicately, where her corsage should have been and her own hands twisted into his hair as if to hold him there—which led to such a harangue about her trouble with the couch that, finally, even her old mother was moved to say that there was a war on, after all.

Later, her best girlfriend joked that maybe she would want to bring that couch along with her on her wedding night. And joked again, nine months to the week later, when her first son was born, that she didn't seem to need that old couch after all.

There were seven children born altogether, the first followed and each of the others preceded by a miscarriage, so that there were thirteen pregnancies in all, every loss mourned so ferociously that both her husband and her mother advised, each time, not to try again, each birth celebrated with a christening party that packed the small house—made smaller by the oversized floral couch and high-backed chairs and elaborate lamps she had chosen—and spilled out into the narrow yard and breezeway, where there would be dancing, if the weather allowed. A phonograph placed behind the screen in the kitchen window and the records going all through the long afternoon, and on into the evening. You'd see her there after the last guest had gone, the baby on her shoulder and maybe another child on her hip, dancing to something slow and reluctant and melancholy ("One for my baby, and one more for the road"). Lipstick and face powder on the white christening gown that night, as well as the scent of the party itself, cigarette smoke and perfume and the cocktails on her breath.

She was a mother forever rubbing a licked finger to her children's cheeks, scrubbing at the pink traces of her own kisses, forever swelling up again with the next birth. Kids in her lap and her arms wrapped around them even after their limbs had grown longer than her own. The boys, before she knew it, lifting her off her feet when she took them in her arms.

10 She was forty-six when she gave birth to the last, and he was eighteen and on a weekend home from college when he recognized, for the first time in his life, what the sighs and the stirrings coming from his parents' bedroom on that Saturday morning actually signified. (He did a quick calculation of their ages, just to be sure he had it right and then thought, Still?, amazed and a little daunted.) For the rest of the weekend, he imagined ways he might rib them about it, although he couldn't bring himself to come out with anything, knowing full well that even the most good-natured mention of what went on behind their bedroom door could get him the back of his father's hand—or, worse yet, cause a blush to rise from his own cheeks well before he'd managed to raise any kind of glow in theirs.

And there was the Christmas, some years later, when one of them had given their parents a nostalgic collection of forties music and, listening to Bing Crosby sing in his slow, sleepy way, "Kiss me once and kiss me twice (and kiss me once again)," hadn't their mother said, for all assembled to hear, "If you don't turn this off, I'm going to have to find a place to be alone with your father." And hadn't he and his siblings, every one of them well versed by then in matters of love and sex, sat dumbfounded, calculating, no doubt . . . seventy-one, seventy-two . . . still?

Shades of the trouble with the couch, she took her husband's hand in his last days and unbuttoned her blouse and didn't seem to care a bit who saw her, doctor or nurse, son or daughter or grandchild—or older sister who'd never married herself and couldn't help but say, out in the waiting room, "Now, really." She leaned forward, now and again, to whisper to him, even after he was well past hearing, her open lips brushing both the surgical tape that secured the respirator in his mouth and the stubbly gray beard of his cheek.

Growing plump in her widowhood, though she was the first to admit she'd never been what you would call thin, she travelled in busloads of retirees—mostly widows, although there was the occasional man or two—only missing a museum trip or a foliage tour or a luncheon (with a cocktail) at this or that historic site or country inn if a grandchild was in need of minding. What she could do best—her own daughters marvelled at it, who else would have the patience—was sit for hours and hours at a time with a colicky baby over her shoulder or a worn-out toddler on her knee and talk or sing. She told nonsense stories, more sound than substance, or sang every tune in her lifetime repertoire, from Beatles songs to ancient hymns, hypnotizing the children somehow (her sons and daughters were sure of it) into sleep, or sometimes just a dazed contentedness, tucked under her arm or under her chin, seconds, minutes, then hours ticking by, the bars of summer or winter, late-afternoon or early-morning sunlight moving across them, across the length of a room, and neither of them, adult or child, seeming to mark the time gone by.

But take a look in your freezer after she's gone, the daughters reported to one another and to the better-liked sisters-in-law as well. Nearly a full gallon eaten—or all but a final spoonful so she didn't have to put the carton in the trash and give herself away. She's welcome to it, of course, but at her age it's a weight thing. She needs to watch her weight. It's the deceptiveness, too, don't you see. What does she eat when she's alone?

15 Alone, in an apartment now, ever since the night a stranger crept up the breezeway, broke the kitchen window, and made off with her purse, the portable TV, and the boxed silver in the dining room which had been her mother's, she licked chocolate pudding from the back of a spoon, sherbet, gelato, sorbet, ice cream, of course. She scraped the sides of the carton, ran a finger around the rim.

On visits to her out-of-state children she'd get up in the night, stand by the light of the refrigerator, take a few tablespoons from the gallon, or a single ice-cream bar, but always end up going back for more. A daughter-in-law found her one morning, 2 a.m., with the last chocolate/vanilla ice-cream cup and a tiny wooden spoon—leftovers from the grandchild's birthday party she had made the trip specifically to attend—and gave her such a lecture, as she put it when she got home, that you'd think she'd been shooting heroin.

It was the weight that concerned them, said her children, conferring. They were afraid it was the weight that was keeping her these days from those senior trips she used to love, from the winter vacations in Florida she'd once looked forward to. Now that the grandchildren were grown out of the need for a sitter, she should be doing more of those things, not fewer. They solicited a talking-to for their mother from her doctor, who instead reminded them all that she was past eighty and healthy enough and free to do, or not do, what she liked.

They took to stopping by to see her, on lunch hours, or before going to the grocery store, keeping their car keys in their hands, and urging her to turn off the television, to plan something, to do something. Her grandchildren, driving cars now, asked her out to their kinds of places, treated her to frothy lattes topped with whipped cream that would repeat on her the rest of the afternoon and on into the evening, despite bicarbs and antacids, until she brought herself to tell them when they called, "Thank you, dear, but I'm quite content at home."

Peach, strawberry, and reliable vanilla. Rocky road and butter pecan and mint chocolate chip. Looking at ninety and still, still, the last thing she feels at the end of each day is that longing to wrap her legs around him, around someone. The pleasure of the taste, of loading up a spoon and finishing it bit by bit, and then taking another spoonful and another—one kind of pleasure, enhanced by stealth and guilt, when it is someone else's carton, someone else's home in the middle of the night, another kind when it's her own and she carries her bowl, in full light, to the couch before the television in the living room. Forbidden youthful passion and domestic married love, something like that, anyway, if you want to extrapolate. If you want to begin with the ice-cream dishes licked clean by a girl who is now the old woman past all usefulness, closing her eyes at the first taste. If you want to make a metaphor out of her lifelong cravings, something she is not inclined to do. Pleasure is pleasure. A remnant of strawberries, a young man's hands, a newborn in your arms, or your own child's changing face. Your lips to the familiar stubble of your husband's cheek. Your tongue to the last vein of fudge in the empty carton. Pleasure is pleasure. If you have an appetite for it, you'll find there's plenty. Plenty to satisfy you—lick the back of the spoon. Take another, and another. Plenty. Never enough.

■ POETRY ■

WILLIAM SHAKESPEARE

The sonnets of William Shakespeare (1564–1616) are the most prolific, most-loved form of his nondramatic poetry. Numbering 154, the sonnets incorporate images from everyday life, nature, the fine arts, business, law, and, of course, love. The characters and situations of Shakespeare's sonnets signaled a departure from the conventional, more restrictive Petrarchan sonnet tradition and enabled Shakespeare to explore themes of time and death, truth and deceit, beauty and decay and permanence, and love in all of its forms. In this poem, Shakespeare (1564–1616) refers to "The Order of Solemnization of Matrimony" in the Anglican Book of Common Prayer: "I require that if either of you know any impediments why ye may not be lawfully joined together in matrimony, ye do now confess it."

1609

LET ME NOT TO THE MARRIAGE OF TRUE MINDS

Let me not to the marriage of true minds
Admit impediments. Love is not love
Which alters when it alteration finds,
Or bends with the remover to remove.
5 O no, it is an ever-fixèd mark
That look on tempests and is never shaken;

It is the star to every wand'ring bark,[1]
Whose worth's unknown, although his height[2] be taken.
Love's not Time's fool,[3] though rosy lips and cheeks

10   Within his bending sickle's compass come;
Love alters not with his brief hours and weeks,
But bears it out[4] even to the edge of doom.[5]
If this be error and upon me proved,
I never writ, nor no man every loved.

■ EXPLORATIONS OF THE TEXT

1. Why does the persona speak of a "marriage of true minds"?
2. Paraphrase the first two lines. What does the first statement mean?
3. Why does love not "[alter]" or "[bend]"? Why is it "an ever-fixèd mark"?
4. What do the navigational images mean?
5. Look at personification in this sonnet. What is personified? Why? What is the relationship of love and time? Why is love not "Time's fool"?
6. Discuss the final **couplet**. Solve the **paradox**.
7. Consider the view of love in this sonnet. Is the persona convincing in his contention that true love lasts "even to the edge of doom"?

■ THE READING/WRITING CONNECTION

1. Define love or another abstract idea by stating what it is not. Begin with: Love is not. . . .
2. "Think" Topic: Do you agree with the persona's view of true love?

■ IDEAS FOR WRITING

1. Some critics consider this poem to be Shakespeare's greatest sonnet. Evaluate "Let Me Not to the Marriage of True Minds." (See checklist in chapter 10.)
2. Contrast this poem with Blake's "Garden of Love."

WILLIAM SHAKESPEARE   1609

SHALL I COMPARE THEE TO A SUMMER'S DAY?

Shall I compare thee to a summer's day?
Thou art more lovely and more temperate.
Rough winds do shake the darling buds of May,
And summer's lease hath all too short a date.

5   Sometimes too hot the eye of heaven shines,
And often is his gold complexion dimmed;

---

[1] Small ship.
[2] Altitude.
[3] Slave.
[4] Endures.
[5] The Last Judgment.

> And every fair from fair sometime declines,
> By chance, or nature's changing course, untrimmed.
> But thy eternal summer shall not fade,
> 10 Nor lose possession of that fair thou ow'st;[1]
> Nor shall death brag thou wand'rest in his shade,
> When in eternal lines to time thou grow'st.
> So long as men can breathe or eyes can see,
> So long lives this, and this gives life to thee.

▪ EXPLORATIONS OF THE TEXT

1. Why does the speaker consider his loved one more lovely than "a summer's day"? What are the positive qualities of the loved one?
2. List ways in which nature and time change beauty. Interpret lines 3–8.
3. Explain the shift in tone and in subject in line 9. Why does the speaker assure the lover that "eternal summer shall not fade"?
4. What is the relation of art and love? Look carefully at the **couplet** at the end. To what does "this" refer?
5. Which syllables are stressed in the last line? How does this rhythm emphasize the meaning?
6. Identify **metaphors** and **similes** in the sonnet. How do they relate to theme?

▪ THE READING/WRITING CONNECTION

1. Write about the timelessness of art and the fragility of beauty in this sonnet. What do you conclude?
2. Freewrite and create a portrait of a loved one through the use of figurative language (e.g., similes and metaphors).

▪ IDEAS FOR WRITING

1. Explicate this sonnet. (Focus on imagery, figurative language, formal elements.)

JOHN DONNE

John Donne (1571–1631), born into a prominent Catholic family in London during a strongly anti-Catholic time, was educated at Oxford and Cambridge Universities. After holding various jobs, Donne converted to Anglicanism, took Anglican orders in 1615 at the age of forty-two, and preached sermons that rank among the greatest of the seventeenth century. He was considered the greatest of the metaphysical poets, whose works combined passion and reason through highly innovative conceits or elaborate metaphors.

1633

A VALEDICTION FORBIDDING MOURNING

> As virtuous men pass mildly away,
> And whisper to their souls to go,
> Whilst some of their sad friends do say
> The breath goes now, and some say, no:

---

[1] Ownest.

5 So let us melt, and make no noise,
 No tear-floods, nor sigh-tempests move;
'Twere profanation[1] of our joys
 To tell the laity our love.

Moving of th' earth[2] brings harms and fears;
10 Men reckon what it did and meant;
But trepidation of the spheres,[3]
 Though greater far, is innocent.

Dull sublunary lovers' love
 (Whose soul is sense)[4] cannot admit
15 Absence, because it doth remove
 Those things which elemented it.

But we, by a love so much refined
 That ourselves know not what it is,
Inter-assured of the mind,
20 Care less, eyes, lips, and hands to miss.

Our two souls, therefore, which are one,
 Though I must go, endure not yet
A breach, but an expansion,[5]
 Like gold to airy thinness beat.

25 If they be two, they are two so
 As stiff twin compasses are two:[6]
Thy soul, the fixed foot, makes no show
 To move, but doth, if th' other do.

And though it in the center sit,
30 Yet when the other far doth roam,
It leans and harkens after it,
 And grows erect as that comes home.

Such wilt thou be to me, who must,
 Like th' other foot, obliquely run;
35 Thy firmness makes my circle just,[7]
 And makes me end where I begun.

---

[1] The lovers are like priests, and their love is a mystery.

[2] Earthquakes.

[3] Prior to Newton's explanation of the equinoxes, people assumed that stars and planets had circular positions. The observation of irregularities (the result of the wobbling of the earth's axis) was explained by the theory of trepidation, a trembling that occurred in outer spheres around the earth.

[4] A completely physical attraction.

[5] Gold is quite malleable.

[6] Compasses used for drawing circles.

[7] Round.

■ EXPLORATIONS OF THE TEXT

1. To what event does the speaker compare his separation from his beloved in the first stanza?
2. What does he mean by the "trepidation of the spheres"?
3. Why can "dull" lovers not part easily? Why can they not tolerate "absence"?
4. What does the "refined" love of the speaker require? (See stanza 5.)
5. How does the gold imagery in lines 21–24 expand the vision of the lovers' communion?
6. Examine the metaphysical **conceit** comparing the lovers to "twin compasses." Is this extended figure effective?
7. Is the speaker's argument against "mourning" persuasive?

■ THE READING/WRITING CONNECTION

1. Many popular songs attest to the difficulty of saying goodbye, of separation. Freewrite about one of these themes.
2. "Think" Topic: Write a letter to the speaker of the poem, responding to his view of love.

■ IDEAS FOR WRITING

1. Both Shakespeare and Donne refer to "the marriage of true minds," a love more refined than ordinary relationship. Take a position on ideal love or on grand passion.
2. Characterize the speaker in the poem; write about his voice, beliefs, attitudes, intelligence, and capacity for love.
3. Compare Plato's concept of union with Donne's ideas.

ANDREW MARVELL

Andrew Marvell (1621–78) was born in Winchester, England, and educated at Cambridge University. In 1659, he became a member of Parliament and wrote pamphlets and satires on politics. His lyric poetry speaks of love, nature, and God. Most of Marvell's poems were published posthumously in 1681, his satires in 1689. "To His Coy Mistress," Marvell's best-known poem, represents a common literary motif called carpe diem, *which means "seize the day." The poet emphasizes that life is fleeting and urges the person addressed by the speaker—usually a virgin—to enjoy the pleasures of life and of love.*

1681

TO HIS COY MISTRESS

Had we but world enough and time,
This coyness, lady, were no crime.
We would sit down and think which way
To walk, and pass our long love's day.
5 Thou by the Indian Ganges'[1] side
Should'st rubies find; I by the tide

---

[1] River in India, sacred to Hindus.

Of Humber[2] would complain.[3] I would
Love you ten years before the flood,
And you should, if you please, refuse
10 Till the conversion of the Jews.
My vegetable love should grow[4]
Vaster than empires, and more slow.
An hundred years should go to praise
Thine eyes, and on thy forehead gaze,
15 Two hundred to adore each breast,
But thirty thousand to the rest.
An age at least to every part,
And the last age should show your heart.
For, lady, you deserve this state,
20 Nor would I love at lower rate.
    But at my back I always hear
Time's wingèd chariot hurrying near,
And yonder all before us lie
Deserts of vast eternity.
25 Thy beauty shall no more be found,
Nor, in thy marble vault, shall sound
My echoing song; then worms shall try
That long-preserved virginity,
And your quaint honor turn to dust,
30 And into ashes all my lust.
The grave's a fine and private place,
But none, I think, do there embrace.
    Now therefore, while the youthful hue
Sits on thy skin like morning dew[5]
35 And while thy willing soul transpires[6]
At every pore with instant fires,
Now let us sport us while we may;
And now, like amorous birds of prey,
Rather at once our time devour
40 Than languish in his slow-chapped[7] power.
Let us roll all our strength and all
Our sweetness up into one ball
And tear our pleasures with rough strife
Thorough the iron gates of life.
45 Thus, though we cannot make our sun
Stand still, yet we will make him run.

---

[2] Small river that flows through Marvell's hometown of Hull.
[3] Compose love songs.
[4] Slow, unconscious development.
[5] Glow.
[6] Breathes.
[7] Slow-jawed.

■ **EXPLORATIONS OF THE TEXT**

1. In what ways does the speaker suggest the lovers might pass their "long love's day" if only they had time?
2. Why is the lady "coy"?
3. Trace the steps in the argument that begin on lines 1, 21, and 33.
4. What concepts of time and of death does the speaker present? What are the consequences to the beloved?
5. What is the speaker's view of "Time's wingèd chariot"?
6. Why does he suggest that "worms" will "try" her "virginity" and her "quaint honor"? Does the image have sexual connotations?
7. In the conclusion, how does his description of proposed acts of love function? How will the lovers make the sun "run"?
8. How does hyperbole add to the humorous and whimsical tone? Contrast the tone of this poem with "The Dover Bitch," "The Garden of Love," and "The Flea."

■ **THE READING/WRITING CONNECTION**

1. In a mini-essay, write a feminist critique of this poem.
2. In a monologue, persuade someone to change his or her attitude or behavior about a love relationship. Use **hyperbole** in an effort to be persuasive.

■ **IDEAS FOR WRITING**

1. Outline and critique the argument in "To His Coy Mistress."
2. Write a paper on virginity. Consider such questions as abstinence, social and cultural values, peer pressure, and marriage.
3. Read Herrick's "To the Virgins, To Make Much of Time." Would Herrick agree with Marvell?

MATTHEW ARNOLD

Matthew Arnold (1822–88), born at Laliham, Middlesex, England, attended Oxford University. He was professor of poetry at Oxford from 1857 to 1867, then an inspector of schools until 1886. His first volume of poetry, The Strayed Reveller and Other Poems, *appeared in 1849, to be followed by* Empedocles and Other Poems *in 1852. In 1853, Arnold withdrew both volumes from circulation and replaced them with* Poems. *Arnold's prose began to circulate after 1860. The most significant of these works were* Essays in Criticism *and* Culture and Anarchy *(1869). He wrote religious criticism as well as social and political analysis and attempted to improve education, in particular secondary education.*

1851

DOVER BEACH

> The sea is calm tonight,
> The tide is full, the moon lies fair
> Upon the straits; on the French coast the light
> Gleams and is gone; the cliffs of England stand,
> 5 Glimmering and vast, out in the tranquil bay.
> Come to the window, sweet is the night-air!
> Only, from the long line of spray

Where the sea meets the moon-blanched land,
Listen! you hear the grating roar
10 Of pebbles which the waves draw back, and fling,
At their return, up the high strand,
Begin, and cease, and then again begin,
With tremulous cadence slow, and bring
The eternal note of sadness in.[1]

15 Sophocles long ago
Heard it on the Aegean, and it brought
Into his mind the turbid ebb and flow
Of human misery; we
Find also in the sound a thought,
20 Hearing it by this distant northern sea.

The Sea of Faith
Was once, too, at the full, and round earth's shore
Lay like the folds of a bright girdle[2] furled.
But now I only hear
25 Its melancholy, long, withdrawing roar,
Retreating, to the breath
Of the night-wind, down the vast edges drear
And naked shingles[3] of the world.

Ah, love, let us be true
30 To one another! for the world, which seems
To lie before us like a land of dreams,
So various, so beautiful, so new,
Hath really neither joy, nor love, nor light,
Nor certitude, nor peace, nor help for pain;
35 And we are here as on a darkling plain
Swept with confused alarms of struggle and flight,
Where ignorant armies clash by night.

■ EXPLORATIONS OF THE TEXT

1. Compare the initial description with the closing lines (33–37). What is the difference? Are both effective?
2. To whom is the poem addressed? Why?
3. What is "the eternal note of sadness"? What creates the motion and sound of the sea?
4. What is the significance of the "withdrawing roar" of the "Sea of Faith"?
5. What can the lovers do to avoid despair? What can anyone do? Is the speaker hopeful?
6. How would you answer the speaker?
7. Discuss the title and the setting. Is the sadness a modern attitude, or has it always been central to the human condition?

---

[1] A reference to *Antigone* where Sophocles alludes to the tragedies that plague the House of Oedipus as a "mourning tide."

[2] Belt or cord.

[3] Beaches covered with small stones or pebbles.

■ **THE READING/WRITING CONNECTION**
1. In a paragraph, describe the setting and its effect on the persona and on the themes.
2. Write about the sea. Imitate the tone of "Dover Beach."
3. "Think:" Topic: Choose the best lines in the poem, and discuss the word choice, sound, and imagery that make them effective.

■ **IDEAS FOR WRITING**
1. M. H. Abrams has called a poem that uses landscape as a prelude to meditation "the greater romantic lyric." The first part creates the setting; the second section presents the meditation; the third transforms the landscape according to the persona's insights. Analyze "Dover Beach" as a lyric in this mode.
2. Write a meditation in lyric or prose form.
3. Explore the sea as setting, character, and/or theme in Arnold and in Paz.

ANTHONY HECHT (1923–2004)   1968

THE DOVER BITCH

A Criticism of Life
for Andrews Wanning

So there stood Matthew Arnold and this girl
With the cliffs of England crumbling away behind them,
And he said to her, "Try to be true to me,
And I'll do the same for you, for things are bad
5   All over, etc., etc."
Well now, I knew this girl. It's true she had read
Sophocles in a fairly good translation
And caught that bitter allusion to the sea,
But all the time he was talking she had in mind
10 The notion of what his whiskers would feel like
On the back of her neck. She told me later on
That after a while she got to looking out
At the lights across the channel, and really felt sad,
Thinking of all the wine and enormous beds
15 And blandishments in French and the perfumes.
And then she got really angry. To have been brought
All the way down from London, and then be addressed
As a sort of mournful cosmic last resort –
Is really tough on a girl, and she was pretty.
20 Anyway, she watched him pace the room
And finger his watch-chain and seem to sweat a bit,
And then she said one or two unprintable things.
But you mustn't judge her by that. What I mean to say is,
She's really all right. I still see her once in a while
25 And she always treats me right. We have a drink
And I give her a good time, and perhaps it's a year
Before I see her again, but there she is,
Running to fat, but dependable as they come.
And sometimes I bring her a bottle of *Nuit d'Amour.*

■ **EXPLORATIONS OF THE TEXT**

1. How does "The Dover Bitch" comment on "Dover Beach"? Consider the change in point of view, tone, setting, plot, and the characterization of the speaker and the loved one.
2. What views of love does "The Dover Bitch" present?
3. Why do you think that Hecht chose the title? Point to specific images and themes of the work to justify your interpretation.

■ **THE READING/WRITING CONNECTION**

1. Characterize the speaker or his paramour.
2. Write a poem in response to a work in this chapter.

■ **IDEAS FOR WRITING**

1. Compare "Dover Beach" and "The Dover Bitch."

WILLIAM BLAKE

William Blake (1757–1827), born in London, began drawing at an early age; at fourteen, he was apprenticed to an engraver. Many of the poems he wrote during this period were eventually printed in Poetical Sketches *(1783), his first book of poems. In 1789, Blake wrote and engraved his great poetic work,* Songs of Innocence, *which was followed in 1790 by the prose* The Marriage of Heaven and Hell. *In 1804, he undertook the engravings of his final pieces,* Milton *(1808) and* Jerusalem *(1820). He also engraved his work on copper with the poems surrounded by illustrations that he painted, a process he called "illuminated printing."*

1794

THE GARDEN OF LOVE

I went to the Garden of Love,
And I saw what I never had seen:
A Chapel was built in the midst,
Where I used to play on the green.

5 And the gates of this Chapel were shut,
And "Thou shalt not" writ over the door:
So I turned to the Garden of Love
That so many sweet flowers bore;

And I saw it was filled with graves,
10 And tomb-stones where flowers should be;
And Priests in black gowns were walking their rounds,
And binding with briars my joys and desires.

■ **EXPLORATIONS OF THE TEXT**

1. What is the speaker's first sense of love when he "used to play on the green"?
2. What are the obstacles to the experience of love?
3. What are the contradictory sides of love suggested in the images of the "green," "the garden," and "graves"?
4. Analyze the rhyme scheme and the form. How do they create meaning?
5. What critique of organized religion appears in this work?

■ THE READING/WRITING CONNECTION

1. "Love is a time of torment" or "Love is a time of bliss." Comment in a journal entry.
2. Choose a character from one of the short stories in this chapter, and create his/her response to the poem.

■ IDEAS FOR WRITING

1. Compare three views of love presented in three poems in this chapter.
2. Demonstrate the relationship of imagery to theme in this poem.

PABLO NERUDA   Translated from the Spanish by Alastair Reid

Pablo Neruda (1904–73), born in Chile, received an appointment to the consular service in his twenties, and he served in India and in other Asian countries. In 1934, he received a post in Spain, where he became deeply involved in the Spanish Civil War. As a result, his poetry, which had expressed a romantic view of life, came to express concerns both personal and political. Among his works are Selected Poems of Pablo Neruda *(1961),* The Heights of Macchu Picchu *(1966), and* Pablo Neruda: A New Decade *(1969). His* Collected Poems *has been translated into numerous languages, including English. Neruda was awarded the Nobel Prize for Literature in 1971.*

1958

SWEETNESS, ALWAYS

Why such harsh machinery?
Why, to write down the stuff
and people of every day,
must poems be dressed up in gold,
5 in old and fearful stone?

I want verses of felt or feather
which scarcely weigh, mild verses
with the intimacy of beds
where people have loved and dreamed.
10 I want poems stained
by hands and everydayness.

Verses of pastry which melt
into milk and sugar in the mouth,
air and water to drink,
15 the bites and kisses of love.
I long for eatable sonnets,
poems of honey and flour.

Vanity keeps prodding us
to lift ourselves skyward
20 or to make deep and useless
tunnels underground.
So we forget the joyous
love-needs of our bodies.
We forget about pastries.
25 We are not feeding the world.

In Madras[1] a long time since,
I saw a sugary pyramid,
a tower of confectionery—
one level after another,
30 and in the construction, rubies,
and other blushing delights,
medieval and yellow.

Someone dirtied his hands
to cook up so much sweetness.
35 Brother poets from here
and there, from earth and sky,
from Medellín,[2] from Veracruz,[3]
Abyssinia,[4] Antofagasta,[5]
do you know the recipe for honeycombs?
40 Let's forget about all that stone.

Let your poetry fill up
the equinoctial pastry shop
our mouths long to devour—
all the children's mouths
45 and the poor adults' also.
Don't go on without seeing,
relishing, understanding
all these hearts of sugar.
Don't be afraid of sweetness.

50 With us or without us,
sweetness will go on living
and is infinitely alive,
forever being revived,
for it's in a man's mouth,
55 whether he's eating or singing,
that sweetness has its place.

■ **EXPLORATIONS OF THE TEXT**

1. Whom does the speaker address in the first stanza? Why does he believe that "the stuff/and people of every day" need not be written in "gold" or in "stone"?
2. What kind of poetry does the persona want? Why?
3. Discuss the extended metaphor of "sweetness." What is the connection between love and sweetness?
4. What are the barriers to the poetry of sweetness, to the "eatable sonnets"? What does the speaker mean when he declares, "We are not feeding the world"?

---

[1] Industrial city in India.
[2] City in Colombia.
[3] Mexican seaport.
[4] Ethiopia.
[5] Coastal city in Chile.

5. Why does he tell about the incident in Madras? Why does he emphasize the cook's dirty hands?
6. Why does he address "brother poets"? Why does he ask the poets to "forget about all that stone"?
7. Why does the speaker say: "Don't be afraid of sweetness"?
8. The speaker contends that sweetness "is infinitely alive," that "it's in a man's mouth." What does he mean?
9. Contrast Neruda's "sweetness" and Arnold's "sadness." What views of life are implied?

■ THE READING/WRITING CONNECTION
1. In a mini-essay, agree or disagree with the speaker's position.
2. Write a short piece in which images of confections represent love. Do *not* be sentimental; control your material.

■ IDEAS FOR WRITING
1. Answer Neruda's "Sweetness, Always." Argue that poetry does not avoid "sweetness" and that poets are not afraid of it.
2. Why does the persona speak only to male poets? Analyze the attitude toward gender presented in the work.
3. Contrast Arnold's vision of "sadness" and Neruda's view of "sweetness." What philosophical stances are suggested?

PABLO NERUDA (1904–1973)   Translated by W. S. Merwin, 1969

1924

TONIGHT I CAN WRITE . . .

Tonight I can write the saddest lines.

Write, for example, "The night is shattered
and the blue stars shiver in the distance."

The night wind revolves in the sky and sings.

5 Tonight I can write the saddest lines.
I loved her, and sometimes she loved me too.

Through nights like this one I held her in my arms.
I kissed her again and again under the endless sky.

She loved me, sometimes I loved her too.
10 How could one not have loved her great still eyes.

Tonight I can write the saddest lines.
To think that I do not have her. To feel that I have lost her.

To hear the immense night, still more immense without her.
And the verse falls to the soul like dew to the pasture.

15 What does it matter that my love could not keep her.
The night is shattered and she is not with me.

This is all. In the distance someone is singing. In the distance.
My soul is not satisfied that it has lost her.

20 My sight searches for her as though to go to her.
My heart looks for her, and she is not with me.

The same night whitening the same trees.
We, of that time, are no longer the same.

I no longer love her, that's certain, but how I loved her.
My voice tried to find the wind to touch her hearing.

25 Another's. She will be another's. Like my kisses before.
Her voice. Her bright body. Her infinite eyes.

I no longer love her, that's certain, but maybe I love her.
Love is so short, forgetting is so long.

Because through nights like this one I held her in my arms
30 my soul is not satisfied that it has lost her.

Though this be the last pain that she makes me suffer
and these the last verses that I write for her.

■ EXPLORATIONS OF THE TEXT

1. Describe the voice and point of view of the persona.
2. Discuss images of night, darkness, and loss in the poem.
3. How do the two-line stanzas deepen mood and heighten themes of the work?
4. Discuss the meaning of this line, "Love is so short, forgetting is so long."

■ THE READING/WRITING CONNECTION

1. What makes this work a powerful love poem? Respond in a freewrite.
2. In a mini-essay, compare the view of love expressed in this poem with your own feelings and experiences.

■ IDEAS FOR WRITING

1. Contrast the view of love in "Sweetness, Always" with the vision of love in this poem.

LÉOPOLD-SÉDAR SENGHOR   Translated by John Reed and Clive Wake

Léopold-Sédar Senghor (1906–2001) was born in French West Africa, now the republic of Senegal. He fought to gain independence for Senegal and in 1960 was elected president of the new independent republic. He served in that post until 1981. In addition to being a renowned statesman, he has also written many volumes of poetry and collections of essays, including Ethiopiques *(1956),* Prose and Poetry *(1965), and* Poems of a Black Orpheus *(1981). He has been a leading spokesperson for the literary movement of* negritude, *arguing the need for crafting a new African tongue, diction, and form, free of imperialism. In 1983, he was elected to the Academie Francaise.*

1945

NUIT DE SINE

Woman, rest on my brow your balsam hands, your hands gentler than fur.
The tall palmtrees swinging in the nightwind
Hardly rustle. Not even cradlesongs,

The rhythmic silence rocks us.
5   Listen to its song, listen to the beating of our dark blood, listen
To the beating of the dark pulse of Africa in the mist of lost villages.
Now the tired moon sinks towards its bed of slack water,
Now the peals of laughter even fall asleep, and the bards themselves
Dandle their heads like children on the banks of their mothers.
10 Now the feet of the dancers grow heavy and heavy grows the tongue of the
    singers.
This is the hour of the stars and of the night that dreams
And reclines on this hill of clouds, draped in her long gown of milk.
The roofs of the houses gleam gently. What are they telling so confidently to
    the stars?
Inside the hearth is extinguished in the intimacy of bitter and sweet scents.
15 Woman, light the lamp of clear oil, and let the children in bed talk about their
    ancestors, like their parents.
Listen to the voice of the ancients of Elissa.[1] Like we, exiled,
They did not want to die, lest their seminal flood be lost in the sand.
Let me listen in the smoky hut for the shadowy visit of propitious souls,
My head on your breast glowing, like a kuskus[2] ball smoking out of the fire,
20 Let me breathe the smell of our dead, let me contemplate and repeat their
    living voice, let me learn
To live before I sink, deeper than the diver, into the lofty depth of sleep.

■ EXPLORATIONS OF THE TEXT

1. Whom does the speaker address?
2. What mood is created by the setting? How is that mood intrinsic to the development of the vision of love?
3. Why are memories of "the ancestors" invoked? Why does the speaker want to "breathe the smell" of the dead and "repeat their living voices"?
4. Discuss the speaker's final wish, expressed in the last line.
5. Isolate and discuss the effect of the poem's sensory images.
6. Discuss the personification in the poem. What is its impact?
7. What vision of Africa emerges from this poem? Is it solely a poem about love?
8. How is Senghor's vision of passion quite different from the views of Neruda and of Snyder? Why?

■ THE READING/WRITING CONNECTION

1. Create a scene in which you include details from all of the senses to evoke the mood of love.
2. Contrast this poem with Snyder's "The Bath." What do you conclude about the poets' uses of point of view, tone, and imagery?

■ IDEAS FOR WRITING

1. Contrast this poem, written as a dramatic monologue, with "The Love Song of J. Alfred Prufrock." Are they solely about love? How do they differ?

---

[1] A village in Guinea.
[2] A spicy dumpling, cooked in soups.

Gary Snyder

Gary Snyder (1930–   ) was born in San Francisco. He attended the University of California at Berkeley and later studied Zen at a monastery in Kyoto, Japan. Snyder has worked as a seaman, logger, trail crew member, and forester. He first received critical attention for his poetry with Riprap *(1959). Other volumes include* Three Worlds, Three Realms, Six Roads *(1966),* Songs for Gaia *(1979), and* Mountains and Rivers Without End *(1996). Snyder was awarded the Pulitzer Prize for Poetry in 1975 for* Turtle Island. *Influenced by the Beat poets, Snyder is recognized as an environmental writer whose work reflects his interest in social and spiritual subjects.*

1974

THE BATH

Washing Kai in the sauna,
The kerosene lantern set on a box
   outside the ground-level window,
Lights up the edge of the iron stove and the
5   washtub down on the slab
Steaming air and crackle of waterdrops
   brushed by on the pile of rocks on top
He stands in warm water
Soap all over the smooth of his thigh and stomach
10   "Gary don't soap my hair!"
   —his eye-sting fear—
   the soapy hand feeling
   through and around the globes and curves of his body
   up in the crotch,
15 And washing-tickling out the scrotum, little anus,
   his penis curving up and getting hard
   as I pull back skin and try to wash it
Laughing and jumping, flinging arms around,
   I squat all naked too,
20   *is this our body?*

Sweating and panting in the stove-steam hot-stone
   cedar-planking wooden bucket water-splashing
   kerosene lantern-flicker wind-in-the-pines-out
   sierra forest ridges night—
25 Masa comes in, letting fresh cool air
   sweep down from the door
   a deep sweet breath
And she tips him over gripping neatly, one knee down
   her hair falling hiding one whole side of
30   shoulder, breast, and belly,
Washes deftly Kai's head-hair
   as he gets mad and yells—
The body of my lady, the winding valley spine,
   the space between the thighs I reach through,
35   cup her curving vulva arch and hold it from behind,
   a soapy tickle   a hand of grail

The gates of Awe
That open back a turning double-mirror world of
    wombs in wombs, in rings,
40   that start in music,
                    is this our body?
The hidden place of seed
The veins net flow across the ribs, that gathers
    milk and peaks up in a nipple—fits
45   our mouth—
The sucking milk from this our body sends through
    jolts of light; the son, the father,
    sharing mother's joy
That brings a softness to the flower of the awesome
50   open curling lotus gate I cup and kiss
As Kai laughs at his mother's breast he now is weaned
    from, we
    wash each other,
                    this our body

55 Kai's little scrotum up close to his groin,
    the seed still tucked away, that moved from us to him
In flows that lifted with the same joys forces
    as his nursing Masa later,
    playing with her breast,
60 Or me within her,
Or him emerging,
                    this is our body:

Clean, and rinsed, and sweating more, we stretch
    out on the redwood benches hearts all beating
65 Quiet to the simmer of the stove,
    the scent of cedar
And then turn over,
    murmuring gossip of the grasses,
    talking firewood,
70 Wondering how Gen's napping, how to bring him in
    soon wash him too—
These boys who love their mother
    who loves men, who passes on
    her sons to other women;

75 The cloud across the sky. The windy pines.
    the trickle gurgle in the swampy meadow

    this is our body.

Fire inside and boiling water on the stove
We sigh and slide ourselves down from the benches
80   wrap the babies, step outside,

    black night & all the stars.

Pour cold water on the back and thighs
Go in the house—stand steaming by the center fire
Kai scampers on the sheepskin
85 Gen standing hanging on and shouting,

"Bao! bao! bao! bao! bao!"

This is our body. Drawn up crosslegged by the flames
  drinking icy water
   hugging babies, kissing bellies,

90 Laughing on the Great Earth

Come out from the bath.

▪ EXPLORATIONS OF THE TEXT

1. Who is the speaker? Who is Kai? What is the nature of the bath in the first section? Describe the setting.
2. What is the speaker's attitude toward Masa in the second section? What images characterize her?
3. Why does Snyder employ such explicit language about bodies and about love? Are the speaker's values different from other peoples'? from other cultures'?
4. How do images of birth and of sexuality function in section 4?
5. What does the speaker reveal about himself in the following lines: "These boys who love their mother/who loves men, who passes on/her sons to other women"?
6. Discuss the refrain and its variations.
7. Describe the scene after the bath—the narrative, the setting, and the personae. What do you conclude?
8. What does the speaker mean by the last line: "Come out from the bath"? To whom does he speak?
9. The poem presents a simple action—a family taking a bath in a sauna—but what larger themes does it also evoke?

▪ THE READING/WRITING CONNECTION

1. Do you like "The Bath"? Write a reader response journal entry about this poem.
2. Gloss and annotate the poem. Analyze the sexual imagery.

▪ IDEAS FOR WRITING

1. Write an essay exploring concepts of the body. Refer to Snyder, to Neruda, to Boyle, to McDermott, and/or to Woolf.
2. Discuss the spiritual meaning of "The Bath."
3. Argue against the speaker's attitudes. Are they sexist?
4. How does the setting function in developing narrative, personae, and theme?

LIZ ROSENBERG

Liz Rosenberg (1955–   ), educated at Bennington College and Johns Hopkins University, teaches at the State University of New York at Binghamton. She is a frequent reviewer of poetry, prose, and children's books for publications including the Chicago Tribune *and the* Philadelphia Inquirer. *She was a Kellogg Foundation Fellow and in 1976 won the Atlantic First Award for her story "Memory."* The Angel Poems (1984) *was followed by* The Fire Music

(1986), which won the 1985 Agnes Lynch Stewart Award from the University of Pittsburgh Press, and Children of Paradise *(1993). Rosenberg has recently edited a collection of poems,* Roots and Flowers: An Anthology of Poems about Family *(2001), that reflect her ongoing interest in children and family.*

1986

IN THE END, WE ARE ALL LIGHT

I love how old men carry purses for their wives,
those stiff light beige or navy wedge-shaped bags
that match the women's pumps,
with small gold clasps that click open and shut.
5 The men drowse off in medical center waiting rooms,
with bags perched in their laps like big tame birds
too worn to flap away. Within, the wives slowly undress,
put on the thin white robes, consult, come out
and wake the husbands dreaming openmouthed.

10 And when they both rise up
to take their constitutional,
walk up and down the block, her arms are free as air,
his right hand dangles down.

So I, desiring to shed this skin
15 for some light silken one,
will tell my husband, "Here, hold this,"
and watch him amble off into the mall among the shining
cans of motor oil, my leather bag
slung over his massive shoulder bone,
20 so prettily slender-waisted, so forgiving of the ways
we hold each other down, that watching him
I see how men love women, and women men,
and how the burden of the other comes to be
light as a feather blown, more quickly vanishing.

■ EXPLORATIONS OF THE TEXT

1. Discuss the characters of the "old men" and "their wives." Focus on the simile of the "big tame birds" and on the images of hands.
2. What does the husbands' carrying of their wives' "purses" suggest about their relationships?
3. What is unexpected in this portrayal of marriage and love?
4. What does the speaker conclude from her observations?
5. Characterize the tone of the poem. Does it shift? Look carefully at the images of "light." What word play is evident in the use of "light"?
6. Discuss the speaker's revelation at "how the burden of the other comes to be/light as a feather blown, more quickly vanishing."
7. What do you learn about long-lasting marriages? about the state of older people in love?
8. Contrast this marriage with that of the couples in *M Butterfly* and in *Trifles*.

■ THE READING/WRITING CONNECTION

1. Journal Entry: Go to a public place. Observe several couples in love. What does their body language reveal about their relationships?

2. Imagine a young couple whom you know. Describe their lives after fifty years of marriage. Write a scene with them in it.

■ IDEAS FOR WRITING

1. Compare and contrast the state of the newly married with that of people who have been married for many years.
2. Use your first journal entry as the basis of portraits of several couples in love. As Rosenberg does, isolate particular details that evoke visions of the people's characters and relationships.
3. Compare the "old men" and Prufrock.

HUDA NAAMANI   Translated from the Arabic by Huda Naamani and Miriam Cooke

Born in Damascus, Syria, Huda Naamani (1930–   ) earned a law degree from Syrian University and became a court attorney for her uncle's firm. She moved to Beirut, Lebanon, in 1968. She writes regularly for Al-Nahar, *the Beirut newspaper and belongs to the Arab Writers Union. She has published two plays concerning the Lebanese civil war. Her poetry includes* To You *(1970) and* I Was a Point I Was a Circle: An Elegiac Ode *(1975), a collection of patriotic poems about peace.*

1970

I TAKE YOU AN ORANGE

I take you an orange and I squeeze you holding you to my face
Spring you blossom in my eyes
A peacock's tail you gaze at me in the dark
I wear you gipsy garb I fold you a nomad's cloak
5   A flute grass and warmth of sheep flow with you
In the arms of mountains you paint the wreaths of heaven
    And the pains of a goddess

A frame for me I carve you I gild you and
    I fill you with roses
10 A fish I slaughter you, or a sun
    I bake you
    A star
Lightning flashes from your ring
Your eyes hang on my face coffee grounds honeycombs
15 Nigerian songs brush my neck, flocks of geese
Your word is suspended on the back of a door a duck's nose

■ EXPLORATIONS OF THE TEXT

1. What images represent the lover and her beloved? Explain the "orange," the "blossom," the "tail," and the "gipsy garb."
2. Why does the beloved "paint the wreaths of heaven/And the pains of a goddess"? What is the meaning of the opposition?
3. What are the changes in the second stanza? Why does the love become increasingly consuming and violent?

4. In the final stanza, the word of the beloved is negated, "a duck's nose." What has happened?
5. Discuss the ironies of the title.
6. Is this poem a declaration of independence or a call to battle? What is the attitude of the speaker?
7. Are the metaphors powerful? effective? Look at word order.

■ THE READING/WRITING CONNECTION
1. List questions that you have about this work.
2. What surprises do you discover in this poem?

■ IDEAS FOR WRITING
1. Why is "the word" of the beloved the most important issue? Explain the power of language in love.
2. Answer one of your questions.

VIRGINIA HAMILTON ADAIR

Virginia Hamilton Adair (1913–2004) was born in New York City, was educated at Mt. Holyoke College and Radcliffe College, and did postgraduate work at the University of Wisconsin, the University of Washington, and Claremont Graduate School. She was granted an Honorary Doctorate from Mt. Holyoke College. Adair has published three volumes of poetry and has contributed more than seventy poems to well-known periodicals, such as the Atlantic Monthly *and* The New Yorker. *Adair, encouraged by her poet father, composed her first poem at the age of two. Her first book of poetry,* Ants on the Melon *(1996), was published when she was eighty-three and blind; she had previously been afraid that publishing would encourage her to write for someone other than herself. The following poem illustrates the detailed attention to the senses that has won her praise from both literary critics and poetry lovers alike.*

1996

PEELING AN ORANGE

Between you and a bowl of oranges I lie nude
Reading *The World's Illusion* through my tears.
You reach across me hungry for global fruit,
Your bare arm hard, furry and warm on my belly.
5 Your fingers pry the skin of a navel orange
Releasing tiny explosions of spicy oil.
You place peeled disks of gold in a bizarre pattern
On my white body. Rearranging, you bend and bite
The disks to release further their eager scent.
10 I say "Stop, you're tickling," my eyes still on the page.
Aromas of groves arise. Through green leaves
Glow the lofty snows. Through red lips
Your white teeth close on a translucent segment.
Your face over my face eclipses *The World's Illusion.*
15 Pulp and juice pass into my mouth from your mouth.
We laugh against each other's lips. I hold my book
Behind your head, still reading, still weeping a little.
You say "Read on, I'm just an illusion," rolling

Over upon me soothingly, gently moving,
20 Smiling greenly through long lashes. And soon
I say "Don't stop. Don't disillusion me."
Snows melt. The mountain silvers into many a stream.
The oranges are golden worlds in a dark dream.

■ **EXPLORATIONS OF THE TEXT**

1. Characterize the speaker's voice and persona.
2. Discuss the use of the imagery of "peeling an orange." What is the significance of the statement: "You reach across me hungry for global fruit."
3. Analyze the juxtaposition of illusion and reality in the work. How does the imagery develop this theme? Why does the speaker state: "'Don't disillusion me.'" What is the irony?
4. Explore the sensuality of the imagery. What is the impact of the word choice?
5. Compare and contrast the character of the speaker in this work with that in Naamani's "I Take You an Orange" or Soto's "Oranges" (chapter 4). How do their experiences of love differ?

■ **THE READING/WRITING CONNECTION**

1. "Think" Topic: Compare and contrast the treatment of passion in this work with that of Neruda's "Sweetness, Always" or McDermott's "Enough."
2. Collins's "Osso Buco," Neruda's "Sweetness, Always," and this poem use food metaphors to suggest passion. Which poem do you think is most effective? Write a paragraph presenting your evaluation of this technique in one work.
3. Compose a journal entry or a monologue for the beloved in this poem or in Collins's work. Use Hecht's "The Dover Bitch" as a model.
4. Freewrite in response to this question: Why do the poets choose oranges as the central symbol in their love poems?

■ **IDEAS FOR WRITING**

1. Compare and contrast the speakers in Snyder's "The Bath," in Collins's "Osso Buco," and in this work.
2. Write your own poem about passion using food as a symbolic motif, and then explicate your work.

MARGE PIERCY

Marge Piercy (1936–   ) was born in Detroit, Michigan, and was educated at the University of Michigan and Northwestern University. She published her first novel, Going Down Fast, *in 1969. She has written fiction, including* Woman on the Edge of Time *(1976),* Braided Lives *(1982),* He, She, and It *(1992), and* Three Women *(1999), as well as poetry, including* The Moon Is Always Female *(1980),* My Mother's Body *(1985), and* Available Light *(1988). In 1987, she edited* Early Ripening: American Women's Poetry Now. *In 2002 she published a memoir,* Sleeping with Cats. *Piercy, a feminist, writes about the oppression of people in society and desires her work to be, ultimately, "useful."*

1973

BARBIE DOLL

This girlchild was born as usual
and presented dolls that did pee-pee
and miniature GE stoves and irons

and wee lipsticks the color of cherry candy.
5 Then in the magic of puberty, a classmate said:
You have a great big nose and fat legs.

She was healthy, tested intelligent,
possessed strong arms and back,
abundant sexual drive and manual dexterity.
10 She went to and fro apologizing.
Everyone saw a fat nose on thick legs.

She was advised to play coy,
exhorted to come on hearty,
exercise, diet, smile and wheedle.
15 Her good nature wore out
like a fan belt.
So she cut off her nose and legs
and offered them up.

In the casket displayed on satin she lay
20 with the undertaker's cosmetics painted on,
a turned-up putty nose,
dressed in a pink and white nightie.
Doesn't she look pretty? everyone said.
Consummation at last.
25 To every woman a happy ending.

■ EXPLORATIONS OF THE TEXT

1. Analyze the point of view and the persona in the poem. Who do you imagine the speaker to be?
2. What does the symbolism of the Barbie doll suggest about girl's socialization? List all the images that relate to the "girlchild['s]" adolescent body. How does the girl conform to gender stereotypes? How does she not fit the stereotypes? What do you conclude?
3. What advice does the girl receive? Discuss its significance.
4. Analyze and interpret the ironies at the conclusion of the poem. What is the "consummation"?
5. Compare the feminist critique in this work with that of Atwood's "Happy Endings."

■ THE READING/WRITING CONNECTION

1. Write a poem for a G.I. Joe doll. What gender stereotypes prevail for adolescent boys?
2. "Think" Topic: Compare the "happy ending" in this work with that of the "happy endings" in Atwood's story, or create alternate endings for both works. Compare and contrast the endings. What do your new endings suggest about options for young women?
3. Write a letter to your body in the voice of your adolescent or adult persona.

■ IDEAS FOR WRITING

1. Argue Pro or Con: Young girls today are less likely to be taken in by media images of the perfect body
2. Compare and contrast the images of the female body in this work, in Atwood's "The Female Body," in Woolf's "Professions for Women," and/or in Kingston's "No Name Woman."
3. How do the female protagonists in Oates's "Where Are You Going, Where Have You Been?" (chapter 4) and Kingsolver's "Rose-Johnny" (chapter 4) relate to their female bodies?

Cherríe Moraga

Cherríe Moraga (1952–   ) was born in Whittier, California, and educated at San Francisco State University. With Gloria Anzaldúa, she edited This Bridge Called My Back: Writings by Women of Color *(1981). Her first book,* Loving in the War Years, *appeared in 1983. Subsequent works include the plays* Giving up the Ghost *(1986) and* Watsonville/Circle in the Dirt: Some Place Not Here/El Pueblo De East Palo Alto *(2002); a collection of prose and poetry,* The Last Generation *(1993); and a memoir,* Waiting in the Wings: Portrait of a Queer Motherhood *(1998). A self-described Chicana lesbian, Moraga focuses on the situations of all minority communities in her work.*

1983

LOVING IN THE WAR YEARS

Loving you is like living
in the war years.
I *do* think of Bogart & Bergman
not clear who's who
5 but still singin a long smoky
mood into the piano bar
drinks straight up
the last bottle in the house
while bombs split
10 outside, a broken
world.

A world war going on
but you and I still insisting
in each our own heads
15 still thinkin how
if I could only make some contact
with that woman across the keyboard
we size each other up
      yes . . .

20 Loving you has this kind of desperation
to it, like do or die, I
having eyed you from the first
time you made the decision to move
from your stool
25 to live dangerously.

All on the hunch
that in our exchange of photos
of old girlfriends, names
of cities and memories
30 back in the states
the fronts we've manned
out here on the continent
all this on the hunch

that *this* time there'll be
35 no need for resistance.

Loving in the war years
calls for this kind of risking
without a home to call our own
I've got to take you as you come
40 to me, each time like a stranger
all over again. Not knowing
what deaths you saw today
I've got to take you
as you come, battle bruised
45 refusing our enemy, fear.

We're all we've got. You and I

maintaining
this wartime morality
where being queer
50 and female is as rude
as we can get.

■ **EXPLORATIONS OF THE TEXT**

1. Why is "loving" "like living/in the war years"? What "world war" is taking place for the speaker?
2. Why does the poem include references to Bogart and to Bergman?
3. Describe the enemy—"fear."
4. What is the view presented of "being queer/and female"?
5. Contrast the persona's state of being in love with that of Neruda's speaker in "Sweetness, Always."

■ **THE READING/WRITING CONNECTION**

1. "Think" Topic: Do love relationships engender fear and vulnerability? Argue pro or con.

■ **IDEAS FOR WRITING**

1. Compare this love poem with Adrienne Rich's sonnet, "[my mouth hovers across your breasts]" in Poems for Comparison/Contrast: Poems of Passion. How do the speakers' senses of love differ?

Poems for Comparison/Contrast: Love and Loss

BILLY COLLINS (1941–)   **1995**

OSSO BUCO

I love the sound of the bone against the plate
and the fortress-like look of it
lying before me in a moat of risotto,
the meat soft as the leg of an angel
5 who has lived a purely airborne existence.
And best of all, the secret marrow,

the invaded privacy of the animal
prized out with a knife and swallowed down
with cold, exhilarating wine.

10 I am swaying now in the hour after dinner,
a citizen tilted back on his chair,
a creature with a full stomach—
something you don't hear much about in poetry,
that sanctuary of hunger and deprivation.
15 You know: the driving rain, the boots by the door,
small birds searching for berries in winter.

But tonight, the lion of contentment
has placed a warm, heavy paw on my chest,
and I can only close my eyes and listen
20 to the drums of woe throbbing in the distance
and the sound of my wife's laughter
on the telephone in the next room,
the woman who cooked the savory osso buco,
who pointed to show the butcher the ones she wanted.
25 She who talks to her faraway friend
while I linger here at the table
with a hot, companionable cup of tea,
feeling like one of the friendly natives,
a reliable guide, maybe even the chief's favorite son.

30 Somewhere, a man is crawling up a rocky hillside
on bleeding knees and palms, an Irish penitent
carrying the stone of the world in his stomach;
and elsewhere people of all nations stare
at one another across a long, empty table.

35 But here, the candles give off their warm glow,
the same light that Shakespeare and Izaak Walton[1] wrote by,
the light that lit and shadowed the faces of history.
Only now it plays on the blue plates,
the crumpled napkins, the crossed knife and fork.

40 In a while, one of us will go up to bed
and the other one will follow.
Then we will slip below the surface of the night
into miles of water, drifting down and down
to the dark, soundless bottom
45 until the weight of dreams pulls us lower still,
below the shale and layered rock,
beneath the strata of hunger and pleasure,
into the broken bones of the earth itself,
into the marrow of the only place we know.

---

[1] (1593–1638), English writer.

ELIZABETH SPIRES (1952–   )   **2003**

LIKE WATER

It hadn't been three months since he had died
when we sat together in your living room,
a green world going on outside, the June wind
blowing hot and hard, bending each leaf and branch,
5   while inside all was still: a still interior where
three women sat in shadow stirring summer drinks,
the room the same as it had always been,

but changed, his absence palpable. You said,
"I thought I'd gradually miss him less, the way
10   a craving for a cigarette lessens a little after weeks
of going without. It's not like that." You paused,
drawing in a breath. "It's like a thirst that deepens
as each day passes. Like water," you finally said.
"I want him back the way I want a drink of water."

ANNA AKHMATOVA (1889–1966)   Translated from the Russian by D. M. Thomas

1922–24

LOT'S WIFE

And the just man trailed God's messenger,
His huge, light shape devoured the black hill.
But uneasiness shadowed his wife and spoke to her:
"It's not too late, you can look back still[1]

5   At the red towers of Sodom,[2] the place that bore you,
The square in which you sang, the spinning-shed,
At the empty windows of that upper storey
Where children blessed your happy marriage-bed."

Her eyes that were still turning when a bolt
10   Of pain shot through them, were instantly blind;
Her body turned into transparent salt,
And her swift legs were rooted to the ground.

Who mourns one woman in a holocaust?
Surely her death has no significance?
15   Yet in my heart she never will be lost,
She who gave up her life to steal one glance.

---

[1] Lot was the nephew of Abraham. His wife was transformed into a pillar of salt for looking back during their flight from Sodom (Genesis 13–19).

[2] An ancient city destroyed by God because of its wickedness (Genesis 18–19).

T. S. ELIOT (1888–1965)   1910–11

THE LOVE SONG OF J. ALFRED PRUFROCK

S'io credessi che mia risposta fosse
A persona che mai tornasse al mondo,
Questa fiamma staria senza piu scosse.
Ma perciocche giammai di questo fondo
Non torno vivo alcun, s'i'odo il vero,
Senza tema d'infamia ti rispondo.[1]

Let us go then, you and I,
When the evening is spread out against the sky
Like a patient etherized upon a table;
Let us go, through certain half-deserted streets,
5   The muttering retreats
Of restless nights in one-night cheap hotels
And sawdust restaurants with oyster-shells:
Streets that follow like a tedious argument
Of insidious intent
10 To lead you to an overwhelming question . . .
Oh, do not ask, "What is it?"
Let us go and make our visit.

      In the room the women come and go
Talking of Michelangelo.

15   The yellow fog that rubs its back upon the window-panes,
The yellow smoke that rubs its muzzle on the window-panes
Licked its tongue into the corners of the evening,
Lingered upon the pools that stand in drains,
Let fall upon its back the soot that falls from chimneys,
20 Slipped by the terrace, made a sudden leap,
And seeing that it was a soft October night,
Curled once about the house, and fell asleep.

      And indeed there will be time
For the yellow smoke that slides along the street,
25 Rubbing its back upon the window-panes;
There will be time, there will be time
To prepare a face to meet the faces that you meet;
There will be time to murder and create,
And time for all the works and days[2] of hands
30 That lift and drop a question on your plate;

---

[1] The epigraph from Dante's *Inferno,* spoken by Guido da Montefeltro, "If I thought that my reply were to someone who could ever return to the world, this flame would shake no more. But since no one has ever returned alive from this place, if what I hear is true, without fear of infamy I answer you," suggests Prufrock's "damnation" and psychological torment.

[2] Reference to a poem by Hesiod, an eighth-century Greek writer.

Time for you and time for me,
And time yet for a hundred indecisions,
And for a hundred visions and revisions,
Before the taking of a toast and tea.

35   In the room the women come and go
Talking of Michelangelo.

    And indeed there will be time
To wonder, "Do I dare?" and, "Do I dare?"
Time to turn back and descend the stair,
40 With a bald spot in the middle of my hair—
(They will say: "How his hair is growing thin!")
My morning coat, my collar mounting firmly to the chin,
My necktie rich and modest, but asserted by a simple pin—
(They will say: "But how his arms and legs are thin!")
45 Do I dare
Disturb the universe?
In a minute there is time
For decisions and revisions which a minute will reverse.

    For I have known them all already, known them all:
50 Have known the evenings, mornings, afternoons,
I have measured out my life with coffee spoons;
I know the voices dying with a dying fall[3]
Beneath the music from a farther room.
    So how should I presume?

55   And I have known the eyes already, known them all—
The eyes that fix you in a formulated phrase,
And when I am formulated, sprawling on a pin,
When I am pinned and wriggling on the wall,
Then how should I begin
60 To spit out all the butt-ends of my days and ways?
    And how should I presume?

    And I have known the arms already, known them all—
Arms that are braceleted and white and bare
(But in the lamplight, downed with light brown hair!)
65 Is it perfume from a dress
That makes me so digress?
Arms that lie along a table, or wrap about a shawl.
    And should I then presume?
    And how should I begin? . . .

∞

70 Shall I say, I have gone at dusk through narrow streets
And watched the smoke that rises from the pipes
Of lonely men in shirt-sleeves, leaning out of windows? . . .

---

[3] Allusion to Orsino's speech in Shakespeare's *Twelfth Night* (I, i), "That strain again! It had a dying fall."

I should have been a pair of ragged claws
Scuttling across the floors of silent seas.

75 And the afternoon, the evening, sleeps so peacefully!
Smoothed by long fingers,
Asleep . . . tired . . . or it malingers,
Stretched on the floor, here beside you and me.
Should I, after tea and cakes and ices,
80 Have the strength to force the moment to its crisis?
But though I have wept and fasted, wept and prayed,
Though I have seen my head (grown slightly bald) brought in upon a platter,[4]
I am no prophet—and here's no great matter;
I have seen the moment of my greatness flicker,
85 And I have seen the eternal Footman[5] hold my coat, and snicker,
And in short, I was afraid.

And would it have been worth it, after all,
After the cups, the marmalade, the tea,
Among the porcelain, among some talk of you and me,
90 Would it have been worth while,
To have bitten off the matter with a smile,
To have squeezed the universe into a ball
To roll it toward some overwhelming question,
To say: "I am Lazarus,[6] come from the dead,
95 Come back to tell you all, I shall tell you all"—
If one, settling a pillow by her head,
        Should say: "That is not what I meant at all.
        That is not it, at all."

And would it have been worth while, after all
100 Would it have been worth while,
After the sunsets and the dooryards and the sprinkled streets,
After the novels, after the teacups, after the skirts that trail along the floor—
And this, and so much more?—
It is impossible to say just what I mean!
105 But as if a magic lantern threw the nerves in patterns on a screen:
Would it have been worth while
If one, settling a pillow or throwing off a shawl,
And turning toward the window, should say:
        "That is not it at all,
110   That is not what I meant, at all."

No! I am not Prince Hamlet, nor was meant to be;
Am an attendant lord, one that will do

---

[4] Reference to John the Baptist, who was beheaded by King Herod (Matthew 14:3–11).
[5] Figure of death or fate.
[6] Lazarus was raised from the dead by Jesus (John 11:1–44).

To swell a progress,[7] start a scene or two,
Advise the prince; no doubt, an easy tool,
115 Deferential, glad to be of use,
Politic, cautious, and meticulous;
Full of high sentence,[8] but a bit obtuse;
At times, indeed, almost ridiculous—
Almost, at times, the Fool.[9]

120   I grow old . . . I grow old . . .
I shall wear the bottoms of my trousers rolled.

        Shall I part my hair behind? Do I dare to eat a peach?
I shall wear white flannel trousers, and walk upon the beach.
I have heard the mermaids singing, each to each.

125 I do not think that they will sing to me.

        I have seen them riding seaward on the waves
Combing the white hair of the waves blown back
When the wind blows the water white and black.

        We have lingered in the chambers of the sea
130 By sea-girls wreathed with seaweed red and brown
Till human voices wake us, and we drown.

Poems for Comparison/Contrast: Poems of Passion

ROBERT HERRICK (1591–1674)   **1648**

TO THE VIRGINS, TO MAKE MUCH OF TIME

Gather ye rosebuds while ye may,
    Old Time is still a-flying;
And this same flower that smiles today,
    Tomorrow will be dying.

5 The glorious lamp of heaven, the sun,
    The higher he's a-getting
The sooner will his race be run,
    And nearer he's to setting.

That age is best which is the first,
10   When youth and blood are warmer;
But being spent, the worse, and worst
    Times still succeed the former.

---

[7] A royal journey (Elizabethan English).

[8] Ideals, sentiments.

[9] Reference to the stock figure of a Fool, appearing in many dramas (e.g., Shakespeare's *King Lear*).

Then be not coy, but use your time,
    And while ye may, go marry;
15 For having lost but once your prime,
    You may forever tarry.

JOHN DONNE (1572–1631)   **1633**

THE FLEA

Mark[1] but this flea, and mark in this,
How little that which thou deniest me is;
It sucked me first, and now sucks thee,
And in this flea our two bloods mingled be;
5 Thou know'st that this cannot be said[2]
A sin, nor shame, nor loss of maidenhead,
    Yet this enjoys before it woo,[3]
    And pampered swells with one blood made of two,
    And this, alas, is more than we would do.

10 Oh stay, three lives in one flea spare,
Where we almost, yea more than married, are.
This flea is you and I, and this
Our marriage bed and marriage temple is;
Though parents grudge, and you, we are met,
15 And cloistered in these living walls of jet.
    Though use[4] make you apt to kill me
    Let not to that, self-murder added be,
    And sacrilege, three sins in killing three.

Cruel and sudden, hast thou since
20 Purpled thy nail, in blood of innocence?
Wherein could this flea guilty be,
Except in that drop which it sucked from thee?
Yet thou triumph'st and say'st that thou
Find'st not thy self nor me the weaker now;
25   'Tis true, then learn how false fears be;
    Just so much honor, when thou yield'st to me,
    Will waste, as this flea's death took life from thee.

---

[1] Note, look at.
[2] Called.
[3] Marry.
[4] Custom.

GEORGE GORDON, LORD BYRON (1788–1824)   **1814**

SHE WALKS IN BEAUTY

> She walks in beauty, like the night
>   Of cloudless climes and starry skies;
> And all that's best of dark and bright
>   Meet in her aspect and her eyes:
> 5 Thus mellow'd to that tender light
>   Which heaven to gaudy day denies.
>
> One shade the more, one ray the less,
>   Had half impaired the nameless grace
> Which waves in every raven tress,
> 10   Or softly lightens o'er her face;
> Where thoughts serenely sweet express
>   How pure, how dear their dwelling-place.
>
> And on that cheek, and o'er that brow,
>   So soft, so calm, yet eloquent,
> 15 The smiles that win, the tints that glow,
>   But tell of days in goodness spent,
> A mind at peace with all below,
>   A heart whose love is innocent!

JOHN KEATS (1795–1821)   **1819**

LA BELLE DAME SANS MERCI[1]

> O what can ail thee, knight-at-arms,
>   Alone and palely loitering?
> The sedge[2] has withered from the lake,
>   And no birds sing.
>
> 5 O what can ail thee, knight-at-arms,
>   So haggard and so woe-begone?
> The squirrel's granary is full,
>   And the harvest's done.
>
> I see a lily on thy brow,
> 10   With anguish moist and fever dew,
> And on thy cheeks a fading rose
>   Fast withereth too.

---

[1] The title taken from a medieval poem means "The Beautiful Lady Without Mercy."
[2] Grasslike or marshlike vegetation growing in wet places.

I met a lady in the meads,[3]
 Full beautiful—a faery's child,
15 Her hair was long, her foot was light,
 And her eyes were wild.

I made a garland for her head,
 And bracelets too, and fragrant zone;[4]
She looked at me as she did love,
20 And made sweet moan.

I set her on my pacing steed,
 And nothing else saw all day long,
For sidelong would she bend, and sing
 A faery's song.

25 She found me roots of relish sweet,
 And honey wild, and manna dew,
And sure in language strange she said,
 "I love thee true."

She took me to her elfin grot,
30 And there she wept, and sighed full sore,
And there I shut her wild wild eyes
 With kisses four.

And there she lullèd me asleep,
 And there I dreamed—Ah! woe betide!
35 The latest[5] dream I ever dreamed
 On the cold hill side.

I saw pale kings and princes too,
 Pale warriors, death-pale were they all;
They cried—"La Belle Dame sans Merci
40 "Hath thee in thrall!"

I saw their starved lips in the gloam,[6]
 With horrid warning gapèd wide,
And I awoke and found me here,
 On the cold hill's side.

45 And this is why I soujourn here,
 Alone and palely loitering,
Though the sedge has withered from the lake,
 And no birds sing.

---

[3] Meadows.
[4] Belt.
[5] Last.
[6] Twilight.

Elizabeth Barrett Browning (1806–61)   **1850**

HOW DO I LOVE THEE?

How do I love thee? Let me count the ways.
I love thee to the depth and breadth and height
My soul can reach, when feeling out of sight
For the ends of Being and ideal Grace.
5 I love thee to the level of everyday's
Most quiet need, by sun and candle-light.
I love thee freely, as men strive for Right;
I love thee purely, as they turn from Praise.
I love thee with the passion put to use
10 In my old griefs, and with my childhood's faith.
I love thee with a love I seemed to lose
With my lost saints,—I love thee with the breath,
Smiles, tears, of all my life!—and, if God choose,
I shall but love thee better after death.

Christina Rossetti (1830–1894)   **(1859, 1862)**

GOBLIN MARKET

Morning and evening
Maids heard the goblins cry:
'Come buy our orchard fruits,
Come buy, come buy:
5 Apples and quinces,
Lemons and oranges,
Plump unpecked cherries,
Melons and raspberries,
Bloom-down-cheeked peaches,
10 Swart-headed mulberries,
Wild free-born cranberries,
Crab-apples, dewberries,
Pine-apples, blackberries,
Apricots, strawberries;—
15 All ripe together
In summer weather,—
Morns that pass by,
Fair eves that fly;
Come buy, come buy:
20 Our grapes fresh from the vine,
Pomegranates full and fine,
Dates and sharp bullaces,[1]

---

[1] European plum.

Rare pears and greengages,
Damsons and bilberries,
25 Taste them and try:
Currants and gooseberries,
Bright-fire-like barberries,
Figs to fill your mouth,
Citrons from the South,
30 Sweet to tongue and sound to eye;
Come buy, come buy.'

Evening by evening
Among the brookside rushes,
Laura bowed her head to hear,
35 Lizzie veiled her blushes:
Crouching close together
In the cooling weather,
With clasping arms and cautioning lips,
With tingling cheeks and finger tips.
40 'Lie close,' Laura said,
Pricking up her golden head:
'We must not look at goblin men,
We must not buy their fruits:
Who knows upon what soil they fed
45 Their hungry thirsty roots?'
'Come buy,' call the goblins
Hobbling down the glen.
'Oh,' cried Lizzie, 'Laura, Laura,
You should not peep at goblin men.'
50 Lizzie covered up her eyes,
Covered close lest they should look;
Laura reared her glossy head,
And whispered like the restless brook:
'Look, Lizzie, look. Lizzie,
55 Down the glen tramp little men.
One hauls a basket,
One bears a plate,
One lugs a golden dish
Of many pounds weight.
60 How fair the vine must grow
Whose grapes are so luscious;
How warm the wind must blow
Thro' those fruit bushes.'
'No,' said Lizzie: 'No, no, no;
65 Their offers should not charm us,
Their evil gifts would harm us.'
She thrust a dimpled finger
In each ear, shut eyes and ran:
Curious Laura chose to linger
70 Wondering at each merchant man.
One had a cat's face,

One whisked a tail,
One tramped at a rat's pace,
One crawled like a snail,
75 One like a wombat prowled obtuse and furry,
One like a ratel[2] tumbled hurry skurry.
She heard a voice like voice of doves
Cooing all together:
They sounded kind and full of loves
80 In the pleasant weather.

Laura stretched her gleaming neck
Like a rush-imbedded swan,
Like a lily from the beck,
Like a moonlit poplar branch,
85 Like a vessel at the launch
When its last restraint is gone.

Backwards up the mossy glen
Turned and trooped the goblin men,
With their shrill repeated cry,
90 'Come buy, come buy.'
When they reached where Laura was
They stood stock still upon the moss,
Leering at each other,
Brother with queer brother;
95 Signalling each other,
Brother with sly brother.
One set his basket down,
One reared his plate;
One began to weave a crown
100 Of tendrils, leaves and rough nuts brown
(Men sell not such in any town);
One heaved the golden weight
Of dish and fruit to offer her;
'Come buy, come buy,' was still their cry.

105 Laura stared but did not stir,
Longed but had no money:
The whisk-tailed merchant bade her taste
In tones as smooth as honey,
The cat-faced purr'd,
110 The rat-paced spoke a word
Of welcome, and the snail-paced even was heard;
One parrot-voiced and jolly
Cried 'Pretty Goblin' still for 'Pretty Polly;'—
One whistled like a bird.

115 But sweet-tooth Laura spoke in haste;
'Good folk, I have no coin;

---

[2] An African or Asian carnivorous mammal resembling the badger.

To take were to purloin:
I have no copper in my purse,
I have no silver either,
120 And all my gold is on the furze
That shakes in windy weather
Above the rusty heather.'
'You have much gold upon your head,'
They answered all together:
125 'Buy from us with a golden curl.'
She clipped a precious golden lock,
She dropped a tear more rare than pearl,
Then sucked their fruit globes fair or red:
Sweeter than honey from the rock,
130 Stronger than man-rejoicing wine,
Clearer than water flowed that juice;
She never tasted such before,
How should it cloy with length of use?
She sucked and sucked and sucked the more
135 Fruits which that unknown orchard bore;
She sucked until her lips were sore;
Then flung the emptied rinds away
But gathered up one kernel-stone,
And knew not was it night or day
140 As she turned home alone.

Lizzie met her at the gate
Full of wise upbraidings:
'Dear, you should not stay so late,
Twilight is not good for maidens;
145 Should not loiter in the glen
In the haunts of goblin men.
Do you not remember Jeanie,
How she met them in the moonlight,
Took their gifts both choice and many,
150 Ate their fruits and wore their flowers
Plucked from bowers
Where summer ripens at all hours?
But ever in the noonlight
She pined and pined away;
155 Sought them by night and day,
Found them no more but dwindled and grew grey;
Then fell with the first snow,
While to this day no grass will grow
Where she lies low:
160 I planted daisies there a year ago
That never blow.
You should not loiter so.'
'Nay, hush,' said Laura:
'Nay, hush, my sister:
165 I ate and ate my fill,

Yet my mouth waters still;
Tomorrow night I will
Buy more:' and kissed her:
'Have done with sorrow;
170 I'll bring you plums tomorrow
Fresh on their mother twigs,
Cherries worth getting;
You cannot think what figs
My teeth have met in,
175 What melons icy-cold.
Piled on a dish of gold
Too huge for me to hold,
What peaches with a velvet nap,
Pellucid grapes without one seed:
180 Odorous indeed must be the mead
Whereon they grow, and pure the wave they drink
With lilies at the brink,
And sugar-sweet their sap.'

Golden head by golden head,
185 Like two pigeons in one nest
Folded in each other's wings,
They lay down in their curtained bed:
Like two blossoms on one stem,
Like two flakes of new-fall'n snow,
190 Like two wands of ivory
Tipped with gold for awful kings.
Moon and stars gazed in at them,
Wind sang to them lullaby,
Lumbering owls forbore to fly,
195 Not a bat flapped to and fro
Round their rest:
Cheek to cheek and breast to breast
Locked together in one nest.

Early in the morning
200 When the first cock crowed his warning,
Neat like bees, as sweet and busy,
Laura rose with Lizzie:
Fetched in honey, milked the cows,
Aired and set to rights the house,
205 Kneaded cakes of whitest wheat,
Cakes for dainty mouths to eat,
Next churned butter, whipped up cream,
Fed their poultry, sat and sewed;
Talked as modest maidens should:
210 Lizzie with an open heart,
Laura in an absent dream,
One content, one sick in part;
One warbling for the mere bright day's delight,
One longing for the night.

215 At length slow evening came:
    They went with pitchers to the reedy brook;
    Lizzie most placid in her look,
    Laura most like a leaping flame.
    They drew the gurgling water from its deep;
220 Lizzie plucked purple and rich golden flags,[3]
    Then turning homewards said: 'The sunset flushes
    Those furthest loftiest crags;
    Come, Laura, not another maiden lags,
    No wilful squirrel wags,
225 The beasts and birds are fast asleep.'
    But Laura loitered still among the rushes
    And said the bank was steep.

    And said the hour was early still,
    The dew not fall'n, the wind not chill:
230 Listening ever, but not catching
    The customary cry,
    'Come buy, come buy,'
    With its iterated jingle
    Of sugar-baited words:
235 Not for all her watching
    Once discerning even one goblin
    Racing, whisking, tumbling, hobbling;
    Let alone the herds
    That used to tramp along the glen,
240 In groups or single,
    Of brisk fruit-merchant men.
    Till Lizzie urged, 'O Laura, come;
    I hear the fruit-call but I dare not look:
    You should not loiter longer at this brook:
245 Come with me home.
    The stars rise, the moon bends her arc,
    Each glowworm winks her spark,
    Let us get home before the night grows dark:
    For clouds may gather
250 Tho' this is summer weather,
    Put out the lights and drench us thro';
    Then if we lost our way what should we do?'

    Laura turned cold as stone
    To find her sister heard that cry alone,
255 That goblin cry,
    'Come buy our fruits, come buy.'
    Must she then buy no more such dainty fruit?
    Must she no more such succous pasture find,
    Gone deaf and blind?
260 Her tree of life drooped from the root:

---

[3] Lilies.

She said not one word in her heart's sore ache;
But peering thro' the dimness, nought discerning,
Trudged home, her pitcher dripping all the way;
So crept to bed, and lay
265 Silent till Lizzie slept;
Then sat up in a passionate yearning,
And gnashed her teeth for baulked desire, and wept
As if her heart would break.

Day after day, night after night,
270 Laura kept watch in vain
In sullen silence of exceeding pain.
She never caught again the goblin cry:
'Come buy, come buy;'—
She never spied the goblin men
275 Hawking their fruits along the glen:
But when the noon waxed bright
Her hair grew thin and gray;
She dwindled, as the fair full moon doth turn
To swift decay and burn
280 Her fire away.

One day remembering her kernel-stone
She set it by a wall that faced the south;
Dewed it with tears, hoped for a root,
Watched for a waxing shoot,
285 But there came none;
It never saw the sun,
It never felt the trickling moisture run:
While with sunk eyes and faded mouth
She dreamed of melons, as a traveller sees
290 False waves in desert drouth
With shade of leaf-crowned trees,
And burns the thirstier in the sandful breeze.

She no more swept the house,
Tended the fowls or cows,
295 Fetched honey, kneaded cakes of wheat,
Brought water from the brook:
But sat down listless in the chimney-nook
And would not eat.

Tender Lizzie could not bear
300 To watch her sister's cankerous care
Yet not to share.
She night and morning
Caught the goblins' cry:
'Come buy our orchard fruits,
305 Come buy, come buy:'—
Beside the brook, along the glen,
She heard the tramp of goblin men,
The voice and stir

Poor Laura could not hear;
310 Longed to buy fruit to comfort her,
But feared to pay too dear.
She thought of Jeanie in her grave,
Who should have been a bride;
But who for joys brides hope to have
315 Fell sick and died
In her gay prime,
In earliest Winter time,
With the first glazing rime,
With the first snow-fall of crisp Winter time.

320 Till Laura dwindling
Seemed knocking at Death's door:
Then Lizzie weighed no more
Better and worse;
But put a silver penny in her purse,
325 Kissed Laura, crossed the heath with clumps of furze
At twilight, halted by the brook:
And for the first time in her life
Began to listen and look.

Laughed every goblin
330 When they spied her peeping:
Came towards her hobbling,
Flying, running, leaping,
Puffing and blowing,
Chuckling, clapping, crowing,
335 Clucking and gobbling,
Mopping and mowing,
Full of airs and graces,
Pulling wry faces,
Demure grimaces,
340 Cat-like and rat-like,
Ratel- and wombat-like,
Snail-paced in a hurry,
Parrot-voiced and whistler,
Helter skelter, hurry skurry,
345 Chattering like magpies,
Fluttering like pigeons,
Gliding like fishes,—
Hugged her and kissed her,
Squeezed and caressed her:
350 Stretched up their dishes,
Panniers, and plates:
'Look at our apples
Russet and dun,
Bob at our cherries,
355 Bite at our peaches,
Citrons and dates,
Grapes for the asking,

Pears red with basking
Out in the sun,
360 Plums on their twigs;
Pluck them and suck them,
Pomegranates, figs.'—

'Good folk,' said Lizzie,
Mindful of Jeanie:
365 'Give me much and many:'—
Held out her apron,
Tossed them her penny.
'Nay, take a seat with us,
Honour and eat with us,'
370 They answered grinning:
'Our feast is but beginning.
Night yet is early,
Warm and dew-pearly,
Wakeful and starry:
375 Such fruits as these
No man can carry;
Half their bloom would fly,
Half their dew would dry,
Half their flavour would pass by.
380 Sit down and feast with us,
Be welcome guest with us,
Cheer you and rest with us.'—
'Thank you,' said Lizzie: 'But one waits
At home alone for me:
385 So without further parleying,
If you will not sell me any
Of your fruits tho' much and many,
Give me back my silver penny
I tossed you for a fee.'—
390 They began to scratch their pates,
No longer wagging, purring,
But visibly demurring,
Grunting and snarling.
One called her proud,
395 Cross-grained, uncivil;
Their tones waxed loud,
Their looks were evil.
Lashing their tails
They trod and hustled her,
400 Elbowed and jostled her,
Clawed with their nails,
Barking, mewing, hissing, mocking,
Tore her gown and soiled her stocking,
Twitched her hair out by the roots,
405 Stamped upon her tender feet,

Held her hands and squeezed their fruits
Against her mouth to make her eat.
White and golden Lizzie stood,
Like a lily in a flood,—
410 Like a rock of blue-veined stone
Lashed by tides obstreperously,—
Like a beacon left alone
In a hoary roaring sea,
Sending up a golden fire,—
415 Like a fruit-crowned orange-tree
White with blossoms honey-sweet
Sore beset by wasp and bee,—
Like a royal virgin town
Topped with gilded dome and spire
420 Close beleaguered by a fleet
Mad to tug her standard down.

One may lead a horse to water,
Twenty cannot make him drink.
Tho' the goblins cuffed and caught her,
425 Coaxed and fought her,
Bullied and besought her,
Scratched her, pinched her black as ink,
Kicked and knocked her,
Mauled and mocked her,
430 Lizzie uttered not a word;
Would not open lip from lip
Lest they should cram a mouthful in:
But laughed in heart to feel the drip
Of juice that syrupped all her face,
435 And lodged in dimples of her chin,
And streaked her neck which quaked like curd.
At last the evil people
Worn out by her resistance
Flung back her penny, kicked their fruit
440 Along whichever road they took,
Not leaving root or stone or shoot;
Some writhed into the ground,
Some dived into the brook
With ring and ripple,
445 Some scudded on the gale without a sound,
Some vanished in the distance.

In a smart, ache, tingle,
Lizzie went her way;
Knew not was it night or day;
450 Sprang up the bank, tore thro' the furze,
Threaded copse and dingle,
And heard her penny jingle

Bouncing in her purse,
Its bounce was music to her ear.
455 She ran and ran
As if she feared some goblin man
Dogged her with gibe or curse
Or something worse:
But not one goblin skurried after,
460 Nor was she pricked by fear;
The kind heart made her windy-paced
That urged her home quite out of breath with haste
And inward laughter.

She cried 'Laura,' up the garden,
465 'Did you miss me?
Come and kiss me.
Never mind my bruises,
Hug me, kiss me, suck my juices
Squeezed from goblin fruits for you,
470 Goblin pulp and goblin dew.
Eat me, drink me, love me;
Laura, make much of me:
For your sake I have braved the glen
And had to do with goblin merchant men.'

475 Laura started from her chair,
Flung her arms up in the air,
Clutched her hair:
'Lizzie, Lizzie, have you tasted
For my sake the fruit forbidden?
480 Must your light like mine be hidden,
Your young life like mine be wasted,
Undone in mine undoing
And ruined in my ruin,
Thirsty, cankered, goblin-ridden?'—
485 She clung about her sister,
Kissed and kissed and kissed her:
Tears once again
Refreshed her shrunken eyes,
Dropping like rain
490 After long sultry drouth;
Shaking with aguish fear, and pain,
She kissed and kissed her with a hungry mouth.

Her lips began to scorch,[4]

---

[4] A European plant that has a bitter oil, used in absinthe; something bitter.

That juice was wormwood to her tongue,
495 She loathed the feast:
Writhing as one possessed she leaped and sung,
Rent all her robe, and wrung
Her hands in lamentable haste,
And beat her breast.
500 Her locks streamed like the torch
Borne by a racer at full speed,
Or like the mane of horses in their flight,
Or like an eagle when she stems the light
Straight toward the sun,
505 Or like a caged thing freed,
Or like a flying flag when armies run.

Swift fire spread thro' her veins, knocked at her heart,
Met the fire smouldering there
And overbore its lesser flame;
510 She gorged on bitterness without a name:
Ah! fool, to choose such part
Of soul-consuming care!
Sense failed in the mortal strife:
Like the watch-tower of a town
515 Which an earthquake shatters down,
Like a lightning-stricken mast,
Like a wind-uprooted tree
Spun about,
Like a foam-topped waterspout
520 Cast down headlong in the sea,
She fell at last;
Pleasure past and anguish past,
Is it death or is it life?

Life out of death.
525 That night long Lizzie watched by her,
Counted her pulse's flagging stir,
Felt for her breath,
Held water to her lips, and cooled her face
With tears and fanning leaves:
530 But when the first birds chirped about their eaves,
And early reapers plodded to the place
Of golden sheaves,
And dew-wet grass
Bowed in the morning winds so brisk to pass,
535 And new buds with new day
Opened of cup-like lilies on the stream,
Laura awoke as from a dream,
Laughed in the innocent old way,
Hugged Lizzie but not twice or thrice;
540 Her gleaming locks showed not one thread of grey,

Her breath was sweet as May
And light danced in her eyes.

Days, weeks, months, years
Afterwards, when both were wives
545 With children of their own;
Their mother-hearts beset with fears,
Their lives bound up in tender lives;
Laura would call the little ones
And tell them of her early prime,
550 Those pleasant days long gone
Of not-returning time:
Would talk about the haunted glen,
The wicked, quaint fruit-merchant men,
Their fruits like honey to the throat
555 But poison in the blood;
(Men sell not such in any town:)
Would tell them how her sister stood
In deadly peril to do her good,
And win the fiery antidote:
560 Then joining hands to little hands
Would bid them cling together,
'For there is no friend like a sister
In calm or stormy weather;
To cheer one on the tedious way,
565 To fetch one if one goes astray,
To lift one if one totters down,
To strengthen whilst one stands.'

EDNA ST. VINCENT MILLAY (1892–1950)   **1923**

WHAT LIPS MY LIPS HAVE KISSED, AND WHERE, AND WHY

What lips my lips have kissed, and where, and why,
I have forgotten, and what arms have lain
Under my head till morning; but the rain
Is full of ghosts tonight, that tap and sigh
5 Upon the glass and listen for reply,
And in my heart there stirs a quiet pain
For unremembered lads that not again
Will turn to me at midnight with a cry.
Thus in the winter stands the lonely tree,
10 Nor knows what birds have vanished one by one,
Yet knows its boughs more silent than before:
I cannot say what loves have come and gone;
I only know that summer sang in me
A little while, that in me sings no more.

E. E. CUMMINGS[1] (1894–1962)   **1931**

LVII

somewhere i have never travelled,gladly beyond
any experience,your eyes have their silence:
in your most frail gesture are things which enclose me,
or which i cannot touch because they are too near

5   your slightest look easily will unclose me
though i have closed myself as fingers,
you open always petal by petal myself as Spring opens
(touching skilfully,mysteriously)her first rose

or if you wish be to close me,i and
10 my life will shut very beautifully,suddenly,
as when the heart of this flower imagines
the snow carefully everywhere descending;

nothing which we are to perceive in this world equals
the power of your intense fragility:whose texture
15 compels me with the colour of its countries,
rendering death and forever with each breathing

(i do not know what it is about you that closes
and opens;only something in me understands
the voice of your eyes is deeper than all roses)
20 nobody,not even the rain,has such small hands

ADRIENNE RICH (1929–   )   **1986**

MY MOUTH HOVERS ACROSS YOUR BREASTS[1]

My mouth hovers across your breasts
in the short grey winter afternoon
in this bed   we are delicate
and tough   so hot with joy we amaze ourselves
5 tough   and delicate we play rings

---

[1] According to Liveright Publishing, a subsidiary of Norton, and the copyright holder for E. E. Cummings, the convention of setting Cummings' name in lowercase has been made in error. Contrary to popular belief, Cummings never had his name legally changed to an all lowercase spelling, nor did he sign his name in lowercase on letters, legal documents, or paintings. The convention arose when contemporary reviewers noted his habit of writing his poems in all lowercase and began referring to him as "the lowercase mr. cummings" or "mr. lowercase." Cummings, who majored in the classics in college, wrote his poems in lowercase to imitate the ancient Greeks, who did not capitalize the first letter of a sentence. The matter seemed final when Harry Moore wrote the introduction to Norman Friedman's *E. E. Cummings: The Growth of a Writer,* saying that Cummings "had his name put legally into lowercase." There is no record that Cummings ever did so.

[1] This poem is taken from Rich's series, "Contradictions: Tracking Poems."

around each other   our daytime candle burns
with its peculiar light   and if the snow
begins to fall outside   filling the branches
and if the night falls   without announcement
10   these are the pleasures of winter
sudden, wild and delicate   your fingers
exact   my tongue exact at the same moment
stopping to laugh at a joke
my love   hot on your scent   on the cusp of winter

■ DRAMA ■

Susan Glaspell

Susan Glaspell (1882–1948), born in Davenport, Iowa, graduated from Drake University. In 1911, she moved to Greenwich Village; in 1913, she married George Cook; and in 1915, with her husband she founded the Provincetown Players on Cape Cod, Massachusetts. She wrote more than twenty plays, numerous short stories, and novels. In 1930, her drama Alison's House *won the Pulitzer Prize. Glaspell's most famous work is* Trifles *(1916), a one-act play she based on a trial that she covered as a reporter in Iowa and later transformed into a short story, "A Jury of Her Peers."*

1916

TRIFLES

Characters

County Attorney	Hale
Mrs. Peters	Mrs. Hale
Sheriff	

(*Scene: The kitchen in the now abandoned farmhouse of John Wright, a gloomy kitchen, and left without having been put in order—unwashed pans under the sink, a loaf of bread outside the bread-box, a dish-towel on the table—other signs of incompleted work. At the rear the outer door opens and the Sheriff comes in followed by the County Attorney and Hale. The Sheriff and Hale are men in middle life, the County Attorney is a young man; all are much bundled up and go at once to the stove. They are followed by two women— the Sheriff's wife first; she is a slight wiry woman, a thin nervous face. Mrs. Hale is larger and would ordinarily be called more comfortable looking, but she is disturbed now and looks fearfully about as she enters. The women have come in slowly, and stand close to- gether near the door.*)

County Attorney: (*Rubbing his hands.*) This feels good. Come up to the fire, ladies.

Mrs. Peters: (*After taking a step forward.*) I'm not—cold.

Sheriff: (*Unbuttoning his overcoat and stepping away from the stove as if to mark the beginning of official business.*) Now, Mr. Hale, before we move things about, you explain to Mr. Henderson just what you saw when you came here yesterday morning.

County Attorney: By the way, has anything been moved? Are things just as you left them yesterday?

5 **Sheriff:** (*Looking about.*) It's just the same. When it dropped below zero last night I thought I'd better send Frank out this morning to make a fire for us—no use getting pneumonia with a big case on, but I told him not to touch anything except the stove—and you know Frank.

County Attorney: Somebody should have been left here yesterday.

Sheriff: Oh—yesterday. When I had to send Frank to Morris Center for that man who went crazy—I want you to know I had my hands full yesterday. I knew you could get back from Omaha by today and as long as I went over everything here myself—

County Attorney: Well, Mr. Hale, tell just what happened when you came here yesterday morning.

Hale: Harry and I had started to town with a load of potatoes. We came along the road from my place and as I got here I said, "I'm going to see if I can't get John Wright to go in with me on a party telephone." I spoke to Wright about it once before and he put me off, saying folks talked too much anyway, and all he asked was peace and quiet—I guess you know about how much he talked himself; but I thought maybe if I went to the house and talked about it before his wife, though I said to Harry that I didn't know as what his wife wanted made much difference to John—

10 **County Attorney:** Let's talk about that later, Mr. Hale. I do want to talk about that, but tell now just what happened when you got to the house.

Hale: I didn't hear or see anything; I knocked at the door, and still it was all quiet inside. I knew they must be up, it was past eight o'clock. So I knocked again, and I thought I heard somebody say, "Come in." I wasn't sure, I'm not sure yet, but I opened the door—this door (*Indicating the door by which the two women are still standing.*) and there in that rocker—(*Pointing to it.*) sat Mrs. Wright.

(*They all look at the rocker.*)

County Attorney: What—was she doing?

Hale: She was rockin' back and forth. She had her apron in her hand and was kind of—pleating it.

County Attorney: And how did she—look?

15 **Hale:** Well, she looked queer.

County Attorney: How do you mean—queer?

Hale: Well, as if she didn't know what she was going to do next. And kind of done up.

County Attorney: How did she seem to feel about your coming?

Hale: Why, I don't think she minded—one way or other. She didn't pay much attention. I said, "How do, Mrs. Wright, it's cold, ain't it?" And she said, "Is it?"—and went on kind of pleating at her apron. Well, I was surprised; she didn't ask me to come up to the stove, or to set down, but just sat there, not even looking at me, so I said, "I want to see John." And then she—laughed. I guess you would call it a laugh. I thought of Harry and the team outside, so I said a little sharp: "Can't I see John?" "No," she says, kind o' dull like. "Ain't he home?" says I. "Yes," says she, "he's home." "Then why can't I see him?" I asked her, out of patience. "'Cause he's dead," says she. "*Dead?*" says I. She just nodded her head, not getting a bit excited, but rockin' back and forth. "Why—where is he?" says I, not knowing what to say. She just pointed upstairs—like that (*Himself pointing to the room above.*). I got up, with the idea of going up there. I walked from there to here—then I says, "Why, what did he die of?" "He died of a rope round his neck," says she, and just went on pleatin' at her apron. Well, I went out and called Harry. I thought I might—need help. We went upstairs and there he was lying—

20 **County Attorney:** I think I'd rather have you go into that upstairs, where you can point it
     all out. Just go on now with the rest of the story.

Hale: Well, my first thought was to get that rope off. It looked . . . (*Stops, his face
     twitches.*) . . . but Harry, he went up to him, and he said, No, he's dead all right, and
     we'd better not touch anything. So we went back down stairs. She was still sitting that
     same way. "Has anybody been notified?" I asked. "No," says she, unconcerned. "Who
     did this, Mrs. Wright?" said Harry. He said it business-like—and she stopped pleatin'
     of her apron. "I don't know," she says. "You don't *know?*" says Harry. "No," says she.
     "Weren't you sleepin' in the bed with him?" says Harry. "Yes," says she, "but I was on
     the inside." "Somebody slipped a rope round his neck and strangled him and you
     didn't wake up?" says Harry. "I didn't wake up," she said after him. We must 'a looked
     as if we didn't see how that could be, for after a minute she said, "I sleep sound."
     Harry was going to ask her more questions but I said maybe we ought to let her tell
     her story first to the coroner, or the sheriff, so Harry went fast as he could to Rivers'
     place, where there's a telephone.

County Attorney: And what did Mrs. Wright do when she knew that you had gone for the
     coroner?

Hale: She moved from that chair to this one over here (*Pointing to a small chair in the corner.*)
     and just sat there with her hands held together and looking down. I got a feeling that I
     ought to make some conversation, so I said I had come in to see if John wanted to put
     in a telephone, and at that she started to laugh, and then she stopped and looked at
     me—scared. (*The County Attorney, who has had his notebook out, makes a note.*) I dunno,
     maybe it wasn't scared. I wouldn't like to say it was. Soon Harry got back, and then
     Dr. Lloyd came, and you, Mr. Peters, and so I guess that's all I know that you don't.

County Attorney: (*Looking around.*) I guess we'll go upstairs first—and then out to the
     barn and around there. (*To the Sheriff.*) You're convinced that there was nothing impor-
     tant here—nothing that would point to any motive.

25 **Sheriff:** Nothing here but kitchen things.

(*The County Attorney, after again looking around the kitchen, opens the door of a cupboard
closet. He gets up on a chair and looks on a shelf. Pulls his hand away, sticky.*)

County Attorney: Here's a nice mess.

(*The women draw nearer.*)

Mrs. Peters: (*To the other woman.*) Oh, her fruit; it did freeze. (*To the County Attorney.*) She
     worried about that when it turned so cold. She said the fire'd go out and her jars
     would break.

Sheriff: Well, can you beat the women! Held for murder and worryin' about her preserves.

County Attorney: I guess before we're through she may have something more serious than
     preserves to worry about.

30 **Hale:** Well, women are used to worrying over trifles.

(*The two women move a little closer together.*)

County Attorney: (*With the gallantry of a young politician.*) And yet, for all their worries,
     what would we do without the ladies? (*The women do not unbend. He goes to the sink,
     takes a dipperful of water from the pail and pouring it into a basin, washes his hands.
     Starts to wipe them on the roller-towel, turns it for a cleaner place.*) Dirty towels! (*Kicks
     his foot against the pans under the sink.*) Not much of a housekeeper, would you say,
     ladies?

Mrs. Hale: (*Stiffly.*) There's a great deal of work to be done on a farm.

County Attorney: To be sure. And yet *(With a little bow to her.)* I know there are some Dickson county farmhouses which do not have such roller towels.

(He gives it a pull to expose its full length again.)

Mrs. Hale: Those towels get dirty awful quick. Men's hands aren't always as clean as they might be.

35   **County Attorney:** Ah, loyal to your sex, I see. But you and Mrs. Wright were neighbors. I suppose you were friends, too.

Mrs. Hale: *(Shaking her head.)* I've not seen much of her of late years. I've not been in this house—it's more than a year.

County Attorney: And why was that? You didn't like her?

Mrs. Hale: I liked her all well enough. Farmers' wives have their hands full, Mr. Henderson. And then—

County Attorney: Yes—?

40   **Mrs. Hale:** *(Looking about.)* It never seemed a very cheerful place.

County Attorney: No—it's not cheerful. I shouldn't say she had the homemaking instinct.

Mrs. Hale: Well, I don't know as Wright had, either.

County Attorney: You mean that they didn't get on very well?

Mrs. Hale: No, I don't mean anything. But I don't think a place'd be any cheerfuller for John Wright's being in it.

45   **County Attorney:** I'd like to talk more of that a little later. I want to get the lay of things upstairs now.

(He goes to the left, where three steps lead to a stair door.)

Sheriff: I suppose anything Mrs. Peters does'll be all right. She was to take in some clothes for her, you know, and a few little things. We left in such a hurry yesterday.

County Attorney: Yes, but I would like to see what you take, Mrs. Peters, and keep an eye out for anything that might be of use to us.

Mrs. Peters: Yes, Mr. Henderson.

(The women listen to the men's steps on the stairs, then look about the kitchen.)

Mrs. Hale: I'd hate to have men coming into my kitchen, snooping around and criticising.

(She arranges the pans under sink which the County Attorney had shoved out of place.)

50   **Mrs. Peters:** Of course it's no more than their duty.

Mrs. Hale: Duty's all right, but I guess that deputy sheriff that came out to make the fire might have got a little of this on. *(Gives the roller towel a pull.)* Wish I'd thought of that sooner. Seems mean to talk about her for not having things slicked up when she had to come away in such a hurry.

Mrs. Peters: *(Who has gone to a small table in the left rear corner of the room, and lifted one end of a towel that covers a pan.)* She had bread set.

(Stands still.)

Mrs. Hale: *(Eyes fixed on a loaf of bread beside the breadbox, which is on a low shelf at the other side of the room. Moves slowly toward it.)* She was going to put this in there. *(Picks up loaf, then abruptly drops it. In a manner of returning to familiar things.)* It's a shame about her fruit. I wonder if it's all gone. *(Gets up on the chair and looks.)* I think there's some here that's all right, Mrs. Peters. Yes—here; *(Holding it toward the window.)* this is cherries, too. *(Looking again.)* I declare I believe that's the only one. *(Gets down, bottle in her hand. Goes to the sink and wipes it off on the outside.)* She'll feel awful bad after all her hard work in the hot weather. I remember the afternoon I put up my cherries last summer.

(She puts the bottle on the big kitchen table, center of the room. With a sigh, is about to sit down in the rocking-chair. Before she is seated realizes what chair it is; with a slow look at it, steps back. The chair, which she has touched, rocks back and forth.)

Mrs. Peters: Well, I must get those things from the front room closet. *(She goes to the door at the right, but after looking into the other room, steps back.)* You coming with me, Mrs. Hale? You could help me carry them.

(They go in the other room; reappear, Mrs. Peters carrying a dress and skirt, Mrs. Hale following with a pair of shoes.)

55   **Mrs. Peters:** My, it's cold in there.

(She puts the clothes on the big table, and hurries to the stove.)

Mrs. Hale: *(Examining her skirt.)* Wright was close. I think maybe that's why she kept so much to herself. She didn't even belong to the Ladies Aid. I suppose she felt she couldn't do her part, and then you don't enjoy things when you feel shabby. She used to wear pretty clothes and be lively, when she was Minnie Foster, one of the town girls singing in the choir. But that—oh, that was thirty years ago. This all you was to take in?

Mrs. Peters: She said she wanted an apron. Funny thing to want, for there isn't much to get you dirty in jail, goodness knows. But I suppose just to make her feel more natural. She said they was in the top drawer in this cupboard. Yes, here. And then her little shawl that always hung behind the door. *(Opens stair door and looks.)* Yes, here it is.

(Quickly shuts door leading upstairs.)

Mrs. Hale: *(Abruptly moving toward her.)* Mrs. Peters?
Mrs. Peters: Yes, Mrs. Hale?
60   **Mrs. Hale:** Do you think she did it?
Mrs. Peters: *(In a frightened voice.)* Oh, I don't know.
Mrs. Hale: Well, I don't think she did. Asking for an apron and her little shawl. Worrying about her fruit.
Mrs. Peters: *(Starts to speak, glances up, where footsteps are heard in the room above. In a low voice.)* Mr. Peters says it looks bad for her. Mr. Henderson is awful sarcastic in a speech and he'll make fun of her sayin' she didn't wake up.
Mrs. Hale: Well, I guess John Wright didn't wake when they was slipping that rope under his neck.
65   **Mrs. Peters:** No, it's strange. It must have been done awful crafty and still. They say it was such a—funny way to kill a man, rigging it all up like that.
Mrs. Hale: That's just what Mr. Hale said. There was a gun in the house. He says that's what he can't understand.
Mrs. Peters: Mr. Henderson said coming out that what was needed for the case was a motive; something to show anger, or—sudden feeling.
Mrs. Hale: *(Who is standing by the table.)* Well, I don't see any signs of anger around here. *(She puts her hand on the dish towel which lies on the table, stands looking down at table, one half of which is clean, the other half messy.)* It's wiped to here. *(Makes a move as if to finish work, then turns and looks at loaf of bread outside the breadbox. Drops towel. In that voice of coming back to familiar things.)* Wonder how they are finding things upstairs. I hope she had it a little more red-up up there. You know, it seems kind of *sneaking.* Locking her up in town and then coming out here and trying to get her own house to turn against her!

Mrs. Peters: But Mrs. Hale, the law is the law.

70 **Mrs. Hale:** I s'pose 'tis. (*Unbuttoning her coat.*) Better loosen up your things, Mrs. Peters. You won't feel them when you go out.

(*Mrs. Peters takes off her fur tippet, goes to hang it on hook at back of room, stands looking at the under part of the small corner table.*)

Mrs. Peters: She was piecing a quilt.

(*She brings the large sewing basket and they look at the bright pieces.*)

Mrs. Hale: It's log cabin pattern. Pretty, isn't it? I wonder if she was goin' to quilt it or just knot it?

(*Footsteps have been heard coming down the stairs. The Sheriff enters followed by Hale and the County Attorney.*)

Sheriff: They wonder if she was going to quilt it or just knot it!

(*The men laugh; the women look abashed.*)

County Attorney: (*Rubbing his hands over the stove.*) Frank's fire didn't do much up there, did it? Well, let's go out to the barn and get that cleared up.

(*The men go outside.*)

75 **Mrs. Hale:** (*Resentfully.*) I don't know as there's anything so strange, our takin' up our time with little things while we're waiting for them to get the evidence. (*She sits down at the big table smoothing out a block with decision.*) I don't see as it's anything to laugh about.

Mrs. Peters: (*Apologetically.*) Of course they've got awful important things on their minds.

(*Pulls up a chair and joins Mrs. Hale at the table.*)

Mrs. Hale: (*Examining another block.*) Mrs. Peters, look at this one. Here, this is the one she was working on, and look at the sewing! All the rest of it has been so nice and even. And look at this! It's all over the place! Why, it looks as if she didn't know what she was about!

(*After she has said this they look at each other, then start to glance back at the door. After an instant Mrs. Hale has pulled at a knot and ripped the sewing.*)

Mrs. Peters: Oh, what are you doing, Mrs. Hale?

Mrs. Hale: (*Mildly.*) Just pulling out a stitch or two that's not sewed very good. (*Threading a needle.*) Bad sewing always made me fidgety.

80 **Mrs. Peters:** (*Nervously.*) I don't think we ought to touch things.

Mrs. Hale: I'll just finish up this end. (*Suddenly stopping and leaning forward.*) Mrs. Peters?

Mrs. Peters: Yes, Mrs. Hale?

Mrs. Hale: What do you suppose she was so nervous about?

Mrs. Peters: Oh—I don't know. I don't know as she was nervous. I sometimes sew awful queer when I'm just tired. (*Mrs. Hale starts to say something, looks at Mrs. Peters, then goes on sewing.*) Well, I must get these things wrapped up. They may be through sooner than we think. (*Putting apron and other things together.*) I wonder where I can find a piece of paper, and string.

85 **Mrs. Hale:** In that cupboard, maybe.

Mrs. Peters: (*Looking in cupboard.*) Why, here's a bird-cage. (*Holds it up.*) Did she have a bird, Mrs. Hale?

Mrs. Hale: Why, I don't know whether she did or not—I've not been here for so long. There was a man around last year selling canaries cheap, but I don't know as she took one; maybe she did. She used to sing real pretty herself.

Mrs. Peters: *(Glancing around.)* Seems funny to think of a bird here. But she must have had one, or why would she have a cage? I wonder what happened to it.

Mrs. Hale: I s'pose maybe the cat got it.

90　**Mrs. Peters:** No, she didn't have a cat. She's got that feeling some people have about cats—being afraid of them. My cat got in her room and she was real upset and asked me to take it out.

Mrs. Hale: My sister Bessie was like that. Queer, ain't it?

Mrs. Peters: *(Examining the cage.)* Why, look at this door. It's broke. One hinge is pulled apart.

Mrs. Hale: *(Looking too.)* Looks as if someone must have been rough with it.

Mrs. Peters: Why, yes.

(She brings the cage forward and puts it on the table.)

95　**Mrs. Hale:** I wish if they're going to find any evidence they'd be about it. I don't like this place.

Mrs. Peters: But I'm awful glad you came with me, Mrs. Hale. It would be lonesome for me sitting here alone.

Mrs. Hale: It would, wouldn't it? *(Dropping her sewing.)* But I tell you what I do wish, Mrs. Peters. I wish I had come over sometimes when *she* was here. I—*(Looking around the room.)*—wish I had.

Mrs. Peters: But of course you were awful busy, Mrs. Hale—your house and your children.

Mrs. Hale: I could've come. I stayed away because it weren't cheerful—and that's why I ought to have come. I—I've never liked this place. Maybe because it's down in a hollow and you don't see the road. I dunno what it is but it's a lonesome place and always was. I wish I had come over to see Minnie Foster sometimes. I can see now—

(Shakes her head.)

100　**Mrs. Peters:** Well, you mustn't reproach yourself, Mrs. Hale. Somehow we just don't see how it is with other folks until—something comes up.

Mrs. Hale: Not having children makes less work—but it makes a quiet house, and Wright out to work all day, and no company when he did come in. Did you know John Wright, Mrs. Peters?

Mrs. Peters: Not to know him; I've seen him in town. They say he was a good man.

Mrs. Hale: Yes—good; he didn't drink, and kept his word as well as most, I guess, and paid his debts. But he was a hard man, Mrs. Peters. Just to pass the time of day with him—*(Shivers.)* Like a raw wind that gets to the bone. *(Pauses, her eye falling on the cage.)* I should think she would 'a wanted a bird. But what do you suppose went with it?

Mrs. Peters: I don't know, unless it got sick and died.

(She reaches over and swings the broken door, swings it again. Both women watch it.)

105　**Mrs. Hale:** You weren't raised round here, were you? *(Mrs. Peters shakes her head.)* You didn't know—her?

Mrs. Peters: Not till they brought her yesterday.

Mrs. Hale: She—come to think of it, she was kind of like a bird herself—real sweet and pretty, but kind of timid and—fluttery. How—she—did—change. *(Silence; then as if* *struck by a happy thought and relieved to get back to everyday things.*) Tell you what, Mrs. Peters, why don't you take the quilt in with you? It might take up her mind.

Mrs. Peters: Why, I think that's a real nice idea, Mrs. Hale. There couldn't possibly be any objection to it, could there? Now, just what would I take? I wonder if her patches are in here—and her things.

(They look in the sewing basket.)

Mrs. Hale: Here's some red. I expect this has got sewing things in it. *(Brings out a fancy box.)* What a pretty box. Looks like something somebody would give you. Maybe her scissors are in here. *(Opens box. Suddenly puts her hand to her nose.)* Why—*(Mrs. Peters bends nearer, then turns her face away.)* There's something wrapped up in this piece of silk.

110 **Mrs. Peters:** Why, this isn't her scissors.

Mrs. Hale: *(Lifting the silk.)* Oh, Mrs. Peters—it's—

(Mrs. Peters bends closer.)

Mrs. Peters: It's the bird.

Mrs. Hale: *(Jumping up.)* But, Mrs. Peters—look at it! Its neck! Look at its neck! It's all—other side *to.*

Mrs. Peters: Somebody—wrung—its—neck.

(Their eyes meet. A look of growing comprehension, of horror. Steps are heard outside. Mrs. Hale slips box under quilt pieces, and sinks into her chair. Enter Sheriff and County Attorney. Mrs. Peters rises.)

115 **County Attorney:** *(As one turning from serious things to little pleasantries.)* Well, ladies, have you decided whether she was going to quilt it or knot it?

Mrs. Peters: We think she was going to—knot it.

County Attorney: Well, that's interesting, I'm sure. *(Seeing the bird-cage.)* Has the bird flown?

Mrs. Hale: *(Putting more quilt pieces over the box.)* We think the—cat got it.

County Attorney: *(Preoccupied.)* Is there a cat?

(Mrs. Hale glances in a quick covert way at Mrs. Peters.)

120 **Mrs. Peters:** Well, not *now.* They're superstitious, you know. They leave.

County Attorney: *(To Sheriff Peters, continuing an interrupted conversation.)* No sign at all of anyone having come from the outside. Their own rope. Now let's go up again and go over it piece by piece. *(They start upstairs.)* It would have to have been someone who knew just the—

(Mrs. Peters sits down. The two women sit there not looking at one another, but as if peering into something and at the same time holding back. When they talk now it is in the manner of feeling their way over strange ground, as if afraid of what they are saying, but as if they can not help saying it.)

Mrs. Hale: She liked the bird. She was going to bury it in that pretty box.

Mrs. Peters: *(In a whisper.)* When I was a girl—my kitten—there was a boy took a hatchet, and before my eyes—and before I could get there—*(Covers her face an instant.)* If they hadn't held me back I would have—*(Catches herself, looks upstairs where steps are heard, falters weakly.)*—hurt him.

Mrs. Hale: *(With a slow look around her.)* I wonder how it would seem never to have had any children around. *(Pause.)* No, Wright wouldn't like the bird—a thing that sang. She used to sing. He killed that, too.

125 **Mrs. Peters:** (*Moving uneasily.*) We don't know who killed the bird.
Mrs. Hale: I knew John Wright.
Mrs. Peters: It was an awful thing was done in this house that night, Mrs. Hale. Killing a man while he slept, slipping a rope around his neck that choked the life out of him.
Mrs. Hale: His neck. Choked the life out of him.

(*Her hand goes out and rests on the bird-cage.*)

Mrs. Peters: (*With rising voice.*) We don't know who killed him. We don't know.
130 **Mrs. Hale:** (*Her own feeling not interrupted.*) If there'd been years and years of nothing, then a bird to sing to you, it would be awful—still, after the bird was still.
Mrs. Peters: (*Something within her speaking.*) I know what stillness is. When we home-steaded in Dakota, and my first baby died—after he was two years old, and me with no other then—
Mrs. Hale: (*Moving.*) How soon do you suppose they'll be through, looking for the evidence?
Mrs. Peters: I know what stillness is. (*Pulling herself back.*) The law has got to punish crime, Mrs. Hale.
Mrs. Hale: (*Not as if answering that.*) I wish you'd seen Minnie Foster when she wore a white dress with blue ribbons and stood up there in the choir and sang. (*A look around the room.*) Oh, I *wish* I'd come over here once in a while! That was a crime! That was a crime! Who's going to punish that?
135 **Mrs. Peters:** (*Looking upstairs.*) We mustn't—take on.
Mrs. Hale: I might have known she needed help! I know how things can be—for women. I tell you, it's queer, Mrs. Peters. We live close together and we live far apart. We all go through the same things—it's all just a different kind of the same thing. (*Brushes her eyes, noticing the bottle of fruit, reaches out for it.*) If I was you I wouldn't tell her her fruit was gone. Tell her it *ain't.* Tell her it's all right. Take this in to prove it to her. She—she may never know whether it was broke or not.
Mrs. Peters: (*Takes the bottle, looks about for something to wrap it in; takes petticoat from the clothes brought from the other room, very nervously begins winding this around the bottle. In a false voice.*) My, it's a good thing the men couldn't hear us. Wouldn't they just laugh! Getting all stirred up over a little thing like a—dead canary. As if that could have any-thing to do with—with—wouldn't they *laugh!*

(*The men are heard coming down stairs.*)

Mrs. Hale: (*Under her breath.*) Maybe they would—maybe they wouldn't.
County Attorney: No, Peters, it's all perfectly clear except a reason for doing it. But you know juries when it comes to women. If there was some definite thing. Something to show—something to make a story about—a thing that would connect up with this strange way of doing it—

(*The women's eyes meet for an instant. Enter Hale from outer door.*)

140 **Hale:** Well, I've got the team around. Pretty cold out there.
County Attorney: I'm going to stay here a while by myself. (*To the Sheriff.*) You can send Frank out for me, can't you? I want to go over everything. I'm not satisfied that we can't do better.
Sheriff: Do you want to see what Mrs. Peters is going to take in?

(*The County Attorney goes to the table, picks up the apron, laughs.*)

County Attorney: Oh, I guess they're not very dangerous things the ladies have picked out. (*Moves a few things about, disturbing the quilt pieces which cover the box. Steps back.*)

No, Mrs. Peters doesn't need supervising. For that matter, a sheriff's wife is married to the law. Ever think of it that way, Mrs. Peters?

Mrs. Peters: Not—just that way.

145 **Sheriff:** (*Chuckling.*) Married to the law. (*Moves toward the other room.*) I just want you to come in here a minute, George. We ought to take a look at these windows.

County Attorney: (*Scoffingly.*) Oh, windows!

Sheriff: We'll be right out, Mr. Hale.

(*Hale goes outside. The Sheriff follows the County Attorney into the other room. Then Mrs. Hale rises, hands tight together, looking intensely at Mrs. Peters, whose eyes make a slow turn, finally meeting Mrs. Hale's. A moment Mrs. Hale holds her, then her own eyes point the way to where the box is concealed. Suddenly Mrs. Peters throws back quilt pieces and tries to put the box in the bag she is wearing. It is too big. She opens box, starts to take bird out, cannot touch it, goes to pieces, stands there helpless. Sound of a knob turning in the other room. Mrs. Hale snatches the box and puts it in the pocket of her big coat. Enter County Attorney and Sheriff.*)

County Attorney: (*Facetiously.*) Well, Henry, at least we found out that she was not going to quilt it. She was going to—what is it you call it, ladies?

Mrs. Hale: (*Her hand against her pocket.*) We call it—knot it, Mr. Henderson.

(*Curtain.*)

■ EXPLORATIONS OF THE TEXT

1. Characterize Mrs. Hale and Mrs. Peters at the beginning of the play. How do they differ?
2. What clues lead the women to conclude that Minnie Wright killed her husband?
3. How do the men differ from the women? from each other?
4. What do the men discover? Why do they conclude "Nothing here but kitchen things"? What do the women discover?
5. Why do the men and women find different clues about the murder? What does Glaspell imply about the ways in which men and women were conditioned to view the world?
6. Do Mrs. Hale and Mrs. Peters change? Why? How? What makes them sympathize with Minnie Wright? Discuss the symbolism of the broken cage and the dead canary.
7. Characterize Minnie Wright and her husband. Describe their relationship. Why is Minnie Wright absent from the play?
8. Interpret the ending and the title. With what "crime" should Minnie Wright be charged?
9. Compare the marriage of the Wrights with those in other works in this chapter.
10. Compare Glaspell's critique of gender roles and of women's place in society with treatments of these issues by Gilman and Chopin.

■ THE READING/WRITING CONNECTION

1. Write a journal entry in Minnie Wright's voice.
2. Are Mrs. Hale and Mrs. Peters justified in withholding evidence concerning John Wright's murder?
3. "Think" Topic: Discuss the symbolism of the cage.

■ IDEAS FOR WRITING

1. Susan Glaspell claimed that the idea for the play came from a story that she covered as a reporter. Construct your version of her article.

2. What are the strengths and weaknesses of *Trifles?* Consider conflict, characters, setting, theme, symbol, irony, emotion, and/or general effect.
3. After the play was produced, Glaspell wrote a short story, "A Jury of Her Peers," about this subject. Read the story, and decide which version is better. Defend your choice.
4. Should Minnie Wright be found guilty for her actions?

REBECCA GILMAN

Rebecca Gilman (1965–) was born in Alabama and educated at Middlebury College, Birmingham Southern College, and the University of Virginia. Gilman began writing plays while in college and was the first American playwright to receive the Evening Standard *Award, for her play* The Glory of Living *(2001).* Boy Gets Girl *(2000) is Gilman's second play. Gilman's work is effective in depicting events that can and do occur in the lives of regular Americans.*

2000

BOY GETS GIRL

Cast of Characters

The world premiere of *Boy Gets Girl* was presented by the Goodman Theatre in Chicago, Illinois, on March 13, 2000. It was directed by Michael Maggio. Sets were designed by Michael Philippi, costumes by Nan Cibula Jenkins, lights by John Culbert, and sound by Michael Bodeen and Rob Milburn. The dramaturg was Susan V. Booth and the production stage manager was Alden Vasquez. The cast was as follows:

Theresa Bedell	*Mary Beth Fisher*
Tony	*Ian Lithgow*
Howard Siegel	*Matt DeCaro*
Mercer Stevens	*David Adkins*
Harriet	*Shayna Ferm*
Madeleine Beck	*Ora Jones*
Les Kennkat	*Howard Witt*

Characters

Theresa Bedel, *thirty-five to forty*
Tony, *thirty to thirty-five*
Howard Siegel, *fifties*
Mercer Stevens, *thirty-five*
Harriet, *twenty-one*
Madeleine Beck, *forty*
Les Kennkat, *seventy-two*

Time and place

Various locales in New York City, in the present

Act 1
Scene 1

A table in a bar, two chairs. TONY *sits alone, a little nervous, waiting for someone. He is an attractive man in his thirties. He is drinking a beer.* THERESA *enters, a bit hesitant. She carries a big bag, looks a little flustered. They stare at each other for a second.*

Theresa: Tony?

Tony: Theresa? (*They laugh awkwardly.*) Hi. (*He rises, offers his hand, she shakes it.*)

Theresa: I'm sorry I'm late.

Tony: It's okay.

5 **Theresa:** No, I just . . . I didn't want you to be sitting here thinking I wasn't going to come. I mean, I wouldn't do that. I tried to call but I can't get my phone to work. They gave me this new phone . . . (*She pulls a cellular phone out of her bag.*) And I don't know. The display thing comes on but then I can't get a dial tone. (*She pushes a button, listens, holds it out to* TONY.) Do you know anything about these?

Tony: No. (*Takes it, listens.*) I don't think it's working.

Theresa: Anyway, I'm really sorry.

Tony: It's okay, really.

Theresa: Well, anyway. Hi.

10 **Tony:** Hi. (*Beat.*) Do you want to sit down?

Theresa: Yeah. I think, though, I might get a beer.

Tony: Let me get you one.

Theresa: No. It's okay.

Tony: Let me get you one. What would you like?

15 **Theresa:** Whatever. Just nothing dark.

Tony: Do you want a Weiss beer?

Theresa: Is that the big tall one?

Tony: Yeah.

Theresa: I don't think so. Just an, you know, an ale or something. (*He starts off.*) Let me give you some money.

20 **Tony:** No, you can get the next one. Okay?

Theresa: Okay. (*He exits. She sits. The phone rings. She quickly answers it.*) What? . . . Oh, hey. Don't call me on the phone . . . (*She looks to where* TONY *exited.*) I lied, I said it was broken and I couldn't call. I was late. (*Beat.*) Well, I was thinking I wouldn't come. I was just sort of walking around. (*Beat.*) Look, I came, I'm here, so don't, you know, get all . . . whatever. (*Beat.*) He's fine, I guess. I've been here two minutes. (*Beat.*) I've been here two minutes and I don't know. All right? (*Beat.*) Okay, you know what? I'm hanging up now. (*Beat.*) I'll call you tonight. (*Beat.*) I'm pretty sure I'll be home in time to call you. (*Beat.*) No, he's fine. I'm not saying that. (TONY *enters with a beer, gives her a slightly puzzled look. She's been watching, knows he's coming. She makes a motion to him for one more second.*) I'm going now. Goodbye. (*Moving the phone away*) Goodbye. (*She looks for a button, hangs up. To* TONY) That was Linda.

Tony: Really?

Theresa: (*Looking at the phone*) I guess people can call in, but I can't call out.

Tony: What did she want?

25 **Theresa:** She wanted to know how it was going.

Tony: You just got here.

Theresa: That's what I told her.

Tony: Oh. (*Small beat.*) I got you an India Pale Ale. Is that okay?

Theresa: That's great, thanks. It used to be a lot easier when everybody just drank Miller High Life.

30 **Tony:** I never had Miller High Life.

Theresa: Well, if you had been living the high life you would have. (*Beat.*) I mean, it's the champagne of beers.

(*Beat.*)

Tony: Maybe I should try it.

Theresa: No. I'm sorry. You know, I have kind of a dumb sense of humor. I'm usually not serious when I say stupid things like that.

Tony: Oh.

35 **Theresa:** I mean, it's obviously not very funny either, so don't feel bad.

Tony: No, I mean . . . I'm sorry, too. I guess I'm a little nervous.

Theresa: Me, too.

Tony: Really?

Theresa: Yes.

40 **Tony:** Oh, good. I mean, not good you're nervous, but good I'm not alone.

Theresa: I understand.

Tony: I've never actually been on a blind date before.

Theresa: Really?

Tony: Have you?

45 **Theresa:** Tons. Nobody who actually knows me will go out with me. (*Beat.*) That was a joke.

Tony: (*Laughs.*) Sorry.

Theresa: I'll just stop trying. No, actually, I had a blind date in high school once, when I was a junior. I was supposed to meet this guy from another school at a party and when I did, he asked me if I wanted to go out to his van and "fool around" and I said I had to go to the bathroom and left with some friends. (*Beat*) I guess I probably shouldn't tell you that, on your first blind date, how I just ditched some guy.

Tony: I think it's good you ditched him. I mean, anybody with a van.

Theresa: (*Smiles.*) Exactly. What'd you drive in high school?

50 **Tony:** A Dodge Dart.

Theresa: Cool. I drove a Chrysler Cordoba.

Tony: With fine Corinthian leather.

Theresa: Exactly.

(*Small beat.*)

Tony: So you know Linda from work?

55 **Theresa:** I do. Before she quit to go off and have babies and everything, she was my research assistant.

Tony: You know, I have to make a confession: I've never read your magazine.

Theresa: Well, first of all, it's not my magazine, and second of all, don't worry about it.

Tony: What sort of stuff do you write?

Theresa: All sorts, really

60 **Tony:** Do you get to pick? I mean, what you write about?

Theresa: Usually. A couple of weeks ago I did a story about Edith Wharton's upstate estate. (*Small beat.*) That was kind of hard to say. Upstate estate.

Tony: I don't . . . I don't know who she is.

Theresa: Oh, she's a writer. She's dead, first of all. But she was a New York writer from the turn of the century.

Tony: Is she really famous?

65 **Theresa:** I guess her most famous book is *Age of Innocence*?

Tony: Oh, with Winona Ryder?

Theresa: Exactly. So, that was interesting. But then, I do get assignments still and it's usually something annoying. Like, on Thursday, I have to go interview Les Kennkat.

Tony: The filmmaker?

Theresa: I think "film" is a generous term.

70 **Tony:** I thought he was dead.

Theresa: So did I, actually. *(They laugh.)* So you met Linda through her sister?

Tony: Right. I met Sarah at Michigan.

Theresa: Right.

Tony: And when I moved here, you know, I looked up everybody I even vaguely knew because I was terrified—this is the first big city I ever lived in—

75 **Theresa:** Where are you from?

Tony: Terre Haute?

Theresa: The home of Eugene Debs.

Tony: Yeah.

Theresa: And Theodore Dreiser and Paul Dresser.

80 **Tony:** I guess so.

Theresa: On the banks of the Wabash.

Tony: It is. Have you been there?

Theresa: No.

Tony: Oh. Well, anyway, I looked up Sarah, and then, my first Thanksgiving here, she took pity on me and took me along to Linda's for turkey. Then, I guess you know, Sarah moved to Boston last spring. But that's how I met Linda. But I have to be honest, I don't know Linda well. I mean, I hardly ever see her.

85 **Theresa:** I don't know her well either and I see her all the time.

Tony: Oh. Is she . . . I mean, do you not get along?

Theresa: No, we get along fine. She just . . . she's certain she knows how I should live my life and she's always telling me what to do next.

Tony: Like, maybe, go on a date with me.

Theresa: Like, maybe that, but that's okay.

90 **Tony:** Good.

(Beat.)

Theresa: How long have you lived here?

Tony: Four years.

Theresa: Do you like it?

Tony: I do now. I really hated it at first. I just thought everybody was so mean and it's so dirty here.

95 **Theresa:** I know.

Tony: But after a while it started to grow on me, and now, I mean, this might sound weird, but part of what I like about it now is how big it is. I like being able to just blend in. There are so many people, I just feel anonymous. I don't know what that says about me . . .

Theresa: I agree. I think it makes you a little less self-involved.

Tony: Right.

Theresa: So what do you do?

100 **Tony:** I do computer work. I work for KCS, and what they do is, they go into a business and design software specifically for the business, and then I go in and train people how to use it.

Theresa: Do you like it?

Tony: I like the work itself, but the thing I don't like is that I move around to a new site every two or three months, so I never really get to know anybody I'm working with. Or even if I do, it's sort of like, what's the point because I'm never going to see them again.

Theresa: I see.

Tony: *(Beat.)* But anyway, I don't want to ramble.

105 **Theresa:** You're not rambling.

Tony: I know we only agreed to have a beer tonight . . .

Theresa: Yeah.

Tony: So if you need to go, or whatever, I understand . . .

Theresa: Oh. Do you want me to go?

110 **Tony:** No, no. I was actually going to ask you before you went . . . I mean, not to be too forward or anything, but I thought I'd just go ahead and ask if you'd like to do something this weekend?

Theresa: Just to get it on the table.

Tony: Yeah, just to get it on the table.

Theresa: Yeah. You know? I would like that.

Tony: Great. We could have dinner maybe.

115 **Theresa:** I can't do anything Friday night because I have to cover this benefit thing, but I'm free on Saturday.

Tony: Saturday would be great. What's the benefit?

Theresa: Some MoMA thing to get some MoMA thing going so MoMA people can give money to MoMA.

Tony: You don't like MoMA?

Theresa: Oh, sure, of course. I just don't like being around rich people. Have you ever noticed how rich people eat a lot when there's free food? Then poor people like me go hungry because we can't get to the buffet?

120 **Tony:** You could stand to eat more, too.

Theresa: Oh. Thank you, I guess.

Tony: You're really thin.

(Pause.)

Theresa: So what do you do when you're not working?

Tony: Well, I run every day, and I like to do all the usual stuff, you know. Go to movies and read and watch TV and all that. Go for long walks. *(Small beat.)* That was a joke.

125 **Theresa:** It was?

Tony: Yeah. You know how, in the personals, everybody says they like to go for long walks. I always figured, if all those desperate single people really went for those long walks, eventually, wouldn't they run into each other?

Theresa: Eventually, wouldn't they all find each other in the park?

Tony: Yeah.

(They laugh.)

Theresa: Do you like baseball?

130 **Tony:** I'm not a big sports guy. I still follow Michigan football.

Theresa: Don't they have the largest college stadium in the country?

Tony: I don't know. Do you like baseball?

Theresa: Oh yeah.

Tony: Yankees or Mets?

135 **Theresa:** Yankees, please.

Tony: The only women I ever knew who liked sports liked them just because their boyfriends did.

Theresa: Oh yeah?

Tony: Did you have a boyfriend who was a big Yankees fan or something?

Theresa: No.

(*Pause.*)

140 **Tony:** My dad was a huge Cardinals fan.

Theresa: Really?

Tony: Yeah, well, any kind of sports, really, he was just a fanatic. Which is where, I guess, the word "fan" comes from, obviously. He was always pushing me to play football, when I was in high school, and I really didn't want to, but my mom talked me into it, because she said . . . well, her reasoning was that we didn't get along, my dad and me, because we didn't have much in common, so this way we would have some sort of connection. But I was really terrible at it, I'm sure in large part because I hated it so much, and so all it really did was give him another excuse to make fun of me. And then, you know, I just felt completely betrayed by my mother.

Theresa: I'm sorry.

Tony: Oh. Well . . . (*Suddenly very self-conscious. Making a joke of it*) "And that's why I'm so fucked up today." (THERESA *laughs.*) I'm sorry, I didn't mean to get into all that.

145 **Theresa:** I won't ever mention the Yankees around you again.

Tony: No, no. Not that. Maybe you could take me to see a Yankees game sometime and I could learn to love them, too.

Theresa: Maybe so.

Tony: When does baseball season end?

Theresa: At the end of September if they don't make the play-offs.

150 **Tony:** Oh.

Theresa: But they will.

Tony: Well, maybe we could go see them now.

Theresa: Well, first of all, they're out of town for a while, and second of all, let's not move that fast.

Tony: Oh. I'm sorry.

155 **Theresa:** It's okay, I just . . . you know.

Tony: Right. (*Beat.*) So tell me, what's your favorite story? That you ever wrote?

Theresa: Boy, that's a hard one. I don't really have a favorite.

Tony: Did you study journalism in college?

Theresa: I was a history major in college, but I wrote for the school paper, and then I went to graduate school in journalism at Indiana Bloomington.

160 **Tony:** Oh! I think Linda mentioned that, but I forgot. So you were in Bloomington.

Theresa: Yeah.

Tony: What years?

Theresa: It was . . . twelve . . . fifteen years ago.

Tony: Then I was actually . . . I was just starting at Michigan then.

165 **Theresa:** Oh, man, I'm older than you.

Tony: You're robbing the cradle.

Theresa: Yeah.

Tony: I had a guy tell me once that men who go out with older women really want to have sex with their mothers. But I don't think that's true. Do you think that's true?

(*Beat.*)

Theresa: I wouldn't know. But I think I'm only about three years older than you are, so . . . (*Beat.*) Was that . . . ? Was that a joke?

(*Small beat.*)

170   **Tony:** *(Lying)* Yeah.

    Theresa: Good, because you scared me there for a second.

    Tony: See? I, too, have a dry sense of humor.

    Theresa: I do see. You might actually outdo me, drynesswise.

    Tony: I think we have a lot in common.

175   **Theresa:** Well, we'll find that out, won't we?

    Tony: We will. *(Pause.* THERESA *finishes her beer.)* Do you want another one?

    Theresa: Um, actually, I do have some work I need to do tonight. I've got a deadline to-morrow. And I was just . . . I was just planning on the one beer actually. So I think I'll go.

    Tony: But we're still on for Saturday?

    Theresa: Absolutely.

180   **Tony:** Can I walk you home, or . . . ?

    Theresa: I think I'm just going to grab a cab.

    Tony: Where do you live?

    Theresa: Upper East Side. It's, you know, dull but quiet.

    Tony: Which street?

185   **Theresa:** Um . . . Seventy-fourth.

    Tony: Near the park?

    Theresa: Near the park, yeah.

    Tony: I live down on Perry. Do you know where that is?

    Theresa: I do. Nice neighborhood.

190   **Tony:** I like it. There are a lot of nice bars and restaurants. Little shops and stuff. There's one place down there called Allison's? (THERESA *shakes her head.)* It's just a little place but they have really good food and it's not too expensive. I go in there enough, they sort of know me there.

    Theresa: That's nice.

    Tony: Maybe we could go there Saturday night.

    Theresa: Sure. That'd be great.

    Tony: I'll call you, then, later this week, and we can set up a time.

195   **Theresa:** Okay.

    Tony: Maybe Thursday or Friday, during the day. Can I call you at work? I mean, is that okay?

    Theresa: That's fine. If I'm not there, just leave me a voice mail message.

    Tony: I don't know if I have your home phone number.

    Theresa: If you don't get me at work, just leave a message and I'll call back.

200   **Tony:** Okay. *(Beat.)* Well, it was very nice to meet you, Theresa.

    Theresa: It was very nice to meet you.

    Tony: I'd say Linda did good.

    Theresa: Yeah. *(He makes a move as if to kiss her; she holds out her hand.)* Thanks for the beer.

    Tony: *(Shaking her hand)* I'll see you Saturday.

Scene 2

The following day; Theresa's office. A large bouquet of flowers is on her desk. Her boss, HOWARD, *is waiting for her, reading something.* THERESA *enters, carrying several pages of manuscript.*

Theresa: Here you go. Thanks for waiting.

Howard: Flowers came.

Theresa: Look at that.

Howard: Who are they from?

5 **Theresa:** You.

Howard: No.

(THERESA *takes the card and opens it, reads.*)

Theresa: They're from this guy.

Howard: Are you dating somebody?

Theresa: No. I had one date with this guy last night. It wasn't even a date. It was a beer.

10 **Howard:** He must have been really taken with you.

Theresa: I guess he was. I don't know. I thought I was pretty unimpressive.

Howard: What does the card say?

Theresa: "It was really nice meeting you—Tony."

Howard: Tony.

15 **Theresa:** Yeah.

Howard: Well, you should be very flattered. He obviously really liked you.

Theresa: I guess so. (*Changing the subject*) So I read the new guy's story.

Howard: Would you stop calling him that? He's been here three months.

Theresa: Sorry. I read *Mercer's* story, and I think it's good, for what's there, but I think it's only half a story.

20 **Howard:** How's that?

Theresa: (*Flipping pages*) Well, he ends with "the term 'literary friendship,' finally, seems an oxymoron, and so much of one that it borders on pretentious ludicrocity." Which . . . okay, first of all, "ludicrocity"? I looked it up and it is a word, but isn't it kind of a stupid word?

Howard: Yeah.

Theresa: And then, to be fair, he doesn't look at any literary friendships that were good. I mean, he only focuses on the ones in which people are betrayed or hurt.

Howard: Are there any good ones?

25 **Theresa:** Sure. I mean, go back just a little ways and start with William Dean Howells and Mark Twain, and Howells and Henry James.

Howard: Who is William Dean Howells?

Theresa: Oh, he's really great. His novels are great. (*Appraising him*) I can't believe you've never heard of William Dean Howells. You're an editor.

Howard: I drank my way through college. Is there somebody else he can look at? Who's still alive?

(*The phone rings.*)

Theresa: I'll let the voice mail get it.

30 **Howard:** You can forward it straight to voice mail and then it doesn't even ring.

Theresa: I know. It's just too much trouble.

Howard: It's a button. You press a button.

(*The phone stops abruptly.*)

Theresa: Okay. I think William Styron and Arthur Miller are friends.

Howard: They're not going to talk to us.

35 **Theresa:** Why not?

Howard: They're just not. There's just an echelon that doesn't return our calls. They'll call *The New Yorker* back, but they won't call us.

Theresa: You have such an inferiority complex.

Howard: It's true, though. (*The phone rings again.*) Just answer it. (*Picking it up*)

Theresa: Yeah? (*Beat.*) Oh, hi, Tony, how are you? (*Beat.*) Yes, I did get the flowers. They're very pretty. Thank you. I was going to call, but, um, I'm in a meeting. (HOWARD *gets up to go, she motions him back.*) I do like irises, too. Maybe they're out of season. (*Beat.*) Eight would be fine. Why don't you give me the address now so I can meet you. (*Beat.*) No, you don't have to pick me up. (*Beat.*) No, Tony, it would be silly to have you come all the way uptown and then just turn around and go back again. I'll just meet you there. (*Beat.*) Look, I'm a big girl, I can take a cab. (*Beat. Writing something*) Okay then. Eight on Saturday. (*Beat*) I had a good time, too. (*Beat. Interrupting*) Look, Tony, I don't want to be rude, but I'm still in that meeting. (*Beat.*) No, no, it's okay, just . . . um, I'll talk to you later, okay? (*Beat.*) You too. Bye. (*She hangs up.*)

40 **Howard:** You should have let him pick you up.

Theresa: Why?

Howard: He was trying to be gallant. You should have let him be gallant.

Theresa: That's like a hundred and fifty blocks worth of gallantry, round trip. That's ridiculous.

Howard: He wouldn't have offered if he didn't want to do it.

45 **Theresa:** I'm not even sure I want to go out with him.

Howard: Why not?

Theresa: I don't know.

Howard: When's the last time you dated somebody?

Theresa: It's been a while.

50 **Howard:** What about that one guy? That Mark guy?

Theresa: Mark Carter?

Howard: He was a nice guy.

Theresa: He got transferred. To Kuala Lumpur.

Howard: Why didn't you go with him?

55 **Theresa:** He didn't ask.

Howard: Oh. I'm sorry.

Theresa: I wouldn't have gone if he had. We weren't that serious. And I don't want to live in Kuala Lumpur.

Howard: Right.

Theresa: I bet a lot of Kuala Lumpurians don't want to live in Kuala Lumpur.

60 **Howard:** You like saying "Kuala Lumpur," don't you?

Theresa: Yeah.

Howard: Anyway, I'm just saying that I think you're not used to the attention. That it makes you uncomfortable.

Theresa: You know what? I don't want to talk about my love life.

Howard: Okay. So you think Mercer should try to balance this ludicrocity?

65 **Theresa:** Yes, I do.

Howard: Okay, then . . . (*Referring to what she handed him*) . . . I'll read this after lunch. When do you talk to Les Kennkat?

Theresa: Next week.

Howard: Good deal.

Theresa: (*Overlapping*) But can't you find somebody else—

70 **Howard:** (*Interrupting*) Don't ask me again, I don't have anybody else to do it. (*Beat.*) Theresa. I honestly don't.

Theresa: (*Beat.*) Look, Howard, it's just that, with certain stories you give me, I feel like I'm writing for *People* magazine and that's not why I went into journalism.

Howard: You have to take the good with the bad—

Theresa: (*Overlapping*) After twelve years?

Howard: Look, if it was up to me we'd only publish stories about saints and we'd print them on a hundred-percent recycled paper and we'd only sell ads to people who paid union wages, but there's this little thing called the bottom line, and if I don't pay attention to it, then I'm out of a job—

75 **Theresa:** Yeah, yeah . . .

Howard: And so, I may add, are you. (*Pause.*) So how many words can you give me on Mr. Kennkat?

Theresa: Five thousand?

Howard: Make it fifteen.

Theresa: Ten.

80 **Howard:** (*Beat.*) It's a deal. (*Indicating pages*) I'll get this back to you by five.

(HOWARD *exits.* THERESA *stands, then looks at the flowers. She is not necessarily pleased.*)

Scene 3

A restaurant. TONY *sits at a table alone. They have finished their meal. He takes a bottle of wine from the ice bucket, refills Theresa's glass, freshens his own.* THERESA *returns to the table.*

Theresa: Sorry it took so long.

Tony: Are you feeling all right?

Theresa: I'm fine. (*Beat.*) They had the TV on in the bar when I walked by. The Yankees are winning.

Tony: Oh yeah? Do they go to the World Series from here?

5 **Theresa:** Well, they have to clinch the division first, then they go to a five-game play-off series. Then a seven-game series for the pennant.

Tony: You're going to have to teach me all this stuff. I don't know any of this stuff.

Theresa: It's not hard, really. Just read the sports page.

(*Beat.*)

Tony: The waitress brought the check while you were in the ladies' room, and she sort of knows me, and she said we make a great-looking couple.

Theresa: Really.

10 **Tony:** I told her that I only looked good because I was with you.

Theresa: That was nice.

Tony: Look, I was sitting here . . . I feel like I've been talking about myself all night. Why don't you tell me about your family.

Theresa: There's not much to tell.

Tony: Brothers? Sisters?

15 **Theresa:** I have a brother.

Tony: Older, younger?

Theresa: He's older.

Tony: Do you not want to talk about him?

Theresa: No, he's just, um . . . he moves around a lot, so it's been hard to really keep in touch with him.

20 **Tony:** What about your parents?

Theresa: They're both dead, actually.

Tony: I'm sorry.

Theresa: Thank you.

Tony: I don't know what I'd do if mine died. I mean, I complain about them all the time, but I think I'd feel so alone or something. Although, if my dad died tomorrow, sometimes I think I wouldn't really care. You know? I mean, I know that sounds harsh, but he treats my mom like shit. I mean, my mom is a saint. When I was growing up, she did so much for me that other kids' moms wouldn't even think of doing. You should have seen the lunches she made me. Everybody else would have peanut butter and jelly sandwiches, right? She'd make me homemade pasties. *(Beat.)* Do you know what a pasty is? *(He pronounces pasty with a short* a.*)*

25   **Theresa:** They're little, like, meat pies, right?

Tony: *(Disappointed she knows.)* Right. But she'd make me these pasties, and every day she'd put something different in it. One day chicken, the next day steak. They were great. And homemade cookies or a big slice of cake. I mean, I was the envy of that lunchroom. People were always trying to trade lunches with me, but there was no way. You know?

Theresa: Sounds like she really . . . spent a lot of time in the kitchen.

Tony: Do you cook?

Theresa: No, I don't.

30   **Tony:** Why not?

Theresa: I've just never enjoyed it.

Tony: I love to cook.

Theresa: That's nice.

Tony: I think one person in a couple should always know how to cook. My mom taught me to cook. But I'm glad she did, because it seems like more and more women don't cook these day.

35   **Theresa:** More and more women have other things to do these days.

(Beat.)

Tony: So are you like a, feminist?

Theresa: I'm like that, yeah.

Tony: I am, too.

Theresa: Good.

40   **Tony:** I mean, there are women I work with who know so much more about programming than I ever will, and I think how they used to not even have the opportunity to get those jobs, you know? I think that's completely unfair.

Theresa: It is.

Tony: But what I don't like are those women who are really strident about it. I mean, this might be a generalization, and I know I shouldn't make it, but it seems to me that some feminists really hate men.

Theresa: Well, I guess it's not technically a generalization to say "some" women hate men. I don't know. I don't know. I don't really want to talk about it.

Tony: You don't?

45   **Theresa:** I mean I just . . . I can't speak for other women.

Tony: But you don't hate men.

Theresa: No.

Tony: Good. Have you ever been married?

Theresa: No, I haven't. Look—

50   **Tony:** I was engaged when I moved to New York. I mean, not when I moved here, before I moved here. Which is why I moved. I was engaged to this girl from college and we were going to get married and I had a job in Detroit. But she broke up with me. I mean, it was before the wedding and everything, she didn't leave me standing at the

altar. But that's really why I took this job in New York. I just didn't want to be hanging around where I would run into her all the time and all that and it was sort of an impulsive decision, but I felt like I really wanted to get out of Michigan.

Theresa: I see.

Tony: It took me a long time, though, after that, to trust anybody again.

(Pause.)

Theresa: Look, Tony, this is really, probably, the most awkward moment for me to tell you this, but I'm going to go home.

Tony: Are you sick?

55 **Theresa:** No, I just, I'm tired, and I think I'm going to go on home.

Tony: Well, let me . . . I'll pay the check and I'll take you.

Theresa: *(Getting her purse)* No, I want to go home by myself. If that's all right. *(Getting out her wallet)* And I'm going to go Dutch on this with you.

Tony: No, this is my treat. Are you sure you're feeling all right?

Theresa: *(Taking out a couple of bills)* I'm fine. I'm just tired.

60 **Tony:** Well, maybe . . . I was thinking, if tomorrow's a nice day, maybe we could take a walk up around your neighborhood. Since you live near the park.

Theresa: Okay. Um, look. I have a confession to make. I've been sitting here listening to you talk and I think you're a very nice guy and funny and smart and very nice.

Tony: I'm glad.

Theresa: But I just, I sort of realized . . . I mean, I don't know if Linda told you this, but I don't really date a lot.

Tony: She didn't mention it.

65 **Theresa:** I haven't dated anybody in a while. And I, I realized, while I was sitting here, that I just can't. I mean, I haven't because of my work, because I spend so much time on my work that it didn't seem fair to anybody to get into a relationship with them and then make them take second place to my work. Do you see?

Tony: I guess.

Theresa: It just wasn't fair. And then I thought, when Linda mentioned you . . . I thought, maybe I've changed. Maybe I could date someone. But I've been sitting here this whole time worrying about an article I have to get in on Monday and I realized I haven't changed. I'm just not a good person to be in a relationship with. I'm too selfish or something. I'm just, I'm not good relationship material. You know?

Tony: I don't think that's true.

Theresa: Well, I do. And I do think you're great, but I just don't think there's any point in pursuing this as long as I feel this way.

70 **Tony:** *(Beat.)* Okay.

Theresa: I'm really sorry.

Tony: No, it's okay, I understand. *(Picking up the check)* But at least let me buy dinner.

Theresa: I can't. It's too much.

Tony: Look, I'm just trying to walk away with a little of my pride here. At least let me pay for the meal.

(Pause.)

75 **Theresa:** All right, then. Thank you.

Tony: You know, last night I turned on the TV and I saw there wasn't a game on. I thought, if there was a game, I'd learn some of the names of the players and then I could impress you tonight. Because, you know, when we first met, I just thought that you must think I'm an idiot.

Theresa: I didn't think that.

Tony: Because I don't read books like you do. I mean, I took a lit class in college and all
that, but I didn't know who you were talking about the other night. That woman.

Theresa: Edith Wharton?

80 **Tony:** Yeah, her. Is it because I didn't know who Edith Wharton was?

Theresa: No. I would never in my whole life not like somebody for not knowing who
Edith Wharton was. It's just me. It's entirely me.

Tony: Well, if you leave now, maybe you can catch the end of the game.

Theresa: That's not . . . Please don't think that way.

Tony: Last night, I even, I called the museum. I called MoMA, and asked about that benefit, because I thought, That's something I never do. I live in New York, I should go to
the museum. I should learn about art. But they said it was a five-hundred-dollar-a-
plate dinner. So . . . (*Beat.*) I was just . . . I think I was feeling really lonely.

85 **Theresa:** I'm sorry. But I really . . . I have to go.

Tony: No, I'm sorry. I shouldn't lay all this on you.

Theresa: It's okay. (*Beat.*) Take care of yourself. Okay?

Tony: It was really nice to meet you. You know? I mean it. I mean, even if things don't
work out. It was nice to meet you.

Theresa: You, too. I mean, for me to meet you. Bye, Tony.

(THERESA *exits.* TONY *sits alone.*)

Scene 4

Theresa's office. MERCER *sits at Theresa's desk while her research assistant,* HARRIET, *takes
notes.*

Mercer: Call his agent and see if he'll do something over the phone.

Harriet: Okay.

Mercer: And then . . . What are you doing for Theresa this week?

Harriet: Um . . . (*Flipping back in her notebook*) I'm supposed to find out something about
Thomas Jefferson.

5 **Mercer:** That's what she said?

Harriet: Yeah.

Mercer: Don't be nervous, Harriet. I know it's hard to be new, I'm fairly new myself. But
everybody here is nice, so just ask when you don't understand something.

Harriet: I don't don't understand anything. I just forgot what she said.

(THERESA *enters, carrying a book.*)

Theresa: (*Handing it to* MERCER) I think this is it.

10 **Mercer:** Thanks. Now Harriet needs some clarification on something.

Theresa: Okay.

Harriet: Um, you wanted me to look up something about Thomas Jefferson?

Theresa: Right. It was an article in *The New York Times* about a Library of Congress exhibi-
tion of his letters. If you go online and look up Jefferson in the *Times* archives—do
you know how to do that?

Harriet: Yeah.

15 **Theresa:** Then that should get you started. I'm sorry I can't be more specific.

Harriet: That's okay, that's . . . thanks, that helps a lot. (*She exits.*)

Mercer: What do you want with Thomas Jefferson?

Theresa: I was thinking of writing an article about conspiracy theories. Can I have my
chair back?

Mercer: (*Moving*) Oh yeah. Your phone kept ringing, so I forwarded it to voice mail.
20 **Theresa:** Thanks.
Mercer: So, I took your advice, and I think you were right. And unlike Howard, I think it's interesting to read about dead people.
Theresa: Me, too.
Mercer: But I do think William Dean Howells is a little obscure.
Theresa: He's not obscure! He's so good . . . !
25 **Mercer:** Okay, okay, just hear me out. I thought, what I'd do is start with the Transcendentalists.
Theresa: Okay. Emerson and Thoreau.
Mercer: And Hawthorne . . .
Theresa: And William Dean Howells. Hawthorne and William Dean Howells!
Mercer: Okay, let's just . . . let's stick to this right now.
30 **Theresa:** Okay, the Alcotts. And then Bronson Alcott introduced Thoreau to Walt Whitman.
Mercer: Really?
Theresa: Yeah. And then Whitman met Oscar Wilde when Wilde toured the U.S. You know, you could start with one author and follow them through their literary friendships—do like a six degrees of separation thing all the way up to the present.
Mercer: I actually just wanted, like, four more inches for the article I have now.
Theresa: It was just a suggestion.
35 **Mercer:** And it's a good idea, but it's not the article I'm writing.
Theresa: (*Smiles.*) I'm sorry. I have a tendency to be . . . prescriptive, so just tell me to shut up.
Mercer: It's okay. I do the same thing.

(HARRIET *enters with* TONY)

Harriet: Theresa:? Mr. Ross is here to see you.
Tony: Hi.

(*Beat.*)

40 **Theresa:** Hi. Did you . . . did you call to get up here?
Harriet: Your phone was forwarded to voice mail so I said he could come up.
Tony: I was just running some errands and I thought maybe you'd like to have lunch.
Mercer: Go on, I'm through. Thanks for all this.

(MERCER *exits, taking* HARRIET *with him. Beat.*)

Tony: I know I should have called first, but I couldn't get through, and I thought, if you had a minute, maybe we could get a sandwich and talk.
45 **Theresa:** I don't. I'm sorry.
Tony: Maybe we could just talk for a minute. I'm not, you know, trying to ask you out or anything, I just wanted to apologize. I feel like I probably came on too strong or something and I was thinking about what you said, about how you didn't think it was fair to ask somebody to take second place in your life, and I thought later, you know, it must have seemed like I wanted you to marry me or something. Which is not true. I just want to get to know you. I just want us to be friends. (*Small beat.*) So I thought I'd just see if you wanted to have lunch and maybe we can be friends.
Theresa: No.
Tony: Sorry?
Theresa: No. I want to make this clear this time. I don't think we have anything in common and I don't want to be friends. I don't want to see you again.
50 **Tony:** Oh. (*Beat.*) Is it . . .

Theresa: What?

Tony: Well, you said you hadn't dated anybody in a long time, and I was wondering, are you afraid of intimacy or something?

Theresa: No.

Tony: Because I know a lot of women who really throw themselves into their work, it's because they're afraid of intimacy. I mean, they're afraid of their own sexual desires or sexual powers.

55 **Theresa:** That's not it. Now, if you don't mind, I need to get back to work.

Tony: You sound really like you're mad at me or something.

Theresa: I just don't think there's any point in discussing this.

Tony: I'm just trying to help you figure it out.

Theresa: There's nothing to figure out. And you don't know me.

60 **Tony:** I guess I hit a nerve.

Theresa: That's not it. Now, if you would leave, I have a lot of work to do.

Tony: (Wryly) So you're not hiding behind your work?

Theresa: No.

Tony: Okay, okay. I get the point. I'm sorry that you're so closed off or whatever that you can't even make room for a new friend. Because I'm a good friend. You can ask anybody. And that's all I want, really. I mean, I'm not one of those guys who pretends to be a friend but is really just waiting for you to fall in love with me. Although I think you would fall in love with me because I'm pretty charming. (Laughs. Stops.) But you don't, because you're too repressed or something to even let anybody near you. So, it was my last shot, but I get what you're saying.

65 **Theresa:** Good. And don't come back here again.

Tony: All right! Don't call security. (Laughing) All right. Have a good life, Theresa.

(TONY exits. THERESA stands for a moment, then goes to her door, watches him leave, then calls.)

Theresa: Harriet?

(HARRIET enters.)

Harriet: Yes, ma'am.

Theresa: I don't . . . don't call me ma'am.

70 **Harriet:** I'm sorry.

Theresa: No, Harriet, don't ever let somebody up here to see me without my permission. Okay? That's rule number one.

Harriet: I'm sorry. He said he was a friend of yours.

Theresa: You didn't know, I know, but for future reference, don't ever let anyone up here without my explicit permission.

Harriet: Okay. (Beat.) He's cute. Who is he?

75 **Theresa:** How old are you?

Harriet: Twenty-one.

Theresa: Okay . . . (As if she wants to tell her so much, but doesn't have the time) Cute isn't everything.

Scene 5

Les Kennkat's office, that night. He is a movie producer and director of low-budget, sixties sexploitation movies. A big couch is in his small office with a clutter of boxes, posters, etc. He is dressed in a suit from the seventies. THERESA is positioning a small tape recorder.

Les: You're going to tape this?

Theresa: With your permission.

Les: Sure, fine. (THERESA *takes out a notepad and pencil.*) You're gonna write it down, too?

Theresa: I've never been accused of misquoting anybody.

5 **Les:** Okay, then, that's good.

Theresa: All right, Mr. Kennkat, what are you working on now?

Les: You're just jumping right in?

Theresa: I'm just jumping right in.

Les: Great. Right now I'm working on videos, mostly. I got that going, but I want to make another feature film as soon as I find the right actress.

10 **Theresa:** What's the film about?

Les: I won't know until I find the actress.

Theresa: So that's where you start?

Les: Oh yeah, I've always done that. Because you have to work with the actress's attributes.

Theresa: And what attributes do you look for?

15 **Les:** Big tits.

Theresa: I see. Anything else?

Les: A nice ass is always good.

Theresa: Anything else?

Les: What else do you have in mind?

20 **Theresa:** I don't know. Acting ability?

Les: No, I don't really care if she can act as long as she has gigantic breasts.

Theresa: Okay. And where do you find your . . . actresses?

Les: They flock to me.

Theresa: They do?

25 **Les:** Sure. You want to know why?

Theresa: Sure.

Les: Because. These women want to show off their breasts. They know they have colossal tits. It's no secret to them. So I just give them the opportunity to do that. And by that, I like to think I do them a service. And I do the guys who want to see these tremendous breasts a service, too, because I give them a good story and a good deal of expert camera work for really showing off these breasts in optimum conditions. What I do is, I'll shoot the breasts from down here, you know, low down with maybe a blue sky in the background. Maybe just a touch of treetops and a blue sky with clouds as a backdrop for these beautiful supple breasts. To me, there's nothing more breathtaking than a gorgeous pair of tits just sort of floating in the treetops.

Theresa: (*Smiling.*) So . . . *Ga-Ga-Girls Galore* . . . ?

Les: *Ga-Ga-Girls Galore* is one of the movies I'm most proud of. Are you laughing at me?

30 **Theresa:** No.

Les: (*Not angry*) I'm very serious about my work.

Theresa: I know, I didn't mean to laugh.

Les: Don't apologize. I can't help it if I make people smile.

Theresa: Okay. You're sort of a cult figure now—

35 **Les:** I don't understand that, what does that mean, "a cult figure"?

Theresa: Just that it's hip to be into your movies now.

Les: The people that read your magazine, they think I'm hip?

Theresa: Yeah.

Les: Well, that's good, I have no problem with that. I like being a hip daddy among the young generation. What is this magazine, anyway?

40 **Theresa:** *The World.*

Les: Never heard of it.

Theresa: Really?

Les: No, is it new?

Theresa: No, it's been around about a hundred years.

45 **Les:** What is it? A fashion magazine?

Theresa: No, it's a magazine on culture and politics and art and . . . crap like that.

Les: Really.

Theresa: Originally it was called *Window to the World.* It was targeted to the new middle class in New York. But after World War One, they dropped the *Window* part and started drumming up subscriptions across the country, trying to broaden its appeal. *(Pulling a card from her pocket)* See? That's our logo. The world in a little window.

Les: Can I keep this?

50 **Theresa:** Sure.

Les: Theresa Bedell. Is that you?

Theresa: Yeah. *(Beat.)* If you don't know the magazine, why did you agree to the interview?

Les: I need the publicity. I don't care where it comes from. So what do I fall under? Culture, art, or crap?

(Beat. THERESA *looks at him.)*

Theresa: Culture.

55 **Les:** That was very diplomatic.

Theresa: Have you always made . . . films about breasts?

Les: Well, I did have a contract with Paramount Pictures when I was a young man.

Theresa: Really?

Les: Yes, and they wanted me to make movies about little orphan boys who live in abandoned buildings and learn to be thugs and then meet priests who reform them. Horse hockey like that. It was completely uninspiring. So I quit. And then, for a long time, I couldn't get any work and that was not fun at all. But then I met this girl who had breasts that defied gravity and I thought, Here's what I've been waiting for. So I sold my car and rented a camera and went to work. We shot the whole movie in ten days. I called it *Succubus.* Do you know what a succubus is?

60 **Theresa:** Yes.

Les: Not many people do, I found out. But that's what I wanted to name the movie, because that's what it was about. She-devils who take on beautiful womanly forms and seduce men and then, when they're satisfied sexually, eat them.

Theresa: Right.

Les: And it was a hit. And then I made *Succubus Meets Incubus.* And that was a bigger hit. And pretty soon I didn't regret leaving Paramount Pictures, and I can proudly say that there is not anywhere in existence some crappy movie about an orphan and a priest with my name on it.

Theresa: Congratulations.

65 **Les:** Not many people can say that. That they're proud of what they do.

Theresa: I guess you're right. I'm usually proud of what I do, but sometimes if I don't think my work's good, I see Ernie Pyle staring down on me, reprovingly.

Les: Ernie Pyle?

Theresa: The World War Two reporter?

Les: Yeah, yeah, I know who he is.

70 **Theresa:** My journalism school was named after him. They keep Ernie Pyle's typewriter in this special window on the side of the building, next to a big picture of him. Sort of like a shrine.

Les: I'm sure it's real nice, but we're not talking about you, are we? Ask me another question.

Theresa: Okay. Well, how do you feel about the way in which your movies encourage men to objectify women?

Les: My movies don't do that.

Theresa: They don't?

75 **Les:** No, my movies celebrate women.

Theresa: By fetishizing their breasts?

Les: See, now you're not smiling anymore. Now you're turning on me.

Theresa: No, I'm not.

Les: Just because I didn't want to listen to your little story about Ernie Pyle.

80 **Theresa:** It's hardly an outrageous question. I can't believe you've never been asked it before.

Les: I've been asked it plenty before and I have a standard answer: my movies celebrate women.

Theresa: Okay. How?

Les: They celebrate their beauty, so men can enjoy their beauty. And, I might add, they teach women how to be beautiful. That's another service I do.

Theresa: That's ridiculous.

85 **Les:** No, it's not. Everyone wants to be attractive to the opposite sex. I help show them how to do it.

Theresa: Then why don't you make movies about penises floating around in treetops?

Les: Nobody wants to see that. That's not what women look at anyway. Women go for tight asses.

Theresa: No, they don't,

Les: What, are you gonna tell me a woman looks at a man's face first? That's just until she can look at his ass.

90 **Theresa:** I don't think that's true.

Les: What do you look for first?

Theresa: A good personality—

Les: Yeah, yeah, if the guy was short and bald and had holes where his ears should be and was fat and stinky, you're gonna tell me that you wouldn't care as long as he had a good personality?

Theresa: I thought we were talking about you.

95 **Les:** It's hard to be high and mighty when you're faced with a guy with no ears, isn't it?

Theresa: No ears is different from an un-tight ass.

Les: But what do you see first? The good personality? Or the tight ass? (*Beat. She thinks.*) This ain't calculus here, it's the simple rules of physical attraction.

Theresa: You see the tight ass first if that's what you're looking for.

Les: Fine. Stick to your story. Be the sainted Virgin Mary if that makes you feel better. But I bet, chances are, you've got a type. Because we've all got a type.

(*Small beat.*)

100 **Theresa:** So how about the fact that your movies perpetuate a stereotype of women as sexual predators?

Les: Forget it, I don't want to get into this. I hear this crap all the time and I'm sick of it. Let's wrap this up. I gotta go.

Theresa: Okay. I need to ask you some background questions. It'll take about ten more minutes.

Les: Nah. I gotta go. (*He hands her a folder.*) Here's a press packet. That should answer anything you got.

Theresa: What's the hurry, exactly?

(*Beat.*)

105 **Les:** The Yankees are on. They could clinch tonight.

Theresa: Oh. It was on in the cab when I came up. They were up by a run.

Les: Then what are we sitting here for, let's go watch the game. Can I buy you a drink?

Theresa: I don't know.

Les: It's not a date or anything. You're not my type, if you know what I mean. (*Beat.* THERESA *regards him.*) I mean, you know, I would never put you in one of my movies.

110 **Theresa:** I understood you the first time. (*Turning off the recorder*) I'll watch the game by myself.

Les: (*Getting his own things to leave*) Suit yourself. Just don't crucify me in that article. I mean, let me speak for myself. I can speak for myself.

Theresa: You sure can.

Les: Are you sure you won't have that drink?

Theresa: I'm sure.

115 **Les:** I won't ask a third time.

Theresa: You just did.

Les: What?

Theresa: You just did. And I'll say it thrice: no, no, no.

Scene 6

Theresa's office, a week later. She is on the phone.

Theresa: Linda, I'm not blaming you. You told me up front that you didn't really know him. And I agreed to go out with him. (*Beat.*) I agree. It would be nice to meet somebody. It would be nice to be in a relationship. I would like that. Things are going well for me and I would like that. But not with him. (HARRIET *enters with a big bouquet of flowers.*) Oh God, more flowers?

Harriet: I know, aren't they beautiful? (*She exits*)

Theresa: (*On phone*) Yes, more flowers. Now will you please call Sarah and ask her to call him and tell him that I'm serious and to leave me alone. (*Beat.*) What do you mean Sarah doesn't like him? Why did you fix me up with somebody Sarah doesn't like? (*Small beat.*) Okay, Linda, you know what, you're right: I am blaming you. How's that? I am blaming you. (*Long pause.* LINDA *is chastising her.*) Okay, I'm sorry. I'm not blaming you. I'm just irritated and I haven't gotten much sleep. (*Beat.*) I know. Go to your play group. I'll talk to you later. (*She hangs up, then takes the card from the flowers and reads it. Disgusted, she calls*) Harriet?

Harriet: (*Enters.*) Yes, ma'am?

5 **Theresa:** I don't want to see any more flowers in my office. I want you to go down to the desk in the lobby and tell the guard not to sign for any more flowers. If any flowers make their way up to your desk, I want you to destroy them before I see them. Do you understand?

Harriet: I guess.

Theresa: You guess?

Harriet: I don't know. If some guy was sending me flowers, I'd be flattered.

Theresa: Do you understand my instructions or not?

10 **Harriet:** I understand.

Theresa: Then just do as I say.

Harriet: Okay.

Theresa: And if you copy an article from the paper for me, please check to see if it's continued on another page, because otherwise I only have the first page and that doesn't do me any good.

Harriet: Oh God, I'm sorry.

15 **Theresa:** Just try and be careful.

Harriet: I will. I'm sorry. *(She starts to go.)*

Theresa: And would you take these flowers with you and throw them in the trash?

Harriet: Okay.

(HARRIET *exits with the flowers.* THERESA *reads the card again, then rips it up and throws it away.* HOWARD *enters.*)

Howard: Do you have that Les Kennkat thing?

20 **Theresa:** Not yet.

Howard: Why not?

Theresa: I need to ask him some more questions. He gave me a press packet, but it's twenty years old. Literally.

Howard: Well, make another appointment with him and finish it.

Theresa: Fine.

(Beat.)

25 **Howard:** *(Motions after* HARRIET, *smiling.)* So I notice you've been getting a lot of flowers lately. Is this thing with this guy getting serious?

Theresa: No. This thing with this guy is over!

Howard: Okay, okay.

Theresa: *(Overlapping)* Jesus.

Howard: Okay. What's the matter?

30 **Theresa:** I don't know. *(Beat.)* Do you think I'm paranoid?

Howard: No. Why?

Theresa: Because I think Tony, the flower guy? I think he's following me.

Howard: Why?

Theresa: Because I wouldn't return any of his calls.

35 **Howard:** But why . . . I mean, what evidence do you have that you're being followed?

Theresa: My home phone number's unlisted, but he got it somehow. Maybe Linda gave it to him. She says she didn't, but maybe she gave it to her sister and her sister gave it to him. I don't know. But anyway, he got it somehow. And last night, I got home about nine o'clock and I walked in the door, and turned on the light, and right when I did the phone rang and it was him.

Howard: What'd he say?

Theresa: He wanted to know if I'd gotten all the flowers. I told him not to send me any more flowers, and to stop calling me. And he said okay, but then I got flowers today with a note apologizing for the flowers.

Howard: He's a shmuck.

40 **Theresa:** What?

Howard: He's a shmuck. He doesn't know what he's supposed to do, obviously. With women. He's probably shy.

Theresa: I don't think he's shy.

Howard: Have you seen him following you?

Theresa: No, but he asked me where I'd been and I lied and said I'd been at work and he said, "Oh really." All sarcastic, like he wanted me to know that he knew I was lying.

45 **Howard:** Where had you been?

Theresa: It doesn't matter.

Howard: But you were lying.

Theresa: I don't have to tell him anything.

Howard: I'm not saying you do. I'm just saying, you're not the greatest liar, so maybe he picked up on that and that's why he was being sarcastic. Not because he was following you.

50 **Theresa:** Maybe. But I still felt like I was being watched.

Howard: Are you feeling guilty about something?

Theresa: What would I feel guilty about?

Howard: Well, did you sleep with him?

Theresa: No! Howard. Jesus.

55 **Howard:** I had to ask.

Theresa: No, you didn't.

(*Pause.*)

Howard: All right, I'm sorry. Here's what I think: I think the guy can't take a hint, is all. I'd say, just pretend he's not there and eventually he'll lose interest.

Theresa: I haven't been hinting. I've been directly stating.

Howard: Well, you know how guys are. It takes a while for things to sink in. For example, I was positive that Claudia and I were going to get back together, until she served me with divorce papers. Probably this guy is the same. He just doesn't want to accept that it's over.

60 **Theresa:** Maybe so.

Howard: I'm not helping, am I?

Theresa: I just don't think the situations are the same.

(*Beat.*)

Howard: I wish I knew what to tell you, but this isn't really my area of expertise. I haven't had a date since the Carter administration.

Theresa: (*Small beat.*) Maybe you're right. Maybe I should just ignore him.

65 **Howard:** Okay.

Theresa: I'll get that Kennkat thing to you by the middle of next week.

Howard: Can you make it Monday?

Theresa: All right. (HOWARD *exits. She stares out the door after him for a moment, then calls*) Harriet! Throw the flowers in the trash. Don't leave them on your desk.

(HARRIET *enters.*)

Harriet: I just thought if you didn't want them . . . they're so pretty. You keep throwing them all away and they're so pretty. It seems like a waste. (*Beat.* THERESA *stares at her.* HARRIET *gets it.*) All right. (*She exits.*)

70 **Theresa:** (*To herself*) It's not a difficult concept. You put them in the trash.

Scene 7

Theresa's apartment: a small apartment with a futon couch/bed, desk, and lots of bookshelves. It is late Saturday night. THERESA *is fully dressed, sitting up in bed, working on a laptop. The phone rings, but she makes no move to answer it. After a couple of rings her machine picks up. Theresa's voice comes on.*

Theresa's voice: You've reached my machine. Leave a message.

(*Tony's voice comes on.*)

Tony: Hi, it's me again. It's past one and I'm just hoping you're all right. It's too late for you to be out by yourself, I think. I know you don't really want to talk to me or anything, but I'm just worried about you. I'm wondering if you've gone out of town or something. I haven't . . . I mean, you haven't answered your phone all night. But like I said, I did what you asked, and I stopped sending you flowers. But what I wanted to tell you, that I forgot to tell you before, is that I had this idea that I would keep sending you flowers until irises were back in season, because I know how much you like irises. And I know you can get the hothouse kind, but I don't think that's the same, really. But then, what do I know? They probably grow them in hothouses all year round. That's probably something you would know. But anyway, I know you've been working hard lately and I want to do something for you, but you won't let me send you flowers, so I was just thinking, maybe you'd let me cook you dinner? Maybe tomorrow night? I mean, you haven't even seen my place yet. So give me a call when you get in, because I'll be up. Okay? . . . Okay. Bye.

(The machine clicks. THERESA, *who has stopped working in the middle of it, starts again. Pause. The phone rings again. Her voice comes on.)*

Theresa's voice: You've reached my machine. Leave a message.

Tony: It's me again. I just . . . I left that message to call me when you got in and then I just had a thought: maybe you're not getting in. Maybe you're sleeping with somebody else right now. And the thought of that just made me feel like I wanted to throw up. I just want to know. If you're seeing somebody else I just want to know. I don't want you to think you have to spare my feelings, because if you think that, then you must think I'm some pathetic jerk. Which would make me very angry, Theresa, because I don't need your pity. I'm not asking for your pity for one fucking second. I just think that you owe me the truth. *(*THERESA, *who has been staring at her computer through this, suddenly loses it and makes a grab for the phone.)* I think you owe me at least that much after everything you—

5 **Theresa:** *(Snatching up the receiver)* Stop calling me! Don't send me things, don't try to see me. Don't ever speak to me again! *(She hangs up.)* Jesus Christ! *(Beat. The phone rings again. Furious, she tries to unplug it, can't get the plug out, then rips the cord from the wall. Silence. She goes back to the bed, sits down. She is shaking. She looks toward the window.)* I mean it. *(She looks toward the window again. Something dawns on her. She quickly reaches over and grabs her bag and searches through it. Her cellular phone starts to ring from inside the bag. She finds the phone and turns it off. She sits for a moment and thinks, then she quickly turns off the lights. In the dark she gets up, goes to the door, and checks it. It's locked. Then she gets a chair and pushes it up under the handle. Then she goes into the kitchen and comes back with a butcher knife. She puts the knife down by the bed, then gets in and starts working again by the light of her laptop.)*

Scene 8

Theresa's office, the following Monday. She is sitting, looking tired, staring into space. MERCER *enters with her article.*

Mercer: Hey.
Theresa: Hey.
Mercer: Do you mind if I close the door?
Theresa: No. Go ahead.

*(*MERCER *closes the door, sits.)*

5 **Mercer:** Howard asked me to read your piece.

Theresa: That's okay.

Mercer: Well, what he really did was, he asked me to rewrite it. I think he didn't want to talk to you himself, because he didn't want to hurt your feelings.

Theresa: Is it that bad?

Mercer: It's, um . . . in places it just seems confused, and there are holes in the narrative. I don't know how we got from A to B.

10 **Theresa:** I need to interview him again, but I don't want to, because he's obnoxious.

Mercer: I thought he was kind of funny. (*Beat.*) I mean, in a totally offensive way.

Theresa: He is kind of funny. (*Beat.*) You know, if you want to rewrite it, you won't hurt my feelings.

Mercer: I don't really want to.

Theresa: Then I'll do it. It's my stupid story. I'll do it.

(*Pause.*)

15 **Mercer:** How do you remember all the things that you remember?

Theresa: What do you mean?

Mercer: I feel like you remember everything you read.

Theresa: I keep notebooks.

Mercer: Really?

20 **Theresa:** Yeah. I write down the title of the book I'm reading at the top of the page, and then I write down what seemed most important to me about the book and what ideas I got from it. And then I number the pages and keep an index at the back of the note-book. So I can find what I want, if I go back. (*Beat.*) I guess I'm really anal.

Mercer: No, I think that's really smart. (*He studies her.*) I guess I'm just wondering if there's something wrong. I know we're not close, or anything, but since I've been here, I've come to think of you as the person who holds up the standard around here. And I guess I was a little shocked to see that you let it slip.

Theresa: You know a standard was actually a staff, that soldiers used to hold. They were called standard-bearers.

Mercer: I know. That's why I . . . that's what I meant. (*Beat.*) Is there something wrong?

Theresa: My voice mail was completely full this morning.

25 **Mercer:** You're really busy.

Theresa: No, it was full of messages from someone I didn't want to hear from. From over the weekend.

Mercer: Who?

Theresa: Can I . . . if I tell you something, do you promise not to tell anybody?

Mercer: Of course.

30 **Theresa:** Because I think Howard wants to understand, but I don't think he does, quite. And my friend Linda and I are not really getting along . . .

Mercer: What's up?

Theresa: Do you remember that guy that came into the office that day?

Mercer: That kind of goofy-looking guy?

Theresa: Yes.

35 **Mercer:** Is he the flower guy?

Theresa: Yes.

Mercer: Is he bugging you?

Theresa: He's stalking me. I think. I mean, I don't know what constitutes stalking legally, but if he's not, then he's coming awfully close. I know now he's following me. I mean, he called me all night, Saturday night, before I . . . Well, I ended up ripping the phone out of the wall.

Mercer: Theresa.

40 **Theresa:** Then I turned the light off because I had the feeling he was watching me somehow. And then the first message here was . . . you know there's that time and date
stamp, on the messages . . .

Mercer: Yeah.

Theresa: The first message was after that, after two in the morning on Sunday, and he said,
"I saw your light was off." So he was watching. I live on the second floor. You can't really see in, I don't think. But it's not that high up.

Mercer: What did he say?

Theresa: Well, I had been screening my calls all night and he had been calling and calling,
and I finally picked up the phone and yelled at him, which I shouldn't have done. But
then he knew I had been home, so he called here to tell me how angry he was, and
every message just gets . . .

45 **Mercer:** What?

Theresa: Angrier and angrier. He keeps saying over and over that he wants to hurt me.
That he wants me to suffer, like him. That he wants . . . he wants to hurt me.

Mercer: Did you save them?

Theresa: Yes.

Mercer: Can I hear one?

50 **Theresa:** (*Picks up the phone, punches in a code. Hands the receiver to* MERCER.) That's the first
one. They go on. (MERCER *listens. The message ends and he punches a button for the next
one. He listens a while longer, then he looks at* THERESA.) Do you think I should be scared?

Mercer: How many of these are there?

Theresa: Twenty.

Mercer: I think you should call the police.

Scene 9

Theresa's office, later that day. MERCER *is there with* THERESA *and* MADELEINE BECK, *a plain-
clothes police officer.* BECK *is listening to the messages while* THERESA *and* MERCER *wait.*

Beck: (*Holding the receiver out*) That's the last one. How do I get out of here? (THERESA *takes
the phone, punches buttons, hangs up. Overlapping*) Don't erase those. Do you have any
other messages or letters or anything?

Theresa: There are messages on my machine at home. And he sent me some e-mails, but I
deleted them all.

Beck: That's okay. Did you keep any of the cards he sent you?

Theresa: No.

5 **Beck:** If he sends you anything else, keep it. And from now on keep a diary of any time he
calls, any time you see him. Any contact at all. Write it down, and write down the date
and time. The more specific the better.

Theresa: What am I doing this for?

Beck: Well, I think with these messages, we can get you a temporary restraining order. But
just in case. For future reference, you should keep the diary.

Theresa: For future reference?

Beck: Well, we can get the restraining order, but I'll tell you up front, it's hard to enforce it.
If he doesn't want to be seen, he won't be. I ran a check on him when you called, and
he doesn't have any priors, so if all he does is call you again, then we couldn't hold
him for that. But if he builds up a record of consistent abuse, then we could definitely
charge him.

10 **Theresa:** Consistent abuse?

Beck: Abuse of the restraining order. Not of you, necessarily.

Theresa: Great.

Beck: In the meantime, you can take some precautions. Get an unlisted phone number.

Theresa: I had one, he got it.

15 **Beck:** Get a new one, and don't give it to anybody except your closest circle. And since he knows where you live, you should go ahead and move.

Theresa: Move?

Beck: Do you have a doorman?

Theresa: No.

Beck: Well, when you move, move to a building with a doorman and get an alarm for your apartment. Also, before you move, I'd go ahead and change your name. Then put the apartment and the phone and everything in your new name.

20 **Theresa:** Okay. I don't want to change my name.

Beck: I know it's a hassle.

Theresa: I'm a writer. I write under this name.

Beck: You'll have to decide that one yourself. Okay, what else. Okay, make sure you vary your route to work and back. Never take the same route two days in a row, but don't fall into a pattern either. And vary your routine as well. If you go to the health club after work, start going before work or during lunch. If you go to church on Sundays, think about changing churches. Some people feel safer buying a gun, but I can't in good conscience recommend that. I've seen too many people shot with their own guns.

(Pause.)

Mercer: Can I clarify something?

25 **Beck:** Sure.

Mercer: Are you telling Theresa to do all these things now? Or are you telling her this just in case she needs to know somewhere down the line.

Beck: I think she should seriously consider doing them now. *(Beat. To* THERESA*)* I don't know. This escalated quickly, and I'll be honest, that concerns me. Most of the time, if somebody's being stalked, it's by somebody they had a substantial relationship with. Or a coworker or somebody who sees them every day and has been harboring a secret obsession.

(Beat. Both BECK *and* THERESA *instinctively look at* MERCER*.)*

Mercer: Hey.

Beck: No. I mean somebody like you, not you. So the rapidity of this concerns me.

30 **Theresa:** I guess I should have called you sooner.

Beck: Well, you could have called, but honestly, I couldn't have done anything, because he didn't threaten you until now. *(Beat.)* Don't beat yourself up, okay? I tell all my complainants that. You don't know. You think you can handle him yourself and then all of a sudden he's whacked out on you.

Theresa: I guess I did think I could handle it myself.

Beck: Unfortunately though, the very things you did to try and stop him from bothering you were probably the very things that egged him on.

Theresa: How's that?

35 **Beck:** Well, like if you pick up the phone and say, "Don't ever call me again," you think you're being clear, but all he's hearing is "She's talking to me. I still have a chance." And I don't know how you broke up with him—

Theresa: I didn't break up with him. You have to have a relationship before you can break up, and there was none.

Beck: Right. I just meant, I don't know how you left it. If you gave any kind of excuse, or left it open in any way, then he didn't hear you saying "No." He heard you saying "Yes, once this one thing changes, then we can be together." Like if you said you were still hung up on some other guy, or you weren't ready for a relationship. Any of those things you say.

Theresa: I said it was my work.

Beck: See? What you should have said was "I thought it over and I don't want to see you again," and not given a reason even if he asked.

40 **Theresa:** This isn't doing me much good right now.

Beck: No, I'm just saying . . . for future reference.

Theresa: I don't need it, because I'm never going out with anybody again.

Beck: That's up to you, of course. (*Beat.*) Okay. I can't think of anything else right now. The restraining order may very well scare him off. But you should be prepared for the opposite reaction, too.

Theresa: Which is what?

45 **Beck:** Well, that it pisses him off and he comes back at you even harder. That happens and it's another reason to take precautions.

Theresa: What if none of this works, then what?

Beck: You mean . . . ?

Theresa: I mean, what's the worst that can happen?

Beck: There's no reason to think about that.

50 **Theresa:** Why not?

Beck: There's just no reason to think about it.

Theresa: Well, what's the worst thing you've ever seen?

Beck: You don't want to know.

Theresa: Have you seen people killed?

55 **Beck:** I've seen that.

Theresa: That wasn't the worst thing? (*Beat.*) Detective?

(*Pause.*)

Beck: You don't want to know.

Act 2
Scene 1

THERESA *is back at Les Kennkat's office, interviewing him.*

Theresa: I appreciate your seeing me again.

Les: Well, you said you wanted to get it right, and I want you to get it right, too.

Theresa: So, I have some questions here. Just biographical stuff. You were in the war?

Les: I was with a film unit. I was stationed in London. But that's all in the press packet. Ask me something else.

5 **Theresa:** Okay. (*Scanning down a list of questions, obviously skipping several.*) Your marriage to Joy Box . . . I assume that wasn't her real name?

Les: No.

Theresa: . . . it ended after a year. What happened?

Les: Her name was Kathy Malone. And she didn't like it that I slept around with other women.

Theresa: Oh.

10 **Les:** I was very fond of Kathy, but I couldn't change my spots, it turned out. She told me she would leave me, but I didn't believe her. But she did. She stuck to her guns, and I've always respected her for that.

Theresa: Why didn't you believe her?

Les: I don't know. I just didn't.

Theresa: But if she said it . . .?

Les: I don't know.

15 **Theresa:** Why don't men take women seriously? Why is that?

Les: I take women very seriously.

Theresa: No. When a woman talks, a man just sees her mouth moving. I could say, "The ceiling's caving in" or "You stepped in gum"—something I could prove, empirically— and you wouldn't believe me.

Les: I would believe you. Is the ceiling caving in? (*He looks up.*)

Theresa: I didn't mean you. I meant, one. One wouldn't believe me.

20 **Les:** The reason I didn't believe Kathy is simple. I didn't want to believe her. Okay? I wish I had. Then I wouldn't be sitting here—seventy plus—all alone. I'd have somebody to take care of me. I have health problems. I have problems with my colon and they might have to take it out. An old man without a colon doesn't attract women to him anymore.

Theresa: Well, what do you expect?

(*Beat.*)

Les: You know, I have been interviewed many times, especially in the old days. And even cub reporters from *Movie News* did a better job than you do. These have been two of the worst interviews of my life. After the last one, I went and got drunk. I couldn't be- lieve how rudely you rejected me and my friendly offer of a drink. And now I want to go get drunk again. You're really a depressing person.

Theresa: Well, so are you.

Les: See, I don't think that's your job. To come in here and tell me I'm depressing. (*Beat.*) How am I depressing?

25 **Theresa:** You're whining because the very women you treated like shit aren't here to take care of you in your old age.

Les: I could always hire a nurse. There's nothing I like better than a voluminous pair of breasts in a tight white uniform.

Theresa: Forget it.

Les: I was just joking! You're so depressing you kill a joke before it even hits the air.

Theresa: I could laugh at that, I guess. But I don't want to encourage you. And it's not funny.

30 **Les:** Last time you thought I was funny.

Theresa: Sometimes you are, I guess. Parts of your movies are funny. Not the breast parts, but the parts where people run over each other with cars and their arms fly off.

Les: The comic relief.

Theresa: Right. So I could say about you, "He's a funny guy, except when it comes to women." And I have said that before, about other men. You know: "He's a good guy, but he does have a problem with women." But I'm not saying that anymore. Because you're not a funny guy, and you're not a good guy, if you can't deal with half the popu- lation of the world. Your problem with women is a problem with more than fifty per- cent of the people on this planet, and that's too high a percentage to make you funny.

Les: (*Nods, beat.*) I see what you're saying. If something offends you, then you're not going to find it funny. No matter what.

35 **Theresa:** But do you see what else I'm saying? About how you can't deal with half the pop- ulation of the world?

Les: Sure, but neither can you.

Theresa: That's not true.

Les: No, you obviously can't deal with me.

Theresa: But that's just because you can't deal with me. If you could deal with me, then I could deal with you.

40 **Les:** Aw, forget it. This is stupid. Don't publish anything about me in your stupid magazine. I don't want you writing anything about me.

Theresa: Well, you can't stop me.

Les: Fine, go ahead. But believe me, you can't say anything worse about me than what I've already said about myself. Trust me. There's nothing in me that's surprising. People hear me talk about my passion for breasts and they think, What a sad old man. And they're right. I am a sad old man.

Theresa: You're not going to make me feel sorry for you.

Les: Obviously. You're heartless.

45 **Theresa:** I'm not heartless.

Les: Then stop tormenting me. I thought you were a reporter. I thought your job was to come here and ask me questions, which I then answer. Not to sit in judgment of me. But that's all you've done. All you've done is yell at me.

(Pause.)

Theresa: Then I apologize for my lack of professionalism.

Les: Apology accepted. You'll find I'm also a very forgiving man. Let's just put this behind us. Okay?

Theresa: Okay. I just have a few more questions.

50 **Les:** Shoot.

Theresa: Your new project, do you have any actresses in mind for that?

Les: I do. I just found a lovely young lady, Deena Delite, but I'm going to ask her to change her name because Deena Delite sounds cheap to me.

Theresa: Do you have another name in mind?

Les: Not yet, but something will come to me. Something always does. I usually come up with a good screen name for a woman by staring at her naked breasts.

55 **Theresa:** I see.

Les: Or fucking her. But I can't always do that anymore because old age has finally caught up with me in the nether regions. But even if I can't penetrate a woman, I can still bring her to orgasm with my tongue or finger.

Theresa: *(Fairly jumping up)* Okay. That's all I need.

Les: No, because what I'm saying is, that in that moment of ecstasy, when she's wet and moaning, that's when a name will come to me.

Theresa: *(Putting her recorder away)* That's it! That's all. I don't need to hear any more.

60 **Les:** When will this come out?

Theresa: Next month.

Les: *(As* THERESA *leaves)* And what's the name of the magazine again?

Theresa: *(Already off)* The World.

Les: *(Alone.)* That's right. Window to the world. The little world in a window.

Scene 2

Theresa's office, a couple of days later. MERCER *is waiting for her.* HOWARD *enters with an article.*

Howard: Did you read this?

Mercer: Yeah.

Howard: I can't run this.

Mercer: I thought it was funny.

5   **Howard:** She never lets up. Every reference. *(Reads from different sentences.)* " 'I always start with the actress,' says Kennkat, the seventy-two-year-old connoisseur of women's breasts." "For the past fourteen years, Kennkat, a die-hard fan of mammary glands . . ." "A breast buff from way back, Kennkat began his film career . . ." *(Trails off, smiles.)* It is sort of funny.

Mercer: Run it. What's he going to do? Sue you for defamation of character? It's all true.

Howard: Maybe I will. *(Beat.)* Where's Theresa?

Mercer: I don't know, I'm waiting for her. We were supposed to meet at ten.

Howard: *(Looks at his watch.)* Should we be worried?

10 **Mercer:** I don't know. She hasn't heard from him in two weeks. I think the police might have been right. I think the restraining order scared him off.

Howard: I hope so. The shmuck.

Mercer: Yeah.

Howard: I thought at first he was just smitten. But I guess what used to pass as smitten, these days, is psychotic.

Mercer: Yeah. I guess.

15 **Howard:** Or maybe that's going too far.

Mercer: No, I think I agree.

Howard: Well, I'm not sure I do.

Mercer: I am. I've been thinking about it since this happened. You know, I was wondering, did I ever do anything to scare a woman before? Not intentionally, but did I ever do anything that came off as scary? And I know, when I was in college, I had a girlfriend who dumped me for another guy and I would call her dorm room, just to see if she was there, or walk out of my way to see if her light was on. But just a couple of times, you know. I didn't make a career of it.

Howard: Everybody's done something like that.

20 **Mercer:** I know. I think that's my point. It's not exactly abnormal behavior. But it's on the same continuum.

Howard: I don't get you.

Mercer: Normal, male, heterosexual behavior is somewhat psychotic. I was going to talk to Theresa about this first, but . . . I want to write about this. Can I write about this?

Howard: Write about what?

Mercer: Tony. Or guys like him. Because, when you look at Tony, he looks like a normal guy. And in a lot of ways, he is a normal guy. Or at least he's doing what normal guys do in movies. It's a classic romantic plot. First the guy sees the girl. He thinks she's beautiful; she has long brown hair and big brown eyes, she's just the sort of woman he's dreamed about, so bang—he falls in love with her. Regardless of the fact that he doesn't know anything about her, he falls madly, deeply in love with her. But there's some obstacle to his love. Like the woman's dating some jerk who's completely wrong for her. So our guy has to prove himself to her. And to do that, he starts following her around. He spies on her, and as he watches her, he becomes convinced that if they could only be together, she would love him. So he gets aggressive. He bombards her with flowers and rents a billboard to declare his love, then bursts in on her wedding and tells her she's making a terrible mistake. And she comes around. She dumps the jerk and at the end of the story she's kissing the guy. Even though the guy has basically been stalking her, his persever-ance pays off. He gets the girl. So this Tony guy is probably wondering, Why don't I get the girl? A lot of guys are out there wondering, Why don't I get the girl?

25 **Howard:** And what are the girls thinking?

Mercer: They're thinking . . . I look great. Everybody's watching me. (*Beat.*) But I can't write that.

Howard: Why not?

Mercer: I'm a man. I can't write that.

Howard: But it's true, isn't it? I mean, don't some women walk around thinking they look good?

30 **Mercer:** I think some women do. I mean, sometimes I see a woman, and I think . . . whatever I think, and I think she wants me to look at her and think that. But I also think that's because she's been told all her life that she should want people to look at her. Just like I've been told that I'm the one who's supposed to do the looking.

Howard: But how can you not look at people?

Mercer: Well, it's not just looking at people. It's looking at people in a certain way. Like I'm checking out her ass.

Howard: That's what I meant. How can you not check people out? It's what you instinctively do.

Mercer: But do you look at a woman and think. There's an attractive woman. Or do you think, Nice ass.

35 **Howard:** What's the difference?

Mercer: I think the difference is in the intent. Maybe "There's an attractive woman" would lead you to try and get to know the person. "Nice ass" would be it. You'd stop there, you wouldn't care about the woman, you'd only care about her ass.

Howard: But I've thought "nice ass" and then later I've gotten to know the woman. Then I know her, I like her, and she has a nice ass.

(*Beat.*)

Mercer: Okay, maybe you would get to know her, but guys like Tony wouldn't. He would just assume that he knows her because he likes her ass. And what I'm saying is that you and me and Tony and all the other guys in the world, we all start in the same place. We all have the same training. We're taught to look at asses. And women are taught that they want to have their asses looked at.

Howard: Who taught us that?

40 **Mercer:** Everybody. Every ad on TV. Every song on the radio. Every *Esquire*. Every *Cosmopolitan*. Every Les Kennkat movie. Everybody.

Howard: Les Kennkat doesn't really show asses, though. His movies are mostly breasts.

Mercer: Asses or breasts, it's really academic.

Howard: Okay. So Les Kennkat tells me to look at breasts.

Mercer: Yes.

45 **Howard:** Or does Les Kennkat know that I'm already looking at breasts, and he just takes advantage of that? I mean, men like breasts, right? It's a biological thing.

Mercer: No, you think it's biological because you've been trained to think that, but it's really cultural. Different cultures like different things. I mean, do you like tiny feet?

Howard: I like a nice foot.

Mercer: But do you like teeny tiny feet?

Howard: I guess not.

50 **Mercer:** See, men in China used to like teeny tiny feet, so women bound their feet. Some tribes in Africa liked very long necks so the women put those rings around their necks, to stretch them out. At the turn of the century, apparently, men liked really huge butts so women wore these giant bustles to make their butts look huge. The size of breasts, even, goes up and down. Literally. You can get these breast implants now that you can inflate or deflate, according to the fashion.

Howard: Where'd you see that?

Mercer: The Internet.

Howard: Huh. (*Beat.*) So you don't like large breasts?

Mercer: Not particularly, no.

55 **Howard:** You like small breasts.

(*Beat.*)

Mercer: The point is, Howard, when I meet a woman with breasts I like—

Howard: Small ones.

Mercer: Whatever. Just because I like her breasts, it does not mean that I love her. And it does not mean that I know her. And if I stop at the breasts, I will never know her.

Howard: Unless you know her in the Biblical sense.

60 **Mercer:** Oh, for God's sake!

Howard: I'm just kidding. It's a joke. Relax. (*Beat.*) So what is your article about?

Mercer: It's about Tony and Theresa. And why the boy thinks he should get the girl, and why the girl thinks she's something to get got.

Howard: (*Thinks.*) I think I see where you're going. I'm not sure I agree a hundred percent, but it's interesting.

Mercer: So I can write it?

65 **Howard:** Give it a try. We'll see how it goes.

Mercer: Great. Thanks.

(*Harriet enters with some letters.*)

Harriet: Theresa's mail. (*She puts it on Theresa's desk.* HOWARD *and* MERCER *instinctively look at her breasts. She notices and looks down at her shirt.*) What?

Howard and Mercer: Nothing.

(*Harriet exits.*)

Howard: (*Watching her leave*) How's she working out?

70 **Mercer:** She makes a lot of mistakes and she talks on the phone all the time. But other than that.

(THERESA *enters.*)

Theresa: Hey.

Howard: Hey, you're late. You're supposed to call me so I don't worry.

Theresa: I got rid of my cell phone. It made me feel too accessible.

Howard: Well, get another one so you can call. What if there's an emergency?

75 **Theresa:** All right. I was looking at apartments. I think I found a place.

Howard: Is it secure? Is there a doorman?

Theresa: Yeah, a doorman, and security cameras. The whole bit. I can't afford it. But I liked it and I really . . . I don't feel comfortable in my place anymore.

Howard: How much more is it a month?

Theresa: Four hundred.

80 **Howard:** We'll work something out.

Theresa: Are you giving me a raise?

Howard: We'll work something out, okay? You take the place, though. Call them now so you don't lose it.

Theresa: Okay, Howard. Thank you. (*She pulls a card from her purse and goes to the phone.*)

Howard: And I read this Kennkat thing and I get the point.

85 **Theresa:** He likes breasts?

Howard: No. I get the point that you are not inclined to write these sorts of pieces any-more. (*Beat.*) You don't have to.

Theresa: What?

Howard: I've taken advantage of your loyalty and your reliability for too long, and you and I are going to sit down and decide on a new direction for the both of us, that pleases the both of us.

Theresa: I want to write about the Yankees. The Yankees are the only thing good in my life right now.

(*Beat.*)

90 **Howard:** Then you write about the Yankees.

Theresa: Okay.

Howard: Now get that apartment. (*He exits, quickly.*)

Theresa: What got into him?

Mercer: Guilt. Can I close the door?

95 **Theresa:** Sure. You know, I think I'll get stalked every day. I get a raise, I get to write about the Yankees. (*Dialing the phone.*) I'm just going to call this realtor and then we'll talk about your story.

Mercer: I'm in no hurry.

Theresa: (*On the phone*) Hi. I was calling for Casey Samples . . . Sure, I'll hold. (*She starts flipping through her mail. To* MERCER) So what's your idea?

Mercer: I'll wait till you get off the phone.

Theresa: (*Still flipping through mail. As she talks, she opens something, glances at it, throws it away. Still to* MERCER) I haven't really left my house, you know, I've basically been going home and hunkering down. So I've been watching a lot of TV, and there's that cable channel, Lifetime? It's the women's network? (*Looking at a letter without opening it*) They play all these made-for-TV movies on there and, I don't know, every other night, I guess, there's one on about stalking. They're all called, like *Poisoned Love* or *Love Hurts*.

100 **Mercer:** Or . . . *The Graduate.*

Theresa: (*Laughs.*) Exactly. Anyway, they all start with a married woman, and her husband's ignoring her. But the tennis pro at her country club thinks she's really hot and he makes a pass at her. And she gives in and has sex with him, but she doesn't want to have a real relationship with the guy because he's a tennis pro, for god sake. But he won't have that and he starts stalking her. Then her husband finds out and leaves her. So she buys a gun to protect herself, and at the last minute, she shoots the stalker in the head. Sometimes it's a pistol, sometimes it's a pump-action rifle. (*Noticing a letter, opening it*) At first I was disgusted, but I found I kept watching the stupid things, be-cause, at the end, I felt this real sense of satisfaction when the stalker got it in the head. (*Pause. She's reading the letter. It is very disturbing. Quietly*) Mercer? (*Someone comes on the line. On the phone. Urgent.*) Yeah, I want to get that apartment on Sixty-eighth. This is Theresa Bedell. (*Beat. Suddenly screaming*) What do you mean?! I was there twenty minutes ago! What do you mean?!

Mercer: Theresa?

Theresa: (*On phone*) Then you have to get me another one!

Mercer: (*Overlapping*) Theresa? (*He goes to* THERESA. *As he rounds the desk, he sees the letter she was looking at, looks at it.*)

105 **Theresa:** No! I don't . . . I can't wait! NO NO! Now! Do you hear me? NOW! You can't— we had a verbal contract! A verbal contract!

Mercer: Oh God. (*Quickly turning over the letter*) Hang up the phone. (*He tries to take the re-ceiver from her.*)

Theresa: No!

Mercer: Hang up the . . . (*He pulls it from* THERESA, *sets it down.*) Hang up the phone. (*She is shaking. He puts his arm around her.*) We'll call the police. It's just a letter. He's not here, he's not here. It's just a letter. (*Pause. He holds* THERESA, *then she gently pushes him away. He steps back.*) Okay.

Theresa: (*Quietly*) I don't know you.

110 **Mercer:** Okay.

Theresa: What's your interest in me?

Mercer: I'm just trying to help. Honestly. I promise I'm just trying to help. (THERESA *doesn't answer.*) Is there someone . . . why don't you let me call your friend Linda.

Theresa: This is Linda's fault.

Mercer: Is there somebody else I can call? Somebody in your family?

115 **Theresa:** No.

Mercer: Okay. I'm going to call the police, then. What's the woman's name?

Theresa: Detective Beck.

Mercer: Is it in your Rolodex?

Theresa: Yes. Under "B." For Beck. (*She backs away from the desk as* MERCER *gets the number, dials. Talking to herself*) The play-offs are on tonight.

120 **Mercer:** (*On the phone*) Can I speak to Detective Beck, please? . . . Thanks. (*Beat.*) Yeah. It's Mercer Stevens calling, it's about Theresa Bedell, it's urgent.

Theresa: If he is watching the Yankees . . . if he is somewhere, watching the Yankees, I'll kill him.

Mercer: (*To* THERESA) It's okay. They're paging her.

Theresa: I mean it.

Mercer: I know.

125 **Theresa:** If the Yankees blow the play-offs, I'll kill them.

(*Beat.*)

Mercer: Look, don't let me freak you out, okay? But if you want to come over to our place tonight, we've got a pull-out couch, and according to other guests, it's very comfortable.

Theresa: We?

Mercer: Me and my wife.

Theresa: You're married?

130 **Mercer:** Yes.

Theresa: I didn't know you were married. You don't wear a ring.

Mercer: I have a contact dermatitis. With metal.

Theresa: You get a rash.

Mercer: I get a rash. Right. (*Beat. Into phone*) Yeah, I'll keep holding. Thanks. (*Back to* THERESA) You know, I told Michelle the other day, though, that we should have you over for dinner or something. But I didn't know how to broach it. I'm not good at that stuff. I don't know how to make friends as an adult.

135 **Theresa:** I see. I mean, I understand.

Mercer: In college you'd meet somebody, and if you both really liked Aerosmith, you were best friends.

Theresa: Right.

Mercer: And I was thinking, maybe that's what happened with Tony. Maybe you said something, on that first date, that made him think you were perfect for each other. It could have been anything, really, because he already had a picture of the ideal woman in his head, and he was just looking for somebody to impose that on. You probably said one little thing that fit the picture. Or you wore your hair a certain way. Or he liked the shape of your *(Theresa is staring at him.)* he liked the way you looked.

(Pause.)

Theresa: Is this it?

140 **Mercer:** What?

Theresa: Is this the idea? For the story? You want to write about me and what's happening to me?

Mercer: *(Hesitates for a moment, decides not to lie.)* It is. I didn't mean . . . I mean this isn't the time to talk about it

Theresa: No. Go ahead. Tell me.

Mercer: Maybe later.

145 **Theresa:** No. Tell me now.

Mercer: Well, I just, I want to write about how men and women see each other, but obviously I'm not qualified to write about this from a woman's perspective. I mean, I can guess, but I don't really know how women perceive themselves. In relation to the ways in which men perceive them. If you know what I mean.

Theresa: I do.

Mercer: So that's where I would need your help. (THERESA *doesn't answer.)* Or your blessing. *(She still doesn't answer.)* Or something. *(She picks up the letter.)*

Theresa: Here are the ways in which I perceive myself, in relation to the ways men perceive me: I perceive myself to be a bitch.

150 **Mercer:** Don't read that.

Theresa: I perceive myself as something to be fucked until I scream.

Mercer: *(Putting down the phone)* This isn't what I meant.

Theresa: *(Overlapping with "meant")* As something to be nailed to the ground and fucked so hard I split in two.

Mercer: Theresa, please don't look at that.

155 **Theresa:** As something to be fucked where I'm small. I don't even know what that means. Something to be fucked where I'm small.

Mercer: *(In spite of himself)* I think he means . . . sodomized.

Theresa: Then add that to your list.

Mercer: *(Holding out his hand for the letter)* Don't keep looking at that. This isn't what I meant.

Theresa: My life is not theoretical.

160 **Mercer:** I know.

Theresa: You don't get to make something theoretical out of my life.

Mercer: *(Taking, a step toward her)* Theresa. Please. Stop.

Theresa: *(She backs away.)* No, you stop.

Mercer: Okay. *(He backs off.)*

165 **Theresa:** You stop.

Mercer: Okay. *(He moves back to the phone, picks it up.)* I'm still on hold.

Theresa: I'm not theoretical. I'm real.

Scene 3

Theresa's office, the following day. THERESA *is talking to* DETECTIVE BECK. *She is wearing the same clothes.*

BECK: Have you gotten any more letters?

Theresa: No.

Beck: Phone calls?

Theresa: None here, but he might have called me at home. I spent last night at my boss's place. I didn't want to be by myself.

5 **Beck:** Can you stay there for a while?

Theresa: I guess so. I also called my friend Linda. She lives out on Long Island. She says I can stay with her for as long as I like. But he knows where she lives, so I didn't know.

Beck: I'd stay where you are for now, if you're comfortable. That way your boss can go with you to and from work. You should take a cab every night and have the driver sort of drive you around first.

(*Beat.*)

Theresa: What's wrong?

Beck: I can't find your guy.

10 **Theresa:** What?

Beck: He moved out of his apartment last week, and when I went by his work, they told me he'd been fired over two months ago. I couldn't get the woman to talk at first, but when I told her why I was there, she let me know that he was fired for activity just like this.

Theresa: He was stalking somebody?

Beck: Yeah. Somebody where he worked. The woman's been transferred. They wouldn't say where. But this is sort of what I was wondering. If maybe he'd been stalking somebody and she evaded him so he was just looking for somebody else to fixate on.

Theresa: So I'm just an understudy.

15 **Beck:** So to speak. But to him, now, it's you he's fixated on.

Theresa: He doesn't even have a job?

Beck: No.

Theresa: So he can stalk me full-time?

Beck: Yeah. Try not to be alone. Try not to go anywhere that's not absolutely necessary. (*Beat.*) He might have gotten out all he wanted to say to you in the letter.

20 **Theresa:** Do you think?

Beck: I don't know. (*Handing her an envelope from her bag*) Here. I got a copy of his picture, from his work ID. You should show it to security here, at your boss's place. Let them know to keep an eye out for the guy.

Theresa: (*Doesn't open the envelope.*) I don't want to look at him.

Beck: Just do it sooner rather than later, okay?

Theresa: (*Putting the envelope in her drawer*) Okay. (*Beat.*) How long have you done this?

25 **Beck:** I've worked on this particular detail for two years now. I worked in a rape response unit before that.

Theresa: Doesn't it depress you?

Beck: It does, but it also makes me feel good about myself, that I can be of some help to people.

Theresa: Is there a pattern? In these cases?

Beck: There are some profiles for stalkers, whether it's a man or a woman—

30 **Theresa:** No, I mean, the people who are stalked. Is there anything about them?

Beck: No. I don't know. They come from all walks of life.

Theresa: (*Beat.*) Do they train you on how to talk to people like me?

Beck: They do.

Theresa: Because I feel like you have a standard way of talking. I mean, your language. The way you phrase things.

35 **Beck:** There are standard procedures. I like to think, though, that I respond to people as individuals. In individual ways.

Theresa: I'm not criticizing you. I find it kind of comforting. That there's a standard reply
    to this. It means I'm not alone.

Beck: Right.

Theresa: But do I seem like a person who would get stalked?

Beck: No. There's never any rhyme or reason to it. It's never anybody's fault.

40 **Theresa:** I keep thinking I did something.

    Beck: That's only because you're human.

Theresa: I am?

Beck: (*Smiles.*) Yeah. (*Small beat.*) That's not really what I mean, though. I just mean . . .
    like I'm from this big family. Five boys and I'm the only girl, and my parents paid for
    my brothers to go to college. But they never even offered to pay for me, because I was
    supposed to get married right out of high school. I was engaged and everything, and
    the guy I was supposed to marry, he won a Pulitzer Prize last year.

Theresa: Who is he?

45 **Beck:** I don't want to tell you.

Theresa: Who does he write for?

Beck: It's not important. I didn't want to marry him. That's all that matters. I went to
    Hunter College instead, and I had to pay my own way because my family thought I
    was making such a huge mistake.

Theresa: Does he write for the *Times*?

Beck: It doesn't matter. My point is that I had to work my way through college. But why?
    Why didn't I demand that my parents pay my tuition? They paid for my brothers.
    Right? So why didn't I demand that they pay for me?

50 **Theresa:** I don't know.

    Beck: Because it didn't occur to me. Because the system of my family and the system of the
    world around my family never laid out that option for me, and so I never thought of it.

Theresa: I don't understand the connection.

Beck: Just that we can't always tell how much is us and how much is the world around us.
    (*Small beat.*) If that makes any sense.

Theresa: Okay. When I was a freshman in college, I dated a guy who was a bartender. I
    would go and sit at the bar and wait for him to get off work. And there was this old
    man there who was always drinking alone and I always felt sorry for him. One night,
    he started talking to me, telling me all about his life and how he had lost his wife and
    how his children didn't speak to him anymore, and I felt really sorry for him and I
    told him I felt bad for him and he told me it would make him feel better to kiss a
    pretty girl. So I let him kiss me. On the mouth. (*Beat.*) I didn't want to at all. He was
    an old drunk and it made me sick. But I did it anyway because it's what I thought I
    was supposed to do. I was supposed to be nice. (*Beat.*) And then later that year, I was
    covering a Take Back the Night Rally for the school paper, and this woman turned to
    me and saw me taking notes, and she asked me if I was there as a reporter, or as a
    woman, and I said as a reporter, and she was disgusted. She wanted a protester, not a
    reporter. But I didn't want to say as a woman, because I hadn't had many good experi-
    ences as a woman, so when she presented me with another option, I jumped at it.
    (*Beat.*) Maybe being a woman, to me, meant tolerating a lot of shit. And maybe I never
    learned otherwise. I still tolerate shit, but I do it as a reporter, so it just seems like part
    of the job. But maybe it's really still me thinking that's what I'm supposed to do, as a
    woman. Sit and listen to some asshole go on and on about himself, and then reward
    him for it. So maybe that's why I told Tony that it was entirely me, when that wasn't
    the truth. It was actually entirely him. (*Beat.*) Is that what you were saying?

55 **Beck:** Um . . . I don't know. I think so.

Theresa: I think it was. *(Beat.)* I'm glad you didn't marry that guy.

Beck: Thanks. *(Beat. She stands.)* Okay, then. I'll call you as soon as I know something.

Theresa: Okay.

Beck: I know it's hard, but try not to worry. (THERESA *nods.* BECK *studies her.)* Come here.

60 **Theresa:** What?

Beck: Just come here.

(BECK *gives* THERESA *a big hug.* THERESA *is surprised at first, then very grateful as she relaxes into it.)*

Scene 4

Theresa's office. HARRIET *enters.*

Theresa: Do you need something, Harriet?

Harriet: Howard told me what was going on, with Tony, and I am so sorry.

Theresa: Oh. Well, thank you.

Harriet: He just wanted me to know. I noticed how you'd been wearing the same clothes the last three days.

5 **Theresa:** Yeah, I guess I have.

Harriet: So I was thinking, maybe you'd like to go out to lunch and then maybe go over to Saks. Tish Cornwall is doing a demonstration. She has a new line of makeup, and she and her team are giving free makeovers. It might be fun.

Theresa: I don't think I can.

Harriet: I just thought, you know, because of what was going on with you, maybe it'd be nice to treat yourself to something. If I had the money, I'd offer to treat you to a day at the salon. That's what my mom would do.

Theresa: Really.

10 **Harriet:** Yeah. When I was in high school, if I ever had anything really upsetting happen to me, she'd take me down for the works. I loved it. All the old ladies there would go on and on about how pretty I was, and I'd order everybody around. Make them bring me juice.

Theresa: I'm sure it was fun.

Harriet: It was. *(Beat.)* I just thought, maybe if you pampered yourself a little bit. I'm a big believer in being good to yourself.

Theresa: Harriet, I'm afraid I'll have to pass. I feel kind of funny walking around, and, I don't know, sort of the last thing I want to do right now is get a makeover. But thank you anyway.

Harriet: Can I do anything else for you?

15 **Theresa:** Um . . . well, you could, actually. But, if this makes you uncomfortable, just say so, okay? I need to go back to my apartment and get some things, but in the meantime, I could really use some underwear. If you're going to Saks anyway . . .

Harriet: Sure.

Theresa: Are you sure?

Harriet: I'm positive.

Theresa: *(Getting money from her wallet)* You can just get me the kind that comes in the packs. Um, I like all cotton.

20 **Harriet:** What size? Five?

Theresa: I think six.

Harriet: I bet you're a five.

Theresa: Go ahead and get a six. I'd rather have them too big.

Harriet: God, me too. (*She takes the money.*)

25 **Theresa:** Thank you so much, Harriet.

Harriet: It's no problem.

Theresa: I know, but it's not something I would ever normally ask you to do. Buy under-wear for your boss.

Harriet: I promise I don't mind. (*Beat.*) You look terrible.

Theresa: Thanks.

30 **Harriet:** No. God, I'm sorry. I just meant, that if there's anything else, let me know. (MERCER enters.) Hey.

Mercer: (*Looks at her.*) How do you walk in those shoes?

Harriet: They're tall, but they're flat. (*To* THERESA) I'll be back around two.

Theresa: Take your time.

(HARRIET *exits.*)

Mercer: Where's she going?

35 **Theresa:** Lunch.

Mercer: She's supposed to . . . (*He turns, she's gone.*) She was supposed to do some *work* this morning. (*Beat.*) Can I talk to you?

Theresa: Sure.

Mercer: Look, I know that I handled this whole thing very badly. I was insensitive and pushy when I shouldn't have been, but . . .

Theresa: But?

40 **Mercer:** When you first asked me to listen to those messages, I honestly wasn't thinking, Oh, here's a story. I was thinking that someone I like and respect was in trouble and that she seemed to need my help. That's all. But when that policewoman came in here and started to talk, I thought, My God, there's a standard protocol here, and that made me wonder what else is standard? A standard personality? A standard play of events? And I couldn't help but be curious then. And I wanted to write about it. But I handled it very badly, and I'm sorry for that.

Theresa: But?

Mercer: But I'm still writing the story.

Theresa: I figured you were. (*Beat.*) Look, I thought all that, too. When I could think again. So I don't blame you for wanting to write the article. But right now I don't think I want to read it.

Mercer: I wasn't going to ask you to. And thank you. (*Small beat.*) So you've been staying at Howard's?

45 **Theresa:** Yeah. (*Beat.*) He's the hugest slob I've ever seen in my whole life. I had no idea. His bathtub has an inch of brown gunk on the bottom. I was sitting on the toilet, I looked at it, and I thought I'd throw up. I already had diarrhea and I thought it would come out the other end, too.

Mercer: I'm sorry.

Theresa: I can't believe I just told you that. I'm sorry.

Mercer: It's okay.

Theresa: Sometimes I don't know what's coming out of my own mouth. I feel like I do . . . you know when you're trying to pack for a long trip and you just keep walking around your apartment with, like a blow-dryer in your hand, and you're not really packing anything? You're just walking around? I feel like that.

50 **Mercer:** You're under a lot of pressure.

Theresa: Everybody's noticed, haven't they? That I've been wearing the same clothes.

Mercer: A couple of people did. I told them your apartment burned up.

Theresa: You did?

Mercer: Yeah.

55 **Theresa:** Thanks.

Mercer: You know, if you don't feel like going back to your place, I'd be happy to pick some things up for you. If you just tell me what you need.

Theresa: Maybe so.

(Beat.)

Mercer: If it would make you more comfortable, I could ask Howard to come with me.

Theresa: Mercer, don't take it personally. It's not you. I just . . . I don't feel comfortable going back myself right now, but for some reason I don't want anybody else there either.

60 **Mercer:** I understand. But let me know if you change your mind. Or you think of anything else. *(He starts to leave.)*

Theresa: Would you mind . . . would you like to sit down and talk for a while?

Mercer: Sure. Of course.

Theresa: It's no big deal, I just—I've been feeling lonely lately.

Mercer: I'm sorry.

65 **Theresa:** It's no big deal.

(Small beat.)

Mercer: So what would you like to talk about?

Theresa: I don't know. Why don't you tell me about your wife? How long have you been together?

Mercer: Sixteen years. We met in college.

Theresa: Did you both like Aerosmith?

70 **Mercer:** *(Laughs.)* No, we met . . . well, we met at a dance. We both got stood up.

Theresa: Oh no.

Mercer: Yeah. Michelle had a date with a rugby player and he got drunk and passed out before the dance. And I had a date with this woman from my poetry class. I thought she was great. She was always quoting "The Wasteland" and smoking clove cigarettes and she seemed really tragic and beautiful. So before the dance I went out and—this is so embarrassing, but I actually bought a beret.

Theresa: Oh God.

Mercer: Yeah. And that night, I spent about an hour getting it situated on my head and, you know, arranging my hair around it. And then I got to the dance and my tragic beauty wasn't there. So I waited. And I waited and waited even though I knew she wasn't coming because that was the tragic thing to do. But then after a while I noticed there was this really cute girl in a green dress, and she was also waiting and waiting. So I went up to her and asked her to dance, and she smiled, and there was nothing tragic in that smile. So I took off the beret and we danced.

75 **Theresa:** That's so sweet.

Mercer: Yeah. Sometimes I want to find that girl from my poetry class and write her a check for not showing up.

(Beat.)

Theresa: When I got ready to go out to dinner with him, that Saturday night, I changed clothes three times. I kept looking at myself in the mirror.

Mercer: You were nervous.

Theresa: No, it's more . . . I was looking in the mirror . . . I was looking in the mirror to see how I would look to him. *(Beat.)* When I think about that now, it makes me physically ill.

80 **Mercer:** You didn't know.

Theresa: It makes me physically ill. How much I wanted to look good.

Scene 5

Les Kennkat's hospital room. LES *is propped up in bed. A few flowers are around. The curtain that separates his bed from his roommate's is drawn and his roommate is hidden. He is awake, not doing anything.* HOWARD *and* THERESA *enter*

Theresa: Here we are.

Howard: I'll be down the hall. (*Exits.*)

Les: You came!

Theresa: I did.

5 **Les:** Who was that?

Theresa: My editor. Howard.

Les: He can come in.

Theresa: He's going to go get a Coke.

(*Beat.*)

Les: You came!

10 **Theresa:** I did. How are you?

Les: Good. Good. They took my colon out.

Theresa: Do you have a . . . bag thing now?

Les: A colostomy bag?

Theresa: Right.

15 **Les:** No. They attached my lower intestine directly to my rectum.

Theresa: Oh

Les: I didn't think you'd come.

Theresa: I didn't know you were so sick. So when you called, I guess I felt bad. I don't know. I don't know why I came.

Les: You felt sorry for me.

20 **Theresa:** I guess.

Les: It's all right if it got you down here. I sent you flowers, but they came back. They said you refused delivery.

Theresa: I didn't know.

Les: You didn't refuse?

Theresa: Well, I did. But it's a blanket refusal. It wasn't meant for you, really.

25 **Les:** You're just morally opposed to flowers?

Theresa: It's a long story. Why'd you send me flowers?

Les: To thank you! For the article! It was brilliant.

Theresa: It was?

Les: Yes. I've never had a better write-up. You captured the quintessential me. Again and again, Les Kennkat, a lover of large breasts. I couldn't have done it better myself. Three days later I had backers for my new movie, and then this kid from MTV called and wants to know, do I want to host some special—they want to call it *Girls Are Go!*—all about the era, the girls, the retro hip kitsch thing with girls in go-go boots and the vinyl miniskirts, dancing in cages and all that. You were right! I am a cult hero. So I sent you the flowers as a thank you, but when they came back, I thought maybe you were angry and I wanted to find out why and set it straight, because I'm a man who repays his obligations and I am now, officially, obliged to you.

30 **Theresa:** You don't have to thank me. I was just doing my job.

Les: Then you're not angry?

Theresa: No. I don't know. Maybe you can't help being a jerk.

Les: I can't. As hard as I try, I can't.

Theresa: Maybe it's generational.

35 **Les:** It could be,

Theresa: Or genetic.

Les: Or bluff.

Theresa: What?

Les: A man's gotta make a living.

40 **Theresa:** There are other ways to make a living.

Les: Not for me. I'm not talented. I'm not smart. I'm just fearless.

Theresa: Or shameless.

Les: Or shameless.

   (*Beat.*)

Theresa: Well, I have to go. Howard's waiting for me.

45 **Les:** Aw, do you have to? I've been sitting here all day by myself.

Theresa: I guess I can stay a minute.

Les: Good. It's spooky here, it's so quiet. I think the guy in the next bed is dead. He never says a word.

Theresa: (*Peeking behind the curtain*) He's not dead.

Les: What is he? A vegetable?

50 **Theresa:** I think he's comatose. Yes.

Les: They keep going behind that curtain with little bags and tubes. I figured he was a vegetable. Hospitals are very depressing places.

Theresa: Who sent the flowers?

Les: My producers.

Theresa: Do you have any family?

55 **Les:** No.

Theresa: Me neither. To speak of.

Les: You never married?

Theresa: No.

Les: I was married.

60 **Theresa:** I know. Joy Box.

Les: Kathy. Kathy was her real name. (*Beat.*) That was the biggest mistake I ever made in my life.

Theresa: Getting married?

Les: No. Losing Kathy.

   (*Pause.*)

Theresa: Well. I should go . . .

65 **Les:** Are you sure you can't stay? The nurses tell me that chair's pretty comfortable. And *Jeopardy!* is coming on. It's no fun watching it by yourself, if you can't impress anybody with how smart you are.

Theresa: You're not going to ask me to kiss you, are you?

Les: No. Why would I do that?

Theresa: I don't know. It's something old men do sometimes.

Les: I promise. That was bluff and bluster for the press. Today you're not working. You're here as a visitor only. Okay? A visiting friend,

70 **Theresa:** Well, I kind of feel like staying.

Les: Then stay.

Theresa: Okay.

(She sits. LES *picks up the remote.)*

Les: I'm not sure how this thing works. I pressed a button here and the sound went away, and then I pressed another and everything was in Spanish. *(He tries to work the remote.)* See, I want Channel 9. In English.

Theresa: Can I try?

75 **Les:** Please. *(He hands her the remote.* THERESA *pushes some buttons, the sound of* Jeopardy! *comes on faintly.)* That's it! Put that thing on the table now, and don't touch it. I don't want it messed up again. *(*THERESA *puts down the remote.)* Good timing! It's just starting. *(Beat. They watch TV.)* We can watch the whole thing.

Scene 6

Theresa's office. THERESA *and* MERCER *enter, talking.* THERESA *is wearing the same pants, but a man's shirt.*

Theresa: He's okay, I guess. It was funny. We watched *Jeopardy!* And he didn't know even the easiest ones. But then, when he did know one, he got so excited, like a little kid. Just so proud of himself. And then he told me he never graduated from high school. That when he was a kid, when he was fourteen, it was during the Depression, and one day his father came to him and told him he had to leave the house. That they didn't have enough food for the whole family and he was the oldest so he would just have to go out and make it on his own. He said he sat in the back yard and cried. And then he went inside and packed a bag and went down to the rail yards and figured out how to hop a freight, and that's what he did for the next three years. He hopped freights and went from town to town and lived like a bum. He said he was lonely and scared all the time. He said he met a girl once, in a town, and he thought she was the prettiest, nicest person he'd ever met, and she agreed to walk with him in the park, but her mother caught them and had him arrested. Just because he was poor.

Mercer: That's terrible.

Theresa: I know. And I thought, if girls were this unattainable thing to him, this prize that he didn't deserve, then sure, he would go on to make movies about breasts in trees.

Mercer: I suppose.

5 **Theresa:** You can understand somebody without excusing them. *(*HARRIET *enters with a little gift bag.)* Not again.

Harriet: Mercer, you have a call on line three.

Mercer: Thanks. *(He exits.)*

Theresa: Harriet. You have to stop buying me presents.

Harriet: They're just little treats. To cheer you up. *(*THERESA *pulls a little bottle of cologne out of the bag.)* It's what I wear. You complimented it one day.

10 **Theresa:** *(Takes off the cap, smells it.)* It's nice. But you should keep it for yourself.

Harriet: No.

Theresa: I know you don't make any money.

Harriet: It's okay. I put it on my mother's card.

Theresa: Then that's double the reason. I don't want your mother buying me presents.

15 **Harriet:** But that's why she gave me the card. She wanted me to use it for just this thing: treats.

Theresa: All right, Harriet. Thank you. But no more.

Harriet: I can't promise that.

(HOWARD *enters. His pants are ripped at the knee and his knee is scraped.*)

Harriet: Oh my God! What happened?

Theresa: *(Overlapping)* Howard!

20 **Howard:** I fell down.

Theresa: Are you okay?

Howard: I'm fine. Listen, this guy, Tony, what does he look like?

Theresa: Tall. Brown hair. Fairly thin. Why?

Howard: *(To Harriet)* Harriet? Can you get me something for my knee? *(Harriet exits.)* I thought I saw this guy yesterday. At lunch. A young guy sitting across from me and Jim Watkins. And I thought he was staring at me, but I tried not to be paranoid. Then this morning there was that reception for Carrie Banks, over at the *Post*, she's retiring. It was a huge thing, and I swear this same guy was there, standing in the corner, sort of. Staring at me again. So I just went up to him. And I said, "Do I know you from somewhere or do you know me?" And he said it was neither. I was mistaken. And then I felt like an idiot. But then, when I was leaving, I saw him going for his coat, like he was going to follow me. So I ran out a side door and down the alley. Like I was Harrison Ford or something. But when I looked back, he was coming out the door, too. He was following me. So I ran out in the street and flagged down a cab. I was so nervous, trying to get to it, I tripped and fell.

25 **Theresa:** Howard . . .

Howard: I'm okay. But by the time I got up, the guy was gone. *(Laughs nervously.)* That cabbie must've thought I was crazy.

Theresa: *(Remembering, opening her drawer)* Wait a minute, the police gave me a picture.

(She hands him the envelope. HOWARD *pulls out the picture.)*

Howard: That's him. *(He hands it back to her.* THERESA *looks at it for the first time.)* What do you think he wants?

Theresa: I don't know. Oh my God, if he did anything to you . . .

30 **Howard:** *(Overlapping)* Hey, hey. Don't worry about me.

Theresa: I'll call Detective Beck *(Starts looking for the number in her Rolodex.)*

Howard: Why do you think he's following me?

Theresa: I wonder if he's seen us together.

Howard: I don't think he could have followed us home. But if he's seen us come into the building together, maybe he's figured out that you're staying with me.

35 **Theresa:** I was so hoping he'd gone away. I was even thinking about going back to my apartment.

Howard: You can't do that.

Theresa: I know. But I miss my things. I'd like to have some of my clothes at least.

Howard: What, you don't like my shirt?

Theresa: *(Fingers her shirt.)* When did you buy this?

40 **Howard:** It's Brooks Brothers. It never goes out of style.

Theresa: I just miss my things.

Howard: Look, ask the police, and if they think it's okay, Mercer and I will go and pack up some stuff for you.

Theresa: Okay.

Howard: I got a meeting upstairs at two, so if that cop comes by before then, see if she'll wait.

45 **Theresa:** All right.

Howard: *(Looks at his pants.)* These are my best pants.

Theresa: Thank you, Howard.

Howard: For what?

Theresa: Just . . . for everything.

50   **Howard:** Hell.

(HOWARD *exits.* THERESA *picks up the phone and dials.*)

Theresa: Can I speak to Detective Beck please?

(MERCER *enters with* HARRIET *right behind him.*)

Mercer: Howard says he saw Tony. (*Sees she's on the phone.*) Sorry.

Theresa: (*On phone*) Could you ask her to call Theresa Bedell, please? She has my number . . . Thanks.

Mercer: What happened?

55   **Theresa:** He was following Howard.

Harriet: Oh God! Is that why he's bleeding?

Theresa: He's okay, Harriet, don't panic.

Harriet Oh God. Theresa . . . I have to tell you something really private. Mercer, will you leave?

Mercer: (*Looks to* THERESA, *who nods.*) Sure.

(MERCER *exits.* HARRIET *closes the door.*)

60   **Harriet:** I am so sorry.

Theresa: Why?

Harriet: I am so sorry.

Theresa: Harriet.

Harriet: I didn't know. I mean, I just thought, you know, you had broken up with your boyfriend and Tony seemed so nice and everything. I didn't know you at all. And then, in all honesty, you seemed sort of mad or mean or something at first. I mean, not mean, but you didn't really tell me anything and he kept calling and I had to deal with him and one day—he called to see if you'd gotten some flowers—and I said you wouldn't take his call and he started crying, and he sounded so sad, so I told him, I knew how he felt, you know? If he wanted to talk. (*Beat.*) And then he really opened up to me. I thought. He really seemed to trust me.

65   **Theresa:** What did you tell him?

Harriet: He just wanted to tell you how much he loved you. He said. (*Beat.*) I gave him your home phone number. And then, when you kept wearing the same clothes to work . . . I think I may have told him that you weren't living at your apartment anymore.

Theresa: That's why you've been buying me all the presents.

Harriet: Yes.

Theresa: How many times did you talk to him?

70   **Harriet:** I don't know. A lot. I guess. But after I found out, I didn't talk to him again. I swear! I told him I knew what he was doing and I wouldn't talk to him again and he stopped calling. I swear.

Theresa: When was that?

Harriet: Like, a week ago?

(*Pause.*)

Theresa: Okay, Harriet. Thank you for telling me. I know that was hard to do . . .

Harriet: I'm so sorry.

75   **Theresa:** But in spite of that, you're fired.

Harriet: But I'm sorry.

Theresa: You're also fired.
Harriet: Oh my God.

(*Pause.* HARRIET *looks as if she will cry.* THERESA *holds out the cologne.*)

Theresa: Here.
80 **Harriet:** I bought it for you.
Theresa: But you need a treat right now.

Scene 7

Theresa's apartment; night. It has been ransacked. Books, papers, clothes are everywhere. Everything is ripped up. Pages are torn from books. The furniture is overturned, the futon gutted. A jangling of keys from outside, then the door opens slightly.

Howard: (*From offstage*) I don't think it was locked.
Mercer: (*From offstage*) Watch out.

(HOWARD *slowly pushes the door open. He and* MERCER *are both carrying an empty box. They look at the apartment.*)

Howard: Oh God. (*He takes a step inside.*)
Mercer: Wait a minute! (*He grabs* HOWARD. *They stand, unsure what to do.*) Do you have your phone with you?
5 **Howard:** I gave it to Theresa.
Mercer: Okay. (*Yells*) We're coming in! We're coming in the door!
Howard: Oh, great. Now he knows where to find us.
Mercer: (*Yells*) We're armed!
Howard: No, we're not.
10 **Mercer:** (*Yells*) It's the police! Whoever's in here, come out with your hands up!

(*Beat. Nothing happens.*)

Howard: He's not here.
Mercer: I smell something.
Howard: (*Sniffs.*) Something rotten.
Mercer: I'm calling the police. (*He picks up the phone and sees it's been ripped from the wall.*)
15 **Howard:** Hang on. (*He goes in, walks down the hall. From offstage we hear him.*) Aw jeez.
Mercer: What? What? Are you okay? (*Long pause. Nothing happens.* MERCER *jumps at nothing.*) Howard?! (*No answer.*) Howard!
Howard: (*Enters.*) There's only three rooms here.
Mercer: What is it?
Howard: He's not here. The kitchen is wrecked. There's food everywhere, roaches. That's what you smell. (*Looks at his fingers.*) I put my hand in something.
20 **Mercer:** What?
Howard: (*Smells his hand.*) Shampoo. It's all over the bath. (*He picks up a shirt lying on the floor. It's been ripped to shreds.*) Look at this. He couldn't just go through everything, he had to ruin it, too.

(MERCER *steps gingerly into the middle of the room, looks around.*)

Mercer: What do you think he was after?
Howard: I don't know.
Mercer: It took a long time to do this.
25 **Howard:** No kidding. (*Small beat.*) Thanks for coming with me.

Mercer: Thanks for coming with *me*.

Howard: We probably shouldn't touch anything, huh?

Mercer: Well, it's not like we don't know who did it.

Howard: True. Do you think we could find some clothes that aren't ruined, at least? So we can take *something* back to her? Let's not tell her exactly what happened. Let's just say we couldn't bring anything back because the police wouldn't let us. Let's not tell her it's all torn up like this.

30 **Mercer:** She's going to have to know sometime.

Howard: But not now. She's too upset, I can tell. She's not sleeping. I never see her eat.

Mercer: It's really good of you to let her stay with you.

Howard: It's great for me. My apartment's never been so clean. She's run out of things to scrub. The other morning, I came in, she'd been up all night arranging my books. By genre and by author. (*Beat.*) Also, I sort of like the company. After my mother died, I thought I didn't want another roommate. But it's not so bad.

Mercer: You lived with your mother?

35 **Howard:** Yeah. She was ill. After my wife and I split up, I moved her in with me.

Mercer: I didn't know you were married.

Howard: Seven years. (*They look around for a moment.*) What a mess. (*Beat.*) I've never been in her apartment before. Have you?

Mercer: No.

Howard: (*They start looking, gingerly picking through things.*) Yeah, after we split up, my mother moved in. You know, my wife, she initiated the split up or separation or whatever. She was unhappy. A lot of things weren't working out. I should have seen it coming, but I didn't. I mean, in retrospect, I understand entirely, but at the time it really took me by surprise. It kind of made me gun-shy. Around women. It didn't show, I don't think, but I had friends who'd try and fix me up with dates and I always made excuses. My mom was sick. I had to work. But basically, I didn't trust anybody. (*Beat.*) Sometimes I'd fantasize I was yelling at my wife.

40 **Mercer:** What was her name?

Howard: Claudia.

Mercer: What would you say?

Howard: "Claudia! What do you expect me to do? Read your mind? How am I supposed to know what you want when you won't tell me?"

Mercer: Maybe she didn't know herself.

45 **Howard:** She didn't.

(*They look around.*)

Mercer: Last year, last New Year's Eve, my wife dragged us to ten different bars. We had to go here, we had to go there. Nothing was quite right. This one was too crowded, this one too empty, this one had cheesy music. We spent most of the night in cabs. Finally I said, "What's the matter? What do you want?" She said she didn't know. She just felt restless and sad. Our best friends had moved out to L.A. We always used to spend New Year's with them. She was feeling lonely.

Howard: At least she didn't turn to you and say, "All I know is I don't want to be with you."

Mercer: No. That wasn't it. Thank God. (*Leans over, picks up a calendar.*) She has a cat calendar. Does she have a cat?

Howard: I don't think so.

50 **Mercer:** (*Flipping through the calendar.*) What's this?

Howard: What?

Mercer: She's got it every month. A little dot with a circle around it.

Howard: I don't know.

Mercer: Different days, once a month. What does that mean?

55 **Howard:** Payday?

Mercer: No. (*Looking. Beat.* HOWARD *picks up a book.*) Oh.

Howard: What?

Mercer: It's her period. It must be . . . when her period starts.

(*They are very uncomfortable. They look around.*)

Howard: This isn't a good idea, I don't think. Let's just leave this stuff here and call the cops.

60 **Mercer:** How could he even think of this. I would never think of this.

Howard: Me neither. Just "Claudia, what do you want?" Just stuff like that.

(*Pause.*)

Mercer: I thought about Theresa once.

Howard: What do you mean?

Mercer: About a month after I started work. I still didn't know her well. You asked me to edit some freelance stuff and I didn't know what I was doing and she gave me some suggestions, and she was standing by her desk, sort of leaning on it. She was wearing what she always wears, slacks and a jacket, it wasn't anything she was doing or wearing, but I just looked at her and I thought, I want to fuck her. Right then, I could just . . . I wanted to close the door to her office and . . . fuck her. I guess I imagined she'd be willing, I mean, I wasn't thinking of jumping on her . . .

65 **Howard:** Sure, sure.

Mercer: I mean, I've never cheated on Michelle and I never will. I don't want to. It wasn't— it was just one of those things that flashes through your mind. I mean now, I can't even imagine it.

Howard: You didn't make a move . . .

Mercer: No. Of course not. I never would.

Howard: Then it's harmless.

70 **Mercer:** I guess. (*Beat.*) I don't know.

Howard: (*They put down the things they're holding and start to leave.*) So how does this fit in?

Mercer: With what?

Howard: With your theory. The guy watches the girl, the guy gets the girl. What's this?

Mercer: (*Looks around.*) The guy hurts the girl.

Scene 8

Theresa's office, the next day. She and OFFICER BECK *are talking.*

Beck: (*Handing her a card*) That's got a 1-800 number on it, so you can reach me from wherever.

Theresa: (*Taking it, looking at it*) Thanks. M. Beck?

Beck: Madeleine.

Theresa: Thanks, Madeleine.

5 **Beck:** Take care of yourself.

Theresa: You too.

(BECK *exits.* MERCER *is waiting outside, and he and* BECK *exchange nods as he comes in.*)

Mercer: What'd she say?

Theresa: They found another letter in my apartment. In the medicine cabinet. They think he wanted me to find it when I was alone. He said he wants to put a wire around my throat and pull it until it . . . until it slices through my throat.

Mercer: Jesus.

10 **Theresa:** There were other details, but I chose not to hear them.

Mercer: Well, what are they going to do?

Theresa: They'll put out a warrant for his arrest, but they probably won't find him unless he messes up somehow and draws attention to himself.

Mercer: Unless he tries to attack you.

Theresa: Pretty much, yeah.

15 **Mercer:** Jesus.

Theresa: It's not her fault. She has a million cases.

Mercer: A million?

Theresa: A hundred. It may as well be a million. *(Beat.)* You know—

Mercer: *(Overlapping)* Theresa, I'm not—*(Stops.)* Sorry, go ahead.

20 **Theresa:** No, you go ahead.

Mercer: Um, I'm not going to write my story after all. About what's been going on. I'm sorry I ever suggested it. It was wrong.

Theresa: Are you sure?

Mercer: Yeah. So what were you going to say? Before?

Theresa: *(Picks up the magazine.)* Did you read my article about the Yankees?

25 **Mercer:** I did. I liked it.

Theresa: Apparently it's pretty good. I don't even know what I wrote.

Mercer: It is good. I read it on the train this morning. It actually made me want to watch the World Series. And I hate baseball.

Theresa: Well, you're not the only one who liked it. The editor of the *Denver Free Press* called me this morning. I kind of know him. I met him at a conference last year, and he told me then, if I ever wanted a job, to call him. But I didn't, so I forgot about it. But he called today and he said he read the story and that he wanted to make an offer again. That he needs a new sports columnist, and he thinks I'd be great at it. So I told him I'd think about it.

Mercer: You did?

30 **Theresa:** I told him as long as all he wanted was a woman. You know, as long as he didn't want me, because I'd have to write under another name—

Mercer: You can't move to Denver.

Theresa: And he said that he would rather it be me, you know, under my own name, but that he understood and I could use any name I wanted. That what he wanted was me, but he'd take a woman if he couldn't have me—

Mercer: What are you going to do in Denver?

Theresa: I'm going to get an apartment and I'm going to live in it. I'm going to walk around outside.

35 **Mercer:** It's not right.

Theresa: What's the difference? Why should I wait around until he decides to kill me?

Mercer: But he'll win.

Theresa: He's already won. Whatever it was he wanted me to feel, I feel it.

Mercer: You're terrified.

40 **Theresa:** No, it's more than that *(Beat.)* It's like when I go running in the park . . . if I still could . . . every week or so, not every day, but every week or two some guy drives by or walks by and says something to me. You know, "Nice ass" or "I want to jog with you" or "Fuck you." Or "Fuck me." It's been happening since I was twelve, so I know

how to ignore it. But every tenth time or so, I still feel it. I feel reduced. I feel like everything that I know about myself—that I'm a good writer and I've read a lot of books, and . . . I like fall better than spring or . . . I haven't had many friends really since my parents died, even though that was a long time ago—everything I know about myself, just gets wiped out. It's like I'm just this thing running down the sidewalk. I'm not me anymore. I'm just this thing. (*Beat.*) And that's how I feel now. All the time.

(*Long pause.*)

Mercer: Well, one thing I can tell you . . . I'm your friend. I see you and I know it's you. I know you're there. I do.

Theresa: I know. (*Small beat.*) It's not enough.

Scene 9

Theresa's apartment, a week later. It is night; a light is on. THERESA *and* MERCER *are going through what's left of her things. A big pile of trash is in one corner, some boxes with books are scattered about.* THERESA *is picking through a pile of torn-up paperbacks.* MERCER *is looking through books as well.*

Theresa: So he called me yesterday, because they'd filmed the MTV thing and he was so excited. I guess they treated him like royalty and everybody thought he was a riot. But he said that when he got to the studios, they took him into this big dressing room and there was this huge spread, just for him, with cookies and sandwich stuff and everything, and he started crying.

Mercer: Poor guy.

Theresa: No, he started crying because he's on a special diet, because of his colon, and he couldn't touch any of it.

Mercer: (*Laughs.*) Oh. Hey, do you want this *Access New York?*

5 **Theresa:** No. Keep it if you want it.

Mercer: Thanks.

Theresa: (*Throwing a bunch of books on the trash pile*) He ripped up all my Shakespeare.

Mercer: He hates the Bard.

Theresa: He ripped up all my pictures. My parents' wedding photos. But he took all the pictures of me. (*Beat.*) I had an old box of letters under the bed, though. He didn't find those.

10 **Mercer:** I'll send you a Riverside Shakespeare. All in one big book.

Theresa: (*Smiles.*) Thanks.

Mercer: So anyway, Les is flying you out . . .

Theresa: Right. I told him I was leaving town and why, and he just made this weird noise and said he had to go and hung up. And I was really upset for a minute. It hurt my feelings. But then he called back five minutes later and he had called one of these producers on his new movie, and the guy has a private plane and Les arranged to have him fly me to Denver.

Mercer: That's nice.

15 **Theresa:** I know. He also intimated that he has ties to the Mafia and if I wanted Tony's knees broken, all I had to do was say the word. (MERCER *picks up an intact book and opens it.*) So Linda's picking me up tonight to take me out to her place for the night, and then tomorrow I'm doing the name-change thing, so I can do everything in Denver with my new name, and then Linda and Chris are taking me to the airport tomorrow night.

Mercer: (*Still looking at the book*) Uh-huh.

(HOWARD *enters, carrying a pot and a pan.*)

Howard: Mercer.

Mercer: What?

Howard: This is what she has in her kitchen. One pot and one pan.

20 **Theresa:** I don't cook.

Howard: (*Throwing the pot and pan in a box*) There. I packed your kitchen.

Theresa: Good. Now do the bathroom. (HOWARD *exits.* MERCER *throws the book he was looking at in the trash pile.*) What's wrong with that one?

Mercer: You don't want it.

Theresa: I do, too, what is it? (*Fetching it*) The Culture of Narcissism. I do, too.

25 **Mercer:** (*Taking it from her*) You don't want it.

Theresa: There's nothing wrong with it.

Mercer: He wrote in it.

Theresa: What?

Mercer: He wrote in the margins. There are gross things in the margins. (THERESA *looks, reads, quickly closes it.* MERCER *takes it and throws it in the trash pile.*) Maybe we should check the other ones.

30 **Theresa:** All of these . . . ? (*She pulls a book from the box, opens it, flips, stops.*) Oh God. (*She starts pulling books from the box. Same thing.*) How long . . . how long was he in here doing this? (*She shoves the box away.*) Goddammit!

Mercer: Leave it all. Even if it's okay, you're going to know he touched it and it's not worth it. Leave it all.

(THERESA *looks around.*)

Theresa: Oh God. My letters. (*She opens the box and pulls out a letter.*) If he . . . (*She pulls a letter out and begins to read it. The buzzer sounds.*)

Mercer: That must be Linda. (*Into buzzer*) Hello? (*No answer.*)

Theresa: (*Flipping the letter over*) I don't think he found these.

(HOWARD *enters.*)

35 **Mercer:** (*Into buzzer*) Hello? (*No answer.*) They must have the wrong door.

Howard: It's kids. They do that to me all the time.

(*A distant pounding on the downstairs door.*)

Mercer: Whoever it is wants in. (*The buzzer sounds again.* THERESA *goes to the window. Into buzzer*) What? (*No answer. Into buzzer*) Linda? (*No answer. The buzzer sounds again. Into buzzer*) Who is it? (*No answer. The pounding again.*)

Theresa: (*Looking out the window*) Oh my God! (*She steps back.*) It's him!

Howard (*Going to the window*) Get away from the window!

40 **Mercer:** (*Overlapping*) Where?

Theresa: I saw him! It's him!

Howard: (*Quickly, jumping back*) Oh Christ, that's the guy!

Theresa: (*Overlapping*) Call the police. Call the police! (*She grabs at Howard's coat pocket for his phone. He extracts it and she grabs it.*)

Howard: We should follow him!

45 **Mercer:** I'll go. (*He grabs the pan from the box and runs out the door.* THERESA *dials 911.*)

Howard: Be careful. (*Overlapping with her call. He closes the door and locks it, then moves between the window and* THERESA.) Stay away from the window.

Theresa: (*Overlapping, on phone*) I want to report an . . . an intruder. I have a protective order, he's violating a protective order . . . 354 East 74th. Second floor . . . Theresa Bedell . . . I don't know! . . . Hurry! (*She hangs up and stands for a second.*) If they . . . if they . . . if they can catch him, if they catch him . . . (*Beat.*) If they catch him I won't have to leave.

Howard: The sorry son of a bitch.

Theresa: I won't have to leave.

50 **Howard:** I know.

(*Long pause.*)

Theresa: When I was in college, my parents were killed in a car wreck. My brother had already graduated. But he drank too much and he lost his job and he couldn't stop drinking. And I let him live with me once, but he stole from me and I had to ask him to leave. And I haven't heard from him in six years. I don't know where he is.

Howard: It's okay.

Theresa: I wanted you to know that about me.

(*Pause. The buzzer sounds.*)

Howard: (*Into buzzer*) Yeah?

55 **Mercer:** (*On speaker*) It's me. Let me up.

(HOWARD *buzzes him up.*)

Theresa: (*Angry*) Why is he back?

Howard: He saw me, I think. When I looked out the window.

Theresa: He can't just get away!

Howard: I should have snuck down the back. I could have caught him out front.

60 **Theresa:** Maybe Mercer saw where he went, though. If the police get here . . .

Howard: I know.

Theresa: If the police get here in time . . .

Howard: I know. Theresa. I know. It's okay.

Theresa: No, it's not.

65 **Howard:** I know. I'm sorry

(*A knock on the door.*)

Mercer: (*From offstage*) It's me.

(HOWARD *lets him in.*)

Howard: Did you see him?

Mercer: (*Out of breath*) He disappeared. I don't know where he went.

Theresa: But did you see him?

70 **Mercer:** I never even saw him. There's . . . he could have gone anywhere.

(*Beat.*)

Howard: What were you going to do with that?

Mercer: What?

Howard: The pan? Fry him an egg? (MERCER *puts the pan down. Beat. They are all on edge, but with no way to release it.*) This is no good. It's no good. (MERCER *goes to the window, looks out. Nothing. Pause.* HOWARD *looks around.*) Leave all this stuff. Theresa? Leave it.

Theresa: I want my letters. (*She walks over to the shoebox and picks it up.*) I don't think he found my letters. (*She pulls out a card in a bright envelope.*) There's nothing in here. Some letters my mom wrote me one summer when I went to camp. (*She looks at the letters and starts to cry.*)

75 **Mercer:** Hey. Hey. *(He goes to her.)* Why don't you look at those later?

(He gently takes the box from her. HOWARD *fishes around in a pocket and pulls out a handkerchief and gives it to her.)*

Howard: It's fairly clean.

*(*THERESA *blows her nose. Pause.* HOWARD *looks for some way to help her.)*

Mercer: What's the new name?
Theresa: What?
Mercer: You're changing your name tomorrow. What did you pick?
80 **Theresa:** Claire.
Howard: That's pretty.
Mercer: Claire what?
Theresa: Howells.
Howard: Howells. Where have I heard that?
85 **Theresa:** William Dean Howells.
Mercer: Of course.
Howard: Claire Howells. It's very nice.

(Beat.)

Theresa: I don't want it.
Howard: You don't like it?
90 **Theresa:** I don't want it. I don't want to change my name. I don't want to go to Denver. I don't want to write sports. I don't like snow. *(*HOWARD *and* MERCER *don't know how to answer.)* I want my old name back.
Howard: Claire is very pretty. *(Sounding it out)* Claire. *(Beat.)* Mercer, this is Claire.
Mercer: *(Extends his hand.)* How do you do? *(*THERESA *doesn't take his hand.)* This is Howard.
Howard: Very pleased. *(Beat.)* You know, I hear in Denver the hot tub comes included in every apartment.
Mercer Really? Well, I hear that they have a major league baseball team there. I believe they're called the Colorado Forty-niners.
95 **Theresa:** Stop it. If you're nice . . . if you're nice, that makes it harder.

(Pause. They stand. Then THERESA *holds out her hand to* MERCER.*)*

Mercer: You want your letters?
Theresa: Yeah.

*(*MERCER *gives them to her. Beat.* THERESA *holds out her hand again.)*

Mercer: What?
Theresa: Claire Howells.
100 **Mercer:** *(Shakes her hand.)* Mercer Stevens.

*(*THERESA *holds out her hand to* HOWARD. *He shakes it.)*

Howard: Howard Siegel.
Theresa: Claire Howells.

*(*HOWARD *picks up the top of the shoebox and hands it to her.)*

Howard: You don't want those to spill. *(Suddenly she hugs him tightly, crying.)* Hey hey. *(For a moment they stand.)* Shhh. Shhh.

(They part, and she turns and hugs MERCER. *He hugs her back, then she steps back.)*

Theresa: It's the Colorado Rockies.
105 **Mercer:** I knew that.
Theresa: Where are the cops?
Howard: They're coming.
Theresa: I don't like it in here. *(Small beat.)* I used to, though. I used to like it in here.
Mercer: Maybe we could wait outside?
110 **Howard:** I don't think we should.

(The buzzer sounds. MERCER *gets it.)*

Mercer: Yeah?
Policewoman: *(On buzzer)* You called the police?
Mercer: *(In buzzer)* We'll be right down. *(To* THERESA*)* It should be okay now.

(They start to leave. HOWARD *waits to turn off the light.)*

Theresa: No. Leave the light on.
115 **Howard:** You think?
Theresa: In case he's watching. I don't want him to know I've left.

(They exit, leaving the light on, closing the door behind them.)

■ **EXPLORATIONS OF THE TEXT**

1. Define Theresa's relationships with the men in her life. Look specifically at her interaction with Tony, Howard, and Mercer. Are these three particular men stereotyped in any obvious way? Develop your thoughts based on concrete evidence from the text. Can they be compared to anyone from real life—the news, the entertainment industry, or your own life?

2. Describe whether Les Kennkat is an important character. What is his purpose in the play? Is he just a breast-loving pig, or does he, in reality, cherish and celebrate women? What does his colon operation add to his character?

3. Do Theresa's opinions of the men stay static throughout the play, or do they change? If so, how? What is her opinion of men at the close of the piece? Is she afraid? Jaded? Liberated? Explain.

4. Trace the pattern of Tony's stalking. Name each instance, from the flowers to the answering machine and so on. Does the rapidity of his behavior heighten the dramatic effect and the tension of the play? When do you think his overly aggressive behavior really begins? Is he a stalker from the very first date at the bar, or does he gradually become unbalanced? Do you think he's a stalker at all?

5. Explore the play's main theme: "boy gets girl." As Mercer explains, it's the classic romantic comedy plotline. A hopeless romantic falls in love with a girl and pursues her until his desire is fulfilled. Why is such behavior acceptable in the movies but scary and abnormal in reality? Does the boy get his girl in this play? Consider all that Theresa goes through over the course of two acts. Where is Tony at the play's close? Who is the victor, and who is the victim?

6. Consider the roles of women in the play. Characterize Theresa. Is she a strong person, or is she weak? How does this depiction of her character define her stalking situation? Does she fit the typical profile of a victim?

7. What does Harriet add as a secondary character? Why is she an important foil against Theresa?

8. How are women in general portrayed or discussed? Consider Tony talking about women with intimacy problems. Consider Howard and Mercer talking about asses and culture. Consider Les Kennkat raving about breasts. Are women objectified or empowered in Gilman's storyline?

9. Compare and contrast the portrayal of men's treatment of women in this work with that in Mar's "Bi Bi Hua" and Gordon's "Violation."

■ THE READING/WRITING CONNECTION

1. Journal Exercise: Choose one scene from the play that you deem to be crucial. You might consider the opening scene important, or maybe when Howard and Mercer find Theresa's apartment torn apart. Read over your scene a few times from beginning to end, and then rewrite it (either in dramatic form or prose). From what you understand of the personalities of the characters, redirect the scene's outcome.

2. Write about a time when you felt threatened (e.g., at Disneyworld's Haunted Mansion, or maybe in a car with a hitchhiker). Make the frightening event come back to life through your narrative. Who wound up prevailing in the end? Are you stronger for having experienced that particular moment? Do you find it comparable to the terror that Theresa felt in Gilman's play?

3. Listen to two or more people have a conversation. Try to follow as closely as possible, and take notes. The subject might be boring or ridiculous, personal or public. After you've gathered a good basis, write a brief dramatic scene starring those two people. Feel free to embellish on the dialogue and to build on their characters; ultimately, make the situation your own. There should be some enticing lure that helps to render the scene important to both readers and audience members.

■ IDEAS FOR WRITING

1. Define "stalking." Compare Gilman's play with an instance of stalking that you have heard of elsewhere. Consider stalkers in the news: celebrity stalkers, cyberstalkers, and child abductors, to name a few. In this instance, does fiction shed further emotional light on a weighty topic, or does it do the topic an injustice?

2. Analyze Tony's character. Why does he qualify as a stalker when he thinks that he is simply being romantic and gentlemanly? Compose a character analysis of Tony. Consider his background, actions, gestures, and dialogue.

3. When does "stalking" become "stalking"? Consider Gurov's obsession with Anna in Chekhov's "Lady with Lapdog" and the husband's spying on his wife in Moravia's "The Chase." In an essay, compare and contrast Tony's, Gurov's and the unnamed husband's behavior.

DAVID IVES

David Ives (1950–   ), born in Chicago, was educated at Northwestern University and the Yale School of Drama. His collection of one-act plays, All in the Timing *(1995), which includes "Sure Thing," won an Outer Circle Award for playwriting and was nominated for a Drama Desk Award. He has written longer plays, including* Don Juan in Chicago *(1995),* The Land of Cockaigne *(1998),* English Made Simple *(1998), and* The Red Address *(1998), and a children's book,* Monsieur Eek *(2001). He wrote the libretto for the opera,* The Secret Garden, *which had its premier at the Pennsylvania Opera Theater. Ives's plays are marked by their wit and invention. In their play with language and their multiple interpretations of and variations on a single moment, Ives's plays exemplify postmodern literature.*

1995

SURE THING

Characters

Bill, in his late twenties
Betty, in her late twenties

Setting

A café table, with a couple of chairs.

Scene

Betty, *reading at the table. An empty chair opposite her. Bill enters.*

Bill: Excuse me. Is this chair taken?
Betty: Excuse me?
Bill: Is this taken?
Betty: Yes, it is.
5   **Bill:** Oh. Sorry.
Betty: Sure thing.

(*A bell rings softly.*)

Bill: Excuse me. Is this chair taken?
Betty: Excuse me?
Bill: Is this taken?
10   **Betty:** No, but I'm expecting somebody in a minute.
Bill: Oh. Thanks anyway.
Betty: Sure thing.

(*A bell rings softly.*)

Bill: Excuse me. Is this chair taken?
Betty: No, but I'm expecting somebody very shortly.
15   **Bill:** Would you mind if I sit here till he or she or it comes?
Betty: (*Glances at her watch.*) They seem to be pretty late . . .
Bill: You never know who you might be turning down.
Betty: Sorry. Nice try, though.
Bill: Sure thing.

(*Bell*)

20   **Bill:** Is this seat taken?
Betty: No, it's not.
Bill: Would you mind if I sit here?
Betty: Yes, I would.
Bill: Oh.

(*Bell*)

25   **Bill:** Is this chair taken?
Betty: No, it's not.
Bill: Would you mind if I sit here?
Betty: No. Go ahead.
Bill: Thanks. (*He sits. She continues reading.*) Everyplace else seems to be taken.
30   **Betty:** Mm-hm.
Bill: Great place.
Betty: Mm-hm.
Bill: What's the book?
Betty: I just wanted to read in quiet, if you don't mind.
35   **Bill:** No. Sure thing.

(*Bell.*)

Bill: Everyplace else seems to be taken.

Betty: Mm-hm.

Bill: Great place for reading.

Betty: Yes, I like it.

40 **Bill:** What's the book?

Betty: "The Sound and the Fury."

Bill: Oh. Hemingway.[1]

(Bell)

Bill: What's the book?

Betty: "The Sound and the Fury."

45 **Bill:** Oh. Faulkner.[2]

Betty: Have you read it?

Bill: Not . . . actually. I've read *about* it, though. It's supposed to be great.

Betty: It is great.

Bill: I hear it's great. *(Small pause.)* Waiter?

(Bell)

50 **Bill:** What's the book?

Betty: "The Sound and the Fury."

Bill: Oh. Faulkner.

Betty: Have you read it?

Bill: I'm a Mets fan, myself.

(Bell.)

55 **Betty:** Have you read it?

Bill: Yeah, I read it in college.

Betty: Where was college?

Bill: I went to Oral Roberts University.

(Bell.)

Betty: Where was college?

60 **Bill:** I was lying. I never really went to college. I just like to party.

(Bell.)

Betty: Where was college?

Bill: Harvard.

Betty: Did you like Faulkner?

Bill: I love Faulkner. I spent a whole winter reading him once.

65 **Betty:** I've just started.

Bill: I was so excited after ten pages that I went out and bought everything else he wrote. One of the greatest reading experiences of my life. I mean, all that incredible psychological understanding. Page after page of gorgeous prose. His profound grasp of the mystery of time and human existence. The smells of the earth . . . What do you think?

Betty: I think it's pretty boring.

(Bell.)

---

[1] Ernest Hemingway (1899–1961). U.S. novelist, short story writer.

[2] William Faulkner (1897–1962). U.S. novelist, short story writer.

Bill: What's the book?

Betty: "The Sound and the Fury."

70 **Bill:** Oh! Faulkner!

Betty: Do you like Faulkner?

Bill: I love Faulkner.

Betty: He's incredible.

Bill: I spent a whole winter reading him once.

75 **Betty:** I was so excited after ten pages that I went out and bought everything else he wrote.

Bill: All that incredible psychological understanding.

Betty: And the prose is so gorgeous.

Bill: And the way he's grasped the mystery of time—

Betty: —and human existence. I can't believe I've waited this long to read him.

80 **Bill:** You never know. You might not have liked him before.

Betty: That's true.

Bill: You might not have been ready for him. You have to hit these things at the right moment or it's no good.

Betty: That's happened to me.

Bill: It's all in the timing. (*Small pause.*) My name's Bill, by the way.

85 **Betty:** I'm Betty.

Bill: Hi.

Betty: Hi.

(*Small pause.*)

Bill: Yes, I thought reading Faulkner was . . . a great experience.

Betty: Yes.

(*Small pause.*)

90 **Bill:** "The Sound and the Fury" . . .

(*Another small pause.*)

Betty: Well. Onwards and upwards. (*She goes back to her book.*)

Bill: Waiter—?

(*Bell.*)

Bill: You have to hit these things at the right moment or it's no good.

Betty: That's happened to me.

95 **Bill:** It's all in the timing. My name's Bill, by the way.

Betty: I'm Betty.

Bill: Hi.

Betty: Hi.

Bill: Do you come in here a lot?

100 **Betty:** Actually I'm just in town for two days from Pakistan.

Bill: Oh. Pakistan.

(*Bell.*)

Bill: My name's Bill, by the way.

Betty: I'm Betty.

Bill: Hi.

105 **Betty:** Hi.

Bill: Do you come in here a lot?

Betty: Every once in a while. Do you?

Bill: No much anymore. Not as much as I used to. Before my nervous breakdown.

    (Bell.)

Bill: Do you come in here a lot?

110 **Betty:** Why are you asking?

    Bill: Just interested.

Betty: Are you really interested, or do you just want to pick me up?

Bill: No, I'm really interested.

Betty: Why would you be interested in whether I come in here a lot?

115 **Bill:** Just . . . getting acquainted.

Betty: Maybe you're only interested for the sake of making small talk long enough to ask
me back to your place to listen to some music, or because you've just rented some
great tape for your VCR, or because you've got some terrific unknown Django Reinhardt[3] record, only all you'll really want to do is fuck—which you won't do very
well—after which you'll go into the bathroom and pee very loudly, then pad into the
kitchen and get yourself a beer from the refrigerator without asking me whether I'd
like anything, and then you'll proceed to lie back down beside me and confess that
you've got a girlfriend named Stephanie who's away at medical school in Belgium for a
year, and that you've been involved with her—*off and on*—in what you'll call a very intricate relationship, for about *seven YEARS*. None of which *interests* me, mister!

Bill: Okay.

    (Bell.)

Bill: Do you come in here a lot?

Betty: Every other day, I think.

120 **Bill:** I come in here quite a lot and I don't remember seeing you.

Betty: I guess we must be on different schedules.

Bill: Missed connections.

Betty: Yes. Different time zones.

Bill: Amazing how you can live right next door to somebody in this town and never even
know it.

125 **Betty:** I know.

Bill: City life.

Betty: It's crazy.

Bill: We probably pass each other in the street every day. Right in front of this place, probably.

Betty: Yep.

130 **Bill:** *(Looks around.)* Well, the waiters here sure seem to be in some different time zone.
I don't see one anywhere . . . Waiter! *(He looks back.)* So what do you . . . *(He sees that
she's gone back to her book.)*

Betty: I beg pardon?

Bill: Nothing. Sorry.

    (Bell.)

Betty: I guess we must be on different schedules.

Bill: Missed connections.

---

[3] Famous jazz guitarist, originally named Jean-Baptiste Reinhardt, (1910–43), of Gypsy origin. One of the
originals of European jazz, he performed with the Duke Ellington orchestra in 1946.

135 **Betty:** Yes. Different time zones.

Bill: Amazing how you can live right next door to somebody in this town and never even know it.

Betty: I know.

Bill: City life.

Betty: It's crazy.

140 **Bill:** You weren't waiting for somebody when I came in, were you?

Betty: Actually I was.

Bill: Oh. Boyfriend?

Betty: Sort of.

Bill: What's a sort-of boyfriend?

145 **Betty:** My husband.

Bill: Ah-ha.

    (Bell.)

Bill: You weren't waiting for somebody when I came in, were you?

Betty: Actually I was.

Bill: Oh. Boyfriend?

150 **Betty:** Sort of.

Bill: What's a sort-of boyfriend?

Betty: We were meeting here to break up.

Bill: Mm-hm . . .

    (Bell.)

Bill: What's a sort-of boyfriend?

155 **Betty:** My lover. Here she comes right now!

    (Bell.)

Bill: You weren't waiting for somebody when I came in, were you?

Betty: No, just reading.

Bill: Sort of a sad occupation for a Friday night, isn't it? Reading here, all by yourself?

Betty: Do you think so?

160 **Bill:** Well sure. I mean, what's a good-looking woman like you doing out alone on a Friday night?

Betty: Trying to keep away from lines like that.

Bill: No, listen—

    (Bell.)

Bill: You weren't waiting for somebody when I came in, were you?

Betty: No, just reading.

165 **Bill:** Sort of a sad occupation for a Friday night, isn't it? Reading here all by yourself?

Betty: I guess it is, in a way.

Bill: What's a good-looking woman like you doing out alone on a Friday night? No offense, but . . .

Betty: I'm out alone on a Friday night for the first time in a very long time.

Bill: Oh.

170 **Betty:** You see, I just recently ended a relationship.

Bill: Oh.

Betty: Of rather long standing.

Bill: I'm sorry—Well listen, since reading by yourself is such a sad occupation for a Friday night, would you like to go elsewhere?

Betty: No . . .

175 **Bill:** Do something else?

Betty: No thanks.

Bill: I was headed out to the movies in a while anyway.

Betty: I don't think so.

Bill: Big chance to let Faulkner catch his breath. All those long sentences get him pretty tired.

180 **Betty:** Thanks anyway.

Bill: Okay.

Betty: I appreciate the invitation.

Bill: Sure thing.

(*Bell.*)

Bill: You weren't waiting for somebody when I came in, were you?

185 **Betty:** No, just reading.

Bill: Sort of a sad occupation for a Friday night, isn't it? Reading here all by yourself?

Betty: I guess I was trying to think of it as existentially romantic. You know—capuccino, great literature, rainy night . . .

Bill: That only works in Paris. We *could* hop the late plane to Paris. Get on a Concorde. Find a café . . .

Betty: I'm a little short on plane fare tonight.

190 **Bill:** Darn it, so am I.

Betty: To tell you the truth, I was headed to the movies after I finished this section. Would you like to come along? Since you can't locate a waiter?

Bill: That's a very nice offer, but—I can't.

Betty: Uh-huh. Girlfriend?

Bill: Two of them, actually. One of them's pregnant, and Stephanie—

(*Bell.*)

195 **Betty:** Girlfriend?

Bill: No, I don't have a girlfriend. Not if you mean the castrating bitch I dumped last night.

(*Bell.*)

Betty: Girlfriend?

Bill: Sort of. Sort of . . .

Betty: What's a sort-of girlfriend?

200 **Bill:** My mother.

(*Bell.*)

Bill: I just ended a relationship, actually.

Betty: Oh.

Bill: Of rather long standing.

Betty: I'm sorry to hear it.

205 **Bill:** This is my first night out alone in a long time. I feel a little bit at sea, to tell you the truth.

Betty: So you didn't stop to talk because you're a Moonie,[4] or you have some weird political affiliation—?

---

[4] Member of a religious cult.

Bill: Nope. Straight-down-the-ticket Republican.

(*Bell.*)

Straight-down-the-ticket Democrat.

(*Bell.*)

Can I tell you something about politics?

(*Bell.*)

I consider myself a citizen of the universe.

(*Bell.*)

I'm unaffiliated.
Betty: That's a relief. So am I.
Bill: I vote my beliefs.
210 **Betty:** Labels are not important.
Bill: Labels are not important, exactly. Like me, for example. I mean, what does it matter if I had a two-point—

(*Bell.*)

—three-point—

(*Bell*)

—four-point at college, or if I did come from Pittsburgh—

(*Bell*)

—Cleveland—

(*Bell*)

—Westchester County?
Betty: Sure.
Bill: I believe that a man is what he is.

(*Bell.*)

A person is what he is.

(*Bell.*)

A person is what they are.
Betty: I think so, too.
215 **Bill:** So what if I admire Trotsky?[5]

(*Bell.*)

So what if I once had a total body liposuction?

(*Bell.*)

So what if I don't have a penis?

(*Bell.*)

So what if I spent a year in the Peace Corps? I was acting on my convictions.

---

[5] Leon Trotsky (1879–1940), Russian revolutionary and writer.

Betty: Convictions are important.

Bill: You just can't hang a sign on a person.

Betty: Absolutely. I'll bet you're a Scorpio.

(*Many bells ring.*)

Betty: Listen, I was headed to the movies after I finished this section. Would you like to come along?

220 **Bill:** That sounds like fun. What's playing?

Betty: A couple of the really early Woody Allen movies.

Bill: Oh.

Betty: Don't you like Woody Allen?

Bill: Sure. I like Woody Allen.

225 **Betty:** But you're not crazy about Woody Allen.

Bill: Those early ones kind of get on my nerves.

Betty: Uh-huh.

(*Bell.*)

Bill: (*Simultaneously.*)	**Betty:**
Y'know, I was headed to the . . .	I was thinking about . . .

Bill: I'm sorry.

230 **Betty:** No, go ahead.

Bill: I was just going to say that I was headed to the movies in a little while, and . . .

Betty: So was I.

Bill: The Woody Allen festival?

Betty: Just up the street.

235 **Bill:** Do you like the early ones?

Betty: I think anybody who doesn't ought to be run off the planet.

Bill: How many times have you seen "Bananas"?[6]

Betty: Eight times.

Bill: Twelve. So are you still interested?

240 **Betty:** Do you like Entenmann's crumb cake?

Bill: I went out at two o'clock this morning to buy one. Did you have an Etch-a-Sketch as a child?

Betty: Yes! Do you like brussel sprouts?

Bill: I think they're gross.

Betty: They *are* gross!

245 **Bill:** Do you still believe in marriage in spite of current sentiments against it?

Betty: Yes.

Bill: And children?

Betty: Three of them.

Bill: Two girls and a boy.

250 **Betty:** Harvard, Vassar, and Brown.

Bill: And will you love me?

Betty: Yes.

Bill: And cherish me forever?

Betty: Yes.

---

[6] A movie produced and directed by Woody Allen.

255 **Bill:** Do you still want to go to the movies?
Betty: Sure thing.
Bill and Betty (*Together.*): Waiter!

    (*Blackout.*)

■ EXPLORATIONS OF THE TEXT

1. Why does Ives choose the names Betty and Bill for his protagonists?
2. What is the significance of the setting—the café? What does the bell signify?
3. Discuss the irony of the repeated line, "Sure thing."
4. How do the interactions between the two characters in each scene differ from one another? How do the scenes build upon one another? Discuss the climactic last interchange.
5. What views of dating and relationships does the play suggest? Are they believable?
6. Discuss the impact of the humor in the play.

■ THE READING/WRITING CONNECTION

1. "Think" Topic: Do you relate to the play's vision of the dating game? Create an argumentative mini-essay presenting your response to this question.
2. Using this work as a model, create a dramatic scene or dialogue that conveys a satiric view of relationships. Then in a short paragraph analyze the themes of your work.

■ IDEAS FOR WRITING

1. Analyze this work as an example of the theater of the absurd (refer to chapter 11).

NTOZAKE SHANGE

Ntozake Shange (1948–) was born in Brooklyn, New York, and educated at Barnard College and the University of California. Shange is best known for her 1977 "chorepoem,"[1] *for* colored girls who have considered suicide / when the rainbow is enuf, *which won an Obie award. Her subsequent publications include more chorepoems,* three pieces *(1981); a poem,* I live in music *(1994); and several books, including a work of fiction,* Liliane: Resurrection of the Daughter *(1994). Shange has taught at colleges including Sonoma College, Mills College, and the University of California at Berkeley. She has been named Woman of the Year by* Mademoiselle *magazine and has received the Audelco Award for Best Playwright from the Black Theater Alliance. Shange's work focuses on African-American women and culture, conveying "what it means for black folks" to live in the United States.*

1977

SORRY

From *for colored girls who have considered suicide / when the rainbow is enuf*

lady in blue

    one thing i dont need
    is any more apologies
    i got sorry greetin me at my front door

---

[1] A form of drama in which poetry, music, and dance are intertwined.

you can keep yrs
5 i dont know what to do wit em
they dont open doors
or bring the sun back
they dont make me happy
or get a morning paper
10 didnt nobody stop usin my tears to wash cars
cuz a sorry

i am simply tired
of collectin
         'i didn't know
15   i was so important to you'
I'm gonna haveta throw some away
i cant get to the clothes in my closet
for alla the sorries
i'm gonna tack a sign to my door
20 leave a message by the phone
         'if you called
           to say yr sorry
           call somebody
           else
25   i dont use em anymore'
i let sorry/didnt meanta/& how cd i know abt that
take a walk down a dark & musty street in brooklyn
i'm gonna do exactly what i want to
& i wont be sorry for none of it
30 letta sorry soothe yr soul/i'm gonna soothe mine

you were always inconsistent
doing something & then bein sorry
beatin my heart to death
talkin bout you sorry
35 well
i will not call
i'm not goin to be nice
i will raise my voice
& scream & holler
40 & break things & race the engine
& tell all yr secrets bout yrself to yr face
& i will list in detail everyone of my wonderful lovers
& their ways
i will play oliver lake
45 loud
& i wont be sorry for none of it

i loved you on purpose
i was open on purpose
i still crave vulnerability & close talk
50 & i'm not even sorry bout you bein sorry

> you can carry all the guilt & grime ya wanna
> just dont give it to me
> i cant use another sorry
> next time
> 55 you should admit
> you're mean/low-down/triflin/& no count straight
>   out
> steada being sorry alla the time
> enjoy being yrself

■ EXPLORATIONS OF THE TEXT

1. Discuss the point of view and the tone of the speaker, the lady in blue.
2. What is the speaker's attitude toward her lover?
3. What is the impact of the informal language, the idiosyncratic spelling, and the verse form?
4. What realization does the speaker experience?

■ THE READING/WRITING CONNECTION

1. In a journal entry, characterize the speaker. Imagine her dress, gestures, and actions.
2. Create a portrait of the speaker's "beloved." Write a monologue in his voice.

■ IDEAS FOR WRITING

1. Compare the speaker's voice and tone with that of the persona in "I Take You an Orange."
2. Contrast Betty in "Sure Thing" with the lady in blue.
3. Compare this performance piece with that of "Twilight Bey" in chapter 7. What do you notice about treatment of persona, voice, action, and gestures?

■ NONFICTION ■

PLATO
Translated by Walter Hamilton

Plato (428–347 B.C.) was born in Athens, Greece, and studied with Socrates. After the latter's execution for heresy in 399 B.C., Plato left Athens for a number of years but returned to found the Academy, often considered the first university. Plato taught philosophy and mathematics there until his death. One of the world's great philosophers, Plato wrote many treatises in the form of dialogues among Socrates and other figures in which the philosopher and his circle debate central, metaphysical questions. In the Symposium, *the dialogue concerns the true nature of love.*

c. 387–367 B.C.

THE SEXES

From *The Symposium*

Well, Eryximachus," began Aristophanes,[1] "it is quite true that I intend to take a different line from you and Pausanias. Men seem to me to be utterly insensible of the power of Love; otherwise he would have had the largest temples and altars and the

---

[1] Aristophanes (448?–385? B.C.), Athenian comic playwright. Eryximachus, Pausanias (following), and Agathon and Socrates (later) are other participants at the banquet, where love is the topic of discussions.

largest sacrifices. As it is, he has none of these things, though he deserves them most of all. For of all the gods he is the most friendly to man, and his helper and physician in those diseases whose cure constitutes the greatest happiness of the human race. I shall therefore try to initiate you into the secret of his power, and you in turn shall teach others.

"First of all, you must learn the constitution of man and the modifications which it has undergone, for originally it was different from what it is now. In the first place there were three sexes, not, as with us, two, male and female; the third partook of the nature of both the others and has vanished, though its name survives. The hermaphrodite was a distinct sex in form as well as in name, with the characteristics of both male and female, but now the name alone remains, and that solely as a term of abuse. Secondly, each human being was a rounded whole, with double back and flanks forming a complete circle; it has four hands and an equal number of legs, and two identically similar faces upon a circular neck, with one head common to both the faces, which were turned in opposite directions. It had four ears and two organs of generation and everything else to correspond. These people could walk upright like us in either direction, backwards or forwards, but when they wanted to run quickly they used all their eight limbs, and turned rapidly over and over in a circle, like tumblers who perform a cart-wheel and return to an upright position. The reason for the existence of three sexes and for their being of such a nature is that originally the male sprang from the sun and the female from the earth, while the sex which was both male and female came from the moon, which partakes of the nature of both sun and earth. Their circular shape and their hoop-like method of progression were both due to the fact that they were like their parents. Their strength and vigour made them very formidable, and their pride was overweening; they attacked the gods, and Homer's story of Ephialtes and Otus attempting to climb up to heaven and set upon the gods is related also of these beings.[2]

"So Zeus and the other gods debated what was to be done with them. For a long time they were at a loss, unable to bring themselves either to kill them by lightning, as they had the giants, and extinguish the race—thus depriving themselves for ever of the honours and sacrifice due from humanity—or to let them go on in their insolence. At last, after much painful thought, Zeus had an idea. "I think," he said, "that I have found a way by which we can allow the human race to continue to exist and also put an end to their wickedness by making them weaker. I will cut each of them in two; in this way they will be weaker, and at the same time more profitable to us by being more numerous. They shall walk upright upon two legs. If there is any sign of wantonness in them after that, and they will not keep quiet, I will bisect them again, and they shall hop on one leg." With these words he cut the members of the human race in half, just like fruit which is to be dried and preserved, or like eggs which are cut with a hair. As he bisected each, he bade Apollo turn round the face and the half-neck attached to it towards the cut side, so that the victim, having the evidence of bisection before his eyes, might behave better in the future. He also bade him heal the wounds. So Apollo turned round the faces, and gathering together the skin, like a purse with drawstrings, on to what is now called the belly, he tied it tightly in the middle of the belly round a single aperture which men call the navel. He smoothed out the other wrinkles, which were numerous, and moulded the chest with a tool like those which cobblers use to smooth wrinkles in the leather on their last. But he left a few on the belly itself round the navel, to remind man of the state from which he had fallen.

"Man's original body having been thus cut in two, each half yearned for the half from which it had been severed. When they met they threw their arms round one another and embraced, in their longing to grow together again, and they perished of hunger and general

---

[2] Giants Ephialtes and Otus tried to climb to heaven by piling mountain upon mountain.

neglect of their concerns, because they would not do anything apart. When one member of a pair died and the other was left, the latter sought after and embraced another partner, which might be the half either of a female whole (what is now called a woman) or a male. So they went on perishing till Zeus took pity on them, and hit upon a second plan. He moved their reproductive organs to the front: hitherto they had been placed on the outer side of their bodies, and the processes of begetting and birth had been carried on not by the physical union of the sexes, but by emission on to the ground, as is the case with grasshoppers. By moving their genitals to the front, as they are now, Zeus made it possible for reproduction to take place by the intercourse of the male with the female. His object in making this change was twofold; if male coupled with female, children might be begotten and the race thus continued, but if male coupled with male, at any rate the desire for inter-course would be satisfied, and men set free from it to turn to other activities and to attend to the rest of the business of life. It is from this distant epoch, then, that we may date the innate love which human beings feel for one another, the love which restores us to our ancient state by attempting to weld two beings into one and to heal the wounds which humanity suffered.

5   "Each of us then is the mere broken tally of a man, the result of a bisection which has reduced us to a condition like that of flat fish, and each of us is perpetually in search of his corresponding tally. Those men who are halves of a being of the common sex, which was called, as I told you, hermaphrodite, are lovers of women, and most adulterers come from this class, as also do women who are mad about men and sexually promiscuous. Women who are halves of a female whole direct their affections towards women and pay little atten-tion to men; Lesbians belong to this category. But those who are halves of a male whole pur-sue males, and being slices, so to speak, of the male, love men throughout their boyhood, and take pleasure in physical contact with men. Such boys and lads are the best of their gen-eration, because they are the most manly. Some people say that they are shameless, but they are wrong. It is not shamelessness which inspires their behaviour, but high spirit and manli-ness and virility, which lead them to welcome the society of their own kind. A striking proof of this is that such boys alone, when they reach maturity, engage in public life. When they grow to be men, they become lovers of boys, and it requires the compulsion of convention to overcome their natural disinclination to marriage and procreation; they are quite content to live with one another unwed. In a word, such persons are devoted to lovers in boyhood and themselves lovers of boys in manhood, because they always cleave to what is akin to themselves.

"Whenever the lover of boys—or any other person for that matter—has the good for-tune to encounter his own actual other half, affection and kinship and love combined in-spire in him an emotion which is quite overwhelming, and such a pair practically refuse ever to be separated even for a moment. It is people like these who form lifelong partner-ships, although they would find it difficult to say what they hope to gain from one another's society. No one can suppose that it is mere physical enjoyment which causes the one to take such intense delight in the company of the other. It is clear that the soul of each has some other longing which it cannot express, but can only surmise and obscurely hint at. Suppose Hephaestus with his tools were to visit them as they lie together, and stand over them and ask: "What is it, mortals, that you hope to gain from one another?" Suppose too that when they could not answer he repeated his question in these terms: "Is the object of your desire to be always together as much as possible, and never to be separated from one another day or night? If that is what you want, I am ready to melt and weld you together, so that, instead of two, you shall be one flesh; as long as you live you shall live a common life, and when you die, you shall suffer a common death, and be still one, not two, even in the next world. Would such a fate as this content you, and satisfy your longings?" We know what their answer would be; no one would refuse the offer; it would be plain that this is what every-body wants, and everybody would regard it as the precise expression of the desire which he had long felt but had been unable to formulate, that he should melt into his beloved, and that henceforth they should be one being instead of two. The reason is that this was our primitive condition when we were wholes, and love is simply the name of the desire and pursuit of the whole. Originally, as I say, we were whole beings, before our wickedness caused us to be split by Zeus, as the Arcadians have been split apart by the Spartans.[3] We have reason to fear that if we do not behave ourselves in the sight of heaven, we may be split in two again, like dice which are bisected for tallies, and go about like the people repre-sented in profile on tombstones, sawn in two vertically down the line of our noses. That is why we ought to exhort everyone to conduct himself reverently towards the gods; we shall thus escape a worse fate, and even win the blessing which Love has in his power to bestow, if we take him for our guide and captain. Let no man set himself in opposition to Love—which is the same thing as incurring the hatred of the gods—for if we are his friends and make our peace with him, we shall succeed, as few at present succeed, in finding the person to love who in the strictest sense belongs to us. I know that Eryximachus is anxious to make fun of my speech, but he is not to suppose that in saying this I am pointing at Pausanias and Agathon. They may, no doubt, belong to this class, for they are both unquestionably halves of male wholes, but I am speaking of men and women in general when I say that the way to happiness for our race lies in fulfilling the behests of Love, and in each finding for himself the mate who properly belongs to him; in a word, in returning to our original condition. If that condition was the best, it follows that it is best for us to come as near to it as our pres-ent circumstances allow; and the way to do that is to find a sympathetic and congenial ob-ject for our affections.

"If we are to praise the god who confers this benefit upon us, it is to Love that our praises should be addressed. It is Love who is the author of our well-being in this present life, by leading us towards what is akin to us, and it is Love who gives us a sure hope that, if we conduct ourselves well in the sight of heaven, he will hereafter make us blessed and happy by restoring us to our former state and healing our wounds.

"There is my speech about Love, Eryximachus, and you will see that it is of quite a dif-ferent type from yours. Remember my request, and don't make fun of it, but let us hear what each of the others has to say. I should have said 'each of the other two,' for only Agathon and Socrates are left."

■ EXPLORATIONS OF THE TEXT

1. Explore the descriptions of the "three sexes," particularly of the "third" sex. How do you react to this description?
2. Describe this myth of the "fall." Compare it to the Biblical creation story and to the fall of Adam and Eve.
3. What is the concept of the "bisection"? How does Aristophanes explain homosexuality and heterosexuality?
4. How does the myth account for love?
5. What will happen if human beings set themselves "in opposition to Love"?
6. According to Aristophanes, what is "the way to happiness" for the race? Why?
7. What are Aristophanes's point of view and tone? Find key words and phrases that re-veal his perspective.

---

[3] The conquering Spartans forced the residents of the Arcadian city of Mantinea to live in four separate villages.

▪ THE READING/WRITING CONNECTION

1. Create a myth or a fable that provides an explanation for one of the following: a) Why people fall in love; b) The nature of love or relationships; c) The nature of gender roles.
2. "Think" Topic: Take issue with one point in this treatise. Construct a counterargument.

▪ IDEAS FOR WRITING

1. Agree or disagree with Aristophanes that happiness lies in "fulfilling the behests of love" and in finding the proper mate.
2. Are we only "half" selves, yearning for completion through our mates or through our love relationships?
3. Compare Aristophanes's (Plato's) views of love with the view in one of the love poems in this chapter.
4. Write in the persona of a character in one of the works in this chapter, and respond to Aristophanes's idea of love.

M. Elaine Mar

M. Elaine Mar was born in Hong Kong and moved to Denver, Colorado, at the age of five. She attended Harvard University and presently resides in Cambridge, Massachusetts. Her parents hoped that Mar would retain the Chinese traditions and culture, whereas Mar attempted to fit into her new American life, a difference that created conflicts within her family. Her novel Paper Daughter *(1999) explores the tensions within her family and herself as she leaves home to attend Harvard University. Mar, however, states that her intent with* Paper Daughter *is not so much to reveal her personal conflicts as to talk about class in the United States.*

2004

BI BI HUA

At the age of thirteen, I realized that my parents intended to arrange a marriage for me. They had not yet chosen a groom; my marriage was not predestined at birth, as in fairy tales or the apocryphal anecdotes that circulate about the friend of a friend from the Far East. But my parents' plans carried weight all the same. Their actions made the message clear: My body and my sexuality did not belong to me. I was not free to explore the tantalizing nether regions of sex, as my non-Chinese peers were.

Imagine my surprise: I was a gawky adolescent entering the eighth grade. In the tradition of American womanhood, I'd already learned to diet. I wore my hair coaxed into some version of the famous Farrah Fawcett 'do. My favorite movies were *Grease* and the PG-rated version of *Saturday Night Fever.* Memories of my immigration from Hong Kong eight years earlier were dim and dream-like. I could not conceive of myself as anything other than American. I could not imagine my future unfurling any differently than the ones depicted in *Teen* magazine—first date, first kiss, first dance, first break-up, first true love.

Early that fall, I was granted one of my firsts—first boyfriend, a red-haired ninth-grader who attended a different school, in a different school district. I got to know him on weekends, working at my family's Chinese restaurant. I was a dishwasher. He was a busboy. Like many hormone-driven teens, we were not terribly discreet about our relationship. We cuddled publicly, in the restaurant's service corridors. We sat on the same side of a dining-room booth and held hands throughout meals. We disappeared on "walks" for embarrassingly long, suggestive periods of time.

My parents objected, of course. They said that my behavior would ruin our family's reputation and demanded that we break up. I refused. A tortured, arduous series of arguments ensued. My father went so far as to hit me. In the end, the red-haired boy bowed out, unable to stand the drama. I was devastated, convinced that my parents had just ruined my life. I didn't know that the real shock was yet to come, delivered by my Uncle Andy.

5   Very calmly one night, sitting across from me in a booth at the family restaurant, Uncle Andy announced that I was not allowed to have boyfriends. My family intended to send me back to Hong Kong after my high school graduation. There, they would arrange an appropriate marriage for me.

Uncle Andy's words lingered like a curse. I hoped to defy my family's wishes. I planned a long line of secret dates. But I was foiled—first by the boys at my junior high, then the boys at my high school, none of whom showed the slightest interest in me sexually. I resigned myself to the stereotype of Oriental geek and worked on suppressing my sexual urges.

As it turned out, my uncle's prophecy was not infallible. Harvard was the key to my freedom. At the recommendation of my high school English teacher (who knew nothing about my family situation), I applied to Harvard—and got in. Initially, my parents refused to let me go. Cambridge, Massachusetts, near Boston? Seventeen hundred miles away? Too far, they said. But the university was so famous and so well respected that even people in my family's highly insular immigrant community had heard of it. Once these people explained its significance to my parents, who didn't know the difference between Harvard and the local community college, they had to relent. I was overjoyed, knowing that no other excuse would have freed me from my parents' house.

So, upon graduation from high school, I was not shipped back to Hong Kong. Instead, I moved from my parents' house in Denver, Colorado, to a dorm room in Cambridge, Massachusetts. I was assigned to Hurlbut Hall, which stood across the street from the Union, the building where freshmen took their meals. Hurlbut was one of the smaller freshman dorms, housing fewer than eighty students on four floors combined. I lived in a "pod"—an arrangement of locking bedrooms around a semi-private common room—on the third floor. There were seven one-room singles and a two-room triple in the pod; I lived in one of the singles.

Within the first week, my podmates and I agreed to treat the pod as one large suite. We set up furniture in our common room, exchanged home phone numbers, and made copies of our bedroom keys for one another to keep in case of emergency. I felt like a member of a typical freshman rooming group, rather than the occupant of a "psycho single." For which I was grateful.

10   I was finding my Harvard experience less than ideal. Back in Denver, I'd imagined all Harvard students as being a little like me—socially inexperienced, slightly eccentric, intellectually passionate. My thinking had not been sophisticated enough to include socioeconomic factors in this portrait, nor had I possessed the self-awareness to understand where on the economic spectrum my family lay. Rather than characterizing us as borderline poor—which would have been accurate—I'd honestly believed that we were middle class.

Given such naivete, I could not have prepared myself for the social realities of a college where one year's tuition roughly equaled my family's total annual income. I could not have anticipated the large number of Harvard students who came from affluent backgrounds and thus shared cultural references that were a mystery to me: prep schools, tennis camp, European vacations, ordinary-sounding peoples names that turned out to be high-end clothing stores. Puzzled and embarrassed, I remained silent about my working-class background while resolving to learn the customs of this strange new land.

I befriended Leah, an activities-oriented student who lived in my pod's triple. She was one of those girls who always knew what was cool and who fit into which clique. Her judgments about Harvard people seemed especially keen, at least to me, because her father was a Harvard alumnus and her sister a Harvard junior. I figured that by watching Leah, I could clue myself in on Harvard's mysteries.

∞

On impulse one night, I began writing verse in ant-sized letters on one of the windowsills in Hurlbut's central landing. It was intended more to test the vigilance of Harvard's custodial staff than as any real literary effort, but that first spontaneous poem got my dorm mates' attention, so I continued writing miniature verse in random, half-hidden places throughout the dorm.

Not long after I began this project, a boy named Evan from the first floor pod started saying hello to me. Coming from Evan, this behavior was strange, since he rarely spoke to anyone. He tended to duck his head rather than exchange hellos when he ran into people on the sidewalk outside of Hurlbut. He was said to be a photographer of genius-level talent, and on faith, without having seen a single photo, I believed it. After all, Evan wore a lot of black. He had a high-pitched voice that was both intense and mocking. His tea-colored eyes were impassive behind a pair of black-rimmed glasses. He always seemed to be sneering. To me, these qualities, combined with Evan's solitary air and hint of neuroticism, suggested that he was an artist. Besides, we were at Harvard. I was ready to believe that anyone was a genius.

15   I was on my way into Hurlbut one day in late September when Evan stopped me. He said, "I found the one under the windowsill on the second floor."

I grinned involuntarily, understanding the reference to a poem I'd written a few days earlier.

"I liked the spiderweb imagery," he continued smoothly. "What does it symbolize?"

I shrugged. "Nothing. I didn't think that hard about it. I was just scribbling some neat images."

Evan stepped closer to me. His eyes remained impassive, but his mouth twitched. "Really?" he breathed. "I thought there might be some hidden sexual meaning."

20   My face grew hot. I couldn't tell whether I was being teased, so I remained silent.

He smiled and murmured, "I thought of you as a black widow waiting for a fly to get caught in your web. I thought of you wrapping the fly in silk and eating him, sucking him dry."

The sexual implication of his words was so obvious that even I understood. I wondered if this was some sort of flirtation. I didn't know how I felt if it was. According to Leah, Evan was not socially acceptable. But her judgment had to be weighed against the rumors of his artistic genius. I didn't have any strong feelings about Evan either way. I just didn't want to make a fool of myself here on the sidewalk in front of Hurlbut for everyone to witness. Trying to sound detached and intellectual, I said, "That's an interesting interpretation."

Evan laughed. He took a step toward me and whispered, "You're tough, little Denver girl. Cold. I like that." His lips grazed my ear. Before I could respond, he walked away.

I watched him cross the street, feeling simultaneously intrigued and repulsed. I wondered who his friends at Harvard were. In my imagination, he was part of some artistic clique I had not yet discovered, a group of photographers and painters and poets who gathered in dimly lit coffeehouses to discuss their quest for an uncorrupted creative vision. I longed to become a part of this group, to have my own talents recognized. The image of this artistic clique, and my need for it to exist, were so strong that I never questioned its reality.

25   I began to see Evan everywhere—at the Union, his pale face and drab clothes shocking in the midst of preppy tan skin and pastel madras shirts; on the path in front of Hurlbut; loitering by the mailboxes in the entryway. He quizzed me about the ant-sized poems. He recited random lines of published poems and demanded that I identify the authors. He asked detailed questions about my day: What time did I usually get up? Did I eat breakfast? When did my lectures meet? When did I eat lunch? When did I eat dinner? I became increasingly confused and uncomfortable in his presence, but I remained uncertain about his intentions.

"Do you think he *likes* me?" I asked Leah after being stopped by him one day.

She looked over her shoulder at his retreating figure and wrinkled her nose. She declared definitively, "No, Elaine, he's just *weird.*"

I felt strangely defeated. Leah disapproved of Evan, so he couldn't improve my standing in her eyes. Still, I'd wanted her to say yes. No one had ever had a crush on me before. I'd hoped that Evan was the first.

I turned eighteen on October first of that year. My podmates threw me an impromptu party with champagne and an ice-cream cake. Various dorm mates and friends from my classes showed up. Peter, who lived in a suite on the first floor, impressed us all by opening the champagne with barely a pop. "It's because he's from Beverly Hills," Leah whispered in my ear. I nodded sagely, trusting her judgement, because I'd never met anyone from Beverly Hills before. I didn't question whether or not she had.

30   Evan didn't attend the party, and I didn't miss him.

I was coming back from dinner on Sunday of the following week when I saw Evan pacing the walk in front of Hurlbut. He ran out into the street grinning when he saw me. "Where are your *podmates*?" he asked, emphasizing the word sarcastically.

I answered him briefly, "They went to get ice cream."

Evan made a face. "Oh, how sweet. All you girls are so *sweet.*"

Accustomed to his routine, I ignored him. I started up the path to the front door. Evan stayed close behind. "Why didn't you go?"

35   I shrugged. "I have reading to do."

Evan leered. "Why don't you read in *my* room?"

I didn't bother to answer him. I turned toward the staircase leading to Hurlbut's upper floors. Evan stepped in front of me. "I'll let you read Marilyn Hacker," he offered.

I paused. During one of our sidewalk encounters, Evan had told me that Marilyn Hacker was his favorite poet. I'd been embarrassed to admit that I'd never heard of her— and I'd been too busy since that conversation to look up any of her work.

Evan noticed my hesitation and insinuated his way sleekly into it, murmuring, "Let's go, Denver girl. Marilyn Hacker. My photographs. Everything you've always wanted."

40   I looked into his tea-colored eyes, startled.

He smiled. "Isn't that what you *really* want? To look at my photos. To spend time with an artist, someone on *your* level, instead of those preppy idiots like Leah and Rob."

I opened my mouth to protest, but no words came. I nodded, embarrassed by the transparency of my motives, my neediness.

Evan unlocked the door to his pod, and wordlessly I followed him inside. We walked past flattened cardboard boxes and an upended bedframe. Evan opened the door to his room.

It was unlike anything I'd seen at Harvard thus far.

45   His room was about the same size as my own, ten or twelve feet square—large for a freshman bedroom. It had the same white walls and pale yellow hardwood floor, the same Harvard-issue furniture—extra-long single bed (or, in this case, the mattress), office-size desk, three-shelf bookcase, and Harvard insignia captain's chair. But there the similarities ended.

Evan had disabled the overhead light fixture. He'd strung a series of professional-quality photographer's studio lamps close to the ceiling. They burned the walls and ceiling an incredible bright white, illuminating every corner, giving the room a spare, loft-like feel. The effect of his adjustments was to obscure almost all suggestions that this was a Harvard dorm room. Although I'd never actually seen a New York artist's studio, I imagined that Evan's room looked like one. It looked like the Greenwich Village poet's quarters that I'd always imagined for myself.

The room was virtually undecorated—no rug on the floor, no posters on the wall. Instead, there were photographs. They were scattered rather than displayed, crowding the desk and the floor, pinned up on a clothesline, tacked to the wall. I scanned the black-and-white prints quickly, absorbing their sharp outlines. When I looked up, I was surprised to see Evan's face, the faintly beige skin, the shocking red hair, the dark amber eyes.

His expression was inscrutable. "What do you think?" he asked softly. "Are the rumors true? Am I a genius, like everyone says?"

I stared back at him silently. I wanted to be mean and tell Evan no, he didn't have any talent at all, but the words stuck in my throat. Instead, I said honestly, "Yes. I think you are."

50   Evan chuckled. "So sweet," he murmured, his voice silky. "My sweet little Denver girl."

I scowled. "Where's the Marilyn Hacker?" I asked impatiently, pointing at my watch. "It's almost seven-thirty. I have, like, two hundred pages of reading to do."

In response, Evan gestured toward his bed, which lay at the far end of the room, by the windows. It had been reduced to its most basic components, a single mattress on the floor, covered with black sheets. He said, "Make yourself comfortable."

I hesitated, uncertain of his intentions.

Evan sneered, "What's wrong, Denver girl? Afraid to sit on my bed? Afraid of what I'll do to you?"

55   "No," I snapped, instinctive bravado kicking in. "I've sat on lots of boys' beds." I crossed the floor and flopped down on the mattress.

"Oh really?" Evan breathed. "Lots of experience with boys' beds? Tell me about it."

My face flushed hot. "Just . . . I mean, I'm good at making beds. Hospital corners. So some of the guys at Harvard, freshman year, they need help . . ." My voice faltered.

Evan laughed.

I heard the challenge, the judgment about my lack of desirability. Just like high school. "Some of these guys *have* come on to me," I told Evan defensively.

60   He made a dismissive sound and said, "That's just because you're Chinese."

I tensed, hating the implication before I knew its exact nature. Up to that moment, I'd almost forgotten the racial difference between us and simply been comfortable in my skin, sparring with him student to student, girl to boy, exploring the boundaries of male-female relationships. What right did he have to take that away from me?

Choking back my anger, I snapped, "What does being Chinese have to do with anything?"

Evan cocked his head, looking amused. "Don't you know? Chinese girls are easy," He spoke casually, as if reporting a benign, well-known fact, like the color of grass.

But I'd never heard this stereotype before. I felt my mouth curve upward in an absurd, defensive smile. My smile faltered, then reappeared. I heard myself giggle. "What are you talking about?"

65   Evan elaborated, making sure that I understood: "*All* Asian women are easy. You should see the sex shops in New York, Chinese girls everywhere, their legs spread wide open, fucking strangers by the hundred, twenty bucks a pop. It's the same here, at Harvard, the rich preppies looking for a taste of Chinese cunt. Guys just come on to you because they know you'll sleep with them."

"No." My throat constricted. My eyes filled with tears. How could he say these things? The last few weeks at Harvard had been the best of my life. For the first time, boys were flirting with me, ignoring—or perhaps even appreciating—the Asian features that I'd always considered ugly. I thought that I might have arrived at a place where the standard for beauty could include me. But here Evan was, providing another explanation. The boys didn't think I was pretty. They only wanted to use me for sex. I didn't want to believe him. Words rushed out of my mouth defensively: "But I don't, I'm not, I've never . . ."

Evan grinned.

My sentence lost force and drifted off. Images of another red-haired boy flashed through my head: A weekend at my family's restaurant. Screaming voices and broken drinking glasses. My body vibrating with desire, insisting that I had a right to date the busboy.

In Evan's room, remembering how young I'd been and how far I'd gone sexually, I was overcome with shame and guilt. But that had been a long time ago, I reminded myself—and I hadn't had a boyfriend since. I forced the memories out of my head. "Marilyn Hacker?" I reminded Evan brusquely.

70   He snorted, dug through a pile of paper on his desk, and handed me a magazine folded to the right page. He sat in the captain's chair by his desk. I proceeded to read.

Silence settled as I made my way into the poem. I read intently, trying hard to formulate an intelligent analysis. Then, after several minutes of quiet, Evan's voice interrupted my concentration: "So when are we going to fuck?"

I looked up in surprise. "What?"

He repeated slowly and clearly, "So when are we going to fuck?"

I heard the words but wasn't able to make sense of them. What was Evan hoping to accomplish? He didn't actually want to have sex with me, did he? We'd never even kissed. I stared into his eyes, searching for a clue. They were opaque, as always. He must be testing me, tricking me into being that easy Asian woman, I decided. Determined to prove him wrong, I said coldly, "Never. Why are you even asking?"

75   He grinned. "Oh come on, Denver girl. Stop pretending. You know that you're attracted to me, and I'm attracted to you."

My heart stopped, mid-beat, startled. Evan was attracted to me. He just said that he was attracted to me. If I weren't so confused, I'd be flattered. Then I focused in on the rest of his sentence. He'd also accused me of being attracted to him. How dare he. My face flushed hot. He was far too quirky, too unwilling to be liked by the mainstream Harvard crowd. I couldn't afford to be attracted to him. If Leah knew that I was in Evan's room now, I'd be humiliated. I opened my mouth to retort.

Before any words came out, Evan spoke again, "You *know* you're attracted to me," he insisted. "Why else would you wear those tight jeans? Why else would you write those poems on the windowsill? You're calling attention to yourself, waiting for me."

The heat in my face intensified. His acknowledgment of my sexuality was so embarrassing it was almost unbearable. "I don't know what you're talking about," I blurted out, lying. "What tight jeans?"

Evan grinned. "Nice trick, Denver girl. Playing innocent. It's sexy." He stood, slinked across the room, sat next to me on his mattress. "Marilyn Hacker," he said, reaching across my body to take hold of the journal. I leaned backward to avoid his touch. His arm moved with me, motioning my body down toward the mattress.

80   I let myself fall, almost experimentally, curiosity fighting nerves over the anticipation of what might come next. No one had ever called me sexy before. No one had ever paid attention to how I dressed. So I'd never had to consider how I might act if someone showed interest in me beyond asking me to make his bed. I was dying to find out not only what *Evan* might do, but how *I* might react.

Evan stretched himself out on the narrow twin mattress alongside me, one arm draped across my torso. I lay motionless beside him, savoring the moment. Would he kiss me now, I wondered, and would I let him? Thoughts flurried, barely conscious memories of high school crushes and rejections, boys who'd fabricated ludicrous excuses for not accompanying me to school dances. I was a changed person now. Lying next to Evan, I felt desired for the first time. Powerful. I imagined all the ways I could tell him "no." I could let him down gently or cruelly. I could string him along for weeks or end it now. I looked into his tea-colored eyes, smiling.

Evan said, "So do you want to take off your own clothes, or should I do it for you?"

Still smiling, I answered haughtily, "Neither. I told you, I don't know what you're talking about."

Evan rolled onto his side, propping himself up on one elbow to look me in the face. Very calmly, he said, "Let's just do this, Denver girl. No more of these games."

85   "Do what?" I asked, my voice lilting flirtatiously.

Evan frowned. "Fuck," he growled. "Let's go ahead and fuck."

"No." I sat up angrily. How dare he use that word, that tone of voice? He should chase after me with promises of dinner and movie dates, not treat me like some prostitute. Fighting back tears, I said, "I need to go."

Evan laughed. "No you don't." He pulled me back down, one deft move barely rougher than the flirtatious wrestling of a Harvard boy congratulating me for a well-made bed.

I inched sideways, squirming out of his grasp. "I do. I have reading for tomorrow, I told you—"

90   "Slip it. You're smart enough to bullshit your way through class without reading."

"Yes, but . . ." I hesitated, taken in by the flattery.

"Wouldn't you rather fuck?"

"No,"

"Why not?"

95   "I—"

"Aren't you a little curious?" he countered, before I could complete the answer. "I can make you feel so, so good."

My body tingled at his words, remembering another red-haired boy, reminded of other words and images, all the fantasy scenarios I'd struggled to suppress throughout my adolescence. "Yes," I blurted out honestly, without thinking. "I am curious."

"So let's do it."

"No." I ignored the tingle and tried to regain control. "This isn't right, this isn't the way it should be."

100   He laughed. "How 'should' it be?"

I shrugged. Turned my head. Mumbled, "I don't know, but . . . I mean, we haven't even kissed."

He put his face close to mine. "Do you want me to kiss you?"

I shook my head. "No."

His face hardened, moved away. "Good. None of that bullshit bourgeois romantic stuff."

105   I tried to sit up again. "I should go."

He yanked me back. "Okay, you win. We won't fuck. Just a blow job."

"No." My voice annoyed.

"Have you ever given a blow job?"

I answered honestly, automatically, "Yes."

110   Evan jerked back slightly, unable to hide his surprise. "Where? At Harvard, making other people's beds?"

I congratulated myself for surprising him. "No," I said, making sure I sounded bored and cavalier. "In Denver. Of course."

Evan seemed to relax, regain his composure. "Denver," he sneered. "What kind of blow job could you give in Denver?"

I shrugged elaborately. Told Evan, "Well, *he* said it was good."

Evan's eyes narrowed. He grinned. "Why don't you show me?"

115   I sighed. We'd looped around again. I twisted my head, looked at the door. "I have reading to do."

Evan made a sound of disgust. "I knew you couldn't do it. You're all talk, Denver girl."

Anger flared in my chest. Evan had no right to call me a liar. The blow job had been all too real. My father had beaten me up for fooling around with the red-haired boy. If only Evan knew—but I didn't dare reveal how provincial, backward, and un-American my family was. I tamped down my anger. "No, I can. I have. It's just . . ." My voice trailed off, embarrassed by the words that were to come: *It's just that I don't love you. I want to have sex, but only with someone I love.* How quaint it would sound to his ears, but how daring to mine—the idea that I could choose to have sex at all.

Evan studied my face with his narrowed eyes. "Are you a virgin?"

I swallowed hard. "No," I lied, hoping to end his prying.

120   Evan sat up and stripped off his t-shirt. "Let's do it then."

I shook my head.

He leaned over me, still propped up on one elbow. "Come on," he wheedled. "At least a blow job. Show me how good you are. We'll fuck like artists on the Left Bank, like artists in New York."[1]

I closed my eyes, blocking out his presence. In the weeks before leaving for college, I'd spent countless hours daydreaming about Harvard boys. I'd imagined intense relationships with artists and writers—but in every fantasy, my Harvard boyfriend was gay, and content to hold me in bed for the closeness, the solid warmth of a human body, making no sexual demands. This paradox had never struck me as strange. Growing up in a family where I had not been held since I learned to walk, the desire for even this amount of contact had seemed subversive, dangerous. I'd felt perverse wanting it and couldn't allow my imagination to go deeper, to think about the places I could be touched, the places I could touch.

I had not met one single openly gay boy since arriving at Harvard.

125   Evan was the only artist I knew.

I didn't know how long I'd been lying on Evan's mattress, but suddenly, I didn't feel desirable or powerful. I felt young, stupid, naïve. I didn't have the prep-school poise of the mainstream Harvard crowd, and I wasn't courageous enough to behave like an artist, either. I was only a backroom restaurant worker wearing her customer's hand-me-downs off to college. A poor girl dressed in designer clothes that had been fashionable a year earlier, only I was too ignorant to know it.

Evan's voice, insistent in my ear: "Just a blow job. What's the big deal? A blow job, and you can go read those pages. You know, it'll relieve tension and help you concentrate."

---

[1] The southern bank of the Seine, a center of artistic and student life.

I opened my eyes. How inevitable Evan's face now seemed, the natural consequence of so many years of repression. For all the images I'd constructed, writing poems on dorm windowsills, I couldn't imagine a way out of this scenario.

I gave in.

130 Time collapsed, events unfolding out of sequence. Evan's voice curled inside my ear. The air filled with the bitterness of his skin, a pungency like copper. His penis scraped the back of my throat. I tasted his stickiness, his bitterness, the thickness of his copper scent. I gagged. His hand pushed down on my head. Fifteen minutes stretched into one hour, two. I was naked.

Evan's torso rose above me, the muscles in his shoulders and arms twitching. He lowered himself onto me, into me. There was a quick, sharp pain. I tensed. I pressed my palms against his chest and pushed, but he was inside me. I heard myself say, "No, you bastard, stop," but he was inside me, pounding away, and I could no longer feel anything, I could only see an impossible vision, the sight of myself and Evan from above as I was suspended from the ceiling; I saw his back above me, his glowing hairless flesh. I saw the cleft of his buttocks, the indent of his spine, the white skin, the impossibly white skin. But I didn't see my body. I had no body.

❧

It was after four in the morning by the time I got back to my room. My eyes felt electric, seared hot and dry. My skin smelled of semen. When I brushed my teeth, I gagged on the viscous mixture of toothpaste and saliva creeping down my throat. I spit. Rinsed. Wiped my mouth. I took off my clothes. Every time I moved, the smell intensified, a smell like rubber, like bleach. I couldn't bear it. I wrapped myself in my bathrobe and slipped out to the shower.

❧

My first class started at ten, but I didn't awake until eleven. I figured that it didn't matter. I could skip the class. I hadn't done the reading, after all. Easing myself gingerly out of bed, I crept to the common room and curled up in a corner of our brown leatherette loveseat. The pod was absolutely silent; all my podmates must have classes of their own. A wedge of sunlight streamed from my open bedroom door. Motionless in the corner of the loveseat, I studied the dust motes floating in the light.

My pelvis ached, proof that I hadn't imagined the previous evening. Even so, I couldn't quite believe what had happened. I had had sex. My body told me this, but I didn't want to believe it. I'd wanted to fall in love, to be in a serious relationship, perhaps one headed toward marriage, before I had sex for the first time. Now that was no longer an option.

135 I wondered what to make of my night with Evan. I'd never considered the possibility that I might have sex with someone that I didn't care about, under circumstances that made me want to throw up. I wanted to think about my loss of virginity the way that I imagined an artist would, as a meaningless but necessary technical procedure, one more marker of adulthood—like college. But the night hadn't been meaningless for me; my body felt paradoxically empty and weighted by it, as if Evan had removed all my viscera and filled that space with a dense, unbreathable air.

I still hadn't come to any conclusions when I was stirred back to awareness by sounds from outside the pod—voices in the hallway, a key scratching the lock. My podmates, returning from class, or was it lunch? What time was it? How long had I been sitting there?

I wanted to get up to greet them, to smile and say hello, I wanted to go to my room and get dressed and comb my hair, I wanted to behave like a normal human being, but the weight was too much, and I couldn't move, I could only sit there.

The pod door opened. Leah and two other podmates, Anna and Ellen, walked in, trailing the faintly metallic scent of cold air behind them.

What would they make of my situation? What did *they* think of sex? I'd never consciously thought about this before, but now I was forced to: I knew that Ellen was a devout Catholic; she was the only pod member who regularly attended religious services of any kind. I guessed that she was against premarital sex. Anna had a boyfriend in California; he was older and worked as a professional model. She'd lived with him the previous summer, in order to escape her parents' marital problems, so they'd *probably* had sex—but we'd never talked about that aspect of their relationship, so I didn't know for sure. I'd spent enough time with Leah to know that she disapproved of premarital sex, or casual sex, anyway. I could tell by the way she sniffed at boys' sex talk and rolled her eyes at the mention of some girls' names—girls who spent the night in boys' dorm rooms.

140   Not expecting my presence, my podmates walked past me without looking.

But I needed their attention. I cleared my throat.

They stopped. Turned. Three automatic hellos.

Then, seeing my nightgown, the glasses heavy on my face, Anna laughed. "Oh, Elaine," she said, mock scolding. "You missed classes *again*?"

I nodded.

145   She shook her head. "I don't know how you do it," she said, already turning away again, headed for her room.

Leah and Ellen followed close behind her, their laughter overlapping hers.

Anna's voice continued, "If I slept in the way you do, I could never keep up."

They were leaving. I didn't want them to go. Without thinking, I opened my mouth. "Wait, you guys . . ." My voice sounded panicked.

They turned.

150   I stared at them, brain stuck mid-sentence, not knowing what came next. For reasons unknown to me, I felt compelled to tell them about Evan. But what would I say? Last night I had sex for the first time? I spent the night with Evan? These sentences sounded so neutral. They didn't describe the queasiness in my stomach, the tightness of my throat, the memory of his copper scent and his hand pushing on the back of my head. Suddenly I recalled a student group presentation from freshman week—"Response," a peer rape crisis counseling group. No means no, they'd said. Date rape is real rape. Last night, I'd said no. I *had* said no, hadn't I? My mind was blank. I couldn't remember. I couldn't remember whether I'd said no. I couldn't remember anything except the whiteness of his body above mine, the dark cleft of his buttocks as he thrust into me, the impossible vision from the night before.

I opened my mouth. I heard myself speak. I heard myself say, "You guys, I think Evan raped me last night."

∞

That one moment came to haunt me for a long time.

First there were the gasps, the ashen faces, the long silence as Ellen, Anna, and Leah took in my words. After a while, Anna said, "Are you sure?"

Their faces helped me realize the full import of what I'd just said, and I wanted to take it back. I strained to say the word *no*, but when I opened my mouth again, I only repeated the sentence: "Yeah. I think Evan raped me last night."

155   Now, instead of silence, there were questions, then after the questions, advice, softly worded commands of the usual sort—you need medical attention, you need counseling, you need to call your parents, you need to report this to the dorm proctor and the police, you need to get this boy out of the dorm—out of *our* lives, as well as your own.

    I followed along as best as I could, submitting to a medical exam with full rape kit, speaking to a University Health Services counselor, calling every person I could think of—excluding my family—to build my "support network." Whenever I became confused about how I was supposed to act, I fell back on the "Response" pamphlets, faithfully trotting to the library to read the recommended books and articles.

    I resisted only on one point, and only until I was worn down by Leah's parents—I refused to report the incident to either the police or university authorities. To do so, in my mind, would mean making it an "official" rape, and I still wasn't sure that the term was warranted.

    Sex with Evan had not been entirely voluntary. Of this I was certain. I'd been coerced and manipulated. But I didn't think that I'd been *forced*—and without force, was there rape? I studied the literature, looking for an answer, searching for a word to encompass the range of my experience—curiosity, confusion, naïveté, coercion, manipulation, fear, submission, an unwilling consent.

    The pamphlets, books, and articles all came back with the same answer—I'd been raped. In its own way, the literature was as close-minded as my family on the topic of sex. My choices were dichotomous, an either-or, with no room for ambiguity. Sex was either sanctioned by marriage or immoral, entirely voluntary or rape. I had to choose one.

160   Leah's parents, the Bauers, presented my dilemma another way: Refusing to report the incident as a rape, they asserted, was selfish. They were sorry for my hurt and confusion, but they couldn't help me with that. In fact, they weren't thinking about me at all; they were concerned for their daughter. According to Leah's father, the most important thing was to report Evan so that he couldn't hurt *her* the way he'd hurt me.

    "He wouldn't do anything to Leah," I protested. "He doesn't even like her."

    "If you don't report him," Dr. Bauer replied, "I'll do it myself."

    Having no other choice, I contacted University officials.

    At about the same time, giving up on seeing the event as anything other than a rape, I called Jim, a friend from a summer program that I'd attended between junior and senior years of high school. That summer, we'd spent one night secluded on a fire escape, talking about the meaninglessness of life until four in the morning. I'd hoped that the conversation might lead to a romance, but Jim had become involved with another girl at the program instead. Since then, Jim and Kirsten had broken up. Beginning this fall, Jim and I had talked by phone almost weekly. We'd discussed the possibility of his coming to visit me at Harvard—leaving open all that such a visit might entail.

165   But as much as I cared about Jim, I hadn't actively encouraged him to make the trip. Knowing what I did about Jim's relationship with Kirsten, I was certain that he'd want to have sex with me if he visited, and while I wanted him to be my boyfriend, I remained ambivalent about a relationship that included sex. Although my parents wouldn't have to find out, because they were half a continent way, my podmates would know, and they were just

outside my bedroom door. My social status at Harvard was too tenuous. Without my pod-mates' explicit approval, which had not been expressed, I couldn't agree to sleep with Jim. Of course, after Evan, none of this mattered anymore. I called Jim.

∞

He came up by train from Princeton a few days later. We hugged. We talked. I told him about Evan again. He took me out to dinner at a Mexican restaurant. We returned to Hurl-but, climbed the stairs to my pod, said a brief hello to my podmates, and locked ourselves in my bedroom. I took off my coat, sat on my bed. Wordlessly, Jim approached me. He bent, lifted my foot, removed my shoe. I lay back on the bed, watching him. He kissed the sole of my foot. I cringed, repulsed by the intimacy—but I didn't protest. Without a single word, he undressed me, then himself, and we had sex.

∞

We lay in bed together in the darkening room. Outside, the sun had set, but a residual bluish light limned the solid dark contours of the objects furnishing my room. When the phone rang, I could see well enough to answer it without flicking on a lamp.

"Hello?" I mumbled, crouched on the floor naked, phone to my ear.

170   Evan's voice slid out the other end, a sinuous murmur: "I really like you." Chuckle. "How about going for a walk and getting some ice cream?"

My breath caught. Against my face, the telephone handset glowed an eerie green, lumi-nescence cast by the push-button numbers. The room seemed to darken, and I was sud-denly, acutely aware of my nakedness. I curled in on myself further, hiding my breasts and genitalia. Although I knew it to be physically impossible, I was sure that he could see me through the telephone line, a pale, solitary figure glowing green in the darkness, illuminated by the push buttons of my phone.

I could hear him breathing. He said my name.

I bit back my panic and said, "Yes?"

"How about going for ice cream?"

175   "No."

"Oh, come on," he wheedled, his voice teasing, oblivious to my panic. "Why not?"

He didn't know yet, I realized. He didn't know that I'd reported him to the Freshman Dean's Office, and I didn't want to be the one to inform him. "I need to study," I lied.

"Awww," he answered sarcastically. "How about some other night?"

"Yeah," I said, then, "I have to go." I barely gave him time to say good-bye before hang-ing up.

180   I stood up, arms crossed over my chest. I couldn't believe that Evan had just asked me out on a date. I'd reported him as a rapist, and he'd asked me out for ice cream. Ice cream, just like the preppy idiots he made fun of. Could it be that he never intended to hurt me at all? I blanked out the thought. I wasn't strong enough to feel sorry for us both. I'd read the literature. I'd been lectured by the Bauers. I'd been raped. There was no going back.

I walked across the room and crawled into bed. Jim pulled my body close to his. "Who was that?"

"Never mind," I whispered. I edged away from him, ending the conversation, alone in the telephone's green light.

∞

Jim was still there on Saturday morning, two days later, when my proctor (the Harvard version of a resident advisor) knocked at my bedroom door.

"I'm not up yet," I told George, the proctor, warily, embarrassed to be caught in bed with a boy.

185 George coughed. "I'm sorry. Can you come out here? I need to talk to you."

Heart racing, I bolted out of bed and tugged on a robe. "What?" I slipped out the door and shut it behind me quickly, blocking Jim from George's view.

George didn't even bother trying to look over my shoulder. His face was drawn, a professional seriousness suppressing any more visceral reaction. He coughed again. Said, "Something's happened to your pod." Stepped aside so that I could take a look.

The pod had been vandalized.

In the middle of the night, someone had rigged a spider's web of string and styrofoam cups across our ceiling. Inside the cups were broken eggs. Strings connected the cups both to each other and to our bedroom doors. This contraption was designed to release the eggs when our doors opened. Fortunately, my podmate Leslie had awakened early, discovered the trap, and untied most of the strings, limiting the damage to the pod. But despite her efforts, we spent the day scrubbing egg yolks off our rug, wiping them from between the cushions of the loveseat, and scooping them out of the corners of our common room closets. We found a total of seven dozen eggs.

190 None of us specifically named Evan when speculating about who might have committed the vandalism, but my podmates' half-finished sentences and sidelong glances communicated their suspicions plainly. In that moment, I realized with the clarity of a premonition how public my story was about to become. Every sentence that remained incomplete in my presence would find its audience once I was out of the room.

∽

Jim walked with me to the convenience store to buy more cleaning supplies—Ajax, Pine-Sol, Murphy's Oil Soap. He got pizzas for the entire pod. He complained only briefly when he realized that we'd mistakenly used—and ruined—one of his towels scrubbing the pod floor.

Holding me in bed that night, he whispered, "What a psycho. I wish there were something I could do." He stroked my hair until I fell asleep.

Unable to bear the confluence of emotional and physical intimacy, I did not invite Jim to visit again.

∽

Two of my podmates, Leah and Becky, tried to gather evidence linking Evan to the vandalism but failed. We were never able to bring charges against him for this incident. We had to be satisfied with our own indignation—and the report of date rape.

195 Harvard's protocol for dealing with date rape was brisk and cerebral: First, I was summoned to the Freshman Dean's Office and asked to write a formal statement describing the events in Evans room. In a separate appointment, Evan provided his own formal account of the same night. We were called back to the FDO individually to read each others statements. We were allowed to furnish a rebuttal. Our statements were then discussed by the college's Administrative Board, who issued a formal recommendation.

The Board suggested mediation.

Mediation.

As if Evan and I had disagreed about the results of an academic research project.

When the Freshman Dean informed me, I laughed—a hot, bitter sound.

200 The Freshman Dean asked why I was so angry.

I said, "I was raped. Why do you think?"

In response, he blinked once, nothing more.

Evan and I never met for mediation. We did not have any further contact, although I occasionally saw him around Hurlbut or in the Union. These instances were rare and fleeting—a glimpse of his wiry form across the dining hall, a flash of his red hair ducking in a door. Each time, I froze momentarily, panicked, short of breath and nauseated.

Evan remained on the edge of my consciousness for the next four years. Almost by instinct, without any effort or will, I stayed apprised of his activities. I knew where he lived, who his friends were, what subjects he studied, what films he made, what awards he won. By the time we graduated, he'd received a fair number of artistic accolades and had a steady girlfriend. I absorbed this information with a mixture of dismay and relief. Part of me found it unfair that neither Harvard nor fate had punished Evan. The other part, still ambivalent about having called the incident rape, was glad that I had not completely ruined Evan's life.

∞

205 I didn't tell my parents about Evan. I didn't want them to know that I was no longer a virgin. Despite my resistance to their traditional ideas about gender roles and arranged marriages, I still wanted to please them to the best of my abilities. Even if my first intercourse had been joyful, I would not have wanted my parents to know about it. I certainly was not going to announce that I'd been coerced into sex, that I'd reported it as a date rape, and that I was now the subject of dorm rumors.

Compounding the problem was Evan's comment, "All Asian women are easy." I wanted to protect my parents from these words, just as I'd protected them from racist remarks throughout my childhood by not translating those particular words. I'd always thought that if my parents didn't understand the words, they wouldn't understand the sneers on the store clerks' faces or the intent behind the beer splashed down our backs the one time my family sat down to watch a men's softball game in the neighborhood park. Despite my teenage rebellion, I never wanted my parents to know about racism. I didn't want them to know that other people could hate them as much as I sometimes did—but without the love I felt to temper my hostility.

I grew up in a household where adults never touched, and no one was ever naked. Even as a young child, I wasn't allowed to leave the bathroom after a bath until I was fully dressed—underwear, undershirt, pajamas, robe, and slippers. My mother still refused to talk about sex; she would only say, "Never be alone in a room with a man. Never let a man touch you." And the only time I'd had a boyfriend, my family had reacted violently. Given these circumstances, it was hard for me to think of myself—or any of my female relatives— as sexual. Evan's characterization of us all as "easy" felt like a violation.

Before my night with Evan, I didn't realize that Asian women could be seen as sexual fetish objects. Growing up, I never saw Asian women portrayed as sex objects in the magazines that I read or the television shows and movies that I watched; I never saw them in these media at all. The boys in high school clearly did not think that I, as an Asian girl, was "easy"—they never asked me out in the hopes of receiving sexual favors, nor even attempted a pass at me during lunch periods. If anyone flirted with me, chances were that he wanted homework help, not sex. In high school, the one Asian stereotype I knew was *science geek*. Once, someone even called me "a typical Oriental" who made the word sex sound "scientific." This, despite the fact that I nearly failed high-school chemistry.

I didn't know what to do about Evan's comment. It bothered me, but I didn't feel comfortable discussing the issue with any of my podmates or even my counselor at University Health Services, a middle-aged white woman who nodded in automatic sympathy every time I paused for breath. We didn't discuss race as an issue in Harvard's mainstream population. It, like money and privilege, was an embarrassing topic. Feeling like I'd caused enough trouble already, I decided to remain silent about Evan's comment, saving my confusion for my journals.

210   I quit counseling after three sessions, feeling like a failure because I didn't know how to answer questions about how I felt, much less explain why I felt that way. I could talk about my situation intellectually, but I didn't have any grasp of my emotional state. Most of the time, unless I was confronted with external clues—physical sensations like the wetness of my own tears or the sound of my raised voice—I had trouble naming my emotions.

I wasn't so much avoiding the issue (consciously or subconsciously) as I was confused by the American concept of an individual self whose feelings and experiences have distinct boundaries from those of family and community. Growing up in a traditional Chinese family, I'd been trained to think of myself not as a separate individual, but as one part of a larger whole, seamlessly connected to my parents, my brother, my aunts and uncles—even in some small way to my classmates and schoolteachers, even now.

At an early age, I learned to define my emotions based on other people's reactions to me. If my mother was happy, I felt happy. If my teacher disapproved of my work, I felt sad. If my friends were angry, I felt bereft. I had trouble understanding myself outside the context of interpersonal relationships, no matter how much I wanted to—no matter how American I believed myself to be.

In fact, I had no idea what it meant to have my own voice, one that was internally, rather than externally, constructed.

I studied the pamphlets handed out by the college rape crisis center. They spoke of depression, anger, anxiety, confusion, guilt. I echoed these feelings back to the University Health Services therapist, trying to be a good date rape victim. My head and throat and chest hurt when she told me I wasn't examining my emotions deeply enough. I wanted to scream, frustrated by the lack of language, angry at the therapist's assumption that I could so easily own myself.

215   My sexuality reeled out of control for a long time after Evan. I became intent on proving that no lasting damage had been done, and used sex as the method to do so. Angry at myself for having been so naïve about sex, and at my parents for having raised me this way, I worked to separate emotion from sex. I made an effort to view the act as insignificant, irrelevant to the rest of my life. "Sport fucking," I laughed, echoing the Harvard boys. Wanting to know how sex felt when it was freely, unambiguously given, I had sex with a lot of men; I didn't realize that my deliberation, in itself, created the ambiguity. Sex during this period was always voluntary but never enjoyable.

Whenever I could be honest with myself, I wished for physical intimacy with someone I loved—or even liked. I wished that my first time had been this way. In these moments, I understood exactly what Evan had taken from me, and the damage *was* irreparable. I kept myself busy, avoiding the flashes of clarity. I told Leah that Evan had not been my first, hoping to delude myself as well as her.

For most of freshman year, after Evan, I didn't care why someone wanted to sleep with me. I collected men like books of poetry, objects for my shelf, within my control. There were men who prowled for random bodies, men who were seen at breakfast with a different Asian woman each week, men who seemed to desire me because they'd heard the rumor that I'd been date raped.

Then I realized that I wasn't in control.

The pornographic avidity of this last group, which comprised three members of Hurlbut's first-floor suite, shocked me to my senses. Initially, I believed these boys to be my friends, because they had the courage to ask me directly about what had happened, rather than whisper as I passed. But over time, their interest took on an obsessive, fetishistic quality. They started challenging me to get over the rape by sleeping with them, singly or as a group. They showed me soft-porn magazines and rubbed against me, asking, "Did he do anything like this?"

220   I finally broke down in the first-floor suite at the end of freshman year, collapsing in a crying fit more profound than any I'd suffered in the previous months. By the time the boys called for help, I was trying to cut myself with a piece of broken glass. The Harvard Police and my proctor intervened. They escorted me to the UHS emergency psychiatric ward, where I spent the night crying uncontrollably.

When I returned for sophomore year, I was placed on disciplinary probation for one semester. I wasn't mandated to attend counseling, and I didn't seek it on my own until junior year, the morning of my *Introduction to Anglo-Saxon Poetry* final. Chris, my boyfriend at the time, had broken up with me a week earlier. I remained devastated. He'd been my first "real" boyfriend, the first sexual partner I'd loved. We'd been together almost a year and a half. I'd expected us to spend our lives together.

I'd been crying non-stop for days, too depressed to get out of bed some mornings. The day of the final, I managed to make it out of bed but couldn't stop crying long enough to attend the exam. That morning, sobbing into a Kleenex while a UHS clinician approved my absence from the final (which I would have to make up later), I realized that I needed to start evaluating the events of the last few years. Otherwise, I wouldn't make it through another semester.

On my way out of the clinic, I scheduled a counseling appointment. It was only a beginning step in the long process of learning to become whole, one that continues still, although the counseling ended years ago.

I used to think that getting over the events of freshman year was like being an alcoholic—I was always in recovery, never recovered. But it's been over fifteen years now, and long stretches pass when I don't think of that period at all. I no longer have nightmares about lying in bed paralyzed while men creep in next to me. I don't worry about being attacked every time I'm alone in an enclosed space with a man.

225   I'm not sure when the memories lost their edge and set me free. There was a point, senior year of college, when I stopped being ashamed of what had happened and started wearing my status as a date rape survivor like a badge of honor. I became politically active in women's issues, particularly with regard to sexual violence. Today, I remain just as passionate about these issues, but I feel less compelled to present my life in such stark, polemic terms.

I think far more about the way I got to Evan's room that night. I try to trace the trajectory from my teen magazines, the red-haired busboy, my family's history of arranged marriages, and my own, conflicting desires, to Evan's room. I try to trace the trajectory from that room to the choices I've made since. I think about my mother, and how she's never been allowed to decide whom to love.

∞

On a recent New Year's Eve, I found myself standing outside a bar on New York's Upper West Side with my friend Kiendel, whom I was visiting from Boston. It was four in the morning, and the party that we'd attended had ended. Now we were trying to get rid of some men—three or four total—who thought it was a good idea for us to have more drinks with all of them at one of their apartments. That night, I was wearing sharp-toed, black patent-leather pumps with four-inch stiletto heels. Kiendel is a natural blonde with hair so pale it glows like filaments of light. She is slender but curvaceous. Between the two of us, we fulfilled the criteria for any number of fetishes. Now that we were in our thirties, we understood this. We knew that these men did not see beyond our physicality. We would never be swayed by their arguments; we were simply trying to leave without being rude.

Mid-discussion, a taxi pulled up at the curb, four or five feet from where we stood. I turned my head, glad for the distraction. Perhaps Kiendel and I could take this, an available cab, as our excuse, I thought. The taxi doors opened, and three men poured out. There were two white men of the same approximate height, both with dark hair, one's curly, the other's straight. Their faces weren't familiar, so I didn't pay attention to them. The third man was black, with soft-looking, pale brown skin. His woolly dark hair was cut close to the scalp. His eyes were heavy lidded, giving him a perpetually sleepy appearance. They were familiar eyes, a familiar face, although I had not seen this man, a college friend, in over five years. I stepped away from Kiendel and said his name uncertainly, "Vaughn?"

He answered with my name. I ran to him, and we hugged. He said, "I think about you every day."

230   "You liar!" I teased. "I haven't seen you for five years, at least—not since I moved out of New York."

"I know," he said, "but the last time I heard from you, you'd left a message on my machine, asking me to come protest the opening of *Miss Saigon*. I didn't come, but now I work in a building across the street from *Miss Saigon*. I think about you every time I look across the street."

I laughed. I could barely remember that protest, it had been so long ago. I'd been twenty-four at the time, in my third year out of college and active with a number of political action groups, Asian and otherwise. I'd protested *Miss Saigon* for two reasons: first, because a white actor was playing an Asian role, one that he'd performed in London with eyes taped back and wearing yellowface makeup. Second, because I believed that the theme of the play—Asian prostitute waiting for rescue from her homeland by a white soldier—was denigrating to women in general and to Asian women specifically. At the protest, I'd carried a sign that said, "No more fuckee fuckee."

Now thirty-two, I told Vaughn, "It's been years since I've been to that kind of protest."

He said, "It still inspires me that you would put yourself out there like that."

235   Embarrassed, I shrugged. I introduced him to Kiendel. He introduced me to his two friends, José, the one with straight hair, and Jeff, the one whose hair was curly. The five of us went around the corner to a diner for breakfast, then upstairs to Vaughn's apartment to drink a very expensive bottle of champagne that Vaughn, until now, had refused to open. We stayed up drinking and talking until eight that morning, when Kiendel and I finally left.

My vacation ended. I returned home to Boston, where I was preparing for the publication of my first book, a memoir. I'd almost forgotten about New Year's Eve when Jeff, Vaughn's curly haired friend, sent me an email several weeks later, inviting me to have dinner with him if I ever happened to be in San Francisco. Uncertain of his intentions, I wrote back cautiously, "I'll be there on book tour in August. I'll let you know if I have time."

He answered, "Tell me when your book comes out, and I'll buy it right away. Will you need a ride from the airport? I can pick you up, play tour guide, take you to your appointments, whatever you need."

Touched by his generosity, I agreed to dinner in August.

I had more fun than I could ever have imagined. The meal stretched into a late-night talk, morning coffee, a day's exploration of San Francisco bookstores, another dinner, another breakfast coffee—and not once did Jeff make a pass at me. Saying good-bye at the airport after thirty-seven and one-half hours together, I confessed my disappointment that he hadn't.

240 Jeff laughed. "Maybe I thought that I didn't need to." I looked at him quizzically, and he elaborated, "I thought that we clicked. I thought that if anything happened between us, it would develop with time. Making a move now would only scare you off."

"Hmm," I said, already turning away. I hoisted my duffel bag over one shoulder, thoughts too full of my fledgling career to consider whether we'd actually clicked. Looking down the terminal, I said, "On to Seattle. Then Denver. Then Boston."

"Can I call you?"

I shrugged. "You have the number in the alumni directory, right?"

Jeff didn't answer. His throat rippled, swallowing hard.

245 We hugged briefly, not knowing whether we'd see each other again.

I didn't anticipate leaving a message on Jeff's machine two days later, asking him to call me in Denver that night, any time, it didn't matter how late. My parents, who could not read English, had nevertheless called me an ungrateful daughter for having written a memoir (in English) about the entrenched poverty of our immigrant community. They'd told me to leave their house and never return, then called me a disrespectful daughter when I tried to check into a hotel for the night. My entire adolescence came hurtling back at me; I remembered sharply, viscerally, exactly why I'd fled for Harvard, for a voice I could call my own. I honestly thought that I might hurt myself.

In the midst of this chaos, Jeff telephoned. He stayed on the line with me for five hours straight, without once trying to hang up. At the end, he said that he'd even had fun. I didn't believe him, but I didn't need to. With his help, I'd made it through the night.

When I got back to Boston two days later, I called to let him know I was okay. We said that we'd keep in touch, and we did—every day. After a week of calls, Jeff bought me a plane ticket to visit him in San Francisco for the Labor Day weekend. We decided that either we'd get sick of each other or we wouldn't.

We didn't.

250 A month later, October 1999, I was in San Francisco visiting Jeff again. He was planning a seven-month trip to Asia that was to begin in December, so I brought him a Hong Kong travel guide with mini-phrasebook included. I promised to teach him Cantonese, although my pronunciation was so corrupted and my vocabulary so poor at this point that I barely knew it myself. I speak *bi bi hua*, I told him—baby language.

Sneaking a sip from my coffee cup, Jeff groaned. "I'll be walking around China asking for something yummy for my tum-tum . . ."

I nodded. "Pretty much."

"Is that why you've never taught anyone else to speak Chinese?"

My smile froze. I knew he was teasing, but there had been too many strangers, too many boyfriends, too many well-meaning teachers, demanding, "Say something in Chinese!" And I always felt like a pet dog. But not with Jeff. Never with Jeff. I stared at him mutely. If I tried to explain, my trust would collapse under the weight of too many words. I would never be able to teach him my *bi bi hua*.

255   The silence stretched. Jeff cleared his throat. "What's wrong?"

I shrugged.

Jeff looked into my eyes for a long time without blinking. He took another sip from my coffee cup. "I like baby language," he said quietly.

I looked away, suddenly aware of the motion of my heart. Jeff and I had agreed not to become too attached, because he would be away for so long. I wondered if we hadn't already breached the agreement. I opened the travel guide and read aloud, *"Ba-see zham hai BEAN doe ah?"* Where is the bus stop?

Jeff bent his head over the book. Our shoulders touching, he repeated after me.

260   We went to Chinatown one day that weekend, and I guided him through grocery-store aisles, pointing out the dried, salted plums and sweet tofu pudding that had been my childhood favorites—that I still sometimes craved. I urged him to eavesdrop on nearby conversations, and, dutifully, he cocked his head in the direction of two middle-aged women nearby, his forehead scrunched in concentration.

"Are you getting any of it?" I asked.

"No," he whispered back. "I don't think they're asking about the bus stop."

I nudged him playfully. "They're talking about the prices. *Gum doh-ah!* 'How expensive!' You know that."

He inclined his head again, listening. "What are they saying now?"

265   I frowned. "They're complaining about their daughters."

Jeff looked at me suspiciously. "I'm getting the feeling that's a common theme for Chinese mothers."

"It is."

Jeff stepped in closer, grazing my hip with his hand. "Then things will get better with *your* mother."

We left the grocery store to wander the sidewalk stalls. We explored an herbalist's shop, where Jeff gazed in wonder at the bins of dried jellyfish, dried scallops, dried sea slug. *"Gum doh-ah!"* he said solemnly, when I confirmed that the price of dried jellyfish—$245 a pound—was not a mistake. Then, taking my hand, he led me out of the shop. "Enough Chinese lessons," he declared. "Time to rest."

270   We found a park nearby, and I sat on a bench with Jeff's head in my lap, my fingers absent-mindedly twisting themselves through his hair. The sun was about to set. The day's heat rose from the concrete beneath my feet, cooled by the incoming night air. All around us there were Chinese people—old men on benches, gossiping; children scrambling down slides on the playground; garishly overdressed Christian Chinese families returning from church. I looked down at Jeff. His eyes were closed and his face relaxed but smiling, looking utterly content. For an instant, I had a sensation of being able to see myself both from the outside and within—I could see my face, as content and relaxed as Jeff's, at ease with both him and the Chinese American community around me. I was no longer struggling, and in that moment, I believed that all my life up to this point had been worthwhile, because it all boiled down to this moment, this understanding that I had a choice. And I chose now to be here.

■ **EXPLORATIONS OF THE TEXT**

1. Explore the narrator's conflict of being an adolescent caught between Chinese and American worlds. Does this conflict continue to manifest itself at Harvard?

2. Examine the narrator's "culture shock" at Harvard. How do class and racial identity shape her experiences there? Compare her reactions to being a freshman at an elite

educational institution with that of the protagonist in Packer's "Drinking Coffee Else-where."

3. Interpret the symbolism of the "ant-sized poems" on the window sill and "bi bi hua," baby language. What do they suggest about the narrator's character?

4. Why is the narrator attracted to Evan? Why is he drawn to her? Do stereotypes of Asian women play a role? Do cultural roles for women?

5. Why does the narrator yield to Evan's initial sexual demand? Examine their sexual en-counter. Is it date rape? Why is the narrator uncertain about whether she was raped?

6. Discuss the aftermath of the rape for the narrator. What is the impact upon her life?

7. Compare and contrast the treatment of seduction and sexual violence in this work with those in Gordon's "Violation," Rossetti's "Goblin Market," and Gilman's *Boy Gets Girl*. How do these works treat the subject in complex ways?

■ THE READING/WRITING CONNECTION

1. "Think" Topic: How is the narrator's gender identity formed by her Chinese upbringing?

2. In a journal entry, write about your first month at college. Compare your experiences with those of the narrator in this work or the protagonist in Packer's "Drinking Coffee Elsewhere."

3. Classify the college "types" depicted in this work. Do they seem familiar to you? Does Mar present a believable portrait of college life?

4. In a journal entry, discuss the desire to "fit in" portrayed in the work. What are the con-sequences of this need for acceptance?

■ IDEAS FOR WRITING

1. Date rape and acquaintance rape, unfortunately, are realities on college campuses. Share this work with your friends, and interview them concerning their responses. What do you conclude? Does this work present a realistic portrayal of a phenomenon that should be discussed? Do the narrator's efforts to deal with the aftermath of the rape send an im-portant message about this problem?

2. This essay presents a complex portrait of a victim of date rape. The writer transforms a statistic or case study into a complex human drama. How does the writer accomplish this? Evaluate the essay, and note the techniques of memoir writing that make it effective.

3. In "Bi Bi Hua," Mar depicts a journey from unconsciousness to consciousness, from fragmentation to wholeness. Referring to Hollis's "The Heroic Journey" (chapter 4), trace the stages of the narrator's growth. As an alternative, compare her journey with Sedaris's in "I Like Guys" (chapter 4) or Nora's in *A Doll's House* (chapter 4).

Kᴉᴍ Fɪᴄᴇʀᴀ (1959–)   **2003**

BI-BYE

I couldn't pick a bisexual woman out of a lineup if she'd just mugged me on a curb outside an Ani DiFranco concert. I can't tell the difference between lesbians and straight women anymore, either. Beautiful, long-nailed women in dresses are now stylish fixtures in gay clubs, and I don't know if they like girls or boys. As a denim-wearing dyke who will never make the transformation to lesbian chic, I sometimes feel like all my years of faithful service to my sisters should be rewarded by a hint here or there.

Okay, so maybe I wasn't always faithful, but someone from those clubs should have no-tified me of the change immediately, by virtue of my seniority, or in acknowledgment of the vast amounts of alcohol I've consumed at their bars in the last twenty-five years, I didn't appreciate the surprise, nor did I enjoy feeling like the only naked woman on the outside of an inside joke at a prison on No-Shower Thursday.

Now that I've grown accustomed to the gorgeous new scenery, however, I have to admit that the change has its benefits. For instance, I didn't see a softball uniform or even a dyke in a knee brace at the last lesbian dance I attended. I also didn't have to dodge darts or pinball machines. The pool table, the final vestige of lesbian tokenism, remained, however. As long as there's chalk, there will be chubby, die-hard dykes claiming the all-important green felt territory in a bar. Like roaches, lesbians with pool cues and pockets full of quarters would likely survive the devastation of nuclear war.

I suspect those dykes won't survive the neo-lesbian mushroom cloud of femininity that's threatening their domain, though. With uniformity hugging them like blinders, they don't know they're an endangered species. They're unaware that a lesbian filmmaker in heels, with a grant from Donna Karan, will net them in the parking lot as they leave, tag their sneakers for future reference, and immediately deliver them to the Discovery Channel, the network that will air her documentary *Neander-Dyke* during Fashion Week. Sadly, they'll die a slow, clueless death of extinction, and no one except Taco Bell shareholders will miss them.

5   I'm too thin to be mourned by fast-food chain executives, that's true, but if I hadn't acted quickly, my outdated wardrobe would have ensured that I'd become one of the fallen. So, because I never want to be the type of lesbian well-dressed anthropologists observe from the tops of trees, I bought a few pairs of slacks and silk shirts with girl buttons. And, after only one jean-less week, a great deal of prodding by a friend, and a particularly moving episode of *ER*, I took my new de-dyked self to a dance club.

With editorial content from both *Jane* and *Girlfriends*[1] under my hair, feeling sufficiently armed and ready to infiltrate the gender muck, I boldly entered the doors, made my way to a stool at the bar, and ordered a drink. As the bartender mixed my gimlet, I looked around for my friend who, since refusing to join in my effort to blend in, would have stood out like Goldilocks at a Black Panther meeting had she been in the room. I was on my own, surrounded by about thirty of the most flawlessly beautiful strangers I'd ever seen.

Alone and in uncomfortable clothing, my self-confidence waned. I was intimidated. The ease with which the women around me approached one another for the purpose of getting a date or, in some cases, I assumed, just to get laid, terrified me but, I admit, also filled me with envy. They danced into one another's lives with little effort, and brazenly dared to scream words like, "I love this song!" over the music and into each other's ears. I was afraid to take such bold steps. I assumed I'd cross the razor thin line that separates a confident person from an asshole.

My fear and jealousy told me that I was witnessing the remnants of a coup. *The new, indie lesbians and bis will likely rule forever,* I thought, *regardless of whether or not I can differentiate between the two troops. I should either resign myself to a life of comfortable and cordial dinner parties, or cross enemy lines and relinquish my cheekbones to the gorgeous garrison at a Macy's cosmetics counter.* But, just as I considered surrendering, I noticed confusion in their ranks. I wasn't the only woman in the room scratching my head.

She was gorgeous and tall, her figure toned. The red lipstick on her full mouth was perfectly applied, her nails professionally manicured, and, from what I observed, her breasts were real. I put her age at around thirty.

10   She walked by me slowly, almost valiantly, to a stool a few feet away, as if the Oscar or some equally fabulous award awaited her there. She sat down, turned to me, and smiled. I smiled back, but my *gaydar* fluctuated. Something wasn't right—the needle on my internal lesbo-meter bobbed between the *S,* the *B,* and the *L.*

I was confused, perplexed, my thoughts were willy-nilly. Nevertheless, I regrouped. I reminded myself of the determination I possessed when I'd first entered the bar. I instructed myself to risk being an asshole, to chance rejection, and to talk to that woman, even though she might be straight or, worse, a man.

So, I walked over to her and introduced myself.

"Hello," I said.

"Hi," she replied with a slight, but polite, smile.

15   "Hi, again. Er . . . hello. My name is . . . uh . . . Kim," I said, nervously.

A very long, uncomfortable pause followed, during which I stared into my drink looking for my better judgment. I was sure it had fallen in there on my way over to her.

"I hope this doesn't sound rude, but I'm waiting for a friend," she said.

Of course you are, I thought. But I didn't give up. "Really? Me, too."

"She's late, as usual."

20   "My friend, too," I said, sitting on the stool beside her.

She nodded slowly, in a way that said, *Yeah, right, loser!*

"She'll be here soon," I assured.

"I hate waiting for people in clubs. I don't like to sit alone at a bar. Do you know what I mean?" she asked.

I didn't know what she meant. Perhaps that was her way of telling me that I didn't meet the height requirement that she'd imposed to determine whether or not she was, in fact, alone. Maybe I was too short to be considered company. But I didn't ask her to confirm my suspicions. "I don't generally mind sitting alone," I told her. "But I hate walking in alone. I don't know what's up with that."

25   "It screams, '*single!*'" she said.

"I guess you're right. But I'm *not* single," I lied.

"I am," she said. "And I hate it."

"You are! You do! I thought when you said that you were waiting for someone it was just a line."

"No, I'm really waiting for someone."

30   "So am I."

"Right, you said that already."

"No, I mean, I'm really single."

"I thought so," she said.

"Is it that obvious?"

35   She nodded.

"I can never guess who's single and who's not."

"I can. I've been alone a long time," she said.

Maybe you should lower the height requirement, I thought.

"I've crashed and burned more than I care to admit," she continued. "But now I get it right most of the time."

40   "I think everyone should be given a color-coded bracelet, button, or even a distinguishing hat when they go into a bar," I said. "You know, pink for single, blue for partnered, white for bi, and green for straight. That way, no one would be confused."

"Maybe," she said.

I shook my head. "No maybes about it. It's a fabulous idea!"

"It would take a lot of the mystery out of the first conversation with someone."

"Only part of the mystery," I said. "The part I hate."

45 "Are you hating *this* conversation?" she asked.

"No." I smiled. "I'm enjoying it, actually."

We each took sips of our drinks and scoped the bar for our friends.

"See those two women over there?" she asked, nodding toward a couple talking in the corner. "The blonde is straight," she said. "But I think the woman she's talking to is bi."

I looked. "I think they're both bi," I said.

50 "What makes you think so?"

"I don't know. Just a feeling, I guess."

"Are you bi?" she bluntly asked.

I laughed. "Don't you know?"

She shook her head. "I'm pretty good at weeding the straight women from the lesbians," she said. "But I don't always have a sense for the bi vibe." She paused. "So, are you bi?"

55 "Something tells me that's a trick question?" I said.

Her eyebrows narrowed. "No. No trick," she replied. "It's just that I don't date bisexual women."

"Ah, I see."

She must have sensed in my voice that I thought her words sharp. "Look, you're really nice. Really," she said. "But if you're bisexual, I think it's important to get that out in the open quickly, so you don't have any false expectations."

I looked at her quizzically—more than a bit put off. If I were bisexual, I would have been offended. I would have wondered why she hadn't just drilled her swizzle stick into my eye. So, in defense of bisexuals everywhere, I couldn't let her get away with it. "You're not leaving much room to get to know me, are you?"

60 After giving her plenty of time to respond, I considered moving on because the night was young. But because the hours ahead would provide plenty of time for me to be insulted by someone much less attractive, I became even more annoyed. So, I continued. "Okay, since you asked, I like dogs, old movies, and Italian food." I smiled.

She nodded righteously. "Well, you must be bi, since you can't even answer the question," she said smugly.

"Ahhh!" I said with feigned enlightenment. "Chinese food and *Twin Peaks* it is!"

She rolled her eyes and probably wished I would go away. But I remained.

"Aw, c'mon. Don't get mad." I smiled. "What about the mystery?"

65 She said nothing. She was apparently no longer interested in mystery.

"Let's say, hypothetically, that I am bisexual," I proposed, beginning to enjoy myself. "Is that a bad thing?"

She shook her head and frowned. "It's not very good." She paused to gather her thoughts and form the most serious expression I'd seen in some time. "You see," she said, "I know that I love women."

"I love women too!"

She smirked. "Maybe, but you also love men."

70 I shook my head. "Did I say that?" I thought for a moment. "I don't think I said that."

"You implied it!" she answered emphatically.

"I did?"

"Your refusal to answer the question," she said slowly and clearly, obviously vexed, "leads me to believe that you are."

She held her impermeability up to me like a mirror, and I felt sorry for her. Suddenly, I wished I'd kept my ugly insecurities to myself. "Honest, I'm not," I said.

75   She shook her head vigorously. "I don't believe you!"

"What?" I was shocked.

"I said I don't believe you." She paused. "And, now that I've lost trust in you, there's no hope for even a friendship."

"You're kidding, right?" I asked.

She didn't immediately answer. I imagined a thought bubble over her head with the words "Not kidding, asshole!" floating inside.

80   "Look," she said curtly, "I think you're bi and you don't want to admit it."

I leaned into her, very close. "You're not charging me for this analysis, are you?" I whispered.

She huffed. "You're not very funny."

"Bummer," I said. "I was hoping we could go back to my place so I could fuck you with my joke books."

She threw her hands in the air. "What's with you bis?"

85   I wasn't sure how to answer that, so I replied as I thought a bisexual might. "I can't tell you. It's a secret."

Her face flushed with a hue of anger only a shade or two lighter than her lipstick. "How is a true lesbian supposed to feel comfortable, safe, and committed in a relationship with you if you might leave her for a man?" she asked me.

Sarcasm or sincerity? Sarcasm or sincerity? Sarcasm or sincerity? Fuck it. "Isn't it just as possible that I could leave her for another woman?" I asked. "Or, would that, in some way, be less painful?"

She got off the stool, grabbed her purse from the bar, and shrieked with great exasperation, "You bisexuals can't commit to anything, not even to your own commitment!"

"Huh? What the hell does that mean?"

90   She turned and walked away. "Whatever!" she yelled, waving the back of her hand at me.

I shrugged my shoulders. "My point exactly!" I said to no one.

■ EXPLORATIONS OF THE TEXT

1. Why does Ficera use humor to tell her personal stories? How does Ficera's humor help the reader to characterize her?
2. Why does Ficera relate the actual conversation in "Bi-Bye" as opposed to merely summarizing it? Is reading the conversation verbatim effective? Why, or why not?
3. Do you sense a difference in Ficera's tone in "All in the Family" and "Bi-Bye"? Why do you think this is?
4. Do you think Ficera's sarcasm and wit are appropriate in her real life? Why, or why not? Do you think that they might get her into trouble at times? Why are the written personalities of writers sometimes different from who they really are?
5. What critique of sexual stereotypes and sexual roles does Ficera present? What critique of body image is implied?
6. What does Ficera mean by "gender muck"? Compare and contrast her view of the blurring of gender roles with the vision in Cooper's "Burl's."

■ THE READING/WRITING CONNECTION

1. Create a sexual stereotype log. Spend a weekend noting your stereotypical responses to others. What do you conclude?
2. Try to remember a conversation in which you and the other person were just not communicating at all, as in "Bi-Bye." Do a freewrite about the conversation, and then write a short essay using the conversation as a springboard.

3. "Think" Topic: Write a paragraph about how Ficera's essays informed or changed you. What did her essays teach you?

■ **IDEAS FOR WRITING**

1. Write an essay about the use of humor. Discuss several ways in which people use humor, such as to quell fears, disguise insecurities, or explain tragedy. Why is using humor sometimes more effective than simply relaying the facts?

2. Write a short personal essay using humor.

3. Take the opposing view in relation to your reaction to Ficera's essay. If you agree with her, write an essay presenting the opposing viewpoint. If you disagree with her, write an essay in support of her ideas.

4. Do you think that this generation of college students is more independent in their thinking, more willing to break out of stereotypical gender roles and ways of behaving? Present your views on this question. You may refer to such works in this chapter as Mar's "Bi Bi Hua," Packer's "Drinking Coffee Elsewhere," and Leavitt's "Territory."

MAXINE HONG KINGSTON

Maxine Hong Kingston (1940–   ) was born in Stockton, California, to parents who immigrated from China. After graduating from the University of California, Kingston moved to Hawaii and taught in secondary schools, colleges, and the University of Hawaii. She is presently a Chancellor's Distinguished Professor at the University of California, Berkeley. The Woman Warrior: Memoirs of a Girlhood Among Ghosts, *published in 1976, won the National Book Critics Circle Award. Her second autobiographical volume,* China Men, *was published in 1980. Kingston released her first novel,* Tripmaster Monkey, *in 1989; her second novel,* The Fifth Book of Peace, *was published in 2003. Kingston's writing interweaves her Chinese heritage with her American upbringing, transplanting the Chinese tradition into a strange American soil.*

1976

NO NAME WOMAN

Y ou must not tell anyone," my mother said, "what I am about to tell you. In China your father had a sister who killed herself. She jumped into the family well. We say that your father has all brothers because it is as if she had never been born.

"In 1924 just a few days after our village celebrated seventeen hurry-up weddings—to make sure that every young man who went 'out on the road' would responsibly come home—your father and his brothers and your grandfather and his brothers and your aunt's new husband sailed for America, the Gold Mountain. It was your grandfather's last trip. Those lucky enough to get contracts waved good-bye from the decks. They fed and guarded the stowaways and helped them off in Cuba, New York, Bali, Hawaii. "We'll meet in California next year," they said. All of them sent money home.

"I remember looking at your aunt one day when she and I were dressing; I had not noticed before that she had such a protruding melon of a stomach. But I did not think, 'She's pregnant,' until she began to look like other pregnant women, her shirt pulling and the white tops of her black pants showing. She could not have been pregnant, you see, because her husband had been gone for years. No one said anything. We did not discuss it. In early summer she was ready to have the child, long after the time when it could have been possible.

"The village had also been counting. On the night the baby was to be born the villagers raided our house. Some were crying. Like a great saw, teeth strung with lights, files of people walked zigzag across our land, tearing the rice. Their lanterns doubled in the disturbed black water, which drained away through the broken bunds. As the villagers closed in, we could see that some of them, probably men and women we knew well, wore white masks. The people with long hair hung it over their faces. Women with short hair made it stand up on end. Some had tied white bands around their foreheads, arms, and legs.

5   "At first they threw mud and rocks at the house. Then they threw eggs and began slaughtering our stock. We could hear the animals scream their deaths—the roosters, the pigs, a last great roar from the ox. Familiar wild heads flared in our night windows; the villagers encircled us. Some of the faces stopped to peer at us, their eyes rushing like searchlights. The hands flattened against the panes, framed heads, and left red prints.

"The villagers broke in the front and the back doors at the same time, even though we had not locked the doors against them. Their knives dripped with the blood of our animals. They smeared blood on the doors and walls. One woman swung a chicken, whose throat she had slit, splattering blood in red arcs about her. We stood together in the middle of our house, in the family hall with the pictures and tables of the ancestors around us, and looked straight ahead.

"At that time the house had only two wings. When the men came back, we would build two more to enclose our courtyard and a third one to begin a second courtyard. The villagers pushed through both wings, even your grandparents' rooms, to find your aunt's, which was also mine until the men returned. From this room a new wing for one of the younger families would grow. They ripped up her clothes and shoes and broke her combs, grinding them underfoot. They tore her work from the loom. They scattered the cooking fire and rolled the new weaving in it. We could hear them in the kitchen breaking our bowls and banging the pots. They overturned the great waist-high earthenware jugs; duck eggs, pickled fruits, vegetables burst out and mixed in acrid torrents. The old woman from the next field swept a broom through the air and loosed the spirits-of-the-broom over our heads. 'Pig.' 'Ghost.' 'Pig,' they sobbed and scolded while they ruined our house.

"When they left, they took sugar and oranges to bless themselves. They cut pieces from the dead animals. Some of them took bowls that were not broken and clothes that were not torn. Afterward we swept up the rice and sewed it back up into sacks. But the smells from the spilled preserves lasted. Your aunt gave birth in the pigsty that night. The next morning when I went for the water, I found her and the baby plugging up the family well.

"Don't let your father know that I told you. He denies her. Now that you have started to menstruate, what happened to her could happen to you. Don't humiliate us. You wouldn't like to be forgotten as if you had never been born. The villagers are watchful."

10   Whenever she had to warn us about life, my mother told stories that ran like this one, a story to grow up on. She tested our strength to establish realities. Those in the emigrant generations who could not reassert brute survival died young and far from home. Those of us in the first American generations have had to figure out how the invisible world the emigrants built around our childhoods fit in solid America.

The emigrants confused the gods by diverting their curses, misleading them with crooked streets and false names. They must try to confuse their offspring as well, who, I suppose, threaten them in similar ways—always trying to get things straight, always trying to name the unspeakable. The Chinese I know hide their names; sojourners take new names when their lives change and guard their real names with silence.

Chinese-Americans, when you try to understand what things in you are Chinese, how do you separate what is peculiar to childhood, to poverty, insanities, one family, your mother who marked your growing with stories, from what is Chinese? What is Chinese tradition and what is the movies?

If I want to learn what clothes my aunt wore, whether flashy or ordinary, I would have to begin, "Remember Father's drowned-in-the-well sister?" I cannot ask that. My mother has told me once and for all the useful parts. She will add nothing unless powered by Necessity, a riverbank that guides her life. She plants vegetable gardens rather than lawns; she carries the odd-shaped tomatoes home from the fields and eats food left for the gods.

Whenever we did frivolous things, we used up energy; we flew high kites. We children came up off the ground over the melting cones our parents brought home from work and the American movie on New Year's Day—*Oh, You Beautiful Doll* with Betty Grable one year, and *She Wore a Yellow Ribbon* with John Wayne another year. After the one carnival ride each, we paid in guilt; our tired father counted his change on the dark walk home.

15   Adultery is extravagance. Could people who hatch their own chicks and eat the embryos and the heads for delicacies and boil the feet in vinegar for party food, leaving only the gravel, eating even the gizzard lining—could such people engender a prodigal aunt? To be a woman, to have a daughter in starvation time was a waste enough. My aunt could not have been the lone romantic who gave up everything for sex. Women in the old China did not choose. Some man had commanded her to lie with him and be his secret evil. I wonder whether he masked himself when he joined the raid on her family.

Perhaps she encountered him in the fields or on the mountain where the daughters-in-law collected fuel. Or perhaps he first noticed her in the marketplace. He was not a stranger because the village housed no strangers. She had to have dealings with him other than sex. Perhaps he worked an adjoining field, or he sold her the cloth for the dress she sewed and wore. His demand must have surprised, then terrified her. She obeyed him; she always did as she was told.

When the family found a young man in the next village to be her husband, she stood tractably beside the best rooster, his proxy, and promised before they met that she would be his forever. She was lucky that he was her age and she would be the first wife, an advantage secure now. The night she first saw him, he had sex with her. Then he left for America. She had almost forgotten what he looked like. When she tried to envision him, she only saw the black and white face in the group photograph the men had had taken before leaving.

The other man was not, after all, much different from her husband. They both gave orders: she followed. "If you tell your family, I'll beat you. I'll kill you. Be here again next week." No one talked sex, ever. And she might have separated the rapes from the rest of living if only she did not have to buy her oil from him or gather wood in the same forest. I want her fear to have lasted just as long as rape lasted so that the fear could have been contained. No drawn-out fear. But women at sex hazarded birth and hence lifetimes. The fear did not stop but permeated everywhere. She told the man, "I think I'm pregnant." He organized the raid against her.

On nights when my mother and father talked about their life back home, sometimes they mentioned an "outcast table" whose business they still seemed to be settling, their voices tight. In a commensal tradition,[1] where food is precious, the powerful older people made wrongdoers eat alone. Instead of letting them start separate new lives like the Japanese, who could become samurais and geishas, the Chinese family, faces averted but eyes glowering sideways, hung on to the offenders and fed them leftovers. My aunt must have lived in the same house as my parents and eaten at an outcast table. My mother spoke about

---

[1] A tradition that values communal meals—people's sharing of meals.

the raid as if she had seen it, when she and my aunt, a daughter-in-law to a different household, should not have been living together at all. Daughters-in-law lived with their husbands' parents, not their own; a synonym for marriage in Chinese is "taking a daughter-in-law." Her husband's parents could have sold her, mortgaged her, stoned her. But they had sent her back to her own mother and father, a mysterious act hinting at disgraces not told me. Perhaps they had thrown her out to deflect the avengers.

20   She was the only daughter; her four brothers went with her father, husband, and uncles "out on the road" and for some years became western men. When the goods were divided among the family, three of the brothers took land, and the youngest, my father, chose an education. After my grandparents gave their daughter away to her husband's family, they had dispensed all the adventure and all the property. They expected her alone to keep the traditional ways, which her brothers, now among the barbarians, could fumble without detection. The heavy, deep-rooted women were to maintain the past against the flood, safe for returning. But the rare urge west had fixed upon our family, and so my aunt crossed boundaries not delineated in space.

The work of preservation demands that the feelings playing about in one's guts not be turned into action. Just watch their passing like cherry blossoms. But perhaps my aunt, my forerunner, caught in a slow life, let dreams grow and fade and after some months or years went toward what persisted. Fear at the enormities of the forbidden kept her desires delicate, wire and bone. She looked at a man because she liked the way the hair was tucked behind his ears, or she liked the question-mark line of a long torso curving at the shoulder and straight at the hip. For warm eyes or a soft voice or a slow walk—that's all—a few hairs, a line, a brightness, a sound, a pace, she gave up family. She offered us up for a charm that vanished with tiredness, a pigtail that didn't toss when the wind died. Why, the wrong lighting could erase the dearest thing about him.

It could very well have been, however, that my aunt did not take subtle enjoyment of her friend, but, a wild woman, kept rollicking company. Imagining her free with sex doesn't fit, though. I don't know any women like that, or men either. Unless I see her life branching into mine, she gives me no ancestral help.

To sustain her being in love, she often worked at herself in the mirror, guessing at the colors and shapes that would interest him, changing them frequently in order to hit on the right combination. She wanted him to look back.

On a farm near the sea, a woman who tended her appearance reaped a reputation for eccentricity. All the married women blunt-cut their hair in flaps about their ears or pulled it back in tight buns. No nonsense. Neither style blew easily into heart-catching tangles. And at their weddings they displayed themselves in their long hair for the last time. "It brushed the backs of my knees," my mother tells me. "It was braided, and even so, it brushed the backs of my knees."

25   At the mirror my aunt combed individuality into her bob. A bun could have been contrived to escape into black streamers blowing in the wind or in quiet wisps about her face, but only the older women in our picture album wear buns. She brushed her hair back from her forehead, tucking the flaps behind her ears. She looped a piece of thread, knotted into a circle between her index fingers and thumbs, and ran the double strand across her forehead. When she closed her fingers as if she were making a pair of shadow geese bite, the string twisted together catching the little hairs. Then she pulled the thread away from her skin, ripping the hairs out neatly, her eyes watering from the needles of pain. Opening her fingers, she cleaned the thread, then rolled it along her hairline and the tops of her eyebrows. My mother did the same to me and my sisters and herself. I used to believe that the expression "caught by the short hairs" meant a captive held with a depilatory string. It especially hurt at the temples, but my mother said we were lucky we didn't have to have our feet

bound when we were seven. Sisters used to sit on their beds and cry together, she said, as their mothers or their slaves removed the bandages for a few minutes each night and let the blood gush back into their veins. I hope that the man my aunt loved appreciated a smooth brow, that he wasn't just a tits-and-ass man.

Once my aunt found a freckle on her chin, at a spot that the almanac said predestined her for unhappiness. She dug it out with a hot needle and washed the wound with peroxide.

More attention to her looks than these pullings of hairs and pickings at spots would have caused gossip among the villagers. They owned work clothes and good clothes, and they wore good clothes for feasting the new seasons. But since a woman combing her hair hexes beginnings, my aunt rarely found an occasion to look her best. Women looked like great sea snails—the corded wood, babies, and laundry they carried were the whorls on their backs. The Chinese did not admire a bent back: goddesses and warriors stood straight. Still there must have been a marvelous freeing of beauty when a worker laid down her burden and stretched and arched.

Such commonplace loveliness, however, was not enough for my aunt. She dreamed of a lover for the fifteen days of New Year's, the time for families to exchange visits, money, and food. She plied her secret comb. And sure enough she cursed the year, the family, the village, and herself.

Even as her hair lured her imminent lover, many other men looked at her. Uncles, cousins, nephews, brothers would have looked, too, had they been home between journeys. Perhaps they had already been restraining their curiosity, and they left, fearful that their glances, like a field of nesting birds, might be startled and caught. Poverty hurt, and that was their first reason for leaving. But another, final reason for leaving the crowded house was the never-said.

30   She may have been unusually beloved, the precious only daughter, spoiled and mirror gazing because of the affection the family lavished on her. When her husband left, they welcomed the chance to take her back from the in-laws; she could live like the little daughter for just a while longer. There are stories that my grandfather was different from other people, "crazy ever since the little Jap bayoneted him in the head." He used to put his naked penis on the dinner table, laughing. And one day he brought home a baby girl, wrapped up inside his brown western-style greatcoat. He had traded one of his sons, probably my father, the youngest, for her. My grandmother made him trade back. When he finally got a daughter of his own, he doted on her. They must have all loved her, except perhaps my father, the only brother who never went back to China, having once been traded for a girl.

Brothers and sisters, newly men and women, had to efface their sexual color and present plain miens.[2] Disturbing hair and eyes, a smile like no other threatened the ideal of five generations living under one roof. To focus blurs, people shouted face to face and yelled from room to room. The immigrants I know have loud voices, unmodulated to American tones even after years away from the village where they called their friendships out across the fields. I have not been able to stop my mother's screams in public libraries or over telephones. Walking erect (knees straight, toes pointed forward, not pigeon-toed, which is Chinese-feminine) and speaking in an inaudible voice, I have tried to turn myself American-feminine. Chinese communication was loud, public. Only sick people had to whisper. But at the dinner table, where the family members came nearest one another, no one could talk, not the outcasts nor any eaters. Every word that falls from the mouth is a coin lost. Silently they gave and accepted food with both hands. A preoccupied child who took his bowl with one hand got a sideways glare. A complete moment of total attention is due everyone alike.

---

[2] Looks.

Children and lovers have no singularity here, but my aunt used a secret voice, a separate attentiveness.

She kept the man's name to herself throughout her labor and dying; she did not accuse him that he be punished with her. To save her inseminator's name she gave silent birth.

He may have been somebody in her own household, but intercourse with a man outside the family would have been no less abhorrent. All the village were kinsmen, and the titles shouted in loud country voices never let kinship be forgotten. Any man within visiting distance would have been neutralized as a lover—"brother," "younger brother," "older brother"—one hundred and fifteen relationship titles. Parents researched birth charts probably not so much to assure good fortune as to circumvent incest in a population that has but one hundred surnames. Everybody has eight million relatives. How useless then sexual mannerisms, how dangerous.

As if it came from an atavism[3] deeper than fear, I used to add "brother" silently to boys' names. It hexed the boys, who would or would not ask me to dance, and made them less scary and as familiar and deserving of benevolence as girls.

35   But, of course, I hexed myself also—no dates. I should have stood up, both arms waving, and shouted out across libraries, "Hey, you! Love me back." I had no idea, though, how to make attraction selective, how to control its direction and magnitude. If I made myself American-pretty so that the five or six Chinese boys in the class fell in love with me, everyone else—the Caucasian, Negro, and Japanese boys—would too. Sisterliness, dignified and honorable, made much more sense.

Attraction eludes control so stubbornly that whole societies designed to organize relationships among people cannot keep order, not even when they bind people to one another from childhood and raise them together. Among the very poor and the wealthy, brothers married their adopted sisters, like doves. Our family allowed some romance, paying adult brides' prices and providing dowries so that their sons and daughters could marry strangers. Marriage promises to turn strangers into friendly relatives—a nation of siblings.

In the village structure, spirits shimmered among the live creatures, balanced and held in equilibrium by time and land. But one human being flaring up into violence could open up a black hole, a maelstrom that pulled in the sky. The frightened villagers, who depended on one another to maintain the real, went to my aunt to show her a personal, physical representation of the break she had made in the "roundness." Misallying couples snapped off the future, which was to be embodied in true offspring. The villagers punished her for acting as if she could have a private life, secret and apart from them.

If my aunt had betrayed the family at a time of large grain yields and peace, when many boys were born, and wings were being built on many houses, perhaps she might have escaped such severe punishment. But the men—hungry, greedy, tired of planting in dry soil, cuckolded—had had to leave the village in order to send food-money home. There were ghost plagues, bandit plagues, wars with the Japanese, floods. My Chinese brother and sister had died of an unknown sickness. Adultery, perhaps only a mistake during good times, became a crime when the village needed food.

The round moon cakes and round doorways, the round tables of graduated size that fit one roundness inside another, round windows and rice bowls—these talismans had lost their power to warn this family of the law: a family must be whole, faithfully keeping the descent line by having sons to feed the old and the dead, who in turn look after the family. The villagers came to show my aunt and her lover-in-hiding a broken house. The villagers were speeding up the circling of events because she was too shortsighted to see that her infidelity

---

[3] Reversion to a primitive or an earlier type (or ancestral form).

had already harmed the village, that waves of consequences would return unpredictably, sometimes in disguise, as now, to hurt her. This roundness had to be made coin-sized so that she would see its circumference: punish her at the birth of her baby. Awaken her to the inexorable. People who refused fatalism because they could invent small resources insisted on culpability. Deny accidents and wrest fault from the stars.

40   After the villagers left, their lanterns now scattering in various directions toward home, the family broke their silence and cursed her. "Aiaa, we're going to die. Death is coming. Death is coming. Look what you've done. You've killed us. Ghost! Dead ghost! You've never been born." She ran out into the fields, far enough from the house so that she could no longer hear their voices, and pressed herself against the earth, her own land no more. When she felt the birth coming, she thought that she had been hurt. Her body seized together. "They've hurt me too much," she thought. "This is gall, and it will kill me." Her forehead and knees against the earth, her body convulsed and then released her onto her back. The black well of sky and stars went out and out and out forever; her body and her complexity seemed to disappear. She was one of the stars, a bright dot in blackness, without home, without a companion, in eternal cold and silence. An agoraphobia rose in her, speeding higher and higher, bigger and bigger; she would not be able to contain it; there would be no end to fear.

Flayed, unprotected against space, she felt pain return, focusing her body. This pain chilled her—a cold, steady kind of surface pain. Inside, spasmodically, the other pain, the pain of the child, heated her. For hours she lay on the ground, alternately body and space. Sometimes a vision of normal comfort obliterated reality: she saw the family in the evening gambling at the dinner table, the young people massaging their elders' backs. She saw them congratulating one another, high joy on the mornings the rice shoots came up. When these pictures burst, the stars drew yet further apart. Black space opened.

She got to her feet to fight better and remembered that old-fashioned women gave birth in their pigsties to fool the jealous, pain-dealing gods, who do not snatch piglets. Before the next spasms could stop her, she ran to the pigsty, each step a rushing out into emptiness. She climbed over the fence and knelt in the dirt. It was good to have a fence enclosing her, a tribal person alone.

Laboring, this woman who had carried her child as a foreign growth that sickened her every day, expelled it at last. She reached down to touch the hot, wet, moving mass, surely smaller than anything human, and could feel that it was human after all—fingers, toes, nails, nose. She pulled it up on to her belly, and it lay curled there, butt in the air, feet precisely tucked one under the other. She opened her loose shirt and buttoned the child inside. After resting, it squirmed and thrashed and she pushed it up to her breast. It turned its head this way and that until it found her nipple. There, it made little snuffling noises. She clenched her teeth at its preciousness, lovely as a young calf, a piglet, a little dog.

She may have gone to the pigsty as a last act of responsibility: she would protect this child as she had protected its father. It would look after her soul, leaving supplies on her grave. But how would this tiny child without family find her grave when there would be no marker for her anywhere, neither in the earth nor the family hall? No one would give her a family hall name. She had taken the child with her into the wastes. At its birth the two of them had felt the same raw pain of separation, a wound that only the family pressing tight could close. A child with no descent line would not soften her life but only trail after her, ghostlike, begging her to give it purpose. At dawn the villagers on their way to the fields would stand around the fence and look.

45   Full of milk, the little ghost slept. When it awoke, she hardened her breasts against the milk that crying loosens. Toward morning she picked up the baby and walked to the well.

Carrying the baby to the well shows loving. Otherwise abandon it. Turn its face into the mud. Mothers who love their children take them along. It was probably a girl; there is some hope of forgiveness for boys.

"Don't tell anyone you had an aunt. Your father does not want to hear her name. She has never been born." I have believed that sex was unspeakable and words so strong and fathers so frail that "aunt" would do my father mysterious harm. I have thought that my family, having settled among immigrants who had also been their neighbors in the ancestral land, needed to clean their name, and a wrong word would incite the kinspeople even here. But there is more to this silence: they want me to participate in her punishment. And I have.

In the twenty years since I heard this story I have not asked for details nor said my aunt's name; I do not know it. People who can comfort the dead can also chase after them to hurt them further—a reverse ancestor worship. The real punishment was not the raid swiftly inflicted by the villagers, but the family's deliberately forgetting her. Her betrayal so maddened them, they saw to it that she would suffer forever, even after death. Always hungry, always needing, she would have to beg food from other ghosts, snatch and steal it from those whose living descendants give them gifts. She would have to fight the ghosts massed at crossroads for the buns a few thoughtful citizens leave to decoy her away from village and home so that the ancestral spirits could feast unharassed. At peace, they could act like gods, not ghosts, their descent lines providing them with paper suits and dresses, spirit money, paper houses, paper automobiles, chicken, meat, and rice into eternity—essences delivered up in smoke and flames, steam and incense rising from each rice bowl. In an attempt to make the Chinese care for people outside the family, Chairman Mao[4] encourages us now to give our paper replicas to the spirits of outstanding soldiers and workers, no matter whose ancestors they may be. My aunt remains forever hungry. Goods are not distributed evenly among the dead.

My aunt haunts me—her ghost drawn to me because now, after fifty years of neglect, I alone devote pages of paper to her, though not origamied[5] into houses and clothes. I do not think she always means me well. I am telling on her, and she was a spite suicide, drowning herself in the drinking water. The Chinese are always very frightened of the drowned one, whose weeping ghost, wet hair hanging and skin bloated, waits silently by the water to pull down a substitute.

■ EXPLORATIONS OF THE TEXT

1. Why does the mother tell her story about the narrator's aunt? Why is the aunt considered to have "never been born"?
2. What are the conditions—social, cultural, economic, and personal—that drive the aunt to another man?
3. Why do the villagers storm and raid the house? What do the actions in the scene suggest about the villagers and their values?
4. What is the purpose of storytelling for these first-generation Chinese American women? What additional motives for the mother's narrative emerge?
5. Why do Chinese "guard their real names with silence"? Why do they want to confuse the gods?
6. Explain: "Adultery is extravagance." Relate the statement to Chinese values and philosophy of life.
7. How does the daughter reinterpret the story of her aunt?

---

[4] Chinese Communist leader (1893–1976).

[5] Origami, the Japanese art of decorative paper folding.

8. How does the daughter view her aunt as her precursor? Look at details of hair and appearance.
9. Why is the aunt's pregnancy so threatening to the society?
10. Why does the aunt give birth in a pigsty? Why does she drown herself and her baby in the well?
11. What are the attitudes toward sexuality, love, marriage, and women's roles in China at the time of this story?
12. Compare the aunt with the narrator in Mar's "Bi Bi Hua."

■ THE READING/WRITING CONNECTION

1. Gloss and annotate the text and explore the theme of silence in "No Name Woman."
2. Explain the imagery of the ghost and of the "No Name Woman." Why does she have no name?

■ IDEAS FOR WRITING

1. Consider the title. What are views of language and of identity in this work? What do words mean to the daughter?
2. Write a short scene for a play in which the aunt and Minnie Wright talk with each other. Write monologues and/or dialogue for each character.
3. Examine the theme of initiation in "No Name Woman," "Violation," and "Bi Bi Hua."

VIRGINIA WOOLF

Virginia Woolf (1882–1941) was born in London. Largely self-educated, Woolf published her first novel, The Voyage Out, *in 1915. She achieved fame with her experimental novels, which include* Mrs. Dalloway *(1925),* To the Lighthouse *(1927), and* The Waves *(1931), and with her essays, which include shorter reviews and critical essays collected in* The Common Reader *(1925) and* The Second Common Reader *(1932) and longer essays concerned with the position of women:* A Room of One's Own *(1929) and* Three Guineas *(1938). With her husband, Leonard, Woolf founded the Hogarth Press in 1917, which published many of the leading writers of the time. Her posthumously published* Letters *(1975–80) and* Diary *(1977–84) give further evidence of her genius.*

1942

PROFESSIONS FOR WOMEN

When your secretary invited me to come here, she told me that your Society is concerned with the employment of women and she suggested that I might tell you something about my own professional experiences. It is true I am a woman; it is true I am employed; but what professional experiences have I had? it is difficult to say. My profession is literature; and in that profession there are fewer experiences for women than in any other, with the exception of the stage—fewer, I mean, that are peculiar to women. For the road was cut many years ago—by Fanny Burney, by Aphra Behn, by Harriet Martineau, by Jane Austen, by George Eliot[1]—many famous women, and many more unknown and forgotten, have been before me, making the path smooth, and regulating my steps. Thus, when I came

---

[1] Famous women writers: Fanny Burney (1752–1840), English novelist and diarist; Aphra Behn (1640–89), English dramatist and novelist; Harriet Martineau (1802–76), English novelist; Jane Austen (1775–1817), English novelist; and George Eliot (1819–80), pen name of Mary Ann Evans, English novelist.

to write, there were very few material obstacles in my way. Writing was a reputable and harmless occupation. The family peace was not broken by the scratching of a pen. No demand was made upon the family purse. For ten and sixpence one can buy paper enough to write all the plays of Shakespeare—if one has a mind that way. Pianos and models, Paris, Vienna and Berlin, masters and mistresses, are not needed by a writer. The cheapness of writing paper is, of course, the reason why women have succeeded as writers before they have succeeded in the other professions.

But to tell you my story—it is a simple one. You have only got to figure to yourselves a girl in a bedroom with a pen in her hand. She had only to move that pen from left to right—from ten o'clock to one. Then it occurred to her to do what is simple and cheap enough after all—to slip a few of those pages into an envelope, fix a penny stamp in the corner, and drop the envelope into the red box at the corner. It was thus that I became a journalist; and my effort was rewarded on the first day of the following month—a very glorious day it was for me—by a letter from an editor containing a cheque for one pound ten shillings and sixpence. But to show you how little I deserve to be called a professional woman, how little I know of the struggles and difficulties of such lives, I have to admit that instead of spending that sum upon bread and butter, rent, shoes and stockings, or butcher's bills, I went out and bought a cat—a beautiful cat, a Persian cat, which very soon involved me in bitter disputes with my neighbours.

What could be easier than to write articles and to buy Persian cats with the profits? But wait a moment. Articles have to be about something. Mine, I seem to remember, was about a novel by a famous man. And while I was writing this review, I discovered that if I were going to review books I should need to do battle with a certain phantom. And the phantom was a woman, and when I came to know her better I called her after the heroine of a famous poem, The Angel in the House.[2] It was she who used to come between me and my paper when I was writing reviews. It was she who bothered me and wasted my time and so tormented me that as last I killed her. You who come of a younger and happier generation may not have heard of her—you may not know what I mean by the Angel in the House. I will describe her as shortly as I can. She was intensely sympathetic. She was immensely charming. She was utterly unselfish. She excelled in the difficult arts of family life. She sacrificed herself daily. If there was chicken, she took the leg; if there was a draught she sat in it—in short she was so constituted that she never had a mind or a wish of her own, but preferred to sympathize always with the minds and wishes of others. Above all—I need not say it— she was pure. Her purity was supposed to be her chief beauty—her blushes, her great grace. In those days—the last of Queen Victoria—every house had its Angel. And when I came to write I encountered her with the very first words. The shadow of her wings fell on my page; I heard the rustling of her skirts in the room. Directly, that is to say, I took my pen in hand to review that novel by a famous man, she slipped behind me and whispered: "My dear, you are a young woman. You are writing about a book that has been written by a man. Be sympathetic; be tender; flatter; deceive; use all the arts and wiles of our sex. Never let anybody guess that you have a mind of your own. Above all, be pure." And she made as if to guide my pen. I now record the one act for which I take some credit to myself, though the credit rightly belongs to some excellent ancestors of mine who left me a certain sum of money— shall we say five hundred pounds a year?—so that it was not necessary for me to depend solely on charm for my living. I turned upon her and caught her by the throat. I did my best to kill her. My excuse, if I were to be had up in a court of law, would be that I acted in self-defence. Had I not killed her she would have killed me. She would have plucked the heart

---

[2] Woolf took the term from a poem by Coventry Patmore, an English poet and essayist (1823–96).

out of my writing. For, as I found, directly I put pen to paper, you cannot review even a novel without having a mind of your own, without expressing what you think to be the truth about human relations, morality, sex. And all these questions, according to the Angel in the House, cannot be dealt with freely and openly by women; they must charm, they must conciliate, they must—to put it bluntly—tell lies if they are to succeed. Thus, whenever I felt the shadow of her wing or the radiance of her halo upon my page, I took up the inkpot and flung it at her. She died hard. Her fictitious nature was of great assistance to her. It is far harder to kill a phantom than a reality. She was always creeping back when I thought I had despatched her. Though I flatter myself that I killed her in the end, the struggle was severe; it took much time that had better have been spent upon learning Greek grammar; or in roaming the world in search of adventures. But it was a real experience; it was an experience that was bound to befall all women writers at that time. Killing the Angel in the House was part of the occupation of a woman writer.

But to continue my story. The Angel was dead; what then remained? You may say that what remained was a simple and common object—a young woman in a bedroom with an inkpot. In other words, now that she had rid herself of falsehood, that young woman had only to be herself. Ah, but what is "herself"? I mean, what is a woman? I assure you, I do not know. I do not believe that you know. I do not believe that anybody can know until she has expressed herself in all the arts and professions open to human skill. That indeed is one of the reasons why I have come here—out of respect for you, who are in process of showing us by your experiments what a woman is, who are in process of providing us, by your failures and successes, with that extremely important piece of information.

5   But to continue the story of my professional experiences. I made one pound ten and six by my first review; and I bought a Persian cat with the proceeds. Then I grew ambitious. A Persian cat is all very well, I said; but a Persian cat is not enough. I must have a motor car. And it was thus that I became a novelist—for it is a very strange thing that people will give you a motor car if you will tell them a story. It is a still stranger thing that there is nothing so delightful in the world as telling stories. It is far pleasanter than writing reviews of famous novels. And yet, if I am to obey your secretary and tell you my professional experiences as a novelist, I must tell you about a very strange experience that befell me as a novelist. And to understand it you must try first to imagine a novelist's state of mind. I hope I am not giving away professional secrets if I say that a novelist's chief desire is to be as unconscious as possible. He has to induce in himself a state of perpetual lethargy. He wants life to proceed with the utmost quiet and regularity. He wants to see the same faces, to read the same books, to do the same things day after day, month after month, while he is writing, so that nothing may break the illusion in which he is living—so that nothing may disturb or disquiet the mysterious nosings about, feelings round, darts, dashes and sudden discoveries of that very shy and illusive spirit, the imagination. I suspect that this state is the same both for men and women. Be that as it may, I want you to imagine me writing a novel in a state of trance. I want you to figure to yourselves a girl sitting with a pen in her hand, which for minutes, and indeed for hours, she never dips into the inkpot. The image that comes to my mind when I think of this girl is the image of a fisherman lying sunk in dreams on the verge of a deep lake with a rod held out over the water. She was letting her imagination sweep unchecked round every rock and cranny of the world that lies submerged in the depths of our unconscious being. Now came the experience, the experience that I believe to be far commoner with women writers than with men. The line raced through the girl's fingers. Her imagination had rushed away. It had sought the pools, and depths, the dark places where the largest fish slumber. And then there was a smash. There was an explosion. There was foam and confusion. The imagination had dashed itself against something hard. The girl was roused from her dream. She was indeed in a state of the most acute and difficult distress. To speak without figure she had thought of something, something

about the body, about the passions which it was unfitting for her as a woman to say. Men, her reason told her, would be shocked. The consciousness of what men will say of a woman who speaks the truth about her passions had roused her from her artist's state of unconsciousness. She could write no more. The trance was over. Her imagination could work no longer. This I believe to be a very common experience with women writers—they are impeded by the extreme conventionality of the other sex. For though men sensibly allow themselves great freedom in these respects, I doubt that they realize or can control the extreme severity with which they condemn such freedom in women.

These then were two very genuine experiences of my own. These were two of the adventures of my professional life. The first—killing the Angel in the House—I think I solved. She died. But the second, telling the truth about my own experiences as a body, I do not think I solved. I doubt that any woman has solved it yet. The obstacles against her are still immensely powerful—and yet they are very difficult to define. Outwardly, what is simpler than to write books? Outwardly, what obstacles are there for a woman rather than for a man? Inwardly, I think, the case is very different; she has still many ghosts to fight, many prejudices to overcome. Indeed it will be a long time still, I think, before a woman can sit down to write a book without finding a phantom to be slain, a rock to be dashed against. And if this is so in literature, the freest of all professions for women, how is it in the new professions which you are now for the first time entering?

Those are the questions that I should like, had I time, to ask you. And indeed, if I have laid stress upon these professional experiences of mine, it is because I believe that they are, though in different forms, yours also. Even when the path is nominally open—when there is nothing to prevent a woman from being a doctor, a lawyer, a civil servant—there are many phantoms and obstacles, as I believe, looming in her way. To discuss and define them is I think of great value and importance; for thus only can the labour be shared, the difficulties be solved. But besides this, it is necessary also to discuss the ends and the aims for which we are fighting, for which we are doing battle with these formidable obstacles. Those aims cannot be taken for granted; they must be perpetually questioned and examined. The whole position, as I see it—here in this hall surrounded by women practising for the first time in history I know not how many different professions—is one of extraordinary interest and importance. You have won rooms of your own in the house hitherto exclusively owned by men. You are able, though not without great labour and effort, to pay the rent. You are earning your five hundred pounds a year. But this freedom is only a beginning; the room is your own, but it is still bare. It has to be furnished; it has to be decorated; it has to be shared. How are you going to furnish it, how are you going to decorate it? With whom are you going to share it, and upon what terms? These, I think are questions of the utmost importance and interest. For the first time in history you are able to ask them; for the first time you are able to decide for yourselves what the answers should be. Willingly would I stay and discuss those questions and answers—but not tonight. My time is up; and I must cease.

■ **EXPLORATIONS OF THE TEXT**

1. How does Woolf view the professions of journalist and writer?
2. Explore the image of the "Angel in the House." What is Woolf's attitude toward this "phantom"? How does the "Angel" affect Woolf's writing career?
3. Discuss Woolf's process of creating a novel. Contrast this process with her work as a journalist.
4. Analyze the "image of a fisherman" and "the girl" extending her line. What is the challenge Woolf faces as a woman writer?

5. Compare Woolf's vision of "telling the truth about [her] own experiences as a body" with the experiences of one or several of the female figures in the thematic cluster, "Venus, Barbie, and Beyond."

■ THE READING/WRITING CONNECTION

1. What does Woolf mean by her "own experiences as a body"? Freewrite in response to this quotation.
2. "Think" Topic: Woolf wrote this essay in 1931. Do you think that women artists today face these same "obstacles"?
3. Write a mini-essay in response to one of the statements or questions in the last paragraph of the essay. Probe the statement or question; relate it to your own observations, experiences, and reading; analyze it; and come to conclusions.

■ IDEAS FOR WRITING

1. Consider Woolf's statement in the last paragraph as a challenge.
2. Explicate the image of a "room of [one's] own."
3. How are women today exercising their "freedom"? "furnish[ing]" "room[s]"?
4. Debate Topic: Do men need to create similar places?
5. Choose a character from this chapter and imagine the kind of "room" this character would create. Create diary entries in the voice of this character.
6. Creative Options: Create a drawing of this room; furnish and decorate it. Or create a poem for a character from this chapter who is now living in a "room of [her] own."

SIMONE DE BEAUVOIR

Simone de Beauvoir (1908–86) had a strict middle class, Catholic upbringing and traced the seeds of her feminism to her repugnance at that restricted social world. She studied philosophy at the Sorbonne, where she met Jean-Paul Sartre and began her career as a writer and as an existential philosopher. A prolific writer, a leftist, an intellectual, and an iconoclast, she wrote philosophical essays and memoirs, chronicling her personal, political, and intellectual development, as well as several novels, of which The Mandarins *(1954) won the* Prix Goncourt. *Her most famous work is* The Second Sex *(1949), one of the most important works of twentieth-century feminism.*

1949

WOMAN AS OTHER

What is a woman?

To state the question is, to me, to suggest, at once, a preliminary answer. The fact that I ask it is in itself significant. A man would never get the notion of writing a book on the peculiar situation of the human male. But if I wish to define myself, I must first of all say: "I am a woman"; on this truth must be based all further discussion. A man never begins by presenting himself as an individual of a certain sex; it goes without saying that he is a man. The terms *masculine* and *feminine* are used symmetrically only as a matter of form, as on legal papers. In actuality the relation of the two sexes is not quite like that of two electrical poles, for man represents both the positive and the neutral, as is indicated by the common use of *man* to designate human beings in general; whereas woman represents only the negative, defined by limiting criteria, without reciprocity. In the midst of an abstract discussion it is vexing to hear a man say: "You think thus and so because you are a woman"; but I know that my only defense is to reply: "I think thus and so because it is true," thereby removing my subjective self from the argument. It would be out of the question to reply: "And you think the contrary because you are a man," for it is understood that the fact of being a man is no peculiarity. A man is in the right in being a man; it is the woman who is in the wrong. It amounts to this: just as for the ancients there was an absolute vertical with reference to which the oblique was defined, so there is an absolute human type, the masculine. Woman has ovaries, a uterus; these peculiarities imprison her in her subjectivity, circumscribe her within the limits of her own nature. It is often said that she thinks with her glands. Man superbly ignores the fact that his anatomy also includes glands, such as the testicles, and that they secrete hormones. He thinks of his body as a direct and normal connection with the world, which he believes he apprehends objectively, whereas he regards the body of woman as a hindrance, a prison, weighed down by everything peculiar to it. "The female is a female by virtue of a certain *lack* of qualities," said Aristotle;[1] "we should regard the female nature as afflicted with a natural defectiveness." And St. Thomas[2] for his part pronounced women to be an "imperfect man," an "incidental" being. This is symbolized in Genesis where Eve is depicted as made from what Bossuet[3] called "a supernumerary bone" of Adam.

Thus humanity is male and man defines woman not in herself but as relative to him; she is not regarded as an autonomous being. Michelet[4] writes: "Woman, the relative being. . . ." And Benda[5] is most positive in his *Rapport d'Uriel:* "The body of man makes sense in itself quite apart from that of woman, whereas the latter seems wanting in significance by itself. . . . Man can think of himself without woman. She cannot think of herself without man." And she is simply what man decrees; thus she is called "the sex," by which is meant that she appears essentially to the male as a sexual being. For him she is sex—absolute sex, no less. She is defined and differentiated with reference to man and not he with reference to her; she is the incidental, the inessential as opposed to the essential. He is the Subject, he is the Absolute—she is the Other.

The category of the *Other* is as primordial as consciousness itself. In the most primitive societies, in the most ancient mythologies, one finds the expression of a duality—that of the Self and the Other. This duality was not originally attached to the division of the sexes; it was not dependent upon any empirical facts. It is revealed in such works as that of Granet[6] on Chinese thought and those of Dumézil[7] on the East Indies and Rome. The feminine element was at first no more involved in such pairs as Varuna-Mitra, Uranus-Zeus, Sun-Moon, and Day-Night[8] than it was in the contrasts between Good and Evil, lucky and unlucky auspices, right and left, God and Lucifer. Otherness is a fundamental category of human thought.

5   Thus it is that no group ever sets itself up as the One without at once setting up the Other over against itself. If three travelers chance to occupy the same compartment, that is enough to make vaguely hostile "others" out of all the rest of the passengers on the train. In small-town eyes all persons not belonging to the village are "strangers" and suspect; to the native of a country all who inhabit other countries are "foreigners"; Jews are "different" for

---

[1] Greek philosopher (384–322 B.C.).

[2] Saint Thomas Aquinas, ecclesiastical writer and philosopher (1224?-1225–1274).

[3] Jacques Bossuet, French bishop, defended the rights of the French church against papal authority. His literary works include *Funeral Panegyrics* and *Four Great Personages* (1627–1704).

[4] French historian (1798–1874).

[5] Julian Benda, French novelist and philosopher (1867–1956).

[6] Francois Marius Granet, French painter and watercolorist (1775–1849).

[7] Expert on mythology.

[8] Varuna—Vedic god of skies and sea; Mitra—Vedic god of moon; Uranus—god/father of the Titans in Greek mythology; Zeus—king of the gods in Greek mythology; oppositions.

the anti-Semite, Negroes are "inferior" for American racists, aborigines are "natives" for colonists, proletarians are the "lower class" for the privileged.

Lévi-Strauss,[9] at the end of a profound work on the various forms of primitive societies, reaches the following conclusion: "Passage from the state of Nature to the state of Culture is marked by man's ability to view biological relations as a series of contrasts; duality, alternation, opposition, and symmetry, whether under definite or vague forms, constitute not so much phenomena to be explained as fundamental and immediately given data of social reality." These phenomena would be incomprehensible if in fact human society were simply a *Mitsein* or fellowship based on solidarity and friendliness. Things become clear, on the contrary, if, following Hegel,[10] we find in consciousness itself a fundamental hostility toward every other consciousness; the subject can be posed only in being opposed—he sets himself up as the essential, as opposed to the other, the inessential, the object.

But the other consciousness, the other ego, sets up a reciprocal claim. The native traveling abroad is shocked to find himself in turn regarded as a "stranger" by the natives of neighboring countries. As a matter of fact, wars, festivals, trading, treaties, and contests among tribes, nations, and classes tend to deprive the concept *Other* of its absolute sense and to make manifest its relativity; willy-nilly, individuals and groups are forced to realize the reciprocity of their relations. How is it, then, that this reciprocity has not been recognized between the sexes, that one of the contrasting terms is set up as the sole essential, denying any relativity in regard to its correlative and defining the latter as pure otherness? Why is it that women do not dispute male sovereignty? No subject will readily volunteer to become the object, the inessential; it is not the Other who, in defining himself as the Other, establishes the One. The Other is posed as such by the One in defining himself as the One. But if the Other is not to regain the status of being the One, he must be submissive enough to accept this alien point of view. Whence comes this submission in the case of woman?

There are, to be sure, other cases in which a certain category has been able to dominate another completely for a time. Very often this privilege depends upon inequality of numbers—the majority imposes its rule upon the minority or persecutes it. But women are not a minority, like the American Negroes or the Jews; there are as many women as men on earth. Again, the two groups concerned have often been originally independent; they may have been formerly unaware of each other's existence, or perhaps they recognized each other's autonomy. But a historical event has resulted in the subjugation of the weaker by the stronger. The scattering of the Jews, the introduction of slavery into America, the conquests of imperialism are examples in point. In these cases the oppressed retained at least the memory of former days; they possessed in common a past, a tradition, sometimes a religion or a culture.

The parallel drawn by Bebel[11] between women and the proletariat is valid in that neither ever formed a minority or a separate collective unit of mankind. And instead of a single historical event it is in both cases a historical development that explains their status as a class and accounts for the membership of *particular individuals* in that class. But proletarians have not always existed, whereas there have always been women. They are women in virtue of their anatomy and physiology. Throughout history they have always been subordinated to men, and hence their dependency is not the result of a historical event or a social change—it was not something that *occurred*. The reason why otherness in this case seems to

---

[9] Claude Lévi-Strauss, French anthropologist (1908–   ).

[10] Georg Wilhelm Friedrich Hegel, German philosopher who developed the theory of dialectic (1770–1831).

[11] August Bebel, German Social Democrat leader and writer (1840–1913).

be an absolute is in part that it lacks the contingent or incidental nature of historical facts. A condition brought about at a certain time can be abolished at some other time, as the Negroes of Haiti[12] and others have proved; but it might seem that a natural condition is beyond the possibility of change. In truth, however, the nature of things is no more immutably given, once for all, than is historical reality. If woman seems to be the inessential which never becomes the essential, it is because she herself fails to bring about this change. Proletarians say "We"; Negroes also. Regarding themselves as subjects, they transform the bourgeois, the whites, into "others." But women do not say "We," except at some congress of feminists or similar formal demonstration; men say "women," and women use the same word in referring to themselves. They do not authentically assume a subjective attitude. The proletarians have accomplished the revolution in Russia, the Negroes in Haiti, the Indochinese are battling for it in Indochina;[13] but the women's effort has never been anything more than a symbolic agitation. They have gained only what men have been willing to grant; they have taken nothing, they have only received.

10   The reason for this is that women lack concrete means for organizing themselves into a unit which can stand face to face with the correlative unit. They have no past, no history, no religion of their own; and they have no such solidarity of work and interest as that of the proletariat. They are not even promiscuously herded together in the way that creates community feeling among the American Negroes, the ghetto Jews, the workers of Saint-Denis,[14] or the factory hands of Renault.[15] They live dispersed among the males, attached through residence, housework, economic condition, and social standing to certain men—fathers or husbands— more firmly than they are to other women. If they belong to the bourgeoisie, they feel solidarity with men of that class, not with proletarian women; if they are white, their allegiance is to white men, not to Negro women. The proletariat can propose to massacre the ruling class, and a sufficiently fanatical Jew or Negro might dream of getting sole possession of the atomic bomb and making humanity wholly Jewish or black; but woman cannot even dream of exterminating the males. The bond that unites her to her oppressors is not comparable to any other. The division of the sexes is a biological fact, not an event in human history. Male and female stand opposed within a primordial *Mitsein,* and woman has not broken it. The couple is a fundamental unity with its two halves riveted together, and the cleavage of society along the line of sex is impossible. Here is to be found the basic trait of woman: she is the Other in a totality of which the two components are necessary to one another.

    One could suppose that this reciprocity might have facilitated the liberation of woman. When Hercules sat at the feet of Omphale[16] and helped with her spinning, his desire for her held him captive; but why did she fail to gain a lasting power? To revenge herself on Jason, Medea[17] killed their children: and this grim legend would seem to suggest that she might have obtained a formidable influence over him through his love for his offspring. In *Lysistrata* Aristophanes[18] gaily depicts a band of women who joined forces to gain social ends

---

[12] Country of the West Indies.

[13] Peninsula of Southeast Asia composed of Vietnam, Laos, Cambodia, Thailand, Burma, and the Malay Peninsula; name given to group of former French colonies.

[14] City in north central France, near Paris.

[15] French car manufacturer.

[16] Hercules—hero of Greek mythology, known for his strength; as punishment, Zeus condemned Hercules to serve as a slave to Queen Omphale, who required him to dress as a woman and to do women's chores.

[17] Jason—Thessalian hero who journeyed with the Argonauts in search of the Golden Fleece. Medea—a magician or sorceress who aided Jason and later murdered their two children when he betrayed her.

[18] Aristophanes—Athenian dramatist (448–380? B.C.). *Lysistrata,* a comedy by Aristophanes, features a rebellion by women who protest war by denying their husbands sexual favors.

through the sexual needs of their men; but this is only a play. In the legend of the Sabine women,[19] the latter soon abandoned their plan of remaining sterile to punish their ravishers. In truth woman has not been socially emancipated through man's need—sexual desire and the desire for offspring—which makes the male dependent for satisfaction upon the female.

Master and slave, also, are united by a reciprocal need, in this case economic, which does not liberate the slave. In the relation of master to slave the master does not make a point of the need that he has for the other; he has in his grasp the power of satisfying this need through his own action; whereas the slave, in his dependent condition, his hope and fear, is quite conscious of the need he has for his master. Even if the need is at bottom equally urgent for both, it always works in favor of the oppressor and against the oppressed. That is why the liberation of the working class, for example, has been slow.

Now, woman has always been man's dependent, if not his slave; the two sexes have never shared the world in equality. And even today woman is heavily handicapped, though her situation is beginning to change. Almost nowhere is her legal status the same as man's, and frequently it is much to her disadvantage. Even when her rights are legally recognized in the abstract, long-standing custom prevents their full expression in the mores. In the economic sphere men and women can almost be said to make up two castes; other things being equal, the former hold the better jobs, get higher wages, and have more opportunity for success than their new competitors. In industry and politics men have a great many more positions and they monopolize the most important posts. In addition to all this, they enjoy a traditional prestige that the education of children tends in every way to support, for the present enshrines the past—and in the past all history has been made by men. At the present time, when women are beginning to take part in the affairs of the world, it is still a world that belongs to men—they have no doubt of it at all and women have scarcely any. To decline to be the Other, to refuse to be a party to the deal—this would be for women to renounce all the advantages conferred upon them by their alliance with the superior caste. Man-the-sovereign will provide woman-the-liege with material protection and will undertake the moral justification of her existence; thus she can evade at once both economic risk and the metaphysical risk of a liberty in which ends and aims must be contrived without assistance. Indeed, along with the ethical urge of each individual to affirm his subjective existence, there is also the temptation to forgo liberty and become a thing. This is an inauspicious road, for he who takes it—passive, lost, ruined—becomes henceforth the creature of another's will, frustrated in his transcendence and deprived of every value. But it is an easy road; on it one avoids the strain involved in undertaking an authentic existence. When man makes of woman the *Other,* he may, then, expect her to manifest deep-seated tendencies toward complicity. Thus, woman may fail to lay claim to the status of subject because she lacks definite resources, because she feels the necessary bond that ties her to man regardless of reciprocity, and because she is often very well pleased with her role as the *Other.*

◼ EXPLORATIONS OF THE TEXT

1. Why does de Beauvoir begin with a question? with the need for definition?
2. Do you agree with her assessment that "man represents both the positive and the neutral . . . whereas woman represents only the negative"?
3. What does de Beauvoir mean when she states that woman is "imprison[ed] in her subjectivity" and that "she thinks with her glands"?

---

[19] Allusion to the abduction of the Sabine women by the Romans (c. 290 B.C.).

4. State in your own words her concept of "the Other." Agree or disagree with her position.
5. Why does de Beauvoir include references to the ideas of "reciprocity" and of "duality"? to master-slave relations?
6. How has woman's sexuality led historically to her position as "Other"? Why have women failed to break out of this position?
7. Outline de Beauvoir's argument. Does she argue through definition, causal analysis, or comparison? Does she argue inductively or deductively? Who is her audience?
8. Why does she include references to Haiti and Indochina, to Jews and African Americans? Why does she include references to Hercules, Jason and Medea, *Lysistrata,* and the Sabine Women? Are the allusions effective?
9. De Beauvoir wrote *The Second Sex* in 1949. Do her ideas still apply to contemporary society? What aspects of women's status have changed?

■ THE READING/WRITING CONNECTION

1. In a short paragraph, define the "Other."
2. "Think" Topic: Do you agree with de Beauvoir's characterization of woman as "Other"?
3. What do you see as a current issue for men and women in North American society? Is de Beauvoir's critique still relevant? Evaluate her arguments. Write a journal response to one of these questions.

■ IDEAS FOR WRITING

1. Compare de Beauvoir's view of the woman as "Other" with the roles of several women in works in this chapter.
2. Conceive of an alternative relationship for men and women. What do you see as ideal?
3. Compare de Beauvoir's argument with Plato's assessment in "The Sexes." How would de Beauvoir respond to Plato?

■ WRITING ASSIGNMENTS ■

1. a. What is platonic or ideal love? Write a definition.
   b. Define your ideal lover.
   c. Discuss platonic or ideal love in Donne, in Shakespeare's "Let Me Not to the Marriage of True Minds," in Senghor, in Snyder, and/or in Rosenberg.
2. a. What is romantic love? Why do people fall in love? Respond in a journal entry.
   b. Explore the vision of romantic love in several works in this chapter.
   c. Compare three views of romantic love and marriage in this chapter.
3. Discuss sexuality in Silko, Snyder, Paz, Senghor, and/or Chekhov.
4. a. What are the major problems in love relationships? Write a journal entry.
   b. Analyze the essay by Woolf. What obstacles does she enumerate?
   c. Write an essay on obstacles in love relationships. Use three works in this chapter to support your points. Refer to Woolf and to your journal entry.
5. Explicate "Let Me Not to the Marriage of True Minds." Concentrate on persona, figurative language, and sonnet form.
6. a. In a journal entry, explore your conceptions of young love, married love, and love in old age.
   b. Categorize kinds of love. Refer to works that represent different states of love.
7. Have any of these works changed your attitude about love? Which ones? Why? Why not?
8. Write about the end of love, the acceptance of loss. Refer to Mason, Akhmatova, Hemingway, Porter, and/or Joyce.

9. a. Trace the phases of a relationship you have experienced or observed.
   b. Trace the phases of the love relationship in one of the texts in this chapter.
   c. Compare your relationship with the view of love in one of the works in the text.

10. a. Interview three people from the same cultural background. Ask about gender roles, socialization, and responsibilities.
    b. Write an essay on roles of men and women in that culture. Have gender roles changed in that culture in the twentieth century?
    c. Write an analysis of gender roles in three works in this chapter. You may choose works in other chapters if you wish.

11. a. Interview men about women; women about men. Ask about conceptions of the opposite sex, relationships, and social roles. Summarize your interviews.
    b. Analyze the results of the interviews. What misconceptions do men have about women? Women about men?
    c. "Men and women are doomed never to understand one another." Develop an argument in response to this quotation.

12. a. Freewrite about ways in which men and women might perceive conflict differently.
    b. Choose one experience, and write a monologue for each person involved in the incident.
    c. Based on a work in this chapter, write an essay about how a man and a woman develop different views of a conflict. How does the conflict resolve itself?

13. a. Have you ever felt like an "Other"? Write about this experience in your journal.
    b. In your own words, define "Other." Use your journal entry as a basis for your definition.
    c. Analyze the experience of the woman as "Other" in three works in this chapter.

14. Compare two dramatic monologues. How do voice, tone, and theme develop the personae?

15. What is most important in the development of characters in three works in this chapter? (Choose one genre, and refer to the checklists in chapters 9–12.)

16. Analyze images of the sea in Arnold, Eliot, and Paz.

17. Examine the conflicts and characters in *Trifles* and in *M Butterfly*. How does symbolism help to create character and theme?

18. In three works in this chapter, discuss how landscape functions in the development of character, conflict, and theme.

19. "Men are conditioned to fear a full expression of intimacy." Do you agree or disagree? Which works in this chapter support your views?

20. a. Interview another person who has read one of the works in this chapter. Ask questions about speaker, conflict, theme, language, and other literary elements. Summarize your interview.
    b. Write an essay about your interview.

21. Analyze views of romantic love in works in this cluster.

22. Discuss the "battle of the sexes" as it is depicted in three works in this chapter.

23. Compare Woolf's views of woman's experiences and the challenges for a woman writer with the portrayal of three female characters from three works in this chapter.

24. Explore the concept of the female body as presented in works in the thematic cluster. You also may refer to other works in the chapter. Do female characters break out of their socially defined roles and experience the fullness of their beings?

25. Compare and contrast the treatment of the pleasures of love and passion as presented in several works in this chapter, such as McDermott's "Enough," T. C. Boyle's "Modern Love," Silko's "Yellow Woman," and Porter's "The Jilting of Granny Weatherall."

26. a. Have gender roles in marriage changed during the last twenty years? Interview several people in long-term marriages. How do they see their defined roles? Do they perceive that roles for men and women have changed over the years?

b. Compare their views of roles in marriage with your observations about your generation's conceptions of roles for men and for women.

c. Examine the treatment of marital relationships on television programs. You may view such situation comedies as *I Love Lucy* from the 1950s, *The Brady Bunch* from the 1970s, *The Simpsons* from the 1990s, or *Everybody Loves Raymond* from the 2000s.

d. Compare and contrast views of men's and women's roles in marriage with that of several relationships portrayed in the literary works, such as Moravia's "The Chase," Gordon's "Violation," and McDermott's "Enough."

27. Focus on the theme of disappointment with love.

a. Write about your own disappointments—a failed love relationship.

b. Compare your sense of loss with that of a character in one of the stories in this chapter, such as Joyce's "Eveline," Chekhov's "Lady with Lapdog," Paz's "My Life with the Wave," Moravia's "The Chase," and Mason's "Shiloh."

28. Find a copy of the old English poem "The Demon Lover." Analyze the symbolism of the figure of the lover, and then explore this psychosexual, symbolic motif in several of the following works: Oates's "Where Are You Going, Where Have You Been?" (chapter 4), Hwang's *M Butterfly,* Faulkner's "A Rose for Emily," Mar's "Bi Bi Hua," Rossetti's "Goblin Market," and Gilman's *Boy Gets Girl.*

29. What does it mean to be a man or a woman in contemporary society? What images of the male and female body are promoted in the media? What are North American society's overt and covert attitudes toward young men and women? How does the society claim to treat young men and women? How does it really treat them? Examine these questions through scrutinizing advertisements, particularly women's or men's magazines, television programs, or films such as *Kids* or *Thirteen.* What do they reveal? What images of men and women are portrayed? After doing this research, write an argumentative essay presenting your position on this issue.

30. a. Freewrite about your relationships to your female or male body.

b. Compare and contrast your views and attitudes toward your body with another work in this chapter.

31. Several writers merge concerns with sexuality and gender with the political motif of the colonizer and the colonized. How does this pattern manifest itself in several works in this chapter such as Hwang's *M Butterfly,* thúy's "The Gangster We Are All Looking For," and Mar's "Bi Bi Hua."

32. a. Focus on a favorite love song. What vision of love is presented?

b. Connect the song with a particular work in the chapter.

33. Create a character analysis for a person in love. See Leigh Grimm's "The Jilting of Granny Weatherall."

■ STUDENT ESSAYS ■

Student Essay: Explication and Character Analysis

Leigh Grimm

The Jilting of Granny Weatherall

In "The Jilting of Granny Weatherall" by Katherine Anne Porter, Granny Weatherall, almost eighty years old, lies in a bed in her daughter's house dying. Granny is not consumed by thoughts of her imminent death but by thoughts of the people in her past. There is the sense that her relationships and people in her life have somehow failed her.

When she thinks about how neat and orderly she always kept her house, unlike her daughter Cornelia, Granny remembers a box of old letters in her attic from the two men in her life, George and John. She plans to do something with those letters the next day so that her children do not find them after she is gone. She is afraid that they will read the letters and know what she was like before she was their mother. These letters are the key to why she drifts into the past.

Granny Weatherall drifts off into the past where she can remember her children when they needed her. She would love to be able to go back and do things over again. She remembers her children coming home out of the chilly night air to get warm. She loved the children huddling around her until the house was all lit up. But once the lights were on, they would leave her because they were no longer afraid of the dark. They had no need to cling to her then just as they have no need to cling to her now. Granny Weatherall repeats in her head, "Never, never, never more." All that she has ever wanted was to be needed by her children, and it makes her sad to know that they do not need her anymore. She is happier to think about the way things used to be before her children betray her by growing up.

All through her life she was a strong and independent woman. She became strong when her husband John died leaving her with a house to run and children to support and nurture. She fenced in one hundred acres of land, cooked dozens of meals, made clothes for her family and kept the garden flourishing year after year.

5   In one of her trips to the past, she wonders if John would recognize her after all she has endured. Having to be strong and independent changed her. She says everything changed her, from "Riding country roads in the winter when women had their babies" to "sitting up nights with sick horses and sick negroes and sick children and hardly ever losing one." John also betrayed her by leaving her.

But her children and her husband are not the only ones to betray her. Before she met and married John, she was jilted by another lover. In her wedding gown Granny was left standing at the altar by George. She remembers the cake that never got eaten and the sorrow and embarrassment that she felt. In her head, she still tries to hide the scars of that day. She begins to act like a teenage girl as she asks her children to find George and to tell him that she has forgotten all about him. She wants him to know that she married a man she loved and had beautiful children with him. But the pain of that day forms a shadow that follows her to her death bed. The final jilting is that the pain of that day does not desert her; she never reaches an acceptance of her past—a reconciliation of her own past. She does not find peace and contentment—fulfillment even at the end of her life.

As the moment of death approaches "her body [is] now only a deeper mass of shadow in an endless darkness. . . . " She asks for God to give her a sign. "For the second time there [is] no sign. Again no bridegroom and the priest in the house. She [can] not remember any other sorrow because this grief [wipes] them all away."

By continually drifting into the past, Granny Weatherall shows dissatisfaction with her life. Every relationship comes to some kind of stasis that she found to be difficult and imprisoning. On her death bed she feels that she has missed something all of her life. What she has missed is life itself.

Student Essay: Thematic Analysis and Movie Review

KIMBERLEY THOMAS

The Concept of Love in The English Patient

There are several types of love, ranging from romantic love to platonic love to parental love, all of which are expressed in Michael Ondaatje's novel, *The English Patient. Oxford's Mini-Reference Dictionary and Thesaurus* states that love is "warm liking or affection" between people. Yet, love is a difficult concept to understand. Emma Goldman, Russian-born writer of the nineteenth and twentieth centuries, once labeled an iconoclast, writes in her essay "Marriage and Love":

> Love, the strongest and deepest element in all life, the harbinger of hope, of joy, of ecstasy; love, the defier of all laws, of all conventions; love, the freest, the most powerful molder of human destiny. (242)

Love is unpredictable. Love is security. "Love needs no protection; it is its own protection" (Goldman 243). Love is perplexing. Love should be, but is not, permanent. Love hurts. "Love has the magic power to make a beggar a king" (Goldman 242). Love has the ability to conquer all people, regardless of age or race.

Where does the concept of love come from? From where does love arise? Greek philosopher Aristophanes explains this strange and unknown concept in Plato's *Symposium:* "I shall therefore try to initiate you in the secret of [the] power" of love (Plato 911). He explains to his audience about the three sexes of the world: males, females, and hermaphrodites. These hermaphrodites, both male and female, were "formidable, and their pride was overweening; they attacked the gods" (Plato 912). As punishment for their sin, the god Zeus decided to split them up. This is the reason why people love others: "Each of us is perpetually in search of his corresponding tally" (Plato 912). Aristophanes explains, "Love . . . restores us to our ancient state by attempting to weld two beings into one" (Plato 912).

Romantic love is the kind of love that exists between the characters Hana and Kip and Almasy and Katharine; however, their affection for one another is not established immediately. Kip, the Indian sapper, stumbles into Hana's life as she is playing the piano in the Villa San Girolamo, "an old nunnery, taken over by the Germans, then converted into a hospital" (Ondaatje 28). Upon hearing the music, the sapper rushes towards the villa, fearing that there is a destructive mine implanted in the piano, a tactic that the Germans tended to use. Kip resides in a tent in the garden of the villa and, over time, Hana begins to realize she is attracted to Kip. Several times, she "suddenly [realizes that] she is watching him" (Ondaatje 73). She watches while he works, noticing insignificant things, such as "the darker brown skin of his wrist" (Ondaatje 74); things most people would not pay much attention to. Hana has a "crush" on Kip, reminding the reader of her child-like ways.

The relationship between Almasy and Katharine Clifton begins when Katharine arrives in the desert with her new husband, Geoffrey Clifton, in 1936. The film version of *The English Patient* depicts Almasy as standoffish upon the arrival of the newlyweds. The reason for his behavior is left untold, but one can speculate that it is one of two things: 1) the fact that she is the only woman among a group of desert explorers; or 2) because Almasy wants to disguise his attraction to her. It is as she recites a poem that he "[falls] in love with a voice" (Ondaatje 144). Almasy states: "This is a story of how I fell in love with a woman . . . I heard the words she spoke across the fire" (Ondaatje 233). For Almasy this is appropriate. He is a man of languages, a man of words. He explains this at one point to Caravaggio: "Words, Caravaggio. They have a power" (Ondaatje 234).

5   Love is unpredictable, because a person cannot help with whom he or she falls in love. Love is blind, overlooking all things such as age, race, or status. Both Katharine and Hana fall in love with "international bastards" (Ondaatje 176). Writer Gloria Anzaldúa expresses ideas similar to this in her poem "To Live in the Borderlands Means You": "To survive in the Borderlands/you must live sin fronteras/be a crossroads" (1269).

How could Hana know that she would fall in love with an Indian sapper? How could Katharine know that she would love someone fifteen years her senior? How could Almasy know that he would love a married woman? Such things are irrelevant when it comes down to loving someone. Some things cannot be resisted. Different in more ways than one in the light, the lovers were "equal in darkness" (Ondaatje 225).

Although romantic love exists between the couples, it seems as though Kip and Hana are more affectionate while Almasy and Katharine are more passionate. In the novel, Hana and Kip are usually depicted as holding each other: "There is the one month when Hana and Kip sleep beside each other. A formal celibacy between them" (Ondaatje 225). Kip also mentions several times that he simply wants to touch Hana:

> He wanted Hana's shoulder, wanted to place his palm over it as he had done in the sunlight when she slept and he had lain there as if in someone's rifle sights, awkward with her. (Ondaatje 114).

On the other hand, Almasy and Katharine have a more physical relationship. In the film, they are constantly keeping their romantic affair to themselves, sneaking around to share their love for one another. Katharine says to Almasy, "I want you to ravish me" (Ondaatje 236).

There is another type of love that exists in *The English Patient* between Hana and Kip and Almasy and Katharine. It is physical love, not sexual intercourse, but a love of the physical body. While observing Kip, Hana is described by the narrator: "She loves most the wet colours of his neck when he bathes . . . and his chest with its sweat" (Ondaatje 127). In return, Kip "loves most her face's smart look . . . he loves her voice . . . and the way she crawls in against his body like a saint" (Ondaatje 128). Another time, Hana comments to Kip, "It's your mouth that I'm most purely in love with" (Ondaatje 128). Almasy and Katharine have the same type of physical love: "This is my shoulder, he thinks, not her husband's, this is my shoulder. As lovers they have offered parts of their bodies to each other, like this" (Ondaatje 156). Almasy loves Katharine's vaccination scar, the "pale aureole on her arm" (Ondaatje 158). He also loves the hollow at the base of a woman's neck that he likes to call the "Bosphorus" and which he later discovers is called the "vascular sizood" (Ondaatje 241).

Is marriage the next step after falling in love? Author Stanley N. Bernard writes "[l]ove, lust, and marriage go hand in hand" (in "Love, Lust, and Marriage"), while feminist author Emma Goldman disagrees, stating in her essay that "marriage and love have nothing in common" (233). She discusses the concept of free love, which is love without church and state, the type of love shared between Almasy and Katharine and Hana and Kip. They were free to love one another without the burden of marriage. Although Goldman was married, divorced, and then remarried, she still believes that "it is utterly false that love results in marriage" (233).

10   A major question to ask is: are the couples in *The English Patient* truly in love? Hana, after the loss of her child, the father of the child, and her own father is seeking love and comfort. She is searching for her "half," her "corresponding tally" (Plato 912). Plato's *Symposium* discusses this idea. He suggests that we yearn for our other half and experience love as a result of this "weld[ing] of two beings into one . . ." (Plato 912). The relationship between Almasy and Katharine is slightly more complicated. Katharine is married to Geoffrey during the affair. Geoffry loves her, but the novel does not describe Katharine's feelings for him in return. Is it possible to be in love with two people at once? In an article found on *Jet Online* ("Which Urge Is Stronger—Sex or Love?"), psychologist Dr. Grace Cornish discusses the age-old belief that "women give sex just to feel love and men will say 'I love you' just to have the sex." Almasy has a burning desire for Katharine, which might be mistaken for lust since "love endears while lust desires" (Bernard); however, the reader is encouraged to believe that Almasy is truly in love with Katharine.

"The strongest human desire for most people is to be loved" ("Which Urge"), and when that love is gone, the lovers's world comes crashing down. As singer Mariah Carey once sang: "Love takes time to heal when you're hurting so much . . . I can't escape the pain inside, 'cause love takes time'." Katharine breaks off the short-lived love affair, because she is "too proud to be a lover, a secret" (Ondaatje 171). Almasy is distraught but remains calm, stating "I don't miss you yet" (Ondaatje 171). Knowing that absence makes the heart grow fonder, Katharine simply replies, "You will" (Ondaatje 158). Unknown by the lovers, however, Geoffrey Clifton has discovered the truth about their relationship and plans a murder-suicide. He deliberately attempts to crash the plane carrying himself and Katharine into Almasy, killing them all.

The tragedy leaves Clifton dead, Katharine severely injured with broken ribs and a broken wrist, and Almasy unharmed. Almasy and Katharine are separated for several months, and during this time Almasy "ha[s] grown bitter" (Ondaatje 172). He believes that Katharine has found another lover and "did not trust her last endearments to him anymore" (Ondaatje 172), but he still loves her enough to take care of her after the accident. Placing her in the Cave of Swimmers, he vows to get help and return for her. He does keep his promise to her, but is unable to return for three years. When he arrives at the cave, he finds his love dead. Almasy, as well as Kip, proves that love is security. He does all that he can to bring aid to the woman he loves, possibly the only woman whom he has ever loved (this fact is not mentioned in the novel).

Kip's actions also suggest that love means security. One day, he discovers a mine hidden in the garden of the villa. Hana comes along, sees what he is doing and offers her help. Kip responds, "You must leave" (Ondaatje 101). He is trying to protect her, but Hana, with her stubborn nature, stays by his side, holding the wire that he must cut in her left hand. Later, Kip is somewhat angry with her for not leaving and going to safety. If Almasy and Kip did not truly love their women,

Katharine and Hana, then they might not have tried to protect them. "Love is your head and heart" ("Which Urge"), and this is what the men seem to believe when their lovers are in danger.

Though the lovers are unable to remain together, due to the unfortunate death of Katharine and the unexpected flight of Kip, they are never forgotten. Almasy, as an amnesiac burn patient, frequently slips into the past, telling his story to those who are around him. At the end of the film, which centers on his memory of the romantic affair between him and Katharine, he requests an overdose of morphine, allowing him to die peacefully and to be reunited with his greatest love. The end of the novel reveals that Kip returns to India after he leaves the villa, marries, and has a family of his own. He still reminisces about the young, Canadian girl, child-like in nature, whom he loved. Both situations imply that love can be found and lost, but never forgotten.

15   In his poem "September 1, 1939," W.H. Auden observes:

> For the error bred in the bone
>
> Of each woman and each man
>
> Craves what it cannot have,
>
> Not universal love
>
> But to be loved alone.

Aristophanes from Plato's *Symposium* believed this concept, too. Men and women simply want their other half:

> The way to happiness for our race lies in fulfilling the behests of Love, and in each finding for himself [herself] the mate who properly belongs to him [her]; in a word, in returning to our original condition. (Plato 913)

Love should never be repelled or taken advantage of. Remember, as another writer once taught, "The greatest thing you'll ever learn is just to love and be loved in return."

Works Cited

Anzaldúa, Gloria. "To Live in the Borderlands Means You." *Legacies*. Eds. Jan Zlotnik Schmidt, Carley Bogarad, and Lynne Crockett. Australia: Thompson, 2005. 1269.

Auden, W. H. "September 1, 1939." 3 April 2002. http://www.auden.com.

Bernard, Stanley N. "Love, Lust, and Marriage." *Humanist*. November 2000. http://www.findarticles.com.

Goldman, Emma. *Anarchism and Other Essays*. Third Revised Edition. New York: Mother Earth Publishing Association, 1917.

Ondaatje, Michael. *The English Patient*. New York: Vintage International, 1992.

Plato. "The Sexes" from *The Symposium*. *Legacies*. Eds. Jan Zlotnik Schmidt, Carley Bogarad, and Lynne Crockett. Australia: Thomson, 2005. 910–913.

"Which Urge is Stronger—Sex or Love?" *Jet Online*. 3 April 2000. http://www.findarticles.com.

· CHAPTER 7 ·

Sites of Conflict

The world is too dangerous to live in—not because of the people who do evil, but because of the people who sit and let it happen.

Albert Einstein

All the people like us are we, and everyone else is they.

Rudyard Kipling

. . . definitions belong . . . to the definers–not the defined.

Toni Morrison, *Beloved*

Contact zones [are] social spaces where cultures meet, clash, and grapple with each other, often in contexts of highly asymmetrical relations of power, such as colonialism, slavery, or their aftermaths as they are lived out in many parts of the world today.

Mary Louise Pratt

Kathe Kullwitz, "Beim Dengein" ("Sharpening the Scythe"), 1921

• Introduction •

There is a cyclone fence between
ourselves and the slaughter and behind it
we hover in a calm, protected world like
netted fish, exactly like netted fish.
It is either the beginning or the end
of the world, and the choice is ourselves
or nothing.

Carolyn Forché, "Ourselves or Nothing"

Whereas once people felt that they perhaps could "hover in a calm, protected world," after 9/11 it seems impossible to escape the presence of the "slaughter." People live with a heightened sense of fear and vulnerability because of the threat of terrorist acts, because of the knowledge of sites of conflict worldwide. No longer may people assume that they will remain untouched by acts of violence. The writers in this chapter explore both the new ideas of threat and those sites of conflict (from the physical to the verbal) that exist within and independent of terrorism.

The works in Crossing the Genres/Terror and Terrorism explore the impact of terrorism on characters in very different parts of the world. In the thematic cluster, "Visions of the Holocaust," another version of the "end" is portrayed: the Nazi genocide during World War II. The Holocaust marked a time in history when concepts of good and evil, moral responsibility, and the idea of civilization itself were challenged.

The poems in the 9/11 cluster attest to the need to commemorate the dead through acts of remembrance and writing.

Another site of conflict explored in this chapter is a way to oppose the "slaughter": the awareness of and fight against racial oppression. In the United States, two of the first advocates for human rights were female slaves who eventually claimed their freedom.

Yet despite advances since, the dream of an ideal—freedom and of a true America— persists. The works in the thematic cluster, "American Dreams Lost and Found," present the tension between the ideal and the real in American life. In these works, images of destruction and renewal are intertwined.

War represents the ultimate form of destruction. Henry Ward Beecher once said, "It is not merely cruelty that leads men to love war; it is excitement." The soldiers in this chapter, however, do not seem to love war. Diverse works attest to the physical and the emotional burdens that soldiers bear. Parents who send their sons and daughters to war do not love the cruelty of war either; they do not find vicarious excitement in their children's service. They often shield themselves from the horrors of war through rationalization and denial, as many of the works in chapter 7 attest.

Acts of violence, however, do not always occur through acts of terror, oppression, or war; they can also manifest themselves when the will of the majority defeats the will of the individual.

964

Opportunities for social transformation still exist. Indeed, the works in this chapter attest to the power of art to incite questioning, awareness, and, hopefully, social change. As Forché reminds us, "all things human take time":

> Time which the damned never seem to have, time for life
> To repair at least the worst of its wounds. . .

"Ourselves or Nothing"

■ *Thematic Clusters* ■

■ *More Themes that Cross the Genres* ■

Alfred Kazin wrote that war is the enduring condition of twentieth-century man. He was only partly right. War is the enduring condition of man, period. Men have gone to war over everything from Helen of Troy to Jenkin's ear. Two million Frenchmen and Englishmen died in muddy trenches in World War I because a student shot an archduke. The truth is, the reasons don't matter. There is a reason for every war and a war for every reason.

For centuries men have hoped that with history would come progress, and with progress, peace. But progress has simply given man the means to make war even more horrible; no wars in our savage past can begin to match the brutality of the wars spawned in this century, in the beautifully ordered, civilized landscape of Europe, where everyone is literate and classical music plays in every village café. War is not an aberration; it is part of the family the crazy uncle we try—in vain—to keep locked in the basement.

William Broyles, Jr., "Why Men Love War"

Crossing the Genres

TERROR AND TERRORISM

LUISA VALENZUELA

Luisa Valenzuela (1938–   ) was born in Buenos Aires, Argentina, and attended the University of Buenos Aires. Since that time, Valenzuela has published nineteen books. Her work is considered to be experimental, going beyond the style of magical realism to convey life's nonlinear reality. Valenzuela left Argentina after the death of dictator Juan Perón in 1974 to escape the military dictatorship that ruled until 1983. Before she fled, she wrote, "Buenos Aires belonged then to violence and to state terrorism, and I could only sit in cafes and brood. Till I decided a book of short stories could be written in a month at those same cafe tables, overhearing scraps of scared conversations, seeping in the general paranoia. Strange Things Happen Here *(1979) was born, and with it a new political awareness. And action."*

1975

I'M YOUR HORSE IN THE NIGHT

The doorbell rang: three short rings and one long one. That was the signal, and I got up, annoyed and a little frightened; it could be them, and then again, maybe not; at these ungodly hours of the night it could be a trap. I opened the door expecting anything except him, face to face, at last.

He came in quickly and locked the door behind him before embracing me. So much in character, so cautious, first and foremost checking his—our—rear guard. Then he took me in his arms without saying a word, not even holding me too tight but letting all the emotions of our new encounter overflow, telling me so much by merely holding me in his arms and kissing me slowly. I think he never had much faith in words, and there he was, as silent as ever, sending me messages in the form of caresses.

We finally stepped back to look at one another from head to foot, not eye to eye, out of focus. And I was able to say Hello showing scarcely any surprise despite all those months when I had no idea where he could have been, and I was able to say

I thought you were fighting up north
I thought you'd been caught
I thought you were in hiding
I thought you'd been tortured and killed
I thought you were theorizing about the revolution in another country

Just one of many ways to tell him I'd been thinking of him, I hadn't stopped thinking of him or felt as if I'd been betrayed. And there he was, always so goddamn cautious, so much the master of his actions.

5   "Quiet, Chiquita.[1] You're much better off not knowing what I've been up to."

---

[1] Small one, little one (female).

Then he pulled out his treasures, potential clues that at the time eluded me: a bottle of cachaça[2] and a Gal Costa[3] record. What had he been up to in Brazil? What was he planning to do next? What had brought him back, risking his life, knowing they were after him? Then I stopped asking myself questions (quiet, Chiquita, he'd say). Come here, Chiquita, he was saying, and I chose to let myself sink into the joy of having him back again, trying not to worry. What would happen to us tomorrow, and the days that followed?

Cachaça's a good drink. It goes down and up and down all the right tracks, and then stops to warm up the corners that need it most. Gal Costa's voice is hot, she envelops us in its sound and half-dancing, half-floating, we reach the bed. We lie down and keep on staring deep into each other's eyes, continue caressing each other without allowing ourselves to give in to the pure senses just yet. We continue recognizing, rediscovering each other.

Beto, I say, looking at him. I know that isn't his real name, but it's the only one I can call him out loud. He replies:

"We'll make it someday, Chiquita. But let's not talk now."

10   It's better that way. Better if he doesn't start talking about how we'll make it someday and ruin the wonder of what we're about to attain right now, the two of us, all alone.

"A noite eu so teu cavalo," Gal Costa suddenly sings from the record player.

"I'm your horse in the night," I translate slowly. And so as to bind him in a spell and stop him from thinking about other things:

"It's a saint's song, like in the *macumba*.[4] Someone who's in a trance says she's the horse of the spirit who's riding her, she's his mount."

"Chiquita, you're always getting carried away with esoteric meanings and witchcraft. You know perfectly well that she isn't talking about spirits. If you're my horse in the night it's because I ride you, like this, see? . . . Like this . . . That's all."

15   It was so long, so deep and so insistent, so charged with affection that we ended up exhausted. I fell asleep with him still on top of me.

I'm your horse in the night.

The goddamn phone pulled me out in waves from a deep well. Making an enormous effort to wake up, I walked over to the receiver, thinking it could be Beto, sure, who was no longer by my side, sure, following his inveterate habit of running away while I'm asleep without a word about where he's gone. To protect me, he says.

From the other end of the line, a voice I thought belonged to Andrés—the one we call Andrés—began to tell me:

"They found Beto dead, floating down the river near the other bank. It looks as if they threw him alive out of a chopper. He's all bloated and decomposed after six days in the water, but I'm almost sure it's him."

20   "No, it can't be Beto," I shouted carelessly. Suddenly the voice no longer sounded like Andrés: it felt foreign, impersonal.

"You think so?"

"Who is this?" Only then did I think to ask. But that very moment they hung up.

Ten, fifteen minutes? How long must I have stayed there staring at the phone like an idiot until the police arrived? I didn't expect them. But, then again, how could I not? Their hands feeling me, their voices insulting and threatening, the house searched, turned inside

---

[2] An alcoholic beverage.

[3] Chanteuse.

[4] A polytheistic religion of African origin, practiced mainly by Brazilian blacks in urban areas. A religion involving spirits.

out. But I already knew. So what did I care if they broke every breakable object and tore apart my dresser?

They wouldn't find a thing. My only real possession was a dream and they can't deprive me of my dreams just like that. My dream the night before, when Beto was there with me and we loved each other. I'd dreamed it, dreamed every bit of it, I was deeply convinced that I'd dreamed it all in the richest detail, even in full color. And dreams are none of the cops' business.

25   They want reality, tangible facts, the kind I couldn't even begin to give them.

Where is he, you saw him, he was here with you, where did he go? Speak up, or you'll be sorry. Let's hear you sing, bitch, we know he came to see you, where is he, where is he holed up? He's in the city, come on, spill it, we know he came to get you.

I haven't heard a word from him in months. He abandoned me, I haven't heard from him in months. He ran away, went underground. What do I know, he ran off with someone else, he's in another country. What do I know, he abandoned me, I hate him, I know nothing.

(Go ahead, burn me with your cigarettes, kick me all you wish, threaten, go ahead, stick a mouse in me so it'll eat my insides out, pull my nails out, do as you please. Would I make something up for that? Would I tell you he was here when a thousand years ago he left me forever?)

I'm not about to tell them my dreams. Why should they care? I haven't seen that so-called Beto in more than six months, and I loved him. The man simply vanished. I only run into him in my dreams, and they're bad dreams that often become nightmares.

30   Beto you know now, if it's true that they killed you, or wherever you may be, Beto, I'm your horse in the night and you can inhabit me whenever you wish, even if I'm behind bars. Beto, now that I'm in jail I know that I dreamed you that night; it was just a dream. And if by some wild chance there's a Gal Costa record and a half-empty bottle of cachaça in my house, I hope they'll forgive me: I will them out of existence.

Bharati Mukherjee

Mukherjee (1940–   ) has published close to ten novels, including Wife *(1975),* Jasmine *(1989), and* Tree Bride *(2004), and several collections of short stories, including* The Middleman and Other Stories *(1988), which received the 1988 National Book Critics Circle Award for Fiction. "The Management of Grief," from* The Middleman and Other Stories, *is based on the 1985 bombing of an Air-India jet traveling from Canada to India. Three hundred and twenty nine people died in the explosion, caused by terrorists who were Indian members of the Sikh religion. In "The Management of Grief," the narrator, Shalia, in dealing with her grief, also must determine how to treat her Sikh friends and neighbors.*

1988

THE MANAGEMENT OF GRIEF

Awoman I don't know is boiling tea the Indian way in my kitchen. There are a lot of women I don't know in my kitchen, whispering, and moving tactfully. They open doors, rummage through the pantry, and try not to ask me where things are kept. They remind me of when my sons were small, on Mother's Day or when Vikram and I were tired, and they would make big, sloppy omelets. I would lie in bed pretending I didn't hear them.

Dr. Sharma, the treasurer of the Indo-Canada Society, pulls me into the hallway. He wants to know if I am worried about money. His wife, who has just come up from the basement with a tray of empty cups and glasses, scolds him. "Don't bother Mrs. Bhave with mundane details." She looks so monstrously pregnant her baby must be days overdue. I tell her she shouldn't be carrying heavy things. "Shaila," she says, smiling, "this is the fifth." Then she grabs a teenager by his shirttails. He slips his Walkman off his head. He has to be one of her four children, they have the same doomed and dented foreheads. "What's the official word now?" she demands. The boy slips the headphones back on. "They're acting evasive, Ma. They're saying it could be an accident or a terrorist bomb."

All morning, the boys have been muttering. Sikh Bomb, Sikh Bomb. The men, not using the word, bow their heads in agreement. Mrs. Sharma touches her forehead at such a word. At least they've stopped talking about space debris and Russian lasers.

Two radios are going in the dining room. They are tuned to different stations. Someone must have brought the radios down from my boys' bedrooms. I haven't gone into their rooms since Kusum came running across the front lawn in her bathrobe. She looked so funny, I was laughing when I opened the door.

5   The big TV in the den is being whizzed through American networks and cable channels.

"Damn!" some man swears bitterly. "How can these preachers carry on like nothing's happened?" I want to tell him we're not that important. You look at the audience, and at the preacher in his blue robe with his beautiful white hair, the potted palm trees under a blue sky, and you know they care about nothing.

The phone rings and rings. Dr. Sharma's taken charge. "We're with her," he keeps saying. "Yes, yes, the doctor has given calming pills. Yes, yes, pills are having necessary effect." I wonder if pills alone explain this calm. Not peace, just a deadening quiet. I was always controlled, but never repressed. Sound can reach me, but my body is tensed, ready to scream. I hear their voices all around me. I hear my boys and Vikram cry, "Mommy, Shaila!" and their screams insulate me, like headphones.

The woman boiling water tells her story again and again. "I got the news first. My cousin called from Halifax before six A.M., can you imagine? He'd gotten up for prayers and his son was studying for medical exams and he heard on a rock channel that something had happened to a plane. They said first it had disappeared from the radar, like a giant eraser just reached out. His father called me, so I said to him, what do you mean, 'something bad'? You mean a hijacking? And he said, *behn*, there is no confirmation of anything yet, but check with your neighbors because a lot of them must be on that plane. So I called poor Kusum straightaway. I knew Kusum's husband and daughter were booked to go yesterday."

Kusum lives across the street from me. She and Satish had moved in less than a month ago. They said they needed a bigger place. All these people, the Sharmas and friends from the Indo-Canada Society, had been there for the housewarming. Satish and Kusum made homemade tandoori on their big gas grill and even the white neighbors piled their plates high with that luridly red, charred, juicy chicken. Their younger daughter had danced, and even our boys had broken away from the Stanley Cup telecast to put in a reluctant appearance. Everyone took pictures for their albums and for the community newspapers—another of our families had made it big in Toronto—and now I wonder how many of those happy faces are gone. "Why does God give us so much if all along He intends to take it away?" Kusum asks me.

10   I nod. We sit on carpeted stairs, holding hands like children. "I never once told him that I loved him," I say. I was too much the well brought up woman. I was so well brought up I never felt comfortable calling my husband by his first name.

"It's all right," Kusum says. "He knew. My husband knew. They felt it. Modern young girls have to say it because what they feel is fake."

Kusum's daughter, Pam, runs in with an overnight case. Pam's in her McDonald's uniform. "Mummy! You have to get dressed!" Panic makes her cranky. "A reporter's on his way here."

"Why?"

"You want to talk to him in your bathrobe?" She starts to brush her mother's long hair. She's the daughter who's always in trouble. She dates Canadian boys and hangs out in the mall, shopping for tight sweaters. The younger one, the goody-goody one according to Pam, the one with a voice so sweet that when she sang *bhajans* for Ethiopian relief even a frugal man like my husband wrote out a hundred dollar check, *she* was on that plane. *She* was going to spend July and August with grandparents because Pam wouldn't go. Pam said she'd rather waitress at McDonald's. "If it's a choice between Bombay and Wonderland, I'm picking Wonderland," she'd said.

15   "Leave me alone," Kusum yells. "You know what I want to do? If I didn't have to look after you now, I'd hang myself."

Pam's young face goes blotchy with pain. "Thanks," she says, "don't let me stop you."

"Hush," pregnant Mrs. Sharma scolds Pam. "Leave your mother alone. Mr. Sharma will tackle the reporters and fill out the forms. He'll say what has to be said."

Pam stands her ground. "You think I don't know what Mummy's thinking? *Why ever?* that's what. That's sick! Mummy wishes my little sister were alive and I were dead."

Kusum's hand in mine is trembly hot. We continue to sit on the stairs.

20   She calls before she arrives, wondering if there's anything I need. Her name is Judith Templeton and she's an appointee of the provincial government. "Multiculturalism?" I ask, and she says, "partially," but that her mandate is bigger. "I've been told you knew many of the people on the flight," she says. "Perhaps if you'd agree to help us reach the others . . . ?"

She gives me time at least to put on tea water and pick up the mess in the front room. I have a few *samosas*[1] from Kusum's housewarming that I could fry up, but then I think, why prolong this visit?

Judith Templeton is much younger than she sounded. She wears a blue suit with a white blouse and a polka dot tie. Her blond hair is cut short, her only jewelry is pearl drop earrings. Her briefcase is new and expensive looking, a gleaming cordovan leather. She sits with it across her lap. When she looks out the front windows onto the street, her contact lenses seem to float in front of her light blue eyes.

"What sort of help do you want from me?" I ask. She has refused the tea, out of politeness, but I insist, along with some slightly stale biscuits.

"I have no experience," she admits. "That is, I have an MSW and I've worked in liaison with accident victims, but I mean I have no experience with a tragedy of this scale—"

25   "Who could?" I ask.

"—and with the complications of culture, language, and customs. Someone mentioned that Mrs. Bhave is a pillar—because you've taken it more calmly."

At this point, perhaps, I frown, for she reaches forward, almost to take my hand. "I hope you understand my meaning, Mrs. Bhave. There are hundreds of people in Metro directly affected, like you, and some of them speak no English. There are some widows who've never handled money or gone on a bus, and there are old parents who still haven't eaten or gone outside their bedrooms. Some houses and apartments have been looted. Some wives are still hysterical. Some husbands are in shock and profound depression. We want to help, but our hands are tied in so many ways. We have to distribute money to some people, and there are legal documents—these things can be done. We have interpreters, but we

---

[1] Small turnover of Indian origin filled with vegetables or meat and fried and served hot.

don't always have the human touch, or maybe the right human touch. We don't want to make mistakes, Mrs. Bhave, and that's why we'd like to ask you to help us."

"More mistakes, you mean," I say.

"Police matters are not in my hands," she answers.

30   "Nothing I can do will make any difference," I say. "We must all grieve in our own way."

"But you are coping very well. All the people said, Mrs. Bhave is the strongest person of all. Perhaps if the others could see you, talk with you, it would help them."

"By the standards of the people you call hysterical, I am behaving very oddly and very badly, Miss Templeton." I want to say to her, *I wish I could scream, starve, walk into Lake Ontario, jump from a bridge.* "They would not see me as a model. I do not see myself as a model."

I am a freak. No one who has ever known me would think of me reacting this way. This terrible calm will not go away.

She asks me if she may call again, after I get back from a long trip that we all must make. "Of course," I say. "Feel free to call, anytime."

∞

35   Four days later, I find Kusum squatting on a rock overlooking a bay in Ireland. It isn't a big rock, but it juts sharply out over the water. This is as close as we'll ever get to them. June breezes balloon out her sari and unpin her knee-length hair. She has the bewildered look of a sea creature whom the tides have stranded.

It's been one hundred hours since Kusum came stumbling and screaming across my lawn. Waiting around the hospital, we've heard many stories. The police, the diplomats, they tell us things thinking that we're strong, that knowledge is helpful to the grieving and maybe it is. Some, I know, prefer ignorance, or their own versions. The plane broke into two, they say. Unconsciousness was instantaneous. No one suffered. My boys must have just finished their breakfasts. They loved eating on planes, they loved the smallness of plates, knives, and forks. Last year they saved the airline salt and pepper shakers. Half an hour more and they would have made it to Heathrow.

Kusum says that we can't escape our fate. She says that all those people—our husbands, my boys, her girl with the nightingale voice, all those Hindus, Christians, Sikhs, Muslims, Parsis[2] and atheists on that plane—were fated to die together off this beautiful bay. She learned this from a swami in Toronto.

I have my Valium.

Six of us "relatives"—two widows and four widowers—chose to spend the day today by the waters instead of sitting in a hospital room and scanning photographs of the dead. That's what they call us now: relatives. I've looked through twenty-seven photos in two days. They're very kind to us, the Irish are very understanding. Sometimes understanding means freeing a tourist bus for this trip to the bay, so we can pretend to spy our loved ones through the glassiness of waves or in sunspeckled cloud shapes.

40   I could die here, too, and be content.

"What is that, out there?" She's standing and flapping her hands and for a moment I see a head shape bobbing in the waves. She's standing in the water, I, on the boulder. The tide is low, and a round, black, head-sized rock has just risen from the waves. She returns, her sari end dripping and ruined, and her face is a twisted remnant of hope, the way mine was a

---

[2] Sikhism, a progressive religion founded 500 years ago; Parsi is a form of Zoroastrian religion (religious sects in India).

hundred hours ago, still laughing but inwardly knowing that nothing but the ultimate tragedy could bring two women together at six o'clock on a Sunday morning. I watch her face sag into blankness.

"That water felt warm, Shaila," she says at length.

"You can't," I say. "We have to wait for our turn to come."

I haven't eaten in four days, haven't brushed my teeth.

45   "I know," she says. "I tell myself I have no right to grieve. They are in a better place than we are. My swami says I should be thrilled for them. My swami says depression is a sign of our selfishness."

Maybe I'm selfish. Selfishly I break away from Kusum and run, sandals slapping against stones, to the water's edge. What if my boys aren't lying pinned under the debris? What if they aren't stuck a mile below that innocent blue chop? What if, given the strong currents. . . .

Now I've ruined my sari, one of my best. Kusum has joined me, knee-deep in water that feels to me like a swimming pool. I could settle in the water, and my husband would take my hand and the boys would slap water in my face just to see me scream.

"Do you remember what good swimmers my boys were, Kusum?"

"I saw the medals," she says.

50   One of the widowers, Dr. Ranganathan from Montreal, walks out to us, carrying his shoes in one hand. He's an electrical engineer. Someone at the hotel mentioned his work is famous around the world, something about the place where physics and electricity come together. He has lost a huge family, something indescribable. "With some luck," Dr. Ranganathan suggests to me, "a good swimmer could make it safely to some island. It is quite possible that there may be many, many microscopic islets scattered around."

"You're not just saying that?" I tell Dr. Ranganathan about Vinod, my elder son. Last year he took diving as well.

"It's a parent's duty to hope," he says. "It is foolish to rule out possibilities that have not been tested. I myself have not surrendered hope."

Kusum is sobbing once again. "Dear lady," he says, laying his free hand on her arm, and she calms down.

"Vinod is how old?" he asks me. He's very careful, as we all are. *Is,* not was.

55   "Fourteen. Yesterday he was fourteen. His father and uncle were going to take him down to the Taj and give him a big birthday party. I couldn't go with them because I couldn't get two weeks off from my stupid job in June." I process bills for a travel agent. June is a big travel month.

Dr. Ranganathan whips the pockets of his suit jacket inside out. Squashed roses, in darkening shades of pink, float on the water. He tore the roses off creepers in somebody's garden. He didn't ask anyone if he could pluck the roses, but now there's been an article about it in the local papers. When you see an Indian person, it says, please give him or her flowers.

"A strong youth of fourteen," he says, "can very likely pull to safety a younger one."

My sons, though four years apart, were very close. Vinod wouldn't let Mithun drown. *Electrical engineering,* I think, foolishly perhaps: this man knows important secrets of the universe, things closed to me. Relief spins me light-headed. No wonder my boys' photographs haven't turned up in the gallery of photos of the recovered dead. "Such pretty roses," I say.

"My wife loved pink roses. Every Friday I had to bring a bunch home. I used to say, why? After twenty-odd years of marriage you're still needing proof positive of my love?" He has identified his wife and three of his children. Then others from Montreal, the lucky ones, intact families with no survivors. He chuckles as he wades back to shore. Then he swings around to ask me a question. "Mrs. Bhave, you are wanting to throw in some roses for your loved ones? I have two big ones left."

60 But I have other things to float: Vinod's pocket calculator; a half-painted model B-52 for my Mithun. They'd want them on their island. And for my husband? For him I let fall into the calm, glassy waters a poem I wrote in the hospital yesterday. Finally he'll know my feelings for him.

"Don't tumble, the rocks are slippery," Dr. Ranganathan cautions. He holds out a hand for me to grab.

Then it's time to get back on the bus, time to rush back to our waiting posts on hospital benches.

∾

Kusum is one of the lucky ones. The lucky ones flew here, identified in multiplicate their loved ones, then will fly to India with the bodies for proper ceremonies. Satish is one of the few males who surfaced. The photos of faces we saw on the walls in an office at Heathrow and here in the hospital are mostly of women. Women have more body fat, a nun said to me matter-of-factly. They float better.

Today I was stopped by a young sailor on the street. He had loaded bodies, he'd gone into the water when—he checks my face for signs of strength—when the sharks were first spotted. I don't blush, and he breaks down. "It's all right," I say. "Thank you." I had heard about the sharks from Dr. Ranganathan. In his orderly mind, science brings understanding, it holds no terror. It is the shark's duty. For every deer there is a hunter, for every fish, a fisherman.

65 The Irish are not shy; they rush to me and give me hugs and some are crying. I cannot imagine reactions like that on the streets of Toronto. Just strangers, and I am touched. Some carry flowers with them and give them to any Indian they see.

After lunch, a policeman I have gotten to know quite well catches hold of me. He says he thinks he has a match for Vinod. I explain what a good swimmer Vinod is.

"You want me with you when you look at photos?" Dr. Ranganathan walks ahead of me into the picture gallery. In these matters, he is a scientist, and I am grateful. It is a new perspective. "They have performed miracles," he says. "We are indebted to them."

The first day or two the policemen showed us relatives only one picture at a time; now they're in a hurry, they're eager to lay out the possibles, and even the probables.

The face on the photo is of a boy much like Vinod; the same intelligent eyes, the same thick brows dipping into a V. But this boy's features, even his cheeks, are puffier, wider, mushier.

70 "No." My gaze is pulled by other pictures. There are five other boys who look like Vinod.

The nun assigned to console me rubs the first picture with a fingertip. "When they've been in the water for a while, love, they look a little heavier." The bones under the skin are broken, they said on the first day—try to adjust your memories. It's important.

"It's not him. I'm his mother. I'd know,"

"I know this one!" Dr. Ranganathan cries out suddenly from the back of the gallery. "And this one!" I think he senses that I don't want to find my boys. "They are the Kutty brothers. They were also from Montreal." I don't mean to be crying. On the contrary, I am ecstatic. My suitcase in the hotel is packed heavy with dry clothes for my boys.

The policeman starts to cry. "I am so sorry, I am so sorry, ma'am. I really thought we had a match."

75 With the nun ahead of us and the policeman behind, we, the unlucky ones without our children's bodies, file out of the makeshift gallery.

∾

From Ireland most of us go on to India. Kusum and I take the same direct flight to Bombay, so I can help her clear customs quickly. But we have to argue with a man in uniform. He has large boils on his face. The boils swell and glow with sweat as we argue with him. He wants Kusum to wait in line and he refuses to take authority because his boss is on a tea break. But Kusum won't let her coffins out of sight, and I shan't desert her though I know that my parents, elderly and diabetic, must be waiting in a stuffy car in a scorching lot.

"You bastard!" I scream at the man with the popping boils. Other passengers press closer. "You think we're smuggling contraband in those coffins!"

Once upon a time we were well brought up women; we were dutiful wives who kept our heads veiled, our voices shy and sweet.

⚮

In India, I become, once again, an only child of rich, ailing parents. Old friends of the family come to pay their respects. Some are Sikh, and inwardly, involuntarily, I cringe. My parents are progressive people; they do not blame communities for a few individuals.

80　In Canada it is a different story now.

"Stay longer," my mother pleads. "Canada is a cold place. Why would you want to be all by yourself?" I stay.

Three months pass. Then another.

"Vikram wouldn't have wanted you to give up things!" they protest. They call my husband by the name he was born with. In Toronto he'd changed to Vik so the men he worked with at this office would find his name as easy as Rod or Chris. "You know, the dead aren't cut off from us!"

My grandmother, the spoiled daughter of a rich *zamindar*[3] shaved her head with rusty blades when she was widowed at sixteen. My grandfather died of childhood diabetes when he was nineteen, and she saw herself as the harbinger of bad luck. My mother grew up without parents, raised indifferently by an uncle, while her true mother slept in a hut behind the main estate house and took her food with the servants. She grew up a rationalist. My parents abhor mindless mortification.

85　The *zamindar's* daughter kept stubborn faith in Vedic rituals; my parents rebelled. I am trapped between two modes of knowledge. At thirty-six, I am too old to start over and too young to give up. Like my husband's spirit. I flutter between two worlds.

⚮

Courting aphasia, we travel. We travel with our phalanx of servants and poor relatives. To hill stations and to beach resorts. We play contract bridge in dusty gymkhana clubs. We ride stubby ponies up crumbly mountain trails. At tea dances, we let ourselves be twirled round the ballroom. We hit the holy spots we hadn't made time for before. In Varanasi, Kalighat, Rishikesh, Hardwar, astrologers and palmists seek me out and for a fee offer me cosmic consolations.

Already the widowers among us are being shown new bride candidates. They cannot resist the call of custom, the authority of their parents and older brothers. They must marry; it is the duty of a man to look after a wife. The new wives will be young widows with their

---

[3] A landholder in British colonial England responsible for collecting and paying to the government taxes on land under his jurisdiction.

children, destitute but of good family. They will make loving wives, but the men will shun them. I've had calls from the men over crackling Indian telephone lines. "Save me," they say, these substantial, educated, successful men of forty. "My parents are arranging a marriage for me." In a month they will have buried one family and returned to Canada with a new bride and partial family.

I am comparatively lucky. No one here thinks of arranging a husband for an unlucky widow.

Then, on the third day of the sixth month into this odyssey, in an abandoned temple in a tiny Himalayan village, as I make my offering of flowers and sweetmeats to the god of a tribe of animists, my husband descends to me. He is squatting next to a scrawny *sadhu* in moth-eaten robes. Vikram wears the vanilla suit he wore the last time I hugged him. The *sadhu* tosses petals on a butter-fed flame, reciting Sanskrit Mantras, and sweeps his face of flies. My husband takes my hands in his.

90   *You're beautiful,* he starts. Then, *What are you doing here?*

Shall I stay? I ask. He only smiles, but already the image is fading. *You must finish alone what we started together.* No seaweed wreathes his mouth. He speaks too fast just as he used to when we were an envied family in our pink split-level. He is gone.

In the windowless altar room, smoky with joss sticks and clarified butter lamps, a sweaty hand gropes for my blouse. I do not shriek. The *sadhu* arranges his robe. The lamps hiss and sputter out.

When we come out of the temple, my mother says, "Did you feel something weird in there?"

My mother has no patience with ghosts, prophetic dreams, holy men, and cults.

95   "No," I lie. "Nothing."

But she knows that she's lost me. She knows that in days I shall be leaving.

∾

Kusum's put her house up for sale. She wants to live in an ashram in Hardwar. Moving to Hardwar was her swami's idea. Her swami runs two ashrams, the one in Hardwar and another here in Toronto.

"Don't run away," I tell her.

"I'm not running away," she says. "I'm pursuing inner peace. You think you or that Ranganathan fellow are better off?"

100   Pam's left for California. She wants to do some modelling, she says. She says when she comes into her share of the insurance money she'll open a yoga-cum-aerobics studio in Hollywood. She sends me postcards so naughty I daren't leave them on the coffee table. Her mother has withdrawn from her and the world.

The rest of us don't lose touch, that's the point. Talk is all we have, says Dr. Ranganathan, who has also resisted his relatives and returned to Montreal and to his job, alone. He says, whom better to talk with than other relatives? We've been melted down and recast as a new tribe.

He calls me twice a week from Montreal. Every Wednesday night and every Saturday afternoon. He is changing jobs, going to Ottawa. But Ottawa is over a hundred miles away, and he is forced to drive two hundred and twenty miles a day. He can't bring himself to sell his house. The house is a temple, he says; the king-sized bed in the master bedroom is a shrine. He sleeps on a folding cot. A devotee.

∾

There are still some hysterical relatives. Judith Templeton's list of those needing help and those who've "accepted" is in nearly perfect balance. Acceptance means you speak of your family in the past tense and you make active plans for moving ahead with your life. There are courses at Seneca and Ryerson we could be taking. Her gleaming leather briefcase is full of college catalogues and lists of cultural societies that need our help. She has done impressive work, I tell her.

"In the textbooks on grief management," she replies—I am her confidante, I realize, one of the few whose grief has not sprung bizarre obsessions—"there are stages to pass through: rejection, depression, acceptance, reconstruction." She has compiled a chart and finds that six months after the tragedy, none of us still reject reality, but only a handful are reconstructing. "Depressed Acceptance" is the plateau we've reached. Remarriage is a major step in reconstruction (though she's a little surprised, even shocked, over *how* quickly some of the men have taken on new families). Selling one's house and changing jobs and cities is healthy.

105   How do I tell Judith Templeton that my family surrounds me, and that like creatures in epics, they've changed shapes? She sees me as calm and accepting but worries that I have no job, no career. My closest friends are worse off than I. I cannot tell her my days, even my nights, are thrilling.

She asks me to help with families she can't reach at all. An elderly couple in Agincourt whose sons were killed just weeks after they had brought their parents over from a village in Punjab. From their names, I know they are Sikh. Judith Templeton and a translator have visited them twice with offers of money for air fare to Ireland, with bank forms, power-of-attorney forms, but they have refused to sign, or to leave their tiny apartment. Their sons' money is frozen in the bank. Their sons' investment apartments have been trashed by tenants, the furnishings sold off. The parents fear that anything they sign or any money they receive will end the company's or the country's obligations to them. They fear they are selling their sons for two airline tickets to a place they've never seen.

The high-rise apartment is a tower of Indians and West Indians, with a sprinkling of Orientals. The nearest bus stop kiosk is lined with women in saris. Boys practice cricket in the parking lot. Inside the building, even I wince a bit from the ferocity of onion fumes, the distinctive and immediate Indianness of frying *ghee*, but Judith Templeton maintains a steady flow of information. These poor old people are in imminent danger of losing their place and all their services.

I say to her, "They are Sikh. They will not open up to a Hindu woman." And what I want to add is, as much as I try not to, I stiffen now at the sight of beards and turbans. I remember a time when we all trusted each other in this new country, it was only the new country we worried about.

The two rooms are dark and stuffy. The lights are off, and an oil lamp sputters on the coffee table. The bent old lady has let us in, and her husband is wrapping a white turban over his oiled, hip-length hair. She immediately goes to the kitchen, and I hear the most familiar sound of an Indian home, tap water hitting and filling a teapot.

110   They have not paid their utility bills, out of fear and the inability to write a check. The telephone is gone; electricity and gas and water are soon to follow. They have told Judith their sons will provide. They are good boys, and they have always earned and looked after their parents.

We converse a bit in Hindi.[4] They do not ask about the crash and I wonder should I bring it up. If they think I am here merely as a translator, then they may feel insulted. There

---

[4] The most widely spoken of modern Indian vernaculars.

are thousands of Punjabi-speakers, Sikhs, in Toronto to do a better job. And so I say to the old lady, "I too have lost my sons, and my husband, in the crash."

Her eyes immediately fill with tears. The man mutters a few words which sound like a blessing. "God provides and God takes away," he says.

I want to say, but only men destroy and give back nothing. "My boys and my husband are not coming back," I say. "We have to understand that."

Now the old woman responds. "But who is to say? Man alone does not decide these things." To this her husband adds his agreement.

115   Judith asks about the bank papers, the release forms. With a stroke of the pen, they will have a provincial trustee to pay their bills, invest their money, send them a monthly pension.

"Do you know this woman?" I ask them.

The man raises his hand from the table, turns it over and seems to regard each finger separately before he answers. "This young lady is always coming here, we make tea for her and she leaves papers for us to sign." His eyes scan a pile of papers in the corner of the room. "Soon we will be out of tea, then will she go away?"

The old lady adds, "I have asked my neighbors and no one else gets *angrezi* visitors. What have we done?"

"It's her job," I try to explain. "The government is worried. Soon you will have no place to stay, no lights, no gas, no water."

120   "Government will get its money. Tell her not to worry, we are honorable people."

I try to explain the government wishes to give money, not take. He raises his hand. "Let them take," he says. "We are accustomed to that. That is no problem."

"We are strong people," says the wife. "Tell her that."

"Who needs all this machinery?" demands the husband. "It is unhealthy, the bright lights, the cold air on a hot day, the cold food, the four gas rings. God will provide, not government."

"When our boys return," the mother says. Her husband sucks his teeth. "Enough talk," he says.

125   Judith breaks in. "Have you convinced them?" The snaps on her cordovan briefcase go off like firecrackers in that quiet apartment. She lays the sheaf of legal papers on the coffee table. "If they can't write their names, an *X* will do—I've told them that."

Now the old lady has shuffled to the kitchen and soon emerges with a pot of tea and two cups. "I think my bladder will go first on a job like this," Judith says to me, smiling. "If only there was some way of reaching them. Please thank her for the tea. Tell her she's very kind."

I nod in Judith's direction and tell them in Hindi, "She thanks you for the tea. She thinks you are being very hospitable but she doesn't have the slightest idea what it means."

I want to say, humor her. I want to say, my boys and my husband are with me too, more than ever. I look in the old man's eyes and I can read his stubborn, peasant's message: *I have protected this woman as best I can. She is the only person I have left. Give to me or take from me what you will, but I will not sign for it. I will not pretend that I accept.*

In the car, Judith says, "You see what I'm up against? I'm sure they're lovely people, but their stubbornness and ignorance are driving me crazy. They think signing a paper is signing their sons' death warrants, don't they?"

130   I am looking out the window. I want to say, *In our culture, it is a parent's duty to hope.*

"Now Shaila, this next woman is a real mess. She cries day and night, and she refuses all medical help. We may have to—"

"—Let me out at the subway," I say.

"I beg your pardon?" I can feel those blue eyes staring at me.

It would not be like her to disobey. She merely disapproves, and slows at a corner to let me out. Her voice is plaintive. "Is there anything I said? Anything I did?"

135 I could answer her suddenly in a dozen ways, but I choose not to. "Shaila? Let's talk about it," I hear, then slam the door.

∞

A wife and mother begins her new life in a new country, and that life is cut short. Yet her husband tells her: Complete what we have started. We, who stayed out of politics and came halfway around the world to avoid religious and political feuding, have been the first in the New World to die from it. I no longer know what we started, nor how to complete it. I write letters to the editors of local papers and to members of Parliament. Now at least they admit it was a bomb. One MP answers back, with sympathy, but with a challenge. You want to make a difference? Work on a campaign. Work on mine. Politicize the Indian voter.

  My husband's old lawyer helps me set up a trust. Vikram was a saver and a careful investor. He had saved the boys' boarding school and college fees. I sell the pink house at four times what we paid for it and take a small apartment downtown. I am looking for a charity to support.

  We are deep in the Toronto winter, gray skies, icy pavements. I stay indoors, watching television. I have tried to assess my situation, how best to live my life, to complete what we began so many years ago. Kusum has written me from Hardwar that her life is now serene. She has seen Satish and has heard her daughter sing again. Kusum was on a pilgrimage, passing through a village, when she heard a young girl's voice singing one of her daughter's favorite *bhajans*.[5] She followed the music through the squalor of a Himalayan village, to a hut where a young girl, an exact replica of her daughter, was fanning coals under the kitchen fire. When she appeared, the girl cried out, "Ma!" and ran away. What did I think of that?

  I think I can only envy her.

140 Pam didn't make it to California, but writes me from Vancouver. She works in a department store, giving make-up hints to Indian and Oriental girls. Dr. Ranganathan has given up his commute, given up his house and job, and accepted an academic position in Texas where no one knows his story and he has vowed not to tell it. He calls me now once a week.

  I wait, I listen, and I pray, but Vikram has not returned to me. The voices and the shapes and the nights filled with visions ended abruptly several weeks ago.

  I take it as a sign.

  One rare, beautiful sunny day last week, returning from a small errand on Yonge Street, I was walking through the park from the subway to my apartment. I live equidistant from the Ontario Houses of Parliament and the University of Toronto. The day was not cold, but something in the bare trees caught my attention. I looked up from the gravel, into the branches and the clear blue sky beyond. I thought I heard the rustling of larger forms, and I waited a moment for voices. Nothing.

  "What?" I asked.

145 Then as I stood in the path looking north to Queen's Park and west to the university, I heard the voices of my family one last time. *Your time has come,* they said. *Go, be brave.*

  I do not know where this voyage I have begun will end. I do not know which direction I will take. I dropped the package on a park bench and started walking.

---

[5] Hindu devotional song.

NATHAN ENGLANDER

Nathan Englander (1970–   ) was born in New York City and has lived in both the United States and Israel. He was educated at Binghamton University, Hebrew University in Jerusalem, and the Iowa Writers' Workshop. His works have appeared in The New Yorker, Story, Atlantic, *and* American Short Fiction. *Englander's collection of short stories,* For the Relief of Unbearable Urges, *was published in 1999. His writing, with its blend of humor and pathos, has been considered by critics to reflect the tradition of Jewish storytelling.*

1999

IN THIS WAY WE ARE WISE

Three blasts. Like birds. They come through the window, wild and lost. They are trapped under the high-domed ceiling of the café, darting round between us, striking walls and glass, knocking the dishes from the shelves. And we know, until they stop their terrible motion, until they cease swooping and darting and banging into the walls, until they alight, come to us, rest, exhausted, spent, there is nothing at all we can do.

Plates in halves and triangles on the floor. A group of ceramic mugs, fat and split, like over-ripe fruit. The chandelier, a pendulum, still swings.

The owner, the waitress, the other few customers, sit. I am up at the windows. I am watching the people pour around the corner, watching them run toward us, mouths un-hinged, pulling at hair, scratching at faces. They collapse and puff up, hop about undirected.

Like wild birds frightened.

5   Like people possessed, tearing at their forms trying to set something free.

Jerusalemites do not spook like horses. They do not fly like moths into the fire.

They have come to abide their climate. Terror as second winter, as part of their weather. Something that comes and then is gone.

Watching plumes of smoke, the low clouds of smoke that follow the people down the street, I suddenly need to be near the fire, to be where the ash still settles and café umbrellas burn.

I make for the door and the waitress stops me. The owner puts a hand on my shoulder.

10   "Calm down, Natan."

"Sit down, Natan,"

"Have a coffee, Natan." The waitress is already on her way to the machine.

I feel an urgency the others dismiss. I can run with a child to a braking ambulance. Can help the barefooted find their shoes. The time, 3:16, my girlfriend late to meet me. I should be turning over bodies searching for her face.

In a chair drinking coffee holding the owner's hand. "There is nothing to do outside. No one to rescue. Who is already there is who's helping, Natan. If you are not in the eye when it happens, it's already too late to put yourself in."

15   I trade a picture of my girlfriend dead for one of her badly wounded.

Inbar with her face burned off, hands blown off, a leg severed near through. I will play the part of the supportive one. I will bunch up and hold the sheet by her arm, smile and tell her how lucky she is to be alive and in a position where, having discussed it in a happy bed, in a lovers' bed, we had both sworn we'd rather die.

The phones are back. The streets secured. Soldiers everywhere, taking up posts and positions. Fingers curled by triggers.

An Arab worker comes out of the kitchen with a broom.

I'm the first to reach the phone, but I can't remember numbers. One woman slams a portable against the table, as if this will release the satellite from the army's grip.

20   I dial nonsense and hang up, unable to recollect even the code to my machine.

"Natan will be OK," I promise before leaving. "Natan is a grown man. He can find his way home."

On the street I am all animal. I am all sense, all smell and taste and touch. I can read every stranger's intentions from scent, from the flex of a muscle, the length of the passing of our eyes.

I'm on the corner and can turn up the block, take a few strides into the closest of kill zones. I can tour the stretch of wounded weeping and dead unmoving, walk past the blackened and burned, still smoldering ghosts.

The Hasidim[1] will soon come to collect scattered bits, partial Christs. Parts of victims nailed up, screwed in, driven to stone and metal.

25   Hand pierced with rusted nail and hung on the base of a tree.

It is with true force, with the bit of higher thought I can muster, that I spare myself a lifetime of dreams.

I follow a street around and then back on trail to Inbar's apartment.

She is there. We kiss and hug. She holds me in the doorway while I pass through the whole of evolution. The millions of years of animal knowing, of understanding without thought, subside.

We exchanges stories of almosts, of near deaths, theories on fate and algorithm, probability and God. Inbar late, on a bus, distant thunder and then traffic. She got off with a few others and walked the rest of the way home.

30   She makes tea and we sit and watch our world on television.

There is the corner. There is a man reporting in front of my café. And then the long shot of the stretch I avoided. The street I walk on a dozen times a day. There is my cash machine, its awning shattered, its frame streaked with blood. There is the bazaar where I buy pens and pencils. The camera lingers over spilled notebooks, school supplies scattered, the implied contrast of death and a new school year. They will seek out distraught classmates, packs of crying-girls, clutching-girls, crawling-all-over-each-other-suckling-at-grief girls. They will get the boyfriends to talk, the parents to talk; they will have for us the complete drama, the house-to-house echo of all three blasts, before the week is through.

We watch our life on every channel. We turn to CNN for a top-of-the-hour translation of our world. Maybe English will make it more real.

It does not help. There is my café. There is my cash machine. There is the tree I wait by when there is waiting to be done.

"Would you recognize your own bedroom," I say, "if you saw it on TV?"

---

[1] Sect of Orthodox Jews who follow the Mosaic law strictly.

35   Inbar makes phone calls, receives phone calls, while I sit and watch the news. A constant cycle of the same story, little bits added each time. The phone calls remind me of America. The news, of America. Like snow days. Hovering around the radio in the morning. A chain list of calls. "Good morning, Mrs. Gold. It's Nathan, speaking. Please tell Beth that school is closed because the buses can't come." The absurdity of the change. Years and miles. A different sort of weather. "Yes, hello Udi. It's Inbar. Another attack. Natan and I are fine."

Inbar tells me Israeli things, shares maxims on fate and luck. "We cannot live in fear," she says. "Of course you're terrified, it's terror after all." She has nonsensical statistics as well. "Five times more likely to be run over. Ten times more likely to die in a car. But you still cross the street don't you?"

She rubs my neck. Slips a hand under my shirt and rubs my back.

"Maybe I shouldn't," I say. A kiss on my ear. A switch of the channel. "Maybe it's time the street crossing stopped."

A biblical Israel, crowded with warriors and prophets, fallen kings and common men conscripted to do God's will. An American boy's Israel. A child raised up on causality and symbol.

40   Holocaust as wrath of God.

Israel the Phoenix rising up from the ashes.

The reporters trot out the odd survivors, the death defiers and nine lived. A girl with a small scratch on her cheek who stood two feet from the bomber, everyone around her dead. An old man with shrapnel buried in the hardcover book he was reading who survived the exact same way when the street blew up fifty years before. A clipping. He searches his wallet for a clipping he always takes with him.

They make themselves known after every tragedy. Serial survivors. People who find themselves on exploding buses but never seem to die.

"Augurs," I say. "Harbingers of doom. They are demons. Dybbuks. We should march to their houses. Drag them to the squares and burn them in front of cheering crowds."

45   "You are stupid with nerves," Inbar says. "They are the unluckiest lucky people in the world. These are hopeful stories from hopeless times. Without them the grief of this nation would tip it into the sea."

I'm swollen with heroism. The sad fact of it. Curled up on the bathroom floor woozy with the makings for a bold rescue, overdosed on my own life-or-death acumen. My body exorcises its charger of burning buildings, its icy-waters diver. The unused hero driven out while I wait patiently inside.

The chandelier, like a pendulum; the day, like a pendulum, swings.

Inbar will turn the corner in her apartment and find her American boyfriend pinned to the floor, immobile, sweating a malarial sweat.

She will discover him suffering the bystander's disease. She'll want to wrap him in a blanket, put him in a cab, and take him to the hospital where all the uninjured victims, the unhurt, uninvolved victims, trickle in for the empty beds, to be placed on the cots in the halls.

50   I do not want the hospital. Do not want treatment for having sat down after, for having sipped coffee after, and held on to the owner's hand.

A call home. Inbar dials the moment she thinks I can pull off a passable calm. My mother's secretary answers. Rita, who never says more than hello and "I'll get your mother." My phone calls precious because of the distance. As if I'm calling from the moon.

Today she is talking. Today Rita has something to share.

"Your mother is in her office crying. She don't say nothing to you, but that woman is miserable with you out in a war. Think about where you live, child. Think about your mom."

There is an element of struggle. Sex that night a matter of life and death. There is much scrambling for leverage and footing. Displays of body language that I've never known. We cling and dig in, as if striving for permanence, laboring for a union that won't come undone.
55 We laugh after. We cackle and roll around, reviewing technique and execution. Hysterical. Absurd. Perfect in its desperation. We make jokes at the expense of ourselves.

"No sex like near-death sex."

We light up a cigarette, naked, twisted up in the sheets. Again we would not recognize ourselves on TV.

Inbar has gone to work and invited Lynn over to make sure that I stay out of bed, that I go into town for coffee and sit at my café. Same time, same table, same cup, if I can manage it.

Nothing can be allowed to interrupt routine.
60 "Part of life here," Lynn says.

This is why Inbar invited her. She respects Lynn as an American with Israeli sensibilities. The hard-news photographer, moving in after every tragedy to shoot up what's left.

The peeper's peep, we call her. The voyeur's eye. Our Lynn, feeding the grumbling image-hungry bellies of America's commuter trains and breakfast nooks.

"A ghost," Lynn says. She is gloomy, but with a sportsman's muted excitement. "Peak invisibility. People moving right through me. I think I even went weightless at some point, pulled off impossible angles. Floated above the pack. My stuff is all over the wire this morning," She pops the top on a used film canister, tips its contents into her palm. "You've got to come out with me one day just for the experience. You can stand in the middle of a god-damn riot, people going down left and right. Arab kids tossing rocks, Molotov cocktails, Israelis firing back tear gas and rubber bullets. Chaos. And you move, you just slide right through it all like a fucking ghost, snatching up souls, freezing time. A boy in the air, his body arched, his face to the sky. He's lobbing back a gas canister, the smoke caught in a long snaking trail. Poetry. Yesterday, though. Yesterday was bad."

"I'm not made for this," I tell her. "I grew up in the suburbs. I own a hot-air popcorn popper. A selection of Mylec Air-Flo street hockey sticks."
65 "Two of these," she says, and drops two orange capsules in my tea. "Drink up." And I do. "Two before I shoot and two right after I dump the film. An image comes back to haunt me, I take another. The trapdoor in my system. If it gets to be too much, I'll just stay asleep. So to show my utter thankfulness upon waking, I make a pass of the Old City the next day. I stop in every quarter, pray at every place of worship I find. That's my secret, a flittingness. I favor no gods. Establish again and again my lack of allegiance.

"That's what keeps me invisible. That's how I get to walk through the heart of a conflict, to watch everything, to see and see and see, then pack up my images and walk away. In return, nothing. A ghost. Sensed but not seen. That's the whole trick.

"Staying alive," she says, "means never blinking and never taking sides."

"I didn't look, didn't want the dreams. I went the long way around so not to see."

"Unimportant. Not how you see, but the distance that counts. The simple fact of exposure to death. Same principle as radiation or chemotherapy. Exposure to all that death is what keeps you alive."
70 "I feel old from this," I say.

"Good," she says. "World-weary is good, just what you should be trying for. Go play the expatriate at your café. Go be the witty war-watching raconteur. Cock an eyebrow and have them spike your coffee. Ignore the weather and put on a big, heavy sweater. Pinch the waitress on her behind."

I was raised on tradition. Pictures of a hallowed Jerusalem nestled away like Eden. A Jerusalem so precious God spared it when he flooded the world.

I can guide you to the valley where David slew Goliath. Recite by heart the love songs written by Solomon, his son. There have been thirteen sieges and twenty downfalls. And I can lead you through the alleys of the Old City, tell you a story about each one.

This is my knowing. Dusty-book knowing. I thought I'd learned everything about Jerusalem only to discover my information was very very old.

75 I move through town, down the street of empty windows and blackened walls. The cobblestones are polished. Even the branches and rooftops have been picked clean. Every spot where a corpse lay is marked by candles. Fifty here, a hundred there. Temporary markers before monuments to come.

I make my way into the café. I nod at the owner, look at all the people out to display for the cameras, for each other, an ability to pass an afternoon at ease.

I sit at my table and order coffee. The waitress goes off to her machine. Cradling my chin, I wrestle images: unhinged mouths and clouds of smoke. Blasts like wild birds.

Today is a day to find religion. To decide that one god is more right than another, to uncover in this sad reality a covenant—some promise of coming good. There are signs if one looks. If one is willing to turn again to his old knowing, to salt over shoulders, prayers before journeys, wrists bound with holy red thread.

Witchery and superstition.

80 Comforts.

A boom that pushes air, that bears down and sweeps the room. My hair goes loose at the roots.

The others talk and eat. One lone woman stares off, page of a magazine held midturn.

"Fighter," the waitress says, watching, smiling, leaning up against the bar.

She's world-weary. Wise. The air force, obviously. The sound barrier broken.

85 I want to smile back at her. In fact, I want to be her. I concentrate, taking deep breaths, studying her style. Noting: How to lean against a bar full of knowing. Must master loud noises, sudden moves.

I reach for my coffee and rattle the cup, burn my fingers, pull my hand away.

The terrible shake trapped in my hands. Yesterday's sounds caught up in my head. I tap an ear, like a swimmer. A minor frequency problem, I'm sure. I've picked up on the congenital ringing in Jerusalem's ears.

The waitress deals with me in a waitress's way. She serves me a big round-headed muffin, poppy seeds trapped in the glaze. The on-the-house offer, a bartering of sorts. Here's a little kindness; now don't lose your mind.

Anchors. Symbols. The owner appears next to me, rubbing my arm. "Round foods are good for mourning," I say. "They symbolize eternity and the unbreakable cycles of life." I point with my free hand. "Cracks in the windows are good too. Each one means another demon has gone."

90 He smiles, as if to say, That's the spirit, and adds one of his own.

"A chip in your mug," he says. "In my family it means good things to come. And from the looks of my kitchen, this place will soon be overflowing with luck."

The waitress pushes the muffin toward me, as if I'd forgotten it was served.

But it's not a day for accepting kindness. Inbar has warned me, Stick with routine. Lynn has warned me, Don't blink your eyes.

And even this place has its own history of warnings. One set accompanying its every destruction and another tied to each rise. The balance that keeps the land from tipping. The traps that cost paradise and freedom, that turn second sons to firstborn. A litany of unburning bushes and smote rocks.

95 A legion of covenants sealed by food and by fire. Sacrifice after sacrifice. I free myself from the owner's hand and run through the biblical models.

Never take a bite out of curiosity.

Never trade your good name out of hunger.

And even if a public bombing strikes you in a private way, hide that from everyone lest you be called out to lead them.

JESSICA HAGEDORN

Jessica Hagedorn (1949–) was born in Manila in the Philippines, moved to the United States in the 1960s, and now resides in New York City. Hagedorn has published three books of poetry, three novels, and has written or edited several other works, including Charlie Chan Is Dead: An Anthology of Contemporary Asian American Fiction *(1993). In 1983 she won the National Book Award and the Before Columbus Foundation Award for her collection of poems,* Pet Food and Tropical Apparitions *(1981). In her writing, Hagedorn confronts disturbing subjects, many of which relate to her life in the Philippines or her experiences as an Asian American. "The Song of Bullets" is taken from her poetry collection,* Danger and Beauty *(1993).*

1993

THE SONG OF BULLETS

   Formalized
   by middle age
   we avoid crowds
   but still
5 love music.

   Day after day
   with less surprise
   we sit
   in apartments
10 and count
   the dead.

   Awake,
   my daughter croons
   her sudden cries
15 and growls

my new language.
While she sleeps
we memorize
a list of casualties:

20 The photographer's brother
the doctor is missing.
Or I could say:
"Victor's brother Oscar
has been gone for two years . . .
25 It's easier for the family
to think of him dead."

Victor sends
a Christmas card
from El Salvador:
30 "Things still the same."

And there are others
who don't play
by the rules—
someone else's brother
35 perhaps mine
languishes in a hospital;
everyone's grown tired
of his nightmares
and pretends
40 he's not there.

Someone else's father
perhaps mine
will be executed
when the time comes.
45 Someone else's mother
perhaps mine
telephones incessantly
her husband is absent
her son has gone mad
50 her lover has committed suicide
she's a survivor
who can't appreciate
herself.

The sight
55 of my daughter's
pink and luscious flesh
undoes me.
I fight
my weakening rage

60 I must remember
to commit
those names to memory
and stay angry.

Friends send postcards:
65 "Alternating between hectic
social Manila life & rural wonders
of Sagata[1] . . . on to Hongkong and Bangkok—
Love . . ."

Assassins cruise the streets
70 in obtrusive limousines
sunbathers idle
on the beach

War is predicted
in five years
75 ten years
any day now
I always thought
it was already happening

snipers and poets locked
80 in a secret embrace
the country
my child may never see

a heritage
of women in heat
85 and men
skilled at betrayal

dancing
to the song
of bullets.

CAROLYN FORCHÉ

Carolyn Forché (1950–   ) was born in Detroit, Michigan. She attended Michigan State University and Bowling Green State University. Her publications include the volumes of poetry Gathering the Tribes *(1976), which won the Yale University Younger Poets Award;* The Country Between Us *(1981), which was named the Lamont Selection of the Academy of American Poets;* The Angel of History *(1994), and* Blue Hour *(2003). Forché lived in El Salvador from 1978 to*

---

[1] Area with caves in the Philippines.

1980, working as a journalist and human rights activist, and she has translated the works of Salvadoran poets. She has edited an anthology of poetry of witness: Against Forgetting *(1993).*

1981

THE COLONEL

What you have heard is true. I was in his house. His wife carried a tray of coffee and sugar. His daughter filed her nails, his son went out for the night. There were daily papers, pet dogs, a pistol on the cushion beside him. The moon swung bare on its black cord over the house. On the television was a cop show. It was in English. Broken bottles were embedded in the walls around the house to scoop the kneecaps from a man's legs or cut his hands to lace. On the windows there were gratings like those in liquor stores. We had dinner, rack of lamb, good wine, a gold bell was on the table for calling the maid. The maid brought green mangoes, salt, a type of bread. I was asked how I enjoyed the country. There was a brief commercial in Spanish. His wife took everything away. There was some talk then of how difficult it had become to govern. The parrot said hello on the terrace. The colonel told it to shut up, and pushed himself from the table. My friend said to me with his eyes: say nothing. The colonel returned with a sack used to bring groceries home. He spilled many human ears on the table. They were like dried peach halves. There is no other way to say this. He took one of them in his hands, shook it in our faces, dropped it into a water glass. It came alive there. I am tired of fooling around he said. As for the rights of anyone, tell your people they can go fuck themselves. He swept the ears to the floor with his arm and held the last of his wine in the air. Something for your poetry, no? he said. Some of the ears on the floor caught this scrap of his voice. Some of the ears on the floor were pressed to the ground.

CAROLYN FORCHÉ

2003

PRAYER

Begin again among the poorest, moments off, in another time and place.
Belongings gathered in the last hour, visible invisible:
Tin spoon, teacup, tremble of tray, carpet hanging from sorrow's balcony.
Say goodbye to everything. With a wave of your hand, gesture to all you
    have known.
5 Begin with bread torn from bread, beans given to the hungriest, a carcass
    of flies.
Take the polished stillness from a locked church, prayer notes left
    between stones.
Answer them and hoist in your net voices from the troubled hours.
Sleep only when the least among them sleeps, and then only until the
    birds.
Make the flatbed truck your time and place. Make the least daily wage
    your value.
10 Language will rise then like language from the mouth of a still river. No
    one's mouth.
Bring night to your imaginings. Bring the darkest passage of your holy
    book.

Laura Blumenfeld

Laura Blumenfeld (1964–   ) received a Master's degree in International Affairs from Colum-bia University. Since 1992 she has been a journalist for The Washington Post *and has con-tributed articles to periodicals such as* The New Yorker, The New York Times Magazine, *and the* Los Angeles Times. *The complete story of Blumenfeld's encounter with the Palestinian terrorist who shot her father is memorialized in her autobiographical work,* Revenge: A Story of Hope *(2002).*

2002

THE APOLOGY: LETTERS FROM A TERRORIST

The gunman was not at home. "Come in," his mother said. "Would you like some orange soda?" My knocking must have shaken her out of a nap; she was wearing slip-pers and a pink embroidered bathrobe. Inside, the living room was full of family members, young and old.

"That's him," the woman said, pointing over her grandchildren's heads to the gunman's photograph. "He tried to kill someone," she said in an easy voice.

"Who?" I asked.

"Some Jew," said a boy, who appeared to be about twelve years old. He smiled crookedly, and added, "I don't know who—a Mossad agent.[1]

5   "I'm not sure he was a Mossad agent," a man who introduced himself as Saed, the gun-man's older brother, said. "He was a person from the outside—a leader from New York. We heard he was doing something against Palestinians. Why else would they choose him to be shot?"

"Why did he fire only once?" I asked.

"It was in the marketplace," Saed said.

"After the shooting, he threw the gun in the air, and it fell to the ground," his mother said. She began to chuckle and the others joined in.

The attack had taken place in the early spring of 1986. It had been a quiet time in Jerusalem: people could walk through the Old City without fear. In March, all that changed when Palestinian terrorists began gunning down foreign tourists—Americans, British, Ger-mans. Their first target was an American man; he had been shot as he strolled through the Arab market shortly after sundown. The gunman had aimed a little too high, and the bullet had grazed his scalp.

10   Twelve years later, I arrived in Israel for an extended honeymoon with my husband. While he did part-time legal work, I took a leave of absence from my job at the *Washington Post* to do research for a book about the culture of vengeance—the thirst for settling scores which has created so much turmoil in the Middle East and throughout the world. My re-search took me to Albania, Sicily, Iran, and other countries; between trips I looked for the gunman who had shot the American in the market. From records in the Jerusalem District Attorney's office, I learned that several Palestinians in a pro-Syria breakaway faction of the Palestine Liberation Organization had been convicted in 1986 for the shooting of foreigners. The man who had shot the American was named Omar Khatib. He had been tried and con-victed in an Israeli court, and was now serving a sentence of twenty-five years in Shikma Prison, in Ashkelon.

---

[1] Intelligence agency in Israel.

The Khatibs lived in the West Bank, in the last house on a narrow, rutted lane, which ended at a limestone quarry. Trash and rusty appliances spilled over the precipice. Their house, which was behind a red gate, was really a number of buildings joined together—cement improvisations with raw concrete steps and half-stacked cinder blocks. In rudimentary Arabic, I introduced myself as an American journalist.

"Why did he do it?" I asked the gunman's father, a tall, bony man in a gray robe.

The father's response was terse. "He did his duty," he said. "Every Palestinian must do it. Then there will be justice."

Another brother of the gunman came into the room. He introduced himself as Imad. His mustache and goatee were dyed burnt orange, and he was wearing a silly red-and-black shirt. He told me that he had been a member of the Popular Front for the Liberation of Palestine, a radical faction of the P.L.O., and that he had returned to Palestine, after twenty-five years of exile in Jordan, in 1994, the summer after the Israelis and the Palestinians signed the Oslo peace accords. "Anybody would do what my brother did under those circumstances," he said. "If you pretend to be a Palestinian for five minutes, you'll feel what we feel."

15   "And what about the man he tried to kill?" I asked.

"It wasn't a personal vendetta," Imad replied. "It was public relations. It was like telling the media to pay attention to us."

"Won't someone from the victim's family kill one of your people?" I asked.

"My brother never met the man," Imad said. "Nothing personal, so no revenge."

For me, however, the shooting was personal. The man whom Imad's brother had tried to kill was my father.

20   In March of 1986, when I was an undergraduate at Harvard, my father, in his capacity as executive director of the New York Holocaust Memorial Commission, went to Israel to look at the country's various Holocaust museums. One evening, after a visit to the Western Wall,[2] in Jerusalem, one of the Holy Land's most sacred sites, he was walking back to his hotel when he was shot by an unseen assailant. He was treated for the head wound in an Israeli hospital, and the story of the shooting made front-page news.

"Did you ever wonder who the gunman was or what he looked like?" I later asked my father. "I never thought about it," he replied. But, for me, putting the incident out of my mind wasn't so easy. I understood that people who commit acts of terrorism are less concerned with what happens to their victims than with advancing their cause, but I had resolved to find a way to make my father human in the gunman's eyes. And I wanted him to see that what he had done was horrible. I thought about introducing myself as the daughter of his victim but discarded the idea, because I did not want him to regard me as "a Jew" or as an adversary. Given the Palestinians' eagerness to get their views out to the world, I reasoned that the best way to gain access to him would be to identify myself to him and his family simply as an American journalist who was interested in hearing his story.

Several weeks after I met Omar's family, I went back to their house to return some clippings about the shooting which they had given me to photocopy. I was greeted by Omar's mother and his brother Imad, and led to an upstairs bedroom. We sat down on the couch where Omar had slept before his imprisonment.

---

[2] The most sacred and holy place in the Jewish religion, the Western Wall in the Old City of Jerusalem is the remaining section of the Temple Mount, which has remained intact since 70 C.E., the destruction of the Second Jerusalem Temple.

"His head was here, his feet were here," his mother said, brushing the upholstery with her fingers. She brought out a black attaché case and opened it. Inside was a karate manual, a picture of Omar in martial-arts dress, executing a kick, and a black-belt certificate that he had won in 1979. The picture showed a slim young man with an angry expression on his face. There was also a copy of the Koran, a book entitled "Theories About Revolution and National Liberation," and a copy of "Measure for Measure."[3]

"He was at Bethlehem University, studying English," Imad pointed out.

25   "And business, too," his mother said. "He got a ninety-five in public relations."

I was shown Omar's report cards, his birth certificate from a hospital on the Mount of Olives, and a high-school certificate of graduation that read, "The school administration certifies that Mr. Omar Kamel Said Al Khatib was a student in 1980–81. His conduct was very good." Before saying goodbye, Imad offered to take a letter from me to his brother in prison. Only immediate relatives were allowed contact with such prisoners, but Imad agreed to deliver whatever I wanted to write.

In my first letter to Omar, I explained that I was an American journalist who was writing a book about the region, and that I was curious about his life in an Israeli prison. I asked him about his hobbies and his plans for the future. At the end of the letter, I wrote, "And finally, I would like to hear about the events that led to your arrest. What happened? When you think back on it, what were your feelings then? How do you feel about it today?"

Six weeks later, Omar wrote back, in an intricate light-blue scrawl, on eight sheets of tissue paper:

Dear Laura,

I would like first to extend my appreciation and regard for your message, which I have read with interest and care. This is not a dream, but a real fact we are seeking to incarnate on land through the long march of our revolution and in accordance with rules of justice and equality and the right of people to liberate their lands, this sacred right which was secured by international law. We, as sons to this people, and part of its past and present, have on our shoulders the burden of holding the difficulty of the liberation road; it's our mission to let the rifles live.

I would like you to know that our choice in the military struggle is a legitimate choice on a historical basis that takes into account the fact that the enemy we are facing is one who stands on a Zionist ideology that is racist in its basis and fascist in its aims and means. It is an enemy with a huge military destructive machine higher in its ability than any other superpower state. It's an enemy that can be faced and defeated only by force. . . .

There is a huge difference, my dear, between "terror" and the right of self-determination, between a criminal and a revolutionary. . . . It is hard for us, as prisoners, to accept a peace process which does not answer all the questions that the Israeli/Palestinian conflict has raised. We continue in our efforts to affect what is going on outside the walls of our prisons.

Sincerely,
Omar Kamel Al Khatib

---

[3] The sacred writing of Islam revealed by God to the prophet Muhannad; *Measure for Measure*, a Shakespeare play.

The letter read more like a manifesto than like an exchange between two people. I wanted to know Omar as he really was, beneath the layers of ideology, and the next day I wrote to him again and inquired about what he was currently reading, what he could tell me about his family's history, and what, in particular, had inflamed his feelings against Israel.

30   A month later, he replied:

> I love English literature, and have been reading it from the first years of my imprisonment; lately I have dedicated my time to the reading of theoretical and philosophical books. . . . I have read the works of Tolstoy and Dostoevsky. I do suggest that you read Dostoevsky's "Memoirs from the House of the Dead"; it will help you in the work you are conducting.

> My chances of being released now are big because of my deteriorating health conditions. I suffer from asthma, an illness which puts me very near death. I'm living in unhealthy conditions, with ten of my friends in a small, cold cell very full of humidity. They smoke, cook, and do all their daily activities, which brings me a hard time. You can't imagine how it feels when you find yourself being chased even by the breath you breathe.

> I don't know if the Israelis consider me as "having blood on my hands," but I do know that there is no meaning in keeping me in prison after more than 13 years. The term "blood on their hands" is a bad term I do not like to hear. It is a racist term used to fulfill some political purpose aimed to distort our identity as freedom fighters.

He went on to say that he had been "chosen" to join the rebel Abu Musa faction of the Palestine Liberation Organization in 1985, with orders to "create a state of unrest," whose objective was to put an end to Israel's occupation of Palestine.

> I was young at that time, but since then I have discovered that violence is not in my personality. Maybe this is the answer to your question of why I shot just one shot at that man, despite the fact that my pistol was very full of bullets.

When Israel became a state, in 1948, Omar said, his mother's family had been forced to leave their home in Jaffa and migrate to Lebanon. Omar's father was born in the West Bank, but after his marriage to Omar's mother he had gone to live in Jerusalem, where the couple had brought up their children.

He continued:

> This city has shaped my identity; she planted in my mind unforgettable memories. I witnessed the Israeli aggression of the Six-Day War. I was four years old then, but enough aware to understand what was going on. I remember when my mother used to hide us with the rest of our neighbors who came to have shelter in our small room. We were so frightened by the darkness and the sound of guns. Six days, and the history entered into a new stage, the stage of the occupation.

> The resistance movement began, and at the end of the '60s my brother was arrested and sent to prison. . . . I saw the painful time that my family went through, searching to know the fate of my brother. I remember visiting him with my mother once or twice, but after that he was expelled to Jordan. . . . There he was sent to prison for no reason but under the pretext of crossing the borders illegally.

> We were such a poor family at the time, we didn't have enough money to eat. . . . I will never forget the exhaustion and pain of the journey when I accompanied my mother to visit my

brother. . . . Do you know when I saw [my brother] next?! It was 25 years later. This time I was the prisoner, and he was the visitor. After the signing of the Oslo agreement he got the chance to return to his home land. He came to visit me at Ashkelon prison. It was a very sad meeting, we both couldn't stop crying. I had no words to say, I had forgotten everything, but felt the need of touching him, and kissing him.

For all its self-justifying tone, the letter was more candid on a personal level, and in my reply I asked Omar to describe how he had felt when he shot the man in the marketplace. I also asked him what he would say to the man if the two of them were to meet again. In his next two letters, he dwelled on the hardships of prison life and the satisfaction he felt in taking a college correspondence course. He said that he had learned French and Hebrew, and that he had written a book of grammar for his fellow-prisoners entitled "The Practical Use of English Structure." He said that he had six more courses to complete before earning his B.A.

35   In my next letter, I again asked Omar why he had shot the American tourist. Omar wrote back:

With regard to David Blumenfeld—I hope he can understand the reasons behind my act. If I were him I would. I have thought a lot about meeting him one day. We have been in a state of war, and now we are passing through a new stage of historical reconciliation where there is no place for hatred and detestation. In this new era and atmosphere, he is welcome to be my guest in Jerusalem.

The letter hinted that Omar was capable of remorse, though an earlier reference to my father as a "chosen military site" had made me wince. And Omar's lofty talk about "historical reconciliation" made me wonder whether we were both involved in an elaborate game of manipulation, each for a different purpose. To give him a better sense of David Blumenfeld, I replied that I had contacted David, and discovered that his grandparents had been killed in the Holocaust, and that he had come to Israel to gather material for building a Holocaust museum in New York. I told him that David was not hostile to the Palestinian cause but that he was concerned about whether Omar would ever again resort to violence against anyone, innocent or not. Omar began his next letter with an account of an examination that he had undergone for his asthma, in the hope of winning a release from prison on medical grounds:

When the van stopped in front of Ramallah hospital, it was as if I were an alien from another world. Each of the guards took his place around my vehicle. Guns were ready for use. The door was opened, and all around me I saw people looking at me strangely. I touched the ground with slow steps because my hands and legs were tied. I took a deep breath and looked at the sky, feeling the need to fly. . . . And all the people looked at me with pity and wonder because of my weak appearance.

They led me to an elevator to the main section of the testing area. We waited till a very beautiful Moroccan girl came to lead us to the examination room. I introduced myself to her and spoke with her a little about the prison while she conducted the test three times. She was shocked to see the bad test results.

In his next letter, he wrote:

Back to David, I do admire his talking to you and I appreciate his understanding, his support for my people. If these feelings are really from the depth of his heart, this may contribute a lot to our friendship. Of course, my answer to his question [about committing an act of violence again] is NO.

∞

A few weeks later, I learned that the parole board had rejected Omar's petition for release. Two months later, his petition came up again, on appeal to a higher court. I asked Imad if I could attend the hearing, and he agreed.

The courtroom was packed with defendants and their families—Israelis and Palestinians together on the benches. Omar's mother and his brother Imad were there, along with nine other relatives. I took a seat directly in front of them. Three judges filed into the room, and finally Omar arrived. Although he was in ankle chains, his entrance was triumphant. He greeted the other prisoners effusively, shaking their hands and clapping them on the back. And yet the effects of his incarceration were visible: the skin on his face was so taut that his cheekbones cast a skeletal shadow under his eyes; there was a noticeable swelling around his mouth. His mother rushed over to him and kissed him. Imad ruffled his hair. Then Imad pointed to me. "Laura is here," he said.

40   "Laura!" Omar said, smiling. "I hoped to meet you one day, but not in this setting." I couldn't keep my hands from shaking as I smiled back.

"I need to know if you're sorry," I said.

"I will write David a long letter," he said.

"No, I need to know now," I said. For a moment our eyes met, and then a court officer led him away.

Several hours passed before Omar's lawyer, an energetic Israeli woman, presented the case to the judges. They listened to the details of Omar's asthma, and then gave orders for the petition to be sent back to the medical-parole committee for further review. As Omar and his family got up to leave, I realized that this was my last chance to confront him. I stood up and said, "I am David Blumenfeld's daughter, Laura Blumenfeld." For a moment, Omar and his family stared at me. Then Omar's mother, Imad, and several other relatives began to weep. I tried to explain why I had concealed my identity for so long. "I did it for one reason," I said. "This conflict is between human beings, and not between disembodied Arabs and Jews. And we're people. Not military targets. We're people with families." I turned to Omar. He looked stunned. "You promised me you would never hurt anyone again," I said. He looked at me and said nothing. As he was led away, his family rushed over to embrace me.

45   A few weeks later, I received another letter from Omar:

A week has passed since the day of the hearing, and all that is in my mind and imagination is the picture of you standing in front of the court, and the echo of your voice.

You made me feel so stupid that once I was the cause of your and your kind mother's pain. Sorry and please understand.

Of course I was shocked to learn that you are David's daughter. I didn't sleep for almost two days. I reread all your precious letters trying to rearrange the whole puzzle again.

∞

My stay in Israel was nearly over. Before leaving for America, I visited Omar's family one last time. The house was full of people, and in honor of my departure Omar's mother had laid out plates of vegetables, bread, and cheese. Arabic music was coming from a tape player, and several of the women and children invited me to dance with them. Imad presented me with gifts from Omar—two gold necklaces, one for me and one for my father, with Omar's name inscribed on it. I felt unsure of this display of warmth: only a short while ago, these same people had condoned the attempted killing of my father, as they might condone other attacks on innocent bystanders in their struggle with Israel, if the fragile peace process broke down.

A few weeks after I had returned to America, my father received a letter from Omar that I have read many times since, in the hope that its sentiments are genuine:

> *Dear David,*
>
> *Thirteen years have passed. Yes, it's so late to come and ask you about your injuries, but I would like you to know that I've prayed a lot for you. I hope you are well today.*
>
> *I admit to having some good feeling toward you from the beginning, a feeling that made me hope to meet you one day. It seems to me that this good feeling is coming to be a reality. . . . I would like first to express to you my deep pain and sorrow for what I caused you. I've learned many things about you. You are supposed to be a very close friend to my people. I hope you believe that we both were victims of this long historical conflict. . . . Laura was the mirror that made me see your face as a human person deserving to be admired and respected. I apologize for not understanding her message from the beginning.*
>
> *If God helps and I get to be released, I hope you accept my invitation to be my guest in the holy city of peace, Jerusalem.*

PHILIP GOUREVITCH

Philip Gourevitch (1961–   ) was born in Philadelphia, raised in New England, and educated at Cornell University and Columbia University, where he received an M.F.A. in fiction writing. Although Gourevitch had intended to become a fiction writer, his first two books are nonfiction. We Wish to Inform You that Tomorrow We Will Be Killed with Our Families *(1998), Gourevitch's first and best-known work, is about the West's refusal to acknowledge and, thus, to prevent the genocide in Rwanda. Gourevitch has received eight awards for this work, including the National Book Club Critics Circle Award for general nonfiction (1999), the George Polk Book Award, the London* Guardian *Prize, and the* Los Angeles Times *Book Award.* We Wish to Inform You, *from which the following chapter is excerpted, tells the story of genocide through the voices of Rwandans who survived the crisis.*

1998

EXCERPT FROM *WE WISH TO INFORM YOU THAT TOMORROW WE WILL BE KILLED WITH OUR FAMILIES*

In the province of Kibungo, in eastern Rwanda, in the swamp- and pastureland near the Tanzanian border, there's a rocky hill called Nyarubuye with a church where many Tutsis were slaughtered in mid-April of 1994. A year after the killing I went to Nyarubuye with two Canadian military officers. We flew in a United Nations helicopter, traveling low over the hills in the morning mists, with the banana trees like green starbursts dense over the slopes. The uncut grass blew back as we dropped into the center of the parish schoolyard.

A lone soldier materialized with his Kalashnikov, and shook our hands with stiff, shy formality. The Canadians presented the paperwork for our visit, and I stepped up into the open doorway of a classroom.

At least fifty mostly decomposed cadavers covered the floor, wadded in clothing, their belongings strewn about and smashed. Macheted skulls had rolled here and there.

The dead looked like pictures of the dead. They did not smell. They did not buzz with flies. They had been killed thirteen months earlier, and they hadn't been moved. Skin stuck here and there over the bones, many of which lay scattered away from the bodies, dismembered by the killers, or by scavengers—birds, dogs, bugs. The more complete figures looked a lot like people, which they were once. A woman in a cloth wrap printed with flowers lay near the door. Her fleshless hip bones were high and her legs slightly spread, and a child's skeleton extended between them. Her torso was hollowed out. Her ribs and spinal column poked through the rotting cloth. Her head was tipped back and her mouth was open; a strange image—half agony, half repose.

I had never been among the dead before. What to do? Look? Yes. I wanted to see them, I suppose; I had come to see them—the dead had been left unburied at Nyarubuye for memorial purposes—and there they were, so intimately exposed. I didn't need to see them. I already knew, and believed, what had happened in Rwanda. Yet looking at the buildings and the bodies, and hearing the silence of the place, with the grand Italianate basilica standing there deserted, and beds of exquisite, decadent, death-fertilized flowers blooming over the corpses, it was still strangely unimaginable. I mean one still had to imagine it.

5   Those dead Rwandans will be with me forever, I expect. That was why I had felt compelled to come to Nyarubuye: to be stuck with them—not with their experience, but with the experience of looking at them. They had been killed there, and they were dead there. What else could you really see at first? The Bible bloated with rain lying on top of one corpse or, littered about, the little woven wreaths of thatch which Rwandan women wear as crowns to balance the enormous loads they carry on their heads, and the water gourds, and the Converse tennis sneaker stuck somehow in a pelvis.

The soldier with the Kalashnikov—Sergeant Francis of the Rwandese Patriotic Army, a Tutsi whose parents had fled to Uganda with him when he was a boy, after similar but less extensive massacres in the early 1960s, and who had fought his way home in 1994 and found it like this—said that the dead in this room were mostly women who had been raped before being murdered. Sergeant Francis had high, rolling girlish hips, and he walked and stood with his butt stuck out behind him, an oddly purposeful posture, tipped forward, driven. He was, at once, candid and briskly official. His English had the punctilious clip of military drill, and after he told me what I was looking at I looked instead at my feet. The rusty head of a hatchet lay beside them in the dirt.

A few weeks earlier, in Bukavu, Zaire, in the giant market of a refugee camp that was home to many Rwandan Hutu militiamen, I had watched a man butchering a cow with a machete. He was quite expert at his work, taking big precise strokes that made a sharp hacking noise. The rallying cry to the killers during the genocide was "Do your work!" And I saw that it *was* work, this butchery; hard work. It took many hacks—two, three, four, five, hard hacks—to chop through the cow's leg. How many hacks to dismember a person?

Considering the enormity of the task, it is tempting to play with theories of collective madness, mob mania, a fever of hatred erupted into a mass crime of passion, and to imagine the blind orgy of the mob, with each member killing one or two people. But at Nyarubuye, and at thousands of other sites in this tiny country, on the same days of a few months in 1994, hundreds of thousands of Hutus had worked as killers in regular shifts. There was always the next victim, and the next. What sustained them, beyond the frenzy of the first attack, through the plain physical exhaustion. and mess of it?

The pygmy in Gikongoro said that humanity is part of nature and that we must go against nature to get along and have peace. But mass violence, too, must be organized; it does not occur aimlessly. Even mobs and riots have a design, and great and sustained destruction requires great ambition. It must be conceived as the means toward achieving a new order, and although the idea behind that new order may be criminal and objectively very stupid, it must also be compellingly simple and at the same time absolute. The ideology of genocide is all of those things, and in Rwanda it went by the bald name of Hutu Power. For those who set about systematically exterminating an entire people—even a fairly small and unresisting subpopulation of perhaps a million and a quarter men, women, and children, like the Tutsis in Rwanda—blood lust surely helps. But the engineers and perpetrators of a slaughter like the one just inside the door where I stood need not enjoy killing, and they may even find it unpleasant. What is required above all is that they want their victims dead. They have to want it so badly that they consider it a necessity.

10   So I still had much to imagine as I entered the classroom and stepped carefully between the remains. These dead and their killers had been neighbors, schoolmates, colleagues, sometimes friends, even in-laws. The dead had seen their killers training as militias in the weeks before the end, and it was well known that they were training to kill Tutsis; it was announced on the radio, it was in the newspapers, people spoke of it openly. The week before the massacre at Nyarubuye, the killing began in Rwanda's capital, Kigali. Hutus who opposed the Hutu Power ideology were publicly denounced as "accomplices" of the Tutsis and were among the first to be killed as the extermination got under way. In Nyarubuye, when Tutsis asked the Hutu Power mayor how they might be spared, he suggested that they seek sanctuary at the church. They did, and a few days later the mayor came to kill them. He came at the head of a pack of soldiers, policemen, militiamen, and villagers; he gave out arms and orders to complete the job well. No more was required of the mayor, but he also was said to have killed a few Tutsis himself.

The killers killed all day at Nyarubuye. At night they cut the Achilles tendons of survivors and went off to feast behind the church, roasting cattle looted from their victims in big fires, and drinking beer. (Bottled beer, banana beer—Rwandans may not drink more beer than other Africans, but they drink prodigious quantities of it around the clock.) And, in the morning, still drunk after whatever sleep they could find beneath the cries of their prey, the killers at Nyarubuye went back and killed again. Day after day, minute to minute, Tutsi by Tutsi: all across Rwanda, they worked like that. "It was a process," Sergeant Francis said. I can see that it happened, I can be told how, and after nearly three years of looking around Rwanda and listening to Rwandans, I can tell you how, and I will. But the horror of it—the idiocy, the waste, the sheer wrongness—remains uncircumscribable.

Like Leontius, the young Athenian in Plato, I presume that you are reading this because you desire a closer look, and that you, too, are properly disturbed by your curiosity. Perhaps, in examining this extremity with me, you hope for some understanding, some insight, some flicker of self-knowledge—a moral, or a lesson, or a clue about how to behave in this world: some such information. I don't discount the possibility, but when it comes to genocide, you already know right from wrong. The best reason I have come up with for looking closely into Rwanda's stories is that ignoring them makes me even more uncomfortable about existence and my place in it. The horror, as horror, interests me only insofar as a precise memory of the offense is necessary to understand its legacy.

The dead at Nyarubuye were, I'm afraid, beautiful. There was no getting around it. The skeleton is a beautiful thing. The randomness of the fallen forms, the strange tranquillity of their rude exposure, the skull here, the arm bent in some uninterpretable gesture there—these things were beautiful, and their beauty only added to the affront of the place. I couldn't settle on any meaningful response: revulsion, alarm, sorrow, grief, shame, incomprehension, sure, but nothing truly meaningful. I just looked, and I took photographs, because I wondered whether I could really see what I was seeing while I saw it, and I wanted also an excuse to look a bit more closely.

We went on through the first room and out the far side. There was another room and another and another and another. They were all full of bodies, and more bodies were scattered in the grass, and there were stray skulls in the grass, which was thick and wonderfully green. Standing outside, I heard a crunch. The old Canadian colonel stumbled in front of me, and I saw, though he did not notice, that his foot had rolled on a skull and broken it. For the first time at Nyarubuye my feelings focused, and what I felt was a small but keen anger at this man. Then I heard another crunch, and felt a vibration underfoot. I had stepped on one, too.

15   Rwanda is spectacular to behold. Throughout its center, a winding succession of steep, tightly terraced slopes radiates out from small roadside settlements and solitary compounds. Gashes of red clay and black loam mark fresh hoe work; eucalyptus trees flash silver against brilliant green tea plantations; banana trees are everywhere. On the theme of hills, Rwanda produces countless variations: jagged rain forests, round-shouldered buttes, undulating moors, broad swells of savanna, volcanic peaks sharp as filed teeth. During the rainy season, the clouds are huge and low and fast, mists cling in highland hollows, lightning flickers through the nights, and by day the land is lustrous. After the rains, the skies lift, the terrain takes on a ragged look beneath the flat unvarying haze of the dry season, and in the savannas of the Akagera Park wildfire blackens the hills.

One day, when I was returning to Kigali from the south, the car mounted a rise between two winding valleys, the windshield filled with purple-bellied clouds, and I asked Joseph, the man who was giving me a ride, whether Rwandans realize what a beautiful country they have. "Beautiful?" he said. "You think so? After the things that happened here? The people aren't good. If the people were good, the country might be OK." Joseph told me that his brother and sister had been killed, and he made a soft hissing click with his tongue against his teeth. "The country is empty," he said. "Empty!"

It was not just the dead who were missing. The genocide had been brought to a halt by the Rwandese Patriotic Front, a rebel army led by Tutsi refugees from past persecutions, and as the RPF advanced through the country in the summer of 1994, some two million Hutus had fled into exile at the behest of the same leaders who had urged them to kill. Yet except in some rural areas in the south, where the desertion of Hutus had left nothing but bush to reclaim the fields around crumbling adobe houses, I, as a newcomer, could not see the emptiness that blinded Joseph to Rwanda's beauty. Yes, there were grenade-flattened buildings, burnt homesteads, shot-up facades, and mortar-pitted roads. But these were the ravages of war, not of genocide, and by the summer of 1995, most of the dead had been buried. Fifteen months earlier, Rwanda had been the most densely populated country in Africa. Now the work of the killers looked just as they had intended: invisible.

From time to time, mass graves were discovered and excavated, and the remains would be transferred to new, properly consecrated mass graves. Yet even the occasionally exposed bones, the conspicuous number of amputees and people with deforming scars, and the superabundance of packed orphanages could not be taken as evidence that what had happened to Rwanda was an attempt to eliminate a people. There were only people's stories.

"Every survivor wonders why he is alive," Abbé Modeste, a priest at the cathedral in Butare, Rwanda's second-largest city, told me. Abbé Modeste had hidden for weeks in his sacristy, eating communion wafers, before moving under the desk in his study, and finally into the rafters at the home of some neighboring nuns. The obvious explanation of his survival was that the RPF had come to the rescue. But the RPF didn't reach Butare till early July, and roughly seventy-five percent of the Tutsis in Rwanda had been killed by early May. In this regard, at least, the genocide had been entirely successful: to those who were targeted, it was not death but life that seemed an accident of fate.

20   "I had eighteen people killed at my house," said Etienne Niyonzima, a former business-man who had become a deputy in the National Assembly. "Everything was totally destroyed—a place of fifty-five meters by fifty meters. In my neighborhood they killed six hundred and forty-seven people. They tortured them, too. You had to see how they killed them. They had the number of everyone's house, and they went through with red paint and marked the homes of all the Tutsis and of the Hutu moderates. My wife was at a friend's, shot with two bullets. She is still alive, only"—he fell quiet for a moment—"she has no arms. The others with her were killed. The militia left her for dead. Her whole family of sixty-five in Gitarama were killed." Niyonzima was in hiding at the time. Only after he had been separated from his wife for three months did he learn that she and four of their children had survived. "Well," he said, "one son was cut in the head with a machete. I don't know where he went." His voice weak-ened, and caught. "He disappeared." Niyonzima clicked his tongue, and said, "But the others are still alive. Quite honestly, I don't understand at all how I was saved."

Laurent Nkongoli attributed his survival to "Providence, and also good neighbors, an old woman who said, 'Run away, we don't want to see your corpse.'" Nkongoli, a lawyer, who had become the vice president of the National Assembly after the genocide, was a ro-bust man, with a taste for double-breasted suit jackets and lively ties, and he moved, as he spoke, with a brisk determination. But before taking his neighbor's advice, and fleeing Kigali in late April of 1994, he said, "I had accepted death. At a certain moment this happens. One hopes not to die cruelly, but one expects to die anyway. Not death by machete, one hopes, but with a bullet. If you were willing to pay for it, you could often ask for a bullet. Death was more or less normal, a resignation. You lose the will to fight. There were four thousand Tutsis killed here at Kacyiru"—a neighborhood of Kigali. "The soldiers brought them here, and told them to sit down because they were going to throw grenades. And they sat.

"Rwandan culture is a culture of fear," Nkongoli went on. "I remember what people said." He adopted a pipey voice, and his face took on a look of disgust: " 'Just let us pray, then kill us,' or 'I don't want to die in the street, I want to die at home.' " He resumed his normal voice, "When you're that resigned and oppressed you're already dead. It shows the genocide was prepared for too long. I detest this fear. These victims of genocide had been psychologically prepared to expect death just for being Tutsi. They were being killed for so long that they were already dead."

I reminded Nkongoli that, for all of his hatred of fear, he had himself accepted death before his neighbor urged him to run away. "Yes," he said. "I got tired in the genocide. You struggle so long, then you get tired."

Every Rwandan I spoke with seemed to have a favorite, unanswerable question. For Nkongoli, it was how so many Tutsis had allowed themselves to be killed. For François Xavier Nkurunziza, a Kigali lawyer, whose father was Hutu and whose mother and wife were Tutsi, the question was how so many Hutus had allowed themselves to kill. Nkurunziza had escaped death only by chance as he moved around the country from one hiding place to an-other, and he had lost many family members. "Conformity is very deep, very developed here," he told me. "In Rwandan history, everyone obeys authority. People revere power, and there isn't enough education. You take a poor, ignorant population, and give them arms, and say, 'It's yours. Kill.' They'll obey. The peasants, who were paid or forced to kill, were looking up to people of higher socio-economic standing to see how to behave. So the people of influ-ence, or the big financiers, are often the big men in the genocide. They may think that they didn't kill because they didn't take life with their own hands, but the people were looking to them for their orders. And, in Rwanda, an order can be given very quietly."

25   As I traveled around the country, collecting accounts of the killing, it almost seemed as if, with the machete, the *masu*—a club studded with nails—a few well-placed grenades, and a few bursts of automatic rifle fire, the quiet orders of Hutu Power had made the neutron bomb obsolete.

"Everyone was called to hunt the enemy," said Theodore Nyilinkwaya, a survivor of the massacres in his home village of Kimbogo, in the southwestern province of Cyangugu. "But let's say someone is reluctant. Say that guy comes with a stick. They tell him, 'No, get a *masu*.' So, OK, he does, and he runs along with the rest, but he doesn't kill. They say, 'Hey, he might denounce us later. He must kill. Everyone must help to kill at least one person.' So this person who is not a killer is made to do it. And the next day it's become a game for him. You don't need to keep pushing him."

At Nyarubuye, even the little terracotta votive statues in the sacristy had been methodically decapitated. "They were associated with Tutsis," Sergeant Francis explained.[1]

■ EXPLORATIONS OF THE TEXT

1. In his "Brief History of Terrorism," Martin Walker states that "well into the twentieth century, terror usually meant state-sponsored terror," evoking images of Nazi Germany and the Soviet secret police. After World War II, however, terror tactics began to be used by such revolutionary groups as the National Liberation Front of Algeria and the Irish Republican army in Northern Ireland to promote their causes. He then contends that suicide bombers represent a third kind of terrorist group, "implacable new fanatics . . . who simply want to blow up the peace table along with everything else." After reading the works in this thematic cluster and considering Walker's categorization of terrorists, create your definition of terrorism. Use evidence from the works to support your points.

2. Explore the mindset of the terrorist or the fanatic as presented in selected works in this cluster. What are the similarities or the differences in these various states of mind?

3. How does terror differ from terrorism? Discuss the aftermath of terror as envisioned by several authors in this cluster. How are the main characters, for example, in Englander's "In This Way We Are Wise" and Mukherjee's "The Management of Grief," affected by terrorist acts?

4. After 9/11, we in the United States certainly live with a heightened sense of fear and vulnerability. How do several writers in this cluster portray the intrusions of terror into everyday life?

5. What do Luisa Valenzuela, Philip Gourevitch, Laura Blumenfeld, and Carolyn Forché present as antidotes to fanaticism?

6. Do any of the authors conceive of a possible resolution of tribal conflicts? Ethnic tensions? What do Blumenfeld and Gourevitch propose as alternatives to demonizing the enemy?

7. When we witness disaster, we often are left speechless. In many ways acts of terrorism are unimaginable. What techniques do several of the writers in this cluster use to portray inconceivable horror (e.g., use of descriptive detail, irony, imagery, etc.)? You also may examine the poems in the 9/11 cluster or the works dealing with the Holocaust.

■ THE READING/WRITING CONNECTION

1. Choose a passage from one of the readings that you find particularly meaningful. In a freewrite, respond to that passage.

---

[1] Between April and August of 1994, at least half a million Tutsis and moderate Hutus were killed in Rwanda.

2. Imagine a dialogue between the main characters in Englander's and Mukherjee's stories or between Laura Blumenfeld and Phillip Gourevitch about the aftermath of horror. You also may write letters or journal entries for the characters or narrators.

3. "Think" Topic: How does Englander use natural imagery to convey his vision of a society living with the constant threat of terrorist actions, with the knowledge of potential destruction?

4. Write a poem in response to one of the works in this cluster. You may start with one of the titles as your first line (e.g., "In this way we are wise . . .").

5. Create a memorial for someone you've lost or for those lost on 9/11 or in the Iraq War—or in another historical event, such as the explosion of the *Challenger* or the tsunami. Describe the design of your memorial and the reasons for your design.

■ IDEAS FOR WRITING

1. For Europeans who survived World War II, the destruction and carnage resulting from war became "natural law," according to Milosz in "American Ignorance of War." We have entered a new era in which the fact of terrorism has reshaped our visions of our world. How do several of the authors envision what has become "natural" in a society threatened by terrorism?

2. What are the human costs of terrorist actions?

3. Compare and contrast the responses by the characters to violence in Mukherjee's "The Management of Grief," Englander's "In This Way We Are Wise," and Hagedorn's "The Song of Bullets."

4. How do several of the writers treat the incomprehensibility of the terrorist act?

5. What do Mukherjee, Forché, and Blumenfeld propose as forces that could combat fanaticism? Do you agree with their positions?

6. In the aftermath of 9/11, acts of witnessing—acts of commemoration—have abounded. What do you learn about aesthetic techniques of witnessing from analyzing several works in this cluster? Explore the role of the writer as witness.

■ FICTION ■

LUIGI PIRANDELLO

Luigi Pirandello (1867–1936), born in Sicily, earned his doctorate in philology from Bonn University. A playwright, novelist, short story writer, essayist, and poet, he created "grotesco," the expressionist theater form that deals with the psychological realities underlying social appearances. Pirandello joined the Fascist party in 1924 and was patronized by Mussolini. He won the Nobel Prize for Literature in 1934. Pirandello wrote more than forty plays, including Six Characters in Search of an Author *(1921). He is famous as a playwright and as a writer of short stories.*

1939

WAR

The passengers who had left Rome by the night express had had to stop until dawn at the small station of Fabriano in order to continue their journey by the small old-fashioned local joining the main line with Sulmona.

At dawn, in a stuffy and smoky second-class carriage in which five people had already spent the night, a bulky woman in deep mourning was hoisted in—almost like a shapeless bundle. Behind her, puffing and moaning, followed her husband—a tiny man, thin and weakly, his face death-white, his eyes small and bright and looking shy and uneasy.

Having at last taken a seat he politely thanked the passengers who had helped his wife and who had made room for her; then he turned round to the woman trying to pull down the collar of her coat, and politely inquired:

"Are you all right, dear?"

5   The wife, instead of answering, pulled up her collar again to her eyes, so as to hide her face.

"Nasty world," muttered the husband with a sad smile.

And he felt it his duty to explain to his traveling companions that the poor woman was to be pitied, for the war was taking away from her her only son, a boy of twenty to whom both had devoted their entire life, even breaking up their home at Sulmona to follow him to Rome, where he had to go as a student, then allowing him to volunteer for war with an assurance, however, that at least for six months he would not be sent to the front and now, all of a sudden, receiving a wire saying that he was due to leave in three days' time and asking them to go and see him off.

The woman under the big coat was twisting and wriggling, at times growling like a wild animal, feeling certain that all those explanations would not have aroused even a shadow of sympathy from those people who—most likely—were in the same plight as herself. One of them, who had been listening with particular attention, said:

"You should thank God that your son is only leaving now for the front. Mine has been sent there the first day of the war. He has already come back twice wounded and been sent back again to the front."

10   "What about me? I have two sons and three nephews at the front," said another passenger.

"Maybe, but in our case it is our *only* son," ventured the husband.

"What difference can it make? You may spoil your only son with excessive attentions, but you cannot love him more than you would all your other children if you had any. Paternal love is not like bread that can be broken into pieces and split amongst the children in equal shares. A father gives *all* his love to each one of his children without discrimination, whether it be one or ten, and if I am suffering now for my two sons, I am not suffering half for each of them but double . . ."

"True . . . true . . ." sighed the embarrassed husband, "but suppose (of course we all hope it will never be your case) a father has two sons at the front and he loses one of them, there is still one left to console him . . . while . . ."

"Yes," answered the other, getting cross, "a son left to console him but also a son left for whom he must survive, while in the case of the father of an only son if the son dies the father can die too and put an end to his distress. Which of the two positions is the worse? Don't you see how my case would be worse than yours?"

15   "Nonsense," interrupted another traveler, a fat, red-faced man with blood-shot eyes of the palest gray.

He was panting. From his bulging eyes seemed to spurt inner violence of an uncontrolled vitality which his weakened body could hardly contain.

"Nonsense," he repeated, trying to cover his mouth with his hand so as to hide the two missing front teeth. "Nonsense. Do we give life to our children for our own benefit?"

The other travelers stared at him in distress. The one who had had his son at the front since the first day of the war sighed: "You are right. Our children do not belong to us, they belong to the Country. . . . "

"Bosh," retorted the fat traveler. "Do we think of the Country when we give life to our children? Our sons are born because . . . well, because they must be born and when they come to life they take our own life with them. This is the truth. We belong to them but they never belong to us. And when they reach twenty they are exactly what we were at their age. We too had a father and mother, but there were so many other things as well . . . girls, cigarettes, illusions, new ties . . . and the Country, of course, whose call we would have answered when we were twenty—even if father and mother had said no. Now at our age, the love of our Country is still great, of course, but stronger than it is the love for our children. Is there any one of us here who wouldn't gladly take his son's place at the front if he could?"

20   There was a silence all round, everybody nodding as to approve.

"Why then," continued the fat man, "shouldn't we consider the feelings of our children when they are twenty? Isn't it natural that at their age they should consider the love for their Country (I am speaking of decent boys, of course) even greater than the love for us? Isn't it natural that it should be so, as after all they must look upon us as upon old boys who cannot move any more and must stay at home? If Country exists, if Country is a natural necessity, like bread, of which each of us must eat in order not to die of hunger, somebody must go to defend it. And our sons go, when they are twenty, and they don't want tears, because if they die, they die inflamed and happy (I am speaking, of course, of decent boys). Now, if one dies young and happy, without having the ugly sides of life, the boredom of it, the pettiness, the bitterness of disillusion . . . what more can we ask for him? Everyone should stop crying; everyone should laugh, as I do . . . or at least thank God—as I do—because my son, before dying, sent me a message saying that he was dying satisfied at having ended his life in the best way he could have wished. That is why, as you see, I do not even wear mourning. . . ."

He shook his light fawn coat as to show it; his livid lip over his missing teeth was trembling, his eyes were watery and motionless, and soon after he ended with a shrill laugh which might well have been a sob.

"Quite so . . . quite so . . ." agreed the others.

The woman who, bundled in a corner under her coat, had been sitting and listening had—for the last three months—tried to find in the words of her husband and her friends something to console her in her deep sorrow, something that might show her how a mother should resign herself to send her son not even to death but to a probably dangerous life. Yet not a word had she found amongst the many which had been said . . . and her grief had been greater in seeing that nobody—as she thought—could share her feelings.

25   But now the words of the traveler amazed and almost stunned her. She suddenly realized that it wasn't the others who were wrong and could not understand her but herself who could not rise up to the same height of those fathers and mothers willing to resign themselves, without crying, not only to the departure of their sons but even to their death.

She lifted her head, she bent over from her corner trying to listen with great attention to the details which the fat man was giving to his companions about the way his son had fallen as a hero, for his King and his Country, happy and without regrets. It seemed to her that she had stumbled into a world she had never dreamt of, a world so far unknown to her and she was so pleased to hear everyone joining in congratulating that brave father who could so stoically speak of his child's death.

Then suddenly, just as if she had heard nothing of what had been said and almost as if waking up from a dream, she turned to the old man, asking him:

"Then . . . is your son really dead?"

Everybody stared at her. The old man, too, turned to look at her, fixing his great, bulging, horribly watery light gray eyes, deep in her face. For some little time he tried to answer, but words failed him. He looked and looked at her, almost as if only then—at that silly, incongruous question—he had suddenly realized at last that his son was really dead—gone for ever—for ever. His face contracted, became horribly distorted, then he snatched in haste a handkerchief from his pocket and, to the amazement of everyone, broke into harrowing, heart-rending, uncontrollable sobs.

■ **EXPLORATIONS OF THE TEXT**
1. Discuss the function and effectiveness of the night train as a setting for the story.
2. Describe each of the passengers. What do their physical and emotional traits reveal about their attitudes toward war?
3. Analyze the conversation between the "husband" and the father with two sons. What do you conclude?
4. Why is "the fat man's" speech about love of country so compelling and persuasive? How does his appearance at the end of his speech foreshadow the conclusion of the story?
5. The grieving mother begins to feel "amazed" and "stunned." What is the source of her question: "Then . . . is your son really dead?"
6. What happens to "the fat man"? What is the meaning of his insight?
7. Consider the economy of Pirandello's style. What do you learn about the value of concise and terse writing?
8. Compare the themes of this story with those in works by O'Brien, Milosz, Ozick, Endō, and/or Delbo.

■ **THE READING/WRITING CONNECTION**
1. What reasons compel "decent" young people to go to war? Would you go to war?
2. "Think" Topic: Why does "the fat man" rationalize his son's death?
3. Assume that you are about to become a soldier. Write a journal entry about your position on war.

■ **IDEAS FOR WRITING**
1. Explore the concept of the train journey. What does Pirandello accomplish with this setting?
2. Compare Hemingway's and Pirandello's styles.
3. Analyze the character of "the fat man."
4. Do young people feel more patriotic and bellicose than older people?

PANOS IOANNIDES

Panos Ioannides (1935–   ) was born in Cyprus and educated in Cyprus, the United States, and Canada. He presently lives in Cyprus, where he is Head of TV Programmes at the Cyprus Broadcasting Corporation. Ioannides has written poems, plays, short stories, novels, and scripts for radio and television documentaries. His novel, Census, *and short story collections,* Epics of Cyprus *and* The Unseen View, *have won national awards. Ioannides wrote "Gregory" (1963) when coming down with the flu and thinking about an incident he had witnessed during the struggle in Cyprus during the 1950s to liberate itself from the British.*

1989

GREGORY

My hand was sweating as I held the pistol. The curve of the trigger was biting against my finger.

Facing me, Gregory trembled.

His whole being was beseeching me, "Don't!"

Only his mouth did not make a sound. His lips were squeezed tight. If it had been me, I would have screamed, shouted, cursed.

5　　　The soldiers were watching. . . .

The day before, during a brief meeting, they had each given their opinions: "It's tough luck, but it has to be done. We've got no choice."

The order from Headquarters was clear: "As soon as Lieutenant Rafel's execution is announced, the hostage Gregory is to be shot and his body must be hanged from a telegraph pole in the main street as an exemplary punishment."

It was not the first time that I had to execute a hostage in this war. I had acquired experience, thanks to Headquarters which had kept entrusting me with these delicate assignments. Gregory's case was precisely the sixth.

The first time, I remember, I vomited. The second time I got sick and had a headache for days. The third time I drank a bottle of rum. The fourth, just two glasses of beer. The fifth time I joked about it, "This little guy, with the big pop-eyes, won't be much of a ghost!"

10　　　But why, dammit, when the day came did I have to start thinking that I'm not so tough, after all? The thought had come at exactly the wrong time and spoiled all my disposition to do my duty.

You see, this Gregory was such a miserable little creature, such a puny thing, such a nobody, damn him.

That very morning, although he had heard over the loudspeakers that Rafel had been executed, he believed that we would spare his life because we had been eating together so long.

"Those who eat from the same mess tins and drink from the same water canteen," he said, "remain good friends no matter what."

And a lot more of the same sort of nonsense.

15　　　He was a silly fool—we had smelled that out the very first day Headquarters gave him to us. The sentry guarding him had got dead drunk and had dozed off. The rest of us with exit permits had gone from the barracks. When we came back, there was Gregory sitting by the sleeping sentry and thumbing through a magazine.

"Why didn't you run away, Gregory?" we asked, laughing at him, several days later.

And he answered, "Where would I go in this freezing weather? I'm O.K. here."

So we started teasing him.

"You're dead right. The accommodations here are splendid. . . ."

20　　　"It's not so bad here," he replied. "The barracks where I used to be are like a sieve. The wind blows in from every side. . . ."

We asked him about his girl. He smiled.

"Maria is a wonderful person," he told us. "Before I met her she was engaged to a no-good fellow, a pig. He gave her up for another girl. Then nobody in the village wanted to marry Maria. I didn't miss my chance. So what if she is second-hand. Nonsense. Peasant ideas, my friend. She's beautiful and good-hearted. What more could I want? And didn't she load me with watermelons and cucumbers every time I passed by her vegetable garden? Well, one day I stole some cucumbers and melons and watermelons and I took them to her. 'Maria,' I said, 'from now on I'm going to take care of you.' She started crying and then me, too. But ever since that day she has given me lots of trouble—jealousy. She wouldn't let me go even to my mother's. Until the day I was recruited, she wouldn't let me go far from her apron strings. But that was just what I wanted. . . ."

He used to tell this story over and over, always with the same words, the same commonplace gestures. At the end he would have a good laugh and start gulping from his water jug.

His tongue was always wagging! When he started talking, nothing could stop him. We used to listen and nod our heads, not saying a word. But sometimes, as he was telling us about his mother and family problems, we couldn't help wondering, "Eh, well, these people have the same headaches in their country as we've got."

25   Strange, isn't it!

Except for his talking too much, Gregory wasn't a bad fellow. He was a marvelous cook. Once he made us some apple tarts, so delicious we licked the platter clean. And he could sew, too. He used to sew on all our buttons, patch our clothes, darn our socks, iron our ties, wash our clothes. . . .

How the devil could you kill such a friend?

Even though his name was Gregory and some people on his side had killed one of ours, even though we had left wives and children to go to war against him and his kind —but how can I explain? He was our friend. He actually liked us! A few days before, hadn't he killed with his own bare hands a scorpion that was climbing up my leg? He could have let it send me to hell!

"Thanks, Gregory!" I said then, "Thank God who made you. . . ."

30   When the order came, it was like a thunderbolt. Gregory was to be shot, it said, and hanged from a telegraph pole as an exemplary punishment.

We got together inside the barracks. We sent Gregory to wash some underwear for us.

"It ain't right."

"What is right?"

"Our duty!"

35   "Shit!"

"If you dare, don't do it! They'll drag you to court-martial and then bang-bang. . . ."

Well, of course. The right thing is to save your skin. That's only logical. It's either your skin or his. His, of course, even if it was Gregory, the fellow you've been sharing the same plate with, eating with your fingers, and who was washing your clothes that very minute.

What could I do? That's war. We had seen worse things.

So we set the hour.

40   We didn't tell him anything when he came back from the washing. He slept peacefully. He snored for the last time. In the morning, he heard the news over the loudspeaker and he saw that we looked gloomy and he began to suspect that something was up. He tried talking to us, but he got no answers and then he stopped talking.

He just stood there and looked at us, stunned and lost. . . .

Now, I'll squeeze the trigger. A tiny bullet will rip through his chest. Maybe I'll lose my sleep tonight but in the morning I'll wake up alive.

Gregory seems to guess my thoughts. He puts out his hand and asks, "You're kidding, friend! Aren't you kidding?"

What a jackass! Doesn't he deserve to be cut to pieces? What a thing to ask at such a time. Your heart is about to burst and he's asking if you're kidding. How can a body be kidding about such a thing? Idiot! This is no time for jokes. And you, if you're such a fine friend, why don't you make things easier for us? Help us kill you with fewer qualms? If you would get angry—curse our Virgin, our God—if you'd try to escape it would be much easier for us and for you.

So it is *now.*

Now, Mr. Gregory, you are going to pay for your stupidities wholesale. Because you didn't escape the day the sentry fell asleep; because you didn't escape yesterday when we sent you all alone to the laundry—we did it on purpose, you idiot! Why didn't you let me die from the sting of the scorpion?

So now don't complain. It's all your fault, nitwit.

Eh? What's happening to him now?

Gregory is crying. Tears flood his eyes and trickle down over his cleanshaven cheeks. He is turning his face and pressing his forehead against the wall. His back is shaking as he sobs. His hands cling, rigid and helpless, to the wall.

Now is my best chance, now that he knows there is no other solution and turns his face from us.

I squeeze the trigger.

Gregory jerks. His back stops shaking up and down.

I think I've finished him! How easy it is. . . . But suddenly he starts crying out loud, his hands claw at the wall and try to pull it down. He screams, "No, no. . . ."

I turn to the others. I expect them to nod, "That's enough."

They nod, "What are you waiting for?"

I squeeze the trigger again.

The bullet smashed into his neck. A thick spray of blood spurts out.

Gregory turns. His eyes are all red. He lunges at me and starts punching me with his fists.

"I hate you, hate you. . . ," he screams.

I emptied the barrel. He fell and grabbed my leg as if he wanted to hold on.

He died with a terrible spasm. His mouth was full of blood and so were my boots and socks.

We stood quietly, looking at him.

When we came to, we stooped and picked him up. His hands were frozen and wouldn't let my legs go.

45   I still have their imprints, red and deep, as if made by a hot knife.

"We will hang him tonight," the men said.

"Tonight or now?" they said.

I turned and looked at them one by one.

"Is that what you all want?" I asked.

50   They gave me no answer.

"Dig a grave," I said.

Headquarters did not ask for a report the next day or the day after. The top brass were sure that we had obeyed them and had left him swinging from a pole.

They didn't care to know what happened to that Gregory, alive or dead.

■ EXPLORATIONS OF THE TEXT

1. The story takes place during the few seconds in which the narrator must decide whether to kill Gregory. Why do you think that Ioannides limited the plot to these few moments? Why does he choose to tell the story from the executioner's rather than from the victim's perspective?

2. Analyze the narrator's character. Focus on his attitude toward his "job," his changing relationship with Gregory, his actions, and his dialogue. Why is it significant that Gregory was his "friend"?

3. Why does the author depict Gregory's relationship with Maria and the other soldiers? What do these details suggest about Gregory's character?

4. How does the narrator change during the course of the story? How does he justify his actions?

5. Explore the symbolism of the "imprints" of Gregory's hands on the narrator's legs?

6. How does the narrator's behavior compare with Hartley's treatment of the prisoner in "I, Jailor"?

■ **THE READING/WRITING CONNECTION**
1. In a journal entry, discuss a moral dilemma that you faced. What did you do?
2. Debate Topic: Is the narrator to be blamed for the killing, or was he just doing his duty as a soldier?

■ **IDEAS FOR WRITING**
1. Discuss the theme of obedience to authority in this work, in *Antigone,* and in Hartley's "I, Jailor."
2. Examine the personal transformation that a solider undergoes as it is depicted in this work, in O'Brien's "How to Tell a True War Story," and in Rivera's "Gas." What happens to soldiers who go to war?

Cynthia Ozick

Cynthia Ozick (1928–   ) was born in New York City. Her writing shows the influence of her extensive reading in Jewish philosophy and the effect of the anti-Semitism that she experienced as a child. Her work includes the novels Trust *(1966),* The Puttermesser Papers *(1997), and* Heir to the Glimmering World: A Novel *(2004); a novella,* The Messiah of Stockholm *(1987); and the volumes of short fiction* The Pagan Rabbi and Other Stories *(1971) and* Bloodshed and Three Novellas *(1976). Several of Ozick's short stories have been chosen for* The Best American Short Stories, *notably "The Shawl" and its companion piece, the novella "Rosa." Her work also won first prize in the annual O. Henry Prize Stories collection in 1975, 1981, and 1984.*

1980

THE SHAWL

Stella, cold, cold, the coldness of hell. How they walked on the roads together, Rosa with Magda curled up between sore breasts, Magda wound up in the shawl. Sometimes Stella carried Magda. But she was jealous of Magda. A thin girl of fourteen, too small, with thin breasts of her own, Stella wanted to be wrapped in a shawl, hidden away, asleep, rocked by the march, a baby, a round infant in arms. Magda took Rosa's nipple, and Rosa never stopped walking, a walking cradle. There was not enough milk; sometimes Magda sucked air; then she screamed. Stella was ravenous. Her knees were tumors on sticks, her elbows chicken bones.

Rosa did not feel hunger; she felt light, not like someone walking but like someone in a faint, in trance, arrested in a fit, someone who is already a floating angel, alert and seeing everything, but in the air, not there, not touching the road. As if teetering on the tips of her fingernails. She looked into Magda's face through a gap in the shawl: a squirrel in a nest, safe, no one could reach her inside the little house of the shawl's windings. The face, very round, a pocket mirror of a face: but it was not Rosa's bleak complexion, dark like cholera, it was another kind of face altogether, eyes blue as air, smooth feathers of hair nearly as yellow as the Star sewn into Rosa's coat. You could think she was one of *their* babies.

Rosa, floating, dreamed of giving Magda away in one of the villages. She could leave the line for a minute and push Magda into the hands of any woman on the side of the road. But if she moved out of line they might shoot. And even if she fled the line for half a second and pushed the shawl-bundle at a stranger, would the woman take it? She might be surprised, or afraid; she might drop the shawl, and Magda would fall out and strike her head and die. The little round head. Such a good child, she gave up screaming, and sucked now only for the taste of the drying nipple itself. The neat grip of the tiny gums. One mite of a tooth tip sticking up in the bottom gum, how shining, an elfin tombstone of white marble, gleaming there. Without complaining, Magda relinquished Rosa's teats, first the left, then the right; both were cracked, not a sniff of milk. The duct crevice extinct, a dead volcano, blind eye, chill hole, so Magda took the corner of the shawl and milked it instead. She sucked and sucked, flooding the threads with wetness. The shawl's good flavor, milk of linen.

It was a magic shawl, it could nourish an infant for three days and three nights. Magda did not die, she stayed alive, although very quiet. A peculiar smell, of cinnamon and almonds, lifted out of her mouth. She held her eyes open every moment, forgetting how to blink or nap, and Rosa and sometimes Stella studied their blueness. On the road they raised one burden of a leg after another and studied Magda's face. "Aryan," Stella said, in a voice grown as thin as a string; and Rosa thought how Stella gazed at Magda like a young cannibal. And the time that Stella said "Aryan," it sounded to Rosa as if Stella had really said, "Let us devour her."

5 But Magda lived to walk. She lived that long, but she did not walk very well, partly because she was only fifteen months old, and partly because the spindles of her legs could not hold up her fat belly. It was fat with air, full and round. Rosa gave almost all her food to Magda, Stella gave nothing; Stella was ravenous, a growing child herself, but not growing much. Stella did not menstruate. Rosa did not menstruate. Rosa was ravenous, but also not; she learned from Magda how to drink the taste of a finger in one's mouth. They were in a place without pity, all pity was annihilated in Rosa, she looked at Stella's bones without pity. She was sure that Stella was waiting for Magda to die so she could put her teeth into the little thighs.

Rosa knew Magda was going to die very soon; she should have been dead already, but she had been buried away deep inside the magic shawl, mistaken there for the shivering mound of Rosa's breasts; Rosa clung to the shawl as if it covered only herself. No one took it away from her. Magda was mute. She never cried. Rosa hid her in the barracks, under the shawl, but she knew that one day someone would inform; or one day someone, not even Stella, would steal Magda to eat her. When Magda began to walk Rosa knew that Magda was going to die very soon, something would happen. She was afraid to fall asleep; she slept with the weight of her thigh on Magda's body; she was afraid she would smother Magda under her thigh. The weight of Rosa was becoming less and less, Rosa and Stella were slowly turning into air.

Magda was quiet, but her eyes were horribly alive, like blue tigers. She watched. Sometimes she laughed—it seemed a laugh, but how could it be? Magda had never seen anyone laugh. Still, Magda laughed at her shawl when the wind blew its corners, the bad wind with pieces of black in it, that made Stella's and Rosa's eyes tear. Magda's eyes were always clear and tearless. She watched like a tiger. She guarded her shawl. No one could touch it; only Rosa could touch it. Stella was not allowed. The shawl was Magda's own baby, her pet, her little sister. She tangled herself up in it and sucked on one of the corners when she wanted to be very still.

Then Stella took the shawl away and made Magda die.

Afterward Stella said: "I was cold."

10 And afterward she was always cold, always. The cold went into her heart: Rosa saw that Stella's heart was cold. Magda flopped onward with her little pencil legs scribbling this way and that, in search of the shawl; the pencils faltered at the barracks opening, where the light began. Rosa saw and pursued. But already Magda was in the square outside the barracks, in the jolly light. It was the roll-call arena. Every morning Rosa had to conceal Magda under the shawl against a wall of the barracks and go out and stand in the arena with Stella and hundreds of others, sometimes for hours, and Magda, deserted, was quiet under the shawl,

sucking on her corner. Every day Magda was silent, and so she did not die. Rosa saw that today Magda was going to die, and at the same time a fearful joy ran in Rosa's two palms, her fingers were on fire, she was astonished, febrile: Magda, in the sunlight, swaying on her pencil legs, was howling. Ever since the drying up of Rosa's nipples, ever since Magda's last scream on the road, Magda had been devoid of any syllable; Magda was a mute. Rosa believed that something had gone wrong with her vocal cords, with her windpipe, with the cave of her larynx; Magda was defective, without a voice; perhaps she was deaf; there might be something amiss with her intelligence; Magda was dumb. Even the laugh that came when the ash-stippled wind made a clown out of Magda's shawl was only the air-blown showing of her teeth. Even when the lice, head lice and body lice, crazed her so that she became as wild as one of the big rats that plundered the barracks at daybreak looking for carrion, she rubbed and scratched and kicked and bit and rolled without a whimper. But now Magda's mouth was spilling a long viscous rope of clamor.

"Maaaa—"

It was the first noise Magda had ever sent out from her throat since the drying up of Rosa's nipples.

"Maaaa . . . aaa!"

Again! Magda was wavering in the perilous sunlight of the arena, scribbling on such pitiful little bent shins. Rosa saw. She saw that Magda was grieving the loss of her shawl, she saw that Magda was going to die. A tide of commands hammered in Rosa's nipples: Fetch, get, bring! But she did not know which to go after first, Magda or the shawl. If she jumped out into the arena to snatch Magda up, the howling would not stop, because Magda would still not have the shawl; but if she ran back into the barracks to find the shawl, and if she found it, and if she came after Magda holding it and shaking it, then she would get Magda back, Magda would put the shawl in her mouth and turn dumb again.

15   Rosa entered the dark. It was easy to discover the shawl. Stella was heaped under it, asleep in her thin bones. Rosa tore the shawl free and flew—she could fly, she was only air—into the arena. The sunheat murmured of another life, of butterflies in summer. The light was placid, mellow. On the other side of the steel fence, far away, there were green meadows speckled with dandelions and deep-colored violets; beyond them, even farther, innocent tiger lilies, tall, lifting their orange bonnets. In the barracks they spoke of "flowers," of "rain": excrement, thick turd-braids, and the slow stinking maroon waterfall that slunk down from the upper bunks, the stink mixed with a bitter fatty floating smoke that greased Rosa's skin. She stood for an instant at the margin of the arena. Sometimes the electricity inside the fence would seem to hum; even Stella said it was only an imagining, but Rosa heard real sounds in the wire: grainy sad voices. The farther she was from the fence, the more clearly the voices crowded at her. The lamenting voices strummed so convincingly, so passionately, it was impossible to suspect them of being phantoms. The voices told her to hold up the shawl, high; the voices told her to shake it, to whip with it, to unfurl it like a flag. Rosa lifted, shook, whipped, unfurled. Far off, very far, Magda leaned across her air-fed belly, reaching out with the rods of her arms. She was high up, elevated, riding someone's shoulder. But the shoulder that carried Magda was not coming toward Rosa and the shawl, it was drifting away, the speck of Magda was moving more and more into the smoky distance. Above the shoulder a helmet glinted. A light tapped the helmet and sparkled it into a goblet. Below the helmet a black body like a domino and a pair of black boots hurled themselves in the direction of the electrified fence. The electric voices began to chatter wildly. "Maamaa, maaamaaa," they all hummed together. How far Magda was from Rosa now, across the whole square, past a dozen barracks, all the way on the other side! She was no bigger than a moth.

All at once Magda was swimming through the air. The whole of Magda traveled through loftiness. She looked like a butterfly touching a silver vine. And the moment

Magda's feathered round head and her pencil legs and balloonish belly and zigzag arms splashed against the fence, the steel voices went mad in their growling, urging Rosa to run and run to the spot where Magda had fallen from her flight against the electrified fence; but of course Rosa did not obey them. She only stood, because if she ran they would shoot, and if she tried to pick up the sticks of Magda's body they would shoot, and if she let the wolf's screech ascending now through the ladder of her skeleton break out, they would shoot; so she took Magda's shawl and filled her own mouth with it, stuffed it in and stuffed it in, until she was swallowing up the wolf's screech and tasting the cinnamon and almond depth of Magda's saliva; and Rosa drank Magda's shawl until it dried.

■ EXPLORATIONS OF THE TEXT

1. Describe the agony of Rosa, Stella, and Magda as they walk to the camp. What is the attitude of each toward the shawl?
2. Why does Magda's existence remain secret?
3. Explore Stella's relationships with Rosa and with Magda.
4. Examine the agony of Magda's first cry. Consider the language that describes Magda's death. What are the major images?
5. Explain the ending: "Rosa drank Magda's shawl until it dried." Has Ozick chosen the right response for Rosa? Why? Why not?
6. Why does the speaker begin her description of Magda's death only to interrupt it with a fantasy of saving her?
7. How does Stella "make" Magda die? Why is Stella's heart "cold"?
8. Compare the fates of the central characters in works by O'Brien, Endō, Pirandello, and Valenzuela.

■ THE READING/WRITING CONNECTION

1. In a paragraph discuss the symbolism of the shawl.
2. React to Stella's character. Freewrite in your journal.
3. "Think" Topic: Is Stella to be blamed for Magda's death? Argue pro or con.

■ IDEAS FOR WRITING

1. Evaluate the descriptive language in this story. Does it enhance and create meaning?
2. Discuss "The Shawl's" portrayal of the inhumanity and cruelty of the concentration camps during the Holocaust. Is it powerful?
3. Analyze Rosa's or Stella's character.

SARA NOMBERG-PRZYTYK

Sara Nomberg-Przytyk (1915–   ) was born in Lublin, Poland, and attended the University of Warsaw. After having spent several years in Polish jails for her leftist political activities, she moved east, near the Russian border, when the Germans invaded Poland in 1939. Nonetheless, she was caught in 1943 and transported first to a camp in Stutthof and then, in 1944, to Auschwitz. After her liberation in 1945, Nomberg-Przytyk worked as a journalist in Lublin and, in her free time, wrote about her experiences in Auschwitz. Nomberg-Przytyk's book, Auschwitz: True Tales from a Grotesque Land, was denied publication by Poland's communist government unless she agreed to eliminate all references to Jews. Nomberg-Przytyk moved to Israel in 1968, and her manuscript was published in English in 1985. "Natasha's Triumph" is taken from Nomberg-Przytyk's book.

1985

NATASHA'S TRIUMPH

Every day deathly undernourished women and hundreds of mortally sick people came through the doors of the infirmary to which was attached a little cottage that housed the personnel who worked in the infirmary. Actually, it was not really a cottage but a little shack without windows. The total area of the shack was about two by six meters. Inside there were two three-decker beds and a small table. We thought that it was the most wonderful habitation in the world. It was our corner, different from the terrible barracks.

One sunny day we received a notice that hit us like a clap of thunder. It was a summer evening in 1944 when Orli brought us the news that we would have to move out of our little shack because Mengele had decided to create a ward for mentally disturbed women. At night we removed our meager possessions. The next morning we waited for the patients. The whole affair looked very suspicious to me. It was difficult to understand why Mengele would create a ward for the mentally sick in the infirmary. Until now there had been no such ward. We had a feeling that Mengele must have a new trick up his sleeve.

First thing in the morning they brought the first patient. Her name was Natasha. The *blokowa* brought her in.

"She has to stay here with you in the infirmary," the *blokowa* said and left.

5   Before me stood a young girl, straight as a tree, with a gloomy, rebellious face. She was nineteen years old and from Leningrad. She would not tell us anything else. Our Jewish doctors were not invited to examine her, since their findings were set at no value. Natasha immediately took an upper bunk. She lay there quietly, saying nothing, but when we brought her some soup she came to life, and a big smile brightened up her face. She ate while she continued to lie there without saying a word.

The same afternoon, five new patients were brought in, including two German, one Dutch, and two French women. They were all very young and very sad. At first we were afraid of them. We imagined that they would cause trouble, maybe have fits. Perhaps we would have to use physical force to subdue them. We had no experience in handling such cases. But the new patients lay quietly in their beds, or else they sat bent over on the edge of the bed.

I remember that I made several attempts to talk to them, but my words did not reach them. That same day, just before roll call, a few more women were brought in. By this time a few of the beds were being shared by two women. A couple of mornings later we prepared the infirmary to receive a visit from Dr. Mengele.[1] We knew that he would come to examine the new "ward." That morning, as we were admitting the sick to the hospital, we did not accept the very sick ones. We sent them back to the blocks. We knew that if he started looking at them he would certainly send them to the ovens. It was with heavy hearts that we sent those women away to do heavy labor, women who were barely alive, with swollen legs and terrible sores all over their bodies. But we well knew the monster in the white coat who had the face of a Romeo. He would assign them to the gas and then would say to us, "You see yourselves that these women are not strong enough to live. Why should they suffer? I am sending them to the gas for their own good."

Mengele arrived about twelve o'clock.

"Achtung," shouted Marusia.

10   The selection of the sick and the signing of the cards started. Everything was going smoothly, without a hitch. All of a sudden, from the next room, we heard a loud, happy voice calling,

---

[1] The Nazi doctor at Auschwitz who determined who lived and died—who was to be sent to the gas chambers—and who performed medical experiments on inmates. He was called the Angel of Death.

"Hey, you! Doctor! Maybe you can come in and see us."

It was Natasha calling to Mengele; she was speaking to him in beautiful German, her voice radiant with happiness.

"What are you afraid of, coward, you who can murder women and children? Come here. We will discuss your Hitler's crimes. Maybe you want to discuss Stalingrad, where you are dying like mad dogs."

We turned to stone. Every one of us pretended to be very busy. We were afraid to look in his direction. We knew that in a minute something terrible would happen. Natasha's ringing, violent voice floated in from the other room.

15   "You will all die in Russia, the way Napoleon did. You are afraid to come to me. You don't want to listen to the truth, you specialist of the gas chambers."

Suddenly we saw Mengele get up and go into the other room. I waited for a shot and automatically covered my ears with my fists.

"Come, sit next to us. We will have a chat."

Mengele did not say a thing. Only the voice of Natasha could be heard.

"Hitler, that human garbage, destroyed Germany. All the nations will hate you through the ages. You will see. Even if you live through the war, you will have to hide from human revenge like a worm."

20   We stood there completely motionless, as though hypnotized. Natasha started to sing. What a wonderful voice she had.

She finished the interview with an abrupt, "Get out of here. I can't stand to look at your shiny mug any more."

Mengele got up and left without a word. Only after he had crossed the threshold of the infirmary and had looked at our pale faces did he shout out the order to dress all the sick, because the orderly would come to pick them up after lunch.

"The Russian is to stay here," he added in closing.

We knew what that meant. The orderly would give them an injection of phenol, and in the evening the *leichenauto* would take them to the gas chambers. Natasha had to remain here. Why? Maybe he was preparing a more agonizing death for her.

25   The next day they brought a new batch of women. They, too, were sad and silent. About lunch time Mengele came in again.

"Come here, hero of the gas chambers," Natasha called again. "We will discuss your death. If you wish, I will tell you how you're going to die."

With wonder we watched him approach Natasha. For an hour she carried on a tirade against Hitler. She sang Russia's praises. Mengele sat on the chair with his head hung low on his chest.

I remember looking at him and not believing my own eyes. What was going on here? What was drawing that predator to his prey? To this very day I cannot understand what secret was lurking behind his behavior. Maybe it was just one more aberration. Perhaps the flagellation he received from Natasha's tongue gave him some sort of satisfaction.

Every day the sanitation worker took the sick for the *szpryce* (injection). That was their term for murder by phenol in Auschwitz. Every day Mengele came to listen to Natasha's speeches. One evening I decided to have a talk with Natasha. I told her everything about myself, waiting for her to get up enough confidence so that she would be willing to tell me about her life. I was not mistaken.

30   Natasha had been a student. Her parents had been professors of German. It was from them that she had learned such elegant German. After that conversation I was certain that Natasha was not mentally ill and that she was feigning mental illness in order to be able to get away with telling the Germans exactly how she felt about them.

"But dear Natasha," I screamed with anguish, "do you know what they do to mentally ill people? They don't heal but kill."

"I know," said Natasha. "But I don't want to live in this rotten world."

The next day Dr. Koenig came for the inspection instead of Mengele. We closed the door to the little room. Maybe we could hide the sick from him.

"Hey, you, Doctor of death," Natasha shouted in a loud voice. "Come here, we will discuss your Hitler."

35 Koenig shuddered. He pushed open the door and went into the little room. The room was almost completely dark. On the beds sat the huddled figures.

"What, you're afraid to come in, you Hitler's coward?"

Then there was a shot. All the sick screamed at the same time, with a terrible, hollow voice.

When we reached Natasha she was already dead.

■ EXPLORATIONS OF THE TEXT

1. Describe the position of the narrator. Who do you imagine her to be?
2. Why does the narrator admire Natasha?
3. Why does Natasha confront Mengele? Why is it important that she speaks to him in "beautiful German"?
4. What does her confrontation symbolize?

■ THE READING/WRITING CONNECTION

1. Discuss the theme of silence and speech in this work. What is the power of language?
2. Debate Topic: Is Natasha insane?
3. Freewrite in response to this question: What is "Natasha's Triumph"?

■ IDEAS FOR WRITING

1. How does Natasha turn victimization into heroism? Why does she inspire others?
2. Compare and contrast Natasha with the protagonist in Valenzuela's "I'm Your Horse in the Night."

Shusaku Endō

Shusaku Endō (1923-1996), born in Tokyo, spent his early childhood in Manchuria, China, then returned to Japan after his parents separated, living with his mother in the home of a Roman Catholic aunt. He received a B.A. from Keio University and studied French literature at Lyon University in France. A playwright, novelist, and short story writer, Endō frequently wrote about the clash between Eastern and Western morals and philosophy. His works include Stained Glass Elegies *(1979),* The Samurai *(1980),* Deep River *(1994), and* The Girl I Left Behind *(1996).*

1979

THE WAR GENERATION

Outside it was raining, and the restaurant was crowded. A steaming pot on a white charcoal brazier in front of them, office workers and various other customers blew on their onions and *kiritanpo*[1] before eating them. A young woman dressed in a dark blue kimono with white splashes went from table to table setting down bottles of *sake*.[2]

---

[1] A kind of stew, pounded into a mortar and served with chicken.
[2] A kind of alcoholic beverage, made of rice and served warm.

"Are these seats taken?" a businessman with a young woman in tow asked Konishi.

"No." With his *sake* cup still at his lips, Konishi shook his head sourly. In truth he had wanted this table all to himself.

"Shall we have the fish broth?"

5   "Anything. I'm starving."

She took a cigarette from her brown handbag and began to smoke. Looking at her, Konishi thought of his wife and daughters waiting for him at home. This woman would be about the same age as his oldest girl, but she brought the cigarette to her lips like a habitual smoker. It was a distressing sight.

"Don't you think they're charging a little too much for the year-end party this time?"

"What can we do? We have to go."

Listening without interest to the whispered conversation between these two, Konishi concluded that they must work in the same section at some company. Their talk shifted from the cost of the year-end party to backbiting against their co-workers.

10   He consumed a good deal of time slowly drinking down his second bottle of *sake*. At home, his wife and daughters had probably already started dinner. He often stopped off for a few drinks on his way home from work, so his family would wait until seven o'clock and then go ahead and eat without him. Konishi felt more comfortable having them do that than making them wait for him.

As intoxication began to settle in, Konishi thought about the funeral of one of his fellow workers that he had attended the previous day. Mimura had been Personnel Director at the company, and was the same age as Konishi—fifty-two. He had heard that Mimura's blood pressure was a little high, but when the two of them had been tested together a year before in the company examination room, Konishi's blood pressure had been 150, Mimura's around 160. They had talked about how, by taking medicine, the pressure could be held below 200, and so there was nothing to worry about. But Mimura had died suddenly of a heart attack.

A photograph of Mimura, smiling and wearing a golfing hat, had been placed above the Buddhist memorial tablet surrounded by chrysanthemums. To one side sat the drooping figures of Mimura's wife, dressed in mourning kimono, and his son, wearing his high-school uniform. As he pressed his hands together reverently and gazed at Mimura's photograph, Konishi thought that this would be happening to him too before very long. Death, which had until now seemed still some distance away, had suddenly closed in on him with a whirr. In fact, two other funerals he had attended this year were for men in their fifties; he had to be on his guard.

"On my guard . . . ?" he muttered to himself. The woman who was sharing his table was putting fish and onions from the broth into a bowl for her date. The man, puffing on a cigarette, watched her as though he expected such treatment. Doubtless they had already slept together.

I must be on my guard. . . . But what was he supposed to do at this point? He was by no means satisfied with his job, but he had no intention of leaving. Eventually he would become an executive. Thereby he would avoid mandatory retirement. These days he had to feel very grateful for the position he was in. In his youth he had never imagined that his declining years would take their present shape. When he entered the Department of Law, he had planned to become a government official. Those plans had been aborted when he was taken out of school and sent off to war.

15   But Konishi had not been the only one that had happened to. All around him in those days were people who had had to change the direction of their lives because of the war. It was a matter of course for Konishi's generation.

He finished off his second bottle, and while he was debating whether to order a third, the glass door of the restaurant opened with a clatter. In the artificial light the rain looked like needles. A tall, thin woman in a black raincoat, around fifty or so, came into the restaurant.

Her nose was as pronounced as a foreigner's. Flecks of silver streaked her hair, like a foreigner's. Droplets of rain glimmered on her black raincoat. She asked the kimono-clad hostess a brief question and disappeared into a room at the back.

Still holding the empty *sake* bottle in his hand, Konishi let out an unintentional gasp. The man at the next table gave him a peculiar look.

None of the other customers in the restaurant knew who the woman was. But Konishi recognized the middle-aged woman as the violinist Ono Mari.

20   There was not a single clear sky over Tokyo in the days just before Konishi went into the army. Each day was leadenly overcast.

Though he knew it couldn't be the case, he wondered if the ashen skies over Tokyo had something to do with the city being as dark as his own feelings at the time. He had been at the university, and his boarding-house was located at Shinano-machi. Even the main road from there to Shinjuku was always deserted, every store had its glass doors tightly shut and displayed signs reading "Closed." Outside the shops, sandbags, buckets and fire blankets had been stacked in preparation for air raids. But there were no signs of human life.

Every day the sky looked as though it had been stuffed full of tattered cotton swabs. He could remember hearing sounds like faint explosions echoing constantly from the sky.

There was no longer anything resembling classes at the university. Instead, students like Konishi were sent to the F. Heavy Industries factory in Kawasaki, where they assembled airplane parts.

On the wintry mornings, factory workers and students dressed in work clothes and gaiters and carrying knapsacks over their shoulders lined up in single file on the square in front of Kawasaki Station. Buffeted by the cold wind, they waited and waited for their bus to come. Inside Konishi's knapsack he had some soya beans wrapped in paper, the only food that would help in some small way to stave off his hunger throughout the entire day.

25   Towards the end of 1944, the factory suffered a shortage of raw materials, and many machines ground to a halt. Even so, Konishi and the other grease-covered students had to stand in front of their drill presses all day long. Supervisors continued to make their rounds, marking down the names of any students whose work was slack. Those whose names were logged were not given any of the watery porridge that was brought around each day at three o'clock. Diluted as it was, the ravenous students coveted the porridge.

They were starved for more than just food. They likewise craved books. They yearned for heated rooms. They were hungry for human conversation, and for love. And so during the noon break, as they lined up in groups of five or six with their backs to the sunlit concrete wall, they discussed food and books. Then with sighs of longing they talked about certain members of the women's volunteer corps, who worked in a separate building. Dressed in their work pantaloons and wearing headbands, these women sorted the various machine parts. Throughout the factory hung posters that read: "Advance to Attu Island!"[3]

As that year drew to a close, however, one after another of the young men who basked in that noonday sun received their draft notices printed on red paper. Each morning at the factory it was easy to tell from the looks on people's faces just who had received their orders. They would try to force a smile, but the dark, heavy circles under their eyes betrayed them.

"It's come," the latest recipient would announce to everyone in a low voice, as though he were confessing some dark secret.

"When do you leave?"

---

[3] Island southwest of Alaska, the most western of the Aleutians.

30   "In two weeks."

Of course, no one mouthed empty phrases like "Congratulations" or "Give it your best!" Sooner or later the same piece of paper would be coming their way. They all stared at the tall factory chimney. Again today the smoke from the chimney swirled straight up into the sombre sky. The scene was unchanged from yesterday or the day before. It seemed as though it would stay that way for eternity.

"When is this war going to end?" No one knew. They felt as though it would linger on and on for ever.

Whenever a new recruit left Tokyo, everyone assembled at Shinjuku or Tokyo Station to see him off. The students formed a circle on the crowded platform and sang their school song in an angry roar. They howled and leaped about, less interested in seeing off their friend than in masking the anxiety and fear that lurked in their own hearts. As the train carrying their comrade vanished from sight, looks of bleak emptiness appeared on the faces of those who had been so boisterous just a few moments before.

1945 came, and still Konishi had not received his induction notice. Around that time the enemy air raids gradually intensified. The previous November the Nakashima Aircraft Plant in Musashino had been bombed, and enemy planes appeared fifteen times the following month. Strangely, F. Factory in Kawasaki was untouched. Often the trains packed with exhausted workers at the end of the day would come to a stop with a groan. Sometimes there appeared to be an attack over the downtown area; from the train windows they could see the sky in that direction glowing a dark red. The train service was often suspended, and Konishi would have to crouch for a long while on a connecting platform at Tokyo Station, staring at the reddened sky, realizing with a start that death was all that lay before them.

35   On 28 February his good friend Inami received his draft notice, and the feeling that his own turn was coming soon struck Konishi with greater force than ever before. The night Inami's orders came, four or five of them gathered in his room for a farewell party. They drank rationed liquor and some watered-down medicinal alcohol they had stolen from the factory. Later that night, the landlord and the owner of an electrical shop who represented the local veterans' association came in and clumsily began to chant some Chinese poetry. "Do your best! Work for your country." They spouted callous words of encouragement. Inami, his face sallow, sat up straight in the student uniform he had not put on for some time.

That night he and Konishi slept in his room under the same blanket. Inami turned over, and Konishi could hear him weeping softly. He listened in silence for a while, then whispered, "I'll be getting drafted too, before long."

"Uh-huh," Inami nodded. He turned so that Konishi could see the profile of his face. "If you want anything of mine, you can have it."

"I don't want any books. My red slip will be coming before I could finish reading any of them."

"Probably. In that case, would you go to a concert in my place? I had to fight to get the ticket. I wanted to go to just one concert before the army got me." He slipped out of bed in his worn-out underwear and rifled through his desk drawer until he found a brown-coloured ticket. Inami was engrossed in music: he had his own record collection, and even had a phonograph in his room.

40   "Whose concert?"

"Ono Mari on the violin. You've heard of her, haven't you—Ono Mari? They say she's a young genius."

"I've heard the name a lot."

In the dim light from the lamp swathed in a black cloth, Konishi looked at the brown ticket. On the coarse paper had been printed the words: "Ono Mari Solo Violin Concert,

March 10." It hardly seemed possible that a concert could be held in Tokyo now that death was everywhere.

"Are you sure I can have this?"

45 "Please go. In my place."

Inami set out from Shinjuku Station the following morning. The usual clusters of students had gathered in circles on the platform to sing. Inami seemed thinner and shorter than the other students who were boarding the trains. He blinked his eyes behind glasses that kept sliding down his nose, and bowed his head repeatedly to his friends.

On the night of 9 March, a large formation of B-29s attacked Tokyo. The hour was approximately 12 a.m.

There was a strong northerly wind that night. A heavy snow had fallen in Tokyo two or three days earlier, and a thick layer of black ice still remained along the sides of the streets. Around six o'clock, Mari finished rehearsing for the following day's performance at the home of her accompanist, a White Russian named Sapholo, who lived nearby. She returned home, but because of the wind that had stirred up around noon, the long hair that was her trademark kept blowing across her face, and she had to stop many times along the way.

At the age of fourteen, she had left all the older violinists in the dust and taken first place in a music competition sponsored by the Mainichi Newspaper Corporation. Thereafter she attracted many fans. As a young child she had been in poor health, and the rowdy children at elementary school had made fun of her. Unable to endure the atmosphere, she had pleaded with her parents not to make her continue in school; they had agreed to let her pursue her violin and other essential studies at home. Perhaps that was why she was fawned upon there.

50 That evening, as she warmed her legs under the *kotatsu*[4] and ate the potato pie and unsweetened black tea her mother had prepared for her, she discussed with her parents the possibility of going to Manchuria.[5] The Musicians' Patriotic Society had proposed a series of concerts in Manchuria, and if possible she wanted her mother to go with her. Her father, wearing a frayed dressing-gown, agreed that they should go for about half a year, treating it as a kind of evacuation; there would be no air raids in Manchuria, and they would probably not have to contend with food shortages.

"This war should be over within half a year anyway." Her artist father, who had studied in France as a young man, hated the military. He took an active part in air-raid drills and went to pay his respects to departing soldiers, but at the dinner table he often shared his grim outlook on the war situation with his wife and daughter.

Mari eventually grew tired and put her hand to her mouth to yawn. The radio had been playing a song called "Look, a Parachute!," but suddenly it was interrupted by a shrill buzzer, and the announcer began to read a report from the Eastern Military Command.

"Enemy planes have been sighted over the ocean south of the city. They are approaching the mainland." The announcer repeated the words three times.

"It's all right," Mari's mother said. "They're probably just reconnaissance planes."

55 "Why don't we just go to bed instead of putting out the lights," her father replied, extinguishing the coals in the *kotatsu*. "I'm not about to do everything the army wants us to do."

---

[4] Heated charcoal, wrapped in cloth or blankets to preserve warmth and often covered with a box. Used only in winter, the *kotatsu* can be placed in a central location at dinner so that everyone seated for the meal can enjoy the comfort of the heat.

[5] A region in Northeast China, including Heilongjiang, Tilin, and Liaoning provinces and part of Inner Mongolia.

Mari fell asleep in her upstairs room. She had placed her violin case, air-raid hood and knapsack by her pillow, ready for an emergency, and had then dropped off to sleep as swiftly as a shower of falling pebbles. Soon in her dreams the orchestra members began to tune their instruments. The reverberations from the instruments were jumbled and confused, and somehow refused to modulate together as they usually did. Someone was beating on the kettledrum.

"Wake up! Mari, wake up!"

Someone was shouting at her bedside. She opened her eyes and dimly saw her father standing there wearing a metal helmet. Her ears still rang with the discordant strains of the orchestra.

"We've got to get away. It's an air raid! The flames are coming closer to us!"

60 For some reason her father's voice seemed to come from far away. She felt no sense of urgency at the words "air raid." Like a marionette she did as she was instructed and stumbled out of bed. It was then that she realized the noises in her ears were not those of an orchestra tuning up, but the crackling of fires somewhere nearby.

They joined her mother at the foot of the stairs and started for the air-raid shelter in the garden. As they hurried along, they looked up and saw that the sky over Honjo and Fukagawa was a flaming red. There was a popping sound like roasting beans, and they could hear the shouting, clamouring voices of many people. When they reached the shelter, their noses were stung by the smells of straw and damp earth.

"We can't stay here. We've got to run!" her father shouted. To her mother, who was carrying a rucksack and her purse, he called, "Leave that. You don't need it." Carrying just one rucksack on his back, he hurried the two women out through the gate. From the neighbouring Yoshimura house came clattering noises of others preparing to flee; on a road nearby a child cried, "Ma-a-ama!"

The main street was already a maelstrom of people. The sky behind them was a sombre red. In the torrent were a man pulling his belongings along in a bicycle trailer, a young man carrying bedding in a hand-cart and a woman with a blanket wrapped around her body. All of them streamed towards the west, as though drawn by some phantom power. Time and again Mari's father shouted, "Stay together!" Mari realized that the only thing she was carrying was her violin case. Another explosion shook the sky. The white bodies of the B-29s, their arms outstretched, appeared in the searchlights. The anti-aircraft guns opened fire, but the B-29s continued to soar calmly overhead. The wind still blew fiercely. From the distance echoed a succession of thunderous noises, as though a pile-driver were pounding the ground.

At his Shinano-machi boarding-house, Konishi was unable to get to sleep until about 2 a.m., thanks to the searchlights that glanced off his window and the explosion of anti-aircraft guns in the distance. The next morning he learned from the Imperial Headquarters bulletin that part of the city had been indiscriminately bombed by a hundred and thirty B-29s. The information bureau of the Headquarters and the newspapers reported without comment that fifty of the enemy planes had been damaged and fifteen shot down. But that day as he set out for the factory on the sporadically paralysed train line, Konishi saw that nearly all of the downtown sector had been consumed by fire in the previous night's raid. At the plant, workers gathered in small groups here and there, talking in subdued voices. Many of the labourers they were used to seeing had not shown up for work. From the student workforce, Taguchi, Ueno and Fujimoto were absent. A supervisor appeared and roared at the group, "Get back to work!"

65 The ticket he had received from Inami was still carefully tucked into his train pass holder, but as he worked, Konishi began to have doubts that the concert would be held under the present circumstances. Besides, even if he tried to go to the concert, and there

was another air raid like the one the night before, he would not be able to get back to his boarding-house. He decided it would be better not to go. When he reached that conclusion, though, he could hear Inami's plaintive voice echoing in his ears: "I had to fight to get the ticket. Please go in my place." He began to feel that wasting the brown ticket would be akin to betraying his friend. Without even asking, Konishi knew full well what sort of trials Inami was now enduring in the army.

At five o'clock the long, heavy siren announcing the end of the working day blared out. Still uncertain whether or not to go to the concert, Konishi crowded into the bus for Kawasaki Station with the other workers, then transferred to the equally packed train. Those who had found seats and those who dangled from the straps all had their eyes closed, and their faces looked as if they belonged to overworked beasts of burden.

It was pitch black at the deserted Yūraku-chō Station when Konishi got off the train and started walking towards Hibiya Public Hall. Along the way he took some of the paper-wrapped soya beans from his knapsack and chewed them. At the end of the day's labours his legs felt heavy and his stomach empty. When the dark hall at last came into view, he had to sit down on a rock in the park and rest for a while. Then he stood up and walked to the steps of the hall, where about fifty people had gathered by the entrance. Each of them wore gaiters and work pants and carried a knapsack on his shoulders.

As it was nearly six o'clock and the doors still hadn't been opened, someone asked his neighbour in the queue, "Is there going to be a concert or not?" Word of mouth had it that the fires caused by the previous night's air raid had driven both Mari and her accompanist Sapholo from their homes; their whereabouts were unknown, and the hall was presently attempting to contact them. Still no one made a move to leave; they all stood patiently at the entrance.

Two men with stern faces, dressed in patriotic uniforms, appeared and bellowed, "Hmph, what are you doing listening to enemy music in times like these? Go home, all of you!" The group lowered their eyes and said nothing. The men shrugged their shoulders and disappeared.

70 Before long a timid, middle-aged employee came out of the hall and announced apologetically, "We have not been able to make contact. The concert is cancelled. I'm very sorry."

No one protested. With shadows of resignation flickering on their backs, they silently began to disperse. Feeling somehow relieved, Konishi started to follow them out of the park. Just then a man at the front of the procession called, "She's here!"

Everyone stopped walking. A weary, long-haired girl dressed in men's trousers and carrying a violin case was walking towards the hall with a look of pain on her face. It was Ono Mari.

"There's going to be a concert!" The shout passed from one person to the next like the baton in a relay race. The music enthusiasts turned on their heels like a flock of ducks and went back to the hall.

It was a peculiar concert, the sort not likely to have been seen before or since. The audience filled only half of Hibiya Public Hall, so the patrons dressed in their working clothes picked out seats to their liking and waited eagerly for Ono Mari to make her appearance.

75 Soon Mari came out onto the dusty stage, clutching her violin and bow in one hand. She had not had time to adjust her make-up, and the pained expression lingered as she stood in the centre of the stage. Exhaustion was etched into her face, and the renowned long hair and the wide, almost European eyes seemed agonizingly incongruous with the tattered men's trousers she was wearing. But no one laughed.

"We were burned out of our house," she apologized, the violin and bow dangling from her hands. "The trains couldn't go any further than Yotsuya . . . I walked here from Yotsuya. I had to come . . . knowing this might be my last concert."

She bit her lip, and the audience knew she was choking down her emotions. There was not even a suggestion of applause. Everyone remained silent, pondering what she had just said.

At that moment, Konishi thought, "This just might be the last concert I'll ever hear."

Mari shook her head vigorously to get the hair out of her face, tucked the violin under her chin, leaned forward, bent her slender wrist sharply, and adjusted her bow.

80   From beneath that wrist the strains of Fauré's *Elegy*[6] began to pour out. Not a single cough came from the audience. The tired, begrimed patrons closed their eyes and listened to the music, absorbed in their own private thoughts and individual griefs. The dark, low melody pierced the hearts of each one. As he followed the music, Konishi thought about the dying city of Tokyo. He thought of the scorched, reddish sky he had seen from the station platform. He thought of the drafted workers and students waiting in the chill winter wind for a bus to pick them up at Kawasaki Station. He remembered the thin face of Inami, the tear-stained face he had buried in his bedcovers the night before his induction. Perhaps the air-raid sirens would whine again tonight, and many more people would die. Tomorrow morning Konishi, the other members of the audience and Ono Mari might be reduced to charred grey corpses. Even if he did not die today, before long he would be carted off to the battlefield. When that happened, only the strains of this melody would remain to reach the ears of those who survived.

When she finished the *Elegy*, Mari played Fauré's *Après un rêve*, then performed the Saint-Saëns "Rondo Capriccioso"[7] and Beethoven's "Romance." No one even considered the possibility that at any moment the alarms might sound, that the sky might be filled with a deafening roar, and that bombs might start to fall with a screeching howl.

Something sticky brushed against his head. A spider had woven its web in the *yatsude* plants in front of his house. Konishi clicked his tongue and opened the glass door.

From the parlour he could hear music playing on the television. As a man in his fifties, he could not begin to comprehend the electric guitar music that so delighted his daughters. It sounded to him like nothing more than someone banging noisily on metal buckets.

He was balancing himself with one hand on the shoe cabinet and removing his shoes when his wife came out of the parlour. "Welcome home," she said, and a moment later his second daughter, a high-school girl, appeared and begrudgingly repeated the greeting.

85   "Clean up the entranceway. How many times do I have to tell you?"

His wife and daughter said nothing. With a sour expression he washed his hands in the bathroom and then gargled, making a sound exactly like a duck. When he had changed his clothes he went into the parlour. The two daughters who had been watching television got abruptly to their feet, looked at him coldly, and muttering, "We've got homework to do," headed for their rooms. Konishi cast a disappointed glance after them.

Konishi's wife chattered as she filled his rice bowl, "Remember I told you that the owner of the Azusa-ya was complaining of stiff shoulders?" The Azusa-ya was a grocery store by the bus stop. "He's gone into hospital. His wife says he's got some kind of growth in his chest. It looks like cancer."

The shop-owner was not much older than Konishi. Once again he felt death closing in on him with a whirring sound. He remembered the funeral of Mimura, his co-worker who had died of a heart attack. No, death was not closing in on them. Since their schooldays, death had always lived alongside the members of his generation. That smouldering red sky

---

[6] François-Félix Fauré, French composer (1843–1924).
[7] Charles Camille Saint-Saëns, French composer (1835–1921).

he had seen from the platform at Tokyo Station. The buzz of enemy planes that constantly filled the clogged grey skies. Inami had died of an illness on the battlefield in Korea. Other friends had been killed in the South Seas or on islands in the Pacific. Somewhere within, he felt as though the postwar period was just an extension of life that he had been granted.

"Toshiko wants to go on a vacation to Guam with some of her friends." Glumly he continued to eat while his wife went on talking. Her face was fleshy around the eyelids and chin. It occurred to him that when he had seen Ono Mari in the restaurant tonight, her hair was streaked with flecks of silver.

90   "I saw Ono Mari today," he said, almost to himself.

"Who's she?" His wife smothered a yawn.

■ EXPLORATIONS OF THE TEXT

1. Describe the occasion and the setting. What do you learn about Konishi in the restaurant?
2. Why does Endō emphasize sky imagery?
3. Discuss Konishi's experience in the factory during the war. Why are the young men so unhappy when the red paper arrives?
4. Analyze the section on Ono Mari and her family. Why is this section in the narrative?
5. Why is Konishi so moved by Ono Mari's appearance in the restaurant many years later? What is the significance of her "hair streaked with flecks of silver"?
6. Examine Konishi's relationships at home. What accounts for his estrangement from his wife and daughters?
7. What are the ironies of the end of the story?
8. Compare the view of the brutality of war in this story with the treatment of the same theme in Pirandello's "War" and in O'Brien's "How to Tell a True War Story."

■ THE READING/WRITING CONNECTION

1. List your preconceptions of the Japanese during World War II. Does this story change your views in any way?
2. React to Konishi's character. What does he fear? Respond to this question in your journal.

■ IDEAS FOR WRITING

1. Characterize Konishi. How does he represent and symbolize the "war generation"?
2. What does the story reveal about life in Japan during World War II? Use exercise 1 in The Reading/Writing Connection as a beginning.
3. What is Ono Mari's role in the story?
4. Compare the attitudes about war and about being a soldier in Endō's story, in Owen's "Dulce et Decorum Est," in O'Brien's "How to Tell a True War Story," and/or in Pirandello's "War."
5. Discuss Endō's use of imagery, tone, and point of view.

TIM O'BRIEN

Tim O'Brien (1946-   ), born in Austin, Minnesota, was educated at Macalester College and Harvard University. He served in the U.S. Army in Vietnam, ultimately attaining the rank of sergeant, and much of his fiction reflects his experiences of the Vietnam War. His work includes Going After Cacciato *(1978), for which he was awarded the National Book Award;* The Things They Carried *(1990), which was nominated for the Pulitzer Prize;* In the Lake of the Woods *(1994);* Tomcat in Love *(1988), and* July, July *(2002). He is a frequent contributor to magazines and literary journals.*

1990

HOW TO TELL A TRUE WAR STORY

This is true.

I had a buddy in Vietnam. His name was Bob Kiley, but everybody called him Rat.

A friend of his gets killed, so about a week later Rat sits down and writes a letter to the guy's sister. Rat tells her what a great brother she had, how together the guy was, a number one pal and comrade. A real soldier's soldier, Rat says. Then he tells a few stories to make the point, how her brother would always volunteer for stuff nobody else would volunteer for in a million years, dangerous stuff, like doing recon or going out on these really badass night patrols. Stainless steel balls, Rat tells her. The guy was a little crazy, for sure, but crazy in a good way, a real daredevil, because he liked the challenge of it, he liked testing himself, just man against gook. A great, great guy, Rat says.

Anyway, it's a terrific letter, very personal and touching. Rat almost bawls writing it. He gets all teary telling about the good times they had together, how her brother made the war seem almost fun, always raising hell and lighting up villes and bringing smoke to bear every which way. A great sense of humor, too. Like the time at this river when he went fishing with a whole damn crate of hand grenades. Probably the funniest thing in world history, Rat says, all that gore, about twenty zillion dead gook fish. Her brother, he had the right attitude. He knew how to have a good time. On Halloween, this real hot spooky night, the dude paints up his body all different colors and puts on this weird mask and hikes over to a ville and goes trick-or-treating almost stark naked, just boots and balls and an M-16. A tremendous human being, Rat says. Pretty nutso sometimes, but you could trust him with your life.

5   And then the letter gets very sad and serious. Rat pours his heart out. He says he loved the guy. He says the guy was his best friend in the world. They were like soul mates, he says, like twins or something, they had a whole lot in common. He tells the guy's sister he'll look her up when the war's over.

So what happens?

Rat mails the letter. He waits two months. The dumb cooze never writes back.

A true war story is never moral. It does not instruct, nor encourage virtue, nor suggest models of proper human behavior, nor restrain men from doing the things men have always done. If a story seems moral, do not believe it. If at the end of a war story you feel uplifted, or if you feel that some small bit of rectitude has been salvaged from the larger waste, then you have been made the victim of a very old and terrible lie. There is no rectitude whatsoever. There is no virtue. As a first rule of thumb, therefore, you can tell a true war story by its absolute and uncompromising allegiance to obscenity and evil. Listen to Rat Kiley. Cooze, he says. He does not say bitch. He certainly does not say woman, or girl. He says cooze. Then he spits and stares. He's nineteen years old —it's too much for him—so he looks at you with those big sad gentle killer eyes and says *cooze,* because his friend is dead, and because it's so incredibly sad and true: she never wrote back.

You can tell a true war story if it embarrasses you. If you don't care for obscenity, you don't care for the truth; if you don't care for the truth, watch how you vote. Send guys to war, they come home talking dirty.

10   Listen to Rat: "Jesus Christ, man, I write this beautiful fuckin' letter, I slave over it, and what happens? The dumb cooze never writes back."

The dead guy's name was Curt Lemon. What happened was, we crossed a muddy river and marched west into the mountains, and on the third day we took a break along a trail junction in deep jungle. Right away, Lemon and Rat Kiley started goofing. They didn't understand about the spookiness. They were kids; they just didn't know. A nature hike, they thought, not even a war, so they went off into the shade of some giant trees—quadruple canopy, no sunlight at all—and they were giggling and calling each other yellow mother and playing a silly game they'd invented. The game involved smoke grenades, which were harmless unless you did stupid things, and what they did was pull out the pin and stand a few feet apart and play catch under the shade of those huge trees. Whoever chickened out was a yellow mother. And if nobody chickened out, the grenade would make a light popping sound and they'd be covered with smoke and they'd laugh and dance around and then do it again.

It's all exactly true.

It happened, to *me*, nearly twenty years ago, and I still remember that trail junction and those giant trees and a soft dripping sound somewhere beyond the trees. I remember the smell of moss. Up in the canopy there were tiny white blossoms, but no sunlight at all, and I remember the shadows spreading out under the trees where Curt Lemon and Rat Kiley were playing catch with smoke grenades. Mitchell Sanders sat flipping his yo-yo. Norman Bowker and Kiowa and Dave Jensen were dozing, or half dozing, and all around us were those ragged green mountains.

Except for the laughter things were quiet.

15   At one point, I remember, Mitchell Sanders turned and looked at me, not quite nodding, as if to warn me about something, as if he already *knew*, then after a while he rolled up his yo-yo and moved away.

It's hard to tell you what happened next.

They were just goofing. There was a noise, I suppose, which must've been the detonator, so I glanced behind me and watched Lemon step from the shade into bright sunlight. His face was suddenly brown and shining. A handsome kid, really. Sharp gray eyes, lean and narrow-waisted, and when he died it was almost beautiful, the way the sunlight came around him and lifted him up and sucked him high into a tree full of moss and vines and white blossoms.

In any war story, but especially a true one, it's difficult to separate what happened from what seemed to happen. What seems to happen becomes its own happening and has to be told that way. The angles of vision are skewed. When a booby trap explodes, you close your eyes and duck and float outside yourself. When a guy dies, like Curt Lemon, you look away and then look back for a moment and then look away again. The pictures get jumbled; you tend to miss a lot. And then afterward, when you go to tell about it, there is always that surreal seemingness, which makes the story seem untrue, but which in fact represents the hard and exact truth as it *seemed.*

In many cases a true war story cannot be believed. If you believe it, be skeptical. It's a question of credibility. Often the crazy stuff is true and the normal stuff isn't, because the normal stuff is necessary to make you believe the truly incredible craziness.

20   In other cases you can't even tell a true war story. Sometimes it's just beyond telling.

I heard this one, for example, from Mitchell Sanders. It was near dusk and we were sitting at my foxhole along a wide muddy river north of Quang Ngai. I remember how peaceful the twilight was. A deep pinkish red spilled out on the river, which moved without sound, and in the morning we would cross the river and march west into the mountains. The occasion was right for a good story.

"God's truth," Mitchell Sanders said. "A six-man patrol goes up into the mountains on a basic listening-post operation. The idea's to spend a week up there, just lie low and listen for enemy movement. They've got a radio along, so if they hear anything suspicious—anything—they're supposed to call in artillery or gunships, whatever it takes. Otherwise they keep strict field discipline. Absolute silence. They just listen."

Sanders glanced at me to make sure I had the scenario. He was playing with his yo-yo, dancing it with short, tight little strokes of the wrist.

His face was blank in the dusk.

25 "We're talking regulation, by-the-book LP. These six guys, they don't say boo for a solid week. They don't got tongues. *All* ears."

"Right," I said.

"Understand me?"

"Invisible."

Sanders nodded.

30 "Affirm," he said. "Invisible. So what happens is, these guys get themselves deep in the bush, all camouflaged up, and they lie down and wait and that's all they do, nothing else, they lie there for seven straight days and just listen. And man, I'll tell you—it's spooky. This is mountains. You don't *know* spooky till you been there. Jungle, sort of, except it's way up in the clouds and there's always this fog—like rain, except it's not raining—everything's all wet and swirly and tangled up and you can't see jack, you can't find your own pecker to piss with. Like you don't even have a body. Serious spooky. You just go with the vapors—the fog sort of takes you in . . . And the sounds, man. The sounds carry forever. You hear stuff no-body should *ever* hear."

Sanders was quiet for a second, just working the yo-yo, then he smiled at me.

"So after a couple days the guys start hearing this real soft, kind of wacked-out music. Weird echoes and stuff. Like a radio or something, but it's not a radio, it's this strange gook music that comes right out of the rocks. Faraway, sort of, but right up close, too. They try to ignore it. But it's a listening post, right? So they listen. And every night they keep hearing that crazyass gook concert. All kinds of chimes and xylophones. I mean, this is wilderness—no way, it can't be real—but there it *is,* like the mountains are tuned in to Radio fucking Hanoi. Naturally they get nervous. One guy sticks Juicy Fruit in his ears. Another guy al-most flips. Thing is, though, they can't report music. They can't get on the horn and call back to base and say, 'Hey, listen, we need some firepower, we got to blow away this weirdo gook rock band.' They can't do that. It wouldn't go down. So they lie there in the fog and keep their mouths shut. And what makes it extra bad, see, is the poor dudes can't horse around like normal. Can't joke it away. Can't even talk to each other except maybe in whis-pers, all hush-hush, and that just revs up the willies. All they do is listen."

Again there was some silence as Mitchell Sanders looked out on the river. The dark was coming on hard now, and off to the west I could see the mountains rising in silhouette, all the mysteries and unknowns.

"This next part," Sanders said quietly, "you won't believe."

35 "Probably not," I said.

"You won't. And you know why?" He gave me a long, tired smile. "Because it hap-pened. Because every word is absolutely dead-on true."

Sanders made a sound in his throat, like a sigh, as if to say he didn't care if I believed him or not. But he did care. He wanted me to feel the truth, to believe by the raw force of feeling. He seemed sad, in a way.

"These six guys," he said, "they're pretty fried out by now, and one night they start hearing voices. Like at a cocktail party. That's what it sounds like, this big swank gook cock-tail party somewhere out there in the fog. Music and chitchat and stuff. It's crazy, I know, but they hear the champagne corks. They hear the actual martini glasses. Real hoity-toity, all very civilized, except this isn't civilization. This is Nam.

"Anyway, the guys try to be cool. They just lie there and groove, but after a while they start hearing—you won't believe this—they hear chamber music. They hear violins and cel-los. They hear this terrific mama-san soprano. Then after a while they hear gook opera and a glee club and the Haiphong Boys Choir and a barbershop quartet and all kinds of weird chanting and Buddha-Buddha stuff. And the whole time, in the background, there's still that cocktail party going on. All these different voices. Not human voices, though. Because it's the mountains. Follow me? The rock—it's *talking*. And the fog, too, and the grass and the goddamn mongooses. Everything talks. The trees talk politics, the monkeys talk religion. The whole country. Vietnam. The place talks. It talks. Understand? Nam—it truly *talks*.

40   "The guys can't cope. They lose it. They get on the radio and report enemy move-ment—a whole army, they say—and they order up the firepower. They get arty and gun-ships. They call in air strikes. And I'll tell you, they fuckin' crash that cocktail party. All night long, they just smoke those mountains. They make jungle juice. They blow away trees and glee clubs and whatever else there is to blow away. Scorch time. They walk napalm up and down the ridges. They bring in the Cobras and F-4s[1], they use Willie Peter and HE and incendiaries. It's all fire. They make those mountains burn.

"Around dawn things finally get quiet. Like you never even *heard* quiet before. One of those real thick, real misty days—just clouds and fog, they're off in this special zone—and the mountains are absolutely dead-flat silent. Like Brigadoon—pure vapor, you know? Everything's all sucked up inside the fog. Not a single sound, except they still *hear* it.

"So they pack up and start humping. They head down the mountain, back to base camp, and when they get there they don't say diddly. They don't talk. Not a word, like they're deaf and dumb. Later on this fat bird colonel comes up and asks what the hell hap-pened out there. What'd they hear? Why all the ordnance? The man's ragged out, he gets down tight on their case. I mean, they spent six trillion dollars on firepower, and this fatass colonel wants answers, he wants to know what the fuckin' story is.

"But the guys don't say zip. They just look at him for a while, sort of funny like, sort of amazed, and the whole war is right there in that stare. It says everything you can't ever say. It says, man, you got *wax* in your ears. It says, poor bastard, you'll never know—wrong fre-quency—you don't *even* want to hear this. Then they salute the fucker and walk away, be-cause certain stories you don't ever tell."

You can tell a true war story by the way it never seems to end. Not then, not ever. Not when Mitchell Sanders stood up and moved off into the dark.

45   It all happened.

Even now, at this instant, I remember that yo-yo. In a way, I suppose, you had to be there, you had to hear it, but I could tell how desperately Sanders wanted me to believe him, his frustration at not quite getting the details right, not quite pinning down the final and definitive truth.

And I remember sitting at my foxhole that night, watching the shadows of Quang Ngai, thinking about the coming day and how we would cross the river and march west into the mountains, all the ways I might die, all the things I did not understand.

Late in the night Mitchell Sanders touched my shoulder.

"Just came to me," he whispered. "The moral, I mean. Nobody listens. Nobody hears nothin'. Like that fatass colonel. The politicians, all the civilian types. Your girlfriend. My girlfriend. Everybody's sweet little virgin girlfriend. What they need is to go out on LP. The vapors, man. Trees and rocks—you got to *listen* to your enemy."

---

[1] Fighter jets.

50   And then again, in the morning, Sanders came up to me. The platoon was preparing to move out, checking weapons, going through all the little rituals that preceded a day's march. Already the lead squad had crossed the river and was filing off toward the west.

"I got a confession to make," Sanders said. "Last night, man, I had to make up a few things."

"I know that."

"The glee club. There wasn't any glee club."

"Right."

55   "No opera."

"Forget it, I understand."

"Yeah, but listen, it's still true. Those six guys, they heard wicked sound out there. They heard sound you just plain won't believe."

Sanders pulled on his rucksack, closed his eyes for a moment, then almost smiled at me. I knew what was coming.

"All right," I said, "what's the moral?"

60   "Forget it.'"

"No, go ahead."

For a long while he was quiet, looking away, and the silence kept stretching out until it was almost embarrassing. Then he shrugged and gave me a stare that lasted all day.

"Hear that quiet, man?" he said. "That quiet—just listen. There's your moral."

In a true war story, if there's a moral at all, it's like the thread that makes the cloth. You can't tease it out. You can't extract the meaning without unraveling the deeper meaning. And in the end, really, there's nothing much to say about a true war story, except maybe "Oh."

65   True war stories do not generalize. They do not indulge in abstraction or analysis.

For example: War is hell. As a moral declaration the old truism seems perfectly true, and yet because it abstracts, because it generalizes, I can't believe it with my stomach. Nothing turns inside.

It comes down to gut instinct. A true war story, if truly told, makes the stomach believe.

This one does it for me. I've told it before—many times, many versions—but here's what actually happened.

We crossed that river and marched west into the mountains. On the third day, Curt Lemon stepped on a booby-trapped 105 round. He was playing catch with Rat Kiley, laughing, and then he was dead. The trees were thick; it took nearly an hour to cut an LZ for the dustoff.

70   Later, higher in the mountains, we came across a baby VC water buffalo. What it was doing there I don't know—no farms or paddies—but we chased it down and got a rope around it and led it along to a deserted village where we set up for the night. After supper Rat Kiley went over and stroked its nose.

He opened up a can of C rations, pork and beans, but the baby buffalo wasn't interested.

Rat shrugged.

He stepped back and shot it through the right front knee. The animal did not make a sound. It went down hard, then got up again, and Rat took careful aim and shot off an ear. He shot it in the hindquarters and in the little hump at its back. He shot it twice in the flanks. It wasn't to kill; it was to hurt. He put the rifle muzzle up against the mouth and shot the mouth away. Nobody said much. The whole platoon stood there watching, feeling all kinds of things, but there wasn't a great deal of pity for the baby water buffalo. Curt Lemon was dead. Rat Kiley had lost his best friend in the world. Later in the week he would write a long personal letter to the guy's sister, who would not write back, but for now it was a question of pain. He shot off the tail. He shot away chunks of meat below the ribs. All around us there was the smell of smoke and filth and deep greenery, and the evening was humid and very hot. Rat went to automatic. He shot randomly, almost casually, quick little spurts in the belly and butt. Then he reloaded, squatted down, and shot it in the left front knee. Again the animal fell hard and tried to get up, but this time it couldn't quite make it. It wobbled and went down sideways. Rat shot it in the nose. He bent forward and whispered something, as if talking to a pet, then he shot it in the throat. All the while the baby buffalo was silent, or almost silent, just a light bubbling sound where the nose had been. It lay very still. Nothing moved except the eyes, which were enormous, the pupils shiny black and dumb.

Rat Kiley was crying. He tried to say something, but then cradled his rifle and went off by himself.

75   The rest of us stood in a ragged circle around the baby buffalo. For a time no one spoke. We had witnessed something essential, something brand-new and profound, a piece of the world so startling there was not yet a name for it.

Somebody kicked the baby buffalo.

It was still alive, though just barely, just in the eyes.

"Amazing," Dave Jensen said. "My whole life, I never seen anything like it."

"Never?"

80   "Not hardly. Not once,"

Kiowa and Mitchell Sanders picked up the baby buffalo. They hauled it across the open square, hoisted it up, and dumped it in the village well.

Afterward, we sat waiting for Rat to get himself together.

"Amazing," Dave Jensen kept saying. "A new wrinkle. I never seen it before."

Mitchell Sanders took out his yo-yo. "Well, that's Nam," he said. "Garden of Evil. Over here, man, every sin's real fresh and original."

85 How do you generalize?

War is hell, but that's not the half of it, because war is also mystery and terror and adventure and courage and discovery and holiness and pity and despair and longing and love. War is nasty; war is fun. War is thrilling; war is drudgery. War makes you a man; war makes you dead.

The truths are contradictory. It can be argued, for instance, that war is grotesque. But in truth war is also beauty. For all its horror, you can't help but gape at the awful majesty of combat. You stare out at tracer rounds unwinding through the dark like brilliant red ribbons. You crouch in ambush as a cool, impassive moon rises over the nighttime paddies. You admire the fluid symmetries of troops on the move, the harmonies of sound and shape and proportion, the great sheets of metal-fire streaming down from a gunship, the illumination rounds, the white phosphorus, the purply orange glow of napalm, the rocket's red glare. It's not pretty, exactly. It's astonishing. It fills the eye. It commands you. You hate it, yes, but your eyes do not. Like a killer forest fire, like cancer under a microscope, any battle or bombing raid or artillery barrage has the aesthetic purity of absolute moral indifference—a powerful, implacable beauty—and a true war story will tell the truth about this, though the truth is ugly.

To generalize about war is like generalizing about peace. Almost everything is true. Almost nothing is true. At its core, perhaps, war is just another name for death, and yet any soldier will tell you, if he tells the truth, that proximity to death brings with it a corresponding proximity to life. After a firefight, there is always the immense pleasure of aliveness. The trees are alive. The grass, the soil—everything. All around you things are purely living, and you among them, and the aliveness makes you tremble. You feel an intense, out-of-the-skin awareness of your living self—your truest self, the human being you want to be and then become by the force of wanting it. In the midst of evil you want to be a good man. You want decency. You want justice and courtesy and human concord, things you never knew you wanted. There is a kind of largeness to it, a kind of godliness. Though it's odd, you're never more alive than when you're almost dead. You recognize what's valuable. Freshly, as if for the first time, you love what's best in yourself and in the world, all that might be lost. At the hour of dusk you sit at your foxhole and look out on a wide river turning pinkish red, and at the mountains beyond, and although in the morning you must cross the river and go into the mountains and do terrible things and maybe die, even so, you find yourself studying the fine colors on the river, you feel wonder and awe at the setting of the sun, and you are filled with a hard, aching love for how the world could be and always should be, but now is not.

Mitchell Sanders was right. For the common soldier, at least, war has the feel—the spiritual texture—of a great ghostly fog, thick and permanent. There is no clarity. Every-thing swirls. The old rules are no longer binding, the old truths no longer true. Right spills over into wrong. Order blends into chaos, love into hate, ugliness into beauty, law into an-archy, civility into savagery. The vapors suck you in. You can't tell where you are, or why you're there, and the only certainty is overwhelming ambiguity.

90 In war you lose your sense of the definite, hence your sense of truth itself, and there-fore it's safe to say that in a true war story nothing is ever absolutely true.

Often in a true war story there is not even a point, or else the point doesn't hit you until twenty years later, in your sleep, and you wake up and shake your wife and start telling the story to her, except when you get to the end you've forgotten the point again. And then for a long time you lie there watching the story happen in your head. You listen to your wife's breathing. The war's over. You close your eyes. You smile and think, Christ, what's the *point*?

This one wakes me up.

In the mountains that day, I watched Lemon turn sideways. He laughed and said some-thing to Rat Kiley. Then he took a peculiar half step, moving from shade into bright sun-light, and the booby-trapped 105 round blew him into a tree. The parts were just hanging there, so Dave Jensen and I were ordered to shinny up and peel him off. I remember the white bone of an arm. I remember pieces of skin and something wet and yellow that must've been the intestines. The gore was horrible, and stays with me. But what wakes me up twenty years later is Dave Jensen singing "Lemon Tree"[2] as we threw down the parts.

You can tell a true war story by the questions you ask. Somebody tells a story, let's say, and afterward you ask, "Is it true?" and if the answer matters, you've got your answer.

95 For example, we've all heard this one. Four guys go down a trail. A grenade sails out. One guy jumps on it and takes the blast and saves his three buddies.

Is it true?

The answer matters.

You'd feel cheated if it never happened. Without the grounding reality, it's just a trite bit of puffery, pure Hollywood, untrue in the way all such stories are untrue. Yet even if it did happen—and maybe it did, anything's possible—even then you know it can't be true, be-cause a true war story does not depend upon that kind of truth. Absolute occurrence is ir-relevant. A thing may happen and be a total lie; another thing may not happen and be truer than the truth. For example: Four guys go down a trail. A grenade sails out. One guy jumps

---

[2] A popular folk song.

on it and takes the blast, but it's a killer grenade and everybody dies anyway. Before they die, though, one of the dead guys says, "The fuck you do *that* for?" and the jumper says, "Story of my life, man," and the other guy starts to smile but he's dead.

That's a true story that never happened.

100 Twenty years later, I can still see the sunlight on Lemon's face. I can see him turning, looking back at Rat Kiley, then he laughed and took that curious half step from shade into sunlight, his face suddenly brown and shining, and when his foot touched down, in that instant, he must've thought it was the sunlight that was killing him. It was not the sunlight. It was a rigged 105 round. But if I could ever get the story right, how the sun seemed to gather around him and pick him up and lift him high into a tree, if I could somehow recreate the fatal whiteness of that light, the quick glare, the obvious cause and effect, then you would believe the last thing Curt Lemon believed, which for him must've been the final truth.

Now and then, when I tell this story, someone will come up to me afterward and say she liked it. It's always a woman. Usually it's an older woman of kindly temperament and humane politics. She'll explain that as a rule she hates war stories; she can't understand why people want to wallow in all the blood and gore. But this one she liked. The poor baby buffalo, it made her sad. Sometimes, even, there are little tears. What I should do, she'll say, is put it all behind me. Find new stories to tell.

I won't say it but I'll think it.

I'll picture Rat Kiley's face, his grief, and I'll think, *You dumb cooze.*

Because she wasn't listening.

105 It *wasn't* a war story. It was a *love* story.

But you can't say that. All you can do is tell it one more time, patiently, adding and subtracting, making up a few things to get at the real truth. No Mitchell Sanders, you tell her. No Lemon, no Rat Riley. No trail junction. No baby buffalo. No vines or moss or white blossoms. Beginning to end, you tell her, it's all made up. Every goddamn detail—the mountains and the river and especially that poor dumb baby buffalo. None of it happened. *None* of it. And even if it did happen, it didn't happen in the mountains, it happened in this little village on the Batangan Peninsula[3] and it was raining like crazy, and one night a guy named Stink Harris woke up screaming with a leech on his tongue. You can tell a true war story if you just keep on telling it.

And in the end, of course, a true war story is never about war. It's about sunlight. It's about the special way that dawn spreads out on a river when you know you must cross the river and march into the mountains and do things you are afraid to do. It's about love and memory. It's about sorrow. It's about sisters who never write back and people who never listen.

■ **EXPLORATIONS OF THE TEXT**

1. What could be the reason why Curt Lemon's sister didn't respond to Rat's letter? Evaluate Rat's reaction. Why did it affect him so deeply?
2. What is innovative about this story? Consider the metafictional elements and distinctive narrative voice.
3. The narrator states: "It's difficult to separate what happened from what seemed to happen." Discuss the relationship between memory and truth.
4. Discuss the moral of Mitchell Sanders' story. Is there one? If so, what is it?

---

[3] Area in central Vietnam, a Viet Cong stronghold during the Vietnam War.

5. What is the attitude toward "truth" in this story? What is the attitude about "generalizations"? What relationship do these abstract concepts share?

6. This story contains a multitude of horrifying images; however, it also offers many images of beauty, which lend a strong sense of hope to the story. Contemplate these images of beauty amid horror. Why are they so important to the narrator?

7. How does this story exemplify the statement, "True war stories do not generalize. They do not indulge in abstraction or analysis."

8. Respond to the following statement: "It wasn't a war story. It was a love story." Why does the narrator view it as such?

9. Contrast the process of depersonalization, of dehumanization, presented in this work with that in Ioannides's "Gregory" and Hartley's "I, Jailor."

■ THE READING/WRITING CONNECTION

1. This story blurs the lines between fact and fiction. Why? What effect does it create? Respond to this question in a paragraph.

2. For some, the process of writing may be therapeutic. Consider O'Brien's involvement as a soldier in the Vietnam War. Write one page on how the author is trying to battle his past through the manner in which he tells a war story and the manner in which this fictional story closely parallels many of his lived experiences.

■ IDEAS FOR WRITING

1. Respond to the narrator's suggestion that fiction sometimes seems truer than the truth because some truths are too hard to believe. How may the narrator be reaching for an emotional truth rather than a factual one?

2. Write about a time when you fabricated a factual truth to tap into a greater emotional truth.

3. As a writer, O'Brien has returned time and time again to his own memories of, and experiences in, the Vietnam War. Do you have certain memories of past experiences that continually resurface in your thoughts? How may writing about them help you to come to terms with, or at least better understand, your past? Experiment with this.

4. Although it seems contradictory, the narrator bends the truth to make it believable. Freewrite about a truth (e.g., personal, political, etc.) that is so horrifying that it appears to be fictional.

FREDERICK BUSCH

The author of more than twenty books, Frederick Busch (1941-   ) was educated at Muhlenberg College and Columbia University. He is currently Fairchild Professor of Literature at Colgate University. His novels include The Mutual Friend *(1978),* Girls *(1997),* The Night Inspector *(1999), and* A Memory of War *(2003). His awards include Guggenheim and Ingram-Merrill Fellowships. Busch's work explores the details of domestic life and the difficulties encountered by ordinary characters. "Ralph the Duck" is the second chapter of Busch's novel,* Girls.

1989

RALPH THE DUCK

I woke at up 5:25 because the dog was vomiting. I carried seventy-five pounds of heaving golden retriever to the door and poured him onto the silver, moonlit snow. "Good boy," I said because he'd done his only trick. Outside he retched, and I went back up, passing the sofa on which Fanny lay. I tiptoed with enough weight on my toes to let her know how considerate I was while she was deserting me. She blinked her eyes. I swear I heard her blink her eyes. Whenever I tell her that I hear her blink her eyes, she tells me I'm lying; but I can hear the damp slap of lash after I have made her weep.

In bed and warm again, noting the red digital numbers (5:29) and certain that I wouldn't sleep, I didn't. I read a book about men who kill each other for pay or for their honor. I forget which, and so did they. It was 5:45, the alarm would buzz at 6:00, and I would make a pot of coffee and start the wood stove; I would call Fanny and pour her coffee into her mug; I would apologize because I always did, and then she would forgive me if I hadn't been too awful—I didn't think I'd been that bad—and we would stagger through the day, exhausted but pretty sure we were all right, and we'd sleep that night, probably after sex, and then we'd waken in the same bed to the alarm at 6:00, or the dog, if he'd returned to the frozen deer carcass he'd been eating in the forest on our land. He loved what made him sick. The alarm went off, I got into jeans and woolen socks and a sweatshirt, and I went downstairs to let the dog in. He'd be hungry, of course.

I was the oldest college student in America, I thought. But of course I wasn't. There were always ancient women with their parchment for skin who graduated at seventy-nine from places like Barnard and the University of Georgia. I was only forty-two, and I hardly qualified as a student. I patrolled the college at night in a Bronco with a leaky exhaust system, and I went from room to room in the classroom buildings, kicking out students who were studying or humping in chairs—they'd do it *anywhere*—and answering emergency calls with my little blue light winking on top of the truck. I didn't carry a gun or a billy, but I had a flashlight that took six batteries and I'd used it twice on some of my overprivileged northeastern-playboy part-time classmates. On Tuesdays and Thursdays I would awaken at 6:00 with my wife, and I'd do my homework, and work around the house, and go to school at 11:30 to sit there for an hour and a half while thirty-five stomachs growled with hunger and boredom, and this guy gave instruction about books. Because I was on the staff, the college let me take a course for nothing every term. I was getting educated, in a kind of slow-motion way—it would have taken me something like fifteen or sixteen years to graduate, and I would no doubt get an F in gym and have to repeat—and there were times when I respected myself for it. Fanny often did, and that was fair incentive.

I am not unintelligent. *You are not an unintelligent writer,* my professor wrote on my paper about Nathaniel Hawthorne.[1] We had to read short stories, I and the other students, and then we had to write little essays about them. I told how I saw Kafka[2] and Hawthorne in a similar light, and I was not unintelligent, he said. He ran into me at dusk one time, when I answered a call about a dead battery and found out it was him. I jumped his Buick from the Bronco's battery, and he was looking me over, I could tell, while I clamped onto the terminals and cranked it up. He was a tall, handsome guy who never wore a suit. He wore khakis and sweaters, loafers or sneakers, and he was always talking to the female students with the brightest hair and best builds. But he couldn't get a Buick going on an ice-cold night, and he didn't know enough to look for cells going bad. I told him he was going to need a new battery and he looked me over the way men sometimes do with other men who fix their cars for them.

5   "Vietnam?"

---

[1] Nathaniel Hawthorne (1804–64), U.S. novelist and short story writer.
[2] Frank Kafka (1883–1924), Austrian novelist and short story writer who wrote nightmarish and surreal fiction.

I said, "Too old."

"Not at the beginning. Not if you were an adviser. So-called. Or one of the Phoenix Project fellas?"

I was wearing a watch cap made of navy wool and an old Marine fatigue jacket. Slick characters like my professor like it if you're a killer or at least a onetime middleweight fighter. I smiled like I knew something. "Take it easy," I said, and I went back to the truck to swing around the cemetery at the top of the campus. They'd been known to screw in down-filled sleeping bags on horizontal stones up there, and the dean of students didn't want anybody dying of frostbite while joined at the hip to a matriculating fellow resident of our northeastern camp for the overindulged.

He blinked his high beams at me as I went. "You are not an unintelligent driver," I said.

10 Fanny had left me a bowl of something made with sausage and sauerkraut and potatoes, and the dog hadn't eaten too much more than his fair share. He watched me eat his leftovers and then make myself a king-sized drink composed of sourmash whiskey and ice. In our back room, which is on the northern end of the house, and cold for sitting in that close to dawn, I sat and watched the texture of the sky change. It was going to snow, and I wanted to see the storm come up the valley. I woke up that way, sitting in the rocker with its loose right arm, holding a watery drink, and thinking right away of the girl I'd convinced to go back inside. She'd been standing outside her dormitory, looking up at a window that was dark in the midst of all those lighted panes—they never turned a light off, and often let the faucets run half the night—crying onto her bathrobe. She was barefoot in shoe-pacs, the brown ones so many of them wore unlaced, and for all I know she was naked under her robe. She was beautiful, I thought, and she was somebody's red-headed daughter, standing in a quadrangle how many miles from home weeping.

"He doesn't love anyone," the kid told me. "He doesn't love his wife—I mean his ex-wife. And he doesn't love the ex-wife before that, or the one before that. And you know what? He doesn't love me. I don't know anyone who *does!*"

"It isn't your fault if he isn't smart enough to love you," I said, steering her toward the truck. She stopped. She turned. "You know him?"

I couldn't help it. I hugged her hard, and she let me, and then she stepped back, and of course I let her go. "Don't you *touch* me! Is this sexual harassment? Do you know the rules? Isn't this sexual harassment?"

15 "I'm sorry," I said at the door to the truck. "But I think I have to be able to give you a grade before it counts as harassment."

She got in. I told her we were driving to the dean of students' house. She smelled like marijuana and something very sweet, maybe one of those coffee-with-cream liqueurs you don't buy unless you hate to drink.

As the heat of the truck struck her, she started going kind of clay-gray-green, and I reached across her to open the window.

"You touched my breast!" she said.

"It's the smallest one I've touched all night, I'm afraid."

20 She leaned out the window and gave her rendition of my dog.

But in my rocker, waking up, at whatever time in the morning in my silent house, I thought of her as someone's child. Which made me think of ours, of course. I went for more ice, and I started on a wet breakfast. At the door of the dean of students' house, she'd turned her chalky face to me and asked, "What grade would you give me, then?"

It was a week composed of two teachers locked out of their offices late at night, a Toyota with a flat and no spare, an attempted rape on a senior girl walking home from the library, a major fight outside a fraternity house (broken wrist and significant concussion), and variations on breaking-and-entering. I was scolded by the director of nonacademic services for embracing a student who was drunk; I told him to keep his job, but he called me back because I was right to hug her, he said, and also wrong, but what the hell, and would I please stay. I thought of the fringe benefits—graduation in only sixteen years—so I went back to work.

My professor assigned a story called "A Rose for Emily,"[3] and I wrote him a paper about the mechanics of corpse fucking, and how, since she clearly couldn't screw her dead boyfriend, she was keeping his rotten body in bed because she truly loved him. I called the paper "True Love." He gave me a B and wrote *See me, pls.* In his office after class, his feet up on his deck, he trimmed a cigar with a giant folding knife he kept in his drawer.

"You got to clean the hole out," he said, "or they don't draw."

25   "I don't smoke," I said.

"Bad habit. Real *habit,* though. I started in smoking 'em in Georgia, in the service. My C.O. smoked 'em. We collaborated on a brothel inspection one time, and we ended up smoking these with a couple of women—" He waggled his eyebrows at me, now that his malehood was established.

"Were the women smoking them too?"

He snorted laughter through his nose while the greasy smoke came curling off his thin, dry lips. "They were pretty smoky, I'll tell ya!" Then he propped his feet—he was wearing cowboy boots that day—and he sat forward. "It's a little hard to explain. But—hell. You just don't say *fuck* when you write an essay for a college prof. Okay?" Like a scoutmaster with a kid he'd caught in the outhouse jerking off: "All right? You don't wanna do that."

"Did it shock you?"

30   "Fuck, no, it didn't shock me. I just told you. It violates certain proprieties."

"But if I'm writing it to you, like a letter—"

"You're writing it for posterity. For some mythical reader someplace, not just me. You're making a *statement.*"

"Right. My statement said how hard it must be for a woman to fuck with a corpse."

"And a point worth making. I said so. Here."

35   "But you said I shouldn't say it."

"No. Listen. Just because you're talking about fucking, you don't have to say *fuck.* Does that make it any clearer?"

"No."

"I wish you'd lied to me just now," he said.

I nodded. I did too.

40   "Where'd you do your service?" he asked.

"Baltimore. Baltimore, Maryland.

"What's in Baltimore?"

"Railroads. I liaised on freight runs of army matériel. I killed a couple of bums on the road with my bare hands, though."

He snorted again, but I could see how disappointed he was. He'd been banking on my having been a murderer. Interesting guy in one of my classes, he must have told some terrific woman at an overpriced meal: I just *know* the guy was a rubout specialist in the Nam, he had to have said. I figured I should come to work wearing my fatigue jacket and a red bandanna tied around my head. Say "Man" to him a couple of times, hang a fist in the air for

---

[3] A story by William Faulkner.

grief and solidarity, and look terribly worn, exhausted by experiences he was fairly certain that he envied me. His dungarees were ironed, I noticed.

45 On Saturday we went back to the campus because Fanny wanted to see a movie called *The Seven Samurai.* I fell asleep, and I'm afraid I snored. She let me sleep until the auditorium was almost empty. Then she kissed me awake. "Who was screaming in my dream?" I asked her.

"Kurosawa," she said.

"Who?"

"Ask your professor friend."

I looked around, but he wasn't there. "Not an un-weird man," I said.

50 We went home and cleaned up after the dog and put him out. We drank a little Spanish brandy and went upstairs and made love. I was fairly premature, you might say, but one way and another by the time we fell asleep we were glad to be there with each other, and glad that it was Sunday coming up the valley toward us, and nobody with it. The dog was howling at another dog someplace, or at the moon, or maybe just his moon-thrown shadow on the snow. I did not strangle him when I opened the back door and he limped happily past me and stumbled up the stairs. I followed him into our bedroom and groaned for just being satisfied as I got into bed. You'll notice I didn't say fuck.

He stopped me in the hall after class on a Thursday, and asked me How's it going, just one of the kickers drinking sour beer and eating pickled eggs and watching the tube in a country bar. How's it goin. I nodded. I wanted a grade from the man, and I did want to learn about expressing myself. I nodded and made what I thought was a smile. He'd let his mustache grow out and his hair grow longer. He was starting to wear dark shirts with lighter ties. I thought he looked like someone in *The Godfather.* He still wore those light little loafers or his high-heeled cowboy boots. His corduroy pants looked baggy. I guess he wanted them to look that way. He motioned me to the wall of the hallway, and he looked and said, "How about the Baltimore stuff?"

I said, "Yeah?"

"Was that really true?" He was almost blinking, he wanted so much for me to be a damaged Vietnam vet just looking for a bell tower to climb into and start firing from. The college didn't have a bell tower you could get up into, though I'd once spent an ugly hour chasing a drunken ATO down from the roof of the observatory. "You were just clocking through boxcars in Baltimore?"

"I said, "Nah."

55 "I thought so!" He gave a kind of sigh.

"I killed people," I said.

"You know, I could have sworn you did," he said.

I nodded, and he nodded back. I'd made him so happy.

The assignment was to write something to influence somebody. He called it Rhetoric and Persuasion. We read an essay by George Orwell and "A Modest Proposal" by Jonathan Swift. I liked the Orwell better, but I wasn't comfortable with it. He talked about "niggers," and I felt him saying it two ways.

60 I wrote "Ralph the Duck."

Once upon a time, there was a duck named Ralph who didn't have any feathers on either wing. So when the cold wind blew, Ralph said, Brr, and shivered and shook.

What's the matter? Ralph's mommy asked.

I'm cold, Ralph said.

Oh, the mommy said. Here. I'll keep you warm.

65   So she spread her big, feathery wings, and hugged Ralph tight, and when the cold wind blew, Ralph was warm and snuggly, and fell fast asleep.

∞

The next Thursday, he was wearing canvas pants and hiking boots. He mentioned kind of casually to some of the girls in the class how whenever there was a storm he wore his Lake District walking outfit. He had a big, hairy sweater on. I kept waiting for him to make a noise like a mountain goat. But the girls seemed to like it. His boots made a creaky squeak on the linoleum of the hall when he caught up with me after class.

"As I told you," he said, "it isn't unappealing. It's just—not a college theme."

"Right," I said. "Okay. You want me to do it over?"

"No," he said. "Not at all. The D will remain your grade. But I'll read something else if you want to write it."

70   "This'll be fine," I said.

"Did you understand the assignment?"

"Write something to influence someone—Rhetoric and Persuasion."

We were at his office door and the redheaded kid who had gotten sick in my truck was waiting for him. She looked at me like one of us was in the wrong place, which struck me as accurate enough. He was interested in getting into his office with the redhead, but he remembered to turn around and flash me a grin he seemed to think he was known for.

Instead of going on shift a few hours after class, the way I'm supposed to, I told my supervisor I was sick, and I went home. Fanny was frightened when I came in, because I don't get sick and I don't miss work. She looked at my face and she grew sad. I kissed her hello and went upstairs to change. I always used to change my clothes when I was a kid, as soon as I came from school. I put on jeans and a flannel shirt and thick wool socks, and I made myself a dark drink of sourmash. Fanny poured herself some wine and came into the cold northern room a few minutes later. I was sitting in the rocker, looking over the valley. The wind was lining up a lot of rows of cloud so that the sky looked like a baked trout when you lift the skin off. "It'll snow," I said to her.

75   She sat on the old sofa and waited. After a while, she said, "I wonder why they always call it a mackerel sky?"

"Good eating, mackerel," I said.

Fanny said, "Shit! You're never that laconic unless you feel crazy. What's wrong? Who'd you punch out at the playground?"

"We had to write a composition," I said.

"Did he like it?"

80   "He gave me a D."

"Well, you're familiar enough with D's. I never saw you get this low over a grade."

"I wrote about Ralph the Duck."

She said, "You did?" She said, "Honey." She came over and stood beside the rocker and leaned into me and hugged my head and neck. "Honey," she said. "Honey."

It was the worst of the winter's storms, and one of the worst in years. That afternoon they closed the college, which they almost never do. But the roads were jammed with snow over ice, and now it was freezing rain on top of that, and the only people working at the school that night were the operator who took emergency calls and me. Everyone else had gone home except the students, and most of them were inside. The ones who weren't were drunk, and I kept on sending them in and telling them to act like grown-ups. A number of them said they were, and I really couldn't argue. I had the bright beams on, the defroster set high, the little blue light winking, and a thermos of sourmash and hot coffee that I sipped from every time I had to get out of the truck or every time I realized how cold all that wetness was out there.

85   About eight o'clock, as the rain was turning back to snow and the cold was worse, the roads impossible, just as I was done helping a county sander on the edge of the campus pull a panel truck out of a snowbank, I got the emergency call from the college operator. We had a student missing. The roommate thought the kid was headed for the quarry. This meant I had to get the Bronco up on a narrow road above the campus, above the old cemetery, into all kinds of woods and rough track that I figured would be chocked with ice and snow. Any kid up there would really have to want to be there, and I couldn't go in on foot, because you'd only want to be there on account of drugs, booze, or craziness, and either way I'd be needing blankets and heat, and then a fast ride down to the hospital in town. So I dropped into four-wheel drive to get me up the hill above the campus, bucking snow and sliding on ice, putting all the heater's warmth up onto the windshield because I couldn't see much more than swarming snow. My feet were still cold from the tow job, and it didn't seem to matter that I had on heavy socks and insulated boots I'd coated with waterproofing. I shivered, and I thought of Ralph the Duck.

I had to grind the rest of the way, from the cemetery, in four-wheel low, and in spite of the cold I was smoking my gearbox by the time I was close enough to the quarry—they really did take a lot of rocks for the campus buildings from there—to see I'd have to make my way on foot to where she was. It was a kind of scooped-out shape, maybe four or five stories high, where she stood—well, wobbled is more like it. She was as chalky as she'd been the last time, and her red hair didn't catch the light anymore. It just lay on her like something that had died on top of her head. She was in a white nightgown that was plastered to her body. She had her arms crossed as if she wanted to be warm. She swayed, kind of, in front of the big, dark, scooped-out rock face, where the trees and brush had been cleared for trucks and earthmovers. She looked tiny against all the darkness. From where I stood, I could see the snow driving down in front of the lights I'd left on, but I couldn't see it near her. All it looked like around her was dark. She was shaking with the cold, and she was crying.

I had a blanket with me, and I shoved it down the front of my coat to keep it dry for her, and because I was so cold. I waved. I stood in the lights and I waved. I don't know what she saw—a big shadow, maybe. I surely didn't reassure her, because when she saw me she backed up, until she was near the face of the quarry. She couldn't go any farther.

I called, "Hello! I brought a blanket. Are you cold? I thought you might want a blanket."

Her roommates had told the operator about pills, so I didn't bring her the coffee laced with mash. I figured I didn't have all that much time, anyway, to get her down and pumped out. The booze with whatever pills she'd taken would make her die that much faster.

90   I hated that word. Die. It made me furious with her. I heard myself seething when I breathed. I pulled my scarf and collar up above my mouth. I didn't want her to see how close I might come to wanting to kill her because she wanted to die.

I called, "Remember me?"

I was closer now. I could see the purple mottling of her skin. I didn't know if it was cold or dying. It probably didn't matter much to distinguish between them right now, I thought. That made me smile. I felt the smile, and I pulled the scarf down so she could look at it. She didn't seem awfully reassured.

"You're the sexual harassment guy," she said. She said it very slowly. Her lips were clumsy. It was like looking at a ventriloquist's dummy.

"I gave you an A," I said.

95   "When?"

"It's a joke," I said. "You don't want me making jokes. You want me to give you a nice warm blanket, though. And then you want me to take you home."

She leaned against the rock face when I approached. I pulled the blanket out, then zipped my jacket back up. The snow had stopped, I realized, and that wasn't really a very good sign. It felt like an arctic cold descending in its place. I held the blanket out to her, but she only looked at it.

"You'll just have to turn me in," I said. "I'm gonna hug you again."

She screamed, "No more! I don't want any more hugs!"

100 But she kept her arms on her chest, and I wrapped the blanket around her and stuffed a piece into each of her tight, small fists. I didn't know what to do for her feet. Finally, I got down on my haunches in front of her. She crouched down too, protecting herself.

"No," I said. "No. You're fine."

I took off the woolen mittens I'd been wearing. Mittens keep you warmer than gloves because they trap your hand's heat around the fingers and palms at once. Fanny had knitted them for me. I put a mitten as far onto each of her feet as I could. She let me. She was going to collapse, I thought.

"Now, let's go home," I said. "Let's get you better."

With her funny, stiff lips, she said. "I've been very self-indulgent and weird and I'm sorry. But I'd really like to die." She sounded so reasonable that I found myself nodding in agreement as she spoke.

105 "You can't just die," I said.

"Aren't I dying already? I took all of them, and then"—she giggled like a child, which of course is what she was—"I borrowed different ones from other people's rooms. See, this isn't some teenage cry for like *help*. Understand? I'm seriously interested in death and I have to like stay out here a little longer and fall asleep. All right?"

"You can't do that," I said. "You ever hear of Vietnam?"

"I saw that movie," she said. "With the opera in it? *Apocalypse*? Whatever."

"I was there!" I said. "I killed people! I helped to kill them! And when they die, you see their bones later on. You dream about their bones and blood on the ends of the splintered ones, and this kind of mucous stuff coming out of their eyes. You probably heard of guys having dreams like that, didn't you? Whacked-out Vietnam vets? That's me, see? So I'm telling you, I know about dead people and their eyeballs and everything falling out. And people keep dreaming about the dead people they knew, see? You can't make people dream about you like that! It isn't fair!"

110 "You dream about me?" She was ready to go. She was ready to fall down, and I was going to lift her up and get her to the truck.

"I will," I said. "If you die."

"I want you to," she said. Her lips were hardly moving now. Her eyes were closed. "I want you all to."

I dropped my shoulder and put it into her waist and picked her up and carried her down to the Bronco. She was talking, but not a lot, and her voice leaked down my back. I jammed her into the truck and wrapped the blanket around her better and then put another one down around her feet. I strapped her in with the seat belt. She was shaking, and her eyes were closed and her mouth open. She was breathing. I checked that twice, once when I strapped her in, and then again when I strapped myself in and backed up hard into a sapling and took it down. I got us into first gear, held the clutch in, leaned over to listen for breathing, heard it—heard it—shallow panting, like a kid asleep on your lap for a nap—and then I put the gear in and howled down the hillside on what I thought might be the road.

We passed the cemetery. I told her that was good sign. She didn't respond. I found myself panting too, as if we were breathing for each other. It made me dizzy, but I couldn't stop. We passed the highest dorm, and I dropped the truck into four-wheel high. The cab smelled like burnt oil and hot metal. We were past the chapel now, and the observatory, the president's house, then the bookstore. I had the blue light winking and the V-6 roaring, and I drove on the edge of out-of-control, sensing the skids just before I slid into them, and getting back out of them as I needed to. I took a little fender off once, and a bit of the corner of a classroom building, but I worked us back on course, and all I needed to do now was negotiate the sharp left turn around the Administration Building past the library, then floor it for the straight run to the town's main street and then the hospital.

115   I was panting into the mike, and the operator kept saying, "Say again?"

I made myself slow down some, and I said we'd need stomach pumping, and to get the names of the pills from her friends in the dorm, and I'd be there in less than five or we were crumpled up someplace and dead.

"Roger," the radio said. "Roger all that." My throat tightened and tears came into my eyes. They were helping us, they'd told me: Roger.

I said to the girl, whose head was slumped and whose face looked too blue all through its whiteness, "You know, I had girl once. My wife, Fanny. She and I had small girl one time."

I reached over and touched her cheek. It was cold. The truck swerved, and I got my hands on the wheel. I'd made the turn past the Ad Building using just my left. "I can do it in the dark," I sang to no tune I'd ever learned. "I can do it with one hand." I said to her, "We had a girl child, very small. Now, I do *not* want you dying."

120   I came to the campus gates doing fifty on the ice and snow, smoking the engine, grinding the clutch, and I bounced off a wrought iron fence to give me the curve going left that I needed. On a pool table, it would have been a bank shot worth applause. The town cop picked me up and got out ahead of me and let the street have all the lights and noise it could want. We banged up to the emergency room entrance and I was out and at the other door before the cop on duty, Elmo St. John, could loosen his seat belt. I loosened hers, and they took her away from me. I tried to talk to them, but they made me sit down and do my shaking on a dirty sofa decorated with drawings of little spinning wheels. Somebody brought me hot coffee, I think it was Elmo, but I couldn't hold it.

"They won't," he kept saying to me. "They won't."

"What?"

"You just been sitting there for a minute and a half like St. Vitus dancing, telling me, 'Don't let her die. Don't let her die.'"

"Oh."

125   "You all *right*?"

"How about the kid?"

"They'll tell us soon."

"She better be all right."

"That's right."

130   "She—somebody's gonna have to tell me plenty if she isn't."

"That's right."

"She better not die this time," I guess I said.

Fanny came downstairs to look for me. I was at the northern windows, looking through the mullions down the valley to the faint red line along the mounds and little peaks of the ridge beyond the valley. The sun was going to come up, and I was looking for it.

Fanny stood behind me. I could hear her. I could smell her hair and the sleep on her. The crimson line widened, and I squinted at it. I heard the dog limp in behind her, catching up. He panted and I knew why his panting sounded familiar. She put her hands on my shoulders and arms. I made muscles to impress her with, and then I let them go, and let my head drop down until my chin was on my chest.

135 "I didn't think you'd be able to sleep after that," Fanny said.

"I brought enough adrenaline home to run a football team."

"But you hate being a hero, huh? You're hiding in here because somebody's going to call, or come over, and want to talk to you—her parents for shooting sure, sooner or later. Or is that supposed to be part of the service up at the playground! Saving their suicidal daughters. Almost dying to find them in the woods and driving too fast for *any* weather, much less what we had last night. Getting their babies home. The bastards." She was crying. I knew she would be, sooner or later. I could hear the soft sound of her lashes. She sniffed and I could feel her arm move as she felt for the tissues on the coffee table.

"I have them over here," I said. "On the windowsill."

"Yes." She blew her nose, and the dog thumped his tail. He seemed to think it one of Fanny's finer tricks, and he had wagged for her for thirteen years whenever she'd done it. "Well, you're going to have to talk to them."

140 "I will," I said. "I will." The sun was in our sky now, climbing. We had built the room so we could watch it climb. "I think that jackass with the smile, my prof? She showed up a lot at his office, the last few weeks. He called her 'my advisee,' you know? The way those guys sound about what they're achieving by getting up and shaving and going to work and saying the same thing every day? Every year? Well, she was his advisee, I bet. He was shoving home the old advice."

"She'll be okay," Fanny said. "Her parents will take her home and love her up and get her some help." She began to cry again, then she stopped. She blew her nose, and the dog's tail thumped. She kept a hand between my shoulder and my neck. "So tell me what you'll tell a waiting world. How'd you talk her out?"

"Well, I didn't, really. I got up close and picked her up and carried her is all."

"You didn't say *anything*?"

"Sure I did. Kid's standing in the snow outside of a lot of pills, you're gonna say something.

145 "So what'd you *say*?"

"I told her stories," I said. "I did Rhetoric and Persuasion."

Fanny said, "Then you go in early on Thursday, you go in half an hour early, and you get that guy to jack up your grade."

■ **EXPLORATIONS OF THE TEXT**

1. What is your first impression of the point of view of the narrator? Is he a reliable narrator? Discuss voice and tone.
2. Summarize the main plot and subplots. How do they connect and reinforce each other?
3. Why does Busch include the hints at the relationship between the professor and the redheaded girl? Is this subplot necessary to the development of the story?
4. Discuss the significance of the story of "Ralph the Duck." What does it mean to the narrator and to his wife? To the reader? Discuss the levels of irony in its presentation.
5. Why does the writer include the description of the dog? What is the significance of this detail?
6. Explore the class critique and criticism of the academy presented in the story.
7. Discuss the significance of the repeated line, "Rhetoric and Persuasion."
8. Do you think that the narrator actually went to war? What is the significance of this detail?
9. How does the dialogue develop theme?
10. Compare visions of compassion and community presented in this work with the treatment of this theme in "How to Tell a True War Story."

▪ **THE READING/WRITING CONNECTION**

1. "Think" Topic: Is the narrator a sympathetic character? Why or why not? Explain your impression in a paragraph.

2. Journal Entry: How would this story change if it were narrated in third person from the point of view of the wife? Write a portion of the story from this perspective and analyze the results. What is the impact of the narrative point of view?

▪ **IDEAS FOR WRITING**

1. Discuss war as the central symbol in the story. How does this symbol connect the layers of the plot and suggest themes of the work?

2. How would the narrator of this work respond to "American Ignorance of War"? Construct a letter written by the narrator to Milosz.

Stories for Comparison/Contrast: In[Visibility]: Minorities vs. Majorities

ALICE WALKER (1944–   )   **1981**

NINETEEN FIFTY-FIVE

1955

The car is a brandnew red Thunderbird convertible, and it's passed the house more than once. It slows down real slow now, and stops at the curb. An older gentleman dressed like a Baptist deacon gets out on the side near the house, and a young fellow who looks about sixteen gets out on the driver's side. They are white, and I wonder what in the world they doing in this neighborhood.

Well, I say to J. T, put your shirt on, anyway, and let me clean these glasses offa the table.

We had been watching the ballgame on TV. I wasn't actually watching, I was sort of daydreaming, with my foots up in J. T.'s lap.

I seen 'em coming on up the walk, brisk, like they coming to sell something, and then they rung the bell, and J. T. declined to put on a shirt but instead disappeared into the bedroom where the other television is. I turned down the one in the living room; I figured I'd be rid of these two double quick and J. T. could come back out again.

5   Are you Gracie Mae Still? asked the old guy, when I opened the door and put my hand on the lock inside the screen.

And I don't need to buy a thing, said I.

What makes you think we're sellin? he asks, in that hearty Southern way that makes my eyeballs ache.

Well, one way or another and they're inside the house, and the first thing the young fellow does is raise the TV a couple of decibels. He's about five feet nine, sort of womanish looking, with real dark white skin and a red pouting mouth. His hair is black and curly and he looks like a Loosianna Creole.

About one of your songs, says the deacon. He is maybe sixty, with white hair and beard, white silk shirt, black linen suit, black tie and black shoes. His cold gray eyes look like they're sweating.

10   One of my songs?

      Traynor here just *loves* your songs. Don't you, Traynor? He nudges Traynor with his elbow. Traynor blinks, says something I can't catch in a pitch I don't register.

      The boy learned to sing and dance livin' round you people out in the country. Practically cut his teeth on you.

      Traynor looks up at me and bites his thumbnail.

      I laugh.

15   Well, one way or another they leave with my agreement that they can record one of my songs. The deacon writes me a check for five hundred dollars, the boy grunts his awareness of the transaction, and I am laughing all over myself by the time I rejoin J. T.

      Just as I am snuggling down beside him though I hear the front door bell going off again.

      Forgit his hat? Asks J. T.

      I hope not, I say.

      The deacon stands there leaning on the door frame and once again I'm thinking of those sweaty-looking eyeballs of his. I wonder if sweat makes your eyeballs pink because his are sure pink. Pink and gray and it strikes me that nobody I'd care to know is behind them.

20   I forgot one little thing, he says pleasantly. I forgot to tell you Traynor and I would like to buy up all of those records you made of the song. I tell you we sure do love it.

      Well, love it or not, I'm not so stupid as to let them do that without making 'em pay. So I says, Well, that's gonna cost you. Because, really, that song never did sell all that good, so I was glad they was going to buy it up. But on the other hand, them two listening to my song by themselves, and nobody else getting to hear me sing it, give me a pause.

      Well, one way or another the deacon showed me where I would come out ahead on any deal he had proposed so far. Didn't I give you five hundred dollars? he asked. What white man—and don't even need to mention colored—would give you more? We buy up all your records of that particular song: first, you git royalties. Let me ask you, how much you sell that song for in the first place? Fifty dollars? A hundred, I say. And no royalties from it yet, right? Right. Well, when we buy up all of them records you gonna git royalties. And that's gonna make all them race record shops sit up and take notice of Gracie Mae Still. And they gonna push all them other records of yourn they got. And you no doubt will become one of the big name colored recording artists. And then we can offer you another five hundred dollars for letting us do all this for you. And by God you'll be sittin' pretty! You can go out and buy you the kind of outfit a star should have. Plenty sequins and yards of red satin.

      I had done unlocked the screen when I saw I could get some more money out of him. Now I held it wide open while he squeezed through the opening between me and the door. He whipped out another piece of paper and I signed it.

      He sort of trotted out to the car and slid in beside Traynor, whose head was back against the seat. They swung around in a u-turn in front of the house and then they was gone.

25   J. T. was putting his shirt on when I got back to the bedroom. Yankees beat the Orioles 10–6, he said. I believe I'll drive out to Paschal's pond and go fishing. Wanta go?

      While I was putting on my pants J. T. was holding the two checks.

      I'm real proud of a woman that can make cash money without leavin' home, he said. And I said *Umph.* Because we met on the road with me singing in first one little low-life jook after another, making ten dollars a night for myself if I was lucky, and sometimes bringin' home nothing but my life. And J. T. just loved them times. The way I was fast and flashy and always on the go from one town to another. He loved the way my singin' made the dirt farmers cry like babies and the womens shout Honey, hush! But that's mens. They loves any style to which you can get 'em accustomed.

1956

My little grandbaby called me one night on the phone: Little Mama, Little Mama, there's a white man on the television singing one of your songs! Turn on channel 5.

Lord, if it wasn't Traynor. Still looking half asleep from the neck up, but kind of awake in a nasty way from the waist down. He wasn't doing too bad with my song either, but it wasn't just the song the people in the audience was screeching and screaming over, it was that nasty little jerk he was doing from the waist down.

30   Well, Lord have mercy, I said, listening to him. If I'da closed my eyes, it could have been me. He had followed every turning of my voice, side streets, avenues, red lights, train crossings and all. It give me a chill.

Everywhere I went I heard Traynor singing my song, and all the little white girls just eating it up. I never had so many ponytails switched across my line of vision in my life. They was so *proud*. He was a *genius*.

Well, all that year I was trying to lose weight anyway and that and high blood pressure and sugar kept me pretty well occupied. Traynor had made a smash from a song of mine, I still had seven hundred dollars of the original one thousand dollars in the bank, and I felt if I could just bring my weight down, life would be sweet.

1957

I lost ten pounds in 1956. That's what I give myself for Christmas. And J. T. and me and the children and their friends and grandkids of all description had just finished dinner—over which I had put on nine and a half of my lost ten—when who should appear at the front door but Traynor. Little Mama, Little Mama! It's that white man who sings —— —— ——. The children didn't call it my song anymore. Nobody did. It was funny how that happened. Traynor and the deacon had bought up all my records, true, but on his record he had put "written by Gracie Mae Still." Bur that was just another name on the label, like "produced by Apex Records."

On the TV he was inclined to dress like the deacon told him. But now he looked presentable.

35   Merry Christmas, said he.

And same to you. Son.

I don't know why I called him Son. Well, one way or another they're all our sons. The only requirement is that they be younger than us. But then again, Traynor seemed to be aging by the minute.

You looks tired, I said. Come on in and have a glass of Christmas cheer.

J. T. ain't never in his life been able to act decent to a white man he wasn't working for, but he poured Traynor a glass of bourbon and water, then he took all the children and grandkids and friends and whatnot out to the den. After while I heard Traynor's voice singing the song, coming from the stereo console. It was just the kind of Christmas present my kids would consider cute.

40   I looked at Traynor, complicit. But he looked like it was the last thing in the world he wanted to hear. His head was pitched forward over his lap, his hands holding his glass and his elbows on his knees.

I done sung that song seem like a million times this year, he said. I sung it on the Grand Ole Opry, I sung it on the Ed Sullivan show. I sung it on Mike Douglas, I sung it at the Cotton Bowl, the Orange Bowl. I sung it at Festivals. I sung it at Fairs. I sung it overseas in Rome, Italy, and once in a submarine *underseas*. I've sung it and sung it, and I'm making forty thousand dollars a day offa it, and you know what, I don't have the faintest notion what that song means.

Whatchumean, what do it mean? It mean what it says. All I could think was: These suckers is making forty thousand a *day* offa my song and now they gonna come back and try to swindle me out of the original thousand.

It's just a song, I said. Cagey. When you fool around with a lot of no count mens you sing a bunch of 'em. I shrugged.

Oh, he said. Well. He started brightening up. I just come by to tell you I think you are a great singer.

45   He didn't blush, saying that. Just said it straight out.

And I brought you a little Christmas present too. Now you take this little box and you hold it until I drive off. Then you take it outside under that first streetlight back up the street aways in front of that green house. Then you open the box and see . . . Well, just *see.*

What had come over this boy, I wondered, holding the box. I looked out the window in time to see another white man come up and get in the car with him and then two more cars full of white mens start out behind him. They was all in long black cars that looked like a funeral procession.

Little Mama, Little Mama, what it is? One of my grandkids come running up and started pulling at the box. It was wrapped in gay Christmas paper—the thick, rich kind that it's hard to picture folks making just to throw away.

J. T. and the rest of the crowd followed me out the house, up the street to the streetlight and in front of the green house. Nothing was there but somebody's gold-grilled white Cadillac. Brandnew and most distracting. We got to looking at it so till I almost forgot the little box in my hand. While the others were busy making 'miration I carefully took off the paper and ribbon and folded them up and put them in my pants pocket. What should I see but a pair of genuine solid gold caddy keys.

50   Dangling the keys in front of everybody's nose, I unlocked the caddy, motioned for J. T. to git in on the other side, and us didn't come back home for two days.

1960

Well, the boy was sure nuff famous by now. He was still a mite shy of twenty but already they was calling him the Emperor of Rock and Roll.

Then what should happen but the draft.

Well, says J. T. There goes all this Emperor of Rock and Roll business.

But even in the army the womens was on him like white on rice. We watched it on the News.

Dear Gracie Mae [he wrote from Germany],

How you? Fine I hope as this leaves me doing real well. Before I come in the army I was gaining a lot of weight and gitting jittery from making all them dumb movies. But now I exercise and eat right and get plenty of rest. I'm more awake than I been in ten years.

I wonder if you are writing any more songs?

Sincerely,
Traynor

55   I wrote him back:

Dear Son,

We is all fine in the Lord's good grace and hope this finds you the same. J. T. and me be out all times of the day and night in that car you give me—which you know you didn't have to do. Oh, and I do appreciate the mink and the new self-cleaning oven.

But if you send anymore stuff to eat from Germany I'm going to have to open up a store in the neighborhood just to get rid of it. Really, we have more than enough of everything. The Lord is good to us and we don't know Want.

Glad to here you is well and gitting your right rest. There ain't nothing like exercising to help that along. J. T. and me work some part of every day that we don't go fishing in the garden.

Well, so long Soldier.

Sincerely,
Gracie Mae

He wrote:

Dear Gracie Mae,

I hope you and J. T. like that automatic power tiller I had one of the stores back home send you. I went through a mountain of catalogs looking for it—I wanted something that even a woman could use.

I've been thinking about writing some songs of my own but every time I finish one it don't seem to be about nothing I've actually lived myself. My agent keeps sending me other people's songs but they just sound mooney. I can hardly git through 'em without gagging.

Everybody still loves that song of yours. They ask me all the time what do I think it means, really. I mean, they want to know just what *I* want to know. Where out of your life did it come from?

Sincerely,
Traynor

1968

I didn't see the boy for seven years. No. Eight. Because just about everybody was dead when I saw him again. Malcolm X, King, the president and his brother, and even J. T. J. T. died of a head cold. It just settled in his head like a block of ice, he said, and nothing we did moved it until one day he just leaned out the bed and died.

His good friend Horace helped me put him away, and then about a year later Horace and me started going together. We was sitting out on the front porch swing one summer night, dusk-dark, and I saw this great procession of lights winding to a stop.

Holy Toledo! said Horace. (He's got a real sexy voice like Ray Charles.) Look *at* it. He meant the long line of flashy cars and the white men in white summer suits jumping out on the drivers' sides and standing at attention. With wings they could pass for angels, with hoods they could be the Klan.

60   Traynor comes waddling up the walk.

And suddenly I know what it is he could pass for. An Arab like the ones you see in storybooks. Plump and soft and with never a care about weight. Because with so much money, who cares? Traynor is almost dressed like someone from a storybook too. He has on, I swear, about ten necklaces. Two sets of bracelets on his arms, at least one ring on every finger, and some kind of shining buckles on his shoes, so that when he walks you get quite a few twinkling lights.

Gracie Mae, he says, coming up to give me a hug. J. T.

I explain that J. T. passed. That this is Horace.

Horace, he says, puzzled but polite, sort of rocking back on his heels, Horace.

65   That's it for Horace. He goes in the house and don't come back.

Looks like you and me is gained a few, I say.

He laughs. The first time I ever heard him laugh. It don't sound much like a laugh and I can't swear that it's better than no laugh a'tall.

He's gitting fat for sure, but he's still slim compared to me. I'll never see three hundred pounds again and I've just about said (excuse me) fuck it. I got to thinking about it one day an' I thought: aside from the fact that they say it's unhealthy, my fat ain't never been no trouble. Mens always have loved me. My kids ain't never complained. Plus they's fat. And fat like I is I looks distinguished. You see me coming and know somebody's *there*.

Gracie Mae, he says, I've come with a personal invitation to you to my house tomorrow for dinner. He laughed. What did it sound like? I couldn't place it. See them men out there? he asked me. I'm sick and tired of eating with them. They don't never have nothing to talk about. That's why I eat so much. But if you come to dinner tomorrow we can talk about the old days. You can tell me about that farm I bought you.

70   I sold it, I said.

You did?

Yeah, I said, I did. Just cause I said I liked to exercise by working in a garden didn't mean I wanted five hundred acres! Anyhow, I'm a city girl now. Raised in the country it's true. Dirt poor—the whole bit—but that's all behind me now.

Oh well, he said, I didn't mean to offend you.

We sat a few minutes listening to the crickets.

75   Then he said: You wrote that song while you was still on the farm, didn't you, or was it right after you left?

You had somebody spying on me? I asked.

You and Bessie Smith got into a fight over it once, he said.

You *is* been spying on me!

But I don't know what the fight was about, he said. Just like I don't know what happened to your second husband. Your first one died in the Texas electric chair. Did you know that? Your third one beat you up, stole your touring costumes and your car and retired with a chorine to Tuskegee. He laughed. He's still there.

80   I had been mad, but suddenly I calmed down. Traynor was talking very dreamily. It was dark but seems like I could tell his eyes weren't right. It was like some*thing* was sitting there talking to me but not necessarily with a person behind it.

You gave up on marrying and seem happier for it. He laughed again. I married but it never went like it was supposed to. I never could squeeze any of my own life either into it or out of it It was like singing somebody else's record. I copied the way it was sposed to be *exactly* but I never had a clue what marriage meant.

I bought her a diamond ring big as your fist. I bought her clothes. I built her a mansion. But right away she didn't want the boys to stay there. Said they smoked up the bottom floor. Hell, there were *five* floors.

No need to grieve, I said. No need to. Plenty more where she come from.

He perked up. That's part of what that song means, ain't it? No need to grieve. Whatever it is, there's plenty more down the line.

85   I never really believed that way back when I wrote that song, I said. It was all bluffing then. The trick is to live long enough to put your young bluffs to use. Now if I was to sing that song today I'd tear it up. 'Cause I done lived long enough to know it's *true*. Them words could hold me up.

I ain't lived that long, he said.

Look like you on your way, I said. I don't know why, but the boy seemed to need some encouraging. And I don't know, seem like one way or another you talk to rich white folks and you end up reassuring *them*. But what the hell, by now I feel something for the boy. I wouldn't be in his bed all alone in the middle of the night for nothing. Couldn't be nothing worse than being famous the world over for something you don't even understand. That's what I tried to tell Bessie. She wanted that same song. Overheard me practicing it one day, said, with her hands on her hips: Gracie Mae, I'ma sing your song tonight. I *likes* it.

Your lips be too swole to sing, I said. She was mean and she was strong, but I trounced her.

Ain't you famous enough with your own stuff? I said. Leave mine alone. Later on, she thanked me. By then she was Miss Bessie Smith to the World, and I was still Miss Gracie Mae Nobody from Notasulga

90 The next day all these limousines arrived to pick me up. Five cars and twelve bodyguards. Horace picked that morning to start painting the kitchen.

Don't paint the kitchen, fool, I said. The only reason that dumb boy of ours is going to show me his mansion is because he intends to present us with a new house.

What you gonna do with it? he asked me, standing there in his shirtsleeves stirring the paint.

Sell it. Give it to the children. Live in it on weekends. It don't matter what I do. He sure don't care.

Horace just stood there shaking his head. Mama you sure looks *good*, he says. Wake me up when you git back.

95 *Fool*, I say, and pat my wig in front of the mirror.

The boy's house is something else. First you come to this mountain, and then you commence to drive and drive up this road that's lined with magnolias. Do magnolias grow on mountains? I was wondering. And you come to lakes and you come to ponds and you come to deer and you come up on some sheep. And I figure these two is sposed to represent England and Wales. Or something out of Europe. And you just keep on coming to stuff. And it's all pretty. Only the man driving my car don't look at nothing but the road. Fool. And then *finally*, after all this time, you begin to go up the driveway. And there's more magnolias— only they're not in such good shape. It's sort of cool up this high and I don't think they're gonna make it. And then I see this building that looks like if it had a name it would be The Tara Hotel. Columns and steps and outdoor chandeliers and rocking chairs. Rocking chairs? Well, and there's the boy on the steps dressed in a dark green satin jacket like you see folks wearing on TV late at night, and he looks sort of like a fat dracula with all that house rising behind him, and standing beside him there's this little white vision of loveliness that he introduces as his wife.

He's nervous when he introduces us and he says to her: This is Gracie Mae Still, I want you to know me. I mean . . . and she gives him a look that would fry meat.

Won't you come in, Gracie Mae, she says, and that's the last I see of her.

He fishes around for something to say or do and decides to escort me to the kitchen. We go through the entry and the parlor and the breakfast room and the dining room and the servants' passage and finally get there. The first thing I notice is that, altogether, there are five stoves. He looks about to introduce me to one.

100 Wait a minute, I say. Kitchens don't do nothing for me. Let's go sit on the front porch.

Well, we hike back and we sit in the rocking chairs rocking until dinner.

Gracie Mae, he says down the table, taking a piece of fried chicken from the woman standing over him, I got a little surprise for you.

It's a house, ain't it? I ask, spearing a chitlin.

You're getting *spoiled*, he says. And the way he says *spoiled* sounds funny. He slurs it. It sounds like his tongue is too thick for his mouth. Just that quick he's finished the chicken and is now eating chitlins *and* a pork chop. *Me* spoiled, I'm thinking.

105   I already got a house. Horace is right this minute painting the kitchen. I bought that house. My kids feel comfortable in that house.

But this one I bought you is just like mine. Only a little smaller.

I still don't need no house. And anyway who would clean it?

He looks surprised.

Really, I think, some peoples advance *so* slowly.

110   I hadn't thought of that. But what the hell, I'll get you somebody to live in.

I don't want other folks living 'round me. Makes me nervous.

You *don't*? It *do*?

What I want to wake up and see folks I don't even know for?

He just sits there downtable staring at me. Some of that feeling is in the song, ain't it? Not the words, the *feeling*. What I want to wake up and see folks I don't even know for? But I see twenty folks a day I don't even know, including my wife.

115   This food wouldn't be bad to wake up to though, I said. The boy had found the genius of corn bread.

He looked at me real hard. He laughed. Short. They want what you got but they don't want you. They want what I got only it ain't mine. That's what makes 'em so hungry for me when I sing. They getting the flavor of something but they ain't getting the thing itself. They like a pack of hound dogs trying to gobble up a scent.

You talking 'bout your fans?

Right. Right. He says.

Don't worry 'bout your fans, I say. They don't know their asses from a hole in the ground. I doubt there's a honest one in the bunch.

120   That's the point. Dammit, that's the point! He hits the table with his fist. It's so solid it don't even quiver. You need a honest audience! You can't have folks that's just gonna lie right back to you.

Yeah, I say, it was small compared to yours, but I had one. It would have been worth my life to try to sing 'em somebody else's stuff that I didn't know nothing about.

He must have pressed a buzzer under the table. One of his flunkies zombies up.

Git Johnny Carson, he says.

On the phone? asks the zombie.

125   On the phone, says Traynor, what you think I mean, git him offa the front porch? Move your ass.

So two weeks later we's on the Johnny Carson show.

Traynor is all corseted down nice and looks a little bit fat but mostly good. And all the women that grew up on him and my song squeal and squeal. Traynor says: The lady who wrote my first hit record is here with us tonight, and she's agreed to sing it for all of us, just like she sung it forty-five years ago. Ladies and Gentlemen, the great Gracie Mae Still!

"Well, I had tried to lose a couple of pounds my own self, but failing that I had me a very big dress made. So I sort of rolls over next to Traynor, who is dwarfed by me, so that when he puts his arm around back of me to try to hug me it looks funny to the audience and they laugh.

I can see this pisses him off. But I smile out there at 'em. Imagine squealing for twenty years and not knowing why you're squealing? No more sense of endings and beginnings than hogs.

130   It don't matter, Son, I say. Don't fret none over me.

I commence to sing. And I sound——wonderful. Being able to sing good ain't all about having a good singing voice a'tall. A good singing voice helps. But when you come up in the Hard Shell Baptist church like I did you understand early that the fellow that sings is the singer. Them that waits for programs and arrangements and letters from home is just good voices occupying body space.

So there I am singing my own song, my own way. And I give it all I got and enjoy every minute of it. When I finish Traynor is standing up clapping and clapping and beaming at first me and then the audience like I'm his mama for true. The audience claps politely for about two seconds.

Traynor looks disgusted

He comes over and tries to hug me again. The audience laughs.

135 Johnny Carson looks at us like we both weird.

Traynor is mad as hell. He's supposed to sing something called a love ballad. But instead he takes the mike, turns to me and says; Now see if my imitation still holds up. He goes into the same song, *our* song, I think, looking out at his flaky audience. And he sings it just the way he always did. My voice, my tone, my inflection, everything. But he forgets a couple of lines. Even before he's finished the matronly squeals begin.

He sits down next to me looking whipped.

It don't matter, Son, I say, patting his hand. You don't even know those people. Try to make the people you know happy.

Is that in the song? he asks.

140 Maybe, I say.

1977

For a few years I hear from him, then nothing. But trying to lose weight takes all the attention I got to spare. I finally faced up to the fact that my fat is the hurt I don't admit, not even to myself, and that I been trying to bury it from the day I was born. But also when you git real old, to tell the truth, it ain't as pleasant. It gits lumpy and slack. Yuck. So one day I said to Horace, I'ma git this shit offa me.

And he fell in with the program like he always try to do and Lord such a procession of salads and cottage cheese and fruit juice!

One night I dreamed Traynor had split up with his fifteenth wife. He said: *You meet 'em for no reason. You date 'em for no reason. You marry 'em for no reason. I do it all but I swear it's just like somebody else doing it. I feel like I can't remember Life.*

The boy's in trouble, I said to Horace.

145 You've always said that, he said.

I have?

Yeah. You always said he looked asleep. You can't sleep through life if you wants to live it.

You not such a fool after all, I said, pushing myself up with my cane and hobbling over to where he was. Let me sit down on your lap, I said, while this salad I ate takes effect.

In the morning we heard Traynor was dead. Some said fat, some said heart, some said alcohol, some said drugs. One of the children called from Detroit. Them dumb fans of his is on a crying rampage, she said. You just ought to turn on the t.v.

150 But I didn't want to see 'em. They was crying and crying and didn't even know what they was crying for. One day this is going to be a pitiful country, I thought.

Tayeb Salih (1929–   ) 1978

A HANDFUL OF DATES

I must have been very young at the time. While I don't remember exactly how old I was, I do remember that when people saw me with my grandfather they would pat me on the head and give my cheek a pinch—things they didn't do to my grandfather. The strange thing was that I never used to go out with my father, rather it was my grandfather who would take me with him wherever he went, except for the mornings when I would go to the mosque to learn the Koran. The mosque, the river and the fields—these were the landmarks in our life. While most of the children of my age grumbled at having to go to the mosque to learn the Koran, I used to love it. The reason was, no doubt, that I was quick at learning by heart and the Sheikh always asked me to stand up and recite the *Chapter of the Merciful* whenever we had visitors, who would pat me on my head and cheek just as people did when they saw me with my grandfather.

Yes, I used to love the mosque, and I loved the river too. Directly we finished our Koran reading in the morning I would throw down my wooden slate and dart off, quick as a genie, to my mother, hurriedly swallow down my breakfast, and run off for a plunge in the river. When tired of swimming about I would sit on the bank and gaze at the strip of water that wound away eastwards and hid behind a thick wood of acacia trees. I loved to give rein to my imagination and picture to myself a tribe of giants living behind that wood, a people tall and thin with white beards and sharp noses, like my grandfather. Before my grandfather ever replied to my many questions he would rub the tip of his nose with his forefinger; as for his beard, it was soft and luxuriant and as white as cotton-wool—never in my life have I seen anything of a purer whiteness or greater beauty. My grandfather must also have been extremely tall, for I never saw anyone in the whole area address him without having to look up at him, nor did I see him enter a house without having to bend so low that I was put in mind of the way the river wound round behind the wood of acacia trees. I loved him and would imagine myself, when I grew to be a man, tall and slender like him, walking along with great strides.

I believe I was his favourite grandchild: no wonder, for my cousins were a stupid bunch and I—so they say—was an intelligent child. I used to know when my grandfather wanted me to laugh, when to be silent; also I would remember the times for his prayers and would bring him his prayer-rug and fill the ewer for his ablutions without his having to ask me. When he had nothing else to do he enjoyed listening to me reciting to him from the Koran in a lilting voice, and I could tell from his face that he was moved.

One day I asked him about our neighbour Masood. I said to my grandfather: 'I fancy you don't like our neighbour Masood?'

5   To which he answered, having rubbed the tip of his nose: 'He's an indolent man and I don't like such people.'

I said to him: 'What's an indolent man?'

My grandfather lowered his head for a moment, then looking across at the wide expanse of field, he said: 'Do you see it stretching out from the edge of the desert up to the Nile bank? A hundred feddans. Do you see all those date palms? And those trees—sant, acacia and sayal? All this fell into Masood's lap, was inherited by him from his father.'

Taking advantage of the silence that had descended upon my grandfather, I turned my gaze from him to the vast area defined by his words. 'I don't care,' I told myself, 'who owns those date palms, those trees or this black, cracked earth—all I know is that it's the arena for my dreams and my playground.'

My grandfather then continued; 'Yes, my boy, forty years ago all this belonged to Masood—two-thirds of it is now mine.'

10   This was news to me for I had imagined that the land had belonged to my grandfather ever since God's Creation.

'I didn't own a single feddan when I first set foot in this village. Masood was then the owner of all these riches. The position has changed now, though, and I think that before Allah calls to Him I shall have bought the remaining third as well.'

I do not know why it was I felt fear at my grandfather's words—and pity for our neighbour Masood. How I wished my grandfather wouldn't do what he'd said! I remembered Masood's singing, his beautiful voice and powerful laugh that resembled the gurgling of water. My grandfather never used to laugh.

I asked my grandfather why Masood had sold his land.

'Women,' and from the way my grandfather pronounced the word I felt that 'women' was something terrible 'Masood, my boy, was a much-married man. Each time he married he sold me a feddan or two.' I made the quick calculation that Masood must have married some ninety women. Then I remembered his three wives, his shabby appearance, his lame donkey and its dilapidated saddle, his djellaba with the torn sleeves. I had all but rid my mind of the thoughts that jostled in it when I saw the man approaching us, and my grandfather and I exchanged glances.

15   'We'll be harvesting the dates today,' said Masood. 'Don't you want to be there?'

I felt, though, that he did not really want my grandfather to attend. My grandfather, however, jumped to his feet and I saw that his eyes sparkled momentarily with an intense brightness. He pulled me by the hand and we went off to the harvesting of Masood's dates,

Someone brought my grandfather a stool covered with an oxhide, while I remained standing. There was a vast number of people there, but though I knew them all, I found myself for some reason, watching Masood: aloof from the great gathering of people he stood as though it were no concern of his, despite the fact that the date palms to be harvested were his own. Sometimes his attention would be caught by the sound of a huge clump of dates crashing down from on high. Once he shouted up at the boy perched on the very summit of the date palm who had begun hacking at a clump with his long, sharp sickle: 'Be careful you don't cut the heart of the palm.'

No one paid any attention to what he said and the boy seated at the very summit of the date palm continued, quickly and energetically, to work away at the branch with his sickle till the clump of dates began to drop like something descending from the heavens.

I, however, had begun to think about Masood's phrase 'the heart of the palm'. I pictured the palm tree as something with feeling, something possessed of a heart that throbbed. I remembered Masood's remark to me when he had once seen me playing about with the branch of a young palm tree: 'Palm trees, my boy, like humans, experience joy and suffering.' And I had felt an inward and unreasoned embarrassment.

20   When I again looked at the expanse of ground stretching before me I saw my young companions swarming like ants around the trunks of the palm trees, gathering up dates and eating most of them. The dates were collected into high mounds. I saw people coming along and weighing them into measuring bins and pouring them into sacks, of which I counted thirty. The crowd of people broke up, except for Hussein the merchant, Mousa the owner of the field next to ours on the east, and two men I'd never seen before.

I heard a low whistling sound and saw that my grandfather had fallen asleep. Then I noticed that Masood had not changed his stance, except that he had placed a stalk in his mouth and was munching at it like someone surfeited with food who doesn't know what to do with the mouthful he still has.

Suddenly my grandfather woke up, jumped to his feet and walked towards the sacks of dates. He was followed by Hussein the merchant, Mousa the owner of the field next to ours, and the two strangers. I glanced at Masood and saw that he was making his way towards us with extreme slowness, like a man who wants to retreat but whose feet insist on going forward. They formed a circle round the sacks of dates and began examining them, some taking a date or two to eat. My grandfather gave me a fistful, which I began munching. I saw Masood filling the palms of both hands with dates and bringing them up close to his nose, then returning them.

Then I saw them dividing up the sacks between them. Hussein the merchant took ten; each of the strangers took five. Mousa the owner of the field next to ours on the eastern side took five, and my grandfather took five. Understanding nothing, I looked at Masood and saw that his eyes were darting about to left and right like two mice that have lost their way home.

'You're still fifty pounds in debt to me,' said my grandfather to Masood. 'We'll talk about it later.'

25   Hussein called his assistants and they brought along donkeys, the two strangers produced camels, and the sacks of dates were loaded on to them. One of the donkeys let out a braying which set the camels frothing at the mouth and complaining noisily. I felt myself drawing close to Masood, felt my hand stretch out towards him as though I wanted to touch the hem of his garment. I heard him make a noise in his throat like the rasping of a lamb being slaughtered. For some unknown reason, I experienced a sharp sensation of pain in my chest.

I ran off into the distance. Hearing my grandfather call after me, I hesitated a little, then continued on my way. I felt at that moment that I hated him. Quickening my pace, it was as though I carried within me a secret I wanted to rid myself of. I reached the river bank near the bend it made behind the wood of acacia trees. Then, without knowing why, I put my finger into my throat and spewed up the dates I'd eaten.

■ POETRY ■

W. H. AUDEN

W. H. Auden (1907–73), born in York, England, received a scholarship to Oxford University, where he studied science and engineering before changing his field of study to English. After immigrating to the United States and living there for a number of years, Auden became a citizen in 1946. He taught at colleges including Bryn Mawr and Barnard. Auden's work includes Poems *(1928), and* Some Poems *(1940); and the plays,* The Dance of Death *(1934) and* No More Peace! A Thoughtful Comedy *(1936). He also wrote introductions to many collections of verse and translated a number of works. His many awards include the King's Gold Medal for poetry in 1937 and the Pulitzer Prize for Poetry in 1948.*

1940

MUSÉE DES BEAUX ARTS

About suffering they were never wrong,
The Old Masters: how well they understood
Its human position; how it takes place
While someone else is eating or opening a window or just walking dully
        along
5 How, when the aged are reverently, passionately waiting
For the miraculous birth, there always must be
Children who did not specially want it to happen, skating
On a pond at the edge of the wood:
They never forgot

10 That even the dreadful martyrdom must run its course
Anyhow in a corner, some untidy spot
Where the dogs go on with their doggy life and the torturer's horse
Scratches its innocent behind on a tree.

In Brueghel's *Icarus*,[1] for instance: how everything turns away
15 Quite leisurely from the disaster; the ploughman may
Have heard the splash, the forsaken cry,
But for him it was not an important failure; the sun shone
As it had to on the white legs disappearing into the green
Water; and the expensive delicate ship that must have seen
20 Something amazing, a boy falling out of the sky,
Had somewhere to get to and sailed calmly on.

■ EXPLORATIONS OF THE TEXT

1. About what were the "Old Masters" correct? What views did the "Old Masters" hold about suffering?
2. Characterize the persona. How does he view suffering? Contrast the speaker's vision with that of the "Old Masters."
3. Discuss the symbolism of Brueghel's painting. How does the symbolism develop themes of the poem?
4. What does the poem suggest about heroism, great deeds, and suffering?
5. How would the father in the story "War" respond to the poem?

■ THE READING/WRITING CONNECTION

1. Respond to the speaker's view of suffering in this poem. Write a letter to the speaker.
2. Compare the views presented in this poem with those in "American Ignorance of War" or in "Gas."

■ IDEAS FOR WRITING

1. Compare the view of suffering presented in this work with that of Charlotte Delbo's persona in "Prayer to the Living to Forgive Them for Being Alive."

W. H. AUDEN (1907–73)   1940

THE UNKNOWN CITIZEN

(To JS/07/M/378
**This Marble Monument
is Erected by the State**)

He was found by the Bureau of Statistics to be
One against whom there was no official complaint,
And all the reports on his conduct agree
That, in the modern sense of an old-fashioned word, he was a saint,

---

[1] Peter Brueghel, Flemish painter (ca. 1525–69), whose painting, "Landscape with the Fall of Icarus," hangs in the Musees Royaux des Beaux-Arts in Brussels, Belgium. Icarus is a classical mythological figure who with his father, Daedalus, designed wings of wax and feathers, which they used to attempt to escape from Crete. Daedalus succeeded, but Icarus flew too close to the sun. The sun melted the boy's wings, and he plunged into the sea and drowned.

5 For in everything he did he served the Greater Community.
Except for the War till the day he retired
He worked in a factory and never got fired,
But satisfied his employers, Fudge Motors Inc.
Yet he wasn't a scab or odd in his views,
10 For his Union reports that he paid his dues,
(Our report on his Union shows it was sound)
And our Social Psychology workers found
That he was popular with his mates and liked a drink.
The Press are convinced that he bought a paper every day
15 And that his reactions to advertisements were normal in every way.
Policies taken out in his name prove that he was fully insured,
And his Health-card shows he was once in hospital but left it cured.
Both Producers Research and High-Grade Living declare
He was fully sensible to the advantages of the Installment Plan
20 And had everything necessary to the Modern Man,
A phonograph, a radio, a car and a frigidaire.
Our researchers into Public Opinion are content
That he held the proper opinions for the time of year;
When there was peace, he was for peace; when there was war, he went.
25 He was married and added five children to the population,
Which our Eugenist[1] says was the right number for a parent of his generation,
And our teachers report that he never interfered with their education.
Was he free? Was he happy? The question is absurd:
Had anything been wrong, we should certainly have heard.

■ EXPLORATIONS OF THE TEXT

1. Identify the **allusion** in the title. Why is it ironic? What is the occasion?
2. Why is the citizen called a "saint" in "the modern sense" of this word? What is "the modern sense" of the word?
3. How does he serve "the Greater Community"? Describe his work and his relationship to his union.
4. In lines 18 to 21, "the unknown citizen" is depicted as a perfect consumer. How? Why?
5. What is the importance of the following line: "And our teachers report that he never interfered with their education"?
6. With all the sources of information on the citzen, "Was he free? Was he happy?" Does it matter? Why was he "unknown"?
7. What critique of modern culture does Auden offer? Is his analysis still relevant?

■ THE READING/WRITING CONNECTION

1. Make a list of ways in which you are a conformist or a nonconformist.
2. Agree or disagree with Auden's arguments.
3. Discuss the **irony** in the closing.

■ IDEAS FOR WRITING

1. Characterize a contemporary unknown citizen.
2. Compare and contrast this poem with Ginsberg's "America."

---

[1] A scientist who studies ways to improve species, especially the human species, through careful selection of offspring by genetic means.

Lao-tzu

Lao-tzu lived during the sixth century b.c. in the ancient state of Ch'u in China. The Tao-te-Ching, *the major document of Taoism, is attributed to his authorship, although it may not be the work of a single person. Some of the* Tao-te-Ching's *sayings may date from the time of Confucius, but others are certainly later, and the book as a whole may date from 300 b.c. Indeed, the name Lao-tzu may represent a type of sage and not a specific person, though the work attributed to him has continued to be respected in China and throughout the world. The* Tao-te-Ching *is a collection of eighty-one poems or segments that present an eloquent expression of withdrawal from action, the way to virtue.*

c. 500–200 b.c.

WEAPONS AT BEST

Weapons at best are tools of bad omen,
Loathed and avoided by those of the Way.

In the usage of men of good breeding,
Honor is had at the left;
5 Good omens belong on the left;
Bad omens belong on the right;
And warriors press to the right!
When the general stands at the right
His lieutenant is placed at the left.
10 So the usage of men of great power
Follows that of the funeral rite.

Weapons are tools of bad omen,
By gentlemen not to be used;
But when it cannot be avoided,
15 They use them with calm and restraint.
Even in victory's hour
These tools are unlovely to see;
For those who admire them truly
Are men who in murder delight.

20 As for those who delight to do murder,
It is certain they never can get
From the world what they sought when ambition
Urged them to power and rule.

A multitude slain!—and their death
25 Is a matter for grief and for tears;
The victory after a conflict
Is a theme for a funeral rite.

■ EXPLORATIONS OF THE TEXT

1. What is the difference between "left" and "right" in stanza 2?
2. Why does Lao-tzu say that one may use arms "when it cannot be avoided?"

3. Why should the victor not rejoice? Why is taking pleasure in "a multitude slain" wrong, according to Lao-tzu?

4. Compare this poem with Owen's "Dulce et Decorum Est."

■ **THE READING/WRITING CONNECTION**

1. Respond to the following quotation from the *Tao-te-Ching:*
   "To quicken but not to own, to make but not to claim.
   To raise but not rule, this is called profound virtue."

2. Explore themes of "Weapons at Best."

■ **IDEAS FOR WRITING**

1. Agree or disagree with the following statements: "Arms are unblest among tools and not the superior man's tools. Only when it is unavoidable he uses them."

2. Compare this work with "Arms and the Boy" by Owen (see chapter 10).

WILFRED OWEN

Wilfred Owen (1893–1918), born in Shropshire, England, attended the University of London. In 1915, he joined the British army and served in a rifle corps during World War I. After seven months, he was injured and sent to a war hospital in Scotland, where he met another patient, poet Siegfried Sassoon, who encouraged him to write. After recovering from his injury, Owen returned to the battlefield in France and was awarded the Military Cross for gallantry under fire. He was killed while leading troops across the Sombre Canal just a week before the Armistice. His work was collected and published by Sassoon in a volume titled Poems *(1920).*

1920

DULCE ET DECORUM EST

    Bent double, like old beggars under sacks,
    Knock-kneed, coughing like hags, we cursed through sludge,
    Till on the haunting flares we turned our backs
    And towards our distant rest began to trudge.
5 Men marched asleep. Many had lost their boots
    But limped on, blood-shod. All went lame; all blind;
    Drunk with fatigue; deaf even to the hoots
    Of tired, outstripped Five-Nines[1] that dropped behind.

    Gas! Gas! Quick, boys!—An ecstasy of fumbling,
10 Fitting the clumsy helmets just in time;
    But someone still was yelling out and stumbling
    And flound'ring like a man in fire or lime . . .
    Dim, through the misty panes and thick green light,
    As under a green sea, I saw him drowning.

15 In all my dreams, before my helpless sight,
    He plunges at me, guttering, choking, drowning.

    If in some smothering dreams you too could pace
    Behind the wagon that we flung him in,

---

[1] Gas shells

And watch the white eyes writhing in his face,
20 His hanging face, like a devil's sick of sin;
If you could hear, at every jolt, the blood
Come gargling from the froth-corrupted lungs,
Obscene as cancer, bitter as the cud
Of vile, incurable sores on innocent tongues,—
25 My friend, you would not tell with such high zest
To children ardent for some desperate glory,
The old Lie: Dulce et decorum est
Pro patria mori.[2]

■ EXPLORATIONS OF THE TEXT

1. Discuss the **similes** in lines 1 and 2. What images of the young soldiers does Owen present?
2. Find the words with negative **connotations** in stanza 1. Why are the men "lame," "blind," "drunk with fatigue," and "deaf"?
3. Why does Owen shift to the **first person** in the second verse? What effect does this highly personal testimony achieve?
4. Whom does the narrator address as "you" in stanza 4? What is his purpose? Who is the audience?
5. Give a synopsis of the narrative in this poem. What is the attitude of the speaker? Describe the tone.
6. Discuss figures of speech, rhyme scheme, and sound. How do they contribute to the effectiveness of this work?
7. Compare "Dulce et Decorum Est" to "How to Tell a True War Story."

■ THE READING/WRITING CONNECTION

1. "Think" Topic: Gloss and annotate the text; identify and react to the similes in this poem.
2. In a mini-essay, respond to the vision of war in stanza 4 or the attitude toward war in stanza 2.

■ IDEAS FOR WRITING

1. Write an essay that takes a position on Horace's quotation. Refer to works in the chapter to support your points.
2. Explicate this poem. Concentrate on point of view, tone, and imagery. (Look at the analysis of Owen's "Arms and the Boy" in chapter 10 as a model.)
3. Does this poem persuade you that "war is Hell"? Why or why not?

MARY JO SALTER

Mary Jo Salter (1954–   ), a graduate of Harvard University, teaches at Mount Holyoke College. Her volumes of poetry include Henry Purcell in Japan *(1985) and* Unfinished Painting *(1989). Recent works include* Sunday Skaters *(1994) and* Kiss in Space *(1999). In the early 1980s, Salter lived in Japan for three years. She also has lived in France, Italy, and Iceland. These locations all figure into her poetry, leading some to regard her as a first-rate travel writer.*

1985

---

[2] "It is sweet and fitting to die for one's country" (Horace).

WELCOME TO HIROSHIMA

is what you first see, stepping off the train:
a billboard brought to you in living English
by Toshiba Electric. While a channel
silent in the TV of the brain

5 projects those flickering re-runs of a cloud
that brims its risen columnful like beer
and, spilling over, hangs its foamy head,[1]
you feel a thirst for history: what year

it started to be safe to breathe the air,
10 and when to drink the blood and scum afloat
on the Ohta River.[2] But no, the water's clear,
they pour it for your morning cup of tea

in one of the countless sunny coffee shops
whose plastic dioramas advertise
15 mutations of cuisine behind the glass:
a pancake sandwich; a pizza someone tops

with a maraschino cherry. Passing by
the Peace Park's floral hypocenter[3] (where
how bravely, or with what mistaken cheer,
20 humanity erased its own erasure),

you enter the memorial museum
and through more glass are served, as on a dish
of blistered grass, three mannequins. Like gloves
a mother clips to coatsleeves, strings of flesh

25 hang from their fingertips; or as if tied
to recall a duty for us, *Reverence
the dead whose mourners too shall soon be dead,*
but all commemoration's swallowed up

in questions of bad taste, how re-created
30 horror mocks the grim original,
and thinking at last *They should have left it all*
you stop. This is the wristwatch of a child.

Jammed on the moment's impact, resolute
to communicate some message, although mute,
35 it gestures with its hands at eight-fifteen
and eight-fifteen and eight-fifteen again

while tables of statistics on the wall
update the news by calling on a roll

---

[1] Reference to the telltale mushroom cloud of the atomic blast.
[2] River in Hiroshima.
[3] Epicenter of the blast.

of tape, death gummed on death, and in the case
40 adjacent, an exhibit under glass

is glass itself: a shard the bomb slammed in
a woman's arm at eight-fifteen, but some
three decades on—as if to make it plain
hope's only as renewable as pain,

45 and as if all the unsung
debasements of the past may one day come
rising to the surface once again—
worked its filthy way out like a tongue.

■ **EXPLORATIONS OF THE TEXT**
1. Why does Salter use the "welcome" sign as the title and the first line of the poem? What impact does this wording have?
2. Discuss the persona's response to the exhibits at Hiroshima. How do the exhibits represent the nuclear holocaust? Focus particularly on stanza 5. What messages do these images convey?
3. How does she use visceral, bodily images?
4. Why do the exhibits of the "wristwatch" and "shard of glass" capture the speaker's attention?
5. Explore the conception of witnessing enunciated in the last two stanzas.
6. How do the rhyme, rhythm, and stanzaic form further themes of the poem?

■ **THE READING/WRITING CONNECTION**
1. Freewrite and respond to the following line: "humanity erased its own erasure . . ." To what other historical events would this statement apply?
2. Gloss and annotate the poem. Explore the contrasting images of naïve hope versus understanding of pain; or present versus past realities.
3. "Think" Topic: What is the speaker's view of the exhibit? Connect her views with human beings' abilities to witness war.

■ **IDEAS FOR WRITING**
1. Compare the vision of witnessing war and genocide presented in this work with themes expressed in "American Ignorance of War," "Prayer to the Living to Forgive Them for Being Alive," and "Song of Bullets."
2. Compare the views of war presented in this work with those suggested in "The War Generation."

MARILYN CHIN

Marilyn Chin (1957–   ) was born in Hong Kong, raised in the United States, and educated at the University of Massachusetts at Amherst and the University of Iowa, where she received an M.F.A. in poetry. Chin has published several collections of her own poems, has translated Chinese poems, and has edited anthologies of literature. She also has published her poems in prestigious anthologies, including The Best American Poetry *(1996) and the* Pushcart Press XX *(1996), and won several awards and fellowships for her writing. Chin's poems explore the often-difficult process of cultural assimilation into mainstream American society.*

1987

LOVE POEM FROM NAGASAKI

To say you are beautiful, to say
trees are, grass is, everything under
the weather—you are not really, no.

But the dark cloud exposing a rim of sun,
5   the river sedge dotted with strange new flowers,
ten thousand dragonflies spinning around the moon . . .

Suddenly, the earth emits a fragrance
deadlier than the teeming of flowers . . .
Tonight I am in love—
10   from the squat houses of Nagaskai,

doves, bats, gnats
fly out
ecumenically.

■ EXPLORATIONS OF THE TEXT

1. Contrast images of the "beautiful" with the aftereffects of the bombing of Nagasaki. According to the speaker, how has that world changed?
2. Discuss the juxtapositions of destruction and creation in the work.
3. Explain the closing lines of the poem. Why do "doves, bats, gnats/fly out/ecumenically"?
4. How does the poem move beyond Nagasaki to present a vision of a post–nuclear holocaust world?
5. Why does Chin entitle the work a "love poem"?

■ THE READING/WRITING CONNECTION

1. Create a love poem in which you juxtapose images of beauty and ugliness or growth and decay.
2. In a journal entry, compare and contrast the vision of Nagasaki in this work with Salter's portrayal of Hiroshima in "Welcome to Hiroshima." Focus on the depiction of setting, the aftermath of the bombing, and the speaker's stance as a witness.

■ IDEAS FOR WRITING

1. Create a portrait of the speaker: her appearance, attitudes, gestures, actions, and background. Imagine the setting that she is in. What do you learn from creating the world of the poem?

YUSEF KOMUNYAKAA

Yusef Komunyakaa (1947–   ) was born in Bogalusa, Louisiana, and was educated at the University of Colorado, Colorado State University, and the University of California, Irvine, where he received an M.F.A. Komunyakaa has published twelve collections of poetry and has edited several others, including the Best American Poetry 2003 *and a translation of the Vietnamese poet Nguyen Quang Thieu,* The Insomnia of Fire *(1995). His many awards include the 1994 Pulitzer Prize for poetry for his collection* Neon Vernacular *(1993). Komunyakaa's poems often reflect his experience as a soldier in Vietnam.*

1988

FACING IT

My black face fades,
hiding inside the black granite.
I said I wouldn't,
dammit: No tears.
5 I'm stone. I'm flesh.
My clouded reflection eyes me
like a bird of prey, the profile of night
slanted against morning. I turn
this way—the stone lets me go.
10 I turn that way—I'm inside
the Vietnam Veterans Memorial
again, depending on the light
to make a difference.
I go down the 58,022 names,
15 half-expecting to find
my own in letters like smoke.
I touch the name Andrew Johnson;
I see the booby trap's white flash.
Names shimmer on a woman's blouse
20 but when she walks away
the names stay on the wall.
Brushstrokes flash, a red bird's
wings cutting across my stare.
The sky. A plane in the sky.
25 A white vet's image floats
closer to me, then his pale eyes
look through mine. I'm a widow.
He's lost his right arm
inside the stone. In the black mirror
30 a woman's trying to erase names;
No, she's brushing a boy's hair.

YUSEF KOMUNYAKAA (1947–)   **1988**

NUDE INTERROGATION

*D*id *you kill anyone over there?* Angela shifts her gaze from the Janis Joplin poster to
the Jimi Hendrix, lifting the pale muslin blouse over her head. The blacklight deepens the blues when the needle drops into the first groove of "All Along the Watchtower." I
don't want to look at the floor. *Did you kill anyone? Did you dig a hole, crawl inside, and*
5 *wait for your target?* Her miniskirt drops into a rainbow at her feet. Sandalwood incense
hangs a slow comet of perfume over the room. I shake my head. She unhooks her bra and
flings it against a bookcase made of plywood and cinderblocks. *Did you use an M-16, a*
handgrenade, a bayonet, or your own two strong hands, both thumbs pressed against that lit-
tle bird in the throat? She stands with her left thumb hooked into the elastic of her sky-blue
10 panties. When she flicks off the blacklight, snowy hills rush up to the windows. *Did you*
kill anyone over there? Are you right-handed or left-handed? Did you drop your gun after-

wards? Did you kneel beside the corpse and turn it over? She's nude against the falling snow. Yes. The record spins like a bull's-eye on the far wall of Xanadu. *Yes,* I say. *I was scared of the silence. The night was too big. And afterwards, I couldn't stop looking up at the sky.*

■ EXPLORATIONS OF THE TEXT

1. How does the speaker respond to the Vietnam Wall? List images that suggest his response.
2. Why does the poet use images of surface, depth, and reflection to depict the experience? What is the impact of portraying the speaker's face as "hiding inside the black granite"? Why is the speaker "inside/the Vietnam Veterans Memorial"?
3. What do the closing lines signify: ". . . In the black mirror/a woman's trying to erase names;/No she's brushing a boy's hair."
4. In "Nude Interrogation," analyze the speaker's character. Examine the conflict between the speaker and Angela.
5. In "Nude Interrogation," what does the italicized dialogue suggest?
6. Why does the poet include allusions to Janis Joplin, Jimi Hendrix, and Xanadu in "Nude Interrogation"?
7. Why does Komunyakaa use a love scene as the setting for a work about war? Is this a poem about love or war? Discuss the significance of the title.
8. Compare and contrast the motif of storytelling in "Nude Interrogation" and in Pirandello's "War."
9. Compare and contrast the motif of war stories in these works, in Rivera's "Gas," in Busch's "Ralph the Duck," and in O'Brien's "How to Tell a True War Story." What do the war stories reveal about the protagonists? What do they reveal about the state of war?

■ THE READING/WRITING CONNECTION

1. "Think" Topic: In O'Brien's "How to Tell a True War Story," the narrator suggests that war stories are, ultimately, "love" stories. How do these poems and Rivera's "Gas" prove or refute this point of view?
2. Choose one or two lines from one of these two poems about war or a line from another work about war in this chapter, and use it as the opening of your own poem about war.
3. In a journal entry, examine why you think that Komunyakaa wrote "Nude Interrogation" as a prose poem. Transform it into stanzaic form, and compare the two versions. What are the differences between the two? You also may examine Forché's "The Colonel," another example of the form.

■ IDEAS FOR WRITING

1. Compare and contrast the speaker's attitude toward war in these poems with that of the protagonist in Busch's "Ralph the Duck" or the autobiographical persona in Hartley's "I, Jailor."
2. In "Making the Memorial," an autobiographical essay published in *The New York Review of Books*, Maya Lin suggests that memorials "should be . . . honest about the reality of war, about the loss of life in war." Do these poems project this sense of honesty? In what ways?
3. Lin also suggests in that essay that she saw "the wall as pure surface, an interface between light and dark," "an interface between the world of the living and the world of the dead." How does her vision of the memorial illuminate the poem?

LANGSTON HUGHES

Langston Hughes (1902–67), born in Joplin, Missouri, wrote more than twenty books—poetry, fiction, drama, and nonfiction—becoming the best-known African American writer of his generation. Hughes, educated at Columbia University, published his first book of poems, The Weary Blues, *in 1926. He was a member of the group of writers and artists known as the Harlem Renaissance, who celebrated African American experience and attempted to find literary forms more suited to it. In 1961, Hughes became a member of the National Academy of Arts and Letters. His works include* Shakespeare in Harlem *(1942),* One Way Ticket *(1949), and* Ask Your Mamma *(1961).*

1938

LET AMERICA BE AMERICA AGAIN

Let America be America again.
Let it be the dream it used to be.
Let it be the pioneer on the plain
Seeking a home where he himself is free.

5 (America never was America to me.)

Let America be the dream the dreamers dreamed—
Let it be that great strong land of love
Where never kings connive nor tyrants scheme
That any man be crushed by one above.

10 (It never was America to me.)

O, let my land be a land where Liberty
Is crowned with no false patriotic wreath,
But opportunity is real, and life is free,
Equality is in the air we breathe.

15 (There's never been equality for me,
Nor freedom in this "homeland of the free.")

Say who are you that mumbles in the dark?
And who are you that draws your veil across the stars?

I am the poor white, fooled and pushed apart,
20 I am the red man driven from the land.
I am the refugee clutching the hope I seek—
But finding only the same old stupid plan

Of dog eat dog, of mighty crush the weak.
I am the Negro, "problem" to you all.
25 I am the people, humble, hungry, mean—
Hungry yet today despite the dream.
Beaten yet today—O, Pioneers!
I am the man who never got ahead,
The poorest worker bartered through the years.
30 Yet I'm the one who dreamt our basic dream
In that Old World while still a serf of kings,
Who dreamt a dream so strong, so brave, so true,
That even yet its mighty daring sings
In every brick and stone, in every furrow turned
35 That's made America the land it has become.
O, I'm the man who sailed those early seas
In search of what I meant to be my home—

For I'm the one who left dark Ireland's shore,
And Poland's plain, and England's grassy lea,
40 And torn from Black Africa's strand I came
To build a "homeland of the free."

The free?
Who said the free? Not me?
Surely not me? The millions on relief today?
45 The millions who have nothing for our pay
For all the dreams we've dreamed
And all the songs we've sung
And all the hopes we've held
And all the flags we've hung,
50 The millions who have nothing for our pay—
Except the dream we keep alive today.

O, let America be America again—
The land that never has been yet—
And yet must be—the land where *every* man is free.
55 The land that's mine—the poor man's, Indian's, Negro's, ME—
Who made America,
Whose sweat and blood, whose faith and pain,
Whose hand at the foundry, whose plow in the rain,
Must bring back our mighty dream again.

60 O, yes,
I say it plain,
America never was America to me,
And yet I swear this oath—
America will be!

■ **EXPLORATIONS OF THE TEXT**

1. What does the title mean? Who is the speaker? For whom does he speak?
2. What dreams of America emerge in the first three stanzas? What is the meaning of America in the refrain?
3. Describe the transformation of the speaker which begins in line 19: "I am the poor white, fooled and pushed apart."
4. What criticisms of America does the speaker make? Compare them to Ginsberg's "America." Are the issues similar?
5. Analyze the **paradox:**
   "O let America be America again—
   The land that never has been yet—"
6. How does the speaker's attitude change in the last stanza?
7. Examine Hughes' use of **irony.** (See chapter 11 for a discussion of irony.)
8. Consider the form of this poem—line length, repetition, stanza divisions—and compare this work with Whitman's "Out of the Cradle Endlessly Rocking" in chapter 4.

■ **THE READING/WRITING CONNECTION**

1. "Think" Topic: Write about one of Hughes' two Americas.
2. Respond to Hughes' poem in a double-entry notebook.

3. Respond to a contemporary event as if you were Hughes. Create a monologue in his voice. Or, how would Twilight Bey respond to Hughes's vision?

■ **IDEAS FOR WRITING**
1. Write about speaker and voice in "Let America Be America Again."
2. Agree or disagree with Hughes' analysis of America.
3. Explicate and evaluate this poem. Focus on imagery, paradox, tone, irony, and/or form.
4. Compare this poem with Ginsberg's "America."

LANGSTON HUGHES   1951

HARLEM

What happens to a dream deferred?

Does it dry up
like a raisin in the sun?
Or fester like a sore—
5   And then run?
Does it stink like rotten meat?
Or crust and sugar over—
like a syrupy sweet?

Maybe it just sags
10 like a heavy load.

Or does it explode?

■ **EXPLORATIONS OF THE TEXT**
1. What is the connection between the title and the opening question?
2. What possible consequences does the speaker suggest?
3. Why does Hughes create so many **similes**? Are they effective? Why does he use so many questions? Are they effective?
4. Why does the persona speak only one declarative sentence?
5. Why is the last question isolated and written in italics? What are the implications? What is the answer?
6. Examine the rhyme scheme and other formal elements in the poem. What makes "Harlem" work?
7. Compare themes in this poem to those in works by Auden, Ginsberg, and Angelou.

■ **THE READING/WRITING CONNECTION**
1. Gloss and annotate the poem, and write an end comment.
2. Journal Entry: Write about "a dream deferred" in your own life. Compare your experience with the lost hopes of the poem.

■ **IDEAS FOR WRITING**
1. Explicate formal elements—figures of speech, sound, rhyme, and rhythm—in "Harlem."
2. Consider each of the similes and paraphrase them. Write a cause-effect analysis of the "dream deferred."

GWENDOLYN BROOKS

Gwendolyn Brooks (1917–2000), born in Topeka, Kansas, graduated from Wilson Junior College. A novelist and poet, she taught at a number of colleges and universities, including Columbia University and the University of Wisconsin. Her many works include the novel Maud Martha *(1953) and volumes of poetry, including* Annie Allen *(1949), which won the Pulitzer Prize for Poetry,* The Bean Eaters *(1960), and* To Disembark *(1981). She was the first African American poet to win the Pulitzer Prize, and she received numerous other awards and honors. She was Distinguished Professor of the Arts at the City College of New York in 1971.*

In 1954, the Supreme Court ordered desegregation of schools "with all deliberate speed" in a landmark decision in the case of Brown v. The Board of Education of Topeka, Kansas.

1960

THE CHICAGO DEFENDER SENDS A MAN TO LITTLE ROCK

In Little Rock[1] the people bear
Babes, and comb and part their hair
And watch the want ads, put repair
To roof and latch. While wheat toast burns
5   A woman waters multiferns.

Time upholds or overturns
The many, tight, and small concerns.

In Little Rock the people sing
Sunday hymns like anything,
10 Through Sunday pomp and polishing.

And after testament and tunes,
Some soften Sunday afternoons
With lemon tea and Lorna Doones.[2]

I forecast
15 And I believe
Come Christmas Little Rock will cleave
To Christmas tree and trifle, weave,
From laugh and tinsel, texture fast.

In Little Rock is baseball; Barcarolle.[3]
20 That hotness in July . . . the uniformed figures raw and implacable
And not intellectual,
Batting the hotness or clawing the suffering dust.
The Open Air Concert, on the special twilight green. . . .

---

[1] Little Rock, Arkansas, scene of one test of the Supreme Court case (*Brown* v. *The Board of Education*) concerning desegregation of schools. Federal troops in 1957 had to be sent to enforce the Supreme Court decision and integrate Little Rock High School.

[2] Cookies.

[3] Venetian boat song with a rowing rhythm or music imitating such songs.

When Beethoven[4] is brutal or whispers to lady-like air.
25 Blanket-sitters are solemn, as Johann[5] troubles to lean
To tell them what to mean. . . .

There is love, too, in Little Rock. Soft women softly
Opening themselves in kindness,
Or, pitying one's blindness,
30 Awaiting one's pleasure
In azure
Glory with anguished rose at the root. . . .
To wash away old semi-discomfitures.
They re-teach purple and unsullen blue.
35 The wispy soils go. And uncertain
Half-havings have they clarified to sures.

In Little Rock they know
Not answering the telephone is a way of rejecting life,
That it is our business to be bothered, is our business
40 To cherish bores or boredom, be polite
To lies and love and many-faceted fuzziness.
I scratch my head, massage the hate-I-had.
I blink across my prim and pencilled pad.
The saga I was sent for is not down.
45 Because there is a puzzle in this town.
The biggest News I do not dare
Telegraph to the Editor's chair:
"They are like people everywhere."

The angry Editor would reply
50 In hundred harryings of Why.

And true, they are hurling spittle, rock,
Garbage and fruit in Little Rock.
And I saw coiling storm a-writhe
On bright madonnas. And a scythe
55 Of men harassing brownish girls.
(The bows and barrettes in the curls
And braids declined away from joy.)

I saw a bleeding brownish boy. . . .

The lariat lynch-wish I deplored.

60 The loveliest lynchee was our Lord.

---

[4] Ludwig van Beethoven, German composer (1770–1827).
[5] Johann Sebastian Bach, German composer (1685–1750).

■ **EXPLORATIONS OF THE TEXT**

1. Examine the first four stanzas, and describe life in Little Rock.
2. Who is the narrator? Why is the narrator in Little Rock?
3. What is the nature of love in Little Rock? Describe the "soft women." Interpret this section carefully.
4. Why is the narrator so puzzled that the citizens of Little Rock "are like people everywhere"? What are the implications of this conclusion?
5. What has the man sent to Little Rock actually seen? What acts of harassment and violence happen there?
6. Why are the last three lines separated into stanzas? What is the effect?
7. What is traditional about the form of this poem?
8. Compare and contrast this poem with works by Hughes, Deavere Smith, and Ginsberg.

■ **THE READING/WRITING CONNECTION**

1. Freewrite. Respond to the idea that the people in Little Rock who opposed desegregation "are like people everywhere."
2. "Think" Topic: Is this poem still relevant, or is it an interesting and powerful description of a singular moment in history? Respond to this question in a paragraph.

■ **IDEAS FOR WRITING**

1. Write a brief research paper on the historical context of this poem.
2. What are the functions of setting in this poem?

ALLEN GINSBERG

Allen Ginsberg (1926–97) was born in Newark, New Jersey. After graduating from Columbia University, Ginsberg went to San Francisco, where he worked on his long poem, Howl, *which was published in 1956 and which distinguished him as a major Beat writer in the company of Jack Kerouac and William S. Burroughs. The Beat writers were characterized by their attempt to combine socially marginal behavior with the quest for spiritual enlightenment. During the early 1960s, he traveled extensively; during the late 1960s, he received a Guggenheim fellowship and visited many colleges and universities. Ginsberg taught at City College in New York and Naropa Institute in Colorado. His work,* Collected Poems *(1984), gives a view of American life over several decades, introducing readers to hundreds of personalities of the times.*

1956

AMERICA

America I've given you all and now I'm nothing.
America two dollars and twentyseven cents January 17, 1956.
I can't stand my own mind.
America when will we end the human war?
5 Go fuck yourself with your atom bomb.
I don't feel good don't bother me.
I won't write my poem till I'm in my right mind.
America when will you be angelic?
When will you take off your clothes?
10 When will you look at yourself through the grave?

When will you be worthy of your million Trotskyites?[1]
America why are your libraries full of tears?
America when will you send your eggs to India?
I'm sick of your insane demands.
15 When can I go into the supermarket and buy what I need with my good looks?
America after all it is you and I who are perfect not the next world.
Your machinery is too much for me.
You made me want to be a saint.
There must be some other way to settle this argument.
20 Burroughs[2] is in Tangiers[3] I don't think he'll come back it's sinister.
Are you being sinister or is this some form of practical joke?
I'm trying to come to the point.
I refuse to give up my obsession.
America stop pushing I know what I'm doing.
25 America the plum blossoms are falling.
I haven't read the newspapers for months, everyday somebody goes on trial
        for murder.
America I feel sentimental about the Wobblies.[4]
America I used to be a communist when I was a kid I'm not sorry.
I smoke marijuana every chance I get.
30 I sit in my house for days on end and stare at the roses in the closet.
When I go to Chinatown I get drunk and never get laid.
My mind is made up there's going to be trouble.
You should have seen me reading Marx.[5]
My psychoanalyst thinks I'm perfectly right.
35 I won't say the Lord's Prayer.
I have mystical visions and cosmic vibrations.

America I still haven't told you what you did to Uncle Max after he came
        over from Russia.
I'm addressing you.
Are you going to let your emotional life be run by Time Magazine?
40 I'm obsessed by Time Magazine.
I read it every week.
Its cover stares at me every time I slink past the corner candystore.
I read it in the basement of the Berkeley Public Library.
It's always telling me about responsibility. Businessmen are serious.
45   Movie producers are serious. Everybody's serious but me.
It occurs to me that I am America.
I am talking to myself again.

Asia is rising against me.
I haven't got a chinaman's chance.

---

[1] Those who believe in principles proposed by Leon Trotsky, especially the adoption of worldwide communism through revolution.

[2] William S. Burroughs, American Beat novelist (1914–97).

[3] Port on the Strait of Gibralter in North Morocco.

[4] Members of the Industrial Workers of the World.

[5] Karl Marx, German philosopher and Socialist (1818–83).

50 I'd better consider my national resources.
   My national resources consist of two joints of marijuana millions of genitals
        an unpublishable private literature that jetplanes 1400 miles
        an hour and twentyfive-thousand mental institutions.
   I say nothing about my prisons nor the millions of underprivileged who
55   live in my flowerpots under the light of five hundred suns.
   I have abolished the whorehouses of France, Tangiers is the next to go.
   My ambition is to be President despite the fact that I'm a Catholic.

   America how can I write a holy litany in your silly mood?
   I will continue like Henry Ford my strophes are as individual as his
60   automobiles more so they're all different sexes.
   America I will sell you strophes $2500 apiece $500 down on your old strophe
   America free Tom Mooney[6]
   America save the Spanish Loyalists[7]
   America Sacco & Vanzetti must not die[8]
65 America I am the Scottsboro boys.[9]
   America when I was seven momma took me to Communist Cell meetings
        they sold us garbanzos a handful per ticket a ticket costs a nickel
        and the speeches were free everybody was angelic and sentimental
        about the workers it was all so sincere you have no idea what a
70   good thing the party was in 1835 Scott Nearing was a grand old
        man a real mensch Mother Bloor the Silk-strikers' Ewig-Weibliche[10]
           made me cry I once saw the Yiddish orator Israel Amter plain.[11]
           Everybody must have been a spy.
   America you don't really want to go to war.
75 America it's them bad Russians.
   Them Russians them Russians and them Chinamen. And them Russians.
   The Russia wants to eat us alive. The Russia's power mad. She wants to take
        our cars from out our garages.
   Her wants to grab Chicago. Her needs a Red *Reader's Digest.* Her wants our
        auto plants in Siberia. Him big bureaucracy running our fillingstations.
80 That no good. Ugh. Him make Indians learn read. Him need big black niggers.
        Hah. Her make us all work sixteen hours a day. Help.
   America this is quite serious.
   America this is the impression I get from looking in the television set.
   America is this correct?
   I'd better get right down to the job.
85 It's true I don't want to join the Army or turn lathes in precision parts
        factories, I'm nearsighted and psychopathic anyway.
   America I'm putting my queer shoulder to the wheel.

---

[6] American Wobbly, convicted for murder in 1916 and pardoned more than twenty years latter.

[7] Spaniards, Republicans, who opposed Franco's Nationalists during the Spanish Civil War (1936–39).

[8] Nicola Sacco (1891–1927) and Bartolemeo Vanzetti (1888–1927), American anarchists who were executed.

[9] Nine African American youths convicted of raping two white women; a controversial case because of lack of evidence.

[10] Ewig-Weibliche: "Eternal feminine" in German.

[11] Nearing, Bloor, and Amter; American leftists.

■ EXPLORATIONS OF THE TEXT

1. Describe the speaker. Focus on his character traits, tone, values, and attitudes.
2. In addressing "America" as his audience, to whom does he speak? What are his criticisms of his culture?
3. Why does he state "It occurs to me that I am America./I am talking to myself again"?
4. Analyze the section beginning: "Asia is rising against me." From whose view is the persona speaking? Is this change of point of view effective?
5. Discuss the speaker's vocation as a writer.
6. How are the historical allusions—Spanish Loyalists, Sacco and Vanzetti, Communist cell meetings—important to the poem?
7. Why does he speak in baby talk, in "Indian" dialect? When does the voice shift?
8. What impact does the humor have? Does it develop themes of the work?
9. In the last line, does the speaker change his point of view and attitude? How?
10. Compare this poem to the poems by Brooks and Hughes.

■ THE READING/WRITING CONNECTION

1. Make a catalogue of the criticisms of America. Are they valid?
2. Write a humorous critique about some aspect of life in the United States. Begin with "America, I . . . ."

■ IDEAS FOR WRITING

1. Analyze the speaker in this poem. How does Ginsberg achieve this characterization? Discuss voice, tone, imagery, humor, word choice, and/or theme. Compose a diary entry in the speaker's voice.
2. Compare themes of this poem with another work in this chapter.
3. Compare this poem with Whitman's "Out of the Cradle Endlessly Rocking" in chapter 4.

GLORIA ANZALDÚA

Gloria Anzaldúa (1942–2004) was born in Jesus Maria in the Rio Grande Valley of South Texas. She was educated at Pan American University and the University of Texas, Austin. Her first book, This Bridge Called My Back: Writings by Radical Women of Color (1981), co-edited by Cherrie Moraga, won the 1986 Before Columbus Foundation American Book Award. Anzaldúa has worked in the migrant farmers movement, and she has taught at colleges including the University of Texas, Austin, and Vermont College of Norwich University. Her other works include Borderlands/La Frontera: The New Mestiza (1987), Making Faces, Making Soul/Haciendo Caras (1990), and The Dark One (1997). Anzaldúa also has written several children's books, including Prietita Has a Friend (1991) and Friends from the Other Side (1993). Anzaldúa's work reflects her commitment as a politically active Chicana feminist and lesbian.

1987

horse
(para la gente de Hargill, Texas)[1]

Great horse running in the fields
come thundering toward

---

[1] For the people of Hargill, Texas.

the outstretched hands
nostrils flaring at the corn
5   only it was knives in the hidden hands
can a horse smell tempered steel?

Anoche[2] some kids cut up a horse
it was night and the *pueblo*[3] slept
the Mexicans mutter among themselves:
10 they hobbled the two front legs
the two hind legs, kids aged sixteen
but they're *gringos*[4]
and the sheriff won't do a thing
he'd just say boys will be boys
15 just following their instincts.

But it's the mind that kills
the animal the *mexicanos* murmur
killing it would have been a mercy
black horse running in the dark
20 came thundering toward
the outstretched hands
nostrils flaring at the smell
only it was knives in the hidden hands
did it pray all night for morning?

25 It was the owner came running
30-30 in his hand
put the *caballo*[5] out of its pain
the Chicanos shake their heads
turn away some rich father
30 fished out his wallet
held out the folds of green
as if green could staunch red

pools dripping from the ribbons
on the horse's flanks
35 could cast up testicles
grow back the ears on the horse's head
no ears of corn but sheaths
hiding blades of steel
earth drinking blood sun rusting it
40 in that small Texas town
the *mexicanos* shuffle their feet
shut their faces stare at the ground.

---

[2] Last night.
[3] Village.
[4] Whites.
[5] Horse.

Dead horse neighing in the night
come thundering toward the open faces
45 hooves iron-shod hurling lightning

only it is red red in the moonlight
in their sleep the *gringos* cry out
the *mexicanos* mumble if you're Mexican
you are born old.

■ **EXPLORATIONS OF THE TEXT**

1. Examine the image of the horse in stanza 1. What is the effect of "the outstretched hands"? of the "knives"? What is the meaning of the corn?
2. Does the story of the boys who cut the horse have symbolic meaning?
3. Explain: "It's the mind that kills."
4. Why does the speaker repeat the image of the horse and the hands with the corn and the knives? Is the repetition effective?
5. Why do the Mexicanos "shuffle their feet/shut their faces stare at the ground" and "mumble"?
6. Examine the **paradox** in the next-to-last stanza. How can the dead horse still thunder "toward the open faces"?
7. Why do the gringos "cry"?
8. How do the last two lines convey themes of the work?
9. Discuss symbolism, imagery, and language in this poem. Is the use of Spanish words and phrases effective?
10. Compare the themes of oppression and bigotry in this poem with similar ideas in "Harlem" or "The Chicago Defender Sends a Man to Little Rock."

■ **THE READING/WRITING CONNECTION**

1. Gloss and annotate the poem, and write an end comment. See the example in chapter 2.
2. React to the situations of the Mexicans and Chicanos. Why are they "born old"? Freewrite.

■ **IDEAS FOR WRITING**

1. What does the story symbolize about the attitudes of the gringos toward other people, animals, land, things? Do you agree?
2. Compare the ending of this poem and the endings of works by Griffin, Angelou, Rose, and Harjo. Discuss the reversals, the anger, and the desire for change and for retribution.

JOY HARJO

Joy Harjo (1951–   ), a member of the Creek Tribe, was born in Tulsa, Oklahoma. Educated at the University of New Mexico and the University of Iowa, Harjo has taught writing at Arizona State University, Tempe, and at the University of American Indian Arts in Santa Fe, New Mexico. Her volumes of poetry include The Last Song *(1975),* She Has Some Horses *(1985),* In Mad Love and War *(1990), and* A Map to the Next World: Poetry and Tales *(2000). She has received numerous awards, including one from the American Academy of Poetry and two from the National Endowment of the Arts. In addition to writing poetry, Harjo's band, Joy Harjo and Poetic Justice, has released several recordings, including* The Woman Who Fell from the Sky *(1994) and* Letter from the End of the Twentieth Century *(1997). Harjo's work is influenced by her respect for nature.*

1990

FOR ANNA MAE AQUASH WHOSE SPIRIT IS PRESENT HERE AND IN THE DAPPLED STARS
For we remember the story and must tell it again so we may all live

Beneath a sky blurred with mist and wind,
            I am amazed as I watch the violet
heads of crocuses erupt from the stiff earth
               after dying for a season,
5 as I have watched my own dark head
            appear each morning after entering
the next world
        to come back to this one,
             amazed.
10 It is the way in the natural world to understand the place
          the ghost dancers[1] named
after the heart breaking destruction.
              Anna Mae,
           everything and nothing changes
15 You are the shimmering young woman
         who found her voice
when you were warned to be silent, or have your body cut away
from you like an elegant weed.
        You are the one whose spirit is present in the dappled stars.
20 (They prance and lope like colored horses who stay with us
      through the streets of these steely cities. And I have seen them
     nuzzling the frozen bodies of tattered drunks
        on the corner.)
This morning when the last star is dimming
25   and the buses grind toward
the middle of the city, I know it is ten years since they buried
you the second time in Lakota, a language that could
          free you.
I heard about it in Oklahoma, or New Mexico
30   how the wind howled and pulled everything down
in a righteous anger.
   (It was the women who told me) and we understood wordlessly
the ripe meaning of your murder.
   As I understand ten years later after the slow changing
35   of the seasons

---

[1] Dancers who performed the Ghost Dance, a group dance begun by late nineteenth-century Native Americans to promote the return of the dead and the restoration of the spiritual life of the tribe.

that we have just begun to touch
<blockquote>the dazzling whirlwind of our anger,</blockquote>
we have just begun to perceive the amazed world the ghost
dancers entered
40 <blockquote>crazily, beautifully.</blockquote>

■ EXPLORATIONS OF THE TEXT

1. Describe the setting and season. What is the attitude of the speaker? Explain the following lines: "as I have watched my own dark head/appear each morning after entering/the next world/to come back to this one,/amazed."
2. What is the place "the ghost dancers named"? How can it be understood?
3. How is Anna Mae invoked and described? Consider the star imagery and the extension of the **metaphor.**
4. What does the speaker mean when she says "I know it is ten years since they buried/you the second time in Lakota, a language that could/free you"?
5. Examine the last five lines. What is "the dazzling whirlwind" of anger? What is "the amazed world the ghost/dancers entered"?
6. Discuss the images of beauty and of destruction in this poem. How do they reveal theme?
7. Compare the political message of this poem to the ideas in Hughes's "Let America Be America Again" and Ginsberg's "America."

■ THE READING/WRITING CONNECTION

1. Imitate this poem, and write to someone who has died for a political cause.
2. Write a double-entry journal on this poem.
3. Freewrite about the line: "everything and nothing changes."

■ IDEAS FOR WRITING

1. Characterize the speaker and Anna Mae.
2. Analyze the imagery in this poem.

Poems for Comparison/Contrast: Injustice

MAYA ANGELOU (1928–)   **1978**

STILL I RISE

You may write me down in history
With your bitter, twisted lies,
You may trod me in the very dirt
But still, like dust, I'll rise.

5 Does my sassiness upset you?
Why are you beset with gloom?
'Cause I walk like I've got oil wells
Pumping in my living room.

Just like moons and like suns,
10 With the certainty of tides,

Just like hopes springing high,
Still I'll rise.

Did you want to see me broken?
Bowed head and lowered eyes?
15 Shoulders falling down like teardrops,
Weakened by my soulful cries.

Does my haughtiness offend you?
Don't you take it awful hard
'Cause I laugh like I've got gold mines
20 Diggin' in my own back yard.

You may shoot me with your words,
You may cut me with your eyes,
You may kill me with your hatefulness,
But still, like air, I'll rise.

25 Does my sexiness upset you?
Does it come as a surprise
That I dance like I've got diamonds
At the meeting of my thighs?

Out of the huts of history's shame
30 I rise
Up from a past that's rooted in pain
I rise
I'm a black ocean, leaping and wide,
Welling and swelling I bear in the tide.

35 Leaving behind nights of terror and fear
I rise
Into a daybreak that's wondrously clear
I rise
Bringing the gifts that my ancestors gave,
40 I am the dream and the hope of the slave.
I rise
I rise
I rise.

LUCILLE CLIFTON (1936–   )   **2000**

JASPER TEXAS 1998
for j. byrd

i am a man's head hunched in the road.
i was chosen to speak by the members
of my body. the arm as it pulled away
pointed toward me, the hand opened once
5 and was gone.

why and why and why
should i call a white man brother?
who is the human in this place,
the thing that is dragged or the dragger?
10 what does my daughter say?

the sun is a blister overhead,
if i were alive i could not bear it.
the townsfolk sing we shall overcome
while hope bleeds slowly from my mouth
15 into the dirt that covers us all.
i am done with this dust. i am done.[1]

NAOMI SHIHAB NYE (1952–)   **1994**

STEPS

A man letters the sign for his grocery
in Arabic and English.
Paint dries more quickly in English.
The thick swoops and curls of Arabic letters
5 stay moist and glistening
till tomorrow when the children
show up jingling their dimes.

They have learned the currency of the New World,
carrying wishes for gum and candies
10 shaped like fish.
They float through the streets,
diving deep to the bottom,
nosing rich layers of crusted shell.

One of these children will tell a story
15 that keeps her people alive.
We don't know yet which one she is.
Girl in the red sweater dangling a book bag,
sister with eyes pinned to the barrel
of pumpkin seeds.
20 They are lettering the sidewalk with their steps.

They are separate and together and a little bit late.
Carrying a creased note, "Don't forget."
Who wrote it? They've already forgotten.
A purple fish sticks to the back of the throat.
25 Their long laughs are boats they will ride and ride,
making the shadows that cross each other's smiles.

---

[1] In Jasper, Texas, on June 7, 1998, three white men, with ties to such hate groups as Aryan Nation, kidnapped James Bryd, Jr., an African-American man, beat him, dragged him behind a truck, and killed him. His head was severed from his body.

WOLE SOYINKA (1934–   )   1967

TELEPHONE CONVERSATION

The price seemed reasonable, location
Indifferent. The landlady swore she lived
Off premises. Nothing remained
But self-confession. "Madam," I warned,
5   "I hate a wasted journey—I am African."
Silence. Silenced transmission of
Pressurized good-breeding. Voice, when it came,
Lipstick coated, long gold-rolled
Cigarette-holder pipped. Caught I was, foully.

10   "HOW DARK?" . . . I had not misheard . . . "ARE YOU LIGHT
OR VERY DARK?" Button B. Button A. Stench
Of rancid breath of public hide-and-speak.
Red booth. Red pillar-box. Red double-tiered
Omnibus squelching tar. It *was* real! Shamed
15   By ill-mannered silence, surrender
Pushed dumbfoundment to beg simplification.
Considerate she was, varying the emphasis—

"ARE YOU DARK? OR VERY LIGHT?" Revelation came.
"You mean—like plain or milk chocolate?"
20   Her assent was clinical, crushing in its light
Impersonality. Rapidly, wave-length adjusted,
I chose. "West African sepia"—and as afterthought,
"Down in my passport." Silence for spectroscopic
Flight of fancy, till truthfulness clanged her accent
25   Hard on the mouthpiece. "WHAT'S THAT?" conceding
"DON'T KNOW WHAT THAT IS." "Like brunette."

"THAT'S DARK, ISN'T IT?" "Not altogether.
Facially, I am brunette, but madam, you should see
The rest of me. Palm of my hand, soles of my feet
30   Are a peroxide blonde. Friction, caused—
Foolishly madam—by sitting down, has turned
My bottom raven black—One moment madam!"—sensing
Her receiver rearing on the thunderclap
About my ears—"Madam," I pleaded, "wouldn't you rather
35   See for yourself?"

CHARLOTTE DELBO (1913–85)   1970

PRAYER TO THE LIVING TO FORGIVE
THEM FOR BEING ALIVE

You who are passing by
well dressed in all your muscles
clothing which suits you well

or badly
5 or just about
you who are passing by
full of tumultuous life within your arteries
glued to your skeleton
as you walk with a sprightly step athletic awkward
10 laughing sullenly, you are all so handsome
so commonplace
so commonplacely like everyone else
so handsome in your commonplaceness
diverse
15 with this excess of life which keep you
from feeling your bust following your leg
your hand raised to your hat
your hand upon your heart
your kneecap rolling softly in your knee
20 how can we forgive you for being alive . . .
You who are passing by
well dressed in all your muscles
how can we forgive you
that all are dead
25 You are walking by and drinking in cafés
you are happy she loves you
or moody worried about money
how how
will you ever be forgiven
30 by those who died
so that you may walk by
dressed in all your muscles
so that you may drink in cafés
be younger every spring
35 I beg you
do something
learn a dance step
something to justify your existence
something that gives you the right
40 to be dressed in your skin in your body hair
learn to walk and to laugh
because it would be too senseless
after all
for so many to have died
45 while you live
doing nothing with your life.

I have returned
from a world beyond knowledge
and now must unlearn
50 for otherwise I clearly see
I can no longer live.

∞

After all
better not to believe
these ghostly tales
55 for if you do
you'll never sleep again
if you believe
these ghostly phantoms
revenants returning
60 yet unable to tell
how.

Poems for 9/11

GALWAY KINNELL (1927–   )   **2002**

WHEN THE TOWERS FELL

From our high window we saw the towers
with their bands and blocks of light
brighten against a fading sunset,
saw them at any hour glitter and live
5 as if the spirits inside them sat up all night
calculating profit and loss, saw them reach up
and steep their tops in the first yellow
of sunrise, grew so used to them
often we didn't see them, and now,
10 not seeing them, we see them.

The banker is talking to London.
Humberto is delivering breakfast sandwiches.
The trader is already working the phone.
The mail sorter has started sorting the mail.

15   . . . *povres et riches*
Sages et folz, prestres et laiz
Nobles, villains, larges et chiches
Petiz et grans et beaulx et laiz . . .[1]

The plane screamed low down lower Fifth Avenue,
20 lifted at the Arch, someone said, shaking the dog walkers

---

[1] Stanza XXXIX of "Le Testament" by Francois Villon (1431–?)
Poor and rich
Wise and fools, priests and laymen
Nobles, serfs, the generous and niggardly
Short and tall, handsome and homely.

in Washington Square Park, drove for the north tower,
struck with a heavy thud, released a huge bright gush
of blackened fire, and vanished, leaving a hole
the size and shape a cartoon plane might make
25 if it had passed harmlessly through and were flying away now,
on the far side, back into the realm of the imaginary.

Some with torn clothing, some bloodied,
some limping at top speed like children in a three-legged race,
some half dragged,
30 some intact in neat suits and dresses,
they walk in silence up the avenues,
all dusted to a ghostly whiteness,
all but their eyes, which are rubbed red as the eyes of a Zahoris,
who can see the dead under the ground.

35 Some died while calling home to say they were O.K.
Some died after over an hour spent learning they would die.
Some died so abruptly they may have seen death from within it.
Some broke windows and leaned out and waited for rescue.
Some were asphyxiated.
40 Some burned, their very faces caught fire.
Some fell, letting gravity speed them through their long
      moment.
Some leapt hand in hand, the elasticity in their last bits of love
      time letting—I wish I could say—their vertical streaks down
      the sky happen more lightly.

At the high window, where I've often stood
to escape a nightmare, I meet
45 the single, unblinking eye
that lights the all-night lifting
and sifting for bodies, for pieces of bodies,
for anything that is not nothing,
in the search that always goes on
50 somewhere, now in New York and Kabul.

On a street corner she holds up a picture—
of a man who is smiling. In the gray air
of today few pass. Sorry sorry sorry.
She startles. Suppose, down the street, that headlong lope . . .
55 Or over there, that hair so black it's purple . . .
And yet, suppose some evening I forgot
The fare and transfer, yet got by that way
Without recall,—lost yet poised in traffic.
Then I might find your eyes . . .
60 It could happen. Sorry sorry good luck thank you.
On this side it is "amnesia"—forgetting the way home—;
on the other, "invisibleness"—never entirely returning.
Hard to see clearly in the metallic mist,
or through the sheet of supposed reality

65 cast over our world, bourne that no creature born
     pokes its way back through, and no love can tear.

     The towers burn and fall, burn and fall—
     in a distant shot, like smokestacks spewing oily earth remnants.
     Schwarze Milch der Frühe wir trinken sie abends
70 *wir trinken sie mittage und morgens wir trinken sie nachts*
     wir trinken und trinken[2]
     Here is not a comparison but a corollary,
     not a likeness but a common lineage
     in the twentieth-century history of violent death—
75 black men in the South castrated and hanged from trees,
     soldiers advancing in mud at 90,000 dead per mile,
     train upon train headed eastward of boxcars shoved full to the
        corners with Jews and Gypsies to be enslaved or gassed,
     state murder of twenty, thirty, forty million of its own,
     atomic blasts wiping cities off the earth, fire bombings the same,
80 death marches, starvations, assassinations, disappearances,
     entire countries turned into rubble, minefields, mass graves.
     Seeing the towers vomit these omens, that the last century
        dumped into this one, for us to dispose of, we know
     they are our futures, that is our own black milk
        crossing the sky: *wir schaufeln ein Grab in den Lüften da*
        liegt man nicht eng[3]

     Burst jet fuel, incinerated aluminum, steel fume, volatized
        marble, exploded granite, pulverized wallboard, berserked
        plastic, mashed concrete, gasified mercury, scoria, vapor
85 of the vaporized—draped over our island up to streets regimented
        into numbers and letters,
     breathed across the great bridges to Brooklyn and the waiting
        sea:
     astringent, sticky, miasmic, empyreumatic,
     air too foul to take in, but we take it in,
     too gruesome for seekers of lost beloveds
90 to breathe, but they breathe it and you breathe it.

     A photograph of a woman hangs
     from his neck. He doesn't look up.
     He stares down at the sidewalk of flagstone slabs
     laid down in Whitman's century, gutter edges
95 iron wheels rasped long ago to a melted roundedness:
     conscious mind envying the stones.

---

[2] References to Paul Celan's "Death Fugue" (see chapter 7):
Black milk of daybreak we drink at nightfall
we drink it at midday, at morning, at night.
We drink it and drink it.
[3] We're digging a grave in the sky
There'll be plenty of room to be down there.

Nie stają się, są
Nic nad to, myślalem,
zbrzydziwszy sobie
100 *wszystko co staje się.*[3]

And I sat down by the waters of the Hudson,
by the North Cove Yacht Harbor, and thought
of what those on the high floors must have suffered: knowing
they would burn alive, and then, burning alive.
105 Could there be a mechanism of death
so mutilating to existence, that no one
gets over it ever, not even the dead?
And then I saw before me, in steel letters welded
to the steel railing posts, Walt Whitman's words
110 written when America plunged into war with itself:
City of the world! . . .
Proud and passionate city—mettlesome, mad, extravagant city!
Words of a time of illusions. And then I remembered
others of his words after the war was over and Lincoln dead:
115 *I saw the debris and debris of all the slain soldiers of the war,*
But I saw they were not as was thought,
They themselves were fully at rest—they suffer'd not,
The living remain'd and suffer'd, the mother suffer'd,
And the wife and the child and the musing comrade suffer'd . . .

120 In our minds the glassy blocks
succumb over and over into themselves,
slam down floor by floor into themselves.
They blow up as if in reverse, explode
downward and outward, billowing
125 through the streets, engulfing the fleeing.

Each tower as it falls concentrates
into itself, as if transforming itself
infinitely slowly into a black hole

infinitesimally small: mass
130 without space, where each light,
each life, put out, lies down within us.

---

[3] They do not become, they are.
Nothing but that, I thought,
Now loathing within myself
everything that becomes.

BRUCE SPRINGSTEEN (1949–   )   **2002**

THE RISING

    Can't see nothin' in front of me
    Can't see nothin' coming up behind
    I make my way through this darkness
    I can't feel nothing but this chain that binds me
5 Lost track of how far I've gone
    How far I've gone, how high I've climbed
    On my back's a sixty pound stone
    On my shoulder a half mile of line

    Come on up for the rising
10 Come on up, lay your hands in mine
    Come on up for the rising
    Come on up for the rising tonight

    Left the house this morning
    Bells ringing filled the air
15 Wearin' the cross of my calling
    On wheels of fire I come rollin' down here

    Come on up for the rising
    Come on up, lay your hands in mine
    Come on up for the rising
20 Come on up for the rising tonight

    Li,li, li,li,li,li, li,li,li

    There's spirits above and behind me
    Faces gone black, eyes burnin' bright
    May their precious blood bind me
25 Lord, as I stand before your fiery light

    Li,li, li,li,li,li, li,li,li

    I see you mary in the garden
    In the garden of a thousand sighs
    There's holy pictures of our children
30 Dancin' in a sky filled with light
    May I feel your arms around me
    May I feel your blood mix with mine
    A dream of life comes to me
    Like a catfish dancin' on the end of my line

35 Sky of blackness and sorrow (a dream of life)
    Sky of love, sky of tears (a dream of life)
    Sky of glory and sadness (a dream of life)
    Sky of mercy, sky of fear (a dream of life)
    Sky of memory and shadow (a dream of life)
40 Your burnin' wind fills my arms tonight

Sky of longing and emptiness (a dream of life)
Sky of fullness, sky of blessed life

Come on up for the rising
Come on up, lay your hands in mine
45 Come on up for the rising
Come on up for the rising tonight

Li,li, li,li,li,li, li,li,li

ADAM ZAGAJEWSKI (1945–   )   Translated, from the Polish, by Clare Cavanagh

2001

TRY TO PRAISE THE MUTILATED WORLD

Try to praise the mutilated world.
Remember June's long days,
and wild strawberries, drops of wine, the dew.
The nettles that methodically overgrow
5 the abandoned homestead of exiles.
You must praise the mutilated world.
You watched the stylish yachts and ships;
one of them had a long trip ahead of it,
while salty oblivion awaited others.
10 You've seen the refugees heading nowhere,
you've heard the executioners sing joyfully.
You should praise the mutilated world.
Remember the moments when we were together
in a white room and the curtain fluttered.
15 Return in thought to the concert where music flared.
You gathered acorns in the park in autumn
and leaves eddied over the earth's scars.
Praise the mutilated world
and the gray feather a thrush lost,
20 and the gentle light that strays and vanishes
and returns.

■ EXPLORATIONS OF THE TEXT

1. What impact does Kinnell's narrative method have—the details of the day interspersed with the literary allusions?
2. How does Kinnell enlarge the scope of 9/11 and envision it as part of a "twentieth century history of violent death"? Analyze the historical allusions.
3. How does the reader become a witness to disaster?
4. Although Zagajewski's "Try to Praise the Mutilated World" was not written in response to 9/11 (Alice Quinn, the poetry editor of *The New Yorker,* chose it as the back page in the edition that came out directly after the date), how is the poem a comment on the tragedy?

5. The refrain in Zagajewski's "Try to Praise the Mutilated World" changes. What do these changes suggest about the perspective of the speaker?
6. Analyze Springsteen's "The Rising" as a commemorative poem, as a prayer for those who died on 9/11.
7. Compare the speakers in Kinnell's "When the Towers Fell," Zagajewski's "Try to Praise the Mutilated World," and Springsteen's "The Rising." How do they view the "mutilated world"? Who is more optimistic? More pessimistic? Do any of the speakers have hope for the future? Compare their stances with that of the speaker in Yeats's "The Second Coming" or Johnson's "Stone Olives" in chapter 8.

■ **THE READING/WRITING CONNECTION**

1. Write your own 9/11 poem, autobiographical narrative, or short story. What do you remember about the day? What helped you to deal with the horror?
2. After 9/11, did you find comfort in any literary works, music, or art? If you had to add another work to this 9/11 cluster, what would it be? Explain your choice.
3. Begin a poem with "Try to . . ."
4. Analyze the use of repetition in the three works. What is the impact of this technique?
5. Write a letter to one of the poets, responding to the work and presenting your reactions to 9/11.

■ **IDEAS FOR WRITING**

1. Compare the attitudes of the speakers toward 9/11 and other historic calamities and tragedies. You may include your own 9/11 work. How do they treat the event? How do they envision the impact on people's daily lives? Do they see themselves living in a changed world? You also may refer to Milosz's "American Ignorance of War."
2. Research the myth of the phoenix. Connect this myth with these works. Discuss images of destruction and creation, of death and rebirth, presented in these works.
3. Using your response to question 2 in the Reading/Writing Connection as a starting point, compose an essay suggesting how a particular text helped you to cope with 9/11 or another tragic event. Focus on the specific elements of the work that proved to be comforting or instructive.

ON THE WEB

Responses to 9/11—Wendell Berry
"Thoughts in the Presence of Fear"
http://www.oriononline.org
Narratives about 9/11
http://www.mrbellersneighborhood.com

Poems for Comparison/Contrast: The Ideal vs. Real World

JONATHAN SWIFT (1667–1745)   1710

A DESCRIPTION OF THE MORNING

Now hardly here and there a hackney-coach
Appearing, showed the ruddy morn's approach.
Now Betty from her master's bed had flown,
And softly stole to discompose her own;
5 The slip-shod 'prentice from his master's door
Had pared the dirt and sprinkled round the floor.
Now Moll had whirled her mop with dext'rous airs,
Prepared to scrub the entry and the stairs.
The youth with broomy stumps began to trace
10 The kennel-edge, where wheels had worn the place.[1]
The small-coal man was heard with cadence deep,
Till drowned in shriller notes of chimney-sweep:
Duns at his lordship's gate began to meet;
And brickdust Moll had screamed through half the street.
15 The turnkey now his flock returning sees,
Duly let out a-nights to steal for fees:[2]
The watchful bailiffs take their silent stands,
And schoolboys lag with satchels in their hands.

WILLIAM BLAKE (1757–1827)   1794

LONDON

I wander through each chartered[1] street,
Near where the chartered Thames does flow,
And mark in every face I meet
Marks of weakness, marks of woe.

5 In every cry of every man,
In every Infant's cry of fear,
In every voice, in every ban,
The mind-forged manacles I hear.

How the Chimney-sweeper's cry
10 Every black'ning Church appalls;
And the hapless Soldier's sigh
Runs in blood down Palace walls.

---

[1] The youths is scavenging in the tracks of wheels in the road.
[2] The "turnkey" (the jailer) has let his incarcerated criminals out in the night to steal.
[1] Pre-empted by the State and leased by royal patent.

But most through midnight streets I hear
How the youthful Harlot's curse
15 Blasts the new-born Infant's tear,
And blights with plagues the Marriage hearse.

FRANCES ELLEN WATKINS HARPER (1825–1911)   1854

THE SLAVE AUCTION

The sale began—young girls were there,
   Defenceless in their wretchedness,
Whose stifled sobs of deep despair
   Revealed their anguish and distress.

5 And mothers stood with streaming eyes,
   And saw their dearest children sold;
Unheeded rose their bitter cries,
   While tyrants bartered them for gold.

And woman, with her love and truth—
10   For these in sable[1] forms may dwell—
Gaz'd on the husband of her youth,
   With anguish none may paint or tell.

And men, whose sole crime was their hue,
   The impress of their Maker's hand,
15 And frail and shrinking children, too,
   Were gathered in that mournful band.

Ye who have laid your love to rest,
   And wept above their lifeless clay,
Know not the anguish of that breast,
20   Whose lov'd are rudely torn away.

Ye may not know how desolate
   Are bosoms rudely forced to part,
And how a dull and heavy weight
   Will press the life-drops from the heart.

THOMAS HARDY (1840–1928)   1902

THE MAN HE KILLED

"Had he and I but met
By some old ancient inn,
We should have sat us down to wet
Right many a nipperkin[1]

---

[1] Black.
[1] Half-pint cup.

5 "But ranged as infantry,
    And staring face to face,
    I shot at him as he at me,
    And killed him in his place.

    "I shot him dead because—
10 Because he was my foe,
    Just so; my foe of course he was;
    That's clear enough; although

    "He thought he'd 'list, perhaps,
    Off-hand like—just as I—
15 Was out of work—had sold his traps[2]—
    No other reason why.

    "Yes; quaint and curious war is!
    You shoot a fellow down
    You'd treat if met where any bar is,
20 Or help to half-a-crown."

PAUL LAURENCE DUNBAR (1872–1906)   1893

SYMPATHY

I know what the caged bird feels, alas!
    When the sun is bright on the upland slopes;
When the wind stirs soft through the springing grass,
And the river flows like a stream of glass;
5   When the first bird sings and the first bud opens,
And the faint perfume from its chalice steals—
I know what the caged bird feels!

I know why the caged bird beats his wing
    Till its blood is red on the cruel bars;
10 For he must fly back to his perch and cling
When he fain would be on the bough a-swing;
    And a pain still throbs in the old, old scars
And they pulse again with a keener sting—
I know why he beats his wing!

15 I know why the caged bird sings, ah me,
    When his wing is bruised and his bosom sore,—
When he beats his bars and he would be free;
It is not a carol of joy or glee,
    But a prayer that he sends from his heart's deep core,
20 But a plea, that upward to Heaven he flings—
I know why the caged bird sings!

---

[2] Personal possessions or property.

EPISODE OF HANDS

The unexpected interest made him flush.
Suddenly he seemed to forget the pain,—
Consented,—and held out
One finger from the others.

5 The gash was bleeding, and a shaft of sun
That glittered in and out among the wheels,
Fell lightly, warmly, down into the wound.

And as the fingers of the factory owner's son,
That knew a grip for books and tennis
10 As well as one for iron and leather,—
As his taut, spare fingers wound the gauze
Around the thick bed of the wound,
His own hands seemed to him
Like wings of butterflies
15 Flickering in sunlight over summer fields.

The knots and notches,—many in the wide
Deep hand that lay in his,—seemed beautiful.
They were like the marks of wild ponies' play,—
Bunches of new green breaking a hard turf.

20 And factory sounds and factory thoughts
Were banished from him by that larger, quieter hand
That lay in his with the sun upon it.
And as the bandage knot was tightened
The two men smiled into each other's eyes.

AMERICAN TUNE

Many's the time I've been mistaken
And many times confused
Yes, and often felt forsaken
And certainly misused
5 But I'm all right, I'm all right
I'm just weary to my bones
Still, you don't expect to be
Bright and bon vivant
So far away from home, so far away from home

10 And I don't know a soul who's not been battered
I don't have a friend who feels at ease
I don't know a dream that's not been shattered
or driven to its knees
But it's all right, it's all right

15 We've lived so well so long
Still, when I think of the road
we're traveling on
I wonder what went wrong
I can't help it, I wonder what went wrong

20 And I dreamed I was dying
And I dreamed that my soul rose unexpectedly
And looking back down at me
Smiled reassuringly
And I dreamed I was flying
25 And high up above my eyes could clearly see
The Statue of Liberty
Sailing away to sea
And I dreamed I was flying

We come on the ship they call the Mayflower
30 We come on the ship that sailed the moon
We come in the age's most uncertain hour
and sing an American tune
But it's all right, it's all right
You can't be forever blessed
35 Still, tomorrow's going to be another working day
And I'm trying to get some rest
That's all I'm trying to get some rest.

I'm trying to get some rest?

SARAH JONES   2000

GOD BLESS AMERICA . . .

(As performed in the play *Bridge and Tunnel,*
by Rose Aimee Sylvince, a Haitian immigrant who experiences
discrimination from a Miami real estate border.)

God Bless America, but not because of you
God Bless the Haitian immigrants, and Cubans too
God Bless the Italians, Koreans, and the
Columbians who came
5 God Bless Jamaicans, the Chinese, the Spanish
Without them, Florida will have no name
God Bless the Polish, the Mexicans, the French
Without them, McDonalds will have no fries
God Bless the Japanese, Senegalese, and Swedish,
10 Without them, no Nobel prize
God Bless the Turkish, the Vietnamese,
the people from Peru
God Bless America, but not because of you

God Bless the Nicaraguans, the Russians,
15 and the ones from Liechtenstein

God Bless the Scottish—without them we would
have no *Auld Lang Syne*
God Bless the Filipinos, Liberians, Iraqis,
and Greeks
20   God Bless the British too, for the language
we all speak
God Bless the Albanians, the Brazilians,
the Egyptians
Without them, no paper for writing
25   the Declaration
God Bless Bosnian, Somali, and Croatian
God Bless the Indians, without them,
no word for shampoo
—it's true, you can look it up
30   God Bless America but not because of you

God Bless all those who are proud of
this colorful nation
God Bless us whether we are first, fifth,
or tenth generation
35   We build our home with others in unity
We love this land of opportunity
So may God bless America and let us not
discriminate
Whether immigration law or just Miami
40   real estate
God Bless your ancestors, real estate man,
once they were new here too
And God Bless this great America,
but not because of you

PAUL CELAN (1920–1970)   Translated by Robert H. Waugh

1952

DEATH FUGUE

Black milk of the morning we drink it at evening
we drink it at noon in the morning we drink it at night
we drink and we drink
we shovel a grave in the winds you don't lie there cramped
5 A man lives in the house he plays with snakes he writes
he writes when it darkens to Germany your gold hair Margaret
he writes and steps from the house the stars spark he whistles up hounds
he whistles his Jews out he has them shovel a grave in the earth
he commands us play for the dance

10 Black milk of the morning we drink you at night
we drink you morning and noon we drink you at evening
we drink and we drink

A man lives in the house he plays with the snakes he writes
he writes when it darkens to Germany your golden hair Margaret[1]
15 Your ashen hair Shulamite[2] we shovel a grave in the winds you don't lie there cramped

He calls dig deeper into earth's kingdom you there you others sing and play
he grabs the iron in his belt he swings it his eyes are blue
dig deeper with your spades you there you others play on for the dance

Black milk of the morning we drink you at night
20 we drink you noon and morning we drink you at evening
we drink and we drink
a man lives in the house your golden hair Margaret
your ashen hair Shulamite he plays with the snakes

He calls play death more sweetly death is a German craftsman
25 he calls play the violins more darkly you will rise like smoke in the wind
you will have a grave in the clouds you won't lie there cramped

Black milk of the morning we drink you at night
we drink you at noon death is a German master
we drink you evenings mornings we drink and we drink
30 death is a German craftsman his eyes are blue
he hits you with a lead bullet he hits you now
a man lives in the house your golden hair Margaret
he sets his hounds on us he gives us a grave in the wind
he plays with the snakes and dreams death is a German master

35 your golden hair Margaret
your ashen hair Shulamite

■ DRAMA ■

SOPHOCLES

Translated by Dudley Fitts and Robert Fitzgerald

Although he wrote more than one hundred and twenty dramas, only seven complete plays of Sophocles (496–406 B.C.) survive. Nonetheless, he is considered, with Aeschylus and Euripides, one of the three great Greek tragic dramatists. His first play won the prize over Aeschylus in 468 B.C. By 450 B.C., Sophocles had written at least twenty-four plays and had initiated significant changes in the form of tragedy, most notably that of introducing a third actor to the stage. He won more victories in the play competition than any other writer. In his Poetics, *Aristotle praised Sophocles above other dramatists.*

---

[1] "Margaret" alludes to Gretchen in Goethe's *Faust.*
[2] "Shulamite" to the name of the beloved in *The Song of Songs.*

(c. 441 B.C.)

ANTIGONE

Characters

ANTIGONE ⎱
ISMENE ⎰ daughters of Oedipus
EURYDICE, *wife of Creon*
CREON, *King of Thebes*
HAIMON, *son of Creon*
TEIRESIAS, *a blind seer*
A SENTRY
A MESSENGER
CHORUS

>Scene: *Before the palace of* CREON, *King of Thebes. A central double door, and two lateral doors. A platform extends the length of the façade, and from this platform three steps lead down into the "orchestra" or chorus-ground.*

>Time: *dawn of the day after the repulse of the Argive army from the assault on Thebes.*

Prologue

ANTIGONE *and* ISMENE *enter from the central door of the Palace.*

Antigone: Ismene, dear sister,
    You would think that we had already suffered enough
    For the curse on Oedipus:[1]
    I cannot imagine any grief
5   That you and I have not gone through. And now—
    Have they told you of the new decree of our King Creon?
Ismene: I have heard nothing: I know
    That two sisters lost two brothers, a double death
    In a single hour; and I know that the Argive army
10   Fled in the night; but beyond this, nothing.
Antigone: I thought so. And that is why I wanted you
    To come out here with me. There is something we must do.
Ismene: Why do you speak so strangely?
Antigone: Listen, Ismene:
15   Creon buried our brother Eteocles
    With military honors, gave him a soldier's funeral,
    And it was right that he should; but Polyneices,
    Who fought as bravely and died as miserably,—
    They say that Creon has sworn
20   No one shall bury him, no one mourn for him,
    But his body must lie in the fields, a sweet treasure

---

[1] **Oedipus:** Oedipus, father of Antigone, Ismene, Polyneices, and Eteocles, was King of Thebes. Unknowingly, he killed his father and married his mother. Upon learning what he had done, he put out his eyes and went into exile. Heirs to the throne, Polyneices and Eteocles eventually quarreled. Eteocles drove out Polyneices, but Polyneices returned to attack Thebes, and both brothers died in battle. Creon became king and ordered that Polyneices's body be left unburied.

For carrion birds to find as they search for food.
That is what they say, and our good Creon is coming here
To announce it publicly; and the penalty—

25   Stoning to death in the public square!

                            There it is,

And now you can prove what you are:
A true sister, or a traitor to your family.

Ismene: Antigone, you are mad! What could I possibly do?

30 **Antigone:** You must decide whether you will help me or not.

Ismene: I do not understand you. Help you in what?

Antigone: Ismene, I am going to bury him. Will you come?

Ismene: Bury him! You have just said the new law forbids it.

Antigone: He is my brother. And he is your brother, too.

35 **Ismene:** But think of the danger! Think what Creon will do!

Antigone: Creon is not strong enough to stand in my way.

Ismene: Ah sister!

    Oedipus died, everyone hating him
For what his own search brought to light, his eyes

40   Ripped out by his own hand; and Iocaste died,
His mother and wife at once: she twisted the cords
That strangled her life; and our two brothers died,
Each killed by the other's sword. And we are left:
But oh, Antigone,

45   Think how much more terrible than these
Our own death would be if we should go against Creon
And do what he has forbidden! We are only women,
We cannot fight with men, Antigone!
The law is strong, we must give in to the law

50   In this thing, and in worse. I beg the Dead
To forgive me, but I am helpless: I must yield
To those in authority. And I think it is dangerous business
To be always meddling.

Antigone: If that is what you think,

55   I should not want you, even if you asked to come.
You have made your choice, you can be what you want to be
But I will bury him; and if I must die,
I say that this crime is holy: I shall lie down
With him in death, and I shall be as dear

60   To him as he to me.

                It is the dead,
Not the living, who make the longest demands:
We die for ever . . .

              You may do as you like,

65   Since apparently the laws of the gods mean nothing to you.

Ismene: They mean a great deal to me; but I have no strength
To break laws that were made for the public good.

Antigone: That must be your excuse, I suppose. But as for me,
I will bury the brother I love.

70 **Ismene:**   Antigone,
I am so afraid for you!

Antigone: You need not be:
> You have yourself to consider, after all.

Ismene: But no one must hear of this, you must tell no one!
75   I will keep it a secret, I promise!

Antigone: Oh tell it! Tell everyone!
> Think how they'll hate you when it all comes out
> If they learn that you knew about it all the time!

Ismene: So fiery! You should be cold, with fear.

80 **Antigone:** Perhaps. But I am doing only what I must.

Ismene: But can you do it? I say that you cannot.

Antigone: Very well: when my strength gives out, I shall do no more.

Ismene: Impossible things should not be tried at all.

Antigone: Go away, Ismene:
85   I shall be hating you soon, and the dead will too,
> For your words are hateful. Leave me my foolish plan:
> I am not afraid of the danger; if it means death,
> It will not be the worst of deaths—death without
> honor.

90 **Ismene:** Go then, if you feel that you must.
> You are unwise,
> But a loyal friend indeed to those who love you.

Exit into the Palace. ANTIGONE *goes off, left. Enter the* CHORUS.

PARODOS[2] I • Strophe[3] 1

Chorus: Now the long blade of the sun, lying
> Level east to west, touches with glory
> Thebes of the Seven Gates. Open, unlidded
> Eye of golden day! O marching light
5   Across the eddy and rush of Dirce's stream[4]
> Striking the white shields of the enemy
> Thrown headlong backward from the blaze of morning!

Choragos:[5] Polyneices their commander
> Roused them with windy phrases,
10   He the wild eagle screaming
> Insults above our land,
> His wings their shields of snow,
> His crest their marshalled helms.

Antistrophe[6] 1

Chorus: Against our seven gates in a yawning ring
15   The famished spears came onward in the night;
> But before his jaws were sated with our blood,

---

[2] **Parodos:** Sung by the Chorus upon entering.
[3] **Stophe:** Sung by the chorus as they move from stage right to stage left.
[4] **Dirce's stream:** Near Thebes
[5] **Choragos:** Leader of the Chorus.
[6] **Antistrophe:** Sung by the chorus as they move from stage left to stage right.

Or pinefire took the garland of our towers,
He was thrown back; and as he turned, great Thebes—
No tender victim for his noisy power—
20   Rose like a dragon behind him, shouting war.

Choragos: For God hates utterly
The bray of bragging tongues;
And when he beheld their smiling,
Their swagger of golden helms,
25   The frown of his thunder blasted
Their first man from our walls.

Strophe 2

Chorus: We heard his shout of triumph high in the air
Turn to a scream; far out in a flaming arc
He fell with his windy torch, and the earth struck him.
30   And others storming in fury no less than his
Found shock of death in the dusty joy of battle.

Choragos: Seven captains at seven gates
Yielded their clanging arms to the god
That bends the battle-line and breaks it.
35   These two only, brothers in blood,
Face to face in matchless rage,
Mirroring each the other's death,
Clashed in long combat.

Antistrophe 2

Chorus: But now in the beautiful morning of victory
40   Let Thebes of the many chariots sing for joy!
With hearts for dancing we'll take leave of war:
Our temples shall be sweet with hymns of praise,
And the long night shall echo with our chorus.

Scene 1

Choragos: But now at last our new King is coming:
Creon of Thebes, Menoikeus' son.
In this auspicious dawn of his reign
What are the new complexities
5   That shifting Fate has woven for him?
What is his counsel? Why has he summoned
The old men to hear him?

Enter CREON *from the Palace, center. He addresses the* CHORUS *from the top step.*

Creon: Gentlemen: I have the honor to inform you that our Ship of State, which recent
storms have threatened to destroy, has come safely to harbor at last, guided by the
10   merciful wisdom of Heaven. I have summoned you here this morning because I know
that I can depend upon you: your devotion to King Laios was absolute; you never
hesitated in your duty to our late ruler Oedipus; and when Oedipus died, your loyalty
was transferred to his children. Unfortunately, as you know, his two sons, the princes
Eteocles and Polyneices, have killed each other in battle; and I, as the next in blood,
15   have succeeded to the full power of the throne.

I am aware, of course, that no Ruler can expect complete loyalty from his subjects until he has been tested in office. Nevertheless, I say to you at the very outset that I have nothing but contempt for the kind of Governor who is afraid, for whatever rea-son, to follow the course that he knows is best for the State; and as for the man who
20   sets private friendship above the public welfare,—I have no use for him, either. I call God to witness that if I saw my country headed for ruin, I should not be afraid to speak out plainly; and I need hardly remind you that I would never have any dealings with an enemy of the people. No one values friendship more highly than I; but we must remember that friends made at the risk of wrecking our Ship are not real friends
25   at all.

These are my principles, at any rate, and that is why I have made the following decision concerning the sons of Oedipus: Eteocles, who died as a man should die, fighting for his country, is to be buried with full military honors, with all the ceremony that is usual when the greatest heroes die; but his brother Polyneices, who broke his
30   exile to come back with fire and sword against his native city and the shrines of his fa-thers' gods, whose one idea was to spill the blood of his blood and sell his own people into slavery—Polyneices, I say, is to have no burial: no man is to touch him or say the least prayer for him; he shall lie on the plain, unburied; and the birds and the scaveng-ing dogs can do with him whatever they like.

35   This is my command, and you can see the wisdom behind it. As long as I am King, no traitor is going to be honored with the loyal man. But whoever shows by word and deed that he is on the side of the State,—he shall have my respect while he is living, and my reverence when he is dead.

Choragos: If that is your will, Creon son of Menoikeus,
40   You have the right to enforce it: we are yours.
Creon: That is my will. Take care that you do your part.
Choragos: We are old men: let the younger ones carry it out.
Creon: I do not mean that: the sentries have been appointed.
Choragos: Then what is it that you would have us do?
45 **Creon:** You will give no support to whoever breaks this law.
Choragos: Only a crazy man is in love with death!
Creon: And death it is; yet money talks, and the wisest
Have sometimes been known to count a few coins too many.

Enter SENTRY *from left.*

Sentry: I'll not say that I'm out of breath from running, King, because every time I stopped
50   to think about what I have to tell you, I felt like going back. And all the time a voice kept saying, "You fool, don't you know you're walking straight into trouble?"; and then another voice: "Yes, but if you let somebody else get the news to Creon first, it will be even worse than that for you!" But good sense won out, at least I hope it was good sense, and here I am with a story that makes no sense at all; but I'll tell it anyhow, be-
55   cause, as they say, what's going to happen's going to happen, and—
Creon: Come to the point. What have you to say?
Sentry: I did not do it. I did not see who did it. You must not punish me for what some-one else has done.
Creon: A comprehensive defense! More effective, perhaps,
60   If I knew its purpose. Come: what is it?
Sentry: A dreadful thing . . . I don't know how to put it—
Creon: Out with it!

Sentry: Well, then;

The dead man—

65 Polyneices—

Pause. The SENTRY *is overcome, fumbles for words.* CREON *waits impassively.*

out there—

someone,—

New dust on the slimy flesh!

Pause. No sign from CREON.

Someone has given it burial that way, and

70 Gone . . .

Long pause. CREON *finally speaks with deadly control:*

Creon: And the man who dared do this ?

Sentry: I swear I

Do not know! You must believe me!

Listen:

75 The ground was dry, not a sign of digging, no,

Not a wheeltrack in the dust, no trace of anyone.

It was when they relieved us this morning: and one of them,

The corporal, pointed to it.

There it was,

80 The strangest—

Look:

The body, just mounded over with light dust: you see?

Not buried really, but as if they'd covered it

Just enough for the ghost's peace. And no sign

85 Of dogs or any wild animal that had been there.

And then what a scene there was! Every man of us

Accusing the other: we all proved the other man did it,

We all had proof that we could not have done it.

We were ready to take hot iron in our hands,

90 Walk through fire, swear by all the gods,

It was not I

I do not know who it was, but it was not I!

CREON'S *rage has been mounting steadily, but the* SENTRY *is too intent upon his story to notice it.*

And then, when this came to nothing, someone said

A thing that silenced us and made us stare

95 Down at the ground: you had to be told the news,

And one of us had to do it! We threw the dice,

And the bad luck fell to me. So here I am,

No happier to be here than you are to have me:

Nobody likes the man who brings bad news.

100 **Choragos:** I have been wondering, King: can it be that the gods have done this?

Creon *(Furiously)*: Stop!

Must you doddering wrecks

Go out of your heads entirely? "The gods!"

Intolerable!

105   The gods favor this corpse? Why? How had he served them?
Tried to loot their temples, burn their images,
Yes, and the whole State, and its laws with it!
Is it your senile opinion that the gods love to honor bad men?
A pious thought!—

110   No, from the very beginning
There have been those who have whispered together,
Stiff-necked anarchists, putting their heads together,
Scheming against me in alleys. These are the men,
And they have bribed my own guard to do this thing.

115   *(Sententiously)* Money!
There's nothing in the world so demoralizing as money,
Down go your cities,
Homes gone, men gone, honest hearts corrupted,
Crookedness of all kinds, and all for money!

120   *(To* SENTRY*)*   But you—!

I swear by God and by the throne of God,
The man who has done this thing shall pay for it!
Find that man, bring him here to me, or your death
Will be the least of your problems: I'll string you up

125   Alive, and there will be certain ways to make you
Discover your employer before you die;
And the process may teach you a lesson you seem to have missed:
The dearest profit is sometimes all too dear:
That depends on the source. Do you understand me?

130   A fortune won is often misfortune.

Sentry: King, may I speak?

Creon: Your very voice distresses me.

Sentry: Are you sure that it is my voice, and not your conscience?

Creon: By God, he wants to analyze me now!

135 **Sentry:** It is not what I say, but what has been done, that hurts you.

Creon: You talk too much.

Sentry: Maybe; but I've done nothing.

Creon: Sold your soul for some silver: that's all you've done.

Sentry: How dreadful it is when the right judge judges wrong!

140 **Creon:** Your figures of speech
May entertain you now; but unless you bring me the man,
You will get little profit from them in the end.

Exit CREON *into the Palace.*

Sentry: "Bring me the man"—!
I'd like nothing better than bringing him the man!

145   But bring him or not, you have seen the last of me here.
At any rate, I am safe!

Exit SENTRY.

ODE I • *Strophe 1*

Chorus: Numberless are the world's wonders, but none
More wonderful than man; the stormgray sea

Yields to his prows, the huge crests bear him high;
Earth, holy and inexhaustible, is graven
5   With shining furrows where his plows have gone
Year after year, the timeless labor of stallions.

Antistrophe 1

The lightboned birds and beasts that cling to cover,
The lithe fish lighting their reaches of dim water,
All are taken, tamed in the net of his mind;
10   The lion on the hill, the wild horse windy-maned,
Resign to him; and his blunt yoke has broken
The sultry shoulders of the mountain bull.

Strophe 2

Words also, and thought as rapid as air,
He fashions to his good use; statecraft is his,
15   And his the skill that deflects the arrows of snow,
The spears of winter rain: from every wind
He has made himself secure—from all but one:
In the late wind of death he cannot stand.

Antistrophe 2

O clear intelligence, force beyond all measure!
20   O fate of man, working both good and evil!
When the laws are kept, how proudly his city stands!
When the laws are broken, what of his city then?
Never may the anarchic man find rest at my hearth,
Never be it said that my thoughts are his thoughts.

Scene II

Re-enter SENTRY *leading* ANTIGONE.

Choragos: What does this mean? Surely this captive woman
    Is the Princess, Antigone. Why should she be taken?
Sentry: Here is the one who did it! We caught her
    In the very act of burying him.—Where is Creon?
5 **Choragos:** Just coming from the house.

Enter CREON, *center.*

Creon: What has happened?
    Why have you come back so soon?
Sentry (*Expansively*):
                   O King,
    A man should never be too sure of anything:
10   I would have sworn
    That you'd not see me here again: your anger
    Frightened me so, and the things you threatened me with;
    But how could I tell then
    That I'd be able to solve the case so soon?
15   No dice-throwing this time: I was only too glad to come!
    Here is this woman. She is the guilty one:

We found her trying to bury him.
Take her, then; question her; judge her as you will.
I am through with the whole thing now, and glad of it.
20 **Creon:** But this is Antigone! Why have you brought her here?
Sentry: She was burying him, I tell you!
Creon (*Severely*):

                Is this the truth?
Sentry: I saw her with my own eyes. Can I say more?
Creon: The details: come, tell me quickly!
25 **Sentry:**   It was like this:
After those terrible threats of yours, King,
We went back and brushed the dust away from the body.
The flesh was soft by now, and stinking,
So we sat on a hill to windward and kept guard.
30 No napping this time! We kept each other awake.
But nothing happened until the white round sun
Whirled in the center of the round sky over us:
Then, suddenly,
A storm of dust roared up from the earth, and the sky
35 Went out, the plain vanished with all its trees
In the stinging dark. We closed our eyes and endured it.
The whirlwind lasted a long time, but it passed;
And then we looked, and there was Antigone!
I have seen
40 A mother bird come back to a stripped nest, heard
Her crying bitterly a broken note or two
For the young ones stolen. Just so, when this girl
Found the bare corpse, and all her love's work wasted,
She wept, and cried on heaven to damn the hands
45 That had done this thing.
                And then she brought more dust
And sprinkled wine three times for her brother's ghost.

We ran and took her at once. She was not afraid,
Not even when we charged her with what she had done.
50 She denied nothing.
              And this was a comfort to me,
And some uneasiness: for it is a good thing
To escape from death, but it is no great pleasure
To bring death to a friend.
55   Yet I always say
There is nothing so comfortable as your own safe skin!
Creon (*Slowly, dangerously*): And you, Antigone,
You with your head hanging,—do you confess this thing?
Antigone: I do. I deny nothing.
60 **Creon** (*To* SENTRY): You may go.

                              (*Exit* SENTRY)

(*To* ANTIGONE) Tell me, tell me briefly:
Had you heard my proclamation touching this matter?
Antigone: It was public. Could I help hearing it?

Creon: And yet you dared defy the law.

65 **Antigone:**   I dared.
    It was not God's proclamation. That final Justice
    That rules the world below makes no such laws.

    Your edict, King, was strong,
    But all your strength is weakness itself against
70   The immortal unrecorded laws of God.
    They are not merely now: they were, and shall be,
    Operative for ever, beyond man utterly.

    I knew I must die, even without your decree:
    I am only mortal. And if I must die
75   Now, before it is my time to die,
    Surely this is no hardship: can anyone
    Living, as I live, with evil all about me,
    Think Death less than a friend? This death of mine
    Is of no importance; but if I had left my brother
80   Lying in death unburied, I should have suffered.
    Now I do not.
               You smile at me. Ah Creon,
    Think me a fool, if you like; but it may well be
    That a fool convicts me of folly.

85 **Choragos:** Like father, like daughter: both headstrong, deaf to reason!
    She has never learned to yield.

Creon: She has much to learn.
    The inflexible heart breaks first, the toughest iron
    Cracks first, and the wildest horses bend their necks
90   At the pull of the smallest curb.
                   Pride? In a slave?
    This girl is guilty of a double insolence,
    Breaking the given laws and boasting of it.
    Who is the man here,
95   She or I, if this crime goes unpunished?
    Sister's child, or more than sister's child,
    Or closer yet in blood—she and her sister
    Win bitter death for this!
    (*To* SERVANTS)   Go, some of you,
100   Arrest Ismene. I accuse her equally.
    Bring her: you will find her sniffling in the house there.

    Her mind's a traitor: crimes kept in the dark
    Cry for light, and the guardian brain shudders;
    But how much worse than this
105   Is brazen boasting of barefaced anarchy!

Antigone: Creon, what more do you want than my death?

Creon: Nothing.
    That gives me everything.

Antigone: Then I beg you: kill me.
110   This talking is a great weariness: your words

Are distasteful to me, and I am sure that mine
Seem so to you. And yet they should not seem so:
I should have praise and honor for what I have done.
All these men here would praise me
115 Were their lips not frozen shut with feat of you.
(*Bitterly*) Ah the good fortune of kings,
Licensed to say and do whatever they please!

Creon: You are alone here in that opinion.

Antigone: No, they are with me. But they keep their tongues in leash.

120 **Creon:** Maybe. But you are guilty, and they are not.

Antigone: There is no guilt in reverence for the dead.

Creon: But Eteocles—was he not your brother too?

Antigone: My brother too.

Creon: And you insult his memory?

125 **Antigone** (*Softly*): The dead man would not say that I insult it.

Creon: He would: for you honor a traitor as much as him.

Antigone: His own brother; traitor or not, and equal in blood.

Creon: He made war on his country. Eteocles defended it.

Antigone: Nevertheless, there are honors due all the dead.

130 **Creon:** But not the same for the wicked as for the just.

Antigone: Ah Creon, Creon,
Which of us can say what the gods hold wicked?

Creon: An enemy is an enemy, even dead.

Antigone: It is my nature to join in love, not hate.

135 **Creon** (*Finally losing patience*): Go join them, then; if you must have your love,
Find it in hell!

Choragos: But see, Ismene comes:

Enter ISMENE, *guarded.*

Those tears are sisterly, the cloud
That shadows her eyes rains down gentle sorrow.

140 **Creon:** You too, Ismene,
Snake in my ordered house, sucking my blood
Stealthily—and all the time I never knew
That these two sisters were aiming at my throne!

Ismene,
145 Do you confess your share in this crime, or deny it?
Answer me.

Ismene: Yes, if she will let me say so. I am guilty.

Antigone (*Coldly*): No, Ismene. You have no right to say so.
You would not help me, and I will not have you help me.

150 **Ismene:** But now I know what you meant; and I am here
To join you, to take my share of punishment.

Antigone: The dead man and the gods who rule the dead
Know whose act this was. Words are not friends.

Ismene: Do you refuse me, Antigone? I want to die with you:
155 I too have a duty that I must discharge to the dead.

Antigone: You shall not lessen my death by sharing it.

Ismene: What do I care for life when you are dead?

Antigone: Ask Creon. You're always hanging on his opinions.

Ismene: You are laughing at me. Why, Antigone?
160 **Antigone:** It's a joyless laughter, Ismene.
   Ismene: But can I do nothing?
   Antigone: Yes. Save yourself. I shall not envy you.
      There are those who will praise you; I shall have honor, too.
   Ismene: But we are equally guilty!
165 **Antigone:**   No more, Ismene.
      You are alive, but I belong to Death.
   Creon (*To the* CHORUS): Gentlemen, I beg you to observe these girls:
      One has just now lost her mind; the other,
      It seems, has never had a mind at all.
170 **Ismene:** Grief teaches the steadiest minds to waver, King.
   Creon: Yours certainly did, when you assumed guilt with the guilty!
   Ismene: But how could I go on living without her?
   Creon: You are.
      She is already dead.
175 **Ismene:**   But your own son's bride!
   Creon: There are places enough for him to push his plow.
      I want no wicked women for my sons!
   Ismene: O dearest Haimon, how your father wrongs you!
   Creon: I've had enough of your childish talk of marriage!
180 **Choragos:** Do you really intend to steal this girl from your son?
   Creon: No; Death will do that for me.
   Choragos: Then she must die?
   Creon : You dazzle me.
                           —But enough of this talk!
185   (*To* GUARDS) You, there, take them away and guard them well:
      For they are but women, and even brave men run
      When they see Death coming.

   Exeunt ISMENE, ANTIGONE, *and* GUARDS

ODE II • *Strophe 1*

Chorus: Fortunate is the man who has never tasted God's vengeance!
      Where once the anger of heaven has struck, that house is shaken
      For ever: damnation rises behind each child
      Like a wave cresting out of the black northeast,
5   When the long darkness under sea roars up
      And bursts drumming death upon the windwhipped sand.

   Antistrophe 1

      I have seen this gathering sorrow from time long past
      Loom upon Oedipus' children: generation from generation
      Takes the compulsive rage of the enemy god.
10   So lately this last flower of Oedipus' line
      Drank the sunlight! but now a passionate word
      And a handful of dust have closed up all its beauty.

   Strophe 2

      What mortal arrogance
      Transcends the wrath of Zeus?

15   Sleep cannot lull him, nor the effortless long months
    Of the timeless gods: but he is young forever,
    And his house is the shining day of high Olympos.
        All that is and shall be,
        And all the past, is his.
20   No pride on earth is free of the curse of heaven.

Antistrophe 2

      The straying dreams of men
        May bring them ghosts of joy:
    But as they drowse, the waking embers bum them;
    Or they walk with fixed eyes, as blind men walk.
25   But the ancient wisdom speaks for our own time:
      Fate works most for woe
      With Folly's fairest show.
    Man's little pleasure is the spring of sorrow.

Scene III

Choragos: But here is Haimon, King, the last of all your sons.
    Is it grief for Antigone that brings him here,
    And bitterness at being robbed of his bride?

    Enter HAIMON.

Creon: We shall soon see, and no need of diviners.
5   —Son,
    You have heard my final judgment on that girl:
    Have you come here hating me, or have you come
    With deference and with love, whatever I do?
Haimon: I am your son, father. You are my guide.
10   You make things clear for me, and I obey you.
    No marriage means more to me than your continuing wisdom.
Creon: Good. That is the way to behave: subordinate
    Everything else, my son, to your father's will.
    This is what a man prays for, that he may get
15   Sons attentive and dutiful in his house,
    Each one hating his father's enemies,
    Honoring his father's friends. But if his sons
    Fail him, if they turn out unprofitably,
    What has he fathered but trouble for himself
20   And amusement for the malicious?
                            So you are right
    Not to lose your head over this woman.
    Your pleasure with her would soon grow cold, Haimon,
    And then you'd have a hellcat in bed and elsewhere.
25   Let her find her husband in Hell!
    Of all the people in this city, only she
    Has had contempt for my law and broken it.

    Do you want me to show myself weak before the people?
    Or to break my sworn word? No, and I will not.

30   The woman dies.
        I suppose she'll plead "family ties." Well, let her,
        If I permit my own family to rebel,
        How shall I earn the world's obedience?
        Show me the man who keeps his house in hand,
35   He's fit for public authority.
                                    I'll have no dealings
        With law-breakers, critics of the government:
        Whoever is chosen to govern should be obeyed—
        Must be obeyed, in all things, great and small,
40   Just and unjust! O Haimon,
        The man who knows how to obey, and that man only,
        Knows how to give commands when the time comes.
        You can depend on him, no matter how fast
        The spears come: he's a good soldier, he'll stick it out.
45   Anarchy, anarchy! Show me a greater evil!
        This is why cities tumble and the great houses rain down,
        This is what scatters armies!
        No, no: good lives are made so by discipline.
        We keep the laws then, and the lawmakers,
50   And no woman shall seduce us. If we must lose,
        Let's lose to a man, at least! Is a woman stronger than we?
   Choragos: Unless time has rusted my wits,
        What you say, King, is said with point and dignity.
   Haimon (*Boyishly earnest*): Father:
55   Reason is God's crowning gift to man, and you are right.
        To warn me against losing mine. I cannot say—
        I hope that I shall never want to say!—that you
        Have reasoned badly. Yet there are other men
        Who can reason, too; and their opinions might be helpful.
60   You are not in a position to know everything
        That people say or do, or what they feel:
        Your temper terrifies them—everyone
        Will tell you only what you like to hear.
        But I, at any rate, can listen; and I have heard them
65   Muttering and whispering in the dark about this girl.
        They say no woman has ever, so unreasonably,
        Died so shameful a death for a generous act:
        "She covered her brother's body. Is this indecent?
        She kept him from dogs and vultures. Is this a crime?
70   Death?—She should have all the honor that we can give her!"

        This is the way they talk out there in the city.

        You must believe me:
        Nothing is closer to me than your happiness.
        What could be closer? Must not any son
75   Value his father's fortune as his father does his?
        I beg you, do not be unchangeable:
        Do not believe that you alone can be right.

The man who thinks that,
The man who maintains that only he has the power
80   To reason correctly, the gift to speak, the soul—
A man like that, when you know him, turns out empty.
It is not reason never to yield to reason!

In flood time you can see how some trees bend,
And because they bend, even their twigs are safe,
85   While stubborn trees are torn up, roots and all.
And the same thing happens in sailing:
Make your sheet fast, never slacken,—and over you go,
Head over heels and under: and there's your voyage.
Forget you are angry! Let yourself be moved!
90   I know I am young; but please let me say this:
The ideal condition
Would be, I admit, that men should be right by instinct;
But since we are all too likely to go astray,
The reasonable thing is to learn from those who can teach.

95 **Choragos:** You will do well to listen to him. King,
If what he says is sensible. And you, Haimon,
Must listen to your father. —Both speak well.
Creon: You consider it right for a man of my years and experience
to go to school to a boy?
100 **Haimon:**   It is not right
If I am wrong. But if I am young, and right,
What does my age matter?
Creon: You think it right to stand up for an anarchist?
Haimon: Not at all. I pay no respect to criminals.
105 **Creon:** Then she is not a criminal?
Haimon: The City would deny it, to a man.
Creon: And the City proposes to teach me how to rule?
Haimon: Ah. Who is it that's talking like a boy now?
Creon: My voice is the one voice giving orders in this City!
110 **Haimon:** It is no City if it takes orders from one voice.
Creon: The State is the King!
Haimon: Yes, if the State is a desert.

Pause

Creon: This boy, it seems, has sold out to a woman.
Haimon: If you are a woman: my concern is only for you.
115 **Creon:** So? Your "concern"! In a public brawl with your father!
Haimon: How about you, in a public brawl with justice?
Creon: With justice, when all that I do is within my rights?
Haimon: You have no right to trample God's right.
Creon (*Completely out of control*): Fool, adolescent fool! Taken in by a woman!
120 **Haimon:** You'll never see me taken in by anything vile.
Creon: Every word you say is for her!
Haimon (*Quietly, darkly*):   And for you.
And for me. And for the gods under the earth.
Creon: You'll never marry her while she lives.

125 **Haimon:** Then she must die.—But her death will cause another.
   Creon: Another?
       Have you lost your senses? Is this an open threat?
   Haimon: There is no threat in speaking to emptiness.
   Creon: I swear you'll regret this superior tone of yours!
130   You are the empty one!
   Haimon: If you were not my father,
       I'd say you were perverse.
   Creon: You girlstruck fool, don't play at words with me!
   Haimon: I am sorry. You prefer silence.
135 **Creon:**   Now, by God—!
       I swear, by all the gods in heaven above us,
       You'll watch it, I swear you shall!
       (*To the* SERVANTS)   Bring her out!
       Bring the woman out! Let her die before his eyes!
140   Here, this instant, with her bridegroom beside her!
   Haimon: Not here, no; she will not die here, King.
       And you will never see my face again.
       Go on raving as long as you've a friend to endure you.

       Exit HAIMON

   Choragos: Gone, gone.
145   Creon, a young man in a rage is dangerous!
   Creon: Let him do, or dream to do, more than a man can.
       He shall not save these girls from death.
   Choragos: These girls
       You have sentenced them both?
150 **Creon:**   No, you are right.
       I will not kill the one whose hands are clean.
   Choragos: But Antigone?
   Creon (*Somberly*): I will carry her far away
       Out there in the wilderness, and lock her
155   Living in a vault of stone. She shall have food,
       As the custom is, to absolve the State of her death.
       And there let her pray to the gods of hell:
       They are her only gods:
       Perhaps they will show her an escape from death,
160   Or she may learn,
                   though late,
       That piety shown the dead is pity in vain.

       Exit CREON.

   ## ODE III • *Strophe*

   Chorus: Love, unconquerable
       Waster of rich men, keeper
       Of warm lights and all-night vigil
       In the soft face of a girl:
5   Sea-wanderer, forest-visitor!
       Even the pure Immortals cannot escape you,

And mortal man, in his one day's dusk,
Trembles before your glory.

Antistrophe

Surely you swerve upon ruin
10   The just man's consenting heart,
As here you have made bright anger
Strike between father and son—
And none has conquered but Love!
A girl's glance working the will of heaven:
15   Pleasure to her alone who mocks us,
Merciless Aphrodite.

Scene IV

Choragos   (*As* ANTIGONE *enters guarded*):
But I can no longer stand in awe of this,
Nor, seeing what I see, keep back my tears.
Here is Antigone, passing to that chamber
Where all find sleep at last.

Strophe 1

5 **Antigone:** Look upon me, friends, and pity me
Turning back at the night's edge to say
Good-by to the sun that shines for me no longer;
Now sleepy Death
Summons me down to Acheron, that cold shore:
10   There is no bridesong there, nor any music.
Chorus: Yet not unpraised, not without a kind of honor,
You walk at last into the underworld;
Untouched by sickness, broken by no sword.
What woman has ever found your way to death?

Antistrophe 1

15 **Antigone:** How often I have heard the story of Niobe,
Tantalos' wretched daughter, how the stone
Clung fast about her, ivy-close: and they say
The rain falls endlessly
And sifting soft snow; her tears are never done.
20   I feel the loneliness of her death in mine.
Chorus: But she was born of heaven, and you
Are woman, woman-born. If her death is yours,
A mortal woman's, is this not for you
Glory in our world and in the world beyond?

Strophe 2

25 **Antigone:** You laugh at me. Ah, friends, friends,
Can you not wait until I am dead? O Thebes,
O men many-charioted, in love with Fortune,
Dear springs of Dirce, sacred Theban grove,
Be witnesses for me, denied all pity,

30 Unjustly judged! and think a word of love
  For her whose path turns
  Under dark earth, where there are no more tears.

 Chorus: You have passed beyond human daring and come at last
  Into a place of stone where Justice sits.
35 I cannot tell
  What shape of your father's guilt appears in this.

 Antistrophe 2

 Antigone: You have touched it at last: that bridal bed
  Unspeakable, horror of son and mother mingling:
  Their crime, infection of all our family!
40 O Oedipus, father and brother!
  Your marriage strikes from the grave to murder mine.
  I have been a stranger here in my own land:
  All my life
  The blasphemy of my birth has followed me.

45 **Chorus:** Reverence is a virtue, but strength
  Lives in established law: that must prevail.
  You have made your choice,
  Your death is the doing of your conscious hand.

 Epode

 Antigone: Then let me go, since all your words are bitter,
50 And the very light of the sun is cold to me.
  Lead me to my vigil, where I must have
  Neither love nor lamentation; no song, but silence.

 CREON *interrupts impatiently.*

 Creon: If dirges and planned lamentations could put off death,
  Men would be singing for ever.
55 (*To the* SERVANTS)   Take her, go!
  You know your orders: take her to the vault
  And leave her alone there. And if she lives or dies,
  That's her affair, not ours: our hands are clean.

 Antigone: O tomb, vaulted bride-bed in eternal rock,
60 Soon I shall be with my own again
  Where Persephone welcomes the thin ghosts underground:
  And I shall see my father again, and you, mother,
  And dearest Polyneices—
         dearest indeed
65 To me, since it was my hand
  That washed him clean and poured the ritual wine:
  And my reward is death before my time!

  And yet, as men's hearts know, I have done no wrong.
  I have not sinned before God. Or if I have,
70 I shall know the truth in death. But if the guilt
  Lies upon Creon who judged me, then, I pray,
  May his punishment equal my own.

Choragos: O passionate heart,
Unyielding, tormented still by the same winds!
75 **Creon:** Her guards shall have good cause to regret their delaying.
Antigone: Ah! That voice is like the voice of death!
Creon: I can give you no reason to think you are mistaken.
Antigone: Thebes, and you my fathers' gods,
And rulers of Thebes, you see me now, the last
80 Unhappy daughter of a line of kings,
Your kings, led away to death. You will remember
What things I suffer, and at what men's hands,
Because I would not transgress the laws of heaven.
(To the GUARDS, *simply)*: Come: let us wait no longer.

Exit ANTIGONE, *left, guarded.*

ODE IV • *Strophe 1*

Chorus: All Danae's beauty was locked away
In a brazen cell where the sunlight could not come:
A small room, still as any grave, enclosed her.
Yet she was a princess too,
5 And Zeus in a rain of gold poured love upon her.
O child, child,
No power in wealth or war
Or tough sea-blackened ships
Can prevail against untiring Destiny!

Antistrophe 1

10 And Dryas' son[1] also, that furious king,
Bore the god's prisoning anger for his pride:
Sealed up by Dionysos in deaf stone,
His madness died among echoes.
So at the last he learned what dreadful power
15 His tongue had mocked:
For he had profaned the revels,
And fired the wrath of the nine
Implacable Sisters[2] that love the sound of the flute.

Strophe 2

And old men tell a half-remembered tale
20 Of horror done where a dark ledge splits the sea
And a double surf beats on the gray shores:
How a king's new woman,[3] sick
With hatred for the queen he had imprisoned,
Ripped out his two sons' eyes with her bloody hands
25 While grinning Ares watched the shuttle plunge

---

[1] **Dryas' son:** Lycurgus, King of Thrace.
[2] **Implacable sisters:** The nine Muses.
[3] **King's new woman:** Reference to Eidothea, wife of King Phineas.

Four times: four blind wounds crying for revenge,

Antistrophe 2

Crying, tears and blood mingled.—Piteously born.
Those sons whose mother was of heavenly birth!
Her father was the god of the North Wind

30   And she was cradled by gales,
She raced with young colts on the glittering hills
And walked untrammeled in the open light:
But in her marriage deathless Fate found means
To build a tomb like yours for all her joy.

Scene V

Enter blind TEIRESIAS, *led by a boy. The opening speeches of* TEIRESIAS *should be in singsong contrast to the realistic* CREON.

Teiresias: This is the way the blind man comes, Princes, Princes,
    Lock-step, two heads lit by the eyes of one.
Creon: What new thing have you to tell us, Old Teiresias?
Teiresias: I have much to tell you: listen to the prophet, Creon.
5 **Creon:** I am not aware that I have ever failed to listen.
Teiresias: Then you have done wisely, King, and ruled well.
Creon: I admit my debt to you. But what have you to say?
Teiresias: This, Creon: you stand once more on the edge of fate.
Creon: What do you mean? Your words are a kind of dread.
10 **Teiresias:** Listen, Creon:
    I was sitting in my chair of augury, at the place
    Where the birds gather about me. They were all a-chatter,
    As is their habit, when suddenly I heard
    A strange note in their jangling, a scream, a
15   Whirring fury; I knew that they were fighting,
    Tearing each other, dying
    In a whirlwind of wings clashing. And I was afraid.
    I began the rites of burnt-offering at the altar,
    But Hephaistos failed me: instead of bright flame,
20   There was only the sputtering slime of the fat thighflesh
    Melting: the entrails dissolved in gray smoke,
    The bare bone burst from the welter. And no blaze!

    This was a sign from heaven. My boy described it,
    Seeing for me as I see for others.

25   I tell you, Creon, you yourself have brought
    This new calamity upon us. Our hearths and altars
    Are stained with the corruption of dogs and carrion birds
    That glut themselves on the corpse of Oedipus' son.
    The gods are deaf when we pray to them, their fire
30   Recoils from our offering, their birds of omen
    Have no cry of comfort, for they are gorged
    With the thick blood of the dead.
                    O my son,

These are no trifles! Think: all men make mistakes,
35   But a good man yields when he knows his course is wrong,
And repairs the evil. The only crime is pride.

Give in to the dead man, then: do not fight with a corpse—
What glory is it to kill a man who is dead?
Think, I beg you:
40   It is for your own good that I speak as I do.
You should be able to yield for your own good.
Creon: It seems that prophets have made me their special province.
All my life long
I have been a kind of butt for the dull arrows
45   Of doddering fortune-tellers!
                                        No, Teiresias:
If your birds—if the great eagles of God himself
Should carry him stinking bit by bit to heaven,
I would not yield. I am not afraid of pollution:
50   No man can defile the gods.
                                        Do what you will,
Go into business, make money, speculate
In India gold or that synthetic gold from Sardis,
Get rich otherwise than by my consent to bury him.
55   Teiresias, it is a sorry thing when a wise man
Sells his wisdom, lets out his words for hire!
Teiresias: Ah Creon! Is there no man left in the world—
Creon: To do what?—Come, let's have the aphorism!
Teiresias: No man who knows that wisdom outweighs any wealth?
60   **Creon:** As surely as bribes are baser than any baseness.
Teiresias: You are sick, Creon! You are deathly sick!
Creon: As you say: it is not my place to challenge a prophet.
Teiresias: Yet you have said my prophecy is for sale.
Creon: The generation of prophets has always loved gold.
65   **Teiresias:** The generation of kings has always loved brass.
Creon: You forget yourself! You are speaking to your King.
Teiresias: I know it. You are a king because of me.
Creon: You have a certain skill; but you have sold out.
Teiresias: King, you will drive me to words that—
70   **Creon:**   Say them, say them!
Only remember: I will not pay you for them.
Teiresias: No, you will find them too costly.
Creon: No doubt. Speak:
Whatever you say, you will not change my will.
75   **Teiresias:** Then take this, and take it to heart!
The time is not far off when you shall pay back
Corpse for corpse, flesh of your own flesh.
You have thrust the child of this world into living night,
You have kept from the gods below the child that is theirs:
80   The one in a grave before her death, the other,
Dead, denied the grave. This is your crime:
And the Furies and the dark gods of Hell

Are swift with terrible punishment for you.

85   Do you want to buy me now, Creon?
                              Not many days,
And your house will be full of men and women weeping.
And curses will be hurled at you from far
Cities grieving for sons unburied, left to rot
Before the walls of Thebes.

90   These are my arrows, Creon: they are all for you.
(*To* BOY): But come, child: lead me home.
Let him waste his fine anger upon younger men.
Maybe he will learn at last
To control a wiser tongue in a better head.

Exit TEIRESIAS.

95 **Choragos:** The old man has gone, King, but his words
      Remain to plague us. I am old, too,
      But I cannot remember that he was ever false.
Creon: That is true. . . . It troubles me.
      Oh it is hard to give in! but it is worse
100   To risk everything for stubborn pride.
Choragos: Creon: take my advice.
Creon: What shall I do?
Choragos: Go quickly: free Antigone from her vault
      And build a tomb for the body of Polyneices.
105 **Creon:** You would have me do this?
Choragos: Creon, yes!
      And it must be done at once: God moves
      Swiftly to cancel the folly of stubborn men.
Creon: It is hard to deny the heart! But I
110   Will do it: I will not fight with destiny.
Choragos: You must go yourself, you cannot leave it to others.
Creon: I will go.
      —Bring axes, servants:
      Come with me to the tomb. I buried her, I
115   Will set her free.
                 Oh quickly!
My mind misgives—
The laws of the gods are mighty, and a man must serve them
To the last day of his life!

Exit CREON.

PAEAN • *Strophe 1*

Choragos: God of many names
Chorus: O Iacchos
                      son
  of Kadmeian Semele
5   O born of the Thunder!

Guardian of the West
                        Regent
        of Eleusis' plain
                        O Prince of maenad Thebes
10   and the Dragon Field by rippling Ismenos:

Antistrophe 1

Choragos: God of many names
Chorus: the flame of torches
        flares on our hills
                        the nymphs of Iacchos
15   dance at the spring of Castalia:
        From the vine-close mountain
                                come ah come in ivy:
        Evohe evohe![1] sings through the streets of Thebes

Strophe 2

Choragos: God of many names
20 **Chorus:**   Iacchos of Thebes
        heavenly Child
                        of Semele bride of the Thunderer!
        The shadow of plague is upon us:
                                come
25   with clement feet
                        oh come from Parnasos
        down the long slopes
                        across the lamenting water

Antistrophe 2

Choragos: Io Fire! Chorister of the throbbing stars!
30   O purest among the voices of the night!
        Thou son of God, blaze for us!
Chorus: Come with choric rapture of circling Maenads
        Who cry *Io Iacche!*
                        God of many names!

EXODUS[1]

Enter MESSENGER, *left.*

Messenger: Men of the line of Kadmos, you who live
        Near Amphion's citadel[2]
                        I cannot say
        Of any condition of human life "This is fixed,
5   This is clearly good, or bad". Fate raises up,
        And Fate casts down the happy and unhappy alike:
        No man can foretell his Fate.
                        Take the case of Creon:

---

[1] *Evohe evohe!:* "Come forth; come forth!"
[1] **Exodos:** Concluding scene.
[2] **Amphion's citadel:** Thebes.

Creon was happy once, as I count happiness:
10 Victorious in battle, sole governor of the land,
Fortunate father of children nobly born.
And now it has all gone from him! Who can say
That a man is still alive when his life's joy fails?
He is a walking dead man. Grant him rich,
15 Let him live like a king in his great house:
If his pleasure is gone, I would not give
So much as the shadow of smoke for all he owns.
Choragos: Your words hint at sorrow: what is your news for us?
Messenger: They are dead. The living are guilty of their death.
20 **Choragos:** Who is guilty? Who is dead? Speak!
Messenger: Haimon.
Haimon is dead; and the hand that killed him
Is his own hand.
Choragos: His father's? or his own?
25 **Messenger:** His own, driven mad by the murder his father had
done.
Choragos: Teiresias, Teiresias, how clearly you saw it all!
Messenger: This is my news: you must draw what conclusions you
can from it.
30 **Choragos:** But look: Eurydice, our Queen:
Has she overheard us?

Enter EURYDICE *from the Palace, center.*

Eurydice: I have heard something, friends:
As I was unlocking the gate of Pallas' shrine,
For I needed her help today, I heard a voice
35 Telling of some new sorrow. And I fainted
There at the temple with all my maidens about me.
But speak again: whatever it is, I can bear it:
Grief and I are no strangers.
Messenger: Dearest Lady,
40 I will tell you plainly all that I have seen.
I shall not try to comfort you: what is the use,
Since comfort could lie only in what is not true?
The truth is always best.
                                    I went with Creon
45 To the outer plain where Polyneices was lying,
No friend to pity him, his body shredded by dogs.
We made our prayers in that place to Hecate
And Pluto, that they would be merciful. And we bathed
The corpse with holy water, and we brought
50 Fresh-broken branches to burn what was left of it,
And upon the urn we heaped up a towering barrow
Of the earth of his own land.
                                    When we were done, we ran
To the vault where Antigone lay on her couch of stone.
55 One of the servants had gone ahead,
And while he was yet far off he heard a.voice
Grieving within the chamber, and he came back
And told Creon. And as the King went.closer,

The air was full of wailing, the words lost,
60 And he begged us to make all haste. "Am I a prophet?"
He said, weeping, "And must I walk this road,
The saddest of all that I have gone before?
My son's voice calls me on. Oh quickly, quickly!
Look through the crevice there, and tell me
65 If it is Haimon, or some deception of the gods!"

We obeyed; and in the cavern's farthest corner
We saw her lying:
She had made a noose of her fine linen veil
And hanged herself. Haimon lay beside her,
70 His arms about her waist, lamenting her,
His love lost under ground, crying out
That his father had stolen her away from him.

When Creon saw him the tears rushed to his eyes
And he called to him: "What have you done, child?
75   Speak to me.
What are you thinking that makes your eyes so strange?
O my son, my son, I come to you on my knees!"
But Haimon spat in his face. He said not a word,
Staring—
80   And suddenly drew his sword
And lunged. Creon shrank back, the blade missed;
and the boy,
Desperate against himself, drove it half its length
Into his own side, and fell. And as he died
85 He gathered Antigone close in his arms again,
Choking, his blood bright red on her white cheek.
And now he lies dead with the dead, and she is his
At last, his bride in the houses of the dead.

Exit EURYDICE *into the Palace.*

Choragos: She has left us without a word. What can this mean?
90 **Messenger:** It troubles me, too; yet she knows what is best,
Her grief is too great for public lamentation,
And doubtless she has gone to her chamber to weep
For her dead son, leading her maidens in his dirge.

Pause.

Choragos: It may be so: but I fear this deep silence
95 **Messenger:** I will. see what she is doing. I will go in.

Exit MESSENGER *into the Palace.*

Enter CREON *with attendants, bearing* HAIMON's *body.*

Choragos: But here is the King himself: oh look at him,
Bearing his own damnation in his arms.
Creon: Nothing you say can touch me any more.

My own blind heart has brought me
100   From darkness to final darkness. Here you see
The father murdering, the murdered son—
And all my civic wisdom!

Haimon my son, so young, so young to die,
I was the fool, not you; and you died for me.
105 **Choragos:** That is the truth; but you were late in learning it.
Creon: This truth is hard to bear. Surely a god
Has crushed me beneath the hugest weight of heaven,
And driven me headlong a barbaric way
To trample out the thing I held most dear.

110   The pains that men will take to come to pain!

Enter MESSENGER *from the Palace.*

Messenger: The burden you carry in your hands is heavy,
But it is not all: you will find more in your house.
Creon: What burden worse than this shall I find there?
Messenger: The Queen is dead.
115 **Creon:** O port of death, deaf world,
Is there no pity for me? And you, Angel of evil,
I was dead, and your words are death again.
Is it true, boy? Can it be true?
Is my wife dead? Has death bred death?
120 **Messenger:** You can see for yourself.

The doors are opened, and the body of EURYDICE *is disclosed within.*

Creon: Oh pity!
All true, all true, and more than I can bear!
O my wife, my son!
Messenger: She stood before the altar, and her heart
125   Welcomed the knife her own hand guided,
And a great cry burst from her lips for Megareus[3] dead,
And for Haimon dead, her sons; and her last breath
Was a curse for their father, the murderer of her sons.
And she fell, and the dark flowed in through her closing eyes.
130 **Creon:** O God, I am sick with fear.
Are there no swords here? Has no one a blow for me?
Messenger: Her curse is upon you for the deaths of both.
Creon: It is right that it should be. I alone am guilty.
I know it, and I say it. Lead me in,
135   Quickly, friends.
I have neither life nor substance. Lead me in.
Choragos: You are right, if there can be right in so much wrong.
The briefest way is best in a world of sorrow.

---

[3] **Megareus:** Son of Creon, killed in the attack on Thebes.

Creon: Let it come,
140   Let death come quickly, and be kind to me.
     I would not ever see the sun again.
Choragos: All that will come when it will; but we, meanwhile,
     Have much to do. Leave the future to itself.
Creon: All my heart was in that prayer!
145   **Choragos:** Then do not pray any more: the sky is deaf.
Creon: Lead me away. I have been rash and foolish.
     I have killed my son and my wife.
     I look for comfort; my comfort lies here dead.
     Whatever my hands have touched has come to nothing.
150   Fate has brought all my pride to a thought of dust.

As CREON *is being led into the house, the* CHORAGOS *advances and speaks directly to the audience.*

Choragos: There is no happiness where there is no wisdom;
     No wisdom but in submission to the gods.
     Big words are always punished,
     And proud men in old age learn to be wise.

■ EXPLORATIONS OF THE TEXT

1. How did Eteocles and Polyneices die? Why is Eteocles buried with honor but Polyneices left to decompose in the open? Why does Antigone believe that they should both be buried? What is Ismene's position?
2. Who helps to convince Creon to free Antigone? Why might Sophocles have made Creon change his mind? What effect does this have on the play's message?
3. Why does Creon's son Haimon die? Give more than one answer—his death can be explained literally but also within the context of the play's deeper meaning. Who else dies?
4. What is the role of the chorus in this play? What is the role of Theiresias?
5. In Greek tragedy, a character often suffers for possessing a tragic flaw. One example of a tragic flaw is *hubris,* or excessive pride. In *Antigone,* who is tragically flawed, Creon or Antigone? Which is the tragic hero?
6. Do you admire Antigone? Why, or why not?
7. Compare/contrast Antigone's sense of moral responsibility with Natasha's in "Natasha's Triumph" or the soldier's in "Gregory."

■ THE READING/WRITING CONNECTION

1. Throughout history, there are times when people have chosen to break the law because it is the "right" thing to do. Write a journal entry explaining under what circumstances you think that following a law would be unethical. Use specific examples.
2. Write about a time that you refused to change your mind. List each of your reasons, and then write from the point of view of the chorus, convincing you to change.

■ IDEAS FOR WRITING

1. Teiresias tells Creon that "a good man yields when he knows his course is wrong." Referring to two other works in this chapter as evidence, argue either for or against this statement.
2. Write about a time when you felt that you were unjustly punished, and then revise it to become a short story. Use characters to fulfill the function of the chorus and the soothsayer.
3. Find Tim O'Brien's "On the Rainy River" in *The Things They Carried.* Compare the moral conflicts of the two main characters, and consider O'Brien's definition of cowardice.

ANNA DEAVERE SMITH

Anna Deavere Smith (1950–   ) is an actress, playwright, and performance artist. A professor at New York University, Smith won an Obie award and was nominated for the 1992 Pulitzer Prize for Drama for Fires in the Mirror: Crown Heights, Brooklyn, and Other Identities. *She also has written* Twilight Los Angeles 1992 *(1994), which addresses the racial situation in Los Angeles after the police trials following the Rodney King beating, and* House Arrest: A Search for American Character in and Around the White House, Past and Present *(2003). Her work is concerned with representing the multiple perspectives of those experiencing contemporary American racial conflicts. According to Smith, "race and class are the big dividing lines in all society."*

1994

LIMBO/TWILIGHT #2
from *Twilight Los Angeles 1992*

(In a Denny's restaurant in a shopping center. Saturday morning, February 1993. He is a gang member. He is short, graceful, very dark skinned. He is soft-spoken and even in his delivery. He is very confident.)

Twilight Bey,
that's my name.
When I was
twelve and thirteen,
5 I stayed out until, they say,
until the sun come up.
Every night, you know,
and that was my thing.
I was a
10 watchdog.
You know, I stayed up in the neighborhood,
make sure we wasn't being rolled on and everything,
and when people
came into light
15 a what I knew,
a lot a people said,
"Well, Twilight, you know,
you a lot smarter and you have a lot more wisdom than those
twice your age."
20 And what I did, you know,
I was
at home writing one night
and I was writing my name
and I just looked at it and it came ta me:
25 "twi,"
abbreviation
of the word "twice."
You take a way the "ce."
You have the last word,
30 "light."

"Light" is a word that symbolizes knowledge, knowing,
wisdom,
within the Koran[1] and the Holy Bible.
Twilight.
35 I have twice the knowledge of those my age,
twice the understanding of those my age.
So twilight
is
that time
40 between day and night.
Limbo,
I call it limbo.
So a lot of times when I've brought up ideas to my homeboys,
they say,
45 "Twilight,
that's before your time,
that's something you can't do now."
When I talked about the truce back in 1988,
that was something they considered before its time,
50 yet
in 1992
we made it
realistic.
So to me it's like I'm stuck in limbo,
55 like the sun is stuck between night and day
in the twilight hours.
You know,
I'm in an area not many people exist.
Nighttime to me
60 is like a lack of sun,
and I don't affiliate
darkness with anything negative.
I affiliate
darkness with what was first,
65 because it was first,
and then relative to my complexion.
I am a dark individual,
and with me stuck in limbo,
I see darkness as myself.
70 I see the light as knowledge and the wisdom of the world
and understanding others,
and in order for me to be a, to be a true human being,
I can't forever dwell in darkness,
I can't forever dwell in the idea,
75 of just identifying with people like me and understanding me and mine.

---

[1] The sacred text of Islam.

So I'm up twenty-four hours, it feels like,
and, you know,
what I see at nighttime
is,
80 like,
little kids
between the ages of
eight and eleven
out at three in the morning.
85 They beatin' up a old man on the bus stop,
a homeless old man.
You know,
I see these things.
I tell 'em, "Hey, man, what ya all doin'?
90 Whyn't ya go on home?
What ya doin' out this time of night?"
You know,
and then when I'm in my own neighborhood, I'm driving through and I
see the living dead, as we call them,
95 the base heads,
the people who are so addicted on crack,
if they need a hit they be up all night doin' whatever they have to do
to make the money to get the hit.
It's like gettin' a total dose
100 of what goes on in the daytime creates at night.

■ **EXPLORATIONS OF THE TEXT**
1. How does Twilight Bey think that he has changed since he was "twelve and thirteen"?
2. What is the significance of his name?
3. Discuss the images of darkness, light, and "limbo" in the work.
4. How does "limbo" represent Bey's state of mind.
5. What do you think Bey's dreams are for his future? For his people's future?

■ **THE READING/WRITING CONNECTION**
1. Journal Entry: Compare Twilight Bey's view of life with your own.
2. "Think" Topic: In a paragraph write about the view of fate and free will presented in this work.

■ **IDEAS FOR WRITING**
1. Create a talk show that focuses on issues for today's people of color. Include Twilight Bey as one of the speakers.
2. Compare Manning Marable's and Twilight Bey's relationship to their ethnic heritage and environment. How do both men react to their ethnic backgrounds and to their present worlds?
3. Examine the performance pieces by Anna Deavere Smith and Ntozake Shange (See chapter 6). What techniques of performance drama do you notice? How does performance drama differ from a one-act play (see, for example, "Trifles" in chapter 6)?

José Rivera

José Rivera (1955–   ) was born in San Juan, Puerto Rico; moved to Long Island, New York, in 1959; and attended Dennison College, where he began writing and producing plays. On a Fullbright fellowship, Rivera worked in London in 1989–90, where he wrote Marisol *(1992), which in 1993 won an Obie Award for best play, a Susan Marton Award, a PEN West Dramatic Writing Award nomination, and the 1993 Joseph Kesselring Award Honorable Mention. After returning to the United States from London, Rivera moved to California to write screenplays. Rivera has written more than twenty plays and screenplays. "Gas" illustrates Rivera's socio-political perspective, presented with a touch of magical realism.*

1997

GAS
For Juan Carlos Rivera

Cast

Cheo

Time

Start of the ground offensive of the Persian Gulf War.

Place

A gas station

(A car at a gas station. CHEO *stands next to the pump about to fill his car with gas. He is a working-class Latino. Before he pumps gas he speaks to the audience.)*

Cheo: His letters were coming once a week. I could feel his fear. It was in his handwriting. He sat in a tank. In the middle of the Saudi Arabian desert. Wrote six, seven, eight hours a day. These brilliant letters of fear. This big Puerto Rican guy! What the fuck's he doing out there? What the fucking hell sense that make? He's out there, in the
5   Saudi sand, writing letters to me about how he's gonna die from an Iraqi fucking missile. And he's got all this time on his hands to think about his own death. And there's nothing to do 'cause of these restrictions on him. No women, no magazines, 'cause the Saudis are afraid of the revolutionary effects of ads for women's lingerie on the population! Allah would have a cow! There's nothing he's allowed to eat even remotely re-
10   minds him of home. Nothing but the fucking time to sit and think about what it's gonna be like to have some fucking towel-head—as he calls them—run a bayonet clean through his guts. He's sitting in the tank playing target practice with the fucking camels. Shooting at the wind. The sand in all the food. Sand in his dreaming. He and his buddies got a camel one day. They shaved that motherfucker clean! Completely
15   shaved its ass! Then they spray-painted the name of their company, in bright American spray-paint, on the side of the camel, and sent it on its way! Scorpion fights in the tents! All those scenes from fucking *Apocalypse Now* in his head. Fucking Marlon Brando decapitating that guy and Martin Sheen going fucking nuts. That's what fills my brother's daily dreams as he sits out there in the desert contemplating his own
20   death. The Vietnam Syndrome those people are trying to eradicate. His early letters were all about that. A chronicle. His way of laying it all down, saying it all for me, so I would know what his last days, and months, and seconds were like. So when he got offed by an Iraqi missile, I would at least know what it was like to be in his soul, if just

for a little while. He couldn't write to save his life at first. Spelled everything totally,
unbelievably wrong. "Enough": e-n-u-f. "Thought": t-h-o-t. "Any": e-n-y. But with
time, he started to write beautifully. This angel started to come out of the desert. This
singing angel of words. Thoughts I honestly never knew he had. Confessions. Ideas.
We started to make plans. We start to be in sync for the first time since I stopped
telling him I loved him. I used to kick his fucking ass! It wasn't hard or nothing. That's
not bragging, just me telling you a simple truth. He was always sick. Always the first
to cry. He played drums in a parade back home. He couldn't even play the fucking instrument, he was so uncoordinated. Spastic. But they let him march in the parade anyway—without drumsticks. He was the last guy in the parade, out of step, banging
make-believe drumsticks, phantom rhythms on this snare drum—playing air drum for
thousands of confused spectators! Then he got into uniforms and the scouts. But I
knew that bullshit was just a cover anyway. He didn't mean it. Though after he joined
the army and was in boot camp, he took particular delight in coming home and
demonstrating the fifty neat new ways he learned to kill a guy. One day he forgot he
weighed twice my weight and nearly snapped my spine like a fucking cucumber! I
thought, in agony, "where's my bro? Where's that peckerhead I used to kick around?
The first one to cry when he saw something beautiful. The first one to say 'I love that'
or 'I love Mom' or 'I love you.'" He never got embarrassed by that, even after I got too
old to deal with my fucking little brother kissing me in front of other people. Even
later, he always, always, always ended every conversation with, "I love you bro," and I
couldn't say, "I love you" back, 'cause I was too hip to do that shit. But he got deeper
in it. The war thing. He wrote to say I'd never understand. He's fighting for my right to
say whatever I want. To disagree. And I just fucking love how they tell you on the
news the fucking temperature in Riyadh, Saudi Arabia! Like I fucking care! And a couple of times the son-of-a-bitch called me collect from Saudi! *I said collect!* And I told
him if Saddam Hussein didn't kill him, I would! He told me about troubles with his
wife back home. He'd just gotten married a month before shipping out. He didn't really know her and was wondering if she still loved him. My brother always loved ugly
women. It was a thing with him. Low self-esteem or something. Like he couldn't love
himself and didn't understand a woman that would. So he sought out the absolute losers of the planet: trucker whores with prison records who liked to tie him up and
whip him, stuff like that. I honestly have trouble contemplating my little brother being
whipped by some trucker whore in leather. Love! He didn't know another way. Then
he met a girl who on their first date confessed she hated spiks—so my brother married
her! This racist looked him in the eye, disrespected his whole race to his face, and my
brother says, "I do." Last night somebody got on TV to say we shouldn't come down
on rich people 'cause rich people are a minority too, and coming down on them was a
form of racism! And I thought, they're fucking afraid of class warfare, and they should
be! And the news showed some little white punk putting up flags all over this dipshit
town in California and this little twirp's story absorbed twenty minutes of the news—
this little, blond Nazi kid with a smile full of teeth—and the protests got shit. And this
billboard went up in my town showing Stalin, Hitler, and Hussein, saying we stopped
him twice before we have to stop him again! This billboard was put up by a local
newspaper! The music, the computer graphics, the generals coming out of retirement
to become media stars, public hard ons. And we gotta fight NAKED AGGRESSION—
like his asshole president should come *to my fucking neighborhood* if he wants to see
naked aggression! I never thought the ideas in the head of some politician would
mean the death of my brother and absolutely kill my mother. I'm telling you, that
woman will not survive the death of my brother no matter how much she believes in

God, no matter how much praying she does. But I keep that from him. I write back
about how it's not going to be another Vietnam. It's not going to be a whole country
that spits on you when you come back. That we don't forget the ones we love and
fight for us. Then his letters stopped. I combed the newspapers trying to figure out
what's going on over there, 'cause his letters said nothing about where he was. He
wasn't allowed to talk about locations, or troop size, or movement, 'cause, like, I was
going to personally transmit this information to the Iraqi fucking Ministry of Defense!
I thought about technology. The new shit Iraq has that was made in the United States,
shit that could penetrate a tank's armour and literally travel through the guts of a tank,
immolating every living human soul inside, turning human Puerto Rican flesh into hot
screaming soup, the molecules of my brother's soul mixing with the metal molecules
of the iron coffin he loved so much. I couldn't sleep. My mother was suicidal. Why
wasn't he writing? The air war's continuing. They're bombing the shit out of that
motherfucking country! And I find myself ashamed. I think, "yeah, bomb it more.
Level it. Send it back to the Stone Age. Make it so every last elite Republican Guard is
dead. So my brother won't get killed." For the first time in my life, I want a lot of people I don't hate to die 'cause I know one of them could kill the man I love most in this
fucked up world. If my brother is killed, I will personally take a gun and blow out the
brains of George Herbert Walker Bush. And I'm sick. I'm sick of rooting for the
bombs. Sick of loving every day the air war continues. Sick of every air strike, every
sortie. And being happy another Iraqi tank got taken out and melted, another Iraqi
bunker was bombed, another bridge can't bring ammunition, can't deliver that one
magic bullet that will incapacitate my brother, bring him back a vegetable, bring him
back dead in his soul, or blinded, or butchered in some Iraqi concentration camp.
That the Iraqi motherfucker that would torture him won't live now 'cause our smart
bombs have killed that towelhead motherfucker in his sleep! They actually got me
wanting this war to be bloody!

(Beat.)

Last night the ground war started. It started. The tanks are rolling. I find my gut
empty now. I don't have thoughts. I don't have dreams. My mother is a shell. She has
deserted herself and left behind a blathering cadaver, this pathetic creature with rosary
beads in her hands looking up to Christ, and CNN, saying words like "Scud,"
"strategic interests," "collateral damage," "target rich environment"—words this
woman from a little town in Puerto Rico has no right to know. So I fight my demons. I
think of the cause. Blood for oil. I NEED MY CAR, DON'T I? I NEED MY CAR TO
GET TO WORK SO I CAN PAY THE RENT AND NOT END UP A HOMELESS
PERSON! DON'T I HAVE A RIGHT TO MY CAR AND MY GAS? AND WHAT ABOUT
FREEING DEMOCRATIC KUWAIT?!

(Beat.)

So I wait for a sign, anything, a prayer, any sign. I'll take it. Just tell me he's okay. Tell
me my brother's gonna kill well and make it through this alive. He's gonna come home
and he's gonna come home the same person he left; the spastic one who couldn't spell
. . . the one who couldn't play the drums.

(CHEO *starts to pump gas. As he pumps the gas, he notices something horrifying. He pulls the
nozzle out of the car. Blood comes out of the gas pump.* CHEO *stares and stares at the bloody
trickle coming out of the gas pump.)*

BLACKOUT

■ EXPLORATIONS OF THE TEXT

1. Gloss and annotate the monologue. Concentrate on the narrator's perceptions of how his brother changed after he enlisted. What do the brother's letters reveal about the experience of being a solider?

2. What is the protagonist's attitude toward the Gulf War?

3. How has the brother's state affected the family?

4. How does the language of war—phrases such as "collateral damage" and "strategic interests"—contrast with the reality? What do they suggest, in general, about the ways in which politicians and the media portray the realities of war?

5. Explore the significance of the symbolism of the gas pump. Is it effective?

6. Compare and contrast the brother's experience of the Gulf War with that of Hartley's experience of the Iraq War in "I, Jailor."

■ THE READING/WRITING CONNECTION

1. Do a double-entry notebook for this work, focusing on the brother's state before and after he enlisted.

2. "Think" Topic: What do you think the speaker's attitude would be toward the Iraq War? Respond in a freewrite, or compose a series of letters between the brother in "Gas" and Hartley.

3. Create a dialogue among the speaker in "Gas," Jason Hartley, and "the fat man" in Pirandello's "War."

■ IDEAS FOR WRITING

1. Write an argumentative essay based on the following statement; "War Is Hell." As an alternative, agree or disagree with O'Brien that the experience of being a soldier in a war cannot be reduced to a single phrase. Use evidence from this play and from several other works.

■ NONFICTION ■

SOJOURNER TRUTH

Born into slavery in Ulster County, New York, Sojourner Truth (1797–1883) originally was named Isabella Van Wagener, after Isaac Van Wagener, who bought her and set her free just before New York State abolished slavery in 1827. In 1829, she went to New York City, where she preached in the streets. Taking the name Sojourner Truth in answer to a divine call, she left the city and began preaching and singing at camp meetings across the country. Although she never abandoned her message of God's goodness, she added to her speeches concern for the abolition of slavery and the rights of women. Her brilliant speeches attracted many listeners and made her famous. In his new biography of Sojourner Truth, Carlton Mabee argues that she never spoke these exact words.[1]

1851

---

[1] Sojourner Truth first gave the speech now referred to as the "Ain't I a Woman?" speech at a women's rights convention in Akron, Ohio, in 1851. However, as Nell Painter, Truth's most recent biographer, has pointed out, the version of the speech that we associate with Truth was not written down until twelve years later by the activist Frances Dena Gage, who added to it considerably. For the popular consciousness, Gage's revision of Truth's speech has become the speech itself, inspiring countless people who have read it. It is for this reason that we print this version of Truth's work.

AIN'T I A WOMAN?

W ell, children, where there is so much racket there must be something out of kilter. I think that 'twixt the negroes of the South and the women at the North, all talking about rights, the white men will be in a fix pretty soon. But what's all this here talking about?

That man over there says that women need to be helped into carriages, and lifted over ditches, and to have the best place everywhere. Nobody ever helps me into carriages, or over mud-puddles, or gives me any best place! And ain't I a woman? Look at me! Look at my arm! I have ploughed and planted, and gathered into barns, and no man could head me! And ain't I a woman? I could work as much and eat as much as a man—when I could get it—and bear the lash as well! And ain't I a woman? I have borne thirteen children, and seen them most all sold off to slavery, and when I cried out with my mother's grief, none but Jesus heard me! And ain't I a woman?

Then they talk about this thing in the head; what's this they call it? [Intellect, someone whispers.] That's it, honey. What's that got to do with women's rights or negro's rights? If my cup won't hold but a pint, and yours holds a quart, wouldn't you be mean not to let me have my little half-measure full?

Then that little man in black there, he says women can't have as much rights as men, 'cause Christ wasn't a woman! Where did your Christ come from? Where did your Christ come from? From God and a woman! Man had nothing to do with Him.

5   If the first woman God ever made was strong enough to turn the world upside down all alone, these women together ought to be able to turn it back, and get it right side up again! And now they is asking to do it, the men better let them.

Obliged to you for hearing me, and now old Sojourner ain't got nothing more to say.

■ EXPLORATIONS OF THE TEXT

1. What is the occasion? Why does Truth connect women's rights with racial issues in the first section of her speech?
2. Examine the vision of woman presented in paragraph 2. What is the effect of the repetition of "ain't I a woman?"
3. What is the argument about intellect?
4. Why does she include religion in her speech? What does she accomplish when she contends that "Man had nothing to do with [Jesus]"? How does she use humor?
5. Consider Truth's version of Eve, "the first woman." Is her argument logical or true?
6. What elements of persuasion does Truth use effectively? (See chapter 12.)
7. Characterize the voice of the speaker.

■ THE READING/WRITING CONNECTION

1. In a journal entry, respond to the vision of "woman" presented in the speech.
2. Why was the speaker doubly vulnerable?

■ IDEAS FOR WRITING

1. Analyze the rhetorical structure of Sojourner Truth's speech. See checklist for nonfiction in chapter 12.
2. Compose a contemporary version of "Ain't I a Woman?"

Harriet Jacobs

Harriet Jacobs (1815–97), born a slave in Edenton, North Carolina, was orphaned as a child. Taught to read and write by her owner/mistress, Jacobs would recount the events of her life in her 1881 Incidents in the Life of a Slave Girl. *Jacob's book was published pseudonymously (under the name Linda Brent) with encouragement from Amy Post, a feminist and abolition-ist, and William C. Nell, an African American abolitionist and writer. During the Civil War, Ja-cobs nursed black solders in Washington, D.C.*

1881

INCIDENTS IN THE LIFE OF A SLAVE GIRL

Childhood

I was born a slave; but I never knew it till six years of happy childhood had passed away. My father was a carpenter, and considered so intelligent and skilful in his trade, that, when buildings out of the common line were to be erected, he was sent for from long dis-tances, to be head workman. On condition of paying his mistress two hundred dollars a year, and supporting himself, he was allowed to work at his trade, and manage his own af-fairs. His strongest wish was to purchase his children; but, though he several times offered his hard earnings for that purpose, he never succeeded. In complexion my parents were a light shade of brownish yellow, and were termed mulattoes. They lived together in a com-fortable home; and, though we were all slaves, I was so fondly shielded that I never dreamed I was a piece of merchandise, trusted to them for safe keeping, and liable to be de-manded of them at any moment. I had one brother, William, who was two years younger than myself—a bright, affectionate child. I had also a great treasure in my maternal grand-mother, who was a remarkable woman in many respects. She was the daughter of a planter in South Carolina, who, at his death, left her mother and his three children free, with money to go to St. Augustine;[1] where they had relatives. It was during the Revolutionary War; and they were captured on their passage, carried back, and sold to different purchasers. Such was the story my grandmother used to tell me; but I do not remember all the particulars. She was a little girl when she was captured and sold to the keeper of a large hotel. I have of-ten heard her tell how hard she fared during childhood. But as she grew older she evinced so much intelligence, and was so faithful, that her master and mistress could not help seeing it was for their interest to take care of such a valuable piece of property. She became an in-dispensable personage in the household, officiating in all capacities, from cook and wet nurse to seamstress. She was much praised for her cooking; and her nice crackers became so famous in the neighborhood that many people were desirous of obtaining them. In con-sequence of numerous requests of this kind, she asked permission of her mistress to bake crackers at night, after all the household work was done; and she obtained leave to do it, provided she would clothe herself and her children from the profits. Upon these terms, after working hard all day for her mistress, she began her midnight bakings, assisted by her two oldest children. The business proved profitable; and each year she laid by a little, which was saved for a fund to purchase her children. Her master died, and the property was divided among his heirs. The widow had her dower in the hotel, which she continued to keep open. My grandmother remained in her service as a slave; but her children were divided among her master's children. As she had five, Benjamin, the youngest one, was sold, in order that each heir might have an equal portion of dollars and cents. There was so little difference in our ages that he seemed more like my brother than my uncle. He was a bright, handsome lad, nearly white; for he inherited the complexion my grandmother had derived from Anglo-Saxon ancestors. Though only ten years old, seven hundred and twenty dollars were

---

[1] City in Florida.

paid for him. His sale was a terrible blow to my grandmother; but she was naturally hope-ful, and she went to work with renewed energy, trusting in time to be able to purchase some of her children. She had laid up three hundred dollars, which her mistress one day begged as a loan, promising to pay her soon. The reader probably knows that no promise or writing given to a slave is legally binding; for, according to Southern laws, a slave, *being* property, can *hold* no property. When my grandmother lent her hard earnings to her mistress, she trusted solely to her honor. The honor of a slaveholder to a slave!

To this good grandmother I was indebted for many comforts. My brother Willie and I often received portions of the crackers, cakes, and preserves, she made to sell; and after we ceased to be children we were indebted to her for many more important services.

Such were the unusually fortunate circumstances of my early childhood. When I was six years old, my mother died; and then, for the first time, I learned, by the talk around me, that I was a slave. My mother's mistress was the daughter of my grandmother's mistress. She was the foster sister of my mother; they were both nourished at my grandmother's breast. In fact, my mother had been weaned at three months old, that the babe of the mistress might obtain sufficient food. They played together as children; and, when they became women, my mother was a most faithful servant to her whiter foster sister. On her death-bed her mistress promised that her children should never suffer for any thing; and during her lifetime she kept her word. They all spoke kindly of my dead mother, who had been a slave merely in name, but in nature was noble and womanly. I grieved for her, and my young mind was trou-bled with the thought who would now take care of me and my little brother. I was told that my home was now to be with her mistress; and I found it a happy one. No toilsome or dis-agreeable duties were imposed upon me. My mistress was so kind to me that I was always glad to do her bidding, and proud to labor for her as much as my young years would permit. I would sit by her side for hours, sewing diligently, with a heart as free from care as that of any free-born white child. When she thought I was tired, she would send me out to run and jump; and away I bounded, to gather berries or flowers to decorate her room. Those were happy days—too happy to last. The slave child had no thought for the morrow; but there came that blight, which too surely waits on every human being born to be a chattel.

When I was nearly twelve years old, my kind mistress sickened and died. As I saw the cheek grow pale and the eye more glassy, how earnestly I prayed in my heart that she might live! I loved her; for she had been almost like a mother to me. My prayers were not answered. She died, and they buried her in the little churchyard, where, day after day, my tears fell upon her grave.

5 I was sent to spend a week with my grandmother. I was now old enough to begin to think of the future; and again and again I asked myself what they would do with me. I felt sure I should never find another mistress so kind as the one who was gone. She had prom-ised my dying mother that her children should never suffer for any thing; and when I re-membered that, and recalled her many proofs of attachment to me, I could not help having some hopes that she had left me free. My friends were almost certain it would be so. They thought she would be sure to do it, on account of my mother's love and faithful service. But, alas! we all know that the memory of a faithful slave does not avail much to save her chil-dren from the auction block.

After a brief period of suspense, the will of my mistress was read, and we learned that she had bequeathed me to her sister's daughter, a child of five years old. So vanished our hopes. My mistress had taught me the precepts of God's Word: "Thou shalt love thy neighbor as thyself." "Whatsoever ye would that men should do unto you, do ye even so unto them." But I was her slave, and I suppose she did not recognize me as her neighbor. I would give much to blot out from my memory that one great wrong. As a child, I loved my mistress; and, looking back on the happy days I spent with her, I try to think with less bitterness of this act of injustice. While I was with her, she taught me to read and spell; and for this privilege, which so rarely falls to the lot of a slave, I bless her memory.

She possessed but few slaves; and at her death those were all distributed among her relatives. Five of them were my grandmother's children, and had shared the same milk that nourished her mother's children. Notwithstanding my grandmother's long and faithful service to her owners, not one of her children escaped the auction block. These God-breathing machines are no more, in the sight of their masters, than the cotton they plant, or the horses they tend.

The New Master and Mistress

Dr. Flint, a physician in the neighborhood, had married the sister of my mistress, and I was now the property of their little daughter. It was not without murmuring that I prepared for my new home; and what added to my unhappiness, was the fact that my brother William was purchased by the same family. My father, by his nature, as well as by the habit of transacting business as a skilful mechanic, had more of the feelings of a freeman than is common among slaves. My brother was a spirited boy; and being brought up under such influences, he early detested the name of master and mistress. One day, when his father and his mistress both happened to call him at the same time, he hesitated between the two; being perplexed to know which had the strongest claim upon his obedience. He finally concluded to go to his mistress. When my father reproved him for it, he said, "You both called me, and I didn't know which I ought to go to first."

"You are *my* child," replied our father, "and when I call you, you should come immediately, if you have to pass through fire and water."

10 　Poor Willie! He was now to learn his first lesson of obedience to a master. Grandmother tried to cheer us with hopeful words, and they found an echo in the credulous hearts of youth.

When we entered our new home we encountered cold looks, cold words, and cold treatment. We were glad when the night came. On my narrow bed I moaned and wept, I felt so desolate and alone.

I had been there nearly a year, when a dear little friend of mine was buried. I heard her mother sob, as the clods fell on the coffin of her only child, and I turned away from the grave, feeling thankful that I still had something left to love. I met my grandmother, who said, "Come with me, Linda;" and from her tone I knew that something sad had happened. She led me apart from the people, and then said, "My child, your father is dead." Dead! How could I believe it? He had died so suddenly I had not even heard that he was sick. I went home with my grandmother. My heart rebelled against God, who had taken from me mother, father, mistress, and friend. The good grandmother tried to comfort me. "Who knows the ways of God?" said she. "Perhaps they have been kindly taken from the evil days to come." Years afterwards I often thought of this. She promised to be a mother to her grandchildren, so far as she might be permitted to do so; and strengthened by her love, I returned to my master's. I thought I should be allowed to go to my father's house the next morning; but I was ordered to go for flowers, that my mistress's house might be decorated for an evening party. I spent the day gathering flowers and weaving them into festoons,[2] while the dead body of my father was lying within a mile of me. What cared my owners for that? he was merely a piece of property. Moreover, they thought he had spoiled his children,

---

[2] A decorative chain or strip hanging between two points.

by teaching them to feel that they were human beings. This was blasphemous doctrine for a slave to teach; presumptuous in him, and dangerous to the masters.

The next day I followed his remains to a humble grave beside that of my dear mother. There were those who knew my father's worth, and respected his memory.

My home now seemed more dreary than ever. The laugh of the little slave children sounded harsh and cruel. It was selfish to feel so about the joy of others. My brother moved about with a very grave face. I tried to comfort him, by saying, "Take courage, Willie; brighter days will come by and by."

15   "You don't know any thing about it, Linda," he replied. "We shall have to stay here all our days; we shall never be free."

I argued that we were growing older and stronger, and that perhaps we might, before long, be allowed to hire our own time, and then we could earn money to buy our freedom. William declared this was much easier to say than to do; moreover, he did not intend to *buy* his freedom. We held daily controversies upon this subject.

Little attention was paid to the slaves' meals in Dr. Flint's house. If they could catch a bit of food while it was going, well and good. I gave myself no trouble on that score, for on my various errands I passed my grandmother's house, where there was always something to spare for me. I was frequently threatened with punishment if I stopped there; and my grandmother, to avoid detaining me, often stood at the gate with something for my breakfast or dinner. I was indebted to *her* for all my comforts, spiritual or temporal. It was *her* labor that supplied my scanty wardrobe. I have a vivid recollection of the linsey-woolsey[3] dress given me every winter by Mrs. Flint. How I hated it! It was one of the badges of slavery.

While my grandmother was thus helping to support me from her hard earnings, the three hundred dollars she had lent her mistress were never repaid. When her mistress died, her son-in-law, Dr. Flint, was appointed executor. When grandmother applied to him for payment, he said the estate was insolvent, and the law prohibited payment. It did not, however, prohibit him from retaining the silver candelabra, which had been purchased with that money. I presume they will be handed down in the family, from generation to generation.

My grandmother's mistress had always promised her that, at her death, she should be free; and it was said that in her will she made good the promise. But when the estate was settled, Dr. Flint told the faithful old servant that, under existing circumstances, it was necessary she should be sold.

20   On the appointed day, the customary advertisement was posted up, proclaiming that there would be a "public sale of negroes, horses, &c." Dr. Flint called to tell my grandmother that he was unwilling to wound her feelings by putting her up at auction, and that he would prefer to dispose of her at private sale. My grandmother saw through his hypocrisy; she understood very well that he was ashamed of the job. She was a very spirited woman, and if he was base enough to sell her, when her mistress intended she should be free, she was determined the public should know it. She had for a long time supplied many families with crackers and preserves; consequently, "Aunt Marthy," as she was called, was generally known, and every body who knew her respected her intelligence and good character. Her long and faithful service in the family was also well known, and the intention of her mistress to leave her free. When the day of sale came, she took her place among the chattels, and at the first call she sprang upon the auction-block. Many voices called out, "Shame! Shame! Who is going to sell *you,* aunt Marthy? Don't stand there! That is no place for *you.*" Without saying a word, she quietly awaited her fate. No one bid for her. At last, a

---

[3] A coarse sturdy fabric of wool and linen or cotton.

feeble voice said, "Fifty dollars." It came from a maiden lady, seventy years old, the sister of my grandmother's deceased mistress. She had lived forty years under the same roof with my grandmother; she knew how faithfully she had served her owners, and how cruelly she had been defrauded of her rights; and she resolved to protect her. The auctioneer waited for a higher bid; but her wishes were respected; no one bid above her. She could neither read nor write; and when the bill of sale was made out, she signed it with a cross. But what consequence was that, when she had a big heart overflowing with human kindness? She gave the old servant her freedom.

At that time, my grandmother was just fifty years old. Laborious years had passed since then; and now my brother and I were slaves to the man who had defrauded her of her money, and tried to defraud her of her freedom. One of my mother's sisters, called Aunt Nancy, was also a slave in his family. She was a kind, good aunt to me; and supplied the place of both housekeeper and waiting maid to her mistress. She was, in fact, at the beginning and end of every thing.

Mrs. Flint, like many southern women, was totally deficient in energy. She had not strength to superintend her household affairs; but her nerves were so strong, that she could sit in her easy chair and see a woman whipped, till the blood trickled from every stroke of the lash. She was a member of the church; but partaking of the Lord's supper did not seem to put her in a Christian frame of mind. If dinner was not served at the exact time on that particular Sunday, she would station herself in the kitchen, and wait till it was dished, and then spit in all the kettles and pans that had been used for cooking. She did this to prevent the cook and her children from eking out their meagre fare with the remains of the gravy and other scrapings. The slaves could get nothing to eat except what she chose to give them. Provisions were weighed out by the pound and ounce, three times a day. I can assure you she gave them no chance to eat wheat bread from her flour barrel. She knew how many biscuits a quart of flour would make, and exactly what size they ought to be.

Dr. Flint was an epicure.[4] The cook never sent a dinner to his table without fear and trembling; for if there happened to be a dish not to his liking, he would either order her to be whipped, or compel her to eat every mouthful of it in his presence. The poor, hungry creature might not have objected to eating it; but she did object to having her master cram it down her throat till she choked.

They had a pet dog, that was a nuisance in the house. The cook was ordered to make some Indian mush[5] for him. He refused to eat, and when his head was held over it, the froth flowed from his mouth into the basin. He died a few minutes after. When Dr. Flint came in, he said the mush had not been well cooked, and that was the reason the animal would not eat it. He sent for the cook, and compelled her to eat it. He thought that the woman's stomach was stronger than the dog's; but her sufferings afterwards proved that he was mistaken. The poor woman endured many cruelties from her master and mistress; sometimes she was locked up, away from her nursing baby, for a whole day and night.

When I had been in the family a few weeks, one of the plantation slaves was brought to town, by order of his master. It was near night when he arrived, and Dr. Flint ordered him to be taken to the work house, and tied up to the joist, so that his feet would just escape the ground. In that situation he was to wait till the doctor had taken his tea. I shall never forget that night. Never before, in my life, had I heard hundreds of blows fall, in succession, on a human being. His piteous groans, and his "O, pray don't, massa," rang in my ear for months afterwards. There were many conjectures as to the cause of this terrible punishment. Some

25

---

[4] A person devoted to sensual pleasure.
[5] Corn meal pudding.

said master accused him of stealing corn; others said the slave had quarrelled with his wife, in presence of the overseer, and had accused his master of being the father of her child. They were both black, and the child was very fair.

I went into the work house next morning, and saw the cowhide still wet with blood, and the boards all covered with gore. The poor man lived, and continued to quarrel with his wife. A few months afterwards Dr. Flint handed them both over to a slavetrader. The guilty man put their value into his pocket, and had the satisfaction of knowing that they were out of sight and hearing. When the mother was delivered into the trader's hands, she said, "You *promised* to treat me well." To which he replied, "You have let your tongue run too far; damn you!" She had forgotten that it was a crime for a slave to tell who was the father of her child.

From others than the master persecution also comes in such cases. I once saw a young slave girl dying soon after the birth of a child nearly white. In her agony she cried out, "O Lord, come and take me!" Her mistress stood by, and mocked at her like an incarnate fiend. "You suffer, do you?" she exclaimed. "I am glad of it. You deserve it all, and more too."

The girl's mother said, "The baby is dead, thank God; and I hope my poor child will soon be in heaven, too."

"Heaven!" retorted the mistress. "There is no such place for the like of her and her bastard."

30   The poor mother turned away, sobbing. Her dying daughter called her, feebly, and as she bent over her, I heard her say, "Don't grieve so, mother; God knows all about it; and HE will have mercy upon me."

Her sufferings, afterwards, became so intense, that her mistress felt unable to stay; but when she left the room, the scornful smile was still on her lips. Seven children called her mother. The poor black woman had but the one child, whose eyes she saw closing in death, while she thanked God for taking her away from the greater bitterness of life.

The Loophole of Retreat
(Linda Brent Escapes)

A small shed had been added to my grandmother's house years ago. Some boards were laid across the joists at the top, and between these boards and the roof was a very small garret, never occupied by any thing but rats and mice. It was a pent roof, covered with nothing but shingles, according to the southern custom for such buildings. The garret was only nine feet long and seven wide. The highest part was three feet high, and sloped down abruptly to the loose board floor. There was no admission for either light or air. My uncle Phillip, who was a carpenter, had very skilfully made a concealed trap-door, which communicated with the storeroom. He had been doing this while I was waiting in the swamp. The storeroom opened upon a piazza. To this hole I was conveyed as soon as I entered the house. The air was stifling; the darkness total. A bed had been spread on the floor. I could sleep quite comfortably on one side; but the slope was so sudden that I could not turn on the other without hitting the roof. The rats and mice ran over my bed; but I was weary, and I slept such sleep as the wretched may, when a tempest has passed over them. Morning came. I knew it only by the noises I heard; for in my small den day and night were all the same. I suffered for air even more than for light. But I was not comfortless. I heard the voices of my children. There was joy and there was sadness in the sound. It made my tears flow. How I longed to speak to them! I was eager to look on their faces; but there was no hole, no crack, through which I could peep. This continued darkness was oppressive. It seemed horrible to sit or lie in a cramped position day after day, without one gleam of light. Yet I would have chosen this, rather than my lot as a slave, though white people considered it an easy one; and it was so compared with the fate of others. I was never cruelly overworked; I was never lacerated with the whip from head to foot; I was never so beaten and bruised that I could not turn from one side to the other; I never had my heel-strings cut to prevent my running away; I was never chained to a log and forced to drag it about, while I toiled in the fields from morning till night; I was never branded with hot iron, or torn by bloodhounds. On the contrary, I had always been kindly treated, and tenderly cared for, until I came into the hands of Dr. Flint. I had never wished for freedom till then. But though my life in slavery was comparatively devoid of hardships, God pity the woman who is compelled to lead such a life! My food was passed up to me through the trap-door my uncle had contrived; and my grandmother, my uncle Phillip, and aunt Nancy would seize such opportunities as they could, to mount up there and chat with me at the opening. But of course this was not safe in the daytime. It must all be done in darkness. It was impossible for me to move in an erect position, but I crawled about my den for exercise. One day I hit my head against something, and found it was a gimlet. My uncle had left it sticking there when he made the trap-door. I was as rejoiced as Robinson Crusoe could have been at finding such a treasure. It put a lucky thought into my head. I said to myself, "Now I will have some light. Now I will see my children." I did not dare to begin my work during the daytime, for fear of attracting attention. But I groped round; and having found the side next the street, where I could frequently see my children, I stuck the gimlet in and waited for evening. I bored three rows of holes, one above another; then I bored out the interstices between. I thus succeeded in making one hole about an inch long and an inch broad. I sat by it till late into the night, to enjoy the little whiff of air that floated in. In the morning I watched for my children. The first person I saw in the street was Dr. Flint. I had a shuddering, superstitious feeling that it was a bad omen. Several familiar faces passed by. At last I heard the merry laugh of children, and presently two sweet little faces were looking up at me, as though they knew I was there, and were conscious of the joy they imparted. How I longed to *tell* them I was there!

My condition was now a little improved. But for weeks I was tormented by hundreds of little red insects, fine as a needle's point, that pierced through my skin, and produced an intolerable burning. The good grandmother gave me herb teas and cooling medicines, and finally I got rid of them. The heat of my den was intense, for nothing but thin shingles protected me from the scorching summer's sun. But I had my consolations. Through my peeping-hole I could watch the children, and when they were near enough, I could hear their talk. Aunt Nancy brought me all the news she could hear at Dr. Flint's. From her I learned that the doctor had written to New York to a colored woman, who had been born and raised in our neighborhood, and had breathed his contaminating atmosphere. He offered her a reward if she could find out any thing about me. I know not what was the nature of her reply; but he soon after started for New York in haste, saying to his family that he had business of importance to transact. I peeped at him as he passed on his way to the steamboat. It was a satisfaction to have miles of land and water between us, even for a little while; and it was a still greater satisfaction to know that he believed me to be in the Free States. My little den seemed less dreary than it had done. He returned, as he did from his former journey to New York, without obtaining any satisfactory information. When he passed our house next morning, Benny[6] was standing at the gate. He had heard them say that he had gone to find me, and he called out, "Dr. Flint, did you bring my mother home? I want to see her." The doctor stamped his foot at him in a rage, and exclaimed, "Get out of the way, you little damned rascal! If you don't, I'll cut off your head."

Benny ran terrified into the house, saying, "You can't put me in jail again. I don't belong to you now." It was well that the wind carried the words away from the doctor's ear. I told

---

[6] Brent's son.

my grandmother of it, when we had our next conference at the trap-door; and begged of her not to allow the children to be impertinent to the irascible old man.

35   Autumn came, with a pleasant abatement of heat. My eyes had become accustomed to the dim light, and by holding my book or work in a certain position near the aperture I contrived to read and sew. That was a great relief to the tedious monotony of my life. But when winter came, the cold penetrated through the thin shingle roof, and I was dreadfully chilled. The winters there are not so long, or so severe, as in northern latitudes; but the houses are not built to shelter from cold, and my little den was peculiarly comfortless. The kind grandmother brought me bed-clothes and warm drinks. Often I was obliged to lie in bed all day to keep comfortable; but with all my precautions, my shoulders and feet were frostbitten. O, those long, gloomy days, with no object for my eye to rest upon, and no thoughts to occupy my mind, except the dreary past and the uncertain future! I was thankful when there came a day sufficiently mild for me to wrap myself up and sit at the loophole to watch the passers by. Southerners have the habit of stopping and talking in the streets, and I heard many conversations not intended to meet my ears. I heard slave-hunters planning how to catch some poor fugitive. Several times I heard allusions to Dr. Flint, myself, and the history of my children, who, perhaps, were playing near the gate. One would say, "I wouldn't move my little finger to catch her, as old Flint's property." Another would say, "I'll catch *any* nigger for the reward. A man ought to have what belongs to him, if he *is* a damned brute." The opinion was often expressed that I was in the Free States. Very rarely did any one suggest that I might be in the vicinity. Had the least suspicion rested on my grandmother's house, it would have been burned to the ground. But it was the last place they thought of. Yet there was no place, where slavery existed, that could have afforded me so good a place of concealment.

Dr. Flint and his family repeatedly tried to coax and bribe my children to tell something they had heard said about me. One day the doctor took them into a shop, and offered them some bright little silver pieces and gay handkerchiefs if they would tell where their mother was. Ellen[7] shrank away from him, and would not speak; but Benny spoke up, and said, "Dr. Flint, I don't know where my mother is. I guess she's in New York; and when you go there again, I wish you'd ask her to come home, for I want to see her; but if you put her in jail, or tell her you'll cut her head off, I'll tell her to go right back."

Preparations for Escape

I hardly expect that the reader will credit me, when I affirm that I lived in that little dismal hole, almost deprived of light and air, and with no space to move my limbs, for nearly seven years. But it is a fact; and to me a sad one, even now; for my body still suffers from the effects of that long imprisonment, to say nothing of my soul. Members of my family, now living in New York and Boston, can testify to the truth of what I say.

Countless were the nights that I sat late at the little loophole scarcely large enough to give me a glimpse of one twinkling star. There, I heard the patrols and slave-hunters conferring together about the capture of runaways, well knowing how rejoiced they would be to catch me.

Season after season, year after year, I peeped at my children's faces, and heard their sweet voices, with a heart yearning all the while to say, "Your mother is here." Sometimes it appeared to me as if ages had rolled away since I entered upon that gloomy, monotonous existence. At times, I was stupefied and listless; at other times I became very impatient to

---

[7] Brent's daughter.

know when these dark years would end, and I should again be allowed to feel the sunshine, and breathe the pure air.

40   After Ellen left us, this feeling increased. Mr. Sands had agreed that Benny might go to the north whenever his uncle Phillip could go with him; and I was anxious to be there also, to watch over my children, and protect them so far as I was able. Moreover, I was likely to be drowned out of my den, if I remained much longer; for the slight roof was getting badly out of repair, and uncle Phillip was afraid to remove the shingles, lest some one should get a glimpse of me. When storms occurred in the night, they spread mats and bits of carpet, which in the morning appeared to have been laid out to dry; but to cover the roof in the daytime might have attracted attention. Consequently, my clothes and bedding were often drenched; a process by which the pains and aches in my cramped and stiffened limbs were greatly increased. I revolved various plans of escape in my mind, which I sometimes imparted to my grandmother, when she came to whisper with me at the trap-door. The kind-hearted old woman had an intense sympathy for runaways. She had known too much of the cruelties inflicted on those who were captured. Her memory always flew back at once to the sufferings of her bright and handsome son, Benjamin, the youngest and dearest of her flock. So, whenever I alluded to the subject, she would groan out, "O, don't think of it, child. You'll break my heart." I had no good old aunt Nancy now to encourage me; but my brother William and my children were continually beckoning me to the north.

And now I must go back a few months in my story. I have stated that the first of January was the time for selling slaves, or leasing them out to new masters. If time were counted by heart-throbs, the poor slaves might reckon years of suffering during that festival so joyous to the free. On the New Year's day preceding my aunt's death, one of my friends, named Fanny, was to be sold at auction, to pay her master's debts. My thoughts were with her during all the day, and at night I anxiously inquired what had been her fate. I was told that she had been sold to one master, and her four little girls to another master, far distant; that she had escaped from her purchaser, and was not to be found. Her mother was the old Aggie I have spoken of. She lived in a small tenement belonging to my grandmother, and built on the same lot with her own house. Her dwelling was searched and watched, and that brought the patrols so near me that I was obliged to keep very close in my den. The hunters were somehow eluded; and not long afterwards Benny accidentally caught sight of Fanny in her mother's hut. He told his grandmother, who charged him never to speak of it, explaining to him the frightful consequences; and he never betrayed the trust. Aggie little dreamed that my grandmother knew where her daughter was concealed, and that the stooping form of her old neighbor was bending under a similar burden of anxiety and fear; but these dangerous secrets deepened the sympathy between the two old persecuted mothers.

My friend Fanny and I remained many weeks hidden within call of each other; but she was unconscious of the fact. I longed to have her share my den, which seemed a more secure retreat than her own; but I had brought so much trouble on my grandmother, that it seemed wrong to ask her to incur greater risks. My restlessness increased. I had lived too long in bodily pain and anguish of spirit. Always I was in dread that by some accident, or some contrivance, slavery would succeed in snatching my children from me. This thought drove me nearly frantic, and I determined to steer for the North Star at all hazards. At this crisis, Providence opened an unexpected way for me to escape. My friend Peter came one evening, and asked to speak with me. "Your day has come, Linda," said he. "I have found a chance for you to go to the Free States. You have a fortnight to decide." The news seemed too good to be true; but Peter explained his arrangements, and told me all that was necessary was for me to say I would go. I was going to answer him with a joyful yes, when the thought of Benny came to my mind. I told him the temptation was exceedingly strong, but I was terribly afraid of Dr. Flint's alleged power over my child, and that I could not go and leave him behind. Peter remonstrated earnestly. He said such a good chance might never occur again; that Benny was free, and could be sent to me; and that for the sake of my children's welfare I ought not to hesitate a moment. I told him I would consult with uncle Phillip. My uncle rejoiced in the plan, and bade me go by all means. He promised, if his life was spared, that he would either bring or send my son to me as soon as I reached a place of safety. I resolved to go, but thought nothing had better be said to my grandmother till very near the time of departure. But my uncle thought she would feel it more keenly if I left her so suddenly. "I will reason with her," said he, "and convince her how necessary it is, not only for your sake, but for hers also. You cannot be blind to the fact that she is sinking under her burdens." I was not blind to it. I knew that my concealment was an ever-present source of anxiety, and that the older she grew the more nervously fearful she was of discovery. My uncle talked with her, and finally succeeded in persuading her that it was absolutely necessary for me to seize the chance so unexpectedly offered.

The anticipation of being a free woman proved almost too much for my weak frame. The excitement stimulated me, and at the same time bewildered me. I made busy preparations for my journey, and for my son to follow me. I resolved to have an interview with him before I went, that I might give him cautions and advice, and tell him how anxiously I should be waiting for him at the north. Grandmother stole up to me as often as possible to whisper words of counsel. She insisted upon my writing to Dr. Flint, as soon as I arrived in the Free States, and asking him to sell me to her. She said she would sacrifice her house, and all she had in the world, for the sake of having me safe with my children in any part of the world. If she could only live to know *that* she could die in peace. I promised the dear old faithful friend that I would write to her as soon as I arrived, and put the letter in a safe way to reach her; but in my own mind I resolved that not another cent of her hard earnings should be spent to pay rapacious slaveholders for what they called their property. And even if I had not been unwilling to buy what I had already a right to possess, common humanity would have prevented me from accepting the generous offer, at the expense of turning my aged relative out of house and home, when she was trembling on the brink of the grave.

I was to escape in a vessel; but I forbear to mention any further particulars. I was in readiness, but the vessel was unexpectedly detained several days. Meantime, news came to town of a most horrible murder committed on a fugitive slave, named James. Charity, the mother of this unfortunate young man, had been an old acquaintance of ours. I have told the shocking particulars of his death, in my description of some of the neighboring slaveholders. My grandmother, always nervously sensitive about runaways, was terribly frightened. She felt sure that a similar fate awaited me, if I did not desist from my enterprise. She sobbed, and groaned, and entreated me not to go. Her excessive fear was somewhat contagious, and my heart was not proof against her extreme agony. I was grievously disappointed, but I promised to relinquish my project.

45   When my friend Peter was apprised of this, he was both disappointed and vexed. He said, that judging from our past experience, it would be a long time before I had such another chance to throw away. I told him it need not be thrown away; that I had a friend concealed near by, who would be glad enough to take the place that had been provided for me. I told him about poor Fanny, and the kind-hearted, noble fellow, who never turned his back upon any body in distress, white or black, expressed his readiness to help her. Aggie was much surprised when she found that we knew her secret. She was rejoiced to hear of such a chance for Fanny, and arrangements were made for her to go on board the vessel the next night. They both supposed that I had long been at the north, therefore my name was not mentioned in the transaction. Fanny was carried on board at the appointed time, and stowed away in a very small cabin. This accommodation had been purchased at a price that would pay for a voyage to England. But when one proposes to go to fine old England, they

stop to calculate whether they can afford the cost of the pleasure; while in making a bargain to escape from slavery, the trembling victim is ready to say, "Take all I have, only don't betray me!"

The next morning I peeped through my loophole, and saw that it was dark and cloudy. At night I received news that the wind was ahead, and the vessel had not sailed. I was exceedingly anxious about Fanny, and Peter too, who was running a tremendous risk at my instigation. Next day the wind and weather remained the same. Poor Fanny had been half dead with fright when they carried her on board, and I could readily imagine how she must be suffering now. Grandmother came often to my den, to say how thankful she was I did not go. On the third morning she rapped for me to come down to the storeroom. The poor old sufferer was breaking down under her weight of trouble. She was easily flurried now. I found her in a nervous, excited state, but I was not aware that she had forgotten to lock the door behind her, as usual. She was exceedingly worried about the detention of the vessel. She was afraid all would be discovered, and then Fanny, and Peter, and I, would all be tortured to death, and Phillip would be utterly ruined, and her house would be torn down. Poor Peter! If he should die such a horrible death as the poor slave James had lately done, and all for his kindness in trying to help me, how dreadful it would be for us all! Alas, the thought was familiar to me, and had sent many a sharp pang through my heart. I tried to suppress my own anxiety, and speak soothingly to her. She brought in some allusion to aunt Nancy, the dear daughter she had recently buried, and then she lost all control of herself. As she stood there, trembling and sobbing, a voice from the piazza called out, "Whar is you, aunt Marthy?" Grandmother was startled, and in her agitation opened the door, without thinking of me. In stepped Jenny, the mischievous housemaid, who had tried to enter my room, when I was concealed in the house of my white benefactress. "I's bin huntin ebery whar for you, aunt Marthy," said she. "My missis wants you to send her some crackers." I had slunk down behind a barrel, which entirely screened me, but I imagined that Jenny was looking directly at the spot, and my heart beat violently. My grandmother immediately thought what she had done, and went out quickly with Jenny to count the crackers, locking the door after her. She returned to me, in a few minutes, the perfect picture of despair. "Poor child!" she exclaimed, "my carelessness has ruined you. The boat ain't gone yet. Get ready immediately, and go with Fanny. I ain't got another word to say against it now; for there's no telling what may happen this day."

Uncle Phillip was sent for, and he agreed with his mother in thinking that Jenny would inform Dr. Flint in less than twenty-four hours. He advised getting me on board the boat, if possible; if not, I had better keep very still in my den, where they could not find me without tearing the house down. He said it would not do for him to move in the matter, because suspicion would be immediately excited; but he promised to communicate with Peter. I felt reluctant to apply to him again, having implicated him too much already; but there seemed to be no alternative. Vexed as Peter had been by my indecision, he was true to his generous nature, and said at once that he would do his best to help me, trusting I should show myself a stronger woman this time.

He immediately proceeded to the wharf, and found that the wind had shifted, and the vessel was slowly beating down stream. On some pretext of urgent necessity, he offered two boatmen a dollar apiece to catch up with her. He was of lighter complexion than the boatmen he hired, and when the captain saw them coming so rapidly, he thought officers were pursuing his vessel in search of the runaway slave he had on board. They hoisted sails, but the boat gained upon them, and the indefatigable Peter sprang on board.

The captain at once recognized him. Peter asked him to go below, to speak about a bad bill he had given him. When he told his errand, the captain replied, "Why, the woman's here already; and I've put her where you or the devil would have a tough job to find her."

50   "But it is another woman I want to bring," said Peter. "*She* is in great distress, too, and you shall be paid any thing within reason, if you'll stop and take her."

"What's her name?" inquired the captain.

"Linda," he replied.

"That's the name of the woman already here," rejoined the captain. "By George! I believe you mean to betray me."

"O!" exclaimed Peter, "God knows I wouldn't harm a hair of your head. I am too grateful to you. But there really *is* another woman in great danger. Do have the humanity to stop and take her!"

55   After a while they came to an understanding. Fanny, not dreaming I was any where about in that region, had assumed my name, though she called herself Johnson. "Linda is a common name," said Peter, "and the woman I want to bring is Linda Brent."

The captain agreed to wait at a certain place till evening, being handsomely paid for his detention.

Of course, the day was an anxious one for us all. But we concluded that if Jenny had seen me, she would be too wise to let her mistress know of it; and that she probably would not get a chance to see Dr. Flint's family till evening, for I knew very well what were the rules in that household. I afterwards believed that she did not see me; for nothing ever came of it, and she was one of those base characters that would have jumped to betray a suffering fellow being for the sake of thirty pieces of silver.

I made all my arrangements to go on board as soon as it was dusk. The intervening time I resolved to spend with my son. I had not spoken to him for seven years, though I had been under the same roof, and seen him every day, when I was well enough to sit at the loophole. I did not dare to venture beyond the storeroom; so they brought him there, and locked us up together, in a place concealed from the piazza door. It was an agitating interview for both of us. After we had talked and wept together for a little while, he said, "Mother, I'm glad you're going away. I wish I could go with you. I knew you was here; and I have been *so* afraid they would come and catch you!"

I was greatly surprised, and asked him how he had found it out.

60   He replied, "I was standing under the eaves, one day, before Ellen went away, and I heard somebody cough up over the wood shed. I don't know what made me think it was you, but I did think so. I missed Ellen, the night before she went away; and grandmother brought her back into the room in the night; and I thought maybe she'd been to see *you*, before she went, for I heard grandmother whisper to her, 'Now go to sleep; and remember never to tell.' "

I asked him if he ever mentioned his suspicions to his sister. He said he never did; but after he heard the cough, if he saw her playing with other children on that side of the house, he always tried to coax her round to the other side, for fear she would hear me cough, too. He said he had kept a close lookout for Dr. Flint, and if he saw him speak to a constable, or a patrol, he always told grandmother. I now recollected that I had seen him manifest uneasiness, when people were on that side of the house, and I had at the time been puzzled to conjecture a motive for his actions. Such prudence may seem extraordinary in a boy of twelve years, but slaves, being surrounded by mysteries, deceptions, and dangers, early learn to be suspicious and watchful, and prematurely cautious and cunning. He had never asked a question of grandmother, or uncle Phillip, and I had often heard him chime in with other children, when they spoke of my being at the north.

I told him I was now really going to the Free States, and if he was a good, honest boy, and a loving child to his dear old grandmother, the Lord would bless him, and bring him to me, and we and Ellen would live together. He began to tell me that grandmother had not eaten any thing all day. While he was speaking, the door was unlocked, and she came in with a small bag of money, which she wanted me to take. I begged her to keep a part of it, at least, to pay for Benny's being sent to the north; but she insisted, while her tears were falling fast, that I should take the whole. "You may be sick among strangers," she said, "and they would send you to the poorhouse to die." Ah, that good grandmother!

For the last time I went up to my nook. Its desolate appearance no longer chilled me, for the light of hope had risen in my soul. Yet, even with the blessed prospect of freedom before me, I felt very sad at leaving forever that old homestead, where I had been sheltered so long by the dear old grandmother; where I had dreamed my first young dream of love; and where, after that had faded away, my children came to twine themselves so closely round my desolate heart. As the hour approached for me to leave, I again descended to the storeroom. My grandmother and Benny were there. She took me by the hand, and said, "Linda, let us pray." We knelt down together, with my child pressed to my heart, and my other arm round the faithful, loving old friend I was about to leave forever. On no other occasion has it ever been my lot to listen to so fervent a supplication for mercy and protection. It thrilled through my heart, and inspired me with trust in God.

Peter was waiting for me in the street. I was soon by his side, faint in body, but strong of purpose. I did not look back upon the old place, though I felt that I should never see it again.

■ EXPLORATIONS OF THE TEXT

1. Describe life in Dr. Flint's home. Explore the treatment of slaves.
2. Characterize the grandmother, Aunt Marthy. What is the importance of the candelabra?
3. Consider the beating of the field slave. What does Jacobs indicate about the cause of the arguments between the man and woman?
4. Characterize Mrs. Flint. What is the position of the jealous mistress? What does Jacobs think of Southern women?
5. Describe the years in the garret. Explain the following quotation: "My body still suffers from the effects of the long imprisonment, to say nothing of my soul."
6. What are the preparations for escape? What aspects of the flight are most memorable?
7. Characterize the narrator. Is she strong? What evidence suggests an answer to the previous question?
8. Determine the point of view, purpose, and audience for this narrative.
9. Compare speakers in this work with those in Sojourner Truth's speech and in Griffin's poem.

■ THE READING/WRITING CONNECTION

1. Write a journal entry in the voice of Dr. Flint, of the grandmother, of Mrs. Flint, or of the narrator.
2. "Think" Topic: Why does sexual exploitation become the central issue of this work?

■ IDEAS FOR WRITING

1. Characterize the narrator.
2. Write about the portraits of slave owners in these excerpts of Jacobs' narrative.

MANNING MARABLE

Manning Marable (1950–   ) was born in Dayton, Ohio. Educated at Earlham College, the University of Wisconsin, and the University of Maryland, Marable was founding director of the Institute for Research in African American Studies at Columbia University from 1993 to 2003. He currently is professor of Public Affairs, History, and Political Science at Columbia University.

Marable has pursued the role of public intellectual, and his weekly public affairs commentary, "Along the Color Line," is published in more than 280 journals and newspapers.

1995

THE PRISM OF RACE

Introduction: The Prism of Race

Black and white. As long as I can remember, the fundamentally defining feature of my life, and the lives of my family, was the stark reality of race. Angular and unforgiving, race was so much more than the background for what occurred or the context for our relationships. It was the social gravity which set into motion our expectations and emotions, our language and dreams. Race seemed far more powerful than distinctions between people based on language, nationality, religion or income. Race seemed granite-like, fixed and permanent, as the center of the social universe. The reality of racial discrimination constantly fed the pessimism and doubts that we as black people felt about the apparent natural order of the world, the inherent unfairness of it all, as well as limiting our hopes for a better life somewhere in the distant future.

I am a child of Middle America. I was born in Dayton, Ohio, on 13 May 1950, at the height of McCarthyism[1] and on the eve of the Korean[2] conflict. One of the few rituals I remember about the anti-Communist hysteria sweeping the nation in the fifties were the obligatory exercises we performed in elementary school, "ducking and covering" ourselves beneath small wooden desks in our classroom to shield ourselves from the fallout and blast of a nuclear explosion. Most of what I now recall of growing up in south-central Ohio had little to do with nuclear war or communism, only the omnipresent reality of race.

In the 1950s, Dayton was a predominantly blue-collar, working-class town, situated on the banks of the Great Miami River. Neighborhoods were divided to some extent by class. Oakwood was the well-to-do, WASP-ish community, filled with the corporate executives and professionals who ran the city's enterprises. Dayton View on the northwest side was becoming increasingly Jewish. Kettering and Centerville were unpretentiously middle class, conservative and Republican. But beneath the divisions of income, religion and political affiliation seemed to be the broad polarization rooted in race. There appeared to be two parallel racial universes which cohabited the same city, each with its own set of religious institutions, cultural activities, social centers, clubs, political organizations and schools. African-Americans generally resided west of the Great Miami River. The central core of the ghetto was located along the corridors of West Third and West Fifth Street. With the great migration of southern blacks to Dayton immediately following World War II, the African-American population became much more dense, and began to spread west, out to the city's furthest boundaries.

The black community existed largely in its own world, within the logic of institutions it had created to sustain itself. We were taught to be proud of our history and literature. Every day, on the way to Edison Elementary School, I would feel a surge of pride as we drove past the home of celebrated African-American poet Paul Lawrence Dunbar. My parents, James

---

[1] The practice of making accusations of disloyalty, especially of pro-Communist sentiments, that often were unsupported or based on doubtful evidence.

[2] The Korean War (1950–53); between North Korea (supported by Communist China) and South Korea (aided by the United States) and other members of the United Nations.

and June Marable, were school teachers, a solidly middle-class profession by the standards of the status-conscious Negro elite. During the fifties, my father taught at predominantly black Dunbar and Roosevelt high schools during the day; after school was dismissed, he worked as a laborer in the second shift at Dayton tire factory. Although my father had a principal's certificate and a Master's degree, which qualified him to be appointed as a principal, he was constantly passed over by white administrators because of his fiercely independent spirit and self-initiative. Frustrated, my father eventually went into business for himself, borrowing the money to build a private nursery and daycare center for black children on the city's West Side.

5   Because of my parent's education and jobs, we were part of Dayton's Negro middle class. Our family attorney, James McGee, was elected the city's first black mayor after the successes and reforms in the wake of the civil-rights movement. Most of my parents' friends were physicians, dentists, lawyers, school teachers, entrepreneurs and professionals of various types. Despite their pretensions, most middle-class Negroes were barely two or three paychecks from poverty. Many of the businesses that sold consumer goods to blacks, which were located on West Third Street, were white-owned. Our own business sector consisted chiefly of funeral parlors, beauty salons, auto repair shops and small restaurants.

The college-educated Negro middle class had begun purchasing comfortable, spacious homes clustered high on the ridge which overlooked the West Side, not far from the mostly German farm families who lived in Jefferson Township. Poorer black families lived closer to the factories and foundries, near the dirt, smoke and industrial stench I vividly recall even today. Social class and income stratification were not unimportant. There seemed to be striking similarities between the houses and the manner in which working and poor people were dressed on "our" side of town and in "their" working-class neighborhoods. But color was the greatest denominator of all.

On Gettysburg Avenue there were a group of small rental properties and boarding houses which were within walking distance of the Veteran's Administration Hospital on the far West Side. In the front windows of most of these buildings were small cardboard signs, reading simply "No Colored." Blacks legally could not be denied entrance into the hotels or best restaurants downtown, but they were certainly not welcomed. White taxicab drivers often avoided picking up black passengers at the train station. Very few blacks were on the local police force. Black children weren't permitted to use the public swimming pool on Germantown Pike. In most aspects of public and private life, whites acted toward African-Americans as "superiors," and usually expected to be treated deferentially. There were exceptions, certainly. At my elementary school, there were white students who were friendly. There were white teachers who displayed kindness and sincerity towards their black students. But there was always an unbridgeable distance separating us. No white students with whom I attended school ever asked to come to my home. Although my parents taught in the Dayton Public School system, most white teachers and administrators maintained a strictly professional rather than personal relationship towards them. Whites were omnipresent in our lives, frequently as authority figures: politicians, police officers, bank-loan officers, school administrators, tax auditors, grocery-store managers. Race existed as a kind of prism through which we understood and saw the world, distorting and coloring everything before us.

Despite these experiences and numerous examples of discrimination, Dayton, Ohio was never the Deep South. Although the largest department stores downtown rarely employed Negroes, I recall that black customers were usually treated with courtesy. Whites were enrolled in every school I attended. Occasionally, whites attended our black church. Public institutions were largely desegregated. The color line was at its worse where it converged with the boundaries of class inequality. Blacks were treated most differently, for example, when it was also clear that they lacked money or material resources. Conversely, middle-class African-Americans certainly experienced prejudicial behavior by whites, but often encountered a less virulent form of hatred than their sisters and brothers who were poor. The recognition of class mobility and higher education gave a small number of blacks a buffer status from the worst forms of discrimination at a day-to-day level. But despite this relative privilege, we never forgot that we were black.

Every summer, we had the opportunity to encounter a far more racially charged society. At the end of the school year, my family packed our 1957 Chevrolet and traveled south, through Cincinnati and Nashville, along highways and narrow, two-lane country roads. Often at nights we were forced to sleep in the cramped confines of the automobile, because we could find no motel which permitted black people to stay overnight. We would stop along the highway to purchase gasoline, never knowing in advance whether we would be allowed to use the gas station's toilet facilities. If we were stopped for any reason by a highway patrol officer, we had to be prepared for some kind of verbal, racist abuse, and we had absolutely no recourse or appeal against his behavior or actions. Finally, we would arrive at my father's family home, Tuskegee, Alabama, where the sense of racial hostility and discrimination against African-Americans was the central theme of local life. I knew that Tuskegee then was in the midst of a major legal struggle initiated by blacks to outlaw the political gerrymandering of the city that had in effect disfranchised African-Americans.[3] We were taught that any open protest or violation of the norms of Jim Crow segregation was to court retaliation and retribution, personally and collectively. We learned that whites, with few exceptions, saw us as subhuman, without the rights to economic development, political expression and participation, and public accommodation which whites accepted and took for granted for themselves.

10   It was in Tuskegee, during my long visits to Alabama's Black Belt as a child, that many of my basic impressions concerning the relative permanence and inflexibility of race were formed. Part of that consciousness was shaped by the experiences and stories of my father. James Marable was the grandson of slaves, and the second son of thirteen children. His father, Manning Marable, had owned and operated a small sawmill, cutting pulpwood for farm households. Along with other black rural families, they experienced the prism of race in hundreds of different ways, which formed the basic framework of their existence. From being denied the right to vote to being confined to unequal, segregated schools; from being harassed and intimidated by local white police officers to being forced to lower one's eyes when being directly addressed by a white man, "race" was ingrained in the smallest aspects of Southern daily life.

My father rarely talked at length about growing up black in the Deep South. But occasionally, and especially when we were visiting his large, extended family in Tuskegee, he would reflect about his own history, and recall the hostility and rudeness of whites toward himself, his family and his people. He was trying to prepare me for what I would surely experience. One of my father's stories I remember best occurred on a cold, early winter day in 1946. World War II had ended only months before, and millions of young people were going home. My father had served as a master sergeant in a segregated unit in the US Army Air Corps. Arriving in the Anniston, Alabama, bus station, he had to transfer to another local bus to make the final forty-mile trek to his family's home outside Wedowee, Alabama.

---

[3] Seat of Macon County, east-central Alabama; home of the Tuskegee Institute, founded by Booker T. Washington in 1881. In 1957 the state legislature approved changes in the city's boundaries that resulted in the disenfranchisement of 400 black voters. In 1960 the U.S. Supreme Court declared that act to be unconstitutional.

My father was wearing his army uniform, proudly displaying his medals. Quietly he purchased his ticket and stood patiently in line to enter the small bus. When my father finally reached the bus driver, the white man was staring intensely at him. With an ugly frown, the driver took a step. "Nigger," he spat at my father, "you look like you're going to give somebody some trouble. You had better wait here for the next bus." My father was immediately confused and angry. "As a soldier, you always felt sort of proud," my dad recalls. This white bus driver's remarks "hit me like a ton of bricks. Here I am, going home, and I'd been away from the South for four years. I wasn't being aggressive."

Dad turned around and saw that he was standing in front of three whites, who had purchased tickets after him. James Marable had forgotten, or had probably repressed, a central rule in the public etiquette of Jim Crow segregation.[4] Black people had to be constantly vigilant not to offend whites in any way. My father was supposed to have stepped out of line immediately, permitting the white patrons to move ahead of him. My father felt a burning sense of rage, which he could barely contain. "You get there some other way, nigger," the driver repeated with a laugh. The bus door shut in my father's face. The bus pulled away into the distance.

There was no other bus going to Wedowee that afternoon. My father wandered from the station into the street, feeling "really disgusted." Nothing he had accomplished in the previous four years, the sacrifices he had made for his country, seemed to matter. The rhetoric of democracy and freedom which had been popularized in the war against fascism rang hollow and empty. Although he eventually obtained a ride home by hitchhiking on the highway, my father never forgot the bitterness and hatred in the bus driver's words. Years later, he still felt his resentment and rage of that winter afternoon in Alabama. "When you go against the grain of racism," he warned me, "you pay for it, one way or another."

15   For both my father and myself, as well as for millions of black people for many generations, the living content of race was simultaneously and continuously created from within and imposed from without. That is, "race" is always an expression of how black people have defined themselves against the system of oppression, as well as a repressive structure of power and privilege which perpetuates an unequal status for African-Americans within a stratified social order. As an identity, race becomes a way of perceiving ourselves within a group. To be black in what seems to be a bipolar racial universe gives one instantly a set of coordinates within space and time, a sense of geographical location along an endless boundary of color. Blackness as a function of the racial superstructure also gives meaning to collective memory; it allows us to place ourselves within a context of racial resistance, within the many struggles for human dignity, for our families and for material resources. This consciousness of racial pride and community awareness gave hope and strength to my grandfather and father; it was also the prime motivation for the Edward Wilmot Blydens, Marcus Garveys and Fannie Lou Hamers throughout black history.[5] In this way, the prism of race structures the community of the imagination, setting parameters for real activity and collective possibility.

But blackness in a racially stratified society is always simultaneously the "negation of whiteness." To be white is not a sign of culture, or a statement of biology or genetics: it is essentially a power relationship, a statement of authority, a social construct which is perpetuated by systems of privilege, the consolidation of property and status. There is no genius behind the idea of whiteness, only an empty husk filled with a mountain of lies about superiority and

---

[4] Laws segregating, discriminating against Negroes.

[5] Activists for equal rights for blacks. Marcus Garvey (1887–1940), for example, organized the first important American-based black nationalist movement (1919–1926).

a series of crimes against "nonwhite" people. To be black in a white-dominated social order, for instance, means that one's life chances are circumscribed and truncated in a thousand different ways. To be black means that when you go to the bank to borrow money, despite the fact that you have a credit profile identical to your white counterpart, you are nevertheless two or three times more likely to be denied the loan than the white. To be black means that when you are taken to the hospital for emergency health-care treatment, the quality of care you receive will be inadequate and substandard. To be black means that your children will not have the same academic experiences and access to higher learning resources as children in the white suburbs and exclusive urban enclaves. To be black means that your mere physical presence and the reality of your being can trigger surveillance cameras at shops, supermarkets, malls and fine stores everywhere. To be black, male, and to live in central Harlem in the 1990s, for example, means that you will have a life expectancy of forty-nine years of age—less than in Bangladesh. Race constantly represents itself to black people as an apparently unending series of moments of inequality, which constantly challenge us, sapping and draining our physical, mental and moral resources.

Perhaps this is what most white Americans have never fully comprehended about "race": the racism is not just social discrimination, political disfranchisement and acts of extra-legal violence and terror which proliferated under the Jim Crow segregation of my father's South. Nor is racism the so-called "silent discrimination" faced by my generation of African-Americans raised during the civil-rights era, who are still denied access to credit and capital by unfair banking practices, or who encounter the "glass ceiling" inside businesses which limits their job advancement. As its essential core, racism is most keenly felt in its smallest manifestations: the white merchant who drops change on the sales counter, rather than touch the hand of a black person; the white salesperson who follows you into the dressing room when you carry several items of clothing to try on, because he or she suspects that you are trying to steal; the white teacher who deliberately avoids the upraised hand of a Latino student in class, giving white pupils an unspoken yet understood advantage; the white woman who wraps the strap of her purse several times tightly around her arm, just before walking past a black man; the white taxicab drivers who speed rapidly past African-Americans or Latinos, picking up whites on the next block. Each of these incidents, no matter how small, constructs the logic for the prism of race for the oppressed. We witness clear, unambiguous changes of behavior or language by whites toward us in public and private situations, and we code or interpret such changes as "racial." These minor actions reflect a structure of power, privilege and violence which most blacks can never forget.

The grandchildren of James Marable have never encountered Jim Crow segregation. They have never experienced signs reading "white" and "colored." They have never been refused service at lunch counters, access to hotel accommodation, restaurants or amusement parks, or admission to quality schools. They have never experienced the widespread unemployment, police brutality, substandard housing and the lack of educational opportunity which constitute the everyday lives of millions of African-American youth. For my children—eighteen-year-old Malaika, and sixteen-year old twins, Sojourner and Joshua—Martin Luther King, Jr., Medgar Evers, Fannie Lou Hamer and Ella Baker[6] are distant figures from the pages of black history books. Malcolm X is the charismatic image of Denzel Washington from Spike Lee's film, or perhaps the cinematic impression from several recent hip-hop music videos. "We shall Overcome" is an interesting but somewhat dated melody of the past, not a hopeful and militant anthem projecting an integrated America.

---

[6] Civil rights activists.

Yet, like my father before them, and like myself, my children are forced to view their world through the racial prism. They complain that their high-school textbooks don't have sufficient information about the activities and events related to African-Americans in the development of American society. In their classrooms, white students who claim to be their friends argue against affirmative action, insisting that the new "victims" of discrimination are overwhelmingly white and male. When Joshua goes to the shopping mall, he is followed and harassed by security guards. If he walks home alone through an affluent white neighborhood, he may be stopped by the police. White children have moved items away from the reach of my son because they have been taught the stereotype that "all blacks steal." Sojourner complains about her white teachers who have been hostile and unsympathetic toward her academic development, or who have given her lower grades for submitting virtually the identical level of work turned in by her white friends. As my daughter Malaika explains: "White people often misjudge you just by the way you look, without getting to know you. This makes me feel angry inside."

20   A new generation of African-Americans who never personally marched for civil rights or Black Power, who never witnessed the crimes of segregation, feel the same rage expressed by my father half a century ago. When they watch the beating of Rodney King on television or the trial of O.J. Simpson, they instantly comprehend the racism of the Los Angeles police officers involved in each case, and the larger racial implications of both incidents. When they listen to members of Congress complain about "welfare dependency" and "crime," they recognize the racial stereotypes which are lurking just behind the code words. They have come to expect hypocritical behavior from the white "friends" who act cordially towards them at school but refuse to acknowledge or recognize them in another context. Race is a social force which still has real meaning to the generation of my children.

But the problem with the prism of race is that it simultaneously clarifies and distorts social reality. It both illuminates and obscures, creating false dichotomies and distinctions between people where none really exists. The constructive identity of race, the conceptual framework which the oppressed create to interpret their experiences of inequality and discrimination, often clouds the concrete reality of class, and blurs the actual structure of power and privilege. It creates tensions between oppressed groups which share common class interests, but which may have different physical appearances or colors. For example, on the recent debates concerning undocumented immigrants, a narrow racial perspective could convince African-Americans that they should be opposed to the civil rights and employment opportunities of Mexican Americans, Central Americans and other Latino people. We could see Latinos as potential competitors in the labor market rather than as allies in a struggle against corporate capital and conservatives within the political establishment. On affirmative action, a strict racist outlook might view the interest of lower-class and working-class whites as directly conflicting with programs which could increase opportunities for blacks and other people of color. The racial prism creates an illusion that "race" is permanent and finite; but, in reality, "race" is a complex expression of unequal relations which are dynamic and ever-changing. The dialectics of racial thinking pushes black people toward the logic and "us" versus "them," rather than a formulation which cuts across the perceived boundaries of color.

This observation is not a criticism of the world-views of my father, my children, or myself as I grew up in Dayton, Ohio. It is only common sense that most African-Americans perceive and interpret the basic struggle for equality and empowerment in distinctly racial terms. This perspective does speak to our experiences and social reality, but only to a portion of what that reality truly is. The parallel universes of race do not stand still. What was "black" and "white" in Booker T. Washington's Tuskegee of 1895 was not identical to categories of color and race in New Orleans a century ago; both are distinctly different from how we perceive and define race in the USA a generation after legal segregation. There is always a distance between our consciousness and the movement of social forces, between perception and historical reality. "Blackness" must inevitably be redefined in material terms ideologically, as millions of black and Hispanic people from the Caribbean, Africa and Latin America immigrate into the USA, assimilating within hundreds of urban centers and thousands of neighborhoods with other people of color. As languages, religions, cultural traditions and kinship networks among blacks in the USA become increasingly diverse and complex, our consciousness and our ideas of historical struggle against the leviathan of race also shift and move in new directions. This does not mean that "race" has declined in significance; it does mean that what we mean by "race" and how "race" is utilized as a means of dividing the oppressed are once again being transformed in many crucial respects.

At the beginning of the African presence in the Americas, an African-American culture, nationality and consciousness was constructed. Against great odds, inside the oppressive context of slavery and later racial segregation, the racial identity and perspective of resistance, a community empowered by imagination, was developed against the weight of institutional racism. That historic leap of collective self-definition and inner faith must once again occur, now inside the very different environment of mature capitalism. We must begin the process of redefining blackness in a manner which not only interprets but also transforms our world.

■ EXPLORATIONS OF THE TEXT

1. What is Marable's purpose in his essay? What is his thesis? Paraphrase his thesis statement.
2. What autobiographical examples of the racial divide, of "the color line," are most powerful? Most persuasive? How does the inclusion of these autobiographical examples enhance the essay?
3. Contrast the world of his childhood—Dayton, Ohio—with that of his father's family home—Tuskegee, Alabama.
4. Contrast James Marable's experiences of growing up during Jim Crow segregation with that of his grandchildren.
5. Do you agree with the following statement: "At its essential core, racism is most keenly felt in its smallest manifestations. . . . These minor actions reflect a structure of power, privilege and violence which most blacks can never forget"?
6. What are Marable's conclusions about the "prism of race"? Does he propose solutions to this problem?

■ THE READING/WRITING CONNECTION

1. "Think" Topic: Do racial politics divide us from one another? Create a dialogue on this subject with the author.
2. Choose one statement from this essay. Agree or disagree with it in a paragraph response.

■ IDEAS FOR WRITING

1. Connect one of Marable's conceptions regarding the "color line" or the "prism of race" with one of the poems about race presented in this chapter.
2. Analyze Marable's essay as a form of creative nonfiction.

ELIE WIESEL   Translated by Rosette C. Lamont

Elie Wiesel (1928–) was born in Sighet, Romania. His childhood world centered around Jewish tradition and the study of the Talmud, the Torah, and the teachings of the Hasidic masters. In 1944, he and his family were deported to Auschwitz where his three sisters and parents were killed. After the war, Wiesel lived in France, eventually studying philosophy at the Sorbonne and writing for a French newspaper. In 1950, he became the chief foreign correspondent for the Tel Aviv daily newspaper, Yedioth Ahronot. More than ten years after his liberation from the camps, he published several autobiographical novels based on his concentration camp and postwar experience: Night *(1956),* Dawn *(1961), and* The Accident *(1962). Wiesel's other published works include a play,* Zalmen: or the Madness of God *(1968);* Legends of Our Time *(1966), a collection of short stories, autobiographical articles, and reflective essays;* A Beggar in Jerusalem *(1970), a novel that focuses on the 1967 Arab-Israeli conflict, and a work of nonfiction,* After the Darkness: Reflections on the Holocaust *(2002). Wiesel, who was awarded the Nobel Peace Prize in 1986, believes that he and other Holocaust survivors have a responsibility to tell their stories; "to remain silent and indifferent," he says, "is the greatest sin of all."*

1985

WHY I WRITE: MAKING NO BECOME YES

Why do I write.
Perhaps in order not to go mad. Or, on the contrary, to touch the bottom of madness. Like Samuel Beckett,[1] the survivor expresses himself "en désepoir de cause"—out of desperation.

Speaking of the solitude of the survivor, the great Yiddish and Hebrew poet and thinker Aaron Zeitlin addresses those—his father, his brother, his friends—who have died and left him: "You have abandoned me," he says to them. "You are together, without me. I am here. Alone. And I make words."

So do I, just like him. I also say words, write words, reluctantly.

5   There are easier occupations, far more pleasant ones. But for the survivor, writing is not a profession, but an occupation, a duty. Camus calls it "an honor." As he puts it: "I entered literature through worship." Other writers have said they did so through anger, through love. Speaking for myself, I would say—through silence.

It was by seeking, by probing silence that I began to discover the perils and power of the word. I never intended to be a philosopher, or a theologian. The only role I sought was that of witness. I believed that, having survived by chance, I was duty-bound to give meaning to my survival, to justify each moment of my life. I knew the story had to be told. Not to transmit an experience is to betray it. This is what Jewish tradition teaches us. But how to do this? "When Israel is in exile, so is the word," says the Zohar.[2] The word has deserted the meaning it was intended to convey—impossible to make them coincide. The displacement, the shift, is irrevocable.

This was never more true than right after the upheaval. We all knew that we could never, never say what had to be said, that we could never express in words, coherent, intelligible words, our experience of madness on an absolute scale. The walk through flaming night, the silence before and after the selection, the monotonous praying of the condemned, the Kaddish of the dying, the fear and hunger of the sick, the shame and suffering, the haunted eyes, the demented stares. I thought that I would never be able to speak of them. All words seemed inadequate, worn, foolish, lifeless, whereas I wanted them to be searing.

Where was I to discover a fresh vocabulary, a primeval language? The language of night was not human, it was primitive, almost animal—hoarse shouting, screams, muffled moaning, savage howling, the sound of beating. A brute strikes out wildly, a body falls. An officer raises his arm and a whole community walks toward a common grave. A soldier shrugs his

---

[1] Irish playwright, essayist, poet, and novelist (1906–1989).
[2] The source of the Kabbalah, Jewish mysticism.

shoulders, and a thousand families are torn apart, to be reunited only by death. This was the concentration camp language. It negated all other language and took its place. Rather than a link, it became a wall. Could it be surmounted? Could the reader be brought to the other side? I knew the answer was negative, and yet knew that "no" had to become "yes." It was the last wish of the dead.

The fear of forgetting remains the main obsession of all those who have passed through the universe of the damned. The enemy counted on people's incredulity and forgetfulness. How could one foil this plot? And if memory grew hollow, empty of substance, what would happen to all we had accumulated along the way? Remember, said the father to his son, and the son to his friend. Gather the names, the faces, the tears. We had all taken an oath: "If, by some miracle, I emerge alive, I will devote my life to testifying on behalf of those whose shadow will fall on mine forever and ever."

10   That is why I write certain things rather than others—to remain faithful.

Of course, there are times of doubt for the survivor, times when one gives in to weakness, or longs for comfort. I hear a voice within me telling me to stop mourning the past. I too want to sing of love and of its magic. I too want to celebrate the sun, and the dawn that heralds the sun. I would like to shout, and shout loudly: "Listen, listen well! I too am capable of victory, do you hear? I too am open to laughter and joy! I want to stride, head high, my face unguarded, without having to point to the ashes over there on the horizon, without having to tamper with facts to hide their tragic ugliness. For a man born blind, God himself is blind, but look, I see, I am not blind." One feels like shouting this, but the shout changes to a murmur. One must make a choice; one must remain faithful. A big word, I know. Nevertheless, I use it, it suits me. Having written the things I have written, I feel I can afford no longer to play with words. If I say that the writer in me wants to remain loyal, it is because it is true. This sentiment moves all survivors; they owe nothing to anyone, but everything to the dead.

I owe them my roots and my memory. I am duty-bound to serve as their emissary, transmitting the history of their disappearance, even if it disturbs, even if it brings pain. Not to do so would be to betray them, and thus myself. And since I am incapable of communicating their cry by shouting, I simply look at them. I see them and I write.

While writing, I question them as I question myself. I believe I have said it before, elsewhere. I write to understand as much as to be understood. Will I succeed one day? Wherever one starts, one reaches darkness. God? He remains the God of darkness. Man? The source of darkness. The killers' derision, their victims' tears, the onlookers' indifference, their complicity and complacency—the divine role in all that I do not understand. A million children massacred—I shall never understand.

Jewish children—they haunt my writings. I see them again and again. I shall always see them. Hounded, humiliated, bent like the old men who surround them as though to protect them, unable to do so. They are thirsty, the children, and there is no one to give them water. They are hungry, but there is no one to give them a crust of bread. They are afraid, and there is no one to reassure them.

15   They walk in the middle of the road, like vagabonds. They are on the way to the station, and they will never return. In sealed cars, without air or food, they travel toward another world. They guess where they are going, they know it, and they keep silent. Tense, thoughtful, they listen to the wind, the call of death in the distance.

All these children, these old people, I see them. I never stop seeing them. I belong to them.

But they, to whom do they belong?

People tend to think that a murderer weakens when facing a child. The child reawakens the killer's lost humanity. The killer can no longer kill the child before him, the child inside him.

But with us it happened differently. Our Jewish children had no effect upon the killers. Nor upon the world. Nor upon God.

20   I think of them, I think of their childhood. Their childhood is a small Jewish town, and this town is no more. They frighten me; they reflect an image of myself, one that I pursue and run from at the same time—the image of a Jewish adolescent who knew no fear, except the fear of God, whose faith was whole, comforting, and not marked by anxiety.

No, I do not understand. And if I write, it is to warn the reader that he will not understand either. "You will not understand, you will never understand," were the words heard everywhere during the reign of night. I can only echo them. You, who never lived under a sky of blood, will never know what it was like. Even if you read all the books ever written, even if you listen to all the testimonies ever given, you will remain on this side of the wall, you will view the agony and death of a people from afar, through the screen of a memory that is not your own.

An admission of impotence and guilt? I do not know. All I know is that Treblinka and Auschwitz cannot be told. And yet I have tried. God knows I have tried.

Have I attempted too much or not enough? Among some twenty-five volumes, only three or four penetrate the phantasmagoric realm of the dead. In my other books, through my other books, I have tried to follow other roads. For it is dangerous to linger among the dead, they hold on to you and you run the risk of speaking only to them. And so I have forced myself to turn away from them and study other periods, explore other destinies and teach other tales—the Bible and the Talmud, Hasidism[3] its fervor, the shtetl[4] and its songs, Jerusalem and its echoes, the Russian Jews and their anguish, their awakening, their courage. At times, it has seemed to me that I was speaking of other things with the sole purpose of keeping the essential—the personal experience—unspoken. At times I have wondered: And what if I was wrong? Perhaps I should not have heeded my own advice and stayed in my own world with the dead.

But then, I have not forgotten the dead. They have their rightful place even in the works about the Hasidic capitals Ruzhany and Korets, and Jerusalem. Even in my biblical and Midrashic tales[5] pursue their presence, mute and motionless. The presence of the dead then beckons in such tangible ways that it affects even the most removed characters. Thus they appear on Mount Moriah, where Abraham is about to sacrifice his son, a burnt offering to their common God. They appear on Mount Nebo, where Moses enters solitude and death. They appear in Hasidic and Talmudic legends in which victims forever need defending against forces that would crush them. Technically, so to speak, they are of course elsewhere, in time and space, but on a deeper, truer plane, the dead are part of every story, of every scene.

25   "But what is the connection?" you will ask. Believe me, there is one. After Auschwitz everything brings us back to Auschwitz. When I speak of Abraham, Isaac and Jacob, when I invoke Rabbi Yohanan ben Zakkai and Rabbi Akiba,[6] it is the better to understand them in the light of Auschwitz. As for the Maggid of Mezeritch[7] and his disciples, it is in order to encounter the followers of their followers that I reconstruct their spellbound, spellbinding

---

[3] Popular Eastern European, Orthodox Jewish religious movement that developed in the 1700s.

[4] A village; usually refers to Jewish towns in Eastern Europe.

[5] Readings and interpretations of biblical texts done by rabbis.

[6] Rabbi Yohanan ben Zakkai, disciple of Rabbi Hillel, responsible for continuation of Jewish scholarship after Jerusalem fell to Rome in 70 C.E.; Rabbi Akiba (250–135 C.E.) became the first of Judaism's scholars.

[7] Hasidic master.

universe. I like to imagine them alive, exuberant, celebrating life and hope. Their happiness is as necessary to me as it was once to themselves.

And yet—how did they manage to keep their faith intact? How did they manage to sing as they went to meet the Angel of Death? I know Hasidim who never vacillated—I respect their strength. I know others who chose rebellion, protest, rage—I respect their courage. For there comes a time when only those who do not believe in God will not cry out to him in wrath and anguish.

Do not judge either group. Even the heroes perished as martyrs, even the martyrs died as heroes. Who would dare oppose knives to prayers? The faith of some matters as much as the strength of others. It is not ours to judge, it is only ours to tell the tale.

But where is one to begin? Whom is one to include? One meets a Hasid in all my novels. And a child. And an old man. And a beggar. And a madman. They are all part of my inner landscape. The reason why? Pursued and persecuted by the killers, I offer them shelter. The enemy wanted to create a society purged of their presence, and I have brought some of them back. The world denied them, repudiated them, so I let them live at least within the feverish dreams of my characters.

It is for them that I write, and yet the survivor may experience remorse. He has tried to bear witness; it was all in vain.

30   After the liberation, we had illusions. We were convinced that a new world would be built upon the ruins of Europe. A new civilization would see the light. No more wars, no more hate, no more intolerance, no fanaticism. And all this because the witnesses would speak. And speak they did, to no avail.

They will continue, for they cannot do otherwise. When man, in his grief, falls silent, Goethe[8] says, then God gives him the strength to sing his sorrows. From that moment on, he may no longer choose not to sing, whether his song is heard or not. What matters is to struggle against silence with words, or through another form of silence. What matters is to gather a smile here and there, a tear here and there, a word here and there, and thus justify the faith placed in you, a long time ago, by so many victims.

Why do I write? To wrench those victims from oblivion. To help the dead vanquish death.

■ EXPLORATIONS OF THE TEXT

1. As a survivor, why does Wiesel think that it is his "duty" to become a witness? What does he mean by witnessing? Give examples of his stance. What are the struggles that he endures as a witness?

2. Why does he state that he "write[s] certain things rather than others—to remain faithful" "to the dead"?

3. Wiesel's essay contains a series of paradoxes. Isolate the paradoxes, and analyze them. Why does Wiesel include so many paradoxical statements? What messages do they convey?

4. The tension between the impossibility of writing about the Holocaust and the necessity of doing so informs Wiesel's stance. Does he succeed in writing about the Holocaust—in making "no become yes"? Does this essay belie his contention that he is unable to probe the darkness?

5. Is Wiesel optimistic that acts of witnessing will create "a new civilization"? Is he optimistic about the future?

---

[8] Johann Wolfgang Goethe (1749–1832); German playwright and poet.

6. Do other writers in the Holocaust cluster effectively portray Holocaust worlds? Are they able to create what Wiesel calls "the language of night"? How do you think that they accomplish this impossible task?

■ THE READING/WRITING CONNECTION

1. "Think" Topic: For Wiesel, "the dead are part of every story, of every scene." Relate this state to Delbo's vision in "Prayer to the Living to Forgive Them for Being Alive."
2. Why do you write? Compare your reasons for writing with Wiesel's.
3. In a journal entry, explore the dangers of forgetting the past.

■ IDEAS FOR WRITING

1. Compare and contrast Wiesel's, and, in chapter 8, Sanders's, Aciman's, and/or Morrison's reasons for writing and your own.
2. In the essay, Wiesel states that he needed to "discover a fresh vocabulary, a primeval language . . . The language of night was not human, it was primitive, almost animal . . ." "This was the concentration camp language." What do you think he means? Are Pryztyk, Delbo, Celan, or Ozick successful in creating this new language? Why, or why not?
3. Discuss the incomprehensibility of horror as it is portrayed by Wiesel, Pryztyk, and Ozick.
4. Compare Wiesel's use of paradox with Celan's in "Death Fugue."

Emma Goldman

Emma Goldman (1869–1940) was born in Kovno, Lithuania, and moved to the United States in 1885 to escape an arranged marriage. Goldman studied nursing and midwifery in Vienna, Austria, during the late 1890s, but she is known primarily for her work as a political activist. Goldman, an anarchist, was the founder and editor of Mother Earth *magazine (1906–1917); lectured about social causes, including free speech and reproductive rights for women; and was deported to Russia in 1919 after having been imprisoned for two years. Goldman wrote eleven books, including collections of essays, lectures, criticism, and memoirs. "Minorities vs. Majorities" is from* Anarchism and Other Essays *(1910), her first published collection.*

1910

MINORITIES VS. MAJORITIES

If I were to give a summary of the tendency of our times, I would say, Quantity. The multitude, the mass spirit, dominates everywhere, destroying quality. Our entire life—production, politics, and education—rests on quantity, on numbers. The worker who once took pride in the thoroughness and quality of his work, has been replaced by brainless, incompetent automatons, who turn out enormous quantities of things, valueless to themselves, and generally injurious to the rest of mankind. Thus quantity, instead of adding to life's comforts and peace, has merely increased man's burden.

In politics, naught but quantity counts. In proportion to its increase, however, principles, ideals, justice, and uprightness are completely swamped by the array of numbers. In the struggle for supremacy the various political parties outdo each other in trickery, deceit, cunning, and shady machinations, confident that the one who succeeds is sure to be hailed by the majority as the victor. That is the only god,—Success. As to what expense, what terrible cost to character, is of no moment. We have not far to go in search of proof to verify this sad fact.

Never before did the corruption, the complete rottenness of our government stand so thoroughly exposed; never before were the American people brought face to face with the Judas nature of that political body, which has claimed for years to be absolutely beyond reproach, as the mainstay of our institutions, the true protector of the rights and liberties of the people.

Yet when the crimes of that party became so brazen that even the blind could see them, it needed but to muster up its minions, and its supremacy was assured. Thus the very victims, duped, betrayed, outraged a hundred times, decided, not against, but in favor of the victor. Bewildered, the few asked how could the majority betray the traditions of American liberty? Where was its judgment, its reasoning capacity? That is just it, the majority cannot reason; it has no judgment. Lacking utterly in originality and moral courage, the majority has always placed its destiny in the hands of others. Incapable of standing responsibilities, it has followed its leaders even unto destruction. Dr. Stockman[1] was right; "The most dangerous enemies of truth and justice in our midst are the compact majorities, the damned compact majority." Without ambition or initiative, the compact mass hates nothing so much as innovation. It has always opposed, condemned, and hounded the innovator, the pioneer of a new truth.

5   The oft repeated slogan of our time is, among all politicians, the Socialists, included, that ours is an era of individualism, of the minority. Only those who do not probe beneath the surface might be led to entertain this view. Have not the few accumulated the wealth of the world? Are they not the masters, the absolute kings of the situation? Their success, however, is due not to individualism, but to the inertia, the cravenness, the utter submission of the mass. The latter wants but to be dominated, to be led, to be coerced. As to individualism, at no time in human history did it have less chance of expression, less opportunity to assert itself in a normal, healthy manner.

Today, as then, public opinion is the omnipresent tyrant; today, as then, the majority represents a mass of cowards, willing to accept him who mirrors its own soul and mind poverty. That accounts for the unprecedented rise of a man like Roosevelt[2] He embodies the very worst element of mob psychology. A politician, he knows that the majority cares little for ideals or integrity. What it craves is display. It matters not whether that be a dog show, a prize fight, the lynching of a "nigger," the rounding up of some petty offender, the marriage exposition of an heiress, or the acrobatic stunts of an ex-president.[3] The more hideous the mental contortions, the greater the delight and bravos of the mass. Thus, poor in ideals and vulgar of soul, Roosevelt continues to be the man of the hour

In the American struggle for liberty, the majority was no less of a stumbling block. Until this very day the ideas of Jefferson, of Patrick Henry, of Thomas Paine,[4] are denied and sold by their posterity. The mass wants none of them. The greatness and courage wor-

---

[1] Medical officer of the Municipal Baths in Henrik Ibsen's play, *An Enemy of the People,* written in 1882. He is full of the spirit of innovation and enterprise and betrays the town by not telling them that the baths are built on a poisonous swamp and that the people using the baths to better their health will be infected with fever.

[2] Theodore Roosevelt (1858–1919) 26th President of U.S. (1901–1909). Called Rough Rider for his escapades and prosecution of the Spanish-American war.

[3] The dog show refers to a birthday party for Lady Astor's dog and the lynching refers to the lynching craze.

[4] Thomas Jefferson (1743–1826) one of the framers of the U.S. Constitution, Patrick Henry (1736–99) American revolutionary and statesman, whose oratorical skills made him famous. Thomas Paine (1737–1809) Revolutionary philosopher and writer. Born in England, he became a sailor. In 1774 he sailed for Philadelphia, where his pamphlet *Common Sense* (1776) argued for complete independence.

shipped in Lincoln have been forgotten in the men who created the background for the panorama of that time. The true patron saints of the black men were represented in that handful of fighters in Boston, Lloyd Garrison, Wendell Phillips, Thoreau, Margaret Fuller,[5] and Theodore Parker, whose great courage and sturdiness culminated in that somber giant, John Brown.[6] Their untiring zeal, their eloquence and perseverance undermined the stronghold of the Southern lords. Lincoln and his minions followed only when abolition had become a practical issue, recognized as such by all.

About fifty years ago, a meteor-like idea made its appearance on the social horizon of the world, an idea so far-reaching, so revolutionary, so all-embracing as to spread terror in the hearts of tyrants everywhere. On the other hand, that idea was a harbinger of joy, of cheer, of hope to the millions. The pioneers knew the difficulties in their way, they knew the opposition, the persecution, the hardships that would meet them, but proud and unafraid they started on their march onward, ever onward. Now that idea has become a popular slogan. Almost everyone is a Socialist today: the rich man, as well as his poor victim; the upholders of law and authority, as well as their unfortunate culprits; the freethinker, as well as the perpetuator of religious falsehoods; the fashionable lady, as well as the shirtwaist girl. Why not? Now that the truth of fifty years ago has become a lie, now that it has been clipped of all its youthful imagination, and been robbed of its vigor, its strength, its revolutionary ideal—why not? Now that it is no longer a beautiful vision, but a "practical, workable scheme," resting on the will of the majority, why not? With the same political cunning and shrewdness the mass is petted, pampered, cheated daily. Its praise is being sung in many keys: the poor majority, the outraged, the abused, the giant majority, if only it would follow us.

Who has not heard this litany before? Who does not know this never-varying refrain of all politicians? That the mass bleeds, that it is being robbed and exploited, I know as well as our vote-baiters. But I insist that not the handful of parasites, but the mass itself is responsible for this horrible state of affairs. It clings to its masters, loves the whip, and is the first to cry Crucify! the moment a protesting voice is raised against the sacredness of capitalistic authority or any other decayed institution. Yet how long would authority and private property exist, if not for the willingness of the mass to become soldiers, policemen, jailers, and hangmen.

10   Yes, power, authority, coercion, and dependence rest on the mass, but never freedom, never the free unfoldment of the individual, never the birth of a free society.

Not because I do not feel with the oppressed, the disinherited of the earth; not because I do not know the shame, the horror, the indignity of the lives the people lead, do I repudiate the majority as a creative force for good. Oh, no, no! But because I know so well that as a compact mass it has never stood for justice or equality. It has suppressed the human voice, subdued the human spirit, chained the human body. As a mass its aim has always been to make life uniform, gray, and monotonous as the desert. As a mass it will always be the annihilator of individuality, of free initiative, of originality. I therefore believe with Emerson[7] that

[5] Garrison (1805–79) Abolitionist; Phillips (1811–84) U.S. orator and reformer; Fuller (1810–50) feminist and revolutionary, author of *Woman in the Nineteenth Century;* Thoreau (1817–62) essayist who wrote *Civil Disobedience.*

[6] An antislavery militant who led a raid on Harper's Ferry on October 16, 1859, in hopes of inciting a slave rebellion.

[7] Ralph Waldo Emerson (1803–82) Poet, essayist, born in Boston. He was a transcendentalist in philosophy, a rationalist in religion, and a bold advocate of spiritual individualism. Quote is from *The Conduct of Life.*

"the masses are crude, lame, pernicious in their demands and influence, and need not to be flattered, but to be schooled. I wish not to concede anything to them, but to drill, divide, and break them up, and draw individuals out of them. Masses! The calamity are the masses. I do not wish any mass at all, but honest men only, lovely, sweet, accomplished women only."

In other words, the living, vital truth of social and economic well-being will become a reality only through the zeal, courage, the non-compromising determination of intelligent minorities, and not through the mass.

■ **EXPLORATIONS OF THE TEXT**

1. What does Goldman mean when she says the following: "Our entire life—production, politics and education—rests on quantity, on numbers"?
2. What does Goldman mean when she speaks about the "struggle for supremacy" of a political party, that "the one hailed by the majority is the victor"? Do you see any comparisons between today's politics and those of 100 years ago?
3. Define Goldman's use of the following: "the mass," "the majority," and Socialism. What does she mean by "mob psychology"?

■ **THE READING/WRITING CONNECTION**

1. How would you characterize the effect of the media on today's mass consciousness with that described in Walker's "Nineteen Fifty-Five" and Goldman's essay? Where do you see mass consciousness in your own life?
2. Characterize the meaning of success in Walker's story and in Goldman's essay. How do we define success today?

■ **IDEAS FOR WRITING**

1. Take a statement from Goldman's essay, and write an argument essay either opposing or supporting it.
2. At the end of Salih's "A Handful of Dates," the protagonist is disillusioned by his grandfather's success. Using Goldman's essay as a critical lens, interpret Salih's story.

Czeslaw Milosz

Czeslaw Milosz (1911–2004) was born in Wilno, Poland. A leader in the Polish literary avant-garde in the 1930s, Milosz immigrated to the United States after the Second World War, settling in California, where he taught at the University of California, Berkeley. He has written essays, including The Captive Mind *(1953) and* Beginning with My Streets: Essays and Recollections *(1992), and poetry, including* Facing the River *(1995). His* Collected Poems *appeared in 1990. He received the Nobel Prize for Literature in 1980.*

1953

AMERICAN IGNORANCE OF WAR

Are Americans *really* stupid? I was asked in Warsaw. In the voice of the man who posed the question, there was despair, as well as the hope that I would contradict him. This question reveals the attitude of the average person in the people's democracies toward the West: It is despair mixed with a residue of hope.

During the last few years, the West has given these people a number of reasons to despair politically. In the case of the intellectual, other, more complicated reasons come into play. Before the countries of Central and Eastern Europe entered the sphere of the

Imperium,[1] they lived through the Second World War. That war was much more devastating there than in the countries of Western Europe. It destroyed not only their economies but also a great many values which had seemed till then unshakable.

Man tends to regard the order he lives in as *natural.* The houses he passes on his way to work seem more like rocks rising out of the earth than like products of human hands. He considers the work he does in his office or factory as essential to the harmonious functioning of the world. The clothes he wears are exactly what they should be, and he laughs at the idea that he might equally well be wearing a Roman toga or medieval armor. He respects and envies a minister of state or a bank director, and regards the possession of a considerable amount of money as the main guarantee of peace and security. He cannot believe that one day a rider may appear on a street he knows well, where cats sleep and children play, and start catching passersby with his lasso. He is accustomed to satisfying those of his physiological needs which are considered private as discreetly as possible, without realizing that such a pattern of behavior is not common to all human societies. In a word, he behaves a little like Charlie Chaplin in *The Gold Rush,* bustling about in a shack poised precariously on the edge of a cliff.

His first stroll along a street littered with glass from bomb-shattered windows shakes his faith in the "naturalness" of his world. The wind scatters papers from hastily evacuated offices, papers labeled "Confidential" or "Top Secret" that evoke visions of safes, keys, conferences, couriers, and secretaries. Now the wind blows them through the street for anyone to read; yet no one does, for each man is more urgently concerned with finding a loaf of bread. Strangely enough, the world goes on even though the offices and secret files have lost all meaning. Farther down the street, he stops before a house split in half by a bomb, the privacy of people's homes—the family smells, the warmth of the beehive life, the furniture preserving the memory of loves and hatreds—cut open to public view. The house itself, no longer a rock, but a scaffolding of plaster, concrete, and brick; and on the third floor, a solitary white bathtub, rain-rinsed of all recollection of those who once bathed in it. Its formerly influential and respected owners, now destitute, walk the fields in search of stray potatoes. Thus overnight money loses its value and becomes a meaningless mass of printed paper. His walk takes him past a little boy poking a stick into a heap of smoking ruins and whistling a song about the great leader who will preserve the nation against all enemies. The song remains, but the leader of yesterday is already part of an extinct past.

5   He finds he acquires new habits quickly. Once, had he stumbled upon a corpse on the street, he would have called the police. A crowd would have gathered, and much talk and comment would have ensued. Now he knows he must avoid the dark body lying the gutter, and refrain from asking unnecessary questions. The man who fired the gun must have had his reasons; he might well have been executing an Underground sentence.

Nor is the average European accustomed to thinking of his native city as divided into segregated living areas, but a single decree can force him to this new pattern of life and thought. Quarter A may suddenly be designated for one race; B, for a second; C, for a third. As the resettlement deadline approaches, the streets become filled with long lines of wagons, carts, wheelbarrows, and people carrying bundles, beds, chests, caldrons, and bird cages. When all the moves are effected, 2,000 people may find themselves in a building that once housed 200, but each man is at last in the proper area. Then high walls are erected around Quarter C, and daily a given lot of men, women, and children are loaded into wagons that take them off to specially constructed factories where they are scientifically slaughtered and their bodies burned.

---

[1] Empire: Sphere of dominance; Soviet Union.

And even the rider with the lasso appears, in the form of a military van waiting at the corner of a street. A man passing that corner meets a leveled rifle, raises his hands, is pushed into the van, and from that moment is lost to his family and friends. He may be sent to a concentration camp, or he may face a firing squad, his lips sealed with plaster lest he cry out against the state; but, in any case, he serves as a warning to his fellow men. Perhaps one might escape such a fate by remaining at home. But the father of a family must go out in order to provide bread and soup for his wife and children; and every night they worry about whether or not he will return. Since these conditions last for years, everyone gradually comes to look upon the city as a jungle, and upon the fate of twentieth-century man as identical with that of a caveman living in the midst of powerful monsters.

It was once thought obvious that a man bears the same name and surname throughout his entire life; now it proves wiser for many reasons to change them and to memorize a new and fabricated biography. As a result, the records of the civilian state become completely confused. Everyone ceases to care about formalities, so that marriage, for example, comes to mean little more than living together.

Respectable citizens used to regard banditry as a crime. Today, bank robbers are heroes because the money they steal is destined for the Underground. Usually they are young boys, mothers' boys, but their appearance is deceiving. The killing of a man presents no great moral problem to them.

10   The nearness of death destroys shame. Men and women change as soon as they know that the date of their execution has been fixed by a fat little man with shiny boots and a riding crop. They copulate in public, on the small bit of ground surrounded by barbed wire— their last home on earth. Boys and girls in their teens, about to go off to the barricades to fight against tanks with pistols and bottles of gasoline, want to enjoy their youth and lose their respect for standards of decency.

Which world is "natural"? That which existed before, or the world of war? Both are natural, if both are within the realm of one's experience. All the concepts men live by are a product of the historic formation in which they find themselves. Fluidity and constant change are the characteristics of phenomena. And man is so plastic a being that one can even conceive of the day when a thoroughly self-respecting citizen will crawl on all fours, sporting a tail of brightly colored feathers as a sign of conformity to the order he lives in.

The man of the East cannot take Americans seriously because they have never undergone the experiences that teach men how relative their judgments and thinking habits are. Their resultant lack of imagination is appalling. Because they were born and raised in a given social order and in a given system of values, they believe that any other order must be "unnatural," and that it cannot last because it is incompatible with human nature. But even they may one day know fire, hunger, and the sword. In all probability this is what will occur; for it is hard to believe that when one half of the world is living through terrible disasters, the other half can continue a nineteenth-century mode of life, learning about the distress of its distant fellow men only from movies and newspapers. Recent examples teach us that this cannot be. An inhabitant of Warsaw or Budapest once looked at newsreels of bombed Spain or burning Shanghai, but in the end he learned how these and many other catastrophes appear in actuality. He read gloomy tales of the NKVD[2] until one day he himself had to deal with it. *If something exists in one place, it will exist everywhere.* This is the conclusion he draws from his observations, and so he has no particular faith in the momentary prosperity of America. He suspects that the years 1933–1945 in Europe[3] prefigure what will

---

[2] The Soviet secret police, 1935–43.

[3] The years of the rise, dominance, and demise of Nazism.

occur elsewhere. A hard school, where ignorance was punished not by bad marks but by death, has taught him to think sociologically and historically. But it has not freed him from irrational feelings. He is apt to believe in theories that foresee violent changes in the countries of the West, for he finds it unjust that they should escape the hardships he had to undergo.

■ **EXPLORATIONS OF THE TEXT**

1. This essay appears in Milosz's first American volume *The Captive Mind* published shortly after World War II and after his defection from Poland in 1951 and thirty-five years before the birth of democracies in Eastern Europe and détente in Soviet Russia. Do you see evidence in the essay of the historical context of this work? To what historical events does the author refer?

2. Why does Milosz begin with the question: "Are Americans really stupid?" What is his perspective in the essay? How does the opening paragraph suggest his point of view, tone, and themes of the essay?

3. Consider Milosz's use of the term "nature." What is "natural" to man? Is he being ironic? Contrast the two views of human nature, modes of living, states of civilization presented in the essay.

4. What does he conclude about the world? Now fifty years after the publication of this essay, do you concur with his views expressed in paragraphs 11 and 12? Have Americans lost their innocence? Their sense of insularity from world events?

5. Compare the view of witnessing expressed in this essay with Creon's growth of awareness.

■ **THE READING/WRITING CONNECTION**

1. "Think" Topic: Do Americans live in a state of willed "ignorance"? Freewrite in response to this question.

2. Choose a statement from this essay that you agree or disagree with. Create a dialogue with the author.

3. Do ordinary citizens bear the responsibility for the living and the dying? Respond in a journal entry.

■ **IDEAS FOR WRITING**

1. Evaluate Milosz's argument. How does Milosz build his argument? What forms of evidence does he use? Are his techniques effective?

2. Compare Milosz's vision of the response to war with one of the short stories presented in this chapter.

3. Imagine that America has been invaded and occupied by another country. Create a short scene that demonstrates the consequences.

4. Debate Topics: Argue pro or con about one of these contentions.
   • Americans' "lack of imagination is appalling."
   • Americans have never experienced "fire, hunger, and the sword."
   • The state of war is "natural."

Jason Hartley

Jason Hartley (1974–   ) was born in Provo, Utah, and lived in Salt Lake City until 1999, when he moved to New York City. Hartley was educated at Utah State University and the State University of New York at New Paltz, where he presently majors in English. Hartley joined the Army National Guard when he was 17, and served in Iraq as an infantryman in the Sunni Triangle until January of 2005. He also served at Ground Zero from September 11 until September 22, 2001. Hartley's work has been published in the Journal of Electronic Defense *(2003) and* Tokion Magazine *(2004). Hartley's essays began as Internet blog entries, but his pene-trating perspective of Army life in Iraq has spread his popularity to offline readers as well. Hartley's weblog,* Just Another Soldier, *was published in 2005.*

2004

I, JAILOR

This morning our battalion conducted several simultaneous pre-dawn raids. The first home my platoon hit went down in a fashion that's becoming the norm for us— moments before the ram is to hit the door for the dynamic entry that turgid grunts salivate over, the door is unlocked and opened from the inside by a man who is probably already on his second cup of Turkish coffee. People here wake up stupid early to get a jump on the long day of chicken herding or dirt farming or whatever. Some of the intel was of dubious credibility resulting in nothing but a lot of wide-eyed and confused detainees, as was the case with my platoon's target building, and some intel is rock solid. There were RPGs and belts of machine gun ammunition found at other target locations today, not a completely fruitless morning of raids.

I missed out on this morning's soiree pulling a twelve-hour shift of gate and jail guard instead. Our forward operations base's jail (detention center?) is right at the front gate, a messy configuration where detainees, local civilian contractors and politicians along with ICDC clowns, Iraqi police officers and all the other random visitors we get are being corralled through the same small area. Anyway, everyone was back by before 0800 at which point they dumped off all the men captured to our reluctant jailor. This "facility" is smaller than my apartment and with twenty-some-odd Ali Babba (the locals' term for evildoers) bound and blindfolded, it can be pretty cramped. One of the first detainees had on his person 3000 dinars (like 2 bucks), an ID card, and a slip of paper with what looked like some sort of apparent code handwritten on it. When the lieutenant in charge of performing ad-hoc in-processing saw this, he thought he might have struck gold by stumbling upon some sort of encrypted message. Looking at it, there were two lines of alpha-numeric text, each line five groups of five English alphabet characters separated by hyphens. Scrawled underneath was what looked like the word, "Word". The code looked incredibly familiar. Then it hit me. I kinda chuckled and told the Lieutenant that at best this implicated our detainee in the crime of software piracy. It was a couple of CD-keys, for Microsoft Word no doubt.

Once everyone had their restraints cut off and was farmed out evenly into the four cells, still blindfolded and seated facing the wall, an interpreter instructed each detainee that he would stay seated, not talk and not remove his blindfold. Each man was also informed that if he followed these rules and acted like a gentleman, he would be treated like a gentleman. Then began the Parade of Piss. "Mister, mister. Toilet, toilet." Once again, Jesus made manifest his displeasure with me for leaving his church. Had I stayed Mormon, gotten married ridiculously young, settled down, made a family, and took on the inevitable tour of duty of running the nursery at church while the other adults attended various meetings and Sunday classes, I would have been able to do my time in this life of taking rascals pee pee. In lieu of this duty I thought I had successfully dodged, I was now taking rascals pee pee that reeked of the body odor only a Middle-Eastern diet can create. So when are you being humane letting detainees urinate (the term this Lieutenant kept using was "titrate") as needed, and when are you just plain being taken advantage of by performing an endless round-robin of urinal runs? (There isn't actually any urinal, just a tube stuck in the dirt behind the jail.) Most of the soldiers I had with me had not worked with detainees yet and seemed to also be searching for a sense of what the right tone to set for a jail was. I felt myself walking a fine line between proper Geneva Convention–esque humane treatment of enemy combatants and being made a fool of by the same guys that have been making fools of us for the past few weeks by hitting our FOB almost nightly with mortars and RPGs who then always slip away into the night before we can catch them. It pretty much came down to the rule of thumb that if he did the pee pee dance for at least a half hour, he was probably legit and was allowed to go.

Once the initial shock and fear among the herd subsided, the chatter and blindfold fidgeting-with began. I'd say that most these guys were model detainees, but just like any Army platoon or company, there's always one or two problem children. First, two guys wouldn't stop whispering to each other. So I put them in separate cells. Then one kept pulling down his blindfold claiming allergy-beset eyes. We compromised and told him we'd loosen the blindfold if he faced the wall and shut up. He only partially complied. He was warned and re-warned by the Lieutenant and the interpreter. But like a child, he kept pushing the limit. The Lieutenant left as did the interpreter. More chatter, more blindfold-slippage. He started eyeballing me and some of the other soldiers. (If I were in East L.A., I'd be compelled to proclaim, "Why you mad doggin' me, yo?!") I yelled at him to shut up and pull the blind fold back up. He just smiled and gave me the thumbs up. I've said that the thumbs up in Iraq is a way of simultaneously telling someone both "okay" and "fuck you" at once, a trick this little bastard was now turning back on me deftly. Something I have to express here is that this childish way of pushing the limit and seeing what you can get away with is a pet peeve of mine. More last warnings, then I got fed up. I removed him from the cell, took his blindfold off and put on tightly a huge one made out of a first-aid cravat. I also flex-cuffed his hands, behind his back, also tight enough to be uncomfortable. A half hour later he had pulled the blindfold down with his teeth somehow. Last straw.

5   Everyone knows that duct tape can fix anything. In the Army, we have six-inch wide green duct tape that we call hundred mile-an-hour tape, a moniker apparently due to its ability to mend tears in the canvas wings of Wright Brothers–era planes, good up to one-hundred miles-an-hour. I put dickhead on his knees in the middle of his cell, removed the blindfold that he was now wearing as a dashing olive-drab scarf and wrapped the top half of his head with about ten layers of 100 MPH tape. Then one last piece across the bridge of his nose and around his head again to seal off the small gap that invariably is present at the bottom of one's field of vision when one is blindfolded. I tried to create as much drama as possible with the event. Our S-2 (intel) Master Sergeant happened to be present at the time, a mean-spirited quasi-sadist, the fulltime El Capitán of the jail, a job that he seems to relish, and was in the process of systematically interrogating the detainees. He kept saying, "Okay Sergeant, that's enough tape. Okay, that's enough. Okay, that's enough Sergeant." The distinct sound of duct tape being applied directly off the roll was loud and satisfying as it reverberated off the six cold concrete planes of wall, floor, and ceiling. I tried my best to seem stern and to disguise the fact that my heart was pounding. One layer or fifty layers, I figured it wouldn't make much difference as far as adhesive blindfolds go, I just wanted to give the impression of an excessive and final response to his juvenile game of tit for tat. I felt like my disciplinarian pious father (a relationship I'll never reconcile); I felt like I was on the wrong side of recurring anxiety dreams I've always had of being imprisoned; I felt stupid and petty and cowardly. I fucking loathe loathe loathe treating people like that. I'd rather be working with exceptional people, not dealing with troublesome people. Antagonistic relationships that have some constructive end or transparent layer of camaraderie, like the relationship a soldier has with a drill sergeant, I have no problem with. I actually endorse this sort of thing openly. But having to assert my assumed authority in front of my prisoners and my peers to make an example of this ne'er-do-well has no positive product as far as I'm concerned. There's a darkly intoxicating aspect to this kind of thing though. I'm over-armed with my rifle and grenade launcher and the veritable ammunition dump that is the vest over my body

armor. Because of this my power over these men is near-absolute, especially if I were to consider spending life in Fort Leavenworth immaterial. I can see how the bully feels, how one could grow fond of this darkly amusing massive imbalance of power. I tried to keep in mind that even simple playful mockery of the detainees could easily be perceived as cold humor. I wanted to maintain order, I wanted to assert a measure of authority that was little to ask considering the situation, but most importantly I did not want to perpetrate something on others that I am deeply phobic of myself, to be imprisoned and tormented.

I let this guy sit and think about what he had done wrong. Isn't that how our parents used to put it? He finally broke his macho stoic silence after about forty-five minutes. "Mister. Mister. I'm sorry. I'm sorry." I was furious at this asshole. Not only was he apparently contrite now, but his English was getting better too. But mostly I was furious that he "made" me do this. I yelled some nonsense at him about how it was too late to be sorry, that he would continue to be sorry before I did anything for him. Not my words, just rhetorical crap I was regurgitating from a lifetime of being caught in a punishment-lecture-punishment-lecture cycle for serial rule-breaking. Working with me at the time was a medic, this forty-something-ish Hispanic specialist with an improbable number of vowels in his name and a thick salt-and-pepper moustache that seemed to exude an avuncular warmth. He had a pleasant and attentive demeanor and looked like he could be a dentist or a good-natured washing machine salesman at Sears. All day he had been eminently respectful to me, everything was a snappy Yes Sergeant, No Sergeant, something that always makes me uncomfortable when coming from someone so clearly my senior. He looked at me now like he had been suffering along with this guy the whole time, maybe empathetic because he's a medic or because he knew it would probably be his job to help separate tape from eyebrows in a few minutes. I assured him that I'd only let the guy stew for five more minutes tops, but after hemming and hawing for about five more seconds I finally just said Fuck it, let's just give this jerk his reprieve. From his knees again we unwrapped tapehead and I absurdly lectured him in an unavoidably paternal (patronizing?) way in a language I knew he couldn't understand but a tone that I knew he would. He looked up at me, his eyes red and watering (had he been crying or were his eyes actually irritated?) and he reverently uttered, "Thank you." After we locked the cell door (padlock on a grille-like door, not quite totally archetypical for a jail), all inside either sat or slept quietly, unmoving.

Hours later it was the problem child's turn to be interrogated and was escorted by several soldiers to an out-of-sight location by the Master Sergeant. I sat outside by the front gate, eating an MRE. My knife, a beloved Spyderco Delica with green handle and black blade, slayer of MRE packages, lay in front of me as I shoveled beef and mushroom into my mouth like the engineer fed coal into the furnace of his engine in the old Popeye cartoon. As they were walking, the Master Sergeant stopped for a moment to talk to someone. My favorite detainee now stood in front of me. He eyed my knife, then eyed me. I looked back at him and he didn't look away, or should I say he wouldn't look away. Honestly I couldn't tell if he was trying to read my eyes like I was trying to read his or if he was just trying to memorize my face, or maybe he just plain hated me and was indulging his fascination with the object of his hate, a thirst that you can never really slake.

Truth be told, I paid little attention to how he looked, not nearly as much attention as he seemed to pay to how I looked. If I saw him on the street right now, I probably wouldn't recognize him. Shame on me I guess. The first step is to remove the person-ness from your enemy. Once you remove his humanity in your mind, distance him from you, the human, it's easier to kill him if it comes down to that. He wore a green camouflage jacket making him stand out from the rest of the white and gray man-dress wearers. In the back of the jacket on the bottom there was a buttoned flap. Ever since the advent of the man-dress (dish dash or pish posh or whatever they call them, I forget), when it came time to go into combat you'd reach between your legs, grab the back hem and pull it up into your belt in the front, creating a big man-diaper. My seminary teacher in junior high said this was called "girding up your loins." My guess is the flap on the back of this jacket was made for the same purpose, to turn the flowing man-dress of would-be fighters into MC Hammer pants. His hair was neat and short-cropped. I only know this really because I had to pull all that tape off his head. He was probably in his early twenties. I'd say if it came down to hand-to-hand, this guy, being most likely in the same weight-class as me, would give me a run for my money. But most non-farmer Iraqis are in absurdly bad shape, so I'd probably prevail. If not, I'd at least bite his nose off or something really dirty like that. So there he was, staring me down again, who knows what machinations going on in his head.

■ EXPLORATIONS OF THE TEXT

1. Czeslaw Milosz talks of the assumption by Americans that their way of seeing the world is "natural," normal. Do you notice this attitude in Hartley's "I, Jailor"? Explain.
2. Milosz asks, "Which world is 'natural'? That which existed before, or the world of war?" Answer this question, referring to Hartley's description of Iraq.
3. The American soldiers call the Iraqis "Ali Babba," and the Iraqis use the thumbs-up signal to simultaneously convey "okay" and "fuck you." How might these uses of spoken and sign language indicate the birth of a new society?
4. Does Hartley seem to be "ignorant" by Milosz's standards? Why, or why not?

■ THE READING/WRITING CONNECTION

1. Why does Hartley duct-tape the detainee's eyes, even though he despises himself for doing so? Write about a time when you felt a similar sense of frustration. How did you act?

■ IDEAS FOR WRITING

1. Hartley explains that "the first step is to remove the person-ness from your enemy." Relate this to Milosz's concern that Americans are "ignorant" and to the soldier's response in "Gregory."
2. In Hartley's experience with the detainee, why might it be good for him not to consider the man as an equal, as human? Conversely, why might it be bad? What do you think might be the long-term result of having an occupying force treating people as subhumans? Write an argument in favor of or opposed to treating others as subhuman during a time of war.

 ## ON THE WEB—CIVIL RIGHTS

Civil Rights Timeline

The Black Freedom Struggle Chronology (Civil Rights Timeline)
http://www.stanford.edu/group/king/about_king/details

William E. B. Du Bois

The Souls of Black Folk
The Avalon Project at Yale Law School
http://www.yale.edu/lawweb/avalon/avalon.htm

Martin Luther King Speeches

The Martin Luther King Jr. Pages Project at Stanford University
http://www.stanford.edu/group/king/popular_requests

Malcolm X

http://www.malcolm-x.org/bio.htm
http://www.webcorp.com/civilrights/malcolm.htm
http://www.brothermalcolm.net/mxwords/whathesaid11.html

Dudley Randall

"Ballad of Birmingham"
http://webinstituteforteachers.org
"Ballad of Birmingham"
http://washingtonart.com/beltway/randall.html
Dudley Randall's Life and Career
http://www.english.uiuc.edu/maps/poets/m_r/randall/randall.htm

■ WRITING ASSIGNMENTS ■

1. a. Write a list of positive and negative aspects of life in the United States.
   b. Write an essay on the criticisms of the United States by Ginsberg, Hughes, Brooks, and Angelou. Do these writers express hope?
2. What is the relationship between identity and politics?
3. a. Write a list of themes about war.
   b. Write about one of the themes. Refer to three works in this chapter.
4. a. Make double-entry notebooks on Forché's poems.
   b. Summarize Valenzuela's "I'm Your Horse in the Night."
   c. Write a paper on political issues in Central and South America. Refer to Forché and to Valenzuela.
5. Compare a work about the Second World War to one about the Vietnam War (e.g., "The War Generation," "How to Tell a True War Story").
6. a. Annotate the works by Endō, Owen, and O'Brien. Concentrate on the soldiers' attitudes concerning war.
   b. Write an essay about the attitudes of soldiers toward war in the works you have annotated.
7. a. Discuss Marable's treatment of racism in the United States.
   b. Connect his view with two of the readings.
8. a. Write about law and justice. When is law just? When is it not?
   b. Is it ever right to disobey the law?
   c. Discuss the disobedience of Sojourner Truth.
9. a. Define cultural history.
   b. Write about your cultural history.
   c. Compare "Jasper Texas, 1998," "horse," and "Prayer to the Living. . . ."
10. a. Gloss and annotate a political protest poem in this chapter. How effectively does the poet convey his/her political message?
    b. Analyze the poem that you have glossed and annotated. How does it achieve its impact? Focus, for example, on tone, imagery, symbolism, word choice, and/or form.

11. Write about parents whose children are endangered by war. Refer to the works by Pirandello and Ozick.
12. a. Write about the horse symbolism in works by Valenzuela, Anzaldúa, and Harjo.
    b. Write about a specific instance of political terrorism. Create a symbol to represent the terror or the hope.
    c. Compare Latino/Latina visions of the United States. Refer to Soto in chapter 4, Espada in chapter 5, and/or Anzaldúa in this chapter.
13. a. Write about the anger and dreams of retribution in the poems by Angelou, Anzaldúa, and Harjo.
    b. Is anger necessary for social change? Refer to three works in this chapter.
14. Write about the strength of the human spirit and the enduring dream of freedom and equality. Refer to works by Hughes, Angelou, Forché, and/or Ginsberg.
15. Write an essay on the statement that "Soldiers are dreamers." Refer to the works by O'Brien, Endō, Hartley and/or Valenzuela.
16. Create an antiwar argument. Use examples from works in this chapter to prove your points.
17. a. Make a list of political injustices presented in works in this chapter.
    b. Write on one writer's presentation of this issue.
    c. Support a point of view that counters the presentation of one of the works in this chapter.
18. Contrast the characters of three rebels presented in this chapter.
19. Write a research paper on one of the following topics:
    a. Langston Hughes and the Harlem Renaissance.
    b. Tim O'Brien and the Vietnam War.
    c. A conflict between a minority group and the police (e.g., the Los Angeles riots, racial profiling).
    d. The use of chemical weapons in World War I or in another conflict.
    e. Ginsberg and the Beat generation.
    f. Taoism.
    g. Some aspect of women's suffrage.
    h. Some aspect of slavery in the United States, (e.g., the Underground Railroad).
    i. The Holocaust or another twentieth-century genocode.
    j. A contemporary site of conflict, civil war, or injustice.
20. Analyze Sophocles's *Antigone* as a political tragedy. How does personal suffering become or cause public suffering?
21. Write about the forms of and responses to injustice in the works in the Terror and Terrorism cluster.
22. Choose three works from this chapter and focus on their visions of the "natural order of the world." (See Milosz's "American Ignorance of War.")
23. Several different writers in this chapter envision their roles as witnesses to injustice.
    a. Referring to Wiesel's essay, define *witness*. Entertain these questions: Why witness injustice? How do you witness injustice? Why is forgetting injustice dangerous?
    b. Then explore three visions of witnessing (e.g., those of Gourevitch, Przytyk, Angelou, Nye, and/or Forché).
24. a. Gloss and annotate O'Brien's "How to Tell a True War Story," noting each definition of a "true war story."
    b. Apply one or several of O'Brien's definitions to other works in this chapter.
25. After reading the works in the cluster depicting terror and terrorism, create your own fictional version of "How to Tell a True Story about Terror." Use evidence from works in the chapter.

26. Examine the theme of "American Dreams: Lost and Found" in several works in the chapter. What dreams and ideals are represented? What is the underside of the American Dream? What dreams are lost?

27. Compare and contrast O'Brien's portrayal of being a soldier in Vietnam in "How to Tell a True War Story" with Rivera's experience of Desert Storm and with Hartley's depiction of the Iraq war.

28. How would the narrator in "Ralph the Duck," the fat man in "War," and Hartley's autobiographical persona respond to this passage from O'Brien's "How to Tell a True War Story": "For the common soldier, at least, war has the feel—the spiritual texture—of a great ghostly fog, thick and permanent. There is no clarity. The old rules are no longer binding, the old truths no longer true. Right spills into wrong." You may create a dialogue among the characters.

29. In "How to Tell a True War Story," O'Brien states the following: "A true war story is never moral. . . ." What does he mean? Do you agree with him? Create a conversation among several characters or speakers in the texts on this subject.

30. Many of the characters in works in this chapter face moral dilemmas. What moral conflicts do they experience? How do they resolve these dilemmas?
    (Suggestions include Antigone, the narrator in "I'm Your Horse in the Night," the narrator in "Gregory," and Jason Hartley.)

31. Imagine a character from one of the works in this chapter visits a museum and reflects on a painting of his or her choosing. Write a monologue in that character's voice, similar to Gloria M. Winter's "Rosa's Final Scream."

■ STUDENT ESSAYS ■

Student Essay: Thematic Analysis and Research Essay

MELANIE CHOPKO

A Mother's Survival

> *"I worry very much that this subject [the Holocaust] is corrupted by fiction and fiction in general corrupts history.*
>
> Cynthia Ozick

Though Cynthia Ozick worries that fiction can blur the essential facts that need to be taught to humanity, her writing does just the opposite. It is through her short story, "The Shawl," that those of us who did not experience the Holocaust are led into its horrors through the experiences of one mother, Rosa. In doing so, Ozick also explores the complex human experience of motherhood in the Holocaust and the incredible ritual of sacrifice. Through her exploration of motherhood, Ozick reveals the process of survival, showing us that temporary sustenance can be found through motherhood but true sustenance is found spiritually.

By placing the lyrical explorations of motherhood in juxtaposition to an unnamed death camp, Ozick emphasizes the very essence of motherhood: the continuity of life (survival) (Scrafford 11). As the story leads the reader on a journey defined by images of death (Rosa's breasts are cracked and dry while her niece's knees are swellings on sticks), the reader is made aware that the only life mentioned is in relation to Rosa and her baby, Magda. Motherhood is the only concept containing life that these marching prisoners are aware of, and it, therefore, defines their existence and offers a source of sustenance.

Ozick describes in great detail the hunger and physical sufferings of Rosa's niece, Stella, but her description of Rosa's presents a distinctly different response to the situation:

> Rosa did not feel hunger; she felt light, not like someone walking but like someone in a faint, in trance, arrested in a fit, someone who is already a floating angel, alert and seeing everything, but in the air, not there touching the ground. As if teetering on the tips of her fingernails. (3-4)

This description reveals that Rosa's existence is no longer defined by her physical presence; it has transcended her body. As her breasts dry from the lack of milk production and she ceases to menstruate, Rosa's body is unable to provide the life that her baby needs. In knowing that Magda's death is eminent, Rosa's existence becomes directed by instinct alone, her body a "walking cradle" (Scrafford 12). She transcends her physical need for survival to find sustenance in the emotional needs of her child.

With her existence defined by the maternal instinct to protect the life of her child, Rosa moves beyond normal human capabilities to provide for Magda. She does not eat but, rather, gives all of her food to her child. The warm shawl that Stella envies wraps the mother and child together like an umbilical cord, providing the wet nourishment Rosa's breasts cannot. Despite the knowledge that Magda will die in the near future from either starvation or discovery, Rosa protects her with this cloth extension of her body, both hiding her presence and vicariously nourishing her with the shawl (Scrafford 15).

The fictional Rosa's sacrifice opens a window to the real-life experiences of mothers who endured such suffering. While death defined nearly every part of existence in the Jewish ghettos and concentration camps, the sacrifices of mothers within these worlds testify that death was not the final victor. Portraits of women in both Lodz and Warsaw reveal that the sufferings of their families filled them with an incredible sense of purpose and strength. Their commitment sustained them as they worked eight to ten hours in factories and offices, as they provided food for their families (often through the dangerous act of smuggling), and as they returned home to fulfill their traditional roles (Ofer and Weitzman 10). Michael Unger's essay, "Women in the Lodz Ghetto," cites the diary entry of an anonymous young woman in response to her mother's sacrifice:

> March 11, 1942 . . . I ate all the honey. I am selfish. What will the family say? I'm not worthy of my mother, who works so hard . . . My mother looks awful, like a shadow. She works very hard. When I wake up at twelve or one o'clock at night she's sewing, and at six a.m. she's back on her feet. I have no heart, I have no pity. I eat anything that lands near me . . . I don't know what she lives on. She works the hardest and eats the least. (134)

Along with finding the strength to support their families through working, the women also were able to cope with hunger to a superhuman extent. In a desperate sacrifice for the lives of their children, mothers constantly deprived themselves of food and gave that sustenance to others despite the sickness it brought (Ofer and Weitzman 10).

Even through this deprivation, statistics show that these women had a higher chance of survival than men. Their care of and responsibility for others protected against despair and violence, for their sacrifices were an extension of their prewar nurturing and responsibility to the family. Many accounts describe this act of extending care to be so essential for survival that it transcended the original ties of the family and led to the formation of surrogate families. The development of "camp sister" and "camp mother" relationships also instructed the men in survival, for the "lone wolf behavior" nearly always guaranteed death (Goldenburg 337).

Though caring for others could lead to survival, the instinct of a mother to live for her child most often began in hunger and ended in death. Mothers often were presented with the choice of a life alone as a worker or of death with their children. At Birkenau, in response to this choice, only two of about six hundred mothers of younger children presented themselves for work selection, while the others died, caring for their children until the end (Bondy 324). This commitment reveals that when faced with death, mothers continued the process of seeking sustenance and, in doing so, reached from emotion to find the spiritual nourishment that lasts for all time.

As shown in these accounts, the maternal instinct is so forceful that it battles the mother's own basic instinct for self-preservation. Because her mothering instinct is what drives her to survive, Rosa's thoughts are all directed toward Magda's life. Even Stella's bones are looked at without pity, only noticed because "[s]he [Rosa] was sure that Stella was waiting for Magda to die so that she could put her teeth into the little thighs" (Ozick 5). When Stella steals Magda's shawl selfishly for her own warmth, Magda is pushed out of the world of Rosa's protection and enters the roll-call arena of the death camp. Reduced to instinct alone, Magda's screams for her shawl are echoed in the buzzing voices of the electric fence around the arena, ordering Rosa, through her breasts, to run for the shawl in the hopes of saving her child.

It is only after Magda is thrown into the electric fence by a Nazi guard that Rosa is free to respond to her "instinct of self-preservation" (Scrafford 14). For the first time, she considers the consequences of following the command of her body to run to Magda's corpse and fights an internal battle to survive. Instead of following the instinct of motherhood, Rosa's scream in reaction to the death of her child is stifled by her pushing the scarf, which has become a symbol for Magda's life, into her mouth. This ingestion reveals the extent to which Rosa is controlled by this battle of instinct, for the action defines her existence as both a mother and an individual. By "swallowing" the shawl (Ozick 10), it becomes physically evident that Rosa has been reduced to a primitive creature (defined by instinct alone), behaving as a mother in the wild would, by consuming her young in a last attempt to save them from their predator (Scrafford 14).

With the emotional sustenance of motherhood unable to be claimed, Rosa is forced to acknowledge her physical needs. Just as the shawl provided nutrients for Magda in its wetness, Rosa now "drinks" the shawl both physically and spiritually (Ozick 10). By consuming that which defined Magda, Rosa makes her child a part of her own being, once again finding survival in motherhood. As "The Shawl" closes with Rosa swallowing the scarf, one is faced with the question of Rosa's survival. This question not only considers the mother's physical but also her emotional survival. Once a life is consumed by one purpose, the instinct of sacrifice over self-preservation, is it possible to meet all levels of need (physical, emotional, and spiritual) and, therefore, return to a balanced existence?

Just as the shawl provides nutrients to Magda, the symbol of the shawl provides more than physical sustenance to Rosa. It provides for her both emotionally and spiritually after the war. According to Lawrence S. Friedman, the shawl first preserves all levels of physical life by giving nourishment to Magda, warmth to Stella, and safety to Rosa. In doing so, the shawl unites the three characters into a symbol of the persecuted millions and alludes to another symbol of Jewish affiliation: the Jewish prayer shawl, the tallit (Friedman 115).

During the ritual of prayer, the believer covers his or her body with the tallit, a shawl with stripes on both ends that is large enough to enclose an entire frame. This action of being enclosed within the shawl represents the believer's communion with God (and with other believers) and His covenant with them. The lines on each end of the shawl are to encourage the wearer even more, for each stripe represents a swaying reed—bent but not broken by the winds of sorrow and suffering. In wrapping both Magda and Rosa's lives in the symbol of the tallit, Ozick assures her readers that even though Rosa, like the Jewish people, is bent nearly to the point of death, she is not broken. She will survive, for she is not alone. Because the use of the tallit was originally withheld from women due to fundamentalist beliefs of their uncleanness, the use of the shawl in Ozick's story has an even greater meaning, for it extends all of these covenantal promises to the gender that had for so long been excluded.

Despite its initial power, the shawl's reminder of the covenant loses its meaning to Rosa. Ozick's companion novella, "Rosa," reveals that Rosa's family was not pious but, rather, universal, denying their heritage as Jews and idolizing instead gentile culture. Rosa reduces the shawl from a Jewish emblem to a personal fetish. In idolizing this portion of her past, Rosa centers her life on idealizing it and creates a heritage separate from that which the Nazis destroyed (Friedman 116–118).

As a result, Rosa is unable to enter the present. She insists on honoring Magda's memory, but she also rejects her Jewishness. Rosa does not allow herself to claim the promises of the covenant promised by her heritage and is left without the ability to enter a postwar existence. The infliction of such inhuman suffering as Rosa experienced cannot be healed by human strength alone; it is only after Rosa moves to invite a character into her life who so blatantly represents the Jewish life she left behind that Ozick begins to speak about a rebirth of existence. As Rosa moves to invite her Jewish friend and all he symbolizes into her home, her emotional need for Magda finds a new source of fulfillment.

When Rosa finds rebirth in the acceptance of the spiritual symbols behind the shawl, Ozick reveals that the strength to survive is found not through the fulfillment of physical or emotional needs but, rather, through the eternal gift of spiritual sustenance. The maternal instinct can overcome the instinct for self-preservation of the body, but the fulfillment of both instincts is found in sustenance for the soul.

Works Consulted

Berger, Alan L. *Crisis and Covenant: The Holocaust in American Jewish Fiction*. Albany: State University of New York Press, 1985. 54.

Bondy, Ruth. "Women in Theresiensdat and the Family Camp in Birkenau." *Women in the Holocaust*. Eds. Dalia Ofer and Lenore J. Weitzman. New Haven: Yale University Press, 1998. 310-326.

Friedman, Lawrence S. *Understanding Cynthia Ozick*. Columbia: University of South Carolina Press, 1991.

Goldenberg, Myrna. "Memoirs of Auschwitz Survivors: The Burden of Gender." *Women in the Holocaust*. Eds. Dalia Ofer and Lenore J. Weitzman. New Haven: Yale University Press, 1998. 327-339.

Ofer, Dalia and Weitzman, Lenore J. "Introduction." *Women in the Holocaust*. Eds. Dalia Ofer and Lenore J. Weitzman. New Haven: Yale University Press, 1998. 1-18.

Ozick, Cynthia. *The Shawl*. New York: Alfred A. Knopf, 1989.

Scrafford, Barbara. "Nature's Silent Scream: A Commentary on Cynthia Ozick's 'The Shawl'." *Critique* 31.1 (1989):11-15.

Unger, Michael. "The Status and Plight of Women in the Lodz Ghetto." *Women in the Holocaust*. Eds. Dalia Ofer and Lenore J. Weitzman. New Haven: Yale University Press, 1998. 123-142.

Student Essay: Creative Response

Gloria M. Winter

Rosa's Final Scream

New York City in springtime holds a certain charm. The air is filled with promises of new life and warmer days to come. People seem to be a little happier and more energetic. Children shed their long winter coats and mittens and play in the park while their mothers watch from the benches. The birds are busy, too, reconstructing their homes and preparing for new arrivals. During this time it is easy to forget about the past winter and the damage that it caused. Winter has a way of keeping people locked inside and out of the cold. For some, though, the past is tucked away and suppressed. Some memories are too painful to relive.

She doesn't exactly remember how she was rescued or when the troops arrived. At that time she was too weak to respond to the miracle at hand and collapsed from exhaustion. Rosa later woke up in a hospital with tubes in every part of her body. She was not afraid, nor was she excited. Rosa knew that Stella and Magda were gone and that she would be alone in this world. It was a bittersweet triumph because she survived and her daughters didn't. A part of Rosa did die, though. Her heart was heavy and her mind was numb. She could not speak about the horrors of the camp or the heinous murder of Magda. Poor Stella died of starvation only a few days before the troops came. Rosa felt that her survival was part of God's plan and that she needed to honor His wishes and carry on. She promised to start over but also to bury the past.

Rosa came to America after the war ended with the hopes of a new life and freedom. She did not let her conscious mind think about her past horrors but thanked

God everyday for giving her the strength to live on. Rosa sailed to New York with other refugees and misplaced souls. They did not have much in tow or any idea where they were going to live. Some only had the clothes on their backs, but that did not matter. They were coming to the land of the free filled with opportunity. Milk and honey for everyone.

Rosa stayed in New York City, where she found a small apartment to live in and a job at the clothing factory. During her spare time she would take English lessons at the community center to learn to read and write. She did not want to work as a seamstress forever. Rosa wanted to take advantage of all this New World had to offer. It was a busy life for her, and some days she really felt at peace. But some days were very lonely. Rosa did not allow herself to think of Magda or Stella. The pain was too much to handle and too confusing to understand. Grieving was not a part of her life. She dreaded the nights when her unconscious mind dragged her back to the past and played a miserable dream of the Nazi soldiers. It was always the same dream about the soldiers taking away her tattered shawl and setting it on fire. They would laugh at her, while in silence she watched it burn. There was nothing she could do. Rosa would wake from this dream and pray for the morning. Somehow the daylight would make it go away.

Rosa also found solace at the art museum. Every Sunday she would take the bus to the Metropolitan Museum of Art. This was a special place for her. This was a place where she could learn about other cultures and see beautiful paintings. Most importantly, this was a place where she felt safe. The museum was always quiet and inviting. The only sounds that could be heard were the whispers of the art students, the occasional cough and sneeze or the clickety-click of high-heeled shoes on the wood floors. The Great Hall was always filled with grand flower arrangements and the most spectacular view of the balcony above. The ceilings seemed to reach Heaven. Rosa would spend all day walking through the galleries and special exhibits. She enjoyed looking at the paintings by Monet and Renoir. She observed how soft the colors were in *Water Lilies* and how happy the people looked in *Le Moulin de la Galette*. She thought that Chagall's paintings were amusing and that Van Gogh was an odd-looking fellow. The paintings were her friends, and she looked forward to visiting them each week. She never tired of the images, because each week she found something new to discover. Her love for art also furthered her English studies. Each week she would try to read the information at the museum library about the artists and their paintings. Rosa wanted to know everything. One day each week she felt special, intelligent, and complete. Her weekly ritual allowed her some temporary happiness. That is, until she saw the painting.

A new exhibit had opened the day before Rosa's usual Sunday visit. It was the Post-Impressionism exhibit. Rosa looked forward to making new friends with Cezanne, Seurat, and Gauguin. The museum was especially busy on this particular Sunday, and the gallery was filled with curious art connoisseurs. The exhibit contained paintings that were on loan from some of Europe's finest art museums. For some people, this would be their only chance to see these rare pieces of art. Rosa was amazed with all the excitement. She was also proud that she fumbled through that morning's *New York Times* article about the exhibit and had learned some interesting facts about the displayed artists. Rosa followed the crowd up the marble stairs and around the Great Hall balcony. She entered the new exhibit gallery and began her tour of the paintings. How wonderful everything looked! The Cezanne paintings hung on the wall with all their still-life glory. Rosa could almost taste the apples he painted. The next room contained her old friend Van Gogh and a new acquaintance named Toulouse-Lautrec. Vibrant colors and fantastic images were enfolded in these rooms. Rosa felt alive and radiant. She lost herself to the world of art, and for a moment in time, she became someone else. She was not a concentration camp survivor or the mother of forgotten children. She was Rosa, woman of the New World, art critic and a champion of life.

The tour was almost over, and there was one room left to view. She admired the Seurat and Picasso and blushed at Rousseau's painting, *The Dream*. The next artist was Munch. His paintings appeared intensely strange and horrifying. Rosa was not sure if she liked his work, and for the first time, she felt uncomfortable in the museum. The image of the *Vampire* frightened her, and *Death in the Sickroom* made her heart beat a little faster. Something uncontrollable was beginning to happen to Rosa, and she could not understand why. But there it was. The painting that brought it all back to her conscious mind. Rosa saw *The Scream*. The splashes of reddish-orange sky and bluish-purple water reminded her of the bloody ground and bruised bodies. The filth and stench and the swollen eyes and bellies. She then looked at the figure in the painting wearing black clothes and a frightened face. She suddenly imagined Stella was in the painting, too. Her poor skeleton body leaning on the figure and looking at Rosa from the canvas. She remembered it all. Once again Rosa saw her beautiful baby girl flying through the air. Her precious Magda had no idea that the fence would eat her body. It occurred to Rosa that she, herself, was the figure. This was her nightmare, her frightened face, and her scream. The sound that she muffled to remain alive by practically swallowing the shawl. Her mouth began to water, and she could taste the cinnamon and almond essence again. Rosa felt that scream in the depths of her soul, and this time she could not remain silent. Without a second thought, she opened her mouth and let herself cry in the middle of the room. She cried and wailed at the top of her lungs. Her scream filled the gallery and traveled through the museum. She screamed for her daughters. She screamed for her family and other camp victims. She screamed for humanity and prayed that this tragedy would never happen again. In an instant the madness was over, and Rosa fell to the ground. People rushed to help her, but it was too late.

Rosa died that afternoon in the museum. Nobody in the gallery could figure out why she screamed or what caused her heart to stop. To them, Rosa was just another visitor to the museum. They did not know about the other life she led or how she finally grieved for the loss of her daughters. Nor did they know how the soldiers stole her right to mourn for Magda when she was killed. How could they know unless they read the numbers on her wrist? Even then they would not truly understand that Rosa would be much happier in the afterlife. She cleansed her soul and lifted her burden by ultimately finding the courage and the voice to scream.

Online Forum and Discussion: Creative Responses to "horse"

In the assignment below, Rachel Rigolino, the instructor, asked her students to compose a creative response to the poem "horse" by Gloria Anzaldúa. The students were given a week and a half to compose their responses and also to critique one another's pieces.

Assignments (choose one):

1. Write a monologue in the voice of one of the boys.
2. Write a last stanza to the poem or a stanza that comes before the first stanza.
3. Write an official police report (or a poetic interpretation of an official police report) about the incident. Remembering the sheriff's attitude, what might actually appear in an "official" report?
4. Imagine that you are an elderly Mexican man or woman who is witness to what happens to the horse. Write a poetic monologue about your experience.

You can use my ideas as a starting point. Use your own creativity and choose another approach if you wish.

Forum: Quest. 5 "HORSE"
Date: 07-07-2004 22:34
Author: GREEN, KATHERINE ANNE
Subject: last stanza

> The blood has sunken deep within the soil
> And the evidence is hard to find
> But the guilty gringos have sown their seeds
> Which nature cannot ignore
> New growth carries gross familiarity
> And the gringos will someday harvest
> Their tainted crops
> Which will materialize beyond their wildest nightmares

Forum: Quest. 5 "HORSE"
Date: 07-14-2004 07:17
Author: DORRIAN, MARY F.
Subject: response last stanza

Hi Katie,

Wow! Great response!! Your response makes me think that even though these "gringo boys" seem to have gotten away with killing this horse and perhaps terrorizing these "Borderland People," retribution is not far behind. I do think that sooner or later we "reap what we sow," and that is what your response made me think about. Very creative, and I loved your choice of words. Your response had a lot of strength, especially the lines "New growth carries gross familiarity/and the gringos will someday harvest/Their tainted crops." I think that these "boys" will perhaps be surprised at what the future brings, and maybe this mighty horse will infiltrate their dreams until they become nightmares. The violence these "boys" commit against these people may very well "taint their crops." Clever way to say that sooner or later their actions will catch up to them, and it may just bleed into every part of their lives in a most uncomfortable fashion.

I have to say that your post is brilliant and extremely well-written. You said a lot in a few lines, which made your response even more powerful!

Great job, Katie!

Forum: Quest. 5 "HORSE"
Date: 07-09-2004 12:14
Author: TAMRAZ, LAUREN JOY
Subject: creative response:Witness

> Rusting blood smell sours the wind
> From the adobe porch I can see the caballo
> No prayers can bring forgiveness to these boys
> But they pray to a different god than I
> They believe their god looks like them, thinks like them
> I believe my god regrets creating them
> Questions why they think they are another man's keeper
> I almost pulled the children away,
> Wanted to call them to the rio to help me with the washings
> So they would not see the broken spirit of the village
> Rusting in the sticky sun
> But this will only become clearer as they grow,
> What good to let them think otherwise?
> I turn away from the scene
> I string chilies for drying
> The caballo and I,
> The old lady,
> rusting in the sun together.

Forum: Quest. 5 "HORSE"
Date: 07-16-2004 23:54
Author: HOEY, CHRISTOPHER ROBERT
Subject: Excellent job Lauren

Wow, excellent poem response, Lauren. I really enjoyed reading your piece. The lines you wrote "They believe their god looks like them, thinks like them/I believe my god regrets creating them" is really powerful and shows the deep racial tensions that Anzaldúa experienced growing up and expressed in her poem "horse." Your choice of words to end your response, "The caballo and I,/The old lady, rusting in the sun together," are very interesting. I wonder why you chose to have the old woman so accepting of the cruel actions against the horse and why she is so accepting of the horses and her fate? Maybe there has been just so much fighting that she just has no strength to fight back anymore, or perhaps she feels powerless in a land of such conflict? Good work on deciphering the meaning of the original poem and incorporating a very thoughtful response!

Forum: Quest. 5 "HORSE"
Date: 07-10-2004 20:36
Author: HERTZBERG, EMILY KATE
Subject: Emily's Last Stanza

> memory like explosives in a feather pillow
> hundreds of missing lines
> horrible months torn from old
> they melted the horse from their minds
> like photographs taken by dead people with cameras without film
> black out-of-tune notes playing a death dirge on a violin strung with barbwire
> at a loss for a reason
> surrounded by danger and uncertainty
> hallucinating that the horse still rode in the night
> breaking the mirror of silence
> badly beaten by invisible things
> water boiling underground
> remember to remember
> time to turn somebody in
> it's now and never
> never seen or heard from again

Forum: Quest. 5 "HORSE"
Date: 07-12-2004 16:50
Author: SORCI, REBECCA MARY
Subject: Re:creative police report

Incident 59089089000283098909090
Type of Incident- Wild Horse
Date- October 30th, 1987
Sheriff Racism of the Hargill Texas Police Dept.

On Monday October 30th, I was called to the town of Hargill, Texas at 1:30 am. Mr. Anzaldúa had called the police station claiming that two white boys killed his horse. When I got to the farm, Mr. Anzaldúa had the boys in his custody waiting for my arrival. The boys had told me that they were coming home from the creek, where they had been fishing all day. They were walking through Mr. Anzaldúa's land when they saw a beautiful black horse. They decided they wanted to take him for a quick ride. As they approached, the horse became wild and started to attack them, they did not know what to do. Tommy (a 16-year-old male) asked Bobby (a 16-year-old male) to hand them the knives they had used early to cut the fishing line. The horse continued to come at the two boys, out of protection the two boys sliced off the horse's legs. Anzaldúa told me he came out when heard noises coming from the barn, he saw the horse in much pain but still alive, he shot the horse to take it out of its misery. The father of the boys was called to the property and was told to take the two boys home. Mr. Anzaldúa was told to keep a better eye out for people on his property; he was also told that if he didn't keep his other animals tamed, he would receive a fine. Mr. Anzaldúa had trouble cooperating with my orders and questioned my authority by asking why the boys were not in trouble for trespassing and killing his horse. I told Mr. Anzaaluda to stop questioning my authority and told him, "boys will be boys, just following their instincts" (897). I then told Mr. Anzaldúa if he wanted to continue to talk back to me or question me, I could take him down to the station. I left the property at about 2:15 am.

Forum: Quest. 5 "HORSE"
Date: 07-12-2004 17:59
Author: LAROBARDIER, JOSEPHINE LOPANE
Subject: Re:Rebecca

        Hi Rebecca,

        Wow, I really like your response! You really capture
        the tone of the poem. The way you turn the situation
        around and put the blame on the poor rancher, Mr.
        Anzaldúa, was superb! I could see the whole event
        happening as I read your "police report," and I felt a
        bit ashamed that the poor man would be ignored by the
        authorities instead of being helped. Those boys really
        deserved to be punished, and it makes me sick that they
        got away scott-free. You made the whole thing very,
        very believable. Great Job!

        JoAnn

Forum: Quest. 5 "HORSE"
Date: 07-12-2004 23:05
Author: REZMOVITS, DANIEL ADAM
Subject: Re: creative response as witness

I sit and watch over the field from my humble little hut
They say I am old, but I know I am young with a mind full of wisdom.
As I sit and watch the horses dance in the moonlight,
Out of the darkness comes a group of young gringos.
I know right away, nothing good will come of this,
With the children these days, nothing ever does.
They approach the beautiful animal at full speed,
As it screams in terror, bucking back and forth.
All I see is red, and it splashes down in bursts
The boys have done it again,
When will this killing stop?

The animal does nothing to deserve such a fate,
Yet all it can do now is wait for its end.
I sit and watch over the field from my humble little hut,
As I have for many years which have passed.
They say I am old, but I say I am young, with a mind full of wisdom,
The same way I have been, since the day I was born.

· CHAPTER 8 ·

Strange New Worlds

We are animals, in search of a home, in relationship to Other, an expanding community with a mosaic of habitats, domestic and wild; there is nothing precious or nostalgic about it.

Terry Tempest Williams

[Exile is] the unhealable rift forced between a human being and a native place, between the self and its true home: its essential sadness can never be surmounted. . . . The achievements of exile are permanently undermined by the loss of something left behind forever.

Edward Said

But in order to speak about all to all, one has to speak of what we know and the reality common to all. The sea, the rain, necessity, desire, and the struggle against death—these are the things that unite us all.

Albert Camus

Francisco José de Goya y Lucientes, "El sueño de la razon produce monstrous," 1799

▪ *Introduction* ▪

> "To survive the Borderlands
> you must live sin fronteras
> be a crossroads."
>
> Gloria Anzaldúa, "To Live in the Borderlands Means You"

The twenty-first century brings with it the dissolution of boundaries that once provided meaning and identity in a world of small communities. With widespread use of the Internet, satellite communication, and air travel, we are now aware of events that occur in countries all around the planet, and we recognize that these seemingly local happenings affect us all. International travel exposes people to different languages, cultures, and foods, leading to the creation of new, hybrid cultures. Travel is not restricted to humans; plants and nonhuman animals move across boundaries as pets, houseplants, or stowaways—sometimes wreaking havoc in their new environments. Both human and nonhuman animals have even traveled into outer space, a feat that was earlier imagined only in science-fiction stories. This elimination of borders brings with it both anxiety and exhilaration. Gloria Anzaldúa challenges us to embrace our strange new world, to "be a crossroads," to live "*sin fronteras*," without borders. If we are unable to accept her challenge, we may fulfill the prediction of science-fiction writers who foresee the world's future as global conflict and extinction.

Perhaps this place at the "crossroads"—a place envisioned by artists across four centuries—offers us the greatest challenge and the greatest possibilities for visions of community for the twenty-first century.

Whatever the situation, the stranger is one who lives on the edge between her unique world and the world of others that she has just entered. The stranger, by her presence, asks something of us: she asks that her heritage or her condition be respected. This requires that those with whom she comes in contact enter into a dialogical relationship with her. Real dialogue allows for the uniqueness of the other to be brought forth. . . .
How the community responds to the stranger will either alienate one from the other or will serve in the work toward peace . . .
If we want to live in a world that will not destroy itself, the stranger has to be drawn in.

Virginia Shabatay, "The Stranger's Story"

What is happening to the world lies, at the moment, just outside the realm of common human understanding. It is the writers, the poets, the artists, the singers, the filmmakers who can make the connections, who can find ways of bringing it into the realm of common understanding. Who can translate cash-flow charts and scintillating boardroom speeches into real stories about real people with real lives. Stories about what it's like to lose your home, your land, your job, your dignity, your past, and your future to an invisible force.

Arundhati Roy

Crossing the Genres

SCIENCE FICTION

OCTAVIA E. BUTLER

Octavia E. Butler (1947–   ) was born in Pasadena, California, and educated at Pasadena City College, California State University in Los Angeles, and the University of California in Los Angeles. Butler has written fourteen books and published short stories and essays in several anthologies. Her story "Bloodchild" won three of the top science-fiction awards in 1985: the Nebula Award, the Hugo Award, and the Locus Award. More recently, her novel, The Parable of the Talents *(1998), won the Nebula Award in 1999. As the only female black science-fiction writer in the United States, Butler frequently is asked what good is science fiction for black people. She responds, "What good is . . . thinking about the present, the future, and the past? What good is [science fiction's] tendency to warn or to consider alternative ways of thinking and doing? What good is its examination of possible effects of science and technology, or social organization and political direction?"*

1984

BLOODCHILD

My last night of childhood began with a visit home. T'Gatoi's sister had given us two sterile eggs. T'Gatoi gave one to my mother, brother, and sisters. She insisted that I eat the other one alone. It didn't matter. There was still enough to leave everyone feeling good. Almost everyone. My mother wouldn't take any. She sat, watching everyone drifting and dreaming without her. Most of the time she watched me.

I lay against T'Gatoi's long, velvet underside, sipping from my egg now and then, wondering why my mother denied herself such a harmless pleasure. Less of her hair would be gray if she indulged now and then. The eggs prolonged life, prolonged vigor. My father, who had never refused one in his life, had lived more than twice as long as he should have. And toward the end of his life, when he should have been slowing down, he had married my mother and fathered four children.

But my mother seemed content to age before she had to. I saw her turn away as several of T'Gatoi's limbs secured me closer. T'Gatoi liked our body heat and took advantage of it whenever she could. When I was little and at home more, my mother used to try to tell me how to behave with T'Gatoi—how to be respectful and always obedient because T'Gatoi was the Tlic[1] government official in charge of the Preserve, and thus the most important of her kind to deal directly with Terrans.[2] It was an honor, my mother said, that such a person had chosen to come into the family. My mother was at her most formal and severe when she was lying.

I had no idea why she was lying, or even what she was lying about. It *was* an honor to have T'Gatoi in the family, but it was hardly a novelty. T'Gatoi and my mother had been friends all my mother's life, and T'Gatoi was not interested in being honored in the house

---

[1] Insect-like creatures native to the planet.
[2] People from Earth.

she considered her second home. She simply came in, climbed onto one of her special couches, and called me over to keep her warm. It was impossible to be formal with her while lying against her and hearing her complain as usual that I was too skinny.

5   "You're better," she said this time, probing me with six or seven of her limbs. "You're gaining weight finally. Thinness is dangerous." The probing changed subtly, became a series of caresses.

"He's still too thin," my mother said sharply.

T'Gatoi lifted her head and perhaps a meter of her body off the couch as though she were sitting up. She looked at my mother, and my mother, her face lined and old looking, turned away.

"Lien, I would like you to have what's left of Gan's egg."

"The eggs are for the children," my mother said.

10   "They are for the family. Please take it."

Unwillingly obedient, my mother took it from me and put it to her mouth. There were only a few drops left in the now-shrunken, elastic shell, but she squeezed them out, swallowed them, and after a few moments some of the lines of tension began to smooth from her face.

"It's good," she whispered. "Sometimes I forget how good it is."

"You should take more," T'Gatoi said. "Why are you in such a hurry to be old?"

My mother said nothing.

15   "I like being able to come here," T'Gatoi said. "This place is a refuge because of you, yet you won't take care of yourself."

T'Gatoi was hounded on the outside. Her people wanted more of us made available. Only she and her political faction stood between us and the hordes who did not understand why there was a Preserve—why any Terran could not be courted, paid, drafted, in some way made available to them. Or they did understand, but in their desperation, they did not care. She parceled us out to the desperate and sold us to the rich and powerful for their political support. Thus, we were necessities, status symbols, and an independent people. She oversaw the joining of families, putting an end to the final remnants of the earlier system of breaking up Terran families to suit impatient Tlic. I had lived outside with her. I had seen the desperate eagerness in the way some people looked at me. It was a little frightening to know that only she stood between us and that desperation that could so easily swallow us. My mother would look at her sometimes and say to me, "Take care of her." And I would remember that she too had been outside, had seen.

Now T'Gatoi used four of her limbs to push me away from her onto the floor. "Go on, Gan," she said. "Sit down there with your sisters and enjoy not being sober. You had most of the egg. Lien, come warm me."

My mother hesitated for no reason that I could see. One of my earliest memories is of my mother stretched alongside T'Gatoi, talking about things I could not understand, picking me up from the floor and laughing as she sat me on one of T'Gatoi's segments. She ate her share of eggs then. I wondered when she had stopped, and why.

She lay down now against T'Gatoi, and the whole left row of T'Gatoi's limbs closed around her, holding her loosely, but securely. I had always found it comfortable to lie that way, but except for my older sister, no one else in the family liked it. They said it made them feel caged.

20   T'Gatoi meant to cage my mother. Once she had, she moved her tail slightly, then spoke. "Not enough egg, Lien. You should have taken it when it was passed to you. You need it badly now."

T'Gatoi's tail moved once more, its whip motion so swift I wouldn't have seen it if I hadn't been watching for it. Her sting drew only a single drop of blood from my mother's bare leg.

My mother cried out—probably in surprise. Being stung doesn't hurt. Then she sighed and I could see her body relax. She moved languidly into a more comfortable position within the cage of T'Gatoi's limbs. "Why did you do that?" she asked, sounding half asleep.

"I could not watch you sitting and suffering any longer."

My mother managed to move her shoulders in a small shrug. "Tomorrow," she said.

25   "Yes. Tomorrow you will resume your suffering—if you must. But just now, just for now, lie here and warm me and let me ease your way a little."

"He's still mine, you know," my mother said suddenly.

"Nothing can buy him from me." Sober, she would not have permitted herself to refer to such things.

"Nothing," T'Gatoi agreed, humoring her.

"Did you think I would sell him for eggs? For long life? My son?"

30   "Not for anything," T'Gatoi said, stroking my mother's shoulders, toying with her long, graying hair.

I would like to have touched my mother, shared that moment with her. She would take my hand if I touched her now. Freed by the egg and the sting, she would smile and perhaps say things long held in. But tomorrow, she would remember all this as a humiliation. I did not want to be part of a remembered humiliation. Best just be still and know she loved me under all the duty and pride and pain.

"Xuan Hoa, take off her shoes," T'Gatoi said. "In a little while I'll sting her again and she can sleep."

My older sister obeyed, swaying drunkenly as she stood up. When she had finished, she sat down beside me and took my hand. We had always been a unit, she and I.

My mother put the back of her head against T'Gatoi's underside and tried from that impossible angle to look up into the broad, round face. "You're going to sting me again?"

35   "Yes, Lien."

"I'll sleep until tomorrow noon."

"Good. You need it. When did you sleep last?"

My mother made a wordless sound of annoyance. "I should have stepped on you when you were small enough," she muttered.

It was an old joke between them. They had grown up together, sort of, though T'Gatoi had not, in my mother's lifetime, been small enough for any Terran to step on. She was nearly three times my mother's present age, yet would still be young when my mother died of age. But T'Gatoi and my mother had met as T'Gatoi was coming into a period of rapid development—a kind of Tlic adolescence. My mother was only a child, but for a while they developed at the same rate and had no better friends than each other.

40   T'Gatoi had even introduced my mother to the man who became my father. My parents, pleased with each other in spite of their different ages, married as T'Gatoi was going into her family's business—politics. She and my mother saw each other less. But sometime before my older sister was born, my mother promised T'Gatoi one of her children. She would have to give one of us to someone, and she preferred T'Gatoi to some stranger.

Years passed. T'Gatoi traveled and increased her influence. The Preserve was hers by the time she came back to my mother to collect what she probably saw as her just reward for her hard work. My older sister took an instant liking to her and wanted to be chosen, but my mother was just coming to term with me and T'Gatoi liked the idea of choosing an infant and watching and taking part in all the phases of development. I'm told I was first caged within T'Gatoi's many limbs only three minutes after my birth. A few days later, I was given my first taste of egg. I tell Terrans that when they ask whether I was ever afraid of her. And I tell it to Tlic when T'Gatoi suggests a young Terran child for them and they, anxious and ignorant, demand an adolescent. Even my brother who had somehow grown up to fear and distrust the Tlic could probably have gone smoothly into one of their families if he had been adopted early enough. Sometimes, I think for his sake he should have been. I looked at him, stretched out on the floor across the room, his eyes open, but glazed as he dreamed his egg dream. No matter what he felt toward the Tlic, he always demanded his share of egg.

"Lien, can you stand up?" T'Gatoi asked suddenly.

"Stand?" my mother said. "I thought I was going to sleep."

"Later. Something sounds wrong outside." The cage was abruptly gone.

45   "What?"

"Up, Lien!"

My mother recognized her tone and got up just in time to avoid being dumped on the floor. T'Gatoi whipped her three meters of body off her couch, toward the door, and out at full speed. She had bones—ribs, a long spine, a skull, four sets of limb bones per segment. But when she moved that way, twisting, hurling herself into controlled falls, landing running, she seemed not only boneless, but aquatic—something swimming through the air as though it were water. I loved watching her move.

I left my sister and started to follow her out the door, though I wasn't very steady on my own feet. It would have been better to sit and dream, better yet to find a girl and share a waking dream with her. Back when the Tlic saw us as not much more than convenient, big, warm-blooded animals, they would pen several of us together, male and female, and feed us only eggs. That way they could be sure of getting another generation of us no matter how we tried to hold out. We were lucky that didn't go on long. A few generations of it and we would have *been* little more than convenient, big animals.

"Hold the door open, Gan," T'Gatoi said. "And tell the family to stay back."

50   "What is it?" I asked

"N'Tlic."[3]

I shrank back against the door. "Here? Alone?"

"He was trying to reach a call box, I suppose." She carried the man past me, unconscious, folded like a coat over some of her limbs. He looked young—my brother's age perhaps—and he was thinner than he should have been. What T'Gatoi would have called dangerously thin.

"Gan, go to the call box," she said. She put the man on the floor and began stripping off his clothing.

55   I did not move.

After a moment, she looked up at me, her sudden stillness a sign of deep impatience.

"Send Qui," I told her. "I'll stay here. Maybe I can help."

She let her limbs begin to move again, lifting the man and pulling his shirt over his head. "You don't want to see this," she said. "It will be hard. I can't help this man the way his Tlic could."

"I know. But send Qui. He won't want to be of any help here. I'm at least willing to try."

60   She looked at my brother—older, bigger, stronger, certainly more able to help her here. He was sitting up now, braced against the wall, staring at the man on the floor with undisguised fear and revulsion. Even she could see that he would be useless.

"Qui, go!" she said.

He didn't argue. He stood up, swayed briefly, then steadied, frightened sober.

"This man's name is Bram Lomas," she told him, reading from the man's armband. I fingered my own armband in sympathy. "He needs T'Khotgif Teh. Do you hear?"

---

[3] Humans impregnated with newly hatched Tlic eggs.

"Bram Lomas, T'Khotgif Teh," my brother said. "I'm going." He edged around Lomas and ran out the door.

65 Lomas began to regain consciousness. He only moaned at first and clutched spasmodically at a pair of T'Gatoi's limbs. My younger sister, finally awake from her egg dream, came close to look at him, until my mother pulled her back.

T'Gatoi removed the man's shoes, then his pants, all the while leaving him two of her limbs to grip. Except for the final few, all her limbs were equally dexterous. "I want no argument from you this time, Gan," she said.

I straightened. "'What shall I do?"

"Go out and slaughter an animal that is at least half your size."

"Slaughter? But I've never—"

70 She knocked me across the room. Her tail was an efficient weapon whether she exposed the sting or not.

I got up, feeling stupid for having ignored her warning, and went into the kitchen. Maybe I could kill something with a knife or an ax. My mother raised a few Terran animals for the table and several thousand local ones for their fur. T'Gatoi would probably prefer something local. An achti, perhaps. Some of those were the right size, though they had about three times as many teeth as I did and a real love of using them. My mother, Hoa, and Qui could kill them with knives. I had never killed one at all, had never slaughtered any animal. I had spent most of my time with T'Gatoi while my brother and sisters were learning the family business. T'Gatoi had been right. I should have been the one to go to the call box. At least I could do that.

I went to the corner cabinet where my mother kept her large house and garden tools. At the back of the cabinet there was a pipe that carried off waste water from the kitchen—except that it didn't anymore. My father had rerouted the waste water below before I was born. Now the pipe could be turned so that one half slid around the other and a rifle could be stored inside. This wasn't our only gun, but it was our most easily accessible one. I would have to use it to shoot one of the biggest of the achti. Then T'Gatoi would probably confiscate it. Firearms were illegal in the Preserve. There had been incidents right after the Preserve was established—Terrans shooting Tlic, shooting N'Tlic. This was before the joining of families began, before everyone had a personal stake in keeping the peace. No one had shot a Tlic in my lifetime or my mother's, but the law still stood—for our protection, we were told. There were stories of whole Terran families wiped out in reprisal back during the assassinations.

I went out to the cages and shot the biggest achti I could find. It was a handsome breeding male, and my mother would not be pleased to see me bring it in. But it was the right size, and I was in a hurry.

I put the achti's long, warm body over my shoulder—glad that some of the weight I'd gained was muscle—and took it to the kitchen. There, I put the gun back in its hiding place. If T'Gatoi noticed the achti's wounds and demanded the gun, I would give it to her. Otherwise, let it stay where my father wanted it.

75 I turned to take the achti to her, then hesitated. For several seconds, I stood in front of the closed door wondering why I was suddenly afraid. I knew what was going to happen. I hadn't seen it before but T'Gatoi had shown me diagrams and drawings. She had made sure I knew the truth as soon as I was old enough to understand it.

Yet I did not want to go into that room. I wasted a little time choosing a knife from the carved, wooden box in which my mother kept them. T'Gatoi might want one, I told myself, for the tough, heavily furred hide of the achti.

"Gan!" T'Gatoi called, her voice harsh with urgency.

I swallowed. I had not imagined a single moving of the feet could be so difficult. I realized I was trembling and that shamed me. Shame impelled me through the door.

I put the achti down near T'Gatoi and saw that Lomas was unconscious again. She, Lomas, and I were alone in the room—my mother and sisters probably sent out so they would not have to watch. I envied them.

80   But my mother came back into the room as T'Gatoi seized the achti. Ignoring the knife I offered her, she extended claws from several of her limbs and slit the achti from throat to anus. She looked at me, her yellow eyes intent. "Hold this man's shoulders, Gan."

I stared at Lomas in panic, realizing that I did not want to touch him, let alone hold him. This would not be like shooting an animal. Not as quick, not as merciful, and, I hoped, not as final, but there was nothing I wanted less than to be part of it.

My mother came forward. "Gan, you hold his right side," she said. "I'll hold his left." And if he came to, he would throw her off without realizing he had done it. She was a tiny woman. She often wondered aloud how she had produced, as she said, such "huge" children.

"Never mind," I told her, taking the man's shoulders. "I'll do it." She hovered nearby.

"Don't worry," I said. "I won't shame you. You don't have to stay and watch."

85   She looked at me uncertainly, then touched my face in a rare caress. Finally, she went back to her bedroom.

T'Gatoi lowered her head in relief. "Thank you, Gan," she said with courtesy more Terran than Tlic. "That one . . . she is always finding new ways for me to make her suffer."

Lomas began to groan and make choked sounds. I had hoped he would stay unconscious. T'Gatoi put her face near his so that he focused on her.

"I've stung you as much as I dare for now," she told him. "When this is over, I'll sting you to sleep and you won't hurt anymore."

"Please," the man begged. "Wait . . ."

90   "There's no more time, Bram. I'll sting you as soon as it's over. When T'Khotgif arrives she'll give you eggs to help you heal. It will be over soon."

"T'Khotgif!" the man shouted, straining against my hands.

"Soon, Bram." T'Gatoi glanced at me, then placed a claw against his abdomen slightly to the right of the middle, just below the left rib. There was movement on the right side—tiny, seemingly random pulsations moving his brown flesh, creating a concavity here, a convexity there, over and over until I could see the rhythm of it and knew where the next pulse would be.

Lomas's entire body stiffened under T'Gatoi's claw, though she merely rested it against him as she wound the rear section of her body around his legs. He might break my grip, but he would not break hers. He wept helplessly as she used his pants to tie his hands, then pushed his hands above his head so that I could kneel on the cloth between them and pin them in place. She rolled up his shirt and gave it to him to bite down on.

And she opened him.

95   His body convulsed with the first cut. He almost tore himself away from me. The sound he made . . . I had never heard such sounds come from anything human. T'Gatoi seemed to pay no attention as she lengthened and deepened the cut, now and then pausing to lick away blood. His blood vessels contracted, reacting to the chemistry of her saliva, and the bleeding slowed.

I felt as though I were helping her torture him, helping her consume him. I knew I would vomit soon, didn't know why I hadn't already. I couldn't possibly last until she was finished.

She found the first grub. It was fat and deep red with his blood—both inside and out. It had already eaten its own egg case but apparently had not yet begun to eat its host. At this stage, it would eat any flesh except its mother's. Let alone, it would have gone on excreting the poisons that had both sickened and alerted Lomas. Eventually it would have begun to eat. By the time it ate its way out of Lomas's flesh, Lomas would be dead or dying—and unable to take revenge on the thing that was killing him. There was always a grace period between the time the host sickened and the time the grubs began to eat him.

T'Gatoi picked up the writhing grub carefully and looked at it, somehow ignoring the terrible groans of the man.

Abruptly, the man lost consciousness.

100 "Good," T'Gatoi looked down at him. "I wish you Terrans could do that at will." She felt nothing. And the thing she held . . .

It was limbless and boneless at this stage, perhaps fifteen centimeters long and two thick, blind and slimy with blood. It was like a large worm. T'Gatoi put it into the belly of the achti, and it began at once to burrow. It would stay there and eat as long as there was anything to eat.

Probing through Lomas's flesh, she found two more, one of them smaller and more vigorous. "A male!" she said happily. He would be dead before I would. He would be through his metamorphosis and screwing everything that would hold still before his sisters even had limbs. He was the only one to make a serious effort to bite T'Gatoi as she placed him in the achti.

Paler worms oozed to visibility in Lomas's flesh. I closed my eyes. It was worse than finding something dead, rotting, and filled with tiny animal grubs. And it was far worse than any drawing or diagram.

"Ah, there are more," T'Gatoi said, plucking out two long, thick grubs. You may have to kill another animal, Gan. Everything lives inside you Terrans."

105 I had been told all my life that this was a good and necessary thing Tlic and Terran did together—a kind of birth. I had believed it until now. I knew birth was painful and bloody, no matter what. But this was something else, something worse. And I wasn't ready to see it. Maybe I never would be. Yet I couldn't not see it. Closing my eyes didn't help.

T'Gatoi found a grub still eating its egg case. The remains of the case were still wired into a blood vessel by their own little tube or hook or whatever. That was the way the grubs were anchored and the way they fed. They took only blood until they were ready to emerge. Then they ate their stretched, elastic egg cases. Then they ate their hosts.

T'Gatoi bit away the egg case, licked away the blood. Did she like the taste? Did childhood habits die hard—or not die at all?

The whole procedure was wrong, alien. I wouldn't have thought anything about her could seem alien to me.

"One more, I think," she said. "Perhaps two. A good family. In a host animal these days, we would be happy to find one or two alive." She glanced at me. "Go outside, Gan, and empty your stomach. Go now while the man is unconscious."

110 I staggered out, barely made it. Beneath the tree just beyond the front door, I vomited until there was nothing left to bring up. Finally, I stood shaking, tears streaming down my face. I did not know why I was crying, but I could not stop. I went further from the house to avoid being seen. Every time I closed my eyes I saw red worms crawling over redder human flesh.

There was a car coming toward the house. Since Terrans were forbidden motorized vehicles except for certain farm equipment, I knew this must be Lomas's Tlic with Qui and perhaps a Terran doctor. I wiped my face on my shirt, struggled for control.

"Gan," Qui called as the car stopped. "What happened?" He crawled out of the low, round, Tlic-convenient car door. Another Terran crawled out the other side and went into the house without speaking to me. The doctor. With his help and a few eggs, Lomas might make it.

"T'Khotgif Teh?" I said.

The Tlic driver surged out of her car, reared up half her length before me. She was paler and smaller than T'Gatoi—probably born from the body of an animal. Tlic from Terran bodies were always larger as well as more numerous.

115   "Six young," I told her. "Maybe seven, all alive. At least one male."

"Lomas?" she said harshly. I liked her for the question and the concern in her voice when she asked it. The last coherent thing he had said was her name.

"He's alive," I said,

She surged away to the house without another word.

"She's been sick," my brother said,, watching her go. "When I called, I could hear people telling her she wasn't well enough to go out even for this."

120   I said nothing. I had extended courtesy to the Tlic. Now I didn't want to talk to anyone. I hoped he would go in—out of curiosity if nothing else.

"Finally found out more than you wanted to know, eh?"

I looked at him.

"Don't give me one of *her* looks," he said. "You're not her. You're just her property."

One of her looks. Had I picked up even an ability to imitate her expressions?

125   "What'd you do, puke?" He sniffed the air. "So now you know what you're in for."

I walked away from him. He and I had been close when we were kids. He would let me follow him around when I was home, and sometimes T'Gatoi would let me bring him along when she took me into the city. But something had happened when he reached adolescence. I never knew what. He began keeping out of T'Gatoi's way. Then he began running away— until he realized there was no "away." Not in the Preserve. Certainly not outside. After that he concentrated on getting his share of every egg that came into the house and on looking out for me in a way that made me all but hate him—a way that clearly said, as long as I was all right, he was safe from the Tlic.

"How was it, really?" he demanded, following me.

"I killed an achti. The young ate it."

"You didn't run out of the house and puke because they ate an achti."

130   "I had . . . never seen a person cut open before." That was true, and enough for him to know. I couldn't talk about the other. Not with him.

"Oh," he said. He glanced at me as though he wanted to say more, but he kept quiet.

We walked, not really headed anywhere. Toward the back, toward the cages, toward the fields.

"Did he say anything?" Qui asked. "Lomas, I mean."

Who else would he mean? "He said 'T'Khotgif.'"

135   Qui shuddered. "If she had done that to me, she'd be the last person I'd call for."

"You'd call for her. Her sting would ease your pain without killing the grubs in you."

"You think I'd care if they died?"

No. Of course he wouldn't. Would I?

"Shit!" He drew a deep breath. "I've seen what they do. You think this thing with Lomas was bad? It was nothing."

140   I didn't argue. He didn't know what he was talking about.

"I saw them eat a man," he said.

I turned to face him. "You're lying!"

"*I saw them eat a man.*" He paused. "It was when I was little. I had been to the Hartmund house and I was on my way home. Halfway here, I saw a man and a Tlic and the man was N'Tlic. The ground was hilly. I was able to hide from them and watch. The Tlic wouldn't open the man because she had nothing to feed the grubs. The man couldn't go any further and there were no houses around. He was in so much pain, he told her to kill him. He begged her to kill him. Finally, she did. She cut his throat. One swipe of one claw. I saw the grubs eat their way out, then burrow in again, still eating."

His words made me see Lomas's flesh again, parasitized, crawling. "Why didn't you tell me that?" I whispered.

145 He looked startled as though he'd forgotten I was listening. "I don't know."

"You started to run away not long after that, didn't you?"

"Yeah. Stupid. Running inside the Preserve. Running in a cage."

I shook my head, said what I should have said to him long ago. "She wouldn't take you, Qui. You don't have to worry."

"She would . . . if anything happened to you."

150 "No. She'd take Xuan Hoa. Hoa . . . wants it." She wouldn't if she had stayed to watch Lomas.

"They don't take women," he said with contempt.

"They do sometimes." I glanced at him. "Actually, they prefer women. You should be around them when they talk among themselves. They say women have more body fat to protect the grubs. But they usually take men to leave the women free to bear their own young."

"To provide the next generation of host animals," he said, switching from contempt to bitterness.

"It's more than that!" I countered. Was it?

155 "If it were going to happen to me, I'd want to believe it was more, too."

"It *is* more!" I felt like a kid. Stupid argument.

"Did you think so while T'Gatoi was picking worms out of that guy's guts?"

"It's not supposed to happen that way."

"Sure it is. You weren't supposed to see it, that's all. And his Tlic was supposed to do it. She could sting him unconscious and the operation wouldn't have been as painful. But she'd still open him, pick out the grubs, and if she missed even one, it would poison him and eat him from the inside out."

160 There was actually a time when my mother told me to show respect for Qui because he was my older brother. I walked away, hating him. In his way, he was gloating. He was safe and I wasn't. I could have hit him, but I didn't think I would be able to stand it when he refused to hit back, when he looked at me with contempt and pity.

He wouldn't let me get away. Longer legged, he swung ahead of me and made me feel as though I were following him.

"I'm sorry," he said.

I strode on, sick and furious.

"Look, it probably won't be that bad with you. T'Gatoi likes you. She'll be careful."

165 I turned back toward the house, almost running from him.

"Has she done it to you yet?" he asked, keeping up easily. "I mean, you're about the right age for implantation. Has she—"

I hit him. I didn't know I was going to do it, but I think I meant to kill him. If he hadn't been bigger and stronger, I think I would have.

He tried to hold me off, but in the end, had to defend himself. He only hit me a couple of times. That was plenty. I don't remember going down, but when I came to, he was gone. It was worth the pain to be rid of him.

I got up and walked slowly toward the house. The back was dark. No one was in the kitchen. My mother and sisters were sleeping in their bedrooms—or pretending to.

170 Once I was in the kitchen, I could hear voices—Tlic and Terran from the next room. I couldn't make out what they were saying—didn't want to make it out.

I sat down at my mother's table, waiting for quiet. The table was smooth and worn, heavy and well crafted. My father had made it for her just before he died. I remembered hanging around underfoot when he built it. He didn't mind. Now I sat leaning on it, missing him. I could have talked to him. He had done it three times in his long life. Three clutches of eggs, three times being opened up and sewed up. How had he done it? How did anyone do it?

I got up, took the rifle from its hiding place, and sat down again with it. It needed cleaning, oiling.

All I did was load it.

"Gan?"

175 She made a lot of little clicking sounds when she walked on bare floor, each limb clicking in succession as it touched down. Waves of little clicks.

She came to the table, raised the front half of her body above it, and surged onto it. Sometimes she moved so smoothly she seemed to flow like water itself. She coiled herself into a small hill in the middle of the table and looked at me.

"That was bad," she said softly. "You should not have seen it. It need not be that way."

"I know."

"T'Khotgif—Ch'Khotgif now—she will die of her disease. She will not live to raise her children. But her sister will provide for them, and for Bram Lomas." Sterile sister. One fertile female in every lot. One to keep the family going. That sister owed Lomas more than she could ever repay.

180 "He'll live then?"

"Yes."

"I wonder if he would do it again."

"No one would ask him to do that again."

I looked into the yellow eyes, wondering how much I saw and understood there, and how much I only imagined. "No one ever asks us," I said. "You never asked me."

185 She moved her head slightly. "What's the matter with your face?"

"Nothing. Nothing important." Human eyes probably wouldn't have noticed the swelling in the darkness. The only light was from one of the moons, shining through a window across the room.

"Did you use the rifle to shoot the achti?"

"Yes."

"And do you mean to use it to shoot me?"

190 I stared at her, outlined in the moonlight—coiled, graceful body. "What does Terran blood taste like to you?"

She said nothing.

"What are you?" I whispered. "What are we to you?"

She lay still, rested her head on her topmost coil. "You know me as no other does," she said softly. "You must decide."

"That's what happened to my face," I told her.

195 "What?"

"Qui goaded me into deciding to do something. It didn't turn out very well." I moved the gun slightly, brought the barrel up diagonally under my own chin. "At least it was a decision I made."

"As this will be."

"Ask me, Gatoi."

"For my children's lives?"

200 She would say something like that. She knew how to manipulate people, Terran and Tlic. But not this time.

"I don't want to be a host animal," I said. "Not even yours."

It took her a long time to answer. "We use almost no host animals these days," she said. "You know that."

"You use us."

"We do. We wait long years for you and teach you and join our families to yours." She moved restlessly. "You know you aren't animals to us."

205   I stared at her, saying nothing.

"The animals we once used began killing most of our eggs after implantation long before your ancestors arrived," she said softly. "You know these things, Gan. Because your people arrived, we are relearning what it means to be a healthy, thriving people. And your ancestors, fleeing from their home-world, from their own kind who would have killed or enslaved them—they survived because of us. We saw them as people and gave them the Preserve when they still tried to kill us as worms."

At the word "worms," I jumped. I couldn't help it, and she couldn't help noticing it.

"I see," she said quietly. "Would you really rather die than bear my young, Gan?"

I didn't answer.

210   "Shall I go to Xuan Hoa?"

"Yes!" Hoa wanted it. Let her have it. She hadn't had to watch Lomas. She'd be proud. . . . Not terrified.

T'Gatoi flowed off the table onto the floor, startling me almost too much.

"I'll sleep in Hoa's room tonight," she said. "And sometime tonight or in the morning, I'll tell her."

This was going too fast. My sister Hoa had had almost as much to do with raising me as my mother. I was still close to her—not like Qui. She could want T'Gatoi and still love me.

215   "Wait! Gatoi!"

She looked back, then raised nearly half her length off the floor and turned to face me. "These are adult things, Gan. This is my life, my family!"

"But she's . . . my sister."

"I have done what you demanded. I have asked you!"

"But—"

220   "It will be easier for Hoa. She has always expected to carry other lives inside her."

Human lives. Human young who should someday drink at her breasts, not at her veins.

I shook my head. "Don't do it to her, Gatoi." I was not Qui. It seemed I could become him, though, with no effort at all. I could make Xuan Hoa my shield. Would it be easier to know that red worms were growing in her flesh instead of mine?

"Don't do it to Hoa," I repeated.

She stared at me, utterly still.

225   I looked away, then back at her. "Do it to me."

I lowered the gun from my throat and she leaned forward to take it.

"No," I told her.

"It's the law," she said.

"Leave it for the family. One of them might use it to save my life someday."

230   She grasped the rifle barrel, but I wouldn't let go. I was pulled into a standing position over her.

"Leave it here!" I repeated. "If we're not your animals, if these are adult things, accept the risk. There is risk, Gatoi, in dealing with a partner."

It was clearly hard for her to let go of the rifle. A shudder went through her and she made a hissing sound of distress. It occurred to me that she was afraid. She was old enough to have seen what guns could do to people. Now her young and this gun would be together in the same house. She did not know about the other guns. In this dispute, they did not matter.

"I will implant the first egg tonight," she said as I put the gun away. "Do you hear, Gan?"

Why else had I been given a whole egg to eat while the rest of the family was left to share one? Why else had my mother kept looking at me as though I were going away from her, going where she could not follow? Did T'Gatoi imagine I hadn't known?

235   "I hear."

"Now!" I let her push me out of the kitchen, then walked ahead of her toward my bedroom. The sudden urgency in her voice sounded real. "You would have done it to Hoa tonight!" I accused.

"I must do it to someone tonight."

I stopped in spite of her urgency and stood in her way. "Don't you care who?"

She flowed around me and into my bedroom, I found her waiting on the couch we shared. There was nothing in Hoa's room that she could have used. She would have done it to Hoa on the floor. The thought of her doing it to Hoa at all disturbed me in a different way now, and I was suddenly angry.

240   Yet I undressed and lay down beside her. I knew what to do, what to expect. I had been told all my life. I felt the familiar sting, narcotic, mildly pleasant. Then the blind probing of her ovipositor.[4] The puncture was painless, easy. So easy going in. She undulated slowly against me, her muscles forcing the egg from her body into mine. I held on to a pair of her limbs until I remembered Lomas holding her that way. Then I let go, moved inadvertently, and hurt her. She gave a low cry of pain and I expected to be caged at once within her limbs. When I wasn't, I held on to her again, feeling oddly ashamed.

"I'm sorry," I whispered.

She rubbed my shoulders with four of her limbs.

"Do you care?" I asked. "Do you care that it's me?"

She did not answer for some time. Finally, "You were the one making the choices tonight, Gan. I made mine long ago."

245   "Would you have gone to Hoa?"

"Yes. How could I put my children into the care of one who hates them?"

"It wasn't . . . hate."

"I know what it was."

"I was afraid."

250   Silence.

"I still am." I could admit it to her here, now.

"But you came to me . . . to save Hoa."

"Yes." I leaned my forehead against her. She was cool velvet, deceptively soft. "And to keep you for myself," I said. It was so. I didn't understand it, but it was so.

She made a soft hum of contentment. "I couldn't believe I had made such a mistake with you," she said. "I chose you. I believed you had grown to choose me."

255   "I had, but . . ."

"Lomas."

"Yes."

"I had never known a Terran to see a birth and take it well. Qui has seen one, hasn't he?"

"Yes."

260   "Terrans should be protected from seeing."

I didn't like the sound of that—and I doubted that it was possible. "Not protected," I said. "Shown. Shown when we're young kids, and shown more than once. Gatol, no Terran ever sees a birth that goes right. All we see is N'Tlic—pain and terror and maybe death."

She looked down at me. "It is a private thing. It has always been a private thing."

Her tone kept me from insisting—that and the knowledge that if she changed her mind, I might be the first public example. But I had planted the thought in her mind. Chances were it would grow, and eventually she would experiment.

"You won't see it again," she said. "I don't want you thinking any more about shooting me."

---

[4] A tube-shaped organ used by some insects to lay eggs.

265   The small amount of fluid that came into me with her egg relaxed me as completely as a sterile egg would have, so that I could remember the rifle in my hands and my feelings of fear and revulsion, anger and despair. I could remember the feelings without reviving them. I could talk about them.

      "I wouldn't have shot you," I said. "Not you." She had been taken from my father's flesh when he was my age.

      "You could have," she insisted.

      "Not you." She stood between us and her own people, protecting, interweaving.

      "Would you have destroyed yourself?"

270   I moved carefully, uncomfortable. "I could have done that. I nearly did. That's Qui's 'away.' I wonder if he knows."

      "What?"

      I did not answer.

      "You will live now."

      "Yes." *Take care of her*, my mother used to say. Yes.

275   "I'm healthy and young," she said. "I won't leave you as Lomas was left—alone, N'Tlic. I'll take care of you."

Afterword

It amazes me that some people have seen "Bloodchild" as a story of slavery. It isn't. It's a number of other things, though. On one level, it's a love story between two very different beings. On another, it's a coming-of-age story in which a boy must absorb disturbing information and use it to make a decision that will affect the rest of his life.

      On a third level, "Bloodchild" is my pregnant man story. I've always wanted to explore what it might be like for a man to be put into that most unlikely of all positions. Could I write a story in which a man chose to become pregnant *not* through some sort of misplaced competitiveness to prove that a man could do anything a woman could do, not because he was forced to, not even out of curiosity? I wanted to see whether I could write a dramatic story of a man becoming pregnant as an act of love—choosing pregnancy in spite of as well as because of surrounding difficulties.

      Also, "Bloodchild" was my effort to ease an old fear of mine. I was going to travel to the Peruvian Amazon to do research for my Xenogenesis books (*Dawn*, *Adulthood Rites*, and *Imago*), and I worried about my possible reactions to some of the insect life of the area. In particular, I worried about the botfly—an insect with, what seemed to me then, horror-movie habits. There was no shortage of botflies in the part of Peru that I intended to visit.

      The botfly lays its eggs in wounds left by the bites of other insects. I found the idea of a maggot living and growing under my skin, eating my flesh as it grew, to be so intolerable, so terrifying that I didn't know how I could stand it if it happened to me. To make matters worse, all that I heard and read advised botfly victims not to try to get rid of their maggot passengers until they got back home to the United States and were able to go to a doctor—or until the fly finished the larval part of its growth cycle, crawled out of its host, and flew away.

      The problem was to do what would seem to be the normal thing, to squeeze out the maggot and throw it away, was to invite infection. The maggot becomes literally attached to its host and leaves part of itself behind, broken off, if it's squeezed or cut out. Of course, the part left behind dies and rots, causing infection. Lovely.

      When I have to deal with something that disturbs me as much as the botfly did, I write about it. I sort out my problems by writing about them. In a high school classroom on November 22, 1963, I remember grabbing a notebook and beginning to write my response to news of John Kennedy's assassination. Whether I write journal pages, an essay, a short story, or weave my problems into a novel, I find the writing helps me get through the trouble and get on with my life. Writing "Bloodchild" didn't make me like botflies, but for a while, it made them seem more interesting than horrifying.

There's one more thing I tried to do in "Bloodchild." I tried to write a story about paying the rent—a story about an isolated colony of human beings on an inhabited, extrasolar world. At best, they would be a lifetime away from reinforcements. It wouldn't be the British Empire in space, and it wouldn't be *Star Trek*. Sooner or later, the humans would have to make some kind of accommodation with their um . . . their hosts. Chances are this would be an unusual accommodation. Who knows what we humans have that others might be willing to take in trade for a livable space on a world not our own?

WILLIAM BUTLER YEATS

William Butler Yeats (1865–1939) was born in Dublin, Ireland. The leader of the Irish Renaissance, he helped found the Abbey Theater in 1904. In 1922, he was elected to a six-year term as senator after the Irish Free State was formed. Yeats's writing displays an imaginative, skillful blend of Eastern and Western cultures and ancient and modern thought. Despite this impressive eclecticism, Yeats always remains an Irish poet. His works include the prose volumes A Vision *(1925) and* Autobiographies *(1926) and the poetic volumes* The Tower *(1928),* The Winding Stair *(1929), and* The Collected Poems *(1933). Yeats was awarded the Nobel Prize for Literature in 1923.*

1919

THE SECOND COMING[1]

Turning and turning in the widening gyre
The falcon cannot hear the falconer;
Things fall apart; the center cannot hold;
Mere anarchy is loosed upon the world,
5   The blood-dimmed tide is loosed, and everywhere
The ceremony of innocence is drowned;
The best lack all conviction, while the worst
Are full of passionate intensity.

Surely some revelation is at hand.
10 Surely the Second Coming is at hand.
The Second Coming! Hardly are those words out
When a vast image out of *Spiritus Mundi*[2]
Troubles my sight: somewhere in sands of the desert
A shape with lion body and the head of a man,[3]
15 A gaze blank and pitiless as the sun,
Is moving its slow thighs, while all about it
Reel shadows of the indignant desert birds.

---

[1] Allusion to Jesus's prediction of his second coming. Written in 1919, the poem refers to the Black and Tan War in Ireland when British soldiers were sent to quell the republicans.

[2] The author's term for divine inspiration or for a place from which images are received, never invented.

[3] The Egyptian sphinx.

The darkness drops again; but now I know
That twenty centuries[4] of stony sleep
20 Were vexed to nightmare[5] by a rocking cradle,
And what rough beast, its hour come round at last,
Slouches towards Bethlehem[6] to be born?

STEPHEN JAY GOULD

Stephen Jay Gould (1941–2002) was born in New York City and educated at Antioch College and Columbia University. A paleontologist and evolutionary biologist, he taught at Harvard University and wrote prolifically about science, particularly evolution theory. He was the au-thor of twenty-nine books and the editor of many more, including The Best American Essays 2002. *Gould was the recipient of many awards, both for his scientific and his literary achieve-ments. Some of the most recent included the Rhone-Poulenc Prize and Pulitzer Prize (finalist, 1991) for* Wonderful Life: The Burgess Shale and the Nature of History; *the Iglesias Prize (1991) for the Italian translation of* The Mismeasure of Man; *the Golden Trilobite Award, Pa-leontological Society (1992); the Homer Smith Medal, New York University School of Medicine (1992); the Commonwealth Award in Interpretative Science, State of Massachusetts (1993); the St. Louis Libraries Literary Award, Univeristy of St. Louis (1994); the Gold Medal for Service to Zoology, Linnaean Society of London; Distinguished Service Medal, Teachers College, Co-lumbia University; and honorary degrees from numerous colleges and universities. Gould's writing is read by many laypeople, perhaps because of his ability to make connections between complex ideas and common subjects with which we are familiar, such as baseball (another of Gould's passions).*

1982

NONMORAL NATURE

When the Right Honorable and Reverend Francis Henry, earl of Bridgewater, died in February, 1829, he left £8,000 to support a series of books "on the power, wisdom and goodness of God, as manifested in the creation." William Buckland,[1] England's first offi-cial academic geologist and later dean of Westminister, was invited to compose one of the nine Bridgewater Treatises.[2] In it he discussed the most pressing problem of natural theol-ogy: If God is benevolent and the Creation displays his "power, wisdom and goodness," then why are we surrounded with pain, suffering, and apparently senseless cruelty in the animal world?

Buckland considered the depredation of "carnivorous races" as the primary challenge to an idealized world in which the lion might dwell with the lamb. He resolved the issue to his satisfaction by arguing that carnivores actually increase "the aggregate of animal enjoy-ment" and "diminish that of pain." The death of victims, after all, is swift and relatively pain-less, victims are spared the ravages of decrepitude and senility, and populations do not

---

[4] Reference to twenty centuries of Christianity.

[5] Implication that Christianity created its opposite.

[6] Birthplace of Jesus.

[1] William Buckland (1784–1856) authored one of the Bridgewater Treatises, "Geology and Minerology," in 1836.

[2] Essays about the moral and religious implications of scientific research.

outrun their food supply to the greater sorrow of all. God knew what he was doing when he made lions. Buckland concluded in hardly concealed rapture:

> The appointment of death by the agency of carnivora, as the ordinary termination of animal existence, appears therefore in its main results to be a dispensation of benevolence; it deducts much from the aggregate amount of the pain of universal death; it abridges, and almost annihilates, throughout the brute creation, the misery of disease, and accidental injuries, and lingering decay; and imposes such salutary restraint upon excessive increase of numbers, that the supply of food maintains perpetually a due ratio to the demand. The result is, that the surface of the land and depths of the waters are ever crowded with myriads of animated beings, the pleasures of whose life are co-existence with its duration; and which throughout the little day of existence that is allotted to them, fulfill with joy the functions for which they were created.

We may find a certain amusing charm in Buckland's vision today, but such arguments did begin to address "the problem of evil" for many of Buckland's contemporaries—how could a benevolent God create such a world of carnage and bloodshed? Yet these claims could not abolish the problem of evil entirely, for nature includes many phenomena far more horrible in our eyes than simple predation. I suspect that nothing evokes greater disgust in most of us than slow destruction of a host by an internal parasite—slow ingestion, bit by bit, from the inside. In no other way can I explain why *Alien,* an uninspired, grade-C, formula horror film, should have won such a following. That single scene of Mr. Alien, popping forth as a baby parasite from the body of a human host, was both sickening and stunning. Our nineteenth-century forebears maintained similar feelings. Their greatest challenge to the concept of a benevolent deity was not simple predation—for one can admire quick and efficient butcheries, especially since we strive to construct them ourselves—but slow death by parasitic ingestion. The classic case, treated at length by all the great naturalists, involved the so-called ichneumon fly. Buckland had sidestepped the major issue.

The ichneumon fly, which provoked such concern among natural theologians, was a composite creature representing the habits of an enormous tribe. The Ichneumonoidea are a group of wasps, not flies, that include more species than all the vertebrates combined (wasps, with ants and bees, constitute the order Hymenoptera; flies, with their two wings—wasps have four—form the order Diptera). In addition, many related wasps of similar habits were often cited for the same grisly details. Thus, the famous story did not merely implicate a single aberrant species (perhaps a perverse leakage from Satan's realm), but perhaps hundreds of thousands of them—a large chunk of what could only be God's creation.

5   The ichneumons, like most wasps, generally live freely as adults but pass their larval life as parasites feeding on the bodies of other animals, almost invariably members of their own phylum, Arthropoda. The most common victims are caterpillars (butterfly and moth larvae), but some ichneumons prefer aphids and others attack spiders. Most hosts are parasitized as larvae, but some adults are attacked, and many tiny ichneumons inject their brood directly into the egg of their host.

The free-flying females locate an appropriate host and then convert it to a food factory for their own young. Parasitologists speak of ectoparasitism when the uninvited guest lives on the surface of its host, and endoparasitism when the parasite dwells within. Among endoparasitic ichneumons, adult females pierce the host with their ovipositor and deposit eggs within it. (The ovipositor, a thin tube extending backward from the wasp's rear end, may be many times as long as the body itself.) Usually, the host is not otherwise inconvenienced for the moment, at least until the eggs hatch and the ichneumon larvae begin their grim work of interior excavation. Among ectoparasites, however, many females lay their eggs directly upon the host's body. Since an active host would easily dislodge the egg, the ichneumon mother often simultaneously injects a toxin that paralyzes the caterpillar or other victim. The paralysis may be permanent, and the caterpillar lies, alive but immobile, with the agent of its future destruction secure on its belly. The egg hatches, the helpless caterpillar twitches, the wasp larva pierces and begins its grisly feast.

Since a dead and decaying caterpillar will do the wasp larva no good, it eats in a pattern that cannot help but recall, in our inappropriate, anthropocentric interpretation, the ancient English penalty for treason—drawing and quartering, with its explicit object of extracting as much torment as possible by keeping the victim alive and sentient. As the king's executioner drew out and burned his client's entrails; so does the ichneumon larva eat fat bodies and digestive organs first, keeping the caterpillar alive by preserving intact the essential heart and central nervous system. Finally, the larva completes its work and kills its victim, leaving behind the caterpillar's empty shell. Is it any wonder that ichneumons, not snakes or lions, stood as the paramount challenge to God's benevolence during the heyday of natural theology?

As I read through the nineteenth- and twentieth-century literature on ichneumons, nothing amused me more than the tension between an intellectual knowledge that wasps should not be described in human terms and a literary or emotional inability to avoid the familiar categories of epic and narrative, pain and destruction, victim and vanquisher. We seem to be caught in the mythic structures of our own cultural sagas, quite unable, even in our basic descriptions, to use any other language than the metaphors of battle and conquest. We cannot render this corner of natural history as anything but story, combining the themes of grim horror and fascination and usually ending not so much with pity for the caterpillar as with admiration for the efficiency of the ichneumon.

I detect two basic themes in most epic descriptions: the struggles of prey and the ruthless efficiency of parasites. Although we acknowledge that we witness little more than automatic instinct or physiological reaction, still we describe the defenses of hosts as though they represented conscious struggles. Thus, aphids kick and caterpillars may wriggle violently as wasps attempt to insert their ovipositors. The pupa of the tortoise-shell butterfly (usually considered an inert creature silently awaiting its conversion from duckling to swan) may contort its abdominal region so sharply that attacking wasps are thrown into the air. The caterpillars of *Hapalia,* when attacked by the wasp *Apanteles machaeralis,* drop suddenly from their leaves and suspend themselves in air by a silken thread. But the wasp may run down the thread and insert its egg nonetheless. Some hosts can encapsulate the injected egg with blood cells that aggregate and harden, thus suffocating the parasite.

10   J.-H. Fabre, the great nineteenth-century French entomologist,[3] who remains to this day the preeminently literate natural historian of insects, made a special study of parasitic wasps and wrote with an unabashed anthropocentrism about the struggles of paralyzed victims (see his books *Insect Life* and *The Wonders of Instinct*). He describes some imperfectly paralyzed caterpillars that struggle so violently every time a parasite approaches that the wasp larvae must feed with unusual caution. They attach themselves to a silken strand from the roof of their burrow and descend upon a safe and exposed part of the caterpillar:

> The grub is at dinner: head downwards, it is digging into the limp belly of one of the caterpillars. . . . At the least sign of danger in the heap of caterpillars, the larva retreats . . . and climbs back to the ceiling, where the swarming rabble cannot reach it. When peace is restored, it slides down [its silken cord] and returns to table, with its head over the viands and its rear upturned and ready to withdraw in case of need.

---

[3] A scientist who specializes in the study of insects.

In another chapter, he describes the fate of a paralyzed cricket:

> One may see the cricket, bitten to the quick, vainly move its antennae and abdominal styles, open and close its empty jaws, and even move a foot, but the larva is safe and searches its vitals with impunity. What an awful nightmare for the paralyzed cricket!

Fabre even learned to feed some paralyzed victims by placing a syrup of sugar and water on their mouthparts—thus showing that they remained alive, sentient, and (by implication) grateful for any palliation of their inevitable fate. If Jesus, immobile and thirsting on the cross, received only vinegar from his tormentors, Fabre at least could make an ending bittersweet.

The second theme, ruthless efficiency of the parasites, leads to the opposite conclusion—grudging admiration for the victors. We learn of their skill in capturing dangerous hosts often many times larger than themselves. Caterpillars may be easy game, but the psammocharid wasps prefer spiders. They must insert their ovipositors in a safe and precise spot. Some leave a paralyzed spider in its own burrow. *Planiceps hirsutus,* for example, parasitizes a California trapdoor spider. It searches for spider tubes on sand dunes, then digs into nearby sand to disturb the spider's home and drive it out. When the spider emerges, the wasp attacks, paralyzes its victim, drags it back into its own tube, shuts and fastens the trapdoor, and deposits a single egg upon the spider's abdomen. Other psammocharids will drag a heavy spider back to a previously prepared cluster of clay or mud cells. Some amputate a spider's legs to make the passage easier. Others fly back over water, skimming a buoyant spider along the surface.

Some wasps must battle with other parasites over a host's body. *Rhyssella curvipes* can detect the larvae of wood wasps deep within alder wood and drill down to its potential victims with its sharply ridged ovipositor. *Pseudorhyssa alpestris,* a related parasite, cannot drill directly into wood since its slender ovipositor bears only rudimentary cutting ridges. It locates the holes made by *Rhyssella,* inserts its ovipositor, and lays an egg on the host (already conveniently paralyzed by *Rhyssella*), right next to the egg deposited by its relative. The two eggs hatch at about the same time, but the larva of *Pseudorhyssa* has a bigger head bearing much larger mandibles. *Pseudorhyssa* seizes the smaller *Rhyssella* larva, destroys it, and proceeds to feast upon a banquet already well prepared.

15   Other praises for the efficiency of mothers invoke the themes of early, quick, and often. Many ichneumons don't even wait for their hosts to develop into larvae, but parasitize the egg directly (larval wasps may then either drain the egg itself or enter the developing host larva). Others simply move fast. *Apanteles militaris* can deposit up to seventy-two eggs in a single second. Still others are doggedly persistent. *Aphidius gomezi* females produce up to 1,500 eggs and can parasitize as many as 600 aphids in a single working day. In a bizarre twist upon "often," some wasps indulge in polyembryony, a kind of iterated supertwinning. A single egg divides into cells that aggregate into as many as 500 individuals. Since some polyembryonic wasps parasitize caterpillars much larger than themselves and may lay up to six eggs in each, as many as 3,000 larvae may develop within, and feed upon, a single host. These wasps are endoparasites and do not paralyze their victims. The caterpillars writhe back and forth, not (one suspects) from pain, but merely in response to the commotion induced by thousands of wasp larvae feeding within.

The efficiency of mothers is matched by their larval offspring. I have already mentioned the pattern of eating less essential parts first, thus keeping the host alive and fresh to its final and merciful dispatch. After the larva digests every edible morsel of its victim (if only to prevent later fouling of its abode by decaying tissue), it may still use the outer shell of its host. One aphid parasite cuts a hole in the belly of its victim's shell, glues the skeleton to a leaf by sticky secretions from its salivary gland, and then spins a cocoon to pupate within the aphid's shell.

In using inappropriate anthropocentric[4] language in this romp through the natural history of ichneumons, I have tried to emphasize just why these wasps became a preeminent challenge to natural theology—the antiquated doctrine that attempted to infer God's essence from the products of his creation. I have used twentieth-century examples for the most part, but all themes were known and stressed by the great nineteenth-century natural theologians. How then did they square the habits of these wasps with the goodness of God? How did they extract themselves from this dilemma of their own making?

The strategies were as varied as the practitioners; they shared only the theme of special pleading for an a priori doctrine[5]—they knew that God's benevolence was lurking somewhere behind all these tales of apparent horror. Charles Lyell,[6] for example, in the first edition of his epochal *Principles of Geology* (1830–1833), decided that caterpillars posed such a threat to vegetation that any natural checks upon them could only reflect well upon a creating deity, for caterpillars would destroy human agriculture "did not Providence put causes in operation to keep them in due bounds."

The Reverend William Kirby,[7] rector of Barham and Britain's foremost entomologist, chose to ignore the plight of caterpillars and focused instead upon the virtue of mother love displayed by wasps in provisioning their young with such care.

> The great object of the female is to discover a proper nidus for her eggs. In search of this she is in constant motion. Is the caterpillar of a butterfly or moth the appropriate food for her young? You see her alight upon the plants where they are most usually to be met with, run quickly over them, carefully examining every leaf, and, having found the unfortunate object of her search, insert her sting into its flesh, and there deposit an egg. . . . The active Ichneumon braves every danger, and does not desist until her courage and address have insured subsistence for one of her future progeny.

20   Kirby found this solicitude all the more remarkable because the female wasp will never see her child and enjoy the pleasures of parenthood. Yet her love compels her to danger nonetheless:

> A very large proportion of them are doomed to die before their young come into existence. But in these the passion is not extinguished. . . . When you witness the solicitude with which they provide for the security and sustenance of their future young, you can scarcely deny to them love for a progeny they are never destined to behold.

Kirby also put in a good word for the marauding larvae, praising them for their forbearance in eating selectively to keep their caterpillar prey alive. Would we all husband our resources with such care!

---

[4] The act of interpreting reality exclusively in terms of human values and experience.

[5] **a priori:** "beforehand." Gould is claiming that scientists who approach scientific research with preconceived ideas are not being objective.

[6] Charles Lyell (1797–1875) was a famous geologist whose work influenced Darwin and who later encouraged Darwin to publish *On the Origin of Species* (1859).

[7] The Reverend William Kirby (1759–1850) authored the Bridgewater Treatise "On the power, wisdom, and goodness of God, as manifested in the creations of animals, and in their history, habits, and instincts" (2 vols., 1835).

In this strange and apparently cruel operation one circumstance is truly remarkable. The larva of the Ichneumon, though every day, perhaps for months, it gnaws the inside of the caterpillar, and though at last it has devoured almost every part of it except the skin and intestines, carefully all this time it avoids injuring the vital organs, as if aware that its own existence depends on that of the insect upon which it preys! . . . What would be the impression which a similar instance amongst the race of quadrupeds would make upon us? If, for example, an animal . . . should be found to feed upon the inside of a dog, devouring only those parts not essential to life, while it cautiously left uninjured the heart, arteries, lungs, and intestines—should we not regard such an instance as a perfect prodigy, as an example of instinctive forebearance almost miraculous? [The last three quotes come from the 1856, and last pre-Darwinian, edition of Kirby and Spence's *Introduction to Entomology*.]

This tradition of attempting to read moral meaning from nature did not cease with the triumph of evolutionary theory after Darwin published *On the Origin of Species* in 1859—for evolution could be read as God's chosen method of peopling our planet, and ethical messages might still populate nature. Thus, St. George Mivart, one of Darwin's most effective evolutionary critics and a devout Catholic, argued that "many amiable and excellent people" had been misled by the apparent suffering of animals for two reasons. First, however much it might hurt, "physical suffering and moral evil are simply incommensurable." Since beasts are not moral agents, their feelings cannot bear any ethical message. But secondly, lest our visceral sensitivities still be aroused, Mivart assures us that animals must feel little, if any, pain. Using a favorite racist argument of the time—that "primitive" people suffer far less than advanced and cultured people—Mivart extrapolated further down the ladder of life into a realm of very limited pain indeed: Physical suffering, he argued,

depends greatly upon the mental condition of the sufferer. Only during consciousness does it exist, and only in the most highly organized men does it reach its acme. The author has been assured that lower races of men appear less keenly sensitive to physical suffering than do more cultivated and refined human beings. Thus only in man can there really be any intense degree of suffering, because only in him is there that intellectual recollection of past moments and that anticipation of future ones, which constitute in great part the bitterness of suffering. The momentary pang, the present pain, which beasts endure, though real enough, is yet, doubtless, not to be compared as to its intensity with the suffering which is produced in man through his high prerogative of self-consciousness [from *Genesis of Species*, 1871].

It took Darwin himself to derail this ancient tradition—in that gentle way so characteristic of his radical intellectual approach to nearly everything. The ichneumons also troubled Darwin greatly and he wrote of them to Asa Gray[8] in 1860:

I own that I cannot see as plainly as others do, and as I should wish to do, evidence of design and beneficence on all sides of us. There seems to me too much misery in the world. I cannot persuade myself that a beneficent and omnipotent God would have designedly created the Ichneumonidae with the express intention of their feeding within the living bodies of Caterpillars, or that a cat should play with mice.

---

[8] Asa Gray (1810–1888) was a famous American botanist.

Indeed, he had written with more passion to Joseph Hooker[9] in 1856: "What a book a devil's chaplain might write on the clumsy, wasteful, blundering, low, and horribly cruel works of nature!"

25   This honest admission—that nature is often (by our standards) cruel and that all previous attempts to find a lurking goodness behind everything represent just so much absurd special pleading—can lead in two directions. One might retain the principle that nature holds moral messages for humans, but reverse the usual perspective and claim that morality consists in understanding the ways of nature and doing the opposite. Thomas Henry Huxley[10] advanced this argument in his famous essay on *Evolution and Ethics* (1893):

> The practice of that which is ethically best—what we call goodness or virtue—involves a course of conduct which, in all respects, is opposed to that which leads to success in the cosmic struggle for existence. In place of ruthless self-assertion it demands self-restraint; in place of thrusting aside, or treading down, all competitors, it requires that the individual shall not merely respect, but shall help his fellows. . . .
> It repudiates the gladiatorial theory of existence. . . . Laws and moral precepts are directed to the end of curbing the cosmic process.

The other argument, more radical in Darwin's day but common now, holds that nature simply is as we find it. Our failure to discern the universal good we once expected does not record our lack of insight or ingenuity but merely demonstrates that nature contains no moral messages framed in human terms. Morality is a subject for philosophers, theologians, students of the humanities, indeed for all thinking people. The answers will not be read passively from nature; they do not, and cannot, arise from the data of science. The factual state of the world does not teach us how we, with our powers for good and evil, should alter or preserve it in the most ethical manner.

Darwin himself tended toward this view, although he could not, as a man of his time, thoroughly abandon the idea that laws of nature might reflect some higher purpose. He clearly recognized that the specific manifestations of those laws—cats playing with mice, and ichneumon larvae eating caterpillars—could not embody ethical messages, but he somehow hoped that unknown higher laws might exist "with the details, whether good or bad, left to the working out of what we may call chance."

Since ichneumons are a detail, and since natural selection is a law regulating details, the answer to the ancient dilemma of why such cruelty (in our terms) exists in nature can only be that there isn't any answer—and that the framing of the question "in our terms" is thoroughly inappropriate in a natural world neither made for us nor ruled by us. It just plain happens. It is a strategy that works for ichneumons and that natural selection has programmed into their behavioral repertoire. Caterpillars are not suffering to teach us something; they have simply been outmaneuvered, for now, in the evolutionary game. Perhaps they will evolve a set of adequate defenses sometime in the future, thus sealing the fate of ichneumons. And perhaps, indeed probably, they will not.

Another Huxley, Thomas's grandson Julian,[11] spoke for this position, using as an example—yes, you guessed it—the ubiquitous ichneumons:

> Natural selection, in fact, though like the mills of God in grinding slowly and grinding small, has few other attributes that a civilized religion would call divine.

---

[9] Joseph Hooker (1817–1911), an English botanist who encouraged Darwin to publish *On the Origin of Species*.

[10] Thomas Henry Huxley (1825–1895), a famous English naturalist.

[11] Julian Huxley (1887–1975), an English biologist.

. . . Its products are just as likely to be aesthetically, morally, or intellectually repulsive to us as they are to be attractive. We need only think of the ugliness of
Sacculina or a bladderworm, the stupidity of a rhinoceros or a stegosaur, the horror of a female mantis devouring its mate or a brood of ichneumon flies slowly eating out a caterpillar.

It is amusing in this context, or rather ironic since it is too serious to be amusing, that modern creationists accuse evolutionists of preaching a specific ethical doctrine called secular
humanism and thereby demand equal time for their unscientific and discredited views. If
nature is nonmoral, then evolution cannot teach any ethical theory at all. The assumption
that it can has abetted a panoply of social evils that ideologues falsely read into nature from
their beliefs—eugenics[12] and (misnamed) social Darwinism[13] prominently among them.
Not only did Darwin eschew any attempt to discover an antireligious ethic in nature, he also
expressly stated his personal bewilderment about such deep issues as the problem of evil.
Just a few sentences after invoking the ichneumons, and in words that express both the
modesty of this splendid man and the compatibility, through lack of contact, between science and true religion, Darwin wrote to Asa Gray,

I feel most deeply that the whole subject is too profound for the human intellect.
A dog might as well speculate on the mind of Newton. Let each man hope and believe what he can.

■ EXPLORATIONS OF THE TEXT

1. Butler says that she is surprised that some readers consider "Bloodchild" to be about
   slavery. Do you think it is? Why, or why not? When read in tandem with Gould's "Nonmoral Nature," does slavery seem more or less likely to be the topic?
2. According to Gould, "[N]othing evokes greater disgust in most of us than slow destruction of a host by an internal parasite." Why might Butler have created her aliens in a
   form that would most "disgust" her readers? Does William Butler Yeats's sphinx seem
   more or less troubling than Butler's aliens? Why?
3. In Butler's "Bloodchild," T'Gatoi tells Gan that humans fled Earth to avoid being killed
   or enslaved by other humans. Gould compares the ichneumon wasp's method of ensur-
   ing the larva's survival to the human act of drawing and quartering other humans. Yeats
   predicts a grim future because of the inability of humans to act appropriately. How
   does knowing these details about human behavior affect your interpretation of these
   works?
4. In Butler's "Bloodchild," the society of Terrans and Tlics is seen by Qui to be a confining
   and negative place and by Gan as a community in which each species serves the other.
   Which do you think is most true, or are both perspectives valid? Why? Do you find
   similar ambiguity in Gould's essay or Yeats's poem? Why do you think some writers
   choose to be ambiguous?
5. In "The Second Coming," William Butler Yeats writes of humans: "The best lack all
   conviction, while the worst/Are full of passionate intensity." Do you find this to be true

---

[12] The science of improving the world by selectively breeding humans for certain genetic traits, such as intelligence or health.

[13] Applying Darwin's theories of evolution to social relationships.

of the humans portrayed in Butler's "Bloodchild" or quoted in Gould's "Nonmoral Nature"? Do you find these qualities to be purely negative? Why, or why not?

■ THE READING/WRITING CONNECTION

1. Freewrite: How does an examination of nonhuman—alien or insect or other—behavior help the reader to better understand human behavior? Why might this indirect approach to examining human issues be more effective than a direct approach?
2. "Think" Topic: Explore Gould's description of the nineteenth-century contention that animals cannot feel pain. Relate this to the attitudes of the humans toward the child in Le Guin's "The Ones Who Walk Away From Omelas" or to the treatment of Blue in Walker's essay.
3. If you were writing a science-fiction story, what Earth creature would your aliens resemble? Why? Write an outline for a science fiction story.

■ IDEAS FOR WRITING

1. In "Nonmoral Nature," Gould explains that nature is not moral and that animals have evolved certain behaviors simply to survive. Relate this idea to the society of Terrans and Tlics described by Butler or to Yeats's poem.
1. Butler says that she wrote "Bloodchild" as a "pregnant man story." List similarities between the birth process described in "Boodchild" and the human birth process, and then list differences. Explain whether you find it to be a successful male birth story. Why, or why not? If you were to write a story about a man giving birth, how would you do it?
3. Butler says that "Bloodchild" is, in part, a "love story between two very different beings."
   a. Is this a love story? Argue pro or con.
   b. Write a love poem from Gan to T'Gatoi, or vice versa. Then, write an essay exploring what the poem reveals about their relationship.
4. What critiques of contemporary societies are implied in Butler's and Gould's visions? Do you agree with their critiques?

■ FICTION ■

Ursula K. Le Guin

Ursula K. Le Guin (1929–) was born in Berkeley, California, and was educated at Radcliffe College (1951) and Columbia University, where she received an M.A. in French and Italian literature in 1952. She currently lives in Portland, Oregon. A prolific writer who has published more than sixty books, Le Guin began writing as a child. Her first novel to receive critical acclaim was The Left Hand of Darkness *(1969), which won the prestigious Hugo and Nebula Awards. She has since won numerous awards, most recently the Mythopoeic Fantasy Award, Adult Literature (finalist), World Fantasy Award in novel category, and Nebula Award nomination in novel category, all in 2002 for* The Other Wind; *the Nebula Award Grand Master, 2002; and the Hugo Award nomination in best novelette category, World Science Fiction Society, 2003, for "The Wild Girls." Le Guin's work is recognized for its important social messages, most recently in the wake of the 9/11 terrorist attack.*

1973

THE ONES WHO WALK AWAY FROM OMELAS
(Variations on a Theme by William James)[1]

With a clamor of bells that set the swallows soaring, the Festival of Summer came to the city Omelas, bright-towered by the sea. The rigging of the boats in harbor sparkled with flags. In the streets between houses with red roofs and painted walls, between old moss-grown gardens and under avenues of trees, past great parks and public buildings, processions moved. Some were decorous: old people in long stiff robes of mauve and grey, grave master workmen, quiet, merry women carrying their babies and chatting as they walked. In other streets, the music beat faster, a shimmering of gong and tambourine, and the people went dancing, the procession was a dance. Children dodged in and out, their high calls rising like the swallows' crossing flights over the music and the singing., All the processions wound towards the north side of the city, where on the great water-meadow called the Green Fields boys and girls, naked in the bright air, with mud-stained feet and ankles and long, lithe arms, exercised their restive horses before the race. The horses wore no gear at all but a halter without bit. Their manes were braided with streamers of silver, gold, and green. They flared their nostrils and pranced and boasted to one another; they were vastly excited, the horse being the only animal who has adopted our ceremonies as his own. Far off to the north and west the mountains stood up half encircling Omelas on her bay. The air of morning was so clear that the snow still crowning the Eighteen Peaks burned with white-gold fire across the miles of sunlit air, under the dark blue of the sky. There was just enough wind to make the banners that marked the racecourse snap and flutter now and then. In the silence of the broad green meadows one could hear the music winding through the city streets, farther and nearer and ever approaching, a cheerful faint sweetness of the air that from time to time trembled and gathered together and broke out into the great joyous clanging of the bells.

Joyous! How is one to tell about joy? How describe the citizens of Omelas?

They were not simple folk, you see, though they were happy. But we do not say the words of cheer much any more. All smiles have become archaic. Given a description such as this one tends to make certain assumptions. Given a description such as this one tends to look next for the King, mounted on a splendid stallion and surrounded by his noble knights, or perhaps in a golden litter borne by great-muscled slaves. But there was no king. They did not use swords, or keep slaves. They were not barbarians. I do not know the rules and laws of their society, but I suspect that they were singularly few. As they did without monarchy and slavery, so they also got on without the stock exchange, the advertisement, the secret police, and the bomb. Yet I repeat that these were not simple folk, not dulcet shepherds, noble savages, bland utopians. They were not less complex than us. The trouble is that we have a bad habit, encouraged by pedants and sophisticates, of considering happiness as something rather stupid. Only pain is intellectual, only evil interesting. This is the treason of the artist: a refusal to admit the banality of evil and the terrible boredom of pain. If you can't lick 'em, join 'em. If it hurts, repeat it. But to praise despair is to condemn delight, to embrace violence is to lose hold of everything else. We have almost lost hold, we can no longer describe a happy man, nor make any celebration of joy. How can I tell you about the people of Omelas? They were not naïve and happy children—though their children were, in fact, happy. They were mature, intelligent, passionate adults whose lives were not wretched. O miracle! but I wish I could describe it better. I wish I could convince you. Omelas sounds in my words like a city in a fairy tale, long ago and far away, once upon a

---

[1] American philosopher and experimental psychologist (1842–1910).

time. Perhaps it would be best if you imagined it as your own fancy bids, assuming it will rise to the occasion, for certainly I cannot suit you all. For instance, how about technology? I think that there would be no cars or helicopters in and above the streets; this follows from the fact that the people of Omelas are happy people. Happiness is based on a just discrimination of what is necessary, what is neither necessary nor destructive, and what is destructive. In the middle category, however—that of the unnecessary but undestructive, that of comfort, luxury, exuberance, etc.—they could perfectly well have central heating, subway trains, washing machines, and all kinds of marvelous devices not yet invented here, floating light-sources, fuelless power, a cure for the common cold. Or they could have none of that: it doesn't matter. As you like it. I incline to think that people from towns up and down the coast have been coming in to Omelas during the last days before the Festival on very fast little trains and double-decked trams, and that the train station of Omelas is actually the handsomest building in town, though plainer than the magnificent Farmers' Market. But even granted trains, I fear that Omelas so far strikes some of you as goody-goody. Smiles, bells, parades, horses, bleh. If so, please add an orgy. If an orgy would help, don't hesitate. Let us not, however, have temples from which issue beautiful nude priests and priestesses already half in ecstasy and ready to copulate with any man or woman, lover or stranger, who desires union with the deep godhead of the blood, although that was my first idea. But really it would be better not to have any temples in Omelas—at least, not manned temples. Religion yes, clergy no. Surely the beautiful nudes can just wander about, offering themselves like divine soufflés to the hunger of the needy and the rapture of the flesh. Let them join the processions. Let tambourines be struck above the copulations, and the glory of desire be proclaimed upon the gongs, and (a not unimportant point) let the offspring of these delightful rituals be beloved and looked after by all. One thing I know there is none of in Omelas is guilt. But what else should there be? I thought at first there were no drugs, but that is puritanical. For those who like it, the faint insistent sweetness of *drooz* may perfume the ways of the city, *drooz* which first brings a great lightness and brilliance to the mind and limbs, and then after some hours a dreamy languor, and wonderful visions at last of the very arcana and inmost secrets of the Universe, as well as exciting the pleasure of sex beyond all belief; and it is not habit-forming. For more modest tastes I think there ought to be beer. What else, what else belongs in the joyous city? The sense of victory, surely, the celebration of courage. But as we did without clergy, let us do without soldiers. The joy built upon successful slaughter is not the right kind of joy; it will not do; it is fearful and it is trivial. A boundless and generous contentment, a magnanimous triumph felt not against some outer enemy but in communion with the finest and fairest in the souls of all men everywhere and the splendor of the world's summer: this is what swells the hearts of the people of Omelas, and the victory they celebrate is that of life. I really don't think many of them need to take *drooz*.

Most of the procession have reached the Green Fields by now. A marvelous smell of cooking goes forth from the red and blue tents of the provisioners. The faces of small children are amiably sticky; in the benign grey beard of a man a couple of crumbs of rich pastry are entangled. The youths and girls have mounted their horses and are beginning to group around the starting line after the course. An old woman, small, fat, and laughing, is passing out flowers from a basket, and tall young men wear her flowers in their shining hair. A child of nine or ten sits at the edge of die crowd, alone, playing on a wooden flute. People pause to listen, and they smile, but they do not speak to him, for he never ceases playing and never sees them, his dark eyes wholly rapt in the sweet, thin magic of the tune.

5   He finishes, and slowly lowers his hands holding the wooden flute.

As if that little private silence were the signal, all at once a trumpet sounds from the pavilion near the starting line: imperious, melancholy, piercing. The horses rear on their slender legs, and some of them neigh in answer. Sober-faced, the young riders stroke the horses' necks and soothe them, whispering. "Quiet, quiet, there my beauty, my hope. . . ." They begin to form in rank along the starting line. The crowds along the racecourse are like a field of grass and flowers in the wind. The Festival of Summer has begun.

Do you believe? Do you accept the festival, the city, the joy? No? Then let me describe one more thing.

In a basement under one of the beautiful public buildings of Omelas, or perhaps in the cellar of one of its more spacious private homes, there is a room. It has one locked door, and no window. A little light seeps in dustily between cracks in the boards, secondhand from a cobwebbed window somewhere across the cellar. In one corner of the little room a couple of mops, with stiff, clotted, foul-smelling heads, stand near a rusty bucket. The floor is dirt, a little damp to the touch, as cellar dirt usually is. The room is about three paces long and two wide: a mere broom closet or disused tool room. In the room a child is sitting. It could be a boy or a girl. It looks about six, but actually is nearly ten. It is feeble-minded. Perhaps it was born defective, or perhaps it has become imbecile through fear, malnutrition, and neglect. It picks its nose and occasionally fumbles vaguely with its toes or genitals, as it sits hunched in the corner farthest from the bucket and the two mops. It is afraid of the mops. It finds them horrible. It shuts its eyes, but it knows the mops are still standing there; and the door is locked; and nobody will come. The door is always locked; and nobody ever comes, except that sometimes—the child has no understanding of time or interval—sometimes the door rattles terribly and opens, and a person, or several people, are there. One of them may come in and kick the child to make it stand up. The others never come close, but peer in at it with frightened, disgusted eyes. The food bowl and the water jug are hastily filled, the door is locked, the eyes disappear. The people at the door never say anything, but the child, who has not always lived in the tool room, and can remember sunlight and its mother's voice, some- times speaks, "I will be good," it says. "Please let me out. I will be good!" They never answer. The child used to scream for help at night, and cry a good deal, but now it only makes a kind of whining, "eh-haa, eh-haa," and it speaks less and less often. It is so thin there are no calves to its legs; its belly protrudes; it lives on a half-bowl of corn meal and grease a day. It is naked. Its buttocks and thighs are a mass of festered sores, as it sits in its own excrement continually.

They all know it is there, all the people of Omelas. Some of them have come to see it, others are content merely to know it is there. They all know that it has to be there. Some of them understand why, and some do not, but they all understand that their happiness, the beauty of their city, the tenderness of their friendships, the health of their children, the wis- dom of their scholars, the skill of their makers, even the abundance of their harvest and the kindly weathers of their skies, depend wholly on this child's abominable misery.

10   This is usually explained to children when they are between eight and twelve, when- ever they seem capable of understanding; and most of those who come to see the child are young people, though often enough an adult comes, or comes back, to see the child. No matter how well the matter has been explained to them, these young spectators are always shocked and sickened at the sight. They feel disgust, which they had thought themselves superior to. They feel anger, outrage, impotence, despite all the explanations. They would like to do something for the child. But there is nothing they can do. If the child were brought up into the sunlight out of the vile place, if it were cleaned and fed and comforted, that would be a good thing, indeed; but if it were done, in that day and hour all the pros- perity and beauty and delight of Omelas would wither and be destroyed. Those are the terms. To exchange all the goodness and grace of every life in Omelas for that single, small improvement: to throw away the happiness of thousands for the chance of the happiness of one: that would be to let guilt within the walls indeed.

The terms are strict and absolute; there may not even be a kind word spoken to the child.

Often the young people go home in tears, or in a tearless rage, when they have seen the child and faced this terrible paradox. They may brood over it for weeks or years. But as time goes on they begin to realize that even if the child could be released, it would not get much good of its freedom: a little vague pleasure of warmth and food, no doubt, but little more. It is too degraded and imbecile to know any real joy. It has been afraid too long ever to be free of fear. Its habits are too uncouth for it to respond to humane treatment. Indeed, after so long it would probably be wretched without walls about it to protect it, and darkness for its eyes, and its own excrement to sit in. Their tears at the bitter injustice dry when they begin to perceive the terrible justice of reality, and to accept it. Yet it is their tears and anger, the trying of their generosity and the acceptance of their helplessness, which are perhaps the true source of the splendor of their lives. Theirs is no vapid, irresponsible happiness. They know that they, like the child, are not free. They know compassion. It is the existence of the child, and their knowledge of its existence, that makes possible the nobility of their architecture, the poignancy of their music, the profundity of their science. It is because of the child that they are so gentle with children. They know that if the wretched one were not there snivelling in the dark, the other one, the flute-player, could make no joyful music as the young riders line up in their beauty for the race in the sunlight of the first morning of summer.

Now do you believe in them? Are they not more credible? But there is one more thing to tell, and this is quite incredible.

At times one of the adolescent girls or boys who go to see the child does not go home to weep or rage, does not, in fact, go home at all. Sometimes also a man or woman much older falls silent for a day or two, and then leaves home. These people go out into the street, and walk down the street alone. They keep walking, and walk straight out of the city of Omelas, through the beautiful gates. They keep walking across the farmlands of Omelas. Each one goes alone, youth or girl, man or woman. Night falls; the traveler must pass down village streets between the houses with yellow-lit windows, and on out into the darkness of the fields. Each alone, they go west or north, towards the mountains. They go on. They leave Omelas, they walk ahead into the darkness, and they do not come back. The place they go towards is a place even less imaginable to most of us than the city of happiness. I cannot describe it at all. It is possible that it does not exist. But they seem to know where they are going, the ones who walk away from Omelas.

▪ EXPLORATIONS OF THE TEXT

1. How does the Festival of Summer set the stage for the narrative? What are its mythic implications?
2. Analyze the narrator's persona. Who do you imagine him/her to be?
3. Explore the symbolism of the flute player. What does he represent?
4. Analyze the character of the adult townspeople, the children, and the ones "who walk away from Omelas." How do they differ from each other? Why does the narrator state the following: "One thing I know there is none of in Omelas is guilt"?
5. What function does the "child" serve in the society? Why is her presence necessary to the survival of the town?
6. Le Guin's story often is classified as a parable (see glossary). What vision of morality and of human nature does it convey?
7. Compare the treatment of themes of obedience and conformity in this work and in Vonnegut's "Harrison Bergeron."

▪ THE READING/WRITING CONNECTION

1. How does this story portray "the banality of evil"? What characterizes the townspeople's behavior? In a journal entry, respond to these questions.

2. Freewrite in answer to this statement: There are others in global history who "walk away from Omelas." Who are they? What have they done?

3. Write a monologue in the voice of the child, a visitor to the town, another young child, or an adult member of the community.

■ IDEAS FOR WRITING

1. Write a parable, science-fiction narrative, or children's story that conveys a truth of human nature, and then interpret your work.

2. Write a conversation about the nature of evil among the following: the narrator in this work, Harrison Bergeron in Vonnegut's "Harrison Bergeron," Hally in Fugol's *"Master Harold" . . . and the Boys,* Elie Wiesel in "Why I Write: Making No Become Yes" (chapter 7), and Rose-Johnny in "Rose-Johnny" (chapter 4).

3. Find Shirley Jackson's "The Lottery" in a short-story anthology. (It is a frequently anthologized work.) Compare the treatment of obedience and conformity in Le Guin's work with that of Jackson's.

Kurt Vonnegut, Jr.

Kurt Vonnegut, Jr. (1922–   ), born in Indianapolis, Indiana, enlisted in the U.S. Army in World War II and was captured by the Germans in 1944. He survived the Allied firebombing of Dresden, after which he and his fellow prisoners were given the task of searching for corpses. This experience was the source for his best-known novel, Slaughterhouse Five *(1969). His other novels include* Cat's Cradle *(1963),* Galapagos *(1985), and* Timequake *(1997), and his short stories are collected in* Canary in a Cathouse *(1961),* Welcome to the Monkey House *(1968),* Bagombo Snuff Box *(1999), and* God Bless You, Dr. Kevorkian *(2000).*

1968

HARRISON BERGERON

The year was 2081, and everybody was finally equal. They weren't only equal before God and the law. They were equal every which way. Nobody was smarter than anybody else. Nobody was better looking than anybody else. Nobody was stronger or quicker than anybody else. All this equality was due to the 211th, 212th, and 213th Amendments to the Constitution, and to the unceasing vigilance of agents of the United States Handicapper General.

Some things about living still weren't quite right, though. April, for instance, still drove people crazy by not being springtime. And it was in that clammy month that the H-G men took George and Hazel Bergeron's fourteen-year-old son, Harrison, away.

It was tragic, all right, but George and Hazel couldn't think about it very hard. Hazel had a perfectly average intelligence, which meant she couldn't think about anything except in short bursts. And George, while his intelligence was way above normal, had a little mental handicap radio in his ear. He was required by law to wear it at all times. It was tuned to a government transmitter. Every twenty seconds or so, the transmitter would send out some sharp noise to keep people like George from taking unfair advantage of their brains.

George and Hazel were watching television. There were tears on Hazel's cheeks, but she'd forgotten for the moment what they were about.

5   On the television screen were ballerinas.

A buzzer sounded in George's head. His thoughts fled in panic, like bandits from a burglar alarm.

"That was a real pretty dance, that dance they just did," said Hazel.

"Huh?" said George.

"That dance—it was nice," said Hazel.

10   "Yup," said George. He tried to think a little about the ballerinas. They weren't really very good—no better than anybody else would have been, anyway. They were burdened with sashweights and bags of birdshot, and their faces were masked, so that no one, seeing a free and graceful gesture or a pretty face, would feel like something the cat drug in. George was toying with the vague notion that maybe dancers shouldn't be handicapped. But he didn't get very far with it before another noise in his ear radio scattered his thoughts.

George winced. So did two out of the eight ballerinas.

Hazel saw him wince. Having no mental handicap herself, she had to ask George what the latest sound had been.

"Sounded like somebody hitting a milk bottle with a ball peen hammer," said George.

"I'd think it would be real interesting, hearing all the different sounds," said Hazel, a little envious. "All the things they think up."

15   "Um," said George.

"Only, if I was Handicapper General, you know what I would do?" said Hazel. Hazel, as a matter of fact, bore a strong resemblance to the Handicapper General, a woman named Diana Moon Glampers. "If I was Diana Moon Glampers," said Hazel, "I'd have chimes on Sunday—just chimes. Kind of in honor of religion."

"I could think, if it was just chimes," said George.

"Well—maybe make 'em real loud," said Hazel. "I think I'd make a good Handicapper General."

"Good as anybody else," said George.

20   "Who knows better'n I do what normal is?" said Hazel.

"Right," said George. He began to think glimmeringly about his abnormal son who was now in jail, about Harrison, but a twenty-one-gun salute in his head stopped that.

"Boy!" said Hazel, "that was a doozy, wasn't it?"

It was such a doozy that George was white and trembling, and tears stood on the rims of his red eyes. Two of the eight ballerinas had collapsed to the studio floor, were holding their temples.

"All of a sudden you look so tired," said Hazel. "Why don't you stretch out on the sofa, so's you can rest your handicap bag on the pillows, honeybunch." She was referring to the forty-seven pounds of birdshot in a canvas bag, which was padlocked around George's neck. "Go on and rest the bag for a little while," she said. "I don't care if you're not equal to me for a while."

25   George weighed the bag with his hands. "I don't mind it," he said. "I don't notice it any more. It's just a part of me."

"You been so tired lately—kind of wore out," said Hazel. "If there was just some way we could make a little hole in the bottom of the bag, and just take out a few of them lead balls. Just a few."

"Two years in prison and two thousand dollars fine for every ball I took out," said George. "I don't call that a bargain."

"If you could just take a few out when you came home from work," said Hazel. "I mean—you don't compete with anybody around here. You just set around."

"If I tried to get away with it," said George, "then other people'd get away with it—and pretty soon we'd be right back to the dark ages again, with everybody competing against everybody else. You wouldn't like that, would you?"

30   "I'd hate it," said Hazel.

"There you are," said George. "The minute people start cheating on laws, what do you think happens to society?"

If Hazel hadn't been able to come up with an answer to this question, George couldn't have supplied one. A siren was going off in his head.

"Reckon it'd fall all apart," said Hazel.

"What would?" said George blankly.

35 "Society," said Hazel uncertainly. "Wasn't that what you just said?"

"Who knows?" said George.

The television program was suddenly interrupted for a news bulletin. It wasn't clear at first as to what the bulletin was about, since the announcer, like all announcers, had a serious speech impediment. For about half a minute, and in a state of high excitement, the announcer tried to say, "Ladies and gentlemen—"

He finally gave up, handed the bulletin to a ballerina to read.

"That's all right—" Hazel said of the announcer, "he tried. That's the big thing. He tried to do the best he could with what God gave him. He should get a nice raise for trying so hard."

40 "Ladies and gentlemen—" said the ballerina, reading the bulletin. She must have been extraordinarily beautiful, because the mask she wore was hideous. And it was easy to see that she was the strongest and most graceful of all the dancers, for her handicap bags were as big as those worn by two-hundred-pound men.

And she had to apologize at once for her voice, which was a very unfair voice for a woman to use. Her voice was a warm, luminous, timeless melody. "Excuse me—" she said, and she began again, making her voice absolutely uncompetitive.

"Harrison Bergeron, age fourteen," she said in a grackle squawk, "has just escaped from jail, where he was held on suspicion of plotting to overthrow the government. He is a genius and an athlete, is under-handicapped, and should be regarded as extremely dangerous."

A police photograph of Harrison Bergeron was flashed on the screen upside down, then sideways, upside down again, then right side up. The picture showed the full length of Harrison against a background calibrated in feet and inches. He was exactly seven feet tall.

The rest of Harrison's appearance was Halloween and hardware. Nobody had ever borne heavier handicaps. He had outgrown hindrances faster than the H-G men could think them up. Instead of a little ear radio for a mental handicap, he wore a tremendous pair of earphones, and spectacles with thick wavy lenses. The spectacles were intended to make him not only half blind, but to give him whanging headaches besides.

45 Scrap metal was hung all over him. Ordinarily, there was a certain symmetry, a military neatness to the handicaps issued to strong people, but Harrison looked like a walking junkyard. In the race of life, Harrison carried three hundred pounds.

And to offset his good looks, the H-G men required that he wear at all times a red rubber ball for a nose, keep his eyebrows shaved off, and cover his even white teeth with black caps at snaggle-tooth random.

"If you see this boy," said the ballerina, "do not—I repeat, do not—try to reason with him."

There was the shriek of a door being torn from its hinges.

Screams and barking cries of consternation came from the television set. The photograph of Harrison Bergeron on the screen jumped again and again, as though dancing to the tune of an earthquake.

50 George Bergeron correctly identified the earthquake, and well he might have—for many was the time his own home had danced to the same crashing tune. "My God—" said George, "that must be Harrison!"

The realization was blasted from his mind instantly by the sound of an automobile collision in his head.

When George could open his eyes again, the photograph of Harrison was gone. A living, breathing Harrison filled the screen.

Clanking, clownish, and huge, Harrison stood in the center of the studio. The knob of the uprooted studio door was still in his hand. Ballerinas, technicians, musicians, and announcers cowered on their knees before him, expecting to die.

"I am the Emperor!" cried Harrison. "Do you hear? I am the Emperor! Everybody must do what I say at once!" He stamped his foot and the studio shook.

55 "Even as I stand here—" he bellowed, "crippled, hobbled, sickened—I am a greater ruler than any man who ever lived! Now watch me become what I *can* become!"

Harrison tore the straps of his handicap harness like wet tissue paper, tore straps guaranteed to support five thousand pounds.

Harrison's scrap-iron handicaps crashed to the floor.

Harrison thrust his thumbs under the bar of the padlock that secured his head harness. The bar snapped like celery. Harrison smashed his headphones and spectacles against the wall.

He flung away his rubber-ball nose, revealed a man that would have awed Thor, the god of thunder.

60 "I shall now select my Empress!" he said, looking down on the cowering people. "Let the first woman who dares rise to her feet claim her mate and her throne!"

A moment passed, and then a ballerina arose, swaying like a willow.

Harrison plucked the mental handicap from her ear, snapped off her physical handicaps with marvelous delicacy. Last of all, he removed her mask.

She was blindingly beautiful.

"Now—" said Harrison, taking her hand, "shall we show the people the meaning of the word dance? Music!" he commanded.

65 The musicians scrambled back into their chairs, and Harrison stripped them of their handicaps, too. "Play your best," he told them, "and I'll make you barons and dukes and earls."

The music began. It was normal at first—cheap, silly, false. But Harrison snatched two musicians from their chairs, waved them like batons as he sang the music as he wanted it played. He slammed them back into their chairs.

The music began again and was much improved.

Harrison and his Empress merely listened to the music for a while—listened gravely, as though synchronizing their heartbeats with it.

They shifted their weights to their toes.

70 Harrison placed his big hands on the girl's tiny waist, letting her sense the weightlessness that would soon be hers.

And then, in an explosion of joy and grace, into the air they sprang!

Not only were the laws of the land abandoned, but the law of gravity and the laws of motion as well.

They reeled, whirled, swiveled, flounced, capered, gamboled, and spun.

They leaped like deer on the moon.

75 The studio ceiling was thirty feet high, but each leap brought the dancers nearer to it. It became their obvious intention to kiss the ceiling.

They kissed it.

And then, neutralizing gravity with love and pure will, they remained suspended in air inches below the ceiling, and they kissed each other for a long, long time.

It was then that Diana Moon Glampers, the Handicapper General, came into the studio with a double-barreled ten-gauge shotgun. She fired twice, and the Emperor and the Empress were dead before they hit the floor.

80 Diana Moon Glampers loaded the gun again. She aimed it at the musicians and told them they had ten seconds to get their handicaps back on.

It was then that the Bergerons' television tube burned out.

Hazel turned to comment about the blackout to George. But George had gone out into the kitchen for a can of beer.

George came back in with the beer, paused while a handicap signal shook him up. And then he sat down again. "You been crying?" he said to Hazel.

"Yup," she said.

85 "What about?" he said.

"I forget," she said. "Something real sad on television."

"What was it?" he said.

"It's all kind of mixed up in my mind," said Hazel.

"Forget sad things," said George.

90 "I always do," said Hazel.

"That's my girl," said George. He winced. There was the sound of a rivetting gun in his head.

"Gee—I could tell that one was a doozy," said Hazel.

"You can say that again," said George.

"Gee—" said Hazel, "I could tell that one was a doozy."

■ EXPLORATIONS OF THE TEXT

1. React to the first paragraph. What associations does the concept of "equality" evoke?
2. Why do people in the story have "handicaps"?
3. Contrast Hazel and George. Why does George's "mental handicap radio" make noise?
4. Analyze Harrison's appearance, character, behavior, and rebellion. Why is he depicted as a fourteen-year-old? Why is Harrison dangerous?
5. Explain the conclusion of the story. Is it **ironic?**
6. Evaluate the **satire** and humor in the story.
7. Why does Vonnegut create a series of short paragraphs to depict Harrison's and the ballerina's dance? What is the effect of this technique?
8. Discuss the world of 2081. What are its collective values? In what ways does Vonnegut criticize North American society and its values?

■ THE READING/WRITING CONNECTION

1. "Think" Topic: React to Vonnegut's vision of equality.
2. Begin a journal entry: "It was 2081 and. . . ." Freewrite. (Imagine that you are a character in a place.)
3. Write a monologue in Diana Moon Glampers's or in Harrison's voice.

■ IDEAS FOR WRITING

1. What critique of North American society is presented?
2. Compare this story's view of individuality with the view of identity in "To live in the Borderlands means you."

CHINUA ACHEBE

"Your personal god fights for you": these words translate the name of Chinua Achebe, born Albert Chinwalumogo Achebe (1930–) in Ogide, Nigeria. In writing about the clash between cultures and the quest for independence, Achebe has celebrated the spirit of Africa by writing essays, children's books, poetry, short stories, and novels. His work includes novels (Things Fall Apart, 1958, which brought him immediate fame; No Longer at Ease, 1960; Anthills of the

Savannah, *1988; and* Home and Exile, *2000), short stories* (Girls at War, *1972), and poetry* (Beware, Soul Brother and Other Poems, *1971; and* Another Africa, *1997).*

1972

GIRLS AT WAR

The first time their paths crossed, nothing happened. That was in the first heady days of warlike preparation, when thousands of young men (and sometimes women, too) were daily turned away from enlistment centers because far too many of them were coming forward burning with readiness to bear arms in defense of the exciting new nation.[1]

The second time they met was at a checkpoint at Awka. Then the war had started and was slowly moving southwards from the distant northern sector. He was driving from Onitsha to Enugu and was in a hurry. Although intellectually he approved of thorough searches at roadblocks, emotionally he was always offended whenever he had to submit to them. He would probably not admit it but the feeling people got was that if you were put through a search then you could not really be one of the big people. Generally he got away without a search by pronouncing in his deep, authoritative voice: "Reginal Nwankwo, Ministry of Justice." That almost always did it. But sometimes either through ignorance or sheer cussedness the crowd at the odd checkpoint would refuse to be impressed. As happened now at Awka. Two constables carrying heavy Mark 4 rifles were watching distantly from the roadside, leaving the actual searching to local vigilantes.

"I am in a hurry," he said to the girl who now came up to his car. "My name is Reginald Nwankwo, Ministry of Justice."

"Good afternoon, sir. I want to see your boot."

5   "Oh Christ! What do you think is in the boot?"

"I don't know, sir."

He got out of the car in suppressed rage, stalked to the back, opened the boot, and holding the lid up with his left hand he motioned with the right as if to say: After you!

"Are you satisfied?" he demanded.

"Yes, sir. Can I see your pigeonhole?"

10   "Christ Almighty!"

"Sorry to delay you, sir. But you people gave us this job to do."

"Never mind. You are damn right. It's just that I happen to be in a hurry. But never mind. That's the glove box. Nothing there as you can see."

"All right, sir, close it." Then she opened the rear door and bent down to inspect under the seats. It was then he took the first real look at her, starting from behind. She was a beautiful girl in a breasty blue jersey, khaki jeans, and canvas shoes with the new-style hair plait which gave a girl a defiant look and which they called—for reasons of their own—"air force base"; and she looked vaguely familiar.

"I am all right, sir," she said at last, meaning she was through with her task. "You don't recognize me?"

15   "No. Should I?"

"You gave me a lift to Enugu that time I left my school to go and join the militia."

"Ah, yes, you were the girl. I told you, didn't I, to go back to school because girls were not required in the militia. What happened?"

---

[1] Nigeria became an independent nation in 1960. Later, civil unrest broke out between the Hausa and Igbo peoples, and the Igbos fled to the east, where they formed the independent nation of Biafra and seceded from Nigeria. The war lasted from 1967 to 1970, when the Biafrans surrendered.

"They told me to go back to my school or join the Red Cross."

"You see, I was right. So, what are you doing now?"

20 "Just patching up with Civil Defense."

"Well, good luck to you. Believe me, you are a great girl."

That was the day he finally believed there might be something in this talk about revolution. He had seen plenty of girls and women marching and demonstrating before now. But somehow he had never been able to give it much thought. He didn't doubt that the girls and the women took themselves seriously, they obviously did. But so did the little kids who marched up and down the streets at the time, drilling with sticks and wearing their mothers' soup bowls for steel helmets. The prime joke of the time among his friends was the contingent of girls from a local secondary school marching behind a banner: WE ARE IMPREGNABLE!

But after that encounter at the Awka checkpoint he simply could not sneer at the girls again, nor at the talk of revolution, for he had seen it in action in that young woman whose devotion had simply and without self-righteousness convicted him of gross levity. What were her words? We are doing the work you asked us to do. She wasn't going to make an exception even for one who once did her a favor. He was sure she would have searched her own father just as rigorously.

When their paths crossed a third time, at least eighteen months later, things had got very bad. Death and starvation, having long chased out the headiness of the early days, now left in some places blank resignation, in others a rock-like, even suicidal, defiance. But surprisingly enough there were many at this time who had no other desire than to corner whatever good things were still going and to enjoy themselves to the limit. For such people a strange normalcy had returned to the world. All those nervous checkpoints disappeared. Girls became girls once more and boys boys. It was a tight, blockaded, and desperate world but nonetheless a world—with some goodness and some badness and plenty of heroism, which, however, happened most times far, far below the eye level of the people in this story—in out-of-the-way refugee camps, in the damp tatters, in the hungry and barehanded courage of the first line of fire.

25 Reginald Nwankwo lived in Owerri then. But that day he had gone to Nkwerri in search of relief. He had got from Caritas in Owerri a few heads of stockfish, some tinned meat, and the dreadful American stuff called Formula Two, which he felt certain was some kind of animal feed. But he always had a vague suspicion that not being a Catholic put one at a disadvantage with Caritas. So he went now to see an old friend who ran the WCC depot at Nkwerri to get other items like rice, beans, and that excellent cereal commonly called *Gabon gari*.[2]

He left Owerri at six in the morning so as to catch his friend at the depot, where he was known never to linger beyond 8:30 for fear of air raids. Nwankwo was very fortunate that day. The depot had received on the previous day large supplies of new stock as a result of an unusual number of plane landings a few nights earlier. As his driver loaded tins and bags and cartons into his car the starved crowds that perpetually hung around relief centers made crude, ungracious remarks like "War Can Continue!" meaning the WCC! Somebody else shouted "*Irevolu!*" and his friends replied "*shum!*" "*Irevolu!*" "*shum!*" "*Isofeli?*" "*shum*" "*Isofeli?*" "*Mba!*"[3]

---

[2] **Gari** is a staple made from a starchy root that when cooked has the consistency of grits. During the civil war, when the Nigerian government imposed a food embargo on Biafra, relief supplies were flown in from Gabon. One supply, farina, was used as a substitute for gari, and hence was called Gabon gari.

[3] **Irevolu** and **shum** are a variation of *revolution*. **Isofeli** means "are you joining them (the revolutionaries) in the feast?" or are the poor people benefiting from the so-called revolution? The final response, "**Mba!**" means "No."

Nwankwo was deeply embarrassed not by the jeers of this scarecrow crowd of rags and floating ribs but by the independent accusation of their wasted bodies and sunken eyes. Indeed, he would probably have felt much worse had they said nothing, simply looked on in silence, as his boot was loaded with milk, and powdered egg and oats and tinned meat and stockfish. By nature such singular good fortune in the midst of a general desolation was certain to embarrass him. But what could a man do? He had a wife and four children living in the remote village of Ogbu and completely dependent on what relief he could find and send them. He couldn't abandon them to kwashiorkor. The best he could do—and did do, as a matter of fact—was to make sure that whenever he got sizable supplies like now he made over some of it to his driver, Johnson, with a wife and six, or was it seven, children and a salary of ten pounds a month when *gari* in the market was climbing to one pound per cigarette cup. In such a situation one could do nothing at all for crowds; at best one could try to be of some use to one's immediate neighbors. That was all.

On his way back to Owerri, a very attractive girl by the roadside waved for a lift. He ordered the driver to stop. Scores of pedestrians, dusty and exhausted, some military, some civilian, swooped down on the car from all directions.

"No, no, no," said Nwankwo firmly. "It's the young woman I stopped for. I have a bad tire and can only take one person. Sorry."

30   "My son, please," cried one old woman in despair, gripping the door handle.

"Old woman, you want to be killed?" shouted the driver as he pulled away, shaking her off. Nwankwo had already opened a book and sunk his eyes there.

For at least a mile after that he did not even look at the girl until she, finding, perhaps, the silence too heavy, said: "You've saved me today. Thank you."

"Not at all. Where are you going?"

"To Owerri. You don't recognize me?"

35   "Oh yes, of course. What a fool I am . . . You are . . ."

"Gladys."

"That's right, the militia girl. You've changed, Gladys. You were always beautiful, of course, but now you are a beauty queen. What do you do these days?"

"I am in the Fuel Directorate."

"That's wonderful."

40   It was wonderful, he thought, but even more it was tragic. She wore a high-tinted wig and a very expensive skirt and low-cut blouse. Her shoes, obviously from Gabon, must have cost a fortune. In short, thought Nwankwo, she had to be in the keep of some well-placed gentleman, one of those piling up money out of the war.

"I broke my rule today to give you a lift. I never give lifts these days."

"Why?"

"How many people can you carry? It is better not to try at all. Look at that old woman."

"I thought you would take her."

45   He said nothing to that and after another spell of silence Gladys thought maybe he was offended and so added: "Thank you for breaking your rule for me." She was scanning his face, turned slightly away.

He smiled, turned, and tapped her on the lap. "What are you going to Owerri to do?"

"I am going to visit my girlfriend."

"Girlfriend? You sure?"

"Why not? . . . If you drop me at her house you can see her. Only I pray God she hasn't gone on weekend today; it will be serious."

50   "Why?"

"Because if she is not at home I will sleep on the road today."

"I pray to God that she is not at home."

"Why?"

"Because if she is not at home I will offer you bed and breakfast . . . What is that? he asked the driver, who had brought the car to an abrupt stop. There was no need for an answer. The small crowd ahead was looking upwards. The three scrambled out of the car and stumbled for the bush, necks twisted in a backward search of the sky. But the alarm was false. The sky was silent and clear except for two high-flying vultures. A humorist in the crowd called them Fighter and Bomber and everyone laughed in relief. The three climbed into their car again and continued their journey.

55   "It is much too early for raids," he said to Gladys, who had both her palms on her breast as though to still a thumping heart. "They rarely come before ten o'clock."

But she remained tongue-tied from her recent fright. Nwankwo saw an opportunity there and took it at once.

"Where does your friend live?"

"250 Douglas Road."

"Ah; that's the very center of town—a terrible place. No bunkers, nothing. I won't advise you to go there before 6 p.m.; it's not safe. If you don't mind I will take you to my place, where there is a good bunker, and then as soon as it is safe, around six, I shall drive you to your friend. How's that?"

60   "It's all right," she said lifelessly. "I am so frightened of this thing. That's why I refused to work in Owerri. I don't even know who asked me to come out today."

"You'll be all right. We are used to it."

"But your family is not there with you?"

"No," he said. "Nobody has his family there. We like to say it is because of air raids but I can assure you there is more to it. Owerri is a real swinging place now, and we live the life of gay bachelors."

"That is what I have heard."

65   "You will not just hear it; you will see it today. I shall take you to a real swinging party. A friend of mine, a lieutenant colonel, is having a birthday party. He's hired the Sound Smashers to play. I'm sure you'll enjoy it."

He was immediately and thoroughly ashamed of himself. He hated the parties and frivolities to which his friends clung like drowning men. And to talk so approvingly of them because he wanted to take a girl home! And this particular girl, too, who had once had such beautiful faith in the struggle and was betrayed (no doubt about it) by some man like him out for a good time. He shook his head sadly.

"What is it?" asked Gladys.

"Nothing. Just my thoughts."

They made the rest of the journey to Owerri practically in silence.

70   She made herself at home very quickly as if she was a regular girlfriend of his. She changed into a housedress and put away her auburn wig.

"That is a lovely hairdo. Why do you hide it with a wig?"

"Thank you," she said, leaving his question unanswered for a while. Then she said: "Men are funny."

"Why do you say that?"

" 'Now you are a beauty queen,' " she mimicked.

75   "Oh, that! I meant every word of it." He pulled her to him and kissed her. She neither refused nor yielded fully, which he liked for a start. Too many girls were simply too easy those days. War sickness, some called it.

He drove off a little later to look in at the office and she busied herself in the kitchen helping his boy with lunch. It must have been literally a look-in, for he was back within half an hour, rubbing his hands and saying he could not stay away too long from his beauty queen.

As they sat down to lunch, she said: "You have nothing in your fridge."

"Like what?" he asked, half offended.

"Like meat," she replied, undaunted.

80 "Do you still eat meat?" he challenged.

"Who am I? But other big men like you eat."

"I don't know which big men you have in mind. But they are not like me. I don't make money trading with the enemy or selling relief or . . ."

"Augusta's boyfriend doesn't do that. He just gets foreign exchange."

"How does he get it? He swindles the government—that's how he gets foreign exchange, whoever he is. Who is Augusta, by the way?"

85 "My girlfriend."

"I see."

"She gave me three dollars last time which I changed to forty-five pounds. The man gave her fifty dollars."

"Well, my dear girl, I don't traffic in foreign exchange and I don't have meat in my fridge. We are fighting a war and I happen to know that some young boys at the front drink *gari* and water once in three days."

"It is true," she said simply. "Monkey de work, baboon de chop."

90 "It is not even that; it is worse," he said, his voice beginning to shake. "People are dying every day. As we talk now somebody is dying."

"It is true," she said again.

"Plane!" screamed his boy from the kitchen.

"My mother!" screamed Gladys. As they scuttled toward the bunker of palm stems and red earth, covering their heads with their hands and stooping slightly in their flight, the entire sky was exploding with the clamor of jets and the huge noise of homemade antiaircraft rockets.

Inside the bunker she clung to him even after the plane had gone and the guns, late to start and also to end, had all died down again.

95 "It was only passing," he told her, his voice a little shaky. "It didn't drop anything. From its direction I should say it was going to the war front. Perhaps our people are pressing them. That's what they always do. Whenever our boys press them, they send an SOS to the Russians and Egyptians to bring the planes." He drew a long breath.

She said nothing, just clung to him. They could hear his boy telling the servant from the next house that there were two of them and one dived like this and the other dived like that.

"I see dem well well," said the other with equal excitement. "If no to say de ting de kill porson e for sweet for eye. To God."

"Imagine!" said Gladys, finding her voice at last. She had a way, he thought, of conveying with a few words or even a single word whole layers of meanings. Now it was at once her astonishment as well as reproof, tinged perhaps with grudging admiration for people who could be so lighthearted about these bringers of death.

"Don't be so scared," he said. She moved closer and he began to kiss her and squeeze her breasts. She yielded more and more and then fully. The bunker was dark and unswept and might harbor crawling things. He thought of bringing a mat from the main house but reluctantly decided against it. Another plane might pass and send a neighbor or simply a chance passerby crashing into them. That would be only slightly better than a certain gentleman in another air raid who was seen in broad daylight fleeing his bedroom for his bunker stark-naked, pursued by a woman in a similar state!

100 Just as Gladys had feared, her friend was not in town. It would seem her powerful boyfriend had wangled for her a flight to Libreville to shop. So her neighbors thought, anyway.

"Great!" said Nwankwo as they drove away. "She will come back on an arms plane loaded with shoes, wigs, pants, bras, cosmetics, and what have you, which she will then sell and make thousands of pounds. You girls are really at war, aren't you?"

She said nothing and he thought he had got through at last to her. Then suddenly she said, "That is what you men want us to do."

"Well," he said, "here is one man who doesn't want you to do that. Do you remember that girl in khaki jeans who searched me without mercy at the checkpoint?"

She began to laugh.

105 That is the girl I want you to become again. Do you remember her? No wig. I don't even think she had any earrings . . ."

"Ah, na lie-o. I had earrings."

"All right. But you know what I mean."

"That time done pass. Now everybody want survival. They call it number six. You put your number six; I put my number six. Everything all right."

The lieutenant colonel's party turned into something quite unexpected. But before it did, things had been going well enough. There was goat meat, some chicken and rice, and plenty of homemade spirits. There was one fiery brand nicknamed "tracer" which indeed sent a flame down your gullet. The funny things was, looked at in the bottle, it had the innocent appearance of an orange drink. But the thing that caused the greatest stir was the bread—one little roll for each person! It was the size of a golf ball and about the same consistency, too! But it was real bread. The band was good, too, and there were many girls. And to improve matters even further two white Red Cross people soon arrived with a bottle of Courvoisier and a bottle of Scotch! The party gave them a standing ovation and then scrambled to get a drop. It soon turned out from his general behavior, however, that one of the white men had probably drunk too much already. And the reason, it would seem, was that a pilot we knew well had been killed in a crash at the airport the night before, flying in relief in awful weather.

110 Few people at the party had heard of the crash by then. So there was an immediate damping of the air. Some dancing couples went back to their seats and the band stopped. Then for some strange reason the drunken Red Cross man just exploded.

"Why should a man, a decent man, throw away his life. For nothing! Charley didn't need to die. Not for this stinking place. Yes, everything stinks here. Even these girls who come here all dolled up and smiling, what are they worth? Don't I know? A head of stockfish, that's all, or one American dollar and they are ready to tumble into bed."

In the threatening silence following the explosion one of the young officers walked up to him and gave him three thundering slaps—right! left! right!—pulled him up from his seat and (there were things like tears in his eyes) shoved him outside. His friend, who had tried in vain to shut him up, followed him out and the silenced party heard them drive off. The officer who did the job returned, dusting his palms.

"Fucking beast!" said he with an impressive coolness. And all the girls showed with their eyes that they rated him a man and a hero.

"Do you know him?" Gladys asked Nwankwo.

115 He didn't answer her. Instead, he spoke generally to the party. "The fellow was clearly drunk," he said.

"I don't care," said the officer. "It is when a man is drunk that he speaks what is on his mind."

"So you beat him for what was on his mind," said the host. "That is the spirit, Joe."

"Thank you, sir," said Joe, saluting.

"His name is Joe," Gladys and the girl on her left said in unison, turning to each other.

120   At the same time Nwankwo and a friend on the other side of him were saying quietly, very quietly, that although the man had been rude and offensive, what he had said about the girls was unfortunately the bitter truth, only he was the wrong man to say it.

When the dancing resumed Captain Joe came to Gladys for a dance. She sprang to her feet even before the word was out of his mouth. Then she remembered immediately and turned round to take permission from Nwankwo. At the same time the captain also turned to him and said "Excuse me."

"Go ahead," said Nwankwo, looking somewhere between the two.

It was a long dance and he followed them with his eyes without appearing to do so. Occasionally a relief plane passed overhead and somebody immediately switched off the lights, saying it might be the Intruder. But it was only an excuse to dance in the dark and make the girls giggle, for the sound of the Intruder was well known.

Gladys came back feeling very self-conscious and asked Nwankwo to dance with her. But he wouldn't. "Don't bother about me," he said. "I am enjoying myself perfectly sitting here and watching those of you who dance."

125   "Then let's go," she said, "if you won't dance."

"But I never dance, believe me. So please enjoy yourself."

She danced next with the lieutenant colonel and again with Captain Joe, and then Nwankwo agreed to take her home.

"I am sorry I didn't dance," he said as they drove away. "But I swore never to dance as long as this war lasts."

She said nothing.

130   "When I think of somebody like that pilot who got killed last night. And he had no hand whatever in the quarrel. All his concern was to bring us food . . ."

"I hope that his friend is not like him," said Gladys.

"The man was just upset by his friend's death. But what I am saying is that with people like that getting killed and our own boys suffering and dying at the war fronts I don't see why we should sit around throwing parties and dancing."

"You took me there," said she in final revolt. "They are your friends. I don't know them before."

"Look, my dear, I am not blaming you. I am merely telling you why I personally refuse to dance. Anyway, let's change the subject . . . Do you still say you want to go back tomorrow? My driver can take you early enough on Monday morning for you to go to work. No? All right, just as you wish. You are the boss."

135   She gave him a shock by the readiness with which she followed him to bed and by her language.

"You want to shell?" she asked. And without waiting for an answer said, "Go ahead but don't pour in troops!"

He didn't want to pour in troops either and so it was all right. But she wanted visual assurance and so he showed her.

One of the ingenious economies taught by the war was that a rubber condom could be used over and over again. All you had to was wash it out, dry it, and shake a lot of talcum powder over it to prevent its sticking; and it was as good as new. It had to be the real British thing, though, not some of the cheap stuff they brought in from Lisbon, which was about as strong as a dry *cocoyam* leaf in the *harmattan*.

He had his pleasure but wrote the girl off. He might just as well have slept with a prostitute, he thought. It was clear as daylight to him now that she was kept by some army officer. What a terrible transformation in the short period of less than two years! Wasn't it a miracle that she still had memories of the other life, that she even remembered her name? If the affair of the drunken Red Cross man should happen again now, he said to himself, he would stand up beside the fellow and tell the party that here was a man of truth. What terrible fate to befall a whole generation! The mothers of tomorrow!

140   By morning he was feeling a little better and more generous in his judgments. Gladys, he thought, was just a mirror reflecting a society that had gone completely rotten and maggoty at the center. The mirror itself was intact; a lot of smudge but no more. All that was needed was a clean duster. "I have a duty to her," he told himself, "the little girl that once revealed to me our situation. Now she is in danger, under some terrible influence."

He wanted to get to the bottom of this deadly influence. It was clearly not just her goodtime girlfriend, Augusta, or whatever her name was. There must be some man at the center of it, perhaps one of these heartless attack traders who traffic in foreign currencies and make their hundreds of thousands by sending young men to hazard their lives bartering looted goods for cigarettes behind enemy lines, or one of those contractors who receive piles of money daily for food they never deliver to the army. Or perhaps some vulgar and cowardly army officer full of filthy barrack talk and fictitious stories of heroism. He decided he had to find out. Last night he had thought of sending his driver alone to take her home. But no, he must go and see for himself where she lived. Something was bound to reveal itself there. Something on which he could anchor his rescue operation. As he prepared for the trip his feeling toward her softened with every passing minute. He assembled for her half of the food he had received at the relief center the day before. Difficult as things were, he thought, a girl who had something to eat would be spared, not all, but some of the temptation. He would arrange with his friend at the WCC to deliver something to her every fortnight.

Tears came to Gladys's eyes when she saw the gifts. Nwankwo didn't have too much cash on him but he got together twenty pounds and handed it over to her.

"I don't have foreign exchange, and I know this won't go far at all, but . . ."

She just came and threw herself at him, sobbing. He kissed her lips and eyes and mumbled something about victims of circumstances, which went over her head. In deference to him, he thought with exultation, she had put away her high-tinted wig in her bag.

145   "I want you to promise me something," he said.

"What?"

"Never use that expression about shelling again."

She smiled with tears in her eyes. "You don't like it? That's what all the girls call it."

"Well, you are different from all the girls. Will you promise?"

150   "O.K."

Naturally their departure had become a little delayed. And when they got into the car it refused to start. After poking around the engine the driver decided that the battery was flat. Nwankwo was aghast. He had that very week paid thirty-four pounds to change two of the cells and the mechanic who performed it had promised him six months' service. A new battery, which was then running at two hundred and fifty pounds, was simply out of the question. The driver must have been careless with something, he thought.

"It must be because of last night," said the driver.

"What happened last night?" asked Nwankwo sharply, wondering what insolence was on the way. But none was intended.

"Because we use the headlight."

155   "Am I supposed not to use my light, then? Go and get some people and try pushing it." He got out again with Gladys and returned to the house while the driver went over to neighboring houses to seek the help of other servants.

After at least half an hour of pushing it up and down the street, and a lot of noisy advice from the pushers, the car finally spluttered to life, shooting out enormous clouds of black smoke from the exhaust.

It was eight-thirty by his watch when they set out. A few miles away a disabled soldier waved for a lift.

"Stop!" screamed Nwankwo. The driver jammed his foot on the brakes and then turned his head toward his master in bewilderment.

"Don't you see the soldier waving? Reverse and pick him up!"

160 "Sorry, sir," said the driver. "I don't know Master want to pick him."

"If you don't know you should ask. Reverse back."

The soldier, a mere boy, in filthy khaki drenched in sweat, lacked his right leg from the knee down. He seemed not only grateful that a car should stop for him but greatly surprised. He first handed in his crude wooden crutches, which the driver arranged between the two front seats, then painfully he levered himself in.

"Thanks, sir," he said, turning to look at the back and completely out of breath.

"I am very grateful. Madame, thank you."

165 "The pleasure is ours," said Nwankwo. "Where did you get your wound?"

"At Azumini, sir. On tenth of January."

"Never mind. Everything will be all right. We are proud of you boys and will make sure you receive your due reward when it is all over."

"I pray God, sir."

They drove in silence for the next half hour or so. Then as the car sped down a slope toward a bridge somebody screamed—perhaps the driver, perhaps the solder—"They have come!" The screech of the brakes merged into the scream and the shattering of the sky overhead. The doors flew open even before the car had come to a stop and they were fleeing blindly to the bush. Gladys was a little ahead of Nwankwo when they heard through the drowning tumult the solder's voice crying: "Please come and open for me!" Vaguely he saw Gladys stop; he pushed past her, shouting to her at the same time to come on. Then a high whistle descended like a spear through the chaos and exploded in a vast noise and motion that smashed up everything. A tree he had embraced flung him through the bush. Then another terrible whistle starting high up and ending again in a monumental crash of the world; and then another, and Nwankwo heard no more.

170 He woke up to human noises and weeping and the smell and smoke of a charred world. He dragged himself up and staggered toward the source of the sounds.

From afar he saw his driver running toward him in tears and blood. He saw the remains of his car smoking and the entangled remains of the girl and the soldier. And he let out a piercing cry and fell down again.

■ EXPLORATIONS OF THE TEXT

1. What view do you gain of Nigeria's civil war (1967–70)?
2. Do you trust the narrator? Is he a reliable narrator? Analyze his character.
3. Analyze Glady's character. How has she changed in the years that the narrator has known her?
4. What is the purpose of the incident of the party? How does the scene reveal aspects of the narrator's and of Glady's characters?
5. Discuss the irony of the phrase, "deadly influence," and the ending.
6. Explore the theme of collision of worlds in this work and in Walcott's "A Far Cry From Africa."

■ THE READING/WRITING CONNECTION

1. "Think" Topic: Is Gladys a "mirror reflecting a society that had gone completely rotten and maggoty at the center"? Create an argumentative response to this question.
2. Journal Entry: Who is a more sympathetic character—Nwankwo or Gladys? Defend your choice.

■ **IDEAS FOR WRITING**
1. Discuss the tension between the traditional and the modern in this story.
2. Analyze Nwankwo's or Glady's character.

GABRIEL GARCÍA MÁRQUEZ   Translated by Gregory Rabassa

Gabriel García Márquez (1928–   ) was born in the coastal village of Aracataca, Colombia.
After studying at the University of Colombia at Bogota and the University of Cartagena, he
traveled throughout South America, the United States, and Europe as a reporter and began
writing short stories. Although he has lived in Mexico City for the past twenty years, García
Márquez returns frequently to Colombia, the setting for most of his work. His most famous
work is One Hundred Years of Solitude *(1972); other works include* Chronicle of a Death
Foretold *(1983) and* Love in the Time of Cholera *(1987). He was awarded the Nobel Prize for*
Literature in 1982. García Márquez is considered to be one of the leading practitioners of the
school of fiction known as magical realism, which combines the fantastic with the realistic.

1971

THE HANDSOMEST DROWNED MAN IN THE WORLD
A Tale for Children

The first children who saw the dark and slinky bulge approaching through the sea let themselves think it was an empty ship. Then they saw it had no flags or masts and they thought it was a whale. But when it washed up on the beach, they removed the clumps of seaweed, the jellyfish tentacles, and the remains of fish and flotsam, and only then did they see that it was a drowned man.

They had been playing with him all afternoon, burying him in the sand and digging him up again, when someone chanced to see them and spread the alarm in the village. The men who carried him to the nearest house noticed that he weighed more than any dead man they had ever known, almost as much as a horse, and they said to each other that maybe he'd been floating too long and the water had got into his bones. When they laid him on the floor they said he'd been taller than all other men because there was barely enough room for him in the house, but they thought that maybe the ability to keep on growing after death was part of the nature of certain drowned men. He had the smell of the sea about him and only his shape gave one to suppose that it was the corpse of a human being, because the skin was covered with a crust of mud and scales.

They did not even have to clean off his face to know that the dead man was a stranger. The village was made up of only twenty-odd wooden houses that had stone courtyards with no flowers and which were spread about on the end of a desertlike cape. There was so little land that mothers always went about with the fear that the wind would carry off their children and the few dead that the years had caused among them had to be thrown off the cliffs. But the sea was calm and bountiful and all the men fit into seven boats. So when they found the drowned man they simply had to look at one another to see that they were all there.

That night they did not go out to work at sea. While the men went to find out if anyone was missing in neighboring villages, the women stayed behind to care for the drowned man. They took the mud off with grass swabs, they removed the underwater stones entangled in his hair, and they scraped the crust off with tools used for scaling fish. As they were doing that they noticed that the vegetation on him came from faraway oceans and deep water and that his clothes were in tatters, as if he had sailed through labyrinths of coral. They noticed too that he bore his death with pride, for he did not have the lonely look of other drowned men who came out of the sea or that haggard, needy look of men who drowned in rivers.

But only when they finished cleaning him off did they become aware of the kind of man he was and it left them breathless. Not only was he the tallest, strongest, most virile, and best built man they had ever seen, but even though they were looking at him there was no room for him in their imagination.

5   They could not find a bed in the village large enough to lay him on nor was there a table solid enough to use for his wake. The tallest men's holiday pants would not fit him, nor the fattest ones' Sunday shirts, nor the shoes of the one with the biggest feet. Fascinated by his huge size and his beauty, the women then decided to make him some pants from a large piece of sail and a shirt from some bridal Brabant[1] linen so that he could continue through his death with dignity. As they sewed, sitting in a circle and gazing at the corpse between stitches, it seemed to them that the wind had never been so steady nor the sea so restless as on that night and they supposed that the change had something to do with the dead man. They thought that if that magnificent man had lived in the village, his house would have had the widest doors, and highest ceiling, and the strongest floor; his bedstead would have been made from a midship frame held together by iron bolts, and his wife would have been the happiest woman. They thought that he would have had so much authority that he could have drawn fish out of the sea simply by calling their names and that he would have put so much work into his land that springs would have burst forth from among the rocks so that he would have been able to plant flowers on the cliffs. They secretly compared him to their own men, thinking that for all their lives theirs were incapable of doing what he could do in one night, and they ended up dismissing them deep in their hearts as the weakest, meanest, and most useless creatures on earth. They were wandering through that maze of fantasy when the oldest woman, who as the oldest had looked upon the drowned man with more compassion than passion, sighed:

"He has the face of someone called Esteban."

It was true. Most of them had only to take another look at him to see that he could not have any other name. The more stubborn among them, who were the youngest, still lived for a few hours with the illusion that when they put his clothes on and he lay among the flowers in patent leather shoes his name might be Lautaro. But it was a vain illusion. There had not been enough canvas, the poorly cut and worse sewn pants were too tight, and the hidden strength of his heart popped the buttons on his shirt. After midnight the whistling of the wind died down and the sea fell into its Wednesday drowsiness. The silence put an end to any last doubts: he was Esteban. The women who had dressed him, who had combed his hair, had cut his nails and shaved him were unable to hold back a shudder of pity when they had to resign themselves to his being dragged along the ground. It was then that they understood how unhappy he must have been with that huge body since it bothered him even after death. They could see him in life, condemned to going through doors sideways cracking his head on crossbeams, remaining on his feet during visits, not knowing what to do with his soft pink, sealion hands while the lady of the house looked for her most resistant chair and begged him, frightened to death, sit here, Esteban, please, and he, leaning against the wall, smiling, don't bother, ma'am, I'm fine where I am, his heels raw and his back roasted from having done the same thing so many times whenever he paid a visit, don't bother, ma'am, I'm fine where I am to avoid the embarrassment of breaking up the chair, and never knowing perhaps that the one who said don't go, Esteban, at least wait till the coffee's ready, were the ones who later on would whisper the big boob finally left, how nice, the handsome fool has gone. That was what the women were thinking beside the body a little before dawn. Later, when they covered his face with a handkerchief so that the light would not bother him, he looked so forever dead, so defenseless, so much like their men

---

[1] Former region of Western Europe including the current Brabant province of the Netherlands and Brabant and Antwerp regions of Belgium.

that the first furrows of tears opened in their hearts. It was one of the younger ones who began the weeping. The others, coming to, went from sighs to wails, and the more they sobbed the more they felt like weeping, because the drowned man was becoming all the more Esteban for them, and so they wept so much, for he was the most destitute, most peaceful, and most obliging man on earth, poor Esteban. So when the men returned with the news that the drowned man was not from the neighboring villages either, the women felt an opening of jubilation in the midst of their tears.

"Praise the Lord," they sighed, "he's ours!"

The men thought the fuss was only womanish frivolity. Fatigued because of the difficult nighttime inquiries, all they wanted was to get rid of the bother of the newcomer once and for all before the sun grew strong on that arid, windless day. They improvised a litter with the remains of foremasts and gaffs, tying it together with rigging so that it would bear the weight of the body until they reached the cliffs. They wanted to tie the anchor from a cargo ship to him so that he would sink easily into the deepest waves, where the fish are blind and divers die of nostalgia, and bad currents would not bring him back to shore, as had happened with other bodies. But the more they hurried, the more the women thought of ways to waste time. They walked about like startled hens, pecking with the sea charms on their breasts, some interfering on one side to put a scapular of the good wind on the drowned man, some on the other side to put a wrist compass on him, and after a great deal of *get away from there, woman, stay out of the way, look, you almost made me fall on top of the dead man,* the men began to feel mistrust in their livers and started grumbling about why so many main-altar decorations for a stranger, because no matter how many nails and holy-water jars he had on him, the sharks would chew him all the same, but the women kept on piling on their junk relics, running back and forth, stumbling, while they released in sighs what they did not in tears, so that the men finally exploded with *since when has there ever been such a fuss over a drifting corpse, a drowned nobody, a piece of cold Wednesday meat.* One of the women, mortified by so much lack of care, then removed the handkerchief from the dead man's face and the men were left breathless too.

10   He was Esteban. It was not necessary to repeat it for them to recognize him. If they had been told Sir Walter Raleigh,[2] even they might have been impressed with his gringo accent, the macaw on his shoulder, his cannibal-killing blunderbuss, but there could be only one Esteban in the world and there he was, stretched out like a sperm whale, shoeless, wearing the pants of an undersized child, and with those stony nails that had to be cut with a knife. They had only to take the handkerchief off his face to see that he was ashamed, that it was not his fault that he was so big or so heavy or so handsome, and if he had known that this was going to happen, he would have looked for a more discreet place to drown in; seriously, I even would have tied the anchor off a galleon around my neck and staggered off a cliff like someone who doesn't like things in order not to be upsetting people now with this Wednesday dead body, as you people say, in order not to be bothering anyone with this filthy piece of cold meat that doesn't have anything to do with me. There was so much truth in his manner that even the most mistrustful men, the ones who felt the bitterness of endless nights at sea fearing that their women would tire of dreaming about them and begin to dream of drowned men, even they and others who were harder still shuddered in the marrow of their bones at Esteban's sincerity.

That was how they came to hold the most splendid funeral they could conceive of for an abandoned drowned man. Some women who had gone to get flowers in the neighboring villages returned with other women who could not believe what they had been told, and

---

[2] English navigator, courtier, and historian (1554–1618).

those women went back for more flowers when they saw the dead man, and they brought more and more until there were so many flowers and so many people that it was hard to walk about. At the final moment it pained them to return him to the waters as an orphan and they chose a father and mother from among the best people, and aunts and uncles and cousins, so that through him all the inhabitants of the village became kinsmen. Some sailors who heard the weeping from a distance went off course, and people heard of one who had himself tied to the mainmast, remembering ancient fables about sirens. While they fought for the privilege of carrying him on their shoulders along the steep escarpment by the cliffs, men and women became aware for the first time of the desolation of their streets, the dryness of their courtyards, the narrowness of their dreams as they faced the splendor and beauty of their drowned man. They let him go without an anchor so that he could come back if he wished and whenever he wished, and they all held their breath for the fraction of centuries the body took to fall into the abyss. They did not need to look to one another to realize that they were no longer all present, that they would never be. But they also knew that everything would be different from then on, that their houses would have wider doors, higher ceilings, and stronger floors so that Esteban's memory could go everywhere without bumping into beams and so that no one in the future would dare whisper the big boob finally died, too bad, the handsome fool has finally died, because they were going to paint their house fronts gay colors to make Esteban's memory eternal and they were going to break their backs digging for springs among the stones and planting flowers on the cliffs so that in future years at dawn the passengers on great liners would awaken, suffocated by the smell of gardens on the high seas, and the captain would have to come down from the bridge in his dress uniform, with his astrolabe,[3] his pole star, and his row of war medals and, pointing to the promontory of roses on the horizon, he would say in fourteen languages, look there, where the wind is so peaceful now that it's gone to sleep beneath the beds, over there, where the sun's so bright that the sunflowers don't know which way to turn, yes, over there, that's Esteban's village.

▪ EXPLORATIONS OF THE TEXT

1. Why does García Márquez subtitle the story "A Tale for Children"? What expectations does the subtitle create in the reader?
2. Why do the children play with the body? What is their attitude toward death?
3. What is the meaning of the symbolism of the vegetation and mud on the drowned man's body?
4. What are the consequences of the women's comparisons to their own men? What is the importance of identifying him as Esteban?
5. Examine the imaginary conversation about his size. How does he become "the big boob" and "the handsome fool"? Why do the villagers feel "jubilation" when Esteban becomes their drowned man?
6. Explore the men's attitudes, the funeral, and the behavior of the women. How does Esteban win the people with his sincerity?
7. Describe the ritual of the "most splendid funeral." How does the experience with the drowned man transform the people and the village?
8. Compare the transformation of the people in this story with the change in the narrator in Wright's "A Blessing."

---

[3] An instrument used to observe and calculate the positions of stars and planets before the invention of the sextant.

■ THE READING/WRITING CONNECTION

1. Write a story that imitates both the style and theme of "The Handsomest Drowned Man in the World."
2. Gloss and annotate the story. Consider the use of **hyperbole**.
3. React to the idea of Esteban as "the stranger" who is taken into the community. Write a short essay on this subject.

■ IDEAS FOR WRITING

1. Analyze the transformation of the people and their village.
2. Discuss the symbolism of the drowned man.
3. How do the settings (village and sea) elucidate theme?
4. Look for elements of fairy tales in this story. How are they effective?
5. Contrast García Márquez's view of death with the attitude of Thomas in "Do Not Go Gentle . . . ."
6. Compare the idea of community in García Márquez, Achebe, Le Guin and Lahiri.
7. Argue: Without imagination, people live constricted, static lives.

Sandra Cisneros

Sandra Cisneros (1954–   ) was born in Chicago to a Mexican-American mother and a Mexican father. She has worked as an arts administrator and college recruiter and has taught both high school dropouts and university students. Her publications include The House on Mango Street *(1984), which won the American Book Award and the Before Columbus Foundation Award (1985), as well as* Woman Hollering Creek and Other Stories *(1991),* Loose Woman *(1994), and* Caramelo *(2002). In spare, poetic language that resembles prose poetry, Cisneros explores issues of the Chicana/o community.*

1991

THERE WAS A MAN, THERE WAS A WOMAN

There was a man and there was a woman. Every payday, every other Friday, the man went to the Friendly Spot Bar to drink and spend his money. Every payday, every other Friday, the woman went to the Friendly Spot Bar to drink and spend her money. The man was paid on the second and fourth Friday of the month. The woman was paid on the first and third Friday. Because of this the man and the woman did not know each other.

The man drank and drank with his friends and believed if he drank and drank, the words for what he was feeling would slip out more readily, but usually he simply drank and said nothing. The woman drank and drank with her friends and believed if she drank and drank, the words for what she was feeling would slip out more readily, but usually she simply drank and said nothing. Every other Friday the man drank his beer and laughed loudly. Every Friday in between the woman drank her beer and laughed loudly.

At home when the night came down and the moon appeared, the woman raised her pale eyes to the moon and cried. The man in his bed contemplated the same moon, and thought about the millions who had looked at the moon before him, those who had worshiped or loved or died before that same moon, mute and lovely. Now blue light streamed inside his window and tangled itself with the glow of the sheets. The moon, the same round O. The man looked and swallowed.

■ EXPLORATIONS OF THE TEXT

1. Why might Cisneros have chosen to portray the man and woman's after-work visits to the bar as a way of introducing them to the reader? What does this detail tell you about the lives of these characters?
2. Why does the story end with the characters looking at the moon? How do they react to this sight? What does the moon symbolize?

■ THE READING/WRITING CONNECTION

1. Read the first paragraph. What do you think the rest of the story will be about? Continue reading. What is the story about? How accurate was your prediction?
2. Journal Entry: Compare the feeling Joan Didion describes when putting her hand against the dam with the feeling of Cisneros's characters as they look at the moon. Try to explain why these objects excite such strong emotions.

■ IDEAS FOR WRITING

1. Compare the characters's view of the moon to Sylvia's view from the pine tree in "A White Heron" (chapter 4). Have you ever had a similar experience? In writing, describe what you saw and how it made you feel.
2. Write an ending to the story. What happens the next day?

Jhumpa Lahiri

Jhumpa Lahiri (1967–) was born in London to Indian parents and raised in Rhode Island. She was educated at Barnard College and Boston University. Her short stories have appeared in The New Yorker, Story, *and* Salamander. *In 1999, she published her first collection of stories,* The Interpreter of Maladies, *which won a Pulitzer Prize, and in 2003, she published her first novel,* The Namesake. *Lahiri, educated in the United States and raised in England, has visited regularly with relatives in Calcutta, India, and her fiction captures the movement between these locations.*

1999

THE THIRD AND FINAL CONTINENT

I left India in 1964 with a certificate in commerce and the equivalent, in those days, of ten dollars to my name. For three weeks I sailed on the SS *Roma,* an Italian cargo vessel, in a cabin next to the ship's engine, across the Arabian Sea, the Red Sea, the Mediterranean, and finally to England. I lived in north London, in Finsbury Park, in a house occupied entirely by penniless Bengali bachelors like myself, at least a dozen and sometimes more, all struggling to educate and establish ourselves abroad.

I attended lectures at LSE[1] and worked at the university library to get by. We lived three or four to a room, shared a single, icy toilet, and took turns cooking pots of egg curry, which we ate with our hands on a table covered with newspapers. Apart from our jobs we had few responsibilities. On weekends we lounged barefoot in drawstring pajamas, drinking tea and smoking Rothmans, or set out to watch cricket at Lord's. Some weekends the house was crammed with still more Bengalis, to whom we had introduced ourselves at the greengrocer,

---

[1] London School of Economics.

or on the Tube, and we made yet more egg curry, and played Mukesh[2] on a Grundig reel-to-reel, and soaked our dirty dishes in the bathtub. Every now and then someone in the house moved out, to live with a woman whom his family back in Calcutta had determined he was to wed. In 1969, when I was thirty-six years old, my own marriage was arranged. Around the same time I was offered a full-time job in America, in the processing department of a library at MIT. The salary was generous enough to support a wife, and I was honored to be hired by a world-famous university, and so I obtained a sixth-preference green card, and prepared to travel farther still.

By now I had enough money to go by plane. I flew first to Calcutta, to attend my wedding, and a week later I flew to Boston, to begin my new job. During the flight I read *The Student Guide to North America,* a paperback volume that I'd bought before leaving London, for seven shillings six pence on Tottenham Court Road, for although I was no longer a student I was on a budget all the same. I learned that Americans drove on the right side of the road, not the left, and that they called a lift an elevator and an engaged phone busy. "The pace of life in North America is different from Britain as you will soon discover," the guidebook informed me. "Everybody feels he must get to the top. Don't expect an English cup of tea." As the plane began its descent over Boston Harbor, the pilot announced the weather and time, and that President Nixon had declared a national holiday: two American men had landed on the moon. Several passengers cheered. "God bless America!" one of them hollered. Across the aisle, I saw a woman praying.

I spent my first night at the YMCA in Central Square, Cambridge, an inexpensive accommodation recommended by my guidebook. It was walking distance from MIT, and steps from the post office and a supermarket called Purity Supreme. The room contained a cot, a desk, and a small wooden cross on one wall. A sign on the door said cooking was strictly forbidden. A bare window overlooked Massachusetts Avenue, a major thoroughfare with traffic in both directions. Car horns, shrill and prolonged, blared one after another. Flashing sirens heralded endless emergencies, and a fleet of buses rumbled past, their doors opening and closing with a powerful hiss, throughout the night. The noise was constantly distracting, at times suffocating. I felt it deep in my ribs, just as I had felt the furious drone of the engine on the SS *Roma.* But there was no ship's deck to escape to, no glittering ocean to thrill my soul, no breeze to cool my face, no one to talk to. I was too tired to pace the gloomy corridors of the YMCA in my drawstring pajamas. Instead I sat at the desk and stared out the window, at the city hall of Cambridge and a row of small shops. In the morning I reported to my job at the Dewey Library, a beige fortlike building by Memorial Drive. I also opened a bank account, rented a post office box, and bought a plastic bowl and a spoon at Woolworth's, a store whose name I recognized from London. I went to Purity Supreme, wandering up and down the aisles, converting ounces to grams and comparing prices to things in England. In the end I bought a small carton of milk and a box of cornflakes. This was my first meal in America. I ate it at my desk. I preferred it to hamburgers or hot dogs, the only alternative I could afford in the coffee shops on Massachusetts Avenue, and, besides, at the time I had yet to consume any beef. Even the simple chore of buying milk was new to me; in London we'd had bottles delivered each morning to our door.

5   In a week I had adjusted, more or less. I ate cornflakes and milk, morning and night, and bought some bananas for variety, slicing them into the bowl with the edge of my spoon. In addition I bought tea bags and a flask, which the salesman in Woolworth's referred to as a

---

[2] Popular playback singer of popular music and classical music in India.

thermos (a flask, he informed me, was used to store whiskey, another thing I had never consumed). For the price of one cup of tea at a coffee shop, I filled the flask with boiling water on my way to work each morning, and brewed the four cups I drank in the course of a day. I bought a larger carton of milk, and learned to leave it on the shaded part of the windowsill, as I had seen another resident at the YMCA do. To pass the time in the evenings I read the *Boston Globe* downstairs, in a spacious room with stained-glass windows. I read every article and advertisement, so that I would grow familiar with things, and when my eyes grew tired I slept. Only I did not sleep well. Each night I had to keep the window wide open; it was the only source of air in the stifling room, and the noise was intolerable. I would lie on the cot with my fingers pressed into my ears, but when I drifted off to sleep my hands fell away, and the noise of the traffic would wake me up again. Pigeon feathers drifted onto the windowsill, and one evening, when I poured milk over my cornflakes, I saw that it had soured. Nevertheless I resolved to stay at the YMCA for six weeks, until my wife's passport and green card were ready. Once she arrived I would have to rent a proper apartment, and from time to time I studied the classified section of the newspaper, or stopped in at the housing office at MIT during my lunch break, to see what was available in my price range. It was in this manner that I discovered a room for immediate occupancy, in a house on a quiet street, the listing said, for eight dollars per week. I copied the number into my guidebook and dialed from a pay telephone, sorting through the coins with which I was still unfamiliar, smaller and lighter than shillings, heavier and brighter than *paisas*.

"Who is speaking?" a woman demanded. Her voice was bold and clamorous.

"Yes, good afternoon, madame. I am calling about the room for rent."

"Harvard or Tech?"

"I beg your pardon?"

10   "Are you from Harvard or Tech?"

Gathering that Tech referred to the Massachusetts Institute of Technology, I replied, "I work at Dewey Library," adding tentatively, "at Tech."

"I only rent rooms to boys from Harvard or Tech!"

"Yes, madame."

I was given an address and an appointment for seven o'clock that evening. Thirty minutes before the hour I set out, my guidebook in my pocket, my breath fresh with Listerine. I turned down a street shaded with trees, perpendicular to Massachusetts Avenue. Stray blades of grass poked between the cracks of the footpath. In spite of the heat I wore a coat and a tie, regarding the event as I would any other interview; I had never lived in the home of a person who was not Indian. The house, surrounded by a chain-link fence, was off-white with dark brown trim. Unlike the stucco row house I'd lived in in London, this house, fully detached, was covered with wooden shingles, with a tangle of forsythia bushes plastered against the front and sides. When I pressed the calling bell, the woman with whom I had spoken on the phone hollered from what seemed to be just the other side of the door, "One minute, please!"

15   Several minutes later the door was opened by a tiny, extremely old woman. A mass of snowy hair was arranged like a small sack on top of her head. As I stepped into the house she sat down on a wooden bench positioned at the bottom of a narrow carpeted staircase. Once she was settled on the bench, in a small pool of light, she peered up at me with undivided attention. She wore a long black skirt that spread like a stiff tent to the floor, and a starched white shirt edged with ruffles at the throat and cuffs. Her hands, folded together in her lap, had long pallid fingers, with swollen knuckles and tough yellow nails. Age had battered her features so that she almost resembled a man, with sharp, shrunken eyes and prominent ceases on either side of her nose. Her lips, chapped and faded, had nearly disappeared, and her eyebrows were missing altogether. Nevertheless she looked fierce.

"Lock up!" she commanded. She shouted even though I stood only a few feet away. "Fasten the chain and firmly press that button on the knob! This is the first thing you shall do when you enter, is that clear?"

I locked the door as directed and examined the house. Next to the bench on which the woman sat was a small round table, its legs fully concealed, much like the woman's, by a skirt of lace. The table held a lamp, a transistor radio, a leather change purse with a silver clasp, and a telephone. A thick wooden cane coated with a layer of dust was propped against one side. There was a parlor to my right, lined with bookcases and filled with shabby claw-footed furniture. In the corner of the parlor I saw a grand piano with its top down, piled with papers. The piano's bench was missing; it seemed to be the one on which the woman was sitting. Somewhere in the house a clock chimed seven times.

"You're punctual!" the woman proclaimed. "I expect you shall be so with the rent!"

"I have a letter, madame." In my jacket pocket was a letter confirming my employment from MIT, which I had brought along to prove that I was indeed from Tech.

20   She stared at the letter, then handed it back to me carefully, gripping it with her fingers as if it were a dinner plate heaped with food instead of a sheet of paper. She did not wear glasses, and I wondered if she'd read a word of it. "The last boy was always late! Still owes me eight dollars! Harvard boys aren't what they used to be! Only Harvard and Tech in this house! How's Tech, boy?"

"It is very well."

"You checked the lock?"

"Yes, madame."

She slapped the space beside her on the bench with one hand, and told me to sit down. For a moment she was silent. Then she intoned as if she alone possessed this knowledge:

25   "There is an American flag on the moon!"

"Yes, madame." Until then I had not thought very much about the moon shot. It was in the newspaper, of course, article upon article. The astronauts had landed on the shores of the Sea of Tranquillity, I had read, traveling farther than anyone in the history of civilization. For a few hours they explored the moon's surface. They gathered rocks in their pockets, described their surroundings (a magnificent desolation, according to one astronaut), spoke by phone to the president, and planted a flag in lunar soil. The voyage was hailed as man's most awesome achievement. I had seen full-page photographs in the *Globe,* of the astronauts in their inflated costumes, and read about what certain people in Boston had been doing at the exact moment the astronauts landed, on a Sunday afternoon. A man said that he was operating a swan boat with a radio pressed to his ear; a woman had been baking rolls for her grandchildren.

The woman bellowed, "A flag on the moon, boy! I heard it on the radio! Isn't that splendid?"

"Yes, madame."

But she was not satisfied with my reply. Instead she commanded, "Say 'splendid'!"

30   I was both baffled and somewhat insulted by the request. It reminded me of the way I was taught multiplication tables as a child, repeating after the master, sitting cross-legged, without shoes or pencils, on the floor of my one-room Tollygunge school. It also reminded me of my wedding, when I had repeated endless Sanskrit verses after the priest, verses I barely understood, which joined me to my wife. I said nothing.

"Say 'splendid'!" the woman bellowed once again.

"Splendid," I murmured. I had to repeat the word a second time at the top of my lungs, so she could hear. I am soft-spoken by nature and was especially reluctant to raise my voice to an elderly woman whom I had met only moments ago, but she did not appear to be offended. If anything the reply pleased her because her next command was:

"Go see the room!"

I rose from the bench and mounted the narrow carpeted staircase. There were five doors, two on either side of an equally narrow hallway, and one at the opposite end. Only one door was partly open. The room contained a twin bed under a sloping ceiling, a brown oval rug, a basin with an exposed pipe, and a chest of drawers. One door, painted white, led to a closet, another to a toilet and a tub. The walls were covered with gray and ivory striped paper. The window was open; net curtains stirred in the breeze. I lifted them away and inspected the view: a small back yard, with a few fruit trees and an empty clothesline. I was satisfied. From the bottom of the stairs I heard the woman demand, "What is your decision?"

35   When I returned to the foyer and told her, she picked up the leather change purse on the table, opened the clasp, fished about with her fingers, and produced a key on a thin wire hoop. She informed me that there was a kitchen at the back of the house, accessible through the parlor. I was welcome to use the stove as long as I left it as I found it. Sheets and towels were provided, but keeping them clean was my own responsibility. The rent was due Friday mornings on the ledge above the piano keys. "And no lady visitors!"

"I am a married man, madame." It was the first time I had announced this fact to anyone.

But she had not heard. "No lady visitors!" she insisted. She introduced herself as Mrs. Croft.

My wife's name was Mala. The marriage had been arranged by my older brother and his wife. I regarded the proposition with neither objection nor enthusiasm. It was a duty expected of me, as it was expected of every man. She was the daughter of a schoolteacher in Beleghata. I was told that she could cook, knit, embroider, sketch landscapes, and recite poems by Tagore, but these talents could not make up for the fact that she did not possess a fair complexion, and so a string of men had rejected her to her face. She was twenty-seven, an age when her parents had begun to fear that she would never marry, and so they were willing to ship their only child halfway across the world in order to save her from spinsterhood.

For five nights we shared a bed. Each of those nights, after applying cold cream and braiding her hair, which she tied up at the end with a black cotton string, she turned from me and wept; she missed her parents. Although I would be leaving the country in a few days, custom dictated that she was now a part of my household, and for the next six weeks she was to live with my brother and his wife, cooking, cleaning, serving tea and sweets to guests. I did nothing to console her. I lay on my own side of the bed, reading my guidebook by flashlight and anticipating my journey. At times I thought of the tiny room on the other side of the wall which had belonged to my mother. Now the room was practically empty; the wooden pallet on which she'd once slept was piled with trunks and old bedding. Nearly six years ago, before leaving for London, I had watched her die on that bed, had found her playing with her excrement in her final days. Before we cremated her I had cleaned each of her fingernails with a hairpin, and then, because my brother could not bear it, I had assumed the role of eldest son, and had touched the flame to her temple to release her tormented soul to heaven.

40   The next morning I moved into the room in Mrs. Croft's house. When I unlocked the door I saw that she was sitting on the piano bench, on the same side as the previous evening. She wore the same black skirt, the same starched white blouse, and had her hands folded together the same way in her lap. She looked so much the same that I wondered if she'd spent the whole night on the bench. I put my suitcase upstairs, filled my flask with boiling water in the kitchen, and headed off to work. That evening when I came home from the university, she was still there.

"Sit down, boy!" She slapped the space beside her.

I perched beside her on the bench. I had a bag of groceries with me—more milk, more cornflakes, and more bananas, for my inspection of the kitchen earlier in the day had revealed no spare pots, pans, or cooking utensils. There were only two saucepans in the refrigerator, both containing some orange broth, and a copper kettle on the stove.

"Good evening, madame."

She asked me if I had checked the lock. I told her I had.

45   For a moment she was silent. Then suddenly she declared, with the equal measures of disbelief and delight as the night before, "There's an American flag on the moon, boy!"

"Yes, madame."

"A flag on the moon! Isn't that splendid?"

I nodded, dreading what I knew was coming. "Yes, madame."

"Say 'splendid'!"

50   This time I paused, looking to either side in case anyone were there to overhear me, though I knew perfectly well that the house was empty. I felt like an idiot. But it was a small enough thing to ask. "Splendid!" I cried out.

Within days it became our routine. In the mornings when I left for the library Mrs. Croft was either hidden away in her bedroom, on the other side of the staircase, or she was sitting on the bench, oblivious to my presence, listening to the news or classical music on the radio. But each evening when I returned the same thing happened: she slapped the bench, ordered me to sit down, declared that there was a flag on the moon, and declared that it was splendid. I said it was splendid, too, and then we sat in silence. As awkward as it was, and as endless as it felt to me then, the nightly encounter lasted only about ten minutes; inevitably she would drift off to sleep, her head falling abruptly toward her chest, leaving me free to retire to my room. By then, of course, there was no flag standing on the moon. The astronauts, I had read in the paper, had seen it fall before they flew back to Earth. But I did not have the heart to tell her.

Friday morning, when my first week's rent was due, I went to the piano in the parlor to place my money on the ledge. The piano keys were dull and discolored. When I pressed one, it made no sound at all. I had put eight one-dollar bills in an envelope and written Mrs. Croft's name on the front of it. I was not in the habit of leaving money unmarked and unattended. From where I stood I could see the profile of her tent-shaped skirt. She was sitting on the bench, listening to the radio. It seemed unnecessary to make her get up and walk all the way to the piano. I never saw her walking about, and assumed, from the cane always propped against the round table at her side, that she did so with difficulty. When I approached the bench she peered up at me and demanded:

"What is your business?"

"The rent, madame."

55   "On the ledge above the piano keys!"

"I have it here." I extended the envelope toward her, but her fingers, folded together in her lap, did not budge. I bowed slightly and lowered the envelope, so that it hovered just above her hands. After a moment she accepted, and nodded her head.

That night when I came home, she did not slap the bench, but out of habit I sat beside her as usual. She asked me if I had checked the lock, but she mentioned nothing about the flag on the moon. Instead she said:

"It was very kind of you!"

"I beg your pardon, madame?"

60   "Very kind of you!"

She was still holding the envelope in her hands.

On Sunday there was a knock on my door. An elderly woman introduced herself: she was Mrs. Croft's daughter, Helen. She walked into the room and looked at each of the walls as if for signs of change, glancing at the shirts that hung in the closet, the neckties draped over the doorknob, the box of cornflakes on the chest of drawers, the dirty bowl and spoon in the basin. She was short and thick-waisted, with cropped silver hair and bright pink lipstick. She wore a sleeveless summer dress, a row of white plastic beads, and spectacles on a chain that hung like a swing against her chest. The backs of her legs were mapped with dark blue veins, and her upper arms sagged like the flesh of a roasted eggplant. She told me she lived in Arlington, a town farther up Massachusetts Avenue. "I come once a week to bring Mother groceries. Has she sent you packing yet?"

"It is very well, madame."

"Some of the boys run screaming. But I think she likes you. You're the first boarder she's ever referred to as a gentleman."

65 "Not at all, madame."

She looked at me, noticing my bare feet (I still felt strange wearing shoes indoors, and always removed them before entering my room). "Are you new to Boston?"

"New to America, madame."

"From?" She raised her eyebrows.

"I am from Calcutta, India."

70 "Is that right? We had a Brazilian fellow, about a year ago. You'll find Cambridge a very international city."

I nodded, and began to wonder how long our conversation would last. But at that moment we heard Mrs. Croft's electrifying voice rising up the stairs. When we stepped into the hallway we heard her hollering:

"You are to come downstairs immediately!"

"What is it?" Helen hollered back.

"Immediately!"

75 I put on my shoes at once. Helen sighed.

We walked down the staircase. It was too narrow for us to descend side by side, so I followed Helen, who seemed to be in no hurry, and complained at one point that she had a bad knee. "Have you been walking without your cane?" Helen called out. "You know you're not supposed to walk without that cane." She paused, resting her hand on the banister, and looked back at me. "She slips sometimes."

For the first time Mrs. Croft seemed vulnerable. I pictured her on the floor in front of the bench, flat on her back, staring at the ceiling, her feet pointing in opposite directions. But when we reached the bottom of the staircase she was sitting there as usual, her hands folded together in her lap. Two grocery bags were at her feet. When we stood before her she did not slap the bench, or ask us to sit down. She glared.

"What is it, Mother?"

"It's improper!"

80 "What's improper?"

"It is improper for a lady and gentleman who are not married to one another to hold a private conversation without a chaperone!"

Helen said she was sixty-eight years old, old enough to be my mother, but Mrs. Croft insisted that Helen and I speak to each other downstairs, in the parlor. She added that it was also improper for a lady of Helen's station to reveal her age, and to wear a dress so high above the ankle.

"For your information, Mother, it's 1969. What would you do if you actually left the house one day and saw a girl in a miniskirt?"

Mrs. Croft sniffed. "I'd have her arrested."

85 Helen shook her head and picked up one of the grocery bags. I picked up the other one, and followed her through the parlor and into the kitchen. The bags were filled with

cans of soup, which Helen opened up one by one with a few cranks of a can opener. She tossed the old soup in the saucepans into the sink, rinsed the pans under the tap, filled them with soup from the newly opened cans, and put them back in the refrigerator. "A few years ago she could still open the cans herself," Helen said. "She hates that I do it for her now. But the piano killed her hands." She put on her spectacles, glanced at the cupboards, and spotted my tea bags. "Shall we have a cup?"

I filled the kettle on the stove. "I beg your pardon, madame. The piano?"

"She used to give lessons. For forty years. It was how she raised us after my father died." Helen put her hands on her hips, staring at the open refrigerator. She reached into the back, pulled out a wrapped stock of butter, frowned, and tossed it into the garbage. "That ought to do it," she said, and put the unopened cans of soup in the cupboard. I sat at the table and watched as Helen washed the dirty dishes, tied up the garbage bag, watered a spider plant over the sink, and poured boiling water into two cups. She handed one to me without milk, the string of the tea bag trailing over the side, and sat down at the table.

"Excuse me, madame, but is it enough?"

Helen took a sip of her tea. Her lipstick left a smiling pink stain on the inside rim of the cup. "Is what enough?"

90   "The soup in the pans. Is it enough food for Mrs. Croft?"

"She won't eat anything else. She stopped eating solids after she turned one hundred. That was, let's see, three years ago."

I was mortified. I had assumed Mrs. Croft was in her eighties, perhaps as old as ninety. I had never known a person who had lived for over a century. That this person was a widow who lived alone mortified me further still. It was widowhood that had driven my own mother insane. My father, who worked as a clerk at the General Post Office of Calcutta, died of encephalitis when I was sixteen. My mother refused to adjust to life without him; instead she sank deeper into a world of darkness from which neither I, nor my brother, nor concerned relatives, nor psychiatric clinics on Rash Behari Avenue could save her. What pained me most was to see her so unguarded, to hear her burp after meals or expel gas in front of company without the slightest embarrassment. After my father's death my brother abandoned his schooling and began to work in the jute mill he would eventually manage, in order to keep the household running. And so it was my job to sit by my mother's feet and study for my exams as she counted and recounted the bracelets on her arm as if they were the beads of an abacus. We tried to keep an eye on her. Once she had wandered half naked to the tram depot before we were able to bring her inside again.

"I am happy to warm Mrs. Croft's soup in the evenings," I suggested, removing the tea bag from my cup and squeezing out the liquor. "It is no trouble."

Helen looked at her watch, stood up, and poured the rest of her tea into the sink. "I wouldn't if I were you. That's the sort of thing that would kill her altogether."

95   That evening, when Helen had gone back to Arlington and Mrs. Croft and I were alone again, I began to worry. Now that I knew how very old she was, I worried that something would happen to her in the middle of the night, or when I was out during the day. As vigorous as her voice was, and imperious as she seemed, I knew that even a scratch or a cough could kill a person that old; each day she lived, I knew, was something of a miracle. Although Helen had seemed friendly enough, a small part of me worried that she might accuse me of negligence if anything were to happen. Helen didn't seem worried. She came and went, bringing soup for Mrs. Croft, one Sunday after the next.

In this manner the six weeks of that summer passed. I came home each evening, after my hours at the library, and spent a few minutes on the piano bench with Mrs. Croft. I gave her a bit of my company, and assured her that I had checked the lock, and told her that the flag on the moon was splendid. Some evenings I sat beside her long after she had drifted off to sleep, still in awe of how many years she had spent on this earth. At times I tried to picture the world she had been born into, in 1866—a world, I imagined, filled with women in long black skirts, and chaste conversations in the parlor. Now, when I looked at her hands, with their swollen knuckles folded together in her lap, I imagined them smooth and slim, striking the piano keys. At times I came downstairs before going to sleep, to make sure she was sitting upright on the bench, or was safe in her bedroom. On Fridays I made sure to put the rent in her hands. There was nothing I could do for her beyond these simple gestures. I was not her son, and apart from those eight dollars, I owed her nothing.

At the end of August, Mala's passport and green card were ready. I received a telegram with her flight information; my brother's house in Calcutta had no telephone. Around that time I also received a letter from her, written only a few days after we had parted. There was no salutation; addressing me by name would have assumed an intimacy we had not yet discovered. It contained only a few lines. "I write in English in preparation for the journey. Here I am very much lonely. Is it very cold there. Is there snow. Yours, Mala."

I was not touched by her words. We had spent only a handful of days in each other's company. And yet we were bound together; for six weeks she had worn an iron bangle on her wrist, and applied vermilion powder to the part in the hair, to signify to the world that she was a bride. In those six weeks I regarded her arrival as I would the arrival of a coming month, or season—something inevitable, but meaningless at the time. So little did I know her that, while details of her face sometimes rose to my memory, I could not conjure up the whole of it.

A few days after receiving the letter, as I was walking to work in the morning, I saw an Indian woman on the other side of Massachusetts Avenue, wearing a sari with its free end nearly dragging on the footpath, and pushing a child in a stroller. An American woman with a small black dog on a leash was walking to one side of her. Suddenly the dog began barking. From the other side of the street I watched as the Indian woman, startled, stopped in her path, at which point the dog leapt up and seized the end of the sari between its teeth. The American woman scolded the dog, appeared to apologize, and walked quickly away, leaving the Indian woman to fix her sari in the middle of the footpath, and quiet her crying child. She did not see me standing there, and eventually she continued on her way. Such a mishap, I realized that morning, would soon be my concern. It was my duty to take care of Mala, to welcome her and protect her. I would have to buy her her first pair of snow boots, her first winter coat. I would have to tell her which streets to avoid, which way the traffic came, tell her to wear her sari so that the free end did not drag on the footpath. A five-mile separation from her parents, I recalled with some irritation, had caused her to weep.

100 Unlike Mala, I was used to it all by then: used to cornflakes and milk, used to Helen's visits, used to sitting on the bench with Mrs. Croft. The only thing I was not used to was Mala. Nevertheless I did what I had to do. I went to the housing office at MIT and found a furnished apartment a few blocks away, with a double bed and a private kitchen and bath, for forty dollars a week. One last Friday I handed Mrs. Croft eight one-dollar bills in an envelope, brought my suitcase downstairs, and informed her that I was moving. She put my key into her change purse. The last thing she asked me to do was hand her the cane propped against the table, so that she could walk to the door and lock it behind me. "Goodbye, then," she said, and retreated back into the house. I did not expect any display of emotion, but I was disappointed all the same. I was only a boarder, a man who paid her a bit of money and passed in and out of her home for six weeks. Compared to a century, it was no time at all.

At the airport I recognized Mala immediately. The free end of her sari did not drag on the floor, but was draped in a sign of bridal modesty over her head, just as it had draped my mother until the day my father died. Her thin brown arms were stacked with gold bracelets, a small red circle was painted on her forehead, and the edges of her feet were tinted with a decorative red dye. I did not embrace her, or kiss her, or take her hand. Instead I asked her, speaking Bengali for the first time in America, if she was hungry.

She hesitated, then nodded yes.

I told her I had prepared some egg curry at home. "What did they give you to eat on the plane?"

"I didn't eat."

105 "All the way from Calcutta?"

"The menu said oxtail soup."

"But surely there were other items."

"The thought of eating an ox's tail made me lose my appetite."

When we arrived home, Mala opened up one of her suitcases, and presented me with two pullover sweaters, both made with bright blue wool, which she had knitted in the course of our separation, one with a V neck, the other covered with cables. I tried them on; both were tight under the arms. She had also brought me two new pairs of drawstring pajamas, a letter from my brother, and a packet of loose Darjeeling tea. I had no present for her apart from the egg curry. We sat at a bare table, each of us staring at our plates. We ate with our hands, another thing I had not yet done in America.

110 "The house is nice," she said. "Also the egg curry." With her left hand she held the end of her sari to her chest, so it would not slip off her head.

"I don't know many recipes."

She nodded, peeling the skin off each of her potatoes before eating them. At one point the sari slipped to her shoulders. She readjusted it at once.

"There is no need to cover your head," I said. "I don't mind. It doesn't matter here."

She kept it covered anyway.

115 I waited to get used to her, to her presence at my side, at my table and in my bed, but a week later we were still strangers. I still was not used to coming home to an apartment that smelled of steamed rice, and finding that the basin in the bathroom was always wiped clean, our two toothbrushes lying side by side, a cake of Pears soap from India resting in the soap dish. I was not used to the fragrance of the coconut oil she rubbed every other night into her scalp, or the delicate sound her bracelets made as she moved about the apartment. In the mornings she was always awake before I was. The first morning when I came into the kitchen she had heated up the leftovers and set a plate with a spoonful of salt on its edge on the table, assuming I would eat rice for breakfast, as most Bengali husbands did. I told her cereal would do, and the next morning when I came into the kitchen she had already poured the cornflakes into my bowl. One morning she walked with me down Massachusetts Avenue to MIT, where I gave her a short tour of the campus. On the way we stopped at a hardware store and I made a copy of the key, so that she could let herself into the apartment. The next morning before I left for work she asked me for a few dollars. I parted with them reluctantly, but I knew that this, too, was now normal. When I came home from work there was a potato peeler in the kitchen drawer, and a tablecloth on the table, and chicken curry made with fresh garlic and ginger on the stove. We did not have a television in those days. After dinner I read the newspaper, while Mala sat at the kitchen table, working on a cardigan for herself with more of the bright blue wool, or writing letters home.

At the end of our first week, on Friday, I suggested going out. Mala set down her knitting and disappeared into the bathroom. When she emerged I regretted the suggestion; she had put on a clean silk sari and extra bracelets, and coiled her hair with a flattering side part on top of her head. She was prepared as if for a party, or at the very least for the cinema, but I had no such destination in mind. The evening air was balmy. We walked several blocks down Massachusetts Avenue, looking into the windows of restaurants and shops. Then, without thinking, I led her down the quiet street where for so many nights I had walked alone.

"This is where I lived before you came," I said, stopping at Mrs. Croft's chain-link fence.

"In such a big house?"

"I had a small room upstairs. At the back."

120 "Who else lives there?"

"A very old woman."

"With her family?"

"Alone."

"But who takes care of her?"

125 I opened the gate. "For the most part she takes care of herself."

I wondered if Mrs. Croft would remember me; I wondered if she had a new boarder to sit with her on the bench each evening. When I pressed the bell I expected the same long wait as that day of our first meeting, when I did not have a key. But this time the door was opened almost immediately, by Helen. Mrs. Croft was not sitting on the bench. The bench was gone.

"Hello there," Helen said, smiling with her bright pink lips at Mala. "Mother's in the parlor. Will you be visiting awhile?"

"As you wish, madame."

"Then I think I'll run to the store, if you don't mind. She had a little accident. We can't leave her alone these days, not even for a minute."

130 I locked the door after Helen and walked into the parlor. Mrs. Croft was lying flat on her back, her head on a peach-colored cushion, a thin white quilt spread over her body. Her hands were folded together on top of her chest. When she saw me she pointed at the sofa, and told me to sit down. I took my place as directed, but Mala wandered over to the piano and sat on the bench, which was now positioned where it belonged.

"I broke my hip!" Mrs. Croft announced, as if no time had passed.

"Oh dear, madame."

"I fell off the bench!"

"I am so sorry, madame."

135 "It was the middle of the night! Do you know what I did, boy?"

I shook my head.

"I called the police!"

She stared up at the ceiling and grinned sedately, exposing a crowded row of long gray teeth. Not one was missing. "What do you say to that, boy?"

As stunned as I was, I knew what I had to say. With no hesitation at all, I cried out, "Splendid!"

140 Mala laughed then. Her voice was full of kindness, her eyes bright with amusement. I had never heard her laugh before, and it was loud enough so that Mrs. Croft had heard, too. She turned to Mala and glared.

"Who is she, boy?"

"She is my wife, madame."

Mrs. Croft pressed her head at an angle against the cushion to get a better look. "Can you play the piano?"

"No, madame," Mala replied.

145 "Then stand up!"

Mala rose to her feet, adjusting the end of her sari over her head and holding it to her chest, and, for the first time since her arrival, I felt sympathy. I remembered my first days in

London, learning how to take the Tube to Russell Square, riding an escalator for the first time, being unable to understand that when the man cried "piper" it meant "paper," being unable to decipher, for a whole year, that the conductor said "mind the gap" as the train pulled away from each station. Like me, Mala had traveled far from home, not knowing where she was going, or what she would find, for no reason other than to be my wife. As strange as it seemed, I knew in my heart that one day her death would affect me, and stranger still, that mine would affect her. I wanted somehow to explain this to Mrs. Croft, who was still scrutinizing Mala from top to toe with what seemed to be placid disdain. I wondered if Mrs. Croft had ever seen a woman in a sari, with a dot painted on her forehead and bracelets stacked on her wrists. I wondered what she would object to. I wondered if she could see the red dye still vivid on Mala's feet, all but obscured by the bottom edge of her sari. At last Mrs. Croft declared, with the equal measures of disbelief and delight I knew well:

"She is a perfect lady!"

Now it was I who laughed. I did so quietly, and Mrs. Croft did not hear me. But Mala had heard, and, for the first time, we looked at each other and smiled.

I like to think of that moment in Mrs. Croft's parlor as the moment when the distance between Mala and me began to lessen. Although we were not yet fully in love, I like to think of the months that followed as a honeymoon of sorts. Together we explored the city and met other Bengalis, some of whom are still friends today. We discovered that a man named Bill sold fresh fish on Prospect Street, and that a shop in Harvard Square called Cardullo's sold bay leaves and cloves. In the evenings we walked to the Charles River to watch sailboats drift across the water, or had ice cream cones in Harvard Yard. We bought an Instamatic camera with which to document our life together, and I took pictures of her posing in front of the Prudential building, so that she could send them to her parents. At night we kissed, shy at first but quickly bold, and discovered pleasure and solace in each other's arms. I told her about my voyage on the SS *Roma,* and about Finsbury Park and the YMCA, and my evenings on the bench with Mrs. Croft. When I told her stories about my mother, she wept. It was Mala who consoled me when, reading the *Globe* one evening, I came across Mrs. Croft's obituary. I had not thought of her in several months—by then those six weeks of the summer were already a remote interlude in my past—but when I learned of her death I was stricken, so much so that when Mala looked up from her knitting she found me staring at the wall, the newspaper neglected in my lap, unable to speak. Mrs. Croft's was the first death I mourned in America, for hers was the first life I had admired; she had left this world at last, ancient and alone, never to return.

150   As for me, I have not strayed much farther. Mala and I live in a town about twenty miles from Boston, on a tree-lined street much like Mrs. Croft's, in a house we own, with a garden that saves us from buying tomatoes in summer, and room for guests. We are American citizens now, so that we can collect social security when it is time. Though we visit Calcutta every few years, and bring back more drawstring pajamas and Darjeeling tea, we have decided to grow old here. I work in a small college library. We have a son who attends Harvard University. Mala no longer drapes the end of her sari over her head, or weeps at night for her parents, but occasionally she weeps for our son. So we drive to Cambridge to visit him, or bring him home for a weekend, so that he can eat rice with us with his hands, and speak in Bengali, things we sometimes worry he will no longer do after we die.

Whenever we make that drive, I always make it a point to take Massachusetts Avenue, in spite of the traffic. I barely recognize the buildings now, but each time I am there I return instantly to those six weeks as if they were only the other day, and I slow down and point to Mrs. Croft's street, saying to my son, here was my first home in America, where I lived with a woman who was 103. "Remember?" Mala says, and smiles, amazed, as I am, that there was ever a time that we were strangers. My son always expresses his astonishment, not at Mrs. Croft's age, but at how little I paid in rent, a fact nearly as inconceivable to him as a flag on the moon was to a woman born in 1866. In my son's eyes I see the ambition that had first hurled me across the world. In a few years he will graduate and pave his way, alone and unprotected. But I remind myself that he has a father who is still living, a mother who is happy and strong. Whenever he is discouraged, I tell him that if I can survive on three continents, then there is no obstacle he cannot conquer. While the astronauts, heroes forever, spent mere hours on the moon, I have remained in this new world for nearly thirty years. I know that my achievement is quite ordinary. I am not the only man to seek his fortune far from home, and certainly I am not the first. Still, there are times I am bewildered by each mile I have traveled, each meal I have eaten, each person I have known, each room in which I have slept. As ordinary as it all appears, there are times when it is beyond my imagination.

■ EXPLORATIONS OF THE TEXT

1. Describe the point of view of the narrator. What impact does this narrative perspective have?
2. What main impression do you gain of the narrator at the beginning of the story? Does your view of him change as the story progresses?
3. Discuss the narrator's interactions with Mrs. Croft. In what ways are they both outsiders in North American society?
4. What does he learn from his experiences with Mrs. Croft? How does his relationship with her prepare him for his marriage? How does the narrator change as the story progresses?
5. What possible interpretations exist for the phrase "the third and final continent"? What views do you gain of the immigrant experience in North America?
6. Explore the significance of the moon landing. How does the symbol develop themes of the story?
7. Compare the vision of exile in this story with Agosín's and Aciman's works.

■ THE READING/WRITING CONNECTION

1. Do a freewrite on the topic of exile.
2. "Think" Topic: Argue for or against arranged marriage.

■ IDEAS FOR WRITING

1. Explore the symbolism of the "third and final continent." How many different "third . . . continents" are there in this story? How do they intersect?

ISABEL ALLENDE   Translated by Margaret Sayers Peden

Isabel Allende (1942–   ) was born in Lima, Peru. Her parents divorced when she was young, and her mother's second husband was a diplomat whose job took the family to Bolivia, the Middle East, and Europe. Allende returned to Chile when she was fifteen, finished high school, and began working as a journalist. In 1973, her uncle, President Salvador Allende, was assassinated during a military coup under the command of General Augusto Pinochet Ugarte. Allende remained in Chile for several months after the takeover to assist those fleeing the new regime, but in 1974, she escaped with her family to Venezuela. She later moved to the United States. In 1982, Allende published The House of the Spirits (La casa de los espíritus), *a fictional story of the political events in Chile. Allende's novels have won awards around the world, including the Panorama Literario Award (Chile) in 1983, the Grand Prix d'Evasion (France) in 1984, the Author of the Year and Book of the Year Awards (Germany) in 1984 and 1986, the Point de Mire (Belgium) in 1985, and the Colima Award for Best Novel (Mexico) in*

1985, all for The House of the Spirits. *More recently,* Eva Luna *(1988) won the Before Colum-bus Foundation Award in 1989. Allende's novels often are told from a woman's perspective, have social or political themes, and weave fantastic events into the real through the use of magical realism.*

1989

AND OF CLAY ARE WE CREATED

They discovered the girl's head protruding from the mudpit, eyes wide open, calling soundlessly. She had a First Communion name, Azucena. Lily. In that vast cemetery where the odor of death was already attracting vultures from far away, and where the weeping of orphans and wails of the injured filled the air, the little girl obstinately clinging to life became the symbol of the tragedy. The television cameras transmitted so often the unbearable image of the head budding like a black squash from the clay that there was no one who did not recognize her and know her name. And every time we saw her on the screen, right behind her was Rolf Carlé, who had gone there on assignment, never suspecting that he would find a fragment of his past, lost thirty years before.

First a subterranean sob rocked the cotton fields, curling them like waves of foam. Geologists had set up their seismographs weeks before and knew that the mountain had awakened again. For some time they had predicted that the heat of the eruption could detach the eternal ice from the slopes of the volcano, but no one heeded their warnings; they sounded like the tales of frightened old women. The towns in the valley went about their daily life, deaf to the moaning of the earth, until that fateful Wednesday night in November when a prolonged roar announced the end of the world, and walls of snow broke loose, rolling in an avalanche of clay, stones, and water that descended on the villages and buried them beneath unfathomable meters of telluric vomit. As soon as the survivors emerged from the paralysis of that first awful terror, they could see that houses, plazas, churches, white cotton plantations, dark coffee forests, cattle pastures—all had disappeared. Much later, after soldiers and volunteers had arrived to rescue the living and try to assess the magnitude of the cataclysm, it was calculated that beneath the mud lay more than twenty thousand human beings and an indefinite number of animals putrefying in a viscous soup. Forests and rivers had also been swept away, and there was nothing to be seen but an immense desert of mire.

When the station called before dawn, Rolf Carlé and I were together. I crawled out of bed, dazed with sleep, and went to prepare coffee while he hurriedly dressed. He stuffed his gear in the green canvas backpack he always carried, and we said goodbye, as we had so many times before. I had no presentiments. I sat in the kitchen, sipping my coffee and planning the long hours without him, sure that he would be back the next day.

He was one of the first to reach the scene, because while other reporters were fighting their way to the edges of that morass in jeeps, bicycles, or on foot, each getting there however he could, Rolf Carlé had the advantage of the television helicopter, which flew him over the avalanche. We watched on our screens the footage captured by his assistant's camera, in which he was up to his knees in muck, a microphone in his hand, in the midst of a bedlam of lost children, wounded survivors, corpses, and devastation. The story came to us in his calm voice. For years he had been a familiar figure in newscasts, reporting live at the scene of battles and catastrophes with awesome tenacity. Nothing could stop him, and I was always amazed at his equanimity in the face of danger and suffering; it seemed as if nothing could shake his fortitude or deter his curiosity. Fear seemed never to touch him, although he had confessed to me that he was not a courageous man, far from it. I believe that the lens of the camera had a strange effect on him; it was as if it transported him to a different time from which he could watch events without actually participating in them. When I knew him better, I came to realize that this fictive distance seemed to protect him from his own emotions.

5   Rolf Carlé was in on the story of Azucena from the beginning. He filmed the volunteers who discovered her, and the first persons who tried to reach her; his camera zoomed in on the girl, her dark face, her large desolate eyes, the plastered-down tangle of her hair. The mud was like quicksand around her, and anyone attempting to reach her was in danger of sinking. They threw a rope to her that she made no effort to grasp until they shouted to her to catch it; then she pulled a hand from the mire and tried to move, but immediately sank a little deeper. Rolf threw down his knapsack and the rest of his equipment and waded into the quagmire, commenting for his assistant's microphone that it was cold and that one could begin to smell the stench of corpses.

"What's your name?" he asked the girl, and she told him her flower name. "Don't move, Azucena," Rolf Carlé directed, and kept talking to her, without a thought for what he was saying, just to distract her, while slowly he worked his way forward in mud up to his waist. The air around him seemed as murky as the mud.

It was impossible to reach her from the approach he was attempting, so he retreated and circled around where there seemed to be firmer footing. When finally he was close enough, he took the rope and tied it beneath her arms, so they could pull her out. He smiled at her with that smile that crinkles his eyes and makes him look like a little boy; he told her that everything was fine, that he was here with her now, that soon they would have her out. He signaled the others to pull, but as soon as the cord tensed, the girl screamed. They tried again, and her shoulders and arms appeared, but they could move her no farther; she was trapped. Someone suggested that her legs might be caught in the collapsed walls of her house, but she said it was not just rubble, that she was also held by the bodies of her brothers and sisters clinging to her legs.

"Don't worry, we'll get you out of here," Rolf promised. Despite the quality of the transmission, I could hear his voice break, and I loved him more than ever. Azucena looked at him, but said nothing.

During those first hours Rolf Carlé exhausted all the resources of his ingenuity to rescue her. He struggled with poles and ropes, but every tug was an intolerable torture for the imprisoned girl. It occurred to him to use one of the poles as a lever but got no result and had to abandon the idea. He talked a couple of soldiers into working with him for a while, but they had to leave because so many other victims were calling for help. The girl could not move, she barely could breathe, but she did not seem desperate, as if an ancestral resignation allowed her to accept her fate. The reporter, on the other hand, was determined to snatch her from death. Someone brought him a tire, which he placed beneath her arms like a life buoy, and then laid a plank near the hole to hold his weight and allow him to stay closer to her. As it was impossible to remove the rubble blindly, he tried once or twice to dive toward her feet, but emerged frustrated, covered with mud, and spitting gravel. He concluded that he would have to have a pump to drain the water, and radioed a request for one, but received in return a message that there was no available transport and it could not be sent until the next morning.

10   "We can't wait that long!" Rolf Carlé shouted, but in the pandemonium no one stopped to commiserate. Many more hours would go by before he accepted that time had stagnated and reality had been irreparably distorted.

A military doctor came to examine the girl, and observed that her heart was functioning well and that if she did not get too cold she could survive the night.

"Hang on, Azucena, we'll have the pump tomorrow," Rolf Carlé tried to console her.

"Don't leave me alone," she begged.

"No, of course I won't leave you."

15   Someone brought him coffee, and he helped the girl drink it, sip by sip. The warm liquid revived her and she began telling him about her small life, about her family and her school, about how things were in that little bit of world before the volcano had erupted. She was thirteen, and she had never been outside her village. Rolf Carlé, buoyed by a premature optimism, was convinced that everything would end well: the pump would arrive, they would drain the water, move the rubble, and Azucena would be transported by helicopter to a hospital where she would recover rapidly and where he could visit her and bring her gifts. He thought, She's already too old for dolls, and I don't know what would please her; maybe a dress. I don't know much about women, he concluded, amused, reflecting that although he had known many women in his lifetime, none had taught him these details. To pass the hours he began to tell Azucena about his travels and adventures as a news hound, and when he exhausted his memory, he called upon imagination, inventing things he thought might entertain her. From time to time she dozed, but he kept talking in the darkness, to assure her that he was still there and to overcome the menace of uncertainty.

That was a long night.

Many miles away, I watched Rolf Carlé and the girl on a television screen. I could not bear the wait at home, so I went to National Television, where I often spent entire nights with Rolf editing programs. There, I was near his world, and I could at least get a feeling of what he lived through during those three decisive days. I called all the important people in the city, senators, commanders of the armed forces, the North American ambassador, and the president of National Petroleum, begging them for a pump to remove the silt, but obtained only vague promises. I began to ask for urgent help on radio and television, to see if there wasn't *someone* who could help us. Between calls I would run to the newsroom to monitor the satellite transmissions that periodically brought new details of the catastrophe. While reporters selected scenes with most impact for the news report, I searched for footage that featured Azucena's mudpit. The screen reduced the disaster to a single plane and accentuated the tremendous distance that separated me from Rolf Carlé; nonetheless, I was there with him. The child's every suffering hurt me as it did him; I felt his frustration, his impotence. Faced with the impossibility of communicating with him, the fantastic idea came to me that if I tried, I could reach him by force of mind and in that way give him encouragement. I concentrated until I was dizzy—a frenzied and futile activity. At times I would be overcome with compassion and burst out crying; at other times, I was so drained I felt as if I were staring through a telescope at the light of a star dead for a million years.

I watched that hell on the first morning broadcast, cadavers of people and animals awash in the current of new rivers formed overnight from the melted snow. Above the mud rose the tops of trees and the bell towers of a church where several people had taken refuge and were patiently awaiting rescue teams. Hundreds of soldiers and volunteers from the Civil Defense were clawing through rubble searching for survivors, while long rows of ragged specters awaited their turn for a cup of hot broth. Radio networks announced that their phones were jammed with calls from families offering shelter to orphaned children. Drinking water was in scarce supply, along with gasoline and food. Doctors, resigned to amputating arms and legs without anesthesia, pled that at least they be sent serum and painkillers and antibiotics; most of the roads, however, were impassable, and worse were the bureaucratic obstacles that stood in the way. To top it all, the clay contaminated by decomposing bodies threatened the living with an outbreak of epidemics.

Azucena was shivering inside the tire that held her above the surface. Immobility and tension had greatly weakened her, but she was conscious and could still be heard when a microphone was held out to her. Her tone was humble, as if apologizing for all the fuss. Rolf

Carlé had a growth of beard, and dark circles beneath his eyes; he looked near exhaustion. Even from that enormous distance I could sense the quality of his weariness, so different from the fatigue of other adventures. He had completely forgotten the camera; he could not look at the girl through a lens any longer. The pictures we were receiving were not his assistant's but those of other reporters who had appropriated Azucena, bestowing on her the pathetic responsibility of embodying the horror of what had happened in that place. With the first light Rolf tried again to dislodge the obstacles that held the girl in her tomb, but he had only his hands to work with; he did not dare use a tool for fear of injuring her. He fed Azucena a cup of the cornmeal mush and bananas the Army was distributing, but she immediately vomited it up. A doctor stated that she had a fever, but added that there was little he could do: antibiotics were being reserved for cases of gangrene. A priest also passed by and blessed her, hanging a medal of the Virgin around her neck. By evening a gentle, persistent drizzle began to fall.

20   "The sky is weeping," Azucena murmured, and she, too, began to cry.

"Don't be afraid," Rolf begged. "You have to keep your strength up and be calm. Everything will be fine. I'm with you, and I'll get you out somehow."

Reporters returned to photograph Azucena and ask her the same questions, which she no longer tried to answer. In the meanwhile, more television and movie teams arrived with spools of cable, tapes, film, videos, precision lenses, recorders, sound consoles, lights, reflecting screens, auxiliary motors, cartons of supplies, electricians, sound technicians, and cameramen: Azucena's face was beamed to millions of screens around the world. And all the while Rolf Carlé kept pleading for a pump. The improved technical facilities bore results, and National Television began receiving sharper pictures and clearer sound; the distance seemed suddenly compressed, and I had the horrible sensation that Azucena and Rolf were by my side, separated from me by impenetrable glass. I was able to follow events hour by hour; I knew everything my love did to wrest the girl from her prison and help her endure her suffering; I overheard fragments of what they said to one another and could guess the rest; I was present when she taught Rolf to pray, and when he distracted her with the stories I had told him in a thousand and one nights beneath the white mosquito netting of our bed.

When darkness came on the second day Rolf tried to sing Azucena to sleep with old Austrian folk songs he had learned from his mother, but she was far beyond sleep. They spent most of the night talking, each in a stupor of exhaustion and hunger, and shaking with cold. That night, imperceptibly, the unyielding floodgates that had contained Rolf Carlé's past for so many years began to open, and the torrent of all that had lain hidden in the deepest and most secret layers of memory poured out, leveling before it the obstacles that had blocked his consciousness for so long. He could not tell it all to Azucena; she perhaps did not know there was a world beyond the sea or time previous to her own; she was not capable of imagining Europe in the years of the war. So he could not tell her of defeat, nor of the afternoon the Russians had led them to the concentration camp to bury prisoners dead from starvation. Why should he describe to her how the naked bodies piled like a mountain of firewood resembled fragile china? How could he tell this dying child about ovens and gallows? Nor did he mention the night that he had seen his mother naked, shod in stiletto-heeled red boots, sobbing with humiliation. There was much he did not tell, but in those hours he relived for the first time all the things his mind had tried to erase. Azucena had surrendered her fear to him and so, without wishing it, had obliged Rolf to confront his own. There, beside that hellhole of mud, it was impossible for Rolf to flee from himself any longer, and the visceral terror he had lived as a boy suddenly invaded him. He reverted to the years when he was the age of Azucena, and younger, and, like her, found himself trapped in a pit without escape, buried in life, his head barely above ground; he saw before his eyes the boots and legs of his father, who had removed his belt and was whipping it in the air with the never-forgotten hiss of a viper coiled to strike. Sorrow flooded through him, intact and precise, as if it had lain always in his mind, waiting. He was once again in the armoire where his father locked him to punish him for imagined misbehavior, there where for eternal hours he had crouched with his eyes closed, not to see the darkness, with his hands over his ears, to shut out the beating of his heart, trembling, huddled like a cornered animal. Wandering in the mist of his memories he found his sister Katharina, a sweet, re-tarded child who spent her life hiding, with the hope that her father would forget the dis-grace of her having been born. With Katharina, Rolf crawled beneath the dining room table, and with her hid there under the long white tablecloth, two children forever embraced, alert to footsteps and voices. Katharina's scent melded with his own sweat, with aromas of cook-ing, garlic, soup, freshly baked bread, and the unexpected odor of putrescent clay. His sis-ter's hand in his, her frightened breathing, her silk hair against his cheek, the candid gaze of her eyes. Katharina . . . Katharina materialized before him, floating on the air like a flag, clothed in the white tablecloth, now a winding sheet, and at last he could weep for her death and for the guilt of having abandoned her. He understood then that all his exploits as a reporter, the feats that had won him such recognition and fame, were merely an attempt to keep his most ancient fears at bay, a stratagem for taking refuge behind a lens to test whether reality was more tolerable from that perspective. He took excessive risks as an exer-cise of courage, training by day to conquer the monsters that tormented him by night. But he had come face to face with the moment of truth; he could not continue to escape his past. He *was* Azucena; he was buried in the clayey mud; his terror was not the distant emo-tion of an almost forgotten childhood, it was a claw sunk in his throat. In the flush of his tears he saw his mother, dressed in black and clutching her imitation-crocodile pocketbook to her bosom, just as he had last seen her on the dock when she had come to put him on the boat to South America. She had not come to dry his tears, but to tell him to pick up a shovel: the war was over and now they must bury the dead.

"Don't cry. I don't hurt anymore. I'm fine," Azucena said when dawn came.

25   "I'm not crying for you," Rolf Carlé smiled. "I'm crying for myself. I hurt all over."

The third day in the valley of the cataclysm began with a pale light filtering through storm clouds. The President of the Republic visited the area in his tailored safari jacket to confirm that this was the worst catastrophe of the century; the country was in mourning; sister nations had offered aid; he had ordered a state of siege; the Armed Forces would be merciless, anyone caught stealing or committing other offenses would be shot on sight. He added that it was impossible to remove all the corpses or count the thousands who had dis-appeared; the entire valley would be declared holy ground, and bishops would come to cel-ebrate a solemn mass for the souls of the victims. He went to the Army field tents to offer relief in the form of vague promises to crowds of the rescued, then to the improvised hospi-tal to offer a word of encouragement to doctors and nurses worn down from so many hours of tribulations. Then he asked to be taken to see Azucena, the little girl the whole world had seen. He waved to her with a limp statesman's hand, and microphones recorded his emo-tional voice and paternal tone as he told her that her courage had served as an example to the nation. Rolf Carlé interrupted to ask for a pump, and the President assured him that he personally would attend to the matter. I caught a glimpse of Rolf for a few seconds kneeling beside the mudpit. On the evening news broadcast, he was still in the same position; and I, glued to the screen like a fortuneteller to her crystal ball, could tell that something funda-mental had changed in him. I knew somehow that during the night his defenses had crum-bled and he had given in to grief; finally he was vulnerable. The girl had touched a part of him that he himself had no access to, a part he had never shared with me. Rolf had wanted to console her, but it was Azucena who had given him consolation.

I recognized the precise moment at which Rolf gave up the fight and surrendered to the torture of watching the girl die. I was with them, three days and two nights, spying on them from the other side of life. I was there when she told him that in all her thirteen years no boy had ever loved her and that it was a pity to leave this world without knowing love. Rolf assured her that he loved her more than he could ever love anyone, more than he loved his mother, more than his sister, more than all the women who had slept in his arms, more than he loved me, his life companion, who would have given anything to be trapped in that well in her place, who would have exchanged her life for Azucena's, and I watched as he leaned down to kiss her poor forehead, consumed by a sweet, sad emotion he could not name. I felt how in that instant both were saved from despair, how they were freed from the clay, how they rose above the vultures and helicopters, how together they flew above the vast swamp of corruption and laments. How, finally, they were able to accept death. Rolf Carlé prayed in silence that she would die quickly, because such pain cannot be borne.

By then I had obtained a pump and was in touch with a general who had agreed to ship it the next morning on a military cargo plane. But on the night of that third day, beneath the unblinking focus of quartz lamps and the lens of a hundred cameras, Azucena gave up, her eyes locked with those of the friend who had sustained her to the end. Rolf Carlé removed the life buoy, closed her eyelids, held her to his chest for a few moments, and then let her go. She sank slowly, a flower in the mud.

You are back with me, but you are not the same man. I often accompany you to the station and we watch the videos of Azucena again; you study them intently, looking for something you could have done to save her, something you did not think of in time. Or maybe you study them to see yourself as if in a mirror, naked. Your cameras lie forgotten in a closet; you do not write or sing; you sit long hours before the window, staring at the mountains. Beside you, I wait for you to complete the voyage into yourself, for the old wounds to heal. I know that when you return from your nightmares, we shall again walk hand in hand, as before.

■ EXPLORATIONS OF THE TEXT

1. Why does the narrator think that Rolf Carlé becomes so involved with the plight of the girl? Why do you think he does?
2. Analyze the relationship between the woman and Carlé. Can you find textual references to support your assertions? For example, do you understand why she "envies" Azucena?
3. Describe the event that begins the tale, and relate it to the title. Explain the symbolism of the earth swallowing the girl.
4. Do you think that memory works in short flashes, as Allende indicates here? What memories does this event stir up for Carlé? How to these memories relate to the girl's plight? What do we readers get from Carlé's brief flashbacks?
5. What role does the woman play in the story? What does she do? How is her passive observation of the events useful to the reader?
6. Discuss whether the ending is optimistic. Why?

■ THE READING/WRITING CONNECTION

1. The narrator explains that as a cameraman, Carlé sees the world through a lens, as a potential picture. Freewrite about the significance of this perspective within the story.
2. Write a brief, stream-of-consciousness piece from three perspectives: Acuzena, Carlé, and the woman. Change voices, content, and perspective.
3. What is trauma (from the German *der traum*, "the dream")? Write a Freudian analysis of Carlé's experience.

4. Compare/contrast the inability of Carlé to save the girl with Didion's recognition of the power of the Hoover Dam. Is nature or humankind ultimately more powerful? What position do you think Allende presents?

■ **IDEAS FOR WRITING**

1. At the end of the story, the narrator realizes that although Carlé has returned, he is not the same man. Write about an experience of your own that changed you. Was the change noticeable to other people?
2. Write a love letter from the woman to Carlé.
3. Write a poem to Carlé or the girl expressing your feelings about the situation. You may write in your own voice or in the voice of Carlé or the girl.
4. Describe a moment in your life that you know you have yet to fully understand and deal with on a psychological level.

Stories for Comparison/Contrast: Facing Death

LORRIE MOORE (1957–)   **1998**

DANCE IN AMERICA

I tell them dance begins when a moment of hurt combines with a moment of boredom. I tell them it's the body's reaching, bringing air to itself. I tell them that it's the heart's triumph, the victory speech of the feet, the refinement of animal lunge and flight, the purest metaphor of tribe and self. It's life flipping death the bird.

I make this stuff up. But then I feel the stray voltage of my rented charisma, hear the jerry-rigged authority in my voice, and I, too, believe. I'm convinced. The troupe dismantled, the choreography commissions dwindling, my body harder to make limber, to make go, I have come here for two weeks—to Pennsylvania Dutch[1] country, as a "Dancer in the Schools." I visit classes, at colleges and elementary schools, spreading Dance's holy word. My head fills with my own yack. What interior life has accrued in me is depleted fast, emptied out my mouth, as I stand before audiences, answering their fearful, forbidding *German* questions about art and my "whorish dances" (the thrusted hip, the sudden bump and grind before an *attitude*). They ask why everything I make seems so "feministic."

"I think the word is *feministical*," I say. I've grown tired. I burned down my life for a few good pieces, and now this.

With only one night left, I've fled the Quality Inn. (CREAMED CHICKEN ON WAFFLE $3.95 reads the sign out front. How could I leave?) The karaoke in the cocktail lounge has kept me up, all those tipsy and bellowing voices just back from the men's room and urged to the front of the lounge to sing "Sexual Healing" or "Alfie." I've accepted an invitation to stay with my old friend Cal, who teaches anthropology at Burkwell, one of the myriad local colleges. He and his wife own a former frat house they've never bothered to renovate. "It was the only way we could live in a house this big," he says. "Besides, we're perversely fascinated

---

[1] German-speaking Swiss or French Huguenots, not Dutch from Holland, who settled in Pennsylvania before 1812.

by the wreckage." It is Fastnacht,[2] the lip of Lent, the night when the locals make hot fried dough and eat it in honor of Christ. We are outside, before dinner, walking Cal's dog, Chappers, in the cold.

5   "The house *is* amazing to look at," I say. "It's beat-up in such an intricate way. Like a Rauschenberg.[3] Like one of those beautiful wind-tattered billboards one sees in the California desert." I'm determined to be agreeable; the house, truth be told, is a shock. Maple seedlings have sprouted up through the dining room floorboards, from where a tree outside has pushed into the foundation. Squirrels the size of collies scrabble in the walls. Paint is chipping everywhere, in scales and blisters and flaps; in the cracked plaster beneath are written the names of women who, in 1972, 1973, and 1974, spent the night during Spring Rush weekend. The kitchen ceiling reads "Sigma power!" and "Wank me with a spoon."

    But I haven't seen Cal in twelve years, not since he left for Belgium on a Fulbright[4] so I must be nice. He seems different to me: shorter, older, cleaner, despite the house. In a burst of candor, he has already confessed that those long years ago, out of friendship for me, he'd been exaggerating his interest in dance. "I didn't get it," he admitted. "I kept trying to figure out the *story*. I'd look at the purple guy who hadn't moved in a while, and I'd think, So what's the issue with *him*?"

    Now Chappers tugs at his leash. "Yeah, the house." Cal sighs. "We did once have a painter give us an estimate, but we were put off by the names of the paints: Myth, Vesper, Snickerdoodle. I didn't want anything called Snickerdoodle in my house."

    "What *is* a Snickerdoodle?"

    "I think they're hunted in Madagascar."

10   I leap to join him, to play. "Or eaten in Vienna," I say.

    "Or worshiped in L.A." I laugh again for him, and then we watch as Chappers sniffs at the roots of an oak.

    "But a myth or a vesper—they're always good," I add.

    "Crucial," he says. "But we didn't need paint for that."

    Cal's son, Eugene, is seven and has cystic fibrosis[5] Eugene's whole life is a race with medical research. "It's not that I'm not for the arts," says Cal. "*You're* here; money for the arts brought you here. That's wonderful. It's wonderful to see you after all these years. It's wonderful to fund the arts. *It's* wonderful; you're wonderful. The arts are so nice and wonderful. But really: I say, let's give all the money, every last fucking dime, to science."

15   Something chokes up in him. There can be optimism in the increments, the bits, the chapters; but I haven't seen him in twelve years and he has had to tell me the whole story, straight from the beginning, and it's the whole story that's just so sad.

    "We both carried the gene but never knew," he says. "That's the way it works. The odds are one in twenty, times one in twenty, and then after that, still only one in four. One in sixteen hundred, total. Bingo! We should move to Vegas."

    When I first knew Cal, we were in New York, just out of graduate school; he was single, and anxious, and struck me as someone who would never actually marry and have a family, or if he did, would marry someone decorative, someone slight. But now, twelve years later, his silver-haired wife, Simone, is nothing like that: she is big and fierce and original, joined with him in grief and courage. She storms out of PTA meetings. She glues little

---

[2] The day before Ash Wednesday, marking the beginning of Lent. "Fastnacht," "the day of the feast," is celebrated by eating doughnuts.

[3] Robert Rauschenberg (1925–   ) is an American contemporary artist.

[4] A fellowship given to graduate students, scholars, and professionals to study abroad.

[5] A genetic disease that affects the lungs.

sequins to her shoes. English is her third language; she was once a French diplomat to Belgium and to Japan. "I miss the caviar" is all she'll say of it. "I miss the caviar so much." Now, in Pennsylvania Dutchland, she paints satirical oils of long-armed handless people. "The locals," she explains in her French accent, giggling. "But I can't paint hands." She and Eugene have made a studio from one of the wrecked rooms upstairs.

"How is Simone through all this?" I ask.

"She's better than I am," he says. "She had a sister who died young. She expects unhappiness."

20   "But isn't there hope?" I ask, stuck for words.

Already, Cal says, Eugene has degenerated, grown worse, too much liquid in his lungs. "Stickiness," he calls it. "If he were three, instead of seven, there'd be *more* hope. The researchers are making some strides; they really are."

"He's a great kid," I say. Across the street, there are old Colonial houses with candles lit in each window; it is a Pennsylvania Dutch custom, or left over from Desert Storm, depending on whom you ask.

Cal stops and turns toward me, and the dog comes up and nuzzles him. "It's not just that Eugene's great," he says. "It's not just the precocity or that he's the only child I'll ever have. It's also that he's such a good person. He accepts things. He's very good at understanding everything."

I cannot imagine anything in my life that contains such sorrow as this, such anticipation of missing someone. Cal falls silent, the dog trots before us, and I place my hand lightly in the middle of Cal's back as we walk like that through the cold, empty streets. Up in the sky, Venus and the thinnest paring of sickle moon, like a cup and saucer, like a nose and mouth, have made the Turkish flag in the sky. "Look at that," I say to Cal as we traipse after the dog, the leash taut as a stick.

25   "Wow," Cal says. "The Turkish flag."

∞

"You're back, you're back!" Eugene shouts from inside, dashing toward the front door as we step up onto the front porch with Chappers. Eugene is in his pajamas already, his body skinny and hunched. His glasses are thick, magnifying, and his eyes, puffed and swimming, seem not to miss a thing. He slides into the front entryway, in his stocking feet, and lands on the floor. He smiles up at me, all charm, like a kid with a crush. He has painted his face with Merthiolate and hopes we'll find that funny.

"Eugene, you look beautiful!" I say.

"No I don't!" he says. "I look *witty*."

"Where's your mother?" asks Cal, unleashing the dog.

30   "In the kitchen. Dad, Mom says you have to go up to the attic and bring down one of the pans for dinner." He gets up and chases after Chappers, to tackle him and bring him back.

"We have a couple pots up there to catch leaks," Cal explains, taking off his coat. "But then we end up needing the pots for cooking, so we fetch them back."

"Do you need some help?" I don't know whether I should be with Simone in the kitchen, Cal in the attic, or Eugene on the floor.

"Oh, no. You stay here with Eugene," he says.

"Yeah. Stay here with me." Eugene races back from the dog and grabs my leg. The dog barks excitedly.

35   "You can show Eugene your video," Cal suggests as he leaves the room.

"Show me your dance video," he says to me in a singsong. "Show me, show me."

"Do we have time?"

"We have fifteen minutes," he says with great authority. I go upstairs and dig it out of my bag, then come back down. We plug it into the VCR and nestle on the couch together. He huddles close, cold in the drafty house, and I extend my long sweater around him like a shawl. I try to explain a few things, in a grown-up way, how this dance came to be, how movement, repeated, breaks through all resistance into a kind of stratosphere: from recalcitrance to ecstasy; from shoe to bird. The tape is one made earlier in the week. It is a demonstration with fourth graders. They each had to invent a character, then design a mask. They came up with various creatures: Miss Ninja Peacock. Mr. Bicycle Spoke Head. Evil Snowman. Saber-toothed Mom: "Half-girl-half-man-half-cat." Then I arranged the kids in a phalanx and led them, with their masks on, in an improvised dance to Kenny Loggins's "This Is It."

He watches, rapt. His brown hair hangs in strings in his face, and he chews on it. "There's Tommy Crowell," he says. He knows the fourth graders as if they were royalty. When it is over, he looks up at me, smiling, but businesslike. His gaze behind his glasses is brilliant and direct. "That was really a wonderful dance," he says. He sounds like an agent.

40 "Do you really think so?"

"Absolutely," he says. "It's colorful and has lots of fun, interesting steps."

"Will you be my agent?" I ask.

He scowls, unsure. "I don't know. Is the agent the person who drives the car?"

"Dinner's ready!" Simone calls from two rooms away, the "Wank me with a spoon" room.

45 "Coming!" shouts Eugene, and he leaps off the couch and slides into the dining room, falling sideways into her chair. *"Whoo,"* he says, out of breath. "1 almost didn't make it."

"Here," says Cal. He places a goblet of pills at Eugene's place setting.

Eugene makes a face, but in the chair, he gets up on his knees, leans forward, glass of water in one hand, and begins the arduous activity of taking all the pills.

I sit in the chair opposite him and place my napkin in my lap.

Simone has made a soup with hard-boiled eggs in it (a regional recipe, she explains), as well as Peking duck, which is ropy and sweet. Cal keeps passing around the basket of bread, anxiously, talking about how modern man has only been around for 45,000 years and probably the bread hasn't changed much since then.

50 "Forty-five thousand years?" says Simone. "That's all? That can't be. I feel like we've been *married* for that long."

There are people who talk with their hands. Then there are people who talk with their arms. Then there are people who talk with their arms over their head. These are the ones I like best. Simone is one of those.

"Nope, that's it," says Cal, chewing. "Forty-five thousand. Though for about two hundred thousand years before that, early man was going through all kinds of anatomical changes to get where we are today. It was a *very* exciting time." He pauses, a little breathlessly. "I wish I could have been there."

"Ha!" exclaims Simone.

"Think of the parties," I say.

55 "Right," says Simone. " 'Joe, how've you been? Your head's so *big* now, and, well, what is this crazy thing you're doing with your thumb?' A lot like the parties in Soda Springs, Idaho."

"Simone used to be married to someone in Soda Springs, Idaho," Cal says to me.

"You re kidding!" I say

"Oh, it was very brief," she says. "He was ridiculous. I got rid of him after about six months. Supposedly, he went off and killed himself." She smiles at me impishly.

"Who killed himself?" asks Eugene. He has swallowed all the pills but one.

60   "Mommy's first husband," says Cal.

"Why did he kill himself?" Eugene is staring at the middle of the table, trying to think about this.

"Eugene, you've lived with your mother for seven years now, and you don't know why someone close to her would want to kill himself?" Simone and Cal look straight across at each other and laugh brightly.

Eugene smiles in an abbreviated and vague way. He understands this is his parents' joke, but he doesn't like or get it. He is bothered they have turned his serious inquiry into a casual laugh. He wants information! But now, instead, he just digs into the duck, poking and looking.

Simone asks about the school visits. What am I finding? Are people nice to me? What is my life like back home? Am I married?

65   "I'm not married," I say.

"But you and Patrick are still together, aren't you?" Cal says in a concerned way.

"Uh, no. We broke up."

"You broke up?" Cal puts his fork down.

"Yes," I say, sighing.

70   "Gee, I thought you guys would never break up!" he says in a genuinely flabbergasted tone.

"*Really*?" I find this reassuring somehow, that my relationship at least looked good from the outside, at least to someone.

"Well, not *really*," admits Cal. "Actually, I thought you guys would break up long ago."

"Oh," I say.

"So *you* could marry her?" says the amazing Eugene to his father, and we all laugh loudly, pour more wine into glasses, and hide our faces in them.

75   "The thing to remember about love affairs," says Simone, "is that they are all like having raccoons in your chimney."

"Oh, not the raccoon story," groans Cal.

"Yes! The raccoons!" cries Eugene.

I'm sawing at my duck.

"We have raccoons sometimes in our chimney," explains Simone.

80   "Hmmm," I say, not surprised.

"And once we tried to smoke them out. We lit a fire, knowing they were there, but we hoped that the smoke would cause them to scurry out the top and never come back. Instead, they caught on fire and came crashing down into our living room, all charred and in flames and running madly around until they dropped dead." Simone swallows some wine. "Love affairs are like that," she says. "They all are like that."

I'm confused. I glance up at the light, an old brass octopus of a chandelier. All I can think of is how Patrick said, when he left, fed up with my "selfishness," that if I were worried about staying on alone at the lake house, with its squirrels and call girl–style lamps, I should just rent the place out—perhaps to a nice lesbian couple like myself.

But Eugene, across from me, nods enthusiastically, looks pleased. He's heard the raccoon story before and likes it. Once again, it's been told right, with flames and gore.

Now there is salad, which we pick and tear at like crows. Afterward, we gaze upon the bowl of fruit at the center of the table, lazily pick a few grapes off their stems. We sip hot tea that Cal brings in from the kitchen. We sip until it's cool, and then until it's gone. Already the time is ten o'clock.

85   "Dance time, dance time!" says Eugene when we're through. Every night, before bed, they all go out into the living room and dance until Eugene is tired and falls asleep on the sofa. Then they carry him upstairs and tuck him in.

     He comes over to my chair and takes my hand, leads me out into the living room.

     "What music shall we dance to?" I ask.

     "You choose," he says, and leads me to the shelf where they keep their compact discs. Perhaps there is some Stravinsky. Perhaps *Petrouchka*, with its rousing salute to Shrovetide.

     "Will you come see me tomorrow when you visit the fourth graders?" he asks as I'm looking through the selection. Too much Joan Baez. Too much Mahler. "I'm in room one oh four" he says. "When you visit the fourth graders, you can just stop by my classroom and wave to me from the door. I sit between the bulletin board and the window."

90   "Sure!" I say, not knowing that, in a rush, I will forget, and that I'll be on the plane home already, leafing through some inane airline magazine, before I remember that I forgot to do it. "Look," I say, finding a Kenny Loggins disc. It has the song he heard earlier, the one from the video. "Let's play this."

     "Goody," he says. "Mom! Dad! Come on!"

     "All right, Eugenie-boy," says Cal, coming in from the dining room. Simone is behind him.

     "I'm Mercury, I'm Neptune, now I'm Pluto so far away," says Eugene, dashing around the room, making up his own dance.

     "They're doing the planets in school," says Simone.

95   "Yes," says Eugene. "We're doing the planets'"

     "And which planet," I ask him, "do you think is the most interesting?" Mars, with its canals? Saturn, with its rings?

     Eugene stands still, looks at me thoughtfully, solemnly. "Earth, of course," he says.

     Cal laughs. "Well, that's the right answer!"

     "This is it!" sings Kenny Loggins. "This is it!" We make a phalanx and march, strut, slide to the music. We crouch, move backward, then burst forward again. We're aiming to create the mildewy, resinous sweat smell of dance, the parsed, repeated movement. Cal and Simone are into it. They jiggle and link arms. "This is it!" In the middle of the song, Eugene suddenly sits down to rest on the sofa, watching the grown-ups. Like the best dancers and audiences in the world, he is determined not to cough until the end.

100   "Come here, honey," I say, going to him. I am thinking not only of my own body here, that unbeguilable, broken basket, that stiff meringue. I am not, Patrick, thinking only of myself, my lost troupe, my empty bed. I am thinking of the dancing body's magnificent and ostentatious scorn. This is how we offer ourselves, enter heaven, enter speaking: we say with motion, in space, This is what life's done so far down here; this is all and what and everything it's managed—this body, these bodies, that body—so what do you think, Heaven? What do you fucking think?

     "Stand next to me," I say, and Eugene does, looking up at me with his orange warrior face. We step in place: knees up, knees down. Knees up, knees down. Dip-glide-slide. Dip-glide-slide. "This is it!" "This is it!" Then we go wild and fling our limbs to the sky.

Ben Okri (1959–)   **1993**

A PRAYER FROM THE LIVING

We entered the town of the dying at sunset. We went from house to house. Everything was as expected, run-down, a desert, luminous with death and hidden life. The gunrunners were everywhere. The world was now at the perfection of chaos. The little godfathers who controlled everything raided the food brought for us. They raided the airlifts and the relief aid and distributed most of the food among themselves and members of their clan.

We no longer cared. Food no longer mattered. I had done without for three weeks. Now I feed on the air and on the quest.

Every day, as I grow leaner, I see more things around us. I see the dead—all who had died of starvation. They are more joyful now; they are happier than we are; and they are everywhere, living their luminous lives as if nothing had happened, or as if they were more alive than we are.

5   The hungrier I became, the more I saw them—my old friends who had died before me, clutching onto flies. Now they feed on the light of the air. And they look at us—the living—with so, much pity and compassion.

I suppose this is what the white ones cannot understand when they come with their TV cameras and their aid. They expect to see us weeping. Instead, they see us staring at them, without begging, and with a bulging placidity in our eyes. Maybe they are secretly horrified that we are not afraid of dying this way.

But after three weeks of hunger the mind no longer notices; you're more dead than alive; and it's the soul wanting to leave that suffers. It suffers because of the body's tenacity.

We should have come into the town at dawn. In the town everyone had died. The horses and cows were dying, too. I could say that the air stank of death, but that wouldn't be true. It smelled of rancid butter and poisoned heat and bad sewage. There was even the faint irony of flowers.

The only people who weren't dead were the dead. Singing golden songs in chorus, jubilant everywhere, they carried on their familiar lives. The only others who weren't dead were the soldiers. And they fought among themselves eternally. It didn't seem to matter to them how many died. All that mattered was how well they handled the grim mathematics of the wars, so that they could win the most important battle of all, which was for the leadership of the fabulous graveyard of this once beautiful and civilized land,

10   I was searching for my family and my lover. I wanted to know if they had died or not. If I didn't find out, I intended to hang on to life by its last tattered thread. If I knew that they, too, were dead and no longer needed me, I would die at peace.

All my information led me to this town. If my lover, my brothers, my family are anywhere, they are here. This is the last town in the world. Beyond its rusted gate lies the desert. The desert stretches all the way into the past; into history, to the Western world, and to the source of drought and famine—the mighty mountain of lovelessness. From its peaks, at night, the grim spirits of negation chant their awesome soul-shrinking songs. Their songs steal hope from us and make us yield to the air our energies. Their songs are cool and make us submit to the clarity of dying.

Behind us, in the past, before all this came to be, there were all the possibilities in the world. There were all the opportunities for starting from small things to create a sweet new history and future, if only we had seen them. But now, ahead, there lie only the songs of the mountain of death.

We search for our loved ones mechanically and with a dryness in our eyes. Our stomachs no longer exist. Nothing exists except the search. We turn the bodies over, looking for familiar faces. All the faces are familiar; death made them all my kin.

I search on, I come across an unfamiliar face; it is my brother. I nod. I pour dust on his flesh. Hours later, near a dry well, I come across the other members of my family. My mother holds on tightly to a bone so dry it wouldn't even nourish the flies. I nod twice. I pour dust on their bodies. I search on. There is one more face whose beautiful unfamiliarity will console me. When I have found the face, then I will submit myself to the mountain songs.

15   Sunset was approaching when, from an unfinished school building, I heard singing. It was the most magical sound I had ever heard and I thought only those who know how sweet life is can sing like that, can sing as if breathing were a prayer.

    The singing was like the joyous beginning of all creation, the holy yes to the breath and light infusing all things, which makes the water shimmer, the plants sprout, the animals jump and play in the fields, and which makes the men and women look out into the first radiance of colors, the green of plants, the blue of sea, the gold of the air, the silver of the stars. It was the true end of my quest, the music to crown this treacherous life of mine, the end I couldn't have hoped for, or imagined.

    It seemed to take an infinity of time to get to the school building. I had no strength left, and it was only the song's last echo, resounding through the vast spaces of my hunger, that sustained me. After maybe a century, when history had repeated itself and brought about exactly the same circumstances, because none of us ever learned our lesson, or loved enough to learn from our pain, I finally made it to the schoolroom door. But a cow, the only living thing left in the town, went in through the door before I did. It, too, must have been drawn by the singing. The cow went into the room, and I followed.

    Inside, all the space was taken up with the dead. But here the air didn't have death in it. The air had prayer in it. The prayers stank more than the deaths. But all the dead here were differently dead from the corpses out side. The dead in the school were—forgive the paradox— *alive.* I have no other word to explain the serenity. I felt they had made the room holy because they had, in their last moments, thought not of themselves but of all people who suffer. I felt that to be the case because I felt myself doing the same thing. I crawled to a corner, sat against a wall, and felt myself praying for the whole human race.

    I prayed—knowing full well that prayers are possibly an utter waste of time—but I prayed for everything that lived, for mountains and trees, for animals and streams, and for human beings, wherever they might be. I heard the great anguished cry of all mankind, its great haunting music as well. And I, too, without moving my mouth, for I had no energy, began to sing in silence. I sang all through the evening. And when I looked at the body next to me and found the luminous unfamiliarity of its face to be that of my lover's—I sang all through the recognition. I sang silently even when a good-hearted white man came into the school building with a television camera and, weeping, recorded the roomful of the dead for the world—and I hoped he recorded my singing, too.

20   And the dead were all about me, smiling, serene. They didn't urge me on; they were just quietly and intensely joyful. They did not ask me to hurry to them, but left it to me. What could I choose? Human life—full of greed and bitterness, dim, low-oxygenated, judgmental and callous, gentle, too, and wonderful as well, but . . . human life had betrayed me. And besides, there was nothing left to save in me. Even my soul was dying of starvation.

    I opened my eyes for the last time. I saw the cameras on us all. To them, we were the dead. As I passed through the agony of the light, I saw them as the dead, marooned in a world without pity or love.

    As the cow wandered about in the apparent desolation of the room, it must have seemed odd to the people recording it all that I should have made myself so comfortable among the dead. I did. I stretched myself out and held the hand of my lover. With a painful breath and a gasp and a smile, I let myself go.

    The smile must have puzzled the reporters. If they had understood my language, they would have known that it was my way of saying goodbye.

▪ POETRY ▪

W. S. MERWIN

W. S. Merwin (1927–   ) was born in New York City and educated at Princeton University. Merwin has written more than thirty collections of poetry and has translated several volumes of poetry and prose. His poetry has been published in Harper's, The Nation, The New Yorker, Atlantic, Kenyon Review, *and* Evergreen Review. *He served as the poetry editor of* The Nation *in 1962. A Pulitzer Prize winner, Merwin's most recent awards include the Lenore Marshall Poetry Prize in 1994 for* Travels, *the Tanning Prize for Poetry in 1994, and the Lila Wallace/ Reader's Digest fellowship in 1994. In 1999, he was named Poetry Consultant to the Library of Congress along with poets Rita Dove and Louise Glück. His most recent book is entitled* Ends of the Earth *(2004). Merwin is well known for his interest in ecological issues and lives on an old pineapple plantation in Hawaii, which he is restoring to its natural rainforest state. "The Chinese Mountain Fox" comes from his collection,* The River Sound *(1999).*

1998

THE CHINESE MOUNTAIN FOX

Now we can tell that there
must once have been a time
when it was always there
and might at any time

5   appear out of nowhere
as they were wont to say
and probably to their
age it did look that way

though how are we to say
10 from the less than certain
evidence of our day
and they referred often

through the centuries when
it may have been a sight
15 they considered common
so that they mentioned it

as a presence they were
sure everyone had seen
and would think familiar
20 they alluded even

then until it became
their unquestioned habit
like a part of the name
to that element it

25 had of complete surprise
of being suddenly

the blaze in widened eyes
that had been turned only

at that moment upon
30 some place quite near that they
all through their lives had known
and passed by every day

perhaps at the same place
where they themselves had just
35 been standing that live face
looking as though it must

have been following them
would have appeared with no
warning they could fathom
40 or ever come to know

though they made studied use
of whatever system
logic calculus ruse
they trusted in their time

45 to tell them where they might
count on it next and when
if once they figured right
as though it traveled in

a pattern they could track
50 like the route of some far
light in the zodiac
comet or migrant star

but it was never where
they had thought it would be
55 and showed the best of their
beliefs successively

to be without substance
shadows they used to cast
old tales and illusions
60 out of some wishful past

each in turn was consigned
to the role of legend
while yet another kind
of legend had wakened

65 to play the animal
even while it was there
the unpredictable
still untaken creature

part lightning and part rust
70 the fiction was passed down
with undiminished trust
while the sightings began

to be unusual
second-hand dubious
75 unverifiable
turning to ghost stories

all the more easily
since when it had been seen
most times that was only
80 by someone all alone

and unlike its cousins
of the lowlands captive
all these generations
and kept that way alive

85 never had it been caught
poisoned or hunted down
by packs of dogs or shot
hung up mounted or worn

never even been seen
90 twice by the same person
in the place it had been
when they looked there again

and whatever they told
of it as long as they
95 still spoke of it revealed
always more of the way

they looked upon the light
while it was theirs to see
and what they thought it might
100 let them glimpse at any

moment than of the life
that they had rarely been
able to catch sight of
in an instant between

105 now and where it had been
at large before they came
when the mountains were green
before it had a name

■ EXPLORATIONS OF THE TEXT

1. Merwin repeats the word "time" twice in the first stanza. What other words in the poem signify time? What words signify definite as opposed to uncertain objects?
2. There is no punctuation in this poem, and, aside from the capitalized first letter, there are no obvious beginnings or endings of sentences. What effect does this produce? How does this add to the poem's meaning?
3. How do we know that the poem is about a fox? Provide more than one answer.
4. Why is the fox described as "unpredictable"? What are the human attitudes toward the fox?
5. The theme of naming, or knowing, runs through the poem. Why is this important?

■ **THE READING/WRITING CONNECTION**

1. The poem begins with the narrator looking back in time, speculating about a time that the fox was always there. Write a journal entry in which you look back in time and describe something that no longer exists. You can write about anything—it does not have to be a living creature.

■ **IDEAS FOR WRITING**

1. "The Chinese Mountain Fox" explores the fading of the real to the mythical. Write a myth of your own, using as the mythical creature an earth animal that is now alive but will someday be extinct.
2. Write an essay about an animal or plant that has gone or is presently going extinct.
3. Compare/contrast the treatment of extinction in this and Oliver's "Ghosts."

JUDITH EMLYN JOHNSON

Judith Emlyn Johnson (1936–   ) is Professor of English at the State University of New York at Albany. Educated at Radcliffe, Barnard, and Columbia, Johnson has been recipient of many awards, including the Yale University Younger Poets Award. She served as President of the Poetry Society of America, 1975–78. Her works include How the Dead Count *(1978) and* The Ice Lizard *(1992). She is editor-in-chief of* 13th Moon: A Feminist Literary Journal. *Commenting on poetry, Johnson says, "Before poetry was anything else, it was a physical act: the act of making sounds in the throat." About fiction she says there was "the current of concentration uniting the storyteller with his or her listeners around the campfire or in the workplace, when the hands moved and the minds moved, and the dancer and the dance were one moving creature." In "Stone Olives," the speaker mourns the death of a student on Pan Am Flight 103, a plane destroyed by a terrorist bomb over Lockerbie, Scotland, in December 1988.*

1992

STONE OLIVES
(in memoriam Melina Hudson, of Albany,
Pan Am Flight 103, December 1988)

Tulip-flowered wind, night-smelling sea,
long swell of desert sands, and the roar of tractors
crawling up from the Hudson,[1] from under water
into Albany's Washington Park:[2] what is that ploughing?

5 It is the sound
      of olive trees.
First one, then two, then the whole grove, they drop
      their small, hard fruits,
  and their tears are gathered up,
10 packed into baskets, then carried
  to the earth-floored rooms.
        Some go into jars.

---

[1] A major river in New York.

[2] Reference to a park where Melina Hudson enjoyed leisure time with her friends, among them the poet's daughter.

Some have their centers plucked out
to be filled with slivered almonds or roasted
15   red peppers. Some go to the press
where they're crushed. From their pulp
oozes the purest gold,
to be strained into jars and sold.
Little dead ones, they sing, *blink blink,*
20   as they fall, *little dead ones, blink blink*
la muerte, ay, los niños, ay, la muerte.[3]
Take my hand, come down, dance with me, take my hand.

Tulip-fluttered wind, night-swelling sea:
in the smell of desert sands, before we were born,
25 the tractors ploughed back time from under Mount Sinai[4]
into Washington Park. There, carved stone
Moses[5] watches his wise God stand hard by
as the father prepares to spill on the quickening sand
his son. No olive trees whisper here. Does Abraham[6]
30 see that no scapegoat waits at hand? His son
and his son's sons and daughters,
sucked down, will sweeten that sand, no matter how many
small, innocent, wordless furs squeak out their lives.
What is dying now, even as we speak, to save us?

35   It is the stand
of apple trees behind the barbed wire.
first one, then two, then the whole grove, the sun
flattens them. Gravid, they droop,
ripen, and men lean ladders,
40   and their treasures are gathered, packed,
into baskets, then ferried out
from the earth-walled rooms.
Some are rendered down,
some peeled of their skins, grated
45   with almonds, and mixed to haroseth that makes sweet
the bitter herbs. Some have their teeth plucked out
for the fillings. Some go to the press.
From their pulped flesh oozes the purest gold,
sweeter, oh Lord their God, than the fruit of the vine
50   to be filtered through cheesecloth and sold.
Little dead ones, they sing, *shalom,*[7]

---

[3] "Death, oh, the children, oh, death" (from the Spanish).

[4] Mountain of northeastern Egypt on the Sinai Peninsula.

[5] Hebrew prophet who led the Israelites out of Egyptian slavery. He delivered to them the commandments of their God's covenant at Mount Sinai.

[6] Allusion to patriarch of the Jews regarded as the founder of the Hebrew people through his son Isaac. This passage refers to God's commanding Abraham to sacrifice Isaac.

[7] Hebrew for "peace."

as they drop, *little dead ones, shalom*
ich sterbe hier,[8] *nicht versteh,*[9] *je crêve,*[10] *nou verbeshti,*[11] *mamaye.*[12]
Take my hand, come down, dance with me, take my hand.

55 Tulip-sequined wind, night-shimmying sea,
long bloom of desert sands, and the roar of the spring
festival onto the grass: tell me the mother,
before our history sprouted, should have thrown
herself under the blades to save her child. Yes, tell me
60 the father should have given to God the Father
his own life, not his son's. Tell me, if all,
man, woman, child, had thrown their lives away
rather than take that dumb, furred sacrifice
still squeaking its lives out under our knives
65 would all our history have borne different fruits?
We planted no orchard here next to City Hall[13]
but the walls still shake. What are we ploughing under
when we do that prime time shimmy?

It is the sands
70 of the pyramids.
One grain, then two, then whole stones, they melt.
Their sharp, unlanded granules
drill from their homeless camps the far away dam.
The wind lifts them, gathers them in, and they ride
75 the red tide's maternal breast
from their hulled earth rooms to their ghost of a promised land.
Stones fall, whole shoulders drop
from the Sphinx[14] who was raised
by forced labor. Eyes run
80 from their heads. Scalps, halves of scalps rain down.
Melina, who once danced
at proms far from Beirut,[15] laughed with my daughter
years after Hiroshima[16] broke into flower, told
her beads in a church the Gulag[17] never touched,
85 now pours down through our air
her young hands full with the seventeen pressed years

---

[8] "I'm dying here." (German).

[9] "I don't understand" (German).

[10] "I'm collapsing"; "I'm being slaughtered"; "I'm dying like a dog." (French)

[11] "Shut up"; "don't talk"; literally "no more words." (Rumanian).

[12] "Mommy." (Rumanian).

[13] In Albany, New York.

[14] Egyptian statue in the form of a lion, having a man's head.

[15] Capital city of Lebanon.

[16] City in Japan. In this case, an allusion to the United States dropping an atomic bomb during World War II, an action that destroyed the city and ended the war in the Pacific.

[17] Network of labor camps in the former USSR.

that are all she can hold
of spring: will the Dead Sea[18]
grow fat with these fragments? Our mouths are being stuffed
90 with our sons and daughters, our centers plucked out
with tongs. From our poor,
pressed through heat, through cold
over vents and gratings, flow simples, poultices, tinctures
to be forced into jars and sold.
95   *Little dead ones,* they sing, *ushh, ushh,*
as they drop, *little dead ones, ushh, ushh.*
d d d kkkkk d d d kkkkk aaaaaaah heart
Take my hand, come down, dance with me, take my hand.

Tulip-grinning wind, night-crying sea,
100 long shudder of desert sands, and the drowned tractors
bubbling up from our bodies, cut from our tongues
deep into Washington Park where Moses holds
his law in his hands: they told me God Himself
gave His Son's life to stop it as Abraham
105 gave Isaac. But what if each father
should give himself? What if we all stand up,
we, who are old enough to have held our lives,
and empty out, not our children, but ourselves?
Why do I hear no such ploughing?

110   Instead, I hear the bend
beyond the asteroids bleed.
First one, then two, then whole planets they fall
and their milk will be pressed out,
their hulled tears, neither water or salt, hold elements
115   we can neither measure nor read
their red shift to name. They carry
no life we know as life in their milled earths.
Their centaurs[19] are long gone
replaced by an airless patience,
120   their languages hot ores,
or frozen metals.
Of their forgiveness nothing remains, not even Aztec
gold to be ferried away
to the galaxies and sold. We know what their silence says.
125 *Little dead ones,* they sing as they shimmy, *aaah nnnnn,*
as they drop, *little dead ones, aaah nnnnnnnn*
eiaa mohsrden, aiee, eiaa khilsderin, aiee, eiaaaa mohsdenn
nnnnhh   *aaaaaqaaaaahhhhh.*[20]
Take my hand, come down, dance with me, take my hand.

---

[18] Salt lake on the boundary between Israel and Jordan.

[19] Creature fabled to be half man and half horse.

[20] Invented language intended to convey the cries of the children; equivalent to "ay, los niños," or "Ick sterbe hier."

■ EXPLORATIONS OF THE TEXT

1. What worlds converge in stanza 1? What does the "ploughing" signify?
2. How does the symbolism of the "olive trees" change throughout the poem? With what are the olives connected?
3. With whom does the speaker identify at the end of stanza 2?
4. Explain the references to Abraham and Isaac. (See Genesis 22.)
5. Analyze the following: "What is dying now, even as we speak, to save us?"
6. What historical allusions are suggested in stanzas 3, 4, and 6?
7. What does the speaker present as the alternative to the sacrifice of "our children"?
8. In the last stanza, why does Johnson enlarge her vision to include the "fall" of the "planets"? What poetic device is used?
9. Discuss the contrasting images of "gold," pressed blood and flesh, and the pressed pulp of fruit.
10. What is the significance of the repetition and variation of the lines: "Tulip-flowered wind, night-smelling sea,/long swell of desert sands"?
11. What is the significance of the repetition of "Little dead ones" and "Take my hand, come down, dance with me, take my hand"?
12. Who is the speaker? What is the speaker's role in the poem?
13. Why does Johnson include lines in different languages?
14. Compare the speaker's view of global issues with Okri's. What futures do these writers imagine?

■ THE READING/WRITING CONNECTION

1. Read this poem aloud, and react to it.
2. Paraphrase the message of each stanza. How does the argument progress?
3. In a short essay, react to the visions of the past, of the present, and of the future. Do you agree with those visions?

■ IDEAS FOR WRITING

1. Gloss and annotate the text. Analyze the symbolism of the "stone olives."
2. Discuss the theme of sacrifice.
3. Who is the speaker? What is the speaker's role?

RABINDRANATH TAGORE

Rabindranath Tagore (1861-1941) was born in Calcutta, India. A mystical experience in 1883 led him to a conception of god as intimate, a wellspring of inspiration that greatly influenced his work. He wrote nearly sixty volumes of verse, more than forty plays, fourteen novels, two hundred short stories, and thousands of songs, in addition to numerous essays, journals, and religious and philosophical tracts. In 1913, shortly after he wrote Gitanjali *("Song Offerings"), a collection of serenely mystical poems inspired by the deaths of his father, wife, two daughters, and youngest son, Tagore became the first Indian writer to win the Nobel Prize for Literature.*

1910

GITANJALI: SONGS I AND II

I

Thou hast made me endless, such is thy pleasure. This frail vessel
thou emptiest again and again, and fillest it ever with fresh life.

This little flute of a reed thou hast carried over hills and dales, and
has breathed through it melodies eternally new.

5   At the immortal touch of thy hands my little heart loses its limits
in joy, and gives birth to utterance ineffable.

Thy infinite gifts come to me only on these very small hands of
mine. Ages pass, and still thou pourest, and still there is room to fill.

II

When thou commandest me to sing, it seems that my heart would
10 break with pride; and I look to thy face, and tears come to my eyes.

All that is harsh and dissonant in my life melts into one sweet
harmony—and my adoration spreads wings like a glad bird on its
flight across the sea.

I know thou takest pleasure in my singing. I know that only as a
15 singer I come before thy presence.

■ EXPLORATIONS OF THE TEXT

Song I
1. What does the speaker experience? Examine the images of the "vessel," the "flute," and
    the "heart."
2. What does the speaker mean when he describes "utterance ineffable"?
3. Interpret the last line. Explain the **paradox.**

Song II
1. What is the commandment "to sing"?
2. Why does "all that is harsh and dissonant" melt? Describe the speaker's version of
    harmony.
3. Explain the bird **simile.**
4. Why can the speaker come into the presence of divinity only as a singer? What does
    the joy of "singing" suggest?
5. Compare Tagore's and Rilke's views of spirit and divinity.

■ THE READING/WRITING CONNECTION
1. Describe the voice in these lyrics.
2. Create your own version of a third song in this sequence. Consider speaker, tone, im-
    agery, and theme.
3. "Think" Topic: What is the source of joy in these works?

■ IDEAS FOR WRITING
1. Write about the concept of divinity in these poems.
2. Characterize the speaker.
3. How does Tagore's poetry differ from other poets?

RAINER MARIA RILKE

*Born in Czechoslovakia, Rainer Maria Rilke (1875–1926) went to military school as a child and
attended university in his native Prague, in Berlin, and in Munich. The work that first gained
him recognition as a poet was* The Book of Images *(1902). Rilke wrote intermittently, in great
prolific bursts that he believed were periods of grace when the poems were "dictated" to him.*

He composed the Sonnets to Orpheus *in 1923 while he lived alone in a tower in Switzerland, but they were not published until eight years after his death from blood poisoning. With Rilke's* Duino Elegies, *the* Sonnets *are considered the greatest poems in modern German literature.*

1923

SONNET 1

There arose a tree. Oh, pure transcension!
Oh, Orpheus sings[1]! Oh, tall tree in the ear!
And all was still. But even in this suspension
new beginnings, signs, and changes were.

5 Animals from the silence, from the clear
now opened wood came forth from nest and den;
and it so came to pass that not from fear
or craftiness were they so quiet then,

but to be listening. Howling, cry, roar
10 seemed little to their hearts. Where scarce a
humble
hut for such reception was before,

a hiding-place of the obscurest yearning,
with entrance shaft whose underpinnings tremble,
15 you made for the beasts temples in the hearing.

■ EXPLORATIONS OF THE TEXT

1. What is the "transcension" in the first **quatrain?** What does the tree symbolize? What is the "tall tree in the ear"?
2. Why do the animals come forth? Why is the silence significant?
3. Explicate: "Howling, cry, roar/seemed little to their hearts."
4. Explain the last line. Who is "you"? Interpret "temples in the hearing."
5. What has Orpheus accomplished?
6. Explore the form of the poem as a version of the **Petrarchan sonnet,** with two **quatrains** (an **octave**) and two **tercets** (a **sestet**). What other formal elements are noteworthy?
7. Compare the tone of this sonnet to the tone in Rich's "Diving into the Wreck" and in Tagore's lyrics.

---

[1]According to Greek mythology, Orpheus was the son of Oeagrus, a river god, and one of the Muses (Polyhymnia, Clio, or Calliope). Born in Thrace, Orpheus may have been king of some Thracian tribes and was famous as a great singer, musician, and poet. In some legends, he supposedly invented the lyre. Because of the magic of his songs, all of nature responded to his music. Wild animals followed him, trees and plants leaned in his direction, and he tamed the souls of the wildest men.

The most famous exploit of Orpheus concerns his descent into the underworld to save his wife, Eurydice, who died when a serpent bit her. Inconsolable, he charmed monsters guarding the gates of hell and the gods of the dead in order to rescue her. For a brief moment, even the damned were relieved of pain by his music. The underworld deities, Hades and Persephone, agreed to allow Eurydice to return to earth with one stipulation: that Orpheus, followed by Eurydice, leave and that he not look back at her. When he could not resist temptation, he turned around, and she disappeared—lost to him forever.

- **THE READING/WRITING CONNECTION**
1. Gloss, annotate, and comment on this sonnet.
2. Create a scene in which music or art transforms animals and/or people.
3. Analyze the **paradoxes** in the poem.
4. Freewrite about silence in this sonnet.

- **IDEAS FOR WRITING**
1. Write about the figure of Orpheus. What are his powers?
2. Explicate and evaluate this sonnet. Use Reading/Writing Connection 1 as a beginning. Focus on imagery and form. (See chapter 10.)
3. Explore the theme of transformation in this poem, in "Diving into the Wreck," and in "My Name Is 'I Am Living.'"

RAINER MARIA RILKE (1875–1926) 1923

SONNET 29

Still friend of many distances, feel yet
how your breathing is augmenting space.
From the beamwork of gloomy belfries let
yourself ring. What devours you will increase

5 more strongly from this food. Explore and win
knowledge of transformation through and
    through.
What experience was the worst for you?
Is drinking bitter, you must turn to wine.

10 Be the magic power of this immense
midnight at the crossroads of your senses,
be the purport of their strange meeting. Though

earth itself forgot your very name,
15 say unto the tranquil earth: I flow.
To the fleeting water speak: I am.

- **EXPLORATIONS OF THE TEXT**
1. Who is the "friend"?
2. How does the poet "win" "transformation"? What is the value of the "worst" "experience"?
3. What does the speaker mean: "Be the magic power of this immense/midnight at the crossroads of your senses"?
4. Interpret the last three lines. What is the meaning of the declarations "I flow" and "I am"?
5. Compare the form of this sonnet with Sonnet 1.

- **THE READING/WRITING CONNECTION**
1. Does a person or poet learn from bitter experiences? Respond to this question in a journal entry.
2. "Think" Topic: Discuss transformation in Rilke's sonnets.

■ **IDEAS FOR WRITING**

1. Analyze the form of the poem. Is it effective?
2. Write a **parody** of this sonnet. Analyze your parody. Focus on point of view, tone, imagery, and form.
3. Can the poet or his or her art change the world?

ADRIENNE RICH

Adrienne Rich (1929–   ), born in Baltimore, Maryland, is one of America's finest poets and most influential feminists. She is also an essayist and teacher. Her works include the poetry collections A Change of World *(1951), selected by W. H. Auden for the Yale Younger Poets Award;* Snapshots of a Daughter-in-Law *(1963);* Facts of a Doorframe *(1984), as well as* On Lies, Secrets, and Silence—Selected Prose 1966–1978 *(1979),* What Is Found There: Notebooks on Poetry and Politics *(1993), and* Fox: Poems, 1998–2000 *(2001). Her awards include the 1974 National Book Award for* Diving into the Wreck.

1972

DIVING INTO THE WRECK

First having read the book of myths,
and loaded the camera,
and checked the edge of the knife-blade,
I put on
5   the body-armor of black rubber
the absurd flippers
the grave and awkward mask.
I am having to do this
not like Cousteau[1] with his
10 assiduous team
aboard the sun-flooded schooner
but here alone.

There is a ladder.
The ladder is always there
15 hanging innocently
close to the side of the schooner.
We know what it is for,
we who have used it.
Otherwise
20 it's a piece of maritime floss
some sundry equipment.

I go down.
Rung after rung and still
the oxygen immerses me
25 the blue light

---

[1] French underwater explorer and film maker (1910–97).

the clear atoms
of our human air.
I go down.
My flippers cripple me,
30 I crawl like an insect down the ladder
and there is no one
to tell me when the ocean
will begin.

First the air is blue and then
35 it is bluer and then green and then
black I am blacking out and yet
my mask is powerful
it pumps my blood with power
the sea is another story
40 the sea is not a question of power
I have to learn alone
to turn my body without force
in the deep element.

And now: it is easy to forget
45 what I came for
among so many who have always
lived here
swaying their crenellated[2] fans
between the reefs
50 and besides
you breathe differently down here.

I came to explore the wreck.
The words are purposes.
The words are maps.
55 I came to see the damage that was done
and the treasures that prevail.
I stroke the beam of my lamp
slowly along the flank
of something more permanent
60 than fish or weed

the thing I came for:
the wreck and not the story of the wreck
the thing itself and not the myth
the drowned face always staring
65 toward the sun
the evidence of damage
worn by salt and sway into this threadbare beauty
the ribs of the disaster
curving their assertion
70 among the tentative haunters.

---

[2] Having notched or scalloped projections.

This is the place.
And I am here, the mermaid whose dark hair
streams black, the merman in his armored body
We circle silently
75 about the wreck
we dive into the hold.
I am she: I am he

whose drowned face sleeps with open eyes
whose breasts still bear the stress
80 whose silver, copper, vermeil[3] cargo lies
obscurely inside barrels
half-wedged and left to rot
we are the half-destroyed instruments
that once held to a course
85 the water-eaten log
the fouled compass

We are, I am, you are
by cowardice or courage
the one who find our way
90 back to this scene
carrying a knife, a camera
a book of myths
in which
our names do not appear.

DEREK WALCOTT

*The first Caribbean writer to win the Nobel Prize for Literature (1992), Derek Walcott (1930–   )
was born on the island of St. Lucia. His first book appeared in 1948 when his mother gave him
two hundred dollars to have* Twenty-Five Poems *published. His volumes of poetry include* Sea
Grapes *(1976),* Midsummer *(1984), the epic* Omeros *(1990), and* Tiepolo's Hound *(2000). Walcott's poetry celebrates the diversity of modern English, Creole pidgin, and slang; he writes, "I had
a sound colonial education. / I have Dutch, nigger and English in me, / and either I'm nobody or
I'm a nation."*

1962

A FAR CRY FROM AFRICA

A wind is ruffling the tawny pelt
Of Africa. Kikuyu,[1] quick as flies,
Batten upon the bloodstreams of the veldt.[2]

---

[3] Metal that is gilded.

[1] African tribe who conducted an eight-year fight against British colonial settlers. They were known as Mau
Mau.

[2] Grassland in southern Africa with sparsely growing trees and shrubs.

Corpses are scattered through a paradise.
5 Only the worm, colonel of carrion, cries:
"Waste no compassion on these separate dead!"
Statistics justify and scholars seize
The salients of colonial policy.
What is that to the white child hacked in bed?
10 To savages, expendable as Jews?

Threshed out by beaters,[3] the long rushes break
In a white dust of ibises whose cries
Have wheeled since civilization's dawn
From the parched river or beast-teeming plain.
15 The violence of beast on beast is read
As natural law, but upright man
Seeks his divinity by inflicting pain.
Delirious as these worried beasts, his wars
Dance to the tightened carcass of a drum,
20 While he calls courage still that native dread
Of the white peace contracted by the dead.

Again brutish necessity wipes its hands
Upon the napkins of a dirty cause, again
A waste of our compassion, as with Spain,[4]
25 The gorilla wrestles with the superman.
I who am poisoned with the blood of both,
Where shall I turn, divided to the vein?
I who have cursed
The drunken officer of British rule, how choose
30 Between this Africa and the English tongue I love?
Betray them both, or give back what they give?
How can I face such slaughter and be cool?
How can I turn from Africa and live?

■ EXPLORATIONS OF THE TEXT

1. What are the double meanings of the title?
2. Analyze the depiction and **personification** of Africa in stanza 1. Examine the questions in lines 9–10. Why does the speaker allude to the Jews?
3. Explain the image of the ibises. How does this scene function?
4. How does the violence of "beast on beast" contrast with that of "upright man"?
5. Why does the speaker mention "a dirty cause"? Interpret the reference to Spain.
6. Explain: "The gorilla wrestles with the superman."
7. Examine the divided loyalties of the speaker. Will he choose?
8. Compare the view of Africa in this poem to that of *"Master Harold" . . . and the Boys.*

■ THE READING/WRITING CONNECTION

1. Describe a conflict, "divided to the vein," that represents your background.
2. Characterize the speaker. Respond to him. Is he "a far cry from Africa"?
3. Explicate a powerful image in the poem.

---

[3] People hired by game hunters to beat the bush in order to chase wild animals.
[4] Allusion to the Spanish Civil War (1936–39).

4. Relate the title of the poem to the effects of "colonial policy."

■ IDEAS FOR WRITING

1. Explicate this poem. Focus on persona, imagery, and formal elements.
2. What are themes of this poem?
3. Create a prose version of the poem. What is lost? What is gained?
4. Explore the image of Africa in this poem and in another work in this chapter.
5. Compare this poem with W. B. Yeats's "The Second Coming."

GLORIA ANZALDÚA (1942–2004)

In this poem, the speaker begins by reflecting on being a "mulata"[1]—Hispanic, Indian, black, Spanish, and white.

1986

TO LIVE IN THE BORDERLANDS MEANS YOU

To live in the Borderlands means you
    are neither *hispana india negra española*[2]
    ni[3] *gabacha,*[4] *eres mestiza,*[5] *mulata,* half-breed
    caught in the crossfire between camps
5   while carrying all five races on your back
    not knowing which side to turn to, run from;

To live in the Borderlands means knowing
    that the *india* in you, betrayed for 500 years,
    is no longer speaking to you,
10   that *mexicanas* call you *rajetas,*[6]
    that denying the Anglo inside you
    is as bad as having denied the Indian or Black;

Cuando vives en la frontera[7]
    people walk through you, the wind steals your voice,
15   you're a *burra,*[8] *buey,*[9] scapegoat,
    forerunner of a new race,
    half and half—both woman and man, neither—
    a new gender;

To live in the Borderlands means to
20   put *chile* in the borscht,

---

[1] A person of mixed racial ancestry.

[2] Spanish, Indian, black, black Spanish woman.

[3] Neither (nor).

[4] A Chicano term for a white woman [Author's note].

[5] You are of mixed blood.

[6] Literally, "Split," that is, having betrayed your word [Author's note].

[7] When you live in the borderlands.

[8] Donkey [Author's note].

[9] Ox [Author's note].

eat whole wheat *tortillas,*
speak Tex-Mex with a Brooklyn accent;
be stopped by *la migra* at the border checkpoints;

Living in the Borderlands means you fight hard to
25   resist the gold elixer beckoning from the bottle,
the pull of the gun barrel,
the rope crushing the hollow of your throat;

In the Borderlands
you are the battleground
30   where enemies are kin to each other;
you are at home, a stranger,
the border disputes have been settled
the volley of shots have shattered the truce
you are wounded, lost in action
35   dead, fighting back;

To live in the Borderlands means
the mill with the razor white teeth wants to shred off
your olive-red skin, crush out the kernel, your heart
pound you pinch you roll you out
40   smelling like white bread but dead;

To survive the Borderlands
you must live *sin fronteras*[10]
be a crossroads.

■ EXPLORATIONS OF THE TEXT

1. Who is "you"? How does the speaker characterize "you"?
2. In the Borderlands, "people walk through you, the wind steals your voice"—why?
3. How does the speaker extend her vision beyond the "mestiza"? Whom does her vision include? What are the other borders?
4. Analyze stanzas 5–8. To what specific historical contexts does Anzaldúa refer in stanzas 5 and 6?
5. Explain the symbolism of "the mill" in stanza 7. What is the central metaphor?
6. Examine the speaker's conclusion. What **paradox** is apparent?
7. Analyze the impact of the Spanish words. What do they add to the poem's effect?
8. Compare views of language, heritage, and naming in this poem with those in Walcott's "A Far Cry from Africa" or Rich's "Diving into the Wreck."

■ THE READING/WRITING CONNECTION

1. Freewrite. Respond to this poem. How do you react to the violent images?
2. Choose one stanza, and write a reader response. Do you agree with the persona's views?
3. "Think" Topic: Analyze the poem's structure as if it were an expository essay. What modes of development does Anzaldúa employ?

■ IDEAS FOR WRITING

1. Compare processes of awakening and revelation in this poem and in "Diving into the Wreck."

---

[10] Without borders [Author's note].

2. How does Anzaldúa envision/re-envision North American ethnic identity? Do you agree?
3. Paraphrase and analyze the political argument of this poem.
4. Compare the clash of traditions in this poem with the conflicts in *"Master Harold"* . . . *and the Boys* and "Girls at War."
5. Contrast Anzaldúa's view of "living in the borderlands" with Tagore's view of a limitless world.

MARJORIE AGOSIN

Marjorie Agosin (1955–) was born in Bethesda, Maryland; lived in Santiago, Chile, as a child; and immigrated to the United States in 1969. Agosin was educated at Indiana University, where she received a Ph.D. in 1982. Agosin's many books include volumes of poetry, short fiction, autobiography, essays, longer works of nonfiction, and collections of other writers, totaling more than seventy publications. She has been awarded a Fullbright fellowship to study in Argentina; the Good Neighbor Award for the National Association for Christians and Jews; the Latino Literature Prize, University of Miami North South Center (1995); the Letras de Oro Prize in Poetry; and the United Nations Leadership Award for Human Rights. Agosin's childhood in Chile and her experiences with anti-Semitism have influenced her writing. Her bilingual collection of poetry, Dear Anne Frank *(1994), is about the Holocaust, and* A Cross and a Star: Memoirs of a Jewish Girl in Chile *(1995), is the story of her mother's life in Chile, where, because she was Jewish, she was barred from the German, Catholic, and English schools. The following two poems, "Far Away" and "The Foreigner," from* At the Threshold of Memory *(2003), reflect on the complex relationship between an individual person and her homeland.*

2003

FAR AWAY

My country is a slender pier
anchored inside me
curving between
my knees and skin
5 still damp from the sun.
My country is a tatter of stars like pockmarks
a rhapsody of useless voices
that come out to mourn the moon
through the ravished pelt
10 of plain daylight.

My country is a blue vial
hidden and radiant as the sea
or the shadow of your eyes
that never will be blue.

15 My country is a man
whom I loved
and when he kissed me
my legs turned to rain
to a grove
20 to a boundary of holy water.

My country is the color of smoke
and coal-heated irons
that drowsily envelop
the houses of adobe.

25 My country
is my house with the keys
hidden waiting for me,
on the beach.

MARJORIE AGOSIN (1955–   )   **2003**

THE FOREIGNER

You will search for another
landscape in which
to speak with
your dead.
5 No words
will respond to the voices of your love.
You will make up another gaze
and you will walk with your head bowed as if wounded
in borrowed cities.

10 You will know that there will be no return for you
and you will name those who made
of your memory
a language of orphanhood.
You will think of other breaths
15 because yours are distant and alone
because your language
carries the shadows of strangers.

■ **EXPLORATIONS OF THE TEXT**

1. In "Far Away," metaphors define the speaker's relationship with her country. Explicate each one. What does each signify? How do the metaphors change? What do they suggest about her state of exile?
2. Explore the significance of the closing stanza.
3. In "The Foreigner," characterize the speaker's persona and voice.
4. In "The Foreigner," explore the significance of the "language of orphanhood." How does language separate her from others? How does it carry the memories of the past?
5. Who are "the strangers"? Discuss the significance of the closing two lines: "your language/ carries the shadows of strangers."
6. A state of exile often is characterized by a sense of never feeling rooted, of being caught between worlds. Revisit Cervantes's "Refugee Ship" in chapter 1 for a vision of this sense of rootlessness. How do these three poems portray this state?

■ **THE READING/WRITING CONNECTION**

1. "Think" Topic: How do these two poems use bodily imagery to suggest the speaker's state of being?

2. Create a monologue in response to the speaker.
3. Create a poem of "return." Create a sequel to "The Foreigner" in the voice of one of her forebears.

▪ **IDEAS FOR WRITING**

1. Compare and contrast Agosin's "search" for roots with that of Aciman's in "Alexandria: The Capital of Memory."

DONALD JUSTICE

Donald Justice (1925–   ) was born in Miami, Florida, and educated at the University of Miami, the University of North Carolina, and Stanford University. He received his Ph.D. from the University of Iowa. Justice has published thirteen volumes of poetry and several books of short fiction, nonfiction, plays, and translations. He also has edited six books. Justice won the Pulitzer Prize for his Selected Poems *in 1979; "The Missing Person" is taken from this volume. Justice is praised by critics for his craftmanship. The "invisible architecture" of his poems, and his use of new techniques and word combinations, create his subtle yet "elegant" verse.*

1967

THE MISSING PERSON

He has come to report himself
A missing person.

The authorities
Hand him the forms.

5 He knows how they have waited
With the learned patience of barbers

In small shops, idle,
Stropping their razors.

But now that these spaces in his life
10 Stare up at him blankly,

Waiting to be filled in,
He does not know how to begin.

Afraid that he may not answer
To his description of himself,

15 He asks for a mirror.
They reassure him

That he can be nowhere
But wherever he finds himself

From moment to moment,
20 Which, for the moment, is here.

And he might like to believe them.
But in the mirror

He sees what is missing.
It is himself

25 He sees there emerging
Slowly, as from the dark

Of a furnished room
Only by darkness,

One who receives no mail
30 And is known to the landlady only

For keeping himself to himself,
And for whom it will be years yet

Before he can trust to the light
This last disguise, himself.

■ EXPLORATIONS OF THE TEXT

1. Discuss the symbolism of the "missing person." Why does he "report himself" missing? Why does he "[ask] for a mirror"? Analyze and interpret the imagery of darkness and light in the poem.
2. Develop a specific portrait of the character of "the missing person." What does he look like? What does he wear? How does he act? Create a few lines of dialogue for him.
3. What is the view of identity depicted in the poem?
4. Analyze the poet's use of paradox and irony.
5. Compare and contrast Justice's "missing person" with Auden's "Unknown Citizen" in chapter 7. Do they share similar traits?

■ THE READING/WRITING CONNECTION

1. Freewrite: Why is this person missing? Speculate.
2. Freewrite: Stare into a mirror, and create a self-portrait.
3. Journal Entry; Respond to the following: "he can be nowhere/But wherever he finds himself."

■ IDEAS FOR WRITING

1. Relate the symbolism of Justice's "The Missing Person" to several other works in this chapter. Which characters or personae in poems are "missing"? Which ones have found themselves?
2. Does contemporary society promote a sense of alienation from self? Using observations and experiences from your own life as well as evidence from works in this chapter, argue pro or con.
3. Imagine the "spaces" in the missing person's life that "stare up at him blankly." List your own blank spaces, and write about them, explaining why these might be blank whereas others are not. Do all people have blank spaces?

Poems for Comparison/Contrast: Utopia/Dystopia

ANNA LEE WALTERS (1946–)   **1975**

MY NAME IS "I AM LIVING"

My name is "I am living."
My home is all directions and is everlasting.

Instructed and carried to you by the wind,
I have felt the feathers in pale clouds and bowed before the Sun
5 who watches me from a blanket of faded blue.
In a gentle whirlwind I was shaken,
made to see on earth in many ways,
And when in awe my mouth fell open,
I tasted a fine red clay.
10 Its flavor has remained after uncounted days.
This gave me cause to drink from a crystal stream
that only I have seen.
So I listened to all its flowing wisdom
and learned from it a Song—
15 This song the wind and I
have since sung together.
Unknowing, I was encircled by its water and cleansed.
Naked and damp, I was embraced and dried
by the warmth of your presence.
20 Dressed forever in the scent of dry cedar,
I am purified and free.
And I will not allow you to ignore me.
I have brought to you a gift.
It is all I have but it is yours.
25 You may reach out and enfold it.
It is only the strength in the caress of a gentle breeze,
But it will carry you to meet the eagle in the sky.
My name is "I am living." I am here.
My name is "I am living." I am here.

MARY OLIVER (1935–   )   **1983**

GHOSTS

1

Have you noticed?

2

Where so many millions of powerful bawling beasts
lay down on the earth and died
it's hard to tell now
5 what's bone, and what merely
was once.

The golden eagle, for instance,
has a bit of heaviness in him;
moreover the huge barns
10 seem ready, sometimes, to ramble off
toward deeper grass.

3

1805
near the Bitterroot Mountains:
a man named Lewis kneels down
15 on the prairie watching

a sparrow's nest cleverly concealed in the wild hyssop
and lined with buffalo hair. The chicks,
not more than a day hatched, lean
quietly into the thick wool as if
20 content, after all,
to have left the perfect world and fallen
helpless and blind
into the flowered fields and the perils
of this one.

4

25 In the book of the earth it is written:
nothing can die.

In the book of the Sioux it is written:
they have gone away into the earth to hide.
Nothing will coax them out again
30 *but the people dancing.*

5

Said the old-timers:
the tongue
is the sweetest meat.

Passengers shooting from train windows
35 could hardly miss, they were
that many.

Afterward the carcasses
stank unbelievably, and sang with flies, ribboned
with slopes of white fat,
40 black ropes of blood—hellhunks
in the prairie heat.

6

Have you noticed? how the rain
falls soft as the fall
of moccasins. *Have you noticed?*
45 how the immense circles still,
stubbornly, after a hundred years,

mark the grass where the rich droppings
from the roaring bulls
fell to the earth as the herd stood
50 day after day, moon after moon
in the tribal circle, outwaiting
the packs of yellow-eyed wolves that are also
have you noticed? gone now.

7

Once only, and then in a dream,
55 I watched while, secretly
and with the tenderness of any caring woman,
a cow gave birth
to a red calf, tongued him dry and nursed him
in a warm corner
60 of the clear night
in the fragrant grass
in the wild domains
of the prairie spring, and I asked them,
in my dream I knelt down and asked them
65 to make room for me.

WISLAWA SZYMBORSKA (1923–   )   **1986**

THE CENTURY'S DECLINE

Our twentieth century was going to improve on the others.
It will never prove it now,
now that its years are numbered,
its gait is shaky,
5 its breath is short.

Too many things have happened
that weren't supposed to happen,
and what was supposed to come about
has not.

10 Happiness and spring, among other things,
were supposed to be getting closer.

Fear was expected to leave the mountains and the valleys.
Truth was supposed to hit home
before a lie.

15 A couple of problems weren't going
to come up anymore:
hunger, for example,
and war, and so forth.

There was going to be respect
20 for helpless people's helplessness,
trust, that kind of stuff.

Anyone who planned to enjoy the world
is now faced
with a hopeless task.

25 Stupidity isn't funny.
Wisdom isn't gay.
Hope
isn't that young girl anymore,
et cetera, alas.

30 God was finally going to believe
in a man both good and strong,
but good and strong
are still two different men.

"How should we live?" someone asked me in a letter.
35 I had meant to ask him
the same question.

Again, and as ever,
as may be seen above,
the most pressing questions
40 are naïve ones.

WISLAWA SZYMBORSKA (1923–   )   **1972**

COULD HAVE

It could have happened.
It had to happen.
It happened earlier. Later.
Nearer. Farther off.
It happened, but not to you.
5

You were saved because you were the first.
You were saved because you were the last.
Alone. With others.
On the right. The left.
10 Because it was raining. Because of the shade.
Because the day was sunny.

You were in luck—there was a forest.
You were in luck—there were no trees.
You were in luck—a rake, a hook, a beam, a brake,
15 a jamb, a turn, a quarter inch, an instant.

You were in luck—just then a straw went floating by.

As a result, because, although, despite.
What would have happened if a hand, a foot,
within an inch, a hairsbreadth from
20 an unfortunate coincidence.

So you're here? Still dizzy from another dodge, close shave,
    reprieve?
One hole in the net and you slipped through?
I couldn't be more shocked or speechless.
Listen,
25 how your heart pounds inside me.

WISLAWA SZYMBORSKA (1923–   )   1993

HATRED

See how efficient it still is,
how it keeps itself in shape—
our century's hatred.
How easily it vaults the tallest obstacles.
5 How rapidly it pounces, tracks us down.

It's not like other feelings.
At once both older and younger.
It gives birth itself to the reasons
that give it life.
10 When it sleeps, it's never eternal rest.
And sleeplessness won't sap its strength; it feeds it.

One religion or another—
whatever gets it ready, in position.
One fatherland or another—
15 whatever helps it get a running start.
Justice also works well at the outset
until hate gets its own momentum going.
Hatred. Hatred.
Its face twisted in a grimace
20 of erotic ecstasy.

Oh these other feelings,
listless weaklings.
Since when does brotherhood
draw crowds?
25 Has compassion
ever finished first?
Does doubt ever really rouse the rabble?
Only hatred has just what it takes.

Gifted, diligent, hardworking.
30 Need we mention all the songs it has composed?
All the pages it has added to our history books?
All the human carpets it has spread
over countless city squares and football fields?

Let's face it:
35 it knows how to make beauty.
The splendid fire-glow in midnight skies.
Magnificent bursting bombs in rosy dawns.
You can't deny the inspiring pathos of ruins
and a certain bawdy humor to be found
40 in the sturdy column jutting from their midst.

Hatred is a master of contrast—
between explosions and dead quiet,
red blood and white snow.
Above all, it never tires
45 of its leitmotif—the impeccable executioner
towering over its soiled victim.

It's always ready for new challenges.
If it has to wait awhile, it will.
They say it's blind. Blind?
50 It has a sniper's keen sight
and gazes unflinchingly at the future
as only it can.

Poems for Comparison/Contrast: Life in the Midst of Death

WILLIAM WORDSWORTH (1770–1850)   **1802**

MY HEART LEAPS UP WHEN I BEHOLD

My heart leaps up when I behold
    A rainbow in the sky:
So was it when my life began;
So is it now I am a man;
5 So be it when I shall grow old,
    Or let me die!
The Child is father of the Man;
And I could wish my days to be
Bound each to each by natural piety.

SAMUEL TAYLOR COLERIDGE (1772–1834)   **1816**

KUBLA KHAN: OR, A VISION IN A DREAM[1]

In Xanadu[2] did Kubla Khan[3]
A stately pleasure-dome decree:
Where Alph, the sacred river, ran
Through caverns measureless to man
5   Down to a sunless sea.
So twice five miles of fertile ground
With walls and towers were girdled round:
And here were gardens bright with sinuous rills
Where blossomed many an incense-bearing tree;
10 And there were forests ancient as the hills,
Enfolding sunny spots of greenery.

But oh! that deep romantic chasm which slanted
Down the green hill athwart a cedarn cover![4]
A savage place! as holy and enchanted
15 As e'er beneath a waning moon was haunted
By woman wailing for her demon-lover!
And from this chasm, with ceaseless turmoil seething,
As if this earth in fast thick pants were breathing,
A mighty fountain momently was forced,
20 Amid whose swift half-intermitted burst
Huge fragments vaulted like rebounding hail,
Or chaffy grain beneath the thresher's flail:
And 'mid these dancing rocks at once and ever
It flung up momently the sacred river.
25 Five miles meandering with a mazy motion
Through wood and dale the sacred river ran,
Then reached the caverns measureless to man,
And sank in tumult to a lifeless ocean:
And 'mid this tumult Kubla heard from far
30 Ancestral voices prophesying war!

    The shadow of the dome of pleasure
    Floated midway on the waves;
    Where was heard the mingled measure
    From the fountain and the caves.
35 It was a miracle of rare device,
A sunny pleasure-dome with caves of ice!

---

[1] The poem resulted from a dream induced by opium. Because he was interrupted, Coleridge remembered only a fragment.

[2] Summer capital of Kubla Khan.

[3] Kubla Khan (1216–1294), grandson of Genghis Khan and founder of the Mongol Empire in China.

[4] Spanning a grove of cedars.

> A damsel with a dulcimer
> In a vision once I saw;
> It was an Abyssinian[5] maid,
40 And on her dulcimer she played,
> Singing of Mount Abora.[6]
> Could I revive within me
> Her symphony and song,
> To such a deep delight 'twould win me,
45 That with music loud and long,
> I would build that dome in air,
> That sunny dome! those caves of ice!
> And all who heard should see them there,
> And all should cry, Beware! Beware!
50 His flashing eyes, his floating hair!
> Weave a circle round him thrice,
> And close your eyes with holy dread,
> For he on honey-dew hath fed,
> And drunk the milk of Paradise.

JOHN KEATS (1795–1821)   **1820**

ODE ON A GRECIAN URN

I

> Thou still unravished bride of quietness,
>   Thou foster child of silence and slow time,
> Sylvan[1] historian, who canst thus express
>   A flowery tale more sweetly than our rhyme:
5 What leaf-fringed legend haunts about thy shape
>   Of deities or mortals, or of both,
>   In Tempe[2] or the dales of Arcady?[3]
>   What men or gods are these? What maidens loath?
> What mad pursuit? What struggle to escape?
10   What pipes and timbrels? What wild ecstasy?

II

> Heard melodies are sweet, but those unheard
>   Are sweeter; therefore, ye soft pipes, play on;

---

[5] Ethiopian.

[6] Mount Abora in Abyssinia, referred to by Milton, *Paradise Lost* 4:28.

[1] Referring to woods or forest.

[2] Valley in Greece.

[3] Valleys of Arcadia, symbolic of pastoral life and beauty.

Not to the sensual ear, but, more endeared,
　　　Pipe to the spirit ditties of no tone:
15　Fair youth, beneath the trees, thou canst not leave
　　　Thy song, nor ever can those trees be bare;
　　　　　Bold Lover, never, never canst thou kiss,
　　　Though winning near the goal—yet, do not grieve;
　　　　　She cannot fade, though thou hast not thy bliss,
20　　　Forever wilt thou love, and she be fair!

III

Ah, happy, happy boughs! that cannot shed
　　　Your leaves, nor ever bid the Spring adieu;
And, happy melodist, unweariéd,
　　　Forever piping songs forever new;
25　More happy love! more happy, happy love!
　　　Forever warm and still to be enjoyed,
　　　　　Forever panting, and forever young;
All breathing human passion far above,
　　　That leaves a heart high-sorrowful and cloyed,
30　　　A burning forehead, and a parching tongue.

IV

Who are these coming to the sacrifice?
　　　To what green altar, O mysterious priest,
Lead'st thou that heifer lowing at the skies,
　　　And all her silken flanks with garlands dressed?
35　What little town by river or sea shore,
　　　Or mountain-built with peaceful citadel,
　　　　　Is emptied of this folk, this pious morn?
And, little town, thy streets forevermore
　　　Will silent be; and not a soul to tell
40　　　Why thou art desolate, can e'er return.

V

O Attic[4] shape! Fair attitude! with brede[5]
　　　Of marble men and maidens overwrought,[6]
With forest branches and the trodden weed;
　　　Thou, silent form, dost tease us out of thought
45　As doth eternity: Cold Pastoral![7]
　　　When old age shall this generation waste,

---

[4] Referring to Athens or Athenians.
[5] Braid.
[6] Elaborate; highly decorated.
[7] An idealized vision of country or rural life.

Thou shalt remain, in midst of other woe
Than ours, a friend to man, to whom thou say'st,
"Beauty is truth, truth beauty,—that is all
50   Ye know on earth, and all ye need to know."

EDGAR ALLAN POE (1809–49)   **1832**

THE HAUNTED PALACE

I

In the greenest of our valleys,
   By good angels tenanted,
Once a fair and stately palace—
   Radiant palace—reared its head.
5 In the monarch Thought's dominion—
   It stood there!
Never seraph spread a pinion
   Over fabric half so fair.

II

Banners yellow, glorious, golden,
10   On its roof did float and flow;
(This—all this—was in the olden
   Time long ago)
And every gentle air that dallied,
   In that sweet day,
15 Along the ramparts plumed and pallid,
   A winged odor went away.

III

Wanderers in that happy valley
   Through two luminous windows saw
Spirits moving musically
20   To a lute's well-tunèd law,
Round about a throne, where sitting
   (Porphyrogene!)[1]
In state his glory well befitting,
   The ruler of the realm was seen.

IV

25 And all with pearl and ruby glowing
   Was the fair palace door,

---

[1] Born to purple, in royal demeanor.

Through which came flowing, flowing, flowing
    And sparkling evermore,
A troop of Echoes whose sweet duty
30   Was but to sing,
In voices of surpassing beauty,
    The wit and wisdom of their king.

V

But evil things, in robes of sorrow,
    Assailed the monarch's high estate;
35 (Ah, let us mourn, for never morrow
    Shall dawn upon him, desolate!)
And, round about his home, the glory
    That blushed and bloomed
Is but a dim-remembered story
40   Of the old time entombed.

VI

And travelers now within that valley,
    Through the red-litten windows see
Vast forms that move fantastically
    To a discordant melody;
45 While, like a rapid ghastly river,
    Through the pale door,
A hideous throng rush out forever,
    And laugh—but smile no more.

WALT WHITMAN (1819–92)   **1860**

FACING WEST FROM CALIFORNIA'S SHORES

Facing west from California's shores,
Inquiring, tireless, seeking what is yet unfound,
I, a child, very old, over waves, towards the house of maternity,
    the land of migrations, look afar,
5 Look off the shores of my Western sea, the circle almost circled;
For starting westward from Hindustan, from the vales of Kashmere,
From Asia, from the north, from the God, the sage, and the
        hero,
From the south, from the flowery peninsulas and the spice islands,
10 Long having wander'd since, round the earth having wander'd,
Now I face home again, very pleas'd and joyous,
(But where is what I started for so long ago?
And why is it yet unfound?)

EMILY DICKINSON (1830–86)   **1862**

I HEARD A FLY BUZZ—WHEN I DIED

> I heard a Fly buzz—when I died—
> The Stillness in the Room
> Was like the Stillness in the Air—
> Between the Heaves of Storm—
>
> 5 The Eyes around—had wrung them dry—
> And Breaths were gathering firm
> For that last Onset—when the King
> Be witnessed—in the Room—
>
> I willed my Keepsakes—Signed away
> 10 What portion of me be
> Assignable—and then it was
> There interposed a Fly—
>
> With Blue—uncertain stumbling Buzz—
> Between the light—and me—
> 15 And then the Windows failed—and then
> I could not see to see—

CHARLOTTE MEW (1870–1928)   **1916**

THE FOREST ROAD

The forest road,
The infinite straight road stretching away
World without end: the breathless road between the walls
Of the black listening trees: the hushed, grey road
5 Beyond the window that you shut to-night
Crying that you would look at it by day—
There is a shadow there that sings and calls
But not for you. Oh! hidden eyes that plead in sleep
Against the lonely dark, if I could touch the fear
10 And leave it kissed away on quiet lids—
If I could hush these hands that are half-awake,
Groping for me in sleep I could go free.
I wish that God would take them out of mine
And fold them like the wings of frightened birds
15 Shot cruelly down, but fluttering into quietness so soon,
Broken, forgotten things; there is no grief for them in the green Spring
When the new birds fly back to the old trees.
But it shall not be so with you. I will look back. I wish I knew that God would stand
Smiling and looking down on you when morning comes,

20 To hold you, when you wake, closer than I,
    So gently though: and not with famished lips or hungry arms:
    He does not hurt the frailest, dearest things
    As we do in the dark. See, dear, your hair—
    I must unloose this hair that sleeps and dreams
25 About my face, and clings like the brown weed
    To drowned, delivered things, tossed by the tired sea
    Back to the beaches. Oh! your hair! If you had lain
    A long time dead on the rough, glistening ledge
    Of some black cliff, forgotten by the tide,
30 The raving winds would tear, the dripping brine would rust away
    Fold after fold of all the loveliness
    That wraps you round, and makes you, lying here,
    The passionate fragrance that the roses are.
    But death would spare the glory of your head
35 In the long sweetness of the hair that does not die:
    The spray would leap to it in every storm,
    The scent of the unsilenced sea would linger on
    In these dark waves, and round the silence that was you—
    Only the nesting gulls would hear—but there would still be whispers in your hair;
40 Keep them for me; keep them for me. What is this singing on the road
    That makes all other music like the music in a dream—
    Dumb to the dancing and the marching feet; you know, in dreams, you see
    Old pipers playing that you cannot hear,
    And ghostly drums that only seem to beat. This seems to climb:
45 Is it the music of a larger place? It makes our room too small: it is like a stair,
    A calling stair that climbs up to a smile you scarcely see,
    Dim but so waited for; and *you* know what a smile is, how it calls,
    How, if I smiled you always ran to me.
    Now you must sleep forgetfully, as children do.
50 There is a Spirit sits by us in sleep
    Nearer than those who walk with us in the bright day.
    I think he has a tranquil, saving face: I think he came
    Straight from the hills: he may have suffered there in time gone by,
    And once, from those forsaken heights, looked down,
55 Lonely himself, on all the lonely sorrows of the earth.
    It is his kingdom—Sleep. If I could leave you there—
    If, without waking you, I could get up and reach the door—!
    We used to go together.—Shut, scared eyes,
    Poor, desolate, desperate hands, it is not I
60 Who thrust you off. No, take your hands away—
    I cannot strike your lonely hands. Yes, I have struck your heart,
    It did not come so near. Then lie you there
    Dear and wild heart behind this quivering snow
    With two red stains on it: and I will strike and tear
65 Mine out, and scatter it to yours. Oh! throbbing dust,
    You that were life, our little wind-blown hearts!
                    The road! the road!
    There is a shadow there: I see my soul,
    I hear my soul, singing among the trees!

WILLIAM BUTLER YEATS (1865–1939)   **1926**

SAILING TO BYZANTIUM[1]

1

That is no country[2] for old men. The young
In one another's arms, birds in the trees
—Those dying generations—at their song,
The salmon-falls, the mackerel-crowded seas,
5 Fish, flesh, or fowl, commend all summer long
Whatever is begotten, born, and dies.
Caught in that sensual music all neglect
Monuments of unageing intellect.

II

An aged man is but a paltry thing,
10 A tattered coat upon a stick, unless
Soul clap its hands and sing, and louder sing
For every tatter in its mortal dress,
Nor is there singing school but studying
Monuments of its own magnificence;
15 And therefore I have sailed the seas and come
To the holy city of Byzantium.

III

O sages standing in God's holy fire
As in the gold mosaic of a wall,
Come from the holy fire, perne in a gyre[3]
20 And be the singing-masters of my soul.
Consume my heart away; sick with desire
And fastened to a dying animal
It knows not what it is; and gather me
Into the artifice of eternity.

IV

25 Once out of nature I shall never take
My bodily form from any natural thing,
But such a form as Grecian goldsmiths make

---

[1] Capital of the Byzantine Empire; revered by Yeats as a place where artistry reached its apex. Now called Istanbul, "Byzantium was the center of European civilization and the source of its spiritual philosophy, so I symbolize the search for spiritual life by a journey to that city." (Yeats, BBC, 1931)

[2] Ireland.

[3] Whirl in spirals. The gyre or cone represented cycles of history and the fate of the individual. The speaker asks the sages in the mosaic to take him from the ordinary world and to the eternal world of art.

Of hammered gold and gold enamelling[4]
To keep a drowsy Emperor awake;
30 Or set upon a golden bough to sing
To lords and ladies of Byzantium
Of what is past, or passing, or to come.

THEODORE ROETHKE (1908–63)   **1953**

THE WAKING

I wake to sleep, and take my waking slow.
I feel my fate in what I cannot fear.
I learn by going where I have to go.

We think by feeling. What is there to know?
5 I hear my being dance from ear to ear.
I wake to sleep, and take my waking slow.

Of those so close beside me, which are you?
God bless the Ground! I shall walk softly there,
And learn by going where I have to go.

10 Light takes the Tree; but who can tell us how?
The lowly worm climbs up a winding stair;
I wake to sleep, and take my waking slow.

Great Nature has another thing to do
To you and me; so take the lively air,
15 And, lovely, learn by going where to go.

This shaking keeps me steady. I should know.
What falls away is always. And is near.
I wake to sleep, and take my waking slow.
I learn by going where I have to go.

DYLAN THOMAS (1914–53)   **1951**

DO NOT GO GENTLE INTO THAT GOOD NIGHT

Do not go gentle into that good night,
Old age should burn and rave at close of day;
Rage, rage against the dying of the light.

Though wise men at their end know dark is right,
5 Because their words had forked no lightning they
Do not go gentle into that good night.

---

[4] Yeats read that the emperor's palace contained a tree of gold and silver and artificial birds that could sing.

Good men, the last wave by, crying how bright
Their frail deeds might have danced in a green bay,
Rage, rage against the dying of the light.

10 Wild men who caught and sang the sun in flight,
And learn, too late, they grieved it on its way,
Do not go gentle into that good night.

Grave men, near death, who see with blinding sight
Blind eyes could blaze like meteors and be gay,
15 Rage, rage against the dying of the light.

And you, my father, there on the sad height,
Curse, bless, me now with your fierce tears, I pray.
Do not go gentle into that good night.
Rage, rage against the dying of the light.

ROBERT FROST (1874–1963)   **1916**

BIRCHES

When I see birches bend to left and right
Across the lines of straighter darker trees,
I like to think some boy's been swinging them.
But swinging doesn't bend them down to stay.
5 Ice-storms do that. Often you must have seen them
Loaded with ice a sunny winter morning
After a rain. They click upon themselves
As the breeze rises, and turn many-colored
As the stir cracks and crazes their enamel.
10 Soon the sun's warmth makes them shed crystal shells
Shattering and avalanching on the snow-crust—
Such heaps of broken glass to sweep away
You'd think the inner dome of heaven had fallen
They are dragged to the withered bracken[1] by the load,
15 And they seem not to break; though once they are bowed
So low for long, they never right themselves:
You may see their trunks arching in the woods
Years afterwards, trailing their leaves on the ground
Like girls on hands and knees that throw their hair
20 Before them over their heads to dry in the sun.
But I was going to say when Truth broke in
With all her matter-of-fact about the ice-storm
I should prefer to have some boy bend them
As he went out and in to fetch the cows—

---

[1] A large fern; a cluster or thicket of ferns.

25 Some boy too far from town to learn baseball,
   Whose only play was that he found himself,
   Summer or winter, and could play alone.
   One by one he subdued his father's trees
   By riding them down over and over again
30 Until he took the stiffness out of them,
   And not one but hung limp, not one was left
   For him to conquer. He learned all there was
   To learn about not launching out too soon
   And so not carrying the tree away
35 Clear to the ground. He always kept his poise
   To the top branches climbing carefully
   With the same pains you use to fill a cup
   Up to the brim, and even above the brim
   Then he flung outward, feet first, with a swish,
40 Kicking his way down through the air to the ground.
   So was I once myself a swinger of birches.
   And so I dream of going back to be.
   It's when I'm weary of considerations,
   And life is too much like a pathless wood
45 Where your face burns and tickles with the cobwebs
   Broken across it, and one eye is weeping
   From a twig's having lashed across it open.
   I'd like to get away from earth awhile
   And then come back to it and begin over.
50 May no fate willfully misunderstand me
   And half grant what I wish and snatch me away
   Not to return. Earth's the right place for love:
   I don't know where it's likely to go better.
   I'd like to go by climbing a birch tree,
55 And climb black branches up a snow-white trunk
   Toward heaven, till the tree could bear no more,
   But dipped its top and set me down again.
   That would be good both going and coming back.
   One could do worse than be a swinger of birches.

JAMES WRIGHT (1927–80)   **1963**

A BLESSING

   Just off the highway to Rochester, Minnesota,
   Twilight bounds softly forth on the grass.
   And the eyes of those two Indian ponies
   Darken with kindness.
5 They have come gladly out of the willows
   To welcome my friend and me.
   We step over the barbed wire into the pasture
   Where they have been grazing all day, alone.

They ripple tensely, they can hardly contain their happiness
10 That we have come.
They bow shyly as wet swans. They love each other.
There is no loneliness like theirs.
At home once more,
They begin munching the young tufts of spring in the darkness.
15 I would like to hold the slenderer one in my arms.
For she has walked over to me
And nuzzled my left hand.
She is black and white,
Her mane falls wild on her forehead,
20 And the light breeze moves me to caress her long ear
That is delicate as the skin over a girl's wrist.
Suddenly I realize
That if I stepped out of my body I would break
Into blossom.

WALLACE STEVENS (1879–1955)   **1935**

THE IDEA OF ORDER AT KEY WEST

She sang beyond the genius of the sea.
The water never formed to mind or voice,
Like a body wholly body, fluttering
Its empty sleeves; and yet its mimic motion
5 Made constant cry, caused constantly a cry,
That was not ours although we understood,
Inhuman, of the veritable ocean.

The sea was not a mask. No more was she.
The song and water were not medleyed sound
10 Even if what she sang was what she heard,
Since what she sang was uttered word by word.
It may be that in all her phrases stirred
The grinding water and the gasping wind;
But it was she and not the sea we heard.

15 For she was the maker of the song she sang.
The ever-hooded, tragic-gestured sea
Was merely a place by which she walked to sing.
Whose spirit is this? we said, because we knew
It was the spirit that we sought and knew
20 That we should ask this often as she sang.

If it was only the dark voice of the sea
That rose, or even colored by many waves;
If it was only the outer voice of sky
And cloud, of the sunken coral water-walled,
25 However clear, it would have been deep air,

The heaving speech of air, a summer sound
Repeated in a summer without end
And sound alone. But it was more than that,
More even than her voice, and ours, among
30 The meaningless plungings of water and the wind,
Theatrical distances, bronze shadows heaped
On high horizons, mountainous atmospheres
Of sky and sea.
                        It was her voice that made
35 The sky acutest at its vanishing.
She measured to the hour its solitude.
She was the single artificer of the world
In which she sang. And when she sang, the sea,
Whatever self it had, because the self
40 That was her song, for she was the maker. Then we,
As we beheld her striding there alone,
Knew that there never was a world for her
Except the one she sang and, singing, made.

Ramon Fernandez,[1] tell me, if you know,
45 Why, when the singing ended and we turned
Toward the town, tell why the glass lights,
The lights in the fishing boats at anchor there,
As the night descended, tilting in the air,
Mastered the night and portioned out the sea,
50 Fixing emblazoned zones and fiery poles,
Arranging, deepening, enchanting night.

Oh! Blessed rage for order, pale Ramon,
The maker's rage to order words of the sea,
Words of the fragrant portals, dimly-starred,
55 And of ourselves and of our origins,
In ghostlier demarcations, keener sounds.

CATHY SONG (1955–)   1988

HEAVEN

He thinks when we die we'll go to China.
Think of it—a Chinese heaven
where, except for his blond hair,
the part that belongs to his father,
5 everyone will look like him.
China, that blue flower on the map,

---

[1] According to information contained in one of his letters, Stevens combined two Spanish names to form this figure's presence in the poem, and he did not mean to refer to French critic Ramon Fernandez.

        bluer than the sea
        his hand must span like a bridge
        to reach it.
10   An octave away.

        I've never seen it.
        It's as if I can't sing that far.
        But look—
        on the map, this black dot.
15   Here is where we live,
        on the pancake plains
        just east of the Rockies,
        on the other side of the clouds.
        A mile above the sea,
20   the air is so thin, you can starve on it.
        No bamboo trees
        But the alpine equivalent,
        reedy aspen with light, fluttering leaves.
        Did a boy in Guangzhou[1] dream of this
25   as his last stop?

        I've heard the trains at night
        whistling past our yards,
        what we've come to own,
        the broken fences, the whiny dog, the rattletrap cars.
30   It's still the wild west,
        mean and grubby,
        the shootouts and fistfights in the back alley.
        With my son the dreamer
        and my daughter, who is too young to walk,
35   I've sat in this spot
        and wondered why here?
        Why in this short life,
        this town, this creek they call a river?

        He had never planned to stay,
40   the boy who helped to build
        the railroads for a dollar a day.[2]
        He had always meant to go back.
        When did he finally know
        that each mile of track led him further away,
45   that he would die in his sleep,
        dispossessed,
        having seen Gold Mountain,
        the icy wind tunneling through it,
        these landlocked, makeshift ghost towns?

---

[1] Canton, a seaport in southeastern China.

[2] In the nineteenth century Chinese laborers and other immigrants laid the railroad tracks.

50 It must be in the blood,
 this notion of returning.
 It skipped two generations, lay fallow,
 the garden an unmarked grave.
 On a spring sweater day
55 it's as if we remember him.
 I call to the children.
 We can see the mountains
 shimmering blue above the air.
 If you look really hard
60 says my son the dreamer,
 leaning out from the laundry's rigging,
 the work shirts fluttering like sails
 you can see all the way to heaven.

JANE KENYON (1947–95)   **1996**

OTHERWISE

I got out of bed
on two strong legs.
It might have been
otherwise. I ate
5 cereal, sweet
milk, ripe, flawless
peach. It might
have been otherwise.
I took the dog uphill
10 to the birch wood.
All morning I did
the work I love.

At noon I lay down
with my mate. It might
15 have been otherwise.
We ate dinner together
at a table with silver
candlesticks. It might
have been otherwise.
20 I slept in a bed
in a room with paintings
on the walls, and
planned another day
just like this day.
25 But one day, I know,
it will be otherwise.

▪ DRAMA ▪

Athol Fugard

*Athol Fugard (1932–   ), born in South Africa, has spent most of his life in Port Elizabeth. His 1961
production of* The Blood Knot *was considered shocking because it was the first time black
and white actors shared the stage in South Africa. In addition to his many award-winning
plays, which include* Boesman and Lena *(1969),* A Lesson from Aloes *(1978), and* The Road to
Mecca *(1984), Fugard has written scripts, including those for* Gandhi *(1982) and* The Killing Fields
(1984). In his Notebooks: 1960–1977, *Fugard describes the relationship between himself and Sam
on which he based* "Master Harold" . . . and the Boys, *recalling that Sam was his best friend during his boyhood. Fugard recounts being overwhelmed with shame at his betrayal of his friend.*

1982

"MASTER HAROLD" . . . AND THE BOYS

The St. George's Park Tea Room on a wet and windy Port Elizabeth[1] afternoon.
   *Tables and chairs have been cleared and are stacked on one side except for one which
stands apart with a single chair. On this table a knife, fork, spoon and side plate in
anticipation of a simple meal, together with a pile of comic books.*
   *Other elements: a serving counter with a few stale cakes under glass and a not very
impressive display of sweets, cigarettes and cool drinks, etc.; a few cardboard advertising
handouts—Cadbury's Chocolate, Coca-Cola—and a blackboard on which an untrained hand
has chalked up the prices of Tea, Coffee, Scones, Milkshakes—all flavors—and Cool Drinks;
a few sad ferns in pots; a telephone; an old-style jukebox.*
   There is an entrance on one side and an exit into a kitchen on the other.
   *Leaning on the solitary table, his head cupped in one hand as he pages through one of the
comic books, is Sam. A black man in his mid-forties. He wears the white coat of a waiter. Behind
him on his knees, mopping down the floor with a bucket of water and a rag, is Willie. Also black
and about the same age as Sam. He has his sleeves and trousers rolled up.*
   The year: 1950

Willie *(Singing as he works.):*
   "She was scandalizin' my name,
   She took my money
   She called me honey
   But she was scandalizin' my name.
   Called it love but was playin' a game . . ."

*(He gets up and moves the bucket. Stands thinking for a moment, then, raising his arms to
hold an imaginary partner, he launches into an intricate ballroom dance step. Although a
mildly comic figure, he reveals a reasonable degree of accomplishment.)*

Hey, Sam.

(Sam, absorbed in the comic book, does not respond.)

Hey, Boet Sam!

---

[1] Southeastern South African city on the Indian Ocean.

(Sam looks up.)

I'm getting it. The quickstep. Look now and tell me. *(He repeats the step.)* Well?

Sam *(Encouragingly.):* Show me again.

Willie: Okay, count for me.

Sam: Ready?

5   **Willie:** Ready.

Sam: Five, six, seven, eight . . . *(Willie starts to dance.)* A-n-d one two three four . . . and one two three four. . . . *(Ad libbing as Willie dances.)* Your shoulders, Willie . . . your shoulders! Don't look down! Look happy, Willie! Relax, Willie!

Willie *(Desperate but still dancing.):* I am relax.

Sam: No, you're not.

Willie *(He falters.):* Ag no man, Sam! Mustn't talk. You make me make mistakes.

10   **Sam:** But you're too stiff.

Willie: Yesterday I'm not straight . . . today I'm too stiff!

Sam: Well, you are. You asked me and I'm telling you.

Willie: Where?

Sam: Everywhere. Try to glide through it.

15   **Willie:** Glide?

Sam: Ja, make it smooth. And give it more style. It must look like you're enjoying yourself.

Willie *(Emphatically.):* I wasn't.

Sam: Exactly.

Willie: How can I enjoy myself? Not straight, too stiff and now it's also glide, give it more style, make it smooth. . . . Haai! Is hard to remember all those things, Boet Sam.

20   **Sam:** That's your trouble. You're trying too hard.

Willie: I try hard because it *is* hard.

Sam: But don't let me see it. The secret is to make it look easy. Ballroom must look happy, Willie, not like hard work. It must . . . Ja! . . . it must look like romance.

Willie: Now another one! What's romance?

Sam: Love story with happy ending. A handsome man in tails, and in his arms, smiling at him, a beautiful lady in evening dress!

25   **Willie:** Fred Astaire, Ginger Rogers.[2]

Sam: You got it. Tapdance or ballroom, it's the same. Romance. In two weeks' time when the judges look at you and Hilda, they must see a man and a woman who are dancing their way to a happy ending. What I saw was you holding her like you were frightened she was going to run away.

Willie: Ja! Because that is what she wants to do! I got no romance left for Hilda anymore, Boet Sam.

Sam: Then pretend. When you put your arms around Hilda, imagine she is Ginger Rogers.

Willie: With no teeth? You try.

30   **Sam:** Well, just remember, there's only two weeks left.

Willie: I know, I know! *(To the jukebox.)* I do it better with music. You got sixpence for Sarah Vaughan?[3]

Sam: That's a slow foxtrot. You're practicing the quickstep.

Willie: I'll practice slow foxtrot.

Sam *(Shaking his head.):* It's your turn to put money in the jukebox.

35   **Willie:** I only got bus fare to go home. *(He returns disconsolately to his work.)* Love story and happy ending! She's doing it all right, Boet Sam, but is not me she's giving happy

---

[2] North American dancers and movies stars.   [3] Jazz singer.

endings. Fuckin' whore! Three nights now she doesn't come practice. I wind up gramophone, I get record ready and I sit and wait. What happens? Nothing. Ten o'clock I start dancing with my pillow. You try and practice romance by yourself, Boet Sam. Struesgod, she doesn't come tonight I take back my dress and ballroom shoes and I find me new partner. Size twenty-six. Shoes size seven. And now she's also making trouble for me with the baby again. Reports me to Child Wellfed, that I'm not giving her money. She lies! Every week I am giving her money for milk. And how do I know is my baby? Only his hair looks like me. She's fucking around all the time I turn my back. Hilda Samuels is a bitch! *(Pause.)* Hey, Sam!

Sam: Ja.

Willie: You listening?

Sam: Ja.

Willie: So what you say?

40 **Sam:** About Hilda?

Willie: Ja.

Sam: When did you last give her a hiding?

Willie *(Reluctantly.):* Sunday night.

Sam: And today is Thursday.

45 **Willie** *(He knows what's coming.):* Okay.

Sam: Hiding on Sunday night, then Monday, Tuesday and Wednesday she doesn't come to practice . . . and you are asking me why?

Willie: I said okay, Boet Sam!

Sam: You hit her too much. One day she's going to leave you for good.

Willie: So? She makes me the hell-in too much.

50 **Sam** *(Emphasizing his point.):* *Too* much and *too* hard. You had the same trouble with Eunice.

Willie: Because she also make the hell-in, Boet Sam. She never got the steps right. Even the waltz.

Sam: Beating her up every time she makes a mistake in the waltz? *(Shaking his head.)* No, Willie! That takes the pleasure out of ballroom dancing.

Willie: Hilda is not too bad with the waltz, Boet Sam. Is the quickstep where the trouble starts.

Sam *(Teasing him gently.):* How's your pillow with the quickstep?

55 **Willie** *(Ignoring the tease.):* Good! And why? Because it got no legs. That's her trouble. She can't move them quick enough, Boet Sam. I start the record and before halfway Count Basie[4] is already winning. Only time we catch up with him is when gramophone runs down.

(Sam laughs.)

Haaikona, Boet Sam, is not funny.

Sam *(Snapping his fingers.):* I got it! Give her a handicap.

Willie: What's that?

Sam: Give her a ten-second start and then let Count Basie go. Then I put my money on her. Hot favorite in the Ballroom Stakes: Hilda Samuels ridden by Willie Malopo.

Willie *(Turning away.):* I'm not talking to you no more.

60 **Sam** *(Relenting.):* Sorry, Willie . . .

---

[4] U.S. jazz musician, composer, and bandleader (1904–84).

Willie: It's finish between us.

Sam: Okay, okay . . . I'll stop.

Willie: You can also fuck off.

Sam: Willie, listen! I want to help you!

65 **Willie:** No more jokes?

Sam: I promise.

Willie: Okay. Help me.

Sam (*His turn to hold an imaginary partner.*)*:* Look and learn. Feet together. Back straight. Body relaxed. Right hand placed gently in the small of her back and wait for the music. Don't start worrying about making mistakes or the judges or the other competitors. It's just you, Hilda and the music, and you're going to have a good time. What Count Basie do you play?

Willie: "You the cream in my coffee, you the salt in my stew."

70 **Sam:** Right. Give it to me in strict tempo.

Willie: Ready?

Sam: Ready.

Willie: A-n-d . . . (*Singing.*)
"You the cream in my coffee.
You the salt in my stew.
You will always be my
     necessity.
I'd be lost without
you. . . . " (*etc.*)

(*Sam launches into the quickstep. He is obviously a much more accomplished dancer than Willie. Hally enters. A seventeen-year-old white boy. Wet raincoat and school case. He stops and watches Sam. The demonstration comes to an end with a flourish. Applause from Hally and Willie.*)

Hally: Bravo! No question about it. First place goes to Mr. Sam Semela.

75 **Willie** (*In total agreement.*)*:* You was gliding with style, Boet Sam.

Hally (*Cheerfully.*)*:* How's it, chaps?

Sam: Okay, Hally.

Willie (*Springing to attention like a soldier and saluting.*)*:* At your service, Master Harold!

Hally: Not long to the big event, hey!

80 **Sam:** Two weeks.

Hally: You nervous?

Sam: No.

Hally: Think you stand a chance?

Sam: Let's just say I'm ready to go out there and dance.

85 **Hally:** It looked like it. What about you, Willie?

(*Willie groans.*)

What's the matter?

Sam: He's got leg trouble.

Hally (*Innocently.*)*:* Oh, sorry to hear that, Willie.

Willie: Boet Sam! You promised. (*Willie returns to his work.*)

(*Hally deposits his school case and takes off his raincoat. His clothes are a little neglected and untidy: black blazer with school badge, gray flannel trousers in need of an ironing, khaki shirt and tie, black shoes. Sam has fetched a towel for Hally to dry his hair.*)

Hally: God, what a lousy bloody day. It's coming down cats and dogs out there. Bad for business, chaps . . . (*Conspiratorial whisper.*) . . . but it also means we're in for a nice quiet afternoon.

90 **Sam:** You can speak loud, your Mom's not here.

Hally: Out shopping?

Sam: No. The hospital.

Hally: But it's Thursday. There's no visiting on Thursday afternoons. Is my Dad okay?

Sam: Sounds like it. In fact, I think he's going home.

95 **Hally** (*Stopped short by Sam's remark.*): What do you mean?

Sam: The hospital phoned.

Hally: To say what?

Sam: I don't know. I just heard your Mom talking.

Hally: So what makes you say he's going home?

100 **Sam:** It sounded as if they were telling her to come and fetch him.

(*Hally thinks about what Sam has said for a few seconds.*)

Hally: When did she leave?

Sam: About an hour ago. She said she would phone you. Want to eat?

(*Hally doesn't respond.*)

      Hally, want your lunch?

Hally: I suppose so. (*His mood has changed.*) What's on the menu? . . . as if I don't know.

Sam: Soup, followed by meat pie and gravy.

105 **Hally:** Today's?

Sam: No.

Hally: And the soup?

Sam: Nourishing pea soup.

Hally: Just the soup. (*The pile of comic books on the table.*) And these?

110 **Sam:** For your Dad. Mr. Kempston brought them.

Hally: You haven't been reading them, have you?

Sam: Just looking.

Hally (*Examining the comics.*): Jungle Jim . . . Batman and Robin . . . Tarzan[5] . . . God, what rubbish! Mental pollution. Take them away.

(*Sam exits waltzing into the kitchen. Hally turns to Willie.*)

Hally: Did you hear my Mom talking on the telephone, Willie?

115 **Willie:** No, Master Hally. I was at the back.

Hally: And she didn't say anything to you before she left?

Willie: She said I must clean the floors.

Hally: I mean about my Dad.

Willie: She didn't say nothing to me about him, Master Hally.

120 **Hally** (*With conviction.*): No! It can't be. They said he needed at least another three weeks of treatment. Sam's definitely made a mistake. (*Rummages through his school case, finds a book and settles down at the table to read.*) So, Willie!

Willie: Yes, Master Hally! Schooling okay today?

Hally: Yes, okay. . . . (*He thinks about it.*) . . . No, not really. Ag, what's the difference? I don't care. And Sam says you've got problems.

---

[5] Comic book characters.

Willie: Big problems.

Hally: Which leg is sore?

(*Willie groans.*)

Both legs.

125 **Willie:** There is nothing wrong with my legs. Sam is just making jokes.

Hally: So then you *will* be in the competition

Willie: Only if I can find me a partner.

Hally: But what about Hilda?

Sam (*Returning with a bowl of soup.*): She's the one who's got trouble with her legs.

130 **Hally:** What sort of trouble, Willie?

Sam: From the way he describes it, I think the lady has gone a bit lame.

Hally: Good God! Have you taken her to see a doctor?

Sam: I think a vet would be better.

Hally: What do you mean?

135 **Sam:** What do you call it again when a racehorse goes very fast?

Hally: Gallop?

Sam: That's it!

Willie: Boet Sam!

Hally: "A gallop down the homestretch to the winning post." But what's that got to do with Hilda?

140 **Sam:** Count Basie always gets there first.

(*Willie lets fly with his slop rag. It misses Sam and hits Hally.*)

Hally (*Furious.*): For Christ's sake, Willie! What the hell do you think you're doing!

Willie: Sorry, Master Hally, but it's him. . . .

Hally: Act your bloody age! (*Hurls the rag back at Willie.*) Cut out the nonsense now and get on with your work. And you too, Sam. Stop fooling around.

(*Sam moves away.*)

No. Hang on. I haven't finished! Tell me exactly what my Mom said.

Sam: I have. "When Hally comes, tell him I've gone to the hospital and I'll phone him."

145 **Hally:** She didn't say anything about taking my Dad home?

Sam: No. It's just that when she was talking on the phone . . .

Hally (*Interrupting him.*): No, Sam. They can't be discharging him. She would have said so if they were. In any case, we saw him last night and he wasn't in good shape at all. Staff nurse even said there was talk about taking more X-rays. And now suddenly to-day he's better? If anything, it sounds more like a bad turn to me . . . which I sincerely hope it isn't. Hang on . . . how long ago did you say she left?

Sam: Just before two . . . (*His wrist watch.*) . . . hour and a half.

Hally: I know how to settle it. (*Behind the counter to the telephone. Talking as he dials.*) Let's give her ten minutes to get to the hospital, ten minutes to load him up, another ten, at the most, to get home and another ten to get him inside. Forty minutes. They should have been home for at least half an hour already. (*Pause—he waits with the receiver to his ear.*) No reply, chaps. And you know why? Because she's at his bedside in hospital helping him pull through a bad turn. You definitely heard wrong.

150 **Sam:** Okay.

(*As far as Hally is concerned, the matter is settled. He returns to his table, sits down and divides his attention between the book and his soup. Sam is at his school case and picks up a textbook,* Modern Graded Mathematics for Standards Nine and Ten. *Opens it at random and laughs at something he sees.)*

Who is this supposed to be?

Hally: Old fart-face Prentice.

Sam: Teacher?

Hally: Thinks he is. And believe me, that is not a bad likeness.

Sam: Has he seen it?

155 **Hally:** Yes.

Sam: What did he say?

Hally: Tried to be clever, as usual. Said I was no Leonardo da Vinci[6] and that bad art had to be punished. So, six of the best, and his are bloody good.

Sam: On your bum?

Hally: Where else? The days when I got them on my hands are gone forever, Sam.

160 **Sam:** With your trousers down!

Hally: No. He's not quite that barbaric.

Sam: That's the way they do it in jail.

Hally *(Flicker of morbid interest.):* Really?

Sam: Ja. When the magistrate sentences you to "strokes with a light cane."

165 **Hally:** Go on.

Sam: They make you lie down on a bench. One policeman pulls down your trousers and holds your ankles, another one pulls your shirt over your head and holds your arms . . .

Hally: Thank you! That's enough.

Sam: . . . and the one that gives you the strokes talks to you gently and for a long time be- tween each one. *(He laughs.)*

Hally: I've heard enough, Sam! Jesus! It's a bloody awful world when you come to think of it. People can be real bastards.

170 **Sam:** That's the way it is, Hally.

Hally: It doesn't *have* to be that way. There is something called progress, you know. We don't exactly burn people at the stake anymore.

Sam: Like Joan of Arc.[7]

Hally: Correct. If she was captured today, she'd be given a fair trial.

Sam: And then the death sentence.

175 **Hally** *(A world-weary sigh.):* I know, I know! I oscillate between hope and despair for this world as well, Sam. But things will change, you wait and see. One day somebody is going to get up and give history a kick up the backside and get it going again.

Sam: Like who?

Hally *(After thought.):* They're called social reformers. Every age, Sam, has got its social re- former. My history book is full of them.

Sam: So where's ours?

Hally: Good question. And I hate to say it, but the answer is: I don't know. Maybe he hasn't even been born yet. Or is still only a babe in arms at his mother's breast. God, what a thought.

180 **Sam:** So we just go on waiting.

Hally: Ja, looks like it. *(Back to his soup and the book.)*

---

[6] Renaissance artist, creator, for example, of the *Mona Lisa* (1452–1519).   [7] French military leader and heroine, later canonized by the Catholic church (1412–31).

Sam (*Reading from the textbook.*): "Introduction: In some mathematical problems only the
magnitude . . ." (*He mispronounces the word "magnitude."*)

Hally (*Correcting him without looking up.*): Magnitude.

Sam: What's it mean?

185 **Hally:** How big it is. The size of the thing.

Sam (*Reading.*): ". . . a magnitude of the quantities is of importance. In other problems we
need to know whether these quantities are negative or positive. For example, whether
there is a debit or credit bank balance . . ."

Hally: Whether you're broke or not.

Sam: ". . . whether the temperature is above or below Zero . . ."

Hally: Naught degrees. Cheerful state of affairs! No cash and you're freezing to death.
Mathematics won't get you out of that one.

190 **Sam:** All these quantities are called . . . (*Spelling the word.*) . . . s-c-a-l . . .

Hally: Scalars.

Sam: Scalars! (*Shaking his head with a laugh.*) You understand all that?

Hally (*Turning a page.*): No. And I don't intend to try.

Sam: So what happens when the exams come?

195 **Hally:** Failing a maths exam isn't the end of the world, Sam. How many times have I told
you that examination results don't measure intelligence?

Sam: I would say about as many times as you've failed one of them.

Hally (*Mirthlessly.*): Ha, ha, ha.

Sam (*Simultaneously.*): Ha, ha, ha.

Hally: Just remember Winston Churchill[8] didn't do particularly well at school.

200 **Sam:** You've also told me that one many times.

Hally: Well, it just so happens to be the truth.

Sam (*Enjoying the word.*): Magnitude! Magnitude! Show me how to use it.

Hally (*After thought.*): An intrepid social reformer will not be daunted by the magnitude of
the task he has undertaken.

Sam (*Impressed.*): Couple of jaw-breakers in there!

205 **Hally:** I gave you three for the price of one. Intrepid, daunted and magnitude. I did that
once in an exam. Put five of the words I had to explain in one sentence. It was half a
page long.

Sam: Well, I'll put my money on you in the English exam.

Hally: Piece of cake. Eighty percent without even trying.

Sam (*Another textbook from Hally's case.*): And history?

Hally: So-so. I'll scrape through. In the fifties if I'm lucky.

210 **Sam:** You didn't do too badly last year.

Hally: Because we had World War One. That at least had some action. You try to find that
in the South African Parliamentary system.

Sam (*Reading from the history textbook.*): "Napoleon[9] and the principle of equality." Hey!
This sounds interesting. "After concluding peace with Britain in 1802, Napoleon used
a brief period of calm to in-sti-tute . . ."

Hally: Introduce.

Sam: ". . . many reforms. Napoleon regarded all people as equal before the law and wanted
them to have equal opportunities for advancement. All ves-ti-ges of the feu-dal system

---

[8] Prime minister of England during World War II (1940–45) and recipient of the Nobel Prize for Peace in
1953 (1874–1965).   [9] French general who declared himself emperor of France from 1804 to 1814
(1769–1821).

with its oppression of the poor were abolished. Vestiges, feudal system and abolished." I'm all right on oppression.

215   **Hally:** I'm thinking. He swept away . . . abolished . . . the last remains . . . vestiges . . . of the bad old days . . . feudal system.

  Sam: Ha! There's the social reformer we're waiting for. He sounds like a man of some magnitude.

  Hally: I'm not so sure about that. It's a damn good title for a book, though. A man of magnitude!

  Sam: He sounds pretty big to me, Hally.

  Hally: Don't confuse historical significance with greatness. But maybe I'm being a bit preju-diced. Have a look in there and you'll see he's two chapters long. And hell! . . . has he only got dates, Sam, all of which you've got to remember! This campaign and that campaign, and then, because of all the fighting, the next thing is we get Peace Treaties all over the place. And what's the end of the story? Battle of Waterloo,[10] which he loses. Wasn't worth it. No, I don't know about him as a man of magnitude.

220   **Sam:** Then who would you say was?

  Hally: To answer that, we need a definition of greatness, and I suppose that would be somebody who . . . somebody who benefited all mankind.

  Sam: Right. But like who?

  Hally *(He speaks with total conviction.):* Charles Darwin.[11] Remember him? That big book from the library. *The Origin of the Species.*

  Sam: Him?

225   **Hally:** Yes. For his Theory of Evolution.

  Sam: You didn't finish it.

  Hally: I ran out of time. I didn't finish it because my two weeks was up. But I'm going to take it out again after I've digested what I read. It's safe. I've hidden it away in the The-ology section. Nobody ever goes in there. And anyway who are you to talk? You hardly even looked at it.

  Sam: I tried. I looked at the chapters in the beginning and I saw one called "The Struggle for an Existence." Ah ha, I thought. At last! But what did I get? Something called the mistletoe which needs the apple tree and there's too many seeds and all are going to die except one . . . ! No, Hally.

  Hally *(Intellectually outraged.):* What do you mean, No! The poor man had to start some-where. For God's sake, Sam, he revolutionized science. Now we know.

230   **Sam:** What?

  Hally: Where we come from and what it all means.

  Sam: And that's a benefit to mankind? Anyway, I still don't believe it.

  Hally: God, you're impossible. I showed it to you in black and white.

  Sam: Doesn't mean I got to believe it.

235   **Hally:** It's the likes of you that kept the Inquisition in business. It's called bigotry. Anyway, that's my man of magnitude. Charles Darwin! Who's yours?

  Sam *(Without hesitation.):* Abraham Lincoln.

  Hally: I might have guessed as much. Don't get sentimental, Sam. You've never been a slave, you know. And anyway we freed your ancestors here in South Africa long before the Americans. But if you want to thank somebody on their behalf, do it to

---

[10] Town in Belgium, site of major battle in which Napoleon was defeated in 1815..   [11] Nineteenth-century British scientist and naturalist who developed the theory of evolution.

Mr. William Wilberforce.[12] Come on. Try again. I want a real genius. (*Now enjoying
himself, and so is Sam. Hally goes behind the counter and helps himself to a chocolate.*)

Sam: William Shakespeare.[13]

Hally (*No enthusiasm.*): Oh. So you're also one of them, are you? You're basing that opinion
on only one play, you know. You've only read my *Julius Caesar* and even I don't understand half of what they're talking about. They should do what they did with the old
Bible: bring the language up to date.

240 **Sam:** That's all you've got. It's also the only one *you've* read.

Hally: I know. I admit it. That's why I suggest we reserve our judgment until we've
checked up on a few others. I've got a feeling, though, that by the end of this year one
is going to be enough for me, and I can give you the names of twenty-nine other chaps
in the Standard Nine class of the Port Elizabeth Technical College who feel the same.
But if you want him, you can have him. My turn now. (*Pacing.*) This is a damned good
exercise, you know! It started off looking like a simple question and here it's got us really probing into the intellectual heritage of our civilization.

Sam: So who is it going to be?

Hally: My next man . . . and he gets the title on two scores: social reform and literary genius . . . is Leo Nikolaevich Tolstoy.[14]

Sam: That Russian.

245 **Hally:** Correct. Remember the picture of him I showed you?

Sam: With the long beard.

Hally (*Trying to look like Tolstoy.*): And those burning, visionary eyes. My God, the face of a
social prophet if ever I saw one! And remember my words when I showed it to you?
Here's a *man*, Sam!

Sam: Those were words, Hally.

Hally: Not many intellectuals are prepared to shovel manure with the peasants and then go
home and write a "little book" called *War and Peace*. Incidentally, Sam, he was somebody else who, to quote, ". . . did not distinguish himself scholastically."

250 **Sam:** Meaning?

Hally: He was also no good at school.

Sam: Like you and Winston Churchill.

Hally (*Mirthlessly.*): Ha, ha, ha.

Sam (*Simultaneously.*): Ha, ha, ha.

255 **Hally:** Don't get clever, Sam. That man freed his serfs of his own free will.

Sam: No argument. He was a somebody, all right. I accept him.

Hally: I'm sure Count Tolstoy will be very pleased to hear that. Your turn. Shoot. (*Another
chocolate from behind the counter.*) I'm waiting, Sam.

Sam: I've got him.

Hally: Good. Submit your candidate for examination.

260 **Sam:** Jesus.

Hally (*Stopped dead in his tracks.*): Who?

Sam: Jesus Christ.

Hally: Oh, come on, Sam!

Sam: The Messiah.

265 **Hally:** Ja, but still . . . No, Sam. Don't let's get started on religion. We'll just spend the
whole afternoon arguing again. Suppose I turn around and say Mohammed?

---

[12] English abolitionist (1759–1833).   [13] English poet and dramatist (1564–1616). See chapter 4.
[14] Russian novelist, author of *Anna Karenina* and *War and Peace* (1828–1910).

Sam: All right.

Hally: You can't have them both on the same list!

Sam: Why not? You like Mohammed, I like Jesus.

Hally: I *don't* like Mohammed. I never have. I was merely being hypothetical. As far as I'm concerned, the Koran is as bad as the Bible. No. Religion is out! I'm not going to waste my time again arguing with you about the existence of God. You know perfectly well I'm an atheist . . . and I've got homework to do.

270 **Sam:** Okay, I take him back.

Hally: You've got time for one more name.

Sam (*After thought.*): I've got one I know we'll agree on. A simple straightforward great Man of Magnitude . . . and no arguments. And *he* really *did* benefit all mankind.

Hally: I wonder. After your last contribution I'm beginning to doubt whether anything in the way of an intellectual agreement is possible between the two of us. Who is he?

Sam: Guess.

275 **Hally:** Socrates?[15] Alexandre Dumas?[16] Karl Marx?[17] Dostoevsky?[18] Nietzsche?[19]

(Sam shakes his head after each name.)

Give me a clue.

Sam: The letter P is important . . .

Hally: Plato!

Sam: . . . and his name begins with an F.

Hally: I've got it. Freud and Psychology.[20]

280 **Sam:** No. I didn't understand him.

Hally: That makes two of us.

Sam: Think of mouldy apricot jam.

Hally (*After a delighted laugh.*): Penicillin and Sir Alexander Fleming![21] And the title of the book: *The Microbe Hunters.* (*Delighted.*) Splendid, Sam! Splendid. For once we are in total agreement. The major breakthrough in medical science in the Twentieth Century. If it wasn't for him, we might have lost the Second World War. It's deeply gratifying, Sam, to know that I haven't been wasting my time in talking to you. (*Strutting around proudly.*) Tolstoy may have educated his peasants, but I've educated you.

Sam: Standard Four to Standard Nine.

285 **Hally:** Have we been at it as long as that?

Sam: Yep. And my first lesson was geography.

Hally (*Intrigued.*): Really? I don't remember.

Sam: My room there at the back of the old Jubilee Boarding House. I had just started working for your Mom. Little boy in short trousers walks in one afternoon and asks me seriously: "Sam, do you want to see South Africa?" Hey man! Sure I wanted to see South Africa!

Hally: Was that me?

290 **Sam:** . . . So the next thing I'm looking at a map you had just done for homework. It was your first one and you were very proud of yourself.

Hally: Go on.

---

[15] Greek philosopher (470–399 B.C.). [16] Nineteenth-century French novelist (1824–95). [17] Nineteenth-century German political philosopher and economist whose thought provided the basis of the socialist state. [18] Nineteenth-century Russian novelist, author of *Crime and Punishment* and *The Brothers Karamazov* (1821–81). [19] German philosopher (1844–1900). [20] Founder of modern psychology; physician and psychiatrist (1856–1939). [21] Physician and scientist who with Sir Howard Florey discovered penicillin in 1929 (1881–1955).

Sam: Then came my first lesson. "Repeat after me, Sam: Gold in the Transvaal, mealies in the Free State, sugar in Natal and grapes in the Cape." I still know it!

Hally: Well, I'll be buggered. So that's how it all started.

Sam: And your next map was one with all the rivers and the mountains they came from. The Orange, the Vaal, the Limpopo, the Zambezi[22] . . .

295 **Hally:** You've got a phenomenal memory!

Sam: You should be grateful. That is why you started passing your exams. You tried to be better than me.

(They laugh together. Willie is attracted by the laughter and joins them.)

Hally: The old Jubilee Boarding House. Sixteen rooms with board and lodging, rent in advance and one week's notice. I haven't thought about it for donkey's years . . . and I don't think that's an accident. God, was I glad when we sold it and moved out. Those years are not remembered as the happiest ones of an unhappy childhood.

Willie *(Knocking on the table and trying to imitate a woman's voice.):* "Hally, are you there?"

Hally: Who's that supposed to be?

300 **Willie:** "What you doing in there, Hally? Come out at once!"

Hally *(To Sam.):* What's he talking about?

Sam: Don't you remember?

Willie: "Sam, Willie . . . is he in there with you boys?"

Sam: Hiding away in our room when your mother was looking for you.

305 **Hally** *(Another good laugh.):* Of course! I used to crawl and hide under your bed! But finish the story, Willie. Then what used to happen? You chaps would give the game away by telling her I was in there with you. So much for friendship.

Sam: We couldn't lie to her. She knew.

Hally: Which meant I got another rowing for hanging around the "servants' quarters."
I think I spent more time in there with you chaps than anywhere else in that dump. And do you blame me? Nothing but bloody misery wherever you went. Somebody was always complaining about the food, or my mother was having a fight with Micky Nash because she'd caught her with a petty officer in her room. Maud Meiring was another one. Remember those two? They were prostitutes, you know. Soldiers and sailors from the troopships. Bottom fell out of the business when the war ended. God, the flotsam and jetsam that life washed up on our shores! No joking, if it wasn't for your room, I would have been the first certified ten-year-old in medical history. Ja, the memories are coming back now. Walking home from school and thinking: "What can I do this afternoon?" Try out a few ideas, but sooner or later I'd end up in there with you fellows. I bet you I could still find my way to your room with my eyes closed. *(He does exactly that.)* Down the corridor . . . telephone on the right, which my Mom keeps locked because sombody is using it on the sly and not paying . . . past the kitchen and unappetizing cooking smells . . .around the corner into the backyard, hold my breath again because there are more smells coming when I pass your lavatory, then into that little passageway, first door on the right and into your room. How's that?

Sam: Good. But, as usual, you forgot to knock.

Hally: Like that time I barged in and caught you and Cynthia . . . at it. Remember? God, was I embarrassed! I didn't know what was going on at first.

310 **Sam:** Ja, that taught you a lesson.

---

[22] Rivers in South Africa.

Hally: And about a lot more than knocking on doors, I'll have you know, and I don't mean
geography either. Hell, Sam, couldn't you have waited until it was dark?

Sam: No.

Hally: Was it that urgent?

Sam: Yes, and if you don't believe me, wait until your time comes.

315 **Hally:** No, thank you. I am not interested in girls. *(Back to his memories . . . Using a few
chairs he recreates the room as he lists the items.)* A gray little room with a cold cement
floor. Your bed against that wall . . . and I now know why the mattress sags so
much! . . . Willie's bed . . . it's propped up on bricks because one leg is broken . . . that
wobbly little table with the washbasin and jug of water . . . Yes! . . . stuck to the wall
above it are some pin-up pictures from magazines. Joe Louis . . .

Willie: Brown Bomber.[23] World Title. *(Boxing pose.)* Three rounds and knockout.

Hally: Against who?

Sam: Max Schmeling.

Hally: Correct. I can also remember Fred Astaire and Ginger Rogers, and Rita Hayworth in
a bathing costume which always made me hot and bothered when I looked at it. Under Willie's bed is an old suitcase with all his clothes in a mess, which is why I never
hide there. Your things are neat and tidy in a trunk next to your bed, and on it there is
a picture of you and Cynthia in your ballroom clothes, your first silver cup for third
place in a competition and an old radio which doesn't work anymore. Have I left out
anything?

320 **Sam:** No.

Hally: Right, so much for the stage directions. Now the characters. *(Sam and Willie move to
their appropriate positions in the bedroom.)* Willie is in bed, under his blankets with his
clothes on, complaining nonstop about something, but we can't make out a word of
what he's saying because he's got his head under the blankets as well. You're on your
bed trimming your toenails with a knife—not a very edifying sight—and as for
me . . . What am I doing?

Sam: You're sitting on the floor giving Willie a lecture about being a good loser while you
get the checker board and pieces ready for a game. Then you go to Willie's bed, pull
off the blankets and make him play with you first because you know you're going to
win, and that gives you the second game with me.

Hally: And you certainly were a bad loser, Willie!

Willie: Haai!

325 **Hally:** Wasn't he, Sam? And so slow! A game with you almost took the whole afternoon.
Thank God I gave up trying to teach you how to play chess.

Willie: You and Sam cheated.

Hally: I never saw Sam cheat, and mine were mostly the mistakes of youth.

Willie: Then how is it you two was always winning?

Hally: Have you ever considered the possibility, Willie, that it was because we were better
than you?

330 **Willie:** Every time better?

Hally: Not every time. There were occasions when we deliberately let you win a game so
that you would stop sulking and go on playing with us. Sam used to wink at me when
you weren't looking to show me it was time to let you win.

Willie: So then you two didn't play fair.

---

[23] Nickname of U.S. prizefighter Joseph Louis, (1914–81), who won the heavyweight boxing championship
in 1938 against German Max Schmeling.

Hally: It was for your benefit, Mr. Malopo, which is more than being fair. It was an act of self-sacrifice. *(To Sam.)* But you know what my best memory is, don't you?

Sam: No.

335 **Hally:** Come on, guess. If your memory is so good, you must remember it as well.

Sam: We got up to a lot of tricks in there, Hally.

Hally: This one was special, Sam.

Sam: I'm listening.

Hally: It started off looking like another of those useless nothing-to-do afternoons. I'd already been down to Main Street looking for adventure, but nothing had happened. I didn't feel like climbing trees in the Donkin Park or pretending I was a private eye and following a stranger . . . so as usual: See what's cooking in Sam's room. This time it was you on the floor. You had two thin pieces of wood and you were smoothing them down with a knife. It didn't look particularly interesting, but when I asked you what you were doing, you just said, "Wait and see, Hally. Wait . . . and see" . . . in that secret sort of way of yours, so I knew there was a surprise coming. You teased me, you bugger, by being deliberately slow and not answering my questions!

(Sam laughs.)

And whistling while you worked away! God, it was infuriating! I could have brained you! It was only when you tied them together in a cross and put that down on the brown paper that I realized what you were doing. "Sam is making a kite?" And when I asked you and you said "Yes . . . !" *(Shaking his head with disbelief.)* The sheer audacity of it took my breath away. I mean, seriously, what the hell does a black man know about flying a kite? I'll be honest with you, Sam, I had no hopes for it. If you think I was excited and happy, you got another guess coming. In fact, I was shit-scared that we were going to make fools of ourselves. When we left the boarding house to go up onto the hill, I was praying quietly that there wouldn't be any other kids around to laugh at us.

340 **Sam** *(Enjoying the memory as much as Hally.):* Ja, I could see that.

Hally: I made it obvious, did I?

Sam: Ja. You refused to carry it.

Hally: Do you blame me? Can you remember what the poor thing looked like? Tomato-box wood and brown paper! Flour and water for glue! Two of my mother's old stockings for a tail, and then all those bits and pieces of string you made me tie together so that we could fly it! Hell, no, that was now only asking for a miracle to happen.

Sam: Then the big argument when I told you to hold the string and run with it when I let go.

345 **Hally:** I was prepared to run, all right, but straight back to the boarding house.

Sam *(Knowing what's coming.):* So what happened?

Hally: Come on, Sam, you remember as well as I do.

Sam: I want to hear it from you.

(Hally pauses. He wants to be as accurate as possible.)

Hally: You went a little distance from me down the hill, you held it up ready to let it go. . . . "This is it," I thought. "Like everything else in my life, here comes another fiasco." Then you shouted, "Go, Hally!" and I started to run. *(Another pause.)* I don't know how to describe it, Sam. Ja! The miracle happened! I was running, waiting for it to crash to the ground, but instead suddenly there was something alive behind me at the end of the string, tugging at it as if it wanted to be free. I looked back . . . *(Shakes his head.)* . . . I still can't believe my eyes. It was flying! Looping around and trying to

climb even higher into the sky. You shouted to me to let it have more string. I did, until there was none left and I was just holding that piece of wood we had tied it to. You
came up and joined me. You were laughing.

350 **Sam:** So were you. And shouting, "It works, Sam! We've done it!"

Hally: And we had! I was so proud of us! It was the most splendid thing I had ever seen. I
wished there were hundreds of kids around to watch us. The part that scared me,
though, was when you showed me how to make it dive down to the ground and then
just when it was on the point of crashing, swoop up again!

Sam: You didn't want to try yourself.

Hally: Of course not! I would have been suicidal if anything had happened to it. Watching
you do it made me nervous enough. I was quite happy just to see it up there with its
tail fluttering behind it. You left me after that, didn't you? You explained how to get
it down, we tied it to the bench so that I could sit and watch it, and you went away.
I wanted you to stay, you know. I was a little scared of having to look after it by
myself.

Sam (*Quietly.*): I had work to do, Hally.

355 **Hally:** It was sort of sad bringing it down, Sam. And it looked sad again when it was lying
there on the ground. Like something that had lost its soul. Just tomato-box wood,
brown paper and two of my mother's old stockings! But, hell, I'll never forget that first
moment when I saw it up there. I had a stiff neck the next day from looking up so
much.

(*Sam laughs. Hally turns to him with a question he never thought of asking before.*)

Why did you make that kite, Sam?

Sam (*Evenly.*): I can't remember.

Hally: Truly?

Sam: Too long ago, Hally.

Hally: Ja, I suppose it was. It's time for another one, you know.

360 **Sam:** Why do you say that?

Hally: Because it feels like that. Wouldn't be a good day to fly it, though.

Sam: No. You can't fly kites on rainy days.

Hally (*He studies Sam. Their memories have made him conscious of the man's presence in his
life.*): How old are you, Sam?

Sam: Two score and five.

365 **Hally:** Strange, isn't it?

Sam: What?

Hally: Me and you.

Sam: What's strange about it?

Hally: Little white boy in short trousers and a black man old enough to be his father flying
a kite. It's not every day you see that.

370 **Sam:** But why strange? Because the one is white and the other black?

Hally: I don't know. Would have been just as strange, I suppose, if it had been me and my
Dad . . . cripple man and a little boy! Nope! There's no chance of me flying a kite without it being strange. (*Simple statement of fact—no self-pity.*) There's a nice little short
story there. "The Kite-Flyers." But we'd have to find a twist in the ending.

Sam: Twist?

Hally: Yes. Something unexpected. The way it ended with us was too straightforward . . .
me on the bench and you going back to work. There's no drama in that.

Willie: And me?

375 **Hally:** You?

Willie: Yes me.

Hally: You want to get into the story as well, do you? I got it! Change the title: "Afternoons in Sam's Room" . . . expand it and tell all the stories. It's on its way to being a novel. Our days in the old Jubilee. Sad in a way that they're over. I almost wish we were still in that little room.

Sam: We're still together.

Hally: That's true. It's just that life felt the right size in there . . . not too big and not too small. Wasn't so hard to work up a bit of courage. It's got so bloody complicated since then.

(The telephone rings. Sam answers it.)

380 **Sam:** St. George's Park Tea Room . . . Hello, Madam . . . Yes, Madam, he's here . . . Hally, it's your mother.

Hally: Where is she phoning from?

Sam: Sounds like the hospital. It's a public telephone.

Hally *(Relieved.):* You see! I told you. *(The telephone.)* Hello, Mom . . .Yes . . . Yes no fine. Everything's under control here. How's things with poor old Dad? . . . Has he had a bad turn? . . . What? . . . Oh, God! . . .Yes, Sam told me, but I was sure he'd made a mistake. But what's this all about, Mom? He didn't look at all good last night. How can he get better so quickly? . . . Then very obviously you must say no. Be firm with him. You're the boss. . . . You know what it's going to be like if he comes home. . . . Well, then, don't blame me when I fail my exams at the end of the year. . . . Yes! How am I expected to be fresh for school when I spend half the night massaging his gammy leg? . . . So am I! . . . So tell him a white lie. Say Dr. Colley wants more X-rays of his stump. Or bribe him. We'll sneak in double tots of brandy in future. . . . What? . . . Order him to get back into bed at once! If he's going to behave like a child, treat him like one. . . . All right, Mom! I was just trying to . . . I'm sorry. . . . I said I'm sorry. . . . Quick, give me your number. I'll phone you back. *(He hangs up and waits a few seconds.)* Here we go again! *(He dials.)* I'm sorry, Mom. . . . Okay . . . But now listen to me carefully. All it needs is for you to put your foot down. Don't take no for an answer. . . . Did you hear me? And whatever you do, don't discuss it with him. . . . Because I'm frightened you'll give in to him. . . . Yes, Sam gave me lunch. . . . I ate all of it! . . . No, Mom not a soul. It's still raining here. . . . Right, I'll tell them. I'll just do some homework and then lock up. . . . But remember now, Mom. Don't listen to anything he says. And phone me back and let me know what happens. . . . Okay. Bye, Mom. *(He hangs up. The men are staring at him.)* My Mom says that when you're finished with the floors you must do the windows. *(Pause.)* Don't misunderstand me, chaps. All I want is for him to get better. And if he was, I'd be the first person to say: "Bring him home." But he's not, and we can't give him the medical care and attention he needs at home. That's what hospitals are there for. *(Brusquely.)* So don't just stand there! Get on with it!

(Sam clears Hally's table.)

You heard right. My Dad wants to go home.

Sam: Is he better?

385 **Hally** *(Sharply.):* No! How the hell can he be better when last night he was groaning with pain? This is not an age of miracles!

Sam: Then he should stay in hospital.

Hally *(Seething with irritation and frustration.):* Tell me something I don't know, Sam. What the hell do you think I was saying to my Mom? All I can say is fuck-it-all.

Sam: I'm sure he'll listen to your Mom.

Hally: You don't know what she's up against. He's already packed his shaving kit and pajamas and is sitting on his bed with his crutches, dressed and ready to go. I know him when he gets in that mood. If she tries to reason with him, we've had it. She's no match for him when it comes to a battle of words. He'll tie her up in knots. (*Trying to hide his true feelings.*)

390 **Sam:** I suppose it gets lonely for him in there.

Hally: With all the patients and nurses around? Regular visits from the Salvation Army? Balls! It's ten times worse for him at home. I'm at school and my mother is here in the business all day.

Sam: He's at least got you at night.

Hally (*Before he can stop himself.*): And we've got him! Please! I don't want to talk about it anymore. (*Unpacks his school case, slamming down books on the table.*) Life is just a plain bloody mess, that's all. And people are fools.

Sam: Come on, Hally.

395 **Hally:** Yes, they are! They bloody well deserve what they get.

Sam: Then don't complain.

Hally: Don't try to be clever, Sam. It doesn't suit you. Anybody who thinks there's nothing wrong with this world needs to have his head examined. Just when things are going along all right, without fail someone or something will come along and spoil everything. Somebody should write that down as a fundamental law of the Universe. The principle of perpetual disappointment. If there is a God who created this world, he should scrap it and try again.

Sam: All right, Hally, all right. What you got for homework?

Hally: Bullshit, as usual. (*Opens an exercise book and reads.*) "Write five hundred words describing an annual event of cultural or historical significance."

400 **Sam:** That should be easy enough for you.

Hally: And also plain bloody boring. You know what he wants, don't you? One of their useless old ceremonies. The commemoration of the landing of the 1820 Settlers,[24] or if it's going to be culture, Carols by Candlelight every Christmas.

Sam: It's an impressive sight. Make a good description, Hally. All those candles glowing in the dark and the people singing hymns.

Hally: And it's called religious hysteria. (*Intense irritation.*) Please, Sam! Just leave me alone and let me get on with it. I'm not in the mood for games this afternoon. And remember my Mom's orders . . . you're to help Willie with the windows. Come on now, I don't want any more nonsense in here.

Sam: Okay, Hally, okay.

(*Hally settles down to his homework; determined preparations . . . pen, ruler, exercise book, dictionary, another cake . . . all of which will lead to nothing.*)

(*Sam waltzes over to Willie and starts to replace tables and chairs. He practices a ballroom step while doing so. Willie watches. When Sam is finished, Willie tries.*) Good! But just a little bit quicker on the turn and only move in to her after she's crossed over. What about this one?

(*Another step. When Sam is finished, Willie again has a go.*)

Much better. See what happens when you just relax and enjoy yourself? Remember that in two weeks' time and you'll be all right.

---

[24] In 1819–20, the British government paid Britons who moved to South Africa 100 acres of land per family.

405 **Willie:** But I haven't got partner, Boet Sam.
Sam: Maybe Hilda will turn up tonight.
Willie: No, Boet Sam. (*Reluctantly.*) I gave her a good hiding.
Sam: You mean a bad one.
Willie: Good bad one.
410 **Sam:** Then you mustn't complain either. Now you pay the price for losing your temper.
Willie: I also pay two pounds ten shilling entrance fee.
Sam: They'll refund you if you withdraw now.
Willie (*Appalled.*): You mean, don't dance?
Sam: Yes.
415 **Willie:** No! I wait too long and I practice too hard. If I find me new partner, you think I
can be ready in two weeks? I ask Madam for my leave now and we practice every day.
Sam: Quickstep non-stop for two weeks. World record, Willie, but you'll be mad at the
end.
Willie: No jokes, Boet Sam.
Sam: I'm not joking.
Willie: So then what?
420 **Sam:** Find Hilda. Say you're sorry and promise you won't beat her again.
Willie: No.
Sam: Then withdraw. Try again next year.
Willie: No.
Sam: Then I give up.
425 **Willie:** Haaikona, Boet Sam, you can't.
Sam: What do you mean, I can't? I'm telling you: I give up.
Willie (*Adamant.*): No! (*Accusingly.*) It was you who start me ballroom dancing.
Sam: So?
Willie: Before that I use to be happy. And is you and Miriam who bring me to Hilda and
say here's partner for you.
430 **Sam:** What are you saying, Willie?
Willie: You!
Sam: But me what? To blame?
Willie: Yes.
Sam: Willie . . . ? (*Bursts into laughter.*)
435 **Willie:** And now all you do is make jokes at me. You wait. When Miriam leaves you is my
turn to laugh. Ha! Ha! Ha!
Sam (*He can't take Willie seriously any longer.*): She can leave me tonight! I know what to do.
(*Bowing before an imaginary partner.*) May I have the pleasure? (*He dances and sings.*)
Just a fellow with his pillow . . .
Dancin' like a willow . . .
In an autumn breeze . . ."
Willie: There you go again!

(*Sam goes on dancing and singing.*)

Boet Sam!
Sam: There's the answer to your problem! Judges' announcement in two weeks' time:
"Ladies and gentlemen, the winner in the open section . . . Mr. Willie Malopo and his
pillow!"

(*This is too much for a now really angry Willie. He goes for Sam, but the latter is too quick
for him and puts Hally's table between the two of them.*)

Hally *(Exploding.):* For Christ's sake, you two!

440 **Willie** *(Still trying to get at Sam.):* I donner you, Sam! Struesgod!

Sam *(Still laughing.):* Sorry, Willie . . . Sorry . . .

Hally: Sam! Willie! *(Grabs his ruler and gives Willie a vicious whack on the bum.)* How the hell am I supposed to concentrate with the two of you behaving like bloody children!

Willie: Hit him too!

Hally: Shut up, Willie.

445 **Willie:** He started jokes again.

Hally: Get back to your work. You too, Sam. *(His ruler.)* Do you want another one, Willie?

> *(Sam and Willie return to their work. Hally uses the opportunity to escape from his unsuccessful attempt at homework. He struts around like a little despot, ruler in hand, giving vent to his anger and frustration.)*

> Suppose a customer had walked in then? Or the Park Superintendent. And seen the two of you behaving like a pair of hooligans. That would have been the end of my mother's license, you know. And your jobs! Well, this is the end of it. From now on there will be no more of your ballroom nonsense in here. This is a business establishment, not a bloody New Brighton dancing school. I've been far too lenient with the two of you. *(Behind the counter for a green cool drink and a dollop of ice cream. He keeps up his tirade as he prepares it.)* But what really makes me bitter is that I allow you chaps a little freedom in here when business is bad and what do you do with it? The foxtrot![25] Specially you, Sam. There's more to life than trotting around a dance floor and I thought at least you knew it.

Sam: It's a harmless pleasure, Hally. It doesn't hurt anybody.

Hally: It's also a rather simple one, you know.

Sam: You reckon so? Have you ever tried?

450 **Hally:** Of course not.

Sam: Why don't you? Now.

Hally: What do you mean? Me dance?

Sam: Yes. I'll show you a simple step—the waltz—then you try it.

Hally: What will that prove?

455 **Sam:** That it might not be as easy as you think.

Hally: I didn't say it was easy. I said it was simple—like in simple-minded, meaning mentally retarded. You can't exactly say it challenges the intellect.

Sam: It does other things.

Hally: Such as?

Sam: Make people happy.

460 **Hally** *(The glass in his hand.):* So do American cream sodas with ice cream. For God's sake, Sam, you're not asking me to take ballroom dancing serious, are you?

Sam: Yes.

Hally *(Sigh of defeat.):* Oh, well, so much for trying to give you a decent education. I've obviously achieved nothing.

Sam: You still haven't told me what's wrong with admiring something that's beautiful and then trying to do it yourself.

Hally: Nothing. But we happen to be talking about a foxtrot, not a thing of beauty.

465 **Sam:** But that is just what I'm saying. If you were to see two champions doing, two masters of the art . . . !

---

[25] A dance characterized by slow, quick steps.

Hally: Oh, God, I give up. So now it's also art!

Sam: Ja.

Hally: There's a limit, Sam. Don't confuse art and entertainment.

Sam: So then what is art?

470 **Hally:** You want a definition?

Sam: Ja.

Hally (*He realizes he has got to be careful. He gives the matter a lot of thought before answering.*): Philosophers have been trying to do that for centuries. What is Art? What is Life? But basically I suppose it's . . . the giving of meaning to matter.

Sam: Nothing to do with beautiful?

Hally: It goes beyond that. It's the giving of form to the formless.

475 **Sam:** Ja, well, maybe it's not art, then. But I still say it's beautiful.

Hally: I'm sure the word you mean to use is "entertaining."

Sam (*Adamant.*): No. Beautiful. And if you want proof, come along to the Centenary Hall in New Brighton in two weeks' time.

(*The mention of the Centenary Hall draws Willie over to them.*)

Hally: What for? I've seen the two of you prancing around in here often enough.

Sam (*He laughs.*): This isn't the real thing, Hally. We're just playing around in here.

480 **Hally:** So? I can use my imagination.

Sam: And what do you get?

Hally: A lot of people dancing around and having a so-called good time.

Sam: That all?

Hally: Well, basically it is that, surely.

485 **Sam:** No, it isn't. Your imagination hasn't helped you at all. There's a lot more to it than that. We're getting ready for the championships, Hally, not just another dance. There's going to be a lot of people, all right, and they're going to have a good time, but they'll only be spectators, sitting around and watching. It's just the competitors out there on the dance floor. Party decorations and fancy lights all around the walls! The ladies in beautiful evening dresses!

Hally: My mother's got one of those, Sam, and quite frankly, it's an embarrassment every time she wears it.

Sam (*Undeterred.*): Your imagination left out the excitement.

(*Hally scoffs.*)

Oh, yes. The finalists are not going to be out there just to have a good time. One of those couples will be the 1950 Eastern Province Champions. And your imagination left out the music.

Willie: Mr. Elijah Gladman Guzana and his Orchestral Jazzonions.

Sam: The sound of the big band, Hally. Trombone, trumpet, tenor and alto sax. And then, finally, your imagination also left out the climax of the evening when the dancing is finished, the judges have stopped whispering among themselves and the Master of Ceremonies collects their scorecards and goes up onto the stage to announce the winners.

490 **Hally:** All right. So you make it sound like a bit of a do. It's an occasion. Satisfied?

Sam (*Victory.*): So you admit that!

Hally: Emotionally yes, intellectually no.

Sam: Well, I don't know what you mean by that, all I'm telling you is that it is going to be the event of the year in New Brighton. It's been sold out for two weeks already. There's only standing room left. We've got competitors coming from Kingwilliamstown, East London, Port Alfred.

(*Hally starts pacing thoughtfully.*)

Hally: Tell me a bit more.

495 **Sam:** I thought you weren't interested . . . intellectually.

Hally (*Mysteriously.*)*:* I've got my reasons.

Sam: What do you want to know?

Hally: It takes place every year?

Sam: Yes. But only every third year in New Brighton. It's East London's turn to have the championships next year.

500 **Hally:** Which, I suppose, makes it an even more significant event.

Sam: Ah ha! We're getting somewhere. Our "occasion" is now a "significant event."

Hally: I wonder.

Sam: What?

Hally: I wonder if I would get away with it.

505 **Sam:** But what?

Hally (*To the table and his exercise book.*)*:* "Write five hundred words describing an annual event of cultural or historical significance." Would I be stretching poetic license a little too far if I called your ballroom championships a cultural event?

Sam: You mean . . . ?

Hally: You think we could get five hundred words out of it, Sam?

Sam: Victor Sylvester has written a whole book on ballroom dancing.

510 **Willie:** You going to write about it, Master Hally?

Hally: Yes, gentlemen, that is precisely what I am considering doing. Old Doc Bromely— he's my English teacher—is going to argue with me, of course. He doesn't like natives. But I'll point out to him that in strict anthropological terms the culture of a primitive black society includes its dancing and singing. To put my thesis in a nutshell: The war-dance has been replaced by the waltz. But it still amounts to the same thing: the re-lease of primitive emotions through movement. Shall we give it a go?

Sam: I'm ready.

Willie: Me also.

Hally: Ha! This will teach the old bugger a lesson. (*Decision taken.*) Right. Let's get our-selves organized. (*This means another cake on the table. He sits.*) I think you've given me enough general atmosphere, Sam, but to build the tension and suspense I need facts. (*Pencil poised.*)

515 **Willie:** Give him facts, Boet Sam.

Hally: What you called the climax . . . how many finalists?

Sam: Six couples.

Hally (*Making notes.*)*:* Go on. Give me the picture.

Sam: Spectators seated right around the hall. (*Willie becomes a spectator.*)

520 **Hally:** . . . and it's a full house.

Sam: At one end, on the stage, Gladman and his Orchestral Jazzonions. At the other end is a long table with the three judges. The six finalists go onto the dance floor and take up their positions. When they are ready and the spectators have settled down, the Master of Ceremonies goes to the microphone. To start with, he makes some jokes to get the people laughing . . .

Hally: Good touch! (*As he writes.*) ". . . creating a relaxed atmosphere which will change to one of tension and drama as the climax is approached."

Sam (*Onto a chair to act out the M.C.*)*:* "Ladies and gentlemen, we come now to the great moment you have all been waiting for this evening. . . . The finals of the 1950 Eastern Province Open Ballroom Dancing Championships. But first let me introduce the final-ists! Mr. and Mrs. Welcome Tchabalala from Kingwilliamstown . . ."

Willie (*He applauds after every name.*): Is when the people clap their hands and whistle and make a lot of noise, Master Hally.

525 **Sam:** Mr. Mulligan Njikelane and Miss Nomhle Nkonyeni of Grahamstown; Mr. and Mrs. Norman Nchinga from Port Alfred; Mr. Fats Bokolane and Miss Dina Plaatjies from East London; Mr. Sipho Dugu and Mrs. Mable Magada from Peddie; and from New Brighton our very own Mr. Willie Malopo and Miss Hilda Samuels.

(*Willie can't believe his ears. He abandons his role as spectator and scrambles into position as a finalist.*)

Willie: Relaxed and ready to romance!

Sam: The applause dies down. When everybody is silent, Gladman lifts up his sax, nods at the Orchestral Jazzonions . . .

Willie: Play the jukebox please, Boet Sam!

Sam: I also only got bus fare, Willie.

530 **Hally:** Hold it, everybody. (*Heads for the cash register behind the counter.*) How much is in the till, Sam?

Sam: Three shillings. Hally . . . your Mom counted it before she left.

(*Hally hesitates.*)

Hally: Sorry, Willie. You know how she carried on the last time I did it. We'll just have to pool our combined imaginations and hope for the best. (*Returns to the table.*) Back to work. How are the points scored, Sam?

Sam: Maximum of ten points each for individual style, deportment, rhythm and general appearance.

Willie: Must I start?

535 **Hally:** Hold it for a second, Willie. And penalties?

Sam: For what?

Hally: For doing something wrong. Say you stumble or bump into somebody . . . do they take off any points?

Sam (*Aghast.*): Hally . . . !

Hally: When you're dancing. If you and your partner collide into another couple.

(*Hally can get no further. Sam has collapsed with laughter. He explains to Willie.*)

540 **Sam:** If me and Miriam bump into you and Hilda . . .

(*Willie joins him in another good laugh.*)

Hally, Hally . . . !

Hally (*Perplexed.*): Why? What did I say?

Sam: There's no collisions out there, Hally. Nobody trips or stumbles or bumps into anybody else. That's what that moment is all about. To be one of those finalists on that dance floor is like . . . like being in a dream about a world in which accidents don't happen.

Hally (*Genuinely moved by Sam's image.*): Jesus, Sam! That's beautiful!

Willie (*Can endure waiting no longer.*): I'm starting! (*Willie dances while Sam talks.*)

545 **Sam:** Of course it is. That's what I've been trying to say to you all afternoon. And it's beautiful because that is what we want life to be like. But instead, like you said, Hally, we're bumping into each other all the time. Look at the three of us this afternoon: I've bumped into Willie, the two of us have bumped into you, you've bumped into your mother, she bumping into your Dad. . . . None of us knows the steps and there's no music playing. And it doesn't stop with us. The whole world is doing it all the time.

Open a newspaper and what do you read? America has bumped into Russia, England is bumping into India, rich man bumps into poor man. Those are big collisions, Hally. They make for a lot of bruises. People get hurt in all that bumping, and we're sick and tired of it now. It's been going on for too long. Are we never going to get it right? . . . Learn to dance life like champions instead of always being just a bunch of beginners at it?

Hally (*Deep and sincere admiration of the man.*): You've got a vision, Sam!

Sam: Not just me. What I'm saying to you is that everybody's got it. That's why there's only standing room left for the Centenary Hall in two weeks' time. For as long as the music lasts, we are going to see six couples get it right, the way we want life to be.

Hally: But is that the best we can do, Sam . . . watch six finalists dreaming about the way it should be?

Sam: I don't know. But it starts with that. Without the dream we won't know what we're going for. And anyway I reckon there are a few people who have got past just dreaming about it and are trying for something real. Remember that thing we read once in the paper about the Mahatma Gandhi?[26] Going without food to stop those riots in India?

550 **Hally:** You're right. He certainly was trying to teach people to get the steps right.

Sam: And the Pope.

Hally: Yes, he's another one. Our old General Smuts as well, you know. He's also out there dancing. You know, Sam, when you come to think of it, that's what the United Nations boils down to . . . a dancing school for politicians!

Sam: And let's hope they learn.

Hally (*A little surge of hope.*): You're right. We mustn't despair. Maybe there's some hope for mankind after all. Keep it up, Willie. (*Back to his table with determination.*) This is a lot bigger than I thought. So what have we got? Yes, our title: "A World Without Collisions."

555 **Sam:** That sounds good! "A World Without Collisions."

Hally: Subtitle: "Global Politics on the Dance Floor." No. A bit too heavy, hey? What about "Ballroom Dancing as a Political Vision"?

(*The telephone rings. Sam answers it.*)

Sam: St. George's Park Tea Room . . . Yes, Madam . . . Hally, it's your Mom.

Hally (*Back to reality.*): Oh, God, yes! I'd forgotten all about that. Shit! Remember my words, Sam? Just when you're enjoying yourself, someone or something will come along and wreck everything.

Sam: You haven't heard what she's got to say yet.

560 **Hally:** Public telephone?

Sam: No.

Hally: Does she sound happy or unhappy?

Sam: I couldn't tell. (*Pause.*) She's waiting, Hally.

Hally (*To the telephone.*): Hello, Mom . . . No, everything is okay here. Just doing my homework. . . . What's your news? . . . You've what? . . . (*Pause. He takes the receiver away from his ear for a few seconds. In the course of Hally's telephone conversation, Sam and Willie discreetly position the stacked tables and chairs. Hally places the receiver back to his ear.*) Yes, I'm still here. Oh, well, I give up now. Why did you do it, Mom? . . . Well, I

---

[26] Indian religious leader and philosopher who developed the idea of *satyagraha*, passive resistance (1869–1948).

just hope you know what you've let us in for. . . . (*Loudly.*) I said I hope you know what you've let us in for! It's the end of the peace and quiet we've been having. (*Softly.*) Where is he? (*Normal voice.*) He can't hear us from in there. But for God's sake, Mom, what happened? I told you to be firm with him. . . . Then you and the nurses should have held him down, taken his crutches away. . . . I know only too well he's my father! . . . I'm not being disrespectful, but I'm sick and tired of emptying stinking chamberpots full of phlegm and piss. . . . Yes, I do! When you're not there, he asks me to do it. . . . If you really want to know the truth, that's why I've got no appetite for my food. . . . Yes! There's a lot of things you don't know about. For your information, I still haven't got that science textbook I need. And you know why? He borrowed the money you gave me for it. . . . Because I didn't want to start another fight between you two. . . . He says that every time. . . . All right, Mom! (*Viciously.*) Then just remember to start hiding your bag away again, because he'll be at your purse before long for money for booze. And when he's well enough to come down here, you better keep an eye on the till as well, because that is also going to develop a leak. . . . Then don't complain to me when he starts his old tricks. . . . Yes, you do. I get it from you on one side and from him on the other, and it makes life hell for me. I'm not going to be the peacemaker anymore. I'm warning you now: when the two of you start fighting again, I'm leaving home. . . . Mom, if you start crying, I'm going to put down the receiver. . . . Okay . . . (*Lowering his voice to a vicious whisper.*) Okay, Mom. I heard you. (*Desperate.*) No. . . . Because I don't want to. I'll see him when I get home! Mom! . . . (*Pause. When he speaks again, his tone changes completely. It is not simply pretense. We sense a genuine emotional conflict.*) Welcome home, chum! . . . What's that? . . .Don't be silly, Dad. You being home is just about the best news in the world. . . . I bet you are. Bloody depressing there with everybody going on about their ailments, hey! . . . How you feeling? . . . Good . . . Here as well, pal. Coming down cats and dogs. . . . That's right. Just the day for a kip and a toss in your old Uncle Ned. . . . Everything's just hunky-dory on my side, Dad. . . . Well, to start with, there's a nice pile of comics for you on the counter. . . . Yes, old Kemple brought them in. *Batman and Robin, Submariner* . . . just your cup of tea . . . I will. . . . Yes, we'll spin a few yarns tonight. . . . Okay, chum, see you in a little while. . . . No, I promise. I'll come straight home. . . . (*Pause—his mother comes back on the phone.*) Mom? Okay. I'll lock up now. . . . What? . . . Oh, the brandy . . . Yes, I'll remember! . . . I'll put it in my suitcase now, for God's sake. I know well enough what will happen if he doesn't get it. . . . (*Places a bottle of brandy on the counter.*) I was kind to him, Mom. I didn't say anything nasty! . . . All right. Bye. (*End of telephone conversation. A desolate Hally doesn't move. A strained silence.*)

565 **Sam** (*Quietly.*): That sounded like a bad bump, Hally.

Hally (*Having a hard time controlling his emotions. He speaks carefully.*): Mind your own business, Sam.

Sam: Sorry. I wasn't trying to interfere. Shall we carry on? Hally? (*He indicates the exercise book. No response from Hally.*)

Willie (*Also trying.*): Tell him about when they give out the cups, Boet Sam.

Sam: Ja! That's another big moment. The presentation of the cups after the winners have been announced. You've got to put that in.

(*Still no response from Hally.*)

570 **Willie:** A big silver one, Master Hally, called floating trophy for the champions.

Sam: We always invite some big-shot personality to hand them over. Guest of honor this year is going to be His Holiness Bishop Jabulani of the All African Free Zionist Church.

(*Hally gets up abruptly, goes to his table and tears up the page he was writing on.*)

Hally: So much for a bloody world without collisions.

Sam: Too bad. It was on its way to being a good composition.

Hally: Let's stop bullshitting ourselves, Sam.

575 **Sam:** Have we been doing that?

Hally: Yes! That's what all our talk about a decent world has been . . . just so much bullshit.

Sam: We did say it was still only a dream.

Hally: And a bloody useless one at that. Life's a fuck-up and it's never going to change.

Sam: Ja, maybe that's true.

580 **Hally:** There's no maybe about it. It's a blunt and brutal fact. All we've done this afternoon is waste our time.

Sam: Not if we'd got your homework done.

Hally: I don't give a shit about my homework, so, for Christ's sake, just shut up about it. (*Slamming books viciously into his school case.*) Hurry up now and finish your work. I want to lock up and get out of here. (*Pause.*) And then go where? Home-sweet-fucking-home. Jesus, I hate that word.

(*Hally goes to the counter to put the brandy bottle and comics in his school case. After a moment's hesitation, he smashes the bottle of brandy. He abandons all further attempts to hide his feelings. Sam and Willie work away as unobtrusively as possible.*)

Do you want to know what is really wrong with your lovely little dream, Sam? It's not just that we are all bad dancers. That does happen to be perfectly true, but there's more to it than just that. You left out the cripples.

Sam: Hally!

Hally (*Now totally reckless.*): Ja! Can't leave them out, Sam. That's why we always end up on our backsides on the dance floor. They're also out there dancing . . . like a bunch of broken spiders trying to do the quickstep! (*An ugly attempt at laughter.*) When you come to think of it, it's a bloody comical sight. I mean, it's bad enough on two legs . . . but one and a pair of crutches! Hell, no, Sam. That's guaranteed to turn that dance floor into a shambles. Why you shaking your head? Picture it, man. For once this afternoon let's use our imaginations sensibly.

585 **Sam:** Be careful, Hally.

Hally: Of what? The truth? I seem to be the only one around here who is prepared to face it. We've had the pretty dream, it's time now to wake up and have a good long look at the way things really are. Nobody knows the steps, there's no music, the cripples are also out there tripping up everybody and trying to get into the act, and it's all called the All-Comers-How-to-Make-a-Fuckup-of-Life Championships. (*Another ugly laugh.*) Hang on, Sam! The best bit is still coming. Do you know what the winner's trophy is? A beautiful big chamber-pot with roses on the side, and it's full to the brim with piss. And guess who I think is going to be this year's winner.

Sam (*Almost shouting.*): Stop now!

Hally (*Suddenly appalled by how far he has gone.*): Why?

Sam: Hally? It's your father you're talking about.

590 **Hally:** So?

Sam: Do you know what you've been saying?

(*Hally can't answer. He is rigid with shame. Sam speaks to him sternly.*)

No, Hally, you mustn't do it. Take back those words and ask for forgiveness! It's a terrible sin for a son to mock his father with jokes like that. You'll be punished if you carry on. Your father is your father, even if he is a . . . cripple man.

Willie: Yes, Master Hally. Is true what Sam say.

Sam: I understand how you are feeling, Hally, but even so . . .

Hally: No, you don't!

595 **Sam:** I think I do.

Hally: And I'm telling you you don't. Nobody does. (*Speaking carefully as his shame turns to rage at Sam.*) It's your turn to be careful, Sam. Very careful! You're treading on dangerous ground. Leave me and my father alone.

Sam: I'm not the one who's been saying things about him.

Hally: What goes on between me and my Dad is none of your business!

Sam: Then don't tell me about it. If that's all you've got to say about him, I don't want to hear.

(*For a moment Hally is at loss for a response.*)

600 **Hally:** Just get on with your bloody work and shut up.

Sam: Swearing at me won't help you.

Hally: Yes, it does! Mind your own fucking business and shut up!

Sam: Okay. If that's the way you want it, I'll stop trying.

(*He turns away. This infuriates Hally even more.*)

Hally: Good. Because what you've been trying to do is meddle in something you know nothing about. All that concerns you in here, Sam, is to try and do what you get paid for—keep the place clean and serve the customers. In plain words, just get on with your job. My mother is right. She's always warning me about allowing you to get too familiar. Well, this time you've gone too far. It's going to stop right now.

(*No response from Sam.*)

You're only a servant in here, and don't forget it.

(*Still no response. Hally is trying hard to get one.*)

And as far as my father is concerned, all you need to remember is that he is your boss.

605 **Sam** (*Needled at last.*): No, he isn't. I get paid by your mother.

Hally: Don't argue with me, Sam!

Sam: Then don't say he's my boss.

Hally: He's a white man and that's good enough for you.

Sam: I'll try to forget you said that.

610 **Hally:** Don't! Because you won't be doing me a favor if you do. I'm telling you to remember it.

(*A pause. Sam pulls himself together and makes one last effort.*)

Sam: Hally, Hally . . . ! Come on now. Let's stop before it's too late. You're right. We *are* on dangerous ground. If we're not careful, somebody is going to get hurt.

Hally: It won't be me.

Sam: Don't be so sure.

Hally: I don't know what you're talking about, Sam.

615 **Sam:** Yes, you do.

Hally (*Furious.*): Jesus, I wish you would stop trying to tell me what I do and what I don't know.

(*Sam gives up. He turns to Willie.*)

Sam: Let's finish up.

Hally: Don't turn your back on me! I haven't finished talking.

(He grabs Sam by the arm and tries to make him turn around. Sam reacts with a flash of anger.)

Sam: Don't do that, Hally! *(Facing the boy.)* All right, I'm listening. Well? What do you want to say to me?

620 **Hally** *(Pause as Hally looks for something to say.)*: To begin with, why don't you also start calling me Master Harold, like Willie.

Sam: Do you mean that?

Hally: Why the hell do you think I said it?

Sam: And if I don't.

Hally: You might just lose your job.

625 **Sam** *(Quietly and very carefully.)*: If you make me say it once, I'll never call you anything else again.

Hally: So? *(The boy confronts the man.)* Is that meant to be a threat?

Sam: Just telling you what will happen if you make me do that. You must decide what it means to you.

Hally: Well, I have. It's good news. Because that is exactly what Master Harold wants from now on. Think of it as a little lesson in respect, Sam, that's long overdue, and I hope you remember it as well as you do your geography. I can tell you now that somebody who will be glad to hear I've finally given it to you will be my Dad. Yes! He agrees with my Mom. He's always going on about it as well. "You must teach the boys to show you more respect, my son."

Sam: So now you can stop complaining about going home. Everybody is going to be happy tonight.

630 **Hally:** That's perfectly correct. You see, you mustn't get the wrong idea about me and my Dad, Sam. We also have our good times together. Some bloody good laughs. He's got a marvelous sense of humor. Want to know what our favorite joke is? He gives out a big groan, you see, and says: "It's not fair, is it, Hally?" Then I have to ask: "What, chum?" And then he says: "A nigger's arse" . . . and we both have a good laugh.

(The men stare at him with disbelief.)

What's the matter, Willie? Don't you catch the joke? You always were a bit slow on the uptake. It's what is called a pun. You see, fair means both light in color and to be just and decent. *(He turns to Sam.)* I thought *you* would catch it, Sam.

Sam: Oh ja, I catch it all right.

Hally: But it doesn't appeal to your sense of humor.

Sam: Do you really laugh?

Hally: Of course.

635 **Sam:** To please him? Make him feel good?

Hally: No, for heaven's sake! I laugh because I think it's a bloody good joke.

Sam: You're really trying hard to be ugly, aren't you? And why drag poor old Willie into it? He's done nothing to you except show you the respect you want so badly. That's also not being fair, you know . . . and I mean just or decent.

Willie: It's all right, Sam. Leave it now.

Sam: It's me you're after. You should just have said "Sam's arse" . . . because that's the one you're trying to kick. Anyway, how do you know it's not fair? You've never seen it. Do you want to? *(He drops his trousers and underpants and presents his backside for Hally's inspection.)* Have a good look. A real Basuto[27] arse . . . which is about as nigger as they

---

[27] A person from Basutoland, South Africa.

can come. Satisfied? (*Trousers up.*) Now you can make your Dad even happier when you go home tonight. Tell him I showed you my arse and he is quite right. It's not fair. And if it will give him an even better laugh next time, I'll also let *him* have a look. Come, Willie, let's finish up and go.

(*Sam and Willie start to tidy up the tea room. Hally doesn't move. He waits for a moment when Sam passes him.*)

640 **Hally** (*Quietly.*): Sam . . .

(*Sam stops and looks expectantly at the boy. Hally spits in his face. A long and heartfelt groan from Willie. For a few seconds Sam doesn't move.*)

Sam (*Taking out a handkerchief and wiping his face.*): It's all right, Willie.

(*To Hally.*)

Ja, well, you've done it . . . Master Harold. Yes, I'll start calling you that from now on. It won't be difficult anymore. You've hurt yourself, Master Harold. I saw it coming. I warned you, but you wouldn't listen. You've just hurt yourself *bad.* And you're a coward, Master Harold. The face you should be spitting in is your father's . . . but you used mine, because you think you're safe inside your fair skin . . . and this time I don't mean just or decent. (*Pause, then moving violently towards Hally.*) Should I hit him, Willie?

Willie (*Stopping Sam.*): No, Boet Sam.

Sam (*Violently.*): Why not?

Willie: It won't help, Boet Sam.

645 **Sam:** I don't want to help! I want to hurt him.

Willie: You also hurt yourself.

Sam: And if he had done it to you, Willie?

Willie: Me? Spit at me like I was a dog? (*A thought that had not occurred to him before. He looks at Hally.*) Ja. Then I want to hit him. I want to hit him hard!

(*A dangerous few seconds as the men stand staring at the boy. Willie turns away, shaking his head.*)

But maybe all I do is go cry at the back. He's little boy, Boet Sam. Little *white* boy. Long trousers now, but he's still little boy.

Sam (*His violence ebbing away into defeat as quickly as it flooded.*): You're right. So go on, then: groan again, Willie. You do it better than me. (*To Hally.*) You don't know all of what you've just done . . . Master Harold. It's not just that you've made me feel dirtier than I've ever been in my life . . . I mean, how do I wash off yours and your father's filth? . . . I've also failed. A long time ago I promised myself I was going to try and do something, but you've just shown me . . . Master Harold . . . that I've failed. (*Pause.*) I've also got a memory of a little white boy when he was still wearing short trousers and a black man, but they're not flying a kite. It was the old Jubilee days, after dinner one night. I was in my room. You came in and just stood against the wall, looking down at the ground, and only after I'd asked you what you wanted, what was wrong, I don't know how many times, did you speak and even then so softly I almost didn't hear you. "Sam, please help me to go and fetch my Dad." Remember? He was dead drunk on the floor of the Central Hotel Bar. They'd phoned for your Mom, but you were the only one at home. And do you remember how we did it? You went in first by yourself to ask permission for me to go into the bar. Then I loaded him onto my back like a baby and carried him back to the boarding house with you following behind carrying his crutches. (*Shaking his head as he remembers.*) A crowded Main Street with all the people watching a little white boy following his drunk father on a nigger's back! I felt for that little boy . . . Master Harold. I felt for him. After that we still had to clean him up, remember? He'd messed in his trousers, so we had to clean him up and get him into bed.

650 **Hally** (*Great pain.*): I love him, Sam.

Sam: I know you do. That's why I tried to stop you from saying these things about him. It would have been so simple if you could have just despised him for being a weak man. But he's your father. You love him and you're ashamed of him. You're ashamed of so much! . . . And now that's going to include yourself. That was the promise I made to myself: to try and stop that happening. (*Pause.*) After we got him to bed you came back with me to my room and sat in a corner and carried on just looking down at the ground. And for days after that! You hadn't done anything wrong, but you went around as if you owed the world an apology for being alive. I didn't like seeing that! That's not the way a boy grows up to be a man! . . . But the one person who should have been teaching you what that means was the cause of your shame. If you really want to know, that's why I made you that kite. I wanted you to look up, be proud of something, of yourself . . . (*Bitter smile at the memory.*) . . . and you certainly were that when I left you with it up there on the hill. Oh, ja . . . something else! . . . If you ever do write it as a short story, there *was* a twist in our ending. I couldn't sit down there and stay with you. It was a "Whites Only" bench. You were too young, too excited to notice then. But not anymore. If you're not careful . . . Master Harold . . . you're going to be sitting up there by yourself for a long time to come, and there won't be a kite in the sky. (*Sam has got nothing more to say. He exits into the kitchen, taking off his waiter's jacket.*)

Willie: Is bad. Is all all bad in here now.

Hally (*Books into his school case, raincoat on.*): Willie . . . (*It is difficult to speak.*) Will you lock up for me and look after the keys?

Willie: Okay.

(*Sam returns. Hally goes behind the counter and collects the few coins in the cash register. As he starts to leave . . .*)

655 **Sam:** Don't forget the comic books.

(*Hally returns to the counter and puts them in his case. He starts to leave again.*)

Sam (*To the retreating back of the boy.*): Stop . . . Hally . . .

(*Hally stops, but doesn't turn to face him.*)

Hally . . . I've got no right to tell you what being a man means if I don't behave like one myself, and I'm not doing so well at that this afternoon. Should we try again, Hally?

Hally: Try what?

Sam: Fly another kite, I suppose. It worked once, and this time I need it as much as you do.

Hally: It's still raining, Sam. You can't fly kites on rainy days, remember.

660 **Sam:** So what do we do? Hope for better weather tomorrow?

Hally (*Helpless gesture.*): I don't know. I don't know anything anymore.

Sam: You sure of that, Hally? Because it would be pretty hopeless if that was true. It would mean nothing has been learnt in here this afternoon, and there was a hell of a lot of teaching going on . . . one way or the other. But anyway, I don't believe you. I reckon there's one thing you know. You don't *have* to sit up there by yourself. You know what that bench means now, and you can leave it any time you choose. All you've got to do is stand up and walk away from it.

(Hally leaves. Willie goes up quietly to Sam.)

Willie: Is okay, Boet Sam. You see. Is . . . *(He can't find any better words.)* . . . is going to be okay tomorrow. *(Changing his tone.)* Hey, Boet Sam! *(He is trying hard.)* You right. I think about it and you right. Tonight I find Hilda and say sorry. And make promise I won't beat her no more. You hear me, Boet Sam?

Sam: I hear you, Willie.

665 **Willie:** And when we practice I relax and romance with her from beginning to end. Non-stop! You watch! Two weeks' time: "First prize for promising newcomers: Mr. Willie Malopo and Miss Hilda Samuels." *(Sudden impulse.)* To hell with it! I walk home. *(He goes to the jukebox, puts in a coin and selects a record. The machine comes to life in the gray twilight, blushing its way through a spectrum of soft, romantic colors.)* How did you say it, Boet Sam? Let's dream. *(Willie sways with the music and gestures for Sam to dance.)*

(Sarah Vaughan sings.)

> "Little man you're crying,
> I know why you're blue,
> Someone took your kiddy car away;
> Better go to sleep now,
> Little man you've had a busy day." *(etc. etc.)*
>> You lead. I follow.

(The men dance together.)

> "Johnny won your marbles,
> Tell you what we'll do;
> Dad will get you new ones
>> right away;
> Better go to sleep now,
> Little man you've had a
>> busy day."

■ EXPLORATIONS OF THE TEXT

1. Describe the characters in the initial scene. What does the dancing symbolize? What is the nature of the relationship between Sam and Willie before Hally enters?

2. Describe Hally. How does his relationship with his father affect him? Analyze his attitudes toward Willie and Sam.

3. To what extent are the relationships in this play determined by South African history, culture, economics, and politics?

4. Why is Hally so pessimistic? Explain: "It's a bloody awful world when you come to think of it. People can be real bastards."

5. Explore the discussion of history, "magnitude," and social reformers. What does it reveal about Hally? about Sam?

6. What does the kite symbolize? How does Hally describe the event? Why does Sam not give a true answer to Hally's question, "Why did you make that kite, Sam?"

7. Why does Hally long to be in the Jubilee again? Why did life "[feel] the right size in there"?

8. What can be inferred from the first telephone conversation? What is Hally's attitude toward his father's returning home from the hospital? How does it affect his attitude about life?

9. Why does Sam believe that ballroom dancing is an art? Why does Hally choose to write about the contest? Is the scene **ironic**?
10. Consider the line: "There's no collisions out there, Hally." What are the big collisions?
11. What does dreaming represent to Sam?
12. Why does Hally not finish his composition on "A World Without Collisions"?
13. Examine the second telephone conversation. Why does Hally say, "Life's a fuck-up and it's never going to change"?
14. Why do "the cripples" trip everyone else? Why does Sam warn Hally to be careful about mocking his father? Why does Hally warn Sam?
15. Why does Hally insult Sam and Willie? Why does Hally insist on being called "Master Harold"?
16. Why does Hally spit in Sam's face? Why does Sam retort, "The face you should be spitting in is your father's"?
17. Discuss the incident in the Central Hotel Bar.
18. Why did Sam build the kite? Why did he want Hally or "Master Harold" not to be ashamed?
19. Will Hally leave "the bench" now that he knows what it means?
20. Discuss the relationships of the characters at the end of the play. Look carefully at the title and the punctuation in the title.
21. Fugard wrote in his notebook about a moment in his childhood that led him to spit in Sam's face. After this action, Fugard stated that he was "overwhelmed" with "shame." Consider this personal revelation in relation to the play and to works by Walcott and Gordimer (see chapter 4).

■ **THE READING/WRITING CONNECTION**
1. Write a journal entry in the voice of Hally, Sam, or Willie.
2. Freewrite in response to the final incident.
3. "Think" Topic: What is Willie's function in the play? Discuss in a paragraph.

■ **IDEAS FOR WRITING**
1. Describe Sam as a spiritual father or as a mentor.
2. Discuss power and powerlessness in the play. Refer to Gordimer (chapter 4) and to Morrison.
3. Write a character analysis of Sam or Hally.
4. Analyze the structure of the play. Why are there no scenes or acts?
5. How does the work portray the challenge of meeting the stranger? What does Hally's behavior suggest about the dimensions of this challenge in a racially divided South African society in the midst of apartheid? What does it reveal about the depth of racist attitudes? What does it reveal about what William E. B. Du Bois defines as the central problem of the twentieth century, "the color line"? You may refer to other works in the thematic cluster, "The Stranger."

■ NONFICTION ■

ANDRE ACIMAN

Andre Aciman (1951–) was born in Alexandria, Egypt; raised in Egypt, Italy, and France; and educated at Lehman College and Harvard University, where he received his Ph.D. Aciman has written or edited seven books, most recently The Proust Project *(2004). His work has been published in* The New Yorker, The New York Times Magazine, The New Republic, The New

York Review of Books, *and* The Best American Essays 1999, 2000, *and* 2003. *He has been awarded the Whiting Foundation Writers's Award and a Guggenheim Fellowship. Aciman's essays explore the relationship between memory and place, exile and home.* "Alexandria: The Capital of Memory" *is from* False Papers *(2000).*

2000

ALEXANDRIA: THE CAPITAL OF MEMORY

To those who asked, I said I went back to touch and breathe the past again, to walk in shoes I hadn't worn in years. This, after all, was what everyone said when they returned from Alexandria—the walk down Memory Lane, the visit to the old house, the knocking at doors history had sealed off but might pry open again. The visit to the old temple, the visit to Uncle So-and-so's house, the old school, the old haunts, the smell of the dirty wooden banister on days you almost glided downstairs on your way to a movie. And then, of course, the tears, the final reckoning, the big themes: the return of the native, the romance of the past, the redemption of time. All of it followed by predictable letdowns: the streets always much narrower than before, buildings grown smaller with time, everything in tatters, the city dirty, in ruins. There are no Europeans left, and the Jews are all gone. Alexandria is Egyptian now.

As I step onto the narrow balcony of my room at the Hotel Cecil and try to take in the endless string of evening lights speckling the eastern bay, I am thinking of Lawrence Durrell[1] and of what he might have felt standing in this very same hotel more than fifty years ago, surveying a magical, beguiling city—the "capital of memory," as he called it, with its "five races, five languages . . . and more than five sexes."

That city no longer exists; perhaps it never did. Nor does the Alexandria I knew: the mock-reliquary[2] of bygone splendor and colonial opulence where my grandmother could still walk with an umbrella on sunny days and not realize she looked quite ridiculous, the way everyone in my family must have looked quite ridiculous, being the last European Jews in a city where anti-Western nationalism and anti-Semitism had managed to reduce the Jewish population from at least fifty thousand to twenty-five hundred by 1960 and put us at the very tail end of those whom history shrugs aside when it changes its mind.

The Alexandria I knew, that part-Victorian, half-decayed, vestigial nerve center of the British Empire, exists in memory alone, the way Carthage and Rome and Constantinople[3] exist as vanished cities only—a city where the dominant languages were English and French, though everyone spoke in a medley of many more, because the principal languages were really Greek and Italian, and in my immediate world Ladino (the Spanish of the Jews who fled the Inquisition in the sixteenth century),[4] with broken Arabic holding everything more or less together. The arrogance of the retired banker, the crafty know-it-all airs of the small shopkeeper, the ways of Greeks and of Jews, all of these were not necessarily compatible, but everyone knew who everyone else was, and on Sundays—at the theater, in restaurants, at the beach, or in clubs—chances were you sat next to each other and had a good chat. My

---

[1] Lawrence Durrell (1912–90), a British writer and author of the *Alexandrian Quartet,* who lived in Alexandria in the 1940s.

[2] A "reliquary" is a receptacle for keeping and displaying sacred objects.

[3] Ancient civilizations in Africa, Italy, and Turkey.

[4] In Spain in 1492, the Catholics expelled the Jews and tortured and killed all who were not Catholic, accusing them of heresy.

grandmother knew Greek well enough to correct native Greeks, she knew every prayer in Latin, and her written French, when she was vexed, would have made the Due de Saint-Simon[5] quite nervous.

5   This is the Alexandria I live with every day, the one I've taken with me, written about, and ultimately superimposed on other cities, the way other cities were originally sketched over the Alexandrian landscape when European builders came, in the middle of the nineteenth century, and fashioned a new city modeled after those they already loved. It was this Alexandria I came looking for—knowing I'd never find it. That did not bother me. For I had come not to recover memories, nor even to recognize those I'd disfigured, nor to toy with the thought that I'd ever live here again; I had come to bury the whole thing, to get it out of my system, to forget, to hate even, the way we learn to hate those who wouldn't have us.

I am, it finally occurs to me, doing the most typical thing a Jew could do. I've come back to Egypt the way only Jews yearn to go back to places they couldn't wait to flee. The Jewish rite of passage, as Passover[6] never tells us, is also the passage back to Egypt, not just away from it.

Until the mid-1950s, Jews had done extremely well in Egypt. They had risen to prominence and dominated almost every profession, and they were among the major financiers who brokered Egypt's passage from a European to a national economy, serving as important conduits for foreign investors. Jews managed a significant share of Egypt's stock exchange and owned some of the biggest banks and almost all the department stores; the country boasted the greatest number of Jewish multimillionaires in the Middle East. Jews, though very few in number, held seats in the Egyptian parliament.

These were, for the most part, observant Jews, but in a cosmopolitan city like Alexandria, where overzealous piety was derided and where friendship was almost never based on creed, many of these Jews were quite relaxed when it came to religion, particularly since most of them, educated in Catholic schools, tended to know more about the religions of others than about their own. Seders,[7] I remember, were rushed affairs; no one wanted to inflict Passover on Christians who happened to be visiting and had been induced to stay for dinner.

Following the Israelis' 1948 defeat of the Arabs, anti-Semitism rose sharply in Egypt, and there were some deadly incidents in the wake of the war. Matters became worse after 1956, when Israel joined forces with France and England in a tripartite attack on Egypt after Nasser nationalized the Suez Canal.[8] British and French residents of Alexandria were summarily expelled from Egypt, as were many Jews; everyone had assets, businesses, and properties seized by the state. Aunts and uncles, friends, grandparents, some of whom hadn't been expelled, read the writing on the wall and left within a few years of the 1956 war, abandoning everything they owned. Most settled in Europe, others in America.

10   Some, like us, simply waited, the way Jews did elsewhere when it was already too late to hope for miracles. We saw the city change and each year watched European shop names come down and be replaced by Egyptian ones, and heard of streets being renamed, until—as is the case now—I didn't know a single one.

---

[5] Duc de Saint-Simon, (1675–1755), a member of the French courts of Louis XIV and Louis XV and famous for his detailed memoirs, which are petty, bitter, and filled with gossip.

[6] The eight-day observance commemorating the freedom and exodus of the Israelites from Egypt during the reign of Pharaoh Ramses II.

[7] The celebratory meal shared during the holiday of Passover.

[8] Gamal Abdul-Nasser (1918–70), the president of Egypt from 1954–1970. Nasser nationalized the Suez Canal, a move that led to the Israeli invasion of the Sinai Peninsula and an Anglo-French invasion of the canal zone.

The only street whose name hasn't changed is the waterfront road known as the Corniche, al-Corniche, a thick bottleneck mass of tottering loud vehicles emitting overpowering gas fumes.

I try to rest both arms on the balustrade outside my hotel room, as I'd envisioned doing on receiving the glossy brochure with the Cecil's picture. But the small, Moorish/Venetian-style balcony is entirely taken over by a giant compressor unit; it's impossible to maneuver around it. Bird droppings litter the floor.

Two men are speaking in Arabic downstairs. One is telling the other about his very bad foot and his pain at night. The other says it might go away. They don't know how surreal mundane talk can seem to someone who's been away for thirty years.

On the main square facing the hotel stands the ungainly statue of the Egyptian patriot Sa'ad Zaghlul, one leg forward in the manner of ancient Egyptian statues, except that this one wears a fez. I used to pass by here every morning on my way to school by bus.

15 Beyond Sa'ad Zaghlul is a villa housing the Italian consulate, and farther yet is the city's main tramway station and to its right the Cinema Strand, all unchanged, though worn by age. To my right is Délices, one of the city's best pastry shops. It hasn't moved either. Nothing, I think, is unfamiliar enough. I haven't forgotten enough.

Across the bay sits the fortress of Kait Bey, its ill-lit, brooding halo guarding the Eastern Harbor. The fortress is said to occupy the site of the ancient Pharos lighthouse, one of the Seven Wonders of the Ancient World. Some say that the fort was built with stones taken from the old lighthouse itself. A French archaeological company has been commissioned to dig here. The area is cordoned off and considered top secret.

Not far from the dig lies the Western Harbor, which the ancients used to call the Harbor of Safe Return, Portus Eunostos, from the Ancient Greek *eu*, meaning good, safe, and *nostos*, meaning return. Nostalgia is the ache to return, to come home; *nostophobia*, the fear of returning; *nostomania*, the obsession with going back; *nostography*, writing about return.

So this is Alexandria, I think, before shutting the window, feeling very much like Freud[9] when, in his early forties, he had finally achieved his lifelong dream of visiting Athens and, standing on the Acropolis,[10] felt strangely disappointed, calling his numbness derealization.

I look at my watch. It is one in the afternoon New York time. I pick up the telephone to call America. After a short wait, I hear my father's voice. In the background, I make out a chorus of children, mine probably—or is it the clamor of a school recess down his block?

20 "How is it?" he asks. I describe the view from my window.

"Yes, but how is it?" he presses. What he means is: has it changed, and am I moved? I can't find the right words.

"It's still the same," I reply. "It's Egypt," I finally say, all else failing.

Each year the city sees many ex-Alexandrians return and wander along its streets. Like revenants[11] and time travelers, some come back from the future, from decades and continents away, A.D. people barging in on B.C. affairs, true anachronoids[12] drifting about the city with no real purpose but to savor a past that, even before arriving, they know they'll neither recapture nor put behind them, but whose spell continues to lure them on these errands in time. The Portuguese have a word: *retornados*, descendants of Portuguese settlers who return to their homeland in Europe centuries after colonizing Africa—except that they are African-born Europeans who return to Africa as tourists, not knowing why they come,

---

[9] Sigmund Freud (1856–1939), the father of modern psychology.

[10] A hill in Athens, Greece, known as the "Sacred Rock" and the site of the Parthenon.

[11] People who return after an absence or after death.

[12] From anachronism, a person or thing that is out of place.

or why they need to come again, or why this city that feels like home and which they can almost touch at every bend of the street can be as foreign as those places they've never seen before but studied in travel books.

The first thing I want to do tonight is roam the streets by myself. The downtown shops are still open, and people are literally spilling out into the streets, an endless procession of cars going up the rue Missallah (Obelisk), renamed rue Saffeyah Zaghlul after the patriot's wife. The same stores stand in exactly the same spots, the same pharmacies, bookstores, restaurants; and everywhere the unbroken chain of shoe stores and third-tier haberdasheries with wares dangling over the sidewalks, and always that muted spill of lights which reminds me of Cavafy's nights[13] and Baudelaire's Paris.[14] I manage to recognize the Gothic-Venetian window sashes of an old restaurant. When I walk into Flückiger's, the pastry shop, and tell the cashier that I am just looking around, she smiles and says, as she must have done to hundreds like me, "*Ah, vous êtes de nos temps,*" as if time could ever belong to anyone. Do I want to buy cakes? I shake my head. "They're still the same. We're still Flückiger," she adds. I nod. One would have thought that I shopped there every day and had stopped now on my way from work, only to change my mind at the last minute. The idea of eating cake to summon my past seems too uncanny and ridiculous. I smile to myself and walk out through the beaded curtain. It hasn't changed either. Nor have the buildings. They are far more beautiful than I remember, the architecture a mix of turn-of-the-century French and floral Italian. But they are also grimier, some of them so rundown it's impossible to tell how long they've got. It's no different with cars here. Many are rickety thirty-plus patched-up jobs, part rust, part tin, part foil; soldered and painted over with the sort of Egyptian ingenuity that knows how to preserve the old and squeeze residual life out of objects which should have perished long ago but whose replacement will neither come from abroad nor be manufactured locally. These are not really cars but, rather, elaborate collages of prostheses.

25   I turn right and walk into a murky street that used to be called rue Fuad. Next to the Amir Cinema looms a strange, large structure I have never seen before. It is the newly dug-up Roman amphitheater I've been reading about. I ignore it completely and turn left, where I spot Durrell's pastry shop, and walk down a narrow street, where I find the Cinema Royale and, right across from it, the old Mohammed Ali, now known as the Sayyed Darwish Theater, the pride of Alexandria's theater elite.

And then it hits me. The Mohammed Ali is my last stop tonight; I now have nowhere else to turn but the Hotel Cecil. To my complete amazement, I have revisited most of my haunts in Alexandria in the space of about eight minutes!

Once on the crowded streets again, I walk the way I have come, along the edge of the sidewalk, my eyes avoiding everyone else's, my gait hurried and determined, everything about me trying to discourage contact with a city that is, after all, the only one I think I love. Like characters in Homer,[15] I want to be wrapped in a cloud and remain invisible, not realizing that, like all revenants, I am perhaps a ghost, a specter already.

The next morning, I head out on another exploratory walk. But in fifteen minutes I have already reached Chatby, the very place I was meaning to see last. This is where most of the cemeteries are located. Perhaps I should pay a visit to my grandfather's tomb now.

I try to find the Jewish cemetery, but am unable to. Instead, I head in a different direction and decide to visit my great-grandmother's house. As soon as I near her neighborhood,

---

[13] Constantine (C. P.) Cavafy (1863–1933), a Greek poet who lived in Alexandria (see Chapter 6).

[14] Charles Baudelaire (1812–67), a French poet.

[15] Homer (750 B.C.–?), author of *The Iliad* and *The Odyssey*.

I find myself almost thrust into the old marketplace. It, too, hasn't changed since my childhood. The pushcarts and open shops are still in place, as is the unforgettable stench of fish and meat, and always the screaming and the masses of people thronging between stacks of food and crates of live chickens.

30   I could go upstairs, I think, once I reach the building on rue Thèbes, but people are watching me fiddle with my camera, and someone actually pops his head out of the window and stares. I decide to leave. Then, having walked to the next block, I change my mind and come back again, trying to let the building come into view gradually, so as to hold that magical moment when remembrance becomes recovery. I am resolved not to be intimidated this time and make my way straight to the main doorway.

A woman appears with a child in her arms; she is the caretaker's wife; the caretaker died a few years ago; she is the caretaker now. A man also shows up. He lives on the street floor, he says in English, and has lived there since the early fifties. I tell him I, too, lived here once, at number 15. He thinks for a moment, then says he doesn't remember who lives there now. I tell the caretaker that I want to knock at apartment 15. She smiles and looks at me with suspicion. She is thinking. "Sit Vivi," she says, Mme Vivi. I am almost on the verge of shaking. Vivi was my great-aunt. "They left," she says. Of course they left, I want to shout, we all left thirty years ago! "May I knock at the door?" I ask. "You may," she replies, with the same smile, "but no one is there." When will they be back? She looks at me with a blank stare. No one has occupied the apartment since.

I know that if I push the matter and tip her well, I might persuade her to show me the apartment. But the thought of a dark apartment where no one's been for three decades frightens me. Who knows what I'd find creeping about the floor, or crawling on the walls. It's all well and good for a German to go digging for the ghost of Troy or sifting through Helen's jewels. But no Trojan ever went back to Troy.[16]

When I point to the elevator and ask her whether it still works, she laughs. It had died long ago. And she adds, with inimitable Egyptian humor, "*Allah yerhamu.*" May God have mercy on its soul.

I step into the main courtyard and look up to our old service entrance: I can almost hear our cook screaming at the maid, my mother screaming at the cook, and the poor maid's heartrending yelp each time the tumor on her liver pressed against her spine. I am trying to decide whether I should insist and ask to be taken upstairs, or perhaps she could show me another apartment in the same line. I see a cat playing in the foyer; next to it is a dead mouse. The caretaker does not notice it. Even the man from the first floor doesn't seem to notice, doesn't care.

35   I know I'll regret not insisting, and also that this is typical of my perfunctory, weak-willed attempts at adventure. But I am tired of these ruins, and the smell of the old wood panels in the foyer is overpowering. Besides, this is how I always travel: not so as to experience anything at the time of my tour, but to plot the itinerary of a possible return trip. This, it occurs to me, is also how I live.

Outside, I spot an old woman with a shopping basket; she looks European. I ask her whether she speaks French. She says she does. She is Greek. I am almost ready to tell her about my entire life, everything about my grandparents, my mother, our apartment that has never been lived in since the day we left so many years ago, and all these ruins scattered everywhere, but I break in mid-sentence, hail a cab, and ask to be taken to the museum—by way of the Corniche, because I want to see the water.

---

[16] Troy was an ancient Greek city. Helen, daughter of Zeus and queen of Sparta, known for her beauty, was abducted by Paris and taken to Troy. This event sparked the Trojan War, depicted in Homer's *The Iliad.*

The Corniche always breaks the spell of monotonous city life, the first and last thing one remembers here. It is what I think of whenever I sight a beckoning patch of blue at the end of a cross street elsewhere in the world. The sky is clear and the sea is stunning, and my cabdriver, who speaks English, tells me how much he loves the city.

The Graeco-Roman Museum was where I would come to be alone on Sunday mornings in 1965, my last year in Alexandria.

I pay the fee and, as usual, rush through the corridors and the quiet garden, where a group of Hungarian tourists are eating potato chips. The Tanagra statuettes,[17] the busts of Jupiter[18] and of Alexander,[19] the reclining statue of a dying Cleopatra,[20] all these I pass in haste. There is only one thing I want to see, a Fayoum portrait[21] of a mummified Christian. I linger in the old, musty room. The painting is exquisite indeed, more so than I remember. But I am astonished that this bearded man looks so young. There was a time when he was older than I. Now I could almost be his father. Otherwise, nothing has changed: I'm standing here, and he's lying there, and it's all as if nothing has happened between one Sunday and the next.

40   I want to buy his picture in the museum shop. There are no postcards of Fayoum portraits. I want to buy E. M. Forster's guide[22] to the city, but they haven't had it in a long time. I ask whether they have any of the Durrell books. They haven't carried those in a long time either. There is, in fact, really very little to buy. And very little else to see. I have seen everything I wanted to see in Alexandria. I could easily leave now.

An entire childhood revisited in a flash. I am a terrible nostographer. Instead of experiencing returns, I rush through them like a tourist on a one-day bus tour. Tomorrow I must try to find the cemetery again.

Outside the museum, I am reminded of my grammar school nearby. I remember coming here in high school hoping to pay a quick visit to my old school and getting lost instead. I know I've strayed into the once-affluent Greek neighborhood. But I also know that I'm lost exactly where I lost my way thirty years earlier. The thought amuses me. I used to come here for private English lessons twice a week. I remembered the teacher, and her sumptuous home, and the luxurious china in which I, at the age of seven, would have to drink tea. I remember a poem by Wordsworth,[23] the dim-lit living room with many flowers and perfumes, and my father coming to pick me up after tutorial, discussing books with her. I would sit and listen, and watch them talk, as other guests kept arriving.

I thought I recognized her building and decided, why not, Mademoiselle Nader might still be there. I look at the names on the mailboxes, but there is no Nader. I see the name *Monsieur et Madame E. Nahas* and assume they are Syrian-Lebanese. Perhaps they might tell me where she lives. As I am ascending the stairs, I happen upon a name on a brass plate; it's the name of a very old school friend. I ring his bell. The Filipino maid speaks good English; I explain I used to know her employer. He is in Europe, she replies. She shows me into a living room streaming in daylight. I sit on the sofa and scribble a note for him, leaning over

---

[17] An ancient territory in Greece, defeated in 426 B.C. by the Athenians.

[18] Greek god Zeus, ruler of Olympus.

[19] Alexander the Great (356–323 B.C.), a Macedonian conquerer, founded the city of Alexandria in Egypt in 331 B.C.

[20] Cleopatra (69–30 B.C.) was born in Alexandria, Egypt, and was Pharaoh from 51 to 30 B.C.

[21] The Fayoum is a lush area in Egypt where the oldest portraits of the world, Greco-Roman mummy paintings from 31 B.C. to 324 A.D., were found.

[22] E. M. Forster (1879–1970), a British writer stationed in Alexandria during World War I (1915–19). Forster wrote history books and travel guides to Alexandria.

[23] William Wordsworth (1770–1850), an English Romantic poet.

to the tea table. Then I hand it to her and ask whether she knows of a certain Mademoiselle Nader. Never heard of her. I say goodbye and continue climbing the stairs until I've reached the Nahas residence. They're not home either, and their maid has never heard of the Naders. A delivery boy, who happens to be coming up the stairs, seems to remember something and asks me to knock at another apartment. An old woman, speaking impeccable French, says that of course she remembers Marcelle Nader, whom she calls Lola. Lola died two years ago, totally alone, impoverished, and broken-spirited. Her family had lost everything during the mass nationalizations of 1961. She and her sister would rent out rooms in their large home, but even then, that hardly constituted an income. When her sister left for Switzerland, Lola was forced to give private lessons to businessmen who, it seems, had other things in mind but who settled for English the more she aged. In the end, she sold her apartment to, of all people, my old school friend downstairs. I hadn't recognized the apartment at all. Perhaps it was on the same sofa and at the same tea table that I'd learned English.

Turb'al Yahud, Alexandria's Jewish cemetery, is located at the opposite end of the Armenian cemetery and lies only a few steps away from the Greek Orthodox. Farther down the quiet, dusty, tree-lined road is the Catholic cemetery. Magdi, a native Alexandrian who is employed by the American school I attended as a child, swears that Turb'al Yahud must be somewhere close by but can't remember where. "I come here only once a year—for my mother," he explains, pointing to the Coptic[24] cemetery not far along the same road.

45   Magdi double-parks and says he will ask directions from the warden of the Armenian cemetery. We have been driving around for more than two hours in search of my parents' old summer beachside home, but here, too, without luck. Either it's been razed or it lies buried in a chaos of concrete high-rises and avenues built on what used to be vast stretches of desert sand. Soon Magdi comes out, looking perplexed. There are, as it turns out, not one but two Jewish cemeteries in the area.

"Which one has a gate on the left?" I say, remembering my very early childhood visits to my grandfather's grave four decades ago. "That's the problem," says Magdi, drawing on his cigarette. "Both have gates to the right."

I am dismayed. I can situate the grave only in relation to the left gate. We decide to try the nearest cemetery.

Magdi starts the car, waits awhile, then immediately speeds ahead, leaving a cloud of dust behind us. In a matter of minutes we have parked on a sidewalk and ambled up to a metal gate that looks locked. Magdi does not knock; he pounds. I hear a bark, and after a series of squeaks, a man in his early fifties appears at the door. I try to explain in broken Arabic the reason for my visit, but Magdi interrupts and takes over, saying I have come to see my grandfather's grave. The warden is at a loss. Do I know where the grave is? he asks. I say no. Do I know the name, then?

I say a name, but it means nothing to him. I try to explain about the gate to the left, but my words are getting all jumbled together. All I seem to remember is a pebbled alleyway that started at the left gate and crossed the breadth of the cemetery.

50   The warden has a three-year-old son wearing a very faded red sweatshirt bearing the initials CCCP—not unusual in a place where ancient relics come in handy. Their dog, fleeced from the neck down, has a large bleeding ulcer on his back.

"Oh, *that* gate," the warden responds when I point to another, much smaller gate at the opposite end of the cemetery. "It's locked, it's never been used." Indeed, the gate at the end

---

[24] The Christian Coptic Orthodox Church of Egypt is based on the teachings of St. Mark, who came to Egypt in the first century.

of the alleyway looks welded in place. I am almost too nervous to hope. But I pick my way to the end of the path and, having reached the area near the left gate, climb over a wild bush whose dried leaves stick to my trousers, turning with a sense of certainty that I am trying to distrust, fearing the worst.

"Is this it?" asks Magdi.

I am reluctant to answer, still doubting that this could be the spot, or this the marble slab, which feels as warm and smooth to the touch as I knew it would each time I rehearsed this moment over the years. Even the name looks dubious.

"Yes," I say, pointing to the letters, which I realize Magdi can't read.

55   The warden knows I am pleased. His son trails behind him. A fly is crawling around his nose. Both of them, as well as the warden's wife, are barefoot, Bedouin style.[25]

I take out my camera. Everyone is staring at me, including the warden's ten-year-old daughter, who has come to see for herself. It turns out that no Jew ever visits here. "No one?" I ask. "*Walla wahid*," answers the daughter emphatically. Not one.

There are, it occurs to me, far more dead Jews in this city than there will ever again be living ones. This reminds me of what I saw in a box at the main temple earlier this morning: more skullcaps than Jews to wear them in all of Egypt.

The warden asks whether I would like to wash the tombstone. I know Magdi has to go back to work; he is a bus driver and school ends soon. I shake my head.

"Why?" asks the warden. "*Lazem.*" You must.

60   I have lived my entire life outside rituals. Now I am being asked to observe one that seems so overplayed and so foreign to me that I almost want to laugh, especially since I feel I'm about to perform it for them, not for me. Even Magdi sides with the warden. "*Lazem*," he echoes.

I am thinking of another ritual, dating back to those days when my father and I would come on quiet early-morning visits to the cemetery. It was a simple ritual. We would stand before my grandfather's grave and talk; then my father would say he wished to be alone awhile and, when he was finished, hoist me up and help me kiss the marble. One day, without reason, I refused to kiss the stone. He didn't insist, but I knew he was hurt.

I pay the warden's family no heed and continue to take pictures, not because I really want to, but because in looking through the viewfinder and pretending to take forever to focus, I can forget the commotion around me, stand still, stop time, stare into the distance, and think of my childhood, and of being here, and of my grandfather, whom I hardly knew and scarcely remember and seldom think of.

I am almost on the point of forgetting those present when the warden appears, lugging a huge tin drum filled with water. He hoists it on a shoulder and then splashes the dried slab, flooding the whole area, wetting my clothes, Magdi's, and the little boy's feet, allowing the stone to glisten for the first time in who knows how many decades. With eager palms, we all go about the motions of wiping the slab clean. I like the ritual. Magdi helps out silently, but I want it to be my job. I don't want it to end. I am even pleased that my clothes are wet and dirty.

I still can't believe I was able to find my grandfather's grave so quickly. Memories are supposed to distort, to lie. I am at once comforted and bewildered.

65   In the distance I can hear the tireless drone of Alexandria's traffic, and farther off the loud clank of metal wheels along the tramway lines—not obtrusive sounds, for they emphasize the silence more—and I am reminded of how far Grandfather is from all this: from all these engines; from the twentieth century; from history; from exile, exodus, and now return;

---

[25] Desert-dwelling, nomadic people of Arabia, the Negev, and the Sinai.

from the nights we spent huddled together in the living room, knowing the end had come; from our years in cities he had never visited, let alone thought some of us might one day call home. Time for him had stopped in the early fifties on this dry, quiet, secluded patch of dust that could turn into desert in no time.

I look around and recognize famous Jewish names on tombstones and mausoleums. They, too, like my grandfather, were lucky not to have seen the end. But they also paid a price: no one ever comes here. The opulent mausoleums, built in Victorian rococo, were meant to house unborn generations that have since grown up elsewhere and don't know the first thing about Egypt.

"Are you happy now?" I want to ask my grandfather, rubbing the stone some more, re-membering a tradition practiced among Muslims of tapping one's finger ever so gently on a tombstone to tell the dead that their loved ones are present, that they miss them and think of them. I want to speak to him, to say something, if only in a whisper. But I am too em-barrassed. Perhaps this is why people say prayers instead. But I don't know any prayers. All I know is that I cannot take him with me—but I don't want to leave him here. What is he doing here anyway? In a hundred years, no one will even know my grandfather had lived or died, here or elsewhere. It's the difference between death and extinction.

I pretend to want to take another picture and ask Magdi, the warden, and his family to pose in front of one of the palm trees, hoping they will stay there after the picture and leave me alone awhile. I can feel my throat tighten, and I want to hide the tears welling up inside me, and I am, once again, glad to cover my eyes with the viewfinder. The warden's daugh-ter comes closer. She wants a picture by herself. I smile and say something about her pretty eyes. I give her father a good tip.

Everyone thinks it's been a good visit. Perhaps all cemetery visits are.

70 On my last evening in Alexandria, I and a group of young teachers from the American school have gathered at a pizzeria to celebrate someone's birthday. We've parked on a narrow al-leyway, halfway on the sidewalk, exactly where my father would park his car. Everyone at the party orders pizza, salad, and beer. It occurs to me that we might easily be in Cambridge or New Haven.

By eleven the party breaks up. Before getting into the car, we take a stroll toward the Church of St. Saba. The streets are very dark, and after spending time in the American bar, I am suddenly confronted with the uncanny thought that we are, after all, very much in Egypt still. Maybe it's the alcohol, but I don't know whether I'm back in Egypt or have never left, or whether this is all a very cruel prank and we're simply stranded in some old neigh-borhood in lower Manhattan. This, I realize, is what happens when one finally comes home: one hardly notices, and it doesn't feel odd at all.

Later that night, as I'm looking out from my balcony, I think of the young man from Fayoum, and of the young man of fourteen I used to be back then, and of myself now, and of the person I might have been had I stayed here thirty years ago. I think of the strange life I'd have led, of the wife I would have, and of my other children. Where would I be living? I suppose in my great-grandmother's apartment—it would have fallen to me. And I think of this imaginary self who never strayed or did the things I probably regret having done but would have done anyway and don't wish to disown; a self who never left Egypt or ever lost ground and who, on nights such as these, still dreams of the world abroad and of faraway America, the way I, over the years, have longed for life right here whenever I find I don't fit anywhere else.

I wonder if this other self would understand about him and me, and being here and now and on the other bank as well—the other life, the one that we never live but conjure up when the one we have is perhaps not the one we want.

This, at least, has never changed, I think, my mind drifting to my father years ago, when we would stop the car and walk along the Corniche at night, thinking of the worst that surely lay ahead, each trying to give up this city and the life that came with it in the way he knew how. This is what I was doing now as well, thinking of the years ahead when I would look back to this very evening and remember how, standing on the cluttered balcony at the Cecil, I had hoped finally to let go of this city, knowing all the while that the longing would start again soon enough, that one never washes anything away, and that this marooned and spectral city, which is no longer home for me and which Durrell once called "a shabby little seaport built upon a sand reef," would eventually find newer, ever more beguiling ways to remind me that here is where my mind always turns, that here, to quote this century's most famous Alexandrian poet, Constantine Cavafy, I'll always end up, even if I never come back:

> For you won't find a new country,
> won't find a new shore,
> the city will always pursue you,
> and no ship will ever take you away from yourself.

75   And then I remembered. With all the tension in the cemetery that afternoon, I had forgotten to ask Magdi to show me Cavafy's home. Worse yet, I had forgotten to kiss my grandfather's grave. Maybe next time.

■ EXPLORATIONS OF THE TEXT

1. Why does Aciman return to Alexandria?
2. Gloss and annotate the text, noting the stages of his journey. How does Aciman respond to each landmark from his childhood? How do his feelings for Alexandria change?
3. How does Aciman characterize Alexandria itself? What was appealing about the city? How has it changed? What has it lost?
4. How is his trip a Jewish "rite of passage," an Exodus story? What is the irony?
5. Discuss the symbolism of cleaning his grandfather's grave.
6. What does the essay reveal about autobiographical acts of reminiscing and reflection? Does autobiographical writing lead to discovery?
7. The diaspora of peoples partially characterizes the world at the millennium. What does the essay teach us about the state of being an exile? About the possibility of the return?
8. Compare and contrast Aciman's autobiographical journey and its discoveries with that of Scott Russell Sanders in "Wayland"? How do they treat the connection to place? The return? The realizations gained through writing?

■ THE READING/WRITING CONNECTION

1. What is your "capital of Memory"? Freewrite in response to this question.
2. Return to a place that you have left: a childhood home, an old school, or a neighborhood. In a journal entry, compare your memories with your present impressions.
3. "Think" Topic: Why does Aciman specifically mention how long it takes him to visit each place? Why does he include those specifics?

■ IDEAS FOR WRITING

1. Write a descriptive essay about your return to a place. Use your journal entry in the Reading/Writing Connection as a basis for your essay.
2. Aciman defines four kinds of nostalgia. Does the work illustrate all four? If so, in what ways? Analyze this portrait of return.
3. Compare and contrast the vision of the divided self in this essay and in Agosin's poems.

Toni Morrison

Toni Morrison (1931–   ) was born in Lorain, Ohio, and was educated at Harvard and Cornell Universities. She published her first novel, The Bluest Eye, *in 1970. Subsequent novels include* Sula *(1974);* Song of Solomon *(1977);* Beloved *(1987), which won the Pulitzer Prize;* Paradise *(1998); and* Love *(2003). Morrison also has co-written six children's books with her son, Slade Morrison. In 1993, Morrison was awarded the Nobel Prize for Literature, the first African American woman to receive it. She serves as the Golheen Professor of the Humanities at Princeton University.*

1993

THE NOBEL PRIZE SPEECH

Members of the Swedish Academy, Ladies and Gentlemen:
Narrative has never been merely entertainment for me. It is, I believe, one of the principal ways in which we absorb knowledge. I hope you will understand, then, why I begin these remarks with the opening phrase of what must be the oldest sentence in the world, and the earliest one we remember from childhood: "Once upon a time . . ."

"Once upon a time there was an old woman. Blind but wise." Or was it an old man? A guru, perhaps. Or a *griot*[1] soothing restless children. I have heard this story, or one exactly like it, in the lore of several cultures.

"Once upon a time there was an old woman. Blind. Wise."

5   In the version I know the woman is the daughter of slaves, black, American, and lives alone in a small house outside of town. Her reputation for wisdom is without peer and without question. Among her people she is both the law and its transgression. The honor she is paid and the awe in which she is held reach beyond her neighborhood to places far away; to the city where the intelligence of rural prophets is the source of much amusement.

One day the woman is visited by some young people who seem to be bent on disproving her clairvoyance and showing her up for the fraud they believe she is. Their plan is simple: they enter her house and ask the one question the answer to which rides solely on her difference from them, a difference they regard as a profound disability: her blindness. They stand before her, and one of them says,

"Old woman, I hold in my hand a bird. Tell me whether it is living or dead."

She does not answer, and the question is repeated. "Is the bird I am holding living or dead?"

Still she does not answer. She is blind and cannot see her visitors, let alone what is in their hands. She does not know their color, gender, or homeland. She knows only their motive.

10   The old woman's silence is so long, the young people have trouble holding their laughter.

Finally she speaks, and her voice is soft but stern. "I don't know," she says. "I don't know whether the bird you are holding is dead or alive, but what I do know is that it is in your hands. It is in your hands."

Her answer can be taken to mean: if it is dead, you have either found it that way or you have killed it. If it is alive, you can still kill it. Whether it is to stay alive is your decision. Whatever the case, it is your responsibility.

For parading their power and her helplessness, the young visitors are reprimanded, told they are responsible not only for the act of mockery but also for the small bundle of life

---

[1] A storyteller in western Africa.

sacrificed to achieve its aims. The blind woman shifts attention away from assertions of power to the instrument through which that power is exercised.

Speculation on what (other than its own frail body) that bird in the hand might signify has always been attractive to me, but especially so now, thinking as I have been about the work I do that has brought me to this company. So I choose to read the bird as language and the woman as a practiced writer.

15   She is worried about how the language she dreams in, given to her at birth, is handled, put into service, even withheld from her for certain nefarious purposes. Being a writer, she thinks of language partly as a system, partly as a living thing over which one has control, but mostly as agency—as an act with consequences. So the question the children put to her, "Is it living or dead?," is not unreal, because she thinks of language as susceptible to death, erasure; certainly imperiled and salvageable only by an effort of the will. She believes that if the bird in the hands of her visitors is dead, the custodians are responsible for the corpse. For her a dead language is not only one no longer spoken or written, it is unyielding language content to admire its own paralysis. Like statist language, censored and censoring. Ruthless in its policing duties, it has no desire or purpose other than to maintain the free range of its own narcotic narcissism, its own exclusivity and dominance. However, moribund, it is not without effect, for it actively thwarts the intellect, stalls conscience, suppresses human potential. Unreceptive to interrogation, it cannot form or tolerate new ideas, shape other thoughts, tell another story, fill baffling silences. Official language smitheried to sanction ignorance and preserve privilege is a suit of armor, polished to shocking glitter, a husk from which the knight departed long ago. Yet there it is; dumb, predatory, sentimental. Exciting reverence in schoolchildren, providing shelter for despots, summoning false memories of stability, harmony among the public.

She is convinced that when language dies, out of carelessness, disuse, indifference, and absence of esteem, or killed by fiat, not only she herself but all users and makers are accountable for its demise. In her country children have bitten their tongues off and use bullets instead to iterate the void of speechlessness, of disabled and disabling language, of language adults have abandoned altogether as a device for grappling with meaning, providing guidance, or expressing love. But she knows tongue-suicide is not only the choice of children. It is common among the infantile heads of state and power merchants whose evacuated language leaves them with no access to what is left of their human instincts, for they speak only to those who obey, or in order to force obedience.

The systematic looting of language can be recognized by the tendency of its users to forgo its nuanced, complex, midwifery properties, replacing them with menace and subjugation. Oppressive language does more than represent violence; it is violence; does more than represent the limits of knowledge; it limits knowledge. Whether it is obscuring state language or the faux language of mindless media; whether it is the proud but calcified language of the academy or the commodity-driven language of science; whether it is the malign language of law-without-ethics, or language designed for the estrangement of minorities, hiding its racist plunder in its literary cheek—it must be rejected, altered, and exposed. It is the language that drinks blood, laps vulnerabilities, tucks its fascist boots under crinolines of respectability and patriotism as it moves relentlessly toward the bottom line and the bottomed-out mind. Sexist language, racist language, theistic language—all are typical of the policing languages of mastery, and cannot, do not, permit new knowledge or encourage the mutual exchange of ideas.

The old woman is keenly aware that no intellectual mercenary or insatiable dictator, no paid-for politician or demagogue, no counterfeit journalist would be persuaded by her thoughts. There is and will be rousing language to keep citizens armed and arming; slaughtered and slaughtering in the mauls, courthouses, post offices, playgrounds, bedrooms, and

and boulevards; stirring, memorializing language to mask the pity and waste of needless death. There will be more diplomatic language to countenance rape, torture, assassination. There is and will be more seductive, mutant language designed to throttle women, to pack their throats like pâté-producing geese with their own unsayable, transgressive words; there will be more of the language of surveillance disguised as research; of politics and history calculated to render the suffering of millions mute; language glamorized to thrill the dissatisfied and bereft into assaulting their neighbors; arrogant pseudo-empirical language crafted to lock creative people into cages of inferiority and hopelessness.

Underneath the eloquence, the glamour, the scholarly associations, however stirring or seductive, the heart of such language is languishing, or perhaps not beating at all—if the bird is already dead.

20   She had thought about what could have been the intellectual history of any discipline if it had not insisted upon, or been forced into, the waste of time and life that rationalizations for and representations of dominance required—lethal discourses of exclusion blocking access to cognition for both the excluder and the excluded.

The conventional wisdom of the Tower of Babel story is that the collapse was a misfortune. That it was the distraction or the weight of many languages that precipitated the tower's failed architecture. That one monolithic language would have expedited the building, and heaven would have been reached. Whose heaven, she wonders? And what kind? Perhaps the achievement of Paradise was premature, a little hasty if no one could take the time to understand other languages, other views, other narratives. Had they, the heaven they imagined might have been found at their feet. Complicated, demanding, yes, but a view of heaven as life; not heaven as post-life.

She would not want to leave her young visitors with the impression that language should be forced to stay alive merely to be. The vitality of language lies in its ability to limn the actual, imagined, and possible lives of its speakers, readers, writers. Although its poise is sometimes in displacing experience, it is not a substitute for it. It arcs toward the place where meaning may lie. When a president of the United States thought about the graveyard his country had become, and said, "The world will little note nor long remember what we say here. But it will never forget what they did here," his simple words were exhilarating in their life-sustaining properties because they refused to encapsulate the reality of 600,000 dead men in a cataclysmic race war. Refusing to monumentalize, disdaining the "final word," the precise "summing up," acknowledging their "poor power to add or detract," his words signal deference to the uncapturability of the life it mourns. It is deference that moves her, that recognition that language can never live up to life once and for all. Nor should it. Language can never "pin down" slavery, genocide, war. Nor should it yearn for the arrogance to be able to do so. Its force, its felicity, is in its reach toward the ineffable.

Be it grand or slender, burrowing, blasting or refusing to sanctify; whether it laughs out loud or is a cry without an alphabet, the choice word or the chosen silence, unmolested language surges toward knowledge, not its destruction. But who does not know of literature banned because it is interrogative; discredited because it is critical; erased because alternate? And how many are outraged by the thought of a self-ravaged tongue?

Word-work is sublime, she thinks, because it is generative; it makes meaning that secures our difference, our human difference—the way in which we are like no other life.

25   We die. That may be the meaning of life. But we *do* language. That may be the measure of our lives.

"Once upon a time . . ." Visitors ask an old woman a question. Who are they, these children? What did they make of that encounter? What did they hear in those final words: "The bird is in your hands"? A sentence that gestures toward possibility, or one that drops a latch?

Perhaps what the children heard was, "It's not my problem. I am old, female, black, blind. What wisdom I have now is in knowing I cannot help you. The future of language is yours."

They stand there. Suppose nothing was in their hands. Suppose the visit was only a ruse, a trick to get to be spoken to, taken seriously as they have not been before. A chance to interrupt, to violate the adult world, its miasma of discourse about them. Urgent questions are at stake, including the one they have asked: "Is the bird we are holding living or dead?" Perhaps the question meant: "Could someone tell us what is life? What is death?" No trick at all; no silliness. A straightforward question worthy of the attention of a wise one. An old one. And if the old and wise who have lived life and faced death cannot describe either, who can?

But she does not; she keeps her secret, her good opinion of herself, her gnomic pronouncements, her art without commitment. She keeps her distance, enforces it and retreats into the singularity of isolation, in sophisticated, privileged space.

Nothing, no word follows her declaration of transfer. That silence is deep, deeper than the meaning available in the words she has spoken. It shivers, this silence, and the children, annoyed, fill it with language invented on the spot.

30   "Is there no speech," they ask her, "no words you can give us that help us break through your dossier of failures" through the education you have just given us that is no education at all because we are paying close attention to what you have done as well as to what you have said? to the barrier you have erected between generosity and wisdom?

"We have no bird in our hands, living or dead. We have only you and our important question. Is the nothing in our hands something you could not bear to contemplate, to even guess? Don't you remember being young, when language was magic without meaning? When what you could say, could not mean? When the invisible was what imagination strove to see? When questions and demands for answers burned so brightly you trembled with fury at not knowing?

"Do we have to begin consciousness with a battle heroes and heroines like you have already fought and lost, leaving us with nothing in our hands except what you imagined is there? Your answer is artful, but its artfulness embarrasses us and ought to embarrass you. Your answer is indecent in its self-congratulation. A made-for-television script that makes no sense if there is nothing in our hands.

"Why didn't you reach out, touch us with your soft fingers, delay the sound bite, the lesson, until you knew who we were? Did you so despise our trick, our modus operandi, that you could not see that we were baffled about how to get your attention? We are young. Unripe. We have heard all our short lives that we have to be responsible. What could that possibly mean in the catastrophe this world has become; where, as a poet said, 'nothing needs to be exposed since it is already barefaced'? Our inheritance is an affront. You want us to have your old, blank eyes and see only cruelty and mediocrity. Do you think we are stupid enough to perjure ourselves again and again with the fiction of nationhood? How dare you talk to us of duty when we stand waist deep in the toxin of our past?

"You trivialize us and trivialize the bird that is not in our hands. Is there no context for our lives? No song, no literature, no poem full of vitamins, no history connected to experience that you can pass along to help us start strong? You are an adult. The old one, the wise one. Stop thinking about saving your face. Think of our lives and tell us your particularized world. Make up a story. Narrative is radical, creating us at the very moment it is being created. We will not blame you if your reach exceeds your grasp; if love so ignites your words that they go down in flames and nothing is left but their scald. Or if, with the reticence of a surgeon's hands, your words suture only the places where blood might flow. We know you can never do it properly—once and for all. Passion is never enough; neither is skill. But try. For our sake and yours forget your name in the street; tell us what the world has been to you in the dark places and in the light. Don't tell us what to believe, what to fear. Show us belief's wide skirt and the stitch that unravels fear's caul. You, old woman, blessed with blindness, can speak the language that tells us what only language can: how to see without pictures. Language alone protects us from the scariness of things with no names. Language alone is meditation.

35 "Tell us what it is to be a woman so that we may know what it is to be a man. What moves at the margin. What it is to have no home in this place. To be set adrift from the one you knew. What it is to live at the edge of towns that cannot bear your company.

"Tell us about ships turned away from shorelines at Easter, placenta in a field. Tell us about a wagonload of slaves, how they sang so softly their breath was indistinguishable from the falling snow. How they knew from the hunch of the nearest shoulder that the next stop would be their last. How, with hands prayered in their sex, they thought of heat, then sun. Lifting their faces as though it was there for the taking. They stop at an inn. The driver and his mate go in with the lamp, leaving them humming in the dark. The horse's void steams into the snow beneath its hooves and the hiss and melt are the envoy of the freezing slaves.

"The inn door opens: a girl and a boy step away from its light. They climb into the wagon bed. The boy will have a gun in three years, but now he carries a lamp and a jug of warm cider. They pass it from mouth to mouth. The girl offers bread, pieces of meat, and something more: a glance into the eyes of the one she serves. One helping for each man, two for each woman. And a look. They look back. The next stop will be their last. But not this one. This one is warmed."

"It's quiet again when the children finish speaking, until the woman breaks into the silence.

"Finally," she says, "I trust you now. I trust you with the bird that is not in your hands because you have truly caught it. Look. How lovely it is, this thing we have done—together."

■ EXPLORATIONS OF THE TEXT

1. Consider aspects of audience for this essay including and beyond: "Members of the Swedish Academy, Ladies and Gentlemen."

2. At one point in the essay we read the following: "Narrative is radical, creating us at the very moment it is being created." Analyze and explain the complex layers of narrative Morrison uses in this essay. What is the function, for example, of the story within a story?

3. Consider the various symbolic references to the bird. How does the symbolism of the bird change? What is the significance of the "bird in . . . [the] hand"?

4. As you interpret the references to the bird, consider the possibility of forms of narrative as a way into symbolic meaning. Is this a parable, a folk story, an allegory, or even a Socratic dialogue? (Refer to chapter 9 on forms of narrative; to the excerpt from *The Symposium* in chapter 6; to "The Allegory of the Cave" in this chapter).

5. Morrison makes numerous powerful, even provocative, statements about language in this essay. Examine and discuss at least three of these statements. Do you agree with her views of language? Possible examples include the following: "The systematic looting of language can be recognized by the tendency of its user to forgo its nuanced, complex, midwifery properties replacing them with menace and subjugation"; or "Official language smitheried to sanction ignorance and preserve privilege is a suit of armor, polished to shocking glitter, a husk from which the knight departed long ago."

6. What does the speech suggest about storytelling, language, and the power of words?

7. Compare her views of the power of words with the treatment of language in *"Master Harold" . . . and the Boys.*

■ THE READING/WRITING CONNECTION

1. Gloss and annotate the text of the speech—concentrate on the symbolism of the bird—in preparation for class discussion of question 3 in Explorations of the Text.
2. Draft a letter from Toni Morrison to Hally in *"Master Harold."* Or imagine that Hally has read Morrison's speech. Write a letter in his voice to Morrison.
3. After reading this speech, list several questions that you have about the work. Then answer one of your questions in the form of a paragraph.

■ IDEAS FOR WRITING

1. Choose one of Morrison's controversial statements about language. Agree or disagree with her. Your response may take the form of a letter to Morrison.
2. Continue exploring question 4 in Explorations of the Text. Is Morrison's essay a parable, allegory, or something else? Defend your choice.
3. Is Morrison's speech effective? Convincing? Evaluate her work. Refer to the student portfolio in chapter 12 for ideas.

ALICE WALKER

Alice Walker (1944–   ) was born in Eatonville, Georgia. After attending Spelman College and Sarah Lawrence College, Walker, influenced by her involvement in voter registration in Georgia and in welfare programs in Mississippi, began to write. Her first volume of poetry, Once: Poems *(1968), contains accounts of her work and her travels to Africa. In 1979, she edited* I Love Myself When I Am Laughing, *a selection from the writings of Zora Neale Hurston that was responsible for new interest in and appreciation of Hurston's work. The author of more than ten books of fiction, Walker won the Pulitzer Prize and the National Book Award in 1982 for her third novel,* The Color Purple. *Her most recent novel is* Now Is the Time to Open Your Heart *(2004). Her essays have been collected in* In Search of Our Mother's Gardens *(1983) and* Living by the Word: Selected Writings 1973–1987 *(1988). Walker, known as a "womanist" with a keen connection to nature, displays in her work a sense of hope even in the midst of despair.*

1986

AM I BLUE?

"Ain't these tears in these eyes tellin' you?"

For about three years my companion and I rented a small house in the country that stood on the edge of a large meadow that appeared to run from the end of our deck straight into the mountains. The mountains, however, were quite far away, and between us and them there was, in fact, a town. It was one of the many pleasant aspects of the house that you never really were aware of this.

It was a house of many windows, low, wide, nearly floor to ceiling in the living room, which faced the meadow, and it was from one of these that I first saw our closest neighbor, a large white horse, cropping grass, flipping its mane, and ambling about—not over the entire meadow, which stretched well out of sight of the house, but over the five or so fenced-in acres that were next to the twenty-odd that we had rented. I soon learned that the horse, whose name was Blue, belonged to a man who lived in another town, but was boarded by our neighbors next door. Occasionally, one of the children, usually a stocky teen-ager, but sometimes a much younger girl or boy, could be seen riding Blue. They would appear in the meadow, climb up on his back, ride furiously for ten or fifteen minutes, then get off, slap Blue on the flanks, and not be seen again for a month or more.

There were many apple trees in our yard, and one by the fence Blue could almost reach. We were soon in the habit of feeding him apples, which he relished, especially because by the middle of summer the meadow grasses—so green and succulent since January—had dried out from lack of rain, and Blue stumbled about munching the dried stalks half-heartedly. Sometimes he would stand very still just by the apple tree, and when one of us came out he would whinny, snort loudly, or stamp the ground. This meant, of course: I want an apple.

It was quite wonderful to pick a few apples, or collect those that had fallen to the ground overnight, and patiently hold them, one by one, up to his large, toothy mouth. I remained as thrilled as a child by his flexible dark lips, huge, cubelike teeth that crunched the apples, core and all, with such finality, and his high, broad-breasted *enormity;* beside which, I felt small indeed. When I was a child, I used to ride horses, and was especially friendly with one named Nan until the day I was riding and my brother deliberately spooked her and I was thrown, head first, against the trunk of a tree. When I came to, I was in bed and my mother was bending worriedly over me; we silently agreed that perhaps horseback riding was not the safest sport for me. Since then I have walked, and prefer walking to horseback riding—but I had forgotten the depth of feeling one could see in horses' eyes.

5   I was therefore unprepared for the expression in Blue's. Blue was lonely. Blue was horribly lonely and bored. I was not shocked that this should be the case; five acres to tramp by yourself, endlessly, even in the most beautiful of meadows—and his was—cannot provide many interesting events, and once rainy season turned to dry that was about it. No, I was shocked that I had forgotten that human animals and nonhuman animals can communicate quite well; if we are brought up around animals as children we take this for granted. By the time we are adults we no longer remember. However, the animals have not changed. They are in fact *completed* creations (at least they seem to be, so much more than we) who are not likely to change; it is their nature to express themselves; What else are they going to express? And they do. And, generally speaking, they are ignored.

After giving Blue the apples, I would wander back to the house, aware that he was observing me. Were more apples not forthcoming then? Was that to be his sole entertainment for the day? My partner's small son had decided he wanted to learn how to piece a quilt; we worked in silence on our respective squares as I thought . . . .

Well, about slavery: about white children, who were raised by black people, who knew their first all-accepting love from black women, and then, when they were twelve or so, were told they must "forget" the deep levels of communication between themselves and "mammy" that they knew. Later they would be able to relate quite calmly, "My old mammy was sold to another good family." "My old mammy was ⎯⎯⎯⎯⎯⎯ ." Fill in the blank. Many more years later a white woman would say: "I can't understand these Negroes, these blacks. What do they want? They're so different from us."

And about the Indians, considered to be "like animals" by the "settlers" (a very benign euphemism for what they actually were), who did not understand their description as a compliment.

And about the thousands of American men who marry Japanese, Korean, Filipina, and other non–English-speaking women and of how happy they report they are, "*blissfully,*" until their brides learn to speak English, at which point the marriages tend to fall apart. What then did the men see, when they looked into the eyes of the women they married, before they could speak English? Apparently only their own reflections.

10   I thought of society's impatience with the young. "Why are they playing the music so loud?" Perhaps the children have listened to much of the music of oppressed people their parents danced to before they were born, with its passionate but soft cries for acceptance and love, and they have wondered why their parents failed to hear.

I do not know how long Blue had inhabited his five beautiful, boring acres before we moved into our house; a year after we had arrived—and had also traveled to other valleys, other cities, other worlds—he was still there.

But then, in our second year at the house, something happened in Blue's life. One morning, looking out the window at the fog that lay like a ribbon over the meadow, I saw another horse, a brown one, at the other end of Blue's field. Blue appeared to be afraid of it, and for several days made no attempt to go near. We went away for a week. When we returned, Blue had decided to make friends and the two horses ambled or galloped along together, and Blue did not come nearly as often to the fence underneath the apple tree.

When he did, bringing his new friend with him, there was a different look in his eyes. A look of independence, of self-possession, of inalienable *horseness*. His friend eventually became pregnant. For months and months there was, it seemed to me, a mutual feeling between me and the horses of justice, of peace. I fed apples to them both. The look in Blue's eyes was one of unabashed "this is *itness*."

It did not, however, last forever. One day, after a visit to the city, I went out to give Blue some apples. He stood waiting, or so I thought, though not beneath the tree. When I shook the tree and jumped back from the shower of apples, he made no move. I carried some over to him. He managed to half-crunch one. The rest he let fall to the ground. I dreaded looking into his eyes—because I had of course noticed that Brown, his partner, had gone—but I did look. If I had been born into slavery, and my partner had been sold or killed, my eyes would have looked like that. The children next door explained that Blue's partner had been "put with him" (the same expression that old people used, I had noticed, when speaking of an ancestor during slavery who had been impregnated by her owner) so that they could mate and she conceive. Since that was accomplished, she had been taken back by her owner, who lived somewhere else.

15 Will she be back? I asked.

They didn't know.

Blue was like a crazed person. Blue *was*, to me, a crazed person. He galloped furiously, as if he were being ridden, around and around his five beautiful acres. He whinnied until he couldn't. He tore at the ground with his hooves. He butted himself against his single shade tree. He looked always and always toward the road down which his partner had gone. And then, occasionally, when he came up for apples, or I took apples to him, he looked at me. It was a look so piercing, so full of grief, a look so *human,* I almost laughed (I felt too sad to cry) to think there are people who do not know that animals suffer. People like me who have forgotten, and daily forget, all that animals try to tell us. "Everything you do to us will happen to you; we are your teachers, as you are ours. We are one lesson" is essentially it, I think. There are those who never once have even considered animals' rights: those who have been taught that animals actually want to be used and abused by us, as small children "love" to be frightened, or women "love" to be mutilated and raped. . . . They are the great-grandchildren of those who honestly thought, because someone taught them this: "Women can't think," and "niggers can't faint." But most disturbing of all, in Blue's large brown eyes was a new look, more painful than the look of hatred: the look of disgust with human beings, with life; the look of hatred. And it was odd what the look of hatred did. It gave him, for the first time, the look of a beast. And what that meant was that he had put up a barrier within to protect himself from further violence; all the apples in the world wouldn't change that fact.

And so Blue remained, a beautiful part of our landscape, very peaceful to look at from the window, white against the grass. Once a friend came to visit and said, looking out on the soothing view: "And it *would* have to be a *white* horse; the very image of freedom." And I thought, yes, the animals are forced to become for us merely "images" of what they once so beautifully expressed. And we are used to drinking milk from containers showing "contented" cows, whose real lives we want to hear nothing about, eating eggs and drumsticks from "happy" hens, and munching hamburgers advertised by bulls of integrity who seem to command their fate.

As we talked of freedom and justice one day for all, we sat down to steaks. I am eating misery, I thought, as I took the first bite. And spit it out.

■ EXPLORATIONS OF THE TEXT

1. React to the opening paragraph. Why does Walker describe the setting? What does the setting reveal about her psyche? Her place in the world?
2. How does Walker characterize "Blue"? Discuss the significance of his name. Why does she refer to his "companion" as "Blue's friend"?
3. What is the relationship of the examples given in paragraphs 7–10 to the main story line? Are these paragraphs tangential or relevant to her argument?
4. Is Walker projecting her own feelings onto the horse?
5. Walker's essay uses an extended analogy as the basis of her argument. Summarize her argument. Is this strategy effective?
6. Discuss the significance of the concluding sentence: "I am eating misery. . . ." Why is she upset?
7. Compare Walker's essay with Anna Lee Walter's poem, "My Name Is 'I Am Living,'" and Scott Russell Sanders's "Wayland."

■ THE READING/WRITING CONNECTION

1. Do you believe that animals "suffer"? Are you an animal rights activist? Respond in a freewrite.
2. "Think" Topic: Interpret the title of the essay. Connect the title with themes of the poem.
3. Journal Entry: Alice Walker recognizes that Blue, a social animal, needs companionship to live happily. She relates this need to that of humans, another social animal. Do you think that humans are similar to other social animals? If so, which ones? Write a journal entry with your thoughts, referring to Walker or Sanders.

■ IDEAS FOR WRITING

1. Create an argument based on an analogy. Use Walker's essay as a model.
2. Discuss Walker's essay and Marquez's story, "The Handsomest Drowned Man" as Utopian visions.

HERMAN MELVILLE

Herman Melville (1819–91) was born in New York City, where he lived until his father's financial difficulties forced the family to move to Albany, New York. Melville attended Columbia College and Albany Academy. His writing career began after the first of many sea voyages in 1839, and in 1841, he joined the crew of a whaling ship, an experience that influenced the writing of his most famous novel, Moby Dick *(1851). Though known for his novels and short fiction, Melville's earliest books were travel narratives, and later in his career, Melville wrote poetry. His first two publications were* Typee: A Peep at Polynesian Life, During a Four Months Residence in a Valley of the Marquesas *(1846) and* Oomo: A Narrative of Adventures in the South Seas *(1848). "The Encantadas" (1854) is believed to be part of a longer work on tortoise hunting that was never completed and is an example of Melville's travel writing.*

1854

THE ENCANTADAS

Sketch First
The Isles at Large

—"That may not be, said then the ferryman,
Least we unweeting hap to be fordonne;
For those same islands seeming now and than,
Are not firme land, nor any certein wonne,
But stragling plots which to and fro do ronne
In the wide waters; therefore are they hight
The Wandering Islands; therefore do them shonne;
For they have oft drawne many a wandring wight
Into most deadly daunger and distressed plight;
For whosoever once hath fastened
His foot thereon may never it recure
But wandreth evermore uncertein and unsure."

"Darke, dolefull, dreary, like a greedy grave,
That still for carrion carcasses doth crave;
On top whereof ay dwelt the ghastly owl,
Shrieking his balefull note, which ever drave
Far from that haunt all other cheerful fowl,
And all about it wandring ghosts did wayle and howl."

Take five-and-twenty heaps of cinders dumped here and there in an outside city lot; imagine some of them magnified into mountains, and the vacant lot the sea; and you will have a fit idea of the general aspect of the Encantadas, or Enchanted Isles. A group rather of extinct volcanoes than of isles; looking much as the world at large might, after a penal conflagration.

It is to be doubted whether any spot of earth can, in desolateness, furnish a parallel to this group. Abandoned cemeteries of long ago, old cities by piecemeal tumbling to their ruin, these are melancholy enough; but, like all else which has but once been associated with humanity they still awaken in us some thoughts of sympathy, however sad. Hence, even the Dead Sea,[1] along with whatever other emotions it may at times inspire, does not fail to touch in the pilgrim some of his less unpleasurable feelings.

And as for solitariness; the great forests of the north, the expanses of unnavigated waters, the Greenland ice-fields, are the profoundest of solitudes to a human observer; still the magic of their changeable tides and seasons mitigates their terror; because, though unvisited by men, those forests are visited by the May; the remotest seas reflect familiar stars even as Lake Erie does; and in the clear air of a fine Polar day, the irradiated, azure ice shows beautifully as malachite.

---

[1] Small, land-locked sea between Jordan, Israel, and Palestine.

But the special curse, as one may call it, of the Encantadas, that which exalts them in desolation above Idumea[2] and the Pole, is that to them change never comes; neither the change of seasons nor of sorrows. Cut by the Equator, they know not autumn and they know not spring; while already reduced to the lees of fire, ruin itself can work little more upon them. The showers refresh the deserts, but in these isles, rain never falls. Like split Syrian gourds left withering in the sun, they are cracked by an everlasting drought beneath a torrid sky. "Have mercy upon me," the wailing spirit of the Encantadas seems to cry, "and send Lazarus[3] that he may dip the tip of his finger in water and cool my tongue, for I am tormented in this flame."

5   Another feature in these isles is their emphatic uninhabitableness. It is deemed a fit type of all-forsaken overthrow, that the jackal should den in the wastes of weedy Babylon,[4] but the Encantadas refuse to harbor even the outcasts of the beasts. Man and wolf alike disown them. Little but reptile life is here found:—tortoises, lizards, immense spiders, snakes, and that strangest anomaly of outlandish nature, the *iguana*. No voice, no low, no howl is heard; the chief sound of life here is a hiss.

On most of the isles where vegetation is found at all, it is more ungrateful than the blankness of Atacama.[5] Tangled thickets of wiry bushes, without fruit and without a name, springing up among deep fissures of calcined rock, and treacherously masking them; or a parched growth of distorted cactus trees.

In many places the coast is rock-bound, or more properly, clinker-bound; tumbled masses of blackish or greenish stuff like the dross of an iron-furnace, forming dark clefts and caves here and there, into which a ceaseless sea pours a fury of foam; overhanging them with a swirl of gray, haggard mist, amidst which sail screaming nights of unearthly birds heightening the dismal din. However calm the sea without, there is no rest for these swells and those rocks; they lash and are lashed, even when the outer ocean is most at peace with itself. On the oppressive, clouded days, such as are peculiar to this part of the watery Equator, the dark, vitrified masses, many of which raise themselves among white whirlpools and breakers in detached and perilous places off the shore, present a most Plutonian sight. In no world but a fallen one could such lands exist.

Those parts of the strand free from the marks of fire, stretch away in wide level beaches of multitudinous dead shells, with here and there decayed bits of sugar-cane, bamboos, and cocoanuts, washed upon this other and darker world from the charming palm isles to the westward and southward; all the way from Paradise to Tartarus[6]; while mixed with the relics of distant beauty you will sometimes see fragments of charred wood and mouldering ribs of wrecks. Neither will any one be surprised at meeting these last, after observing the conflicting currents which eddy throughout nearly all the wide channels of the entire group. The capriciousness of the tides of air sympathizes with those of the sea. Nowhere is the wind so light, baffling, and every way unreliable, and so given to perplexing calms, as at the Encantadas. Nigh a month has been spent by a ship going from one isle to. another, though but ninety miles between; for owing to the force of the current, the boats employed to tow barely suffice to keep the craft from sweeping upon the cliffs, but do nothing towards accelerating

---

[2] In ancient times, the country inhabited by the descendants of Edom, south of Judea and the Dead Sea.

[3] In the New Testament, the brother of Mary and Martha whom Jesus raised from the dead.

[4] An ancient kingdom in Mesopotamia, the oldest known civilization, said to be the place of the Garden of Eden. It was located between Iran and the Arabian Peninsula, by the Tigris and Euphrates Rivers.

[5] A desert in Chile, running from the Pacific to the Andes.

[6] From Greek mythology, the region Hades—Hell.

her voyage. Sometimes it is impossible for a vessel from afar to fetch up with the group it-self, unless large allowances for prospective lee-way have been made ere its coming in sight. And yet, at other times, there is a mysterious indraft, which irresistibly draws a passing ves-sel among the isles, though not bound to them.

True, at one period, as to some extent at the present day, large fleets of whalemen cruised for Spermaceti[7] upon what some seamen call the Enchanted Ground. But this, as in due place will be described, was off the great outer isle of Albemarle,[8] away from the intrica-cies of the smaller isles, where there is plenty of sea-room; and hence, to that vicinity, the above remarks do not altogether apply; though even there the current runs at times with singular force, shifting, too, with as singular a caprice. Indeed, there are seasons when cur-rents quite unaccountable prevail for a great distance round about the total group, and are so strong and irregular as to change a vessel's course against the helm, though sailing at the rate of four or five miles the hour. The difference in the reckonings of navigators produced by these causes, along with the light and variable winds, long nourished a persuasion that there existed two distinct clusters of isles in the parallel of the Encantadas, about a hundred leagues apart. Such was the idea of their earlier visitors, the Buccaneers,[9] and as late as 1750, the charts of that part of the Pacific accorded with the strange delusion. And this ap-parent fleetingness and unreality of the locality of the isles was most probably one reason for the Spaniards calling them the Encantada, or Enchanted Group.

10   But not uninfluenced by their character, as they now confessedly exist, the modern voyager will be inclined to fancy that the bestowal of this name might have in part origi-nated in that air of spell-bound desertness which so significantly invests the isles. Nothing can better suggest the aspect of once living things malignly crumbled from ruddiness into ashes. Apples of Sodom,[10] after touching, seem these isles.

However wavering their place may seem by reason of the currents, they themselves, at least to one upon the shore, appear invariably the same: fixed, cast, glued into the very body of cadaverous death.

Nor would the appellation, enchanted, seem misapplied in still another sense. For con-cerning the peculiar reptile inhabitant of these wilds—whose presence gives the group its second Spanish name, Gallipagos[11]—concerning the tortoises found here, most mariners have long cherished a superstition, not more frightful than grotesque. They earnestly believe that all wicked sea-officers, more especially commodores and captains, are at death (and in some cases, before death) transformed into tortoises; thenceforth dwelling upon these hot aridities, sole solitary Lords of Asphaltum.[12]

Doubtless so quaintly dolorous a thought was originally inspired by the woe-begone landscape itself, but more particularly, perhaps, by the tortoises. For apart from their strictly physical features, there is something strangely self-condemned in the appearance of these creatures. Lasting sorrow and penal hopelessness are in no animal form so suppliantly ex-pressed as in theirs; while the thought of their wonderful longevity does not fail to enhance the impression.

---

[7] A white, waxy substance obtained from cavities in the head of a sperm whale and used for making candles, oils, and cosmetics.

[8] One of the Galapagos Islands.

[9] Pirates.

[10] A fruit that is physically beatiful but dissolves into smoke and ash when plucked.

[11] The Galapagos Archipelago is a cluster of islands in the Pacific Ocean 650 miles off the coast of Ecuador.

[12] Melville is calling the tortoises the rulers of the bare, rocky land—the "asphaltum," or pavement of the Galapagos.

Nor even at the risk of meriting the charge of absurdly believing in enchantments, can I restrain the admission that sometimes, even now, when leaving the crowded city to wander out July and August among the Adirondack Mountains, far from the influences of towns and proportionally nigh to the mysterious ones of nature; when at such times I sit me down in the mossy head of some deep-wooded gorge, surrounded by prostrate trunks of blasted pines, and recall, as in a dream, my other and far-distant rovings in the baked heart of the charmed isles; and remember the sudden glimpses of dusky shells, and long languid necks protruded from the leafless thickets; and again have beheld the vitreous inland rocks worn down and grooved into deep ruts by ages and ages of the slow draggings of tortoises in quest of pools of scanty water; I can hardly resist the feeling that in my time I have indeed slept upon evilly enchanted ground.

15   Nay, such is the vividness of my memory, or the magic of my fancy, that I know not whether I am not the occasional victim of optical delusion concerning the Gallipagos. For often in scenes of social merriment, and especially at revels held by candle-light in old-fashioned mansions, so that shadows are thrown into the further recesses of an angular and spacious room, making them put on a look of haunted undergrowth of lonely woods, I have drawn the attention of my comrades by my fixed gaze and sudden change of air, as I have seemed to see, slowly emerging from those imagined solitudes, and heavily crawling along the floor, the ghost of a gigantic tortoise, with "Memento ****" burning in live letters upon his back.

Sketch Second
Two Sides to a Tortoise

"Most ugly shapes and horrible aspects,
Such as Dame Nature selfe mote feare to see,
Or shame, that ever should so fowle defects
From her most cunning hand escaped bee;
All dreadfull pourtraicts of deformitee.
Ne wonder if these do a man appall;
For all that here at home we dreadfull hold
Be but as bugs to fearen babes withall
Compared to the creatures in these isles' entrall.

∞

Fear naught, then said the palmer, well avized,
For these same monsters are not these indeed,
But are into these fearful shapes disguized.

∞

And lifting up his vertuous staffe on high,
Then all that dreadful armie fast gan flye
Into great Tethys' bosom, where they hidden lye."

In view of the description given, may one be gay upon the Encantadas? Yes: that is, find one the gayety, and he will be gay. And indeed, sackcloth and ashes as they are, the isles are not perhaps unmitigated gloom. For while no spectator can deny their claims to a most solemn and superstitious consideration, no more than my firmest resolutions can decline to behold the spectre-tortoise when emerging from its shadowy recess; yet even the tortoise, dark and melancholy as it is upon the back, still possesses a bright side; its calapee or breast-plate being sometimes of a faint yellowish or golden tinge. Moreover, every one knows that tortoises as well as turtle are of such a make, that if you but put them on their backs you thereby expose their bright sides without the possibility of their recovering themselves, and turning into view the other. But after you have done this, and because you have done this, you should not swear that the tortoise has no dark side. Enjoy the bright, keep it turned up perpetually if you can, but be honest and don't deny the black. Neither should he who cannot turn the tortoise from its natural position so as to hide the darker and expose his livelier aspect, like a great October pumpkin in the sun, for that cause declare the creature to be one total inky blot. The tortoise is both black and bright. But let us to particulars.

Some months before my first stepping ashore upon the group, my ship was cruising in its close vicinity. One noon we found ourselves off the South Head of Albemarle, and not very far from the land. Partly by way of freak, and partly by way of spying out so strange a country, a boat's crew was sent ashore, with orders to see all they could, and besides, bring back whatever tortoises they could conveniently transport.

It was after sunset when the adventurers returned. I looked down over the ship's high side as if looking down over the curb of a well, and dimly saw the damp boat deep in the sea with some unwonted weight. Ropes were dropt over, and presently three huge antediluvian-looking[13] tortoises after much straining were landed on deck. They seemed hardly of the seed of earth. We had been broad upon the waters for five long months, a period amply sufficient to make all things of the land wear a fabulous hue to the dreamy mind. Had three Spanish custom-house officers boarded us then, it is not unlikely that I should have curiously stared at them, felt of them, and stroked them much as savages serve civilized guests. But instead of three custom-house officers, behold these really wondrous tortoises—none of your schoolboy mud-turtles—but black as widower's weeds, heavy as chests of plate, with vast shells medallioned and orbed like shields, and dented and blistered like shields that have breasted a battle, shaggy too, here and there, with dark green moss, and slimy with the spray of the sea. These mystic creatures suddenly translated by night from unutterable solitudes to our peopled deck, affected me in a manner not easy to unfold. They seemed newly crawled forth from beneath the foundations of the world. Yea, they seemed the identical tortoises whereon the Hindoo[14] plants this total sphere. With a lantern I inspected them more closely. Such worshipful venerableness of aspect! Such furry greenness mantling the rude peelings and healing the fissures of their shattered shells. I no more saw three tortoises. They expanded—became transfigured. I seemed to see three Roman Coliseums in magnificent decay.

Ye oldest inhabitants of this, or any other isle, said I, pray, give me the freedom of your three walled towns.

20 The great feeling inspired by these creatures was that of age:—dateless, indefinite endurance. And in fact that any other creature can live and breathe as long as the tortoise of the Encantadas, I will not readily believe. Not to hint of their known capacity of sustaining life, while going without food for an entire year, consider that impregnable armor of their living mail. What other bodily being possesses such a citadel wherein to resist the assaults of Time?

---

[13] Ancient, dating back to the time before the flood described in the Bible.
[14] Archaic spelling of Hindu.

■ **EXPLORATIONS OF THE TEXT**

1. Melville describes the Encantadas as bleak and gloomy, yet he also notes their powerful influence on him; he cannot forget them. In what lies the power of these islands?

2. In this brief sketch of the Encantadas, Melville refers to many historical events. Why? What is the effect of these references?

3. Melville describes the tortoises of the Encantadas as "grotesque." What is his attitude toward these ancient creatures? Why?

4. What, or who, are the ghosts named in the opening verse of Herman Melville's "The Encantadas"? Compare/contrast to the ghosts in Oliver's "Ghosts" or to Merwin's "The Chinese Mountain Fox."

■ **THE READING/WRITING CONNECTION**

1. Without looking at the text, list three words that to you describe the Encantadas. Then, look again at Melville's essay, and see what led to your impression. Were your words accurate?

2. Freewrite: Using Melville as an example, describe a place that is important to you.

■ **IDEAS FOR WRITING**

1. Write a journal entry about a place that did not impress you the first time you visited it but that you later could not forget. Then, using your journal and two other works from this chapter, write an essay about this place, explaining why you think it strongly impressed your memory.

2. Referring to Sanders's "Wayland," Aciman's "Alexandria: The Capital of Memory," or Didion's "At the Dam," write an essay about the techniques the authors use to describe places. Do you find these techniques to be powerful? How do the descriptions of place help to create the work's meaning?

3. Soon after Melville visited the Encantadas, Charles Darwin arrived to study the creatures that inhabited the islands. These same islands are now tourist attractions, and the human traffic is destroying the habitat of these creatures. Write an essay explaining your attitude toward human encroachment of animal habitat. Refer to at least one other work in the Wilderness or Wasteland? cluster.

JOAN DIDION

Joan Didion was born in Sacramento, California, and was educated at the University of California, Berkeley. Didion's work includes novels, essays, and screenplays, totaling more than twenty publications, and has been published in Vogue, Saturday Evening Post, Holiday, Harper's Bazaar, The New York Times Book Review, The New Yorker, *and* The New York Review of Books. *Didion's first book of collected essays,* Slouching Toward Bethlehem *(1968), was widely acclaimed, as was her later volume,* The White Album *(1979); both works examine the confusing period of the 1960s and 1970s. Her book* Salvador, *which was based on a trip that Didion made to El Salvador in 1982, was nominated for a Pulitzer Prize. Didion's writing generally explores the social and political conditions within the United States; and her two most recent books,* Where I Was From *(2003) and* Fixed Ideas: America Since 9.11 *(2003), examine the myths and realities of her home state of California and criticize the political actions taken after September 11, 2001.*

1970

AT THE DAM

Since the afternoon in 1967 when I first saw Hoover Dam,[1] its image has never been entirely absent from my inner eye. I will be talking to someone in Los Angeles, say, or New York, and suddenly the dam will materialize, its pristine concave face gleaming white against the harsh rusts and taupes and mauves of that rock canyon hundreds or thousands of miles from where I am. I will be driving down Sunset Boulevard, or about to enter a freeway, and abruptly those power transmission towers will appear before me, canted vertiginously over the tailrace. Sometimes I am confronted by the intakes and sometimes by the shadow of the heavy cable that spans the canyon and sometimes by the ominous outlets to unused spillways, black in the lunar clarity of the desert light. Quite often I hear the turbines. Frequently I wonder what is happening at the dam this instant, at this precise intersection of time and space, how much water is being released to fill downstream orders and what lights are flashing and which generators are in full use and which just spinning free.

I used to wonder what it was about the dam that made me think of it at times and in places where I once thought of the Mindanao Trench,[2] or of the stars wheeling in their courses, or of the words *As it was in the beginning, is now and ever shall be, world without end, amen.* Dams, after all, are commonplace: we have all seen one. This particular dam had existed as an idea in the world's mind for almost forty years before I saw it. Hoover Dam, showpiece of the Boulder Canyon project[3]the several million tons of concrete that made the Southwest plausible, the *fait accompli* that was to convey, in the innocent time of its construction, the notion that mankind's brightest promise lay in American engineering.

Of course the dam derives some of its emotional effect from precisely that aspect, that sense of being a monument to a faith since misplaced. "They died to make the desert bloom," reads a plaque dedicated to the 96 men who died building this first of the great high dams, and in context the worn phrase touches, suggests all of that trust in harnessing resources, in the meliorative power of the dynamo, so central to the early Thirties. Boulder City built in 1931 as the construction town for the dam, retains the ambience of a model city, a new town, a toy triangular grid of green lawns and trim bungalows, all fanning out from the Reclamation building. The bronze sculptures at the dam itself evoke muscular citizens of a tomorrow that never came, sheaves of wheat clutched heavenward, thunderbolts defied. Winged Victories guard the flagpole. The flag whips in the canyon wind. An empty Pepsi-Cola can clatters across the terrazzo. The place is perfectly frozen in time.

But history does not explain it all, does not entirely suggest what makes the dam so affecting. Nor, even, does energy, the massive involvement with power and pressure and the transparent sexual overtones to that involvement. Once when I revisited the dam I walked through it with a man from the Bureau of Reclamation.[4] For a while we trailed behind a guided tour, and then we went on, went into parts of the dam where visitors do not generally go. Once in a while he would explain something, usually in that recondite language having to do with "peaking power," with "outages" and "dewatering," but on the whole we spent the afternoon in a world so alien, so complete and so beautiful unto itself that it was scarcely necessary to speak at all. We saw almost no one. Cranes moved above us as if under their own volition. Generators roared. Transformers hummed. The gratings on which we

---

[1] Built in Black Canyon, Colorado, during the 1930s to control the Colorado River's seasonal flooding and drought cycles. It is the highest and third largest dam in the United States.

[2] The deepest part of the ocean in the western Pacific, near the Mariana Islands.

[3] Authorized in 1928 to build the dam and power plant.

[4] Under the U. S. Department of the Interior and in charge of water management.

stood vibrated. We watched a hundred-ton steel shaft plunging down to that place where the water was. And finally we got down to that place where the water was, where the water sucked out of Lake Mead roared through thirty-foot penstocks and then into thirteen-foot penstocks and finally into the turbines themselves. "Touch it," the Reclamation man said, and I did, and for a long time I just stood there with my hands on the turbine. It was a peculiar moment, but so explicit as to suggest nothing beyond itself.

5   There was something beyond all that, something beyond energy, beyond history, something I could not fix in my mind. When I came up from the dam that day the wind was blowing harder, through the canyon and all across the Mojave. Later, toward Henderson and Las Vegas, there would be dust blowing, blowing past the Country-Western Casino FRI & SAT NITES and blowing past the Shrine of Our Lady of Safe Journey STOP & PRAY, but out at the dam there was no dust, only the rock and the dam and a little greasewood and a few garbage cans, their tops chained, banging against a fence. I walked across the marble star map that traces a sidereal revolution of the equinox and fixes forever, the Reclamation man had told me, for all time and for all people who can read the stars, the date the dam was dedicated. The star map was, he had said, for when we were all gone and the dam was left. I had not thought much of it when he said it, but I thought of it then, with the wind whining and the sun dropping behind a mesa with the finality of a sunset in space. Of course that was the image I had seen always, seen it without quite realizing what I saw, a dynamo[5] finally free of man, splendid at last in its absolute isolation, transmitting power and releasing water to a world where no one is.

■ EXPLORATIONS OF THE TEXT

1. Didion begins the essay by explaining her inability to forget the dam. Why is she so impressed by it?
2. Although the dam still exists in the present, Didion writes about it using references to history, to a time past. Why?
3. Didion refers to a plaque that honors the men who died building the dam. What historical structures also claimed many lives in their construction? Explain the dam's symbolism.
4. Didion is awed by the power of the Hoover Dam, much as Melville is entranced by the "evil . . . enchantment" of the Encantadas. Is there a similarity between the power of man-made and nature-made objects? Explain.
5. Didion envisions the "dynamo" in the dam as a symbol of the expertise and success of American engineering. What today would be a symbol of technological expertise?

■ THE READING/WRITING CONNECTION

1. Didion is moved by the physical power of the dam. Write a journal entry about a force, physical or man made, that has moved you with its power.
2. Compare/contrast Didion's inability to forget the dam with Melville's inability to forget the Encantadas. Neither the dam nor the islands are beautiful in a conventional way. Describe something you have seen or a place you have visited that struck your imagination even though it was not lovely.

■ IDEAS FOR WRITING

1. Many dams are being dismantled in the Southwest because they have damaged the environment and exacerbate drought. Didion says of the Hoover Dam that "it made the Southwest possible," that when it was built, people were hopeful they could conquer

---

[5] A generator of power, electricity.

nature through engineering. Write about this statement, explaining what the dam "made possible" and describing present attitudes toward technology.

2. Didion imagines the dam as functioning in a post-human world, alone and completely independent. Write about this image. What comes to mind? What do you imagine as outliving humanity?

SCOTT RUSSELL SANDERS

Scott Russell Sanders (1945–) was born in Memphis, Tennessee; received his Ph.D. from Cambridge University; and presently resides in Bloomington, Indiana, where he is a Distinguished Professor at Indiana University. Sanders is the author of twenty-six books as well as numerous essays and stories that have been anthologized in collections such as The Best American Essays 1987, 1993, 1999, *and* 2000 *and many distinguished literary journals and magazines. He has won several fellowships and awards for his writing, including the National Endowment of the Arts (1983–84), the PEN Syndicated Fiction Award (1988), and more recently, the Great Lakes Book Award (1996) for* Writing from the Center *(1995) and the John Burroughs Award for best natural history essay (2000). Sanders is known as an environmentalist and nature writer whose sense of wonder about the natural world often is portrayed through his recognition of family ties as an instinctive and primitive human bond.*

1993

WAYLAND

Two blacktop roads, broken by frost and mended with tar, running from nowhere to nowhere, cross at right angles in the rumpled farm country of northeastern Ohio. The neighborhood where they intersect is called Wayland—not a village, not even a hamlet, only a cluster of barns and silos and frame houses and a white steepled Methodist church. Just north of Wayland, the Army fenced in fifty square miles of ground for a bomb factory, and just to the south the Corps of Engineers built a dam and flooded even more square miles for a reservoir. I grew up behind those government fences in the shadows of bunkers, and on farms that have since vanished beneath those government waters. Family visits to church began carrying me to Wayland when I was five, romance was carrying me there still at seventeen, and in the years between I was drawn there often by duty or desire. Thus it happened that within shouting distance of the Wayland crossroads I met seven of the great mysteries.

Even as a boy, oblivious much of the time to all save my own sensations, I knew by the tingle in my spine when I had bumped into something utterly new. I groped for words to describe what I had felt, as I grope still. Since we give labels to all that puzzles us, as we name every blank space on the map, I could say that what I stumbled into in Wayland were the mysteries of death, life, beasts, food, mind, sex, and God. But these seven words are only tokens, worn coins that I drop onto the page, hoping to bribe you, coins I finger as reminders of those awful encounters.

The roads that cross at Wayland are too humble to show on the Ohio map, too small even to wear numbers. And yet, without maps or mistakes, without quite meaning to, I recently found my way back there from half a thousand miles away, after an absence of twenty-five years, led along the grooves of memory.

The grooves are deep, and they set me vibrating well before I reached the place, as the spinal cuts in phonograph records will shake music from a needle. I was heading toward Cleveland when I took a notion to veer off the interstate and see what had become of Akron, which led me to see what had become of Kent, which led me to Ravenna, the seat of Portage County. Nothing aside from stoplights made me pause. Not sure what I was looking for, I drove east from the county seat along a highway hurtling with trucks. Soon the rusted chain link fence of the Ravenna Arsenal came whipping by on my left and the raised bed of the Baltimore & Ohio tracks surged by on the right. Then I realized where I was going. My knuckles whitened on the steering wheel as I turned from the highway, put my back toward the trucks and bombs, and passed under the railroad through a concrete arch. Beyond the arch, the woods and fields and houses of Wayland shimmered in the October sunlight, appearing to my jealous eye scarcely changed after a quarter of a century.

5   I knew the place had changed, of course, if only because in the years since I had come here last—drawn in those days like a moth to the flame of a girl—the population of the earth had nearly doubled. Every crossroads, every woods, every field on the planet is warping under the pressure of our terrible hunger. So I knew that Wayland had changed, for all its pastoral shimmer in the autumn light. Yet I was grateful that on the surface it so much resembled my childhood memories, for in my effort to live adequately in the present, I had come here to conduct some business with the past. What had brought me back to Wayland was a need to dig through the fluff and debris of ordinary life, down to some bedrock of feeling and belief.

I left my car in the graveled parking lot of the church and set out walking. Without planning my steps, I meandered where memory led, and where it led was from station to station of my childhood astonishment. Not yet ready for the church, I went next door to the parsonage, where I had first caught a whiff of death. The white clapboard house, a two-story box with a porch across the front and a green hipped roof, could have belonged to any of the neighboring farms. That was appropriate, for the ministers who succeeded one another in the house often preached as though they were farmers, weeding out sins, harvesting souls.

The minister whom I knew first was the Reverend Mr. Knipe, a bulky man sunken with age, his hair as white as the clapboards on the parsonage, his voice like the cooing of pigeons in the barn. Much in life amused him. Whenever he told you something that struck him as funny, he would cover his mouth with a hand to hide his smile. Despite the raised hand, often his laugh burst free and rolled over you. I began listening to him preach and pray and lead hymns when I was five, and for the next two years I heard Reverend Knipe every Sunday, until his voice became for me that of the Bible itself, even the voice of God. Then one Sunday when I was seven, I shook his great hand after the service as usual, suffering him to bend down and pat my head, and I went home to my dinner and he went home to his. While his wife set the table in the parsonage, Reverend Knipe rested on the front porch in his caned rocking chair, drifted off to sleep, and never woke up.

When Mother told me of this, the skin prickled on my neck. To sleep and never wake! To be a white-haired man with a voice like a barnful of pigeons, and the next minute to be nothing at all! Since my parents considered me too young to attend the funeral, I could only imagine what had become of his body, and I imagined not decay but evaporation—the flesh dispersing into thin air like morning mist from a pond.

The following Sunday, while a visitor preached, I stole from church and crept over to the parsonage. I drew to the edge of the porch, wrapped my fingers around the spindles of the railing, and stared at the empty rocker. Reverend Knipe will never sit in that chair again, I told myself. Never, never, never. I tried to imagine how long forever would last. I tried to imagine how it would feel to be nothing. No thing. Suddenly chair and house and daylight vanished, and I was gazing into a dark hole, I was falling, I was gone. I caught a whiff of death, the damp earthly smell seeping from beneath the porch. It was also the smell of mud, of leaping grass, of spring. Clinging to that sensation, I pulled myself up out of the hole. There was the house again, the chair. I let go of the railing, swung away, and ran back to the church, chanting to myself: *He was old and I am young. He was old and I am young.*

10   Nights, often, and sometimes in the broad light of day, I still have to scrabble up out of that hole. We all do. Sometime in childhood, each of us bangs head-on into the blank fact we call death. Once that collision takes place, the shock of it never wears off. We may find ourselves returning to the spot where it occurred as to the scene of an accident, the way I found myself drawn, half a lifetime later, to the front steps of this parsonage. I was a stranger to the family who lived there now. Not wishing to intrude on them, I paused by the steps and surveyed the porch. Vinyl siding had covered the clapboard. An aluminum folding chair had replaced the rocker. I squatted by the railing, lowering my face to the height of a seven-year-old, closed my eyes against the shadows, and sniffed. From below the sill of the porch came the earth's dank perennial breath, fetid and fertile. Yet, I thought, filling myself with the smell: this abides, this is real; no matter the name we give it, life or death, it is a fact as rough and solid as a stone squeezed in the palm of the hand.

     A dog yapped inside the parsonage. I stood up hurriedly and backed away, before anyone could appear at the door to ask me what in tarnation I was looking for under that porch.

     Still following the grooves of memory, I crossed the road to stand in the driveway of another white frame house. It was not so much the house that drew me as it was the side yard, where, about this time each fall, we brought our apples for pressing. The old press with its wooden vat and iron gears used to balance on concrete blocks in the shade of a willow. We would pick apples in the military reservation, from orchards that had been allowed to go wild after the government bulldozed the farmsteads. Unsprayed, blotched and wormy, these apples were also wonderfully sweet. We kept them in bushel baskets and cardboard boxes in the cellar, their fragrance filling the house, until we had accumulated enough to load our station wagon. Then we drove here, parked beside the willow, and fed our fruit into the press.

     On this mild October day, the willow looked as I remembered it, thick in the trunk and gold in the leaves. There was no sign of a press, but that did not keep me from remembering what it was like to squeeze apples. First we pulped them in a mill, then we wrapped them in cheesecloth and tamped them down, layer by layer, into the slotted wooden vat. To mash them, we spun a cast iron wheel. It was easy to begin with, so easy that my brother and sister and I could make the spokes whirl. Later, the cranking would become too hard for us, and our mother would take her turn, then our father, then both of them together. The moment that set me trembling, however, came early on, while my hand was still on the iron wheel, the moment when cider began to ooze through the cheesecloth, between the slats, and down the spout into a waiting bucket. Out of the dirt, out of the gnarled trunks and wide-flung branches, out of the ripe red fruit had come this tawny juice. When my arms grew tired, I held a Mason jar under the spout, caught a glassful, and drank it down. It was as though we had squeezed the planet and out had poured sweetness.

     What came back to me, musing there by the willow all these years later, was the sound of cider trickling into the bucket, the honeyed taste of it, and my bewilderment that rain and wood and dirt and sun had yielded this juice. Amazing, that we can drink the earth! Amazing, that it quenches our thirst, answers our hunger! Who would have predicted such an outlandish thing? Who, having sipped, can forget that it is the earth we swallow?

15   Well, I had forgotten; or at least I had buried under the habits of casual eating that primal awareness of the meaning of food. And so here was another fundamental perception, renewed for me by my sojourn in Wayland. This image of cider gushing from a spout was my cornucopia, proof of the dazzling abundance that sustains us.

From the cider house I walked downhill to the crossroads. One corner was still a pasture, browsed by three horses, another was a scrubby field grown up in brush and weeds, and the other two corners were expansive lawns. Through the brushy field meandered a creek where I used to hunt frogs with a flashlight and bucket. As in all the Octobers I could remember, the maples in the yards were scarlet, the pasture oaks were butterscotch, and the sycamores along the creek were stripped down to their voluptuous white limbs. Yellow mums and bright red pokers of salvia were still thriving in flowerbeds. A portly older man on a riding mower was cutting one of the lawns, while from a stump beside the driveway an older woman observed his progress, a hand shading her eyes. I knew them from childhood, but their names would not come. I waved, and they waved back. That was conversation enough. I had no desire to speak with them or with anyone in Wayland, since I would have been hard put to explain who I was or why I had come back. Maybe I also wanted to keep the past pure, unmixed with the present.

Because the crossroads are laid out on the grid of survey lines, the blacktop runs due north and south, east and west. The roads were so little traveled that I could stand in the intersection, the tar gummy beneath my boots, and gaze along the pavement in each of the cardinal directions. I had just come from the south, where the church gleamed on its hill. My view to the north was cut off by the railroad, except for the arched opening of the underpass, through which I could see the rusted fence of the Arsenal. Memories of a girl I had courted were beckoning from the west; but less feverish memories beckoned from the opposite direction, and that is where I chose to go next.

A quarter mile east of the crossroads I came to a farm where the Richards family used to breed and board and train horses. Although the name of the mailbox had changed, ten or twelve horses were grazing, as before, in a paddock beside the barn. I leaned against the fence and admired them.

In boyhood I had raised and ridden horses of my own, a stocky mixture of Shetland pony and the high-stepping carriage breed known as hackney. They all came out of a single ornery mare called Belle, and they all had her color, a sorrel coat that grew sleek in summer and shaggy in winter. We used to bring Belle here to the Richards place for mating with a hackney stallion. Years before the voltage of sex began to make my own limbs jerk, I had been amazed by the stallion's urgency and the mare's skittishness. He nipped and nuzzled and pursued her; she dance and wheeled. Their energy seemed too great for the paddock to hold. Surely the fence would give way, the barn itself would fall! Then at length Belle shivered to a standstill and allowed the stallion to lift his forelegs onto her rump, his back legs jigging, hoofs scrambling for purchase, her legs opening to his dark pizzle, the two of them momentarily one great plunging beast. And then, if luck held, twelve months later Belle would open her legs once more and drop a foal. Within minutes of entering the world, the foal would be tottering about on its wobbly stilts, drunk on air, and it would be ramming its muzzle into Belle's belly in search of milk. What a world, that the shivering union of mare and stallion in the barnyard should lead to this new urgency!

20   Musing there by the paddock on this October afternoon, I felt toward the grazing horses a huge affection. Each filled its hide so gloriously. I gave a low whistle. Several massive heads bobbed up and swung toward me, jaws working on grass, ears pricked forward. Their black eyes regarded me soberly, then all but one of the heads returned to grazing. The exception was a palomino gelding, who tossed his white mane, switched his white tail, and started ambling in my direction. As he drew near, I stretched my right arm toward him, palm open. Had I known I would be coming here, I would have brought apples or sugar cubes. My father would have pulled a cigarette from his pocket and offered that. But all I had to offer was the salt on my skin. The palomino lowered his muzzle to my palm, sniffed cautiously, then curled out his rasping red tongue and licked.

I knew that sandpapery stroke on my hand as I knew few other sensations. Just so, my own horses had nibbled oats and sugar and sweat from my palm. The pressure of their tongues made my whole body sway. There by the fence, past and present merged, and I was boy and man, swaying. I reveled in the muscular touch, animal to animal. Contact! It assured me that I was not alone in the world. I was a creature among creatures.

When the palomino lost interest in my right hand, I offered my left. He sniffed idly, and, finding it empty, turned back to the greater temptation of grass. But the rasp of his tongue on my palm stayed with me, another clean, hard fact, another piece of bedrock on which to build a life.

∞

The field across the road from the Richards place was grown up into a young woods, mostly staghorn sumac and cedar and oak. When I had seen it last, twenty-five years earlier, this had been a meadow luxuriant with grasses and wildflowers. Back where the far edge of the field ran up against the sinuous line of willows bordering the creek, there had been a cottage, low and brown, moss growing on the roof, weeds lapping at the windows, a place that looked from a distance more like a forgotten woodpile than a house. Today, no cottage showed above the vigorous trees. But near my feet I could see the twin ruts of the dirt track that used to lead back to the place. I followed them, my boots knocking seeds from thistle and wild rye.

I knew the meadow and the cottage because the woman who used to live here was my science teacher in high school. Fay Givens must have been in her early sixties when I met her in my freshman year. Many students mocked her for being so unthinkably old, for looking like a schoolmarm, for loving science, for trembling when she spoke about nature. She would gaze fervently into a beaker as though an entire galaxy spun before her. She grew so excited while recounting the habits of molecules that she would skip about the lab and clap her spotted hands. She would weep for joy over what swam before her in a microscope. Mrs. Givens wept easily, more often than not because of a wisecrack or prank from one of the students. Our cruelty was a defense against the claim she made on us. For she was inviting us to share her passionate curiosity. She called us to hunger and thirst after knowledge of the universe.

25   I would not join the others in mocking her. I supposed it was pity that held me back, or an ingrained respect for my elders. Only in the fall of my freshman year, on a day when Mrs. Givens brought us here to this field for a botany class, did I realize that I could not mock her because I loved her. She led us through her meadow, naming every plant, twirling the bright fallen leaves, telling which birds ate which berries, opening milkweed pods, disclosing the burrows of groundhogs, parting the weeds to reveal caterpillars and crickets, showing where mice had severed blades of grass. Much of the meadow she had planted, with seeds carried in her pockets from the neighboring countryside. Every few years she burned it, as the Indians had burned the prairies, to keep the woods from reclaiming it.

While Mrs. Givens told us these things in her quavery voice, students kept sidling away to smoke or joke or dabble their hands in the creek, until there were only three of us following her. I stayed with her not from a sense of obedience but from wonder. To know this patch of land, I dimly realized, would be the work of a lifetime. But in knowing it deeply, right down to the foundations, you would comprehend a great deal more, perhaps everything. As she touched the feathery plants of her meadow, as she murmured the names and histories of the creatures who shared the place with her, I came to feel that this was holy ground. And if the meadow was holy, why not the entire earth?

At one point, Mrs. Givens knelt amid the bristly spikes of a tall russet grass. "You see why it's called foxtail, don't you?" she said. "Livestock won't eat it, but you can twist the stalks together and make a fair rope. Farmers used to bind up corn fodder with hanks of foxtail." She grasped one of the spikes, and, with a rake of her thumb, brushed seeds into her palm. She poured a few seeds into my hand and a few into the hands of the other two students who had remained with her. "Now what do you have there?" she ask us.

We stared at the barbed grains in our palms. "Seeds," one of us replied.

"That's the universe unfolding," she told us, "right there in your hands. The same as in every cell of our bodies. Now *why?* That's the question I can't ever get behind. Why should the universe be alive? Why does it obey laws? And why these particular laws? For that matter, why is there a universe at all?" She gave a rollicking laugh. "And isn't it curious that there should be creatures like us who can walk in this beautiful field and puzzle over things?"

30 She asked her questions gaily, and I have carried them with me all these years in the same spirit. They rose in me again on this October afternoon as I followed the dirt track to the spot where her cottage used to be. Stones marked the cellar hole and the front stoop. Brush grew up through the space left by her death. The woods had reclaimed her meadow. Yet the ground still felt holy. Her marveling gaze had disclosed for me the force and shapeliness of things, and that power survived her passing. She taught me that genius is not in our looking but in what we see. If only we could be adequate to the given world, we need not dream of paradise.

Reversing my steps, I walked back to the crossroads and kept going west for a hundred yards or so, until I fetched up before the house where, as a simmering teenager, I had wooed a girl. Let me call her Veronica. She and her family moved from Wayland soon after the Army Corps of Engineers built that needless dam, and so on this October day her house was for me another shell filled only with memory. The present kept abrading the past, however, because during the few minutes while I stood there a grown man in a go-cart kept zooming around the yard, following a deeply gouged path. Every time he roared past, he peered at me from beneath his crash helmet. I nodded, assuming the look of one who is infatuated with loud machines, and that appeared to satisfy him.

Veronica had the face of a queen on the deck of cards with which I learned to play poker, a face I considered perfect. Words tumbled from her lush lips, impulsively, like rabbits fleeing a burrow. Black wavy hair tumbled down her back, twitching nearly to her slender hips. Having learned in marriage what it means to love a woman, I cannot say that what I felt for Veronica was quite love. Nor was it simply lust, although for much of my seventeenth year the mere thought of her set me aching. At that age, I would have been reluctant to see myself as the urgent stallion and Veronica as the skittish mare. Later, I would realize that horseflesh and humanflesh dance to the same ardent music, even though our human dance is constrained by rules that horses never know. During the season of our affection, Veronica was a chased girl but also a chaste one, and I was a polite boy, both of us keenly aware of boundaries.

In her backyard there was a sycamore tree that loomed high over the house, its fat trunk a patchwork of peeling bark and its crooked upper branches as creamy as whole milk. Wooden crossbars nailed to the trunk formed a ladder up to a treehouse. Veronica and I often sat beneath the sycamore on a stone bench, talking and falling silent, aware of parental eyes watching us from the kitchen. With our backs to the house, our sides pressed together, I could risk brushing a hand over her knee, she could run a fingernail under my chin. But even a kiss, our mouths so visibly meeting, would have prompted a visit from the kitchen.

One October day, a day very like this one of my return to Wayland, Veronica and I were sitting on the bench, hunting for words to shape our confusion, when suddenly she leapt to her feet and said, "Let's go up to the treehouse."

35   "We'll get filthy," I said. I glanced with misgiving at my white knit shirt and chino pants, so carefully pressed. Her lemony blouse was protected by a green corduroy jumper.

"It'll wash out," she said, tugging me by the hand.

I stood. Without waiting for me, she kicked off her shoes and clambered up the wooden rungs, but instead of halting at the rickety platform of the treehouse, she kept on, swaying from limb to limb. I watched until the flashing of her bare legs made me look away. When she had gone as high as she dared, high enough to escape the view from the kitchen, she balanced on a branch and called to me, "Come on up! Are you afraid?"

I was afraid—but not of the tree. I stepped onto a crossbrace and started climbing, and as I climbed there was nowhere else to look but up, and there was nothing else to see above me except those white legs parted within the green hoop of her skirt. Her creamy forked limbs and the creamy forked limbs of the sycamore merged in my sight, as they merge now in memory, and I was drawn upward into the pale shadows between her thighs. My knowledge of what I was climbing toward would remain abstract for a number of years. I understood only that where her legs joined there was an opening, a gateway for life coming and going. When I reached Veronica I put my hand, briefly, where my gaze had gone, just far enough to feel the surprising warmth of that secret, satiny place. Then I withdrew my hand and she smoothed her skirt, neither of us risking a word, and we teetered there for a hundred heartbeats on those swaying branches, shaken by inner as well as outer winds. Then the kitchen door creaked open and her mother's voice inquired as to our sanity, and we climbed down. I went first, as though to catch Veronica should she fall, my eyes toward the ground.

The buzzing of the go-cart eventually wore through the husk of memory, and my lungs filled with the present. I became again what I was, a man long married, a man with a daughter the age Veronica had been on that day of our climb into the tree. The sycamore still rose behind the house, twenty-five years taller, crisp brown leaves rattling in the wind, the pale upper limbs as pale and silky as ever.

40   I had a choice of returning to the church by the road or across the stubble of a cornfield. I chose the field. All the way, I could see the white steepled box gleaming on its rise. The only car in the parking lot was mine. Beyond a treeline to the southwest, beyond the annihilating waters of the reservoir that I could not bear to look at, the sun wallowed down toward dusk. The church might already be locked, I thought, so late on a weekday afternoon. Still I did not hurry. My boots scuffed the ridges where corn had stood. Raccoons and crows would find little to feast on in this stubble, for the harvester had plucked it clean. I recalled the biblical injunction to farmers, that they leave the margins of their fields unpicked, for the poor and the beasts. I thought of the margins in a life, in my life, the untended zones beyond the borders of clarity, the encircling wilderness out of which new powers and visions come.

A cornfield is a good approach to a church, for you arrive with dirt on your boots, the smell of greenery in your nostrils, dust on your tongue. The door would be locked, I figured, and the main door was, the broad entrance through which the Methodist women carried their piety and their pies, through which men carried mortgages and mortality, through which children like myself carried headfuls of questions. But the rear door was unlocked. I left my boots on the stoop and went inside.

The back room I entered had the familiarity of a place one returns to in dream: the squeaky pine boards of the floor, the dwarf tables where children would sit on Sundays to color pictures of Jesus, the brass hooks where the choir would hang their robes and the minister his hat, the folding chairs collapsed into a corner, the asthmatic furnace, and on a counter the stack of lathe-turned walnut plates for the offering.

Every few paces I halted, listening. The joints of the church cricked as the sun let go. Birds fussed beyond the windows. But no one else was about; this relieved me; for here least of all was I prepared to explain myself. I had moved too long in circles where to confess an interest in religious things marked one as a charlatan, a sentimentalist, or a fool. No doubt I have all three qualities in my character. But I also have another quality, and that is an unshakable hunger to know who I am, where I am, and into what sort of cosmos I have been so briefly and astonishingly sprung. Whatever combination of shady motives might have led me here, the impulse that shook me right then was a craving to glimpse the very source and circumference of things.

I made my way out through the choir door into the sanctuary. Cushionless pews in somber ranks, uncarpeted floor, exposed beams in the vault overhead and whitewashed plaster on the walls: it was a room fashioned by men and women who knew barns, for preachers who lived out of saddlebags, in honor of a God who cares nothing for ornament. No tapestries, no shrines, no racks of candles, no gold on the alter, no bragging memorials to vanished patrons. The window glass, unstained, let in the plain light of day.

45   I sat in a pew midway along the central aisle and looked out through those clear windows. My reasons for coming here were entwined with that sky full of light. As a boy I had looked out, Sunday after Sunday, to see corn grow and clouds blow, to watch crows bustle among the tops of trees, to follow hawks, unmindful of the Sabbath, on their spiraling hunts, and to sense in all this radiant surge the same rush I felt under my fingers when I pressed a hand to my throat. There was no gulf between outside and inside. We gathered in this room not to withdraw, but more fully to enter the world.

On this day of my return, I kept watching the sky as the light thinned and the darkness thickened. I became afraid. Afraid of dying, yes, but even more of not having lived, afraid of passing my days in a stupor, afraid of squandering my moment in the light. I gripped the pew in front of me to still my trembling. I wanted to dive down to the center of being, touch bedrock, open my eyes and truly, finally, unmistakably see. I shifted my gaze from the darkening window to the altar, to the wooden cross, to the black lip of the Bible showing from the pulpit. But those were only props for a play that was forever in rehearsal, the actors clumsy, the script obscure. I was myself one of the actors, sustained in my own clumsy efforts by the hope that one day the performance would be prefect, and everything would at last come clear.

One cannot summon grace with a whistle. The pew beneath me, the air around me, the darkening windows did not turn to fire. The clouds of unknowing did not part. I sat there for a long while, and then I rose and made my way down the aisle, past the organ, through the choir door and back room, out into the freshening night. On the stoop I drew on my boots and laced them up. The chrome latch of my car was already cool. I drove back through the crossroads with headlights glaring, alert for animals that might dash before me in the confusion of dusk.

There is more to be seen at any crossroads than one can see in a lifetime of looking. My return visit to Wayland was less than two hours long. Once again half a thousand miles distant from that place, making this model from slippery words, I cannot be sure where the pressure of mind has warped the surface of things. If you were to go there, you would not find every detail exactly as I have described it. How could you, bearing as you do a past quite different from mine? No doubt my memory, welling up through these lines, has played tricks with time and space.

What memory is made of I cannot say; my body, at least, is made of atoms on loan from the earth. How implausible, that these atoms should have gathered to form this *I*, this envelope of skin that walks about and strokes horses and tastes apples and trembles with desire in the branches of a sycamore and gazes through the windows of a church at the ordinary sky. Certain moments in one's life cast their influence forward over all the moments that follow. My encounters in Wayland shaped me first as I lived through them, then again as I recalled them during my visit, and now as I write them down. That is of course why I write them down. The self is a fiction. I make up the story of myself with scraps of memory, sensation, reading, and hearsay. It is a tale I whisper against the dark. Only in rare moments of luck or courage do I hush, forget myself entirely, and listen to the silence that precedes and surrounds and follows all speech.

50   If you have been keeping count, you may have toted up seven mysteries, or maybe seven times seven, or maybe seven to the seventh power. My hunch is that, however we count, there is only one mystery. In our nearsightedness, we merely glimpse the light scintillating off the numberless scales of Leviathan, and we take each spark for a separate wonder.

Could we bear to see all the light at once? Could we bear the roar of infinite silence? I sympathize with science, where, in order to answer a question, you limit the variables. You draw a circle within which everything can be measured, and you shut out the rest of the universe. But every enclosure is a makeshift, every boundary an illusion. With great ingenuity, we decipher some of the rules that govern this vast shining dance, but all our efforts could not change the least of them.

Nothing less than the undivided universe can be our true home. Yet how can one speak or even think about the whole of things? Language is of only modest help. Every sentence is a wispy net, capturing a few flecks of meaning. The sun shines without vocabulary. The salmon has no name for the desire that drives it upstream. The newborn groping for the nipple knows hunger long before it knows a single word. Even with an entire dictionary in one's head, one eventually comes to the end of words. Then what? Then drink deep like the baby, swim like the salmon, burn like any brief star.

▪ EXPLORATIONS OF THE TEXT
1. Why does Sanders return to Wayland? He says he arrived there "without quite meaning to." Do you believe him?
2. Why is Sanders "grateful" that Wayland has not changed dramatically since he left? Do you think the story would be different if it had—if, for example, there was a large shopping mall where the parsonage once stood?
3. Sanders recalls his first experience with death. Why did the minister's death affect him so strongly? How does he comfort himself?
4. Sanders mentions several times that Wayland lies on a crossroads. Why is this important? Explain the symbolism.
5. Why is Sanders emotionally affected by the horse's rough tongue on his hand?
6. What impresses Sanders about his biology teacher? Why do the other children laugh at her? What does Sanders have in common with her?

▪ THE READING/WRITING CONNECTION
1. Sanders returns to Wayland twenty-five years after he left. Write a journal entry to yourself twenty-five years in the future. As an alternative, imagine yourself twenty-five years from now returning to your hometown. What would you want to find?
2. Sanders remembers making apple cider and being amazed that food can come from the Earth. List the foods you have eaten recently that have come from the Earth. (This does not include processed items like corn chips!) What do you conclude?

▪ IDEAS FOR WRITING
1. Scott Russell Sanders lists life's seven mysteries as "death, life, beasts, food, mind, sex, and God." Create your own list of life's mysteries, and then write an essay explaining your encounter with two or more of them.

2. Write about a memory from your youth that strongly affected you. Connect this memory to a place, using details to help create a mood to enhance the memory.

3. Compare Sanders's return to his homeland with Aciman's. How are their journeys similar? How do they differ?

PLATO (428–347 B.C.) Translated by Benjamin Jowett

The "Allegory of the Cave" appears in Plato's Republic.

c. 387–367 B.C.

THE ALLEGORY OF THE CAVE

And now, I[1] said, let me show in a figure how far our nature is enlightened or unenlightened:[2]—Behold! human beings housed in an underground cave, which has a long entrance open towards the light and as wide as the interior of the cave; here they have been from their childhood, and have their legs and necks chained, so that they cannot move and can only see before them, being prevented by the chains from turning round their heads. Above and behind them a fire is blazing at a distance, and between the fire and the prisoners there is a raised way; and you will see, if you look, a low wall built along the way, like the screen which marionette players have in front of them, over which they show the puppets.

I see.

And do you see, I said, men passing along the wall carrying all sorts of vessels, and statues and figures of animals made of wood and stone and various materials, which appear over the wall? While carrying their burdens, some of them, as you would expect, are talking, others silent.

You have shown me a strange image, and they are strange prisoners.

5 Like ourselves, I replied; for in the first place do you think they have seen anything of themselves, and of one another, except the shadows which the fire throws on the opposite wall of the cave?

How could they do so, he asked, if throughout their lives they were never allowed to move their heads?

And of the objects which are being carried in like manner they would only see the shadows?

Yes, he said.

And if they were able to converse with one another, would they not suppose that the things they saw were the real things?

10 Very true.

And suppose further that the prison had an echo which came from the other side, would they not be sure to fancy when one of the passers-by spoke that the voice which they heard came from the passing shadow?

No question, he replied.

To them, I said, the truth would be literally nothing but the shadows of the images.

That is certain.

---

[1] From *The Republic*, Book 7. Socrates speaks to Glaucon.

[2] In the original Greek, the words for enlightened and unenlightened are *paideia* and *apaideusia*. The former, depending on context, also may be understood as "education," "culture," or "knowledge." [Translator's note.]

15   And now look again, and see in what manner they would be released from their bonds, and cured of their error, whether the process would naturally be as follows. At first, when any of them is liberated and compelled suddenly to stand up and turn his neck round and walk and look towards the light, he will suffer sharp pains; the glare will distress him, and he will be unable to see the realities of which in his former state he had seen the shadows; and then conceive someone saying to him that what he saw before was an illusion, but that now, when he is approaching nearer to being and his eye is turned towards more real existence, he has a clearer vision,—what will be his reply? And you may further imagine that his instructor is pointing to the objects as they pass and requiring him to name them,—will he not be perplexed? Will he not fancy that the shadows which he formerly saw are truer than the objects which are now shown to him?

    Far truer.

    And if he is compelled to look straight at the light, will he not have a pain in his eyes which will make him turn away to take refuge in the objects of vision which he can see, and which he will conceive to be in reality clearer than the things which are now being shown to him?

    True, he said.

    And suppose once more, that he is reluctantly dragged up that steep and rugged ascent, and held fast until he is forced into the presence of the sun himself, is he not likely to be pained and irritated? When he approaches the light his eyes will be dazzled, and he will not be able to see anything at all of what are now called realities.

20   Not all in a moment, he said.

    He will require to grow accustomed to the sight of the upper world. And first he will see the shadows best, next the reflections of men and other objects in the water, and then the objects themselves; and, when he turned to the heavenly bodies and the heaven itself, he would find it easier to gaze upon the light of the moon and the stars at night than to see the sun or the light of the sun by day?

    Certainly.

    Last of all he will be able to see the sun, not turning aside to the illusory reflections of him in the water, but gazing directly at him in his own proper place, and contemplating him as he is.

    Certainly.

25   He will then proceed to argue that this is he who gives the seasons and the years, and is the guardian of all that is in the visible world, and in a certain way the cause of all things which he and his fellows have been accustomed to behold?

    Clearly, he said, he would arrive at this conclusion after what he had seen.

    And when he remembered his old habitation, and the wisdom of the cave and his fellow-prisoners, do you not suppose that he would felicitate himself on the change, and pity them?

    Certainly, he would.

    And if they were in the habit of conferring honours among themselves on those who were quickest to observe the passing shadows and to remark which of them went before and which followed after and which were together, and who were best able from these observations to divine the future do you think that he would be eager for such honours and glories, or envy those who attained honour and sovereignty among those men? Would he not say with Homer,[3]

    "Better to be a serf, labouring for a landless master,"

---

[3] Greek epic poet (c. ninth–eighth centuries B.C.).

and to endure anything, rather than think as they do and live after their manner?

30　　Yes, he said, I think that he would consent to suffer anything rather than live in this miserable manner.

Imagine once more, I said, such a one coming down suddenly out of the sunlight, and being replaced in his old seat; would he not be certain to have his eyes full of darkness?

To be sure, he said.

And if there were a contest, and he had to compete in measuring the shadows with the prisoners who had never moved out of the cave, while his sight was still weak, and before his eyes had become steady (and the time which would be needed to acquire this new habit of sight might be very considerable), would he not make himself ridiculous? Men would say of him that he had returned from the place above with his eyes ruined; and that it was better not even to think of ascending; and if anyone tried to loose another and lead him up to the light, let them only catch the offender, and they would put him to death.

No question, he said.

35　　This entire allegory, I said, you may now append, dear Glaucon, to the previous argument; the prison-house is the world of sight, the light of the fire is the power of the sun, and you will not misapprehend me if you interpret the journey upwards to be the ascent of the soul into the intellectual world according to my surmise, which, at your desire, I have expressed—whether rightly or wrongly God knows. But, whether true or false, my opinion is that in the world of knowledge the Idea of good appears last of all, and is seen only with an effort; although, when seen, it is inferred to be the universal author of all things beautiful and right, parent of light and of the lord of light in the visible world, and the immediate and supreme source of reason and truth in the intellectual; and that this is the power upon which he who would act rationally either in public or private life must have his eye fixed.

I agree, he said, as far as I am able to understand you.

Moreover, I said, you must agree once more, and not wonder that those who attain to this vision are unwilling to take any part in human affairs; for their souls are ever hastening into the upper world where they desire to dwell; which desire of theirs is very natural, if our allegory may be trusted.

Yes, very natural.

Then, I said, the business of us who are the founders of the State will be to compel the best minds to attain that knowledge which we have already shown to be the greatest of all, namely, the vision of the good; they must make the ascent which we have described; but when they have ascended and seen enough we must now allow them to do as they do now.

40　　What do you mean?

They are permitted to remain in the upper world, refusing to descend again among the prisoners in the cave, and partake of their labours and honours, whether they are worth having or not.

But is not this unjust? he said; ought we to give them a worse life, when they might have a better?

You have again forgotten, my friend, I said, the intention of our law, which does not aim at making any one class in the State happy above the rest; it seeks rather to spread happiness over the whole State, and to hold the citizens together by persuasion and necessity, making each share with others any benefit which he can confer upon the State; and the law aims at producing such citizens, not that they may be left to please themselves, but that they may serve in binding the State together.

True, he said, I had forgotten.

45　　Observe, Glaucon, that we shall do no wrong to our philosophers but rather make a just demand, when we oblige them to have a care and providence of others; we shall explain to them that in other States, men of their class are not obliged to share in the toils of politics; and this is reasonable, for they grow up spontaneously, against the will of the governments in their several States; and things which grow up of themselves, and are indebted to no one for their nurture, cannot fairly be expected to pay dues for a culture which they have never received. But we have brought you into the world to be rulers of the hive, kings of yourselves and of the other citizens, and have educated you far better and more perfectly than they have been educated, and you are better able to share in the double duty. Wherefore each of you, when his turn comes, must go down to rejoin his companions, and acquire with them the habit of seeing things in the dark. As you acquire that habit, you will see ten thousand times better than the inhabitants of the cave, and you will know what the several images are and what they represent, because you have seen the beautiful and just and good in their truth. And thus our State, which is also yours, will be a reality and not a dream only, and will be administered in a spirit unlike that of other States, in which men fight with one another about shadows only and are distracted in the struggle for power, which in their eyes is a great good. Whereas the truth is that the State in which those who are to govern have least ambition to do so is always the best and most quietly governed, and the State in which they are most eager, the worst.

Quite true, he replied.

And will our pupils, when they hear this, refuse to take their turn at the toils of State, when they are allowed to spend the greater part of their time with one another in the heavenly light?

Impossible, he answered; for they are just men, and the commands which we impose upon them are just. But there can be no doubt that every one of them will take office as a stern necessity, contrary to the spirit of our present rulers of State.

Yes, my friend, I said; and there lies the point. You must contrive for your future rulers another and a better life than that of a ruler, and then you may have a well-ordered State; for only in the State which offers this, will they rule who are truly rich, not in gold, but in virtue and wisdom, which are the true blessings of life. Whereas if men who are destitute and starved of such personal goods go to the administration of public affairs, thinking to enrich themselves at the public expense, order there can never be; for they will be fighting about office, and the civil and domestic broils which thus arise will be the ruin of the rulers themselves and of the whole State.

50   Most true, he replied.

And the only life which looks down upon the life of political ambition is that of true philosophy. Do you know of any other?

Indeed, I do not, he said.

And those who govern should not "make love to their employment?" For, if they do there will be rival lovers, and they will fight.

No question.

55   Whom, then, will you compel to become guardians of the State? Surely those who excel in jugement of the means by which a State is administered, and who at the same time have other honours and another and a better life than that of politics?

None but these, he replied.

■ EXPLORATIONS OF THE TEXT

1. Describe or sketch the scene in the cave. Where are the "prisoners," "fire," and "screen"? What do the elements of the allegory represent?
2. What does the "light" signify? Why is it difficult for the prisoners to adjust to the "light"?
3. Describe the stages of illumination presented by Socrates.
4. According to Socrates, how can the "uneducated" and the unenlightened become enlightened?

5. What is the role of the "best minds" of the State? Who are the true rulers? What is the goal of the State? Do you agree to Plato's views?

6. Plato creates a dialogue that is supposed to instruct. Does it? What are the effects of this technique?

■ THE READING/WRITING CONNECTION

1. "Think" Topic: Agree or disagree: "The state in which rulers are most reluctant to govern is always the best . . . and the State in which they are most eager, the worst."

2. Does learning something or changing one's mind cause pain? Cite an incident or experience from your own life.

3. List your own examples and descriptions of Plato's worlds of "shadows" and "light."

4. Create a list of questions you have about this work.

■ IDEAS FOR WRITING

1. Connect Plato's concept of conversion with another experience of awakening, of knowledge, or of faith (e.g., Carver's "Cathedral" in chapter 4).

2. Argue for or against Plato's view of the ideal ruler and the nature of politics.

3. Explore the definitions of the word "see" or "light" in this essay. How do they advance Plato's argument?

4. Write an allegory or a fable to explain an abstraction (death, love, faith).

Albert Camus

Albert Camus (1913–60) was born in Algeria when it was still a French colony. While studying philosophy at the University of Algiers, he organized and directed a small theater company and became involved in political causes. During World War II, he was active in the French Resistance and also wrote The Stranger *(1942), a novel, and* The Myth of Sisyphus *(1942), a philosophical essay, both important works in existential thought and the literature of the absurd. His other works include a novel,* The Plague *(1948), a short story collection,* Exile and the Kingdom *(1958), and a collection of plays,* Caligula and Three Other Plays *(1958). Camus's work earned him the Nobel Prize for Literature in 1957.*

1942

THE MYTH OF SISYPHUS

The gods had condemned Sisyphus to ceaselessly rolling a rock to the top of a mountain, whence the stone would fall back of its own weight. They had thought with some reason that there is no more dreadful punishment than futile and hopeless labor.

If one believes Homer,[1] Sisyphus was the wisest and most prudent of mortals. According to another tradition, however, he was disposed to practice the profession of highwayman. I see no contradiction in this. Opinions differ as to the reasons why he became the futile laborer of the underworld. To begin with, he is accused of a certain levity in regard to the gods. He stole their secrets. Ægina,[2] the daughter of Æsopus, was carried off by Jupiter. The father was shocked by that disappearance and complained to Sisyphus. He, who knew of the abduction, offered to tell about it on condition that Æsopus would give water to the

---

[1] Greek epic poet (c. ninth to eighth centuries B.C.) who wrote about Sisyphus in *The Iliad.*

[2] A story from Greek mythology.

citadel of Corinth. To the celestial thunderbolts he preferred the benediction of water. He was punished for this in the underworld. Homer tells us also that Sisyphus had put Death in chains. Pluto[3] could not endure the sight of his deserted, silent empire. He dispatched the god of war, who liberated Death from the hands of her conqueror.

It is said also that Sisyphus, being near to death, rashly wanted to test his wife's love. He ordered her to cast his unburied body into the middle of the public square. Sisyphus woke up in the underworld. And there, annoyed by an obedience so contrary to human love, he obtained from Pluto permission to return to earth in order to chastise his wife. But when he had seen again the face of this world, enjoyed water and sun, warm stones and the sea, he no longer wanted to go back to the infernal darkness. Recalls, signs of anger, warnings were of no avail. Many years more he lived facing the curve of the gulf, the sparkling sea, and the smiles of earth. A decree of the gods was necessary. Mercury[4] came and seized the impudent man by the collar and, snatching him from his joys, led him forcibly back to the underworld, where his rock was ready for him.

You have already grasped that Sisyphus is the absurd hero. He *is*, as much through his passions as through his torture. His scorn of the gods, his hatred of death, and his passion for life won him that unspeakable penalty in which the whole being is exerted toward accomplishing nothing. This is the price that must be paid for the passions of this earth. Nothing is told us about Sisyphus in the underworld. Myths are made for the imagination to breathe life into them. As for this myth, one sees merely the whole effort of a body straining to raise the huge stone, to roll it and push it up a slope a hundred times over; one sees the face screwed up, the cheek tight against the stone, the shoulder bracing the clay-covered mass, the foot wedging it, the fresh start with arms outstretched, the wholly human security of two earth-clotted hands. At the very end of his long effort measured by skyless space and time without depth, the purpose is achieved. Then Sisyphus watches the stone rush down in a few moments toward that lower world whence he will have to push it up again toward the summit. He goes back down to the plain.

5   It is during that return, that pause, that Sisyphus interests me. A face that toils so close to stones is already stone itself! I see that man going back down with a heavy yet measured step toward the torment of which he will never know the end. That hour like a breathing space which returns as surely as his suffering, that is the hour of consciousness. At each of those moments when he leaves the heights and gradually sinks toward the lairs of the gods, he is superior to his fate. He is stronger than his rock.

If this myth is tragic, that is because its hero is conscious. Where would his torture be, indeed, if at every step the hope of succeeding upheld him? The workman of today works every day in his life at the same tasks, and this fate is no less absurd. But it is tragic only at the rare moments when it becomes conscious. Sisyphus, proletarian of the gods, powerless and rebellious, knows the whole extent of his wretched condition: it is what he thinks of during his descent. The lucidity that was to constitute his torture at the same time crowns his victory. There is no fate that cannot be surmounted by scorn.

If the descent is thus sometimes performed in sorrow, it can also take place in joy. This word is not too much. Again I fancy Sisyphus returning toward his rock, and the sorrow was in the beginning. When the images of earth cling too tightly to memory, when the call of happiness becomes too insistent, it happens that melancholy rises in man's heart: this is the rock's victory, this is the rock itself. The boundless grief is too heavy to bear. These are

---

[3] Greek god of the underworld.
[4] Roman god; messenger to the other gods.

our nights of Gethsemane.[5] But crushing truths perish from being acknowledged. Thus, Oedipus at the outset obeys fate without knowing it. But from the moment he knows, his tragedy begins. Yet at the same moment, blind and desperate, he realizes that the only bond linking him to the world is the cool hand of a girl. Then a tremendous remark rings out: "Despite so many ordeals, my advanced age and the nobility of my soul make me conclude that all is well." Sophocles' Oedipus, like Dostoevsky's Kirilov,[6] thus gives the recipe for the absurd victory. Ancient wisdom confirms modern heroism.

One does not discover the absurd without being tempted to write a manual of happiness. "What! by such narrow ways—?" There is but one world, however. Happiness and the absurd are two sons of the same earth. They are inseparable. It would be a mistake to say that happiness necessarily springs from the absurd discovery. It happens as well that the feeling of the absurd springs from happiness. "I conclude that all is well," says Oedipus, and that remark is sacred. It echoes in the wild and limited universe of man. It teaches that all is not, has not been, exhausted. It drives out of this world a god who had come into it with dissatisfaction and a preference for futile sufferings. It makes a fate a human matter, which must be settled among men.

All Sisyphus' silent joy is contained therein. His fate belongs to him. His rock is his thing. Likewise, the absurd man, when he contemplates his torment, silences all the idols. In the universe suddenly restored to its silence, the myriad wondering little voices of the earth rise up. Unconscious, secret calls, invitations from all the faces, they are the necessary reverse and price of victory. There is no sun without shadow, and it is essential to know the night. The absurd man says yes and his effort will henceforth be unceasing. If there is a personal fate, there is no higher destiny, or at least there is but one which he concludes is inevitable and despicable. For the rest, he knows himself to be the master of his days. At that subtle moment when man glances backward over his life, Sisyphus returning toward his rock, in that slight pivoting he contemplates that series of unrelated actions which becomes his fate, created by him, combined under his memory's eye and soon sealed by his death. Thus, convinced of the wholly human origin of all that is human, a blind man eager to see who knows that the night has no end, he is still on the go. The rock is still rolling.

10   I leave Sisyphus at the foot of the mountain! One always finds one's burden again. But Sisyphus teaches the higher fidelity that negates the gods and raises rocks. He too concludes that all is well. This universe henceforth without a master seems to him neither sterile nor futile. Each atom of that stone, each mineral flake of that night-filled mountain, in itself forms a world. The struggle itself toward the heights is enough to fill a man's heart. One must imagine Sisyphus happy.

■ **EXPLORATIONS OF THE TEXT**

1. Why does Camus include two different versions of Sisyphus's fate? What common thread connects them? What does Sisyphus represent to Camus?
2. Explain: "When he leaves the heights and gradually sinks toward the lairs of the gods, he is superior to his fate."
3. What does Camus mean by consciousness? Why does the "tragic" occur at the point of being "conscious"?

---

[5] Garden outside Jerusalem. A reference to Jesus's discussion with his disciples the night before his crucifixion.

[6] Character who kills himself in Dostoevsky's novel, *The Possessed* (1871).

4. What does Camus mean by the "absurd"? Why is Sisyphus "the absurd hero"? What is the "absurd" man's fate?

5. This excerpt is part of Camus's longer essay considered by critics to be a meditation on suicide. What arguments does Camus offer to oppose suicide?

6. Characterize the voice of the persona in the essay and his approach to the audience.

7. Compare Camus's and Plato's views of enlightenment.

■ **THE READING/WRITING CONNECTION**

1. In a paragraph explore contemporary parallels for each aspect of the allegory (Sisyphus, his meaningless labor, his act of defiance, the gods).

2. "Think" Topic: Do you agree with Camus's view of the absurd universe? his vision of people's fates in such a world?

■ **IDEAS FOR WRITING**

1. How does Camus define tragedy?

2. Write an essay discussing Camus's concept of the absurd.

3. Do you agree with Camus's statement: "The absurd man says yes, and his effort will henceforth be unceasing. If there is a personal fate, there is no higher destiny"?

■ WRITING ASSIGNMENTS ■

1. Compare views of the future in "Bloodchild," "Harrison Bergeron," "The Handsomest Drowned Man in the World" and "The Ones Who Walk Away from Omelas."

2. Compare views of obedience and conformity suggested in Vonnegut's "Harrison Bergeron," in Butler's "Bloodchild," and in Le Guin's "The Ones Who Walk Away from Omelas."

3. Examine the views of global and environmental issues presented in the following: "Stone Olives"; "My Name Is 'I Am Living'"; and "Ghosts."

4. a. What does Anzaldúa mean by "borderland"?
   b. Describe a "borderland" in which you live.
   c. Compare your "borderland" with a work in this chapter that presents a "borderland."
   d. Compare Anzaldúa's view of "the borderland" with Agosín's conception of exile in her poetry.

5. Discuss the concept of exile presented in three works in this chapter.

6. a. Explain the concept of renewal in one work in this chapter.
   b. The possibility and impossibility of renewal and rebirth in a global world are recurring themes in this chapter. Compare and contrast three visions of renewal.
   c. Which works present the most convincing and/or believable visions?

7. Explicate "Diving into the Wreck" or one of Rilke's sonnets. Focus on point of view, imagery, figurative language, and form. (See chapter 10.)

8. a. Explore the water or natural imagery in three works in this chapter.
   b. Explain kite imagery in *"Master Harold" . . . and the Boys.*

9. Compare the points of view of three speakers in three poems. How does point of view relate to tone, imagery, and theme?

10. a. What new myths of the future emerge in "Diving into the Wreck," "The Second Coming" and "The Chinese Mountain Fox"?
    b. Create your own myth or allegory for a view of the future.

11. Contrast Walker's vision in "Am I Blue?" with the themes of Szymborska's poems.

12. a. Ask several people to envision the world in 2102. What do they fear about the future, and what do they wish for the future?
    b. Analyze your results. What patterns do you perceive?
    c. Use one interview as the basis for an essay.
    d. Compare one of your interviewee's views of the future with a work in this chapter.
13. Create a science fiction short story. Develop a view of a utopian or dystopian society.
14. Choose one of the following topics as the basis for research: genocide, AIDS, terrorism, ecological issues (global warming, decimation of the rain forests, acid rain, extinction of species, overpopulation), stem cell research, genetic engineering, world hunger, world drought, nuclear war or holocaust, a contemporary Middle Eastern poet or novelist, Utopian or dystopian literature, existentialism, or science fiction.
15. Write a character analysis of Hally or Sam from *"Master Harold" . . . and the Boys.* (Refer to the model in chapter 11.)
16. Compare two works that present hopeful views of the future.
17. a. Evaluate your favorite work in this chapter. Argue for its inclusion in the next edition of this text. Write a letter to the authors.
    b. Evaluate your favorite work in this book. Assume that your audience is the publisher of this anthology.
    c. Select one work from *Legacies* that has changed your views. Explain your reaction to it. How did it change your perspective?
18. Write an argument, agreeing or disagreeing with Yeats's "The Second Coming." You may refer to other works in this chapter.
19. Create comments for several characters from works in this chapter about the following: "the secrets/of never having a home" (Linda Hogan, "Heritage").
20. Discuss the ideal versus the reality of harmony among people of different races and/or cultures in the works in this chapter.
21. Compare the views of Plato, Camus, and Márquez on the cosmos and on human beings and their destinies. Compare the philosophies of life depicted in the works.
22. Discuss the collision of the Old and the New Worlds presented in "Bloodchild," "Harrison Bergeron," "Prayer for the Living," and "The Ones Who Walk Away from Omelas."
23. a. What is your view of the relationship between the individual and the community? The community may include nonhuman creatures.
    b. Discuss the sense of community represented in three works in this chapter.
    c. Which work exemplifies your view of the interrelationship between the individual and the community?
24. Many stories in this chapter, as in the last chapter, portray humans as being violent toward one another. Meanwhile, most of us seek to live in a peaceful community. Do you consider this to be a basic human contradiction? Explain.
25. In Lahiri's story, "The Third and Final Continent," the protagonist reads in a guidebook, "The pace of life in North America is different from Britain . . . Everybody feels he must get to the top." Do you think this is an accurate depiction of the United States? Explain by referring to two stories in this or another chapter.
26. *Legacies* begins with an examination of identity in chapter 4. Explain in an essay how one person can shape events, leading to the conflicts portrayed in chapter 7 or to the bridging of barriers as seen in chapter 8. Refer to three works as examples.
27. The theme of the stranger is ancient; it has been captured in Old English poetry, science fiction, and in other genres. Why might this idea be so compelling to writers and readers? Explain using examples from your own experience and from two works in this volume.
28. Joan Didion, Mary Oliver, Herman Melville, W. S. Merwin, and Scott Russell Sanders all perceive of organic life as fleeting, while the rocks and bones of the planet alone have

lasting substance. Why might this perspective be significant when thinking of planetary history? Human history? Is this idea meant to be comforting or frightening?

29. Sylvia, in Sarah Orne Jewett's "A White Heron" (chapter 4), is treated to a larger perspective of the world when she climbs the large pine tree. Choose one of the selections in this chapter, and explain how the author, like Jewett, changes a character's or the reader's perspective through the use of imagery, symbolism, or metaphor.

30. Melville's "The Encantadas" and Oliver's "Ghosts" refer to the timelessness of nature. Write about this topic, using examples from your own experience.

31. In "Wayland," Sanders explains that we live on a whole earth, yet the largeness of it is too overwhelming for us to comprehend. Referring to two other works in this chapter, show how people attempt to comprehend wholeness or to fragment our environment as a way to control it.

32. In Keats's "Ode on a Grecian Urn," the speaker states, "beauty is truth, truth beauty,— that is all/Ye know on earth, and all ye need to know," suggesting that the urge to conquer death through art is universal. Discuss this portrayal of this theme in Okri's "A Prayer from the Living," Moore's "Dance in America," Yeats's "Sailing to Byzantium," or Stevens's "The Idea of Order at Key West." Does art transcend death?

33. Virginia Shabatay contends that "strangers in literature offer us images of individuals who live in some ways separate from the community." These stories lead us "to imagine an event from the side of another person, to grasp his or her uniqueness." "The ability to appreciate otherness in individuals and communicate is a way of redeeming the stranger and of redeeming the world."

a. Write an essay explaining your personal and literary encounters with the stranger. What have they taught you?

b. Compare your state of "strangerhood" with that of a character in a work in this chapter. See Michael Mei's "Lost in Transition."

◼ STUDENT ESSAYS ◼

Student Essay: Cultural Analysis

MICHAEL MEI

Lost in Transition

Despite the subtle different transitional problems encountered by immigrants, the variables ultimately remain the same. They must assimilate themselves into a society with common, indelible goals inspired by the American dream or face the possibility of alienation. Jhumpa Lahiri's "The Third and Final Continent," from the short-story collection *Interpreter of Maladies*, reminds audiences that immigrants establish the diverse cultural society of the United States, but at a personal cost. Lahiri exposes the exploitation of the malleability and vulnerabilities of immigrants who are quick to conform for the purposes of adaptation and survival. Slowly but gradually, Lahiri's narrator epitomizes people who do not understand the intrinsic value of what they give up until it becomes irrevocably lost.

The title, "The Third and Final Continent," implies a long journey from one culture and society to the next—in this case, only to end up in America, a place where theoretically all identities cohesively weld. The narrator travels from the subcontinent of India (named because of its geographical placement and geological shape) to England, and then finally to the third and final continent, the United States. The narrator traverses three continents, representative of the three stages of the transition from his native Indian roots to a new American lifestyle. Just as a day is characterized by morning, afternoon, and night, the narrator's transition begins with light, hopes, and aspirations, but ends in the night, when he finds himself submerged by the darkness of a culture he has yet to understand or adapt to. The third *and* final continent represents two ideas: The narrator will finally stop moving from one impermanent situation to the next perceived destination and settle into a land where he can nurture his identity. On the pessimistic end of this spectrum, the narrator will settle into a melting-pot culture that will annihilate what remains of his ethnic roots from years of travel into and through three culturally different atmospheres.

Upon his arrival, the narrator (nameless by intention to represent all of the immigrants or former immigrants on U.S. soil who come knowing who they were but end up not knowing where they fit in because of their dual identities) willfully accepts the challenges and adversities of cultural adaptation. When he learns that "Americans [drive] on the right side of the road, not the left (India), and that they call a lift an elevator and an engaged phone busy (England)" (1228), he accepts and begins feeling comfortable with his new culture, expressions, and traditions. Prior to his Massachusetts Avenue apartment, he had "never lived in the home of a person who was not Indian" (1229), but now, he finds himself becoming familiarized with the infrastructure of developed North American society (i.e., post office and banks) in addition to the ubiquitous burgers and hotdogs on diner menus (1228). Having his cultural roots cultivated in India, his identity thus continues an aggravated process of decomposition since his arduous travels have considerably weakened his native Indian identity.

The protagonist learns quickly that American culture is characterized by the notion that "everybody feels he must get to the top" (1228), his first exposure to the American dream. Although an elusive ideal, many immigrants center their daily routines around the goal of seeing their version of the dream come to fruition. The actions of his landlady, Mrs. Croft, symbolize the habitual routines imposed on immigrant citizens. Each evening when the narrator returns home, he finds her sitting on the same bench inviting him to sit down and revel in the fact that an American man had landed and placed a United States flag on the moon (1230, 1232). Landing on the moon was without doubt one of humanity's greatest accomplishments but, on the consequential end, fueled the development of America's arrogance as a culture. Immigrants became seduced by a culture that yielded prosperity and a proud sense of nationalism.

Not only was there nationalism, there was also a growing sense of the affirmation in being nurtured in a capitalist economy. As a result, immigrants began considering themselves, in the context of this story, as American Indians rather than Indian Americans. Despite the subtle difference, and only in title, the distinction stands unequivocally. Upon realizing his uprooting, the narrator attempts to save his ethnic roots and cultural identity by complying with his arranged marriage to Mala. Despite resorting to an unorthodox method of preservation, the narrator persists in balancing his newly acquired American habits with his native Indian traditions.

Through the narrator's marriage, Lahiri explicitly reveals the innumerable cultural traditions that must continue, even if partially, to be practiced and/or implemented despite entering countries embedded with contrasting practices and/or traditions. The persistent notion of arranged marriages illuminates the often incomplete (accidental or engineered) cultural assimilation of immigrants. As a young Indian immigrant, he has been immersed into American society so much that his breakfast consists of cereal and milk, contrary to his traditional curry eggs and rice. Yet, when the discussion moves to marriage, a lifelong and life-altering event, he passively expresses his contentment with the arrangements already made for him by his brother and sister-in-law in India. "[He regards] the proposition with neither objection nor enthusiasm. It was a duty expected of [him], as it was expected of every man" (1231). Although merely acquiescing to tradition, the narrator expresses his contentment to preserve his heritage and background on a subconscious level of reality. For many Americans with backgrounds in foreign cultures, life becomes a matter of maintaining cultural values and traditions as a means of resisting cultural hegemony and preserving vestiges of their cultural identities. The narrator thus understands that the benefits of this arranged marriage far exceed any conceivable harm accompanying this institution. After arriving in the United States, Mala offers him a lifelong companion who shares similar cultural values and traditions from their native homeland. She also provides a character with whom the narrator can identify his immigrant struggles (1238). Her presence (even though the relationship between the two is not constructed on the foundations of love) offers the narrator a compassionate reminder that his roots are from India and that it is in his best interests to preserve such intrinsic aspects of his social life, even if it means having to conform to such a, by American standards, vehemently frowned upon institution. While the idea of an arranged marriage stands far from being a liberating experience, it is a comparatively small price to pay for the sake of cultural maintenance.

The narrator's relationship with Mrs. Croft, though vicariously, presents him another opportunity (consciously or unconsciously) to preserve his ethnic roots. Helen (Mrs. Croft's daughter) visits only on a sporadic basis and leaves the elderly woman confined to her apartment. And even with her presence, the relationship between mother and daughter does not have deep intimacy, but the companionship that Helen fails to offer her mother, the protagonist succeeds in providing. He thinks back to how his mother died after years of widowhood-induced insanity and how he never had the chance to fulfill any notion of filial piety. This prompts him to acquiesce to each of Mrs. Croft's demands (1234). He checks the lock, accompanies her on her bench for conversations, professes the flag on the moon is "splendid," and always remembers to heat up her soup in the evenings (1231, 1232, 1234). "Although Helen had seemed friendly enough, a small part of [him] worried that she might accuse [him] of negligence if anything were to happen. Helen didn't seem worried" (1234). Helen, whose focus manifests itself in her self-interests demonstrated by her occasional and lack of perfunctory interest in such visits, typifies the American lifestyle that the narrator acknowledges he must resist. He does so by willingly acquiring the job that Helen fails to complete. Available to Mrs. Croft, he shows the respect with which a child should honor his or her parents, respect that he did not have the chance to pay his mother. However, his responsibility towards the landlady clearly illustrates that while he has acclimatized to physical elements of North American society like food, his cultural ethics and expectations have never been neglected.

However, the vast difficulties of transmitting and maintaining a native culture, especially in the successive generations, resurface when the narrator introduces his son. The United States continues to be a unique home to many immigrants who are able to survive only by the ethnic-American identities and social adjustments they are coerced into developing and making. Thus, for individuals like the narrator and his wife, as much as they are able to preserve parts of their cultural identities by implementing cultural practices and complying with traditional codes of conduct, the generations that they will watch grow up will retain even less of what they have accomplished. With every ensuing generation, immigrants experience a habitual decline in awareness of ethnic principles and practices of ancestral traditions. Typically, by the third or fourth generation, immigrant roots are so far removed that children like the narrator's son's children will begin to drop the title of Indian from Indian American altogether in pursuit of the American Dream and the rewards of a material culture. The narrator's son, if imbued with a sense of get-rich-now, will inevitably sacrifice his identity, discovering that to prosper in a racially and ethnically conscious country, he must become strictly American.

"The Third and Final Continent" reflects on the cultural transition from a native Indian culture based on subsistence to a culture of constant material acquisition. The narrator acknowledges in his final lines that

> [w]hile the astronauts, heroes forever, spent more hours on the moon, [he has] remained in this new world for nearly thirty years. [He] knows [his] achievement is quite ordinary. [He is] not the only man to seek his fortune far from home, and certainly not the first. Still, there are times [he is] bewildered by each mile [he has] traveled, each meal [he has] eaten, each person [he has] known and each room in which [he has] slept. As ordinary as it all appears, there are times when it is beyond [his] imagination. (1239)

The narrator humbly admits that his experiences cannot compare to the extraordinary first men and women who exchanged lives of familiarity in their native lands for lives isolated in unfamiliar territory and circumstances. He leads by example in pursuit of new dreams and aspirations in America, but he warns readers of the complementary but, potentially, overwhelming process of assimilation that, if continued at the current pace, threatens to dry out his cultural identity. People's infatuation with the prospects of financial stability and economic prosperity causes people to forget their need for native culture and identity. The American ethos inspires and reminds people of the foundation of motivation and persistence on which the original thirteen colonies rose, but today it has transpired into an oppressive hegemonic force that obliterates diverse cultures and ethnicities rather than encourage acceptance or tolerance for cultural multiplicity.

Lahiri's short stories remind me of just how much immigrants of one nation do, in actuality, face the same adversities and joys that immigrants of another country experience. Despite being born a citizen of the United States, I was raised in a sheltered, traditional Chinese household by Chinese immigrant parents. Until I reached the public school system of New York, I was utterly oblivious to the functions of American society. Thus, when I entered a classroom with students of all colors for the first time, I felt foreign in an atmosphere that required a considerable amount of time for me to become acclimated to. However, after tedious repetitions of daily routines that included making the Pledge of Allegiance to the United States each day at 10 A.M., like the narrator gets used to the fact that he needed to express how "splendid" a spectacle America's flag being stabbed on the moon was, I grew more and more accustomed to the American traditions that constituted the way of life in the United States. And like the narrator's preferences for food, I, too, went from eating traditional Chinese breakfasts to having cereal and milk in the mornings. Once I was exposed to the American lifestyles that I had been sheltered from as a child, I began to associate "an ends justifies the means" mentality in adapting to a new style of life. I found myself practicing less and less of the Chinese traditions, which included praying on every first and fifteenth of the Chinese Lunar Calendar. I even had the audacity to end my enrollment at Chinese school on the weekends in addition to neglecting to practice my calligraphy of Chinese characters altogether. The result? I am now an English major with Chinese roots that are so close to decimation that if I do not do something to revive these roots soon, the bridge that connects my children to my parents will be completely obliterated. However, for the sake of cultural maintenance, I will continue to practice Chinese traditions and cultural practices that remind me from time to time that I am a Chinese American and not that "Banana" everyone refers to me as.

Jhumpa Lahiri reminds us that whether we are immigrants or the children of immigrants, we must learn to weigh both the intrinsic and extrinsic benefits of assimilating into a new culture, especially one as pervasive as America's. There are always fringe benefits that possess the potential to be a curse in disguise. While she implicitly requests American citizens to be tolerant of foreign ethnic groups and cultures, she also asserts that immigrants like the protagonist must learn to resist the temptations of American hegemony.

Works Cited

Lahiri, Jhumpa. "The Third and Final Continent." *Legacies,* 3rd ed. Eds. Jan Zlotnik
    Schmidt, Carley Bogarad, and Lynne Crockett. Australia: Thomson, 2005. 1227–
    1239.

··PART THREE··

Reading and Writing
about the Genres

· CHAPTER 9 ·

Fiction

Fiction is the imagined creation of character and action for the purpose of conveying a vision of life. Like forms of nonfictional narration (storytelling), fiction depends on a recording of a sequence of events (as in historical rendering) and on an organization of incident and action (as in reporting). Fiction also requires a colorful, vivid depiction of characters and action (as in oral storytelling).

Fundamental to short fiction are a concentration on characters and the changes in characters brought about by events. Discussing the components of plot in *Aspects of the Novel,* E. M. Forster differentiates between an account of incidents and plot. He states that "The king died, and then the queen died" does not form a story line for fiction; however, the following presents the kernel of a tale, "The king died, and the queen died of grief." In the second version, the fiction emerges from the effect of the husband's death on the wife; a vision of mourning and loss is implied.

FORMS OF NARRATIVE

The earliest forms of narrative stories are the **myths** that ancient people conceived to explain their worlds—natural phenomena, human behavior, beliefs, and values—and to satisfy their need for transcendent experiences and meanings. Creation myths appear in the Old Testament, in Norse legends, and in Native American tribal lore. Greek and Roman myths of gods and goddesses and the creation of the world are written in such works as Thesiod's *Theogeny* and Ovid's *Metamorphoses.* The *Vedas,* the sacred Sanskrit texts of the Hindus, explore the origins of the gods of India.

Many myths explain facts of life, death, and immortality. "Coyote and the Shadow People," a Nez Percé myth, for example, relates the story of Coyote, who longs for his wife's return from the dead. The Death Spirit permits Coyote's wife to live in the world as a shadow for a three-day trial, but, because Coyote touches his wife's shadow, he loses the opportunity to regain his wife permanently. In "This Is What It Mean to Say Phoenix, Arizona," Sherman Alexie intertwines Native American myth and legend in the story of two young men's journey of self-discovery.

Some stories, called **parables,** provide moral instruction or convey moral, religious, or spiritual truths. Consider the story of the prodigal son in the New Testament, a story in which the younger son squanders his share of his father's wealth in riotous living, while his older brother stays and works with the father. The prodigal son endures hard times and returns to his father to ask for mercy, and the father joyously welcomes him and celebrates his homecoming. When the elder son protests, the father replies, "Be glad: for this thy brother was dead and is alive again and was lost and is found." This tale teaches the need for charity, compassion, and forgiveness. Ursula Le Guin's "The Ones Who Walk Away

1378

from Omelas," a short story in parabolic form, suggests the impact of scapegoating in an imagined society.

A **fable,** another kind of moralizing story, commonly features animals or inanimate objects endowed with human qualities. Their experiences and behavior teach a lesson, stated explicitly at the conclusion of the tale. Some of the oldest fables may be traced to Aesop, a sixth-century Roman. In his story, "The Tortoise and the Hare," for instance, the hare, conceited and overly confident, falls asleep during a race while the slower tortoise plods ahead and wins. The moral of the tale is "slow but steady wins the race." In "My Life with the Wave," Octavio Paz, working out of the tradition of the fable, creates a male character who falls in love with a wave, a female lover (chapter 6). The lesson of the story concerns the power and consequences of romantic love.

Every culture also has its epics—stories of the exploits of heroes and mythical creatures—and folk tales that provide entertainment and present moral truths. Like myths, **epic poems** were passed from generation to generation as strictly oral entertainment before being written down and read as literature. *The Iliad* and *The Odyssey,* the oldest known Western epics, recount the exploits of the warriors of the Trojan War and the wanderings of the Greek hero Odysseus after the war. The *Mahabharata,* a monumental Hindu epic, depicts the strife of two Indian royal families and the spiritual development of the Indian hero, Krishna.

Each culture enjoys folk tales. The fairy tales we learned as children from Hans Christian Andersen or from the Brothers Grimm were actually Danish and German stories. *Cinderella,* for example, has many incarnations as a French folk tale transcribed by Perrault; as a German story recorded by the Brothers Grimm; as Algonquin Indian and Chinese tales. Although each version transmits different cultural values, fairy tales around the world convey recurring and familiar motifs: they portray the struggle between parents and children, between innocence and corruption, between good and evil, and between life and death. Short story writers often draw on folk and fairy tales in the development of character, plot, and theme. Gabriel Garciá Márquez deliberately titles "The Handsomest Drowned Man in the World" (chapter 8) a "Tale for Children" to highlight its fairy tale elements. In chapter 4, the thematic cluster, "Fairy Tales," includes short fiction that incorporates fairy-tale motifs.

Other forms of narrative emerged in the Middle Ages and the Renaissance. The epic, the tale of the hero, became transformed into romances in which knights fought battles for the love of their ladies. Sometimes the quest for romance also became a quest for spiritual salvation, as in many of the stories of King Arthur, his knights of the Round Table, and their search for the Holy Grail, as in the poem, *Sir Gawain and the Green Knight.*

The word **novella** came into existence to describe the short tales of Boccacio written in the fourteenth century. Now the term signifies a work of fiction longer than and more expansive than a short story but less complex than a novel. They were stories of love, designed as courtly entertainment. Boccacio's *The Decameron* is a collection of one hundred short stories told by ten residents of Florence who attempted to escape the plague.

Lady Murasaki of Japan wrote the first **novel,** *The Tale of Genji,* in 1022. The novel emerged as a form of fictional prose narrative in the seventeenth century in England with the advent of a middle class that had both the leisure and a level of literacy to read and to support magazines. The first English protonovels were Aphra Behn's *Oroonoko* (1688) and Daniel Defoe's *Robinson Crusoe* (1719), a tale of a man abandoned on an island. The reading public and the demand for novels grew in the eighteenth century. The nineteenth century, however, became the great age of the British novel. The fullest representation of a story line, the novel captures a moment in time, a moment in a culture. This form incorporates the breadth and depth created by development of many characters, plots, subplots, and themes.

The invention of the modern **short story** is often attributed to Edgar Allen Poe. His most famous works include "The Masque of the Red Death," "The Pit and the Pendulum," and "The

Telltale Heart." Poe suggested that a reader should be able complete a story in a single sitting. In the nineteenth century, the tradition of the American short story began with the publication of works by Poe, Nathaniel Hawthorne, Herman Melville, Mary Wilkins Freeman, Sarah Orne Jewett, and Kate Chopin. See, for example, Jewett's "A White Heron" (chapter 4).

A single concentrated story line, a single plot that involves a conflict or crisis that leads to a climax and to a resolution, and a limited number of characters distinguish the short story. Another usual feature of the genre is that it, like poetry, is compressed so that all elements may develop character, plot, and theme.

The modern short story was influenced by James Joyce's conception that a central character should be involved in a conflict or momentary experience that leads to discovery or to an awakening—in Joyce's term—an epiphany. However, contemporary short stories portray characters caught in experiences that may not lead to a climax, resolution, or realization. The stories conclude without the characters undergoing any change or gaining any great insight. The characters—in stasis—remain in a cycle of sterility. According to its creators, this form of development mirrors the absurdity and lack of meaning in the modern world. Finally, many fiction writers today, aware of the history of the genre, mix narrative techniques and modes to create new forms of the short story. One new form is the metafiction in which the story itself reflects on the process of writing a story. Margaret Atwood's "Happy Endings" (chapter 6) is an example of this form.

ELEMENTS OF FICTION

Point of View

Many elements of fiction—**point of view, setting, plot, characters, conflict, symbolism,** and **theme**—combine to create a work. We use these elements when we create even a simple, informal narrative, as when we recount a tragedy reported in the news or describe the previous night's party. Read this ghost story:

> I woke up in the middle of the night because I thought someone was watching me. When I awakened, a girl, dressed in a white nightgown, stood at the foot of my bed. She had long, yellow hair and large, luminous eyes, staring at me. I was petrified. I freaked. I closed my eyes. She was still there. I pulled the pillow over my head. When I lifted the pillow, she had disappeared. Only later, much later, did I tell my husband this story. He told me that he had shared the same experience. Later, much later, I learned that a little girl had died in our house in Kentucky, in the house where we experienced those nightmares.

Many elements of fiction are prevalent in this short tale, including a certain **point of view,** a narrative perspective. The choice of narrative perspective shapes the direction of the tale and is intertwined with plot, character, and theme. In this case, the story presents a first-person, singular point of view—"I." Writers create a sense of immediacy and personal involvement with first-person narrators.

An alternative to the first-person point of view is third-person narrative. To recognize the third-person point of view, look for the use of "he," "she," and "they." In third-person, the narrative perspective presents the characters and action and tells the tale from a certain distance. Recast the ghost story into third-person, using *she* and *her* in place of *I* and *me.* Such a change may result in a loss of intimacy, immediacy, and urgency.

There are several forms of third-person narration. An omniscient narrator assumes the vantage point of knowing everything in his or her characters' minds. Readers gain insights into the consciousness of all characters in the story. A narrator with limited knowledge discloses information about one or several, but not all, of the narrative points of view. In detached or dramatic narrative point of view, the speaker describes the characters and actions with no insight into characters' feelings. If the ghost story appeared in third-person, the narrator could develop his or her perspective, or possibly the husband's, or even the ghost's point of view. The story would progress differently. Consider this excerpt from Joyce Carol Oates' "Where Are You Going, Where Have You Been?" (chapter 4):

> Her name was Connie. She was fifteen and she had a quick nervous giggling habit of craning her neck to glance into mirrors, or checking other people's faces to make sure her own was all right. Her mother, who noticed everything and knew everything and who hadn't much reason any longer to look at her own face, always scolded Connie about it. "Stop gawking at yourself, who are you? You think you're so pretty?" she would say. Connie would raise her eyebrows at these familiar complaints and look right through her mother, into a shadowy vision of herself as she was right at that moment: she knew she was pretty and that was everything. Her mother had been pretty once too, if you could believe those old snapshots in the album, but now her looks were gone and that was why she was always after Connie.

Oates creates a limited third-person narrative perspective to depict her main character's struggles in adolescence. The reader gains insight into Connie's feelings about her appearance and about her disdainful attitudes toward her mother, but does not learn anything about Connie from the mother's point of view.

We also may characterize a narrator as participant or as nonparticipant. A participant narrator is a presence within the story who creates and engages in the action. A nonparticipant narrator observes the action. In the ghost story, a participant first-person narrator tells her own tale. Imagine this first-person narrator as a nonparticipant in the action, a woman who recounts a tale she heard from her friend. The story would have a different dramatic impact.

A participant narrator also may be trustworthy or untrustworthy. We consider a narrator trustworthy when we accept his or her view of the situation, when we think it is credible or, perhaps, represents the position of the author. In a story with an untrustworthy narrator, we question the narrative's stance and ask if it is credible, biased, or even, perhaps, delusional or hysterical. We question the validity of the point of view and realize that a distinction exists between the narrative and authorial point of view. In the ghost story, the narrator is trustworthy because her responses seem skeptical and because she qualifies her discussion. We accept her version of the truth. Imagine an untrustworthy narrator, extremely overwrought, talking to the ghost—we would not believe her version.

Setting

Setting is the location, time, place, and/or environment in which the story takes place. In the ghost story, the location is the bedroom of a house, the time is night and the present; and the environment is a middle-class household in the 1980s in Kentucky. The setting creates a particular mood, sense of place, and context. The ghost story would have little impact if the event occurred in broad daylight, in a city, and in a less scientific and skeptical age.

Plot

A **plot** presents the sequence of events in a story. In a short story the sequence of events is concentrated and does not necessarily represent actual time. Events in daily life, perhaps having taken place over a period of time, or events that appear random or fragmentary are often shaped, developed, and given cohesive form. For example, routine trips to work on the bus may become the basis for a central episode in a story, or a chance encounter with an old friend may be transformed into the central action of a tale. In the case of the ghost story, the sighting may represent many nights of uneasy feelings or partial glimpses.

Since a short story is so compressed, usually the sequence of events narrows to a single moment, a series of moments, or action that reveals a larger truth of character and life. The sequence builds to a **climax,** a high point of action. In an adventure or horror short story, the climax may be an apex of suspense; in a short story focused on character, the climactic point may be a moment of discovery, awakening, or revelation. For example, in the ghost story, the most important event is not the appearance of the spirit, but the discovery that a child had died in the house, and, indeed, that the apparition could be a real ghost; in short, the narrator begins to recognize the possibility of supernatural occurrences.

Short story writers also manipulate the sequence of events in a story; they may not present the events in chronological (time) order. For example, the story may begin in the middle of the action or at the end of the sequence, and then the narrator may *flash back*—move back in time—to the beginning of the action. The ghost story, for instance, could have begun with the sighting of the ghost and then could have returned to the beginning of the night's sleep. Flashback techniques add dramatic impact and meaning to the unfolding events since the reader already knows what will transpire; the technique also may shift the focus from the plot to character development since attention moves away from the rendering of the action. *Flash forward* is another method of manipulating time in which the narrator relates the beginning of the tale, then moves quickly to the ending, and then returns to the beginning of the story. This technique adds dramatic impact and irony (double meanings) to each stage of the action since the reader is aware of the contribution of each moment to the unfolding of the action. In a rendering of the ghost story, the narrator could have quickly moved to the sighting, then returned to see partial, mysterious glimpses of the face, hair, clothes, and eyes of a figure—these glimpses would have dramatic impact for a reader. Short stories also may unfold through associations and may move backward and forward in time.

Conflict

Conflict is the tension between two forces; the exposition of a problem; an internal battle between two forces, psychic or external. Major conflicts in fiction arise between people and nature, between people and their environments, among people, or within a person. In the ghost story, the conflict, an internal struggle, centers on whether the narrator believes that she has seen a ghost. The plot of the short story concentrates on and develops such a conflict until it is resolved after a moment of crisis. In conventional short stories, the climax prompts the resolution through a moment of reckoning, recognition, awakening, or discovery. However, many contemporary short stories do not present resolutions of conflict. Again in the ghost story, no answers exist to test the validity of the reported sighting of the apparition. The story leaves questions open. The story ends in an ambivalent, mysterious way.

Character

The short story primarily concentrates on the presentation of **characters:** the people in the story and their conflicts. In the ghost story, the characters are the first-person narrator, the apparition, and the husband. The conflict concerns the tension within the narrator between believing and negating the presence of the little girl. We learn about characters through action, dialogue, and physical appearance. Their personalities evolve through events and through interaction with others.

In fiction, E. M. Forster has distinguished between **round** and **flat** characters. Round characters are multidimensional, capable of growth and change. Flat characters, according to Forster, are one-dimensional and often stereotypical. The effective short story concentrates on presenting at least one round character in conflict with others. Because of the length and complicated texture of a short story, the writer of this genre cannot develop as many characters in depth as can writers of such longer forms as the novella or novel. In a further draft of the ghost story, the narrator could become the round character and the ghost of the little girl, the flat, one-dimensional character.

Language

The **language** in a short story is compressed. Each word is well chosen and contributes to the impact of the whole. Sharp, vivid sensory details involve the reader in the world of the narrator, in setting, in characters, in the unfolding drama of the plot. In addition, short story writers often choose elements of poetic diction: images, figurative language, symbolism, allusion, and irony to create their worlds (see chapter 3).

Short story writers also work with the **denotations** (dictionary definitions) and **connotations** (associations) of words to create effect. Because the form is concentrated, each word must have impact and add to the presentation of theme (messages of the work). Think of the word "luminous" in the ghost story as it alludes to the physical presence of the ghost as transparent and also refers to the girl's wide-eyed stare. The connotations lead readers to form a picture of a ghost: mysterious, innocent, and yet scary.

Another element of language is the texture of the prose: the sounds and the rhythms of the language. Storytelling, originally oral entertainment, does exist as "music." Think of the tension between the liquid "l" sounds and the staccato "e" words, which reflects the narrator's state of mind. The repetition of the "s" and the "d" sounds evoke feelings of sharpness and of hardness, appropriate to a confrontation with the supernatural.

In addition, aspects of style that create the rhythm of language are repetition and parallelism (repeated and balanced wording). The short, simple sentences evoke the fear felt by the narrator.

For stories to be powerful, writers also avoid **clichés** (hackneyed or overused expressions and figures of speech). Clichés detract from impact because they belong to everyday conversational speech, not to the heightened language of fiction; and, therefore, they are jarring and destructive to the mood. They also do not add descriptive detail or image because they cannot evoke word pictures since their meanings are predictable and often taken for granted. In the ghost story, the narrator reverts to a level of colloquial language: "freaked." This shift is jarring. She could have used a stronger verb to convey both her fear and astonishment.

Tone

Tone, the sense of the narrator, emerges from the connotations, the inferences, of every word. Tone also conveys the attitude of the narrator toward his or her subject, for example, characters and events in the work. Apparent from the first word, tone colors every detail of the work—dialogue, imagery, symbol, and setting. In the ghost story, the tone shifts from fear to puzzlement to mystery as the narrator learns about the death of the child.

Symbolism

A **symbol** is a person, place, object, thing, name, title, aspect of setting that suggests something beyond itself and has a range of meanings. Since a short story, like poetry, is compressed, all aspects of the story—title, setting, characters' names, appearance, dialogue, and events of the plot—may contain symbolic meanings and create the theme. For example, even in the informal telling of the ghost story, the girl's yellow hair and white dress suggest her innocence; the head under the pillow, the denial of truth.

Theme

The **theme** of the short story is the message presented by the work. No story has a single central idea; there may be several themes. As he or she is crafting the story, the writer may be conscious of several themes of the work and may shape it with these ideas in mind. In addition, readers may discover other messages from careful analyses of the text. In the ghost story, one theme certainly is the mystery of supernatural occurrences. Another theme concerns the omnipresence of death and the human drive to negate that reality.

All aspects of an effective short story may create themes: point of view, setting, plot, character, conflict, tone, and symbolism. In the narrator's story one theme centers on the impossibility of escaping death. The point of view—first person—gives the reader the thoughts of the woman facing the appearance of the ghost and the fact of death itself. The setting also develops this theme: it is the "middle of the night," a time of dream and unreality that contrasts with the stark presence of the apparition. The tension and conflict in the plot center on the narrator's vision of the ghost—is she real? The stark, simple language builds the confrontation and mood of the work. The gesture of "[pulling] the pillow over [her] head" symbolically suggests the narrator's need for denial. This short story then becomes a tightly woven anecdote about facing the supernatural and the irrefutable fact of death.

THE READING/WRITING PROCESS: FICTION

In addition to critical reading responses, we recommend a process for understanding fiction. First, read the story. Involve yourself on the level of point of view and plot. Ask yourself who is telling the story, and explore your reactions to the narrative point of view. Is the narrator part of the story? Is the narrator objective about the events? Is the narrator trustworthy? As you read, remember the main events and follow the sequence of action. Who are the main characters? With whom do you sympathize? Locate the problems and conflicts. As you read, notice the shifts in conflict and the development of crisis. At the story's conclusion, ask yourself if the conflicts are resolved. Ask if any of the characters have changed. How have they developed? Ask if your sympathies and involvement with certain characters have shifted. What messages have you discovered in the text? Explore the emotional impact of the work. Ask how you felt after finishing the story. In a second or third reading, analyze the function of point of view, setting, tone, symbolism, word choice, detail, imagery, and figurative language used by the writer in building the story. Throughout your reading, explore your own reactions and associations with the story. Assess your reactions to the themes of the narrative.

CHECKLIST FOR READING SHORT FICTION

1. What point of view is apparent? first person? third person? omniscient? limited? detached? What is the impact of this choice of narrative perspective? Participant or nonparticipant narrative point of view?

2. What is the setting of the story? time? place? environment? What moods are created by the setting in the story? What social, cultural, historical contexts are established by setting?

3. What are the key events of the plot? Does the plot build to a climax? What are the conflicts in the story? Are the conflicts resolved? Is there a moment of awakening or discovery?

4. Who are the main characters? Are they round? flat? With whom do you relate? Sympathize? How are they related to each other? What is the role of minor characters?

5. What is the tone of the story? What can you tell about the tone from the opening? Why? From key descriptions and details?

6. Characterize word choice. Is there vivid detail? Figurative language? Irony?

7. What are the symbolic details (title, names, setting, gesture, objects, events)? How does symbolism create theme?

8. What are the themes of the work? Do all elements of the story contribute to the theme?

▪ STUDENT PORTFOLIO ▪

Response to Kate Chopin's "The Story of an Hour"

KATE CHOPIN

THE STORY OF AN HOUR

Knowing that Mrs. Mallard was afflicted with a heart trouble, great care was taken to break to her as gently as possible the news of her husband's death.

It was her sister Josephine who told her, in broken sentences; veiled hints that revealed in half concealing. Her husband's friend Richards was there, too, near her. It was he who had been in the newspaper office when intelligence of the railroad disaster was received, with Brently Mallard's name leading the list of "killed." He had only taken the time to assure himself of its truth by a second telegram, and had hastened to forestall any less careful, less tender friend in bearing the sad message.

She did not hear the story as many women have heard the same, with a paralyzed inability to accept its significance. She wept at once, with sudden, wild abandonment, in her sister's arms. When the storm of grief had spent itself she went away to her room alone. She would have no one follow her.

There stood, facing the open window, a comfortable, roomy armchair. Into this she sank, pressed down by a physical exhaustion that haunted her body and seemed to reach into her soul.

5   She could see in the open square before her house the tops of trees that were all aquiver with the new spring life. The delicious breath of rain was in the air. In the street below a peddler was crying his wares. The notes of a distant song which some one was singing reached her faintly, and countless sparrows were twittering in the eaves.

There were patches of blue sky showing here and there through the clouds that had met and piled one above the other in the west facing her window.

She sat with her head thrown back upon the cushion of the chair, quite motionless, except when a sob came up into her throat and shook her, as a child who had cried itself to sleep continues to sob in its dreams.

She was young, with a fair, calm face, whose lines bespoke repression and even a certain strength. But now there was a dull stare in her eyes, whose gaze was fixed away off yonder on one of those patches of blue sky. It was not a glance of reflection, but rather indicated a suspension of intelligent thought.

There was something coming to her and she was waiting for it, fearfully. What was it? She did not know; it was too subtle and elusive to name. But she felt it, creeping out of the sky, reaching toward her through the sounds, the scents, the color that filled the air.

10   Now her bosom rose and fell tumultuously. She was beginning to recognize this thing that was approaching to possess her, and she was striving to beat it back with her will—as powerless as her two white slender hands would have been.

When she abandoned herself a little whispered word escaped her slightly parted lips. She said it over and over under her breath: "free, free, free!" The vacant stare and the look of terror that had followed it went from her eyes. They stayed keen and bright. Her pulses beat fast, and the cursing blood warmed and relaxed every inch of her body.

She did not stop to ask if it were or were not a monstrous joy that held her. A clear and exalted perception enabled her to dismiss the suggestion as trivial.

She knew that she would weep again when she saw the kind, tender hands folded in death; the face that had never looked save with love upon her, fixed and gray and dead. But she saw beyond that bitter moment a long procession of years to come that would belong to her absolutely. And she opened and spread her arms out to them in welcome.

There would be no one to live for her during those coming years; she would live for herself. There would be no powerful will bending hers in that blind persistence with which men and women believe they have a right to impose a private will upon a fellow-creature. A kind intention or a cruel intention made the act seem no less a crime as she looked upon it in that brief moment of illumination.

15   And yet she had loved him—sometimes. Often she had not. What did it matter! What could love, the unsolved mystery, count for in face of this possession of self-assertion which she suddenly recognized as the strongest impulse of her being!

"Free! Body and soul free!" she kept whispering.

Josephine was kneeling before the closed door with her lips to the keyhole, imploring for admission. "Louise, open the door! I beg; open the door—you will make yourself ill. What are you doing, Louise? For heaven's sake open the door."

"Go away. I am not making myself ill." No; she was drinking in a very elixir of life through that open window.

Her fancy was running riot along those days ahead of her. Spring days, and summer days, and all sorts of days that would be her own. She breathed a quick prayer that life might be long. It was only yesterday she had thought with a shudder that life might be long.

20   She arose at length and opened the door to her sister's importunities. There was a feverish triumph in her eyes, and she carried herself unwittingly like a goddess of Victory. She clasped her sister's waist, and together they descended the stairs. Richards stood waiting for them at the bottom.

Someone was opening the front door with a latchkey. It was Brently Mallard who entered, a little travel-stained, composedly carrying his grip-sack and umbrella. He had been far from the scene of the accident, and did not even know there had been one. He stood amazed at Josephine's piercing cry; at Richards' quick motion to screen him from the view of his wife.

But Richards was too late.

When the doctors came they said she had died of heart disease—of joy that kills.

∞

The following works present a student's reaction responses to Kate Chopin's "The Story of an Hour." To demonstrate the process of constructing a response essay to a work, we include Maria Taylor's initial journal entry and three drafts of her essay.

The thesis of the essay evolved from Taylor's freewrite (composed in her journal), designed to spur personal connections with the work. Students in the class were asked to write a monologue in the voice of Mrs. Mallard. After the completion of her assignment, Taylor discovered that she empathized with Mrs. Mallard and shared her feelings of imprisonment. Taylor's position is voiced in the lines: "I want to be free to be for me, only me." She begins with Mrs. Mallard's exclamations (" 'free, free, free. . . . ' ") and moves to her own: "I never really felt free," and "It was the only house I knew as woman." She shifts from speaking in Mrs. Mallard's voice to voicing her own ideas and experiences. The discovery gained from the freewrite became the kernel of the first draft of the reaction essay. In this version, she expresses her yearning.

A collage writer, Taylor jumps from association to association: household duties, her relationship with her husband, the memories of his goodness and his abuse, her need for "balance," her panic, eating disorder, and fear. In her next two drafts, she more freely articulates her connections with Mrs. Mallard, organizes her thoughts, treats her responses in a systematic manner, and arranges them in stages that follow Mrs. Mallard's process of discovering her desire to be free. She also includes the quotations from the work that spark her insights.

Journal Entry

Freewrite: A Monologue Spoken by Mrs. Mallard
By Maria Taylor

I've said it over and over under my breath, "I want to be free, free, free." I want to be free to be for me, only me. To be no-one's mother, daughter, wife. I want to be free to come and go as I please, when I please, how I please. The words "free, free, free" speak to my longing soul.

I never really felt free. I went from Dad's household to my husband's control. The transition was easy for me; it was a role I always wanted. It was expected of me. It was the only role I knew as woman.

As a female, I was to be wife, mother, daughter, depending on "man" in all roles. I never realized then, in playing out my role I was always depending on a man for my well being. If I needed nurturing, I went to him. If I needed money, I went to him.

Note following reading of the story:

I could see so clearly the truth in the quotation "free." I see the dichotomy in her.

Taylor's First Draft

I want to enjoy a relationship based on equality. Do I sound selfish? Well—it may be—but maybe it's my time, huh? I don't want to cook, clean, do laundry, shop, have to be home, say when I'll be home, where I'll be etc., be questioned about anything—anymore. I want to be free, and yet, I want to be connected. I suppose that would be with and to him. He is my husband, and he has been a good one. He is the father of my four incredible children, and he has been a good father. But there are the horrendous memories of his drinking and emotional and psychological abuse, all of which he denies to this day. He's demeaning of me and my role as woman, wife, person. I want out. I feel selfish and wrong and guilty, but I cannot continue to be a wife anymore. I want a balance in my life. No, this isn't even true. I want it all to be for me now. I know I cannot fulfill my roles anymore because my own health is beginning to fail. I have "panic attacks" regularly, and they are the most painful, terrorizing feelings I have ever experienced. I cannot control my food intake, anymore. Food has become my friend, lover, consoler, comforter. All things except what it truly is—I feel my own life has been fused to others for so long, and in that fusion, I've become lost. I am so frightened. I wonder how I can go on and on and what is left for me? Would I have been better off never knowing him or any man and just be for me?

Conclusion?

Is there ever a relationship between man and woman that is based on true equality and true freedom? Isn't love supposed to give these gifts? Will I, like Mrs. Mallard, have to die before I am truly free?

In the next draft, Taylor creates paragraphs to explore each topic.

Taylor's Second Draft

It's almost too difficult to write, to express on paper, but I know this story. I have in many ways lived it.

I suppose you would have to be married for a while to understand Mrs. Mallard. I have been married for thirty-one years, so I understand her. (We can only really understand someone when we have walked in her shoes.)

I like Chopin's Mrs. Mallard's wish to be free. Free to be, for me—only me, no-one else. Free to sleep and eat, come and go—do, not do, whatever I want, when I want, for a while.

And yet am I afraid of this? Yes, for I have never lived for myself, lived by myself. I have never taken care of myself financially. I always took care of others and was taken care of financially by others.

I went from Dad's home living under his jurisdiction to my husband's home living under his jurisdiction. This sounds so cynical; doesn't it? But this is how I feel and how it was.

I never felt "free." Their control was always so subtle and elusive, but I knew it was there like Mr. Mallard and that I had to walk within the lines of their boundaries. If not, I would be abandoned, emotionally, physically and financially. Then how would I exist? I was programmed to believe I could not live without them.

And yet I love him. I believe I do anyway. But I so want to be free. I want to be like Mrs. Mallard looking out the window. I want to continue to love him, but I do not want to live within the confines of what he believes that love should be.

In the final draft, Taylor develops substantial responses and connection to the work.

Taylor's Final Draft "Free, Free, Free": Chopin's "The Story of an Hour"

Under her breath, Mrs. Mallard says, "free, free, free!" Over and over again. I have said the same words over and over again under my breath. I want to be free. Free to be for me, only me, to be no one's daughter, wife, or mother. I do not want to be caregiver, support, keeper. I want to live only for myself. I want to be free to come and go as I please, when I please, how I please.

The adjectives, "free, free, free," speak to my longing soul. And yet I am afraid. Yes, for I have never lived for myself, lived by myself. I have never taken care of myself financially. In many ways, I am like Mrs. Mallard's sobbing child. I always took care of others and was taken care of financially by others. I took care of both my parents when they were ill. Then I became a wife and mother. Emotionally, all of my energies were out there, caring for others all my life, leaving very little energy for nurturing myself. Consequently, I feel uncomfortable and I question whether or not I can be free. At fifty-one, this is a sorry commentary. Like Mrs. Mallard, I have never lived for myself.

I went from Dad's house, living under his jurisdiction, to my husband's home, living under his jurisdiction. Coming from a patriarchal home and environment, I thought that this simply was the way that it was for all women. I thought that the "powerful will bending [mine] in that blind persistence with which men and women believe they have a right to impose a private will upon a fellow-creature" was to be expected and the way it should be.

I never felt free. Their control was always so subtle and elusive, but I knew it was there and that I had to walk within the lines of their boundaries. If not, I would be abandoned, emotionally, physically and financially. Then how would I exist, survive? I was programmed to believe I could not live without them. As a result, I felt as if I danced around this big bear that lived in the center of the living room for most of my life. I do not want to dance anymore. Like Mrs. Mallard, who said "she would live for herself," I too wish for autonomy.

I want to continue a relationship with him, but I do not want to live within the confines of what he believes that love should be. I want to feel "spring days, and summer days . . . that would be [my] own."

5   My husband is a domineering man. He often treats me in a way that suffocates me. His constant questions, his lack of trust, his knee-jerk anger oppress and fatigue me. I understand his fear, that he will lose me, that he doesn't understand me any more, and I empathize with him. But I no longer can claim this shattering as my own. When I do, I become shattered myself. I love my husband, and yet I want to be free.

I want to enjoy a relationship based on equality and freedom. Can a relationship between a man and a woman be based on these things? Is it possible? Is it possible with my relationship with him? Has he snatched that away from me, too? Would I have been happier never knowing my love or any man and just be, for me? Will I, like Mrs. Mallard, have to die before I feel free, before I feel that "monstrous joy"—the "joy that kills?"

In the introduction to this last draft, Taylor states her thesis, the yearning "to be free" that she shares with Mrs. Mallard. In the middle paragraphs, she explains the origins of that desire, tracing her need for autonomy to her family background (paragraph 2), and to her marriage, an extension of that "patriarchal home and environment" (paragraph 3). She next presents (in paragraphs 5 and 6) her desire for autonomy; finally, she articulates her dilemma: the conflict between her love and loyalty to her husband and her need to find a "relationship based on equality and freedom." Her conclusion contains her pessimistic assessment: "Will I, like Mrs. Mallard, have to die before I feel free, before I feel that 'monstrous joy'—the 'joy that kills'?" She builds the essay to its dramatic conclusion.

Taylor also strives to include more quotations from the story so that the progression in her thinking mirrors, in some ways, the logic and progression of the plot of "The Story of An Hour." She begins by citing Mrs. Mallard's wish to be "free, free, free," which appears midway in Chopin's story. In the description of her relationship to her husband, she includes Mrs. Mallard's realization that after her husband's death, there will be no "powerful will bending [her]" into submission. By following the pattern of Mrs. Mallard's recognition, Taylor makes their situations analogous and strengthens the comparison of her situation with the character's plight. They both came to similar despairing assessments of the possibility of "true equality" in the relation of men and women. Chopin's character dies . . . death is her only release. Taylor despairs of the possibility of finding relationships based on a "true balance" between the sexes.

Taylor's connections with "The Story of an Hour" are made explicit: her understanding of Mrs. Mallard's imprisonment caused by her social role; Mrs. Mallard's inability to change her circumstances; the protagonist's inhibited desire for freedom and her ambivalent feelings toward her husband; her desire for release from a marriage that denies her autonomy.

· CHAPTER 10 ·

Poetry

When asked to define poetry, a student responded, "Poems make words dance." This brief reply stimulates many provocative ideas and images concerning a difficult question. The excellent answer implies that poems are metaphorical, paradoxical, and dynamic. In poetry the images do not work if they do not inspire sudden connection and insight. The words must "dance," or they cannot create effective and astonishing meanings. This definition also suggests the necessity of rhythm, beat, and accent. If the work lacks these intrinsic qualities, it is not poetry.

What else does this definition signify? It indicates that poems create themes, character, and contexts through compressed language, through figures of speech, through economy of form, and through sound. If academic definitions always require appropriate language, then the student's answer insists upon such words. If academic definitions insist upon rhythm or meter, then the student's answer alludes to rhythm through the word "dance." If academic definitions require that poetry elicit feelings and imagination, the student's answer implies that poetry creates these responses in the reader or the listener.

The word "make," above all, connotes *art* and insists that words have the power of the visual to imitate, signify, please, mean, and construct new realities and truths. In ancient cultures, chants and religious rituals were poetry; epics and dramas were poetry. We appreciate the enduring value of the genre as an accessible source of wisdom and pleasure, a significant form of enrichment and of redemption, and an expression of the deepest experiences and truths of human existence.

KINDS OF POETRY

In general, every poem falls into one of three broad categories: **narrative poetry** tells a story, **lyric poetry** gives a brief account of the person's feelings, ideas, or moods, and **dramatic poetry** presents monologues and soliloquies.

Narrative Poetry

Any poem that spins a tale may be defined as a *narrative* work. In Gwendolyn Brooks' "The Chicago Defender Sends a Man to Little Rock" (chapter 7), the speaker catalogues the daily actions of citizens who bear children, celebrate holidays, play baseball, attend concerts, and love each other. The persona wants to report that "they are like people everywhere." Another story, however, exists in Little Rock; people are "hurling spittle, rocks, garbage, and fruit." The speaker must recount this conflict. Why? The Supreme Court had ordered desegregation of the schools in an historic decision in the case of *Brown* vs. *The Board of Education,*

1391

a case never directly mentioned in Brooks' narrative. Because of its political context, "The Chicago Defender Sends a Man to Little Rock" may be called a *protest poem.*

Other forms of narrative poetry include the epic and the ballad. **Epics,** written in many eras and in many cultures, derive from oral tradition and describe the adventures and accomplishments of great heroes. The story assumes grand proportions and often includes supernatural beings and their actions that create monumental consequences. The language of epics is formal and figurative, and almost all epics share similar conventions. *The Iliad* and *The Odyssey* by Homer (Greek), *The Epic of Gilgamesh* (Babylonian), *Sundiata* (Mali), and *Beowulf* (Anglo-Saxon) represent works in this tradition.

Ballads, another form of narrative poetry, also derive from oral tradition since originally they were songs. Literary ballads include most features of the oral form: repetition and refrain—phrases or lines reappearing at certain places in the poem. Ballads alternate lines of eight and six syllables, with rhymes in the second and fourth lines. Not every ballad must be written in the standard stanzaic pattern. Not every ballad contains a refrain. The Beatles, for example, wrote a humorous song about "Rocky Raccoon" that mimics "Frankie and Johnny"; both are ballads. More serious works tell stories of young women such as Thomas Hardy's "The Ruined Maid."

Lyric Poetry

Lyrics are short and subjective; in these poems, the speakers describe their thoughts or feelings. The original definition of the lyric meant a song accompanied by a lyre. This category includes the following forms:

1. An **elegy** mourns the death of a particular person, or sometimes, the inexorable fate of humans, their mortality. Ben Jonson's "On My First Son" presents a father's grief, a sorrow so deep that it renders his identity as a poet meaningless (see chapter 5).

2. A **meditation** centers on a particular object as a method for consideration of metaphysical ideas. (see "Dover Beach" by Mathew Arnold in chapter 6.)

3. An **ode,** a song of praise, is long, serious, and formal in all of its aspects. It always has a complex stanzaic pattern. Keats' "Ode on a Grecian Urn" is an example of this form (see chapter 8).

4. A **pastoral** celebrates the idyllic nature of country life. James Wright's "A Blessing" represents a modern version of the pastoral (see chapter 8).

Matsuo Bashō, a Japanese poet who lived in the seventeenth century, wrote haiku, unrhymed three-line poems with seventeen syllables. Haiku also may be considered lyrical in nature:

Sleeping at noon
the body of the blue heron
poised in nobility
(hiru neburu / aosagi no mi no / tōtosayo)
(translated by Earl Miner)

Notice that Bashō has compressed a strong image into three lines. The meaning depends on sudden insight and a connection between the heron's pose and a spiritual stance. At first glance, the poem seems to celebrate the serene immobility of the heron, "sleeping at noon." The closing line, however, implies a moment of spiritual awareness that transcends the physical.

Dramatic Poetry

In **dramatic poetry**, the speaker becomes an actor. In "Girl," (see chapter 5), for example, Jamaica Kincaid creates a **monologue** for a mother who is attempting to inculcate gender roles into her young daughter.

Other forms of dramatic poems include epistolary monologues—letters written as poems. In the most familiar example of this kind of work, Ezra Pound's "The River Merchant's Wife: A Letter," loosely translated from a poem in Chinese written by Rihaku (also known as Li Po), the speaker has loved her husband deeply since childhood. The young Chinese wife waits patiently for his return and expresses her loneliness and longing in the letter. Admired as a model of dignity and of marital love, this eighth-century poem by Li Po presents great autobiographical detail in highly controlled and terse language.

Performance poetry, another kind of dramatic verse, has its roots in the oral tradition—in oral storytelling—particularly in its use of anaphora, in its conversational tone, and in its direct interaction with an audience. The form also developed out of the Dadaist artistic movement of the 1920s that advocated stream-of-consciousness writing, out of the works of the Beats of the 1950s who experimented with forms of spontaneous prose and poetry, and out of the improvisational structure of jazz. The form also was influenced by rap music and hip-hop—with their emphasis on word play, rhyme, street slang, and political messages. Performance poetry got its start at New York City's Nuyorican Café, founded by Miguel Algarin and Miguel Piñero, and was popularized by Russell Simmons's *Def Poetry Jam*, a dramatic enactment of a poetry slam that was featured on Broadway. Sarah Jones's poem, "God Bless America" (see chapter 7), is an example of the form.

Although readers wish to designate strict categories for poems, some works defy such classification. Contemporary poetry often combines narrative and lyric modes; poets often extend the limits of traditional forms; and in their experiments, they create new language and images; they step into the borderland between narration and lyric, a place where new voices may sing and be heard.

ELEMENTS OF POETRY

Voice

Poems, like fiction, present speakers who tell about events, experiences, emotions, or ideas. The poet remains separate from the persona or speaker, although in some works little distance exists between the two. In all cases, however, the reader should assume that poet and speaker have distinct identities. Often the poet creates a voice exceedingly different from him or herself. The speaker may even be anonymous.

One of the best methods of interpreting poetry is to define the voice, to discover as much as possible about its quality, mood, and concerns. In "Danaë," a voice poem based on Greek myth, the anonymous poet alludes to the imprisonment of the virgin, Danaë, by her father, a crime that he committed to circumvent the fulfillment of a prophecy that predicted the death of Acrisius at the hands of his grandson. Zeus, however, seduced Danaë in a shower of gold; and from this magical union, Perseus was born. Eventually the curse was fulfilled. Listen to the voice of Danaë. Consider the poem, and answer the following questions:

1. Who is the speaker?
2. What is the point of view?
3. What can you tell about the speaker? What is the situation of the speaker?
4. How is the story told? What story is being told?

5. What details and words characterize the speaker?
6. To whom does the speaker talk? Who is the audience?

DANAË

to be born to a curse
is all of history
that dark will
is all I knew
5 in the dark cavern
I lived
I saw just the
immediate edge of my body
the dark shadings and contours
10 of that shell
and you live in it
as if it were light
as if it gave you light
then one day
15 a rain came
a gold rain
a sheen of rain
a cool yellow breeze
a shimmer of gold
20 a sift of gold all over my skin
a wash of yellow light
and in this way
he came
my child
25 came as rain fell
came as silently
to life
came to me
a rinse of yellow gold
30 that boy child
my words
my history
my unsaid self
a blessing
35 too fragile
to be dreamt

The poet retells the story of Danaë with a first-person point of view and adds some new details to the ancient Greek myth. The persona expresses her sadness and loneliness as she considers her body as something to "live in." Subject to "the dark will," she exists in shadow "as if it were light." She seems concerned about the body, its history; and she feels resignation. She does not speak in anger, but she acknowledges indirectly that men and gods have power over her body. Yet the men are completely absent from the speaker's story.

The poet devotes half of the poem to the gold rain that impregnates Danaë and gives her a son. The repetition of "rain," "gold," "yellow," and "light" introduces a sense of quiet joy into the poem. These details about the conception of the child allow the speaker to claim herself, her history, and her child through words. In this connection between language and the body, the poet transforms Danaë into a contemporary woman.

Tone

The **tone** of a poem establishes the mood of the piece, the changing emotions of the speaker, or the attitude of the persona toward the subject. The poem may be sad, angry, shocking, nostalgic, or humorous. In "Daddy" by Sylvia Plath, the speaker begins with a mildly angry tone as she announces her rejection of her father, but the voice quickly becomes sad as she admits, "you died before I had time" (chapter 5). In the monologue, the young woman, the persona, calls her father a god, a Nazi, and the devil. At the end, she attempts to exorcise him through a darkly humorous allusion to Dracula in vampire movies:

> There's a stake in your fat black heart
> And the villagers never liked you.
> They are dancing and stamping on you.
> They always knew it was you.
> 5 Daddy, daddy, you bastard, I'm through.

Here the speaker refers to the only method that kills a vampire: a stake in the heart. She indicates that the villagers in Transylvania always knew that the vampire really was Count Dracula who lived in the eerie castle above the town. As a final shock, the speaker calls "Daddy" a "bastard" and declares wildly that she is "through." Some critics find the tone too exaggerated and do not believe that the ending convinces; others praise the poem for its devastating truth about the impact of the death of a parent and about the overwhelming anger of the betrayed and bereaved child.

Theme

Poems can explore any **theme**, any central idea. The poet can write about the terror of war, the ecstasy of love or religion, the mysteries or certainties of life or ideas. A poem may protest injustice, define itself, or mourn the death of a particular person. Many of these themes recur frequently. In every culture, poets write about time, death, love, and art. They celebrate achievements and laugh at and satirize human error and folly.

In order to determine the theme of a poem, look at images, voice, symbols, form, and sound. Combined, these aspects create the conceptions central to meaning. Because poetry is allusive and highly compressed, however, many interpretations become possible. Each reader may discover a different theme; but most of the time, a poem, rich in language and content, leads to certain agreements about thematic intent.

CHASING FIRE ENGINES

> The women in my family
> always chase fire engines,
> sirens wailing in their ears,

long funnels down and in,
5 a throb in their arms—
the urge to touch men,
the big hoses, eyes on the stream
arching toward smoke.
I was born with arson
10 in my heart, the desire
to light fires, to set
aflame every hand
that brushes my wrist,
to incinerate.

15 Now I dream of a stranger,
incendiary fingers on my breast.
I rise toward shadow,
light a match to identify
the face, to reach
20 the tender place;
and I smell ashes,
push the hand aside,
heat cooling

as I wake, women
25 in my family running
after fire engines, watching
men dowse flames,
water arching and arching:
the spray, the spray.

30 Then you turn to me in sleep,
move your leg over mine,
easy in your skin,
and I slide under you,
old luminations surround us,
35 the longing for arson
rising in my throat,
a moan subsides
as I chase the engines.
Fires, burning everywhere,
40 light the pillow where
your head circles mine.

In "Chasing Fire Engines," the persona speaks of natural curiosity and obsessions about sexuality; she feels the "heat cooling" and fantasizes about strangers; finally, she embraces her lover, familiar fires circling their heads on the pillow. Traditional themes about love and loss are deflated, but they remain relevant. The themes in this work center on the highly sexual nature of men and women, represented by the fire, the hoses, the spray. The heat cools in relationships, but every person eventually discovers that familiarity and "old luminations" in love remain more important than initial and easy incendiary impulses.

Setting

Every poem presents a persona and a theme or themes; every poem takes place in a **setting**—the place, location, or atmosphere. Consider the various places in "Chasing Fire Engines." At first, the persona remembers the world of her childhood, a time when all of the men in the family served in the volunteer fire department and when the women and children hurried to watch the men in action. Of necessity, the town must have been small—perhaps, a village located in the South or Midwest. The setting also becomes a dream where a stranger touches the speaker, and the place seems shadowy and dark. As the third setting, the speaker alludes to a bed where she and her lover sleep; and, as they awaken, fire circles their heads on a pillow. Through an examination of setting, you can discover new aspects of meaning in every poem. By carefully describing locations in "Chasing Fire Engines," for example, you learn that the shifts in settings create important complications in the poem, complications that enrich its texture and significance.

Imagery

Everyone's first experience with reality begins with an **image**—a message from the world that comes to consciousness through the senses. It may enter through the eye as shape and shade; it may enter the nose as odor; it may enter the ear as sound; it may tingle the tongue as taste; it may caress the skin as touch. Every strong memory exists as an image or as a series or composite of images. Every dream emerges as vivid, often surreal, imagery. Scientists and poets confirm the inextricable relationship between ideas and images. Einstein arrived at his theory of relativity by picturing a man traveling on a wave of light. Goethe complained that he no sooner had an idea before "it [turned] into an image."

Certainly poetry cannot exist without **imagery**. Those things that appear as physical sensation are called **concrete images**; those that represent ideas may be **abstract images**. Consider this short poem by Margaret Atwood:

YOU FIT INTO ME

you fit into me
like a hook into an eye.

a fish hook
an open eye

The first two lines create the picture of the fitting together of the two parts of a familiar household fastener to connote a couple's embracing, caressing, or making love. The next two images twist the meaning—the hook becomes a fish hook penetrating a literal, not a metaphorical, eye—and they shock the reader with the deliberate announcement of pain. The relationship is an agonizing, not a loving, one.

Economy and brevity represent the advantages of images in poetry. They suggest; they enable readers to imagine experiences or sensations. They provide emotional connotations that color responses and evoke feelings in readers. William Carlos Williams's poem, "The Red Wheelbarrow," represents the compressed nature of poetry:

so much depends
upon

> a red wheel
> barrow
>
> 5 glazed with rain
> water
>
> beside the white
> chickens.

What does the picture suggest? For a moment, the wet wheelbarrow beside the white chickens composes the world in a particular order, one that ascribes harmony and beauty to an ordinary scene. Through the first two lines Williams takes his representation of a bucolic scene and transforms it into a vision of the pleasures and purposes of perception. Williams suggests that the ability to perceive the relationship of images gives meaning to life. This poem exemplifies the tenets of the Imagist movement of the early twentieth century. Ezra Pound, who created such poetry, stated, "In a poem of this sort, one is trying to record the precise instant when a thing outward and objective transforms itself, or darts into a thing inward and subjective."

Poems often present highly complicated series of images that are woven through the entire work, strands that become a fabric of meaning. In this extension of imagery lies much of the pleasure of poetic form. In Walt Whitman's "When I Heard the Learn'd Astronomer," the speaker sits in a classroom and listens to a lecture. The first six lines of the poem introduce the astronomer and extend the images associated with him: "proofs," "figures," "charts and diagrams." The speaker, "sick" from the aridity of technical explanations, glides outside to enjoy the "mystical" experience of looking at the stars. The final lines emphasize and elaborate images of freedom in the natural world.

When I heard the learn'd astronomer,
When the proofs, the figures, were 'ranged in columns before me,
When I was shown the charts and diagrams, to add, divide and measure them,
When I sitting heard the astronomer where he lectured with much applause in the lecture-
    room,
5 How soon unaccountable I became tired and sick
Till rising and gliding out I wander'd off by myself,
In the mystical moist night-air, and from time to time,
Look'd up in perfect silence at the stars.

Note the passivity of the persona who listens, who "heard," and who "was shown," as the astronomer teaches in a "lecture-room." The speaker must perform calculations—"add, divide and measure"—in order to understand the "columns" placed before him. The proliferation and repetition ("when") of images denigrate the concrete, scientific atmosphere of the academy. The beautiful, abstract, active quality of the imagery that evokes the natural world, the world of "mystical moist night-air" and "stars," creates a "perfect" and silent contrast to the confinement of the lecture and the lecture-room. Whitman demonstrates the value of human experience and his view of the dangers of science by weaving images of a boring, sickening astronomy lecture and active perception of a starry night as threads through his work.

Figures of Speech

Figures of speech, expressions that suggest more than their literal meanings, present implied or direct comparisons that give readers the experience of an abstraction or of an emotion. Some figures are **metaphor, simile, personification, synecdoche, metonymy,** and **hyperbole.** In this famous section from Keats' "Endymion," the first line contains a metaphor:

> A thing of beauty is a joy for ever.
> Its loveliness increases; it will never
> Pass into nothingness; but still will keep
> A bower quiet for us, and a sleep
> 5 Full of sweet dreams, and health, and quiet breathing.
> Therefore, on the morrow, are we wreathing
> A flowery band to bind us to the earth,
> Spite of despondence, of the inhuman death
> Of noble natures, of the gloomy days,
> 10 Of all the unhealthy and o'er-darkened ways
> Made for our searching; yes, in spite of all,
> Some shape of beauty moves away the pall
> From our dark spirits.

Metaphor and Simile

The **metaphor** equates "A thing of beauty" with eternal joy and expresses Keats' belief that beauty transcends time, space, and matter, that beauty redeems the darkness in human life. A metaphor pictures a thing or an idea, "thing of beauty," and juxtaposes it with something different, "a joy forever," and implies an analogy between them. Look at the passage, and notice the additional comparisons that Keats creates. The "thing of beauty" becomes a "flowery band" and "some shape" that "moves away the pall." In fact, Keats extends the metaphor of beauty beyond the first line and elaborates the idea with numerous images. **Extended metaphors,** sometimes called conceits, often appear in poetry and serve to complicate its form and meaning, to create depth. In "The Love Song of J. Alfred Prufrock," T. S. Eliot describes the fog as a cat in stanzas two and three (chapter 6). This extraordinary extended metaphor presents the fog in such a catlike manner that the comparison becomes obvious—even though Eliot never mentions the word *cat.*

Similes make a direct comparison of one thing to another; usually the words "like" or "as" serve to create connections. Keats, for example, could have written the first line of the passage from "Endymion" as a simile, "A thing of beauty is [like] a joy for ever." Think of William Wordsworth's "I Wandered Lonely as a Cloud." In this title, Wordsworth's speaker convinces the reader of his loneliness through a concrete object, a cloud. Its solitary movement in the sky suddenly illuminates the emotional state of the persona.

Personification, Synecdoche, Metonymy, and Hyperbole

These figures of speech appear frequently in poetry:

Personification is the attribution of human traits to objects, ideas, or creatures. In Keats's "Endymion" beauty possesses human powers to "keep" and to "move." Keats endows beautiful things with noble human qualities that can negate the dark nature of life.

Synecdoche, sometimes considered a special type of metonymy, is a figure of speech in which part of a thing is used to represent the whole. References to a monarch as the crown and to sailors as hands provide familiar samples of this technique.

Metonymy is a figure of speech in which a single name of a person, place, or thing stands for a more complex situation or experience with which the name is associated. Washington sometimes represents all branches of the government of the United States.

Hyperbole or **exaggeration** is overstatement of the situation, idea, person in order to shock, to create humor, to command attention. In Nikki Giovanni's "Ego Tripping," the entire poem becomes an exercise in hyperbole (chapter 4). The speaker makes wild claims that she "gives oil to the Arab World," that her son is Hannibal, that she "cannot be comprehended."

Symbol, Myth, and Allusion

SYMBOL

A **symbol** is an object or event that represents something else or that has meaning beyond itself. Everyday objects become symbols when a red cross signifies an international relief organization, when ram's horns symbolize a football team, or when a swastika stands as a Nazi emblem.

In many cultures, poetic symbols have conventional meanings: cherry blossoms, jade, birds, and roses all have well-established significance in Japanese, Chinese, or English poetry. Many contemporary poets, however, create private symbols that readers may interpret from a close reading of the work. This development can make symbols more difficult to discover and to comprehend. Adrienne Rich's "Diving into the Wreck" presents a complex system of symbols that can be read simply as a dive to a sunken ship for treasure and as a personal search through the wreckage of a life (chapter 8). In the end, however, the poet shifts from the first-person singular "I" to plural and multiple points of view:

> We are, I am, you are
> by cowardice or courage
> the one who finds our way
> back to this scene
> 5 carrying a knife, a camera
> a book of myths
> in which our names do not appear

The "we" who dive into the wreck become an androgynous "one who finds our way/back" to a place where "a book of myths" denies existence through the absence of names. Rich seems to proclaim that none can have identity if the "book of myths" is not replaced by the recognition of personhood and autonomy for women as well as for men, for the oppressed as well as for the oppressors, by a merging, in fact, of these categories.

MYTH

A **myth** is similar to a symbol, but it includes a story that stands for something else. In many cultures and traditions, myths explain the inexplicable and the mysterious; they preserve history, culture, customs; they describe the actions of supernatural beings. Some of these beings symbolize natural forces—fertility, harvest, the sea. Some of them represent abstract qualities—love, wisdom, cunning, evil. A **mythology,** a system or collection of myths, represents the beliefs of a culture or a particular group; these myths often originated in religious belief and ritual. Among the mythologies most commonly found in poetry are Greek, Roman, Germanic, Native American, and Egyptian.

Rilke's "Sonnets to Orpheus" incorporate the Orpheus myth; this myth provides the symbolic subtexts of the poems.

ALLUSION

An **allusion** refers to a well-known literary work, person, event, or place. Whether it is implicit or explicit, the allusion enlarges the world of the poem. In "Sailing to Byzantium," for example, Yeats refers to the city where the beauty and culture of the Byzantine empire reached its height in the fifth and sixth centuries (chapter 8). Judith Johnson writes about Abraham and Isaac and the divine command that Abraham sacrifice his son in her poem, "Stone Olives" (chapter 8). She also alludes to the terrorists who killed the passengers on Pan Am Flight 103, the plane that exploded near Lockerbie, Scotland, in December 1988. In particular, the speaker mourns the death of Melina Hudson of Albany, New York:

> Melina, who once danced
> at proms far from Beirut, laughed with my daughter
> years after Hiroshima broke into flower, told
> her beads in a church the Gulag never touched
> 5 now pours down through our air.

Johnson traces the senseless deaths of children in Beirut, Lebanon, in the atomic bomb blast in Hiroshima, in the Soviet Gulag camps as she pictures the fragments of Melina's body raining to the ground. In "Stone Olives," the persona suggests that fathers allow and cause the sacrifice of children.

STRUCTURE

Stanzas

Historically poems originated as oral expression. Poets accompanied their songs with instruments, or they performed with choral or instrumental groups. The first aspect of the poem in any analysis of sound should be the visual picture of lines arranged on a page. The lines of a poem may be divided into separate groups or units called **stanzas** that function like paragraphs in fiction and in essays. Some questions to pose about stanzaic patterns include: How are the poetic groups or stanzas divided? Where do they begin and end? How does the punctuation provide cues for reading? The strong marks of punctuation—periods, semicolons, dashes, question marks, colons, exclamation points—require longer pauses than a comma. Examine Gwendolyn Brooks's poem:

WE REAL COOL
THE POOL PLAYERS
SEVEN AT THE GOLDEN SHOVEL

We real cool. We
Left school. We

Lurk late. We
Strike straight. We

5 Sing sin. We
Thin gin. We

Jazz June. We
Die soon.

The short sentences, each three words long, require a fast pace and regular beat. The two-line stanzas, called **couplets,** are open because each line and each couplet ends with "we." A line of poetry that ends without punctuation or pause is known as a run-on line, also as an **enjamb-ment.** The internal periods command pauses, and the repetitions and positions of the pronoun "we" also demand emphasis. Read the poem as eight short sentences, and then read it according to stanzaic and line arrangements. What is the connection between sound and meaning?

Rhyme and Sound

Rhyme, the repetition of sounds usually at the ends of lines in regular patterns, represents a traditional technique that pleases the ear and enhances the effects of images and symbols. In Brooks's poem, each line rhymes because all except the last line end with the same word. In each couplet, Brooks has used internal rhyme: cool, school; late, straight; sin, gin; June, soon. If these rhymes were **end rhymes,** the **rhyme scheme** would read aa, bb, cc, dd. To determine the scheme of any rhymed poem, simply assign letters of the alphabet to each new rhyming sound, and begin with *a*.

Another good example of rhyme is Shakespeare's "Shall I Compare Thee to a Summer's Day?" (See page 789.) Its form, called a **Shakespearean** or **Elizabethan sonnet,** divides the traditional fourteen lines into three four-line verses or quatrains and a final couplet. The rhyme scheme reads abab, cdcd, efef, gg. Sonnets also may take **Petrarchan** form, named for the famous Italian poet, Petrarch. In this kind of sonnet, the poet writes two **quatrains,** called the **octave** (eight lines), and two **tercets,** three-line verses, called the **sestet** (six lines). The theme shifts radically at the ninth line in Petrarchan sonnets; this turn is known as the volta. The rhyme scheme in the octave usually reads abba abba. The sestet may rhyme in a number of ways: cdecde, cdccdc, cdedce. Another technique for rhyming in free verse or formal poetry includes slant or half rhyme, one in which words almost rhyme.

The sounds of the words contribute to the meaning of the poem. The repetition of the initial sounds of accented consonant syllables at close intervals, called **alliteration,** may create effects that enlarge, reinforce, or contradict the ideas and mood of the poem. In Brooks's work, for example, the alliteration begins with the identification of the speakers as *p*ool *p*layers, and she continues this pattern in *l*urk *l*ate, in *str*ike *str*aight, in *s*ing *s*in, in *j*azz *J*une. This frequent use of alliteration in such a short poem heightens the sense of jazz and music. Brooks also em-ploys **assonance,** the repetition of vowel sounds of stressed syllables or important words at close intervals: c*oo*l sch*oo*l. Notice that this poem relies heavily on sound for meaning. Notice that the long, sighing vowel in d*ie* in the last line stands alone, a jarring conclusion.

Rhythm

One of the indispensable elements distinguishing poetry is **rhythm.** Like song or dance, no poem can exist without a beat that augments its meaning and beauty or contradicts and conflicts with its themes and images to create tension. Poets choose rhythms from four basic categories: *traditional meters, strong stress rhythms, syllabic counts,* and *free verse.*

Meter

Meter is a rhythmic pattern of stressed (/) and unstressed (◡) syllables in a poem. Each unit, called a *foot,* has either two or three syllables. The most common feet in poetry follow:

Foot	Designation	Example
iamb or iambic	(◡ /)	dĕlíght
trochee or trochaic	(/ ◡)	córăl
spondee or spondaic	(/ /)	hó húm
pyrrhus or pyrrhic	(◡ ◡)	advántăge ŏf
anapest or anapestic	(◡ ◡ /)	ĭn ă flásh
dactyl or dactylic	(/ ◡ ◡)	níght cŏmĭng

Line lengths can be measured in number of feet.

Line Length	Number of Feet
monometer	one foot
dimeter	two feet
trimeter	three feet
tetrameter	four feet
pentameter	five feet
hexameter	six feet
heptameter	seven feet
octometer	eight feet

Scansion

In order to discover the meter of a poem, each line is scanned for accented and unaccented syllables. This process, called **scansion,** enables you to examine the effects of rhythm in the work. Look at this scansion of Shakespeare's parody of the conceits in the sonnet tradition. Note that each syllable is marked to indicate stressed or unstressed pronunciations.

> Mў místress' eýes, ăre nóthĭng líke thĕ Sún;
>
> Córăl ĭs fár mŏre réd, thăn hĕr líps' réd:
>
> If snów bĕ whíte, whу thĕn hĕr bréasts ăre dún;
>
> If haírs bĕ wíres, blăck wíres grów ŏn hĕr heád.

I have seen Roses damasked, red and white,

But no such Roses see I in her cheeks;

And in some perfumes is there more delight

Than in the breath that from my Mistress reeks.

I love to hear her speak, yet well I know

That music hath a far more pleasing sound:

I grant I never saw a goddess go,

My Mistress, when she walks treads on the ground.

And yet, by heaven, I think my love as rare

As any she belied with false compare.

With very little variation, this poem's meter is iambic pentameter (five iambic feet), the most frequent and natural rhythm in English. Line 2 contains a trochee (coral), as does line 6 (Í in). Such variety prevents boredom, a sing-song quality, and commands attention. In this sonnet, Shakespeare makes little attempt to provide alternate rhythm. The boring regularity suits the purposes of his parody.

Strong Stress Meter

Early Anglo-Saxon and Germanic rhythms featured only strong stresses or **accents,** each line containing four stressed syllables. *Beowulf* and some Middle English poetry exemplify accentual meter. Strong stress rhythms still appear in such children's rhymes as "Hickory Dickory Dock." Gerard Manley Hopkins, an English poet, developed sprung rhythm, a variant of accentual meter, in the nineteenth century. In his poems, each line begins with a stressed syllable that may be followed by one, two, or three unaccented syllables or that may stand alone.

Syllabic Rhythm

Poetry also may receive its beat from patterns of **counted syllables,** a method that disregards accentual feet. In this mode, the poet chooses any combination of syllables and repeats the pattern. In Sylvia Plath's "Metaphors," she writes a riddle in nine lines, each containing nine syllables:

1 2 3 4 5 6 7 8 9
I'm a riddle in nine syllables

1 2 3 4 5 6 7 8 9
An elephant, a ponderous house

This clever poem catalogues metaphors about pregnancy. Japanese haiku also represents a form in which syllabic count is fixed and traditional: five syllables; seven; five syllables. Remember Bashō's lyric, "On New Year's Day."

Free Verse

More than eighty years ago, Ezra Pound theorized about composing "in the sequence of the metrical phrase, not in the sequence of a metronome. . . ." Pound noted that some poets had abandoned traditional meters and explored natural rhythms, and he advocated **free**

verse as an exciting alternative to traditional meters. Pound was not the first poet to recognize the value of this approach, but his description certainly provides an apt definition.

Free verse has no strict meter or line length. Traditional feet appear but in natural order. Such rising feet as iambs and anapests may occur together; such falling feet as trochees and dactyls may occur together. One of the most famous examples of free verse is Walt Whitman's great poem of love and death, "Out of the Cradle Endlessly Rocking" (chapter 4). Read the first few lines without any attempt at analysis; follow the surge of the sea.

> Out of the cradle endlessly rocking,
> Out of the mocking-bird's throat, the musical shuttle,
> Out of the Ninth-month midnight,
> Over the sterile sands and the fields beyond, where the child
>   leaving his bed wander'd alone, bareheaded, barefoot,
> 5 Down from the shower'd halo, ...

Anaphora—the repetition of phrases—in this case, adverbial phrases as "Out of" and biblical rhythm characterize this poem.

Needless to say, poets change and combine all of these categories. Every culture's poetic tradition recognizes rhythm as essential to the enjoyment and meaning of poetry because rhythm remains central to all natural movement: the beating of the heart, the rocking of the cradle, the swaying of the sea.

THE READING/WRITING PROCESS: POETRY

A poem requires more than one reading. Several examinations of the text may be necessary simply to understand the general idea of the piece. Any work of art worth attention—a Verdi opera, a Rembrandt painting, Lady Murasaki's *The Tale of Genji*—becomes more exciting and more valuable after careful examination.

The second task in understanding poetry should become the constant use of a dictionary. The multiple meanings of words in each poem result from the compression that characterizes this form. Any dictionary will suffice, but the *Oxford English Dictionary* presents the most comprehensive history of the meanings of words in English. A reader also should have access to other reference books on world mythology and to religious texts.

Listen to the sounds of poetry. Since poems originated in song and in oral tradition, the meaning resides in the sounds as well as in the words. Read poems aloud, and begin with your favorites. In your interpretation, be animated. Muriel Rukeyser once stated that fear of poetry is a fear of emotion. The feelings and meaning already exist in a poem; they will express themselves. In any attempt to render the work as an oral interpretation, find the patterns of rhythm, grammar, and punctuation. Try not to swallow the last lines or important words.

The central purpose of the poem becomes the next question. To comprehend the poem's purpose, characterize the voice of the speaker and paraphrase the action of the poem. Ask yourself: Who is speaking? What is happening in the poem? The speaker in "Daddy" feels angry and concludes: "Daddy, you bastard, I'm through." Victimized like the Jews in Nazi concentration camps, she transforms her father from God into a devil and later into a vampire. The purpose of the poem appears to reside in the speaker's desire to resolve her feelings about her father's death.

Ask, then, about the achievement of purpose. How is it achieved? Find the answer by describing the organization of ideas in the poem. In Plath's soliloquy, she begins with fairy tale; then she describes Daddy as "a bag full of God." Her speaker relates his roots, his language, to German history; and she contends that every woman wants a brutal father and that her speaker marries a "man in black with a Meinkampf look" (like Hitler) in order to recover her father. Finally, both men are symbolically killed, and Daddy becomes the villain in a Dracula movie. The purpose is achieved. Readers find the poem powerful; not everyone likes it or believes that the speaker has resolved her losses.

When reading a poem, give it what Shakespeare called "passionate attention." Consider voice, tone, theme, setting, imagery, figures of speech, symbols, sounds, and rhythm. These elements of poetry will reveal the richness of meaning and evoke responses and evaluation.

CHECKLIST FOR WRITING ABOUT POETRY

1. What is the category for the poem? Is it lyrical, narrative, or dramatic?
2. Who is the speaker? What is the point of view? What is the speaker's attitude toward the subject? What details, images, and uses of language give information about the persona?
3. What is the tone, and does it change? Why?
4. What is happening in the poem?
5. What are the significant figures of speech? How do they function?
6. Describe the setting.
7. Which senses do the images evoke? Does the poem have one image or a series of images? Are the images related? Is there a pattern? What concepts do the images represent? How do the images support the theme? How effective is the use of imagery?
8. What is the central symbol? Are the symbols universal or private? How does symbolism function in the poem?
9. Does the poem refer to mythological figures? Does the poet change the myth?
10. Are there any allusions? What are the specific historical events, names, and/or literary references in the poem? How do the allusions work? Are they effective?
11. What sounds are important? Does the poem contain alliteration or assonance? How does the poet arrange the lines?
12. What is the rhythm of the poem? How does rhythm function?
13. Does the poem have a conventional form? Is the poem a sonnet, villanelle, or sestina? Is the poem an open form?
14. Is the poem effective? What is best about this work? What are its flaws? What is the final evaluation of this work?

■ STUDENT PORTFOLIO ■

Response to Wilfred Owen's "Arms and the Boy"

Ursula Lebris's work presents a model of an explication of Wilfred Owen's "Arms and the Boy" and evolves from a gloss of the text, from notes, from freewriting, and from several drafts. An explication offers a careful analysis of a poem. The methodology requires an examination of the work to gain knowledge of each of its aspects and parts, and it attempts to determine the relation of all of the elements in the poem to the meaning of the whole. Note that the first draft of "Let the Boy Try" is articulate and structured but also seriously underdeveloped and lacking in precision. The final draft overcomes these deficiencies and demonstrates outstanding mastery of this poem.

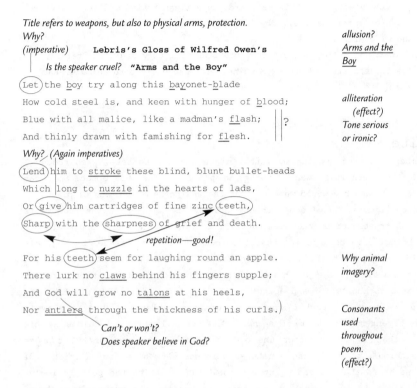

Title refers to weapons, but also to physical arms, protection.
Why?
(imperative)   **Lebris's Gloss of Wilfred Owen's**

  Is the speaker cruel? **"Arms and the Boy"**

allusion?
Arms and the Boy

Let the boy try along this bayonet-blade
How cold steel is, and keen with hunger of blood;
Blue with all malice, like a madman's flash; ?
And thinly drawn with famishing for flesh.

alliteration
 (effect?)
Tone serious or ironic?

Why? (Again imperatives)
Lend him to stroke these blind, blunt bullet-heads
Which long to nuzzle in the hearts of lads,
Or give him cartridges of fine zinc teeth,
Sharp with the sharpness of grief and death.
      repetition—good!

For his teeth seem for laughing round an apple.
There lurk no claws behind his fingers supple;
And God will grow no talons at his heels,
Nor antlers through the thickness of his curls.

Why animal imagery?

    Can't or won't?
    Does speaker believe in God?

Consonants used throughout poem. (effect?)

Notes

bayonet—a weapon attached to the muzzle of a rifle
keen—eager and sharp
malice—intention to injure others
thinly drawn—a sword is "drawn" in order to fight; the shape of the bayonet is
    like a thin line; also can mean drawn in (i.e., with hunger)
famishing—suffering extreme hunger
zinc—bluish white metallic element
talons—claws, esp. of a bird of prey
antlers—the horns of a stag or deer

Personification—the bayonet is starving to death ("famishing for flesh") and
    capable of emotion ("blue with all malice."). The bullets "long to nuzzle" and
    the cartridges feel "grief and death." The poem is divided into three
    quatrains; the first two discuss human weapons; the third introduces "natural"
    (animal) weapons. I don't think the poem uses a particular meter, but in the
    first two quatrains each line ends with a heavily stressed syllable. I really

hear this when I read the poem aloud. The emphasis (e.g., on "blade" and
"blood") makes the weapons seem more threatening.

Alliteration—the hard "b" sounds are like explosions and the "sh" sounds are like
the hiss of bullets through the air.

What about consonance (half-rhyme)? The words seem to rhyme at first but there is
a jarring effect. Is this significant?

Simile—"like a madman's flash." This is weird. Is a flash a kind of fit? I suppose
like a flash of anger (malice). Why *blue*? Metal can look bluish. Ok. Also the
blue flash of gunfire.

Metaphor—"blind, blunt bullet-heads." They are blunt but they are not literally
blind. The bullets are made to seem vulnerable like newly born animals, but
all they want to do is kill young "lads." They do not see their targets; they
are not meant to see.

Freewrite

I remember years ago taking my father's gun out of its case, even though I
was forbidden to touch it. I wanted to see what all the fuss was about. So I can
understand why a young boy would want to test the sharpness of a blade or play with
bullets and cartridges. But I don't understand why the speaker in the poem wants
him to. I feel frustrated by the poem overall. I like the way the weapons are described as being alive because it makes them seem even more threatening. But allowing a kid to play with things which intend to kill him is pretty sadistic. I
suppose it's the final verse which really throws me. Ok, the boy's teeth are innocent compared to the "grief and death" of the cartridge teeth, but why does the
poet then go on to talk about claws and talons and antlers? Maybe the claw is
meant to represent the trigger of a gun. "And God will grow no talons at his
heels"—is it that God can protect the boy, but won't? Why "talons"? I suppose
that unlike animals the boy has no natural defenses. So "give him cartridges of
fine zinc teeth" so that he can protect himself. But I think the poet is imply-
ing that to fight is to go against God—human beings are not naturally equipped
for battle ("Thou shalt not kill"). Anyway the poem is deliberately shocking because Owen wants to show how vulnerable the young boy is. Let him touch these
weapons, and maybe he will realize how sick war is before it is too late.

Essay: First Draft: "Let the Boy Try"

At first "Arms and the Boy" may seem to be a cruel, even sadistic, poem, for
in the first two stanzas a young boy is encouraged to play with potentially lethal
weapons. However, in the final stanza the poet's compassion for the young lives lost
in World War I is revealed. Although the poem is only twelve lines long, Owen makes
the reader vividly aware of the vulnerability of youth by using several techniques
to emphasize the horror of war.

The technique of personification is perhaps the most important. The bayonet is
not only some starving animal "famishing for flesh." This simile likens the blue flash
of gunfire to the indiscriminate malice of a madman. The bullets are also personified
but in a different way. Far from being evil madmen, they are like the new-born young
of some animal which "long to nuzzle in the hearts of lads." This perverse image is
intended to shock: Owen wants the reader to realize how sick and unnatural war is.

The disturbing images of the first two quatrains are intensified through alliteration. The repetition of consonants in "blade," "blood," "blind," and "blunt" creates a hard, explosive effect like that of gunfire, while the "s," "f," and "sh" sounds suggest the hiss of blades or bullets through the air. These sounds, along with the strongly stressed syllables at the end of each line, give the poem a threatening tone, as though the speaker is talking through clenched teeth. The use of half-rhyme combines certain key images in the reader's mind while giving a jarring effect that adds to the tension in these first two quatrains.

The sinister effects created by personification, alliteration, and meter disappear in the final quatrain. The boy's youthful innocence is shown in the comparison between his laughing teeth and the "grief and death" of the cartridge teeth and by references to "his fingers supple" and "the thickness of his curls." These images emphasize how vulnerable he is. The boy has no natural defenses, and since "God will grow no talons at his heels" perhaps it is necessary to "give him cartridges of fine zinc teeth" so that he may survive. However, this is no answer because the weapons intended to protect him are bent on his destruction.

The figurative language and the several possible readings of the final quatrain make "Arms and the Boy" a somewhat difficult poem. But despite this the reader cannot help but share the poet's compassion for the young victims of armed conflict. And there is a more hopeful interpretation—perhaps if the boy experiences the 'grief and death' of the weapons now, he will decide against becoming part of the horror and insanity that is war.

Lebris' Final Draft: "Let the Boy Try"

"Arms and the Boy" is a short lyric poem of great power, comprising three quatrains and employing the rhyme scheme AABB CCDD EEFF. The alliteration used throughout is an important feature, as it creates a tension appropriate to the subject matter. At first "Arms and the Boy" may seem to be a cruel, even sadistic, poem, for in the initial two stanzas, the speaker encourages another to give potentially lethal weapons to a young boy. The final stanza, however, reveals the deep compassion felt for the young lives lost on the battlefield. As an officer in the First World War, Wilfred Owen witnessed firsthand the atrocities inflicted by men upon other men. Although the poem is only twelve lines long, he succeeds in making the reader vividly aware of the vulnerability of youth and of the horror and perversity of war.

It is significant that the poem begins with an imperative statement: "Let the boy try along this bayonet-blade/ How cold steel is, and keen with hunger of blood." The note of challenge introduced here quickly becomes one of menace as the description of the bayonet shifts rapidly from the literal "cold steel" to the figurative "keen with hunger of blood." This personification of the weaponry is one of the most important devices used in the poem, as it transforms them from inanimate objects into evil personalities with conscious intentions. The bayonet, "keen" in the sense of both eager *and* sharp, is not only like a starving animal but also "Blue with all malice, like a madman's flash." This startling simile takes the blue flash of gunfire and likens it to the indiscriminate malice of a psychopath, a telling indication of how Owen himself had come to view military action. Note that "blue" also suggests the hue of cold steel and the pallor of death.

The second quatrain continues the menacing tone with another imperative statement: "Led him to stroke these blind, blunt bullet-heads/Which long to nuzzle in the hearts of lads." Again personification is used, but this time in a slightly different way. Far from being like evil madmen, the bullets are described as being like the new-born young of some animal. Paradoxically, it is they who seem vulnerable rather than the young boy who is being allowed to play with them. The use of the casual, inoffensive "lads" here is also significant; it strikes an even more chilling note into the metaphor. The sexual connotations of "stroke" and "nuzzle," in conjunction with the phallic symbolism of the bayonet and the bullets, create a very unsettling undercurrent in an already disturbing poem. That instruments of death should be described in sexual, hence creative, terms does, however, highlight the poem's main theme—that war is something perverse and unnatural.

The second quatrain concludes with the third imperative statement: "Or give him cartridges of fine zinc teeth,/Sharp with the sharpness of grief and death." There is an important progression here in the level of involvement implied: the boy was initially allowed to touch the bayonet, was then lent bullets, and is now *given* cartridges. Although it is never made clear whom the speaker in the poem is addressing, there is a note of accusation here which implicates a far wider group of people than just a few soldiers on sentry duty. That the boy should be encouraged to play with weapons which actively seek to harm him is the key paradox in the poem, and it is this action which gives the final quatrain its power.

5   The sinister mood of the first two quatrains is intensified through a variety of poetic devices. The alliteration in "blood," "blade," "blind," and "blunt" creates a hard, exploding effect like that of gunfire, while the softer "s," "f," and "sh" sounds suggest the hiss of blades or bullets through the air. These sounds, along with the strongly stressed syllables at the end of each line, further contribute to the threatening tone, as though the speaker is talking through clenched teeth. Although the poem does not employ any fixed metrical pattern, the groups of unstressed syllables followed by several stressed syllables ("Blue with all malice, like a madman's flash") seem to mimic the stabbing motion of a bayonet. Certain key images are combined in the reader's mind through consonance ("blade"/"blood"), while the jarring effect of the half-rhyme adds an appropriate air of tension to the first eight lines.

In the final quatrain, however, the tone changes, and the sinister effects created by personification, alliteration, and meter disappear. Consonance is still used, but weak rhyme replaces the strong, heavily stressed rhyme of the first two quatrains, giving the last four lines a much more gentle mood. The boy's youthful innocence is shown in the comparison between his teeth "laughing round an apple" and the "grief and death" of the cartridge teeth. It is at this point that the disturbing images of the first two quatrains are justified, and the apparent sadism of the speaker is now revealed as compassion. The poet emphasizes the boy's vulnerability through references to "his finger supple" and "the thickness of his curls," while his complete lack of aggression is expressed through a series of negative statements ("no claws," "no talons," "nor antlers"). The boy, unlike animals, has no natural defenses, and since "God will grow no talons at his heels," perhaps it is necessary to "give him cartridges of fine zinc teeth" so that he may survive. But the meaning of the poem cannot be quite as straightforward as this, because the implication is that for any human being to fight, whether boy or man, is to go against God. The poem's power comes from its tragic irony—that the weapons meant to protect the boy are intent only on his destruction.

The several possible readings of the final quatrain, along with the figurative language used throughout, make "Arms and the Boy" a somewhat difficult poem. It is also a shocking poem, and intentionally so, for Owen seems to have had in mind an audience of complacent armchair patriots. The poem's message is, of course, not limited to his contemporaries of the First World War but is, regrettably, still very relevant today. The knowledge that Owen himself was killed on the front lines at the age of twenty-five adds another dimension to the poem, but even without this fact, the reader cannot help but feel sadness and anger at the young lives which were, and still are, wasted on the battlefield. But there is a more hopeful interpretation—perhaps if the boy experiences the "grief and death" of weaponry secondhand, he will decide against becoming involved in the horror and insanity that is war.

The gloss and notes identify and explore the grammar, figurative language, sounds, and meaning of Owen's poem. The writer focuses on the formal elements of "Arms and the Boy" and on the connection between form and meaning. The journal entry describes a personal experience of touching a weapon and reveals the writer's attitudes toward violence, toward the poem, and toward war. In the journal the initial ideas for the essay are formulated.

The first draft contains an excellent introduction. The explication analyzes personification and alliteration in the first two stanzas or quatrains. The third paragraph discusses the meaning of the last verse, and the conclusion is excellent.

In the final version of "Let the Boy Try," the writer enlarges the vision of the poem and announces her view in the introduction that seems slightly cluttered with the rhyme scheme and with a comment concerning alliteration. Although the paper is well organized, the introduction fails to focus exclusively on the writer's plan. The beginning, however, engages the reader's interest and expresses the major ideas. The paragraphs on the three quatrains are brilliantly conceived and brilliantly illustrated. The careful reading of imagery, significant figures of speech, grammatical constructions (imperative statements), sounds, tone, speaker, and theme result in an exemplary performance. The introduction of biographical details about Wilfred Owen emphasizes the dramatic conclusion about the "insanity that is war."

· CHAPTER 11 ·

Drama

In *As You Like It,* Shakespeare claims that "all the world's a stage." His declaration captures the deep connection between dramatic literature and life; and, by extension, Shakespeare captures the human fascination with all of the imaginative arts. Every person views his or her experience as dramatic; each views the world as a setting for personal and public actions and ideas, for triumphs and crises, for the ordinary and the sublime. Plays and other forms of literature, therefore, are not simply imitations of life; they represent much more. They order, concentrate, and elevate acts of interpretation that may be crucial to daily life.

Theater existed in human cultures long before recorded history. Societies developed dramatic rituals with characters, costumes, makeup, masks, settings, and special effects to inspire, educate, entertain, initiate, worship the gods, and control the environment. Music became the universal accompaniment. In the rain dance of the Dieri in Australia, for instance, a lodge was constructed; and then, at the end of the ritual, it was destroyed by dancers who knocked it down with their heads. This ceremony signified the elimination of clouds so that rain could fall. In the drama of the Great Serpent held to celebrate the March moon, the Hopis burned fires in the kivas (ceremonial chambers) that they built; a prop person smothered the blazes to produce smoke curtains at certain intervals to facilitate changes in scenes and actors. They also devised sets with painted backdrops containing holes through which symbols of dancing serpents appeared. These performances exemplify the complexity of the drama before the practice of writing scripts. Some early comedies appeared as animal impersonations. For entertainment, one society in the Philippines created a comic play in which a searcher for honey experienced many outrageous indignations. Religious expression was central to many of these productions, but secular concerns also provided subject matter and impetus for public spectacles. Except for written scripts, the elements of modern drama—setting, character, action, plot—existed in prototype in these ceremonies.

The oldest evidences of scripts for drama are the fifty-five Pyramid Texts (3000 B.C.) of Egypt. Written on the walls of tombs and pyramids, they contain stage directions and lines for different characters. The major theme of these dramas was resurrection. Scholars estimate that more than four thousand texts once existed, developed, perhaps, from rituals celebrating the return of spring. The Egyptians also performed coronation festival plays that hailed the crowning of a new monarch.

FORMS OF DRAMA

Much of the theater, as it exists today, originated in Greece. Performances to honor gods or to commemorate rites of spring developed into formal productions. The most famous playwrights, Aeschylus (525–426 B.C.), Sophocles (496–406 B.C.), and Euripedes (c. 480–406

B.C.) composed plays for the annual Dionysian festivals. Presented to a selection group and later evaluated by judges, the plays—three tragedies and one comedy by each playwright— were performed in a semicircular theater.

Tragedy is a form of drama about fortunes and misfortunes, about disaster. Broadly defined, tragedy refers to dramatic representations of serious and significant actions that result in disaster for the protagonist or main character. In classical plays, these disasters happened to human beings with high position and great power such as Oedipus, Agamemnon, and Antigone. These characters possessed noble qualities and high passion. In tragedy, these attributes could not, however, save them from self-destruction or from fate.

Aristotle's classic theory in the *Poetics* (fourth century B.C.) describes tragedy as "the imitation of an action that is serious and also, as having magnitude, complete in itself," written in dramatic form and in poetic language. The tragic drama features "incidents arousing pity and fear, wherewith to accomplish the catharsis of such emotion." This **catharsis**, or purging of emotion, implies that the play will leave the audience or reader with feelings of relief or even exaltation. According to Aristotle, the play focuses on a **tragic hero** who has higher than ordinary moral values. This hero suffers a change or reversal of fortune, caused by his or her **tragic flaw, hamartia,** an "error in judgment." One common expression of hamartia in Greek drama is **hubris** or excessive pride.

According to Aristotle, every successful drama must possess the three unities: action, time and place. By this, Aristotle means that a drama must be organic and continuous to be considered serious and believable. The action, therefore, must arise out of a clearly stated conflict, and the time and place must be logical and consistent to the action. Rarely is there a change of place or time in Greek drama because it would disturb the unity of the whole play. Elaborate set changes and special effects were not employed by the ancient Greek dramatists. Because the sets were simple and the power of the plays was largely psychological, violence in Greek tragedies occurs off stage.

To assure unity of action, time, and place, playwrights often employ the chorus to create a transition from one scene to another. The chorus serves as spectators and commentators who elaborate on events as they unfold within the drama. They also provide background information and note the passage of time. The choral odes frequently are divided into strophes, recited as the chorus moves across the stage in one direction, and antistrophes, recited while moving in the opposite direction. In the tragedies, comic relief can be provided by the chorus.

Greek **comedy** first appeared in fertility rites and in the worship of Dionysus. From the time of Aristophanes (c. 448–c. 380 B.C.), the greatest Greek comic playwright, the form has been associated primarily with drama. Aristophanes wrote a variety of comedies combining lyrics, dance, satire, social comment, fantasy, and buffoonery. He attempted to reveal truth by exposing political deceit and pretense in such plays as *Lysistrata, The Wasps,* and *The Peace.* His more philosophical works include *The Clouds, The Frogs,* and *The Birds.* Aristotle distinguished comedy from tragedy by suggesting that it features ordinary people in amusing, everyday situations. It derives from the word **komos** or revel.

While both tragedies and comedies deliver moral messages, tragedies do so by focusing on the downfall of the tragic hero, a superior individual, whereas comedies portray the actions of an ordinary person. The behavior of the tragic hero often leads not only to his own downfall but to the disintegration of his society, whereas the comic hero is responsible for the reinstitution of social order. In tragedies catharsis consists of pity and fear, whereas the emotions in comedies inspire the feelings of sympathy and ridicule.

Few of the early tragedies or comedies still exist, but those that have survived convey the beauty and wisdom, the bawdy humor, the awe and wonder of classical Greece. They establish without a doubt the incredible influence of the Greek theater on world drama during the past two thousand years.

Fifteen years after the death of Aristophanes, scenic entertainments to appease the gods began in Rome (364 B.C.). Like Greek theater, Roman drama also originated in ritual ceremonies and secular entertainment. The most famous Roman dramatist was Seneca (3 B.C.–A.D. 65), although his tragedies may never have been performed in public.

During the Roman Empire, comedy employed two kinds of subjects: one derived from Greek dramas and the other concerned Roman materials. Seventy works from the Roman-based comedies are recorded, but the two best known Roman dramatists who wrote comedies depended on Greek plays. They are Maccius Plautus and Publius Terentius Afer, known as Terence. Plautus created the form known as **tragicomedy** by referring to the unconventional mixture of kings and servants in his play *Amphitrus,* as *tragico-comedia.* Choosing elements of both comedy and tragedy, the playwright attempted to balance a conflict of vision. The extant plays of both Plautus and Terence greatly influenced Elizabethan theater and, in turn, modern theater. Mime and pantomime, which developed as elaborate performances separate from dramas, also represent an original contribution of the Romans to the art.

The theater did not die with the fall of Rome. Until the twelfth century, it survived in public entertainment and in religious performances, in particular, in cycles and in noncyclical plays. In England, Elizabethan drama developed from religious plays performed at medieval festivals during the twelfth and thirteenth centuries. These **mystery plays,** as they were called, presented Biblical stories—Noah and the ark, Jonah and the whale, the passion of Jesus—in town squares or in churches. As the dramas grew in popularity, platforms, called **pageants,** were wheeled from city to city; and the plays often expanded into a series that was enacted over a period of several days.

The **miracle play,** another dramatic genre related to the mystery play, presented saints' lives and miracles. It often centered on the divine acts of the Virgin Mary. A famous cycle of forty-two plays, the *Miracles de Notre Dame,* is extant in France. Other European examples are the German *Marienklage* (*The Complaint of Mary*), and the Dutch *Mariken Van Nieumaghen* (*Mary of Nieumaghen*). In England, where the cult of the Virgin Mary did not flourish, most miracle plays dramatized the lives of saints.

During the fourteenth and fifteenth centuries, **morality plays** allegorized Christian values. Characters symbolized Christian virtues and vices. The most famous play, *Everyman* (1500), presented positive and negative human qualities in a single representative figure whose conflicts mirrored all life processes.

In the sixteenth century, Greek and Roman drama began to influence English theater. Secular plays became popular as interest in religious dramatizations waned. At first the new plays, based on classic Greek models, focused on murder and revenge. Roman dramatists, Seneca and Menander, also influenced the writers of these plays. Professional actors performed plays in courtyards and later in theaters. Audiences were composed of both educated and illiterate spectators.

From the defeat of the Spanish Armada in 1588 until 1642 when all theaters were closed during the Civil War, the English theater reached its highest development through the genius of such playwrights as Christopher Marlowe, Ben Jonson, Thomas Kyd, Thomas Dekker, John Webster, and William Shakespeare. In *Tamburlaine* and *Dr. Faustus,* Marlowe (1564–93) invented blank verse, or unrhymed iambic pentameter, a rhythm that became the dominant meter of Elizabethan drama.

The greatest genius of the reigns of Queen Elizabeth I and James I was William Shakespeare. A writer of comedies, tragedies, and histories, Shakespeare was the best of many astonishingly fine dramatists. A member of the Lord Chamberlain's company (1594), he joined a group that constructed the Globe Theater (1599), a most successful structure, small enough to fit into the orchestra area of the Greek Theater of Dionysius. At most, the Globe could have accommodated two thousand people.

The stage was a platform that projected into the audience. In the rear was an area with a curtain for intimate scenes; above was a balcony. There was a trap door for such purposes as the gravedigger scene in *Hamlet,* and ghosts descended on ropes from a canopy. The theater had no painted sets, and props were minimal. As in Greek drama, all actors were male. Elizabethan theaters were designed like courtyards. Six hundred "groundlings" sat or stood in the open yards. More privileged spectators occupied tiers of covered balconies.

In *Hamlet,* the prince lectures the actors who perform the play-within the play and defines the purpose of drama: "to hold, as 'twere, the mirror up to nature." This blossoming of dramas in England focused on imitation of reality. At the same time, the performances of plays in the open theaters created a wonderful and wild public life—real entertainment.

The excitement of the Renaissance renewed interest in drama in Italy, France, and Germany; and audiences enjoyed many kinds of theater. No great dramatic literature emerged during the Renaissance in these countries. However, innovations in theater architecture influenced the development and form of modern drama: horseshoe seating, the **proscenium arch** (a frame enclosing the stage area behind which the front curtain hangs), painted sets, indoor lighting, and spectacular costumes.

In Spain, Lope de Vega and Calderón wrote spectacular plays, the most famous in Spanish literature. More than two thousand actors are listed in public records, and public playhouses in Spain developed in the same patterns as English theaters. They accommodated the same kind of enthusiastic audiences. Complete professionalization of theater and establishment of repertory groups represent significant accomplishments during this period.

In the seventeenth century, French theater was greatly influenced by Greek and Roman drama. During this time, the most significant drama was written by Molière, Racine, and Corneille. The actors developed revolutionary performing styles, and the first national European theater, the Comèdie Francaise, began.

During the Restoration in England (after 1688), the great achievement became the comedy of manners—hard, brilliant, accomplished. The major playwrights were George Etherege, William Wycherley, and William Congreve. In the eighteenth century in England, theater did not occupy a primary place. Oliver Goldsmith and Richard Brinsley Sheridan are notable exceptions. The art of acting, however, reached new heights; the best performer was the legendary David Garrick. This period also produced the **picture frame stage** and very large theaters.

On the European continent, Voltaire and Diderot in France and Goethe and Lessing in Germany wrote memorable and classic works. Dramatic theory and criticism received great attention. Many great actors emerged, and the number of theaters increased. Spectacular effects appeared in stage design. All of these developments received more attention in the nineteenth and twentieth centuries.

NINETEENTH- AND TWENTIETH-CENTURY DRAMA

In Europe and in North America, three major movements in drama have developed in the last century: realism, Theater of the Absurd, and Symbolist Drama.

Realism

At the end of the nineteenth century, writers began to create realistic dramas that presented accurate versions of the world and of human nature, of ordinary people leading ordinary lives. In dramatic literature, realism avoided all that was visionary and unbelievable. These dramatists chose serious, often tragic themes and well-developed characters who did not possess special status. They reacted against the spirit of Romanticism in England and in

Europe, which emphasized the emotions and imagination above reason and intellect. They also reacted against melodrama, plays that depend on spectacle, action, and extravagant emotional appeal.

Realism, as it is defined and recognized today, is primarily the invention of Henrik Ibsen, a nineteenth century Norwegian playwright (see *A Doll's House* in chapter 4). This dramatic movement corresponded to great cultural upheavals—the Napoleonic Wars, the Industrial Revolution, the rise of the middle class. People longed for critical analysis of social institutions.

In Russia, Anton Chekhov, Leo Tolstoy, and Maxim Gorki wrote realistic plays and fiction. In France, Émile Zola and Guy de Maupassant provided analysis of a movement that they called naturalism. The bases for this theory were Charles Darwin's idea of the survival of the fittest and Karl Marx's contention that economic conditions shape human life.

Ibsen influenced George Bernard Shaw, August Strindberg, and, subsequently, an entire generation of famous dramatists. Ibsen's work deeply affected Stanislavsky's teaching of method acting. Many North American playwrights—Eugene O'Neill, Arthur Miller, and Tennessee Williams—adopted fundamental tenets of realism. Lorraine Hansberry's *A Raisin in the Sun* (chapter 5) is an example of realist drama.

Theater of the Absurd

The notion that life is absurd is not new, but it has acquired more specific meaning in the past century. Philosophers have defined the purposeless role of humans in a purposeless universe as absurd—mathematically, a *surd* is that which cannot be expressed in finite terms of ordinary numbers or quantities. It is in this mathematical sense that the philosophy of the absurd has been defined. (See Camus' "The Myth of Sisyphus" in chapter 8.). The theatrical phrase was coined by Martin Esslin, who wrote *The Theatre of the Absurd* in 1961. Scholars trace the lineage of this form from Roman mime plays to the comic techniques of medieval and Renaissance drama, especially commedia dell'arte, comedy originating in the Italian Renaissance that featured improvisation, stock characters, and masks. Finally, Esslin cites the influence of August Strindberg and of Bertolt Brecht.

In the 1950s, this concept was expressed in a number of plays that focus on characters struggling with existential angst, anxiety, and anguish. The human condition is presented as essentially meaningless. The plays have no formal logic and lack conventional structure. The following dramatists and works represent this tradition: Samuel Beckett, *Waiting for Godot, Endgame;* Jean Genet, *Les Negres* (The Blacks), *Le Balcon* (The Balcony); Eugene Ionesco, *La Leçon* (The Lesson), *La Cantatrice Chauve* (The Bald Soprano), *Rhinoceros;* Harold Pinter, *The Birthday Party, The Homecoming;* Edward Albee, *The Zoo Story* and *The Sandbox*. David Ives's *Sure Thing* (see chapter 6) is a comic representation of Theater of the Absurd.

Symbolist Drama

With the advent of realism, twentieth-century theater relinquished many traditional sources of dramatic tension—poetic language, symbols, illusions, such as the ghost in *Hamlet*. Like symbols in poetry and fiction, the actions and characters in symbolist drama refer to eternal ideas, abstract concepts. In such a play, a woman might encounter an abandoned child. The situation would not be presented as criticism of a particular society. Instead, the event might indicate the woman's discovery of her real and autonomous self; it might mean that humans are always abandoned in life.

Most plays contain symbols, but most dramatists do not intend that all action be interpreted as symbolic. **Symbolist dramas,** however, may feature many traditional poetic symbols and allegorical names, and they employ dreamlike atmospheres. This mode traces its roots to Kabuki theater, to Nō plays, to morality plays, and to the folk dramas of William

Butler Yeats and of John Millington Synge. (See *Riders to the Sea* in chapter 5.) Contemporary Chinese American playwright David Henry Hwang has written such symbolist dramas as *The Sound of a Voice* and *M. Butterfly* (see chapter 6).

Performance Drama

Performance drama has its roots in such diverse traditions as the oral narratives told by African griots and Native American seers; as the soliloquies of Shakespearean drama; as the surreal cabaret performances of the Dadaists and Surrealists of the 1920s (e.g., Andre Breton); as the monologues of stand-up comics; and as the performance art of the 1970s, which drew on forms of different media and often incorporated lighting, music, visuals, dance, and written text.

Performance drama combines elements of drama, poetry, and the short story as the genre also breaks down the boundaries between art forms. The central figure is a speaker, a solo artist who often creates an autobiographical persona or impersonates a collection of characters. The speaker presents interior monologues—a combination of inner thoughts, remembrance, and, often, social commentary. The approach is open and personal; the audience feels as if the persona is conversing in an intimate way with the public or letting the audience overhear his/her inner thoughts. The structure of the drama is open-ended and fluid. The script does not adhere to traditional forms of narrative or of dramatic structure, often following a stream-of-consciousness logic and using symbolism, dream, and anecdote to convey state of mind, character, and theme. The script, sometimes spontaneously improvised, also may draw on such poetic techniques as imagery, symbolism, and figurative language. One element of the form resembles the structure of the modern short story, created by James Joyce. The speaker often experiences a realization—an epiphany—by the end of the monologue, as does a protagonist in Joyce-ian short fiction. The performance also may include décor, costumes, settings, music, art, graphics, lighting, video—elements of other art forms. Finally, performance texts challenge orthodox notions of drama because they may be performed in such alternative spaces as cafes, coffeehouses, or art galleries instead of theaters, and therefore, attract public audiences who may not attend theatrical performances.

Like other forms of literature, the work also conveys a message—oftentimes a critique of everyday life or a vision of social protest. Some performance artists are noted for their comic, outrageous, or iconoclastic productions that challenge societal norms of appropriate behavior and North American cultural and social values. For example, in 1981, Laurie Anderson, combining elements of music, narrative, and visuals, created an eight-hour montage of song, story, and spectacle that critiqued the media culture of North America. In another performance scenario, "Constant State of Desire (1986)," Karen Finlay rebels quite vividly against the constraints of urban domesticity. Two important performance artists whose work expands the narrative and dramatic possibilities of the form are Spalding Gray, who in "Swimming to Cambodia" explores autobiographical landscapes of his life, and Eric Bogosian, who in several performance pieces critiques the character of men in America and what he views as an apathetic American society.

Anna Deavere Smith's *Twilight Los Angeles: 1992* portrays many characters who witnessed the Los Angeles riots. Her monologues, based on interviews, give readers multiple perspectives and visions of this moment in history. Her monologue, based on a interview with gang leader, Twilight Bey, is included in chapter 7.

Film and Television

An important twentieth-century development that influences public interest in theater is the moving image—film. The advent of moving pictures and of television has changed the viewing habits of human beings forever.

FILM

Film shares many characteristics with drama: setting, plot, character, conflict, dialogue, images, symbolism, and theme. The image adds new dimensions to language on screen; in drama, the work retains a more powerful position. Films, like drama, require conventions. For example, movies generally have music in the background—a score that helps to determine tone or mood.

One advantage of film is the capacity to change settings and locations. Since movies are shot in small scenes and out of sequence, the screenwriter can defy all of the dramatic unities. A film can span centuries and continents. Now digital imaging and computer software can create virtual realities, computer-morphed images, and special effects.

Like fiction writers, screenwriters have enormous freedom with point of view. The camera lens can determine viewer response: a wide-angle lens gives a panoramic shot, a normal-angle lens what we can imagine as a realistic view, and a telephoto lens, a close-up, detailed image. A close-up can create the illusion of intimacy just as a first-person narrator in a novel may achieve the same effect. A wide angle provides distance, objectivity, and a sweeping view. A zoom can accomplish both purposes. Not only the camera lens but also the point of view from which the subject is filmed results in a change of perspective; you can manipulate point of view through camera angles. A high-angle shot has the scene viewed from above and from a distance, an eye-level angle from normal viewing distance, a low-angle shot from below, and a bird's eye view from above the subject. The camera also can film a shot from the perspective or gaze of a character in the film; this kind of shot creates a particular point of view. Films depend on cinematography, lighting, and music to create effects and to heighten the visual drama. For example, a wide-angle shot of helicopters in the air accompanied by Richard Wagner's "Ride of the Valkyries" playing in the background in Francis Ford Coppola's *Apocalypse Now* gives the viewer an idea of the idiocy of war and of the powerful exhilaration of battle before it subsides inescapably into horror. A close-up of Martin Sheen's face as he witnesses his friend's severed head renders the terror personal and human.

CHECKLIST FOR WRITING ABOUT FILM

1. What is the function of the setting and props? Of the objects in the film?
2. Who are the main subjects? The main characters? Are they developed? What role do the minor characters play in the film?
3. How does the film handle plot? Are there flashbacks? Flash-forwards?
4. How does the director use composition (i.e., the placement of the image in the frame)?
5. How do the lens types, shots, and camera angles develop the story?
6. What is the impact of the cinematography?
7. Does the editing seem to be smooth?
8. What is the effect of the lighting? Is it dark? Is it soft?
9. What is the impact of the music? Does the music heighten the action? Develop character? Develop the theme?
10. How do all the elements of the film develop the theme?
11. Evaluate the film. Consider screenplay, acting, directing, editing, and cinematography.

SIMILARITIES AND DIFFERENCES BETWEEN DRAMA AND FILM

The elements that will be compared are those that are defined in terms of the "mise-en-scene" of a text, a term from drama that means those elements that the director manipulates to create a unified work. These elements include the following: scene, subjects, story, perspective, continuity, visuals, sound effects and music, symbolism, verbal or visual impact, and relationship with an audience. Understanding the similarities and differences between these two forms will help you to analyze and to write an essay about each genre or an essay comparing a dramatic and a filmed version of a text. For example, your instructor may ask you to compare two filmed versions of Hamlet with the original or the text and the film version of *A Raisin in the Sun*.

The following chart provides you with some points of comparison and contrast between drama and film.

Drama	Film
Scene	
Similarities:	
Scene—physical location of a play	Settings where film occurs
Stage sets	Stage sets
Illusion of reality on stage	Illusion of reality
Symbolic role of scenes	Symbolic role of setting
Differences:	
Constructed sense of reality	On location sets
Illusion of reality on stage	Ability to have multiple settings and locations
	Visual impact of settings to create images, moods, and theme
	More expansive sense of setting
Subjects	
Similarities:	
Main characters	Main characters
Round or flat characters	Round or flat characters
Major and minor protagonists	Major or minor protagonists
Character foils	Character foils
Character revealed through appearance, gesture, action, dialogue, and relationships with others	Character revealed through appearance, gesture, action, dialogue, and relationships with others
Differences:	
Emphasis on character revelation through monologues and dialogue	More emphasis on physical presence on screen
Story	
Similarity:	
Script includes setting, characters, plot conflict, dialogue, and symbolism	Script includes setting, characters, plot, conflict, dialogue, and symbolism
Differences:	
Concentrated plot line	Multiple plot lines; ability to develop simultaneous stories through split-screen editing

Drama	Film
Stage directions may include instructions for character gestures, lighting, and music	Shooting script includes shots, camera placement, and angles

Perspective

Differences:

Limited ability to manipulate perspective	Perspective established by use of camera lens, shots, and by camera angles
Perspective dependant on use of parts of the stage (i.e., foreground and background); different sets; staging— movement of actors on the stage and in parts of the theater (i.e., actors speaking from balconies in the theater)	

Continuity

Similarity:

Continuity determined by sequence of plot and textual editing to create unity	Continuity determined by sequence of plot

Difference:

Plot devices, structural elements, and dialogue create unity	Editing of shots and film sequences to create unity; cuts to create transitions from one shot to the next

Visuals

Similarity:

Visuals include stage sets, costumes, props, and lighting	Visuals include settings, stage sets, props, costumes, and lighting

Difference:

Effects emanate from physical placement on stage and impact of lighting	Cinematography includes kind of film, texture of film, lighting, color, light and shadow

Sound Effects and Music

Similarity:

Use of sound effects and background music to create mood and theme	Use of sound effects and music to create mood and theme

Differences:

Limited use of sound effects	Heightened use of sound effects and music; more continuous use of sound effects and music
	Use of music as an underlying thread to develop themes and to unify work

Symbolism

Similarity:

Elements of setting, props, costumes, and lighting serve as symbols and develop the meanings of the work	Elements of setting, props, objects in film, characters' dress, and lighting serve as symbols and develop the meanings of the work

Difference:

Dialogue creates irony and symbolism	Cinematography and editing create symbolism

Theme

Similiarity:

All elements develop the themes of the work	All elements develop the themes of the work

Verbal/Visual Medium

Difference:

Primarily a verbal medium; impact based on staged version of a text	Primarily a visual medium; impact arises from visual images, from cinematography

Impact on Audience

Difference:

Play's impact is from live performance and interaction with an audience	Audience is in a darkened theater, watching controlled moving images on a screen
Performances of a play may change based upon audience's reaction	The audience is passive
	The medium suggests larger-than-life images

TELEVISION

Television shares many techniques with film; the great difference, of course, is the size of the screen. Because the viewing area is confined, television employs more close-up shots. Programs are shaped by segments and by commercials, and series require twenty-six episodes each season. These constraints determine character, theme, conflict, and quality.

With the expansion of cable and pay per view television, specialty networks—news, music, science fiction, cartoons, movie, sports—make the possibilities endless. At the same time, Bruce Springsteen still sings that he has "fifty-seven channels and nothing to watch." Surely, more exciting productions will come from artists in the future as they explore the full potential of television.

ELEMENTS OF DRAMA

Character

Imagined people stand at the center of almost all of the forms of literature. Anyone who appears in a work is called a **character,** a term chosen carefully for its meaning—those innate faculties that give a person identity and that distinguish him or her from others. Plays present a special framework for characters because the genre differs from fiction and from poetry since most dramas function without narration and narrators.

The *major* characters tend to be round, dynamic, and well-developed, whereas *minor* characters remain flat, static, and slightly developed. Often a character appears in order to illuminate, double, or contradict a main character—a foil. Because they are easily recognized types, some characters are known as **stereotypes** or **stock** characters. In commedia dell'arte, for example, the harlequin always plays the same part—always acts in a predictable manner. All of the characters in this kind of drama are stereotypes by definition. This comfortable recognition allows the playwright to create characters easily.

The personae in most plays, however, grow and change; the development of the characters leads to important knowledge concerning the meaning of the drama. For example, at the end of *Antigone*, Creon recognizes his responsibility for the tragedy that has ruined both his life and the city of Thebes.

Soliloquy, Monologue, and Dialogue

A character's language reveals his or her feelings, values, situation, and/or beliefs. In a **soliloquy**—a long speech by one character, the speaker communicates special information to the audience. Think of Hamlet's famous words on suicide, "To be or not to be." Through this eloquent aside, the audience learns of Hamlet's pain as he contemplates his duty to exact revenge for his father's death, a pain that makes life unbearable. Hamlet resents his situation, his mother, his uncle; he feels increasingly angry, desperate, sad, and suicidal. Indeed, he cannot decide on an adequate response to the unreasonable demands of life (chapter 4). Unlike a soliloquy, a **monologue** may be addressed to other characters as well as to the audience. It serves the same function; it permits an extended discussion of information, attitudes, or ideas by one character.

Most words in a play, however, are spoken between two characters. This exchange, called **dialogue**, demonstrates agreements, conflicts, relationships, differing or similar beliefs and motives between personae. Dialogue becomes the main element in the play for the development of character, plot, and theme. Consider the following lines from Synge's *Riders to the Sea* (chapter 5), in which Synge writes about the power of family ties and about the power of the sea. The mother, Maurya, fears that her son, Michael, is dead; and she awaits news of his being washed ashore after buying wood to build a coffin for his burial. She entreats Bartley, her remaining son, not to leave the island. Examine the language:

Bartley*(Beginning to work with the rope.)*: I've no halter the way I can ride down on the mare, and I must go now quickly. This is the one boat going for two weeks or beyond it, and the fair will be a good fair for horses I heard them saying below.

Maurya: It's a hard thing they'll be saying below if the body is washed up and there's no man in it[1] to make the coffin, and I after giving a big price for the finest white boards you'd find in Connemara.

Bartley: How would it be washed up, and we after looking[2] each day for nine days, and a strong wind blowing a while back from the west and south?

Maurya: If it isn't found itself,[3] that wind is raising the sea, and there was a star up against the moon, and it rising in the night. If it was a hundred horses, or a thousand horses you had itself, what is the price of a thousand horses against a son where there is one son only?

---

[1] i.e., the house.   [2] when we have been looking.   [3] even if it isn't found.

The poetry of Maurya's language, the persuasive quality of her description of the landscape and of the horses, and the value that she places on her love for and need of her sons make the difference. Bartley leaves wishing "the Blessing of God" on his family. Ironically, the audience knows at the moment of Bartley's departure that he, too, will ride to the sea and drown. Synge's use of accent, dialect, ungrammatical constructions, figurative language, and poetic style are examples of effective use of dialogue to create meaning.

Action

Every character, played by an actor, not only speaks, but also acts and reacts to others and to events. A character may portray motivation through action. In *"Master Harold" . . . and the Boys,* Hally's action of spitting on Sam reveals his motive. Sam is African, but Sam represents Hally's spiritual father. Hally's action, in many ways, is unexplicable and unforgivable. His motives, however, arise from a lifetime of subtle bigotry and personal frustration.

The audience also can learn about characters when they refuse to act according to normal expectations. Mrs. Hale and Mrs. Peters do not reveal their knowledge about the Wright murder to the sheriff. They realize that Mrs. Wright was motivated to commit such violence by actions which the men would consider *Trifles* (chapter 6). In this play, Susan Glaspell artfully portrays character through inaction.

Much of the interaction in drama becomes quite complicated. Hamlet kills Polonius by mistake; Ophelia kills herself because she erroneously believes that Hamlet does not love her; Laertes agrees to kill Hamlet with a foil dipped in poison because he thinks that Hamlet has deliberately caused the deaths of his father and sister. All of these actions involve misunderstandings, and they represent only a small proportion of the intricate events in the play. Such complexity in relationships among characters deepens the texture and meaning of drama.

Plot

The **plot** in a dramatic or narrative work is the structure of its actions, ordered to achieve emotional and aesthetic effects. This definition becomes complicated by the relationship between plot and character. The actions, both verbal and physical, are performed by characters; they provide the vehicle through which characters reveal their moral and personal traits. Plot is more, much more, than the "story" of a play, which is a simple synopsis of the temporal events. Only when the story becomes related to discussions of relationships and organization of actions in order to produce meaning does it become part of the definition of plot.

Numerous patterns for plots exist; each depends on the mode of drama and its purposes. Is it tragedy? comedy? romance? satire? ritual? melodrama? Whatever the genre, all plots share certain elements in traditional forms of dramatic literature.

In any play, the interest centers on the **protagonist,** the hero or heroine. Usually this character struggles against an opponent or enemy, the character designated as the **antagonist.** The relation between them becomes the **conflict.** Many, but not all, plays contain one or more conflicts. In Shakespeare's *Hamlet,* the prince is the protagonist, and King Claudius, the antagonist. As Hamlet seeks revenge for his father's murder, a conflict between them escalates and complicates until both men die. Often the protagonist struggles in conflict with fate or circumstance; often the conflict resides within the main character.

Sometimes a character concocts a scheme that entraps another person, one who is naïve, trusting, and vulnerable. This scheme is called **intrigue.** Rosencrantz and Guildenstern agree to assist Claudius in his plans against Hamlet; this intrigue fails. Many comedies also depend upon this device.

As the audience or reader begins to follow and to sympathize with characters, the plot builds **suspense** about its events and resolutions. If the action contradicts readers' expectations, the result becomes **surprise.** The relationship of suspense and surprise provides the essential dynamism in a play and must be predicated on the effectiveness of motive and of previous action.

A traditional plot has what Aristotle called **unity of action,** by which he meant that every part or event becomes necessary and integral to the whole and that the loss of any part destroys the whole. In *Antigone,* the recognition of Antigone as the guilty person sought by Creon, Creon's inflexibility, Haimon's betrothal to Antigone, and Creon's final change of heart, incident by incident, clue by clue, exemplifies this quality (chapter 7).

Other plays include **double plots,** as in Elizabethan drama. Such plays involve a second story that becomes fascinating on its own merits and that enlarges understanding of the main plot. Such a **subplot** exists in *Hamlet* in the relationship between Hamlet and Ophelia. Plays may have multiple subplots.

In this traditional definition of plot, a sequence of events provides a *beginning* that establishes the situation and introduces characters, a *middle* that complicates the actions and develops character and an *end* that completes the action. The beginning of Hamlet captures attention with the appearance of the ghost and an exposition that implies that "something is rotten in the state of Denmark." The middle reveals Claudius as murderer, Hamlet as a pretended madman with a plan "to capture the conscience of a king." At this moment, the conflict reaches its highest point of tension for the protagonist, a point called the **apex.** By the end, Claudius has plotted the death of Hamlet; Ophelia has committed suicide; Hamlet has killed Polonius; Gertrude has swallowed poison; Laertes has killed Hamlet. Only Horatio remains to mourn the death of his "sweet prince" and to welcome Fortinbras.

In *Technique of the Drama* (1863), Gustav Freytag described plot in a configuration known as **Freytag's Pyramid.** According to this schema, a plot begins with rising action. In *Hamlet* this complication includes the appearance of the ghost; it includes the conflict between Claudius and Hamlet and events that eventually lead to Hamlet's success in achieving control. This rising action reaches a **climax** or **apex** for the hero. In *Hamlet* it becomes the proof of Claudius's crime through the play-within-the-play. Then comes the crisis where Hamlet fails to kill Claudius because the latter is praying. Then the **falling action** leads to the ascendance of Claudius until a **catastrophe** happens, as in the deaths of the main characters. This catastrophe may also be called the **denouement,** for not all plays end in tragic circumstances. Contemporary dramas often deliberately defy expectations of conventional plots, and some attempt to eliminate plot entirely.

Setting

In drama, **setting** differs greatly from other forms of literature because of the imperative for performance. In stage directions and in dialogue, the dramatist describes the place and time for the play. A designer creates stage sets that suggest the background for each scene. Shakespeare, for example, places Hamlet in Denmark; yet the stage can be transformed only into semblances of rooms in a castle, a graveyard, or a ship. The audience or reader must imagine the drowning of Ophelia and the battle won by Fortinbras. Still, the stage adds a dimension to drama that other forms of literature lack—visual and auditory images, live action, and spatial and temporal realities.

Props, scenery, costumes, and lights can change as the play progresses; but the setting on stage remains both limited and central to all productions. For instance, the set for *Riders to the Sea* should indicate the poverty of the modest cottage. One entrance must lead to the external world, to the sea that gives each family work and that claims each family's sons. Setting in drama may reveal economic status, geographic location, time period, and personal taste. Unlike fiction writers and poets, the playwright does not describe place in great detail, and he or she leaves much more to the imagination or to the stage.

Symbolism

In dramatic literature, **symbols** often are not subtle. They appear on stage as visual reminders of their central place in the meaning of the play. In "Trifles," one of the symbols, the dead canary, suggests the husband's cruelty and Minnie Wright's caged and broken state of self.

Irony

Dramatic irony appears in a play or in fiction when a situation or action becomes apparent to the audience but remains unknown to a character or to characters. Consequently, the persona acts in ignorance and often inappropriately. The Greek tragedians, whose conflicts and stories were already known to their audiences, based their works on a constant use of this technique.

Other kinds of irony:

- **Verbal irony** is a statement in which the meaning is different from the message that is expressed. Jonathan Swift's "A Modest Proposal" for eating children as a solution to the problem caused by the potato famine in Ireland depends greatly on this device.
- **Structural irony** sustains double meaning throughout the work. In drama, this technique requires a naïve protagonist; in fiction an unreliable narrator often serves this purpose.

Theme

The themes of a play are not its subjects, but rather its central idea or ideas. One theme of *Antigone* concerns the idea of individual moral responsibility versus obedience to authority. Should Antigone obey the dictates of conscience or submit to Creon's decree that her brother remain unburied? This question directs the action. The theme centers on the tension between an individual code of ethics and a socially sanctioned moral code.

THE READING/WRITING PROCESS: DRAMA

Interpreting drama begins with impressions about a play. Feelings often provide guidelines to intellectual analysis and responses. Reread the drama and examine its parts—character, plot, theme—to determine their relationship to the whole. Grasping the wholeness in a drama depends on looking carefully at all of its elements. Consider characters and their development; consider the conflicts and their complications and possible resolutions. Consider how themes emerge. Evaluate how well the play comes together.

Take notes, and be careful to pay close attention to stage directions, prologues, epilogues, and important quotations. Determine the play's meaning, and assess its ability to force a reader or audience to face matters of enduring value.

CHECKLIST FOR WRITING ABOUT DRAMA

1. Does the play have a **narrator?** How does this character function? Is he or she reliable?

2. Are the main characters fully developed? How do they change? What actions or words demonstrate such change? How do minor characters function in the play? What do you learn about characters from the dialogue of others? Is the character sympathetic? How would an audience react? What different interpretations of these characters are possible?

3. What is the central conflict? How is it resolved? Are there subplots? Which acts or scenes represent the **rising action?** Identify the **climax.** Is there suspense? Which acts or scenes represent the falling action? How are the **subplots** resolved?

4. How does the **dialogue** contribute to the **plot?** How do characters advance the plot or plots? How does **setting** function in relation to plot? Does offstage action contribute to the development of conflict? How?

5. Does the play contain **irony?** What kinds of irony are present? Is the irony effective?

6. Are there symbols that suggest the theme?

7. What information about production is included in the stage directions? What information does the play give about costume, set, lighting, sound effects?

8. What are central themes? What are other significant issues? How do characters and conflicts illuminate themes?

9. Discuss conflict, character, language, theme in relation to the total effect of the play. Does it work? What does it mean?

10. What is the best feature of the play? What is the weakest feature of the play? What is the final evaluation?

■ STUDENT PORTFOLIO ■

Response to Rebecca Gilman's *Boy Gets Girl*

Students in Kathena Hasbrouck's Composition II class were asked to write a character analysis essay for Gilman's *Boy Gets Girl*. The main goal of the assignment was to strengthen critical understanding of the characters and their motives. Instead of simply coming to a broad conclusion about a figure, students were encouraged to consider every facet and detail about a character's personality. Consider: How might he or she react to a situation emotionally? Physically? Intellectually? Drawing on evidence from the text to support these conclusions, students were able to formulate detailed analyses.

After listing topics of interest and freewriting about the various people in Gilman's play, Rob Dexter chose to focus on Theresa Bedell. He found her relationships with men to be intriguing, and he wondered mostly whether they were positive and if they ever evolved over the course of the drama. After opting to focus on Theresa's involvement with men, Rob read the play again, highlighting sections that clearly depict the way her particular character deals with situations and people. Meanwhile, during class, students worked collaboratively to dig beneath each character's surface. Exercises were done to examine how one character might respond to a character from a different play. For instance, how would Nora from Ibsen's *A Doll's House* cope with Tony's stalking? By gathering textual evidence, students were able to defend their interpretation of a character as well as posit an explanation for his or her actions.

After further thinking about Theresa, Rob wrote the first draft of his essay. His main guide for this process was a basic outline that explored the main male characters in the play—Howard, Mercer, Les, and Tony. When the draft was complete, one of his peers reviewed it. The main issues that his classmate found with the character analysis included a weak introduction and conclusion as well as a lack of textual evidence and transitions between thoughts. Rob returned to his copy of the play. He further developed his introduction, integrated more quotes, and found ways to segue smoothly from topic to topic.

The next draft showed vast improvement. Now that Rob had made the introduction more specific, the thesis became clearer and more insightful. Having a stronger thesis made the paper easier to follow as a whole. In addition, precise details and quotes were applied to each of the main claims. With each example of textual evidence, Rob further explained his ideas. The teacher had only one main qualm with that draft: the conclusion was still ambiguous. The process Rob went through in arguing for his interpretation came to a standstill in the conclusion, because there was no final epiphany. After another revision, the final paper includes a more fully developed conclusion, one that explains directly to the reader exactly who Theresa Bedell is in relation to the men in her life. Rob's final draft reveals a precise, careful examination of the relationship of characters in a dramatic work.

Notes

Theresa is involved in different types of relationships with different men over the course of the play. Most of these relationships evolve as the play goes on.

Howard—her boss—not friends, but they do get along—discuss outside lives—after the stalking begins, they grow closer—offers her a raise so she can afford apartment—allows her to stay at his house—visits her apartment to pick up clothes and other stuff for her—throws himself between window and her to be sure that she is not harmed by Tony

Mercer—work acquaintance at first—calls him "new guy"—begins to ask for his advice with personal problems—he asks her if she wants to stay at his house when she can't get the apartment she wants—visits apartment with Howard—when Tony shows up, he chases after him

Les—Initially turned off by his obnoxious behavior and womanizing movies—he grows on her after they watch Jeopardy in his hotel room—he tells her about his past, and he understands why he is how he is—offers to break Tony's legs—flies her to Denver on a private jet

Tony—starts off as nice guy who seems to be desperate for a girlfriend—gets a little ahead of himself on second date—her termination of the relationship sends him into a downward spiral—shows up at office, trying to get her to see him again—sends flowers, bombs her answering machine—sends a threatening note—trashes her apartment and steals from her

First Draft: Peer Review

Rob Dexter

Kathena Hasbrouck

Composition 2

March 2004

                    Insert Title Here

    Theresa has relationships of different types with the men in the play Boy Gets Girl. All of these relationships evolve throughout the course of the play.

Where's the rest of your intro? Try to introduce the essay in an interesting way.

Theresa mentions two relationships she has had with men that occurred before the beginning of the play: one with a former boyfriend named Mark (Gilman 22), and one with her estranged brother (Gilman 25). Not much information is given about these relationships, but neither ended on good terms. Mark was transferred to Kuala Lumpur and did not ask her to go. Though she says she would not have gone with him, it must have hurt that he did not even ask her to go with him (25). Her relationship with her brother also ended poorly. After their mother died, he began drinking and lost his job. Theresa moved him in with her, but he stole from her and she was forced to kick him out. She has not seen him in six years. These were <u>both dysfunctional</u> relationships.

For these two, put in quotes to back up your information.

Same comment on the intro. You need more of it.

How does this relate to evolving relationships?

Theresa also has a relationship with her boss, Howard. Early on, they are not close friends, but they are at least friendly with each other. They talk about Theresa's date with Tony, showing that they sometimes discuss their lives outside of work (Gilman 19). At one point, Howard asks about Theresa's ex-boyfriend, Mark. He does not remember much about him, but the fact that he remembers the name shows that he and Theresa have discussed their personal lives in the past (22). Later on in their discussion, Theresa says, "You know what? I don't want to talk about my love life" (23). Because she and Howard are not close friends, she is uncomfortable discussing her love life with him.

I kind of agree, but I feel like you are using these to perhaps support the reasons for her evolving relationships w/the other men in her life.

The relationship between Howard and Theresa grows stronger as the story progresses. After her second date with Tony, she tells him that she thinks Tony is following her (46). She would not have told him this if she did not feel that they had a good friendship. After Tony's harassment becomes severe and Theresa has found a new apartment that she cannot afford, Howard offers her a raise (74). His concern for her safety has caused him to do something he may not ordinarily have done. Around the same time, he says, "I've taken advantage of your loyalty and your reliability for too long, and you and I are going to sit down and decide on a new direction for the both of us, that pleases the both of us" (74). This is another gesture he would not have <u>made</u> if

did it ever seem like he didn't care about her?

he <u>did not care about</u> her. When Theresa is unable to find a new apartment, Howard allows her to move in with him and (88). Again, he would not have done this if he *? where did the rest go? And what?* did not feel close to Theresa.

By the end, the two have become close enough that Howard is willing to help Theresa at the expense of his own safety. When she says that she misses her things, he offers to go to her apartment with Mercer to pick up a few things for her (100). This is taking a risk because of the possibility of Tony being there. He takes another risk when he and Mercer arrive and find the door unlocked. Instead of leaving to call for help, he stays and pretends to be the police (103). In doing this, he is potentially putting himself in harm's way in order to help her. In the final scene, when Tony is seen trying to get in, he goes as far as to place himself between a window and Theresa in order to act as a human shield. Here, their relationship is strong enough that Howard is willing to take a bullet for Theresa.

Put in the name. The he's can get confusing.

Transition?

Theresa also has a relationship with her coworker, Mercer. In the beginning, they are little more than work acquaintances. When talking to Howard, Theresa calls Mercer "the new guy" despite the fact that he has worked there for three months (20). Their conversations are mainly work related (32-33) and rarely drift into their personal lives, as evidenced by the fact that she does not know that he was married (78).

As time goes on, the relationship between Theresa and Mercer grows tighter. Though it may be because she does not have anyone else to really talk to, Theresa begins to confide in Mercer and seek his advice. When she asks him, "If I tell you something, do you promise not to tell anybody?" she is showing a willingness to tell him something that she would not tell a casual work acquaintance (54). Upon hearing that she is unable to get the apartment she wants, Mercer immediately asks if Theresa wants to stay with him and his wife for the night, another indiction of the closeness of their friendship (78).

Good! I like this sentence.

Mercer also puts himself in harm's way in order to help Theresa. He goes along with Howard on the trip to her apartment, and also does not run away when they find the door unlocked (103). He goes a step further by chasing after Tony when they see him trying to get into Theresa's apartment building (115). He has no idea if

Seems repetitive.

Maybe put in either

Tony has a weapon, but still decides to chase after him because of his closeness with Theresa.

The strangest relationship Theresa has is with Les Kennkat. She is initially reluctant to talk to him (23), but does not dislike him at the beginning of their first interview. They share an interest in the Yankees, and he offers to buy her a drink. She considers this offer until he says, "You're not my type, if you know what I mean. I mean, you know, I would never put you in one of my movies." Offended, she rejects his offer (43-44). She still has not completely soured on him, as she tells Mercer that "he is kind of funny" (52).

During the second interview, however, she becomes offended at his repeated womanizing. She says:

> So I could say about you, "He's a funny guy, except when it comes to women." And I have said that before, about other men. You know: "He's a good guy, but he does have a problem with women." But I'm not saying that anymore. Because you're not a funny guy, and you're not a good guy, if you can't deal with half the population of the world (65).

Their relationship takes a surprising twist after Theresa's story is published. She visits Les in the hospital, and her opinion of him changes. When she enters his room, he is thrilled to see her (92). After telling her how much he loved her story, he convinces her to stay and watch <u>Jeopardy</u> with him (96). [Her decision to stay shows that she is no longer disgusted with him as she once was, and that she may be beginning to enjoy his company.] Theresa later tells Mercer that during this time, Les told her about his past, and that she is beginning to understand why he is the way he is (98). Their relationship further solidifies when Les arranges for Theresa to fly to Denver on a private jet and offers to have Tony's knees broken (113).

This sentence shows clear evolution of their relationship! Good!

Theresa's most unhealthy relationship is with Tony. Even in the beginning, Tony showed signs of being a stalker. He tries to move the relationship along quickly. On their first date, he says, "Maybe you could take me to see a Yankees game some time and I could learn to love them too" (16). This implies that he is already planning on having a future relationship with her. Later on, he says, "I think we have a lot in common" (17).

More on Tony? Conclusion?

At this point, it is impossible for him to know how much they have in common. They simply have not spent enough time together. He is so desperate to be in a relationship, that he has found similarities where none exist.

When you write the conclusion, make it longer than your current intro ☺

In response to the peer-review comments that Rob received, he revised the first draft of his paper and turned the second in to his instructor. After revising again based on his instructor's comments, Rob was able to turn in a final draft for a grade.

Final Draft

Rob Dexter

Kathena Hasbrouck

Composition 2

March 2004

Theresa's Relationships with Men

In the play <u>Boy Gets Girl</u> by Rebecca Gilman, the main character Theresa is involved in several types of relationships with men. While seemingly a strong, independent woman, she finds herself being swept along due to the action of one man in her life. During the course of the story, Theresa ranges from being the victim of a frightening stalker and a colleague in need of protection to the unlikely friend of a man who is neither close to her age nor a person with the same values. The play ends with her having to give up unwillingly her former life and name, never having found a mutually satisfying relationship with a male peer and not able to stop the terror any other way.

While not a prominent part of the story, Theresa mentions two relationships she has had with men that occurred before the beginning of the play: one with a former boyfriend named Mark (22), and one with her estranged brother (25). Not much information is given about these relationships, but neither ended on good terms. Mark was transferred to Kuala Lumpur and did not ask her to go. Though she says she would not have gone with him, it must have hurt that he did not even ask her to go with him (25). Her relationship with her brother also ended poorly. After their mother died, he began drinking and lost his job. Theresa moved him in with her, but he stole from her and she was forced to kick him out. She has not seen him in six years. These were both dysfunctional relationships. It is interesting to note that in both of these early relationships, Theresa must have been frustrated that she was not able to steer the men in the direction she had hoped for.

Theresa also has a relationship with her boss, Howard. Early on, they are not close friends, but they are at least friendly with each other. They talk about Theresa's date with Tony, showing that they sometimes discuss their lives outside of work (19). At one point, Howard asks about Theresa's ex-boyfriend, Mark. He does not remember much about him, but the fact that he remembers the name shows that he and Theresa have discussed their personal lives in the past (22). Later on in their discussion, Theresa says, "You know what? I don't want to talk about my love life" (23). Because she and Howard are not close friends, she is uncomfortable discussing her love life with him.

The relationship between Howard and Theresa grows stronger as the story progresses as a result of her being stalked. After her second date with Tony, she tells Howard that she thinks Tony is following her (46). She would not have told him this if she did not feel that they had a good friendship. After Tony's harassment becomes severe and Theresa has found a new apartment that she cannot afford, Howard offers her a raise (74). His concern for her safety has caused him to do something he may not ordinarily have done. Around the same time, he says, "I've taken advantage of your loyalty and your reliability for too long, and you and I are going to sit down and decide on a new direction for the both of us, that pleases the both of us" (74). This is another gesture he would not have made if she was not being harassed by Tony. When Theresa is unable to find a new apartment, Howard allows her to move in with him (88). There would have been no need for this if Tony had not entered Theresa's life.

By the end, the two have become close enough that Howard is willing to help Theresa at the expense of his own safety. When she says that she misses her things, he offers to go to her apartment with Mercer to pick up a few things for her (100). This is taking a risk because of the possibility of Tony being there. He takes another risk when he and Mercer arrive and find the door unlocked. Instead of leaving to call for help, he stays and pretends to be the police (103). In doing this, he is potentially putting himself in harm's way in order to help her. In the final scene, when Tony is seen trying to get in, Howard goes as far as to place himself between a window and Theresa in order to act as a human shield. Here, their relationship is strong enough that Howard is willing to take a bullet for Theresa. While she is an independent woman, she is in a dangerous situation and in need of protection for a situation that is out of her hands.

Theresa also has a relationship with her coworker, Mercer. In the beginning, they are little more than work acquaintances. When talking to Howard, Theresa calls Mercer "the new guy" despite the fact that he has worked there for three months. Their conversations are mainly work related and rarely drift into their personal lives, as evidenced by the fact that she does not know that he was married.

As time goes on, the relationship between Theresa and Mercer grows tighter. Though it may be because she does not have anyone else to really talk to, Theresa begins to confide in Mercer and seek his advice. When she asks him, "If I tell you something, do you promise not to tell anybody?" she is showing a willingness to tell him something that she would not tell a casual work acquaintance (54). Upon hearing that she is unable to get the apartment she wants, Mercer immediately asks if Theresa wants to stay with he and his wife for the night, another indication of the closeness of their friendship (78).

Mercer, like Howard, also puts himself in harm's way in order to help Theresa. He goes along with Howard on the trip to her apartment and does not run away when they find the door unlocked (103). He goes a step further by chasing after Tony when they see him trying to get into Theresa's apartment building (115). He has no idea if Tony has a weapon, but he still decides to chase after him because of his closeness with Theresa. Here, again, Theresa takes the role of a woman needing protection in a situation that she is unable to stop on her own.

The strangest relationship Theresa has is with Les Kennkat. She is initially reluctant to talk to him (23), but she does not dislike him at the beginning of their first interview. They share an interest in the Yankees, and he offers to buy her a drink. She considers this offer until he says, "You're not my type, if you know what I mean. I mean, you know, I would never put you in one of my movies." Offended, she rejects his offer (43–44). She still has not completely soured on him, though, as she tells Mercer that "he is kind of funny" (52).

During the second interview, however, she becomes offended at his repeated womanizing. She says:

> So I could say about you, "He's a funny guy, ex-
> cept when it comes to women." And I have said
> that before, about other men. You know: "He's a
> good guy, but he does have a problem with
> women." But I'm not saying that anymore. Be-
> cause you're not a funny guy, and you're not a
> good guy, if you can't deal with half the popu-
> lation of the world. (65)

Their relationship takes a surprising twist after Theresa's story is published. She visits Les in the hospital, and her opinion of him changes. When she enters his room, he is thrilled to see her (92). After telling her how much he loved her story, he convinces her to stay and watch Jeopardy with him (96). Her decision to stay shows that she is no longer disgusted with him, as she once was, and that she may be beginning to enjoy his company. Theresa later tells Mercer that during this time, Les told her about his past, and that she is beginning to understand why he is the way he is (98). Their relationship further solidifies when Les arranges for Theresa to fly to Denver on a private jet and offers to have Tony's knees broken (113).

Theresa's most unhealthy relationship is with Tony, and it gets worse as time progresses. Even in the beginning, Tony shows signs of being a stalker. He tries to move the relationship along quickly. On their first date, he says, "Maybe you could take me to see a Yankees game sometime and I could learn to love them too" (16). This implies that he is already planning on having a future relationship with her. Later on, he says, "I think we have a lot in common" (17). At this point, it is impossible for him to know how much they have in common. They simply have not spent enough time together. He is so desperate to be in a relationship that he has found similarities where none exist.

Theresa and Tony's relationship gets even worse on the second date. After Theresa says that she saw the

Yankees on TV at the restaurant bar, she explains to him how the playoffs are structured. After hearing this, Tony says, "You're going to have to teach me all this stuff. I don't know any of this stuff (25-26)." Here again he is already planning for a future relationship. Later, after Theresa says she is going home, Tony tells her, "Last night, I even, I called the museum. I called MoMA and asked about that benefit" (30). This is yet another instance in which Tony has overstepped the bounds of a young relationship.

After Theresa cuts the second date short, her relationship with Tony rapidly deteriorates until it reaches a frightening level. One day, he shows up at her office and tries to convince her to see him again. When she refuses, he asks her if she is afraid of intimacy (34-35), a highly inappropriate question given their situation. Soon, he is sending her flowers (44) and bombarding her answering machine with messages (50). After she tells him not to call her anymore, he escalates his messages to threats of violence (55). Shortly after that, he sends her a letter threatening her with rape (80). Finally, he breaks into her house, destroys the place (104), and writes awful messages in the margins of her books (114). In a short period of time, Tony has gone from being the guy trying to win the girl's heart to being the guy trying to destroy the girl's life.

Theresa has different types of relationships with several different men that evolve over the course of the play. Howard and Mercer both become her friends by the end after having been only casual work acquaintances at the beginning. Les Kenkatt becomes a friend despite the fact that she finds him to be an obnoxious womanizer in their first few meetings. Tony changes from being a harmless, slightly overzealous suitor to a dangerous stalker intent on ruining Theresa's life. Even with the support of the friends she develops along the way, Tony's harassment ultimately forces Theresa to change her name and start her life anew.

Works Cited

Gilman, Rebecca. *Boy Gets Girl:* New York: Faber and Faber, Farrar, Straus and Giroux, 2000.

· CHAPTER 12 ·

Nonfiction

When we think of nonfiction prose, we envision objective **expository** writing designed to convey information to an audience: newswriting, for example, or scientific and business communications. Nonfiction also may be creative, evocative essays replete with a sense of voice and power. Imaginative reaction, passionate commitment, and the urgency of personal perspective play a role in some kinds of nonfiction. Many forms have features of fiction, poetry, and drama: vivid, descriptive detail, narrative example, metaphoric language, and dialogue.

In nonfiction, we may be drawn into the world of the writing just as we are in fiction, in poetry, or in drama. However, we become involved in different ways. We read to absorb, to react, perhaps to be moved and enlightened by facts, arguments, issues, and ideas. As Susan Sontag suggests, "an essay could be as much an event, a transforming event, as a novel or a poem."

FORMS OF NONFICTION

Speech

As major civilizations and communal life flourished, public discourse evolved. The **speech,** oral communication designed to be delivered to an audience, became a popular form of public communication in Greek times, particularly during the fifth century B.C., the age of Pericles, at the height of Athenian democracy. In his treatise, *The Rhetoric,* Aristotle (384–322 B.C.), a Greek philosopher, categorized the three kinds of speeches prevalent in his society: orations delivered in the law courts, in the political arena, at ceremonial occasions. Many examples of these declamations, of course, did not survive because they were not transcribed. One famous speech is Pericles's funeral oration for the Athenian dead (430 B.C.), which appears in Thucydides's *History of the Peloponnesian Wars.* Among other arguments, Pericles praises the Athenian democratic "system of government" as a "model to others." Many famous Greek orators and teachers developed the form of the speech between the fifth and fourth centuries B.C., including Isocrates and Demosthenes whose political works are notable examples. Roman rhetoric was patterned after Greek models. Cicero (106–43 B.C.), a Roman statesman, politician, and rhetorician, excelled at oratory and published his own speeches, which still serve as exemplars of classical argument. (See chapter 3.) Examples of speeches in *Legacies* include Sojourner Truth's "Ain't I a Woman?" (chapter 7) and Martin Luther King's "Letter from Birmingham Jail" (chapter 12).

1436

Philosophical Treatise

Another human imperative has been to speculate on the state of the world and on human nature. One of the earliest forms of nonfiction has been the **philosophical treatise,** an extended formal meditation on a philosophical, religious, or political subject. Such treatises convey the central ideas, beliefs, and values of many Western and Eastern societies. Interestingly, at approximately the same time (c. 600 B.C.), Pythagoras wrote about mathematics in ancient Greece, Confucius was a teacher in China, and Hindu sages created the *Upanishads,* the central documents of Hindu thought in India.

Plato (428–347 B.C.), one of the foremost Greek philosophers, wrote tracts on such subjects as the nature of love, "The Symposium" (chapter 6) and the ideal state, *The Republic* (chapter 8). The wisdom of Confucius (551–479(?) B.C.), a Chinese scholar and teacher, instructed people to live a good life in harmony with others. Confucius suggests, for example, that a ruler must "govern by virtue. . . .": "Govern the people by virtue . . . and the people . . . will be reformed of themselves." Another Chinese philosopher, known as Lao-tzu (575–485(?) B.C.), assumes a different religious stance: withdrawal from the world, meditation, mysticism, and the cultivation of silence as the way of the spirit. Lao-tzu is considered responsible for the *Tao te Ching,* the opening line of which states, "The way that can be spoken of is not the way. . . ."

Examples of political, philosophical, and or religious treatises abound in world history. Think of the documents of the American or the French revolution; the Communist Manifesto; Chairman Mao's sayings; the sacred texts of world religions. The poem of Lao-tzu (chapter 7) and the reflections of Albert Camus (chapter 8) also exemplify this form of nonfiction.

Autobiography

One structured type of personal writing is **autobiography,** defined as writing about one's life. Autobiography became prevalent with the rise of Christianity as people had the urge to document their spiritual conversions. One of the earliest stories of such a conversion, St. Augustine's *Confessions,* written between A.D. 397 and 400, describes the author's childhood, his conversion to Christianity at thirty-two, and his transformation from sinner to Christian.

The desires to fashion a story of one's life, to create from memories—from inchoate reminiscences—an ordered vision of one's past, and to seek personal meaning from one's past are deep needs in human beings. The autobiographical impulse has taken hold of writers throughout the ages as diverse as Machiavelli, Helen Keller, and Maya Angelou. Autobiography becomes a particularly powerful means of expression for those groups who feel disenfranchised because this form of writing defines and asserts selfhood in response to the lack of recognition of ethnic identity. Alice Walker has written many autobiographical essays that explore her stance as an African American woman, for example, "Am I Blue?" (chapter 8). One particularly North American form of autobiography is the *slave narrative,* a story that portrays the slave's efforts to secure release from bondage and to gain freedom. Read Harriet Jacobs's autobiography, *Incidents in the Life of a Slave Girl* in chapter 7.

Memoir

As eras of conquest and travel progressed during the Middle Ages and the Renaissance, another autobiographical form emerged. **Memoir** presents the remembrances of a public figure and the events of an historical era. Perhaps, one of the earliest examples of such a document is Julius Caesar's record of his military campaigns in Gaul 102–44 B.C. Other examples of memoir include Marco Polo's travels in China and India (*The Travels of Marco Polo,* 1293), Leo Africanus's account of Africa written when he was taken captive and held as a slave by pirates (1526), and Babur's (Zahir Ud-Din Mohammed's) recounting of his battles in India (1526). Contemporary memoirists include Winston Churchill and Richard Nixon.

Journal

The **journal**, another form of personal writing, concerns the self exclusively, and the presumed audience is the author. Some of the earliest examples include the lists of Sei Shonogan—a form of a diary kept by a woman in the court of the emperor in tenth-century Japan. Titles from Shonogan's diary reveal "Things That Make One's Heart Beat Faster"; "Things That Arouse a Fond Memory of the Past"; "Hateful Things"; and "Depressing Things."

As journals developed, many types emerged: travel diaries, diaries of spiritual life, journals kept during the settlement of the frontier by the pioneers in North America, and diaries kept by women during the Civil War. Throughout literary history, numerous artists and writers were inveterate journal keepers: Leonardo da Vinci wrote and drew in sketchbooks; Henry David Thoreau composed more than 60,000 pages of journals; Anaïs Nin had at least sixteen volumes of journals.

Letter writing represents another form of personal expression; often in letter writing, the assumption of a public as well as a private audience exists. Benjamin Franklin composed letters to his son; F. Scott Fitzgerald communicated by letter with his daughter, Scottie (see Chapter 5). Martin Luther King's "Letter from Birmingham Jail" presents a complex political argument that suggests the fusion of both the public and the private self and the impossibility of separating these selves in the response to political oppression.

Essay

During the Renaissance, with its emphasis on individual will and consciousness, the **essay** developed, a form of prose that presented a person's reflections and ideas on a specific topic. The essay (derived from the French verb *assayer*—meaning to try, to attempt) presents a concise, prose discussion of a limited topic and of limited length, designed for a general audience. Although the origin of the essay can be traced to ancient Rome—to Seneca and to Plutarch who wrote works with such titles as "On Envy and Hate," "On the Control of Anger," and "On Having Many Friends,"—Francis Bacon, the English scientist and philosopher (1561–1628), often receives credit for inventing the modern form of the genre. He wrote volumes of essays on subjects as varied as the relation of parents and children, death, truth, adversity, anger, revenge, atheism, suspicion, and cunning. During the 1600s and 1700s, many writers experimented with this form, including Blaise Pascal, who produced his *Pensées* (Thoughts, 1670), a collection of his thoughts; Montaigne, who penned his Essais (1580), his meditations; and in England in the 1700s Joseph Addison and Richard Steele, who wrote essays for their literary journal, *The Spectator.* The essay flourished in the hands of such eighteenth-century British writers as Jonathan Swift, Samuel Johnson, and William Hazlitt and such nineteenth-century North American writers as Henry David Thoreau and Ralph Waldo Emerson who wrote "Civil Disobedience" and "The American Scholar," respectively. Essay writing reached its apex in Britain and in North America in the eighteenth and nineteenth centuries.

Kinds of Essays

EXPOSITION

Exposition, the main form of nonfiction, explains or conveys information to a particular audience. Exposition may have a range of approaches—objective, subjective, factual, or reflective. An expository essay may describe, explain, give examples, compare, define, analyze, or demonstrate cause and effect. David Elkind's "Hurried Children" (chapter 4) explores the impact of our "hurried" lifestyle on today's children. Elkind uses several rhetorical modes, including definition, exemplification, and cause and effect to develop his points.

Expository essays may fall into two classes: *formal* and *informal* writing. In a formal expository essay, the writing may be organized with an introduction, middle paragraphs, and conclusion. The essay is carefully and tightly developed: a thesis and subtopics exist; the writer orders ideas into supporting paragraphs with clear topic sentences and supporting evidence; a direct and logical progression of points moves toward the conclusion. The point of view and tone may be more objective and less personal. Gould's "Nonmoral Nature" (chapter 8) represents a superb example of a tightly and formally organized essay. The informal essay may be organized by associations and may use techniques of fiction (personal, symbolic detail, dialogue, narrative excerpts) and of poetry (imagery, figurative language, repetition). Witness Maxine Hong Kingston's mix of description, reminiscence, narration, character sketch, and reflection in "No Name Woman" (chapter 6).

ARGUMENTATION

In **argumentation,** one of the primary forms of nonfiction prose, the writer presents a personal opinion with the intention of convincing an audience about his or her point of view, constructs reasons for that position, and develops supporting evidence. Informal and formal modes of structuring argument exist. Informal argument may take the form of persuasive writing in which emotional appeals, detail, narrative and personal examples provide the proof designed to convince a reader. For instance, if a writer composed an essay for a local paper to convince the audience that eighteen-year-olds' drunken driving poses a serious threat to others, he or she refers to the experience of witnessing a violent and fatal accident caused by an eighteen-year-old. Or the writer may recount a tale about his or her child or another teenager in order to persuade readers. The intent is to convince an audience of the validity of the position or to persuade people to take some action.

In formal argument, the writer also will develop an argumentative thesis (a position) and reason with his or her audience in mind. However, the position and the thesis will be more objectively stated; the reasons supported with proofs, data, statistics, examples. One option is to shape an argument in classic, Aristotelian style (see chapter 3). Martin Luther King's "Letter from Birmingham Jail" (chapter 12) is an excellent example of a formally structured, complex argumentative essay.

At the heart of argumentative writing remains a solid statement of thesis (position), development of reasons and supporting evidence, and sound, logical reasoning. Compare Toni Morrison's exploratory, allusive, lyrical, narrative political argument in "The Nobel Prize Speech" (chapter 8) with Simone de Beauvoir's logically structured presentation of women's position as "object" in "Woman as Other" (chapter 6).

FORMS OF CREATIVE NONFICTION

Creative nonfiction, once classified as the personal essay, is characterized by a strong sense of a personal voice and slant; an intimacy of tone—as if the writer is conversing with an imagined audience; experimental structure as opposed to academic essay form; and the use of literary devices. The literary techniques borrowed from fiction include shifts in point of view, setting, characterization, descriptive detail, and plot; from drama, character, conflict, and dialogue; and from poetry, imagery, figurative language, and symbolism. Creative nonfiction writers also balance the subjective and objective, showing and telling, narration and reflection. The essay embodies a process of discovery, moving from the personal to larger meanings and issues. As Janet Burroway suggests, "the essay begins in personal experiences but reaches out to a larger idea or area of thought about the human condition." Examples of this form include Scott Russell Sanders's "Wayland" and Joan Didion's "At the Dam" (both in chapter 8).

ELEMENTS OF NONFICTION

All forms of nonfiction share some similarities. A writer thinks of the audience, of the occasion for writing, of the reasons for the writing; he or she then shapes the writing with audience in mind. The writer becomes aware of purposes, intentions and overall goals and chooses relevant details, examples, facts, and reasons. Furthermore, he or she considers **point of view,** voice, the attitude and relationship to material and to audience, and thinks about the relationship between point of view and the persona in the work. This relationship provides readers with a sense of the writer as the character, the person behind the writing. Is the person honest? Does the voice sound real? truthful? distant? impassioned? angry? The persona and point of view of the writer influence the slant of the piece, the main idea, the thesis, the organization, the details, and the word choice. Rhetoricians label this consciousness of audience, occasion, purpose, goals, intent, and point of view the *rhetorical situation.*

Tone involves the feeling, mood, and attitude that readers infer from the content of the essay. In Alice Walker's "Am I Blue?" part of the tone emanates from a sense of righteous anger at the ways in which people treat animals.

The crux of effective nonfiction prose, detail and specific example, makes the piece come alive. The power of nonfiction rests in the interplay of the general and of the specific, of the abstract and of the concrete. Return to the drunken driving example. Just saying eighteen-year-olds should not drive when they are drunk will not convince a reader. An example of a car accident or a statistic regarding the number of eighteen-year-olds involved in drunken-driving accidents and the consequence for others—death, injury of passengers—is much more persuasive.

A college freshman, Jody Levy, wrote the following paragraph. The sensory details, including "as a calm river, soon interrupted by rapids," intensify the description of a commonplace object.

Incense

I watched a stick of incense burn. It was a pale brown colored stick of musk incense, with a red hot tip that slowly smoldered downward. A stream of smoke rose from it, and moved with the wind. It was relaxing to watch the dreamy mist. It was calm and controlled, mesmerizing and hypnotic. The smoke ascended straight towards the ceiling, and, then broke its flow; it spurt, swirled, waved, and curled. It started as a calm river, soon interrupted by rapids. Ashes fell, and, crumbled on the tissue underneath, creating a pile of dirt. Dead and used. I let out a deep breath, and, the smoke scrambled. More ashes formed on the top as the red dot moved down. The ashes bent, and then broke, but they did not fall. They hung like a dead leaf on a tree. I followed the smoke with my eyes—thin, thick, straight, smooth, wavy, curly, spiral, fast, slow, short, long,—always moving and changing—floating lines and forms. A continuous flow of greyish, whitish, bluish smoke. Beautiful, like silk thread. . . . As the stick became shorter, the room smelled nicer; the smoke spiraled off with its musk scent. I liked the smell. The scent obscured the smell of my roommate's fat and odorous boyfriend. My roommate walked in; she hates the smell of incense. And the smoke rose in circles, like a horn shouting out scent. Two lines streamed from the stick, sometimes synchronized, cooperating to make forms. Other times, they crossed and waved in opposition, independently creating their own design, and then coming together again. The smoke formed a tunnel, and, then a spiral shell. . . . The incense neared its end, and spurted its last breaths of smoke that slowly floated away and disappeared; but they wafted somewhere in the air. For hours after the final stream of smoke was gone. The red glow faded and left the stick, solitary and lifeless, with a head of ashes. It died and left a lasting memory

In this piece, the reader senses the persona of the observer: her awe as the stick of incense assumes a life of its own as a "river," as "dirt," as "a dead leaf," then as smoke "like silk thread." The details—color, shape, texture, and smell—of the concrete comparisons and figurative language give this vision of incense its "lasting" place in our minds.

The **organization** of an essay remains crucial. The introduction attracts readers and involves them in the world of the writing and the main idea (the thesis); the middle paragraphs compel through their treatment of evidence (the interplay of generalization and specifics, details and example); and the conclusion reinforces the thesis and leaves the reader with a view to contemplate, feeling enriched, enlivened, convinced, and intellectually aware.

Word choice and *style* are crucial in nonfiction. The writer selects words as carefully as a novelist, poet, or dramatist. He or she plays with words: ironic, witty, comic, lyrical; evocative wordplay and figurative language become crucial to nonfiction. Inexact or diffuse wording leads readers astray; and the work loses its impact. In "Incense" Jody Levy occasionally undermines vivid descriptions by the use of vague words and clichés. For example, after describing the "smoke" as "silk thread," Levy then depicts the room, which "smelled nicer." The "nicer" smell, vague, not at all suggestive of any odor, causes the piece to lose some of its power. The work also loses impact at the end because "lasting memory" is a cliché, a hackneyed means of stating the effect of a moment. Levy easily could have omitted the last sentence.

The total effect of a piece of nonfiction prose is its message: the total meaning of a work. As parts of a short story, drama, poem, build themes, so parts of a nonfiction essay build the message or thesis.

THE READING/WRITING RESPONSE: NONFICTION

When you read nonfiction prose, a checklist of questions will help you analyze the text.

CHECKLIST OF QUESTIONS FOR NONFICTION PROSE

1. What form of nonfiction prose am I reading: speech, treatise, autobiography, memoir, journal, essay, or creative nonfiction?
2. Is it exposition or argument?
3. What is the rhetorical situation (purpose, occasion, audience)?
4. What is the writer's point of view? Persona?
5. What is the writer's tone?
6. How do I, as a reader, respond to the point of view and tone?
7. What is the thesis? Supporting points?
8. What are significant details? Examples?
9. How is the essay organized? Formally? Informally? Experimentally?
10. What do I notice about style? Word choice?

11. What literary devices are used?

12. What have I learned from reading this work?

▪ STUDENT PORTFOLIO ▪

Response to King's "Letter from Birmingham Jail"[1]

The portfolio presents a model that demonstrates the stages in the process of writing an evaluation essay. Because King's work is so complex, Jack Ferguson created both a gloss and an outline of the essay to make sure that he grasped the structure of the argument. He next wrote a double-entry notebook. Finally, he composed first and final drafts of his essay. In the final draft, the writer tightened the introduction, clarified King's use of appeals, and analyzed his style.

Ferguson's Gloss

My Dear Fellow Clergymen:

While confined here in the Birmingham city jail, I came across your recent statement calling my present activities "unwise and untimely." Seldom do I pause to answer criticism of my work and ideas. If I sought to answer all the criticisms that cross my desk, my secretaries would have little time for anything other than such correspondence in the course of the day, and I would have no time for constructive work. But since I feel that you are men of genuine good will and that your criticisms are sincerely set forth, I want to try to answer your statements in what I hope will be patient and reasonable terms.

King adopts a non-confrontational "Rogerian" stance.

Appeal to character— King wants to appear trustworthy.

opposing argument #1 Refutation a)

I think I should indicate why I am here in Birmingham, since you have been influenced by the view which argues against "outsiders coming in." I have the honor of serving as president of the Southern Christian Leadership Conference, an organization operating in every southern state, with headquarters in Atlanta, Georgia. We have some eighty-five affiliated organizations

Appeal to character— establishes credibility.

---

[1] This response to a published statement by eight fellow clergymen from Alabama (Bishop C. C. J. Carpenter, Bishop Joseph A. Durick, Rabbi Hilton L. Grafman, Bishop Paul Hardin, Bishop Holan B. Harmon, the Reverend George M. Murray, the Reverend Edward V. Ramage and the Reverend Earl Stallings) was composed under somewhat constricting circumstances. Begun on the margins of the newspaper in which the statement appeared while I was in jail, the letter was continued on scraps of writing paper supplied by a friendly Negro trusty, and concluded on a pad my attorneys were eventually permitted to leave me. Although the text remains in substance unaltered, I have indulged in the author's prerogative of polishing it for publication. [King's note.]

across the South, and one of them is the Alabama Christian Movement for Human Rights. Frequently we share staff, educational and financial resources with our affiliates. Several months ago the affiliate here in Birmingham asked us to be on call to engage in a nonviolent direct-action program if such were deemed necessary. We readily consented, and when the hour came we lived up to our promise. So I, along with several members of my staff, am here because I was invited here I am here because I have organizational ties here.

b)

But more basically, I am in Birmingham because injustice is here. Just as the prophets of the eighth century B.C. left their villages and carried their "thus saith the Lord" far beyond the boundaries of their home towns, and just as the Apostle Paul left his village of Tarsus and carried the gospel of Jesus Christ to the far corners of the Greco-Roman world, so am I (compelled) to carry the gospel of freedom beyond my own home town. Like Paul, I must constantly respond to the Macedonian call for aid.

Biblical allusions indicate his audience.

c)

Moreover, I am (cognizant) of the interrelatedness of all communities and states. I cannot sit idly by in Atlanta and not be concerned about what happens in Birmingham. Injustice anywhere is a threat to justice everywhere. We are caught in an inescapable network of mutuality, tied in a single garment of destiny. Whatever affects one directly, affects all indirectly. Never again can we afford to live with the narrow, provincial "outside agitator" idea. Anyone who lives inside the United States can never be considered an outsider anywhere within its bounds.

opposing argument #2

You deplore the demonstrations taking place in Birmingham. But your statement, I am sorry to say, fails to express a similar concern for the conditions that brought about the demonstrations. I am sure that none of you would want to rest content with the superficial kind of social analysis that deals merely with effects and does not grapple with underlying causes. It is unfortunate that demonstrations are taking place in Birmingham, but it is even more unfortunate that the city's white power structure left the Negro community with no alternative.

Rogerian approach to opponents.

Refutation

a)

In any nonviolent campaign there are four basic steps: collection of the facts to determine whether injustices exist; negotiation; self-purification; and direct action. We have gone through all these steps in Birmingham. There can be no (gainsaying) the fact that racial injustice engulfs this community. Birmingham is probably the most thoroughly segregated city in the United States. Its ugly record of brutality is widely known. Negroes have experienced grossly unjust treatment in the courts. There have been more unsolved bombings of Negro homes and churches in Birmingham than in any other city in the nation. These are the hard, brutal facts of the case. On the basis of these conditions, Negro leaders sought to negotiate with the city fathers. But the latter consistently refused to engage in good-faith negotiation.

Evidence—but maybe this could have been more specific.

b)

Then, last September, came the opportunity to talk with leaders of Birmingham's economic community. In the course of the negotiations, certain promises were made by the merchants—for example, to remove the stores' humiliating racial signs. On the basis of these promises, the Reverend Fred Shuttlesworth and the leaders of the Alabama Christian Movement for Human Rights agreed to a moratorium on all demonstrations. As the weeks and months went by, we realized that we were the victims of a broken promise. A few signs, briefly removed, returned; the others remained.

c)

As in so many past experiences, our hopes had been blasted, and the shadow of deep disappointment settled upon us. We had no alternative except to prepare for direct action, whereby we would present our very bodies as a means of laying our case before the conscience of the local and the national community. Mindful of the difficulties involved, we decided to undertake a process of self-purification. We began a series of workshops on nonviolence, and we repeatedly asked ourselves : "Are you able to accept blows without retaliating?" "Are you able to endure the ordeal of jail?" We decided to schedule our direct-action program for the Easter season, realizing that except for Christmas, this is the main shopping period of the year. Knowing that a strong economic-withdrawal program would be the by-product of direct action, we felt that this would be the best time to bring pressure to bear on the merchants for the needed change.

Then it occurred to us that Birmingham's mayoral election was coming up in March, and we speedily decided to postpone action until after election day. When we discovered that the Commissioner of Public Safety, Eugene "Bull" Connor, had piled up enough votes to be in the run-off we decided again to postpone action until the day after the run-off so that the demonstrations could not be used to cloud the issues. Like many others, we wanted to see Mr. Connor defeated, and to this end we endured postponement after postponement. Having aided in this community need, we felt that our direct-action program could be delayed no longer.

Appeal to character.

d)   You may well ask: "Why direct action? Why sit-ins, marches and so forth? Isn't negotiation a better path?" You are quite right in calling for negotiation. Indeed, this is the very purpose of direct action. Nonviolent direct action seeks to create such a crisis and foster such a tension that a community which has constantly refused to negotiate is forced to confront the issue. It seeks so to dramatize the issue that it can no longer be ignored. My citing the creation of tension as part of the work of the nonviolent-resister may sound rather shocking. But I must confess that I am not afraid of the word "tension." I have earnestly opposed violent tension, but there is a type of constructive, nonviolent tension which is necessary for growth. Just as Socrates felt that it was necessary to create a tension in the mind so that individuals could rise from the bondage of myths and half-truths to the unfettered realm of creative analysis and objective appraisal, we must we see the need for nonviolent gadflies to create the kind of tension in society that will help men rise from the dark depths of prejudice and racism to the majestic heights of understanding and brotherhood.

Appeal to reason.

Interesting!

King seeks to establish common ground.

The purpose of our direct-action program is to create a situation so crisis-packed that it will inevitably open the door to negotiation. I therefore concur with you in your call for negotiation. Too long has our beloved Southland been bogged down in a tragic effort to live in monologue rather than dialogue.

"Our" implies unity.

opposing argument #3

One of the basic points in your statement is that the action that I and my associates have taken in Birmingham is untimely. Some have asked: "Why didn't you give the new city administration time to act?" The only answer that I can give to this query is that the new Birmingham administration must be prodded about as much as the outgoing one, before it will act. We are sadly mistaken if we feel that the election of Albert

Refutation

Appeal to reason.

Boutwell as mayor will bring the millennium to Birmingham. While Mr. Boutwell is a much more gentle person than Mr. Connor, they are both segregationists, dedicated to maintenance of the status quo. I have hoped that Mr. Boutwell will be reasonable enough to see the futility of massive resistance to desegregation. But he will not see this without pressure from devotees of civil rights. My friends, I must say to you that we have not made a single gain in civil rights without determined legal and nonviolent pressure. <u>Lamentably, it</u> <u>is an historical fact that privileged groups seldom</u> <u>give up their privileges voluntarily.</u> Individuals may <u>see the moral light and voluntarily give up their un-</u> <u>just posture; but, as Reinhold Niebuhr has reminded us,</u> <u>groups tend to be more immoral than individuals.</u>

Uses outside authority to support his argument.

We know through painful experience that freedom is never voluntarily given by the oppressor; it must be demanded by the oppressed. Frankly, I have yet to engage in a direct-action campaign that was "well timed" in the view of those who have not suffered unduly from the disease of segregation. For years now I have heard the word "Wait!" It rings in the ear of every Negro with piercing familiarity. This "Wait" has almost always meant "Never." <u>We must come to see, with one of</u> <u>our distinguished jurists, that "justice too long de-</u> <u>layed is justice denied."</u>

✓

We have waited for more than 340 years for our constitutional and God-given rights. <u>The nations of Asia</u> <u>and Africa are moving with jetlike speed toward gaining</u> <u>political independence, but we still creep at horse-</u> <u>and-buggy pace toward gaining a cup of coffee at a</u> <u>lunch counter.</u> Perhaps it is easy for those who have never felt the stinging darts of segregation to say, "Wait." But <u>when you have seen</u> vicious mobs lynch your mothers and fathers at will and drown your sisters and brothers at whim; <u>when you have seen hate</u>-filled policemen curse, kick and even kill your black brothers and sisters; <u>when you see</u> the vast majority of your twenty million Negro brothers smothering in an airtight cage of poverty in the midst of an affluent society; <u>when you suddenly find your</u> tongue twisted and your speech stammering as you seek to explain to your six-year-old daughter why she can't go to the public amusement park that has just been advertised on television, and see tears welling up in her eyes when she is

good contrast

Appeal to emotion.

parallelism and repetition

told that Funtown is closed to colored children, and
see ominous clouds of inferiority beginning to form in
her little mental sky, and see her beginning to distort
her personality by developing an unconscious bitterness toward white people; when you have to concoct an
answer for a five-year-old son who is asking: "Daddy,
why do white people treat colored people so mean?";
when you take a cross-country drive and find it necessary to sleep night after night in the uncomfortable
corners of your automobile because no motel will accept
you; when you are humiliated day in and day out by nagging signs reading "white" and "colored"; when your
first name becomes "nigger," your middle name becomes
"boy" (however old you are) and your last name becomes
"John," and your wife and mother are never given the
respected title "Mrs."; when you are harried by day and
haunted by night by the fact that you are a Negro, living constantly at tiptoe stance, never quite knowing
what to expect next, and are plagued with inner fears
and outer resentments; when you are forever fighting a
degenerating sense of "nobodiness"—then you will understand why we find it difficult to wait. There comes
a time when the cup of endurance runs over, and men are
no longer willing to be plunged into the abyss of despair. I hope, sirs, you can understand our legitimate
and unavoidable impatience.

*Personal
examples—
very
persuasive*

You express a great deal of anxiety over our willingness to break laws. This is certainly a legitimate
concern. Since we so (diligently) urge people to obey the
Supreme Court's decision of 1954 outlawing segregation
in the public schools, at first glance it may seem
rather paradoxical for us consciously to break laws.
One may well ask: "How can you advocate breaking some
laws and obeying others?" The answer lies in the fact
that there are two types of laws: just and unjust. I
would be the first to advocate obeying just laws. One
has not only a legal but a moral responsibility to obey
just laws. Conversely, one has a moral responsibility
to disobey unjust laws. I would agree with St. Augustine that "an unjust law is no law at all."

*"Sirs"
indicates
respect—
King does
not want to
alienate
his audience.*

*opposing
argument #4*

Refutation

*Appeal to
reason.*

Now, what is the difference between the two? How
does one determine whether a law is just or unjust? A
just law is a man-made code that squares with the moral
law or the law of God. An unjust law is a code that is
out of harmony with the moral law. To put it in the

terms of St. Thomas Aquinas: An unjust law is a human law that is not rooted in eternal law and natural law. Any law that uplifts human personality is just. Any law that degrades human personality is unjust. All segregation statutes are unjust because segregation distorts the soul and damages the personality. It gives the segregator a false sense of superiority and the segregated a false sense of inferiority. Segregation, to use the terminology of the Jewish philosopher Martin Buber, substitutes an "I-it" relationship for an "I-thou" relationship and ends up relegating persons to the status of things. Hence segregation is not only politically, economically and sociologically unsound, it is morally wrong and sinful. Paul Tillich has said that sin is separation. Is not segregation an existential expression of man's tragic separation, his awful estrangement, his terrible sinfulness? Thus it is that I can urge men to obey the 1954 decision of the Supreme Court, for it is morally right; and I can urge them to disobey segregation ordinances, for they are morally wrong.

Again King refers to a respected authority to support his argument.

Let us consider a more concrete example of just and unjust laws. An unjust law is a code that a numerical or power majority group compels a minority group to obey but does not make binding on itself. This is difference made legal. By the same token, a just law is a code that a majority compels a minority to follow and that it is willing to follow itself. This is sameness made legal.

Let me give another explanation. A law is unjust if it is inflicted on a minority that, as a result of being denied the right to vote, had no part in enacting or devising the law. Who can say that the legislature of Alabama which set up that state's segregation laws was democratically elected? Throughout Alabama all sorts of devious methods are used to prevent Negroes from becoming registered voters, and there are some counties in which, even though Negroes constitute a majority of the population, not a single Negro is registered. Can any law enacted under such circumstances be considered democratically structured?

Again I think his evidence could be more specific —what methods?

Sometimes a law is just on its face and unjust in its application. For instance, I have been arrested on a charge of parading without a permit. Now, there is nothing wrong in having an ordinance which requires a

permit for a parade. But such an ordinance becomes unjust when it is used to maintain segregation and to
deny citizens the First-Amendment privilege of peaceful assembly and protest.

I hope you are able to see the distinction I am
trying to point out. In no sense do I advocate evading
or defying the law, as would the rabid segregationist.
That would lead to anarchy. One who breaks an unjust
law must do so openly, lovingly, and with a willingness
to accept the penalty. I submit that an individual who
breaks a law that conscience tells him is unjust and
who willingly accepts the penalty of imprisonment in
order to arouse the conscience of the community over
its injustice, is in reality expressing the highest respect for law.

Of course, there is nothing new about this kind of
civil disobedience. It was evidenced sublimely in the
refusal of Shadrach, Meshach and Abednego to obey the
laws of Nebuchadnezzar, on the ground that a higher
moral law was at stake. It was practiced superbly by
the early Christians, who were willing to face hungry
lions and the excruciating pain of chopping blocks
rather than submit to certain unjust laws of the Roman
Empire. To a degree, academic freedom is a reality today because Socrates practiced civil disobedience. In
our own nation, the Boston Tea Party represented a massive act of civil disobedience.

We should never forget that everything Adolf
Hitler did in Germany was "legal" and everything the
Hungarian fighters did in Hungary was "illegal." It was
"illegal" to aid and comfort a Jew in Hitler's Germany.
Even so, I am sure that, had I lived in Germany at the
time, I would have aided and comforted my Jewish brothers. If today I lived in a Communist country where
certain principles dear to the Christian faith are
suppressed, I would openly advocate disobeying that
country's antireligious laws.

I must make two honest confessions to you, my
Christian and Jewish brothers. First, I must confess
that over the past few years I have been gravely disappointed with the white moderate. I have almost reached
the regrettable conclusion that the Negro's great
stumbling block in his stride toward freedom is not the
White Citizen's Counciler or the Ku Klux Klanner, but
the white moderate, who is more devoted to "order" than

*These biblica
allusions
create a
common
ground
between King
and his
audience.*

*Wasn't
Thoreau a
big influence
on M. L. King?*

*This is a
pretty
challenging
parallel to
draw.*

parallelism

to justice; who prefers a negative peace which is the absence of tension to a positive peace which is the presence of justice; who constantly says, "I agree with you in the goal you seek, but I cannot agree with your methods of direct action"; who paternalistically believes he can set the timetable for another man's freedom; who lives by a mythical concept of time and who constantly advises the Negro to wait for a "more convenient season." Shallow understanding from people of good will is more frustrating than absolute misunderstanding from people of ill will. Lukewarm acceptance is much more bewildering than outright rejection.

I had hoped that the white moderate would understand that law and order exist for the purpose of establishing justice and that when they fail in this

strong metaphor

purpose they become the dangerously structured dams that block the flow of social progress. I had hoped that the white moderate would understand that the present tension in the South is a necessary phase of the transition from an obnoxious negative peace, in which the Negro passively accepted his unjust plight, to a substantive and positive peace, in which all men will respect the dignity and worth of human personality. Actually, we who engage in nonviolent direct action are not the creators of tension. We merely bring to the surface the hidden tension that is already alive. We bring it out in the open, where it can be seen and dealt with. Like a boil that can never be cured so long as it is covered up but must be opened with all its ugliness to the natural medicines of air and light, injustice must be exposed, with all the tension its exposure creates, to the light of human conscience and the air of national opinion, before it can be cured.

This is a great analogy— racism is something that festers beneath the surface.

opposing argument #5

In your statement you assert that our actions, even though peaceful, must be condemned because they precipitate violence. But is this a logical assertion? Isn't this like condemning a robbed man because his possession of money precipitated the evil act of robbery? Isn't this like condemning Socrates because his unswerving commitment to truth and his philosophical inquiries precipitated the act by the misguided populace in which they made him drink hemlock? Isn't this like condemning Jesus because his unique God-consciousness and never-ceasing devotion to God's will precipitated the evil act of crucifixion? We must come

False analogy maybe?

Isn't this a little weak? He uses rhetorical questions instead of specific evidence.

to see that, as the federal courts have consistently affirmed, it is wrong to urge an individual to cease his efforts to gain his basic constitutional rights because the quest may precipitate violence. Society must protect the robbed and punish the robber.

I had also hoped that the white moderate would reject the myth concerning time in relation to the struggle for freedom. I have just received a letter from a white brother in Texas. He writes: "All Christians know that the colored people will receive equal rights eventually, but it is possible that you are in too great a religious hurry. It has taken Christianity almost two thousand years to accomplish what it has. The teachings of Christ take time to come to earth." Such an attitude stems from a tragic misconception of time, from the strangely irrational notion that there is something in the very flow of time that will inevitably cure all ills. Actually, time itself is neutral; it can be used either destructively or constructively. More and more I feel that the people of ill will have used time much more effectively than have the people of good will. We will have to repent in this generation not merely for the hateful words and actions of the bad people, but for the appalling silence of the good people. Human progress never rolls in on wheels of inevitability; it comes through the tireless efforts of men willing to be co-workers with God, and without this hard work, time itself becomes an ally of the forces of social stagnation. We must use time creatively, in the knowledge that the time is always ripe to do right. Now is the time to make real the promise of democracy and transform our pending national elegy into a creative psalm of brotherhood. Now is the time to lift our national policy from the quicksand of racial injustice to the solid rock of human dignity.

opposing argument #6

You speak of our activity in Birmingham as extreme. At first I was rather disappointed that fellow clergymen would see my nonviolent efforts as those of an extremist. I began thinking about the fact that

Refutation

stand in the middle of two opposing forces in the Negro community. One is a force of complacency, made up in part of Negroes who, as a result of long years of oppression, are so drained of self-respect and a sense of "somebodiness" that they have adjusted to segregation; and in part of a few middle-class Negroes who, because

of a degree of academic and economic security and because in some ways they profit by segregation, have become insensitive to the problems of the masses. The
other force is one of bitterness and hatred, and it
comes perilously close to advocating violence. It is
expressed in the various black nationalist groups that
are springing up across the nation, the largest and
best-known being Elijah Muhammad's Muslim movement.
Nourished by the Negro's frustration over the continued existence of racial discrimination, this movement
is made up of people who have lost faith in America,
who have absolutely (repudiated) Christianity, and who
have concluded that the white man is an (incorrigible)
"devil."

I have tried to stand between these two forces,
saying that we need (emulate) neither the "do-
nothingism" of the complacent nor the hatred and despair of the black nationalist. For there is the more
excellent way of love and nonviolent protest. I am
grateful to God that, through the influence of the Negro church, the way of nonviolence became an integral
part of our struggle.

He constantly reminds his audience of this.

If this philosophy had not emerged, by now many
streets of the South would, I am convinced, be flowing
with blood. And I am further convinced that if our
white brothers dismiss as "rabble-rousers" and "outside agitators" those of us who employ nonviolent direct action, and if they refuse to support our
nonviolent efforts, millions of Negroes will, out of
frustration and despair, seek (solace) and security in
black-nationalist (ideologies)—a development that would
inevitably lead to a frightening racial nightmare.

Oppressed people cannot remain oppressed forever.
The yearning for freedom eventually manifests itself,
and that is what has happened to the American Negro.
Something within has reminded him of his birthright of
freedom, and something without has reminded him that it
can be gained. Consciously or unconsciously, he has
been caught up by the Zeitgeist, and with his black
brothers of Africa and his brown and yellow brothers of
Asia, South America, and the Caribbean, the United
States Negro is moving with a sense of great urgency
toward the promised land of racial justice. If one recognizes this vital urge that has engulfed the Negro
community, one should readily understand why public
demonstrations are taking place. The Negro has many

pent-up resentments and (latent) frustrations, and <u>he</u> must release them. So let <u>him</u> march; let <u>him</u> make prayer pilgrimages to the city hall; let <u>him</u> go on freedom rides—and try to understand why he must do so. <u>If his repressed emotions are not released in nonviolent ways, they will seek expression through violence; this is not a threat but a fact of history.</u> So I have not said to my people, "Get rid of your discontent." Rather, I have tried to say that this normal and healthy discontent can be channeled into the creative outlet of nonviolent direct action. And now this approach is being termed extremist.

Rhetorical qeustions create strong tone.

But though I was initially disappointed at being categorized as an extremist, as I continued to think about the matter I gradually gained a measure of satisfaction from the label. <u>Was not Jesus</u> an extremist for love: "Love your enemies, bless them that curse you, do good to them that hate you, and pray for them which despitefully use you, and persecute you." <u>Was not Amos</u> an extremist for justice: "Let justice roll down like waters and righteousness like an everflowing stream." <u>Was not Paul</u> an extremist for the Christian gospel: "I bear in my body the marks of the Lord Jesus." Was not Martin Luther an extremist: "Here I stand; I cannot do otherwise, so help me God." <u>And John Bunyan:</u> "I will stay in jail to the end of my days before I make a butchery of my conscience." <u>And Abraham Lincoln:</u> "This nation cannot survive half slave and half free." <u>And Thomas Jefferson:</u> "We hold these truths to be self-evident, that all men are created equal...." So the question is not whether we will be extremists, but what kind of extremists we will be. Will we be extremists for hate or for love? Will we be extremists for the preservation of injustice or for the extension of justice? In that dramatic scene on Calvary's hill three men were crucified. We must never forget that all three were crucified for the same crime—the crime of extremism. Two were extremists for immorality, and thus fell below their environment. The other, Jeans Christ, was an extremist for love, truth, and goodness, and thereby rose above his environment. <u>Perhaps the South, the nation, and the world are in dire need of creative extremists.</u>

Again parallism is used for emotional emphasis.

King wants to connect Christian tradition with American history.

I had hoped that the white moderate would see this need. Perhaps I was too optimistic; perhaps I expected too much. I suppose I should have realized that few members of the oppressor race can understand the <u>deep groans</u> and <u>passionate yearnings</u> of the oppressed race, and still fewer have the vision to see that injustice must be rooted out by strong, persistent, and determined action. I am thankful, however, that some of our white brothers in the South have grasped the meaning of this social revolution and committed themselves to it. They are still too few in quantity, but they are big in quality. Some—such as Ralph McGill, Lillian Smith, Harry Golden, James McBride Dabbs, Ann Braden, and Sarah Patton Boyle—have written about our struggle in eloquent and prophetic terms. Others have marched with us down nameless streets of the South. They have languished in filthy, roach-infested jails, suffering the abuse and brutality of policemen who view them as "dirty nigger-lovers." Unlike so many of their moderate brothers and sisters, they have recognized the urgency of the moment and sensed the need for powerful "action" antidotes to combat the disease of segregation.

Let me take note of my other major disappointment. I have been so greatly disappointed with the white church and its leadership. Of course, there are some notable exceptions. I am not unmindful of the fact that each of you has taken some significant stands on this issue. I commend you, Reverend Stallings, for your Christian stand on this past Sunday, in welcoming Negroes to your worship service on a nonsegregational basis. I commend the Catholic leaders of this state for integrating Spring Hill College several years ago.

But despite these notable exceptions, I must honestly (reiterate) that I have been disappointed with the church. I do not say this as one of those negative critics who can always find something wrong with the church. I say this as a minister of the gospel, <u>who loves</u> the church; <u>who was nurtured</u> in its bosom; <u>who has been</u> sustained by its spiritual blessings and <u>who will remain true</u> to it as long as the cord of life shall lengthen.

When I was suddenly catapulted into the leadership of the bus protest in Montgomery, Alabama, a few years ago, I felt we would be supported by the white church felt that the white ministers, priests, and rabbis of the South would be among our strongest allies. Instead, some have been outright opponents, refusing to understand the freedom movement and misrepresenting its

*

leaders; <u>all too many others have been more cautious
than courageous and have remained silent behind the
anesthetizing security of stained-glass windows.</u>

In spite of my shattered dreams, I came to Birmingham with the hope that the white religious leadership of this community would see the justice of our
cause and, with deep moral concern, would serve as the
channel through which our just grievances could reach
the power structure. I had hoped that each of you would
understand. But again I have been disappointed.

I have heard numerous southern religious leaders
(admonish) their worshipers to comply with a desegregation decision because it is the law, but I have longed
to hear white ministers declare: "Follow this decree
because integration is morally right and because the
Negro is your brother." In the midst of blatant injustices inflicted upon the Negro, I have watched white
churchmen stand on the sideline and mouth pious irrel-
evancies and (sanctimonious) trivialities. In the midst
of a mighty struggle to rid our nation of racial and
economic injustice, I have heard many ministers say:
"Those are social issues, with which the gospel has no
real concern." And I have watched many churches commit
themselves to a completely otherworldly religion which
makes a strange, un-Biblical distinction between body
and soul, between the sacred and the secular.

I have traveled the length and breadth of Alabama,
Mississippi and all the other southern states. On sweltering summer days and crisp autumn mornings I have
looked at the South's beautiful churches with their
lofty spires pointing heavenward. I have beheld the impressive outlines of her massive religious-education
buildings. Over and over I have found myself asking:

*Again, series
of questions
creates
strong tone.*

"What kind of people worship here? Who is their God?
Where were their voices when the lips of Governor Barnett dripped with words of (interposition) and nullifi-
cation? Where were they when Governor Wallace gave a
clarion call for defiance and hatred? Where were their
voices of support when bruised and weary Negro men and

opposition

women decided to rise from the <u>dark dungeons of compla-
cency</u> to the <u>bright hills of creative protest?</u>"

Yes, these questions are still in my mind. In <u>deep
disappointment</u> I have wept over the (laxity) of the
church. But be assured that my tears have been tears of
love. There can be no <u>deep disappointment</u> where there

is not deep love. Yes, I love the church. How could I
do otherwise? l am in the rather unique position of being the son, the grandson and the great-grandson of
preachers. Yes, I see the church as the body of Christ.
But, oh! How we have blemished and scarred that body
through social neglect and through fear of being non-
conformists.

There was a time when the church was very powerful—in the time when the early Christians rejoiced at
being deemed worthy to suffer for what they believed.
In those days the church was not merely a thermometer
that recorded the ideas and principles of popular opinion; it was a thermostat that transformed the mores of
society. Whenever the early Christians entered a town,
the people in power became disturbed and immediately
sought to convict the Christians for being "disturbers
of the peace" and "outside agitators." But the Christians pressed on, in the conviction that they were "a
colony of heaven," called to obey God rather than man.
Small in number, they were big in commitment. They were
too God intoxicated to be "astronomically intimidated." By their effort and example they brought an end
to such ancient evils as infanticide. and gladiatorial
contests.

Things are different now. So often the contemporary church is a weak, ineffectual voice with an uncertain sound. So often it is an archdefender of the
status quo. Far from being disturbed by the presence of
the church, the power structure of the average community is consoled by the church's silent—and often even
vocal—sanction of things as they are.

But the judgment of God is upon the church as never
before. If today's church does not recapture the sacrificial spirit of the early church, it will lose its au-
thenticity, forfeit the loyalty of millions, and be
dismissed as an irrelevant social club with no meaning
for the twentieth century. Every day I meet young people whose disappointment with the church has turned
into outright disgust.

Perhaps I have once again been too optimistic. Is
organized religion too inextricably bound to the status quo to save our nation and the world? Perhaps I
must turn my faith to the inner spiritual church, the
church within the church, as the true ekklesia and the
hope of the world. But again I am thankful to God that

Note use of "we" here— King wants to create an impression of unity, rather than one of alienation.

some noble souls from the ranks of organized religion have broken loose from the paralyzing chains of conformity and joined us as active partners in the struggle for freedom, They have left their secure congregations and walked the streets of Albany, Georgia, with us. They have gone down the highways of the South on tortuous rides for freedom. Yes, they have gone to jail with us. Some have been dismissed from their churches, have lost the support of their bishops and fellow ministers. But they have acted in the faith that right defeated is stronger than evil triumphant. Their witness has been the spiritual salt that has preserved the true meaning of the gospel in these troubled times. They have carved a tunnel of hope through the dark mountain of disappointment.

I hope the church as a whole will meet the challenge of this decisive hour. But even if the church does not come to the aid of justice, I have no despair about the future. I have no fear about the outcome of our struggle in Birmingham, even if our motives are at present misunderstood. We will reach the goal of freedom in Birmingham and all over the nation, because the goal of America is freedom. Abused and scorned though we may be, our destiny is tied up with America's destiny. Before the pilgrims landed at Plymouth, we were here. Before the pen of Jefferson etched the majestic words of the Declaration of Independence across the pages of history, we were here. For more than two centuries our forebears labored in this country without wages; they made cotton king; they built the homes of their masters while suffering gross injustice and shameful humiliation—and yet out of a bottomless vitality they continued to thrive and develop. If the inexpressible cruelties of slavery could not stop us, the opposition we now face will surely fail. We will win our freedom because the sacred heritage of our nation and the eternal will of God are embodied in our echoing demands.

Before closing I feel impelled to mention one other point in your statement that has troubled me profoundly. You warmly commended the Birmingham police force for keeping "order" and "preventing violence." I doubt that you would have so warmly commended the police force if you had seen its dogs sinking their teeth into unarmed, nonviolent Negroes. I doubt that you

This is an important aspect of his argument—the fate of the black Americans is linked with the fate of the nation as a whole.

more parallelism

would so quickly commend the policemen <u>if you were to</u> <u>observe</u> their ugly and inhumane treatment of Negroes here in the city jail; <u>if you were to watch</u> them push and curse old Negro women and young Negro girls; if you were to see them slap and kick old Negro men and young boys; <u>if you were to observe them,</u> as they did on two occasions, refuse to give us food because we wanted to sing our grace together. I cannot join you in your praise of the Birmingham police department.

emotional language

<u>It is true that the police have exercised a degree</u> <u>of discipline in handing the demonstrators.</u> In this sense they have conducted themselves rather "nonviolently" in pubic. But for what purpose? To preserve the evil system of segregation. Over the past few years I have consistently preached that nonviolence demands that the means we use must be as pure as the ends we seek. I have tried to make clear that it is wrong to use immoral means to attain moral ends. But now I must affirm that it is just as wrong, or perhaps even more so, to use moral means to preserve immoral ends. Perhaps Mr. Connor and his policemen have been rather nonviolent in public, as was Chief Pritchett in Albany, Georgia, but they have used the moral means of nonviolence to maintain the immoral end of racial injustice. <u>As T. S. Eliot has said: "The last temptation is the</u> <u>greatest treason: To do the right deed for the wrong</u> <u>reason."</u>

Concedes opposing point of view but immediately modifies it.

I wish you had commended the Negro sit-inners and demonstrators of Birmingham for their sublime courage, their willingness to suffer and their amazing discipline in the midst of great provocation. One day the South will recognize its real heroes. <u>They will be</u> the James Merediths, with the noble sense of purpose that enables them to face jeering, and hostile mobs, and with the agonizing loneliness that characterizes the life of the pioneer. <u>They will be</u> old, oppressed, battered Negro women, symbolized in a seventy-two-year-old woman in Montgomery, Alabama, who rose up with a sense of dignity and with her people decided not to ride segregated buses, and who responded with ungrammatical profundity to one who inquired about her weariness: "My feets is tired, but my soul is at rest." <u>They</u> <u>will be</u> the young high school and college students, the young ministers of the gospel and a host of their elders, courageously and nonviolently sitting in at lunch counters and willingly going to jail for conscience'

sake. <u>One day the South will know that when these dis-</u>
<u>inherited children of God sat down at lunch counters,</u>
<u>they were in reality standing up for what is best in</u>
<u>the American dream and for the most sacred values in</u>
<u>our Judaeo-Christian heritage, thereby bringing our</u>
<u>nation back to those</u> great <u>wells of democracy which</u>
<u>were dug deep by the founding fathers in their formu-</u>
<u>lation of the Constitution and the Declaration of</u>
<u>Independence.</u>

Never before have I written so long a letter. I'm
afraid it is much too long to take your precious time.
I can assure you that it would have been much shorter
if I had been writing from a comfortable desk, but what

*appeal to
emotion*

else can one do when he is alone in a narrow jail cell,
other than write long letters, think long thoughts, and
pray long prayers?

*appeal to
character*

If I have said anything in this letter that over-
states the truth and indicates an unreasonable impatience, I beg you to forgive me. If I have said
anything that understates the truth and indicates my
having a patience that allows me to settle for anything
less than brotherhood, I beg God to forgive me.

*King
addresses
his audience
directly to
establish
personal tone.*

I hope this letter finds you strong in the faith. I
also hope that circumstances will soon make it possible
for me to meet each of you, not as an integrationist or
a civil-rights leader but as a fellow clergyman and a

*Figurative
language
here—to stir
his readers'
imaginations
by reminding
his audience
of their common
national identity.*

Christian brother. Let us all hope that <u>the dark clouds</u>
<u>of racial prejudice</u> will soon pass away and the <u>deep</u>
<u>fog of misunderstanding will be lifted</u> from our <u>fear-</u>
<u>drenched communities,</u> and in some not too distant to-
morrow the <u>radiant stars</u> of love and brotherhood will
shine over our great nation with all their scintillating beauty.

Yours for the cause of Peace and Brotherhood,
MARTIN LUTHER KING, JR.

This letter was written by King as a direct answer to the criticisms made by
eight clergymen that his involvement in the Birmingham demonstrations was "unwise
and untimely." For the most part, the essay consists of a point-by-point refutation
of his opponents' arguments.

POINT 1: As an "outsider," King has no right to be in Birmingham.
Refutation:
(a) As president of the Southern Christian Leadership Conference, King was invited
by the Birmingham affiliate to take part in the demonstrations.

(b) As a Christian, King cannot ignore injustice, but must respond to any "call for aid" no matter where it comes from.

(c) The term "outside agitator" is dated and narrow-minded. "Injustice anywhere is a threat to justice everywhere."

POINT 2: The demonstrations in Birmingham were deplorable and cannot be justified.
Refutation:

(a) The Negro community had no choice. Birmingham is one of the most segregated cities in the country.

(b) Previous attempts at negotiation had failed.

(c) Self-purification workshops were held to ensure that the demonstrations were peaceful.

(d) Direct action is the only way to force a complacent system to face the issue.

POINT 3: The new Boutwell administration should have been given time to act.
Refutation:

The new administration is also segregationist and will not act without direct pressure from the Negro community.

POINT 4: The civil rights movement is hypocritical in its willingness to break certain laws while upholding others.
Refutation:

Only just laws should be obeyed.

POINT 5: Direct action leads to violence.
Refutation:

It is illogical to condemn peaceful protestors for precipitating violence. The fault lies with those who seek to disrupt the demonstrations. Those seeking their constitutional rights should be protected from violence by law.

POINT 6: King's activity in Birmingham has been extreme.
Refutation:

King does, in fact, occupy a moderate position between the two extremes of violence and passivity. Without this moderate position, the streets of the South would be "flowing with blood."

King then expresses his disappointment with both the white moderates and the white church. He criticizes the church in particular for its lack of moral initiative, its lack of strong leadership, and its failure to support the civil rights movement.

King's last main point is that it is the demonstrators who should be commended for their self-control, not the police. He calls for the recognition of the "real heroes" of the civil rights movement, such as the "James Merediths."

The essay concludes on a uplifting note as King expresses his hope that "the dark clouds of racial prejudice will soon pass away . . . and in some not too distant tomorrow the radiant stars of love and brotherhood will shine over our great nation with all their scintillating beauty."

Excerpt from Ferguson's Double-Entry Note

Quotes and Summaries	Reactions
"I doubt you would have so warmly commended the police force if you	King really knows how to use language to involve the reader emotionally. His

Quotes and Summaries	Reactions

had seen its dogs sinking their teeth into unarmed, nonviolent Negroes."

reasonable tone allows him to do this without losing his reader's trust. So rather than just saying 'dogs attacking Negroes' he says "dogs *sinking* their teeth into *unarmed, nonviolent* Negroes." He's making an appeal to emotion here and uses parallelism to increase the effect ("if you were to watch," "if you were to see" etc.). His use of the word "Negro" makes me kind of uncomfortable. It seems so dated now. At first it makes it seem as though a lot has changed since King wrote this essay. But how much is different, really? We hardly live in an equitable society. Maybe that's why "Negro" bothers me so much. We've made the terminology "politically correct" but the injustices remain.

King concedes that the police officers may have appeared restrained in public, but argued that their behavior is still indefensible. No actions can be considered moral if they are used for immoral purposes.

King doesn't want to antagonize his audience, so he sometimes concedes the opposing point of view. Here he quickly turns the point around so that his own argument doesn't lose any ground. Nonviolent law enforcement cannot be commended if it is used to enforce unjust laws. It's important that King addresses this point because otherwise he might seem to be avoiding the issue. I mean, ignoring evidence in favor of the police would make him look biased. Instead, he makes this possible weakness into one of his strengths.

As T. S. Eliot has said, "The last temptation is the greatest treason: To do the right deed for the wrong reason."

King does this a lot—brings in some respected individual to support his argument. It shows that he is writing for a literate audience, and also that King himself is well educated (appeal to character again).

King suggests that his fellow clergymen commend the demonstrators for their self-control, not the police.

I admire King for his forthright criticisms of the white church. He's not afraid to say what he really thinks, despite his non-confrontational approach. I wonder how these clergymen reacted to the letter. I imagine it made them pretty uncomfortable. I hope so.

Quotes and Summaries	Reactions
"One day the South will recognize its real heroes."	I've come to realize through studying this this essay that there is a reason for everything King does. Here I think he is deliberately bringing the focus back to ordinary people after a lot of fairly abstract discussion. The "My feets is tired but my soul is at rest" quote suddenly makes it all real. You can feel the struggle and frustration. Again King uses parallelism for emphasis.
One day the South will know that when these disinherited children of God sat down at lunch counters, they were in reality standing up for what is best in the American dream and for the most sacred values in our Judaeo-Christian heritage, thereby bringing our nation back to those great wells of democracy which were dug deep by the founding fathers in their formulations of the Constitution and the Declaration of Independence.	I've quoted this whole passage because I think it's one of the most important in the whole essay. It gives the civil rights movement an historical context—this is not just about one town in the South; it's about American and Christian traditions. This prevents people from seeing the protest movement as "outside agitation." In referring to the Constitution, etc. King is playing on his audience's patriotic feelings and trying to stir their emotions. I think this is a legitimate tactic. He's not distorting anything—the American dream is meant to be about freedom and equality for all. But he is being quite clever here—these patriotic references ensure that no one can accuse him of being "un-American." I like the opposition between "sat down" and "standing up."
"Let us all hope that the dark clouds of racial prejudice will soon pass away and the deep fog of misunderstanding will be lifted from our fear-drenched communities, and in some not too distant tomorrow the radiant stars of love and brotherhood will shine over our great nation with all their scintillating beauty."	King really likes long sentences. The repetition of "hope" is important—King wants to lift the tone of the essay and end on a positive note. He wants to involve the reader emotionally so he uses a lot of figurative language. The "dark clouds" and "deep fog" are contrasted with the "radiant stars." (Religious imagery here? Dark vs light etc.) The reference to "our great nation" reminds the audience again of common national identity. These final sentences are uplifting and inspiring, but they rather depress me, too. We are still waiting for those "radiant stars of love and brother-hood" to shine. Has King's "not too distant tomorrow" come much closer in the past forty years, or not?

Ferguson's First Draft

"Letter from Birmingham Jail" is a powerful, persuasive essay which argues for the necessity of direct, nonviolent action to end racial segregation in the city of Birmingham in 1963. King wrote it while in solitary confinement, in response to the published criticisms of eight white clergymen, but its scope goes far beyond that of a personal letter. In the course of the essay's pages, King demonstrates the most important aspects of argument, such as the use of appeals to character, emotion, and reason, logical structure and development, and the effective refutation of the op-position. Through reading "Letter from Birmingham Jail" I have a greater apprecia-tion of persuasive writing and also of Martin Luther King himself.

King begins by establishing his own credibility—as the president of the South-ern Christian Leadership Conference, he has a great deal of experience in the civil rights movement. This is part of the appeal to character which King maintains all the way through the essay. Aware that his audience is not sympathetic to his posi-tion, King also seeks to establish common ground between them by emphasizing their mutual involvement in the church. Himself a preacher, King draws attention to his thoroughly respectable background, "I am in the rather unique position of being the son, the grandson, and the great-grandson of preachers." By making a great many Bib-lical allusions, King hopes to win the trust of his opponents and so lead them to-wards his way of thinking. For the same reason, he presents their point of view in a calm and reasonable manner, "It is true that the police have exercised a degree of discipline in handling the demonstrators. In this sense, they have conducted themselves nonviolently in public. But for what purpose? To preserve the vile sys-tem of segregation." By fairly presenting the opposing point of view, which King does through the essay, he shows that he is unbiased and objective and, therefore, trustworthy.

The reasonable tone and the strong appeal to character allow King to manipulate his audience emotionally without losing his own credibility. He does this through the skillful use of such devices as vivid detail, metaphorical language, paral-lelism, and repetition. For instance, in response to the criticism that the campaign was "untimely," King creates a sharp metaphorical contrast to emphasize the natural impatience of the African American community,

> We have waited more than 340 years for our constitutional and God-given rights. The nations of Africa and Asia are moving with jetlike speed toward gaining po-litical independence, but we still creep at horse-and-buggy pace toward gaining a cup of coffee at a lunch counter." King builds on this point by using a great deal of vivid detail, as in "when you have seen hate-filled policemen curse, kick, and even kill your Negro brothers and sisters; when you see the vast ma-jority of your Negro brothers smothering in an airtight cage of poverty in the midst of an affluent society . . .

This appeal to emotion is further strengthened through parallelism and repetition as King lists examples of his own personal humiliations. The reader cannot help but feel shocked and disgusted by these many injustices and must agree with King's fi-nal comment, "I hope, sirs, you can understand our legitimate and unavoidable impatience."

King also makes constant appeals to reason when refuting the opposing point of view, most notably when answering the criticism that the movement was too ready to break the law. While King agrees that this is "certainly a legitimate concern," he points out that "there are two types of law—just and unjust." In an extended appeal to reason, King argues that "An unjust law is a code that a numerical or power majority group compels a minority group to obey but does not make binding on itself." He then illustrates this by referring to the segregation laws of Alabama and further supports his argument by bringing in the opinions of respected individuals such as Paul Tillich and Martin Buber. King deliberately and methodically makes the distinction between just and unjust laws, and again draws on the Bible to remind his audience of the common ground between them.

In his powerful and moving conclusion, King expresses his hope that "the dark clouds of racial prejudice will soon pass away." A great deal may have changed in the forty years since King wrote "Letter from Birmingham Jail," but we are still waiting for "the radiant stars of love and brotherhood" to shine over "our great nation." Racism is still a "hidden tension" in our society, and we desperately need "creative extremists" such as Martin Luther King to bring it to the surface and cure it. The value of this essay is not just that it demonstrates the most important features of persuasive writing, but that it reminds us that racism is something that affects us all in our common identity as American citizens. As King said of himself and his followers, "our destiny is tied up with America's destiny."

An Analysis of "Letter from Birmingham Jail"

Ferguson's Final Draft

"Letter from Birmingham Jail" was written by Martin Luther King in 1963 while he was being held in solitary confinement for daring to lead a protest march against the city's segregationist policies. It is a direct response to the statement published by eight white clergymen criticizing King's direct action campaign, but its scope goes far beyond that of a personal letter. Rather than being simply a justification of his own actions, King's carefully constructed and eloquently worded argument is a justification of the civil rights movement itself. In his lengthy essay, King systematically addresses each of his opponents' points, refutes them in turn, and concludes with a series of his own criticisms of white moderates and church leaders. "Letter from Birmingham Jail" is a remarkable piece of persuasive writing which demonstrates both the principal features of argument and those individual aspects of King's style which made him such a powerful preacher and political activist.

Perhaps, the essay's greatest strength is King's non-confrontational or Rogerian approach to the argument. To avoid antagonizing an unsympathetic audience, King must appear to be a reasonable, well-informed individual whose views on this sensitive issue can be trusted. This is done very effectively in a number of ways. For instance, at the start of the essay he establishes his own credibility by describing his involvement in the Southern Christian Leadership Conference. As the president of this respected organization, it can be assumed that he has a great deal of experience in the civil rights movement. Furthermore, King constantly emphasizes his own involvement in the Church, pointing out that he is "the son, the grandson, and the great-grandson of preachers." He also compares himself with famous Christian figures, "Like Paul, I must constantly respond to the Macedonian call for aid." These somewhat obscure Biblical allusions not only show that King is thoroughly familiar with the Scriptures, but also establish a common ground between two adversaries who have little else in common but the Church. To further lessen any sense of conflict King refers to his fellow clergymen as "my friends" and "my Christian and Jewish brothers" and calls them "men of genuine good faith." Finally, King presents the opposing point of view in a calm and reasonable manner, often conceding its validity before presenting his own case: "It is true that the police have exercised a degree of discipline in handling the demonstrators. In this sense they have conducted themselves "nonviolently" in public. But for what purpose? To preserve the vile system of segregation." By fairly addressing the opposition, King shows that he is unbiased and capable of viewing the situation objectively. Therefore, when he attacks the white church for its lack of leadership and moral initiative, his criticisms carry real weight.

This strong appeal to character is maintained throughout and allows King to play on his audience's emotions without losing his own credibility. He proceeds through the constant use of metaphorical language, vivid detail, parallelism, and repetition, all of which combine to create his own unique style. For instance, in response to the criticism that the direct action campaign was "untimely" King stresses the natural impatience of his people:

We have waited more than 340 years for our constitutional and God-given rights. The nations of Africa and Asia are moving with jetlike speed toward gaining political independence, but we still creep at horse-and-buggy pace toward gaining a cup of coffee at a lunch counter.

The contrast of these metaphors causes the reader to feel the frustration and humiliation of segregation. King builds on this by combining further metaphor with vivid detail, as in "when you have seen hate-filled policemen curse, kick, and even kill your Negro brothers and sisters; when you see the vast majority of your Negro brothers smothering in an airtight cage of poverty in the midst of an affluent society. . . ." This appeal to emotion is given even more impact through the skillful parallelism and repetition of "when you have seen . . . when you see . . . when you suddenly find . . . when you have to concoct . . ." The effect on the reader of this catalog of social injustice is one of shock and disgust, so that even the most conservative individual would have to concur with King's final comment, "I hope, sirs, you can understand our legitimate and unavoidable impatience." It is noteworthy that, despite the emotional intensity of this long passage, King never loses his self-control. With the simple insertion of "sirs" he maintains the modest and respectful tone which characterizes the whole essay.

While the appeals to character and emotion are arguably the most memorable aspects of the essay, King also makes constant appeals to reason in his defense of the direct action campaign in Birmingham. One of the best examples of his use of logic is his refutation of one of the most damaging criticisms of the movement—its "willingness to break laws." King concedes that this is "certainly a legitimate concern" but points out that "there are two types of law: just and unjust." In an extended appeal to reason, King argues that "An unjust law is a code that a numerical or power majority group compels a minority group to obey but does not make binding on itself." He then illustrates this general statement with a specific example:

Who can say that the legislature of Alabama which set up that state's segregation laws was democratically elected? Throughout Alabama all sorts of devious methods are used to prevent Negroes from becoming registered voters, and there are even some counties in which, even though Negroes constitute a majority of the population, not a single Negro is registered.

Perhaps King could have given more detailed evidence here, by describing the "devious methods" used and identifying the counties in question. He does, however, refer repeatedly to respected intellectuals such as Paul Tillich and Martin Buber to support his points, and it must be remembered that his essay was composed in a jail cell where there were no reference books.

In his powerful and moving conclusion, King expresses his hope that "the dark clouds of racial prejudice will soon pass away." The highly figurative language in this final paragraph creates another strong appeal to emotion, but this time the effect is one of promise and elation rather than shock and disgust. Throughout the letter, King has made references to the American Dream, the Constitution, and symbolic figures such as Thomas Jefferson and Abraham Lincoln, and this is continued in "our great nation." These references not only stir positive, patriotic feelings in his audience but also create a feeling of a shared national identity. For me, the value of this essay is not just in its tone, its skillful use of appeals, or its powerful language, but in its reminder that racism is something which affects us all in our common cultural identity. As King said of himself and of his followers, "our destiny is tied up with America's destiny." This is something none of us should forget. A great deal may have changed in the forty years since King wrote "Letter from Birmingham Jail," but we are still waiting for "the radiant stars of love and brotherhood" to shine. Racism is still a "hidden tension" in our society, and more than ever we need "creative extremists" such as Martin Luther King to bring it to the surface and to cure it.

In the final draft, the writer moves from a diffuse focus on imagery to a concentration on the three forms of appeal and the stylistic devices that create the appeals and that make them persuasive.

·· PART FOUR ··

Appendixes

· APPENDIX A ·

The Research Process and MLA Documentation

The reason for doing research is to attain information that will enlarge your understanding and analysis of a subject or topic. In your research, you may conceive of yourself as a detective, posing problems, deciphering the mysteries in the text or texts that need to be solved. You begin with clues, the words on a page; the clues reveal patterns. You discard false leads, red herrings, and develop a vision of a work or topic—your interpretation—expanded by information that you have gained from reading sources other than the work itself (if your subject concerns one particular text). The technical term in the research process for the work itself is the primary source. Other primary or original sources include autobiography, letters, journals, documents, and manuscripts. After you examine primary documents, then you study secondary sources that give you commentary about the topic. These materials may be biographical, historical, or critical.

An instructor may assign a specific subject for the research paper, for example, the role of the ghost or the play within the play in *Hamlet*. Other instructors may offer you the opportunity to determine the topic. If no particular assignment is given, you may want to concentrate on one of these areas:

- The biography of the author.
- The relationship between the writer's life and works.
- The artistic influences upon the writer.
- Analysis of the process of the writer through examination of drafts.
- Features of a particular work, characteristics of the genre, such as point of view and symbolism in a short story, imagery and tone in a poem, character and conflict in a play.
- The social, historical, and political contexts of a work.
- A particular critical approach, such as a formalist analysis of Keats's "Ode on a Grecian Urn"; a feminist reading of "The Yellow Wallpaper."

These key topic areas may be posed as beginning questions for research:

- What biographical facts do I need to know about the writer that will help me understand the topic?
- What are the connections between the life and works?
- How did the writer develop his or her work? What can I learn by examining successive drafts of a work or by reading about the writer's artistic techniques?
- What features of the genre do I want to explore? Refer to the checklists for the evaluation of short fiction, poetry, drama, and nonfiction in chapters 9 through 12.

- What themes seem most important?
- How did the historical, social, political, and cultural realities of the time influence the writer?
- How are the intellectual movements of the writer's time evident in his or her work?
- How will my reading of criticism enlarge my vision of the topic?
- What aspects of the subject do I find most puzzling?
- What interpretations of the topic do I find most debatable?
- What schools of thought will enlarge my understanding and provide new intellectual contexts and directions for further analysis?

Any one of these questions may provide a starting point.

THE RESEARCH PROCESS

For the sake of discussion, assume that you have chosen a particular work that interests or intrigues you. Before you begin your research project, you need to develop an understanding of the work. Perhaps you have discussed it in class. Perhaps you have talked about the reading in collaborative learning groups or with friends. Perhaps you have determined your own topic and have selected and studied a work not assigned or discussed in the course. After you analyze the text, you are ready to begin your research. Some suggested stages of the process follow. As you become more comfortable with the process, you may adapt or modify these stages to fit your needs.

Begin with a full exploration of the work. Engage in forms of reader response: annotate the text, brainstorm, freewrite, compose a double-entry notebook, and write several journal entries. Determine your interpretation, analyze your interpretation, and identify questions that remain. Discover the most puzzling areas concerning the topic. Then formulate a list of research questions. Check the most interesting queries. Have potential directions for research before you go to the library.

Next, explore other primary and secondary sources that will provide you with further information about the work. In the reference section of the library, you may want to consult a general encyclopedia for information on the writer and his or her work. Often the encyclopedia will have a signed entry by an expert and additional bibliographic sources. You may assume that the author of the encyclopedia entry is a reliable expert on the topic as are the other writers of cited secondary references. You now have a beginning point for research. After you complete this overview of a writer's life and works, you may choose a specialized biographical source, including the *Dictionary of National Biography, Dictionary of American Biography, Contemporary Authors, Twentieth-Century Authors,* the *Oxford Companion to American Literature,* and the *Oxford Companion to English Literature.* The Oxford Companion series also includes guides to other areas of literary study besides British and American literature (e.g., *The Oxford Companion to African American Literature, to American Theater,* etc). Cambridge University Press also publishes literary reference guides. One title, for example, is *The Cambridge Guide to Asian Theatre* (1993). Other valuable resources for background information include the following: *The Bloomsbury Guide to Women's Literature, The Feminist Companion to Literature in English: Women Writers from the Middle Ages to the Present,* and *The Penguin Companion to World Literature.* These reference books will give you a more comprehensive view of the writer and his or her work and additional sources for research.

After you gather information about a writer's life and works, you may narrow your focus to a single research area. At this point, you also will consult the computerized catalog

|or computer indices of information to discover and gain additional secondary sources concerning biography and criticism. Other specialized indices in print form for research in journals and periodicals include the *Arts and Humanities Citation Index, Biography Index, Book Review Index,* and *Essay and General Literature Index.* Electronic databases include ProQuest, Wilson, JSTAR, Expanded Academic Index, Lexis-Nexis (abstracts and full texts from newspapers and journals), Info-Trac-One File, and Opposing Viewpoints. A very productive source of information for the study of literary texts is the Gale Literature Resource Center. The "Center" includes biographical, critical, and scholarly sources. Online indices include the Academic Index and Expanded Humanities Index. Note: First Search, a commercial database service to which many schools subscribe, allows you to find information on a broad range of subject areas. In many cases, collections of essays on the author and substantial critical treatments of the writer's life and works exist. You then survey and skim your materials with a slant or idea in mind. Before writing, in order to determine a focus, review biographical and critical materials so that you do not take too many preliminary notes.

As you consult sources, you write bibliographic entries. Each source may appear on a separate card, or you may devise some other system. The entry should contain the following information for a book: Author, Title, Publication Information (Place Published, Publisher, Date), and Library of Congress reference number so that you can find the book again without searching for it in the catalog. A bibliographic entry for a journal should contain the following: Author, Title of the Article, Journal, Publication Source, Volume, Year, Date, and Page. Include a brief evaluation of the source.

BOOK

Bundtzen, Lynda K.	PS 3566
Plath's Incarnations: A Woman and the Creative Process	.L27 Z588 1983
Ann Arbor: University of Michigan Press, 1983	
Good evidence and analysis of theme of transcendence.	

JOURNAL

Pollitt, Katha	PMLA Bibliography
"A Note of Triumph" *Nation.*	
16 January 1982: 52–55.	
Excellent review of *Collected Poems* by Plath	

Both biographical and critical treatments of the author and collections of essays may provide additional reference materials. You also may want to consult such general indices as *The Reader's Guide to Periodical Literature* (for information on current writers), *The New York Times Index,* and *The Book Review Digest* as well as computerized general subject indices for information in periodicals, magazines, journals, and newspapers and for reviews of current authors. The reference room also contains specialized bibliographies. For example, there are several bibliographies of women's studies materials (e.g., see *American Women Writers: A Critical Reference Guide from Colonial Times to the Present*). A standard bibliography for information on literature is the *Modern Language Association International Bibliography of Books and Articles on Modern Language and Literature.* This bibliography indexes the major scholarship in the discipline and lists entries for authors according to field of literature, nationality, and time period. For example, Ernest Hemingway's name would appear in the Twentieth Century American Literature section. Other specialized bibliographies include *American Literary Scholarship, American Literature and Language: A Guide to Information Sources, The New Cambridge Bibliography of English Literature,* and *The Oxford History of English Literature.* Also particularly helpful reference sources are the *Literary Criticism Index, Contemporary Literary Criticism, Contemporary Authors,* and *Gale Literary Criticism Series.*

After you have decided on a research question and after you have narrowed your focus and established a preliminary direction for research, isolate the materials that you plan to study. At this point, you have an initial list of "works consulted" and a working bibliography of those books and articles from which you genuinely intend to gather information. Your instructor may want to check your bibliography and to offer further directions for research. As you shape your bibliography, examine your sources of information. You want to be aware of the publication date of your secondary sources so that you do not rely on outdated materials or interpretations of works.

Now, the notetaking phase of the research process begins. Before you start taking notes, however, keep your research questions and possible subtopics or subheadings for analysis on a separate sheet of paper so that they are foremost in your mind. You also may draft a potential thesis and determine a tentative purpose and audience for your essay. The purposes of research essays about literature are informative, argumentative, or evaluative; that is, the writer explains an interpretation, argues a point of view, or evaluates the effectiveness of a work or a writer's use of a particular technique. You may assume that your audience is your instructor and a community of knowledgeable peers. Having a beginning idea of questions, of topics, of thesis, of purpose, and of audience will direct your thinking and notetaking and will help you to assess the information from your sources. As you take notes, be aware that you may change your approach, thesis, topics, purpose, and audience.

Read and review your secondary sources carefully. Some people prefer to take notes on index cards; others use sheets of paper; others take minimal notes on cards or paper and create a system of notes that refers to photocopied information. You may put notes in the margins of duplicated information. In addition, you may wish to enter data into a computer. Whatever method you use, as you take notes, you engage in a combination of summarizing, paraphrasing, and quoting. When you summarize, you compress the central idea and main points in a work. When you paraphrase, you "translate" a passage from a work into your own words. Paraphrasing keeps the length, spirit, tone, logic, and ideas of the original passage, but the wording is different. When you quote, you are recording the author's statement exactly. Be certain not to include any words from the original work within your summary or paraphrase without using quotation marks. Any material from a source in the words of the author must be quoted. For this reason, take notes meticulously. Summarize, paraphrase, and quote accurately on the front of a note card or page. Then write your reaction and comments on the back of the card or paper or photocopy so that you have carefully documented and differentiated between your words and the language in the source, between your view and the critic's interpretations.

Each note also should contain an abbreviated annotation for source and page and a heading so that you may arrange your notes into categories of discussion and reshuffle them as your thesis and topics evolve.

THE RESEARCH PROCESS ONLINE

The stages of researching online are similar to traditional research methods: gain an overview of your topic by using an online encyclopedia (e.g., Encyclopedia Britannica on CD-ROM); develop a search strategy—narrow your topic; define and then refine your search terms and key words; and then limit your search and isolate appropriate online resources (CD-ROM; databases; indices; works online; other World Wide Web resources—public posting, home pages, etc).

Consider carefully the search engine. Some search engines index general information according to subject areas (e.g., Google, Yahoo!) and compile information from other search engines, while others are more appropriate for literary research (e.g., AltaVista). What follows are some important procedures for doing research online once you have chosen a search engine:

- Define the terms of your search (author, title, work, phrase).
- Identify a phrase or subject area by using parentheses or quotation marks.
- Limit your search by combining key words with Boolean operators. Remember that "and" narrows your search, "or" widens the search, and "not" excludes information.
- Check each search engine for appropriate field indicators and for directions as to how to search.
- Once you find sources, bookmark them.
- Create a list of viable sources. You may create a hyperlinked bibliography.
- Print out the most important information.

It is especially important when you are doing research on the Web that you evaluate your sources carefully and that you verify your information by using print sources. To assess Web sources, consider these important questions about a Web site:

- Who is the author? Is he or she an expert in the field? What is the intended audience? Do you detect bias on the part of the authors?
- In what format is the site? a personal home page? newsgroup? article online? (Be aware that information from online dialogues and online forums may not be useful. The people are not likely to be authorities on a subject, so the information may be inaccurate.)
- What organization is sponsoring the Web site? Is the site a reputable one? an academic site? These abbreviations commonly indicate the kind of group sponsoring the site: .com = commercial site; .org = organization; .edu = educational institution; .gov = government site. (Be careful to distinguish between a personal home page and authorized sites for authors or for organizations.)
- Is the information accurate? current? verifiable?
- Is the treatment of subject comprehensive? balanced?
- What is the date of the entry?

As you download material, be selective. Note the date that you accessed the material as well as the URL and information about the site.

Here is a list of selected search engines and helpful web sites for literary research:

- Yahoo!—http://www.yahoo.com (a subject guide to the Web with links to other sites and search engines).
- Google—http://www.google.com (a comprehensive search engine with links to more than a billion Web pages).
- Ask Jeeves—http://www.ask.com (a resource for general information).
- Galaxy—http://www.galaxy.com (a resource for humanities and literature research).
- AltaVista—http://www.altavista.com (a search engine for humanities and literature topics).
- Lycos—http://www.lycos.com (another useful search engine).
- The Argus Clearinghouse—http://www.clearinghouse.net (a directory of subject guides, helpful to scholars).
- MLA on the Web—http://www.mla.org (the site of the Modern Language Association with a link to guidelines for documenting sources in MLA format).
- The Voice of the Shuttle: Web Pages for Humanities Research—http://www.vos.ucsb.edu/ (guide to Web sites on literary studies).
- The EServer (University of Washington)—http://eserver.org.

PRINCIPLES OF DOCUMENTATION

You need to follow principles of documentation in your research process. Documentation indicates the sources of your information to a reader and demonstrates that you have absorbed and synthesized the materials from your secondary sources. Information that you should document in the text of your research paper includes the following:

- Facts that are not common knowledge (that could not be verified in several sources).
- Paraphrased information from a source (information from a source that you have put into your own words).
- Quoted material.
- Other people's views—even when they are paraphrased, not quoted—interviews, and other sources of information.

All of the above forms of information must be documented. If you do not document thoroughly or if you inadequately paraphrase the source, you will be plagiarizing. **Plagiarism** is the taking of someone else's ideas or words and representing them as your own. This act, which constitutes academic "theft," is a serious matter.

Once you have refined your research question, decided upon a focus for your research, a preliminary approach, thesis, and subtopics, and conducted research, you are ready to revise your thesis, to create an outline, and to draft your essay. The final stage in the research process is actually composing the essay. During this phase, you may repeat the acts of the writing process although you already have done considerable prewriting and planning: brainstorming, shaping, drafting, revising, and writing several versions of your paper. In this research-writing process, however, you must document carefully from all your sources.

For students, another issue in the research process becomes the value of their own opinions and thinking. During the drafting of a research essay, you focus on an original thesis and idea. Your thesis emerges from your thinking, reading, and research. The exploration, evaluation, and synthesis of evidence from sources also emanate from your own thinking. When you piece together your opinions, analysis, and information from primary and secondary sources, you may discover that you experience the satisfaction of exploring and validating your thesis and of sharing your findings with others.

FORM OF MLA DOCUMENTATION—CITATION WITHIN THE TEXT

All sources must be cited; that is, you must give the reader information about the material to which you refer. The accepted method of documenting information in research is MLA citation form that requires three steps: (1) use parenthetical references within your research essay; (2) include a "Works Cited" page that contains an alphabetized list of all of the primary and secondary sources that you have used in the development of your essay; and (3) include explanatory endnotes, if necessary.

The parenthetical reference involves two parts: an indication of author and of page. If the author's name is mentioned in the discussion, then you only need to indicate page number. If the author has written two books and if the title of the book is not given, then you should include an abbreviated title in the citation.

The common forms of parenthetical citation for papers about literature appear in the following examples. Examine these manuscript and punctuation forms—the conventions for citations:

1. Discussion (author and page)
   (Alexander 200).
2. Discussion—author already mentioned
   (79).
3. Two Works by Same Author whose name is mentioned
   ("Hope" 265) (*Ariel* 54).
4. Paraphrased and Summarized Material—author not mentioned
   (Alexander 302).
5. Direct Quotation—author mentioned
   Kroll states that "it is uncertain how seriously the speaker will entertain the theme of purity, and its related theme of transcendence" (178).
   Note: Citation appears after quotation mark and before final punctuation.
6. Indented quotation—more than two lines of poetry and four lines of prose:
   This poem is about two kinds of fire—
   the fires of hell, which merely
   agonize, and the fires of hell which
   purify. During the poem, the first
   suffers into the second. (Newman 62)

If you interpret only one literary work, you may indicate the paragraphs or pages of a short story, the lines of a poem, or the acts and scenes of a drama in a citation rather than the author and title since they previously have appeared in the introduction to the essay.

"WORKS CITED" PAGE

The "Works Cited" page also has a specific format, a particular pattern for each form of reference, dictated by the conventions of the MLA documentation system. The following are the most common bibliographic forms for the "Works Cited" page. Consult the handbook used in your school's freshman composition program for further information.

Common Forms of Bibliographic Entries for the "Works Cited" Page

FOR A BOOK

> Gilligan, Carol. *In a Different Voice: Psychological Theory and Women's Development.* Cambridge: Harvard University Press, 1982.

> Kincaid, Jamaica. *Annie John.* New York: Farrar, Straus, Giroux, 1985.

> Morrison, Toni. *Beloved.* New York: Knopf, 1987.

The citation is double-spaced, the author's name is placed at the margin, and the second line indented (five spaces). There are periods between parts of the entry. The citation includes author's name, the title of the work and publication information—place published, publisher, and date.

FOR A BOOK WITH TWO AUTHORS

> Flynn, Elizabeth A. and Patrocino Schweickart, eds. *Gender and Reading: Essays on Readers, Texts and Contexts.* Baltimore: John Hopkins Press, 1986.

When there are two authors, the second author's name is presented first name and then last name.

FOR AN AUTHOR WITH TWO WORKS

> Rich, Adrienne. *An Atlas of a Difficult World: Poems 1988–1991.* New York: W.W. Norton, 1991.

> — .*On Lies, Secrets and Silence: Selected Prose 1966–1978.* New York: W.W. Norton, 1979.

Note the alphabetical order of books for the author and a long (em) dash or three hyphens with a period to indicate the repeated name.

FOR THREE OR MORE AUTHORS

> Belenky, Mary Field, et al. *Women's Ways of Knowing: The Development of Self, Voice, and Mind.* New York: Basic Books, 1986.

Notice the use of "et al." to indicate the additional authors.

TRANSLATION

> Wolf, Christa. *The Quest for Christa T.* Trans. Christopher Middletown. New York: Farrar, Straus, and Giroux, 1970.

Note that the translator's name appears after title and before publication information.

A Work Within an Anthology of Works

Mukherjee, Bharati. "Courtly Vision." *Sudden Fiction International: Sixty Short-Short Stories.* Eds. Robert Shapard and James Thomas. New York: W.W. Norton, 1989. 215–219.

The author's name and work appear before the title of the anthology. The names of the authors of the anthology are acknowledged, with the abbreviation indicating that they are the editors. Finally, the publication information is given.

Additional Entries for Works in an Anthology

Schmidt, Jan Zlotnik, and Carley Bogarad, eds. *Legacies.* Boston: Wadsworth, 2006.

Shakespeare, William. *Hamlet.* Schmidt and Bogarad, eds. 174–261.

Keats, John. "Ode on a Grecian Urn." Schmidt and Bogarad, eds. 1094–1095.

If you cite more than one selection from the same anthology, list the anthology as a separate entry with all publication information. If you use more than one work from the same anthology, also list each selection. Give the author's name and title of the selection, but mention only the name(s) of the editor(s) of the anthology and the page numbers.

Other Examples of a Short Story, Poem, or Play in an Edited Anthology

Borowski, Tadeusz. "Silence." *Literature: Reading, Reacting, Writing.* Eds. Laurie G. Kirzner and Stephen R. Mandell. Fort Worth: Harcourt Brace, 1993. 315–316.

Note the indication of page numbers.

Kumin, Maxine. "The Envelope." *Tangled Vines: A Collection of Mother and Daughter Poems.* Ed. Lyn Lifshin. New York: Harcourt, Brace, Jovanovich, 1992. 143.

Childress, Alice. *Wedding Band. 9 Plays by Black Women.* Ed. Margaret B. Wilkerson. New York: New American Library, 1986. 69–133.

Note that titles of short stories, poems, and essays require quotation marks and that titles of plays are underlined or italicized. As a general rule, complete works are underlined, and shorter works appear in quotation marks.

Work in Several Volumes

Eagleton, T. Allston. *A History of the New York Stage.* 3 vols. New York: Prentice Hall, 1987.

Note the indication of volumes.

One Work in a Several Volume Work

Eagleton, T. Allston. *A History of the New York Stage.* New York: Prentice Hall, 1987. Vol. 2.

Note the indication of the particular volume cited in the essay at the end of the note.

An Edited Anthology Cited as a Whole Work, Not as a Single Citation of a Particular Selection

Halpern, Daniel, ed. *The American Poetry Anthology.* New York: Avon, 1975.

Note the indication that Halpern is the editor.

An Article in a Critical Anthology

Volpe, Edmond L. "The Wasteland of Nathanael West." *Nathanael West: A Collection of Critical Essays.* Ed. Jay Martin. Englewood Cliffs, NJ: Prentice Hall, 1971. 91–101.

An Article or Selection in a Weekly Magazine for General Audiences, Paginated Anew in Each Issue

Barthelme, Frederick. "Law of Averages." *The New Yorker,* 5 October 1987: 36–39.

Notice the format for presentation of articles: Author, Title of Work, Name of Magazine, Date, a colon, and then pages.

An Article in an Academic Journal Paginated Continuously Throughout the Volume Year

Wilentz, Gay. "Toward a Diaspora Literature: Black Women Writers from Africa, the Caribbean and the United States." *College English* 54 (1992): 385–445.

Note the addition of volume number after the title of the journal and the placement of year within parentheses.

An Article in a Journal That Comes Out Once a Month, That Is Paginated Anew Each Month, and That Has a Volume and Issue Number

Muscatine, Charles. "Faculty Responsibility for the Curriculum." *Academe* 71.5 (1985): 18–21.

Notice that 71 is the volume number and that 5 is the issue number.

An Encyclopedia

Blotner, Joseph L. "James Joyce." *The Webster Family Encyclopedia,* 1984 ed.

You do not need to include publication information for well-known reference sources.

An Article in a Newspaper

Sontag, Deborah. "Making 'Refugee Experience' Less Daunting." *New York Times* 27 September 1992: Sec.1:1,35.

A Film or Book Review

Rafferty, Terrence. "Closing Time." Rev. of *Leaving Las Vegas,* dir. Mike Figgis with Nicholas Cage and Elizabeth Shue. *The New Yorker.* 6 Nov. 1995: 176–178.

Note: The reviewer's name and the title of the review precede the film or publication information.

A Film, Videotape, or DVD

The Manchurian Candidate. Screenplay by George Axelrod. Dir. John Frankenheimer. Prod. George Axelrod. Perf. Frank Sinatra, Laurence Harvey, Janet Leigh, and Angela Lansbury. MGM. 1962.

Artwork

Matisse, Henri. *Goldfish.* Museum of Modern Art. 1914–1915.

Interview

Dove, Rita. "An Interview with Helen Vendler." The National Humanities Center, January 16, 1989.

Bogarad, Carley. "Sylvia Plath's and Ted Hughes' Poetry." Talk given at State University of New York College at New Paltz. New Paltz, October 24, 1990.

PRINCIPLES OF ONLINE DOCUMENTATION

When you document online sources, follow these general guidelines. Begin with the author's name, title of the work, and publication information as you would for a print source. Next list the electronic publication date and then the date you accessed the information. Finally, include the URL (uniform resource locator). If the URL takes more than one line of text, split the citation following a slash. Do not break the URL with a hyphen.

What follows is a list of online resources for teaching Sherman Alexie's "This Is What It Means to Say Phoenix, Arizona" that Vika Shock, an ESL instructor at the State University of New York at New Paltz, compiled as background material for teaching the story.

Common Forms of Bibliographic Entries for Internet Sources on the "Works Cited" Page

Online Newspaper

"Sherman Alexie, Indian Country's Favorite Writer." *Oklahoma Indian Times Online: The Native American Resources.* 5 July 2000. <http://www.okit.com/news/2000/September/Best/shermanalexie.htm>

Online Not-for-Profit Organization

Soneda, Brian. "Sherman and the Heavy Hitters." *ALKI: The Washington Library Association Journal* December 1998. WLA Online. 5 July 2000.<http://www.wla.org/alki/dec98/soneda.html>

Online Article from an Education Source

Luscher, Robert M. *Anthology of Modern American Poetry.* Book. *Modern American Poetry: Sherman Alexie (1966–   )* Multimedia Companion Online. University of Illinois at Urbana-Champaign. 1999. <http://www.english.uiuc.edu/maps/poets/a-f/alexie/alexie.htm>

HOME PAGE

> Rani. "The Official Sherman Alexie Site." Home page. January 1999. 5 July 2000. <http://www.fallsapart.com/>

ONLINE INTERVIEW

> West, Dennis and Joan M. West. Interview. "Sending Cinematic Smoke Signals: An Interview with Sherman Alexie." *Cineaste* v23, n4 (Fall, 1998) :28 (5 pages) 5 July 2000. <http://www.lib.berkeley.edu/MRC/alexie.html>

ENDNOTES

When you use parenthetical citation form, you may create endnotes to include explanatory information that is not necessary to the text. This information may be additional sources, added biographical data, or an opposing critical view. Endnotes are numbered, follow in numerical order in the essay, and are indicated by a number in superscript above the line:[1] The "Endnote" page, labeled "Notes," is doubled-spaced, appears after the last page of your paper, and is your last numbered page. The "Works Cited" page is the last page of your research essay.

Here is an example of an endnote designed to provide additional bibliographic information:

Text of Essay

In recent years, there have been many attempts to define women's separate ways of knowing and developing moral consciousness.[1]

Notes

[1] See, for example, Belenky et al. and Gilligan.

Here is an endnote designed to provide a differing critical view:

Text of Essay

House on Mango Street is considered by many critics to be Cisneros's best work. This first, autobiographical work brought her critical acclaim.[1]

Notes

[1] *Although House on Mango Street* brought Cisneros acclaim, I would contend that *Woman Hollering Creek* is a more complex and subtle work.

AN EXAMPLE OF THE RESEARCH PROCESS— MLA DOCUMENTATION

This case study presents the research and writing process of a student, Kevin Stoffel. It includes a journal entry, an outline, and the final version of the essay with annotations by the editors. The assignment for the research paper offered the option of literary analysis, and Stoffel immediately chose to write about Sylvia Plath. The instructor required eight typewritten pages and a variety of sources. The paper was due in six weeks. In order to ensure success, the instructor established deadlines for parts of the work. She encouraged her students to conduct research and writing according to the processes described in this chapter. Stoffel created a work schedule, chose and defined a topic, thought about the rhetorical situation, took notes, kept a journal, and made careful copies of sources to avoid plagiarism. When he submitted his complete portfolio, it contained far more work than the instructor had assigned. In the folder, he placed copies of original drafts of Plath's poems, an essay on "Lady Lazarus," several handwritten versions of the paper, many articles on the topic, note cards, and copious written notes and summaries of articles and of books, and his final research project.

In many ways, Kevin Stoffel began his college composition research project in high school when he watched a segment of the PBS series on American poets, *Voices and Visions.* The program on Sylvia Plath sparked his interest in her poetry and impelled him to purchase, to read, and to memorize *Ariel,* her most famous single volume. In the first conference with his composition professor, he discussed his desire to write about Plath; and he presented a number of ideas in order to choose an original thesis for his research paper. Possible ideas included Plath's marriage and her poetry; *The Bell Jar;* Plath's suicide; her obsession with death. As he prepared his bibliography, read primary and secondary sources, and took notes, he received critiques and suggestions from other students in the class.

His instructor then encouraged him to consult a member of the English department faculty whose research focused on Plath; and she, in turn, called Ruth Mortimer, curator of the Rare Book Room of the Neilson Library at Smith College which owns the manuscripts of sixty-six of the lyrics known as the "Ariel Poems" by Sylvia Plath. At this point, Stoffel's term paper became an adventure. He drove to Smith College, a long journey, and worked extensively in the Sylvia Plath Collection.

He began with three research questions:

1. What is the relation between Plath's life and her poems?
2. Is the poetry totally personal, depressing, and suicidal?
3. What is the connection between death and transformation?

These questions led him to a thematic consideration of several poems in *Ariel,* and he began to focus on the theme of transcendence in Plath's draft versions. His research in the original manuscripts clarified some of his questions and suggested a new problem: What do the draft versions reveal about themes of the works? He wanted to answer these questions, and he wanted to explore Plath's revisions.

During his visit to Smith, he copied by hand all drafts of "Lady Lazarus," "Stings," "Edge," "Fever 103°," and "Ariel" since the Plath estate permitted no duplication of manuscripts. He also wrote all significant emendations in pencil (no pens permitted) in the margins and between the lines of his battered copy of *Ariel.* In the following journal entry, he records his responses to his encounter with the original drafts of these poems:

> I have just returned from Smith College where I worked in the Sylvia Plath Collection. For such a long time, I have admired Plath's poems, and I can hardly believe that the facsimiles of the manuscript lay in my hands, that I touched her books, that I scrutinized her list of submissions. I am in awe of Plath's poetic powers, and I feel exhilarated, happy, great.
>
> In high school, I became fascinated by her poems when I watched the Plath segment of PBS' *Voices and Visions* on American poets. I began reading her books over and over, and eventually my interest resulted in a paper on "Daddy" that my

teacher really liked. He encouraged me to continue my research. When I took the Regents examination in English, Plath's poem "Mirror" appeared in a major question. My passion for Plath paid off in a truly unexpected moment.

Now after studying the manuscripts of "Lady Lazarus," "Edge," "Ariel," and "Fever 103°" closely, I believe that my idea about her search for transcendence holds validity and that the drafts have exciting new information in them, information that seems, at first glance, to support my thesis. I feel certain that I can write an original paper because no one has published any materials from these drafts and all important scholars seem to have divided opinions on the question of transcendence.

After a number of drafts of his essay, Stoffel submitted a version to the class and to his professor. In order to assist him with his revisions, they asked these questions about his tentative paper:

Do you want to include the texts of the poems so that readers may refer to them?

Where is your thesis?

What is the connection between the biographical details and your paper?

How does the theme of transcendence connect to the draft versions of the poems?

What is the organizing principle (the thesis) of the paper? of the paragraphs?

How does "Edge" become transcendent?

Why does the analysis of "Edge" focus on the drafts and *not* on the theme?

Who is your audience?

They praised Stoffel's intention and passion for his subject, his command of the research process, and his enormous portfolio. Everyone expressed a sense of enrichment and excitement that he or she attributed to Stoffel's conception of himself as a scholar.

Stoffel then reorganized and revised his essay according to the suggestions given by his instructor and his peers. On the basis of their critiques, he clarified his thesis and decided to limit his interpretations to "Fever 103°" and to "Ariel." He realized that he could not complete his ambitious project successfully unless he concentrated more fully on his two best examples. He eliminated "Lady Lazarus" because of the length of the poem and because of the number of draft versions. Since he believed that the analysis of the manuscripts of "Edge" in his rough draft included new material about Plath's attitude toward the dead children in the poem, he reluctantly chose to omit that section. A careful reading of his first essay, however, convinced him that he had lost the thematic emphasis in his interpretation of "Edge" and that his description of the drafts lacked specificity. He concluded that his paper changed focus at that point and that the analysis was not necessary for the final revision of his paper.

His instructor asked him to review MLA notation form since his draft contained inaccurate citations and to revise his "Works Cited" list to include his primary sources, *Ariel* and the Sylvia Plath Collection at Smith College. She requested that he include copies of the poems with his essay. His outline and final research paper, which follow, offer clarity of organization, a revised thesis, and expanded interpretations of the theme of transcendence in "Fever 103°" and "Ariel." Notice the inclusion of secondary sources and of interesting examples from the manuscripts of the drafts. The citations, the Notes, and the "Works Cited" list now are correct, and they provide models for MLA documentation. Kevin Stoffel selected an extremely difficult topic, and he received high praise for his original project. His paper represents an excellent example of the value of research and of writing.

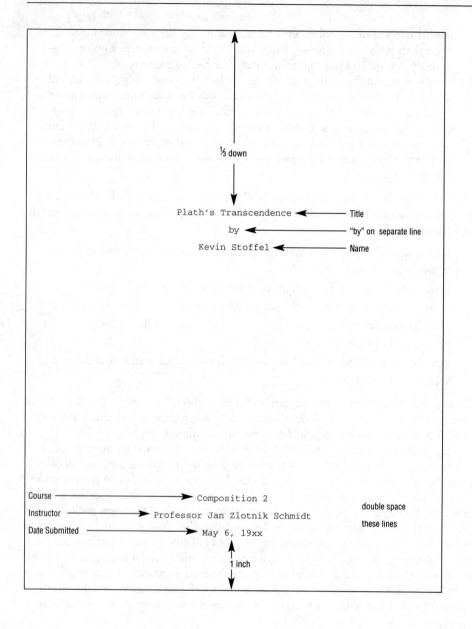

⅓ down

Plath's Transcendence ◄——————— Title

by ◄——————— "by" on separate line

Kevin Stoffel ◄——————— Name

Course ————————————► Composition 2

Instructor ————————————► Professor Jan Zlotnik Schmidt

Date Submitted ————————————► May 6, 19xx

double space

these lines

1 inch

½ inch

Stoffel i

OUTLINE

I. Introduction

   A. Critics interpret Plath's poems as autobiography.

   B. Theme of transcendence is central to Plath's poems, and draft versions reveal Plath's movement away from autobiography toward universal experience of transcendence.

   C. "Fever 103°" and "Ariel" are two versions of transcendence and prove hypothesis about revisions.

II. Autobiography in "Fever 103°" and in "Ariel":

   A. "Fever 103°" versions show omission of materials on Ted Hughes in order to focus on transformation.

   B. "Ariel" recounts a real event on a runaway horse, but experience becomes transcendent.

III. Interpretation of "Fever 103°"

   A. Plath's statement on two kinds of fire.

   B. Purity defined by opposite images of hell, sexual sin.

   C. Universal death from radiation (Hiroshima) caused by adultery.

   D. Purgation by retching.

Name, number. (Number appears in lowercase Roman numerals.) Center the word "Outline." Place one inch from top of page. Double space outline.

Thesis statement

Stoffel writes a topic outline.

Divide major sections with Roman numerals.

Each part in a major section of the outline should be numbered A, B, C, etc.

Strive for parallel constructions.

All verbs should be in the present tense.

Stoffel ii

E. Transformations:

   1. lantern.

   2. camellia.

   3. acetylene virgin.

F. Draft versions.

IV. Transition

A. Use of sexual imagery in "Fever 103'"—it is the sin.

B. Use of sexual imagery as metaphor for ecstatic transformation in "Ariel."

V. Interpretation of "Ariel"

A. The ride on the horse:

   1. sexual imagery

   2. out-of-control

   3. the hooks

B. "Something else hauls me through air"—the beginning of merging, of transformation.

C. White Godiva:

   1. She "unpeels"

   2. "Dead hands, dead stringencies."

D. Arrow and dew—evaporated into the sun/annihilation:

   1. Creative energy.

   2. Unification with sun.

E. Draft versions.

Stoffel iii

VI. Conclusion
    A. Summary of thesis and proofs.
    B. Quote from Katha Pollitt.

ARIEL
Sylvia Plath

Stasis in darkness.
Then the substanceless blue
Pour of tor and distances.

God's lioness,
How one we grow,
Pivot of heels and knees!—The furrow

Splits and passes, sister to
The brown arc
Of the neck I cannot catch,

Nigger-eye
Berries cast dark
Hooks—

Black sweet blood mouthfuls,
Shadows,
Something else

Hauls me through air—
Thighs, hair;
Flakes from my heels.

                                                  Stoffel iv

White
Godiva, I unpeel—
Dead hands, dead stringencies

And now I
Foam to wheat, a glitter of seas.
The child's cry

Melts in the wall,
And I
Am the arrow,

The dew that flies
Suicidal, at one with the drive
Into the red

Eye, the cauldron of morning.
                                        (27 October 1962)

                        FEVER 103°
                        Sylvia Plath

Pure? What does it mean?
The tongues of hell
Are dull, dull as the triple

Tongues of dull, fat Cerberus
Who wheezes at the gate. Incapable
Of licking clean

Stoffel v

The aguey tendon, the sin, the sin.
The tinder cries.
The indelible smell

Of a snuffed candle!
Love, Love, the low smokes roll
From me like Isadora's scarves, I'm in a
    fright

One scarf will catch and anchor in the wheel
Such yellow sullen smokes
Make their own element. They will not rise,

But trundle round the globe
Choking the aged and the meek,
The weak

Hothouse baby in its crib,
The ghastly orchid
Hanging its hanging garden in the air,

Devilish leopard!
Radiation turned it white
And killed it in an hour.

Greasing the bodies of adulterers
Like Hiroshima ash and eating in.
The sin. The sin.

Stoffel vi

Darling, all night
I have been flickering, off, on, off, on.
The sheets grow heavy as a lecher's kiss.

Three days. Three nights.
Lemon water, chicken
Water, water make me retch.

I am too pure for you or anyone.
Your body
Hurts me as the world hurts God. I am a
    lantern—

My head a moon
Of Japanese paper, my gold beaten skin
Infinitely delicate and infinitely expensive.

Does not my heat astound you. And my light.
All by myself I am a huge camellia
Glowing and coming and going, flush on flush.

I think I am going up,
I think I may rise—
The beads of hot metal fly, and I, love, I

Am a pure acetylene
Virgin
Attended by roses,

Stoffel vii

By kisses, by cherubim,
By whatever these pink things mean.
Not you, nor him

Not him, nor him
(My selves dissolving, old whore petticoats)—
To Paradise.

(20 October 1962)

½ inch 1

PLATH'S TRANSCENDENCE

Sylvia Plath's suicide in 1963 casts a shadow over her poems, a long shadow which seems to encourage readers and critics to interpret her work as autobiography. Her writing certainly includes details from her life, and no one can challenge M. L. Rosenthal's definition of her poetry as "confessional" in *The New Poets* (79). However, strong evidence of Plath's emphasis on transformation and of her control of both form and content which consistently made her poems less personal appears in her late poetry[1] and in the draft versions of the poems from *Ariel* in the Sylvia Plath Collection in the Neilson Library at Smith College.[2]

In "Fever 103°" and in "Ariel," Plath creates two kinds of transcendent visions, and drafts of both poems reveal her careful revisions through handwritten and typed versions—each draft a movement away from personal anger and outrage, from desire for revenge, and from confession.

Both poems begin in personal suffering, and both poems refer to events in her life. "Fever 103°" alludes to Plath's separation from her husband, Ted Hughes, former Poet Laureate of England, and to his affair with Assia Wevill which ended their marriage in 1962 (Alexander 290). The poem's preoccupation with sexuality and with sin and its emphasis on "adulterers" may stem from

Stoffel 2

On every sheet, except page 1, Stoffel inserts his name before the number.

Plath's experience with Hughes, but the drafts demonstrate repeated efforts to eliminate direct references to him. "Ariel" recounts a wild ride on a horse, Sam, which galloped out of control (Alexander 302), but the drafts transform the incident into "something else." Sylvia Plath begins with her own pain and despair, with the concrete details of her daily life, but she often focuses on transcendence, and she often revises autobiography into stunning and symbolic figures including the "pure acetylene/virgin" (*Ariel* 54)[3] of "Fever 103˙" and the "White/Godiva" (*Ariel* 26) of "Ariel."

  In a statement prepared for a BBC reading, Plath describes "Fever 103˙": "This poem is about two kinds of fire—the fires of hell, which merely agonize, and the fires of heaven which purify. During the poem, the first sort suffers into the second" (Newman 62). "Fever 103˙" is one of several poems by Plath in which fire serves to create a sense of purity equivalent to a type of transcendence, a movement to a higher plane. However, in the beginning of the poem, Judith Kroll suggests that "it is uncertain how seriously the speaker will entertain the theme of purity, and its related theme of transcendence" (178). The speaker inquires about the meaning of the term "pure," but she defines it through descriptions of its opposite, images of hell—all evil, impure images. The speaker, in her feverish state, descends into the classical underworld. In order for

PARENTHETICAL REFERENCE TO SOURCE.

PARAPHRASE OF SOURCE— To avoid too many quotations, Stoffel paraphrases central events from Alexander's biography of Plath.

Parenthetical reference to author not named in the text. The source (author and page) is added in parentheses.
TOPIC SENTENCE—Stoffel analyzes theme in "Fever 103˙."

Stoffel 3

its fires to purify and for death, rebirth, and
transcendence to occur, she must confront sexual sins,
lust, and the "full images of hell" (Bassnett 127).
These depths include Cerberus, the mythological three-
headed dog that guards the gates of Hades. His
disgusting tongues cannot ". . . clean/The aguey tendon,
the sin, the sin" (*Ariel* 53). Nothing can clean the sin.
This image blends into the sulfurous smell of a "snuffed
candle" (Ariel 53) and into the speaker's illness
rolling from her like the scarves of Isadora Duncan,
scarves that can choke and kill. The smokes "will not
rise" (*Ariel* 53). Instead, they reach a universal level
as they "trundle round the globe" (*Ariel* 53). This
sexual circle of hell with the smell and smoke and taste
of sin engulfs the world and seems "dull" and "sullen"
(*Ariel* 53), a parody of its Biblical and classical
counterparts.

> Evidence of purifying fires in poem. Quotation within sentence. Stoffel quotes Bassnett and fits her description into his sentence.

The smoke of hell murders the old and the young. The
speaker ceases her concern for her own plight and for
the sins committed against her which render her impure,
and she moves to a global level as the smokes choke "The
weak/ Hothouse baby in its crib" (*Ariel* 53), and "The
ghastly orchid" (*Ariel* 53). The smokes transform into
radiation which kills the "Devilish leopard" (*Ariel* 53).
The nuclear fall-out from the destruction of Hiroshima—a
version of hell on earth—greases ". . . the bodies of
adulterers/ Like Hiroshima ash. . ." (*Ariel* 54). Even

> Evidence of sexual sin, impurity.

Stoffel 4

in this form, the radiation becomes a punishment for
adultery and for sexual sin. Some of its victims are not
innocent like those upon whom the atomic bomb was dropped.

Thus, the speaker, by being impure, takes on the
role of a Hiroshima radiation victim:

> Darling, all night
> I have been flickering, off,
>   on, off, on,
> The sheets grow heavy as a
>   lecher's kiss
>
> Three days. Three nights.
> Lemon water, chicken
> Water, water makes me retch. (*Ariel* 54)

An apt and accurate description of a feverish state, the
flickering clearly connotes sexuality—the rhythm of the
lines, the lecher. The speaker begins to experience
purgation through retching.

After being a victim of the bombing of Hiroshima,
the speaker becomes ". . . a huge camellia/Glowing and
coming and going, flush on flush" (*Ariel* 54). This
orgasmic blossom creates its own metamorphosis, "all by
[it]self" (*Ariel* 54). Then the speaker enters a state of
purity. The first fire "suffers into the second." Plath
alludes to the Ascension of Mary: "I think I am going

LONG QUOTATION—A quotation of more than four typewritten lines is separated from the rest of the text.

Stoffel indents ten spaces and double spaces the quotation.

The reference for the quotation is given in parentheses after the quotation. Since Stoffel uses two Plath references in his paper, he gives the name of the volume to indicate which primary source by Plath serves as the text.

Stoffel 5

up,/I think I may rise" (*Ariel* 54). (Note the sexual
implications of her language.) The speaker transforms
herself into a virgin, not because she wants this
persona, but because she still retains the "glow"
and the "heat" of the radiation. She "emerges from
her suffering as an infinitely desirable, but
untouchable virgin" (Bundtzen 199)—too hot for any man
to touch or to enjoy. All men are pushed aside as
she rises. She needs no one as she ascends to heaven,
as she overflows with purity. She turns all men away
from her "unquenchable fire" (Bundtzen 199). All of
the sins, "old whore petticoats" (*Ariel* 54),
dissolve as she ascends, through purification, into
Paradise.

   This transcendence becomes a kind of purification
of the fiery "acetylene/Virgin" (*Ariel* 54) in three
draft versions of this poem written on October 20,
1962. In the first two drafts of this poem, Plath
refers to the devilish leopard as "you": "Oh that
devilish leopard!/ Radiation turned you white/And
killed you in an hour" (Plath Collection, Smith
College). Here she reveals her anger about Hughes'
affair with Assia Wevill. However, in the third and
final version, she changes the "you" to "it" in order
to depersonalize the image and to move the poem from a
personal to a general level. The lover, the man, the
darling is not killed, simply left behind.

QUOTATION FROM DRAFT
VERSIONS—Stoffel indicates
the source of the quotation
from Plath because he has
used two entries for Plath:
Ariel and the Sylvia Plath
Collection.

Movement to more general
level of interpretation.

Paraphrase of third draft.

Stoffel 6

In both poems, Plath creates sexual imagery, but the imagery serves different purposes. In "Fever 103˙," the illness clearly serves as metaphor for the speaker's pain, for her descent into hell because of adultery and because of sexual sin. "Your Body/Hurts me as the world hurts God. . . ." (*Ariel* 54). The purgation of illness leads to transcendence, even though the virgin in this case rises to Paradise from "hot beads" and from fire. She is not the image of a Renaissance madonna. Still, she transcends her experience of impurity and suffering; and she reaches Paradise, the ultimate state of blessedness. In "Ariel," however, the sexual imagery stands for transformation of the speaker into a bare, "White Godiva" from whom things drop away, and the speaker's annihilation becomes a unification of personal and artistic energy through evaporation into the source of all human life, the sun, ". . . the red/eye, the cauldron of morning" (*Ariel* 27). The sexual ride and the connotations represent "something else" which "hauls [her] through air" (*Ariel* 26). The sexual imagery is *not* the subject matter here as it is in "Fever 103˙." The subject matter is "something else" (*Ariel* 26).

"Ariel" begins in a motionless and black state— "Stasis in darkness" (*Ariel* 26)—as the persona describes the commencement of a ride on a horse that gallops out of control. The name, Ariel, refers to a favorite horse that Plath rode in Devonshire (Butscher 377). The name

TRANSITION—Sexual imagery in both poems.

Transition to interpretation of theme in "Ariel."

Paraphrase of numerous primary and secondary sources. Plath, the *Bible*, and Shakespeare represent primary sources. Kroll is a secondary source.

Stoffel 7

also conveys a key to the poem. It refers to Jerusalem
(Isaiah 29:1-3). The derivation may be either "lioness
of God," which was underlined in her dictionary and
which was written at the top of the first page of the
first draft of the poem (Plath Collection, Smith
College), or "altar of God" (Isaiah 29:1-3). In forming
a connection between the horse and the Biblical
allusions, Plath also infers that the horse is an altar
upon which the speaker can be consumed. The horse is the
"scrobis" upon which the speaker can shed all of the
"inessentials of life, thus becoming free and pure"
(Kroll 181). Plath also invokes the air spirit, Ariel,
from Shakespeare's *The Tempest,* the spirit who seeks
only to be free.

In the first two tercets of the poem, the speaker
becomes one with the runaway horse, God's lioness. The
violent ride itself merges woman and horse, female and
male. In every image, the reader discovers sexual
connotations: "Pivot of heels and knees!—The
furrow/Splits and passes. . ." (*Ariel* 26). Yet the
concrete details of the "brown arc/of the neck. . ."
(*Ariel* 26) and of the "Black sweet blood mouthfuls"
(*Ariel* 26) of the berries eventually become "Shadows"
(*Ariel* 26). The wild galloping ends, and the speaker is
"Haul[ed]. . . through air" (*Ariel* 26) by "Something
else" (*Ariel* 26) as she transforms into a symbolic figure
like Lady Godiva as she sheds her body and her past:

Paraphrase of action of the
poem. The horse and woman
merge. The speaker becomes
one with the horse.

Stoffel 8

White

Godiva, I unpeel—

Dead hands, dead stringencies. (*Ariel* 27)

When she experiences the orgasmic "foam[ing] to wheat"
(*Ariel* 26), she transforms again. "Thus the identity not
only of the rider but also of the horse is dissolved: the
newly created self is an 'arrow'. . ." (Wagner 116).
After this merging with the landscape, "seas" of "wheat"
(*Ariel* 26), the speaker becomes one with the horse, even
though, at the beginning of the poem, she is restrained
from this unity. The berries "still tried to catch her
with their hooks" (Kroll 182). Thus, just as "the child's
cry/Melts in the wall" (*Ariel* 26-27), the speaker blends
with the horse and the landscape, escapes her body and
her suffering (the "White/Godiva" (*Ariel* 26)), and
"flies" as the "arrow" and "the dew" (*Ariel* 27)—pure
energy—into the sun. The flight is both suicidal and
ecstatic since the transcendence leads to the creative
source. The poem, which begins in motionless darkness,
ends in infinite motion and light. The speaker enters a
"revelation of a new world. It is a transcendence into a
new world written at no one's expense but her
own. . . . 'Ariel' is Plath's most triumphant assertion
of her poetic powers. . ." (Bundtzen 256).[4]

> Endnote acknowledges
> alternative interpretations of
> the ending.

　　How does Plath create the amazing transformations in
"Ariel"? To what degree does she control autobiographical

Stoffel 9

detail for artistic and thematic purposes? She writes
about a real event and a real horse. She changes the
name of the horse for symbolic reasons. (Sam becomes
Ariel.) She invents an extended sexual metaphor for the
experience, and an examination of draft versions reveals
that she controls the erotic imagery through revision.
In the first three drafts of "Ariel," Plath calls the
horse "crude mover whom I move/And burn to love," "oh,
bright beast," "lover," "the plunging/Hooves" (Plath
Collection, Smith College). The fourth draft consists
mainly of versions of one tercet, the pivotal stanza
about the unpeeling Godiva. Here she presents the same
tendency to kill the lover (Hughes) that appears in the
drafts of "Fever 103˙."

> Hands, hearts, dead men,
>
> Dead men,
>
> Hands, heads, peel off. (Plath
>
>> Collection, Smith College)

Plath attempts six different revisions of the above
stanza before she writes:

> White
>
> Godiva, I unpeel—
>
> Dead hands, dead stringencies. (Plath
>
>> Collection, Smith College)

Evidence of control of personal materials for thematic purposes.

Use of primary source. Draft versions of poems.

Stoffel 10

Note that she eliminates the desire for revenge, the
thinly veiled details of her life. She had written the
same lines which appear in the above stanza in the first
three versions, but she had not ordered them as a
separate tercet. In the fourth draft, she attempts

Analysis of theme in draft of
"Ariel."

numerous revisions of the idea before she returns to her
original language and rearranges it as a distinct
stanza. Once again, the reader discovers that Plath
controls her personal anger in order to enhance the
effect of her poem and to attain a larger meaning. These
draft versions reveal a tightening of the language which
creates a fast tempo and an ecstatic tone, the idea of
transcending, of changing to another form, of merging
with the sun.

    Plath fully develops the theme of transcendence

CONCLUSION

in "Fever 103˚" and in "Ariel." Through revision, she
crafts great poems and often eliminates her private
angers and desire for revenge in order to create deeply
human themes. Through rising and blending images, the
ideas of rebirth and of transcendence to a higher plane
are expressed with great intensity. The strength of her
poetic vision emerges and begins to balance the widely
held conception of her negativity. These poems—
wonderfully controlled, brilliantly worded, deeply felt,
wisely conceived—earn her an important place in
twentieth century poetry. As Katha Pollitt writes in the

Stoffel 11

Nation: "She was always becoming more distinctly
herself, and by the time she came to write her last
seventy or eighty poems, there was no other voice like
hers on earth" (53).

Quotation with author and
source named in the text.

Stoffel 12

NOTES

¹ See Susan R. Van Dyne's essay, " 'More Terrible Than She Ever Was': The Manuscripts of Sylvia Plath's Bee Poems" in Wagner's Collection for confirmation of this thesis.

² I wish to acknowledge the assistance of Ruth Mortimer and her staff at the Rare Book Room of Neilson Library at Smith College and to express my gratitude for permission to quote from the manuscripts to the library and to the Plath Estate through Faber and Faber.

³ All future references to the two poems are taken from Sylvia Plath. *Ariel*. New York: Harper and Row, 1973 or from draft versions in the Plath Collection at Smith College.

⁴ Such critics as Alvarez and Rosenthal interpret this poem pessimistically.

"Notes" appear on separate numbered page, the last numbered page of the essay. The endnotes give material that does not fit into the text. The note begins with number in superscript and is indented five spaces for the first line. All notes are double spaced. Stoffel offers comparison with his thesis. Stoffel acknowledges the assistance of Ruth Mortimer at Smith College and permission to quote from Plath material.

Stoffel acknowledges alternatives to his interpretations.

Stoffel 12

WORKS CITED

Alexander, Paul. *Rough Magic: A Biography of Sylvia
    Plath*. New York: Viking Press, 1991.

Alvarez, A., *The Savage God*. New York: Random House,
    1972.

Bassnett, Susan. *Sylvia Plath*. Totowa, New Jersey:
    Barnes and Noble Books, 1987.

Bundtzen, Lynda K. *Plath's Incarnations: A Woman and the
    Creative Process*. Ann Arbor: University of Michigan
    Press, 1983.

Butscher, Edward. *Sylvia Plath: Method and Madness*. New
    York: Simon and Schuster, 1977.

Kroll, Judith. *Chapters in a Mythology: The Poetry of
    Sylvia Plath*. New York: Harper and Row, 1976.

Newman, Charles. *The Art of Sylvia Plath*. Bloomington:
    Indiana University Press, 1970.

Perloff, Marjorie. "Angst and Animism in the Poetry of
    Sylvia Plath." *Critical Essays on Sylvia Plath*. Ed.
    Linda W. Wagner. Boston: G. K. Hall and Company,
    1984. 109–124.

Plath, Sylvia. *Ariel*. New York: Harper and Row, 1973.

---. Unpublished Manuscripts. Sylvia Plath Collection.
    Rare Book Room, Neilson Library, Smith College.

Pollitt, Katha. "A Note of Triumph." *Nation* 16 January
    1982:52–55.

Rosenthal, M. L. *The New Poets*. New York: Oxford
    University Press, 1967.

Bibliography, named "Works Cited," appears at the end of the paper. Entries are alphabetized by author's last name, with a five-space indentation after the first line of each citation. Double space entries, and double space between entries.

Entry for a book by a single author.

Essay in an edited book.

Second work by the same author. Three hyphens and a period represent the author's name. Works are listed in alphabetical order by title.

Entry for an essay in a journal. Essay title is in quotation marks; the journal, date, and year appear, and page numbers are denoted without pp. designation.

Please note: Another model of a research paper follows: Erik Schoonebeek's "Literature as History." Another example is Melanie Chopko's "A Mother's Survival" (chapter 7).

■ STUDENT ESSAY ■

Historical and Cultural Analysis and Argument

ERIK SCHOONEBEEK

Literature as History

> In the barracks they spoke of 'flowers,' of
> 'rain': excrement, thick turd-braids, and the
> slow stinking maroon waterfall that sunk from
> the upper bunks, the stink mixed with bitter
> fatty floating smoke that greased Rosa's skin
> (Ozick 8–9).

What kind of wicked hell is this? What is this place where a steel fence is the division between a stinking, floating, greasy death and "green meadows speckled with dandelions and deep-colored violets . . . innocent tiger lilies lifting their orange bonnets" (Ozick 8)? This is the arena of dehumanization and the trivialization of life: the Nazi concentration camps of World War II, through the words of Cynthia Ozick.

Ozick's *The Shawl* is a historical narrative, surrounded by massive amounts of Holocaust documentation that historians have cemented in human chronology forever. But, how can one human fathom 6 million deaths? It is as much beyond the grasp of all imagination as the mind-set of the monster that ordered this mass murder. Without any personal experience in something that was so personal to so many people, we can only attempt to relate the Holocaust to our own consciousness through what is left behind. With the number of Holocaust survivors dwindling, eventually all that will be left behind are documents and Holocaust literature.

"The Shawl" falls in the category of Holocaust literature and attempts to call to mind the humanity (or lack there of) of the Holocaust through the use of fiction. With Holocaust literature holding so much importance to the future understanding of history, Cynthia Ozick's piece becomes controversial, because it is fictional. One must ask if fiction, in the case of the Holocaust, is credible as a tool for understanding and preventing atrocity or if it merely portrays the imagination of the author, becoming a sort of folk tale, over time perverting the truth of documentation and first-hand accounts. To fully understand the role that "The Shawl" takes in relation to Holocaust history we must first define what it is not.

"The Shawl" is not a memoir of Cynthia Ozick (she was not a victim of the Holocaust), nor is it a memoir of Rosa, the main character. Ozick chooses an omniscient narrator to stay at a distance to factual history throughout the story. She distances "The Shawl" from being tied to history to the point of refraining from using the terms "Holocaust," "Nazi," or even "concentration camp." Much of the documented history of WWII Germany is based around these terms, so frequently repeated that they begin to lose their meaning and the gravity of their associations.

Hayden White observes that such terms begin to be "associated with metaphysical concepts, religious beliefs or story forms" (398) and in becoming so, ironically, start to lose their true identity as we attempt to identify with them. To further this disassociation with history, it can also be observed that with the changing value of these terms history can take on an exotic quality simply due to the distance in time from our modern era. By these means we begin to associate documented history with cultures, people, and places that seem very different from our own. We overestimate the difference in the state of human consciousness from age to age, and documented Holocaust history (even in its greatest detail) becomes quite foreign as the reader makes assumptions and associations in the context of his own era.

Extensively detailed histories can be seen to contain some qualities not usually associated with such strict observation. Many classic histories contain a sort of filler that is based on hypothesis as logical progression. This can happen when documentation of an era is lacking, and a history of this era can only be presumed by its context. Thus, detailed history (accepted as non-fiction) can take on a touch of the fictional. In *Fables of Identity,* Northrup Frye states that "when a historian's scheme gets to a certain point of comprehensiveness it becomes mythical in shape, and so approaches the poetic in structure" (as quoted in White 396). To say that the Holocaust documented history has become "mythical in shape" would come as quite a stretch to most. However, a minority has been swayed by the mythical capability of history in this case. "The number of books published that seek to deny the existence of the Nazi death camps now exceeds one hundred," states Czeslaw Milosz in his 1980 Nobel Peace Prize speech (as quoted in Hampl 632). This fact draws attention to one of the most basic, but most important, differences between documented history and narrative history.

History is constructive on two levels. First, as stated before, history can construct a public view that is either accurate or false, depending on who holds the power and the pen. Second, the historian is constructing history itself, from a sea of nothing but fact. There is no preconception to work from. Historians construct the concept. In contrast, narrative history works from the foundation laid down by historians. Narrative history can construct a public view, but it is not the goal. Much of narrative history appeals to the human aspects of history, making them tangible to the senses and, in effect, giving documentation a new solidity in the human consciousness. Hayden White aptly describes this relationship which is especially apparent in "The Shawl": ". . . the historical narrative does not reproduce the events it describes; it tells us in what direction to think about the events and charges our thought about events with different emotional valences" (White 402). To see whether "The Shawl" truly does justice to the Holocaust in respect to White's comment, one must examine the images, symbols, and characterization Ozick chooses.

The most widely used and important device in "The Shawl" is imagery. Ozick attempts to call to mind the feelings of loathing, shock, and desperation through the use of imagination, abstraction, and embellishment. Ozick assaults the senses to create a sense of tangibility and truth. Thirty-five years after the Holocaust, in "Rosa," Ozick describes Miami: "The streets were a furnace, the sun an executioner" (Ozick 14). "They [the citizens] were all scarecrows, blown about under the murdering sunball with empty rib cages" (Ozick 16). With this imagery, Miami takes on the likeness of a barren valley of decay, or a desert, suggesting that Rosa (now described as a "madwoman" and a "scavenger") is not free of her past in the death camp, but that it follows her like a black cloud. Ozick also plays with our senses in the description of the barracks and the beauty that lies outside (see epigraph). Again, in "Rosa," Rosa walks on a beach at night: "In the dark . . . hotel roofs held up their merciless teeth. Across the water the sky breathed a starless black; behind her, where the hotels bit down on the city, a dusty glow of brownish red lowered. Mud clouds. The sand was littered with bodies. Photograph of Pompeii: prone in the volcanic ash" (Ozick 47). All senses are involved in these bold and effectively graphic descriptions. Ozick also uses specific imagery and aptly unique descriptions in her construction of characters.

Ozick embellishes some physical traits of Rosa, Magda, and Stella in "The Shawl" to create vital, weighty characters in a work that is only seven pages in length. Rosa's characterization in "The Shawl" is close to that of nonexistence. "Rosa did not feel hunger; she felt light. . . like someone in a faint, in trance . . . a floating angel, alert and seeing everything, but in the air, not there, not touching the road. As if teetering on the tips of her fingernails" (Ozick 4–5). Rosa becomes ethereal and ghost-like in quality with the embellishment of her emaciated state. Later, in "Rosa," Rosa takes on more human qualities as she interacts with people but is still described as a "scavenger" amongst death and decay as the sheets on her bed are described as "an umbilical cord. A shipwreck" (Ozick 30). Rosa tugs her dress out of the sheets "like a coarse colored worm . . " (Ozick 33). Magda, Rosa's infant daughter, is also characterized by images, coupled with animal personification. Magda is surrounded by and compared to everything from a squirrel in a nest to having the eyes of a tiger and, most often, a butterfly. Ozick gives Magda "pencil legs," "zigzag arms," and a "balloonish belly" (10) as she flies through the air like a butterfly but as far away as a moth toward the electric fence. Stella has "knees like tumors on sticks, her elbows chicken bones" (Ozick 3). Some of this imagery is unclear if taken literally, but "historical narrative does not image the things it indicates; it calls to mind images of the things it indicates, in the same way metaphor does" (Ozick 402). Ozick's images conjure up different associations between the Holocaust and each reader's own life, and the work becomes personal. However, "The Shawl" not only is personal but also contains some key symbols that are universal in quality and of historical and traditional Jewish origin.

The entirety of "The Shawl" is inspired by one line from William Shirer's massive *The Rise and Fall of the Third Reich:* "that spoke about babies being thrown against the electrified fences" (Friedman 113). Ozick's short story stands upon a fifteen-hundred page foundation, which Shirer built, from 485 tons of documented fact. Ozick also uses symbols from Jewish mysticism. Magda's breath smelled of cinnamon and almonds, even though she hadn't been near anything of the sort. This smell calls to mind that of the Jewish besamin (spice box), which is sniffed at the havadalah ceremony, ending the Sabbath. To smell the scent of this box is to sustain one from any tribulations they may cross during the ordinary days of the week (Friedman 115). Rosa is sustained by Magda's meager survival, as if only her breath will guard her from evil.

The most important symbol in "The Shawl" is, of course, the shawl of the title. The shawl represents the one image of life in a sea of excrement and death. Magda "milks" the shawl, as it can suffice as a magical source of nourishment. Later, in "Rosa," Stella sends Rosa the shawl as it again brings about life, this time in Rosa's disillusionment as Magda fills the room "like a butterfly in this corner and that" upon the arrival of the shawl (Ozick 64). It converts to a dead baby to a "Queen of Bloom and Blossom" and Stella into the "Angel of Death" (Ozick 66). The shawl is not only a universal symbol of life but also affiliated with Judaism. The Jewish prayer shawl, or tallit, is worn at times of prayer when Jews are closer with their God and become a community (Friedman 115). When Magda is on her way to certain death, voices tell Rosa to "hold up the shawl, high . . . to shake it, to whip with it, to unfurl it like a flag" (Ozick 9). Rosa does so, in a declaration of surrender, desperation, and a Jewish prayer for life. Following Magda's death, the shawl saves Rosa's own life as she stuffs her mouth with it, "swallowing the wolf's screech" so she would not be shot (Ozick 10).

Remaining consistent with Jewish symbolism, the "grainy sad voices" that Rosa hears emanating from the electric fence are most likely those of Jewish history (Ozick 8), telling Rosa to wave the shawl and attempt to save her baby (Lowin 109). The voices begin to take on the howling of Magda as she reaches the fence; "Maa-maa, maaamaaa, they all hummed together" (Ozick 9). The symbols of the tallit, the besamin, and the electric fence are solid because they are rooted in history and tradition, giving "The Shawl" a strong basis for valid-ity as an important historical narrative, with both its personal and historical qualities.

Cynthia Ozick is best represented in her writing philosophy: "History is the ground of our being, and together with imagination, that is what makes writing" By her own philosophy, "The Shawl" is great writing. Ozick doesn't use imagination so much as she uses the Jewish tradition of memory, although the relationship between the two are very close: " . . memory impul-sively reaches out its arms and embraces imagination. That is the resort to invention. It isn't a lie, but an act of necessity, as the innate urge to locate personal truth always is" (Hampl 631). Documented history fo-cuses on the awareness of the masses, and historical narrative sets its sights on the necessity of a created version of the past on a more personal level as to be easily identifiable. And, in the most basic function of imagination and memory, "we can only know the actual by contrasting it with the imaginable" (White 406), as to create our own valid consciousness. Historical narra-tives serve this purpose.

Tim O'Brien and Elie Wiesel, authors of *The Things They Carried* and *Night*, respectively, wrote their his-torical narratives in the form of memoir, differing from Ozick. Even though each work consists primarily of the author's own personal experience, both authors see imagination as a necessity because both use fiction to make their work more accessible and malleable to the mind of the reader for means of more personal under-standing while remaining in the realm of truth.

Two testimonials by Holocaust survivors, Brandla Small and Victor Frankl, are historical narratives that also aim for personal understanding by the reader. Both are completely nonfictional. But both do tug at the heart because they are very personal, with Frankl giving light to the invincibility of spirituality and Small to the importance of family as an undying source of healing. Both authors incorporate their stories into universal themes to make them familiar while providing vital information about the atrocity that was the Holocaust.

"The Shawl" is just as successful as memoir and the nonfictional testimonials of Holocaust survivors due to its historical foundation and, most importantly, its appeal to the human senses and heart through imagery. "The Shawl," with its conformity to the reader becomes more truthful than the hard fact of 6 million Holocaust victims. Ozick's writing can be smelled, tasted, seen, heard, and felt. As horrible as it may be, 6 million victims is simply unimaginable. Cynthia Ozick shows us a small piece as to better understand the whole.

Works Consulted

Bolick, Katie. "The Many Faces of Cynthia Ozick," *The Atlantic Online* 15 May 1997. *http://www.theatlantic.com/unbound/factfict/ozick.html*

Frankl, Viktor E. "Man's Search for Meaning." *Images from the Holocaust.* Ed. Jean Braun. NTC, 1997. 267–270.

Friedman, Lawrence S. *Understanding Cynthia Ozick.* Columbia: University of South Carolina Press, 1991.

Hampl, Patricia. "Memory and Imagination." *The Dolphin Reader.* Eds. Douglas Hunt and Carolyn Perry. Houghton Mifflin, 1999. 591–601.

Lowin, Joseph. *Cynthia Ozick.* Twayne' United States Authors Series 545. Boston: Twayne Publishers, 1988.

O'Brien, Tim. *The Things They Carried.* New York: Broadway Books, 1990.

Ozick, Cynthia. *The Shawl.* New York: Alfred A. Knopf, 1989.

Small, Brandla. "Brandla Small," *Mothers, Sisters, Resisters.* Ed. Brana Gurewitsch. Tuscaloosa: University Press of Alabama, 1998.

White, Hayden. "The Historical Text as Literary Artifact." *Critical Theory Since 1965.* Eds. Hazard Adams and Leroy Searle. Tallahassee: Florida State University Press, 1986. 395–407.

Wiesel, Elie. *Night.* New York: Bantam Books, 1986.

· APPENDIX B ·

Critical Approaches to Literature

We approach literary texts with presuppositions, often undefined, about what literature is, about what it means, and about what determines its worth. Critical theories enable us to articulate assumptions and to devise methodologies for reading, for analyzing, for interpreting, for evaluating, and for writing about literary works. A number of theories offer sometimes complementary, often competing, views of the literary text, of language itself, of the meaning or meanings of the text, of the process of creating meaning, and of the question concerning who or what creates meaning—the work, the writer, the reader, the culture.

Some critics think of a work of literature as fixed—a thing in itself with little if any relationship to the author or to his or her purpose or experiences, with no relationship to the reader, or with no relationship to the culture of the writer. The work, according to such a view, is objective and, consequently, free from the subjectivity of the writer or the reader. We begin with these theories that focus on the text; then we move to critical approaches that center on the writer, the reader, or the culture.

FORMALISM/NEW CRITICISM

Formalism in English language literary criticism began with I. A. Richards's *Practical Criticism* (1929) in England. It was picked up and developed in the 1940s by a group of American literary critics including Cleanth Brooks, Robert Penn Warren, and Rene Wellek, who came to be known as the New Critics. Formalist criticism considers formal elements of literature (organization, structure, language, etc.) in order to determine meaning. Each work is independent, complete in itself, and everything external to the work is of secondary importance. The formalist is less concerned with the state of mind of the writer, with any biographical, economic, political, or social information than with such intrinsic features as plot, character, narrative technique, irony, and paradox.

Both the underlying assumptions and something of the methodology of formalism can be glimpsed in a quotation from Cleanth Brooks: "The language of poetry is the language of paradox." Brooks's use of the word "paradox" is key: a paradox is an apparent contradiction that is resolved on a deeper level. Perhaps the simplest example of this is the metaphor. Consider the statement, "my love is a red rose." Taken literally, such a statement is nonsensical: unless the speaker actually is in love with a flower, there is no way for it to be factually true. Taken nonliterally (as of course we do take it), the statement is easily understood: the speaker is comparing his beloved to a particular kind of flower. What seems contradiction is revealed to be coherent meaning. We find similar examples of such conflict and tension at the level of character and plot: consider the character of Hamlet, whose attitudes toward Ophelia include both callous indifference to her love for him and overwhelming grief at her death; or the conclusion of "The Story of an Hour," where we are told that Mrs. Mallard, who has spent the story awakening to the freedom her husband's death brings her, has died of "joy" at the sight of him still alive. For this reason, formalist critics are interested in irony, since irony is another means to reconcile seemingly contradictory meanings.

Formalist critics judge the use of language in a literary work as a special situation in which the way the substance of a work is conveyed is as important as the substance itself. For this reason, Cleanth Brooks writes of "the heresy of paraphrase," the mistaken belief that a summary of the literary work could be equivalent to the work itself. For the formalist, method and message are intimately connected—another example of Formalism's concern with textual unity—and so there is no substitute for the literary text itself.

For the formalist critic, then, literature is an art form that always appears to be in tension with itself, but that ultimately resolves into a unified whole. It is the task of the formalist critic to demonstrate how that resolution is achieved, to identify the move from contradiction to coherence. To do so, the critic employs a strategy of "close reading," in which the work is subjected to close, even minute consideration and analysis, its moments of tension studied to reveal its underlying unity. A formalist reading of a literary work will attempt to demonstrate how its seemingly diverse components add up to a coherent whole.

In formalist criticism, the reader can make assumptions about the validity of interpretation and about the worth of the work of art; that is, some interpretations, based on evidence from the text, are better than others, while some works of art, based on their complexity, beauty, and depth, may be considered greater than others.

A formalist reading of "The Story of an Hour" by Kate Chopin (chapter 9) might begin by focusing on the story's last line: "When the doctors came they said she had died of heart disease—of joy that kills." From having read the story, which has given us access to Mrs. Mallard's inner experience, we know that the doctors' assessment is incorrect. Mrs. Mallard has experienced "joy," but not the "joy" the doctors assume. Why, then, does the story conclude with their diagnosis? Is this ending a carefully planned, unifying culmination of the story's events, or is it merely a trick, a simple surprise? To answer this question, the formalist critic would seek to resolve the tension between what we know of Mrs. Mallard and the doctors' diagnosis. The critic would ask if there is a level of meaning on which the doctors' assessment could be true, if Mrs. Mallard could be described accurately as the victim "of joy that kills"? The critic might consider the descriptions of Mrs. Mallard's happiness at the freedom her husband's death brings her, of the way her "fancy . . . [runs] riot along those days ahead of her." The critic might hypothesize that it is this joy at her liberation from the constraints of marriage that stops her heart, as it turns to despair that she will not be free from marriage after all. Mrs. Mallard must be free, and if she cannot be free in life, then she will be free in death. Thus, the formalist critic would argue, the doctors are correct in their diagnosis, but they are so ironically. Through such an exploration, the formalist critic would begin to determine the unifying principle of the story's ending.

Although formalism has been superceded by more recent theories of literary criticism, its methodology of close reading remains the bedrock for beginning students of literary criticism and for most of the critical schools that come after it. If formalism has taught and continues to teach anything, it is that nothing substitutes for close attention to the literary text.

STRUCTURALISM

Like formalism, *structuralism* attempts to offer objective analysis of the meaning of literature. The structuralist critic also seeks to minimize considerations of history, economics,
and politics. The theory aspires to scientific inquiry through ideas and methods borrowed
from linguistics and from anthropology. Each work becomes a system, and the critic's task
becomes the discovery of the laws that pertain to the interaction of elements in the system.
The structuralist examines surface phenomena in order to uncover "a deep structure." For
example, the structuralist attempts to define conventions of literary form, perhaps aspiring
to understand the features or elements that identify a text as a poem or drama.

Because structuralism developed from linguistics, some critics apply linguistic approaches to literature. In *Course in General Linguistics* (1915), Ferdinand de Saussure, a
French linguist, called the relationship between an object and the name by which the object
is designated (i.e., a sign) arbitrary. A word makes sense only within the system of an entire
language, and it signifies meaning only to those who know that particular language system.
Saussure further assumes that signs or words are useful when they emphasize difference: a
hand and a foot are both appendages, but a hand has fingers and a foot has toes. A hand is
attached to an arm, a foot to a leg, and so on.

Saussure theorized about the rules that govern the complex system of signs in language. He claimed that a *semiotic* (a science of signs) principle, which enables humans to
communicate through a system of signs, governs the structure of language. Literary critics
who apply linguistics to texts assume that poems, fiction, and drama are part of a larger system. Any analysis of a work requires the comprehension of the system in which the work
operates and of the difference between that system and other systems. Structuralism also requires readers to discover the way in which sign systems create meaning.

A structuralist approach, then, requires the critic to think about the way that a story
functions as a story, as opposed to a poem or drama. Structuralism looks to establish categories: for kinds of plot, for occurrences within plots, for kinds of characters, and so on. In
the case of "The Story of an Hour," a structuralist would seek to reduce the story to its es-
sentials in order to understand how it functions. It begins with Mrs. Mallard's learning of the
death of her husband. It has a middle that complicates the action—she uncharacteristically
finds herself joyful because of her newly acquired freedom. The end, which has a surprising
twist, is also Mrs. Mallard's end since she suffers a fatal coronary when she learns that her
husband still lives. The structuralist would recognize conventions of plot, theme, and character that appear in similar stories: the surprise O. Henry ending, for example, which began
as a device in mystery stories and remains a recognizable feature in short fiction. The structuralist would compare the story to others in which characters gain autonomy and happiness only to suffer a tragic reversal of fortune, a reversal both surprising and ironic. The
structuralist would note that Mrs. Mallard is made happy by an event that should make her
unhappy and made unhappy by an event that should make her happy. A scheme for the
structure of this story, then, might be that a character undergoes a pair of reversals, each of
which is received in a manner the reverse of what one might expect.

Structuralist criticism lost favor in the 1970s, and many new theories that borrowed
from Saussure or that contradicted the objectivist approach appeared. Scholars often consider contemporary criticism to be "poststructuralism."

DECONSTRUCTION

Deconstruction contends that literary works do not contain unified or stable meanings. Unlike formalist critics, who seek to reconcile tensions in a text in order to establish the relation of the parts to the whole work, deconstructionists argue that any close reading of a text

uncovers contradictions that inevitably "deconstruct" or dissolve the possibility of unity. Underlying and motivating deconstructive criticism is a belief that what we accept as truth, especially as it is conveyed through language, is nothing of the kind. Because they believe that language can never truly convey single, fixed messages, deconstructionists postulate that language creates endless meanings that destabilize a text and that create contradictions that cannot be reconciled.

Deconstruction begins with the assertion that there is nothing outside language, that language shapes and orders our perceptions. As described by its most prominent theorist, philosopher Jacques Derrida, language (and all linguistic constructions) operates through *différance,* a term that contains two meanings: "to be different" and "to defer." We do not understand a word, Derrida argues, because of any inherent qualities in it. Rather, we understand a word because of its difference from other words (e.g., "cat" is not the same as "cut" or "cap"). We also understand it in terms of other words (i.e., its dictionary definition), which we in turn understand in terms of other words (i.e., the dictionary definitions of the words that make up the dictionary definitions), and so on. Thus, meaning in language is always provisional and endlessly deferred. Deconstruction assumes that since the word that signifies an object is separate from that object, the word stands for the object in a metaphorical way, and so all language is metaphorical. Because words can only signify, they cannot serve as reality or truth. Because they cannot serve as truth, there is nothing to stop them from tangling and/or contradicting. If we read a text attentively, Derrida argues, we will see that this is exactly what happens. Every written text contains elements that will destabilize it. The appearance of stable, unitary meaning in a literary work is just that, an appearance: every work contains a multiplicity of meaning that undermines any notion of a stable, unitary literary text. Literary criticism that claims to find a single meaning in a text, deconstructionists argue, is, in fact, imposing that meaning onto it, choosing one of its competing meanings and focusing on it to the exclusion of all others.

Like formalists and structuralists, deconstructionists focus on the text. In deconstructing a work, however, the reader examines ambiguities, wordplay, competing meanings. The task of the critic becomes to expose the text's contradictions, to show the way that it does not add up to a unified achievement. One of deconstruction's favorite techniques is to take a text that has been understood as saying one thing and then to demonstrate how it can be read as saying exactly the opposite. The critic does so by examining the elements in the story that seem to be encouraging us to interpret it in one way and then demonstrating how those elements could as easily be understood as asking us to interpret it in exactly the opposite way. The purpose of such an interpretation is not to replace the old reading with the new, but to show how both readings exist within the text simultaneously, thus foreclosing any chance of achieving a unitary interpretation of it.

A deconstructive reading of "The Story of an Hour" might begin by considering the opposition the story appears to set up between freedom and captivity. Mrs. Mallard, it seems, moves from the captivity of marriage to the freedom of widowhood. The deconstructive critic might focus on the language the story uses to present that movement. After hearing the news of her husband's death, brought by "her sister Josephine," Mrs. Mallard sits facing an "open window." She is "reached" by the "notes of a distant song." She is "motionless, except when a sob . . . [shakes] her." Gradually, "something . . . [approaches] to possess her." Accepting her joy at her new freedom, Mrs. Mallard "[drinks] in a very elixir of life through that open window." The deconstructive critic would note that although these images ostensibly refer to Mrs. Mallard's becoming free, they do so using language that relentlessly emphasizes freedom as external to Mrs. Mallard. Freedom is something that is visited upon her, as much outside her control as was her marriage. Such language suggests that Mrs. Mallard still is not acting as an autonomous being and that she remains under the sway of external forces. Although, pragmatically speaking, Mrs. Mallard may be free of her marriage, at the level at which she experiences life she remains passive. Thus, the critic would argue, while the story appears to be telling us about Mrs. Mallard's moment of liberation, it does so in language that emphasizes her subjection. Mrs. Mallard is at once free and not free. The deconstructive critic would find another level of irony to the story's ending: namely, that Mrs. Mallard is killed by external forces, just as her entire life—even what has appeared to be her one moment of liberation—has been dominated by external forces.

Although not all critics accept deconstruction's insistence on the ultimate indeterminacy of meaning, a number of critical schools have employed deconstructive techniques in order to advance their own concerns. Feminist, gender, and postcolonial theorists, to name a few, have used deconstructive techniques to destabilize prevailing assumptions about sexuality and race.

PSYCHOLOGICAL CRITICISM

Psychological criticism applies the insights offered by such psychologists as Sigmund Freud, Jacques Lacan, and Julia Kristeva to the interpretation of literary works. Most psychological criticism has drawn on Freud's writing; although many of his insights into and assertions concerning consciousness have been superceded by more recent developments within the field, his ideas remain fruitful for the interpretation of literary works. A number of Freud's ideas—the Oedipus complex, the concept of repression, the significance of dreams—have entered popular discourse to the extent that we employ them unaware that they originated with him. We might find ourselves discussing the significance of Hamlet's attachment to his mother without being fully aware that our interpretation is informed by Freud's notion of the Oedipus complex. The responsible psychological critic makes an effort to understand Freud's (or Lacan's or Kristeva's) theories before attempting to apply them to a literary work. This is not to say that the psychological critic must be a practicing psychologist, only that a certain level of competency with the psychological concepts is necessary.

Psychological criticism tends to fall into one of three categories: the *biographical,* the *character oriented,* and the *structural.* In *biographical* criticism, the critic assumes a reasonably straightforward connection between events and forces in the author's personal life and the concerns, subject matter, and themes of her/his art. The artwork becomes a rather complex symptom through which the critic attempts to diagnose the writer. Such "psychobiographical" critics consider the connections they explore as being central to an understanding of the work.

Thus, in Kate Chopin's "Story of an Hour," the critic might assert similarities between Chopin's life and her heroine's existence: Chopin represented her own traditional marriage in which her role as a woman was restricted in her depiction of Mrs. Mallard's relationship to Brently. She recreated her genteel, bourgeois existence as the wife of a Creole cotton trader in her portrayal of Mrs. Mallard's domestic situation. The biographical critic might note that Chopin suppressed her own needs and desires until her husband died, as does Mrs. Mallard. Chopin subsequently chose to pursue a career as a writer to support her six children; a choice Mrs. Mallard never has. The biographical critic might suggest that Chopin created versions of her own life not only in this story, but again and again in her fiction.

Beyond psychobiography, the psychological critic may choose to *analyze the behavior of a character or characters in a literary work.* Such a critical approach assumes that since literary characters are meant to be representations of real people, they may be analyzed in the same manner as real people. The psychological critic approaching "The Story of an Hour" might notice the description of the "repression" in Mrs. Mallard's face. That same term is used in Freudian psychology to indicate the mechanism whereby the conscious mind suppresses unacceptable desires into the unconscious, whence they cannot arise directly without great trauma. Equipped with this definition, the critic might see that it describes Mrs. Mallard's character quite accurately: in order to fulfill her own expectations of what a good wife should be, Mrs. Mallard has repressed any feelings of dissatisfaction with her husband in particular and marriage in general. It is only through the unexpected shock of her husband's death that Mrs. Mallard's repressed feelings can surface, and their appearance is traumatic, heralded by "her bosom . . . [rising and falling] . . . tumultuously." The critic might note that Mrs. Mallard experiences the return of these repressed feelings as if they come from outside herself, as "something coming to her," as "this thing that was approaching to posses her," and that she struggles "to beat it back with her will." Her feelings are so unacceptable to Mrs. Mallard that she projects them outside herself and contests them to the end. The critic might note that it is not until Mrs. Mallard has accepted her feelings (or been overwhelmed by them) that she can articulate them: "free, free, free!" Having accepted what she had repressed, Mrs. Mallard achieves a new level of personal wholeness, indicated by her speaking of herself as free in "[b]ody and soul," that is, in a manner that emphasizes her integration physically and mentally. Like other critics, the psychological critic would recognize the irony of the story's ending: Mrs. Mallard integrates what she has so long repressed, and in so doing makes herself susceptible to the fatal shock of her husband's reappearance.

Finally, the psychological critic may choose to examine the way in which the literary work itself enacts psychological concepts. Such *structuralist psychological criticism* attempts to psychologize the literary text, treating it as a psychologist might treat a patient. The psychological critic looks to find the psychological principles at work in the construction of a given work. The critic approaching "The Story of an Hour" might find that, in addition to presenting a protagonist who represses information from herself, the story itself represses information from the reader. While the story wants to be about Mrs. Mallard's dawning realization of freedom, its language indicates that she is not free, that she is still acted upon by outside forces. It, therefore, contains a series of rhetorical Freudian slips. Mrs. Mallard is not in control of her own body: she sits "motionless, except when a sob . . . [shakes] her." Her awareness of her own freedom is "something . . . [approaching] to possess her." Even when she accepts her joy at her new freedom, Mrs. Mallard "[drinks] in a very elixir of life through that open window," taking it into herself from the outside. Such an interpretation has much in common with that offered by deconstruction; both critical approaches look to discover what other meanings may be present in the literary text than the seemingly obvious one.

The examples we have considered have employed principles drawn from Freudian psychology. They need not have: we could as easily have used the work of Lacan, Kristeva, or any number of other psychologists (and psychological critics) to analyze "The Story of an Hour." The benefit to psychological criticism is that it allows us to speak of dimensions of the work neglected by the critical schools we have considered thus far. As is always the case with literary criticism, however, the best psychological criticism is that which remains rooted in the text, drawing its insights from the words on the page.

READER RESPONSE CRITICISM

Reader response criticism is grounded in certain assumptions about literary texts and their readers. The first is that texts have their existence in the reading: until a reader is engaged with the words on the page, we cannot speak of them as having meaning. Therefore, literary texts must be understood rhetorically, which is to say, for the effect they have on an audience.

As Stanley Fish, one of the leading proponents of this school, has claimed, the critic should describe not what a poem is, but what it does. The reader response critic seeks to analyze the ways in which a given text arouses expectations that it then fulfills or frustrates. The emphasis is on understanding the text as a site where readers may produce meaning. Reader response critics differ in terms of how much independence they give to the text as a separate object of study. Louise Rosenblatt, for example, views the reading process as interactive, as "transitive," as an interaction between the world of the reader and the world of the text. Norman Holland envisions the reading process as a re-creation based on a dynamic interaction between a reader who has a particular "identity theme," a particular personality pattern, and a text that is re-created and shaped by the demands of the reader's identity theme. Holland theorizes that identity replicates itself—in all acts of living and of reading. David Bleich, another reader response theorist, contends in his early works, *Reading and Feeling* (1975) and *Subjective Criticism* (1978), that the reader response process primarily is individual and subjective and that the interpretation of a work is based on the reader's subjective response to it: the reader's "resymbolization" of that work. In his more recent work, *The Double Perspective: Language, Literacy, and Social Relations* (1988), Bleich acknowledges the role of gender and social context in shaping the reader's "resymbolization" of a work. What finally accounts for and governs response? Are there only totally idiosyncratic, subjective individual responses to works? For reader response critics, the reading process always will be personal; this is not to say, however, that such an approach must lapse into hopeless relativism and subjectivism. Reader response criticism is, as its name indicates, not only about the reader, but also about the response to a specific text. The best reader response criticism describes the reactions evoked by specific features of the text. In addition, the totality of response depends on what Stanley Fish labels "the interpretive community of readers." That is, part of the process is influenced by the intellectual community and concerns of readers. The community helps shape the intellectual background—the approach, views, and values—of the reader. Reader response critics also maintain that interpretation of a text may change depending on when a person reads a work. People read differently at different phases of their lives. Part of this process is determined by cultural context. The world of the 2000s in the United States, for example, contrasts drastically with the world of the 1950s in the United States.

The student's essay in chapter 9 is a reader response to "The Story of an Hour." The writer compares Mrs. Mallard's entrapment and desire for freedom with her own situation: her own marriage and yearning for autonomy. Reader response criticism may begin with highly personal responses, as the freewrites that follow demonstrate. In them, the writer reflects on the changes in her view of "The Story of an Hour" at varying stages of her life.

> When I first read "The Story of an Hour," I thought about how entrapped Mrs. Mallard was and how limited her life and her options were. She seemed totally cowed by the authority figures in her life: her sister, her husband. She seemed spineless.

> I tasted her single delightful moment of freedom and felt sorry for her. I truly felt pity. As a young twenty-two year old, I couldn't imagine a life without infinite possibility.

> I reread the story in my thirties when I taught it in a creative writing class to a group of older, returning women students. I saw it as a story of awakenings. I saw it as a reflection of changing values. She recognized her own oppression. She realized a possibility for freedom. That opening up was vividly depicted in her looking out the window.

> That view of the story very much seemed to go with the times, with the burgeoning of the women's movement in the mid 1970s, with the faith that roles for

women could be, as Adrienne Rich said, "reenvision(ed)." It was all in the recognition of oppression and the opening up. Writing was an act of consciousness. Mrs. Mallard's opening up of consciousness seemed the center of the work and her death—just at the point of dawning awareness—seemed tragic.

As I reread the work to teach it again in my forties, what strikes me anew is imprisonment. Roles are still being redefined—but not as quickly or as easily. Women are still trapped. Women are still not able to let go of traditional roles. Many women are still caught in the same bind: the struggle between duty and responsibility and self-fulfillment.

Mrs. Mallard's imprisonment and her only way out—death—seem more poignant— and even more realistic—now.

These responses represent the reader exploring her own changing response to the story. The next step in developing a critical essay would be for the writer to establish how her feelings are grounded in specific features of the text.

As criticism moves away from concentrating solely on the text and toward embracing both the writer and the reader, it also moves toward suggesting the place of the text within the larger social order. Sociological critics analyze the work within its cultural context. Treatment is given to the ways in which the text both mirrors and is defined by the social and cultural concerns of the age.

FEMINIST CRITICISM

One important form of sociological criticism is *feminist theory*, which views the work in terms of sexual politics. To talk about "sexual politics" is to talk about how the unequal distribution of power operates in male/female relationships and how this imbalance structures many unspoken assumptions about the roles that men and women are expected to play within society. That these roles have traditionally been oppressive for women is the basic foundation of feminist thought. Feminist critics assert that throughout history, men have exercised political, social, and economic authority in ways that have privileged their own needs and interests while making the needs and interests of women secondary. Women's roles have been defined in ways that tend to support the patriarchal system; moreover, the male perspective is presented as the norm for humankind while the female perspective is presented as being somehow intrinsically "feminine" rather than simply "human." Simone de Beauvior describes this eloquently in "Woman as Other," where she says, "Thus humanity is male and man defines woman not in herself but as relative to him; she is not regarded as an autonomous being." Taking this unequal power dynamic as their basic starting point, feminist critics have raised many challenging questions about the ways in which literature is both written and read.

In the 1960s, feminist criticism sought to expose the patriarchal assumptions embedded in society by analyzing the representation of women in literary works written by men. In *Sexual Politics* (1970), Kate Millet took on the literary establishment by critiquing a number of canonical male novelists for the chauvinist assumptions underlying their characters. For instance, Millet claims that D. H. Lawrence associates activity and intellect with the masculine realm and sees any attempt by women to enter that realm as both unnatural and threatening to men. For Millet, literary criticism must address such chauvinism, because "sexual distinctions are political definitions." In *Thinking About Women* (1968), Mary Ellman considered the reader as well as the writer, noting that "the working rule is simple, basic: there must always be two literatures like two public toilets, one for Men and one for Women." The underlying claim in much feminist criticism of this period was that literature, no matter how "great" it might be, implicitly socializes men and women according to established categories of masculine and feminine.

In the 1970s, much feminist criticism was concerned with rediscovering and reevaluating women writers who had previously been excluded from the predominantly male canon of "great works." The Feminist Press in the United States and the Women's Press in Britain were committed to reprinting neglected works by women (for example, Rebecca Harding Davis's 1861 novel *Life in the Iron Mills*) and were instrumental in furthering feminist scholarship. One landmark study from this period is *A Literature of Their Own: British Women Novelists from Brontë to Lessing* (1977) by Elaine Showalter. Showalter charts the struggle of female writers to establish themselves in a predominantly male tradition. Bringing together famous and less well-known writers, Showalter describes an alternative female tradition that first imitated male models, then challenged them, and finally established its own agenda. Showalter also coined the term "gynocriticism," a new approach that would specifically address "the psychodynamics of female creativity; linguistics and the problem of a female language; the trajectory of the individual or collective female literary career; literary history; and, of course, studies of particular writers and works." By focusing on issues such as female creativity and female language, Showalter raised a question that preoccupied feminist critics of the 1980s: Is there a particularly female mode of writing?

In the 1980s, a number of poststructuralist feminists came to the forefront of literary theory. Influenced, like other poststructuralists, by the French philosopher Michel Foucault, these critics saw language not as a transparent medium that reflects reality, but at a system of meanings that partially construct what we understand as reality. And, like Foucault, these critics saw language as one of the fundamental means by which power relations are maintained in a society. Therefore, challenging the accepted ways of speaking and writing can be a means of challenging inequitable power relations. According to Luce Irigaray, feminists have to work within patriarchal discourses, whether literary, philosophical, or scientific, and challenge the assumptions of those discourses, in the process "leaving open the possibility of a different language." Similarly, Hélène Cixous advocated an *écriture féminine,* or "feminine writing," that would provide an alternative to the "phallocentric" language of Western culture—language that, in privileging reason and logic, privileged principles associated with the masculine intellect. Cixous sought a nonlinear, fluid form of writing that allowed for instability and excess of meaning; she also insisted on the connection between women's creativity and their sexuality: "Write your self. Your body must be heard." Other feminists, however, have critiqued this strong identification between feminine writing and the female body. For some, to define female writing as unstructured and diffuse is to revert to the biological essentialism that for so many centuries has categorized women as not intellectual, not logical, not coherent.

Current feminism continues to work with all of the preceding issues, but has also become more interested in race and class in relation to gender, resisting the idea of a universal female nature or experience. Postcolonial feminism, for instance, considers the assumptions at work within a predominantly white, middle-class, and academic feminist tradition, and whether the terms and concepts used by such feminists are relevant to those in minority or non-Western cultures. A woman can have multiple identities in terms of race, class, and sexual preference, and the tendency now is to talk about "feminisms" rather than simply "feminism."

A basic feminist reading of "The Story of an Hour" would foreground the tragedy inherent in the plot: that in order to feel empowered and emotionally connected, a woman must suffer the death of her husband. This is a harsh statement to make, but a feminist critic would argue that for the Victorian woman, marriage was such an oppressive institution that most women had to sacrifice their own needs and ambitions, even their identities as autonomous individuals. The pain of such sacrifice could be so acute that the death of a husband, while traumatic, could also represent tremendous freedom—the kind of freedom that would not be available to a young single woman whose sole purpose in life, in this era, was to marry and have children. By analyzing the process of change in Mrs. Mallard, the feminist critic might note the initial negativity of her portrayal: she is weak, emotionally and physically, even before the news of her husband's death. She sinks into a "comfortable, roomy armchair"—the symbol of her domestic entrapment—and is "pressed down by a physical exhaustion that seemed haunted her body and seemed to reach into her soul." Her dawning consciousness, however, is expressed positively in terms of the natural world, with images of spring and renewal: "the tops of the trees that were all aquiver with the new spring life." In this way, the text affirms Mrs. Mallard's process of self-empowerment, which becomes fully realized when she whispers, "Free! Body and soul free!" By encouraging the reader to empathize with Mrs. Mallard, this text communicates a powerful feminist message. But the feminist critic might also question the text's underlying assumption: that Mrs. Mallard is so much the victim of social institutions that only the death of her husband can free her. This is not, perhaps, such an inspiring message for women seeking to challenge those institutions.

GENDER CRITICISM

Gender criticism is related to feminist criticism in that both are interested in how sexual difference functions socially and politically. However, gender criticism has several important differences. Firstly, gender criticism is not as woman-centered as feminist criticism. As Myra Jehlen puts it, *"The Adventures of Huckleberry Finn* is a man's book about a boy, and just as likely an object of gender criticism as writing by or about women." Jehlen focuses on the scene in which Huck, disguised as a girl, is discovered by the motherly Judith Loftus, who contrives a series of tests to prove that Huck is (as she suspects) actually a boy. By performing the tests of throwing, catching, and threading a needle like a boy, Huck shows that being a boy is largely a matter of performance—of playing a role according to certain learned behaviors. Jehlen describes this scene as "the reversal of feminity from nature to nurture—from sex to gender" and relates it to the broader themes of the novel: Huck learns through Jim that racial categories are also socially constructed, and he comes (however imperfectly) to learn another way of relating to Jim—as another person rather than as a black slave.

Secondly, gender criticism is also specifically interested in gay and lesbian issues, and many critics have adopted the term *queer theory* to describe their approach. Some of the issues they address are similar to those of feminist critics, but with a different emphasis. If there is a female tradition in literature, is there also a gay tradition? What happens when one rereads canonical authors from a perspective outside the category of heterosexual love? Are there identifiably gay strategies for reading and writing? How should a critic address homophobia in a literary text? How do we talk about these issues in the classroom? Such questions have motivated gender critics to reread such authors as Herman Melville, Emily Dickinson, Henry James, Willa Cather, and Virginia Woolf, writers whose conservative social contexts did not allow them to explore their sexual identities openly in their work. Other writers who were more open can now be appreciated for this openness. Walt Whitman, for instance, whose celebrations of male love were previously interpreted as asexual comradeship, can now be recognized as a great poet who was also a gay poet.

Within gender criticism there are those who wish to distinguish between male and female homosexuality. Some see women and men as essentially different regardless of their sexual preference. Some argue that society marginalizes the male homosexual differently from the female lesbian, and that, therefore, their lived experiences are different. Important questions are raised by this division. Is sexual preference or physiology the primary factor in identity formation? Are gay men psychologically more like women than other men? Does the biological fact of maternity create a distinctively feminine sensibility, regardless of whether the woman is straight or gay? Some critics, however, completely eschew the notion of innate male/female essences. According to Teresa de Lauretis, "sexuality, commonly thought to be a natural as well as a private matter, is in fact completely constructed in culture according to the political aims of the society's dominant class." But for all gender critics, the process of literary analysis is conceived of as a liberating project that can open up scholarly and classroom discussion to issues that have serious implications from all individuals and their communities. A readiness to explore the intersection of personal and social realities from the perspective of gender not only enriches the reading of literature, but also builds an understanding of the ways in which all cultures create categories of identification and difference that often need to be interrogated.

A gender critic would consider how individual characters in "The Story of an Hour" suggest particular things about the categories of "female" and "male" in Chopin's own social milieu. Several patterns emerge quite clearly: women are associated with the domestic sphere, with fragility and passivity, while men are associated with the public sphere, with control and activity. Thus, it is Richards who first learns about Brently Mallard's death in the newspaper office and brings that information back to Mrs. Mallard at home. She shuts herself away in her room and sinks into her "comfortable, roomy armchair," where, through the open window, she hears a peddler "crying his wares in the street below." The world through the open window is not one in which Mrs. Mallard can actively participate, but it calls to her powerfully as the implications of her husband's death begin to sink in: "she was drinking in a very elixir of life through that open window." When her husband appears at the end of the story, his entrance into the domestic sphere of the house is described so as to emphasize both his masculine activity and his self-control: "Somebody was opening the front door with a latchkey. It was Brently Mallard who entered, a little travel-stained, composedly carrying his gripsack and umbrella." The other male character, Richards, automatically moves to protect Mrs. Mallard—unsuccessfully, of course, but nonetheless reinforcing the role of men as active and women as passive. Such a reading need not undermine the effectiveness of the story, but would simply emphasize the extent to which all art, regardless of its aesthetic achievements, inevitably carries with it a sociological dimension.

NEW HISTORICISM

The *new historicism* represents another variant of sociological criticism. By reading a literary work through its historical and social context, the new historicist seeks to reconnect the text with the complexity of lived experience during its own time. In doing so, the new historicist emphasizes issues of social power and considers how a particular text dramatizes the social and political struggles of certain groups. In this way new historicism is quite different from "old" or traditional historicism, which tended to explored the thematic unity of a work against the backdrop of "official" history—that is, the broad sweep of famous personages and noteworthy events. In contrast, new historicism is concerned less with thematic unity and more with the contesting voices in a work, voices that, when we allow ourselves to hear them, may destabilize thematic unity rather than reinforce it. The new historicist considers how a literary work speaks to the power struggles of its own time, struggles that often involve the ordinary people that traditional historicism had marginalized or silenced. This impulse to make the marginal the center of study arises from the assumption that all forms of writing embody cultural realities. The new historicist considers newspaper articles, legal documents, letters, advertisements, and popular entertainment in relation to literary texts, arguing that all are equally important as representations of social reality.

New historicism has been significantly influenced by French philosopher Michel Foucault and his ideas about power and language. For Foucault (and many other poststructural theorists), language and meaning are unstable and constantly being contested. When we learn language, we also learn the complex network of values and codes that maintain our culture. For although every society has concrete ways of maintaining order—such as police and prison systems—every society also uses religious, educational, and mass media systems to maintain its status quo. In this way, power is dispersed through a culture in innumerable subtle ways. One might ask, how is it that we don't all see the world in exactly the same way? Certain charismatic dictators have indeed striven for such uniformity. But in democracies, where freedom of speech is upheld, surely language cannot work to control us in the same way? Foucault would argue that the diversity in democratic systems often conceals the operations of power. For instance, advertising teaches us from an early age that material possessions equal social status, and hence we grow up into earning and spending citizens who participate in and support the capitalist economy. We might even say that the mass media produce desires in us that we satisfy through consumer goods. In this way, power is productive as well as repressive and says, "Yes, do this" as well as "No, don't do that." New historicists are interested in Foucault's claim that "Power is everywhere; not because it embraces everything, but because it comes from everywhere." Power is everywhere because language is everywhere, and new historicists want to read literary texts as cultural sites where meaning, and hence power, is contested. And like Foucault, new historicists favor an interdisciplinary approach that combines a variety of cultural documents in order to explore how a particular period constructs its own versions of "truth" and "reality."

The new historicist would read "The Story of an Hour," written in 1894, as articulating women's growing anger at their imprisonment within rigid social roles. Contemporaneous documents, such as articles from *Ladies Home Journal* or *Revolution,* the newspaper of the National Woman Suffrage Association, would be read alongside Chopin's story in order to illustrate the conflict for women of that time between a traditional marriage, in which the women belonged both sexually and economically to their husbands, and the independence advocated by such activists as Matilda Gage and Elizabeth Cady Stanton. In 1892 Stanton had given a speech, "The Solitude of Self," which argued for full civil rights for women, and other feminists of the time likewise argued that women should enjoy the privilege of "self-ownership" even within marriage, with the power to control their own reproductive destinies regardless of the marital "rights" of the husband. The new historicist might also look at the many medical documents of the time on the subject of female hysteria, at the dress and behavior codes that rendered women both fragile and nervous, and from such connections argue that Mrs. Mallard's "heart trouble" is a socially produced condition that manifests physically her mental suffering. In interpreting the text, a new historicist would consider how "The Story of an Hour" intersects with other cultural discourses on women and marriage, and how, in exposing the tyranny of a patriarchal social system, the story also demonstrates the seeming invincibility of that system. A new historicist might also be interested in the way that the medical discourse of the (undoubtedly) male doctors at the end fixes the meaning of Mrs. Mallard's death in a way that implicitly supports the existing patriarchy—she has died "of joy" at her husband's return.

MARXIST CRITICISM

Marxist criticism resembles new historicism in its focus on how works mirror complex historical, social, and cultural realities and in its concentration on the plight of the marginalized in society. However, this school of literary critics examines works through the lens of Marxist social and economic theory. Karl Marx (*Das Kapital,* 1867–1891) proposed that the most important aspect of material reality was the economic realm, the means of production. In other words, the means by which a society produces both goods and services determines the relation of one class of people to another. Some are primarily producers, and others are primarily consumers—as was the case in slave and feudal systems. During the Industrial Revolution, a working class arose that was exploited by the middle class (or bourgeois) bosses who controlled the means of production (i.e., owned the mines and the factories). Marx argued that all social structures are primarily created by (i.e., determined by) the economic base. The economic base determines the superstructure (e.g., government, religious, educational, and family practices). For Marx, this economic determinism affects the way people think to such an extent that they cannot imagine living any other way. What keeps them in their place is ideology, a structured belief system, which Marx defines as "false consciousness." This ideology, which is circulated through educational, religious, and political systems, presents various justifications for the existing class structure and obscures the exploitation. For example, during Marx's time, and until quite recently, the prevailing opinion was that higher education was the right of a select, highly gifted few and that all others should "know their place" and remain manual laborers. When the workers were demystified, Marx argued, they would refuse to participate in the capitalist system, and this would trigger class warfare—a proletarian revolution that would overthrow the bourgeois exploiters, leading to a utopian, classless society in which the workers themselves owned the means of production.

Later Marxist critics argued that ideology was not simply the "false consciousness" of the proletariat but that all societies and all classes have their own set of structured beliefs that seem like common sense to them. Therefore, people have an "ideology" that provides a basis for their actions and the way they conduct themselves. Undoubtedly, though, societies have a ruling class—even in the supposedly classless society of the United States or those societies based on Marxism, in which the means of production are supposedly owned by the workers. How, then, does the ruling class remain in a dominant position? In totalitarian systems, force often is openly used through military, police, or judicial agencies, but democracies rely more on maintaining a dominant ideology through what the Italian theorist Antonio Gramsci in the 1930s called "hegemony." Direct force is not effective if used too often, because direct force may initiate direct resistance. Instead, if people can be persuaded to accept certain ideas, then they also will accept certain social and economic conditions and will consent to the dominant ideology and to the ruling class. This process of winning consent is what Gramsci calls hegemony; it can be understood as the maintenance of existing power relations not only through "official" channels but also through all aspects of lived experience, including family and marital relations and popular culture. Hegemony, however, is not unassailable—it can be challenged, sometimes successfully, and social conditions can change for the better. For Gramsci, it was important always to critique and to question reality and to work toward changing the hegemonic structure so that the marginalized and the exploited could achieve autonomy and more equitable living and working conditions.

Marxist critics often focus on works that overtly treat the fate of the working class or expose the underlying economic and social motifs in texts that are not necessarily considered to be political. For example, a Marxist film critic would explore the treatment of the autoworkers in filmmaker Michael Moore's *Roger and Me.* Or a Marxist critic would concentrate on the underlying treatment of the working class in Tillie Olsen's "I Stand Here Ironing," a short story more often studied in terms of the mother-daughter dynamic.

In Kate Chopin's "The Story of an Hour," a Marxist critic would concentrate on the pattern of economic domination and submission represented in the work, suggesting that Brently Mallard's power in the marriage results from his status as the provider while Mrs. Mallard's weakened physical state and her passivity suggest her economic disenfranchisement. In addition, her inability to imagine a way to live independently other than through the route of her husband's death arises from her "false consciousness"; that is, she sees no way to escape from the hegemonic structures—her economic subservience and her socialized gender role. That realization crushes her.

POSTCOLONIAL CRITICISM

Postcolonial criticism considers the legacy of European colonialism as it is represented in literature. Drawing its inspiration and methodologies from other schools of literary criticism including deconstruction, psychological criticism, feminism, new historicism, and Marxist criticism, and postcolonial criticism focuses its attention in two directions: at literary texts currently being produced in former colonial regions, to discover the ways in which they respond to the impact of colonialism and its aftermath on their cultures, and at canonical texts to discover evidence of colonial themes. Postcolonial critics consider the ways in which such contemporary writers as Chinua Achebe, Gabriel García Márquez, and Nadine Gordimer represent the legacy of colonialism in their work; they also consider the ways in which such canonical texts as Defoe's *Robinson Crusoe* and Shakespeare's *The Tempest* represent colonial situations. Although the work of such writers as Aime Cesaire and Franz Fanon is important to the establishment of postcolonial criticism, probably the most important text to the movement is Edward Said's *Orientalism* (1978). Said extensively explores the link between English and French colonialism in the Middle East and the representation of the Middle East in scholarly and creative literature. Sometimes intentionally, sometimes unintentionally, Said concludes, scholarly and creative writers worked in collusion with colonial powers to construct an image of the Middle East as "the Orient," a decadent, culturally backward region in need of the steadying hand of European rule. Subsequent critics have built on Said's work, developing the connection between history and literature. Homi Bhabha, in particular, has sought to develop a critical language adequate to describing postcolonial literature. In *The Location of Culture* (1994), Bhabha offers a number of terms to describe postcolonial works, among them mimicry and hybridity. By mimicry, Bhabha refers to postcolonial writers' retelling of such canonical narratives as *Robinson Crusoe*, through their mimicry of those sources causing us to understand them in new ways. By hybridity, Bhabha refers to postcolonial literature's drawing on sources from both the indigenous culture and the culture of its former colonizers. Postcolonial critics might apply Bhabha's ideas to a poem such as Derek Walcott's "Far Cry from Africa," finding in the poem a combination of poetic techniques drawn from European (and especially English-language) sources, and subject matter drawn from the colonial history of Africa and the Caribbean.

CONCLUSION

If one views a work through the lenses of many critical interpretations, the work becomes kaleidoscopic. The fear may arise that the text will disintegrate and not bear the pressure of so many critical approaches. The work, however, is a pattern of many layers, and one may focus on one layer without hopelessly smearing the whole design.

Moreover, not all works yield themselves to particular interpretations, and each framework for critical interpretation is not equally justified. In one class some years ago, for example, a student suggested that William Carlos Williams's "The Red Wheelbarrow" reveals the pervasive influence of a communist threat, foreshadowing the eventual takeover of the United States by communist forces. After all, the student contended, "the red wheelbarrow" was next to "the white chickens." This assertion was challenged by the other students, who argued that a political interpretation of the bucolic country scene seemed implausible, given what they knew of Williams's poetry, his motivations for writing, his artistic technique, and the relationship of that section of the poem to the themes of the work. In other words, this intellectual community of readers cited biographical, historical, and new critical bases for their response to the first student's interpretation. The community of readers pointed out more applicable interpretations of the poem. For this reason, it is also worth recognizing that the best critics tend to be eclectic, drawing on a variety of critical approaches in whatever combination seems most appropriate to the work at hand.

Critical interpretation leads ultimately to an enriched vision of the text: a pluralistic one in which many meanings coexist. Each interpretation must be contextualized. Each literary work is a particular confluence of linguistic, biographical, cultural realities—a single artifact of language that exhibits and represents those realities. This artifact has the power to sensitize a reader to the forces shaping values, to the ways in which interpretations of the world are based on these systems of values, and to prompt investigations of both the texts and the world in new and expansive ways.

Glossary

abstract and concrete abstract language uses a high proportion of abstract nouns, which refer to concepts, qualities, or general conditions ("truth," "honesty," "poverty"). Concrete language, on the other hand, uses more concrete nouns, which refer to things perceptible through the senses ("house," "rain," "tree"). Effective writing balances the two, using specific details to illustrate abstract ideas.

act a major division in a play; each act normally is composed of several scenes.

aesthetic distance the emotional closeness of either writer or reader to a work of art.

affective responses the emotional responses, including feeling, remembering, and associating.

allegory a story in verse or prose that can be understood on both a literal and symbolic level. In *The Pilgrim's Progress* by John Bunyan (1678), Christian, the hero, embarks on a pilgrimage that takes him through the Slough of Despond, the Valley of the Shadow of Death, and so forth, until finally he reaches the Celestial City. Christian represents everyman, and his journey is an allegory of Christian salvation.

alliteration the repetition of consonant sounds for poetic effect, particularly at the beginnings of words. A famous example is Coleridge's description of the River Alph in "Kubla Khan": "Five miles meandering with a mazy motion" (chapter 8).

allusion a reference to historical events or figures, used to develop and deepen the meaning of a work (e.g., Plath's "Daddy").

ambiguity the state that exists when there are several legitimate interpretations of a literary work.

anaphora repetition of a word at the beginning of successive clauses or verses (e.g., Whitman's "Out of the Cradle").

anecdote a brief account of a story about an individual or an incident.

antagonist the character or force opposing the protagonist in a play.

anthropomorphism the endowment of animals with human thoughts and feelings.

anticlimax a move—in a sentence, stanza, paragraph, or literary work—from a noble tone to a less elevated one.

antihero a protagonist who is deliberately unheroic, i.e., often passive, ineffectual, or self-interested.

apex the height of the action in a drama.

archetype a theme, emblem, or character that reoccurs so frequently in all literature that it is accepted as universal. Examples include the theme of the quest, in which the protagonist sets out on a journey of self-discovery; the character of the femme fatale, or deadly woman; and the emblem of the rose, the symbol for romantic love.

argument a basic rhetorical mode that seeks, through logic and reason, to convince an audience by providing factual evidence to support a certain point of view.

aside in drama, words spoken in an undertone to the audience that are assumed to be inaudible to the other characters on stage.

assonance the repetition of similar vowel sounds, usually close together, for poetic effect. The first lines of Keats's "Ode on a Grecian Urn" contain a number of long /i/ sounds, creating a sensual, unhurried effect: "Thou still unravished bride of quietness,/ Thou foster child of silence and slow time."

atmosphere the emotional ambience created by a writer through setting, action, and word choice. The opening scene of *Hamlet,* in which the ghost appears, has a forbidding, fearful atmosphere.

authorial intrusion when the author of a narrative seems to step out of the story and address the reader directly.

autobiography a biography written by the subject about herself or himself.

ballad a narrative poem, usually arranged in quatrains, that employs the rhyme scheme ABCB. There are two types. The folk ballad, a form of great antiquity, is composed and transmitted orally. It tells a dramatic story vividly and is anonymous. A literary ballad is a conscious imitation of this form by a poet. Many of the most famous literary ballads were written during the Romantic period, such as Coleridge's *Rime of the Ancient Mariner* and Keats's "La Belle Dame sans Merci."

bathos a pejorative term that describes what happens when a writer describes an honestly tragic situation in such an overblown way that the situation becomes unintentionally comic.

Beat movement a literary movement centered in the United States in the 1950s and distinguished by its attempt to combine socially marginal behavior with the quest for spiritual enlightenment (e.g., Ginsberg's "America").

Bildungsroman a German term meaning "novel of education," in which the fortunes of the protagonist are traced from early years to adulthood.

blank verse unrhymed iambic pentameter.

canon the group of literary works a given culture judges to possess special merit.

caricature the exaggeration of aspects or features of a character, usually for humorous or satiric purposes.

catastrophe the tragic conclusion of action in a play.

catharsis Aristotle's term for the therapeutic sense of emotional release supposedly felt by an audience that witnesses the tragic or terrifying onstage.

cause and effect a form of process analysis that explains the factors creating a certain situation or the consequences of a particular event. The downfall of Creon, for example, can be analyzed in terms of cause and effect.

character any person represented in a literary work. Characters are commonly described as being *round* (psychologically complex and convincing), *flat* (simplistic and often stereotypical), or *foils* (existing only to highlight certain aspects of the protagonist). It is also useful to distinguish between *dynamic* characters (those undergoing change) and *static* characters (those remaining unchanged).

chorus a group of players in Greek drama who provide a collective commentary on the action and the main characters. Although an essential part of Greek tragedy, a full chorus has rarely been used in English or American drama; two notable exceptions to this are Milton's *Samson Agonistes* (1671) and T. S. Eliot's *Murder in the Cathedral* (1935).

classification the process of grouping items together based on their similarities. Thus, poetry can be classified according to such categories as the sonnet, the ballad, or the ode.

cliché an overused, and hence ineffective, figure of speech such as "pretty as a picture" or "white as snow." Since the purpose of figurative language is to surprise the reader into a new way of seeing, writers should avoid clichés.

climax the point in a narrative or play at which a crisis is reached and resolution achieved.

colloquial expressions informal words and phrases that are a normal part of everyday speech but that are inappropriate in formal writing.

comedy a term usually applied to drama, although any work may have comic elements. There are many types of comedy (high, low, romantic, satiric, etc.), but overall the genre is characterized by its use of humor and the "happy ending." The comedy moves from complication to resolution, frequently resolving individual and social problems through marriage.

comic relief the insertion of a comic scene or character into a serious or tragic work in order to temporarily release some of the work's tension.

commedia dell'arte a sixteenth-century form of drama with mimes, skits, buffoonery, and such stereotypical characters as the harlequin and the young lover.

comparison-contrast the process of analyzing and determining similarities and differences in objects, phenomena, literary works, and so forth; often essays on literature compare character, theme, style. For organization of essays, see chapter 3.

conceit a figure of speech comparing two dissimilar things or states; an elaborate and extended metaphor. See chapter 10.

Confessional poets a group of American poets of the 1950s and 1960s distinguished by their concern with intensely personal subject matter (e.g., Sexton's "My Little Girl").

conflict an aspect of plot that concerns the tensions between opposing forces. Conflicts exist within characters, between or among characters, and between characters and such forces as nature, society, and the cosmos.

connotation the meanings or emotional associations evoked by a word.

couplets in poetry, two-line stanzas.

denotation the dictionary definition(s) of a word.

denouement the part of a narrative that follows the climax, in which any remaining unresolved plot elements are resolved.

deus ex machina literally "god from the machine," this term from classical Greek drama is applied to plot complications that are resolved through unnatural or strained means.

dialect a manner of speaking peculiar to an individual, class, or region that may differ considerably from the standard language of the country. While perfectly acceptable within its own context, dialect should be avoided in most formal writing, as the writer cannot assume a knowing audience. Dialect is most frequently found in fiction or drama, where it is used to make individual characters more realistic.

dialogue the direct speech of characters in any literary context.

Dirty Realism an American school of fiction of the 1970s and 1980s that focused on the minute, and frequently unpleasant, details of people's daily lives (e.g., Carver's "Cathedral").

double plot a second story that becomes fascinating on its own merits and enlarges the meaning of the main plot.

drafting composing and concentrating on organization, development, and fluency in the early stages of the writing process.

drama any work meant to be performed on a stage by actors. Usually, the work is divided into acts and scenes.

dramatic irony See *irony*.

dramatic poetry poetry in which the speaker becomes an actor, as in a monologue or a soliloquy.

editing the stage of the writing process concerned with sharpening word choice and style to clarify meaning and to strengthen presentation of message.

elegy a poem that expresses mourning for the death of a particular person and/or for mortality in general.

Elizabethan or Shakespearean sonnet a fourteen-line poem comprising three quatrains and a final couplet. The quatrains express and develop a dilemma or proposition to which the couplet offers a response (e.g., Shakespeare's "Let Me Not to the Marriage of True Minds").

end rhymes rhymes that occur at the end of verse lines.

enjambment in poetry, a statement that runs on into the next line.

epic poetry poems derived from oral tradition that describe the adventures and accomplishments of great heroes.

epigram a short, pithy, generally humorous observation presented as a general truth.

epigraph the inscription on the title page of a book, which may be a quotation from another literary work or an original remark by the author and which calls attention to the book's theme.

epiphany in a short story, a sudden moment of insight when a character discovers a truth important to the story (e.g., Joyce's "Eveline").

essay a concise prose discussion of a limited topic for a general audience.

evidence the use of facts, statistics, personal experiences, or the opinions of authorities to support a writer's claims or conclusions.

explication the close reading of a text, usually involving line-by-line analysis.

exposition intended primarily to inform, this rhetorical mode can take a variety of forms, such as classification, definition, process analysis, comparison/contrast, and cause and effect.

extended metaphor see *conceit.*

fable a short tale told to illustrate a moral, in which the characters are animals whose character traits represent human traits.

figurative language language that includes figures of speech.

figures of speech expressions that are based on comparisons, either explicit or implied, and that are intended to be interpreted imaginatively rather than literally. Their purpose is to surprise the reader into a new way of seeing. Among the most common are *simile, metaphor, personification, hyperbole,* and *litotes.*

first person narrative point of view in which the narrator speaks as "I" and is a participant in the narrative (e.g., Baldwin's "Sonny's Blues").

flashback a term derived from cinema, referring to any scene inserted into a literary work in order to show an earlier event.

foreshadowing using the current action in a literary work to anticipate later events.

free verse verse with no regular meter or line length. Although it may appear haphazard at first, free verse can acquire rhythms and melodies of its own.

Freytag's Pyramid Gustav Freytag conceived of plot in drama as rising action, climax, and falling action that leads to a dénouement. His conception took the shape of a pyramid.

generalization a broad statement that may well be true but that is not supported by concrete evidence. Generalizations lack substance, and so essays should not rely on them.

genre a literary type or class. The major classical genres are *tragedy, comedy, satire, epic,* and *lyric.*

hamartia a tragic error in judgment in classical Greek drama (e.g., Sophocles's *Antigone*).

Harlem Renaissance a cultural movement of the 1920s centered in Harlem, New York, which celebrated African American experience and attempted to find literary forms suited to it (e.g., Hughes's "Let America Be America Again").

hubris in classical Greek drama, overweening pride (e.g., Sophocles's *Antigone*).

hyperbole a figure of speech that uses deliberate exaggeration, usually for comic effect.

iamb a poetic foot consisting of an unstressed syllable followed by a stressed syllable, as in "bĕhóld."

illustration the use of concrete examples to support a generalization.

imagery concrete language that appeals to the senses. An image does not have to be interpreted literally; indeed, many are conveyed by figurative language. (See *figures of speech*.)

in media res literally "in the middle of things," beginning a story in the midst of the action.

inductive and deductive reasoning two forms of everyday thinking. Inductive reasoning uses specific examples to formulate a general truth; deductive reasoning takes a general truth and seeks to demonstrate it through examples.

interior monologue in a work of fiction, an extended passage relating a character's thoughts (e.g., Busch's "Ralph the Duck").

intrigue scheme in a drama in which a character entraps another person who is naïve, trusting, and vulnerable.

introduction the first section of a paper, which should get the reader's attention, state the thesis, and establish the tone and point of view. In most college writing assignments, one paragraph will be sufficient. In longer papers, the introductory material may consist of several paragraphs.

irony a complex attitude that relies on contrast for its effect. There are three basic types. *Verbal irony* occurs when what is said contrasts with what is meant (e.g., "You are really too kind" said with great bitterness). *Dramatic irony* contrasts what is expected with what actually happens (e.g., a character laughs at another's misfortune, unaware that the same misfortune is happening to her). *Structural irony* used a particular device to sustain irony through-

out the entire work, i.e., the naïve hero who constantly misinterprets events.

jargon the specialized vocabulary of a particular field or trade, which the general reader is unlikely to understand.

journal a form of personal writing concerning the self. The presumed audience is the author.

Kmart Realism a school of American fiction during the 1980s distinguished by its use of the icons of popular culture to make serious points (e.g., Mason's "Shiloh").

komos revel in classical Greek drama, from which we derive the word *comedy.*

literary theory/criticism a conceptual framework for understanding and interpreting a work of art. (See Appendix A.)

litotes the opposite of *hyperbole,* this figure of speech uses understatement for humorous effect.

lyric any short, non-narrative poem that deals subjectively with the thoughts and feelings of a single speaker. Although written in the first person, its sentiments are not necessarily those of the poet, but may be those of an adopted *persona.*

Magical Realism a twentieth-century literary movement associated with Central and South America in which the fantastical and the everyday are presented as equally "real" (e.g., García Márquez's, "The Handsomest Drowned Man in the World").

meditation a reflection on a scene that moves from observation of the object to consideration of metaphysical ideas.

memoir the remembrances of a public figure and/or of an historical era; an autobiographical form.

metafiction fiction that reflects on the subject and writing of fiction.

metaphor an implied comparison that brings together two dissimilar things without the use of "like" or "as." For instance, the metaphorical equivalent of Burns's famous simile "My love is like a red, red rose" would be "My love is a red, red rose."

Metaphysical poets a seventeenth-century English literary movement, whose poetry combined passion and reason through highly innovative conceits (e.g., Donne's "The Flea"). (See *conceit*.)

meter the pattern of stressed and unstressed syllables in lines of verse, each unit being termed a *foot*. / denotes a long or *stressed* syllable; ˘ denotes a short or *unstressed* syllable. The most common feet in English verse are:

iamb:	˘ /	e.g., dĕsíre
trochee:	/ ˘	e.g., wómĕn
anapest:	˘ ˘ /	e.g., ĭn ă flásh
dactyl:	/ ˘ ˘	e.g., yéstĕrdăy
spondee:	/ /	e.g., oútwíth

In addition, lines are named according to the number of feet they contain:

> monometer: one foot
> dimeter: two feet
> trimeter: three feet
> tetrameter: four feet
> pentameter: five feet
> hexameter: six feet
> heptameter: seven feet
> octameter: eight feet

metonymy the substitution of one thing for another with which it is closely associated, such as using "the White House" to refer to the president.

mimesis the literary process of attempting to create a convincing and uninterrupted illusion of real life.

miracle plays a dramatic genre presenting Christian saints' lives and miracles.

modernism A European and American literary movement of the first half of the twentieth century, distinguished by its use of experimental techniques, its concern with individual psychology, and its concern with the decay of civilization (e.g., Eliot's "Love Song of J. Alfred Prufrock").

monologue a sustained speech by a single character, either with or without a direct audience (e.g., Shakespeare's *Hamlet*, III, ii).

mood the atmosphere or tone of a literary work, created not only by the characters and events but also by the author's style and choice of language.

morality plays a dramatic genre that allegorized Christian values.

motif a theme or image that occurs repeatedly within a literary work and thus acquires symbolic value.

motivation the reason a character performs an action.

multiculturalism the increasing emphasis on race, class, and gender in education. In recognition of the diversity of most classrooms, the traditional curriculum is being modified to encompass the achievements and experiences of many groups.

mystery plays dramas presenting biblical stories.

myth a story involving supernatural beings that usually explains the cosmos and the mysteries of life and death.

narration essay form that seeks to recreate a series of events (i.e., a "story") as vividly as possible using descriptive detail.

narrative poetry form of poetry that tells a story.

narrator person telling a story.

novel an extended work of prose fiction that, although traditionally realistic, can be highly experimental.

novella an extended work of fiction, longer and more expansive than a short story, but shorter than a novel.

objective and subjective terms used to describe the extent and type of the author's involvement with her or his work. *Objective* writing is primarily factual and maintains a detached, impersonal tone. *Subjective* writing reveals the author's feelings and attitudes and often seeks to involve the reader emotionally.

octave see *Petrarchan sonnet.*

ode a formal and elaborate lyric poem that praises either a person or a thing. The *Pindaric Ode,* named after the classical Greek poet Pindar, traditionally celebrates a noteworthy individual upon some public occasion. The *Horatian Ode,* named after the classical Roman poet Horace, is in contrast private and personal (e.g., Keats's "Ode on a Grecian Urn").

onomatopoeia the use of words that imitate the sounds they represent, such as "crash" and "buzz."

organization the way a writer chooses to develop ideas in both paragraphs and essays, according to the purpose and audience. The five main methods are: (1) *deductive,* from general statement to specific example, (2) *inductive,* from specific example to general statement, (3) *climactic,* from least to most important, (4) *chronological,* according to time sequence, (5) *spatial,* according to physical organization.

oxymoron a word or phrase composed of two words that apparently contradict each other, such as "bittersweet."

pageants the platforms used in productions of mystery, miracle, and morality plays.

parable a story with a moral, often religious, the purpose of which is instruction. See discussion of the prodigal son in chapter 9.

paradox an apparent contradiction that resolves itself on a deeper level.

paragraph a group of logically related sentences that together develop a central idea. This idea is stated broadly in a topic sentence and illustrated with supporting detail. Paragraphs break information down into smaller units, which the reader can assimilate more easily.

paraphrase a detailed restatement of information in words other than those of the original source.

parody the imitation of a certain author's style, tone, or attitude with the intent to ridicule. The technique is one of exaggeration.

pastoral a poem celebrating the idyllic nature of country life.

pathetic fallacy the attribution of human emotions to the nonhuman, used particularly when the writing is clichéd or melodramatic.

pathos the aspect of a narrative that causes its reader to feel pity or sorrow for the various characters.

performance art a form of American art of the 1980s and 1990s, distinguished by its combination of aspects of drama and improvisation (e.g., Smith's "Twilight Los Angeles").

persona from the Latin for "mask," this term originally referred to the false face of clay worn by actors. It now denotes the identity adopted by an author for any literary work.

personification the attribution of human qualities to inanimate things for poetic effect.

Petrarchan sonnet named for a famous Italian poet, Petrarch, this sonnet is composed of an eight-line *octave* (composed of two *quatrains*) and a six-line *sestet* (composed of two *tercets*). The octave states a problem or proposition to which the sestet replies; the shift from octave to sestet in the ninth line is called the *volta.*

philosophical treatise an extended formal meditation on a philosophical, religious, or political subject (see chapter 12).

picture frame stage an innovation in European drama that created the effect of framing the stage.

plagiarism the representation of another's words or ideas as though they were the writer's own. This academic theft, whether conscious or unconscious, is a serious offense. To avoid plagiarism, document all outside information.

plot the arrangement of events in a narrative or dramatic work. When two story lines are developed in equal length, the work is said to have a *double plot*. When one story line dominates the other, the latter is said to be the *subplot*.

point of view the perspective from which a story is told. Events can be narrated in the *first person* (the narrator is part of the action), or the *third person* (the narrator is outside the action). Narration in the *second person* is rare. An *omniscient narrator* uses the third person and is all-knowing.

postmodernism A European and American literary movement of the second half of the twentieth century distinguished by its conspicuous irony and its self-conscious concern with the nature of art (e.g., Busch's "Ralph the Duck").

premises supporting statements.

prewriting the generating of ideas prior to the initial drafting of a paper. The common strategies are *freewriting* and *brainstorming*. Freewriting involves writing nonstop for a short period of time. The writer is not concerned with grammar or spelling but with the free association of ideas. Brainstorming involves quickly listing anything and everything related to the topic. Ideas can then be grouped or subdivided to establish what is relevant.

primary and secondary sources *primary sources* are original materials, whether novels, speeches, scientific reports, or government documents. *Secondary sources* are studies of those materials. Thus, Wilfred Owen's poem "Arms and the Boy" is a primary source; a critical analysis of its themes is a secondary source.

proofreading the final stage of the writing process, in which the writer rereads the finished draft carefully for grammatical, spelling, or mechanical errors.

proscenium arch a frame enclosing the stage area behind which the front curtain hangs.

protagonist the principal character in a work of drama or fiction.

purpose and audience a writer's purpose, generally speaking, can be *to entertain, to explain, to explore,* or *to persuade.* Often several purposes will overlap, but the writer's overall intention will be closely tied to the audience being addressed. This can be any individual or group, whether the self, as in a journal entry, or the general public, as in a newspaper article.

quatrains in poetry, four-line stanzas.

realism although all literature is clearly artificial, certain works can be said to represent life more accurately than others. Such works attend to the minutiae of everyday experience and present characters and events realistically rather than romantically.

revision this stage of the writing process involves rewriting a rough draft to improve both form and content. *Purpose* and *audience* should be reconsidered, as should the overall focus and development of the paper. Material may be cut, expanded, or moved around, while the language itself should be reworked for clarity and conciseness.

rhetorical question a question to which no answer is expected, or to which the answer is assumed to be self-evident. Used primarily for stylistic effect, this device encourages an emotional response from the reader and, thus, is often used in persuasive writing.

rhetorical situation purpose, audience, occasion, and point of view for the generation of a piece of writing. It is mainly a term used for the analysis of nonfiction. See, for example, the speech by Sojourner Truth .

rhyme in English poetry, the repetition of the last accented vowel and all succeeding sounds (e.g., boy–joy).

rhyme scheme fixed pattern of rhymes characterizing a poem or its stanzas.

rhythm in poetry or prose, the patterns of beats that establish the rise and fall of sounds; cadence. See the analysis of rhythm in Shakespeare's sonnet, "My Mistress' Eyes Are Nothing Like the Sun" and the chanting patterns in Anna Lee Walters's "My Name Is 'I Am Living' "

Romanticism a European literary movement of the late eighteenth and early nineteenth centuries distinguished by its concern with the free and subjective expression of passion, pathos, and personal feelings (e.g., Coleridge's "Kubla Khan").

satire literature that exposes folly and seeks to correct it through ridicule. While the irony employed in satire may be amusing, the intent is not simply to entertain but to enlighten an audience. Jonathan Swift's essay "A Modest Proposal" is a classic example.

scansion the process of measuring poetry, of marking accented and unaccented syllables, and of dividing lines into feet in order to discern the metrical pattern of the poem and to notice deviations from the pattern.

scene a unit of continuous action in a play in which the setting remains unchanged. Groups of interrelated scenes comprise larger units of the work, known as *acts*.

sestet See *Petrarchan sonnet*.

setting the time, place, and/or environment in which a literary work occurs.

sexist language the misrepresentation or exclusion of either sex. One of the most common forms of sexist language is the use of the male pronoun "he" for an individual of unknown gender.

Shakespearean sonnet see *Elizabethan sonnet*.

short story a fictional narrative of more limited scope than the novel, often focusing on a single incident or character. It is a challenging medium, as the theme must be developed and brought to a satisfactory conclusion within approximately thirty pages.

simile a figure of speech that compares two unlike things using "like" or "as." See *metaphor*.

slave narrative a form of nineteenth century autobiography that documents a slave's journey from bondage to freedom.

soliloquy a dramatic convention in which a character, alone on the stage, voices her or his private thoughts. It is generally assumed that the feelings expressed are sincere (e.g., *Hamlet*, III, i).

sonnet a lyric poem of fourteen lines, usually in iambic pentameter, that employs a highly formal pattern of organization. Although there are a great number of possible rhyme schemes, the two most common are the *English* (also known as the *Elizabethan* and the *Shakespearean*) and the *Italian* (also known as the *Petrarchan*). The English consists of three quatrains and a concluding couplet and deploys the rhyme scheme ABAB/CDCD/EFEF/GG. The Italian consists of an octave and a sestet and deploys the rhyme scheme ABBA/ABBA/ CDC/CDC.

stanza the basic unit of structure in a poem. Each unit consists of a group of interrelated lines arranged in a pattern that is usually repeated throughout the poem.

stereotypes easily recognized types of characters, such as the fool.

stock characters see *stereotypes*.

subplots secondary plot or plots in drama or fiction.

summary a concise restatement of a longer piece of writing, containing only the essential information.

surprise essential element of plot that contradicts the audience's or reader's expectations.

Surrealism a European literary movement of the 1920s and 1930s that emphasizes the author's imaginative expression of dreams and other psychic states reached through the unconscious mind.

suspense element of plot that builds excitement and uncertainty about the resolution of events.

syllabic verse a method of composing poetry that disregards accentual feet and creates rhythm through a regularized pattern of counted syllables.

syllogism a deductive argument in three parts that moves from a major and minor premise to a logical conclusion. For example: a) water is wet; b) rain is water; therefore c) rain is wet.

symbol an object, character, or action that stands for something more than itself. In *"Master Harold" . . . and the Boys,* ballroom dancing symbolizes social harmony.

symbolist dramas form of drama that features many traditional poetic symbols, allegorical names, and a dreamlike atmosphere. All of the action would be interpreted symbolically.

synecdoche the use of a part of something to stand for its whole, i.e., saying "My heart belongs to you" to indicate that the entire self belongs to the beloved.

synonyms words that are close enough in meaning to be interchangeable. Exact synonyms are rare, however, since all words have slightly different connotations.

syntax the arrangement of words within a sentence and the way this arrangement can affect meaning.

tercets three-line stanzas.

Theater of the Absurd a form of drama prevalent in the 1950s and associated with such playwrights as Pinter, Ionesco, and Beckett. Although literature has always explored the potentially comic aspects of humankind, the Theater of the Absurd reflects explicitly the twentieth-century philosophical view of a meaningless universe in which there is no coherence and little dignity. The plays themselves are, therefore, intentionally meaningless.

theme the central idea or message in a work. It can be expressed either directly or indirectly.

thesis statement usually contained in the introduction, the thesis statement establishes the focus of the essay—what it is about—in one or two sentences. Experienced writers sometimes use an *implied thesis statement,* where the purpose of the essay is clear without being directly stated. Student writers, however, should ensure that the thesis statement is identifiable.

tone created by both word choice and syntax, tone reflects the author's attitude toward the subject matter, which can be humorous, sarcastic, and so forth.

topic sentence the concise statement of the idea being developed within a paragraph. The topic sentence focuses the paragraph in the same way that the thesis statement focuses the essay.

tragedy a term usually applied to drama, tragedy traditionally traces the downfall of an initially noble character in a serious and elevated manner. In classical Greek drama, this downfall is invariably attributed to some tragic flaw in the protagonist, a device also seen frequently in Shakespearean tragedy (e.g., *Hamlet*). Modern tragedy is often said to lack the grandeur of classical tragedy, perhaps because it aims at broader social commentary and deals more with ordinary people in everyday situations.

tragic flaw see *hamartia.*

tragic hero protagonist in a tragedy; a person of high moral stature whose downfall is, nonetheless, the result of some tragic flaw (e.g., Shakespeare's *Hamlet*).

tragicomedy a mixture of tragedy and comedy created by the classical Roman dramatist Plautus.

transitional expressions essential to effective writing, these signal connections between ideas, thus allowing fluency between sentences and paragraphs. Some common transitional expressions are *however, therefore, consequently,* and *on the other hand.*

triplets in poetry, three-line stanzas.

unity of action in the *Poetics,* the classical Greek philosopher Aristotle wrote that every part of the action in a play must be integral to the whole. Any missing or extraneous part destroys the play's integrity.

vignette a sketch or a short scene in a larger work written with great skill for the purpose of either creating a vivid, resonant picture or illuminating some larger aspect of a work's theme.

villanelle a poem consisting of five *tercets* and a *quatrain,* based on two rhymes and with systematic repetitions of lines one and three of the first tercet (e.g., Thomas's "Do Not Go Gentle into That Good Night").

voice the individual personality of the author. Although a work may have many characters and may shift in tone according to the subject matter, there will remain a distinct authorial presence beyond even a first-person narrator. Student writers should recognize the importance of allowing their own voices to develop in their writing.

Literary Credits

Chinua Achebe "Girls at War" from *Girls at War and Other Stories* by Chinua Achebe, copyright © 1972, 1973 by Chinua Achebe. Used by permission of Doubleday, a division of Random House, Inc. and Harold Ober Associates, Inc.

Andre Aciman "Alexandria: The Capital of Memory" from *False Papers* by Andre Aciman. Copyright © 2000 by Andre Aciman. Reprinted by permission of Farrar, Straus and Giroux, LLC.

Virginia Hamilton Adair "Peeling an Orange" copyright © 1996 by Virginia Hamilton Adair, from *Ants on the Melon* by Virginia Hamilton Adair. Used by permission of Random House, Inc.

Marjorie Agosin "Far Away" translated by Cola Franzen and "The Foreigner" translated by Monica Bruno Galmozzi from *At the Threshold of Memory: Selected and New Poems.* Copyright © 2003 by Marjorie Agosin. Translations copyright © 2003 by Cola Franzen and Monica Bruno Galmozzi. Reprinted with the permission of White Pine Press, Buffalo, New York.

Anna Akhmatova "Lot's Wife" by Anna Akhmatova from *Selected Poems* translated by D.M. Thomas. Rerpinted by permission of John Johnson Ltd.

Harry Akst and **Grant Clarke** *Am I Blue?* By Harry Akst and Grant Clarke. Copyright 1929 (renewed) Warner Bros. Inc. All Rights Reserved. Used by permission. Warner Bros. Publications U.S. Inc., Miami, FL 33014.

Sherman Alexie Excerpt from *Smoke Signals* by Sherman Alexie, p. 148. Courtesy of Hyperion. "This Is What It Means to Say Phoenix, Arizona" from *The Lone Ranger and Tonto Fistfight in Heaven* by Sherman Alexie. Copyright © 1993 by Sherman Alexie. Used by permission of Grove/Atlantic, Inc.

Agha Shahid Ali "Snowmen" from *The Half-Inch Himalayas* © 1987 by Agha Shahid Ali and reprinted by permission of Wesleyan University Press.

Isabel Allende "And of Clay We Are Created" reprinted with the permission of Scribner, an imprint of Simon & Schuster Adult Publishing Group, from *The Stories of Eva Luna* by Isabel Allende. Copyright © 1989 by Isabel Allende. English Translation Copyright © 1991 by Macmillan Publishing Company.

Julia Alvarez "Homecoming" by Julia Alvarez from *Homecoming.* Copyright © 1984, 1996 by Julia Alvarez. Published by Plume, an imprint of Dutton Signet, a division of Penguin USA; originally published by Grove Press. Reprinted by permission of Susan Bergholz Literary Services, New York. All rights reserved.

Maya Angelou "Still I Rise" copyright © 1978 by Maya Angelou, from *And Still I Rise* by Maya Angelou. Used by permission of Random House, Inc.

Athol Fugard *"Master Harold" . . . and the Boys* by Athol Fugard, copyright © 1982 by Athol Fugard. Used by permission of Alfred A. Knopf, a division of Random House, Inc.

Rebecca Gilman "Boy Gets Girl" by Rebecca Gilman.

Allen Ginsberg "America" from *Collected Poems 1947-1980* by Allen Ginsberg. Copyright © 1956, 1959 by Allen Ginsberg. Reprinted by permission of HarperCollins Publishers Inc.

Nikki Giovanni "Ego Tripping' from *The Selected Poems of Nikki Giovanni* by Nikki Giovanni. Compilation copyright © 1996 by Nikki Giovanni. Reprinted by permission of HarperCollins Publishers, Inc.

Susan Glaspell *Trifles* by Susan Glaspell. Reprinted by permission. Copyright 1951 by Walter H. Baker Co. For all rights contact: Baker's Plays, 100 Chauncy Street, Boston, MA 02111.

Louise Glück "Summer at the Beach" from *The Seven Ages* by Louise Gluck. Copyright © 2001 by Louise Gluck. Reprinted by permission of HarperCollins Publishers Inc.

Emma Goldman "Minorities vs. Majorities" by Emma Goldman from *Anarchism and Other Essays.*

Nadine Gordimer "Once Upon a Time" from *Jump and Other Stories* by Nadine Gordimer. Copyright © Felix Licensing B.V., 1992. Reprinted by permission of Farrar, Straus and Giroux, LLC and Penguin Group (Canada), a Division of Pearson Penguin Canada Inc.

Mary Gordon "Violation" from *Temporary Shelter* by Mary Gordon, copyright © 1987 by Mary Gordon. Used by permission of Random House, Inc.

Stephen Jay Gould "Non-Moral Nature" by Stephen Jay Gould from *Natural History,* February 1982. Reprinted by permission.

Philip Gourevitch Chapter 1 from *We Wish to Inform You That Tomorrow We Will Be Killed with Our Families: Stories from Rwanda* by Philip Gourevitch. Copyright © 1998 by Philip Gourevitch. Reprinted by permission of Farrar, Straus and Giroux, LLC.

Jessica Hagedorn "The Song of Bullets" from *Danger and Beauty* by Jessica Hagedorn. Copyright © 2003 by Jessica Hagedorn. Reprinted by permission of City Lights Books.

Lorraine Hansberry *A Raisin in the Sun* by Lorraine Hansberry, copyright © 1958 by Robert Nemiroff, as an unpublished work. Copyright © 1959, 1966, 1984 by Robert Nemiroff. Used by permission of Random House, Inc.

Joy Harjo "For Anna Mae Aquash Whose Spirit is Present Here and in the Dappled Stars" from *In Mad Love and War* © 1990 by Joy Harjo and reprinted by permission of Wesleyan University Press.

G.B. Harrison "Hamlet" from *Shakespeare: The Complete Works* by G.B. Harrison, copyright 1952 by Harcourt, Inc. and renewed 1980 by G.B. Harrison, reprinted by permission of the publisher.

Jason Hartley "I, Jailor" by Jason Hartley. Reprinted by permission of the author.

Ntozake Shange Reprinted with the permission of Scribner, an imprint of Simon & Schuster Adult Publishing Group, from *For Colored Girls Who Have Considered Suicide When the Rainbow is Enuf* by Ntozake Shange. Copyright © 1975, 1976, 1977 by Ntozake Shange.

Leslie Marmon Silko "Yellow Woman" by Leslie Marmon Silko. Copyright © 1981 by Leslie Marmon Silko, Reprinted with the permission of the Wylie Agency Inc.

Paul Simon "American Tune" by Paul Simon. Copyright © 1973 by Paul Simon. Paul Simon Music, NY.

Anna Deavere Smith "Limbo/Twilight #2/Twilight Bey/Organizer of Gang Truce" from *Twilight: Los ANGELES 1992* by Anna Deavere Smith, copyright © 1994 by Anna Deavere Smith. Used by permission of Doubleday, a division of Random House, Inc.

Gary Snyder "The Bath" by Gary Snyder, from *Turtle Island,* copyright © 1974 by Gary Snyder. Reprinted by permission of New Directions Publishing Corp.

Cathy Song "Lost Sister" from *Picture Bride* by Cathy Song. Copyright © 1983 by and reprinted by permission of Yale University Press. "Heaven" from *Frameless Windows, Squares of Light: Poems* by Cathy Song. Copyright © 1988 by Cathy Song. Used by permission of W. W. Norton & Company, Inc.

Gary Soto "Black Hair" and "Oranges" by Gary Soto from *New and Selected Poems* by Gary Soto. Copyright © 1995 by Gary Soto. Reprinted by permission of Chronicle Books LLC, San Francisco. Visit ChronicleBooks.com.

Wole Soyinka "Telephone Conversation" by Wole Soyinka. Copyright © 1962, 1990 by Wole Soyinka. Reprinted by permission of Melanie Jackson Agency, L. L. C.

Elizabeth Spires "Like Water" by Elizabeth Spires from *New Criterion,* Vol. 21. Reprinted by permission of New Criterion.

Bruce Springsteen "The Rising" by Bruce Springsteen. Copyright © 2002 by Bruce Springsteen. All rights reserved. Reprinted by permission.

John Steinbeck "Flight" from *The Long Valley* by John Steinbeck, copyright 1938, renewed © 1966 by John Steinbeck. Used by permission of Viking Penguin, a division of Penguin Group (USA) Inc.

Gloria Steinem "Ruth's Song" from *Outrageous Acts and Everyday Rebellions,* 2nd edition, by Gloria Steinem. Copyright © 1983 by Gloria Steinem, 1984 by East Toledo Productions, Inc., 1995 by Gloria Steinem. Reprinted by permission of Henry Holt and Company, LLC.

Wallace Stevens "The Idea of Order at Key West" from *The Collected Poems of Wallace Stevens* by Wallace Stevens, copyright 1954 by Wallace Stevens and renewed 1982 by Holly Stevens. Used by permission of Alfred A. Knopf, a division of Random House, Inc.

Wislawa Szymborska "Hatred", "Could Have" and "The Century's Decline" from *View with a Grain of Sand,* copyright © 1993 by Wislawa Szymborka, English translation by Stanislaw Baranczak and Clare Cavanagh copyright © 1995 by Harcourt, Inc., reprinted by permission of the publisher.

Amy Tan "Scar" from *The Joy Luck Club* by Amy Tan, copyright © 1989 by Amy Tan. Used by permission of G.P. Putnam's Sons, a division of Penguin Group (USA) Inc.

Index of Authors, Titles, and First Lines of Poetry

Subject Index